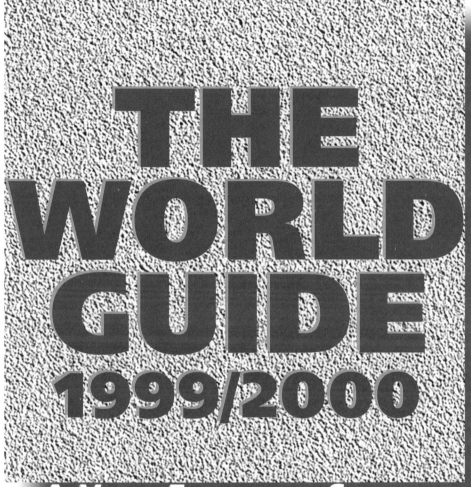

THE WORLD GUIDE 1999/2000

A VIEW FROM THE SOUTH

I Te M

INSTITUTO DEL TERCER MUNDO

The World Guide 1999/2000

Third World Guide (English language edition) 1986, 1988, 1990, 1992.
The World Guide (English language edition) 1995, 1997.

Paperback ISBN 1-869847 - 68 - 7
Hardback ISBN 1-869847 - 67 - 9

A catalogue record for this book is available from the British Library.

New Internationalist Publications Ltd.,
Registered Office: 55 Rectory Road,
Oxford OX4 1BW, United Kingdom.
Fax: 01865 793152
E-mail: ni@newint.org

Printed by C&C Offset Printing Co. Ltd., Hong Kong.

Contents
WORLD GUIDE 1999/2000

General Index:

Global Issues

AN OVERVIEW OF THE 20th CENTURY

I. The Earth and its peoples

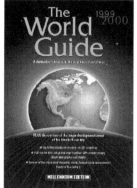

SINCE 1997, THROUGH THE INTERNET AND TOGETHER WITH ITS UPDATING SERVICE — GUÍA DE LA SEMANA — THE SPANISH VERSION OF THE WORLD GUIDE IS AVAILABLE IN WEB PAGES.

19 BIODIVERSITY
The destruction of life

The planet's biological resources, which also encompass their historical, geographical and cultural sustenance, have this century suffered accelerated destruction. International negotiations have sought to establish a new regulatory framework but in the meantime local communities have often become the front-line defenders of biodiversity - thereby also defending their identities.

21 DEFORESTATION
Underlying causes of deforestation and forest degradation

Deforestation rates during the 1980s were as high as 15 million hectares per year for tropical forests alone and the phenomenon accelerated in the following decade in most parts of the world. Forests were not disappearing because people and their governments were ignorant but because a number of interconnected international and national policies prepared the ground for it to happen.

23 CLIMATIC CHANGES
Lack of responsibility or lack of foresight?

Towards the end of the 20th century devastating climatic changes - like those caused by the "El Niño" sea current, or increasing desertification - showed that insufficient action had been taken by the international community to counter the serious problems of human-caused environmental deterioration.

24 WATER

A new source of conflict

Increasingly scarce and vulnerable to destructive human activity, water has become a strategic resource and a determining factor in new conflicts - as can be seen in some regions of Africa and the Middle East, particularly in the territories occupied by Israel.

26 DEMOGRAPHY

The debate around population

The world's population has reached nearly 6 billion. Meanwhile, the debate on demographic growth and the distribution of the earth's resources which began two centuries ago has not changed.

(TABLE) **POPULATION DENSITY** (p 25)

- **Indicator:** Population per sq km, 1994.

Source: Statistical Yearbook 41st issue, CD-ROM, United Nations, 1997.

(TABLE) **FERTILITY IN FIGURES**

- **Indicators:** percentage of married women of childbearing age using contraceptives, 1990-97; crude death rate per thousand people, 1996; crude birth rate per thousand people, 1996; children per woman, 1996.

Source: The State of the World's Children 1998, UNICEF, 1998.

28 INDIGENOUS PEOPLES

America: five centuries of manipulation

Since the colonization of America, all the projects which sought to integrate, absorb or represent indigenous people did nothing more than prolong Eurocentrism. When these peoples started to make themselves heard on their own account, hitherto unquestioned concepts of power, state and nation were shaken up.

29 MISKITO BOX

IT WOULD BE BENEFICIAL IF THE INTERNATIONAL BODIES PREPARED TO DECLARE YEARS AND DECADES OF INDIGENOUS RIGHTS, WOULD OPEN THEIR EARS AND REALLY LISTEN TO WHAT THESE PEOPLES HAVE TO SAY. FOR AMONGST OTHER MATTERS, THESE PEOPLE KNEW HOW TO LIVE IN HARMONY WITH NATURE - A HARMONY THE REST OF THE PLANET APPEARS TO HAVE LOST.

II. SOCIETY

30 SOCIAL MODELS

The search for Utopia

The hopes and dreams of technological and philosophical optimists have often been presented as utopian - but the flipside of the dreams are the nightmares, which challenge the concept of unending, linear progress, common to liberals and Marxists alike.

31 GLOBAL POLL BOX

32 WOMEN

Building upon diversity

At the end of the millennium, women in the world (almost 2.87 billion) are living in widely differing situations in terms of material wealth. However, what they all have in common is that they hold the most unfavourable positions, and that they are involved in constant and diverse battles in the quest for greater equality.

(TABLE) WOMEN IN HIGH LEVEL JOBS

- **Indicators:** percentage of administration and managerial posts occupied by women; percentage of professional women and women technicians; salaries of women as a percentage of men's income (data refers to latest available year).

Source: Human Development Report 1997, UNDP, 1997.

(TABLE) WOMEN IN POLITICAL LIFE

- **Indicators:** percentage of parliamentary seats occupied by women, 1997; percentage of governmental posts occupied by women (ministerial level and total), 1995.

Source: Human Development Report 1997, UNDP, 1997.

35 ECOLOGY

30 years on

The ecological movement, which some thought would be short-lived and limited to the rich countries, has not only expanded across the globe but has also managed to evade attempts to undermine it or incorporate it into the establishment.

37 TOXICITY BOX

(TABLE) FOOD IN FIGURES

- **Indicators:** food production per capita index (1979-81=100), 1993; food imports as a percentage of merchandise imports, 1994; cereal imports (1,000 metric tons), 1994.

Sources: Human Development Report 1997, UNDP, 1997; World Development Indicators 1997, World Bank 1997.

38 EDUCATION

The levelling out of culture

Education is in crisis. Transformed by scientific and technological revolutions into a means of adapting individuals to the globalized market, it has strayed from its original principles of forming citizens fully capable of participating in communities.

40 RITES OF PASSAGE BOX

(TABLE) EDUCATION ENROLMENT IN FIGURES

- **Indicators:** percentage of students across the school-age population (gross enrolment rate is the number of children enrolled at a level - primary or secondary - regardless of age, divided by the population of that age group): male and female at primary and secondary level (1990/95) and total at tertiary level (1995).

Sources: The State of the World's Children 1998, UNICEF, 1998; World Development Indicators 1998, World Bank, 1998.

(TABLE) EDUCATION IMBALANCES

- **Indicators:** primary pupil to teacher ratio, 1995.

Source: World Development Indicators 1998, World Bank, 1998.

(TABLE) LITERACY

- **Indicator:** adult literacy rate (total, female, male), 1995.

Source: The State of the World's Children 1998, UNICEF, 1998.

42 HEALTH

The limits of biomedicine

The idea of the human body as a machine composed of myriad separate micro-mechanisms and of illnesses caused by specific pathogenic agents allowed for the great progress of 20th century medicine. But criticism of such thinking is on the increase and is calling into question the bases of the so-called biomedicine.

(TABLE) HEALTH SERVICES

- **Indicators:** percentage of population with access to safe water, 1990-96; percentage of population with access to health services, 1990-96.

Source: The State of the World's Children 1997 and 1998, UNICEF, 1997 and 1998.

45 BATTLE AGAINST CANCER BOX

(TABLE) HEALTH IN FIGURES

- **Indicators:** population per doctor and per nurse, 1988-91.

Source: Human Development Report 1997, UNDP, 1997.

46 CHILDHOOD
Poverty and discrimination: the biggest causes of death

The number of children immunized against the six major childhood illnesses grew from 5 per cent in 1974 to 80 per cent in 1995. However, millions of children still die each year from preventable infectious diseases like diarrhoea, and poorer countries still suffer from a lack of basic health-care provision.

(TABLE) BREAST IS BEST

- **Indicator:** percentage of mothers breastfeeding at six months, 1980-92.

Source: Human Development Report 1997, UNDP, 1997.

(TABLE) CHILDREN'S HEALTH

- **Indicators:** percentage of births attended by health personnel, 1990-96; life expectancy at birth (years), 1996; percentage of low birth-weight babies (2,500 gr), 1990-94; infant mortality rate (per 1,000 live births), 1996; underweight children under-five, percentage, 1990-97; maternal mortality rate (per 100,000 live births), 1990

Source: The State of the World's Children 1998, UNICEF, 1998.

48 LABOUR

Rights in a deregulated world

The nations of the industrialized North are debating ways of reducing the working day in the face of persistent unemployment - but a large number of the world's workers, mainly in the poor countries, have not yet gained access to basic labour rights.

(TABLE) WORKERS IN FIGURES (P 50)

- **Indicators:** labour force (percentage of total population), 1990; percentage of women in labour force, 1996; percentage of the labour force in agriculture, industrial and services sectors, 1990; unemployment rate, 1996.

Sources: Yearbook of Labor Statistics 1997, ILO, 1997; World Development Indicators 1998, World Bank, 1998.

49 DEREGULATION BOX   51 WORKERS' RIGHTS BOX

51 Child labour

All over the world, children continue to work, putting at stake their education, health, their normal development to adulthood, and even their lives.

III. SCIENCE AND TECHNOLOGY

52 SCIENCE AND TECHNOLOGY
The relativity of science

The historical and social relativity of Western science and technology is being increasingly recognized. Even accepting the usual premise that these are the forces behind progress and the well-being of the human race, the possibility that they could also become the instrument of their own destruction is becoming difficult to ignore.

52 INDUSTRIALIZATION
The magic and danger of plastic

Plastic had demonstrated very attractive qualities in the age of technological optimism: adaptability, lightness, flexibility. But with the experience and research of recent years, the undesirable effects are also known: contamination, toxicity, uncontrollable waste and, in packaging, the transference of certain substances to the things contained.

(TABLE) URBAN POPULATION

- **Indicators:** percentage of urban population over total, 1996; rate of annual growth up to the year 2000 (1994).

Sources: UN Population Division, United Nations Web site, 1998; Human Development Report 1997, UNDP, 1997.

56 The car: dream turned nightmare

The desire for greater speed and independence of movement far pre-dates the arrival of the automobile. The invention of the car has granted this wish, but with mass-production, the dream has begun to turn into a nightmare.

57 COMMUNICATIONS

From telephones to satellites

The utopian dream that technology could help people return to a local or clan level of communication, where common problems could be discussed virtually face to face, is still far from reality. Increasingly we realize that these technologies are mere tools and cannot solve human problems.

(TABLE) TELEPHONES

- **Indicator:** main telephone lines per 1,000 people, 1994.

Source: Human Development Report 1997, UNDP, 1997.

60 NUCLEAR ENERGY

Present and future costs

It will take millennia for current levels of toxic nuclear waste to break down naturally, to say nothing of the potential dangers of accidents, leaks and nuclear warfare. This means an inevitable toxic legacy for the generations to come.

61 ACCIDENTS BOX

UP TILL 1986, DEFENDERS OF NUCLEAR ENERGY CLAIMED IT WAS THE MOST BENEVOLENT SOURCE OF ENERGY KNOWN - BOTH CLEAN AND SILENT - AND COMPARED FIGURES OF DEATHS AT WORK IN COAL MINES, OIL WELLS AND DAMS WITH THOSE REGISTERED IN NUCLEAR PLANTS. UNTIL THEN THERE HAD BEEN NO DEATHS IN NUCLEAR PLANTS.

IV. ECONOMICS

62 DEVELOPMENT

The fiction of development

As the millennium draws to a close, the concepts of modernization, progress and development - central to the aims and frustrations of the international community during the 19th and 20th centuries - are increasingly being questioned not only for their cultural assumptions but also in view of the economic system they have fostered.

63 GLOBALIZATION

What is globalization?

Globalization is an euphemism for 'transnationalization' - the unfettered expansion of transnational corporations into the world economy, particularly into the economies of the poor countries. The multilateral organizations such as the World Trade Organization, the IMF and the World Bank are playing a key role in this process.

(TABLE) INTERNATIONAL TRADE

- **Indicators:** exports and imports by country ($ millions), 1996.

Source: World Development Indicators 1998, World Bank, 1998.

66 TRANSNATIONALS

The new international powers

Transnational corporations are the powerful players in the "global village" beyond the frontiers established in previous centuries by the nation-states. Centralization of decision-making, increasing take-overs and mergers allow them to expand geographically in search of lower production costs and bigger markets.

67 INTERNET BOX

(TABLE) THE TOP 100 CORPORATIONS

- **Indicators:** the world's 100 largest corporations, revenues and employees, 1996.

Source: The Global 500, Fortune, 1998.

69 SPECULATIVE ECONOMY

The speculative economy takes control

In recent years 97.5 per cent of international monetary transactions were of a speculative nature, that is, money was exchanged for money. The potential consequences threatened global financial agreements, the sovereignty of nation-states and the futures of millions of people.

73 THE WORLD ACCORDING TO THE WORLD BANK, UNDP AND UNICEF

(TABLE) GROSS NATIONAL PRODUCT

- **Indicator:** countries ranked by Gross National Product (GNP) per capita (US$), 1996.

Source: World Development Indicators 1998, World Bank, 1998.

(TABLE) UNDER-FIVE MORTALITY

- **Indicator:** countries ranked by under-five mortality rate (per 1,000 live births), 1996.

Source: The State of the World's Children 1998, UNICEF, 1998.

(TABLE) HUMAN DEVELOPMENT INDEX

- **Indicator:** countries ranked by Human Development Index (HDI) value, 1994. (The HDI value indicates how far a country has to go to attain certain goals: an average life span of 85 years, access to education for all and a decent income).

Source: Human Development Report 1997, UNDP, 1997.

74 DEBT

The infinite debt spiral

International negotiations to reduce and eliminate Third World debt have only led to increasing exports of capital and further indebtedness of the countries affected (as with sub-Saharan Africa). The wealthy North has established a new form of economic colonialism, a new version of the old "debt bondage".

(TABLE) DEBT IN FIGURES

- **Indicators:** total external debt ($ millions), 1996; debt service as percentage of exports of goods and services, 1996; external debt per capita ($) calculated from total external debt and total population, 1996.

Source: World Development Indicators 1998, World Bank, 1998.

76 AID
Contradictory policies

So-called development aid is just one aspect of the relationship between poor and rich countries. It is closely linked to the policies of international financial organizations, international trade relationships and, increasingly in recent years, the choices of multinational corporations.

(TABLE) **AID IN FIGURES**

- **Indicators:** total net official development assistance (ODA) disbursed, in $ millions and as a percentage of donors' GNP, 1995.

Source: Human Development Report 1997, UNDP, 1997.

(TABLE) **RECIPIENTS**

- **Indicators:** net official development assistance (ODA) received: total in $ millions, per capita $ and as a percentage of receivers' GNP, 1995.

Source: Human Development Report 1997, UNDP, 1997.

V. INTERNATIONAL RELATIONS

78 THE UN
Taken by the great powers

The United Nations organization is over 50 years old, but still has not proved entirely effective as a moderating agency in international relations. Its faults and fiascos are shared by the global community it is a part of, and particularly of its most influential members.

78 Restructure and Budget

79 REFUGEES
Victims of human catastrophes

The words "globalization" and "liberalization", fashionable in late-20th century political speeches, do not appear remotely related to the situation of tens of millions of refugees, who are subject to ever tougher restrictions in their attempts to achieve the most basic right to life and peace.

THE COUNTRIES MOST AFFECTED BY THE CURRENTS OF ENFORCED MIGRATION ARE, IN TURN, THE POOREST IN THE WORLD. THE TWENTY NATIONS WITH THE HIGHEST PROPORTION OF REFUGEES HAVE PER CAPITA INCOME OF NO MORE THAN $700 PER YEAR.

80 ARMS
The expansion of NATO

The end of the Cold War in the 1990s did not bring with it the end of NATO, despite its founding principles. For the United States and its main Western partners, NATO's military structures were still the best way to group and, above all, control the allies.

81 ARMS CONTROL BOX   81 NATO AND THE ENVIRONMENT

(TABLE) **ARMS IN FIGURES**

- **Indicators:** defence expenditure as a percentage of GDP, 1995; imports of conventional weapons ($ millions, 1990 prices), 1995.

Source: Human Development Report 1997, UNDP, 1997.

Countries

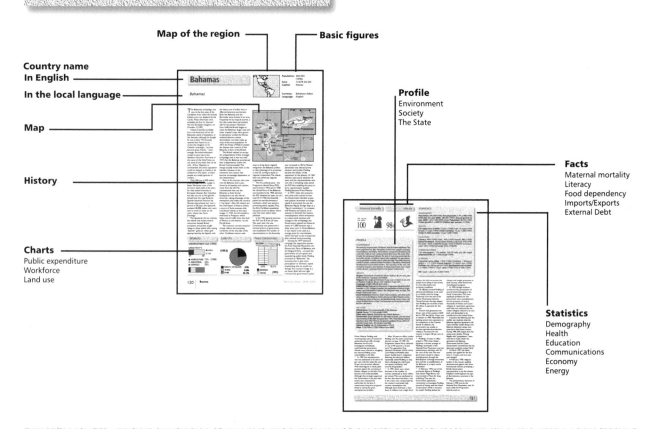

Map of the region ———

Basic figures ———

Country name
In English ———

In the local language ———

Map ———

History ———

Charts
Public expenditure
Workforce
Land use

Profile
Environment
Society
The State

Facts
Maternal mortality
Literacy
Food dependency
Imports/Exports
External Debt

Statistics
Demography
Health
Education
Communications
Economy
Energy

PROFILE

ENVIRONMENT

Estimates of area are based on UN official estimates according to internationally recognized borders; these include inland waters but not territorial ocean waters. Except where otherwise specified, territories claimed by certain countries but not under their effective jurisdiction are not taken into account, though this implies no judgment as to the validity of the claims. Geographical descriptions and data on environmental problems are based on the sources listed in the general bibliography at the end of this Guide.

SOCIETY

Peoples, Languages and Religions: Very few countries keep official ethnic and religious data, and UN-related institutions definitely do not do so. The ethnic and religious make-up of a society is a historical-cultural factor which is in constant change. Certain forces promote tribal or ethnic divisions to favour their own plans of domination, while others favour whatever makes for integration and national unity. In many countries the political and social problems cannot be grasped without reference to these factors. When including them here, we have sought to consult the most reliable sources (mentioned in the general bibliography) and to avoid the racist connotations often associated with such information.

Political parties and Social movements: It is practically impossible to make a complete listing of all parties and other movements of any country, since they are permanently changing and in most cases would add up to several hundred names. Thus only major organizations are mentioned, even though 'major' is subjective when votes, parliamentary representation or number of members cannot be verified, where parties are outlawed or the right to associate is restricted.

THE STATE

Official Name: Complete name of the state in the official language.

Administrative divisions, the capital and other cities: Population figures are for the most recent available year. The legal limits of a city frequently do not match its real borders. Thus the information may refer only to the core area, which is a minor part of the whole city.

Government: Names of the major authorities and institutional bodies as of June 1998.

National Holiday: When more than one holiday is commemorated, Independence Day (if it is a holiday) is indicated.

Armed Forces and Others: The total number of personnel for the year indicated. 'Other' forces are those trained and equipped beyond the level of a Police Force (though some fulfill this role) and whose constitution and control means they can be used as regular troops. The source used is the most reliable available on military statistics, but the data is based on government information which is not always explicit as to the total number of troops and military expenditure.

PUBLIC EXPENDITURE

Government expenditure: Percentage of total social and defence expenditure (1995). **The military expenditure** figure is given as a percentage of health and education expenditure (1990-91).

Sources: b, i.

PUBLIC EXPENDITURE

16.8% 58%
1995 ■ DEFENCE □ SOCIAL

In **1990/91** Military as % of health
& education expenditure was 24%.

WORKERS

WORKERS

The male and female labour force, excluding care-givers at home and other unpaid workers (1996), and by activity sector (agriculture, industry and services, 1990). **Unemployment rate** (1996).

Sources: b, f, g.

UNEMPLOYMENT 6.1% (1996)

Labour force %

■ WOMEN
□ MEN

44   56

■ AGRICULTURE 10% (1990)
□ INDUSTRIAL   25%
■ SERVICES   65%

LAND USE

LAND USE RATE:

Forest and **woodland** as percentage of land area (1993).

Arable land as percentage of land area (1993).

Irrigated area as percentage of arable land area (1993). **Annual rate of deforestation** (1981-90).

Source: b.

DEFORESTATION -0.7 % annual (81/90)
IRRIGATED 1.6 % of arable

(1993)

■ FOREST & WOODLAND 49.5%
□ ARABLE   4.6%
■ OTHER   45.9%

HISTORY

1. A range of sources has been used to update the texts on each country. In many cases this meant checking with local sources and contributors, documentation centers linked to electronic mail networks and grass-roots organizations throughout the world. This input went into our database in Montevideo, where the final editing was done.

2. Efforts were made to avoid the most frequent bias of Western reference books, such as to appearing to make history start with the arrival of the Europeans (particularly in the case of African and Latin American countries) or ignoring the role of women.

3. The last overall updating of the database before printing was done in June 1998, but in several cases events as late as August were included.

STATISTICS

DEMOGRAPHY

Population: Total population, according to 1996 United Nations Population Division. In a few cases, where the UN does not supply a figure, other sources have been used.

Source: a.

Annual growth: Average annual rate of population growth during the period 1980/1996.

Source: c.

Estimates for the year 2000: The population projections for the year 2000 are calculations based on current data on population, rates of growth, and trends of these rates to increase or decrease (1994-2000).

Source: b.

Annual growth to year 2000: Average annual rate of population growth during the period 1994/2000.

Source: b.

Urban population: Percentage of total population living in urban areas (1996). Figures are to be treated with care since definitions of «urban zones» differ from country to country.

Source: a.

Urban Growth: Average rate of annual growth of the urban population in the period 1980-1995.

Source: i.

Children per woman: Total fertility rate - the number of children that would be born per woman were she to live to the end of her child-bearing years and bear children at each age in accordance with prevailing age-specific fertility rates (1996).

Source: c.

HEALTH

Life expectancy at birth: The number of years a newborn infant, male or female, would live if prevailing patterns of mortality at the time of birth were to stay the same throughout child's life (1994, 1996).

Source: b, c.

Infant mortality: The annual number of deaths of infants under one year of age per 1,000 live births (1996).

Source: c.

Under-5 child mortality: Number of children dying between birth and exactly five years of age per 1,000 live births (1996).

Source: c.

Calorie supply: Daily per capita calorie supply as a percentage of the minimum requirement (1988/90). Shown as a national average, though a country's income distribution may create a wide gap between the average, the highest and the lowest strata. Minimum calorie requirements vary in different countries, depending on climate and nature of the main activities.

Source: d.

People per doctor: Traditional medicine and community health care practised by health personnel who are not officially recognized are not included in these statistics, although these may be the only health service available for the majority of the population in many countries.

Source: b.

Safe water: The United Nations includes the percentage of population with "reasonable" access to safe water sources. These include treated surface water and untreated but uncontaminated water from springs, wells and protected boreholes in the 'reasonably safe' water category (1990-96).

Source: c.

EDUCATION

Literacy: Indicates the estimated percentage of people, male or female, over the age of fifteen who can read and write (1995).

Source: c.

CONTINUES ON NEXT PAGE

School enrolment: Gross enrolment ratio by level of education. Number of people, male or female, enrolled in a schooling level (primary, secondary or tertiary), regardless of age, divided by the population of the age group officially corresponding to that level (1990/95).

Sources: c, g.

Primary school teachers: Primary school teachers/students ratio (students per teacher, 1995).

Source: g.

COMMUNICATIONS

Mass media: Estimate of the number of copies of daily newspapers per 1,000 people, and the number of radios and TVs per 1,000 people. The latter figure may rely on the number of licences granted or the number of radios and TVs declared (1994).

Source: b.

Telephones: Number of main telephone lines per 1,000 people (1994).

Source: b.

Books: Number of new titles published per 100,000 people (1992-94).

Source: b.

ECONOMY

Per capita GNP: GDP (Gross Domestic Product) is the value of the total production of goods and services of a country's economy within the national territory. GNP (Gross National Product) is GDP plus the income received from abroad by residents in the country (such as remittances from migrant workers and income from investments abroad), minus income obtained in the domestic economy which goes abroad (such as profits remitted by foreign companies). The data is calculated in local currencies. Converting them into US dollars (or into any other currency) may lead to distortions. For example, if a country devalues its currency, conversion into US dollars would seem to cut its GDP or GNP while actual production was not reduced. The World Bank corrects such distortions by calculating per capita GNP on the basis of the purchasing power of the local currency and converting it into US dollar purchasing power, and this is the figure used in The World Guide 1999/2000.

Source: g.

Annual growth of GNP: Average annual growth in per capita GNP during the period 1995-1996.

Source: g.

Annual inflation: Average annual inflation rate calculated in the national currency for each year of the period 1985-1995.

Source: i.

Consumer price index: Variation in 1994 in relation to base year (1990 = 100).

Source: e.

Currency: Name and exchange rate in relation to US dollar in 1995.

Source: e.

Cereal imports:

The cereals are wheat, flour, rice, unprocessed grains and the cereal components of combined foods. This figure includes cereals donated by other countries, and those distributed by international agencies (1994).

Source: h.

Food import dependency:

Imported food in relation to the food available for internal distribution (the total of food production, plus food imports, minus food exports), for 1994.

Source: b.

Fertilizer use: Refers to purchases of nitrate, potassium and phosphate based fertilizers used on arable land (1994).

Source: h.

Exports and Imports: Annual value in US dollars f.o.b. (free on board) for exports and c.i.f. (costs, insurance and freight) for imports (1996).

Source: g.

External debt (total and per capita): Public state guaranteed and private foreign debt accumulated by 1996. Per capita debt was calculated from total 1996 external debt and total 1996 population.

Sources: a, g.

Debt service: The service of a foreign debt is the sum of interest payments and repayment of principal (capital loaned, regardless of yield). The relation between debt service and exports of goods and services is a practical measurement commonly used to evaluate capacity to pay the debt or obtain new credits. These coefficients do not include private foreign debts without state guarantees - a considerable amount in some countries (1996).

Source: g.

Development aid received: Official development assistance (ODA) consists of money flows from official governmental or international institutions for the purpose of promoting economic development or social welfare in developing countries. These funds are supplied in the form of grants or soft' loans, i.e. long-maturity loans at interest rates lower than those prevailing on the international market. We included the total and per capita net ODA received in dollars (1995) and as a percentage of 1994 recipient country's GNP.

Source: b.

ENERGY

These statistics refer only to commercial energy, and do not include for example energy produced by rural people in poor countries (mainly firewood). Energy consumption of the country is measured in kilograms of 'oil-equivalent' per capita. Energy imports are given as a percentage of energy consumption. Figures are negative in those countries that are net exporters of energy products (1994).

Source: i.

Human Development Index (HDI) Since 1990 the United Nations Development Programme (UNDP) has presented the HDI to capture as many aspects of human development as possible in one simple composite index. It is an index of achievements in basic human potential in three fundamental dimensions: a long and healthy life, knowledge, and a decent standard of living. Three variables have been chosen to represent these three dimensions: life expectancy, educational attainment and income.

Source: b.

SOURCES

a) Population Division, Web site, United Nations, 1998.

b) Human Development Report 1997, UNDP, 1997.

c) The State of the World's Children 1998, UNICEF, 1998.

d) The State of the World's Children 1997, UNICEF, 1997.

e) Statistical Yearbook 41st issue, CD-ROM, United Nations, 1997.

f) Yearbook of Labour Statistics 1997, ILO, 1997.

g) World Development Indicators 1998, World Bank, 1998

h) World Development Indicators 1997, CD-ROM, World Bank, 1997.

i) World Development Report 1997, World Bank, 1997.

Index to countries

Index to Special Boxes

PREFACE

One day, powerful Mongolian king Tamerlane invited the wise Hodja to his palace for dinner. The royal chef prepared, among others, a cabbage recipe for the occasion.

After the dinner, Tamerlane asked,
- How did you like the cabbage?
- It was very delicious, complimented Hodja.
- I thought it tasted awful, said Tamerlane.
- You're right, added Hodja, it was very bland.
- But you just said it tasted delicious, Tamerlane noted.
- Yes, but I'm the servant of His Majesty, not of the cabbage, he replied.

Almost a millennium has gone by since this episode happened (or is supposed to have happened). People still look for advice and opinion, not only asking old wise persons, but now also querying reference books, encyclopedias and the Internet. Few of these sources are as honest as Hodja in admitting whose servant they are and whose opinions they express, and would rather claim "objectivity". Yet, while we can avoid the use of adjectives and not state our opinions in every paragraph, the very selection of what to speak about is not value-free.

Instead of expressing the likes and dislikes of those in power, the World Guide has chosen since its first edition in 1979 to be the servant of the poor, the discriminated, the neglected. Those majorities that, at the times when the French revolution exploded, lacked any privilege and were called "tiers état" and later, by analogy, "third world".

The World Guide is the only major reference work of its kind whose editorial and research team is entirely based in a Southern country (Uruguay), hosted by the Third World Institute. In this "kitchen" the editorial and research team works as a demanding chef with original information coming from its own correspondents. Other major "ingredients" are the daily reports of Third World Network (the most influential Southern international advocacy group), the news generated by the cooperative news agency Inter Press Service, and the input of dozens of citizen groups around the world that form the Social Watch monitoring system of social development and the advancement of women.

The "secret recipe" is to process those components in a way that does not overwhelm the reader with unnecessary data but helps her or him to understand the trends as they evolve. For those who just can't wait another two years to have the information updated with a new edition of the book, the World Guide is now being updated on-line in Spanish over the Internet. Tamerlane would have loved it. News took weeks to reach him from the corners of his huge empire. And, who knows, maybe a source that didn't hide unpleasant information from his eyes would have been even more useful.

Roberto Bissio
EDITOR-IN-CHIEF

THE WORLD GUIDE 1999/2000
A VIEW FROM THE SOUTH

By Instituto del Tercer Mundo

Editor-in-Chief: Roberto Bissio.

Managing Editor: Víctor Bacchetta.

Co-editor: Daniel Martínez.

Research and editing: Amir Hamed, Javier Lyonnet, Marcelo Falca, María Isabel Sans, Santiago Gilles and Mario Maciel.

Contributors: Jorge Barreiro, Levan Butkhuzi, Mariana Cabrera, Ricardo Carrere, Ricardo Cayssials, Roberto Elissalde, Mariela Farías, Alina González, Alvaro González, Alexander Krylov, Martha Long, Simone Lovera, Gustavo Nagy, Andrew Nette, Katerina Oridjanska, Chakravarthi Raghavan, Mikhail Roshchin, Susana Rostagnol, Luis Sabini and Alexandre Sokolov.

Statistics: Daniel Macadar and Roberto Volfovics.

Translators: Alvaro Queiruga, Sarah Mason, Beatriz Sosa Martínez and Raquel Nuñez.

Graphic Designer: Mario Burgueño.

Information and communication technologies: Mauricio León, Pablo Alsina and Red Telemática Chasque.

Marketing: Hersilia Fonseca.

Administration: Rosario Lema, Walter Sena and Elizabeth Díaz Borra.

By New Internationalist Publications Ltd (English language edition)

Editor: Troth Wells.

Production: F Harvey, A Kokotka and I Nixon.

Marketing & Distribution: Dexter Tiranti, Jo Lateu.

This book is the result of documentation, research, writing, editing and design work done by the Instituto del Tercer Mundo (Third World Institute), a non-profit institution, devoted to information, communication and education, based in Montevideo, Uruguay.

The World Guide 1999/2000 is an updated, corrected and expanded edition of the World Guide 1997/98. This reference book was published for the first time in Mexico in 1979, on the initiative of Neiva Moreira, to complement the dissemination work of the Third World magazine he had begun publishing. In 1980 the first Portuguese version of the Guide was published. The first English version was published in 1984. New Internationalist Publications Ltd, in Oxford, has been in charge of the English version and its distribution among English-speaking countries since 1996. In 1999 SERMIS-EMI (Editrice Missionaria Italiana), from Bologna, launched the Italian version of the World Guide. Since 1992, the World Guide has been published on CD-ROM. Since 1997, through the Internet and together with its updating service, Guía de la Semana, the Spanish version of the World Guide has been available in Web Pages.

The World Guide is a cumulative work, building on the efforts of former staff members. We would like to mention the contributions of: Mohiuddin Ahmad, Claude Alvares, Iván Alves, Juan José Argeriz, Maria Teresa Armas, Marcos Arruda, Iqbal Asaria, Gonzalo Abella, Susana de Avila, Edouard Balby, Artur Baptista, Roberto Bardini, Luis Barrios, Alicia Bidegaray, Beatriz Bissio, Ricardo de Bittencourt, Samuel Blixen, Gerardo Bocco, José Bottaro, José Cabral, Luis Caldera, Juan Cammá, Altair Campos, Paulo Cannabrava Filho, Carmen Canoura, Cristina Canoura, Gerónimo Cardozo, Diana Cariboni, Gustavo Carrier, Virgilio Caturra, Macário Costa, Carlos María Domínguez, Wáshington Estellano, Marta Etcheverrigaray, Carlos Fabião, Marcelo Falca, Helena Falcão, Wilson Fernández, Alejandro Flores, Lidia Freitas, Sonia Freitas, Marc Fried, Héctor García, José Carlos Gondim, Mario Handler, David Hathaway, Ann Heidenreich, Bill Hinchberger, Etevaldo Hipólito, Heraclio Labandera, Peter Lenny, Cecilia Lombardo, Linda Llosa, Geoffrey Lloyd Gilbert, Fernando López, Hakan Lundgren, Pablo Mazzini, Daniel Mazzone, Carol Milk, João Murteira, Abdul Naffey, Claudia Neiva, Ruben Olivera, Hattie Ortega, Pablo Piacentini, Ana Pérez, Christopher Peterson, Virginia Piera, Carlos Pinto Santos, Sieni C. Platino, Artur José Poerner, Graciela Pujol, Roberto Raposo, Felisberto Reigado, Maria da Gloria Rodrigues, Julio Rosiello, Ash Narain Roy, Ana Sadetzky, Alexandru Savulescu, John Sayer, Dieter Schonebohm, Irene Selser, Eunice H. Senna, Baptista da Silva, Yesse Jane V. de Souza, José Steinleger, Firiel Suijker, Carolina Trujillo, Pedro Velozo, Horacio Verbitsky, Amelia Villaverde, Anatoli Voronov and Asa Zatz.

We have received the help, encouragement and support of Carlos Abín, Carlos Afonso, Cedric Belfrage, Max van den Berg, Dirk-Jan Broertjes, Alberto Brusa, Anne-Pieter van Dijk, Rodrigo Egaña, Cecilia Ferraría, Goran Hammer, Mohammed Idris, Sytse Kujik, Arne Lindquist, Carlos Mañosa, Fernando Molina, Hans Poelgrom, Malva Rodríguez, John Schlanger, Gregorio Selser, Herbet de Souza, Sjef Theunis and Germán Wettstein. Leo van Grunsven gave us editorial suggestions, together with his confidence in the project.

The editorial staff acknowledges the valuable contributions made by the libraries of the following institutions: UNDE, UNESCO, CLASH, FE, the UN Information Center in Montevideo, Impala in Madrid and the UNCLAD in Geneva.

The Third World Network, Penang, Malaysia provided ideas, documents and links with many contributors.

To all of them we offer our thanks. Thanks are also due to the hundreds of readers who have given us their comments, suggestions and detailed information.

The judgements and values contained in this book are the exclusive responsibility of the editors and do not represent the opinion of any of the people or institutions listed, except for the Third World Institute.

Instituto del Tercer Mundo
Juan D. Jackson 1136, Montevideo 11200, Uruguay
Phone: 598 2 4096192; Fax: 598 2 401 9222.
E-mail: item@chasque.apc.org.
Website: http://www.item.org.uy/

New Internationalist Publications Ltd
55 Rectory Road, Oxford OX4 1BW, United Kingdom
Tel: (44) 01865 728181; Fax: (44) 01865 793152
E-mail: newint@newint.org
Website: http://www.newint.org/

© Copyright 1999 by Instituto del Tercer Mundo

New Internationalist Publications Ltd has an exclusive licence to publish and distribute the English language print editions of The World Guide throughout the world.

Third World Guide (English language edition) 1984, 1985, 1986, 1988, 1990 and 1992.
The World Guide (English language edition) 1995, 1997 and 1999.

No part of this book may be stored, reproduced, photocopied or transmitted in any form, by any means, electronic or mechanical including photocopying, recording or as information on storage and retrieval systems without prior consent from either New Internationalist Publications Ltd or the Instituto del Tercer Mundo. Both publishers are keen to facilitate the use of this material by non-profit institutions of the South and educational institutions.

INSTITUTO DEL TERCER MUNDO

Global Issues

An overview
of the
20th Century

The destruction of life

The planet's biological resources or "biodiversity", which also refers to their historical, geographical and cultural sustenance, have this century suffered accelerated destruction. International summits and negotiations have sought to establish a new regulatory framework. However, as any positive outcome is still out of sight, local communities have become the direct defenders of biodiversity, thereby also defending their identities

The term "biodiversity" appeared in the North in the 1960s, at a time when some governments and civil society started to become concerned about the rapid disappearance of species. The economic interests of the big biotechnology companies also played their part in this interest in the fate of the species.

However, one important fact particularly marks our century: the will of nation-states to dispose of the components of biodiversity as they please, calling them "wealth", or "lands" or "dominions". This was one of the main motives behind 19th century European expansion in Africa, of the US extending its dominion over formerly indigenous lands in the West and the behaviour of post-colonial governments in South America.

The definition of biodiversity has deep political and economic implications. The interests of governments and communities are in play along with those of powerful industries, like the pharmaceutical, food and agro-chemical sectors.

The ill-defined use of concepts such as natural, biological or genetic resources, when referring to biodiversity have done little to clarify the issue. Therefore, it is worthwhile differentiating them. We will take "biological resources" to cover the group of known or yet to be discovered living beings, used by or which may possibly be used by human societies.

Silvia Rodrguez, researcher at the National University of Costa Rica said these include "organic resources" like wild or domesticated plants and animals used directly for their qualities as a whole - as

with rice used as food; "biochemical resources" such as organisms useful for their molecular information or their active components for the development of synthetic materials - for example, a plant which provides a substance of pharmaceutical use; and "genetic resources", used for conventional improvement of crops and domestic animals by crossing and selection or for biotechnological manipulation, as is the case with any plant containing a gene of particular interest.

Meanwhile, the "official" definition of biodiversity (contained in the text of the Biodiversity Convention signed in Rio de Janeiro, Brazil in 1992) concentrates on resources reproduced in the wild, their potential use and genetic properties. It also includes a territorial dimension, as it refers to land and maritime ecosystems. However it fails to consider any cultural dimension.

A useful tool for vindicating the rights of the peoples - as much in the North as in the South - could be gained by emphasizing the territorial, dynamic and cultural nature of biodiversity.

Biological wealth and poverty

Factors like the time needed for natural processes, environmental stability, spatial heterogeneity, competition and predation amongst species have determined that the South possesses the greater part of the world's biological and geographical diversity. The so-called "countries with rich biodiversity" - Brazil, Colombia, Mexico, Madagascar and Malaysia - are all found here.

Furthermore, there is another, less-publicized kind of biodiversity: - agricultural biodiversity, the product of millennia of natural and cultural co-evolution. Some 90 per cent of the supply of calories for the world population depends on the 20 most widespread crops. As with wild biodiversity, it is in the South that humanity's treasury of agricultural resources lie.

After World War II, the "Green Revolution" raised hopes of a world without hunger. However, the fact that the main cause of hunger is usually political and not related to the technology of agriculture was overlooked. The initially promising "high-yield varieties" rapidly reached their highest yield, bringing declining returns thereafter.

The standardization of crops and techniques brought about by the Green Revolution caused an impoverishment of agricultural biodiversity, which affected both North and South. "In the United States for example, only 3 per cent of the total vegetable varieties registered by the Ministry of Agriculture in 1900 survive today", said US vice-president Al Gore in his book *Earth in the Balance*.

The Indian researcher Vandana Shiva points out that out of the more than 30,000 native varieties of rice cultivated in India at the beginning of the 19th only 50 remain, of which barely 10 would be used in three-quarters of the paddy fields of the nation in a few years' time. "Genetic erosion" has been a rapid process.

The "countries with poor biodiversity" - paradoxically those which dominate world trade and industry - today continue to look to the genetic wealth of the remote mountains of the Andes, the dry plains of the Middle East and fertile valleys of India in search of the resistant genotype which will save their crops from the threat of pests, or the carrier of a gene with a desired characteristic. It is the Southern countries which have made the greatest contributions of reproductive material to the germplasm banks kept in the International Agricultural Research Centres.

Cultural biodiversity

"Cultural biodiversity" is the most neglected aspect of the issue even though it is of fundamental importance. Practically the entire world is inhabited by people. The regions thought of as "natural" are in reality areas modified to a greater or lesser degree by human societies. From the coastline of the seas and oceans, the fertile valleys suitable for human settlement, to the inhospitable deserts of sand or ice.

Sometimes humans are represented as naturally predatory - without considering their cultures, territories and particular histories. However, neither a large part of wild biodiversity nor the total of agricultural biodiversity can be explained without taking into account and valuing human intervention. The conservationist forestry practised by rural and indigenous communities in Latin America is an example of this.

Victor Toledo, Mexican ethno-ecologist, mentioned examples from Brazil, Bolivia, Peru, Mexico, Costa Rica and Honduras. In addition there have been experiments in the Chaco forest of Argentina and equatorial Amazonia. The expulsions of indigenous populations from areas declared National Parks, which have taken place for example in Brazil, Kenya and Thailand, do not conserve biodiversity as these displaced people were usually the force maintaining the ecological balance.

Traditional farming methods, for example the framing of corn and chinapopo beans in Honduras, have contributed greatly to agricultural biodiversity and the growth and stockpiling of agricultural resources.

End of century perspectives

Genetic engineering - the main branch of modern biotechnology - is especially relevant amongst the threats to biodiversity. The biotechnological revolution, a part of the scientific-technical revolution which is producing accelerated changes in our lives, appears destined to replace the Green Revolution. But its consequences are uncertain and appear to be, for the most part, harmful.

As the German sociologist Elmer Rompczky explained, the situation is compounded by the concentration of biotechnological research in the hands of powerful transnational consortia, the accidental dissemination of pathogenic material produced by genetic manipulation in natural environments, the uncontrolled multiplication of genetically manipulated organisms and the possible military implications of this technology.

Even if biotechnology is supplied by traditionally-maintained genetic diversity this does not necessarily mean it can support it. Its aim is not to broaden the genetic base of crops and livestock but simply to isolate and make use of a few genes with determined characteristics.

At the level of wild biodiversity, one important threat can be seen in how the current system of international aid and credit supports destructive activities. The replacing of natural forests with monoculture forestry plantations - promoted by the Food and Agriculture Organization (FAO) - are a prime example of this. Thus, Thailand, which lost nearly 80 per cent of its forests this century, is starting a reforestation plan to increase its "forestry cover", a plan which, paradoxically, does not aim to regenerate its natural forest ecosystems, but to cover the country with mainly eucalyptus plantations.

The increasing tendency to privatize biodiversity resources both wild and agricultural is another threat. Agrochemical and food transnationals, for example, benefit hugely from the patenting of new plant varieties.

It is worth remembering that no biodiversity is divorced from its cultural, historical or geographical context. Hence the importance of territorial claims. Genetic biodiversity and that of the species requires diversity of ecosystems - that is, of territory - in which to develop.

It is fundamental then to listen and support the territorial claims of the indigenous and rural communities who have proven, in the vast majority of cases throughout history, their capacity to manage territory without destroying it, maintaining and increasing its biodiversity. The claims of the Iban in Sarawak (Malaysia), the Tupinikim of Espiritu Santo (Brazil) and the Kolla in Salta (Argentina) constitute examples of these battles at the end of the 20th century.

In parallel, it would be worth rescuing experiences of sustainable use of wild - both on land and at sea - and agricultural biodiversity. Cases like the domestication of wild mammals in the Puyo region of Ecuador, the management of estuary and coastal waters by the fisherfolk of the tropical forests, or even the example of the so-called "analogue forestry" (a kind of forestry that imitates nature) in Sri Lanka.

These issues need to be reconsidered by the world scientific community, especially the biological disciplines and geosciences directly linked to the biodiversity issue.

Source: World Rainforest Movement (WRM)

Map of the genetic diversity centers based on those identified by VI Vavilov. It shows the main diversity sources and centers of the 20 most disseminated crops which account for around 90 per cent of world food provision (in calorie supply).

MEDITERRANEAN
Oats
Rape

SOUTHWEST ASIA
Rye
Barley
Wheat
Pea

CENTRAL AMERICA
Maize
Bean
Sweet potato

CHINA
Millet
Soybean
Rice

ANDES
Potato
Lima bean
Peanut

SOUTHEAST ASIA
Banana
Sugar cane
Yam
Rice

ABYSSINIA
(Region of Ethiopia, Eritrea and Djibouti)
Barley
Sorghum
Millet

HINDU MYANMAR
Rice
Dwarf wheat

SOUTHERN BRAZIL-PARAGUAY
Manioc
(Cassava)

CENTRAL ASIA
Wheat

Deforestation

The underlying causes

Forests are one of the most valuable eco-systems in the world, containing over 60 per cent of the world's biodiversity. This biodiversity has multiple social and economic values, apart from its intrinsic value, varying from the important ecological functions of forests in terms of soil and watershed protection to the economic value of the numerous products which can be extracted from the forest

For many indigenous and other forest-dependent peoples, forests are their livelihood. They provide them with edible and medicinal plants, bushmeat, fruits, honey, shelter, firewood and many other goods, as well as with cultural and spiritual values. On a global scale, all forests play a crucial role in climate regulation and constitute one of the major carbon sinks on earth, their survival thus preventing an increase in the greenhouse effect.

Forests have already disappeared in many parts of the world and deforestation rates worldwide during the 1980s were as high as 15 million hectares per year for tropical forests alone. In most parts of the world deforestation accelerated during the 1990s. It should be noted in this respect that deforestation rates tend to be obscured by the fact that there is no clear definition of forests. The latest definition given by the UN Food and Agriculture Organization (FAO), formally the main body responsible for forests within the UN system, is so broad that most green urban areas can be considered major forest eco-systems. Thus, the replacement of valuable primary forest eco-systems by monoculture plantations - of in many cases, an alien species such as eucalyptus or pine - or by biologically-poor forests, is seldom taken into account. Europe, for example, lost most of its primary forests during the 19th century. Yet, the latest FAO reports state enthusiastically that there is an increase of boreal and temperate forests in this region. A substantial part of these "forests" are biologically-poor production forests, lacking undergrowth, original soil biodiversity, and most original bird, mammal and reptile species. They are in fact more akin to monoculture plantations than to true forests.

The direct causes of deforestation

The most important direct causes of deforestation include logging, the conversion of forested lands for agriculture and cattle-raising, urbanization, mining and oil exploitation, acid rain and fire. However, there has been a tendency of highlighting small-scale migratory farmers or "poverty" as the major cause of forest loss. Such farmers tend to settle along roads through the forest, to clear a patch of land and to use it for growing subsistence or cash crops. In tropical forests, such practices tend to lead to rapid soil degradation as most soils are too poor to sustain agriculture. Consequently, the farmer is forced to clear another patch of forest after a few years. The degraded agricultural land is often used for a few years more for cattle raising. This is a death sentence for the soil, as cattle remove the last scarce traces of fertility. The result is an entirely degraded piece of land which will be unable to recover its original biomass for many years. It is a major mistake to think that such unsustainable agricultural practices only take place in tropical countries. Many parts of North America and western Europe have become deforested due to unsustainable agriculture, leading to severe soil degradation and in many cases abandonment of the area by the farmers.

In other countries, clearcut logging practices have been the main reason for forest loss. In the early 1990s, Canada and Malaysia were famous examples of countries where logging companies ruthlessly cleared mile upon mile of precious primary forests. Here too, the historical perspective should not be overlooked. Countries like Ireland and Scotland used to be almost entirely forested, but were nearly completely cleared under British rule to provide timber for English shipbuilders. Today, logging still forms the most important direct threat to forests in regions like the Guianan shield (stable area of low relief in the Earth's crust), Central Africa, East Siberia and British Columbia.

The underlying causes

During the last few decades, the forest crisis has prompted many international, regional and national preservation initiatives, yet many have had little success. There is general agreement that this is due to the fact that these strategies were too focused on the immediate causes of deforestation, and neglected the underlying causes which are multiple and interrelated. In some cases they are related to major international economic phenomena, such as macro-economic strategies which provide a strong incentive for short-term profit-making instead of long-term sustainability. Also important are deep-rooted social structures, which result in inequalities in land tenure, discrimination against indigenous peoples, subsistence farmers and poor people in general. In other cases they include political factors such as the lack of participatory democracy, the influence of the military and the exploitation of rural areas by urban elites. Overconsumption by consumers in high-income countries constitutes another of the major underlying causes of deforestation, while in some regions uncontrolled industrialization is at the heart of forest degradation with widespread pollution resulting in acid rain.

The causes of deforestation are many and varied, and it is impossible to cover them all. However some examples can show how these causes are closely interrelated one to each other.

The forces behind unsustainable agriculture

According to the FAO, 90 per cent of deforestation is caused by unsustainable agricultural practices, while logging and plantation forestry play a greater role in forest degradation. However debatable these figures may be, unsustainable agriculture is undoubtedly one of the major direct causes of deforestation and forest degradation in many countries of the world. A simplistic approach to the problem would imply blaming the "ignorance" of the farmers involved in this process. The process is however more complex. Few people actually decide that they want to leave their native land, go to the forest, cut it and convert it into agricultural land. They are driven to such actions by national and international forces with interests different to theirs. In some countries, forests act as safety-valves to avoid social uprisings, in the following way. The concentration of power and land in few hands results in large groups of dispossessed people, which may lead to confrontation. To avoid conflict, some of these people are offered free land within the forests. Access to forests is made possible through government-promoted road projects, either built to open up and "develop" the forests or resulting from the commercial activities of logging, mining, and energy generation. In the above example, it is clear that deforestation can take place only because a number of government policies - social and economic - indirectly promote it. Whilst the poor may operate the chainsaws or set the forest on fire, it is mostly governments and corporations who are behind such actions.

Far-reaching consequences of globalization

In other cases, forests are opened up for modern large-scale agriculture or cattle-raising aimed at the export market. For example, forests have been converted for cattle in Central America, for soy bean production in Brazil and for pulpwood in Indonesia. In the first case, the process originated in the explosive development of a fast food - hamburger - market in the US which required vast amounts of low-quality cheap meat which could be produced in nearby tropical countries. The result was widespread deforestation in Central America. Subsidized and highly intensive meat production in Europe requires an ever-increasing supply of grains to feed livestock. Soy bean is one of the major inputs for such production and enormous patches of forest have been opened up in Brazil - and in many other Southern countries - to ensure the economic sustainability of that sector through the supply of cheap grain. A similar situation occurs with paper: the continued growth of paper consumption, particularly in high income countries, depends on the availability of cheap wood or pulp to feed the paper mills. Forests are thus being cleared in Indonesia - and many other parts of the world - to give way to eucalyptus plantations aimed at supplying that market with increasing amounts of cheap raw material.

In the above cases, it is clear that the production of hamburgers in the US, of meat in Europe and of paper in high-income countries are a contributory cause of deforestation in Central America, Brazil and Indonesia.

Land tenure policies and inequalities

It should be emphasized that it is seldom the production of food for the poor which causes deforestation, as the largest areas of forests converted to other uses are currently being dedicated to the production of cash crops and cattle. These products, which vary from coffee and beef to coca and soy bean, are in many cases almost exclusively produced for export markets in OECD countries. It is absurd to defend the production of these goods with arguments about food security, as some governments and international institutions (including the FAO) do, since Northern countries have excessively high levels of consumption.

Under the current free-trade oriented ideology, the standard solution of institutions like the International Monetary Fund for these problems is increasing exports, instead of decreasing imports. Meanwhile, it is the import of luxury goods for the wealthy, as well as weapons, which often lie at the roots of trade balance and balance of payments distortions, both in industrialized and in low income countries. One of the major contributory factors in deforestation is the failure of macro-economic bodies like the Bretton Woods Institutions to recognize this relationship between consumption patterns and macro-economic problems.

A global problem with many actors

Deforestation and forest degradation occurs both in Northern and Southern countries and its underlying causes also originate in both, although with varying degrees of responsibility. Industrialized countries have not only cut down or degraded their own forests in the past; many are still doing so today. This occurs either through large-scale clear-cutting - as in many areas of Canada, the US or Australia - or through the thinning and therefore degradation of forests, reducing them to a few commercially valuable species at the expense of biodiversity - such as in Sweden, France or Finland. At the same time, problems resulting from industrialization - such as acid rain - are having a strong impact. In the South, some forests are being clear-felled - mostly for unsustainable export-oriented agriculture, tree and oil-palm plantations and cattle - or are being degraded as a result of the selective logging of the more commercial species - such as mahogany.

Some underlying causes originate within the country while others can be found outside national boundaries. In this latter situation, the main responsibility usually lies in the North. Macro-economic policies imposed on the South through a number of mechanisms can also contribute to deforestation. One of the more obvious results of such policies has been the increasing incorporation of Southern agricultural exports to markets in Northern countries, usually at the expense of forests. The same macro-economic policies have resulted in the concentration of wealth in the North which, coupled with strong incentives to consumerism, have created unsustainable consumption patterns which have a strong impact particularly - though not exclusively - on Southern forests.

Southern governments and elites also hold responsibility for some deeper causes of deforestation. Government policies on indigenous peoples' rights - particularly those affecting territorial rights - have been the cause of much deforestation which would not have occurred if those rights had been acknowledged. Policies over land tenure rights in general have resulted in the concentration of the best agricultural lands in a few hands and the consequent migration of poor peasants into the forests, resulting in large-scale felling of trees. In most cases however government policies are linked to external actors such as multilateral institutions, "co-operation" agencies and transnational corporations who must share the blame. Building access roads means that trees are chopped down. The road then opens up the forest to loggers, landless peasants, mining companies and many other actors, resulting in tree clearance. Road-building is one of the activities promoted and funded by multilateral institutions such as the World Bank and other regional multilateral banks and it allows governments to comply with the International Monetary Fund's policies to increase exports. Road-building is also linked to transnational corporations' interests, as they can thereby access natural resources and incorporate them into the global market.

The role of the military

Weapons imports constitute an important socio-economic, and thus ecological, burden in many countries. Every dollar spent on weapons is one dollar less spent on education, health-care, sustainable technology development and sustainable development in general. It is also one dollar on the wrong side of the balance of payments. The export of weapons constitutes big business for many - particularly Northern - countries. Naturally, war and violence themselves place a major direct and indirect burden upon forests. In some cases, the military have direct interests in logging concessions or the production of cash-crops like coca. The influence of the military on governmental policies in many countries is profound. For the military, the inaccessibility of forests is a strategic problem. Indigenous peoples and other isolated groups of society can pose a threat. Opening up the forest and stimulating migration of people from the centre of the country to these isolated areas serves a strategic purpose. Oil and mineral exploitation within the nation is strategically important, even when one has to attract foreign companies with conditions which allows all profits to flow out of the country.

More indirectly, the continuing dominance of Cold War mentalities cause some of the world's macro-economic institutions to be ruthlessly free-market oriented. Despite these obvious and not-so-obvious relationships, there seems to be a strong taboo on discussing the influence of the military on deforestation and other social and ecological problems. Clear figures are absent and little research has been done.

Moving forward

The international community - at least within the framework of the Commission for Sustainable Development's Intergovernmental Forum on Forests - has recognized the need for identifying the underlying causes of deforestation in order to find ways to save the remaining forests of the world. The Non-Governmental Organizations which participate in the Forum have offered to work in collaboration with governments and international agencies to identify the major underlying causes of deforestation in all regions of the world and to work out solutions.

It is important, however, to realize that deforestation and forest degradation are not "technical" issues. Forests are not disappearing because people and their governments are ignorant or because there are no proper management plans. Forests are disappearing because a number of interlinked international and national policies prepare the ground for it to happen. It is therefore at that level that solutions must be found. In addition, it is crucial to reach out to the public at large in order to ensure that such changes are actually implemented in a way that both humanity as a whole and the people living in the forest areas benefit from them equally. This is obviously a huge and difficult challenge, but one which opens up some hope for the future.

Source: World Rainforest Movement

Climatic changes:
lack of responsibility or lack of foresight?

Devastating climatic changes - like those caused by the "El Niño" sea current and increasing desertification - show that insufficient action has been taken by the international community to alleviate the environmental deterioration brought about by human activities.

Devastating climatic changes - like those caused by the "El Niño" sea current and increasing desertification - show that insufficient action has been taken by the international community to alleviate the environmental deterioration brought about by human activities.

The state of the environment is largely determined by the interaction between people and nature. Its current state is a result of the historical process of the occupation and transformation of spaces by human societies.

When studying the changes in the earth's total environment, the atmosphere, hydrosphere, geosphere and biosphere, two types of different but related phenomena can be distinguished: systemic and cumulative changes.

Systemic changes occur at a global level - the increase in CO_2 and global warming, rising sea levels, the reduction of ozone in the stratosphere and so on.

Cumulative changes take place in smaller spaces, but have a "global" effect when, combined with other factors, they modify the biosphere capacity to store CO_2.

Systemic change: El Niño

The weather and climate are basically affected by the same things, for while the weather changes from hour to hour, day to day, and month to month, climate is the average of such variations.

Extraordinary events like floods occur every 20 to 100 years, and can be part of long-term natural variability. The challenge for the scientific community is to figure out whether this "anomalous weather" is part of natural variability or of a tendency to change, and to what extent humans are responsible.

At the beginning of the 20th century, when studying the monsoon phenomenon, which determines rainfall in India, scientists observed a relationship between pressure systems around the world, which they termed the Southern Oscillation.

When the low pressures associated with this phenomenon predominate in the Central Pacific, a warm ocean current is produced which reaches the Peruvian coast around Christmas time. Hence its name   El Niño (the boy-Christ child). This warm current, which replaces usually cold waters, strongly reduces fish stocks and causes widespread rainfall, about twice every decade.

Its opposite, the "La Niña" (the girl child) cold phase, occurs one or two years later, but its impact is somewhat less strong. El Niño leads to rains in various zones, while causing severe drought in others. La Niña has the opposite effects in these zones. During these phases climatic extremes are produced on a global scale, but affecting the South of the planet more than the North.

The frequency and intensity of these episodes has increased since the 1970s, but it is uncertain whether this is due to an increase in natural variability or whether there are human causes (for example, global warming).

Interest in the phenomenon increased following the catastrophic El Niño of 1982-83, commonly known as "the mother of all Niños." In 1998 a particularly catastrophic El Niño was registered again.

Cumulative change: desertification

The term desertification was used for the first time to refer to areas in Africa which were being progressively degraded due to unsuitable use of resources." The conference of the International Union of Geographers, held in Rio de Janeiro in 1956, addressed the problems faced by countries affected by desertification. In the conferences in Montreal (1972), Moscow (1976) and Nairobi (1977), discussions about the serious deterioration of the arid and semi-arid zones led to the first attempts to draw up a global battle-plan against desertification. At the Earth Summit (1992) a Convention was approved on this theme.

Life on earth depends on the fragile, thin layer of soil covering the continents. This living blanket, which varies in thickness from between a few centimetres in rocky areas to four or five metres in some tropical regions, takes millions of years to form.

Errors made in the course of the human management of natural resources can unleash processes of degradation which can lead to its total destruction in a few years' time.

Nutrients and organic matter (humus) are concentrated in the first few centimetres of soil. Therefore soil degradation over a very short period of time can result in a significant reduction in biological productivity and a corresponding reduction in the fixing of atmospheric CO_2.

According to the Convention, desertification affects a third of the Earth's total land surface. It has been caused by various factors, chief among which are climatic variations and predatory human activities.

Poor soil-use is not only due to the inappropriate use of farming technology, but is also caused by complex socio-economic, educational and cultural factors - with poverty often acting as the spur to over-use of these naturally fragile dry lands.

Since the meeting in Nairobi, several countries have argued that the battle against desertification should not be restricted to specific regions. All the land ecosystems could conceivably be suffering a reduction in biological productivity and taking the first steps towards destruction due to natural or human-induced causes.

This is the case in many wet tropical zones where deforestation has generated desert areas in the space of a few years. Consider also the erosion of soil by water in temperate, sub-humid and humid zones, where the most fertile lands of the planet are found.

The Convention's battle-plan against desertification stresses the real participation of populations affected by the process and the raising of awareness by governments.

Human responsibility

Some catastrophic climatic episodes like El Niño can, up to a certain degree, be reliably predicted. Their occurrence and their environmental and social consequences should be no surprise, as they have already been known of for a long time.

Humanity changes nature at its own peril, using up the soils, grasslands and forests, destroying biodiversity and causing excessive nutrient levels in water. All of this leads to a greater amount of CO_2 entering the atmosphere, contributing to global warming and sea-level rise.

The only valid way forward in confronting global environmental changes is education at all levels and an increasingly responsible approach to environmental problems so that available scientific knowledge can be used to serve society. ❑

Water

A new source of conflict

As the end of the century approaches, water – increasingly scarce and vulnerable to destructive human activity – has become a strategic resource and a determining factor in new conflicts, as can be seen in some regions of Africa and the Middle East, particularly in the occupied territories held by Israel

Water covers more than 70 per cent of the Earth's surface, but only three per cent is freshwater. The degradation of freshwater ecosystems is becoming a problem which could cause numerous conflicts both within countries and between them, affecting regions like the Middle East where this resource is scarce.

Although water is a renewable resource, the quantity of natural water on Earth is also limited and highly vulnerable to the effects of human action. Until recently it was considered an endless resource with access limited only by engineering techniques, and it was therefore consumed irresponsibly. The world consumption of water spiralled upwards from the 1950s.

The agricultural sector uses 69 per cent of the water supply, industry 21 per cent, urban uses account for 6 per cent and leaks from reservoirs are calculated at 4 per cent. The greatest amount is used for irrigation, and this has been on the increase. During the course of the 20th century, the quantity of water used in agriculture has increased tenfold. In the next 30 years, 80 per cent of all food is expected to come from irrigated agriculture.

More than 1 billion of the world's 5.6 billion or so people do not have access to clean and healthy water, while a further 1.7 billion do not have access to adequate sanitation.

According to the World Health Organization (WHO), unhealthy water caused the deaths of 27,000 people per day in 1986. Twenty-six countries, mostly in Africa and the Middle East – although also some in Europe, like the Netherlands – are short of water.

In some regions, the availability of this resource has reached "the water barrier", calculated at 1,000 cubic metres per person per year – the approximate minimum of water required for an acceptable standard of living.

The water crisis especially affects North Africa, the Middle East and China. The megacities of the Third World suffer from great sanitation and health problems, while in other places the lack of water impedes industrial growth.

People tend to settle close to sources of freshwater - 47 per cent of the world's inhabited land is in river valleys and nearly 50 countries have more than three-quarters of their total land areas in these valleys. There are 217 international river valleys which are shared by various countries, including 57 in Africa and 48 in Europe. That is, nearly 40 per cent of the world population lives alongside international rivers. Two billion people depend on some sort of co-operation to assure them the shared supply of this vital resource, and often the co-operation is not forthcoming or denied altogether.

As the most important river valleys of the world run through several countries, agreements on the management and protection of freshwater resources tend to occur at an international level.

The states whose supply of water depends purely on the goodwill of their neighbours, as the source is beyond their frontiers, have a weaker negotiating position. In the European Union there are regulations on shared water resources, especially on the quality of the water, which restrict the rights of countries even within their frontiers. In the light of this experience, it is possible similar initiatives can be made to work in other parts of the world.

The Middle East and Africa

The difficulties of access to water have become both a cause and a weapon of war. The hydraulic installations of the enemy are strategic objectives and, the greater the scarcity of water in a region or a country, the greater the military importance of its hydraulic systems. Several Middle Eastern and North African countries are immersed in the water crisis.

There are three great river axes which, being shared by many states, constitute permanent sources of tension. In the Nile river valley disputes over water involve Egypt, Sudan and Ethiopia. The waters of the rivers Tigris and Euphrates are shared by Turkey, Iraq and Syria. The river Jordan (with its tributaries, the Yarmuk, Banias and Hasbani) and the Litani river are a source of instability between Lebanon, Syria, Israel and Jordan.

The International Centre of Strategic Studies in Washington stated "toward the early 21st century the pressure for water resources could aggravate the already fragile links between the states of the region (Middle East), creating a climate of unprecedented agitation".

In 1979, then President of Egypt, Anwar Sadat declared, "the only issue which could lead Egypt into war again, is water". And in 1990, King Hussein of Jordan said the same of his own country.

The Nile

While Ethiopia controls 85 per cent of the sources of the Nile, Sudan and especially Egypt are in a less favourable geographical situation. But Egypt, with greater political and economic stability than its neighbours can get round its physical vulnerability to take a dominant position in the region.

The high indices of population growth in these countries – a population of 75 million in the year 2000 is predicted for Egypt – mean water supplies will continue to fall.

But the most complex problem to be faced by these countries, according to some experts, is the unpredictable flow of the river, which alternates long periods of drought with periods of floods.

In any case, this is the only region where a bilateral agreement has been signed on the management of shared resources between two riverside countries, Egypt and Sudan. The agreement signed on November 8, 1959 distributed the estimated flow of the river. A special Binational Commission deals with any disputes.

The Tigris and Euphrates

The sources of these two rivers lie in Turkey, the only country of the region with no water supply crisis to date. Syria and Iraq share the river valley, but there is no treaty on the shared management of water resources in this zone.

There is a large-scale hydraulic project underway in Southeast Anatolia, the only region of Turkey with a water shortage. This plan is made up of 13 sub-projects: six on the Tigris and seven on the Euphrates; and includes the building of 21 dams and 19 hydro-electric centres all paid for by Turkey. This plan would increase the dependence of Syria and Iraq on Turkey.

The Arab countries consider the construction of the large-scale Ataturk dam a belligerent act.

The Jordan and the Litani

The Jordan river valley accounts for part of the territories occupied by Israel (the West Bank and the Golan Heights), Jordanian territory and the south-eastern part of Syria. The area suffers from a serious water shortage and a crisis in management and preservation, in a complex context of conflict: the political, economic and strategic occupation of territories by Israel. This country jealously protects its water supplies, gained in constant confrontations with Syria, Jordan and Lebanon.

The Unity Dam is a significant example of the scale of the problems. This was proposed as a joint project to use the waters of the Yarmuk river, the main river of Jordan, to benefit Jordan and Syria. Israel threatened to bomb it if it was built.

The Litani river rises and flows only in Lebanon and is used by this country to generate hydro-electric power. Due to its low degree of salinity it is also an attractive source of drinking water. But as it contributes to the waters of the Hasbani river, which flows into Jordan and the Israeli security zone in southern Lebanon, its use is no straightforward matter.

Lebanon has not yet faced serious water shortages and Syria acquires large quantities of water from the rivers Euphrates and Yarmuk. But Israel, Jordan and the occupied territories are in a critical situation, having used up practically all their conventional resources.

Israel: the key to occupation

In Israel, the main problems are the over-exploitation of the resource and bad management. Having used up freshwater supplies, they have had to develop the biggest waste water recycling system in the world. Israel dedicates a large percentage of the water it consumes to irrigation activities.

The situation on the West Bank is different. The Arab population is totally dependent on underground water and the distribution of the resource between Palestinians and Israelis is not at all equitable. Israel imposed a control system on the exploitation of aquifers: giving all power over water to its authorities, allowing them to set bans and grant authorizations. Since 1967, the authorities have only given 34 permits for new wells to be drilled. This situation meant that many of the Palestinians on the West Bank were forced to abandon agriculture and move to the cities.

According to Palestinian sources, they consume only a fifth of their own water supplies.

While the Israeli colonists are allowed to drill wells of up to 800 metres in depth, the Palestinians are not allowed to go beyond 120 metres, a depth where the salinity of the water is far higher. In 1990, according to figures from the Israeli authorities themselves, the Palestinians of the West Bank consumed 119 cubic metres of water per head, while the Israelis consumed 354 cubic metres.

The water consumption tariffs system in Israel and the occupied territories also affects Palestinians and Jews differently. The management and maintenance of the water resources has been controlled by the Israeli company Mekorot since 1982. According to Israeli sources, Palestinians pay twice the Israeli rate, and Palestinian sources claim this is really five times as much.

The situation is critical in the Gaza Strip. The aquifer exploitation quotas for Palestinians have remained frozen at 1967 levels, when Israel occupied the area. Furthermore, the inequality in the payment of tariffs is alarming; the Palestinians pay 20 times more than the Israeli colonisers, who also receive government subsidies. Most of the drinking water in Gaza comes from its underground aquifer, which has been over-exploited for more than 20 years, leading to high levels of salinization from the seepage of sea water. The low quality of the water has become a public health problem.

Gaza is up against the need to obtain additional supplies, be that from outside the area or through desalinization and/or re-use. In the year 2000, when the Gaza population reaches a million inhabitants, the water may no longer be drinkable.

In the Golan Heights, Syrian territory annexed by Israel in 1967, water distribution is also monopolized by Mekorot, with the ensuing inequalities in access to the resource between the Israeli colonisers and Arabs.

Source: Centro de Investigación para la Paz, Madrid, Spain.

Population density (people per sq km) 1994

Country	Density	Country	Density	Country	Density
Afghanistan	29	Ghana	71	Oman	10
Albania	119	Gibraltar	4,667	Pakistan	159
Algeria	11	Greece	79	Palau	37
Andorra	143	Greenland	0.03	Palestine	444
Angola	9	Grenada	267	Panama	34
Anguilla	83	Guadeloupe	247	Papua New Guinea	9
Antigua	147	Guam	266	Paraguay	12
Aotearoa/N. Z.	13	Guatemala	95	Peru	18
Argentina	13	Guinea	26	Philippines	223
Armenia	119	Guinea-Bissau	29	Pitcairn	14
Aruba	358	Guyana	4	Poland	119
Australia	2	Haiti	254	Portugal	107
Austria	96	Honduras	51	Puerto Rico	410
Azerbaijan	86	Hungary	110	Qatar	49
Bahamas	20	Iceland	3	Reunion	257
Bahrain	791	India	279	Romania	95
Bangladesh	818	Indonesia	101	Russia	9
Barbados	607	Iran	37	Rwanda	294
Belarus	50	Iraq	45	Sahara (Western)	1
Belgium	330	Ireland	51	Samoa	58
Belize	9	Israel	256	Samoa, American	266
Benin	48	Italy	190	San Marino	402
Bermuda	1,189	Jamaica	227	São Tome & Principe	129
Bhutan	34	Japan	331	Saudi Arabia	8
Bolivia	7	Jordan	53	Senegal	41
Bosnia-Herzeg.	69	Kanaky/New Cal.	10	Seychelles	162
Botswana	2	Kazakhstan	6	Sierra Leone	61
Brazil	18	Kenya	50	Singapore	4,741
Brunei	49	Kiribati	106	Slovakia	109
Bulgaria	76	Korea, North	195	Slovenia	96
Burkina Faso	36	Korea, South	448	Solomon Is.	13
Burundi	220	Kuwait	91	Somalia	14
Cambodia	53	Kyrgyzstan	23	South Africa	33
Cameroon	27	Laos	20	Spain	77
Canada	3	Latvia	39	Sri Lanka	272
Cape Verde	94	Lebanon	280	St Helena	54
Cayman Is.	114	Lesotho	66	St Kitts-Nevis	157
Central Afr. Rep.	5	Liberia	24	St Lucia	227
Ceuta	3,737	Libya	3	St Pierre & Miquelon	25
Chad	5	Liechtenstein	192	St Vincent	286
Chile	18	Lithuania	57	Sudan	12
China	126	Luxembourg	155	Suriname	3
Christmas Is	7	Macau	22,111	Swaziland	48
Cocos	43	Macedonia, TFYR	83	Sweden	20
Colombia	30	Madagascar	24	Switzerland	169
Comoros	282	Malawi	80	Syria	75
Congo D.R.	18	Malaysia	59	Taiwan	569
Congo R.	7	Maldives	825	Tajikistan	41
Cook Is.	81	Mali	8	Tanzania	33
Costa Rica	60	Malta	1,152	Thailand	116
Côte d'Ivoire	42	Malvinas/Falklands	0.18	Togo	69
Croatia	51	Marshall Is.	299	Tokelau	167
Cuba	99	Martinique	340	Tonga	131
Cyprus	79	Mauritania	2	Trinidad & Tobago	245
Czech Rep.	131	Mauritius	541	Tunisia	53
Denmark	121	Mayotte Is.	259	Turkey	79
Diego García Is	19	Melilla	4,833	Turkmenistan	8
Djibouti	24	Mexico	47	Turks and Caicos	33
Dominica	95	Micronesia	149	Tuvalu	346
Dominican Rep.	159	Moldova	129	Uganda	86
East Timor	54	Monaco	20,805	Ukraine	86
Ecuador	40	Mongolia	2	United Arab Emirates	22
Egypt	58	Montserrat	108	United Kingdom	238
El Salvador	268	Morocco	60	United States	28
Equatorial Guinea	14	Mozambique	21	Uruguay	18
Eritrea	29	Myanmar/Burma	67	Uzbekistan	50
Estonia	33	Namibia	2	Vanuatu	14
Ethiopia	50	Nauru	524	Vatican	2,273
Faeroe Is.	34	Nepal	145	Venezuela	23
Fiji	43	Netherlands	377	Vietnam	219
Finland	15	Netherlands Antilles	246	Virgin Is. (Am.)	300
France	105	Nicaragua	34	Virgin Is. (Br.)	118
French Guiana	2	Niger	7	Wallis and Futuna Is.	70
French Polynesia	54	Nigeria	117	Yemen	24
Gabon	5	Niue	8	Yugoslavia Fed. Rep.	103
Gambia	96	Norfolk Is.	75	Zambia	12
Georgia	78	Northern Marianas	101	Zimbabwe	29
Germany	228	Norway	13		

Source: Statistical Yearbook 41st issue, CD-ROM, United Nations, 1997.

Demography

The debate around population growth

The world's population has reached nearly six billion people. The debate on demographic growth and the distribution of the earth's resources which began two centuries ago has not changed.

Since the 18th century when Thomas Malthus wrote his *Essay on Population* there have been two opposed views of the advantages and disadvantages of population growth and its link to resource availability on the planet.

Malthus was inclined toward birth control, considering that there were only limited resources to supply the needs of an ever bigger population. In the opposite camp, the populationist theory stated demographic growth should be left completely free as this was believed to be the motor of increased economic production.

Up until the first half of the 20th century, the debates centred upon the spatial distribution of the population. The situation changed following World War II, when demographic growth rates were used to justify the poverty of the Third World.

Population increase was held up as one of the main causes of the underdevelopment affecting two-thirds of the planet and 80 per cent of its population.

The international bodies, working under the assumptions of the developmentalist theories of the 1950s, recommended that governments of poorer countries apply demographic control or "family planning" policies. This was considered a prerequisite for development.

Reductionists in Africa and Asia

The first Third World country to establish a family planning programme was India, in 1952. It was later followed by other countries with high percentages of rural workers, like Egypt and China.

Several countries argued that aid for family planning programmes from the rich countries could have been more effectively spent on other areas. This issue was first proposed at an international level at the 1974 UN Conference in Bucharest.

Some Third World countries accused the rich nations of insisting more on demographic than economic solutions for the mismatch between population and resources. Their central argument was that population increase was a consequence, and not the cause, of underdevelopment.

China is the only case of a large, populous country where birth control policies have worked (figures went from 40 births per 1,000 inhabitants in 1955 to 17 per 1,000 in 1996). However this success was achieved by coercion, with families limited to one child only.

Meanwhile, India after years of harsh birth-control measures still has a fairly high birth rate with an average of 26 births per 1,000 population (down from 39 per 1,000 in 1970). While India's birth rate is lower than the average for South Asia (28 per 1,000 in 1996) and much lower than the average for Sub-Saharan Africa (43 per 1,000) it was achieved at a cost. In the mid-1970s mass vasectomy campaigns sterilized thousands of people in return for a small payment.

Pro-natalists in Europe

At the other end of the scale, some European countries applied pro-natalist measures like discouraging contraception and offering economic support for large families - in response to declining fertility rates. These measures were implemented, for example, in Nazi Germany in the 1930s, with the aim of increasing the numbers of the "pure races."

Other states like Belgium, Sweden, the United Kingdom and France, also adopted pro-natalist measures in response to falling birth rates.

In some Third World countries, pro-natalist policies were also applied following independence, in order to swell the workforce in agricultural areas.

The fertility rates of the poor countries are still high, but are not geographically uniform. The economically better off, more urbanized regions have seen a falling-off in recent decades.

Countries with a large rural population and traditional farming methods still have high birth rates. Countries like Senegal, Sierra Leone, Afghanistan and Laos have rates of more than 40 per 1000.

In the more industrialized countries, rates began to fall again after 1964, reaching their lowest levels in Germany and Denmark which have practically no annual growth.

Infant mortality

Infant mortality rates (IMR) (see p.47) are also a determining factor in the total growth of the world population.

The rates are generally low in the rich world and the variation between these countries is moderate. The industrialized world - including United States, Japan, Australia, Aotearoa/New Zealand and the nations of Northern and Western Europe - has an infant mortality rate average of 6 per 1,000 live births (1996 figures). In some countries of Southern and Eastern Europe the rates are higher.

In the Third World, infant mortality rates are much higher and present more contrasts. Sub-Saharan Africa has the highest average (105 per 1,000 live births), followed by South Asia with an average of 80 per 1,000 live births, while Latin America is generally lower at 35 per 1,000 live births. ❑

Notes for a debate

The debate on the demographic question is centered at the end of the 20th century on unequal distribution of income, rather than lowering the birth-rate. What matters is the control of resources and what threatens its depletion is not the consumption by the poor majorities of the South, but the waste of wealthy societies in the North.

Some facts confirm this statement:

1 - The average annual growth rate of world production of foodstuffs in the last 20 years was above 3%, while global demographic growth is merely above 2%. This shows the falseness of the idea extended in the 1960s that, in order to defeat hunger, demographic growth has to be controlled.

2 - If Third World nations had control over the food they produce, those countries would not suffer malnutrition nor death by hunger. At present, the nutritional needs of local populations do not count when the economic policies imposed by international financial institutions decide what to produce or when to produce it.

3 - Commonly, we hear how scarce arable land is. It is estimated the world has 1.5 billion hectares of land fit for agriculture. However, less than half are used to produce food. Although the farmed land of some countries has been reduced, due to rural emigration to large cities and the incorporation of these arable lands for urbanization purposes, the biggest problem which affects the soil of the world is its degradation. Above all as a consequence of the impact of technology and intensification, especially in poor countries, of commercial crop plantations.

4 - The technology encouraged since the 1960s by the North to fight hunger, insted of accomplishing its objective: a) has encouraged the concentration of rural property by large companies and displaced small farmers who are not able to afford the costs of agricultural modernization (tractors, seeds, fertilizers, pesticides); b) has harmed biodiversity, substituting indigenous varieties intended for local use, with high nutritional value, resistant to local weather and plagues, for hybrids produced by laboratories in the North and intended for foreign markets; c) has favoured the dependence of imported elements which increase the costs of production and, therefore, the value of products in local markets, increasingly separating the farmer from the harvest. ❑

Source: The State of the World's Children 1998, UNICEF, 1998.

	Contraceptive prevalence % 1990/97	Crude death rate per thousand people 1996	Crude birth rate per thousand people 1996	Children per woman 1996
Afghanistan	2	21	52	6.9
Albania	..	6	22	2.7
Algeria	57	6	30	4.0
Angola	1	19	49	6.8
Antigua	53	6	17	..
Aotearoa/New Z.	70	8	16	2.1
Argentina	74	8	20	2.7
Armenia	..	7	15	1.8
Australia	76	7	14	1.9
Austria	71	10	11	1.4
Azerbaijan	..	7	20	2.4
Bahamas	62	5	18	2.0
Bahrain	54	4	22	3.1
Bangladesh	49	10	27	3.2
Barbados	55	9	15	1.7
Belarus	50	12	11	1.5
Belgium	79	11	11	1.6
Belize	47	4	32	3.8
Benin	9	13	43	6.0
Bhutan	19	14	41	5.9
Bolivia	45	9	34	4.5
Bosnia-Herzegovina	..	7	11	1.4
Botswana	33	12	36	4.6
Brazil	77	7	20	2.3
Brunei	..	3	23	2.8
Bulgaria	76	13	10	1.5
Burkina Faso	8	18	46	6.7
Burundi	9	18	44	6.4
Cambodia	..	13	35	4.6
Cameroon	16	12	40	5.4
Canada	73	7	13	1.6
Cape Verde	15	8	32	3.7
Central African Rep.	15	17	38	5.1
Chad	1	18	42	5.6
Chile	43	6	20	2.5
China	83	7	17	1.8
Colombia	72	6	24	2.8
Comoros	21	11	42	5.7
Congo D.R.	8	14	46	6.4
Congo R.	..	15	43	6.0
Cook Is.	50	..	..	..
Costa Rica	75	4	25	3.0
Côte d'Ivoire	11	14	38	5.3
Croatia	..	12	11	1.6
Cuba	70	7	14	1.6
Cyprus	..	8	17	2.3
Czech Republic	69	12	11	1.5
Denmark	78	12	13	1.8
Djibouti	..	15	39	5.5
Dominica	50	6	23	..
Dominican Republic	64	5	25	2.9
East Timor	..	17	36	4.9
Ecuador	57	6	26	3.2
Egypt	48	7	27	3.5
El Salvador	53	6	29	3.2
Equatorial Guinea	..	17	42	5.6
Eritrea	8	15	41	5.5
Estonia	70	13	10	1.4
Ethiopia	4	17	48	7.0
Fiji	32	5	23	2.8
Finland	80	10	12	1.8
France	75	9	12	1.7
Gabon	..	15	37	5.3
Gambia	12	18	41	5.3
Georgia	..	9	14	2.0
Germany	75	11	9	1.3
Ghana	20	11	39	5.4
Greece	..	10	10	1.4
Grenada	54	..	..	..
Guatemala	31	7	37	5.0
Guinea	2	19	49	6.7
Guinea-Bissau	1	21	41	5.5
Guyana	..	8	23	2.4
Haiti	18	13	34	4.7
Honduras	47	6	35	4.5
Hungary	73	15	11	1.5
Iceland	..	7	17	2.2
India	41	9	26	3.2
Indonesia	55	8	24	2.7
Iran	73	6	35	4.9
Iraq	18	9	37	5.4
Ireland	..	9	13	1.9
Israel	..	6	21	2.8
Italy	78	10	9	1.2
Jamaica	62	6	22	2.5
Japan	59	8	10	1.5
Jordan	35	5	38	5.3
Kazakhstan	59	8	19	2.4
Kenya	33	11	37	5.0
Kiribati	28	9	28	..
Korea, North	..	6	21	2.1
Korea, South	79	6	15	1.7
Kuwait	35	2	22	2.9

	Contraceptive prevalence % 1990/97	Crude death rate per thousand people 1996	Crude birth rate per thousand people 1996	Children per woman 1996
Kyrgyzstan	..	7	26	3.3
Laos	19	14	45	6.7
Latvia	..	14	10	1.5
Lebanon	55	7	25	2.9
Lesotho	23	11	36	5.0
Liberia	6	19	48	6.5
Libya	..	7	41	6.1
Lithuania	..	12	11	1.6
Luxembourg	..	10	13	1.7
Macedonia, TFYR	..	7	15	2.0
Madagascar	17	10	42	5.8
Malawi	22	22	49	6.8
Malaysia	48	5	26	3.4
Maldives	10	8	42	6.8
Mali	7	18	48	6.8
Marshall Is.	27	..	..	..
Mauritania	4	13	39	5.1
Mauritius	75	7	20	2.3
Mexico	53	5	25	2.9
Micronesia	..	7	33	..
Moldova	..	11	14	1.9
Mongolia	..	7	28	3.4
Morocco	50	7	26	3.3
Mozambique	4	18	43	6.2
Myanmar/Burma	17	10	28	3.4
Namibia	29	12	36	5.0
Nepal	29	12	37	5.1
Netherlands	80	9	12	1.6
Nicaragua	49	6	34	4.0
Niger	4	18	51	7.2
Nigeria	6	14	43	6.1
Norway	76	11	14	1.9
Oman	9	4	44	7.2
Pakistan	12	8	37	5.2
Palau	38	..	..	..
Palestine	..	..	..	6.1
Panama	58	5	23	2.7
Papua New Guinea	4	10	33	4.8
Paraguay	50	6	32	4.3
Peru	64	7	26	3.1
Philippines	40	6	29	3.7
Poland	75	11	12	1.7
Portugal	66	11	11	1.5
Qatar	32	4	19	3.9
Romania	57	11	11	1.4
Russia	..	14	10	1.4
Rwanda	21	27	43	6.2
Samoa	21	6	27	3.9
São Tomé and Principe	10	7	35	..
Saudi Arabia	..	4	35	6.0
Senegal	13	15	42	5.8
Seychelles	..	7	22	..
Sierra Leone	4	27	47	6.2
Singapore	74	5	16	1.8
Slovakia	74	11	12	1.6
Slovenia	..	11	10	1.3
Solomon Is.	25	4	37	5.1
Somalia	1	17	50	7.0
South Africa	50	8	30	3.9
Spain	59	9	10	1.2
Sri Lanka	66	6	18	2.1
St Kitts-Nevis	41	12	20	..
St Lucia	47	6	28	..
St Vincent	58	7	22	..
Sudan	8	12	34	4.7
Suriname	..	6	23	2.5
Swaziland	21	10	37	4.6
Sweden	78	11	12	1.9
Switzerland	71	9	11	1.5
Syria	36	5	31	4.2
Tajikistan	..	7	31	4.0
Tanzania	16	14	42	5.6
Thailand	74	6	17	1.8
Togo	12	15	43	6.2
Tonga	39	6	28	..
Trinidad and Tobago	53	6	17	2.2
Tunisia	60	6	24	3.0
Turkey	63	7	22	2.6
Turkmenistan	..	8	30	3.7
Uganda	15	21	51	7.1
Ukraine	..	14	10	1.5
United Arab Emirates	..	3	19	3.6
United Kingdom	82	11	12	1.7
United States	74	9	14	2.0
Uruguay	84	10	17	2.3
Uzbekistan	56	7	29	3.6
Vanuatu	15	6	34	4.5
Venezuela	49	5	26	3.1
Vietnam	65	7	26	3.1
Yemen	7	11	48	7.6
Yugoslavia Fed. Rep.	..	10	13	1.8
Zambia	15	18	43	5.6
Zimbabwe	48	14	38	4.8

America:
Five centuries of manipulation

Since the colonization of the Americas, all projects which sought to integrate, absorb or represent indigenous people did little more than prolong Eurocentrism. When these peoples started to make themselves heard on their own account, the hitherto unquestioned concepts of power, state and nation were shaken up.

Although it cannot be scientifically calculated how many people lived on the continents that are present day North and South America when Christopher Columbus arrived in 1492, the number is generally estimated at around 40 million.

By the end of the 16th century the figure plummeted to less than a million. Amongst the factors responsible were the battles of European conquest, forced labour, and epidemics against which indigenous Americans lacked immunity. Entire tribes committed collective suicide because they could not withstand the loss of the cultural values which had maintained them in harmony with their habitat. This, undoubtedly, added up to genocide a cultural genocide, rather than the massacre of individuals in a war. But beyond the historical and moral judgement this deserves, the European powers reacted to the unusual experience of confronting totally new cultures in the manner to which they were accustomed. They maintained their old values and, instead of being enriched by this contact with the new, they simply denied the existence of the Other.

Demons and angels

It can be said that the Eurocentric vision finally resulted in two ways of seeing the American indigenous people:

1. Demonization, which led to them being considered, in the words of Ginés de Sepúlveda, less than human, comparing them with other supposedly 'subhuman' beings like children, women and monkeys. In the Europe of the time, only adult males were considered fully human.

2. A euphoric view, like that of Columbus, who spoke of sin-free civilisations a vision shared by the priest Bartolome de las Casas, and which would lead Thomas More to writing his Utopia.

Eurocentric blindness to the concerns of indigenous people has changed little, as accounts of the conquest and colonization of what the Europeans termed the New World (even though it was as old at theirs was) remain more or less the same more than five centuries later. The only difference is the guilt felt by some contemporary descendants of European settlers.

However, despite the unprecedented catastrophe experienced by the native peoples of America, their population has once again climbed back to 40 million. And it appears that in the fifth century of conquest (euphemistically called "the meeting of two cultures" by some), indigenous Americans have started cornering some space for themselves.

Cultures versus the State

The complaints lodged by Las Casas in the 16th century led to the Spanish Crown providing more beneficial laws for the indigenous people of the Indies, the name by which South America was commonly known at the time. This legislation was almost never followed by the conquistadors or colonizers, and led the conquistador Hernán Cortés to speak his famous line: "The law is obeyed but not complied with."

On another front, Las Casas' complaints formed the basis for the famous Black Legend of the Spaniards, used by the French and British to justify their own imperial practices in America.

In any case, for the native American peoples, once the cataclysm of the conquest was over, the colonial period was more benign than what was to follow with the decolonization of the American states - from the independence of the 13 colonies forming the basis of the United States of America, through to the secession of countries in Latin America.

Indigenous people were regularly used as troops in wars of independence, but once American nation-states saw the need to consolidate their frontiers, these peoples were systematically expelled. It is no coincidence that the late 20th century crisis of the nation-state, exactly five centuries after the conquest of the Americas, would be accompanied by protests and uprisings demanding rights for indigenous peoples.

The mask of rural work

Latin American revolutionary movements active until only a few years ago relied on totalitarian Marxist ideology and camouflaged indigenous identities by declaring them to be rural workers.

This ideology did not make inroads amongst indigenous people, who generally remained on the sidelines of the revolutionary movements, but were massacred by battles between the guerrillas and counter-guerrillas of Central America (in Nicaragua, El Salvador and Guatemala) during 1970s and 1980s.

Being on the margins of the power struggle the indigenous people of the region became the victims in the crossfire. Tens of thousands of Maya were initially considered to be a "social base" by the Guatemalan guerrillas, but ended up in southern Mexico, refugees from a terrifyingly cruel counter-revolutionary campaign. The migration of the Maya once again showed that these people had little or nothing to do with the frontiers established by the American nation-states.

Seeking their own voice

One exception to this rule occurred in Nicaragua, under the Sandinista Government of the 1980s, which took the indigenous communities seriously, providing them with political openings. In 1987, following several proposals and counter-proposals, two independent regions were established - one in the south, predominantly Miskito and Sumu, and another in the north, mixed-race and Creole, establishing the first independent indigenous territories of the American continent.

In 1991 an indigenous uprising in Ecuador shook the Government as the rebels demanded the transformation of society, the recognition of cultural diversity, and a new form of territoriality which would defend the various indigenous nationalities. If this was not forthcoming, they said, the indigenous peoples would break off from the Ecuadorian State.

In Peru the native populations suffered in the cross-fire between guerrillas and the Government, neither of whose notions of the state they could claim as their own.

State versus nations

A few romantic pseudo-vindications of indigenous peoples have appeared in literary works like *Aves sin nido* by Clorinda Matto de Turner of Peru or *Tabaré* by Zorrilla de San Martín of Uruguay, which displaced their indigenous protagonists from their contemporary reality to an idealised past. Only recently have the bulk of the Guatemalan people been able to reclaim a "true" Mayan heritage.

In 1995 the uprising in Chiapas, Mexico demonstrated how indigenous peoples claims operate in a framework different from that of the nation-state. Just as Mexico joined the North American Free Trade Agreement (NAFTA) on January 1 1995, opening up its "northern frontier," the Zapatista National Liberation Army (EZLN) rose up in Chiapas.

As the fiction of the centralist state fell, an opening was created for indigenous people to make their voices heard. The Zapatistas, who had followed the old Latin American guerrilla model and hidden in the Lacandona jungle, found that the indigenous people they had tried to lead into rebellion pleaded with them to represent their case.

"To give the orders....obeying"

The Zapatistas ended up assuming the role of indigenous representatives (although a large part of the region's indigenous population had nothing to do with this movement). Thus, Subcomandante Marcos coined the slogan "to give the orders....obeying", by which he meant obeying the wishes of the indigenous people of Chiapas and protecting them. The Zapatistas had also been supported and protected by ordinary Mexicans who had become alienated from their Government and the state-machinary it represented.

None of these uprisings have been through chance. What they indicate is that Western proposals aimed at shaping their lives and worlds are completely inadequate.

It would also be beneficial if the international bodies that declare years and decades nominally dedicated to indigenous rights, would open their ears and really listen to what these peoples have to say. For amongst other matters, these people knew how to live in harmony with nature - a harmony the rest of the planet appears to have lost ❑

The Miskito: a troubled history

Following their involvement in the political battles of Nicaragua and the region in which they live, the Miskito were granted territorial independence — the first such case in the post-colonial history of South America. However, their desire to be left to live in peace is far from guaranteed

The history of the Miskito, who live on the Atlantic coast of what is now Nicaragua, is an example of the complexity of the relations between an indigenous group, their colonizers, and the nation-state.

The first Westerners to come into close contact with the Miskito were pirates who traded Jamaican rum and mirrors for tiger skins, antelopes and cochineal. In 1633, the Miskito fell into rank alongside the British in their first battles against the Spaniards, and the British crowned a Miskito king in order to ensure control over the riches of the region. In 1860, London abandoned the colony, leaving a Miskito reserve with indigenous self-government.

The liberal presidency of Jos Santos Zelaya "incorporated" the Miskito into Nicaragua in 1884, annexing their land to the national territory, and later governments encouraged big foreign companies into this region, including Standard Fruit and the Bragmanns Bluff Company, which spent many years over-exploiting and exhausting the land concessions granted them.

Under the governments of Anastasio Somoza and his sons, who dominated Nicaragua's politics from 1933 to 1979, colonization programmes were launched in the supposedly 'unoccupied' territories, invading the land of poor rural farmers of the Atlantic region where the Miskito lived.

In 1972, the Alliance for the Progress of the Miskito and Sumo (Alpromisu) was created. It campaigned for administrative decentralization, the control of municipal governments and seats in the National Congress, but the Somoza Government virtually ignored their efforts.

When the last Somoza fell in July 1979, the new Sandinista National Liberation Front (FSLN) Government which replaced it took the view that the Atlantic coast was a large marginalized zone. The official Sandinista vision described the Miskito as living isolated from the rest of the country in a supposedly utopian, harmonious community. In reality, Miskito people had lived in contact with foreign cultures and the capitalist national and transnational economy for centuries, which had brought about radica<

The new regime provided political openings for indigenous peoples which had not previously existed, setting up the *Misurasata*, or "Miskitos, Sumos, Ramas, Sandinistas asla Takanta" (Miskito, Sumo, Rama and Sandinistas working together).

However, the FSLN did not exactly view the indigenous people as agents of their own destiny. The projects for agrarian reform, agricultural co-operatives and the Sandinista Defence Committees (CDS) were a far cry from the traditional organization of the Miskito, and led to confrontations.

The problems could have been overcome if two old Misurasata leaders had not reappeared on the scene: Brooklyn Rivera and Steadman Fagoth, the latter a former member of the Somoza national security cabinet.

The stage was set for the US-backed "plan 81" which aimed at controlling most of the Nicaraguan Caribbean - the ancient Miskito kingdom. The plan was implemented with the creation of a regional council made up of one Miskito, one Creole and one Sumu, but ignoring the mixed-race communities as they had not been present in ancient times

The indigenous peoples united under the slogan "*Indian baman indian swaki sakisa*" - only the Indian can save the Indian - with the Yspa-Yul (Spaniards) as the enemy. In 1982, in the face of a possible indigenous uprising, the "Spaniards", in this case the Sandinistas, swiftly imprisoned the indigenous leaders.

International pressure soon led to the liberation of the leaders, and once out of prison, they headed off in different directions. Steadman Fagoth fled to Honduras, where the United States was organizing an anti-Sandinista guerrilla force - the Counter-revolutionaries or Contras. Brooklyn Rivera went to Costa Rica while the third Misurata leader, Hazel Lau, decided to support the Sandinistas.

While the Contras were reinforced and increased, an *ipso facto* war began between the United States and Nicaragua in the Coco river region on the frontier with Honduras. Heavily armed groups from both sides began to abduct, rape and kill indiscriminately. Their victims were doctors, nurses, teachers and rural farmers, along with members of the Miskito communities.

The Sandinistas proceeded to arrest those suspected of collaborating with the Contras, often hastily sentencing them to long terms of imprisonment, spurring the Miskito exodus from their ranks. In 1982, when Fagoth's attacks intensified, war broke out between armed Miskito groups and government soldiers.

In 1984, the Sandinistas changed previous policy and started a Bilingual Intercultural Education Programme (PEBI). Despite the war, the PEBI of Miskito, Creoles and Mayangna was considered a success. Distances were reduced between the school, the family and the community and education levels rose.

In spring 1987, as a result of negotiations, the Government created two independent regions: one in the south, predominantly Miskito and Sumu, and another in the north, mixed-race and Creole, establishing the first independent post-colonial indigenous territories in the Americas.

In 1990, the Sandinistas were defeated and replaced by the Violeta Chamorro administration, and new problems appeared. Little by little, the PEBI was given the squeeze, as the Government saw the scheme as an instrument for pro-independence and separatist tendencies. The Government did what it could to put obstacles in the path of the educational programme and the most effective members of the programme staff were removed from their posts, accused of pro-Sandinism.

By mid-1992, the PEBI was on its last legs. Discouraged by the systematically negative attitude of the Government and the obstacle course they were forced to run, the majority of supporting NGOs withdrew.

Despite these problems, when the conservative Arnoldo Aleman was elected President in 1996, the PEBI project schools still made up 31.8 per cent of all schools on the Atlantic coast.

Aleman's right-wing backers were particularly hostile to the PEBI. The Government criticized the programme because it did not offer bilingual education, but a monolingual curriculum in native languages. As a response to such "unacceptable" indigenous monolingualism, the Government decided to reinstate education in Spanish alone.

In 1997, President Aleman visited the region: when he arrived, the Miskito flag was flying - just as it had in the 18th and 19th centuries, under the British protectorate. The President ordered its immediate removal. Nicodema Serapio, Representative of the Council of Elders, angered by the attitude of the regional government which played down the incident, declared, "Due to the lack of respect of central government, we have agreed that if the Spaniards will not respect the flag, we will not participate in the next elections. We have decided, just as in 1636, that the indigenous law must be respected".

Meanwhile, local leader Juan P. López said "There are many people who want the National Assembly to suppress regional autonomy. And this would be a dangerous move, as in this case it would unleash a war for independence". If that was the case, by supressing the Miskitos' autonomy the National Assembly would be re-igniting a 500 year old struggle. ❑

Social Model in the West

The search for utopia

The hopes and dreams of technological and philosophical optimists have often been presented as utopias, but the flipside of the dreams are the nightmares, questioning the concept of unending, linear progress common to liberals and Marxists alike

The tale published by Thomas More in 1516 of his imaginary visit to a paradisaical island called Utopia provided the name for a key concept in politics. It has been central to the imagination and destiny of Western societies starting with 19th century socialism and continuing up until the present day.

More was shrewd enough to make "utopia" (which means "nowhere" in Greek) the destination of his supposed trip, a name which revealed his political intentions. By presenting what he valued as good as something non-existent he was criticizing the actual political situation of his time.

Plato's perfect society

Utopian thinking is nothing new in literature or politics. Plato envisioned a perfect society in The Republic written around the 4th century BC. This was not the only utopian vision produced by the Greek world. Besides such affirmative and serious visions, we can already observe dystopias, or counter-utopias, even in the Greek world. Aristophanes for example parodied the utopias of his time.

In the 6th century AD, Ireland's St Brendan recounted the tale of his journey to a perfect society with "crystal cathedrals". Such tales appear intermittently throughout all periods of history.

In the Renaissance era of More's Utopia, there were also many others, generally strictly political, religious or social projects, like Tommasso Campanella's City of the Sun written in the early 17th century and Francis Bacon's New Atlantis in 1624. This period also had its dystopia: the Aristophanes of the Renaissance was François Rabelais who wrote the Abbey of Thelema about Thelemites who lived without watches, obligations, or laws.

Desirable and undesirable utopias

Classic utopian thought has had two dominant characteristics: 1) the definition of utopia as something desirable, as a target worth reaching and 2) that the world described there is a perfect world, blemish-free, with a network of extremely fair laws making it a highly regimented world, regulated even in its smallest details, and therefore lacking the most minimal notions or expressions of liberty.

"There are fifty-four cities on the island (of Utopia), all big and well-built; the customs, laws and ways of life are as similar both in disposition and aspect as is allowed by the terrain.

"If anyone leaves the city and is found outside this, without the authorization needed to travel, they are treated with great severity, punished as a fugitive and sent home with the consequent humiliation. If they should commit the same fault twice, they will be condemned to slavery.

"In Utopia, slavery is the punishment meted out for all crime, even the most serious; because apart from being no less terrible than death for those condemned to it, the Utopians also believe that keeping them in a state of servitude is more beneficial for the State (...)"

These passages give some idea of the aim of More's particular project and also the utopian plan in general: highly rationalist, functionalist, but divorced from all notion of individual freedom or autonomy. There are, however, exceptions; utopias where the spirit of control and geometry have not entered, which are eulogies to the non-regimented lifestyle, like William Morris' 1861 work News from Nowhere (which with the simple addition of a comma would read News from now, here).

In any case, anti-individualist or individualist, arch-regimented or libertarian, these were all conceived as positive utopias.

Utopian literature, as a genre, overlaps with science fiction. Perhaps the most representative examples of this crossing over are HG Wells' A Modern Utopia (1905) and Men as Gods (1923). Jules Verne, one of the predecessors of science fiction, and

the utopian Edward Bellamy, wrote of scientific development as a prop in building a whole model society.

Dangerous utopias

From 1920, utopian thinking suffered a revealing change of direction with the emergence of utopian descriptions which, unlike those mentioned above, describe a utopia achieved, but which instead of constituting a desirable universe, is presented as an unliveable nightmare.

The Russian Eugeny Zamyatin, with his Us, the Others describes a totally socialist world in a thousand years' time, with transparency in behaviour which allows for permanent control. The houses have glass walls, power lies with "the Benefactor" who makes use of guardians who work as "guardian angels"; election day is known as "the day of unanimity" and the supreme objective is for human beings to be "as perfect as machines".

In the 20th century such negative utopias or dystopias have proliferated. Nikolai Berdiaev, another Russian thinker, aptly sums up the reason for this: "Utopias today are so much easier to make reality than in the past. And we find ourselves up against an incomparably more worrying problem: how can we stop them from happening?"

Karin Boye's Kallocain (1928), an invented word translatable as "Coldcain", Aldous Huxley's Brave New World (1931) and George Orwell's 1984 (1948) are all responses to this concern.

However, positive utopias have certainly not disappeared. In the same year as Orwell presented his nightmare vision of English socialism, the US writer Burrhus Skinner came up with Walden Two a eulogy of behaviourism and positive conditioning for the building of a truly happy world. Skinner described a highly pleasant world without conflict, basically achieved through conditioning human beings from their infancy.

Skinner reflects as few others the moment of unlimited glory for his country shortly after the collapse of the enemy industrial centres - the Japanese-German axis - in the recent war and the decisive fracturing of the friendly industrial centres - the United Kingdom, France and the Netherlands.

It is interesting to point out that the Skinner utopia, founded on a very different doctrine from other utopias, is responsible for the most radical manipulation of the "fortunate" human beings living there.

The notion of utopia thus raises various problematic questions.

Ally or enemy?

There is a basic contradiction. Utopias provide a fresh vision, a project, the hope of modifying and improving unjust and unacceptable social situations. Practically all utopian descriptions have a strong critical tone, often accurate and incisive, in relation to contemporary conditions. At the same time, utopian hopes for change for the good of humanity, get betrayed in the attempt to make them a reality.

This is because the will to predict and foreshadow the future of any utopia can only suffocate it. It is easy to trace arch-authoritarian traits in attempts to turn utopias into reality.

Charles Fourier, in many aspects original and joyful in his utopian design, turned out in reality to be exasperatingly rigid. His *falansterios* - the housing structure which was the building block of his utopia - had to have 810 humans: 405 men and 405 women. Similarly, Etienne Cabet even

laid down the design of the flowerbeds in Icaria, his land of promise. As a result, attempts to make such dreams reality ended in arguments over variations from the original design.

Those who make such attempts generally prefer to work with "simple hardworking people", that is people whose thinking can be shaped - often young people.

The world without utopia

The utopian attitude is far from being the only problem-riddled way of thinking: non-utopian thinking is similarly full of pitfalls. Constructing utopias is about offering an alternative to reality. As such it can be a galvanizing process, providing creative options. When political thinking

and action have no room for the utopian, what remains is pure positivity, the factual, the given.

This is, for example, the main characteristic of the business world, a world which is totally real. But a world of pure reality, a world with no alternatives, is also only a step away from the most absolute tyranny. Conservative thinking has no need for anything "beyond reality" because it is satisfied with things as they are.

And this is a substantial difference: the person with a utopian vision can compare action with values. But the person who lacks such a vision need not consider any contradiction between proposals and the reality he or she constructs. His or her world can be built *ad infinitum* without even the smallest critical consideration. ❏

Citizens Want Teeth Added to Environmental Laws

The majority of people in the world's most populous countries want sharper teeth put into laws to protect the environment, according to the largest-ever international survey of public opinion on the environment done in June 1998

Majorities in 28 of 30 countries surveyed, ranging from 91% in Greece to 54% in India, say environmental laws as currently applied in their country "don't go far enough". Two thirds or more of people in countries such as China, Japan, France, Italy, Spain, Mexico, Canada, Australia, Chile, Argentina, and South Korea, are dissatisfied with environmental laws, while six of every 10 people feel that way in Russia, Brazil, Germany, the U.S. and elsewhere.

Only in Nigeria and Finland do the majority of citizens feel environmental laws "strike the right balance", or "go too far," according to the 1998 International Environmental Monitor survey, co-ordinated by Environics International Ltd. of Toronto, Canada.

"In the face of rising environmental concerns and dissatisfaction with pollution laws, it will be increasingly difficult for government and industry leaders to continue to emphasize voluntary corporate environmental targets," said Doug Miller, President of Environics International Ltd. "Most citizens want to see legal teeth around the words."

This second annual International Environmental Monitor survey was conducted by associated polling firms in 30 countries, the largest-ever survey of its kind. In March and April 1998, more than 35,000 in person or telephone interviews (at least 1,000 per country) were conducted in India, China, Japan, South Korea, Indonesia, the United States,

Canada, Mexico, Argentina, Brazil, Chile, Colombia, Uruguay, Venezuela, France, Italy, Spain, Germany, Finland, UK, Greece, Turkey, Poland, Hungary, Russia, Kazakhstan, Australia, New Zealand, Nigeria, and South Africa.

Together, the countries surveyed contain two-thirds of the world's population. Each national survey is considered accurate to within plus or minus 3%, 19 times out of 20.

Environmental concerns are in the forefront

The survey found the environment to be a major concern, particularly in urban China and India.

The first question (without a choice of responses) asked interviewees to name the most important problems facing their nation. Some 40% of urban citizens of China and 27% in India volunteered an environment-related response (e.g. air, water pollution, ozone layer depletion, climate change) most often or second most often. The question posed was identical to that used in an international Gallup poll before the 1992 Earth Summit. The 27% result in India this year is up 21 points from the 6% result obtained by Gallup six years ago. (China was not surveyed in 1992).

The environment is also an important concern in Germany (23%, up 14 points from 1992), Australia (23%, 1992 n/a); UK (22%, up 19 points), Japan (20%, up 8 points), Korea (19%, up 8 points) and Italy

(17%, 1992 n/a). The environment is a top-of-mind concern of between 10% and 15% of respondents in Russia, Kazakstan, Spain, Turkey, Mexico, Canada, Chile, Colombia, Greece and New Zealand.

In North America, the environment is less of a top-of-mind concern than it was in 1992. Today, 12% of Canadians (down 5 points) and 8% of Americans (down 8 points) cite environmental issues as their nation's first or second most important problem.

Rising levels of environmental concern

Prompted to describe their level of concern about the environment, those answering "a great deal" ranged from 69% (Venezuela) to 22% (Finland). When those answering "a fair amount" are added, the percentage of those expressing concern in most countries adds up to over 75%.

In 15 of the countries surveyed this year, an identical question had been asked by Gallup in 1992. Comparing results, the percentage of people expressing "a great deal" of concern is higher in 13 of the 15 countries: Mexico (62%, up 12 points), Chile (56%, up 26 points), India (52%, up 18 points), Turkey (51%, up 39 points), Russia (48%, up 7 points), Uruguay (43%, up 5 points), U.S. (39%, up 1 point), Korea (38%, up 16 points), Hungary (33%, up 1 point), UK (31%, up 3 points), Japan (27%, up 4 points), Germany (23%, up 9 points) and Finland (22%, up 6 points).

Only in Nigeria (56%, down 15 points) and Canada (36%, down 1 point) is there a smaller percentage of people expressing a "great deal" of concern about the environment this year compared with 1992.

Source: 1998 International Environmental Monitor Survey

Women

Building upon diversity

At this end of the millennium, women in the world (almost 2.87 billion) are living in widely differing situations in terms of material wealth. However, what women world-wide have in common is that they hold the most unfavourable positions, and that they are involved in constant and diverse battles in the quest for greater equality

In some countries, women may seek an abortion when they learn they are expecting a girl, thinking that life will not be kind to a daughter. In some instances the pregnancy reaches term but a female infant may be done away with; in others girl babies are simply fed less well and receive little health care, conditions which lead to greater female mortality. Pakistan is a prime example of the latter with just 906 women to every 1,000 men, according to the 1981 Census. (The world average is 111 women to every 100 men.) In the 15-40 years-old bracket, 75 per cent more women die than men. This is attributed to the nutritional anaemia which affects more women than men as a result of the food discrimination they are subject to. Meanwhile, their culture denies them much access to sun and fresh air which also makes them more vulnerable to illnesses.

A long road

At the beginning of the century, Western women fought for universal suffrage eventually gaining the vote by means of their radical protests. The 1960s saw new women's movements emerging with new goals ranging from revolutionary changes in social and production relations, access to public spaces, debate and decision-making, to a new vision of their own bodies and sexuality, prompted by use of the contraceptive pill and a new position in the family.

These movements were precursors of women's movements today. The issues, the ideological perspectives and the organizational methods show significant differences from one country to the next, depending on their historical and cultural contexts.

The First World Conference of Women held in Mexico in 1975 made clear the social inequality engendered by legal and de facto discrimination. The Decade for Women was inaugurated in 1985, and it ended with a Conference in Nairobi. Toward the end of the millennium, in 1995, the Beijing Conference demonstrated the cultural diversity of women and the difficulty of constructing real citizenship, understood as the right to have rights.

Tackling the varied situations women are in implies dealing with two key issues: one is related to women's participation in the production of goods and services in an increasingly capitalist framework; the other is related to reproductive aspects and sexuality. These are central preoccupations of societies the world over.

The labour market and globalization

'Work' is frequently spoken of in the same terms as 'employment' - normally taken to mean the carrying out of a paid task outside the home within a stipulated time schedule. Since the industrial revolution, this has been the most common work situation for urban men. This century has seen a wide-scale increase in the entry of women to the labour market, adding paid work to their domestic tasks, giving them, in the vast majority of cases, long hours and 'double days' as they juggle job and family.

So, even if the end of this century finds women participating more actively in the labour market than 50 years ago, this increase does not necessarily mean an improvement in their living conditions. Women in poorer countries are frequently driven by poverty into the labour market.

Micro-economic studies indicate poverty is one of the leading reasons for women entering the job market, often creating additional pressures in the organization of their domestic and extra-domestic activities. It is also well-known that poverty affects women more than men.

Rural differences

Meanwhile, the entry of women into the job market has been unequal in different countries, due to particular employment policies as well as cultural differences.

The first big difference depends on the degree of integration into the capitalist economy. Thus, for example, towards the end of the 1980s the Chayahuita women of the central Peruvian forest worked in the most important activity of this ethnic group: agriculture. Despite general collective land ownership, small patches growing food for family subsistence are privately owned. This is both men and women's work, although some crops are preferentially farmed by women, like yucca and forest vegetables. In commercial agriculture, women contribute materially from the sowing to the harvest, but as "assistants" because all the decisions and management are handled by their husbands.

The situation of women in certain regions of Africa is very similar. Here, they are the main producers of food for family meals, while the men produce crops for export. Such is the situation of many women in communities which move between traditional and capitalist forms of production.

Especially in the rural community and smallholding economies, women carry out what has been called enlarged housework, which includes feeding the domestic livestock, collecting eggs, baking bread and preparing the harvested goods for market, amongst many other tasks such as fetching fuel and water. This frequently ends up being 'invisible' labour, which does not appear in national accounts.

Invisible work with no rules

In the urban setting, many women with informal and insecure employment are often performing invisible labour. One of the greatest difficulties in studying the role of women in the informal sector is the lack of statistics and reliable data. However, informal labour is continually on the increase in the countries of the South. The largest percentage of the female workforce in these countries is employed in the service sector, mainly as domestic workers.

The situation of domestic employees and the extent of their rights varies. In some countries they are treated like any other worker, while in others, they are totally dependent on their bosses. In all cases, pay is low and in live-in arrangements, the working week is very long and their private lives practically non-existent.

Finally, many women world-wide are sex workers. Southeast Asia is perhaps the zone most affected by sexual trafficking. Given the widespread poverty of this region, young girls may be 'sold' by families, taken with no passport to faraway places, often living in conditions not far removed from slavery.

The impact of structural adjustment

Structural adjustment measures which many Southern countries have been forced to adopt appear to have affected women more than men, as many functions previously assumed by the state started to be carried out by women. In many countries women must shoulder the burden of activities and work which was the responsibility of society in general or the state.

In some cases, international co-operation contributed to this kind of privatization through programmes of self-managed childcare centres, where women took on the care of their own and others' children free of charge, or health programmes where women were trained to work as health volunteers.

These activities allowed some women to develop their organizational and leadership capacity establishing truly important popular movements, as is the case in Lima.

Economic internationalization - globalization - affects men and women differently, especially in terms of the displacement of population to areas of employment. For example, the expansion of the clothing industry in Bangladesh caused thousands of young, mainly single, women to migrate from rural to urban areas. Although the working conditions are bad, research amongst female clothing workers showed the women considered the alternatives to this type of work even worse.

The sexual division of labour

In many countries, in the North as well as the South, women are increasingly entering areas previously reserved exclusively for men, although access to decision-making posts continues to be scarce. Although the number of professional women has increased , women continue to be the majority in work which is badly paid: services, especially domestic service, and manual labour which requires dexterity, such as electronics.

New possibilities

Their entry into the labour market with the possibility of earning a cash income has allowed many women to see things from a different standpoint, and afforded them new possibilities for negotiation in day to day relationships. For many women, income from paid work has been the first step on the road to some kind of independence. "Of course my house was kept up by me alone when he was laid off", said one Peruvian mother. "And the cars, I bought them myself, with my savings, my business. I worked until 11 at night doing overtime, I worked Saturdays too, Sundays. And sometimes when I start to think, its seems impossible to me."

Women, sexuality and independence

The International Conference on Population and Development (Cairo, 1994) and the Fourth World Conference on Women (Beijing, 1995) included long debates on the sexual and reproductive health of women, and their sexuality in general. Sexuality, it is recognized, is both a private and a public affair. Although defined in the privacy of a room, its implications are public, involving control over future lineage, honour and domination. It is in these aspects where perhaps there is the greatest cultural diversity.

The safeguarding of female virginity continues to be a central issue of state policies for women in many countries. In Turkey, for example - although not widely practised - clinical examinations for virginity are still carried out on young women suspected of having had sexual relations. Virginity is seen as a matter of honour. Women's and human rights groups lobby against these practices, as they can jeopardise young women's futures. Conversely in the early part of this century, the young Trobriand Islanders of Papua New Guinea were free to have sexual relations with whomever they desired until they found someone they wanted to marry.

Control over the sexuality of women continues after marriage in many societies. In 1994, Reuters carried a story of an Iranian woman convicted for adultery who was stoned to death. In Pakistan, for example, there is the "Zina" - a classification of extramarital sex, covering adultery, fornication and rape - with the toughest sentence being the stoning to death of adulterous married women. For single women the punishment for sex is a hundred lashes and ten years imprisonment. However, things were not always like this: in 1947, Mohammed Ali Jinnah wanted Pakistan to be a secular state. "We are the victims of terrible customs", he said. "It is a crime against humanity that our women are shut inside the four walls of their houses as though they were prisoners." Years later, in 1977, under the dictatorship of Zia, who was backed by the United States, the status of women in Pakistan changed for the worse. At times customs which appear to be remnants of old traditions can in reality be modern "re-inventions". In many parts of Latin America, female adultery is considered immoral and criminal, leading to the "justification" of frenzies of male domestic violence.

Visions and values

In southern Africa, in the Kalahari desert of the 1970s, a 50-year-old Kung woman was tallying up her past: "I have told you of my lovers, but I have not told you of all of them, there are as many as I have fingers and toes (referring to her entire adult life). Some have died, others are still alive (...) When you are a woman, you don't simply sit around, doing nothing - you have lovers. You don't merely stay with the man in your hut, simply with one man. One man can give you very little."

The value systems surrounding female sexuality are complex and diverse. Women have realized that to live their sexuality fully

Women in high level jobs (1994)

A = Salaries of women as a percentage of men's income (*)
B = % of administration and managerial posts (*)
C = % of professional and technical workers (*)

Country	A	B	C	Country	A	B	C	Country	A	B	C
Algeria	19	6	28	Finland	41	26	62	Panama	28	28	49
Aotearoa/New Z.	39	32	48	France	39	9	41	Papua New Guinea	35	12	30
Australia	40	43	25	Germany	35	19	43	Paraguay	23	15	51
Austria	34	19	49	Greece	31	12	44	Peru	23	20	41
Bahamas	39	26	57	Guatemala	21	32	45	Philippines	31	34	63
Bangladesh	23	5	23	Guyana	26	13	48	Poland	39	16	60
Barbados	40	37	52	Haiti	36	33	39	Portugal	34	37	52
Belgium	33	19	51	Honduras	24	31	50	Sierra Leone	30	8	32
Belize	18	37	39	Hungary	40	58	49	Singapore	31	34	16
Bolivia	27	17	42	India	26	2	21	Solomon Is.	40	3	27
Botswana	39	36	61	Indonesia	33	7	41	South Africa	31	17	47
Brazil	29	17	57	Iran	19	4	33	Spain	29	12	48
Bulgaria	41	29	57	Ireland	26	17	48	Sri Lanka	34	17	25
Burkina Faso	40	14	26	Israel	33	19	54	Sudan	23	2	29
Cameroon	31	10	24	Italy	31	38	46	Suriname	26	22	70
Canada	38	42	56	Japan	34	9	42	Swaziland	35	15	54
Cape Verde	32	23	48	Korea, South	28	4	45	Sweden	45	39	64
Central African Rep.	39	9	19	Kuwait	25	5	37	Switzerland	30	28	24
Chile	22	17	34	Lesotho	30	33	57	Thailand	37	22	52
China	38	12	45	Luxembourg	25	9	38	Togo	33	8	21
Colombia	33	27	42	Malawi	42	5	35	Trinidad and Tobago	30	23	53
Congo D.R.	37	9	17	Malaysia	30	12	45	Tunisia	25	7	18
Congo R.	36	6	29	Maldives	35	14	35	Turkey	33	7	29
Costa Rica	27	21	45	Mali	39	20	19	United Arab Emirates	10	2	25
Cuba	31	19	48	Mauritania	37	8	21	United Kingdom	35	33	44
Cyprus	27	10	41	Mauritius	25	14	41	United States	41	42	53
Denmark	42	20	63	Mexico	25	20	44	Uruguay	33	25	63
Dominican Republic	23	21	50	Morocco	28	26	31	Venezuela	27	18	55
Egypt	25	16	29	Mozambique	41	11	20	Zambia	39	6	32
El Salvador	28	25	45	Netherlands	34	15	44	Zimbabwe	37	15	40
Equatorial Guinea	29	2	27	Norway	42	31	58				
Fiji	21	10	45	Pakistan	21	3	20				

(*) Data refers to 1994 or latest available year.

Source: Human Development Report 1997, UNDP, 1997.

is a right, according to their ethnic and religious values, and there are numerous women's and feminist organizations which hold workshops on these issues.

The most heated arguments revolve around the reproductive aspects of sexuality. Should individuals be free to decide how many children they have and when? Or is this the business of the state, as is the case in China and others nations which have implemented sterilization policies for segments of their populations? Various ethical positions immediately appear in the discussion of contraceptive methods. The consequences of unwanted

pregnancies are abortions - generally carried out in terrible conditions - or the birth of unwanted children. Abortion is an important issue in relation to the sexual and reproductive health of women. Latin America and the Caribbean together present the highest incidence of unsafe abortions in the world and the second highest percentage of maternal deaths as a result. Faced with this situation, women's movements have demanded the right to decide on the interruption of unwanted pregnancies, and, if abortion is the option chosen, to have suitable hygiene, health and technical facilities available.

All in all, given the inequality encountered by women in most countries, they are slowly managing to improve their situation by following their own paths. Thus, while many groups of Muslim women seek arguments from the Koran and the life of the prophet with which to confront the fundamentalists, others formulate their own arguments and activities. In every case, women have struggled bravely to change gender relations in the quest for a more equitable world. ❑

Women in political life

A = % OF GOVERNMENTAL POSTS OCCUPIED BY WOMEN, TOTAL (1995)
B = % OF MINISTERIAL POSTS OCCUPIED BY WOMEN (1995)
C = % OF PARLIAMENTARY SEATS OCCUPIED BY WOMEN (1997)

COUNTRY	A	B	C
Albania	12	0	..
Algeria	2	0	7
Angola	6	7	.
Antigua	30	0	..
Aotearoa/New Z.	17	7	29
Argentina	3	0	..
Armenia	2	0	..
Australia	24	13	21
Austria	7	21	25
Azerbaijan	5	4	..
Bahamas	34	20	11
Bahrain	0	0	..
Bangladesh	3	5	9
Barbados	23	33	18
Belarus	4	8	..
Belgium	8	11	15
Belize	10	0	11
Benin	10	15	..
Bhutan	5	13	..
Bolivia	9	0	6
Botswana	11	0	9
Brazil	13	4	7
Brunei	2	0	..
Bulgaria	9	9	13
Burkina Faso	10	11	9
Burundi	4	8	..
Cambodia	5	0	..
Cameroon	5	3	12
Canada	19	19	19
Cape Verde	12	13	11
Central African Rep.	5	5	4
Chad	3	5	..
Chile	12	16	7
China	4	6	21
Colombia	25	11	10
Comoros	3	7	..
Congo D.R.	2	3	5
Congo R.	4	6	2
Costa Rica	21	15	16
Côte d'Ivoire	3	6	..
Cuba	8	4	23
Cyprus	5	8	5
Czech Republic	1	0	..
Denmark	19	30	33
Djibouti	1	0	..
Dominica	31	8	..
Dominican Republic	12	3	10
Ecuador	10	7	..
Egypt	2	3	2
El Salvador	18	6	11
Equatorial Guinea	3	4	9
Estonia	10	6	..
Ethiopia	11	12	..
Fiji	10	9	6
Finland	16	35	34
France	9	7	6
Gabon	6	3	..

COUNTRY	A	B	C
Gambia	7	22	..
Georgia	3	0	..
Germany	7	16	26
Ghana	11	11	..
Greece	6	0	6
Grenada	19	10	..
Guatemala	18	19	13
Guinea	5	15	..
Guinea-Bissau	12	8	..
Guyana	16	11	20
Haiti	14	17	3
Honduras	17	11	8
Hungary	8	5	11
Iceland	8	13	..
India	6	4	7
Indonesia	2	4	13
Iran	0	0	4
Iraq	0	0	..
Ireland	11	18	14
Israel	10	13	8
Italy	10	3	10
Jamaica	13	6	..
Japan	8	7	8
Jordan	7	3	..
Kazakhstan	1	3	..
Kenya	5	0	..
Korea, North	1	1	..
Korea, South	2	3	3
Kuwait	6	0	0
Kyrgyzstan	8	4	..
Laos	3	0	..
Latvia	16	6	..
Lebanon	0	0	..
Lesotho	14	7	11
Libya	0	0	..
Lithuania	9	0	..
Luxembourg	8	17	20
Madagascar	0	0	..
Malawi	6	5	6
Malaysia	6	8	10
Maldives	10	5	6
Mali	7	10	2
Malta	2	0	..
Mauritania	5	4	1
Mauritius	7	4	8
Mexico	7	14	14
Moldova	4	0	..
Mongolia	5	0	..
Morocco	1	0	1
Mozambique	13	4	25
Myanmar/Burma	0	0	..
Namibia	7	10	..
Nepal	0	0	..
Netherlands	20	26	28
Nicaragua	11	11	..
Niger	9	10	..
Nigeria	4	4	..

COUNTRY	A	B	C
Norway	44	41	39
Oman	4	0	..
Pakistan	2	4	3
Panama	11	11	10
Papua New Guinea	2	0	..
Paraguay	3	0	6
Peru	10	6	11
Philippines	24	8	12
Poland	8	6	13
Portugal	18	9	13
Qatar	2	0	..
Romania	3	0	..
Russia	2	3	..
Rwanda	10	8	..
Samoa	7	7	..
São Tomé and Príncipe	4	0	..
Saudi Arabia	0	0	..
Senegal	2	4	..
Seychelles	21	31	..
Sierra Leone	5	4	6
Singapore	5	0	3
Slovakia	13	14	..
Solomon Is.	0	0	2
South Africa	7	9	24
Spain	10	15	20
Sri Lanka	9	13	5
St Kitts-Nevis	21	10	..
St Lucia	5	8	..
St Vincent	25	10	..
Sudan	1	0	5
Suriname	14	0	16
Swaziland	7	0	8
Sweden	33	48	40
Switzerland	7	17	20
Syria	4	7	..
Tajikistan	4	7	..
Tanzania	9	16	..
Thailand	4	4	7
Togo	3	4	1
Trinidad and Tobago	14	20	19
Tunisia	5	3	7
Turkey	5	3	2
Turkmenistan	4	4	..
Uganda	10	13	..
Ukraine	1	0	..
United Arab Emirates	0	0	0
United Kingdom	8	9	8
United States	30	21	11
Uruguay	3	0	7
Uzbekistan	3	3	..
Vanuatu	0	0	..
Venezuela	6	4	6
Vietnam	4	7	..
Yemen	0	0	..
Zambia	9	7	10
Zimbabwe	11	3	15

Source: Human Development Report 1997, UNDP, 1997.

Ecology

Thirty years on

The ecological movement, which some considered would be short-lived and limited to the rich countries, has not only expanded across the entire world, but has also managed to evade attempts to undermine it or incorporate it into the establishment

At the end of the 1960s, when a fledgling movement to defend the environment emerged in the industrialized countries, some predicted it would short-lived.

Nearly 30 years later, the heterogeneous "green", ecological or environmental movement has become, to a greater or lesser degree depending on the country, a main player in political, social and intellectual life.

In some cases, its representatives work in government, or are leading cultural figures, university experts or leaders of grass roots social movements.

Growth of ecology movement

Two factors have been decisive in making the ecological movement a very influential factor in many countries.

In the first place, the concept of progress has lost its power to convince and there is an increasingly widespread consciousness that current levels of 'development' are unsustainable in the medium-term, given that the dominant economic rationale tends to behave as though there are endless natural resources. Thus, it is not surprising that the ecological movement was born and gained its first supporters precisely in those countries where this rationale had reached its apogee.

The movement has been most influential where the environmentally damaging consequences of capitalist progress are most evident. This is partly due to the fact that in these countries, the consequences of modernisation are at least as undesirable as notions of "social and economic backwardness" in the eyes of the citizens.

This helps explain why, along with campaigns for the protection of endangered species, non-renewable natural resources and opposition to forms of international trade they consider unjust, the ecological movements of the developed countries have incorporated other concerns into their programmes.

They question: certain models of consumption (something hardly thinkable for Southern countries until only a few years ago); the predominant energy model (a model that includes, amongst other things, the use of nuclear energy) and the structure of society, including the organization of work and leisure within it.

The fact that the ecology movement and culture, or what is commonly understood as these, have spread across the countries of Western Europe and North America in the 1970s and 1980s, is proof that these concerns were close to the hearts of these citizens.

The two most important environmental groups in the world (Greenpeace and Friends of the Earth) have hundreds of thousands of collaborators and associates in the developed countries and, more importantly, have extended their cultural influence over most of society. In the 1990s, with the dissolution of communism, it is the Eastern European national Greenpeace and Friends of the Earth groups which have grown most.

In poor countries as well

The second point is that the emergence of the ecology movement in the developing countries - even in some particularly poor ones - also counters the view that the ecology movement would be short-lived.

If up until ten or fifteen years ago, ecological criticism was thought to be a "luxury", the last years of the 1980s and the 1990s have seen the rise of ecological thinking in developing countries as well.

Environmental destruction is commonplace in the countries of Latin America, Africa and Asia as well - although it occurs as a consequence of reasons perhaps opposite to those of the more developed countries.

One explanation offered by ecologists is that poverty constitutes at least as serious a threat to the environment as industrial progress. If the economic rationale behind consumerist notions of progress is a threat to the environment, so is poverty. Poor people's battle for survival can also damage natural resources.

The growth of the "green" movements can also be seen in Latin America, Asia and Africa, partly due to the fact that these countries became involved in the increasing globalization of markets without seeing any of the benefits the advocates of globalization had promised.

The politicization of the movement

But if the 30 years of the ecological movement have resulted in maturity, there is also a schism at its heart.

There is a division between pure and social ecologists, on the one hand, and between those talking in terms of political intervention, on the another.

With the passage of time and the deepening of the environmental crisis, "green" activists have realized that preventing further deterioration of the environment and living conditions is more difficult than was initially thought. Thus, many have abandoned the illusion that the ecological crisis could be confronted with calls for consciousness from the political decision makers, or by lobbying in the corridors of ministries and parliaments.

These frustrations helped reinforce a wing of the ecologist movement dedicated today to sharp criticism of the current development model, claiming that certain forms of organizing production, trade, work and social life, are directly responsible for the environmental crisis of the planet. To overcome this, they argue, the interests benefiting from the current established order will have to undergo changes.

Sustainability and/or social justice

Many ecologists agree the crisis cannot be overcome from a purely ecological point of view, so they have coined the term "sustainability" to define the sort of society they would like.

They say that it is possible (although not desirable) for a society to exist which respects the environment, but which is unsustainable from the economic and political point of view. For instance, an authoritarian "green" regime could impose the military protection of nature without this guaranteeing a sustainable society.

Thus, Friends of the Earth no longer defines itself as a purely environmental organization, but campaigns for a democratic and socially just model of sustainable development. Hence the close relationships between these ecologists and other social movements, like the unions, rural workers and marginalized urban people, and endorsement of their struggles to improve the quality of life. In many cases, this brought the group into contact with issues the movement had not considered in the early days, like transport, food, waste management, working or housing conditions.

A = **Food production per capita index (1979-81=100) 1993**
B = **Food imports (as % of merchandise imports) 1994**
C = **Cereal imports (1,000 metric tons) 1994**

Country	A	B	C
Afghanistan	..	..	182
Albania	..	..	270
Algeria	119	26	7,760
Angola	72	15	475
Antigua	..	..	5
Aotearoa/New Z.	..	..	316
Argentina	94	4	28
Armenia	..	..	300
Aruba	..	..	7
Australia	..	..	66
Austria	..	..	233
Azerbaijan	..	..	275
Bahamas	..	..	14
Bahrain	..	7	122
Bangladesh	97	14	952
Barbados	64	..	57
Belize	95	13	15
Benin	119	18	107
Bermuda	..	..	2
Bhutan	..	11	41
Bolivia	107	13	434
Botswana	69	13	175
Brazil	114	9	8,971
Brunei	100	..	32
Bulgaria	..	..	58
Burkina Faso	132	14	110
Burundi	92	19	105
Cambodia	141	9	58
Cameroon	79	11	226
Canada	..	..	1,022
Cape Verde	..	32	87
Cayman Is.	..	..	1
Central African Rep.	94	24	52
Chad	99	6	50
Chile	118	5	1,277
China	145	3	16,331
Colombia	114	7	2,353
Comoros	83	37	34
Congo D.R.	100	42	253
Congo R.	79	17	86
Costa Rica	104	6	453
Côte d'Ivoire	89	16	466
Croatia	..	..	82
Cuba	65	21	1,464
Cyprus	94	7	551
Czech Republic	..	..	287
Denmark	..	..	480
Djibouti	..	27	52
Dominica	..	..	8
Dominican Rep.	104	14	895
Ecuador	110	5	486
Egypt	114	22	9,200
El Salvador	95	11	448
Equatorial Guinea	..	13	9
Eritrea	..	..	281
Estonia	..	..	82
Ethiopia	86	20	928
Faeroe Is.	..	..	3
Fiji	97	12	126
Finland	..	..	130
France	..	..	1,228
French Guiana	..	..	10
French Polynesia	..	..	38
Gabon	78	13	64
Gambia	76	32	97
Georgia	..	..	713
Germany	..	..	3,321
Ghana	115	9	311
Greece	..	..	570
Greenland	..	..	2
Grenada	78	..	21
Guadeloupe	..	..	80
Guam	..	..	9
Guatemala	94	11	517
Guinea	98	23	384
Guinea-Bissau	110	46	68
Guyana	94	7	50
Haiti	67	77	311
Honduras	89	16	278
Hungary	..	..	305
Iceland	..	..	32
India	123	5	12
Indonesia	145	6	5,113
Iran	126	16	5,450
Iraq	87	32	1,099
Ireland	..	..	444
Israel	..	..	2,311
Italy	..	..	6,014
Jamaica	111	10	335
Japan	..	..	29,937
Jordan	121	20	1,347
Kanaky/N.Caledonia	..	..	40
Kenya	83	15	622
Kiribati	..	..	8
Korea, North	76	15	310
Korea, South	94	4	11,936
Kuwait	..	14	455
Laos	..	4	22
Latvia	..	..	65
Lebanon	186	14	577
Lesotho	70	12	99
Liberia	..	..	121
Libya	81	19	1,790
Lithuania	..	..	19
Macau	..	..	37
Macedonia, TFYR	..	..	133
Madagascar	86	14	140
Malawi	70	35	506
Malaysia	203	4	3,509
Maldives	84	..	22
Mali	91	15	70
Malta	..	..	133
Martinique	..	..	66
Mauritania	81	49	206
Mauritius	99	12	255
Mexico	94	9	8,100
Moldova	..	..	120
Mongolia	63	23	63
Morocco	106	11	1,678
Mozambique	77	16	496
Myanmar/Burma	107	15	49
Namibia	72	9	112
Nepal	114	9	62
Netherlands	..	..	6,676
Netherlands Antilles	..	..	60
Nicaragua	64	19	174
Niger	77	22	155
Nigeria	129	13	1,078
Norway	..	..	668
Oman	..	13	460
Pakistan	118	11	1,916
Panama	87	8	273
Papua New Guinea	103	14	275
Paraguay	109	7	31
Peru	..	13	2,289
Philippines	88	6	2,219
Poland	..	..	505
Portugal	..	..	2,351
Qatar	..	12	142
Reunion	..	..	189
Romania	..	..	529
Rwanda	70	25	97
Samoa, American	..	..	3
São Tome & Principe	..	..	11
Saudi Arabia	340	12	6,182
Senegal	111	29	579
Seychelles	..	..	11
Sierra Leone	86	57	141
Singapore	47	3	776
Slovakia	..	..	201
Slovenia	..	..	512
Solomon Is.	88	14	..
Somalia	..	..	129
South Africa	74	5	913
Spain	..	..	5,047
Sri Lanka	81	7	927
Sudan	76	22	1,022
Suriname	81	13	36
Swaziland	82	8	75
Sweden	..	..	211
Switzerland	..	..	380
Syria	89	10	952
Tanzania	76	8	195
Thailand	102	2	740
Togo	106	10	69
Tonga	..	..	8
Trinidad & Tobago	85	17	162
Tunisia	123	7	1,592
Turkey	102	3	878
Uganda	109	4	56
United Arab Emirates	..	6	759
United Kingdom	..	..	3,321
United States	..	..	7,363
Uruguay	113	8	277
Vanuatu	80	..	11
Venezuela	101	11	2,015
Vietnam	133	5	387
Yemen	75	25	..
Zambia	99	3	35
Zimbabwe	78	3	100

Sources: Human Development Report 1997, UNDP, 1997; World Development Indicators 1997, World Bank, 1997.

Meanwhile, at the other extreme of the movement are the "deep ecologists", who claim the ecosystems and the living beings who constitute them all have rights as valid as those of humanity. They follow a sort of social Darwinism, which states that society is ruled by laws similar to those of nature. Many of them claim there is no reason to lament the loss of human life in natural catastrophes, as the survival of the fittest is the way nature has of tackling demographic growth. These "ecologists" believe any sort of action is legitimate in imposing the protection of nature.

The diversity of battle strategies

The entry of some ecological groups into institutional politics also produced serious fragmentation in the movement. During its first decade of life, ecology incarnated criticism of traditional politics, a system they viewed as deepening the division between governors and the governed and blocking direct citizen participation. But 30 years on, this debate appears to have broadened in the face of the events which have occurred.

While some ecological movements prefer to keep themselves "uncontaminated" and concentrate their activity on denunciation campaigns, direct action and monitoring government conduct (Greenpeace is the best example of this), others present their own candidates in national elections, either supporting their respective governments, or forming a part of them.

Such has been the case with the German "Greens", who in the 1980s and 1990s have formed, and continue to form, part of Government coalitions in various regions of the country, or of the Italian ecologists, who have been part of the "Ulivo" coalition in Italy for more than a year.

The risk of trivialization

The factor which will decisively influence the future of environmental movements on all five continents is the "trivialization" of the ecological theme. For if during the initial years ecology presupposed a more radical criticism of the social order and hegemonic ideas, today many of its proposals have been "integrated" by companies, governments, educational systems and citizens of all social categories.

Thus ecological consciousness has extended to the most unpredictable corners of social and cultural life (including green marketing), but has in many cases become a paradoxically innocuous and standardized idea.

Increasingly care of the environment is being seen as an area of individual responsibility rather than a reason to dismantle a model of social organisation which inevitably leads to environmental destruction.

The movement will be confronted by new challenges in the next few years which could certainly never have been foreseen by its founders. ❏

Toxicity: moving the goalposts

The principle behind setting toxicity limits is called ALARA - As Low As Reasonably Achievable. The crudeness of this phrase reveals that limits are determined by practical situations rather than scientific principles.

The limits of toxicity caused by lead in gasoline were set in the United States in 1970 at 60 ug (micrograms) for every 100 cubic centimetres of blood. In 1975, however, those limits were lowered by the same authorities to 30 ug for the same amount of blood.

LIMITS OF LEAD TOXICITY IN BLOOD		
1970	60	^{ug} per every 100 cc of blood
1971	40	^{ug} per every 100 cc of blood
1975	30	^{ug} per every 100 cc of blood
1985	25	^{ug} per every 100 cc of blood
1986	15	^{ug} per every 100 cc of blood
1989	00	^{ug} per every 100 cc of blood

Source: United States and Canada Health Bureau

The zero threshold for lead in gasoline was set in 1989. There is no safe limit for lead in the blood. It is always harmful even though it may not be traceable. Is the issue then that what was harmful in 1970 had quadrupled its ability to harm in 1986? Or is it rather that the toxicity of lead had been underestimated until 1989, when its absolute toxicity was discovered?

This does not ring true, however, as in the 1920s US doctor Alice Hamilton had already warned about the toxicity of lead in gasoline and had listed precisely the medical consequences which justified the ban of the product more than 60 years later.

Food researcher Frances Moore Lappé, also an American, has observed: "The limit of tolerance for mercury in the United States was zero until December 30 1970. But since American agriculture and industries used over 400 tonnes of mercury per year, the ministries of Health and Agriculture agreed to abandon that limit of tolerance on December 31 1970." And she adds: "The limits of tolerance of organic compounds which contain phosphoric acid - such as malathion and parathion - had to be raised when it was proven that, in the state of Montana, the traces of these pesticides in milk had begun to increase."

Regarding radioactivity, the limits in the 1980s set by the then European Economic Community were 370 becquerel (becq.) for a kilogramme of food for adults and 600 becq. for children. But then, on April 1986, Chernobyl happened. The European Union (EU) considered it appropriate to raise the thresholds, unmovable until then, and set limits at 1,000 becq. for milk and 1,250 for adult foodstuffs. But these limits were not the same throughout Europe. After Chernobyl, the legal limit of radioactive caesium in milk was set at different limits in different countries and regions in Europe (not all of which were member states of the EU).

TOLERANCE TO THE PRESENCE OF RADIOACTIVE CAESIUM IN MILK		
GERMANY	(FRG) 500	BECQ
HESSEN*	20	"
NORWAY	1000	"
FINLAND	2000	"
SWEDEN	2000	"
AUSTRIA	74	"

* IN THE GERMAN STATE OF HESSEN, THE GREENS ARE IN POWER AT THE LOCAL GOVERNMENT LEVEL.

The daily limit of radioactivity accepted a few years ago was 5 rem*. About 600 rem per day would be fatal for a human. New studies on the effects of radioactivity have led several environmentalist and medical organizations, the latter interested in radioactivity used in medical procedures, to set a limit of two rem a day: another substantial change to the limits.

*rem: 'roentgen equivalent man', a unit of effective absorbed dose of ionizing radiation in human tissue, roughly equivalent to the effect of one roentgen unit of X-rays. (Roentgen from the discoverer of X-rays, Wilhelm Roentgen).

Source: Revista del Sur.

Education

The levelling out of culture

Education is in crisis. Transformed by scientific and technological revolutions into a means of adapting individuals to the globalized market, it has strayed from its original principles of forming citizens fully capable of participating in communities

After the French Revolution and throughout the 19th century, industrialized countries of the North believed in the power of education as a means to change society. The prevalent idea was that future citizens would be formed by centres of education.

This belief rested upon the assumptions of the 18th century scientific revolution that science, helped by reason, was in the service of "progress" which, according to the ideology of modernism, would bring happiness to humankind.

The industrial revolution in the 19th century, and the political changes which led to the formation of nation-states, brought about the need to make "productive" individuals who could work as cogs in the machine of capitalist production.

Literacy became a priority for the industrialized countries of Europe and North America. In the 20th century it was championed in the rest of the world as well. Literacy became also a national objective for many countries newly-freed from colonialism.

It was considered a prerequisite of "development" and equity. Education was promoted as the ideal means for people who were discriminated against, for reasons of gender, race or ethnic origin, to claim their place in society.

In educational terms, "progress" was measured by a simple yardstick - that the "child knows more than its parents".

The model in crisis

In the second half of the 20th century, the developmental paradigm of the North was transferred to the South almost without modification. Thus, during the period from 1950 to 1970, when development programmes and projects were at their peak, the number of universities world-wide mushroomed.

Towards the end of the 20th century, along with the computer revolution and the transition towards a global market, this Western model continued to be considered indispensable for the formation of highly competitive individuals, capable of functioning efficiently in the "global village".

In this manner, education throughout the world adapted itself to the Northern paradigm. But this model is in crisis.

The large growth of the student population has taken education systems to the brink of their capacity, while serious problems have arisen regarding the goals and means of education for students from increasingly diverse cultural and economic contexts.

In the cities of the North, for example, successive immigration waves have formed an increasingly heterogeneous population, difficult to teach according to traditional parameters. Throughout the world, emigration of rural inhabitants to the cities has created a similar problem.

The transmission of knowledge

The Northern education system is based, by and large, on the expectation that today's student is capable of storing more information than his or her predecessors. In this model, the teacher becomes the instrument of a society which seems to "manufacture" its young. Young people may be seen as boxes to be filled with knowledge according to a particular programme and, when filled, the programme is considered complete. It is then assumed that the youngster has become an adult.

This Western transmission of knowledge is based on two assumptions. The first is immediate comprehension - that is, if things are clearly expressed they will be instantly and totally understood. The other is the idea that knowledge, once learnt, can be stored indefinitely.

Changes introduced by computers represent the peak of this accumulative aspiration. More and more complex data, which has to be constantly reviewed and renewed, is stored in increasingly smaller electronic units.

This emphasis on the mechanical transmission of knowledge has led to a new conception of the individual. It is almost as if the citizen of today could be replaced by an automoton.

20th century automatons

Education intended to create citizens for the nation-state attempted to level out differences. It was meant to erase differences of background and produce individuals capable of reaching an undifferentiated civic behaviour.

However, the failure of these models is apparent in the more computerized societies. One extreme aspect is technical illiteracy, where individuals are incapable of conceptually understanding, in the traditional way, chains or lines of words when they read.

In some cases, this failure to understand the linear aspect of phrases results from the confrontation between the oral culture from which the students come and the "literate" culture which is imposed upon them. The collision between the education model and the cultural background of the student is amplified in the countries of the South, since they have incorporated an educational model which is completely alien to them. The educational system in these countries is trying and failing to transmit its knowledge in a cultural vacuum, with the sole purpose of incorporating the individual to the market.

Ultimately education has to be built upon the moral and cultural bases of a community. With the loss of these it looks unrealistic to think in terms of a "global citizenship".

The idea of producing citizens for nationalist democracies which appeared after the French Revolution was based on a credible morality and ideology. But nowadays, for the Algerians in Paris, the Pakistanis in London or the Turks in Germany, the values they learn at home clash with those promoted by the education system.

At the same time, the notion of belonging to a nation becomes more and more hazy as globalization and the new political, economic and linguistic blocs displace the sense of identity and roots.

In regions where initiation ceremonies take place, such as in non-Islamic Africa, the transmission of knowledge is commonly signified by a visible mark on the body of the initiate. That mark is the indelible inscription of society and its values upon the body of the individual.

In Western societies changed by technological revolutions, this mark, whether concrete or abstract, has nowadays virtually disappeared. Instead of knowledge and values, the individual learns functional codes of behaviour. In this context, society produces individuals capable of functioning within society and labour like machines, but without the values which render their functioning meaningful. It may be said that this type of individual resembles a sociopath: a cipher behind which there is no meaning, no

PERCENTAGE OF STUDENTS ACROSS THE SCHOOL-AGE POPULATION
(GROSS ENROLMENT RATE IS THE NUMBER OF CHILDREN ENROLLED AT A LEVEL – PRIMARY OR SECONDARY – REGARDLESS OF AGE, DIVIDED BY THE POPULATION OF THAT AGE GROUP)

	Primary (1990-95)		Secondary (1990-95)		Tertiary (1995)
	Male	Female	Male	Female	Total
Afghanistan	63	32	32	11	..
Albania	98	99	36	37	10
Algeria	111	98	66	58	11
Angola	95	87	..	..	1
Aotearoa/New Zealand	103	101	111	114	58
Argentina	108	107	70	75	38
Armenia	87	93	80	90	49
Australia	107	106	83	86	72
Austria	103	103	109	104	45
Azerbaijan	120	115	87	85	20
Bahamas	100	103	95	95	..
Bahrain	110	113	97	100	..
Bangladesh	84	73	25	13	..
Barbados	90	91	90	80	..
Belarus	98	95	92	97	..
Belgium	99	100	103	104	49
Belize	113	109	46	52	..
Benin	88	44	17	7	3
Bhutan	31	19	7	2	..
Bolivia	99	90	40	34	..
Botswana	114	115	54	58	4
Brazil	..	..	..	..	11
Brunei	113	106	67	73	..
Bulgaria	88	84	68	72	39
Burkina Faso	48	31	12	6	1
Burundi	76	62	8	5	1
Cambodia	130	106	31	18	2
Cameroon	93	84	32	22	..
Canada	104	102	106	106	103
Cape Verde	132	130	28	26	..
Central African Rep.	88	55	17	6	1
Chad	75	36	13	3	1
Chile	100	98	66	70	28
China	120	116	60	51	5
Colombia	118	120	57	68	17
Comoros	81	69	21	17	..
Congo D.R.	78	58	33	15	2
Costa Rica	107	105	47	51	32
Côte d'Ivoire	78	59	33	17	4
Croatia	87	86	75	81	28
Cuba	104	103	70	79	14
Cyprus	100	100	96	98	..
Czech Republic	100	100	90	94	21
Denmark	99	99	113	117	45
Djibouti	43	33	15	10	..
Dominican Republic	103	104	34	47	..
Ecuador	124	122	54	56	..
Egypt	105	91	82	71	18
El Salvador	79	80	27	30	18
Eritrea	54	43	19	13	1
Estonia	103	100	92	90	38
Ethiopia	33	21	11	10	1
Fiji	128	127	64	65	..
Finland	100	100	110	130	67
France	107	105	104	107	50
Gambia	79	56	25	13	2
Georgia	82	81	82	76	38
Germany	97	98	101	100	43
Ghana	83	70	45	29	..
Greece	95	95	99	96	38
Guatemala	89	78	25	23	8
Guinea	61	30	18	6	..
Guinea-Bissau	77	42	9	4	..
Guyana	113	111	56	59	..
Haiti	58	54	22	21	..
Honduras	111	112	29	37	10
Hungary	97	97	79	83	19
Iceland	100	96	105	105	..
India	113	91	59	38	6
Indonesia	117	113	49	41	11
Iran	104	97	76	62	15
Iraq	98	83	53	34	..
Ireland	104	104	110	115	37
Israel	95	95	83	89	41
Italy	98	99	81	82	41
Jamaica	109	108	62	70	6
Japan	102	102	98	99	40
Jordan	94	95	52	54	..
Kazakhstan	86	86	89	92	33
Kenya	92	91	28	23	..
Korea, North	108	101	..	..	..
Korea, South	95	96	100	99	52
Kuwait	69	69	65	64	25
Kyrgyzstan	110	111	84	89	14
Laos	123	92	31	19	2
Latvia	85	81	84	89	26
Lebanon	114	110	75	83	27
Lesotho	93	104	23	34	2
Libya	110	110	95	95	16
Lithuania	97	95	80	84	28
Luxembourg	88	94	78	78	..
Macedonia, TFYR	88	87	55	56	18
Madagascar	75	72	14	14	3
Malawi	126	114	6	4	2
Malaysia	93	94	58	64	11
Maldives	136	133	49	49	..
Mali	39	25	11	6	..
Malta	110	107	93	83	..
Mauritania	81	66	19	11	4
Mauritius	107	106	58	60	6
Mexico	114	110	57	58	14
Moldova	95	94	71	74	25
Mongolia	82	87	50	70	15
Morocco	92	68	43	32	11
Mozambique	75	54	10	6	1
Myanmar/Burma	112	108	23	23	5
Namibia	136	138	57	69	8
Nepal	129	88	46	23	5
Netherlands	96	98	129	118	49
Nicaragua	102	105	40	47	9
Niger	35	21	9	5	..
Nigeria	100	79	33	28	4
Norway	99	99	118	114	55
Oman	85	80	67	61	5
Pakistan	94	42	33	17	3
Panama	108	104	60	65	30
Papua New Guinea	88	75	17	11	3
Paraguay	111	108	38	40	10
Peru	..	..	..	..	31
Philippines	110	111	..	..	27
Poland	100	98	95	96	27
Portugal	122	118	63	74	34
Qatar	89	84	82	82	..
Romania	94	93	77	78	18
Russia	109	108	84	91	43
Rwanda	78	76	11	9	..
Saudi Arabia	79	75	57	47	15
Senegal	68	51	21	11	3
Sierra Leone	60	42	22	12	..
Singapore	109	107	69	71	34
Slovakia	101	101	88	93	20
Slovenia	100	100	89	91	32
Solomon Is.	104	90	21	14	..
South Africa	119	115	76	88	17
Spain	104	105	107	120	46
Sri Lanka	106	104	71	79	5
Sudan	61	48	24	19	..
Suriname	129	125	50	58	..
Swaziland	125	119	53	51	..
Sweden	100	100	99	100	43
Switzerland	100	102	93	89	32
Syria	108	97	50	41	18
Tajikistan	91	88	83	75	20
Tanzania	71	69	6	5	1
Thailand	98	97	38	37	20
Togo	122	81	34	12	3
Trinidad and Tobago	94	94	74	78	8
Tunisia	123	113	58	53	13
Turkey	101	94	76	50	18
Uganda	74	59	14	8	2
Ukraine	87	87	88	95	41
United Arab Emirates	112	108	88	97	9
United Kingdom	114	114	93	95	48
United States	107	106	98	97	81
Uruguay	110	109	74	88	27
Uzbekistan	78	76	99	87	32
Vanuatu	105	107	23	18	..
Venezuela	93	96	29	41	29
Vietnam	..	..	..	..	4
Yemen	118	47	37	9	4
Yugoslavia Fed. Rep.	68	71	61	63	21
Zambia	85	79	31	19	3
Zimbabwe	119	111	49	39	7

Sources: The State of the World's Children 1998, UNICEF, 1998; World Development Indicators 1998, World Bank, 1998.

feelings nor a socially viable interpretation of the world.

The uprooted individual, who no longer finds moral bases at home or in society, often finds refuge in artificial paradises such as drugs or with groups that seek an identity alien to society's model. In the end, social harmony is at risk if education cannot value differences and use them to enrich knowledge. ❑

Country	Ratio	Country	Ratio
Albania	18	Latvia	14
Algeria	27	Lebanon	12
Aotearoa/New Zealand	18	Lesotho	49
Armenia	22	Lithuania	17
Australia	16	Macedonia, TFYR	20
Austria	12	Madagascar	40
Azerbaijan	20	Malawi	62
Belarus	20	Malaysia	20
Belgium	12	Mali	66
Benin	49	Mauritania	52
Botswana	26	Mauritius	22
Brazil	23	Mexico	29
Bulgaria	17	Moldova	23
Burkina Faso	58	Mongolia	25
Burundi	65	Morocco	28
Cambodia	45	Mozambique	58
Cameroon	46	Myanmar/Burma	48
Canada	16	Namibia	32
Chad	62	Nepal	39
Chile	27	Netherlands	19
China	24	Nicaragua	38
Colombia	25	Niger	37
Congo D.R.	45	Nigeria	37
Congo R.	70	Norway	9
Costa Rica	31	Oman	26
Côte d'Ivoire	45	Palestine	42
Croatia	20	Papua New Guinea	33
Cuba	14	Paraguay	24
Czech Republic	20	Peru	28
Denmark	10	Philippines	35
Dominican Republic	35	Poland	16
Ecuador	26	Portugal	12
Egypt	24	Romania	20
El Salvador	28	Russia	20
Eritrea	41	Saudi Arabia	13
Estonia	17	Senegal	58
Ethiopia	33	Slovakia	24
France	19	Slovenia	14
Gabon	52	South Africa	37
Gambia	30	Spain	18
Georgia	16	Sri Lanka	28
Germany	18	Sudan	36
Ghana	28	Sweden	11
Greece	16	Switzerland	12
Guatemala	34	Syria	24
Guinea	49	Tajikistan	23
Honduras	35	Tanzania	37
Hungary	11	Thailand	20
India	63	Togo	51
Indonesia	23	Trinidad and Tobago	25
Iran	32	Tunisia	25
Iraq	22	Turkey	28
Ireland	23	Uganda	35
Israel	16	Ukraine	20
Italy	11	United Arab Emirates	17
Jamaica	37	United Kingdom	19
Japan	18	United States	16
Jordan	21	Uruguay	20
Kazakhstan	20	Uzbekistan	21
Kenya	31	Venezuela	23
Korea, South	32	Vietnam	34
Kuwait	15	Yugoslavia Fed. Rep.	22
Kyrgyzstan	20	Zambia	39
Laos	30	Zimbabwe	39

Source: World Development Indicators 1998, World Bank, 1998.

Rites of passage

Many societies accord deep significance to their rites of transition or passage which allow youngsters to gain admission into adulthood as full members of their community.

For societies which practise them, rites of transition or initiation are an essential characteristic, and all social and religious life of the community is organized around them.

The body of the initiated is of primary importance in such rituals. The body is the only place considered appropriate to hold the sign of a particular time of life, the mark of a transition and the determination of a destiny.

Why is it necessary for the individual body to be the repository of ethnic identity? Why should knowledge to be gained only be communicated through the social action of a ritual on the bodies of the young?

European chroniclers at the time of the American conquest revealed their horror at these indigenous ceremonies. The way in which the community took over the body of the inititated often involved torture.

"One by one, the youngsters, after three days of fasting and three nights without sleep, walk towards their executioners", wrote chronicler George Catlin. Then he described the piercing, wounds, amputations and torn flesh of the young bodies. He added: "The impassiveness, even the serenity with which these youngsters endured their martyrdom, was much more extraordinary even than the torment itself".

The techniques and means differ from one group or society to another, from one region to another, but the goal is always the same: to cause suffering. One common interpretation has been to consider the initiation only as a test of the courage or bravery of the young people in their transition to adulthood.

To suffer in silence is, undoubtedly, proof of individual courage, but there is something else which the community wants to teach and, once the marks and scars are engraved on the body, it turns into indelible memory.

The rite emphasizes keeping the memory of the secret entrusted by the clan. In possessing the memory of that knowledge, initates are transformed into full members of the community. "Now you are one of us and you will not forget that".

That is the secret: each one of you is like us, you have the same name and will not change it, each one of you holds the same place as us, not one of you is inferior, nor superior to us, you cannot forget this.

Source: *Society against the State*, Pierre Clastres.

ADULT LITERACY RATE % 1995

	Total	Male	Female		Total	Male	Female
Afghanistan	32	47	15	Liechtenstein	100	100	100
Algeria	62	74	49	Lithuania	99	100	99
Angola	42	56	29	Madagascar	46	60	32
Antigua	95	..	..	Malawi	56	72	42
Argentina	96	96	96	Malaysia	84	89	78
Armenia	100	100	99	Maldives	93	93	93
Azerbaijan	100	100	99	Mali	31	39	23
Bahamas	98	99	98	Malta	91	91	92
Bahrain	85	89	79	Marshall Is.	91	..	90
Bangladesh	38	49	26	Mauritania	38	50	26
Barbados	97	98	97	Mauritius	83	87	79
Belarus	99	100	99	Mexico	90	92	87
Belize	80	70	70	Micronesia	81	..	79
Benin	37	49	26	Moldova	99	98	99
Bhutan	42	56	28	Mongolia	83	89	77
Bolivia	83	91	76	Morocco	44	57	31
Botswana	70	81	60	Mozambique	40	58	23
Brazil	83	83	83	Myanmar/Burma	83	89	78
Brunei	88	93	83	Namibia	76	78	74
Bulgaria	98	99	98	Nepal	28	41	14
Burkina Faso	19	30	9	Nicaragua	66	65	67
Burundi	35	49	23	Niger	14	21	7
Cambodia	65	80	53	Nigeria	57	67	47
Cameroon	63	75	52	Niue	99	..	99
Canada	97	..	..	Oman	59	71	46
Cape Verde	72	81	64	Pakistan	38	50	24
Central African Rep.	60	69	52	Palau	98	..	97
Chad	48	62	35	Palestine	84	92	77
Chile	95	95	95	Panama	91	91	90
China	82	90	73	Papua New Guinea	72	81	63
Colombia	91	91	91	Paraguay	92	94	91
Comoros	57	64	50	Peru	89	95	83
Congo D.R.	77	87	68	Philippines	95	95	94
Congo R.	75	83	67	Poland	..	99	98
Cook Is.	99	..	99	Portugal	90	92	87
Costa Rica	95	95	95	Qatar	79	79	80
Côte d'Ivoire	40	50	30	Romania	98	99	97
Croatia	98	98	97	Russia	99	100	99
Cuba	96	96	95	Rwanda	61	70	52
Cyprus	94	98	91	Samoa	98	..	98
Djibouti	46	60	33	São Tome and Principe	57	73	42
Dominican Republic	82	82	82	Saudi Arabia	63	72	50
Ecuador	90	92	88	Senegal	33	43	23
Egypt	51	64	39	Seychelles	84	83	86
El Salvador	72	74	70	Sierra Leone	31	45	18
Equatorial Guinea	79	90	68	Singapore	91	96	86
Estonia	98	98	98	Slovenia	99	100	99
Ethiopia	36	46	25	Solomon Is.	62	..	56
Fiji	92	94	89	Somalia	24	36	14
Gabon	63	74	53	South Africa	82	82	82
Gambia	39	53	25	Spain	97	98	96
Georgia	99	100	99	Sri Lanka	90	93	87
Ghana	65	76	54	St Kitts-Nevis	90	..	..
Greece	97	98	95	St Vincent	82	..	..
Grenada	96	..	..	Sudan	46	58	35
Guatemala	56	63	49	Suriname	93	95	91
Guinea	36	50	22	Swaziland	77	78	76
Guinea-Bissau	55	68	43	Syria	71	86	56
Guyana	98	99	98	Tajikistan	100	100	100
Haiti	45	48	42	Tanzania	68	79	57
Honduras	73	73	73	Thailand	94	96	92
Hungary	99	99	99	Togo	52	67	37
India	52	66	38	Tonga	99	..	99
Indonesia	84	90	78	Trinidad and Tobago	98	99	97
Iran	69	78	59	Tunisia	67	79	55
Iraq	58	71	45	Turkey	82	92	72
Israel	95	97	93	Turkmenistan	98	99	97
Italy	98	99	98	Tuvalu	99	..	..
Jamaica	85	81	89	Uganda	62	74	50
Jordan	87	93	79	Ukraine	99	98	99
Kazakhstan	100	100	99	United Arab Emirates	79	79	80
Kenya	78	86	70	United States	99	..	..
Kiribati	93	..	92	Uruguay	97	97	98
Korea, South	98	99	97	Uzbekistan	100	100	100
Kuwait	79	82	75	Vanuatu	64	..	60
Kyrgyzstan	97	99	95	Venezuela	91	92	90
Laos	57	69	44	Vietnam	94	97	91
Latvia	100	100	100	Yemen	33	53	26
Lebanon	92	95	90	Yugoslavia Fed. Rep.	98	99	97
Lesotho	71	81	62	Zambia	78	86	71
Liberia	38	54	22	Zimbabwe	85	90	80
Libya	76	88	63				

Source: The State of the World's Children 1998, UNICEF, 1998.

The limits of biomedicine

The idea of the human body as a machine composed of myriad separate micro-mechanisms and of illnesses caused by specific pathogenic agents allowed for the great progress of 20th century medicine. But criticism of such thinking is on the increase and is calling into question the bases of so-called biomedicine

Throughout the history of Western science, the development of biology has been parallel to that of medicine. It is therefore natural that the mechanistic view of life, after it was firmly established in the field of biology, also conquered the interpretation of health and disease by physicians. The human body was considered as a machine whose separate parts could be analysed and illness as a defective activity of cellular and molecular biology mechanisms. The task of doctors was to intervene, physically or chemically, to correct the dysfunctional activity of a specific mechanism. This view, prevalent today at an institutional level, has led medicine to focus on increasingly smaller fragments of the human body. When health was reduced to a mechanical function, the ability to deal with the phenomenon of healing was lost.

Complete well-being

According to the World Health Organization (WHO), health is a "state of complete physical, mental and social well-being and not simply an absence of illness". This suggests the holistic nature of health, which should be taken into account when healing is attempted.

This approach is more akin to the modes of healing which traditional healers have practised from time immemorial, guided by popular wisdom. Illness is viewed as a disorder of the whole person, including body and soul, the patient's self-image, dependence on physical and social environs, and relation with the cosmos and gods.

Healers, who still treat the majority of the world's ill people, follow holistic criteria and use a wide range of therapeutical techniques. But the thing they have in common is that they never restrict themselves to purely physical phenomena, as the biomedical model does.

Through rituals and ceremonies, they try to dissipate fear in the patient's mind, always a significant component of illness, and help to enhance the patient's own natural healing powers.

Modern medicine

The beginning of the 19th century saw Western medicine at its peak, with major discoveries in the field of biology. Early in the century, practically the whole structure of the human body was already known in its most minute details. Also, fast progress was being made in the understanding of physiological processes, mainly due to the elaborate experiments of Claude Bernard. Therefore, physicians and virologists focused their attention on smaller entities. This trend followed two paths. The first was promoted by Rudolf Virchow for whom all sickness indicated a series of structural changes within the cells, and he proposed cellular biology as the basis of medicine. The second path was taken by Louis Pasteur, founder of the study of micro-organisms which has since been adopted by biomedical researchers.

Pasteur clearly showed the relationship between bacteria and illness and that is why his theories had a decisive impact. Throughout the history of modern medicine, physicians had debated whether diseases were caused only by one factor or were the result of several factors acting simultaneously.

In the 19th century, these two views were represented respectively by Pasteur and Bernard. The latter pointed out the importance of environmental factors, external and internal, and stressed the idea of illnesses produced by a loss of internal balance which supposed the occurrence of a great number of factors.

Pasteur centred his efforts on explaining the role played by bacteria in the emergence of illnesses, relating different illnesses with certain microbes.

Pasteur and his followers won the debate and as a result germ theory, according to which each illness is caused by a specific microbe, was rapidly accepted by medical professionals.

The concept of scientific aetiology was introduced by physician Robert Koch who formulated a series of criteria to prove without a doubt if a certain microbe caused a specific disease.

In the 20th century the progress of biology was linked to the development of medical technology. New diagnostic instruments were invented, among them the stethoscope and devices to measure blood pressure, and surgical technology became more sophisticated.

From the patient to the illness

Physicians began shifting their attention from the patient to the illness. Pathologies were located, diagnosed and labelled according to a defined system of classification, and were studied in hospitals which were no longer medieval homes of mercy but centres of diagnosis, therapy and learning. This is how the trend towards specialization began in medicine, which would reach its peak in the 20th century.

The same emphasis on the localization and precise definition of pathologies was used in the medical analysis of mental disorders, for which the term psychiatry was coined. Instead of trying to understand the psychological aspects, psychiatrists focused their efforts towards finding organic causes - infections, nutritional deficiencies, brain injuries - for all mental ills.

New trends appeared as a reaction to this. In fact, already in the 19th century, the limited success of the biomedical approach towards mental illness had inspired an alternative movement - the psychological approach - which led to the dynamic psychiatry and psychotherapy of Sigmund Freud.

Vaccines, antibiotics, hormones

Modern medicine is characterized by the gradual orientation of biology towards the molecular level and the understanding of several biological phenomena at this level. The first significant progress was the emergence of a large number of drugs and vaccines which fought against diseases caused by bacteria - typhus, tetanus, diphtheria and many more - and then against those caused by viruses. In tropical medicine, the joint action of immunization and pesticides to control disease-transmitting mosquitoes has made significant inroads towards the eradication of the three most common diseases of the tropics: malaria, yellow fever and leprosy.

The discovery of penicillin in 1928 marked the beginning of the era of antibiotics, one of the most spectacular periods in modern medicine, which would peak in the 1950s with the emergence of several germ-killing compounds able to tackle a wide range of micro-organisms.

A great victory for modern medicine was the development of endocrinology, the study of the endocrine glands and their fluids, called hormones, which flow in the bloodstream and regulate many physiological functions. Endocrinology's greatest breakthrough was the discovery of insulin. The extraction of this hormone, along with the discovery of the link between diabetes and insulin deficiency, saved many diabetics from a sure death and enabled them to carry on a normal life, sustained by periodical injections.

Another significant advance in the study of hormones was the discovery of cortisone, a substance extracted from the envelope of suprarenal glands which is a powerful anti-inflammatory agent.

All these examples reveal cases in which biomedical problems were reduced to molecular phenomena in order to combat them with drugs.

One unfortunate result of this is that physicians only have a partial view of the ills they research and the drugs they invent. Aspects which go beyond this view are considered irrelevant to the disease and are classified as "side-effects".

Surgery

The detailed knowledge of biological functions at cellular and molecular levels was also of great assistance to surgery. Three blood groups were discovered, blood transfusions became possible and a substance was developed which prevents blood from clotting. These breakthroughs, along with progress in anaesthesia, gave surgeons greater leeway in their operating procedures.

With the emergence of antibiotics, risk of post-operative infection was reduced, and it became possible to replace injured bone and tissue with other materials, especially plastic.

In the 1960s, Christian Barnard performed the first successful heart transplant operation, followed by other transplants which had varying degrees of success. With these developments, medical technology not only reached an unprecedented degree of complexity but also became an essential part of modern health care.

Health and lifestyle

In spite of these medical breakthroughs, the crisis of health care in Europe and North America is deep. People are discontented with medical institutions due to, among other things, the lack of access to services, the lack of understanding and care, and negligence amongst some physicians. But it is the disproportion between costs and the efficiency of medicine which comes in for the most criticism. In spite of the huge rise in medical costs in the last three decades, it does not seem that the general health of the population has improved in a significant way.

It is difficult to judge the relationship between medicine and health, since most statistics on health define it as the absence of disease. A meaningful evaluation would have to enclose both individual health and social health, and would include mental illness and social pathologies. A wider view would argue that although medicine has helped in the eradication of several diseases, this does not necessarily mean it has restored health in its broadest sense. If health is regarded from a holistic point of view, physical disease is an expression of a basic imbalance within the organism.

Health in figures

A = Population per doctor 1988-91
B = Population per nurse 1988-91

COUNTRY	A	B	COUNTRY	A	B
Albania	730	..	Korea, South	1,205	1,538
Algeria	1,064	..	Laos	4,545	..
Angola	25,000	..	Lebanon	413	2,174
Aotearoa/New Zealand	521	..	Lesotho	25,000	2,000
Argentina	329	1,786	Libya	962	328
Bahrain	775	..	Madagascar	8,333	3,846
Bangladesh	12,500	20,000	Malawi	50,000	33,333
Belarus	282	..	Malaysia	2,564	..
Belgium	298	..	Mali	20,000	5,882
Benin	14,286	3,226	Mauritania	16,667	2,273
Bhutan	11,111	6,667	Mauritius	1,176	398
Bolivia	2,564	7,692	Mexico	621	..
Botswana	4,762	469	Mongolia	389	209
Brazil	847	3,448	Mozambique	33,333	5,000
Bulgaria	315	..	Myanmar/Burma	12,500	..
Burkina Faso	33,333	10,000	Namibia	4,545	339
Burundi	16,667	..	Nepal	16,667	33,333
Cameroon	12,500	1,852	Netherlands	398	..
Canada	446	..	Nicaragua	2,000	3,125
Central African Rep.	25,000	11,111	Niger	50,000	3,846
Chad	33,333	50,000	Nigeria	5,882	1,639
Chile	943	3,846	Norway	309	..
Colombia	1,064	2,632	Pakistan	2,000	3,448
Comoros	10,000	3,448	Panama	562	1,064
Congo D.R.	14,286	1,351	Papua New Guinea	..	1,587
Congo R.	3,571	1,370	Paraguay	1,587	7,143
Costa Rica	1,136	2,222	Peru	1,031	..
Côte d'Ivoire	11,111	3,226	Philippines	8,333	..
Cuba	332	180	Poland	467	..
Cyprus	585	..	Portugal	352	..
Denmark	360	..	Romania	552	..
Dominican Republic	935	9,091	Rwanda	25,000	8,333
Ecuador	671	1,818	Saudi Arabia	704	310
El Salvador	1,563	3,333	Senegal	16,667	12,500
Ethiopia	33,333	14,286	Singapore	725	..
Finland	405	..	Spain	262	..
France	333	..	Sri Lanka	7,143	1,754
Gabon	2,500	1,471	Swaziland	9,091	595
Ghana	25,000	3,704	Sweden	395	..
Greece	313	..	Switzerland	585	..
Guatemala	4,000	7,143	Syria	1,220	1,031
Guinea	7,692	..	Thailand	4,762	1,064
Haiti	7,143	9,091	Togo	11,111	3,030
Honduras	1,266	4,545	Trinidad and Tobago	1,370	..
Hungary	312	..	Tunisia	1,852	407
India	2,439	3,333	Turkey	1,176	..
Indonesia	7,143	2,857	Uganda	25,000	7,143
Iraq	1,667	1,370	Ukraine	259	..
Ireland	633	..	United Arab Emirates	1,042	568
Italy	211	..	Vietnam	247	1,149
Jamaica	7,143	..	Yemen	4,348	1,818
Jordan	649	641	Zambia	11,111	5,000
Kenya	20,000	9,091	Zimbabwe	7,692	1,639

Source: Human Development Report 1997, UNDP, 1997.

	% OF POPULATION WITH ACCESS TO SAFE WATER 1990-96	% OF POPULATION WITH ACCESS TO HEALTH SERVICES 1990-96
Afghanistan	12	29
Algeria	78	98
Angola	32	..
Aotearoa/New Zealand	97	..
Argentina	71	71
Bangladesh	97	45
Barbados	100	..
Belize	89	..
Benin	50	18
Bhutan	58	65
Bolivia	63	67
Botswana	93	..
Brazil	76	..
Burkina Faso	42	90
Burundi	52	80
Cambodia	36	53
Cameroon	50	80
Cape Verde	51	..
Central African Rep.	38	52
Chad	24	30
Chile	95	97
China	67	88
Colombia	85	81
Comoros	53	..
Congo D.R.	42	26
Congo R.	34	83
Cook Is.	100	..
Costa Rica	96	..
Côte d'Ivoire	42	..
Cuba	93	100
Djibouti	90	..
Dominica	96	..
Dominican Republic	65	78
Ecuador	68	..
Egypt	87	99
El Salvador	69	40
Equatorial Guinea	95	..
Eritrea	22	..
Ethiopia	25	46
Fiji	100	..
Gabon	68	..
Gambia	48	93
Ghana	65	60
Guatemala	77	57
Guinea	46	80
Guinea-Bissau	59	40
Guyana	61	..
Haiti	37	60
Honduras	87	69
India	81	85
Indonesia	62	93
Iran	90	88
Iraq	78	93
Jamaica	86	90
Japan	97	..
Jordan	98	97
Kazakhstan	93	..
Kenya	53	77
Kiribati	100	..
Korea, North	81	..
Korea, South	93	100
Kuwait	..	100
Kyrgyzstan	71	..
Laos	44	67
Lebanon	94	95
Lesotho	62	80
Liberia	46	39

	% OF POPULATION WITH ACCESS TO SAFE WATER 1990-96	% OF POPULATION WITH ACCESS TO HEALTH SERVICES 1990-96
Libya	97	95
Madagascar	34	38
Malawi	37	35
Malaysia	78	..
Maldives	96	..
Mali	66	40
Marshall Is.	74	..
Mauritania	74	63
Mauritius	98	100
Mexico	83	93
Micronesia	100	..
Moldova	55	..
Mongolia	40	95
Morocco	65	70
Mozambique	63	39
Myanmar/Burma	60	60
Namibia	57	59
Nepal	63	..
Nicaragua	61	83
Niger	48	99
Nigeria	50	51
Niue	100	..
Oman	82	96
Pakistan	74	55
Palau	88	..
Panama	93	70
Papua New Guinea	28	96
Paraguay	60	63
Peru	67	44
Philippines	84	71
Rwanda	..	80
Samoa	82	..
São Tome and Principe	82	..
Saudi Arabia	95	97
Senegal	63	90
Sierra Leone	34	38
Singapore	100	..
Solomon Is.	61	..
Somalia	31	..
South Africa	99	..
Sri Lanka	57	..
St Kitts-Nevis	100	..
St Vincent	89	..
Sudan	50	70
Swaziland	60	..
Syria	86	90
Tajikistan	60	..
Tanzania	38	42
Thailand	89	90
Togo	55	..
Tonga	100	..
Trinidad and Tobago	97	100
Tunisia	98	..
Turkey	49	..
Turkmenistan	74	100
Tuvalu	97	..
Uganda	46	49
United Arab Emirates	95	99
Uruguay	99	82
Uzbekistan	62	..
Vanuatu	87	..
Venezuela	79	..
Vietnam	43	90
Yemen	61	38
Zambia	27	..
Zimbabwe	79	85

Sources: The State of the World's Children, UNICEF, 1997 and 1998.

Psychological and social pathologies cannot be discounted, for when the physical symptoms of a disease are suppressed through medical intervention, the illness can express itself through other means. In fact, psychological and social pathologies have become a major issue for public health systems. According to several surveys up to 25 per cent of the population can be considered as seriously affected by psychological problems and in need of therapeutic care.

There has also been an alarming increase in alcoholism and other addictions, violent crimes, accidents and suicides, all of them symptoms of social unease.

What then is the relation between medicine and health? How far has Western medicine gone towards curing disease and easing suffering?

Stress

The key factors which define the health of human beings are not medical intervention, but behaviour, nutrition, and their environment. Since these factors vary from culture to culture, each civilization has distinctive diseases and, since food, behaviour, and environmental situations change, pathological models also differ.

That explains why acute infections, which plagued Europe and North America in the 19th century and which are still the main killers in the Third World, have been replaced in developed countries by diseases which are no longer linked to poverty and deficient lifestyles, but related to material well-being and over-consumption.

These are chronic and degenerative illnesses - heart disease, cancer, diabetes - which are often referred to as the "ills of civilization", since they are closely related to stress, a diet rich in fats and proteins, drug abuse, smoking, a sedentary life and environmental pollution.

Modern Western medicine is the less effective because it does not consider the philosophical and holistic questions which arise in relation to all illness.

It is ironic that doctors themselves may be the ones that suffer most from a mechanistic or allopathic view of health, by neglecting the stressful circumstances of their own professional lives.

The life expectancy of a physician is today between 10 and 15 years below that of an average individual. In addition, medical staff not only suffer from a high rate of physical illnesses but they are also susceptible to alcoholism, drug abuse, suicide and other social pathologies. Many doctors acquire these unhealthy habits when they enter medical school, where learning turns into an experience loaded with stress.

Social pathologies

In order to adopt a holistic and ecological concept of health it is necessary to radically change current ideas of medicine and public perceptions. Many people support the biomedical model typical of Western health care because they fear changing their lifestyles and confronting their unhealthy behaviour. Instead of facing up to a situation which is often embarrassing and painful, these people insist in delegating all responsibility for their health to doctors and drugs. There is also a trend to use medical diagnoses to conceal social problems.

It is easier to talk about hyperactivity or of learning difficulties among children than to analyze school failures. We prefer to suffer from high blood pressure than changing the competitive way in which we conduct our business; we accept the high rates of deaths related to cancer instead of investigating food manufacturers' use of chemicals in food, or giving up smoking.

These health problems reach beyond the concerns of the medical profession but they inevitably become the centre of attention when we seriously attempt to go beyond current medical care. Overcoming the biological model will only be possible when we are willing to transform the whole of culture and society.

Source: *The crucial time*, Fritjof Capra.

The battle against cancer

The questionable safety of drugs

According to the World Health Organization (WHO), more than 10 million people developed cancer and more than six million died from this illness in 1996. With progress being made in the fight against other fatal diseases and increases in life expectancies, the risks of developing cancer continue to rise

Health institutions and the media have bombarded us with information on the risks of getting cancer and AIDS and the amount of investment involved in searching for cures is astronomical. However, hopes of really curing cancers and AIDS do not depend so much on new medical research, as on the treatment strategies of the medical establishment and the power of the companies interested in continuing to trade in the drugs and equipment developed for this kind of treatment.

Here are two cases of new research in the treatment of these illnesses:

* Dr. Ryke Geerd Hamer from the University of Tubingen, Germany, created a new psycho-neurosomatic therapy for cancer. Hamer was the head of the Radiology Service of the institution, specializing in intern medicine and psychiatry, as well as being a member of the University hospital teaching staff.

Hamer's studies attributed the origin of cancer to a shock or serious conflict, provoking an encoding error in the brain. His method of diagnosis and therapy allows the patient to adopt a positive and responsible attitude, instead of putting up with the aggressive treatments normally used which ignore the self-regulating mechanisms and processes of the human organism. This system also allows for the costs of treatment to be reduced.

Struck off the medical list for opposing the use of chemotherapy and radiotherapy, he was sentenced to more than a year in prison in 1997. The judge repeatedly refused to let him out on bail. Hamer had been asking for his discoveries to be verified for the last 15 years.

* Products for the treatment of cancer and AIDS developed in France by Doctors Mirko and Monique Beljanski suffered serious restrictions in distribution and both researchers were forced to leave the Pasteur Institute, because the conclusions of their research contradicted the views of the director, Nobel prize winner Jacques Monod.

The drugs they developed are plant extracts which work selectively for certain types of cancer and viruses. They had gathered evidence that these drugs protect healthy cells, while increasing the effectiveness of radio- and chemotherapy.

The Beljanskis have questioned traditional treatments on two counts - their invasive nature and the rapid resistance they trigger in viruses and cancerous cells. In the case of AIDS, they also question AZT, one of the first drugs to be widely prescribed to people with AIDS. They emphasize that this drug - produced by the Wellcome pharmaceutical company and now widely used to fight AIDS - was first discovered as a cancer treatment in the 1960s, but did not pass the health tests needed before it could be marketed.

However, during the Reagan administration in the US, AZT was recognised as valid by the US health agencies and triumphantly entered the market. Wellcome shares increased and the company expanded. ❏

Childhood

Poverty and discrimination: the biggest causes of death

The number of children immunized against the six most important childhood illnesses grew from 5 per cent in 1974 to 80 per cent in 1995. However, millions of children still die each year from preventable infectious diseases like diarrhoea, and poorer countries still suffer from a lack of basic health-care provision

U p until the middle of this century most people died before reaching 50; now the vast majority live longer. The 1955 average life span was 48, rising to 59 in 1975. The world's population has been steadily ageing. In 1997, there were more than 380 million people aged 65 or more and forecasts indicated the number would reach more than 690 million by the year 2020.

More than 52 million people died in 1996, 40 million in the Third World, 9 million of these in the poorest countries. The main causes were infectious or parasitic illnesses, which together accounted for 43 per cent of deaths, and chronic illnesses like respiratory and circulatory conditions and cancer, which accounted for 40 per cent.

Nearly 10 per cent of the deaths were of babies under a month old and under-fives made up a similar percentage. Chronic malnutrition is to blame for most of these deaths. Causes of the malnutrition affecting half the under-fives of Asia and a third of those of sub-Saharan Africa include poor eating habits, the shortage of health services, the lack of clean drinking water and insufficient maternal care.

Breast-feeding is the key to good child nutrition and development. In countries with high or moderately high mortality indices the risk of death from diarrhoea of a baby fed exclusively on its mother's milk is 14 times lower than that of a non-breast-fed baby.

According to UNICEF, between 30 per cent and 50 per cent of the population of the 35 poorest countries in the world had no access to health centres in early 1998. More than 1.1 billion people lacked clean drinking water and 2.9 billion had no sanitation. These conditions provide fertile ground for the spread of infectious diseases: in 1996, tuberculosis killed 3 million people, diarrhoea 2.5 million children, and malaria between 1.5 and 2.7 million people.

Discrimination against women is another of the basic causes of malnutrition and low birth weight. Women's limited access to education and employment as well as their often lower social status has a negative affect on their own health and that of their children.

Despite the infant mortality indices having fallen by 50 per cent in the last 50 years and the nutritional status of infants improving world-wide since 1980, the British NGO Save the Children reported that over the last 20 years there have never been so many children excluded from health-care as there are at present.

According to data from this organization, 800 million people lack health-care, including 200 million in sub-Saharan Africa, 300 million in the rural zones of India, another 200 million on its urban margins and at least 100 million more in the poorest countries of South-east Asia, like Nepal, Bangladesh and Laos. ❑

Breast is best

% OF MOTHERS BREAST FEEDING AT 6 MONTHS (1980-92)

Guinea-Bissau	100	Egypt	83
Congo D.R.	99	Jamaica	82
Nigeria	99	Mauritania	82
Papua New Guinea	99	Côte d'Ivoire	81
Zambia	99	Sri Lanka	81
Burkina Faso	98	Thailand	80
Congo R.	98	Guatemala	79
Laos	98	El Salvador	77
Bangladesh	97	India	75
Rwanda	97	Ecuador	73
Cameroon	95	Jordan	72
Indonesia	95	Guinea	70
Madagascar	95	Paraguay	69
Mali	95	Colombia	65
Cambodia	93	China	60
Mozambique	93	Saudi Arabia	57
Burundi	92	Mauritius	55
Ghana	92	Seychelles	55
Kenya	92	Panama	53
Zimbabwe	92	Mexico	50
Senegal	91	Trinidad and Tobago	49
Turkey	91	Dominican Republic	45
Botswana	90	Iraq	45
Sudan	90	Brazil	43
Tanzania	90	Lebanon	40
Benin	89	Costa Rica	38
Pakistan	88	Argentina	36
Uganda	88	Cuba	33
Vietnam	88	Uruguay	33
Peru	87	Honduras	28
Swaziland	87	Nicaragua	25
Togo	87	Chile	18
Namibia	86	Barbados	17
Bolivia	84	St Kitts-Nevis	3

Source: Human Development Report 1997, UNDP, 1997.

Children's health

A = Births attended by health personnel (%)
B = Life expectancy at birth (years)
C = % of low birth weight babies (2,500 gr)
D = Infant mortality (per 1,000 live births)
E = Underweight children under-5, %
F = Maternal mortality (per 100,000 live births)

	A 1990-96	B 1996	C 1990-94	D 1996	E 1990-97	F 1990
Afghanistan	9	45	20	165	..	1,700
Albania	99	71	7	34	..	65
Algeria	77	68	9	34	13	160
Andorra	..	..	..	5	..	..
Angola	15	47	19	170	..	1,500
Antigua	90	75	8	18	10	..
Aotearoa/New Z.	99	77	6	7	..	25
Argentina	97	73	7	22	..	100
Armenia	..	71	..	25	..	50
Australia	100	78	6	6	..	9
Austria	100	77	6	5	..	10
Azerbaijan	..	71	..	34	..	22
Bahamas	100	73	..	19	..	100
Bahrain	97	73	6	18	..	60
Bangladesh	14	57	50	83	56	850
Barbados	98	76	10	11	5	43
Belarus	100	70	..	14	..	37
Belgium	100	77	6	6	..	10
Belize	77	74	10	36	..	..
Benin	45	54	..	84	..	990
Bhutan	15	52	..	90	38	1,600
Bolivia	47	61	12	71	8	650
Bosnia-Herzegovina	..	73	..	15	..	..
Botswana	78	52	8	40	15	250
Brazil	88	67	11	44	6	220
Brunei	98	75	..	9	..	60
Bulgaria	100	71	6	16	..	27
Burkina Faso	42	46	21	82	30	930
Burundi	19	46	..	106	37	1,300
Cambodia	47	53	..	108	40	900
Cameroon	64	56	13	63	14	550
Canada	99	79	6	6	..	6
Cape Verde	30	66	11	54	19	..
Central African Rep.	46	49	15	103	27	700
Chad	15	47	..	92	..	1,500
Chile	98	75	5	11	1	65
China	84	69	9	38	16	95
Colombia	85	71	9	26	8	100
Comoros	52	57	8	83	26	950
Congo D.R.	..	53	15	128	34	870
Congo R.	..	51	16	81	24	890
Cook Is.	99	..	3	26	..	..
Costa Rica	93	77	7	13	2	55
Côte d'Ivoire	45	51	14	90	24	810
Croatia	..	72	..	10	..	..
Cuba	90	76	8	10	..	95
Cyprus	100	77	..	9	..	5
Czech Republic	..	73	6	6	..	15
Denmark	100	75	6	6	..	9
Djibouti	79	50	11	112	23	570
Dominica	96	73	10	17	5	..
Dominican Republic	96	71	11	45	6	110
East Timor	..	45	..	149	..	..
Ecuador	64	70	13	31	17	150
Egypt	46	65	10	57	15	170
El Salvador	87	69	11	34	11	300
Equatorial Guinea	58	49	..	111	..	820
Eritrea	21	50	13	78	44	1,400
Estonia	..	69	..	13	..	41
Ethiopia	14	49	16	113	48	1,400
Fiji	96	72	12	20	..	90
Finland	100	76	4	4	..	11
France	99	79	5	5	..	15
Gabon	80	55	..	87	..	500
Gambia	44	46	..	78	..	1,100
Georgia	..	73	..	23	..	33
Germany	99	76	..	5	..	22
Ghana	44	57	7	70	27	740
Greece	97	78	6	8	..	10
Grenada	81	..	9	25	..	..
Guatemala	35	66	15	43	27	200
Guinea	31	46	21	130	26	1,600
Guinea-Bissau	27	44	20	132	23	910
Guyana	90	64	19	60	18	..
Haiti	21	54	15	94	28	1,000
Honduras	88	69	9	29	18	220
Hungary	99	69	9	11	..	30
Iceland	100	79	..	5	..	0
India	34	62	33	73	53	570
Indonesia	36	64	14	47	11	650
Iran	77	69	9	33	16	120
Iraq	54	61	15	94	12	310
Ireland	..	76	4	6	..	10
Israel	99	77	7	8	..	7
Italy	..	78	5	6	..	12
Jamaica	82	74	10	10	10	120
Japan	100	80	7	4	..	18
Jordan	87	69	7	21	9	150
Kazakhstan	99	68	..	38	8	80
Kenya	45	54	16	61	23	650
Kiribati	72	58	6	56	..	..
Korea, North	100	72	..	23	..	70
Korea, South	98	72	9	6	..	130
Kuwait	99	76	7	13	6	29
Kyrgyzstan	..	68	..	39	..	110
Laos	..	53	18	102	40	650
Latvia	..	68	..	16	..	40
Lebanon	45	69	10	33	..	300
Lesotho	40	58	11	96	16	610
Liberia	58	48	..	157	..	560
Libya	76	65	..	50	5	220
Liechtenstein	..	..	..	6	..	..
Lithuania	..	70	..	14	..	36
Luxembourg	99	76	..	7	..	0
Macedonia, TFYR	..	72	..	26	..	..
Madagascar	57	58	17	100	34	490
Malawi	55	41	20	137	30	560
Malaysia	94	72	8	11	23	80
Maldives	90	64	20	54	39	..
Mali	24	47	17	134	27	1,200
Malta	..	77	..	10	..	0
Marshall Is.	..	..	15	63	..	..
Mauritania	40	53	11	124	23	930
Mauritius	97	71	13	20	16	120
Mexico	77	72	8	27	14	110
Micronesia	90	..	9	21	..	..
Moldova	..	68	4	26	..	60
Monaco	..	..	..	5	..	..
Mongolia	99	65	6	55	12	65
Morocco	40	66	9	64	9	610
Mozambique	25	47	20	133	27	1,500
Myanmar/Burma	57	59	16	105	43	580
Namibia	68	56	16	60	26	370
Nauru	..	..	..	25	..	..
Nepal	9	56	..	82	47	1,500
Netherlands	100	78	..	5	..	12
Nicaragua	61	68	15	44	12	160
Niger	15	48	15	191	36	1,200
Nigeria	31	52	16	114	36	1,000
Norway	100	77	4	5	..	6
Oman	87	70	8	15	23	190
Pakistan	19	63	25	95	38	340
Palau	90	..	8	25	..	..
Palestine	..	..	..	30	..	..
Panama	86	74	9	18	7	55
Papua New Guinea	20	57	23	79	35	930
Paraguay	66	69	5	28	4	160
Peru	56	68	11	45	8	280
Philippines	53	68	15	32	30	280
Poland	99	71	..	12	..	19
Portugal	90	75	5	7	..	15
Qatar	97	71	..	17	..	..
Romania	100	70	11	21	..	130
Russia	..	65	..	20	..	75
Rwanda	26	36	17	105	29	1,300
Samoa	95	69	6	42	..	35
San Marino	..	..	..	12	..	..
São Tome & Principe	86	69	7	62	17	..
Saudi Arabia	82	71	7	25	..	130
Senegal	46	51	11	74	22	1,200
Seychelles	99	72	10	15	6	..
Sierra Leone	25	37	11	164	29	1,800
Singapore	100	77	7	4	..	10
Slovakia	..	71	..	10	..	..
Slovenia	..	73	..	6	..	13
Solomon Is.	87	71	20	24	..	..
Somalia	2	48	16	125	..	1,600
South Africa	82	65	..	50	9	230
Spain	96	78	4	5	..	7
Sri Lanka	94	73	25	17	38	140
St Kitts-Nevis	100	69	9	31	..	..
St Lucia	99	71	8	18	..	..
St Vincent	73	72	8	19	..	..
Sudan	69	54	15	73	34	660
Suriname	91	71	13	25	..	..
Swaziland	55	59	10	68	10	560
Sweden	100	78	5	4	..	7
Switzerland	99	78	5	5	..	6
Syria	67	68	11	28	13	180
Tajikistan	..	67	..	56	..	130
Tanzania	53	51	14	93	27	770
Thailand	71	69	13	31	26	200
Togo	54	50	20	78	19	640
Tonga	92	69	2	19	..	..
Trinidad & Tobago	98	73	10	15	7	90
Tunisia	69	69	8	28	9	170
Turkey	76	68	8	41	10	180
Turkmenistan	..	65	5	57	..	55
Tuvalu	..	..	2	40	..	..
Uganda	38	41	..	88	26	1,200
Ukraine	100	69	..	18	..	50
Un. Arab Emirates	96	75	6	15	..	26
United Kingdom	100	77	7	6	..	9
United States	99	76	7	8	..	12
Uruguay	96	73	8	20	7	85
Uzbekistan	..	68	..	46	..	55
Vanuatu	86	67	7	41	20	280
Venezuela	69	72	9	24	6	120
Vietnam	95	67	17	33	45	160
Yemen	16	57	19	78	39	1,400
Yugoslavia Fed. Rep.	..	72	..	19	..	..
Zambia	51	43	13	112	28	940
Zimbabwe	69	49	14	49	16	570

Source: The State of the World's Children 1998, UNICEF, 1998.

Labour

Rights in a deregulated world

The nations of the industrialized North are debating ways of reducing the working day in the face of persistent unemployment, but a large number of the world's workers, above all in the poor nations, have not yet gained access to basic labour rights. Meanwhile, neoliberal propositions for the deregulation of the labour market predominate in various regions, proposing that working conditions be negotiated on an individual basis between employers and workers

At the beginning of the 20th century, workers in the countries with the highest industrial development were still fighting for an eight hour day. A growing union movement managed to unite workers groups in a call for more humane working conditions. The employers' associations were forced to recognize the presence of these new players and negotiate labour norms. Governments, although with different profiles depending on the country, intervened increasingly in the resolution of these conflicts.

In 1919, the International Labour Organization (ILO) - created following World War I and the October 1917 Russian Revolution - drew up an international convention, limiting working hours in industrial companies to eight hours a day and a forty-eight hour week. This norm was gradually adopted by most developed nations and some other areas of the world where industrialization was underway.

The 1929 economic crisis created large masses of unemployed people and led to trials of new macro-economic policies aiming to achieve full employment. In some countries this included the reduction of the working week to 40 hours. The 1935 ILO Convention said: "Considering that unemployment has spread so much and has become so persistent ..., it would be convenient, as far as possible, to encourage worker participation in the benefits of technical progress, the rapid development of which characterizes modern industry; ... a continuous effort is essential in order to reduce the working hours of all classes of job as far as possible".

The economic recovery of the following decades allowed for working conditions to improve and for the strengthening of the union movement. Industry grew in giant steps, but so did the tertiary sector, commerce and private and public services. The

employment structure in the industrialized countries changed profoundly; workers in the primary sector became only a small part of the economically active population, while employees in commerce and services, increased significantly in number.

However, the economic crisis of the 1970s once again jeopardized the development achieved in the Northern countries. Profound changes have been seen in the last 25 years, with some regions undergoing rapid industrialization, the development of new technologies and the absolute predominance of the capitalist productive system following the collapse of the socialist economies. At present, unemployment persists despite economic growth. Increased automation in modern industry has resulted in reductions of the workforce. The enormous development of the commerce and service sectors, on the other hand, has not made up for the loss of employment in industry.

On the threshold of the new century, the reduction of the working day has returned to the negotiating table as a possible option given the incapacity of the economies to generate sufficient jobs.

This time round, the negotiation presents a dilemma for both workers and employers. Each has a lot to lose if the mechanisms used to implement this do not serve their ends.

In a situation where the union movement has been weakened, further reduction of the working day must be obtained at a collective level, avoiding a loss of salary and maintaining some control over companies which might try to propose unrealistic intensification of work.

While workers are concerned they might be on the way to swelling the ranks of the unemployed and there is an increasing tendency toward individual

agreements with employers, the unions are on the horns of a dilemma between the needs of those who are working and those who are not. On another front, the changes in and the increasing complexity of the employment structure challenge the capacity of the unions to represent the workers as a whole.

Meanwhile, for the company bosses, the reduction of working hours must be accompanied by other methods of liberalizing the workforce in order to manage the use of working time more rationally. The increase in number of jobs is possible if companies can reduce costs - a fundamental issue in a globalized market, where they have to compete with foreign companies often operating with lower labour costs. Thus, negotiation of the working day must be carried out in each individual company, between workers and employers, taking into account the organizational necessities of each.

This means the role of the state becomes of crucial importance to both groups of players, pulling in two practically opposite directions. This makes it extremely difficult for the solutions to reach the consensus required for them to be implemented.

The political process of France in the late 1990s gives a good example of this *impasse*: following months of protests over high rates of unemployment, a socialist government tried to generate between 200,000-700,000 new jobs with a law reducing the working week to 35 hours, with no loss of salary. The project had the support of the workers, and was opposed by employers' organizations. The centre and right-wing parties proposed alternative legislation which would give the companies greater freedom of action, avoiding the obligatory nature of the measure.

The "unregulated" workers of the world

While this discussion is underway in the more developed nations, many workers, mainly in the less industrialized countries, continue to work in insecure conditions with no possibility of changing their situation. The average working day is more than eight hours and the working week longer than 48 hours.

International agreements and national legislation have only protected part of the workforce during this century. Today, the 1919 ILO Convention is still awaiting recognition by some countries. The legislation is still lax or is simply not applied in some nations.

Furthermore, millions of people are employed in small companies or the informal sector, with no legal protection, in extremely insecure or even dangerous conditions, generally working very long hours. One extreme case is that of the child workers, mostly working unprotected, with adult work schedules, despite international agreements which establish special conditions for children's work.

The co-existence of sectors with different degrees of protection within one country, also generates strong differences between groups of workers. This phenomenon, present all over the world, is most visible in underdeveloped nations, in many of which it is possible to talk of dual economies, with the persistence of pre-capitalist production systems alongside ultra-modern sectors.

In Latin America, the informal sector continues to generate most of the jobs. In 1990, 51.6 per cent of the economically active population was working in this sector, and this had risen to 56 per cent in 1995, a tendency which has continued since. In Asia, millions of people work in insecure or informal jobs. One in five children works in this region. In Africa, only one in ten workers has a regular, paid job in the modern industry and service sectors. Many workers, especially women, are self-employed, with low levels of income and no legal protection. Meanwhile, in sub-Saharan Africa, around 75 per cent of the workforce (some 314 million workers) work on the margins of the formal economy, while 16 million children aged between 10 and 14 years old are economically active in this region.

Labour regulations in transition

Today labour regulations the world over are being reassessed.

In the last two decades, economic and social policies have turned towards neoliberal views which claim the state must withdraw from its role as regulator of economic activity. The present labour regulations, which impede the liberalization of the work market, are being called into question. In an environment of globalization, the structural changes needed to adapt national economies to competition become more difficult, as some countries have lower labour costs, in many cases as a result of less rigid or more permissive labour regimes, or lower welfare contributions.

Such conditions, often present in structural adjustment programmes, get strongly established in the less developed nations, where offering a flexible market can attract or maintain the entry of foreign capital for productive investments.

However, deregulation in the strict sense of the term is unthinkable: these "deregulation" proposals aim in fact toward a new type of regulation, where

negotiation guidelines are drawn up, but with few actual rules, as these will be decided at an individual company, or in some cases, branch level.

No answers forthcoming

The 20th century is notable for gains in the labour rights field. The application of these regulations over increasingly wide geographical areas has even allowed the conditions of workers with no legal protection to be improved, or has at least made their situations more visible.

However, the outlook at the end of the century is not optimistic. The

difficulties of employment generation are compounded by demands on companies for increased competitiveness in a world context where labour regulations - still not available to a large part of the workforce - are being questioned.

For the unions, the challenge lies in achieving viable rules, without having to backslide on the basic rights obtained.

Without doubt, labour regulations will continue to play an important role in market regulation, but perhaps we will see significant changes in their content over the next few years. The direction they take will depend above all on the vision and negotiating ability of the employers' and workers' organizations.

Source: La Sociedad del Trabajo.

Deregulation and social inequalities

Labour flexibility and wage deflation sum up the economic strategy of the industrialized countries' 'club', the OECD. To improve competitiveness, this organization openly promotes a policy which leads to increasing social inequalities

In 1994, the Organization for Economic Co-operation and Development (OECD) made several recommendations regarding labour. From 1996 to 1998, it insisted in "creating a favourable climate for the private company, increasing the flexibility of working hours and wage costs and reviewing regulations regarding employment security which restrain the expansion of the private sector".

In most countries of the world, the rise in inequality of income has been remarkable. The OECD considers the growth of inequalities as the product of "economic sense", and relies on "powerful lobbies" to maintain adequate social protection.

In its view a higher "rotation rate" in the labour market is encouraging. The OECD explains the persistence of permanent unemployment as a phenomenon caused by "the excessive rigour of regulations which protect employment, the exaggerated generosity of subsidy systems, the exceedingly high level of minimum wages and the administrative extension mechanism of wage agreements".

The organization also claims that "if work does not reap benefits, people will not want to work" and proposes to restore to "idle people" the "desire to work" through the spike of poverty. In other words, it suggests they should be freed from state assistance which keeps them within a "culture of dependency".

In order for social benefits not to compete with lower wages, the OECD believes "the generosity of compensation systems for the unemployed and related benefits should be reduced". Likewise, adds the organization, an excessive level of social protection "risks increasing wage demands and, therefore, unemployment, reducing the cost which the loss of their job represents for the workers".

In order for wage earners to remain in their jobs or accept all working conditions, it is necessary to make them understand that any period of inactivity will be financially unbearable.

The United Kingdom has already taken many "measures in the good direction" since the beginning of the 1980s and currently has one of the least regulated labour markets with lower levels of social benefits, compared to other wealthy countries.

According to the OECD, the most competitive countries are those with "small open economies, where the State plays a modest role and taxes are low". ❑

A = Labour force (% of total population) D = industrial sector
B = % of women in labour force E = services sector
C = agriculture sector F = % unemployment

	A	B	C	D	E	F
	1990	1996	1990	1990	1990	1996
Albania	48	41	55	23	22	..
Algeria	28	25	26	31	43	..
Angola	47	46	75	8	17	..
Aotearoa/New Zealand	48	44	10	25	65	6.1
Argentina	38	31	12	32	55	16.3
Armenia	48	48	18	43	39	..
Australia	50	43	6	26	68	8.6
Austria	46	41	8	38	55	4.1
Azerbaijan	42	44	31	29	40	..
Bahamas	49	..	5	15	79	..
Bahrain	44	..	2	30	68	..
Bangladesh	49	42	65	16	18	2.5
Barbados	50	..	7	23	70	..
Belarus	52	49	20	40	40	..
Belgium	40	40	3	28	70	9.6
Belize	31	..	34	19	48	..
Benin	46	48	64	8	28	..
Bhutan	51	..	94	1	5	..
Bolivia	40	37	47	18	36	..
Botswana	44	46	46	20	33	..
Brazil	44	35	23	23	54	..
Bulgaria	51	48	13	48	38	..
Burkina Faso	54	47	92	2	6	..
Burundi	54	49	92	3	6	..
Cambodia	50	53	74	8	19	..
Cameroon	40	38	70	9	21	..
Canada	53	45	3	25	71	9.7
Cape Verde	37	..	31	30	40	..
Central African Rep.	49	47	80	4	16	..
Chad	49	44	83	4	13	..
Chile	38	32	19	25	56	5.4
China	59	45	72	15	13	..
Colombia	40	38	27	23	50	..
Comoros	44	..	77	9	13	..
Congo D.R.	42	44	68	13	19	..
Congo R.	42	43	49	15	37	..
Costa Rica	38	30	26	27	47	6.2
Côte d'Ivoire	37	33	60	10	30	..
Croatia	47	44	16	34	50	..
Cuba	45	38	18	30	51	..
Cyprus	48	..	14	30	56	..
Czech Republic	53	47	11	45	43	3.9
Denmark	57	46	6	28	66	6.9
Dominican Republic	40	29	25	29	46	..
Ecuador	35	27	33	19	48	10.4
Egypt	35	29	..	..	..	..
El Salvador	36	35	36	21	43	7.7
Equatorial Guinea	43	..	75	5	20	..
Eritrea	50	47	80	5	15	..
Estonia	54	49	14	41	44	..
Ethiopia	44	41	86	2	12	..
Fiji	34	..	46	15	39	..
Finland	52	48	8	31	61	16.1
France	44	44	5	29	66	12.4
Gabon	49	44	52	16	33	..
Gambia	50	45	82	8	11	..
Georgia	49	46	26	31	43	..
Germany	50	42	4	38	58	8.8
Ghana	47	51	59	13	28	..
Greece	42	37	23	27	50	..
Guatemala	35	27	52	17	30	..
Guinea	49	47	87	2	11	..
Guinea-Bissau	48	40	85	2	13	..
Guyana	40	..	22	25	53	..
Haiti	45	43	68	9	23	..
Honduras	34	30	41	20	39	..
Hungary	46	44	15	38	47	9.9
Iceland	55	..	11	27	62	3.7
India	43	32	64	16	20	..
Indonesia	44	40	55	14	31	4.0
Iran	29	25	32	25	43	..
Iraq	26	18	16	18	66	..
Ireland	37	33	14	29	57	11.9
Israel	39	40	4	29	67	6.7
Italy	43	38	9	31	60	12.1
Jamaica	49	46	25	23	52	..
Japan	52	41	7	34	59	3.4
Jordan	27	22	15	23	61	..
Kazakhstan	47	47	22	32	46	..
Kenya	48	46	80	7	13	..
Korea, North	50	45	38	31	31	..
Korea, South	46	41	18	35	47	2.0
Kuwait	42	29	1	25	74	..
Kyrgyzstan	41	47	32	27	41	..
Laos	50	47	78	6	16	..
Latvia	55	50	16	40	44	18.3
Lebanon	31	28	7	31	62	..
Lesotho	40	37	40	28	32	..
Libya	29	21	11	23	66	..
Lithuania	52	48	18	41	41	..
Luxembourg	43	..	4	27	69	..
Macau	..	..	..	..	..	4.3
Macedonia, TFYR	45	41	22	40	38	..
Madagascar	48	45	78	7	15	..
Malawi	49	49	87	5	8	..
Malaysia	39	37	27	23	50	..
Maldives	41	..	32	31	37	..
Mali	50	46	86	2	12	..
Malta	37	..	3	35	63	..
Mauritania	45	44	55	10	34	..
Mauritius	41	32	17	43	40	..
Mexico	37	31	28	24	48	3.7
Moldova	49	49	33	30	37	..
Mongolia	47	46	32	23	45	..
Morocco	38	35	45	25	31	..
Mozambique	53	48	83	8	9	..
Myanmar/Burma	51	43	73	10	17	..
Namibia	42	41	49	15	36	..
Nepal	47	40	94	0	6	..
Netherlands	46	40	5	26	70	6.6
Netherlands Antilles	..	..	..	..	..	14
Nicaragua	34	36	28	26	46	..
Niger	49	44	90	4	6	..
Nigeria	40	36	43	7	50	..
Norway	50	46	6	25	68	4.9
Oman	26	15	45	24	32	..
Pakistan	35	27	52	19	30	..
Palestine	..	..	13	34	53	21.5
Panama	39	34	26	16	58	13.9
Papua New Guinea	49	42	79	7	14	..
Paraguay	37	29	39	22	39	..
Peru	35	29	36	18	46	7.0
Philippines	40	37	46	15	39	7.4
Poland	49	46	27	36	37	12.3
Portugal	49	43	18	34	48	7.2
Puerto Rico	..	36	..	..	..	13.4
Qatar	57	..	3	32	65	..
Romania	46	44	24	47	29	6.7
Russia	52	49	14	42	45	9.3
Rwanda	52	49	92	3	5	..
Saudi Arabia	34	14	19	20	61	..
Senegal	45	43	77	8	16	..
Sierra Leone	37	36	67	15	17	..
Singapore	49	38	0	36	64	3.0
Slovakia	51	48	12	33	55	..
Slovenia	49	46	6	46	48	7.3
Solomon Is.	51	..	..	..	..	..
South Africa	39	37	14	32	55	..
Spain	41	36	12	33	55	22.2
Sri Lanka	40	35	48	21	31	11.3
Sudan	36	29	69	8	22	..
Suriname	34	..	21	18	61	..
Swaziland	34	..	39	22	38	..
Sweden	54	48	4	30	66	8.0
Switzerland	53	40	6	35	60	3.7
Syria	28	26	33	24	43	..
Tajikistan	36	44	41	23	36	..
Tanzania	52	49	..	..	..	..
Thailand	57	46	64	14	22	..
Togo	42	40	66	10	24	..
Trinidad and Tobago	39	37	11	32	57	..
Tunisia	35	31	28	33	39	..
Turkey	44	36	53	18	29	5.8
Turkmenistan	41	45	37	23	40	..
Uganda	51	48	85	5	11	..
Ukraine	50	49	20	40	40	..
United Arab Emirates	51	14	8	27	65	..
United Kingdom	50	43	2	29	69	8.2
United States	50	46	3	26	71	5.4
Uruguay	44	41	14	27	59	..
Uzbekistan	39	46	35	25	40	..
Vanuatu	37	..	12	27	61	..
Venezuela	..	33	..	..	..	..
Vietnam	51	49	71	14	15	..
Yemen	30	29	61	17	22	..
Yugoslavia Fed. Rep.	..	42	..	..	..	..
Zambia	42	45	75	8	17	..
Zimbabwe	46	44	68	8	24	..

Sources: Yearbook of Labour Statistics 1997, ILO, 1997; World Development Indicators 1998, World Bank, 1998.

Child labour

All over the world, children continue to work, putting at stake their education, health, their normal development to adulthood, and even their lives

According to the ILO's latest estimates, about 250 million children between the ages of 5 and 14 are working full or part-time in developing countries. Sixty-one per cent are found in Asia, 32 per cent in Africa, and 7 per cent in Latin America.

Millions are working in hazardous occupations, in prostitution and pornography, or are exploited as slaves and bonded labourers.

Table 1 Distribution of economically active children 5-14 years of age in developing countries, by regions and sex, 1995.

REGION	BOTH SEXES	BOYS	GIRLS
WORLD (ESTIMATES IN MILLIONS)	250	140	110
REGIONS	%	%	%
AFRICA	32	56	44
ASIA (EXCLUDING JAPAN)	61	54	46
LATIN AMERICA & CARIBBEAN	7	67	33
OCEANIA (EXCLUDING AUSTRALIA & AOTEAROA/N.Z.)	0.2	57	43
SEX RATIO (WORLD)	100	56	44

Source: ILO Bureau of Statistics (Geneva, 1996)

Although Asia has the largest number of child workers, Africa has the highest incidence at around 41 per cent of children between 5 and 14 years old. The corresponding proportion in Asia is approximately one-half of the level in Africa (22 per cent) and it is 17 per cent in Latin America.

Table 2 Economic activity participation rate of children 5-14 years of age, by region and sex, 1995.

REGION	BOTH SEXES	BOYS	GIRLS
	%	%	%
WORLD	24.7	27.0	22.3
REGIONS			
AFRICA	41.4	46.0	36.7
ASIA (EXCLUDING JAPAN)	21.5	22.5	20.4
LATIN AMERICA & CARIBBEAN	16.5	21.8	11.1
OCEANIA (EXCLUDING AUSTRALIA AND AOTEAROA/N.Z.)	29.3	32.7	25.8

Source: ILO Bureau of Statistics (Geneva, 1996)

While most child labour is found in developing countries, industrialized economies are not entirely free of it either. In Eastern and Central Europe, for example, child labour has been reappearing in the wake of social and economic dislocation caused by the transition to a market economy.

The data so far obtained show that more boys than girls work - about three boys to two girls, on average. Africa has the highest participation rate of girls among the developing regions of the world (37 per cent) (see table 2). It should be borne in mind that the number of working girls is often underestimated by statistical surveys which usually do not take into account unpaid economic activity carried out in and around the household, including household enterprises. Also more girls – many of them between 8-12 years old – than boys perform full-time housework of a non-economic nature, e.g., housekeeping in their own parents' household in order to enable their parents or guardians to go to work, or to take care of sick or handicapped members in the household. If such full-time housework were taken into account, there would be little or no variation between the sexes in the total size of working children and the number of girls could even exceed that of boys.

Most statistical surveys cover only children aged 10 and above. But many children begin work at an earlier age. Rural children, in particular girls, tend to begin their economic activity at 5, 6 or 7 years of age. In some countries, children under 10 years of age are estimated to account for 20 per cent of child labour in the rural areas and around 5 per cent in urban centres. Their number can be much higher in certain occupations and industries, for example, in domestic service and home-based industries.

Source: ILO, 1998.

A reduction of workers' rights

The business point of view can offer several arguments against the reduction of the working day

Reductions in working hours can only contribute minimally to the elimination of unemployment, as often unemployment is due to other factors - such as lack of qualifications or the fact that the unemployed are in a location that is geographically distant from where the jobs are.

Any general reduction of workinghours creates a heavy burden on company costs. Further, it would be impossible to maintain full pay for reduced hours - workers unhappy with the reduced schedule (and the additional free time thus gained) would try to improve their income by working illegally.

Thus collective reductions of working hours would not only limit worker freedom, but would negatively affect possible productive profit, depriving the state of taxes and social contributions.

Business can also benefit from unemployment especially in situations when the average salary is low. Such conditions offer better recruitment possibilities, less resistance when the amount of work is intensified, weakened pay claims and so on. For the situation to continue benefiting business, the consequences of unemployment must remain below the threshold of becoming a threat to the system.

Unions have shown scepticism over regulations which make working hours and conditions largely dependent on company interests. Existing part-time posts are mainly made up of openings requiring low levels of qualification and rarely offer chances for promotion or the acquisition of additional qualifications.

Flexible working hour regulations can often be seen as a business strategy allowing the rationalization and intensification of work, one that can do away with idle time.

The type of workers who normally take on these shorter-than-normal working days generally as temporary employment or for a second income - show a greater propensity to accept intensification, the insecurities of the post, lower salaries, and so on than to organize a union and act collectively.

Conventional regulations can be side-stepped through individual working-hour agreements, avoiding the sort of collective action aimed at reducing the working day. Part-time jobs in reality constitute an abbreviation of the working day; workers thus end up attempting to do a day's work in the hours allotted. Hence, the individual liberalization of working hours does not appear to be a solution for unemployment, nor does is contribute to the creation of workers' "sovereignty over their own time." ❑

Science and Technology

The relativity of science

The historical and social relativity of Western science and technology is being increasingly recognized. Even accepting the usual premise that these are the forces behind progress and the well-being of the human race, the possibility that they could also become the instrument of its self-destruction is becoming difficult to ignore

An overview, however brief, of the evolution of science in the 20th century needs to take into account the fact that the concept of science itself is susceptible to change. It changes due to historical, philosophical and cultural factors, and due to changing conceptions of the world and the accumulation of knowledge. Even the evolving solutions it offers to immediate practical tasks change the way in which science is perceived.

Science has accounted for diverse forms of classification. During the 20th century, scientific arguments have been distinguished in terms of their 'styles', 'models', 'forms of organization' and an unending list of criteria. Distinctions have been drawn between pre-scientific and scientific status, between 'the modern' and 'post-modernity', between 'idealism' and 'scientific materialism', and between various 'types' of 'rationality'

Even so a general definition of science would be that it is the knowledge of reality or being. It is a regular type of knowledge - in the sense that it is interested in the regularities or interactions which take place between various aspects of reality - of a theoretical nature - because it is expressed by a conjunction of concepts and laws. It is also predictive as it predicts the behaviour of the processes it studies under certain specific conditions.

In the 20th century science has seen unprecedented development. An enormous field of investigation has opened up with the objective of studying science itself; its nature as a form of knowledge, its methods and research and demonstration procedures, and the laws which dominate its functioning and change.

In the 1950s, a point of view emerged, emphasizing not so much the definition of science as objective or true thought which crystallises in the form of a theory, but its quality as a human social activity aimed at the production, dissemination and application of new knowledge.

This outlook emphasizes that "scientific activity" does not take place in a vacuum, but within the limits of a certain "ethos", in its own space which does not arise "naturally" but is socially and culturally subject to numerous determining factors.

Scientific activity takes place in conditions imposed by the social division of labour and within the limits of an institutional framework which is permeated by cultural and social values, as well as by power relationships.

Traditionally the notion of scientific "truth" was perceived as an ideal to be defended at all costs as many social institutions rested upon it. However, in the last few decades, post-modernist thinking has undertaken a process of cultural dismantling which questions scientific truth, and thus threatens the stability of the culture built upon it.

An important change has been the introduction of relativism as a fundamental element of the truth and science. Relativism sets limits to scientific knowledge and postulates that truth is relative and hence imperfect. The fact that truth can be improved upon and even refuted confirms its historical nature.

The social problems of science are at the forefront of current reflection on the subject. The take-over of scientific knowledge by corporations and governments has prompted a rethink on notions of progress. Scientific progress is being viewed with increasing ambivalence, as science comes to be seen not just as a discipline promising well-being and liberation, but also possible self-destruction.

Thus, the notion of scientific-technical progress has lost its mythic quality insofar as it has accompanied the processes of the deterioration of human health and the environment, the robotization or automation of humanity and the increase in inequality in the world.

Coupled with this is the increasing fragmentation of knowledge. Science is no longer monolithic, it is becoming "secular", and can no longer set itself above other forms of consciousness or attempt, alone, the organization of a global society. ❏

Industrialization

The magic and danger of plastic

Plastic materials have been around for a hundred years, although the research which led to their production came much earlier. As with the automobile, the aeroplane and computers, plastics - though relative newcomers to human use - have become almost indispensable

Plastics have had two eras of production: the first was when they were made from naturally existing fibres and the second when they were synthesized from materials that do not occur naturally.

In the last third of the 19th century in Germany and Britain, processes were developed almost simultaneously to manufacture plastic materials as a substitute for scarce tortoiseshell and ivory. In Britain around 1865, E Parkes ended his experiments with cellulose (derived from cottonseed) by producing celluloid. This was an important part of the great cultural revolution heralded by the cinema as celluloid was used to make film from 1895 onwards.

In 1887, research with resins led the German, E Berliner, to produce the material used for 78 rpm records (which would not be replaced until half way through the 20th century). In the first decade of this century, the Belgian chemist LH Baekeland made the first rigid plastic, named Bakelite in his honour. This product helped the expanding electrical industry tremendously because Bakelite, like all plastics, is a bad conductor and therefore an excellent insulator. Plugs, handles and switches began to be made of this material.

World War I (1914-1918) intensified the use of celluloid and its derivatives, like cellulose acetate, which had applications in the military air vehicles of the period. The end of the War allowed this research to be redirected into the so-called "artificial silk" or rayon.

In 1929, new, rigid, heat-resistant plastics appeared, still based on natural raw materials like urea. They brought about an aesthetic revolution as they could be made in a variety of colours unlike Bakelite and ebonite: yellows and reds burst out in household and industrial articles.

The golden age

But it was in the 1930s, with the creation of nylon, that plastics really took off again. Nylon is a completely synthetic product, made from amides which are synthetic materials.

Hard on its heels came acrylic, a thermo-rigid plastic with enormous possibilities due to its hardness and transparency, and polyvinylchloride (PVC). The 1940s brought polyester and the most commonly used plastic of the present day, polyethylene. In 1943 chlorofluorocarbons (CFCs) were produced achieving a series of technological coups in refrigeration, aerosols and other applications. Silicones also date from this time.

The period from around 1930 until the mid-1940s was a sort of 'golden age' for plastics when most of those known today were invented.

All plastics take their form and consistency when the raw materials used are subjected to high temperatures and pressure. Once the critical moment in this process is past and the cooling begins, two main groups of plastics can be produced: the thermo-stable and the thermo-plastic. The first, also known as thermo-rigid, are those which harden and any further process of heating only ruins or destroys them; the second are characterized by a return to a state of plasticity upon further heating during which they can be reconstructed and reshaped. In the latter, the presence of plasticizers - substances which soften with great ease, like pthalates (derived from an oil acid) - is decisive. The unexpected consequences of their presence is discussed later on.

The key to the production of plastic materials is polymerization, a process through which monomer molecules are joined together establishing long intermolecular chains, hence the names polyamide, polystyrene and so on.

The most common process for making products with the polymerized material is extrusion, by which plastic material of a pasty, almost liquid consistency, is injected into moulds which are then cooled and removed, leaving the object cast.

Since the 'golden age' only one major new plastic has appeared: polypropylene, created at the end of the 1950s. Its most notable characteristic is its resistance to heat, which is also its weak point.

Expansion

The plastics industry saw impressive expansion after the end of World War II. In Britain, between 1950 and 1961, production quadrupled: going from 150,000 tons per year to 600,000 tons.

The volume of the annual world production of plastics in the 1990s is drawing even with that of metals. The 1950s and 1960s saw the most accelerated expansion in the use of plastics, with growth rates of more than 20 per cent a year. This was due to two factors - technological optimism, which allowed talk of the "odd resistance" of CFCs "to nearly all chemical and solvent products" and the extraordinary cheapness of the raw materials involved.

This second aspect was explained by the absurdly low price of oil, a product used as fuel since ancient times. Production, from the beginning of its industrial exploitation at the end of the 19th century until 1945, had never exceeded 300,000 tons per year. However, from 1945 to 1973 its use was multiplied sevenfold, constituting a quarter of the world's energy supply from the end of the War (a time of low demand), to half in 1973 (when demand was high).

Why was this oil (of which the petrochemical industry consumes a tenth) so generously available? The companies of this sector, almost all of US, British and Dutch origin set themselves up, via concessions of varying generosity, in the most remote corners of the planet, wherever the existence of oil fields was proven. And, during these decades, extraction was carried out with minimum costs as the countries owning the oil fields were hardly paid anything for the resource. The main producers were developing countries: Mexico, Venezuela, Iraq, Iran, Saudi Arabia, Libya, and Kuwait the United States and the former USSR, but the latter were not great oil exporters.

This explains the colossal expansion in the areas 'conquered' by plastics in the 1950s and 1960s: pipes and tubing, objects for domestic use, like buckets, dustpans or combs, the automobile industry (bodywork, switchboards, gear box meshes), expansion toward the construction industry and the take-over of the packaging industry. In 1973 the petroleum exporting countries decided not to keep oil prices frozen, as over decades they had seen prices for their imports rising. Their 'terms of trade' (the difference between what they paid for imports and what they received for exports) had deteriorated to a critical point. That year also marked a relative slowing down in the use of oil; plastic products stopped being "dirt cheap".

This phase of expansion was motivated by profit and high economic remuneration for the designers of new compounds and articles. In time, the purely monetary calculation of the short term costs gave over to other considerations, such as the "end production" of rubbish or waste. The petrochemical industry began to be scrutinized for the first time. In this respect 1974 was a key year: it was finally accepted that the deaths of dozens of workers on the PVC polymerization production lines in the United States were due to intoxication from these productive processes. In this year the first report appeared from researchers linking the "ozone hole" to the effect of CFCs in the stratosphere, demonstrating that not only were they extraordinarily resistant to other chemicals but actually attacked some of them - in this case the vital ozone.

Rubbish

Until the beginning of the 20th century, human rubbish had been mainly biodegradable and recyclable allowing for a series of linked economic activities dedicated to the recovery of materials.

The incorporation of plastic into daily life created a new phenomenon: rubbish that kept growing without perishing. The mixture of plastics and organic waste is a form of squandering which burdens the planet in a way increasing numbers of scientists and ecologists consider suicidal. Plastic does not biodegrade and is not easily eroded. Jacques Yves-Cousteau has left us impressive testimony of how the seas of the planet are contaminated with plastic molecules.

Recycling, the latest watchword of the petrochemical industry, has purely propaganda value: in the United States 1.5 per cent of all the plastic produced is recycled (1995 data). The remaining 98.5 per cent is unusable.

Toxicity

Plastics had shown very attractive qualities in the time of technological optimism: adaptability, lightness, flexibility. With the experience and research of recent years, their undesirable effects are also known: contamination, toxicity, uncontrollable waste and, in relation to packaging, "migrations".. Plastic packaging contains softeners which get transferred to the things contained given time and heat. This phenomenon, which could be considered of secondary importance for packaging of non-foodstuffs, is highly dangerous in the case of foodstuffs, primarily because these migrations occur

PRODUCTION OF PLASTICS (in thousands of tons)		
Years	US	Whole world
1930	1485	
1945	400	
1955	1700	2870
1960	2800	
1966	6200	
1993	90000	

Sources: The Story of the Plastics Industry, Don Masson (ed.), New York: The Society of the Plastics Industry, 1966, Panorama de la ciencia. Los Plásticos en perspectiva, Arthur Garratt (ed.) Buenos Aires: Eudeba, 1963.

at fairly low temperatures (barely 40 degrees centigrade is enough for a marked migration) and because they are generally toxic, and even carcinogenic.

In the happy ignorance of the 1960s, PVC was recorded as offering "high resistance to acids, alkalis and alcohol". Today, conclusive research shows PVC is soluble in alcohol and fats due to its chlorine content, and so its use is not recommended for the packaging of fatty or alcoholic goods.

In the early 1980s, once it was proven that laminated plastics (PVC) migrate to foodstuffs wrapped in them, like cheese (which contains fat), the Swedish National Food Department published "recommendations to the population" advising them to throw away the first slice of cheese, while tests were carried out for substitute packaging.

Plastic as an expression of the dominant culture

Plastic is a manifestation of the cultural network we are living in, as are the increasingly rapid communication and transport media. Plastic appears to fulfil the dream of creative polymorphism, of the unlimited capacity of humanity to shape reality. A current of contemporary thought, linked to behaviourism, which has been centred in the United States throughout the 20th century, holds 'human plasticity' as the basis of a modern society not tied to tradition, and which presents the boundlessly 'plastic' human being as the greatest achievement of humanity.

Similarly, technological development has imbued the dominant culture with the idea that nature is infinitely malleable. Scientists may not be prepared to admit as much but it also reveals their presumptions of omnipotence.

The production and consumption of plastic material in an indiscriminate manner could be causing more problems than solutions.

We have to learn to rethink costs, not based solely on the sale price which varies according to supply and demand, but including also environmental factors and future costs. It is no easy task, because state involvement in plastic production has been low from the beginning and the industry is in the hands of private enterprise which is motivated by the search for profit. ❏

Urban Population

	AS % OF TOTAL POPULATION 1996	% OF ANNUAL GROWTH TO YEAR 2000
Afghanistan	20.3	..
Albania	37.5	2.1
Algeria	56.4	3.6
Andorra	95.4	..
Angola	31.6	6.0
Anguilla	11.2	..
Antigua	36.0	1.2
Aotearoa/New Zealand	86.1	1.4
Argentina	88.4	1.5
Armenia	68.8	1.7
Australia	84.7	1.2
Austria	64.3	0.8
Azerbaijan	55.9	1.7
Bahamas	86.9	1.9
Bahrain	90.8	2.9
Bangladesh	18.9	5.4
Barbados	47.8	1.7
Belarus	71.8	0.9
Belgium	97.1	0.4
Belize	46.4	2.5
Benin	39.2	4.7
Bermuda	100.0	..
Bhutan	6.2	6.0
Bolivia	61.5	3.9
Bosnia-Herzegovina	41.5	..
Botswana	63.2	6.6
Brazil	79.0	2.4
Brunei	69.9	2.2
Bulgaria	68.6	0.3
Burkina Faso	16.4	9.8
Burundi	7.8	6.7
Cambodia	21.0	5.9
Cameroon	45.6	4.9
Canada	76.7	1.2
Cape Verde	56.0	5.9
Cayman Is.	100.0	..
Central African Rep.	39.5	3.6
Chad	22.5	4.1
Chile	84.0	1.6
China	31.0	3.8
Colombia	73.1	2.2
Comoros	31.0	5.8
Congo D.R.	29.0	4.4
Congo R.	59.3	4.4
Cook Is.	60.9	..
Costa Rica	49.8	3.3
Côte d'Ivoire	44.0	4.9
Croatia	56.2	..
Cuba	76.3	1.2
Cyprus	54.6	2.0
Czech Republic	65.6	0.3
Denmark	85.3	0.2
Djibouti	82.4	2.5
Dominica	69.7	..
Dominican Republic	62.6	2.9
East Timor	7.5	..
Ecuador	59.6	3.3
Egypt	44.8	2.6
El Salvador	45.3	2.9
Equatorial Guinea	43.4	5.5
Eritrea	17.4	..
Estonia	73.2	-0.2
Ethiopia	15.8	5.2
Faeroe Is.	32.6	..
Fiji	40.9	2.5
Finland	63.5	1.0
France	74.8	0.5
French Guiana	76.8	..
French Polynesia	56.4	..
Gabon	51.2	4.4
Gambia	29.7	5.6
Georgia	58.8	1.1
Germany	86.7	0.4
Ghana	36.3	4.5
Gibraltar	100.0	..

	AS % OF TOTAL POPULATION 1996	% OF ANNUAL GROWTH TO YEAR 2000		AS % OF TOTAL POPULATION 1996	% OF ANNUAL GROWTH TO YEAR 2000
Greece	59.4	1.1	Palau	71.5	..
Greenland	81.3	..	Panama	56.0	2.4
Grenada	36.2	..	Papua New Guinea	16.3	4.0
Guadeloupe	99.5	..	Paraguay	53.2	4.0
Guam	38.4	..	Peru	71.3	2.5
Guatemala	39.1	4.1	Philippines	55.0	3.9
Guinea	29.9	5.7	Pitcairn	0.0	..
Guinea-Bissau	22.1	4.6	Poland	64.0	0.9
Guyana	35.9	2.9	Portugal	36.0	1.3
Haiti	32.4	4.1	Puerto Rico	73.7	..
Honduras	44.4	4.4	Qatar	91.6	2.2
Hungary	65.0	0.4	Reunion	68.3	..
Iceland	91.7	1.2	Romania	56.3	0.6
India	27.1	3.0	Russia	76.3	0.3
Indonesia	36.4	4.2	Rwanda	5.8	4.7
Iran	59.5	3.1	Sahara (Western)	93.5	..
Iraq	75.0	3.6	Samoa	21.1	1.9
Ireland	57.7	0.7	São Tome and Principe	43.7	3.6
Israel	90.8	2.1	Samoa, American	50.8	..
Italy	66.7	0.1	San Marino	94.6	..
Jamaica	54.2	1.7	Saudi Arabia	83.5	3.6
Japan	78.2	0.4	Senegal	44.3	4.0
Jordan	72.0	4.7	Seychelles	55.3	2.4
Kanaky/New Caledonia	62.4	..	Sierra Leone	33.9	4.6
Kazakhstan	60.0	1.4	Singapore	100.0	0.9
Kenya	29.5	6.0	Slovakia	59.2	1.2
Kiribati	36.0	..	Slovenia	51.5	..
Korea, North	61.5	2.3	Solomon Is.	17.5	6.4
Korea, South	82.5	2.3	Somalia	26.0	..
Kuwait	97.1	0.5	South Africa	49.5	3.1
Kyrgyzstan	39.0	2.4	Spain	76.7	0.4
Laos	21.2	5.9	Sri Lanka	22.3	2.7
Latvia	73.1	-0.3	St Helena	64.5	..
Lebanon	88.0	2.9	St Kitts-Nevis	33.9	0.8
Lesotho	24.8	6.0	St Lucia	37.2	2.0
Liberia	45.5	..	St Pierre and Miquelon	91.6	..
Libya	85.9	4.0	St Vincent	49.5	2.9
Liechtenstein	21.3	..	Sudan	32.3	4.7
Lithuania	72.6	0.7	Suriname	49.7	2.5
Luxembourg	89.5	1.5	Swaziland	32.0	5.9
Macau	98.8	..	Sweden	83.1	0.5
Macedonia, TFYR	60.3	..	Switzerland	61.3	1.4
Madagascar	27.0	5.8	Syria	52.7	4.4
Malawi	13.8	5.0	Taiwan	95.2	..
Malaysia	54.4	3.6	Tajikistan	32.3	3.2
Maldives	27.1	4.2	Tanzania	25.0	5.9
Mali	27.5	5.7	Thailand	20.2	2.8
Malta	89.6	0.9	Togo	31.2	4.9
Malvinas/Falklands	85.5	..	Tokelau	0.0	..
Marshall Is.	69.6	..	Tonga	42.1	..
Martinique	93.7	..	Trinidad and Tobago	72.2	1.8
Mauritania	52.7	4.6	Tunisia	62.7	2.7
Mauritius	40.6	1.5	Turkey	70.6	3.7
Mexico	73.6	2.5	Turkmenistan	45.0	2.5
Micronesia	28.0	..	Turks and Caicos	43.9	..
Moldova	52.3	1.8	Tuvalu	47.9	..
Monaco	100.0	..	Uganda	12.8	5.6
Mongolia	61.3	3.0	Ukraine	70.7	0.6
Montserrat	16.7	..	United Arab Emirates	84.3	2.7
Morocco	52.6	3.0	United Kingdom	89.3	0.4
Mozambique	35.2	7.4	United States	76.3	1.2
Myanmar/Burma	26.2	3.7	Uruguay	90.5	0.8
Namibia	37.0	5.6	Uzbekistan	41.3	2.8
Nauru	100.0	..	Vanuatu	19.1	3.8
Nepal	10.6	6.9	Vatican	100.0	..
Netherlands	89.0	0.7	Venezuela	86.2	2.5
Netherlands Antilles	69.4	..	Vietnam	19.4	3.5
Nicaragua	62.7	4.3	Virgin Is. (Am.)	45.3	..
Niger	18.6	5.9	Vírgin Is. (Br.)	57.1	..
Nigeria	40.5	5.0	Wallis and Futuna Is.	0.0	..
Niue	29.3	..	Yemen	34.4	6.6
Northern Marianas	53.8	..	Yugoslavia Fed. Rep.	57.3	..
Norway	73.4	0.7	Zambia	43.3	3.4
Oman	77.7	7.7	Zimbabwe	32.5	..
Pakistan	34.8	4.6			

Sources: Population Division Web site, United Nations, 1998; Human Development Report 1997, UNDP, 1997.

The car: dream turned nightmare

The desire for greater speed and independence of movement far pre-dates the arrival of the automobile. The invention of the car has granted this wish, but with mass-production, the dream has begun to turn into a nightmare

Speed has been a human obsession since time immemorial - from faithful steeds to horse-drawn coaches to, eventually, a metal vehicle moved by gentle pressure from the driver's right foot.

The car promised independent movement - people would no longer have to rely on other human beings, public train services or coaches. However, the "democratization" of the automobile - with more than 100,000 cars produced in the world each day - has altered this supposed independence of movement into a crazy form of dependence.

Relative independence

In the first place, a driver is dependent on all other road users, as the speed at which one's vehicle may travel is governed by others. The increasing number of automobiles has reduced the average speed of movement in big cities.

In a city like Montevideo, Uruguay, whose car/inhabitant ratio is lower than any city in the developed world, the average speed of movement has been gradually slowing down over the last 20 years, and is currently no more than 15 kilometres per hour. Around London in the 1980s and 1990s, tailbacks of several kilometres were common, creating traffic chaos for several hours, and paralyzing the city. But speed of movement is not the only unfulfilled promise.

The supposed independence gained by the individual driver has also disappeared. Drivers must now choose their journey time and route carefully in order not to come up against the unpleasant realization that - at least in certain urban spaces - the individual car no longer represents an advantage over collective systems of transport.

Finally, car drivers are also dependent on a battalion of technicians and specialists for the maintenance and repair of their vehicles.

A privilege suffered by everyone

The automobile remains an appendage to the lifestyles of a privileged few and is far beyond the reach of the majority of citizens of the five continents. At present, nearly 600 million motorized vehicles run along the highways and streets of the planet - nearly 500 million private cars and 100 million goods and collective transport vehicles.

More than 85 per cent of the cars produced in the world by 1990 had been sold in North America, Western Europe and Japan. The Peoples Republic of China, with around a fifth of the world's population, had 300,000 cars in the 1980s, amounting to barely double the number of cars in Luxembourg.

The harm done by the car however is suffered by everyone, drivers and pedestrians alike. The most obvious examples are traffic accidents: more than 250,000 people die as a result every year world-wide. This figure does not include those who were behind the wheel. A million wounded or permanently disabled people must be added to the casualty list, creating costs which are paid for by the whole community.

Further, entire cities have had to be redesigned to facilitate the movement of motorized vehicles. In the era of the automobile, the public spaces of yesteryear were reorganized to suit the needs of this urban despot.

The tyrant of the cities

The broadening of streets and access roads, the reduction of space for pedestrians, public spaces used for parking, financial resources invested in traffic lights, road repair, security systems and the salaries of municipal officials dedicated to the control and management of automobiles - money which could be used for other social ends - are some of the more evident consequences of a transport system which has favoured the use of the private car.

Despite the fact that in most countries car owners pay extra taxes towards the costs they impose on society, experts agree the former do not, in fact, cover the latter. The irrationality of this system is clear when we consider that a car takes up 22.1m^2 of space, compared to 0.8 for a pedestrian, 2.1 for a bus passenger and 9.7 for a bicycle.

The mass production of the automobile has been more of a problem than a solution. Urban planners in many countries of the world have been forced into reverse, closing off areas to cars and imposing parking fees. In Los Angeles lone drivers or those using certain routes or driving at certain times of day are made to pay.

Environmental impacts and...

The consequences of the increase in number of automobiles on the global environment have been much discussed in recent years. Although experts still argue over the extent of the impact, no one now questions the generation of sulphur dioxide, nitrogen oxide, carbon monoxide (CO), unburned hydrocarbons and solid particles which are partially responsible for acid rain and global climate change.

According to the US Environmental Protection Act (EPA), automobiles are responsible for 16 per cent of acid rain and 10 per cent of emissions of greenhouse gases. Even one source which cannot be suspected of "complicity" with the ecological movements - the Ford company - admitted in a recent leaflet that "although the individual polluting capacity of automobiles is not alarming, it can become so if its global impact is considered, as, at present, automobile emissions account for 4.5 per cent of total atmospheric contamination".

A car with four people consumes 90 per cent more energy per person and per kilometre than a bus carrying 50 passengers. This figure must be quadrupled if the car contains only the driver, a fairly routine occurrence, as the average number of vehicle occupants is between 1.2 and 1.3 at peak times.

Despite the fact that modern cars consume increasingly less fuel, and that in many developed countries the use of exhaust gas reducing catalytic converters is obligatory, the squandering of energy and atmospheric contamination follow the automobile like a shadow.

...effects on human health

The most local environmental effects of car use are on human health. A great deal of research by the World Health Organization (WHO) and other health institutions has concluded without a shadow of a doubt that the carbon monoxide emitted by the burning of oil derivatives has toxic effects in blood, as it blocks the oxygenation process; that unburned hydrocarbons are powerful carcinogens and that lead contained in some fuels causes central nervous system disorders and affects the normal development of the skeleton, by disturbing calcium fixation.

Another undesirable effect not always taken into account is noise pollution. According to the WHO, the maximum level of noise tolerable by humans is equivalent to 65 decibels. Moderate automobile traffic 20 metres away produces 55 decibels, while more intense traffic at closer quarters increases this to 85 decibels.

Car manufacturers are aware of all these shortcomings and their engineers have been searching for substitutes - generally powered by electricity or solar energy - but up until now they have not succeeded and it is doubtful they will do so in the short term without losing the most seductive aspect of the automobile - its speed.

Showing-off

Although it may not appear so at first, the omnipresence of the automobile is a political question, as the rationales behind contemporary transport systems are not just technological, but economic, political and cultural as well.

The irrationality of the current transport system cannot be attributed to the automobile itself - which continues to offer some notable advantages over other means of transport in long distance or inter-city travel - but to a culture which values the private car as an indicator of status and progress. Other factors include the distances between home, work and leisure. ❏

Communications

From telephones to satellites

The utopian dream that technology could help people return to a tribal or clan level of communication, where common problems can be discussed virtually face to face, is still far from reality. Increasingly we realize that these technologies are mere tools and do not possess the power to solve human problems

Information has become the 'key strategic resource' on which the world economic structure rests.

This sentence, plucked from one of the many authors who have analyzed political and social development in recent years, reflects a fairly widespread view amongst intellectuals in the developed world. It predominates the mass communications media world-wide. Such a perception of the increasing importance of information is based on the enormous development in communications media in recent years and justifies it.

In its most limited sense "communication" means the exchange of ideas, information or attitudes between people. Over time the concept also came to include the movement of people or goods, that is, transport. Today's complex communications system is made up of a gigantic network of physical components, like highways, bridges, aeroplanes, cars, telephones, telegraphs, satellites, computers, cables, airwaves, images, books and sounds. It is also regulated by a series of conventions, agreements, languages, codes and institutions.

Some of these components were invented this century, others have undergone important developments. All constitute the basis for the transmission (or non-transmission) of information.

Crossing the Atlantic

In 1901, Guglielmo Marconi sent the first message across the Atlantic Ocean without using a cable. This experiment, using radio waves, showed communication between two distant points was possible without the use of a physical link. It opened the way for wireless communication, still predominant today.

The 19th century had witnessed many inventions which heralded the birth of many important communications media. Photography, cinema, the linotype, the rotary press, railways and steamboats had changed the way people operated in the world. But the advances which resulted in the most spectacular uses came via electrical implements: the telephone and the telegraph.

These permitted immediate communication over long distances, outperforming - although not replacing - more traditional media like the mail system which required physical movement of objects (letters and parcels). The development of wireless communication was to change the nature of navigation, trade and the flow of information in the 20th century.

These new forms of communication did not develop in a uniform way around the world. The most powerful European countries on one side of the Atlantic, and the United States on the other were at the forefront of the new developments.

Britain kicked off with the commercial exploitation of the first underwater cables beneath the Atlantic. In the years before World War I it had twice the amount of kilometres of cable installed in the United States. The US companies, meanwhile, installed more than double the number of point-to-point telegraph lines, in a strategic decision which led to their domination of the telecommunications sector in later years.

Preparations for the War intensified research into communications systems and faster means of transport — like the aeroplane. Once the war was over, adaptations for civilian use were immediately apparent. In the 1920s it was discovered images could be transmitted by waves, and in 1930 there was already a regular commercial television service. In 1922 the first portable radio went on sale in the US. Within a few years automobile manufacturers started to incorporate radios into their new designs. Commercial airlines were also established in various parts of the world around this time.

The preparations for World War II produced a similar effect. The major advances of the early period were honed and perfected and put into service by the armed forces of the industrialized countries.

During World War II, aeronautics was far more significant than it had been during the previous conflict. Radar was

especially important and research got underway which would lead to ballistics, and later form the basis of the aerospace industry.

The invention of the transistor in 1947 was the watershed which marked the beginning of a new series of developments.

Technical progress in communications had been driven by commercial and war interests in Europe and the United States. Other players, like the Soviet Union, China and Japan, only started to make their influence felt in the second half of the century.

Meanwhile, Southern countries also started to join the world-wide communication networks, but mainly as recipients rather than as broadcasters.

The broadcasting centres

In an increasingly communicative world, the content of broadcasts and newspapers became consumer items which would have to be paid for as never before. During the 19th century four news agencies had divided the world into rigidly defined areas. The enormous volume of newsprint which arose because of advances in the rotary press needed news from the rest of the world to help guide exporters, importers and politicians. Paul Julius Reuter, a German, was given the support of the British Government and his agency supplied the whole Empire, some Asian and Mediterranean countries. France's Charles-Louis Havas had established his control over the dominions of the French Empire, south-west Europe and South America. The German service, Wolff, had the rest of Europe, including Austria-Hungary, Scandinavia and the Slav countries. Meanwhile, United Press (UP) had been created in the United States to compete against the European predominance. But the combined strength of the other three great agencies kept UP confined to its own territory until World War I.

The defeat of Germany after World War I meant Wolff's part of the business passed into the hands of Havas and Reuters. Despite many attempts to break through the wall built by the big agencies, these continued to control the core of the business, transmitting their own perspectives along with the news. Alliances with the governments and the socio-political systems of the Northern countries were - and are still - reflected in the focus of the news.

After World War II, the victorious powers also managed to control the content and information offered by most of the world's newspapers. Reuters, AP and the US United Press International (UPI) were joined by the Soviet Tass and France's Agence France Press (AFP), which emerged from the ruins of Havas. The five companies then became the new rulers of the market.

The post-war period

The allied victory led to changes in international relations, which also affected communications. The colonial system in place until 1945 started to crumble and several nations gained independence in the 1950s and 1960s.

One of the main tasks of the new states was to find their place within the international community and thus the issue of communications became a priority.

Investments in transport allowed the new countries to develop new road systems or to upgrade old ones according to their needs rather than those of the old colonial powers. These countries started to establish airlines, railway networks and port systems suited to their new requirements.

But entry into the world-wide flow of information was beyond the reach of these countries. The technical know-how, and the particular format of any sort of communication had already been determined by wealthier countries. The concessions for television or radio waves and the protocol for the transmission stations was controlled by the industrialized nations who also produced the receivers. The codes for writing and sending messages were also already set out. But the content of the information was readily available, provided they purchased the services of the big agencies. It was practically impossible to find alternative information from other parts of the world.

The old post-war political order, broken by the wave of decolonization, started to see its deterioration reflected in the content of the news. In the 1970s attempts were made, particularly through UNESCO, to create a "New International Information Order" capable of unblocking the "unidirectional, vertical and monopolistic communication system", and promoting the right to information on a global level. The 1980 MacBride Report suggested the creation of communication alternatives, both in the structure and ownership of the media, alternatives to the monopoly of the news agencies and their flow of information. This task was seen as something which would benefit humanity and was thus adopted by these forums.

This initiative was received with enthusiasm by many and silence by others. But the desire for a change of status - full recognition for the new nations - could not be achieved through a New Information Order alone. This initiative formed part of a project which was more ambitious and perhaps, as a result, more difficult to achieve: the creation of a New Economic Order, contemplating fairer trade rules for all nations. The inability to achieve a new economic order also reduced hopes of a change in the information order.

The other way

The invention of the transistor in 1947 opened the way for the innovations which ended in the widespread availability of televisions, portable radios, electronic calculators and computers.

At the end of World War II, there were only a few computers in the world, each of which occupied several rooms and could only be operated by experts. The following 50 years have shown how the transistor converted these giants into a mass-produced machine, which fits on a desk, in a small case, or even in the palm of a hand. The power and speed of these machines in processing data is hundreds of times better than their pre-war predecessors.

The establishment of world-wide networks linking computers have caused an enormously important turnaround in the access to and exchange of information. With more than 40 million users and exponential growth, the Internet has become an irreplaceable tool. Immediate access to databases and sources of information, the possibility of making links through electronic mail and news groups has made it more possible for groups to side-step the one-way flow of information imposed by the big news agencies. Thousands of non-governmental organizations, civil associations, and other groups have opened new routes for rapid, reliable and reasonably priced communication. Citizens in different parts of the world have made their voices heard together, supporting diverse causes, while at the same time making their knowledge available to others.

This capacity to link up networks convinced many people that the democratization of access to sources of information is now an indisputable and irreversible fact. However, this development also has its flaws.

Due to the high levels of standardization needed for such networks to function, languages which use non-Roman characters, used by people with little economic clout, have had serious difficulties in joining the tide of world information. Be that as it may, it is still possible to find programmes with Arabic, Chinese, Hebrew, Cyrillic, and other characters. But English remains the doorway to the "information super-highway" as it is known. Most of the servers putting information at the disposal

of network users, like the Internet, are in the developed countries, particularly in the United States.

The world has become dependent on information which travels almost as fast as light, making it a 'key strategic resource' in some people's eyes. Without doubt it is a vital asset for the functioning of all the world's stock exchanges and for the companies that operate within them, as also for armies, credit companies, insurers and almost all companies whose interests go beyond their home-ground.

The convergence of the fields of communication and information has led to the emergence of a powerful computer industry. Here, the interests of commerce, military, entertainment, electronics and programming industries converge, leading to the creation of new monopolies, like Microsoft, which uses its power over 90 per cent of the market to eliminate competition and impose its own standards on users and providers of services.

Seen from a more general perspective, the global village foreseen by Marshall MacLuhan has not been built. Even though the media needed for the integration of a global community are available, the majority of the world's people do not have the material resources needed to join.

On another front, those who are able to join the information community do not - as yet - fulfil the vision implied in the words 'global village'. Cables, television, satellite and the Internet have all been considered elements which could unite society, but so far they have contributed an explosive diversity that is in fact aggravating social fragmentation in the poorer nations of the Third World as much as in the industrialized societies of the North. Much as diversity is to be valued, the information world has yet to learn how not to let it turn into divisiveness. ❑

MAIN TELEPHONE LINES PER 1,000 PEOPLE (1994)

Albania	12		Kyrgyzstan	73
Algeria	41		Laos	4
Anguilla	308		Latvia	258
Aotearoa/New Zealand	468		Lebanon	84
Argentina	141		Lesotho	8
Armenia	156		Libya	51
Australia	496		Lithuania	241
Austria	465		Luxembourg	553
Azerbaijan	85		Macedonia, TFYR	161
Bahamas	283		Madagascar	3
Bahrain	248		Malawi	3
Bangladesh	2		Malaysia	147
Barbados	327		Maldives	48
Belarus	186		Mali	2
Belgium	449		Malta	448
Belize	134		Mauritania	4
Benin	5		Mauritius	117
Bhutan	7		Mexico	93
Bolivia	35		Moldova	126
Botswana	35		Mongolia	29
Brazil	74		Morocco	38
Brunei	221		Mozambique	3
Bulgaria	295		Myanmar/Burma	3
Burkina Faso	3		Namibia	47
Burundi	3		Nepal	4
Cambodia	1		Netherlands	511
Cameroon	4		Nicaragua	20
Canada	590		Niger	1
Cape Verde	49		Nigeria	3
Central African Rep.	2		Norway	550
Colombia	92		Oman	76
Comoros	9		Pakistan	15
Congo D.R.	1		Panama	111
Congo R.	8		Papua New Guinea	9
Costa Rica	130		Paraguay	31
Côte d'Ivoire	8		Peru	33
Croatia	252		Philippines	17
Cuba	32		Poland	131
Cyprus	518		Portugal	348
Czech Republic	212		Qatar	215
Chad	1		Romania	123
Chile	110		Russia	162
China	23		Rwanda	2
Denmark	600		São Tome and Principe	20
Djibouti	13		Saudi Arabia	96
Dominica	235		Senegal	9
Dominican Republic	79		Seychelles	170
Ecuador	59		Sierra Leone	3
Egypt	43		Singapore	455
El Salvador	44		Slovakia	187
Equatorial Guinea	6		Slovenia	287
Eritrea	4		Solomon Is.	15
Estonia	252		South Africa	91
Ethiopia	3		Spain	375
Fiji	77		Sri Lanka	10
Finland	551		St Kitts-Nevis	332
France	547		St Lucia	172
Gabon	30		St Vincent	155
Gambia	17		Sudan	2
Georgia	96		Suriname	120
Germany	483		Swaziland	20
Ghana	3		Sweden	683
Greece	478		Switzerland	597
Grenada	228		Syria	48
Guatemala	24		Tajikistan	45
Guinea	1		Tanzania	3
Guinea-Bissau	9		Thailand	47
Guyana	53		Togo	5
Haiti	7		Trinidad and Tobago	158
Honduras	24		Tunisia	54
Hungary	169		Turkey	200
Iceland	557		Turkmenistan	76
India	11		Uganda	2
Indonesia	13		Ukraine	157
Iran	66		United Arab Emirates	276
Iraq	34		United Kingdom	488
Ireland	350		United States	602
Israel	394		Uruguay	184
Italy	428		Uzbekistan	69
Jamaica	100		Vanuatu	27
Japan	480		Venezuela	108
Jordan	72		Vietnam	6
Kazakhstan	117		Yemen	12
Kenya	9		Zambia	9
Korea, North	47		Zimbabwe	12
Korea, South	396			
Kuwait	226			

Source: Human Development Report 1997, UNDP, 1997.

Nuclear Energy

Present and future costs

It will take millennia for current levels of toxic nuclear waste to break down naturally, to say nothing of the potential dangers of accidents, leaks and nuclear warfare. This results in a toxic legacy for generations to come

At the end of the 19th century, a type of wave or energy was discovered: radioactivity. Invisible to the naked eye, it could penetrate solid tissue. In 1895, a short, hard radiation wave - gamma - and a long, soft type - ultraviolet - began to be distinguished.

When around 1900, scientists announced the effects of radiation on living beings, the chemist Pierre Curie exposed himself to it in order to observe the biological reactions. His wife and colleague, Marie Curie, noted the effects of this experiment: "a lesion similar to a burn was produced which developed progressively and took some months to heal".

In 1901, the chemist Henri Becquerel also showed a burn on his body caused by a radioactive substance he had carried in a test tube to a scientific meeting. Becquerel confided his passion for the new discoveries to the Curies, but spoke also about his "mania" against them. Becquerel's ambivalent attitude to radioactivity set the tone for discussion of both it and its close relation, nuclear energy. This could be called the "Becquerel effect": the conquest of a new field of knowledge with medical, economic and military applications, coupled with apprehension about a form of poisoning which could not be seen, heard, felt nor smelt.

In 1901, Becquerel discovered uranium, the natural radioactive element.

The radioactivity of unnatural elements - elements which do not occur naturally but are processed in the laboratory, allowing for far greater degrees of radioactivity - was discovered 30 years later by Irene, daughter of the two pioneers of radiation, Marie and Pierre Curie, along with her husband Frderic Joliot.

Both Marie Curie, her daughter and son-in-law died relatively young from leukaemia, undoubtedly due to their handling the minimal but repeated doses of radioactivity which constituted their main field of research. Pierre Curie died in a road accident.

The era of optimism

The discovery of the enormous discharge of energy from nuclear fission - the bombarding of a radioactive nucleus until it splits ('splitting the atom') - coincided with the run up to World War II.

Most of this research broke away from scientific tradition, and remained unpublished for fear the Nazi war machine would make use of it.

Meanwhile, the US military establishment fostered this research and funded the first nuclear fission experiments under the Italian scientist Enrico Fermi, resident in the US, and the German scientist Franz Oppenheimer, a naturalized US citizen. Fermi carried out his first experiments in 1942 and Oppenheimer put the finishing touches to the first atomic bomb which was dropped by the US on Hiroshima, Japan, in August 1945.

After the War, the United States carried out a series of nuclear explosions with no direct military purpose, merely to improve techniques and accumulate experience. Recruits were taken to the state of Nevada as an end-of-course visit. The instructors, to "familiarize" the soldiers with the new weapon, displayed the small cylinders in their bare hands which would explode minutes later producing an atomic mushroom cloud several kilometres in diameter.

Handling nuclear material was thought to be scientifically regulated and therefore 'safe'. But the authorities were prompted to take the issue more seriously with the birth of calves with two heads, plants with unknown colours or properties, and the occurrence of leukaemia in humans, not only amongst rural people in the area but also amongst the conscripts taken to see the "fireworks" (as their sergeants jokingly called the explosions).

Ignorance about the toxic effects of radiation was not only a problem in the field of nuclear energy and nuclear fission. There were also difficulties in its medical application. At the beginning of the century, weak radioactivity began to be used to "photograph" bones inside previously opaque bodies - x-rays. The dosage used was far higher than the limit acceptable today.

Around the middle of the 1950s, atomic energy first began being used for peaceful purposes as a source of domestic power.

Opinions about this energy, and the way it has been employed, differed before and after April 1986, when extremely high temperature nuclear material was released in Chernobyl, Ukraine, melting the protective barriers and causing a blaze which forced the evacuation of the plant and nearby towns. In the following days, 31 people died trying to put out the fire.

Up till 1986, defenders of nuclear energy claimed it was the most benevolent source of energy known - both clean and silent - and compared figures of deaths at work in coal mines, oil wells and dams with those registered in nuclear plants. Until then there had been no deaths in nuclear plants.

This was a biased comparison because the nuclear industry was still "young" and because death by radiation tends to be a slow process. Initially the link between radiation and consequent illness and death was not as well established as it is today and there was, and remains, a tendency to register fewer cases than actually present.

The consequences of Chernobyl

The worst aspect of Chernobyl however came after the tragic initial fire. Successive measurements of radioactivity led to the complete evacuation of an area of some 5,000 km^2 (half the size of Lebanon). The evacuation was permanent for most of those affected, as it was suggested the area be left unpopulated for several decades, and the numbers of people affected increased every year. Today, official estimates state between eight and ten thousand people died in the first decade following the explosion, as a result of radiation, but environmentalists reckon the true figure is more like tens of thousands.

The UN estimated the catastrophe had affected the health of around 2.2 million Ukrainians, while several million people received an abnormally high dose of radioactivity in the rest of Europe. The long-term effects of the radiation released are unknown.

The Chernobyl tragedy could not fit in with the optimistic "scientific" forecasts given in the table above. Chernobyl alone made the risk of death by an accident in a nuclear plant 20 times more likely than previously assumed.

Since 1986, there has been a crisis of confidence which has brought into question the nuclear programmes of most of the countries of the so-called First World: only Japan and France went ahead with their nuclear energy development plans and some, like Austria and Italy, decided to dismantle their plants. In Sweden, a plebiscite decided that nuclear energy must be phased out before 2010. For years more acceptable energy options have been sought, although there has been opposition to this decision. The first Swedish reactor was shut down in 1997.

Making the most of a bad lot

Chernobyl also made scientists reconsider radiation exposure safety limits. What were once considered maximum limits of radioactivity by the European regulatory agencies, were ironically revised upwards.

The Chernobyl accident released radioactivity across an extensive swathe of Europe. Countries like Poland and regions of Germany, Sweden, Finland and Russia received unprecedented quantities of radioactivity. Zones as far away as Lapland, in the north of Finland, Sweden and Norway, registered levels of caesium which made the consumption of exposed meats and vegetables completely unacceptable. In Poland tons of vegetables were dumped, in

---

Risk of death for the world population due to the accident in Chernobyl during the first decade

1/500,000.

Source: Coefficient of the total world population according to official Soviet data on the number of dead.

Lapland, tons of reindeer meat buried. In Denmark and Sweden livestock was kept inside for a whole year as it was proven that the level of radioactivity in milk increased if the animals lived and ate outside.

The monitoring organizations in Europe set lower acceptable levels or dosages. Thus, a litre of milk which was previously allowed to contain up to 100 becquerels (becq.) was, after Chernobyl, allowed a higher threshold in various countries, with up to 500 becq. in Germany, 1,000 in Norway, and 2,000 in Finland and Sweden.

The nuclear economy

Another argument for the promotion of nuclear energy was its relative cost, which was said to be lower than other forms of energy. However, this is a far from simple issue.

At current rates it is more expensive than hydroelectricity, although still cheaper than coal or oil-produced power and many alternative energy sources wind, sun and wave power. The calculation of the energy costs include inputs and infrastructure. In the case of nuclear energy the cost of the final dumping of nuclear waste should be included, for up until now - nearly 50 years after the plants came on stream - there are no satisfactory nuclear waste dumps. The construction costs for these, if it ever becomes possible to build them, have never been calculated, but what is certain is that they will be very expensive. Nor are the incalculable medical, social and environmental costs of accidents like Chernobyl taken into account.

Meddling with the future

There have been many problems encountered with nuclear reactors. The latest of these relates to their life-span which is 30-40 years.

The number of deaths from radiation has increased in some countries during recent years. Russian scientists consider unregulated sources - for example stolen or obsolete material - of radioactive contamination to be one of the main causes of the declining life expectancy of the Russian population in the 1990s. In the area of Moscow alone there are estimated to be around 500 such sources of radioactivity.

At the same time, the International Commission of Radiological Protection has proposed to reduce the security threshold on radiation from 5 rem. (unit of radiation dosage applied to humans, derived from "Roentgen equivalent man") per year to 2, thereby acknowledging that up until now its poisonous effects had been underestimated.

Many scientists are more worried by the future consequences of nuclear energy, especially radioactive waste, and the potential danger of toxic accidents than by the threat of nuclear weapon explosions.

It will take millennia rather than centuries for current amounts of toxic nuclear waste to biodegrade. This is meddling with future life carried to an extreme. ❑

Accidents and measurements

Atomic energy installations are shrouded in secrecy, officially for security reasons. In practice, the secrets so closely guarded concern mainly the difficulties involved in fulfilling security regulations, the dangers of contamination and accidents.

A case in point was Chernobyl, where a leak of radiation 90 times more powerful than the atomic explosion in Hiroshima in 1945 went undeclared for nearly three days, until routine radioactivity monitoring around the reactors in Forsmark, Sweden one Monday gave unusually high readings. The Forsmark plant personnel were immediately evacuated and readings taken inside the building - these were almost exactly the same as outside, proving the leak did not originate there. Readings were then taken across the nation and radioactivity of an inconceivably and unacceptably high level through its length and breadth was revealed. Neighbouring Finland was consulted, and similar levels were found there. Only when other nearby countries were also consulted did the Soviet authorities admit there had been an accident in Ukraine...the previous Friday.

Dozens of entries have been added to the list of fires, radioactive leaks and accidents in atomic plants since the first accidents at Chalk River, Ontario, Canada in September 1952, and the spillage of radioactive plutonium at Windscale (now Seascale) on the north-west coast of England in October 1957. The current level of leukaemia in children in the Windscale area is ten times the national average.

NUMBER OF ACCIDENTS PER DECADE	
1952 - 1961	5
1962 - 1971	2
1972 - 1981	14
1982 - 1991	32

NUMBER OF ACCIDENTS PER COUNTRY	
UNITED STATES	18
FRANCE	17
CANADA	4
JAPAN	4
USSR	3
UNITED KINGDOM	2
GERMANY	1
ARGENTINA	1
BULGARIA	1
SPAIN	1
FINLAND	1

Source: Greenpeace

The statistics, available up to 1991 and with only partial information for Third World countries, show that the first decade of nuclear power had more accidents than the second. This supports criticism that the initial security thresholds were deficient and that there was a general lack of awareness about the potential dangers of radioactivity. However, there was a considerable increase in the number of accidents in the third decade - possibly related to the larger number of reactors in operation once the industry had been consolidated. But this does not explain the increase from the third to the fourth decade, as the Chernobyl tragedy caused the scrapping of some nuclear projects around the world. In fact the increase may be due to the fact that many reactors are reaching the end of their useful working lives after thirty or forty years, and to a greater sensitivity in noting leaks from 1986 onwards. ❑

The fiction of development

As the millennium draws to a close, the concepts of modernization, progress and development - central to the aims and frustrations of the international community of nations during the 19th and 20th centuries, are increasingly being questioned not only for their cultural assumptions but also in view of the economic system they have fostered

Throughout the 20th century, documents outlining global policies rested on concepts like "modernization", "progress" or "development", which took it as given that human societies all follow a single course on the subject of "general well-being", without sufficiently taking into account the disparate levels of advancement of different nations.

At the end of the 1940s, the word development came to serve a function similar to the earlier terms modernization and progress which, along with the optimism born of the Industrial Revolution, expressed the need of the dominant powers to subordinate other states.

In Africa, Asia and Latin America, for example, the term modernization was used of at the end of the 19th century and in the early 20th century. In the 1950s however, with the emergence of the Cold War between the capitalist and communist blocs, development became the paradigm from which other terms like "underdevelopment", "developing countries", and so on took their meaning.

Impossible independence

Despite their differences, the liberal and Marxist ideologies share a linear concept of history which states that progress and general well-being are unavoidably reached, be this due to the stimulus of capital or the advance of productive forces (workers, technology, and so on).

The concept of development inherent in such assumptions was particularly emphasized, to adjust the international division of labour to the new post-war situations, and above all to align the newly independent countries of Asia and Africa in a new world order.

The nations of capitalist Europe, the United States and Japan were seen as "developed" states and the poor countries were "under", "pre" or "little" developed. The term "Third World" was coined at this time, to include those countries which did not belong to the First 'capitalist' World, nor the Second 'communist' World, with the implication that the latter two were superior.

Within this framework, the capitalist camp's interest in maintaining control over its former areas of influence (Latin America for the United States, and the former colonies of Asia and Africa for the European powers) was translated into the promise of progress and development, which would come to these countries through financial aid and investments.

In the early 1960s, the economists and sociologists of the Third World formulated Dependency Theory, where development and underdevelopment are seen as two sides of the same coin: one could not exist without the other. This interpretation has served as a basis for the most radical movements of the following years, postulating "independent development" and an escape from the capitalist system.

The Dependency Theory continued to be based on the generic possibility of development, but this supposition was shot down in flames when it became evident that not even the communist bloc, the former Soviet Union, could survive outside the world economy. Some of those who had formulated it later criticised the theory and started to talk of "non-development" instead.

With the collapse of the communist bloc, the ideological confrontation between the two systems disappeared. In fact, the flow of international investment took on the hard-nosed purpose of the simple pursuit of maximum profits, while development aid decreased year on year. However, the terminology of development did not disappear. It now meant that the entire world had to follow a single capitalist path.

Unsustainable development

In 1992, governments and thousands of non-governmental organizations met in Rio de Janeiro to discuss the environment. The Earth Summit was called to seek solutions to the increasing ecological damage inflicted on the planet by humans. However, Agenda 21, which arose from this meeting, did no more than reactivate the notion of development, now with the help of a new adjective: "sustainable".

A world commitment was drawn up aiming to achieve "sustainable development" which would not further damage ecosystems. The rich governments of the North committed themselves to providing financial and technological aid to the poor states of the South, which in turn promised plans to eradicate poverty and satisfy the basic needs of their populations.

The common objective was to achieve a world development system making it possible to "satisfy the needs of current generations without sacrificing the possibilities of future generations".

Due either to a lack of capacity or political will to fight the real forces behind the capitalist system, the Rio commitment could not be fulfilled. This made the shortfalls of the developmentalist proposals even more evident. And while the term "globalization" was being born to explain the new course of events, the inescapable crisis of the nation-state and the unstoppable triumph of the speculative economy made the old patterns of comparison appear increasingly ridiculous.

The crisis of the nation-state

The ethnocentric prejudice locked into the very origin of the term development - the aim of which was to impose a certain model of Western capitalist democracy on the different cultures of the world - was shown up by the real situation which revealed the argument's complete lack of economic and political validity.

At the end of the 20th century, the

idea of the nation-state was being shaken up by the rapacious growth of transnational companies and the supra-state political entities (like the EC, NAFTA, Mercosur, ASEAN) which served them.

At the same time, with the abandonment of the gold standard, financial activity went completely out of control. The old relation between investor and producer countries no longer existed, replaced by the indiscriminate flow of speculative capital, investing in any region of the world and above all in the financial markets.

It then became extremely difficult to determine how the global economy was sustained. Just as the informal economy provided the greatest part of the income of many countries, the multimillion-dollar flow of illicit capital (from drugs, arms and diamond trafficking, for example) made it very difficult to detect where and how to aim in order to achieve the proclaimed target of development.

To re-think the paradigms

Electronic money, which could be deposited instantaneously in the various stock exchanges of the world and was constantly changing hands, was hidden, and forced a rethinking of the old schemes of development and international trade. In an effort to make coherent the speed and uncertainty of speculative activity and the knock-on local effects on other countries, the world began to be thought of in terms of "interdependence".

But this interdependence, far from being manageable, in fact appeared to designate the uncontrollable flow of capital and to what extent the consequences of this flow were immeasurable. The financial bubble which burst in Mexico and Singapore, had already provided signs that the fragile balance of interdependence was already on the point of exploding.

Despite its capacitiy for renewal within discourses, the idea of a feasible, unified and global development was losing its legitimacy. In fact, it became an unreasonable goal - that was not to be reached by everybody. It became necessary then to re-think the paradigms of development which had led to such a state of stagnation. ❏

Globalization

What is globalization?

Globalization is really a euphemism for 'transnationalization' - the unfettered expansion of transnational corporations (TNCs) into the world economy, particularly into the economies of the poor countries. Multilateral organizations such as the World Trade Organization (WTO), the International Monetary Fund (IMF) and the World Bank are playing a key role in this process

As the latest buzz-word, globalization is used in any and every context. In international discourses, both official and non-official, and more so within the last decade or so, the term is often used in an adjectival form - 'this phenomenon of globalization' - and in the context of the 'interdependence' of economies and nations.

Globalization is acquiring a connotation akin to age-old terms like *karma* or *kismet* (or fate) used by people to explain their current difficult situation or some hardship that cannot be overcome, but has to be borne.

Even "rational" people who otherwise believe that science and technology can solve or cure anything (including economists who insist that their discipline is scientific and logical) use the term 'globalization' in such a way as to appear to attribute (and blame) everything that happens in the broad social and economic sectors, on this phenomenon. Governments and governmental institutions, and a host of national and international elites, use the term to disown their own responsibilities for certain unwelcome developments.

Economic development

'Globalization' is clearly not a natural phenomenon like an earthquake, or hurricane - occurrences in nature which, whether they can be foretold or not, cannot be averted.

While the term is being increasingly used by various people - and journalists and the media are often to blame - to describe wide-ranging and dramatic changes in the world, in its true sense globalization describes certain economic developments.

Within the realm of the new economic order, 'globalization' is acquiring a wide variety of uses, referring to the emergence of a new asymmetric international division of labour as well as a greater dispersion of economic activity directed by corporate strategic planning that has replaced governmental or state efforts in various countries. It is also being increasingly used in terms of the current world economic situation - the erosion of the post-war US dominance of the world

economy by the rising competitiveness of Western Europe and Japan and the rise of regional spheres of influence.

Globalization is also used to describe the worldwide spread of capitalism. Recent years have seen the collapse of centrally planned economies and the capitalist system dominates most of the world. Even in countries like China where the political system is still being maintained, there are increasing moves away from the command economy towards a market economy or as the Chinese call it a 'social market economy'.

'Liberalization'

Globalization is also being used synonymously for the 'liberalization' and 'greater openness' of economies - implying liberalization both of the domestic external economies. Thus, in October last year, the head of the World Trade Organization, Mr Renato Ruggiero, speaking at the Telecom-95 conference to heads of the major telecommunication enterprises of the G-7 countries, said that while "liberalization of capital and trade flows is creating a global economy, the liberalization of telecommunications, which can bring high quality, medical, education and business services to every village in the world, will globalize human society itself".

When one talks of globalization in the economic sector, one is thus talking about economic and economic-related structures knit together and across the world of nations. Globalization (and the term 'integration' often used with it), is the outcome of several elements of politics, economics, industrial processes and the way human society is organised and run, both within and among countries.

Advances in technology

No doubt the advances in the technology of transport and communication and information technology have contributed to and helped this process. The major corporations of the world in the pursuit of profit-maximization and capital accumulation objectives have been exerting their pressures and influence on their governments to facilitate this type of integration, through the process of globalization, that is, the transnationalization of the world economy.

The term integration, at international levels, is used to describe governmental actions - regionally or multilaterally across the world - to reduce the barriers to trade and economic exchanges and to the mobility factors of production, and also harmonizing national economic policies for common world good. But increasingly, the concept of international economic integration and interdependence is being used to explain the interdependence of national economies, irrespective of whether it is brought about by acts of governments or by the independently conceived and executed actions of micro-economic agents. (M Panic, 1988, *National Management of the International Economy*, Macmillan).

The current talk, since the late 1980s and early 1990s, of globalization and integration is really a smokescreen to hide the efforts of transnational corporations (TNCs) to expand their activities to developing countries.

Transnational corporations

This was made clear by Sylvia Ostrey, former Chief Economist of the Organization for Economic Co-operation and Development (OECD) and former Canadian Trade Policy official, in 1990, when the Uruguay Round of the General Agreement on Tariffs and Trade (GATT) negotiations was being stalled by US and European differences over agriculture. Ostrey wrote then ('Help the Three Systems sing in Harmony', *International Herald Tribune*, 19 April 1990): 'The primary agent of globalization is the transnational enterprise. The primary driving force is the revolution in information and communications technology.... In a globalizing world, competition among transnational enterprises in sophisticated products and services... is also competition among systems... For the global corporation competing in the international economy, it means competing under the same set of rules - that is the same set of domestic rules in different countries".

It was a plea for governments to act, agree upon a set of trading rules in the Uruguay Round negotiations, and facilitate the globalization of the world economy by the TNCs: a call for governmental or intergovernmental actions to transnationalize the world economy. The globalization she was advocating was not a spontaneous force, but a deliberate set of policies to be adopted by governments to further the transnationalization of the world economy.

Initially, the GATT, through successive rounds of tariff negotiations - from the initial Geneva and Torquay tariff negotiation rounds right through the Dillon and Kennedy rounds - embarked on a course of gradual tariff reductions and liberalization of trade between the US and Europe, subsequently involving Japan. The

rest of the membership, mostly developing countries, were onlookers, benefitting to some extent from the concessions exchanged among the industrial nations, through the most favoured nation (MFN) principle, but gaining no direct rights through trade liberalization in areas of interest to them.

Until the Tokyo Round of negotiations and accords, the aims of the industrialized countries were basically to facilitate and accommodate new production, in existing or new sectors and lines, within the industrialized world.

Changing perceptions

The industrialized countries in all these earlier negotiations did not focus on the markets of the developing world, but rather on each other's markets. Trade liberalization measures were designed to further the intra-industry trade among themselves. Their more or less equal technological and other capabilities resulted in intense product differentiation and intra-industry trade as well as intra-firm trade. All the successive tariff cuts and other measures were aimed at facilitating this, with the corporations in effect lobbying their governments.

For a long time within the GATT, the developing countries which were not major markets, were allowed to benefit from the concessions exchanged by the industrialized countries among themselves, without having to give any reciprocal concessions or benefits.

But the rise of competition from the newly industrialized countries (NICs) of the Far East (South Korea, Hong Kong, Singapore and Taiwan) and the second tier of NICs (Malaysia and other ASEAN members) began to change the perceptions of the North. Also, with slower growth and stagnation in their own countries, and the change of stance in macro-economics in 1980 (with financial assets and their protection taking precedence over, and to the detriment of, manufacturing capital) the transnational corporations began to eye the markets of the major developing countries.

No more Koreas or Taiwans

In the North there were moves to protect domestic markets (through non-tariff measures) against the new competition from the NICs, as well to penetrate those markets, and those of the major developing countries. Thus Northern TNCs pushed to break down the trade barriers in the South against imports, as well as establish themselves within those countries to compete with domestic enterprises.

The Uruguay Round was really about this. The US objectives spelt out in Congressional hearings were very clear: ensure that there are no more Koreas or Taiwans to challenge and compete with the US.

There was a push to end the differential treatment of the developing

countries, to tighten terms in the traditional goods area and ensure that the developing countries were bound by them. There were moves to extend the ambit of the GATT negotiations to include new areas such as services, agriculture and intellectual property rights (in the parlance of GATT, Trade-related Intellectual Property Rights or TRIPS) and liberalize them.

This liberalization drive in services which is currently being continued through the World Trade Organization (WTO), the successor of GATT, embraces service sectors such as financial services and basic telecommunications and is aimed at facilitating the control by foreign capital of the key sectors of domestic economies of these developing countries.

Secure framework

The TRIPs, while motivated and pushed by the pressures of the US film and music industry (against copying and sale of video- and audio-cassettes and compact discs) are designed to establish a secure framework for TNCs to supply a distant market with their products, or to licence a local producer.

Side by side with the trading rules to promote transnationalization, the major industrialized countries, particularly the US which really controls the International Monetary Fund (IMF) and the World Bank, has been pushing these institutions to further this same goal of globalization through their policies. This has come to be known as the Washington Consensus.

The TNCs, however, still do not have unrestrained rights to invest and set up enterprises in the developing world. Hence the efforts now to set up an investment treaty inside the WTO and enforce the right through trade retaliation.

All these moves which come under the umbrella of 'globalization' are pushing 'free market' and 'free trade' theories on to the developing countries.

Source: Thirld World Network.

	EXPORTS (MILLIONS $) 1996	IMPORTS (MILLIONS $) 1996		EXPORTS (MILLIONS $) 1996	IMPORTS (MILLIONS $) 1996
Albania	296	1,283	Latvia	1,443	2,319
Algeria	12,609	8,372	Lebanon	1,153	7,560
Angola	4,472	2,039	Libya	10,126	5,191
Aotearoa/New Zealand	13,789	14,716	Lithuania	3,356	4,559
Argentina	23,810	23,762	Macedonia, TFYR	1,119	1,941
Armenia	290	862	Madagascar	616	671
Australia	53,252	60,897	Malawi	501	687
Austria	57,822	67,142	Malaysia	78,151	76,082
Azerbaijan	618	1,255	Mali	288	1,159
Bangladesh	3,297	6,898	Mauritania	574	616
Belarus	5,122	6,778	Mauritius	1,699	2,255
Belgium	168,010	157,860	Mexico	95,199	97,630
Benin	255	869	Moldova	1,104	1,522
Bolivia	1,087	1,601	Mongolia	424	451
Brazil	47,164	53,736	Morocco	4,742	8,254
Bulgaria	4,543	4,313	Mozambique	226	783
Burkina Faso	216	783	Myanmar/Burma	1,187	2,524
Burundi	37	125	Nepal	358	664
Cambodia	300	1,647	Netherlands	177,228	160,700
Cameroon	1,758	1,204	Nicaragua	653	1,076
Canada	199,071	170,265	Niger	79	567
Central African Rep.	115	180	Nigeria	15,610	6,433
Chad	125	217	Norway	48,922	34,290
Chile	14,979	16,810	Oman	6,395	4,610
China	151,047	138,833	Pakistan	9,266	11,812
Colombia	10,976	13,863	Panama	558	2,778
Congo D.R.	1,461	1,331	Papua New Guinea	2,554	1,866
Congo R.	1,833	1,590	Paraguay	1,043	3,107
Costa Rica	2,882	3,871	Peru	5,226	7,947
Côte d'Ivoire	4,996	2,909	Philippines	20,328	34,663
Croatia	4,512	7,788	Poland	24,387	37,092
Cuba	1,834	3,004	Portugal	23,184	33,979
Czech Republic	21,882	27,709	Romania	8,084	11,435
Denmark	48,868	43,093	Russia	81,438	43,318
Dominican Republic	3,893	6,300	Rwanda	168	385
Ecuador	4,762	3,733	Saudi Arabia	58,117	27,764
Egypt	3,534	13,020	Senegal	655	1,672
El Salvador	1,023	2,670	Sierra Leone	214	334
Estonia	2,074	3,196	Singapore	124,794	131,083
Ethiopia	494	1,492	Slovakia	8,824	10,924
Finland	40,520	30,853	Slovenia	8,308	9,412
France	283,318	274,088	South Africa	18,132	26,861
Gabon	3,146	898	Spain	101,417	122,842
Gambia	22	272	Sri Lanka	4,097	5,028
Georgia	261	884	Sudan	468	1,439
Germany	511,728	443,043	Sweden	82,704	63,970
Ghana	1,684	3,219	Switzerland	80,756	79,192
Greece	9,558	26,881	Syria	3,980	6,399
Guatemala	2,031	3,146	Taiwan	115,646	101,338
Guinea	774	810	Tajikistan	770	668
Guinea-Bissau	56	107	Tanzania	828	1,642
Haiti	180	865	Thailand	55,789	73,289
Honduras	845	1,922	Togo	363	1,032
Hungary	13,138	16,207	Trinidad and Tobago	2,456	2,204
India	32,325	36,055	Tunisia	5,517	7,681
Indonesia	49,727	42,925	Turkey	23,045	42,733
Iran	22,102	13,926	Turkmenistan	1,693	1,313
Iraq	502	492	Uganda	568	725
Ireland	45,565	35,750	Ukraine	16,040	24,042
Israel	20,504	29,796	United Arab Emirates	28,096	30,374
Italy	250,718	202,908	United Kingdom	259,039	283,682
Jamaica	1,347	2,916	United States	575,477	814,888
Japan	410,481	347,496	Uruguay	2,391	3,322
Jordan	1,466	4,293	Uzbekistan	2,671	4,761
Kazakhstan	6,230	4,261	Venezuela	22,633	8,902
Kenya	2,203	3,480	Vietnam	7,016	13,910
Korea, North	1,007	2,201	Yemen	4,538	3,443
Korea, South	124,404	144,724	Yugoslavia Fed. Rep.	1,842	4,101
Kuwait	13,420	8,113	Zambia	1,020	1,106
Kyrgyzstan	507	838	Zimbabwe	2,094	2,808
Laos	334	642			

Source: World Development Indicators 1998, World Bank, 1998.

Transnationals

The new international power

Transnational corporations are the powerful players in the "global village". Centralization of decision-making and increasing take-overs and mergers allow them to expand unhindered by national boundaries in search of lower production costs and bigger markets.

At the beginning of the 1990s there were some 37,000 major transnational corporations with 170,000 subsidiaries in the international economy. However, around 200 of them covered the bulk of world trade. These 200 have been undergoing a metamorphosis since the 1980s, constantly expanding through mergers and take-overs.

The speed of the transnationalization of capital, measured as a proportion of the world Gross Domestic Product, is astonishing: from 17 per cent in the mid-1960s through 24 per cent in 1982 to more than 32 per cent in 1995. The top 200 are conglomerates which cross the classic divisions between the primary, secondary and tertiary sectors: from manufacturing and financial services to large-scale agricultural production and commerce.

Geographical location

These 200 corporations are headquartered in nine countries: Japan (62), the United States (53), Germany (23), France (19), Britain (11), Switzerland (8), South Korea (6), Italy (5) and the Netherlands (4). If one counts joint ventures between Britain and the Netherlands as a single entity, in reality eight countries dominate 96.5 per cent of the 200 biggest transnationals, and 96 per cent of their profits.

But the concentration is even greater than these figures show, as the 200 biggest are often not independent firms, as is the case of the five Mitsubishi corporations, with sales worth more than $320 billion. While the feuds between the largely independent branches of the Mitsubishi empire continue, they remain strategically interlinked through common policies on administration, price-setting, production and marketing, along with networks of economic and political intelligence. Their common political agent is Japan's Liberal Democratic Party, 37 per cent of whose expenses are funded by the Mitsubishi empire.

The distribution of power

In the last two decades the top 200 corporations grew impressively, and so did the inequality in the power distribution between them, pitching them into a constant war for larger and better sectors of the world market.

The number of US transnationals fell from 80 in 1982 to 53 in 1995, while in Japan they number grew from 35 to 62 in the same period. There was also a notable emergence of big corporations in Switzerland and a reduction in Britain, from 18 to 11.

However, the most noticeable factor was the mushrooming of transnationals in South Korea - from one to six in a relatively short period or time. These are led by Daewoo, one of the most aggressive expansionists. With sales of more than $52 billion, Daewoo towers over other giants like Nichimen, Kanematsu, Unilever and Nestlé.

The roots of Korean expansionism

The world-wide expansion of Daewoo is a symptom of the power of the Chaebol (conglomerates). The assets of the 30 main Chaebol catapulted from $223 billion in 1992 to $367 billion in 1996, and currently constitute more than 80 per cent of South Korean GDP. But the four biggest Daewoo, Sangong, Samsung and Hyundai - account for half ($184 billion) of these assets. The capital accumulation of the South Korean transnationals would not have been possible without billions of US dollars in the crucial period of growth in South Korea, between 1947 and 1955, and tens of billions in state subsidies since. Where the Chaebol end and the state begins is impossible to determine.

Many prominent politicians and high-ranking members of the military are big shareholders, creating a closed fraternity, where even their children inter-marry.

The directors of the Chaebol and their interactions bring to mind German industrialist Walter Rathenau wise words in 1909: "300 men who know each other direct the economic destiny of Europe and choose their successors from amongst their numbers." The only thing which has changed since then is that the number of members of this elite caste has shrunk.

The economies of scale

Given the slowing down of economic growth and decreasing share markets, the transnationals cannot expand by creating new factories and more jobs, but through the take-over of competitors and the acquisition of a larger portion of the market.

Take-overs allow transnationals to maximize the economies of scale in the world market. Some have already done this: Boeing, the three large US automobile builders, the Japanese and Korean electronics corporations, and car and ship-building giants. Five companies monopolise half the markets for aerospace and electrical goods, electronic components and software; two fast foods, and five tobacco and alcoholic and non alcoholic beverages.

The transnationals are not only backed by their governments, but the host governments are also given sweeteners to aid their advances. The governments of Britain and Ireland, not to mention those of Eastern Europe, agreed to colossal subsidies and welcomed the transnationals in with privatizations and fiscal stimuli of various types.

Investment banks: catalysts

Corporate mergers and alliances   for example Shell and BP (British Petroleum) - are all part of the game with slogans like "liberalization" "privatization," "deregulation" and "free and multilateral trade". Amongst the main promoters of these mergers are the big investment banks and mutual and pension funds. Pressure for increased profits or "share values" from Wall Streets provide enormous incentive for the concentration of corporations. Not only are the mergers vigorously promoted by the Wall Street investment banks, but their promoters are generously rewarded. The profits of Goldman Sachs, one of the biggest investment banks and world leader in the consolidation of transnational corporations, after the El Dorado and M&A (Mergers & Acquisitions) megaagreements went from $931 million to $1.9 billion in a year. Furthermore, Goldman Sachs practices what it preaches: the bank is not burdened with "excessive" labour costs, as it has cut 20 per cent of its workforce in recent years. The annexing of the corporations yielded abundant dividends: their 175 general partners receive more than $200,000 per year, on top of their share of the capital.

Novartis

The 1996 merger of Sandoz and Ciba-Geigy was the biggest corporate merger in history, leading to the creation of Novartis, the second biggest pharmaceutical company in the world.

This merger generated profits, in commissions and legal rights, of $ 95 million which were split between JP Morgan, Morgan Stanley and the Swiss Union Bank. Their capital increased from $63 billion to $82 billion overnight.

The creation of Novartis was followed by mass redundancies. As with other transnationals, the dismissals were carried out swiftly in the name of "restructuring" and "cost reduction". Consequently, the value of the shares of both companies saw an unprecedented increase.

Boeing

As with Novartis, Wall Street and all the financial markets were pleased when Boeing took over McDonnel Douglas. As with Novartis, there was a clear process of strengthening within the transnational. There was no difference at all in the take-over strategies. The acquisition of McDonnel Douglas for $14 billion was not just thought up by the Boeing board of directors, but was also strongly encouraged by the Pentagon and the Department of Trade, who argued that the deal would broaden the US-owned sector of the aerospace industry in international markets. It caused mass redundancies. Since 1992, the 32 defence establishments have been reduced to nine, and more than a million posts have been eliminated.

Such the strategic considerations are linked to the profitability of the big companies. What the owners of Boeing, the Pentagon and the Trade Department hope for is rather more than extending the US share of the world market; they also want to push out the main competitor, Europe's Airbus, until they have annihilated the last vestiges of its power in the market.

Backed by McDonnel Douglas, Boeing's proportion of the market increased to 64 per cent. The acquisition of McDonnel trebled defence orders for Boeing and considerably increased its access to the public sector.

This take-over provides Boeing with an enormous subsidy and at the same time increases its capacity to subsidize civil aircraft. Boeing has been selling its products and services at far below market costs. Its R&D have received billions of dollars of subsidies from the Pentagon since the end of the {Second World}war The empire-building of Novartis and Boeing highlights the usual trajectory of the transnationalization of capital.

Source: Revista del Sur

A new Internet conglomerate

The $37 billion deal by which WorldCom acquired telecommunications multinational MCI shows that the battle for the control of the Internet follows the familiar patterns of the 'free' market.

A press release by WorldCom on the Internet (www.wcom.com) announced the emergence of one of the most important Net service providers. "We will be present in 2,000 points throughout the world," stated WorldCom, promising a wide range of services.

In 1997, WorldCom carried out a series of purchases and mergers before acquiring MCI which revealed the extent of its plans for the Internet, since it involved the acquisition of some of the most powerful providers of network infrastructure.

WorldCom, once a small Mississippi-based company, had already purchased UUNet, which formed the backbone of connections on the Net, and Compuserve, one of the largest suppliers in the world of on-line services.

With the incorporation of MCI-Internet, the company was set to control 60 per cent of access to the Net in the United States, the most connected country in the world.

In the early 1990s, WorldCom began a retail business of long-distance services in the United States. Since then, the company has grown with the purchase of some 50 telecommunications firms, issuing stock to use as capital.

The $37 billion MCI deal makes it the world's second largest telecommunications company, after AT&T. MCI-WorldCom will have 22 million customers and 70,000 employees throughout the world. This makes it the best placed in a $670 billion market, boasts the company.

To achieve this, WorldCom made great efforts to leave powerful competitors behind. British Telecom (BT) made the first offer for MCI. It was willing to pay $18 billion and create an alliance called Concert, with the participation of Telefónica of Spain, joint owner of several Latin American telecommunications companies.

WorldCom joined the race with a higher offer which swept aside BT's aspirations, but competition turned tough when the US company GTE decided to offer $27 billion. WorldCom then raised its offer to $37 billion and won.

Afterwards, US commercial authorities gave the go-ahead to the $1.2 billion purchase of Compuserve, a deal with major consequences for the Internet. WorldCom decided to keep the connection structure of Compuserve and linked itself with the huge America-On-Line (AOL) corporation. WorldCom paid AOL $175 million in order to achieve this link, and gave it Compuserve's interactive services with some three million customers. Although the new telecommunications giant has no overt partnership with AOL, the network infrastructure has linked it with this Internet provider which, with 12 million customers, has become the largest in the world after the current deal.

With the UUNet, Compuserve and AOL nodes in place and the MCI-Internet deal, WorldCom now has a powerful connections infrastructure which includes more than 10,000 kilometres of fibre-optic cable.

The Internet had 19.5 million servers in 1997, according to Network Wizards (www.nw.com), a company which has been measuring information about the Net for over 20 years. Each one of these servers has an average of six or seven connections. The optimistic Internet Society (www.isoc.org) believes the number is closer to 10. In any case, the web today reaches over a 100 million people.

Source: Revista del Sur

Corporation name	Revenues $ millions	Employees	Country
GENERAL MOTORS	168,369	647,000	U.S.
FORD MOTOR CO.	146,991	371,702	U.S.
MITSUI	144,942	41,694	JAPAN
MITSUBISHI	140,203	35,000	JAPAN
ITOCHU	135,542	6,999	JAPAN
ROYAL DUTCH/SHELL GROUP	128,174	101,000	U.K./NETH.
MARUBENI	124,026	65,000	JAPAN
EXXON	119,434	79,000	U.S.
SUMITOMO	119,281	26,200	JAPAN
TOYOTA MOTOR CO.	108,702	150,736	JAPAN
WAL-MART STORES	106,147	675,000	U.S.
GENERAL ELECTRIC	79,179	239,000	U.S.
NISSHO IWAI	78,921	17,497	JAPAN
NIPPON TELEGRAPH & TELEPHONE	78,320	230,300	JAPAN
INTL. BUSINESS MACHINES	75,947	268,648	U.S.
HITACHI	75,669	330,152	JAPAN
AT&T	74,525	130,400	U.S.
NIPPON LIFE INSURANCE	72,575	86,695	JAPAN
MOBIL	72,267	43,000	U.S.
DAIMLER-BENZ	71,589	290,029	GERMANY
BRITISH PETROLEUM	69,851	53,150	UNITED KINGDOM
MATSUSHITA ELECTRIC INDUSTRIAL	68,147	270,651	JAPAN
VOLKSWAGEN	66,527	260,811	GERMANY
DAEWOO	65,160	186,314	SOUTH KOREA
SIEMENS	63,704	379,000	GERMANY
CHRYSLER	61,397	126,000	U.S.
NISSAN MOTOR	59,118	135,331	JAPAN
ALLIANZ	56,577	65,836	GERMANY
U.S. POSTAL SERVICE	56,402	887,546	U.S.
PHILIP MORRIS	54,553	154,000	U.S.
UNILEVER	52,067	306,000	U.K./NETH.
FIAT	50,509	237,865	ITALY
SONY	50,277	163,000	JAPAN
DAI-ICHI MUTUAL LIFE INSURANCE	49,144	66,953	JAPAN
IRI	49,055	132,489	ITALY
NESTLÉ	48,932	221,144	SWITZERLAND
TOSHIBA	48,415	186,000	JAPAN
HONDA MOTOR	46,994	101,100	JAPAN
ELF AQUITAINE	46,818	85,400	FRANCE
TOMEN	46,506	11,500	JAPAN
BANK OF TOKYO - MITSUBISHI	46,451	19,304	JAPAN
VEBA GROUP	45,246	122,110	GERMANY
TOKYO ELECTRIC POWER	44,735	43,166	JAPAN
TEXACO	44,561	28,957	U.S.
SUMITOMO LIFE INSURANCE	44,063	67,027	JAPAN
SUNKYONG	44,031	33,299	SOUTH KOREA
NEC	43,932	151,966	JAPAN
ÉLECTRICITÉ DE FRANCE	43,658	116,919	FRANCE
STATE FARM INSURANCE COS.	42,781	71,612	U.S.
DEUTSCHE TELEKOM	41,910	201,000	GERMANY
PHILIPS ELECTRONICS	41,036	262,500	NETHERLANDS
UNION DES ASSURANCES DE PARIS	40,736	50,810	FRANCE
PRUDENTIAL INS. CO. OF AMERICA	40,175	83,000	U.S.
FUJITSU	39,982	167,000	JAPAN
E.I. DU PONT DE NEMOURS	39,689	97,000	U.S.
DEUTSCHE BANK	39,413	74,356	GERMANY
RWE GROUP	39,289	132,658	GERMANY
ENI	38,843	83,424	ITALY
CHEVRON	38,691	40,820	U.S..
HEWLETT-PACKARD	38,420	112,000	U.S.
SEARS ROEBUCK	38,236	335,000	U.S.
METRO HOLDING	36,567	176,518	SWITZERLAND
RENAULT	35,979	140,905	FRANCE
ING GROUP	35,912	58,106	NETHERLANDS
PROCTER & GAMBLE	35,284	103,000	U.S.
BMW (BAYERISCHE MOTOREN WERKE)	34,727	116,112	GERMANY
CRÉDIT AGRICOLE	34,619	85,240	FRANCE
ABB ASEA BROWN BOVERI	34,574	214,894	SWITZERLAND
NICHIMEN	34,545	18,715	JAPAN
TOTAL	34,513	57,555	FRANCE
SAMSUNG	34,286	11,904	SOUTH KOREA
PEUGEOT	33,914	139,100	FRANCE
PDVSA	33,855	53,206	VENEZUELA
HOECHST	33,838	147,862	GERMANY
MEIJI LIFE INSURANCE	33,175	44,365	JAPAN
MITSUBISHI ELECTRIC	33,072	113,353	JAPAN
AMOCO	32,726	41,723	U.S.
AXA	32,681	36,695	FRANCE
CITICORP	32,605	89,400	U.S.
MITSUBISHI MOTORS	32,601	27,827	JAPAN
CIE GÉNÉRALE DES EAUX	32,428	217,300	FRANCE
BASF	32,409	103,406	GERMANY
BAYER	32,298	142,200	GERMANY
GAN	32,259	35,083	FRANCE
ALCATEL ALSTHOM GROUP	31,683	190,600	FRANCE
PEPSICO	31,645	486,000	U.S.
KMART	31,437	275,000	U.S.
KANEMATSU	30,868	12,000	JAPAN
ZURICH INSURANCE	30,760	40,981	SWITZERLAND
SSANGYONG	30,530	33,000	SOUTH KOREA
CARREFOUR	30,277	109,300	FRANCE
INDUSTRIAL BANK OF JAPAN	30,208	5,175	JAPAN
ASSICURAZIONI GENERALI	29,618	40,003	ITALY
FRANCE TÉLÉCOM	29,564	165,200	FRANCE
NOVARTIS	29,310	116,178	SWITZERLAND
HSBC HOLDINGS	28,859	102,470	UNITED KINGDOM
PEMEX (PETRÓLEOS MEXICANOS)	28,429	120,945	MEXICO
DAIEI	28,281	16,686	JAPAN
VIAG	28,207	88,014	GERMANY
AMERICAN INTERNATIONAL GROUP	28,205	36,600	U.S.

Source: The Global 500, Fortune, 1998.

Economics

The speculative economy takes control

In recent years 97.5 per cent of international monetary transactions were of a speculative nature, that is, money was exchanged for money. The potential consequences threatened global financial agreements, the sovereignty of nation-states and the futures of millions of people

In 1975, around 80 per cent of currency transactions - where one national currency is exchanged for another - were directed towards carrying out business in the real economy. The money changed hands, for example, to import oil, export cars, invest in companies or portfolios or to build factories. Such real transactions refer to commerce in actual goods and services.

The remaining 20 per cent of the transactions in 1975 were of a speculative type, which means their only aim was to profit from the buying and selling of currencies, dependent on their changing values. Thus, even in the days when the real economy was dominant, there was already a certain degree of monetary speculation underway.

At present, currency transactions in the real economy have fallen to 2.5 per cent and 97.5 per cent of transactions are of the speculative kind.

The causes

In 1997 there were nearly $2 billion worth of monetary transactions per day. This is equivalent to pouring the entire volume of the annual Gross Domestic Product (GDP) of the United States into monetary transactions every three days. There are three causes of this explosive increase in speculation:

- **Systemic redefinition:** The first important action was the liberation of the dollar from the gold standard in 1973, by then President of the United States Richard Nixon. The "floating" of the dollar allowed the value of currencies to be determined by the agents of the foreign exchange market. This gave a higher value to the currencies of nations with strong economies and healthy fiscal sectors, than to those of countries with unstable or weak economies or policies. This "liberalizing" of the system created the framework for increased speculation.
- **Legal deregulation:** In the 1980s, former President of the United States Ronald Reagan, and Britain's former Prime Minister Margaret Thatcher, introduced strategies for deregulation. The Baker Plan, applied by the World Bank and the International Monetary Fund (IMF), introduced these changes to a dozen key countries in the Third World. This provided more room for international movements of capital.
- **Technology:** one of the structural phenomena which underlie the system is technological change; the computerization of market systems and the electronic transferability of money.

The changing face of enterprise

The economics text books say companies and individuals compete for markets and resources. This is arguable to say the least. Companies and individuals compete for money using markets and resources. The liberalization of the system, which led to the "floating of currencies", also created a new kind of asset. Traditional assets include real estate, bonds, shares. In the present day we also have currencies.

This means that money, the tool of trade, has become an asset which intervenes in investment. This change has various repercussions, depending upon whether we are dealing with an investor or a "real" trader. From the point of view of an investor, this new class of assets - currencies - has the following important advantages:

- Extraordinarily low transaction costs. It is ten or twenty times cheaper to make a currency transaction than a share transaction.
- A market which operates 24 hours per day.
- A currency market is, by far, the best market. The placing of some billions of dollars in the share market implies a change in the value of the shares and is visible to other investors. This is so in the majority of share markets, except in the United States and some European markets due to their large size. In the currency market, even five or ten billion dollars make no impression. This is the ideal place for those who have a large quantity of money to mobilize. It can be invested and removed without affecting the market.

Due to these advantages, loans of money to people - to buy houses, cars or anything else - are no longer the best way to make money. The currency market is ideal. The banks are no longer the biggest agents in terms of providing credit. In the last 25 years, the percentage of total credit loans of the banks as a source of financing in the United States fell from 75 per cent to 26.5 per cent.

For the big international banks, like Chase Manhattan, Citicorp, Bank of America, Barclays or Simitomo, trade in currencies represents at least 20 per cent of total income. In a good year it will be more than 50 per cent.

When considering so-called "real" deals - the manufacture of goods - the "exchange risk" has come to be the biggest risk in international commercial activity, often above political or market risk. For example, if a German chemical company invests in a factory in India, it makes the investment in German marks. The chemical products of this factory sold on a local scale will be paid for in rupees, the Indian currency. If the value of the rupee falls in relation to the German mark, then the profitability of the original investment will also fall.

Therefore, the greatest risk of such investments is not whether the Indians will buy the chemical products (market risk) or whether the government will nationalize the factory (political risk), but changes in value of the currencies involved (exchange risk). One strategy of dealing with this risk is the reorganization of the business conglomerate. The production and marketing sectors are decentralizing because adaptation to local circumstances can be managed better on a local level. .

But while on the one hand production and marketing are decentralizing, on the other the financial and equity functions are being centralized.

Twenty or thirty years ago, when a US company had a factory in Germany, the factory managed its own finances. Now they would be managed from the company headquarters.

Another strategy pursued by the big companies is to change the make-up of their executives. In the 1940s and 1950s, anyone who could make a product could sell it. Thus, a manager with experience in production or engineering, would, without doubt, be a candidate for an executive post. In the 1960s and 1970s this changed. Experience in marketing became a key, obligatory element for executive posts. In the 1980s and 1990s, the financial specialists are the decision makers.

The biggest private financial institution in the United States at present is General Electric. The biggest earning sector within General Electric is not the defence sector, nor electric light bulbs, nor power stations. It is the finance department, due to its multiple financial transactions.

Those who deal in only one currency shoulder the greatest exchange risk. Most

(See also p.73)

		GNP per capita (US$) 1996				GNP per capita (US$) 1996
1	Switzerland	44,350		66	Morocco	1,290
2	Japan	40,940		67	Ukraine	1,200
3	Norway	34,510		68	Bulgaria	1,190
4	Denmark	32,100		69	Philippines	1,160
5	Singapore	30,550		70	Syria	1,160
6	Germany	28,870		71	Papua New Guinea	1,150
7	Austria	28,110		72	Egypt	1,080
8	United States	28,020		73	Indonesia	1,080
9	Belgium	26,440		74	Uzbekistan	1,010
10	France	26,270		75	Macedonia, TFYR	990
11	Netherlands	25,940		76	Turkmenistan	940
12	Sweden	25,710		77	Georgia	850
13	Finland	23,240		78	Bolivia	830
14	Australia	20,090		79	Albania	820
15	Italy	19,880		80	China	750
16	United Kingdom	19,600		81	Sri Lanka	740
17	Canada	19,020		82	Congo R.	670
18	Ireland	17,110		83	Côte d'Ivoire	660
19	Israel	15,870		84	Honduras	660
20	Aotearoa/New Zealand	15,720		85	Lesotho	660
21	Spain	14,350		86	Armenia	630
22	Greece	11,460		87	Cameroon	610
23	Korea, South	10,610		88	Zimbabwe	610
24	Portugal	10,160		89	Moldova	590
25	Slovenia	9,240		90	Senegal	570
26	Argentina	8,380		91	Guinea	560
27	Uruguay	5,760		92	Kyrgyzstan	550
28	Chile	4,860		93	Azerbaijan	480
29	Czech Republic	4,740		94	Pakistan	480
30	Brazil	4,400		95	Mauritania	470
31	Malaysia	4,370		96	Laos	400
32	Hungary	4,340		97	India	380
33	Gabon	3,950		98	Nicaragua	380
34	Trinidad and Tobago	3,870		99	Yemen	380
35	Croatia	3,800		100	Ghana	360
36	Mauritius	3,710		101	Mongolia	360
37	Mexico	3,670		102	Zambia	360
38	South Africa	3,520		103	Benin	350
39	Slovakia	3,410		104	Tajikistan	340
40	Poland	3,230		105	Kenya	320
41	Estonia	3,080		106	Central African Rep.	310
42	Panama	3,080		107	Haiti	310
43	Venezuela	3,020		108	Cambodia	300
44	Lebanon	2,970		109	Togo	300
45	Thailand	2,960		110	Uganda	300
46	Turkey	2,830		111	Vietnam	290
47	Costa Rica	2,640		112	Angola	270
48	Peru	2,420		113	Bangladesh	260
49	Russia	2,410		114	Guinea-Bissau	250
50	Latvia	2,300		115	Madagascar	250
51	Lithuania	2,280		116	Mali	240
52	Namibia	2,250		117	Nigeria	240
53	Colombia	2,140		118	Burkina Faso	230
54	Belarus	2,070		119	Nepal	210
55	Tunisia	1,930		120	Niger	200
56	Paraguay	1,850		121	Sierra Leone	200
57	El Salvador	1,700		122	Rwanda	190
58	Jordan	1,650		123	Malawi	180
59	Dominican Republic	1,600		124	Burundi	170
60	Jamaica	1,600		125	Tanzania	170
61	Romania	1,600		126	Chad	160
62	Algeria	1,520		127	Congo D.R.	130
63	Ecuador	1,500		128	Ethiopia	100
64	Guatemala	1,470		129	Mozambique	80
65	Kazakhstan	1,350				

Source: World Development Indicators 1998, World Bank, 1998.

people fall into this category. All those who own their own homes use only one currency - be it dollars, German marks or yen - and have their savings and income in the same currency. They risk all their assets losing value if the currency falls. In a world of floating currencies, not diversifying in currencies is like having a portfolio of shares in only one concern.

The weakening of the nation-state

The first consequence of this situation is that national governments are losing power. The nation-state is the only entity which cannot renegotiate its situation in this new environment. It has no way of gaining power against global capital and computer science. Those who deal on the exchange markets effectively influence governments by selling the currency of a given nation each time they are not satisfied with the policies of its government.

If a large enough number of speculators act together, the value of a currency can collapse, creating a consequent "monetary crisis". These sudden large-scale sales can occur in a very short period of time, in days or even hours, thanks to the new world-wide communications system. There are no negotiations or discussions, nor anyone proposing "this is what we are going to do" or "what if we renegotiate this part?"

Instead there is a sudden currency crisis. Such was the case with the fall of British sterling in 1991, the Scandinavian currencies in 1992 and 1993, the Mexican peso in 1993 and various Asian currencies in 1997. In the future there could be a devaluation of this type - an "attack" - on the US dollar, the kingpin of the entire system.

But would speculators want to change the kingpin? From the point of view of an individual agent, it doesn't matter which currency provides the benefits. The agent only speculates. If a sufficient quantity of agents in the exchange market consider there is a chance of profit in fluctuations of the dollar, they would speculate, because no one would think that their individual action could topple the entire system.

Interest in instability

The central banks can often intervene when a currency is attacked, to counteract the action of speculators by buying or selling. But the volumes of money which are traded are so enormous that not even central banks can avoid a strong impact being felt. All the reserves of all the central banks together total around $640 billion. They could be emptied in a third of a normal day of speculative activity.

This supports an increasing interest in the instability of the market, because that is where opportunities for extraordinary profits lie. Large fluctuations in the value of currencies provide juicy profits to those trading them.

"The biggest current preoccupation is the increasing interest created in instability", said Paul Volcker, former governor of the Federal Reserve in the magazine Changing Fortunes. "Instability is cumulative, such that the possible bankruptcy of the free floating currencies is possible", wrote George Soros, the biggest present-day exchange speculator, in 'The Alchemy of Finance.' Both agree more people are now interested in benefiting from instability.

In an unstable system, it is only a question of time when things spin out of control. It would explode the moment the US dollar went into crisis. At present there is no gold standard to lean on, so there is no precedent for a collapse of this nature. It would be a truly global collapse as all the currencies in the world are pegged to the dollar.

Growth no longer means production

While a large proportion of national currencies - around $2000 billion per day - are spinning around in the financial cybereconomy, there is no satisfactory medium of exchange available to the people on the lowest rung of the economic ladder. Various national currencies are not at the disposition of the poorest sectors of the population.

The era of work as an essential component of production is over. It is important as a source for "money", that is, national currency. Even when structural unemployment increases, the economy can "grow" perfectly well, and technology accentuates this tendency.

On the other hand, a new phenomenon is arising in the developed countries: an explosion of "local currencies" - money which is not the national currency. This had not been seen since the Great Depression, when there were literally thousands of local currencies in the United States and other countries affected by mass unemployment.

Supporting the development of local currency schemes would perhaps amount to preparing the ground for the next monetary system. This could become one of the most powerful instruments available to ordinary citizens to control their monetary destiny.

Source: IFG News

Human Development Index

(THE HDI VALUE INDICATES HOW FAR A COUNTRY HAS TO GO TO ATTAIN CERTAIN GOALS: AN AVERAGE LIFE SPAN OF 85 YEARS, ACCESS TO EDUCATION FOR ALL AND A DECENT INCOME)

(See also p.73)

COUNTRIES RANKED BY HDI VALUE, 1994

1	Canada	0.960
2	France	0.946
3	Norway	0.943
4	United States	0.942
5	Iceland	0.942
6	Netherlands	0.940
7	Japan	0.940
8	Finland	0.940
9	Aotearoa/New Zealand	0.937
10	Sweden	0.936
11	Spain	0.934
12	Austria	0.932
13	Belgium	0.932
14	Australia	0.931
15	United Kingdom	0.931
16	Switzerland	0.930
17	Ireland	0.929
18	Denmark	0.927
19	Germany	0.924
20	Greece	0.923
21	Italy	0.921
23	Israel	0.913
24	Cyprus	0.907
25	Barbados	0.907
26	Singapore	0.900
27	Luxembourg	0.899
28	Bahamas	0.894
29	Antigua	0.892
30	Chile	0.891
31	Portugal	0.890
32	Korea, South	0.890
33	Costa Rica	0.889
34	Malta	0.887
35	Slovenia	0.886
36	Argentina	0.884
37	Uruguay	0.883
38	Brunei	0.882
39	Czech Republic	0.882
40	Trinidad and Tobago	0.880
41	Dominica	0.873
42	Slovakia	0.873
43	Bahrain	0.870
44	United Arab Emirates	0.866
45	Panama	0.864
46	Fiji	0.863
47	Venezuela	0.861
48	Hungary	0.857
49	St Kitts-Nevis	0.853
50	Mexico	0.853
51	Colombia	0.848
52	Seychelles	0.845
53	Kuwait	0.844
54	Grenada	0.843
55	Qatar	0.840
56	St Lucia	0.838
57	St Vincent	0.836
58	Poland	0.834
59	Thailand	0.833
60	Malaysia	0.832

COUNTRIES RANKED BY HDI VALUE, 1994

61	Mauritius	0.831
62	Belarus	0.806
63	Belize	0.806
64	Libya	0.801
65	Lebanon	0.794
66	Suriname	0.792
67	Russia	0.792
68	Brazil	0.783
69	Bulgaria	0.780
70	Iran	0.780
71	Estonia	0.776
72	Ecuador	0.775
73	Saudi Arabia	0.774
74	Turkey	0.772
75	Korea, North	0.765
76	Lithuania	0.762
77	Croatia	0.760
78	Syria	0.755
79	Romania	0.748
80	Macedonia, TFYR	0.748
81	Tunisia	0.748
82	Algeria	0.737
83	Jamaica	0.736
84	Jordan	0.730
85	Turkmenistan	0.723
86	Cuba	0.723
87	Dominican Republic	0.718
88	Oman	0.718
89	Peru	0.717
90	South Africa	0.716
91	Sri Lanka	0.711
92	Latvia	0.711
93	Kazakhstan	0.709
94	Paraguay	0.706
95	Ukraine	0.689
96	Samoa	0.684
97	Botswana	0.673
98	Philippines	0.672
99	Indonesia	0.668
100	Uzbekistan	0.662
101	Mongolia	0.661
102	Albania	0.655
103	Armenia	0.651
104	Guyana	0.649
105	Georgia	0.637
106	Azerbaijan	0.636
107	Kyrgyzstan	0.635
108	China	0.626
109	Egypt	0.614
110	Moldova	0.612
111	Maldives	0.611
112	El Salvador	0.592
113	Bolivia	0.589
114	Swaziland	0.582
115	Tajikistan	0.580
116	Honduras	0.575
117	Guatemala	0.572
118	Namibia	0.570
119	Morocco	0.566

COUNTRIES RANKED BY HDI VALUE, 1994

120	Gabon	0.562
121	Vietnam	0.557
122	Solomon Is.	0.556
123	Cape Verde	0.547
124	Vanuatu	0.547
125	São Tome and Principe	0.534
126	Iraq	0.531
127	Nicaragua	0.530
128	Papua New Guinea	0.525
129	Zimbabwe	0.513
130	Congo R.	0.500
131	Myanmar/Burma	0.475
132	Ghana	0.468
133	Cameroon	0.468
134	Kenya	0.463
135	Equatorial Guinea	0.462
136	Laos	0.459
137	Lesotho	0.457
138	India	0.446
139	Pakistan	0.445
140	Comoros	0.412
141	Nigeria	0.393
142	Congo D.R.	0.381
143	Zambia	0.369
144	Bangladesh	0.368
145	Côte d'Ivoire	0.368
146	Benin	0.368
147	Togo	0.365
148	Yemen	0.361
149	Tanzania	0.357
150	Mauritania	0.355
151	Central African Rep.	0.355
152	Madagascar	0.350
153	Cambodia	0.348
154	Nepal	0.347
155	Bhutan	0.338
156	Haiti	0.338
157	Angola	0.335
158	Sudan	0.333
159	Uganda	0.328
160	Senegal	0.326
161	Malawi	0.320
162	Djibouti	0.319
163	Guinea-Bissau	0.291
164	Chad	0.288
165	Gambia	0.281
166	Mozambique	0.281
167	Guinea	0.271
168	Eritrea	0.269
169	Burundi	0.247
170	Ethiopia	0.244
171	Mali	0.229
172	Burkina Faso	0.221
173	Niger	0.206
174	Rwanda	0.187
175	Sierra Leone	0.176

Source: Human Development Report 1997, UNDP, 1997.

Under-five mortality

Under-5 mortality rate (per 1,000 live births), 1996

Rank		Mortality rate	Rank		Mortality rate	Rank		Mortality rate
1	Niger	320	65	Cape Verde	73	128	Bahrain	22
2	Angola	292	65	Zimbabwe	73	128	St Lucia	22
3	Sierra Leone	284	67	Indonesia	71	128	Uruguay	22
4	Afghanistan	257	67	Mongolia	71	128	Yugoslavia Fed. Rep.	22
5	Liberia	235	69	South Africa	66	138	Qatar	21
6	Guinea-Bissau	223	70	Libya	61	134	Dominica	20
7	Mali	220	71	Uzbekistan	60	134	Latvia	20
8	Malawi	217	72	Peru	58	134	Panama	20
9	Mozambique	214	73	Nicaragua	57	137	Bulgaria	19
10	Somalia	211	74	Dominican Republic	56	137	Seychelles	19
11	Guinea	210	74	Guatemala	56	137	Sri Lanka	19
12	Congo D.R.	207	74	Tuvalu	56	140	Belarus	18
13	Zambia	202	77	Samoa	53	140	Lithuania	18
14	Nigeria	191	77	Vanuatu	53	140	Oman	18
15	Mauritania	183	79	Brazil	52	140	United Arab Emirates	18
16	Ethiopia	177	80	Botswana	50	144	Bosnia-Herzegovina	17
17	Burundi	176	80	Kyrgyzstan	50	144	Trinidad and Tobago	17
18	Equatorial Guinea	173	82	China	47	146	Estonia	16
19	Cambodia	170	82	Turkey	47	147	Costa Rica	15
19	Rwanda	170	84	Kazakhstan	45	148	Kuwait	14
21	Central African Rep.	164	85	Azerbaijan	44	148	Poland	14
21	Madagascar	164	85	Belize	44	150	Chile	13
23	Burkina Faso	158	85	Vietnam	44	150	Malaysia	13
24	Djibouti	157	88	Albania	40	150	San Marino	13
25	Côte d'Ivoire	150	88	Ecuador	40	153	Barbados	12
25	Myanmar/Burma	150	88	El Salvador	40	153	Hungary	12
27	Chad	149	88	Lebanon	40	155	Brunei	11
28	Gabon	145	92	Algeria	39	155	Croatia	11
29	Tanzania	144	93	Philippines	38	155	Jamaica	11
30	Uganda	141	93	St Kitts-Nevis	38	155	Malta	11
31	Benin	140	93	Thailand	38	155	Slovakia	11
32	Lesotho	139	96	Iran	37	160	Cuba	10
33	Pakistan	136	98	Palestine	36	160	Cyprus	10
34	Haiti	134	98	Honduras	35	162	Greece	9
35	Laos	128	98	Palau	35	162	Israel	9
36	Bhutan	127	98	Tunisia	35	164	United States	8
36	Senegal	127	101	Paraguay	34	165	Aotearoa/New Zealand	7
38	Togo	125	101	Syria	34	165	Belgium	7
39	Comoros	122	103	Mexico	32	165	Canada	7
39	Iraq	122	103	Moldova	32	165	Czech Republic	7
41	Eritrea	120	105	Colombia	31	165	Ireland	7
42	Nepal	116	105	Grenada	31	165	Italy	7
42	Sudan	116	105	Nauru	31	165	Korea, South	7
44	Bangladesh	112	105	Suriname	31	165	Liechtenstein	7
44	Papua New Guinea	112	109	Armenia	30	165	Luxembourg	7
46	India	111	109	Cook Is.	30	165	Portugal	7
47	Ghana	110	109	Korea, North	30	165	United Kingdom	7
48	Congo R.	108	109	Macedonia, TFYR	30	176	Andorra	6
49	Gambia	107	109	Saudi Arabia	30	176	Australia	6
50	Yemen	105	114	Georgia	29	176	Austria	6
51	Bolivia	102	114	Solomon Is.	29	176	Denmark	6
51	Cameroon	102	116	Venezuela	28	176	France	6
53	Swaziland	97	117	Micronesia	27	176	Germany	6
54	Marshall Is.	92	118	Argentina	25	176	Japan	6
55	Kenya	90	118	Jordan	25	176	Monaco	6
56	Guyana	83	118	Romania	25	176	Netherlands	6
57	São Tome and Principe	80	118	Russia	25	176	Norway	6
58	Egypt	78	122	Fiji	24	176	Slovenia	6
58	Turkmenistan	78	122	Ukraine	24	187	Iceland	5
60	Namibia	77	124	Bahamas	23	187	Spain	5
61	Kiribati	76	124	Mauritius	23	187	Switzerland	5
61	Maldives	76	124	St Vincent	23	190	Finland	4
61	Tajikistan	76	124	Tonga	23	190	Singapore	4
64	Morocco	74	128	Antigua	22	190	Sweden	4

Source: The State of the World's Children 1998; UNICEF, 1998.

The World according to ...

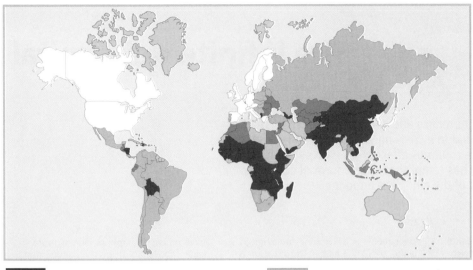

... The World Bank -
Ranked by income
(GNP per capita).
See page 70

■ Low-income economies

■ Middle-income economies

▨ Upper middle income economies

☐ High-income economies

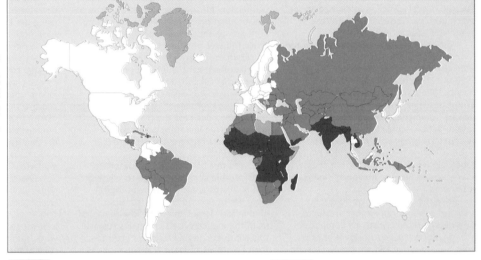

... UNDP
(UN Development
Programm)
Ranked by Human
Development Index.
See page 71

■ Low "human development"

■ Medium "human development"

☐ High "human development"

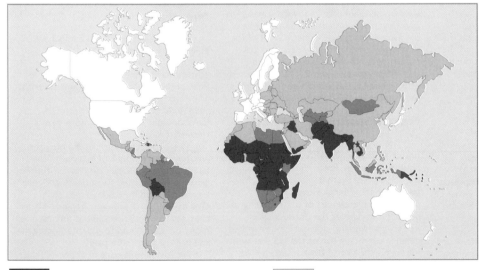

... UNICEF
(UN children's agency)
Ranked by under-5
mortality rate.
See page 72

■ Very high under-5 mortality rate

■ High under-5 mortality rate

▨ Medium under-5 mortality rate

☐ Low under-5 mortality rate

Debt

The infinite debt spiral

International negotiations to reduce and eliminate the foreign debt of the Third World have only led to increasing exports of capital and the further indebtedness of the countries affected (as with sub-Saharan Africa). The wealthy North has established a new form of economic colonialism, a new version of the old "debt bondage"

Even though sub-Saharan Africa paid back the total amount of its foreign debt twice over between 1980 and 1996, today it is still three times more in debt than it was 16 years ago. In 1997 it owed creditors $235.4 billion compared with the $84.3 billion it owed in 1980. Meanwhile, it has paid out $170 billion in debt servicing which each year costs four times the health and education budgets.

In spite of this, the 48 countries of the African region have accumulated enormous debts: $48 billion in 1994. In 1996, 31 of these countries - six more than in 1994 - were included in the World Bank category of 'low-income seriously-indebted countries.' In order to pay foreign debt in hard currency, they must discount a large part of their export income. To free themselves of the entire debt, they would have to pay out their entire export income for more than three years.

Since the 1980s, the world market prices of sub-Saharan export products have deteriorated constantly compared with products the subcontinent imports from the industrialized countries. Despite the fleeting price increase of some raw materials in 1995/96 - coffee, cocoa- the general trend is downward. Products exported have lost half their value compared to products imported from the North.

Africa has reacted by attempting to increase the volume of its exports on the world market. But this has not solved the problem, as the prices of these products fall faster than the prices of imported goods.

An account with a permanent deficit

In reality, under the current system of world trade, the Southern countries, especially those of sub-Saharan Arica which export fewer manufactured products, are at a disadvantage: any increase in the volume of their exports tends to reduce their value. Consequently, their trade balance has an increasing deficit.

More than 10 years of World Bank and IMF dictated policies aimed at achieving a trade surplus have patently failed.

In 1995, sub-Saharan Africa received barely 1 per cent of direct foreign

investments in developing countries: $2.2 billion of $240.3 billion. The situation is even more critical considering the fact that a small number of states receive more than 90 per cent of these loans: South Africa and some oil and mineral producing countries, like Nigeria, Angola, Gabon and Cameroon. Meanwhile, the head offices of the multinationals installed in the region continue to repatriate profits, which are twice the size of their investments.

Favourable reports by the media and international financial institutions do not reflect the real situation: in reality we are witnessing an increasing indebtedness despite the payment of large sums; unequal trade which deepens the trade deficit; scarce foreign investment and the repatriation of profits toward Northern multinationals.

"You must be aware that despite the considerable sums dedicated to bilateral and multilateral aid, the flow of capital from Africa toward the industrialized countries is larger than the flow of capital from the industrialized countries toward this continent", said François Mitterand, then President of France, at the meeting of the seven most industrialized countries (G7) in July 1994.

This is only a half truth, as it cannot be said that the sums assigned to bilateral and multilateral aid are considerable. Public development aid is at its lowest for the last 45 years, at less than 0.33 per cent of the Gross National Product (GNP) of the developed countries, when the objective set by the United Nations at the end of the 1960s was to reach 0.7 per cent, a figure the heads of State meeting at the Rio Summit in 1992 promised to treble.

North-South corruption

The process of African indebtedness is similar to that which affects other Southern regions. From the second half of the 1960s, Northern bankers looked for takers for their surplus cash. The phenomenon grew out of the recycling of petrodollars. Under the presidency of Robert McNamara - former United States defence secretary during the US war with Vietnam - the World Bank multiplied its loans tenfold between 1968 and 1973.

The economic crisis which struck industrialized countries in 1973 led their

governments to attempt lending more capital to the South, on the condition these countries buy their products. World Bank envoys, bankers and foreign co-operation ministers from the Northern countries bombarded African governments persuading them to request loans, then carrying out large infrastructure works using the equipment and know-how of the Northern countries.

Given that the interest rates were extremely low, that they were accompanied by large commissions paid by companies and governments in the industrialized countries fighting for clients, and that the projects were presitigious, many of African countries accepted willingly. Northern corruption fed corrupt regimes in the South and reinforced their kleptocracy. The sub-Saharan African debt multiplied twelvefold between 1970 and 1980.

The crisis exploded in the early 1980s when interest rates shot up, pushed by the US Federal Reserve. Suddenly debtor countries, saw themselves up against interest rates which had trebled at a time when the price of their exports began to fall and the hellish cycle took over. The countries asked for further loans to repay debts and, despite repayments, their foreign debt increased.

"Protect me from my friends"

In recent years, private banks have collected their loans to the debtor countries and to the Northern governments, which own nearly half the debt of the sub-Saharan African countries. The international financial institutions – the World Bank, IMF and African Development Bank - hold more than a third of the debt.

The poorer the African country, the greater is the amount of its debt in the hands of international financial institutions: Burundi 79 per cent, Rwanda 81 per cent, Central African Republic 77 per cent, Guinea-Bissau 61 per cent, Uganda 77 per cent. The World Bank and the IMF receive more than they lend to indebted countries and are the first to be paid.

A considerable part of public development aid granted by the Northern countries is used by indebted countries to pay the international financial institutions.

	Total external debt (millions $) 1996	Debt service as % of exports 1996	External debt $ per capita * 1996		Total external debt (millions $) 1996	Debt service as % of exports 1996	External debt $ per capita * 1996
Albania	781	3.5	230	Lesotho	654	6.1	315
Algeria	33,260	27.7	1,156	Lithuania	1,286	2.9	345
Angola	10,612	13.3	949	Macedonia, TFYR	1,659	3.9	763
Argentina	93,841	44.2	2,664	Madagascar	4,175	9.4	272
Armenia	552	10.7	152	Malawi	2,312	18.6	235
Azerbaijan	435	1.3	57	Malaysia	39,777	8.2	1,933
Bangladesh	16,083	11.7	134	Mali	3,020	17.9	271
Belarus	1,071	2.0	103	Mauritania	2,363	21.7	1,013
Benin	1,594	6.8	287	Mauritius	1,818	7.2	1,610
Bolivia	5,174	30.9	681	Mexico	157,125	35.4	1,695
Botswana	613	4.9	413	Moldova	834	6.2	188
Brazil	179,047	41.1	1,111	Mongolia	524	9.7	208
Bulgaria	9,819	20.5	1,160	Morocco	21,767	27.7	806
Burkina Faso	1,294	10.8	120	Mozambique	5,842	32.3	328
Burundi	1,127	54.6	181	Myanmar/Burma	5,184	..	113
Cambodia	2,111	1.2	205	Nepal	2,414	7.7	110
Cameroon	9,515	23.6	702	Nicaragua	5,929	24.2	1,399
Central African Rep.	928	6.3	278	Niger	1,557	17.3	165
Chad	997	9.5	153	Nigeria	31,407	16.0	273
Chile	27,411	32.3	1,901	Oman	3,415	9.9	1,483
China	128,817	8.7	105	Pakistan	29,901	27.4	214
Colombia	28,859	34.6	792	Panama	6,990	10.7	2,611
Congo D.R.	12,826	2.4	274	Papua New Guinea	2,359	12.6	536
Congo R.	5,240	21.3	1,964	Paraguay	2,141	5.5	432
Costa Rica	3,454	14.1	987	Peru	29,176	35.4	1,219
Côte d'Ivoire	19,713	26.2	1,407	Philippines	41,214	13.7	595
Croatia	4,634	5.5	1,030	Poland	40,895	6.4	1,059
Czech Republic	20,094	8.3	1,960	Romania	8,291	12.6	366
Dominican Republic	4,310	11.4	541	Russia	124,785	6.6	842
Ecuador	14,491	22.6	1,239	Rwanda	1,034	20.3	192
Egypt	31,407	11.6	496	Senegal	3,663	15.9	429
El Salvador	2,894	9.5	499	Sierra Leone	1,167	52.6	272
Eritrea	46	0.0	14	Slovakia	7,704	11.9	1,441
Estonia	405	1.3	275	Slovenia	4,031	8.7	2,095
Ethiopia	10,077	42.2	173	South Africa	23,590	11.1	556
Gabon	4,213	11.1	3,809	Sri Lanka	7,995	7.3	442
Gambia	452	12.7	396	Sudan	16,972	5.0	622
Georgia	1,356	..	249	Syria	21,420	3.8	1,470
Ghana	6,202	26.4	348	Tajikistan	707	0.1	119
Guatemala	3,785	11.0	346	Tanzania	7,412	18.7	241
Guinea	3,240	14.7	431	Thailand	90,824	11.5	1,547
Guinea-Bissau	937	48.7	859	Togo	1,463	10.8	348
Haiti	897	13.8	124	Trinidad and Tobago	2,242	15.6	1,729
Honduras	4,453	28.8	766	Tunisia	9,887	16.5	1,080
Hungary	26,958	41.0	2,683	Turkey	79,789	21.7	1,291
India	89,827	24.1	95	Turkmenistan	825	10.6	199
Indonesia	129,033	36.8	644	Uganda	3,674	20.0	181
Iran	21,183	..	303	Ukraine	9,335	6.1	181
Jamaica	4,041	18.0	1,622	Uruguay	5,899	15.6	1,841
Jordan	8,118	12.3	1,455	Uzbekistan	2,319	8.1	100
Kazakhstan	2,920	9.9	174	Venezuela	35,344	16.8	1,584
Kenya	6,893	27.5	248	Vietnam	26,764	3.5	356
Kyrgyzstan	789	9.2	177	Yemen	6,356	2.4	405
Laos	2,263	6.3	449	Yugoslavia Fed. Rep.	13,439	..	1,306
Latvia	472	2.3	188	Zambia	7,113	24.6	860
Lebanon	3,996	6.4	1,296	Zimbabwe	5,005	21.2	438

(*) Calculated from total 1996 external debt and total 1996 population.

Source: World Development Indicators 1998, World Bank, 1998.

Apart from South Africa (due to the strength of its economy) and Sudan (which broke off relations with these institutions), sub-Saharan governments are dependent on the IMF, the World Bank and the Paris Club, which dictate policies to the governments.

Nearly 15 years later, structural adjustment plans were imposed on most sub-Saharan countries. The IMF and World Bank use an effective blackmail mechanism: credit is suspended if the authorities reject the plan. The social and economic effects of adjustment are regularly disastrous: a reduction in State controlled income redistribution, a drop in production in the agricultural and semi-industrial sectors, and worse living conditions for most of the population. In Zambia, for example, between 1990 and 1993, the Government invested $37 million in primary education, whilst paying $1.3 billion in debt servicing. Put another way, for each dollar invested in primary education, the Government pays $35 to the club of rich countries. In 1995, the Government spent six times less per inhabitant on primary education than ten years earlier and 30 per cent less on the health budget. As a result 80 per cent of the cost of primary schooling fell back on families. Infant mortality increased 20 per cent in the same period.

Touching generosity

Since 1994, the Paris Club, endorsed by the IMF, has been negotiating reductions in debt with African countries and has proclaimed its intention to reduce the amount of bilateral debt of the most indebted nations to 67 per cent of its present total. In reality, the requirements for access to these benefits are so difficult to fulfil that the promised reduction is severely limited. The first country which benefited from the generosity of the Paris Club - Uganda - obtained only a 3 per cent reduction in its debt, and the total cancellations and facilities agreed for all the countries of sub-Saharan Africa in 1995 represented less than 1 per cent of the value of their debt.

In 1996, the World Bank, the IMF and the Paris Club launched a new proposal, seeking to make the payment of debt servicing "sustainable" for the poorest and most indebted nations, whose debt totalled $200 billion. The first reductions have already been announced, but most of them will not come into force until after the year 2000.

The World Bank and the IMF announced they would collect up to $7 billion to fund the initiative, that is "almost as much as the building of the Eurodisney park in France", and 30 times less than the 200 billion which evaporated on the Asian stock exchange in the month of August 1997 alone.

The foreign debt of sub-Saharan Africa - home to more than 10 per cent of the world's inhabitants - represents less than 1 per cent of dollar debts in the world. Refusing to cancel this is equivalent to refusing help to people in danger of dying.

Source: Le Monde Diplomatique

Aid

Contradictory policies

So-called development aid is just one aspect of the relationship between poor and rich countries. It is closely linked to the policies of international financial organizations, international trade relationships and, increasingly in recent years, the choices of multinational corporations

International trade, investment, conflict prevention and debt reduction are much more important in the creation of opportunities for fair human development than much of development aid. The arms trade, environmental policies and foreign policy are also essential factors.

What sense is there, for example, in using aid funds to support indigenous peoples in their sustainable management of forests if commercial agents can at the same time cut down all the trees they want and export the wood to rich countries?

In many cases, co-operation for development is linked more to the support of rights and claims than to economic development, modernization and any transfer of resources. There are several cases of contradictory policies. With regard to the arms trade, it is obvious that development aid cannot be used efficiently to reduce poverty in regions devastated by war: for example, Swiss aeroplanes were used against Burmese refugee camps funded by Switzerland.

Kerala: a positive case

However, this is not to say that there has been no progress whatsoever. An example of successful people-targeted development can be found in India's state of Kerala. According to analyst Govindan Parayil, "Kerala was able, in spite of huge adversity, to eliminate acute poverty without a swift growth of its per capita GDP, as is expected of all models and theories of economic development".

Kerala's success is due to several factors which include extensive land reform, literacy - specially among women - through free primary education for all, and social movements to promote the preservation of the environment. The involvement of peasants and low-paid workers also played an important role.

It cannot be said that Kerala has eradicated poverty and it is still unknown whether it will be able to sustain its accomplishments. However, it is clear that these were achieved in a manner different to those usually recommended by Northern countries.

Meanwhile, poverty continues to rise in the rich countries of the North. More than 100 million people live below the poverty line (set at half the average income), five million are homeless and 37 million are unemployed in the highly industrialized countries.

The work done by NGOs

Many NGOs promote sustainable human development with a view to creating an ethics of global citizenship. At the root of their efforts lies the belief that human beings are agents of change and that people must define their own development.

NGOs play an essential role in this regard, supplying resources, training and helping to inform public opinion. Global citizenship promotes collective action linking people from North and South.

In the South, new social movements are developing alternatives to state and corporate power. They promote and practice development which is focused on individuals. In the North, NGOs with extensive international experience are acquiring increasing political influence by informing the public about the realities of the South. NGOs and other social agents of the North and South have sought out a path of unity which includes joint networks, campaigns and policies.

Source: ACTIONAID

Aid in figures

Total net official development assistance (ODA) disbursed, 1995

	As % of GNP	Millions $
Aotearoa/New Zealand	0.23	123
Australia	0.36	1,194
Austria	0.33	767
Belgium	0.38	1,034
Canada	0.38	2,067
Denmark	0.96	1,623
Finland	0.32	388
France	0.55	8,443
Germany	0.31	7,524
Ireland	0.29	153
Italy	0.15	1,623
Japan	0.28	14,489
Luxembourg	0.36	65
Netherlands	0.81	3,226
Norway	0.87	1,244
Portugal	0.27	271
Spain	0.24	1,348
Sweden	0.77	1,704
Switzerland	0.34	1,084
United Kingdom	0.28	3,157
United States	0.10	7,367

Source: Human Development Report, UNDP, 1997.

Government commitments

A significant number of governments from the North promised in 1969 to spend no less than 0.7 per cent of their GNP on development aid and, recently, the governments of the South agreed to contribute 20 per cent of their resources to basic services for their poorest citizens. There was an increase in goal-related government commitments at international summits in the 1990s, such as the Earth Summit (Rio de Janeiro, 1992), the International Conference on Population and Development (Cairo, 1994), the World Conference on Women (Beijing, 1995), the Conference on Human Settlements (Istanbul, 1996), the World Food Summit (Rome, 1996) and the failed Second Earth Summit (New York, 1997).

Shaping the 21st century

In the "Shaping the 21st century: contribution to development co-operation" report, Development Assistance Committee (DAC) member countries confirmed several specific objectives agreed at UN conferences. These included a 50 per cent reduction of the number of people living in absolute poverty by the year 2015, real progress towards gender equality, the empowerment of women through the elimination of gender disparity in primary and secondary education by 2005, and a two-thirds reduction in the mortality rate of children under five and a three-quarter reduction of maternal mortality rates by 2015.

The 20:20 proposal

In the 1995 World Summit on Social Development, governments voluntarily committed themselves to the so-called "20:20 proposal". The proposal requests donors to set apart 20 per cent of their aid for development and receiving governments to allocate 20 per cent of their public spending to guarantee basic services.

At the summit, NGOs agreed on an initiative which increased the share spent on the social sector to 50 per cent, with special focus on primary education and primary health-care, nutrition and drinking water programmes, support for income generating activities for the poor in rural and informal urban sectors, and the strengthening of social and civilian organizations. In 1969, DAC member countries had set a goal of setting apart 0.7 per cent of their GDP for development aid to the Third World. Since then, very few countries have honoured this commitment. In spite of the reduction of aid in recent years, the DAC member countries, with the exception of the United States, frequently confirm their commitment to the 0.7 per cent goal. The latest confirmation was done in June 1997, at a special meeting of the UN General Assembly.

Unconditional aid

Although donor governments have not made a collective commitment to remove conditions from their assistance, there is a strong campaign underway for countries to adopt unilateral measures in order to remove conditionality in development aid and target it for the reduction of poverty. However, there has not been any significant progress. France, for example, has blocked efforts to reach a multilateral agreement on non-conditionality. As for Britain, a recent report by the Overseas Development Administration (ODA) revealed that the unilateral elimination of conditionality would favour the British economy. Britain has not taken any measures towards that goal, although the new government has indicated its plan to put an end to conditional aid. ❑

Official aid: recipients

TOTAL NET OFFICIAL DEVELOPMENT ASSISTANCE (ODA) RECEIVED (NET DISBURSEMENTS)

	As % of GNP 1994	Millions $ 1995	Per capita $ 1995		As % of GNP 1994	Millions $ 1995	Per capita $ 1995
Algeria	0.8	310	11	Laos	20.3	311	66
Angola	..	423	40	Lebanon	2.0	188	48
Antigua	2.7	2	200	Lesotho	8.4	114	57
Argentina	0.1	222	7	Libya	..	7	1
Bahamas	0.1	4	15	Madagascar	16.4	301	23
Bahrain	1.2	49	89	Malawi	34.1	429	40
Bangladesh	4.8	1,269	11	Malaysia	0.2	114	6
Barbados	-0.1	-1	-4	Maldives	22.1	55	220
Belize	3.0	16	76	Mali	29.6	542	57
Benin	18.6	276	53	Mauritania	22.6	220	99
Bhutan	26.8	73	107	Mauritius	0.7	23	21
Bolivia	13.0	692	96	Mexico	0.1	379	4
Botswana	2.3	92	64	Mongolia	28.8	208	88
Brazil	0.1	366	2	Morocco	1.7	494	19
Brunei	0.1	4	133	Mozambique	90.4	1,102	66
Burkina Faso	16.6	483	48	Myanmar/ Burma	0.2	152	3
Burundi	32.1	288	46	Namibia	6.4	188	125
Cambodia	24.4	567	57	Nepal	..	430	21
Cameroon	6.5	444	35	Nicaragua	48.1	662	155
Cape Verde	33.6	111	292	Niger	17.8	268	30
Central African Rep.	18.4	161	50	Nigeria	0.6	208	2
Chad	26.4	237	38	Oman	0.6	59	29
Chile	0.3	159	11	Pakistan	1.5	805	6
China	0.7	3,521	3	Panama	0.8	50	19
Colombia	3.7	231	6	Papua New Guinea	7.4	372	88
Comoros	20.4	43	88	Paraguay	1.9	146	30
Congo D.R.	..	189	4	Peru	0.9	428	18
Congo R.	10.8	125	50	Philippines	23.8	884	109
Costa Rica	0.3	25	8	Qatar	..	3	6
Côte d'Ivoire	22.0	1,200	87	Rwanda	122.8	711	92
Cuba	..	64	6	Samoa	24.3	43	253
Cyprus	..	22	30	São Tome & Principe	339.1	78	600
Djibouti	..	103	181	Saudi Arabia	..	21	1
Dominica	12.1	24	343	Senegal	17.9	663	82
Dominican Rep.	1.2	124	16	Seychelles	2.8	13	186
Ecuador	1.5	235	21	Sierra Leone	27.7	205	45
Egypt	4.8	2,017	35	Singapore	..	16	6
El Salvador	3.7	304	54	Solomon Is.	15.1	47	127
Equatorial Guinea	20.5	33	85	South Africa	..	384	10
Eritrea	..	145	42	Sri Lanka	48.0	553	31
Ethiopia	18.7	876	16	St Kitts-Nevis	2.1	4	100
Fiji	2.5	43	56	St Lucia	9.6	47	313
Gabon	4.4	143	138	St Vincent	20.5	47	427
Gambia	12.3	46	43	Sudan	..	225	8
Ghana	12.1	644	38	Suriname	27.6	77	183
Grenada	4.2	10	111	Swaziland	5.6	54	59
Guatemala	1.6	213	21	Syria	..	347	25
Guinea	12.0	392	62	Tanzania	..	875	30
Guinea-Bissau	49.6	119	113	Thailand	0.6	863	15
Guyana	19.2	88	106	Togo	20.2	188	47
Haiti	45.5	733	104	Trinidad & Tobago	0.6	26	20
Honduras	14.1	411	75	Tunisia	0.4	69	8
India	0.6	1,738	2	Turkey	0.2	303	5
Indonesia	0.8	1,389	7	Uganda	20.4	805	43
Iran	0.2	183	3	United Arab Emirates	..	8	4
Iraq	1.6	326	16	Uruguay	0.5	81	26
Jamaica	2.7	108	43	Vanuatu	24.5	46	288
Jordan	9.3	536	127	Venezuela	0.1	81	4
Kenya	3.9	707	42	Vietnam	5.3	826	..
Korea, North	..	14	1	Yemen	4.7	173	13
Korea, South	..	58	1	Zambia	62.9	2,029	221
Kuwait	..	6	4	Zimbabwe	9.6	490	45

Source: Human Development Report 1997, UNDP, 1997.

UN taken by the great powers

The United Nations organization is more than 50 years old, but still has not proved effective as a moderating agency in international relations. Its faults and fiascos are shared by the global community, particularly its most influential members

When created in 1945, the United Nations (UN) expressed member states' commitment to peacekeeping and more widespread international justice, but until 1989 it was in fact ruled by the ups and downs of the great powers of the Cold War - the US and the USSR.

Once the Berlin Wall had fallen, pleading the pretext of a new international order, the US took control of the UN. Confused by rapid geopolitical changes and beset by an economic crisis, the organization went into a tailspin of failures that wiped out all the reform projects promised for its 50th anniversary, sumptuously celebrated in its New York headquarters in 1995.

The UN is seriously undermined by its deficit. The balance of unpaid contributions in August 1995 amounted to some $3.9 billion ($858 million of the ordinary budget and $3 billion of the peacekeeping budget). The most powerful countries have refused to pay their contributions, an amount which is insignificant compared to their military expenses or public sector transactions.

Every time war breaks out, the UN implements ineffective and expensive plans to stop it. But the organization is not invited to major peace negotiations undertaken behind its back by the US (as in Palestine or Bosnia).

By way of compensation, Washington uses it as an instrument to crush certain peoples with highly dubious coercive measures such as those which maintain conditions of poverty for the people of Iraq and punish Libya for its part in an aircraft bomb which has not yet been given a formal trial.

In fact, the weakest states, the most threatened peoples and the most persecuted individuals have not found that the UN offers any guarantee of providing justice in the face of national and international power relations.

Controlled by governments closely linked to the world financial players, the UN cannot act as a countervailing power. During the 1970s arguments arose favourable to a new framework for the world economy, but the future new international economic order glimpsed at that time failed to materialize.

Arms sales versus collective security

The UN crisis cannot be kept hidden any longer, and, in the absence of action, discussions of the need to reform the organization are afoot. The cornerstone of reform would be equitable representation in the Security Council by increasing the number of members. The last change was made in 1963, when seats were increased from 11 to 15.

Most countries consider wider representation of the developing countries essential in making the Council more democratic and representative. But the working party in charge of examining this issue merely concluded there are "important differences".

In fact, the present situation does not allow for true reform, as revision of the UN Charter is only possible if two-thirds of UN members, including all the permanent members of the Security Council, support the move.

The present composition of the Security Council reflects the criterion used for choosing the permanent members, basically, the winners of World War II. Therefore, peacekeeping responsibility was left up to countries with the political, financial and military means to ensure it.

But this view overlooks the involvement of these states in arms production and their failure to establish collective security.

The war in Chechnya and the repression in Tiananmen Square showed the nature of Russia and China's notions of internal peace, and the democratic traditions of the three remaining members do not actually make them any more creditable.

The ban on the use of force binding the Security Council should be combined with its mission of ensuring "only the lesser part of the world's human and economic resources be used in armaments". But the great powers are fierce competitors in the arms market and their defence ministers are effective sales representatives for their products.

The US and its allies have said that they could accept the inclusion of Germany and Japan as permanent members, considering their "wish to act in the prevention of conflict and that they have the means to do this". But beyond the official statements, behind the scenes, the prevalent idea is that the decisions must be up to those who pick up the tab. This idea of a "democracy amongst the rich" would lead to the UN adopting the weighted suffrage which already exists in its financial institutions (the IMF and the World Bank).

This would mean an about turn on the original ideals of the organization, founded on the basis of equality amongst nations regardless of their financial contribution, military capacity or any conjecture about their predisposition towards peace.

Source: Le Monde Diplomatique

Restructure and budget

The United Nations organization (UN) was founded in 1945 by the 51 representatives of the Allied Nations of World War II. It was conceived as the successor to the League of Nations which had been unable to prevent the War and committed itself to maintaining international peace and security

At present there are 185 member countries, which have embarked upon a process of structural reform to make the organization more effective. The size of the UN, its lack of effective leadership, of unified purpose and flexibility to react to the challenges of the international community led to deep questioning at the time of its 50th anniversary in 1995.

Secretary-General Kofi Annan's proposals for reform include some of the criteria the United States demanded before supporting Annan's candidacy in December 1996, criteria which were not shared by his predecessor, Egypt's Boutros Boutros-Ghali, and which ruined his re-election chances.

Amongst other measures, Annan proposed the elimination of 1,000 of the UN's 9,000 jobs, two-thirds of the higher management posts and the merger of some of the agencies, like UNICEF, UNDP and UNFPA - which work on the issues regarding children, development and population respectively.

These measures meant savings of up to $1.3 billion per year, taking administrative costs from 38 per cent down to 25 per cent of the total budget. In an effort to gain the support of the Third World, Annan said the money saved would be spent on aid programmes for poorer countries.

In late 1997, for the first time in the UN's history, the Secretary-General's Office presented a zero growth administrative budget for 1998-1999. One of the most serious financial problems faced by the UN is debt in contributions amounting to $4 billion. The United States is responsible for 30 per cent of this debt. ❏

Refugees

Victims of human catastrophes

The words "globalization" and "liberalization" - fashionable in late-20th century political speeches - do not appear remotely related to the situation of tens of millions of refugees, who are subject to ever tougher restrictions in their attempts to achieve the most basic rights to life and peace

According to the 1951 Convention on the Status of Refugees, a refugee is a person who "obeying duly founded fear of persecution for motives of race, religion, nationality or political opinion, finds him/herself outside his/her country of origin, which does not offer him/her security."

But emigration also comes about through other circumstances. "Environmental" refugees are forced to move through the lack of access to land, the desertification of their habitat or the imposition of economic systems which do not allow them to satisfy their basic needs.

The United Nations High Commissioner for Refugees (UNHCR) is responsible for guaranteeing the security of refugees in the countries where they seek asylum and aiding the governments of these nations in this task. It is also concerned with supervising conditions for the return of refugees to their home countries.

According to the biennial UNHCR report published in December 1997, the number of people dealt with by the body fell from 27.4 million in 1995 to 22.7 million in 1997. But this does not mean the situation has improved. The document predicts that the number of people forced to leave their homes will increase again, and that an increasingly smaller number will find refuge.

The countries most affected by the currents of enforced migration are the poorest in the world. The 20 nations with the highest proportion of refugees have per capita incomes of no more than $700 per year.

Conflicts continue

The changing nature of conflicts, which in some cases aim to disperse or expel broad sectors of the population, and the closing of frontiers in the industrialized

countries as in the poorest are the main sources of the new refugee crisis.

Even though 10 million people have returned to their homes since 1990, the amount of displaced people who remain trapped in war zones unable to cross frontiers is growing. According to UNHCR estimates, around 30 million people are in this situation.

The fact they cannot leave their countries implies they have no access to international aid while their rights are completely ignored. In Africa there are more than 16 million internally-displaced people, in Asia 7 million, in Europe 5 million with a further 3 million in the Americas.

Original UNHCR commitments did not include the internal displaced. However, in 1997 it aided 4.9 billion people in this situation. Another type of situation also assigned to this agency is that of those who have lost their nationality due to large scale political changes in their home country. This is the case of many people living in Russia and other republics which formed part of the former Soviet Union before it was dismembered.

Up until December 1997, there were 29 countries with more than 100,000 refugees, a list headed by Iran with 2 million (mainly Afghans), Germany with 1.26 million (it received half of all asylum requests in Western Europe) and Pakistan with 1.2 million (also mostly Afghans).

Expelled by the wars

The Afghan refugees, who began fleeing their country in 1979 following the invasion of Afghanistan by the army of the former Soviet Union, are still the largest group dealt with by the UNHCR: 1.4 million in Iraq, 820,000 in Pakistan and several thousands in Russia, despite the

fact that 130,000 people returned to Afghanistan in 1996, increasing the number of returns to 3.89 million since the beginning of the exodus. When the Taliban imposed Islamic law in the city of Kabul and the east of the country, population displacements started again, both within Afghanistan and to Pakistan. Liberia with 778,000 refugees and Bosnia-Herzegovina with 673,000 are the other two countries with the largest numbers of foreign refugees.

An important problem is the security of refugees during exile and guaranteeing that they return home only once the stabilization processes have been completed in their countries of origin.

The attacks on refugee camps in the African Great Lakes region following the exodus of 1.75 million Rwandans to Tanzania, DR Congo (formerly Zaire) and Burundi, and of 160,000 Burundians to DR Congo and Tanzania were partly resolved with the return of most of these refugees.

Hundreds of thousands of people have been forced to return to their countries before the conflict which had forced them to emigrate had ended or due to confrontations in the countries they had fled to - as with the Rwandans in Zaire (DR Congo) when Laurent Kabila and his Alliance of Democratic Forces for the Liberation of Congo-Zaire launched an offensive to oust President Mobutu.

New stumbling blocks for refugees

The refugee problem reached such proportions in the 1990s that international and local aid systems were unable to deal with all the situations. The tightening of the laws on the admission of foreigners and asylum made it increasingly difficult for refugees to find asylum.

In the countries of Western Europe, in the midst of the crisis in former Yugoslavia, asylum petitions fell from 690,000 in 1992 to 250,000 in 1996, as foreigners found it increasingly difficult to cross frontiers. The countries of the more industrialized regions (Western Europe, North America, Japan and Australia) received 5 million asylum requests between 1985 and 1995. Nearly a fifth of these applicants were still waiting for an answer in 1998.

"The challenge of the 21st century will be for countries to be able to ensure human security. The security of states will be threatened until people feel safe in their own countries," said UN High Commissioner for Refugees Sadako Ogata. ❏

Return to the former USSR

In the last four years, more than three million people from other countries have entered the nations of the Community of Independent States (CIS), the group of republics that arose after the collapse of the former Soviet Union

The main migrant groups are Russian-speakers returning to Russia from the countries of Central Asia; natives of other former Soviet countries escaping from the war in the Caucasus; illegal immigrants in transit, mostly Chinese, and asylum-seekers from Africa, the Middle East and other Asian countries. Following the collapse of the Soviet bloc, population movements in the region have become more noticeable and unprecedented situations have occurred.

Not all of the 287 million people who lost their Soviet citizenship found another to replace it. For example, in the Baltic states of Latvia, Estonia and Lithuania, only two-thirds of the 1.6 million Russians who live there were recognized as citizens.

The United Nations High Commissioner for Refugees (UNHCR) stated in early 1998 that 25 million Russians were living beyond the frontiers of the Russian Federation.

Between 1990 and 1996, between three and four million Russians returned to their country from other former Soviet States. The majority of people in movement within the CIS had no recognized refugee status.

The Moscow branch of UNHCR - established in 1992 - has recently concentrated on attending to the roughly 200,000 people displaced by the war in Chechnya. The issue of foreign immigrants is not given priority at the government level. It ranks low amongst the many problems of social and political reconstruction that the CIS countries face.

Up until 1993, the Russian Federation had no immigration department. The Government only processed between 600 and 800 of the 12,000 asylum requests it received, arguing that the presence of foreigners was intimately linked to increasing crime rates.

Around 65 per cent of asylum-seekers come from Afghanistan. Most of them are adult males, speak Russian and are familiar with the culture of the country, setting them apart from the 7,000 people in a similar situation who come from Angola, Ethiopia, Iraq, Rwanda, Somalia, Sri Lanka and Zaire any case, only 80 people have been authorised as refugees, mostly Afghanis and Ethiopians.

The intention of many of the immigrants entering Russia is to use the country as a springboard to Western Europe or the United States either legally or illegally. The restrictive immigration policies of the Western countries - which criticized the former USSR for not allowing its citizens to leave the country - have pushed up the number of refugees who remain in the Russian Federation. ❑

Arms

The expansion of NATO

The end of the Cold War in the 1990s did not bring with it the end of NATO, despite its founding principles. For the United States and its main Western partners, NATO's military structures were still the best way to group and, above all, control the allies

The North Atlantic Treaty Organization (NATO) was created in 1949 to protect Western Europe from possible invasion by the Soviet Union. With the disintegration of the communist bloc, the demise of NATO could have been expected. But instead, the military alliance extended towards Eastern Europe, incorporating Poland, Hungary and the Czech Republic, at an estimated cost of $100 billion, funded by the United States.

US President Bill Clinton said the extension of NATO was essential for the construction of a "democratic and undivided Europe". But, noted David Krieger, head of the Nuclear Era Foundation for Peace, "the President did not say how the expansion of NATO would promote this aim", nor why it should be extended before 1999, nor why the countries which were once enemies of the United States cannot now be allies without belonging to the Atlantic alliance.

George Kennan, former United States ambassador to the Soviet Union, qualified the expansion of NATO as "the biggest political mistake of the United States in the post-Cold War period" and a measure which threatens to "have an adverse effect on the development of democracy in Russia". Similarly, the Defence Information Center in Washington warned that the expansion "could ruin a whole decade of arms control treaties".

In fact, the expansion of NATO led the Russians to hold up the nuclear arms reduction treaty Start II. Furthermore, Russia established a dangerous military policy allowing the "first strike" use of nuclear weapons. This went back on the commitment made by Mikhail Gorbachev in 1993 to not use nuclear weapons against countries without nuclear weapons. The Russian policy is similar to the US-backed NATO protocol of the Cold War era.

The benefits of expansion

One of the undeclared functions of the military exercises is to assure the health of the arms industry. Every time a rifle is fired, a missile is launched or a million-dollar fighter plane crashes, arms industry contracts become more secure. The Defense Information Center warned that the expansion of NATO cloaks the hidden intention of opening markets for the US arms industry.

The military exercises in the Czech Republic and other NATO hopefuls have another important aim: the Westernization of the armed forces of Eastern Europe.

The arms of the Warsaw Pact - T-72 tanks and MIG fighter planes of the Soviet era - are obsolete now, and the existing communications systems must be replaced by NATO - compatible digital technology. The integration of the armed forces of Eastern Europe to the military alliance will require the new members to invest in hundreds of millions of dollars worth of rifles, munitions of NATO-standard calibre and up-to-date communications and air defence systems.

Washington is predicting investment of $27 to $35 billion in the expansion of NATO over the next 13 years. The Rand Corporation and the Congress Budget Office calculated the costs at between $30 and $125 billion by the year 2010. Independent estimates put these at around $1.4 billion per year. Whatever the amount, the greatest beneficiaries will be the arms manufacturers.

The US dollars paid to Poland, Hungary and the Czech Republic to "NATO-ize" their armies are subject to the condition the money be invested in US-produced arms. Thus, the expansion of NATO will be transformed into another example of the use of military aid programmes outside the United States to channel millions of tax payers' dollars into the coffers of a handful of US companies, and consequently towards the politicians in the form of contributions to their election campaigns.

Thomas L. Friedman said in *The New York Times* that Western Europe is not afraid of Russia, but of Eastern Europe. The threat comes from "the new free market economies of Eastern Europe, whose factories and farmers want to export to the West at more competitive prices, and whose workers want to look for jobs in Western Europe, which would reduce rates of pay. The Russian missiles and tanks are a distant and dark danger, but Polish ham and workers are a clear and real threat".

Friedman confirmed that the expansion of NATO is "the ideal way of impeding the Eastern Europeans from becoming members of the European Union without feeling guilty for it". As Mandelbaum said, "We are holding out the NATO umbrella towards Eastern Europe, in such a way that the Western Europeans don't have to buy their tomatoes".

Fortress Europe

If NATO membership protects democracy and the free market, why did Belgium, France, Germany, Luxembourg, the Netherlands, Portugal and Spain, all Alliance members, sign the Schengen Accords to create a European economic "fortress"? Although these countries support the opening of their common frontiers, they argue they must toughen their eastern borders to protect themselves from drugs and organized crime.

A new Iron Curtain, the Schengen curtain, is coming down in the West as countries hasten to join fortress Europe before 1998. On advice from Germany, Austria invested $140 million in securing its eastern frontiers with new watchtowers, helicopters, armed guards and infra-red detectors.

While NATO is opening its doors to Hungary, Poland and the Czech Republic, the Schengen Accord is closing them. And while the citizens of fortress Europe will move easily through the frontier posts, all others will be subject to long waits and computer controls of the Interpol type, with a control centre in Strasbourg, France, designed to keep 10 million records and keep track of a million names.

"Once they have finished with this project, Europe will once again be divided into half for years to come", complained a Hungarian driver to journalist Eric Geiger, during a wait at the new frontier post near Nickelsdorf, Austria. According to a German magazine, this economic neo-isolationism constitutes "an example of how, furtively, new anti-democratic structures are created. The day that Schengen came into effect, Europe took a large step, but in the wrong direction".

Source: Gar Smith, Earth Island Journal

Arms-control developments

The most influential arms-control event of 1997 was the US-Russia summit held in Helsinki in March. Presidents Bill Clinton and Boris Yeltsin set out their understandings on the Strategic Arms Reduction Treaty (START) in their joint declaration. The main elements were:

— Once Russia ratifies START II, negotiations on START III should begin. START III aims to reach lower aggregate levels of 2,000-2,500 strategic warheads for each side.

— START II reductions to below 3,500 warheads on each side are to be phased over a longer period to 2007 instead of 2003. This would coincide with the proposed target date for START III reductions.

Dovetailing the dates for START II and III reductions will allow Russia to retain parity with the US once both are left with only the single-warhead intercontinental ballistic missile (ICBM) systems required by START II.

This concession was intended to help ease the ratification of START II in the Russian Duma. The understandings were affirmed in an agreement signed by the two governments in New York on 26 September 1997, thus further enhancing the chances of early ratification in Russia. The two sides agreed that all warheads on strategic delivery vehicles due to be eliminated by 2007 should be either 'removed or by other means (jointly agreed) placed in a deactivated status' by 31 December 2003. The US is to provide funds through the Nunn-Lugar Cooperative Threat Reduction programme to assist early de-activation.

At the Helsinki summit, the US and Russia also came to an understanding on the Anti-Ballistic Missile (ABM) Treaty which has cleared the way to an agreed distinction between strategic and theatre missile defences. This understanding was affirmed in the US-Russia agreement signed on 26 September.

Other arms-control developments 1997/98 included:

— Comprehensive Test Ban Treaty (CTBT) – the administering organization (CTBO) was established in March 1997. Although over 140 states have signed the Treaty, it cannot come into force until 44 designated countries (including India, Pakistan and North Korea) have ratified it. This was unlikely to happen in the near future.

— Treaty on the Non-Proliferation of Nuclear Weapons (NPT) – Brazil joined in June 1997 bringing the total membership to 186 states. The International Atomic Energy Agency (IAEA) completed its strengthened 'safeguards' (verification) system, although it would not be fully implemented for some time as members must first complete bilateral agreements with the IAEA.

— Chemical Weapons Convention (CWC) – the Treaty came into force in April 1997 and verification inspections have begun. Russia, which possesses one of the world's largest CW arsenals, had yet to ratify the Convention. India, however, did so and, to the surprise of many (including Indian citizens), declared a CW arsenal which it will now destroy.

— Biological Weapons Convention (BWC) – progress on developing a verification protocol remained slow.

Source: The Military Balance 1997/98, IISS, London, 1998.

NATO and the environment

The NATO Committee on the Challenges of Modern Society identified some of the problems caused by more than 25 years' activity by the military alliance. These included leaks of toxic substances during the transportation of military materials; atmospheric pollution over coastal areas; air pollution from ship engines; the transportation of contaminating agents along rivers, via deltas and estuaries; the dumping of radioactive waste; noise pollution; and chemical accidents.

The German example

Following its incorporation into NATO, Germany had to put up with 600,000 military flights per year, one sixth of which took place at a height of only 225 feet. In addition to their kerosene, the F-16 jets deployed carried almost 27 litres of hydrazine, a highly toxic and corrosive fuel. The lethal dose of hydrazine for humans is only one gram.

Between 1965 and 1988, the aeroplanes emitted around 220,000 tons of exhaust gases like nitrogen oxide, carbon dioxide, hydrogen carbide, sulphur dioxide and soot over West Germany. The kerosene expelled by the jets caused forest fires near the US base in Ramstein.

There were many plane crashes due to collisions with birds. In 1988, nearly 120 people died in air accidents, mostly in US planes. The low-level flights made chickens stop laying. Wild birds abandoned their nests when the planes came near, and the shock waves in their wake destroyed nests. Low-level flights were also associated with an increase in the number of heart attacks and spontaneous abortions. Children exposed to the noise of the planes suffered hearing problems. Some were so terrified they refused to go outside on sunny days when the planes were flying, and others became afraid of birds' shadows.

Source: Gar Smith, Earth Island Journal

Arms in figures

	IMPORTS OF CONVENTIONAL WEAPONS ($ MILLIONS, 1990 PRICES) 1995	DEFENCE EXPENDITURE AS % OF GDP 1995		IMPORTS OF CONVENTIONAL WEAPONS ($ MILLIONS, 1990 PRICES) 1995	DEFENCE EXPENDITURE AS % OF GDP 1995		IMPORTS OF CONVENTIONAL WEAPONS ($ MILLIONS, 1990 PRICES) 1995	DEFENCE EXPENDITURE AS % OF GDP 1995
Albania	..	2.8	Finland	..	2.0	Netherlands	..	2.2
Algeria	165	2.5	France	..	3.1	Nicaragua	..	1.8
Angola	..	4.8	Gabon	..	1.7	Niger	..	0.9
Antigua	..	0.8	Gambia	..	3.8	Nigeria	..	2.9
Aotearoa/N. Zealand	..	1.7	Georgia	..	3.4	Norway	..	2.6
Argentina	515	1.7	Germany	..	2.0	Oman	..	15.1
Armenia	..	4.4	Ghana	..	1.2	Pakistan	391	6.5
Australia	..	2.5	Greece	..	4.6	Panama	..	1.3
Austria	..	1.0	Guatemala	..	1.4	Papua New Guinea	..	1.3
Azerbaijan	..	5.0	Guinea	..	1.4	Paraguay	..	1.4
Bahamas	..	0.6	Guinea-Bissau	..	3.0	Peru	..	1.6
Bahrain	353	5.2	Guyana	..	1.1	Philippines	..	1.6
Bangladesh	118	1.8	Haiti	..	2.1	Poland	..	2.5
Barbados	..	0.7	Honduras	..	1.3	Portugal	..	2.9
Belarus	..	3.3	Hungary	..	1.4	Qatar	..	4.4
Belgium	..	1.7	India	770	2.5	Romania	..	3.1
Belize	..	2.6	Indonesia	711	1.6	Russia	..	7.4
Benin	..	1.3	Iran	187	3.9	Rwanda	..	4.4
Bolivia	..	2.6	Iraq	..	14.8	Saudi Arabia	961	10.6
Botswana	..	7.1	Ireland	..	1.2	Senegal	..	1.9
Brazil	237	1.5	Israel	..	9.2	Seychelles	..	3.9
Brunei	..	6.0	Italy	..	1.8	Sierra Leone	..	5.7
Bulgaria	..	3.3	Jamaica	..	0.6	Singapore	91	5.9
Burkina Faso	..	2.4	Japan	..	1.1	Slovakia	..	2.8
Burundi	..	5.3	Jordan	..	6.7	Slovenia	..	1.5
Cambodia	..	4.7	Kazakhstan	..	3.0	South Africa	39	2.9
Cameroon	..	1.8	Kenya	..	2.3	Spain	..	1.5
Canada	..	1.6	Korea, North	..	25.2	Sri Lanka	..	4.9
Cape Verde	..	1.8	Korea, South	1,677	3.4	Sudan	..	4.3
Cent. African Rep.	..	1.8	Kuwait	1,117	11.8	Suriname	..	3.9
Chad	..	2.6	Kyrgyzstan	..	3.5	Sweden	..	2.9
Chile	386	3.8	Laos	..	4.2	Switzerland	..	1.9
China	1,696	5.7	Latvia	..	3.2	Syria	185	6.8
Colombia	..	2.0	Lebanon	..	5.3	Tajikistan	..	6.9
Congo D.R.	..	2.0	Lesotho	..	5.5	Tanzania	..	2.7
Congo R.	..	1.7	Libya	..	5.5	Thailand	888	2.5
Costa Rica	..	0.3	Lithuania	..	2.4	Togo	..	2.5
Côte d'Ivoire	..	1.0	Luxembourg	..	0.9	Trinidad & Tobago	..	1.3
Croatia	..	12.6	Madagascar	..	1.1	Tunisia	..	2.0
Cuba	..	2.8	Malawi	..	1.2	Turkey	1,125	3.6
Cyprus	..	4.5	Malaysia	1,120	4.5	Turkmenistan	..	1.9
Czech Republic	..	2.8	Mali	..	2.4	Uganda	..	2.6
Denmark	..	1.8	Malta	..	1.1	Ukraine	..	3.0
Djibouti	..	5.3	Mauritania	..	1.9	United Arab Emirates	427	4.8
Dominican Rep.	..	1.3	Mauritius	..	0.5	United Kingdom	..	3.1
Ecuador	..	3.4	Mexico	..	0.9	United States	..	3.8
Egypt	1,555	4.3	Moldova	..	3.7	Uruguay	..	2.6
El Salvador	..	1.8	Mongolia	..	2.4	Uzbekistan	..	3.6
Equatorial Guinea	..	1.3	Morocco	50	4.3	Venezuela	..	1.1
Eritrea	55	5.7	Mozambique	..	3.7	Vietnam	..	4.3
Estonia	..	5.3	Myanmar/Burma	310	6.2	Yemen	..	3.9
Ethiopia	..	2.1	Namibia	..	2.7	Zambia	..	1.9
Fiji	..	1.5	Nepal	..	1.0	Zimbabwe	..	4.2

Source: Human Development Report 1997, UNDP, 1997.

INSTITUTO DEL TERCER MUNDO

Countries of the World

Afghanistan

Afghanestan

Population: 20,883,000
(1996)
Area: 652,090 SQ KM
Capital: Kabul

Currency: Afghanis
Language: Pushtu

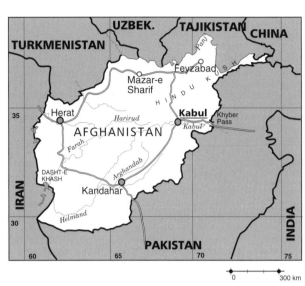

The group of mountains currently known as the Hindu Kush (called the Caucasus by the Greeks and Paropamisos by the Persians) were sparsely populated until the agricultural revolution. During this period the region was a passageway for frequent migrations of displaced peoples, and the Khyber Pass became the gateway to northern India.

2   The Hindu Kush was incorporated into the Persian Empire of Cyrus the Great in the sixth century BC, and 300 years later became part of the Hellenic world, as a result of the military campaigns of Alexander of Macedonia who founded Alexandropolis (present-day Kandahar). An armistice between the Greeks and Indians made it a province of the Mauryan Empire, and unified all of northern India.

3   Between the first century BC and the third century AD, an invading nation of Scythian origin (speaking an Indo-European language) founded the state of Kusana, on the trade line between Rome, India and China, known as the "silk route". Following this trail, along the Tarim River basin, Buddhism found its way into China. In 240 AD, Kusana was annexed to the new Sassanian Persian Empire until the beginning of the 8th century and the succession of Caliph Walid, who extended his rule, and the Islamic faith, as far as the Indus.

4   Towards the 13th century, the Mongol invasion caused great upheaval in the Old World. Afghanistan became part of the empire ruled by Genghis Khan from Karakoram. In 1360, the empire disintegrated as a result of constant dynastic strife and the Afghan region was ruled by Tamerlane, whose descendents governed until the beginning of the 16th century.

5   With the rise of the third Persian Shi'a Empire (1502) and the Empire of the Great Mogul in India (1526), the region became the scene of constant battles between the Mongols of India who dominated Kabul, the Saffavid Persians who controlled the southern region, and the Uzbek descendents of Tamerlane who ruled the northwest.

6   The unification of the country in 1747 came about through battles and political upheaval - when an assembly of local chieftains elected Shah Ahmad Durrani, a military commander who previously served Persian sovereigns. Ruling by military might, the new shah consolidated the national borders. Nevertheless, due to its geopolitical relevance, the region would be prone to attacks and its frontiers would suffer radical transformations.

7   Since the beginning of the 18th century the Russians had arrived in the area, eager to gain access to the sea ports of the Persian Gulf and the Arabian Sea, in order to maintain a closer watch on their main enemy there, the Ottoman Empire. On the other hand, the British were intent on controlling the Indus Valley area, where nomadic migrations and sanctuaries sheltering Indian rebels threatened their incipient colonial domain.

8   Consequently, geopolitical conditions in the region were as turbulent as they are today in Afghanistan, Iran and Pakistan. These regions held the geographic key to the colonial designs of both Russia and Britain. However, the two countries used divergent tactics: in Afghanistan, the Russians relied on diplomacy and bribery whilst the British used force.

9   The British defeat in the first British-Afghan War (1839-1842) reinforced Dost Muhammad Shah's slightly pro-Russian sympathies. He increased his influence in northern India by encouraging anti-British movements. His son Sher Ali Shah continued this policy, which led to a British invasion of the country once again.

10   As a result of the second British-Afghan War (1878-1880), the Durrani dynasty was overthrown, Afghanistan lost its territories south of the Khyber (including the Pass itself) and under the rule of the British-imposed Emir, lost control over its foreign relations. Eventually, the British granted Afghanistan a narrow strip of land extending Afghan territory as far as the Chinese border. This closed off a common frontier between Russian and British territories.

11   Afghanistan's borders, established artificially to create a buffer state between two empires, were never recognized by the peoples they were supposed to divide, who routinely crossed with their herds of cattle in search of pastures. In 1919, after a third British-Afghan war, lasting four months, the country was free from British "protection". Independence leader Emir Amanullah Khan (the heir and grandson of the British-imposed ruler) came to power, modernized the country and became the first head of state to recognize the revolutionary government of the Soviet Union. He was overthrown in 1929 by the Mohammedzai clan (descendents of the dynasty ousted in 1879) which crowned Mohamed Nadir Shah. Constitutional guarantees in 1931 recognized the autonomy of local leaders and created a system which remained unchallenged until 1953.

12   In that year, Muhammad Daud Khan, the Shah's cousin and brother-in-law, became Prime Minister and launched a new modernization process: he nationalized utilities, built roads, irrigation systems, schools and hydroelectric facilities (with US funding); he abolished the obligatory use of the *chador* (veil) by women; reorganized the armed forces (with Soviet assistance); and maintained neutrality throughout the Cold War. Unfortunately, land reform was never attempted and he was forced to abdicate in 1963.

13   The following period was dominated by traditional forces. The People's Democratic Party of Afghanistan (PDPA), founded as an underground organization, staged its first anti-government demonstrations in 1965, as Zahir Shah and his council were drawing up a new constitution. The PDPA split into two factions: the Khalk advocated revolution through a worker-peasant alliance, and the Parcham, who sought to find a broad-based front involving the intellectuals, national bourgeoisie, urban middle class and military. The military finally overthrew the monarchy and Zahir Shah in 1973, installing Muhammad Daud as president with PDPA support.

14   In April 1977, the murder of PDPA leader Mir Akhbar Khyber triggered a popular uprising. The Parcham military reacted by deposing President Daud, replacing him with Nur Muhammad Taraki. Hafizulah Amin and Babrak Karmal were appointed vice premiers but conflicts arose and in April 1979, Amin was appointed Prime Minister, a position previously vacant. In September, Amin succeeded in a conspiracy to overthrow the President, who was subsequently murdered.

15   As the new leader, Amin introduced reforms: a compulsory literacy campaign; abolition of the

32%

PROFILE

ENVIRONMENT
The country consists of a system of highland plains and plateaus, separated by east-west mountain ranges (principally the Hindu Kush) which converge on the Himalayan Pamir. The main cities are located in the eastern valleys. The country is dry and rocky though there are many fertile lowlands and valleys where cotton, fruit and grain are grown. Coal, natural gas and iron ore are the main mineral resources. The rapid increase in the rate of deforestation (which relates with desertification and soil degradation) constitutes the main environmental problem. The shortage of drinking water has contributed to the increase in infectious diseases.

SOCIETY
Peoples: The Pushtus (Pathans) are a majority of the population, the Tajiks one third; also Uzbeks, Hazaras and nomads of Mongol origin.
Religions: 99 per cent of the population is Muslim (Sunni and Shi'a).
Languages: Pushtu is the national language. Persian (Dari) is widely used; also Turkic and dozens of other languages.
Political Parties:
The Taliban party (whose name means "students") controls two thirds of the country and governs according to the party's interpretation of the Koran. Former Defence Minister, Ahmed Shah Massud, controls the north-east part of Afghanistan, which functions as a virtually independent republic.

THE STATE
Official Name: Doulat i Islami-ye Afghánistan (Islamic State of Afghanistan).
Administrative divisions: 31 provinces.
Capital: Kabul, 700,000 people in 1988.
Other cities: Kandahar, 225,000 people; Herat, 177,000 people; Mazar-e-Sharif, 130,000 people (1988).
Government: Mohammed Omar Akhunzada was elected "Commandant of Believers" ("amir ol momumin ").
National Holiday: May 27, Independence Day (1919).

dowry system and other traditional customs; and radical land reforms. All of which brought predictable opposition from traditional local leaders and religious authorities. In February 1979, the US ambassador to Kabul was kidnapped and murdered; consequently the US withdrew economic assistance and increased hostilities towards what they considered a pro-Soviet government. The period between April 1978 and September 1979 saw 25 different cabinets. Amin survived several assasination attempts until in late 1979 he was finally murdered.
[16] He was replaced by Babrak Karmal, who had been placed in power by the Soviet troops that had entered the country in December 1979. Karmal himself had legitimized their presence, citing a treaty of friendship and cooperation between the two states. Soviet intervention served as a pretext for the intensification of the "Second Cold War", initiated several months earlier with the US decision to freeze SALT, the Strategic Arms Limitation Treaty. The presence of the Soviets also triggered a sense of solidarity among Islamic fundamentalists, who travelled into Afghan territory to fight "Satan", in volunteer expeditions financed by Saudi Arabia. Afghan peasants who supported the mujahedin, or Islamic guerrillas, migrated to the cities or to neighboring Pakistan or Iran.
[17] In April 1986, heavy fighting near the border with Pakistan left an estimated 2,000 insurgents and 200 Pakistani soldiers dead (although no official figures were available), and a combined Afghan-Soviet force captured the main opposition base. On May 4, President Babrak Karmal returned from several weeks of medical treatment in Moscow and requested to be relieved of his party post.
[18] New PDPA Secretary-General Najibullah, a young doctor (born in 1947) of Pushtu origin was made president. He announced a unilateral ceasefire in January 1987, with guarantees for guerrilla leaders willing to negotiate with the government, an amnesty for rebel prisoners, and the promise of a prompt withdrawal of Soviet troops.
[19] In 1988, after six years of negotiations, an Afghan-Pakistani accord was signed in Geneva, guaranteed by both the US and USSR. The agreement set the terms of mutual relations specifying the principles of non-interference and non-intervention, and guaranteeing the voluntary return of refugees. Another document, signed by Afghanistan and the USSR, provided for the withdrawal of Soviet troops a month later.
[20] Three thousand Jamiat-i-Islami fighters announced they would take advantage of the amnesty law, but turned the disarmament ceremony into an ambush, killing several members of the Kabul military high command. The PDPA was renamed the Watan Party, the Party of the Homeland.
[21] In September 1991, the US and USSR stopped sending arms to the Afghan guerrillas. The US-USSR pact unleashed the confrontation between Saudi Arabia and Iran, countries that financed the Afghan "mujahedin" groups. The Kabul regime had no foreign support since the break-up of the USSR.
[22] President Najibullah was replaced in mid-April 1992, after he took refuge in the UN headquarters in Kabul. The Government remained in the hands of the four vice-presidents. The authorities immediately announced the Government's willingness to negotiate with the rebel groups and met commander Ahmed Shah Massud - of the Jamiat-i-Islami - at the city gates. Massud was a Tajik leader, known as the "Lion of Panjshir", due to the fierce battles that he had waged in the northern region against the army and the Soviet occupation troops. Massud's presence in Kabul triggered protest demonstrations among the guerrilla groups who belong to the Pushtu majority in the south and east of the country. From Pakistan, Gulbuddin Hekhmatyar, the head of fundamenstalist group Hezb-i-Islami, threatened to start bombing the capital if Massud did not surrender to the government. Provisional president Abdul Rahim Hatif stated that the government would be transferred to a coalition of all the rebel groups and to none in particular. In the days that followed, the forces of Massud and Hekhmatyar fought in Kabul itself.
[23] In March, the president of the Central Bank fled the country, taking with him all the country's foreign reserves.
[24] An interim government under the leadership of Sibgatullah Mojadidi took power, toward the end of April. The alliance of moderate Muslim groups, under the leadership of Ahmed Shah Massud - the new minister of defence - gained control of the capital, expelling the Islamic fundamentalists led by Gulbuddin Hekhmatyar. Pakistan, Iran, Turkey and Russia were the first countries to recognize the new Afghan government.
[25] On May 6 1992, the Interim Council formally dissolved the communist Watan Party, whose various factions had governed the country since 1978. The Council set up a special court to try the former communist officials who had violated either Islamic or national laws. The KHAD, the country's secret police, and the National Assembly were also dissolved.
[26] Some of the changes which were carried out showed the government's intention of imposing Islamic law: the sale of alcohol was outlawed, and an attempt was made to enforce new rules requiring women to cover their heads and wear traditional Islamic dress.
[27] Towards the end of May 1992, most of the rebel Afghan groups, including the Hezb-i-Islami and the Jamiat-i-Islami, announced a

Maternal Mortality

1990

PER 100,000
LIVE BIRTHS

1,700

peace agreement. The main points were the decision to hold elections within a year, and the withdrawal of some militia.

[28] A few days after the agreement, interim president Modjadidi miraculously escaped an attempt on his life. On May 31, the truce between the two main factions of guerrillas was broken. During the first few days of June, the Afghan capital once again became a battleground for Hezb-i-Islami and Jamiat-i-Islami troops. In a week of fierce fighting, the death toll reached 5,000, and Kabul took on the look of a city devastated by war.

[29] On June 28, Mojadidi turned over the presidency to the leader of Jamiat-i-Islami, Burhanuddin Rabbani. The latter declared, upon assuming the presidency, "We have only one condition in our program: unity. We will not take a single step without consensus".

[30] Hekhmatyar continued fighting against Kabul, demanding the withdrawal of Massud, as well as the militia loyal to Abdel Rashid Dostam. The latter had been a member of the communist government, but had defected in order to join the Muslim guerrillas that took power.

[31] The UN announced a $10 million aid program, to provide food and medication to the civilian population that had been forced to leave Kabul because of the violence. As a result of the war, the country's economy had come to a standstill and 60 per cent of its productive structure had been destroyed. Afghanistan had also become the world's largest producer of opium.

[32] The Pakistani Government, a long-term supplier of the mujahedin, decided to put a stop to the arms and food contraband across its border with Afghanistan, in order to weaken Hekhmatyar, whom it accused of being responsible for a deterioration in relations between the two countries. The United Nations High Commissioner for Refugees declared the existence of 4.5 million Afghan war refugees. Almost 3 million of these were in Iran, and the Iranian Government announced its desire to expel the refugees. Most of these were Shi'ia muslims, an Afghan minority.

[33] In March 1993, the leaders of eight rival factions announced the signing of a peace agreement in Islamabad, Pakistan. The accord, sponsored by Pakistan's prime minister, resulted in Nawaz Sharif-Rabbani and Hekhmatyar agreeing to share power for an 18-month period, until elections could be held. Rabbani was to continue as president, while Hekhmatyar was to be prime minister. Abdul Rashid Dostam, the powerful general whose militia controlled most of the northern part of the country, did not take part in the peace conference.

[34] In June, Hekhmatyar became prime minister and Massud resigned from the Ministry of Defence. In September, Russian and Tajik government forces confronted Tajik rebels allied to Afghan fighters along the border with Tajikistan. In spite of accusations from Moscow and the Tajik capital, Dushanbe, Afghan authorities denied any participation in the conflict and demanded the withdrawal of Russian forces from their territory.

[35] In January 1994, Dostam's militias, allied to Prime Minister Hekhmatyar, launched an offensive against the capital. Kabul remained divided in zones controlled by rival groups, while 75 per cent of the capital's 2 million population took refuge in other regions. In June, Rabbani refused to hand over the government at the end of his term, which was finally extended by the supreme court.

[36] The division of Afghanistan was partly a result of rivalry between various countries of the region, including Iran, Saudi Arabia, Uzbekistan, Pakistan and Russia, which intervened directly or indirectly in the civil war. In 1995, the emergence of the armed Taliban group ("students" in Persian), in the south of Afghanistan, changed the course of the war. These guerrillas, trained in Pakistan, aimed to create a united Islamic government in Afghanistan and were supported by broad swathes of society.

[37] In February, the Taliban occupied Hekhmatyar's general barracks in the centre of the country, while the Dostam

militias continued reinforcing their positions in the north-west. Following the destruction of Kabul, some two thirds of the population resided in zones controlled by the Uzbek militias. At a time when no solution could be seen for the civil war, in mid-1996, some 8,000 Taliban guerrillas started to bombard the centre of Kabul from the suburbs, tightening the siege on the capital. In September, the capital fell into Taliban hands, while the Government headed to the north of the country.

[38] During the first months of 1997, the situation remained unchanged but at the end of May, Dostam tried to break his alliance with the displaced president Burhanuddin Rabbani and join with the Taliban militia. The new alliance barely lasted two weeks and the gains made by the Kabul forces were rapidly lost. Ahmed Shah Massud, Rabbani's former military chief became the focal point of the new anti-Taliban alliance and took control of the north-east, which virtually started to function as an independent republic.

[39] The Taliban were supported by Pakistan, Saudi Arabia and the United States in taking over most of the Afghan territory. Once they had taken Kabul, the Taliban - following their decision to govern

according to their interpretation of the Koran - banished women from the public sphere and from the education system. Meanwhile, they banned music and singing (except for hymns), cinema, theatre and alcohol, declaring them "non-Islamic". Following the taking of Kabul, the Taliban regime passed a series of decrees which sought to impose its form of Koranic law on sport. In October 1997, in commemoration of the fall of Kabul, a great sporting event was held here with 3,000 participating male athletes (women were also banished from the sporting world), covered from the neck to below the knees. Applause was also prohibited, and the spectators were informed they were to encourage the athletes by shouting "Allah u Akbar" (God is great).

[40] On February 4 1998, an earthquake shook Rustaq, a city under the control of Massud's opposition forces. The Kabul Government, classing this "a tragedy for all Afghans," sent dozens of truck-loads of medicine and food.

[41] In August 1998 US missiles bombed the Afghani base of Saudi millionaire Osama bin Laden, whose World Islam Front was suspected of bombing the US embassies in Kenya and Tanzania.

Albania

Shqipërí

Population: 3,401,000
(1996)
Area: 28,748 SQ KM
Capital: Tirana
(Tiranë)

Currency: New Leks
Language: Albanian

The Albanians are descendents of the ancient Illirians, an Indo-European people who had migrated southward from Central Europe to the north of Greece by the beginning of the Iron Age. The southern Illirians were much in contact with Greek colonies, while the northern Albanian tribes were united at various times under local kings. The most important of them was Argon, whose kingdom (second half of the 3rd century BC) expanded from Dalmatia in the north to the Vijose river in the south.

[2] By the year 168 BC the Romans conquered all of Illiria and then the Albanians became part of the prosperous Roman province of Illyricum. After 395 AD, with the decline of the Roman empire, the area was administered from Constantinople. Despite the Hun incursions during the 3rd to 5th centuries, and the Slavic invasions during the 6th and 7th centuries, the Albanians were one of the few peoples in the Balkans who kept their own language and customs.

[3] When the Turks invaded in 1431, the Albanians put up stiff resistance, finally being occupied 47 years later. In the years which followed, the Ottomans imposed Islam upon the country. A popular uprising ended foreign domination in 1912, and independence was officially proclaimed at the end of World War I.

[4] In 1927, Ahmed Zogu, who had become President in 1925, signed a treaty with Mussolini, turning the country into a virtual Italian protectorate. A year later, Zogu proclaimed the country a monarchy. In April 1939, Italy occupied and formally annexed Albania to the kingdom of Victor Emmanuel III.

[5] The communists, under the leadership of Enver Hoxha, organized guerrilla resistance and a wide anti-Fascist front, receiving support from the allies during World War II. The occupation forces withdrew on November 29 1944, and the People's Republic was declared on January 11 1945.

[6] When the neighbouring Yugoslavian leader Tito and the Soviet Union's Josef Stalin split in 1948 (see Yugoslavia), the Albanian Workers' Party sided with the KOMINFORM (communist parties allied with the Soviet Union). When the Soviet Union started "de-Stalinization" in the 1960s, Albania

broke with Moscow and established close ties with the People's Republic of China, with which it eventually broke ties in 1981, when the Cultural Revolution came to an end and the Maoists fell from power. This break with China became official at the Eighth Workers' Party Congress, where a party line was put forth "against US imperialism, Soviet socialist-imperialism, Chinese and Yugoslavian revisionism, Eurocommunism and social democracy". By condemning the policies of non-alignment and European detente, as set forth in the Helsinki accords, this party line virtually isolated the country from any international alliance.

[7] Until Albania's liberation from Italian Fascist occupation in 1944, 85 per cent of the population lived in the country, and 53 per cent lacked even a place to grow their own vegetables. In 1967 collective farming was established. In 1977, Albania proclaimed self-sufficiency in wheat. According to official figures, between 1939 and 1992 industrial output grew by 12,500 per cent, building materials by 26,200 per cent, and electricity by 32,200.

[8] In 1989, Ramiz Alia, the Albanian head of state since Hoxha's death in April 1985, initiated a reorganization process aimed at improving the economy, and breaking the country's international isolation.

[9] The pace of the reforms picked up during 1989 and 1990. Border immigration procedures were simplified to encourage tourism; talks were initiated with the aim of resuming relations with both the US and the USSR; freedom of religion was declared; capital punishment was abolished for women; the number of crimes punishable by death was reduced from 34 to 11 and guidelines were established in the area of civil rights.

[10] Other innovations included the right to own a home, the opening of the economy to foreign investment and the election of workplace managers by employees through secret ballot. In February 1990, amnesty was granted to political and common prisoners. In November of the same year, Alia also announced that the constitution, which had been in effect since 1976, would be

revised. In December, independent political parties were authorized.

[11] That same month free, direct elections were announced, the first to be held in Albania in 46 years. Although originally planned for February 1991, the election had to be postponed until March 31 due to the instability produced by a mass exodus of thousands of Albanians to Italy. Almost 2 million voters were faced with a choice of more than a 1,000 candidates from 11 political parties, under the scrutiny of about a 100 international observers, and more than 250 foreign journalists.

[12] Despite the overwhelming defeat of Ramiz Alia in Tirana - 18 of the 19 posts to be filled went to the Democratic Party led by the hitherto unknown engineer, Franko Karogi - the Communists managed to obtain 156 of the 250 parliamentary seats. The election, in which 95 per cent of all registered voters participated, gave the Democratic Party (of social democratic orientation) 67 seats. The rest of the offices were won by small political groups like the Association for the Defence of the Greek Minority (OMONIA). Former King Leka I issued a statement from Paris, denouncing electoral fraud and opposition leader Gramoz Pashko stated that evidence was being collected which

would prove the illegitimacy of the electoral proceedings.

[13] In May 1991, more than 300,000 workers went on strike, demanding the resignation of the communist government, as well as a 50 per cent salary increase. Prime Minister Fatos Nano dissolved his cabinet to form an alliance with the opposition. This, in turn, provoked angry protests from orthodox communists; at the party conference held in June, President Alia was accused of being a traitor.

[14] After deliberating the issue, the Albanian Workers' Party decided to change its name to the Socialist Party, naming Nano as president and Spiro Dede - a liberal - vice-president. A new government was formed with a communist majority, led by Ylli Bufi, with the opposition holding key positions, such as the defence ministry.

[15] On June 19 1991, the Conference on Security and Cooperation in Europe announced the admission of Albania, the last European country remaining outside this group. In 1991, Albania received $77 million in aid from the European Community. Albania pays for its food imports by exporting chrome, agricultural goods, oil and copper. It also provides Greece and Yugoslavia with electricity.

[16] At the end of 1991 the Democratic Party accused the

PROFILE

ENVIRONMENT
A Balkan state on the Adriatic Sea, Albania's seacoast is comprised of distinct regions. Alluvial plains, which become partially swampy in the winter, extend from the Yugoslavian border to the Bay of Vlöre. Further to the south, the coast is surrounded by mountains and has a Mediterranean climate. The soil of the mountainous inner region is very poor. Cattle-raising predominates there, while cotton, tobacco and corn are grown on the plains. Irrigated valleys produce rice, olives, grapes and wheat. The country has large areas of forest and is rich in mineral resources, including oil deposits.

SOCIETY
Peoples: Albanians are a homogeneous ethnic group; there is a Greek minority. **Languages:** Albanian (official) and Albanian dialects. **Religions:** Freedom of worship was authorized in 1989, having been banned since 1967. Pre-1967 estimates placed Islam as the largest religion (70 per cent), with the Albanian Orthodox Church in second place (20 per cent) and the Catholic Church (10 per cent) in third. **Political Parties:** A multiparty system was established by the constitution which has been in effect since April 30 1991. Socialist Party (PS), formerly communist; today, it advocates a democratic socialism within a free market economy. The Democratic Party (PDA), a liberal democratic party, in favor of a free market economy. **Social Organizations:** The Central Council of Albanian Trade Unions has 610,000 members.

THE STATE
Official Name: Republíka e Shqipërisë. **Administrative divisions:** 26 districts. **Capital:** Tirana (Tiranë), 244,200 people (1990). **Other cities:** Durrës, 85,400 people; Elbasan, 83,300 people; Vlöre, 73,800 people (1990). **Government:** Parliamentary republic. Rexhep Mejdani, President of the Popular Assembly since June 1997. Fatos Nano, Prime Minister and Head of Government, since June 1997 (second time). Single-chamber legislature: People's Assembly, made up of 140 deputies elected by universal suffrage every four years. **National Holiday:** November 28, Liberation Day (1944). **Armed Forces:** 73,000 (22,400 conscripts). **Other:** 16,000; International Security Force: 5,000; People's Militia: 3,500.

STATISTICS

DEMOGRAPHY
Population: 3,401,000 (1996). **Annual growth:** 1.5% (1980/1996). **Estimates for year 2000:** 4,000,000. **Annual growth to year 2000:** 0.6% (1994/2000). **Urban Population:** 37.5% (1996). **Urban growth:** 2.1% (1980/95). **Children per woman:** 2.7 (1996).

HEALTH
Life expectancy at birth: 71 years (1996) male: 68 years (1994) female: 74 years (1994). **Infant mortality:** 34 per 1,000 (1996). **Under-5 child mortality:** 40 per 1,000 (1996). **Calorie consumption:** 107% (1988/90). 730 **people per doctor** (1988/91).

EDUCATION
School enrolment: Primary total: 98% (1990/95) male : 98% (1990/95) female: 99% (1990/95). Secondary: male : 36% (1990/95) female: 37% (1990/95). Tertiary: 10% (1995). **Primary school teachers:** one for every 18 students (1995).

COMMUNICATIONS
50 **newspapers**, 190 **radios** 90 **TV sets** and 12 **main telephone lines** per 1,000 people (1994).

ECONOMY
Per capita, GNP: $ 820 (1996). **Annual inflation:** 27.34% (1985/95). **Consumer price index:** 226.7 (1994). **Currency:** 90.8 new leks = $ 1 (1995). **Cereal imports:** 270 metric tons (1994). **Fertilizer use:** 253 kgs per ha (1994). **Exports:** $ 296 million (1996). **Imports:** $ 1,283 million (1996). **External debt:** $ 781 million (1996). $ 230 **per capita:** (1996). **Debt service:** 3.5% of exports (1996).

ENERGY
Consumption: 341.34 Kgs of Oil equivalent per capita yearly (1994). 2.65% imported (1994). **HDI** (rank / value) 102 / 0.655 (1994)

government of paralyzing the reforms and withdrew its ministers from the cabinet. The Socialist Party could not handle the crisis. In the aftermath of a collapse of the economy, the parliamentary elections of March 1992 gave the Democratic Party a spectacular success (65.6 per cent) over the Socialist Party (22.6 per cent). 80 per cent of the voters abstained.

[17] On April 4 1992 Sali Berisha, leader of the Democratic party, replaced Ramiz Alia as President of Albania. He won the parliamentary vote 96 to 35, becoming the first non-Marxist president since the end of World War II.

[18] The trials of the main political figures of the previous regime began in mid-1993. Naxhmija Hoxha, widow of the historic communist leader Enver Hoxha, the ex-President Ramiz Alia, and the ex-Premier Fatos Nano among others, were sent to prison convicted of misuse of public funds.

[19] During 1994 and 1995 laws about private property were sanctioned, and this stimulated national and foreign investors. The gross internal income grew by an average of 7 per cent due to the development of the building industry, services and agriculture. Inflation and public deficit were reduced. Despite the fact that half a million Albanians live and work outside the country, unemployment remained as high as 18 per cent. Foreign debt was refinanced by the Western banks and reduced from $700 to $300 million.

[20] Concerning foreign politics, Albania was accepted as the 36th member of the European Council, and relations with neighboring countries improved. An agreement of military cooperation with the United States was signed, which included the establishment of air bases on Albanian territory for intelligence flights over Bosnia-Herzegovina.

[21] A state of conflict prevailed through 1995 and 1996. The press denounced the censorship and intimidatory practices, and the relationships among the political parties remained difficult. Legislation approved during this period reflects those tensions. The so-called "Verification Bill" made it possible for the Government to decide on the accessibility to public office for journalists and other people according to the reports of Sigurimi, ex-secret police of the communist regime. The Bill about "Genocide and Communist Crimes" forbids notorious ex-political leaders access to public office until the year 2002, and the new electoral law forbids coalitions among the smaller parties.

[22] On May 26 1996 parliamentary elections took place, in which the main leaders of the opposition were not allowed to participate. The Democratic Party won 122 out of 140 places. On the day of the elections the Socialist Party, the Democratic Alliance (center right), the Social Democratic Party, and the Human Rights Party withdrew their candidacies. The Socialist Party accused the Government of controlling the voting through the police and party groups, and demanded the annulment of the elections. President Berisha, on the other hand, accused the socialists of organizing terrorist gangs. Observers sent by Washington verified the existence of pressure from above.

[23] In the following months, the legitimacy of the elections was questioned by the United States and several European countries, interested in investing in Albania. In response to a recommendation by the European Council, the Parliament formed an ad hoc commission to investigate the accusations, mainly the violence against opposition leaders.

[24] In late January 1997, the collapse of a series of investment funds, called "fast wealth pyramids" and guaranteed by the State, led to a bloody social and political uprising. One out of every six Albanians was left penniless and the main cities, including Tirana, rose in arms. This situation caused the virtual disintegration of the Albanian state. Eighty per cent of weapons were in the hands of civilians, after they sacked forts and barracks abandoned by the army and the police, who had joined the rebels. Armed confrontations caused 1,500 deaths. Berisha was forced to bring forward parliamentary elections to June 1997. The Socialist Party, led by Fatos Nano, won the elections.

[25] Berisha resigned in July and the Government was headed by Nano as prime minister. In September, due to a disagreement with a Socialist deputy, the National Council of the Democratic Party withdrew from the Parliament. By the end of the year, the Nano administration had resumed control over the country and was able to reduce inflation. The Socialist government pledged to carry out reforms which included the revitalization of the economy through an extensive privatization plan. In March 1998, the IMF lauded Nano's management and promised funding for three years to support Albania's economic reforms.

[26] The political atmosphere remained extremely tense due to the developments in Yugoslavia. The province of Kosovo, geographically belonging to the Federal Republic of Yugoslavia, but ethnically made up of a majority of Albanians, had requested its independence and guerrilla groups fought against Serbian forces. In March, major protests were held outside the Yugoslav embassy in Tirana, while the Albanian army in the northern region, on the border with Yugoslavia, was put on red alert.

Algeria

Algerie

Population : 28,784,000 (1996)
Area: 2,381,741 SQ KM
Capital: Algiers (Alger)

Currency: Dinars
Language: Arabic

From ancient times, the states that arose in what is now Algeria developed links with the two power nuclei in that part of the world: Tunisia, beginning in the Carthaginian period (10th century BC), and Morocco, after the conquest of the Iberian Peninsula by the Arabs (711 AD). Those who resented the fact that long-time Muslims and recent converts were taxed differently, settled in this area. These "dissidents" would later embrace the Jariyite sect, a religious group which was characterized by its egalitarian principles. It maintained, for example, that caliphs did not have to be descended from Muhammad or his relatives; thus, any Muslim could become caliph regardless of race, colour or social position. This tenet fitted in well with the Berbers' social reality, given their subordinate position in relation to the Arabs (although the latter were a minority, they nevertheless exercised greater political power). Variations of this doctrine spread widely among the Berbers, contributing to the formation of many North African empires.

[2] With the downfall of the Almohad Empire, Yaglimorossen ibn Ziane founded a new state on the Algerian coast. Its borders were consolidated as economic prosperity and cultural development led nomadic peoples to settle down. Ziane and his successors governed the country between 1235 and 1518. After the Christians had put an end to seven centuries of Moslem domination, in 1492, the Zianids were confronted with a series of Spanish military incursions in which various strategic sites, like Oran, were taken.

[3] Algeria and Tunisia both became part of the Ottoman Empire in the 16th century. The Arroudj and Kheireddine brothers drove the Spanish from the Algerian coast and expanded the state's authority over a sizeable territory. Its mighty fleet won respect for the nation, and its sovereignty was acknowledged in a series of treaties (with the Low Countries in 1663, France in 1670, Britain in 1681, and the US in 1815).

[4] Wheat production gradually increased until it became an export crop once again, for the first time since the Hilalian invasion (see Mauritania). Wheat exports would eventually be the indirect cause of European intervention. At the end of the 18th century, the French revolutionary government bought large amounts of wheat from Algeria but failed to pay. Napoleon, and later the Restoration monarchy, delayed payment until the Dey of Algiers demanded that the debt be paid. Reacting to further excuses and delays, he slapped a perplexed French official in the face - a show of temper that would cost the Turkish Pasha dearly. 36,000 French soldiers disembarked to "avenge the offence", a pretext used by the French to carry out a long-standing project: to re-establish a colony on the African coast opposite their own shores. However, the French encountered heavy resistance, and were defeated.

[5] In 1840, disembarking with 115,000 troops, the French set out once again to conquer Algeria. Successive rebellions were launched against the French. In the South, however, the nomadic groups remained virtually independent and fought the French until well into the 20th century (see Sahara). In 1873, France decided to expropriate land for French settlers, or pieds-noirs as they were known, who wished to live in the colonies (500,000 by 1900, and over a million after World War II). As a result, the French pieds-noirs came to monopolize the fertile land, and the country's economy was restructured to meet French interests.

[6] Nationalist resistance grew stronger from the 1920s onwards, until in 1945 it exploded when celebration of the victory over Nazi-Fascism turned into a popular rebellion. The French forces tried to put down the rebellion and according to official French reports, 45,000 Algerians and 108 Europeans were killed in the ensuing massacre.

[7] Shortly thereafter, the Algerian People's Party, founded in 1937, was restructured as the Movement for the Triumph of Democratic Liberties (MTLD), which was to participate in the 1948 and 1951 elections called by the colonialists.

[8] Convinced of the futility of elections under colonial control, nine leaders of the OS (Special Organization, the military wing of the MTLD) founded the Revolutionary Committee for Unity and Action (CRUA). In November 1954, this committee became the National Liberation Front (FLN) that led the armed rebellion. Franz Fanon, a doctor from Martinique, who had fought in the liberation of France during World War II, joined the FLN and came to exert great theoretical influence not only in Algeria, but also throughout the Sub-Saharan region. 9 In order to maintain "French Algeria" and the pieds-noirs, the French colonial system destroyed 8,000 villages, eliminated more than a million civilians, made systematic use of torture and deployed more than 500,000 troops. Right-wing French residents of Algeria formed the feared Secret Army Organization (OAS), a terrorist group which blended Neo-Fascism with the demands of the French colonials, who resented the growing power of the Algerians. Finally, on March 18 1962, French President De

Gaulle signed the Evian Agreement, agreeing to a cease-fire and a plebiscite on the proposal for self-determination.
[10] Independence was declared on July 5 1962, and a Constituent Assembly was elected later that year. Ahmed Ben Bella was named prime minister. Almost all foreign companies were nationalized, 600,000 French nationals abandoned the country taking everything they could with them, and 500,000 Algerians returned, to share the lot of 150,000 landless and hungry peasants. A system of local agricultural and industrial operations was introduced by the new government.
[11] However, Ben Bella's self-management program came up against the reality of a government with little administrative expertise. In June 1965 a revolutionary council headed by Houari Boumedienne took power and jailed Ben Bella. A new emphasis on organization, centralization, and state power began to prevail over Ben Bella's self-management notions. Under Boumedienne, there were further nationalizations and a program of rapid industrialization based on revenues from oil and liquid natural gas. The country entered a period of economic expansion, which was not reflected in the countryside. Population grew more rapidly than agricultural production, and Algeria went from exporting to importing food.
[12] Houari Boumedienne died in December 1978, after a long illness, just as the country's political institutions were beginning to consolidate. In 1976, a new National Charter was approved and, in 1977, the new members of the National People's Assembly were elected, with Colonel Chadli Ben Jedid being designated president.
[13] Ben Jedid received almost unanimous support at the fourth FLN congress in January 1979, and was sworn in with full presidential powers.
[14] The new president initiated a policy of reconciliation by releasing Ahmed Ben Bella, who had been imprisoned for 14 years. Restrictions on travel abroad were lifted, taxes reduced and prohibitions lifted on private housing. Over-large public enterprises gradually shrank and the restructuring of inefficient public enterprises gave an impulse to private companies.
[15] Ben Jedid was re-elected in January 1984. In October 1988, a

wave of protests broke out in several cities due to the lack of water and basic consumer goods; the legitimacy of the FLN and the military was called into question. Among the main groups participating in these mass protests were militant Muslim fundamentalists. Some mosques - above all, those in poorer neighborhoods - became the site of political demonstrations, particularly on Friday afternoons, when mosque prayers ended in political declarations voicing economic and social demands.
[16] Some sectors of the most radical forms of Islam, influenced by Iran, began sending volunteers to fight in Afghanistan, to carry out the jihad or "holy war" against the Soviet-backed Kabul regime. In mid-1989, against a background of protest and upheaval, Ben Jedid presented a new constitution which introduced a modified multiparty system, breaking the monopoly which the FLN had held.
[17] More than 20 opposition groups - including Muslims - openly expressed their views. The most significant were the Islamic Salvation Front (FIS), the Da'wa Islamic League, the communist Socialist Avant Garde Party (PAGS) and the strongly Kabbyle (ethnic minority of Berber origin) Pro-Democracy and Culture Group (RDC). Mouloud Hamrouche, a leading reformer, was appointed prime minister. In the first multiparty elections since Algeria's independence from France in 1962, the FIS defeated the FLN in the June elections.
[18] Hamrouche and his cabinet resigned in June 1991, against a background of social agitation promoted by the mullahs. In early June, a state of siege was declared throughout the country, in the face of massive protests pitting the country's military and police forces against FIS agitators who demanded that presidential elections be held ahead of schedule and that an Islamic state be proclaimed. Sid Ahmed Ghozali, an oil technician who had been prime minister during the previous government, was designated as the new prime minister. Legislative and presidential elections were scheduled for later in the year, and the FIS suspended its campaign of social and political agitation.

PROFILE

ENVIRONMENT
South of the fertile lands on the Mediterranean coast lie the Tellian and Saharan Atlas mountain ranges, with a plateau extending between them. Further south is the Sahara desert, rich in oil, natural gas and iron deposits. Different altitudes and climates in the north make for agricultural diversity, with Mediterranean-type crops (vines, citrus fruits, olives, etc.) predominating. The country's flora and fauna are seriously threatened. More than 30 mammal, 8 reptile and 70 bird species are in danger of extinction. Desertification affects primarily the pre-Saharan regions. However, erosion also poses a serious threat to 45 per cent of all agricultural land (12 million hectares).

SOCIETY
Peoples: Algerians are mostly Arab (80 per cent) and Berber (17 per cent). Nomadic groups linked to the Tuareg of Nigeria and Mali live in the south. Nearly a million Algerians live in France.
Religion: Islam
Languages: Arabic (official), and Berber in some areas. Many people speak French, but Arabic has gradually been replacing it in education and public administration.
Political Parties: National Liberation Front (FLN); Vanguard Socialist Party (PAGS); Front for Socialist Forces (FFS); Movement for Democracy in Algeria (MDA); Reunion of Culture and Democracy (RCD); Islamic Salvation Front (FIS); Hamas; Movement for a Peaceful Society.
Social Organizations: General Union of Algerian Workers (UGTA), National Union of Algerian Peasants, National Union of Algerian Women, National Youth Union.

THE STATE
Official Name: Al-Jumjuriya al -Jazairia ash-Shaabiya
Capital: Algiers (Alger), 1,721,607 people (1987)
Other cities: Oran, 609,823 people; Constantine, 440,842; Annaba, 348,322 (1987).
Government: Lamine Zeroual, President.
National Holiday: November 1st, Anniversary of the Revolution (1954).
Armed Forces: 121,700 (65,000 conscripts).
Other: 180,000 (Gendarmerie, National Security Forces, Republican Guard)

[19] The country turned to the IMF for loans, to offset the effects of the fluctuation in the price of oil. Ghozali submitted a series of reforms to the National Assembly, to ensure the fairness of the election. However, these reforms - which included doing away with a man's right to vote in his wife's name - were rejected by the FLN, which had a parliamentary majority.
[20] In the December elections, 40 per cent of the country's 13 million voters abstained. The FIS won the first round of voting, winning 188 of the 430 seats contested in Parliament, with the support of 3.2 million voters. The Socialist Forces Front (FFS), a secular party dominated by Berbers, obtained 25 seats, while the FLN obtained 15.

[21] Anti-fundamentalists - led by the General Union of Algerian Workers (UGTA) and the FFS - were alarmed by the FIS victory in the first round of voting. They called a massive demonstration in the center of Algiers, which was attended by 100,000 people. Women's groups, professionals and intellectuals also participated in the demonstration.
[22] President Chadli Ben Jedid resigned, under strong pressure from the military and from political figures who feared an FIS victory. A Supreme Council of Security, made up of 3 military officers and the prime minister, took over. Shortly afterwards, the High Council of State was appointed, headed by Mohamed Boudiaf, dissident leader of the

1990

PER 100,000
LIVE BIRTHS

160

MILLIONS $ 1996

IMPORTS
8,372
EXPORTS
12,609

STATISTICS

DEMOGRAPHY
Population: 28,784,000 (1996). **Annual growth**: 2.7% (1980/1996).
Estimates for year 2000: 31,600,000. **Annual growth to year 2000**:
2.4% (1994/2000). **Urban Population**: 56.4% (1996). **Urban growth**:
4.48% (1980/95). **Children per woman**: 4 (1996).

HEALTH
Life expectancy at birth: 68 years (1996) male: 67 years (1994)
female: 69 years (1994). **Infant mortality**: 34 per 1,000 (1996).
Under-5 child mortality: 39 per 1,000 (1996). **Calorie Consumption**:
123% (1988/90). 1,064 **people per doctor** (1988/91). **Safe water**:
78% (1990/96).

EDUCATION
Literacy: 62% (1995) male : 74% (1995) female: 49% (1995). **School
enrolment** : Primary total: 105% (1990/95) male : 111% (1990/95)
female: 98% (1990/95). Secondary: male : 66% (1990/95) female:
58% (1990/95). Tertiary: 11% (1995). **Primary school teachers**: one
for every 27 students (1995)

COMMUNICATIONS
50 **newspapers**, 236 **radios**, 70 **TV sets** and 41 **main telephone
lines** per 1,000 people (1994). **Books**: 1 new titles per 100,000 people
(1992/94).

ECONOMY
Per capita, GNP: $ 1,520 (1996). **Annual growth, GNP**: 1.8% (1995/
96). **Annual inflation**: 22.94% (1985/95). **Consumer price index**:
257.8 (1994). **Currency**: 52.18 dinars = $ 1 (1995). Cereal imports:
7,760 metric tons (1994). **Food import dependency**: 26% (1994).
Fertilizer use: 152 kgs per ha (1994). **Exports**: $ 12,609 million
(1996). **Imports**: $ 8,372 million (1996). **External debt**: $ 33,260
million (1996). $ 1,156 **per capita**: (1996). **Debt service**: 27.7% of
exports (1996). **Development aid received**: $ 310 million (1995). $
11 per capita (1995) 0.8% of GNP (1994).

ENERGY
Consumption: 905.62 Kgs of Oil equivalent per capita yearly (1994).
-318.10% imported (1994).

HDI (rank / value) 82 / 0.737 (1994)

FLN, in exile since 1964. All FIS leaders were arrested and the vote was invalidated. On February, the High Council of State declared a state of emergency throughout the country, to remain in effect for a year. The army was opposed to any form of power-sharing with the FIS.
[23] In March 1992, the FIS was dissolved. In early April, the Government dissolved nearly 400 city and town councils controlled by FIS members since the June 1990 municipal elections. In late April 1992, the Supreme Court ratified the banning of the FIS.
[24] Violence kept on the increase among both factions, the Government and Islamic extremists. In June, Boudiaf was assassinated by one of his bodyguards while delivering a public speech. He was replaced by Ali Kafi. Both Boudiaf's death and Ghozali's resignation led to the increasing inflexibility of the Government towards the opposition.
[25] In September, a series of anti-terrorist measures were decreed by Prime Minister Belaid Abdelsalam's government, among them the increased enforcement of the death penalty. Amnesty International estimated that more than 2,000 people lost their lives in this first year of civil war. In February 1993 the High Council of State extended the state of emergency indefinitely and established a curfew in Algiers and five provinces. In addition, all associations linked to the FIS were dissolved.
[26] At that point, the army hesitated between the option of a negotiated solution and the pursuit of a military victory over Islamic armed groups. Towards late 1993, the FIS announced its intention of initiating talks with the Government, which responded by freeing some 60 FIS prisoners and calling for a conference to begin negotiations.
[27] However, the initiative was the first of a long series of failures caused by disagreement among the different political sectors. The Government refused to invite certain Islamic sectors and the FLN and the Socialist Forces Front (FFS), led by Hocine Ait Ahmed, stated that no president appointed by that conference would be

considered legitimate. After this failed attempt, the administration named Minister of Defense Lamine Zeroual as president of the country for three years.
[28] The defeat of Abdelsalam, who had been opposed to widescale privatizations, facilitated the signature of an agreement between the IMF and the new government of Redha Malek in early 1994. The growth of foreign debt coincided with higher unemployment, which covered 22 per cent of the economically active population. Malek was replaced by another advocate of economic liberalization, Mokdad Sifi, considered more open towards a dialogue with the Islamic fundamentalists.
[29] In what marked the beginning of a growing schism among all political sectors, the Islamic guerrillas split into the Armed Islamic Group (GIA) and the Armed Islamic Movement. The violent ways of the Government and the Islamic guerrillas continued throughout the year, none of them being able to obtain a military victory. In one of its most impressive actions, the guerrillas forced the escape of 1,000 prisoners from a high-security prison in Tazoult.
[30] Civil war continued in 1995 and, in spite of a certain military advantage by the government, the defeat of Islamic opposition did not seem possible. Political attempts to find a way out of the conflict were fruitless. Early in the year, after meeting in Rome, the FIS, FLN, FFS and moderate Islamic representatives belonging to Hamas proposed an end of violence, the liberation of political prisoners and the formation of a government of national unity which would hold elections. In spite of the support of Spain, United States, France and Italy, the proposal was rejected by Zeroual.
[31] President Zeroual continued the war against Islamic guerrillas and held presidential elections in November 1995. The FIS, FLN, and the FFS boycotted the elections, won by Zeroual with 61 per cent of the vote, compared with 25 per cent for moderate Mahfoud Nahnah. The elections were tainted by accusations of fraud, in spite of the presence of international monitors.

[32] In the first months of 1996, the Zeroual administration, with the apparent support of the FLN's new leadership, achieved major military victories and continued the structural adjustment program prescribed by the IMF. This intensified the pauperization of a large part of the middle class and the poorest sectors of the population.
[33] January 1997 was particularly violent and the GIA showed it still had a strong operational capacity. More than 200 people died in several attacks, including 50 whose throats had been cut. As a result the Government was on full alert.
[34] Violence grew as the date of the legislative elections, expected for June 5, drew closer. The government party obtained overall majority of the vote with 155 of the 380 seats in stake. The moderate Islamic group Movement for a Peaceful Society won 69 seats while the FLN retained 64 and the Socialist Forces Front 19, the same number as the Reunion of Culture and Democracy party. The FIS, which had called for the boycott of the elections, stated its satisfaction with the abstention, which amounted to 34 per cent.
[35] In August 1997, FIS leader

Abasi Madani, recently freed, confirmed his movement's intention to put an end to violence through dialogue with the Government. However, that same month, the massacre of 300 people in a small town south of Algiers, unprecedented since 1992, impaired the possibility of a solution. Witnesses claimed army officers could have prevented the massacre, but chose not to get involved. In October, the Government's victory in the municipal elections ratified the supremacy of the ruling coalition, but brought about little or no hopes for change.
[36] A group of Islamic Algerian militants was arrested in Belgium, in March 1998 - a move which the Belgian authorities considered the first step towards the breaking up of the European supporters of the GIA.
[37] According to Amnesty International, the responsibility for the death and disappearance of hundreds of people lies both with government security forces as well as with armed opposition groups. The organization reported torture and ill-treatment of prisoners in 1997, as well as abuses in the time a person can legally be detained.

Angola

Angola

Population: 11,185,000 (1996)
Area: 1,246,700 SQ KM
Capital: Luanda

Currency: New kwanzas
Language: Portuguese

The original inhabitants of what is now Angola were probably Khoisan-speaking hunters and gatherers. During the first millennium AD, large-scale Bantu-speaking migrations (possibly originating in central Africa) into southern Africa absorbed the older population and expanded iron technology and cereal cultivation in the area. Eventually, they came to constitute the dominant ethnolinguistic group of southern Africa. Their occupation of the area that is now Angola was complete by 1600. The most significant Bantu kingdom in Angola was the Kongo, with its capital at Mbanza Kongo (called by the Portuguese São Salvador do Congo). This kingdom was a highly centralized and complex state that was divided into six provinces. South of the Kongo, the Mbundu people formed the Ndongo, an equally centralized kingdom that gave Angola its name from the title of its king, the *Ngola*.
[2] In 1483 Portuguese explorers reached Angola, Christianized the ruling family of the Kongo, and engaged in trade and missionary work. However, increasing Portuguese involvement in the slave trade eventually turned the Kongo against Portugal, which in turn led to Portugal's destruction of the Ndongo kingdom to the south. Portugal's colonization of the area was slow, but its slave trade flourished, so much so that by the early 17th century some 5,000 to 10,000 slaves were being exported annually from Luanda. All the kingdoms in the area vigorously resisted foreign occupation until the mid-18th century. War and slavery decimated the population. It dropped from 18 million in 1450, to barely 8 million in 1850. Even so, Angolan resistance to Portuguese

colonization continued, led by figures like Ngola Kiluange, Nzinga Mbandi, Ngola Kanini, Mandume and others.
[3] Portugal intensified its military incursions following the 1884 Berlin Conference which divided Africa among the European colonial powers. Nonetheless, it took 30 years of military campaigns (1890-1921) to "pacify" the colony. From then on, Portuguese settlers arrived in ever-increasing numbers. In 1900, there were an estimated 10,000; in 1950, 50,000; and in 1974, less than a year before independence, 350,000. Only one per cent lived on farms inland. The colonial economy was parasitic, built upon the exploitation of mineral and agricultural wealth (diamonds and coffee), with the bulk of profits going to Portuguese merchants.
[4] On December 10 1956, several small nationalist groups fused to form the Popular Movement for the Liberation of Angola (MPLA). Their aim was to pressure the Portuguese Government into recognizing the Angolan people's right to self-determination and independence. When Britain and France began to withdraw from their overseas colonies in the 1960s, Portugal did not follow suit and frustrated all Angolan attempts to win independence by peaceful means.
[5] On February 4 1961, a group of MPLA militants from the most underprivileged classes stormed Luanda's prisons and other strategic points in the capital. This acted as a spur to resistance in other Portuguese colonies. Their manifesto was clear: they were fighting not just colonialism but also the international power system which sustained it. In addition, they were fighting racism and tribal chauvinism.
[6] In the years that followed, other independence movements with different regional origins sprang up: the National Front for the Liberation of Angola (FNLA) led by Holden Roberto, the Cabinda Liberation Front (FLEC), and the Union for the Total Independence of Angola (UNITA) led by Jonas Savimbi.
[7] Under the direction of Agostinho Neto, the MPLA militants held a conference in January 1964 to discuss and define

their strategy of a prolonged people's war.
[8] Portugal's domestic problems, coupled with military setbacks in Angola, Mozambique and Guinea-Bissau and repeated shows of international solidarity with the independence fighters, dashed Portuguese army hopes of a military solution. An uprising led by the Armed Forces Movement (MFA) overthrew the Portuguese regime of Oliveira Salazar and Marcelo Caetano on April 25 1974. The MFA expressly recognized the African colonies' right to self determination and independence.
[9] The MFA immediately invited the MPLA, FNLA and UNITA to participate with Portugal in a transitional government for Angola in the interim period, the mechanisms of which were established in the Alvor Accords, signed in January 1975. By this time, political and ideological divergences among the three groups had become irreconcilable; the FNLA was directly assisted by US intelligence services and received military aid from Zaire (now People's Democratic Republic of Congo). UNITA received overt backing from South Africa and Portuguese settlers; while the MPLA was aligned ideologically with the socialist

countries. The accords were never implemented.
[10] The FNLA and UNITA unleashed a series of attacks on MPLA strongholds in Luanda, and a bloody battle for control of the capital ensued. Between September and October 1975, Angola was attacked on all sides: Zaire invaded from the north while South Africa, with the complicity of UNITA, attacked from the south to prevent a Marxist government.
[11] On November 11 1975, the date agreed upon to end colonial rule, the MPLA unilaterally declared independence in Luanda, pre-empting the formal transfer of sovereignty. Some 15,000 Cuban troops aided the new government in fighting off the South African invasion. In 1976, the United Nations recognized the MPLA government as the legitimate representative of Angola.
[12] The Angolan economy was severely debilitated. The war had paralyzed production in the far north and south of the country. The Europeans had emigrated en masse, taking all that they could with them and effectively destroying the productive capacity.
[13] Under these circumstances, the Angolan Government began to restore the chief production centres, and to train the largely

ENVIRONMENT

The 150 kilometre-wide strip of coastal plains is fertile and dry. The extensive inland plateaus, higher to the west, are covered by tropical rainforests in the north, grasslands at the center and dry plains in the south. In the more densely populated areas (the north and central west) diversified subsistence farming is practiced. Coffee, the main export crop, is grown in the north; sisal is cultivated on the Benguela and Huambo plateaus; sugar-cane and oil palm along the coast. The country has abundant mineral reserves: diamonds in Luanda, petroleum in Cabinda and Luanda, iron ore in Cassinga and Cassala. The port of Lobito is linked by railway to the mining centers of Zaire and Zambia. There are a number of environmental problems aggravated by the civil war, the lack of drinking water (in 1987 there was a cholera epidemic in Luanda), soil erosion and deforestation as a result of the export of valuable timber.

SOCIETY

Peoples: As a consequence of centuries of slave trade the population density is still very low. To maintain control over the country, the Portuguese colonizers fostered local divisions between the various ethnic groups; Bakondo, Kimbundu, Ovimbundu and others.
Religions: The majority practise traditional African religions. 38 per cent Catholic, and 15 per cent Protestant. However, there are forms of syncretism which make it impossible to establish strict boundaries between one religion and another.
Languages: Portuguese (official) and African languages derived from Bantu; Ovidumbo, Kimbundu, Kikongo and others.
Political Parties: The People's Movement for the Liberation of Angola (MPLA), founded by Agostinho Neto on December 10 1956; the National Union for the Total Independence of Angola (UNITA); and the National Front for the Liberation of Angola (FNLA).
Social Organizations: National Union of Angolan Workers (UNTA); Organization of Angolan Women (OMA).

THE STATE

Official Name: República Popular de Angola.
Administrative Divisions: 18 Districts.
Capital: Luanda, 1,134,000 people (1988).
Other cities: Huambo (Nova Lisboa), 203,000 people; Lobito, 150,000; Benguela, 155,000 (1988).
Government: José Eduardo dos Santos, president; Fernando Franca Van Dunem, prime Minister. Unicameral Legislature. 223-member National Assembly, elected by direct popular vote.
National Holiday: November 11, Independence Day (1975).
Armed Forces: 82,000.
Other: 20,000 Internal Security Police.

unskilled and illiterate workforce. In this way, a large public sector emerged which was to become the economy's driving force, and banking and strategic activities were nationalized.

[14] In May 1977, Nito Alves led a faction of the MPLA committed to "active revolt", in a coup attempt. Six leading MPLA members were killed but the conspiracy was successfully put down within hours. Seven months later, at its first congress, the MPLA declared itself Marxist-Leninist and adopted the name of MPLA-Labor Party. In 1978, closer political and economic links were established with the countries of the socialist Council for Mutual Economic Assistance.

[15] The country's first president, Agostinho Neto, died of cancer in Moscow on September 10 1979 and was succeeded by Planning Minister José Eduardo dos Santos.

[16] In August 1981, South Africa launched "Operation Smokeshell", in which 15,000 soldiers, with tanks

and air support, advanced 200 kilometers into Cunene province. Pretoria justified this aggression as an operation against guerrilla bases belonging to the Namibian liberation movement, the South West African Peoples Organization (SWAPO). The undeclared aim seems to have been to establish a "liberated zone" where UNITA could install a parallel government inside Angolan territory capable of obtaining some degree of international recognition.

[17] This incursion and successive attacks in the years that followed were contained by effective Angolan and Cuban military resistance. The cost of the war, plus international pressure and the mounting anti-apartheid campaign at home, obliged South Africans to resume diplomatic discussions with the MPLA government. In December 1988, Angola, South Africa and Cuba signed a Tripartite Accord in New York which put an end to the war between Luanda

African Cultures

U ntil a comparatively short time ago, Europeans knew little about Africa. Scholars of the 15th century summed up their knowledge of that continent writing on the maps "Ibi sunt leones" (Here there are lions). The 19th century philosopher Hegel, described blacks as a childish race, and Africa as "the unhistorical spirit, the non-developed spirit, still submerged in the conditions of the natural... situated on the threshold of the history of the world".

[2] Such notions corresponded with a lack of knowledge about the continent, and the subordination of its peoples to subjugation and slavery. But decolonization in the second half of the 20th century opened a period in which African peoples were confronted with the complex tasks of social and cultural change and development. Part of it consists of a reassessment and a revaluing of the African past. "The history of Africa," Ki Zerbo has said, "is the history of the awakening of its consciousness."

[3] The knowledge that the West has accumulated about Africa is littered with myths. Among them, the myth of the impossibility of a scientific history, or the myth of the inaccessibility of its past, or the myth of the absence of written testimonies and writing itself, or the myth of the stagnation of the black peoples - which reduced historical interest about Africa to its connections with the Mediterranean world and to isolated subjects, such as Egypt, the Maghreb, or Christian Ethiopia.

[4] If these myths are not overturned, the true history of Africa cannot be born. The task involves the double operation of deconstructing traditional African history - written under the light of the prejudices of a domineering Eurocentric perspective - and of critically investigating an ample and ignored past.

[5] In any case, the object of study should not be to wonder about the fate of Africa if colonialism had not existed, but to consider its autonomous contribution to the history of human culture and its promise for the future.

[6] Charles Darwin wrote: "It is likely that our first fathers had lived in Africa more than anywhere else." This intuition is apparently being confirmed by contemporary science. Present research supports the view that conditions favourable for the essential phases in the evolution to the human form existed. Africa supposedly holds the most complete spectrum of prehistorical human remains.

[7] Archaeological discoveries indicate the pre-eminence of African prehistory over the prehistory of other civilizations. Advanced techniques of tool-making - quarries and workshops, manufacture of double-edged axes, the use of stones as heat accumulators, and pottery making - became differentiated as they extended over wider geographical areas, but "the initiative, the great tradition, and the 'fashion' came from Africa".

[8] The Neolithic era began in Africa three thousand years earlier than in Europe. Not in Egypt as has been supposed, but in the Sahara, which was then an attractive area with wide rivers and abundant vegetation. The exchange of techniques between different communities made possible diversified agricultural activities. Corn, barley, sorghum, millet, palms, textile plants and so on, were cultivated. There were modest improvements in cattle-breeding. These practices evolved in an autonomous and parallel way to those of other Asian and Indo-American peoples.

[9] Neolithic African peoples of the Sahara created one of the first technical revolutions through their agricultural

Before Colonization

practices. This allowed them to lead stable lives and to carry on technical and cultural exchanges with peoples from other areas. The development came from the south upwards through the communities living in the Sahara and then reached the north of Africa. The civilization which flourished later in the Nile valley cannot be accounted for solely as a result of the changes that were made possible there because of the extraordinary fertility of the land, and the population pressure which finally led to the desertification of the Sahara. The cultural riches created and transmitted by the black peoples of the South were also a factor in this process. The Egyptians recognized that those peoples shared their ancestry.

[10] The Egyptians organized an agricultural civilization with artisanal skills and a consistent governing and military structure which triumphed over the neighbouring populations, among them the kingdoms of Nubia. They developed commercial relations along the river, and exported towards the south bronze manufactures and other products. They also invented their own writing. They drew hieroglyphs on papyrus, which evolved and became partly alphabetical.

[11] Women had a significant role in Egyptian civilization. The mother figure was foremost in their culture. There was also a female clergy. Landed property was inherited by women, and a dowry was given to the parents of the wife. Their imposing works of art had a profound religious inspiration. Their world-view did not underline the value of progress but rather of equilibrium and peace in opposition to the forces of decay and chaos.

[12] In the centuries immediately before and after the first century AD, migration and mingling took place among the peoples established south of the Sahara. Several languages were born then, and achievements include an indigenous iron culture which had a revolutionary impact. Iron was abundant in the region. The making of iron tools augmented the productive abilities and the military capabilities of those peoples, and allowed their expansion and their subjugation of less advanced groups. Ironsmiths and craftspeople gained the uppermost positions in these societies. This is the origin of a tradition which recognizes the king-smiths as the African ancestors. From the point of view of social organization, this era represents the passage from clan organization to the formation of kingdoms.

[13] Between the 7th and the 12th Centuries the majority of the bigger African kingdoms were founded. The Arab-Muslim conquest of North Africa began in the 7th Century. From then on commerce through the Sahara became easier, as did commerce from the coasts towards the kingdoms of sub-Saharan Africa. The Arabs acted as intermediaries.

[14] The empires of Ghana and Awdaghost to the west, and those of Nubia and Aksum to the north-east dominated several other kingdoms and won territories rich in gold mines. Thanks to the commerce in gold and slaves, they acquired considerable economic power. They created cities as market centres for agricultural products and cattle. Courts headed by black kings admitted civilian councils which, more frequently than not, included Muslim ministers, because of their technical competence. Powerful armies were organized for campaigns of expansion which led either to success, or the decline of those kingdoms.

[15] Today it is recognized that the period between the 12th and the 16th centuries were the "great centuries" of Black Africa. African countries reached well-balanced positions, were socio-politically well integrated and developed strong economies. The strongest were the empires of Mali, which at the time of Mahmud Ali had 400 cities in what is now west Sudan; the states of Hausa, Yoruba and Benin, respectively towards the south-east and the south-west of Nigeria; the Bantu Kingdom and the Kongo in Central Africa; and the Zimbabwe and Monomotapa in the South.

[16] These empires derived revenue from taxes on harvests and cattle, from tributes, customs houses, gold nuggets (which were by law the property of the government), and war booty. They integrated politically different peoples through a government compounded of high officers whose competence was either functional - such as the ministers - or territorial - the chiefs who controlled the provinces - and whose mandates were revocable, not hereditary. Almost all of them had professional armies. Their lands were worked by peasants, compelled to pay a tribute, and by slaves. There was a distinction between war slaves and house slaves, who respectively served in the court and in households, and who had certain civil rights, and were eligible for eventual emancipation. But in some communities and ethnic groups, such as those of Equatorial Africa, there were no slaves.

[17] Sometimes, as in Timbuktu, cities had centres of religious studies which evolved into universities of sorts. The empires fostered art and architecture, such as the prodigious buildings of Great Zimbabwe, which were heard about in Europe through reports by the Portuguese colonists.

[18] From the 16th century onwards the independent life of the African empires began to be eroded. The Muslim states were not happy with being mere intermediaries anymore, and they launched expansionist policies which demolished the inner empires. In this they were gradually replaced by the Europeans who, after initial exploration, organized slave traffic in order to satisfy the needs of the New World for cheap manual labour. The slave trade was organized from coastal stations and involved a total of some 10-15 million slaves. Some African kings and leaders collaborated.

[19] The economic involvement of Europe was not limited to the slave trade. An economy based on the export of grain was developed, but it did not include, at least at the beginning, direct political control, or the loss of sovereignty on the part of the African states.

[20] These decisive historical changes entrenched a situation of general dependency and contributed to the later underdevelopment of Africa. In the 20 years between 1890 and 1910, the European powers conquered, occupied and finally subjugated a continent whose territory (or rather 80 per cent of it) had been previously governed by autonomous leaders. Most of them resisted this imposition in order to defend their sovereignty and independence, their religions, and their traditional lifestyles.

[21] Despite this resistance, colonization destroyed the social and cultural balance of subjugated countries and established relationships of dependence. European capital and a world economy robbed African peoples of their resources through mining firms, commercial and financial institutions, compelling them to work for European development.

[22] However, these cultures did not disappear. Today, African traditions have not only helped to shape the culture of the European countries which once subjugated them, but also have seen a renaissance in their own native soil over the last years.

PER 100,000 LIVE BIRTHS
1,500

42%

1994
15%

PER CAPITA
$949

STATISTICS

DEMOGRAPHY
Population: 11,185,000 (1996). **Annual growth**: 2.9% (1980/1996). **Estimates for year 2000**: 12,800,000. Annual growth to year 2000: 3.4% (1994/2000). **Urban Population**: 31.6% (1996). **Urban growth**: 5.87% (1980/95). Children per woman: 6.8 (1996).

HEALTH
Life expectancy at birth: 47 years (1996) **Infant mortality**: 170 per 1,000 (1996). **Under-5 child mortality**: 292 per 1,000 (1996). **Calorie Consumption**: 80% (1988/90). 25,000 **people per doctor** (1988/91). **Safe water**: 32% (1990/96).

EDUCATION
Literacy: 42% (1995) male : 56% (1995) female: 29% (1995). **School enrolment** : Primary total: 88% (1990/95) male : 95% (1990/95) female: 87% (1990/95). Tertiary: 1% (1995).

COMMUNICATIONS
10 **newspapers**, 30 **radios** and 30 **TV sets** per 1,000 people.

ECONOMY
Per capita, GNP: $ 270 (1996). **Annual growth, GNP**: -1.7% (1995/96). **Annual inflation**: 169.46% (1985/95). **Consumer price index**: 61,981.8 (1994). **Currency**: new kwanzas = $ 1 (1995). **Cereal imports**: 475 metric tons (1994). **Food import dependency**: 15% (1994). **Fertilizer use**: 28 kgs per ha (1994). **Exports**: $ 4,472 million (1996). **Imports**: $ 2,039 million (1996). **External debt**: $ 10,612 million (1996). $ 949 **per capita**: (1996). **Debt service**: 13.3% of exports (1996). **Development aid received**: $ 423 million (1995). $ 40 per capita (1995).

ENERGY
Consumption: 89.10 Kgs of Oil equivalent per capita yearly (1994). -2,576.04% imported (1994).

HDI (rank / value) 157 / 0.335 (1994).

and Pretoria, and provided for the independence of Namibia and withdrawal of South African and Cuban troops from Angola.

[18] In June 1989, UNITA signed a truce in the presence of 20 African heads of state at Gbadolite, Zaire. However, the ceasefire was broken barely two months later. At the end of April 1990, Angolan authorities announced in Lisbon, Portugal, that direct negotiations with UNITA would be resumed to achieve a lasting ceasefire. A month later, UNITA leader Jonas Savimbi officially recognized José Eduardo dos Santos as head of state.

[19] At the end of 1990, the MPLA announced the introduction of reforms geared towards democratic socialism. On May 11 1991, a law on political parties was published, which brought one-party rule (under the MPLA) to an end. In addition, the law banned political participation by active members of the armed forces, the police or the judiciary. On May 23, the last Cubans left Angola. After 16 years of civil war, a peace settlement was signed on May 31 by the Angolan Government and UNITA, in Estoril, Portugal. This agreement included an immediate cease-fire, as well as a promise to hold democratic elections in 1992 and the creation of a Joint Politico-Military Commission (CCPM), charged with establishing a national army made up of soldiers from both opposition groups. The governments of Portugal, the United States and the Soviet Union were involved in the discussion and drawing up of the agreement, as was the United Nations, which was put in charge of supervising compliance with the terms of the peace agreement.

[20] Holden Roberto, leader of the National Front for the Liberation of Angola (FNLA) and Jonas Savimbi, president of UNITA, returned to Luanda in August and September 1991 respectively - after 15 years of exile - to launch their election campaigns. The United States continued to support UNITA, and as a result tensions increased as the 1992 elections drew near.

[21] The changes of the nineties went far beyond the agreements on a political and diplomatic level and were reflected in the mobilisation and transformation of the Angolan society. The Organisation of Angolan Women (OMA), founded in 1961, separated from the MPLA to become a non governmental organisation (NGO). In its first Congress, in August 1991, the OMA established a common platform between church groups, intellectuals and professional associations.

[22] Plagued by a foreign debt of more than six billion dollars, the government appealed to the international community for economic aid. The United States refused to suspend the economic and diplomatic blockade, alleging that Angola was a Marxist nation and announcing it would not grant diplomatic recognition until after the 1992. Consequently, the US companies in Angola were unable to get loans from banks in their own country.

[23] Following intense negotiations between the government and UNITA, elections were set for September 1992. The governing MPLA took nearly 50 per cent of the vote, to UNITAs 40 per cent. Savimbi refused to recognize defeat and ordered hostilities to start up again. In their advance, the UNITA troops occupied the diamond mines of the interior, leaving the government with oil as the only stable source of income (between 1.6 and 1.7 billion dollars per year).

[24] In November 1993, peace talks were re-started in Lusaka, the capital of Zambia. A year later - November 1994 - a peace agreement was signed. The main points - a cease-fire and constitutional changes so that Savimbi could become vice president - were not put into practice until late 1995 and the fighting continued.

[25] Some progress was seen during 1996. In May, an amnesty law was approved and UNITA troops started to be absorbed by the armed forces. Savimbi withdrew most of his troops to barracks and handed over some of the weapons. The civil war caused the most serious social and economic crisis in Angolan history. The adoption of IMF and World Bank set of economic liberalization measures did not produce the desired results.

[26] In April 1997, harsh negotiations ended with UNITA accepting to join the government on executive, legislative and military levels. Even though its position in the capital was weak, Savimbi's troops still controlled 40 per cent of the territory. The fall of Mobuto Sese Seko in Zaire (now DR Congo), in May, weakened UNITA even further, and they were forced to abandon areas of the northern frontier. The Angolans wanted to avoid the infiltration of Mobutus troops formerly allied to Savimbi - into their territory fleeing from the government of Laurent Kabila - a former ally of dos Santos.

[27] In March 1998, thousands of demobilised soldiers mostly with little or no education encountered serious difficulties in returning to their home villages, given the scarce employment possibilities in the small rural villages and the slow arrival of economic aid. Since 1994, only 300,000 of the 4.5 million people uprooted by the civil war had been able to resettle according to the United Nations figures. The presence of large numbers of land mines, spread across the entire territory increased the insecurity of the population.

[28] Despite the agreement, the skirmishes continued. The United Nations, and even Washington, his old ally, pressured Savimbi to fulfil the agreements and abandon hostilities. Certain UNITA members - particularly those who had gained government posts- tended to be in favour of lasting peace. Savimbi's group had four ministers, seven deputy-ministers, and 77 representatives in the Peoples Assembly. Meanwhile, it was estimated an rebel uprising, with official armed forces better equipped than a few years ago, meant little possibility of the UNITA leader winning.

Anguilla

Anguilla

Population: 8,000 (1996)
Area: 96 SQ KM
Capital: The Valley

Currency: E.C. dollars
Language: English

A nguilla is the most northerly of the Leeward Islands. Its small size, barely 96 sq km including the neighboring Sombrero Island, and the lack of fresh water for agriculture, made the island unattractive to the British Empire. From 1816 to 1871 Anguilla, St Kitts-Nevis and the Virgin Islands were administered together as one colony. The Virgin Islands were split off in 1871, leaving the others as a colonial unit ruled from St Kitts.

[2] Colonialism lasted until the group became one of the five Caribbean "States in Association with the United Kingdom". Anguillans opposed the agreement and rebelled against the St Kitts government. Under the leadership of local entrepreneur Ronald Webster, Anguilla demanded a separate constitution. In March 1969, British troops disembarked on the island to supervise the installation of its colonial Commissioner, but the separatist movement continued its struggle.

[3] In 1976 a new constitution was approved by Britain, establishing a parliamentary system of government under the patronage of the British Commissioner. But it was not until 1980 that Anguilla was able to formally withdraw from the Associated State arrangement with St Kitts-Nevis, gaining the status of "British Dependent Territory".

[4] The 1976 constitution provided for a governor appointed by the British Crown, responsible for defence, foreign relations, internal security (including the police), utilities, justice and the public audit. The Governor presides over the Executive Council.

[5] The first legislative elections held in March 1976 voted in the Anguilla United Party leader, Ronald Webster, as Chief Minister. A year later he failed to win a vote of confidence and was replaced by opposition leader Emile Gumbs. In the 1980 general elections, the United Party of Anguilla, led by Webster, won by a landslide majority, obtaining six out of the seven seats. A year later, the Government suffered internal divisions and Webster created the Popular Party of Anguilla (PPA). In the elections of June 1981, he won 5 seats, while the remaining 2 went to the Anguilla National Alliance (ANA), led by Emile Gumbs.

[6] In September, the Constitution was changed leading to home rule on internal matters.

[7] On March 9 1984 in accordance with the new constitution of 1982 requiring a parliamentary government, elections were held and Emile Gumbs became Chief Minister once more. The ANA received 53.8 per cent of the vote.

[8] The new ANA government requested greater power for the Executive Council and an increase in British investment in the island's economic infrastructure. After the Council called for constitutional changes, particularly with reference to the situation of women and people born outside the island who had relatives there, the Governor appointed a Committee to review the Constitution.

[9] Through the 1980s the building industry for tourism reduced unemployment from 26 per cent to 1 per cent, but at the beginning of the 1990s this trend stopped and the US recession brought a reduction of tourists.

[10] In 1991 Prime Minister Gumbs tried to bring about closer cooperation between the British possessions and the Organization of East Caribbean States.

[11] The income generated by cattle-breeding, salt production, lobster fishing, boat building and the money sent by nationals working abroad (located mainly in the US), lost its former predominant role to the profit made by the building industry, tourism, and financial offshore services. In 1992 legislation gave then Governor Alan W Shave the task of granting permits to foreign firms, in an effort to control them more tightly.

[12] In March 1994, the legislative elections were won by Hubert Hughes, of the United Party of Anguilla. In November, the new legislative assembly proclaimed a law regulating the activities of transnational companies. In 1995, the economy suffered with Hurricane Luis. Throughout 1997 and part of 1998, there was an average annual growth of 7 per cent as a result of increased tourism from the United States and Britain.

Map

Atlantic Ocean 20
DOMINICAN REPUBLIC
PUERTO RICO
VIRGIN IS.
ANGUILLA
NETHERLANDS ANTILLES
ST. KITTS
NEVIS
ANTIGUA 16
MONTSERRAT
GUADELOUPE
DOMINICA
MARTINIQUE
ST LUCIA
ST VINCENT
BARBADOS 12
GRENADA
TRINIDAD AND TOBAGO 60
Sombrero
0   20 km
Caribbean Sea
Prickly Pear Cays
Scrub Island
The Valley ANGUILLA
Blowing Point
0   300 km

PROFILE

ENVIRONMENT

Anguilla covers 91 sq km and 5 sq km on its dependency, the island of Sombrero. They are part of the Leeward Islands of the Lesser Antilles. The climate is tropical with heavy rainfall. There are considerable salt deposits on the island.

SOCIETY

Peoples: Most inhabitants are descendants of African slaves integrated with European settlers. There is a British minority. Many Anguillans live permanently in the Virgin Islands or other US possessions.
Religions: Anglican 40 per cent; Methodist 33 per cent; Adventist 7 per cent; Baptist 5 per cent; Roman Catholic 3 per cent. Other 12 per cent.
Languages: English (official).
Political Parties: The Anguillan National Alliance; The Anguilla United Party; The Democratic Party of Anguilla.

THE STATE

Official Name: Anguilla.
Capital: The Valley, 1,042 people (1984).
Government: Hubert Hughes, Chief Minister, elected in March 1994. Robert Harris, Governor-General appointed by the British Crown in 1997. The single chamber Legislative Assembly has 11 members, 7 of them elected by direct vote.

DEMOGRAPHY

Population: 8,000 (1996)
Urban population: 11.2% (1996)

COMMUNICATIONS

308 **main telephone lines** per 1,000 people (1994)

LAND USE

DEFORESTATION -0.7 % annual (81/90)
IRRIGATED 2.5 % of arable

(1993)

■ FOREST & WOODLAND	11.4%
□ ARABLE	18.2%
▨ OTHER	70.4%

Antigua

Antigua and Barbuda

Population: 66,000 (1996)
Area: 422 SQ KM
Capital: St Johns

Currency: E.C. dollars
Language: English

The Caribs inhabited most of the islands in the sea which took their name, but abandoned many of them, including Antigua, in the 16th century due to the lack of fresh water.

[2] In 1493 the name Antigua was given to one of the Antilles by Christopher Columbus in honor of a church in Seville. Other Europeans settled later (the Spanish in 1520, the French in 1629) but again left because of the scarcity of water. However, a few English were able to settle by using appropriate techniques to store rainwater.

[3] By 1640, the number of English families on the island had increased to 30. The few indians who dared to stay were eventually murdered by the settlers, who imported African slaves to work the tobacco plantations and later sugar plantations.

[4] In 1666, the French governor of Martinique invaded the island, kidnapping all the African slaves. When England regained control in 1676, a rich colonist from Barbados, Colonel Codrington, acquired large quantities of land and brought new African slaves. Thus sugar production was reinstated on the island.

[5] Slavery was abolished in the British colonies in 1838. The workers' situation did not noticeably change and quasi-slavery continued for several decades, until the early 20th century when trade unions began to appear.

[6] The first trade union, led by Vere Bird, was formed on January 16 1939. The Antigua Labor Party (ALP), the first political party, originated within a trade union. It was also led by Vere Bird.

[7] In the elections of April 1960, Bird's party won and he became Prime Minister. In 1966, a new constitution introduced self-government with a Parliament elected by Antiguans and Barbudans. Britain remained responsible for defence and foreign relations. Bird was again successful in the 1967 elections.

[8] In 1979, opposition leader George Walter charged the Government with human rights abuses, citing brutal repression of a teachers' strike as an example, and claimed repression could only become worse with independence.

[9] On November 1 1981, Antigua and Barbuda became independent as a "sovereign, democratic and united state" and were admitted into the United Nations and the Caribbean Community (Caricom). Independence also gave the islands the right to become indebted to the IMF and the World Bank. The foreign debt grew dramatically and reached almost half of the GDP by the end of that year.

[10] In foreign affairs the Prime Minister maintained close relations with the US, who used part of the island's territory for military purposes and pay an annual rent. The alliance with the US was further consolidated in 1983, when Antigua participated in the American invasion of Grenada. Parliamentary elections were held in April 1984, and despite accusations during the electoral campaign, Bird was re-elected. His victory was attributed to approval of his stance on the Grenada issue.

[11] In 1987 opposition leaders demanded the Prime Minister's resignation, citing as one of the reasons the misappropriation of funds in the St Johns Airport modernization project.

[12] In 1994, Vere Bird retired from public life and his son Lester replaced him at the head of ALP. In the March elections, Labour lost 4 seats but retained an absolute majority at the Chamber of Representatives, with 11 seats out of 17.

[13] In September 1995, Hurricane Luis caused losses which amounted to $300 million, damaging 60 per cent of the country's buildings, whether partially or completely, including several main hotels, seriously affecting the country's tourism infrastructure.

[14] The catastrophic situation led the Government to apply an economic austerity programme in 1996, including severe spending cuts. Civil servants pay was frozen for two years and government ministers lost 10 per cent of their income. The Government tried to raise money by privatizing some State assets.

[15] That year the Government in Barbuda was taken over by the so-called People's Movement which took five seats in the local Council.

[16] In February 1997, the Government closed four banks, when irregularities were found in their accounts.

PROFILE

ENVIRONMENT

The islands - Antigua with 280 sq km and its dependencies Barbuda with 160 sq km and Redonda with 2 sq km - belong to the Leeward group of the Lesser Antilles. Antigua is endowed with beautiful coral reefs and large dunes. Its wide bays distinguish it from the rest of the Caribbean because they provide safe havens. Barbuda is a coral island with a large lagoon on the west side. It consists of a small volcano joined to a calcareous plain. Redonda is a small uninhabited rocky island, and is now a flora and fauna reserve. Sugar cane and cotton are grown along with tropical fruits; sea foods are exported. The reduction of habitats due to the reforestation of native forests with imported species is the main environmental problem of most of the Caribbean islands.

SOCIETY

Peoples: The majority of Antiguans and Barbudans are of African origin (91.3 per cent); Europeans (2.4 per cent); Mestizo (3.7 per cent); Syrian-Lebanese (0.6 per cent); Indo-Pakistanis (0.4 per cent). Other (1.3 per cent). **Religions:** Protestants 73.7 per cent (Anglicans 32.1 per cent, Moravians 12 per cent; Methodists 9.1 per cent; Adventists of the Seventh Day 8.8 per cent; Cahtolics 10.8 per cent; Witnesses of Jehova 1.2 per cent). Rastafarians 0.8 per cent. **Languages:** English is the official language, but in daily life a local Patois dialect is spoken. **Political Parties:** The Antigua Labour Party (ALP). The Antigua Caribbean Liberation Movement (ACLM). The United National Democratic Party (UNDP). The United Progressive Party (UPP). **Social Organizations:** The labor movement is divided into two groups: the Antigua Workers' Union, linked to the UNDP, and the Antigua Trades and Labour Union, with ALP leadership.

THE STATE

Official Name: Associated State of Antigua and Barbuda. **Capital:** St Johns, 21,500 people (1987). **Other cities:** Parham, Liberta. **Government:** James Carlisle, Governor-General, representative of Queen Elizabeth II, who is formally the Head of State; Prime Minister, Lester Bird, since March, 1994. The British-style bicameral legislature is composed of a 17-member Senate appointed by the Governor-General and a 17-member House of Representatives elected by universal suffrage for a 5-year term. **National Holiday:** November 1, Independence Day (1981).

HEALTH

Life expectancy at birth: 75 years (1996) **Infant mortality:** 18 per 1,000 (1996) **Under-5 child mortality:** 22 per 1,000 (1996)

EDUCATION

Literacy: 95% (1995) **School enrolment:** Primary total: 100% (1990/95)

Aotearoa/New Zealand

Aotearoa/New Zealand

Population: 3,602,000 (1996)
Area: 270,534 SQ KM
Capital: Wellington

Currency: NZ dollars
Language: English and Maori

Aotearoa, "the land of the long white cloud", was settled around the 9th century by Maori, who arrived there from Polynesia. Over the years a distinct culture developed, based on tribal organisation and a strong affinity with the land. Maori appointed themselves as guardians of the land for future generations.

[2] In 1642 Abel Tasman, from Holland, reached the South Island, the larger of Aotearoa's two main islands. However, the resistance of the indigenous population prevented him from going ashore. It was not until 1769 that James Cook, an Englishman, surveyed the shores of the two most important islands, thus opening the door for a growing colonization of the country which Abel Tasman had named "New Zealand". Whalers, sealers and traders, along with a few deserters from the navy and fugitives from Australian jails, established themselves on the islands.

[3] In the early 19th century, colonization increased with the arrival of British immigrants and missionaries. They brought with them new diseases, values, and beliefs, which affected the traditional Maori way of life. Christianity weakened the traditions which gave substance and cohesion to the tribal society, and the introduction of commercial practices by the Europeans seriously damaged the material basis of Maori lifestyle.

[4] In 1840 the territory of New Zealand was formally annexed by the British crown as a colony. The two larger islands were occupied under different legal arrangements: the South Island was incorporated by virtue of the right of "discovery", and the North Island through the Treaty of Waitangi, signed in 1840 by Maori chiefs and representatives of the British Government. According to the text of the treaty - which is somewhat confusing and different in its English and Maori versions - Maori chiefs accepted the presence of British settlers and the establishment of a government by the Crown to rule the settlers. In exchange, Maori were assured absolute respect of their national sovereignty.

[5] However, 20 years after the signing of the Treaty an extremely violent process of expropriation of Maori lands began. The so-called "land wars" between Maori and the Europeans were essentially for sovereignty and guaranteed rights to the lands, forests, fisheries and other taonga (treasures).

[6] Massive immigration, land confiscation and legal decisions led to the gradual annexation of Maori land. The magnitude of their loss becomes clearer if one considers that, out of the 27 million hectares they owned in 1840, they now have a little over a million left.

[7] While the north of the

country was involved in a series of wars, the South Island settlers went through a period of prosperity because of the discovery of gold. This discovery brought a massive flow of British, Chinese and Australian immigrants, which energized the region's economy.

[8] After 1840 colonization increased. The Pakeha (non-Maori) assumed the right to fish in the area, thus depriving the Maori of one of their main activities.

[9] Maori opposition to Pakeha colonization found new expression by the end of the 19th

---

PROFILE

ENVIRONMENT
Aotearoa is situated in Oceania. Its two principal islands are relatively mountainous. The North Island is volcanic and has plateaus and geysers. The South Island is crossed by the Southern Alps, a mountain chain with peaks of over 3,000 metres. The climate is moderately rainy, with temperatures cooler in the south. The native rainforests have been devastated by early colonization, replaced by agricultural land and pastures. The economic base of the country is agricultural, with advanced techniques being used in pastoral and agricultural by-products. Tourism is becoming increasingly important.

SOCIETY
Peoples: Much of the population is descended from European settlers. 12.9 per cent are Maori (a figure rapidly increasing), and 3.5 per cent are from Pacific Islands descent.
Religions: Anglican and other Protestant denominations dominate. There are also Catholic and various Maori church minorities.
Languages: English and Maori are the official languages, with English dominant.
Political Parties: A multi-party system in change due to the adoption of a proportional representation voting system. The major parties are National Party, Labour Party, New Zealand First, ACT and the Alliance Party.
Social Organizations: The Trade Union Federation and the Council of Trade Unions.

THE STATE
Official Name: Aotearoa (Maori); New Zealand (English).
Administrative divisions: Divided into 15 town and 58 district authorities.
Capital: Wellington, 336,858 people (1996).
Other cities: Auckland, 967,404 people; Christchurch, 336,858; Dunedin 118,143; Hamilton, 108,426; Palmerston North 73,095; Timaru 42,630; Nelson 40,242 (1996).
Government: A parliamentary monarchy and member of the British Commonwealth. Governor-General: Michael Hardie Boys. Prime Minister: Jenny Shipley and Head of Government (since December 1997). Aotearoa has a parliamentary system, with a unicameral legislative body of 120 members. The elected members of the Government form a cabinet chaired by the Prime Minister.
On occasions this cabinet acts as the Executive Council presided over by the Governor-General. The Governor-General appoints cabinet on the recommendations of the Prime Minister, and has the power to dissolve Parliament.
National holiday: February 6, Waitangi Day.
Armed Forces: 9,611 (1996).

DEMOGRAPHY

Population: 3,602,000 (1996). **Annual growth:** 0.9 % (1980/
1996). **Estimates for year 2000:** 4,000,000. **Annual growth to
year 2000:** 1.1 % (1994/2000). **Urban Population:** 86.1 % (1996).
Urban growth: 1 % (1980/95). **Children per woman:** 2.1 (1996).

HEALTH

Life expectancy at birth: 77 years (1996) male: 74 years (1994)
female: 79 years (1994). **Infant mortality:** 7 per 1,000 (1996).
Under-5 child mortality: 7 per 1,000 (1996). **Calorie
consumption:** 131 % (1988/90). 521 **people per doctor** (1988/
91). **Safe water:** 97 % (1990/96).

EDUCATION

School enrolment : Primary total: 102 % (1990/95) male : 103%
(1990/95) female: 101% (1990/95). Secondary: male : 111% (1990/
95) female: 114% (1990/95). Tertiary: 58% (1995). **Primary school
teachers:** one for every 18 students (1995).

COMMUNICATIONS

300 **newspapers,** 991 **radios,** 510 **TV sets** and 468 **main
telephone lines** per 1,000 people (1994).

ECONOMY

Per capita, GNP: $ 15,720 (1996). **Annual growth, GNP:**
-0.6 % (1995/96). **Annual inflation:** 3.87 % (1985/95). **Consumer
price index:** 106.8 (1994). **Currency:** 1.53 NZ dollars = $ 1 (1995).
Cereal imports: 316 metric tons (1994). **Food import
dependency:** % (1994). **Fertilizer use:** 1,607 kgs per ha (1994).
Exports: $ 13,789 million (1996). **Imports:** $ 14,716 million
(1996).

ENERGY

Consumption: 4,245.07 Kgs of Oil equivalent per capita yearly
(1994). 14.86 % imported (1994).

HDI (rank / value) 9 / 0.937 (1994)

Cook Islands

Cook Islands

Population: 19,000 (1996)
Area: 236 SQ KM
Capital: Avarua
Currency: NZ Dollar
Language: English

The islands, which had already been explored and settled by Polynesians and Spaniards, received their name from the English navigator Captain James Cook, who drew up the first map of the archipelago in 1770.

[2] In 1821, Tahitian missionaries were sent to the islands by the London Missionary Society; a Protestant theocracy was established and all "pagan" structures were destroyed, as were many of the traditional forms of social organization. The islands were declared a British Protectorate in 1888 and became part of Aotearoa/New Zealand in 1901. The land rights of the native Maori were recognized, and the sale of real estate to foreigners was prohibited. In 1965, the United Nations promoted and supervised a plebiscite, and the population voted against independence, and in favour of maintaining its ties to Aotearoa.

[3] Prime Minister Geoffrey Henry governed the country with an iron hand for 15 years before being replaced in 1978 by Thomas Davis, of the Democratic Party, who gave incentives to private fruit planters. However he was dismissed from office by Parliament in 1987, being replaced by Pupuke Robati, also of the DP. In the 1990 elections, Geoffrey Henry's Cook Islands Party was returned to office, and re-elected in 1994.

[4] From 1991 on, when Aotearoa's economic injections to the Cook Islands fell to 17 per cent of the local budget, both governments decided the auditors' in the Cook Islands would take charge of the State finances in place of the Aotearoa office.

[5] The public debt stood at around $900 million as the second half of the 1990s began. Prime Minister, Geoffrey Henry announced a series of drastic measures including a 50 per cent reduction in State

employees, a 15 per cent pay reduction for the remaining personnel and a privatization plan. In late 1997, some ministries were closed due to the lack of funds and the budget of the remaining entities was reduced by 10 per cent.

ENVIRONMENT:

Area: 236.6 sq km
Archipelago located in the South Pacific 2,700 km northeast of Aotearoa/New Zealand, made up of 15 islands which extend over an ocean area of 2 million sq km They are divided into 2 groups. The northern group is made up of 6 small coral atolls, which are low and arid, with a total area of 25.5 sq km. The southern group comprises 8 larger and more fertile volcanic islands (211 sq km). The capital, Avarua, is located on Rarotonga, the largest of the islands. Every 5 years, for the past 2 decades, the islands have suffered terrible droughts.

SOCIETY

Peoples: The people of Cook Islands are of Polynesian origin.
Religions: Christian.
Languages: English (official), Cook Island Maori. Language and traditions similar to Maori in Aotearoa/New Zealand.
Political Parties: The Cook Islands Party (CIP); the Democratic Party (DP), the main opposition force; the Tumu Democratic Party; the Alliance Party.

THE STATE

Official Name: The Cook Islands.
Capital: Avarua.
Government: Autonomous associated state. Tim Caughley, Representative of Aotearoa. Geoffrey Henry, Prime Minister since January 1990. Single-chamber legislature; there is a Legislative Assembly, with 25 members elected by direct vote every five years.

---

century. They organized petitions, delegations and submitted their claims before local courts and even before the British Crown itself, demanding compliance with the Treaty of Waitangi. These efforts were fruitless. The lands that had once belonged to Maori were now used for farming, which had started to play a central role not only in the life of the settlers but also in the whole economy. New markets for dairy and meat products opened up in the 1880s, with the appearance of cold-storage systems which made long-distance shipping possible. These products constituted the basis of the country's economic development.

[10] For Maori, British rule also meant the beginning of a process of cultural assimilation, through the imposition of European language, religion, and customs. Thus, Maori language which was in theory protected by the Treaty of Waitangi, was given less and less importance.

[11] By the end of the century, the country's political scene was dominated by the Liberal government. They were the first in the world to grant the vote to women (1893) and to establish measures to protect the rights of industrial workers, a group which was growing parallel to the

development of cities and manufacturing industries.

[12] In the 20th century new political movements appeared to oppose the power of the Liberals who had become a coherent, organized political party after 20 years in power. The Labour Party, with ample working-class and urban middle-class support, became one of the country's main political forces.

[13] During the 1930s, Maori demands acquired new strength thanks to an alliance between the groups representing Maori interests and the Labour Party, which came to power for the first time in 1935 with Maori support. But there was still no legislative recognition of the Treaty of Waitangi.

[14] World War II marked the beginning of a new era for the country. During the War Britain's inability to guarantee the security of its former colony led to closer ties between Aotearoa/New Zealand and the US. Through a series of political and military alliances, US presence was consolidated in the region. In the 1950s and 1960s Aotearoa had to pay the price for this relationship, particularly when it found itself involved in the Vietnam War, a conflict which touched the political life of the country very deeply.

Niue

Niue

Population : 2,000 (1996)
Area: 260 SQ KM
Capital: Alofi
Currency: NZ dollars
Language: English

[15] Legislation in the 1950s forced many Maori from their land and the 1960s saw their increasing urbanization. This brought them into greater contact with the Pakeha lifestyle and institutions, and Maori gained better access to the Pakeha education system.

[16] In the 1970s, Aotearoa attempted, with limited success, to diversify its production and gain access to markets other than Britain and the US. Unemployment rose and inflation reached unprecedented levels due to the failure of the diversification scheme, the rise in the price of oil and massive external loans to finance "think big" projects. 1975 saw a drastic fall in the purchasing power earned from primary exports. This fall, combined with the foreign loans, provoked a period of rising foreign debt. After 12 years in opposition, the Labour Party held power from 1972 until it was defeated by the conservative National Party in the 1975 elections. The new government closed the doors on Pacific immigrants, whom it blamed for increasing unemployment

[17] In 1975, growing Maori activism led to the formation of the Waitangi Tribunal to investigate Treaty claims. In 1986 the Labour government gave it the power to hear claims dating back to the 1840 signing. The Tribunal had no binding powers over the Crown, so that settlement of claims for compensation was slow.

[18] In the mid-1980s, the Labour Party regained office, and introduced a monetarist economic policy which included privatization of a number of public enterprises. These policies alienated many traditional Labour supporters.

[19] A 1987 law prohibited the entry of nuclear arms or vessels to the nation's ports, thus questioning the military presence of France and the United States, which used the South Pacific as a nuclear weapons testing ground. This decision eliminated the defence treaties between the US and Aotearoa/New Zealand.

[20] The National Party won the October 1990 elections, but the change in the governing team did not change the economic model of the country. There was an increase in privatizations, protectionism was dismantled even further, and there were large cut-backs in funding for health, education and contributions to social benefits. The result was falling inflation, but unemployment also rose.

[21] The reduced popularity of the Government was not reflected in the electoral results of 1993, when the National Party (NP) took 50 of the 99 seats in parliament and Jim Bolger was re-elected Prime Minister. The Labour Party (LP), the main opposition force, took 45 seats.

[22] Aotearoa achieved its first budget surplus in 17 years in 1994; the currency became more robust, unemployment fell and inflation settled at 2 per cent.

[23] Between 1994 and 1995, the Government compensated the Tainui of the North Island both with NZ$180 million and 15,400 hectares of land, for their claims over land colonised last century. Even Britain's Queen Elizabeth apologized for the loss of life during the colonization of the islands. In 1997, the Government reached an agreement with Ngai Tahu of the South Island, to pay compensation of NZ$170 million and land. The actual settlement has yet to take place.

[24] The general unemployment indices continued to fall, settling at 6 per cent in 1995. Young people, Maori and immigrants from other South Pacific islands constituted the bulk of the unemployed and nearly 10 per cent of the population received State subsidies. Citizen concern for the environment strengthened Bolger's position in the run-up to the October 1996 elections, as he was firmly opposed to the French nuclear trials on the Mururoa atoll.

[25] Bolger's National Party dominated the Labour Party, although most both majority parties lost seats to the minorities. The first parliament elected by proportional representation doubled the number of Maori representatives and the number of women increased from 14 to 21 of the 120 seats.

[26] Between 1988 and 1996, the number of civil servants fell from 71,000 to 32,900. Aotearoa strengthened its profile as an international showcase for neoliberalism. The effects of the reforms implemented from the mid-1980s were followed attentively by the Western governments. The economic growth did not prevent the reduction of health and education budgets from continuing to be questioned.

Niue was settled by Samoans and Tongans. Captain James Cook named it "Savage Island" when he visited it in 1774. The indigenous peoples' reputation for fierceness kept missionaries away (the island's first permanent mission dates from 1861), as well as the slave traders who caused much suffering in other areas of the Pacific. Emigration to the phosphate mines on other islands of the area initiated an outflow which has since continued to the present. In 1900 the island was declared a British protectorate and was annexed by Aotearoa /New Zealand in 1901. It was administered along with the Cook Islands until 1904, when it separated to form a separate possession. In 1974 it became an Associated Territory of Aotearoa. The United Nations recognized this as a legitimate decision and eliminated the "Niue case" from the Decolonization Committee agenda. As well as economic support from Aotearoa, Niue also received help with defence and international affairs.

[2] In April 1989, questions arose over the management of economic aid received from Aotearoa by Prime Minister Robert Rex's government. Despite this, the opposition lacked the votes necessary to approve a parliamentary motion to censure Rex's administration.

[3] In 1991, Aotearoa announced a reduction of financial aid. Niue and Australia established diplomatic links during 1992.

Prime Minister Roberto Rex died on December 12 and was substituted by Young Vivian, who was in turn defeated in the elections to be succeeded by Frank Lui in March 1993. In February 1996, Frank Lui was re-elected for a further three years.

ENVIRONMENT
Located in the South Pacific in southern Polynesia, 2,300 km northeast of Aotearoa, west of the Cook Islands and east of the Tonga Islands. Of coral origin, the island is flat and the soil relatively fertile. Its rainy, tropical climate is tempered by sea winds.

SOCIETY
Peoples: The people of Niue are of Polynesian origin. Religions: Protestant. Languages: English (official), local Niue language (national). Political Parties: Niue People's Action Party (NPAP).

THE STATE
Official name: Niue. Capital: Alofi. **Government**: Autonomous associated state. Kurt Meyer, Representative of Aotearoa. Frank F Lui, Prime Minister, since March 9, 1993. Single-chamber legislature - National Assembly, made up of 20 members (14 village representatives). Since October 1974, the island has had an autonomous local government. There is a 20-member Legislative Assembly which is headed by the Prime Minister. Aotearoa/New Zealand controls defence and foreign affairs.

[27] In December 1997, Bolger resigned after being challenged by members of his own caucus. Jenny Shipley, former transport minister, became the first woman Prime Minister.

[28] The fragility of the government coalition and its unpopularity were seen as symptoms of weakness for the NP as a choice of government.

Tokelau

Tokelau Islands

Population: 2,000 (1994)
Area: 12 SQ KM
Capital: Fakaofo

Currency: NZ dollars
Language: Samoan

From ancient times, the islands were inhabited by Polynesian peoples who lived by subsistence fishing and farming. The first European to set foot on the islands was English explorer John Byron, who arrived in 1765. However, the absence of great riches meant that the islands did not arouse the colonial interests of the British Crown.

[2] In 1877, these islands became a British protectorate. Britain annexed them for the Crown in 1916, and included them as part of the colonial territory of the Gilbert and Ellice Islands (now Kiribati and Tuvalu). In 1925, Britain transferred administrative control of the islands to Aotearoa (New Zealand). In 1946, the group was officially designated the Tokelau Islands, and in 1958 full sovereignty passed to Aotearoa.

[3] Like the Cook Islands, Tokelau was claimed by the United States until 1980, when the US signed a Friendship Treaty with Aotearoa and dropped its claims.

[4] The Government of Aotearoa adopted policies intended to maintain traditional customs, institutions and communal relations in Tokelau. The population lives in relative isolation; with a single ship reaching the islands from Apia (Samoa) every two or three months. The ocean and lagoons provide fish and seafood which are the islanders' staple subsistence foods. There are no tourist facilities.

[5] In the 1980s, farming underwent a crisis due to a number of adverse climatic conditions. As a consequence, emigration to Aotearoa rose considerably. The Government of Aotearoa tried to encourage Tokelau immigrants to return to their homeland, but its policies have not been successful.

[6] In 1976 and 1981 the UN sent delegations to Tokelau. On both occasions the envoys reported that the inhabitants of the islands did not wish to change their relations with Aotearoa/NZ.

[7] In December 1984, the UN Assembly discussed Tokelau's situation and decided that Aotearoa should continue to report on the state of the islands. However, in the report submitted before the UN Special Committee in June 1987, Tokelau expressed a wish to achieve greater political autonomy, while maintaining unchanged relations with Aotearoa.

[8] In 1989, Tokelau's motion to apply sanctions on those states fishing in its territorial waters was supported by the South Pacific Forum. In November of that year, Aotearoa banned fishing in a 200-nautical-mile exclusion zone, in order to protect the fishing reserves which constitute the islands' main wealth.

[9] In 1989, a UN report on the consequences of the greenhouse effect (the warming of the atmosphere as a result of pollution), included Tokelau among the islands which could disappear under the sea in the 21st century, unless drastic measures are taken to halt pollution.

[10] In February 1990, the three groups of islands which make up the country's territory were devastated by hurricane Ofa, which destroyed all the banana trees and 80 per cent of the coconut plantations, as well as hospitals, schools, houses, and bridges. As a result, emigration to Aotearoa/NZ increased once again.

[11] Aotearoa established the first regular maritime transport service between the three atolls during 1991.

[12] In 1993, the Samoan Government announced that it had agreed to the transfer of the Office of Tokelau Affairs, from Apia, Western Samoa, to the islands themselves.

[13] In May 1995, Aotearoa's parliament approved extended powers for the local assembly.

[14] In 1997, the island was linked to the satellite telephone system.

PROFILE

ENVIRONMENT

A group of coral islands, comprising three atolls: Atafu, 2,02 sq km and 577 people, Nakunono, 5,46 sq km and 374 people, Fakaofo, 2,63 sq km and 664 people. Geographically, Sivains atoll belongs to the group but is an administrative dependency of American Samoa. The group is located in Polynesia in the South Pacific, to the east of the Tuvalu islands. The islands are flat, with thin, not very fertile soil. Rainfall is erratic and there are frequent droughts. Fishing constitutes the traditional economic activity.

SOCIETY

Peoples: The population is of Polynesian origin.
Religions: Mostly Protestant, 70 per cent.
Languages: Samoan (official) and local dialects.

THE STATE

Official Name: Tokelau.
Capital: Fakaofo.
Other cities: Fenua Fala, and small villages on every island.
Government: The Governor-General of Aotearoa/NZ has legislative power over the islands, and their administration has been entrusted to the Aotearoan Secretary of Foreign Affairs. Brian Absolum, Administrator since 1994. Each atoll has a *Taupulega* (Council of Elders) formed by the heads of family groups, plus a *Faipule* (who represents the village in its dealings with the Aotearoan administration) and a *Pulenuku* (responsible for local administration). Twice a year, 15 delegates from each Taupulega attend the Fono.

Argentina

Argentina

Population: 35,219,000 (1996)
Area: 2,791,810 SQ KM
Capital: Buenos Aires

Currency: Pesos
Language: Spanish

The Patagonians and the Andeans were the two largest groups living in what is now Argentina at the beginning of the 16th century. Patagonians included Tehuelch, Rehuelche, Rampa, Mataco and Guaycure peoples. The latter two constituted stable, agrarian civilizations, while the others were nomadic hunters and gatherers. They settled in the south, center and north of the country. The principal Andean groups were the Ancient Rehuenche, Algarrobero Rehuelche, Huerpe, Diaguita, Capayane, Omahuaca and Patama. Through contact with the Inkas, they perfected their agricultural system introducing terracing and artificial irrigation. They raised llamas, and traded in the northwest and west of the country.

[2] In the 17th and 18th centuries during the Spanish conquest, the Araucans migrated from Chile toward the central and southwestern regions of what is now Argentina, with the resulting "Araucanization" of the region's inhabitants.

[3] Explorations organized by Spain in the 16th century led Amerigo Vespucci, in 1502, and Juan Díaz de Solís, in 1516, to enter the estuary which they named Río de la Plata (River Plate, meaning silver river) in honor of the much sought after precious metal. In 1526, Sebastián Cabot built a fort on the banks of the Carcarañá River, the first settlement of present-day Argentina.

[4] To check Portugal's advance, Spain sent Pedro de Mendoza to the region with terms of political and economic advantages for the conqueror. In 1536, Mendoza founded Santa María del Buen Aire (Buenos Aires), but this small town was abandoned in 1541, after attacks by the native population became too numerous.

[5] Using Asunción (in today's Paraguay) as the center for colonization, the Spaniards founded several cities in Argentina (Santiago del Estero, Córdoba, Santa Fé), refounding Buenos Aires in 1580. This port soon became Spain's strategic, political and commercial base in the region.

[6] In 1776 the Viceroyalty of Río de la Plata was created - including today's Chile, Paraguay, Argentina, Uruguay and part of Bolivia - with Buenos Aires as its capital. A strong commercial bourgeoisie, based in the port area, became the initiators of the 1810 revolutionary movement. They created the United Provinces of Río de la Plata and ousted the Viceroy, accusing him of disloyalty to Spain, then occupied by Napoleon's troops. Independence for the United Provinces of Río de la Plata was first initiated in 1816, when the governing Junta of Buenos Aires - which aspired to institutional and commercial liberalism - found the ideas of the restored Spanish monarch Fernando VII and his servile party incompatible with their aims.

[7] General José de San Martín organized the armies that defeated the royalists and contributed decisively to the independence of Chile and Peru. During the same period, the United Provinces, as an exporter of hides and import market for manufactured goods, fell under British influence. In two decades this ruined the craftspeople of the upland provinces and increased benefits to the Buenos Aires port oligarchy who controlled import trade. In 1829, when Juan Manuel de Rosas came to power, he reconciled the interests of both parties by creating customs laws and other restrictions primarily to resist French and British penetration. Both powers resorted to military aggression when they blockaded the port of Buenos Aires in an attempt to overcome the Government. Their efforts were thwarted. These first attempts to bring Argentina into the international market were successful after the "Great War" (waged in Argentina and Uruguay 1839-52), involving Argentina, Uruguay and Brazil, with direct intervention from Britain and France.

[8] In 1833 Britain occupied the Malvinas/Falklands Islands, with the blessing of the United States. After Rosas' defeat, Argentina became an importer of British manufactured goods and capital, and exporter of beef and cereals. In the name of economic and political liberalism, President Bartolomé Mitre - together with the Brazilian Empire of Pedro II and Venancio Flores' Uruguay - waged the War of the Triple Alliance (1865-1870) against Paraguay. This war of extermination against their neighbor's prosperous economic experiment began in 1865 and ended with the death of Paraguayan president Francisco Solano López in 1870. (See box The Triple Alliance). At the time of

BOLIVIA · PARAGUAY · CHILE · Salta · Tucumán · Formosa · Resistencia · Posadas · Santiago del Estero · Corrientes · ARGENTINA · BRAZIL · Córdoba · Santa Fé · San Juan · Rosario · URUGUAY · Mendoza · Buenos Aires · La Plata · Colorado · Neuquén · Mar del Plata · Bahía Blanca · Negro · San Carlos de Bariloche · Atlantic Ocean · Trelew · Comodoro Rivadavia · Pto. Deseado · Chico · Río Gallegos · Magellan Strait · Ushuaia · Falkland Is. (Is. Malvinas) Territory occupied by UK, claimed by Argentina · Pacific Ocean · CORDILLERA DE LOS ANDES · PATAGONIA · GRAN CHACO · Paraná · Uruguay · Paraguay · Pilcomayo

0   300 km

WORKERS

UNEMPLOYMENT 16.3% (1996)

Labour force %

■ WOMEN
□ MEN

31   69

■ AGRICULTURE 12% (1990)
□ INDUSTRIAL 32%
■ SERVICES 55%

LAND USE

DEFORESTATION -0.6 % annual (81/90)
IRRIGATED 6.8 % of arable

(1993)

■ FOREST & WOODLAND 18.4%
□ ARABLE 9%
■ OTHER 72.6%

Maternal Mortality
1990
PER 100,000
LIVE BIRTHS
100

Literacy
1995
96%

Foreign Trade
MILLIONS $ 1996
IMPORTS
23,762
EXPORTS
23,810

"victory", Faustino Domingo Sarmiento had already replaced Mitre.

[9] After the war, technological upgrading was necessary to meet new world market requirements. Railroads and ports were built to transfer the country's wealth to London, while the indigenous peoples of the Patagonian and Chaco regions were exterminated to make way for new settlers. There was massive immigration of European labor, mainly Italian and Spanish.

[10] In 1916, Radical Civic Union leader Hipólito Irigoyen was elected president with the vote of the middle class and the emerging proletariat. This election ended a succession of governments dominated by landed interests. Favorable conditions during World War I - in which Irigoyen maintained a position of active neutrality - generated some industrial development and brought new social groups and conflicts of interest to the fore. These built up to the "Tragic Week" of 1919, when troops machine-gunned striking workers in the streets, and extreme rightist opposition vigilantes ransacked the Jewish quarter in search of "Bolsheviks".

[11] The inadequacy of the agro-export model was revealed during the great depression of 1929. Irigoyen was overthrown by the ruling classes, who drew closer to Britain and consolidated their own economic privileges.

[12] World War II stimulated rapid industrial development based on import substitution. An alliance between the bourgeoisie, the working class and the armed forces dominated the political scene. Mass uprisings on October 17 1945 sparked events that carried the then Colonel Juan Domingo Perón to the presidency in 1946. Perón nationalized foreign trade, banks, railroads, oil and telephones, expanded the shipping fleet and set up an airline, increased the workers' share of national income by 50 per cent, and passed progressive social legislation. He also organized workers' and employers' associations into national confederations where economic and social policies were negotiated. In foreign relations, he argued for a "third position", independent of the contending

blocs in the Cold War. Perón's wife, Evita, cultivated a charismatic relationship with the workers, and used her influence to secure female suffrage.

[13] US interests triggered a coup in 1955. Military dictator Pedro Aramburu repudiated Perón's "third position" and embraced the National Security doctrine. Regional defence against "the enemies of democracy" was delegated entirely to the United States. Aramburu's grossly misnamed "Liberating Revolution" was an attempted reversion to the 1940s, with the US playing Britain's former role. The dictatorial regime imposed a reactionary income redistribution. Military and civilian opposition members faced firing squads in the 1956 Operation Massacre, a precursor of decades of political violence.

[14] Though outlawed, Peronism helped Arturo Frondizi win the 1958 presidential election. An advocate of development theories, Frondizi brought multinational oil and automobile concerns into the country and followed a model of economic growth and income concentration, causing subsequent social confrontations. In 1962, Frondizi was forced out of office. Two periods of violent struggle between the "blue" and "red" factions of the armed forces, saw General Juan Carlos Onganía emerge as the new leading force.

[15] With Peronism once again banned, the Radical Party's Arturo Illía was elected. For the first time in four decades Argentina was not subject to the "state of siege" or other extraordinary measures of repression or cultural censorship.

[16] Illía revoked oil contracts signed by Frondizi and paid indemnity to the affected foreign companies. Several good harvests and trade with socialist markets helped to overcome the economic crisis bequeathed by the military interregnum. The Illía administration refused to send Argentinean troops to assist the US invasion of the Dominican Republic. Confrontations with Peronist-led labor unions, which staged strikes, factory take-overs, and anti-government campaigns, continued to plague Illía's administration.

[17] In June 1966, Illía was overthrown by the "Argentinean

PROFILE

ENVIRONMENT

Argentina claims sovereignty over the Malvinas (Falkland) Islands and a 1,250,000 sq km portion of Antarctica. There are four major geographical regions. The Andes mountain range marks the country's western limits. The sub-Andean region consists of a series of irrigated enclaves where sugarcane, citrus fruits (in the North) and grapes (central) are grown. A system of plains extends east of the Andes: in the North, the Chaco plain with sub-tropical vegetation and cotton farms; in the center, the Pampa with deep, fertile soil and a mild climate where cattle and sheep are raised, and wheat, corn, forage and soybeans are grown, and to the South stretches Patagonia, a low, arid, cold plateau with steppe vegetation where sheep are extensively raised and oil is extracted. Untreated domestic waste has raised the levels of contamination of many rivers, especially the Matanza-Riachuelo in Buenos Aires. Another problem is increasing soil erosion, especially in the damp northern Pampas.

SOCIETY

Peoples: Most Argentinians are descendents of European immigrants (mostly Spaniards and Italians) who arrived in large migrations between 1870 and 1950. Among them is found the largest Jewish community in Latin America. According to unofficial figures, the indigenous population of 447,300, is made up of 15 indigenous and 3 mestizo peoples mainly in the north and southeast of the country, and in the marginal settlements around the major cities. Mapuche, Kolla, and Toba constitute the largest ethnic groups. The indigenous peoples in the east, center and southern-most tip are in decline.
Religions: Catholic (92 per cent, official); Protestant, Evangelical, Jewish and Islamic minorities.
Languages: Spanish. Minor groups maintain their indigenous languages: Quechua, Guarani and others.
Political Parties: "Justicialist" or "Peronist" Party (PJ), in power; Electoral Alliance is a coalition composed of the Radical Civic Union (UCR), and the; Frepaso (a coalition made up of former communists, socialists, independents, members of the Intransigent Party and former Peronists, including the head of the alliance, José Octavio Bordón; Socialist Unity; People's Socialist Party; Modin (nationalist); the Center Alliance, liberal, made up of the Progressive Democratic, Autonomist, Federal, Democratic and Union of the Democratic Center (UCeDé) parties; Republican Force, linked to the last military dictatorship.
Social Organizations: The General Labor Confederation (CGT), Peronist in orientation, founded in 1930. In reaction to the current Government's economic and labor policies, the confederation has split into three factions.

THE STATE

Official Name: República Argentina.
Administrative divisions: 5 Regions with 22 Provinces, Federal District of Buenos Aires, National Territory of Tierra del Fuego.
Capital: Greater Buenos Aires, 12,582,300 people (1991).
Other cities: Cordoba, 1,179,100 people; Rosario, 1,078.400; Mendoza, 801,900; La Plata, 542,600 (1991).
Government: Presidential system; Carlos Saúl Menem, President since July 8 1989. Legislature: made up of the Chamber of Deputies and the Senate. Each province has 2 seats in the 48-member Senate.
National Holidays: May 25, Revolution (1810); July 9, Independence Day (1816).
Armed Forces: 67,300: army 60 per cent, navy 26.8 per cent, air force 13.2 per cent (18,100 conscripts).
Other: (Gendarmes) 18,000.

Revolution" of Onganía. This new authoritarian plan, clerical and corporatist in its politics, advocated outright economic liberalism and pursued a foreign policy based on the defence of "ideological borders". Onganía consecrated the country to the holy spirit, banned political parties, and intervened in universities and the Trade Union Confederation (CGT). Control of the economy passed from national companies to US, British and German consortiums with the ability to buy bankrupt Argentinean firms, very cheaply.

[18] The ensuing economic stagnation led to serious social unrest, particularly in 1969, when violent demonstrations and rioting paralyzed Córdoba, the nation's second largest city. The uprising, nicknamed "El Cordobazo", was organized by the Argentinean CGT, led by Raimundo Ongaro (Peronist), Antonio Scipione (Radical) and Agustín Tosco (Marxist). The Cordobazo and other outbreaks of guerrilla warfare, ended Onganía's plans for an "Argentinean Revolution". General Agustín Lanusse came to power in 1971. In order to pacify the country, Lanusse called elections but banned the candidacy of Perón, then in exile in Madrid.

[19] Héctor Cámpora, the "Justicialista" Liberation Front candidate - a Peronist electoral coalition - received 49 per cent of the vote in the March 1973 elections, taking office in May 1973, and resigning two months later to allow new elections after Perón's return to the country. On September 23, Perón was re-elected in a new contest with 62 per cent of the vote, and the vice-presidency went to María Estela ("Isabelita") Martínez de Perón, his wife. He resumed diplomatic relations with Cuba, proposed a reorganization of the Organization of American States (OAS) to serve Latin America's interests, promoted Argentina's participation in the Non-Aligned Movement and increased trade with socialist countries. After the Ezeiza massacre on June 23 1973, the day Perón returned to Argentina, friction grew among various Peronist factions and a situation of open warfare broke out between the old-time labor leaders and the "special squads", as Perón used to

call the guerrillas. When Perón died, his widow took office. Her Social Welfare Minister (Perón's former secretary), José López Rega, set up the "Triple A" (Argentine Anticommunist Alliance), a paramilitary hit squad that murdered Marxist opponents and left-wing Peronists.

[20] On March 25 1976, a military coup put an end to "Isabelita's" inefficient and corrupt administration. A military junta led by General Jorge Videla suspended all civil liberties and set in motion a cycle of kidnapping, torture, betrayal and murder. The term "missing person" became ominously commonplace, and government priorities were dictated by the newly adopted "National Security" doctrine. Human rights organizations drew up a list of over 7,000 missing persons, 80 per cent of whom had been arrested by the police in front of witnesses. Their fate has never been determined with certainty, but a 1983 Armed Forces communiqué stated that the desaparecidos (disappeared) should be considered "killed in action" with counter-insurgency troops.

[21] The Junta encouraged imports to the point of liquidating a third of the country's productive capacity. Fifty years of labor gains were wiped out, real wages lost half of their purchasing power, and regional economies were choked by high interest rates. The country's cattle herds decreased by 10 million head and the foreign debt climbed to $60 billion, a quarter of which had been spent on arms. It was the era of what Argentines called the "patria financiera" (financial fatherland), when governmental economic policies encouraged most of the country's productive sector to turn to speculation. In 1980, a wave of bankruptcies hit banks and financial institutions.

[22] In 1981, General Leopoldo Galtieri became president and Army Commander-in-Chief. He agreed on Argentinean military participation in the US intervention in Central America. Thinking that this was enough to secure US president Reagan's unconditional support, Galtieri decided to ward off the domestic crisis by recovering the Malvinas Islands, in British hands since 1833, and

troops landed there on April 2 1982. Galtieri's error soon became evident. The UN Security Council opposed the invasion, Britain deployed a powerful fleet that included nuclear submarines, and the United States firmly supported its North Atlantic ally. After 45 days of fighting Argentina surrendered on June 15; 750 Argentineans and 250 British soldiers had been killed during the conflict. Two days later Galtieri was forced to resign from both his military and presidential posts.

[23] Seventeen member countries in the OAS acknowledged Argentina's right to the Malvinas. They also voted against Washington for having violated the Interamerican Reciprocal Assistance Treaty by supporting Britain, a non-American nation, in acts of aggression against American territory.

[24] Soon after Galtieri resigned, the upper echelons of the Armed Forces underwent a series of purges. The junta set elections for October 30 1983 and the Army, without consulting the Navy and the Air Force, appointed retired General Reynaldo Bignone acting president until January 30 1984.

[25] The Radical Civic Union's new leader, Raul Alfonsín, won the election with 52 per cent of the vote, well ahead of the Peronists' 40 per cent. During his campaign, Alfonsín denounced the existence of a pact between the military and trade unions, and he offered himself as the candidate of law and life, standing against tyranny and death. This won him the election, even in the Greater Buenos Aires industrial belt, a traditional Peronist stronghold.

[26] Economic efforts concentrated

1970
6%

1994
4%

1994

PER CAPITA
$2,664

on inflation, where forecasts were gloomy. It stood at 688 per cent by the end of 1984. For 1985, it seemed reasonable to expect a monthly rate of 25 per cent. Government expenditure was cut drastically and the military budget shrank to 18 per cent of the total as compared to a previous 30 per cent. The budget deficit spiralled to an annual $70 million. Meanwhile, speculative investments yielded the highest interests paid anywhere in the world.

[27] Workers discovered that their share of national income had decreased from 48 to 35 per cent, and the Peronist CGT wavered towards a variety of mixed political alliances. It reached the point of endorsing a stockbreeders' strike in exchange for an increase in rural wages and support for union control over social spending, especially on public health and domestic tourism.

[28] In mid-June 1985, the government introduced the Austral Plan which froze prices, service tariffs and a new currency, the Austral, was put into circulation, linked to the US dollar.

[29] Relations with Chile improved, after having been extremely tense due to a border dispute in the South (over the Beagle Canal). A treaty was signed, following a plebiscite in which a Vatican peace proposal, backed by the Argentine government, was supported by 80 per cent of the voters.

[30] CONADEP, the National Commission on Missing Persons, continued to reveal horrendous findings at the trials of the nine Commanders-in-Chief of the dictatorship, accused of crimes during that period. The indictment of several high-ranking military officers (including former president Videla) and the subsequent extension of the trials to lower-ranking officers created tension within the military. During Easter 1987, some units occupied their barracks to demand an end to the trials, and amnesty for those who had been indicted. Although the rebels represented a minority, many people doubted the willingness of the "loyal" troops to contain the rebellion.

[31] In response to President Alfonsín's appeal, more than a million people flocked to the Plaza de Mayo in defence of democracy.

The crisis was dispelled on Easter Sunday when Alfonsín personally went to the Campo de Mayo barracks to meet with the rebels, who agreed to accord with the constitution. Consequently, several military officers were relieved of their commands, and the President sent Congress a bill on "due obedience", exempting the majority of the military personnel from prosecution, on the grounds that they had been following orders.

[32] In the years that followed, the majority of the population saw their real earnings steadily eroded by inflation. Resistance to the government's economic strategy was led by trade unions of the General Labor Confederation (CGT). Between December 1983 and April 1989, thousands of jobs were lost, wages came to be just one more "adjustable variable" and recession aggravated the already difficult situation of small and medium sized businesses. In this period there were 14 general strikes.

[33] The social cost of this process spiralled to the point where it is estimated that some 10 million people, nearly 10 per cent of the total population, lived outside the consumer market.

[34] In the summer of 1988 there was a second, but hardly significant, military uprising at Monte Caseros in Corrientes province. Its leader, Lieutenant Colonel Aldo Rico, was tried and subsequently expelled from the army. In the winter of that same year, Colonel Mohamed Ali Seineldin led a third insurrection with the declared aim of settling an internal army matter. The forces were split into "nationalists" loyal to Seineldin and "liberals" who followed army orders. Even though the country survived both episodes, the internal divisions continued to exist.

[35] In February 1989, an armed group from the All for Our Country "movement", which had acted legally until then, attacked an army barracks, allegedly in order to prevent a military coup. The response was disproportionately violent and those fighters who survived received heavy sentences. It is claimed that some prisoners were summarily executed after surrendering, and others "disappeared".

[36] The final 3 months of the

Alfonsín government were marked by hyperinflation of between 100 and 200 per cent a month. The economy was wracked by recession and the president's prestige demolished. Stores in suburbs of the capital and in the interior were sacked once again, with looters stealing food and basic consumer goods.

[37] In the 1989 presidential elections the Peronist governor of La Rioja, Carlos Saúl Menem, received 47.6 per cent of the vote, and the radical candidate, Eduardo César Angeloz, 38.4 per cent. The economic collapse was so drastic that the new president was invited to take office a couple of months earlier than scheduled. Menem passed a State Reform Law in August 1989 starting the privatization of state enterprises, the deregulation of markets, and the decentralization of public administration. Within the year the main oilfields, communications media, the national telecommunications company and the state airline were all privatized.

[38] Menem re-established diplomatic relations with Britain, leaving the key issue of the Malvinas under a dubious "protective umbrella", and in two stages, pardoned all the military responsible for human rights violations during the "dirty war".

[39] The persistent economic and social crisis caused Menem to change the traditional Peronist doctrine, wreaking havoc on the country's main institutions. The CGT split into two sectors: one pro-government and the other, opposition. The Army and political parties were also divided, the Church criticized the political leadership, whose public prestige waned.

[40] In December 1990, the warrant officers rose in arms in Buenos Aires. The uprising lasted for 24 hours and claimed the lives of several civilians and military. Colonel Seineldin, in custody at the time, accepted full responsibility for these events.

[41] During the Gulf War, the Argentinean government sent troops to join the US-commanded anti-Iraq coalition, without waiting for parliamentary approval. In 1991, Argentina announced its withdrawal from the Non-Aligned Movement, and in early 1992, it

joined the United States in denouncing the human rights situation in Cuba, thereby breaking with its traditional non-intervention policy.

[42] From the start, Menem's government was beset by scandal. Several of his top advisors had to resign, accused of drug money laundering or accepting bribes to favor companies in bids or privatization take-overs.

[43] In spite of the corruption, Menem succeeded in keeping his image intact and in the 1991 elections the Justicialista Party retained 13 of the 23 provinces, while 4 were won by the Radicals and 6 by local parties. Voters throughout the country gave 40 per cent of the vote to the ruling party, only 7 per cent less than in 1989.

[44] This political victory was attributed to economic stability attained by the conversion plan which drastically reduced public spending and set a new currency, the peso, equivalent to one US dollar. Inflation fell, reaching record lows, standing at 7.4 per cent in 1993.

[45] In December 1992, Argentina, Brazil, Paraguay and Uruguay signed the agreement leading to Mercosur, a regional common market scheduled to go into effect in January 1995.

[46] In the 1993 parliamentary elections, the Peronists obtained their fourth consecutive electoral victory with 43.2 per cent of the vote, while the Radicals received 30 per cent. Afterwards, the Radicals agreed to support a constitutional reform to enable presidential re-election - which would directly benefit Menem - in exchange for the reduction of the government term from six to four years.

[47] In the economic field, the Gross Domestic Product increased significantly. However, industrial activity remained below 1987 levels. Inequality of wealth distribution between the country's different regions widened. By the end of the year, civil servants in several provinces staged protests over unpaid back wages and in some cases, they set fire to public buildings and looted the homes of politicians and government officials.

[48] In the 1994 constitutional elections, the great surprise was the outcome of the left-wing

"Frente Grande" (Large Front) coalition, which became the country's third most important political force, winning the election in the Federal Capital with 37.6 per cent of the vote. It also won in the southern province of Neuquen. In Buenos Aires, it became the second most important political force with 16.4 per cent of the vote. However, Peronistas and Radicals obtained a sufficient majority to ensure the reform.

[49] 1995 opened with the Mexican crisis threatening possible impacts on the Argentine economy. Economy Minister Domingo Cavallo slashed the budget and applied austerity measures. The political sphere was made tense in March by the mysterious death of Menem's son, Carlos junior, who died in a helicopter crash. Menem's former wife and the son's mother, Zulema Yoma, claimed her son had been murdered, while the federal police classed it as an accident. In the May 14 elections, Menem was re-elected with 50 per cent of the vote, while former Peronist and Frepaso candidate, José Bordón, took 29 per cent and the Radical, Horacio Massaccesi, 17 per cent. In August, Cavallo denounced postal entrepreneur Alfredo Yabrán as a "Mafia leader" attempting to monopolise the Postal service and carry out million-dollar deals with State coverage.

[50] In mid-1996, unemployment topped the two million mark and the underemployed a million and a half, according to official statistics. Unemployment reached a national average of 17.1 per cent, and stood at more than 20 per cent in some provinces. The foreign debt was up 57 per cent on its 1991 level at the beginning of the government imposed anti-inflationary plan. Menem dismissed Cavallo in the first quarter of 1996. The new economy minister, Roque Fernández, with a doctorate from Chicago, declared he was committed to maintaining the policy of his predecessor and overcoming the fiscal deficit, unemployment and recession.

[51] The murder of José Luis Cabezas, photographer for a magazine critical of the government, created tension in late January 1997. Governor of the province of Buenos Aires, Eduardo Duhalde, offered a large reward for anyone providing information on the case and even called the US FBI in on the investigation. This effort led to the hypothesis Cabezas could have been killed for investigating Yabrán s business.

[52] In April and May, the education unions held extensive protests in Buenos Aires and several provinces in the interior. In one of these demonstrations in the province of Neuquén, the police mortally wounded a woman. In July, former minister Cavallo received a four month suspended sentence for slander, which did not bar him from holding public posts. The case had been presented by the lawyer Jorge Kolon, a former official from the National Customs Administration. Cavallo had stated on television that Kolon was "an obstacle in the battle against corruption in the customs sector". Furthermore, Cavallo, who faced another 20 lawsuits, argued that the trials were being held by judges hand-picked by Menem and Justice Minister Carlos Corach, whom Cavallo defined as another of his personal enemies.

[53] The elections for the chamber of deputies in October saw the victory of the Electoral Alliance (of the Radical Party and Frepaso), which took 46 per cent of the vote, while the Justicialist Party took only 36 per cent. The Justicialists experienced electoral defeat while in government on a national level for the first time in 51 years, although they maintained control over the Senate, which was not renewed.

[54] In early 1998, public declarations by Captain Alfredo Astiz, vindicating illegal acts under the military dictatorship (1976-1983), increased the political tension. Astiz, sought by the French courts on charges of murdering two French nuns, and by Interpol, after failing to respond to a summons from a Spanish court investigating the disappearance of Spanish-Argentines, is a symbol of the repression of the military dictatorship. Following his declarations, Astiz was ousted from his post by President Menem, while the military courts condemned him to 60 days house arrest. This created a division in the opposition Electoral Alliance, as Astiz was protected by the Laws of the "Full stop" and "Due obedience" approved during the presidency of the Radical Raúl Alfonsín.

[55] In March, as part of her investigation into the crimes and illegal enrichment of certain Argentine military officers with goods robbed from the "disappeared" in the 1970s, Swiss Attorney General, Carla del Ponte, revealed Astiz had bank accounts in Switzerland. Del Ponte also said she had discovered various accounts belonging to other former officials accused of having participated in the repression during the military dictatorship in Argentina. In the same month, a new report from the Argentine federal police stated that the death of Carlos Menem junior could have been murder. The Gendarmerie confirmed there were shotgun bullet holes in the remains of the helicopter, along with traces of lead and antimony.

Malvinas

Falkland Islands

Population: 2,000 (1996)
Area: 11,410 SQ KM
Capital: Port Stanley (Puerto Argentino)
Currency: Pound Sterling
Language: English

When the islands were sighted for the first time in 1520 by a Spanish ship, they were uninhabited. In the 18th century, they were baptized the "Malouines" in honor of Saint Malo, port of origin of the French fishermen and seal hunters who settled there. In 1764, Louis Antoine Bougainville founded Port Louis on Soledad Island. This move brought Spanish protests, and France recognized Spain's prior claim. That same year the British, who since 1690 had called the islands "Falkland" (after the treasurer of the British Navy), founded Port Egmont. This was later returned to Spain in exchange for £24,000, and renamed Puerto Soledad.

[2] In 1820, shortly after independence, Argentina appointed Daniel Jewit as first Governor of the Malvinas. In 1831, Governor Vernet impounded two US ships on charges of illegal fishing. A US fleet that was visiting South America avenged this act of "piracy" by destroying houses and military facilities at Port Soledad. On January 3, 1833, the English corvette Clio landed a contingent of settlers which the small local force was unable to repel.

[3] After World War II, the United Nations Decolonization Committee included the Malvinas and their dependencies on the list of "non-autonomous" territories and established that, as the inhabitants were British, the principle of self-determination was not applicable. The only juridically valid solution to the problem was to recognize Argentinian sovereignty.

[4] On April 2 1982, Argentinian forces occupied the Malvinas. Two months later, at the cost of more than 1,000 lives, the Union Jack was once again hoisted over the islands.

[5] Diplomatic relations between Britain and Argentina were placed on hold. At the beginning of his administration, Menem renewed relations with London, but the intractable issue of the Malvinas' sovereignty was left pending. During his first official visit to Malvinas, British Foreign Minister Douglas Hurd emphasized London's determination to maintain the islands under British sovereignty.

[6] In November 1991 Britain authorized the Governor of the Malvinas to award contracts, for the exploration for and exploitation of possible underwater oil deposits around the islands.

[7] In March 1994, the Argentinian Minister of Defence reported that in 1982, at least 9 Argentinian soldiers had died at the hands of British forces, in circumstances that violated the Geneva Convention on the treatment of prisoners of war. There were still some 15,000 live mines scattered across the islands.

[8] Understanding agreed between President Carlos Menem and Prime Minister John Major at the United Nations, in September 1995, established that. Argentina and the United Kingdom will explore and exploit jointly the west of the islands, where border lines overlap.

[9] The giant US oil company Amerada Hess announced on May 1998 the presence of "minor hydrocarbons" while drilling a pilot well 120 miles off the north of the islands.

PROFILE

ENVIRONMENT
An archipelago with nearly 100 islands located in the South Atlantic. It includes Georgia, Sandwich and Shetland Islands. There are two main islands - Soledad to the east and Gran Malvina to the west -separated by the San Carlos Channel. The coast is rough and mountainous. More than half of the population lives in the capital on Soledad. The main economic activity is sheep raising. The islands' territorial waters are believed to contain oil reserves. There is also hope that krill (a microscopic crustacean rich in protein) can be marketed. Its proximity to Antarctica also gives the archipelago strategic importance.

SOCIETY
Peoples: Since June 1982, the British have maintained a 4,000-strong garrison on the islands.
Language: English.
THE STATE
Capital: Port Stanley (Puerto Argentino), 1,620 people in 1986.
Government: Richard Ralph, Governor since January 1996, appointed by Britain.
DEMOGRAPHY
Population: 2,000 (1996)
Urban population: 85.5% (1996)

Armenia

Hayastán

Population	: 3,638,000 (1996)
Area:	29,800 SQ KM
Capital:	Yerevan
Currency:	Drams
Language:	Armenian

The first historical reference to the country "Armina" (Armenia) was made in the cuneiform writings from the era of King Darius I of Persia (6th-5th centuries BC). But the name Hayk, as the Armenians are called, comes from the name of the country, Hayasa, mentioned in the Hittite ceramic writings from the 12th century BC. The Urartians, direct ancestors of the Armenians, founded a powerful state in the 9th to 6th centuries BC; its capital was the city of Tushpa (today Van, Turkey). In the year 782 BC, they founded the fortress of Erebuni, in the north of the country (today Yerevan, capital of Armenia).

2 With the collapse of Ur, the ancient Kingdom of Armenia emerged in its territory. The first rulers of Armenia were the satraps (viceroys) of the shahs of Persia. This period was recorded in the works of Xenophon and Herodotus. In "Anabasis", Xenophon described how the Armenians turned back 10,000 Greek mercenaries in 400 BC. His writings also describe Armenia's prosperous production, its wheat, fruit and delicious wines.

3 After the expeditions of Alexander the Great and the rise of the Seleucid Empire, Armenia came under extensive Greek influence which had an important effect upon the cultural life of the country. The Seleucid State fell into the hands of the Romans in 190 BC, and Armenia became independent. The local government named Artashes (Artaxias) King of Greater Armenia.

4 Armenia reached the pinnacle of its prosperity during the reign of Tigranes the Great (95-55 BC). King Tigranes united all Armenian-speaking regions and annexed several neighboring regions. Armenia's borders extended as far as the Mediterranean to the south, the Black Sea to the north and the Caspian Sea to the east. Tigranes' empire soon fell, and Armenia was proclaimed "friend and ally of the Roman people", a euphemism for the vassals of Rome.

5 Armenia began to disintegrate over a 400-year period until it finally disappeared as a state in the year 428, when the Roman Empire and the new kingdom of Persia divided it up between them.

6 In 301, Armenia became the first country in the world officially to adopt Christianity as a state religion At that time, St Gregory the Illuminator, the first Armenian patriarch, founded the monastery at Echmiadzin, still extant as the headquarters for the patriarchs of the Armenian Church. Ever since the 4th century, the Church has been identified with Armenian national feeling as religion made it possible to maintain the unity of the people over the long period during which the country lacked any actual state organization.

7 In 405, a monk, Mesrop Mashtots, devised an alphabet which formed the basis of the Armenian writing system. The characters of this alphabet have remained unchanged, achieving a continuity which spans the centuries and links ancient, medieval and modern cultures. The 5th century was the golden age of religious and secular literature and of Armenian historiography; the natural sciences also developed during a later period. In the 7th century, Ananias Shirakatsi wrote that the world was round and formulated the hypothesis that there were several worlds inhabited by beings endowed with some form of intelligence.

8 In the 5th and 6th centuries, Armenia was divided between Byzantium and Persia. The Persians tried to stamp out all traces of Christianity in the eastern Armenian regions triggering a massive rebellion. Prince Vartan Mamikonian, commander of the Armenian army, assumed the leadership of the rebellion. In the year 452, he led an army of 60,000 troops into battle against a vastly superior Persian force, in the Avaraev valley. The Armenians were defeated and Prince Vartan was killed, but the Persians also suffered heavy losses, and subsequently gave up all attempts to convert the Armenians to Islam. All those who lost their lives in this battle were later canonized by the Armenian Church.

9 In the 7th century, Arab forces invaded Persia, bringing about the collapse of the Persian Empire. The new Muslim leaders also established control over the Armenian regions. The people resisted, fighting for their independence until the late 9th century, when Prince Ashot Bagratuni was named King of Armenia, and established an independent government. The epic novel "David of Sasun" describes this long struggle for independence.

10 The prosperity of the Bagratids' reign was short-lived, for in the 11th century the Byzantines and Seleucids began bearing down on the Transcaucasian region, from Central Asia. Many Armenian princes ceded their lands to the Byzantine emperor, in exchange for lands in Cilicia. The inhabitants of other Armenian regions began flocking to Cilicia, fleeing the Turkish raids.

11 At the end of the 11th century, the Rubenid dynasty founded a new Armenian state in Cilicia, which lasted 300 years. Cilicia had close ties to the western European states; Armenian troops took part in the Crusades, and intermarriage with other ruling dynasties introduced

PROFILE

ENVIRONMENT

Armenia is a mountainous country, which is bounded on the north by Georgia, on the east by Azerbaijan and on the south, by Turkey and Iran. With an average altitude of 1,800 meters, high Caucasian peaks - like Mount Aragats (4,095 meters) - alternate with volcanic plateaus and deep river valleys, where there are a number of important rivers. The most important of these is the Aras River, which is in turn a tributary of the Kura River, which forms a natural boundary with Turkey and Iran. The climate is dry and continental; the summers are long and hot and the winters, extremely cold. On the plains, wheat, grain, cotton, tobacco and sugar beets are grown. There are also vineyards, from which good-quality wine is made. Cattle-raising is generally limited to the mountains. There are important copper, aluminum and molybdenum deposits.

SOCIETY

Peoples: 93.3 per cent Armenian; 2.6 per cent Azeri; 2.3 per cent Russian; 1.7 per cent Kurd.
Religions: Armenian Church (a branch of the Christian Orthodox Church), the vast majority.
Languages: Armenian (official), Russian, Azerbaijani and Kurdish.
Political Parties: Armenian National Movement (ANM); Dashnaktusiun Party (DP).

THE STATE

Capital: Yerevan (Jerevan), 1,283,000 people (1994).
Other cities: Gyumri 163,000 people; Leninakan 218,000 people Kirovakan, 76,000 people; Alavrdi, Dilijan, Razdan, Kamo, Goris.
Government: Robert Kocharyan, President since 1998.
National Holiday: May 28, Independence (1918).
Armed Forces: 57,400 (1996)
Other: Police Squads 1,000.

the Rubenids to the circle of European rulers. In 1375, Armenian Cilicia fell to the Mamelukes of Egypt, who retained Cilician science, culture and literature. In the meantime, the region that had originally been Armenia was devastated by invasions and wars.

[12] In the 13th century the Ottoman Turks replaced the Seleucids and began their conquest of Asia Minor. In 1453, they took Constantinople and marched eastwards, invading Persia. Armenia was the scene of numerous wars between Turkey and Persia, until the 17th century, when the country was divided between the two Islamic empires. During this period, the Church carried out secular functions and also called the attention of fellow-Christian European countries to the plight of the Armenians, who were forced to emigrate and settle far from their home country. Many of these expatriate Armenian "colonies" exist to this day.

[13] In 1722, Russian troops carried out an expedition to Transcaucasia, occupying the city of Baku and other territories belonging to Persia. Armenian princes in Nagorno-Karabakh and other neighboring areas seized the opportunity to join forces with the Russians, and organized a revolution against the Persians. The uprising was led by the Armenian national hero David-bek. However, Armenian hopes were dashed when the Russian czar, Peter the Great, died. He had promised to support the Armenians, but on his death, Russia signed a peace treaty with Persia. Another war between Russia and Persia, a hundred years later, ended in 1813 with the Treaty of Gulistan. According to the terms of this peace treaty, Karabakh and other territories which had historically belonged to Armenia became part of the Russian Empire.

[14] Russia was at war with either Turkey or Persia during the major part of the 19th century; with each war, Russia annexed more and more Armenian territory. Finally, almost the entire eastern part of Armenia - home to more than two million Armenians - was swallowed up. However, the major part of Armenia's historic lands - with a population of more than 4 million - belonged to Turkey.

[15] Protected by Russia against wars and invasions, Eastern Armenia prospered, while within the Ottoman Empire the Armenians were the object of abuse and persecution. There were frequent disturbances and riots, which were cruelly suppressed by the Turks in 1915. During World War I, citing the Armenians' pro-Russian sympathies, the Young Turk government perpetrated the massacre of more than a million Armenians. While the men were executed in the villages, the women and children were sent to the Syrian deserts, where they starved to death. Survivors of these atrocities sought refuge in Armenian expatriate communities.

[16] Upon the fall of the Russian Empire, Armenia's independence was proclaimed in Yerevan. Turkey attacked Armenia in 1918 and again in 1920. In spite of some resounding victories on the part of the Armenian troops, the young republic's economy suffered and it also lost a significant part of its territory. In late 1920, a coalition of communists and nationalists proclaimed the Soviet Republic of Armenia. The nationalists were eased out of power and in February 1921 the communist government was brought down. However, with the help of the Red Army - which came into Armenia from Azerbaijan - the communists were back in power after three months of fighting.

[17] In 1922, Armenia, Georgia and Azerbaijan formed the Transcaucasian Soviet Federated Socialist Republic, which became a part of the USSR at the end of the year. In order to avoid ethnic friction between Christian Armenians and Muslim Azeris, the Soviet regime adopted the policy of the separation of nationalities into different political/administrative entities, which implied the relocation of large segments of the population. In 1923, the Nakhichevan (Nachicevan) Autonomous Soviet Socialist Republic was created as a dependency of Azerbaijan, from which the entire Armenian population had been removed. Azerbaijan was also given Upper Nagorno-Karabakh, a region which had historically been Armenian and which Azerbaijan had previously relinquished in 1920. In 1936, the Transcaucasian Federation was dissolved, and the republics joined the Soviet Union as separate constituent republics.

[18] In 1965, Armenians around the world commemorated the 1915 genocide for the first time. In the Armenian capital, demonstrators clamoured for the return of their lands, referring to the region of Upper Karabakh. The first petition for the reunification of Nagorno-Karabakh and Armenia - signed by 2,500 inhabitants of the former - was submitted to the president of the USSR, Nikita Krushchev, in May 1963. Ever since that time, there have been two diametrically opposed positions: Armenia, in favor of reunification, and Azerbaijan, against. In 1968, fighting broke out between Armenians and Azeris in Stepanakert, the capital of Nagorno-Karabakh.

[19] In February 1988, within the framework of perestroika initiated in the USSR, Nagorno-Karabakh Armenians (80 per cent of the local population) decided to join Armenia. Karabakh's Regional soviet

STATISTICS

DEMOGRAPHY.
Population: 3,638,000 (1996). **Annual growth**: 1% (1980/1996). **Estimates for year 2000**: 4,000,000. **Annual growth to year 2000**: 0.2 % (1994/2000). **Urban Population**: 68.8% (1996). **Urban growth**: 1.64% (1980/95). **Children per woman**: 1.8 (1996).

HEALTH.
Life expectancy at birth: 71 years (1996). male: 67 years (1994). female: 75 years (1994). **Infant mortality**: 25 per 1,000 (1996). **Under-5 child mortality**: 30 per 1,000 (1996).

EDUCATION.
Literacy: 100% (1995) male : 100 % (1995) female: 99 % (1995). **School enrolment** :. Primary total: 90% (1990/95). male : 87% (1990/95). female: 93% (1990/95). Secondary:. male : 80% (1990/95). female: 90% (1990/95). Tertiary: 49 % (1995). **Primary school teachers**: one for every 22 students (1995).

COMMUNICATIONS.
20 **newspapers**, 240 **TV sets** and 156 **main telephone lines** per 1,000 people (1994). **Books**: 6 new titles per 100,000 people (1992/94).

ECONOMY.
Per capita, GNP: $ 630 (1996). **Annual growth, GNP**: 7.4 % (1995/96). **Annual inflation**: 183.06 % (1985/95). **Currency**: 405 dram = $ 1 (1995). **Cereal imports**: 300 metric tons (1994). **Exports**: $ 290 million (1996). **Imports**: $ 862 million (1996). **External debt**: $ 552 million (1996). $ 152 **per capita**: (1996). **Debt service**: 10.7% of exports (1996).
ENERGY.
Consumption: 384.47 Kgs of Oil equivalent per capita yearly (1994). 79.04 % imported (1994).

HDI (rank / value) 103 / 0.651 (1994)

(Parliament) approved the resolution and in Armenia, the Karabakh petition for reunification was received enthusiastically. Moscow reacted violently and sent in Russian troops to crush the demonstrations in Yerevan and Stepanakert.

[20] In the Armenian elections of August 1990, the National Pan-Armenian Movement won, determined to achieve independence by legal means. In the September 1991 referendum, 99.3 per cent of the electorate voted for separation from the USSR. The Armenian soviet proclaimed independence and in October Levon Ter-Petrosian was elected president with 83 per cent of the vote.

[21] Nagorno-Karabakh also declared independence after 90 per cent of the voters approved the separation. Azerbaijan responded with an economic and military blockade around Nagorno-Karabakh, causing war between these republics. In December 1991 Armenia joined the Commonwealth of Independent States (CIS) and in February 1992 was admitted to the UN.

[22] From early 1993, while the pro-Armenian forces made important victories on the Nagorno-Karabakh front, Yerevan started to withdraw its unconditional support - at least officially. In September, Azerbaijan imposed an economic blockade on Armenia.

[23] The Armenian economy grew once again in 1994 and 1995, partly because good relations with Iran cushioned the consequences of the Azerbaijani embargo. In May 1994 - when, according to Azerbaijan, the Armenian forces had taken 12,000 square kilometres of disputed territory - Russian pressure made a cease-fire possible in Nagorno-Karabakh. Some 20,000 people had been killed by the war and a million displaced. In 1995 and early 1996, negotiations continued between the warring parties.

[24] Ter-Petrosian started a second term in office, after winning the elections in September 1996. Despite accusations of fraud and violent protests, the President managed to remain in his post. In August 1997, the Yerevan and Moscow Governments signed political, economic, scientific, cultural and defence co-operation agreements.

[25] Discontent over the social situation - with unemployment affecting 20 per cent of the active population - and pressure from the opposition forced Ter-Petrosian to stand down in March 1998, after the main figures of his governing team resigned. On March 30, Robert Kocharyan, a native of Nagorno-Karabakh, won the second round of presidential elections, defeating Karen Demirchian, leader of the Communist Party during the Soviet era.

Aruba

Aruba

Population: 71,000 (1996)
Area: 193 SQ KM
Capital: Oranjestad

Currency: Florin
Language: Dutch

The Caiquetios were the first inhabitants of Aruba, one of the Lesser Antilles islands. In 1634, some European colonists settled on the island to raise horses, the only economically feasible activity in an archipelago that had been declared worthless by Spain. The Caiquetios were conquered by the Spaniards and sold to Hispaniola as slaves.

[2] According to the Treaty of Westfalia (1648), the Netherlands ruled over Aruba, Curaçao and Bonaire. Aruba required little labor to support its horse and cattle-raising industry, which explains why only 12 per cent of the population was of African origin by the time slavery was abolished.

[3] The installation of large oil refineries on Aruba at the end of the 1920s generated a wave of immigration of specialized, high income workers, particularly from the US. Many Arubans began to resent the administrative dominance of Curaçao.

[4] In 1971, the Aruba People's Party (AVP), led by Prime Minister Henny Eman, an anti-Dutch, anti-Curaçao nationalist, split into two separate parties. One was the Aruban Patriotic Party (PPA), which opposed the separation of Aruba. The other was the People's Electoral Movement (MEP), radical wing, led by Gilberto "Betico" Croes, which supported each island's freedom to choose its own constitution and even become an autonomous republic. After the Netherlands' refusal to accept this proposal, Croes threatened a unilateral declaration of independence.

[5] In 1979 the Antiyas Nobo Movement (MAN), active on 16 islands, won a significant electoral victory in Curaçao. With the MEP and the Bonaire Patriotic Union (UPB), it established a left-of-center coalition government. But while MAN favored a federation with broad autonomy for each island, the MEP insisted on the secession of Aruba. These differences led to the disintegration of the governmental alliance in 1981.

[6] In 1983, the Dutch government granted Aruba separate status, effective from January 1986, establishing a governor appointed by the Dutch queen, a single-chamber parliament with 21 members and its own national symbols. In the 1985 election, eight seats were won by the MEP, seven by the AVP and the remaining six by three minor parties who entered a coalition with the AVP. Henny Eman was Prime Minister. Croes died in 1986 in suspicious circumstances.

[7] In the 1989 elections the MEP won ten seats, the AVP won eight, and each of the three remaining parties, National Democratic Action (ADN), New Patriotic Party (PPN), and PPA, gained one seat. The new prime minister Nelson Odaber, defended continued association with the Netherlands.

[8] The economy of Aruba has the support of Dutch credit. It exports rum and tobacco, but 98.9 per cent of its exports came from refining Venezuelan oil. In 1985 Exxon, the owners of the refinery, withdrew from the country, leaving the island's economy in serious difficulties. With unemployment at 20 per cent, the Government turned to the tourist industry, which has provided 35 per cent of GDP. In recent years the authorities have tried to reduce the dependence on tourism by promoting industrial activities.

[9] In 1986 Aruba split off from the Netherlands Antilles as a first step towards what was to be total independence in 1996. The Netherlands revoked this resolution in 1990, but Aruba has autonomy over its internal affairs. After a faltering start, the economy grew at an average of 10 per cent annually between 1987 and 1993. Its strength was based on tourism, offshore finance and the resumption of oil refining.

[10] During 1990 the hotel capacity of Aruba doubled and the refinery was reopened in 1990-91. Unemployment fell to 0.6 per cent in 1992. However, the financial crisis led to the bankruptcy of many tourism related foreign companies.

[11] The MEP won the elections again in 1993 and started to implement an economic diversification policy, but the coalition faltered and was replaced in 1994 by the AVP.

[12] In September 1997, the legislative assembly was dissolved, due to disagreements between two of the main parties in the governing coalition. However, the December elections did not change the balance of power in the legislative body.

Australia

Australia

Population:	18,053,000 (1996)
Area:	7,741,220 SQ KM
Capital:	Canberra
Currency:	Australian dollars
Language:	English

The first inhabitants of Australia came from Southeast Asia some 50,000 years ago, but it is not possible to determine precisely whether at the time of their arrival they constituted one homogeneous ethnic group.

2   These peoples, named "Aborigines" by the Europeans, spoke over 260 different languages and had distinctive cultures, though they were all semi-nomadic hunters and gatherers. Their daily life was linked to a universal scheme through rituals which guaranteed the ordered changing of the seasons and the community's food supply.

3   Land was held in common, and there was no social stratification, other than the prestige gained by practising religious rites.

4   In 1606, the Spaniard Vaez de Torres explored the strait which today bears his name, located between Australia and Papua-New Guinea. Three years later, Fernández de Quirós, also Spanish, became the first European to set eyes on Australian territory. However, colonization did not begin until after the arrival of Captain James Cook, in the late 18th century.

5   In 1788, the first British settlers arrived, and established a penal colony. This was the beginning of an assault on the way of life and customs of the Aborigines. The two fundamental objectives were: to take over the best lands and to obtain a supply of labour.

6   At first, the British settled in coastal areas, but the process of inland expansion soon began, with the settlers acting as though the land were uninhabited. While British and international law recognized the prior rights of indigenous peoples, Australia was simply declared *terra nullius* (uninhabited).

7   The wars to gain control of the land claimed the lives of 80 per cent of the Aborigines. The "Aborigine problem" was dealt with by genocide. Entire families were poisoned and others were forcibly removed from their lands onto reservations administered by the British.

8   In 1830 more than 58,000 convicts were "transported" to Australia, most of them petty thieves, deserters from the Royal Navy and members of Irish opposition groups. Known by the British as "the human refuse of the Thames", most of them served out their sentences by providing inexpensive labour for European landowners.

9   Australia served as a safety valve for social tensions generated by Britain's rapid industrialization. Most of the wealth accumulated in the colony returned to England, representing an important influx of capital. Finally, Australia's strategic location was important for British trade, in order to control its world-wide maritime network.

10   Australian society was marked by a strong authoritarian streak, a legacy of its original function as a penal colony. Local government was normally limited to a high-ranking military officer, appointed by the Crown to oversee the prison population and take charge of the defence against possible attack by other European powers.

11   The Aboriginal religion, based on a strong spiritual link between each human being and the earth, was given no credence by the settlers. As a result, the religion and language were debased and the people persecuted. The Aborigines lost lands rich in natural resources, fishing areas and any land that the settlers considered suitable for cultivation or grazing. Once the land was in the hands of settlers, it was stocked with sheep to provide the growing British textile industry with both an abundant supply of raw materials, and a cheap source of food for the industry's workforce.

12   The development of the cattle industry and the subsequent discovery of gold and other precious metals, boosted economic development between 1830 and 1860. The possibility of getting rich quickly led to increased European settlement. As resistance was

LAND USE

IRRIGATED 59.1% of arable

(1993)

■	FOREST & WOODLAND	18.8%
☐	ARABLE	6%
▨	OTHER	75.2%

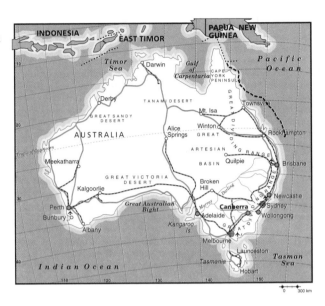

Christmas Island

Population	: 900 (1994)
Area:	130 SQ KM
Capital:	Flying Fish Cove
Currency:	Australian Dollars
Language:	English

1   The island, formerly a dependency of the British colony of Singapore, was transferred to Australia on October 1 1958. Nearly all the island's population work in the Phosphate Mining Commission.

2   As of 1981, the residents of the island were granted the right to become Australian citizens. In 1984, the Australian Government extended social security, health and education benefits to the island, also granting the citizens political rights. There has been an income tax since 1985.

3   In 1987, the authorities closed the mine, which was reopened in 1990 by private investors but under strict guidelines for the preservation of the environment. In 1991 investments were made to develop the island's tourist potential.

ENVIRONMENT

An island in the Indian Ocean, 2,500 km northeast of Perth, Australia, and 380 km south of Java, Indonesia. Mountainous and arid, it has a dry climate.

SOCIETY

Peoples: Nearly two-thirds of the population are of Chinese origin. There are some Malays and a minority of Australians. There are no native inhabitants.
Religions: Christianity (Protestants), Confucianism and Taoism.
Languages: English, Malay, Mandarin and Cantonese.
Capital: Flying Fish Cove.
Government: A D Taylor, Administrator appointed by the Australian Government.

Foreign Trade

MILLIONS $ 1996

IMPORTS
60,897
EXPORTS
53,252

broken, the Aborigines were progressively relegated to Australia's desert areas.

[13] For many years, rural settlers occasionally had to deal with armed Aboriginal resistance. Driven by their desire to free land from the Europeans, they fought the settlers and tried to disrupt their farming.

[14] Once suppressed, Aborigines were forced to sign "work contracts" written in English. These contracts committed them to the status of unpaid workers, household slaves or concubines, often subject to extremely severe disciplinary measures.

[15] In the meantime, a dynamic labour movement was beginning to appear in the cities, and it soon had a significant following. From the mid-19th century onwards, the unions obtained important victories and concessions which Europe's working classes were still a long way from obtaining.

[16] In the latter part of the 19th century, Australia's growing urbanization process went hand-in-hand with an accelerated rate of industrial development, especially in Sydney and Melbourne, which took on the characteristics of any large urban centre.

[17] Successive waves of immigration also helped change the face of Australian society. The low cost of land and a demand for Australia's products on the world market, provided large numbers of mostly British people with the means for achieving rapid social mobility.

[18] A vast middle class developed alongside a wealthy urban industrial bourgeoisie, utterly transforming Australian life. The liberal governments which dominated the country's political scene between 1860 and 1900 accelerated this political, social and economic transformation.

[19] After an uneasy period of consolidation, in 1901 the six British colonies (New South Wales, Victoria, South Australia, Western Australia, Queensland and Tasmania) became independent states united in the "Commonwealth of Australia". The Northern Territory and the Australian Capital Territory did not join until 1911.

[20] A prolonged period of economic prosperity made it possible for the country to finance a series of social reforms. Australia

was a relatively open society, in which social mobility was possible for certain sectors of the population, and there was protective legislation for workers before most European countries. In 1902, Australia became one of the first countries to grant women the right to vote.

[21] World War II loosened the ties between Britain and Australia, as Britain was unable to guarantee the security of its former colonies, in the face of the threat of Japanese attack. The US assumed the role of guaranteeing the region's security, as it has done ever since.

[22] The Korean War triggered a sharp increase in the price of wool on the world market, reinforcing Australia's economic growth. It also helped to avoid creating a gap between urban prosperity and the relative stagnation of the rural areas.

[23] With the onset of the Cold War, the ANZUS military assistance treaty was signed in 1951 by Australia, Aotearoa/New Zealand and the US. The aim of the treaty was to guarantee the security of US and allied interests in the region. This military alliance also committed the Australians to participate in the Vietnam War, which damaged the treaty's image internationally, and triggered an important anti-war movement.

[24] Japan became the main market for Australian minerals, financing coal exploration in Australia in the 60s. The large coal deposits discovered have supplied local industry ever since, and have also met Japan's huge industrial needs.

[25] In the 1960s, the Labor Party became the platform for Aborigine groups, helping to publicize and sensitize public opinion to their grievances and demands.

[26] A plebiscite held in 1967 - supported by the Labor Party - granted Australian Aborigines full citizenship rights. The Aboriginal issue was also placed under the jurisdiction of the federal government. However, the Aborigines still did not gain recognition of their land rights.

[27] There are currently 200,000 Aborigines in Australia, many retaining their original languages. Two-thirds of them no longer live in tribes, living instead in urban areas. A minority continues to live in areas which Europeans consider to

be inhospitable, like the central desert or the wetlands which lie in the northern part of the country, where they have managed to keep their own religious and social traditions alive.

[28] In 1983, powerful transnational corporations interested in

developing mineral resources launched a campaign aimed at convincing the population that the Aborigines' defence of their territorial claims actually compromised the country's economic growth. As a result of this campaign, the Government's

PROFILE

ENVIRONMENT

Australia occupies the continental part of Oceania and the island of Tasmania, and has a predominantly flat terrain. The Great Dividing Range runs along the eastern coast. Inland lies the Central Basin, a desert plateau surrounded by plains and savannahs. The desert region runs west to the huge Western Plateau. Rainfall is greatest in the north where the climate is tropical, with dense rainforests. 75 per cent of the population is concentrated in the southeast, which has a subtropical climate and year-round rainfall. Oats, rye, sugar cane and wheat are grown there; Australia is one of the world's largest producers of the latter. Australia has the largest number of sheep of any country in the world, located in the inland steppes and savannahs, and is also the world's largest exporter of wool. It also exports meat and dairy products and is one of the world's largest producers of minerals: iron ore, bauxite, coal, lead, zinc, copper, nickel and uranium. It is self-sufficient in oil and has a large industrial zone concentrated in the southeast. The soil has undergone increasing salinization. Many unique species, both plant and animal, are in danger of extinction due to the destruction of their habitats.

SOCIETY

Peoples: When the British "discovered" Australia in 1788, there were 250,000 Aborigines in approximately 500 different tribes. In 1901, only 66,000 of their descendents were still alive. Today, there are 200,000, representing just 1 per cent of the national population. Descendents of British immigrants make up two-thirds of the population. The rest are immigrants from Asia, Europe and Latin America, a process which continues today.
Religions: Christians 74 per cent (Catholic 27 per cent, Anglican 24 per cent, Methodist 8 per cent and others). Buddhist, Muslim, Confucian and other, 13 per cent.
Languages: English.
Political Parties: Liberal (conservative) Party, a right-of-centre power (aligned with the National Party (NP), which represents the interests of pastoralists); Labor Party, a centre-left group; Australian Democrats (moderate); Party of the New Left, founded in 1989 after the dissolution of the Communist Party; Socialist Party; Marxist-Leninist Communist Party and Green Party.
Social Organizations: The Australian Council of Trade Unions (ACTU) is the largest labour confederation, with 133 union affiliates.

THE STATE

Official Name: Commonwealth of Australia.
Administrative divisions: 6 states and 2 territories.
Capital: Canberra, 331,800 people (1995).
Other cities: Sydney 3,772,00 people; Melbourne 3,218,100; Brisbane 1,489,100; Perth 1,262,600; Adelaide 1,081,000 (1995).
Government: Parliamentary monarchy. William Deane, Governor General, appointed by the Queen of England. John Howard, Prime Minister since March 1996.
National Holiday: January 26, Australia Day.
Armed Forces: 56,100 (7,500 women included).
Dependencies: Cocos, Coral Islands, Christmas, Norfolk.

STATISTICS

DEMOGRAPHY
Population: 18,053,000 (1996) **Annual growth**: 1.3% (1980/1996) **Estimates for year 2000**: 19,000,000. **Annual growth to year 2000**: 1.1% (1994/2000) **Urban Population**: 84.7% (1996) **Urban growth**: 1.32% (1980/95) **Children per woman**: 1.9 (1996).

HEALTH
Life expectancy at birth: 78 years (1996) male: 75 years (1994) female: 81 years (1994) **Infant mortality**: 6 per 1,000 (1996) **Under-5 child mortality**: 6 per 1,000 (1996) **Calorie consumption**: 124% (1988/90).

EDUCATION
School enrolment: Primary total: 107 % (1990/95) male : 107 % (1990/95) female: 106 % (1990/95) Secondary: male : 83 % (1990/95) female: 86 % (1990/95) Tertiary: 72 % (1995) **Primary school teachers**: one for every 16 students (1995)

COMMUNICATIONS
260 **newspapers**, 1,291 **radios**, 480 **TV sets** and 496 **main telephone lines** per 1,000 people (1994) **Books**: 61 new titles per 100,000 people (1992/94).

ECONOMY
Per capita, GNP: $ 20,090 (1996) **Annual growth, GNP**: 2.6 % (1995/96) **Annual inflation**: 3.73 % (1985/95) **Consumer price index**: 108.1 (1994) **Currency**: 1.34 Australian dollars = $ 1 (1995) **Cereal imports**: 66 metric tons (1994) **Fertilizer use**: 351 kgs per ha (1994) **Exports**: $ 53,252 million (1996) **Imports**: $ 60,897 million (1996).

ENERGY
Consumption: 5,341.28 Kgs of Oil equivalent per capita yearly (1994) -82.64 % imported (1994).

HDI (rank / value) 14 / 0.931 (1994)

Norfolk Island

Population	: 2,700 (1996)
Area:	36 SQ KM
Capital:	Kingston
Currency:	Australian dollars
Language:	English

There are no records on the existence of a native population before the arrival of the Europeans. Discovered by Cook in 1774, it was used as a prison site between 1825 and 1855.

In 1913, the island was transferred to Australia as an overseas territory. In November 1976, two thirds of the Norfolk electorate opposed annexation to Australia. Since 1979, the island has had internal autonomy.

[2] In December 1991, the local population rejected a new proposal to become part of Australia's federal electorate.

ENVIRONMENT
The island is located in Southern Melanesia, northwest of the North Island of Aotearoa/NZ. The subtropical climate is tempered by sea winds.

SOCIETY
Peoples: 2,700 inhabitants in 1996. A large part of the population are descended from the mutineers of the British vessel HMS Bounty, who came from Pitcairn Island in 1856.
Religions: Protestant.
Languages: English (official).

THE STATE
Official name: Norfolk Island.
Capital: Kingston.
Government: Cdr John A Matthew, Administrator appointed by the Governor General of Australia. The office of prime minister was replaced by that of President of the Legislative Assembly. In the May 1992 elections, David Ernest Buffett was elected to this new office.

---

promise of passing federal legislation on territorial rights of the Aborigines was shelved.

[29] In many cases the Aborigines found themselves forced to give in to pressure from mining companies, and sign land use agreements, even though they knew that it could well adversely affect their sacred sites, the environment, and their traditional life style.

[30] Although some aspects of the Aborigines' situation are uniform throughout the country, their legal status nevertheless varies from one state to another. The state of the Northern Territory, for example, has relatively progressive legislation, with regard to the recognition of the rights of Aborigines. Other states, like Tasmania, have only recently begun to study proposals aimed at safeguarding some of the Aborigines' rights, as well as ways of combating the discrimination to which they are subjected.

[31] According to local and international human rights organizations, in 1987, the death rate of Aboriginal prisoners was two per month. In terms of the total prison population, this would be the equivalent of 100 deaths of prisoners of European descent, in the same amount of time.

[32] Australian Aborigines are probably the people with the largest prison population in the world. In 1981, the rate was 775 per 100,000 inhabitants. Among the population of European descent, the proportion was 67 per 100,000. In Queensland, in the northeast of the country, Aborigines make up only 2 per cent of the population, yet account for 35 per cent of the prison population. In Western Australia, where they also make up 2 per cent of the population, 44 per cent of the prison population are Aborigines.

[33] Given this situation, the federal government created a Royal Commission charged with investigating the deaths of Aborigines in prison. After several years of work and research, the commission presented a provisional report which did not clearly establish what the actual causes of these events were, nor who was responsible for them. This report was harshly criticized by spokespersons of different groups, who called it a "sham" for all the country's citizens.

[34] In the area of health, the Aborigines are also at a clear disadvantage with relation to the rest of the population. Thus, they continue to contract diseases which have almost disappeared among the European population, and for which total immunization is available.

[35] Although Australia agreed with Aotearoa/NZ in opposing British and French nuclear tests in the region, the virtual withdrawal of Aotearoa/NZ from ANZUS has made it necessary for the Australian government to redefine its role within this alliance, and within the region. The United States is in the process of negotiating new agreements allowing the maintenance of troops and a telecommunications centre in Australian territory.

[36] In 1989, in order to meet this new international reality head-on, Australia proposed the creation of the Asian Pacific Economic Cooperation (APEC). The project proposes the formation of a common market among the countries of the region, with Australia taking a leading role. At the same time, Australia hoped to become the representative of food-exporting countries. To achieve this goal, it proposed the creation of the so-called "Cairns Group", which includes Argentina, Colombia, Thailand, Uruguay and other countries within the Uruguay Round of the GATT.

[37] In 1989, data supplied by Australian National University research damaged the Labor Government's image. The figures pointed to the fact that 1 percent of all Australians owns more than 20 percent of the total national wealth, and 13 percent of all Australian homes live below the poverty line.

[38] The social and economic crisis worsened, with unemployment figures totalling more than a million in 1991. This put pressure on Bob Hawke's Labor government, which found itself under growing opposition from other political parties, and from within the party as well.

[39] Hawke had been elected in 1983, after 11 years as president of ACTU (the country's largest labour unon), a fact which had given him a huge amount of popular support at the beginning of his term.

[40] Toward the end of the 1980s, with the support of the more conservative elements within his party, Hawke embarked upon a series of economic reforms aimed at liberalizing the economy, including an accelerated program for privatizing public enterprises.

[41] There was growing discontent among the population at large, and opposition to the government began to emerge within the Labor

Coral Sea

Created in 1969 as a separate administrative entity, the territory consists of several islets located east of Queensland (Eastern Australia). The major ones are Cato and Chilcott in the Coringa group, and the Willis archipelago. With the exception of a weather station, on one of the Willis islands, the rest of the islands are uninhabited.

2 The Constitutional Act by which the territory was created did not provide for Australian administration of the islands, but only for control over foreign visitors by the Canberra government. However, this situation may change in view of the possible exploitation of hydrocarbons and the good prospects for fisheries development.

Party itself. In addition, a power struggle developed between Hawke and his former Treasurer (Economics Minister), Paul Keating. In December 1991, the Labor Government held internal elections in order resolve these conflicts once and for all, and also to open up the possibility of improving the government's image. Keating, representing the Labor Party, obtained a slim victory which made him Prime Minister.

42 Shortly after assuming his post as head of the government, Keating announced that further measures would go into effect to liberalize the economy. Keating himself had initiated these measures between 1983 and June 1991, when he had been in charge of economic policy for Hawke's government. These measures were firmly rejected by the unions and the left wing of the Labor Party.

43 In 1992, unemployment reached 11.1 per cent. The Government approved legislation aimed at increasing employment, by reducing immigration by 27 per cent.

44 In the 1993 general elections, Labor won by a narrow margin, with 50.5 per cent of the vote. One of Keating's campaign promises was to give the rights of indigenous Australians a high priority.

45 An important decision on native land rights was made by the Australian High Court in June 1993. Known as the Mabo decision, it effectively overturned the notion of *terra nullius*, which had assumed that when the British colonists arrived in 1788, the Aborigines had neither right of law nor ownership of the land. Mabo was one of Australia's most significant legal decisions since federation in 1901. The decision drew on the history of the Murray Islands north of Queensland and to their Meriam people, whose rules of inheritance were crucial in the final judgement. Following this Mabo decision, the federal Labor government passed revised Native Title legislation. So far only one claim by indigenous Australians has been successful - that of the Dunghutti people in northern NSW in October 1996. There are also concerns over other matters affecting Aborigines and Torres Strait Islanders, including infant mortality, health, education and the country's terrible record of black deaths in custody. Progress Australia had been making in multiculturalism has also slowed, despite it being one of the most ethnically diverse countries in the world.

46 The Government started to develop links with the Asian Pacific nations, through trade and dialogue with regional groups such as ASEAN . But their relations with Cambodia, North Korea, Vietnam, Indonesia, Malaysia and China advanced with greater difficulty.

47 The independence debate intensified in 1995 when Prime Minister Keating announced that Sir William Deane, a Supreme Court judge, would replace Bill Hayden as Governor General. Keating's plans included replacing the post of governor with that of president (for the first time in the nation's history) before the year 2001.

48 Privatization continued to be the Government's main concern, with the sale of the Qantas, the Commonwealth Bank and the partial sale of telecommunications company Telstra.

49 The French nuclear tests on Mururoa atoll caused public protests throughout Australia. The Keating and Chirac Governments were at loggerheads and broke off diplomatic relations. The Australian delegation which went to Europe with the Pacific Islands' Minister of Affairs did not gain the support of the British Government, which refused to confront France. The British decision strengthened Australia's pro-independence stance.

50 In the general elections held on March, 1996, John Howard, leader of the Liberal Party, defeated his

Cocos

Population: 600 (1994)
Area: 14 SQ KM
Capital: West Island
Currency: Australian Dollars
Language: English

The Clunies Ross Company, founded by John Clunies Ross in the early 1800s, was the real owner of the islands, despite their formal status as a British (1857) and later Australian (after 1955) colony. Ross brought in Malayan laborers to work the coconut groves.

2 In 1978, after many years of negotiations, Australia bought the islands from the company. However, the company kept a monopoly on the production and commercialization of copra. The transfer was designed to give Home Island residents formal ownership of their plots of land, in order to alleviate social tensions. On West Island, Australia also has a military base, purchased in 1951.

3 In a 1984 referendum, the population voted in favour of Australian nationality for the islanders and full annexation of the territory to Australia. In December of that year the UN General Assembly validated the results of the plebiscite and Australia was freed from the obligation of reporting to the Decolonisation Committee.

ENVIRONMENT

A group of coral atolls in the Indian Ocean, southwest of Java, Indonesia. Of the 27 islets, only two are inhabited, West and Home. The climate is tropical and rainy, and the land is flat and covered with the coconut groves that give the islands their name.

SOCIETY

Peoples: The inhabitants of Home Island are descended from Malayan workers. Australians predominate on West Island.
Religions: Mainly Protestant
Languages: English.
The State
Capital: West Island, 208 people (1984).
Government: D Lawrie, administrator appointed by the Australian Government.

Labor predecessor. Howard became Prime Minister after pledging the "moralization" of his country's leadership.

51 In early 1996, the High Court of Australia authorized indigenous peoples to claim the use of land leased for grazing or mining activities. In August 1997, the eventual beginning of new uranium extraction activities, in the north, caused a strong sentiment of rejection among aboriginal groups. The leaders of the protest, among them several women, claimed the extraction would contaminate their land and the money would devastate their culture. By the end of the year, several native groups filed suits for the recognition of their property over vast coast and sea areas. The issue of Aboriginal land rights remains politically controversial and undecided.

52 Amnesty International reported in 1997 an increase in the death rate of native peoples held in jails or in police detention operations, as well as ill treatment and intimidation in the enforcement of the law. In October, it was revealed Victoria state police had spied, infiltrated and kept files on ethnic groups, natives, journalists and organizations such as Greenpeace or groups fighting against Aids. Although this shocked some Australians, senior Intelligence officials justified these proceedings and assured it was an essential factor to maintain public order.

53 Despite government opposition to union activity, the unions struggled to retain bargaining power. In April 1998, the Patrick Stevedores company dismissed 1,400 dockers with the implicit support of the Government. This led the Maritime Union of Australia to call a strike which became one of the biggest in the 1990s.

54 The Howard Government provoked widespread controversy over their economic liberalization program; including increased banking fees for small account holders and substantial welfare cuts. New regulations deny immigrants access to social security until they have been in Australia for 2 years. In Queensland, anti-immigration politician Pauline Hanson gained popularity. Her One Nation Party won 23 per cent of the votes in the 1998 state election.

Austria

Österreich

Population: 8,106,000 (1996)
Area: 83,859 SQ KM
Capital: Vienna (Wien)

Currency: Schillings
Language: German

The first traces of human settlement in the Austrian Republic date back to the Early Paleolithic age. From then on, the territory was occupied by various ethnic groups. The Austrian region of Hallstat gave its name to the main culture in the Iron Age, from 800-450 BC.

[2] Celtic tribes moved into the Eastern Alps in the 5th century BC, and it is thought that they founded the kingdom of Noricum. Later, the Romans also settled here, attracted by the iron in the area and by its strategic military importance.

[3] After peaceful penetration, the Roman troops conquered the whole of the country around the year 15 BC. Raetia, Noricum and Pannonia became Roman provinces, extending the Empire's dominions as far as the Danube. The provinces were subdivided into municipalities and a vast network of roads was built.

[4] The Pax Romana ended with the arrival of the Germanic tribes between 166 and 180 AD. This invasion was repulsed, but the region did not recover its prosperity. Between the 4th and 6th centuries, the Huns and the Germans raided the area pushing back the Empire's borders on the Danube.

[5] According to the only written records of the time, the Germanic tribes of the Rugii, the Goths, the Heruli and the Langobardi settled on Austrian territory. In the year 488 part of the population of the devastated province of Noricum was forced to emigrate to Italy.

[6] After a succession of battles between the Germans and the Slavs, the Bavarian lands reached the border with the Avars in the 7th century. Upon the death of King Dagobert I, the Bavarian dukes became virtually independent. Christianity spread in the region, and it was practised by the Romans who had remained in the territory.

[7] Bavarian military expansion and wealth were central to the advance of Christianity. Under their protection, the churches of Salzburg and Passau opposed the missions of the East, led by the Slav apostles, Cyril and Methodius.

[8] During the 9th century the Magyars raided the area and ruled over Austrian territory until they were expelled in 960. The earliest evidence of a developed legal system was found in the region of Burchard, east of the river Enns, in this period. Later on, this legislation was extended as far as the forests of Vienna.

[9] On several occasions Austria was the object of investiture disputes between the Pope and the Holy Roman Emperor, who were struggling over control of the German Church. Meanwhile, the reformists gained ground, with the foundation of the monasteries of Gottmelg, Lambach, and Admont in Styria.

[10] Between the 10th and 13th centuries the dispute over the territories continued and new peoples settled in Germanic and non-Germanic areas. Apart from short interruptions, the Babenbergs kept their sovereignty over the duchies of Austria and Styria and expanded them both north and south.

[11] Upon the death of Frederick II, the Babenberg dominions were coveted by their neighbors. The main beneficiary was Premysl Otakar II, from Bohemia, until Rudolf IV of Hapsburg occupied the German throne in 1273, using Hungarian help to displace him.

[12] At first the Hapsburgs were rejected by the local nobility and their neighbors, but apart from a few minor defeats they succeeded in keeping control over their dominions. During the 14th and 15th centuries the Austrian territories were ruled by the Hapsburgs.

[13] In 1490, after several crises, the Hapsburgs lost everything except Lower Austria. Upon the death of Frederick II, Maximilian I inherited the House of Austria and the German Empire; his son Philip I married Infanta Juana and became king of Spain.

[14] By the end of the Middle Ages, the Hapsburg monarchy held an extent of Alpine land comparable in size to modern Austria. The House of Hapsburg had always wanted to rule over Bohemia and Hungary, an aspiration that Maximilian kept rekindled.

[15] After unification, territories maintained their individuality and their own legal codes. Cities prospered, while rural settlement regressed, particularly in Lower Austria, because of the growing interest in mining.

[16] Martin Luther's reforming ideas penetrated Austria, supported by the noble families, especially in the south and centre of the country. In 1521, Protestant pamphlets were printed in Vienna, and bans on their dissemination had no practical effect.

[17] There were peasant revolts in Tyrol, Salzburg and Innerösterreich. Many peasants were joining the Anabaptists rather than the Lutherans. Their name came from the Greek meaning "to baptize again", as they considered the christening of children ineffectual, subjecting followers to a second christening. As they were more radical, and had no support from the powerful, they suffered greater persecution from the outset.

[18] In 1528, in Vienna, Balthasar Hubmaier, leader of the Anabaptists in the Danube valley and southern Moravia, was burned at the stake. In 1536, in Innsbruck, Jakob Hutter, a Tyrolian, was sentenced to the same fate after he had led his followers into Moravia.

[19] When King Jagiellon of Bohemia and Hungary died, Vienna saw an opportunity to broaden the power of the Hapsburgs. Ferdinand I was proclaimed king of Bohemia in 1526, but his troops were repulsed with the aid of the Turks, when he tried to impose himself over the Hungarians.

[20] At the end of the dispute in 1562, the treaty of Constantinople divided Hungary into three regions: the north and the west went to the Hapsburgs; the centre, to the Turks; and Transylvania, with its surrounding territories, to Hungarian Hanos Zapolya and his successors.

[21] Maximilian II succeeded Ferdinand I as emperor of Bohemia, which was a part of Hungary and the Austrian Danube. The heir had Protestant leanings, although he promised his father

WORKERS

UNEMPLOYMENT 4.1% (1996)

Labour force %
- ■ WOMEN
- □ MEN

41 59

- ■ AGRICULTURE 8% (1990)
- □ INDUSTRIAL 38%
- ■ SERVICES 55%

LAND USE

IRRIGATED 0.3 % of arable

(1993)

- ■ FOREST & WOODLAND 38.6%
- □ ARABLE 16.9%
- ■ OTHER 44.5%

PROFILE

ENVIRONMENT

Austria is a landlocked country in central Europe. The Alps stretch over most of its territory. Tourism, milk by-products and textiles are the main economic activities in the western mountain provinces of Vorarlberg and Tyrol. Rye and potatoes are farmed in the lower woodlands of the Eastern Alps. The rich agricultural basins of Klagenfurt and Styria, in the eastern Alps produce corn, wheat, fruit, cattle and poultry. Austria's iron ore and coal mines feed its large iron and steel industry. The Danube river valley runs across the northern foothills of the Alps and is a major route for river, highway and rail transportation. The gas emissions from industrial plants and cars in large cities, and the use of agrochemicals are the main causes of environmental degradation.

SOCIETY

Peoples: Mostly of Germanic origin. There are Slav, Polish and Hungarian minorities.
Religions: Mainly Catholic.
Languages: German.
Political Parties: The Austrian People's Party (ÖVP); the Austrian Social Democratic Party (SPÖ); the Liberal Party (FPÖ); the Green Alternative and the United Green Party of Austria; the Communist Party and the extreme-right National Democratic Party of Austria.
Social Movements: The Austrian Trade Union Federation.

THE STATE

Official Name: Republik Österreich.
Capital: Vienna (Wien), 1,540,000 people (1996).
Other cities: Graz, 237,000 people; Linz, 203,000; Salzburg, 143,000 (1991).
Government: Thomas Klestil, President, since May, 1992; Viktor Klima, Chancellor (Prime Minister), since January, 1997. A federal Republic of 9 provinces; bicameral parliamentary system.
Armed Forces: some 52,000.

Maternal Mortality

1990

PER 100,000
LIVE BIRTHS

10

Foreign Trade

MILLIONS $ 1994

IMPORTS
67,142
EXPORTS
57,822

---

that he would uphold the Catholic faith. The Counter-reformation started with the Jesuits, who were strong in Vienna, Graz and Innsbruck.

[22] Maximilian's successor, Rudolf II, had been strictly educated in Spain, in the Catholic faith. He removed all the Protestants who served at court and entrusted the conversion of cities and markets to Melchior Klesl, the Apostolic Administrator of Vienna, later to be bishop and cardinal.

[23] The Catholic-Protestant controversy had ups and downs in the House of Hapsburg until the death of Emperor Matthias, in 1619, and the accession of Ferdinand II, who was the least involved with the Counter-reformation. Bohemia and Moravia rebelled, and war became inevitable.

[24] The conflict went beyond the empire's borders: Spain, Bavaria and Saxony joined Ferdinand II; Bohemia was subjected, and Protestants emigrated to Germany in massive numbers. Germany was invaded, and the Protestant backlash came from Sweden in 1630, causing the Thirty Years War that followed.

[25] Between the 17th and 19th centuries, the Hapsburgs were involved in all the European conflicts. The Napoleonic Wars virtually dismantled the Austrian

Empire, and it was only after Napoleon's abdication in 1814 that the House of Austria recovered most of its territory.

[26] The Austrian Chancellor Clemens Metternich was the creator of the Holy Alliance of the European powers in 1815. It upheld the principles of Christian authoritarianism and foreign intervention against the liberal and revolutionary movements of the time.

[27] In 1848, the repercussions of the Paris Commune reached Austria. A revolt broke out in Vienna, led by crowds demanding the liberalization of the regime. Metternich's resignation, rather than bringing peace, unleashed a revolution throughout the empire.

[28] In spite of their active presence in the street fights of Vienna, the workers had little significance in the society of the time, due to the country's lack of industrial development. The most important social consequence of the revolution was the liberation of peasants, sanctioned by the Emperor in 1849.

[29] At the same time the liberal government of Hungary demanded independence. In Germany the revolution installed a National Assembly in Frankfurt, which incorporated Austrian-German liberals and conservatives interested in

separation from the Hapsburg Empire.

[30] The Emperor accepted the Budapest petitions, except on two key points: budget and military autonomy. The Hungarian Parliament declared the power of the Hapsburgs null and void, and proclaimed a republic in April 1849. The revolution was crushed four months later.

[31] Counter-revolution also annulled the Frankfurt Assembly, but the Austrian-Prussian dispute persisted. From then on, the Hapsburg Empire weakened inexorably. It lost, ceded and decentralized its dominions until its final disintegration in 1918, at the end of World War I.

[32] In October of that year, a National Assembly declared German Austria an independent state. In November, after the abdication of the Emperor, it proclaimed a republic. Socialist Karl Renner led the first coalition government of the main parties.

[33] Amidst the economic chaos and the hunger resulting from the war, the Austrian Social Democrats decided to use their strength to confront social unrest and growing Communist activism, inspired by the Soviet revolution in Russia in 1917 and in Hungary in 1919.

[34] Unlike the German Socialists, who made alliances with the old order, Austrian Socialists organised a People's Guard, which thwarted two coup attempts. Otto Bauer and Frederick Adler consolidated their strength when they defeated the communists in the workers' and soldiers' councils.

[35] Once political and social order were re-established in Vienna, the problem moved to the interior, where some states were demanding secession. The 1920 Constitution guaranteed a loose federal system, whereby the capital was governed by the Socialists and the rest of the country by the Conservatives.

[36] The new Constitution granted women the vote, something which had been guaranteed from the moment the republic was proclaimed in 1918.

[37] The Social Democrats had an unquestionable majority in Vienna, where one-third of the population lived. Social Christians had guaranteed support among the

peasants and the Conservatives, while German nationalism fed on popular discontent, with the support of the urban middle classes.

[38] The League of Nations supported Austrian economic recovery during the postwar period, on the condition that the country would remain independent and would not join Germany. In 1922, the Government was granted a loan which enabled complete stabilization of the country's finances.

[39] The great depression of 1929 brought the Austrian economy to the verge of collapse. The Government tried to arrange a customs agreement with Germany which was harshly opposed by the rest of Europe. Together with the rise of Nazism, German nationalism in Austria was showing signs of strengthening.

[40] In 1932, the Social Christian government of Engelbert Dollfuss attempted to take an authoritarian stance against the Social Democrats and the Nazis simultaneously. The Social Democrats rebelled and were declared illegal, and in 1934, the Nazis murdered Dollfuss in a failed coup d'etat.

[41] Taking advantage of the internal crisis and the government's weakness, German troops invaded Austria in 1938, unchallenged by the European powers. A plebiscite carried out that same year in greater Germany recorded a vote of more than 99 per cent in favour of Hitler.

[42] In 1945, after Hitler's defeat, Austria was divided into 4 zones, occupied by US, French, British and Soviet troops. In the November elections, out of the 165 seats in the National Council, the conservatives obtained 85 and the Social Democrats 76 seats.

[43] The Austrian economy recovered with difficulty after the war, with the aid of the United Nations and the United States, through the implementation of the Marshall Plan. Heavy industry and banking were nationalized in 1946, and inflation was controlled by price and salary agreements.

[44] Conservatives and Socialists shared the government of the Second Austrian Republic, which

only recovered full independence in 1955, with the Treaty of State and the withdrawal of the allied troops. The coalition held until 1966, when the People's Party were elected to govern alone.

45 During the postwar period, Austria did not become a member of international organizations. During the Cold War, the country was liberal in the acceptance of political refugees from Poland, and it was a transit station for Soviet Jewish émigrés.

46 Austria became a member of the United Nations in 1955 and of the Council of Europe in 1956. Since then, Austrian foreign policy has centered on the dispute with Italy over Sudtirol (Bolzano), resolved in 1969, and its association with the European Economic Community (EEC).

47 In 1958, Vienna joined the European Free Trade Association, establishing a special agreement with the EEC. It established negotiations with the neighboring countries belonging to the Common Economic Assistance Council. In this way it remained a neutral nation.

48 The Socialist Party (SPÖ) obtained a close victory in 1970 forming a minority government led by Bruno Kreisky. In 1971 and 1975, the SPÖ obtained an absolute majority and monopolized government,

supported by great economic stability and a policy of moderate social reforms.

49 The Austrian Government was a guest at the meetings of the Movement of Non-Aligned Countries and acted as a bridge between the Palestine Liberation Organization (PLO) and Western Europe. Vienna was energetic in its condemnation of the Israeli invasion of Lebanon in 1982.

50 In 1978, the Government lost a plebiscite over the installation of a nuclear power plant, but the SPÖ confirmed its support of the Prime Minister and held power until the 1979 elections. Kreisky resigned after 1983, when the SPÖ lost its majority and had to form a coalition government.

51 The fall of the SPÖ was attributed to the rise of two green parties, which gathered more than 3 per cent of the vote but did not obtain any parliamentary seats. In a coalition with the Freedom Party (FPÖ), the SPÖ maintained its policies of social welfare and active neutrality.

52 In the presidential election of 1986, the SPÖ was defeated by the former Secretary General of the United Nations, Kurt Waldheim, who was an independent candidate with the support of the Austrian People's Party (ÖVP, Social Christian). However, the socialists maintained

their majority in parliament until 1990.

53 During the electoral campaign Waldheim was accused of having been an officer in the Nazi army. After taking office the questioning continued, when evidence of his involvement in the German campaign against the Yugoslav guerrillas was disclosed. This fact had negative repercussions on the country's relations with both the United States and Israel.

54 The governor of the southern province of Carincia, Joerg Haider, leader of the ultra-nationalist Liberal Party (FPÖ), was deposed in June 1991 after he praised the full employment policy of the Third Reich. In the November 1991 municipal elections, after a campaign in which he accused foreigners living in Austria of "stealing" Austrians' jobs, the FPÖ obtained 22.6 per cent of the vote becoming the second largest political party in Vienna.

55 In 1992, amidst growing attacks against foreign residents, the Government passed a law aimed at punishing neo-Nazi activities. In May, Thomas Klestil, from the ÖVP, was elected President with almost 57 per cent of the vote, after Waldheim decided not to stand for re-election and thus put an end to six years of Austrian international isolation.

56 The changes which took place in Europe with the fall of the Berlin Wall had a significant impact on the Austrian economy. The first two years of German reunification, for example, caused a deficit in Austria's trade balance.

57 In 1993, Haider intensified his racist rhetoric, blaming the increase in crime and unemployment on the lack of immigration controls. In February, 200,000 people demonstrated in the streets of Vienna against racism. A bill sponsored by Haider, aimed at reducing the number of foreigners and limiting their rights, failed to receive the amount of signatures required for its approval.

58 A referendum in 1994 decided Austria would join the European Union, which, in theory, did not affect the country's neutrality, as stated by the Constitution. In the March regional elections, the FPÖ improved its electoral outcome once again. In the October parliamentary elections, Haider's party received 23 per cent of the vote, while the SPÖ lost seven points, with 35 per cent and the ÖVP lost more than four points, with almost 28 per cent.

59 The growing number of foreigners living in Austria - some 300,000 in mid-1994 - led to new terrorist attacks against immigrants. Haider officially disapproved of this type of attacks. However, in a widely read book,

Hans Henning Scharsach revealed the similarities between Haider and Hitler, who "was also a populist at first". The rise of the FPÖ leader took place along with a debate on the responsibility held by the Austrians during World War II.

60 On October 12 1995, the coalition between the SPÖ and OVP was broken and Vranitsky called for new elections. On December 17, the SPÖ won 38 per cent of the vote, the OVP 28 per cent and Haider suffered his first electoral setback since 1986, with 22 per cent of the ballots cast. After the elections, Vranitsky formed a new coalition government with the ÖVP.

61 Unemployment rose in the first semester of 1996 to 4.4 per cent of the economically active population, or 300,000 people. More than 1600 companies were declared bankrupt in the first nine months of the year. This situation was linked to the rise of competitive pressure on the economy due to the incorporation into the European Union. In February, 1998 the president of the Austrian Federation of Labour Unions demanded the reduction of the labour week to 35 hours, in order to create supplementary jobs.

62 Social discontent favoured the growth of ultranationalist groups. In June, 1996 the so-called Freedom Alliance, previously the FPÖ, obtained six seats in the European Parliament, the same number, for the first time, as the SPÖ. In the October provincial elections, the Freedom Alliance won seven seats in the Vienna government, traditionally a socialist bulwark, the SPÖ lost 10 places and the majority it previously held, and the ÖVP lost two.

63 The Foreign Minister and Head of Government, Franz Vranitzky, waited for a moment of political tranquility to resign, in view of his party's interest in renewing the leadership. In January, 1997, he was replaced by Finance Minister Viktor Klima, brilliant negotiator and architect of an austerity plan for that year. Klima's new government paved the way for closer links between the SPÖ and Haider's party. On April, a referendum forced the State to end genetic manipulation of foods.

64 In March 1998, while on an official visit to Israel, Klima vowed to compensate victims of Nazism and admitted Austria's role in the massacre of millions of Jews. For years, Vienna had denied any responsibility in the matter, claiming it had been a victim of Germany since annexation by that country in 1938. Austria took over the rotating presidency of the European Union in July.

Azerbaijan

Azerbaidzhan

Population: 7,594,000 (1996)
Area: 86,600 SQ KM
Capital: Baku

Currency: Manat
Language: Azeri

The Azeris came from the mix of ancient peoples of eastern Caucasus. In the 9th century BC, the States of Mana, Media, Caucasian Albania and Atropatene (the name "Azerbaijan" being derived from the latter) emerged in the area corresponding to modern Azerbaijan. General Atropates proclaimed the independence of this province in the year 328 BC, when Persia was conquered by Alexander the Great.

[2] Later, these states were incorporated to the Persian Arsacid and Sassanid kingdoms. There were a number of anti-Sassanid revolts, such as the Mazdokite rebellion. In the year 642, the Arab caliphate conquered Azerbaijan, which was still inhabited by tribes of different ethnic groups. The Arabs unified the country under Shi'a Islam, despite a certain degree of resistance. Between 816 and 837, an anti-Arab revolt was led by Babek.

[3] Between the 7th and 10th centuries, an important trade route passed through Azerbaijan, uniting the Near East with Eastern Europe. From the 11th to the 14th centuries the Seleucid Turks occupied Transcaucasia and the north of Persia. All the peoples of the region adopted the Turkish language, and the Azeris' ethnic identity was forged during this period. In the 15th and 16th centuries, the region of Sirvan, in the north of Azerbaijan, became an independent State.

[4] Between the 15th and 16th centuries, the Setevid State emerged. Shah Ishmael I, founder of the dynasty, was supported by the nomadic Azeri tribes who became the main power behind the State. In the late 16th century, Azeri nobility transferred its support to the Iranians.

[5] In the 16th to 18th centuries, East Transcaucasia was the scene of Iranian-Turkish rivalry. In the 18th century, the Russian Empire began its expansion toward Azerbaijan and by the middle of this century more than 15 Azerbaijani Khanates were dependent upon Iran. After several Russian wars against Turkey and Persia, the peace treaties of Gulistan (1813) and Turkmenchai (1828) were signed, granting Russia Northern Azerbaijan (the provinces of Baku and Yelisavetpol, corresponding to modern Gyanja).

[6] The peasant reform carried out in Russia in 1879 accelerated the development of Azerbaijan, which was attractive because of the abundance of oil in the region. After the Russian Revolution of 1905, the nationalist Musavat (Equality) Party was founded in Baku in 1911. Its base was the country's bourgeoisie, and had a pan-Turkish, and pan-Islamic platform. After the triumph of the Bolsheviks in October 1917, Soviet power was established in Azerbaijan by the Commune of Baku.

[7] In the summer of 1918, joint Turkish-British intervention ousted the Commune of Baku and brought the Musavatists to power. However, two years later the Red Army reconquered Baku and re-established Soviet power throughout Azerbaijan. It was proclaimed the Soviet Socialist Republic (SSR) of Azerbaijan and in March 1922, became part of the Transcaucasian Federation of Soviet Socialist Republics, along with Armenia and Georgia.

[8] In the early 1920s, in an attempt to ease inter-ethnic tensions, Moscow decided to incorporate the regions of Upper Nagorno-Karabakh and Nakhichevan into Azerbaijan. These had previously belonged to Armenia as the ancient khanates of Karabakh and Nakhichevan. In July 1923, the Autonomous Region of Nagorno-Karabakh was founded, and in February of the following year, the Autonomous Region of Nakhichevan; both had formerly belonged to the SSR of Azerbaijan. In December 1936, the Transcaucasian Federation was dissolved, and the SSR of Azerbaijan joined the USSR on its own. In 1929 an attempt was made to substitute the Latin alphabet for Azeri script, which used Arabic characters. In January 1940, the Cyrillic alphabet was introduced.

[9] Between 1969 and 1982, the leadership of the Communist Party of Azerbaijan was in the hands of Gueidar Aliev, a former KGB (Soviet secret police) agent who was known and trusted by the Secretary of the Soviet Communist Party, Leonid Brezhnev.

[10] By the end of the 1980s, socio-economic, political and ethnic problems exacerbated the feeling of discontent among the Azeris. In 1986, the new Soviet leader Mikhail Gorbachev initiated a period of economic reforms (perestroika) and

Nagorno-Karabakh (Under Armenian control)
0   100 km

openness in the administration of the country (glasnost) which channelled popular discontent throughout the Soviet Union.

[11] In the republic of Azerbaijan, there was a wave of strikes, political rallies and demonstrations. New political movements came into being, like the leading People's Front of Azerbaijan (PFA) with a platform stressing civil rights, free elections and political and economic independence for the country. The PFA opposed the long-standing aspiration of the Armenian population of Nagorno-Karabakh (90 per cent of that region's inhabitants) to rejoin the Armenian republic.

[12] On September 25, 1989 Azerbaijan was proclaimed a sovereign state within the USSR. The worsening of ethnic conflicts between Azeris and Armenians led to the formation of extremist groups. In 1989, Armenians were massacred in Sumgait and in 1990, in Baku. After the events in Baku, the Communist Government decreed a state of emergency and called in troops from the USSR to re-establish order; a total of 100 people were killed in the ensuing violence.

[13] The Nagorno-Karabakh issue increased friction with Armenia, triggering an escalation of armed conflicts between Armenian and Azerbaijani guerrilla groups. The Autonomous Region of Nagorno-Karabakh proclaimed its independence from Azerbaijan. In

December 1989, Armenia's Soviet approved reunification with Nagorno-Karabakh and Azerbaijan denounced this decision as interference in its internal affairs. In September 1991, the Republic of Nagorno-Karabakh declared independence from both Azerbaijan and Armenia. In November 1991, the Azerbaijani Soviet annulled the status of Nagorno-Karabakh as an "autonomous region".

[14] On August 30 1991, the USSR's Soviet Presidium approved Azerbaijan's declaration of independence. The state of emergency was lifted in Baku and on September 8, presidential elections were held. The Communist Party of Azerbaijan was dissolved. Former Azeri Communist leader, Ayaz Mutalibov, who had supported the aborted coup against Gorbachev, was the only candidate, and was elected President. The PFA called the elections "undemocratic" because they were held under a state of emergency, and withdrew their candidate. The Autonomous Republic of Nakhichevan, with Gueidar Aliev, abstained from the voting.

[15] On December 22 1991, Azerbaijan joined the new Commonwealth of Independent States (CIS) which replaced the Soviet Union, and on February 2 1992, it was admitted to the UN as a new member.

[16] On December 10, 1991, besieged by Azeri troops and with bombs going off intermittently, the

PROFILE

ENVIRONMENT
Located in the eastern part of Transcaucasia, Azerbaijan is bordered by Iran to the south, Armenia to the west, Georgia to the northwest, Dagestan (an autonomous region of the Russian Federation) to the north, and the Caspian Sea to the east. The mountains of the Caucasus Range occupy half of its territory; the Kura-Araks valley lies in the center of the country; and in the southeast, the Lenkoran Valley. The climate is moderate and subtropical, dry in the mountains and humid on the plains. Its principal rivers are the Kura and the Araks. The vegetation ranges from arid steppes and semi-deserts to Alpine-like meadows. The mountains are covered with forests. The country has important deposits of oil, copper and iron. Like Armenia, Azerbaijan has problems with soil pollution from pesticide use. Highly toxic defoliants have been used extensively on cotton crops. Water pollution is another serious problem: approximately half the population lacks sewage facilities, while only a quarter of all water is treated.

SOCIETY
Peoples: Azeris, 82.7 per cent; Russians, 5.6 per cent; Armenians, 5.6 per cent; Ukrainians and Georgians.
Religions: Muslim.
Languages: Azeri (official) and Russian.
Political Parties: New Azerbaijan, Musavit.

THE STATE
Official Name: Azerbayan Respublikasi.
Capital: Baku, 1,080,000 people (1991).
Other cities: Gyanja (ex Kirovabad), 282,000 people (1990); Sumgait, 236,000; Mingechaur, 90,000.
Government: Heydar Aliev, President since October 1993; Artur Rasizade, Prime Minister since November 1996.
National Holiday: May 28, Independence (1918).
Armed Forces: 86,700.
Other: Militia (Ministry of Internal Affairs): 20,000; Popular Front: Karabakh People's Defence: up to 12,000 claimed.

STATISTICS

DEMOGRAPHY
Population: 7,594,000 (1996) **Annual growth:** 1.3 % (1980/1996) **Estimates for year 2000:** 8,000,000. **Annual growth to year 2000:** 0.8 % (1994/2000) **Urban Population:** 55.9 % (1996) **Urban growth:** 1.72 % (1980/95) **Children per woman:** 2.4 (1996).

HEALTH
Life expectancy at birth: 71 years (1996) male: 67 years (1994) female: 75 years (1994) **Infant mortality:** 34 per 1,000 (1996) **Under-5 child mortality:** 44 per 1,000 (1996).

EDUCATION
Literacy: 100 % (1995) male : 100 % (1995) female: 99 % (1995) **School enrolment :** Primary total: 117 % (1990/95) male : 120 % (1990/95) female: 115 % (1990/95) Secondary: male : 87 % (1990/95) female: 85 % (1990/95) Tertiary: 20 % (1995) **Primary school teachers:** one for every 20 students (1995).

COMMUNICATIONS.
30 **newspapers,** 210 **TV sets** and 85 **main telephone lines** per 1,000 people (1994) **Books:** 5 new titles per 100,000 people (1992/94).

ECONOMY
Per capita, GNP: $ 480 (1996) **Annual growth, GNP:** -1.3 % (1995/96) **Consumer price index:** 453,422.5 (1994) **Currency:** 4,560 manat = $ 1 (1995) **Cereal imports:** 275 metric tons (1994) (1994) **Fertilizer use:** 195 kgs per ha (1994) **Exports:** $ 618 million (1996) **Imports:** $ 1,255 million (1996) **External debt:** $ 435 million (1996) $ 57 **per capita:** (1996) **Debt service:** 1.3 % of exports (1996).

ENERGY
Consumption: 2,181.79 Kgs of Oil equivalent per capita yearly (1994) 1.28 % imported (1994).

HDI (rank / value) 106 / 0.636 (1994).

---

people of Nagorno-Karabakh participated in a plebiscite in which 99 per cent of the electorate voted for independence. The Azeri minority abstained from voting. CIS troops began withdrawing from Nagorno-Karabakh, but fighting between Azeri and Armenian guerrillas intensified.

[17] The People's Front of Azerbaijan accused the Government of ineptitude in handling the Karabakh issue, and demanded that the Government speed up the creation of an Azeri national army. Baku, in turn, accused CIS troops of facilitating the union of Armenia and Nagorno-Karabakh. On March 6 1992, Ayaz Mutalibov resigned and Yuri Mamedov, the acting President of the Soviet, assumed presidential powers.

[18] In April, fighting between Armenians and Azeris extended to Nakhichevan. Turkey warned that it would not accept any changes in its borders, which have been in effect since 1921.

[19] On May 14 1992, Azerbaijan's Parliament, controlled by former Communists, reinstated deposed President Ayaz Mutalibov. He subsequently suspended the June 7 presidential elections, banned all political activity, and imposed censorship of the press and a curfew. The leaders of the Popular Front, with the support of most of the leaders of the national militia,

seized the Parliament building in Baku, declaring the reinstatement of Mutalibov illegal. After two days of street demonstrations and clashes in the capital between supporters of both factions, the opposition consolidated its position and ratified Mamedov as president. The Popular Front assumed key posts in the new government, such as the directorship of the security services and of the official media.

[20] In December 1992, President Mutalibov was forced to resign after the repeated defeat of Azeri troops and the forces of the Popular Front besieged Parliament. In the following weeks, Armenian attacks intensified and, in May 1993, an offensive was launched on Stepanakert, the administrative centre of Nagorno-Karabakh.

[21] In mid-May, Parliament reinstated Mutalibov as President but the Popular Front ousted him once again in an armed uprising. The fighting extended beyond Nagorno-Karabakh and after occupying Stepanakert, Armenian forces fanned out to several other Azerbaijani regions.

[22] In June, Albufaz Elchibei, leader of the Popular Front, won the presidential elections, facilitating the return of Heydar Aliev, former leader of the Communist Party of the Soviet Union, to a leading position. However, a new Armenian attack in Nagorno-Karabakh was

followed by a coup. Its leader, Colonel Guseinov, seized control of five of the country's regions. When the attack on Baku began, Elchibei fled the country and Aliev remained as interim president.

[23] In September 1993, Parliament agreed to Azerbaijan joining the CIS. A month later, Aliev won the presidential elections and launched a successful attack on Nagorno-Karabakh. In May 1994, under pressure from Russia, a ceasefire was agreed and negotiations between rival parties began. These contacts continued throughout 1995 and the first months of 1996, but progress was not made toward a definite agreement.

[24] In October, 1994, followers of Prime Minister Surat Husseynov seized several cities but were swiftly expelled by loyal forces to Aliev. Major demonstrations of support for Aliev, who dismissed Husseynov, were held in Baku. The President decreed a two-month state of emergency and several members of government were arrested, accused of involvement in the failed coup.

[25] Parliamentary elections were held in November, 1995, without the participation of the influential Musavat party, or that of Communist or Islamic groups, whose presence was banned by the Government. New Azerbaijan, Aliev's party, won the elections. The gross domestic product in 1995 fell

20 per cent, a contraction similar to the previous year, while inflation fell from 880 per cent to 790 per cent in the same period.

[26] In November 1996, Artur Rasizade replaced prime minister Fuad Guliyev, who left his post for "medical reasons" according to official explanations. Several ministers responsible for economic affairs, including privatizations, were sacked for their incompetence.

[27] For the second consecutive year, the borders with Russia remained closed. Bilateral relations had deteriorated since the Russian invasion of Chechnya, in December 1994. In April, diplomatic relations with Iran were deadlocked due to the detention of members of the pro-Iranian Islamic Party of Azerbaijan. In June, Azerbaijan and Turkey signed a bilateral agreement of military cooperation.

[28] In 1997, Amnesty International urged the authorities to commute death sentences to prison terms and adopt the necessary steps for the abolition of capital punishment.

[29] Late that year, Azerbaijan celebrated the inauguration of its oil fields in the Caspian sea. The initiative was a result of a contract between the Azeri Government and a 12-company consortium with a 40 per cent stake by US capital. It is estimated Azerbaijan, Kazakhstan and Turkmenistan together possess the third largest oil reserve in the world.

Bahamas

Bahamas

Population: 284,000 (1996)
Area: 13,878 SQ KM
Capital: Nassau

Currency: Bahaman dollars
Language: English

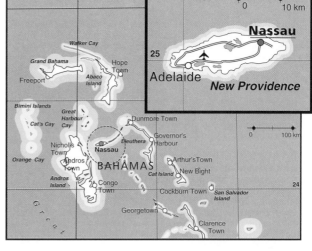

The Bahamian archipelago was one of the few areas of the Caribbean from which the Arawak Indians were not displaced by the Caribs. These Americans were probably the first to "discover" the lost European navigators, on October 12 1492.

[2] Indeed Columbus probably first trod American soil on the Bahamian island of Guanahani, or San Salvador, although he thought he was in Asia. "The Arawaks opened their hearts to us...", wrote the navigator to his Catholic sovereigns..."we have become great friends...". Soon enough, the initial enthusiasm cooled to give way to less idealistic concerns: "from here, in the name of the Holy Trinity we can send all the slaves that can be sold... If Your Majesties so commanded, the entire population could be shipped to Castile or be enslaved on the island... as these people are totally ignorant of warfare...".

[3] Only 300 out of 500 indians lived through the first voyage to Spain. Moreover, most of the survivors died within a few years for they lacked immunity to European diseases. But Columbus had also set out to find gold for himself and the royal family. As Spanish historian Francisco de Gomara has pointed out, "over a period of 20 years, the Spaniards enslaved 40,000 indians who were sent to work in mines on the other islands, like, Santo Domingo".

[4] The Spaniards did not colonize the islands that lacked mineral resources. Instead, British privateers and pirates sought refuge in these islands after seizing "Spanish" gold (or rather, gold appropriated by the Spanish with the heavy cost of indian lives in different American territories). Both the Bahamas and the Bermudas were located in an area frequently hit by tropical storms, a fact that made them particularly safe for buccaneers. However from 1640 the British began to settle the Bahamas. Sugar cane and other tropical crops were grown in plantations worked by African enslaved laborers whose descendants currently make up most of the local population. In 1873, the Treaty of Madrid settled the dispute over control of the Bahamas in favor of the British.

[5] The British refused to accept the independence of this strategic archipelago, and it was not until 1973 that the Bahamas proclaimed their independence within the British Commonwealth. This change actually meant little to the islanders because, in the meantime, the country had become increasingly dependent on the United States.

[6] Most of the tourists who now visit the Bahamas every year, drawn by its beaches and casinos, come from the US. The transnationals that use the Bahamas as their formal headquarters are also North American, taking advantage of the exemptions that make the country a "tax-haven". Also, US citizens are the chief buyers of lottery tickets, a source of fiscal revenue that contributes heavily to the state budget. In 1942, the US installed a naval base at Freeport, which helps control traffic from the Gulf of Mexico to the Atlantic, via the Florida Strait.

[7] The country's current situation closely reflects the prevailing conditions of the area. But while other Caribbean nations seek ways to bring about regional integration, the Bahamas prefers to take advantage of its proximity to the US, turning its back on regional cooperation. The islands have not joined any regional organization.

[8] The first political party - the Progressive Liberal Party (PLP) - was formed in 1953, and in 1958 the United Party of the Bahamas was founded. In the 1954 elections the PLP obtained six seats out of a total 29. In 1956 the Assembly passed an anti-discriminatory resolution, which was aimed at promoting ethnic equality. Thus, the Afro-Caribbean population was given access to places where they had never before been admitted.

[9] In the 1962 general elections the PLP won 8 of the 29 seats. Two years later the new Constitution was passed and a ministerial form of government was established. The number of representatives to the Assembly was increased to 38. Sir Roland Symonette was elected prime minister and Lynden Pindling became the leader of the opposition. In the January 10 1967 election, each party obtained 18 seats, and the representatives who won the 2 remaining seats joined the PLP, thus enabling this party to form a government. Lynden Pindling became Prime Minister.

[10] In 1977, when the economic and social crisis started to bite, the Government decided to give even greater incentives to foreign capital. It promoted the use the Bahamian flag by foreign ships as a "flag of convenience", to compete with Panama and Liberia. In an attempt to diminish the massive unemployment which threatened to create social tensions and changes in the archipelago, the Government opened an industrial estate of 1,200 hectares near a deep water port in Grand Bahama. It was meant to be used as a storage point for merchandise which was later to be re-exported after minimal local processing.

[11] During the 1977 electoral campaign the opposition parties - the Free National Movement, the Democratic Party of Bahamas, and the Vanguard Party - accused the government of corruption and squandering public funds. Pindling promised to "Bahamize" the economy, that is, give more participation to domestic capital, emphasizing that he would not damage the country's image as a tax haven. Both left and right criticized the government's policy towards transnationals, the former because they considered it complacent, the latter because they thought that excessive taxation was driving foreign investment away. However, Pindling again won by a landslide and promised to lower unemployment. He opened the country's coasts to the "seven sisters" (the seven companies that control the world oil industry) which started oil prospecting in 1979.

[12] In 1984, the political scene was further upset when the US NBC Network News directly charged Prime Minister Pindling with receiving large sums of money for authorizing drug traffic through Bahamian territory. An investigation immediately confirmed that government officials were involved in smuggling but cleared Pindling of any responsibility in the affair.

[13] In 1987, the unemployment rate was estimated to be above 18 per cent, with the under-25s and 35 per cent of women affected. With these figures in mind, public protests against the recruiting of Haitian refugees to the labor force

Maternal Mortality
1990

PER 100,000
LIVE BIRTHS
100

Literacy
1995

98%

STATISTICS

DEMOGRAPHY
Population: 284,000 (1996) **Annual growth:** 1.9% (1980/1996) **Estimates for year 2000:** 300,000. **Annual growth to year 2000:** 1.6% (1994/2000) Urban **Population:** 86.9% (1996) **Urban growth:**% (1980/95) **Children per woman:** 2 (1996).

HEALTH
Life expectancy at birth: 73 years (1996) male: 70 years (1994) female: 77 years (1994) **Infant mortality:** 19 per 1,000 (1996) **Under-5 child mortality:** 23 per 1,000 (1996)

EDUCATION
Literacy: 98% (1995) male : 99% (1995) female: 98% (1995) **School enrolment :** Primary total: 97% (1990/95) male : 100% (1990/95) female: 103% (1990/95) Secondary: male : 95% (1990/95) female: 95% (1990/95)

COMMUNICATIONS
130 **newspapers**, 735 **radios**, 240 **TV sets** and 283 **main telephone lines** per 1,000 people (1994)

ECONOMY
Consumer price index: 118.0 (1994) **Currency:** 1 Bahaman dollar= $ 1 (1995) **Cereal imports:** 14 metric tons (1994) **Fertilizer use:** 200 kgs per ha (1994). **Development aid received:** $ 4 million (1995) $ 15 per capita (1995) 0.1% of GNP (1994).

HDI (rank / value) 28 / 0.894 (1994)

PROFILE

ENVIRONMENT
The territory comprises over 750 islands, only 30 of them inhabited. The most important are: New Providence (where the capital is located), Grand Bahama, and Andros. These islands, composed of limestone and coral reefs, built up over a long period of time from the ocean floor. Despite the subtropical climate, the lack of rivers has prevented the favorable climatic conditions being fully exploited for agriculture. Farming is limited to small crops of cotton and sisal. The main economic activity is tourism, centered on New Providence. The effects of industrial development beyond their borders, the warming of the seas, the increasing frequency and intensity of tropical hurricanes and coastal erosion all pose a growing threat to the islands' environment.

SOCIETY
Peoples: Descendants of enslaved African workers, 85 per cent, plus North Americans, Canadians and British.
Religions: Non-Anglican Protestants 55 per cent, of which 32 per cent are Baptists; Anglicans 20 per cent; Catholics 19 per cent.
Languages: English (official) and Creole.
Political Parties: National Free Movement. Progressive Liberal Party (PLP) founded in 1953; bringing together the population of African origin, under a pro-independence banner. The Vanguard Party, socialist. The People's Democratic Force.
Social Movements: There is a Trade Union Congress, and other trade unions such as the Bahamas Hotel Catering and Allied Workers Union, the Bahamas Union of Teachers, the Bahamas Public Service Union, the Airport & Allied Workers Union, the Musicians and Entertainers Union, the Taxi Cabs Union.

THE STATE
Official Name: The Commonwealth of the Bahamas.
Capital: Nassau, 171,542 people (1990).
Other cities: Adelaide, Freeport/Lucaya, Marsh Harbour.
Government: Queen Elizabeth II is the Head of State, and has been represented by Orville Alton Turnquest since 1995. Prime Minister Hubert Ingraham, since 1992. There is a bicameral Legislative Power, with a 16-member Senate and a 49-member Assembly.
National Holiday: July 10, Independence (1973).
Other: 2,550: Police (1,700); Defence Force (850).

became more understandable. Although they strongly supported the Government in the past, labor unions now criticized the authorities for the lack of constructive, long-term programs aimed at solving the grave unemployment problem.
[14] After 20 years in office, Lynden Pindling won his sixth consecutive election on June 19 1987. His

WORKERS

- ■ AGRICULTURE 5% (1990)
- ☐ INDUSTRIAL 15%
- ▨ SERVICES 79%

Progressive Liberal Party obtained 31 out of 49 seats for a 5-year term. The opposition Free National Movement (FNM), led by Cecil Wallace Whitfield (after lawyer Kendal Isaac's resignation following the electoral defeat) repeatedly asked Pindling to step down, charging him with fraud, corruption, and being "soft" towards drug dealers.
[15] In 1991, there was a sharp decrease in the number of tourists, estimated at three million per annum. This was attributed to the fact that there had been a rise in the crime rate, compounded by the country's extremely high cocaine consumption rate. Although there had been a slow-down in inflation and a slight fiscal surplus, this did not prevent the people from taking to the streets,

to voice discontent over economic conditions.
[16] US officials accused Pindling of allowing the Bahamas to be used as a transfer point for drugs. Testimony from the trial of the former Panamanian General, Manuel Antonio Noriega, alleged that Pindling had received at least $5 million in payments for this service.
[17] Tourism had generated over 65 per cent of the country's GDP, but in 1992 this fell by 10 per cent in relation to 1990. Meanwhile the banking system lost customers to its competitors in the Cayman Islands. In addition, the government was unable to increase agricultural production, making it necessary for the country to import 80 per cent of its food.
[18] Pindling's 25 years in office ended in 1992, when Hubert Ingraham, a former protege of Pindling's and leader of the National Free Movement, won the parliamentary elections with 55 per cent of the vote. The new government aimed to reduce unemployment through the liberalization of foreign investment laws and the re-establishment of the Bahamas as a major tourist destination.
[19] In February 1994, one of the prominent figures in Pindling's time, lawyer Nigel Bowe, was incarcerated in Miami for drug trafficking. That year, the Government appointed a commission to investigate Pindling, accused of having used the Hotel Corporation's funds to increase his wealth. Pindling denied the charges and sought protection in

bank secrecy, which limited the Commission's progress.
[20] In 1995, foreign investors carried out the privatization of several hotels belonging to the Hotel Corporation. The most significant problems for the government were unemployment and the presence of several thousands of Haitian and Cuban refugees. A repatriation agreement with Haiti was achieved, but the Cuban refugees refused to be sent back, and demanded to be transferred to the United States.
[21] In January the following year the conflict was resolved, when the Bahamas signed an agreement with Cuba, whereby Cubans living in the Bahaman detention camps were returned to their home country. During 1996, 250 Cubans from the camps, and a further 70 living illegally with "sympathisers," were returned to Cuba. Under the agreement, the Bahamas Government had the Cuban Government's commitment that the deportees would be treated "fairly."
[22] In March 1997, the death penalty was applied for the first time in 12 years, and two men were hanged.
[23] In February 1998, religious leaders in the country publicly demonstrated against visits from homosexual tourists, prompting a British Government representative to say the United Kingdom would oppose any type of discriminatory practices in the Bahamas.
[24] The parliamentary elections of February 1998 won by the National Free Movement, with 34 seats, while the Progressive Liberals took six.

Bahrain

Bahrayn

Population: 570,000 (1996)
Area: 94 SQ KM
Capital: Manama (Al-Manamah)

Currency: Dinars
Language: Arabic

Since the time of the Sumerians, the area now called Bahrain was central to the intense maritime trade between Mesopotamia and India. This trade became particularly prosperous between the 11th and 15th centuries, as Islamic civilization expanded over all the territory from the Atlantic Ocean to the South Pacific.

2 Portuguese sailors occupied the island in 1507 and stayed there for a century until the Persians expelled them. Iran's claim to sovereignty over this part of the Persian or Arab Gulf dates from this period. Sheikh al-Khalifah took power in 1782, displacing the Persians the following year; his descendants are still in power. Independence lasted until 1861, when another Khalifah, afraid of Persian annexation, agreed to declare a "protectorate" under the British.

3 During the two World Wars Bahrain was an important British military base. In 1932 the first oil wells were opened. Nationalist movements demanding labor rights, democracy and independence grew during the 1950s, as they did in other parts of the Arab world.

4 In 1954, a strike broke out in the oil fields, and, in 1956, colonial administrative offices were attacked. British troops were sent to quash the rebellion, and opposition leaders were arrested and exiled. Slowly, some reforms were carried out and local participation in public administration increased.

5 Finally, beginning in the early 1970s, the British decided to withdraw from their last colonies "east of Suez", though they maintained their economic and strategic interests in Bahrain. Bahrain and Qatar refused to join the United Arab Emirates, so in

1971, the country became independent under Sheikh Isa ibn-Sulman al-Khalifah.

6 The new nation authorized Washington to set up naval bases in its ports. These were dismantled in 1973 following the Arab-Israeli conflict. Local elections were held the same year and the National Assembly came under the control of progressive candidates calling for freedom to organize political parties and greater electoral representation. The British felt their interests were being threatened, and, in August 1975, they backed al-Khalifah's decision to dissolve Parliament.

7 In the 1970s, Iran managed to eclipse Saudi control of the Emirates, forcing a virtual protectorate over them. Meanwhile, heavy migration towards Bahrain threatened to create an Iranian majority, or at least a large Iranian minority on the islands.

8 Shortly before his assassination, King Faisal of Saudi Arabia reacted against growing Iranian influence by embarking on a diplomatic campaign that his successors continued to implement. Riyadh, the Saudi capital, put pressure on Qatar, the only Emirate that has traditionally been loyal to the Saudis, to solve their dispute with Bahrain over territorial waters. Faisal appealed to the "Arab sentiment" that supposedly united them (Iran is Muslim, but not Arab). This attempt at solidarity lost ground in 1976 when Saudi Arabia increased its oil prices less than the other OPEC countries, including Iran.

9 The fall of the Shah of Iran in 1979 made matters worse, as the unofficial representatives of the new Islamic Republic declared publicly that Iran maintained its claim to the Gulf islands. The Emir retaliated by cracking down even harder on both Iranian (or Shi'a) immigrants and on all progressive movements in general. At the same time he drew closer to the other Arab governments, rejecting the Camp David agreement and signing mutual defence treaties with Kuwait and Saudi Arabia.

10 Bahrain is the "least rich" oil producer in the Gulf. Its known

total reserves (300 million barrels) will soon be exhausted if it continues the present rate of production. Aware that dry oil wells, and competition to Bahraini pearl-diving from Japanese oyster farms may leave this desert country with fishing as its only resource, the government decided to slow down oil production in 1980 taking advantage of the islands' strategic location to turn them into a trade and financial center.

11 In May 1975, Bahrain obtained a controlling interest in its oil industry, and in 1978 announced that all concessions would be cancelled.

12 The State also promoted the establishment of industries, especially for copper and aluminium production. Generous tax exemptions and unrestricted facilities for profit remittance encouraged transnational corporations to set up subsidiaries. The country became a base for the re-export of all kinds of goods to other ports in the area. Bahrain also houses the second largest refinery in the Middle East, BAPCO, which

processes local as well as a large part of Saudi crude oil.

13 In 1981, the country joined the Gulf Cooperation Council. This organization was set up, with US help, to guarantee military and political control over the area, to counteract spreading Iranian influence, and to keep an eye on opposition groups in the member states.

14 One of the most closely watched movements was the Bahrain National Liberation Front, supported mainly by oil workers, students and professionals. This group was a member of the Gulf Liberation Front until 1981.

15 Toward the end of 1986, Bahrain bought ground-to-air missiles and warplanes from the United States to defend itself in the event of Iranian aggression. In exchange, the US won authorization for the construction of a military airport and the right to use Bahrainian naval bases for its Gulf fleet, which "patrolled" the Gulf during the last few months of the Iran-Iraq war.

16 In November 1986, a super-highway was opened between

PER 100,000
LIVE BIRTHS

60

85%

STATISTICS

DEMOGRAPHY
Population: 570,000 (1996) **Annual growth:** 3.1% (1980/1996)
Estimates for year 2000: 600,000. **Annual growth to year 2000:**
2.2% (1994/2000) **Urban Population:** 90.8% (1996) **Children per
woman:** 3.1 (1996).

HEALTH
Life expectancy at birth: 73 years (1996) male: 70 years (1994)
female: 75 years (1994) **Infant mortality:** 18 per 1,000 (1996)
Under-5 child mortality: 22 per 1,000 (1996).

EDUCATION
Literacy: 85% (1995) male : 89% (1995) female: 79% (1995)
School enrolment : Primary total: 111% (1990/95) male : 110%
(1990/95) female: 113% (1990/95) Secondary: male : 97% (1990/
95) female: 100% (1990/95).

COMMUNICATIONS
130 **newspapers,** 556 **radios,** 420 **TV sets** and 248 **main
telephone lines** per 1,000 people (1994).

ECONOMY
Consumer price index: 103.6 (1994) **Currency:** 0.38 dinars = $
1 (1995) **Cereal imports:** 122 metric tons (1994) **Food import
dependency:** 7% (1994) **Fertilizer use:** 3,000 kgs per ha (1994)
Development aid received: $49 million (1995) $89 per capita
(1995) 1.2% of GNP (1994).

HDI (rank / value) 43 / 0.87 (1994)

PROFILE

ENVIRONMENT
This flat, sandy archipelago consists of 33 islands in the Arab Gulf
between Saudi Arabia and the Qatar Peninsula. The largest
island, also called Bahrain, is 48 km long and 15 km wide. The
climate is warm, moderately humid in summer and slightly dry
in winter. Manama, the capital and main trade center, is located
on the island of Bahrain. Bahrain has the same environmental
problems that are characteristic of all the Gulf countries. The
need to industrialize the country led to the occupation of what
few fertile lands there were, in the northern part of the main
island. In addition, industries were located very near residential
areas. The extraction of oil in this region accounts for 4.7 per cent
of all pollution caused by the oil industry.

SOCIETY
Peoples: The Bahrainis are Arab people. The petroleum industry
has attracted a number of Iranian, Indian and Pakistani
immigrants.
Religions: Islamic, predominantly of the Sunni sect in the urban
areas and Shi'a in the rural areas.
Languages: Arabic.
Political Parties: There are neither legal political parties nor trade
unions. Some opposition forces are the Liberation Front of
Bahrain, the Baath Arab Socialist Party and the Arab Nationalist
Movement.

THE STATE
Official Name: Daulat al-Bahrayn.
Capital: Manama (Al-Manamah) 140,000 people (1992).
Other cities: Al-Muharraq, 45,000 people (1991).
Government: Isa ibn-Sulman al-Khalifah, Emir since 1961;
Khalifah ibn-Sulman al-Khalifah, Prime Minister since1970,
assisted by an 11-member cabinet. The National Assembly,
partially elected by popular vote, was dissolved in August 1975.
National Holidays: August 15, Independence (1971); December
16, National Day.
Armed Forces: 10,700.
Other: (Ministry of Interior): Coast Guard: 400; Police: 9,000.

Saudi Arabia and Bahrain. As a
result, Bahrain is, in practice, no
longer an island. During the first
year alone, the highway was used
by more than a million vehicles.
Such grandiose building projects
may be a thing of the past, as the
fall in world oil prices has plunged
the country into a serious crisis.
[17] In 1989, Bahrain was forced to
seek credit in order to balance its
budget. Kuwait and Saudi Arabia
contribute $100 million per year
to ensure the stability of the
Manama government.
[18] In March 1991, after the Iraqi

MILITARY EXPENDITURE

MILITARY (as % of health and
education expenditures-1990/91) **41%**

defeat in the Gulf War, the foreign
ministers of Egypt, Syria and the
six Arab member States of the
Council for Cooperation signed
an agreement with the United
States in Riyadh in order to
"preserve the regional security".
[19] In July 1991, the Government
announced that it would allow
foreign companies to have full
control of the local businesses
they bought. Previously, all
business interests on the island
had to have a minimum of 51
percent of national capital. The
change in policy was aimed at
attracting foreign investment to
compensate for economic losses
caused by the Gulf War.
[20] After Kuwait, Bahrain was the
emirate most affected by the
conflict. The country was
threatened by the oil slick, and
Bahrain's skies were blackened
for several months by Kuwait's

burning oil wells. In the economic
field, the effects of Kuwait's
invasion and the subsequent war
against Iraq were also felt. For
instance, private bank deposits
dropped by 30 to 40 per cent.
The number of foreign banks fell
from 75 in 1981 to 51 by the end
of 1991.
[21] As from 1992, foreign capital
slowly began to return to Bahrain.
Also that year, the country played
an important role in the Middle
East Peace Conference held in
Moscow, which was attended by
ten Arab nations, as well as Israel.
[22] In October 1994, Israeli
Minister Yoosi Sarid's visit to
Manama - the first high level
public contact between Israel and
a Gulf State - was a clear
indication of the economic
liberalization policy of the regime.
[23] In December 1994, Shi'a
leader Sheik Al-Jamri was
arrested, after signing a claim for
the restoration of the
Constitution and the Parliament,
dissolved in 1975. His arrest
provoked anti-governmental
demonstrations, in which two
students and a police officer died.
In April 1995, Emir Isa ibn-Sulman
al-Khalifa met with 20 opposition
leaders in an attempt to put an
end to growing violence. In
August, both parties reached an
agreement which concluded with
the liberation of 1,000 political
prisoners.
[24] In June, Al-Jamri and another
six opposition leaders denounced
the lack of government
commitment to the agreement
reached and a hunger strike

started which ended on
November 1. A large opposition
demonstration was countered by
closing mosques, a measure which
only heightened the tension.
[25] In 1996, the demonstrations
spread across the country, and
some ended in violent
confrontations with the police.
The Government decided to use
the death penalty to punish
those "responsible", a measure
endorsed by the Courts. The UN
Working Group on Arbitrary
Detentions issued three
declarations on the situation of
the inmates of Bahrain's prisons
in September. The international
organizations were not allowed
to see the prisoners, who were
in many cases denied the right to
trial. In July, Amnesty
International reported that many
women and children suffered
severe abuse in the nation's
penitentiaries.
[26] Due to the situation of social
conflict, some financial bodies like
the Core State Bank of the
United States, abandoned the
country to set up shop in Dubai.
In March 1998, Bahrain and the
other five member nations of the
Gulf Co-operation Council (Saudi
Arabia, Oman, Kuwait, Qatar and
the United Arab Emirates) looked
into the possibility of freeing their
currencies from the dollar to
protect themselves from
persistent fluctuations and to
prevent greater losses in oil
income.

Bangladesh

Bangladesh

Population: 120,073,000 (1996)
Area: 143,998 SQ KM
Capital: Dhaka (Dacca)

Currency: Taka
Language: Bengali

Though Bangladesh is a newly formed state, it is an old nation, with roots in the ancient state of Banga. The country has a written history of several thousand years, dating back to the ancient epic, the Mahabharat.

[2] The British East India Company called it "Bengal" in the 17th century. It was renamed East Bengal after the partition of Bengal and India in 1947, and then East Pakistan when it joined the newly created state of Pakistan in 1956. It emerged as an independent state in 1971, earning its current name (meaning "the land of the Bengali-speaking people") from the national language.

[3] Hindu beliefs flourished in the region with the arrival of the Indo-Aryan peoples between 3,000 and 4,000 years ago. The country was subsequently occupied by Muslims during the 13th century, paving the way for a series of Afghan dynasties, which cut the ties with the ruling Muslim dynasties in Delhi. The country was periodically annexed by the Delhi empire, but these occupations were relatively brief. The Mughals conquered the territory in the 16th century and declared it an autonomous region. Later under Mughal rule, the country became virtually independent.

[4] The Portuguese, Armenians, French and British came to Bangladesh in succession during the 17th and 18th centuries, establishing military and trade outposts. The British purchased three villages - Colikata, Sutanoti and Govindapur - from the landowners, and soon challenged the local authorities on trade and military issues. In June 1757, at the Battle of Plassy, 500 British soldiers led by Robert Clive defeated a much larger enemy force under the command of local ruler Nawab Siraj-ud-Dwola. The defeat of the local army amounted to the British conquering the country. This was the beginning of 190 years of British rule.

[5] When the British partitioned India, transforming part of its territory into Pakistan in August 1947, Bengal was also partitioned. The Muslim majority areas, known as East Bengal, became part of Pakistan, and the Hindu majority areas became part of India. The people of East Pakistan became impatient when they became aware that massive amounts of resources were being transferred from their part of the country to West Pakistan. They also lost patience with the bureaucratic military oligarchy in West Pakistan, and began to demand regional autonomy.

[6] As a result, East Pakistan elected its own political leadership in 1970. The Pakistani Government refused to recognize this secession; the military blocked all attempts to form a government and began campaigns of aggression against East Pakistani civilians on March 25 1971.

[7] The people of East Pakistan declared independence and launched an armed resistance movement. They formed a government-in-exile in India with Sheikh Mujibur Rahman as president, and finally succeeded in ousting the occupation forces. About 3 million lives were lost during the war and 10 million refugees were reported to have crossed the border into India.

[8] On December 16 1972, Bangladesh adopted a constitution providing for parliamentary democracy. Large industries, banks and insurance companies were nationalized. Democracy, secularism, socialism and nationalism were declared as the state's basic principles.

[9] But the task of recuperating the problematic war-torn economy proved too great a challenge for the inexperienced leadership of the ruling party, the Awami League. Nationalist fervour soon died down, giving way to widespread feelings of disappointment. Bangladeshi politics degenerated into confusion as insurgency and armed political movements erupted throughout the country.

[10] In December 1974, the Government declared a state of National Emergency, and in January 1975 fundamental civil rights were suspended. All opposition political parties and trade unions were banned leaving a single party, Bakshal, mainly made up of Awami League members and pro-Moscow communists. Newspapers were banned - except for four national dailies controlled by the Government - and a new press and publication law suppressed all opposition views. On August 15 1975, against this backdrop, a group of active and retired army officers assassinated President Sheikh Mujibur Rahman and his family, and declared martial law.

[11] On November 7 1975, General Zia ur Rahman emerged as the leading force in the opposition, following a series of coups and counter-coups. He founded the Bangladesh Nationalist Party (BNP) which included many members who had opposed Bangladesh's initial independence in 1971. The BNP won the 1978 and 1979 elections, and the Awami League went into opposition.

[12] The country went through a brief period of relative stability. But in May 1981, Zia ur Rahman was killed in an abortive coup attempt. Almost a year later, on March 24 1982, the army engineered a successful coup, placing General Ershad in the presidency.

[13] In 1985, General Ershad

Map

NEPAL · BHUTAN · INDIA · Rangpur · Brahmaputra · Sylhet · Rajshahi · Jamuna · Pabna · Meghna · Dhaka · Ganges · Narayanganj · BANGLADESH · Padma · Tropic of Cancer · Khulna · Noakhali · Rangamati · Chittagong · Dakhin Shahbazpur · Maiskhal · BURMA · Gulf of Bengal

0   100 km

WORKERS

UNEMPLOYMENT 2.5% (1996)

Labour force %

- WOMEN
- MEN

42   58

- AGRICULTURE 65% (1990)
- INDUSTRIAL 16%
- SERVICES 18%

LAND USE

DEFORESTATION -3.3% annual (81/90)
IRRIGATED 32.8% of arable

(1993)

- FOREST & WOODLAND 13.2%
- ARABLE 65.6%
- OTHER 21.2%

Literacy	Food Dependency	External Debt
1995	1970	1994
38%	23%	
	1992	PER CAPITA
	14%	$134

PROFILE

ENVIRONMENT
Located on the Padma River Delta, formed by the confluence of the Meghna with the Ganges and the Brahmaputra, Bangladesh is a fertile, alluvial plain where rice, tea and jute are grown. There are vast rain forests and swamps. A tropical monsoon climate predominates, with heavy summer rains from June to September generally accompanied by hurricanes and floods of catastrophic consequences. Low-quality coal and natural gas are the only mineral resources. The increase in sea level poses a growing threat to the country. The coastal area along the Bay of Bengal has been severely affected by the discharge of sewage and industrial waste. This pollution, together with indiscriminate fishing to supply both internal and export markets, is leading to the destruction of one of the country's main resources with sea-borne pollution threatening to irreversibly damage the coastal ecosystem.

SOCIETY
Peoples:. The people of Bangladesh are ethnically and culturally homogeneous, as a result of 25 centuries of integration between the local Bengali population and immigrants from Central Asia. There are small Urdu and Indian minorities. Of the present ethnic groups, the Chakma are known to have migrated from the hills of Chittagong to border states of India in 1981.
Religions: Mostly Islamic (83 per cent) and Hindu (16 per cent), with Buddhist and Christian minorities.
Languages: Bengali.
Political Parties: Awami League (AL), in favor of a socialist economy with the intervention of the private sector; Bangladesh Nationalist Party, right of center (Bangladesh Jatiyatabadi Dal, BNP); National Party (coalition), an Islamic-inspired alliance of five nationalist parties; Islamic Assembly; Jamaat-I-Islami, Islamic fundamentalists; Communist Party and other minor parties.

THE STATE
Official Name: Gana Prajatantri Bangladesh.
Capital: Dhaka (Dacca), 7,832,000 people (1995).
Other cities: Chittagong 2,040,663 people; Khulna 877,388; Rajshahi 517,136 people (1991).
Government: Parliamentary republic. Sheikh Hasina Wajed, Prime Minister and head of Government since June 1996. Single-chamber legislature: Parliament made up of 330 members (300 elected by direct vote and 30 reserved for women, nominated by Parliament, for 5-year terms).
National Holidays: March 26, Independence Day (1971); December 16, Victory Day (1971).
Armed Forces: 115,500 (1995).
Other: Bangladesh Rifles: 30,000 (border guard); Ansars (Security Guards): 20,000.

necessary for agricultural production sufficient to feed the population. However, as the majority of the quality land is concentrated in the hands of a few large landowners, the low productivity and enormous privations faced by the rural population are not altogether surprising.

[16] Prior to the "green revolution" of the 1970s and 1980s, over 7,000 varieties of rice were commonly cultivated in Bangladesh. Now only one is widely cultivated. This new high-yield variety promised to meet all the country's rice needs, but the only real achievement was to open a new market for the manufacturers of chemical fertilizers, upon which the production of this new variety of rice depends.

[17] In 1982, "administrative decentralization" was initiated, leading to huge unproductive spending in rural areas and a growing alliance between bureaucrats and the rural elite to control public resources.

[18] Economic performance has been very poor, complicated by indiscriminate privatization, increasing military expenditure, low growth rates in manufacturing, falling agricultural production and the material damage caused by recurrent floods.

[19] On April 30 1991, the worst storm to hit Bangladesh since 1970 killed nearly 100,000 people. Prime Minister Khaleda Zia reported that it had caused several million dollars' worth of damage and left millions of people homeless. The most devastated areas were along the coast and on islands of the Ganges delta.

[20] Bangladesh has also suffered from man-made disasters. The Asian Development Bank has $5 million in aid reserved to end the pollution of Bangladesh's waters. Leaks from oil tankers and the disposal of industrial waste along the coast are destroying the coastal ecosystem. Marine life has been decimated, and it is believed that the sea here will soon be completely dead. Bangladeshi fisherfolk are having to go increasingly far out to sea in order to obtain a satisfactory catch. Fishing accounts for six per cent of the GNP, and the export of fish

products earns over $150 million per year.

[21] The district of Khulna is among the world's most polluted areas, with the destruction in recent years of forest worth over $110 million. There are more than a thousand offending industries, known by the Government, which continue to operate in the knowledge that they cannot be closed without further aggravating an already serious unemployment situation.

[22] Bangladesh has always been a predominantly rural society. Agriculture accounts for about half of the gross domestic product, compared to just 10 per cent from manufacturing. About four-fifths of the labor force is employed in agriculture or related activities. Participation by women in the formal labor market is small: only seven per cent of the work force is female.

[23] Women's social status is very low, and under the fundamentalist inspired constitution, a woman may inherit only half as much as her brother, and in practice, this fraction goes to her husband or is saved as a dowry. Bengali feminists complain that women are treated as goods rather than individuals as they belong to their fathers in childhood, to their husbands in marriage (most marry at 13), and to their sons in old age. Their work in the home and the fields is not included in official production statistics, and divorce, a male prerogative under Islamic law, can be easily obtained if a woman's productivity drops. Unfortunately this frequently occurs as many women are seriously undernourished.

[24] Bangladesh joined the UN in 1974 after two earlier attempts were blocked by Chinese vetoes. It is a founding member of the Non-Aligned Movement and also of the Organization of the Islamic Conference. A gradual Islamization of politics has been evident in recent years. A 1989 constitutional amendment declared Islam the official religion, a move opposed by secular forces.

[25] In 1991, Ershad was deposed, and elections were called, in which the Awami League (AL) opposed the Bangladesh Nationalist Party (BNP). Both political alliances launched women as their major

formed the Jatiya Party (JP), going on to win the 1986 general election with what the opposition saw as widespread fraud. As a result of this, massive popular uprisings forced Ershad to dissolve the parliament. Confidence in political integrity was so low that the 1988 elections, were boycotted by all the major political parties and a large percentage of the electorate as well.

[14] Since Sheikh Mujibur Rahman's death in 1975, socialism and secularism have been discarded as state policy. Public sector budgets were gradually reduced and the military became a strong contender for political power.

[15] Bangladesh is one of the poorest and most densely populated countries in the world and has suffered many famines, an occurrence that seems hardly explicable in a country with extremely rich soil and plentiful water and sun - all the elements

Foreign Trade
MILLIONS $ 1996

IMPORTS
6,898
EXPORTS
3,297

Maternal Mortality
1990

PER 100,000
LIVE BIRTHS
850

candidates; in both cases the widow of the leader of the alliance.

26 On March 2 1991, Begum Khaleda Zia of the BNP was elected prime minister. Khaleda Zia declared that she supported the establishment of a parliamentary regime, thereby stripping the AL of one of its traditional platforms. Five months after her triumph in the general election, and with the unanimous approval of the legislative representatives of the 2 major parties, the Congress of Bangladesh replaced the country's presidential system with a parliamentary system.

27 The previous president, Hussain Mohammad Ershad, had been sentenced in 1991 to 10 years in prison for abuse of power, unlawful wealth and possession of illegal weapons. However, he was able to run for the 1996 elections after appealing against the sentence.

28 In mid-August 1991, the political reform was approved when, in a climate of great tension, President Shahabuddin Ahmed threatened to resign unless the system was modified.

29 Bangladesh continues to rely heavily upon international aid; 95 per cent of its development programs are financed from abroad. The United States, Japan, the Asian Development Bank (ADB) and the World Bank contributed $2.3 billion in 1991, 10 million more than the previous year. 95 per cent of the country's budget is taken up in interest payments on its foreign debt.

30 Bangladeshis have an average per capita annual income of $240. Fifty per cent of housing is of mud brick construction and has no plumbing: one toilet may be shared by as many as 50 families. More than 13 million people live in the shanty towns surrounding the cities, which continue to grow at a rapid rate.

31 Among its measures to shore up the fragile economy, the

government declared all-out war against smuggling, in December 1991. Smuggling is a big business in Bangladesh, and involves important financial institutions, the nouveau riche, and corrupt political and government officials.

32 The IMF- and World Bank-backed privatization scheme, which included the sale of 42 public enterprises, came to a standstill in 1991. Since then, Minister of Finance Saifur Rahman has faced the opposition of organized labor, especially in the jute industry (one of the main sources of export earnings), as well as textile and railway unions that fear the loss of jobs. General strikes - demanding a national minimum wage - have become commonplace.

33 The Gulf War (1990-1991) prompted Bangladesh to reaffirm its identity as a Muslim community. This feeling was intensified in 1992, when the repatriation of Muslim refugees began. Early in that year, Bangladesh received several groups of some 250,000 Bihari Muslims, who had supported Pakistan in 1971. In June, another 270,000 Rohingya Muslims arrived, fleeing persecution in Burma, a predominantly Buddhist country. The repatriation agreements signed between the two countries in 1992 failed to stem the flow of refugees.

34 In 1994, writer Taslima Nasrin became famous for her book "Shame", which condemned the alleged oppression of Hindus and other minorities by Muslims. Nasrin was detained for requesting a greater respect by Islamic law of women's rights: this was regarded as criticism against the Koran. Throughout 1994, some 154 MP's opposed to the Kaleda Zia administration boycotted parliamentary activity up to their massive resignation in December. Sheikh Hasina, female leader of the Awani League (AL), led a series of protests by peasants, demanding elections under a neutral administration, which were held through 1994 and 1995.

35 In the 1996 general elections held on February 15, women voted for the first time in the history of Bangladesh. Prime Minister Kaleda Zia, from the

STATISTICS

DEMOGRAPHY
Population: 120,073,000 (1996) **Annual growth:** 1.9% (1980/1996) **Estimates for year 2000:** 128,300,000. **Annual growth to year 2000:** 1.6% (1994/2000) **Urban Population:** 18.9% (1996) **Urban growth:** 5.57% (1980/95) **Children per woman:** 3.2 (1996).

HEALTH
Life expectancy at birth: 57 years (1996) male: 56 years (1994) female: 57 years (1994) **Infant mortality:** 83 per 1,000 (1996) **Under-5 child mortality:** 112 per 1,000 (1996) **Calorie consumption:** 88% (1988/90) 12,500 **people per doctor** (1988/91) **Safe water:** 97% (1990/96).

EDUCATION
Literacy: 38% (1995) male : 49% (1995) female: 26% (1995) **School enrolment :** Primary total: 79% (1990/95) male : 84% (1990/95) female: 73% (1990/95) Secondary: male : 25% (1990/95) female: 13% (1990/95).

COMMUNICATIONS
10 **newspapers**, 47 **radios**, 10 **TV sets** and 2 **main telephone lines** per 1,000 people (1994).

ECONOMY
Per capita, GNP: $ 260 (1996) **Annual growth, GNP:** 3.8% (1995/96) **Annual inflation:** 6.41% (1985/95) **Consumer price index:** 115.8 (1994) **Currency:** 40.75 taka = $ 1 (1995) **Cereal imports:** 952 metric tons (1994) **Food import dependency:** 14% (1994) **Fertilizer use:** 1,081 kgs per ha (1994) **Exports:** $ 3,297 million (1996) **Imports:** $ 6,898 million (1996) **External debt:** $ 16,083 million (1996) $ 134 per capita: (1996) **Debt service:** 11.7% of exports (1996) **Development aid received:** $ 1,269 million (1995) $ 11 per capita (1995) 4.8% of GNP (1994).

ENERGY
Consumption: 64.15 Kgs of Oil equivalent per capita yearly (1994) 27.83% imported (1994)

HDI (rank / value) 144 / 0.368 (1994)

PNB, kept her position but the elections, held under army control, were considered fraudulent. A general strike called by the AL was followed by confrontations between the police and opposition activists. Violence did not end with Zia's fall on March 30. On June 23, the former head of the Supreme Court of Justice, Mohammad Habibur Rahman, who had led the neutral government before the elections held from June 12 to 19, handed over the administration to Prime Minister Sheikh Hasina, chosen in the second elections over a four-month period.

36 Social confrontation continued throughout 1997 and increased in December with a string of strikes called by opposition parties, after the agreement signed by the

Government to put an end to armed rebels in the southeast. For several days, those who supported the strikes and those who were against them held marches in cities - Dhaka, Chittagong, Barisal, Syleht and Rajsani, among others - and in many small towns, which almost paralyzed the country.

37 In 1998, 15 million people were subject to the risk posed by polluted wells, the main source of water supply for the population. The water, laced with naturally-occuring arsenic, had been dug in the last two decades after major mobilization campaigns. This contamination threatened to aggravate the situation of the poorest sectors of the population in a country where 50 per cent of newborn children were underweight.

MILITARY EXPENDITURE

MILITARY (as % of health and education expenditures-1990/91) **41%**

Barbados

Barbados

Population: 261,000 (1996)
Area: 430 SQ KM
Capital: Bridgetown

Currency: Barbadian dollars
Language: English

The peaceful and nomadic Arawak people expanded throughout the Caribbean region, and although they were dislodged from many islands by the Caribs, they remained on others, as in the case of Barbados.

2   The Spanish landed on the island early in the 16th century and christened it the "island of the bearded fig tree". Satisfied that the island lacked natural wealth, they withdrew, but not before massacring the native population, taking a few survivors with them to amuse the Spanish court. In 1625 the British arrived and found a fertile, uninhabited territory.

3   Around 1640 the island had close to 30,000 inhabitants. The majority were farmers and their families, and some were political and religious dissidents from Britain. The settlers grew tobacco, cotton, pepper and fruit on small plots of land, raising cattle, pigs and poultry.

4   Sugar cane was introduced, with the support of the British, and caused extensive social change: plantation owners purchased large plots of land which the new crop required in order to be profitable, and small landowners, most of them in debt, sold off their plots to the plantation owners. The importation of slaves from Africa to work the sugar plantations began during this period.

5   In 1667, 12,000 farmers emigrated to other Caribbean islands or to the 13 colonies of North America. Nonetheless, the island had a commercial fleet of 600 vessels and, as recorded by a French traveller in 1696, was "the most powerful island colony in America".

6   Towards the end of the 18th century, the island was one huge sugar-producing complex which included 745 plantations and over 80,000 African slaves. By this time there was no woodland left on an island described in a 16th century account as "entirely covered with trees". Its ecological balance seriously impaired, the island fell victim to drought in the early 19th century and parts of it suffered soil exhaustion.

7   The pursuit of increased profitability and an economy oriented toward foreign trade resulted in underdevelopment in Barbados. A different approach might have led to development along the lines of the other North American colonies.

8   Slavery was abolished in 1834 but the plantation economy still dominates the island's fiscal system. European landowners dominated local politics until well into the 20th century.

9   In 1938, following the gradual extension of political rights, the Labor Party, led by Grantley Adams, developed from within the existing labor unions. Universal suffrage was declared in 1951, and Adams became leader of the local Government.

10   In 1961, internal autonomy was granted, and in 1966 independence was proclaimed within the British Commonwealth. Errol Barrow was elected Prime Minister. Unlike the rest of the West Indies, Barbados never severed its links with the colonial capital in spite of its political independence.

11   After 1966, Errol Barrow's Democratic Labor Party (DLP) contributed to the creation of the Caribbean Free Trade Association which, in 1973, became CARICOM, involving 12 islands of the region. Barrow showed great interest in the Non-Aligned Countries movement.

12   Free education and new electoral laws were not followed by any significant change in DLP policies towards the owners of sugar refining plants. The rise in unemployment diminished DLP support and resulted in the party's electoral defeat. In 1970, the country became a member of the International Monetary Fund (IMF).

13   The BLP won 17 of the 24 available seats in 1976. Tom Adams, Grantley Adams' son, was elected Prime Minister. He promised to fight corruption and described himself as a social democrat (the BLP became a member of the Socialist International in 1978). However, the Government protected the interest of investors in sugar and tourism transnationals, while encouraging foreign investment.

14   Adams pressured Washington to withdraw from its naval base in St Lucia, which they did in 1979. In 1981, Adams was re-elected and consolidated relations with Washington. Barbados supported the US invasion of Grenada.

15   In order to attract foreign capital, the Government passed new tax exemption laws and liberalized ship registration. In 1986, an agreement between the United States and Barbados led to 650 new companies registering in the off-shore sector. Unemployment and inflation within Barbados continued to grow.

16   The 1986 election was won by the DLP. Prime Minister Errol Barrow committed the Government to changing the foreign policy toward the US which had been followed by the BLP Government in the preceding 10 years. In 1987, Barrow died of a sudden heart attack and was succeeded as Prime Minister by Erskine Sandiford. Two years later, as a result of a split within the DLP, a new opposition group was founded, the National Democratic Party, under the leadership of Richard Heynes.

17   In 1989, steadily falling sugar prices and rising interest rates fuelled inflation. The Government's resolve to cut its budget deficit aroused fears of further unemployment and there were several strikes. Nonetheless, industry recovered, exchange reserves increased, and about a hundred Panamanian offshore concerns expressed

LAND USE

(1993)

- ■ FOREST & WOODLAND   11.6%
- □ ARABLE   37.2%
- ▨ OTHER   51.2%

PROFILE

ENVIRONMENT

Of volcanic origin, it is the eastern-most island of the Lesser Antilles. The fertile soil and rainy tropical climate favor intensive farming of sugarcane, rotated with cotton and corn. The most serious environmental problems are the disposal of sewage and refuse, water consumption, and soil and coastal erosion. From a regional perspective the Caribbean Sea is increasingly contaminated and its resources are over-exploited.

SOCIETY

Peoples: Most are of African origin (92.5 per cent), with a minority of Europeans (3.2 per cent) and mestizos (2.8 per cent). It is one of the most densely populated countries in the world, with an average of 616 people per sq km.
Religions: 33 per cent Anglican. There are also Catholics (4.4 per cent), Methodists and Moravians (29.8 per cent).
Languages: English (official). Creole is also spoken.
Political Parties: The Barbados Labor Party (BLP), in power since 1994. The Democratic Labor Party (DLP); the right-wing National Democratic Party.
Social Organizations: Barbados Workers' Trade Union.

THE STATE

Official Name: Barbados.
Capital: Bridgetown, 110,000 people (1994 est).
Other cities: Speightstown; Holetown; Bathsheba.
Government: Owen Arthur, Prime Minister since September 7 1994; Sir Clifford Husbands, Governor-General, appointed in1996. The bicameral Parliament has been shaped on the British model. The Legislative power is constituted by a Parliament, with a Low Chamber, the Senate and the post of Governor General.
National Holiday: November 30, Independence Day (1966).

STATISTICS

DEMOGRAPHY

Population: 261,000 (1996) **Annual growth:** 0.3% (1980/1996) **Estimates for year 2000:** 300,000. **Annual growth to year 2000:** 0.2% (1994/2000) **Urban Population:** 47.8% (1996) **Children per woman:** 1.7 (1996).

HEALTH

Life expectancy at birth: 76 years (1996) male: 73 years (1994) female: 78 years (1994) **Infant mortality:** 11 per 1,000 (1996) **Under-5 child mortality:** 12 per 1,000 (1996). **Safe water:** 100% (1990/96).

EDUCATION

Literacy: 97% (1995) male : 98% (1995) female: 97% (1995) **School enrolment :** Primary total: 90% (1990/95) male : 90% (1990/95) female: 91% (1990/95) Secondary: male : 90% (1990/ 95) female: 80% (1990/95).

COMMUNICATIONS

160 **newspapers**, 877 **radios**, 260 **TV sets** and 327 **main telephone lines** per 1,000 people (1994).

ECONOMY

Consumer price index: 114.1 (1994) **Currency:** 2.01 Barbadian dollars = $ 1 (1995) **Cereal imports:** 57 metric tons (1994) **Fertilizer use:** 1,687 kgs per ha (1994)

HDI (rank / value) 25 / 0.907 (1994)

interest in Barbados. Japan signed agreements to invest in tourism on the island.
[18] In 1989, Barbados requested a review of the CARICOM charter as it was felt that the constraints were too limiting. In order to favor local agriculture, Government import restrictions were introduced, particularly on vegetables from Guyana.
[19] In 1990, serious controversies arose over sugar cane prices between the sugar mills and the Government; demands from workers threatened to end in strike action. The tourist industry employed 15 per cent of the workforce of the island and 450,000 tourists visited Barbados in 1988.
[20] In 1990 the Government

WORKERS

- AGRICULTURE 7% (1990)
- INDUSTRIAL 23%
- SERVICES 70%

MILITARY EXPENDITURE

MILITARY (as % of health and education expenditures-1990/91) **5%**

endorsed the use of solar power as electricity is very expensive on the islands.
[21] According to the Inter-American Development Bank, Barbados's economy has registered a negative growth rate since 1990, although inflation has been reduced. While overall unemployment remained constant, there was an increase in unemployment among female workers in the garment, electronics and tourism industries, the country's main sources of foreign exchange. In the tourist sector, there was a 6.3 per cent decline in the number of tourists, as well as a reduction in the length of their stay on the island.
[22] In 1991, the DLP was re-elected with 49 per cent of the vote although it lost 2 of its 20 seats. In November, riots and protests due to an eight per cent cutback on civil servants' wages, led to a general strike. In spite of having been questioned, Sandiford managed to remain in office.
[23] In 1992 the Government obtained an IMF loan amounting to $ 64.9 million and the Prime Minister announced further wage reductions in the public sector, a rise of interest rates and cutbacks in the social system, as well as the privatization of oil and cement production and the tourism industry.
[24] After two successive finance ministers resigned, Sandiford

himself assumed the post in late 1992, attempting to transform the country into a financial center. Tourist activity has flourished since 1993. That year, tourism revenues reached $500 million, equivalent to one third of the country's GDP.
[25] In June 1994, the Barbados Liberal Party (BLP) withdrew its support for the Prime Minister and won the elections held on September 7. Owen Arthur, the new Prime Minister, cancelled planned wage reductions, which was passed as law in February 1995.
[26] Arthur introduced a deficit budget in April, arguing expenditure was needed to tackle unemployment, which had reached 21.2 per cent. The IMF had advised caution in the management of public funds, but Arthur chose to overlook these prescriptions.
[27] The island's Governor General, Dame Nita Barrow, sister of former Prime Minister Errol Barrow, died on December 19 1995. She had held the post since June 1990.
[28] The legislative assembly voted

in February 1996 for civil servant salaries to be brought back up over a two-year period. The measure, promoted by the Labor Party of Barbados, was a response to the salary reduction policy applied in 1994 by the Democratic Labor Party.
[29] In May, the Government signed a contract with a US company to explore possible offshore oil fields.
[30] In 1997, tourism continued to be the main source of income for Barbados. The Government managed to further increase that income, even though the infrastructure was not considered the most adequate for large-scale expansion of the sector.
[31] In April 1998, during the summit of American Presidents in Santiago, Chile, Prime Minister of Barbados, Owen Arthur, said he was in favour of Cuba's inclusion from the next meeting.

Belarus

Belarus

Population: 10,348,000 (1996)
Area: 207,600 SQ KM
Capital: Minsk (Mensk)

Currency: Rouble
Language: Belarusian

The territory known today as Belarus (formerly Belorussia) was inhabited from the 1st century AD by the Krivich, Radimich and Dregovich Slavc peoples. The first principalities were those of Polotsk and Turov-Pinsk. In the 9th century, Eastern Slav tribes belonging to the Western Rus joined other Eastern Slav peoples to form the Kiev Rus, the ancient Russian State (see history of Russia) which gave rise to modern Russia, Ukraine and Belarus. The major cities of the area, Polotsk, Turov, Brest, Vitebsk, Orsha, Pinsk and Minsk date from the 9th and 10th centuries.

2 In the 14th century, Lithuanian principalities annexed themselves to the Western Rus. As the Lithuanians lacked their own writing system, the language of the Belarusians (which was the only Russian language at the time) became the official language of the State.

3 Between the 14th and 16th centuries, the Belarusian culture began to differentiate itself from that of the Russians and the Ukrainians.

4 In 1569, according to the terms of the Union Treaty between Poland and Lithuania, Belarus became a part of Poland. The Belarusians resisted domination by the Catholic Poles, and maintained their linguistic and cultural identity.

5 With the first partition of Poland in 1772, Russia kept the eastern part of Belarus. Between 1793-95, the rest of Belarus became part of the Russian Empire. The abolition of serfdom in Russia in 1861 accelerated the development of Belarus. Important railways were built, including the Moscow-Brest and the Libava-Romni lines. By the end of the 19th century, Belarus had Russia's second most important railway system.

WORKERS

(1996)

Labour force %

■ WOMEN
□ MEN

49 | 51

■ AGRICULTURE 20% (1990)
□ INDUSTRIAL 40%
□ SERVICES 40%

6 The Russian Czar's abolition of the serf system also put an end to the peasants' feudal bondage to the landed nobility. However, this failed to solve the land tenure problem, as in Belarus only 35 per cent of the land was handed over to the peasants. This triggered a number of uprisings, the most important of which took place in 1863 under the leadership of Kalinovski.

7 In March 1899, the 1st Congress of the Social Democratic Workers' Party of Russia (SDWPR) was held secretly in Minsk. This group was inspired by Marxist socialism and was determined to bring down the czar. Other sectors of the intelligentsia took their cue from the peasants' discontent, and founded an autonomous Belarusian movement in 1902, which sought to revive the nation's culture. During this period, the Czarist regime deported Russian Jews to Belarus, where they came to account for a fifth of the local population.

8 During World War I (1914-1917) part of Belarus was occupied by German troops. After the Russian Revolution of February 1917, councils (soviets) made up of workers' representatives were formed in Minsk, Gomel, Vitebsk, Bobruisk and Orsha.

9 Soviet power began to be established at the end of 1917, and in February 1918 the large land holdings were nationalized. A few months later, land began to be distributed to the peasants. At the insistence of the Bolsheviks (socialist revolutionaries of the SDWPR), the first collective farms (koljoses) were set up. In reality, however, the land gradually went into State control.

10 The 6th Party Conference of the Russian Communists (Bolsheviks), the former SDWPR, held in Smolensk, approved the decision to found the Soviet Socialist Republic of Belarus (SSRB). In January 1918, the decision to join Lithuania was made at the 1st Congress of the SSRB Soviets. The Congress of the Soviets of Lithuania endorsed the same motion.

11 On February 28 1919 in the city of Vilno (today Vilnius, the capital of Lithuania) the Government of the Soviet Socialist Republic of Lithuania and Belarus was elected, with Mickevicius-Kapsukas as head of state.

12 In February 1919, Poland, which had become independent from Russia after the Bolsheviks had seized power in St Petersburg, occupied a large part of Belarus. According to the Treaty of Riga, signed between Soviet Russia and Poland (1921), Western Belarus became part of Poland.

13 On August 1st 1920 the Assembly of representatives of the Lithuanian and Belarusian Communist Parties and of labor organizations in Minsk and its surrounding areas approved the declaration of the foundation of the independent Belarusian republic.

14 On December 30 1922, Belarus joined the Union of Soviet Socialist Republics (USSR) as one of its official founders, along with the Russian Federation, Ukraine and the Transcaucasian Federation (Armenia, Georgia and Azerbaijan).

15 The industrialization and collectivization of agriculture began in the second half of the 1920s. On February 19 1937 the 12th Congress of the Soviets of Belarus approved the new constitution. In November 1939, as a result of the Molotov-Ribbentrop Pact - signed between the USSR and Germany - Western Belarus was reincorporated into the Soviet Union.

16 In June 1941 Belarus became the first of the Soviet republics to suffer Hitler's aggression against the Soviet Union. The fortress at

Brest offered fierce resistance, becoming a symbol of Belarus's heroic defence. Guerrilla warfare extended throughout the country for the duration of the war, a conflict in which more than 2 million Belarusians lost their lives.

17 After Germany's defeat in 1945, Belarus's current borders were established. It became a charter member of the United Nations that same year; like Ukraine, it had its own delegation, independent of the USSR.

18 It took Belarus almost two decades to restore its economy, becoming in the process an important producer of heavy trucks, electrical appliances, radios and television sets. Between the 1920s and the 1980s, Belarus ceased to be a rural country - in which 90 per cent of the population lived from traditional farming and livestock raising - becoming an urban, industrialized country with nearly 70 per cent of its population living in cities.

19 Belarus is one of the few republics that has managed to maintain an ample majority of its local population - more than 80 per cent - with slight influence from Russian or other immigration.

20 Until 1985, the Communist Party and the Belarusian Government followed the course established by the Communist Party of the Soviet Union. Among the outstanding communist leaders of this period was Piotr Masherov.

PROFILE

ENVIRONMENT

Belarus is located between the Dnepr (Dnieper), Western Dvina, Niemen and Western Bug rivers. It is bounded in the west by Poland, in the northwest by Latvia and Lithuania, in the northeast by Russia and in the south by Ukraine. It is a flat country, with many swamps and lakes, and with forests covering a third of its territory. Its climate is continental and cool, with an average summer temperature of 17-19 degrees, and 4-7 degrees below zero in winter. Due to its geographical proximity to Ukraine, Belarus received intense radioactive fall-out following the disaster at the Chernobyl nuclear plant in 1986. A quarter of the country's arable land shows signs of chemical pollution from the overuse of pesticides.

SOCIETY

Peoples: Belarusians, 77.9 per cent; Russians, 13.2 per cent; Poles, 4.1 per cent; Ukrainians, 4.1 per cent; Hebrew, 1.1 per cent (1989). **Religions:** Christian Orthodox; in the west, Catholic. **Languages:** Belarusian (official); Russian (spoken as a second language by most of the population) and Polish. **Political Parties:** Communist Party, Belarusian Popular Front, Agrarian Party. **Social Organizations:** Labor Union Federation of Belarus; Free Union.

THE STATE

Official name: Respublika Belarus. **Administrative divisions:** Six regions (Brest, Gomel, Grodno, Mensk, Moguiliov and Vitebsk). **Capital:** Minsk (Mensk), 1,671,000 people (1992). **Other cities:** Gomel, 506,000 people; Mogilov, 363,000; Vitebsk, 373,000; Grodno, 291,000; Brest, 269,000 (1992). **Government:** Executive power: President, Aleksander Lukashenka, since 1994; Prime Minister, Syarhei Linh, since 1996. The Supreme Soviet is the maximum legislative body; Myachaslau Hryb, President. **National Holiday:** June 27, Independence (1991). **Armed Forces:** 102,600. **Other:** Border Guards (Ministry of Interior): 8,000.

Foreign Trade
MILLIONS $ 1996
IMPORTS
6,778
EXPORTS
5,122

STATISTICS

DEMOGRAPHY

Population: 10,348,000 (1996) **Annual growth:** 0.4% (1980/1996) **Estimates for year 2000:** 10,000,000. **Annual growth to year 2000:** -0.1% (1994/2000) **Urban Population:** 71.8% (1996) **Urban growth:** 2% (1980/95) **Children per woman:** 1.5 (1996).

HEALTH

Life expectancy at birth: 70 years (1996) male: 64 years (1994) female: 75 years (1994) **Infant mortality:** 14 per 1,000 (1996) **Under-5 child mortality:** 18 per 1,000 (1996) 282 **people per doctor** (1988/91).

EDUCATION

Literacy: 99% (1995) male: 100% (1995) female: 99% (1995) **School enrolment:** Primary total: 97% (1990/95) male: 98% (1990/95) female: 95% (1990/95) Secondary: male: 92% (1990/95) female: 97% (1990/95) **Primary school teachers:** one for every 20 students (1995).

COMMUNICATIONS

190 **newspapers**, 285 **radios**, 260 **TV sets** and 186 **main telephone lines** per 1,000 people (1994) **Books:** 32 new titles per 100,000 people (1992/94).

ECONOMY

Per capita, GNP: $ 2,070 (1996) **Annual growth, GNP:** 2.9% (1995/96) **Consumer price index:** 622,202.6 (1994) **Currency:** 11,500 roubles = $ 1 (1995) **Fertilizer use:** 995 kgs per ha (1994) **Exports:** $ 5,122 million (1996) **Imports:** $ 6,778 million (1996) **Extenal debt:** $ 1,071 million (1996) $ 103 per capita: (1996) **Debt service:** 2% of exports (1996).

ENERGY

Consumption: 2,392.04 Kgs of Oil equivalent per capita yearly (1994) 88.18% imported (1994)

HDI (rank / value) 62 / 0.806 (1994)

---

[21] Because of the policies of glasnost (openness) and *perestroika* (restructuring) initiated by President Mikhail Gorbachev, there was no strong pressure within Belarus to secede immediately from the USSR, although there were movements favoring a multi-party political system, as well as protest demonstrations against high food prices.

[22] Belarus was the region outside of Ukraine most affected by the 1986 catastrophe at the Chernobyl nuclear plant. According to foreign researchers, in the following years there was a rapid increase in cases of cancer, leukemia and birth defects in the areas affected by the disaster: Ukraine, Belarus and western Russia.

[23] In June 1991, Belarus declared its independence and in October signed an economic integration agreement with Kazakhstan and Uzbekistan. On December 8, the presidents of the Russian federation, Boris Yeltsin, of Ukraine, Leonid Kravchuk, and the Belarus Parliament, Stanislav Sushkevich, signed an historic agreement which put an end to the USSR. Opposing president Gorbachev s idea of signing a new Union Treaty, the presidents decided to create an association of sovereign states. On the June 21, in Alma-Ata (Kazakhstan), 11 republics signed an agreement creating the Commonwealth of Independent States (CIS), whose members

requested admission to the UN as separate countries. Belarus and 7 of the republics pledged to implement structural reforms which would convert them into market economies.

[24] In September 1993, tensions between the prime minister and the Parliament chairman were coming to a head and there were rumours of a possible coup. In January 1994, Sushkevich was replaced by Mecheslav Grib. On March, Parliament passed the new Constitution, which replaced the previous one from 1977, when Belarus still belonged to the former USSR.

[25] The country became a presidential republic with a 260-seat Parliament. In July, Lukashenka, after a campaign in which he lambasted the corruption of his predecessors, obtained 80 per cent of the vote issued on the second round.

[26] In spite of having criticized it in his electoral campaign, the president continued the policy of rapprochement which led to a monetary union with Russia on April 1994. In August, he met with Russian president Boris Yeltsin and in November decreed a state of emergency, with the excuse of slowing down inflation.

[27] On February 1995, Minsk and Moscow signed a treaty of friendship and cooperation which enables Russia to keep its troops deployed in the country. Insufficient

participation in the May parliamentary elections, which Lukashenka held along with a referendum regarding his rapprochement policy toward Moscow, did not allow for the elections of all deputies, which led to a second by-election in November.

[28] During the first months of 1996, opposition to Lukashenka and his "pro-Russian" policy, as well as the pressure he put on opposition groups, such as the Popular Front, led to major demonstrations. On March, at the conmemoration of the independent republic established in Belarus in 1917, tens of thousands protested against the union with the Russian Federation.

[29] In April, amid mass protests, Russia and Belarus strengthened their relations by signing a political and economic integration agreement. Several opposition leaders went into exile in the United States. By the end of the

year, a constitutional reform granted more powers to Lukashenka. Among those arrested were the former Central Bank chairman and other senior officials. The opposition denounced the establishment of a dictatorship.

[30] The economy was in chaos in 1997. Over 70 per cent of the population was living below the poverty line. The value of the national currency, the ruble, fell against the dollar and inflation grew. Lukashenka dismissed foreign minister Vladimir Syanko and replaced him with Ivan Antanovich. Parliament confirmed the appointment of Syarhei Linh as prime minister.

[31] Amnesty International reported executions and arbitrary arrests and demanded the abolition of the death penalty. In February 1998, Belarus summoned its ambassador in Poland, in midst of accusations of Polish interference in domestic affairs.

Belgium

België / Belgique

Population: 10,159,000
(1996)
Area: 30,519 SQ KM
Capital: Brussels
(Bruxelles/Brussel)
Currency: Belgian francs
Language: French, Dutch
and German

Belgium, Holland, Luxembourg and a part of northern France make up the Low Countries, which had a common history until 1579 (see Netherlands). The linguistic separation which took place between the Roman and Germanic languages coincided with the borders of the Holy Roman Empire, which divided the Low Countries in two.

2   In 1519 Emperor Charles V, who was born in Ghent, ascended the throne, inheriting the Holy Roman Empire from his father and Spain from his mother. This was the beginning of 200 years of Spanish rule. In 1579, the creation of the Union of Arras (achieved by joining together the Catholic provinces of Artois and Hainaut) led Spain to resume its war against the Dutch Protestants. According to the terms of the Treaty of Utrecht, signed in 1713, the southern provinces and Luxembourg were left in the hands of Charles VI, head of the Holy Roman Empire and of the Austrian branch of the Habsburgs.

3   The region's economy was based on the production of linen and textiles. Industrialization was facilitated by the fact that manufacturers and landowners were often one and the same, and that textile mills were concentrated in the hands of a few owners. Factories each employing more than 100 low-paid workers sprang up in Ghent, Antwerp, and Tournai.

4   Fearing the spread of the French Revolution, the House of Austria attempted some progressive reforms, but the conservative revolt of 1789 put an end to these. After French Republican troops invaded in 1794, France did away with the region's autonomy and the privileges of the

local aristocracy, while encouraging the industrial revolution. After the fall of Napoleon in 1814, the European powers enforced reunification with the north. The southern provinces had already forged an identity of their own, and were unwilling to accept Dutch authority.

5   In 1830, the Belgian bourgeoisie, along with urban labourers from Brussels and Lièges, took up arms against the Dutch authorities. When the conflict spread and proved substantial, European powers recognized the independence of the southern provinces, which were henceforth known as Belgium. Congress adopted a parliamentary monarchy, with an electing body made up of property owners. The duchies of Luxembourg and Limburg were divided between Belgium and Holland.

6   By the end of the 19th century, workers forced the government to pass laws aimed at providing housing for working class people, and improving conditions in the workplace, especially for women and children. At the same time, Parliament changed the Constitution and in 1893, established limited male suffrage.

7   Between 1880 and 1885, Leopold II financed international expeditions to the Congo, making it effectively his 'private' colony. Substantial deficits and protests from several European nations against the severe repression and exploitation occurring in the Congo, forced the Belgian government to take it as a colony in 1908. With this, the worst excesses ended, but the Belgian Government, businesses and the church increased their influence over the following years.

8   In 1914, Germany wanted to cross Belgian territory, in order to invade France. Belgium refused to give way to the Germans and was drawn into war. The Treaty of Versailles granted the territories of Eupen and Malmedy to Belgium. In Africa, Belgium colonized the former German colonies of Rwanda and Burundi after the League of Nations granted them a mandate. But Belgium failed to realize any of its other territorial demands. In 1920 Belgium signed a military assistance treaty with France, and the following year, it

formed an economic alliance with Luxembourg.

9   After the war, the government established universal male suffrage. Parliament approved an eight-hour workday, a graduated income tax, and a retirement pension plan. From 1930, increased pressure was put on the government to tackle discrimination against the Flemish people and the Dutch language. This resulted in several "linguistic laws" and two regions: Flanders and Wallonia. In the former, Dutch is the official language, while in the latter it is French.

10   During World War II Belgium remained neutral, but it was occupied by Germany in 1940, until liberation in 1944. The return of King Leopold III, who had been held prisoner by the Germans, unleashed a major controversy. In a plebiscite, 57 per cent of the population voted in favor of his return to the throne, but continuing tension in Wallonia forced Leopold to abdicate in favor of his son Baudouin (1950).

11   In 1947, Belgium, the Netherlands, and Luxembourg formed an economic association known as the Benelux, still extant within the European Union. Belgium also became a member of NATO in 1949. In 1960 the Belgian Congo became independent, but soon had to deal with secessionist

movements in the southern province of Katanga. Belgium tactitly took side with the secessionists, but UN-troops eventually restored national unity. Later on Belgium and the western powers continued to intervene in the former colony (which became Zaire, and is now the Democratic Republic of Congo). In 1962 Rwanda and Burundi became independent.

12   Female suffrage was granted in 1949. In 1975, Belgian women gained the right to equal pay. During the 1960s and 1970s questions about linguisitic communities became increasingly important. In 1970, they were granted autonomy in cultural matters. In 1980, a new federal structure was approved by Parliament, made up of Flanders, Wallonia, and Brussels as the bilingual capital district.

13   In 1983, hundreds of thousandss gathered in the streets of Brussels to protest against the installation of NATO atomic missiles on Belgian soil. The missiles were withdrawn in 1988, after an arms reduction agreement was signed between the United States and the USSR.

14   In April 1990, despite the opposition of Christian Democrats within the coalition government, Parliament approved an abortion law. In order to avoid having to sign

WORKERS

UNEMPLOYMENT 9.6%   (1996)

Labour force %

■ WOMEN	
□ MEN	

| 40 | 60 |

■ AGRICULTURE	2%	(1990)
□ INDUSTRIAL	28%	
■ SERVICES	70%	

PROFILE

ENVIRONMENT

Northwestern Belgium is a lowland, the Plains of Flanders, composed of sand and clay deposited by its rivers. In southern Belgium the southern highlands rise to 700 m on the Ardennes Plateau. One of the most densely populated European countries, its prosperity rests on trade, helped by its geography and by the transport network covering the northern plains, converging at the port of Antwerp. Belgium has highly intensive agriculture, and a major industrial center. Heavy industry was located near the coal fields of the Sambre-Meuse valley, and textiles were traditionally concentrated in Flanders, where new industries have developed since the late 1960s. Water protection laws were approved in 1971. However, the Meuse River, supplying 5 million people with drinking water, is contaminated by industrial waste. Pollution, by the excessive use of both animal wastes and chemical fertilizers, has increased the nitrate concentration in many rivers and accounts for the presence of algae. Belgian smokestack industries contribute to air pollution in Europe, and are responsible for acid rain in neighboring countries.

SOCIETY

Peoples: The country's two major language-based groups are the Flemish (55 per cent) and the Walloons (44 per cent). There is also a German minority (1 per cent). Many industrial workers are immigrants (Italian, Moroccan and, in lesser numbers, Turkish and African). Foreigners represent about 9 per cent of the whole population. **Religions:** Mainly Catholic. **Languages:** French, Dutch and German are the official languages. French is the main language spoken in the south and east, and Dutch in the north and west, while German is spoken by 0.6 per cent of the population. Brussels is bilingual. **Political Parties:** Flemish Christian People's Party (CVP); French-speaking Social Christians (PSC); French-speaking Socialists (PS); Flemish Socialists (SP); Flemish Liberal Party (VLD); French-speaking Liberal Party (PRL); Green parties (AGALEV/ECOLO); Flemish nationalists (VU); and extreme right parties (Vlaams Blok, FN). **Social Organizations:** The General Labor Federation of Belgium (ABVV/FGTB), Confederation of Christian Labor Unions of Belgium (ACV/CSC).

THE STATE

Official Name: Royaume de Belgique/ Koninkrijk België. **Capital:** Brussels (Bruxelles/Brussel) 949,000 people (1994). Brussels is also the capital of the European Union. **Other cities:** Antwerp 463,000 people; Liège, 196,000; Ghent 228,000 (1994). **Government:** Parliamentary monarchy. The Head of State is King Albert II, since August 1 1993. Prime Minister, Jean-Luc Dehaene, Christian Democrat (CVP), since May 1995. **National Holiday:** July 21, National Day (date King Leopold I ascended to the throne); (1831). **Armed Forces:** 53,000. Conscription was abolished in 1994 and there is now only the professional army.

STATISTICS

DEMOGRAPHY

Population: 10,159,000 (1996) **Annual growth:** 0.2% (1980/ 1996) **Estimates for year 2000:** 10,300,000. **Annual growth to year 2000:** 0.3% (1994/2000) **Urban Population:** 97.1% (1996) **Urban growth:** 0.31% (1980/95) **Children per woman:** 1.6 (1996).

HEALTH

Life expectancy at birth: 77 years (1996) male: 73 years (1994) female: 80 years (1994) **Infant mortality:** 6 per 1,000 (1996) **Under-5 child mortality:** 7 per 1,000 (1996) **Calorie consumption:** 149% (1988/90) 298 **people per doctor** (1988/91).

EDUCATION

School enrolment : Primary total: 99% (1990/95) male : 99% (1990/95) female: 100% (1990/95) Secondary: male : 103% (1990/ 95) female: 104% (1990/95) Tertiary: 49% (1995).

COMMUNICATIONS

320 **newspapers**, 774 **radios**, 460 **TV sets** and 449 **main telephone lines** per 1,000 people (1994).

ECONOMY

Per capita, GNP: $ 26,440 (1996) **Annual growth, GNP:** 1.4% (1995/96) **Annual inflation:** 3.15% (1985/95) **Consumer price index:** 111.2 (1994) **Currency:** 29.42 Belgian francs = $ 1 (1995) **Fertilizer use:** 4,105 kgs per ha (1994) **Exports:** $ 168,010 million (1996) **Imports:** $ 157,860 million (1996).

ENERGY

Consumption: 5,119.81 Kgs of Oil equivalent per capita yearly (1994) 78.21% imported (1994) **HDI** (rank / value) 13 / 0.932 (1994)

---

the proposed legislation, King Baudouin stepped down temporarily from the throne, while the bill went through Parliament.

[15] Between 1983 and 1988, Belgium had an average unemployment rate of 11.3 per cent, the third highest in Western Europe, after Spain and Ireland. The economic situation improved in 1989, but after falling significantly in 1990, unemployment began to rise again in 1991. In October 1996 it stood at 13.8 per cent.

[16] In 1988, Belgium reaffirmed its support to the maintenance of NATO as a short reaching nuclear force, but extended the support

MILITARY EXPENDITURE

MILITARY (as % of health and education expenditures-1990/91) **20%**

to its modernization until 1992, a position which was going to be adopted by other Nato members. In the elections held in November 1991, the Vlaams Blok (Flemish Bloc), a xenophobic group which had geared its campaign around the expulsion of immigrants, experienced a six-fold increase in its parliamentary representation. The gains by the far Right and the Greens provoked the resignation of Prime Minister Wilfried Martens.

[17] Wilfried Martens, who had been premier for 10 years was succeeded by his party colleague Jean-Luc Dehaene, who formed a new government with the Christian Democrats and socialists in March 1992. Dehaene immediately announced a plan to reduce the national deficit, in line with the requirements of the European Treaty of Maastricht. This included drastic curbs on public spending.

[18] On July 31 1993, King Baudouin died after a reign of 42 years. He was succeeded by his brother Albert, who was crowned as Albert II. At the same time, Dehaene began negotiations with unions to produce a "comprehensive plan" against unemployment, which had reached 9.8 per cent in May 1994. Charges of corruption forced three leading socialist politicians to resign as ministers.

[19] The 1994 European elections reflected the population's lack of confidence towards the governing coalition. French-speaking socialists went from 38.5 per cent of the vote in 1989 to 30.4 per cent in 1994. In the municipal elections of October, the socialists lost votes once again, while the Vlaams Blok became the second party in Antwerp, by winning 18 out of the 55 seats at stake on the city council.

[20] Meanwhile, Parliament had agreed on major constitutional changes that turned the country into a federal state. Therefore, on May 21 1995, voters not only elected their members of Parliament, but also three new regional assemblies of Brussels, Flanders and Wallonia. The government alliance led by Premier Dehaene reached clear victory in the national elections, allowing him to continue as head of government.

[21] The 1996 budget, which sought to limit the national deficit to 3 per cent of the GDP, was the cause of severe discussions between the Government and labour unions, which contested the reduction of public spending and purchasing-power. However, the unions' resistance gradually decreased, and supported by a significant economic growth and a resumption of private consumption, the Belgian Government managed to close the 1997 budget with a deficit of 2.7 per cent of the GDP. In spite of its enormous public debt, which clearly exceeded the criteria of the Maastricht-treaty, Belgium was allowed to join the European Monetary Union from its very beginning.

[22] The investigation of Marc Dutroux, accused of the kidnapping and murder of several children and teenagers, was to move the attention to the judicial system. Questions were raised about incompetence, nepotism and rivalry among police forces and prosecutors. A parliamentary inquiry unveiled serious faults and shortcomings, but failed to give evidence of any kind of deliberate protection of Dutroux or his fellows by politicians and prosecutors. In April 1998, the short-lived escape of Dutroux from a courthouse unleashed a fresh wave of indignation. Multi-party talks were held, in order to find the broadest possible agreement on substantial reforms of police and justice.

Belize

Population: 219,000 (1996)
Area: 22,696 SQ KM
Capital: Belmopan

Currency: Belize dollars
Language: English

Belize

A Native American people known as the Itzae were the original occupants of what is now Belize (formerly British Honduras). Belize, together with Guatemala and southern Mexico, formed part of the Mayan empire. In Belize, the Mayas built the cities of Lubaatún, Pusilhá, and a third which archaeologists call San José (its original name is unknown).

2 In 1504 Columbus sailed into the bay naming it the Gulf of Honduras. Spain was nominally the colonial power in the region, but it never pushed further into Belize, because it encountered tough resistance from the natives. According to the terms of the Treaty of Paris (1763) Spain allowed the British to start exploiting timber in the area. This authorization was later confirmed in the Treaty of Versailles (1783). From the Captaincy General of Yucatan (now Mexico) the Spaniards tried on several occasions to drive out the British, many of whom were involved in piracy. In 1798 the British gained control of the colony, although Spain retained sovereignty until it became a British colony in 1862. As of 1871 the Crown took charge of local government with the territory administered by the governor of Jamaica until 1884.

3 By the second half of the 17th century, some British entrepreneurs attracted in particular by cedar, campeche wood, and logwood, started establishing themselves in the depopulated coastal areas, importing African slaves to work their estates. Shortly afterwards, slaves outnumbered Europeans, and in 1784 only 10 per cent of the population was of European extraction, a ratio which has been steadily decreasing.

4 The ethnic base became more heterogeneous in the early 19th century. By that time, Garifuna migrants had settled on the Southern coast of Belize. The War of Castes in Yucatan between 1847 and 1853 displaced thousands of Spanish-speaking inhabitants to the northern coast of Belize, while several Maya communities re-settled in the northern and western areas of the country. These immigrants introduced changes in agricultural techniques which set the pattern for subsistence farming and set the basis of sugar, banana and citrus production. During the 1860s and 1870s, sugar-cane plantation owners sponsored the migration of several thousand workers from China and India. By the end of that century, Maya and Kekchi indigenous peoples, who had escaped oppression in Guatemala, established self-sufficient communities in the south and west of Belize.

5 By the early 20th century, this ethnic mixture had become settled in Belize. However, the economy was stagnant and the British colonial administration prevented any democratic participation. In 1931, a hurricane destroyed a major part of Belize City. A number of strikes and demonstrations by workers and the unemployed gave rise to union formation and increasing demands for democracy. Eligibility was legally introduced in 1936, but it was seriously restricted by literacy, land titles and gender requirements. In 1949 when the Governor devalued the national currency, union leaders and the native middle class joined in a People's Committee which demanded constitutional changes.

6 In 1950 the People's United Party (PUP) was founded, led by George Price. First organized as a "people's committee" to fight against arbitrary treatment by the colonial administration, the PUP won its first elections by a landslide majority. In 1954 universal suffrage was granted, and the majority of the legislative representatives were elected directly. In 1961 a ministerial system of government was established, and in 1964 the country was granted internal autonomy, with George Price becoming Prime Minister. On June 1 1973 the country changed its name from British Honduras to Belize.

LAND USE

DEFORESTATION -0.2% annual (81/90)
IRRIGATED 4.4 % of arable

(1993)

- ■ FOREST & WOODLAND 91.5%
- □ ARABLE 2%
- ▧ OTHER 6.5%

7 Guatemala claimed to have inherited sovereignty over Belize from Spain, and did not recognize the Guatemala-Belize border. In March 1981, Guatemala and Britain signed a 16-point agreement. Britain assured the future independence of Belize in exchange for some concessions to the Guatemalan regime, such as free and permanent access to the Atlantic, joint exploitation of the marine resources, the building of a pipeline, and an "anti-terrorist" agreement.

8 Tourism brought in $4 million in 1983, but this was way behind the $36 million earned by sugar.

9 Price and the PUP were accused of partiality towards Cuba and Nicaragua, an issue exploited by the right-wing opposition, the United Democratic Party (UDP), which won 21 out of 28 seats in the December 1984 elections.

10 The new Prime Minister, Manuel Esquivel, a US-educated physics professor, adopted a liberal economic policy and supported the private import-export sector, which was in the hands of inexperienced family business ventures. He also encouraged foreign investment and sought to attract US, Jamaican, and Mexican investments in tourism, energy, and agriculture. The previous government had bequeathed Belize one of the most liberal Third World set of laws concerning foreign investment.

11 Sugar-cane generated 50 per cent of the country's revenue, but a fall in international prices badly affected the economy. The industry only survived because of import quotas guaranteed by the US and EEC markets, which took 60 per cent of the sugar output, with the remainder being sold at a loss.

12 In March 1986, Prime Minister Esquivel proposed a plan for the sale of Belizean citizenship, aimed primarily at Hong Kong business-people, as Hong Kong was due to revert to China in 1997. Anyone investing $25,000 in Government bonds - really worth only $12,500 - would be granted immediate citizenship of Belize.

13 During the 1980s, the country received approximately 40,000 Salvadoran, Guatemalan, Honduran and Nicaraguan refugees. In spite of

ENVIRONMENT

Belize covers the southeastern tip of the Yucatan Peninsula. The land is low, and the climate warm and rainy in the north. In southern Belize, the hillsides sustain a variety of crops. The northern coastline is marshy and flanked by low islands. In the south there are excellent natural harbors between reefs. Significant oil and gas deposits are believed to exist off the coast. The country shares many of the problems of the Caribbean region, including the deterioration of its water-quality and soil erosion. Close to the cities, the surface of the water is covered with residual wastes and by-products of sugar cane production. Industrial waste, dumped in the water, has generated public health problems and killed fish stocks.

SOCIETY

Peoples: Spanish-Indian descendants 43.6 per cent; Creole (predominantly black) 29.8 per cent; Mayan Indian 11.0%; Garifuna (African-Carib Indian) 6.7 per cent; white 3.9 per cent; East Indian 3.5 per cent; other or not stated 1.5%. **Religions:** 60 per cent are Catholic, most of the rest are Protestant (34 per cent). **Languages:** English (official); Spanish; Mayan dialects are also spoken. **Political Parties:** The United Democratic Party (UDP; The People's United Party (PUP), founded in 1950; The National Alliance for the Rights of Belize, founded in 1992 by members of the UDP opposed to compromise with Guatemala. **Social Organizations:** The General Workers' Union, the Christian Workers' Union (CWU), the United General Federation, the General Federation of Workers and the Public Service Union of Belize.

THE STATE

Official Name: Belize. **Administrative divisions:** 6 districts. **Capital:** Belmopan 3,900 people (est. 1996). **Other cities:** Belize City 47,700 people; Orange Walk 12,155; San Ignacio/Santa Elena 9,890; Corozal 8,158 (1996). **Government:** Parliamentary Monarchy, Queen Elizabeth II of England is Head of State. Colville Young, Governor-General since 1993. Manuel Esquivel, Prime Minister since June 1993. Legislative power lies with the House of Representatives, which has 28 members and is elected by universal suffrage, and an 8-member Senate appointed by the Governor-General. **National Holidays:** September 10, National Day; September 21, Independence Day (1981). **Armed Forces:** 1,065 (1995).

DEMOGRAPHY

Population: 219,000 (1996) **Annual growth:** 2.5% (1980/1996) **Estimates for year 2000:** 242,000. **Annual growth to year 2000:** 2.6% (1994/2000) **Urban Population:** 46.4% (1996). **Children per woman:** 3.8 (1996)

HEALTH

Life expectancy at birth: 74 years (1996) **Infant mortality:** 36 per 1,000 (1996) **Under-5 child mortality:** 44 per 1,000 (1996). **Safe water:** 89% (1990/96).

EDUCATION

Literacy: 80% (1995) male : 70% (1995) female: 70% (1995) **School enrolment :** Primary total: 111% (1990/95) male : 113% (1990/95) female: 109% (1990/95) Secondary: male : 46% (1990/95) female: 52% (1990/95).

COMMUNICATIONS

581 **radios**, 170 **TV sets** and 134 **main telephone lines** per 1,000 people (1994) **Books:** 34 new titles per 100,000 people (1992/94)

ECONOMY

Consumer price index: 106.3 (1994) **Currency:** 2 Belize dollars = $ 1 (1995) **Cereal imports:** 15 metric tons (1994) **Food import dependency:** 13% (1994) **Fertilizer use:** 1,087 kgs per ha (1994) **Development aid received:** $ 16 million (1995) $ 76 per capita (1995) 3% of GNP (1994)

HDI (rank / value) 63 / 0.806 (1994)

official tolerance, some officials blamed immigrants for the dramatic rise in marijuana trafficking and crime.

[14] When Vinicio Cerezo became President of Guatemala, relations between the countries changed substantially. In December 1986, Cerezo's government re-established diplomatic relations with Britain, broken over two decades before, due to Guatemalan claims to Belizean territory. A Permanent Joint Commission was formed, with Belizean, Guatemalan and British representatives, to find a peaceful solution to the issue.

[15] In spite of the existence of the commission, Belize feared a Guatemalan invasion and kept a standing army of 1,800 British troops. However Esquivel declared in Mexico that he "would not allow the installation of US military bases", stressing that he did not wish to become involved in the Central American crisis.

[16] However, the number of US embassy personnel grew sixfold since independence, and the number of Peace Corps volunteers was ten times higher. Dean Barrow, Minister of Foreign Affairs and Economic Development, admitted that he was aware of the country's dependence upon the US. But he also stated that Belize can defend its territorial integrity through the Non-Aligned Movement.

[17] Drug-trafficking - or the sale of "Belize breeze", as marijuana is known - has shown spectacular growth. According to some foreign economists, it has become the country's main export, and it is estimated that some 700 tons, worth at least $100 million have been brought into the US, where the resale price is at least ten times this sum. The area under cultivation increased by at least 20 per cent, in spite of a US-sponsored herbicide-spraying campaign carried out with Mexican helicopters.

[18] George Price was returned to power when the PUP won the September 1989 elections with 15 of the 28 seats. The 13 remaining seats went to Esquivel's UDP.

[19] In September 1991

Guatemalan President Jorge Serrano Elias finally recognized Belize's sovereignty and right to self-determination. The Government of Belize, in turn, gave Guatemala free access to the Gulf of Honduras, thereby reducing its own territorial waters.

[20] At the end of the 1980s and early 1990s a large number of Haitians went to Belize as agricultural laborers, attracted by higher wages than at home. Lower inflation rates and more equal income distribution were incentives for immigration, and they also had access to health and education services. The social services consequently became overloaded, triggering a backlash from Belizeans, who demanded that the Haitians be repatriated.

[21] A 1992 census revealed that the Spanish-speaking mestizo population had outgrown the English-speaking population of African origin who, together with the European descendants, had historically been the dominant group.

[22] Banana, sugar and citrus production increased, representing 40 per cent of the country's total production and four-fifths of its exports. Tourism became the sector with the greatest potential. Several environmental organizations cooperated in protecting nature reserves and attempts to improve the quality of the Caribbean waters. Mayan archeological discoveries attracted many visitors.

[23] Hours after President Serrano of Guatemala was ousted, on June 1 1993, Price brought the election date forward 15 months, counting on a new PUP victory to ratify

agreements made with this neighbor. His opponent Manuel Esquivel questioned the validity of Price's concessions to Guatemala, and proposed that these be legitimized by a referendum.

[24] In the June 1993 elections the PUP was pushed out by the UDP, led by Esquivel's mestizo-dominated UDP. In March 1994, the UDP also won the elections for the nation's 7 local councils. The Government formed a group of economic advisors to look into establishing facilities for the capital and tourist markets, and the development of one or more free zones. The fear of new territorial demands from Guatemala and the withdrawal of British troops led to an increase in defence spending and new recruitment for the armed forces.

[25] In January 1995 Prime Minister Esquivel reshuffled his cabinet in an attempt to control the recession and the crime wave. The Government founded a committee to renew the economic citizenship programme (closed in June 1994) in order to attract investors and reduce the foreign debt. It also froze public sector salaries for the 1995-1996 period to reduce the fiscal deficit.

[26] In the March 1997 municipal elections, the opposition PUP took the majority of the seven local councils for the first time in the history of the country. In April, Esquivel made further changes to the cabinet; some ministers were given new portfolios and others were made ambassadors abroad.

[27] In mid-1997 the electoral roll was finally brought up to date and general elections announced for 1998.

WORKERS

■ AGRICULTURE	34%	(1990)
□ INDUSTRIAL	19%	
■ SERVICES	48%	

Benin

Benin

Population: 5,563,000 (1996)
Area: 112,622 SQ KM
Capital: Porto Novo
Currency: CFA francs
Language: French

Benin (known as Dahomey until 1975) is considered one of the poorest countries in the world. It lies in the region of the Yoruba culture, which developed at the ancient city of Ife. It was here that the Ewe peoples, who came from the same linguistic family developed into two distinct kingdoms during the 17th century: Hogbonu (today known as Porto Novo) and Abomey, further inland. These states developed around the booming slave trade, serving as intermediaries.

2 The traditional rulers of Abomey, the Fon, built a centralized state that extended east and west beyond Benin's present-day frontiers. A well-disciplined army, with European rifles and a large contingent of female soldiers enabled them to end the patronage of the Alafin of Oyo (Nigeria) and capture various Yoruba cities. After the 17th century, Ouidah became the main port for British, French and Portuguese slave traders receiving their human cargo.

3 The ruling group of Abomey suffered a setback in 1818 when Britain banned the slave trade, although Ghezo who ruled between 1818 and 1856 maintained a thriving clandestine traffic with Brazil and Cuba. He also promoted the development of agriculture and established a strict state monopoly on foreign trade.

4 In 1889, Ghezo's grandson Benhanzin inherited a prosperous state, but one already threatened by colonialism. In 1891, Fon troops resisted the French invasion only to be defeated a year later. The King and his army retreated to the forests, where they held out until 1894. Benhanzin, who became a symbol of anti-colonial resistance, died in exile in Martinique in 1906.

5 The colonists destroyed the centralized political structure of the ancient Fon state. Traditional Fon society was dismantled and replaced with a system based on the exploitation of farm labor. The French also declared a monopoly on the palm-oil trade and ruined families that had resisted foreign penetration for nearly a century.

6 By the beginning of the 20th century, the colony of Dahomey (as the French called it), was no longer self-sufficient. When it gained independence in August 1960, oil-seed exports stood at 1850 levels, while the population had tripled.

7 Independence came as a direct consequence both of France's weakness at the end of World War II and the activities of European-educated nationalists, led by Louis Hunkanrin, who waged a stubborn 20-year struggle against the compulsory labor imposed by the French. All forms of political organization were banned and in retaliation, Hunkanrin created the Human Rights League. A period of ruthless repression followed: hundreds of villages were burned down, nearly 5,000 people were killed, and Hunkanrin took refuge in Mauritania.

8 By 1960, Dahomey had become an unbearable economic burden and France agreed to independence. The new Government inherited a bankrupt economy and a corrupt infrastructure. A series of 12 military and civilian governments marked a 16-year period of instability.

9 The neocolonial elite collapsed when then-Major Mathieu Kerekou headed a coup by a group of young officers opposed to political corruption and official despotism. Two years later, a Marxist-Leninist

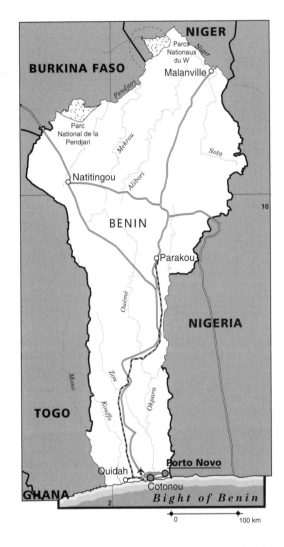

state was proclaimed and its name changed to Benin, with a communitarian political and economic system: all foreign property was nationalized, and a single-party system was introduced with the creation of the People's Revolutionary Party.

10 The revolutionary Government became the target of several conspiracies plotted abroad. There was an unsuccessful invasion in January 1977 with the participation of French mercenaries and the support of Gabon and Morocco.

11 In 1980, a new Revolutionary Assembly was elected through direct vote. The Government switched to a more pragmatic foreign policy and diplomatic relations with France were resumed. Although palm-oil

production continued to drop as the trees grew older, cotton and sugar sales rose. High unemployment continued, but in 1982 offshore oil was discovered thus guaranteeing energy self-sufficiency. In addition large phosphate deposits were discovered in the Mekrou region.

12 Hopes of recovery dimmed as drought reached the northern provinces. Desertification was exacerbated, and the region was unable to supply its own food even in traditional subsistence crops such as manioc, yams, corn and sorghum.

13 To make matters worse, Nigeria cracked down on immigrants, expelling thousands back to Benin and closing the border.

14 The economic crisis forced the

WORKERS

(1996)

Labour force %

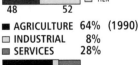

■ WOMEN
□ MEN

48   52

■ AGRICULTURE 64% (1990)
□ INDUSTRIAL   8%
■ SERVICES   28%

LAND USE

DEFORESTATION -1.2% annual (81/90)
IRRIGATED 0.7% of arable

(1993)

■ FOREST & WOODLAND 30.2%
□ ARABLE   12.7%
■ OTHER   57.1%

PER 100,000
LIVE BIRTHS

990

37%

18%

1994

18%

PER CAPITA

$207

PROFILE

ENVIRONMENT

Benin is a narrow strip of land which extends north from the Gulf of Guinea. Its 120-km sandy coast lacks natural ports. Several natural regions cut across the country from south to north: the coastal belt where oil palms are cultivated; the tropical wooded lowlands; and the plateau which rises gradually towards the headwaters of the Queme, Mekrou, Alibori and Pendjari rivers, in a region of tropical hills. One of the major environmental problems is that of desertification, which has been aggravated in recent years by a significant decrease in rainfall.

SOCIETY

Peoples: Benin's people stem from 60 ethnic groups. The Fon (47 per cent), Adja, Yoruba and Bariba groups are the most numerous and before French colonization they had already developed very stable political institutions. **Religion:** 70 per cent practise traditional African religions, 15 per cent are Muslim and 15 per cent Catholic. **Languages:** French (official). Other widely spoken languages are Fon, Fulani, Mine, Yoruba and Massi. **Political parties:** Democratic Renewal Party (PRD); Renaissance Party of Benin (RPB).
Social organizations: The Benin Workers' National Trade Union (UNSTB).

THE STATE

Official name: République Populaire du Bénin. **Capital:** Porto Novo, 177,000 people (1992). **Other cities:** Cotonou 533,000 people; Djougou 132,000; Abomey-Calavi 125,000; Parakou 106,000 (1992). **Government:** Presidential republic. Mathieu Kerekou, President elected in March 1996. Single chamber parliament. **National Holidays:** July 1, Independence (1960); November 30, Revolution Day (1974).
Armed Forces: 4,800. **Other:** Gendarmerie: 2,000; People's Militia: 1,500-2,000.

STATISTICS

DEMOGRAPHY

Population: 5,563,000 (1996) **Annual growth:** 3% (1980/1996) **Estimates for year 2000:** 6,200,000. **Annual growth to year 2000:** 2.8% (1994/2000) **Urban Population:** 39.2% (1996) **Urban growth:** 5.08% (1980/95) **Children per woman:** 6 (1996).

HEALTH

Life expectancy at birth: 54 years (1996) male: 52 years (1994) female: 57 years (1994) **Infant mortality:** 84 per 1,000 (1996) **Under-5 child mortality:** 140 per 1,000 (1996) **Calorie consumption:** 104% (1988/90) 14,286 **people per doctor** (1988/91) **Safe water:** 50% (1990/96).

EDUCATION

Literacy: 37% (1995) male : 49% (1995) female: 26% (1995) **School enrolment :** Primary total: 72% (1990/95) male : 88% (1990/95) female: 44% (1990/95) Secondary: male : 17% (1990/95) female: 7% (1990/95) Tertiary: 3% (1995) **Primary school teachers:** one for every 49 students (1995).

COMMUNICATIONS

91 **radios**, 20 **TV sets** and 5 **main telephone lines** per 1,000 people (1994) **Books:** 2 new titles per 100,000 people (1992/94).

ECONOMY

Per capita, GNP: $ 350 (1996) **Annual growth, GNP:** 3.2% (1995/96) **Consumer price index:** 112.5 (1994) **Currency:** 490 CFA francs = $ 1 (1995) **Cereal imports:** 107 metric tons (1994) **Food import dependency:** 18% (1994) **Fertilizer use:** 90 kgs per ha (1994) **Exports:** $ 255 million (1996) **Imports:** $ 869 million (1996) Extenal debt: $ 1,594 million (1996) $ 287 per capita: (1996) **Debt service:** 6.8% of exports (1996) **Development aid received:** $ 276 million (1995) $ 53 per capita (1995) 18.6% of GNP (1994).

ENERGY

Consumption: 20.09 Kgs of Oil equivalent per capita yearly (1994) - 194.39% imported (1994)

HDI (rank / value) 146 / 0.368 (1994).

Government to accept the terms of the International Monetary Fund, including a 10 per cent income tax and a 50 per cent reduction in non-wage social benefits. In January 1989 students, teachers and other educational bodies staged a strike demanding back pay and scholarship payments which had not been honored.
[15] On December 8 1989, disappointed with results and besieged by street demonstrations, President Kerekou announced that he was abandoning his Marxist-Leninism. A new constitution was drawn up, providing for a series of political and economic reforms, especially the promotion of free enterprise.
[16] On March 24 1991 Prime Minister Nicéphore Soglo defeated President Kerekou with 68 per cent of the votes in the country's first presidential election in 30 years. In 1992, former President Kerekou, prosecuted for his activities following the 1972 coup

was granted an amnesty, and political prisoners were released.
[17] Soglo continued the economic liberalization and privatization policy initiated by Kerekou in 1986. Debt servicing still represented a high percentage of the resources annually obtained (in 1992 debt service was equivalent to 27 per cent of the country's income).
[18] The 100 per cent devaluation of the CFA franc decreed by France in January 1994 provoked contradictory effects in Benin's economy. GDP continued to grow at a 4 per cent annual rate and cotton exports increased. However, public expenditure retrenchment - aimed among other things at curbing inflation after the devaluation - brought about drastic cuts in social spending schemes.
[19] In July 1994, Soglo assumed the leadership of the Renaissance Party of Benin (RPB), founded by his wife Rosine in 1992. The RPB was defeated in the legislative and municipal elections of March 1995

by the opposition Democratic Renewal Party (DRP). In May 1995 the Government banned food exports to reduce local sale prices and curb inflation, at the same time that it refused to increase salaries.
[20] Soglo's "clannish" style and his tendency to rule together with his family not only angered the political class in Benin. In the general elections held in March 1996, Soglo suffered a narrow defeat to Kerekou, the former leader of the Marxist regime. In April, the World Bank stated that Benin's economic reform had made little progress and refused to renegotiate the $98 million loan which the National Assembly had rejected late in 1995.
[21] Between August and October 1997, a disease killed some 60,000 pigs, 10 per cent of the country's stock of swine. In November, labour unions held a 72 hour

strike to "warn" the government of their dissatisfaction with the budget agreed for the following year. In February 1998, social unease reached its peak after the country's five main labour unions launched a strike against "the antisocial 1998 budget, the precepts of the IMF, World Bank and European Union, as well as widespread and systematic corruption by the Kerekou government". In view of the extent of this mobilization, the Government decided to increase public spending by $10 million, which was considered too little by the unions which called for the strike.
[22] Some studies estimated that due to the spread of the AIDS virus, life expectancy in Benin has been reduced by 10 years.

Bermuda

Bermuda

Population: 64,000 (1996)
Area: 53 SQ KM
Capital: Hamilton

Currency: Bermuda dollars
Language: English

The Bermuda archipelago was the first colony of the British Empire. Sighted by the Spanish navigator Juan Bermúdez in 1503, it was settled in 1609 when British emigrants on their way to America were shipwrecked nearby.

2 From 1612, the colony welcomed religious and political dissidents. In 1684, it began to be administrated by the British Crown, and the first parliament was installed. Even though African slaves formed the majority, only plantation owners could elect representatives.

3 Agriculture almost disappeared in the 20th century, being replaced by tourism, gambling and transnational corporations lured by numerous tax exemptions. During the Prohibition (1919-1933) traffickers living in Bermuda smuggled rum into the United States. From 1941, Washington set up air and naval bases on the islands and has completely replaced British military presence since 1957.

4 After the creation of the Bermuda Industrial Union (BIU), in 1963 workers founded the Progessive Labor Party (PLP), which favored the country's total independence and the introduction of an income tax. The following year, the Right organized the United Bermuda Party (UBP).

5 In 1968, Britain granted the islands greater administrative autonomy, and the majority party was given the right to name the prime minister. The period leading up to the elections was marked by racial and political violence. The assassination of the governor led to intervention by British troops. When the election was held, the UBP won by a large margin.

6 In the 1976 election, the PLP increased its number of seats. From its position in opposition, the PLP continued to demand greater autonomy for the island.

7 In 1977, two members of the "Black Cadre" were sentenced to death, for participating in armed anticolonial activities. The execution unleashed a wave of protests, with British troops intervening once again. The Minister of Communal (Race) Relations was withdrawn from his post, and his duties were delegated to the Bermuda Regiment, responsible for putting down protest and discontent.

8 In spite of charges of racism, the European population supported the Government, while the black population opted for the PLP or more radical organizations.

9 The 1979 Bermuda Constitutional Convention failed to reach a consensus on representation and the minimum voting age. However, a reduction in the number of non-Bermudan voters went into effect in that December.

10 The UBP won both the 1980 and 1983 elections, although the opposition increased its representation. With the UBP in power, the country continued without self-determination as the government claimed that the majority was against this.

11 The islands' strategic location along North Atlantic routes explains the continued presence of British, Canadian and US troops.

12 In 1989 Prime Minister John Swan of the UBP was re-elected and his party gained 23 seats. The PLP obtained 15 seats; one seat went to the National Liberal Party (NLP), a center party, and the Environmental Party won one seat.

13 In 1989 and 1990, unemployment rose by 0.5 per cent and 2 per cent, respectively. Employment within the industrial sector was 3.1 per cent. The US recession continued to affect tourism in the first few months of 1992. London rejected plans for independence.

14 In 1992, Sir John Waddington was nominated Governor-General.

15 Intense drug-trafficking in 1993 reulted in a major diversion of investment away from Bermuda. That year, measures also went into effect to control offshore banking operations.

16 In the October 5 1993 elections, J Irving Pearman was elected vice-premier. The UBP retained its majority in the Assembly with 22 seats while the PLP, led by Frederick Wade, confirmed its growth with 18 seats.

17 In August 1995, a plebiscite was held regarding the Prime Minister's proposal on independence. The result was negative and so Bermuda remained a British colony.

18 In March 1997, following the resignation of David Saul, Pamela Gordon took over as Prime Minister. In June, Thorold Masefield was appointed governor.

PROFILE

ENVIRONMENT
This Atlantic archipelago is made up of 360 small coral islands, characterized by chalky, permeable soil. Bermuda includes 150 of these islands, of which 20 are uninhabited. The warm Gulf Stream current produces a mild climate which attracts tourists, mainly from the US.

SOCIETY
Peoples: Approximately 60 per cent descend from Africans; there are also descendents of Portuguese from Madeira and the Azores; mixed European and Indian descendants and a minority who are of European origin.
Religions: Anglican majority (28 per cent), in addition to Methodists (12 per cent), Adventists (6 per cent), Catholics (15 per cent) and members of other religions.
Languages: English (official).
Political parties: The United Bermuda Party (UBP); Progressive Labor Party (PLP); National Liberal Party; Environmental Party.
Social organizations: Bermuda Industrial Union (5,202 members); Bermuda Public Service Association (2,300 members).

THE STATE
Official Name: Bermuda.
Capital: Hamilton, 6,000 people (1991).
Other cities: St George's, 3,000 people (1991).
Government: British dependency. Thorold Masefield, Governor since June 1997; nominated by Queen Elizabeth II. Pamela Gordon, Prime Minister since March 1997. The Prime Minister appoints the cabinet on approval by the Governor. Bicameral parliament: Senate has 11 members, 5 elected by the Prime Minister, 3 by the opposition leader and 3 by the Governor. Assembly has 40 members elected for a 5-year term.
National Holiday: May 24, Bermuda Day.

DEMOGRAPHY
Population: 64,000 (1996). **Urban population:** 100.0 % (1996)

ECONOMY
Consumer price index: 113.0 (1994). **Cereal imports:** 2 metric tons (1994)

Bhutan

Druk Yul

Population: 1,812,000 (1996)
Area: 47,000 SQ KM
Capital: Thimbu

Currency: Ngultrum
Language: Dzongkha

B hutan lies in the heart of the vast Himalayan mountains. Early explorers and envoys of the British colonial Government called it Bootan, land of the Booteas, or sometimes Bhotan. Wedged between giant neighbors China and India and secluded by some of the world's highest peaks, it was little known to the rest of the world. Even today, the origin of its name remains unknown. Perhaps it came from the Sanskrit Bhot'ante ("the end of Tibet") or from another Sanskrit word Bhu'nthan ("high land"). To the people of Bhutan it is Druk or Druk Yul, land of the Thunder Dragon. It was here that the Drukpa Kargyud sect of Buddhism flourished in the 7th century.

2 From the 12th century, the Drukpa Kargyud tradition became dominant. After a long period of rivalry among various groups, the country was united by a Drukpa Kargyud Lama named Ngawang Namgyal in the 17th century. Druk, the country's original name, is derived from the Kargyud Sect of Mahayana Buddhism (Drukpa), now the state religion. Namgyal, popularly known as Shabdrung ("at whose feet one submits"), was both the country's spiritual and secular ruler. Factionalism gradually eroded the power of the subsequent Shabdrungs. On December 17 1907 Ugen Wangchuk united the country and established Bhutan's first hereditary monarchy.

3 The British colonial administration in India signed important treaties with Bhutan in 1774 and 1865. The 1910 Treaty of Punakha stipulated that the British would not interfere in Bhutan's internal affairs, but made the country a British protectorate in terms of external relations. Similar provisions were included in the 1949 treaty signed between Bhutan and independent India.

4 Bhutan emerged from its self-imposed isolation in the 1960s, by joining the Colombo Plan in 1962 and the Universal Postal Union in 1969. A department of foreign affairs established in 1970 was upgraded to ministerial rank in 1971. That same year, Bhutan became a member of the United Nations, opened a diplomatic mission in New Delhi and a permanent mission to the UN in New York; it also became a member of the Non-Aligned Movement.

5 Present King Jigme Singye Wangchuk, fourth in line to the throne, was crowned in 1972. His father, the late King Jigme Dorji Wangchuk, was considered the architect of modern Bhutan. Under his rule, the political and administrative machinery were restructured and modernized, and successive 5-year development plans were initiated.

6 Agriculture and animal husbandry are the predominant means of livelihood in the country. As Bhutan opened up, the development of an economic infrastructure became a priority. A road network, particularly imperative with the closing of the Tibetan border in 1960, is now in place across the country, with important arterial routes heading south toward India.

7 Many rivers and water falls have been exploited as sources of hydroelectric energy. The massive Chukha project lies on the main route between Phuntsholing and Thimbu. With a potential of 8,000 megawatts, it supplies electricity not only within Bhutan, but also to adjacent parts of India. Parts of southern Bhutan have been linked with the Indian grid system, but 80 per cent of Bhutan's population lack electricity.

8 The first chemical industry, Bhutan Carbide and Chemicals Ltd, launched production in June 1988. The Bhutan Development Finance Corporation (BDFC) was also established in 1988 to encourage rapid expansion of the private sector. A rural credit scheme introduced in 1982 under the Royal Monetary Authority has been brought under the auspices of the BDFC.

9 The semblance of political stability which the Government attempts to project abroad has been seriously affected by the campaigns of the various opposition groups, who clamor for the democratization of the country. The main agitator among these movements is a group representing the Nepalese minority which has been extremely active in recent years.

10 Ethnic friction has been on the increase since the 1988 census, when the King stepped up his "Bhutanization" campaign, decreeing the public use of the national dress - the ko for men and the kira for women - as well as use of the Dzonga language. Teaching in Nepalese was prohibited, tourists were barred from sacred sites, and television signals from India were blocked. Work visas for foreigners were also outlawed.

11 These measures infuriated the Nepalese minority (25 per cent of the population), who immediately rejected them. However, their demands were met with intransigence on the part of the monarchy, on various occasions.

12 In September 1990, demonstrations and street protests by the banned Bhutan People's Party were repressed by Government forces in the city of Thimphu. Opposition groups claimed that 300 people were killed in the incidents.

13 The BPP was founded by a group of students of Nepalese origin to represent the Nepalese minority and fight for an end to Drukpa domination, to achieve a more democratic constitution, and legalization of the political parties.

14 Since September 1990, social agitation has increased: Nepalese commandos have set fire to schools and destroyed bridges, they have also carried out kidnappings to raise money, and the Government has blamed them for no fewer than 30 violent deaths.

15 Bhutan depends on India for its imports of consumer goods, fuel, grain, machinery, replacement parts, vehicles and exports with 93 per cent of its produce sold to India. The main Bhutanese exports are hydroelectric energy, cement, handcrafts, fruits and spices such as cardamoms.

16 In the past few years, Bhutan has tried to diversify foreign trade. At the same time, a number of development programs are in effect with financing from India, Norway, Kuwait, Japan and Switzerland amongst other countries.

17 Attempts to introduce a market economy system constantly come up against the fact that Bhutan is among the world's 42 least developed countries. In addition, the mountains make it difficult to

LAND USE

DEFORESTATION -0.6% annual (81/90)
IRRIGATED 29.6% of arable

(1993)

■ FOREST & WOODLAND	66%
□ ARABLE	2.4%
▨ OTHER	31.6%

Maternal Mortality
1990

PER 100,000
LIVE BIRTHS

1,600

Literacy
1995

42%

STATISTICS

DEMOGRAPHY
Population: 1,812,000 (1996) **Annual growth:** 2.1% (1980/1996) **Estimates for year 2000:** 2,000,000. **Annual growth to year 2000:** 2.6% (1994/2000) **Urban Population:** 6.2% (1996) **Children per woman:** 5.9 (1996) .

HEALTH
Life expectancy at birth: 52 years (1996) male: 50 years (1994) female: 53 years (1994) **Infant mortality:** 90 per 1,000 (1996) **Under-5 child mortality:** 127 per 1,000 (1996) **Calorie consumption:** 128% (1988/90) 11,111 **people per doctor** (1988/91) **Safe water:** 58% (1990/96) .

EDUCATION
Literacy: 42% (1995) male : 56% (1995) female: 28% (1995) **School enrolment :** Primary total: 25% (1990/95) male : 31% (1990/95) female: 19% (1990/95) Secondary: male : 7% (1990/95) female: 2% (1990/95).

COMMUNICATIONS
17 **radios** and 7 **main telephone lines** per 1,000 people (1994).

ECONOMY
Currency: 35.18 Ngultrum = $ 1 (1995) **Cereal imports:** 41 metric tons (1994) **Food import dependency:** 11% (1994) **Fertilizer use:** 7 kgs per ha (1994). **Development aid received:** $ 73 million (1995) $ 107 per capita (1995) 26.8% of GNP (1994) .

HDI (rank / value) 155 / 0.338 (1994)

PROFILE

ENVIRONMENT
This Himalayan country is made up of three distinct climatic and geographical regions: the Duar plain in the south, humid and tropical, is densely wooded and ranges in height from 300 to 2,000 metres; at the centre lies a temperate region with heights of up to 3,000 metres. Finally, there are the great northern heights, with year-round snow and peaks that climb 8,000 metres high. Forests are the country's mainstay. Rivers and waterfalls have been exploited and they supply energy to the country and neighbouring areas. There are graphite, marble, granite and limestone deposits. Approximately half of the arable land lies on steep slopes; of this, nearly 15 per cent is merely topsoil. The combination of these two factors makes the terrain very susceptible to erosion.

SOCIETY
Peoples: Bhutia (Ngalops) 50 per cent; Nepalese (Gurung) 35 per cent; Sharchops 15 per cent. There are also Lepchas, native people, and Santal, descended from Indian immigrants. 95 per cent of the teachers and 55 per cent of public servants are of Indian origin. **Religions:** Buddhist 69.6 per cent; Hindu 24.6 per cent; Muslim 5.0 per cent; other 0.8 per cent (1980). **Languages:** Dzongkha (official). Nepalese and other dialects are also spoken. **Political Parties:** The Bhutan People's Party (BPP), founded in Nepal in 1990; the National Bhutanese Congress founded in 1992, in Nepal and India; the People's Forum of Human Rights (PFHR), started in 1990, covering five refugee camps in Nepal; the United People's Liberation Front (UPLF), also founded in 1990.

THE STATE
Official Name: Druk-Yul. **Administrative Divisions:** 18 Districts. **Capital:** Thimbu, 30,400 people (1993). **Government:** Jigme Singye Wangchuk, king since July 21 1972. The hereditary monarch is assisted by a council of 9 members, of whom 5 are elected by the people, 2 are appointed by the autocratic ruler and 2 by the Buddhist religious dignitaries whose 6,000 lamas (monks) are headed by the Je Khempo. There is also a consultative assembly (Tsogdu) of 150 members 101 of whom are elected and 49 appointed, most being Buddhist monks. The ruler also dispenses justice. **National Holidays:** August 2, Buddhist Lent; October 30, end of Buddhist Lent.

build highways and providing an adequate infrastructure is both costly and difficult. Peasants are forced to work in infrastructure projects without remuneration.
[18] Despite these problems, the country's five-year plans have been followed and their timetables respected. As a result, the country's GNP grew in real terms by an annual average of 7.5 per cent between 1980 and

WORKERS

- ■ **AGRICULTURE** 94% (1990)
- ☐ **INDUSTRIAL** 1%
- ▨ **SERVICES** 5%

1990. Since 1992, the seventh plan has been implemented aiming to increase exports, conserve the environment, decentralize and promote women's rights. To achieve these aims the Government has encouraged foreign investment, receiving technical assistance from India. Likewise a cautious privatization plan was introduced, with shares in state enterprises offered to the general public.
[19] Drastic cuts in public spending, the drive against nepotism and the voluntary reduction of the King's personal wealth - including moving from the royal palace into a modest home - encouraged international agencies to provide financing for development projects. Dependence upon

foreign aid was consequently reduced from 50 per cent in 1982, to 20 per cent in 1992. The budget for 1994-95 revealed a new growth of international financial support: 41.6 per cent was contributions from the United Nations and other agencies and 21.2 per cent came from the Government of India.
[20] The country had frontier disputes with China and India. With China the argument was over the sovereignty of the region of Arunachal Pradesh, while with India, it concerned a small zone between Sarbhang and Gueyilegfug.
[21] In a country where neither political parties nor unions are permitted, the National Women s Association, one of the few social organizations in Bhutan, tried to encourage the "promotion" of Bhutanese women, seeking to make them branch out from their traditional agricultural activities into textile handcrafts.
[22] Up until 1996, the Nepalese Government had held seven fruitless meetings with the Bhutanese authorities over the problem of the 100,000 or so immigrants - Nepalese and Bhutanese of Nepalese origin - forced to flee or expelled from Bhutan, living in refugee camps. Since 1990, Bhutan has classed the refugees, called Lhotsampas, as not having a nationality.
[23] In 1995, Nepalese activists claimed that over half the population of Bhutan was Nepalese, but government

estimates said it was no more than a third. Most of the civil servants are of Indian origin.
[24] In 1996, the European Parliament condemned the Thimbu Government's human rights policies. Nepal proposed a survey to reveal the Lhotsampas' nationality, but Bhutan did not accept.
[25] On several occasions the government in New Delhi collaborated with Bhutan to keep opponents exiled in northern India under control, repressing several demonstrations against the Thimbu Government. Bhutan in turn supported India in international bodies. In the UN, in September 1996, for example, Bhutan voted against the suspension of nuclear tests alongside India and Libya.
[26] In early 1998, Amnesty International denounced a systematic government campaign against the opposition. Sympathizers of the National Bhutanese Congress (DNC), a party directed from exile, in Nepal, had been illegally detained. According to Amnesty, most of these were Buddhist monks and religious teachers. The DNC was calling for a democratic system of government and respect for human rights.

Bolivia

Bolivia

Population:	7,593,000 (1996)
Area:	1,098,581 SQ KM
Capital:	La Paz
Currency:	Bolivianos
Language:	Spanish

In 2000 BC the region of modern-day Bolivia was inhabited by farmers in the Andes, and forest hunter-gatherers in the east. Their terrain ranged from high mountain areas, *puna*, to hot valleys and forests. They raised livestock and grew potatoes, cotton, maize, and coca; they also fished and mined. This region, rich in natural resources, sustained several kingdoms and fiefs around Lake Titicaca, with the Tiahuanaco-Huari (600 BC-1000 AC) civilization at their center.

2 The basic social unit was the *ayllu* kinship group, in which there was no private land ownership. The society was stratified into farmers, artisans and the ruling ayllu, of priests and warriors, who appointed the *malku* (chief).

3 By 800 AD, Tiahuanaco formed the first Pan-Andean empire. By 1100, the ayllu of the Inkas, from the Cusco Valley in Peru, had colonized the other Andean peoples and formed a confederation of states called the Tahuantinsuyo. Also known as the Inka empire, it adopted elements of Tiahuanaco culture, technology, religion and economics, particularly the ayllu social unit.

4 Through the mita, a mutual cooperation commitment between the different ayllus, each worker would render service to the centralized state; this system was later cruelly exploited by the Spaniards. The social structure was rigid; at the top was the Inka (son of the Sun), followed by the nobility and the priests. Then came the *capac*, governors of the regions into which the empire was divided, and lastly came the *curacas* (leaders of the ayllus) and the farmers. Social organization was based on self-sufficient, communal production.

5 When the Spaniards arrived at the beginning of the 16th century, the Tahuantinsuyo extended from southern Colombia, through Ecuador and Peru, to northern Chile, and from Lake Titicaca and the *altiplano* highlands to northern Argentina, embracing the mountain valleys and the eastern plains. One million people are estimated to have been living within the area of the present Bolivia, and from twelve to thirteen million in the Tahuantinsuyo as a whole, making it the most densely populated area of South America. This society included a number of ethnic groups, predominantly Aymara (around Lake Titicaca) and Quechua. The eastern plains were inhabited by dispersed groups of Tupi and Guarani, with no central nucleus. To this day, Aymara and Quechua are the most widespread languages in Bolivia.

6 In 1545 the Spanish discovered silver at Potosi. They extracted immense quantities which contributed to the capital accumulation of several European powers. Millions of native Americans died there, cruelly exploited to the point of exhaustion. Potosi was one of the three largest cities of the 17th century, growing up at the foot of the hill. It became the economic nerve center for vast regions of Chile and Argentina, and nurtured a rich mining bourgeoisie, guilty of corruption, ostentation and squandering.

7 Decades of popular struggle against the Spanish reached their peak in the successive failed rebellions of Tupac Katari (1780-82), the Protective Board of La Paz (1809), headed by mestizo Pedro Domingo Murillo, and the

'independence guerrillas'. The pro-independence movement was subsequently taken up by the creoles (Spaniards born in America), who distorted it by advocating social, economic and political systems based not on native models but on those of emerging European capitalist powers. A British blockade interrupted the supply of mercury, essential for treating the silver, and the Bolivian mining industry went into decline. The Buenos Aires based trading bourgeoisie soon lost interest in Upper Peru (Bolivia) and offered little resistance when it fell under the influence of the independence leader Simon Bolivar. The country was renamed after him when the Assembly of Representatives

proclaimed independence in Chuquisaca, in 1825.

8 Peru exerted great influence over the independent Bolivia until 1841. Bolivian president Marshall Andrés de Santa Cruz, tried to modernize Bolivia, founding universities and the Supreme Court of Justice, and compiling law codes.

9 A mine-owning oligarchy, including Patiño, Aramayo, and Hochschild, worked with the politicians and generals, who were their associates, handling the Bolivian republic as if it were part of the tin business. British imperialist interest, initially in the saltpeter at Antofagasta and later in Bolivia's southern oil reserves, triggered two wars in South America: the Pacific War (Chile against Bolivia and Peru from 1879-83), and the Chaco War (Paraguay and Bolivia, from 1932-35). As a result of these conflicts, Bolivia lost its coast and three-quarters of its territory in the Chaco region. The ceding of Amazonian Acre to Brazil, in 1904, completed the country's dismemberment.

10 On July 21 1946 Bolivian president Gualberto Villaroel was overthrown, assassinated, and his body hung from a lamp-post in downtown La Paz. His predecessor, German Busch, from

PUBLIC EXPENDITURE

8.2%   52.3%
1995 ■ DEFENCE □ SOCIAL

In **1990/91** Military as % of health & education expenditure was **23%**.

WORKERS

(1996)

Labour force %

■ WOMEN
□ MEN

37   63

■ AGRICULTURE 47% (1990)
□ INDUSTRIAL 18%
■ SERVICES 36%

LAND USE

DEFORESTATION -1.1% annual (81/90)
IRRIGATED 8.3% of arable

(1993)

■ FOREST & WOODLAND 52.8%
□ ARABLE 1.9%
■ OTHER 45.3%

Foreign Trade
MILLIONS $ 1996

IMPORTS

1,601

EXPORTS

1,087

Maternal Mortality
       1990

PER 100,000
LIVE BIRTHS

650

PROFILE

ENVIRONMENT
A landlocked country with three geographic regions. 70 per cent of the population live in the cold, dry climate of the *altiplano*, an Andean highland plateau with an average altitude of 4,000 meters. This region holds the country's mineral resources: tin (second largest producer in the world), silver, zinc, lead and copper. The subtropical valleys (*yungas*) of the eastern slopes of the Andes form the country's main farming area, where coffee, cocoa, sugar cane, coca and bananas are grown. The tropical plains of the East and North, a region of jungles and grasslands, produce cattle, rice, corn, and sugar cane. The area is also rich in oil. Bolivia is made up of three drainage basins which empty into Lake Titicaca, the Amazon and the Rio de la Plata. Unconstrained exploitation of lumber threatens the country's forest resources, as well as water supplies and fauna. In "El Alto" (a high district of La Paz), air pollution has risen in direct proportion to the number of motor vehicles.

SOCIETY
Peoples: 57 per cent of Bolivians belong to the Quechua and Aymara nations. *Mestizos* and *Cholos* account for 25 per cent of the population. A minority of European descent has ruled the country since the Spanish conquest. The Tupí and Guaraní peoples live in the eastern forests.
Religions: Mainly Catholic. Freedom of religion.
Languages: Spanish (official). More than half of the populatin speak native languages (Quechua, Guarani and Aymara); there are 33 ethnic-linguistic groups.
Political Parties: The parties with parliamentary representation are the Nationalist Democratic Action (ADN), headed by General Hugo Bánzer Suárez; the Nationalist Revolutionary Movement, of President Gonzalo Sanchez de Losada; the new Patriotic Conscience Party (CONDEPA), directed by media businessman Carlos Palenque; the Solidary Civic Union (UCS); the Free Bolivia Movement; the Socialist Democratic Group (ASD); the Revolutionary Movement of the Left (MIR); the Pachacuti-Axis, supported by *campesinos* engaged in coca cultivation; and the MRTK-L (the political wing - albeit small in number - of the Tupac Katari Movement).
Social Organizations: The Bolivian Workers' Confederation (COB); the Sole Labor Union Confederation of Farm Workers of Bolivia (CSUTCB). There are also important ethnic and environmental organizations like the Indigenous Confederation of the Eastern region, Chaco and Bolivian Amazon Area (CIDOB); the Guaraní People's Assembly (APG); the Federation of Campesino Women; the Federation of Neighborhood Commissions; and the Bolivian Forum on Environment and Development (FOBOMADE).

THE STATE
Official Name: República de Bolivia.
Administrative Divisions: 9 Departments.
Capital: La Paz, 1,246,000 people (1995) - including El Alto (404,400 people) which became a separate city in 1988 - and functions as the seat of the Government. Sucre is the constitutional capital, and seat of the judiciary.
Other cities: Santa Cruz de la Sierra, 697,000 people; Cochabamba, 408,000 people (1992).
Government: Hugo Bánzer Suárez, President and Head of the Government since June 1 1997. Bicameral legislature: Chamber of Deputies, made up of 130 members; Senate, 27 members.
National Holiday: August 6, Independence Day (1825).
Armed Forces: 25,000 (1993).
Other: 23,000 Police.

the military generation of the Chaco War, had nationalized Bolivia's oil reserves, and he was accused of being a Nazi by US State Department propaganda.

[11] Nationwide frustration at these humiliations gave way to a powerful current of reformism and anti-imperialism. The Nationalist Revolutionary Movement (MNR) grew up alongside progressive labor and peasant movements. After several uprisings, and a 1951 electoral victory which was not honoured, the MNR led a popular insurrection in 1952. Civilians defeated seven regular army regiments in the streets, and they carried first Victor Paz Estenssoro, and then Hernan Siles Zuazo, to the presidency. The Bolivian revolution nationalized the tin mines, carried out agrarian reform and proclaimed universal suffrage. Workers' and peasant militias were organized and, together with the Bolivian Workers' Confederation (COB), formed a coalition with the MNR. The army was eliminated after the insurrection, but was later reorganized under US pressure.

[12] Troubled by internal divisions, the MNR gradually lost its drive and was defeated in November 1964 by a military junta led by René Barrientos. Ernesto 'Che' Guevara tried to establish a guerrilla nucleus in the Andes to spread revolutionary war throughout South America, but he was caught by US-trained counter-insurgency troops, and assassinated on October 8 1967.

[13] Division within the army, coupled with pressure from the grassroots level, led to an anti-imperialist faction taking over government in 1969, with General Juan José Torres as the leader. During his short time in office, there was a significant increase in the number of grassroots organizations. The People's Assembly was formed, with links to the COB and the parties of the left. In August 1971 he was ousted by Colonel Hugo Banzer Suarez, who formed a government with MNR support. The civilian-military coalition government remained in power until July 1978, with an authoritarian but development-oriented administration encouraging agribusiness and

stressing infrastructure projects, bolstered by the high price of oil and other minerals.

[14] Military uprisings and disregard for election results occurred repeatedly between 1978 and 1980. Juan Pereda Asbun, David Padilla Arancibia, Walter Guevara Arce, Alberto Natusch Busch and Lidia Gueiler all had fleeting presidencies, ended either by coups or parliamentary appointments. On June 29 1980, the elections were won by the Democratic Popular Union (UDP), a center-left coalition whose candidate, Hernan Siles Zuazo, was prevented from taking office by another bloody coup engineered by General Luis Garcia Meza.

[15] According to reports received by Amnesty International, thousands of people were killed or tortured, including Socialist leader Marcelo Quiroga Santa Cruz, Trotskyist parliamentary deputy Carlos Flores Bedregal, and miners' leader Gualberto Vega.

[16] By 1982, the army was seething with internal dissent. Government links with paramilitary groups and drug trafficking were eroding its international prestige, and it was facing dogged popular resistance led by the Bolivian Workers' Confederation (COB), leading to its destruction. In September, the military command decided to convene the government which had been democratically elected in 1980. On October 10, after 18 years of military rule, a civilian, Hernan Siles Zuazo took office in a legal constitutional model that has continued ever since. Siles Zuazo, with a populist/nationalistic outlook, gave administration of the state-owned mines to the labor unions. He also announced the 'non-payment' of Bolivia's foreign debt. The labor movement and the peasants exerted pressure on the government through demonstrations, and several laws passed by his administration allowed these groups to participate in the economic policy decisions of large businesses, and in local committees dealing with food, health and education issues. The Peasant Agricultural Corporation took partial control of the markets and set up collective machinery pools and work teams. In response to these

measures, creditor banks, the IMF and the World Bank blocked credits to Bolivia placing an embargo on its international trade. These measures provoked a fiscal crisis and uncontrolled hyperinflation, with the average wage falling to $13 per month.

[17] Under heavy pressure from all social sectors, the Government cut short its term and called elections for July 14 1985. As neither candidate secured over 50 per cent of the vote, the decision was put to Congress, who elected Paz Estenssoro as constitutional president, though

Hugo Banzer had marginally more votes.

[18] The Estenssoro government decreed a program of neo-liberal measures to end subsidies and close down state enterprises. It eliminated price controls and the official listing of the dollar against the local currency. Mines were closed down, and others rented out, leaving thousands of miners jobless.

[19] There was a drastic cut in real wages, with massive redundancies, while investment ground to a standstill. Inflation increased to four figures.

1970
20%

1994
13%

1996

PER CAPITA
$681

STATISTICS

DEMOGRAPHY
Population: 7,593,000 (1996) **Annual growth:** 2.2% (1980/1996) **Estimates for year 2000:** 8,300,000. **Annual growth to year 2000:** 2.4% (1994/2000) **Urban Population:** 61.5% (1996) **Urban growth:** 3.91% (1980/95) **Children per woman:** 4.5 (1996).

HEALTH
Life expectancy at birth: 61 years (1996) male: 59 years (1994) female: 62 years (1994) **Infant mortality:** 71 per 1,000 (1996) **Under-5 child mortality:** 102 per 1,000 (1996) **Calorie consumption:** 84% (1988/90) 2,564 **people per doctor** (1988/91) **Safe water:** 63% (1990/96).

EDUCATION
Literacy: 83% (1995) male : 91% (1995) female: 76% (1995) **School enrolment** : Primary total: 95% (1990/95) male : 99% (1990/95) female: 90% (1990/95) Secondary: male : 40% (1990/95) female: 34% (1990/95).

COMMUNICATIONS
70 **newspapers**, 670 **radios**, 140 **TV sets** and 35 **main telephone lines** per 1,000 people (1994)

ECONOMY
Per capita, GNP: $ 830 (1996) **Annual growth, GNP:** 2.6% (1995/96) **Annual inflation:** 18.41% (1985/95) **Consumer price index:** 132.2 (1994) **Currency:** 4.94 bolivianos = $ 1 (1995) **Cereal imports:** 434 metric tons (1994) **Food import dependency:** 13% (1994) **Fertilizer use:** 45 kgs per ha (1994) **Exports:** $ 1,087 million (1996) **Imports:** $ 1,601 million (1996) External debt: $ 5,174 million (1996) $ 681 per capita: (1996) **Debt service:** 30.9% of exports (1996) **Development aid received:** $ 692 million (1995) $ 96 per capita (1995) 13% of GNP (1994).

ENERGY
Consumption: 372.80 Kgs of Oil equivalent per capita yearly (1994) -60.82% imported (1994).

HDI (rank / value) 113 / 0.589 (1994)

[20] In the 1989 national elections, Jaime Paz Zamora's Revolutionary Movement of the Left (MIR) proved itself a potent new political force, coming in third with 19 per cent of the votes (double that of previous elections). The MNR candidate, Gonzalo Sanchez de Lozada, obtained 23 per cent and Banzer's Nationalist Democratic Action (ADN), 22.6 per cent. As no party had achieved a majority, an agreement between the MIR and the ADN, known as the Patriotic Accord made it possible for Paz Zamora to be nominated president by the National Congress.

[21] The so-called Patriotic Accord (AP) continued Paz Estenssoro's neo-liberal economic policy. In 1991, the Government embarked upon a transformation of the state, which entailed initiating privatization. Congress passed a law permitting the state to sell off 22 of the existing 64 public enterprises, though the Supreme Court ruled it unconstitutional. The Government promoted joint ventures between the state-owned Mining Corporation (COMIBOL) and private companies. The Federation of Mining Workers (FSTMB) launched a series of hunger strikes and threatened to occupy the mines, defending the principle of continued state ownership.

[22] In April 1991, Bolivia's Congress authorized US military officers to come to Bolivia to train local personnel in the war against drugs. Despite military action and the policy of crop substitution - a program called 'development for coca' - the area under coca cultivation has increased. It has been estimated that in 1992 there were some 463,000 people involved in coca-cocaine production, and that the national net earnings from this crop reached $950 million per year.

[23] The loss of power in the workers' movement was compensated for by new organizations of indigenous peoples and communities. In October 1991, the 9th Congress of the Confederation of Indigenous Peoples of the Eastern Region, the Chaco and the Bolivian Amazon Region (CIDOB) met in Santa Cruz. 340 representatives approved a series

of demands, including claims to lands lost during the Spanish invasion, and the use of their native languages in the educational system.

[24] The population of Bolivia's eastern region includes 250,000 people of 10 linguistic groups and 35 ethnic groups. In September 1990, a group of peoples from this region carried out a 750 km march from the east to the capital with the slogan Land and Dignity. Paz Zamora's government approved a National Plan for the Defence and Development of the Indigenous Peoples, and in August 1991, recognized the Santa Ana de Horachi Mosetana Community's right to 8,000 hectares of land, which they consider collective property. These resolutions have been opposed by companies which have been exploiting the region's vast forestry resources.

[25] In January 1992, Presidents Paz Zamora and Alberto Fujimori (of Peru) signed an agreement whereby Peru ceded an area of 327 hectares to Bolivia for it to develop a free zone at the port of Ilo in southern Peru. In this way Bolivia gained a way out to the sea - that is, a free port for its international trade.

[26] The MNR won the national elections of June 1993, with 36 per cent of the vote. Its presidential candidate was Gonzalo Sanchez Losada, and the vice-presidential candidate was Victor Hugo Cardenas, an Aymara sociologist and leader of the Tupac Katari Movement. While the ADN and MIR suffered significant losses, the new populist and nationalist movements, such as CONDEPA and UCS, led by Carlos Palenque and Max Fernandez retained their support among mestizos and the poorer neighbourhoods.

[27] In its first year the Government established the right to education in the native languages (Aymara, Quecha, Guarani). The Capitalization Bill aimed to privatize 50 per cent of the main public industries (telecommunications, electricity, oil, gas, railways, airlines) on the basis of transferring half the shares to the Bolivian citizens as pension funds. The aim was to attract foreign investment, reduce unemployment and increase GDP.

[28] Many local movements reacted

against the importing of toxic waste from Europe and the environmental deterioration caused by mining, while others protested against the closure of these same mines and the consequent job losses. The burning of coca plantations by the United States led to continuous confrontations between the rural workers and the military. Meanwhile, the World Bank reported that 97 per cent of the rural population were living in poverty.

[29] In 1994, the YPBF oil corporation, on the brink of privatization, was made even more attractive by an agreement with Brazil for the construction of a $2 billion gas pipeline to join Santa Cruz de la Sierra with São Paulo. The Capitalization Bill, unpopular amongst workers fearful of losing their jobs, led to a series of strikes in 1995. The Government declared a state of emergency on two occasions, granting the police special powers and imposing a curfew. Public meetings were banned and more than 100 leaders were imprisoned.

[30] As part of its regional campaign to control the northward flow of cocaine, the United States demanded that the Bolivian parliament approve a law against the drug-money laundering in February 1997.

[31] In the national elections in June, Nationalist Democratic Action won with 22 per cent of the vote, followed by the MNR, MIR, UCS and Patriotic Conscience, with 18, 17, 16 and 16 per cent of the vote respectively. Parliamentary negotiation to make Hugo Banzer the new president was difficult due to the fragmentation of the parties.

[32] The 100 coca-growers' unions agreed with the Government in August to voluntarily reduce coca production in order to fulfil the US demands, in return for $40 million for the fight against drug trafficking.

[33] In early 1998, the Banzer Government faced a serious social crisis when COB demonstrations in favour of improvements for small businesses, rural people and coca-growers were joined by the pensioners. The Government had suspended payment of the solidarity bond (Bonosol), a pension for life for people aged over 65 years old, provided by the Sánchez de Losada administration, with the funds from the privatization of six big public companies. The MNR warned that the agreement between the Government and the private pension funds (AFP) not to pay the Bonosol could cause a social explosion.

Bosnia-Herzegovina

Bosna I Hercegovina

Population: 3,628,000 (1996)
Area: 51,129 SQ KM
Capital: Sarajevo

Currency: Dinars
Language: Serb and Croatian

The earliest inhabitants of what is now Bosnia-Herzegovina were Illyrian tribes. After the Roman conquest in the mid-2nd century BC, this region became a part of the province of Illyria, although the Sava river basin remained within the province of Pannonia. Serbs settled in the area in the 7th century AD. Except for a brief interregnum (1081-1101), Bosnia remained politically separate from Serbia.

2 Hungarian control over Bosnia began in the mid-12th century. The combined efforts of the papacy and of the Hungarians to impose their religious authority over Bosnia gave rise to strong national resistance. Although war was avoided, the region came under the jurisdiction of the Hungarian archbishop of Kalocsa.

3 During this period, Bosnia was looked upon as a bastion of the Bogomils (or Cathari), one of southern Europe's main heretical movements, who found support among the local population, and from the State, as well. Neighboring Christians - both Orthodox Serbs and Catholic Croats - organized several crusades against this heresy. The Bogomils defeated the crusaders, but some parts of Bosnia were converted to Christianity

4 Ban Prijezda founded the Kotromanic dynasty (1254-1395), under which Bosnia conquered the province of Hum (Herzegovina). In 1377, Tvrtko crowned himself king of Serbia, Bosnia and the coastlands. With the Turkish invasion, in 1386, the Serbs were defeated at Kosovo (1389), but Tvrtko carried out further conquests in the west, and in 1390 was crowned king of Rashka, Bosnia, Dalmatia, Croatia and the coastlands.

5 The Ottoman Empire occupied Serbia in 1459 and Bosnia became a province of the Ottoman Empire in 1463. Hum resisted longer, but in 1482, the port of Novi fell (now called Hercegovini), and Herzegovina also became a province of the Ottoman Empire.

6 After the Turkish conquest, a massive campaign began to convert Bosnian Bogomils to Islam. Thus, in addition to Catholic Slavs and Christian Orthodox Slavs, there were now Muslim Slavs. Ever since, relations between the three communities have been strained, and religion became the decisive social factor in the region.

7 At first, the Turkish governor (Pasha) had his headquarters in Banja Luka, but later transferred them to Sarajevo. In 1580, Bosnia was divided into 8 sanjaks (sub-regions), under the jurisdiction of 48 hereditary Kapetans, who exercised a feudal power over their territories. Mining and trade began to decline; only the manufacture of weapons and wrought metals survived.

8 In the 16th and 17th centuries, Bosnia played an important role in the Turkish wars against Austria and Venice. In 1697, Prince Eugene of Savoy captured Sarajevo. By the Treaty of Karlowitz (1699) the Sava river, which formed Bosnia's northern border, also became the northern boundary of the Ottoman Empire. Herzegovina and the part of Bosnia east of the Una river were ceded to Austria in 1718, and returned to Turkey in 1739.

9 In the 19th century, Bosnia's nobility resisted Turkish interference. In 1837, Herzegovina's regent declared independence. Uprisings became chronic, bringing Christians and Muslims together, despite their differences, against the bureaucracy and corruption of the Empire.

10 In 1875, a local Herzegovinian conflict unleashed a rebellion, which spilled over into Bosnia. Austria, Russia and Germany tried unsuccessfully to mediate between Turkey and the rebels. The Sultan's promise to reduce taxes, grant religious freedom and install a provincial assembly was also rejected.

11 By a secret agreement, in 1877, Russia authorized Austria-Hungary to occupy Bosnia-Herzegovina, in exchange for its neutrality in Russia's upcoming war against Turkey. After the Russo-Turkish War of 1877-78, the Congress of Berlin disregarded Serbian wishes, and assigned Bosnia and Herzegovina to Austria-Hungary (although nominally they continued to be under Turkish control).

12 In 1878, Vienna put down armed resistance from Bosnia-Herzegovina. The revolution launched by the Young Turks in 1908 brought on a crisis within the Ottoman Empire.

13 The Turkish Government asked Bosnia-Herzegovina to participate in the new parliament at Istanbul but Austria-Hungary annexed the two provinces in 1908, with Russian consent. Vienna established a provincial assembly (*Sabor*) and special laws of association, without representation in Vienna or Budapest.

14 The 1910 Constitution consolidated social and religious differences by establishing three electoral colleges - Orthodox, Catholic and Muslim - each with a fixed number of seats in the *Sabor*.

15 The influence of the Young Bosnia (Mlada Bosna) movement and other revolutionary groups led the empire's authorities to close Bosnia's *Sabor*, and dissolve several Serbian political groups. The assassination of Archduke Francis Ferdinand and his wife, the Duchess of Hohenberg, in Sarajevo in 1914 by a Bosnian Serb student, triggered World War I.

16 After the collapse of the Austro-Hungarian empire in the Balkans in 1918, Bosnia-Herzegovina became a part of Serbia.

17 During the Nazi occupation, Bosnia-Herzegovina was subjected to the puppet administration established in Croatia. In the two provinces, Croat *Ustashes* (Fascists) massacred the Serbs. The rivalry which had always existed between Muslim, Serb and Croat degenerated into deep hostility.

18 After the war, Bosnia-Herzegovina became a Yugoslav republic. The slogan of the Yugoslav federated socialists was "Brotherhood and Unity", but ethnic confrontation was visible in the arts, the humanities and literature.

19 In April 1990 the Yugoslav Communist League rescinded its total control, and in the first multiparty legislative elections to be held since the War, the nationalist parties elected 73 Serbs and 44 Croats. This resulted in heavy losses for the Democratic Reform Party (ex-Communist) candidates and the liberal technocrats.

20 The Muslims were represented by the Democratic Action Party (DAP) and its leader, Alija Izetbegovic, was elected president of the republic. The DAP held an absolute

majority in 37 communities (administrative units) and a relative majority in 52 others. The Croatian Democratic Community, based in Zagreb, controlled 13 local communities and held a relative majority in 17 others.

[21] In October 1991, Bosnia-Herzegovina's Sabor approved a declaration of independence from the Yugoslav federation. In January 1992, Parliament agreed to hold a plebiscite on the issue of separation. The Serbian communities of Bosnia wanted to remain within a Yugoslav federation, while the Croat and Muslim communities clamored for independence.

[22] Bosnian President Izetbegovic wanted to maintain the unity and integrity of the republic, promising that Bosnia-Herzegovina would not become a Muslim state, and guaranteed that the rights of all nationalities would be respected. In early March, conflict broke out when the referendum was supported by 99.4 per cent of the Muslims and Croats, who ratified the republic's independence.

[23] On April 7, the European Community and the US recognized the independence of Bosnia-Herzegovina. The Bosnian republic was accepted as a member state in the Conference of Security and Cooperation in Europe; in May it became a member of the UN.

[24] At the same time, the Serbian community proclaimed the independence of the "Serbian Republic of Bosnia-Herzegovina" in the areas under Serbian control (Bosnian Krajina, with its center at Banja Luka). The conflict quickly extended throughout the entire region.

[25] Local Croat forces also controlled certain areas of the Republic; there were sporadic confrontations with Bosnian government troops. In late July, Croatia and Bosnia signed a mutual recognition pact.

[26] In January 1993, Serbian troops killed Bosnian deputy prime minister, Hakija Turajlic, in Sarajevo. In March the UN decreed a cease-fire in that city, which was under siege. There were numerous reports on the existence of Serbian

concentration camps, as well as an "ethnic cleansing" campaign. The latter involved the expulsion of all members of rival ethnic groups, especially from the smaller villages.

[27] According to Amnesty International, thousands of civilians, as well as soldiers that had been captured or wounded, were executed. In addition, prisoners were systematically submitted to torture and harsh treatment. According to UN figures, a total of 40,000 women had been raped. Although excesses were committed by all sides, the Serbians bore the major responsibility, while the Muslims were the main victims.

[28] The UN Protection Forces (UNPROFOR) sent in some 20,000 peacekeeping troops. The US refused to send troops to Bosnia, despite pressure from the UN and European countries. Several security zones were decreed in such cities as Tuzla, Zepa, Gorazde, Bihac and Sarajevo. However, these were not always observed, just as

> According to Amnesty International, thousands of civilians, as well as soldiers that had been captured or wounded, were executed. In addition, prisoners were systematically submitted to torture and harsh treatment.

successive cease-fires were consistently violated.

[29] In October, Serbian occupation of Bosanki Brod opened up a corridor between Serbia and Bosnian Krajina. Serbians controlled 70 per cent of the territory, as a result of their superior artillery and armoured vehicles, as well as their control of the bridges over the Drina river - on the border between Serbia and Bosnia - which allowed them to receive arms and other supplies from

the Yugoslav Federation. As a result of their support of the Serbians, the UN called for an economic blockade of the Federation, and an arms embargo aimed at Bosnians and Croats.

[30] The Muslims found themselves cornered in Sarajevo and a few other minor sites, receiving what little financial and

moral support they could from a few Islamic countries.

[31] In June 1993, Serbian President Slobodan Milosevic and his Croatian counterpart, Franjo Tudjman, announced the partition of Bosnia into three ethnic entities (Serbian, Croatian and Muslim), within the framework of a federal state.

Their scheme coincided with a UN-EU peace proposal which provided for a division into semi-autonomous provinces, controlled by each of the ethnic groups.
[32] The Croats, faced with the partition of Bosnia, sought to gain an upper hand, so as to negotiate from a position of strength. In July they launched an offensive against Mostar, capital of Herzegovina. The UN Human Rights Commission reported that 10,000 Muslims had been held in Croatian concentration camps, where they were submitted to torture and in some cases, to summary executions.
[33] In the meantime, the situation in Sarajevo grew progressively worse: there was a lack of electricity, water and food. Besieged by a series of epidemics, the city's estimated 300,000 inhabitants managed to survive on minimal rations, while international aid agencies tried to reach the city under mounting difficulties. In early 1994, the UN appealed to the Serbians to stop their attacks on Sarajevo and withdraw the heavy artillery

The UN's Human Rights Commission for the former Yugoslavia criticized the creation of ethnic boundaries and defended a reform of the democratic system.

surrounding the city. Despite resistance from the Russians, NATO threatened to bomb Serbian positions. When the formal deadline expired, the Serbians withdrew.
[34] The peace conference sponsored by the UN and the EU proposed the territory be divided into Bosnian, Muslim, and Croatian areas as ethnically homogeneous republics. This option called for the transfer of people from one sector to another. The UN's Human Rights

Commission for the former Yugoslavia criticized the creation of ethnic boundaries and defended a reform of the democratic system.
[35] In 1994, the US and Russia exerted growing pressure upon the Serbs to accept the proposal. Croatians and Muslims approved a federal agreement between the two communities: 51 per cent of the territory would remain among Bosnians and Croatians while Serbs would be in control of 49 per cent, without the need of separating Bosnia into three ethnically distinct states.
[36] With support from the EU, Washington and Moscow, the federal agreement was signed by presidents Franjo Tudjman of Croatia and Alija Izetbegovic of Bosnia, but the Serbs rejected it. Negotiations were hampered because Yugoslav president Slobodan Milosevic - who was the Serbs' diplomatic representative - stated he had no authority over the self-proclaimed Bosnian-Serb Republic of Sprska.
[37] In 1995, the Bosnian-Serbs held several UN troops hostage and took Bihac. In August, the situation was radically changed by NATO's bombing of Bosnian-Serb positions in the siege on Sarajevo. Almost at the same time, Croatia expelled Serb-Croat forces from the eastern side of the country forcing their delegates to negotiate.
[38] According to the Dayton Accords, elections were to be held in September 1996, with the aim of promoting more tolerant leaders among each of the nationalities in conflict. The agreement was carried out under US military pressure, with the underlying objective of influencing President Clinton's campaign for re-election in November. The presence of American troops forced a peaceful settlement and, at the same time, froze the political situation.
[39] The Dayton Accords acknowledge the existence of two ethnically pure mini-states due to the physical elimination or expulsion of ethnic minorities: the Bosnian-Serb Republic (Sprska) and the Croatian-Muslim Federation.

[40] The International Criminal Tribunal for the Former Yugoslavia at the Hague convicted Radovan Karadzic, leader of the Sprska Republic and his military commander Ratko Mladic, for genocide. In spite of being convicted, neither was incarcerated. They retained great influence in the republic's political life even though the Dayton Accords had banned electoral participation of individuals accused of committing war crimes.
[41] In June 1996, power, water and transport services began to be reinstated and Sarajevo regained part of its former vitality. The environment of political tranquillity considered necessary for the run-up to the September elections was hindered by the refugees' inability to return to their homes unless their fellow citizens ruled over the area, the limitations of journalists' movements and the difficulties imposed on the activities of several NGOs.
[42] Since the September 1996 elections, Bosnia had a three-member presidency ranked according to their share of the vote. Bosnia's Muslim President, Alija Izetbegovic, is first chairman; the Serb nationalist Momcilo Krajisnik came second and the Croat leader, Kresimir Zubak was third. These three were the most nationalist among the candidates in each federated republic.
[43] In 1997, Bosnian-Serb leader Karadzic was at the heart of several controversies. The European Union pressured for him to submit to the ruling of the International Court in the Hague and it was rumoured that

The International Criminal Tribunal for the Former Yugoslavia at the Hague convicted Radovan Karadzic, leader of the Sprska Republic and his military commander Ratko Mladic, for genocide.

US, French and British commandos were preparing a lightning strike to abduct him. In August, the Croat and Bosnian presidents met in Split to re-launch the Croat-Muslim federation, committing themselves once again to facilitating the return of refugees.
[44] Karadzic questioned the legislative elections of December, accusing the Western representatives of fixing the outcome in favour of the Croat and Muslim parties. Representation of the PDS, led by Karadzic, fell from 45 to 24 seats. The European observers confirmed the election result. On March 2 1998, the United States announced its aim to reduce the size of its contingent within the NATO peacekeeping forces. Mid month, the international commission deciding on the fate of the port city of Brcko - fiercely disputed by the Bosnian Serbs and Bosnian Muslims and Croats - decided to postpone its judgement until the end of the year.

Botswana

Botswana

Population:	1,484,000 (1996)
Area:	581,730 SQ KM
Capital:	Gaborone
Currency:	Pulas
Language:	Setswana

In the course of its history the "Bechuanaland", (English corruption of *ba'tswana*, "Tswana people") now Botswana, was also known as the "fatal crossroads" on account of its position in the heart of southern Africa, providing a passageway for pre-colonial movement and settlement. Later, the British used the "missionary route" from the south of Africa to Sudan and Egypt, whereas the Portuguese sought to unite their colonies of Angola and Mozambique by controlling "Bechuanaland".

2   Since the 18th century therefore this land has been a crossroads for various strategic colonial interests, as well as for the Tswana who had lived in the area since the 17th century. Around 1830, Botswana was penetrated by Boer colonists of Dutch origin, fleeing northward from the Cape to escape the British. These farmers fought with the local people for possession of the scant fertile lands, while the Tswana also clashed with Ndebele who had been driven from Zululand by the Zulu kings (see South Africa: "Zulu expansion"). Tswanas and Boers united to withstand Ndebele invasion. In 1894, leaders of Botswana's three major kingdoms travelled to London to seek support. The British promptly complied, and Botswana soon became a protectorate.

3   British trusteeship prevented political absorption by South Africa but paved the way for white economic supremacy. Consequently, when the first nationalist movements arose they aimed at putting an end to both situations.

4   Although Botswana has a large semi-arid area, it came to be one of southern Africa's major cattle and meat exporters. At the beginning of this century, 97 per cent of the population lived in rural areas, every family owned several cows, and the richest had oxen to plough their fields. By the 1960s, 15 per cent of the population had migrated to the cities and at least 40 per cent of the rural population had lost their cattle.

5   The struggle for independence became entangled with the wedding of Seretse Khama, a leader of the major chiefdom, Bamagwato, who went to England to study law. He married Ruth Williams, a European white-collar worker. This upset both the British and the Afrikaners, who prevented Seretse from returning home. He withstood every pressure including offers of money from the British and, firmly supported by his people, he retained leadership of the country's main ethnic group. Seretse finally returned home in 1956, nine years before the general elections in which his Botswana Democratic Party (BDP) polled 80 per cent of the vote.

6   In September 1966, Botswana gained independence and Seretse was elected first president. A year later he was knighted by the British. The BDP pursued a conciliatory policy towards Europeans, who controlled many of the country's economic resources, and Botswana continued to be highly dependent upon South Africa. Almost all its imports came through Cape Town, and 60 per cent of its exports were purchased by South Africa. Nevertheless, in the political arena, Seretse maintained his distance from South Africa, and supported the region's anti-racist movements. Botswana was one of the "frontline nations" fighting apartheid (see South Africa), and a member of the SADCC (see Organizations) seeking to end the economic dependence on South Africa of the nine southernmost African countries.

7   Seretse Khama died of cancer in July 1980 and was succeeded by the Vice-President, Quett Masire. Strong pressures were exerted on Masire by revolutionary socialist groups to limit the concentration of arable land in Tswana and white hands and to increase the area allotted to cooperatives. The rural poor accused large landowners of overgrazing, causing a deterioration in the quality of the land, and threatening their future. A movement also arose demanding the nationalization of rich diamond, iron, copper and nickel deposits exploited by South African companies.

8   In 1982, the country faced balance of payments problems resulting from a drought that affected cattle farming and exports. By early 1983, and the end of the drought, the difficulties had subsided. Government austerity measures also contributed to increasing farm production and mineral exports grew. The deficit became a surplus in the first half of 1983, enabling the Government to ease the austerity program, giving wage increases and tax cuts.

9   However, 60 per cent of the population still depend on subsistence crops or engage in informal economic activities (occupations which escape official records, taxation, and the trade circuit). The informal labor market includes approximately 15,000 San and Kgaligadi people.

10 Botswana is the world's third largest producer of diamonds, after Australia and DR Congo (formerly Zaire). In recent years, the Government has associated itself with South African mining companies in order to prospect for gold, platinum, and other non-precious metals such as nickel. This effort produced record annual economic growth of 12 per cent between 1978 and 1988.

11 In 1985, South Africa withdrew claims for a non-aggression treaty with Botswana. There had been repeated skirmishes in the border areas due to the Botswana Government's support of the African National Congress in its struggle against apartheid. In 1987 South Africa put pressure on the country by blocking roads leading to the capital Gaborone. In March 1989 nine South Africans were

PUBLIC EXPENDITURE

35.6%

1995 ■ DEFENCE □ SOCIAL

In 1990/91 Military as % of health & education expenditure was 22%.

WORKERS

(1996)

Labour force %

■ WOMEN   □ MEN

46   54

■ AGRICULTURE   46% (1990)
□ INDUSTRIAL   20%
■ SERVICES   33%

Maternal Mortality	Food Dependency	External Debt	Literacy
1990		1994	1995

PER 100,000 LIVE BIRTHS
250

1994
13%

PER CAPITA
$413

70%

PROFILE

ENVIRONMENT
An extensive and sparsely populated country, Botswana is divided into three large regions. In the centre and southwest, the Kalahari basin is a desert steppe where grazing is only possible in certain seasons. The Okavango River basin in the northeast has a tropical climate suitable for agriculture. 80 per cent of the population lives within a strip in the east, stretching along the railroad. Traditionally pastoral, the country is beginning to exploit its mineral resources (manganese, copper, nickel and diamonds). Intensive cattle-raising has meant a reduction in the areas originally set aside for wildlife, and is also rapidly depleting the soil.

SOCIETY
Peoples: Tswana make up 90 per cent of the population.
Religions: Some are Catholic and Protestant, while the rest practice African religions.
Languages: Setswana (national) and English (official).
Political Parties: The Botswana Democratic Party (BDP), founded by Seretse Khama in 1961; the Botswana National Front (BNF) was founded in 1991 as a coalition of leftist and center-left parties.
Social Organizations: 5 of the 13 local trade unions form the Botswana Federation of Trade Unions, founded in 1976.

THE STATE
Official Name: Republic of Botswana.
Administrative Divisions: 4 Districts.
Capital: Gaborone, 180,000 people in 1994.
Other cities: Francistown, 65,026 people; Selebi-Phikwe, 39,769 (1994). **Government:** Sir Quett Masire, President since July 18, 1980 (last re-elected in 1994). The single chamber National Assembly has 46 members.
National Holiday: September 30, Independence Day (1966).
Armed Forces: 7,500 (1994).
Other: 1,000 Transport Police.

STATISTICS

DEMOGRAPHY
Population: 1,484,000 (1996) **Annual growth:** 3.1% (1980/1996) **Estimates for year 2000:** 1,600,000. **Annual growth to year 2000:** 2.3% (1994/2000) **Urban Population:** 63.2% (1996) **Urban growth:** 8.36% (1980/95) **Children per woman:** 4.6 (1996).

HEALTH
Life expectancy at birth: 52 years (1996) male: 51 years (1994) female: 54 years (1994) **Infant mortality:** 40 per 1,000 (1996) **Under-5 child mortality:** 50 per 1,000 (1996) **Calorie consumption:** 97% (1988/90) 4,762 **people per doctor** (1988/91) **Safe water:** 93% (1990/96).

EDUCATION
Literacy: 70% (1995) male : 81% (1995) female: 60% (1995) **School enrolment :** Primary total: 115% (1990/95) male : 114% (1990/95) female: 115% (1990/95) Secondary: male : 54% (1990/95) female: 58% (1990/95) Tertiary: 4% (1995) **Primary school teachers:** one for every 26 students (1995).

COMMUNICATIONS
20 **newspapers**, 125 **radios**, 20 **TV sets** and 35 **main telephone lines** per 1,000 people (1994)

ECONOMY
Annual inflation: 11.48% (1985/95) **Consumer price index:** 164.2 (1994) **Currency:** 2.82 pula = $ 1 (1995) **Cereal imports:** 175 metric tons (1994) **Food import dependency:** 13% (1994) **Fertilizer use:** 23 kgs per ha (1994) External debt: $613 million (1996) $ 413 per capita: (1996) **Debt service:** 4.9% of exports (1996) **Development aid received:** $ 92 million (1995) $ 64 per capita (1995) 2.3% of GNP (1994).

ENERGY
Consumption: 386.54 Kgs of Oil equivalent per capita yearly (1994) 54.82% imported (1994)

HDI (rank / value) 97 / 0.673 (1994).

---

expelled from the country for "security reasons" and in May five ANC members were arrested by Botswana troops, accused of illegal possession of arms.
[12] Elections were held for the National Assembly in 1989. They were won by the Botswana Democratic Party, which obtained 31 of the 34 seats in dispute, with the Botswana National Front obtaining 3 seats. Quett Masire was consequently re-elected President.
[13] The economy slowed down after boom years in the 1980s. Unemployment hit 35 per cent, while in the private sector many jobs were held by foreigners, particularly at the managerial and technical levels.
[14] In spite of the economic crisis, the country was not eligible for loans from the African Development Bank, due to the fact that its national currency, the *pula*, was considered to be one of the strongest in the region.

[15] A profound conflict of political and economic interests led to an increase in Government corruption, culminating in the resignation of several ministers. In 1991, three of the seven opposition parties created a political front to oppose the ruling Botswana Democratic Party.
[16] In spite of the almost constant economic expansion of the last few decades, in 1991 the country faced the most serious strikes since independence. Public sector workers demanded a salary rise of 154 per cent, and the Government responded by dismissing 18,000 public employees.
[17] In 1992, unemployment came close to 25 per cent. In an attempt to increase employment and raise the GDP, the Government launched a series of incentives for opening industries not linked to the mining sector. As a result of the drought, a state of emergency was declared by Government

authorities. Public spending was drastically reduced, which meant that a third of the staff employed directly or indirectly by the State was laid off.
[18] In parliamentary elections held in October 1994, the BDP hung on to its majority, in spite of losing nine seats. For the BNF, social inequalities and unemployment were the real cause of the outburst.
[19] Meanwhile, in 1996 the country continued to depend mostly on the sale price of export minerals, which accounted for 47 per cent of foreign currency earnings. Thanks to tourism and the export of diamonds - which in the 1990s turned Botswana into the second exporter in the world, after Russia - the country reached a surplus budget which, however, did not solve the most urgent problems of the population.

[20] According to UN studies, in 1998, 30 per cent of Botswanan adults were HIV positive.
[21] In February, a new attempt to buy Belgian weapons led to strong pressure from Germany to prevent this deal. In 1996, Germany blocked the sale of Dutch weapons to Botswana. In spite of these obstacles, Gaborone seemed determined to purchase this type of weapons in the future.
[22] Partly as a result of its diamond wealth, Botswana's economy has flourished over the last three decades. According to the World Bank, it had the fastest-growing economy in the world during the period 1965-1996, when per capita income grew at 9.2 per cent. The rapid growth has led to increasing disparities between rich and poor people but this seemed unlikely to produce any political upsets in the 1999 elections.

Brasil

Population: 161,087,000 (1996)
Area: 8,511,965 SQ KM
Capital: Brasilia

Currency: Reals
Language: Portuguese

Small tribal groups belonging mainly to the Tupi Guarani, Carib and Arawak linguistic groups initially inhabited the huge tracts of land that were to become today's Brazil. The indigenous peoples from the Amazon basin fished and practised elementary farming while the inhabitants of the dry savannah were hunter-gatherers. When the first Portuguese ships arrived at the coast of what today is Bahia de todos os Santos in 1500, more than two million people inhabited these lands.

[2] Under the Tordesillas Treaty (1494) which divided the non-European world between Spain and Portugal, the latter was assured its rights over these lands. Sailing towards India, Pedro Alvarez Cabral landed at Bahia de todos os Santos in 1500 and christened the area the Island of Vera Cruz. Between 1501 and 1502 a naval expedition headed by Gaspar de Lemos covered the region between Rio Grande and the Río de la Plata. This is how Cabral's mistake (he thought he had reached an island) was corrected and the region came to be known by the Europeans as Santa Cruz Land.

[3] For the Portuguese, these lands were far less lucrative than Africa and India. The strip of coast did not reveal major deposits of precious metals. It was inhabited by semi-sedentary indigenous peoples, the Tupis, related to the Guaranís, whom the Spanish would later find in Paraguay. At first the Portuguese crown only valued those lands as places to trade slaves or barter metals and trifles with the indians in exchange for brazilwood. The pulp from this tree, used to make a fire-coloured dye, would give the country its final name - *brasa* in Portuguese means embers.

[4] Wood production was quite significant for a time although the industry did not lead to the creation of major cities or other signs of European development. Although the indians were used to felling trees in order to clear the forests, they lacked a commercial tradition in wood and could not cut trees on a large scale. The Portuguese supplied axes and saws and trading agents had the timber ready for shipment. Trading posts were often established on islands on the Atlantic ocean and, shortly after, the first Portuguese settlements were also established on these islands. Only a few Portuguese exiles inhabited the continent by that time, together with the indigenous communities. On several occasions, these exiles helped their European countrymen to make fruitful alliances with the natives.

[5] Around 1530, the Portuguese were forced to increase their involvement with Brazil. Other European traders, particularly the French, started to travel to these lands; commerce with India had slumped and the achievements of Spanish conquistadors in other parts of the continent represented both an incentive and a threat. The Portuguese

PUBLIC EXPENDITURE

n/a

34.5%

1995 ■ DEFENCE □ SOCIAL

In 1990/91 Military as % of health & education expenditure was 23%.

WORKERS

(1996)

Labour force %

■ WOMEN
□ MEN

35   65

■ AGRICULTURE 23% (1990)
□ INDUSTRIAL 23%
■ SERVICES 54%

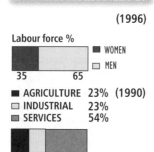

LAND USE

DEFORESTATION -0.6% annual (81/90)
IRRIGATED 6.7 % of arable

(1993)

■ FOREST & WOODLAND 57.3%
□ ARABLE 4.9%
■ OTHER 37.8%

PER 100,000
LIVE BIRTHS
220

83%

1994
9%

crown sent an expedition to expel the French and establish its authority, along with some settlers. Thus, in 1532, the first official Portuguese settlement, São Vicente, was established on an island close to São Paulo.

6   The Spanish expanded their empire through the conquest of lands under the strict control of the Crown. The Portuguese however, in accordance with their maritime commercial tradition, divided the Brazilian coast into captaincies which were awarded to *donatarios*, prominent individuals who supposedly had the wealth required to carry out the occupation and exploitation of the lands. The captaincies were hereditary, with extensive judicial and administrative powers, although several were never occupied and others survived for a brief time. However, four of them became permanent settlements and two (Pernambuco to the north and San Vicente to the south) turned out to be viable and lucrative.

7   As happened in the Spanish colonial outposts, the first Portuguese settlements had to be fortified to defend them from American attacks. Procurement of supplies was difficult and for a while the Portuguese obtained most of their food by trading with the indigenous peoples and eating cassava instead of wheat, which was hard to grow in most of the region.

8   Two agricultural systems developed, the *rozas* or farms and the large *fazendas*, given over to exports, mainly of sugar-cane. In spite of favourable conditions, the *fazendas* took a long time to prosper, due to the lack of capital and labour. Agriculture and the discipline imposed on the plantations was foreign to the local peoples, whom the Portuguese forced to toil in exchange for European products. The settlers soon decided to obtain slave workers through expeditions which hunted for indians or through other indians acting as intermediaries.

9   During the second half of the 16th century, many indians of the region had been decimated by illnesses (influenza, smallpox, measles) or had fled to other areas. African slaves were then imported to grow sugar. This trade grew and it is estimated that from 3 to 4 million Africans arrived in Brazil between the 16th and 19th century. In 1848, as a result of pressures similar to those of 1530, the Crown appointed a general governor, who with 1,000 men carried out an expedition to Brazil, establishing the capital in Bahia on the north-eastern coast. A bishopric was created in 1551. Only 50 years after the first contact, Brazil had reached the same degree of European institutionalization which characterized the Spanish territories.

10   The Jesuits had started coming to the country by that time, and soon became the strongest branch of the Catholic Church, unlike what happened in Spanish America, where they arrived much later than other orders. The Jesuits were very active, learnt the Guarani language to convert indians to Catholicism and established villages very similar to the missions in the Spanish areas. The main contacts between indians and Europeans (war, trade, slavery and missions) were the same as in the Spanish areas. Due to these contacts, Guaraní became the language used in that century for all kinds of exchanges.

11   Brazil carried out major expansions towards the west of the Tordesillas line, whose meridian was drawn up 370 leagues to the west of Cape Verde. This expansion reached the slopes of the Andes mountain range and, from north to south, from the Amazon to the Río de la Plata. In the north, the movement was led by the Jesuits who established several missions along the Amazon. In the northeast, cattle farmers from sugar crop areas of Pernambuco and Bahia ventured to the heart of the continent, looking for new grazing lands and reached today's Piauí, Goiás and Maranhao regions.

12   The westward march was led by the *paulistas*, as São Paulo settlers were known. In the search for indian slaves, gold and precious stones, the paulistas set up major expeditions to the interior, known as *bandeiras*. The incorporation of Portugal into the Spanish kingdom in 1580 facilitated the *paulistas'* incursions, since inner borders were broken down and the Tordesillas division became ineffective. The *bandeiras* took the *paulistas* to Peru's mining regions and even to Bogota, Colombia. They also explored the region of Matto Grosso and to the south attacked local *reducciones* (missions), particularly those of Guaira. Here the guarani people were already relatively immune to disease and were accustomed to collective agricultural work. In most cases, they found resistance among the indians and from the Jesuits who protected them. The human hunts were so devastating that the missions were gradually pushed further and further south until they reached the "Seven Towns", in today's Rio Grande state.

13   It was not just the *paulistas* who penetrated the dense forests. Thousands of Africans also sought refuge there, fleeing from the coastal plantations where they were kept as slaves. Africans, indigenous Americans and their mixed descendants joined forces in constant war against the colonial military expeditions. They also founded villages known by the African terms *quilombo* or *mokambo*, the most famous of which were at Palmares (1630-1695), in northeastern Brazil, where the legendary Zumbi led the struggle. The Brazilian anti-racist movement still commemorates the date of Zumbi's death in battle, November 20, as Negro Consciousness Day.

14   Meanwhile, Brazil found itself involved in a war of independence between the Netherlands and Spain. Flanders and the Netherlands had been 'inherited' by the Spanish Crown. Between 1630 and 1654, the Dutch reasserted their control over Pernambuco after a failed attempt to conquer Bahia, which was repulsed by the joint efforts of native Americans, Africans and Portuguese.

15   When Spain and Portugal subsequently separated, their colonial borders had shifted and the Tordesillas line could not be reinstated. In 1696, a bandeirantes expedition struck the first gold in what is now Minas Gerais. Gold mining peaked in the 18th century. The viceroyal capital was transferred from Salvador to Rio de Janeiro in 1763 mostly due to the effect of these mines on the Brazilian economy.

16   In a way, the local ruling class began to benefit from an expanding export economy and soon expressed a growing desire to dispense with the Portuguese role as intermediaries in their trade with Europe. The first moves towards independence came in the late 18th century and were rapidly crushed by the colonial power. Brazil's main figure of freedom, Ensign Tiradentes, was executed in 1792 as a result of his leading role in the Minas Conspiracy three years earlier.

17   When Napoleon invaded the Iberian peninsula in 1808, Portuguese King Dom João VI had to transfer his court to Brazil, making the country semi-independent. Portugal ceased to be an intermediary and Brazil dealt directly with its main customer, Britain. In this way, the Brazilian merchants prospered at the expense of other sectors linked to the Portuguese monopoly. The 1821 Oporto revolution in Portugal was an attempt to reinstate the old colonial system based on monopoly. When the King returned to Lisbon, the local merchants, determined to secure their gains, declared independence with British blessing. Brazil became an empire and Pedro I, formerly prince-regent, became its emperor.

18   The following decade was one of the most turbulent in Brazilian history. From 1831 to 1835, a regency unsuccessfully tried to put an end to the civil war in the provinces and to the army's insubordination. In 1834, the Constitution was amended to decentralize the government, with the creation of provincial assemblies with considerable local powers, and to choose a regent for a period of four years. In 1835, Diego Antonio Feijóo, a priest, was elected and fought for two years against the break-up - with rebellions in the south, fought by the *gaúchos*, such as the Farrapos War (1835-1845). He was forced to resign in 1837. He

was replaced by Pedro Araújo Lima. Impatient with the regency, Brazilians hoped to find in an Emperor the figurehead that would unite them. In 1840, Pedro de Alcántara was declared of age and was enthroned with the name of Pedro II.

[19] The Empire lasted from 1822 to 1889. During this time Brazil consolidated its national unity and extended its borders over the areas settled by bandeirantes in the 17th and 18th centuries. This period of territorial expansion included the annexation of the Cisplatine Province (now Uruguay), the war of the Triple Alliance against Paraguay, in which Brazil annexed 90,000 square kilometers of Paraguayan territory (see The Triple Alliance); and, towards the end of the century, the annexation of Bolivia's Acre territory.

[20] Under the rule of Pedro II, the population grew from 4 to 14 million, but the economy continued to depend on large estates and the export of tropical agricultural products, mainly coffee. The abolition of slavery in 1888 accelerated the fall of the monarchy, but brought little change in the social and political conditions of blacks. As illiterate people, they were denied the right to vote and, therefore, political freedom.

[21] The gap between urban and rural areas widened in the last decades of the century. The urban middle class, the military and coffee growers pressed for the country's speedy modernization. For them, the monarchy was excessively linked to the old systems of production and to cattle-raising landowners. A republic was seen as a more convenient model for the modernization pursued by these three groups. In 1889, a conspiracy of modernists was supported by the army. Pedro II abdicated and was exiled in Europe.

[22] The abolition of slavery and the fall of the monarchy gave rise to a period of social, political and economic changes which accelerated modernization, although not without political, social and religious woes.

[23] The consolidation and establishment of republican institutions experienced serious difficulties. Prudente de Morais was elected first civilian President in 1894. The Federal Republican Party had been founded in 1893, but the Navy rebelled both that year and the following. From 1893 to 1895, Brazil suffered a federalist rebellion in Rio Grande do Sul. From 1896 to 1897, the Canudos war, in which a religious community was wiped out by the republic's troops, took place in the northeastern provinces. This war was due to a clash between the interior - poor, illiterate and desperate - and the coast-literate, with a developed economy and seeking modernization.

[24] Uprisings, outbursts of authoritarianism and fights among the regional oligarchies were frequent. Neither electoral justice or the secret ballot were instituted yet and dissatisfaction with election results was widespread. Elections were rigged since the electoral rolls often included deceased voters.

[25] In the economic sphere, coffee became the major export. Between 1914 and 1918, World War I brought an economic boom to Brazil, since the country was one of the main suppliers of commodities to the powers at war. Between 1920 and 1930, coffee prices slumped as international competition reduced sales and, in 1929, due to that year's world crisis, 29 million bags of coffee were left unsold.

[26] In 1930 a coup resulted in the appointment of Getulio Vargas as president. The Revolution of 1930 marked the end of the landowners' predominance, already weakened by the 1929 slump which had destroyed the coffee economy.

[27] Getulio Vargas introduced the "import substitution" model which gave priority to national industrial development, especially in iron and steel during World War II. Vargas held power from 1937 to 1945 as dictator of the New State and in 1950 was elected constitutional president. Nationalism and reformist defence of workers' rights, *trabalhismo* (labourism), the name of his movement, were the two outstanding features of his government.

[28] In 1953 the state oil monopoly was created and social security laws were passed. Verges committed suicide in August 1954 leaving a letter accusing "dark forces" (referring to imperialism and its local accomplices) of blocking his efforts to govern according to popular and national aspirations.

[29] Juscelino Kubitschek's administration (1956-61) promoted development and admitted transnationals to the Brazilian market, granting them exceptional privileges. Brasilia was built during his term in office to mark a new era in the country's economic development. In 1960, the federal capital, previously at Rio de Janeiro, was transferred to the new city. Kubitschek's successor, Janio Quadros, initiated some changes in foreign policy but resigned in

PROFILE

ENVIRONMENT

There are five major regions in Brazil. The Amazon Basin, in the North, is the largest tropical rainforest in the world. It consists of lowlands covered with rainforest and rivers. The Carajás mountain range contains one of the world's largest mineral reserves, rich in iron, manganese, copper, nickel and bauxite. The economy is mainly extractive. The northeastern "sertao" consists of rocky plateaus with a semi-arid climate and scrub vegetation. Cattle raising is the main economic activity. The more humid coastal strip, situated on the "Serra do mar" (Coastal Sierra), has numerous sugarcane and cocoa plantations. In the southeast, the terrain consists of huge plateaus bordered in the east by the Serra do Mar mountain range. The main crops are coffee, cotton, corn and sugarcane. The southern plateau, with sub-tropical climate, is the country's main agricultural region, where coffee, soybeans, corn and wheat are grown. In the far south, on the Rio Grande do Sul plains, cattle raising is the main economic activity. Finally, the mid-west region is made up of vast plains where cattle raising predominates. With the devastation of the Amazon region, caused by unrestrained felling of trees and forest fires, the habitats of many species have been destroyed.

SOCIETY

Peoples: Brazilians come from the ethnic and cultural integration of native inhabitants (mainly Guaraní), African slaves and European (mostly Portuguese) immigrants. Arab and Japanese minorities have also settled in the Rio-Sao Paulo area. Contrary to what is commonly admitted, racial discrimination does exist and the groups fighting it are rapidly gaining strength.
Religion: Most are baptized Catholic; but there is considerable merging into syncretic Afro-Brazilian cults *(candomblé and umbanda)*.
Language: Portuguese is the official and predominant language.
Political Parties: Brazilian Social Democratic Party (PSDB), led by senator Artur da Távora and President Fernando Henrique Cardoso; Party of the Liberal Alliance (PFL), led by Jorge Bornhausen; Party of the Brazilian Democratic Movement (PMDB), led by Luís Henrique da Silveira; Worker's Party (PT), led by Rui Falcao; People's Reform Party (PPR), led by senator Espiridião Amin; Democratic Labor Party (PDT), led by Leonel Brizola; Brazilian Labor Party (PTB), led by Jose E. de Andrade Vieira; the Communist Party split into two groups: orthodox communists (PC), led by Oscar Niemeyer, and the People's Socialist Party, led by senator Roberto Freire. In addition, there are countless other minor national or provincial organizations.
Social Organizations: Workers are grouped together primarily in the Consolidated Union of Workers (CUT), the General Confederation of Workers (CGT) and the Labor Union Forum. Many labor unions do not belong to any of these, preferring to remain independent. Movement of the Landless (MST), an association of workers without land whose agenda is agrarian reform in rural areas, and land for the construction of housing, in urban areas. National Union of Indigenous Peoples (UNI), an association of Brazil's different indigenous groups. Pastoral Commission of the Earth (CPT) and Indigenous Missionary Council (CIMI), pastoral groups of the Catholic Church involved in social action in these areas. Defence Network of the Human Race (REDEH), an eco-feminist organization. "Torture No More", state groups committed to the defence of human rights.

THE STATE

Official Name: República Federativa do Brasil.
Administrative Divisions: 26 States, 1 Federal District.
Capital: Brasilia, 1,492,500 people (1994).
Other cities: São Paulo 16,417,000 people (1995); Rio de Janeiro 5,473,900 (1994); Salvador 2,070,300; Belo Horizonte 3,000,000 (1994); Recife 1,297,000; Porto Alegre 1,500,000 (1994); Manaus 1,005,600 (1994).
Government: Fernando Henrique Cardoso, President since 1995. Bicameral legislature.
National Holiday: September 7, Independence Day (1822).
Armed Forces: 295,000 troops (1995).
Other: 243,000 Public Security Forces.

unclear circumstances barely seven months after taking office.
[30] In September 1961, Vice-President João Goulart, the Labor Party leader and Getulio Vargas' political heir, assumed the presidency. High-ranking military officers opposed his appointment but the new President was backed by a civilian/military movement which wanted a legal government, led by Leonel Brizola, governor of Rio Grande do Sul. A compromise parliamentary solution was adopted, with Tancredo Neves becoming Prime Minister. The presidential system was reinstated in January 1963 after a national plebiscite. Goulart then tried to introduce a series of "basic reforms", including agrarian reform and legislation to regulate profit transfers abroad by foreign companies. A US-backed military coup deposed him on April 1 1964.
[31] The new government passed Institutional Act No. 1, which repealed the 1946 liberal constitution, allowing the revocation of parliamentary mandates and the suspension of political rights. A string of arrests all over the country forced major political leaders such as João Goulart, Leonel Brizola, Miguel Arraes and later even Juscelino Kubitschek into exile or to keep up their fight underground.
[32] The military junta appointed general Humberto de Alencar Castello Branco head of government for the remainder of the constitutional period, but his mandate was later extended until 1967. In the October 1965 state elections, opposition candidates won in Rio de Janeiro and Minas Gerais. The military retaliated with Institutional Act No. 2, stating that the President would henceforth be appointed by an electoral college and banning existing political parties. A two-party system was created guaranteeing a majority to the pro-government National Renewal Alliance (ARENA), virtually excluding the opposition Party of the Brazilian Democratic Movement (PMDB) from power.
[33] In January 1967, a new Constitution came into effect and two months later General Arthur da Costa e Silva was appointed President. In December 1968, to confront growing electoral support for the popular opposition, Institutional Act No. 5 was passed, granting full autocratic powers to the military regime. In August 1969, Costa e Silva was replaced by a Military Junta that remained in power until the following October, when another army general, Emilio Garrastazú Médici, former head of the National Information

Services (SNI), was brought into presidential office. The Médici administration was marked by extremely violent repression of both the legal and illegal opposition, while his economic ministers fed middle class consumerism. In 1974, General Ernesto Geisel was appointed President by the Junta. He put an end to the state oil monopoly, signed a controversial nuclear agreement with West Germany and granted further prerogatives to foreign investors. Its arms industry placed Brazil fifth among the world's main arms exporters.
[34] Under the Geisel administration there was a gradual relaxation of political controls, which allowed the democratic process to evolve. In 1974 and 1978, despite media censorship, the PMDB achieved significant victories at the polls. At the end of his mandate, Geisel delivered the reins of government to General João Baptista Figueiredo, also former SNI head.
[35] Figueiredo came to power in March 1979, announcing that he intended to complete the softening of political restrictions. A month later, a strike by 180,000 metalworkers in Sao Paulo led by Luis Inácio "Lula" da Silva was settled without violence, as a result of negotiations between the Labor Ministry and the Union. In November, the Brazilian Congress passed a bill granting a far broader amnesty to political opponents than the Executive had originally intended. As a result, political prisoners were released and exiles began to return.
[36] In the economic-financial arena, the after-effects of the monetary policies applied by successive military governments were felt during the Figueiredo administration. Foreign debt spiralled and in the early 1980s, Brazil went on to become an exporter instead of importer of capital, in its efforts to find funds to pay off the interest on its $100 billion debt.
[37] In 1985, official statistics registered six million unemployed and 13 million under-employed, out of a population of more than 130 million, of which over 50 per cent lived below the poverty line and outside formal economy, in cities alone. In July 1985, Ministry of Labor officials stated that "not even seven per cent growth per year for two consecutive decades would be enough to improve these peoples' living conditions".
[38] The opposition's electoral victory in 1983 reflected enormous popular discontent. The central government held only 12 states while the opposition won 10, including the

economically decisive states of São Paulo, Rio de Janeiro and Minas Gerais which accounted for 59 per cent of the population and 75 per cent of the country's GDP.
[39] Tancredo de Almeida Neves, governor of Minas Gerais, was the chief co-ordinator of the opposition front. A popular campaign for direct elections in 1984 failed, but the opposition won the Electoral College due to divisions within the ruling party. Tancredo Neves was elected President and José Sarney, who a few weeks earlier had been president of the government party, became Vice President. Tancredo announced plans for a new social order: the New Republic.
[40] In this context, agrarian reform, renegotiation of the foreign debt and economic growth were seen as the most effective means towards modernization and democratization. The day before his inauguration, Tancredo Neves was hospitalized and rushed into surgery. José Sarney was sworn in as interim president but stayed on after Tancredo died on April 21 1985. Sarney legalized the Communist Party and other left-wing organizations, some after 20 or even 40 years of illegal

existence. Democratization began to take place with the approval of direct election for President of the Republic and mayors of state capitals. A national assembly was convened for January 1987 to draft a new constitution and illiterate people were granted the right to vote.
[41] In 1986 Sarney declared a moratorium on the foreign debt and launched the Cruzado Plan to fight inflation. The plan produced impressive short-term results: a boom in consumption and economic growth. This startling prosperity coincided with the November 1987 parliamentary and state governmental elections which the PMDB won by a landslide. The new Congress faced the task of drafting a new constitution which would formally inaugurate the return to democratic government. It set Sarney's term at five years, after considerable pressure from the Executive to ignore the groups who wanted to honor Tancredo's promise of reducing the term to four years.
[42] But the Cruzado Plan could not be maintained without fighting financial speculation and halting pressure from the financial sector. Two days after the election, the price freeze came to an end and inflation leapt to a

Foreign Trade

MILLIONS $ 1996

IMPORTS
53,736
EXPORTS
47,164

monthly rate in double figures. The planned agrarian reform was gradually reduced.

[43] In the 1988 municipal elections, the left-wing and center-left PDT, PT, and PSDB parties began to make inroads on the PMDB's popularity.

[44] In December 1988, landowners from the Acre region murdered Chico Mendes, leader of the *seringueiro* (rubber tappers) movement and the Amazonian indigenous peoples. They had organized an *empates* struggle (linking arms to prevent trees being felled) to prevent the clearing of the forests, and proposed the creation of reserves, to guarantee their right to live and work in the forest without destroying it.

[45] Direct presidential elections - the first in 29 years - were held in November and December 1989. Nearly 80 million people voted and the final round was fought between conservative candidate Fernando Collor de Mello and Workers' Party leader, Luiz Inacio "Lula" da Silva. Collor de Mello, a young politician who had begun his career under the military regime, won the second round with 42.75 per cent to his opponent's 37.86 per cent of the vote.

[46] On taking office, on March 16 1990, Collor de Mello announced the New Brazil Plan, an attempt to stem inflation by confiscating 80 per cent of the country's available financial assets.

[47] Collor adopted the neo-liberal model of opening up the economy, with the privatization of state enterprises and the reduction of tariff barriers controlling the import of foreign products. However, he failed to control inflation, to hold off a recession and to reduce unemployment.

[48] In this complex economic setting, the Government faced a critical social situation and the escalation of violence. In 1991, more than 350 street children were murdered in Rio de Janeiro. The parliamentary commission set up to investigate these murders estimated that over 5,000 children had been killed in this way over the past three years. The same commission reported that the persecution of

homeless children - seven million according to estimates of the Brazilian Center for Childhood and Adolescence - was carried out by paramilitary groups financed by shop owners.

[49] The indigenous peoples are under the constant threat of "progress". They have suffered epidemics, the degradation or loss of natural resources, pollution and a systematic fall in their standard of living. They are being decimated by disease, high suicide rates, murders and other violence committed by miners and by the police. Many also refrain from having children as they feel too threatened to do so.

[50] The disappearance of indigenous cultures is linked to the accelerated destruction of the tropical forest in order to exploit its logging potential or to turn it into grassland or mining areas (especially for gold, which pollutes the rivers with mercury). This predatory policy prevents the regeneration of natural resources and so they become depleted. The so-called "Amazonia Legal" is an area considered strategic by the army, which in 1995 began to invest several billions of dollars to monitor it by a satellital tracking system.

[51] In September 1991, thousands of people belonging to the Landless Movement of Brazil (MST) staged a march in the state of Rio Grande do Sul, where there were 150,000 families of landless farmers alongside 9 million hectares of land not in production. The protesters demanded settlements to work and that the 4,700 million cruzeiros earmarked for agrarian reform should be spent. Up till then, only 800 million had actually been used.

[52] Late in September 1991, a 400 per cent inflation rate and an increase in bank interest rates to almost 1,000 per cent a year, triggered wide-scale redundancies in the industrial sector which, in São Paulo alone, left more than one million jobless.

[53] In May 1992, a Parliamentary Investigating Commission was formed to study corruption within the Government, which took the form of influence-peddling in exchange for deposits

made to the President's personal account. Protest demonstrations against corruption and the discovery of evidence implicating other government figures in these schemes led all the country's political parties to vote for the President's impeachment.

[54] In September, Congress voted to relieve the President of his duties, so that he could be tried. Vice-President Itamar Franco became interim President. In December 1992, Collor was found guilty by the Senate of "criminal responsibility" and sentenced. His presidential mandate was removed and his political rights suspended until the year 2000. Franco officially assumed the presidency until the end of that presidential term.

[55] The President tried to project an image of austerity and ethics upon the management of public affairs. After several changes in the Ministry of Economics, Fernando Henrique Cardoso was appointed to this cabinet position.

[56] According to figures provided by the Pastoral Commission of the Earth, in 1992 there were 15,042 rural slaves - triple the number recorded the previous year. According to data gathered by the Federal Bureau of Statistics, nearly four million people living in rural areas work under conditions of virtual slavery. Collor's administration had zoned 20 million hectares as new land for indigenous peoples. This alleviated but did not fully solve the desperate situation of the indians.

[57] In late 1992, 111 inmates of São Paulo's Carandiru prison were killed by members of the Military Police who had entered the premises to deal with a dispute between rival groups of prisoners. Post-mortem examinations found that 85 of the prisoners had been executed after having surrendered. In July 1993, police members murdered 8 street children while they were sleeping on the doorsteps of the Church of the Candelaria, in Rio de Janeiro. The following month, 50 men entered the *favela* (shantytown) of Vigario Geral and killed 21 innocent people, to avenge the death of four military police who had been killed in a confrontation with drug dealers.

[58] The general outcry over these incidents led to some official response. In Rio de Janeiro, for the first time ever, a judge handed down prison sentences to the leaders of *jogo do bicho*, an illegal lottery intrinsically linked to drug dealers and the police. In São Paulo, a police investigator received the maximum prison sentence (516 years) for causing the death of 18 prisoners who had died of asphyxiation in a police cell in 1992.

[59] The Citizens' Action Against Hunger and for Life group, founded in 1993 by Herbert de Souza, organized tens of thousands of committees throughout the country to collect and distribute food and obtain more jobs. Two million people, mostly women, priests and trade unions joined this grassroots movement. By August 1994, over four million families had received food aid.

[60] Towards the end of 1993, Minister Cardoso presented the Plan Real, an economic stabilization project which ended index-linking and created a new currency, the Real, in July 1994. The success of this anti-inflationary policy rapidly made Cardoso the most popular candidate for the October elections. In the first round he beat the previous favourite Luis Ignacio "Lula" da Silva, of the PT.

[61] Cardoso began the privatization of state companies, including part of the operations of Petrobras and the telecommunications sector, but economic recession rose along with stabilization which led to the rise of unemployment, urban labour conflicts, crime and land seizures by poor peasants.

[62] In September 1995, the President announced a government Multi-Year Plan with investments amounting to $153.39 billion, mainly focused on economic infrastructure. According to statistics issued in August, ten per cent of the population received 48 per cent of the income, four times the amount earned by the poor half of the country. According to the World Bank, 43 per cent of fertile land belonged to 0.83 per cent of land owners in 1997. These figures placed Brazil among countries with extreme social inequality. In June, Parliament passed a constitutional reform which enabled presidential reelection.

[63] In September, Cardoso issued a presidential decree which guarantees indigenous peoples the exclusive use of 23 plots of land covering 8.4 million hectares, some 10 per cent of Brazilian territory. The marches and seizures of the Landless received the implicit support of the Vatican s Pontifical Council of Justice and Peace in February 1998, in the document "For better land distribution: the land reform challenge".

[64] In the early part of 1998, the worst fires in the history of the Amazon displaced peasants and entire indigenous communities. By March, more than a quarter of the northern state of Roraima had been devastated by the fires.

Broadening the Mercosur

On October 29 1991, the Treaty of Asunción was ratified by Argentina, Brazil, Paraguay and Uruguay. It had been signed that same year on March 26 in the Paraguayan capital by presidents Carlos Menem, Fernando Collor, Andrés Rodríguez and Luis A. Lacalle. This was the first step in the creation of the Southern Common Market (Mercosur), an economic integration zone effective since January 1 1995, aimed at freeing up the circulation of goods and services within these countries.

[2] The four countries, with a total population of almost 200 million inhabitants and a combined GDP of almost $550 billion, committed themselves to a gradual elimination of tariffs (taxes on imported goods) for merchandise from Mercosur countries. In principle, internal barriers were to be totally eliminated; free circulation of goods and services was scheduled within four years. Exceptions were made for the less powerful members (Uruguay and Paraguay).

[3] The Mercosur countries also agreed to eliminate non-tariff barriers, such as laws protecting national products or protectionist tax breaks to certain industries, which create unfair competition for imported goods. The aim of this measure is to give Mercosur greater power in negotiating with other countries or economic blocs, as well ensuring more favourable prices for national consumers.

[5] The treaty also establishes a common external tariff for importing products from non-member countries, as well as the possibility of dealing as a united economic bloc with other countries, economic communities and even world negotiation entities such as the General Agreement on Trade and Tariffs (GATT).

[6] Two administrative levels operate within Mercosur: the Common Market Council and the Common Market Group. The former is the more important of the two, and is made up of the ministers of Foreign Affairs and of the Economy from the member countries. The latter is the executive branch and is made up of representatives of the aforementioned ministries and of the Central Banks of the four countries.

[6] For Mercosur's smaller members it is difficult to carry out the reconversion of industry which is essential for the scheme to work, given the fact that the two larger nations are in a position to place more competitive products throughout the Mercosur region. Uruguay's labour union group (PIT-CNT) called for meetings to be held with labour union organizations from all Mercosur countries with the aim of seeking solutions to the real possibility of Argentine and Brazilian products "flooding" Uruguayan and Paraguayan markets, and thereby affecting their economies.

[7] In mid-1994 the four governments, upon consideration of the rleative differences in their countries' development, decided to readjust the timetable which had been announced in 1991, so that the common external tariff would come into effect in 2001. Uruguay and Paraguay will have an additional five years to adapt their tariffs to the 14 per cent which has been agreed upon. At the time of this renegotiation, these two countries maintained certain advantages with regard to their free zones and trade agreements with their major trading partners. These will, in some cases, remain in effect until the year 2001, and in others, until 2006.

[8] Chile signed the first document confirming its decision to join the group in June 1995. Two months later, during the tenth presidential meeting of the alliance in San Luis, Argentina, the four Presidents invited their colleagues from Chile and Bolivia, Eduardo Frei and Gonzalo Sánchez de Lozada, to participate in the debates.

[9] In December 1995, Mercosur signed a framework agreement with the European Union. The United States and the World Bank, worried by what they consider to be a desire for economic independence, criticized this policy as being "discriminatory" to third countries. Meanwhile, Washington was proposing the establishment of a free trade area stretching from Alaska to Tierra del Fuego.

[10] On October 1 1996, Chile signed an agreement with Mercosur, but not as a full member. Customs tariffs were reduced 40 per cent, increasing trade

Andean Pact countries · Mercosur countries · Chile

possibilities and preparing the way for access to the Pacific and Atlantic markets. Its exports to Mercosur in 1995 were worth $1.77 million, a 31 per cent increase on the previous year and the equivalent of 11 per cent of all its exports. Some 70 per cent of Chilean foreign investment was aimed toward countries in Mercosur, and on June 30 1996 the value of this reached $7.53 million.

[11] The volume of trade within Mercosur also increased greatly, particularly between Argentina and Brazil: the flow of trade between the two countries increased by 484 per cent between 1990 and 1996, reaching $6.7 million in the first six months of 1997. Some 30 per cent of all Argentine exports went to Brazil, especially in industrial sectors like automobiles, agricultural machinery, textiles, dairy products and fuels.

[12] In April 1998, Mercosur signed a framework agreement with the Andean Pact countries – made up of Bolivia, Ecuador, Peru, Venezuela and Colombia - to open negotiations for the formation of a free trade zone. This would place both bodies in a more favourable position for negotiating the Free Trade Area of the Americas with the United States.

Brunei

Brunei

Population: 300,000 (1996)
Area: 5,765 SQ KM
Capital: Bandar Seri Begawan
Currency: Brunei dollars
Language: Malay

Today's Sultanate of Brunei is what remains of a 13th century Islamic empire that once covered most of the island of Borneo, from which it derives its name. Portuguese, Spanish and Dutch presence in the area occurred virtually uninterrupted from the 16th century. The colonial powers only attempted full occupation of this huge island at the beginning of the 19th century. While the Dutch were making inroads from the south, the Sultan of Brunei sought British support, and succeeded in retaining autonomy.

[2] In 1841, as payment for help in quelling a two year long rebellion, the sultan had to turn the province of Sarawak over to James Brooke, a strange figure who became a European "Rajah" over a Malayan state. In 1846 the British annexed the strategic island of Labuan, and in following years paved the way for the secession of the province of Sabah. In 1888, the British consolidated their position and established separate protectorates over Brunei, Sarawak and Sabah.

[3] Following World War II, despite Britain's efforts, the island began the decolonization process. An agreement signed with Rajah Brooke in 1946 made Sarawak and Sabah into British colonies while Kalimantan (former Dutch Borneo) gained independence in 1954 as part of Indonesia.

[4] All that was left of the British protectorate was the Sultanate of Brunei, reduced to a tiny territorial enclave between two Malaysian provinces, scarcely 40 km from the border with Indonesia. In 1929, the transnational company Shell discovered oil deposits in the area.

In the following decades, drilling for oil and natural gas began, reaching current production rates of 175,000 barrels a day.

[5] In 1962, Sultan Omar Ali Saiffudin accepted a proposal from Malaysian Premier Abdul Rahman to join the Federation of Malaysia, which at the time included Sabah, Sarawak, Singapore, and the provinces of the Malayan peninsula. The Brunei People's Party, (Rakyat) which held 16 seats in the 33-member Legislative Council, was not keen on the idea and opposed the move, proposing instead the creation of a unified state comprising Northern Borneo, Sarawak and Sabah, but excluding peninsular Malaya.

[6] A mass uprising broke out in December 1962, staged by the Rakyat, backed by the Barisan Sosialis (Socialist Party) of Singapore, with support from the anticolonialist Sukarno regime in Indonesia. The rebels opposed integration to the Federation of Malaysia, demanding participation in administration and the end of the autocratic regime. The rebellion was rapidly stifled, the party outlawed and the leaders arrested or forced into exile.

[7] Finally, in spite of ethnic, historical, and cultural ties with Malaya, Sultan Omar decided to keep his sultanate out of the Federation. He was not satisfied with arrangements for power-sharing with the other Malayan rulers and least of all with Federation hopes of a share in his territory's oil resources.

[8] In 1976, with Malaysian prompting and UN support, an opportunity arose to renegotiate the anachronistic colonial statute, when the newly-elected Malaysian prime minister Datuk Hussain Onn promised to respect Brunei's independence. In 1977, Brunei finally accepted independence, but postponed implementation until January 1 1984.

[9] Power was formally transferred on schedule but celebrations were postponed until February 23 1985, so that foreign guests could attend. One month later independence was formally proclaimed, and Hassanal Bokiah, son of Sultan Omar, who had abdicated in his favor in 1967, dissolved the Legislative Council and went on to govern by decree.

[10] Brunei embarked on independent existence in particularly favorable conditions for a Third World country. It had a relatively small population, a high per capita income, low unemployment, a generous social security system and considerable foreign exchange reserves. These reserves stood at $14 billion in 1984.

[11] The main sources of tension were the power struggle within the ruling family and the presence of foreigners in all the key positions of public office, the economy and the armed forces.

[12] Problems on the domestic front included poor basic education. In spite of advanced legislation for education, including a student transport allowance and free accommodation, the illiteracy rate kept climbing; it was estimated at 45 per cent in 1982, posing a serious obstacle to filling civil service posts with Brunei nationals.

[13] The Sultan was aware that the country depended on a non-renewable resource, and Brunei imported nearly 80 per cent of the foodstuffs it consumed. Consequently, with a view to achieving self-sufficiency in food production, he attempted to diversify the economy and promote a new land-owning class. Only 10 per cent of the arable land was cultivated, and small farmers, especially rubber-tree growers, tended to emigrate to the city where they believed a higher standard of living awaited for them.

[14] Economically, Brunei depended upon the complex interplay of transnational interests. The Government's partnership in exploiting natural gas reserves with Brunei Shell Petroleum and Mitsubishi, a shipping contract with Royal Dutch Shell and recent oil field concessions to Woods Petroleum and Sunray Borneo, introduced powerful new parties

LAND USE

IRRIGATED 33.3 % of arable

(1993)

- FOREST & WOODLAND 78%
- ARABLE 0.5%
- OTHER 21.5%

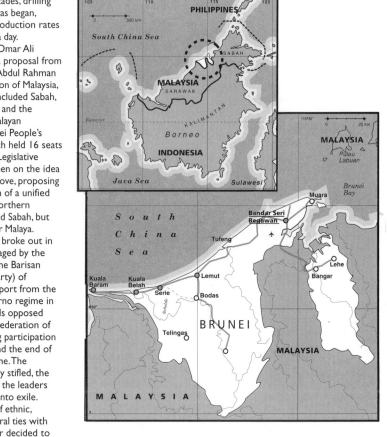

Maternal Mortality
1990

PER 100,000
LIVE BIRTHS
60

Literacy
1995

88%

PROFILE

ENVIRONMENT
Brunei comprises two tracts of land located on the northwestern coast of Borneo, in the Indonesian Archipelago. It has a tropical, rainy climate slightly tempered by the sea. Rubber is harvested in the dense forests. There are major petroleum deposits along the coast. The country is one of the world's main exporters of liquid gas.

SOCIETY
Peoples: Malay 67 per cent; Chinese 15 per cent; Indian and other 18 per cent.
Religions: Islam (official), Buddhism and Christianity.
Languages: Malay (official), Chinese and English.
Political Parties: Brunei Solidarity National Party

THE STATE
Official Name: Islamic Sultanate of Brunei.
Administrative divisions: 4 districts.
Capital: Bandar Seri Begawan, 65,000 people (1994).
Other Cities: Kuala Belait 21,200 people; Seria 21,000 people; Tutong 13,000 people
Government: Hassanal Bolkiah Muizzaddin Waddaulah, Sultan and Prime Minister since 1967.
National Holiday: January 1, Independence Day; July 16, the Sultan's birthday.
Armed Forces: 4,900 (1995).

STATISTICS

DEMOGRAPHY
Population: 300,000 (1996) **Annual growth:** 2.8% (1980/1996) **Estimates for year 2000:** 330,000 **Annual growth to year 2000:** 2.2% (1994/2000) **Urban Population:** 69.9% (1996) **Children per woman:** 2.8 (1996).

HEALTH
Life expectancy at birth: 75 years (1996) **Infant mortality:** 9 per 1,000 (1996) **Under-5 child mortality:** 11 per 1,000 (1996).

EDUCATION
Literacy: 88% (1995) male : 93% (1995) female: 83% (1995) **School enrolment :** Primary total: 109% (1990/95) male : 113% (1990/95) female: 106% (1990/95) Secondary: male : 67% (1990/95) female: 73% (1990/95).

COMMUNICATIONS
70 **newspapers**, 271 **radios**, 320 **TV sets** and 221 **main telephone lines** per 1,000 people (1994) **Books:** 16 new titles per 100,000 people (1992/94).

ECONOMY
Consumer Price index: 109.9 (1994) **Cereal imports:** 32 metric tons (1994) **Fertilizer use:** 5,000 kgs per ha (1994) **Development aid received:** $ 4 million (1995) $ 133 per capita (1995) 0.1% of GNP (1994).

HDI (rank/value) 38 / 0.882 (1994).

---

into the process of national decision-making.

[15] In March 1985, the Government announced the creation of an Energy Control Board to supervise the activities of the Brunei Shell Petroleum Company, a company funded equally by the Government and Shell.

[16] Membership of ASEAN and the UN, obtained in 1984, meant greater international support for the new nation.

[17] At this time 20 per cent of the population was living below the poverty line of $500 a month. Also, 90 per cent of all consumer goods - including basic foodstuffs - were imported, as the country produces little other than oil. The vast amount of imports explains the extremely high cost of living.

[18] In early 1987, it was reported that a request from US colonel Oliver North for "non-lethal" aid to the Nicaraguan contras led the

Sultan of Brunei to deposit a $10 million donation in a Swiss bank account.

[19] The country's military dependence on Britain and the US increased. Under economic restructuring policies applied in recent years, only the military budget grew.

[20] While foreign investment in other areas remained unchanged or fallen, such investment in the military sector also increased. In August 1988, 3,000 British soldiers and Hong Kong Gurkhas carried out joint manoeuvres in the Sultanate's tropical forests

[21] In early 1991, Sultan Hassanal Bolkiah freed 6 political prisoners who had been detained after the failed 1962 revolt. The liberation was ascribed to political pressure by the British Government. This same year Brunei signed a contract for almost $150 million with the United Kingdom in order to modernize its army.

[22] In mid-1992, Brunei joined the Non-Aligned Movement, together with Vietnam and India. The commemoration of the 25th anniversary of Hassanal Bolkiah's reign stressed the role of the monarchy in affirming Brunei's national identity. Brunei's sultan,

the only absolute monarch in the Far East, is also the richest person in the world.

[23] In September 1992, Brunei signed with other members of the Association of South East Asian Nations (ASEAN) - Indonesia, Singapore, Thailand, Malaysia and Philippines - an agreement to create the first integrated market in Asia in 2007. This project stipulated the creation of "growth triangles" - association between some ASEAN members to deregulate trade in certain economic sectors, as a preparation for the overall liberalization planned for the year 2007. Thus, in March 1994, Brunei created - together with Philippines, Malaysia and Indonesia - a sub-regional market to intensify trade in tourism, fishing, and transport by sea and air.

[24] In February 1995, the Solidarity National Party of Brunei - the sole political organization in the country - organized its opening congress and declared its total support for the Sultan. Its leader, Abdul Latif Chuchu also spoke about a royal decree of 1984 which asserted that Brunei's nation-building was

based on the principle of a democratic Malayan-Muslim monarchy. The Sultan's announcement that the state of emergency would be extended was interpreted as a sign of "openness" by the monarch. In October 1995, Brunei joined the World Bank and the IMF.

[25] During 1996, the sultanate continued policies aimed at making Brunei an attractive proposition as a service country. Negotiations with the Southeast Asian leaders were intensified following the regional stock market crisis in 1997, in order to co-ordinate policies to stabilize the regional economy and establish a recovery strategy. In the negotiations, the possibility was discussed of using local currencies instead of the US dollar for trade transactions within the area.

[26] In early 1998, uncontrolled fires in the Indonesian part of the island of Borneo spread dense smoke clouds over Brunei, affecting the daily life of the sultanate. In March, the Sultan led mass prayers for rains to put out the fires. As the situation continued to worsen, he sacked his Health Minister.

MILITARY EXPENDITURE

MILITARY (as % of health and education expenditures-1990/91) **125%**

A VIEW FROM THE SOUTH

BRUNEI   155

Bulgaria

Bulgaria

Population:	8,468,000 (1996)
Area:	110,912 SQ KM
Capital:	Sofia (Sofija)
Currency:	Leva
Language:	Bulgarian

Bulgaria was occupied by the Slav people who spread across the area between the Danube and the Aegean Sea in the 7th and 6th centuries BC. Some of the old Thraco-Illyrian population were expelled, and the rest were assimilated by the invaders. The Slavs worked the land in small organized communities.

[2] The Bulgarians were among the non-European tribes who followed Attila. They were fierce warriors living from warfare and plunder. They first appeared in the region towards the end of the 5th century AD when they settled temporarily on the steppes north of the Black Sea and northeast of the Danube.

[3] Some tribes disappeared and others were enslaved by the Turks. Those tribes led by Kubrat remained in this region until the mid-7th century when the Kazars bore down on them, forcing them into crossing the Danube. They reached as far as Moesia, at that time a province of the Byzantine Empire. Emperor Constantine IV formally recognized the State of Bulgaria in the year 681.

[4] Constant invasions by foreign tribes, led to the new State consolidating its power in the center and southwest. Bulgarian leaders adopted the Slav language and culture. Prince Boris was initially baptized Roman Catholic, but in 870 he turned to the Orthodox Church.

[5] While the Patriarch of Byzantium recognized the independence of the Bulgarian Church Rome refused to appoint a national patriarch. This support helped to consolidate the kingdom's power. Under Simeon (893-927), the Bulgarian State extended its domain as far as the

Adriatic, subduing the Serbs, and becoming the most powerful kingdom of Eastern Europe.

[6] Bulgaria's power declined after Simeon's death. Internal disputes among the nobility, the opposition of the peasants and renewed attacks from abroad led to its downfall. In 1014, Bulgaria lost all of its territory to the Byzantine Empire, which kept control for more than 150 years. After a massive uprising in 1185, the northern part of Bulgaria recovered its independence.

[7] During the reign of Ivan Asen II (1218-41) Bulgaria regained power and territory, including Albania, Epirus, Macedonia and Thracia. However, none of his successors ever managed to impose a central authority over these diverse areas where feudalism was the norm. By 1393 the whole of Bulgaria had fallen under Ottoman rule.

[8] In the 17th and 18th centuries, after the wars with Austria and the unsuccessful siege of Vienna, the Ottoman Empire began to decline, though it still retained much of its territory. In the early 19th century, Bulgaria was still unheard of in Europe, despite the participation of Bulgarian volunteers in the Serbian and Greek uprisings. The former Bulgarian State was twice invaded by Russia in 1810 and 1828.

[9] Throughout the invasion period the Bulgarians maintained their cultural identity; keeping their language, music and folklore alive. Under Turkish domination, the Greek Orthodox Church assumed religious leadership, suppressing the independent patriarch. Hence, Bulgarian monks were among the precursors of the national liberation movement.

[10] The Bulgarian church fought for 40 years to recover its independence. In 1870, the Sultan gave permission for the church to create an exarchate with 15 dioceses under its jurisdiction. The first exarch (deputy patriarch) and his successors were declared schismatic and were excommunicated by the Greek patriarch; this further strengthened Bulgarian nationalism.

[11] From 1876 onwards, a series of Bulgarian revolts were cruelly put down. Some Bulgarian volunteers joined the ranks of the Serbian and Russian armies, who

went to war against the empire. One of Moscow's conditions for the Treaty of St Stephen, was the creation of a Bulgarian State. The European powers feared the creation of a Russian satellite in the Balkans so they blocked the motion.

[12] In the 1878 Berlin Congress, the "autonomous province" of Rumelia was created in the south, and the State of Bulgaria in the north. Rumble was nominally under the sultan's control, and Macedonia was to continue as part of the Ottoman Empire. The legal framework and the election of a governor for the new state remained in the hands of an assembly of selected people.

[13] The assembly approved a liberal Constitution, establishing a constitutional monarchy. Prince Alexander of Battenberg, grandson of Alexander II of Russia, was subsequently elected. He assumed the Bulgarian throne in July 1878, swearing to uphold the Constitution. He suspended it two years later.

[14] The prince set up a dictatorship, headed by the Russian general, LN Sobolev and other conservatives. The Russian emperor's death modified Alexander's behaviour, making him more attuned to Bulgarian issues. In 1885, he supported the liberal rebellion in Rumelia, the governor there was replaced and union with Bulgaria was proclaimed.

[15] The treaties of Bucharest and Top-Khane, signed in 1886, recognized Prince Alexander as the ruler of Rumelia and Bulgaria.

However, he was subsequently taken to Russia against his will and forced to abdicate. Looking for someone who would be acceptable to Russia, as well as the rest of Europe, the Bulgarians finally appointed Ferdinand of Saxe-Coburg-Gotha as his replacement.

[16] Although initially distrusted, Ferdinand was able to gain the support of Vienna, London, Rome and Russia. He then concentrated on the reunification of the Bulgarians whose territory had been divided under the terms of the Treaty of Berlin. Prince Ferdinand proclaimed Bulgaria's independence in 1908, thereby breaking its nominal dependence upon Turkey.

[17] In 1912, Bulgaria signed secret military agreements with Greece and Serbia. In October of that year, Montenegro, accompanied by its Balkan allies, declared war on Istanbul. In May, Turkey ceded its European dominions, north of a line between Enos, in the Aegean Sea, and Midia, on the Black Sea.

[18] The allies did not agree with the distribution; Bulgaria confronted Greece and Serbia over the issue and Romania joined Serbia as its ally. The Second Balkan War quickly ended in Bulgarian defeat. In Bucharest, in August 1913, Macedonia was divided between Greece and Serbia, and Romania gained an area of northern Bulgaria, rich in natural resources.

[19] In 1913, the Bulgarian government abandoned its traditionally pro-Russian stance, seeking closer ties with Germany. When World War I broke out the

PROFILE

ENVIRONMENT

Located on the Balkan Peninsula, Bulgaria comprises four different natural regions. The fertile Danubian plains in the north are wheat and corn-producing areas.

South of these plains are the wooded Balkan Mountains, where cereals and potatoes are cultivated, cattle and sheep are raised, and the country's major mineral resources - iron ore, zinc and copper, are found.

Cattle are also raised on the Rhodope Mountains in southern Bulgaria. South of the Balkan mountains there is a region of grassland, crossed by the Maritza River, where tobacco, cotton, rice, flowers and grapes are cultivated.

Heavy metals, nitrates, petroleum derivatives and detergents have damaged the lower and mid-tributaries of the most important rivers. These flow into the Black Sea, which is highly polluted. About one quarter of the country's woodland is affected by air pollution.

SOCIETY

Peoples: Most of the Bulgarian population is of Slav origin, but there are also people of Turkish, Armenian and Greek origins.
Religions: Orthodox Christian and Muslim.
Languages: Bulgarian (official); Turkish, Greek, and Armenian are also spoken.
Political Parties: Union of Democratic Forces (a coalition made up of 16 parties); Bulgarian Socialist Party (formerly the Communist Party); Movement for Freedom and Human Rights (of the Turkish minority); Bulgarian Agrarian Party.

THE STATE

Official Name: Narodna Republika Balgaria.
Capital: Sofia (Sofija), 1,200,000 people (1994).
Other cities: Plovdiv, 364,000 people; Varna, 306,000 (1994).
Government: Petar Stoyanov, President since January, 1997; Ivan Kostov, Prime Minister since 1997.
National Holiday: March 3, National Liberation Day.
Armed Forces: 102,000.
Other: Border Guards (Ministry of Interior): 12,000; Security Police: 4,000; Railway and Construction Troops: 18,000.

Bulgarian people and the army disapproved of the official policy, even though Serbia was beaten. Ferdinand surrendered to the Allies in 1918 and abdicated in favor of his son Boris.

[20] Having lost much territory, Bulgaria was disarmed and forced to pay extensive war damages. With the restoration of the 1878 Constitution, elections were held in 1920. The anti-war reaction gave the Agrarian Party a wide margin. Working on a Soviet model, the government started radical agrarian reforms. The government was not pro-soviet, however, and local communists were persecuted.

[21] Bulgaria joined the League of Nations and followed a conciliatory line of diplomacy for some time. However, its territorial losses and the pressure exerted by Bulgarians living abroad soon led to new tensions with its neighbors. Aleksandur Stamboliyski, the leader of the Agrarian Party and head of the government, was ousted from power and assassinated by a conspiracy of Macedonians and opposition figures in 1923.

[22] Aleksandur Tsankov assumed control of the government, heading a multi-party alliance which excluded the Liberal, Communist and Agrarian parties. Uprisings and armed activity by the opposition led to hundreds of executions and assassinatons. The government declared martial law and reinforced the army in order to avoid outright rebellion.

[23] In 1926, Tsankov resigned in favor of Andrei Liapchev, leader of the Democratic Party, to make way for more liberal policies. The Government approved a partial amnesty, and permitted a reorganization of the Agrarian Party. In 1932, Liapchev's cabinet was made up of members of the Democratic, Liberal and Agrarian parties, known as the National Bloc.

[24] In 1934, fearing the effects of the worldwide economic depression and taking a cue from his neighbors, King Boris III supported the action of the conservative group, Zveno, which deposed Liapchev and set up a dictatorship. All political parties were proscribed, there was censorship of the press, the universities were closed and an ultra-right youth movement was established.

[25] Tension with Turkey eased, and in 1937 a peace and friendship treaty was signed with Yugoslavia. The following year, Bulgaria signed a non-aggression pact with the Balkan alliance, in exchange for the rearmament of the Bulgarian army.

While the king was once again seeking rapprochement with Germany, the Bulgarian dream of re-establishing its former borders was gathering strength.

[26] In 1940, Germany made Romania return the parts of Bulgaria which it had won in the second Balkan War. Bulgaria signed the Antikomintern pact and German troops set up bases aimed at Greece and Yugoslavia on Bulgarian soil. In exchange, Bulgarian troops were allowed to occupy the part of Thracia belonging to Greece, and the part of Macedonia belonging to Yugoslavia, and part of Serbia.

[27] When Bulgaria refused to declare war on the Soviet Union, King Boris was assassinated, and a new pro-German government was formed. Growing anti-Nazi resistance, led by the communists, contributed to the formation of the Patriotic Front in 1942. The Republicans, left-wing Agrarians, Democrats and independents all subsequently joined.

[28] In May 1944, paralyzed by the civil war, the pro-German Boshilov resigned, and was replaced by Bagrianov. While Soviet troops advanced toward the Danube, Bagrianov sought an agreement with the Allies. In August, Bulgaria proclaimed its neutrality, and ordered the disarmament of the German troops on its soil.

[29] Ignoring the Sofia Declaration, the Red Army entered Bulgarian territory. The resistance fanned local insurrection. On September 8, General Kyril Stanchev's troops took the capital, and the Patriotic Front formed a government headed by the Republican Kimon Georgiev.

[30] Sofia signed a treaty with the allies in October 1944. Bulgarian troops, under Soviet command, collaborated in the defeat of the German forces in Hungary, Yugoslavia and Austria. During 1945, war trials led to the imprisonment of 6,870 people, and the execution of 2,680 others.

[31] In March 1945, communist leader Giorgi Dimitrov returned to Bulgaria after several years at the Komintern headquarters, in Moscow. A few months later a crisis arose when Georgiev failed to have the electoral lists drawn up in time, postponing the approaching election.

[32] In a referendum held in September 1946, 92 per cent of the electorate approved of the creation of the Republic of Bulgaria. In the October election, the Patriotic Front won 364 seats with 70.8 per cent of the vote, 277 seats went to the Communist Party (BCP). In November, Dimitrov became Prime Minister.

[33] In 1947, Britain and the US recognized the government, the National Assembly ratified the peace treaty with the Allies, the new Constitution went into effect and, at the end of the year, the Soviet troops withdrew from the country. After joining the opposition, some of the Patriotic Front's former leaders were arrested and sentenced to death for conspiracy.

[34] Under the leadership of the BCP, the Bulgarian State adopted the Soviet socio-economic model. A process of accelerated economic growth was set into motion, without taking into account the lack of raw materials or the technical preparation of the labor force. In the countryside, collective farming was enforced.

[35] Dimitrov resigned from the government in March 1949, and died a few months later. Vulko Chervenkov succeeded him, first as leader of the government, and then as party premier. In March 1954, Todor Zhivkov was named First Secretary of the BCP, becoming prime minister in 1962. Bulgaria was the USSR's closest ally among the Warsaw Pact countries, and in 1968 Bulgarian troops accompanied Soviet troops in the invasion of Czechoslovakia.

[36] In the 1980s Bulgaria was accused of imposing a policy of forced assimilation, upon the country's 10 per cent Turkish minority. In 1986, Sofia refuted Amnesty International's accusation that more than 250 Turks had been detained or imprisoned for refusing to accept new identity cards.

[37] In 1988, Bulgaria and Turkey signed a protocol governing bilateral economic relations. The dialogue was interrupted in the following year, when it was revealed that the Bulgarian militia had used violence to put down a protest by 30,000 Turks, who had been demonstrating against the government's policy of assimilation.

[38] In June 1989, more than 80,000 Turks were expelled from Bulgaria. Turkey promised to accommodate them all, but towards the end of August, after receiving 310,000 Bulgarian Turks, it closed its borders. 30,000 of these refugees subsequently returned to Bulgaria.

[39] The largest protest meeting since the war was held in November in front of the National Assembly. A group known as "Eco-glasnost" demonstrated against a proposed nuclear power plant on an island in the Danube, citing the fact that it lay in an earthquake-zone. They also protested against the construction of a reservoir in one of the country's largest nature reserves.

[40] In December, some 6,000 members of the Pomak community - a Muslim minority group with an estimated 300,000 members - demanded religious and cultural freedom.

[41] The Central Committee of the

1990

1995

PER 100,000
LIVE BIRTHS
27

98%

STATISTICS

DEMOGRAPHY
Population: 8,468,000 (1996) **Annual growth:** -0.3% (1980/1996) **Estimates for year 2000:** 8,000,000 **Annual growth to year 2000:** -0.5% (1994/2000) **Urban Population:** 68.6% (1996) **Urban growth:** 0.56% (1980/95) **Children per woman:** 1.5 (1996).

HEALTH
Life expectancy at birth: 71 years (1996) male: 68 years (1994) female: 75 years (1994) **Infant mortality:** 16 per 1,000 (1996) **Under-5 child mortality:** 19 per 1,000 (1996) **Calorie consumption:** 148% (1988/90) 315 **people per doctor** (1988/91).

EDUCATION
Literacy: 98% (1995) male : 99% (1995) female: 98% (1995) **School enrolment :** Primary total: 86% (1990/95) male : 88% (1990/95) female: 84% (1990/95) Secondary: male : 68% (1990/95) female: 72% (1990/95) Tertiary: 39% (1995) **Primary school teachers:** one for every 17 students (1995).

COMMUNICATIONS
210 **newspapers,** 454 **radios,** 260 **TV sets** and 295 **main telephone lines** per 1,000 people (1994) **Books:** 69 new titles per 100,000 people (1992/94).

ECONOMY
Per capita, GNP: $ 1,190 (1996) **Annual growth, GNP:** -8.8% (1995/96) **Annual inflation:** 45.89% (1985/95) **Consumer price index:** 2,841.7 (1994) **Currency:** 67.6 leva = $ 1 (1995) **Cereal imports:** 58 metric tons (1994) **Fertilizer use:** 449 kgs per ha (1994) **Exports:** $ 4,543 million (1996) Imports: $ 4,313 million (1996) **External debt:** $ 9,819 million (1996) $ 1,160 **per capita:** (1996) **Debt service:** 20.5% of exports (1996)

ENERGY
Consumption: 2,438.41 Kgs of Oil equivalent per capita yearly (1994) 56.39% imported (1994)

HDI (rank / value) 69 / 0.78 (1994)

BCP replaced Zhivkov as Secretary General, a post he had held for 35 years. He was succeeded by Petur Mladenov, who had been prime minister since 1971 and was considered to be a proponent of liberalization of the regime. In December, Mladenov also replaced Zhivkov as president of the State Council.

[42] The National Assembly lifted the ban against anti-government demonstrations, and granted amnesty to political prisoners. There was an immediate increase in the number of political demonstrations demanding reforms and elections.

[43] In March 1990, the Union of Democratic Forces (UDF), made up of 16 opposition parties, and the official party agreed to the election of a Constitutional Assembly. The July election was won by the Bulgarian Socialist Party, BSP (formerly BCP). In October, the BCP was forced to enter a new coalition Government, led by Yelio Yelev, a dissident during the 1970s and leader of the Social Democratic wing of the UDF.

[44] The new coalition government adopted a program of economic reforms in consultation with the IMF and the World Bank. They reached an agreement with the labor unions for a 200-day "social peace" until the reforms could go into effect.

[45] In July 1991, the new Constitution was approved, establishing a parliamentary system of government, allowing personal property, and freedom of opinion. After the October election, Parliament named Filip Dimitrov as prime minister. Virtually alienated from the Social Democrats and the "Greens", co-founders of the UDF, Dimitrov was chosen because of the support he had from the right-wing of the opposition coalition and the Movement for Freedom and Human Rights (of the Turkish minority).

[46] In the January 1992 election, in which 75 per cent of registered voters participated, Yelev was elected president of the republic. As leader of the political transition period and author of the rapprochement toward the West, he received 54.4 per cent of the vote in the second round of voting, defeating the BSP candidate, Velko Valkanov.

[47] With a general strike protesting low wages and unemployment, Podkrepa - the national labor union - and the government parted company. The unemployment rate reached 17 per cent, and retirement pensions came to an average of $25 per month.

[48] In June 1992, Bulgaria joined the Council of Europe. During this year, former Communist leader Todor Zhivkov, three former prime ministers and another former member of governments prior to 1991, were arrested charged with corruption in the exercise of their duties. The economic situation led the MDL to withdraw its support of Dimitrov, which caused the downfall of his cabinet.

[49] Dimitrov was replaced by Liuben Berov from the MDL. The new prime minister stated he was willing to restore the lands confiscated by the communists to the Turkish minority. Transition from a centralized planned economy to a free market economy continued to be difficult and caused paradoxical situations. Thus, when agricultural cooperatives were dismantled, two million cattle were slaughtered as they could not be managed by the new private farms.

[50] When former USSR stopped buying two thirds of Bulgarian exports, foreign trade was significantly reduced. UN sanctions imposed on neighbouring former Yugoslavia caused losses of $1.5 million to Bulgaria. In 1993, Berov went on with the reforms to install a market economy at a rate considered excessively slow by the IMF, which caused a certain amount of tension between Sofia and the international organization.

[51] However, Berov held on to power until mid 1994, thanks to the support of the MDL, the BSP and the New Union for Democracy, a breakaway group from the UDF. Members of this opposing coalition frequently accused the prime minister of wanting to "restore socialism". Disagreements between Berov and the MDL in matters related to human rights and the social condition of Bulgarians of Turkish background, further weakened the Government.

[52] In June 1994, Berov was able to pass the privatization law and in September he presented his

resignation. After three failed attempts to form a new government, President Yelev dissolved Parliament and called new elections. The BSP won an absolute majority in the National Assembly - 125 seats over a total of 240 - in the December elections, while the anti-communist UDF gained 69 seats.

[53] In January 1995, socialist leader Zhan Videnov formed a new government which included members from the BSP, the Bulgarian Agrarian National Union and the Eco-glasnost Political Club. His cabinet was the first in the history of post-communist Bulgaria with an absolute majority at the National Assembly. Differences between the new government and Yelev were frequent. In July, the President criticized the Government because he believed reforms leading toward a market economy were not being implemented swiftly enough, suggesting the BSP was "genetically connected" to organized crime and that the Videnov administration was incapable of eliminating it.

[54] Petar Stoyanov s Union of Democratic Forces won the first round of the presidential elections in November 1996 and one month later beat the Socialist candidate, Ivan Marazov in the final round by 59.7 per cent of the vote. Pursued by his political rivals, prime minister Zhan Videnov resigned in

December. The conservative groups which supported Stoyanov requested the resignation of the cabinet, sustained by the parliamentary majority of Socialists and their allies. A series of large demonstrations in the capital and other cities pressed for new legislative elections. Stoyanov became president in January 1997, after vowing to bring forward the 1998 elections.

[55] The Union of Democratic Forces won the by-elections on April 1997 and obtained 137 seats of the National Assembly, compared to 58 from the Socialists and 19 from the Union of National Salvation, formed by the monarchists. The new government adopted a neoliberal economic policy, following the IMF guidelines with provision for the privatization of debt-ridden state companies and the scrapping of 60,000 jobs in the public sector. Services were also liberalized in order to reduce inflation.

[56] In late 1997, Bulgaria toughened its stance in the conflict with the government of Macedonia. Sofia denied the nationhood of Macedonia and did not accept the use of Macedonian as a national language. For this reason, Bulgaria refused to sign any documents in that language. This attitude prevented the implementation of 20 economic and cultural agreements between the states.

Burkina Faso

Population: 10,780,000 (1996)
Area: 274,000 SQ KM
Capital: Ouagadougou

Currency: CFA francs
Language: French

Burkina Faso

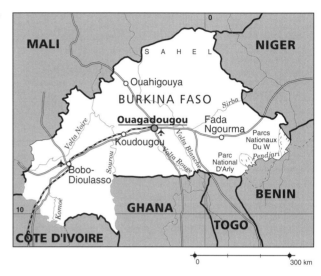

During the 11th century, the Mossi martial caste subdued the neighboring peoples in the region where the Volta rivers (Volta Noire, Volta Blanche and Volta Rouge) rise. In the following two centuries, they established a series of highly organized kingdoms, the most notable being Yatenga and Ouagadougou. In the latter group, rulers were chosen from the royal family by four officials with ministerial rank, whose role was to seek a balance between the Mossi aristocracy and the Mande base. This electoral system persisted into the 20th century.

2 The Mossi and Mande tenaciously resisted attempts at annexation by the Mali and Songhai empires (see Mali and Guinea) and remained independent throughout the Fulah invasions of the 18th and 19th centuries. In a series of military incursions between 1896 and 1904, the French laid waste the central plains, burning houses, and slaughtering humans and animals. The ensuing reign of terror finally sparked off an insurrection in 1916, which met with such violent repression that millions were forced to emigrate, mostly to Ghana.

3 By then the country had been incorporated into the colony of Haute Sénégal-Niger. It was reconstituted as the separate colony of Upper Volta in 1947.

4 Upper Volta had no directly productive role in the international division of labor. Its task was to produce people: forced labor on plantations in Côte d'Ivoire, or cannon fodder for French armies at war in Europe or the colonies.

5 Finally, in line with French neo-colonial strategy, the country was declared independent in 1960. The 1960 elections were won by the Voltese Democratic Union (UDV), a party backed by landowners and private enterprise. Maurice Yameogo was elected president and was re-elected in 1965 amidst intense trade-union agitation, which occurred in response to economic crisis, administrative chaos and austerity measures. Yameogo was overthrown a year later in a military coup led by army chief-of-staff, Colonel Sangoulé Lamizana.

6 The 1970s witnessed a succession of elections, military coups, and more or less fraudulent re-elections orchestrated by Colonel Lamizana. Starvation was widespread, herds were dwindling and an estimated quarter of the population had emigrated to neighboring states. In 1980 Lamizana was ousted in a coup by another colonel, Saye Zerbo, and there were further coups in November 1982, May 1983 and on August 4 1983.

7 The last of these changes was much more than just the latest game of musical chairs among the military élite. The new leader, a young army captain called Thomas Sankara, saw it as a revolution. He launched into a program of radical change which aimed to chart an entirely new course for poor African countries, and this brought him to international notice. He was popular among soldiers and the rural poor as he brought in an anti-corruption campaign and organized brigades to assist victims of the prolonged drought and deforestation.

8 In the first year of Sankara's government: Upper Volta was renamed Burkina Faso - "land of the incorruptible"; the national anthem was sung in African languages; land reform was carried out and popular courts were set up to dispense justice. Sankara set a target of two meals and 10 litres of water per person per day.

9 The implementation of such measures presented a considerable challenge in a country where 82 per cent of adults were illiterate and absolute poverty was the norm. There were practically no bank accounts held within the country. Kerosene was the energy source for lighting. Cutting wood, the main fuel, contributed some 50,000 to 100,000 hectares to the total annual deforestation. Encroachment by the Sahel arid area further aggravated the lack of firewood.

10 On December 15 1987, Sankara was overthrown and executed along with 12 of his supporters in a coup led by his second-in-command, Blaise Compaoré, who pledged to continue the Popular Front and "rectify" the regime internally.

11 Contrasting with the image of Sankara, a man of austere habits who shunned personal property, Compaoré built a government palace and purchased a presidential plane. His economic strategy included encouragement of private enterprise and foreign capital, and consideration of denationalization, deregulation and agreements with international lending institutions.

12 In September 1989, four high-ranking officers were accused of plotting to kill the head of state, and were shot.

13 The 4th Republic adopted a new constitution, which was approved by referendum on June 2 1991 (90 per cent voting in favor, with 50 per cent of registered voters participating). The new constitution, which was put into effect by de facto President Compaoré, re-established a multiparty system and the division of powers, while reducing presidential powers. The office of prime minister was created, and general elections were to be held every seven years.

14 In the May 1992 elections, the official party won 78 of the 107 National Assembly seats. The main opposition force, concentrated in the National Convention of Progressive Patriots-Social Democratic Party (CNPP-PSD) won 13 seats. Blaise Compaoré, who ran unopposed, became the first president of the 4th Republic, with 21.6 per cent of the vote.

15 Prime Minister Yussuf Ouedraogo promised to prioritize agriculture and provide incentives for the creation of small- and medium- sized enterprises in order to create new jobs. International pressure made Ouedraogo pledge to

WORKERS

(1996)

Labour force %

- ■ WOMEN
- □ MEN

47   53

- ■ AGRICULTURE 92% (1990)
- □ INDUSTRIAL 2%
- ■ SERVICES 6%

LAND USE

DEFORESTATION -0.7 % annual (81/90)
IRRIGATED 0.6 % of arable

(1993)

- ■ FOREST & WOODLAND 50.4%
- □ ARABLE 13%
- ■ OTHER 36.6%

1990

PER 100,000
LIVE BIRTHS

930

1995

19%

STATISTICS

DEMOGRAPHY
Population: 10,780,000 (1996) **Annual growth:** 2.8% (1980/1996) **Estimates for year 2000:** 12,100,000 **Annual growth to year 2000:** 2.8% (1994/2000) **Urban Population:** 16.4% (1996) **Urban growth:** 11.29% (1980/95) **Children per woman:** 6.7 (1996).

HEALTH
Life expectancy at birth: 46 years (1996) male: 45 years (1994) female: 48 years (1994) **Infant mortality:** 82 per 1,000 (1996) **Under-5 child mortality:** 158 per 1,000 (1996) **Calorie consumption:** 94% (1988/90) 33,333 **people per doctor** (1988/91) **Safe water:** 42% (1990/96).

EDUCATION
Literacy: 19% (1995) male : 30% (1995) female: 9% (1995) **School enrolment :** Primary total: 39% (1990/95) male : 48% (1990/95) female: 31% (1990/95) Secondary: male : 12% (1990/95) female: 6% (1990/95) Tertiary: 1% (1995) **Primary school teachers:** one for every 58 students (1995).

COMMUNICATIONS
28 **radios,** 10 **TV sets** and 3 **main telephone lines** per 1,000 people (1994).

ECONOMY
Per capita, GNP: $ 230 (1996) **Annual growth, GNP:** 3.3% (1995/96) **Annual inflation:** 2.59% (1985/95) **Consumer price index:** 126.0 (1994) **Currency:** 490 CFA francs = $ 1 (1995) **Cereal imports:** 110 metric tons (1994) **Food import dependency:** 14% (1994) **Fertilizer use:** 65 kgs per ha (1994) **Exports:** $ 216 million (1996) Imports: $ 783 million (1996) **External debt:** $ 1,294 million (1996) $ 120 **per capita:** (1996) **Debt service:** 10.8% of exports (1996) **Development aid received:** $ 483 million (1995) $ 48 per capita (1995) 16.6% of GNP (1994).

ENERGY
Consumption: 15.86 Kgs of Oil equivalent per capita yearly (1994) 100.00% imported (1994)

HDI (rank / value) 172 / 0.221 (1994)

PROFILE

ENVIRONMENT
A landlocked country, Burkina Faso is one of the most densely populated areas of the African Sahel (the semi-arid southern rim of the Sahara).
The Mossi plateau slopes gently southwards and is traversed by the valleys of the three Volta Rivers (Black Volta, White Volta and Red Volta). Though more fertile, these lands are plagued with tsetse flies.
As in the whole Sahel region, this nation suffers from mounting aridity caused by inappropriate farming techniques introduced to produce peanuts and cotton for export. Wood, a popular energy source, is becoming scarce as a result of deforestation.

SOCIETY
Peoples: Over half of the population are Mossi. Pouhi herders and the Tamajek clans with their vassals, the Bellah, amount to around 20 per cent.
Djula peasants and traders are indigenous minorities. The language of these three population groups is the linguistic bridge among the various regions.
Senufo and Bobo-Fing cultures inhabit the western plains where the savannah merges into the forest. In the south, the predominant Lebi, Bobo-Ule, Gurunsi and Bisa cultures extend into several states. The savannah to the east holds the great Gurmantehé civilization, while the Sampo, Rurumba and Marko cultures live in the desert regions to the north and northeast.
Religions: The majority of the population profess traditional African religions; 30 per cent are Muslim and 10 per cent are Christian.
Languages: French (official); Mossi, Bobo and Gurma are the most widely spoken languages.
Political Parties: Organization for the People's Democracy-Workers' Movement (ODP/MT); National Convention of Progressive Patriots-Social Democrats (CNPP-PSD); Burkinabe Socialist Party (PSB).
Social organizations: Voltenese Free Unions Organization, Confederation of Voltanese Unions.

THE STATE
Official Name: République de Burkina Faso.
Administrative division: 30 provinces, 300 departments and 7200 villages.
Capital: Ouagadougou, 730,000 people (1994).
Other cities: Bobo-Dioulasso, 250,000 people; Koudougou, 51,925; Ouahigouya, 38,902 (1990).
Government: Republican parliamentary system, with a strong head of state. Blaise Compaoré, President in power since 1987. Single-chamber legislature: National Assembly (107 members elected by direct vote for a 7-year term). Judiciary: judges responsible to a Superior Council, under the authority of the president of the republic.
National Holiday: August 5, Independence (1960).
Armed Forces: 5,800 (1995).
Other: Gendarmerie: 1,500; Security Company (CRG): 250; People's Militia (R): 45,000 trained.

MILITARY (as % of health and education expenditures-1990/91) **30%**

reduce the country's bureaucracy; Burkina Faso had 36,000 public employees, most of them on pensions.
[16] In December 1992 and March 1993 there were two general strikes against the implementation of the structural-adjustment plan recommended by the IMF. Devaluation of the CFA franc in January 1994 led to Ouedraogo's resignation and his replacement by Marc-Christian Kabore in March that year. In July, in spite of protests from the opposition, Parliament passed a law which allowed the Government to privatize 19 national companies.
[17] In February 1995, the opposition boycotted municipal elections since it considered they were being organized by a non-independent electoral commission. The ruling Organization for the People's Democracy-Workers' Movement won in 26 of the country's largest 33 cities. At a social level, conditions remained tense since indirect consequences from the 1994 devaluation led the cost of living to rise 30 per cent in the first half of 1995.
[18] The Government continued its policy of economic liberalization and officially entered Burkina Faso into the World Trade Organization in June 1995. A project to restructure the recently privatized railways, resulting in 500 lay-offs, caused a new strike which led the country once again toward a tense situation, typical of the early 1990s.
[19] The economy grew 5 per cent in 1996. In June, the IMF approved a new $57 million loan to support the implementation of a structural-adjustment program in the subsequent three years. In 1997, a drought decimated food production and left the country in a critical situation. The deficit in food production, which added up to 32 per cent of the GDP and employed 90 per cent of the population, was estimated at in 156,000 tonnes for the 1997-1998 period. In December 1997, Ouagadogou had to call on the international community for 67,000 tonnes of grain to tackle the crisis.
[20] Marijuana plantations grew swiftly in Burkina Faso, as well as in other countries of the region. Marijuana replaced some "traditional" cash crops whose price had fallen. The devaluation of the CFA franc caused a reduction in the import of medicines, which further complicated the fight against the two major diseases that ravage the population: malaria and Aids. In 1998, there was only one doctor for every 25,000 people in Burkina Faso.

Burundi

Burundi

Population: 6,221,000 (1996)
Area: 27,834 SQ KM
Capital: Bujumbura

Currency: Burundi francs
Languages: Rundi, Kirundi and French

Burundi is one of the poorest countries in the world and one of the most densely populated in Africa. For five centuries it has been torn by ethnic and economic struggles involving the Hutu majority and the Tutsi (or Watusi, as the Germans dubbed them). At least five major massacres affecting one or the other community have occurred since the 15th century.

[2] The Hutu, a Bantu group, were communal farmers. Five hundred years ago they were overrun by the Tutsi, who migrated south from Uganda and Ethiopia in search of fertile grazing land for their cattle. The Tutsi had more sophisticated weapons and were thus able to subdue the Hutu and enslave their people. Tutsi rulers held considerable power during the 17th and 18th centuries, but rivalry between the various local groups weakened the central power structure in the 19th century. This paved the way for German colonization around 1890. The Europeans upheld Tutsi domination and in turn forced the traditional ruler (Mwami) to accept German tutelage. In 1899, Burundi and Rwanda (see Rwanda) were merged into a single colony, Rwanda-Urundi, which became famous for its ivory exports controlled by a German trade monopoly.

[3] Following the defeat of Germany in World War I, Belgium took over the colony and separated Burundi from Rwanda again only to merge the former with Zaire (now DR Congo). The Belgian system of indirect rule assigned Tutsi elites a privileged role and gave rise to nationalist movements in the 1950s. This process bred the Union for National Progress (UNAPRO) led by Louis Rwagasore, elected prime minister in 1960. The Belgians feared that Rwagasore might become a Burundian Lumumba (see DR Congo) and he was therefore assassinated before independence was granted. Burundi gained independence on July 1 1962, governed by a puppet Tutsi ruler under Belgian control.

[4] Violence marked the first four years of autonomous rule under five different prime ministers. Instability predominated until November 1966, when the Prime Minister Captain Michael Micombero, staged a coup and proclaimed the Republic of Burundi. The new president carried out a massive purge of all Hutu government officials. In 1971, 350,000 Hutus were killed through government repression and an additional 70,000 went into exile.

[5] In 1976, Lt-Col Jean Baptiste Bagaza took power promising to end ethnic persecution and set up a reformist government. Bagaza broadened the UNAPRO, put a land reform program into practice, and rehabilitated labor unions, all in blatant defiance of the Tutsi elite and their foreign capitalist allies. In foreign policy, the new government drew closer to Tanzania, and China sent aid to develop Burundi's mineral resources.

[6] In 1979, the first post-independence congress of UNAPRO was held and a new constitution drafted, effective in 1981. The new constitution prevented the exploitation of the Hutu majority by the Tutsi minority, prompted the modernization of the political structure, and gave women equal rights. Reforms stirred up strong feelings between the Government and the conservative Catholic hierarchy, leading to confiscation of properties and deportation of 63 missionaries.

[7] Elections held in 1982, 20 years after independence, upheld President Bagaza's policies and brought about a swift stabilization of the young nation's political situation.

[8] Despite Burundi's established political independence, the country faced serious problems due mostly to economic dependence and its geographical location. Being a landlocked country raised the price of both imports and exports. Population density is high and unevenly distributed geographically; 70 per cent live in the north where overuse of the land has caused massive soil erosion. Wood is the main source of domestic fuel and unfortunately the high demand outstrips the forest production of the country. Ninety per cent of agricultural products were consumed by the domestic market. Burundi's economic hopes lay in the rich nickel deposits and in its hydroelectric potential. Belgian and US companies are currently developing the Musongati mines which also have large cobalt and uranium deposits.

[9] In September 1987, while attending a summit meeting of French-speaking countries in Quebec, Bagaza was overthrown by army major Pierre Buyoya in a bloodless coup.

[10] In August 1988, strife between Hutus and Tutsis broke out in Dtega and Marangana, in the north of the country, leaving several thousand dead, most of them Hutus. The rebellion against Tutsi landowners was cruelly dealt with by an army made up mostly of Tutsis. Over 60,000 Hutus sought refuge in Rwanda. The Government responded by designating a Hutu prime minister, Adrien Sibomana, with a new cabinet in which half the ministers were Hutus.

[11] In 1989, most refugees returned and there was reconciliation between the military government and the Catholic Church, who had regained their property. A structural adjustment program was initiated which included the privatization of public enterprises and the creation of a "watchdog" tribunal to combat corruption.

[12] Burundi depended largely on the export of its main crop, coffee, and on its fluctuating prices. Poverty and high population density added to the environment's degradation. The high rate of deforestation is in part due to the transformation of forests into farming lands for landless peasants.

[13] In 1992, Buyoya enacted a

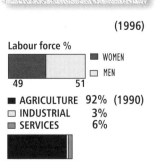

WORKERS

(1996)

Labour force %
- ■ WOMEN
- ☐ MEN

49 | 51

- ■ AGRICULTURE 92% (1990)
- ☐ INDUSTRIAL 3%
- ■ SERVICES 6%

LAND USE

DEFORESTATION -0.6% annual (81/90)
IRRIGATED 1.2% of arable

(1993)

- ■ FOREST & WOODLAND 3.1%
- ☐ ARABLE 40.8%
- ■ OTHER 56.1%

1990

PER 100,000
LIVE BIRTHS

1,300

1995

35%

STATISTICS

DEMOGRAPHY
Population: 6,221,000 (1996) **Annual growth:** 2.6% (1980/1996) **Estimates for year 2000:** 7,000,000 **Annual growth to year 2000:** 2.7% (1994/2000) **Urban Population:** 7.8% (1996) **Urban growth:** 6.76% (1980/95) **Children per woman:** 6.4 (1996)

HEALTH
Life expectancy at birth: 46 years (1996) male: 42 years (1994) female: 45 years (1994) **Infant mortality:** 106 per 1,000 (1996) **Under-5 child mortality:** 176 per 1,000 (1996) **Calorie consumption:** 84% (1988/90) 16,667 **people per doctor** (1988/91) **Safe water:** 52% (1990/96)

EDUCATION
Literacy: 35% (1995) male : 49% (1995) female: 23% (1995) **School enrolment** : Primary total: 69% (1990/95) male : 76% (1990/95) female: 62% (1990/95) Secondary: male : 8% (1990/95) female: 5% (1990/95) Tertiary: 1% (1995) **Primary school teachers:** one for every 65 students (1995)

COMMUNICATIONS
64 **radios**, 10 **TV sets** and 3 **main telephone lines** per 100 people.

ECONOMY
Per capita, GNP: $ 170 (1996) **Annual growth, GNP:** -11.1% (1995/96) **Annual inflation:** 6.05% (1985/95) **Consumer price index:** 128.3 (1994) **Currency:** 277.92 Burundi francs = $ 1 (1995) **Cereal imports:** 105 metric tons (1994) **Food import dependency:** 19% (1994) **Fertilizer use:** 26 kgs per ha (1994) **Exports:** $ 37 million (1996) **Imports:** $ 125 million (1996) **External debt:** $ 1,127 million (1996) $ 181 **per capita:** (1996) **Debt service:** 54.6% of exports (1996) **Development aid received:** $ 288 million (1995) $ 46 per capita (1995) 32.1% of GNP (1994)

ENERGY
Consumption: 23.40 Kgs of Oil equivalent per capita yearly (1994) 96.50% imported (1994)

HDI (rank / value) 169 / 0.247 (1994)

PROFILE

ENVIRONMENT
Most of the land is made up of flat plateaus and relatively low hills covered with natural pastures. Located in the African zone of the Great Lakes (Tanganyika, Victoria), the Ruvubu River valley stretches through the country from north to south. Tropical forests are found in the low, western regions. Most inhabitants engage in subsistence agriculture (corn, cassava, sorghum, beans). Coffee is the main export product. Internal communications are hampered by natural barriers and the nearest sea outlet is 1,400 km beyond the border, a fact which makes foreign trade even more difficult. The forests are fundamental in maintaining climatic balance, and deforestation is one of the country's worst problems, aggravated by the growing incidence of farming on unsuitable lands.

SOCIETY
Peoples: Most Burundians (86 per cent) belong to the Hutu ethnic group, an agricultural people of Bantu origin. They were traditionally dominated by the Tutsi or Watusi (13 per cent), shepherds of Hamitic descent. There is a small minority (1 per cent) of Twa pygmies.
Religions: 67 per cent Christian; 32 per cent follow traditional African religions and 1 per cent are Muslim.
Languages: Rundi, Kirundi and French, official, with Swahili the business language.
Political Parties: Burundi Democratic Front; Unity for National Progress, led by president Pierre Buyoya.
Social Organizations: Workers' Union of Burundi (UTB)

THE STATE
Official Name: Républika y'Uburundi.
Administrative divisions: 15 Provinces.
Capital: Bujumbura, 272,000 people (1992).
Other cities: Muhinga; Gitega, 21,000 people (1990).
Government: Pierre Buyoya, President since July 1996.
National Holiday: July 1, Independence (1962).
Armed Forces: 12,600.

multiparty constitution and called elections to be held in 1993. Buyoya, leading the Union for National Progress (UNAPRO) - with a majority of Tutsi leaders - was defeated by Melchior Ndadaye, from the opposing Democratic Front of Burundi (DEFROBU) composed mainly of Hutus.
[14] On October 24 1993, three months after he was elected, Ndadaye was assassinated during an attempted coup. Prime Minister Sylvie Kinigi, who sought asylum in the French embassy, managed to keep the situation under control. The leaders of the rebellion were either arrested or fled to Zaire. Cyprien Ntaryamira - a Hutu like Ndadaye - was appointed president by the Parliament.
[15] In spite of the failed coup, the assassination of Ndadaye led to one of the worst massacres in

Burundi's history. Supporters of the ex-president attacked UNAPRO members - Tutsis or Hutus - causing the death of tens of thousands of people and the flight of some 700,000. The so-called "extremist armed militias" - hostile to cohabiting with the other ethnic group - were consolidated by this time, as were the "Undefeated" Tutsis or the "Intagohekas" ("those who never sleep") Hutus. Violence began to spread.
[16] On April 6 1994, Ntaryamira died along with Rwandan president Juvenal Habyarimana when their plane was shot down in Kigali, capital of Rwanda. Another Hutu, Sylvestre Ntibantunganya, replaced the assassinated president. Violence was intensified, especially between militias in favour of "Hutu power" and the army, controlled by Tutsi officers.

[17] In February 1995, UNAPRO left the government to force Prime Minister Anatole Kanyenkiko to resign. His resignation enabled the nomination of Tutsi Antoine Nduwayo and the return of UNAPRO to the coalition government which it had been part of along with DEFROBU.
[18] The number of "domestic refugees" continued on the rise in 1996. Many Tutsis fled to the cities, seeking protection from the army, while thousands of Hutu peasants - willingly or not - left with the guerrillas toward mountain or jungle regions. Pierre Buyoya led a successful coup in July 1996 to become Burundi's new president.
[19] Fearing that the Burundian conflict would extend to neighbouring countries, the UN and the Organization for African Unity decided to intervene. Buyoya, claiming the need to prevent an intervention by inter-African forces in the country, staged a successful coup in July 1996 and became the new president of Burundi. After this action, Ethiopia, Kenya, Rwanda, Tanzania, Uganda and Zaire (now DR Congo) imposed sanctions on Bujumbura. In mid-September,

Hutu rebels reported the killing by the army of 10,000 civilians after the coup. A similar number was killed the following year, although Amnesty International considered it was very difficult to distinguish between government and rebel responsibility in these massacres.
[20] In late 1997, Sergio Pinheiro, special UN monitor, confirmed that international sanctions had had devastating effects, significantly degrading the life conditions of poor Burundians and requested the revision of the embargo's usefulness. Meanwhile, peace negotiations promoted by mediator Julius Nyerere, former Tanzanian president, had reached a stalemate. Relations between Burundi and Tanzania were significantly impaired and both accused each other of trespassing across their respective frontiers. In September, Buyoya accused Tanzania of protecting more than 200,000 Hutu rebels and of intending to "annex" Burundi. In October, Bujumbura reported the attacks of Tanzanian forces in the southern towns of Kubonga and Mugina. In February 1998, the number of victims of the civil war was estimated at more than 250,000.

Cambodia

Cambodia

Population: 10,273,000 (1996)
Area: 181,035 SQ KM
Capital: Phnom Penh (Phnum Pénh)

Currency: Riels
Language: Khmer

The land of Cambodia takes its name from a *rishi* (sage), for the first Cambodian kings proclaimed themselves descendents from the great sage Cambu Svayambhuva. The first kingdom of Cambodia was known, in Chinese texts, under the name of Funan and was founded by the Mon and Khmer peoples who migrated from the North in the first century AD. During these first centuries, there was high Indian influence. By that time, Indian and Chinese pilgrims used to stop in today's Cambodian coasts to exchange silk and metals for spices and aromatic wood and gold.

2   During the 2nd and 3rd century Khmer rulers used to offer presents to Chinese emperors. Chinese sources reveal the scope of Indian influence by the example of the sage Kaundimnya, who married princess Soma, of Nagi origin (that is, semi-divine) and transformed the Khmer institutions along Indian lines. One of the modifications was probably the introduction of large-scale irrigation, which allowed the production of up to three rice harvests a year. Also the worship of the Indian god Shiva, who was considered a guardian ancestor and the spirit of land by the Khmer.

3   According to Chinese writings, the Funan created a centralized state machinery, headed by an absolute ruler. This ruler ran agricultural labor and used farming surpluses to maintain his life style and that of a caste of priests, and also to build fortresses, palaces and temples.

4   The first Sanskrit writings date from the 6th century and the first ones found in the Khmer language are from the 7th century. The

developments between the decline of Funan and the foundation, three centuries later, of a new centralized State in the Cambodian north-eastern region (called Chenla in Chinese texts of that period) have not been fully documented as yet. Chinese sources point out the existence of at least two Cambodian kingdoms, which - under the sovereignty of the Java kingdom - requested recognition from China. In the meantime, Sanskrit and Khmer sources cite the existence, during the 7th, 8th and 9th century, of multiple kingdoms that paid homage and fealty to the Java kingdom.

5   In 790 AD, a Cambodian prince, born and raised in the Javanese court of the Sailendra dynasty, proclaimed himself descendant of the Funan rulers. He declared the Khmer territory independent from Java and was crowned Prince Jayavarman II. During the following decade, Jayavarman extended his power north, controlling vassal states. In 802, he was named again, this time Chakravartin (a Sanskrit term meaning 'world ruler'). Jayavarman was the first "national" king of Cambodia.

6   In the year of 887 Indravarman I usurped the throne that belonged to his cousin Jayavarman III. During his reign, a large dam surrounding the capital city Roluos was built. This was the first of a vast system of dams, channels and irrigation canals that turned these lands productive and which would later allow the Khmer to maintain a densely populated and centralized state in the area, which otherwise would have become infertile. Two years later, Yasovarman I became the king of Khmer and commenced the construction of Angkor city (then called Yasodharapura), which turned into the capital of the Khmer empire. In 1002, Suryavarman I usurped the throne and extended the kingdom of Angkor to parts of today's territories of Thailand and Laos. In 1080, after Angkor had been conquered by the kingdom of Champa, a Khmer ruler of a northern province proclaimed himself king under the name of Javayarman VI, ruling the kingdom from his home province rather than from Angkor.

7   In 1177 Angkor was conquered once again by Champa forces.

Jayavarman XII became king in 1181 and conquered Vijaya, capital of Champa (in present-day Vietnam). Under his rule, the Khmer kingdom reached its height, virtually including the whole of today's Thailand and Laos and even reaching Myanmar/Burma, Malaysia and Vietnam. Jayavarman XII converted from Hinduism to Buddhism, which became the national religion.

8   In 1200, work began on building the new capital city of Angkor Thom. This undertaking depleted the royal coffers and the kingdom experienced economic problems during the subsequent decades. The decline of Angkor coincided with the rise of the Thai kingdom to the west and the Vietnamese one to the east. Turned into a small buffer state between both, the Khmer kingdom alternately depended on the power of the Thais or the Vietnamese. In order to free itself from the domination of one conqueror it needed the help of the other, who in turn demanded the subjugation of the Khmer people in compensation. In 1432, after the Thais conquered Angkor once again, the Khmer abandoned the city.

9   During more than 400 years,

the kingdom was alternately conquered by the Thai and Vietnamese forces. This changed in 1864, when Cambodian king Norodom accepted the status of French "protectorate" for his country, in the hope that the French would prevent further annexations. The French were not able to prevent the Siamese (Thais) from temporarily annexing some west Cambodian areas, including the city of Battambang. However, by recognizing the French authority, King Norodom managed to prevent the country from being divided and distributed between Vietnamese and Siam (Thailand). During the previous centuries, Vietnam had taken control of large tracts of Cambodia. The Mekong Delta and the area around Ho Chi Minh City (formerly Saigon) had been inhabited by Cambodians until the 18th century.

10   In 1884, with the consent of King Norodom, Cambodia became a French colony. France's political influence increased and, together with Vietnam and Laos, Cambodia became a part of the Indo-Chinese Union. During the following decades, the colonial empire installed a European administrative system in Cambodia and developed

PER 100,000
LIVE BIRTHS

900

65%

STATISTICS

DEMOGRAPHY
Population: 10,273,000 (1996) **Annual growth:** 2.9% (1980/1996) **Estimates for year 2000:** 11,200,000 **Annual growth to year 2000:** 2.3% (1994/2000) **Urban Population:** 21.0% (1996) **Urban growth:** 6.66% (1980/95) **Children per woman:** 4.6 (1996).

HEALTH
Life expectancy at birth: 53 years (1996) **Infant mortality:** 108 per 1,000 (1996) **Under-5 child mortality:** 170 per 1,000 (1996) **Calorie consumption:** 96% (1988/90) **Safe water:** 36% (1990/96).

EDUCATION
Literacy: 65% (1995) male : 80% (1995) female: 53% (1995) **School enrolment** : Primary total: 118% (1990/95) male : 130% (1990/95) female: 106% (1990/95) Secondary: male : 31% (1990/95) female: 18% (1990/95) Tertiary: 2% (1995) **Primary school teachers:** one for every 45 students (1995).

COMMUNICATIONS
108 **radios**, 10 **TV sets** and 1 **main telephone lines** per 1,000 people (1994).

ECONOMY
Per capita, GNP: $ 300 (1996) **Annual growth, GNP:** 3.9% (1995/96) **Currency:** 2,526 riels = $ 1 (1995) **Cereal imports:** 58 metric tons (1994) **Food import dependency:** 9% (1994) **Fertilizer use:** 33 kgs per ha (1994) **Exports:** $ 300 million (1996) **Imports:** $ 1,647 million (1996) **External debt:** $ 2,111 million (1996) $ 205 **per capita:** (1996) **Debt service:** 1.2% of exports (1996) **Development aid received:** $ 567 million (1995) $ 57 per capita (1995) 24.4% of GNP (1994).

ENERGY
Consumption: 52.43 Kgs of Oil equivalent per capita yearly (1994) 95.70% imported (1994)

HDI (rank / value) 153 / 0.348 (1994)

PROFILE

Environment
The territory is mainly a plain surrounded by mountains, like the Cardamour Mountains in the southwest. In the north, the Dangrek range rises abruptly from the plain. The central basin of the country, occupied by the Tonle Sap (Great Lake) depression, is the point of confluence into the Mekong, one of the largest rivers in Asia. The country has a sub-tropical climate with monsoon rains. The population is concentrated in the central basin where rice, the mainstay of the diet and principal export crop, is grown. The country also exports rubber. The mineral reserves: phosphate, iron ore and limestone, are as yet unexploited. The main environmental problem is massive logging being carried out by foreign companies and the media, which if unchecked destroy all the remaining forests in under a decade.

SOCIETY
Peoples: Mostly Khmers. The Khmers inhabit an area that extends beyond the present boundaries of Cambodia. There are Vietnamese and Chinese minorities.
Religions: In 1986 Buddhism - the religion of the majority - became the country's official religion. There is an Islamic minority (Cham).
Languages: Khmer, official and predominant.
Political Parties: United National Front for an Independent, Neutral, Peaceful and Cooperative Cambodia (Funcinpec); Cambodian People's Party; Liberal Democratic Buddhist Party; National Liberation Movement of Cambodia.

THE STATE
Official Name: Preach Reach Ana Pak Kampuchea
Administrative divisions: 22 provinces.
Capital: Phnom Penh (Phnum Pénh), est. 540,000 people (1994).
Other cities: Battambang 45,000; Kompong Cham 33,000 (1989).
Government: Parliamentary monarchy. Norodom Sihanouk, King. Ung Hout, First Prime Minister; since 1997. Hun Sen, Second Prime Minister. The legislature is made up of a 120-member National Assembly, in which representatives hold 5-year terms.
National Holiday: November 9, Independence Day (1953).
Armed Forces: 88,500.

the country's infrastructure. However the economic development - or exploitation - of the French Indo-Chinese Union did not reach the levels attained by Burma or India under British rule.
[11] After France was invaded by Germany during World War II, Japanese forces occupied Indochina in September 1940. What this actually meant was that the Japanese were able to use the military facilities in exchange for allowing France to maintain administrative control. As a result Cambodia suffered less damage duirng the War than the South Pacific islands, which were fiercely disputed by opposing forces.
[12] In 1941, French authorities appointed the 18-year-old prince Norodom Sihanouk as king of Cambodia, in the hope of easily controlling the politics of an inexperienced youngster. However, when the Japanese invaders withdrew, on March 12 1945, Norodom Sihanouk declared independence. But the French occupied Indochina again. While Vietnam began an anti-colonial war, in Cambodia the King managed to gain greater autonomy from France.
[13] In 1947, a new constitution kept King Sihanouk on the throne. However his power was limited by parliament. In 1949, negotiations with France resulted in Cambodian independence "within the French union", with Paris retaining control over military and foreign affairs. In 1953, the Vietnamese offensive forced French troops to withdraw from Cambodia, leaving the country fully independent. In 1955, Sihanouk abdicated in favor of his father, changing his name to Prince Sihanouk so that he could participate in political life. From 1960 onwards, Sihanouk became head of state.
[14] During the first years of US aggression against Vietnam, the Cambodian Government sought to maintain political and territorial neutrality. In 1965 however, following air raids by US-controlled South Vietnamese forces against North Vietnamese troop sanctuaries, Cambodia broke off relations with the US and moved closer towards the Chinese/Russian camp. Prince Sihanouk lost the 1966 elections to right-winger General Lon Nol who was later toppled during left-wing demonstrations. Sihanouk resumed power. In 1968 the US began launching regular air raids on the so-called "Ho Chi Minh trail" through Cambodian territory, allegedly supplying the Viet Cong from North Vietnam.
[15] While taking diplomatic action abroad to protect his country's sovereignty, Sihanouk was ousted in a coup and replaced again by Lon Nol. During his five-year rule, Lon Nol received $1.6 billion in aid from Washington. During that period, US forces intervened in Cambodia to bomb the Communist Khmer Rouge guerrillas and Vietnamese sanctuaries. In four years of bombing about 50,000 were killed. Sihanouk went into exile in China.
[16] From exile in Beijing, and supported by the Khmer Rouge, Sihanouk organized the National United Front of Kampuchea (NUFK) using the name of the country in Khmer language. By 1972, the NUFK was in control of 85 per cent of Cambodian territory, and its forces closed in on the capital, Phnom Penh (Phnum Pénh).
[17] In 1975, the Khmer Rouge seized power. Lon Nol fled and the kingdom became the the Democratic Republic of Kampuchea with Sihanouk as head of government. In 1976, while a new Constitution was being approved, the People's Congress confirmed Khieu Sampham as head of state with Pol Pot as Prime Minister. However, on his return from exile, Sihanouk was forced to resign and kept under house arrest, while Pol Pot rose to the fore as the regime's new leading force.
[18] Under Pol Pot, the country was completely sealed off from the outside world. Borders were closed and diplomats were not allowed to leave their embassies. Determined to build an unprecedented social system, Pol Pot eliminated money and transferred large numbers of

the urban population to the countryside, enforcing the return to an agricultural lifestyle. Mass purges and executions, hunger and illness, left at least a million people dead.

[19] The Pol Pot regime strengthened ties with China, broke off diplomatic relations with Hanoi, refused to recognize borders "established by colonialism" and sent Khmer Rouge troops to invade Vietnamese territory in late 1977. The disputed borders had been established in 1973 by agreement between Vietnam and Sihanouk, as historical records could provide no exact basis for establishing boundaries.

[20] The UN recognized the Khmer Rouge Government in 1978. The same year, Vietnam invaded to try and oust Pol Pot. In December 1978, when this border war was on the verge of being won by Vietnam, the United Front for the Salvation of Kampuchea was created under the presidency of General Heng Samrin. On January 11 1979, the Vietnamese forces and those of the United Front entered Phnom Penh and proclaimed the People's Republic of Kampuchea (PRK). A People's Revolutionary Council was established, and the Government began the enormous task of rebuilding a hungry and devastated nation.

[21] Heng Samrin's government defined its policy as being one of "independence, non-alignment and democracy directed toward socialism". Pol Pot was tried in absentia for war crimes, and his forces turned to guerrilla warfare. With the support of China and the United States, the Khmer Rouge managed to maintain UN recognition as the country's legitimate government. In 1982, Sihanouk and the Khmer Serei, led by Son Sann, joined former head of state Khieu Samphan's opposition government-in-exile.

[22] One of the main goals of Heng Samrim's government was to reactivate the industrial, agricultural and transportation sectors. The Soviet Union, and other socialist countries gave aid which was focused on the reconstruction of power sources and the formation of a very basic industrial infrastructure.

[23] In March and April 1981 municipal and legislative elections were held, with many candidates for each post. The Non-Aligned Movement summit meeting at the time in New Delhi did not support any of the contending groups. Faced with a wide set of electoral options, Cambodia's seat in the movement was left vacant.

[24] In July 1985, the Vietnamese announced that their 150,000 troops would gradually be withdrawn from Cambodia over the following five years.

[25] Difficulties stemming from the war affected the Phnom Penh Government, and it was only officially recognized by some 30 countries. Still, it managed to bring about a steady increase in the production of rice, cattle, pigs and poultry.

[26] In 1986, the Government began overtures toward Sihanouk within the context of a general agreement, offering him the position of head of state in a government from which the Khmer Rouge would be excluded. From the end of 1987 to mid-1989, Hun Sen, who had become prime minister, met with Sihanouk on six different occasions. The main disagreement each time was whether the Khmer Rouge would be admitted to a new provisional government or not.

[27] During the course of 1989, a curfew in effect since 1979 was lifted and private ownership of some "non-strategic" enterprises was permitted. In addition, collective farms passed into the hands of peasant families, with the assurance that the land could henceforth be passed on from generation to generation, and transportation services were privatized. On June 1 1989, to complete the diplomatic offensive and improve its image, the country changed its name to the State of Cambodia. After a meeting between Hun Sen and the new Thai prime minister, Chatichai Choonhavan, the possibilities of regional agreement and economic relations between the countries improved.

[28] The International Conference for Peace in Cambodia, held in Paris in July 1989, ended in failure as the three factions of the armed opposition could not come to any agreement. The two main points of disagreement were UN monitoring of the Vietnamese withdrawal and Khmer Rouge participation in government. Even without this agreement, Vietnamese troops withdrew completely in September, as planned, followed by an advance in the position of rebel forces.

[29] In April 1990, after a military offensive by Heng Samrin and Hun Sen's government soldiers, the opposition forces retreated to the Thai border. With this development, the Thai Premier, Chatichai Choonhavan, sponsored a new meeting between Sihanouk and Hun Sen. In Bangkok, both leaders agreed to the installation of a supranational agency which would symbolize the sovereignty and national unity of Cambodia. An "adequate" UN presence was also agreed to by both parties.

[30] In July 1990, the US announced they would recognize the State of Cambodia and would initiate negotiations with Vietnam over a peace settlement.

[31] In October 1991, a peace treaty was signed. The Supreme National Council was created, with representatives of the Phnom Penh government and part of the opposition, it was chaired by Sihanouk and was to govern the country until elections in 1993. In 1992, the UN sent a peacekeeping force consisting of 20,000 troops to enforce the cease-fire and organize the elections. To many observers' horror, the Khmer Rouge was included in the UN operation as a legitimate 'warring faction'. This enabled them to gain respectability over time, rehabilitating their reputation.

[32] In the constituent elections of May 1993, boycotted by the Khmer Rouge, the United National Front for an Independent, Neutral, Peaceful and Cooperative Cambodia (Funcinpec) party supporters led by Sihanouk's son Norodom Ranariddh won 58 seats. The former Cambodian People's Communist Party gained 51, the Liberal Democratic Party 10, and the National Liberation Movement of Cambodia, one. In the new government, Ranariddh and Hun Sen shared the post of prime minister.

[33] In September 1993, a new Constitution was enacted. It turned the National Assembly into a Parliament and established a parliamentary monarchy. Sihanouk was appointed king, "independent" of all political parties. But he continued to advocate a "national reconciliation" government, with the inclusion of the Khmer Rouge.

[34] In 1995, fighting intensified between the official army and the Khmer Rouge, which controlled about 15 per cent of the territory. The IMF expressed its faith in the country's economy, which grew 7 per cent in 1995 according to the government.

[35] In 1996, the Khmer Rouge began to show signs of weakness. The rumours of Pol Pot's death in June were construed as an indication of the existence of significant divisions within the guerrilla movement. Many defections - like Ieng Sary's (a leader of the armed group) in August - suggested that the government policy aim of splitting the Khmer Rouge was proving successful.

[36] Accused of treason and of planning a civil war alongside the Khmer Rouge, Prince Ranariddh was ousted in July 1997 by Cambodian army officials loyal to the second prime minister Hun Sen. From China, King Sihanouk approved Hun Sen's proposal to appoint foreign minister Ung Huot, from Funcinpec, to the position of first prime minister, in place of Ranariddh. In March, 1998 the monarch pardoned his son - who had been sentenced to a 30-year prison term - a decision regarded as an attempt to delay the political chaos which followed Ranariddh's expulsion and as a means to secure international financial aid which had been interrupted since the July 1997 coup.

[37] In spite of international efforts to rebuild Cambodian society, the lack of punishment of officials involved in serious human rights violations remained unchanged. Amnesty International reported the killing of hundreds of opposition members and the persistence of an incompetent, weak and corrupt judicial system.

[38] Pol Pot died in Thailand on April 15 1998, never having stood trial. He left behind a devastated country which was still recovering from his years in power. Peaceful elections returned Hun Sen's party to power in July 1998.

Cameroon

Cameroun

Population:	13,560,000 (1996)
Area:	475,442 SQ KM
Capital:	Yaoundé
Currency:	CFA francs
Language:	French and English

The area known as Cameroon is the birthplace and original homeland of the Bantu ethnic group, which after 200 BC migrated east and south, spreading new crop varieties and methods for working iron. In 1472 Fernando Po named a river Camarones (Portugese for shrimp) because of the crustaceans swarming at its mouth. The name eventually became Cameroon.

[2] The Fulah migration (see Niger: Routes of the Sahara; also, Senegal: The Fulah States) helped transform the local economies into part of a regional circuit which later gave rise to the Emirate of Adamaua in the north central region.

[3] German penetration began in June 1884 when German envoy Gustav Nachtigal signed an agreement with the ruler of the Doualas, a coastal group, making the region a protectorate. A year later, the Berlin Conference awarded Cameroon to Germany. But the Emirate of Adamaua, which the British wanted, was not given to the Germans until 1894.

[4] This protectorate did not survive very long. The Doualas dominated trade that the Germans wanted to control between the coast and Yaoundé, the trade center between Adamaua and the south. In 1897, the Doualas resisted German interference, and a bloody four-year war ensued.

[5] The Germans appropriated the most fertile lands, and the Africans began to die of hunger by the thousands, in an area where stable agriculture had existed for centuries. In 1918 France and Britain invaded Cameroon: the French taking three-fourths, and the English taking the rest. The pro-independence organizations found their cause was facilitated by the tensions among the colonial

powers. In 1945, the People's Union of Cameroon (UPC) was founded, headed by Rubem Um Nyobé. The UPC earned popular support and launched a series of legal campaigns between 1948 and 1956, when it was outlawed.

[6] Nationalist leaders fled to the British held western sector and organized a guerrilla movement. The UPC established liberated zones in the southern forests, where they set up their own administration, a first for sub-Saharan Africa. The efficiency of the guerrillas made it possible for them to resist constant French attacks, until 1960. Two years later, Rubem Um Nyobé died, but the revolution continued.

[7] UPC resistance forced the French to adopt a new strategy, adding political manoeuvres to their repressive tactics. Paris created the National Union of Cameroon (UNC), merging two conservative, predominantly Islamic, northern-based parties. UNC leader Alhaji Ahmadou Ahidjo gained power after the French granted the country independence, remaining so after a British plebiscite approved reunification. UPC nationalists were unable to help shape their long-held dream of an independent Cameroon as they were mostly underground or in exile.

[8] Ahidjo stepped up persecution of the opposition in the 1960s, developing one of sub-Saharan Africa's most efficient repressive systems. European human rights groups revealed the existence of thousands of political prisoners in the country. In 1982, Ahidjo suddenly resigned, and was succeeded by his former prime minister, Paul Biya.

[9] Biya maintained his

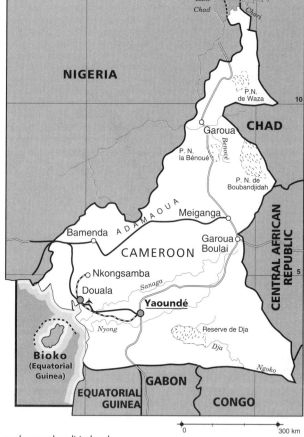

predecessor's political and economic policies, though many of Adhidjo's followers supported a coup attempt by a group of military officers. Young people, especially students, resisted the coup attempt by taking to the streets.

[10] Growing unemployment and food shortages undermined Cameroon's traditionally prosperous image. Biya attempted to reinforce his control by calling early elections for April 1984. With

democratic organizations prohibited, he was re-elected. Nevertheless, the overall instability of the country led to a new coup attempt, followed by a series of bloody incidents in which 200 people were killed.

[11] In the 1980s, the UNC changed its name to "Democratic Group of the People of Cameroon" (RDPC), but its political line remained the same.

[12] The UPC later adopted a more flexible stance in order to broaden its social scope, and Biya created new northern provinces to give the Muslims greater economic and political power. Disagreements over oil revenues aggravated inter-ethnic and inter-regional friction. Economic problems stemming from a drop in world commodity prices for coffee, rubber and cotton were aggravated by Cameroon's dependence on French companies which controlled almost 44 per cent of the export market.

PUBLIC EXPENDITURE

9.4%   29%

1995 ■ DEFENCE □ SOCIAL

In 1990/91 Military as % of health & education expenditure was 48%.

WORKERS

(1996)

Labour force %

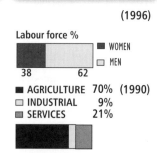

■ WOMEN	
□ MEN	
38	62

■ AGRICULTURE	70%	(1990)
□ INDUSTRIAL	9%	
■ SERVICES	21%	

LAND USE

DEFORESTATION -0.6% annual (81/90)
IRRIGATED 0.4 % of arable

(1993)

■ FOREST & WOODLAND	75.5%
□ ARABLE	12.5%
■ OTHER	12%

PROFILE

ENVIRONMENT

The country is divided into three regions: the plains of the Lake Chad basin in the northern region (savannas where cattle are raised and corn and cotton are grown); the central part, made up of humid grasslands; and the southern part, an area with rich volcanic soil where the main cash crops (coffee, bananas, cocoa and palm oil) are grown. It is in the latter that most of the population lives. Drought and desertification are the main concerns in the southern region, which covers 25 per cent of the nation's land area, and houses over a quarter of the population.

SOCIETY

Peoples: There are some 200 ethnic groups, the main ones being the Dualas, Bamilekes, Tikars and Bamauns in the south; the Euondos and Fulbes in the west, and the Fulanis in the north. In the southeast live the Baka Pygmies, who live by hunting and fishing. **Religions:** Half the population practice traditional African cults. Christians are a majority in the south while Muslims predominate in the north. **Languages:** French and English are the official languages. There are nearly one hundred African languages and dialects. **Political Parties:** Democratic Alliance of the People of Cameroon (RDPC); Movement for the Defense of the Republic; Social Democratic Front (FSD); National Union for Democracy and Progress (UNDP); Front of Allies for Change (FAC). **Social Organizations:** National Workers' Union of Cameroon.

THE STATE

Official Name: République du Cameroun. **Capital:** Yaoundé, 800,000 people (1993). **Other cities:** Douala, 1,000,600 people; Garoua 102,000 (1993). **Government:** Parliamentary republic. Paul Biya, President since 1982, re-elected in October 1997. Peter Musonge Mafani, Prime Minister since 1996. **National Holidays:** January 1, Independence Day (1960); October 1, Reunification (1961), May 20, proclamation of the Republic (1972). **Armed Forces:** 14,600.

STATISTICS

DEMOGRAPHY

Population: 13,560,000 (1996) **Annual growth:** 2.8% (1980/1996) **Estimates for year 2000:** 15,100,000 **Annual growth to year 2000:** 2.8% (1994/2000) **Urban Population:** 45.6% (1996) **Urban growth:** 5.33% (1980/95) **Children per woman:** 5.4 (1996).

HEALTH

Life expectancy at birth: 56 years (1996) male: 54 years (1994) female: 57 years (1994) **Infant mortality:** 63 per 1,000 (1996) **Under-5 child mortality:** 102 per 1,000 (1996) **Calorie consumption:** 95% (1988/90) 12,500 **people per doctor** (1988/91) **Safe water:** 50% (1990/96).

EDUCATION

Literacy: 63% (1995) male : 75% (1995) female: 52% (1995) **School enrolment :** Primary total: 89% (1990/95) male : 93% (1990/95) female: 84% (1990/95) Secondary: male : 32% (1990/95) female: 22% (1990/95) **Primary school teachers:** one for every 46 students (1995).

COMMUNICATIONS

148 **radios,** 80 **TV sets** and 4 **main telephone lines** per 1,000 people (1994)

ECONOMY

Per capita, GNP: $ 610 (1996) **Annual growth, GNP:** 4.5% (1995/96) **Annual inflation:** 1.95% (1985/95) **Currency:** 490 CFA francs = $ 1 (1995) **Cereal imports:** 226 metric tons (1994) **Food import dependency:** 11% (1994) **Fertilizer use:** 42 kgs per ha (1994) **Exports:** $ 1,758 million (1996) **Imports:** $ 1,204 million (1996) **External debt:** $ 9,515 million (1996) $ 702 **per capita:** (1996) **Debt service:** 23.6% of exports (1996) **Development aid received:** $ 444 million (1995) $ 35 per capita (1995) 6.5% of GNP (1994).

ENERGY

Consumption: 103.42 Kgs of Oil equivalent per capita yearly (1994) -333.10% imported (1994)

HDI (rank / value) 133 / 0.468 (1994)

[13] Biya was re-elected in 1988. Censorship increased, journalists were arrested and the post of prime minister was eliminated.

[14] Faced with the fall in oil prices on the world market and foreign debt payments, the Government sought World Bank and IMF support for a structural adjustment program to stabilize its finances. By reducing imports and state expenditure, privatizing public enterprises and reorganizing the banking system, the country's debts were renegotiated with the Paris Club.

[15] In 1990, social and political organizations reported an increase in government repression of hundreds of citizens.

[16] A few months later, the government authorized the creation of political parties: some 70 political organizations were granted legal recognition.

[17] In November 1991, opposition leaders demanded constitutional reform and a return to the federal system abolished in 1972. The political crisis deepened, strikes and pro-democracy demonstrations proliferated, 40 demonstrators were killed by the police.

[18] In December, the Government set the legislative elections for February 16 1992. The opposition wanted the constitution and electoral law be modified prior to the elections, nonetheless, several parties participated in the elections on March 1 1992.

[19] The RDPC won 88 of the 180 parliamentary seats. The National Union for Democracy and Progress (UNDP) came in second, with 68 representatives. According to the official report, 61 per cent of the four million registered electorate voted.

[20] Biya advanced the presidential election to October 11 1992. Seven parties fielded candidates: among them, the Social Democratic Front (FSD) led by John Fru Ndi, the main opposition party representing the English-speaking community. Both the FSD and the Democratic Union of Cameroon, led by Adamu Ndam Njoya, had boycotted the March elections.

[21] Amid widespread accusations of fraud, the Government's victory with 39.98 per cent over the FSD's 35.97, provoked incidents in the English-speaking Northwestern Province, Fru Ndi's territory.

[22] International observers confirmed the fraud, but the Supreme Court refused to annul the election. Fru Ndi proclaimed himself president, and the government decreed a state of emergency in the Northwest. Fru Ndi and his supporters were immediately placed under house arrest.

[23] In November a "coalition" government of the RDPC and minor groups was formed. Government repression intensified, bringing international condemnation. In December, four members of the Bar Association were arrested for leading a protest, one dying after being tortured. When the US suspended foreign aid, Biya cancelled the state of emergency and freed Fru Ndi.

[24] In January 1993, Finance Minister Antoine Ntsimi announced the reduction of civil servants' pay by between 4 and 20 per cent in order, he said, to avoid job cuts for 50,000 employees.

[25] A third of the nation's foreign trade depended on France. The maintenance of this trade link led the opposition to suggest a boycott on French products, stating that France supported Biya.

[26] In January 1993, Benjamin Menga, vice-president of the UDC, was assassinated. Several political leaders were imprisoned and press censorship was stepped up. In 1994, the schism in the opposition helped Biya's "firm hand" policy.

[27] On the economic front, Biya ignored opposition requests remaining in the CFA economic zone, despite the 100 per cent devaluation of the CFA imposed by Paris. Cameroon received funds from the IMF and the Paris Club after announcing far-reaching economic adjustment.

[28] In 1995, the opposition continued dividing. In May, Siga Assanga, former secretary general of Fru Ndi's Social Democratic Front abandoned this group to found the Social Democratic Movement. Meanwhile, the UNDP also suffered a split, following the expulsion of two members who had participated in Biya's governments.

[29] The results of the municipal elections in January 1996 consolidated Biya's power. In October 1997, Biya was re-elected, in elections questioned by the opposition parties, some of whom had called for a boycott on the election. Only three of the six million registered voters were called on to vote, as the others were excluded by the government which insisted they were "foreigners."

[30] In late 1997, opposition increased to a World Bank project to extract oil in southern Chad and to transport it to the Atlantic through Cameroon. Dozens of Non-Governmental Organizations called on the Bank to back social development projects instead.

[31] In March 1998, Cameroon and Nigeria appeared before the International Court in the Hague in a dispute over the Bakassi peninsula, with its rich fishing resources and supposedly extensive oil fields. The disagreement between the two States had led to several armed confrontations.

Canada

Canada

Population: 29,680,000 (1996)
Area: 9,970,610 SQ KM
Capital: Ottawa

Currency: Canadian dollars
Language: English and French

The first inhabitants of present-day Canada were Inuit and other people that had come from the Asian continent across the Bering Strait. The European colonists who came to North America in the 16th century estimated the indigenous population of the entire continent to be between 10 and 12 million.

[2] Between the 17th and 19th centuries, these territories were colonized by Britain and France. Some areas changed hands several times until 1763, when the Peace of Paris which ended the Seven Years' War granted Canada to Britain. Colonization increased thanks to the profitable fur trade, with the local population growing to almost half a million by the end of the 19th century.

[3] The British North America Act of 1867 determined that the Canadian constitution would be similar to Britain's, with executive power vested in the King and delegated to a Governor General and Council. The legislative function would, meanwhile, be carried out by a Parliament composed of a Senate and a House of Commons.

[4] In 1931, the Statute of Westminster released Britain's dominions from the colonial laws under which they had been governed, giving Canada legislative autonomy. That same year, Norway recognized Canadian sovereignty over the Arctic regions to the north of the main part of its territory.

[5] In 1981, the Canadian Government reached an agreement with the British Parliament over the initiation of a constitutional transition. The following year, the 1867 Constitution was replaced by the Act of Canada, which granted Canada the autonomy to reform the constitution.

[6] The Constitution Act of 1982 included a Charter of Rights and Freedoms, which recognized the country's pluralistic heritage and the rights of its indigenous peoples. It set forth the principle of equal benefits among the country's ten provinces, and the sovereignty of each province over its own natural resources, though Quebec did not sign the agreement.

[7] When Quebec was occupied by English Protestants in 1760, its predominantly French population sought to maintain a separate Quebecois identity, marked by both religious and political nationalism. Quebec thus assumed a special role as guardian of the Catholic faith, the French language and the French heritage in North America. It was a role which it performed well. From a French population of 6,000 in 1769, the number of "Québecois" had increased to 6 million by 1960.

[8] In Quebec, four-fifths of the population speak French as a first language and are fiercely proud of their cultural identity, and provincial autonomy has always been a delicate issue. In 1977, the government of the separatist Parti Québécois (PQ), led by René Lévesque, adopted French as the official language of education, business and local public administration.

[9] Lévesque discarded the possibility of a unilateral separation proposing instead a concept of "sovereignty-association", with a monetary and customs union. However, voters rejected this proposal by 59.5 to 40.5 per cent, in a plebiscite held in 1980. Fifteen years later, in a new plebiscite favoured by the Parti Québécois, the margin was narrowed down: 50.4 per cent of voters opposed separation and 49.6 per cent approved it.

[10] Antiquated British law governed relations between the sexes in North America for a long time, and it was not until October 1929 that Canadian women obtained full legal rights, and it was only under the 1982 Constitution that true legal sexual equality was established.

[11] In addition to the federal law, each province has an equal rights law, guaranteeing access to housing, jobs, services and other facilities, without discrimination on the basis of race, religion, age, nationality or sex, though Quebec is the only province which prohibits discrimination on the basis of "sexual inversion", their terminology for homosexuality. A regent supreme court decision extended protection against discrimination based on sexual preference.

[12] Nevertheless, women are still the victims of much discrimination. Not all professions are open to them, and in a great many professional fields they must accept lower salaries. Between 1969 and 1979, there was a 62 per cent increase in the number of women working outside the home. By 1981, this figure represented 49 per cent of all women, and 39 per cent of the economically active population.

[13] Liberal governments, led by Pierre Trudeau, were elected in 1968, 1972, 1974 and again in 1980, after a brief Conservative interlude. Trudeau loosened Canada's traditional ties with Western Europe and the United States, and strengthened those with the Far East, Africa and Latin America. In addition, he refused to participate in the economic blockade against Cuba.

[14] Economic difficulties stemming from the worldwide recession triggered a sharp drop in the Liberal Party's popularity, in favour of the Conservative Party. In 1983, Conservative leader Brian Mulroney, a labour relations

PUBLIC EXPENDITURE

10.8%
n/a
1995 ■ DEFENCE □ SOCIAL

In **1990/91** Military as % of health & education expenditure was 15%.

WORKERS

UNEMPLOYMENT 9.7% (1996)

Labour force %
■ WOMEN
□ MEN
45   55

■ AGRICULTURE   3% (1990)
□ INDUSTRIAL   25%
■ SERVICES   71%

LAND USE

IRRIGATED   1.6 %   of arable

(1993)

■ FOREST & WOODLAND 49.5%
□ ARABLE   4.6%
■ OTHER   45.9%

Maternal Mortality	Foreign Trade
1990	MILLIONS $ 1996

PER 100,000
LIVE BIRTHS

6

IMPORTS
170,265
EXPORTS
199,071

PROFILE

ENVIRONMENT
Canada is the second largest country in the world in land area, divided into five natural regions. The Maritime Provinces along the Atlantic coast are a mixture of rich agricultural land and forests. The Canadian Shield is a rocky region which is covered with woods and is rich in minerals.
To the south, along the shores of the Great Lakes and the St Lawrence River, there is a large plain with fertile farmlands, where over 60 per cent of the population is concentrated, and the major urban centres are located. Farming (wheat, oats and rye), is the mainstay of the Central Prairie Provinces. The Pacific Coast is a mountainous region with vast forests. The "Great North" is almost uninhabited, with very cold climate and tundra. There are ten provinces, and two territories; the Yukon and Northwest. These are working towards provincial status, but this is complicated by Native Land claims. Canada has immense mineral resources; it is the world's largest producer of asbestos, nickel, zinc and silver and the second largest of uranium. There are also major lead, copper, gold, iron ore, gas and oil deposits. Its industry is highly developed. Industrial emissions from Canadian and US plants contribute to the "acid rain" which has affected thousands of lakes. The construction of a number of hydroelectric plants in Quebec is threatening to destroy the lands and livelihood of the indigenous population.

SOCIETY
Peoples: There are about 850,000 Native Americans, "Metis" (mixed race) and Inuit ("Eskimos") ranging from highly acculturated city-dwellers to traditional hunters and trappers living in isolated northern communities. There are six distinct culture areas and ten language families; many native languages such as Cree and Ojibwa are still widely spoken. About 350,000 native people are classified as such: that is, they belong to one of 573 registered groups and can live on a federally protected reserve (though only about 70 per cent actually do so). "Metis" and those who do not have official status as "native people" have historically enjoyed no separate legal recognition, but attempts are now being made to secure them special rights under the law. The original European settlers came from France, England and Scotland. Today Canada is multicultural with many people from Asia, the Caribbean and southern Europe.
Languages: English and French, both official. 13 per cent of the population is bilingual, 67 per cent speak only English, 18 per cent only French, and 2 per cent speak other languages (Italian, German and Ukranian).
Religions: Roman Catholic 45.7 per cent; Protestant 36.3 per cent; Eastern Orthodox 1.5 per cent; Jewish 1.2 per cent; Muslim 1.0 per cent; Buddhist 0.7 per cent; Hindu 0.6 per cent; nonreligious 12.4 per cent; other 0.6 per cent.
Political Parties: The Liberal Party; the Conservative Party; Bloque Québecois; the New Democratic Party, and the Reform Party.
Social Organizations: The Canadian Labour Congress, with over two million members, is the largest trade union; The Assembly of First Nations; the Council of Canadians; National Status of Women Committee.

THE STATE
Official Name: Canada.
Administrative Divisions: 10 Provinces and 2 Territories.
Capital: Ottawa, 780,000 people (1994).
Other cities: Toronto, 4,500,000 people; Montreal, 2,950,000; Vancouver, 1,500,000 (1994).
Government: Roméo LeBlanc, Governor-General. Jean Chrétien, Prime Minister and Head of Government since November 1993. Canada is a federation of ten provinces and a member of the British Commonwealth. The system of Government is parliamentary.
National Holiday: July 1, Canada Day (1867).

lawyer and businessman from Quebec became prime minister, replacing John Turner, who had succeeded Trudeau as head of the Liberal Party.
[15] Mulroney re-established a "special relationship" between Canada and the United States, with the initiation of negotiations for a free trade agreement in 1985. This agreement, which went into effect in January 1989, provoked criticism from the Liberals and other members of the opposition, who claimed that the terms of the agreement were overly favourable to the US. Nevertheless, it received majority support from the voters in the 1988 election.
[16] The Conservative victory was made possible by the Québecois votes, reflecting the growing economic importance of French-speaking voters. This victory also reflected the impact of the Meech Lake Accord, initiated by Mulroney and signed in 1987, in which the federal government ceded important powers to the provinces, granting Quebec recognition of its unique cultural status, for the first time in order for it to accept the constitution and Charter of Rights and Freedoms.
[17] To go into effect, the Meech Lake Accord had to be ratified by the unanimous consent of each of the provinces, and it was blocked by Newfoundland and Manitoba. In Manitoba the one vote against came from a Native American who would not accept the "distinct society" clause for Quebec, saying native people were every bit as distinct.
[18] The Northwest Territories (NWT) - which make up one-third of the country's land area with only 52,000 inhabitants, half of whom are Inuit or members of other indigenous groups - were considering the possibility of splitting into two regions, Nunavut and Denendeh, each with an autonomous government. While this plan was approved by the provincial legislature in 1987, it is subject to ratification by a plebiscite of its residents, and the Federal Government.
[19] The Federal Government declared its willingness to accept the right of the Inuit and other native peoples of the NWT to self-government, incorporating this

right into the Constitution if approved by the provincial governments and by organizations representing the interests of these peoples. In 1988, it transferred 673,000 sq km to the other native peoples and the Inuit. In 1992, representatives from the Federal and provincial governments signed an agreement on the land claims of 17,500 native peoples from the Northwest Territories. The way was paved for the creation of "Nunavut" ("Our Land" in Inuit), a project approved in a plebiscite held on April 4. Nunavut, which includes the area west of Hudson Bay and the Arctic archipelago, covers an area of 2.2 million sq km, equal to one fifth of the country. The agreement also included the transference of 350,000 sq km to the Inuit and the payment of $580 million as a counterpart for the waiver of future land claims.
[20] The Inuit from northwestern Canada have been working with other indigenous groups of Greenland and Alaska to deal with ecological, cultural, social and political problems which affect their nation. The Fifth Circumpolar Conference of the Inuit (CCI) in 1989 reaffirmed Inuit rights to lands which Canada considers government property, and leases out to large mining interests.
[21] Canada's first trading partner is the United States, and vice versa, but while the volume of Canada's sales to the US accounts for one-fifth of its total production, American exports to Canada represent less than 3 per cent. No other major Western economy maintains a trade imbalance of such magnitude; only comparable to the dependence of Southern countries with relation to the industrialized countries.
[22] With the free trade agreement which went into effect in 1989, Canada's integration with the American economy has been accentuated. Through trade, the extension of credit, and investments in Canada, the US has secured ever greater control over Canadian natural resources, and majority control over shares in some Canadian industries.
[23] A recession in the US means a recession in Canada; Ottawa's monetary policy is essentially defined by its neighbour's. This

degree of dependence has been labelled "colonial", despite the fact that Canada is the world's eighth largest industrial power, and that its standard of living is one of the highest in the world.
[24] The Canadian Armed Forces (CF) are charged with protecting

national interests both inside and outside the country, with defending North America in cooperation with the United States, and complying with its NATO commitments; in addition, it has participated in the UN Peacekeeping Forces.

²⁵ The Canadian Forces Europe (CFE) supplied the NATO Supreme Command with troops which were permanently stationed in Germany, including four Mobile Command Brigades and an air division, all of which maintained maximum operational readiness. They also participated in the United States intervention in Haiti in 1994.

²⁶ Relations between Canada and the United States became tense in 1985, when a US Coast Guard vessel passed through the Northwest Passage without Canadian authorization. The US recognizes Canadian sovereignty over the Arctic islands but not over its waters; a similar dispute exists with relation to the waters surrounding the French islands of St Pierre and Miquelon.

²⁷ Canada has made little headway in getting the US to control industrial gas emissions, which drift over Canadian territory, bringing with them acid rain, or in reaching agreement on catch limits for the shared west coast salmon fishery.

²⁸ The Canadian Government has made a commitment to reduce its own industrial emissions by half. This program, which has already gone into effect, anticipates a reduction in industrial pollution of 20 per cent by the year 2005.

²⁹ In 1991, Quebec's premier Robert Bourassa initiated the second phase of the huge James Bay Power Project, which involves damming or diverting nine rivers which flow along 350,000 km of the northwestern part of the province, emptying into the James and Hudson Bays.

³⁰ The first phase, called "La Grande", is capable of generating 10,282 megawatts of hydro-electric power, and once the project is completed, it will reach a capacity of 27,000 megawatts, far greater than the output of Itaipu Dam, in Brazil, or that of Three Gorges Dam in China.

³¹ The region affected by the projects is located in the hunting and fishing grounds of approximately 11,000 Cree and 7,000 Inuit, peoples who have lived in the area for over 5,000 years. This region contains the largest beluga whale population in the world, as well as the largest caribou herds and most of the world's fresh-water seals. Vast numbers of migratory birds make the extensive wetlands their home for several months each year.

³² In order to divert four of the rivers and build the dams and reservoirs, 13,000 sq km of land has been submerged. In 1984, 10,000 caribou died when water was released from one of La Grande's reservoirs.

³³ The completion of the second phase of the project will dam the rivers which empty into the aforementioned bays and will flood an additional 10,000 sq km of land. The project will allow Canada to sell electricity to the United States, set up plants for aluminium production in Quebec and guarantee an energy supply for Canadian consumption, which is among the highest in the world. The ecological consequences of this project on the regional ecosystem are unforeseeable.

³⁴ In 1973, hunting and fishing provided two-thirds of the local population's food, with this percentage dropping to one-fourth, twenty years later. A 1975 treaty allowed local people to retain a small part of their lands, granting some economic compensation for the loss of the rest of their territory. Even so, the chances of the local indigenous culture surviving the nationalistic ecocide of Quebec are severely limited.

³⁵ The Inuit, who inhabit the Belcher Islands in the Hudson Bay and navigate the frozen waters in search of fish and game, were not taken into account in these agreements, and they are very concerned about what effect these major changes will have upon the ecosystem, and their way of life.

³⁶ Canada's original inhabitants have been gradually becoming more organized and, between the 1960s and 1970s, these efforts culminated in the creation of the National Indian Brotherhood (NIB). The aim of this organization is to represent the indigenous peoples point of view to the general public, and also in making their grievances known to the federal government. Recently, the NIB was replaced by the Assembly of First Nations.

³⁷ The indigenous peoples are fighting for government respect of

The effects of the NAFTA

On January 1 1994, the governments of Canada, Mexico and the United States signed the document which brought NAFTA, the North American Free Trade Agreement, into existence. According to the terms of the agreement, the three countries would eliminate all customs and tariff restrictions between them, forming a common economic zone.

² The three partners, with a joint population of 370 million and a combined GNP of more than $6 trillion per year, pledged to eliminate some trade tariffs immediately, gradually doing away with the rest over a 15-year period. They also decided that the United States' and Mexico's most vulnerable industries would be eligible for protection for a longer period of time. According to the treaty, any of the members may withdraw from NAFTA, after giving six months' prior notice.

³ In the lead-up to the signing of the treaty US labour unions, fearful of job losses, demonstrated their resistance. There was a split vote in Congress between members of Bill Clinton's Democratic Party, with unions belonging to the AFL-CIO accusing the President of allowing the causes of unemployment to continue to grow. The majority of the Republican congress supported the agreement, which passed by a narrow margin in Congress.

⁴ The unions' fears were based on the fact that mean wages are 15 per cent lower in Mexico than in the United States. The large transnational companies receive enormous benefits by taking advantage of a labour force capable of operating First World technology at Third World wages.

⁵ Since the treaty went into effect, several Latin American countries have asked to join NAFTA: Chile, Colombia and Argentina have repeatedly offered to sign bilateral agreements with the new common market. There have been job losses in Canada associated with the NAFTA agreement.

⁶ Within NAFTA's projected framework, the three countries agreed to create the North American Development Bank. With funds totalling more than $3 billion, it will join other existing international credit agencies.

⁷ The common economic space created by NAFTA also meant a change in the hierarchy of relations between the United States and Latin America. Just as the European Community and Japan have clear, and almost exclusive, areas of commercial influence, the treaty offered the United States the possibility of privileged access to the mining and oil resources of Mexico.

⁸ In mid-1998, just when the United States was trying to extend NAFTA to all the Americas, opposition sectors in Mexico complained of the de-structuring of the nation's economy. Mexico had doubled the value of its exports, which had grown to $123 billion in 1997, exceeding the $116 billion of the Mercosur countries (Argentina, Brazil, Paraguay and Uruguay) and Chile. However, 80 per cent of the value of these exports was controlled by less than 300 companies, mostly transnationals, minimizing the impact of these exports in the local economy. Thus, in order for exports to reach the $123 billion sum the country was forced to import heavily, to a value of $121 billion that same year.

the treaties which affirm their rights to their land and resources. Those who live from hunting and fishing, like the Cree, the Dene, the Innu, the Inuit and the Haida, are especially vulnerable, facing multiple threats to their lands and traditional way of life.

[38] After World War II, the Government tried to restrict the Innu in Labrador to small reservations, and by the 1970s, most of them were living in areas designated for this purpose. Although Canada officially recognizes the claims of indigenous peoples over their lands, it has sought to reach agreements with individual groups, to set them up in smaller areas in exchange for economic compensation.

[39] The experience that has occurred in one generation of the Innu people has demonstrated that it is a mistake to accept these government propositions. A 1984 report revealed that the suicide rate among the communities in the North of Labrador is five times the national average. In 1988, in retribution, the Innu invaded the military base at Goose Bay, setting up a "peace camp".

[40] Four Innu charged with invading the base were unexpectedly released under the argument that, since land ownership is a concept which is alien to Canada's original inhabitants, it was not reasonable for the court to consider evidence based on British or Canadian legal norms. The Canadian government filed an immediate injunction, calling into question the validity of the judge's ruling, when it became obvious that this decision could set a precedent for land claims of the region's indigenous groups. In mid-1991, the International Task Force for Indian Affairs declared that the Canadian government was not respecting the rights of the Mohawk people to practise their religion, and denounced specific acts of cultural aggression such as the construction of a golf course on their communal lands.

[41] In late 1990, the Federal Parliament approved restrictive legislation with regard to the granting of refugee status, effective as of January 1991. The new legislation establishes that people fleeing persecution can now be returned to their country of origin if that country is considered to be "safe". Both the opposition and humanitarian organizations have accused the government of going "from one extreme to the other". The Government claimed that it had not closed its borders completely, as it authorized the selection of 13,000 refugees by its embassies abroad and also allowed

10,000 family members of foreign residents to enter. Canada remains a major destination for political refugees.

[42] In October 1991, Ottawa announced its decision to earmark some $700 million for the agricultural sector; however, farmers were not satisfied with this amount, considering it insufficient to compensate for the losses of the previous year. Farm subsidies by the governments of the United States and European countries have left Canadian farmers at a distinct disadvantage, as present policy is to pursue liberalized trade under the GATT agreement.

[43] In December 1991, the Canadian Minister of Finance stated that the country had registered its first trade deficit in 15 years (in September, the trade deficit was $275 million). The year was characterized by economic recession, high taxes, corruption scandals, increasing separatism and a decline in Mulroney's popularity.

[44] In early 1992, there was an intense debate over Quebec's growing demands for autonomy. In August, this province rejected the government's scheme for granting it "special" status, as the terms were considered "insufficient".

[45] On August 12 1992, after 18 months of negotiations, Canada, the United States and Mexico signed an agreement creating a free trade zone (North American Free Trade Agreement, NAFTA, see Box).

[46] In February 1993, Prime Minister Brian Mulroney decided to resign from the Conservative Party (and therefore from the Government) with the lowest popularity ratings ever. Earlier, in June, he had tried to take advantage of his 10-seat parliamentary majority to obtain ratification of NAFTA. But his resignation gave credit to the opposition's argument that key issues should be decided on before new elections.

[47] In June of the same year, Parliament ratified the NAFTA treaty. Two months later, the new prime minister travelled all over the country promoting the adoption of austerity measures to combat the budget deficit. In the meantime, her rival, Liberal Jean Chrétien, promised to give high priority to the creation of new jobs.

[48] In the October 1993 general elections, the Liberal Party (opposition) regained power after nine years, with a landslide victory over the Conservative Party, whose representation in the House of Commons dropped from 155 seats to 2. The Liberals won 178 seats, against 79 in the previous legislature. The separatist Bloque Québecois (54 seats) and

the right-of-center Reform Party (52 seats) both made significant gains. This was the worst defeat for a governing party in Canada's 126-year history.

[49] The new Prime Minister, Jean Chrétien, took office on November 4 1993. The following month, former prime minister Kim Campbell resigned from her post as leader of the Conservative Party.

[50] The reduction in the public deficit and State spending, the increase in unemployment to more than 10 per cent and the separatist tendencies in Quebec were the main Government concerns during 1994 and 1995.

[51] The Parti Québecois (PQ) brought up the possible secession of Quebec from Canada again in 1994. The popularity of Prime Minister Chrétien had increased 13 per cent since the 1993 elections, but the PQ triumphed in the province of Quebec. The new provincial Premier, Jacques Parizeau, promised to do everything possible to make Quebec a sovereign state.

[52] The geopolitical context of NAFTA, which came into force on January 1 1994, meant that the Quebec issue was followed with great attention in Mexico and the US, even though the PQ had

promised that the province would meet the obligations assumed by Canada. However on October 30 1995, separation was rejected by 50.6 per cent of the electorate.

[53] The Quebec secession threat faded in 1996, despite the high number of votes received by the separatist option. The federal government transferred some powers to the provinces in an attempt to calm the nationalist movement. Lucien Bouchard, leader of the separatist forces, replaced Parizeau as Premier of Quebec when the latter resigned following the referendum defeat. Unemployment continued to rise in 1996, despite the economic growth. Disagreements continued throughout the year with the United States over Canadian companies dealing with Cuba.

[54] In June 1997, Chrétien's Party won the parliamentary elections, gaining 155 of the 301 seats, followed by the Reform Party and the PQ, then the New Democratic Party with 21 and the Conservatives with 20. In March 1998, under pressure from Quebec nationalists, the Government banned flag-waving by right-wing Reform Party MPs that was disrupting debate in the House of Commons.

STATISTICS

DEMOGRAPHY
Population: 29,680,000 (1996) **Annual growth:** 1.2% (1980/1996) **Estimates for year 2000:** 31,000,000 **Annual growth to year 2000:** 0.9% (1994/2000) **Urban Population:** 76.7% (1996) **Urban growth:** 1.38% (1980/95) **Children per woman:** 1.6 (1996).

HEALTH
Life expectancy at birth: 79 years (1996) male: 76 years (1994) female: 82 years (1994) **Infant mortality:** 6 per 1,000 (1996) **Under-5 child mortality:** 7 per 1,000 (1996) **Calorie consumption:** 122% (1988/90) 446 **people per doctor** (1988/91).

EDUCATION
Literacy: 97% (1995) **School enrolment :** Primary total: 103% (1990/95) male : 104% (1990/95) female: 102% (1990/95) Secondary: male : 106% (1990/95) female: 106% (1990/95) Tertiary: 103% (1995) **Primary school teachers:** one for every 16 students (1995).

COMMUNICATIONS
190 **newspapers,** 1,051 **radios,** 650 **TV sets** and 590 **main telephone lines** per 1,000 people (1994) **Books:** 76 new titles per 100,000 people (1992/94).

ECONOMY
Per capita, GNP: $ 19,020 (1996) **Annual growth, GNP:** 0.5% (1995/96) **Annual inflation:** 2.88% (1985/95) **Consumer price index:** 109.4 (1994) **Currency:** 1.37 Canadian dollars = $ 1 (1995) **Cereal imports:** 1,022 metric tons (1994) **Fertilizer use:** 489 kgs per ha (1994) **Exports:** $ 199,071 million (1996) **Imports:** $ 170,265 million (1996).

ENERGY
Consumption: 7,853.74 Kgs of Oil equivalent per capita yearly (1994) -47.01% imported (1994)

HDI (rank / value) 1 / 0.96 (1994)

Cape Verde

Cabo Verde

Population: 396,000 (1996)
Area: 4,033 SQ KM
Capital: Praia

Currency: Escudo
Language: Portuguese and Creole

When the Portuguese settled on the Cape Verde archipelago in the 15th century, the islands were deserving of their descriptive name (Green Cape). They were covered by lush tropical vegetation that stood out against the black volcanic rock and the blue sea. Some 400 years later, Portuguese colonization had wrought devastation and transformed the islands into a "floating desert". Most of the population emigrated to escape starvation, while those who stayed depended upon foreign aid.

[2] Cape Verde was a very important 16th century port of call for ships carrying slaves to America. Incursions by French, British and Dutch pirates were so frequent that Portugal brought farmers to the islands from the Alentejo region to ensure a more permanent presence. The agriculture practised by the new settlers quickly eroded the thin layer of fertile soil and periodic droughts have struck the country since the 18th century.

[3] Falling farm production caused massive emigration of Cape Verdeans; many went to Guinea-Bissau, another former Portuguese colony with close ties to the archipelago. In later years, there was further emigration to Angola, Mozambique, Senegal, Brazil, and the US.

[4] During the independence struggle, Cape Verde developed closer ties to Guinea-Bissau (see Guinea-Bissau). One major reason was the formation of the African Party for the Independence of Guinea and Cape Verde (PAIGC) in 1956, supported by both colonies. Amilcar Cabral, the PAIGC's founder and ideologist, planned that the two economically similar countries, could fight together for freedom and development, once independence was achieved.

[5] In 1961, guerrilla warfare broke out on the continent, and hundreds of Cape Verdean patriots joined the fight. Portugal's colonial government was overthrown in 1974, a transition government was installed and in 1975 the islands proclaimed independence. The PAIGC set an unusual precedent, as for the first time ever one political party took office in two different countries at the same time. Aristides Pereira was elected president and commander Pedro Pires became prime minister. The PAIGC leadership took the first steps toward establishing a federation between Cape Verde and Guinea-Bissau, and the national assemblies of the two countries sat together as the Council of the Union.

[6] In 1968 the Cape Verde Government faced the devastating effects of a drought that left 80 per cent of the population of the archipelago without food. However, the prudent action of civilian organizations supplemented by foreign assistance averted a major catastrophe.

[7] From 1975 onwards, the forested areas of Cape Verde increased from 3,000 to 45,000 hectares. The government predicted that in the next 10 years a further 75,000 hectares would be planted making the islands self-sufficient in firewood. Early in the rainy season, the population of Cape Verde voluntarily spend a week planting trees.

[8] The Government implemented land reform, giving priority to subsistence farming to replace the export crops of the colonial period, when barely five per cent of food needs was met by local production. The drastic decline in agricultural production led the government to invest in fisheries.

[9] Cape Verde supported Angola during its "second liberation war" (see Angola) by allowing Cuban planes to land on the archipelago during the airlift that helped defeat the invasion of Angola by former Zaire and South Africa. Cape Verde adopted a policy of non-alignment, declaring that no foreign military bases would be allowed in their territory.

[10] In 1981, while the PAIGC was negotiating a new constitution for Guinea-Bissau and Cape Verde, Guinea-Bissau's president Luis Cabral was overthrown. Joao Bernardo Vieira took office, and was initially hostile to integration with Cape Verde. An emergency meeting of PAIGC members in Cape Verde discussed the political developments in Guinea-Bissau. This reaffirmation of support for the principles of Amílcar Cabral led the party congress to adopt a new name "the African Party for the Independence of Cape Verde" (PAICV) stressing their independence from Guinea.

[11] Relations between the two governments became tense, but mediation efforts, particularly by Angola and Mozambique paid off. Reconciliation came in August 1982, in Maputo, when President Machel brought Aristides Pereira and Joao Bernardo Vieira together. Further progress was made at the Conference of Former Portuguese Colonies in Africa, held in Cape Verde in November 1982. In Praia, President Joao Bernardo Vieira met with colleagues from Angola, Mozambique, Cape Verde, and Sao Tomé. Diplomatic relations returned to normal, but plans for reunification were abandoned.

[12] Political stability, defiance and perseverance helped Cape Verde avoid famine and the other drastic consequences of the drought which afflicted Africa. In 1984, crop yields fell by 25 per cent, the trade deficit stood at $70 million and the foreign debt reached $98 million. However, the food distribution system, and efficient state and resource management have prevented famine, although the country has been ravaged by droughts for 19 years. Despite these positive factors, some sectors of the population are still severely undernourished.

[13] The paucity of resources made Cape Verde dependent upon foreign assistance, submitting to a number of projects which were doomed to failure, including the nation's First Development Plan.

[14] The Second Development Plan, launched in 1986, prioritized private enterprise, especially in the informal sector. In agriculture, concentrated efforts were made in the fight against desertification. In

LAND USE

IRRIGATED 7 % of arable

(1993)

■ FOREST & WOODLAND	0.2%
□ ARABLE	10.7%
▨ OTHER	89.1%

Literacy
1995

Food Dependency

72%

1994
32%

PROFILE

ENVIRONMENT
An archipelago of volcanic origin, composed of Windward Islands Santo Antao, Sao Vicente, Sao Nicolau, Santa Luzia, Sal, Boa Vista, Branco and Raso, and Leeward Islands Fogo, Santiago, Maio, Rombo and Brava. The islands are mountainous (heights of up to 2,800 meters) without permanent rivers. The climate is arid, influenced by the cold Canary Islands current. Agriculture is poor; nonetheless it employs most of the population. Cape Verde lies within the Sahel region, which is undergoing increased desertification, with periodic droughts. This phenomenon is aggravated by the islands' small size, topography of rolling hills and the prevalence of high winds.

SOCIETY
Peoples: Cape Verdeans are Africans.
Religions: Roman Catholic 93.2 per cent; Protestant and other 6.8 per cent.
Languages: Portuguese is the official language, but the national language is Creole, based on old Portuguese with African vocabulary and structures.
Political Parties: African Party for the Independence of Cape Verde (PAICV); Movement for Democracy (MPD).
Social Organizations: Organized workers belong to the National Cape Verde Workers' Union-Central Trade Union Committee (UNTC-CS).

THE STATE
Official Name: República do Cabo Verde.
Administrative divisions: 9 islands and 14 counties.
Capital: Praia, 61,000 people (1990).
Other cities: Mindelo, 47,000 (1990).
Government: Parliamentary republic. Antonio Mascarenhas Monteiro, President, and Carlos Alberto de Carvalho Veiga, Prime Minister, since February 1991
National Holiday: July 5, Independence Day (1975).
Armed Forces: 1,100.

STATISTICS

DEMOGRAPHY
Population: 396,000 (1996) **Annual growth:** 2% (1980/1996) **Estimates for year 2000:** 400,000 **Annual growth to year 2000:** 2.5% (1994/2000) **Urban Population:** 56.0% (1996) **Children per woman:** 3.7 (1996)

HEALTH
Life expectancy at birth: 66 years (1996) male: 64 years (1994) female: 66 years (1994) **Infant mortality:** 54 per 1,000 (1996) **Under-5 child mortality:** 73 per 1,000 (1996) **Safe water:** 51% (1990/96)

EDUCATION
Literacy: 72% (1995) male : 81% (1995) female: 64% (1995) **School enrolment :** Primary total: 131% (1990/95) male : 132% (1990/95) female: 130% (1990/95) Secondary: male : 28% (1990/95) female: 26% (1990/95).

COMMUNICATIONS
176 **radios** and 49 **main telephone lines** per 1,000 people (1994).

ECONOMY
Consumer price index: 141.0 (1994) **Currency:** 77.46 escudos = $ 1 (1995) **Cereal imports:** 87 metric tons (1994) **Food import dependency:** 32% (1994) **Development aid received:** $ 111 million (1995) $ 292 per capita (1995) 33.6% of GNP (1994)

HDI (rank / value) 123 / 0.547 (1994)

1990, the plan was to recover more than 500 sq km, and establish a centralized system of administering water reserves for the whole country. During the first phase of the plan, more than 15,000 dams were built to store rainwater, and 231 sq km were forested.
[15] Despite adverse climatic conditions, farm production has gradually increased to the point where the country is practically

WORKERS

- ■ AGRICULTURE 31% (1990)
- □ INDUSTRIAL 30%
- ■ SERVICES 40%

self-sufficient in meat and vegetable requirements.
[16] Amidst the political decline linked to the crisis of socialism worldwide, the PAICV lost the first pluralist parliamentary elections, held in February 1991. The Movement for Democracy (MPD), led by Carlos Veiga, won the elections with over 65 per cent of the vote, though 38 per cent of the electorate abstained from voting. Antonio Mascarenhas Monteiro, a legal expert educated at the University of Louvain, Belgium, and President of the Supreme Court of Cape Verde during the previous decade, was elected president.
[17] In September 1992, the new constitution went into effect. It ratified a multiparty system and banned the formation of parties on the basis of religious doctrines, tribal or regional divisions.
[18] The new government began

the transition to a free-market economy with the privatization of insurance companies, fishing and banking, in line with the requirements of international agencies on which the country greatly depended on. Foreign aid accounted for 46 per cent of the GDP, while money remittances from the 700,000 Cape Verdeans residing abroad, constituted another 15 per cent of it.
[19] The liberal government, faced with a 25 per cent unemployment rate, declared its goal to restructure the State. In the first quarter of 1993, Government authorities announced a 50 per cent reduction of the country's 12,000 civil servants and a gradual deregulation of prices was initiated.
[20] The 1994 budget, despite establishing a retrenchment of the public expenditure, included an increase of public investment, from $80 million in 1993 to $138 million in 1994. The priority sectors for state investment were transport, telecommunications and rural development.
[21] In January 1995, Prime

Minister Carlos Veiga introduced significant changes in government in order to "facilitate the country's transition to a free-market economy". One of the most important changes was the merger of the Ministries of Finance, Economic Coordination and Tourism, and Industry and Commerce into a sole Ministry of Economic Coordination. Inflation in 1995 was six per cent and Cape Verdean economy is still greatly dependent upon foreign aid, particularly from the European Union.
[22] In 1997, unemployment remained at 25 per cent. Midway through the year, the Prime Minister announced the signing of an agreement with Italy to increase investment in tourism. The African Development Bank granted a $4.9 million loan to fund the reconstruction of roads. Cape Verde also received economic support from China and agreed a plan with the Angolan Government for joint ventures in areas like health and social welfare.

Cayman Islands

Cayman Islands

Population:	32,000 (1994)
Area:	264 SQ KM
Capital:	George Town
Currency:	Cayman Dollar
Language:	English

In 1503, Christopher Columbus sighted the Cayman Islands and named them the "Turtles" because of the vast numbers of turtles, iguanas and alligators which were their sole inhabitants. The Cayman Islands include Grand Cayman, which is the largest, Cayman Brac and Little Cayman, and all three are surrounded by coral reefs.

[2] Shortly afterwards, the islands came under French control or more accurately, under the control of buccaneers and privateers: "the fathers of the French colonies in the West Indies". For a good part of the 17th century, the Caymans were the pirate headquarters of the Antilles.

[3] The first permanent colonial settlement was established in Grand Cayman, and most of the settlers came from Jamaica; it was not until around the year 1833 that they started to live on the other two islands. The Antilles were all affected by power struggles between the European colonialists. When Jamaica was ceded to the British Crown in 1670, under the Treaty of Madrid, the Cayman Islands became a Jamaican dependency. In 1959 they were given the status of British dependent territory.

[4] In 1972, a new constitution was passed granting some local autonomy on domestic matters. The Governor is appointed by the Crown and is responsible for defence, foreign affairs, internal security, and some social services. There is also an Executive Council and Legislative Assembly. The new Executive Council, created after the 1988 general elections, has two new members and two who were already appointed.

[5] The Cayman Islands have few natural resources other than the sea and sand, which make them popular tourist resorts. With the exception of turtle farming, local industry and agriculture only meet domestic needs. The Caymanese are renowned schooner builders and sailors. One of the country's main sources of revenue is the money sent home by sailors.

[6] Their tax-exempt status has attracted a growing number of offshore banking and trust companies. In 1987, there were 515 banks in the Cayman Islands.

[7] A quarter of the economically active population works in tourism; there are hotels throughout the islands, with a total of 5,200 beds. The influx of visitors has produced considerable immigration, which currently accounts for 35 per cent of the population. In 1989, the Caymans were visited by 618,000 tourists. Fishing declined seriously in the 1970s and has not recovered. Turtle farming is being developed to replace traditional turtle fishing.

[8] The Cayman issue is considered regularly by the UN Decolonization Committee, which asserts the legitimate right of the inhabitants to self-determination and independence. On the islands however the people do not seem anxious to sever links with Britain. In 1982, when the Malvinas/Falklands War broke out, the islands made a contribution of $1 million to the British forces.

[9] In August 1991, McKeeva Bush, a member of the Assembly, founded the first political party in the Caymans. The DPP (Democratic Progressive Party) aimed to change the legal status of the islands from their current one of British dependencies. The DPP promoted constitutional reform, seeking the creation of a party system, a rise in the number of members of the Executive Council, the creation of the post of prime minister, and an increase in the number of seats in the Legislative Assembly. The Governor would become the president of the extended Executive Council.

[10] The Bank of Credit and Commerce International (BCCI) scandal disclosed the peculiar banking and speculation conditions of the Cayman Islands. In 1991 five countries took legal steps to close the BCCI, which they accused of systematic fraud. When the fraud was revealed, the Bank of England explained that the irregularities included the concealment of losses, the drawing up of false balance sheets and other serious alterations to documents. The two most important offices of the BCCI were in Luxembourg and on the Cayman Islands; both of which provided for tax exemption and bank secrecy.

[11] In January 1996, the capture of a Mexican drug trafficker - the third largest cocaine supplier to the United States - demonstrated the part played by the Cayman Islands in a money-laundering circuit between Texas and the final destination of Switzerland.

[12] In 1997, the Government was forced to abandon a series of tax increases planned in that year's budget, due to the strength of public objections.

[13] In January 1998, the Government denied a cruiser carrying 910 gay tourists, mostly US citizens, the right to dock on the islands, saying they "did not fulfil the behaviour requirements". The British Government made it known they did not agree with these "discriminatory" practices.

PROFILE

ENVIRONMENT
Located west of Jamaica and south of Cuba, this small archipelago is part of the Greater Antilles. It comprises the Grand Cayman islands, where most of the population live, the Small Cayman, and Cayman Brac. The archipelago is of volcanic origin, and has rocky hills and considerable coral formations. The climate is tropical and rainy, tempered by oceanic influences.

SOCIETY
Peoples: 40 per cent of the population are of mixed European and indian descent; 20 per cent are of European descent; 20 per cent are of African origin.
Religions: Protestant.
Languages: English.
Political parties: Democratic Progressive Party (DPP). Groups of independent citizens are formed to elect the local government.

THE STATE
Official Name: Cayman Islands.
Administrative divisions: There are eight districts (Creek, Eastern, Midland, South Rown, Spot Bay, Stake Bay, West End, Western).
Capital: George Town, 12,921 people (1991).
Other cities: West Bay, 5,362 people, Bodden Town 3,407 people.
Government: John Wynne Owen, Governor since 1995. There is an 18 member Legislative Assembly (15 elected by direct, popular vote and 3 named by the governor).

Central African Republic

République Centrafricaine

Population: 3,344,000 (1996)
Area: 622,984 SQ KM
Capital: Bangui

Currency: CFA francs
Language: French

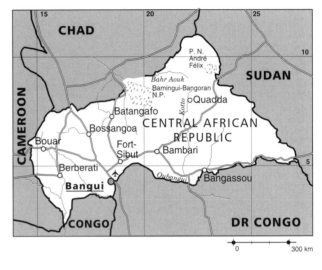

The old Ubangui-Chari empire was associated with other neighboring countries, such as Chad, Gabon and Congo during the colonial period. It has been ruled by tribal chiefs, a sultan, colonial traders, French civil servants, a president, a military dictator, an emperor, and a corrupt politician. This process of unstable leadership started late in the last century and has continued since the Central African Republic proclaimed independence, in August 1960.

2   The region suffered one of the most savage and devastating colonial regimes ever imposed by European powers in Africa. France took an interest in the Central African highlands in the late 19th century, when the coast had already been colonized. Occupation of the interior was begun by three military expeditions directed against Sultan Rabah, the governor of the territory now known as Sudan. The occupation provided an opening for about 40 trading companies which took over rubber and ivory operations in the region, later adding coffee, cotton and diamond mining to their production. This inaugurated a period of nearly 30 years in which the enslavement of native peoples, killings and persecution were widely used by the companies which controlled 70 per cent of the colonized area, renamed Ubangui-Chari in 1908.

3   After World War II, France was short of the financial resources necessary for maintaining a complete colonial administration, so it granted partial autonomy to the Bangui Government. The Europeanized local elite became an instrument of neocolonialism, by which the French retained control of foreign trade, defence and tax collection.

4   Violence and oppression were on the increase in 1949 when a former minister, Barthelemy Boganda, founded the Movement for the Social Evolution of Black Africa (MESAN) to fight for the independence of the Central African Republic. Boganda's prestige grew enormously despite the French attempts to discredit him. In 1956, the French secret service infiltrated MESAN in an attempt to bribe two of Boganda's main advisers, David Dacko and Abel Goumba. Boganda died a year before independence in a suspicious airplane crash, in March 1959.

5   David Dacko took over the post vacated by MESAN's founder, using the position to unleash a purge of the party's more progressive elements. He drew increasingly closer to the French as the US began to show an interest in exploiting the country's uranium and cobalt reserves. Dacko lost the support he had inherited from Boganda, and his government became increasingly corrupt, while the country plunged into deep economic crisis.

6 In December 1965, Dacko was ousted in a coup led by his cousin, Colonel Jean Bedel Bokassa who was pro-France, having served in the French Army for 22 years. Bokassa belonged to a small bourgeois group of M'Baka landowners from Lobaye, where France had recruited agents for its colonial administration. In 1972, he proclaimed himself president-for-life, later taking the rank of field marshal, and finally renaming the country the Central African Empire, crowning himself emperor. The coronation ceremony in December 1977 cost $28 million and was financed by France, Israel and South Africa.

7   In 1978, Bokassa gave 30,000 sq km rich in diamonds to the Israeli army, hiring a notorious international arms dealer as his military adviser. He sent troops to Zaire (now DR Congo) to help Mobutu put down a rebellion in the province of Shaba (see DR Congo).

8   Popular discontent finally erupted in a series of workers' and student rebellions, stifled with the support of Zairean troops. In April 1979, the students refused to comply with regulations specifying that uniforms had to be bought in stores owned by the emperor, and in the ensuing street demonstrations, 100 youths were arrested and taken to the infamous Ngaragba prison, where they were tortured and most of them killed under Bokassa's personal supervision.

9   Resorting to neocolonial manipulations, France decided to depose the emperor, attempting to erase the negative image it had created in supporting his crowning. On September 20 1979, while Bokassa was travelling in Libya, France sent a military plane to bring former president David Dacko back to Bangui. He took power, making no effort to hide his status as a colonial envoy, protected by a thousand French troops. Dacko dissolved the Empire and reinstated a republic, granting France a ten-year lease on the enormous Bouar air base.

10   Dacko's return amounted to no more than a change of name as corruption and repression continued. In 1980, the Central African Government broke off relations with the USSR and Libya, expelling all their technical advisers and diplomats. Political opposition was ruthlessly repressed, and almost all opposition leaders were sent to prison or exiled. Amidst countless conspiracies, Dacko was overthrown by another military coup in September 1981, bringing General Kolingba to power.

11   The new government's first measures were to ask the French to pay the salaries of 24,000 civil servants, and to grant new economic concessions to the US, allowing them to exploit uranium resources. Meanwhile, the return to normality, initially set for 1982, was postponed until 1986. On November 21 of that year, in an election barred to the opposition, Kolingba was elected president with the support of his Central African Party of Democratic Recovery (PCRD). A constitution was passed establishing a one-party system, and on July 21 1987, the members of the General Assembly were chosen from PCRD members.

12   The Government launched a structural adjustment plan, following IMF guidelines. Nevertheless, the economy as a whole showed no signs of recovery.

13   In 1986 Bokassa returned from exile in France. Sentenced to death, during his absence, the former "emperor" was imprisoned.

14   Within the framework of the democratization process, direct municipal elections were held in May 1988, with universal suffrage. It was hoped that this would help to improve trade relations with the developed countries. Seeking popular support for a return to democratic institutions, the government tried to address the question of self-sufficiency in food production, although the country still figures among the world's poorest.

15   Senegal, Côte d'Ivoire, Gabon, Djibouti and the Central African

WORKERS

(1996)

Labour force %

■ WOMEN
□ MEN

47   53

■ AGRICULTURE 80% (1990)
□ INDUSTRIAL   4%
■ SERVICES   16%

PROFILE

ENVIRONMENT

The Central African Republic is a landlocked country in the heart of Africa. It is located on a plateau irrigated by tributaries of the Congo River, such as the Ubangui, the main export route, and of Lake Chad. The southwestern part of the country is covered by a dense tropical forest. Cotton, coffee and tobacco are the basic cash crops. Diamond mining is a major source of revenue. Inadequate methods of cultivation have increased soil erosion and led to a loss of fertility. The scarcity of water and pollution of important rivers pose a serious problem.

SOCIETY

Peoples: Baya (Gbaya) 23.7 per cent; Banda 23.4 per cent; Mandjia 14.7 per cent; Sara 6.5 per cent; Mbum 6.3 per cent; Mbaka 4.3 per cent; Kare 2.4 per cent; other 18.6 per cent. **Religions:** Protestant 25.0 per cent; Roman Catholic 25.0 per cent; traditional African religions 24.0 per cent; Muslim 15.0 per cent. **Languages:** French (official); Sango is the national language, used for intercommunication between the various ethnic groups. **Political Parties:** Central African People's Liberation Party; Democratic Movement for the Rebirth and Evolution of the Central African Republic (MDRERC).

THE STATE

Official Name: République Centrafricaine. **Administrative Divisions:** 16 Prefectures, 52 Sub-prefectures. **Capital:** Bangui, 524,000 people (1994). **Other cities:** Bouar 43,000 people; Berberati 47,000; Bambari 41,000; Carnot 41,000 (1994). **Government:** Ange-Félix Patassé, President, elected in September, 1993. Michel Gbezera-Bria, Prime Minister since January, 1997. Bicameral legislature. **National Holiday:** December 1, Independence Day (1960). **Armed Forces:** 2,650 (1996). **Other:** 2,700 Gendarmes.

STATISTICS

DEMOGRAPHY

Population: 3,344,000 (1996) **Annual growth:** 2.3% (1980/1996) **Estimates for year 2000:** 3,600,000 **Annual growth to year 2000:** 2.2% (1994/2000) **Urban Population:** 39.5% (1996) **Urban growth:** 3.12% (1980/95) **Children per woman:** 5.1 (1996)

HEALTH

Life expectancy at birth: 49 years (1996) male: 46 years (1994) female: 51 years (1994) **Infant mortality:** 103 per 1,000 (1996) **Under-5 child mortality:** 164 per 1,000 (1996) **Calorie consumption:** 82% (1988/90) 25,000 **people per doctor** (1988/91) **Safe water:** 38% (1990/96)

EDUCATION

Literacy: 60% (1995) male : 69% (1995) female: 52% (1995) **School enrolment :** Primary total: 71% (1990/95) male : 88% (1990/95) female: 55% (1990/95) Secondary: male : 17% (1990/95) female: 6% (1990/95) Tertiary: 1% (1995).

COMMUNICATIONS

73 **radios,** 10 **TV sets** and 2 **main telephone lines** per 1,000 people (1994).

ECONOMY

Per capita, GNP: $ 310 (1996) **Annual growth, GNP:** -5% (1995/96) **Annual inflation:** 3.75% (1985/95) **Consumer price index:** 116.6 (1994) **Currency:** 490 CFA francs = $ 1 (1995) **Cereal imports:** 52 metric tons (1994) **Food import dependency:** 24% (1994) **Fertilizer use:** 5 kgs per ha (1994) **Exports:** $ 115 million (1996) **Imports:** $ 180 million (1996) **External debt:** $ 928 million (1996) $ 278 **per capita:** (1996) **Debt service:** 6.3% of exports (1996) **Development aid received:** $ 161 million (1995) $ 50 per capita (1995) 18.4% of GNP (1994)

ENERGY

Consumption: 28.99 Kgs of Oil equivalent per capita yearly (1994) 76.34% imported (1994)

HDI (rank / value) 151 / 0.355 (1994)

Republic (CAR) are the key areas of French foreign policy in Africa.

[16] In July 1991 a plan was approved for Constitutional reform and for the adoption of a multiparty system. Elections were scheduled for October 1992, but shortly after the voting started, Kolingba annulled the process claiming there had been irregularities. After the annulment a Provisional National Council of the Republic was formed, made up of the five presidential candidates. This council announced new elections for April 1993, but these were also postponed on several occasions.

[17] In May, a group of soldiers took the presidential palace and the Bangui radio station by force, demanding payment of eight months of backpay, though they agreed to return to barracks after two salaries were paid. The first round of the presidential elections finally took place on August 11 1993. Kolingba, who came in fourth, annulled the result by decree once again. However, France threatened to suspend its military and financial aid, forcing him to allow the second round to go ahead.

[18] On September 1, Kolingba ordered the political prisoners to be freed, including former emperor Bokassa, who had been accused of cannibalism, murder and the misappropriation of public funds. On September 19, Ange-Felix Patassé, Bokassa's former prime minister, was returned as president with 52.47 per cent of the vote.

[19] In 1994, Patassé continued the rapprochement with Paris, which had supported the candidacy of former president Dacko in 1993. The economy continued to give signs of weakness. The payment of civil servants returned to normal, but the Government continued to owe large sums of backpay. In August 1994, a parliamentary delegation from Kuwait visited Bangui to thank the Central African Republic for its support during the Gulf War.

[20] On December 28 1994, a new constitution was approved by referendum. However, the opposition considered this a defeat for Patassé, as only 46 per cent of the electorate turned out to vote. The increase in international prices for cotton and diamonds produced economic growth, estimated at seven per cent for 1995. Nonetheless, inflation caused by the French imposed 100 per cent devaluation of the CFA continued to affect a large part of the population.

[21] In May 1996, Patassé requested the military intervention of France to crush a new group of rebel soldiers. Direct involvement of French soldiers in street brawls led to a series of demonstrations against French interventionism. Bangui was paralyzed after the rebellions, the looting and the French military action. The CAR economy became even more dependent on France.

[22] In June, the president announced a new government of national unity and named former ambassador in France, Jean Paul Ngoupande, Prime Minister. Social unrest was not appeased and caused the third rebellion in less than a year.

[23] In spite of a truce, in early 1997, France launched an offensive against rebel troops in Bangui in retaliation for the death of two French soldiers. This led Patassé and the rebel leader Anicet Saulet to agree the replacement of French troops by a guard from African countries, although funded by Paris.

[24] In January, Patassé appointed Michel Gbezera-Bria as Prime Minister. In February, a new Government was formed, including some opposition members. Most of the rebels returned to the barracks. In May, new armed confrontations caused a political crisis which led the opposition to leave the Government. New negotiations between the Government and rebel forces, with the mediation of foreign troops, settled the new crisis.

[25] Anti-France hostility was increasingly evident. In October, the CAR president demanded French withdrawal from the military bases. At the same time, he tried to strengthen links with the United States, whose influence over the region had not stopped increasing at the expense of France.

[26] In March 1998, the UN Security Council authorized the deployment of a United Nations mission in the Central African Republic, known as UNMICAR, with 1,400 troops.

Chad

Tchad

Population:	6,515,000 (1996)
Area:	1,284,000 SQ KM
Capital:	N'Djamena
Currency:	CFA francs
Language:	Arabic and French

The Sahel region, of which the Republic of Chad forms part, has been inhabited from time immemorial. Artefacts dating from 4,900 BC have been found in several tombs in the Tibesti mountain region, in the northern part of the country. The southern region around Chad has been under settlement since about 500 BC. In the 8th century AD, increased desiccation of Saharan borderlands stimulated Berber migrations into the area. At that time, the kingdom of Kanem was founded; it converted to Islam in 1085. By the early 1200s the borders of Kanem had been expanded to Fezzan in the north, Quaddaï in the west, and north of Lake Chad into the Bornu kingdom. The new kingdom of Kanem-Bornu was established through merger, its power and prosperity peaking in the sixteenth century because of its command of the southern terminus of the trans-Sahara route to Tripoli.

2 At this point the rival kingdoms of Baguirmi and Ouaddaï evolved in the south. At the height of their power in the 17th century, the Baguirmi made an unsuccesful attempt to expand their territory into Kanem-Bornu. Eventually, in the years 1883-93, all three kingdoms (Ouaddaï, Kanem-Bornu and Baguirmi) were to fall to the Sudanese adventurer Rabih az-Zubayr during 1883-1893.

3 Towards the end of the 18th century, European missionaries converted some of the southern Sara to Christianity and gave them a European-style education. These converts subsequently sided with the Europeans against the native peoples of the north and by 1900 Rabih az-Zubayr was overthrown. The French "acquired" Chad in 1885 during the Berlin Conference, but did not establish themselves in the territory until a 1920 invasion by the notorious French Foreign Legion which defeated the northern Muslim groups.

4 The colonizers introduced cotton farming in 1930, and small parcels of land were distributed to peasants to grow this crop, while the French monopolized its commercialization. In the south, forced changes in the land tenure system replaced a communal practice of self-sufficient agriculture with large-scale farming. The result was a cotton surplus and a food shortage, accompanied by famine.

5 In August 1960 when France granted Chad its independence, southern leaders who had been negotiating with the colonizers since 1956 assumed power. However Chad's first president, François Tombalbaye, leader of the Chad Progressive Party, was unable to unite the country whose frontiers reflected the arbitrary colonial divisions.

6 The Chad Liberation Front (FROLINAT), was founded in 1966 and heavily put down by the French troops. The Front became fully active about the time that southern peasants rebelled against a cotton marketing system introduced by the French company Cotonfran, which controlled the cotton industry. Northerners provided FROLINAT's main political support.

7 In 1970, the Front controlled two-thirds of the national territory, and by 1972 FROLINAT guerrillas were within range of N'Djamena, the capital. In 1975 Tombalbaye was ousted and killed in a French-staged coup which put General Felix Malloum in power. The guerrilla offensive continued, and France began to take advantage of the split within the Front, which had divided into more than 10 groups.

8 Paris supported Hissene Habré's faction because he opposed Goukouni Oueddei, FROLINAT's president, who was receiving support from Muammar Khaddafi's government in Libya. At the time, Habré was at the helm of the Armed Forces of the North (AFN), and Oueddei was the leader of the People's Armed Forces (PAF). Two years later, France dispatched an additional force of 3,000 soldiers, along with fighter planes.

9 The French announced that their troops would maintain neutrality in the struggle between FROLINAT factions, while Hissene Habré accepted the post of prime minister in Malloum's government.

10 Towards the end of 1979 Chad's 11 major political groups formed a Provisional Government of National Unity (PGNU). Habré was named Minister of Defence.

However, the French were displeased with the make-up of the Cabinet because of their strategic interest in Chad - linked to the Maghreb and to the uranium and oil discoveries in the 1960s. In March 1980 Habré resigned, broke the alliance, and unleashed civil war that enabled him to consolidate his power in the south.

11 The ruling coalition split into three factions. In May 1980, Oueddei requested military aid from Libya, and Khaddafi sent 2,000 troops.

12 That same year, over 100,000 refugees fled the country, after the bombing of N'Djamena by Habré's forces. In October, Libyan troops reached the capital, mediation efforts by the Organization for African Unity (OAU) failed, and the defeated Habré fled to Cameroon in December 1980.

13 France led an international campaign against Libyan expansionism in Africa, with support from the United States, Egypt, Sudan, and other African countries, fearful that Khaddafi's revolutionary thrust would eventually "infect" poor Islamic populations of the Sahel region, south of the Sahara.

14 Habré was accused of being opportunistic and corrupt; however, Libyan support made it possible for France to divide Oueddei's allies. In April 1981, backed by France, Habré reorganized his followers in Sudan. In July, in Nairobi, the OAU decided to send a peacekeeping force to Chad, with the help of the French and troops from six African countries. Oueddei, yielding to foreign pressure and tensions within the PGNU, requested the withdrawal of Khaddafi's troops in November.

15 After his defeat by Habré's forces in June 1982, the exiled Oueddei set up a Provisional National Salvation Government in October with 8 of the 11 groups

Map: LIBYA, Aozou, S A H A R A, TIBESTI, NIGER, Faya-Largeau, ENNEDI, Fada, S A H E L, CHAD, Lac Tchad, Bahr el Gazal, Abéché, SUDAN, NIGERIA, N'Djamena, Zakouma N.P., Reserve of Siniaka-Minia, Chari, Bahr Salamat, Bongor, Sarh, CAMEROON, Moundou, CENTRAL AFRICAN REPUBLIC. Area claimed by Libya. 0 — 300 km

PROFILE

ENVIRONMENT

The northern part of Chad is desert, and 40 per cent of its territory is part of the Sahara Desert, with the great Tibesti volcanic highlands. The central region, the Sahel, which stretches to the banks of Lake Chad, is a transition plain where nomadic pastoralism is common. The lake, only half of which lies within Chad's borders, is shallow and mostly covered with swamps. Thought to be the remnant of an ancient inland sea, its waters are fed by two rivers, the Logane and the Chari, which descend from the plateau that separates this basin from that of the Congo River. The banks of these rivers in southern Chad, fertilized by flooding, contain the country's richest agricultural lands and are the most densely populated areas. In colonial times, economic activity was concentrated there. Cotton is the main export product but subsistence agriculture, though hampered by droughts, still predominates. In recent years, mineral reserves of uranium, tungsten and oil have attracted the attention of the transnationals. Desertification and drought are endemic to the region and affect all aspects of daily life.

SOCIETY

Peoples: Northern Chadians are basically nomadic shepherds of Berber and Tuareg origin; Tubu, Quadainee, while southerners (Sara, Massa, Mundani and Hakka) are mainly traditional farmers. Famines have periodically driven people from the Sahel, in the north to the fertile southern regions.
Religions: Around 50 per cent of Chadians are Muslim, 27 per cent practise traditional African religions and 23 per cent are Christian.
Languages: Arabic and French are the official languages. There are many local languages, the most widely spoken being Sara (in the southern region). **Political Parties:** Patriotic Salvation Movement; National Union for Democracy and Socialism; Chad National Liberation Front (FROLINAT); National Front of Chad (FNT); Movement for Democracy and Development (MDD). **Social Organizations:** Chad Federation of Labor Unions.

THE STATE

Official Name: République du Tchad. **Administrative Divisions:** 14 Prefectures. **Capital:** N'Djamena, 530,000 people (1993). **Other cities:** Sarh 198,000 people; Moundou 281,000; Abéché 187,000 (1993). **Government:** Idriss Deby, President, elected in July 1996. Nassour Guelengdoussia Ouaiso, Prime Minister since 1997. Council of the Republic with 31 members, appointed by the President. **Armed Forces:** 25,200. **Other:** 4,500 Gendarmes.

STATISTICS

DEMOGRAPHY

Population: 6,515,000 (1996) **Annual growth:** 2.3% (1980/1996) **Estimates for year 2000:** 7,300,000 **Annual growth to year 2000:** 2.8% (1994/2000) **Urban Population:** 22.5% (1996) **Urban growth:** 3.4% (1980/95) **Children per woman:** 5.6 (1996).

HEALTH

Life expectancy at birth: 47 years (1996) male: 45 years (1994) female: 49 years (1994) **Infant mortality:** 92 per 1,000 (1996) **Under-5 child mortality:** 149 per 1,000 (1996) **Calorie consumption:** 73% (1988/90) 33,333 **people per doctor** (1988/91) **Safe water:** 24% (1990/96).

EDUCATION

Literacy: 48% (1995) male : 62% (1995) female: 35% (1995) **School enrolment :** Primary total: 55% (1990/95) male : 75% (1990/95) female: 36% (1990/95) Secondary: male : 13% (1990/95) female: 3% (1990/95) Tertiary: 1% (1995) **Primary school teachers:** one for every 62 students (1995).

COMMUNICATIONS

246 **radios** and 1 **main telephone line** per 1,000 people (1994)

ECONOMY

Per capita, GNP: $ 160 (1996) **Annual growth, GNP:** 0.5% (1995/96) **Annual inflation:** 3.05% (1985/95) **Currency:** 490 CFA francs = $ 1 (1995) **Cereal imports:** 50 metric tons (1994) **Food import dependency:** 6% (1994) **Fertilizer use:** 21 kgs per ha (1994) **Exports:** $ 125 million (1996) Imports: $ 217 million (1996) **External debt:** $ 997 million (1996) $ 153 **per capita:** (1996) **Debt service:** 9.5% of exports (1996) **Development aid received:** $ 237 million (1995) $ 38 per capita (1995) 26.4% of GNP (1994).

ENERGY

Consumption: 15.90 Kgs of Oil equivalent per capita yearly (1994) 100.00% imported (1994)

HDI (rank / value) 164 / 0.288 (1994)

---

that had opposed Habré in the civil war. The new civil war practically split the country in two: northern Chad, under the control of a recently formed National Liberation Council with Libyan logistical support; and southern Chad, with the Habré Government dependent on French military support.
[16] When Habré seized power, bringing this phase of the civil war to an end, the country was in ruins. The population of the capital, N'Djamena, had dropped to 40,000, and half of its businesses and small enterprises had closed. Outside the cities, 2,000 wells and all the country's water towers had been destroyed, and the health and educational infrastructures were practically non-existent.
[17] An intense drought triggered widespread famine, despite French and American food aid. As hunger spread, massive protests and peasant uprisings occurred in the south. Repression by the Habré Government forced 25,000 Chadians to flee across the border into the Central African Republic.
[18] In 1987, the southern forces supported by France, announced

they had taken Fada, Faya Largeau and the frontier strip of Aozou, claimed by Libya. In 1989, Chad and Libya signed an agreement on this 114,000 sq km territory, which included the return of prisoners and the presentation of a territorial lawsuit before the International Court in The Hague.
[19] In 1990, Idriss Deby (leader of the Patriotic Salvation Movement, supported by France, defeated Habré after a three month military campaign. During the deposed president's term in office in the 1980s, some 40,000 people were executed or "disappeared."
[20] Habré fled to Senegal, where he began to plan a new insurrection. Some 5,000 of his rebel supporters assembled in the N'Guigmi region, near Lake Chad, from where they launched several offensives. In 1992, 400 rebels died and 100 were captured when government forces, with French support, put down an uprising by troops loyal to Habré.
[21] In 1993, Deby officially inaugurated a national conference to "democratize" Chad, with the participation of some 40 opposition parties, another 20

organizations and six armed rebel groups. Adoum Maurice El-Bongo was designated president of the conference, and this meeting called a special court to judge Habré and chose Fidele Moungar to take the role of prime minister during the transition period.
[22] In February 1994, the International Court in The Hague ruled the Aozou strip belonged to Chad. In April, after Chad and the IMF signed an agreement to implement an annual growth programme, the Transition High Council postponed the elections for one more year. In May, Libya officially returned the Aozou strip to N'Djamena.
[23] In March 1995, the Transition High Council once again postponed the elections for 12 months. At the same time, it considered as inadequate the government measures to limit the impact of the devaluation of the CFA, decreed by France in 1994. In the presidential elections, finally held in June and July 1996, Deby was elected constitutional President with 69 per cent of the vote.
[24] That was a year of "reconciliation", as in January the Government had signed a peace agreement with the Action of Union and Development, which was legalized as a party once it abandoned the armed struggle. In a meeting in Gabon, in March,

several rebel groups signed peace agreements with the Government and in August, Deby signed an agreement with the armed forces of the south to establish a federal republic, and the fighting was brought to a close.
[25] The situation remained tense during 1997. At the end of the year, Amnesty International announced that there had been at least 80 people killed in confrontations between the Chad rebel forces and the regular army in the south of the country.
[26] Southern Chad was at the heart of an international controversy in December when the Campaign for the Reform of the World Bank, supported by dozens of NGOs, opposed a megaproject planned by the Bank in this zone. The project included digging 300 oil wells and transporting the product to the Atlantic Ocean through Cameroon. The NGOs considered that funds for fighting poverty should not be used for this type of project.
[27] In March 1998, the director and editor of the "N'Djamena Hebdo" newspaper were sentenced to two years' imprisonment for "slandering the President of Chad" in an article published in December of the previous year. However, the sentence remained suspended.

Chile

Chile

Population:	14,421,000 (1996)
Area:	756,626 SQ KM
Capital:	Santiago
Currency:	Pesos
Language:	Spanish

At the beginning of the 16th Century, the north of Chile formed the southernmost part of the Inka empire (see: Peru, Bolivia and Ecuador). The area between Copiapo to the north and Puerto Montt to the south, was populated by the Mapuche, later called Araucanians by the Europeans. Further south lived the fishing peoples: the Yamana and the Alacalufe.

[2] Diego de Almagro set off from Peru in 1536, to begin the conquest of Chile. With an expeditionary force of Spanish soldiers and enslaved native Americans, he covered nearly 2,500 km, reaching central Chile when a mutiny in Lima forced him to turn back.

[3] Between 1540 and 1558, Pedro de Valdivia settled in what is now the port of Valparaiso, and founded several cities, including Santiago. The Mapuche, headed by their traditional leader Lautaro, put up fierce resistance. They defeated the invaders on several occasions, using war strategies learned from the European enemy. Valdivia died in one of these battles, and his successor Francisco de Villagran caught and killed Lautaro in 1557. Spanish governor Garcia de Hurtado sought out the Mapuche, who were now led by an old warrior, Caupolican, and defeated them. The rebellions continued off and on, and Spanish-Creole domination did not extend over all of the territory until the middle of the 19th century.

[4] In 1811 the governing Junta headed by Jose Miguel Carrera instigated the independence process. General Bernardo O'Higgins, the son of a former viceroy in Peru, joined this movement. War broke out between the independence army and the royalist forces, with their strongholds in Valdivia and Concepción. Helped by the army of José de San Martín, which crossed the Andes to fight the royalists, the independence army finally defeated the Europeans on April 5 1818 in the Battle of Maipú.

[5] In 1817, O'Higgins was designated Supreme Head of State, while the royalist troops still maintained pockets of resistance. He lay the political foundations of the country, which were reinforced in the 1833 Constitution, during the presidential term of Diego Portales. This "aristocratic republic", denied all forms of political expression to the new urban sectors, the middle class and the rising proletariat. English companies, in alliance with the creole oligarchy, organized an export economy based on the rich saltpetre deposits of the north. These deposits extended along the maritime coast of Bolivia and reached as far as the southernmost regions of Peru. Soon the English controlled 49 per cent of Chile's foreign trade. Chilean and British capital owned 33 per cent of Peru's saltpetre, but they wanted total control.

[6] The "Nitrate War" or Pacific War, 1879-1884, was caused by this Chilean-British alliance. Chilean territory increased by a third and left Bolivia in its present landlocked state. The victory brought about the rapid growth of the saltpetre industry and its labor force.

[7] Jose Manuel Balmaceda, was elected president in 1886, and he tried to break the oligarchic order. The nationalism fostered by war, economic growth, social diversification and the education of the wealthy helped to gain him support. He encouraged protectionism to develop national industry. The oligarchy reacted violently, supported by the English. The army defeated the President's partisans, and Balmaceda committed suicide in the Argentine embassy in 1891.

[8] In 1900, the first union was founded in Iquique; in 1904, 15 unions with 20,000 members, joined to form a federation; the National Convention. That year the unions came into conflict with military in Valparaíso, and three years later, automatic weapons supplied by the US, were used to massacre 2,500 workers and their families in a school in Iquique.

[9] Housing, railroads and new mines continued to expand, stimulating trade, new services, and public administration. In 1920, populist politician Arturo

PUBLIC EXPENDITURE

8.8% 77.9%
1995 ■ DEFENCE □ SOCIAL

In 1990/91 Military as % of health & education expenditure was 68%.

WORKERS

UNEMPLOYMENT 5.4% (1996)

Labour force %
■ WOMEN
□ MEN

32   68

■ AGRICULTURE 19% (1990)
□ INDUSTRIAL 25%
■ SERVICES 56%

LAND USE

DEFORESTATION -0.8% annual (81/90)
IRRIGATED 31.8% of arable

(1993)

■ FOREST & WOODLAND 21.8%
□ ARABLE 5.3%
■ OTHER 72.9%

Map labels: PERU, Brazil, BOLIVIA, PARAGUAY, ARGENTINA, Arica, Iquique, Antofagasta, ATACAMA DESERT, CHILE, Pacific Ocean, CORDILLERA DE LOS ANDES, Viña del Mar, Valparaíso, Santiago, Juan Fernandez Is., Talcahuano, Concepción, Valdivia, Osorno, Puerto Montt, Chiloé, Atlantic Ocean, TAITAO PENÍNSULA, Punta Arenas, Tierra del Fuego, 0 300 km.

PROFILE

Environment
Flanked by the Andes mountain range in the east and the Pacific in the west, the country is a thin strip of land 3,500 km long and never wider than 402 km. Its length explains its variety of climates and regions. Due to the cold ocean currents, the northern territory is a desert. The central region has a mild climate which makes it good for agriculture. The southern part of the country is colder and heavily wooded. The major salt and copper mines are located in northern Chile. 65 per cent of the population live in the central valleys. During the military regime, some 40 thousand hectares of native forests were cut down each year, and replaced by other tree species, causing the displacement and death of wildlife.

SOCIETY
Peoples: Chileans result from ethnic and cultural integration between the native American population and European immigrants. 300,000 Mapuche live mainly in southern Chile.
Religions: Mainly Catholic (77 per cent), Protestant 13 per cent.
Languages: Spanish. **Political Parties:** Concertación Democrática is a coalition made of the Christian Democratic Party (PDC), the Democratic Party (PPD), the Socialist Party (PS) and the Radical Party (RP). The National Renovation Party (RN). The Independent Democratic Union (UDI). Democratic Alliance; Union of Center Center (UCC); National Party (PN); Communist Party of Chile (PCCh); Revolutionary Movement of the Left (MIR); the Manuel Rodríguez Patriotic Movement (MPMR); Humanistic Party (PH); Green Party. **Social Organizations:** The Central Workers' Union (CUT), the main labor organization until 1973, had been banned during the dictatorship, and became legal again in 1990. Other trade unions are: the Copper Workers' Confederation (CTC) led by Rodolfo Seguel; the Confederation of Civil Servants of Chile (CEPCH), led by Federico Mujica; the National Association of Civil Servants; the United Workers' Front (FUT); the National Labor Co-ordination Board (CNS); the National Federation of Taxi Drivers, and unions representing artists, petroleum workers professionals and truck drivers; the Democratic Workers' Union (UDT), and the National Union of Civil Servants.

THE STATE
Official Name: República de Chile.
Administrative divisions: 13 Regions and the Metropolitan Area of Santiago. **Capital:** Santiago, 5,076,800 people (1995). **Other cities:** Viña del Mar 322,220 people; Concepción 350,000; Valparaíso 282,000; Temuco 239,300 (1995). **Government:** Eduardo Frei, President since March 11 1994. **National Holiday:** September 18, Independence Day (1810). **Armed Forces:** 89,700 troops (1996). **Other:** Carabineros, 31,000.

Maternal Mortality
1990

PER 100,000 LIVE BIRTHS

65

Literacy
1995

95%

Alessandri became the leader of the new social factions that sought to subvert the oligarchic order and achieve representation in politics. Alessandri's government promoted constitutional reform and welfare legislation with electoral rights for literate men over 21, direct presidential election, an 8 hour working day, social security, and labor regulations.

[10] Chile's economy, based on farm and mineral exports, was severely affected by the 1929-30 depression. Recovery did not come until the Chilean bourgeoisie was able to impose an industrialization program to produce previously imported goods. Their proposal served as a base for the 1936 Popular Front, which marshalled support from Communists and Socialists. The front was led by Pedro Aguirre Cerda, who later became president. The armed forces were purged and withdrew from the political scene for almost forty years. Although the oligarchy was weakened, it made a pact with the government on agrarian policies, and Aguirre Cerda never allowed land reform or the formation of rural workers' unions.

[11] The alliance worked out in the thirties broke down during González Videla's term of office, 1946-1952. The atmosphere created by the Cold War legitimized the Law for the Permanent Defence of Democracy which banned the Communist Party and deprived its members of the vote. On January 9 1949, to compensate for these measures, the government brought in female suffrage. The Radical Party's repressive and de-nationalizing policies, and the disabling of the left enabled the Populist Carlos Ibáñez to win the 1952 election.

[12] Economic deterioration rapidly eroded the strength of the populist government. In 1957, offshoots from the National Falange (populist) and from the old Conservative Party (oligarchic), founded the Christian Democratic Party. The Communist Party was legalized and the left rebuilt its alliances, forming the Popular Action Front. The people wanted change, but, sensitive to an aggressive anti-communist campaign, voted for Eduardo Frei's "revolution in freedom", which initiated agrarian reform in 1964.

[13] The UP (Popular Unity), a coalition formed by the Socialist Party, the Communist Party, the United Popular Action Movement (MAPU), and the Christian Left led by Salvador Allende won the 1970 election, obtaining 35 per cent of the vote, while the rest of the electorate was split between the Christian Democrats and the conservative parties. The following year the UP won almost 50 per cent of the vote in the legislative elections, leading the right to fear a definitive loss of its majority.

[14] Allende nationalized copper and other strategic sectors, together with private banks and foreign trade. He increased land reform, promoted collective production and created a "social sector" in the economy, managed by workers.

[15] The traditional elite, now displaced from government, conspired with the Pentagon, the CIA and transnational corporations, particularly ITT, to topple the Government. The Christian Democrats were indecisive, and finally supported the coup. Inflation, a shortage of goods and internal differences within Popular Unity contributed to the climate of instability.

[16] On September 11 1973 General Augusto Pinochet led a coup. The Presidential Palace at La Moneda was bombed by the air force, and President Allende died during the fighting. Violent repression ensued: people were shot without trial, sent to concentration camps, tortured, or simply "disappeared".

[17] The Chilean military dictatorship was one of many that ravaged the Southern Cone of South America during the 1970s, inspired by the National Security Doctrine. This was supported by the Chilean oligarchy and the middle classes, as well as by transnational corporations who recovered the companies which had escaped their control.

[18] After the coup, Chile's economic policy started to be based on neo-liberal doctrines. Inflation dropped below 10 per cent per year, unemployment practically disappeared and imported manufactured goods flooded the market. Alongside this ran a loss of earning power in workers' salaries and an overall impoverishment of the poorer classes.

[19] The deteriorating influence of these neo liberal economic policies became evident in 1983, two years after a constitution containing a mandate for "continuity" was approved in a plebiscite by 60 per cent of the voters. Unemployment reached 30 per cent, 60 per cent of the population were malnourished, protein consumption had dropped by 30 per cent, real salaries had been reduced by 22 per cent in just two years and 55 per cent of all families were living below the poverty line. This situation provided the background for the violent popular uprising which took place in November 1983, led by the National Labor Co-ordination Board and the National Workers' Command.

[20] In 1984 the Church started talks. To participate in these talks, the opposition formed the Democratic Alliance, led by the PDC. The talks with Home Minister Sergio Onofre Jarpa failed, and from September 1984, the break with the Church became evident. After this date, the Vicarate for Solidarity of the Archbishopric of Santiago played a key role in defending human rights.

[21] The political left joined together under the Popular Democratic Movement (MDP), vindicating all forms of struggle against the dictatorship. One faction of the left formed the "Manuel Rodriguez Patriotic Movement", an armed group which carried out numerous attacks, the most important being an attempted assassination of Pinochet on September 7, 1986.

[22] The international isolation of Chilean Government during the Carter administration eased a little with the election of Ronald Reagan in the US, and Margaret

Food Dependency

1970

15%

1994

5%

External Debt

1996

PER CAPITA

$1,901

STATISTICS

DEMOGRAPHY
Population: 14,421,000 (1996) **Annual growth:** 1.6% (1980/1996) **Estimates for year 2000:** 15,200,000 **Annual growth to year 2000:** 1.4% (1994/2000) **Urban Population:** 84.0% (1996) **Urban growth:** 2.03% (1980/95) **Children per woman:** 2.5 (1996).

HEALTH
Life expectancy at birth: 75 years (1996) male: 72 years (1994) female: 78 years (1994) **Infant mortality:** 11 per 1,000 (1996) **Under-5 child mortality:** 13 per 1,000 (1996) **Calorie consumption:** 102% (1988/90) 943 **people per doctor** (1988/91) **Safe water:** 95% (1990/96).

EDUCATION
Literacy: 95% (1995) male : 95% (1995) female: 95% (1995) **School enrolment :** Primary total: 99% (1990/95) male : 100% (1990/95) female: 98% (1990/95) Secondary: male : 66% (1990/95) female: 70% (1990/95) Tertiary: 28% (1995) **Primary school teachers:** one for every 27 students (1995).

COMMUNICATIONS
100 **newspapers**, 345 **radios**, 250 **TV sets** and 110 **main telephone lines** per 1,000 people (1994) **Books:** 13 new titles per 100,000 people (1992/94).

ECONOMY
Per capita, GNP: $ 4,860 (1996) **Annual growth, GNP:** 8.5% (1995/96) **Annual inflation:** 17.85% (1985/95) **Consumer price index:** 176.6 (1994) **Currency:** 406.91 pesos = $ 1 (1995) **Cereal imports:** 1,277 metric tons (1994) **Food import dependency:** 5% (1994) **Fertilizer use:** 978 kgs per ha (1994) **Exports:** $ 14,979 million (1996) Imports: $ 16,810 million (1996) **External debt:** $ 27,411 million (1996) $ 1,901 **per capita:** (1996) **Debt service:** 32.3% of exports (1996) **Development aid received:** $ 159 million (1995) $ 11 per capita (1995) 0.3% of GNP (1994).

ENERGY
Consumption: 1,011.50 Kgs of Oil equivalent per capita yearly (1994) 67.51% imported (1994)

HDI (rank / value) 30 / 0.891 (1994)

Thatcher in the UK. In August 1985 Chile authorized American space shuttle landings on Easter Island. At the beginning of 1986 an American delegation proposed that Chile be condemned before the UN Human Rights Commission, thereby avoiding having to take more drastic action against Chile.

[23] On October 5 1988, an eight-year extension of Pinochet's rule was submitted to a plebiscite, and a wide opposition alliance ended his government, bringing elections the following year.

[24] Facing up to the fact that change was inevitable, Pinochet negotiated constitutional reform. Proposed changes included further restrictions of the power of future governments, an increase in the number of senators, shortening the presidential term from eight years to four and a liberalization of the proscription of left-wing parties. The reform was approved by referendum on July 30 1989.

[25] Elections were held on December 14 1989, Patricio Aylwin, leader of the Christian Democrats, gained 55.2 per cent of the vote, taking office on March 11, 1990.

[26] In April, Aylwin appointed a Truth and Reconciliation commission to investigate the issue of missing people. The Commission confirmed that there were at least 2,229 missing people, who were assumed dead. It also made a detailed study of repression during the dictatorship. When the facts were made public in March 1991 the president asked the nation for forgiveness in the name of the State. He announced that judicial procedures would follow, and he requested the co-operation of the armed forces in these proceedings

[27] Official recognition virtually brought about an institutional crisis. The armed forces and the Supreme Court reaffirmed their conduct during the Pinochet dictatorship, and denied the validity of the government report, thus discrediting the president. The crisis was defused when the government accepted the prerequisites of "Chilean transition", preserving the judicial system of the previous regime and guaranteeing impunity from human rights violations.

[28] On April 2, senator Jaime Guzman, former adviser and ideologue of the military regime, was murdered and the assassination was attributed to radical left wing groups, enabling the right-wing to raise the issue of terrorism once more. Political life was slowly brought back to normal. On April 23, the MRPM announced its decision to abandon armed struggle.

[29] The Chilean economy maintained a ten year expansion, with annual growth rates of over six per cent, mainly due to high levels of investment (especially fixed capital), and the expansion of the external sector. Direct foreign investment remained at significant levels: $3.5 and $2.9 billion in 1992 and 1993, respectively.

[30] During Aylwin's presidency, social indicators improved. In 1993, real salaries increased 5 five per cent, the unemployment rate fell to 4.5 per cent, and social spending increased 14 per cent.

[31] In August 1993, the Special Commission on Indigenous Peoples, a government agency, proposed introducing indigenous language instruction in Mapuche, Aymara and Rapa Nui at primary school level. This measure was considered to be of utmost importance by Mapuche educators, to reduce the loss of cultural identity indigenous children experience when thrown into a school system where Spanish is the sole medium of instruction.

[32] In the 1993 elections, Eduardo Frei, candidate for the Christian Democratic Party and the *Concertacion* (agreement) coalition, won the presidency with 58 per cent of the vote. However, he did not achieve the parliamentary majority needed to do away with authoritarian habits. Eight "designated" seats remained in the Senate which made opposition to the necessary reforms a majority.

[33] Shortly before handing over the presidency, President Aylwin pardoned four MRPM activists, sentenced to death for the assassination attempt against Pinochet in 1986.

[34] The Frei government announced a plan to reduce the poverty which affected nearly a quarter of the population. In May 1995, the minimum salary was increased 13 per cent. Taxes were introduced on the sale of cigarettes and motor vehicles to fund a 10 per cent increase in the lowest pensions and a 5 per cent increase in the education budget. In June, Chile requested associate membership of the Mercosur and negotiated entry into the North American Free Trade Association (NAFTA).

[35] Brigadier Pedro Espinoza and retired general Manuel Contreras were sentenced to imprisonment for their parts in the murder of former foreign minister Orlando Letelier, in Washington, in 1976. Pinochet reiterated his support to the sentenced officers, but then called for respect for the civil authorities. At the same time, the Government suspended investigations into corruption charges against the former dictator's son. In a later hearing, in February 1998, Contreras stated that the true leader of the DINA (the political police during the dictatorship) was Pinochet himself.

[36] The Chamber of Deputies approved the trade agreement with Mercosur member nations by 76 votes to 26. Two right-wing parties the UDI and RN, came out against the agreement. The signing of the free trade agreement took place on June 25 1996, establishing the "four plus one" association between Argentina, Brazil, Paraguay, Uruguay and Chile. This formula was to remain in place until Chile became a full member of the agreement. The treaty with Mercosur came into operation on October 1 1996.

[37] A report from the National Society of Farmers (SNA) said the agreement would mean annual losses of $460 million for the Chilean agricultural sector, but, balancing this, the country would become integrated into a market of more than 200 million people.

[38] In the October municipal elections, the ruling Concertación Nacional took the majority of the votes. Representation of the Democratic Christians, the Socialist Party (PS), the Democratic Party (PPD) and the Radical Party (RP), increased in the municipal councils. However, the number of Concertación Nacional mayors fell compared with the previous elections in 1992.

[39] Within Concertación, the Democratic Christians lost

95%

support to the increasingly popular PS and PPD, who were more successful in local councils and mayorships. This political advantage allowed them to strengthen their position within the coalition.

40 Various studies in 1996 suggested the average economic growth of 6 per cent in the last 11 years had led to a reduction in "extreme poverty" - but not in social inequality. Thus 20 per cent of the population still controlled 57 per cent of the national wealth, while the poorest 20 per cent handled only 3.9 per cent. During the first half of 1996, military and civil tribunals closed 21 cases of disappearances and extra-judicial killings involving 56 victims, without finding anyone responsible.

41 In May 1997, demonstrations by the miners' union - a bastion of the union movement and the Communist Party - in central Santiago were put down violently.

42 Concertación retained the majority in the December 11 legislative elections, but lost ground to the right. The government coalition took 50.6 per cent of the vote (compared with 56.1 per cent in the 1996 municipal elections), while the right took 39 per cent (35 per cent in 1996).

43 After passing on the post of Commander-in-Chief of the armed forces to General Ricardo Izurieta, Pinochet entered the Senate on March 11 1998, amidst general indignation. During the former dictator's first appearance in the Senate, several senators wielded photographs of people who had disappeared in the dictatorship. One member of parliament hung a sign saying "murderers not admitted" on the window of his office.

44 After his plan for a plebiscite to eliminate the post of 'senator for life', which included Pinochet, was vetoed in the Senate, Frei once again suggested a referendum. At the same time, 21 members of the Congress presented a document which stated the constitutional clause granting former presidents a seat in the Senate for life should not be applied to Pinochet, as he had not been an elected leader.

The ideological discovery of America

The American continent was actually inhabited by humans many millennia before the arrival of Christopher Columbus in the year 1492. The so-called "Discovery of America" reflects Western civilization's obsession with shaping history after its own image

In fact, it took Europeans several years after their first voyages to perceive America as a continent, a huge territory that was already completely inhabited by people. Upon comprehending this situation European intellectuals of the time began to look at ways by which they could ideologically 'invent' America.

In the first few decades following initial contact, various theories attempted to explain the presence of human beings on this continent. It was said, for example, that they were of Semitic origin (one of the lost tribes of Israel). Later, other thinkers would trace their origin to the Phoenicians or Carthaginians - great sailors of ancient times - or to other major civilizations of the Mediterranean, such as Egypt, or even to the mythical Atlantis. However, also in the 15th century, Father Acosta became the first to suggest that hunters came to the continent by land.

Two main methods of study are used to establish the origins of people in America: history and archaeology. The former, based on written documents, covers the last 500 years. The latter goes back to the traces left behind by the first settlers, including those from the prehistoric period. Both disciplines, created by Western thought, cannot distance themselves from the paradigms of Judeo-Christian culture.

The idea of linear time, for example, is based on an evolutionist precept which insists upon the passage from simple to complex. Other cultures have notions of time in which events do not take place in a linear progression, but in a circular or cyclical way. The prototype of a universal history conceived according to these parameters is quite different.

American indian cultures were thus framed within the European concept of history. First, the Europeans denied the indigenous peoples any innovative capacity. All inventions, like agriculture, pottery, metallurgy and civilization itself were credited to the world and history known to the Europeans. America was a marginal region.

Although these assumptions would be proved false, the classification of cultural groups into more evolved or less evolved continues to this day.

Starting from the "center-periphery" precept, each group was categorized in the evolutionist continuum of history as follows:

a) the High Cultures of Mesoamerican (Aztecs, Mayas) and Andean (Inkas) regions, which were granted the status of civilization;

b) the Periphery Cultures of Civilizing Centres or Intermediate Regions, covering all those groups influenced by the above ones (e.g., Caribbean and the surrounding areas), and

c) the Marginal Groups (e.g., hunter-gatherers of South and North American lowlands, some Amazon groups, and so on).

Starting from this evolutionist concept of history, Europeans convinced themselves that the peak of civilization had been reached by Western Europe and that every expansionist action they took was just an attempt to save the rest of the world from taking the wrong steps on the path of progress.

China

Zhonghua

Population:	1,232,083,000 (1996)
Area:	9,562,036 SQ KM
Capital:	Beijing
Currency:	Yuan renminbi
Language:	Chinese

China has one of the world's oldest civilizations, which achieved an unparalleled degree of cultural and social homogeneity several thousand years before most modern nations were formed.

2   Although the nation disintegrated into warring kingdoms at various points in its history, the development of Chinese civilization can be traced back 5,000 years to its emergence in the Yellow River (Huanghe) basin.

3   Territory was consolidated early on, and a single writing system was established by emperor Qin Shihuang some 2,200 years ago, in 221-206 BC; the same system is still in use today. In his determination to consolidate Chinese thinking he also ordered the burning of all previous books, and the execution of many scholars.

4   By the time of the Tang Dynasty, 618-907AD, China had developed a cultured civilization, and during the Song Dynasty, 960-1279 AD, the nation was more developed than Europe in every field.

5   Construction of the 5,000-km Great Wall of China was started in the third century BC, in an attempt to repel invaders from the north. The wall ultimately failed, and China fell to Mongolian invaders; Genghis Khan and his grandson Kublai Khan ruled China from 1276 to 1368.

6   One of the most influential figures in Chinese culture was the scholar Confucius who lived about 2,500 years ago. As a philosopher, he emphasized respect for one's elders, the

ぐ゚ゎ゚ゎ゚ Great Wall

▨ Area claimed by India

importance of unquestioning loyalty and responsibility to superiors in the social hierarchy and the central role of the family. Other philosophers such as Lao Zi emphasized a more imaginative role for individuals in society, but Confucian thinking is most accurately reflected in the partially surviving social structures of China, Korea, Japan and Vietnam.

7   With their highly developed culture, the Chinese soon developed a disdain for the "barbarians" beyond their borders. This attitude was often

combined with the corruption of imperial dynasties, leading to eras of isolationism and social stagnation.

8   Regular contact with Europeans began when the Portuguese opened up maritime routes in the 15th century. The Chinese allowed Europeans to use a limited number of trading ports under strict conditions and granted the tiny enclave of Macau to the Portuguese in 1557. But the Chinese still refused to take foreign powers seriously.

9   The British eventually found a

commodity that could be traded with China to pay for the Chinese silk, tea and porcelain products so fashionable in Europe. They began to import opium from India. When China tried to outlaw the drug trade, and later, to stop smuggling, Britain declared war in the name of free trade.

10   Modern European weapons easily defeated the Chinese imperial armies in the First Opium War, 1839-42. The victorious British demanded that five ports be opened to their trade, that low customs duties be imposed, and that the territory of Xianggang (Hong Kong) be given to them

11   The tottering Chinese Empire suffered another type of defeat with the Taiping rebellion in 1853. The rebel empire controlled much of southern China for 11 years before being crushed with the help of Western troops.

12   Massive imports of opium were now being paid for in Chinese silver, impoverishing the nation as it was weakened by widespread drug addiction. Another war from 1856-1860,

PUBLIC EXPENDITURE

n/a

12.4%
1995 ■ DEFENCE □ SOCIAL

In **1990/91** Military as % of health & education expenditure was 114%.

WORKERS

(1996)

Labour force %

■ WOMEN
□ MEN

45   55

■ AGRICULTURE 72% (1990)
□ INDUSTRIAL 15%
■ SERVICES 13%

LAND USE

DEFORESTATION -0.4% annual (81/90)
IRRIGATED 53.6% of arable

(1993)

■ FOREST & WOODLAND 13.5%
□ ARABLE 9.6%
■ OTHER 76.9%

Food Dependency	External Debt

1970
7%

1992
3%

1994

PER CAPITA
$105

PROFILE

ENVIRONMENT
The terrain of the country is divided into three large areas. Central Asian China, comprising Lower Mongolia, Sin Kiang and Tibet, is made up of high plateaus, snow-covered in winter but sporting steppe and prairie vegetation in summer. North China has vast plains, such as those of Manchuria and Hoang-Ho, which boast large wheat, barley, sorghum, soybean and cotton plantations, and coal and iron ore deposits. Manchuria is the country's main metallurgical center. South China is a hilly area crossed by the Yangtse Kiang and Si-kiang rivers, this area has a hot, humid monsoon climate, and most of the nation's rice plantations. The country possesses great mineral wealth: coal, oil, iron ore and non-ferrous metals. The use of coal as the main source of energy produces acid rain. Less than 13 per cent of the land is covered by forest. The construction of the Three Gorges dam is considered a potential environmental disaster.

SOCIETY
Peoples: There are 56 official recognised nationalities. Han (91.96 per cent), Chuang (1.37 per cent), Manchu (0.87 per cent), Hui (0.76 per cent), Miao (0.65 per cent), Uighur (0.64 per cent), Yi (0.58 per cent), Tuchia (0.50 per cent), Mongol (0.42 per cent), Tibetan (0.41 per cent), Puyi (0.23 per cent), Tung (0.22 per cent), Yao (0.18 per cent), Korean (0.17 per cent), Pai (0.14 per cent), Hani (0.11 per cent), Kazak (0.1 per cent), Tai (0.09 per cent), Li (0.09 per cent), other (0.51 per cent).
Religions: nonreligious 59.2 per cent. Confucianism (a moral code, not a religion), combined with mystical elements from Taoism and Buddhism, are what could be labelled as the predominant "belief". Buddhist 6.0 per cent; Muslim 2.4 per cent; Christian 0.2 per cent; other 0.1 per cent.
Languages: Chinese (official), is a modernized version of northern Mandarin. Variants of this language can be found in the rest of the country, the most widespread being Cantonese, in the south. Ethnic minorities speak their own languages.
Political Parties: The Chinese constitution states that the Communist Party is "the leading nucleus of all the Chinese people".

THE STATE
Official name: Zhonghua Renmin Gongheguo.
Administrative divisions: 23 provinces, 5 autonomous regions and 3 municipalities.
Capital: Beijing, 10,900,000 people (1994).
Other cities: Shanghai, 13,400,000 people; Xianggang (Hong Kong), 5,574,000 (1995); Shenyang, 4,500,000 people (1994).
Government: Jiang Zemin, President and General Secretary of the Communist Party since 1992, re-elected in March 1998. Zu Rongji, Prime Minister since March 1998. The 3,000-member National People's Congress (NPC) sits for about two weeks a year to ratify laws. NPC delegates are drawn from various geographical areas and social sectors (army, minorities, women, religious groups).
National Holiday: October 1 and 2, proclamation of the People's Republic.
Armed Forces: 2,930,000 (1995).
Other: 1,200,000 Armed Peoples' Police, Defense Department.

this time against Anglo-French forces, ended with the capture of Beijing and a new round of concessions, including the admission of missionaries.
[13] In 1895, China suffered an even more humiliating defeat at the hands of its former tributary state Japan, which overran part of the Korean peninsula and the island of Taiwan.
[14] An anti-Western rebellion broke out in 1898 led by the Boxers, and a joint British, Russian, German, French, Japanese and US expedition intervened to put down the uprising. The victorious armies divided the country into "zones of influence" and demanded that the Chinese pay huge war reparations.
[15] The most spectacular example of foreign involvement in China was in Shanghai, where the port was developed for trading, and foreign companies invested in hundreds of factories, located within foreign "concessions", to take advantage of cheap Chinese labor.
[16] Foreign exploitation also brought new ideas and concepts to China. The Government belatedly allowed small groups of students to study overseas. Nationalist groups emerged to focus and articulate the massive anti-foreign sentiment. In 1911, nationalists led by Sun Yat-sen, won the support of several imperial generals. A number of garrisons mutinied, and a Republic was proclaimed.
[17] Most of the generals who had joined the uprising wanted power and had no intention of instituting democratic reforms. Simmering rivalries soon burst into the open and China was thrust into an era of civil war as local "warlords," backed by various foreign powers, fought over the fragmented country.
[18] In 1921, 13 people from all over China gathered in a small house in the French concession of Shanghai to hold the first national congress of the Chinese Communist Party (CCP).
[19] The new party prioritized the organization of workers and it enjoyed considerable success. By 1926 it was involved with 700 trade unions representing 1.24 million members. They formed an alliance with Chiang Kai-Shek's Kuomintang (KMT) nationalist party to oppose the warlords. In 1927, the KMT turned on their allies and massacred some 40,000 communist labor leaders.
[20] In the face of such a defeat, a communist leader, Mao Zedong (Mao Tse Tung), argued that the Chinese peasantry should be mobilized as a revolutionary force. He led most of the Communist Party leadership into rural China, where they carried out political organizing and raised a peasant-based army.
[21] When the KMT armies tried to surround the CCP's remote bases in 1934, the communist army, their leaders and supporters began a march in search of an alternative site. They travelled for over a year, their numbers dwindling under frequent attacks and severe conditions, but they were eventually able to regroup. This legendary journey became known as the "long march."
[22] In 1937 a full-scale Japanese invasion of China forced the CCP and the KMT to set aside their differences and form a second United Front against the common enemy. While fighting against the Japanese, the Communists were also able to extend their influence among the workers in KMT-controlled areas. Chiang Kai-Shek showed more interest in fighting the Communists than the Japanese and broke the pact on several occasions. On one occasion, his own generals arrested him and forced him to negotiate with the CCP to continue joint resistance to the Japanese.
[23] When the allies defeated the Japanese in 1945, the CCP-KMT front collapsed into civil war. The corrupt and autocratic KMT proved no match for the highly-motivated CCP armies and their supporters. On October 1 1949, the communist leadership declared the foundation of the People's Republic of China. An era of foreign control and humiliation went out and an era of social and economic reform came in.
[24] The remnants of the KMT Government and army fled to the island of Taiwan. There, under US protection, they claimed to represent all of China and laid plans to eventually "reconquer" the mainland.
[25] The Chinese Communists instituted far-reaching land reforms, adding to those already carried out in their own liberated zones before the final victory. They also nationalized all foreign-controlled property and initiated widespread education and health programs.
[26] The first five-year development plan incorporated many aspects of the Soviet model; the emphasis was on industrial investment rather than consumption, and heavy industry

Hong Kong (Xianggang): "One country, two systems"

Hong Kong (Xianggang) island was ceded to Britain "in perpetuity" in 1842, when the British attacked China in the first Opium War. Eighteen years later, the British gained the rights over Kowloon, the mainland peninsula facing the island. In 1898, the British forced the Chinese to give them a 99-year lease on the rural zone north of Kowloon, known as the "New Territories."

[2] Hong Kong was initially used as a trade centre, constituting a point of entry to China. But in the fifties, following the Communist victory in China, the United States and Britain imposed a trade embargo. Deprived of its supplies, Hong Kong was forced to import all its basic goods from overseas, therefore having to develop exports, rapidly transforming itself into a light industry centre, exporting textiles, clothing, plastic and electronic goods. Just as in Taiwan and South Korea, this development was generously supported by Western powers interested in these "bastions" of the Cold War.

[3] Growth of trade and the export industry also converted Hong Kong into a financial, communications and transport centre. The Government policy also contributed, setting low taxes and minimal customs tariffs, offering trustworthiness and freedom in movements of capital.

[4] When China announced a stage of liberalization toward foreign trade and investment in the late seventies, Hong Kong - armed with one of the best natural ports in the world, sophisticated international investment and trade systems, big, modern container port facilities - was ready to take advantage of the situation. Between 30 and 50 per cent of China's foreign trade of was carried out through Hong Kong, which was also the source of almost 90 per cent of foreign investment in the Chinese province of Kwangtung.

[5] Almost the entire population of Chinese origin had settled in the enclave following successive migratory waves resulting from political and economic events in their Communist neighbour.

[6] London and Beijing began negotiations on the future of the colony in the early 1980s, as the 99-year lease was due to end in 1997. The people of Hong Kong were not represented in these discussions.

[7] Agreement was reached in 1984, giving China sovereignty over the entire territory, but allowing Hong Kong "a high degree of independence" as a Special Administrative Area.

[8] In September 1991, the people of Hong Kong elected the members of the Legislative Council for the first time in 150 years. The United Democrats of Hong Kong (UDHK), candidates - critical of the colonial government of Hong Kong and of China and supporting stronger democracy - won most of the seats.

[9] The last British Governor, Chris Patten, reformed the electoral system, totally separating the economic and legislative powers. China said this reform contradicted the principles of the Basic Law. In 1998, China appointed a Preparatory Committee for the Administrative Region of Hong Kong, made up of leading figures of Hong Kong, and consultants from the colonial government.

[10] In 1994, Chris Patten proposed a plan to increase the number of voters in the 1995 elections, causing further confrontations with Beijing. In September 1995 the Democrat Party, opposed to the official Chinese interpretation of the Basic Law, triumphed in the Legislative Council elections. Beijing repeated its intention to dissolve the Council in 1997, alleging that it did not take the interests of all the social strata of Hong Kong into account.

[11] The British Governor publicly upbraided the Chinese authorities for only negotiating with "multi-millionaires". Patten referred to the alliance made in 1996 between leading Hong Kong business people and the Government in Beijing.

[12] At 00:00 hours, on Tuesday July 1 1997, China recovered control over Hong Kong after 155 years of British colonial dominion. Businessman Tung Chi Hua was appointed head of the new Executive with the support of a Legislative Council.

[13] According to the new law, Hong Kong retains its rights and liberties, its legal independence and nature as an international financial and trade centre, along with its way of life, for 50 years. The zone mints its own currency and is ruled by its own immigration and customs laws. Beijing will only handle defence and foreign relations during this period.

[14] Reunification put China in a "one country, two systems" situation, combining the free market economy of Hong Kong with rigid political control over the rest of the country, a totally unprecedented situation.

[15] The transferral took place against a backdrop of spectacular growth in the Chinese economy, which gave no signs of slowing. The Hong Kong economy, meanwhile, is considered the third most powerful in the world, and the former enclave is also the third most important international financial centre behind New York and London. In late 1997 rumours of financial difficulties in certain banks were denied by the local monetary authority.

rather than light, all under a centralized economic plan. The creation of a strong industrial base could only be achieved by extracting a large surplus from rural areas, but by 1957 agricultural production was badly stagnating.

[27] In the name of open debate, and in search of solutions to the nation's problems, the party launched a campaign to "let a hundred flowers bloom, let a hundred schools of thought contend," inviting people to criticize the system and suggest alternatives. When citizens began to complain about the lack of democracy and question party rule, the leadership turned about-face and, cracked down on those who had spoken out.

[28] In 1958, Mao launched the Great Leap Forward, aimed at accelerating rural collectivization and urban industrialization. This heavy-handed, dogmatic and inflexible plan led the country down a disastrous path, sparking widespread famine in the countryside. The official Chinese figure for deaths between 1959 and 1961 is 20 million; one of the greatest human tragedies of the century, and one of the least widely reported.

[29] In 1962, Mao was forced to deliver a public self-criticism of his economic policies and was replaced by Liu Shaoqi as state chairman. Mao still enjoyed support among many radicals and, most importantly, from the People's Liberation Army.

[30] During this period, relations with the Soviet Union were souring due to ideological differences. This was highlighted in a 1956 speech by Soviet leader Nikita Khruschev. The split came in 1963, and USSR advisors left China taking plans and blueprints with them.

[31] In 1966, the army and young people, the "Red Guards", armed with the Little Red Book of

82%

STATISTICS

DEMOGRAPHY
Population: 1,232,083,000 (1996) **Annual growth:** 1.3% (1980/1996) **Estimates for year 2000:** 1,276,300,000 **Annual growth to year 2000:** 0.9% (1994/2000) **Urban Population:** 31.0% (1996) **Urban growth:** 4.22% (1980/95) **Children per woman:** 1.8 (1996).

HEALTH
Life expectancy at birth: 69 years (1996) male: 67 years (1994) female: 71 years (1994) **Infant mortality:** 38 per 1,000 (1996) **Under-5 child mortality:** 47 per 1,000 (1996) **Calorie consumption:** 112% (1988/90) **Safe water:** 67% (1990/96).

EDUCATION
Literacy: 82% (1995) male : 90% (1995) female: 73% (1995) **School enrolment :** Primary total: 118% (1990/95) male : 120% (1990/95) female: 116% (1990/95) Secondary: male : 60% (1990/95) female: 51% (1990/95) Tertiary: 5% (1995) **Primary school teachers:** one for every 24 students (1995).

COMMUNICATIONS
20 **newspapers**, 184 **radios**, 230 **TV sets** and 23 **main telephone lines** per 1,000 people (1994) **Books:** 8 new titles per 100,000 people (1992/94).

ECONOMY
Per capita, GNP: $ 750 (1996) **Annual growth, GNP:** 8.9% (1995/96) **Annual inflation:** 9.26% (1985/95) **Consumer price index:** 165.6 (1994) **Currency:** 8.32 renminbi (yuan) = $ 1 (1995) **Cereal imports:** 16,331 metric tons (1994) **Food import dependency:** 3% (1994) **Fertilizer use:** 3,087 kgs per ha (1994) **Exports:** $ 151,047 million (1996) **Imports:** $ 138,833 million (1996) **External debt:** $ 128,817 million (1996) $ 105 **per capita:** (1996) **Debt service:** 8.7% of exports (1996) **Development aid received:** $ 3,521 million (1995) $ 3 per capita (1995) 0.7% of GNP (1994).

ENERGY
Consumption: 664.22 Kgs of Oil equivalent per capita yearly (1994) -0.98% imported (1994)

HDI (rank / value) 108 / 0.626 (1994).

Mao's thoughts, initiated campaigns throughout China attacking bureaucrats and university professors as reactionaries and "capitalist followers". The Great Proletarian Cultural Revolution had begun.

[32] There are many interpretations of the Cultural Revolution, and the upheaval occurred on many levels.

[33] At some stages during the Cultural Revolution, with the internal "struggle between two lines" attaining civil war proportions, production suffered severely with many factories and universities closing altogether. An estimated 10 million people died during the years of turmoil, including Liu Shaoqi, Mao's chief opponent.

[34] At the same time, China took a leading role in founding the Non-Aligned Movement, and sent large numbers of workers abroad on high-profile development projects such as the Tanzam railway, linking Zambia to the coast via Tanzania in Africa. Liberation movements in many countries were inspired by China, adopting the peasant war strategies outlined in the works of Mao Zedong and Lin Piao.

[35] In the early 1970s Prime Minister Zhou Enlai started talks with the US, and Liu Shaoqi's protégé, Deng Xiaoping, was returned to power.

[36] In 1971 the mainland communist Government won sufficient support to replace Taiwan as the representative of China in the United Nations. Unlike earlier occasions, this time the US refrained from exercising its veto because it saw distinct advantages in improving relations with China. In 1976, the US and China re-established diplomatic relations.

[37] Internationally, China seemed to oppose all Soviet allies. This led to Chinese support for movements like UNITA in Angola and the PAC in South Africa. It also caused a growing rift with Vietnam after it defeated the US in 1975. In 1979, China invaded Vietnam to "teach it a lesson" over its military contribution to the Khmer Rouge defeat in Cambodia.

[38] In 1975, Zhou and revolutionary veteran Zhu De both died, with Mao following in 1976. The pragmatists and reformists prevailed, taking advantage of support among party bureaucrats.

[39] The leaders of the Maoist faction - Mao's widow Jiang Qing, Zhang Chunqiao, Yao Wenyuan and Wang Hongwen, dubbed the "Gang of Four" - were arrested and charged with plotting to usurp state and party power. They became scapegoats for the failures and excesses of the Cultural Revolution. In 1981 they were put on public trial as a final symbolic gesture that the era of "revolutionary struggle" was over.

[40] Deng Xiaoping was rehabilitated by the new leadership, and he was universally acknowledged as its leading authority.

[41] The new leadership announced an ambitious economic development program. It envisioned significant advances in agriculture, industry, defence and science and technology.

[42] 1978 and 1979, were marked by the Government's acceptance of greater popular expression and criticism. They knew that this would be directed against the turmoil of the Cultural Revolution and the radicals responsible for it. The "Beijing Spring" was centered on the "Democracy Wall", where common citizens could display posters expressing their opinions. The wall also served as a spot where dissidents distributed unofficial magazines. When criticism began to focus on the country's core political structure, the leadership stopped the movement. The Democracy Wall, a continuing institution throughout the Cultural Revolution, was discontinued. One dissident, Wei Jingshen, who published a magazine calling for a "Fifth Modernization" - democracy - was tried and sentenced to a 15-year prison sentence.

[43] In December 1978, at the 3rd plenary of the 11th Party Central Committee, Deng was fully rehabilitated and sweeping economic reforms were announced.

[44] In the countryside, the People's Communes were disbanded and land was redistributed into family-size units leased from the State. Production quotas were replaced by taxes, and peasants were permitted to sell their surpluses for cash in the towns and cities.

[45] China also announced a dramatic new openness to foreign trade, investment and borrowing. To attract foreign industry, Special Economic Zones were established near Hong Kong (Xianggang) and Macau, offering a range of incentives; such as tax breaks, and cheap land and labor, similar to free trade zones elsewhere.

[46] In industry, a good deal of decision-making power was passed from the ministries to individual plant managers, who were now free to plan production and distribution, and choose the sources of their raw materials. Young workers were offered a contract system of employment instead of lifetime assignment to a production unit. Individuals and families were given permission to start small businesses such as restaurants and shops.

[47] The Government began a phased program of removing price subsidies on consumer goods, allowing the market to determine the price of such basics as food and clothing, to spur economic growth and encourage consumption.

Tibet: high plateau

Tibet was invaded by China in 1950 and today its population is roughly half Chinese and Tibetan with some Hui (Chinese Muslims), Hu, Monba, and other minority nationalities. Most of the inhabitants of this high plateau at the east of the Himalayas have the same ethnic origin. They also have traditionally practised the same religion, and spoken the same language.

[2] The first known religion in the region was Bon, which combined a belief in gods, demons, and ancestral spirits who were responsive to priests, or shamans. Chinese Buddhism was introduced in ancient times - the first scriptures date back to the 3rd century - but the mainstream Buddhist teachings came to Tibet from India in the 7th century. The blend of both produced the particular Lamaist Buddhism of the region and its many different sects. The principal monks of the many monasteries spread over the country became also temporal rulers and began to compete against each other. At different times the Mongols and Chinese took advantage of these conflicts, favouring one or another to suit their own purposes, setting up pendulum-like policy that lasted centuries.

[3] The Tibetans developed a phonetic alphabet about AD 600 and, after centuries of rivalry, a theocratic kind of feudal state was established in the early 10th century. Both political and religious power was conferred on the lamas, and monasteries who, along with the ruling class, controlled the peasants and the produce of the land.

[4] In 1240, the Mongols marched on central Tibet and attacked many important monasteries. In 1247, Köden, the younger brother of Güyük Khan, symbolically invested the Sa-skya lama with temporal authority over Tibet. Kublai Khan, grandson of Genghis Khan, appointed the lama Phags-pa as his "Imperial preceptor". The politico-religious relationship between Tibet and the Mongol Empire was characterized as a personal bond between the Emperor as patron and the lama as priest. During the century, many Sa-skya lamas, living at the Mongol court, became viceroys of Tibet on behalf of the Mongol emperors.

[5] The Dre-lugs-pa hierarchies set a new alliance with the Mongols in 1578. This re-established the framework that shared religious authority - assigned to Tibetan lamas - and political dominance - resting with Mongolian leaders. Atlan conferred on the Bsod-nams-rgya-mtsho - third in the lamas' hierarchy - the title of Dalai ("oceanwide") Lama. In 1640, the Mongols invaded Tibet and two years later the Güüshi Khan enthroned the fourth Dalai Lama as ruler of Tibet, keeping for himself the military protection of the region.

[6] The assassination of two Chinese high commissioners in 1751 - instigated by the Dalai Lama - brought an immediate and bloody response from the Manchu dynasty in power in Beijing: the Emperor sent in a military expedition to Lhasa. Since that time, the Dalai Lama's relationship with China became more difficult than that of the Panchens - the other leaders of the religious hierarchy. Worldly competition between the two heads of the Lamaist Buddhism often fostered division and sectarianism.

[7] In the 17th century, the fifth Dalai Lama declared that his tutor, Blo-bzang chos-kyi-rgyal-mtshan (1570-1662), who was the current Panchen Lama, would be reincarnated in a child.

[8] In 1904 a British military expedition headed by Colonel Younghusband invaded Tibet and forced the Tibetans into making a treaty.

[9] In 1910 Chinese troops entered Lhasa. The Dalai Lama appealed to the British to help expel them - and was refused. But the Chinese empire was in its death throes and fell to the Nationalists in 1911. Tibetans seized the chance to expel the invaders and in June 1912 the Dalai Lama proclaimed Tibetan independence. About ten years later, disagreements between the Dalai Lama and the Panchen Lama ended in the flight of the latter to Beijing. A boy born of Tibetan parents about 1938 in Tsinghai province, China, Bskal-bzang Tshe-brtan, was recognized as his successor by the Chinese Government and brought to Tibet in 1952. Eventually, he entered Lhasa under Communist military escort and was enthroned as head monk of the Tashilhunpo Monastery.

[10] In 1949 the Communists came to power in China and the following year the Government declared its intention to 'liberate' Tibet from feudalism. Some 84,000 troops invaded Tibet's eastern province of Kham and met resistance from Tibetan Khampa horseriders, but they were crushed. In 1951 the present Dalai Lama, Tenzin Gyatso, then aged 15, signed an agreement with China.

[11] In 1959 Tibetan resistance exploded into an uprising which was put down by the Chinese. Chinese figures record 87,000 deaths; Tibetan sources suggest as many as 430,000 were killed. When the 1959 revolt collapsed, the Panchen Lama remained in Tibet, while the Dalai Lama fled into exile. The Panchen Lama's refusal to denounce the Dalai Lama as a traitor brought him into disfavour with the Chinese Government, which imprisoned him in Peking in 1964. He was released in the late 1970s and died in 1989.

[12] The Dalai Lama and the Tibetan government-in-exile, established in India in 1959, continue to fight for the independence of Tibet and the return to traditional society. In 1994 the Chinese declared a five-year-old boy to be the next Panchen Lama instead of the boy found by Tibetan religious authorities. The Dalai Lama and Tibetan government-in-exile has rejected the legitimacy of the nomination.

[13] In the following years, growing tension between Chinese and Tibetans weakened support for the Dalai Lama's "peaceful coexistence" policy. In the beginning of 1998, the religious leader admitted that even his own followers were more and more hostile to that policy, demanding a more active opposition to the Chinese presence in Tibet.

---

[48] As the changes took hold, more goods and foodstuffs appeared in shops, and wages increased for several years. The long-standing problem of unemployment and underemployment diminished as more people became self-employed. Restrictions on the freedom of travel inside and outside China were loosened, greater artistic diversity and expression were tolerated and a greater diversity of information was made available.

[49] These economic reforms began to accelerate inflation, especially on such basic items as food and clothing, and in the late 1980s, workers found that their buying power was falling.

[50] In the countryside, peasants with easy access to urban centers benefited as they were able to supply large markets. Those in more remote areas fell behind. The use of chemical pesticides and fertilizers soared, and production initially rose as well. But production levels began to fall, prompting farmers to apply greater quantities of chemicals, approaching danger levels. Pesticide and fertilizer prices rose sharply.

[51] Workers' welfare deteriorated, and the new employment systems generated insecurity. While managers were given more power, even to hire and fire workers and set production targets, trade unions were not granted any corresponding freedom to act.

[52] High-level debate over the scale and pace of economic reforms included discussion of a clearer division between party and state.

[53] In 1986 students demonstrated in Shanghai, calling for freedom of the press and political reform. As a result, Hu Yaobang, then a relatively young Party General Secretary, was forced to step down, and a campaign against "bourgeois liberalism" was launched by hard-

liners. This aimed to root out what they called "western" ideas; most importantly political pluralism, though consumerism and corruption were also mentioned. Many viewed this campaign as a veiled attack on Deng's economic reform policies, given that Hu Yaobang was one of Deng's protégés.

[54] In March 1989, police in what is known as Central Asian China fired on Tibetan demonstrators who were protesting against cultural and religious persecution and demanding greater political rights. The shooting triggered three days of widespread rioting which resulted in the imposition of Martial Law, lifted only in April 1990. Tibetan exiles reported the detention of many dissidents and several executions. Tibet was officially annexed to China in 1950 and converted into an autonomous region in 1965.

[55] In April 1989, the death of Hu Yaobang served as a pretext for thousands of students to assemble in Tiananmen Square in downtown Beijing. In addition to mourning the death of the man who to them symbolized liberal reform, the students called for an end to corruption and changes in both society and the party.

[56] The students camped in the square and their numbers grew, buoyed by the anniversary of the student demonstrations of May 4 1919. Hundreds of thousands of citizens and workers in Beijing began to demonstrate support for the reform movement, bringing food and other supplies to the students, marching, and blockading intersections when it seemed likely that troops would move against the students.

[57] Students, citizens and workers began similar demonstrations in other cities, and the banners of groups of workers from the official media, trade unions, and various party sections began to appear in the daily demonstrations. Various autonomous bodies were set up by demonstrators, challenging four decades of complete party control over all social organizations.

[58] Finally, on June 4 1989, the Government moved decisively and violently, sending troops into downtown Beijing to clear out the citizens and students. Many hundreds were killed and

thousands wounded. Many Beijing residents and students were killed as the troops forced their way past barricades in armored vehicles and opened fire on the crowds. The pro-democracy demonstrations were smashed. The assault on Tiananmen was followed by a nationwide hunt for leaders of the autonomous student and workers movements, thousands were arrested and badly beaten; many others were executed. There were important political changes, and Li Peng became Prime Minister.

[59] The first Western Government to send representatives to the capital after the Tiananmen massacre was Britain, in September 1991. They signed an agreement with Beijing on the construction of a new airport in Xianggang (Hong Kong), within the constraints of the negotiations to return the British colony to China, in 1997.

[60] With one-third of all public enterprises operating at that time at a deficit, and less and less possibility of balancing the State budget, structural reforms seemed all but inevitable in state enterprises. The Chinese Communist Party was paving the way for a return to the economic liberalization program initiated by Deng Xiaoping, who had reappeared on the political scene at the age of 87. At the same time, there were other indicators of changing attitudes: Jiang Zemin, Deng's successor as Communist Party Secretary, called for "free thinking", and charges against former Secretary Zhao Zhiyang were reduced. Shortly afterwards, however, he was blamed for events leading to the Tiananmen massacre, rendering impossible his chances of rehabilitation.

[61] The Paris Accords on Cambodia (see Cambodia), signed in October 1991, and the end of the Soviet Union accelerated a rapprochement between China and Vietnam. In November 1991, diplomatic relations between the two countries were re-established.

[62] In late November 1991, the Government freed the student leaders from the Tiananmen demonstrations. However, there were an estimated 70,000 political prisoners in various provinces of the the Xinjiang and Qinghai region.

[63] In 1992, China signed the Nuclear Non-Proliferation Treaty. In the annual session of the People's National Congress, Jiang Zemin was designated president of the republic, becoming the first person since Mao to combine the functions of head of state, the party and commander of the armed forces. Prime Minister Li Peng was confirmed in his post.

[64] In April 1992, the decision was made to build the giant Three Gorges dam on the Yangtse river. This controversial project was to be completed in 2009, flooding lands inhabited by 1.3 million people, drowning 10 cities and more than 800 towns. Ecologists immediately opposed the project, saying it would destroy the habitats of endangered species and would leave millions of people exposed to the danger of earthquakes, avalanches and floods. They also considered the dam would not be profitable.

[65] In September, the Government said the pro-independence action in Tibet would be "implacably repressed". On the economic front, an austerity plan was launched in the State apparatus and taxes on the rural population were increased. However, a series of protests and demonstrations forced the Government to remove the new charge from a sector of the population which totalled around 800 million people.

[66] The GDP increased by 12.8 per cent in 1992, a figure unprecedented in the previous decade. However, this growth (the economy nearly doubled since 1990) had its first undesirable effects in 1993, when inflation hit 20 per cent in the first half year. In March 1994, Li Peng proposed limiting the economic expansion to 9 per cent in order to limit inflation despite protests from the coastal provinces like Guandong, the main beneficiaries of the Chinese "boom".

[67] The social inequalities between the new rich in the cities and the vast majority of the workers and rural population continued to increase along with the migration of millions of people from the countryside to the cities. This led the Government to be prudent in closing and privatizing unprofitable State enterprises, as a sharp rise in unemployment would only worsen

an already tense and precarious social situation.

[68] However, another project which planned to limit the social effects of the economic reforms was postponed. The plan was to establish a redundancy payment for workers laid off from closed State companies, but the total lack of a State-run social security system in the nation - without so much as unemployment benefit - made the Government back off from launching excessively radical reforms.

[69] In 1995, Jiang Zemin consolidated his power to continue ruling the nation in the "post-Deng" era. The authorities continued to be concerned about the social effects of the reforms, hence they maintained the large subsidies for State enterprises.

[70] In that year, inflation reached only 13 per cent, and the 1996-2000 five-year plan forecast annual growth of "only" 8-9 per cent. The number of corruption scandals increased dramatically. The CCP first secretary in Beijing, Chen Xitong, was forced to leave his post when it became clear he had been misappropriating funds along with important communal leaders and a large municipal metallurgical company. In April, the deputy-mayor of Beijing, Wang Daosen, accused of having embezzled 37 million dollars of Government funds, committed suicide.

[71] As in previous years, trade relations with the United States strengthened, despite the constant public disagreements between the nations, like the situation provoked by military manoeuvres in the waters around Taiwan (see Taiwan) or the nuclear tests carried out by Beijing. In November, Jiang made the first ever visit of a Chinese president to South Korea, in another demonstration of the commercial and political rapprochement of China with countries it had classed as anti-Communist during the Cold War.

[72] In May 1996 Amnesty International condemned the repression of Buddhist monks in Tibet by the Chinese authorities. According to AI, 80 monks were injured for refusing to respect a ban on the public exhibition of pictures of the Dalai Lama.

[73] Two student leaders of the 1989 uprising were sentenced to

prison sentences of 11 and 3 years, accused of promoting the overthrow of the Government. Another student gained political asylum in the United States. The regime continued with the psychological harassment of Taiwan carrying out large-scale military exercises around the island.

74 The economy continued to do well in 1996, with GDP growth of above 10 per cent, while inflation fell to below 6 per cent. At the same time, industrial yield increased as did foreign investment - considered the motor of economic growth -

which rose 20 per cent. Several foreign companies established in China were authorised to exchange the local currency for dollars or yens.

75 The death of Deng Xiaoping, in February 1997 at the end of a long illness, created some concern amongst investors and diplomats, but the highest government and Communist Party authorities stated the direction of the economic reforms would not change.

76 The 15th Communist Party Congress, in October of this year, consolidated reform policy, particularly as applied to the

State companies, and reaffirmed the traditional political system.

77 In March 1998, the People's National Congress ratified the changes decided by the Communist Party. Jiang Zemin was re-elected head of State and commander of the armed forces, with 98 per cent of the vote. Some 2,882 deputies voted in favour, 36 against and 29 abstained.

78 Hu Jintao, mentioned as a possible successor to Zemin, was elected Vice-President, while outgoing prime minister, Li Peng, became Head of Parliament. The Constitution prevented him from

serving a third term as Head of Government.

79 Zhu Rongji, former deputy prime minister in charge of the economy, was elected Prime Minister. The new cabinet, made up mostly of economic experts, faced the preparation of the 370,000 State companies for free market rules, a process which had already cost between 20 and 30 million jobs.

80 Continuing the reform process started in 1978 by Deng Xiaoping, the new aim of Zhu's administration was to re-structure the financial system.

Macau: a delayed hand-over

The tiny Portuguese enclave of Macau is located across the Pearl River estuary from Hong Kong.

The Portuguese set it up in 1557 as an important link in their chain of trading ports which stretched from Europe, along the coasts of Africa and India, past Melaka in Malaysia, and on to Nagasaki in Japan. Rent was paid for the territory until 1849 when Portugal declared it independent. China accepted this in 1887, after Portugal pledged never to alienate Macau and its dependencies without agreement with China. It was declared an Overseas Province of Portugal in 1951.

2 For several hundred years, Macau represented the main point of contact for economic and cultural links between Europeans and the vast Chinese empire. With the development of Hong Kong next door, and the decline of Portugal as a colonial power, Macau lost its importance.

3 During the height of the Cultural Revolution in China, Macau experienced serious anti-Portuguese rioting, and the Government reportedly offered to abandon the territory within a month, but China refused the offer.

4 In 1974, after the fall of the regime of Antonio de Oliveira Salazar, the Portuguese Government again offered to return the colony to China. Anxious not to alarm Hong Kong or Taiwan, China refused. The Portuguese Government unilaterally declared Macau to be Chinese territory under Portuguese administration.

5 In 1985, once negotiations between China and Britain on the future of Hong Kong had been successfully completed,

Beijing turned its attention to Macau, and negotiated a settlement with the Portuguese under which Macau was to be returned to China in 1999, with arrangements for retaining some local autonomy as in Hong Kong.

6 Macau is an impracticably small enclave, isolated from a central government thousands of miles away and with an administration reluctantly serving out its time. Not surprisingly, corruption is widespread. In 1988 senior officials were implicated in a scandal over privatization of the colony's television station.

7 Much of Macau is separated from China by only a narrow river, preventing the authorities from stopping the large flow of illegal immigrants into the city. These people arrive with no legal means of support and often turn to crime.

8 In 1988 the Government began to allow workers from China into Macau. The move was criticized by labor groups as a means of keeping wages down.

9 Macau has few natural resources: for some time, China has provided part of its water, and since 1984, part of its electricity. However, as of 1989, more than 90 per cent of the electricity used has been produced within the territory. In the past, the colony depended upon tourism, a certain amount of trade with China and light industry (especially toys and textiles). Recently, however, since China began its economic liberalization program and created a Special Economic Zone on the other side of the border, construction was begun on a hotel and a new airport.

10 Between 1985 and 1989, the GNP grew at an annual rate of 8.1 per cent. Most of Macau's tourists come from Hong Kong. The casinos

are the main tourist attraction, and account for 62 per cent of the Government's income. The construction of the airport has attracted investment from Taiwan and other countries, who have benefited from the low cost of labor.

11 In 1989, Portuguese passports were issued to around 100,000 Macau residents of Chinese origin. Macau's "old-time" residents were always considered to be Portuguese citizens, enjoying all the rights of citizenship, including automatic entry to Portugal and, as of 1993, to the rest of the European Community.

12 In 1991, Governor Vasco Rocha Vieira allowed Chinese citizens to work as civil servants and declared Cantonese an official language along with Portuguese. In the September 1992 legislative elections, pro-Chinese organizations won a majority of seats.

13 In 1993, a law was approved to serve as a constitution when the territory became a Special Administrative Region of China from 1999, with a government designated by a local electoral college and a Legislative Council in power until 2001.

14 This document guaranteed the future of the market economy and the casinos, at least over this transition period, banning the imposition of Chinese tariffs, along with death penalties and life sentences of the type applied in the rest of the country.

15 As of December 20 1999, Macau is to be added to the list of Special Economic Zones created by Deng Xiaoping in the provinces of Canton, Shenzhen, Zhuhai and Shantou, where some aspects of the market economy operate.

Taiwan

Taiwan

Population: 21,035,000 (1994)
Area: 36,960 SQ KM
Capital: Taipei

Currency: New dollars
Language: Chinese (Mandarin)

The island of Taiwan's government insists that it represents all of China. It calls itself the Republic of China, and for four decades has pledged itself to the cause of recovering the mainland, from which it is separated by the 200-km wide Taiwan Strait.

[2] China's Qing (Manchu) emperors incorporated Taiwan into the empire in 1683, and the island was proclaimed a separate province of China in 1887. During this time, the political and administrative systems of mainland China were extended to Taiwan, and many people migrated there from the mainland.

[3] After China's defeat in the 1895 Sino-Japanese war, Taiwan became a Japanese colony, but was returned to China after the defeat of Japan at the end of World War II. At first, the people of Taiwan rejoiced at the end of Japanese colonialism, but they soon discovered that life under the ruthlessly authoritarian, corrupt and vehemently anti-Communist Kuomintang (KMT) party led by Chiang Kai-Shek resembled nothing less than a different kind of colonialism.

[4] On February 28, 1947, there was a major demonstration against the KMT authorities. The KMT reacted at first by lifting martial law, and inviting the opposition to form a Settlement Committee of politicians, trade unionists and student groups to discuss possible political reforms. Meanwhile, they drafted in 13,000 additional troops, and when the opposition came forward, the KMT massacred large numbers of them, imprisoning others.

[5] In 1949, the entire KMT government, the remnants of its armies, and their relatives and supporters, fled to Taiwan after losing the mainland civil war to the Communist armies. From its refuge, backed by the United States, the KMT declared Taiwan to be the temporary base of the Republic of China pending recovery of the mainland. Most Western nations continued to recognize the KMT as the representatives of all China.

[6] When the Korean War erupted, with China supporting the North Koreans, the United States redoubled its military and economic commitment to Taiwan, protecting it as a front-line state in the battle to defend the "free world".

[7] Democracy disappeared. Human rights were violated, demonstrations, strikes and political parties banned, and martial law imposed, all in the name of the battle to reconquer the mainland. The KMT set up a governmental system which claimed to represent the whole of China, with legislators representing each mainland province.

[8] Taiwan's remarkable industrialization began in the 1960s, when World Bank and US technocrats helped the government apply an export-oriented development strategy. The era of Japanese colonialism had left Taiwan with only partially-developed transport and an education system. The US granted ideologically-motivated financial, trade and aid advantages to bolster an authoritarian political regime which, in turn, hectored Taiwan's disenfranchised, and politically disorganized workforce.

[9] Taiwanese output grew at an average of 8.6 per cent each year between 1953 and 1985, and became one of the four newly-industrialized dragons of East Asia. Growth was entirely export-oriented, and the island developed the world's second-largest trade surplus with the US, following Japan. Today, Taiwan has highly developed plastics, chemical, ship-building, clothing and electronics industries.

[10] Sweatshop conditions were common in the 1960s and 1970s, and many workers put in long shifts, often exposed to toxic substances.

[11] In 1971, the United States decided to seek closer ties with China, no longer vetoing the latter's admission to the UN. Taiwan therefore lost its representation in that world body. A few years later, in 1979, the United States officially broke off diplomatic relations with Taiwan.

[12] The country found itself at an economic crossroads. The island was over-dependent on a few export markets and labor-intensive industries, importing nations were pressuring for more balanced trade and Taiwan's labor was no longer as cheap as that of many of its Asian neighbors. Technocrats argued that, in order to compete, Taiwan should develop a more open political system. The KMT also faced an internal succession crisis as ageing politicians from the civil war era clung precariously to power.

[13] In this climate, social movements were proliferating, with ecological groups protesting against pollution and nuclear power, farmers' groups demanding higher prices, and students calling for more academic freedom and an end to human rights abuses.

[14] In addition, a significant portion of the population does not consider their country to be a part of China, and rejects both the authoritarian policies of the KMT and Deng Xiaoping's unification proposal of "one nation, two systems" with Taiwan becoming a Chinese dependency.

[15] In September 1986 the Democratic Progress Party (DPP) was formed as the first opposition party to challenge the KMT's political stranglehold. Although technically illegal, the party was allowed to survive, and Martial Law was formally lifted on July 15 1987.

[16] A huge upsurge in union activity took place in 1987. Strong independent sections were formed in the trade union system and supporters founded parallel political structures in the Labor Party and Workers' Party.

[17] Elections were held in December 1989. The KMT won 53 per cent of the vote, against the DPP's 38 per cent. The DPP also fared well in municipal and council elections, winning the mayorship of Taipei.

[18] While the KMT is resolutely opposed to independence, some DPP members formed the New Wave group proposing that Taiwan declare self-rule, and other groups advocate a referendum for self-determination.

[19] The KMT achieved yet another victory over the opposition DPP in the National Assembly elections in December 1991. The results were regarded as a plebiscite on the independence issue. The DPP's electoral platform, favoring a definitive separation from China, was supported by a mere 21 per cent of the electorate, against KMT's 71 per cent.

[20] In 1992, fourteen members of the World Union of Formosans for Independence - a party which had been banned by the Government - were arrested. In addition, diplomatic ties were broken with South Korea, which established relations with China. In December, in the first open elections since 1949, the DPP obtained 31 per cent of the vote, and 50 of the 161 legislative seats.

PROFILE

ENVIRONMENT

Located 160 km Southeast of continental China, Taiwan is part of a chain of volcanic islands in the West Pacific which also includes the Japanese islands. A mountain range runs across Taiwan stretching from north to south along the centre of the country.

A narrow plain along the island's western coast constitutes its main agricultural area where rice, sugar cane, bananas and tobacco are cultivated. More than two-thirds of the island's area is densely wooded.

Taiwan has considerable mineral resources: coal, natural gas, marble, limestone and minor deposits of copper, gold, and oil. The country is suffering the consequences of its enormous industrial explosion, with high levels of water, air and land pollution.

SOCIETY

Peoples: Most inhabitants are Chinese who have migrated from the mainland since the 17th century and are known as "Taiwanese". Hundreds of thousands of Kuomintang Chinese fled to Taiwan during 1949-50. The island's indigenous inhabitants are of Malayo-Polynesian origin, and currently do not exceed 1.7 per cent of the population. They are concentrated on the east coast, where they make up 25 per cent of the population.

Religions: More than half of the population are Chinese Buddhist. There are also Muslim and Christian minorities.

Languages: Chinese (Mandarin), official. Taiwanese, a derivative of the Chinese dialect from Fujian province, is the language of the majority.

Political Parties: Kuomintang (Chinese Nationalist Party), founded in China in 1919, took political monopoly of Taiwan when it fled from the continent in 1949 and ruled under martial law up to 1987; Democratic Progressive Party (DPP), formed in 1986 with a very broad platform to restore political democracy in Taiwan; New Trend split from the DPP with claims for Taiwan independence; Labour Party, centrist, and Workers' Party, socialist, appeared after the resurgence of trade unions in 1987. Among the pro-independence groups there is the illegal World Union of Formosans for Independence.

Social Organizations: Every trade union has to be a member of the Chinese Federation of Labour, controlled by the Kuomintang, but in 1987 appeared a few independent trade union who organised in several federations, including the National Federation of Independent Unions and Tao-Chu-Miao Brotherhood.

THE STATE

Official name: Republic of China.

Administrative divisions: 7 municipalities and 16 counties.

Capital: Taipei (T'aipei), 2,595,699 people (1997).

Other cities: Kaohsiung, 1,434,907 people; Taichung, 881,870; Tainan, 712,172 (1997).

Government: President, Lee Teng-hui, re-elected in 1996. Prime Minister, Vincent Siew, since September 1 1997. The National Assembly has 720 members, is in charge of appointing the president for a six-year-period and is empowered to amend the Constitution. The President heads the legislative "Yuan", with 240 members, and appoints the Prime Minister who heads the executive "Yuan". Internal affairs are under the control of a Provincial Assembly of 77 members which deals with administrative matters.

National holiday: January 1st, Day of the Republic; February 25th, Constitution Day.

Armed Forces: 376,000 troops.

Other: Militarised police, 25,000.

STATISTICS

DEMOGRAPHY

Population: 21,035,000 (1994)*. **Urban population:** 95.2 % (1996).

ECONOMY

Exports: $ 115,646 million (1996). **Imports:** $ 101,338 million (1996).

* Source: Handbook of International Trade and Development Statistics 1995, UNCTAD, 1995.

[21] In early 1993, and as a direct consequence of the electoral results, there were two significant resignations by members of the KMT leadership: that of Prime Minister Hau Pei-tsu, and that of Secretary General James Sung, both of the conservative wing of the party. Lien Chan, the first government leader to have been born in Taiwan, was named prime minister. Shortly afterwards, the governing party experienced its first major division. Thirty deputies broke with the KMT to found the Party of the New Nationalist Alliance.

[22] Starting from 1994, distinctive voices are making themselves heard demanding an independent way for Taiwan, leaving behind the assumption of being a government representative of all Chinese. However, due to Beijing's opposition to any measure which could further lead the island toward independence, Taipei's efforts to be accepted into the United Nations were in vain.

[23] The first multiparty municipal elections were held in December. Most of the vote went to the ruling Kuomintang and the DPP. Meanwhile, in spite of opposition from environmentalists and anti-nuclear activists and DPP objections, the KMT sponsored the approval for the construction of a fourth nuclear plant on the island.

[24] In 1995, economic relations with Beijing intensified. Taiwan became the second "foreign" investor in the People's Republic after Hong Kong, placing approximately $22 billion in China. In spite of this exchange, political relations between the two countries deteriorated after a private visit from Taiwanese president Lee Teng to the US in June. Heedless of US warnings, Beijing carried out a series of missile launchings in July and August on waters just 140 kilometres from Taiwan.

[25] In spite of losing ground from previous elections, the Kuomintang won the December legislative elections with 46 per cent of the vote and 33 per cent by the DPP. In the campaign prior to the March 1996 presidential elections, new Chinese military manoeuvres near the coasts of Taiwan led Washington to send warships in defence of Taiwan's alleged threatened territorial integrity.

[26] Lee Teng, of the Kuomintang, triumphed on March 20 in the first presidential elections with direct suffrage in the history of the island, taking 54 per cent of the vote. The defeated Peng Ming-min, of the Democratic Progressive Party, took 21 per cent. Lee repeated his decision to improve Taiwan's international profile through an energetic diplomatic offensive.

[27] In July, China made a show of military force off the coast of Taiwan, timed to coincide with the return of Hong Kong from British to Chinese control.

[28] In August the Government announced the closure of its embassy on the island of St Lucia, following the Caribbean island's decision to strengthen links with China. The severing of diplomatic relations reduced the number of countries recognizing the Taipei Government to 30. Also that month, Prime Minister Lien Chan handed in his resignation and was replaced by Vincent Siew from September 1.

[29] The triumph of the pro-independence movements in 12 mayorships, signalled clear defeat of the Nationalist Party in the October 1997 municipal elections. The result was poorly received by the government party, in power since 1949, less than a year away from legislative elections.

[30] In April 1998, China and Taiwan decided to restart direct negotiations, having broken off relations in June 1995.

Colombia

Colombia

Population: 36,444,000 (1996)
Area: 1,138,914 SQ KM
Capital: Santa Fé de Bogotá

Currency: Pesos
Language: Spanish

The best known of Colombia's indigenous cultures is that of the Chibchas or "Muiscas", as they called themselves. They lived in the northern Colombia and Panama, farming and mining.

[2] In America, colonization resulted in the plundering of native wealth and the population was subjected to thinly disguised forms of slavery. After 300 years of colonialism, a large part of the indigenous population had disappeared.

[3] Spain conquered Colombia between 1536 and 1539. Gonzalo Giménez de Quesada decimated the Chibchas and founded the city of Santa Fe de Bogotá which became the center of the Viceroyalty of New Granada in 1718.

[4] Extensive, export-oriented agriculture (coffee, bananas, cotton and tobacco) replaced traditional crops (potatoes, cassava, corn, wood and medicinal plants) with African slaves replacing the more rebellious indigenous population.

[5] The Revolt of the Comuneros started the process leading to the declaration of independence in Cundinamarca, in 1813. The road to independence was marked by constant struggles between the advocates of centralized government and the federalists, headed by Camilo Torres. Antonio Nariño (who had drafted the declaration of independence) represented the urban bourgeoisie, linked to European interests, while Torres presided over the Congress of the United Provinces, representing the less privileged.

[6] In 1816, Pablo Morillo reconquered this territory, executing Torres. Three years later, Simon Bolívar counter-attacked from Venezuela, liberated Colombia and founded the Republic of Greater Colombia, including Venezuela, Ecuador and the province of Panama. Regionalism and strong British pressure brought about the secession of Venezuela and Ecuador in 1829-30. The Republic of New Granada was then proclaimed and in 1886 Colombia adopted its current name.

[7] From 1830 to the early 20th century, the country went through civil wars, local wars (including two with Ecuador), three military uprisings and 11 constitutions. The Liberals and Conservatives have kept a permanent hold on the Colombian political situation, separated by a mutual hatred passed down from generation to generation, despite having similar platforms for governing the country.

[8] Between 1921 and 1957, over-production of the country's oil reserves led to a depletion of this resource, leaving American oil companies with a profit of $1 billion, and Colombia with no oil. American companies control 80 to 90 per cent of banana production and mining, and 98 per cent of energy production.

[9] In 1948, in Bogotá, Mayor Jorge Eliecer Gaitan of the Liberal Party was assassinated, and public indignation over his death triggered widespread riots, known as El Bogotazo. That same year, a Liberal mayor organized a guerrilla group, the first of 36 which were active during the presidencies of Ospina Pérez, Laureano Gómez and Rojas Pinilla. In 1957, a constitutional reform ensured the alternation of Liberals and Conservatives in the Government, every 12 years.

[10] The Revolutionary Armed Forces of Colombia (FARC), led by Manuel "Tiro Fijo" (Sure Shot) Marulanda and Jacobo Arenas, appeared on the scene in 1964. Guerrilla strategists included Camilo Torres Restrepo, a priest and co-founder of the National Liberation Army (ELN), who was killed in combat in 1965.

[11] Large landowners organized, armed and paid "self-defence" groups to fight these rural-based guerrilla movements. These were supported by members of the army and, in some cases, by foreign mercenaries. Closed out of official circles, the army also created paramilitary groups, later condemned by Amnesty International.

[12] From 1974, President Alfonso López Michelsen, a Liberal, tried to give greater attention to popular demands, but vested economic interests led to the failure of this policy. Figures for 1978 reveal that only 30 per cent of industrial workers and 11 per cent of the rural workforce had social security benefits. Colombia is dependent on international coffee prices on the American and German markets, for its foreign exchange, as these countries consume 56 per cent of the Colombian product.

[13] Guerrilla movements, particularly the FARC and the April 19 Revolutionary Movement (M-19), continued their activities into the late 1970s. Military repression grew during the government of President Julio C Turbay Ayala (1978-82).

[14] In 1982, a divided Liberal Party nominated two candidates, thus handing over the victory to the Conservative Party's Belisario Betancur, a journalist, poet and humanist, who had actively participated in the peace process in Central America. Betancur proposed that Colombia join the Non-Aligned Movement and reaffirmed the right of debtor nations to negotiate collectively with creditor banks. Also, in 1983

PUBLIC EXPENDITURE

8.7% 40.8%
1995 ■ DEFENCE □ SOCIAL

In 1990/91 Military as % of health & education expenditure was 57%.

WORKERS

(1996)

Labour force %

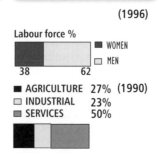

■ WOMEN
□ MEN
38   62

■ AGRICULTURE 27% (1990)
□ INDUSTRIAL 23%
■ SERVICES 50%

LAND USE

DEFORESTATION -0.6% annual (81/90)
IRRIGATED 13.5% of arable

(1993)

■ FOREST & WOODLAND 43.9%
□ ARABLE 3.4%
■ OTHER 52.7%

Maternal Mortality
1990

PER 100,000
LIVE BIRTHS

100

Foreign Trade
MILLIONS $ 1996

IMPORTS
13,863
EXPORTS
10,976

PROFILE

ENVIRONMENT
The Andes cross the country from north to south, in three ranges: the western range on the Pacific coast, and further inland, the central and eastern ranges, separated by the large valleys of the Cauca and Magdalena Rivers. North of the Andes, the swampy delta of the Magdalena River opens up, leaving flat coastal lowlands to the west - along the Pacific coast - and to the east, plains covered by jungle and savannas extend downward to the Orinoco and Amazon Rivers. This diversity results in great climatic variety, from perpetual snows on Andean peaks to tropical Amazon rain forests. The country's Andean region houses most of the population. Coffee is the main export item, followed by bananas. Abundant mineral resources include petroleum, coal, gold, platinum, silver and emeralds. Intensive agriculture and mining have contributed to soil depletion. There is significant deforestation, and two-thirds of the country's bird species are in danger of extinction.

SOCIETY
Peoples: Colombians are the result of cultural and ethnic integration among three groups: native Americans, Africans and Europeans.
Religions: 93 per cent of Colombians are Catholic. Although this is the country's official religion, there is religious freedom.
Language: Spanish (official).
Political Parties: The Liberal Party (LP); the Social Conservative Party (SCP); the New Democratic Force (NFD), led by Andrés Pastrana, conservative; M-19 Democratic Alliance (ADM-19); National Salvation Movement (MSN), which broke away from the PSC; Patriotic Union, formed by the military.
Social Organizations: There are four major labor organizations: the Confederation of Colombian Workers; the Confederation of Workers' Unions of Colombia; and the General Labor Confederation. The Colombian United Labor Federation (CUT), founded on 26 September 1986, and 80 per cent of all salaried workers affiliated to trade unions are members.

THE STATE
Official Name: República de Colombia.
Administrative divisions: 32 departments and the capital district.
Capital: Santa Fé de Bogotá, 5,614,000 people (1995).
Other cities: Cali 1,718,900 people; Medellín 1,621,400; Barranquilla1,064,300; Cartagena 745,700 (1995).
Government: Andrés Pastrana, President since June 1998.
National Holiday: July 20, Independence Day (1810).
Armed Forces: 146,400 troops (1994).
Other: National Police Force, with 85,000 members. Coast Guard: 1,500 (1993).

---

he entered into peace talks with leaders of the M-19.

[15] The M-19 had initiated the peace process in 1980, when guerrilla leader Jaime Bateman proposed a high-level meeting in Panama. Bateman subsequently died in a suspicious airline accident and talks were suspended. In the meantime, the FARC and the government reached an agreement which led to a ceasefire between them and to the adoption of political, social and economic reforms.

[16] Large landowners fiercely opposed talks between the government and the guerrillas. The rural oligarchy, holding 67 per cent of the country's productive land, denounced the pacification process as "a concession to subversion" and proposed the creation of private armies. Paramilitary action started up again; subsequent investigations revealed the hand of the MAS, "Death to the Kidnappers", which had opposed the withdrawal of the army from guerrilla-controlled areas. A one-year truce went into effect but M-19 withdrew five months later, claiming that the army had violated the cease-fire.

[17] In January 1985, the Government passed a series of unpopular economic measures: drastic cuts in public spending, a salary freeze for civil servants, substantial fuel and transport price rises, increased taxes on over 200 products including some basic consumer goods, limited salary increases which lowered real purchasing power, and a currency devaluation. The object was to increase exports and reduce the $2 billion fiscal deficit by 30 per cent.

[18] Rejected by the labor unions and the parties of the left, the plan also failed to satisfy the country's creditors. A commission of 14 banks, presided over by the Chemical Bank, stated that the Government would have to sign a letter of intent and reach a formal agreement with the IMF, two steps which Betancur had wanted to avoid.

[19] According to the Human Rights Commission, 80 prisoners had disappeared in one year, political prisoners had been tortured and 300 clandestine executions were confirmed. The

number of political activists who had disappeared rose to 325.

[20] On November 6 1985, 35 guerrillas from M-19 took over the Palace of Justice in Bogotá. The army attacked, causing a massacre. All the guerrillas were killed, along with 53 civilian victims, including magistrates and employees. A guerrilla commander known as Alonso insisted that those who had been killed "were deliberately sacrificed by the army".

[21] Taking advantage of this panorama of violence, the drug lords, and their traffickers, have created a secure power base for themselves.

[22] Over 2,000 left wing activists were killed by terrorists, and in 1987 Jaime Pardo Leal, a member of the Patriotic Union, was assassinated. Liberal senator and presidential candidate in the 1990 election, Luis Carlos Galán - who had promised to dismantle the paramilitary groups and fight drugs - was assassinated in August 1989. War broke out between the Government and the drug mafia. In March 1990, Bernardo Jaramillo, the Patriotic unions' presidential candidate, was assassinated, with Carlos Pizarro (replacing Jaramillo) being killed 20 days later.

[23] Official figures indicate that there are more than 140 paramilitary groups in Colombia, most financed by the drug mafia. Meanwhile, as part of its "War on Drugs", the United States Drug Enforcement Administration is allegedly bombarding coca plantations with chemical herbicides.

[24] Despite the huge profits generated by the planting, processing and export of drug products (which have given rise to an underground economy), agriculture continues to be the backbone of Colombia's legal economy. Despite using only 5 per cent of the land it represents 23 per cent of the GNP, and in 1981, it employed 21 per cent of the workforce.

[25] The presidential elections of May 27 1990 were won by Liberal Party candidate Cesar Gaviria, who received 48 per cent of the vote in an election where the abstention rate was 58 per cent. The Movement for National Salvation obtained 23.7 per cent of the vote, the Democratic

Alliance of the M-19 (ADM-19) 12.56 per cent, and the Conservative Party, 11.90 per cent.

[26] In December 1990, elections were held to form a constituent assembly with a 65 per cent abstention rate. The number of votes received by ADM-19 was significant, as they won 19 seats, 4 fewer than the Liberal Party (the party in power).

[27] In June 1991, members of Gaviria's government met in Caracas with representatives of the Revolutionary Armed Forces of Colombia (FARC), the National Liberation Army (ELN) and the People's Liberation Army (EPL) - members of the Simon Bolivar Guerrilla Coordinating Committee, which controlled 35 per cent of the country. Talks dealt with the demobilization of guerrillas, the subordination of the armed forces to civilian authority, the dismantling of paramilitary groups and the reintegration of

guerrilla fighters into areas where they could exert political influence.

[28] On July 5 1991, the new constitution created the office of vice-president, eliminated the possibility of presidential re-election and included some major gains: civil divorce for Catholic marriages, direct election of local authorities, autonomy for indigenous peoples, the democratic tools of referendum and grassroots legislative initiatives, and guarantees of equal opportunities for women.

[29] The Constitution met with criticisim from the left for failing to give civilian courts jurisdiction over members of the military accused of committing crimes against civilians and for granting judicial powers to State security agencies.

[30] On October 27, an agreement between the President and the three major political forces participating in the constituent assembly reduced the number of

DEMOGRAPHY
Population: 36,444,000 (1996) **Annual growth:** 2% (1980/1996) **Estimates for year 2000:** 38,900,000 **Annual growth to year 2000:** 1.7% (1994/2000) **Urban Population:** 73.1% (1996) **Urban growth:** 2.74% (1980/95) **Children per woman:** 2.8 (1996).

HEALTH
Life expectancy at birth: 71 years (1996) **male:** 67 years (1994) **female:** 73 years (1994) **Infant mortality:** 26 per 1,000 (1996) **Under-5 child mortality:** 31 per 1,000 (1996) **Calorie consumption:** 106% (1988/90) 1,064 **people per doctor** (1988/91) **Safe water:** 85% (1990/96).

EDUCATION
Literacy: 91% (1995) male : 91% (1995) female: 91% (1995) **School enrolment :** Primary total: 121% (1990/95) male : 118% (1990/95) female: 120% (1990/95) Secondary: male : 57% (1990/95) female: 68% (1990/95) Tertiary: 17% (1995) **Primary school teachers:** one for every 25 students (1995).

COMMUNICATIONS
60 **newspapers,** 178 **radios,** 220 **TV sets** and 92 **main telephone lines** per 1,000 people (1994).

ECONOMY
Per capita, GNP: $ 2,140 (1996) **Annual growth, GNP:** -0.5% (1995/96) **Annual inflation:** 25.17% (1985/95) **Consumer price index:** 250.0 (1994) **Currency:** 987.65 pesos = $ 1 (1995) **Cereal imports:** 2,353 metric tons (1994) **Food import dependency:** 7% (1994) **Fertilizer use:** 1,076 kgs per ha (1994) **Exports:** $ 10,976 million (1996) **Imports:** $ 13,863 million (1996) **External debt:** $ 28,859 million (1996) $ 792 **per capita:** (1996) **Debt service:** 34.6% of exports (1996) **Development aid received:** $ 231 million (1995) $ 6 per capita (1995) 3.7% of GNP (1994).

ENERGY
Consumption: 621.57 Kgs of Oil equivalent per capita yearly (1994) -99.48% imported (1994)

HDI (rank / value) 51 / 0.848 (1994)

External Debt

1996

PER CAPITA

$*792*

trade and transport were increased by 5 per cent each. Unemployment went down to below than 9 per cent in the country's seven largest cities and wages maintained a positive trend. However, 45 per cent of the population were still living in abject poverty.

37 President Gaviria was elected secretary general of the OAS, with the support of the United States, which favoured the victory of his party's candidate, Ernesto Samper, in the 1994 elections defeating Conservative Andrés Pastrana by 50 per cent to 48.6 per cent of the vote. Support for the ADM-19 dropped to 4 per cent of the vote, while the abstention rate was slightly decreased to 65 per cent.

38 The Samper Government began with a series of succesful blows on drug-trafficking, but in September 1995 political scandal broke out when a Cali Cartel spokesman revealed details of that organization's contributions to both the Samper and Pastrana campaigns. Defense Minister Fernando Botero, Samper's former campaign director, was sent to prison for embezzlement.

39 In August 1996, Samper decreed a state of emergency to curb a wave of violence and kidnappings, a move considered an attempt to protect himself from drug-linked scandals. However, the murders of several opposition leaders and actions by the FARC and the ELN, which attacked high-tension power lines, oilpipes, police and military facilities, continued. With fighting in almost 100 places, these two groups controlled growing areas in the economically powerful coffee region, the Caribbean and even in the vicinity of Bogota or Medellin.

40 Efforts to eradicate coca and opium poppy plantations continued, as well as armed operations against the Cartel's bases. Some of the Cali Cartel's main leaders, responsible for 70 per cent of cocaine traffic worldwide, gave themselves up. In March 1996 the United States withdrew Colombia from its list of countries which cooperate in the fight against drugs. This measure ended bilateral aid to Colombia and blocked its access to foreign financial sources. Washington denied an entry visa to Samper, in

an attempt to corner him diplomatically.

41 Some 1,900 candidates decided not to run for the October 26 local elections because 49 mayors and city councillors had been killed and more than 180 kidnapped since the beginning of the year. In spite of the traditionally low turnout, over 5 million people enclosed symbolic "vote for peace" slogans onto their ballot papers.

42 The prosecutor in charge of Human Rights revealed in November that since August 1995 his office had ordered disciplinary measures, including 50 dismissals, against 126 military and police officers for human rights abuses. In the same period, more than 600 cases were investigated against security forces members, related with 1,338 victims of murder, torture or disappearance. Some 500 kidnappings, mainly by FARC and ELN members, were reported in the period.

43 Several organizations estimated that, since early 1997, one million Colombians had been displaced from their homes in conflict areas, mainly due to the activity of paramilitary groups. According to the Government, guerrilla groups obtained an annual net income $750 million, substantially more than that earned by coffee. The only sectors with higher earnings were the drug cartels of Medellin and Cali.

44 US President Bill Clinton decided in February 1998 to "recertify" Bogota, based on "national interest" reasons. According to the World Bank, high homicide rates decreased the gross domestic product growth in 2 per cent per year.

45 The worst defeat suffered by the armed forces in its 35-year fight against the guerrillas took place in March 1998, in Caqueta. Between 60 and 80 soldiers died in confrontation with the FARC. The Government's military inferiority was revealed, causing the administration's worst crisis.

46 In June 1998, former Bogotá Mayor Andrés Pastrana was elected as new President. The winner, from the conservative New Democratic Force party, obtained 50.4 per cent of the vote, ending the Liberal Party's 12-year grip on the presidency.

representatives. After the dissolution of Congress, parliamentary elections were held. The Liberal Party, split into several groups, obtained 60 per cent of the vote and support for the ADM-19 dropped to 10 per cent. In the March 1992 municipal elections, marked by a 70 per cent abstention rate among voters, this trend was confirmed.

31 The peace process reached a low point in 1992. After talks had been discontinued, the Government promoted its so called "Integral War", which authorized intervention in civilian organizations with suspected links to rebel groups.

32 The Simón Bolívar Coordinating Committee resisted the army offensive continuing its campaign. In response, paramilitary groups resumed their activities, primarily in the Mid-Magdalena (River Valley) region, Boyaca and Medellin. Violence caused massive population displacement from conflict areas to other regions in the interior.

33 In November, the Government decreed a state of emergency when Pablo Escobar Gaviria - head of the Medellin Cartel, a powerful drug-trafficking ring - escaped from prison in mid-1992, stepping up the cartel's violent actions. In January

1993 appeared a group known as "PEPES" or People Persecuted by Pablo Escobar. Within a two-month period, they killed 30 cartel members, destroyed several of Escobar's properties and harassed members of his family. The confrontation reached serious proportions, with car-bombs causing dozens of deaths.

34 Finally, on December 2, Escobar was killed in a shoot-out with police forces in downtown Medellin. Although his death was a heavy blow to the political and social power of the Medellin Cartel, the drug-trafficking mafia still had many other operations, including the more discreet Cali Cartel, which emerged stronger.

35 The Supreme Court of Justice decriminalized the use of cocaine, marijuana and other drugs, with the radical opposition of several political and religious circles, headed by President Gaviria.

36 The coffee market crisis and the 1993 drought, as well as the reduction of banana quotas exported to the European Union, affected exports. However, with $2 billion per year from drug-trafficking and the discovery of oil in Casanare province, the country achieved a sustained growth of 2.8 per cent per capita. Construction grew 8 per cent in 1993, while

Comoros

Comoros

Population: 632,000 (1996)
Area: 2,235 SQ KM
Capital: Moroni

Currency: Comorian francs
Language: Arabic and French

Comoros was populated around the 5th century by one of the last Indonesian migrations (see Madagascar). The Comoros Islands remained isolated from the continent until the 12th century when Muslim traders from Kilwa settled on the islands, founded ports and reproduced the civilization of the eastern African coast (see Tanzania: The Zandj Culture in East Africa).

2 In the 16th century the Comoros had a prosperous economy but the Portuguese seized the islands and destroyed their active trade. When the Sultan of Oman finally drove the Portuguese from the region, the Comoros came under the influence of Zanzibar. The Bantu population, originally brought from the continent to work on the islands, increased considerably as a result of the slave trade.

3 In the 19th century, Zanzibar split from the sultanate of Oman and the French occupied Mayotte in 1843. Colonial domination eventually spread to the entire archipelago as, the islands' position on the Cape route gave them strategic value.

4 The Comoros National Liberation Movement (MOLINACO) was created in the context of successful anti-colonial struggles throughout Africa. It joined forces with the local Socialist Party (PASOCO) to form the United National Front (FNU) which pressured the French Government into holding a plebiscite in 1974. A large majority, 154,182 people, voted in favor of the islands' independence, and only 8,854 voted against.

5 Most of those who wished to remain under French rule were Mayotte residents (63 per cent of its voters). France has air and naval bases on Mayotte and the economy is controlled by a few dozen Catholic families, sympathetic to France and politically represented by the "Mahorés People's Movement", led by Marcel Henry.

6 Ahmed Abdallah, the archipelago's leading rice exporter and prime minister of the semi-autonomous local government, proclaimed the independence of Comoros in July 1975, before the French announced the result of the referendum. Abdallah was afraid that his Udzima (Unity) Party would lose out to the FNU in a future assembly to draft a new constitution. The Mahorés People's Movement took advantage of the situation to declare that Mayotte would continue under French rule. Paris supported the secession in order to maintain its military presence in the Indian Ocean, violating its previous commitment to respect the territorial integrity of Comoros and the result of the referendum. France did not oppose the islands' membership in the UN but vetoed specific Security Council resolutions to reincorporate Mayotte into the archipelago.

7 Less than a month before the declaration of independence, a small group of FNU youths seized the national palace in Moroni and appointed their leader, the socialist Ali Soilih, as president, in place of Ahmed Abdallah. France immediately reacted by sending a task force of three warships and 10,000 soldiers to Mayotte; one soldier for every three inhabitants.

8 In May 1978, a mercenary force, under the command of Ahmed Abdallah, in exile in Paris, landed on Grand Comoro overthrowing Ali Soilih, who was assassinated three days later. At the head of the operation was the notorious French mercenary Bob Denard, who had been tried in 1977 for mercenary acts of war against the government of Benin. His presence in Comoros triggered international protests, to the point of the Comoros Islands' delegation being expelled from a ministerial meeting of the Organization for African Unity in Khartoum.

9 From then on, Denard became a key figure in the archipelago's politics, and Abdallah's control of the government came to depend on support from Denard and his 650 troops.

10 On November 26 1989, a coup, led by Bob Denard succeeded in

PROFILE

ENVIRONMENT

The Comoros Islands are located at the entrance of the strategic Mozambique Channel, on the oil tanker route between the Arab Gulf and western consumer nations. The four major islands of this volcanic archipelago are: Njazidja, formerly Grand Comoro; Nzwani, formerly Anjouan; Mwali, formerly Moheli; and Mahore, also known by its former name of Mayotte. Njazidja has an active volcano, Karthala, 2,500 meters in altitude. The mountainous island is covered by tropical forests. Only 37 per cent of the cultivated land is used to grow cash crops; vanilla and other spices, the rest is devoted to subsistence farming which is carried out without permanent rivers. The rainwater, which is stored in reservoirs, is easily polluted.

SOCIETY

Peoples: The original Malay-Polynesian inhabitants were absorbed by waves of Bantu and Arab migrations. Today, the latter groups predominate, co-existing with minor Indian and Malagasay communities.
Religions: Islam (official). There is one mosque for every 500 inhabitants.
Languages: Arabic and French are official. Most people speak Comoran, a Swahili dialect, and some groups speak Malagasay.
Political Parties: Comorian Union for Progress, formerly "Udzima"; National Union for Democracy in Comoros; Democratic Alliance; People's Democratic Movement; Comoros Party for Democracy and Progress; Socialist Party.
Social Organizations: The main organization is the Comoran Workers' Union.

THE STATE

Official Name: République Féderal et Islamique des Comores.
Capital: Moroni, 30,000 people (1991).
Other cities: Mutsamudu, 20,000 people; Domoni, 8,000; Fomboni, 5,600 (1991).
Government: Parliamentary republic. Mohamed Taki Abdoulkarim, President since 1996. Tajidine Ben Said Massomde, Prime Minister since 1996.
National Holiday: July 6, Independence Day (1975).

- ■ AGRICULTURE 77% (1990)
- □ INDUSTRIAL 9%
- ▨ SERVICES 13%

STATISTICS

DEMOGRAPHY
Population: 632,000 (1996) **Annual growth:** 3.1% (1980/1996) **Estimates for year 2000:** 700,000 **Annual growth to year 2000:** 3.1% (1994/2000) **Urban Population:** 31.0% (1996) **Children per woman:** 5.7 (1996).

HEALTH
Life expectancy at birth: 57 years (1996) male: 56 years (1994) female: 57 years (1994) **Infant mortality:** 83 per 1,000 (1996) **Under-5 child mortality:** 122 per 1,000 (1996) 10,000 **people per doctor** (1988/91) **Safe water:** 53% (1990/96).

EDUCATION
Literacy: 57% (1995) male : 64% (1995) female: 50% (1995) **School enrolment** : Primary total: 75% (1990/95) male : 81% (1990/95) female: 69% (1990/95) Secondary: male : 21% (1990/95) female: 17% (1990/95)).

COMMUNICATIONS
129 **radios**, 10 **TV sets** and 9 **main telephone lines** per 1,000 people (1994).

ECONOMY
Currency: 367.5 Comorian francs = $ 1 (1995) **Cereal imports:** 34 metric tons (1994) **Food import dependency:** 37% (1994) **Fertilizer use:** 10 kgs per ha (1994) **Development aid received:** $ 43 million (1995) $ 88 per capita (1995) 20.4% of GNP (1994).

HDI (rank / value) 140 / 0.412 (1994)

---

ousting President Ahmed Abdallah, who was killed in the fighting.

[11] The European mercenaries were financed by South Africa and the Comoros were also said to have served as a supply base for RENAMO, the Mozambican South African-backed rebel group.

[12] In the days following this coup, the French Government suspended all economic aid to the islands and initiated negotiations designed to oust Denard and his mercenaries from the island. The mercenaries left the islands in mid-December, heading for South Africa, which allegedly had political and economic links to the former Comoran presidential guard. Prior to his departure, Denard is said to have turned the responsibility for the island's armed forces over to a French army contingent. The interim president of the Comoros permitted the French troops to stay on the islands for a further year or two.

[13] Legal restrictions on the formation of political parties ceased after Abdallah's death, and a number of opposition groups returned from exile.

[14] The IMF demanded a reduction of the number of civil servants. This instruction was carried out by the government as of 1989 and has been extended in the last years. France continues to be the main source of international credit, with Japan close behind.

[15] In August 1991, the Supreme Court of the Islamic Federal Republic of the Comoros found President Said Mohamed Yohar unfit to govern and guilty of serious negligence.

[16] An alliance of all the political parties of the Island of Mwali (25,000 inhabitants) demanded that central government divide civil service jobs and economic benefits, more fairly among the islands.

[17] After a failed attempt to oust the president in late 1991, the political parties and Yohar signed a national reconciliation pact. In January a new government was formed, headed by Mohammed Taki Abdoulkarim, leader of the National Union for Democracy in Comoros. At the same time, a National Conference drafted a new constitution, which was approved by referendum, in June 1992.

[18] In July 1992, President Yohar dismissed Taki Abdoulkarim and his government, accusing him of appointing a former French mercenary to his cabinet.

[19] In September, there was a failed coup against Yohar, led by two sons of former president Ahmed Abdallah. Several opposition leaders accused of conspiring against the government were arrested and at least six civilians were killed.

[20] Due to irregularities, the first legislative elections were held between November and December. The opposition obtained 25 seats in the Assembly while the ruling party won 17. In June 1993, Ahmed Ben Cheikh Attoumane was named Prime Minister, but less than a year later was forced to leave his position due to widespread protests.

[21] Denard attempted a new coup in September but - along with 1,000 followers - he ended up surrendering to French troops who arrived from Mayotte a few days later. The President was immediately freed. In October, when 80-year old Yohar had gone to Reunion for medical treatment, Prime Minister Caabi el Yachourtu Mohamed proclaimed himself "interim president", refusing to hand over the government upon the head of State's return.

[22] Yohar recovered a "symbolic" presidency in January 1996 and general elections were held on March 6-17, won by Taki Abdoulkarim's National Union for Democracy in Comoros (NUDC).

[23] A month after becoming president, Taki Abdoulkarim dissolved the National Assembly and called for new elections to be held on October 6. The NUDC obtained 36 of the 43 seats in stake, in elections boycotted by the opposition.

[24] The 1996 Constitution, which replaced that of 1992, included among other innovations the creation of a Council of Ulemas to supervise respect of Islamic principles by future legislation. The death penalty, suspended in 1975, was restored.

[25] The World Bank financed a program to reduce communicable diseases. Malaria was the first cause of death in the country, affecting 20 per cent of children who died before their fifth birthday.

[26] In August 1997, a secessionist movement headed by Abdallah Ibrahim called for the independence of Anjouan island, where half the population of Comoros lived. The intervention of the national army and a series of violent acts caused dozens of deaths in the following months.

[27] In March 1998, over 99 per cent of Anjouan citizens voted for independence in a referendum. The vote was tainted by the arrest in Moroni of a secession movement leader.

[28] Moheli island also demanded independence. The Organization of African Unity stated its wish that Comoros remain united and sent a delegation to both islands to monitor the situation.

Mayotte

Population: 97,000 (1994)
Area: 375 SQ KM

The Eighth Conference of Non Aligned Countries, held in Harare (Zimbabwe), issued the following statement on France's failure to honor its commitment to respect Comoran territorial integrity: "The Heads of State or Government of the Non Aligned Countries reaffirmed the fact that the Comoran island of Mayotte, still under French occupation, is an integral part of the sovereign territory of the Federal Islamic Republic of the Comoros. They regret that the Government of France, despite repeated promises, has not, to date, adopted any measure or initiative that could lead to an acceptable solution of the problem of the Comoran Island of Mayotte."

In October 1991, the UN General Assembly reaffirmed the sovereignty of the Comoros over Mayotte by an overwhelming majority.

ENVIRONMENT
A mountainous island with tropical climate and heavy rainfall throughout the year. The island is of volcanic origin, has dense vegetation and is located at the entrance to the Mozambique Channel.

SOCIETY
Peoples: Native Mayotte inhabitants are of the same origin as Comorans. There is an influential community of French origin that controls the island's commerce.
Religions: 98 per cent Muslim. There is a Roman Catholic minority.
Languages: Arabic, Swahili, Comoran, and French (official).
Political Parties: the Mayotte Federation for the Organization of the Republic (RPR); the Mahorais People's Movement (MPM); the Party for the Democratic Organization of the Mahorais (PRDM), which seeks unification with the Comoros; the Union for French Democracy (UDF); the Social Democratic Center (CDS).

THE STATE
Official name: Collectivité Territoriale de Mayotte.
Capital: Dzaoudzi, 5,865 inhab. in 1985.
Other cities: Mamoutzou, 12,026 inhab in 1985.
Government: Jean-Jacques Debacq, prefect, appointed by the French government.

ECONOMY
Currency: CFA francs.

Congo, Dem. Rep.

République Démocratique du Congo

Population: 46,812,000 (1996)
Area: 2,344,858 SQ KM
Capital: Kinshasa

Currency: New Zaires
Language: French

The first known state to emerge in what is now DR Congo was the Luba kingdom, located in the Katanga (Shaba) region. The Luba Kingdom was created in the 16th century when a warrior named Kongolo subdued the small chiefdoms in the area and established a highly centralized state. To the northwest was the Kuba, a federation of numerous chiefdoms that reached its peak in the 18th century. Dr Livingstone brought the region to the notice of the Western world through the journalistic coverage of his explorations in Africa, between 1840 and 1870. In 1876, King Leopold II of Belgium founded the International African Association (later, the International Association of Congo), a private organization that financed Henry Stanley's expeditions. Stanley, a journalist and adventurer, succeeded in signing more than 400 trade and/or protectorate agreements with local leaders along the Congo River. These treaties, and the Belgian trading posts established at the mouth of the river, were used to devise a system for the economic exploitation of the Congo. The Berlin Conference, 1884 to 1885, decided that the "Free State of Congo" was the Belgian King's personal property. Consequently, Leopold's "Compagnie du Katanga" stopped British colonialist Cecil Rhodes' northward expansion.

[2] The Congolese population was subjected to extremely harsh working conditions, which did not change when they formally became a Belgian colony in 1908. Military force was systematically employed to suppress anticolonial opposition and to protect the flourishing copper mining industry in Katanga (now Shaba).

[3] In 1957, liberalizing measures permitted the formation of African political parties. This led countless tribal-based movements to enter the political arena, all trying to benefit from the general discontent. Only the National Congolese Movement, led by Patrice Lumumba, had a national outlook, opposing secessionist tendencies and supporting independence claims.

[4] In 1959, the police suppressed a peaceful political rally triggering a series of bloody confrontations. King Baudouin of Belgium tried to appease the demonstrators by promising independence in the near future, but European residents of the Congo reacted with more oppressive measures. Independence was finally achieved in 1960, with Joseph Kasavubu as President and Lumumba as Prime Minister. A few days later, Moses Tshombe, then Prime Minister of the Province of Katanga, initiated a secessionist movement.

[5] Belgium sent in paratroopers and the United Nations, acting under US influence, intervened with a "peacekeeping force". Kasavubu staged a coup and arrested Lumumba, delivering him to Belgian mercenaries in Katanga who killed him. The civil war continued until 1963. Secessionist activity ceased when Tshombe, who represented the neo-colonial interests, was appointed Prime Minister. With the help of mercenaries, Belgian troops and US logistical support, the Tshombe regime was able to stifle the nationalist opposition movement. In 1965, he was forced to resign by Kasavubu who was in turn overthrown by army commander Joseph Desiré Mobutu. According to representatives of transnationals, Mobutu was seen as the only person in a position to restore the conditions required for them to continue operating there.

[6] Under the doctrine of "African authenticity", Mobutu changed the name of the country to Zaire and his own to Mobutu Sese Seko. However, his nationalism went little further than this, and the "Zairization" of copper, which he declared in 1975, only benefited an already wealthy economic elite and the state bureaucracy.

[7] These measures caused some discomfort among US diplomats as Mobutu had offered Washington his services in the region.

[8] Zaire sheltered and actively supported the so-called National Front for the Liberation of Angola (FNLA). Mobutu encouraged secessionist groups in the oil-rich Angolan province of Cabinda, and Zaire's troops effectively cooperated with the South African racist forces in their war against the Angolan nationalists.

[9] Meanwhile, in Zaire guerrillas continued the struggle in the interior. In 1978 and 1979, the major offensive launched by the Congolese Liberation Front was checked with the aid of French and Belgian paratroopers and Moroccan and Egyptian troops, again with US logistical support.

[10] At the end of 1977, international pressure led to parliamentary elections being held for an institution which had been given limited legislative functions. This helped to divert international attention from human rights violations against students and intellectuals in the cities, the establishment of concentration camps for Mobutu's opponents and the brutal reception given to refugees who returned under an "amnesty" decreed in 1979.

[11] Zaire was the world's largest cobalt exporter, the fourth biggest diamond exporter and ranked among the top ten world producers of uranium, copper, manganese and tin. Ninety per cent of the cobalt used in the US aerospace industry came from Zaire. But corruption was rampant throughout the country's administration, worsening the already unstable economic situation, and leading to soaring rates of unemployment.

[12] During 1980 and 1981, the major Western powers decided to seize direct control of the strategic mineral reserves in the country. The International Monetary Fund (IMF) took special interest in Zaire's economy, facilitating the

WORKERS

(1996)

Labour force %

- ■ WOMEN
- □ MEN

44   56

- ■ AGRICULTURE 68% (1990)
- □ INDUSTRIAL 13%
- ■ SERVICES 19%

LAND USE

DEFORESTATION -0.6% annual (81/90)
IRRIGATED 0.1 % of arable

(1993)

- ■ FOREST & WOODLAND 74.1%
- □ ARABLE 3.1%
- ■ OTHER 22.8%

PROFILE

ENVIRONMENT

Located in the heart of the African continent, DR Congo's territory covers most of the Congo River basin and has a narrow outlet into the Atlantic. The center and northern regions are covered with rain forests and are sparsely populated. Small plots of subsistence farming are found here. In the southeast, a plateau climbs to 1,000 meters in the Shaba region (former Katanga). Most of the nation's resources and population are located in the southern grasslands, where cotton, peanuts, coffee and sugar cane are grown. There are also large palm-oil and rubber tree plantations. The country's mineral wealth is concentrated in the Shaba region: copper, zinc, tin, gold, cobalt and uranium. Local industry is found in the mining areas too. In urban areas, polluted water is a source of infectious diseases. Once abundant forest resources have declined at a rapid rate. Wildlife is threatened by poaching and the lack of resources for protection of wildlife.

SOCIETY

Peoples: The people of Congo come from several major African ethnic groups. West African groups live in the northwest, while Nilo-Hamite descendants live in the northeast and a large pygmy minority live in the eastern center. There are more than 200 ethnic groups, mainly: Luba (18 per cent), Mongo (13.5 per cent), Azande (6.1 per cent), Bangi and Ngale (5.8 per cent), Rundi (3.8 per cent), Teke (2.7 per cent), Boa (2.3 per cent), Chokwe 1.8 per cent), Lugbara (1.6 per cent), Banda (1.4 per cent), other (16.6 per cent).
Religions: Most of the population follow traditional African religions: 41 per cent Catholics, 32 per cent Protestants. There are Muslim groups in the north (1.2 per cent).
Languages: French (official). The most widely spoken local languages are Swahili, Shiluba, Kikongo and Lingala (the army's official language).
Political Parties: Peoples' Revolutionary Movement (MPR); Union for Democracy and Social Progress; Movement of Farmers and Workers.

THE STATE

Official Name: République Démocratique du Congo.
Capital: Kinshasa 4,655,000 people (1994).
Other cities: Lubumbashi, 851,000 people; Mbuyi-Mayi, 806,000; Kisangani, 418,000; Kananga 393,000 (1994).
Government: Laurent Kabila, President since September 1997. Likulia Bolonocongo, Prime Minister since April 1997.
National Holiday: June 30, Independence Day (1960).
Armed Forces: Between 20,000 and 40,000 of Kabila s troops constitute the new Armed Forces of the country. Zaire s old Armed Forces were disbanded in 1997.
Other: Gendarmerie, 21,000; Civil Guard, 19,000.

renegotiation of its foreign debt, while at the same time imposing drastic measures against corruption. The economy of Zaire fell under direct IMF control, and the Fund's representatives in Kinshasa began to supervise the country's accounts personally.
[13] At the end of 1982, positive results were visible to international creditors and European investors. Internally, however, the situation had deteriorated even further because of austere measures imposed by the IMF.
[14] In April 1981, Prime Minister Nguza Karl I-Bond sought political asylum in Belgium; he presented himself to the western powers as a "decent alternative" in view of the official corruption in Zaire.
[15] During the elections of June 1984, Mobutu obtained 99.16 per cent of the vote.
[16] In February 1985, Zaire signed a security pact with Angola to improve relations between the two countries. These had deteriorated by the end of the previous decade

because of Zaire's support of the FNLA and the Congolese Liberation Front, which operated from Angolan territory.
[17] In July 1984, Mobutu attempted to create a League of Black African States. The idea was emphatically rejected by all progressive African governments.
[18] In September 1986, it was discovered that the Reagan administration in the US had channelled $15 million of covert aid for Angolan mercenaries through Zaire, virtually transforming the country into an arms repository.
[19] In June 1989, Mobutu visited the United States and Zaire obtained a loan of $20 million from the World Bank. A few days earlier, Mobutu had hosted a historic meeting in his native city of Gbadolite, at which the President of Angola, Jose Eduardo dos Santos, and the leader of the counter-revolutionary UNITA, Jonas Savimbi, had accepted a cease-fire to negotiate a peaceful solution to the country's conflict.

[20] In April 1990, anticipating the process of democratization which he considered imminent, Mobutu decided to take an even bolder step. He ended the one-party system, opened up the labor movement and promised to hold free elections within a year. A rapid process of political organization began. Hundreds of associations and political groups of all kinds demanded legal recognition from the Government. The extent of the popular reaction frightened the authorities, and on May 3, Mobutu issued a statement saying that no party had yet been legalized and that it would be necessary to modify the constitution before holding elections, because the head of state wished to "preserve his authority without exposing himself to criticism".
[21] Students initiated demonstrations throughout the country, especially at the university in Lubumbashi, capital of the province of Shaba. The students began calling for the resignation of Mobutu, who reacted by sending in his presidential guard to stifle the protests.
[22] The troops stormed the university campus at dawn on May 11. More than 100 students were assassinated and the terrified survivors fled to other provinces and Zambia, from where they condemned the massacre.
[23] President Mobutu managed to muffle the repercussions of the killings, but the European Community demanded an international investigation, and Belgium cut off all economic aid. The plan for opening up the country was shelved, at least for the time being.
[24] The massacre at Lubumbashi University generated an anti-Mobutu wave which led to a series of strikes, like that at Gecamina, the country's most important mining company, a state-owned enterprise. In the United States there were repeated calls for the cessation of aid to Mobutu.
[25] In October 1990, under growing internal and external pressure, Mobutu decided to carry out a new political "democratization" process and he authorized the unrestricted creation of new political parties. In December, the opposition -

grouped together under the Holy Union, a front made up of nine parties (including the four largest) - demanded Mobutu's resignation and called for a national conference to decide on the political future of Zaire without presidential intervention.
[26] In September 1991, Mobutu faced major popular uprisings throughout the country, triggered by a general price increase and the failure of a conference in August which had aimed to introduce democratic reforms. The uprisings caused several deaths and the intervention of hundreds of French and Belgian soldiers, allegedly to "protect foreign citizens residing in Zaire".
[27] In November 1991, the Holy Union formed a "shadow government", and appealed to the armed forces to depose Mobutu. The same month, the President appointed Nguza Karl I-Bond as his new Prime Minister (his fifth in 1991). Nguza, a former opposition leader who had been Mobutu's head of government ten years earlier, took office amidst a worsening economic crisis and growing international pressures, especially from the US.
[28] Early in 1992, the National Conference was set up. The opposition had long been awaiting this opportunity to press for constitutional reform and transition to democracy. In February of the same year, Prime Minister Nguza Karl-I Bond suspended the Conference, causing a faction of the army to rebel, taking over a state-run radio station and demanding President Mobutu's resignation. Some hours later the rebels were defeated by troops loyal to the Government. Thousands of demonstrators demanding the president's resignation and the reopening of the Conference were harshly repressed by the army, resulting in several deaths and many injuries.
[29] The European Community suspended financial aid to Zaire immediately, until the reinstatement of the National Conference. Meanwhile, representatives from the US, France, and Belgium agreed to increase the pressure on the Mobutu government to speed up political change.
[30] In March 1992, after meetings with Archbishop Monsegwo Pasinya, the Conference president, President Mobutu appeared on radio and television to announce the reopening of the National Conference. Etienne Tshisekedi, leader of the Holy Union, was made Prime Minister, to replace Nguza Karl-I Bond. The delegates representing the Government and almost 160 groups resolved to return to the country's former name of the Congo Republic, which had been changed by Mobutu.

[31] In a patent display of US displeasure with the Mobutu regime, Monsegwo Pasinya was received in Washington by Secretary of State James Baker, and by the Senate Foreign Relations Committee.

[32] Inter-ethnic strife erupted again in 1992. In Shaba, in the southwest of the country, there were outbreaks of violence after Karl-I Bond's dismissal from government. Lunda people, Karl-I Bond's group, attacked members of the Luba community, Tshisekedi's people. Some 2,000 people were killed, and thousands of Luba left Shaba as their homes had been destroyed. Security forces eventually intervened several weeks after the fighting broke out.

[33] The twelve commercial banks operating in Zaire closed indefinitely in 1992, due to a lack of funds. Inflation reached 16,500 per cent. According to a report by the Washington-based Population Crisis Committee, in 1992 Zaire was among the ten poorest countries in the world, in 88th place on a scale of one to a hundred.

[34] The Government confiscated oil company funds, claiming that this was necessary in order to prevent a collapse of the national economy.

[35] In December 1992, galloping inflation caused the prime minister to announce that the zaire would no longer be legal tender, placing a new currency in circulation. Regardless of this Mobutu ordered that troops receive their back pay in the old currency.

[36] In early 1993, battles broke out between the soldiers, furious over having been paid in worthless bills, and Mobutu's personal guard. This confrontation caused over 1,000 deaths in Kinshasa, and the capital suffered looting, arson and attacks by irate soldiers.

[37] The French ambassador, Philippe Bernard, was killed when the embassy was hit by tank fire. The French minister of defence insisted that the event was a deliberate hostile act.

[38] On February 24, Mobutu's soldiers and tanks surrounded the building housing the High Council of the Republic, a transitional body formed by the National Conference, demanding that the 800 legislators approve the old currency which Mobutu had returned to circulation.

[39] With the worsening situation, the US, Belgium and France sent a letter to Mobutu demanding that he resign in favor of a provisional government headed by Tshisekedi. Mobutu responded by dismissing Prime Minister Tshisekedi, in March 1993. Faustin Birindwa replaced him.

[40] Though Tshisekedi had not legally been appointed Prime Minister by the President, it was a moot point whether Mobutu was entitled to dismiss him. However the Prime Minister never had any real power anyway, controlling neither the army nor any of the state agencies. Mobutu maintained control of the country from Gbadolite, near the border with the Central African Republic. He did not return to Kinshasa for several months, as it was reported that he feared for his personal safety.

[41] The United States suggested Belgium and France embargo Mobutu's property - his personal fortune was estimated at around $4 billion. Meanwhile, amidst the monetary disorder and suspended foreign debt repayments, the informal economy took over in the urban areas.

[42] The economic and political uncertainty continued throughout 1994. The genocide in Rwanda and the arrival of masses of refugees - amongst whom were found thousands of members of the militias responsible for the massacre - created great tension in eastern Zaire.

[43] When the Rwandan Patriotic Front (FPR) guerrillas came to power in Rwanda, several Western nations, like France, began to reduce the pressure on Mobutu, newly considered as a potential ally following the victory of "the English-speaking Tutsis" in the neighboring country. This reinforced the President's power, facilitating the nomination of Léon Kengo Wa Dondo as prime minister, though this was immediately questioned by the opposition.

[44] The announcement in mid-1995, that the transition government would remain in power for two more years provoked a new wave of protests. In late July, the confrontations between police and demonstrators calling for Tshisekedi to be nominated Prime Minister left 10 people dead.

[45] The tension between Zaire and Rwanda increased in 1996, after the Rwandan Hutu militias, supported by members of the Zairian armed forces, began ethnic cleansing in the Masisi region, ousting and killing Tutsis who had lived in this zone of eastern Zaire for generations.

[46] At the end of that year, the conflict between armed Tutsi groups and the remnants of the Rwandan army, (mostly Hutu) assumed civil war proportions. The confrontation spread with government forces participating to put a stop to the advance of the Tutsi rebels, who had taken several cities in the east of the country. The Mobutu regime became seriously threatened when various opposition forces formed an alliance led by the veteran guerrilla leader Laurent Kabila. After convalescing in Switzerland for four months, Mobutu returned to face the situation in December. After a few weeks in the country during which he declared a general increase in army salaries, Mobutu returned to Switzerland.

[47] In the first few months of 1997, opposition forces easily took over practically the whole country, and a group of states - South Africa, the United States, France and Belgium included - attempted to mediate and seek a solution. Nelson Mandela arranged a meeting between Mobutu and Kabila on a ship in international waters to negotiate the transition. However, the attempt was a failure, as Kabila demanded Mobutu stand down as a pre-condition to the talks.

[48] In March, Parliament sacked Prime Minister Kengo Wa Dondo, and a month later Étienne Tshisekedi was appointed as a replacement for his third term in office, with Mobutu s approval. Tshisekedi offered Kabila six posts in the cabinet, including defence and the foreign office, but he rejected the offer. Barely a week later, disagreements between the government parties led to Tshisekedi being replaced by Likulia Bolongo. Foreseeing the final outcome, the powerful mining companies began to negotiate with Kabila to protect their interests in Zaire.

[49] On May 16, Mobutu fled to Morocco and opposition troops entered Kinshasa the following day. Kabila declared himself president. Mobutu died in Rabat on September 7. The new strongman took over as President that month with full military, legislative and administrative powers. The new government changed the name of Zaire to the Democratic Republic of Congo and announced a series of economic recovery measures. Switzerland reopened an investigation into Mobutu's bank accounts in the country.

[50] A study by Medecins Sans Frontières (MSF) in late 1997 revealed the massacres committed by Kabila's troops and the Rwandan forces which supported him in defeating Mobutu. In April 1998, Kabila said he was prepared to allow United Nations inspectors back into the country to investigate the atrocities, although he disagreed with the procedures used by the international entity. The UN had ordered the withdrawal of the previous mission after Kabila had accused the delegation of desecrating graves.

[51] That month the nation was hit by the worst floods in the last 35 years. In July 1998 forces led by the Banyamulenge (Congolese Tutsis) rebelled against Kabila's regime.

STATISTICS

DEMOGRAPHY
Population: 46,812,000 (1996). **Annual growth:** 3.4% (1980/1996). **Estimates for year 2000:** 51,700,000. **Annual growth to year 2000:** 2.8% (1994/2000). **Urban Population:** 29.0% (1996). **Children per woman:** 6.4 (1996).

HEALTH
Life expectancy at birth: 53 years (1996). **Infant mortality:** 128 per 1,000 (1996). **Under-5 child mortality:** 207 per 1,000 (1996). **Calorie consumption:** 96% (1988/90). 14,286 **people per doctor** (1988/91). **Safe water:** 42% (1990/96).

EDUCATION
Literacy: 77% (1995). male : 87% (1995). female: 68% (1995). **School enrolment** :. Primary total: 68% (1990/95). male : 78% (1990/95). female: 58% (1990/95). Secondary:. male : 33% (1990/95). female: 15% (1990/95). Tertiary: 2% (1995). **Primary school teachers:** one for every 45 students (1995).

COMMUNICATIONS
98 **radios**, 1 **main telephone line** per 1,000 people (1994).

ECONOMY
Per capita, GNP: $ 130 (1996). **Annual growth, GNP:** -0.1% (1995/96). **Currency:** 14,831 New Zaires = $ 1 (1995). **Cereal imports:** 253 metric tons (1994). **Food import dependency:** 42% (1994). **Fertilizer use:** 5 kgs per ha (1994). **Exports:** $ 1,461 million (1996). **Imports:** $ 1,331 million (1996). **External debt:** $ 12,826 million (1996). $ 274 **per capita:** (1996). **Debt service:** 2.4% of exports (1996). **Development aid received:** $ 189 million (1995). $ 4 per capita (1995).

HDI (rank / value) 142 / 0.381 (1994)

Congo Republic

République du Congo

Population: 2,668,000 (1996)
Area: 342,000 SQ KM
Capital: Brazzaville

Currency: CFA francs
Language: French

Today's Congo was originally populated by Pygmies and Bushmen (San). By the 16th century it comprised the Bantu states of Luango and Kacongo, for many years ruled by the Manicongo. These nations managed to stave off early Portuguese attempts at colonization. Instead, for three centuries, under the Batekes of Anzico, they acted as suppliers and intermediaries of British and French slave dealers.

2 Towards the end of the 19th century, trade in rubber and palm oil replaced slave traffic. The new trade brought with it French colonization.

3 In 1880 French troops led by Savorgnan de Brazza began to colonize the Congo by force, and by the 1920s two-thirds of the local population had been killed. This genocide, along with the use of forced labor to build the Brazzaville-Pointe Noire railroad, resulted in the early emergence of semi-religious independence movements, under the leadership of Matswa.

4 After World War II, labor and student movements inspired by socialist ideas formed the backbone of resistance.

5 Sponsored by the French, Friar Fulbert Youlou led the Democratic Union for the Defence of African Interests and was the first president of independent Congo in 1960. Mass participation grew, however, and Youlou's neo-colonialist policies were rejected. A wave of demonstrations against corruption and the banning of trade unions ended in a popular uprising during the "three glorious days" (August 13-15) of 1963.

6 Youlou resigned and the president of the National Assembly, socialist Alphonse Massemba-Debat,

took office and forced the French troops stationed in the country to withdraw. He then founded the National Movement of the Revolution (MNR) as the country's sole party.

7 This force could not coexist with the neo-colonial army, equipped and trained by the French, and the consequent crisis led Massemba-Debat to resign on January 1 1969. He was replaced by a young major, Marien N'Gouabi, backed by leftwing army officers. N'Gouabi founded a Marxist-Leninist party called the Congolese Worker's Party (PCT).

8 In 1973, a new constitution was approved, proclaiming the Congo a people's republic, and the State took control of energy, water, major industrial firms, and petroleum.

9 In December 1975, N'Gouabi made a public self-appraisal, issued a call "to extend the revolution," and launched a general review of party structures, the state apparatus and mass organizations.

10 To afford greater public participation in the running of the State, an ambitious educational reform was begun and the structure of the government was reformed. Until then all the school textbooks had come from France and were therefore Eurocentric.

11 When Angola gained independence in 1975, Congo lost no time recognizing Agostinho Neto's government. His clear position on the problem of Cabinda was decisive in frustrating attempts to have this oil-rich province break away from Angola, a scheme which was being promoted by transnational companies with interests in the Congo.

12 On March 18 1977, N'Gouabi was assassinated by followers of ex-president Massemba-Debat. The

conspirators failed in their efforts to seize power, however, and Massemba-Debat was executed.

13 The new president, Colonel Joachim Yombi Opango, did not maintain N'Gouabi's austere style and was forced to resign on February 6 1979, charged with corruption and abuse of power. Denis Sassou N'Guesso replaced him.

14 N'Guesso launched a campaign against corruption in the public sector, as well as a broad administrative and ministerial

reform. Toward the end of 1981, the Congo faced foreign trade difficulties directly linked to inefficiency in state enterprises which the government refused to close.

15 In 1982, the Congo's finances improved. Part of the recovery can be attributed to oil exports, which financed 49.44 per cent of the budget.

16 Congolese oil is exploited in partnership with French, US and Italian firms. Annual exports approached eight million tons of crude in 1988.

17 President N'Guesso's foreign policy has been pragmatic; he sought closer relations with Eastern Europe, while maintaining commercial ties with the United States and France. He played a leading role in negotiations between Angola, South Africa and Cuba, which culminated in the signing of a peace settlement for the region in December 1988, in Brazzaville, paving the way for Namibia's independence.

18 The fall of the Berlin Wall and

PUBLIC EXPENDITURE

n/a

16.1%
1995 ■ DEFENCE □ SOCIAL

In 1990/91 Military as % of health & education expenditure was 37%.

WORKERS

(1996)

Labour force %

■ WOMEN
□ MEN

43%   57%

■ AGRICULTURE 49% (1990)
□ INDUSTRIAL 15%
■ SERVICES 37%

LAND USE

DEFORESTATION -0.2% annual (81/90)
IRRIGATED 0.7% of arable

(1993)

■ FOREST & WOODLAND 61.7%
□ ARABLE 0.4%
■ OTHER 37.9%

Maternal Mortality	Literacy	Food Dependency	Foreign Trade
1990	1995		MILLIONS $ 1996
PER 100,000 LIVE BIRTHS 890	75%	1994 17%	IMPORTS 1,590 EXPORTS 1,833

PROFILE

ENVIRONMENT

The country comprises four distinct regions: coastal plains; a central plateau (separated from the coast by a range of mountains rising to 800 meters); the Congo River basin in the northeast; and a large area of marshland. The central region is covered with dense rain forests and is sparsely populated. Two-thirds of the population live in the south, along the Brazzaville-Pointe Noire railroad. Lumber and agriculture employ more than one third of the population. The country has considerable mineral resources including oil, lead, gold, zinc, copper and diamonds. The environmental situation is characterized by haphazard urban development, the accumulation of refuse, a lack of sewage facilities, the proliferation of contagious diseases, pollution, deforestation and the disappearance of native fauna.

SOCIETY

Peoples: The Congolese are of Bantu origin; the Bakongo prevail in the South, the Teke (or Bateke) at the center; the Sanga and Vilil in the North.
Religions: The vast majority of the population practice traditional African cults. Chrisitian elements are assimilated into these cults.
Languages: French (official), Kongo and various local dialects.
Political Parties: Pan-African Union for Social Democracy; Congolese Workers' Party (PCT); Congolese Movement for Democracy and Integral Development.
Social Organizations: The four existing labor organizations merged in 1964 to form the Congolese Labor Confederation (CSC).

THE STATE

Official Name: République du Congo.
Administrative divisions: 8 regions and 6 communes.
Capital: Brazzaville, 1,009,000 people in 1995.
Other cities: Pointe Noire, 576,200 people; Loubomo, 83,600 people (1992).
Government: Parliamentary republic. Denis Sassou N'Guesso, President since November 1997. Bernard Koleas, Prime Minister since November 1997.
National Holiday: August 15, Independence Day (1960).
Armed Forces: 10,000.
Other: 6,100: Gendarmerie (1,400); People's Militia (4,700).

STATISTICS

DEMOGRAPHY

Population: 2,668,000 (1996) **Annual growth:** 2.9% (1980/1996) **Estimates for year 2000:** 3,000,000 **Annual growth to year 2000:** 2.9% (1994/2000) **Urban Population:** 59.3% (1996) **Urban growth:** 5.63% (1980/95) **Children per woman:** 6 (1996).

HEALTH

Life expectancy at birth: 51 years (1996) **Infant mortality:** 81 per 1,000 (1996) **Under-5 child mortality:** 108 per 1,000 (1996) **Calorie consumption:** 103% (1988/90) 3,571 **people per doctor** (1988/91) **Safe water:** 34% (1990/96).

EDUCATION

Literacy: 75% (1995) male : 83% (1995) female: 67% (1995) **Primary school teachers:** one for every 70 students (1995).

COMMUNICATIONS

10 **newspapers**, 115 **radios**, 10 **TV sets** and 8 **main telephone lines** per 1,000 people (1994).

ECONOMY

Per capita, GNP: $ 670 (1996) **Annual growth, GNP:** 4.7% (1995/96) **Annual inflation:** 2.21% (1985/95) **Consumer price index:** 141.1 (1994) **Currency:** 490 CFA francs = $ 1 (1995) **Cereal imports:** 86 metric tons (1994) **Food import dependency:** 17% (1994) **Fertilizer use:** 111 kgs per ha (1994) **Exports:** $ 1,833 million (1996) **Imports:** $ 1,590 million (1996) **External debt:** $ 5,240 million (1996) $ 1,964 **per capita:** (1996) **Debt service:** 21.3% of exports (1996) **Development aid received:** $ 125 million (1995) $ 50 per capita (1995) 10.8% of GNP (1994).

ENERGY

Consumption: 330.55 Kgs of Oil equivalent per capita yearly (1994) -1,013.10% imported (1994)

HDI (rank / value) 130 / 0.5 (1994)

---

the demise of Soviet perestroika precipitated political and economic changes. In December 1990, the country adopted a multiparty system. In July 1991, André Milongo took the post of Prime Minister until presidential elections could be held. This decision caused confrontation in the streets and the formation of a transition Government with army participation.
[19] In the early legislative elections of May 1993, the ruling party won 62 seats against the opposition coalition's 49. The opposition accused the Government of fraud and further clashes between demonstrators and the military left six people dead.
[20] Lissouba named retired military officer, Jacques Yhombi-Opango, as

Prime Minister, which led the opposition to form a parallel government led by Bernard Kolelas. In July and December, fresh disturbances caused the death of some 80 people. Meanwhile, the Government continued in bankruptcy and only paid civil servants 7 of their 12 pay packets in 1993.
[21] In January 1994, the army called in the artillery to counteract attacks from armed opposition groups. The disturbances caused the death of more than 100 people. An agreement between the opposition and the Government in mid-March, marked the beginning of a cease-fire. Later, in July, the election of Kolelas as mayor of Brazzaville further calmed the situation, allowing for a public

reconciliation ceremony the following month.
[22] During 1994 Lissouba accepted the IMF structural adjustment programme, including the reduction of the number of civil servants. Competition between various oil multinationals threatened the dominance of the French Elf in Congo, leading the company to increase the amount of profit reinvested in the country from 17 to 31 per cent.
[23] 1995 was dominated by the quest for a definitive agreement to disarm the anti-government urban militias and to eventually integrate them into the official army. On February 19 a general strike was started calling for the payment of overdue salaries. On March 1, an agreement was made including a

reduction in salaries in return for a drop in working hours, but this was rejected by the civil servants.
[24] Fighting started in June 1997 when the Government aimed to disarm and arrest Denis Sassou N'Guesso and some of his followers. In November, following four months of civil war, the opposition forces defeated President Lissouba, with the help of Angolan troops. The fighting often degenerated into pillaging from the local population. N'Guesso formed a new government in Brazzaville and announced his intention to call the presidential elections that had been postponed in July.
[25] In January 1998, Congo and DR Congo started negotiations to demarcate their 2,410 kilometre common frontier.

The settling of America

Over 9,000 years ago, the first Americans began to settle in the continent's vast regions, developing their own kinds of cohabitation with their natural environment and forming social groupings. The Europeans who arrived in the 15th century ignored the great diversity and cultural wealth of the peoples already living there and unleashed devastating wars of conquest

The debate over the origin and settling of the American peoples is inconclusive. There are two major positions. One claims the first settlers came to America through the Bering Strait which, some 12,000 years ago, was a corridor of land between Alaska and Siberia. These settlers brought with them a culture called 'PaleoIndian' similar to that of the Old World's Higher Paleolithic culture. The other position holds that the settlement had begun more than 12,000 years ago. However suggested dates vary very widely depending upon the expert: some have proposed dates as far back as 100,000 years ago. The most widely accepted scientific opinions place the arrival somewhere between 12,000 and 20,000 years ago, at the end of the last glacial period. The first groups of hunters who came to America found a climate, fauna (including large mammals or megafauna), and even a geography substantially different to those we know today. The glacial period finished some 10,000 years ago, the ice masses withdrew, temperatures rose and sea levels grew to levels similar to those we know today.

We do know for certain that, as of 9,000 years ago, all of the American territory was inhabited. The disappearance of megafauna and climatic changes influenced the economic and demographic adaptation of the groups. Throughout the different environmental regions of America there occur unique adaptations. While hunting was the main economic activity in the large plains of North and South America, there are various adaptations in the economic, technological and social spheres in the forested areas, mountains, ocean coasts, and the great rivers. The complexity of the continent led to highly regionalized cultures with their own ritual objects, funerary offerings, ceremonial sites, etc.

Agriculture, settlement and social stratification

Gradually, agriculture became the main economic activity in a process that probably lasted thousands of years. More or less all of the groups were familiar with edible vegetable species since early times. However, the farming and development of certain species by some Amerindian groups (such as corn, beans and pumpkins) led to important changes as early as 7,000 years ago. Economies increasingly dependent on agriculture have larger populations and are more sedentary and socially complex. A dominant social group usually appears, which controls productive forces.

In American prehistory, the period between 1,500 BC and the beginning of our era (with slight differences according to the authors and regions), is considered to have borne the so-called 'High Cultures', although only the Andes and Mesoamerica had strongly stratified societies with complex state organizations. Throughout the rest of America, a tribal social structure (horticulturist or hunter-gatherer), more or less egalitarian, lasted for a longer period of time, in some cases until the European conquest.

The evolution of stratified societies, throughout the 3,000 years from their origins to the arrival of the Spanish, was characterized by a prevailing group learning to control society and by the difficulties implicit in an unequal development of productive forces. This can be seen in the successive appearances of regional cultures, with swift growth and disintegration stages. Take for example the pre-Inca Andean cultures, such as the Chavin (2,500 years ago) and the Tiahuanaco-Huari (1,500 years ago), both of which spread in a comparitively short time.

Then there were smaller regional cultures, such as the Andean cultures of Paracas, Nazca, Moche and Chimu., whose scattered cultural developments contributed to more complex processes of political unification such as the ones led by the Incas and Aztecs.

In other parts of the continent there were several population movements which are not adequately understood yet, such as the Guarani expansion in South America. For several millennia, the groups varied in ways also found on other continents. Different languages were consolidated and the isolation of some groups enabled slight genetic differences. However, these processes were not lasting enough as to conceal the existence of an American racial and ethnic unity.

Disintegrating impact of the conquest

At the time of the conquest, the situation in America was varied. In the most populated and agriculturally productive regions, colonization was based mostly on the exploitation of indigenous labour.

The European conquest was made easier in regions where it was possible to replace a leading class with representatives of the colonial powers.

In the more scattered populations, colonization was characterized by expulsion, destruction and extermination, and in a secondary way, by the integration of the Amerindians.

American indigenous communities were exposed early on to factors which would destroy their socio-cultural bases. The violent passage from their traditional economies to forms of mercantilism in the 16th century was at the forefront of this destruction.

The process by which indigenous cultures disintegrated was complex - mercantilism, high death rates due to appalling working conditions, epidemics of hitherto unknown diseases and the imposition of other worldviews through religion are only its most visible features.

Costa Rica

Costa Rica

Population:	3,500,000 (1996)
Area:	51,100 SQ KM
Capital:	San José
Currency:	Colones
Language:	Spanish

When the first Europeans arrived on its coasts, the territory of present-day Costa Rica was populated by a number of small tribes of the Chorotega, Cobici, Caribe and Boruca nations. Christopher Columbus reached the coast of Costa Rica in his last voyage, in 1502. Although the first contact was friendly, these American tribes were not easily dominated by the Europeans, and it took nearly 60 years for a permanent settlement to be established in the region.

2 Gaspar de Espinosa, Hernán Ponce de León and Juan de Castañeda travelled along the coast of the territory between 1514 and 1516. Between 1560 and 1564, their lead was followed by Juan de Cavallón, Juan de Estrada Rabago and Juan Vásquez de Coronado. The conquest of the territory was consolidated in the second half of the 16th century.

3 The Spanish established the first permanent settlement, the town of Cartago, on the central plain in 1564. This was assigned to the political jurisdiction of the Captaincy-General of Guatemala, while remaining under the spiritual guidance of the bishop of Nicaragua.

4 The indians' resistance kept the colonizers isolated for a long time. They were unable to establish a system of *encomiendas* - the virtual enslavement of the indian work force. In this way a patriarchal society of small landowners was formed, with no powerful land-owning oligarchy, unlike in the neighbouring countries. Perhaps this explains how, instead of becoming a nation scourged by civil wars and military dictatorships, modern Costa Rica has maintained greater democratic stability and has not established a regular army like the rest of the regional countries.

5 When Mexico declared independence from Spain in 1821, Costa Rica, along with other former Spanish colonies in Central America, formed part of the Mexican empire. In 1823, Costa Rica helped create the United Provinces of Central America and remained a part of this federation until its dissolution in 1840. A persistent opponent to the "Balkanization" brought about by British imperialism, Costa Rica's territory was used as a base of operations by Francisco Morazán - an advocate of Central American unity - until 1848, when Costa Rica became an independent state.

6 In the mid-19th century, William Walker - a US national who had taken control of Nicaragua - tried to extend his dominion over the Central American isthmus. He was defeated by forces commanded by the Costa Rican President Juan Rafael Mora. Material progress reached Costa Rica during the regime of General Tomás Guardia, who ruled the nation from 1870 to 1882. While his administration took away some liberties and increased foreign debt, coffee and sugar production rose and more schools were built. The constitution adopted in 1871 remained in place until 1949.

7 The last decades of the 19th century were marked by a gradual reduction of Church influence in secular affairs. Cemeteries were secularized and the Jesuits expelled from the country for a few years. In 1886, primary education became obligatory and free. Schools were founded, along with a museum and a national library. In 1890, José Joaquín Rodríguez was elected President in what were considered the first free and fair elections in Central America.

8 In 1916, Nicaragua gave the

United States permission to use the San Juan river, which forms the frontier with Costa Rica. The San José Government protested that its rights had been overlooked and the complaint was taken to the Central American Court of Justice which ruled in favour of Costa Rica. Nicaragua rejected the verdict and withdrew from the Court. This was one of the main reasons for the dissolution of the Court a year later.

9 Costa Ricans had their first elections with direct voting in 1913. There was no outright winner and the Legislative Assembly designated Alfredo González Flores as President. General Federico Tinoco Granados, unhappy with the reforms proposed by González, led one of the few coups experienced by the nation, in 1917. But the lack of US

recognition for his government and the threat of intervention forced Tinoco to resign in 1919.

10 Between 1940 and 1948 the Government was backed by coffee plantation owners and bankers. However in 1948 opposition leader Otilio Ulate, nominated by the National Unity Party, won a presidential election which was annulled by Congress. This unleashed civil war which ended with a junta seizing power, presided over by José Figueres. The junta issued a call for the election of new representatives, who in turn confirmed Ulate's victory. A year later, a new constitution was ratified, establishing a presidential system of government and prohibiting the formation of armies.

11 The populist revolution led by Figueres spread anti-dictatorial ideas throughout Central America.

12 José Figueres was elected President in 1954 and during his administration Costa Rica became a strongly anti-communist welfare state. In 1958, the conservatives defeated Figueres and imposed an import-substitution development model.

13 The traditional antagonism between liberals and conservatives gave way to new tensions between the National Liberation Party (PLN), led by Figueres, and a heterogeneous group consisting of various small parties. In 1966, the

A VIEW FROM THE SOUTH

PUBLIC EXPENDITURE

n/a

63%
1995 ■ DEFENCE ☐ SOCIAL

In 1990/91 Military as % of health & education expenditure was 5%.

WORKERS

UNEMPLOYMENT 6.2% (1996)

Labour force %

■ WOMEN
☐ MEN

30   70

■ AGRICULTURE 26% (1990)
☐ INDUSTRIAL 27%
▨ SERVICES 47%

LAND USE

DEFORESTATION -2.6% annual (81/90)
IRRIGATED 42.1% of arable

(1993)

■ FOREST & WOODLAND 30.7%
☐ ARABLE 5.6%
▨ OTHER 63.7%

Foreign Trade

MILLIONS $ 1996

IMPORTS

3,871

EXPORTS

2,882

STATISTICS

DEMOGRAPHY
Population: 3,500,000 (1996) **Annual growth:** 2.7% (1980/1996) **Estimates for year 2000:** 3,800,000. **Annual growth to year 2000:** 2.1% (1994/2000) **Urban Population:** 49.8% (1996) **Urban growth:** 3.65% (1980/95) **Children per woman:** 3 (1996).

HEALTH
Life expectancy at birth: 77 years (1996) male: 74 years (1994) female: 79 years (1994) **Infant mortality:** 13 per 1,000 (1996) **Under-5 child mortality:** 15 per 1,000 (1996) **Calorie consumption:** 121% (1988/90) 1,136 **people per doctor** (1988/91) **Safe water:** 96% (1990/96).

EDUCATION
Literacy: 95% (1995) male : 95% (1995) female: 95% (1995) **School enrolment :** Primary total: 106% (1990/95) male : 107% (1990/95) female: 105% (1990/95) Secondary: male : 47% (1990/95) female: 51% (1990/95) Tertiary: 32% (1995) **Primary school teachers:** one for every 31 students (1995).

COMMUNICATIONS
100 **newspapers**, 260 **radios**, 220 **TV sets** and 130 **main telephone lines** per 1,000 people (1994) **Books:** 29 new titles per 100,000 people (1992/94).

ECONOMY
Per capita, GNP: $ 2,640 (1996) **Annual growth, GNP:** -2% (1995/96) **Annual inflation:** 18.43% (1985/95) **Consumer price index:** 195.4 (1994) **Currency:** 194.9 colones = $ 1 (1995) **Cereal imports:** 453 metric tons (1994) **Food import dependency:** 6% (1994) **Fertilizer use:** 2,584 kgs per ha (1994) **Exports:** $ 2,882 million (1996) **Imports:** $ 3,871 million (1996) **External debt:** $ 3,454 million (1996) $ 987 **per capita:** (1996) **Debt service:** 14.1% of exports (1996) **Development aid received:** $ 25 million (1995) $ 8 per capita (1995) 0.3% of GNP (1994).

ENERGY
Consumption: 557.80 Kgs of Oil equivalent per capita yearly (1994) 67.39% imported (1994)

HDI (rank / value) 33 / 0.889 (1994).

PROFILE

ENVIRONMENT
A mountain range with major volcanic peaks stretches across the country from northwest to southeast. Costa Rica has the highest rural population density in Latin America, with small and medium sized farmers who use modern agricultural techniques. Coffee is the main export crop. The lowlands along the Pacific and the Caribbean have different climate and vegetation. Along the Caribbean coast there is dense, tropical rainforest vegetation. Cocoa is grown in that region. The Pacific side is drier; extensive cattle raising is practised along with artificially irrigated sugar cane and rice plantations. Deforestation has been partially responsible for soil erosion and reduced fertility.

SOCIETY
Peoples: Costa Ricans, usually called ticos in Central America, are the result of ethnic integration between native Americas and European migrants, mainly Spanish. African descendants, brought in from Jamaica, make up 3 per cent of the population and are concentrated along the eastern coast. Indigenous peoples, 1 per cent.
Religions: 81.3 per cent of the population are Catholic; Evangelical Protestant 15 per cent.
Languages: Spanish is the official language, spoken by the majority. Mekaiteliu, a language derived from English, is spoken in the province of Limón (east coast). Several indigenous languages.
Political Parties: Social Christian Unity Party (PUSC); National Liberation Party (NLP), social democrat; Democratic Force, centre left coalition; "Cargagines" Agricultural Union, regional: the Agrarian Party.
Social Organizations: The Unitary Workers' Union (CUT); the 50,000-member CUT groups both workers and peasants from the National Federation of Civil Servants, the National Peasant Federation; the Federation of Industrial Workers, regional federations and smaller unions. 375 cooperatives.

THE STATE
Official Name: República de Costa Rica. **Administrative Divisions:** 7 Provinces. **Capital:** San José, 321,193 people (1995). **Other cities:** Limón, 56,525 people; Alajuela, 49,190; Cartago, 109,000 (1992). **Government:** Miguel Angel Rodríguez, president since February 1, 1998. Legislature, single-chamber Assembly, made up of 57 members. **National Holiday:** September 15, Independence Day (1821). **Armed Forces:** Abolished in 1949. **Others:** 7,500 Civil Guard, Frontier Guard and Rural Guard (1994).

opposition managed to form an electoral coalition, the United National Opposition which elected José Joaquín Trejos to the presidency.
[14] After the 1970 election, the PLN returned to power with Figueres, who remained in office until 1974, when Daniel Odúber Quirós, co-founder of the Party in 1950, was elected President.
[15] Odúber tried to restore unity to the Central American Common Market, left in a critical situation after the 1969 war between El Salvador and Honduras. However, his obvious pro-democracy stance did not meet with the approval of Somoza's regime in Nicaragua. Costa Rica was constantly harassed by its neighbour and

became a safe haven for thousands of political refugees.
[16] 1975 saw a rise in wages due to favourable conditions resulting from the nationalization of transnational oil companies and the rise in coffee prices on the world market .
[17] In 1978, contrary to all expectations, presidential elections gave the victory to a conservative coalition which had been critical of the previous government's administration. The leftist bloc, grouped in the United People's Coalition, increased considerably and became the third most important political force. However they remained isolated and unable to propose social changes within

the democratic and pluralist system favored by the majority.
[18] The new President, Rodrigo Carazo Odio, imposed an unpopular economic policy prescribed by the International Monetary Fund (IMF), which resulted in growing confrontation with labour and left groups. In 1979 however, encouraged by popular sympathy towards the Sandinista rebels, and under threat of invasion by neighboring dictator Anastasio Somoza, the Costa Rican Government decided actively to support the Nicaraguan Sandinistas.
[19] A radically different attitude was taken in 1980 with regard to El Salvador's insurgency. In spite of grave and continuous human rights violations in that country, the San José Government supported the Salvadoran military junta. In 1981 President Carazo broke off diplomatic relations with Cuba.
[20] In January 1982, the US-backed Central American Democratic Community was set up in San José with the main objective of isolating revolutionary Nicaragua.
[21] Luis Alberto Monge, a right-wing PLN candidate, became President in February 1982. When he took office in May, Monge

proclaimed his alignment with Western democracies, and announced economic austerity measures. At the same time, he fostered closer ties with the governments of El Salvador, Guatemala and Honduras, thus aggravating relations with Nicaragua.
[22] Costa Rica's hostile attitude towards its neighbour was clearly demonstrated when the US declared a commercial embargo on Nicaragua's revolutionary Government. A series of border incidents brought relations between the two countries to breaking point during July and August 1985. However, prompt action taken by the Contadora Group checked mounting tension in the area; both governments agreed to place neutral observers along the common frontier to arbitrate any further border clashes.
[23] The winner of the February 1986 presidential election was Social Democrat Oscar Arias, who won a tight victory with 52 per cent of the vote.
[24] Arias devoted himself to the task of designing a policy which would break both the logic of war and the escalating tension within the region. In August 1987 he presented a peace plan at a summit meeting held in Esquipulas, Guatemala. This

The Mystery of the Maya

In their writings, the Maya dated their origins back to a mythical year 3113, a date no one has been able to explain. According to archaeologists, their society was "in formation" about 2,000 to 3,000 years ago, when they lived in small huts with palm leaf roofs.

But were these "proto-Maya" - around at the same time as the Olmeca - the ancient people of the Gulf of Mexico? No one knows. Fuller Mayan history begins in the "pre-classical" period, around 300 to 250 BC.

The Maya built impressive pyramids, temples and began sculpting signs, or "glyphs" in stone. The civilization reached its artistic, astronomical, mathematical and architectural apogee in the "classical" period, from the 3rd to 6th centuries AD.

They built true cities which were, in fact, small kingdoms that fought endlessly amongst themselves. Then, strangely, between the 9th and 10th centuries the battles came to an end and the ritual centres were abandoned. Why?

Epidemics, earthquakes, invasions, drought, or even an order to flee from their gods, are all theories which have been suggested, but none of them can be confirmed.

In any case, when the Spaniards landed in the 16th century, the Maya civilization was already in decline. As a result, the chroniclers of the time concentrate almost exclusively on the Aztecs.

---

was accepted and signed by the presidents of El Salvador, Nicaragua, Guatemala, and Honduras. The focal points of the plan were: a simultaneous cease-fire in Nicaragua and El Salvador, an immediate end to American aid to the Nicaraguan "contras", a democratization time-table for Nicaragua which included holding free elections and putting an end to the use of foreign territory as supply or attack bases.

[25] The signing of this peace plan, known as "Esquipulas II", earned Costa Rica a special place in international relations, and constituted a personal triumph for President Arias, who received the Nobel Peace Prize in October 1987 in recognition of his efforts.

[26] During his term, Arias instituted the first phase, and later the second, of a structural adjustment programme, with World Bank support. The objective of this programme was the transformation of industry through technological modernization, increased efficiency and greater productivity. Neo-liberal formulas were applied, following the dictates of international financial organizations. However, according to the labour unions, these "prescriptions" were formulated without looking at their social repercussions.

[27] In July 1989, an investigation into drug trafficking was carried out by a parliamentary commission. The report produced by the commission found both of the main political parties, the PLN and the PUSC, guilty of receiving drug money during the 1986 electoral campaign.

At the same time, another scandal broke out over the financing of electoral campaigns, with accusations that both parties - and Oscar Arias in particular - had received money from Panamanian General Noriega in 1986.

[28] Between March and July, 1988, the structural adjustment policy of the Arias Government led to public discontent and demonstrations by many sectors of the population. Public employees protested against the concessions made to the IMF and the World Bank. The peasant unions staged a one-week strike to protest against the agrarian policy, and farmers went on strike several times.

[29] In 1989 this situation worsened and in August a coalition of regional trade union federations, professional guilds, and citizens' groups called for a strike in the province of Limón. The strike paralyzed sea traffic on the Caribbean coast for four days. Some sectors on the Atlantic coast also joined the protests. In September, teachers staged a nationwide strike.

[30] In 1990, women officially made up 29.9 per cent of the economically active population, but their number on the informal job market was estimated at 41 per cent. In the political arena women held only 15 per cent of posts. Women's organizations observed an increase in teenage prostitution through prostitution rings, which have become multi-million-dollar businesses for their owners.

[31] Under the slogan of "change", and focusing specifically on low-income groups with lower educational levels, the social Christian candidate Rafael Angel Calderón won the election held in February 1990 by a wide margin. In addition, he obtained an absolute majority in the legislature.

[32] The application of a severe economic adjustment program led to a reduction in the State apparatus as well as in the fiscal deficit, which had reached 3.3 per cent of GDP. As a result of these cuts, unemployment rose and popular discontent increased.

[33] In the 1994 elections, social democrat candidate Jose Maria Figueres defeated government candidate Miguel Rodriguez by a slight margin, after a campaign with few differences in their political positions but with notably harsh speeches from the rival parties.

[34] A free trade agreement was signed with Mexico in January 1995. However, the deterioration of the economy, with rising inflation and a fiscal deficit led the Government to increase taxes in order to balance the budget. The World Bank rejected the economic plan and refused to finance the structural adjustment schedule.

[35] In 1996, the governing PLN agreed a budget plan with the opposition which limited the government deficit to 1 per cent of the Gross Domestic Product. In late July, Hurricane Caesar struck Costa Rica, especially the South, causing some 30 deaths. The damage was estimated at some $100 million. The kidnappings of one German and another Swiss tourist dealt a blow to the tourist industry. Both were freed two and a half months later.

Many tourist operators preferred not to run the risk and took Costa Rica off their list of destinations.

[36] In June 1997, San Jose ratified the Interamerican Convention on Forced Detentions. Amnesty International urged the Government to put an end to police abuse against prisoners and refugees, who were mostly Nicaraguans.

[37] On February 1 1998, Miguel Angel Rodríguez, the Social Christian Unity Party (PUSC) candidate was elected President with 46.9 per cent of the vote. The PLN candidate José Miguel Corrales Bolaños, came in second with 44.4 per cent. The PUSC also took the absolute overall majority of seats in the parliamentary elections (29 of the 57 total seats), followed by the PLN (22) and the Democratic Force (2). Rodríguez repeatedly stressed that during his government, Costa Rica would not follow political integration mechanisms, like the Central American Parliament, although it would respect the economic integration devices.

[38] In March, US ambassador Thomas Dodd was accused of interfering in Costa Rica's affairs by the Commission for the Defence of Human Rights in Central America (Codehuca). Following the death of a US citizen in a private dispute, Dodd had declared his government could even impose economic sanctions on the country.

[39] The use of pesticides in banana plantations was questioned by studies warning of possible environmental damage and organic upsets in humans.

Côte d'Ivoire

Côte d'Ivoire

Population: 14,015,000 (1996)
Area: 322,463 SQ KM
Capital: Abidjan

Currency: CFA francs
Language: French

According to Baulé tradition, in 1730 Queen Aura Poka (sister of a defeated pretender to the Ashanti throne) emigrated westwards with her people. They founded a new state in the center of a territory known to Europeans since the 15th century as the Côte d'Ivoire. (or Ivory Coast) because of the active trade in elephant tusks. This Ashanti state soon grew and became a threat to the small states of Aigini, on the coast, and Atokpora, inland. In 1843, these states requested French protection, thus enabling France to obtain exclusive rights over the coastal trade centres.

[2] Fifty years later, French troops moved up the coast aiming to join Côte d'Ivoire. to Guinea, Mali and Senegal. However, they met with stiff resistance from Samori Touré, a Fulani leader who had risen through the social ranks because of outstanding leadership ability. He had set up a state in the heart of the region which the Europeans were planning to unify under a central colonial administration (See Guinea).

[3] After three decades of bloody fighting (1870-1898), Touré was defeated and the leaders of the dominant Fulani groups were forced to sign colonial agreements with the French.

[4] In 1895 the area became known as French West Africa, comprising Senegal, French Sudan (now Mali), Guinea and Côte d'Ivoire. Later, what are now Chad, Burkina Faso and Mauritania were also annexed. The French hoped to balance the poorer regions of Chad and Burkina Faso with the better off Senegal and Côte d'Ivoire. This

centralized administration failed after independence.

[5] Several attempts at economic integration were made, with different degrees of success, but real progress was made only recently with the creation of the Economic Community of West Africa, which includes 15 former colonies of France, Britain and Portugal.

[6] In French West Africa, modern political activities began in 1946 with the creation of the African Democratic Union (ADU), a political party with branches in Senegal, Mali and Guinea. The ADU promoted independence and unity for French colonies in the area. Felix Houphouet-Boigny, hereditary leader of the Baulé ethnic group, and also a physician and well-to-do farmer, was appointed party president, based on his experience leading a farmers' association which had fought against colonial policies.

[7] Tactically allied to the French Communist Party, the only anti-colonial French party at the time, the ADU staged strikes, demonstrations and boycotts of European businesses. The nationalist cause was savagely suppressed, leaving dozens of activists dead and thousands imprisoned, giving Boigny grounds for ending his alliance with the French communists in 1950. He soon reached a new agreement with François Mitterrand, then Minister for Overseas Territories. This move undermined the ADU's standing, and Boigny was only just able to maintain his prestige in his native land.

[8] Between 1958 and 1960 all of French West Africa became independent and the new-born

states joined the UN. Aware of their meagre economic prospects, the political leaders proposed to form a federation. Boigny, however, confident in the relative prosperity of his country and his privileged neo-colonial relations with France, opposed the idea. "We are not saying 'goodbye' to France, but 'see you later'", he had declared when announcing independence.

[9] As a major producer of cocoa, coffee, rubber and diamonds, Côte d'Ivoire. was able to attract transnational investors. In addition to the political stability produced by Boigny's paternalistic, authoritarian rule, Côte d'Ivoire. offered extremely cheap labour, mostly supplied by neighbouring countries. In the ten-year period (1966-76) the economic growth rate remained between 8 and 10 per cent a year. But prosperity withered as the West went into a recession after 1979. Agricultural exports fell from $4 billion to barely $1 billion between 1980 and 1983. Half the industries set up between 1966 and 1976 closed down, pushing unemployment figures up to 45 per cent of the active population. By 1985, the

foreign debt was five times that of 1981.

[10] Following International Monetary Fund recommendations, President Boigny made severe budget cuts, paralyzed nearly all public projects and slashed food subsidies. These decisions did not spark social unrest immediately, but only because of the weakness of the labour unions and the lack of fresh political leadership. The only groups which retained potential for opposition were students and liberal professionals, and they organized mass demonstrations and strikes.

[11] In May 1984, following negotiations with the Paris Club and other sources of financing, Côte d'Ivoire. was allowed to restructure its foreign debt. The economy has continued to deteriorate, however, particularly as coffee and cocoa export prices have fallen steadily.

[12] In October 1985, the 8th congress of the Côte d'Ivoire. Democratic Party (PDCI) issued a resolution nominating octogenarian Houphouet-Boigny for a sixth presidential term. The appointment was confirmed that same month by 99 per cent of

WORKERS

(1996)

Labour force %
■ WOMEN
□ MEN
33   67

■ AGRICULTURE 60% (1990)
□ INDUSTRIAL 10%
■ SERVICES 30%

LAND USE

DEFORESTATION -1% annual (81/90)
IRRIGATED 2.8 % of arable

(1993)

■ FOREST & WOODLAND 22%
□ ARABLE 7.6%
■ OTHER 70.4%

PROFILE

ENVIRONMENT
Located on the Gulf of Guinea, the country is divided into two major natural regions: the South, with heavy rainfall and lush rain forests, where foreign investors have large plantations of cash crops like coffee, cocoa and bananas; and the North, a granite plain characterized by its savannas, where small landowners raise sorghum, corn and peanuts. Côte d'Ivoire. has one of the fastest rates of deforestation in the world.

SOCIETY
Peoples: The population includes five major ethnic groups, the Kru, Akan, Volta, Mande and Malinke, some from the savannas and others from the rain forests, sub-divided into approximately 80 smaller groups.
Religions: Nearly two thirds of the population practice traditional African religions, 23 per cent are Moslem and 12 per cent Christian.
Languages: French (official). There are as many languages as ethnic groups; the most widely spoken are Diula, in the North; Baule, centre and West; and Bete in the Southeast.
Political parties: Côte d'Ivoire Democratic Party (PDCI), in power since independence in 1960; D'Ivoire People's Alliance (FPI), the major opposition force.
Social Organizations: General Workers' Union.

THE STATE
Official Name:
République de Côte d'Ivoire.
Administrative divisions: 49 departments.
Capital: Abidjan (economic centre), 2,600,000 people; Yamoussoukro (political centre since 1983) 100,000 (1994).
Other cities: Bouaké, 600,000 people; Daloa 100,000; Korhogo 60,000; (1994).
Government: Henry Konan Bédié, President since December 8 1993. Daniel Kablan Duncan, Prime Minister since December 11 1993. Single-chamber legislature: National Assembly with 175 members, elected by direct popular vote every 5 years. National Holiday: August 7, Independence (1960). Armed Forces: 8,400. Other: 7,800: Presidential Guard: 1,100; Gendarmerie: 4,400; Militia: 1,500; Military Fire Service: 800.

STATISTICS

DEMOGRAPHY
Population: 14,015,000 (1996) **Annual growth**: 3.4% (1980/1996) **Estimates for year 2000**: 15,100,000 **Annual growth to year 2000**: 2.2% (1994/2000) **Urban Population**: 44.0% (1996) **Urban growth**: 5.24% (1980/95) **Children per woman**: 5.3 (1996).

HEALTH
Life expectancy at birth: 51 years (1996) male: 51 years (1994) female: 54 years (1994) **Infant mortality**: 90 per 1,000 (1996) **Under-5 child mortality**: 150 per 1,000 (1996) **Calorie consumption**: 111% (1988/90) 11,111 **people per doctor** (1988/91) **Safe water**: 42% (1990/96).

EDUCATION
Literacy: 40% (1995) male: 50% (1995) female: 30% (1995) **School enrolment**: Primary total: 68% (1990/95) male: 78% (1990/95) female: 59% (1990/95) Secondary: male: 33% (1990/95) female: 17% (1990/95) Tertiary: 4% (1995) **Primary school teachers**: one for every 45 students (1995).

COMMUNICATIONS
10 **newspapers**, 143 **radios**, 60 **TV sets** and 8 **main telephone lines** per 1,000 people (1994).

ECONOMY
Per capita, GNP: $ 660 (1996) **Annual growth, GNP**: 4.6% (1995/96) **Annual inflation**: 4.01% (1985/95) **Currency**: 490 CFA francs = $ 1 (1995) **Cereal imports**: 466 metric tons (1994) **Food import dependency**: 16% (1994) **Fertilizer use**: 169 kgs per ha (1994) **Exports**: $ 4,996 million (1996) **Imports**: $ 2,909 million (1996) **External debt**: $ 19,713 million (1996) $ 1,407 **per capita**: (1996) **Debt service**: 26.2% of exports (1996) **Development aid received**: $ 1,200 million (1995) $ 87 per capita (1995) 22% of GNP (1994).

ENERGY
Consumption: 103.36 Kgs of Oil equivalent per capita yearly (1994) 69.77% imported (1994)

HDI (rank / value) 145 / 0.368 (1994)

---

the electorate. In November, however, elections for the General Assembly were marked by a very low turnout of 25 per cent.
[13] The Boigny regime's grandiose building schemes stood in stark contrast to African realities. In the face of severe economic hardship, he built Africa's largest cathedral, a project offensive to many people, and also to the 23 per cent Muslim population.
[14] Côte d'Ivoire is one of the world's largest producer of cocoa and, like all Third World producers of raw materials, it suffered from falling commodity prices. From July to October 1987, the price of cocoa dropped 50 per cent on the world market.
[15] In 1990, a government austerity plan went into effect with IMF and World Bank support. These economic measures resulted in decreases in worker salaries in both public and private sectors.

[16] Public reaction, particularly by students, brought about a reduction in the price of staple goods. In the meantime, the government decided not to carry out a planned 11 per cent wage cut, calling the measure a "contribution to national solidarity".
[17] In 1990, a multiparty system was established and presidential elections were held. Houphouet-Boigny was re-elected with 81 per cent of the vote.
[18] By 1991, the Government had not managed to fully apply its three year programme to put its public finances in order, privatize some of the public companies and stimulate the "competitiveness" of the private corporations.
[19] The death of the President in December 1993 triggered a succession dispute. He was replaced by Henri Konan-Bédié, leader of the National Assembly, who consolidated his power within the ruling Democratic Party, despite the opposition of former prime minister Ouattara.
[20] In 1994, the Government faced a strong union movement demanding compensation after the 100% devaluation of the CFA imposed by France and the IMF in January. In what was seen as a reward for having accepted the

devaluation half of Côte d'Ivoire's debt with the Paris Club was cancelled. However, the country continued having the highest per capita foreign debt in the world.
[21] In October 1995, Bédié won a controversial presidential election, boycotted by the opposition. For the first time since the country's independence, residing foreigners were not allowed to vote, neither were those whose parents were not Ivorian. This allowed Bédié to dispose of Ouattara, whose father was from Burkina Faso.
[22] Prime Minister Daniel Kablan Duncan formed a new 31-member cabinet in January 1996. Contrary to expectations of significant change, 25 of the previous government ministers were included in the new cabinet. The economy showed signs of

growth thanks to an increase in international cocoa and coffee prices.
[23] Following World Bank and the IMF guidelines, Côte d'Ivoire. promoted its plan for economic reforms and privatization. These two international financial institutions agreed to grant the country loans for a total of $385 million. The adjustments in the public sector brought enormous problems in healthcare and life expectancy fell to below 50 years. Furthermore, AIDS spread, and other killer diseases like yellow fever and tuberculosis underwent strong resurgence.
[24] In March 1998, the US State Department said Côte d'Ivoire. was not only an important springboard for narcotics like heroin, but that there were also marijuana crops hidden amongst the cocoa plantations.

Croatia

Hrvatska

Population: 4,501,000 (1996)
Area: 88,117 SQ KM
Capital: Zagreb

Currency: Kuna
Language: Croatian

The Croats migrated in the 6th century AD, from White Croatia, a region that now belongs to Ukraine, to the lower Danube Valley. From there they continued moving toward the Adriatic, where they conquered the Roman stronghold Salona in the year 614. After settling in the former Roman provinces of Pannonia and Dalmatia, the Croats freed themselves from the Avars and began developing independently.

[2] The Croatians were a farming people, and maintained their old way of life, uniting under their tribal chieftains. In the 7th century, the Croats were converted to Roman Catholicism; a bishopric was established at Nin for this region, and the Croats obtained the right to use their own language in their religious services.

[3] In the 8th century, Croatian tribes organized themselves into larger units, made up of two Duchies, Pannonia and Dalmatia. By the Peace of 812 between the Franks and the Byzantines, the former became a part of the Frankish Empire, and the latter, of Dalmatia. Both Duchies freed themselves in the mid-9th century, uniting to form the first independent Croatian kingdom toward the end of the century.

[4] Tomislav and his heirs had to defend themselves against both the Bulgarian Empire in Pannonia, and Venetian expansion along the Dalmatian coast. The Byzantine Empire helped Stjepan Drzislav (969-97) defend himself against Venice but in exchange, the Byzantines were allowed to re-establish its influence in the Adriatic. Peter Kresimir (1058-74) broke off relations with Byzantium, and strengthened his links with the papacy. During this period,

Croatia reached the peak of its power, as well as expanding its territory.

[5] However, during Kresimir's Government, the country split in two, with a Latin group favoring the king, and an opposition national group, backed up by broad popular support. When the Pope invited Dimitrije Zvonimir to involve the Kingdom in a war against the Seljuk Turks, the opposition accused him of being the Pope's vassal and assassinated him in 1089. The civil war which was then unleashed marked the beginning of the decline of the Croatian Kingdom.

[6] The Byzantines recovered Dalmatia, and in the meantime, Lazlo I of Hungary conquered Pannonia in 1091, laying claim to the Croatian crown. Lazlo founded a bishopric at Zagreb in 1094, which became the center of the Church's power in the region. Petar Svacic was crowned King by the Dalmatians, but the Pope considered him a rebel, and turned to King Kalman of Hungary to unseat him. Kalman invaded the country; Svacic - the last king of Croat blood - fell in 1097.

[7] After an extended war Kalman signed a treaty, called the Pacta Conventa, with the Croat representatives. Only Bosnia, then a part of the Croatian kingdom, refused to submit to a foreign monarch. For the next eight centuries, Croatia was linked to Hungary. In the 14th century, Dalmatia became a part of Venice, which ruled over it for 400 years.

[8] After the defeat of the Croatian and Hungarian forces in the battles of Krbavsko Polje (1493) and Mohacs (1526), most of Pannonia and Hungary fell into Turkish hands.

[9] Turkish domination altered the ethnic composition of Pannonia, as many Croats migrated northwards, some even going into Austria. In the meantime, the Turks brought in German and Hungarian settlers, and gave incentives for Serbians fleeing the Balkans to settle in the Vojna Krajina.

[10] When the Turks were driven back, in the 17th century, Austria tried to limit Croatia and Hungary's state rights, to make them mere provinces of the Austrian Empire. The Croatian and Hungarian nobility conspired

together to organize an independence movement, which failed. The Croatian leaders were executed and their lands were distributed among foreign nobles.

[11] After the annexation of Rijeka (Fiume) in the 1770s, Hungary tried to impose its language, but this triggered a nationalist reaction among the Croatians. In the meantime, the French Revolution and the Napoleonic Wars which had incorporated Dalmatia, Pannonia and the area south of the Sava river to the French Empire, further stimulated Croatian nationalism. Upon the fall of Napoleon, relations between Hungary and Croatia rapidly deteriorated.

[12] In April 1848, the Hungarian Parliament adopted a series of measures severely limiting Croatian autonomy. The Croatian Diet declared its separation from Hungary, abolishing serfdom and approving equal rights for all its citizens. Hungary's troops were weakened by this conflict, making it easier for the Hapsburgs to put down the Hungarian Revolt and regain power later that year.

[13] The Croatian Diet was dissolved in 1865, and two years later, with the division of the crown, Germany and Hungary became the major nations of the Austro-Hungarian Empire. In 1868, Hungary accepted the union of Croatia, Slavonia and Dalmatia as a separate political entity, though Austria refused to relinquish its claim to Dalmatia.

[14] In the early 20th century, Croatian nationalist groups intensified their activity. An alliance of Croatian and Serbian leaders adopted the "Rijeka resolution", a plan of action which enabled them to win the 1906 elections. In the meantime, the Croatian Peasant Party began political activity among the peasants. The Crown responded by increasing repression.

[15] In 1915, Croatian, Serbian and Slovenian leaders organized the Yugoslav Committee in Paris to push for separation from the empire and union with an independent Serbia. Austria-Hungary's defeat accelerated the creation of the Yugoslav kingdom in 1918.

WORKERS

(1996)

Labour force %

■ WOMEN	
□ MEN	

44   56

■ AGRICULTURE   16% (1990)
□ INDUSTRIAL   34%
▨ SERVICES   50%

External Debt	Foreign Trade
1996	MILLIONS $ 1996

PER CAPITA
$1,030

IMPORTS
7,788
EXPORTS
4,512

PROFILE

ENVIRONMENT

Croatia is bounded to the north by Slovenia and Hungary and to the east by Serbia. The Dalmatian coast - a 1,778-kilometer coastline on the Adriatic, with numerous ports and seaside resorts - lies in southern and western Croatia. The territory is made up of three regions with different landscapes: rolling hills in the north, around Zagreb; rocky mountains along the Adriatic coast and the inland valleys of the Pannonian Basin. The Pannonian Basin, under the influence of masses of continental air, is colder and not as rainy as the coast. The climate along the Dalmatian coast is Mediterranean, with an average temperature of 4°C in winter, and 24°C in summer. The country's traditional economic activities have been agriculture and cattle raising. After World War II, light industry was developed, and the discovery of rich deposits of oil changed the country's economy. The Government is in the process of reconstructing the country's productive apparatus, as well as vast areas of the country which were devastated by the conflict. Likewise, it has begun to assess the impact of the civil war upon the environment.

SOCIETY

Languages: Croatian (official).
Religions: Roman Catholic 76 per cent; Orthodox 11 per cent; Muslims 1 per cent.
Political Parties: The Croatian Democratic Union, right-of-center; the Croat Socio-Liberal Party (CSLP); the Croat Peasant Party.
Social Organizations: These are in the process of being reorganized, after recent political and institutional changes.

THE STATE

Official Name: Republika Hrvatska.
Administrative Divisions: 102 Districts.
Capital: Zagreb, 706,770 people (1991).
Other Cities: Rijeka, 167,964 people (1991).
Government: Franjo Tudjman, President since April,1990 and re-elected in June, 1997. Zlatko Matesa, Prime Minister since November 4 1995. The bicameral parliament (called *Sabor*) is one of Europe's oldest: the Chamber of Deputies has 127 members and the Chamber of Districts has 68 members, elected for a 4 years term.
National Holiday: June 25, Independence (1991).
Armed Forces: 105,000 (1995).
Other: 24,000 Police (1,000 deployed in Bosnia).

[16] The Serbian dynasty's policy of amalgamating the regions immediately came into conflict with Croatian desires for independence. Croatia demanded the creation of a Yugoslav federation. As of 1920, the Peasant Party, led by Stjepan Radic headed the Croatian opposition. The assassination of Radic and other members of the opposition, in 1928 provoked a serious crisis.

[17] When World War II broke out, Yugoslavia was divided internally, so it was easily occupied by Hitler in 1941. The German army set up a puppet regime made up of Croatia, Slavonia, parts of Dalmatia and Bosnia-Herzegovina. A racist campaign was launched in which Serbians, Jews, Gypsies and Croats opposed to Fascism were massacred in concentration camps or forced into exile.

[18] After the Anti-Nazi guerrillas had occupied Zagreb in May 1945, the Anti-Fascist Council of National Liberation of Croatia assumed control of the Government. By the end of the year, Croatia was one of the constituent republics of the new People's Federated Republic of Yugoslavia.

[19] Within the Yugoslav socialist system (see Yugoslavia), Croatia maintained and strengthened its national independence, although this worked against its ethnic minorities. In 1972, a purge within the Croatian League of Communists led to the suspension of the Matica Hrvatska, the Croatian cultural organization.

[20] At the end of the 1980s, Yugoslavia modified its political system; the Yugoslav League of Communists (YLC) renounced the monopoly and leading role assigned to it by the constitution, and in April 1990, the first multiparty elections since World War II were held in the different regions.

[21] In Croatia, parliamentary elections gave a majority to the Croatian Democratic Union (CDU), a center-right party which favored making Yugoslavia a confederation of sovereign states. The leader of the CDU, retired General Franjo Tudjman, was elected President of the republic. In December, Parliament ratified a new constitution which endorsed the right to separate from the federation.

[22] In June 1991, Croatia proclaimed its independence from the federation, while the Serbians in Krajina declared their intention of separating from Croatia. The United States and the European Community held back from recognizing Croatia and Slovenia, which had also declared their independence.

[23] The federal army, whose high command answered primarily to Serbia, intervened in Croatia and Slovenia, claiming that separation constituted a threat to Yugoslavia's integrity. War broke out, with many victims on both sides.

[24] In November, Tudjman's Government arrested the leaders of the ultra-right-wing Croatian *Ustasha* (Fascist) Party (CUP), and dissolved its militia, under the accusation of conspiring against the country's legal authorities. Founded in February 1990, the CUP adopted the name of a nationalist party of the past, whose leader had been the leader of the Croatian puppet Government during Nazi occupation in World War II.

[25] In December, Germany recognized Croatia's independence, accelerating the process whereby the EC would do the same. A few days earlier, the Serbs of Krajina (in southern Croatia), Slavonia, Baranja and western Serm (to the east) proclaimed the republic of Krajina, as a new federated Yugoslav entity, an alliance of Serbian states.

[26] In January 1992, through EC mediation, Serbia and Croatia accepted a peace plan, and agreed to allow the UN to station 15,000 troops in the war zone; however, Krajina's representatives objected to the agreement. Almost a third of Croatia's territory was controlled by federal troops and Serbian irregulars. Both forces accused each other of violating the cease-fire, and of committing war crimes.

[27] In February, after overcoming Krajina's opposition, the UN Security Council unanimously ratified sending a multinational force to Croatia. UN troops were charged with keeping the peace and protecting Croatia's Serbian minority, which maintained civilian guerrilla groups. All parties agreed to the UN peacekeeping force remaining in the region for a one-year period.

[28] In May, the General Assembly of the UN, meeting in New York, formally admitted the former Yugoslav republics of Croatia, Slovenia and Bosnia-Herzegovina, increasing the number of its members to 178.

[29] After his re-election on August, President Franjo Tudjman managed to reopen the main highway link between Zagreb and Belgrade, through an agreement with the New Yugoslav Federation (Serbia and Montenegro). This agreement was engineered through UN mediation, with former US Secretary of State Cyrus Vance acting as chief negotiator.

[30] In Geneva, in October, presidents Tudjman and Cosic, of the Yugoslav Federation, announced their opposition to "ethnic cleansing". They agreed to provide more humane treatment of refugees.

[31] In November, Radovan Karadzic, leader of the Bosnian Serbs, announced the formation of a confederation between the "Serbian Republic of Bosnia and Herzegovina" and the "Serbian Republic of Krajina", in Croatia.

[32] According to official sources, 99 per cent of the Krajina electorate favored unification with the Bosnian Serbs at the time; however, a year went by following Karadzic's announcement and, at

STATISTICS

DEMOGRAPHY
Population: 4,501,000 (1996) **Annual growth:** 0.2% (1980/1996)
Estimates for year 2000: 4,500,000 **Annual growth to year 2000:** -0.1% (1994/2000) **Urban Population:** 56.2% (1996) **Urban growth:** 1.97% (1980/95) **Children per woman:** 1.6 (1996).

HEALTH
Life expectancy at birth: 72 years (1996) male: 67 years (1994) female: 76 years (1994) **Infant mortality:** 10 per 1,000 (1996) **Under-5 child mortality:** 11 per 1,000 (1996).

EDUCATION
Literacy: 98% (1995) male : 98% (1995) female: 97% (1995) **School enrolment :** Primary total: 86% (1990/95) male : 87% (1990/95) female: 86% (1990/95) Secondary: male : 75% (1990/95) female: 81% (1990/95) Tertiary: 28% (1995) **Primary school teachers:** one for every 20 students (1995).

COMMUNICATIONS
580 **newspapers**, 261 **radios**, 230 **TV sets** and 252 **main telephone lines** per 1,000 people (1994) **Books:** 59 new titles per 100,000 people (1992/94).

ECONOMY
Per capita, GNP: $ 3,800 (1996) **Annual growth, GNP:** 4.7% (1995/96) **Consumer price index:** 53,818.2 (1994) **Currency:** 5.32 kune = $ 1 (1995) **Cereal imports:** 82 metric tons (1994) **Fertilizer use:** 1,482 kgs per ha (1994) **Exports:** $ 4,512 million (1996) Imports: $ 7,788 million (1996) **External debt:** $ 4,634 million (1996) $ 1,030 **per capita:** (1996) **Debt service:** 5.5% of exports (1996) .

ENERGY
Consumption: 1,395.35 Kgs of Oil equivalent per capita yearly (1994) 42.68% imported (1994)

HDI (rank / value) 77 / 0.76 (1994)

the end of 1993, nothing had yet been done to bring about such a union.

[33] This situation intensified tensions in Croatia. Tudjman, concerned about avoiding the proliferation of separatist feelings, offered an amnesty and relative autonomy to the Serbs of Croatian Krajina. Likewise, the latter allowed the bridge at Maslenica - which linked the northern and southern parts of the country - to be rebuilt.

[34] However, subsequent discrepancies led to a resumption of hostilities by the Serbs; not even mediation by the UN was able to ensure security of the bridge.

[35] Amnesty reported that thousands of people, most of them Serbs, were accused of armed rebellion or of constituting a threat to the territorial unity of Croatia. Among them were those whom AI considered to be prisoners of conscience, given the fact that they were arrested because of their ethnic origin. AI also received reports of summary executions perpetrated by members of the Croatian army.

[36] The conflict in Croatia, although less bloody than that of Bosnia-Herzegovina, has caused thousands of deaths and injuries among the civilian population.

[37] Toward the end of 1993, Tudjman and Izetbegovic, the president of Bosnia-Herzegovina, signed a cease-fire agreement which also provided for the dismantling of the prisoner of war camps.

[38] In January 1994, Croatia and Serbia agreed in Geneva to a full restoration of transportation and communication links between the two republics. Likewise, offices were opened in Zagreb and Belgrade which were to function as diplomatic representations, although with lesser rank than embassies.

[39] However, there has been no solution to the situation of the enclave of Krajina, still under Serbian control. Croatia attempted to win Serbian recognition of its territorial demands, but Slobodan Milosevic opposed it.

[40] UN and US mediators Thorvald Stoltenberg and Lord Owen welcomed the understanding, which diffused the tension between the two former Yugoslav republics.

[41] Towards the end of January, Croatia made an unsuccessful bid to recover the Krajina enclave by force, thereby violating the cease-fire with Serbia. In February, the UN Security Council unanimously approved an extension of the UN peacekeeping force mandate in Croatia.

[42] In June 1994, Croatia launched the *kuna,* the currency used in that country during World War II by the Government which had been installed by Hitler's troops. The kuna replaced the dinar, which had been adopted after independence.

[43] The new currency was rejected by the opposition. However, Tudjman pointed out that the kuna, which in Croatian means "marten" (the animal), dates back to the 11th century, when the fur of the marten was used as currency.

[44] The opposition also questioned the Government's decision to change the names of streets, schools and plaques dedicated to the memory of famous anti-Fascist war heroes.

[45] Pope John Paul II's visit to Croatia on September 10 and 11, helped to raise the international profile of the nation. The Serb rebels and the Croat Government reached an agreement on opening the Zagreb-Belgrade road, the Adria oil pipeline and for the supply of water and electricity to Serbs in the occupied territories.

[46] Croatia conquered inflation in 1994, though industrial production fell and unemployment remained at around 20 per cent. The emigration of university professionals and qualified workers increased significantly during this year.

[47] In January 1995, Croatia informed the UN that authorization for the peacekeeping troops would not be extended beyond March 31, the date the agreement ended. According to Tudjman, the 12,000 blue helmets legitimised the Serb presence in Krajina, occupying 27 per cent of Croat territory. The Serb and Croat forces took offensive action. The UN said the withdrawal of its troops could cause the most dangerous situation in Europe since 1945.

[48] On April 13, Serbian forces bombarded Dubrovnik airport and 10 days later again blocked the road between Zagreb and Belgrade, in eastern Slavonia. The Croat army regained control in this area in a swift operation in May. Zagreb was immediately shelled by Serbian troops.

[49] President of the Yugoslav Federation, Slobodan Milosevic said that if the UN lifted its sanctions on Yugoslavia, peace would return to the Balkans in a matter of months. An agreement between Franco Tudjman and the United States allowed the international force to remain but to withdraw gradually, with help from NATO troops.

[50] In early August 1995, the Serbs suffered their worst defeat since the break-up of the former Yugoslavia. The Krajina region, in central Croatia, was taken by the Croats, who forced Serb troops and civilians to leave.

[51] Allegations of torture and pillage were lodged against the Croats who occupied Krajina. Some 250,000 Serbs joined the mass of more than 700,000 refugees already uprooted in the Balkans. The Croat occupation of Krajina was considered the biggest ethnic cleansing operation of the Balkan war. By May 1996, only eight Croats had been tried in their absence by the International Criminal Tribunal at the Hague

[52] In October, representatives of the Croat Government and the Serb leaders of eastern Slavonia agreed the basis for the peaceful restructuring of the region. On October 29, Tudjman won the elections but did not receive the two-thirds majority necessary for reforming the Constitution and increasing presidential powers.

[53] The signing of an agreement between the presidents of Croatia, Serbia and Bosnia-Herzegovina at an airbase near Dayton, in the United States, marked the end of hostilities, though civilians maintained the aggression towards UN and NATO troops during 1996.

[54] From August, negotiations between Zagreb and Belgrade allowed the refugees to return and for elections to be held in 1997. Tudjman, accused of obstructing the return of the refugees, allowed a limited number of Serbian Croats to settle in the country again. In June, he was re-elected with 61.4 per cent of the vote. In late 1997 and early 1998, fresh accusations arose about abuses committed by the Croats in their counter-offensive for the Krajina region.

Cuba

Cuba

Population: 11,018,000 (1996)
Area: 110,861SQ KM
Capital: Havana (La Habana)

Currency: Pesos
Language: Spanish

Until the 16th century the island of Cuba was inhabited by the Taino and Ciboney. In 1492, the Spanish emissary to the Indies arrived, but it was not until 1509 that a voyage was made around the coast proving that Cuba was an island. In 1514, the conquest begun in 1510 was completed. This was a violent period in the island's history, with a number of uprisings, like those led by native chieftains Hatuey and Guama.

2   In fact, the Spanish expeditions which would subsequently conquer a large part of the Caribbean, Mexico and Central America, departed from Cuba, which a mid-16th century document described as "high and mountainous" with small rivers "rich in gold and fish". In 1511, colonists from Santo Domingo started mining Cuban gold. It was a short-lived economic cycle, probably because the indian population was rapidly exterminated. As the number of African enslaved workers on the island was insufficient, economic life soon declined and did not recover until the end of the 16th century, with the advent of sugar production.

3   As early as the 17th century, economic diversification was achieved through shipbuilding and the developing leather and copper industries. The economic center of the island gradually moved from Santiago, on the southern coast, to Havana, in the north, a port of great importance in the mid-17th century.

4   Sugar cane plantations in colonial America used slave labor and caused economic dependence. There were periods, during 1840 for example, when slave labor represented 77 per cent of the total Cuban workforce. There is also evidence that there were *palenques*, settlements of escaped slaves (see Brazil, paragraph 6) on the island, and there was an abortive slave revolt in 1843. It took a long, complex process to change this situation, comparable only with that of Brazil, the last American country to abolish slavery. British pressure against the slave trade, and the contribution of the enslaved workers during the Ten Year War, contributed decisively to the abolition of slavery in 1886.

5   The struggle for independence began in the first few decades of the 19th century, but the decisive battle, with José Martí, Antonio Maceo and Máximo Gómez was not fought until 1895. In 1898, aware that the victory of the Cuban patriots was inevitable, the US declared war on Spain and invaded Cuba to guarantee their continued influence in the Caribbean.

6   US occupation forces ruled the country from 1899 to 1902, imposing a constitution including the so-called "Platt Amendment". This secured the US rights to intervene in Cuba and to retain a portion of its territory. Guantánamo became a powerful air and naval base that is still maintained. The "right" to intervene has been exercised on various occasions, with US Marines remaining on Cuban soil for extended periods of time.

7   With the fall of the dictator Machado in 1933, Carlos Manuel de Céspedes came to power. Several months later there was a military coup and the rebelling sergeants established a short-lived "Pentarchy". A few days later, Grau formed the "Government of a Hundred Days" with Fulgencio Batista and Antonio Guiteras, and several anti-imperialist measures were implemented. In January 1934, Batista led a reactionary counter-coup, and Guiteras was assassinated. Elections were held, ushering in a series of governments presided over by Batista's Authentic Party, dominating a period characterized by corruption and gangsterism under the auspices of the United States. On March 10 1952, Batista engineered yet another coup, establishing a dictatorial regime which was responsible for the death of 20,000 Cubans.

8   On July 26 1953, Fidel Castro and a group of revolutionaries attacked the Moncada Army Base in Santiago de Cuba. Although the attack itself failed, it marked the beginning of the revolution. After a short period of imprisonment, Castro went into exile in Mexico only to return in December 1956. Castro's revolutionary program had been defined during his trial after the failed initial uprising, ending with his well-known words: "History will absolve me".

9   On December 31 1958, Batista fled from Cuba as guerrilla columns led by Ernesto "Che" Guevara and Camilo Cienfuegos, closed on Havana. They were the vanguard of the Rebel Army. In just over two years, the guerrillas of the "26th of July" Movement, organized by Fidel Castro, broke the morale of Batista's corrupt army.

10   In 1961, counter-revolutionaries disembarked at Playa Giron (Giron Beach), in the Bay of Pigs, in an attempt to bring down the regime which had carried out Agrarian Reforms and expropriated various American enterprises. They had counted on a popular uprising against the revolutionary government, but this did not materialize. After 72 hours of fierce fighting, the Bay of Pigs invasion ended in the defeat of the invading forces. Two days before the invasion, on April 15, while the victims of the Havana Airport bombing were being buried, Castro proclaimed the socialist nature of the revolution.

11   Also in that year, all the pro-government organizations joined together in a common structure. This was initially known as the Integrated Revolutionary Organizations, and later became the United Party of the Socialist Cuban Revolution (PURSC). The United States had Cuba excluded from the Organization of American States (OAS). It also put pressure on other countries to sever diplomatic relations with Cuba, engineering an economic blockade of the island. That year the October Crisis made the possibility of a third World War into a near-probability. The United States photographed Soviet nuclear missile launching sites on the island, and began preparations for another invasion. However, a peaceful solution was reached as the Soviet Union and the United States came to an agreement. The US pledged not to invade Cuba, but disregarded the Cuban Government's demands for an end to the blockade, the withdrawal of US troops from Guantanamo and an end to US-managed terrorist activities.

12   The literacy campaign during these years soon bore fruit, and by 1964, Cuba was free of illiteracy. Improvements in health were also one of the Government's priorities. In October 1965, the People's Socialist Party, the Revolutionary Directory and the 26 of July Movement (led by Castro himself) dropped the name

PROFILE

Environment
The Cuban archipelago includes the island of Cuba, the Isle of Youth (formerly the Isle of Pines) and about 1,600 nearby keys and islets. Cuba, the largest island of the Antilles, has rainy, tropical climate. With the exception of the southeastern Sierra Maestra highlands, wide and fertile plains predominate in the country. Sugar cane farming takes up over 60 per cent of the cultivated land, particularly in the northern plains. Nickel is the main mineral resource.

SOCIETY
Peoples: Cubans call themselves "Afro-Latin Americans" on account of their mixed Afro-European-American ethnic background. There are also approximately 30,000 Asian natives, mainly Chinese. **Religions:** Catholic 39.6%; atheist 6.4%; Protestant 3.3%; Afro-Cuban syncretists. **Languages:** Spanish.
Political Parties: The Cuban Communist Party is defined by the constitution as the "supreme leading force of society and the state". Founded in October 1965, it replaced the United Party of the Socialist Revolution (PURS). This group had been in existence since 1962, when the Integrated Revolutionary Organizations (ORI) were reorganized and renamed. The ORI, a political front formed in 1961, resulted from a merger of the Revolutionary Movement July 26, the Revolutionary Leadership March 13, and the People's Socialist Party. **Social Organizations:** Cuban Workers' Union (CTC). The CTC had 2,984,393 members in 1988, and represented more than 80 per cent of the Cuban labor force; the National Association of Small Farmers, 167.461 members (1988) with 3,500 grass roots organizations; the Federation of Cuban Women (FMC), 2,420,000 members; the University Student Federation (FEU) and the Federation of Secondary School Students (FEEM), 450,000 student members; the José Martí Pioneers' Union, 2,200,000 children and young people; the Revolution Defense Comitees.

THE STATE
Official Name: República de Cuba. **Administrative Divisions:** 14 Provinces, 169 Municipalities including the special municipality of Isla de Pinos. **Capital:** Havana (la Habana), 2,241,000 people (1995). **Other cities:** Santiago de Cuba 440,100 people; Camaguey 294,000; Holguín 242,100; Guantánamo 207,800 (1993). **Government:** Fidel Castro Ruz, President of the Council of State and the Council of Ministers. The constitution, approved in a plebiscite on November 15 1976, states that the power is exercised through the Assemblies of People's Power. The local Assemblies delegate power to successively more encompassing representative bodies until a pyramid is formed which peaks in the National Assembly. Representatives are subject to recall by the voters. **National Holidays:** January 1, Liberation Day (1959); July 26, Assault on the Moncada military barracks (1953). **Armed Forces:** 105,000 (1995). **Other:** 1,369,000 Civil Defense Force, Territorial Militia, State Security, Border Guard.

PURSC and created the Cuban Communist Party (PCC). This was just one more step closer to the Soviet Union, a relationship which had been strengthened by the economic blockade.
[13] With the consolidation of the socialist regime, Cuba began lending technical assistance to like-minded peoples and governments of the Third World. It sent troops to countries like Ethiopia and Angola, who requested help to resist invading forces.
[14] The revolution began to be institutionalized after the first PCC congress, in 1975. A new constitution was approved in 1976 and there were subsequent elections of representatives for the governing bodies at municipal, provincial and national levels. In 1979, Castro and the leaders of the PCC launched a campaign of revolutionary requirements to correct weaknesses in the administrative and political management areas of the revolutionary process.
[15] Tension between Cuba and the US had increased when Ronald Reagan came to the White House in 1979.
[16] In the mid-1980s, some 120,000 people left Mariel bound for Florida taking advantage of a clause offering automatic US residency to any Cuban arriving in the United States - brought in when emigration from Cuba was practically impossible.
[17] Cuba's relations with many Latin American countries improved as a consequence of the Cuban attitude during the Malvinas/Falklands war. Anxious to put a halt to Cuban-Latin American rapprochement, the United States took a series of measures against Havana. In August 1982 the US Senate passed a resolution allowing the Government to use the armed forces to halt "Marxist-Leninist subversion" in Central America.
[18] In the midst of mounting tension in Central America, Fidel Castro proposed to remove all foreign troops and advisors from the region. Meanwhile on the domestic scene, he outlined a new development strategy aimed at achieving greater economic autonomy. He aimed to make the island less dependent upon external factors and less vulnerable to manipulation by its creditors in the socialist bloc.
[19] These proposals were largely due to open threats of military aggression from the US during Reagan's second term. Consequently, defence had top priority, and efforts to strengthen the economy were made in order to fund the defence budget. Unavoidable imports were to be financed through exports.
[20] Cuba depended on capitalist countries for 15 per cent of its imports, and had foreign debts of some $3 billion, to non-socialist countries and private banks. It had to guarantee the availability of hard currency. To meet the debt payments there were two choices open. One was to save on oil imports and the other was to produce more and better goods, both for export and to replace imported goods in the domestic market.
[21] As economic difficulties increased, the upper echelons of the PCC and the Government proposed a series of new measures. Several party leaders were removed from their posts for failing to adapt to the new situation; a new Office for Religious Affairs was charged with strengthening links between the churches and the State, and state control over the media was relaxed.
[22] The results of the Third Congress were formalized in April 1986 and the so-called "process of the rectification of errors and negative tendencies" was initiated. This coincided with the changes which were taking place in the Soviet Union, but the Cubans avoided adopting the eastern European model.
[23] In June 1989, a high-ranking group of Army officers and officials of the Ministry of the Interior were brought to trial and executed for being involved in drug trafficking.
[24] From the time George Bush took office as US President there was an increase in American pressure on Cuba. In the first few months of 1990 there were important military manoeuvres at Guantanamo Base and in the Caribbean. The US also violated Cuban television airspace with transmissions by "Televisión Martí", which was supported by "The voice of America". However, this broadcast was only picked up on the island for one day, after which it was jammed.
[25] At this time, the last of Cuba's troops returned home from the Congo and Angola. More than 300,000 Cubans had served in Angola, with the loss of 2,016 lives.
[26] After a seven-month delay, the 4th PCC congress took place in October 1991. It was decided to reform the Constitution so that members of the National Assembly could be elected directly, a major ratification of the single-party system. People with religious beliefs were also admitted, and the Government recognized the need for joint ventures, especially with Latin American investors.
[27] With the changes in Eastern Europe, and the disappearance of its former Council for Mutual Economic Assistance allies, some of Cuba's basic supplies dropped to critical levels. To ease this crisis, the Government strengthened its ties with China, Vietnam and North Korea, and looked for ways to capitalize on its recent technological advances.
[28] Biotechnological research has made Cuba a Third World leader in this area. (They recently developed an anti-meningitis vaccine).
[29] The Government decided to ration fuel when the former USSR cut oil shipments by 25 per cent between 1989 and 1991. They also decided to strengthen the tourist industry. The Cuban Government has initiated joint ventures with Spanish companies. The investors maintain 50 per cent ownership of the enterprise once it enters operation.
[30] The loss of its main trading

Food Dependency

1994
21%

Foreign Trade

MILLIONS $ 1996

IMPORTS
3,004
EXPORTS
1,834

STATISTICS

DEMOGRAPHY
Population: 11,018,000 (1996) **Annual growth:** 0.8% (1980/1996) **Estimates for year 2000:** 11,200,000 **Annual growth to year 2000:** 0.4% (1994/2000) **Urban Population:** 76.3% (1996) **Children per woman:** 1.6 (1996).

HEALTH
Life expectancy at birth: 76 years (1996) male: 74 years (1994) female: 78 years (1994) **Infant mortality:** 10 per 1,000 (1996) **Under-5 child mortality:** 10 per 1,000 (1996) **Calorie consumption:** 135% (1988/90) 332 **people per doctor** (1988/91) **Safe water:** 93% (1990/96).

EDUCATION
Literacy: 96% (1995) male : 96% (1995) female: 95% (1995) **School enrolment :** Primary total: 104% (1990/95) male : 104% (1990/95) female: 103% (1990/95) Secondary: male : 70% (1990/95) female: 79% (1990/95) Tertiary: 14% (1995) **Primary school teachers:** one for every 14 students (1995).

COMMUNICATIONS
120 **newspapers,** 347 **radios,** 190 **TV sets** and 32 **main telephone lines** per 1,000 people (1994) **Books:** 9 new titles per 100,000 people (1992/94).

ECONOMY
Currency: 1 pesos = $ 1 (1995) **Cereal imports:** 1,464 metric tons (1994) **Food import dependency:** 21% (1994) **Fertilizer use:** 367 kgs per ha (1994) **Exports:** $ 1,834 million (1996) **Imports:** $ 3,004 million (1996) **Development aid received:** $ 64 million (1995) $ 6 per capita (1995).

HDI (rank / value) 86 / 0.723 (1994)

---

partners, and the re-enforcement of the US blockade led to the creation of a Special Plan, aimed at distributing scarce resources equitably. In 1990, bread was rationed at 100 grams per person per day, three newspapers ceased publication, and the official newspaper, "Granma", was forced to cut its circulation by more than two thirds. Alternative proposals included the possibility of offering more sugar, tobacco and coffee on the international market, an overall strengthening of the agricultural sector, and the possibility of oil purchase agreements with Mexico and Venezuela.

[31] The severe shortage of food forced the authorities to carry out an emergency food program. This scheme sought to increase agricultural production rapidly, maximizing sugar production so that sugar cane derivatives can be used as animal feed. The emergency program also aims to create new sources of employment.

[32] With the break-up of the Soviet Union, the United States urged Russia to take a tougher stand in its relations with the island, and this trend became evident during Mikhail Gorbachev's last months in power. Gorbachev's decision to withdraw 3,000 Soviet soldiers stationed in Cienfuegos and Havana, took the Cubans completely by surprise as the issue had never even been discussed.

WORKERS

(1996)

Labour force %

■ WOMEN
□ MEN

38   62

■ **AGRICULTURE** 18% (1990)
□ **INDUSTRIAL** 30%
■ **SERVICES** 51%

MILITARY EXPENDITURE

MILITARY (as % of health and education expenditures-1990/91) **125%**

[33] In August 1991, through its representative at the United Nations, Cuba presented a motion that the UN should debate ending the American economic blockade. The Cubans quickly withdrew the motion, when they realized what they were up against; the US had put pressure on all the other delegations.

[34] In early 1993, National Assembly (parliament) elections were held, and deputies were elected directly for the first time. Ricardo Alarcón, foreign minister, was designated president of the National Assembly, and Roberto Robaina, secretary general of the Communist Youth organization, became foreign minister.

[35] On July 26 1993, in his speech for the commemoration of the 40th anniversary of the attack on Moncada Army Post, Castro explained the difficult situation which the country was facing, and the need to adopt special measures. He announced that it would henceforth be legal for Cubans to possess and use foreign currency, and to be self-employed.

[36] Towards the end of the same year, the National Assembly met to discuss the country's critical situation, especially its internal finances. The Assembly decided to take no measures for the time being, but to discuss the issue and collect opinions and ideas in workplaces throughout the country. These "Workers' Parliaments" were held during the first quarter of 1994.

[37] In April 1994, a meeting entitled "The Nation and Emigration" was held in Havana on the initiative of Foreign Minister Roberto Robaina, and it was attended by some groups of Cuban émigrés living abroad. Shortly afterwards, there were a series of incidents in Havana involving people who wanted to leave the country illegally in rickety boats. When Cuba announced it would not stop the "boat people" from leaving, the United States started official negotiations to regulate the illegal departure of the immigrants.

[38] In July, Cuba entered the Association of Caribbean States as a full member. Cuban participation in the ACS, a group which is emerging as a new economic bloc, will encourage greater integration of the Cuban economy in the region, offering tariff benefits and trade facilities.

[39] In 1995, the fiscal deficit fell for the third year running, due to the reduction of public services and cutbacks in subsidies. A system of convertibility of the peso with the dollar was introduced and the holding of US currency was legalized. The Cuban parliament approved a new investment law, allowing for totally foreign-owned companies to be established, including by Cubans resident abroad. US Congress approved the Helms-Burton law, penalizing companies dealing with Cuba through third countries. The international community, especially the EU, harshly criticised this measure for violating the WTO and GATT agreements.

[40] In February 1996, the Cuban air force shot down two small civilian planes from an exile group known as "Brothers to the Rescue" in Miami, who, according to Havana, had violated Cuban air space to distribute anti-Castro leaflets. The incident opened a new controversy with the United States, which claimed the incident had occurred over international waters. Amnesty International denounced the imprisonment of several people linked to the Cuban Council. According to Amnesty, the Council included 140 groups of opposition journalists, professionals and unionists, while the Cuban government linked it to the US intervention campaign.

[41] The Helms-Burton law barred Cuban access to loans from international institutions like the World Bank or the IMF. However, the foreign companies continued to invest in Cuba, using various subterfuges, like not using their own names, and the economic reforms continued to be implemented. Banks were allowed to extend their offer of services and tax-free trading areas were created by a decree in June. In mid 1996, productivity was up 8 per cent on 1995 figures, while the GDP had increased 9.6 per cent.

[42] The Cuban exiles in Miami and radical enemies of Castro suffered two heavy blows in late 1997. The first was the death of Alejandro Más Canosa, leader of the Cuban dissidents in Miami, on November 23, and the second was the political coup pulled off by Castro with Pope John Paul II's visit to Cuba, from January 21 to 25 1998. As a run-up to the arrival of the Pope, who had condemned the US embargo on the island, Castro declared Christmas 1997 - normally a working day - as a public holiday.

Cyprus

Kipros Kibris

Population: 756,000 (1996)
Area: 9,251 SQ KM
Capital: Nicosia (Levkosía)

Currency: pounds
Language: Greek and Turkish

The first civilization on Cyprus may be 3,000 years old. Hittites, Phoenicians, Greeks, Assyrians, Persians, Egyptians, Romans, Arabs and Turks trooped through its valleys and over its hills until 1878, when the British negotiated the island with Turkey in exchange for protection against Czarist Russia. Cyprus became a bridgehead of the British expansion eastward.

[2] In 1930, movements favoring *enosis* (annexation) by Greece, gained ground stimulated by the incorporation of Crete to Greece in 1913. Enosis was promoted by the Greek Orthodox Church, the spiritual guide of Greek-Cypriots, who make up the majority of the island's population. But Turkey, Greece's perennial rival, was averse to being completely surrounded by a hostile neighbour on its Mediterranean coast. The British sent many Greek-Cypriot priests into exile. After World War II the country's most important political figure was Archbishop Vaneziz Makarios, who led the Cypriot anti-colonial movement from exile.

[3] In 1959, representatives of the Greek and Turkish communities, of Makarios' Democratic Party and of British colonial interests, approved a plan whereby Cyprus was to become an independent republic with constitutional guarantees for the Turkish minority, and British sovereignty over the island's military bases. Independence was proclaimed on August 16 1960, and Makarios took office as president. An active supporter of anti-colonialism, the President played an important role in the Movement of Non-Aligned Countries. Makarios was re-elected in 1968 and 1973. Tensions between Greece and Turkey persisted and had frequent repercussions in Cyprus where conflicts erupted between the Greek and Turkish communities.

[4] The US Government was not friendly toward Makarios, either, considering him the "Fidel Castro of the Mediterranean". In 1963 there was an unsuccessful coup attempt by members of the radical right, who supported enosis. On July 15 1974, the crisis came to a head when the Cypriot National Guard, under the command of Greek army officers, ousted the President-Archbishop, who fled to Britain. Nikos Sampson, who favored annexation by Greece was appointed. Five days later, Turkey invaded northern Cyprus, bombed Nicosia, and drove 200,000 Greek Cypriots southward, under the pretext of protecting the Turkish minority.

[5] Sampson turned the presidency over to the president of the Lower House, Glafkos Clerides, on July 23. That same day, the Greek military junta also stepped down, unable to face the prospect of a war with Turkey, domestic opposition, and world-wide repudiation.

[6] The Turkish forces, who were occupying 40 per cent of the island, refused to return to the situation which had prevailed prior to the coup, and continued to occupy the north of the country. On August 16 1974 a Turkish-Cypriot Federal state was proclaimed in the northern part of the island - the part under Turkish control - under the presidency of Rauf Denktash.

[7] Makarios returned to Cyprus in December 1974 and held the presidential office until his death in 1977. Spyros Kyprianou succeeded Makarios one month later and followed the same policy, refusing to recognize the division of Cyprus. He also remained a member of the Non-Aligned Movement.

[8] A pact between Makarios and Denktash had set four basic conditions for a negotiated settlement: the establishment of a communal, non-aligned, independent and federal republic; an exact delimitation of the territories that each community would administrate; the discussion of internal restrictions on travelling, ownership rights and other important issues within the frame of a federal system with equal rights for both communities; and sufficient federal power to ensure unity.

[9] The Turkish refusal to withdraw the troops, meant that no substantial progress was made. On November 15 1983, the Turkish Republic of North Cyprus was proclaimed, but only Turkey recognized the new state.

[10] In the 1980s, Cyprus enjoyed a period of economic prosperity brought by tourism, foreign aid, and international business that made the island a financial centre, replacing the city of Beirut, whose money markets had been paralyzed by the Lebanese civil war. The main beneficiary of this was the Greek-Cypriot bourgeoisie. In the northern part of the island there had been a large influx of 40,000 new Turkish immigrants. Added to the 35,000 Turkish soldiers stationed in the area, and the migration of 20,000 Turkish-Cypriots from the south, the area population profile was substantially altered, as the Turkish population in the area tripled.

[11] On May 5 1985, in northern Cyprus, a constitution for the Turkish-Cypriot Republic was submitted to a referendum. The turnout was 70 per cent, of which 65 per cent voted in favour. The low turnout was a political setback for the legitimacy of the Government.

[12] In February 1987, the Greek premier cancelled a visit to the US, because the US had favorable relations with Turkey and installed US arms in the Turkish part of Cyprus.

[13] Giorgis Vassiliu was elected president of Cyprus in 1988,. He re-established negotiations with Denktash, which had been suspended in 1985. Political leaders on both sides and representatives of the 350,000 Cypriots in exile called for constructive flexibility on the part of both leaders. The Greek community - backed by their economic prosperity and the fact that they were numerically in the majority - wanted independence to be guaranteed by the United Nations. They also sought freedom of movement and property ownership throughout the island. The Turkish-Cypriots, on the other hand - based on the status quo and the superiority of the Turkish army - demanded a binational federation, under Ankara protection.

[14] The economy of the island grew by 6.9 per cent in 1989. In

LAND USE

IRRIGATED 35.5% of arable

(1993)

■ FOREST & WOODLAND 13.3%
☐ ARABLE 11.9%
▨ OTHER 74.8%

Maternal Mortality

1990

PER 100,000
LIVE BIRTHS

5

Literacy

1995

94%

STATISTICS

DEMOGRAPHY
Population: 756,000 (1996) **Annual growth:** 1.3% (1980/1996) **Estimates for year 2000:** 800,000 **Annual growth to year 2000:** 1.3% (1994/2000) **Urban Population:** 54.6% (1996) **Children per woman:** 2.3 (1996).

HEALTH
Life expectancy at birth: 77 years (1996) male: 75 years (1994) female: 79 years (1994) **Infant mortality:** 9 per 1,000 (1996) **Under-5 child mortality:** 10 per 1,000 (1996) 585 **people per doctor** (1988/91)

EDUCATION
Literacy: 94% (1995) male : 98% (1995) female: 91% (1995) **School enrolment :** Primary total: 100% (1990/95) male : 100% (1990/95) female: 100% (1990/95) Secondary: male : 96% (1990/95) female: 98% (1990/95)

COMMUNICATIONS
110 **newspapers**, 300 **radios**, 160 **TV sets** and 518 **main telephone lines** per 1,000 people (1994) **Books:** 142 new titles per 100,000 people (1992/94).

ECONOMY
Consumer price index: 122.8 (1994) **Currency:** 0.46 pounds = $ 1 (1995) **Cereal imports:** 551 metric tons (1994) **Food import dependency:** 7% (1994) **Fertilizer use:** 1,841 kgs per ha (1994) **Development aid received:** $ 22 million (1995) $ 30 per capita (1995).

HDI (rank / value) 24 / 0.907 (1994)

PROFILE

ENVIRONMENT
Once a part of continental Europe, the island of Cyprus is located in the eastern Mediterranean, close to Turkey. Two mountain ranges -the Troodos in the southwestern region, and the Kyrenia in northern Cyprus - enclose a fertile central plain. The temperate Mediterranean climate, with hot, dry summers and mild, rainy winters, is good for agriculture. The growing levels of atmospheric pollution rise even higher during peak hours of urban activity, with the combined effect of industrial pollution and traffic. However, though the quality of the air has been affected by pollution, it still lies within acceptable limits. Soil degradation is the result of natural causes and human abuse, particularly where there has been an excessive use of agrochemicals. The coastal ecosystem has felt the effects of tourism, particularly the construction of large hotels and high-rise apartment blocks.

SOCIETY
Peoples: Cypriots are divided into Greek (80 per cent) and Turkish (18 per cent) communities, within which they have separate political, cultural and religious organizations.
Religions: Greek Orthodox and Muslim.
Languages: Greek and Turkish (official).
Political Parties: Democratic Party (Greek sector) and National Unity (Turkish sector), are the main parties.
Social Organizations: There are two major labor organizations, the Pancyprian Federation of Labour, and the Cyprus Worker's Confederation. They group approximately 30 unions.

THE STATE
Official Name: Kypriaki Dimokratia-Kibris Caemhuriyeti.
Capital: Levkosia (Nicosia), 178,000 people (1994).
Other cities: Limassol, 137,000; Larnaca, 61,000 (1992).
Government: Greek sector: presidential republic, constitution in effect since August 16 1960. Glafkos Klerides, Head of State and of the Government since January 28 1993, re-elected in February 1998. Single-chamber legislature: House of Representatives with 71 members (56 from the Greek community and 15 from the Turkish community). Turkish sector: parliamentary republic, constitution in effect since May 5 1985. Rauf Denktash, Head of State since February 13 1975. Single-chamber legislature: 50-member Assembly, elected every five years. The 'Turkish Federated State of Cyprus' based upon Turkish occupation and recognized only by Turkey, exercises an independent administration, including a judicial system and a Legislative Assembly.
National Holiday: October 1 Independence Day (1960).
Armed Forces: 10,000.
Other: Armed Police: 3,700.

April 1990, Denktash was re-elected as President of the "Turkish Republic", in the north of the island. In 1991, with the support of US President George Bush, Turkey proposed a summit with representatives from Ankara, Athens and both Cypriot communities. Washington's support for the initiative was considered compensation for the help given to Turkey during the Gulf War by Greece and the Greek Cypriots.

[15] Nicosia demanded participation in the UN and the European Community, while rejecting the presence of Turkish Cypriot representatives. In April 1992, the UN declared Cyprus a bi-communitarian and bi-regional country, with equal political rights for both communities. In early 1993, Glafkos Klerides defeated Giorgis Vassiliu in the presidential elections.

[16] In the north of the island, Denktash formed a new coalition government in December 1993. In 1994, the Cypriot courts ratified the "legitimacy" of the British military bases on the island, while the European Court ordered an embargo on Turkish Cypriot exports. Despite help from Ankara, this embargo seriously damaged the economy in the north of the island.

[17] In 1995, the idea of Cyprus joining the European Union began to be considered as a way of overcoming the division on the island. Meanwhile, the island received more than two million tourists and its economy continued to grow. Massive investments from Eastern Europe led to accusations of laundering money.

[18] In the May 1996 elections, the Workers' Party won a third of the votes, robbing parliamentary support from President Klerides' government. In August, a series of demonstrations along the internal frontier of the island left several people dead. Amnesty International accused the Turkish Cypriot police of being directly or indirectly responsible for at least two of these deaths.

[19] In efforts to join the European Union, Klerides and the Turkish Cypriot leader Rauf Denktash held repeated meetings throughout 1997. These meetings, backed by the United Nations, aimed for the medium-term reunification of the island prior to entry into the EU. However, direct negotiations between the EU and Greek Cypriot authorities bogged down dialogue within Cyprus and the reunification drive got nowhere. The rivalry between Greece and Turkey on this point also helped slow the negotiations.

[20] Given this impasse, the European Union said if the island were not reunited, the Greek part of the island could be admitted as an independent state, leaving the Turkish section out. Meanwhile, Denktash said the EU should also recognize the political legitimacy of the Turkish Cypriot part and allow all of Cyprus to enter the Union.

[21] In March 1998, following three days of tough decision-making, the Foreign Ministers of the 15 EU member nations agreed to authorize the opening of negotiations for the incorporation of the Greek part of Cyprus to the Union, leaving out the Turkish section.

[22] In the hard-fought February presidential elections, Klerides was re-elected Greek Cypriot President, with 50.8 per cent of the vote to the 49.2 per cent obtained by his rival George lavacu, of the centre-right IKOS party.

WORKERS

- ■ AGRICULTURE 14% (1990)
- □ INDUSTRIAL 30%
- ■ SERVICES 56%

Czech Republic

Ceska Republika

Population: 10,251,000 (1996)
Area: 78,864 SQ KM
Capital: Prague

Currency: Koruny
Language: Czech

No one knows the exact origin of the first inhabitants of the Mid-Danube region, apart from the signs left by the Boii, a Celtic people whose name gave rise to the Latin name "Bohemia". The Celts were displaced, without major conflict, by Germanic tribes and later, in the 6th century, by the Slavs, while the former continued their migration southward.

[2] The inhabitants of mountain and forest areas had the natural protection of these areas. However, the lowlands were repeatedly invaded by the Avars. The Slavs were able to repel these invasions when they had leaders strong enough to unite the tribes. In the 8th century, calm was restored to Bohemia with the defeat of the Avars at the hands of Charlemagne.

[3] In the early 9th century, three potential political centers emerged: the plains of Nitra, the Lower Morava Basin and Central Bohemia. The Slavs of Bohemia gained the upper hand in most of the region. The first Moravian King was Mojmir I, who extended his realm as far as Nitra. His successor, Rostislav I, institutionalized the State and consolidated political relations with the Eastern Frankish empire, as a way of maintaining his own sovereignty.

[4] The Christian Franks organized the first missions at Nitra and in Bohemia, but Rostislav would not allow Latin to be taught, and asked the Byzantine emperor to send preachers who spoke the Slavic language. Religious texts were also translated into Slav. Constantine and Methodius arrived in 863, leading a group of Greek missionaries.

[5] Methodius won recognition from Rome for his work in Moravia and in Panonia (Croatia), which became an ecclesiastical province linked to the Archbishop of Sirmium. The Franks came to consider Methodius an enemy; he was captured and kept prisoner until 873, when he returned to Moravia.

[6] Rostislav was the founder of Great Moravia, uniting the territories inhabited by the Slavs of the region for the first time. Slovakia, bordered by the northern ring of the Carpathian Mountains and by the Morava River, was a natural member of Great Moravia.

[7] Religious rivalry between the Latin and Slav languages continued throughout the period of expansion of the Bohemian principality. The death of Methodius in 885 strengthened the position of the Frankish Bishop Wiching, his life-long enemy. Wiching displaced Methodius's disciples, and convinced the new Pope to outlaw the Slavic liturgy.

[8] Some years later the Czech expansion clashed with the kingdom of Germania. King Arnulf sent a military expedition to Moravia in 892, allying himself later with the Magyars to defeat the principality. Between 905 and 908, Great Moravia went through several foreign occupations, until an agreement was reached between Mojmir II and Arnulf.

[9] In the 10th century, between the strengthening of Germania and the restoration of the Holy Roman Empire, Bohemia lost the major part of its possessions. When Bfetislav I ascended the throne in 1034, the principality recovered part of Moravia and invaded Poland in 1039. However, King Henry III of Germania forced a retreat, and the Hungarian Crown kept Slovakia.

[10] In order to maintain its independence, Bohemia found it necessary to be actively involved in the campaigns of the Holy Roman Empire. Thus, the situation arose whereby the Bohemian princes were being crowned king by both of the rival powers.

[11] In the early 13th century the Church separated from the State, and the feudal lords began demanding greater political participation. At the same time, Germanic immigration was responsible for an increase in population. A series of incentives to build new urban centers and develop mineral resources gave rise to a new class of tradesmen and entrepreneurs.

[12] Under the Przemysl dynasty, which lasted until 1306, Bohemia controlled part of Austria and the Alps; at one point there was even a single king ruling over Bohemia and Poland. This dynasty was succeeded by the Luxembourgs in 1310. With the coronation of Emperor Charles I in 1455, Bohemia and the Holy Roman Empire were joined together. As the capital of the Kingdom and the Empire, this was Prague's greatest moment.

[13] The high level of corruption among the clergy triggered a religious reform movement in the 14th century, which became even more radical under the influence of Father John Huss of Prague's Bethlehem Chapel. Excommunicated by the Pope, Huss was later tried for heresy and sedition by the Council of Constance, and was burned alive in 1415 after refusing to recant.

[14] The anger which followed Huss's execution marked the birth of the Hussite movement in Bohemia and Moravia. The Germanic peoples remained faithful to Rome, however, and in addition to these religious differences, the ethnic issue remained, triggering political conflict between them. The Holy Roman Empire, allied with the German princes, launched several military campaigns in Bohemia, but they were repulsed by the Hussites.

[15] Religious differences prevented political union between Bohemia and its former possessions for many years. Vladislav II reigned over Bohemia from 1471 but Moravia, Silesia and Lusacia were ruled by Mathias, of Hungary. Only when Vladislav II was elected king of Hungary, upon Mathias's death in 1490, were the territories reunited.

[16] The death of Vladislav II's son Louis II in 1526, paved the way for

PUBLIC EXPENDITURE

5.7% 65.7%
1995 ■ DEFENCE □ SOCIAL

In 1990/91 Military as % of health & education expenditure was 17%.

WORKERS

UNEMPLOYMENT 3.9% (1996)

Labour force %
■ WOMEN
□ MEN
47% 53%

■ AGRICULTURE 11% (1990)
□ INDUSTRIAL 45%
■ SERVICES 43%

LAND USE

IRRIGATED 0.8 % of arable

(1993)

■ FOREST & WOODLAND 33.3%
□ ARABLE 40.2%
■ OTHER 26.5%

the rise of the Hapsburgs. Ferdinand I, Louis' brother-in-law, became king by currying favor with the nobility. Austria's victory over the Protestant Society of Schmalkaldica in 1547 permitted Ferdinand to impose the right of hereditary succession to the throne upon Bohemia and its states.

[17] The Hapsburgs strengthened the Counter-reformation throughout the region. Slovakia remained within its realm because the Hapsburgs had retained it when Hungary was invaded by the Ottoman Empire, in 1526.

[18] Rudolf II (1576-1612) transferred the seat of the empire to Prague, making it once again one of the continent's most important political and cultural centers. Many key positions of the kingdom were filled by Catholics during Rudolf's reign, as he himself was Catholic. However, this triggered a rebellion by the non-Catholic (Reformed church) majority, and the king was deposed in 1611.

[19] After a stormy succession, Ferdinand II of Styria, with the support of Maximilian I of Bavaria, defeated the Protestants and ruled with a strong hand. The Diet lost its power to initiate legislation, being reduced to merely approving the king's petitions. The German language was added to the traditional use of Czech, and only the Catholic religion was authorized.

[20] Unlike Bohemia, Moravia did not become involved in the fight against the Hapsburgs and therefore did not suffer the effects of civil and religious strife as severely. In Moravia there was religious tolerance allowing the growth of Protestantism in the state, which remained separate from the Austrian Crown until 1848.

[21] Despite the hegemony of the Germans and the prohibition of political activity, the Czechs conserved their ethnic identity, their language and their culture. Something similar had also occurred in the Hungarian counties inhabited by Slovaks. This set the scene for a resurgence of nationalism in the early 19th century, which strengthened the traditional ties between these two peoples.

Czechs and Slovaks

[22] Czechs and Slovaks, together with the inhabitants of the German republics, helped put a stop to the absolutist doctrine, amidst a revolutionary wave which swept Europe in 1848. In 1867, the empire split in two: Austria, where ethnic Germans outnumbered the Czechs, Poles and other nationalities; and Hungary, where the Magyars subdued the Slovaks.

[23] With World War I the fall of the Austro-Hungarian Empire finally brought about the recognition of the Republic of Czechoslovakia. The new state's borders established in 1919 by the victorious powers included parts of Poland, Hungary and the Sudetenland, all home to ethnic minorities, and all sources of potential conflict.

[24] Czech and Slovak leaders charged the National Assembly with drawing up a Constitution. The Assembly opted for a strict parliamentary system, in which the President and his cabinet would be responsible to two legislative chambers. Women's right to vote or to be elected was granted for the first time.

[25] The 1930s world-wide depression affected the Sudetenland intensely, as it was a highly industrialized region. It also accentuated nationalistic feeling among the German people there, who developed a separatist movement alongside Hitler's rise to power in 1933. Britain, France and Italy negotiated the ceding of the Sudetenland to Germany in 1938, thus paving the way for the German occupation of Czechoslovakia in 1939.

[26] After Hitler's defeat, Czechoslovakia recovered its 1919 borders, while the German population was almost entirely expelled from the country.

[27] The Communist Party (CKC) obtained 38 per cent of the vote in the 1946 election, increasing to 51 per cent in 1948. In June, a People's Republic was proclaimed, and the CKC applied the economic model in effect at the time in the USSR.

Czechoslovakia joined the Council for Mutual Economic Assistance (CMEA) and the Warsaw Pact.

[28] In 1960, the People's Republic of Czechoslovakia added "socialist" to its name. In political terms, this decade was a turning point. Slovak leaders, expelled from the party in the 50s, were rehabilitated. The Slovak struggle for autonomy (which had been even further restricted by the new socialist constitution) together with the 1967 student strikes brought an end to Antony Novotny's leadership of the CKC.

[29] In early 1968, the election of Alexander Dubcek as Secretary of the CKC, and of Ludwik Svoboda as the country's president led to the implementation of a program to decentralize the economy, and affirm national sovereignty, against a background of broad popular support.

[30] Moscow viewed the possibility of Czechoslovakian reforms as a threat to the integrity of the socialist camp; in August 1968, it used Warsaw Pact Forces to intervene in the country and crush the movement. The leaders of the "Prague Spring" were expelled from the CKC and political alignment with the USSR was re-established.

[31] From the time Mikhail Gorbachev was named Communist Party Secretary in the USSR, the reform process there brought about changes in Czechoslovakia, with the CKC trying to keep its hold on power. In 1989, despite violent repression, anti-Government protests continued, precipitating a crisis within the regime.

[32] The Government was forced to negotiate with the Civic Forum, an alliance of several opposition groups. Among other reforms, Parliament approved the elimination of the CKC's leadership role, issuing a condemnation of the 1968 Soviet intervention. In late 1989, a provisional Government was formed, with a non-communist majority.

[33] In December 1989, the Civic Forum declared that the CKC had

redistributed cabinet positions in such a way as to keep its own people in the key positions. 200,000 people gathered in Prague to demand a greater opposition representation in the cabinet. Gustav Husak resigned the presidency of the federation and was replaced by Vaclav Havel, who immediately granted amnesty to all political prisoners and called elections for June 1990.

[34] In late 1989, the Soviet and Czech governments agreed on a gradual withdrawal of the 70,000 Red Army troops stationed within the country. In October 1991, after the dissolution of the Warsaw Pact, president Havel and his Hungarian and Polish counterparts requested some kind of association with the Atlantic alliance.

[35] After the June 1990 elections Havel was confirmed in the presidency and the Czech and Slovak Federal Republic was proclaimed. In September, the Republic joined the World Bank and the IMF.

[36] Following the elections, the Forum divided into the Civic Democratic Party, the self-proclaimed "right with a conservative programme," and the Civic Movement.

[37] In the June legislative elections, the Czech Civic Democratic Party and the Slovak group, Democratic Slovakia, won in their respective republics. When negotiations over the statutes of the new federation came to an impasse, Czech and Slovak leaders meeting in the Moravian city of Brno admitted that separation was inevitable.

[38] On July 17 1992, Czechoslovakian President Vaclav Havel announced his resignation after the declaration of sovereignty in the Slovakian National Assembly. Czechoslovakia disappeared from the world map, replaced by the Czech Republic, with its capital Prague (Praha), and the Republic of Slovakia, with its capital Bratislava.

PER CAPITA
$1,960

IMPORTS
27,709
EXPORTS
21,882

PROFILE

ENVIRONMENT

The Bohemian massif occupies the western region, bounded to the southeast by the Moravian plains. Cereals and sugar beet are cultivated in the lowlands of Bohemia and Moravia, where cattle and pigs are also raised. Rye and potatoes are grown in the Bohemian valleys. The country has rich mineral deposits: coal, lignite, graphite and uranium in the Bohemian massif; coal in Moravia. Sulphur dioxide emissions-produced in the generation of electrical energy are very high, causing acid rain. Air pollution has destroyed or damaged large areas of forest. Approximately three-quarters of all the country's trees show a high degree of defoliation. Water pollution levels are also very high, especially in rural areas. Waste from industry, mining and intensive farms threaten the purity of the water, both above and below the ground.

SOCIETY

Peoples: Czechs, 81.2 per cent; Moravians, 13.2 per cent; Slovaks, 3 per cent.
Religions: Mainly Catholic.
Languages: Czech (official).
Political parties: Civic Democratic Party; Communist Party of Bohemia and Moravia; Social Democratic Party, Socialist Party; Agrarian Party, Green Party, Christian Democratic Union-Czechoslovakian People's Party, Association for the Republic-Republican Party, Democratic Civic Alliance; Movement for Autonomous Democracy of Moravia and Silesia.
Social Organizations: Central Trade Union Council

THE STATE

Official Name: Ceska Republika.
Administrative divisions: 8 regions subdivided into municipalities.
Capital: Prague, 1,217,000 people (1994).
Other cities: Ostrava, 326,000 people; Brno, 390,000; Olomouc, 106,000.
Government: Parliamentary republic. Vaclav Havel, President since January 1993; Josef Tosovsky Prime Minister since November 1997.
National holiday: October 28, Independence Day.
Armed Forces: 92,900 in 1994.
Other: Border Guards: 7,000; Internal Security Forces: 2,000; Civil Defence Troops: 2,000.

STATISTICS

DEMOGRAPHY

Population: 10,251,000 (1996) **Annual growth:** 0% (1980/1996) **Estimates for year 2000:** 10,000,000 **Annual growth to year 2000:** -0.1% (1994/2000) **Urban Population:** 65.6% (1996) **Urban growth:** 0.22% (1980/95) **Children per woman:** 1.5 (1996).

HEALTH

Life expectancy at birth: 73 years (1996) male: 69 years (1994) female: 75 years (1994) **Infant mortality:** 6 per 1,000 (1996) **Under-5 child mortality:** 7 per 1,000 (1996).

EDUCATION

School enrolment: Primary total: 100% (1990/95) male: 100% (1990/95) female: 100% (1990/95) Secondary: male: 90% (1990/95) female: 94% (1990/95) Tertiary: 21% (1995) **Primary school teachers:** one for every 20 students (1995).

COMMUNICATIONS

220 **newspapers**, 631 **radios**, 380 **TV sets** and 212 **main telephone lines** per 1,000 people (1994) **Books:** 91 new titles per 100,000 people (1992/94).

ECONOMY

Per capita, GNP: $4,740 (1996) **Annual growth, GNP:** 4.6% (1995/96) **Annual inflation:** 12.22% (1985/95) **Consumer price index:** 147.7 (1994) **Currency:** 26.6 koruny = $ 1 (1995) **Cereal imports:** 287 metric tons (1994) **Fertilizer use:** 887 kgs per ha (1994) **Exports:** $ 21,882 million (1996) **Imports:** $ 27,709 million (1996) **External debt:** $ 20,094 million (1996) $ 1,960 **per capita:** (1996) **Debt service:** 8.3% of exports (1996)

ENERGY

Consumption: 3,868.22 Kgs of Oil equivalent per capita yearly (1994) 7.10% imported (1994)

HDI (rank / value) 39 / 0.882 (1994)

[39] As soon as Slovakia became independent, in January 1993, the country began a rapid process of integration with Western Europe. On January 26, Vaclav Havel, the former president of Czechoslovakia, was elected President of the Czech Republic, with the support of a parliamentary majority led by the right wing Civic Party,

[40] As Prime Minister, the leader of the Civic Party, Vaclav Klaus, adopted a market economy with less negative results than the other former socialist republics. As for the rest of the region, the freeing of prices and the introduction of consumer taxes had limited inflationary effects:

the price increase was 17 per cent in 1993. Unemployment remained at 2.5 per cent and per capita income continued to be one of the highest in Eastern Europe.

[41] The Czech Republic became the eleventh signatory of the Peace Association in March 1994, an organization which developed out of NATO to progressively include the nations of the former socialist bloc in the alliance.

[42] The national debt continued lower than that of other former communist countries of the region, while foreign investment was amongst the highest. Prime

Minister Klaus planned an economic reform based on a rapid privatization campaign. In 1995, the banking system saw a high number of deposits, many of which came from illegal economic activities. This same year, the Czech Republic became the first former Communist OECD member.

[43] In June 1996, the electoral success of the Social Democrats left Klaus without an absolute majority in Parliament.

[44] In December, the Czech Republic and Germany signed a reconciliation document, in which Germany asked forgiveness for the behaviour of the Nazi regime during World War II, while the Czech Government apologized for the expulsion of three million Germans from the Sudetenland following the war.

[45] During 1997, the devaluation

of the national currency, the crown, brought political chaos. The Civic Party led by Klaus was accused of encouraging financial groups which bribed several of its members with "hidden commissions" during the privatization process. Havel publicly called for Klaus' resignation, which was received in November. Josef Tosovsky became the new prime minister.

[46] The economic crisis coincided with increasing in xenophobia, displayed in racist attacks against minority groups, such as the Gypsies. This violence appeared to be supported by a large and increasing percentage of the population.

[47] In April 1998, the Czech Republic was admitted to NATO.

Denmark

Population:	5,237,000 (1996)
Area:	43,094 SQ KM
Capital:	Copenhagen
Currency:	Kroner
Language:	Danish

Danmark

The first hunters established themselves in Denmark in about 10,000 BC as the Neolithic period drew to a close. This was followed by a flourishing Bronze Age civilization, about 1000 BC Around the year 500 AD, northern Germanic peoples began settling on the islands as fishermen and navigators. Certain place names bear witness to the worship of Scandinavian gods, such as Odin, Thor and Frey.

[2] The first evidence of hierarchical society in Denmark comes from the Viking age, mostly from cemeteries and settlement sites. The Vikings were Scandinavian farmers, navigators, merchants and above all raiders who ruled the northern seas between the 8th and 10th centuries AD.

[3] Archeological remains indicate that Roskilde on the island of Sjaelland; Hedeby, in the south of Jutland, and Jelling in the centre, were the most intensely populated areas. After the Danish victory over the Germans the Eider River became the final southern border. A huge wall was built to the south and west of Hedeby.

[4] In the 10th century, after continuous conflict with rival kingdoms, the center of the kingdom's power was transferred to Jelling, where Gorm became king of Jutland. His son Harald Bluetooth (Blatand) is credited with uniting Denmark and conquering parts of Norway.

[5] Subsequent Viking reigns extended Danish possessions as far as modern-day England and Sweden. In 1397 King Margrethe managed to unite Denmark, Norway, Iceland, Greenland, Sweden and Finland in the "Union of Kalmar".

[6] The introduction and spread of Christianity and strengthening of the Hanseatic League went hand-in-hand with the weakening of Denmark's military power.

[7] The Danish kings were involved in successive wars between themselves, campaigns which were interspersed with peasant rebellions and bourgeois revolts; a large and powerful middle class had developed as a result of growing mercantile activity. These conflicts ceased in the 17th century, when a weakened nobility gave the King power as absolute sovereign. He was then able to create laws to be imposed throughout the land.

[8] During the 18th century, Denmark colonized the Virgin Islands. The Danish colonists organized local production using African slave labor and in 1917 the islands and their population were sold to the United States. (See "American" Virgin Islands)

[9] Peace existed in Denmark and Norway from 1720 until the Napoleonic Wars. After Napoleon's defeat, Sweden attacked Denmark and, under the Kiel Peace Treaty, annexed Norway in 1814.

[10] The loss of Norway, combined with British trading impositions brought on an economic collapse which worsened as a result of low wheat prices. The ensuing agricultural crisis forced land reform to a standstill. The situation later improved when agricultural prices stabilized, trade increased and

PROFILE

ENVIRONMENT
With an average altitude of only 35 meters above sea level, Denmark is one of the flattest countries in Europe. The nation is divided between the mainland of the Jutland (Jylland) Peninsula and islands, which constitute one third of the total territory. Summers are relatively warm and rainy, and winters are very cold. Intensive agriculture is practised. Denmark produces meat products and has large fishing and shipping industries. Pollution of the North Sea has reached significant levels.

SOCIETY
Languages: Danish (official and used throughout the country).
Political Parties: Social Democratic Party, People's Conservative Party, People's Socialist Party, Liberal (Venstre) Party, Progress Party and Danish People's Party (both extreme right-wing), Moderate Democratic Party, social-liberal (Venstre Radical) Party, People's Christian Party.
Social Organizations: The powerful Danish Federation of Trade Unions has 1,200,000 members from 40 different unions. Organization of Technical Personnel and Employees (FTF), 360,000 members, and Central Organization of Academics (AC), 97,000 members.

THE STATE
Official Name: Kongeriget Danmark.
Administrative divisions: 14 departments (Amtskommuner), Frederiksberg, Copenhague.
Capital: Copenhagen, 1,339,395 people(1994).
Other cities : Århus, 274,535 people; Odense, 181,824; Ålborg, 158,000; Frederiksberg, 87,466 (1994).
Government: A constitutional parliamentary monarchy. Margaret II, Queen since 1972. The Prime Minister is Poul Nyrup Rasmussen, re-elected in 1998. The one-chamber parliament has 179 members, including 2 from Greenland and 2 from the Faeroe Islands.
National holiday: June 5 (Constitution of 1953).

WORKERS

UNEMPLOYMENT 6.9% (1996)

Labour force %

■ WOMEN
□ MEN

46	54

■ AGRICULTURE	6%	(1990)
□ INDUSTRIAL	28%	
■ SERVICES	66%	

IMPORTS
43,093
EXPORTS
48,868

Faeroe Is.

Population: 47,000
(1996)
Area: 1,399 SQ KM
Capital: Torshavn

STATISTICS

DEMOGRAPHY
Population: 5,237,000 (1996) **Annual growth:** 0.1% (1980/1996) **Estimates for year 2000:** 5,300,000 (1997) **Annual growth to year 2000:** 0.2% (1994/2000) **Urban Population:** 85.3% (1996) **Urban growth:** 0.23% (1980/95) **Children per woman:** 1.8 (1996).

HEALTH
Life expectancy at birth: 75 years (1996) male: 73 years (1994) female: 78 years (1994) **Infant mortality:** 6 per 1,000 (1996) **Under-5 child mortality:** 6 per 1,000 (1996) **Calorie consumption:** 135% (1988/90) 360 **people per doctor** (1988/91) **Safe water:**% (1990/96).

EDUCATION
School enrolment : Primary total: 99% (1990/95) male : 99% (1990/95) female: 99% (1990/95) Secondary: male : 113% (1990/95) female: 117% (1990/95) Tertiary: 45% (1995) **Primary school teachers:** one for every 10 students (1995).

COMMUNICATIONS
360 **newspapers,** 1,036 **radios,** 540 **TV sets** and 600 **main telephone lines** per 1,000 people (1994) **Books:** 230 new titles per 100,000 people (1992/94).

ECONOMY
Per capita, GNP: $ 32,100 (1996) **Annual growth, GNP:** 1.8% (1995/96) **Annual inflation:** 2.84% (1985/95) **Consumer price index:** 108.0 (1994) **Currency:** 5.55 kroner = $ 1 (1995) **Cereal imports:** 480 metric tons (1994) **Fertilizer use:** 1,971 kgs per ha (1994) **Exports:** $ 48,868 million (1996) **Imports:** $ 43,093 million (1996).

ENERGY
Consumption: 3,976.94 Kgs of Oil equivalent per capita yearly (1994) 28.01% imported (1994)

HDI (rank / value) 18 / 0.927 (1994)

The climate is generally rainy and cloudy, with mild temperatures both in summer and winter. Only 6 per cent of the land is cultivated. Most of the production consists of vegetables as the land is not suitable for grain. Sheep are raised throughout the islands and there is mining in Suderoy. 20 per cent of the population are employed in handicraft production and 21 per cent in fisheries, which provide 90 per cent of the islands' exports.

SOCIETY
Peoples: The population is of Scandinavian origin.
Religions: Lutheran. There are a large number of Baptists and a small Catholic community.
Languages: Danish (official) and the Faeroese dialect.
Political Parties: Social Democratic and Union (liberal) parties, which favor ties with Denmark; the Republican "Left", Popular and Progressive parties, favor independence.

THE STATE
Capital: Thorshavn, 16,000 people in 1992.
Government: The parliament (*Lagtinget*) has up to 30 members, elected on a basis of proportional representation. Parliament names a national cabinet (*Landstyret*) of 6 ministers. After the 1990 elections, the latter was a coalition between the Social Democratic and Popular parties. A high commissioner (*Rigsombudsman*) represents the Crown. The islands elect 2 representatives to the Danish Parliament.
Diplomacy: In January 1974, the *Lagtinget* decided not to join the EEC. To protect the fishing industry, a 200-mile fishing zone was established in 1977. Modernization of the island's fishing fleet and methods was financed trhough a seies of foreign loans, which totalled $839 million in 1990, that is, $18,000 per capita.

DEMOGRAPHY
Urban Population: 32.6% (1996)

industrialization began. In 1814 an educational reform made schooling obligatory.

[11] After the European revolutions of 1848, King Frederick VII called an assembly. A parliamentary monarchy was established and absolutism was abolished. The 1849 Constitution guaranteed freedom of the press, of religion and of association, as well as the right to hold public meetings. The main trends of the period were nationalism and liberalism.

[12] A territorial dispute with Germany over the Duchies of Schleswig and Holstein reinforced nationalistic sentiment. In 1864, when Denmark was defeated by Prussia and Austria, it lost its claim to these lands and the national-liberal government was brought down.

[13] The 1866 Constitution maintained the monarchy. In 1871, Louis Pio, a former military officer, attempted to form a socialist party. A series of strikes and demonstrations organized by the socialists was put down by the army, and Pio was deported to the United States. The Social Democratic Party, mainly supported by intellectuals and workers, was formed in 1876.

[14] The peasants and emerging middle class weakened the monarchy on three fronts: the farm co-operative movement, a liberal bourgeois party (popularly referred to as "leftist") and the social democrat party.

[15] In 1901 the United Left (Liberal) came to power establishing a new government. The emergence of the UL and the Social Democrats as a leading force at the turn of the century was the result of agrarian reform, industrialization and the development of railroads. The growth of urbanization and overseas trade (accelerating the formation of labor unions throughout the country and the rise of co-operatives in the countryside) was the main reason for these changes.

[16] In 1915, the Constitution was revised. The voting age of 35 was maintained, but the right to vote was extended to women, servants and farm hands. There were judicial reforms, bringing in trial by jury, and land distribution in the largest states.

[17] Also in 1915 women were granted the right to stand for election, a right they had not enjoyed since Viking times. The first woman was appointed to the cabinet in 1924.

[18] After the 1870-71 Franco-German War, Denmark adopted a neutral international stance. World War I provided Copenhagen with favorable trading opportunities with the warring nations, but at the same time affected its supplies. During World War II Denmark was invaded by Germany, although it officially maintained its independence until 1943.

[19] When Hitler attacked the USSR, Denmark created a volunteer army and outlawed communist activity. The 1943 election was an anti-Nazi plebiscite, with the electorate throwing its support behind the democratic parties. Resistance to the Nazi regime, strikes, and the Government's refusal to enforce Nazi rule, led the German occupation forces to declare a state of emergency dissolving Denmark's police and armed forces.

[20] In September 1943, the Danish Freedom Council was created to co-ordinate the anti-Nazi opposition. When Germany finally surrendered, a transition government was formed, with representatives from the Council and the traditional parties. The 1945 election was won by the liberals.

[21] The Faeroe Islands, under

Greenland

Population: 58,000 (1996)
Area: 2,175,600 SQ KM
Capital: Nuuk (ex-Godhaab)
Currency: Kroner
Language: Greenlandic Danisf and Inuit

Located in the Arctic Ocean, the island is the second largest tract of frozen land on the planet. Nearly four fifths of its surface is covered by an ice cap. In the month of June, soon after the rapid thaw, moss and lichen vegetation appears on certain parts of the coast. Most of the population is concentrated in the western region, where the climate is less severe. Fishing forms the basis of the economy; whale oil and salted or frozen fish are exported. The country has lead, zinc, and tungsten deposits. Cryolite from the large reserves in Ivigtut is also exported.

SOCIETY
Peoples: 80 per cent are Inuit. The remaining 20 per cent are Danish or other short-term European residents.
Religions: Lutheran. The Greenlandic Church comes under the jurisdiction of the Bishop of Copenhagen and the minister of ecclesiastical affairs.

Languages: Greenlandic, Danish and Inuit
Political Parties: Siumut, Social Democratic; Atassut, liberal-conservative; Inuit Atgatigiit, nationalist federation.

THE STATE
Capital: Nuuk (ex-Godhaab), 12,426 people (1989).
Government: Jonathan Motsfeld, Prime Minister since 1997. Greenland elects two representatives to the Danish *Folketing*, and has one representative on the Nordic Council.
Diplomacy: On January 1 1985 the island withdrew from the European Economic Community. However, EEC countries can still fish in Greenland's territorial waters upon payment of $ 20 million.

DEMOGRAPHY
Population: 58,000 (1996)
Urban population: 81.3 % (1996)

Danish control since 1380, were occupied by Britain during the war and subsequently returned to Denmark. The 1948 Constitution gave the islands greater autonomy, though the Danish Parliament retained control of defence and foreign affairs. Denmark is currently disputing the control of resources under the sea bed in island waters.

[22] In Greenland, also under Danish control since 1380, Denmark was responsible for foreign policy and justice. In 1979, the island obtained the right to have its own legislative assembly (Landsting), which has power over internal affairs. Other areas are dealt with by the Danish Parliament which has two representatives from the island.

[23] Since 1947, there has always been at least one woman in the cabinet. That same year, Protestant women achieved the right to be priests.

[24] In the post-war period, a proposed Nordic Defence Alliance did not come about, as Norway did not agree with Denmark and Sweden. Denmark joined NATO in 1949, increasing its military power with the help of the United States. A US proposal for setting up air bases on Danish soil was turned down.

[25] In 1953, the Constitution was amended reducing the Legislature to a single chamber (Folketing). In 1954 the post of 'ombudsman' was created to ensure that municipal and national government complied with the law, and to protect "ordinary" citizens from the misuse of power on the part of government officials or agencies.

[26] In 1959, Denmark became the founding member of the European Free Trade Association (EFTA). In 1972, 63.7 per cent of the electorate voted yes in a referendum asking whether the country should join the European Economic Community. In 1973, the oil crisis seriously affected the Danish economy and unemployment rose to over 14 per cent.

[27] In the 1973 election, the traditional parties were ousted in favour of two new parties; the extreme right Progressive Party

and the Democratic Center, the right-wing of the Social Democratic Party. In 1975, the Social Democrats were voted back into power. They lost a significant number of votes in subsequent elections because of high unemployment and unpopular economic measures. The Socialists were voted out in 1982, and the Conservatives won office for the first time since 1894. Their victory was due to their alliance with the Liberals, the Democratic Center and the Christian People's Party.

[28] In the 1980s, 23 per cent of the seats in Parliament were held by women.

[29] In 1982, the Government appointed two female ministers responsible for Labor and Religious affairs. In that year 43.9 per cent of the economically active population were women, and they were protected by specific legislation. A woman can interrupt her career for up to two years to raise her children. The average Danish family has four members.

[30] In 1986, Parliament approved a strict environmental protection law which proved costly for both the industrial and agricultural sectors, in a country without nuclear plants.

[31] Denmark was one of the few countries that complied with the UN's recommendation to contribute at least 1 per cent of the GNP to development. The country recycled 72 per cent of all paper used and recovers more than 100,000 tons of industrial waste per year.

[32] Marriage between people of the same sex was authorized by law in 1989.

[33] In 1993, unemployment stood at 12.5 per cent of the economically active population. The Progress Party demanded that foreigners no longer be allowed to enter the country. These account for a mere 3.3 per cent of the population, including 30,000 Turks, 30,000 Europeans from EU countries, 22,000 Scandinavians and other European nationalities, as well as Pakistanis and Sri Lankans.

[34] In 1993, the people of Denmark finally approved the Maastricht Treaty, which formed the European Union, after

rejecting it the previous year, upon condition that the country shall not join the Economic and Monetary Union.

[35] Social Democratic Prime Minister Poul Nyrup Rasmussen was reelected in 1994, after having been chosen for office the previous year, due to the fall of the liberal-conservative government which broke refugee laws. Former Justice minister Erik Ninn Hansen was found guilty of having prevented the family reunion of Tamil refugees from Sri Lanka.

[36] Rasmussen achieved the majority in Parliament through alliances with center and left-wing parties. Economic growth reached its peak in 1994, with 4.4 per cent GDP growth and a 2 per cent rise in inflation. Economic expansion slowed down in 1995 and 1996. Reduction of extended social benefits enabled unemployment to fall from 12.5 per cent to 10 per cent in two years

[37] The country's domestic tranquility was startled by a conflict between rival motorcycle bands in 1996. The bands attacked bars where their rivals met in

urban areas with anti-tank missiles, causing panic and damage to private property. The Government decided to tackle the matter with emergency legislation.

[38] The same year, Denmark had a disagreement with Iceland over fishing rights in the strait located between Greenland and Iceland.

[39] The Danish People's Party, split from the Progress Party - both ultra right-wing - obtained over 6 per cent of the vote in the Copenhagen local elections in November 1997. Its leader, Pia Kjaersgaard, based her campaign on the "threat" Third World immigrants meant to Denmark. However, the unemployment rate - 8 per cent of the economically active population, and the number of foreigners - 4.5 per cent of population - were the lowest in Western Europe.

[40] In legislative elections held on March 11 1998, the ruling Social Democratic coalition retained a majority, although it defeated the centre-right coalition by only one seat, obtaining 90 of the 179 seats at stake, while the opposition received 89 seats.

Djibouti

Djibouti

Population: 617,000 (1996)
Area: 23,200 SQ KM
Capital: Djibouti

Currency: Francs
Language: French

In about the 3rd century BC Ablé immigrants came from Arabia and settled in the north and parts of the south. The Afars, or Danakil, are descendants of these peoples. Later the Somali Issas pushed the Afars out of the south and settled in the coastal regions. In AD 825 Islam was brought to the area by missionaries. Arabs controlled the trade in this region until the 16th century, when the Portuguese competed for it. In 1862, Tadjoura, one of the Sultanates on the Somalian coast (see Somalia), sold the port of Obock and adjoining lands to the French for 52,000 francs and in 1888 French Somaliland (Côte Française des Somalis) was established.

[2] Djibouti became the official capital of this French territory in 1892. A treaty with Ethiopia in 1897 reduced the territory in size. A railway was built to connect Djibouti with the Ethiopian hinterland, reaching Dire Dawa in 1903 and Addis Ababa in 1917. The interior of the area was effectively opened up between 1924 and 1934 by the construction of roads and administrative posts. After World War II Djibouti port lost trade to the Ethiopian port of Aseb (now in Eritrea). In 1946 French Somaliland acquired the status of an overseas territory (from 1967 called the French Territory of the Afars and Issas), and in 1958 it voted to become an overseas territorial member of the French Community under the Fifth Republic.

[3] Independence and the reunification of neighboring Somalia stimulated the emergence of anti-colonialist movements such as the Somaliland Liberation Front and the African League for Independence, both of which used the legal and armed branches.

[4] During the 1970s, renewed resistance forced acting governor Ali Aref to resign. France called a plebiscite on May 8 1977, and 85 per cent of the population voted for independence. Hassan Gouled Aptidon, main leader of the African League for Independence, became president of the fledgling Republic.

[5] The Government of the new state had to deal with tension between the Afar and Issa peoples and with refugees from the war zones in Ethiopia and Somalia. In an attempt to overcome old ethnic divisions, Gouled granted governmental participation to various groups. He even appointed several Afar ministers. Though French remained the official language, Djibouti was admitted into the Arab League.

[6] Ethiopia and Somalia, its two neighbors, both had territorial designs on Djibouti. Ethiopia's interest in Djibouti was basically geopolitical. In the event of Eritrean nationalists achieving independence, Ethiopia would become a landlocked territory - if an agreement could not be reached for the use of Eritrean ports, Djibouti would be their only available harbour. For Somalia it was mainly a historical aim to unify the Somali nation.

[7] In mid-1979, President Hassan Gouled resumed relations with Ethiopia and Somalia, signing trade and transportation agreements with them. The participation of Afars in the government and in the newly-formed army was encouraged as a way of securing some semblance of national unity.

[8] A ruling party was organized and municipal administrations were created to encourage political participation. Foreign aid was basically used for irrigation works and to improve the situation of refugees from the Ogaden war.

[9] The Gouled administration received aid from Saudi Arabia, Kuwait, Iraq and Libya. Gouled skilfully administered his country, playing upon its only valuable resource: its strategic position at the mouth of the Red Sea. Contrary to expectations which foretold a rapid annexation by Ethiopia or Somalia, Djibouti stressed its determination to remain independent.

[10] In spite of a successful performance in diplomatic relations, Gouled faced serious domestic problems, the most pressing of which result from ethnic rivalries between Afars and Issas. Afars, who account for 35 per cent of the population, complained of political and economic discrimination. The Issas, who constituted 60 per cent of the population and hold key positions in the Government, refuted all accusations of group

favouritism, and supported Gouled's radical policies to neutralize the opposition. After the prohibition of the Popular Liberation Movement in 1979, the Afars tried to reorganize as the Djibouti Popular Party in 1981, but this was also banned.

[11] In October 1981, President Gouled amended the Constitution to introduce a single-party system. The official Popular Association for Progress (RPP) became the sole legal party and the other groups were banned. It was argued that they had racial or religious aims and in consequence were potentially harmful to national unity.

[12] During 1983, the first steps were taken in a project planned to radically change Djibouti's economy. Incentives were to be given to transform the country into a financial center and free trading port, a sort of Middle Eastern Hong Kong. Six foreign banks opened offices in Djibouti, mainly attracted by a solid national currency backed by dollar deposits in the US.

[13] By the end of 1984, the first results were not encouraging: the number of passengers and goods in transit to Ethiopia and Somalia had dropped considerably and, therefore, customs revenues and

bank activities had decreased. The continuing conflict in the area has been seen as the major cause for the withdrawal of European capital.

[14] With the support of the UN High Commissioner, the Government of Hassam Gouled resumed the voluntary repatriation of more than a hundred thousand refugees, a process which had been interrupted in 1983.

[15] At the same time, bilateral agreements were signed with Ethiopia to combat contraband and promote peace in the border areas. These had been closed in 1977, at the outset of the conflict with Somalia over the Ogaden region.

[16] In August 1987, foreign military presence in Djibouti grew as French bases started to be used by US and British forces participating in manoeuvres in the Persian Gulf. Relations with the former colonial power were reinforced by President François Mitterand's visit, in December.

[17] Djibouti depends on French economic aid to a large extent, estimated at $200 million per year, a figure which is several times the total of its exports. This dependence on foreign aid

PROFILE

Environment
Located in the Afar triangle, facing Yemen, it is one of the hottest countries in the world (average annual temperature: 30oC). The land is mostly desert, its only green area is found in the basalt ranges of the northern region. Agriculture, confined to oases and to a few spots along the coast, satisfies only 25 per cent of the domestic food demand. Extensive cattle raising is practised by nomads. Economic activity is concentrated around the port.

SOCIETY
Peoples: Djiboutians are divided into two major ethnic groups of equal size; the Afar, scattered throughout the country, and the Issa, of Somalian origin, who populate most of the southern territory and predominate in the capital.
Religions: Muslims. There is a small Christian minority (5 per cent).
Languages: Afar and Issa (Somali), French (official) and Arabic (religious).
Political Parties: People's Assembly for Progress (RPP), which emerged in 1979 from the African People's League for Independence, founded in 1975 by Hassan Gouled. Democratic Renovation Party (PRD); Democratic Front for the Liberation of Djibouti; Movement for the Liberation of Djibouti and the Front for the Restoration of Unity and Democracy (FRUD).

THE STATE
Official Name: République de Djibouti.
Administrative divisions: 5 districts.
Capital: Djibouti, 450,000 people (1989).
Other cities: Ali-Sabieh 4,000 people; Tadjoura 3,500; Dikhil 3,000 (1989).
Government: Hassan Gouled Aptidon, President since June 1977, re-elected in the May 1993 elections. Barkad Gourad Hamadou, Prime Minister. The prime minister is traditionally Afar to counterbalance the power of Gouled, who is Issa.
National Holiday: June 27, Independence Day (1977).
Armed Forces: some 3,900.
Other: Gendarmerie (Ministry of Defence): 600; National Security Force (Ministry of Interior): 3,000.

STATISTICS

DEMOGRAPHY
Population: 617,000 (1996) **Annual growth:** 4.9% (1980/1996) **Estimates for year 2000:** 700,000 **Annual growth to year 2000:** 2.7% (1994/2000) **Urban Population:** 82.4% (1996) **Children per woman:** 5.5 (1996).

HEALTH
Life expectancy at birth: 50 years (1996) **Infant mortality:** 112 per 1,000 (1996) **Under-5 child mortality:** 157 per 1,000 (1996) **Safe water:** 90% (1990/96).

EDUCATION
Literacy: 46% (1995) male : 60% (1995) female: 33% (1995) **School enrolment :** Primary total: 38% (1990/95) male : 43% (1990/95) female: 33% (1990/95) Secondary: male : 15% (1990/95) female: 10% (1990/95)

COMMUNICATIONS
81 **radios**, 50 **TV sets** and 13 **main telephone lines** per 1,000 people (1994).

ECONOMY
Currency: 177.72 francs = $ 1 (1995) **Cereal imports:** 52 metric tons (1994) **Food import dependency:** 27% (1994) **Development aid received:** $ 103 million (1995) $ 181 per capita (1995).

HDI (rank / value) 162 / 0.319 (1994)

worried local authorities, who were making every effort to diversify the country's commercial relations. With this in mind, Prime Minister Barkad Gourad Hamadou signed an economic and technical aid agreement with Turkey in June 1989.

[18] In 1990 France wrote off Djibouti's debt by granting it $40,000,000 as a way of public development aid. In 1991, confrontations between the Government and the Front for the Restoration of Unity and Democracy (FRUD) guerrillas were renewed. In November, Amnesty International accused the Government of Djibouti of the torture of 300 prisoners. Due to mounting pressure France pressed Gouled to begin talks with the opposition.

[19] In September 1992, amid harsh combat against the FRUD, the Government introduced a constitutional reform which established a multiparty system. In the May 1993 presidential elections, Gouled was once again re-elected with over 60.8 per cent of the vote. However, encouraged by the FRUD, half of the electorate abstained from voting and the opposition considered the elections a "fraud".

[20] Armed confrontations between government troops and guerrillas escalated in the weeks following the elections, which led thousands to seek refuge in Ethiopia. Acting as mediator, the French Government sought a cease-fire and negotiations began. Meanwhile, Gouled believed the rebellion was part of a plan orchestrated by Ethiopia.

[21] In March 1994, the FRUD was divided due to a possible agreement with the Government. The movement's Politburo, led by Ahmad Dini Ahmad, who opposed the agreement, was replaced by an executive council headed by Ahmad Ougoureh Kible. In June, Gouled and the FRUD jointly decided to end the war.

[22] In June, a demonstration of mostly Afar residents from the Arhiba district, opposed to the demolition of their homes for "security" reasons, was quelled by government forces. Police intervention left four dead, 20 injured and 300 arrests, including that of Muhammad Ahmad Issa, United Opposition Front president.

[23] In October, dissent within the FRUD had grown and the movement's leaders banned Ahmad Dini Ahmad and Muhammad Adoyta Yussuf, another breakaway leader, from holding any "activity or responsibility" in the FRUD. In 1995, after the Constitution was revised, a section of the FRUD formed an alliance with the ruling party. Ahmad Dini Ahmad said this alliance amounted to "treason".

[24] In mid-1995 under pressure from the IMF, the Government substantially reduced public spending and took a series of measures to increase fiscal income. The following year, the IMF granted Djibouti a $6.7 million credit to support the government reform programme. In March 1996, President Gouled dismissed two ministers: defence and justice post-holder, Ahmed Boulaleh Barreh, and Moumin Bahon Farah of prisons and Islamic affairs. The departure of these ministers consolidated the position of Prime Minister Barkat Gourad Hamadou and the Head of Cabinet Ismael Omar Guelleh, a close relative of Gouled.

[25] Farah, who had announced the formation of a new political party in April, was imprisoned for a month, accused of having insulted Gouled. In August, Farah started a hunger strike protesting over his imprisonment. On September 26, in Addis Ababa, Ethiopia, 17 opponents to the Gouled regime were abducted and made prisoners of the government of Djibouti. The prisoners included human rights campaigner Aicha Debalé, who had moved to the Ethiopian capital on the request of the French NGO Mission Enfance, to help children fleeing the war and repression in Djibouti.

[26] In December, legislative elections, classed as "a masquerade" by the opposition, were won by the People's Assembly for Progress (RPP) with 25 seats, followed by the Front for the Restoration of Unity and Democracy (FRUD) with 11 seats.

[27] In February 1998, thanks to pressure from organizations like Women's Solidarity and the International Democratic Federation of Women, Debalé was freed. Her husband who had also been abducted, remained in prison. On February 17, despite Djibouti having signed the African Human Rights Charter, guaranteeing freedom of speech and information, director of the bi-monthly Al Wahda publication, Ahmed Abdi Farah, and a journalist on the paper, Kamil Hassan Ali, were arrested for an article which had criticized the Government a year earlier.

Dominica

Dominica

Population: 71,000 (1996)
Area: 751 SQ KM
Capital: Roseau

Currency: E.C. Dollars
Language: English

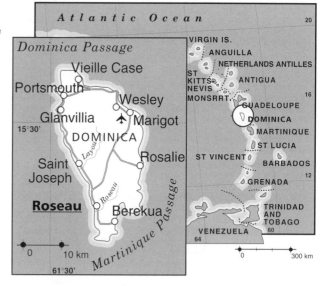

On Sunday, November 3 1493, Italian navigator Christopher Columbus reached an island which he named Dominica. He planted a cross to claim Spanish sovereignty over the newly discovered territory in the name of Queen Isabella and King Ferdinand of Spain.

[2] This territory was actually already populated by Carib peoples, peaceful and friendly indigenous groups. They watched the claiming ceremony from a distance, but could not have understood its significance. Soon afterwards, the Spanish returned in a more aggressive frame of mind, searching for the vast stores of gold that they believed the Caribs were hiding from them. They rapidly exterminated all but a few of the island's people, a pattern of destruction and despoilment that would be repeated throughout the colonial possessions in the new continent.

[3] By 1632 there were an estimated 1,000 Caribs on the island. These few people had only managed to survive through continual resistance. Today, there are only 500 of their descendants left living in the reservations.

[4] The landscape of present-day Dominica has changed greatly since their ancestors' days. In colonial times, the forests were felled to clear the land for extensive sugar plantations. The Carib peoples could not provide a sufficiently robust and reliable workforce, so the plantations were worked by thousands of slave labourers transported from Africa.

[5] In the 17th century, the Spanish withdrew and the French took their place. They introduced cotton and coffee production to complement the sugar trade. In the following two centuries, frequent British attempts to seize the island from French hands culminated in Dominica becoming a British colony in 1805.

[6] French influence still persists. The Catholic religion predominates despite strong competition from well-financed Protestant sects, and Creole, the language spoken by the people, is based on French mixed with African languages.

[7] After five centuries of colonization, the Dominicans inherited a rudimentary agrarian economy based on the monoculture of bananas for export. These are the only significant export item, because most of the land went over to banana production when sugar cane became unprofitable at the end of the 19th century.

[8] The political system adopted on achieving internal autonomy in 1967 was a copy of the British model. The Constitution established the "free association" of the Associated States of the West Indies with Britain. Britain retained responsibility for defence and foreign relations and each member island elected its own state government. The seat of the federal government was in Barbados.

[9] From 1975, independence was negotiated separately by each State. In the case of Dominica the negotiations were conducted by Labor Party premier, Patrick John. In 1978, the British Parliament approved a new statute for the island and on November 3 1978, exactly 485 years after the arrival of Columbus, Dominica became an independent country once more.

[10] The protest rallies that took place during the celebrations were an indication of the difficulties that lay ahead. Political division immediately became evident: a conservative group of veteran politicians opposed independence and a progressive sector supported by young people disagreed with the Labor Government which had done the negotiating.

[11] Since the island lacked the natural resources to attract transnationals and tourism, Dominica could not compete with its neighbors. Vast numbers of young people emigrated to neighboring Guadeloupe, while others who were more radical found political inspiration in the "black power" ideology of US black activists.

[12] In May 1979, the police fired at demonstrators protesting against two decrees limiting union activities and press freedom. At the same time, secret agreements between John and the Government of South Africa were revealed. The Dominican premier had helped to plan a mercenary attack on Barbados and intended to supply Pretoria with oil refined in Dominica. Patrick John was forced to resign. His successor, Oliver Seraphine, from the progressive wing of the Labor Party, called elections and strengthened Dominica's ties with progressive neighboring governments. In September 1979, Hurricane David devastated the island. The Conservative opposition skilfully associated the catastrophe with the Labor administration and gained electoral support.

[13] In the July 1980 election, Mary Eugenia Charles won a landslide victory and became the first woman to head a Caribbean government. She was the daughter of a wealthy and influential landowner and described herself as "liberal, democratic and anti-communist".

[14] In the 1985 election, Charles' party (DFP) obtained 15 of the 21 Parliamentary seats; the Labor Party, led by Michael Douglas, won only 5 seats and the United Dominican Labor Party (UDLP) won the remaining seat for its leader. During the electoral campaign, the opposition called for an investigation into a $100,000 donation made to the Government. It was believed that the donation had been made by the CIA to confirm Dominican collaboration in the US invasion of Grenada.

[15] In August 1986, Air Force commander Frederick Newton was sentenced to death by hanging for his participation in a plot to topple the conservative government in 1981. Former Prime Minister Patrick John and Michael Reid, captain of the Defense Forces, were found guilty of similar charges, and of involvement in a minor Ku Klux Klan conspiracy. They were sentenced to 12 years in prison.

[16] After the May 28 1990 parliamentary election, the third government since independence took office. Of the 21 seats up for election, Charles's DFP (Dominica Freedom Party) won by a slim majority of 11 seats, while the Labor Party (led by Douglas) won 4 and the United Labor Party, a newcomer in the

LAND USE

(1993)

- ■ FOREST & WOODLAND 66.7%
- ▢ ARABLE 9.3%
- ▨ OTHER 24%

PROFILE

ENVIRONMENT

The largest Windward Island of the Lesser Antilles, located between Guadeloupe to the north and Martinique to the south, Dominica is a volcanic island. Its highest peak is Morne Diablotin, at 2,000 meters. The climate is tropical with heavy summer rains. The volcanic soil allows for some agricultural activity, especially banana and cocoa plantations.

SOCIETY

Peoples: Descendants of Africans 89 per cent; descendants of Europeans and Africans 7.2 per cent; Caribs living in reservations 2.4 per cent; Europeans 0.4 per cent; Other 0.7 per cent.
Languages: English (official). Creole, a local French patois, with African elements, is widely spoken.
Religions: Roman Catholic 70.1 per cent; six largest Protestant groups 17.2 per cent.
Political parties: United Dominican Labor Party (UDLP); Dominica Revolutionary Party (PRD); Social Christian Reformist Party (PRSC), led by Jacinto Peynado; Dominican Liberation Party (PLD); Democratic Unity (UD); Dominican Freedom Party (DFP).

THE STATE

Official Name: Commonwealth of Dominica.
Administrative divisions: 10 parishes.
Capital: Roseau, 15,850 people (1991).
Other cities: Portsmouth, 3,621 people, Marigot, 2,372 people (1991).
Government: Crispin Sorhaindo, President; Edison James, Prime Minister since 1995.
National Holidays: November 3, Independence Day (1978) and Discovery by Christopher Columbus (1493).

STATISTICS

DEMOGRAPHY

Population: 71,000 (1996) **Annual growth:** -0.3% (1980/1996) **Estimates for year 2000:** 100,000 **Urban Population:** 69.7% (1996)

HEALTH

Life expectancy at birth: 73 years (1996) **Infant mortality:** 17 per 1,000 (1996) **Under-5 child mortality:** 20 per 1,000 (1996) **Safe water:** 96% (1990/96).

COMMUNICATIONS

0 **newspapers**, 600 **radios**, 70 **TV sets** and 235 **main telephone lines** per 1,000 people (1994)

ECONOMY

Consumer price index: 114.9 (1994) **Currency:** 2.7 E.C. dollars = $ 1 (1995) **Cereal imports:** 8 metric tons (1994) **Fertilizer use:** 2,705 kgs per ha (1994) **Development aid received:** $ 24 million (1995) $ 343 per capita (1995) 12.1% of GNP (1994).

HDI (rank /value) 41/0.873 (1994)

---

electoral process and led by Edison James, won 6 seats. Leonard Baptist's Progressive Force did not win any seats.

[17] The day after the election, which gave the 71-year-old lawyer Charles her third consecutive term, Patrick John and Michael Reid were freed.

[18] In 1990, Prime Minister Charles signed an agreement with her counterparts James Mitchell of St Vincent, John Compton of St Lucia and Nicholas Braithwaite of Grenada, for the four islands to form a new state.

[19] In the same year the Regional Constitutional Assembly of the Eastern Caribbean was set up. It comprised government officials, religious authorities and representatives from social organizations. In a second meeting, in St Lucia in April 1991, the Assembly studied various proposals for the establishment of the future State.

[20] This integration project concorded with the Chaguaramas Treaty, which aimed at the unification of the entire English-speaking Caribbean community, although the three islands of St Kitts, Montserrat and Antigua refused to commit themselves to the process. The opposition parties of Grenada and St Lucia also stated they were against it. The seven mini-States of the Eastern Caribbean have a common Central Bank, which coins their shared currency.

[21] In 1991, the Government decided on a series of measures to stimulate the national economy, centring its efforts on the development of agriculture and communications.

[22] The Prime Minister narrowly escaped censure in April through a motion presented by the United Workers' Party. At the end of 1991, Charles attempted to enact legislation making it illegal for civil servants to protest against the Government.

[23] In 1993, Prime Minister Charles raised the rates on several services, suspended government investment and proposed a wage freeze, in an attempt to deal with the budget deficit. Thanks to her total support of US policies, the island obtained American foreign aid, earmarked for the revitalization of its agriculture.

[24] Charles proposed offering Dominican passports to 1,200 Asians, on the condition that each one invested at least $35,000 in the country, but resistance to this idea increased during 1992-3. In mid-1993 the Prime Minister modified the project, raising the amount of the investment to $60,000 and imposing restrictions on the voting rights of the new citizens.

[25] In April 1994, the Government decision to increase the number of transport vehicle licenses caused protests and public disorder in Roseau. The Prime Minister accused the opposition of trying to bring forward the elections, and the crisis continued until an agreement was signed on May 6.

[26] In the same year, Dominica decided to vote against the establishment of a whale sanctuary in the South Atlantic. This attitude resulted in threatened tourism ban from the International Wildlife Coalition. This measure, which would have seriously affected a national economy heavily dependent on tourism, was not put into practice.

[27] In June 1995, the United Dominican Labour Party (UDLP) won the election, taking 11 of the 21 seats in Parliament. The Freedom Party and Liberal Party took five seats each. The new Prime Minister, Edison James, decided to promote the banana industry and privatize State enterprises in order to invest in the social infrastructure.

[28] In August and September 1995, Government plans were severely shaken. A succession of hurricanes and tropical storms destroyed the plantations and export projects. Houses, bridges, roads, hotels and public facilities were also destroyed and had to be rebuilt, absorbing vast amounts of resources.

[29] The external debt reached EC$ 320 million and the internal EC$ 80 million in January 1996. That year, the Government went ahead with a plan to privatize large public companies in an attempt to impose order on the financial sector. The Companies which passed into private hands were: Dominican Electricity Services, the Industrial and Agricultural Development Bank, the Import-Export Agency of Dominica and other services at the port of Roseau.

[30] Cuban Foreign Minister Roberto Robaina visited the country in May 1996, marking the re-establishment of diplomatic relations between Dominica and Cuba.

[31] In early 1997, the opposition parties severely criticised the privatizations, especially the sale of the Dominican Electricity Services to a British company, claiming the reasons behind this had not been sufficiently explained. On top of the $5 million received from the British Government for development projects, Dominica was awarded another million in April for a project to protect its coasts from erosion.

[32] Finance Minister Julius Timothy announced in 1998 that the international sector was going to be extended by enlarging the registration of foreign vessels and giving new incentives for the installation of insurance companies in the country.

Dominican Republic

República Dominicana

Population: 7,961,000 (1996)
Area: 48,734 SQ KM
Capital: Santo Domingo

Currency: Pesos
Language: Spanish

The island of Quisqueya was made up of two present-day countries: Haiti and the Dominican Republic. The first inhabitants belonged to several ethnic groups; the Lucayo, the Ciguayo, the Taino and the Carib. They were communities of fishers and gatherers who practised basic agriculture. There was always a great deal of contact between the Caribbean islands and trade between the groups.

[2] In December 1492, Christopher Columbus reached the island of Quisqueya, which he renamed Hispaniola. With the wood from one of his vessels he built a fort; initiating the European colonization of America. Within a few years, the Europeans had appropriated the whole island becoming owners of the land and the native Carib population. The terrible living and working conditions imposed by the Spaniards nearly exterminated the indians. Faced with this shameful situation, Bishop Bartolomé de Las Casas proposed that they replace local slave labor with Africans, millions of whom were distributed throughout the American continent.

[3] Dominican Republic historical records show that in 1523 a group of rebel African slave workers, founded the first quilombo (former slave settlement) on the island. Subsequent rebel groups, in 1537 and 1548, set up their own quilombos. The replacement of native American labor with African labor, accompanied a change in economic focus, from panning for gold to plantations of sugar cane and extensive cattle raising. As historian Pierre Vilar points out, the gold cycle in Hispaniola was "destructive, not of raw materials,

but rather, of the labor force". During the colonial period the extraordinary economic potential of the Dominican Republic was comparable only to that of Brazil. The island was successively the greatest gold producer in the Antilles, one of the largest producers of sugar in the New World, between 1570 and 1630, and finally, such an important cattle producer that, there were 40 cattle per person on the island.

[4] As major sugar producer with a key position on the trade route from Mexico and Peru to Spain, Hispaniola was coveted by the other colonial powers. In 1586, the English buccaneer Francis Drake raided the capital and in 1697 the French occupied the island's western half. When they were given official ownership under the Treaty of Ryswick, they renamed it Haiti. Later, the whole island fell under French rule but was partially recovered by Spain in 1809, after the first Afro-American republic had been established.

[5] Haiti's government regained control over the whole island in 1822. The Spanish descendants' (criollo), resistance came to a head after an uprising in Santo Domingo. The independence of the Dominican Republic was proclaimed, but in 1861 the government asked Spain to renew colonial status, in an attempt to gain support for the criollos, whose dominance was threatened by the black and mulatto majorities.

[6] However, Spain did not defend its colony effectively and the Dominican Republic became independent again in 1865 after a mulatto uprising. The economic system remained unchanged.

[7] By that time the US, fully recovered from its civil war, began to gain influence in the West Indies. In 1907 the US imposed an economic and political treaty on the Dominican Republic prefiguring "dollar diplomacy". This treaty helped the US to invade the Dominican Republic and impose a protectorate that lasted until 1924.

[8] In 1930, when the country was autonomous again, Rafael Leónidas Trujillo seized power. He was Chief of Staff of the National Guard, elected and trained by the American occupation forces. He

set up a dictatorial regime, with US backing, without nominally occupying the presidency. His crimes were so numerous and so monstrous that he finally became too embarrassing, even for the US, and the CIA planned his assassination which was carried out in May 1961.

[9] One extreme example of his crimes was the case of Jesús de Galíndez, a Spanish Republican professor, labor leader, and member of the Basque Nationalist Party. He was kidnapped by assassins, on Trujillo's payroll, and was subsequently killed, although his body was never found. Trujillo had the gunmen killed some time later which proved to be a fatal mistake; among the assassins was an American with relatives in the CIA, and they settled the score by killing Trujillo. On his death, Trujillo owned 71 per cent of the country's arable land and 90 per cent of its industry.

[10] In 1963, following a popular rebellion, the first democratic elections were held and writer Juan Bosch was elected president. Seven months later, he was overthrown by military officers from the Trujillo regime. In April 1965, Colonel Francisco Cameo De led a constitutionals armed uprising. Accusing the nationalists of having "Pro-Castro/communist" sympathies, the US intervened once again, sending in 35,000 Marines who suppressed the insurgency.

[11] Before leaving the country, the

US occupation force paved the way for an unconditional Trujillo supporter, Joaquín Balaguer, to rise to power. In return, he opened the country to transnationals; especially Gulf and Western. The sugar industry fell under Gulf control. The corporation also bought shares in local banking, agro-industry, hotels and cattle raising, consequently, becoming very influential in Dominican Republic.

[12] The nationalist opposition kept up its resistance and in 1973 Francisco Cameo was killed while leading a guerrilla group. The Dominican Revolutionary Party, originally led by Juan Bosch, split with the right wing (led by landowner Antonio Guzmán) eliminating the main reformist measures from its program. This action made it acceptable to the State Department, and in 1978, when the PRD won the elections, the US used its influence, in the name of human rights, to ensure that the results would be respected.

[13] The PRD program promised to re-establish democratic freedoms and to follow an economic policy of income redistribution favoring the majority. The first promise was fulfilled and popular organizations took advantage of the new situation to reorganize their weakened structures after decades of harsh repression.

[14] New presidential elections were held on May 16, 1981, and Salvador Jorge Blanco became

Foreign Trade

Food Dependency

MILLIONS $ 1996

IMPORTS
6,300

EXPORTS
3,893

1970
18%

1994
14%

PROFILE

ENVIRONMENT

The Dominican Republic comprises the eastern part of the island of Hispaniola, the second largest of the Antilles. The Cordillera Central, the central mountain range, crosses the territory from northwest to south east. Between the central and northern ranges, lies the fertile region of the Cibao. Sea winds and ocean currents contribute to the tropical, rainy climate. Between 1962 and 1990, the country lost a significant portion of its woodlands. Coral reefs are suffering the effects of pollution, which has harmed marine habitats and reduced fish populations.

SOCIETY

Peoples: Most Dominican Republicans are of Spanish and African descent, with a small native American component.
Languages: Spanish.
Religions: Roman Catholic 91.3 per cent; other 8.7 per cent.
Political Parties: Dominican Liberation Party; Social Christian Reformist Party; Dominican Revolutionary Party.
Social Organizations: Most workers are represented by the General Workers' Union (CGT) and the Unity Workers' Union (CUT). In March 1991, 4 major labor groups, 57 federations and 366 labor unions merged within the CUT.

THE STATE

Official Name: República Dominicana.
Administrative Divisions: 26 Provinces, 1 National District.
Capital: Santo Domingo, 2,100,000 people (1993).
Other cities: Santiago de Los Caballeros, 690,000 people; La Vega, 189,000; San Pedro de Marcorís, 137,000 (1993).
Government: Leonel Fernández Reyna, President since August, 1996.
National Holiday: February 27, Independence (1844).
Armed forces: 24,500 (1995)
Other: National Police, 15,000.

president in PRD's second successive victory. José Francisco Peña Gómez, one of the Latin American leaders in the Socialist International, was elected mayor of Santo Domingo. On July 4, departing president Antonio Guzmán, killed himself, generating political tension, which ended with the announcement of the electoral result.

[15] When president Blanco took office the trade deficit amounted to $562 million. In 1982, sugar prices fell and oil prices rose causing foreign debt to climb to $2 billion. Unemployment affected 25 per cent of the active population.

[16] Blanco tried to tackle the situation by applying IMF-tailored austerity measures. But during 1983, the international price of sugar fell 50 per cent below the cost of production, and sugar accounted for 44 per cent of Dominican Republic exports. In 1984, the government withdrew the subsidies on several products,

and imposed a 200 per cent price increase on staple and medical goods. These measures brought about protest rallies led by leftist organizations and labor unions. In return, the Union headquarters were occupied by soldiers leaving 100 dead, 400 injured, and over 5,000 imprisoned.

[17] In 1985, the US reduced its Dominican Republic sugar quota again, causing another decrease in exports. Unemployment rose abruptly, provoking yet another wave of social unrest. The Government continued to toe the IMF line, harshly repressing all the strikes and protests against its policies.

[18] Internal struggles at the PRD convention led to armed confrontations in which two people were killed; Jacobo Majluta was finally designated party candidate for the 1986 election.

[19] In that year, the gravity of the economic crisis became evident. The judges went on strike and paralyzed the courts for three months. In May,

the powerful Dominican Republic Medical Association began a new round of conflicts, accompanied by the nurses of the Social Security system, the Association of Agriculture Professionals and the Veterinary Association. In August, the Association of Engineers followed suit, supported by the architects and surveyors, who demanded a minimum wage of $260. The Dominican Republic Association of Economists wrote that since 1980 poverty had been "initially limited to the low-income groups, (but) had spread to the point of affecting the middle classes".

[20] In the lower income categories, the situation was untenable. Committees for Popular Struggle began to appear and grass roots movements organized to resist price rises on basic goods and services. In April, dockworkers found 28 young Dominican Republic girls asphyxiated in a ship's container. They could not find work and had expected to find a way of making a living on another island. It was disclosed that every two weeks a "cargo" of Dominican Republic girls left for the Franco-Dutch island of St Martin, where a brothel manager sold them to other Caribbean islands for between 800 and 1,000 German marks.

[21] On May 16, the national election was held with three candidates: Jacobo Majluta for the PRD, Joaquín Balaguer for the Social Christian Reform Party (PRSC) and Juan Bosch for the Marxist Dominican Liberation Party (PLD). The post-election climate was marked by confusion and the vote count was interrupted. Eventually Joaquín Balaguer's PRSC won with 41 per cent of the votes.

[22] The conditions surrounding Balaguer's inauguration were very difficult. Clearly a conservative, without a parliamentary majority and faced with highly organized social opposition, his hands were virtually tied. He did not even have the necessary power to impose a more restrictive economic program to get new loans from the IMF.

[23] The situation worsened when the US further restricted the Dominican Republic's sugar quota. This led to 17,000 redundancies in

an administration that was already suffering 27 per cent unemployment.

[24] In July 1988, former president Jorge Blanco was found guilty of illegal dealings. Despite judicial restrictions prohibiting such activities, he had sold weapons to the armed forces at inflated prices.

[25] The May 16 1990 general election went to President Joaquín Balaguer. His rival, Juan Bosch, leader of the PLD, accused him of an electoral fraud of monumental proportions. In the last opinion poll carried out before the election, Bosch was leading, with 36 per cent of surveyed voters saying that they intended to vote for him, as opposed to the 26 per cent committed to Balaguer. The third candidate, PRD's Peña Gómez, suggested a recount which was held at the polling stations. This recount confirmed Balaguer's victory, with 35 per cent, to Bosch's 34 and Peña Gómez's 23.

[26] For the first time, the tone of campaign programs and speeches gave major attention to women's issues.

[27] In 1991 two of the country's main political leaders, Joaquín Balaguer, aged 85, and Juan Bosch, aged 82, announced their resignations from politics.

[28] In the meantime, the social and economic situation continued to deteriorate. The recession which had begun in 1990 continued throughout the following year: unemployment rose and inflation soared, while agricultural production dropped as did mineral production. The combined effect of a fall in the price of Dominican Republic goods on the world market, and an increase in the price of imported oil (caused by the Gulf War), led to a worsening of the country's foreign trade situation.

[29] From 1990 to 1991 there were hundreds of thousands of Haitian immigrants working as sugar cane cutters in the Dominican Republic sugar industry. In June 1991, Balaguer expelled illegal immigrants.

[30] In 1984, those classified as "poor" represented 31 per cent of the country's population, and the "seriously deprived" made up 16 per cent. In late 1991, the Economic and Social Council of

PER 100,000
LIVE BIRTHS
110

82%

STATISTICS

DEMOGRAPHY
Population: 7,961,000 (1996) **Annual growth:** 2.1% (1980/1996) **Estimates for year 2000:** 8,500,000 **Annual growth to year 2000:** 1.7% (1994/2000) **Urban Population:** 62.6% (1996) **Urban growth:** 3.83% (1980/95) **Children per woman:** 2.9 (1996).

HEALTH
Life expectancy at birth: 71 years (1996) male: 68 years (1994) female: 72 years (1994) **Infant mortality:** 45 per 1,000 (1996) **Under-5 child mortality:** 56 per 1,000 (1996) **Calorie consumption:** 102% (1988/90) 935 **people per doctor** (1988/91) **Safe water:** 65% (1990/96).

EDUCATION
Literacy: 82% (1995) male : 82% (1995) female: 82% (1995) **School enrolment :** Primary total: 103% (1990/95) male : 103% (1990/95) female: 104% (1990/95) Secondary: male : 34% (1990/95) female: 47% (1990/95) **Primary school teachers:** one for every 35 students (1995).

COMMUNICATIONS
30 **newspapers**, 173 **radios**, 90 **TV sets** and 79 **main telephone lines** per 1,000 people (1994).

ECONOMY
Per capita, GNP: $ 1,600 (1996) **Annual growth, GNP:** 5.7% (1995/96) **Annual inflation:** 26.38% (1985/95) **Currency:** 13.47 pesos = $ 1 (1995) **Cereal imports:** 895 metric tons (1994) **Food import dependency:** 14% (1994) **Fertilizer use:** 641 kgs per ha (1994) **Exports:** $ 3,893 million (1996) **Imports:** $ 6,300 million (1996) **External debt:** $ 4,310 million (1996) $ 541 **per capita:** (1996) **Debt service:** 11.4% of exports (1996) **Development aid received:** $ 124 million (1995) $ 16 per capita (1995) 1.2% of GNP (1994).

ENERGY
Consumption: 337.15 Kgs of Oil equivalent per capita yearly (1994) 93.78% imported (1994)

HDI (rank / value) 87 / 0.718 (1994)

the United Nations reprimanded the Dominican Republic Government, as it had done on a previous occasion, for allowing the authorities to evict hundreds of poor families. Between 1986 and 1991, more than 100,000 people lost their homes.

[31] Between 1990 and 1991, labor conflict reached one of the highest levels registered in recent years. The Government was faced with a series of general strikes, which were brutally repressed; in 1990, 15 people died and thousands were detained.

[32] Negotiations carried out by Balaguer made it possible to refinance the foreign debt. In 1933 tourism grew, making the country the fourth most important tourist destination in the Caribbean.

[33] As a result of the political crisis in neighboring Haiti, the Dominican Republic supplied contraband across the Haitian border. This practice foiled the international embargo against the Haitian regime. Oil was the main product smuggled into the country.

[34] Economic problems caused hundreds of Dominican Republicans to leave the country each year with forged visas and documents. Many sail in unseaworthy vessels, bound for Puerto Rico, normally as a "stopover" on their way to New York.

[35] More than a million expatriates in the United States, and half are illegal. There are also an estimated 20,000 in Spain, half of them illegal. The majority are women who work as domestic helpers, while

another 25,000 women work as prostitutes throughout Europe, most of them lured by false promises of employment.

[36] Although he had announced his retirement, Balaguer sought re-election. His perennial opponent Juan Bosch also ran in the 1994 election. According to opinion polls, José Francisco Peña Gómez, of the Dominican Revolutionary Party (PDR) held a slight lead over Balaguer. Intent upon avoiding another case of electoral fraud, four of the five participating parties signed a "civility pact", with the Catholic Church acting as warrantor. In spite of this, the electoral campaign turned violent, with hundreds of people injured and 12 people killed.

[37] International observers were called in to supervise the elections, denouncing irregularities, especially in the interior. The PRD condemned the election, stating that some 200,000 voters were remained unable to vote as a result of official party manipulation. According to official figures, Balaguer obtained 43 per cent of the vote, leading Peña Gómez by 1.5 per cent, while Juan Bosch obtained 31.2 per cent.

[38] The US Government, anxious to win Balaguer's support in enforcing the trade embargo on Haiti, gave assurances that it would approve the final decision of the special commission set up to clarify the electoral results. However, three months after the August 1994 election, the special commission had still not reached a verdict. Finally, the Central Electoral Committee declared Balaguer the winner.

[39] But in mid-August, Peña Gómez and Balaguer agreed to hold elections on November 16 1995. Both leaders decided to reform the constitution in order to bar presidential re-election. In the meantime, Balaguer was proclaimed president. Official returns gave him a 22,281 vote lead.

[40] During 1995, the drought affected the country's electricity supply. The power utility reported that 40 per cent of electricity consumed was not paid for; moreover, a fourth of power production was lost due to technical faults.

[41] The Dominican Revolutionary Party (DRP) candidate, José Francisco Peña Gómez was the most popular candidate (48.75 per cent), but did not win an absolute majority. The ruling party candidate, Jacinto Peinaldo, did not reach the second round of voting. On June 30 1996, Leonel Fernández Reyna, of the DLP, won the second round of elections after forming an alliance with the conservative Social Christian Reformist Party (SCRP). On August 18 he succeeded Joaquín

Balaguer, who had served seven terms as president.

[42] After the election, the SCRP signed an agreement with the DRP giving them control of the Senate, and the DRP dominated the Chamber of Deputies. The DLP remained in a minority in both chambers, preventing the President from implementing several of the initiatives announced in his electoral campaign.

[43] In 1997 a dispute developed over the budget. The controversial budget package included increases in indirect taxes, cutbacks in direct taxation, higher wages for Government officials and reductions in import tariffs.

[44] Given the lack of support in the chambers, the President opted for introducing two controversial measures which did not require approval from the legislative body: the unification of exchange rates and increases in fuel prices. He also vetoed some modifications made by the chambers and issued a decree increasing the number of public employees.

[45] Increasing prices, unemployment of more than 30 per cent, and the poverty which affected 70 per cent of the population led to an increase in social tension. There were many demonstrations in the streets, some violent. Despite this, the economy in general saw exceptional growth of 6.9 per cent in the first half of the year.

[46] A law approved in June allowed private capital to invest in State companies, including the sugar and electricity sectors. The Government aimed to thus balance the State accounts.

[47] Towards the end of 1997, the Presidents of the Dominican Republic and Haiti agreed to stop the large-scale repatriation of Haitians and to respect human rights. The Haitians often worked in the worst conditions, and so the state sugar company had announced a plan to employ 16,000 Haitian cane cutters. This cheap workforce was transported from the frontier to the various sugar plantations to work and then taken directly back to Haiti. However, pressure against the arrival of more Haitians did not stop: anti-immigrant protests led to the expulsion of some 2,500 undocumented Haitians and the strengthening of frontier controls.

[48] On April 16 1998, the Dominican Republic and Cuba reopened diplomatic relations. The Government sent a consular representative to Havana, later followed by a delegation of ministers which formally inaugurated the diplomatic headquarters. The United States protested against the measure, which it deemed "inappropriate."

East Timor

Timor Leste

Population:	829,000 (1996)
Area:	14,874 SQ KM
Capital:	Dili
Currency:	Indonesian rupiahs
Language:	Tetum

Long before the arrival of the Portuguese, the Chinese and Arabs knew Timor as an "inexhaustible" source of precious woods which were exchanged for axes, pottery, lead and other goods of use to the local inhabitants.

[2] Timor's traditional Maubere society consisted of five major categories: the Liurari (kings and chiefs), the Dato (lesser nobles and warriors), the Ema-reino (freemen) the Ata (slaves) and the Lutum (nomadic shepherds).

[3] In 1859, Portugal and the Netherlands agreed to divide the territory between them. The Portuguese kept the eastern part, under an accord ratified in 1904. Resistance to colonialism included armed insurrections in 1719, 1895 and 1959, all of which were put down. Passive resistance by the Maubere enabled their culture to survive five centuries of colonialism. It fared better than the forests of precious woods: species like sandalwood were exhausted very early, or replaced with coffee plantations which are still Timor's economic mainstay.

[4] The independence movement began later than in other Portuguese colonies, but in the mid-1970s a national liberation front was formed, bringing together nationalist forces and all sectors of society.

[5] In April 1974, when the clandestine struggle against colonial rule had already grown and gained broad support, the "Carnation Revolution" took place in Lisbon. With the fall of the fascist colonial regime in the metropolis the political scene in Timor changed and the patriotic movement was legalized. In September, the Revolutionary Front for the Independence of East Timor (FRETILIN) was created.

[6] The new Portuguese Government promised independence but the colonial administration favored the creation of the Timor Democratic Union (UDT), which supported the colonial status quo and "federation" with Portugal. At the same time, the Indonesian consulate in Dili, Timor's capital, encouraged a group of Timorese to organize the Timor Popular Democratic Association

(APODETI) which wanted full independence from Portugal, and supported integration with Indonesia.

[7] A period of conflict ensued between Portuguese neocolonial interests, Indonesian annexationists and the independence movement. In August, the UDT attempted a coup causing FRETILIN to issue a call for general armed insurrection, and the Portuguese administration withdrew from the country. FRETILIN achieved territorial control and declared independence on November 28 1975, proclaiming the Democratic Republic of East Timor. To this day, however, Portugal's withholding of official recognition continues to have important diplomatic and political implications.

[8] On December 7 1975, Indonesia invaded the new republic. A few hours earlier, US President Gerald Ford had visited Jakarta where he had probably learned of, and endorsed, Suharto's expansionist plans. FRETILIN was forced to withdraw from the capital, Dili, and from the major ports. On June 2 1976, a so-called "People's Assembly", made up of UDT and APODETI members, approved Timor's annexation as a province of Indonesia. However, this illegal resolution was not recognized by the United Nations Decolonization Committee, which still regards Portugal as the colonial power responsible for Timor.

[9] Meanwhile, the Democratic Republic of East Timor established diplomatic relations with numerous former Portuguese colonies and socialist states.

[10] In December 1978, FRETILIN president Nicolau dos Reis Lobato died in combat. Despite this great loss, the liberation movement reorganized and continued resistance. According to reliable sources, Indonesia has adopted a policy of extermination on the island, to date killing off nearly 20 per cent of the population.

[11] Tactics used in the war varied. In 1978, in a peculiar decision, the Front organized the massive surrender of civilians, who then moved into the Indonesian-

controlled cities. Young men were armed and trained by the Indonesian army in an attempt to "Timorize" the war and set the Maubere against each other. But acting on FRETILIN instructions, now well-armed and equipped recruits, rebelled and rejoined the revolutionary forces. The Front became active in both the countryside and the cities.

[12] Indonesia's responses to the war were erratic. In 1983, FRETILIN commander-in-chief, Xanana Gusmao, signed a cease-fire with the chief of the expeditionary force, Colonel Purwanto. However, President Suharto objected to this agreement and the guerrilla war continued.

[13] The region is well renowned for its mineral reserves and in April 1985, an international consortium was formed to explore oil and natural gas reserves in Timor territorial waters off the coast of Australia.

[14] FRETILIN sought closer ties with the Timor Democratic Union (UDT), and in 1986 established a coordinating body, the National Convergence. This union helped Portugal to actively resume its role. The internal structure of the nationalist movement was reorganized, to become politically independent and more locally based. Gusmao was confirmed as commander-in-chief of Timor's liberation army.

[15] Portugal won an important

diplomatic victory when the European Parliament and the European Commission adopted a position on the East Timor issue. They defended the Maubere people's right to self-determination, recognized the need for a negotiated settlement, and condemned the Indonesian occupation.

[16] In October 1989, the United Nations Human Rights Subcommission passed a motion condemning Indonesian occupation and repression in East Timor. The disturbances had spread throughout the island, above all in Dili where students took to the streets, burned cars and destroyed the houses of several Indonesian officers.

[17] Repression increased after this. Foreign correspondents were forbidden entry, isolating Dili from the rest of the world. There were no telephone lines out of the country, nor any diplomatic representatives in the capital.

[18] When Pope John Paul II visited Dili in October 1989, a group of young people unfurled a FRETILIN banner 20 meters from the altar where mass was celebrated. Of the 80,000 people who attended the ceremony, 13,000 were thought to have been members of the Indonesian security forces. The young protesters shouted independence slogans while the army waded in to prevent them. Reporters

PROFILE

ENVIRONMENT
Located between Australia and Indonesia, East Timor comprises the eastern portion of Timor Island, the dependency of Oecusse, located on the northwestern part of the island, the island of Atauro to the North, and the islet of Yaco to the East. Of volcanic origin, the island is mountainous and covered with dense rainforest. The climate is tropical with heavy rainfall, which accounts for the extensive river system. The southern region is flat and suitable for farming. Agriculture is the basis of its export-oriented economy, and copra, coffee, rice, cotton, tobacco and sandal are its main crops.

SOCIETY
Peoples: The Maubere people result from the integration between Melanesian and Malayan populations. In 1975 there was a Chinese minority of 20,000 as well as 4,000 Portuguese. Amnesty International estimates that 210,000 people have died as a result of the Indonesian occupation. There are 6,000 Maubere refugees in Australia and 1,500 in Portugal.
Religions: Most of the population profess traditional religions. 50-75 per cent are Catholic.
Languages: Tetum is the national language. There are some forty dialects. Indonesian occupation has banned the use of these languages in education, and virtually all the teaching is done in Bahasa, the main Indonesian language. A minority also speaks Portuguese.
Political Parties: On 31 December 1988, the Front for the Liberation of East Timor (FRETILIN) and the Democratic Union of Timor (UDT) formed the National Convergence.

THE STATE
Official Name: República de Timor Leste.
Capital: Dili, 67,000 people (1980).
Government: The country has been occupied by Indonesia since 1975. Mario Carrascalao is the Governor appointed by the Indonesian Government. Xanana Gusmao, head of the National Liberation Armed Forces for Convergence, is currently in prison in Jakarta.
National Holiday: November 28, Independence Day (1975).

[23] Late in 1991, Portugal reported that Jakarta and Canberra had signed a contract with 12 companies to extract around a billion barrels of oil from the sea around Timor. The list of companies is led by Royal Dutch Shell (British and Dutch), and Chevron (US). They are followed by six Australian companies, Nippon Oil (Japan), Phillips Petroleum, Marathon, and the Enterprise Oil Company. Meanwhile, representatives of the Australian Government announced that they would not support the sanctions against Jakarta.

[24] In Timor, the leaders of Nationalist Convergence urged Portugal to break off negotiations with Indonesia and to take the harsher measures needed for a diplomatic solution to the conflict, through UN intervention. Nationalist Convergence hoped that conditions to put pressure on the Indonesian government would be more favourable in 1992, when Portugal took up the EC presidency, both at EC, and UN, level. The Timorese demanded compliance with the UN resolutions: the withdrawal of occupation troops, and a referendum to decide on the country's political future.

[25] In March 1992, the ship "Lusitania Expresso" left Port Darwin, in Australia. On board were human rights activists from over 23 countries, and well-known Portuguese politicians, including president Ramalho Eanes. "The Peace Boat", left with the aim of commemorating the Dili massacre of November 1991. The Indonesian authorities immediately announced that the ship would be diverted from its course to a nearby island; where the Government would decide which members of the committee would be authorized to enter Timor.

[26] Reports from the island in early 1994 indicated that the families of the dead, "disappeared" and prisoners met in the main square of Dili every Saturday to pray and protest. In November, some 100 people were arrested after a series of public demonstrations. The tension continued, and a year later, in October 1995, between 50 and 100 people were arrested following three days of disturbances in Dili.

[27] In early 1996, shortly before the seventh meeting between the Indonesian and Portuguese foreign ministers to seek a solution to the situation in East Timor, Amnesty International asked for free access for human rights observers to the occupied nation. Other specialist reports insist there are social inequalities between the occupied and occupiers, despite the well-publicized investments made by the Indonesian Government in sectors like education.

[28] In December 1996, the exiled activist Jose Ramos Horta and the Catholic Bishop Carlos Felipe Ximenes Belo were awarded the Nobel Peace prize in Oslo. The Indonesian authorities tried to boycott the ceremony, but the topic East Timor reached the headlines of world media.

[29] In April 1997, Ramos Horta presented a documentary on the 20 years of Indonesian occupation to the United Nations Human Rights Commission in Geneva. And in July, South African president, Nelson Mandela, on a visit to Indonesia, said "the liberation of Xanana Gusmao, the Timorese resistance leader, would be a fundamental gesture in seeking a solution to the problem of East Timor".

[30] In July, a high ranking military officer of the occupying forces, announced he would soon be receiving 18 French-built armed combat vehicles. Two months later, the British Government ended a military aid agreement with Indonesia, claiming the arms might be used in East Timor.

[31] In November, occupying army troops opened fire on university students holding a vigil in Dili in remembrance of the 1991 massacre here, killing one student and wounding another sixteen. Ximenes Belo, denounced the "outrageous brutality" of the military and stated the Indonesian occupation forces had entered the university campus without permission, breaking through windows and doors.

[32] The overthrow of Indonesia's President Suharto in 1998, and the withdrawal of some troops by his successor Habibie, led to speculation that some form of independence could be forthcoming.

---

accompanying the Pope, some of whom had their cameras confiscated, witnessed at first hand the political oppression operating in East Timor, and were able to inform the rest of the world.

[19] Repression has however, continued: every family is required to hang a list on their door naming the family members living in the house, and this list can be checked at any time by occupation forces. Thousands of Maubere women have been compulsorily sterilized, and Tetum, the national language, is banned from schools. The transmigration policy enforced by the Indonesian authorities is reducing the Maubere people to the status of a minority within their own country. Also mass graves have been discovered in different parts of the country, containing corpses which showed signs of having suffered mass execution at the hands of the occupation forces.

[20] In early November 1991, during a massive peaceful funeral procession accompanying the body of a young man who had been murdered, the army opened fire on the crowd, 200 people were killed, and countless more were injured. Media coverage of this event, caused the Portuguese Government to appeal to the EC countries to break trading relations with Indonesia. Indonesia has a preferential trading agreement with the EC, being a member of the six countries of the Association of South East Asian Nations (ASEAN). Portugal also requested a meeting of the UN Security Council, criticizing them harshly because they did not react to Indonesia as they had to Iraq on the invasion of Kuwait in August 1990.

[21] A visit to the island by Portuguese members of parliament, scheduled for November 1991, was cancelled after the Indonesians refused to allow entry to an Australian journalist accompanying the delegation.

[22] Opposition leaders accused the US, Australia, the Netherlands, Japan and other countries with important economic interests in Indonesia, of co-operating with Jakarta in its attempt to play down the genocide and silence the international press.

Ecuador

Ecuador

Population: 11,699,000 (1996)
Area: 283,561 SQ KM
Capital: Quito

Currency: Sucre
Language: Spanish

In 1478, Inka Tupac Yupanqui united the agricultural peoples who had inhabited the territory that is now Ecuador since 2,000 BC, within the Tahuantinsuyu (Inka empire). Within a few years the northern region of the Quechua territory, of which Quito was the center, acquired great economic importance and became the commercial and cultural center of a great civilization. But the rivalry for succession between Atahualpa (from Quito) and Huascar (from Cuzco) weakened the power of the Empire.

2 he Spanish conquistadors commanded by Sebastián de Benalcázar took advantage of the situation to capture Quito in 1534. Indigenous South Americans, who had been free people working the land and living in communities characterized by a high level of social organization and mutual help (*ayllus*) were enslaved and cruelly exploited.

3 At first, the country formed part of the Viceroyalty of Peru as an administrative dependency known as the Real Audiencia de Quito (Royal District of Quito). In 1717, Quito was transferred by the Bourbons to the Viceroyalty of Nueva Granada, which also comprised present-day Colombia, Venezuela and Panama.

4 In 1822, General Antonio José de Sucre, Bolívar's deputy, defeated the royalist forces in the Battle of Pichincha, thus ending Spanish domination and incorporating Ecuador into Bolívar's Greater Colombia scheme.

5 The Royal District of Quito seceded from Greater Colombia in 1830 and adopted the name Republic of Ecuador. The change in name probably meant little to the peasant majority, as nothing

changed with regard to the land tenure system.

6 In 1895, the Liberal Revolution led by Eloy Alfaro rekindled the people's hopes for real land reform. Church property was nationalized although large landowners were not affected. Alfaro was killed and the country, like other parts of the continent, came under the influence of British imperialism.

7 Ecuador successively lost one part of its territory after another, due to the ruling oligarchy's lack of political capacity. Under Spanish domination, Ecuador had covered 1,038,000 sq km, shrinking to 283,560 sq km by 1942 through successive agreements with external powers.

8 In 1944 a popular revolt ousted President Carlos Alberto Arroyo, ushering in a populist government headed by José María Velazco Ibarra and comprising conservatives, communists and socialists, under the common banner of the Democratic Alliance. The Cold War made it impossible for this alliance to continue, and the left began to be the object of repression. In 1962, under pressure from the United States, President Carlos Arosemena broke off diplomatic relations with Cuba.

9 In the early 1970s, bananas, coffee and cocoa exports were replaced by crude oil. That year the political situation also changed. Veteran populist leader, José María Velasco Ibarra was ousted for the fourth time by the armed forces. Under the government of General Guillermo Rodríguez Lara, the country joined OPEC. The Government purchased 25 per cent of the shares of Texaco-Gulf and affirmed its rights over 200

miles of territorial waters. The "tuna war" ensued when this claim was disputed by US fishing interests.

10 Jaime Roldós, nominated by the Convergence of People's Forces (CPF) and the People's Democratic Party, became president in August 1979. Ecuador renewed diplomatic relations with Cuba, China and Albania. The Government also initiated a program aimed at integrating marginalized rural and urban populations into the economy. However, it encountered a hostile Congress, as well as opposition from the United States, which did not take kindly to its human rights policies and its antagonism to the dictatorships in the southern cone.

11 Toward the end of January 1981, the Five Day War broke out between Ecuador and Peru, with skirmishes along borders which had not been clearly delineated by the 1942 Protocol.

12 In May of the same year, Roldós died in a suspicious airplane accident, whereupon Vice President, Osvaldo Hurtado took office. The following year was marked by the most severe social crisis since the military had left power. It was triggered, on the one

hand, by the application of IMF formulas, and on the other, by an overt drive to build up military power to achieve parity with the Peruvian armed forces.

13 The 1984 election was won by conservative León Febres Cordero, of the Social Christian Party. For the most part, Febres Cordero was able to fulfil his campaign promises: to encourage free enterprise, develop agriculture and mining, attract foreign investment and establish relations with the IMF. The agreement with 400 creditor banks entailed assigning 34 per cent of estimated export revenues to meet new commitments.

14 Febres was an ardent defender of US President Reagan's Central American policy. In October 1985 he broke off diplomatic relations with Nicaragua, and on several occasions helped finance Nicaraguan "contra" leaders' travel and expenses.

15 The May 1988 election was won by Social Democrat Rodrigo Borja, inaugurated in August of that year with the support of a coalition made up of the Democratic Left, Osvaldo Hurtado's Christian Democrats and a dozen parties of the left.

WORKERS

UNEMPLOYMENT 10.4% (1996)

Labour force %

- ■ WOMEN
- □ MEN

27% | 73%

- ■ AGRICULTURE 33% (1990)
- □ INDUSTRIAL 19%
- ▣ SERVICES 48%

LAND USE

DEFORESTATION -1.7% annual (81/90)
IRRIGATED 34.1% of arable

(1993)

- ■ FOREST & WOODLAND 55%
- □ ARABLE 5.7%
- ▦ OTHER 39.3%

PROFILE

Environment

The country is divided into three natural regions: the coast, the mountains and the rainforest. Due to the influence of the cold Humboldt current, the climate of the coastal region is mild. More than half of the population lives along the coast, where cash crops of bananas, cocoa, rice and coffee are grown. In the highlands, extending between two separate ranges of the Andes, the climate varies according to altitude, and subsistence crops are grown. In the eastern Amazon region, recent oil finds supply internal demand, leaving a small surplus for export. The Colón or Galapagos archipelago belongs to Ecuador. The country also lays claim to 200,000 sq km of Amazon territory presently controlled by Peru, as well as the air space over its territory, where communication satellites are stationed. In the coastal region, 95 per cent of the woodlands have been felled. Soil depletion has increased by 30 per cent over the past 25 years.

SOCIETY

Peoples: Most Ecuadoreans descend from the Quechua people who made up the kingdom of Quito. A break-down of the current population shows a high percentage of mestizos, the result of intermarriage with the Spaniards and their descendants, in addition to descendants of African slaves. There are also indigenous nationalities: Huaorani, Shuar, Achar, Siona-Secoya, Cofan, Quechua, Tsachila and Chachi. There are over 1.5 million Quechua living in the inter-Andean valley.

Religions: Mainly Catholic.

Languages: Spanish (official), although 40 per cent of the population speaks Quechua.

Political Parties: The Social Christian Party of Jaime Nebot; the United Republican Party, conservative; the Ecuadorean Roldosista Party; the Democratic Left, social democratic, affiliated to the Socialist International; the Conservative Party; People's Democracy; the Christian Democratic Union; the Democratic People's Movement; the Ecuadorean Socialist Party; the Convergence of Popular Forces; the Radical Liberal Party; the Broad Front of the Left; the Radical Alfarista Front; the National Patriotic Front, of Frank Vargas; the Ecuadorean People's Revolutionary Action; the National Liberation Party.

Social Organizations: The major union federations are the Ecuadorean Central Organization of Class Unions (CEDOC), and the Central Organization of Ecuadorean Workers (CTE) coordinated with the United Worker's Front (FUT). In the last few years the Confederation of Indigenous Nationalities of Ecuador (CONAIE) has gained importance; the National Federation of Small Producers (FNPA).

THE STATE

Official Name: República del Ecuador.

Administrative divisions: 21 Provinces.

Capital: Quito, 1,401,000 people (1995).

Other cities: Guayaquil, 1,877,000; Cuenca, 329,000 people (1995).

Government: Fabián Alarcón, President since 1997. The constitution approved by plebiscite in 1978 established a presidential system and granted the right to vote to illiterate people for the first time in 1984.

National Holiday: August 10, Independence Day (1809).

Armed Forces: 57,000 troops (conscripts). 100,000 reserves (1996).

Other: 200 Coast Guard and 6 coastal patrol units (1993).

Foreign Trade

MILLIONS $ 1996

IMPORTS
3,733

EXPORTS
4,762

Food Dependency

1970
8%

1994
5%

STATISTICS

DEMOGRAPHY
Population: 11,699,000 (1996) **Annual growth:** 2.4 % (1980/1996) **Estimates for year 2000:** 12,600,000 Annual growth to year 2000: 2 % (1994/2000) **Urban Population:** 59.6% (1996) **Urban growth:** 3.94 % (1980/95) **Children per woman:** 3.2 (1996).

HEALTH
Life expectancy at birth: 70 years (1996) male: 67 years (1994) female: 72 years (1994) **Infant mortality:** 31 per 1,000 (1996) **Under-5 child mortality:** 40 per 1,000 (1996) **Calorie consumption:** 105 % (1988/90) 671 **people per doctor** (1988/91) **Safe water:** 68 % (1990/96).

EDUCATION
Literacy: 90 % (1995) male : 92 % (1995) female: 88 % (1995) **School enrolment :** Primary total: 123 % (1990/95) male: 124 % (1990/95) female: 122 % (1990/95) Secondary: male: 54 % (1990/95) female: 56 % (1990/95) **Primary school teachers:** one for every 26 students (1995).

COMMUNICATIONS
70 **newspapers,** 327 **radios,** 130 **TV sets** and 59 **main telephone lines** per 1,000 people (1994).

ECONOMY
Per capita, GNP: $ 1,500 (1996) **Annual growth, GNP:** 1.2 % (1995/96) **Annual inflation:** 45.52 % (1985/95) **Consumer price index:** 424.4 (1994) **Currency:** 2,924 sucres = $ 1 (1995) **Cereal imports:** 486 metric tons (1994) **Food import dependency:** 5 % (1994) **Fertilizer use:** 545 kgs per ha (1994) **Exports:** $ 4,762 million (1996) **Imports:** $ 3,733 million (1996) **External debt:** $ 14,491 million (1996) $ 1,239 **per capita:** (1996) **Debt service:** 22.6 % of exports (1996) Development aid received: $ 235 million (1995) $ 21 per capita (1995) 1.5 % of GNP (1994).

ENERGY
Consumption: 565.15 Kgs of Oil equivalent per capita yearly (1994) -231.34 % imported (1994).

HDI (rank / value) 72 / 0.775 (1994)

---

[16] From the time Borja took office, his government was confronted by high rates of inflation and a disastrous economic situation. Compounding a foreign debt of $11 billion, was a fiscal deficit equalling 17 per cent of the GDP, negative monetary reserves of $330 million, and nearly 15 per cent unemployment.

[17] In 1990, the increase in international oil prices, accounting for 54 per cent of the country's exports, economic reform and the drastic limitation of public spending contributed to a mild economic recovery. The GDP rose 1.5 per cent, and inflation fell, as did the country's balance of payments deficit; however, real wages declined. The foreign debt burden clearly had a negative effect upon Ecuador's economic recovery.

[18] Under Borja, important gains were made on the domestic front: the Taura Commandos, who had kidnapped Febres Cordero in January 1987, were deactivated and the guerrilla movement Alfaro Vive ("Alfaro Lives") was integrated into the political mainstream.

[19] On the international scene, under Borja, Ecuador participated actively in the different groups involved in subregional integration. In addition, it supported the Group of Eight, which replaced the Contadora Group (charged with mediating the Central American political crisis). In addition, it was a member of the Rio Group, it rejoined the Movement of Non-Aligned Countries, and became the site of numerous high-level international meetings and forums.

[20] In May 1990, the presidents of Bolivia, Colombia, Peru and Venezuela agreed to begin eliminating tariff barriers between their countries as of January 1 1992, as a first step toward the creation of an Andean Common Market by 1995. In addition, the Andean leaders underscored the importance of collective cooperation with the United States in the war against drugs.

[21] On May 28 1990, a group of indians from the coast took over Santo Domingo Church in Quito, demanding that they be allowed to own land and that their human rights be respected. Shortly thereafter, several highways were closed by other indigenous groups from the highlands and the eastern part of the country.

[22] Dozens of middle-sized cities in the Andean region were symbolically taken over by tens of thousands of indigenous peoples from neighboring villages. Subsequently, native peoples from the Amazon region marched on Quito. In the ensuing police action, one person was killed and several injured, although the large-scale

violence which had marked previous incidents was avoided.

23 In the June 1990 legislative election, President Borja's party was badly defeated, with the winning share going to the conservatives, represented by the Social Christian Party, and the left, by the Socialist Party.

24 On May 28 1991, more than a thousand indians peacefully occupied the assembly room of the National Congress, demanding amnesty for some thousand indians who had been tried in connection with the 1990 uprising.

25 In the April 1992 elections, the Social Christian Party and the United Republican Party were the most successful participants. They obtained 19 and 13 of the 77 seats in Congress, respectively. The ex-president Febres Cordero was elected mayor of Guayaquil with 70 per cent of the returned votes. The turnout for the election was 73 per cent, six points higher than traditional level. None of the presidential candidates managed to achieve 50 per cent of the vote, so the election went to a second round between the two most popular nominees. In the second ballot on July 5, Sixto Durán Ballén of the PUR gained 56 per cent of the vote over Jaime Nebot of the PSC who achieved 43 per cent.

26 The left-of-center and the left contributed to the electoral victory of Sixto Durán, considered the "lesser of two evils", when compared with Nebot's authoritarianism.

27 The new Government proposed a program based on the "modernization of the State", including a plan for privatizing state enterprises and a rigorous structural adjustment plan. This meant eliminating subsidies, increasing or floating the prices of basic goods (including gasoline and other hydrocarbon derivatives) and keeping wage adjustments below the accumulated inflation rate.

28 After a year in office, Vice-President Dahik, considered the real power behind the throne, proclaimed the Government's adjustment policies to be a success. They had achieved a 60 per cent reduction of inflation in 1992 and 32 per cent in 1993, an increase in monetary reserves and a reduction of the fiscal deficit, especially in the public sector, and reduction of public spending to a mere 26 per cent of the GDP in 1993.

29 The opposition, the Confederation of Indigenous Nationalities of Ecuador (CONAIE) and the United Workers' Front (FUT) questioned these policies, citing increased poverty and unemployment, and the total absence of social policies. In actual fact, the mean urban

wage had continued to fall being worth only a fifth of the average 1980 value in 1993.

30 The main conflict stemmed from privatization of the social security system, electricity, telecommunications and oil. The opposition was strengthened by the creation of a National Sovereignty Defense alliance, bringing together strategic labor unions, CONAIE and other social organizations.

31 The legislative package authorizing the privatizations underwent several modifications. The attitude of the Social Christian Party, the main parliamentary force, proved decisive. Although the Party was ideologically in favor of privatization policies, it had to operate with an eye on its electoral prospects for 1996, so the Government proposals were eventually passed in much reduced versions to avoid having to pay a high political cost.

32 Throughout this period the Government committed a number of faux pas, including the Ingenio Azucarero Aztra (a sugar mill) and Ecuatoriana de Aviación (the national airline) scandals. Both of these companies were allowed to go bankrupt before the privatization process began.

33 The damage to the Government was extensive. In the May 1994 elections, the PUR did not obtain a single parliamentary seat, and the Conservative Party only won 6 of a total 77. Together, they obtained less than 10 per cent of the vote. The main beneficiary was the Social Christian Party, with 22 deputies, 25 per cent of the vote, and a candidate, Jaime Nebot, was the main contender for presidential succession.

34 The two left and left-of-center parties, the Democratic Left and Christian Democrats suffered serious setbacks, winning fewer than 15 legislative seats and 15 per cent of the vote. The surprise element was the increase in strength of the MPD - a party with a strong base in the educational sector - and the triumph in Quito of General Frank Vargas Pazzos, whose platform was marked by strong nationalism.

35 Meanwhile, the economy went through a period of deep recession. The PBI and exports decreased, specially banana exports, due to the restrictions of the European Community. The building industry and oil exports were the exceptions. The Government gave new licences for oil prospecting and planned the building of an oil pipeline. The measure was heavily criticised by the opposition, worried, so they said, about the possible exhaustion of the deposits.

36 In April 1994, a fire broke out on Isabela, one of the Galapagos islands, and destroyed 6,000 hectares of land and endangered the life and habitat of giant turtles. This led to a decree which restricted local tourism, immigration and illegal fishing. However, only in January 1998 did the country ban industrial fishing in the area as a way to protect the archipelago's fragile ecosystem.

37 In June 1994, President Durán Ballén reversed the land reform carried out in 1964 and 1973, which had put an end to large haciendas and, for the first time, turned land over to indigenous peoples and small-scale farmers. CONAIE reacted to the legislation by blocking roads in a number of cities and towns. The Government declared the state of emergency and sent the army to control the situation. Forty eight per cent of rural lands belonged to peasant communities, mostly indigenous, and 41 per cent belonged to individuals.

38 In early 1995, new armed struggles took place with Peru in the Condor mountain range. The border had never been precisely set in the area, which is thought to contain gold, uranium and oil reserves. Durán Ballén declared once again a state of emergency and, in spite of international mediation, the conflict caused dozens of victims, especially among the Peruvian army.

39 Late that year, many ministers were questioned by Congress for embezzling state funds. This led to the arrest of several ministers and the flight from the country of Vice-President Alberto Dahík.

40 After harsh debate, Congress passed the sale of 35 per cent of the telecommunications state company. The Government had been determined to arrange this first major privatization before ending its term in August 1996.

41 Populist Abdalá Bucaram won the elections with 54 per cent of the vote over his rival from the Social Christian Party, Jaime Nebot, who obtained 46 per cent. His first government task was to appease the fears of business and finance circles, worried about the fulfillment of his electoral promises to the poorer sectors of the population. Meanwhile, press stories which predicted a military coup in the event of Bucaram's

electoral victory turned out to be without foundation.

42 During a meeting held in September 1996 with his Chilean counterpart Eduardo Frei, Bucaram stated his admiration for the social welfare and housing system in Chile. At the same time, he invited the controversial former economy minister of Argentina, Domingo Cavallo, to join his government team.

43 The fiscal adjustment package imposed by the Government complicated Bucaram's situation. The labor movement called for a national strike day on February 5, 1997 and Bucaram responded by saying the initiative was just and had the Government's support. This unexpected political move did not stop the fall of the President's popularity, in part due to strong price increases: 1,000 per cent in telephone rates, 300 per cent in electricity, 245 per cent in gas and 60 per cent in urban transportation.

44 Parliament declared the president "insane" and did not recognize his authority, through a measure not included among its powers by the Constitution. After three days of uncertainty, with the coexistence of three presidents, Fabián Alarcón obtained the support of Parliament and the military to become president.

45 In late May, a plebiscite gave full support to president Alarcón and confirmed the legitimacy of his presidency with 65 per cent of the vote, against 28 per cent. Meanwhile, a National Assembly elected by universal suffrage was called to modify the Constitution.

46 The Supreme Court of Quito accused Bucaram of corruption and ordered his arrest. The former president, exiled in Panama, was sentenced in December to a two-year prison term for slander.

47 The National Assembly elected on November 29 1997, started to write a new constitution. The opposition's Social Christian Party obtained a majority of seats, with a campaign based on descentralization, the fight against corruption and the need for dramatic economic reforms. Members of indigenous organizations demanded the recognition of the country's multi-ethnic and multicultural status in the new constitution.

Tahuantinsuyo: the Inca empire

The Tahuantinsuyo or Inca empire had a brilliant, if brief, life - its evolution being interrupted by the Spanish invasion of 1532, at a time when it was weakened by in-fighting. The empire once covered almost all of the Andes region.

The beginning of Tahuantinsuyo is estimated around the year 1300, its expansion around 1450 and its end in 1532. Its founders, probably emigrants from lake Titicaca led tribes from the Cuzco valley in order to unify all of the Andes region. If we refer to current political divisions, Tahuantinsuyo included a small part of southern Colombia, the high plateau and desert coast of Peru, the high plateau of Bolivia, northwest Argentina and all of the dry north and fertile lands of central Chile up to the Maule river.

The empire covered two major areas: the mountains or high plateau, where Tahuantinsuyo was founded, and the tropical, marshy and humid coast of Ecuador, as well as the deserted and rainless coast of Peru and Chile. The Inkas failed to conquer the jungle.

Two north-south roads were the backbone of communications. The first, along the coast, measured 4,050 kilometers and the second, through the mountains, 5,180 kilometers. Estimates of the Empire's population vary. Most experts calculate it at between 10 and 16 million. Recent research has placed the figure at over 12 million inhabitants, which would give a population density of 13 inhabitants per square kilometer. By comparison, population density in the Roman Empire's Asian provinces under Augustus amounted to 30 per sq km and to 10 in the European provinces.

Some experts claim Tahuantinsuyo had organized armies of 200,000 to 300,000 soldiers, which does not seem far-fetched if we accept the 13 million population figure. The Roman empire had an army of 300,000 in the late second century.

Qozqo, the centre of the world

Like other great empires, the Inkas built upon knowledge acquired from previous cultures, such as the Chavin, Tiahuanaco-Huari, Nazca, Moche and Chimu. The Inkas also stood out for their political and military efficiency, as well as their economic planning and social control. Cuzco (Qozqo to its founders), the capital of the Empire, had a population of 200,000 in 1532. At the time, only London and Naples in Europe were larger. Antwerp, Amsterdam, Lisbon, Rome and Seville had around 100,000 inhabitants each.

Located in an Andean valley blessed with fertile land and a beautiful landscape, Cuzco was specially developed to become a capital. With an area of some six square kilometers, the city had the shape of a puma, a sacred animal for the Inkas. As centre of the empire, Cuzco was thought of as the intersection point of a sundial - Antisuyo was called the northeast quadrant, Contisuyo the southwest, Collasuyo the southeast and Chinchaysuyo the northwest, according to a tetragonal model.

A solar calendar was followed, which dictated agriculture and religious ceremonies, and which provided a mythical chronology.

It was believed history was ruled by a pattern of four pasts, each one with its own creation and a sudden violent end. The fifth age belonged to the time of Tahuantinsuyo and would also end in cosmic extermination.

Social structure

The social structure of Tahuantinsuyo resembled a pyramid, with multiple rigid classes. Mobility from one class to another was exceptional and individual status was preordained. There were three distinct social classes.

The aristocracy included a reigning family group and descendants of monarchs, the clergy, military bosses, intellectuals and senior officials. At the summit was the Sapainka, Son of the Sun.

The middle class, the Jatunrunakuna, was a large mass of inhabitants which helped to support the state apparatus. Lastly, the Yanakuna, compared by some with Roman plebeians, who were relegated to menial jobs.

The monarch was not a mere autocrat, but a type of high priest and father, who had to conduct himself according to a code set down by tradition.

There were nine kinds of crimes: of status, high treason, against religion, against the administration and official duties, against taxes and property, and against life and health. Three principles were to be followed by everyone to prevent such crimes: *ama suwa*, *ama qella* and *ama llulla* (do not be a thief, a liar, or idle).

Everywhere, the empire was strictly organized. The population was ordered into communities (ayllus) according to the decimal system, ranging from smaller to larger units. Labour was divided into age categories, from childhood to old age, with an additional division for the disabled.

A truly American achievement

Capital was accumulated, mainly in the form of agricultural products, and its concentration enabled it to be used for social purposes. The system was based on the surplus production of the community.

The state and religious organization were maintained by this surplus. Planning was a key feature of the state.

One-third of arable land was allocated for religious purposes, another to the monarch and the rest to the community. The use of the land was distributed once a year among the members of the ayllu.

Artisanal production also had a significant role. The most important skills were weaving, metallurgy, pottery and woodcarving. State, communal and private property co-existed in a unique way.

Western observers have classified Tahuantinsuyo in different ways: primitive communist, socialist, totalitarianist, collectivist, paternalist, a softer version of oriental despotism, a mix of theocracy, monarchy and socialism, and so on.

However, a close analysis shows that the Inka empire did not fit in with Old World paradigms because, although certain features were similar on the surface to those European contexts, it did not wholly resemble any of them.

In spite of its short existence and of the efforts to underrate it, Tahuantinsuyo was a vast and original achievement of the South American peoples, and has earned its place amongst the major human cultures.

Egypt

Misr

Population:	63,271,000 (1996)
Area:	1,001,449 SQ KM
Capital:	Cairo (Al-Qahirah)
Currency:	Pounds
Language:	Arabic

Six thousand years ago, the inhabitants of the Nile valley, Nahr-an Nil, formed a civilization that eventually developed into a centralized state. While struggling to control the periodic flooding of the Nile, the Egyptians built the pyramids and created a culture which was used as an inspiration for the later "western civilization". They succeeded in feeding a large population for such a small area of land, and became a busy center of economic, diplomatic and cultural relations. In the last millennium BC, during the decline of this remarkable civilization, the country was ruled by Libyan and Sudanese Pharaohs and then directly by the Assyrian, Persian, Greek and Roman empires.

[2] During the period of Greco-Roman domination, Alexandria (Al-Iskandariyah) was one of the most influential cultural centers in the classical world, and its famous library was the largest in existence until it was burned down under the Roman emperor Aurelian in the late 3rd century AD. It brought together the most outstanding philosophers, scientists and scholars of the era. In 642, when the Arabs conquered the country, little remained of its highly developed past and the Egyptians adopted Islam and the Arabian language.

[3] Three centuries later, under the government of the Fatimid Caliphs, the new capital, Cairo (Al-Qahirah), became one of the major intellectual centres in the Islamic world and scholars, particularly African Muslims, were attracted by its university.

[4] Between the 10th and 15th centuries, Egypt benefited from its geographic location, becoming the trade center between Asia and the Mediterranean. The Venetians and Genoese came to trade here, and even the constant warfare provoked by the European Crusades in Palestine, in the 11th to 13th centuries, did not stop active trade.

[5] Once the Crusaders were driven out, it seemed that Egypt would naturally become the center of the ancient Arab empire. However the Sultanate of the Ottoman Turks was the rising power in the Islamic world at the beginning of the 16th century, and it soon conquered Egypt. The opening of the sea route between Europe and the Far East had already put an end to Egypt's previous trade monopoly, reliant on its dominion over the Red Sea, and Egypt had begun its economic decline.

[6] Until the 19th century, Turkish domination was little more than nominal and the real power lay in the hands of Mameluke leaders. In 1805, Muhammad Ali, an Albanian military leader, took power. He forcibly eliminated local Mameluke leaders, established a centralized regime, reorganized the army, declared a state monopoly on foreign trade of sugar cane and cotton and achieved increasing autonomy from the Sultan of Istanbul laying the foundations of a modern economy.

[7] The economy was poorly managed by Muhammad Ali's successors, the crisis deepened and dependency on Europe increased. In 1874, Egypt was forced to sell all its shares in the Suez Canal, built as a joint Egyptian-French project between 1860 and 1870, to pay its debts to the British.

[8] The situation continued to deteriorate, loans piled up and in 1879 the creditors imposed a Bureau of Public Debt formed by three ministers, one English, one French and one Egyptian. This bureau assumed the management of the country's finances.

[9] This degree of interference awakened an intense nationalistic reaction, supported by the army. That year, the military overthrew Muhammad Ali's successor Khedive Ismail, forcing his son, Tawfiq, to expel the foreign ministers and appoint a nationalist cabinet. The colonial power reacted promptly: in 1882 an Anglo-French fleet landed English troops in Alexandria, seizing military control of the country.

[10] The occupation was "legalized" in 1914, when Egypt was formally declared a protectorate. This situation continued until 1922, when an Egyptian committee negotiated independence in London. This independence was negotiated in such a way that the resulting conditions really meant the continuation of the protectorate.

[11] During World War II, Egypt was used as a British military base again. Anticolonial feeling reached its height in 1948, when the state of Israel was created in Palestine.

[12] Egypt and other Arab nations launched an unsuccessful war against the new state, and the frustration of defeat brought about massive demonstrations against the royal government.

[13] Against a background of widespread government corruption, a nationalist group known as the "Free Officials" was formed within the Egyptian Army, led by General Mohammed Naguib and Colonel Gamal Abdel Nasser.

[14] On July 23 1952 this group ousted King Faruk and, in June 1953, proclaimed a Republic. Three years later, Nasser became President.

[15] The new regime declared itself nationalist and socialist, deciding to improve the living conditions of the fellahin, the country's impoverished peasants. Land reform was started, limiting the landowners' monopoly of the majority of the land.

[16] Nasser gave priority to the construction of the Aswan dam, one of the world's largest dam projects. The construction was carried out by the Soviet Union, after the western powers had refused to take it on. The dam, which had been hailed as the key to the country's industrialization and "development", in fact caused serious environmental disruption.

[17] In 1955, Nasser was one of the leading organizers of the Bandung Conference, a forerunner of the neutralist Afro-Asian movement which preceded the Movement of Non-Aligned Countries. Twenty-nine Afro-Asian countries condemned colonialism, racial discrimination and nuclear armament.

[18] In October 1956, after the nationalization of the Suez Canal,

PUBLIC EXPENDITURE

8.7% **39.1%**
1995 ■ DEFENCE □ SOCIAL

In **1990/91** Military as % of health & education expenditure was 52%.

Foreign Trade

MILLIONS $ 1996

IMPORTS
13,020

EXPORTS
3,534

Food Dependency

1970
23%

1994
22%

PROFILE

ENVIRONMENT
99 per cent of the population live in the Nile valley and the delta although this constitutes only 30 per cent of the land. The remaining land is covered by deserts except for a few isolated oases. The floods of the Nile set a pattern for the country's economic life thousands of years ago. There are several dams, the major one being the Aswan dam in the south. This has enabled farmers to add new crops such as cotton and sugar cane to the traditional crops; wheat, rice and corn. The hydroelectric power supply, together with the northeastern oil wells, in the Sinai Peninsula, favored industrial development and the disproportionate growth of the cities. Problems which remain unsolved include the unchecked growth of the cities, which has swallowed up fertile lands; erosion of the soil and the use of fertilizers; and water pollution.

SOCIETY
Peoples: Egyptians are Arabs of Hamite origin with East Asian communities in the north and central regions and African groups in the Upper Nile area.
Religions: Muslim, majority Sunni. There is a 10 per cent Coptic minority and other smaller Christian groups.
Languages: Arabic (official), English and French in business, Nubian and Oromo in daily use.
Political Parties: Liberal Party (LP), National Democratic Party (NDP); the New Delegation - Wafd - Party (NWP); National Union Progressive party (NPUP); Nasserist Party; the Muslim Brotherhood; Al Wasat.
Social Organizations: The Egyptian Labor Federation is the only central labor organization, and the Union of Egyptian Students represents the university students.

THE STATE
Official Name: Jumhuriyah Misr al-'Arabiyah.
Administrative divisions: 26 provinces.
Capital: Cairo (Al-Qahirah), 8,900,000 people (1995).
Other cities: Alexandria (Al-Iskandariyah) 3,382,000 people; El Giza (Al-Jizah), 2,144,000 (1994).
Government: Hosni Mubarak, President since 1991. Kamal al-Ganzouri, Prime Minister since January 1996. The Majlis (single-chamber legislature) has 454 members, of which 10 are named by the President.
National Holiday: July 23, Revolution Day (1952).
Armed Forces: 440,000 (incl. 270,000 conscripts).
Other: Coast Guard, National Guard and Border Guards, 74,000.

French, British and Israeli troops invaded Egypt. The Government responded by distributing weapons to civilians. A diplomatic battle was also launched; as a result of UN intervention and joint US-Soviet disapproval, France, Britain and Israel were forced to withdraw and the Canal finally came under Egyptian control.

[19] On February 1 1958, the union of Egypt and Syria was officially announced, under the name of the United Arab Republic (UAR). This lasted until September 1961, when Syria decided to separate from Egypt, although Egypt continued to call itself the United Arab Republic.

[20] After Nasser's re-election in 1965, Egypt gave high priority to the conflict with Israel. However, its attempt to economically paralyze Israel by blockading the Gulf of Aqaba failed during the Arab-Israeli conflict, the "Six-Day War" of June 1967. This ended in another defeat of the Arab countries - Egypt, Syria and Jordan - when Israeli forces occupied the Sinai Peninsula, the Gaza strip, the West Bank, and the Syrian Golan Heights. The cost of the war aggravated Egypt's financial problems and only Soviet aid prevented its total collapse.

[21] Nasser died in 1970, and Vice-President Anwar Sadat, a member of the right wing of Nasser's Arab Socialist Party, took his place. Sadat put the *infitah* into practice. This was a government plan which meant an opening to western influence, the de-nationalization of the Egyptian economy and the end of the single-party system. Furthermore, the new Government broke off relations with the Soviet Union and US economic and military aid flowed into Egypt.

[22] In 1973, Egyptian troops crossed the Suez Canal, beginning the fourth Arab-Israeli war. The

Egyptians were not defeated, and their success resulted in OPEC substantially increasing oil prices. This move did not produce the desired effect, and Israel retained the rest of the occupied territories.

[23] Substantial price rises and unemployment worsened the living conditions of workers and resulted in massive anti-government demonstrations in 1976 and 1977. Peasants rebelled against the land redistribution of 1952, and the Islamic parties began to conspire openly against Sadat, accusing him of paving the road for a new period of foreign domination.

[24] Sadat's visit to Jerusalem in November 1977 raised a wave of protest in the Arab world. The process of rapprochement with Israel reached its apex in March 1979, with the signing of the Camp David Agreement, wherein the US negotiated the return of Sinai to Egypt. From then on, Egypt became the main beneficiary of US military aid, aimed at turning the country into the new US watchdog in the Arab World, as Shah Pahlevi of Iran had recently been deposed.

[25] In October 1981, Sadat was killed in a conspiracy organized by certain sectors of the military opposed to infitah and the repression of fundamentalist Islamic movements. Vice-President Hosni Mubarak became President on October 14.

[26] Repression, corruption and increasing poverty led to widespread popular discontent. To distract public attention Mubarak ordered an inquiry into the wealth accumulated by the Sadat family. He also extended further concessions to foreign companies.

[27] There were some improvements in Egyptian foreign affairs during 1984. Egyptian diplomacy managed to overcome the most adverse reactions to the Camp David agreements. Their new position on the Palestinian question argued that any fair settlement of the Middle East crisis had to contemplate the rights of the Palestinian people and that Arab solidarity was "the only way to recover the usurped rights".

[28] From early 1985 the economic situation became more

difficult as revenues from the four economic pillars: oil, emigrants' repatriated pay, canal fees and tourism shrank considerably. Islamic Fundamentalism was very powerful in opposition and became increasingly so as the Government's popularity plummeted.

[29] Between 1980 and 1986 there was a dramatic increase in the role of foreign capital in the national economy and US aid continued to be a very important source of income. The Government received almost $3 billion per year, $1.3 billion of which was spent on defence. The IMF granted a further $1.5 billion loan in October 1986.

[30] The Egyptian foreign debt went from $2.4 billion in 1970 to $35 billion in 1986; the figure for military aid alone multiplying seven times. Military expenditure and losses caused by war had understandably negative effects upon the economy.

[31] Parliamentary elections, originally scheduled for 1989, were called two years early, and

in April 1987 the National Democratic Party (NDP) was elected with 75 per cent of the vote.

[32] In September 1989, in the United Nations General Assembly, Mubarak, representing contact between the Arab countries and the United States, proposed arranging an Israeli-Palestinian dialogue, with no prior conditions. In October of that year relations with Libya were renewed.

[33] In the 1980s, Egyptian emigration to the Gulf countries reached very high levels. In some villages in the province of Sohag, in Upper Egypt, up to 60 per cent of the men left their homes, mainly to seek work in Kuwait and Lybia. This situation, which continues today, has forced Egyptian women to take sole responsibility for their families, generating conflict and tension between the mothers and their children. Emigrants manage to earn large amounts, but at the expense of weakening the links with and unity of their families.

WORKERS

(1996)

Labour force %
- ■ WOMEN
- □ MEN

29%   71%

PER CAPITA
$496

51%

STATISTICS

DEMOGRAPHY
Population: 63,271,000 (1996) **Annual growth:** 2.3 % (1980/1996) **Estimates for year 2000:** 68,100,000 **Annual growth to year 2000:** 1.9 % (1994/2000) **Urban Population:** 44.8 % (1996) **Urban growth:** 2.48 % (1980/95) **Children per woman:** 3.5 (1996).

HEALTH
Life expectancy at birth: 65 years (1996) male: 63 years (1994) female: 66 years (1994) **Infant mortality:** 57 per 1,000 (1996) **Under-5 child mortality:** 78 per 1,000 (1996) **Calorie consumption:** 132 % (1988/90) **Safe water:** 87 % (1990/96).

EDUCATION
Literacy: 51 % (1995) male : 64 % (1995) female: 39 % (1995) **School enrolment :** Primary total: 98 % (1990/95) male : 105 % (1990/95) female: 91 % (1990/95) Secondary: male : 82 % (1990/95) female: 71 % (1990/95) Tertiary: 18 % (1995) **Primary school teachers:** one for every 24 students (1995).

COMMUNICATIONS
60 **newspapers,** 307 **radios,** 90 **TV sets** and 43 **main telephone lines** per 1,000 people (1994) **Books:** 5 new titles per 100,000 people (1992/94).

ECONOMY
Per capita, GNP: $ 1,080 (1996) **Annual growth, GNP:** 3.5 % (1995/96) **Annual inflation:** 15.67 % (1985/95) **Consumer price index:** 164.9 (1994) **Currency:** 3.39 pounds = $ 1 (1995) **Cereal imports:** 9,200 metric tons (1994) **Food import dependency:** 22 % (1994) **Fertilizer use:** 2,432 kgs per ha (1994) **Exports:** $ 3,534 million (1996) **Imports:** $ 13,020 million (1996) **External debt:** $ 31,407 million (1996) $ 496 **per capita:** (1996) **Debt service:** 11.6 % of exports (1996) Development aid received: $ 2,017 million (1995) $ 35 per capita (1995) 4.8 % of GNP (1994).

ENERGY
Consumption: 599.78 Kgs of Oil equivalent per capita yearly (1994) -78.83 % imported (1994)

HDI (rank / value) 109 / 0.614 (1994)

[34] In August 1990 Iraqi troops invaded Kuwait; Egypt was among the first Arab countries to condemn the action, sending troops to the Gulf immediately.
[35] When the land offensive started in January 1991, the US announced the cancellation of the Egyptian military debt, which amounted to $7 billion.
[36] Egypt's alignment with the West in the war against Iraq was not supported by the majority of the country's population. In February 1991 a demonstration to end the hostilities and seek a peaceful solution to the war in the Persian Gulf was staged in Cairo.
[37] There was great opposition to war against Iraq, despite the fact that Iraqi president Saddam Hussein had expelled nearly two million migrant workers from Iraq and Kuwait during the two previous years, and had attempted to forcibly recruit Egyptians to the army.
[38] In 1990, the foreign debt reached a record $40 billion. Per capita income averaged some $600 per year, with over a third of the population living below the poverty line.
[39] In May 1991, the IMF approved a stand-by loan of $372 million to Egypt, conditional on an economic "structural adjustment plan". Cairo committed itself to privatizing State-run companies, to eliminating controls on production and investment and to reducing the current fiscal deficit from 21 per cent to 6.5 per cent of the GNP. In order to achieve these goals the government decided to cut back subsidies on food and other staples and to reduce the program of aid for the needy.
[40] On May 15 1991, foreign minister and deputy minister Esmat Abdel Meguid was named the new secretary general of the Arab League. Coming upon the heels of the return of Arab League headquarters to Cairo (from Tunis) this appointment signified Egypt's recovery of its leadership role within the Arab world.
[41] The escalation of violence from Islamic fundamentalists led the Government to enact an anti-terrorist law and extend for another three years the state of emergency which had been in effect for the past ten years. According to official statistics, this violence caused 175 deaths between February 1992 and August 1993. Thousands of Islamic followers were arrested and in June and July 1993, 15 people were executed.
[42] The Government continued its economic liberalization policies by facilitating foreign banks' operations. In March 1993, the IMF supported a privatization plan with the cancellation of $3 billion in foreign debt. In October, after being re-elected in a plebiscite, Mubarak continued his iron hand policy with Islamic fundamentalists. However, attempts against the lives of foreign tourists multiplied in 1994.
[43] In April, lawyers' associations denounced the suspicious death in a police station of an Islamic activists' defender. After a week of demonstrations the movement concluded with a general strike which revealed the influence had by Islamic fundamentalists among lawyers' associations. In October, the number of dead reached 460 since March 1992 when the rebellion of Islamic fundamentalists against Mubarak began.
[44] In May, the President formed a committee to organize political talks between the Government and opposition with the exclusion of communists, the Muslim Brotherhood and groups representing the Coptic minority. Simultaneously, relations with the IMF were hampered due to an alleged government slowness in implementing the planned economic liberalization.
[45] In the international sphere, Egypt recovered its main role in the Middle East peace talks and in political exchanges between Arab countries. This was shown by a meeting held in Alexandria in December with the participation of leaders from Egypt, Saudi Arabia and Syria. In February 1995, a summit joined leaders in El Cairo from Egypt, Jordan, Israel and Palestine.
[46] In 1995, Mubarak was unable to find a solution to the confrontation with Islamic fundamentalists. In January, secretary al-Alfi attended a meeting of Arab countries' interior ministers to attempt to coordinate the fight against violent Islamic movements.
[47] In November, the ruling National Democratic Party won the parliamentary elections with the participation of all the parties acknowledged by the Government. Elections, held amid a violent atmosphere, granted 416 of the 444 seats at stake to the ruling party which provoked several accusations of fraud. In January 1996, Mubarak appointed Kamal al-Ganzouri as Prime Minister, replacing Atef Sedki.
[48] In July, the former health minister banned female circumcision - the removal of the clitoris, or part of it and, in some cases, the labia of the vagina - a practice common in some regions of the country.
[49] Attacks by the armed Islamic fundamentalist groups continued throughout 1996 and 1997, along with government repression of all these factions, even those like the Muslim Brotherhood who were opposed to the use of violence. In November 1997, a group of 17 fundamentalists killed 60 foreign tourists in Luxor, partly aiming to stem the growth of tourism. Income from the sector was estimated to have increased to $3 billion in the last year.
[50] In early 1998, there were an estimated 1,251 victims of political attacks and murders, while the number of political prisoners stood at somewhere between 10,000 and 30,000, depending on the source.

El Salvador

El Salvador

Population:	5,796,000 (1996)
Area:	21,041 SQ KM
Capital:	San Salvador
Currency:	Colón
Language:	Spanish

The region of El Salvador was inhabited from early times by Chibcha people (muisca; see Colombia), most of whom were Pipile and Lenca. The Maya also lived within the region, but they were not very influential here.

[2] The Spaniards subdued the Aztecs in Mexico, and subsequently began the conquest of Central America under the leadership of Pedro de Alvarado. In 1525, Alvarado founded the city of El Salvador de Cuscatlan. The territory formed part of the Captaincy-General of Guatemala, a dependency of the Viceroyalty of Mexico. Central America became independent from Spain in 1821 and organized itself into a federation.

[3] In 1827, internal rivalries between "imperialists" and "republicans" led to civil war. In 1839, General Francisco Morazan, president of the Central American Republic, tried to prevent the break-up of the federation. From El Salvador, Morazan struggled to preserve the union with the support of some Nonulco natives, headed by Anastasio Aquino. Morazan was defeated in 1840 and sent into exile, and Anastasio Aquino was arrested and executed.

[4] When the federation was dissolved, Britain took advantage of the situation dominating the isthmus. In 1848, President Doroteo Vasconcelos refused to bow under British pressure, and the British blockaded Salvadoran ports. Over the last three decades of the 19th century, the US began to push the British out.

[5] At the end of the century, the invention of artificial coloring destroyed the demand for indigo, El Salvador's principal export product, and its price fell to rock bottom.

Indigo was replaced with coffee. Coffee required larger and more extensive farming areas, and the Liberal Revolution of 1880 drove thousands of peasants from their communal lands, forming a rural working class and a countryside full of anger and conflict. The coffee plantation owners became the dominant oligarchy and the ruling class of El Salvador.

[6] The 1929 financial crash caused the coffee market to collapse, crops were left unharvested, and thousands of sharecroppers and poor peasants starved. This led to a mass uprising headed by the Communist Party of El Salvador and Farabundo Martí, a former secretary of Augusto C Sandino in his campaign against the US invasion of Nicaragua.

[7] The January 1932 rebellion was ruthlessly crushed, around 30,000 Salvadorans were massacred by the troops of General Maximiliano Hernández Martínez, who had taken power in 1931. This started a series of military regimes which lasted half a century. Twelve thousand people died as a consequence of the repression.

[8] In 1960, the Alliance for Progress sponsored an industrialization program, within the Central American Common Market. High economic growth rates were attained without reducing the rampant unemployment which had caused 300,000 landless peasants to emigrate to neighboring Honduras. Population growth and competition between the local industrial interests, led to war between El Salvador and Honduras in June 1969. The regional common market collapsed after the 100-hour conflict, severely damaging Salvadoran industry.

[9] In the early 1970s unions and other civilian movements took on new life. Guerrilla fighters appeared in El Salvador and the legal opposition parties joined into a national front; the UNO, formed by the Christian Democrats (PDC), the Communists (UDN) and the Social Democrats (MNR). Colonel Arturo Molina, presidential candidate for the official National Conciliation Party, defeated the UNO's candidate Napoleón Duarte in a fixed election in 1972.

[10] In 1977, another fraudulent election made General Carlos Humberto Romero president. Mass riots broke out in protest but social unrest was suppressed leaving 7,000 dead.

[11] The elimination of the legal political opposition encouraged the growth of guerrilla organizations who began to co-ordinate their armed action with the democratic opposition. In response, the US State Department, afraid of a repeat of the Nicaraguan situation, supported a coup by reformist military officers.

[12] On October 15 1979, a civilian/military junta seized power. It included representatives of the Social Democracy and the Christian Democracy. The Junta lacked real power and had no control over the ruthless repression campaigns carried out by police and military forces. Civilian members resigned and were replaced by right-wing Christian Democrats from Duarte's party.

[13] On March 24 1980, the Archbishop of San Salvador, Monsignor Oscar A Romero, was assassinated while performing mass in a clear reprisal for his constant defence of human rights. The leading guerrilla organizations, democratic parties and mass organizations united under the policy of a common program of "popular revolutionary democracy".

[14] In October 1980, the five anti-regime political-military organizations agreed to form the Farabundo Martí Front for National Liberation (FMLN). On January 10 1981 the FMLN launched a "general offensive" throughout most of the country. However, the Front was unable to seize power.

[15] In August 1981, the Mexican and French governments signed a joint agreement recognizing the FMLN and the Democratic Revolutionary Front (FDR) as "a representative political force".

[16] The US administration, led by President Ronald Reagan, saw the situation in El Salvador as a national security issue. The US became directly involved in the political and social conflict, and was the military and economic mainstay of the "counter-insurgency" war which the Salvadoran Army was unsuccessfully waging.

PUBLIC EXPENDITURE

5.2% **37.2%**
1995 ■ **DEFENCE** □ **SOCIAL**

In 1990/91 Military as % of health & education expenditure was 129%.

WORKERS

UNEMPLOYMENT 7.7% (1996)

Labour force %

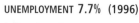

■ WOMEN
□ MEN
35% **65%**

■ AGRICULTURE **36%** (1990)
□ INDUSTRIAL **21%**
■ SERVICES **43%**

LAND USE

DEFORESTATION **-2.1%** annual (81/90)
IRRIGATED **21.2%** of arable

(1993)

■ FOREST & WOODLAND **4.9%**
□ ARABLE **26.9%**
■ OTHER **68.2%**

PROFILE

ENVIRONMENT

It is the smallest and most densely populated country in Central America. A chain of volcanos runs across the country from east to west and the altitude makes the climate mild. Coffee is the main cash crop in the highlands. Subsistence crops such as corn, beans and rice are also grown. Along the Pacific Coast, where the weather is warmer, there are sugar cane plantations. It is the country with the greatest problems of deforestation in Latin America.

SOCIETY

Peoples: 89 per cent of the Salvadoran population are mixed descendants of American natives and Spanish colonizers, 10 per cent are indigenous peoples, and 1 per cent are European.
Religions: Mainly Catholic (75 per cent), Protestant, Mormon, Jehovah's Witness.
Languages: Spanish is the official and predominant language. Indigenous minority groups speak Nahuatl.
Political Parties: The Nationalist Republican Alliance (ARENA); the Christian Democratic Party; the left-wing Democratic Convergence, the Party of National Reconciliation (PCN). The Farabundo Marti; National Liberation Front (FMLN), founded in October 1980, is made up of five political-military organizations; the Farabundo Marti; People's Liberation Forces (FPL), the El Salvador Communist Party (PCS), the National Resistance Armed Forces (FARN), the People's Revolutionary Army (ERP) and the Central American Workers' Revolutionary Party (PRTC).
Social Organizations: the National Union of Salvadoran Workers (UNTS), the United Union and Guild Movement (USIGES) and the National Confederation against Hunger and Repression (CNHR) created in 1988.

THE STATE

Official Name: República de El Salvador. **Administrative division**: 14 Departments. **Capital**: San Salvador, 422,600 people; 1,522,100 metropolitan area (1992). **Other cities**: Soyapango 251,800 people; Santa Ana 202,300; San Miguel, 182,800; Mejicanos 145,000 (1992). **Government**: Armando Calderon Sol, President since May 1994. **National Holiday**: September 15, Independence Day (1821). **Armed Forces**: 30,700 troops (1994). **Other**: National Civilian Police, made up of former guerrillas, soldiers and police.

External Debt
1996

PER CAPITA
$**499**

Literacy
1995

72%

[17] On March 28 1982, as instructed by Washington, the regime held an election for a Constituent Assembly. In response, the rebels launched an offensive ending in a one-week siege of Usulatán, a provincial capital.
[18] After continuous internal tussling for power, the presidency of the constitutional convention went to Roberto D'Aubuisson, the main leader of the ultra-right Nationalist Republican Alliance (ARENA) and the power behind the assassination of Monsignor Romero.
[19] Against a background of an upsurge in fighting, general elections were held on March 25 1984. These were boycotted by the FDR-FMLN; the abstention rate by voters was 51 per cent. Ostensibly supported by the US, the PDC - led by Napoleon Duarte - obtained 43 per cent of the vote, against the 30 per cent won by ultra-right candidate Major Roberto D'Aubuisson.
[20] The extreme right parties disputed the election, but quick responses from the Minister of Defence and the High Command, in support of Duarte, quashed any further reaction. It was the first time that the armed forces had publicly supported the reformists. The only contacts between the two parties took place in La Palma and Ayagualo, in 1984.
[21] In October 1986, a strong earthquake brought about a virtual cease-fire, which eventually led to the renewal of negotiations in October 1987. These talks took place within the new framework of regional peace making. The Central American governments had signed the Esquipulas agreements in August 1987, agreeing to strive for peace.
[22] Between 1987 and 1989, the US supported the Duarte administration's search for a political solution to the conflict with the FDR-FMLN. Internal disputes, and pressure from the ultra-right-wing sectors and the armed forces, blocked such a solution.
[23] Elections were held in October 1989; these were boycotted by some of the guerrillas, but civilian sectors of the FDR (members of the social democratic and Social Christian parties) participated, with Guillermo Ungo as their presidential candidate. Alfredo Cristiani, the ARENA (right-wing) party's candidate, won the election.
[24] In November 1989, the FMLN launched an offensive occupying several areas of the capital and surrounding regions. The Government responded by bombing several densely populated areas of the capital. Six Jesuits, including the rector of the University of Central America, Ignacio Ellacuria, were tortured and killed by heavily armed soldiers. This provoked a world-wide outcry, especially from the Catholic Church, and American economic aid was threatened.
[25] According to the El Salvador Human Rights Commission, a non-governmental organization, women, especially students and members of labor unions are the people who have suffered most from repression. During the last 12 years, the human rights movement has been led by mothers, wives, daughters and relatives of the thousands of victims of repression, and by the National Union of Salvadoran Workers (UNTS). It has challenged the harsh military regime and has denounced the continuous human rights violations.
[26] On March 10 1991, the legislative and local elections reflected a new spirit of negotiation. For the first time in 10 years the FMLN did not call for the boycott of the elections, instead they decreed a 3-day unilateral truce. Abstention was still above 50 per cent, and there were acts of paramilitary violence immediately prior to the polls. The voters narrowly elected the ruling party with 43 out of 84 seats. On March 12 the fighting resumed.
[27] In Mexico on April 4 1991 delegates of the Cristiani Government and the FMLN started negotiations for a cease fire agreement. On April 19, 10,000 demonstrators, from 70 social organizations, gathered in the Permanent Committee for National Debate (CPDN), demanding that the Constitution be reformed. This was two weeks before both the end of the parliamentary term and the deadline given by the FMLN for the signing of the peace agreement.
[28] On April 27, after several attempts, representatives of the Government and the Farabundo Marti Front signed the "Mexico Agreements" restricting the function of the Armed Forces to the defence of national sovereignty and territorial integrity. The formation of paramilitary groups was banned, and it was agreed to reform article 83 of the constitution to say that sovereignty "resides in the people, and that it is from the people that public power emerges". In New York , in June, another agreement was reached; the Salvadoran Government committed itself to dismantling the National Guard and the Rural Police (Policia de Hacienda), replacing it with Civilian Police including FMLN-members.
[29] On November 16, new talks began in the UN headquarters. This time, the FMLN declared an indefinite unilateral truce until a new, definite, cease-fire was signed. Then, a Spanish parliamentary delegation wrote a report on the murders of the six Spanish Jesuits from the Central American University (UCA). The report, submitted to the Spanish, European, Salvadoran, and American parliaments, accused the Salvadoran government and the army of concealing evidence which could help to clarify the facts.
[30] On January 1 1992, after 21 weeks of negotiation and 12 years of civil war, both parties met in New York to sign agreements and covenants establishing peace in El Salvador. The war left 75,000 people dead, 8,000 missing, and nearly 1 million in exile. The two parties fixed a cessation of hostilities period from February 1 until October 3 1992, for all armed conflict to cease, and for an atmosphere to develop that would be propitious for the agreements to go into effect, and for UN and OAS-sponsored negotiations to continue.
[31] The final agreements were signed in the Mexican city of Chapultepec on January 16 1992. They include substantial modifications to the Constitution and to the structure, organization, regulation, and form of the Armed Forces. They guarantee to change rural land tenure and to alter the terms of employee participation in the privatization of State companies; they establish the creation of bodies for the protection of human rights, and guarantee the legal status of the FMLN.
[32] According to the peace accords the Government would have to reduce its troops by half by 1994, bringing the number down to

STATISTICS

DEMOGRAPHY
Population: 5,796,000 (1996) **Annual growth:** 1.5 % (1980/1996) **Estimates for year 2000:** 6,300,000 **Annual growth to year 2000:** 2.2 % (1994/2000) **Urban Population:** 45.3 % (1996) **Urban growth:** 1.95 % (1980/95) **Children per woman:** 3.2 (1996).

HEALTH
Life expectancy at birth: 69 years (1996) male: 66 years (1994) female: 73 years (1994) **Infant mortality:** 34 per 1,000 (1996) **Under-5 child mortality:** 40 per 1,000 (1996) **Calorie consumption:** 102 % (1988/90) 1,563 **people per doctor** (1988/91) **Safe water:** 69 % (1990/96).

EDUCATION
Literacy: 72 % (1995) male : 74 % (1995) female: 70 % (1995) **School enrolment :** Primary total: 79 % (1990/95) male : 79 % (1990/95) female: 80 % (1990/95) Secondary: male : 27 % (1990/95) female: 30 % (1990/95) Tertiary: 18 % (1995) **Primary school teachers:** one for every 28 students (1995).

COMMUNICATIONS
50 **newspapers,** 443 **radios,** 230 **TV sets** and 44 **main telephone lines** per 1,000 people (1994).

ECONOMY
Per capita, GNP: $ 1,700 (1996) **Annual growth, GNP:** 0 % (1995/96) **Annual inflation:** 14.87 % (1985/95) **Consumer price index:** 166.8 (1994) **Currency:** 8.76 colones = $ 1 (1995) **Cereal imports:** 448 metric tons (1994) **Food import dependency:** 11 % (1994) **Fertilizer use:** 1,324 kgs per ha (1994) **Exports:** $ 1,023 million (1996) **Imports:** $ 2,670 million (1996) **External debt:** $ 2,894 million (1996) $ 499 **per capita:** (1996) **Debt service:** 9.5% of exports (1996) **Development aid received:** $ 304 million (1995) $ 54 per capita (1995) 3.7 % of GNP (1994).

ENERGY
Consumption: 370.17 Kgs of Oil equivalent per capita yearly (1994) 70.07 % imported (1994)

HDI (rank / value) 112 / 0.592 (1994).

30,000; in addition, it would have to disband its intelligence service. As of March 3, a new civilian police would be created, made up in part by former members of the FMLN. In January 1992, according to the terms of the Law of National Reconciliation, amnesty was granted to all political prisoners.

[33] In addition, the Government pledged to turn over lands to the combatants and provide assistance to campesinos belonging to both bands. The FMLN became a political party as of April 30 1991, and held its first public meeting on February 1 1992. After years of being underground, it was presided over by guerrilla commanders Shafick Handal, Joaquin Villalobos, Fernan Cienfuegos, Francisco Jovel and Leonel Gonzalez; they called for the unification of all opposition forces for the 1994 elections.

[34] In early March 1992, the first implementation difficulties began to be seen. Several leaders of the National Union of Salvadoran Workers accused the government of violating the accords, and launching a propaganda campaign against grassroots organizations.

[35] On February 15 1993, the last 1,700 armed rebels turned over their weapons in a ceremony which was attended by several Central American heads of State and by UN Secretary-General Boutros Boutros-Ghali. The National Civil Police was created, as well as a Human Rights Defence Commission and a Supreme Electoral Court.

[36] The result of the investigation of human rights violations, carried out by the Truth Commission created by the UN, led to the resignation of Defence Minister General Rene Emilio Ponce, singled out in that investigation as being the one who ordered the assassination of six Jesuits at the University of San Salvador in 1989. According to the Commission's final document, the military, the death squads linked to these and the State were responsible for 85 per cent of the civil rights violations committed during the war.

[37] The Truth Commission recommended the dismissal of 102 military leaders and that some former guerrilla leaders be deprived of their political rights. President Cristiani proposed a general amnesty for cases where excesses had been committed; this proposal was approved on March 20 1993, only 5 days after the document drawn up by the Truth Commission had been made public.

With this measure, the most serious crimes committed during the war met with total impunity.

[38] A year later on March 20 1994, the first elections since the civil war were held. The candidate of the left coalition, Democratic Convergence - made up of the FMLN and other groups - won 25.5 per cent in the first round of voting, against 49.2 per cent for the right-wing candidate, Armando Calderón Sol, from the ARENA party. Although the Left declared the existence of fraud, UN observers in the country (ONUSAL) insisted that the voting had been fair. After the elections, the FMLN faced an internal crisis triggered by discrepancies between the groups that make up the alliance.

[39] According to ONUSAL, the peace accords did not bring an end to the violence. In addition to the existence of intelligence activities within the Armed Forces, members of the military were linked to organized crime. Likewise, the fact that nothing was done to create viable employment opportunities for discharged troops (from both bands) led to an increase in petty crime.

[40] The prisons were overflowing. Built for a total capacity of 3,000 prisoners, they were holding twice that number. In addition, the abominable prison conditions and the delays in bringing cases to trial generated discontent which vented itself in multiple prison riots, in which 70 people were killed and more than a hundred were injured.

[41] The long-promised award of land to demobilized fighters was slow and inefficient. By mid-1994, only one-third of the potential beneficiaries -12,000 of a total 37,000 former members of the army or the guerrillas - had obtained their plots. The rest remained inactive, living in substandard temporary housing and often drifting into organized crime.

[42] On the regional scene, Calderón Sol's administration intensified talks with neighboring Honduras, to resolve long-standing border disputes.

[43] The Government managed to raise the country's annual economic growth to 5 per cent, although 29 per cent of the population live in poverty and 15 per cent of children under 5 years old showed signs of malnutrition, according to official figures.

[44] According to official studies, 90 per cent of El Salvador's vegetation was depleted, two-thirds of the land was deeply eroded and subjected to inadequate agricultural techniques and a mere 2 per cent of the virgin forests remaied intact. Also, 90 per cent of the rivers were polluted by sewage and chemical

waste and more than half the population drinked untreated water.

[45] An agreement between ARENA and the Democratic Party - split from the FMLN - concluded on May 1995 enabled a 3 per cent rise of the valued added tax from 10 to 13 per cent. This raise was explained on the need to collect funds to finance land reform, infrastructure works and reconstruction of the country's electoral and judicial apparatus.

[46] The National Civilian Police was unable to control criminal bands which, according to the local press, committed an average of one crime per hour. The Government sent 5,000 troops to bolster the patrol of roads and rural areas. Three police agents were sentenced for belonging to the paramilitary organization "Black Shadow". Military raids also revealed a sophisticated arsenal belonging to the organization "The Benedictines", whose leader was supposedly linked to a Central American network of criminal organizations.

[47] A UN mission in charge of monitoring the enforcement of agreements between the guerrilla and the Government operated in the country from April to October. In August 1996, demonstrators who considered themselves affected by the slowness of the process, which included the transfer of plots of land and payment of retribution to war veterans, occupied streets and government buildings in downtown San Salvador. In May, the Democratic Party withdrew from its deal with ARENA, which left the Government without a parliamentary majority.

[48] In March 1997, the opposition's FMLN obtained an important victory in municipal elections, after winning in the capital and dozens of provincial cities. In Parliament, ARENA, with 33.3 per cent of the vote, won 28 seats while FMLN with 32.1 per cent ended up with 27 deputies. Electoral turnout amounted to just 40 per cent of those eligible to vote.

[49] In December the Supreme Court ordered businessman Orlando de Sola, who had been removed by the Government, to be reinstated as Electricity and Communications Superintendent. The Court considered the dismissal - decided after a disagreement between president Calderón and de Sola regarding the sale of a television channel - had been arranged in an arbitrary and unlawful way.

[50] A study by the Interamerican Development Bank, issued in March 1998, estimated that 25 per cent of El Salvador's potential economic growth was lost every year due to political and criminal violence.

Equatorial Guinea

Guinea Equatorial

Population: 410,000 (1996)
Area: 28,051 SQ KM
Capital: Malabo

Currency: CFA Francs
Language: English

Around the 13th century, Fang and Ndowe people settled in the Rio Muni area, south of Gabon, subduing the Bayele pygmy population, who now only exist in a few isolated groups. From the continental coast, these nations expanded onto the nearby islands which were described as "densely populated" in the 15th century. In the colonial division of Africa, the Rio Muni area and the islands received the name of Equatorial Guinea.

[2] he Ndowe became allies and intermediaries of Portuguese, Spanish, Dutch and English slave traders. The Fang, whose social organization did not include slavery, withdrew into the forests, convinced that the Europeans were cannibals.

[3] The kings of Portugal, proclaiming themselves the lords of Guinea, ceded the entire "District of Biafra" to Spain under the treaties of San Ildefonso and Pardo in 1777 and 1778, in exchange for Spanish territory in southern Brazil. In 1778, an expedition sailed out from Montevideo to occupy the islands. They lost their commanding officer, Argelejos, in a battle against the Annoboneuses, and the survivors, under their new leader, Lieutenant Primo de Rivera, turned back. The French and British gradually took over sections of the territory, with the British finally occupying it, founding the first settlements. They used it as a base for their conquest of Nigeria and turned the freed slaves, or "Fernandinos", into their agents, creating a ruling group that, in many aspects, still exists today.

[4] Between 1843 and 1858, the District was militarily reconquered by Spain, re-establishing their "rights" over the area. At that time, economic activity centred on cacao, coffee

WORKERS

■ AGRICULTURE	75%	(1990)
□ INDUSTRIAL	5%	
▤ SERVICES	20%	

and timber, but the territory was ineffectively controlled from a distance. The Spanish colonists, led by Fernando Po, supported Franco in the 1936 civil war and were later granted almost full powers over the archipelago. Admiral Carrero Blanco, Franco's prime minister, owned the colony's largest cocoa plantations.

[5] In 1963, the colony obtained a degree of internal autonomy, and three legal political organizations were formed: MONALIGE (the Equatorial Guinean National Liberation Movement), MUNGE (the Equatorial Guinean National Unity Movement), and IPGE (the Equatorial Guinean Popular Ideal). Mounting international pressure forced Spain to grant the colony independence and this was officially proclaimed on October 12, 1968.

[6] Francisco Macías Nguema assumed the presidency with the support of Atanasio Ndongo, of MONALIGE and Edmundo Bosio, leader of the Bubi Union of Fernando Po. He headed a coalition government formed by IPGE and sizeable dissident groups from MUNGE and MONALIGE; movements that had emerged during the struggle for independence.

[7] Within a year, on the pretext of foiling an alleged coup attempt, Macías began a violent campaign to eliminate the opposition killing thousands of political prisoners, murdering opponents, causing disappearances and exiling 160,000 people. Amnesty International reported that two thirds of the National Assembly had mysteriously vanished.

[8] Proceeding with the repression, Macías Nguema dissolved all political parties, and created the Sole Traditional Workers' Party (PUNT), proclaiming himself president for life and "grand master of popular education, science and culture". His reign of terror was kept going by the "Youth on the March with Macías" organization, who extended persecution to Catholic priests and Protestant missionaries.

[9] In August 1979, the rule of Macías Nguema ended in a coup led by his nephew, Lieutenant-Colonel Teodoro Obiang Mba Nzago. Macías was arrested, tried

and executed for crimes against humanity.

[10] Persecution, indiscriminate arrests and corruption were soon rampant, reminiscent of the previous regime. In August 1982, legislative elections were held but the list of candidates was drawn up by the official party. The National Alliance for the Recovery of Democracy formed in exile, sought to negotiate with Obiang but accomplished little.

[11] A coup attempt in June 1986 sparked off another wave of arrests. Among those detained was the deputy prime minister, Fructuoso Mba Onana.

[12] In September 1984, Obiang joined the Customs and Economic Union of Central Africa (UDEAC), linking the Ekwele (the national currency) to the central banks of the region. Stronger ties with the West resulted in a drastic reduction of facilities offered by the Soviet Union and East Germany. The US, France and Spain dominated the economy, controlling the extraction of oil, iron ore and lumber. Meanwhile, Morocco sent troops to guarantee the stability of the new government.

[13] Teodoro Obiang was re-elected in June 1988 and he continued to apply IMF prescriptions, thus obtaining a $16 million loan to improve public investments, restructure the banking system, and accelerate growth. At a meeting of international loan agencies in November 1988, the regime obtained additional loans of $58 million to be spread over three years.

[14] Obiang's visit to France in September 1988 produced closer ties between the two countries, and Equatorial Guinea later called for the integration of all French-speaking countries. At the same time, he obtained an amnesty for two-thirds of his country's foreign debt to Spain.

[15] There was no easing of the repression. Two members of the armed forces were executed in September 1988 on the charge of conspiring against the Government. Around the same time, an opposition leader, José Luis Jones, was arrested on his return to the country, and condemned to a 17-year prison term. He was eventually pardoned.

[16] In June 1989, Obiang was re-elected in elections where the

PER 100,000
LIVE BIRTHS
820

79%

PROFILE

ENVIRONMENT
The country consists of mainland territory on the Gulf of Guinea (Rio Muni, 26,017 sq km) and the islands of Bioko (formerly Fernando Po, and Macias Nguema) and Pigalu (formerly Annobon, Corisco, Greater Elobey and Lesser Elobey). The islands are of volcanic origin and extremely fertile; Rio Muni is a coastal plain covered with tropical rain-forests but without natural harbors. It is one of the most humid and rainy countries of the world, a characteristic which limits the variety of possible crops.

SOCIETY
Peoples: The population is mostly of Bantu origin. In the islands there are also Ibo and Efik peoples who migrated from Nigeria, subduing the local Bubi population. In Rio Muni the inhabitants are mainly Fang and Ndowe. Nearly all of the Europeans and a third of the local population emigrated during the Macías regime.
Religions: Mainly Christian on the islands; traditional African beliefs in Rio Muni.
Languages: Spanish is the official and predominant language. In Rio Muni, Fang is also spoken, and on the islands, Bubi, Ibo and English.
Political Parties: Democratic Party for Equatorial Guinea (PDGE), Joint Opposition Platform, Movement for the Self-Determination of Bioko.

THE STATE
Official Name: República de Guinea Ecuatorial.
Administrative divisions: 4 continental and 3 island regions.
Capital: Malabo, 30,000 people in 1983.
Other cities: Bata, 24,300 people (1983).
Government: Teodoro Obiang Mba Nzago, President since August 25 1979.
National Holiday: October 12, Independence Day (1968).
Armed Forces: 1,300.

STATISTICS

DEMOGRAPHY
Population: 410,000 (1996) **Annual growth:** 4 % (1980/1996) **Estimates for year 2000:** 500,000 **Annual growth to year 2000:** 2.5 % (1994/2000) **Urban Population:** 43.4 % (1996) **Children per woman:** 5.6 (1996).

HEALTH
Life expectancy at birth: 49 years (1996) male: 47 years (1994) female: 50 years (1994) **Infant mortality:** 111 per 1,000 (1996) **Under-5 child mortality:** 173 per 1,000 (1996) **Safe water:** 95% (1990/96).

EDUCATION
Literacy: 79 % (1995) male : 90 % (1995) female: 68 % (1995) **School enrolment :** Primary total: 149 % (1990/95).

COMMUNICATIONS
424 **radios**, 90 **TV sets** and 6 **main telephone lines** per 1,000 people (1994).

ECONOMY
Currency: 490 CFA francs = $ 1 (1995) **Cereal imports:** 9 metric tons (1994) **Food import dependency:** 13 % (1994) **Development aid received:** $ 33 million (1995) $ 85 per capita (1995) 20.5 % of GNP (1994).

HDI (rank / value) 135 / 0.462 (1994)

Democratic Party for Equatorial Guinea was the only legal party. After election the same political line continued to be applied.
[17] In early 1991, the Democratic Co-ordination of Opposition Parties (DCOP) was founded in Gabon and in May, Feliciano Moto, one of the main opposition leaders, was assassinated.
[18] In early 1992, the Government declared a general amnesty. The political parties law banned those based on "tribal, regional or provincial" grounds, demanding the payment of 158,000 dollars as a legalisation fee; furthermore, presidential candidates were obliged to have ten years residence in the country, thus ruling out all those who had lived in exile.
[19] Despite the obstacles, ten political parties were legalized in early 1993. During this period the UN issued a report denouncing the systematic violation of the

basic liberties of opposition politicians.
[20] At the same time, the UN accused the Obiang Government of involvement in the failed attack on US ambassador John Bennett, after the US State Department had criticized the nation for illegal imprisonment, torture and intimidation.
[21] In March, the Government and the Joint Opposition Platform (a coalition of ten legalized parties, formed in November 1992) signed the National Democratic Pact including a clause stating all political prisoners would be freed at the end of the month.
[22] The transparency of the legislative elections toward the end of 1993 was thrown into doubt by international observers. According to official results, the governing Democratic Party took 68 of the 80 seats in play. The expulsion of the Spanish consul-general from the city of Bata, in

January 1994, prompted Spain to reduce the amount of aid granted to Equatorial Guinea by half.
[23] In March 1995, Severo Moto, leader of the opposition Progressive Party, was sentenced to two and a half years in prison for allegedly bribing a police officer and for having "damaged the reputation" of Obiang. In April, Moto was sentenced again - this time to 28 years in prison for treason and conspiracy - earning disapproval from the Western countries, especially Spain.
[24] In July, several members of the Movement for the Self-Determination of Bioko, one of the islands belonging to Equatorial Guinea, were arrested. The Government set the presidential elections for early 1996 amidst accusations of arbitrary arrests and torture. In February the same year, just before the elections, the Government dissolved the Joint Opposition Platform and arrested several of its members. On February 25, Obiang won a

victory - described as a "farce" by the opposition - with 99 per cent of the vote.
[25] Amnesty received many complaints over arrests for political reasons, torture and murder, where the victims included Catholic priests and soldiers accused of conspiring against the Government.
[26] In January 1998 security forces arrested hundreds of members of the Bubi ethnic group on the island of Bioko. They were accused of having attacked military installations and of belonging to the Movement for the Self-Determination of Bioko. According to Amnesty, they were arrested only on ethnic grounds.
[27] Angel Serafin Seriche Dougan, Obiang's Prime Minister, resigned from his post in early 1998 as had been planned at the beginning of his term and the President formed a new cabinet.

Eritrea

Eritrea

Population:	3,280,000 (1996)
Area:	117,600 SQ KM
Capital:	Asmara
Currency:	Nafka
Language:	Tigrinya

As the site of the most important ports of the Aksumite empire (flourished 4th-6th century AD), Eritrea was linked to the beginnings of the Ethiopian kingdom, but it retained much of its independence until it fell under Ottoman rule in the 16th century. From the 17th to the 19th century control over the territory was disputed among Ethiopia, the Ottomans, the kingdom of Tigray, Egypt, and Italy. In 1890, the treaty of Wichale between Italy and Menilek II of Ethiopia recognized Italian possessions on the Red Sea, and the colony, created on January 1 1890, was named by the Italians for the Mare Erythraeum ("Red Sea" in Latin) of the Romans.

2   Eritrea was used as the main base for the Italian invasions of Ethiopia (1896 and 1935-36) and it became one of the six provinces of Italian East Africa. In 1941 the area came under British administration and remained so until Eritrea was federated as an autonomous unit to Ethiopia in 1952.

3   The common struggle against the Italians had brought a reasonable degree of unity to almost one million Eritreans. On December 2 1950, United Nations Resolution 390A declared that Eritrea should become a federated state within the Ethiopian Empire. The resolution rejected Ethiopian demands for outright incorporation, but also left the process of Eritrean self-determination undefined.

4   In Eritrea, a national assembly was elected which enjoyed some autonomy until 1962, when Haile Selassie forced a group of Eritrean congressmen to vote for its complete incorporation into Ethiopia. The decision was contested by nationalist groups and immediately sparked a rebellion.

5   The Eritrean Liberation Front (ELF) began guerrilla activities in September 1961. In 1966, a split produced the Eritrean Popular Liberation Front (EFPL). In 1974, with Sudanese mediation, the two groups agreed to coordinate their actions and in the next few years, the EFPL imposed its leadership upon the rebel movement.

6   In February 1990, the EFPL captured the port of Massewa, and nearly all of the Eritrean territory. The rebels entered Asmara on May 25, and the port of Aseb on the following day. The highway from Aseb to Addis-Ababa is the only land supply route to the Ethiopian capital.

7   At the end of May, the EFPL announced the formation of a Provisional Government, and in July, in the Ethiopian capital, an agreement was reached to hold a UN supervised referendum within a two-year period.

8   From 1991, Asmara and Addis-Ababa started State to State relations. The Red Sea ports were reopened allowing international aid to enter. The rains also reappeared in Eritrea, ending two years of drought.

9   In a plebiscite in April 1993, 99.8 per cent of the voters were in favour of independence. The EPLF, already the de facto government, formed a provisional government led by Isaias Afwerki, charged with drawing up a new Constitution within four years and calling multiparty elections. In this year Eritrea joined the UN.

10   In February 1994, the EPLF held its third congress and became a political party, the Peoples Front for Democracy and Justice (PFDJ). Meanwhile, Eritrea joined the IMF.

11   In December 1994, deteriorating relations with Sudan obstructed the repatriation of 500,000 refugees. In October 1995, Afwerki declared his government would supply arms to any group prepared to overthrow the Khartoum regime.

12   In 1996, a project aiming to give land to foreign investors was obstructed by ownership disputes. That year, restrictions continued on the formation of opposition parties. The Government controlled the media and restricted press freedoms.

13   In late 1997, Eritrea abandoned the common currency and introduced the *nafka*, to replace the Ethiopian *birr*. As a counter measure, Ethiopia announced trade between the two nations should be carried out exclusively in US dollars.

14   The Government could not meet the political transition schedule and postponed the multiparty elections announced for 1997. Territorial disputes worsened with the neighbouring Djibouti and Yemen. Against a backdrop of extreme poverty, tourism, mainly on the islands and coral reefs, gained greater importance as a source of hard currency.

WORKERS

(1996)

Labour force %

■ WOMEN	
□ MEN	
47	53

■ AGRICULTURE 80% (1990)
□ INDUSTRIAL   5%
■ SERVICES   15%

PROFILE

ENVIRONMENT
Eritrea is in the horn of Africa. The northeast coast, all 1,000 km of it, is bordered by the Red Sea; to the northeast lies Sudan; to the south, Ethiopia and to the southeast, Djibouti. The dry plains and extremely hot desert steppes are inhabited by pastoralists. Deforestation and the consequent erosion are partly responsible for the frequent droughts.

SOCIETY
Peoples: The nine ethnic groups are the Tigrinya, Tigre, Bilen, Afar, Saho, Kunama, Nara, Hidareb and Rashaida. The majority are pastoralists or farmers; 20 per cent are urban workers. Half a million Eritrean refugees live in Sudan, 40,000 in Europe and 14,000 in the US.
Religions: Almost half of all Eritreans are Coptic Christians; most of the rest are Muslim, although there are Catholic and Protestant minorities.
Languages: Tigrinya and at least nine local languages.
Political Parties: People's Front for Democracy and Justice (former Eritrean People's Liberation Front).

THE STATE
Capital: Asmara, 400,000 people (1992).
Other cities: Asseb 50,000 people; Keren 40,000; Massaua (Mesewa) 80,000 (1996).
Government: Parliamentary Republic. Isaias Afwerki, President since 1993.
National holiday: May 24, Independence (1993).

Estonia

Eesti

Population: 1,471,000 (1996)
Area: 45,100 SQ KM
Capital: Tallinn

Currency: Krona
Language: Estonian

Despite historical and political links with their southern neighbors, Lithuania and Latvia, the Estonian people have always been known for their spiritual and cultural independence. Belonging to a branch of the Finno-Ugric nations, Estonians have greater cultural and linguistic ties with the Finns to the north than with the Indo-European Balts to the south.

[2] The region was settled some 6,000 years ago. Around the year 400 AD, the semi-nomadic peoples' hunting and fishing activity began to be replaced by agriculture and cattle raising. At the same time, navigation and trade with neighboring countries along the Baltic Sea intensified. In the 11th and 12th centuries, combined Estonian forces successfully repelled Russia's attempts to invade the territory.

[3] The Germans, Russians and Danes, invading Estonia in the 13th century, found a federation of states with a high level of social development and a strong sense of independence, keeping them united against foreign conquerors.

[4] In the 13th century, the Knights of the Sword, a Germanic order which was created during the Crusades, conquered the southern part of Estonia and the north of Latvia, creating the kingdom of Livonia and converting the inhabitants to Christianity. German traders and landowners brought the Protestant Reformation to Estonia in the first half of the 16th century.

[5] The northern part of Estonia remained under Danish control. Livonia was much disputed between 1558 and 1583; it was repeatedly attacked by Russia before being dismembered in 1561. Poland conquered Livonia in 1569; a hundred years later, it ceded the major part of the kingdom to Sweden. In the Nordic Wars (1700-1721), Russia took Livonia away from Sweden, and kept these lands under the Treaty of Nystad.

[6] Russia received the Polish part of Livonia in 1772, with the first partition of Poland. The former kingdom of Livonia became a Russian province in 1783. Power was shared between the czar of Russia and local German nobles, who owned most of the lands and the peasants lived in serfdom.

[7] The abolition of serfdom in Russia and peasant land ownership rights (1804), strengthened the Estonian national consciousness. During the second half of the 19th century, the Society of Estonian Literati developed the written language, and the preservation of national folklore, enabling the people to withstand the czar's Russification campaigns.

[8] In 1904, Estonian nationalists seized control of Tallinn, ousting the German-Baltic rulers. After the fall of the czar in February 1917, a demonstration by 40,000 Estonians in Petrograd forced the Provisional Government to grant them autonomy, maintained even after the Bolshevik Revolution.

[9] In November 1917, with the election of a constituent assembly, the Estonian Bolsheviks only obtained 35.5 per cent of the votes. On February 24 1918, Estonia declared its independence from the Soviet Union and set up a provisional government. The following day, German troops occupied Tallinn and the Estonian government was forced to go into exile.

[10] After World War I, the Estonians successfully fought both the Red Army and the Germans. On February 2 1920, the Soviet Union recognized Estonia's independence.

[11] Estonia, Latvia and Lithuania, joined the League of Nations in 1921. Following the Swiss model, the Estonian constitution established a parliamentary democracy. The Government began the reconstruction of the country and initiated agrarian reform. In the 1920s, Estonia established the world's first shale-oil distillery.

[12] Estonia passed legislation guaranteeing the rights of minorities, and ensuring that all ethnic groups had access to schools in their own languages. The economic depression of the 1930s led to a modification of the Estonian constitution; in 1933, it became a virtual dictatorship before adopting a presidential-parliamentary system in 1937.

[13] The secret protocols of the Molotov-Ribbentrop pact, signed in 1939 determined that Estonia - like its two Baltic neighbors - would remain within the Soviet sphere of influence. At the same time, Tallinn signed a mutual assistance treaty with Moscow giving the USSR the right to install naval bases on Estonian soil.

[14] In June 1940, after demanding the right for his troops to enter Estonian territory under the pretext of searching for missing soldiers, Stalin deposed the Tallinn Government and replaced it with members of the local Communist Party. Elections were held during the Soviet occupation, after which the Communist Party seized power.

[15] Following the examples of Latvia and Lithuania, the new Government adopted the name "Soviet Socialist Republic of Estonia", joining the USSR. According to the official record, all three Baltic States voluntarily became a part of the USSR. In 1941, around 60,000 Estonians were deported to Siberia.

[16] When the German offensive against the USSR began in 1941, Nazi troops invaded Estonia, establishing a reign of terror which was especially directed against Jews, gypsies and Estonian nationalists. The USSR recovered the Baltic States in 1944; Estonian groups began pro-independence guerrilla activity, but had little impact against Soviet military might.

[17] Industrialization was established by the Soviet regime, and collective farming was forced upon the national population. Some 80,000 Estonians emigrated to the West, while Russian colonization gradually altered the traditional ethnic composition of the population. The history of Estonia was rewritten, and its national symbols replaced, with Russian language and culture replacing those of Estonia.

[18] Around 20,000 Estonians were deported between 1945 and 1946. The third wave of mass deportations took place in 1949, when another 40,000 Estonians were sent to the farthest regions of the USSR, most of them farmers who refused to accept collectivization of the land, imposed by Soviet authorities.

[19] In 1982-83, toward the end of the Brezhnev era, a number of underground publications appeared in Estonia, including The Democrat. In addition, several new movements emerged, including the Democratic Movement, the Estonian National Front and others; members of these movements were arrested and sent to forced labor camps.

[20] The reforms set in motion in 1985 by Soviet President, Mikhail Gorbachev stimulated social and political activity within Estonia. In August 1987, a demonstration in Tallinn demanded the publication of the Molotov-Ribbentrop pact. Latvians and Lithuanians also asked that the contents of the protocols be revealed.

[21] In January 1988, former Estonian political prisoners founded the Estonian Independence Party, defending the country's right to self-determination. In addition, this group called for the re-establishment of multiparty democracy, and the restoration of Estonian as the country's official language. Another group, the Estonian Heritage Society, began trying to locate and restore the country's historical monuments.

[22] The Popular Front of Estonia (FPE), founded in April by nationalists and communists, organized a rally in June 1988 which was attended by 150,000 people. The outlawed Estonian flag was displayed on this occasion. In September, some 300,000 Estonians held another rally; a few days later, the ban on the flag was lifted.

[23] In October, the first FPE congress reaffirmed Estonia's demand for autonomy, and asked Moscow for an admission of the fact that Estonia had been occupied against its will in 1940. The following month, Estonia's soviet (parliament) declared the country's sovereignty, and affirmed its right to veto laws

PROFILE

ENVIRONMENT
Located on the northeastern coast of the Baltic Sea, Estonia is bounded by the Gulf of Finland in the north, the Russian Federation in the east and Latvia in the south. The Estonian landscape - with its numerous lakes and river - bears witness to its glacial origin. There are more than 1,500 lakes, the largest of which are Lake Peipsi (Europe's fourth largest) and Lake Vorts. Forests make up 38 per cent of Estonia's territory; the highest elevation is Mount Suur Muna Magi (317 m). The climate is temperate, with average temperatures of 28° C in summer and around 0ºC in winter. The Baltic coast is 1,240 km long and includes a number of fjords. Some 1,500 islands close to the Baltic coast make up around one-tenth of Estonia's territory. The Gulf of Finland has numerous ice-free bays, of which Tallinn is the largest. Estonia's most important mineral resources are bituminous shale (which meets most of Estonia's energy needs), and phosphates. Estonia also has an important fishing industry, although its fleet has had to begin fishing far from its coastal waters due to the polluted state of the Baltic Sea, which contains toxic waste dumped by industries in several countries with Baltic coastlines. Neither Tallinn nor other minor cities have satisfactory sewerage systems.

SOCIETY
Peoples: Estonians, 64.2 per cent; Russians, 28.7 per cent; Ukranians, 2.6 per cent; Belarusians, 1.5 per cent Finnish, and others 3.3 per cent (1998). **Religions:** Lutheran (majority), Orthodox, Baptist. **Languages:** Estonian (official); Russian and others. **Political Parties:** Country Coalition Party; Royalist Party of Estonia; Rural Union of Estonia; Greens of Estonia; Citizen's Union of Estonia; Reform Party; Pro Patria Party.

THE STATE
Official Name: Eesti Vabariik. **Administrative divisions:** 15 districts and 6 cities. **Capital:** Tallinn, 443,000 people (1994). **Other cities:** Tartu, 106,000 people; Narva, 79,000; Kohtla-Jarve, 73,000; Pärnu, 52,000 (1994). **Government:**Parliamentary republic. Lennart Meri, President and Head of State since October 1992, reelected in 1996. Legislature: single-chamber assembly (*Riigikogu*), with 101 members, elected every 4 years. **National Holiday:** February 24, Independence (1918). **Armed Forces:** 2,500 (1993). **Other:** 2,000 (Coast Guard).

STATISTICS

DEMOGRAPHY
Population: 1,471,000 (1996) **Annual growth:** 0 % (1980/1996) **Estimates for year 2000:** 1,000,000 **Annual growth to year 2000:** -1 % (1994/2000) **Urban Population:** 73.2 % (1996) **Urban growth:** 0.42 % (1980/95) **Children per woman:** 1.4 (1996).

HEALTH
Life expectancy at birth: 69 years (1996) male: 63 years (1994) female: 75 years (1994) **Infant mortality:** 13 per 1,000 (1996) **Under-5 child mortality:** 16 per 1,000 (1996).

EDUCATION
Literacy: 98 % (1995) male : 98 % (1995) female: 98 % (1995) **School enrolment :** Primary total: 101 % (1990/95) male : 103 % (1990/95) female: 100 % (1990/95) Secondary: male : 92 % (1990/95) female: 90 % (1990/95) Tertiary: 38 % (1995) **Primary school teachers:** one for every 17 students (1995).

COMMUNICATION
240 **newspapers**, 467 **radios**, 360 **TV sets** and 252 **main telephone lines** per 1,000 people (1994) **Books:** 152 new titles per 100,000 people (1992/94).

ECONOMY
Per capita, GNP: $ 3,080 (1996) **Annual growth, GNP:** 5.2 % (1995/96) **Annual inflation:** 77.18 % (1985/95) **Consumer price index:** 9,960.0 (1994) **Currency:** 11.46 krona = $ 1 (1995) **Cereal imports:** 82 metric tons (1994) **Fertilizer use:** 361 kgs per ha (1994) **Exports:** $ 2,074 million (1996) **Imports:** $ 3,196 million (1996) **External debt:** $ 405 million (1996) $ 275 **per capita:** (1996) **Debt service:** 1.3 % of exports (1996).

ENERGY
Consumption: 3,709.13 Kgs of Oil equivalent per capita yearly (1994) 38.77 % imported (1994)

HDI (rank / value) 71 / 0.776 (1994)

---

imposed by Moscow without consent.

24 In August 1989, some two million Estonians, Latvians and Lithuanians formed a 560-km human chain from Tallinn to Vilnius to demand the independence of the Baltic States. In February 1990, a convention of Estonian representatives approved the Declaration of Independence, based on the 1920 Peace Treaty of Tartu between the Soviet Union and the newly independent Estonian republic.

25 In the May 1990 elections, the FPE and other nationalist groups won an ample majority within parliament. Moderate nationalist leader Edgar Savisaar was named as the leader of the first elected government since 1940. In August, parliament proclaimed the independence of Estonia, but Moscow did not consider it to be valid.

26 In late 1990-early 1991, Moscow threatened to impede Estonia's separation from the USSR, by force, and skirmishes took place between Soviet troops and nationalist groups. In September, the USSR recognized the independence of the three Baltic States, and that same month, they were admitted to the United Nations.

27 In January, Savisaar and his government resigned in the face of growing criticism over his economic policy. Parliament named former transportation minister Tiit Vahi to head the new government. Estonia has had to ration food and fuel ever since the Russian Federation began restricting and raising the price of its products.

28 The Russian Federation, which is Estonia's main trading partner and its chief supplier of fuel, began charging international prices for its exports of crude oil. At the same time, given the limitations on its own consumption, Russia reduced its wheat exports and its importation of clothing and electrical appliances from Estonia.

29 On June 20 1992, the new constitution (based on the 1938 Constitution) was ratified by referendum.

30 In September, the *Rligikogu* (parliament) of the 7th Legislature was elected. On October 7, it issued a declaration announcing the end of the transitional government, and re-invoking the constitution.

31 The following month, Estonia initiated negotiations with the Russian Government for the withdrawal of former Red Army troops. In addition, the Government has territorial claims over part of the Russian region of Pskov, with a land area of 2,000 sq km.

32 Lennart Meri, of the National Country Coalition Party, was elected president of Estonia by parliament on October 5 by 59 votes to 31.

33 In 1992, Estonia became the first Eastern European country to abandon the rouble, and create its own currency, the krona.

34 The privatization process came to a halt in December as a result of the resignation of the official in charge, who had been accused of negligence and fraud. In early 1993, privatizations resumed, although these basically entailed returning properties and goods confiscated during the Communist regime to their former owners.

35 In June, a blatantly nationalistic law was approved, aimed at foreigners, especially those of Russian origin who make up 39 per cent of the total population. The law obliges foreigners to apply for a discretionary residence permit.

36 Russian troops concluded their withdrawal from Estonia in August 1994 while Tallinn had an active participation in NATO's Partnership for Peace. On the domestic side, a former Communist Party leader, Indrek Toome, was arrested two months later charged with alleged corruption.

37 The March 1995 elections led to the defeat of the coalition which had ruled Estonia since the former Soviet republic broke away from the USSR. The new Prime Minister, Tiit Vahi, caused a controversy when he named a supposed "disproportionate" number of former communist ministers in his government. In October his cabinet was forced to resign due to corruption charges against the minister of the Interior. The new government was formed with the inclusion of Reform Party members.

38 On September 20 1996, after a close vote from the Electoral College, Lennart Meri was re-elected as President. A report from the European Bank for Reconstruction and Development - created to favour the transition of former Socialist countries toward a market economy - estimated on December 1997 that reforms carried out by Estonia in its financial sector, which led to the highest foreign investment per capita in the region, favoured its swift incorporation into the European Union.

39 In February 1998, Estonia, Latvia and Lithuania signed a Charter of Association with the United States, in which Washington vowed to support the entry of the three states into NATO. Immediately, Russia announced the normalization of relations with the Baltic nations, as long as they regularized the situation of the Russian-speaking minorities.

Ethipia

Yaitopya

Population: 58,243,000 (1996)
Area: 1,104,300 SQ KM
Capital: Addis Ababa (Adis-Abeba)

Currency: Birr
Language: Amharic

In ancient times, the Greek term "Ethiopian", meaning "burnt face" in Greek, was applied indiscriminately to all Africans. Ethiopia's other name, Abyssinia, came from the Arabic "Habbashat", which was the name of one of the groups that emigrated from Yemen to Africa around 2000 BC.

2 Axum, in the north of present-day Ethiopia, was the center of trade between the Upper Nile valley and the Red Sea ports which traded with Arabia and India. It reached its height in the first centuries AD. Ethiopia was a rich and prosperous state, which was able to subdue present-day Yemen, but which went through a crisis in the 7th century. Trade routes moved as Arab unification and expansion dominated the area, conquering Egypt. The Ethiopian ruling elite had converted to Christianity in the 4th century, further contributing to their isolation. Expansion towards the south, excessive growth of the clergy, and declining trade led to a process of social and economic stratification similar to that in feudal western Europe. By the 16th century, one third of the land belonged to the "king of kings"; another third belonged to the monasteries and the rest was divided among the nobility and the rest of the population.

3 The Muslim population that had developed a powerful trade economy on the coast of the Red Sea (see Tanzania: "The Zandj Culture of East Africa"), instigated an insurrection, leading Ethiopia to resume its relations with Europe to request assistance. The aid took almost a century to arrive, but the Portuguese fleet, when it finally arrived in 1541, was decisive in destroying the Sultanate of Adal (See Somalia).

4 For 150 years, Ethiopian emperors focused their efforts on the coast, giving the Galla (a nation akin to the Haussa) a chance to gradually penetrate from the west until they outnumbered the local population. Their influence grew so great that a Galla became emperor, between 1755 and 1769; though the Ahmara ruling elite took great pains to oust him.

5 This state of affairs continued until 1889 when Menelik II came to power. Designated heir to the throne in 1869, he spent the next 20 years training an army (with British and Italian assistance) and organizing the administration of his own territory, the state of Choa. His efficiency was fortunate; in 1895 his former allies, the Italians, invaded the country claiming that previous commitments had not been honoured. The final battle was fought in Adua in 1896 where, 4,000 of the 10,000 Italian soldiers were killed. It was the most devastating defeat suffered by European troops on African soil until the Algerian War. In the diplomatic negotiations that followed their defeat, the Italians succeeded in obtaining two territories that Ethiopia did not really control: Eritrea and the southern Somalian coast. In 1906, the world powers recognized the independence and territorial integrity of what was then known as Abyssinia, in exchange for certain economic privileges.

6 This arrangement saved Ethiopia from direct colonization until 1936, when Italian Fascist dictator Benito Mussolini invaded the country, taking advantage of internal strife among Menelik's would-be successors. Despite his pleas to the League of Nations, Haile Selassie, heir to the throne, got no concrete help. During the five-year occupation, several basic industries and coffee plantations were started, and a system of racial discrimination was installed, similar to that of apartheid in South Africa.

7 In 1948, Ethiopians won their autonomy back from Britain, which had taken over the country after Mussolini's defeat in 1941. When Selassie returned to the throne, his country was floundering in unprecedented crisis: foreign occupation had disrupted production; nationalist political movements had strengthened in the struggle for autonomy and rejected a return to feudalism; and poverty in the interior had grown considerably.

8 Selassie denounced colonialism, favored non-alignment and supported the creation of the Organization for African Unity, which finally set up headquarters in Addis-Ababa. He also maintained close links with Israel. On the domestic front, the crisis deepened as his government was dominated by a corrupt oligarchy and the Orthodox Church, which between them held 80 per cent of the country's fertile lands. The domestic crisis came to a head in 1956 when Eritrean separatist rebels intensified their attacks. In 1974, after a series of strikes, student rallies and widespread protests against absolutism and food shortages, Haile Selassie was overthrown.

9 In 1975, an Armed Forces Coordination Committee, the *Dergue* ("committee" in Amharic), headed by General Aman Andom abolished the monarchy and proclaimed a republic, suspending the Constitution and dissolving Parliament.

10 Popular movements became more radical, leading to a series of disputes among the military, and a subsequent crisis. Colonel Mengistu Haile Mariam rose to power in December 1977. He managed to hold the Dergue together and put an end to the military's internal struggles.

11 The military government managed to carry out agrarian reform and to nationalize foreign banks and heavy industry. US military bases were closed down. Right-wing groups carried out assassinations and bombings. Left-

WORKERS

(1996)

Labour force %
■ WOMEN
□ MEN

41   59

■ AGRICULTURE 86% (1990)
□ INDUSTRIAL 2%
■ SERVICES 12%

LAND USE

DEFORESTATION -0.3% annual (81/90)
IRRIGATED 1.6 % of arable

(1993)

■ FOREST & WOODLAND 22.7%
□ ARABLE 10.9%
■ OTHER 66.4%

wing organizations retaliated by killing conspirators and monarchists on sight. Between December 1977 and April 1978, the violence left over 5,000 people dead.

[12] Once the military crisis was resolved, a struggle broke out for the control of grassroots organizations. At first the Dergue supported the Pan-Ethiopian Socialist Movement (Meison), which set up neighbourhood committees (*kebeles*) as a basis for mass organization. The Meison grew stronger and proposed a system of self-controlled civilian units. This set them on a collision course with the Dergue, which rejected the creation of autonomous military groups.

[13] Mengistu declared the Meison illegal and backed the Revolutionary Flame, a group of officers and civilians who had studied in socialist Europe and were loyal to the president of the Dergue. After settling this latest crisis, the Government was able to confront the two separatist movements which had been gaining strength since 1977, in Eritrea and the Ogaden desert. The Eritrean rebels considered that their independence struggle was valid, regardless of the existence of a progressive government in Addis-Ababa, and the Somali population of the Ogaden desert (claimed by Somalia) took advantage of the domestic crisis in Addis-Ababa to further their own separatist cause.

[14] Mengistu rejected Eritrean separatist demands. He alleged that their struggle had only been reasonable when they had confronted the feudal monarchy, and not when they had opposed the pro-soviet regime.

[15] Faced with the Somalian intention of annexing the Ogaden, the Soviet Union broke its military treaties with Siad Barre. In this modern armed war, Soviet and Cuban support was decisive in his defeat. With the situation resolved on both battle fronts, Mengistu turned his attention back to domestic policy.

[16] In 1979 the Government set up the Ethiopian Workers' Party Organization Committee (COPWE), and their first general congress was held in 1980. In that year, there was a 15 per cent increase in cultivated land, which raised the GNP by 6 per cent.

[17] In 1984, the country was struggling under the effects of a prolonged drought which had begun in 1982, causing thousands

of deaths from starvation. The drought affected twelve provinces, threatened five million lives and killed over half a million people.

[18] The Ethiopian Workers' Party (PWE) held their founding congress in 1984, approving a program to transform the country into a socialist state.

[19] The newly-elected Assembly (the *Shengo,* or parliament) proclaimed the People's Democratic Republic of Ethiopia on September 12, ratifying Mengistu Haile Mariam as head of state. Separatists extended operations in Eritrea and Tigre, as well as in Wollo, Gondar and Oromo in the south.

[20] The new constitution provided for the creation of five autonomous regions and 25 administrative regions. Eritrea was able to legislate on all matters except defence, national security, foreign relations and its legal status in relation to central government. The separatists rejected the proposal, calling it "colonial".

[21] In December 1987, after a bloody battle, the Eritreans took Af Abed. 18,000 Ethiopian troops, three Soviet advisors and the army commander of the northern region were taken prisoner.

[22] The Tigre People's Liberation Front (Tigray) captured important cities like Wukro, a distribution center for international aid to drought victims. Building on these victories, the rebels from Eritrea and Tigre signed cooperation agreements and began to plan joint military strategies.

[23] Increased rebel activity took a heavy toll on the Ethiopian army and, in 1989, 12 divisions (150,000 troops) stationed in the front line attempted a coup. Mengistu returned hastily from West Germany and managed to abort the coup. He executed dozens of officers, among them Generals Amha Desta, airforce commander-in-chief, and Merrid Negusie, chief-of-staff of the armed forces.

[24] By the end of the 1980s, the war was consuming 60 per cent of Ethiopia's national budget, and agricultural production was slumping. In 1989, former US President Jimmy Carter's mediation brought together delegations from the Government and FPLE in Atlanta, in the US. The FPLE condensed its demands into one: a plebiscite for Eritrea's future. Mengistu refused.

[25] In September 1989, the last Cuban soldiers withdrew from Ethiopia. The Government had signed a peace agreement with Somalia in April 1988, and no longer needed their services.

[26] Ethiopia re-established contact with Israel, as relations had been interrupted after the 1973 war. Mengistu looked to Tel Aviv for

PROFILE

ENVIRONMENT
A mountainous country with altitudes of over 4,000 meters. Ethiopia is isolated from neighboring regions by its geography. In the North, the Eritrean plain, a desert steppe, extends alongside the Red Sea. In the mountains and plateaus, vegetation and climate vary with altitude. The Dega are cool, rainy highlands, above 2,500 meters, where grain is grown and cattle raised. The deep valleys which traverse the highlands are warm and rainy with tropical vegetation, known as the Kolla (up to 1,500 m). The drier, cooler, medium-range plateaus where coffee and cotton are grown,(1,500 to 2,500 m) are the most densely populated parts of the country. To the East lies the Ogaden, a semi-desert plateau inhabited by nomadic shepherds of Somali origin. Many regions which were once rich in vegetation are now rocky, desert areas. Desertification and erosion have increased within the past decade.

SOCIETY
Peoples: Two thirds are of Amhara or Oromo descent. There are many other ethnic groups including the Tigre, Gurage, Niloti, Somali and Danakil.
Religions: Most Ethiopians are Coptic Christians. Traditional African religions are also practiced.
Languages: Amharic; Arabic; and at least 100 local languages.
Political Parties: Ethiopian People's Revolutionary Democratic Front; All Amhara People's Organization; Oromo Liberation Front; Ogaden National Liberation Front.

THE STATE
Official Name: Federal Democratic Republic of Ethiopia.
Administrative Divisions: 25 Administrative Regions, 5 Regions.
Capital: Addis Ababa (Adis-Abeba), 2,209,000 people (1995).
Other city: Dire Dawa 117,700 people (1988).
Government: Negasso Gidada, President since August 1995; Meles Zenawi, Prime Minister since August 1995.
National Holidays: March 21, Proclamation of the Republic (1975).
Armed Forces: 120,000 (1995).

substantial military aid and facilities for 17,000 Ethiopian Jews to emigrate to Israel. Meanwhile, in Eritrea and Tigre, where the drought had reduced the grain harvest by nearly 80 per cent, the situation of millions steadily worsened. International agencies warned of the danger of yet another famine.

[27] In 1990, the Central Committee of the Ethiopian Workers' Party decided to restructure the party and change its name to the Democratic Ethiopian Unity Party (PDUE). While excluding the possibility of a multiparty system, the changes sought to lay the basis of "a party of all Ethiopians", open to "opposition groups". The Marxist-Leninist tag was dropped. The Government established a mixed economy, including state enterprises,

cooperatives and private businesses.

[28] Within one month, the former USSR withdrew its military advisors from Eritrea, and the FPLE took the port of Massawa, thus controlling all of Eritrea, except Asmara, which was totally cut off from the rest of Ethiopia by occupied land.

[29] In May 1991, Mengistu Mariam unexpectedly fled the country, overwhelmed by the repeated guerrilla victories in the north. The Government was left in the hands of Vice-President Tesfaye Gabre Kidane, considered a moderate, who initiated his transitional government by negotiating a cease-fire with the Eritrean rebels.

[30] Kidane's government took part in peace talks in London, presided over by the US, with the participation of the most important rebel groups. They aimed at

Food Dependency	External Debt	Literacy
1970 **9%** 1994 **20%**	1996 PER CAPITA **$173**	1995 **36%**

STATISTICS

DEMOGRAPHY
Population: 58,243,000 (1996) **Annual growth:** 2.9 % (1980/1996) **Estimates for year 2000:** 66,200,000 **Annual growth to year 2000:** 3.2 % (1994/2000) **Urban Population:** 15.8 % (1996) **Urban growth:** 4.48 % (1980/95) **Children per woman:** 7 (1996).

HEALTH
Life expectancy at birth: 49 years (1996) male: 47 years (1994) female: 50 years (1994) **Infant mortality:** 113 per 1,000 (1996) **Under-5 child mortality:** 177 per 1,000 (1996) **Calorie consumption:** 73 % (1988/90) 33,333 **people per doctor** (1988/91) **Safe water:** 25 % (1990/96).

EDUCATION
Literacy: 36 % (1995) male : 46 % (1995) female: 25 % (1995) **School enrolment :** Primary total: 27 % (1990/95) male : 33 % (1990/95) female: 21 % (1990/95) Secondary: male : 11 % (1990/95) female: 10% (1990/95) Tertiary: 1 % (1995) **Primary school teachers:** one for every 33 students (1995).

COMMUNICATIONS
197 **radios**, 3 **main telephone lines** per 1,000 people (1994).

ECONOMY
Per capita, GNP: $ 100 (1996) **Annual growth, GNP:** 7.2 % (1995/96) **Consumer price index:** 167.1 (1994) **Currency:** 6.32 birr = $ 1 (1995) **Cereal imports:** 928 metric tons (1994) **Food import dependency:** 20 % (1994) **Fertilizer use:** 42 kgs per ha (1994) **Exports:** $ 494 million (1996) Imports: $ 1,492 million (1996) **External debt:** $ 10,077 million (1996) $ 173 **per capita:** (1996) **Debt service:** 42.2 % of exports (1996) **Development aid received:** $ 876 million (1995) $ 16 per capita (1995) 18.7% of GNP (1994).

ENERGY
Consumption: 21.73 Kgs of Oil equivalent per capita yearly (1994) 86.92 % imported (1994)

HDI (rank / value) 170 / 0.244 (1994).

reaching an agreement which would stave off civil war. Kidane resigned in late May, when the US advised the forces of the Revolutionary Democratic Front of the People of Ethiopia (FRDPE) to take control of Addis-Ababa.

[31] Ata Meles Zenawi, the 36-year-old leader of the FRDPE became interim president, until a multi-party conference could be held. He promised to bring the civil war to an end, re-establish democracy and conquer the problem of hunger. Three months later, upon reopening Parliament and passing a new Constitution, Zenawi pledged to hold elections within a year.

[32] The interim president also promised to honour economic commitments assumed by the deposed government, and to respect the will of the Eritrean people. The Eritreans had announced the formation of an autonomous government, and

scheduled a referendum to decide the issue of independence (see Eritrea).

[33] The new government confronted two practically insoluble problems: reconciling the various guerrilla groups, and hunger. Ethiopia became one of the poorest countries in the world. In recent years it has been simultaneously confronted with severe drought and civil war on at least four fronts.

[34] It is estimated that within the past 20 years, more than a million Ethiopians have died of starvation, and another million have become refugees in neighboring countries. After an agreement was signed with the Eritreans, international aid was once more transported through the ports of Aseb and Massawa on the Red Sea.

[35] On July 9, for the first time in 17 years, residents of Addis-Ababa elected their representatives to the

kebeles which were outside the control of any political organization. The voters' main concerns were to achieve peace and security within the capital, and to elect a local administration.

[36] In March 1992, the minister of Insurance and Rehabilitation declared that if international aid did not arrive quickly, the transition to democracy would be jeopardized by the instability caused by the extreme poverty of a large number of Ethiopians. Population displacements and ethnic conflicts worsen the situation, events which are reminiscent of the 1984-85 famine.

[37] The transition government promised to promote the market economy, stimulate agricultural production and reduce poverty, within a five year programme co-ordinated by United Nations organizations and the World Bank. In January 1993, large-scale student demonstrations during a visit from the UN Secretary-General Boutros Boutros-Ghali, once again reflected the tense social situation in the nation.

[38] In 1994, the delivery of the $1.2 billion in five years planned in the economic programme, slowed down considerably as the international organizationss decided the Ethiopian government was privatizing too slowly. In a criticism of the structural adjustment plan proposed by the IMF and the World Bank, humanitarian organizations supporting Ethiopia said there should be greater investment in seeds, tools and livestock in order to fight famine.

[39] Ten years after the 1984 famine, the situation became critical again in the first six months of 1994, with 5,000 deaths in the Wolayata district in the south of the country. In May, the Council of Representatives, a temporary 87-member body, approved a draft Constitution which created the Federal Democratic Republic of Ethiopia. This draft was based on the "ethnic federalism" doctrine, which put an end to the previous official unitarian vision of the nation. According to the approved document, the "sovereignty resides in the nations, nationalities and peoples of Ethiopia" and not the people as a whole.

[40] In June, elections were held for a Constituent Assembly, but were

boycotted by main opposition parties, like the Oromo Liberation Front and the Ogaden National Liberation Front. In September, the police carried out mass arrests in the west of the country, a zone mainly inhabited by Oromos. Several human rights organisations, like Amnesty International, expressed concern over the situation of the country.

[41] In May and June 1995, parliamentary elections were held, also boycotted by most of the opposition parties. The new federal republic was officially established in August, when Negasso Gidada, a Christian Oromo from the Welega region in the west of Ethiopia, took over the presidency. The outgoing president, Meles Zenawi, became Prime Minister and the 17 members of government were carefully selected to reflect "the ethnic balance" of the country.

[42] The trial of representatives of the old Mengistu regime was proposed for the second time, and attempts to extradite the former president from Zimbabwe were unfruitful. Amnesty condemned the Ethiopian government once again, following the arrest of five opposition politicians in June.

[43] The Government went ahead with the privatization of state companies - 144 were sold in 1995 - and the annual grain deficit stood at around a million tons. In 1996, there was an abortive assassination attempt against Mengistu. Many of his former supporters were still in prison. The rainy period started well and increased expectations of food self-sufficiency. The World Bank announced a large reduction in the Ethiopian debt. In 1997, Amnesty repeated its plea for the liberation of members of the opposition and called for an end to arbitrary arrests, torture and disappearances.

[44] In early 1998, food shortages threatened millions of Ethiopians. Due to the price increases set by the Government (13 per cent between August and December 1997) the satisfaction of basic needs become increasingly difficult for the poorer sectors of society. The rains trailed off due to the climatic upset related to the El Niño phenomenon. The Ethiopian Catastrophe Prevention Commission formally called on the international bodies for help to avoid another famine.

European Ministates

Andorra

Population: 71,000 (1996)
Area: 453 SQ KM
Capital: Andorra la Vella
Language: Catalan

Located in the eastern Pyrenees, the co-principality of Andorra is made up of deep ravines and narrow valleys surrounded by mountains with altitudes varying between 1,800 to 3,000 meters. The Valira de Ordino and Valira de Carrillo rivers join in Andorran territory under the name of the Valira river. Wheat is grown in the valleys, but livestock (especially sheep-raising) has given way to tourism as the primary economic activity.

SOCIETY

Peoples: Spanish 44.4 per cent; Andorran 20.2 per cent; Portuguese 10.7 per cent; French 6.8 per cent; other 6.6 per cent (1993).
Religions: Catholic 92 per cent; Protestant 0,5 per cent; Jewish 0.4 per cent: other 7.1 per cent (1992).
Languages: Catalan (official), French and Spanish.
Political Parties: Liberal Union Party (Unió Liberal, UL), Liberal Group (Grup Liberal), the National Andorran Coalition (Coalició Nacional Andorrana), and the Canillo-La Massana Grouping (Agrupació Canillo-La Massana). National Democratic Grouping.
Social Organizations: There are no organized trade unions. Many workers have joined French trade unions.

THE STATE

Official Name: Principat d'Andorra.
Administrative divisions: 18 provinces.
Capital: Andorra la Vella, 21,984 people (1997).
Other cities: Les Escaldes, 15,182 people; Encamp, 9,800 people (1997).
Government: Parliamentary republic. Constitution in effect since March 14 1993. The Bishop of Urgel (Spanish jurisdiction) and the President of France, represented by Franceso Badia-Batalla and Louis Deblé, respectively, are "co-princes" of the territory. Oscar Ribas is President of the Executive Council and Head of Government. Single-chamber legislature (General Council), with 28 members elected by direct popular vote, every four years. At some point in the future, total independence from France and the Spanish bishopric is foreseen.
National Holiday: September 8.

Liechtenstein

Population: 31,000 (1996)
Area: 160 SQ KM
Capital: Vaduz
Language: German

This small principality lies between Switzerland and Austria, in the Rhine valley. Wheat, oats, rye, corn, grapes and fruit are produced. 38 per cent of the land is pasture. In recent years, the principality has transformed into a highly industrialized country, producing textiles, pharmaceutical products, precision instruments, refrigerators, among other items.

SOCIETY

Peoples: German 95 per cent; Italian and other 5 per cent.
Capital: Vaduz, 5,085 people (1996).
Religions: Catholic 80 per cent; Protestant 6.9 per cent; other 5.6 per cent.
Languages: German (official).
Political Parties: The Progressive Citizens' Party (FBP); Patriotic Union (VU); Free List, green.
Social Organizations: The Trades Union Association (artisans and traders), and the Agricultural Union.

THE STATE

Official Name: Fürstentum Liechtenstein.
Administrative divisions: 11 communes.
Capital: Vaduz 5,067 people (1995).
Other cities: Schaan, 5,143 people; Balzers, 3,752 people; Triesen, 3,586 people (1995).
Government: Liechtenstein is a constitutional monarchy. Prince Hans Adam II, Head of State since November 13 1989. Mario Frick, Prime Minister, Head of Government. Government functions are carried out by a FBP and VU coalition. Cornelia Gassner (FBP), Minister of Construction, the first woman to be named to a cabinet post. Single-chamber legislature: Parliament with 25 members elected every four years.
Diplomacy: A member of the European Council, Liechtenstein has a customs and monetary alliance with Switzerland, which is its representative abroad.
National holiday: February 14.

Monaco

Population: 32,000 (1996)
Area: 1 SQ KM
Currency: French Francs
Language: French

A small principality on the Mediterranean coast, with a 3.5 km coastline, surrounded by the French department of the Maritime Alps. The territory is made up of three urban centers: Monaco-Ville, the capital, built upon an isolated cliff; Condamine, a residential center; and Montecarlo, to the northeast of the port of Monaco, home of the famous casino and consequently the most often visited location. Olives and citrus fruits are cultivated in the narrow inland strip. Tourism is the country's basic source of revenue.

SOCIETY

Peoples: 47 per cent French, 17 per cent Monacoan, 16 per cent Italian, 4 per cent English, 2 per cent Belgian and 1 per cent Swiss.
Religions: 95 per cent Catholic (1997).
Languages: French (official), Monegasque, English, Italian.
Political Parties: There are no political parties. Candidates form lists to run for election in the National Council (CN). Until 1992, the CN was dominated by the National Democratic Union. In 1993, the main groups were the Cámpora List and the Médecin List. In the last CN election, in January 1997, Michel Leveque was elected Minister of State.

THE STATE

Official Name: Principauté de Monaco.
Administrative divisions: 1 commune.
Government: Parliamentary monarchy. Constitution in effect since December 17 1962. Prince Rainier III, sovereign since May 9 1949, Head of State and of the government. Single-chamber legislature: National Council, with 18 members elected by direct vote every 5 years.

San Marino

Population: 25,000 (1996)
Area: 61 SQ KM
Capital: San Marino
Currency: Lire
Language: Italian

The Republic of San Marino, founded in 1866 and located between the Italian provinces of Romana and Marca, is the world's smallest republican state. Its mountainous terrain is part of Mount Titano, an eastern branch of the Apennines; the La Rocca peak, 749 m, is the highest point in the city-state. Grapes and grain are grown in the farmlands, and sheep are also raised. Tourism is the country's major source of income since the small republic is linked to the port of Rimini, on the Adriatic.

SOCIETY

Peoples: Sammarinesi 75.4 per cent; Italian 23.3 per cent; other 1.3 per cent (1996).
Religions: 95.2 per cent Catholic (1980).
Languages: Italian (official) and a local dialect.
Political Parties: Multiparty system. The Christian Democrat Party (PDC), 26 seats; Socialist Party (PS), 14 seats; Progressive Democratic Party (PDP) formerly communist, 11 seats; Popular Alliance (AP), 4 seats; Democratic Movement, (MD), 3 seats; Communist Refoundation (RC), 2 seats.
Social Organizations: The Unitarian Trade Union Central, the General Democratic Confederation of Workers and the General Confederation of Labor.

THE STATE

Official Name: Serenissima Repubblica di San Marino.
Capital: San Marino, 2,316 people (1996).
Other cities: Serravalle/Dogano 4,726 people; Borgo Maggiore 2,366 people (1996).
Government: Presidential republic. The Executive of the Council of State, with ten members elected every six months (dominated by the PS and the PDC) is presided over by two regent Captains: Maurizio Rattini and Giancarlo Venturini, head of State and head of Government, respectively, elected in between 1996 and 1997. Single-chamber legislature of the General Grand Council, with 60 members elected every five years by direct popular vote.
Diplomacy: At the beginning of 1992, San Marino joined the United Nations and the IMF. It has had a Friendship Treaty with Italy since 1862. As a neutral European country, it is a Non-Aligned Movement observer.

Vatican City

Population: 1,000 (1996)
Area: 0.44 SQ KM
Language: Italian and Latin

The Vatican State dates back to the 9th century when Charlemagne, emperor of the Franks, legalized its existence. The Vatican ceased to exist in 1870 when the first king of Italy, Victor Emmanuel of Savoy, seeking national unification, formally occupied the territory and proclaimed Rome its capital. The 1871 Guarantees Law established the inviolability of the Pope and recognized his ownership of the Vatican, but the Roman pontiffs did not accept the situation until February 11 1929, when the Holy See signed the Treaty of Letran with Benito Mussolini, establishing the current State's borders and privileges.

[2] Originally, the state's revenues derived from the financial investment of 1.75 billion lire indemnity established in the Treaty of Lateran as payment for the territories lost in 1870. Later they were increased by contributions and donations from all over the world, especially from the United States and West Germany. At present, these resources are administered by the Institute for Religious Works - known popularly as Bank of Vatican - re-organized following banking scandals originated in the bankruptcy of the Ambrosiano Bank. Allegedly the Institute has reserves exceeding US$11 billion, participate in numerous other banks and enterprises, and own countless real-estate properties throughout the world.

[3] In 1993, the estimated budget deficit (US$91.7 million) surpassed the projected deficit (US$86.1 million), and there were two unprecedented events. Firstly, Vatican workers organized the first ever protest, demanding wage increases and pensions, and secondly the commercialization of the Pope's image was authorized, during his visit to the United States in June, allowing the sale of posters and T-shirts. Two years later, the Vatican produced a compact disc of prayers recited by the Pope which sold more than 20 million copies. In 1995, the Vatican economy went back into the black, leaving the financial troubles behind.

[4] In January 1998 the Pope made a visit to Cuba.

ENVIRONMENT

Located within the city of Rome, not far from the banks of the Tiber river, the Vatican comprises St Peter's square and basilica, the palaces and gardens of the Vatican itself, the palace and basilica of St John Lateran, the papal villa at Castelgandolfo and another 13 off-limit buildings which enjoy diplomatic privileges because they house congregations of the Catholic Church

SOCIETY

Peoples: Church members whose functions require residence, become Vatican citizens. Most permanent members are Italian, but there is also a large number of Swiss residents, and some other nationalities.
Religions: Catholic.
Languages: Italian (official language of the State) and Latin (official language of the Church).

THE STATE

Official Name: Stato della Città del Vaticano.
Administrative divisions: Two parallel administrations: Holy See (supreme body of the Catholic Church) and Vatican City (site of the Church).
Capital: Vatican City, 1,000 (1995).
Government: Elected lifelong monarchy. Monarch: John Paul II (Karol Wojtyla, of polish origin), elected on October 16, 1978 by the cardinals' conclave (secret meeting), the first non-Italian Pope in 456 years. Secretary of State (a position equivalent to prime minister): Cardinal Angelo Sodano. The state government is exercised by a 5-member pontifical commission appointed by the Pope and headed by the Secretary of State. The Pope is also the Bishop of Rome and the supreme ruler of the Catholic Church. In Church government, he is assisted by the College of Cardinals and the Synods of Bishops, which meet when so instructed by the Pope. The Church's administrative departments comprise 9 holy congregations, 3 Secretariats and several commissions, mayoralties and tribunals, known collectively as the Roman Curia.

Fiji

Fiji

Population: 797,000 (1996)
Area: 18,274 SQ KM
Capital: Suva City

Currency: Fiji dollars
Language: English

Four thousand years ago the Fijian archipelago was already populated. Melanesian migrations first reached the islands in the 6th century BC, and the Fijians had one of the leading Pacific cultures. In 1789, British Captain William Bligh visited the islands, writing the first detailed account of Fijian life.

2   Social life on the islands was organized in families and clans which gradually formed larger communities. One of these, ruled by traditional leader Na Ulivau, extended its influence from Ngau over the rest of the islands, achieving unification.

3   Early in the 19th century, British adventurers and merchants exploited the forests of Fiji, rich in sandalwood and other aromatic species highly prized in China. To settle their rivalries, Europeans sought support from local leaders. In 1830, the first Christian missionaries arrived from Tonga and 24 years later achieved a major victory by christening ruler Thakombau, son of Na Ulivau. Contemporary accounts report a "refined, courteous and honourable gentleman", and this "king" (formerly reported to be a "cannibal") became an enthusiastic admirer of the Western world. He offered to annex Fiji to the US, though this may have been more due to the Fijian ruler's heavy debts after prolonged wars with rival leaders. The White House, caught up in the turmoil of the Secession War, missed the opportunity to tack another star on the flag. The British, faced with a shortage of sugar, "discovered" the archipelago's potential for growing cane and, with Thakombau's consent, officially annexed the islands on October 10 1874.

LAND USE

DEFORESTATION -0.4% annual (81/90)
IRRIGATED 0.6 % of arable

(1993)

■ FOREST & WOODLAND 64.9%
□ ARABLE 9.9%
▨ OTHER 25.2%

4   Fijian officials raised no objections to the purchase or expropriation of large tracts of land for the new crops, though the peasants were unwilling to leave their communal estates to work on the plantations. Consequently, a massive influx of bond workers were brought in, first from the Solomon islands, and then from India. Following the abolition of slavery, the British used this same system of transferring Indian workers to Africa and the Caribbean to curb the labor shortage and ease the population squeeze in India.

5   At the end of their contracts, the workers brought their families to Fiji and became small shop owners, craftspeople or bureaucrats in the colonial administration, and though far from India, they retained their language, religion and caste system. Colonial regulations meant that they were restricted from buying land from native Fijians; a law ostensibly designed to prevent inter-ethnic conflict.

6   Initial moves toward local autonomy resulted in a complicated electoral system securing political control by the "natives" who were in the minority. Prime Minister Sir Kamisese Mara initiated an elaborate scheme of representation, where each electoral category was allotted a quota for governmental representation: Fijians, 22, Indians,

22 and General, 8. A peculiar system that nonetheless proved useful in preventing major disruptions during the transition to independence in 1970. His Alliance Party claimed to be multiracial, and marshalled support from some Indians and other minor groups, in addition to the Fijian electorate.

7   In 1976, the Government turned down a constitutional reform project which would have required multi-group cooperation in the country's administration.

8   Inter-ethnic coexistence has been successful except for two fierce clashes in 1959 and 1968; however, potential conflict situations could still erupt. The recent "back-to-the-roots" trend, centred mainly around the University of the Pacific in Suva, has encouraged young people to honour their Melanesian, Polynesian, Hindu, Islamic or Chinese cultural heritage, thus widening the existing gap between coexistent but and miscible cultures. Indians predominate in trade and the liberal professions. Fijians, in turn, own the arable land and lease it on very advantageous terms to poor Indians.

9   In the 1970s economic difficulties forced thousands of Fijians to emigrate to Aotearoa/ New Zealand in search of job opportunities. Tourism, possibly the single industry which could improve the deficit balance of payments, requires Melanesians to

remain "genuine" to satisfy Australian and Aotearoa's visitors' thirst for exoticism. Individualism and private land ownership were encouraged, seeking to bolster the economic situation of "natives" over that of the Indians. However, under these conditions, the rural workers' gained few improvements; urban income increased by 3.5 per cent in 1978, but rural income increased only 0.3 per cent.

10   The difficult economic situation swelled the number of "racist" groups, such as the Nationalist Party, who militate against Indian majority, though Indians have been on the islands for four or five generations.

11   Former prime minister Kamisese Mara's conservative administration was deeply marked by racial and ideological trends. His government was the only one in the Commonwealth to maintain relations with the racist Rhodesian and South African regimes and to welcome Chilean dictator Augusto Pinochet on an official visit in early 1980. Mass demonstrations during Pinochet's visit demonstrated the growing progressive movement in Fiji.

12   In the 1982 election, the incumbent Alliance Party retained office with a small margin over the opposition NFP, which had unified its two rival factions despite growing conflict within the party.

13   In the April 11 1987 election, the Indian majority won and Timoci

PROFILE

ENVIRONMENT
Fiji consists of nine large islands and 300 volcanic and coral islets and atolls, of which only 100 are inhabited. The group is located in Melanesia, in the Koro Sea, between Vanuatu (former New Hebrides) to the west and Tonga to the east, five degrees north of the Tropic of Capricorn. The largest islands are Viti Levu, where the capital is located, Vanua Levu, Taveuni, Lau, Kandavu, Asua, Karo, Ngau and Ovalau. The terrain is mainly mountainous. Fertile soils in flatland zones plus tropical rainy climate, mildly tempered by sea winds, make the islands suitable for plantation crops, sugar cane and copra. The marine environment is threatened by overfishing and the pollution of its coastal waters.

SOCIETY
Peoples: Half of Fijians are natives of Melanesian origin with some Polynesian components, the other half are descendants of Indian workers who came to the archipelago early in the 20th century; while the others are of European and Chinese origin. Most of the population live in Viti Levu (73 per cent) and Vanua Levu (18 per cent). Banabans (see Kiribati) have bought the island of Rambi, between Vanua Levu and Taveuni, with the purpose of settling there since their native island was left uninhabitable by phosphate mining. **Religions:** 53 per cent of Fijians are Christian (mainly methodist and other protestant sects)38 per cent are Hindu and 8 per cent Muslim. **Languages:** English (official), Urdu, Hindi, Fijian, Chinese. **Political Parties:** Fijian Political Party and United National Front, representing the Fijians; National Federation Party and Fiji Labour Party, depending on the Indo-Fijian support; the General Vote Party representing the remaining minorities. **Social Organizations:** The Association of Fijian Young People and Students.

THE STATE
Official Name: Sovereign Democratic Republic of Fiji. **Administrative Divisions:** 5 Regions divided into 15 Provinces. **Capital:** Suva City, 160,000 people (1994). **Other cities:** Lautoka 28,700 people; Nadi 7,709 (1986). **Government:** Kamisese Mara, head of State since December 16 1993; Sitiveni Rabuka, head of Government since June 1992. **Legislature:** bicameral Parliament: the Chamber of Representatives has 70 members; 37 Fijian, 27 Hindi, 1 from Rotuma Island and 5 others. The Senate is made up of 34 members; 24 named by the Grand Council of the Chieftains, 9 by the president and 1 by the council of Rotuma. **National Holiday:** October 10, Independence (1970). **Armed Forces:** 3,900 (1995).

STATISTICS

DEMOGRAPHY
Population: 797,000 (1996) **Annual growth:** 1.4 % (1980/1996) **Estimates for year 2000:** 800,000 **Annual growth to year 2000:** 1.6 % (1994/2000) **Urban Population:** 40.9 % (1996) **Children per woman:** 2.8 (1996).

HEALTH
Life expectancy at birth: 72 years (1996) male: 70 years (1994) female: 74 years (1994) **Infant mortality:** 20 per 1,000 (1996) **Under-5 child mortality:** 24 per 1,000 (1996) **Safe water:** 100 % (1990/96).

EDUCATION
Literacy: 92 % (1995) male : 94 % (1995) female: 89 % (1995) **School enrolment :** Primary total: 128 % (1990/95) male : 128 % (1990/95) female: 127 % (1990/95) Secondary: male : 64 % (1990/95) female: 65 % (1990/95).

COMMUNICATION
50 **newspapers**, 607 **radios**, 70 **TV sets** and 77 **main telephone lines** per 1,000 people (1994) **Books:** 52 new titles per 100,000 people (1992/94).

ECONOMY
Consumer price index: 119.0 (1994) **Currency:** 1.43 Fiji dollars = $ 1 (1995) **Cereal imports:** 126 metric tons (1994) **Food import dependency:** 12 % (1994) **Fertilizer use:** 692 kgs per ha (1994) **Development aid received:** $ 43 million (1995) $ 56 per capita (1995) 2.5 % of GNP (1994).

HDI (rank / value) 46 / 0.863 (1994).

Bavadra became premier, ending 16 years of Polynesian Government. In May, a few short weeks after the election, Bavadra's labor government was overthrown by a military coup led by Colonel Sitiveni Rabuka. The colonel justified himself as "attempting to solve the ethnic problem", though the real objective seemed to be the removal of the Indian Government, who believed in an independent foreign policy, and planned to join the treaty of Rarotonga. The treaty promoted

WORKERS

- ■ AGRICULTURE   46%   (1990)
- ☐ INDUSTRIAL   15%
- ■ SERVICES   39%

MILITARY EXPENDITURE

MILITARY (as % of health and education expenditures-1990/91) **37%**

regional denuclearization; endorsed by Australia and Aotearoa, but criticized by Britain and the US.
[14] In 1987 Bavadra, who had been imprisoned by the military during the coup, was freed. He rejected the idea of new elections proposed by the military for the end of 1988, ostensibly to draw up a new constitution. The main Indian and Melanesian political parties reached an agreement, with added pressure from the Commonwealth, which appeared to appease the military. However, on October 6 1987, Rabuka retaliated proclaiming a Republic, a move intended to disavow the authority of the head of state, the British appointed governor.
[15] In December 1987, Rabuka resigned as Head of State, in an attempt to create an image of a joint civilian-military government, aimed at improving its foreign image. Penaia Ganilau was named President and Camisese Mara, Prime Minister, a regime never subjected to the approval of the electorate.
[16] In July 1990 a new constitutional decree based on apartheid went

into effect, assuring the native 37 of the Chamber of Representatives' 70 seats and 24 of the Senate's 34 seats. A constitutional referendum announced for 1992 was finally cancelled. The following year, the apartheid model was denounced by the UN's General Assembly, Mauritius and India. In November, the Association of Fijian Young People and Students organized a public burning of the new constitution's text. Demonstrators were harshly subdued.
[17] Rabuka founded the Fijian Political Party and in 1992, amid growing political and social strains, a military officer was named Prime Minister.
[18] Fiji has not been able to overcome its chronic balance of payments deficit: almost all of its fuel and manufactured products are imported and its main sources of income - sugar exports and tourism - are not enough to balance the budget.
[19] In November 1993 six FPP members voted together with the opposition against the budget, forcing general elections. Rabuka retained power with 31 of the 37 Fijian seats and support from independent and General Vote Party members. Dissidents formed a Fijian Association obtaining only 5 seats.
[20] In November 1994, the Government began a timid revision of the racist constitution. In 1995, Rabuka had to reorganize his Cabinet several times due to internal divisions in the coalition. He took legal steps to challenge a

commission's findings which involved him in unlawful management linked to the Central Bank's deficit. The Government's plan to allow 28,000 Chinese from Hong Kong to settle in the country also led to a wave of criticism. According to the official plan, each one of the future immigrants would have to pay $130,000 to legally reside in the country.
[21] In September 1996, a commission completed a report on the new constitution, which created a "multiracial council" and reserved a certain number of seats in parliament for certain ethnic groups. The document was approved in July 1997, coming into operation a year later.
[22] In September 1997, Fiji was readmitted into the British Commonwealth, ten years after the coup which took it out.
[23] The Asian crisis forced the Government to devalue the currency 20 per cent against the dollar and to lower customs barriers.
[24] At the end of that year, a study revealed that 40 per cent of pregnant women on Suva suffered from sexually transmitted diseases. In early 1998, the Government launched a health plan to combat an outbreak of dengue fever (similar to malaria) which had killed four children.
[25] In February 1998, Prime Minister Rabuka spoke publicly of his fear of being deposed in a new coup, accusing members of the clergy and army of plotting against him.

Finland

Süomi

Population: 5,126,000 (1996)
Area: 338,145 SQ KM
Capital: Helsinki
Currency: Markkaa
Language: Finnish

Finland was inhabited from 7500 BC onwards, and the first settlers were the Sami (later also called "Lapps" by other people). The Sami were essentially hunters, fishers and gatherers. Over the centuries they began domesticating animals and practising subsistence agriculture, remaining isolated from the rest of Europe. Much later - in the 1st century AD - descendants of the Finno-Ugrics entered from the south, and they pushed the Sami to the north, taking control of the major part of the territory. By the year 1000 AD, the Finns had established many settlements in the south.

2   The ancestors of the *tavastlanders* came from the southwest across the Gulf of Finland, and the Carelians arrived from the southeast. Scandinavian peoples occupied the west coast, the archipelagos and also the Aland Islands (Ahvenanmaa).

3   From the 12th century onwards, Finland was claimed by both the Russian and Swedish empires. In 1172, the Pope advised the Swedes to control the Finns, to avoid their being proselytized by the Russian Orthodox Church. With the Protestant Reformation, Lutheranism became Sweden's official religion.

4   In 1809 Finland became a grand duchy of Imperial Russia, although it was allowed to maintain its own parliament, army and judicial system.

5   In 1889 the Social Democratic Party was founded, a party which was to play a leading role in Finnish political life from that moment onward. The presence of Lenin and other Bolshevik exiles also helped to strengthen the country's socialist leanings. In 1906

WORKERS

UNEMPLOYMENT 16.1% (1996)

Labour force %

- ■ WOMEN
- □ MEN

48%   52%

- ■ AGRICULTURE   8%   (1990)
- □ INDUSTRIAL   31%
- ▦ SERVICES   61%

a single-chamber parliament was created, and universal suffrage was established. Finland became the third country in the world to recognize female suffrage.

6   Finland declared independence in December 1917. Spurred on by the example of the Russian Revolution, Finnish Socialists tried to seize power by means of a revolution. In January 1918, the Social Democratic Party (SDP) took Helsinki and the major industrial centres. The government counterattacked, backed by the White Army and German troops under the command of General Mannerheim. In May, the civil war came to an end and the Socialist leaders were tried and given harsh sentences.

7   Finland became a monarchy, and German Prince Frederick Charles of Hessen was elected king. After Germany's defeat in World War I, the monarchy collapsed and General Mannerheim was appointed regent, while new republican institutions were established.

8   The 1919 Constitution established a parliamentary system with a strong presidential figure. In addition, it made the prime minister the head of the government, and the president head of state. Although the constitution recognized both Finnish and Swedish as official languages, nationalist youth groups later demanded that Finnish be given priority. This led to the creation of the Swedish People's Party. Subsequent constitutional reforms maintained the right of the Swedish minority to its own language.

9   In 1918, 70 per cent of all Finns depended upon agriculture and forestry for a living. The importance of this segment of the population led to the formation of the Rural Party, which became the Center Party.

10   The country has been governed almost uninterruptedly since its independence by alliances between the Social Democrats and the Centrists. From 1920 to 1930, these two political forces backed an ambitious program of social and economic reforms. Agricultural production was modernized, and the exploitation of the country's lumber resources was intensified. Likewise, the

Government fostered industrialization in the cities, and sponsored progressive legislation, aimed at protecting the emerging working class and agricultural workers.

11   The growth of the Communist Party (FCP) gave rise to the ultra-right-wing Lapua (Lappo) Movement, whose terrorist acts and mass protests were supported by conservative groups and by some Rural Party members. In 1930, the FCP was banned by law, with the support of these parties. In 1931 the Lappo movement began to carry out attacks against the Social Democrats. After an attempted coup the following year, they were finally arrested by the Government.

12   After the German invasion of Poland, the USSR demanded part of the Karelian Islands, a naval base on the Hanko peninsula and other islands of the Gulf of Finland, as a means of defending themselves against imminent German attack. Given the refusal of the Finns to cede the lands, the USSR seized these areas by force, giving rise to

a brief conflict. The 1940 Treaty of Moscow forced Finland to cede these territories.

13   Finland had declared its neutrality at the beginning of World War II, but since it had become involved in a conflict with the USSR, it permitted German troops to use its territory to launch an attack again their mutual enemy. Thus, Finland was briefly able to recover the territories lost in 1940.

14   The 1944 Soviet counter-offensive and subsequent German retreat strengthened the Finnish peace movement. The Karelian Islands once again came under the control of the Red Army, causing the resignation of President Retie, the architect of the alliance with Germany. He was succeeded by General Mannerheim, who negotiated an armistice with Moscow, recognized the 1940 Treaty of Moscow and organized the fight to expel German troops from the country. During the war nearly 500,000 Finns had died.

15   When the war ended, the country's political life was once

PROFILE

ENVIRONMENT

Finland is a flat country (the average altitude is 150 meters above sea level) with vast marine clay plains, low plateaus and numerous hills and lakes formed by glaciers. The population is concentrated mainly on the coastal plains, the country's main farming area. Lumbering of coniferous forests is the central economic activity and provides the main export products: lumber, paper pulp and paper. Sulphur dioxide emissions and the dumping of contaminated water into the Baltic Sea pose serious threats to the environment.

SOCIETY

Peoples: Ethnic make-up: 92.1 per cent of the population is Finnish and 7.5 per cent Swedish. There are Romany (gipsy) and Sami minorities.

Religions: over 86 per cent of the population belongs to the Lutheran Church and 1 per cent to the Finnish Orthodox Church (official churches). 12 per cent are non religious.

Languages: Finnish (official and spoken by 93.2 per cent). Swedish, spoken by 6 per cent of the population, is also an official language. Lapp is spoken by a minority of around 1,700 people.

Political Parties: The Social Democratic Party (SDP), center-left; Center Party (KP), formerly the Finnish Rural Party; the People's Democratic League; the National Coalition Party (KOK), moderate conservative; the People's Liberal Party; the People's Swedish Party, liberal, represents interests of the Swedish-speaking minority; the Green Party; the Christian League of Finland; the Rural Party.

Social Organizations: Central Organization of Finnish Unions, with 1,086,000 members and 28 member unions.

THE STATE

Official Name: Suomen Tasavalta.

Administrative divisions: 12 provinces.

Capital: Helsinki, 515,800 people; metropolitan area 874,900 (1995).

Other cities: Espoo 186,500 people; Tampere 179,200 people; Vantaa 164,400 people; Turku (Abo) 162,400 people (1995).

Government: Unicameral parliamentary democracy. Martti Ahtisaari, President since March 1, 1994; Paavo Lipponen, Prime Minister since April 1995.

National holiday: December 6 (Proclamation of independence).

Armed Forces: Total: 31,200 (1994).

Other: Border guards: 4,400.

STATISTICS

DEMOGRAPHY

Population: 5,126,000 (1996) **Annual growth:** 0.4 % (1980/1996) **Estimates for year 2000:** 5,200,000. **Annual growth to year 2000:** 0.3 % (1994/2000) **Urban Population:** 63.5 % (1996) **Urban growth:** 0.82 % (1980/95) **Children per woman:** 1.8 (1996).

HEALTH

Life expectancy at birth: 76 years (1996) male: 72 years (1994) female: 80 years (1994) **Infant mortality:** 4 per 1,000 (1996) **Under-5 child mortality:** 4 per 1,000 (1996) **Calorie consumption:** 113 % (1988/90) 405 **people per doctor** (1988/91).

EDUCATION

School enrolment : Primary total: 100 % (1990/95) male : 100 % (1990/95) female: 100 % (1990/95) Secondary: male : 110 % (1990/95) female: 130 % (1990/95) Tertiary: 67 % (1995).

COMMUNICATIONS

470 **newspapers**, 1,003 **radios**, 500 **TV sets** and 551 **main telephone lines** per 1,000 people (1994) **Books:** 247 new titles per 100,000 people (1992/94).

ECONOMY

Per capita, GNP: $ 23,240 (1996) **Annual growth, GNP:** 3.5 % (1995/96) **Annual inflation:** 3.82 % (1985/95) **Consumer price index:** 110.9 (1994) **Currency:** 4.36 markkaa = $ 1 (1995) **Cereal imports:** 130 metric tons (1994) **Fertilizer use:** 1,484 kgs per ha (1994) **Exports:** $ 40,520 million (1996) **Imports:** $ 30,853 million (1996).

ENERGY

Consumption: 5,997.24 Kgs of Oil equivalent per capita yearly (1994) 58.25 % imported (1994)

HDI (rank / value) 8 / 0.94 (1994)

---

again controlled by the Social Democratic-Finnish Rural Party alliance and the leader of the Finnish Rural Party, Urho Kekkonen, occupied the presidency from 1956-1982. The office of prime minister was also held by SDP figures for most of that same period.

[16] During the post-war period, Finland was faced with a critical social and economic situation. Production had come to a standstill, there were thousands of unemployed and more than 300,000 refugees from the occupied areas.

[17] Neutrality became the cornerstone of Finnish foreign policy. In 1948, Helsinki and Moscow signed the Finno-Soviet Pact of Friendship, Cooperation and Mutual Assistance. Seven years later, the USSR returned the naval base at Porkkala and the treaty was again ratified in 1970 and 1983. In 1955, Finland joined the European Free Trade Association (EFTA), the United Nations and the Nordic Council, but blocked the creation of a customs union within the framework of the

Council. Finland was the only member of the OECD which simultaneously maintained relations with the EC and the socialist bloc CMEA. This situation explains the country's relatively rapid economic recovery.

[18] The Finnish Government offered incentives to develop the lumber industry, axis of the economy. It promoted industrialization and took advantage of the profits generated by its lucrative foreign trade.

[19] However, with the disintegration of the USSR, which had provided the market for over 25 per cent of its exports, economic growth came to a standstill.

[20] In 1991, Prime Minister Esko Aho, politically moderate, launched a drastic structural adjustment program which was resisted by workers. Economic stagnation caused a decline in Finnish standards of living, and unemployment went from 3.5 to over 20 per cent in December 1993.

[21] Finland requested EU membership in 1992. A plebiscite

in 1994 supported the initiative, which was confirmed in early 1995. The internal impact of this measure was softened by special subsidies for the farming sector, disadvantaged compared with its community partners, because of the cold climate. Part of the State monopoly on public health and the sale of alcoholic beverages was also maintained.

[22] Once the nation had effectively entered the EU, President Ahtisaari declared Finland would not enter the Western European Union, which could have been a step toward NATO membership. The Finnish Government considered a common defence policy should be based on consensus and that their traditional neutrality was obsolete since the fall of the iron curtain. It also warned the West of the risk of isolating Russia and of the environmental danger posed by the nuclear plants and industries of this country.

[23] In the March elections the Social Democratic Party, led by Paavo Lipponen, pushed out the rural-based Centre Party, which

had been the ruling force in Parliament up until then. In October, the Government proposed a plan to reduce unemployment, which oscillated at around 17 per cent. Lipponen was designated Prime Minister, replacing Esko Aho. The Finnish paper industry reduced its emissions of sulphur dioxide, but more than half the contamination continued to come from the neighbouring countries.

[24] In 1996, the Government reiterated its policy of non-alliance on military matters, although it repeated its interest in the economic and monetary union planned for 1999. Inflation stood at just under 1 per cent throughout 1997. The growth in industrial production was amongst the highest in the European Union at 3.2 per cent. In October, unemployment fell to 12.6 per cent.

[25] In early 1998, Lipponen increased contacts with his Western partners in efforts to gain greater economic support for Russian development.

France

France

Population: 58,333,000 (1996)
Area: 551,500 SQ KM
Capital: Paris
Currency: French Franc
Language: French

The two regions occupied by the Celts were known to the Romans as Gaul. The region between the Alps and Rome was Cisalpine Gaul, and beyond the Alps was Transalpine Gaul. With natural borders on all sides; the Alps, the Pyrénées, the Atlantic Ocean and the Rhine, Gaul occupied not only what is now France, but also Belgium, Switzerland and the western banks of the Rhine.

2   Gallic society was essentially agricultural, with almost no urban life. The few cities, were used as fortresses, where the peasants sought refuge when under attack. Society was divided into the nobles (who were also warriors), the people and the Druids, keepers of Celtic wisdom and religious traditions.

3   The Romans came to Gaul in 125 BC. They conquered the area along the Mediterranean, the Rhone valley and Languedoc, calling the combined area "Provincia". Caesar divided Gaul into two regions; Provincia and Free Gaul. Free Gaul was subdivided into ; Belgian Gaul in the north, between the Rhine and the Seine; Celtic Gaul in the center, between the Seine, the Garonne and the lower Rhine; and Aquitaine, in the southwest.

4   In 27 BC, Augustus Caesar set up administrative centres in Gaul, to manage Rome's affairs encouraging urbanization. Bridges and an extensive road network were built throughout the region, facilitating an increase in trade. Wheat production was increased and vineyards were planted, with wine replacing beer as the traditional beverage. After a series of invasions by the Visigoths in the south and the

Burgundians along the Saone and the Rhone, the northern Gauls conquered the rest of Gaul under the leadership of Clovis, adopting the name, "Franks".

5   Between the 5th and the 9th centuries France emerged as the Merovingian and Carolingian dynasties brought the entire region under the influence of Christianity. With the Islamic expansion and the fall of the Roman Empire, trade ceased, urban civilization was almost completely wiped out, population decreased and the culture fell into decadence.

6   By the 9th century, feudalism had become firmly established. Centralized authority practically disappeared, as local people were unable to repel the Scandinavians, Hungarians, Saracens, and other invaders of this era. By the end of the century, the previously united land was a conglomerate of more than 300 independent counties.

7   From the 10th century onward, the royal dynasties slowly recovered their power. They established hereditary succession to the throne, they shared power with the Church and became the main feudal landowners.

8   In the 13th century, an increase in commercial activity led to a remarkable rebirth of the cities, and agricultural techniques were improved, as the population increased. The Crusades led to a greater circulation of people and goods, and the gradual disappearance of serfdom gave rise to greater social mobility. This was the "Golden Age" of the French Middle Ages, when France had great power over, and influence upon Western civilization.

9   Paris was one of Europe's most important cities, and the prestige of its University was linked to its cultural pre-eminence. The University trained lawyers in Roman law, and their influence helped form a new concept of the State where the king was no longer a feudal lord, but rather the embodiment of the law. Over a period of time, nationalistic feelings began to develop.

10   Before the 18th century, France suffered from the Hundred Years' War with England, the Thirty Years' War with Spain;

France - dependencies

Overseas Departments: Guadeloupe; Martinique; French Guyana; Reunion (see each section).

Overseas Territories: Mayotte (see Comoros), St Pierre and Miquelon (text follows); New Caledonia (see Kanaky); Wallis and Futuna (text follows); French Polynesia (see corresponding section).

Southern and Antarctic Territories: Comprising two archipelagos: Kerguelen (7,000 sq km, with 80 people in Port-Aux-Français) and Crozet (500 sq km, with 20 inhab.); two islands: New Amsterdam (60 sq km, with 35 inhab.) and St Paul (7 sq km, uninhabited), located in the southern Indian Ocean; the Land of Adélie (500,000 sq km with 27 inhab. at the Dumont Durville Base), in Antarctica. The territories are governed by an Administrator-General advised by a seven-member Consultative Council appointed by the French government. Technical personnel at weather stations are the only inhabitants.

PUBLIC EXPENDITURE

n/a
72.5%
1995 ■ DEFENCE □ SOCIAL

In **1990/91** Military as % of health & education expenditure was 29%.

WORKERS

UNEMPLOYMENT 12.4% (1996)

Labour force %

■ WOMEN
□ MEN
44%   56%

■ AGRICULTURE	5%	(1990)
□ INDUSTRIAL	29%	
■ SERVICES	66%	

PROFILE

ENVIRONMENT
In the north is the Paris Basin, which spreads out into fields and plains. The Massif Central, in the center of France, is made up of vast plateaus. In the southeast, the Alps rise up. The southern region includes the Mediterranean coast, with mountain ranges, like the Pyrénées, and plains. Grain farming is the main agricultural activity; wheat is grown all over the country, especially in the north. Grapes are grown in the Mediterranean region for wine exports. The main mineral resources are coal, iron ore and bauxite. Dependence on nuclear energy poses a serious problem. Atomic reactors operating in the country generate three quarters of the national consumption of electricity, making France the second largest producer of nuclear energy, after the United States. There is also a nuclear reprocessing plant, as well as one which generates plutonium.

SOCIETY
Peoples: Most of the population stem from the integration of three basic European groups: Nordic, Alpine and Mediterranean. Approximately 7% of the population has a foreign descent. Portuguese 1.1%; Algerian 1.1%; Moroccan 1.0%; Italian 0.4%; Spanish 0.4%; Turkish 0.3%; other 2.1%.
Religions: Mainly Catholic (76%); Calvinism 2 per cent; Muslim 2 per cent, Judaism 1 per cent.
Languages: French is the official and predominant language. There are also regional languages: Breton in Brittany, a German dialect in Alsace and Lorraine, Flemish in the northeast, Catalan and Basque in the Southwest, Provençal in the South-East, Corsican on the island of Corsica. Immigrants speak their own languages, particularly Portuguese, Arab, Berber, Spanish, Italian and diverse African languages.
Political Parties: Socialist Party; Rally for the Republic (RPR); Union for French Democracy (UDF); National Front; Communist Party; the Greens.
Social Organizations: General Labor Confederation (CGT); French Democratic Labor Confederation (CFDT); Workers' Force (FO) ; French Confederation of Christian Workers (CFTC). France has the lowest level of unionization in the European Community (8 per cent in 1990).

THE STATE
Official Name: République Française.
Administrative divisions: 22 Regions with 96 Departments in France and 5 possessions, called "Overseas Departments".
Capital: Paris, 9,500,000 people (1994).
Other cities: Marseille, 1,230,000 people; Lyon, 1,260,000; Toulouse, 608,000; Nice 1,300,000.
Government: President: Jacques Chirac, since May 1995. Lionel Jospin, Prime Minister since June 1997. Bicameral legislature: Chamber of Deputies, 577 members; Senate, 317 members.
Armed Forces: 409,000 (1995) **Other**: 96,300 Gendarmes.

---

several wars with Italy, over a hundred revolts, wars between Catholics and Protestants, and the Black Death which scoured the country in the 14th and 15th centuries. Over the following century, the social and economic structures of the country changed, making conditions ripe for revolution.

[11] All forms of servitude disappeared and many feudal lords had to sell their property. The country's mercantile structures stabilized with the rise of manufacturing and trade, triggering population growth and urbanization.

[12] Louis XIV, the "Sun King", personified the concept of absolute monarchy. He came to the throne in 1661, and established the "Divine Right of Kings". He consolidated the unity of France, giving rise to the concept of the modern State.

During his reign, French cultural influence reached its apogee.

[13] The 1789 Revolution opened up a new era in the history of France. The National Assembly, convened in July of that year, replaced the absolute monarch with a constitutional monarchy. The fall of the Bastille on July 14 and the Declaration of the Rights of Man, on August 27, brought the old regime to an end, thus paving the way for the rise of the bourgeoisie - the prevailing class of the towns - whose reforms came into direct conflict with the Church and the King. Finally, the Assembly overthrew the monarchy and proclaimed the First French Republic.

[14] The rest of Europe joined forces against revolutionary France. Danton and Robespierre declared the nation "to be in peril" and formed a citizen army. This Committee of Public

Salvation was able to forestall foreign invasion but internal confrontations resulted in the "Reign of Terror". Robespierre and his companions were overthrown and executed by the liberal, more moderate bourgeoisie in July 1794.

[15] For the next five years, the revolutionaries tried to regain control of the country, which had fallen victim to corruption, internal strife and instability. Napoleon Bonaparte's coup (1799) brought an end to the dying regime. Seizing power, he had himself named Consul for Life in 1802 and then Emperor in 1804.

[16] Although Napoleon's reign represented a return to absolutism, it preserved the main achievements of the Revolution. Legal, administrative, religious, financial and educational reorganization changed the country irrevocably. Napoleon strove hard to bring the rest of Europe under his control and his armies occupied the whole of the continent from Madrid to the outskirts of Moscow. Finally, exhausted by war, France was defeated at Waterloo in 1815.

[17] France was rocked by rebellions in 1830, 1848 and 1871, and constant disturbance. In spite of this, the Industrial Revolution brought factories, railroads, large companies and credit institutions to France. The Third Republic, beginning in 1870, was to be France's longest-lasting regime in almost a century and a half.

[18] With the establishment of universal male suffrage in 1848, the peasants and the urban middle class had the greatest electoral power. The Government managed to win their support by protectionism and the establishment of free, secular and mandatory primary education, which raised aspirations of greater social mobility.

[19] Under the Republic, France had a period of colonial expansion, beginning with the conquest of Algeria in 1830, and continuing with other territories in Africa and the Far East. A large empire was built, with colonies in the Caribbean, Africa, the Middle East, the Indochinese peninsula and the Pacific.

[20] World War I enabled France to recover Alsace and Lorraine,

which had been annexed by Germany in 1870. The war left France devastated. More than 1.5 million people had been killed. Property damage coupled with the internal and foreign debt added up to more than 150 billion gold francs, and the nation's currency lost its traditional stability. Neither the right-wing bloc nor the radical party was able to bring the economic and political situation under control.

[21] The world-wide recession reached France in 1931. In 1936, the parties of the left, who had joined together to form the Popular Front, had won the legislative elections. They had carried out important social reforms, such as paid vacations and the 40-hour working week, but they were unable to hold back unemployment or the looming economic crisis. Government became polarized between supporters of Italian Fascism and those of Communism. This split led to an impasse until 1939, when Germany invaded Poland.

[22] Germany went on to occupy almost one-third of France. In 1940, Marshall Petain signed an armistice proclaiming the "national revolution" transforming non-occupied France into a satellite of Berlin. From London, General de Gaulle urged the French people to continue the fight.

[23] France was liberated in 1944. The French participated in the liberation and the invasion of Germany, with the resistance movement (especially the communists and socialists), the Free French Forces (liberal nationalists) and French troops fighting alongside the Allies. In October 1946, the Fourth Republic was proclaimed. This period was characterized by political instability and bitter opposition between the French Communist Party (PCF) and General de Gaulle's party.

[24] Funds from the US Marshall Plan, led to the economic and social reconstruction of the country. Production reached a six per cent annual growth rate. Per capita income increased 47 per cent between 1949 and 1959; women were granted the right to

STATISTICS

DEMOGRAPHY
Population: 58,333,000 (1996) **Annual growth:** 0.5 % (1980/1996) **Estimates for year 2000:** 59,000,000 **Annual growth to year 2000:** 0.3 % (1994/2000) **Urban Population:** 74.8 % (1996) **Urban growth:** 0.45 % (1980/95) **Children per woman:** 1.7 (1996).

HEALTH
Life expectancy at birth: 79 years (1996) male: 74 years (1994) female: 83 years (1994) **Infant mortality:** 5 per 1,000 (1996) **Under-5 child mortality:** 6 per 1,000 (1996) **Calorie consumption:** 143 % (1988/90) 333 **people per doctor** (1988/91).

EDUCATION
School enrolment : Primary total: 105 % (1990/95) male : 107 % (1990/95) female: 105 % (1990/95) Secondary: male : 104 % (1990/95) female: 107 % (1990/95) Tertiary: 50 % (1995) **Primary school teachers:** one for every 19 students (1995).

COMMUNICATIONS
240 **newspapers**, 891 **radios**, 580 **TV sets** and 547 **main telephone lines** per 1,000 people (1994) **Books:** 78 new titles per 100,000 people (1992/94).

ECONOMY
Per capita, GNP: $ 26,270 (1996) **Annual growth, GNP:** 1 % (1995/96) **Annual inflation:** 2.75 % (1985/95) **Consumer price index:** 109.7 (1994) **Currency:** 4.9 french francs = $ 1 (1995) **Cereal imports:** 1,228 metric tons (1994) **Fertilizer use:** 2,418 kgs per ha (1994) **Exports:** $ 283,318 million (1996) Imports: $ 274,088 million (1996).

ENERGY
Consumption: 4,042.25 Kgs of Oil equivalent per capita yearly (1994) 94.67 % imported (1994)

HDI (rank / value) 2 / 0.946 (1994).

vote; the banks were nationalized and a social security program went into effect. In 1957 France was one of the six signatories of the Treaty of Rome, which created the European Economic Community (EEC).

[25] After 1945, France was unable to re-establish its pre-war control over its colonies. The spirit of democracy and increasing awareness of universal human rights, was consolidated by the anti-Fascist alliance and the creation of the United Nations. Colonization had not allowed local identity to influence policy, so decolonization took place through fierce pro-independence movements, with little room for negotiation.

[26] In 1945, Syria and Libya were the first countries to become independent, followed by Morocco, Tunisia and Madagascar. Vietnam, Laos and Cambodia became independent only in 1954, after a long and bloody war. In May 1958, four years after the Algerian revolution began, the pieds-noirs - French people residing in the colony - revolted. They made the army promise not to leave the country. This dealt a mortal blow to the Fourth Republic, and the Government called in General de Gaulle to deal with the crisis.

[27] The establishment of the Fifth Republic in 1958 and the 1962 decision to elect the president by direct universal suffrage laid the foundation for a regime with strong presidential powers. After the independence of Algeria and the last remaining African colonies, the country sought to achieve greater stability. With national independence as the primary aim of their foreign policy, France made use of "deterrent" atomic power and withdrew from the military structure of the North Atlantic Treaty Organization (NATO), in 1966.

[28] France continued to be a member of the Atlantic alliance, and maintained enormous economic, cultural and political influence over its former African colonies, south of the Sahara. Diplomatic relations with Algeria, Vietnam, and other countries that had fought bloody wars for independence were not restored until 1982.

[29] In May 1968, the greatest social and political crisis of the Fifth Republic took place. Huge student protests and labor strikes throughout the country were brought on by the regime's growing authoritarianism in the educational and social sectors. For a whole month, the

Wallis and Futuna

Population:	15,000 (1996)
Area:	300 SQ KM
Capital:	Mata-Utu
Currency:	CFP Franc
Language:	French

Wallis was named after Samuel Wallis, a navigator who "discovered" it in 1767. Marist missionaries arrived in the archipelago in 1837 and converted the inhabitants to Catholicism. It became a French protectorate in 1888, and in December 1959, after a referendum, the country adopted the status of French Overseas Territory.

[2] Unlike other French dependencies in the Pacific, there are no pro-independence movements on the islands. In 1983, the two kingdoms of Futuna achieved separation from Wallis, but maintained their relationship with France. The islands' economic prospects are poor: in addition to the devastating effect of cyclones which periodically hit the islands, the only bank on the islands was closed. Wallis and Futuna received FF55 million in aid from France in 1987. Approximately 50 per cent of the economically active population has had to emigrate to other parts of Polynesia in search of work; their remittances, together with public works projects, constitute the main source of income for the islands.

[3] In the 1992 elections for the Territorial Assembly, the left managed to defeat the neo-Gaullist RPR, a party of the right, for the first time in twenty years. In 1997, the neo-gaullist candidate Victor Brial gained the bench of deputy for Wallis in the French National Assembly.

ENVIRONMENT
The territory consists of the Wallis archipelago (159 sq km), formed by Uvea Island - where the capital is located - and 22 islets, plus the Futuna (64 sq km) and Alofi Islands (51 sq km). This group is located in western Polynesia, surrounded by Tuvalu to the north, Fiji to the south and the Samoa archipelago to the east. With a rainy and tropical climate, the major commercial activities are copra and fishing.

SOCIETY
Peoples: Of Polynesian origin. Approximately two thirds of the population live on Wallis and the rest on Futuna. Nearly 12,000 inhabitants live in Kanaky and Vanuatu.
Religions: Catholic.
Languages: French (official) and Polynesian languages.

THE STATE
Capital: Mata-Utu, (located on Uvea) 815 people (1983).
Government: Overseas territory administered by a French-appointed Chief Administrator, Robert Pommies since 1990, assisted by a 20-member Assembly elected for a 5-year term.
The kingdoms of Wallis and Futuna (in Sigave and Alo) from which the country was formed, have very limited powers. They send one deputy to the French National Assembly, and another to the Senate.

government seemed to be seriously threatened. Apart from the student leaders, however, there were no other political forces capable of toppling the government, and the general strike was called off when a salary increase was promised.

[30] The years which followed saw the birth of other groups based around social issues, such as the feminist, ecological and antinuclear movements. In 1972 the Socialist Party and the Communist Party created the Union of the Left, and François Mitterrand, the Socialist candidate, was elected President in 1981 because of the Communist votes; his was the first left-wing cabinet since 1958.

[31] The new government carried out reforms: the nationalization of important industrial and banking groups, new labor rights for workers, the 39-hour working week, an increase in social benefits, retirement at the age of 60 and a decentralization of power. However, unemployment, the economic crisis and an increase in imports led the government to enforce a harsh economic policy and to carry out restructuring of the industrial sector. This led communist ministers to resign from the Government, in 1984. In 1981, a Ministry of Women's Rights had been created, charged to enforce existing legislation.

[32] In mid-1994, Prime Minister Pierre Mauroy, a symbol of the Left's union, was replaced by Laurent Fabius, a young technocrat, considered a loyal friend of Mitterrand's. Fabius formed a more centrist government than Mauroy's, in which the communists refused to take part.

[33] In 1985, relations between France and several South Pacific countries like Australia and New Zealand were deteriorated when it was discovered the French were responsible for sinking a Greenpeace ship which caused the death of a militant ecologist when it was headed for the Mururoa atoll to demonstrate against French nuclear tests.

[34] In 1986, expecting a defeat of the Left, Mitterrand substituted the majority electoral system by a proportional system which gave more seats to the losers than the

previous one. In March, a right-wing coalition made up mainly of the Group for the Republic (RPR), a party led by neo-Gaullist Jacques Chirac and by former president (1974-1981) Valery Giscard D'Estaing's Union for the French Democracy (UDF), defeated the Left in the legislative elections. The elections confirmed a clear progress of Jean Marie Le Pen's ultra-right National Front. Chirac had to form a new government and for two years the country experienced its first 'cohabitation' between a left-wing president and a conservative council of ministers.

[35] Chirac's government wiped out some of the 1981 and 1982 reforms with the privatization of several companies nationalized by the left but kept most of the social gains. In the meantime, it continued a liberalization policy of the economy and finances begun in the socialist government's last years. In the field of individual liberties, the strong hand of Interior minister Charles Pasqua, especially regarding legislation concerning foreigners living in France, was criticized by several humanitarian organizations.

[36] In 1988, Mitterrand defeated Chirac in presidential elections. The elected President called for new legislative elections. After a new victory of the Socialist Party, socialist Michel Rocard was appointed Prime Minister.

[37] The Socialist economic policy did not differ substantially from that of the right. Unemployment kept on the rise, with a 9.5 per cent rate of the economically active population in 1991. That year, Rocard was replaced by Edith Cresson, who was the first woman to become head of government in modern France. Nine months later, Mitterrand replaced Cresson with former Economy minister Pierre Bérégovoy, with the backing of industrial and financial circles.

[38] In 1993, the Left was defeated in legislative elections once again and Mitterrand named conservative Edouard Balladur as prime minister. The corruption scandals, whose main targets had been socialist leaders, affected this time renowned right-wing politicians and caused three of Balladur's ministers to resign in 1994.

St Pierre and Miquelon

Population: 7,000 (1996)
Area: 242 SQ KM
Capital: St Pierre
Currency: French Franc
Language: French

An archipelago of 8 small islands, near the Canadian coast, in the north Atlantic, economically dependent on fishing.

SOCIETY
The People: The majority are descendants of French settlers.
Religion: Catholic.
Language: French.

THE STATE
Capital: St Pierre, 5,663 people (1990).
Other towns: Miquelon, 709 people (1990).

Government: A French overseas department administered by a 19-member Conseil Général elected a 6-year term, and a Commissioner appointed by the **French Government**. In the French National Assembly, the area is represented by one deputy and has one senator and one representative in the European Parliament.

DEMOGRAPHY:
Urban Population: 91.6 (1996)

[39] In the April 1995 presidential elections Chirac defeated socialist Lionel Jospin and appointed conservative Alain Juppé as prime minister.

[40] In December, the largest civil servants' strike since 1968 paralyzed the country for over three weeks. The social situation remained tense in 1996, which some observers linked with unfair income distribution - 20 per cent of the population received 44 per cent of total personal income - and property distribution, since 20 per cent of the French owned 69 per cent of national wealth.

[41] The Juppé administration continued its austerity policy which caused confrontation with labour unions in 1996. A new law was passed in 1997 to restrict the entrance and residence of immigrants in the country. In February there were demonstrations against the measure which mobilized over 150,000 people in one day.

[42] Unexpectedly, Chirac called for early legislative elections. In the second round, on May 25, the

leftist opposition obtained an important victory after running united in the elections. The Socialist Party obtained 241 deputies and became the country's largest party once more. Together with the Communists, with 38 seats, the Greens, with seven, and other 33 deputies from the left, the Socialist Party achieved a comfortable majority in parliament. The right wing coalition obtained 256 deputies, while the National Front only got only one seat.

[43] Lionel Jospin became the new Prime Minister and the Communists had two ministries while the Greens held one, by former presidential candidate Dominique Voynet.

[44] In 1997, in order to address unemployment, Jospin proposed the reduction of the working week to 35 hours. Many demonstrations, both by workers and unemployed, which continued through to 1998, demanded the immediate adoption of this measure.

French Guiana

Guyane Française

Population:	153,000 (1994)
Area:	90,000 SQ KM
Capital:	Cayenne
Currency:	French Franc
Language:	French

The Arawaks were short, copper-skinned people with straight, black hair. They grew corn, cotton, yams and sweet potatoes. They built round huts with thatched, cone-shaped roofs, and slept in hammocks, an Arawak word which survived the culture which gave rise to it. The Caribs displaced them from the area and later resisted the Spaniards who began to arrive toward the beginning of the 16th century.

2   In 1604 the French occupied Guyana, despite Carib resistance. The colony passed successively into Dutch, English and Portuguese hands, until the beginning of French domination in 1676. Towards the end of the 18th century, France sent more than 3,000 colonists to settle the interior. Few survived the tropical diseases, but those who did sought refuge in a group of islands off the coast which they named Health Islands. After a brief period of prosperity brought about by the discovery of gold in the Appranage River basin, the colony gradually fell into decline.

3   In 1946, Guiana became a French 'Overseas Department'. Nine-tenths of the country is covered by forests, and although the country is fertile, most of the food is imported. The creole (African and mestizo) 80 per cent of the population are limited to minor positions in the local bureaucracy or police. The country is heavily reliant on French funding which provided 70 per cent of the GNP in 1989. Imports are worth ten times the exports of wood, rum, coffee and gold.

4   In 1967, the National Center for Space Studies was established. Over 1,300 foreign technicians work there, earning First World salaries, as well as 1,500 French Guianan nationals. Thirty Ariane voyages have been launched from the base at Kourou, with all the satellites sent into space financed by European consortia.

5   During the 1970s, the autonomist Socialist Party of Guiana (PSG) became the majority party at the local level. Early in the 1980s, armed groups attacked 'colonialist' targets, but tensions were defused with the victory in France of the French Socialist Party in 1981.

6   At the "First Conference of the Last French Colonies", held in Guadeloupe in 1985, there was severe criticism of the availability of French visas and citizenship for east Asians, while Haitians, Brazilians and Guyanans, with closer cultural ties, underwent persecution and discrimination.

7   In 1986, Guiana's representation in the French National Assembly increased to two members. In the 1989 municipal elections, Cayenne and 12 other districts, out of the 19 at stake, were won by the left. Georges Othily, a PSG dissident was elected for the French Senate.

8   In 1990, France announced a regional co-operation plan with the Caribbean, including financial aid of only 2.8 million dollars.

9   In 1992, the persistent economic crisis caused a week-long general strike, called by unions and the business sector. As a result, Paris agreed to fund a plan to improve infrastructure and education. In 1994, French Guyana entered the Association of Caribbean States as an associate member.

10   Per capita income is the highest in South America, but the economy is dependent on income generated by the space studies centre in Kourou, French subsidies and imports of food from France.

11   In November 1997, French President Jacques Chirac announced a development plan for French Guiana, after recognizing the critical economic situation of this South American possession. The announcement did not raise many expectations, with the local authorities let down by previous promises.

12   On April 1 1998, André Lecante, was designated president of the Guiana General Council, one of the two main legislative bodies in French Guiana. The growth of the independence movements was reflected in March in the elections for the Regional Council, the other legislative body. The governing Socialist party suffered a serious setback, losing its absolute majority when its representation shrank from 16 to 11 members, while the De-Colonization Movement of Guiana took three seats.

PROFILE

ENVIRONMENT
French Guiana is located slightly north of the Equator. Due to its hot and rainy climate, only the coastal alluvial lowlands are suitable for agriculture (cocoa, bananas, sugar cane, rice and corn). The hinterland mountains are covered with rainforests. The country has large reserves of bauxite and gold.

SOCIETY
Peoples: Mostly from native and European roots. There are Carib and Tupi Guarani ethnic groups, and Cimarrones, descendents of African slaves. In the cities there are Chinese, Indian and French minorities.
Religions: Mainly Catholic, also Hindu.
Languages: French (official), Creole.
Political Parties: The Union for the Republic (RPR); the Socialist Party of Guiana (PSG); the De-Colonization Movement of Guiana; the Union for French Democracy (UDF).

THE STATE
Official Name: Département d'Outre-Mer de la Guyane française.
Administrative Divisions: 2 Districts.
Capital: Cayenne, 55,000 people (1994 est).
Other Cities: Kourou, 135,000 people, St Laurent-du-Maroni, 14,000 people.
Government: Jacques Chirac, Chief of State since May, 1995. Pierre Dartout, prefect designated by France. Regional parliament (consultative body): General Council, made up of 19 members, and Regional Council, with 31 members. The department has 2 representatives in the National Assembly and 2 in the French Senate.
National Holiday: All French holidays.
Armed Forces: 8,400 French troops.

DEMOGRAPHY
Population: 153,000 (1996). **Urban population:** 76.8 % (1996).

French Polynesia

Polynésie Française

Population: 223,000 (1996)
Area: 4,000 SQ KM
Capital: Papeete

Currency: CFP Franc
Language: French

P olynesia's first inhabitants either came from America or Indonesia, but the evidence is inconclusive.

[2] In 1840 the islands were occupied by France and in 1880, despite native resistance, the archipelago was officially made a colony under the name of "the French Establishments of Oceania". In 1958, they became an Overseas Territory.

[3] Except for some concessions on the domestic front, France continued to maintain its control over the islands, with a hard-line policy because of the strategic location of the islands and the atomic tests which have taken place on the Mururoa atoll since 1966. In 1975 France also carried out tests on the Fangataufa atoll for tests, despite strong opposition to the growing militarization of the islands from the population of the territory and other countries in the area, especially New Zealand,.

[4] In the face of French intransigence, there was increasing resistance from separatist groups, who took their case to the UN Decolonization Committee, though few concrete resolutions were made.

[5] The "nuclearization" of the area rapidly resulted in the destruction of French Polynesia's traditional economic base, as the island was currently dependent upon the French military budget. In less than one generation, the economy went from self-sufficiency to dependence upon imported goods. By the end of 1980, 80 per cent of basic foodstuffs were imported.

[6] Both the environment and the health of the islands' inhabitants has deteriorated over the last decades, and there was dramatic increases in the incidence of brain tumors, leukemia and thyroid cancer. The scale of these illnesses is hard to evaluate, as the French Government refused to divulge medical statistics in recent years.

[7] In 1985, the explosion of a bomb planted by two French secret agents killed an ecology activist and destroyed a Greenpeace ship that was heading for Mururoa in order to protest against nuclear testing. In 1992, French President François Mitterrand decided a temporary suspension of nuclear tests and Paris began negotiations with Papeete for an economic plan to be carried out after the permanent closure of the experiment centers in Mururoa and Fangataufa.

[8] The "Progress Pact" between Paris and "French" Polynesia was based in assumptions similar to those in structural adjustment programs advocated by the IMF, i.e. economic liberalization, privatizations and "major balancing" in public finance. For the 1994-1998 period, Paris planned a slight increase in financial contributions for the pact to attain its goals. However, the main pro-autonomy political party, Tavini Uiraatira (that means "serving the people" in the Polynesian language) led by Oscar

> The "nuclearization" of the area rapidly resulted in the destruction of French Polynesia's traditional economic base, as the island was currently dependent upon the French military budget.

Temaru and representing 15 per cent of the voters, proposed nationalizations and the extension of free services.

[9] French President Chirac carried out further nuclear tests in 1995. After the first one of these explosions, there were disturbances and fighting in French Polynesia. In January 1996, he announced the permanent suspension of nuclear tests.

[10] In May 1997, the legislative elections were won by the conservative candidates of the Tahoeraa Huiraatira-RPR, followed by the pro-independence tendencies.

[11] In February 1998, it was revealed that tourism, above all from Japan and Italy, had increased 35 per cent during 1997. This was partly due to the suspension of nuclear tests.

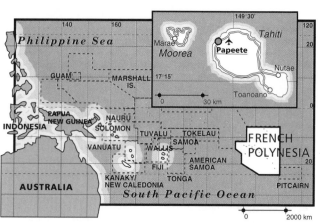

PROFILE

ENVIRONMENT
The territory is located in the southeast portion of Polynesia. Most of the French Polynesian islands are of volcanic origin but they also have major coral formations. The islands are largely mountainous, with tropical climate and heavy rainfall. Relatively fertile soils favor agricultural development. The Windward and Leeward Islands form the Society Archipelago. Nuclear tests carried out by France over a 26-year period have caused damage to the environment and people that is difficult to evaluate.

SOCIETY
Peoples: Polynesian 78 per cent, Chinese 12 per cent, French descendants 6 per cent.
Religions: Mostly Christian, 54 per cent Protestant, 30 per cent Catholic.
Languages: French (official), Tahitian (national).
Political Parties: Tahoeraa Huiraatira (RPR), conservative; Pupu Here Ai'a, pro autonomy; Ai'a Api, a coalition of parties; Tavini Huiraatira, an anti-nuclear and independence movement.
Social Organizations: The Pacific Christian Workers Central (CTCP), the Federation of French Polynesian Unions (FSPF) and the Territorial Union of the General Labor Confederation "Workers' Force" (UTSCGT).

THE STATE
Official Name: Territoire d'Outre-Mer de la Polynésie française.
Administrative Divisions: Windward Islands, which include Tahiti, Murea, Maio; Papeete constitutes the center of the district. Leeward Islands, with the capital in Utoroa on Ralatea island. It also includes the islands of Huahine, Tahaa, Bora-Bora and Maupiti. Tuamotu and Gambier Archipelagos, the Austral Islands and the Marquesas Islands.
Capital: Papeete, 115,000 people (1994).
Government: The French Government is represented by a High Commissioner, who controls the areas of defence, foreign relations and justice. President of the Council of Ministers: Gaston Flosse. A local 41-member Territorial Assembly is elected by universal suffrage for a 5-year term. This assembly, in turn, elects the President of the Council of Ministers, an executive body which is made up of 5 to 10 members of the Territorial Assembly, selected by the President.

DEMOGRAPHY
Population: 223,000 (1996) **Urban population:** 56.4%(1996)

ECONOMY
Cereal imports: 38 metric tons (1994) **Fertilizer use:** 370 kgs per ha (1994)

Gabon

Population:	1,106,000 (1996)
Area:	267,668 SQ KM
Capital:	Libreville
Currency:	CFA francs
Language:	French

Gabon

Tools found in the Gabon forests indicate that this region has been inhabited since the Palaeolithic age. Nothing else is known about life in the area until the 16th century, when the migrations that triggered the crisis in the ancient state of Congo (see "Congo: The Bantu states of Congo") brought the Myene and, in the 17th century, the Fang to Gabon. Thereafter, they monopolized the slave and ivory trade together with the Europeans.

2   The Portuguese arrived in 1472. Around the middle of the 19th century, the French, Dutch and British established a permanent trade of ivory, precious woods and slaves. In 1849, Libreville was founded and established as a settlement for freed slaves from other French colonies. The territory was of little economic interest to the French, who used it as a base for expeditions into the heart of the continent.

3   The quest for independence was relatively uneventful because the two local parties (the Joint Mixed Gabonese Movement of Leon M'Ba and the Democratic and Social Union of Jean-Hillaire Aubame) were willing to accept neo-colonialism.

4   Gabon has abundant resources: iron ore, uranium, manganese, timber and oil. The transnational oil company Shell discovered oil in Rabikuna, near Port Gentil. These oil reserves contain enough crude to last for 50 years and the oil wells are already in operation. Shell holds an 80 per cent interest in the wells already in operation and French company ELF the remaining 20 per cent; Amoco (an American company) and

Braspetro (Brazilian) have been authorized to continue oil exploration in the Port Gentil area.

5   Until recently, timber mills were the only local industry of any size, but a few years ago, French and US transnationals discovered that Gabon could serve as a spearhead to penetrate the markets of central Africa, and they initiated its industrialization. This "development", relying on foreign capital has only exacerbated social conflicts and the promise of jobs in the cities has encouraged urban migration. Gabon's social structure is changing as independent producers become suppliers of cheap labor for transnational industries. Economically, the breakdown of the rural economy has completely blocked the way to food self-sufficiency, destroying the only social sector which remained independent of foreign capital.

6   The neo-colonial system has been guaranteed by a military treaty signed between Libreville and Paris in 1960. Its effectiveness was proved in 1964 when M'Ba was deposed by a group of progressive officers.

7   When M'Ba died in 1967, he was succeeded by Omar Bongo, head of cabinet, who faithfully followed and even refined his predecessor's style, becoming Giscard D'Estaing's "privileged spokesman" in Africa. Applying the US thesis of "sub-imperialisms" to French interests, Bongo became its watchdog in central Africa, with Gabon a base for aggression against neighboring progressive regimes. In January 1977, Gabon provided the planes and arms used by a mercenary group in an unsuccessful attack on Benin.

8   Bongo's foreign policy

continued to evolve and he maintains good relations with several states in the region, without altering the country's privileged relationship with France. Like Senegal, Ivory Coast, Chad, and the Central African Republic, Gabon also had French troops on its soil.

9   In 1979 and again in 1986, Bongo was re-elected with 99 per cent of the vote, in presidential elections in which he was the only candidate.

10   His outrageous squandering led to violent protests from the Gabonese in the early 1980s. The revolt spread to the police who, in 1982, organized an unheard-of demonstration, demanding an increase in wages and the withdrawal of French advisors. The protests were brutally repressed by Gabon's secret police, officially known as the "Documentation Center".

11   The Government repressed the National Reorientation Movement (MORENA), formed by intellectuals, workers, students and nationalist politicians. The movement was accused of having expropriated 30 tons of weapons in October 1982. At that time, the Bongo family and French military installations were the target of

armed attacks. At least 28 top MORENA leaders were sentenced to 15 years' imprisonment. The French Socialist Party criticized the rulings, thus seriously upsetting Bongo's relations with president François Mitterrand.

12   This episode did not stop Bongo from visiting France in March 1984. The friendly greeting at the presidential palace received as much criticism as the decision to allow the French government to build a nuclear plant in Gabon.

13   In late 1989 there were signs of democratic participation for Gabon's opposition forces. After violent confrontations in the streets the President had the constitution amended, introducing a multiparty system and lifting censorship of the press. In the meantime, he invited six opposition leaders to join the cabinet.

14   There was a period of calm after all this social upheaval. However in May, Joseph Redjambe, president of the Gabonese Progressive Party was murdered in a Libreville hotel. His death provoked strong reactions against the Government, thought to be associated with the murder. A state of rebellion through the entire Port Gentil region lasted ten days and

WORKERS

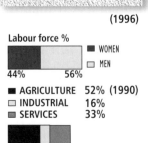

(1996)

Labour force %

■ WOMEN
□ MEN

44%   56%

■ AGRICULTURE   52% (1990)
□ INDUSTRIAL   16%
▨ SERVICES   33%

LAND USE

DEFORESTATION -0.6% annual (81/90)
IRRIGATED 1.4 % of arable

(1993)

■ FOREST & WOODLAND 74.3%
□ ARABLE   1.1%
▨ OTHER   24.6%

PROFILE

ENVIRONMENT

Irrigated by the Ogooue River basin, the country has an equatorial climate with year-round rainfall. The land is covered by dense rainforest and a large part of the population work in the local timber industry. The country has manganese, uranium, iron and petroleum reserves. Deforestation is one of the most serious environmental problems, together with the depredation of the country's wildlife.

SOCIETY

Peoples: Gabon was populated by pygmy hunters. In the 16th century it was invaded by Myene and other ethnic groups. Today over half of the population are Bantu, divided into more than 40 different groups including Galoa, Nkomi, and Irungu. One third of the population are Fang and Kwele, while in the northern and southern parts of Gabon there are Punu and Nzabi minorities.

Religions: Mainly Christian. More than one third practice traditional African religions and there is a small Muslim minority.

Languages: French (official). Bantu languages are spoken along the coast; Fang is used in northern Gabon; local languages and dialects are used in the rest of the country.

Political Parties: Gabonese Democratic Party (PDG), pro-government. Gabonese Progress Party and National Union of Timberworkers, in the opposition.

THE STATE

Official Name: République Gabonaise.

Administrative divisions: 9 provinces and 37 prefectures.

Capital: Libreville, 419,600 people (1993).

Other cities: Port Gentil 178,200 people (1993); Franceville 75,000 people (1988).

Government: Parliamentary republic with strong head of State. Omar (Albert-Bernard) Bongo, President and head of State since December 1967. Paulin Obame-Nguema, Head of Government and Prime Minister since November 1994. Single-chamber legislature:National Assembly, with 120 members elected every five years.

National Holiday: July 17, Independence Day (1960).

Armed Forces: 4,700 (1995).

Other: Coast Guard: 2,800; Gendarmerie: 2,000.

STATISTICS

DEMOGRAPHY

Population: 1,106,000 (1996) **Annual growth:** 2.9% (1980/1996) **Estimates for year 2000:** 1,200,000 **Annual growth to year 2000:** 2.8% (1994/2000) **Urban Population:** 51.2% (1996) **Urban growth:** 5.43% (1980/95) **Children per woman:** 5.3 (1996).

HEALTH

Life expectancy at birth: 55 years (1996) male: 53 years (1994) female: 56 years (1994) **Infant mortality:** 87 per 1,000 (1996) **Under-5 child mortality:** 145 per 1,000 (1996) **Calorie consumption:** 104% (1988/90) 2,500 **people per doctor** (1988/91) **Safe water:** 68% (1990/96).

EDUCATION

Literacy: 63% (1995) male : 74% (1995) female: 53% (1995) **Primary school teachers:** one for every 52 students (1995).

COMMUNICATIONS

20 **newspapers,** 147 **radios,** 50 **TV sets** and 30 **main telephone lines** per 1,000 people (1994).

ECONOMY

Per capita, GNP: $ 3,950 (1996) **Annual growth, GNP:** -1.2% (1995/96) **Annual inflation:** 5.01% (1985/95) **Consumer price index:** 123.8 (1994) **Currency:** 490 CFA francs = $ 1 (1995) **Cereal imports:** 64 metric tons (1994) **Food import dependency:** 13% (1994) **Fertilizer use:** 8 kgs per ha (1994) **Exports:** $ 3,146 million (1996) **Imports:** $ 898 million (1996) **External debt:** $ 4,213 million (1996) $ 3,809 **per capita:** (1996) **Debt service:** 11.1% of exports (1996) Development aid received: $ 143 million (1995) $ 138 per capita (1995) 4.4% of GNP (1994).

ENERGY

Consumption: 651.80 Kgs of Oil equivalent per capita yearly (1994) -2,211.84% imported (1994)

HDI (rank / value) 120 / 0.562 (1994).

---

the French Government evacuated 5,000 French residents, charging the presidential guard with re-establishing order. According to information confirmed by Amnesty International, the incidents left a toll of six dead and a hundred wounded.

[15] Once calm had been restored, the political and social groups met on June 6, in a National Conference and an agreement was reached whereby presidential elections would be held. This was undoubtedly a major victory for the opposition, who extracted promises of multiparty elections from the president. But Bongo advanced the election date from 1992 to late 1990, a tactic meaning that he could use the power base he had built up over the past 20 years in office to carry out his campaign, while the opposition had no time to organize itself adequately or overcome its internal divisions.

[16] In September 1990, President Bongo's Gabonese Democratic Party (PDG), obtained a majority in the National Assembly. The new constitution, approved in March 1991, formally established a multiparty system.

[17] In 1991, the country was rocked by a new outbreak of political and social violence. The economic crisis continued to worsen and the economic stabilization program launched in September under IMF guidelines, and the structural adjustment plan promoted by the World Bank failed to generate much hope.

[18] The absence of an electoral timetable and student agitation demanding greater resources for the university increased tension even further. The President closed the university, called off the elections and banned all political meetings. The opposition called a general strike, which paralyzed

Port Gentil, the center of the oil industry. Concerned by the extent of the protests, Bongo reopened the university and lifted the ban on demonstrations.

[19] The presidential elections of December 1993, which brought Bongo to power again, were questioned by the opposition. In February, the protests continued and were harshly repressed leaving 30 dead. In negotiations in Paris between September and November 1994, a coalition government was formed until new elections could be held.

[20] In July 1995, the President gained the support of 96 per cent of the voters in a referendum for constitutional reform in order for presidential and legislative elections to be held. The National Assembly elections in December 1996 gave the Democratic Party led by Bongo 47 of the 55 seats. Meanwhile, the opposition leader Paul Mba-Abessole, scored a

sizeable victory in the municipal elections, becoming mayor of the capital Libreville.

[21] Despite the fact Gabon had per capita income of $3,490per year thanks to oil income, the poverty indicators provided an alarming picture. In 1997, life expectancy was less than 55years, literacy barely reached 63 per cent of adults and the infant mortality rate stood at 87 per thousand.

[22] In early 1998, Mayor Mba-Abessole asked the United Nations to supervise the presidential elections slated for that year, to prevent "the fraudulent re-election of Omar Bongo." The request from Bongo for European embassies to provide ballot boxes for the election gave some idea of the reigning disorder, as it suggested that the Government had lost the boxes used in the previous elections.

Gambia

Population:	1,141,000 (1996)
Area:	11,295 SQ KM
Capital:	Banjul
Currency:	Dalasis
Language:	English

Gambia

The earliest settlers of the Gambia river valley came from what is now Senegal. Attracted by Gambia's coast, which lent itself to trade and navigation, they settled along the river, carrying out subsistence farming.

2   In the 15th century, the region was colonized by the Mandingo who, together with the Mali Empire, established their authority in the Gambia Valley. They also founded several kingdoms in the area, which controlled coastal trade and enabled them to develop economically and culturally.

3   With the arrival of the Portuguese in 1455, most of the region's domestic trade was displaced toward the Atlantic coast, bringing about the decline of the local kingdoms which had prospered under this trade. For the Portuguese, Gambia became the point of departure for a large quantity of precious metals.

4   Gambia was also important to them as a prosperous port of call on their route to the Orient. However, in 1618 the Portuguese Crown sold its commercial and territorial rights to the British Empire which at the height of its naval prowess was trying to assert its dominance as a colonial power by acquiring a foothold in Africa.

5   At that time, a war began between Britain and France (controlling all of what is now Senegal) which was to last for more than 200 years. From 1644, the British used this coastal area as a source of slaves, setting up alliances with inland tribal princes to provide them with human merchandise.

6   Throughout the 17th century, Gambia was nothing more than a source of slave labor for Britain's colonies and for its slave trade with other colonial powers. The British therefore limited themselves to establishing a rudimentary trading post in the area, founded in 1660. Border disputes between the British and French increased during the 18th century.

7   Throughout the 19th century a series of religious wars in the interior resulted in the complete Islamization of the country, with an increase in Muslim immigration from other parts of Africa. In the meantime, the region lost its international economic significance when the slave trade was abolished in Britain.

8   It did however gain strategic importance by being a British enclave inserted into the heart of Senegal, a region instrumental in France's designs on sub-Saharan Africa. Slavery actually continued within the colony until the 20th century, not being outlawed until 1906.

9   In 1889, France and Britain reached an agreement as to the boundaries of their respective colonies, ensuring peace in the region and the formal recognition of British sovereignty over Gambia by other European powers.

10   Gambia's status as a British colony remained unchanged throughout the first half of the 20th century. Although the decolonization process in Africa began after World War II - resulting in the creation of a number of independent states in what had formerly been European colonies - Gambia did not receive administrative autonomy from Britain until 1963. Two years later, Gambia obtained full independence and joined the British Commonwealth. At the time of its independence, Gambia did not seem to constitute a nation as such because of its ethnic, cultural and economic complexity.

11   After independence, the territory's social and economic structures remained unchanged. Exports continued to be based on a single crop, peanuts, while traditional social structures remained so unassailable that they were finally legitimized by the 1970 constitution. Thus, although some legislative seats were determined by the election of deputies, others were assigned to the 5 regional leaders.

12   Dawda Jawara, founder of the People's Progressive Party (PPP), has dominated Gambian politics since the 1960s. He won the 1962 elections, but failed to assume office because of a vote of no-confidence from the opposition. However, he yet again won the election in 1970 when the country was proclaimed a republic, with a presidential system of government.

13   Around 1975, the success of Alex Haley's book "Roots" turned Gambia into an important tourism center; but alongside this, prostitution and drug trafficking also increased while organized Islamic opposition emerged.

14   The lack of border controls in Gambia led to it becoming a sort of paradise for West African smuggling and a large part of Senegal's agricultural produce was illegally shipped through the port of Banjul.

15   The close economic relationship between the countries led the government of Dawda Jawara to accept a project for union in 1973.

16   In July 1981, Muslim dissidents attempted to overthrow Jawara, aiming to end official corruption through the establishment of a revolutionary Islamic regime. The revolt was crushed by Senegalese troops who entered Gambia at the request of President Dawda, who was in London at the time.

17   The proposed union with Senegal had been planned for 1982, but the coup attempt against Gambia's government accelerated plans for creating the Senegambian federation.

18   The 1980s were marked by a worsening of the country's economic situation, and a severe drought led to a sudden drop in the production of agricultural exports. The most obvious consequences were an increase in unemployment, migration from rural areas to the capital and increasing foreign debt to finance food imports.

19   Senegambia was officially established in February 1982 with Abdou Diouf of Senegal as its first president, assisted by a council of ministers and a bi-national parliament. The federation did not totally unite Senegal and Gambia, as both states retained their autonomous character and internal organization. The treaty ensured that Dawda Jawara gained protection against internal rebellions and Senegal gained greater control over the leak of export tax revenues through smuggling.

20   Gambia became unhappy with this alliance and its dissatisfaction became apparent in mid-1985, with its reluctance to sign the treaties aimed at strengthening ties with Senegal. Jawara subsequently failed to comply with the terms of the agreements promising Senegal military and

WORKERS

(1996)

Labour force %

45%	55%
■ WOMEN	□ MEN

■ AGRICULTURE 82% (1990)
□ INDUSTRIAL 8%
■ SERVICES 11%

LAND USE

DEFORESTATION -0.8% annual (81/90)
IRRIGATED 8.3 % of arable

(1993)

■ FOREST & WOODLAND	24.8%
□ ARABLE	15.9%
■ OTHER	59.3%

PER 100,000 LIVE BIRTHS

1,100

PER CAPITA

$396

39%

PROFILE

Environment
One of the smallest African countries, Gambia stretches 320 km along the Gambia River, which is fully navigable and one of the main waterways in the area. The climate is tropical; there are rainforests along the river-banks and wooded savannah further inland. The economy is based on peanut exports and tourism. Because of the use of firewood as a main energy source and the production of export crops large areas of forest have been felled.

SOCIETY
Peoples: The majority of Gambians belong to the Mandingo ethnic group, 40 per cent; 14 per cent are Futa, 13 per cent are Wolof who belong to the same root and 7 per cent are Diula. There are minor ethnic groups inland (Serahuilis, Akus). Five to ten thousand laborers migrate from Mali, Senegal and Guinea-Bissau every year only to return home after the harvest. **Religions:** The majority of Gambians practise the Islamic faith; a minority practise traditional religions and Christianity, mostly Protestant. **Languages:** English (official); the most widespread local languages are Mandingo, Fulani and Wolof (the Wolof form a majority in the main trade center). **Political Parties:** The People's Progressive Party (PPP), founded by Dawda Jawara in the 1960s; the National Convention Party (NCP) from a PPP split in the 1970s; the People's Party of Gambia (PPG). **Social Organizations:** There are three trade union federations: the Gambia Workers' Union (linked to the PPP); the Gambia Labor Union; and the Gambia Salesmen's and Merchants' Union.

THE STATE
Official Name: Republic of The Gambia. **Administrative Divisions:** 5 Provinces and the Capital. **Capital:** Banjul, 240,000 people (1994). **Other cities:** Brikama 24,300 people; Bakau 23,600 people (1986). **Government:** Presidential republic. Yahya Jammeh, President since September 1996. Legislature. Single-chamber Parliament: Chamber of Deputies, with 50 members, 36 of whom are elected by universal suffrage, 9 special members and 5 tribal chieftains. **National Holiday:** February 18, Independence (1965). **Armed Forces:** 800 troops (1994).

STATISTICS

DEMOGRAPHY
Population: 1,141,000 (1996) **Annual growth:** 3.6% (1980/1996) **Estimates for year 2000:** 1,200,000 **Annual growth to year 2000:** 2.4% (1994/2000) **Urban Population:** 29.7% (1996) **Urban growth:** 6.29% (1980/95) **Children per woman:** 5.3 (1996).

HEALTH
Life expectancy at birth: 46 years (1996) male: 44 years (1994) female: 47 years (1994) **Infant mortality:** 78 per 1,000 (1996) **Under-5 child mortality:** 107 per 1,000 (1996) **Safe water:** 48% (1990/96).

EDUCATION
Literacy: 39% (1995) male: 53% (1995) female: 25% (1995) **School enrolment:** Primary total: 67% (1990/95) male: 79% (1990/95) female: 56% (1990/95) Secondary: male: 25% (1990/95) female: 13% (1990/95) Tertiary: 2% (1995) **Primary school teachers:** one for every 30 students (1995).

COMMUNICATIONS
163 **radios** and 17 **main telephone lines** per 1,000 people (1994) **Books:** 2 new titles per 100,000 people (1992/94).

ECONOMY
Annual inflation: 9.01% (1985/95) **Consumer price index:** 128.8 (1994) **Currency:** 9.64 dalasis = $ 1 (1995) **Cereal imports:** 97 metric tons (1994) **Food import dependency:** 32% (1994) **Fertilizer use:** 46 kgs per ha (1994) **Exports:** $ 22 million (1996) **Imports:** $ 272 million (1996) **External debt:** $ 452 million (1996) $ 396 **per capita:** (1996) **Debt service:** 12.7% of exports (1996) **Development aid received:** $ 46 million (1995) $ 43 per capita (1995) 12.3% of GNP (1994).

ENERGY
Consumption: 55.58 Kgs of Oil equivalent per capita yearly (1994) 100.00% imported (1994)

HDI (rank / value) 165 / 0.281 (1994).

---

diplomatic support in case of external or internal conflicts.
[21] In the 1991-92 budget, the Minister of Finance announced a 6 per cent increase in the salaries of civil servants and reinstated a series of benefits eliminated when a structural adjustment program went into effect. Gambia has one of the world's highest infant mortality rates.
[22] In May 1991, Gambia and Senegal took the first step toward reconciliation by signing a good-will and cooperation treaty. The agreement foresaw an annual

MILITARY (as % of health and education expenditures-1990/91) **11%**

meeting between the two heads of state and the creation of a joint commission presided over by the Foreign Ministers of both countries.
[23] In 1993, agriculture and tourism were hit by the consequences of the European economic crisis. Gambia's trade with Senegal was damaged when the Central Bank of the Western Africa States decided to stop financing trade based upon the African franc (CFA) outside the area comprised by countries using this monetary system.
[24] The Government took measures to initiate a national reconciliation process, including an amnesty granted to rebel movements fighting to oust the regime.
[25] In July 1994, a military coup overthrew President Dawda

Jawara who sought asylum in Senegal after taking refuge in a US warship visiting the country. The presence of this ship in Banjul suggested complicity of the United States with the military. The coup, headed by Yahya Jammeh, began with the protests of soldiers who demanded payment for their peace mission carried out in Liberia.
[26] Two members of the Provisional Armed Forces Council were arrested in January 1995 after trying to hand the government over to civilians. In March, Jammeh also arrested the former Justice minister and general prosecutor for promoting the return of civilian rule. In November, the military junta expanded the powers of the security forces.
[27] The Government announced

legislative and presidential elections would be held in June 1996, but the vote was postponed. In August, after a referendum, a new Constitution was approved. Jammeh described this event as the first step toward the restoration of national political life. In September 1996, Jammeh, up to then chief of the Armed Forces Government Junta, became Gambia's second elected president.
[28] In August 1997, the Government lifted other restrictions which limited political activity since the 1994 military coup. In March 1998, Jammeh reduced the number of members in his cabinet. At the time, Gambia was a non-permanent member of the United Nations Security Council.

Georgia

Sakartvelo

Population: 5,442,000
(1996)
Area: 69,700 SQ KM
Capital: Tbilisi

Currency: Kupon
Language: Georgian

The peoples of the Caucasian Isthmus, considered to be the creators of metallurgy, entered the Bronze Age around 2000 BC. The ancestors of modern Georgians are thought to have formed the first tribes in that region about this time. The kingdom of Kolkhida - which dates back to the 6th century BC - is mentioned in Homer's poems and in traditional Greek mythology.

2 Two centuries later, a legendary chieftain, Farnavaz, created the kingdom of Iberia, in what is now eastern Georgia. These two kingdoms were the first Georgian States, the result of a fusion of ancient agricultural and iron-smelting tribes of the region.

3 Kolkhida and Iberia were subdued by Greece and then by Rome, as the result of Pompei's campaigns, in the 1st century BC. In the year 337 AD, King Mirian of Iberia adopted Christianity, making it the country's official religion. Like the Armenian church, the Georgian church separated from Rome in 506, to form the national Church of St George, with its headquarters at Tiflis (today Tbilisi).

4 From a minor city, Tiflis became first the capital of Iberia, and later of all Georgia, after the unification of the 8th and 9th centuries. Both kingdoms fell under Iranian (Sasanid), then Byzantine and finally Arab control, between the 6th and 10th centuries. Feudal Georgia prospered under King David "the Builder", 1089-1125 and Queen Tamara, 1184-1213.

5 In the 13th and 14th centuries Georgia was invaded by the Tatars and Tamerlane. In the 15th century it dissolved into small fiefdoms, becoming the object of territorial disputes between Turkey and Iran from the 16th to the 18th centuries and there were a number of anti-Turkish and anti-Iranian revolts.

6 Through the Treaty of Georgievsk (1783) Russia established its protection over eastern Georgia, annexing it in 1801. In the second half of the 19th century, Western Georgia (Tiblisi and Kutaisi) met the same fate. The Georgian provinces were incorporated into Transcaucasia, where the Government was in the hands of a viceroy designated by the Czar.

7 Annexation to Russia had a number of negative effects on Georgian life. The local language was eliminated from administrative documents, and it was replaced by Russian in literature and in schools. The Catholic Church of St George was outlawed and its patriarchs deported, to be replaced by Russian Orthodox bishops and Russians were encouraged to come and settle in all of Georgia's cities, a fact which explains why the revolutionary movement was so strong in Georgia, in all of its Marxist, nationalist, populist and social democratic forms. It was here that Josef Dzhugashvili, known as Stalin, began his political career. After frequent rebellions during this period, Georgians played an important part in the revolution which shook the empire in 1905.

8 When World War I broke out, the Caucasus saw fighting between Russia and Turkey. The Georgians formed a legion to fight alongside the Turks. In February 1917, a new wave of uprisings was unleashed by war policies and by hunger, and the peoples of the Caucasus brought down the czarist regime.

9 In November, after the Bolshevik triumph in Petrograd, power in Transcaucasia fell into the hands of the Mensheviks (who wanted gradual change rather than revolution). Confronted with this situation, Stalin's group allowed the Caucasus to join the Bolsheviks led by Lenin. In April 1918, in Tbilisi, the United Government of Transcaucasia announced its separation from Soviet Russia. On May 26, 1918, Georgia proclaimed independence, which was recognized by Moscow two years later.

10 Between 1918 and 1920, German, Turkish and British troops entered Georgia, all intent upon bringing down the socialist regime. In February 1921, the Red Army occupied Georgia and established Soviet power. On February 25, 1921, the Soviet Socialist Republic of Georgia was proclaimed, with the Abkhaz Autonomous Region as an administrative division of this republic. In March 1921, a peace treaty between the Russian Federation and Turkey was finalized, with the latter ceding Batumi and the northern part of Adzharistan, which became an autonomous republic within the Georgian SSR.

11 In March 1922, Georgia, Azerbaijan and Armenia were reorganized as the Transcaucasian Federation. The following month, the South Ossetian Autonomous Region was formed, as a part of Georgia. On December 5 1936 the federation was dissolved and Georgia became one of the 15 republics of the Soviet Union (USSR).

12 Stalin became Secretary General of the Communist Party of the Soviet Union in 1922, and after Lenin's death he became party leader. From 1928, he was leader of the USSR. Georgia witnessed many purges and suffered the effects of centralization and the repression of Stalinism, although to a lesser degree than other republics. In 1924, the Red Army intervened to put down a peasant uprising against forced land collectivization.

13 In the following years the country benefited from the cultural and economic development promoted by the Soviet Union. Many Georgians - apart from Stalin - were in the leadership circle of the Soviet Union's CP, including Sergo Ordzhonikidzegv, the USSR's Minister of Heavy Industry, and Lavrenti Beria, head of the secret police (NKVD) who was executed after Stalin's death, in 1953. When Krushchev denounced his predecessor's crimes at the 20th Party Congress in 1956, it hurt Georgian national pride.

14 In 1953, Moscow made Eduard Shevardnadze chief of police in Tbilisi; a Georgian, he had been head of the Communist Youth (Konsomol) during Vasili Mzhavanadze's period as first secretary of the Georgian Communist Party. Implicated in cases of corruption and fraud, Mzhavanadze was replaced by Shevardnadze in 1972. A new nationalist feeling began to emerge with declarations in defence of the Georgian language and violent acts of sabotage.

15 In 1978, the new constitution of the USSR triggered a wave of protest, as it made Russian the official language of the Soviet Union. However, Shevardnadze managed to have the measure abolished and allowed an anti-Stalin movie, "Repent", to be screened. This marked the development of glasnost and perestroika process in Georgia.

16 Shevardnadze remained at the head of Georgia's Communist Party and government until 1985, when he was made Foreign Minister of the Soviet Union. After the political changes made by Mikhail Gorbachev, several movements and parties emerged in Georgia, clamouring for the independence which Georgia claimed to have lost in 1921, with the establishment of Soviet power. On April 9 1989 in Tbilisi, Red Army units dispersed a crowd meeting in the main square to demand the secession of Georgia, citing Article 72 of the Constitution of the USSR. Nineteen people were killed, most of them women or adolescents.

17 In the mid 1980s, a Green Party emerged in Georgia amid the first ever open debates on the country's ecological problems. The Greens combined their concern for the environment with a defence of non-violence, democracy and human rights. Georgia was the second former Soviet republic - after Estonia - to join the European "Green" Parliament.

PROFILE

ENVIRONMENT:
Located in the central western part of Transcaucasia, Georgia is bounded in the north by Russia, in the east by Azerbaijan and in the south by Armenia and Turkey, with the Black Sea to the west. Most of its territory is occupied by mountains. Between the Little and the Great Caucasus lies the Kolkhida lowland and the Kartalinian Plain; the Alazan Valley lies to the east. Subtropical climate in the west, moderate in the east. Principal rivers Kura, Rioni. Heavy precipitation in the western area, along the shores of the Black Sea. 40 per cent of the republic is covered by forests. Georgia is well-known for its wine. Bacterial pollution of 70 per cent of the Black Sea constitutes a serious problem. Only 18 per cent of the residual waters in the main port of Batumi undergo adequate treatment. The abuse of pesticides has resulted a high level of chemical toxicity in the soil.

SOCIETY
Peoples: Georgians, 70 per cent; Armenians, 8.1 per cent; Russians, 6.3 per cent; Azeris, 5.7 per cent; Ossetes, Abkhazians and Adzharians. **Religions:** Georgian Orthodox (65 per cent), Muslims (11 per cent), Russian Orthodox (10 per cent), and Armenian Orthodox (8 per cent). **Languages:** Georgian (official), Russian and Abkhazian. **Political Parties:** Union of Citizens of Georgia, Georgian Communist Party, National Democratic Party, Aidguilara (national movement of the Abkhazians), Admon Nyjas (national movement of the South Ossetians).

THE STATE
Official Name: Sakartvelos Respublika. **Capital** Tbilisi, 1,253,000 people (1994). **Other cities** Batumi, 137,000 people; Sukhumi, 112,000, Kutaisi, 240,000; Rustavi, 155,500 (1994). **Government** Eduard Shevardnadze, President of Parliament and Head of State between 1992-1995 and President since 1995; Niko Lekishvili, Secretary of State since 1995. **National Holiday** May 26, Independence (1918). **Armed Forces** 13,000.

STATISTICS

DEMOGRAPHY
Population: 5,442,000 (1996) **Annual growth:** 0.4% (1980/1996) **Estimates for year 2000:** 5,000,000 **Annual growth to year 2000:** -0.1% (1994/2000) **Urban Population:** 58.8% (1996) **Urban growth:** 1.3% (1980/95) **Children per woman:** 2 (1996).

HEALTH
Life expectancy at birth: 73 years (1996) male: 69 years (1994) female: 77 years (1994) **Infant mortality:** 23 per 1,000 (1996) **Under-5 child mortality:** 29 per 1,000 (1996).

EDUCATION
Literacy: 99% (1995) male : 100% (1995) female: 99% (1995) **School enrolment :** Primary total: 82% (1990/95) male : 82% (1990/95) female: 81% (1990/95) Secondary: male : 82% (1990/95) female: 76% (1990/95) Tertiary: 38% (1995) **Primary school teachers:** one for every 16 students (1995).

COMMUNICATIONS
550 **radios**, 220 **TV sets** and 96 **main telephone lines** per 1,000 people (1994) **Books:** 6 new titles per 100,000 people (1992/94).

ECONOMY
Per capita, GNP: $ 850 (1996) **Annual inflation:** 310.04% (1985/95) **Cereal imports:** 713 metric tons (1994) **Fertilizer use:** 275 kgs per ha (1994) **Exports:** $ 261 million (1996) **Imports:** $ 884 million (1996) **External debt:** $ 1,356 million (1996) $ 249 **per capita:** (1996).

ENERGY
Consumption: 613.69 Kgs of Oil equivalent per capita yearly (1994) 84.90% imported (1994).

HDI (rank / value) 105 / 0.637 (1994).

---

[18] On October 28 1990, elections were held for the Soviet (parliament) of the Georgian SSR, and the "Free Georgia Round Table" coalition won. Zviad Gamsakhurdia, a well-known political dissident who had been proscribed during the Soviet regime, became the leader of the coalition. The Georgian Soviet decided to change the country's name to the Republic of Georgia.

[19] Ethnic tensions increased, and the South Ossetian Autonomous Region claimed republican status. Georgia's Soviet annulled this decision, declared a state of emergency in South Ossetia and organized a blockade of this region. In April 1991, after fighting broke out between Ossetian guerrillas and Georgian troops, the Soviet approved the region's independence.

[20] On May 27, Gamsakhurdia was elected President. In September, a struggle began between Gamsakhurdia's supporters and the opposition, led by Dzhaba Ioseliani and Tenguiz Kitovani, commander of the National Guard. Repeated protest demonstrations ended in violence on January 6 1992, when government forces (following Kitovani's orders) stormed government headquarters. Gamsakhurdia fled first to Armenia, and then to the Chechen Autonomous Republic.

[21] A Military Council led by Kitovani seized power in Tbilisi and suspended the constitution. Gamsakhurdia loyalists continued to fight against the new regime's forces in western Georgia.

[22] In March, former USSR foreign minister, Eduard Shevardnadze, returned to Georgia to take charge of the presidency of the Council of State, the most powerful governing body. Chosen by the Military Council, he held this post until democratic elections took place. Shevardnadze declared that his country would normalize relations with the international community, giving preference to relations with the former USSR republics, though for the moment not joining the Commonwealth of Independent States (CIS).

[23] On June 28 of the same year, a cease-fire was called in South Ossetia, supervised by a peacekeeping force of Russians, Georgians and Ossetians. From their capital in Sukhumi, the Abkhazian authorities resolved to limit the jurisdiction of Georgia's central government within the autonomous region. On August 14, government troops entered Abkhazia and occupied Sukhumi. Local authorities fled to the city of Gudauta, which became a center of resistance.

[24] In early October, with the support of Russian volunteers and army regulars, they managed to extend their control over a large part of Abkhazia, coming close to Sukhumi.

[25] In early 1993, the Russian air force began regular bombing of Sukhumi, and by mid-March fighting had reached the outskirts of the city. On June 28, a Russian-mediated armistice went into effect, with both parties agreeing to demobilize their troops.

[26] In mid-September 1993, a strong Abkhazian offensive began, taking the Georgians by surprise and culminating in the capture of Sukhumi by the Abkhazian army. Eduard Shevardnadze remained in Sukhumi until the last moment, leaving on the last flight out of the city.

[27] In November, supporters of former President Gamsakhurdia launched a broad offensive, but were defeated with the help of Russian troops. In the same month, Georgia entered the CIS. In early 1994, Gamsakhurdia died in a suicide attempt, according to official reports. In February, Georgia signed a friendship treaty with Russia, and in April a peace treaty was signed with the Abkhazian rebels in Moscow. Despite the rapprochement with Russia, Tbilisi entered the Partnership for Peace program promoted by NATO.

[28] In the first 10 months of the year, industrial production fell by 42 per cent. The inability to repay a debt to the Turkmenistan Government led to a reduction in gas sales - the main Georgian source of energy. In late November, Tbilisi had neither heating, electricity nor running water. In the first 11 months of 1995, industrial production increased 20 per cent.

[29] In August 1995, the Parliament approved a new constitution, which defined Georgia as a presidential republic. In November, Shevardnadze won the presidential elections, while his party, the Citizens' Alliance, won 124 of the 235 seats in Parliament.

[30] The GDP registered an increase of 8 per cent and industrial production 10 per cent in 1996. Annual inflation stood at 30 per cent and the currency maintained its value against the dollar. However, unemployment remained high at 20 per cent. The IMF and the World Bank provided funds to support the economic plan. Despite protests from Russia, Georgia agreed the construction of an oil pipeline in Georgian territory to facilitate the export of Azerbaijan's oil.

[31] In November 1997, Georgia became the first former soviet republic to abolish the death penalty. The Russian and Ukrainian parliaments opposed similar measures promoted by their respective governments.

[32] In February 1998, President Shevardnadze was almost killed in an attack. Parliament called for an investigation into the Russian military bases on Georgian territory. Some members of parliament believed Moscow to have been involved in the incident, with the supposed objective of obstructing the construction of the oil pipeline in Georgia for oil from Azerbaijan. When choosing this project, Azerbaijan had turned down a Russian proposal to route the pipeline through Chechnya. In recent years, the Russian army crushed diverse revolts led by Chechnian independence groups and ravaged entire cities in this region.

Germany

Deutschland

Population: 81,922,000 (1996)
Area: 356,733 SQ KM
Capital: Berlin

Currency: Marks
Language: German

The first reference to the Germanic tribes comes from between 58 and 51 BC when the Romans under Julius Caesar invaded a part of Gaul north of the Alps and west of the Rhine. The Germans descended from the Teutoni and the Cimbri, who had in turn descended from the Danes. Between 113 and 101 BC. Teutoni and Cimbri tribes invaded the Mediterranean regions including the Italian peninsula

[2] In 9 AD Arminius, a Germanic chief and the earliest recognised national hero, led a revolt which defeated three Roman legions in the Teutoburger Wald. By the second half of the 3rd century, the Germanic tribes had fused into larger political units; the Saxons, Franks and Germans.

[3] The Romans found it increasingly difficult to keep their dominion over the region and withdrew gradually. In the 4th century Attila's Huns invaded, and a long period of Migrations followed throughout Europe. In 455, the Germans defeated the Mongols at the battle of the river Nedao and the Mongol Empire subsequently collapsed. Clovis and Charlemagne later subjected the Germanic and Saxon tribes to the Frankish Empire.

[4] After the Treaty of Verdun and the division of the Carolingian empire in 843, the first entirely Germanic kingdom was established under Louis the German. Under Otto I, crowned in Rome in 936, Germania became Europe's most powerful kingdom.

[5] During the 12th and 13th centuries Germany experienced a rapid growth in population, and continuous expansion.

[6] The instability of royal dynasties encouraged the strengthening of secular and religious principalities. Princes were free to build fortresses, exploit natural resources and administer justice in their dominions.

[7] In 1356, the authority of the king in relation to the papacy was consolidated in the Golden Bull of Charles IV (1346-1378) establishing the right to designate the king without the Pope's approval, and strengthened the hand of the principalities, on whose support the king depended.

[8] During the 15th and 16th centuries internal instability persisted. In 1517 Martin Luther led the Protestant Reformation, which coupled with political rivalries frustrated reunification efforts.

[9] The Reformation provided a forum for criticisms of secularisation and corruption in the German Church, which had become an increasingly prosperous economic and financial institution. It owned a third of the land in some districts and profited from selling indulgences. It was the scandal over indulgences that finally led to its downfall. After a succession of internal wars, including peasant uprisings, the Peace of Augsburg was reached in 1555, giving equal rights to both Catholics and Lutherans.

[10] Political and religious factions combined their strengths; in 1608 the Protestant Union was created, and the Catholic League a year later. The Bohemian rebellion triggered the Thirty Year War (1618-1648), which spread to the entire continent, and ultimately reduced the population of central Europe by around 30 per cent, ending with the Peace of Westfalia (1648).

[11] In the 18th century, the Kingdom of Prussia emerged as a dynamic economic and political unit, responsible for creating tensions among the German states. Napoleon's victories over Prussia in 1806 and the formation of the Confederation of the Rhine put an end to the Holy Roman Empire.

[12] In Central Europe during the 18th century, culture formed an outlet for intellectual energies which could not be expressed through politics, as political life itself was dominated by the autocratic rulers. Philosophers like Kant and Herder, and writers like Goethe and Schiller, expressed the idealism and spiritualism which characterized German art and literature of this time.

[13] When Napoleon fell, the German princes created a confederation of 39 states, which were independent except for external policy. Austrian and Prussian opposition to broader forms of representation increased popular unrest, leading to 1830 revolts and increased repression.

[14] In 1834, Prussia threw its growing economic weight into the political realm, with the establishment of the German Customs Union, from which Austria was excluded. The main consequences of the Union were the duplication of trade among its members over the next ten years, as well as the formation of industrial centres and the emergence of a working class. Due to the rapid growth of the urban population, the supply of labour greatly exceeded the demand. The resulting impoverishment of industrial workers and artisans served as a breeding ground for the rebellions of subsequent years, culminating in the revolutionary wave of 1848-49.

[15] A National Assembly first met in Frankfurt on May 18, 1848; its representatives belonged mostly to liberal democratic sectors. They campaigned for German unity, and guarantees of political freedom. However, internal divisions facilitated the regrouping of the forces of the former regime, leading finally to the dissolution of Parliament in June 1849 and the repression of opposition organizations.

[16] With the revolutionary tendencies crushed, Austria and Prussia were free to dispute their respective roles in German unification. The issue was settled in 1866 with Prussia's victory in the Seven Weeks' War. The union was forged around the North German Confederation, a creation of the Prussian chancellor, Otto von Bismarck, that aimed to halt liberalism. The Parliament (*Reichstag*) was inaugurated in February 1867.

[17] Three years later, war broke out with France. Prussia's victory in 1871 was the last step in Bismarck's scheme to unite

LAND USE

IRRIGATED 3.9 % of arable

(1993)

■ FOREST & WOODLAND	30%
□ ARABLE	32.7%
▨ OTHER	37.3%

PROFILE

ENVIRONMENT

The northern part of the country is a vast plain. The Baltic coast is jagged, with deep, narrow gulfs. The center of the country is made up of very old mountain ranges, plateaus and sedimentary river basins. Of the ancient massifs, the most important are the Black Forest region and the Rhineland. The southern region begins in the Danube Valley, and is made up of plateaus (the Bavarian Plateau), bordered to the south by the Bavarian Alps. There are large deposits of coal and lignite along the banks of the Ruhr and Ens rivers, which provided the backbone of Germany's industrial development. Heavy industry is concentrated in the Ruhr Valley, mid-Rhineland and Lower Saxony. The south of the former German Democratic Republic is rich in coal, lignite, lead, tin, silver and uranium deposits. The chemical, electrochemical, metallurgical and steel industries are concentrated there. This region suffers severe air pollution as a result of the carbon output of the industries. The emission of sulphur dioxide in eastern Germany is 15 times that in the west, compounding the problem of acid rain. Untreated industrial effluents carrying heavy metals and toxic chemicals have contaminated many east German rivers, ending up in the highly polluted Baltic Sea.

SOCIETY

Peoples: German 91.8 per cent; Turkish 2.5 per cent, of which Kurdish 0.2 per cent; Yugoslav 1.6 per cent; Italian 0.2 per cent; Greek 0.4 per cent; Polish 0.4 per cent; Spanish 0.2 per cent; other 2.0 per cent. **Religions:** Christian; a Catholic majority in the South and Protestant in the North. There are approximately 28 million Catholics and, before reunification, Catholics constituted a majority in West Germany.
Languages: German (official) and local dialects which, in spite of restrictions, are regaining popularity. Turkish, Kurdish.
Political Parties: Christian Democratic Union (CDU); Christian Social Union (CSU), Liberal Party (FDP), Social Democratic Party (SPD); the Greens/Alliance-90; Democratic Socialist Party (PDS), the Republicans (REP).
Social Organizations Workers' Federation (DGB).

THE STATE

Official Name Bundesrepublik Deutschland.
Administrative divisions Federal parliamentary State made up of 16 *Länder* (federated states), as of October 3, 1990. Eleven *Länder* made up what was formerly West Germany (Schleswig-Holstein, Hamburg, Bremen, Niedersachsen, Nordrhein-Westfalen, Hessen, Rheinland-Pfalz, Saarland, Baden-Wättemberg, Bayern and Berlin) while the former German Democratic Republic was divided into five *Länder*(Mecklemburg, Brandemburg, Sachsen-Anhalt, Sachsen and Thuringen).
Capital Berlin, 3,471,418 people (1995).
Other cities Hamburg, 1,707,901 people; München (Munich), 1,244,676; Köln (Cologne), 963,817; Frankfurt am Main, 652,412; Dresden, 500,000; Leipzig, 481,112 (1995).
Government Roman Herzog, President; Helmut Kohl, Chancellor, appointed by the federal parliament.
Armed Forces 340,000 **Other** Federal Border Guard (Ministry of Interior) 24,800; Coast Guard 535.

Germany under a single monarch, and Prussian domination.

[18] The Empire had to deal with opposing internal forces, namely, the Church and Social Democracy. Bismarck passed the May Laws, secularizing education and some other activities. Bismarck was later to reverse this, securing the Church as an ally against socialism. Alarmed at the growth of Social Democracy, the regime used repression and social reform to neutralize the latter's potential.

[19] Bismarck's government introduced commercial protectionism to increase domestic income and foster national industry and the German economy grew substantially, especially in heavy industry and production. The creation of the Triple Alliance with Austria and Italy, and the acquisition of colonies in Africa and Asia after 1884, placed the German Empire as a leading world power.

[20] However, Germany's imperial venture was not highly successful, either in its African possessions (Tanganyika, Cameroun, Togo and South West Africa - now Namibia) or those in Asia (New Guinea, the Carolina, Mariana, Marshall and Samoan Islands). At the end of World War I, these were all transferred to the victorious powers.

[21] German rivalry with France and Britain in the west, and Russia and Serbia in the east, triggered World War I. The capitulation of the Austro-Hungarian Empire and Turkey in November 1918, led to Germany's final defeat. The crisis was aggravated by an internal revolution which led to the abdication of the Emperor. Government was handed over to the socialist Friedrich Ebert, who was to call a National Constituent Assembly.

[22] German Social Democracy split into a moderate tendency favouring a gradual evolution to socialism, and a radical tendency favouring revolutionary change. The radical group, "the Spartacists", headed by Karl Liebknecht and Rosa Luxemburg, identified with the Russian revolution of October 1917 and wanted to set up a system similar to that of the Soviets.

[23] In December 1918, the Government called constituent elections for a month later. The army was called in to put down a radical socialist coup, and in January 1919 the Spartacist leaders were arrested and executed. A few days later, the electorate returned a moderate socialist majority to power.

[24] In February 1919, in Weimar, the Assembly appointed Ebert as the first president of the Republic. In June of that year, after some hesitation, the government of socialist Gustav Bauer signed the Treaty of Versailles.

[25] In 1921, the victorious powers fixed German reparations at 132,000 million marks, an amount that the country was in no position to pay.

[26] Germany was declared bankrupt by the Commission of Reparations of the victorious powers, and in January 1923, Belgian and French troops occupied the industrial Ruhr region. Economic and financial instability caused hyperinflation, affecting most of the petite bourgeoisie. A fiscal reform in late 1924, managed to stabilize the country's finances.

[27] When Ebert died in 1925, Marshall Paul von Hindenburg was elected President. His main concern was to re-establish Germany's position among the great powers. He supported the ancient landed oligarchy's desire to return to power.

[28] The German economy expanded until the Wall Street crash of 1929, when a lack of foreign credit threw it into recession. In 1930 Hindenburg dissolved Parliament, and that year the vote for both Communists and National Socialists (Nazis) rose sharply. The Nazi Party, led by Adolf Hitler, became the second largest political force behind the Social Democrats.

[29] The middle classes and the impoverished masses became increasingly attracted to the Nazi promise of rebuilding the Great Germany. Humiliated by the postwar treaties they seized on the campaign that blamed Jews and Communists for the economic crisis. The Communists and Socialists held a majority in Parliament, but due to differences they did not join forces against Hitler. By the time they realized the danger he embodied it was too late to stop him.

[30] In the 1932 elections, amidst violent clashes with the Communists, the Nazi Party doubled its support, obtaining 37 per cent of the total vote. The President, who had banned the Nazis from holding public demonstrations, offered Hitler participation in a coalition government led by the right-wing Franz von Papen. He did not yet accept Hitler's demand to be head of government.

[31] Between 1932 and 1933, in international negotiations, Germany attempted to make up for war losses and recover its right to rearm. On the domestic scene, one crisis followed another and the number of unemployed exceeded six million.

[32] In January 1933, at the urging of representatives of the upper bourgeoisie, the President turned over the government to Hitler, who dissolved Parliament in February. He also called elections, in which his NSDAP obtained an absolute majority.

[33] In Potsdam in March 1933, the new parliament granted Hitler the power to issue decrees outside the Constitution without the approval of the legislative body or the President. For four years Hitler had the power to fix the annual budget, request loans and sign agreements with other countries, re-organize both his cabinet and the supreme ranks of

the armed forces, and proclaim martial law.

[34] In July 1933 Hitler abolished the German Federation and set up absolute central power. He outlawed all parties except his own, as well as trade unions and strikes. Germany also withdrew from the Disarmament Conference and the League of Nations.

[35] The Hitler regime installed its first concentration camps to confine thousands of political opponents, gypsies (Sinti and Roma ethnic groups) and homosexuals. In addition, it launched a scheme to eliminate disabled people. Protests from the churches, whose support was still important to the regime, put a temporary halt to these policies.

[36] After the death of President Hindenburg in August 1934, the cabinet was forced to swear personal allegiance to the Chancellor, Adolf Hitler. In 1935, in violation of the Treaty of Versailles, he began to re-arm Germany. The European powers protested, but were unable to stop him.

[37] With the 1935 "Nuremberg Laws", the regime provided a legal framework for its racist ideology, laying the foundation for its subsequent policies of ethnic and religious extermination.

[38] In October 1936 Germany and Italy signed a co-operation agreement which included support for General Franco in the Spanish Civil War. The following month Germany and Japan (the Axis powers) agreed to set up a military exchange, and in November 1937 Germany, Italy and Japan signed the Anti-communist Pact in Rome.

[39] In March 1938, German troops invaded Austria, and Hitler proclaimed its annexation. That same year, the pressure of Hitler and German nationalism on the Sudetenland forced the European powers to cede this Czechoslovakian region to Germany. On "Kristallnacht", November 9-10, the government carried out a systematic destruction of Jewish commercial property and religious and cultural institutions.

[40] In 1939, taking advantage of the disagreements between Czechs and Slovaks, German troops advanced into Prague; Bohemia, Moravia, and Slovakia became protectorates.

[41] Britain assured Poland, Romania, Greece and Turkey that it would protect their independence, and Britain and France attempted to establish an alliance with the Soviet Union. In August 1939, however, the USSR signed a nonaggression treaty with Germany. On September 1, German troops invaded Poland. Britain and France issued Germany an ultimatum and World War II broke out.

[42] By 1940, Germany had invaded Norway, Denmark, Belgium, the Netherlands, Luxembourg, and France. In 1941 Hitler started his offensive against the USSR, but German troops were halted a few miles outside Moscow. They were finally defeated after the siege of Stalingrad (Volgograd) in 1943.

[43] From the outset, German aggression against its neighbours was accompanied by the systematic extermination of the Jewish population in concentration camps, primarily in Poland. Over six million Jews, and a million other people were killed.

[44] The advance of the Red Army on the eastern front - culminating in the capture of Berlin - and the 1944 Allied landing in Normandy on the Western Front forced Germany to surrender in May 1945.

[45] Four million Germans from neighbouring countries, and from the territories annexed by Poland and the USSR, were forced to move to the four zones Germany was divided into, while it remained occupied by the United States, France, Britain and the USSR. In 1949, discord between the ex-allies over the future governing of Germany led to the creation of the Federal Republic of Germany, in the West, and the German Democratic Republic, in the East. The issue of the two Germanies became a bone of contention in postwar relations between the USSR and the United States.

[46] In 1955, the sovereignty of both Germanies was recognized by their occupying forces. During the Cold War, West Germany became a member of NATO (the North Atlantic Treaty Organization) while East Germany joined the Warsaw Pact. Foreign forces continued to be based in their territories and the two republics were still subject to limitations on their armed forces and a ban on nuclear weapons.

[47] The United Socialist Party (SED), formed from the union of Communists and Social Democrats in 1946, took over the government of East Germany. The USSR partly compensated them for war losses with money, equipment and cattle, and a social system similar to that in the USSR was set up. In 1953, the political and economic situation of the German Democratic Republic (GDR) led to a series of protests, which were put down by Soviet troops. In the meantime, emigration to the Federal Republic of Germany (FRG) increased.

[48] Between the state's creation and 1961, when the East German Government forbade all emigrations to the West, some three million East Germans emigrated to West Germany. To enforce their resolution, the East closed its borders and built the Berlin Wall between the eastern and the western sections of the city. In 1971, Erich Honecker took over the leadership of the SED party, and later the GDR Government.

[49] Between 1949 and 1963, Chancellor Konrad Adenauer, a conservative Christian Democrat, oversaw the reconstruction of the FRG, under the slogan "[establishing] a social market economy". With US support (the Marshall Plan) and huge amounts of foreign capital, the FRG became one of the most developed capitalist economies, playing a key role in the founding of the European Community (EC).

[50] With the victory of the Social Democratic Party (SPD) in the 1969 elections, the government of Chancellor Willy Brandt launched a policy of rapprochement toward Eastern Europe and the German Democratic Republic. In 1970 the first formal talks between the FRG and the GDR began, and in 1971 the occupying powers agreed to free access of FRG citizens to the GDR. A Basic Treaty of bilateral relations was signed by both Germanies in 1973; in September they were admitted to the United Nations.

[51] In the 1970s, the number of power stations producing nuclear

MILITARY EXPENDITURE

MILITARY (as % of health and education expenditures-1990/91) **29%**

PER 100,000
LIVE BIRTHS
22

energy increased. In response to this, a strong environmental movement was formed, with a network of hundreds of grassroots groups throughout the country.

[52] In 1974, after the discovery that his private secretary was an East German spy, Brandt resigned as head of the government, and was succeeded by Helmut Schmidt. The modernization of Soviet medium-range missiles in the GDR, and the December 1979 NATO decision to do the same with its arsenal in the FRG, gave a strong impetus to the anti-nuclear movement in both states, with massive protests in the FRG.

[53] In 1982, the SPD had to leave power when the Liberal Party withdrew from the government alliance after 13 years. It was succeeded by the liberal-conservative alliance (CDU/CSU, FDP) led by Chancellor Helmut Kohl (CDU). In the 1983 elections, the environmental party (the Greens) won parliamentary representation on a national level for the first time. Approximately half of its Members of Parliament were women.

[54] In mid-1989, Hungary liberalized regulations regarding transit across the border with Austria. Within a few weeks, some 350,000 Germans from the GDR had emigrated to the FRG. Street demonstrations demanding change brought on a crisis in the GDR. In August, Honecker resigned and was replaced by Egon Krenz. On November 9, the GDR opened up its borders and the Berlin Wall fell.

[55] Kohl immediately proposed the creation of a confederation of East and West Germany. In December 1989, during his first visit to East Germany, Kohl insisted on this proposal and committees were set up to develop bilateral relations. In the meantime, demonstrators began clamouring for reunification of the GDR and the FRG.

[56] In February 1990, the East German Government agreed to German unification and the withdrawal of all foreign troops from its territory. Kohl supported the plan and proposed starting negotiations after the March elections in the East. After the Christian Democrat victory,

promising rapid re-unification, monetary union was achieved in July. The exchange rate was very favourable to East German investors.

[57] The fusion of the two states was officially recognized in August 1990, as the Federal Republic of Germany. Political union was made possible when the USSR accepted the East German entry into NATO. An important difference between the two Germanies is the East's preservation of a more liberal abortion law.

[58] Industrial plants in the East, working with obsolete technology and generating serious pollution, were closed down by the end of 1990, triggering several strikes. At the time of re-unification, 50 per cent of women in the West worked outside the home, as compared to 83 per cent in the East.

[59] In the first parliamentary elections of the new Federal Republic, in December 1990, the governing coalition of Social Christians and Liberals obtained 54 per cent of the vote, Social Democrats had 35 per cent, the Greens 5 per cent, while the Democratic Socialists (descendants of the old Democratic Republic Socialist Party) also obtained 5 per cent. Women make up 20.54 per cent of MPs, 4.5 per cent more than in the former FRG and 12.5 per cent less than in the former GDR.

[60] In 1991, the extreme right made important gains at a local level. In Bremen, they increased their share of the vote by 7 per cent. The elections took place against a background of racist demonstrations and increasing xenophobia. The victims of this violence were mainly citizens of Third World countries, but some were immigrants from the old European socialist bloc. These eastern European people had been coming to Germany in large numbers since 1989, with over 100,000 arriving in 1991 alone.

[61] During 1992, there were 2,280 attacks on foreigners and Jewish monuments, which left 17 people dead. After one incident which caused the death of a Turkish woman and two children, the Government outlawed three neo-Nazi organizations.

[62] Massive demonstrations against racist violence and anti-Semitism were held all over the country. The deliberate burning of a house in the western city of Solingen, which killed two Turkish women and three small girls once again demonstrated the strength of the ultra-right in Germany.

[63] In May 1993, the Supreme Court annulled the law liberalizing abortion as it was considered unconstitutional. It was one of the few dispensations inherited from the GDR. The closure of most of the industry in the east of the country, the economic recession - the worst since 1945 - and the increase in productivity, caused a constant increase in unemployment. In March 1994, more than four million people were out of work.

[64] On May 23, the conservative, Roman Herzog, backed by Kohl, was designated president of Germany by a special electoral assembly, after defeating the Social Democrat Johannes Rau. In the second half of the year, a cycle of economic expansion began, which allowed a level of 2.8 per cent growth to be reached during the 1994 financial year. Unemployment had already fallen to around 3.5 million people by the end of the year.

[65] Kohl triumphed again in the October general elections, although his majority fell to only 10 seats of the 672 in play (in the previous parliament, the difference between the government and opposition had been 134 seats). The conservative alliance which backed Kohl, the CDU-CSU, took 41.5 per cent of the vote, including the 6.9 per cent of their allies in government, the FDP liberals. Meanwhile, the Social Democratic SPD took 36.4 per cent, the ecologists 7.3 per cent and the former East German Communist PDS 4.4 per cent, due to good support in several parts of the former GDR. In 1995, the constant weakening of the FDP in various local elections prompted the resignation of Foreign Minister Klaus Kinkel.

[66] On the social front, Parliament adopted a new law which, despite again permitting abortion during the first 12 weeks of pregnancy, was in fact more restrictive than the one

annulled in 1993, as it obliged women to be "assessed" before any intervention.

[67] The discontent of many foreigners resident in Germany led to the formation of the Democratic Party of Germany, which stood for greater access to the electoral role and citizenship - often restricted to people of German origin - for the children of immigrants.

[68] The economic expansion continued, with growth estimated at 3 per cent in 1995, which led to a rash of pay claims from the unions. In 1996, five years after unification and three years after the frontiers fell for workers of the European Union, unemployment stood at around 10.6 per cent on a national level, and up to 16 per cent in the states of the former East Germany. Five million people were out of work.

[69] On September 1996, Parliament approved an increase in the female retirement age from 60 to 65 years old from the year 2000. But the measure which caused most controversy and led to major protests was the 80 per cent reduction in sickness pay. Workers had gained the right to six weeks sick leave on full pay per year following 16 weeks of strikes in 1957.

[70] Racism and anti-Semitism continued to be issues for the Kohl administration. Not only the young neo-Nazis were expressing their racist 'nostalgia': in October 1997, a television broadcast showed an army battalion giving Nazi salutes and shouting anti-Semitic and anti-US slogans.

[71] In its 1997 report on the country, Amnesty International indicated that police abuse to foreigners could not be seen as isolated cases, due to the systematic repetition of the offences.

[72] In early 1998, the Deutsche Bank paid back Jewish organizations the money made from the sale of gold suspected to have been robbed from the Jews by the Nazis. At the same time, a Swiss foundation began to provide economic compensation - although with "token" sums of money - to gypsies resident in Germany who had survived the Nazi holocaust.

Ghana

Ghana

Population:	17,832,000 (1996)
Area:	238,533 SQ KM
Capital:	Accra
Currency:	Cedis
Language:	English

In about 1300, the Akans or Ashantis moved into Ghana from the north. The powerful and organized Fanti State of Denkyira was already established on the coast so the Akans settled in the inland jungles. Here, they founded a series of small cities that paid tribute to the coastal nation.

2　In the 15th century the Ashantis began to trade in the markets of Begho, on the border of present-day Côte d'Ivoire. They traded slaves and gold for fabrics and other goods from North Africa and further afield. An ornate pitcher that had once belonged to Richard II, king of England between 1367 and 1400, was discovered in the treasure of a Kumasi ruler.

3　In the 17th century, new waves of migration threatened the existence of the small jungle states. This crisis forced the Akans to unite in confronting the Doma invaders. The Doma were defeated.

4　With the decline of the Songhai, the Moroccan incursions and the beginning of the Fulah expansion, the North African trade network collapsed with serious repercussions for the inland economy. The Ashanti were also deprived of access to the coastal trading posts as these were in Denkyira Territory. Instead of paying taxes, they declared war on the Denkyira and defeated them. They then organized a centralized state, ruled by the "Ashantihene" (leader of the Ashanti nation) endowed with a powerful army. By 1700, the Ashanti had control of the slave trade to the coast and the flow of European goods to the interior.

5　When the British stopped trading in slaves, the Ashanti reacted by attempting to seize the shoreline from the Fanti, who still retained a significant share of the coastal trade. English backing of the Fanti led to the Anglo-Ashanti wars, 1806-1816, 1825-28 and 1874. After the last war, the British turned the Fanti territory into a colony. In 1895 under the pretext of defending the region from Samori Turé (see Guinea) they also proclaimed a protectorate over the northern territories.

6　While the coastal and northern regions were under British rule, the central region belonged to the autonomous Ashanti nation. It did not take long for friction to build up and another Anglo-Ashanti war broke out in 1896. The capital, Kumasi, was razed by cannon fire, and the ruler was deposed and exiled. The Ashanti were then told that they owed 50,000 ounces of gold in compensation for "war damages". An attempt to collect the debt coupled with the British Governor's culturally insensitive desire to sit on the gold throne, led to a general rebellion four years later. This was immediately put down with a great loss of lives. In 1902 the Ashanti state was formally annexed to the Gold Coast Colony.

7　During the first half of the 20th century, a strong nationalist current developed in spite of the ethnic and religious differences within Ghana. Economic opposition to the British also grew at this time both in the north, where the traditional structures had remained intact, and in the south, where a Westernized middle class and a relatively significant working class had developed.

8　Popular pressure on the colonial administration led to

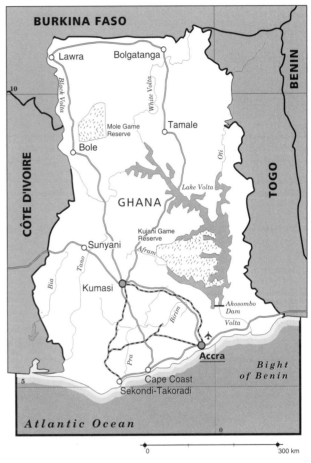

political concessions. In 1946, London admitted a few Africans into the colonial administration and in 1949 Kwame Nkrumah formed the Convention People's Party (CCP) to campaign for greater reform.

9　Nkrumah is known as one of the founding fathers of Pan-Africanism and African nationalism. He established a solid rural and urban party structure and, in 1952, he became Prime Minister of the colony. In his inaugural speech, he proclaimed himself a "socialist, Marxist and Christian", promising to fight against imperialism.

10　Nkrumah represented Ghana at the Bandung Conference in 1955. This conference marked the birth of the Movement of Non-Aligned Countries, and together with Tito, Nasser, Nehru and Sukarno, Nkrumah played an important part (See Non-Aligned Countries). In 1957 he achieved a major victory and Ghana became the first country in West Africa to gain independence. Known as Osagyefo (redeemer), Nkrumah enthusiastically embraced the Pan-African anti-colonialism. He initiated a series of internal changes based on industrialization, agrarian reform and socialist education.

11　These new measures, however, did not suit everybody. Traditional

PUBLIC EXPENDITURE

4.9%　42.3%
1995 ■ DEFENCE □ SOCIAL

In 1990/91 Military as % of health & education expenditure was 12%.

WORKERS

(1996)

Labour force %
■ WOMEN
□ MEN

51　　49

■ AGRICULTURE 59% (1990)
□ INDUSTRIAL 13%
■ SERVICES 28%

LAND USE

DEFORESTATION -1.3% annual (81/90)
IRRIGATED 0.2 % of arable

(1993)

■ FOREST & WOODLAND 33.1%
□ ARABLE 11.7%
■ OTHER 55.2%

1990

PER 100,000
LIVE BIRTHS
740

1970
21%

1994
9%

PROFILE

ENVIRONMENT
The southern region is covered with dense rainforest, partially cleared to plant cocoa, coffee, banana and oil palm trees. Wide savannahs extend to the north. The rest of the territory is low-lying, with a few high points near the border with Togo. The Volta, Ghana's main river, has an artificial lake formed by the Akossombo dam. The climate is tropical, with summer rains. The subsoil is rich in gold, diamonds, manganese and bauxite. Desertification in the northwest and deforestation are the main environmental problems.

SOCIETY
Peoples: Ghanaians come from six main ethnic groups the Akan (Ashanti and Fanti), 44 per cent, located in the mid southern part of the country; the Ewe, 13 per cent, and Ga-Adangbe, 8 per cent, on both sides of the Volta in southern and southeastern Ghana; the Mole-Dagbane, 16 per cent, in the northern savannahs; the Guan, 4 per cent, and the Gurma, 3 per cent, in the valleys and plateaus of the northeastern territory.
Religions: 50 per cent Christian, 32 per cent traditional religions, 13 per cent Muslim.
Languages: English (official); Ga is the main native language, Fanti, Haussa, Fantéewe, Gaadanhe, Akan, Dagbandim and Mampusi are also spoken.
Political Parties: Progressive Alliance, coalition made up of the National Democratic Conference (NDC); the National Convention Party (NCP); and the Every Ghanaian Living Everywhere (EGLE); People's National Convention; National Independence Party (NIP); New Patriotic Party (NPP); People's Heritage Party (PHP).
Social Organizations: Ghana Trade Union Congress.

THE STATE
Official Name: Republic of Ghana.
Administrative divisions: 10 regions, subdivided into 110 districts.
Capital: Accra, 1,560,000 people (1994).
Other cities: Kumasi, 600,000 people; Tamale, 265,000 people.
Government: Jerry Rawlings, President since 1981, re-elected in 1996. Legislature: Parliament (single-chamber), with 200 members elected by direct popular vote for 4-year terms.
National Holiday: March 6, independence (1957).
Armed Forces: 7,000.
Other: People's Militia 5,000.

and neo-colonial interests conspired against the Government and Nkrumah was overthrown. The coup leaders drew up a parliamentary constitution and in 1969 held elections for a civilian government. The CPP was not allowed to participate. Nkrumah died in exile in Bucharest in 1972.

[12] Also in 1969, Colonel Ignatius Acheampong led a new coup replacing the government of Dr Kofi Busia. Acheampong dropped the ambitious industrialization and development plans, substituting an essentially agrarian policy which favored the owners of large cocoa plantations.

[13] Acheampong survived eight coup attempts in five years, but his economic policy was not as successful. In 1977, Ghana had an inflation rate of 36 per cent, an oppressive foreign debt, a devalued currency and hundreds of imprisoned intellectuals and students, condemned for questioning government policy.

[14] In July 1977, the so-called revolt of the middle class occurred. The period of social unrest came to a head in July 1978 and Acheampong resigned. A new military regime was established, lead by General William Frederick Akuffo. The opposition claimed

this was simply a continuation of the previous government under a different figurehead. On June 4 1979, a coup led by Lt Jerry Rawlings overthrew Akuffo and called fresh elections. The People's National Party, which included Nkrumah's followers, won a large majority. A transitional government took power promising an eventual return to a constitutional system.

[15] On October 1 1979, with the acquiescence of the Revolutionary Council of the Armed Forces, Hilla Limann, a PNP leader, took over the presidency. Limann abandoned many of Nkrumah's nationalistic economic policies, replacing them with International Monetary Fund policies, in an attempt to reduce the fiscal deficit. To attract foreign investors and overcome the sharp fall in cocoa export revenues, the Ghanaian Government drastically reduced all imports, including food. As a result, food prices escalated wildly while the purchasing power of workers fell drastically. This inevitably led to a series of strikes in 1980 and 1981.

[16] Support for Rawlings remained high among the poor. He accused the Government of being indecisive and preoccupied with foreign capital. Inflation exceeded 140 per cent and the unemployment rate was more than 25 per cent. This created an unstable situation which culminated in a further coup, led by Rawlings on January 1 1982.

[17] The first concern of the new group of officers was to launch a campaign against corruption in the public sector. They committed themselves to nothing short of a revolution for social justice in the country. Within a few months they were able to increase the amount of taxes collected, and greatly reduce cocoa smuggling (kalabule) to neighboring countries. People's Courts were set up to pass judgement on irregularities committed by the authorities of the previous government.

[18] To deal with the economic crisis it was necessary to straighten out economic policy, and look for sources of foreign capital. Rawlings had already expressed his willingness to carry out an austerity program dictated by the IMF. He intensified relations with them in 1983, and generous

loans were granted to Ghana on the basis that IMF prescriptions would be followed religiously and that Ghana would serve as a model for other countries in the region.

[19] To increase national income and bring contraband under control Ghana devalued its currency (the cedi). This went from 2.74 per $1 in 1982, to 183 per $1 in 1988. Taxes were increased, subsidies were removed, the government salaries budget was reduced, financing for inefficient private enterprises was eliminated and the printing of currency was virtually suspended.

[20] However there were some positive results. Inflation fell from 200 to 25 per cent, the banking system improved and better prices were obtained for cocoa producers.

[21] By applying this economic policy Ghana obtained loans on extremely generous terms; $500 million to be repaid in two instalments, the first in 1994, at 5 percent annual interest, and the second in 1999, at 0.5 per cent. The major drawback of this scheme was that Ghana's finances are under rigid IMF control. Ghana's foreign debt approached $4 billion and the servicing of the debt used up two-thirds of the country's export earnings.

[22] The social cost of this readjustment program has been high. Consumer prices rose by some 30 per cent between 1983 and 1987; 45,000 public employees have lived under the constant threat of losing their jobs and there was a general loss of earning power leading to an increase in hunger, infant mortality and illiteracy.

[23] In 1900 there were only 8 urban centres in the whole of the country, but by 1984 the number had risen to 180. In the past few years there has been a migration towards the major cities, resulting in the creation of shantytowns with no drinking water or sanitation. In the poorest quarters of Takoradi there are only 16 public toilets per 3,250 people. If current rates of rural exodus continue, by the year 2020 over half the population of Ghana will be living in urban centres. In order to ameliorate this situation a Program of Action to Mitigate the

External Debt
1996

Literacy
1995

PER CAPITA
$348

65%

Social Costs of Adjustment (PAMSCAD) was established. A program to transfer 12,000 people per year to rural areas was also put into practice.

[24] The economic upheaval had environmental costs as well. Tropical forest used to cover 34 per cent of the country's surface. This forest is now only a quarter of its original size; and 42 per cent of the area which is officially considered " forest ", is in fact covered with timber plantations, secondary vegetation, or immature trees. For the people who live in the country, and for most of those who live in the cities, forest plants constitute the basis of their traditional medicine. 75 per cent of the population rely on bush meat for their basic source of protein and forests also provide firewood, a basic household necessity.

[25] All of these activities are ignored by official plans, which see the forest merely as a source of timber for export. In Ghana at present some 70,000 people are employed in the timber industry.

[26] A National Forestry Administration Program (NFAP) was established, supported by international bodies like USAID, the FAO and countries such as Canada and the UK. Such programs however lay the blame for deforestation, desertification and soil degradation on the poor population and its search for new areas of farmland. In this thinking the very people who are the victims of an economic model which encourages exports at any price are held responsible for environmental degradation.

[27] Ghana considerably increased its production of cocoa, gold, wood and bauxite, but the fall in the world market price of cocoa generated a loss of $200 million, and many industries were forced to close down. In meetings at the Paris Club in January and February of 1989, further loans of $900 million were granted.

[28] In 1990 in, spite of monetary infusions, the hopes of growth collapsed. The GDP growth fell from 6.1 to 2.7 per cent. Inflation at 25 per cent in 1989, went up to 37 per cent. The current account deficit almost doubled and earnings for exports were lower than in 1988. Between 1988 and 1989, around 120 industries closed down because their products could not compete with cheaper and higher-quality goods from China, South Korea, and Taiwan.

[29] In December 1991, the World Bank announced that Ghana would receive two more loans, totalling $155 million, for the Government to reform the financial system and improve the rural road network.

[30] The Rawlings Government initiated a democratization program and a devolution plan, favoring local administrations. In June 1991, an advisory assembly of 260 members was elected to draft a new constitution. The National Council for Women and Development, a body with ministerial status, won 10 seats and the Organization of Graduate Nurses and Midwives was also represented.

[31] In December 1991, Amnesty International denounced the Ghanaian policy of silencing or intimidating its opponents. In view of such serious and constant human rights violations, the Ghana Committee for Human and Popular Rights was created in January 1992, the first such organization in the country.

[32] In that year, a new constitution was approved and elections were held. Rawlings took 58.3 per cent of the vote in the November presidential elections and the three parties which supported him took 197 of the 200 seats in the December legislative elections.

[33] In spite of alleged election irregularities, 80 countries and international organizations attended Rawlings' investiture in January 1993. This foreign support was attributed to the rigorous application of the IMF imposed structural adjustment plans in the previous decade and the prompt payment of servicing on the foreign debt, which represented some 35 per cent of export earnings.

[34] In February 1994, confrontations over land ownership caused the death of more than a thousand people and the migration of 150,000. The Government declared a state of emergency and in June an agreement was reached to bring an end to the violence. The budget for that year had a surplus of $80 million, following two years of deficit. In May, demonstrations against the new value-added tax left five people dead. Economy Minister, Kwesi Botchwey, withdrew the new tax from the budget, and after 13 years in the post - coinciding with the implementation of the IMF plans - resigned from his job.

[35] Despite the New Patriotic Party and the People's Convention trying to settle their differences and form an alliance to present a common electoral platform, Rawlings won the December 1996 elections with 57.2 per cent of the vote.

[36] The country faced a serious drop in water level in the Akosombo dam, producing a severe energy crisis. In March 1998, the Ministry of Science and Technology said Ghana could not pay the initial investment needed to develop a possible nuclear energy-based project. The crisis was partly resolved with help from Côte d'Ivoire, which increased the amount of electricity supplied to Ghana from 20 to 35 megawatts per day.

STATISTICS

DEMOGRAPHY
Population: 17,832,000 (1996) **Annual growth:** 3.1% (1980/1996) **Estimates for year 2000:** 19,900,000 **Annual growth to year 2000:** 2.8% (1994/2000) **Urban Population:** 36.3% (1996) **Urban growth:** 4.27% (1980/95) **Children per woman:** 5.4 (1996).

HEALTH
Life expectancy at birth: 57 years (1996) male: 55 years (1994) female: 59 years (1994) **Infant mortality:** 70 per 1,000 (1996) **Under-5 child mortality:** 110 per 1,000 (1996) **Calorie consumption:** 93% (1988/90) 25,000 **people per doctor** (1988/91) **Safe water:** 65% (1990/96).

EDUCATION
Literacy: 65% (1995) male : 76% (1995) female: 54% (1995) **School enrolment :** Primary total: 76% (1990/95) male : 83% (1990/95) female: 70% (1990/95) Secondary: male : 45% (1990/95) female: 29% (1990/95) **Primary school teachers:** one for every 28 students (1995).

COMMUNICATIONS
20 **newspapers**, 229 **radios**, 20 **TV sets** and 3 **main telephone lines** per 1,000 people (1994).

ECONOMY
Per capita, GNP: $ 360 (1996) **Annual growth, GNP:** 2.3% (1995/96) **Annual inflation:** 28.57% (1985/95) **Consumer price index:** 202.7 (1994) **Currency:** 1,449 cedis = $ 1 (1995) **Cereal imports:** 311 metric tons (1994) **Food import dependency:** 9% (1994) **Fertilizer use:** 23 kgs per ha (1994) **Exports:** $ 1,684 million (1996) Imports: $ 3,219 million (1996) **External debt:** $ 6,202 million (1996) $ 348 **per capita:** (1996) **Debt service:** 26.4% of exports (1996) Development aid received: $ 644 million (1995) $ 38 per capita (1995) 12.1% of GNP (1994).

ENERGY
Consumption: 92.67 Kgs of Oil equivalent per capita yearly (1994) 66.08% imported (1994)

HDI (rank / value) 132 / 0.468 (1994).

Greece

Ellás

Population:	10,490,000 (1996)
Area:	131,990 SQ KM
Capital:	Athens (Athínai)
Currency:	Drachmas
Language:	Greek

Between 5,000 and 3,000 BC, the Greek peninsula was inhabited by maritime peoples from Asia. In Thessaly, central Greece and Crete traces have been found of previous inhabitants, nomadic and agricultural peoples. From the second millennium BC the Achaeans, an Indo-European people, started to expand throughout the peninsula.

[2] The Achaeans founded Mycenae, Tyrins and Argos, later conquering Athens and the eastern Peloponnese, invading Crete and raiding Troy. They were warriors, with an economy based on agriculture and cattle-breeding. The hierarchical social organization had kings, nobles, and warriors dominating farmers, artisans and peasants.

[3] By the first millennium BC, Mycenian civilization had succumbed to Dorian invasions. The Dorians used iron weapons, unknown to the Achaeans, and they soon mixed with the subject population, bringing linguistic unity to the region.

[4] The peninsula's topography favored the appearance of city-states (*polis*), ruled by a king or tyrant, supported by the military aristocracy. The peasants were forced to pay tributes in kind, and if they could not produce sufficient crops they became serfs or their whole family was sold into slavery.

[5] Despite the social differentiation, the Greeks had an original concept of the human being. All previous civilizations had seen humans as a mere instruments of the will of the gods or the monarchs, whereas in Greek philosophy they acquired the value of individuals. The concept of a male citizen, as an individual who belongs to the polis regardless of his nobility, was one Greek culture's main contributions to Western civilization.

[6] The city states alternately established alliances and fought each other. However, Hellenic groups started to feel they belonged to a common nationality bound by factors like the Olympic games, and a common religion and language.

[7] In the 8th century BC most city-states went through crises, due to the decline in power of the monarchs (who were progressively replaced by magistrates appointed by the nobility), to the lack of fertile soil, and to demographic growth. This produced great social tension spurring the Greeks to colonize the Mediterranean, creating active trade routes and expanding the use of Greek as the language of commerce.

[8] Around 760 BC the Greeks established colonies in southern Italy, in the bay of Naples and in Sicily. The Phoenicians and the Etruscans prevented them from ruling the whole of Sicily and the south of Italy, but their culture was deeply influential in later developments on the Italian peninsula.

[9] When colonization started, the social and political structure of the polis underwent transformations. Merchants, wealthy as a result of maritime expansion, were not ready to leave government to the nobility. They joined the peasants in pressing for political participation. Between the 7th and 6th centuries BC, Athens one of the most prosperous cities in the peninsula started a process of political transformations which led to the gradual democratization of its governmental structures. In 594 BC a reformer called Solon took the first steps in this direction with the establishment of written law, a court of justice and an assembly of 400 members, elected from among the wealthy, which was in charge of legislating on city matters.

[10] Sparta, the other great city-state in the region, evolved in a completely different way. It consolidated an oligarchic state, with a strict social and political structure. Spartan society was completely militarized because of the central importance of the army, which had been a determining factor in expansion and annexation of neighboring territories.

[11] In 540 BC the Persians started advancing on Asia Minor, conquering some Greek cities. These cities revolted, backed first by Athens and then by Sparta, resulting in several wars until the Persians were defeated around 449 BC. These wars served to consolidate Athenian power in the region, exerting its political and economic influence over the other city-states through the League of Delos.

[12] The Athenian triremes (galleys) played a key role in the wars against the Persians. The oarsmen, who belonged to the lowest strata of Athenian society, became an indispensable tool in the defence of Athens, and were thus in a position to demand improvements in their living conditions and increased political rights. In 508 BC, after a period when the Athenian oligarchy had succeeded in recovering its political power, a reformer called Cleisthenes raised the number of assembly members to 500, turning this body into the main governmental structure. Participation in the Assembly was open to all free citizens in the polis. However, these constituted a minority of the population; Athenian prosperity was actually based on the exploitation of huge numbers of slaves. Athenian society of this period is therefore

PUBLIC EXPENDITURE

8.9% **34.1%**
1995 ■ DEFENCE □ SOCIAL

In **1990/91** Military as % of health & education expenditure was 71%.

WORKERS

(1996)

Labour force %
■ WOMEN
□ MEN
37% **63%**

■ AGRICULTURE 23% (1990)
□ INDUSTRIAL 27%
■ SERVICES 50%

LAND USE

IRRIGATED **54.4 %** of arable

(1993)

■ FOREST & WOODLAND 19.8%
□ ARABLE 18.3%
■ OTHER 61.9%

referred to as a "slave holding democracy" by historians.

[13] In 446 BC the *archon* or governor of Athens, Pericles, agreed the Thirty Years' Peace with Sparta, recognizing each city's areas of influence in the Athenian League and the League of the Peloponnese.

[14] Under Pericles' rule, Athens became the trading, political, and cultural centre of the region. The domination of maritime trade and the prosperity this created enabled Pericles to start new democratic reforms. This was the period of scholars such as Anaxagoras, of dramatists such as Sophocles, Aeschylus, Euripides, Aristophanes, and of sculptors like Phidias. The Greeks achieved great scientific knowledge, much of which has now been altered, particularly in the fields of medicine or astronomy, but their contributions to geometry and mathematics are still indispensable for most of present-day science.

[15] A long period of continuous struggles over who should control the region ensued between the Spartans and Athenians. This mutual attrition enabled the Macedonians to conquer this domain under the rule of Philip II, 359-336 BC. Philip's son, Alexander the Great, 336-323 BC, continued to spread Hellenic influence over the north of Africa and the Arabian Peninsula, through Mesopotamia, and as far as India. This empire, built over 11 years, contributed to the dissemination of Greek culture in the East. During the years of conquest, many trading cities were founded. Alexander promoted the fusion of Greek culture with that of the conquered peoples, giving rise to what is known as Hellenism. Upon his death, the Macedonian Empire collapsed and wars and rebellions continued to shake the peninsula.

[16] These internal disputes resulted in a decline in the Greek civilization, leading to devastation and impoverishment which enabled the Romans to move in. The Macedonian wars lasted from 215 to 168 BC, ending with the Romans establishing their rule over Greece by 146 BC.

[17] Under the Romans, Greece was acquainted with Christianity in the 3rd century, and it became a more rural society which was

subjected to several invasions. From 395 to 1204, it belonged to the Eastern Empire, whose domination ended with the formation of the Eastern Roman Empire and the region's division into feudal possessions. In 1054, as a consequence of the Schism of the Roman Church, Greek Christians pledged obedience to the Orthodox Church in Constantinople.

[18] The Turks invaded and conquered in 1460, dividing Greece into six provinces which were forced to pay taxes. The Turks kept an army of occupation in the country for 400 years. External attempts to expel the Turks, in particular incursions led by Venice - eager to acquire this strategic territory for trade with the East - and internal revolts all failed. The Peace of Passarowitz incorporated Greece into the Ottoman Empire in 1718.

[19] In 1821 a Greek uprising succeeded in freeing Tripolitza, and a national assembly drafted a

constitution, declaring independence. In 1825 the attempt ended in a bloodbath when the Turks, aided by Egypt, regained control of the city.

[20] In 1827 Russia, France and Britain, eager to keep the Turks away from their borders, signed the Treaty of London, which demanded Greek autonomy. The Turks refused it, and that year the allied fleet defeated the Turkish-Egyptian navy. In 1830, the London Convention declared the total independence of Greece, although the country had to sacrifice the region of Thessaly.

[21] In later years the European powers fought to control the peninsula, intervening in its domestic affairs and supporting kings who complied with their interests. Otto of Bavaria, 1831-1862, who favored the Russians, was followed by George I, 1864-1913, who was backed by the British.

[22] In 1910, a coup led by Eleutherios Vinizelos resulted in

the enactment of a constitution (1911) establishing a parliamentary monarchy. Throughout the two World Wars and the interwar years, subsequent military coups brought sympathizers of each side alternately to power.

[23] Once the German occupation was ended in 1944, an important part of the country remained under the control of communist guerrillas. They were led by Markos Vafiades, and had been crucial in Nazi resistance. The British and Americans supported the Government in repressing the guerrillas until they were totally destroyed in 1949.

[24] Greece remained under American influence, becoming a member of the Council of Europe in 1949 and of NATO in 1951. In the 1956 elections women voted for the first time. After the War, Greece existed in a state of almost perpetual political instability.

[25] In April 1967, a group of colonels staged a coup. Martial law was enforced, the Constitution was suspended, democratic movements harshly repressed, and socialist leader Andreas Papandreou was sentenced to nine years' imprisonment. In December the King attempted to oust the military junta, but he failed and fled to Rome. The military appointed General Zoitakis president, and Papadopoulos prime minister.

[26] The "colonels'" regime, as it was known, was supported by the United States and by tycoons such as Onassis and Niarchos. Attempts were made to mask the dictatorship behind a unicameral Parliament in 1968, but in reality the military junta ruled by decree.

[27] Between 1973 and 1974 the military government grew weaker. In November, student demonstrations at the Polytechnic University of Athens were harshly repressed, leaving hundreds of casualties, and attracting international condemnation.

[28] In July 1974, the Greek military junta promoted a coup in Cyprus by collaborating with the Cypriot National Guard. The coup succeeded in deposing president Archbishop Vaneziz Makarios, who was forced into exile in London. A minister in favor of Greek annexation was appointed. The Turkish army immediately invaded

IMPORTS
26,881
EXPORTS
9,558

97%

STATISTICS

DEMOGRAPHY
Population: 10,490,000 (1996) **Annual growth:** 0.5% (1980/1996) **Estimates for year 2000:** 11,000,000 **Annual growth to year 2000:** 0.3% (1994/2000) **Urban Population:** 59.4% (1996) **Urban growth:** 1.35% (1980/95) **Children per woman:** 1.4 (1996).

HEALTH
Life expectancy at birth: 78 years (1996) male: 75 years (1994) female: 80 years (1994) **Infant mortality:** 8 per 1,000 (1996) **Under-5 child mortality:** 9 per 1,000 (1996) **Calorie consumption:** 151% (1988/90) 313 **people per doctor** (1988/91).

EDUCATION
Literacy: 97% (1995) male : 98% (1995) female: 95% (1995) **School enrolment :** Primary total: 95% (1990/95) male : 95% (1990/95) female: 95% (1990/95) Secondary: male : 99% (1990/95) female: 96% (1990/95) Tertiary: 38% (1995) **Primary school teachers:** one for every 16 students (1995).

COMMUNICATIONS
160 **newspapers,** 418 **radios,** 210 **TV sets** and 478 **main telephone lines** per 1,000 people (1994).

ECONOMY
Per capita, GNP: $ 11,460 (1996) **Annual growth, GNP:** 2.2% (1995/96) **Annual inflation:** 15.38% (1985/95) **Consumer price index:** 175.7 (1994) **Currency:** 237.04 drachmas = $ 1 (1995) **Cereal imports:** 570 metric tons (1994) **Fertilizer use:** 1,527 kgs per ha (1994) **Exports:** $ 9,558 million (1996) **Imports:** $ 26,881 million (1996).

ENERGY
Consumption: 2,259.73 Kgs of Oil equivalent per capita yearly (1994) 62.43% imported (1994)

HDI (rank / value) 20 / 0.923 (1994)

Cyprus, allegedly defending the Turkish minority in the country. The Greek military government became even more discredited and internationally condemned, and they relinquished power immediately at the prospect of war with Turkey.

[29] In that month, former conservative prime minister Konstantin Karamanlis returned from exile and took over the government. In the 1974 elections his party won a parliamentary majority and a later referendum abolished the monarchy. In June 1975, Parliament adopted a new constitution and Konstantinos Tsatsos, a Karamanlis partisan, was elected first president of the republic.

[30] From 1974 Greece decided not to take part in NATO military exercises after conflict with Turkey, another member of the Organization.

[31] In the 1981 parliamentary elections, Pasok (Pan-Hellenic Socialist Movement) led by Papandreou, gained an absolute majority, and the first socialist government in the history of Greece took office. The country also became the 10th member of the European Economic Community (EEC).

[32] The socialist government approached Third World countries, in particular the Arab nations, recognized the PLO and led a worldwide campaign in favor of handing back works of art that had been stolen during colonial domination.

[33] In 1983, salaries were frozen, provoking a wave of protests and strikes. Trade unions were granted greater participation in the public sector, but their right to strike was curtailed.

[34] The 1983 census revealed that women constituted one-third of the economically active population. Most of them worked in the service sector and their pay was lower than that of their male counterparts. Peasant women accounted for 40 per cent of the active female population, not counting the 400,000 women who worked unpaid on family plots.

[35] In the 1984 elections the PASOK won again, by an even greater margin than it had held in 1981. The 1986 constitutional amendment gave more power to the parliament at the expense of the President. Successive austerity plans and salary freezes fuelled new protests and strikes.

[36] In November 1988, details of embezzlement in the Bank of Crete, involving several government members were disclosed. This scandal caused several ministerial crises. In June of the following year, the Greek Left and the Communist Party formed the Left Alliance.

[37] In the 1989 elections PASOK lost its majority, and the conservative New Democracy party received a large part of the vote. As there was no adequate parliamentary majority and no agreement to form a government, the presidency went to the leader of the left-wing coalition, the communist Charilaos Florakis. He formed a temporary government with New Democracy, aiming to investigate the financial scandals.

[38] The results of the November 1989 elections, and the subsequent ones, did not give any of the parties a significant majority. This led to the formation of a coalition government.

[39] Between 1983 and 1989, Greece and the United States signed various co-operation agreements including, amongst other aspects, the maintenance of four US military bases in the country, in return for economic and military assistance. This also guaranteed US diplomatic support for Greece in its disputes with Turkey, particularly over Cyprus.

[40] In January 1990, Washington and Athens publicised a new agreement, closing two military bases, as part of the US plan to reduce its military presence in the region.

[41] On March 7, a law was passed on collective work agreements for the private sector, public companies and services. The new law established free negotiations between workers and bosses, putting an end to 50 years of State intervention, and including norms for the organisation of the company and union committees, as well as worker participation in company decisions.

[42] Following Karamanlis's triumph in the April presidential elections, a new government was formed headed by the conservative Constantinos Mitsotakis. In 1991, Mitsotakis promoted public spending cuts, price liberalization and privatizations.

[43] The social cost of these measures contributed to the defeat of the conservative government in the 1993 legislative elections. On October 12, Papandreou's PASOK gained the support of 47 per cent of the voters - compared with the 40 per cent of New Democracy - and the absolute majority in Parliament.

[44] The public debt and pressures from the European Union for a more "rigorous" economic policy complicated Papandreou's leadership. In the 1994 European elections PASOK and above all New Democracy, lost votes to the smaller parties like Political Spring, the Communist Party and the Progressive Left Coalition.

[45] In 1995, amidst permanent rumours of Papandreou's retirement on health grounds and fresh accusations of the misappropriation of public funds against him, Finance Minister Alexandros Papadopoulos implemented unpopular fiscal reforms and launched a policy of "strict (budgetary) rigour".

[46] Ill, and increasingly criticized even within his own party, Papandreou resigned from his post in January 1996 and was replaced by his former industry minister, Konstantinos Simitis. The historic leader of Greek Socialism died in June. In September, the Socialist Party, led by the new Prime Minister, won the legislative elections with 41.5 per cent of the vote.

[47] The tensions between Greece and Turkey continued, partly as a consequence of the situation in Cyprus. This did not prevent both countries participating in a regional meeting in Athens, along with the rest of the Balkan governments. Simitis said the idea of the summit was to attack the image of "disorder" which prevented the region from integrating with the rest of Europe.

[48] In January 1998, backing its pro-regional integration stance, Athens decided to abolish a discriminatory constitutional article allowing citizenship to be stripped from "non-ethnic Greeks" wanting to leave the country. This article had been used mainly against the Muslim minority, mostly of Turkish origin. Some 60,000 people had lost their Greek nationality since this much-criticized measure was imposed under the dictatorship of the colonels.

Grenada

Grenada

Population:	92,000
	(1996)
Area:	344 SQ KM
Capital:	St George's
Currency:	E.C. dollars
Language:	English

The Carib Indians inhabited Grenada when Christopher Columbus arrived, around 1498, and named the island "Concepción". This European visit did not disrupt the island's peace, but two centuries later in 1650, the governor of the French possession of Martinique, Du Parquet, decided to occupy the island. By 1674, France had already established control over Grenada, despite fierce resistance from the Caribs.

[2] In 1753, French settlers from Martinique had around a 100 sugar mills and 12,000 slaves on Grenada. The native population had been exterminated.

[3] The British took control of the island towards the end of the 18th century and introduced the cultivation of cocoa, cotton and nutmeg, using slave labor. In 1788 there were 24,000 slaves, a number which remained stable until the abolition of slavery in the following century.

[4] The severe living conditions of workers resulted in the creation of the first union in the mid-20th century, the Grenada Manual and Metal Workers Union. In 1951, a strike broke out and the labor struggle won considerable wage increases. Eric Matthew Gairy, a young adventurer who had lived away from the island most of his life, formed the first local political party, the Grenada United Labor Party (GULP) which favored independence. In 1951, GULP won a legislative election and Gairy became leader of the assembly.

[5] In 1958 Grenada joined the Federation of the British West Indies, which was dissolved in 1962. The country became part of the Associated State of the British Antilles in 1967. That year, Gairy was appointed prime minister when his party won the August elections. Their main objective was total independence from Britain.

[6] GULP soon obtained semi-independence which gradually led to full independence. By that time, left-wing groups such as the New Jewel Movement (NJM) had appeared on the island, opposing separation from Britain. Though apparently paradoxical, many Grenadians considered that Gairy was seeking independence for his personal benefit, manipulating a politically unprepared population.

[7] In January 1974, an "anti-independence" strike broke out to prevent Gairy from seizing power. After some weeks of total paralysis of the country "Mongoose squads", similar to the Haitian Tonton-Macoutes appeared. They were on the prime minister's payroll and brutal repression was used to end the strike. Independence was proclaimed the following week.

[8] As feared, Gairy exploited power for his own personal benefit. He distributed government jobs among the members of his party, while promoting the paramilitary squad to the level of a "Defence Force", making it the only military body on the island. The "Mongoose Squad" received military training from Chilean advisers and increased its numbers considerably by incorporating ex-inmates of St George's Prison.

[9] In the December 1976 election, the People's Alliance, made up of the NJM, the National Party of Grenada and the United Popular Party, gained new ground in Parliament, moving from one to six representatives in a total of 15 parliamentary seats. On March 13 1979, while Gairy was out of the country, the opposition carried out a bloodless coup and seized power. Thanks to widespread popular support, they were able to establish a provisional revolutionary government, under the leadership of Maurice Bishop, a lawyer.

[10] In four years, the People's Revolutionary Government stimulated the formation of grass roots organizations, and they created a mixed economy, expanding the public sector through agro-industries and state farms. Private enterprise was encouraged making Grenada more compatible with global economic policy.

[11] However, because of the Government's socialist ideology, the NJM was under constant harassment from the United States and Grenada's conservative neighbors, who did everything possible to destabilize the Grenadian Government. Claiming that Grenada's modern airport at Point Saline might be used as a stopover for Cuban troops en route to Africa, the United States began a co-ordinated campaign to crush Grenada's economy.

[12] The Government based its foreign policy on the principles of anti-imperialism and non-alignment. Special attention was given to the development of ties with the socialist world. Cuba agreed to collaborate in the construction of an international airport. The project was conceived as a way to stimulate tourism, which employed 25 per cent of the country's work force.

[13] Prime Minister Bishop faced constant pressure from the NJM's extreme left wing. This faction, led by the deputy prime minister, was intent upon radicalizing the political process. On October 10 1983, upon his return from a short state visit to Hungary, Czechoslovakia and Cuba, Bishop was placed under house arrest, while General Hudson Austin, head of the army, seized power. Bishop was freed by a crowd of sympathizers, only to be shot dead by troops. A number of others were killed along with him, including his wife Jacqueline Creft - Minister of Education, the Foreign and Housing Ministers, two union leaders and 13 members of the crowd.

[14] The US then began to take definite steps towards military intervention, a move which had been decided upon and planned for over a year; troop-landing had been rehearsed in manoeuvres. Early in the morning of October 25 1983, 5,000 marines and Green Berets landed on the island. They were followed several hours later by a symbolic contingent of 300 police from six Caribbean countries; Antigua, Barbados, Dominica, Jamaica, St Lucia and St Vincent, who joined the farce of a "multinational intervention for humanitarian reasons".

[15] Resistance from the Grenadian militia and some Cuban technicians and workers, meant that the operation lasted much longer than expected. The US suffered combat casualties, and the press was barred from

LAND USE

(1993)

■	FOREST & WOODLAND	8.8%
□	ARABLE	32.4%
▨	OTHER	58.8%

PROFILE

ENVIRONMENT

Grenada is the southernmost Windward island of the Lesser Antilles. The island is almost entirely volcanic. Lake Grand Etang and Lake Antoine are extinct volcanic craters. The rainy, tropical, climate, tempered by sea winds, is fit for agriculture which constitutes the country's major source of income. It is famous for its spices, and is known as "the Spice Island of the West". The territory includes the islands of Carriacou (34 sq km) and Petite Martinique (2 sq km), which belong to the Grenadines.

SOCIETY

Peoples: Most are descended from African slaves (84 per cent), although there are a large number of mestizos (11 per cent) and European (0.7 per cent) and Indo-Pakistani (3 per cent) minorities.
Religions: Mainly Catholic (53.1 per cent). Protestant (38.1 per cent). Other (7.4 per cent).
Languages: English (official and predominant). A patois dialect derived from French, and another from English are also spoken.
Political Parties: The National Democratic Congress (NDC. The New National Party (NNP).Grenada United Labor Party (GULP). The Maurice Bishop Patriotic Movement.

THE STATE

Official Name: Grenada.
Administrative divisions: 7 zones.
Capital: St George's, 4,361 people (1991).
Government: Reginald Palmer has been the representative of the British Crown since August 1992. Keith Mitchell, Prime Minister from June 1995. Legislature: the bicameral Parliament is made up of the 15-member Chamber of Deputies and the 13-member Senate. Deputies are elected by direct popular vote, while 7 of the senators are appointed by the governor, 3 by the prime minister and 3 by the leader of the opposition.
National holiday: February 7, Independence (1974).

96%

STATISTICS

DEMOGRAPHY
Population: 92,000 (1996) **Annual growth:** 0.2% (1980/1996) **Estimates for year 2000:** 100,000 **Annual growth to year 2000:** 0.4% (1994/2000) **Urban Population:** 36.2% (1996).

HEALTH
Infant mortality: 25 per 1,000 (1996) **Under-5 child mortality:** 31 per 1,000 (1996).

EDUCATION
Literacy: 96% (1995) **School enrolment** : Primary total: 88% (1990/95).

COMMUNICATIONS
595 **radios,** 160 **TV sets** and 228 **main telephone lines** per 1,000 people (1994).

ECONOMY
Consumer price index: 112.3 (1994) **Currency:** 2.7 E.C. dollars = $ 1 (1995) **Cereal imports:** 21 metric tons (1994) **Development aid received:** $ 10 million (1995) $ 111 per capita (1995) 4.2% of GNP (1994).

HDI (rank / value) 54 / 0.843 (1994)

---

entering Grenada until all resistance had been eliminated. This made it impossible to verify how many civilians had been killed in attacks on a psychiatric hospital and other non-military targets.
[16] While strict US military control continued, Sir Paul Scoon, official British crown representative in Grenada, assumed the leadership of an interim government with the task of organizing an election within a period of 6 to 11 months. Under the discreet surveillance of the invaders, voting was held on December 3 1984 to elect the members of a unicameral parliament. In turn, the representatives appointed Herbert Blaize prime minister. Blaize led a coalition of parties that was presented to public opinion as the New National Party (NNP) and received support from the US.
[17] Neither NATO nor the OAS

> The US suffered combat casualties, and the press was barred from entering Grenada until all resistance had been eliminated.

dared to condone the aggression. Twenty days later, Barbados was rewarded for its "co-operation" in the invasion with a $18.5 million aid program.
[18] The new government reached a classic agreement with the International Monetary Fund including a reduction of the civil service, a wage-freeze and incentives to private enterprise.
[19] The System of Regional Security (SSR) permitting the Prime Minister to call on troops from neighboring Caribbean islands if Grenada was threatened, was established by Blaize in December 1986, under the pretext that the trial of those involved in the 1983 coup was coming to an end. Bernard Coard, his wife Phyllis, and former army commander Hudson Austin were sentenced to death, along with 11 soldiers. Three others were tried, receiving prison sentences of 30 to 45 years.
[20] During his first years in government, Blaize achieved considerable economic growth, at between five and six per cent per year, basically from tourism. However, youth unemployment continued to increase, along with crime and drug addiction.
[21] Blaize died in 1989. He was replaced by Ben Jones of the National Party, who was backed by big business and the landowners. On March 13 1990 -

the anniversary of the coup which ousted Eric Gairy in 1979 - the general elections were won by Nicholas Braithwaite, the interim head of government after the invasion, and warmly regarded by the United States.
[22] Studies carried out in 1994 revealed unemployment of 30 per cent and a marked pattern of emigration. The fall in international prices of bananas, coconuts, wood and nutmeg influenced this trend. Between March and April 1995, there were strikes in key sectors of the economy, like the hotels, and sugar and cocoa production. Although tourism is the second most important source of income for the nation, Grenada cannot compete with the other Caribbean islands on this front.
[23] In the June 1995 general elections, the governing NDC was pushed out by Keith Mitchell, former mathematics professor at the Howard University in Washington and leader of the NNP. His victory was attributed to his promise to remove income tax, which had been revoked in 1986 and reimposed by the NDC in 1994.
[24] Despite the agreement made between Indonesia and Grenada - the leading world nutmeg producer - in 1994, the

international prices continued to tumble in 1995.
[25] In early 1996, the ruling NNP objected against the privatization process in the State electricity company alleging "misuse of funds".
[26] The Government announced income on cocoa sales had fallen due to a leading US buyer suspending its imports from Grenada.
[27] In May, Grenada signed an extradition and legal co-operation agreement with the United States. The treaties formed part of the campaign against narco-trafficking which Washington was implementing in the region.
[28] In March 1997, the Government rejected a request from the Grenada Conference of Churches to free the two men serving life sentences for the 1993 murder of former prime minister Maurice Bishop, his wife and a group of ministers and union leaders.
[29] In April, Grenada and Cuba re-established diplomatic relations, broken off during the invasion of Grenada by US troops in 1983. Prime Minister Keith Mitchell made an official visit to Cuba, during which he signed an economic co-operation agreement.

Guadeloupe

Guadeloupe

Population: 431,000 (1996)
Area: 1,705 SQ KM
Capital: Basse Terre
Currency: French Franc
Language: French

The entire archipelago of present-day Guadeloupe was inhabited by the Caribs. Originally from South America, they dispersed throughout the islands after overpowering the Arawak people. They resisted the Spanish invasion in 1493 but were defeated by the French two centuries later.

2 The French colonizers built the first sugar mill on the island in 1633 and began importing African slave labourers. By the end of the 17th century, Guadeloupe had become one of the world's main sugar producers. The colonists killed the last of the archipelago's surviving Caribs in the early 18th century.

3 With the abolition of the slave trade in 1815, France restructured its formal links with the Caribbean islands, giving them the status of colonies. In 1946, with the initiation of the new French constitution, Guadeloupe achieved greater political autonomy, as an Overseas Department.

4 French Government subsidies increased per capita income and the consumption of imported goods, but ruined the local economy.

5 In 1981, in a country where 90 per cent of the population was of African or racially mixed origin, racism made the social climate more tense.

6 In 1985 there were violent clashes between pro-independence demonstrations and the police. Several disruptive actions led to the imprisonment of members of the Revolutionary Caribbean Alliance (ARC).

7 In the 1988 election, François Mitterrand received 70 per cent of the vote on Guadeloupe, although two-thirds of the voters abstained. In the regional elections of October 1988, the Left already in the majority within the General Council was further strengthened, gaining another seat.

8 In 1989, ARC members sentenced in 1985 were granted amnesty. The ARC took part in the elections for the first time, and their failure was taken as a show of support for the present situation.

9 In 1989 Hurricane Hugo left 12,000 people homeless. The French Government announced that it would freeze the interest on the foreign debt, and would send $5.4 million in aid to the island.

10 In 1992 the European Community decision to reduce banana import quotas from the "French" Antilles to benefit imports from Africa and Latin America triggered strong protests in Guadeloupe. In the elections for the Regional Council - one of the two main assemblies in the island - the Guadeloupe Federation of the Union for the Republic (RPR) won. The RPR is a conservative, neo-Gaullist party, led by current French president Jacques Chirac. The RPR obtained 15 of the 41 seats, followed by the Socialist Party with 9.

11 In 1993, the reduction in tourism aggravated the economic crisis. The unemployment rate reached 24 per cent of the active population and the informal sector of the economy increased.

12 An important reduction of productive activities increased the trade balance deficit:

exports, which represented just 9.9 per cent of imports in 1995, were reduced to 5.2 per cent in 1996. Due to the reduction of external demand and the competition from United States' corporations, banana exports in 1996 fell to half the quantity exported in 1993.

13 In late 1997, a massive strike of banana workers was launched. Union representatives accused plantation owners of creating militias which threatened to kill workers to force them to lift the strike. In February 1998, in a country with 40 per cent of unemployment and increasing social inequalities, the strike extended to other sectors.

PROFILE

ENVIRONMENT
Includes the dependencies of Marie Galante, La Désirade, Les Saintes, Petite-Terre, Saint Berthélemy and the French section of Saint Martin forming part of the Windward Islands of the Lesser Antilles. The tropical, rainy climate is tempered by sea winds, and sugar cane is grown.

SOCIETY
Peoples: A majority of descendants of native Africans with a small European minority.
Religions: Mainly Catholic.
Languages: French (official).
Political Parties: Guadeloupe Federation of the Union for the Republic (RPR), and Guadeloupe Federation of the Union in French Democracy (UDF), are the local branches of the colonial parties; Guadeloupe Federation of the Socialist Party (PS); the Communist Party of Guadeloupe (PCG); the Guadeloupe Democrats; the Popular Union for the Liberation of Guadeloupe (UPLG), the largest of the radical pro-independence groups; the Revolutionary Caribbean Alliance (ARC), founded in Point-a-Pitre in 1983, has carried out several armed attacks.
Social Organizations: The Guadeloupe General Labor Confederation, with 15,000 members; the Department Union of Christian Workers' French Confederation, with 3.500 members; the Department Organization of Trade Unions (CGT-FO), with 1,500 members.

THE STATE
Official Name: Département d'Outre-Mer de la Guadeloupe.
Administrative Divisions: 3 Arondissements, 36 Cantons
Capital: Basse-Terre, 15,000 people (1995).
Government: Jean Fedini (since 1997), commissioner appointed by the French Government. Legislative power: a 42-member General Council, and 41-member regional Council. Guadeloupe has 4 deputies and 2 senators in the French parliament.

DEMOGRAPHY
Population: 431,000 (1996) **Urban population:** 99.5 % (1996)

ECONOMY
Consumer price index: 110.1 (1994) **Cereal imports:** 80 metric tons (1994) **Fertilizer use:** 2,592 kgs per ha (1994)

Guam

Guam

Population:	153,000 (1996)
Area:	549 SQ KM
Capital:	Agaña
Currency:	US Dollar
Language:	English

Guam shares a common history with the rest of the Micronesian archipelago (see Micronesia). The population, who settled on the island thousands of years ago, became the victim of extermination campaigns at the hands of Spanish colonizers, between 1668 and 1695.

2   As a result of armed aggression and epidemics (the people lacked immunity against European illnesses), the population declined from 100,000 at the beginning of the 17th century to fewer than 5,000 in 1741.

3 The few survivors intermarried with Spanish and Filipino immigrants, producing the Chamorro people who presently populate the island.

4   For three centuries, Guam was a port of call on the Spanish galleon route between the Philippines and Acapulco (Mexico), a major depot on the trade route to Spain.

5   Under the terms of the Treaty of Paris of 1898, Guam changed hands from Spain to the United States, together with the Philippines. The island continued to serve as a stopover until it was invaded by the Japanese in 1941. Recovered in 1944, it became a US military base.

6   Since 1973, the United Nations has unsuccessfully urged Washington to permit the islanders to exercise their right to self-determination. In January 1982, a plebiscite on a new statute did not achieve the majority required.

7   In a self-determination plebiscite, 75 per cent of the electorate favored a system of association with the United States. As a result of this the UN General Assembly recommended that the US implement Guam's decolonization in December 1984. The UN also reiterated its conviction that military bases are a major obstacle to self-determination and independence, two principles established in the UN Charter.

8   In February 1987, former governor Ricardo Borballo, who had been elected in 1984, was found guilty of bribery, extortion and conspiracy.

9   In November 1987, the High Commission initiated a self-determination referendum for Guam, and voters supported negotiation of a new relationship with the US. In February 1988 Guam received US economic aid, or more precisely, disaster relief, to repair the damage done by the typhoon in January.

10   In November 1994, the democrat Carl Gutiérrez was elected governor with 54.6 per cent of the vote.

11   Negotiations over political self-determination and the creation of a Free Associated State with the United Nations and the United States were restarted in 1996. A landowners' organization demanded the Government include the territory occupied by the US military in the discussions. Washington considered Guam an extremely important geo-strategical enclave.

12   In September 1996, the island formed the operations base for US bombers which carried out a "limited attack" on Iraq.

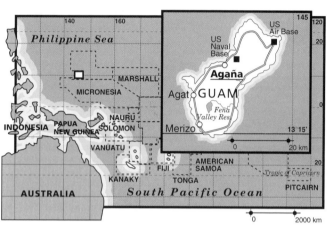

13   In the November 1996 legislative elections, the Republican Party took 11 seats in the legislative chamber, while the Democrat Party took 10.

14   In early 1998, the economy was partly sustained by tourism, mostly from Japan, South Korea and Taiwan. These tourists spent some $300 million in the island each season. Governor Gutiérrez aimed to increase this figure by 50 per cent in the next five years.

> Washington considered Guam an extremely important geo-strategical enclave. In September 1996, the island formed the operations base for US bombers which carried out a "limited attack" on Iraq.

PROFILE

ENVIRONMENT
Guam is the southernmost island of the Marianas archipelago, located east of the Philippines and south of Japan. Of volcanic origin, its contours are mountainous except for the coastal plain in the northern region. The climate is tropical, rainy from June to November (over 300 mm a month) and drier and colder from December to May. It has rainforest vegetation. One-third of the island is occupied by military installations.

SOCIETY
Peoples: Chamorro natives account for approximately 47 per cent of the population; Filippino, 25 per cent; US troops and dependents, 10 per cent; Japanese, Chinese, Korean and other, 18 per cent.
Religions: 98 per cent of all Guamanians are Catholic.
Languages: English (official), Chamorro (a dialect derived from Indonesian), and Japanese.
Political Parties: Republican and Democrat, as in the US.

THE STATE
Official Name: Territory of Guam.
Capital: Agaña, 10,000 people (est 1994).
Government: Carl T C Gutierrez, Governor, elected on November 8 1994. His office responds to the US Interior Department and actually has less autonomy than the local military commander, as one-third of the island is under control of the US Navy and Air force. Although Guamanians formally possess US citizenship they have no representation in the US Congress nor do they participate in the US presidential elections.

DEMOGRAPHY
Population: 153,000 (1996) **Urban population:** 38.4 % (1996).

ECONOMY
Cereal imports: 9 metric tons (1994).

Guatemala

Guatemala

Population: 10,928,000 (1996)
Area: 108,889 SQ KM
Capital: Guatemala

Currency: Quetzales
Language: Spanish

The Maya civilization flourished during the first ten centuries AD in what is now Guatemala and parts of Mexico, Honduras and El Salvador.

[2] Spanish troops, under the command of Pedro de Alvarado, entered the country in 1524, founding the city of Guatemala and gaining total control over the country two years later. This process was facilitated by the fact that the country was undergoing a gradual transition and readjustment among its various ethnic groups - the K'iche', Kaqchi', Mam, Q'eqchi, Poqomchi', Q'anjob'al, Tz'utujiil and others - all of which stemmed from a common Mayan ancestry. Though the situation favored the invaders, there were nevertheless frequent incidents in which they faced stiff resistance.

[3] On September 15 1821, large landowners and local businessmen joined forces with colonial officials, to peacefully proclaim the independence of the Viceroyalty of New Spain, including the five countries of Central America.

[4] The new political and administrative union, called the Federation of Central American States, was dissolved in 1839 as a result of internal struggles prompted by the British policy of "divide and conquer".

[5] In 1831, under tremendous debt pressure, the Government yielded large portions of territory to Britain for timber. This later became British Honduras, now the independent nation of Belize.

[6] The discovery of synthetic dyes in Europe in the mid-18th century caused a serious economic crisis in Guatemala, where the main export products were vegetable dyes. Coffee replaced dyes as the country's main cash crop, and plantation owners deprived the indians of most of their communal lands through the Liberal Reform of 1871. During the late 19th century, Guatemalan politics were dominated by the antagonism between liberals and conservatives. German settlers in Guatemala developed ties with German companies and initiated an import-export business which damaged the interests of the incipient national bourgeoisie.

[7] Toward the end of the 19th century, Manuel Estrada Cabrera rose to power and governed Guatemala until 1920. He began an "open door policy" for US transnationals, who eventually owned the railroads, ports, hydroelectric plants, shipping, international mailing services and the enormous banana plantations of the United Fruit Company.

[8] General Jorge Ubico Castañeda, the last of a generation of military leaders, was elected president in 1931. However, a popular uprising known as the "October Revolution" toppled him in 1944 calling fresh elections. The winner was reformist Juan José Arévalo, who launched a process of economic and social reform.

[9] Arévalo's government heralded a climate of political and economic liberalization. In 1945, literate women were granted the right to vote. That same year the first campesino labor union was formed. The land reform program, under which extensive tracts of unused United Fruit Company land were expropriated, was considered "a threat to US interests" by Washington. An aggressive anti-communist campaign was launched, with the sole aim of harassing Arévalo and his successor, president Jacobo Arbenz.

[10] John Foster Dulles, US Secretary of State, but also a United Fruit Company (UFCO) share-holder and company lawyer pressured the OAS to condemn the reforms being carried out by Jacobo Arbenz's government. Allen Dulles, director of the CIA and former president of the company was the one who organized the invasion carried out by Castillo Armas in June 1954. With the fall of Arbenz, UFCO managed to get back its lands, and subsequently changed its name to United Brands.

[11] Two decades of military regimes followed. Most Guatemalans felt that the four elections which followed, in 1970, 1974, 1978 and 1982, were rigged - with the top military candidates invariably elected.

[12] This kind of political atmosphere bred armed insurgency. The Rebel Armed Forces (FAR) entered the scene in 1962, followed by the Poor People's Guerrilla Army (EGP) and the Organization of the People in Arms (ORPA) in 1975 and 1979, respectively.

[13] According to estimates from several humanitarian organizations, official repression took some 80,000 lives between 1954 and 1982. The Guatemalan National Revolutionary Unity (URNG) was founded in February 1982, uniting the Poor People's Guerrilla Army, the Rebel Armed Forces, the Organization of the People in Arms, and the Guatemalan Labor Party (PGT, National Leadership Committee).

[14] On March 23 1982, only a few days after a rigged election, a military coup ousted Lucas García from office and replaced him with General Efraín Ríos Montt.

[15] Ríos Montt's counter-

PUBLIC EXPENDITURE

15.2%   38.4%
1995 ■ DEFENCE □ SOCIAL

In 1990/91 Military as % of health & education expenditure was 31%.

WORKERS

(1996)
Labour force %
■ WOMEN
□ MEN
27%   73%

■ AGRICULTURE 52% (1990)
□ INDUSTRIAL   17%
■ SERVICES   30%

LAND USE

DEFORESTATION -1.6% annual (81/90)
IRRIGATED 9.4 % of arable

(1993)

■ FOREST & WOODLAND 53.4%
□ ARABLE   12.2%
■ OTHER   34.4%

ENVIRONMENT

The Sierra Madre and the Cuchumatanes Mountains cross the country from east to west, and these are the areas of volcanic activity and earthquakes. Between the mountain ranges there is a high plateau with sandy soil and easily eroded slopes. Although the plateau occupies only 26 per cent of the country's territory, 53 per cent of the population is concentrated there. The long Atlantic coastline is covered with forests and is less populated. In the valleys along the Caribbean coast and in the Pacific lowlands there are banana and sugar cane plantations. In 1980, 41.9 per cent of the country's land area was covered by forests; in 1990, that figure had been reduced to 33.8 per cent, threatening the exceptionally diverse ecosystems, with a great variety of species.

SOCIETY

Peoples: Approximately 90 per cent are of Mayan descent. Amid the country's great cultural and linguistic diversity, four major peoples can be distinguished: the Ladino (descendants of Amerindians and Spaniards), the Maya, the Garifuna (of the Caribbean region) and the Xinca.
Religions: Mainly Catholic. In recent years a number of Protestant groups have appeared. The Mayan Religion has also survived.
Languages: Spanish is official but most of the population speak one of the 22 Maya dialects.
Political Parties: National Advancement Party, conservative; Guatemalan Republican Alliance (FRG), ultra-right-wing led by former dictator Efrain Rios Montt; Christian Democracy of Guatemala (DCG); Union of the National Center (UCN); New Guatemala Democratic Front, a new left wing coalition; Solidarity Action Movement (MAS). The National Revolutionary Unity of Guatemala (URNG) is a coalition of different armed groups.
Social Organizations: Union of Labor and Popular Associations; National Labor Union Alliance; National Workers' Coordinating Committee; Labor Union of Guatemalan Workers; Committee for Campesino Unity; National Coordinating Committee of Indigenous Campesinos; Communities of Peoples Resistance; Permanent Commissions of Refugees in Mexico; National Commission of Widows of Guatemala; Mutual Support Group; "Runujel Junam" Council of Ethnic Communities; Office of Human Rights of the Archbishopric; Coordinating Committee of Mayan Women; Academy of Mayan Languages of Guatemala; "Majawil Q'uij" Coordinating Committee and Council of Mayan Organizations of Guatemala.

THE STATE

Official Name: República de Guatemala.
Administrative Divisions: 22 Departments.
Capital: Guatemala, 1,167,495 people (1995).
Other cities: Mixco, 436,668 people; Villa Nueva, 165,567; Chinautla, 61,335; (1995).
Government: Alvaro Arzú, President since January 1996. Independence Day (1821).
Armed Forces: 44,200 troops (1994).
Other: 10,000 National Police, 2,500 Hacienda Guard; 500,000 Territorial Militia.

insurgency campaign surpassed that of his predecessor's in terms of aggressiveness. Over 15,000 Guatemalans were killed in the first year of Ríos Montt's administration. 70,000 took refuge in neighboring countries, especially Mexico, and 500,000 fled to the mountains to escape the army. Hundreds of villages were razed, while the number of "model hamlets" increased systematically. Peasants were taken by force to these hamlets, where they were required to produce cash crops for export, rather than growing subsistence crops.

[16] In August 1983, another coup staged by the CIA deposed Ríos Montt and General Oscar Mejía Víctores came into power,

promising a quick return to a democratic system.

[17] An 88-seat Constituent Assembly was elected on July 18, 1984, to replace the legal framework in effect since 1965, and annulled after the 1982 coup. The Assembly offered new constitutional guarantees, habeas corpus and electoral regulations. Seventeen parties ran candidates; however, lack of guarantees forced the left to abstain from running yet another time.

[18] The Constituent Assembly approved the right to strike for civil servants, authorized the return from exile of leaders of the Socialist Democratic Party and called for elections in November 1985.

[19] The election, boycotted by the URNG, gave a clear victory to the Christian Democratic candidate, Vinicio Cerezo. One of the first measures was the "total and definitive" suspension of secret police activities.

[20] In October 1987, representatives of the URGN and Vinicio Cerezo's government met in Madrid, the first direct negotiations between the government and guerrilla forces in 27 years of conflict. That year, the National Reconciliation Commission (CNR) played a decisive role in the rapprochement process. The commission was created as a result of the Esquipulas II peace plan for Central America, signed by 6 countries in the region.

[21] On March 30, in Oslo, guerrillas and government agreed on an operational pattern for the meetings and the role of CNR and UN mediators. Despite the persistence of political persecution and assassination, on June 1, 1990 a basic agreement was signed in Madrid by the National Commission for Reconciliation, the political parties and the URGN. The overall aim of the accord was to continue the search for peace in Guatemala.

[22] During the last few months of 1990, negotiations came to a standstill and a high degree of skepticism developed among voters, which led to a 70 per cent abstention rate in the November 11, 1990 presidential elections. During the second round of the elections, held on January 6 1991, Jorge Serrano Elías, of the Solidary Action Movement (MAS), was elected president.

[23] The Serrano Government and the URNG decided to take up peace negotiations. A fortnight later, in Cuernavaca, Mexico, a three-day meeting was held. After three decades of violence, during which over 100,000 people were murdered and 50,000 went missing, the government and the guerrillas committed themselves to the negotiation process, attended by top level delegates and with the aim of achieving a firm and lasting peace agreement in the shortest possible time. The agenda included topics such as: democratization, human rights, the strengthening of civil empowerment, the function of the army in a democratic society, the identity and rights of the indigenous peoples, constitutional reforms and the electoral system, socio-economics and the agrarian situation, the resettlement of the landless as a result of the armed struggle, the incorporation of the URNG into legal political life.

[24] In July, the US Senate suspended military aid to Guatemala. The URNG demanded that human rights violations cease

immediately. Human rights organizations found that in the first 9 months of Serrano's rule there had been 1,760 human rights violations, 650 of them executions without trial. Several deaths of street children below the age of six, were also reported.

[25] Also in September 1991, the Guatemalan president recognized the sovereignty and self-determination of Belize, the ex-British colony which proclaimed its independence in 1981. The announcement caused the resignation of chancellor Alvaro Arzú, the leader of the National Advancement Party (PAN), and one of the ruling party's main allies.

[26] In 1992, a national debate began on the existence of government armed civilian groups, such as the Civilian Self-Defence Patrols (PAC). The Catholic Church criticized the government's economic policy and spoke out in favor of agrarian reform. In the meantime, organizations representing the indigenous peoples demanded the ratification of ILO Agreement 169, dealing with indigenous and tribal peoples.

[27] The government created the "Hunapú" force, made up of the Army, the National Police and the "Hacienda Guard", replacing the former PACs. In April, members of the "Hunapú" provoked an incident during a student demonstration demanding improvements in the education policy. One student was killed and 7 injured. The World Bank, the US Government and the European Parliament urged the Guatemalan government to end political violence.

[28] In October, while the quincentenary of Columbus's arrival on the continent was celebrated, Rigoberta Menchú Tum, an indigenous leader from the Quiché ethnic group, won the Nobel Peace Prize. Menchú has travelled world-wide, denouncing the situation of her country's indigenous peoples.

[29] On May 25, 1993, President Serrano, backed by a group of military officers, carried out an "auto-coup", revoking several articles of the constitution and dissolving Congress and the Supreme Court. On June 1, national and international rejection of this measure - including pressure from the United States - made Serrano abandon office. On June 6, after several days of uncertainty, former Human Rights attorney Ramiro De León Carpio was elected head of the Executive, to finish Serrano's term.

[30] De León Carpio began by purging the officers that had supported Serrano, changing five

1990

PER 100,000
LIVE BIRTHS
200

1995

56%

STATISTICS

DEMOGRAPHY
Population: 10,928,000 (1996) **Annual growth:** 2.9% (1980/1996) **Estimates for year 2000:** 12,200,000 **Annual growth to year 2000:** 2.9% (1994/2000) **Urban Population:** 39.1% (1996) **Urban growth:** 3.62% (1980/95) **Children per woman:** 5 (1996).

HEALTH
Life expectancy at birth: 66 years (1996) male: 63 years (1994) female: 68 years (1994) **Infant mortality:** 43 per 1,000 (1996) **Under-5 child mortality:** 56 per 1,000 (1996) **Calorie consumption:** 103% (1988/90) 4,000 **people per doctor** (1988/91) **Safe water:** 77% (1990/96).

EDUCATION
Literacy: 56% (1995) male : 63% (1995) female: 49% (1995) **School enrolment :** Primary total: 84% (1990/95) male : 89% (1990/95) female: 78% (1990/95) Secondary: male : 25% (1990/95) female: 23% (1990/95) Tertiary: 8% (1995) **Primary school teachers:** one for every 34 students (1995).

COMMUNICATIONS
20 **newspapers,** 68 **radios,** 50 **TV sets** and 24 **main telephone lines** per 1,000 people (1994).
ECONOMY
Per capita, GNP: $ 1,470 (1996) **Annual growth, GNP:** 8.6% (1995/96) **Annual inflation:** 18.64% (1985/95) **Consumer price index:** 181.7 (1994) **Currency:** 6.04 quetzales = $ 1 (1995) **Cereal imports:** 517 metric tons (1994) **Food import dependency:** 11% (1994) **Fertilizer use:** 958 kgs per ha (1994) **Exports:** $ 2,031 million (1994) **Imports:** $ 3,146 million (1996) **External debt:** $ 3,785 million (1996) $ 346 **per capita:** (1996) **Debt service:** 11% of exports (1996) Development aid received: $ 213 million (1995) $ 21 per capita (1995) 1.6% of GNP (1994).

ENERGY
Consumption: 209.74 Kgs of Oil equivalent per capita yearly (1994) 73.71% imported (1994)

HDI (rank / value) 117 / 0.572 (1994)

military commands. Shortly afterwards, Jorge Carpio Nicolle, leader of the Union of the National Center and the president's cousin, was assassinated.

[31] Despite the intense campaign against the PACs and compulsory military service, President De León Carpio stated that he would maintain both institutions as long as the situation of armed conflict persisted, a U-turn on his previously stated opinion. On August 5, the government announced that the "Files" - records kept on citizens considered a "danger" to State security - had disappeared. However, the loss of these papers also implied the elimination of evidence against those responsible for human rights violations. In November, excavations in several clandestine cemeteries uncovered the remains of 177 women and children assassinated by the military in the 1982 "Rio Negro Massacre".

[32] The 1994-95 Government Plan, presented in August, reaffirmed the structural adjustment program already in effect, prioritizing the end of state intervention in the economy, along with fiscal reform and the privatization of enterprises.

[33] De León Carpio's stated goal was to fight corruption in the public sector. On August 26, the president called for the resignation of legislative deputies and members of the Supreme Court, causing a confrontation between the president and Congress. This led to a clash of economic and political interests, culminating in the Executive and Congress agreeing on constitutional reform.

[34] A plebiscite was scheduled for January 30, 1994, for nation's voters to decide on reforms to public administration and in the constitution.

[35] Following a 22-day occupation of the local OAS office by members of the Committee for Campesino Unity and the National Commission of Widows of Guatemala, some 5,000 members of indigenous groups carried out a march demanding the dissolution of the PACs.

[36] In January 1994, the Government and guerrillas signed agreements for the resettlement of the population displaced by the armed conflict, without a mediated cease fire. As a result of the accords 870 people were able to settle in the zones of Chacula, Nenton and Huehuetenango, but the majority of the resettlement areas were still under army control.

[37] Around the same date, a referendum for constitutional reform registered an abstention rate of 85 per cent. Of those who did vote, 69 per cent supported the moves for a new Congress and a new Supreme Court. In general elections with a similar abstention rate, the Guatemalan Republican Alliance led by former dictator Efrain Rios Montt took the majority. The National Vanguard Party came second.

[38] Monica Pinto, the UN Human Rights observer, recommended the demilitarization of society through the gradual reduction in size of the army, the disbanding of the PACs and the Presidential Staff, along with the creation of a Truth Commission.

[39] Following a prolonged silence in early 1994, the foreign minister recognized Belize as an independent State, but maintained its territorial claim, meaning no frontier could be established.

[40] In March, the government and the URNG ratified an agreement related to the disbanding of the PACs and the international verification of human rights by the UN. Three days later the president of the Court of Constitutionality, Epaminondas González, was murdered.

[41] In April, the police evicted 300 rural workers' families from an estate they had occupied in Escuintla. In May a new contingent of nearly 2,000 refugees returned, heading for the Quiche area, which was still occupied by the military.

[42] The URNG and the government signed a draft agreement for the "Resettlement of the People Uprooted by the Armed Confrontation," in Oslo, Norway, in June. The Communities of Peoples were recognized as non fighting civilians and the vital importance of land for these uprooted populations was explicitly stated. The second agreement in Oslo enshrined the principle of not individualizing responsibility for human rights violations as a way of neutralizing the action of sectors opposed to a negotiated outcome.

[43] Income from tourism fell by $100 million due to the hunger strike by a US citizen protesting for the liberty of her husband, who had been detained in 1992 for alleged links with left-wing organizations, and because another US citizen, suspected of involvement in a baby-trafficking network, was brutally flogged before a crowd.

[44] The peace negotiations between the guerrillas and the Government reached stalemate during 1995, due to the elections and the lack of interest by the army and landowners, and the government weakness in face of them. The UN mission reported that impunity continued to be the main obstacle to the respect for human rights, and described hundreds of cases of torture, illegal detentions and extrajudicial executions.

[45] In August 1995, Congress leader Efrain Rios Montt and another two members of the FRG lost their legal immunity and were tried by the Supreme Court on charges of bugging telephones, falsifying documents and abuse of power.

[46] In the November general elections, Alvaro Arzú, the National Advancement Party candidate, took 42 per cent of the vote, while his closest rival, Alfonso Portillo Cabrera, of the FRG, only managed half this. In a second round, on January 7 1996, Arzú was elected president. Abstentions stood at a record 63 per cent.

[47] In December - first in Europe and then in Mexico and Guatemala - the new government and the URNG signed a series of peace agreements putting an end to a civil war which cost more than 100,000 lives. The cease fire was respected and coincided with a considerable increase in crime. Around 80 per cent of the population is estimated to live below the poverty line.

[48] In December 1997, Guatemala was amongst the five Latin American countries most affected by climatic changes caused by the El Niño phenomenon. The FAO sent food aid to this and other countries of the region. One year after the signing of the peace agreements, Guatemala was still facing the challenges of transforming the military structures and the reintegration of thousands of former guerrillas into civilian life.

The colonization of America

The victory of the Spanish invaders over the Inca Empire (Tahuantinsuyo) in the 15th century paved the way in South America for one of the most ferocious colonial regimes, which pillaged precious metals and decimated the native population.

At first glance it seems inexplicable how the handful of men arriving in the Peruvian Andes region from Spain in 1532 could come to dominate the Inca empire, but the Spanish had several powerful forces at their command: superior weaponry, gunpowder and iron, and the cavalry - which had an important psychological impact - to name a few.

Their skill at subtle intrigue, using the wiles of Renaissance politics, was also greatly effective. The Spaniards took advantage of internal rivalries, getting local allies to support their intrusion.

When they arrived, Tahuantinsuyo was riven by civil war, with Huascar and Attahualpa at loggerheads, fighting it out to succeed Inca Wayna Qhápaq. Thus the greatest Inca forces were divided into two opposed blocs and at the critical moment they were unable to form a united front.

Similarly, the interpretations of the Inca oracle before the invasion meant the Spaniards were confused with gods expected to return from the sea to start off a new historical cycle. This meant the invaders were given an exceedingly warm welcome, and their real intentions were discovered too late.

Finally, the measles epidemic they provoked wiped out massive numbers of Amerindians, who lacked immune defences to a disease which had hitherto been unknown on the continent. Thus a regime of oppression and cruel exploitation was rapidly installed, and it lasted for nearly 300 years.

The introduction of mercantilism

The Spanish conquest of the Americas occurred during the time of mercantilism. Villey defined this economic doctrine in the following terms:

"Etymologically [mercantilism] indicates the doctrine which exalts the development of markets, of merchants, of trade. This idea was born at the beginning of the 16th century like a reflection of the sun on the gold of the New World. It was mainly there

- in Portugal and Spain - that the gold entered Europe, where the magic of the precious metals was felt, making the accumulation of these the supreme object of the action of individuals, and the politics of the princes.... In these eras the precious metals of the New World came almost exclusively from the Spanish and Portuguese colonies. The other countries did not have gold mines: for them the question was not how to keep hold of gold, but how to attract it. This is what the French mercantilists tried to do, stimulating above all the production of manufactured goods, and the English developing trade."

The systematic pillaging provided a continuous flow of precious metals (gold and silver) to the colonial centres, a seemingly inexhaustible booty. But this did not benefit Spain as much as the more advanced European countries, which accumulated the capital that would later allow them to undergo industrialization. The resources wrenched out of the Americas in immense quantities barely sufficed to pay for the metropolitan consumption of manufactured and non-manufactured goods from other areas, and to maintain their armies. The sea connection required massive ships and fleets, making dominion of the waves essential.

The colonial economy

In return for metal , the colonial elite received luxury articles, but had to pay heavily for them. No interest at all was taken in improving the living conditions of the population which produced the metal.

The indigenous workforce that powered the production of metals received no benefits for their toil. A chain of economic relations were formed between the silver-producing regions of present day Bolivia, the mercury-producing area of Peru, the Arica region where silver was loaded into ships, the wheat, dried meat and wine supplying regions of Chile and Cordoba and the regions of Tucumán in Argentina which supplied draught animals.

Amongst all the vast silver seams in production, it was Potosí which gained greatest world-wide prestige. In 1772, Potosí's Cerro Rico (Rich Mountain) was described as "a

beehive" of activity. But the technology used was antiquated even for the time. The rise of silver eclipsed gold mining. In the middle of the 17th century, silver made up nearly 99 per cent of exports from Spanish America. This meant the annihilation of the indigenous population in the 5,000 pitheads and foundries of Potosí, which rapidly fell into disuse in the 19th century.

Exploitation of the Amerindians

The human resources needed for the mines were obtained through forced labour, known as the mita. Sixteen indigenous provinces were obliged to supply the workforce with men aged between 18 and 50 years old.

This term of service lasted a year, to be repeated every seven years. The first work group raised by this system in 1573 by Viceroy Toledo, numbered 13,500. In the following centuries the numbers fell markedly, due mainly to the excessively tough conditions of the mita itself. It was almost impossible for any individual to live through three terms of service, as one year in the mines was enough to irreparably ruin the health of any worker.

The indigenous workers ended up physically exhausted and were often plagued by illnesses which killed them. The Imperial Villa of Potosí needed more than 90,000 natives to operate its mines, and simple arithmetic can show us the massive proportions of the undertaking: if we take each of the men to have been the head of a family of five people, then half a million people suffered the consequences of this system.

Descriptions of Potosí in 1603 mention data like the consumption of 1,600,000 bottles of chicha, a local alcoholic drink, and 21,900 packs of cards, giving some idea of what the lifestyle of the city was like at the time.

Genocide

Between the time when conquest first began and 1754, the population of Tahuantinsuyo fell by more than 95 per cent, from more than thirteen million to 612,780. An eloquent example of this genocide is that of Tiahuanaco in Bolivia, which had 868 taxpayers in 1583 of which a mere nine remained by 1658. This drastic reduction of the indigenous population through subhuman working conditions and the spread of epidemics affected mining production, as it became impossible to find workers, causing a terminal decline at the dawn of the 19th century.

Guinea

Guinée

Population:	7,518,000 (1996)
Area:	245,857 SQ KM
Capital:	Conakry
Currency:	Francs
Language:	French

Guinea was initially inhabited by pygmies who were driven towards the more inhospitable regions by the Mande peoples. The country was originally connected to the great states of Sudan and their trade system. The Bambuk gold mines that fed the Mediterranean economy for centuries were located on the ridges of the Futa Dyalon massif (see Mali and Morocco). The same region witnessed the rise and fall of the Fulah states between the 16th and 19th centuries (see Senegal: "The Fulah States").

[2] In 1870, against this background, Samor became the local political and spiritual leader (Almamy) of a state that included the greater part of Guinea and parts of present-day Mali and Ivory Coast. He had first confronted the French troops in 1886, as they were advancing from Senegal, and he had continued to fight constantly until 1898 when he was taken prisoner and exiled to Gabon. He died there two years later.

[3] This episode had been kept alive in the people's memory until 1947 when a small group of activists led by Ahmed Sekou Touré founded the Guinea Democratic Party (GDP). Supported by labor unions, the GDP soon became a very influential political organization.

[4] Overwhelmed by the loss of Indochina in 1954, the independence of Tunisia and Morocco in 1956, and the uprising of Algeria which began in 1954, French President de Gaulle attempted to salvage his interests in West Africa by creating the French Community in 1958. Through agreements and covenants he attempted a neo-colonialist project, to guarantee continued French hegemony in the area, in particular through its large monopolies. When the population of Guinea was consulted, 1,200,000 opposed de Gaulle's proposal for a French Community and only 57,000 supported it.

[5] Four days later, the country proclaimed independence. Sekou Touré stated: "We'd rather be poor and free than rich and enslaved". It was the first time that such a thing had happened in "French" West Africa, and in retaliation, Paris withdrew its technical advisers, paralyzed the few industries that there were, and blocked Guinean trade.

[6] In 1959, the State took over the main economic activities and Guinea immediately created its own currency, becoming independent from the French franc. Industry and farming were diversified in an attempt to attain self-sufficiency, and aluminium production surpassed one million tons per year.

[7] French aggression mounted. In 1965, Guinea's bank accounts in Paris were blocked, large-scale smuggling was fostered and counterfeit currency introduced. In 1970, Portuguese mercenaries invaded the country in an attempt to overthrow the Government and destroy the PAIGC, which was fighting for the independence of neighboring "Portuguese" Guinea (Bissau). In response to the ever more frequent destabilization campaigns, Local Revolutionary Powers (LRPs) were created in every neighbourhood or village with the aim of fighting against corruption, mismanagement and contraband.

[8] In November 1978, the Congress decided to change the country's name to the People's and Revolutionary Republic of Guinea, and to re-open relations with France. After a long period of isolation, Sekou Touré visited African and Arab countries in search of new sources of foreign capital to exploit the country's mineral wealth and to attract investments which might help to pay the foreign debt.

[9] The rapprochement between France and Guinea brought new agreements. The exploitation of the Mount Nimba iron ore reserves was granted to a French firm while the French Oil Company started offshore oil prospecting and the exploitation of rich bauxite deposits discovered in the 1970s. Guinea became the world's second largest bauxite producer. At that time Guinea and Mali signed an agreement envisaging the merger of the two neighbors into an economic and political federation.

[10] At the end of March 1984, Sekou Touré died in a US hospital while undergoing treatment for an old ailment. A week later, Colonel Lansana Conté headed a military coup which overthrew interim president Louis Beavogui.

[11] The new regime dismantled the political structure, the grassroots organizations and the Assembly; the Constitution was abolished too. The Democratic Party of Guinea was banned and the name of the country was changed, eliminating the words "People's" and "Revolutionary". The military government stimulated private enterprise, eliminated mixed companies and applied for economic aid to France, the US and the African States.

[12] Under the burden of an $800 million foreign debt, the Government decreed a 100 per cent devaluation of the *syli* (the national currency), and reduced public expenditure, a precondition of Guinea's entry into the French franc monetary scheme.

[13] In December 1984, the number of cabinet members was reduced, as was the number serving on the Reconstruction Committee. In addition, Colonel Conté consolidated power by simultaneously taking on the positions of head of state, prime minister and minister of defence.

[14] In December 1985, an Economic Recovery program was introduced, where agriculture, especially the cultivation of rice, was given top priority. Industrial and agricultural enterprises were also to be privatized. Self-sufficiency in food is still an unattained goal.

[15] To meet the country's serious economic problems head-on, in 1987 there were mass dismissals of public officials. In 1988, Conté moved a group of military officers away from the capital, as their discontent over low salaries constituted a threat to his government. In January of the same year, the 80 per cent increase in all salaries caused a price explosion with prices tripling over a few days. The

WORKERS

(1996)

Labour force %

- ■ WOMEN
- ☐ MEN

47%   53%

- ■ AGRICULTURE 87% (1990)
- ☐ INDUSTRIAL 2%
- ■ SERVICES 11%

LAND USE

DEFORESTATION 1.1% annual (81/90)
IRRIGATED 15.2 % of arable

(1993)

- ■ FOREST & WOODLAND 58.8%
- ☐ ARABLE 2.5%
- ■ OTHER 38.7%

PROFILE

Environment
The central massif of Futa-Dyalon, where cattle are raised, separates a humid and densely populated coastal plain, where rice, bananas and coconuts are grown, from a dryer northeastern region, where corn and manioc/cassava are cultivated. Rainfall reaches 3,000-4,000 mm per year along the coast. The country has extensive iron and bauxite deposits.

SOCIETY
Peoples: Guineans comprise 16 ethnic groups, of which Fulah, Mandingo, Malinke and Sussu are the most numerous.
Religions: 65 per cent are Muslim, 33 per cent practise traditional religions, and 2 per cent are Christian.
Languages: French (official). The most widely-spoken local languages are Malinke and Sussu.
Political Parties: Party for Unity and Progress; Guinean People's Union; Union for National Prosperity; Democratic Party of Guinea/African Democratic Union.
Social Organizations: National Confederation of Guinean Workers.

THE STATE
Official Name: République de Guinée.
Administrative divisions: 33 regions.
Capital: Conakry, 1,100,000 people (1994).
Other Cities: Kankan, 60,000 people; Labe; N'Zerekore.
Government: General Lansana Conté, President since April 1984. Sidia Touré, Prime Minister since 1996.
National Holiday: October 2, Republic Day.
Armed Forces: 9,700 (1996).
Other: People's Militia: 7,000; Gendarmerie: 1,000; Republican Guard: 1,600.

Maternal Mortality
1990

PER 100,000
LIVE BIRTHS
1,600

Literacy
1995

36%

STATISTICS

DEMOGRAPHY
Population: 7,518,000 (1996) **Annual growth:** 3.3% (1980/1996) **Estimates for year 2000:** 7,900,000 **Annual growth to year 2000:** 1.7% (1994/2000) **Urban Population:** 29.9% (1996) **Urban growth:** 5.76% (1980/95) **Children per woman:** 6.7 (1996).

HEALTH
Life expectancy at birth: 46 years (1996) male: 45 years (1994) female: 46 years (1994) **Infant mortality:** 130 per 1,000 (1996) **Under-5 child mortality:** 210 per 1,000 (1996) **Calorie consumption:** 97% (1988/90) 7,692 **people per doctor** (1988/91) **Safe water:** 46% (1990/96).

EDUCATION
Literacy: 36% (1995) male : 50% (1995) female: 22% (1995) **School enrolment :** Primary total: 46% (1990/95) male : 61% (1990/95) female: 30% (1990/95) Secondary: male : 18% (1990/95) female: 6% (1990/95) **Primary school teachers:** one for every 49 students (1995).

COMMUNICATIONS
43 **radios**, 10 **TV sets** and 1 **main telephone line** per 1,000 people (1994).

ECONOMY
Per capita, GNP: $ 560 (1996) **Annual growth, GNP:** 1.8% (1995/96) **Consumer price index:** 155.6 (1994) **Currency:** 997.98 francs = $ 1 (1995) **Cereal imports:** 384 metric tons (1994) **Food import dependency:** 23% (1994) **Fertilizer use:** 15 kgs per ha (1994) **Exports:** $ 774 million (1996) **Imports:** $ 810 million (1996) **External debt:** $ 3,240 million (1996) $ 431 **per capita:** (1996) **Debt service:** 14.7% of exports (1996) **Development aid received:** $ 392 million (1995) $ 62 per capita (1995) 12% of GNP (1994).

ENERGY
Consumption: 65.05 Kgs of Oil equivalent per capita yearly (1994) 86.36% imported (1994)

HDI (rank / value) 167 / 0.271 (1994)

---

demonstrations which took place at the time forced the Government to freeze the prices of consumer good and rents.
[16] In February 1990 the Government announced an amnesty for political prisoners and exiles. In December, a referendum approved by a vast majority modified the Constitution and created a Temporary Council for National Development (CTDN) in charge of leading the transition to democracy. President Conté announced that legislative elections would be held in 1992, with the participation of several parties.
[17] The drop in the international price of bauxite, which accounted for 60 per cent of the country's earnings and 96 per cent of its exports, aggravated the state of the economy. According to international credit agencies, official corruption was so widespread that a structural adjustment program would be impossible to implement without first eradicating these practices. In 1992, the World Bank demanded that the Government fire 40,000 civil servants.
[18] The country's economic problems were reflected in the quality of life of its inhabitants. Nutritional deficiencies and

diseases resulted in a short life expectancy of 42 years, as well as a high infant mortality rate. The most serious environmental problems were water pollution and the lack of sanitation, which result in the spreading of parasitic diseases like ancylotomiasis and amebiasis.
[19] In 1992, 650,000 refugees crossed the border from Sierra Leone and Liberia, setting up makeshift camps. The Government increased the number of peacekeeping troops sent to both countries by the Southwest African Economic Community, to patrol the borders and prevent more refugees from entering the country.
[20] When the multiparty system was approved, opposition leader Alpha Conde returned from exile and sponsored the creation of the National Democratic Forum (FND) which enclosed 30 opposition groups. However, tension and political persecution continued.
[21] Lansana Conté was re-elected in the December 1993 presidential elections with almost 51 per cent of the vote. Alpha Conde accused him of having staged a coup which led to confrontations between the police and opposition followers. In January 1994, dozens of people died in riots in Macenta near the border with Liberia.
[22] In June 1995, the ruling parties won 76 seats out of 114 in parliamentary elections which the opposition deemed fraudulent. Estimated annual GDP growth

reached almost five per cent and, in recognition of what it considered to be good economic results, the Paris Club cancelled $85 million of Guinea's foreign debt, refinancing another $85 million still owed by Conakry.
[23] In February 1996, a sector of the army rebelled when pay increases were not forthcoming. The mutiny ended in an attempt to overthrow the Government. The rebellion was put down in two days despite the fact that the mutineers, around 2,000 troops and some officers, had taken control of the urban centre of the capital and used artillery to bombard the presidential palace. Several Government officials were accused of encouraging the revolt, and were sent to prison. In July, the economist Sidia Touré was named Prime Minister. Touré announced

the Government priority would be reactivating the economy.
[24] Sierra Leone s President Ahmad Tejan Kabbah, was ousted from power in May 1997 and fled to Guinea with most of the members of his government. The political instability in that country meant thousands of people sought refuge in Guinea fearing attacks against their towns and villages. Kabbah's restoration in 1998 appeared to some confidence, but it was feared that this would be short-lived.
[25] AIDS continued to strike the African continent, and in November 1997, 1.5 per cent of the Guinean population was estimated to carry the virus. This percentage, one of the lowest in Africa, was several times higher than that of rich countries like France.

MILITARYEXPENDITURE

MILITARY (as % of health and education expenditures-1990/91) **37%**

Guinea-Bissau

Guinea-Bissau

Population: 1,091,000 (1996)
Area: 36,125 SQ KM
Capital: Bissau

Currency: Pesos
Language: Portuguese

Guinea-Bissau was the first Portuguese colony to gain independence in Africa. This was achieved even before the fall of the Portuguese dictatorship, in a successful political and military struggle led by Amilcar Cabral's African Party for the Independence of Guinea and Cape Verde (PAIGC).

[2] After belonging to the Mali and Songhai empires, the peoples in the Geba river valley became independent. This independence was soon threatened by the Portuguese, who had been settled on the coast from the end of the 15th century, and by the Fulah, coming from the interior in the 16th century. Inland, the state of Gabu remained autonomous until the 19th century (see Senegal: The Fulah States) while the coastal population suffered the consequences of the slave trade and forced displacement to the Cape Verde Islands.

[3] Resistance against the European colonists began in 1500 when the Portuguese arrived in Guinea. At that time, the country was inhabited by several different groups, immigrants from the state of Mali along with the Fulah and Mandingo groups, who lived in organized autocratic societies in the savannahs. During the 17th century Guineans made their first contact with the inhabitants of the Cape Verde islands, a mandatory stopover for the ships carrying slaves to Brazil.

[4] As the country was small and poor the monopoly on trade and agriculture was dealt with by a private company, the Uniao Fabril. Guineans were forced to cultivate export crops while massively reducing the acreage available for subsistence farming. In the 1950s,

infant mortality reached the remarkable rate of 600 deaths per 1,000 births. There were only 11 doctors in the country and only one per cent of the rural population was literate. In the early 1960s, only 11 Guineans had completed secondary education.

[5] It was against this setting of misery and exploitation that Amilcar Cabral founded the Athletics and Recreational Association, in 1954. This organization developed into the PAIGC two years later. The Party called on all Guineans and inhabitants of Cape Verde to unite in anti-colonial resistance, regardless of colour, race or religion. In September 1959, after trying fruitlessly to engage the Portuguese in negotiations for three years, the PAIGC embarked upon guerrilla warfare. The fighting spread quickly and by 1968 the Portuguese were confined to the capital, Bissau, and a few coastal strongholds. Four years later, the PAIGC had taken two-thirds of the nation's territory under their control. In September and October 1972, the first free elections were held in the liberated areas. A Popular National Assembly was elected and a year later, on September 24 1973, the 'democratic, anti-imperialist and anti-colonialist republic of Guinea' was proclaimed. Two months later the UN General Assembly recognized the independent state.

[6] Amilcar Cabral was assassinated in Conakry, Guinea, in February 1973, by Portuguese agents. He left many books and studies on the struggles for freedom in the African colonies. His successor, Luis Cabral, set up the Government Council of

Guinea-Bissau in a small village called Madina do Boé, in the heart of the liberated area.

[7] The impact of the unilateral independence of Guinea-Bissau and its immediate recognition by the UN shook the infrastructure of Portuguese colonialism. General Spinola, commander of the 55,000 colonial soldiers, came to the realization that his army could not be successful in the war against the PAIGC and argued for political changes in Portugal. It was as a result of these conditions in Bissau that the Captains' Movement was born. This movement later became the Armed Forces' Movement, the group which was responsible for the coup that overthrew the dictatorial regime in Portugal on April 25, 1974. Four months after the coup, Portugal recognized the independence of Guinea-Bissau.

[8] The PAIGC Government diversified agriculture giving priority to feeding the population and reducing the emphasis on export crops. Foreign companies were nationalized, agrarian reform was implemented together with a mass literacy campaign. In foreign relations, the new government opted for non-alignment and unconditional support for the struggle against apartheid and colonialism in Africa. The PAIGC congress also gave top priority to economic integration with the archipelago of Cape Verde, with a view towards uniting the two countries.

[9] In 1980, a military conspiracy led by Joao Bernardino (Niño) Vieira, a former guerrilla commander, overthrew Luis Cabral replacing all the government bodies with a centralized Revolutionary Council, headed by Bernardino Vieira.

[10] Talks with Cape Verde were abruptly cut short while the two countries were discussing a unified constitution (See Cape Verde). The new government in Bissau was immediately recognized by the neighboring Republic of Guinea, which had been at loggerheads with the former president Cabral in a dispute over offshore oil rights in an area presumed to be rich in petroleum deposits.

[11] Contact between the two Guineas was intensified in September 1982, and in February 1983 diplomatic missions were exchanged.

[12] The first development plan of 1983-86 proposed an initial investment of $118.6 million, of which 75 per cent would be financed by international funds. In 1984, the construction of five ports was started at an estimated cost of $40 million, and the construction of the Bisalanca Airport was completed. The Government started a campaign against corruption and inefficiency in public administration, and as a result, in 1984, Vice-President Victor Saude Maria was asked to resign. Shortly afterwards, the Popular Assembly

WORKERS

(1996)

Labour force %
- ■ WOMEN
- □ MEN

40%   60%

- ■ AGRICULTURE 85% (1990)
- □ INDUSTRIAL 2%
- ■ SERVICES 13%

LAND USE

DEFORESTATION -0.7 % annual (81/90)
IRRIGATED 5.7 % of arable

(1993)

- ■ FOREST & WOODLAND 29.6%
- □ ARABLE 8.3%
- ▨ OTHER 62.1%

Literacy

1995

55%

Maternal Mortality

1990

PER 100,000
LIVE BIRTHS

910

STATISTICS

DEMOGRAPHY
Population: 1,091,000 (1996) **Annual growth:** 2% (1980/1996) **Estimates for year 2000:** 1,200,000 **Annual growth to year 2000:** 2% (1994/2000) **Urban Population:** 22.1% (1996) **Urban growth:** 3.74% (1980/95) **Children per woman:** 5.5 (1996)

HEALTH
Life expectancy at birth: 44 years (1996) male: 42 years (1994) female: 45 years (1994) **Infant mortality:** 132 per 1,000 (1996) **Under-5 child mortality:** 223 per 1,000 (1996) **Calorie consumption:** 97% (1988/90) **Safe water:** 59% (1990/96)

EDUCATION
Literacy: 55% (1995) male : 68% (1995) female: 43% (1995) **School enrolment :** Primary total: 60% (1990/95) male : 77% (1990/95) female: 42% (1990/95) Secondary: male : 9% (1990/95) female: 4% (1990/95).

COMMUNICATIONS
10 **newspapers**, 40 **radios** and 9 **main telephone lines** per 1,000 people (1994).

ECONOMY
Per capita, GNP: $ 250 (1996) **Annual growth, GNP:** 3.7% (1995/96) **Annual inflation:** 62.47% (1985/95) **Currency:** 21,929 pesos = $ 1 (1995) **Cereal imports:** 68 metric tons (1994) **Food import dependency:** 46% (1994) **Fertilizer use:** 17 kgs per ha (1994) **Exports:** $ 56 million (1996) Imports: $ 107 million (1996) **External debt:** $ 937 million (1996) $ 859 **per capita:** (1996) **Debt service:** 48.7% of exports (1996) Development aid received: $ 119 million (1995) $ 113 per capita (1995) 49.6% of GNP (1994)

ENERGY
Consumption: 37.31 Kgs of Oil equivalent per capita yearly (1994) 100.00% imported (1994)

HDI (rank / value) 163 / 0.291 (1994)

PROFILE

ENVIRONMENT
The land is flat with slight elevations in the southeast and abundant irrigation from rivers and canals. The coastal area is swampy, suitable for rice. Rice, peanuts, palm oil and cattle are produced in the drier eastern region. The need to increase exports led to over-cultivation of the soil; in addition, rice plantations are replacing part of the coastal woodlands. Slash-and-burn techniques, as well as numerous forest fires, have contributed to deforestation.

SOCIETY
Peoples: Balante 27.2%; Fulani 22.9%;Malinke 12.2%; Mandyako 10.6%; Pepel 10.0%; other 17.1%.
Religions: Two-thirds profess traditional African religions; nearly one-third are Muslim and there is a small Catholic minority.
Languages: Portuguese (official). The crioulo dialect, a mixture of Portuguese and African languages, is used as the lingua franca. The most widely spoken native languages are Mande and Fulah.
Political Parties: The African Party for the Independence of Guinea and Cape Verde (PAIGC) was the country's sole political party until the end of 1991; since that date 10 political groups were registered, among them the Party for Social Renovation, formed by dissidents from the PAIGC.

THE STATE
Official Name: República da Guiné-Bissau.
Administrative Divisions: 8 Regions and 1 Autonomous Sector.
Capital: Bissau, 200,000 people (1994).
Other cities: Bafatá, 13,429 people; Gabu, 7,803 people (1979).
Government: Gen. Joao Bernardino Vieira, President since 1984. Carlos Correia, Prime Minister since 1997. National People's Assembly, parliament of 100 seats.
National Holiday: September 24, Independence Day (1973).
Armed Forces: 7,250 (1996). Other: 2,000 Gendarmes.

eliminated the position of prime minister, and the Revolutionary Council became the Council of State.

[13] In November 1984, the vice-president of the Council of State, Colonel Paulo Correia, led an unsuccessful coup against President Vieira. Correia was executed on July 21 1986.

[14] The 1984 stabilization plan failed, causing further deterioration of the economic and financial situation. The international economic crisis increased, the price of Guinea-Bissau's oil exports lost market value. The Government adopted a 'corrective' policy, including freezing salaries and reducing public investment. This was an attempt to bring it into line with IMF conditions for refinancing the servicing of the foreign debt. The economy was subsequently opened up to foreign capital in the hope of attracting resources from Portugal and France,

particularly in the high-priority areas of telecommunications. In 1989, Portugal participated in the creation of a commercial bank.

[15] In 1986, the Government granted an amnesty to political prisoners. Two years later, in June 1988, the Central Committee of the PAIGC began discussing a proposal for separating the executive and legislative powers. At that time Guinea-Bissau spent more on its military budget than on education and health combined.

[16] In February 1991, the PAIGC approved a political reform which anticipated elections for 1992. The IMF cancelled several loans granted to Guinea-Bissau after the resignation of Economy Minister Manuel dos Santos. Meanwhile, the World Bank deferred the payment of $6.5 million belonging to the structural adjustment program begun in 1987, to force Bissau to pay its foreign debt on time.

[17] Dependence on agricultural exports - especially on peanuts, whose price had fallen abruptly - caused significant social and economic imbalances along with political tensions in 1992 and 1993. The 1992 elections were not held due to a government decision and after the murder in March 1993 of a high military commander they were delayed once more.

[18] Finally, in 1994 Joao Bernardo Vieira defeated Kumba Iala of the Party for Social Renovation. After he obtained 46 per cent of the vote in the first round in July - Iala had less than 22 per cent - Vieira obtained 52 per cent in the second round and was elected president. During the campaign, Iala accused him of supporting tribalism and racism. In the parliamentary elections, Vieira's PAIGC took 64 of the 100 seats at stake. Believing that the ruling party had 'bought' votes, Iala refused to take part in a national unity government.

[19] In January 1995, the IMF granted a new $14 million loan in support of economic reforms. In June, the visit of Senegalese president Abdou Diouf led to a rapprochement with Dakar after a period of relative hostility. Both countries agreed to exploit joint energy and mineral resources. In August, Iala denounced Vieira's

closer ties with France, the rise in the price of basic items like rice, and human rights violations by the government.

[20] In late 1995, Guinea-Bissau ratified the border agreement signed with Senegal in 1993, resetting its maritime frontiers and stipulating the joint exploitation of an area which was supposedly rich in oil.

[21] In August 1996, the Government accepted 44 illegal African immigrants expelled from Spain. The League of Human Rights of Guinea-Bissau said the Government had agreed to the Spanish request in return for payment. In the UN Security Council, Guinea-Bissau supported an air embargo against Sudan for refusing to extradite three individuals suspected of a murder attempt against Egyptian president, Hosni Mubarak.

[22] In 1998, Guinea-Bissau continued to house pro-independence rebels from the Senegalese Movement of Democratic Forces of Casamance (MFDC). However, Guinea-Bissau's army intervention against a refugee camp on the frontier with Senegal, in January that year, fed rumours of rapprochement between Bissau and Dakar, which was to lead to a more severe attitude towards the Casamance refugees.

Guyana

Guyana

Population:	838,000 (1996)
Area:	214,969 SQ KM
Capital:	Georgetown
Currency:	Guyana dollars
Language:	English

The original inhabitants of what is now Guyana were the Arawaks, but they did not increase substantially in number due to the humid lands and the mangrove-covered coasts, which were mostly swamps. The Arawaks were displaced from the area by the Caribs, warriors who dominated the region before moving on to the nearby which were later called after them.

[2] Both the Arawaks and the Caribs were nomads. Organized into families of 15 to 20 people, they lived by fishing and hunting. There are thought to have been half a million inhabitants at the time of the arrival of Europeans in Guyana; there are presently 45,000 indians, divided into nine ethnic groups, of which seven maintain their cultural identity and traditions.

[3] Led on by the legend of El Dorado, in 1616 the Dutch built the first fort. Guyana was made up of three colonies: Demerara, Berbice and Essequibo. But in 1796, the Dutch colony was taken over by the Britlish, who had already begun a wide-scale introduction of slaves. A slave, Cuffy, led a rebellion in 1763 which was brutally put down. To this day, Cuffy is considered a national hero.

[4] Those slaves that escaped from the plantations went into the forests to live with the indigenous peoples, giving rise to the "bush blacks". The English brought in Chinese, Javanese and Indian workers as cheap labor. In the second half of the 20th century, Guyana's population managed to channel independence politics into a single movement, the People's Progressive Party (PPP), with policies of national independence and social improvements, with long term aims for a socialist country. Cheddi Jagan, the first prime minister of the colony, was in power for three successive terms.

[5] After years of struggle and periods of great violence, Britain recognized Guyana's independence within the Commonwealth on May 26 1966. By that time, the PPP had split; the Afro-Guyanese population joined the People's National Congress (PNC), while indigenous people remained loyal to Jagan. Forbes Burnham, leader of the PNC took office, supported by other ethnic minorities.

[6] This process was influenced by ethnic conflict and by foreign interests, particularly from the US, which felt its hegemony in the Caribbean threatened by Jagan's socialism.

[7] Even though Burnham came to power with Washington's blessing, he kept his distance. He declared himself in favor of non-alignment and proclaimed a Cooperative Republic in 1970. The bauxite, timber and sugar industries were nationalized in the first half of the 1970s, and by 1976 the State controlled 75 per cent of the country's economy. At the same time, regional integration was implemented through CARICOM, the Latin American Economic System (SELA), and the Caribbean Merchant Fleet. During the first decade after independence, Burnham and Jagan defended the same political platform.

[8] In May 1976, Cheddi Jagan stated the need to "achieve national anti-imperialist unity", when disputes broke out with Brazil over the border. The PPP representatives returned to Parliament, from which they had withdrawn three years earlier to protest over electoral corruption. Shortly afterwards, Burnham announced the creation of a Popular Militia.

[9] Elections were postponed in order to hold a constitutional referendum, with Parliament drawing up a new constitution. This gave way to harsh criticism by the PPP, which withdrew from legislative activity for the second time. In 1980 Burnham was elected President. However, according to international observers, the election had been plagued by fraud. In 1980 Burnham granted authorization for transnational corporations to carry out oil and uranium operations. In addition, he turned to the IMF to obtain credit.

[10] In June of the same year, Walter Rodney, a world famous intellectual and founder of the opposition "Working People's Alliance" (WPA) was killed by a car bomb. The culprits were never found.

[11] In the post-election period, border disputes escalated. Venezuela claimed the Essequibo region, approximately 159,000 sq km (three quarters) of Guyanese territory, arguing that British imperialism illegally deprived Venezuela of that area in the 19th century.

[12] In 1983, both countries turned to the UN. In 1985 direct negotiations started again to settle the dispute "within a framework of cordiality and goodwill". Negotiations were focused on an outlet to the Atlantic Ocean for Venezuela.

[13] While financial difficulties increased during 1984 and the Government faced a new crisis in its relations with labor unions, Burnham resumed contacts with the IMF to obtain a $150 million loan. Burnham considered the conditions on the loan "unacceptable". The American invasion of Grenada - and Guyana's criticism of this action - led to a deterioration of the relations between the two countries. Guyana made overtures to the socialist countries.

[14] Burnham died in August 1985 and was replaced by Desmond Hoyte. The PNC won the general elections this year with 78 per cent of the vote, but the opposition complained of alleged fraud. In 1986, five of the six opposition parties formed the Patriotic Coalition for Democracy, which chose to boycott the 1986 municipal elections, whereby all the seats went to the PNC. Hoyte, who was chosen President, announced in January 1987 his Government would return to "Co-operative Socialism."

[15] Parliament met on December 3 1991, five days after the Government declared a state of emergency in order to postpone

LAND USE

DEFORESTATION -0.1% annual (81/90)
IRRIGATED 27.1 % of arable

(1993)

■ FOREST & WOODLAND	76.8%
□ ARABLE	2.2%
▨ OTHER	21%

PROFILE

ENVIRONMENT
90 per cent of the population and most of the country's agriculture are concentrated on the coastal plane which ranges between 15 and 90 km in width. Rice and sugar cane are the main crops. As most of the shore is below sea level, dams and canals have been built to prevent flooding. The inner land consists of a 150 km-wide rainforest where the country's mineral resources are concentrated (bauxite, gold, and diamonds). To the west and south, the rest of the country is occupied by an ancient geological formation, the Guyana mountain range. Guyana is a native word meaning "land of waters". There are many rivers, as a result of the tropical climate and year-round rains. In comparison world-wide deforestation, the Guyanas have suffered little, and until 1990, only a small fraction of the extensive forests had been felled. However, foreign agencies are pressing for the intensification of lumber exploitation. In some areas, reforestation after logging has not been carrried out, leading to soil erosion.

SOCIETY
Peoples: Half the population are descended from Indian workers, one-third from African natives and the rest are native Americans, mixed European and indian descendants, Chinese and Europeans.
Religions: Protestant 34 per cent; Catholic 18 per cent; Hindu 34 per cent; Muslim 9 per cent.
Languages: English is official, Hindi and Urdu are used in religious ceremonies.
Political Parties: People's Progressive Party (PPP); People's National Congress (PNC).
Social Organizations: Trade Union Congress (TUC).

THE STATE
Official Name: Cooperative Republic of Guyana.
Administrative Divisions: 10 Regions.
Capital: Georgetown, 248,000 people (1992).
Other cities: Linden 27,200 people; New Amsterdam 17,700.
Government: Janet Jagan, President and Head of State since December 1997, Sam Hinds, Prime Minister and Chief of Goverment since October 1992. Parliament is composed of a unicameral assembly with 65 members, of which 12 are regional representatives and 53 are elected through direct vote and proportional representation. National Holiday: February 23, Proclamation of the Republic (1970).
Armed Forces: 1,600 (1995).
Other: 4,500 People's Militia, national service.

STATISTICS

DEMOGRAPHY
Population: 838,000 (1996) **Annual growth:** 0.6% (1980/1996) **Estimates for year 2000:** 900,000 **Annual growth to year 2000:** 1% (1994/2000) **Urban Population:** 35.9% (1996) **Children per woman:** 2.4 (1996).

HEALTH
Life expectancy at birth: 64 years (1996) male: 60 years (1994) female: 67 years (1994) **Infant mortality:** 60 per 1,000 (1996) **Under-5 child mortality:** 83 per 1,000 (1996) **Safe water:** 61% (1990/96).

EDUCATION
Literacy: 98% (1995) male : 99% (1995) female: 98% (1995) **School enrolment :** Primary total: 112% (1990/95) male : 113% (1990/95) female: 111% (1990/95) Secondary: male : 56% (1990/95) female: 59% (1990/95)

COMMUNICATIONS
100 **newspapers**, 491 **radios**, 40 **TV sets** and 53 **main telephone lines** per 1,000 people (1994) **Books:** 4 new titles per 100,000 people (1992/94).

ECONOMY
Currency: 140.5 Guyana dollars = $ 1 (1995) **Cereal imports:** 50 metric tons (1994) **Food import dependency:** 7% (1994) **Fertilizer use:** 302 kgs per ha (1994) Development aid received: $ 88 million (1995) $ 106 per capita (1995) 19.2% of GNP (1994).

HDI (rank / value) 104 / 0.649 (1994)

---

the elections planned for this month. The Government ignored the opposition objections and extended the state of emergency until June 1992. On October 5 1992, Cheddi Jagan defeated President Desmond Hoyte (54 per cent to 41 per cent respectively) in the general elections. The Progressive People's Party took 32 seats in the National Assembly, while the PNC took 31.

[16] One of the first Latin American leaders to wield the flag of Marxism in the 1950s, Jagan returned to power, putting an end to 28 years of PNC dominion.

[17] In early 1993, unlike his neighbours including Brazil, President Cheddi Jagan allowed US troops to be deployed for training in the forests. He accepted US military collaboration to combat drug-trafficking and aid to develop sanitation in the interior.

[18] Guyana had frequent border disputes with the neighbouring Venezuela and Suriname, although it maintained good relations with Brazil, especially on the trade front.

[19] Jagan intended to modify the adjustment plan launched by his predecessor, Desmond Hoyte, in agreement with the IMF. His government defended "non-conventional" methods of problems solving in land distribution, transport, health, housing and education.

[20] He proposed a market economy strategy to resolve the problem of the poverty of 80 per cent of the population. The emigration rate exceeded the demographic growth index, so that the population diminished from 1,020,000 in 1989 to 808,000 in 1992.

[21] The nation's wealth still remained nearly intact with large reserves of gold, diamonds, bauxite, forests and great agricultural potential. The fiscal deficit, which caused high inflation, was related to the smuggling of minerals, along with the price policy on exports of sugar, rice and other agricultural products.

[22] The celebration of the first anniversary of Jagan's Government was tarnished by a strike in the national electricity company as the Government had failed to implement its promise to increase State workers' pay by 300 per cent. The Government claimed the conditions imposed by the IMF prevented it from being this "generous".

[23] In June 1994, Jagan rejected the ambassador to Georgetown nominated by the United States, accusing him of "subversive activities" during the last few years of British colonial administration.

[24] In 1995, the worst environmental accident in the history of the country occurred, when four million cubic metres of cyanide-contaminated waste fell into the Omai river, a tributary of the Essequibo, the nation's main river.

[25] In February 1996, the human rights organization Amnesty International denounced the use of the death penalty by hanging in Guyana for the first time since 1990. This same year the Government had $500 million of its foreign debt pardoned, nearly a quarter of the total.

[26] Following Jagan's death in 1997, his wife Janet took over as interim Prime Minister. In the December 15 elections, she was elected president with 55.5 per cent against the 40.6 per cent of Hoyte's PNC. Despite threats of civil disobedience incited by Hoyte, the 77 year-old, US-born Jagan took office on December 19. Sam Hinds was designated Prime Minister.

[27] In her first few months in office, Janet Jagan had to deal with a drought which affected the nation's production (especially of gold), reduced trade, generated problems for transport and encouraged forest fires. The price increases caused protest demonstrations. The most important of these took place outside the State telephone company complaining against tariff increases of between 400 and 1,000 per cent.

WORKERS

- ■ AGRICULTURE 22% (1990)
- □ INDUSTRIAL 25%
- ▪ SERVICES 53%

MILITARY EXPENDITURE

MILITARY (as % of health and education expenditures-1990/91) **21%**

Haiti

Haïti

Population: 7,259,000 (1996)
Area: 27,750 SQ KM
Capital: Port-au-Prince

Currency: Gourdes
Language: French

When Quisqueya, as the local population named it, was "discovered" by Christopher Columbus in 1492, the island was inhabited by numerous Arawak peoples. The contact with Europeans was devastating for the Arawaks, who almost entirely disappeared from the island over the next few decades. Spanish colonists, supported by the Dominican missionaries, called the islands after their patron saint, St Dominic.

2 The island was later colonized by the French and other European settlers who were attracted by the sugar plantations. Disputes arose among the Europeans and in 1697 Spain ceded the west of the island to France, under the Treaty of Ryswick.

3 After gaining control of the island, France began to exploit it, introducing about 20,000 African slaves per year, leading to rapid racial mixing. Sugar soon became the principal export product of the region, and during the 18th century Haiti became the most important French possession in the Americas.

4 This prosperity was based on African slave labor. By 1789, the number of African slaves in the colony had reached 480,000, there were 60,000 mulattos and free "coloured" people, while the rich land-owning Europeans constituted a minority of no more than 20,000. The Haitians were influenced by the revolutionary movement that had started in the colonial capitals and they waged a revolutionary war, led by former slave Toussaint L'Ouverture, lasting for 12 years, from 1791 to 1803, ending in the proclamation of the first black republic in the world.

5 Haiti's struggle for independence went through several stages. Initially, the large landowners joined the revolutionary movement, along with the slaves, merchants and poor Europeans (called petit blancs), forming a local Assembly to demand an end to colonial rule. In the second stage, the free mulattos supported the French revolution, under the assumption that it would give equal rights to all people, regardless of the colour of their skin. However, in 1790 the European planters fiercely rejected the demands of the freed slaves, leaving them no alternative but to ally themselves with the *marrons,* two groups of rebel slaves, a year later.

6 It was L'Ouverture who gave the marrons their direction, rallying them to the call of "general freedom for all", transforming the different groups into a disciplined army. On February 4 1794, taking advantage of the splits in the French colonial system, he succeeded in getting the French National Convention to ratify a decree abolishing slavery in Santo Domingo and appointing himself as a general.

7 After the coup of the Brumaire 18, Napoleon Bonaparte sent a large military expedition to reconquer the colony and re-establish slavery. L'Ouverture responded with a general uprising, but he was imprisoned and died in exile in France in 1803.

8 Jean-Jacques Dessalines, took over leadership of the war of independence, aided by Henri Christophe and mulatto Alexandre Pétion, who together radicalized L'Ouvertures's legacy. They succeeded in uniting the Africans and mulattos and after a series of heroic campaigns, they forced the French troops to capitulate. Independence was proclaimed on November 28 1803, and Haiti became the first independent state in Latin America.

9 Dessalines gave his government a strong nationalist direction, trying to consolidate his personal power by creating an autocratic State, similar to the one emerging in France. Like Napoleon, Dessalines proclaimed himself emperor, calling himself Jacques I. Pétion and Christophe immediately started to plot against him, and he was murdered during a revolt in 1806.

10 The east of the island was recovered by the Spaniards under the Treaty of Paris in 1814, while in the west Christophe and Pétion fought for the leadership, dividing the territory. Henri Christophe established a republic in the north, later making it a kingdom with himself as King Henri I from 1811 to 1820. In the south, Alexandre Pétion ruled over a separate republic, from 1808 to 1818, supporting Simon Bolívar with weapons and funding. Pétion was convinced that only total American independence could guarantee that of Haiti, as the country was being harassed by European powers and the US.

11 In 1818, JP Boyer was elected president instead of Pétion. Boyer recovered the north of the country in 1820, putting an end to Christophe's monarchic experiment. Two years later he conquered Santo Domingo in the east of the island, thus achieving a fragile reunification, which lasted for a quarter of a century. In 1843, a revolution led by the Santo Domingan Creoles divided the island into two definite, independent States: the Dominican Republic in the east, and the Republic of Haiti in the west.

12 In spite of the permanent political violence throughout the 19th century, foreign investors gained access to the Haitian market by building ports and railways and by buying profitable plantations. The new transport and communications led to a faster and more effective extraction of the island's riches, with the profits going to the industrialized countries. The unfavourable trading exchange led the country into debt, until it became wholly dependent on its creditors, who were mostly American.

13 From 1867, a bloody civil war launched a period of political instability and economic crisis which lasted until 1915, when the country was occupied by US marines for non-compliance with "its commitments". A year later the US invaded the Dominican Republic, gaining control of the whole island.

WORKERS

(1996)

Labour force %

■ WOMEN
□ MEN

43   57

■ AGRICULTURE 68% (1990)
□ INDUSTRIAL 9%
■ SERVICES 23%

LAND USE

DEFORESTATION -4% annual (81/90)
IRRIGATED 13.4 % of arable

(1993)

■ FOREST & WOODLAND 5%
□ ARABLE 20.2%
■ OTHER 74.8%

PROFILE

ENVIRONMENT

Haiti occupies the western third of the island of Hispaniola, the second largest of the Greater Antilles. Two main mountain ranges run from east to west, extending along the country's northern and southern peninsulas, contributing to their shape. The hills and river basins in between form the center of Haiti. The flatlands that open up to the sea in the west, are protected from the humid trade winds by the mountains to the north and east. Coffee is the main export product. Copper extraction ceased in 1976 and bauxite deposits are almost exhausted. The northern coastline has the heaviest rainfall and contains the country's most developed area, though the land there is suffering from serious erosion. Forests make up less than 2 per cent of the land area.

SOCIETY

Peoples: Nearly 95 per cent of Haitians are descendents of African slaves. There are also minorities of European and Asian origin, and integration has produced a small mestizo group. Thousands of Haitians have emigrated in recent years, especially to Colombia, Venezuela and the United States.

Religions: Voodoo, a mixture of Christianity and various African beliefs. Catholicism.

Languages: French (official), spoken by less than 20 per cent of the population. Most people speak creole, a local dialect of combined Spanish, English, French and African languages.

Political Parties: National Front for Change and Democracy (FNCD); National Alliance for Democracy and Progress (ANDP); National Committee of the Democratic Movements (Konakom); National People's Assembly (APN); Agricultural Industrial Party (PAIN); Unified Party of Haitian Communists (PUCH) ; Union for National Reconciliation (UNR); Lavalas Political Organization.

Social Organizations: The "Grassroots" Church groups, of Catholic origin; Movement in Favor of the Creole Language; Solidarity of the Women of Haiti (SOFA).

THE STATE

Official name: Repiblik Dayti.
Administrative divisions: 5 departments.
Capital: Port-au-Prince, est.1,500,000 people (1994).
Other Cities: Carrefour, 241,000; Delmas, 200,000 (1992).
Government: President René Préval, President since 1996.
National Holiday: January 1, Independence Day (1804).
Armed Forces: 1,500.

[14] The invasion of Haiti was heroically resisted by Charlemagne Péralte's "Revolutionary Army". Péralte was treacherously murdered in 1919. The US troops finally defeated the resistance and controlled the country until 1934, turning it into a virtual colony. That year, President Vincent succeeded in getting the US troops to withdraw from the island, but he could not eliminate US influence from the country's domestic affairs.

[15] The national army, or Garde d'Haiti, took a central role in national politics, staging coups against presidents Lescot, 1941-1946; Estime, 1946-1950; and Magloire, 1950-1957. In 1957, François Duvalier, a middle-class doctor, seized power supported by the army and the US.

[16] The elite mestizo group which was in power repressed the African-based culture until François Duvalier recognized the strategic power he could achieve by manipulating it. Over time he succeeded in building two great supports for his domination. The first was voodoo, the syncretic and distinctive religion of Haiti that combines African and Catholic rites. The second was the Tonton-Macoutes, a group of some 300,000 "national security volunteers".

[17] The army, the commercial bourgeoisie, the ecclesiastic authorities, the state bureaucracy, and the US State Department used Duvalier to control the country for over 30 years. With Washington's backing, Duvalier or "Papa Doc" proclaimed himself President-for-life in 1964, passing on the title to his son Jean-Claude or "Baby Doc" on his death in 1971.

[18] In the meantime Haiti fell from being a rich sugar and coffee producer to being the only Latin American country to rank among the 25 poorest nations in the world.

[19] Assailed on the international level by continual condemnations of human rights violations, and on the domestic level by active opposition, Duvalier's government called elections in 1984. Sixty-one per cent of the population abstained. Organizations opposed to Duvalier renewed their underground activities and the opposition grew, organizing itself into parties and trade unions, while the regime was becoming a burden to the US.

[20] Repression grew, and by 1985 it was estimated that Baby Doc's regime had been responsible for 40,000 murders. The country was enveloped by a growing wave of protests and strikes. Duvalier fled the country in a US air force airplane and received temporary asylum in France.

[21] A National Governing Council (CNG) led by General Henri Namphu assumed control of the government, promising "free and direct" elections by the end of 1987. However, the opposition leaders denounced the continuation of the regime, which was confirmed by Duvalier upon his arrival in France.

[22] The dictator's flight did not end the mobilization of the people. Mass lynching by Tonton-Macoutes forced the National Governing Council to dissolve this repressive force and to free all the prisoners.

[23] In October 1986, the CNG called elections to elect a Constituent Assembly to draw up a new constitution. Less than 10 per cent of the 3 million Haitians participated in the election and, on March 29 1987 a referendum approved the new constitution with 99.8 per cent of the vote. The new constitution limited the presidential term to 5 years, prohibited re-election and divided the power with a prime minister chosen by Parliament.

[24] The elections were to be held in November 1987, but a few hours after the polling stations were opened, they were sabotaged by factions of the armed forces and by ex-Tonton Macoutes, and the elections were suspended, finally taking place in January 1988. In a very volatile atmosphere, Leslie Manigat, the "official" candidate, was elected, only to be deposed in June, in a coup led by General Namphu.

[25] In September 1988, a movement of sergeants and soldiers deposed General Namphu, putting Prosper Avril, the eminence grise of the Duvalier period, into power.

[26] In March 1990, during a period of intense popular protest, General Avril was ousted by General Abraham, who relinquished control to a provisional civilian government headed by Judge Ertha Pascal-Trouillot, the first woman to occupy the presidency in Haiti. The provisional government created suitable conditions to put the Constitution into practice, and called elections for December 1990.

[27] These elections were won by a priest, Jean-Bertrand Aristide, who obtained 67 per cent of the vote as the leader of the National Front for Change and Democracy. He was voted in mostly by the poor urban sectors, and he took office on February 7 1991.

[28] Aristide, a Liberation Theology activist, had been censured in 1988 by the church authorities and expelled from the Salesian order. His governmental program was based on a war against corruption and drug trafficking, including a thorough literacy

PER CAPITA

$124

45%

campaign, and a project to move from "extreme poverty to poverty with dignity".

29 On September 30, General Raoul Cédras staged a bloody coup. In protest the Organization of American States (OAS), declared a trade embargo, starting diplomatic negotiations in the region and in the UN. Meanwhile, the rebels tried to avoid international isolation by officially recognizing the sovereignty and operation of parliament.

30 In February 1992, OAS representatives, Haitian members of parliament, and the deposed Aristide signed an agreement in Washington to re-establish democracy and reinstate the former president. By the end of April 1992 there had been over 4,000 reports of political assassinations, and thousands were leaving the country for fear of further repression.

31 Since Aristide's fall, more than 40,000 Haitians were picked up at sea by the US Navy. In May, the US Government ordered that the Coast Guard stop all boats coming from Haiti, and return them to their country of origin. Two months later, a US Court of Appeal upheld the refugees' claims, declaring that this policy of interdiction violated the 1980 Refugees Act.

32 In June 1992, the military government named Marc Bazin as Prime Minister. He was the founder of the liberal Movement for the Restoration of Democracy.

33 In January 1993, the de facto government held legislative elections which many people considered illegitimate as they were designed only to partially replace Parliament. Less than 3 per cent of those registered to vote took part. Months later, Marc Bazin resigned as prime minister.

34 On June 27, indirect talks began in New York between General Cedras and ousted president Aristide. Meanwhile, the UN Security Council imposed a financial, oil and arms embargo on Haiti. In July, Aristide and Cedras signed an agreement which guaranteed the return of the President as well as an

amnesty for all military leaders involved in the coup. In accordance with the agreement, Aristide named Robert Malval prime minister.

35 However, a new wave of violence soon broke out in Haiti, to prevent the agreement from going into effect. In October, a US warship patrolled the coast near the capital. An armed mob threatened the American troops, so US President Clinton ordered the ship back to US Guantanamo military base in Cuba. In the meantime, the Security Council reinstated the naval embargo.

36 Malval's Justice Minister, Guy Malary, was assassinated. The attack was carried out almost in the same place where Antoine Izmery, a pro-Aristide businessman, had been killed a month earlier. Those responsible for the killings were members of the pro-military Front for the Advancement and Progress of Haiti, who used the same tactics as the Tonton-Macoutes.

37 The embargo destroyed the formal economy and increased poverty, although it did not substantially affect the lifestyle of the country's wealthy families. Violence rose: according to a UN report, 426 Aristide supporters were murdered between May 1993 and February 1994. Aristide called Clinton's sanctions policy "a floating Berlin Wall".

38 On October 15, Aristide returned after the coup leaders had gone into exile and the country was occupied by a multinational force led by the United States. While in exile, the President had promised to implement a structural adjustment program prescribed by the IMF. In December, troops were demobilized in order to create a new national police force.

39 In spite of meaning to punish those responsible for human rights abuses, Aristide - under sustained pressure from Washington - was forced to offer merely symbolic gestures in most cases, such as a gravestone in memory of the victims of death squads.

40 In 1995, a contingent of UN troops replaced the multinational forces. In

STATISTICS

DEMOGRAPHY
Population: 7,259,000 (1996) **Annual growth:** 1.9% (1980/1996) **Estimates for year 2000:** 7,800,000 **Annual growth to year 2000:** 1.9% (1994/2000) **Urban Population:** 32.4% (1996) **Urban growth:** 3.92% (1980/95) **Children per woman:** 4.7 (1996).

HEALTH
Life expectancy at birth: 54 years (1996) male: 53 years (1994) female: 56 years (1994) **Infant mortality:** 94 per 1,000 (1996) **Under-5 child mortality:** 134 per 1,000 (1996) **Calorie consumption:** 89% (1988/90) 7,143 **people per doctor** (1988/91) **Safe water:** 37% (1990/96).

EDUCATION
Literacy: 45% (1995) male : 48% (1995) female: 42% (1995) **School enrolment** : Primary total: 56% (1990/95) male : 58% (1990/95) female: 54% (1990/95) Secondary: male : 22% (1990/95) female: 21% (1990/95)

COMMUNICATIONS
10 **newspapers,** 50 **radios,** 10 **TV sets** and 7 **main telephone lines** per 1,000 people (1994).

ECONOMY
Per capita, GNP: $ 310 (1996) **Annual growth, GNP:** 0% (1995/96) **Annual inflation:** 14.71% (1985/95) **Consumer price index:** 248.7 (1994) **Currency:** 16.16 gourdes = $ 1 (1995) **Cereal imports:** 311 metric tons (1994) **Food import dependency:** 77% (1994) **Fertilizer use:** 56 kgs per ha (1994) **Exports:** $ 180 million (1996) **Imports:** $ 865 million (1996) **External debt:** $ 897 million (1996) $ 124 **per capita:** (1996) **Debt service:** 13.8% of exports (1996) **Development aid received:** $ 733 million (1995) $ 104 per capita (1995) 45.5% of GNP (1994).

ENERGY
Consumption: 28.53 Kgs of Oil equivalent per capita yearly (1994) 93.00% imported (1994)

HDI (rank / value) 156 / 0.338 (1994)

November, René Préval, an Aristide supporter, won the elections with 88 per cent of the vote and took office on February 7 1996. Préval requested the UN peace forces to remain for an additional period of time due to the numerous conflicts and acts of violence which involved national police. Kidnappings and murders - including those of eight policemen out of duty - did not stop, while popular uprisings were violently repressed.

41 On July 16, Claude Raymond, general and minister in Duvalier's cabinet, was arrested for terrorist activities. Four days later, André Armand, former Army sergeant and leader of the retired soldiers lobby group, was killed by unknown assailants after having publicly stated that

retired army members were conspiring to assassinate Préval and former president Aristide.

42 The UN Security Council replaced the peace-keeping troops in September 1997 with a 300-strong civilian police force. In November, a home-made bomb was detonated near a primary school, killing a woman and injuring 14 people, including four children.

Honduras

Honduras

Population:	5,816,000 (1996)
Area:	112,088 SQ KM
Capital:	Tegucigalpa
Currency:	Lempiras
Language:	Spanish

Before the arrival of the Spanish, the region of present-day Honduras was inhabited by Chibcha (see Colombia), Lenca and Maya Indians. In the north of Honduras lies the city of Copan, which belonged to the ancient Mayan Empire. Copan's splendour lasted until the 9th century AD, ending with the downfall of the Mayan Empire.

[2] The first European to reach Honduras appears to have been Amerigo Vespuccio in 1498, but Pedro de Alvarado was in charge of the final Spanish conquest of Honduran territory, joining it to the Captaincy-General of Guatemala, despite strong resistance from the Indians under Lempira's command.

[3] In 1821, Honduras gained independence from Spain. Together with the other Central American provinces it joined the short-lived Mexican Empire of Iturbide, which collapsed two years later. Francisco Morazán and other Honduran leaders of the last century, sought in vain to set up an independent Central American federation. Their efforts were no match for Britain's "Balkanization" tactics.

[4] With the liberal reform of 1880, mining became the backbone of the economy. To encourage the development of this sector the country was opened to foreign investment and technology. In 1898, another "empire" managed to penetrate Honduras: the notorious US United Fruit Company (Unifruco). The Company took over vast tracts of land, it produced almost the entire fruit output of the country, it ruled railroads, ships and ports, and dictated many key political decisions.

[5] US Marines invaded Honduras in 1924, imposing a formal democracy, allowing Unifruco to establish a monopoly in banana production by buying out its main competitor, the Cuyamel Fruit Company. Washington eventually handed power over to Tiburcio Carias Andino, and he governed Honduras from 1933 to 1949.

[6] Border disputes with Guatemala led to US arbitration in 1930. In 1969, friction developed with El Salvador when the number of Salvadoran peasants emigrating to Honduras reached a critical level. This led to a further war, which was triggered by a soccer

game, and was finally ended with mediation by the Organization of American States (see El Salvador).

[7] In 1971, nationalists and liberals signed the Unity Pact. General Osvaldo López Arellano, in power since 1963, permitted elections and Ramón Ernesto Cruz of the National Party, was elected President.

[8] However in 1972 López Arellano overthrew the Cruz administration. He demonstrated his sensitivity to peasant demands for land reform and began to impose controls upon United Brands (as Unifruco was now called). This resulted in López Arellano's resignation and his replacement by Colonel Juan A Melgar Castro.

[9] The army commander-in-chief, General Policarpo Paz García, took power in August 1978. This regime became closely allied to that of the dictator Anastasio Somoza in neighboring Nicaragua. Nicaragua's Sandinista Revolution in 1979 hastened the election of a constituent assembly which promptly ratified Paz García as President. General elections were held in 1981, but leftist parties were banned. Liberal Party candidate, Roberto Suazo Córdova, won the presidency and was inaugurated in January 1982.

[10] The price of consumer goods immediately rose and an anti-terrorist law was passed forbidding strikes as intrinsically subversive. Death squads acted with impunity and opposition political figures disappeared daily.

[11] Honduras tolerated the presence of US troops and the installation of Nicaraguan "contras" in its territory. It was estimated that the Pentagon had 1,200 soldiers there in 1983. They participated in some military operations, gave military instruction and logistical support, and established a military infrastructure. The "contras", had some 15,000 soldiers within Honduran territory, alongside "Nica" camps, holding around 30,000 refugees.

[12] In April 1985, 7,000 US soldiers were on manoeuvres near the Nicaraguan border. Washington offered the Honduran air force the renewal of all its combat planes. With almost $300 million in military aid, the Honduran army doubled its number of troops and

renewed the Air Force combat fleet.

[13] Jose Azcona Hoyo, of the Liberal Party, won the 1985 elections. The new president requested help from Washington so that the "contras" could leave the country; he also tried to stimulate foreign investment.

[14] Poor management of US aid unleashed a wave of corruption, especially within the armed forces. The Government's privatization plan failed, as did its scheme for reducing public spending; in the agricultural sector, seasonal unemployment reached 90 per cent.

[15] In 1989, Rafael Callejas, the National Party candidate, won by a wide margin, although the elections were marked by fraud. Supported by the US and by the business community, Callejas launched an overall liberalization of the economy.

[16] In 1990, after the Sandinista defeat in neighboring Nicaragua's elections, US President Bush's administration made significant cuts in its economic aid to Honduras. Callejas sought closer ties with the armed forces, in the hopes of keeping growing social discontent under control.

[17] In early 1990, the Government raised taxes, increased fuel prices by 50 per cent and devalued the national currency.

[18] In December, the Government extended an amnesty to all political prisoners or victims of political persecution. The anti-terrorism law was abolished and a forum for political discussion was set up, with no group excluded.

[19] On January 12 1991, after eight years in exile, four leftist political leaders returned to Honduras, announcing the end of their armed struggle. In October 1991, the "Lorenzo Zelaya" People's Revolutionary Forces accepted the government's peace declaration and renounced armed conflict.

[20] Armed forces commander, General Arnulfo Cantarera, accused of human rights violations, was relieved of his command and replaced by General Luis Discua, who favored increased intervention by the military in the country's political life. Political assassination and other abuses committed by the military were denounced by the Honduran Committee for the Defense of Human Rights.

[21] The Callejas administration's structural adjustment program permitted the renegotiation of the country's $3.6 billion foreign debt. New agrarian laws authorized the sale of expropriated lands, which led to speculation by transnational agribusiness.

[22] The increase in military power and the country's overall political instability compounded the weakness of the economy, which was suffering the effects of losing dollars previously provided by US military aid.

[23] Voters registered their discontent in the ballots, bringing about the triumph of opposition candidate Carlos Roberto Reina, a social democrat, in the November 1993 elections.

[24] One of the new government's first decisions was the abolition of the mandatory military service.

PROFILE

ENVIRONMENT:
80 per cent of the land is covered by mountains and rainforests. Both population and economic acvtivity are concentrated along the Caribbean coast and in the southern highlands, close to the border with El Salvador. The coastal plains have the largest banana plantations in Central America. Coffee, tobacco and corn are grown in the southern part of the country. Deforestation, misuse of the soil and uncontrolled development have led to soil depletion.

THE SOCIETY
Peoples: Honduran people are of mixed Mayan and European descent. There is a 10 per cent minority of native Americans; 2 per cent are Afro-American. Garifunas, descendants of fugitive slaves and native Americans, live along the Caribbean coast and on the nearby islands, maintaining their traditional lifestyles.
Languages: Spanish is the official and most widely spoken language; Garifuna, various indian languages (as Lenca and Miskito).
Religions: Roman Catholic 85 per cent; Protestant 10 per cent.
Political Parties: People's Liberal Alliance (ALIPO), of social democratic orientation; National Party, conservative; Liberal Party; «Rodista» National Movement (MNR), led by former president Suazo Córdova; Revolutionary Democratic Movement; Innovation and Unity Party (PINU); Christian Democratic Party; Socialist Action Party of Honduras (PASOH); Marxist-Leninist Communist Party (PCML); The Unified National Direction (DNU) is made up of the People's Revolutionary Forces (FPR), the «Morazanista», Alliance for the Liberation of Honduras, the «Cinchonero» People's Liberation Movement (MPLC), the United Revolutionary Movement (MUR), the Communist Party of Honduras (PCH), and the Revolutionary Party of Central American Workers of Honduras.
Social Organizations: The Confederation of Honduran Workers (CTH) founded in 1964 and affiliated to the ORIT (Regional Interamerican Labour Organization), is the only officially recognized labor federation. The General Workers' Central Union (CGT) social-christian, the United Federation of Workers (FUT) the Federation of Honduran Workers' Unions (FESITRAH)the Independent Workers' Federation and the United National Peasants' Front of Honduras (FUNACAMPH.

THE STATE
Official Name: República de Honduras. Administrative divisions: 18 Departments. **Capital:** Tegucigalpa, 775,300 people (1994). Other cities: San Pedro Sula, 368,500 people; La Ceiba, 86,000; El Progreso 81,200; Choluteca, 72,800 (1994). **Government:** Carlos Flores, President since January, 1998. **National Holiday:** September 15, Independence Day (1821).**Armed Forces:** 18.800 troops, 13.200 conscripts (1995). **Other:** 5,500 members of the Public Security Force.

STATISTICS

DEMOGRAPHY
Population: 5,816,000 (1996) **Annual growth:** 3.1% (1980/1996) **Estimates for year 2000:** 6,500,000 **Annual growth to year 2000:** 2.8% (1994/2000) **Urban Population:** 44.4% (1996) **Urban growth:** 5.19% (1980/95) **Children per woman:** 4.5 (1996).

HEALTH
Life expectancy at birth: 69 years (1996) male: 66 years (1994) female: 71 years (1994) **Infant mortality:** 29 per 1,000 (1996) **Under-5 child mortality:** 35 per 1,000 (1996) **Calorie consumption:** 98% (1988/90) 1,266 **people per doctor** (1988/91) **Safe water:** 87% (1990/96).

EDUCATION
Literacy: 73% (1995) male : 73% (1995) female: 73% (1995) **School enrolment :** Primary total: 112% (1990/95) male : 111% (1990/95) female: 112% (1990/95) Secondary: male : 29% (1990/95) female: 37% (1990/95) Tertiary: 10% (1995) **Primary school teachers:** one for every 35 students (1995).

COMMUNICATIONS
40 **newspapers**, 408 **radios**, 80 **TV sets** and 24 **main telephone lines** per 1,000 people (1994).

ECONOMY
Per capita, GNP: $ 660 (1996) **Annual growth, GNP:** -0.3% (1995/96) **Annual inflation:** 14.29% (1985/95) **Consumer price index:** 196.4 (1994) **Currency:** 10.34 lempiras = $ 1 (1995) **Cereal imports:** 278 metric tons (1994) **Food import dependency:** 16% (1994) **Fertilizer use:** 280 kgs per ha (1994) **Exports:** $ 845 million (1996) **Imports:** $ 1,922 million (1996) **External debt:** $ 4,453 million (1996) $ 766 **per capita:** (1996) **Debt service:** 28.8% of exports (1996) Development aid received: $ 411 million (1995) $ 75 per capita (1995) 14.1% of GNP (1994).

ENERGY
Consumption: 203.99 Kgs of Oil equivalent per capita yearly (1994) 82.01% imported (1994)

HDI (rank / value) 116 / 0.575 (1994)

This measure was approved by Parliament in May 1994 and ratified by the legislature in April 1995. However, in August 1994, giving in to pressure from the military the Government agreed to a temporary draft call to fill 7,000 openings in the armed forces. In mid-1994, the Government dissolved the infamous National Bureau of Investigations, which had once been the torture section of the armed forces.

[25] As a result of the fall in banana exports to the EC, the Tela Railroad Company (formerly part of the United Fruit Company) closed four plantations, claiming that they were no longer profitable. They also laid off 3,000 employees for three months. Union workers went on strike and after several days of tension, the Government called off the strike and forced the Company to reopen the banana plantations and rehire the workers who had been laid off. After negotiating directly with the Union - SITRATERCO - the Company reinstated 1,200 workers, though nearly 1,000 female employees were not re-employed.

[26] As a result of the drought which hit the country during the first half of 1994, 90 villages throughout the country lost over 60 per cent of their subsistence crops. Given the danger of famine, which threatened more than 1.5 million people, the Government requested aid from the UN's food agency, FAO. The latter provided $900 million for agricultural development of the declared emergency areas. However, 73 per cent of the population of Honduras were still living in conditions of poverty or extreme poverty.

[27] While the armed forces continued with police assignments in the cities, the Legislative Assembly began to work on amendments to the constitution that handed control of public security forces over to civilians. In January 1995 the new Crime Investigations Unit began to act, led by civilians, replacing the secret police that had been dismantled the previous year. The new body, initially of 1,500 agents, was trained by the Israeli police and the FBI from the US. At that time, more than 50 people were murdered each day in the country.

[28] Senior government officials were imprisoned in 1995 for their involvement in trafficking official passports. The Supreme Court revoked the immunity of former president Callejas to testify on the falsification of documents and the appropriation of public funds. President Reina himself was touched by the offensive against corruption, being investigated for using State funds for private ends.

[29] In early 1996, a 25 per cent pay rise coincided with a 30 per cent increase in the basic products. Demonstrations calling for pay increases became increasingly frequent, especially in the public sector. The IMF imposed strict restrictions on State spending. The Government pruned military power with a series of measures - like removing control of the police force from their hands - and downsized the army. A bomb attack on the presidential palace was attributed to grieved military personnel. In July, the Commander in Chief of the armed forces stopped an attempted military rebellion from occurring.

[30] In October 1997, the police prevented some 400 people erecting a statue of Lempira - an indigenous resistance leader of the Spanish conquest era - in a public thoroughfare in Tegucigalpa. A statue of Christopher Columbus previously on this spot had been pulled off its pedestal and destroyed by demonstrators.

[31] On November 23, the general elections returned the Liberal Party of outgoing President Carlos Reina to power. His successor, Carlos Flores, took 53 per cent of the vote, 11 points more than the ultra-right National Party candidate, Nora Castro. The legislative elections confirmed the exclusion of Left from parliament. Flores announced he would continue with the economic liberalisation.

[32] When sworn in, in January 1998, the new President said he was willing to appoint a national unity government and to make a non-aggression pact with the military-linked opposition. Flores took over a country in crisis where 80 per cent of the population lived in extreme poverty and 228 landowners controlled more than 75 per cent of the land. The international financial bodies pressed for the urgent implementation of a new adjustment programme.

Hungary

Magyarország

Population: 10,049,000 (1996)
Area: 93,032 SQ KM
Capital: Budapest

Currency: Forint
Language: Hungarian

The territory of Hungary belonged to the Roman provinces of Pannonia and Dacia. By the end of the 4th century Rome had lost Pannonia which had been occupied by Germans, Slavs, Huns and Avars. The latter ruled over the Danube basin during the 7th and 8th centuries, until they were conquered by Charlemagne.

[2] Charlemagne's successors set up a series of Duchies in the western and northern parts of the basin, while the southern and eastern parts were under the sphere of influence of the Byzantine Empire and Bulgaria. The Duchy of Croatia became independent in 869 and Moravia put up stiff resistance to the Carolingians until the appearance of the Magyars.

[3] The Magyars had organized a federation of tribes west of the lower Don. These were made up by several clans led by a hereditary chieftain. The federation was called On-Ogur (Ten Arrows); "Hungarian" is a derivation of this term in the Slav language. In 982 Emperor Rudolf turned to the Magyars to break Moravian resistance.

[4] Led by Arpad, the Magyars crossed the Carpathians and conquered the inhabitants of the central plateau. Moravia was defeated in 906 and Pannonia a year later. The Hungarians then expanded northwards and repeatedly raided the rest of Europe.

[5] The German Emperor Otto I defeated Arpad in 955 and halted Magyar expansion. Arpad's heirs reunified the tribes and adopted Western Christianity. Stephen I was crowned by Rome, subsequently laying the foundations of the Hungarian State.

[6] The question of succession upon Stephen's death triggered two centuries of instability, but Hungary consolidated its dominions as far as the Carpathian mountains and Transylvania in the north, and the region between the Sava and Drava rivers in the south. In addition, it ruled over Croatia, Bosnia, and Northern Dalmatia (although the latter remained a separate state).

[7] With the Mongol invasion of the 13th century, Hungary lost half of its population. This prompted the Kingdom to reorganize and open its doors to new settlers; however, it had to make important concessions to the Cuman overlords and immigrants, who further weakened the Kingdom. Finally, the succession of foreigner Charles Robert of Anjou to the throne, stabilized the country.

[8] As the struggles between the Holy Roman Empire and the Papacy did not involve Hungary, the 14th century was the country's golden age. The Kingdom established friendly relations with Austria, Bohemia and Poland, and strong links with Bosnia. However, during this period the country seized Dalmatia from Venice, and other territories from Serbia.

[9] Sigismund of Luxembourg (1387-1437) was both a German and Czech king. His long absences and arbitrary rule enabled the Hungarian Diet (parliament), which was made up of nobles, to expand its power. The Diet's consent was required in order for laws to be passed. Taxes were continually being exacted from the peasants, who started revolts in the north and in Transylvania.

[10] After another controversial succession, Matthias Corvinus of Prague was elected king of Hungary in 1458. He ruled over his country with an iron fist. With the help of the Black Army, an army of mercenaries, Matthias subdued his enemies inside the country and expanded his dominion over Bosnia, Serbia, Walachia, and Moldova. He also carried out a series of campaigns against Bohemia and Austria.

[11] Upon Matthias' death in 1490 the magnates - the richest nobles - appointed Vladislav II, who was King of Bohemia and whose weak personality was well known. The Black Army was disbanded but the oppressed peasants rebelled again in 1514; the rebellion was ruthlessly put down. Meanwhile, Austria recovered the southern provinces and established its authority over Hungary.

[12] Hungary was conquered by the Ottoman empire in 1526. At first the Sultan supported Zapolya to succeed the King who had been killed in battle. However, upon Zapoyla's death he occupied Budapest himself, and annexed a large portion to the south and centre of the country. Croatia and the western and northern strip of the country remained under the rule of Ferdinand of Hapsburg, who had to pay tribute to the Turkish Empire.

[13] During the 17th and 18th centuries Hungary was under two empires whose only interest in the country lay in the tributes it paid. The situation became more volatile when the majority of the population embraced the Reformation, while Vienna attempted to re-establish Catholicism. Even the nobles began to react against absolutism, peasant oppression and stagnation.

[14] During the 1848 revolution, the Hungarian Diet passed the April Laws, which brought changes in agricultural and fiscal matters. They reorganized on a more representative basis and proposed the reunification of the country and the creation of a separate administration in Budapest. The reform was met with distrust on the part of large landowners and Serbian, Romanian, and Croatian minorities.

[15] When the revolution was defeated, Austria, aided by Russia, annulled all reforms and regained control over Hungary. When Austria was defeated by Prussia in 1866, Vienna decided to subdivide its empire and accepted Hungary´s April Laws. A "Nationalities Law" guaranteed respect for the rights of minorities, giving way to the establishment of the Austro-Hungarian Empire in 1867.

[16] In the early 20th century, Hungarian politics was still dominated by conservative landowners, as most business people were foreigners, Jewish or German, and the majority of the population remained excluded from political activity. Minorities continued to be oppressed and the country lacked a strong sense of autonomy.

[17] With the collapse of the Hapsburg empire during World War I, a provisional government

PER 100,000
LIVE BIRTHS
30

PER CAPITA
$2,683

PROFILE

ENVIRONMENT
The country is a vast plain with a maximum altitude of 1,000 m partially ringed by the Carpathian Mountains. The mountainous region has abundant mineral resources (manganese, bauxite, coal). Between the Danube and its tributary, the Tisza, lies a very fertile plain, site of most of the country's farming activity. Cattle are raised on the grasslands east of the Tisza. In the past 30 years there has been rapid industrial expansion, particularly in the production of steel, non-ferrous metals, chemicals and railway equipment. Oil and natural gas deposits have been found in the Szegia and Zala river basins. 41 per cent of the population is exposed to sulphur dioxide and nitrogen dioxide in the air. The sulphurous emissions are greater than in most eastern European countries.

SOCIETY
Peoples: Magyar 92 per cent; Gypsy/Roma 3 per cent; German 1 per cent; Slovak 1 per cent; Jewish 1 per cent; Southern Slav 1 per cent; other 1 per cent.
Religions: Christian 92.9 per cent, of which Roman Catholic 67.8 per cent, Protestant 25.1 per cent; atheist and agnostic 4.8 per cent; other 2.3 per cent.
Languages: Hungarian (official)
Political Parties: Hungarian Socialist Party (HSP); Hungarian Democratic Forum (MDF); Alliance of Free Democrats (SZDSZ); Smallholders' Party; Federation of Young Democrats (FIDESZ); Popular Christian Democratic Party; Social Democratic Party of Hungary; Agrarian Party; Hungarian Socialist Workers' Party (communist).
Social Organizations: Central Council of Hungarian Trade Unions (SZOT); Hungarian Women's Network.

THE STATE
Official Name: Magyar Köztársaság.
Administrative Divisions: 19 Counties and the Capital.
Capital: Budapest, 1,909,000 people (1996).
Other cities: Miskolc, 180,000; Debrecen, 211,000; Szeged, 167,000 (1996).
Government: Arpad Göncz, President. Gyula Horn, Prime Minister since June 1994. The single-chamber National Assembly (386 representatives elected for five-year terms) is the supreme authority in the Republic. Eight seats in the Assembly are reserved for each of the country's minorities.
National Holiday: March 15, Independence (1848), April 4, Anniversary of the Liberation (1945).
Armed Forces: 64,300 (1996).
Other: Border Guard, 15,900. Civil Defence Troops, 2,000. Internal Security Troops, 2,500.

took power and proclaimed the Republic of Hungary. But Serbians, Czechs and Romanians seized two-thirds of the country and the central government was paralyzed. In 1919 a communist rebellion was followed by the formation of a "Soviet" republic.

[18] Bela Kun's Bolsheviks expected Moscow to support them, but they were forced to flee when the Romanian troops took over the capital. The European powers pushed Romania into withdrawing and installed a provisional government. The 1920 Parliament restored monarchy and appointed Admiral Milkos Horthy as provisional ruler.

[19] In the Trianon Treaty, the victorious allies recognized Hungarian independence, but Yugoslavia, Romania, and Czechoslovakia remained in possession of most of the country's territory and 60 per cent of its population. Austria, Poland, and Italy also benefited from the partition of Hungary.

[20] Hungary was forced to pay heavy reparations; its industry and production were left in a shambles. Unemployment rose to unprecedented figures and nearly 400,000 refugees arrived from the territories it had lost. The middle classes and the refugees set up right-wing armed groups, blaming the left for their ruin.

[21] Funds granted by the League of Nations, followed by private investments and credits, alleviated domestic tension, but the depression of the 1930s had serious effects on Hungary. Horthy formed an extreme-right government which sided with Germany, while anti-Semitism grew within the country.

[22] The alliance with Berlin enabled Budapest to recover part of Slovakia, Ruthenia, and the north of Transylvania. Hungary cooperated in the German attacks on Romania, Yugoslavia and the USSR, but nothing could stop the Red Army counter-offensive. In the Treaty of Paris, Hungary was

MILITARY (as % of health and education expenditures-1990/91) **18%**

forced to retreat to the borders fixed in the Treaty of Trianon.

[23] In 1944 a provisional assembly formed a coalition government and took up a program proposed by communist leaders and backed by the USSR. This program included the expropriation of large estates, the nationalization of banking and heavy industry, as well as guarantees for small landowners and private initiative, democratic rights and liberties.

[24] The Communists, at that time represented by the Workers' Party, assumed control of the government. In 1946 the Constitution of the Peoples' Republic of Hungary was established.

[25] In 1948, the Communist Government forcibly collectivized agriculture and started a series of development plans which stressed the development of heavy industry. Upon Stalin's death in 1953, Matyas Rakosi, head of government, was replaced by Imre Nagy, who promised political changes.

[26] In 1955, Nagy was deposed and expelled from the party. Rakosi returned for a short period, until 1956, when he handed power over to Erno Gero, who had similar political views to his own.

[27] Students staged a demonstration in Budapest, and were joined by the rest of the population. Gero reacted harshly: the police were instructed to shoot into the crowd, and the demonstration turned into a popular revolution, backed by the Army. The Government was handed back to Nagy, heading a broad national coalition.

[28] In November 1956, Nagy announced the withdrawal of Hungary from the Warsaw Pact, and requested that the United Nations recognize its neutrality. The Red Army, which had withdrawn during the revolution, occupied the country again and reinstated the communist government, led by Janos Kadar.

[29] Kadar followed Soviet guidelines, where foreign policy was concerned. As for domestic policy, central planning was partly liberalized from 1968 onwards, the standard of living rose, but bureaucracy and corruption increased.

[30] Sexual discrimination continued on all fronts. In 1981, while women made up 45 per cent of all workers, they were systematically paid less than men and their job opportunities were restricted to specific fields of traditionally female labor.

[31] Kadar was elected First Secretary of the Hungarian Workers' Socialist Party and head of government, and he ruled without serious opposition until March 1986, when a youth protest march was heavily crushed. Two years later some 10,000 people demanded freedom and reforms in a demonstration in Budapest.

[32] The Government relaxed press censorship and permitted the formation of trade unions and independent political groups - such as the newly constituted Hungarian Democratic Forum - to be formed.

[33] Between 1986 and 1988 Hungarian and Austrian environmentalists protested against the construction of a dam

on the Danube; part of a Hungarian-Czechoslovakian project supported by Austria. The Budapest Government resisted the pressure but in the end the project was shelved.

[34] In January 1989 Parliament passed a law legalizing strikes, public demonstrations and political associations. Meanwhile, it adopted an austerity plan which reduced subsidies and devalued the currency. Unemployment was expected to rise to 100,000 and annual inflation to 30 per cent.

[35] The Workers' Party also approved the elimination of the single party system and agreed to celebrate Independence Day on March 15, the date of the 1848 revolt against Austria. In March 1989, 100,000 people demonstrated in Budapest, demanding elections and the withdrawal of Soviet troops.

[36] The opposition candidates won the provincial elections held in 1989. In August, two million workers went on strike, protesting

against price increases. In October, after an agreement between the Workers' Party and the opposition, Parliament proclaimed the Republic of Hungary and eliminated the single-party system.

[37] Hungary was the first country in the Warsaw Pact to break its Cold War alliances. Within two years, Budapest established relations with Israel, South Korea, and South Africa.

[38] By the end of the year, the Workers' Party had become the Hungarian Socialist Party, with one faction deciding to keep its old name. In the 1990 elections, the Hungarian Democratic Front obtained 43 per cent of the vote, forming a coalition government with two smaller parties: the Socialist Party and the Workers' party. These received 10.3 and 3.5 per cent of the vote, respectively.

[39] In late 1991, the Hungarian prime minister met with the Czechoslovakian and Polish presidents in the city of Krakow, Poland. The three leaders expressed their wish to establish formal relations with NATO and the West European Union. The Krakow declaration also stressed the importance of associating with the European Community.

[40] Hungary had a foreign debt of $21 billion, the largest in Europe. Its agricultural and industrial production fell by 10 per cent - a situation aggravated by IMF policies-preventing domestic capital accumulation and favoring foreign investors. In 1990, inflation reached 30 per cent, with the average family spending 75 per cent of its income on basic consumer goods. The following year, the figure was 90 per cent, for the same goods. Of its 10 million inhabitants, 2 million were living below the poverty line.

[41] In this new era in Hungary, women's representation in politics declined. In the 1990 elections, women won 7.5 per cent of the seats, while in 1985 they had held 21 per cent. Women constitute 46 per cent of the active workforce, but this is also beginning to change with the increasingly popular ideological position of restoring the "natural order". The idea of women staying at home clashes with the new economic reality of the country, where two salaries are needed to cover even the most basic needs of a nuclear family.

[42] The women's struggle was also heavily involved in the abortion issue. Over 4 million legal abortions have been carried out in Hungary over the past 25 years. However, nearly all the current political parties, except for the Federation of Young Democrats and the Free Democrats, have come out against the practice. Meanwhile, the Hungarian Womens' Network campaigned against the criminalization of abortion and in defence of the living standards, working rights and health of women.

[43] In January 1992, the Government announced its decision to reduce the public deficit, which stood at a level in excess of $900 million in 1991. They hoped to achieve this by imposing a four per cent reduction in public spending. Growing popular discontent, which was reflected in a reduced turn-out for elections and in repeated union strikes, have forced Joszef Lantall's right-of-center government to take a more cautious position.

[44] The economic crisis encouraged nationalistic and xenophobic demonstrations, including the notorious publication of a manifesto signed by the writer and vice-president of the Democratic Forum, Istvçn Csurka, blaming the ex-communists, the "westernized" liberals, the gipsies and the Jews for "the deterioration of the social climate".

[45] The liberal wing of the MDF immediately repudiated the declaration, and a few days later 70,000 people from various political groups took part in a demonstration - a march for democracy - through the city, to "chase the ghost of radicalism out of the country". After this event 48 skinheads were brought to face charges in court.

[46] In October 1993 the Prime Minister, Jozef Antall, was hospitalized when he became seriously ill. Minister of the Interior Peter Boross replaced him, later being confirmed in the post upon Antall's death the following December.

[47] In the winter of that year, a television report revealed high levels of air pollution in Budapest over a 10-day period, recommending that children should not be allowed to play outside. In March 1994, in the middle of the electoral campaign, the Government sacked 129 radio reporters. This action was condemned by international press and human rights organizations. This measure meant the end of 30 cultural and political programs in the three state radio stations.

[48] In the general elections of May 1994, the Hungarian Socialist Party led by Gyula Horn won in the second round. The ex-communists won 54 per cent of the vote and 208 of the 386 seats. In second place came the Free Democrats, with 70 seats compared with 90 in the 1990 election. The Democratic Forum was the largest loser, only retaining 37 of its previous 165 seats.

[49] Horn was sworn in as Prime Minister and the electoral supremacy of the former communists was confirmed in local elections toward the end of the year. In March 1995, his "idyll" with the electorate came to an end, when an unpopular package of economic measures was approved. The Government drastically reduced the education budget, funding for unemployment and maternity benefits, in order to cut back the fiscal deficit.

[50] Horn continued his rapprochement with the Western countries and negotiation with neighbouring countries in order to help the Hungarian minorities living abroad to "preserve their cultural identity." In May 1996, Hungary signed an agreement with Slovakia for the protection of ethnic minorities and, in September that year, a similar accord with Romania was signed.

[51] In early 1997, Hungary started negotiating NATO membership. Budapest accepted the installation of nuclear weapons and NATO troops in Hungarian territory as a pre-condition to joining the military alliance. In November, membership was approved in a referendum where 85 per cent of those who voted supported the integration. Half the electorate (around 4 million people) abstained.

[52] Bilateral relations with Romania - home to a large Hungarian minority - improved after the former communist Iliescu was defeated and the ultra-nationalist Romanian parties were ousted from government. These had been hostile to the Hungarian and Gypsy /Roma minorities. In 1998, Hungary continued to work towards admission to the European Union.

Iceland

Island

Population:	271,000 (1996)
Area:	103,000 SQ KM
Capital:	ReykjaviK
Currency:	Kronur
Language:	Icelandic

In 874, immigrants of European origin began settling in Iceland: Norwegians, Scots and Irish. Iceland was an independent state between 930 and 1264, but under the terms of the "Old Treaty" of 1263, the country became part of the kingdom of Norway.

[2] In 1381, Iceland and Norway were conquered by Denmark, but when Norway separated from the Danish Crown in 1814, Iceland remained under its protection. In 1918, Iceland became an associated state of Denmark, until it recovered its independence and a republic was proclaimed in June 1944.

[3] Until the end of the 19th century, Iceland had no roads or bridges in the interior, and trade was entirely in the hands of Danish companies.

[4] In 1915, Icelandic women acquired equal rights with men, being granted the right to vote and to hold elected office. This was attained through the same legislation which granted these rights to Danish women, as at the time, the country was a Danish colony.

[5] After World War I, local agriculture was revitalized through a series of laws aimed at the agrarian sector, and the introduction of modern equipment. From 1920 onwards, the fishing industry grew steadily. In addition, communication throughout the island improved with the building of a new network of inland roads and bridges, and the creation of a coast guard.

[6] Iceland joined the Council of Europe and NATO in 1949. It had no army or navy, and the United States provided the country with defence forces, within NATO's strategic framework. Iceland had only three coast guard ships, one airplane and two helicopters to protect itself against illegal fishing in its territorial waters.

[7] In 1952, Iceland founded the Nordic Council, including Sweden, Norway, Finland and Denmark.

[8] Due to the importance of fishing for Iceland, and the fear of overfishing near the island by foreign fleets, Reykjavik extended its territorial waters to 12 nautical miles in 1964, and in 1972 to 50 miles. This triggered two serious conflicts known as the "cod wars" with the United Kingdom. They were resolved by a treaty signed in 1973.

[9] In October 1975, Iceland announced the extension of its territorial waters to 200 nautical miles, citing the protection of the environment and of its economic interests. The failure of the 1973 treaty with the UK, and the impossibility of reaching a new agreement led to the third and most serious "cod war".

[10] In February 1976, Iceland briefly broke off relations with the UK, the first breaking of diplomatic ties to occur between NATO members. In June, the two countries reached an agreement and in December, English trawlers withdrew from Icelandic waters. In July 1979, Iceland re-affirmed its 200 mile claim.

[11] NATO membership became a controversial issue in Iceland in the 1970s. In the 1978 election, the joint victory of the Popular Alliance, who favored renouncing the treaty, and the Social Democratic Party (SDP), who were more moderate, caused a two-month delay in the formation of a new government, which depended upon the alliance of the two political groups.

[12] According to 1980 figures, women made up 43.4 per cent of the country's economically active population.

[13] In 1980, Vigdis Finnbogadottir, an independent candidate campaigning against the retention of American military bases on the island, won the presidential election with the support of the left, making her the country's first female head of state. This post did not confer the power for her significantly to alter government policy, so she was unable to carry out her campaign commitment. In 1984 she was re-elected with no opposition candidates.

WORKERS

UNEMPLOYMENT 3.7% (1996)

- AGRICULTURE 11% (1990)
- INDUSTRIAL 27%
- SERVICES 62%

[14] A strict austerity plan was implemented in 1983, aimed at reducing inflation. Trade unions accepted the conditions, and the inflation rate consequently fell from 130 per cent at the beginning of the year, to 27 per cent by December.

[15] In May 1985, Parliament approved a resolution declaring Iceland a "nuclear-free zone", thereby prohibiting nuclear weapons from being brought into the country. Iceland was chosen as the site for the important summit meeting between United States president Ronald Reagan and his Soviet counterpart Mikhail Gorbachev in October 1986.

[16] Although Iceland's continuing NATO membership has not really been threatened, the air base at Keflavik continued to cause controversy. With 2,200 troops, the base is a part of the US "early warning" system. In September 1988, Iceland's executive power formally declared that there would be no new military projects initiated in the country.

[17] That same year, relations between Reykjavik and Washington became tense. The US claimed that Iceland's decision to catch 80 fin whales and 40 sei whales violated the moratorium imposed by the International Whaling Commission. Iceland replied that it was a scientific program and did not modify its decision.

[18] The United States threatened to boycott Icelandic fish products and two Icelandic whaleboats were sunk by ecological activists in Reykjavik Bay. In 1987, Iceland announced the reduction of its catch to 20 whales. The threats of sanctions continued, and the following year it reduced this quota even further.

[19] In June 1988, President Finnbogadottir was re-elected for her third four-year term, with the backing of the main parties and a margin of over 90 per cent of the electorate. This victory was obtained in spite of the existence of an electoral rival, who had proposed increasing presidential power during the campaign.

[20] In September of 1988, Steingrimur Hermannsson became prime minister, as head of a coalition including center and left wing groups, made up of the SDP and the Popular Alliance. The new government promised to initiate an austerity program for Iceland's economy, which was suffering from high inflation and recession, accompanied by currency devaluations.

[21] In August 1989, as a result of growing international pressure, including an international boycott of Icelandic products organized by Greenpeace, Reykjavik

PROFILE

ENVIRONMENT
Located between the North Atlantic and the Arctic Ocean, Iceland is an enormous plateau with an average altitude of 500 meters. A mountain range crosses the country from east to west passing through an extensive ice-covered region; source of the main rivers. The coastline falls sharply from the plateau forming fjords. Most of the population live in the coastal area in the south and west, where ocean currents temper the climate. Reykjavik, the capital and economic center, is located in a fertile plain where the largest cities are found. The northern coast is much colder as a result of Arctic Ocean currents. Geysers and active volcanoes are used as a source of energy. Agricultural output is poor; fishing accounts for 80 per cent of all exports.

SOCIETY
Peoples: 96 per cent of Icelanders are descendants of Norwegian, Scottish and Irish immigrants. **Religions**: Mainly Lutheran (91.5 per cent) Other protestants 4.3 per cent. Catholics 0.9 per cent. Languages: Icelandic. **Political Parties**: Independence Party, conservative; Popular Alliance, socialist; Progress Party, left-of-center); Social Democratic Party. Other parties with parliamentry representation are: the Women's Party and the People's Movement. **Social Organizations**: Icelandic Federation of Workers, with 47,000 members.

THE STATE
Official Name: Lydhveldid Island.
Administrative divisions: 7 districts. Capital: Reykjavik 103,036 people (1994).
Other cities: Kopavogur 17,660 people; Hafnarfjordhur 17,538 people (1996).
Government: Olafur Ragnar Grimsson, President and Head of State since August 1st,1996. David Oddson, Prime Minister and Head of Government since September 1991. Unicameral parliament composed of 63 members, elected by popular vote for a 4 years term.
National Holiday: June, 17.
Other: 130 coast guard (1994); 2.200 NATO troops.

STATISTICS

DEMOGRAPHY
Population: 271,000 (1996) **Annual growth**: 1.1% (1980/1996) **Estimates for year 2000**: 300,000 **Annual growth to year 2000**: 1% (1994/2000) **Urban Population**: 91.7% (1996) **Children per woman**: 2.2 (1996).

HEALTH
Life expectancy at birth: 79 years (1996) male: 77 years (1994) female: 81 years (1994) **Infant mortality**: 5 per 1,000 (1996) **Under-5 child mortality**: 5 per 1,000 (1996)

EDUCATION
School enrolment : Primary total: 98% (1990/95) male : 100% (1990/95) female: 96% (1990/95) Secondary: male ; 105% (1990/95) female: 105% (1990/95)

COMMUNICATIONS
520 **newspapers**, 793 **radios**, 320 **TV sets** and 557 **main telephone lines** per 1,000 people (1994) **Books**: 537 new titles per 100,000 people (1992/94).

ECONOMY
Consumer price index: 117.0 (1994) **Currency**: 65.23 kronur = $ 1 (1995) **Cereal imports**: 32 metric tons (1994) **Fertilizer use**: 36,666 kgs per ha (1994)

HDI (rank / value) 5 / 0.942 (1994)

---

announced a two-year suspension of its whale hunting.
[22] In 1989 Iceland faced economic difficulties, like its Arctic neighbors, the Faeroe Islands, Greenland and northern Norway, affected by a sudden reduction in the international price of fish, due to over-production.
[23] As a result of these economic difficulties, the country's labor unions signed a wage agreement for 1990, accepting an eight per cent drop in purchasing power. One indication of the reduction in consumer demand was the fact that the total number of registered motor vehicles - the world's largest in proportion to its population - decreased that year for the first time ever.
[24] In 1990 the Government created the new post of environment minister, and Julius Solnes was appointed.
[25] In the parliamentary elections of April 1991, the majority again went to the center-left coalition of Prime Minister Hermannsson.
[26] From November 1992, discussion of the potential benefits of joining the European market, with its 380 million consumers, divided the political scene. The opposition Popular Alliance, including socialists and dissident Social Democrats, was against joining. Jon Baldvin

Hannibalsson, foreign minister and minister of foreign trade, on the other hand, claimed that joining the EC would bring a flow of capital and new foreign investment to the island.
[27] Fishing, the most important source of employment, went into crisis as reserves of certain species, especially cod, suffered from over-fishing. This situation led to new laws restricting the foreign access to territorial waters, causing friction in commercial relations with other countries.
[28] Iceland produces abundant electric power and in the early 1990s it had hoped to develop its non-ferrous metal industry. This sector faced stiff competition from Russia, which depressed prices on the international market.
[29] The tourist industry expanded amid hopes that income from this will entail economic recovery for the island. A series of laws was passed in 1993 to protect polar bears which were being systematically exterminated.
[30] Iceland's entry into the European Union was approved by the Althing on January 1 1993. The preparations for unification caused excitement during that year and 1994. There was a feeling that unification would not be achieved and a debate was triggered on whether joining the

European Union was convenient or not.
[31] In 1994 a number of Iceland's fishing boats entered an area of the Barents sea near Russian and Norwegian territorial waters, causing friction in relations with these two countries. Both nations had undertaken a process to recover fish reserves in the area by reducing capture. By the end of 1995, diplomatic negotiations were considered the only solution for the difference.
[32] In the parliamentary elections of April 8 1995, the Independence Party won 25 of the 63 seats and was forced to create an alliance with the Progress Party - with 15 seats - in order to reach a majority in the Althing. The representation of the Popular Alliance and the Women's Alliance dropped, while the new Popular Movement obtained 4 seats.
[33] Iceland's economy managed a slight recovery in 1995 after a slow growth in the previous years. The gross domestic product increased 3 per cent and inflation did not exceed 2 per cent. Unemployment - aggravated by redundancies at the NATO base - reached 5 per cent.
[34] After having governed the country for 16 years, President Vigdis Finnbogadottir did not stand in the June 29 elections in 1996. Olafur Ragnar Grimsson, former finance minister and

member of the Popular Alliance, won the election with 41.4 per cent of the vote, taking office on August 1 of that year.
[35] In 1996, marine resources began to be exploited again and fishing quotas were increased after several years of restrictions imposed to preserve the species, and this stimulated economic growth. That year, the GDP increased 5.7 per cent, unemployment fell to 4 per cent and inflation stood at around 3 per cent.
[36] The economy continued to grow in 1997, partly due to expanding internal consumption, as exports increased only 3 per cent on the previous year's figures. The bulk of investments were aimed at aluminium production. Several foreign companies, mostly from Switzerland, the United States and Norway, intensified exploitation of this mineral resource.
[37] At the end of that year, Iceland participated in the negotiations for reductions in toxic gas emissions in Kyoto, Japan. Due to its economic characteristics, Iceland, along with Australia and Norway, was authorized to increase emissions, unlike "highly contaminating" countries such as the United States or the European Union.

India

Bharat

Population: 944,580,000 (1996)
Area: 3,287,590 SQ KM
Capital: New Delhi

Currency: Rupee
Language: Hindi

Around 3000 BC, the Dravidian inhabitants of the Indus Valley, in present-day Pakistan, built about a hundred cities, erected huge temples in larger urban centres, like Harappa and Mohenjo Daro, created a written language, that has yet to be deciphered, and carved cylindrical seals of rare perfection. With their irrigated agriculture they developed a prosperous economy and maintained active trade from the Indian Ocean to the spurs of the Himalayas, using the Indus River as their main means of communication. Little is known about their culture, their political organization or development except that, after five centuries of existence, invaders devastated the whole region, exterminating the population and destroying their civilization.

[2] Towards 1600 BC, waves of Indo-Europeans arrived from Afghanistan, gradually conquering the subcontinent. Armed with iron weapons, protected by armour and using war chariots, they subdued the local population and established numerous states. The civilization they created, later called Vedic, was based on a rigid caste system in which the conquerors constituted the dominant nobility. They were called the *ariana* or *ayriana* - nobility - giving rise to the term Aryan which was later generically used to designate all Indo-Europeans.

[3] The Iranian-Greek invasions of the 6th-4th centuries BC (see Iran) did not reach Magadha in the Ganges River valley, the most powerful state in India. Under the rule of Ashoka, 274-232 BC, Magadha occupied the entire subcontinent, except for the extreme south. Indian civilization proper dates from this period. Ashoka and his descendants were the driving force behind a cultural unification that included the organization and diffusion of Buddhism, based on the preaching of Gautama Siddhartha, who lived from 563 to 483 BC, and was later known as Buddha. Between the 1st and 3rd centuries AD, this civilization began to break up, fragmented by the development of the Seythian Kusana (see Afghanistan) and Ksatrapa states in the northeast.

[4] When the Guptas of Magadha seized power in the 3rd-6th centuries AD, a new process of unification ushered in one of the most brilliant periods of Indian culture. The 8th century spread of Islam failed to take hold in India, but it was more successful four centuries later, when the Turks of Mahmud of Ghazni reintroduced the faith. Successive groups of Islamic migrants from central Asia invaded the subcontinent, ending with the Tartars of Timur Lenk (Tamburlaine). Between 1505 and 1525, one of their descendants, Babur, founded what later came to be known as the Empire of the Grand Mogul, with its capital in Delhi.

[5] Babur's descendants consolidated Islam, particularly in the northwest and northeast (see Pakistan and Bangladesh). Culture and the arts developed remarkably, the Taj Mahal was built around 1650, but the European presence, that had been limited to coastal trading posts, began to be felt. In 1687, the British East India Company settled in Bombay. In 1696, it built Fort William in Calcutta, and throughout the 18th century, the Company's private army waged war against the French competition, emerging victorious in 1784. From 1798, Company troops led by a brother of the Duke of Wellington methodically conquered Indian territory in various campaigns. By 1820, the English were in control of almost all of India, except for the Punjab, Kashmir and Peshawar, which were governed by their Sikh ally, Ranjit Singh. After his death in 1849, the British annexed these territories. The 'loyal allies' retained nominal autonomy and were allowed to keep their courts, great palaces and immoderate luxury, much to the satisfaction of European visitors.

[6] The Indian economy was completely dismantled. Its textile industry, whose exports of high-quality cloth had reached half the globe, was an obstacle to the growth of the British cotton industry.

[7] The ruin of this industry, based on individual weavers, brought widespread impoverishment to the countryside. Peasants were also hard hit by the reorganization of agriculture for export crops. The early results of British domination were lower incomes and greater unemployment. Public accounts were conveniently arranged. All military spending, including the campaigns in Afghanistan, Burma and Malaya, was covered by the Indian treasury, 70 per cent of whose budget was earmarked for these 'defence expenses'. All British spending, however remotely connected with India, was entered as expenditures of the 'Indian Empire'.

[8] 'Divide and rule' was a motto of British domination. Mercenaries recruited in one region were used to subdue others. Such was the case with Nepalese Gurkhas and Punjabi Sikhs. Religious strife was also fomented; an electoral reform at the beginning of the 20th century stated that Muslims, Hindus and Buddhists could each vote only for candidates of their own faiths. Throughout the colonial period all this manipulation generated innumerable uprisings, both large

1 Territory under Pakistan control 2 Territory under China's control
3 Territory claimed by Pakistan

0   300 km

PUBLIC EXPENDITURE

4.9%   42.3%
1995 ■ DEFENCE □ SOCIAL

In **1990/91** Military as % of health & education expenditure was 65%.

WORKERS

(1996)

Labour force %
■ WOMEN
□ MEN
32   68

■ AGRICULTURE 64% **(1990)**
□ INDUSTRIAL 16%
▨ SERVICES 20%

Foreign Trade

MILLIONS $ 1996

IMPORTS
36,055
EXPORTS
32,325

PROFILE

ENVIRONMENT

The nation is divided into three large natural regions: the Himalayas, along the northern border; the fertile, densely populated Ganges plain immediately to the south, and the Deccan plateau in the center and south.

The Himalayas shelter the country from cold north winds. The climate is subject to monsoon influence; hot and dry for eight months of the year, and raining heavily from June to September. Rice farming is widespread.

Coal and iron ore are the main mineral resources. There is a long-standing territorial dispute with Pakistan over Kashmir, in the northwest.

SOCIETY

Peoples: The population of India contains a multitude of racial, cultural and ethnic groups. Most are descendants of the Aryan peoples who developed the Vedic civilization and created a caste system so robust that it has survived until the present. The influence of Arab invasions, in the 7th and 12th centuries, and Mongolian incursions, in the 13th century, is still felt in the north. Peoples of Dravidian origin still predominate on the Deccan plateau in the centre and south of India.

Religions: 83 per cent Hindu, 11 per cent Muslim, 2.5 per cent Sikh. There are Christian and Buddhist minorities.

Languages: There are 18 officially recognized languages of which Hindi is the most widely spoken.

English is an associated language, widely spoken for official purposes. There are 16 official regional languages and infinity of local dialects.

Political Parties: The Indian National Congress (INC), founded in 1885. Under the leadership of Mahatma Gandhi they fought for independence from Britain.

The United Front, former National Front-Left Front. The Bharatiya Janata Party is a rightwing nationalist party which supposedly has connections with the Rashtriya Swayan Sevak Sangh (RSSS), a paramilitary communal organization, considered responsible for a series of violent acts, especially against Muslims. The Communist Party of India-Marxist (CPI-M).

The Lok Dal claims to be the party of the poor peasants and aims to have considerable influence in northern India. Its main support comes from the middle castes.

Amongst the most important regional parties are the all-India Anna Dravida Munetva Kazhagam (AIA-DMK), the National Conference of Jammu and Kashmir, the Asom Ghana Parishad, ruling in Assam, the Telegu Desam, and the Akali Dal which leads a struggle for greater Punjabi autonomy.

Social Organizations: The most important are the Indian National Trade Union Congress (INTUC), with over 4 million members; the Bharatiya Mazdoor Sangh, with approximately 2 million members; the All-India Trade Union Congress (AITUC), with 1.5 million members; and the Center of Indian Trade Unions (CITU), with 1 million members.

THE STATE

Official name: Bharat (Hindi).

Capital: Delhi and New Delhi, 9,882,000 people (1995).

Other cities: Greater Mumbai/Bombay, 15,093,000 people; Calcutta, 11,673,000; Madras, 5,343,000; Bangalore, 4,749,000; Hyderabad, 5,343,000 (1995).

Government: KR Narayanan, President since July 1997. Atal Bihari Vajpayee, Prime Minister since March 1998.

National Holidays: August 15, Independence Day (1947); January 26, Day of the Republic (1950).

Armed Forces: 1,145,000 troops (1995).

Other: 1,421,800.

and small, on local and national levels.

9   The most serious of these were the 1857-1858 rebellions by sepoys, Indian soldiers in the British army. These began as a barracks movement, eventually incorporating a range of grievances and growing into a nationwide revolt. Hindus and Muslims joined forces and even proposed the restoration of the ancient Moghul empire. This movement demonstrated that the East India Company was incapable of administering such a large domain and led the British crown, after violent repression, to assume direct government of India.

10   The educational system was based on the classic British model and was conceived to train natives for colonial administration in the civil service. However, it did not exactly fulfill this purpose. What it did do was create an intellectual elite fully conversant with European culture and thinking. The British had certainly never planned that the first association of civil servants in India, created in 1876 by Surendranath Banerjee, would take the Italian revolutionary Giuseppe Mazzini as its patron and inspiration and not just quietly follow the government line. Years later in 1885, it was this intelligentsia that formed the Indian National Congress which included British liberals and, for a long time, limited itself to proposing superficial reforms to improve British administration.

11   When Mohandas K Gandhi, a lawyer educated in England with experience of colonial methods in South Africa, returned to India in 1915, he became aware of the need to break out of the straitjacket of Anglo-Indian 'cooperation'. Gandhi tried to win Muslims over to the autonomist cause. He reintroduced Hindu teachings that Ram Mohan Roy had reinterpreted in the 19th century, giving particular importance to mass mobilization. His ties with the Indian National Congress strengthened the movement's most radical wing where young Jawaharlal Nehru was an activist. In 1919, the Amritsar massacre occurred; a demonstration was savagely repressed leaving, according to British sources, 380 dead and 1200 wounded. In 1920, in response to the Amritsar massacre, at Gandhi's urging, the Indian Congress launched a campaign which showed the effectiveness of unarmed civilian opposition. The campaign tactics included the boycotting of colonial institutions; non-participation in elections or administrative bodies, non-attendance at British schools, refusal to consume British products, and passive acceptance

of the ensuing legal consequences. The movement spread nationwide at all levels. Gandhi came to be called Mahatma (Great Soul) in recognition of his leadership.

12   A new campaign between 1930 and 1934 aimed to attain full independence and denounce the state salt monopoly. This demonstrated Gandhi's ability to combine a key political goal with a specific demand affecting all the poor; one they would understand and support. For the first time the British saw women flocking to demonstrations. Jails overflowed with prisoners who did not resist arrest posing an immense problem to the colonial authorities. It was impossible not to negotiate with Gandhi, and after World War II the British were left with no option but to rapidly grant independence.

13   With the British withdrawal in 1947, the subcontinent was divided into two states; the Indian Union, and Pakistan, which was created to concentrate the Muslim population into one area (see Pakistan and Bangladesh). This 'Partition' as it was called was a painful and often violent separation. The Indian Union brought together an enormous diversity of ethnic, linguistic, and cultural groups in a single federated state, consolidating the sentiment of national unity forged in the independence struggle that the British had never managed to stifle. The excitement of independence was clouded by the assassination of Gandhi less than a year later, on 30 January 1948.

14   After independence, Prime Minister Jawaharlal Nehru, along with Sukarno of Indonesia, Gamal Abdel Nasser of Egypt and Tito of Yugoslavia, advanced the concept of political non-alignment for newly decolonized countries. In India, he applied development policies based on the notion that the industrialization of the society would bring prosperity.

15   In a few decades India made rapid technological progress, which enabled it to place satellites in orbit and, in 1974, to detonate an atom bomb, making India the first nuclear power in the non-aligned movement. However, the relevance of this kind of project to a country which had yet to feed all its people was widely questioned. Pakistan's civil war and conflict with India over East Pakistan eventually led to the independence of this portion as Bangladesh, in 1971.

16   The Indian economy was severely hit by the oil crisis of the early 1970s as it was dependent on oil imports. Industrial exports could not grow fast enough to offset increases in import prices, nor to meet the demand for food from a population growing at a rate of 15 million per year. In 1975,

the economic crisis, and popular resistance to the government's mass sterilization campaigns, led Indira Gandhi, Nehru's daughter, who had taken over as prime minister when her father died in 1966) to declare a state of emergency and impose press censorship.

[17] Abandoning the Congress Party's traditional populist policies, Mrs Gandhi followed World Bank economic guidelines, losing mass support for the government, without winning wholehearted backing from business sectors (particularly those linked to foreign capital), which demanded even greater concessions. The British tradition of respect for democratic freedoms instilled in mass organizations, big business and the middle class, led them (for different reasons) to close ranks in opposition and force the government to call parliamentary elections for March 1977. The Congress Party was roundly defeated by the Janata Party, a heterogeneous coalition formed by a splinter group of rightwing Congress Party members, the Socialist Party headed by trade union leader George Fernandes, and the Congress for Democracy, led by Jagjivan Ram, leader of the *Harijans* (Children of God, as Gandhi had renamed the out-castes or 'untouchables') and former minister in Indira Gandhi's cabinet.

[18] India's foreign policy of non-alignment remained basically unchanged under ageing prime minister Morarji Desai. In his time in power he was also unable to fulfill his promises of full employment and economic improvement. By mid-1979, disagreements within the party caused groups led by Charan Singh and Jagjivan Ram to split from the Janata Party. Desai had to resign and, unable to form a cabinet with a stable parliamentary majority, the Prime Minister called early elections, which returned Indira Gandhi to power in January 1980.

[19] Indira's second term was marked by a growing concentration of power, and accusations of unnecessary bureaucracy and corruption in the government, which gradually blemished her image. The problems in the Punjab, where the government faced increasingly strident demands from Sikh separatists, exemplified regionalism at its worst. Small groups of militant Sikhs harassed Hindus, to drive them out of the Punjab and create an absolute Sikh majority in the province. After that, the next step would be secession and the formation of independent 'Khalistan'. Indira accused 'forces from abroad' (namely Pakistan and the US) of destabilizing the country.

[20] On June 6 1984, the Prime Minister called in the army to evict hundreds of militant Sikhs from their most sacred shrine, the Golden Temple at Amritsar, which they had transformed into a command post for their separatist war. Hundreds of Sikh extremists were killed within the temple, including prominent Sikh leader, Jarnail Singh Bhindranwale. This bloody confrontation left moderate Sikh leaders with no room for negotiation. The atmosphere which prevailed throughout the region after the incident led to Indira Gandhi's assassination by two of her Sikh bodyguards, on October 31 1984.

[21] After the assassination, thousands of Sikhs fell victim to indiscriminate retaliation by Hindu paramilitary groups. Bypassing party and institutional formalities, Indira's son Rajiv was rapidly promoted to the office of prime minister and leader of the Congress Party.

[22] Elections in January 1985 gave him overwhelming support: he obtained 401 of Parliament's 508 seats. None of the other parties reached the 50 seats needed to be officially recognized as the opposition. Despite the landslide victory, some strongly regionalist areas such as the states of Karnataka and Andhra Pradesh turned their backs on Gandhi, influenced by Rama Rao, a charismatic former actor. Gandhi also lost in Sikkim, a Himalayan kingdom annexed to India in the 1970s, where the separatist Sikkim Sangram Parishad party won.

[23] The new premier took several steps to deal with Punjab's problems. He appointed a conciliatory figure as governor of the area, released political prisoners including opposition leaders, and directed that militants within his own party who had participated in the anti-Sikh violence be tried and punished. These measures paved the way for dialogue with Akali Dal, the regional majority party of Sikhs and other dissident groups. In spite of radically different stands, progress was made. The Punjab autonomists proposed the Indian central government should maintain its responsibility for defence and foreign affairs, the issuing of currency, mail, highways and telecommunications. Meanwhile, local government would have greater autonomy than in India's other states.

[24] In 1987, India intervened in the conflict in Sri Lanka, pressing for a cease-fire and an agreement between Sinhalese and Tamils by sending in troops. Three years later, the Indian Peace Forces had to discreetly withdraw, having suffered many casualties.

[25] Rajiv Gandhi was an active participant in the group of six neutral countries (Argentina, India, Sweden, Tanzania, Mexico and Greece) which appealed to the superpowers to curtail the arms race. The prime minister announced India would not relinquish nuclear weapons in the future if Pakistan persisted in making the atomic bomb.

[26] India's foreign policy remained loyal to non-alignment but some domestic changes were announced. Rajiv made the personal computer the symbol of his swift 'modernization' policy. He promised the private sector he would lift restrictions on imports and on the purchase of foreign technology, while relaxing fiscal controls. Labor unions feared that sophisticated technology would lead to unemployment and that Indian industry would not survive the competition from foreign products.

[27] Elections in November 1989 were held amidst a violent atmosphere which left more than 100 dead and revealed the opposition's progress. The Congress Party's representation went down to 192 seats while Janata Dal's went up to 141. Although a minority, this party succeeded in forming a government coalition with the National Front which appointed Vishwanath Pratap Singh as prime minister. This was possible because of the unusual simultaneous support from the right-wing Bharatiya Janata Party (BJP) and several left-wing groups.

[28] In March 1990, tensions between India and Pakistan mounted as Pakistan increased its

External Debt
1996

PER CAPITA
$95

Literacy
1995

52%

STATISTICS

DEMOGRAPHY
Population: 944,580,000 (1996) **Annual growth:** 2% (1980/1996) **Estimates for year 2000:** 1,006,800,000 **Annual growth to year 2000:** 1.6% (1994/2000) **Urban Population:** 27.1% (1996) **Urban growth:** 3.05% (1980/95) **Children per woman:** 3.2 (1996).

HEALTH
Life expectancy at birth: 62 years (1996) male: 61 years (1994) female: 61 years (1994) **Infant mortality:** 73 per 1,000 (1996) **Under-5 child mortality:** 111 per 1,000 (1996) **Calorie consumption:** 101% (1988/90) 2,439 **people per doctor** (1988/91) **Safe water:** 81% (1990/96).

EDUCATION
Literacy: 52% (1995) male : 66% (1995) female: 38% (1995) **School enrolment** : Primary total: 102% (1990/95) male : 113% (1990/95) female: 91% (1990/95) Secondary: male : 59% (1990/95) female: 38% (1990/95) Tertiary: 6% (1995) **Primary school teachers:** one for every 63 students (1995).

COMMUNICATIONS
81 **radios,** 60 **TV sets** and 11 **main telephone lines** per 1,000 people (1994) **Books:** 1 new titles per 100,000 people (1992/94).

ECONOMY
Per capita, GNP: $ 380 (1996) **Annual growth, GNP:** 5.1% (1995/96) **Annual inflation:** 9.77% (1985/95) **Consumer price index:** 149.5 (1994) **Currency:** 35.18 rupees = $ 1 (1995) **Cereal imports:** 12 metric tons (1994) **Food import dependency:** 5% (1994) **Fertilizer use:** 796 kgs per ha (1994) **Exports:** $ 32,325 million (1996) **Imports:** $ 36,055 million (1996) **External debt:** $89,827 million (1996) $ 95 **per capita:** (1996) **Debt service:** 24.1% of exports (1996) **Development aid received:** $ 1,738 million (1995) $ 2 per capita (1995) 0.6% of GNP (1994).

ENERGY
Consumption: 248.07 Kgs of Oil equivalent per capita yearly (1994) 20.54% imported (1994)

HDI (rank / value) 138 / 0.446 (1994)

Food Dependency

1970
21%

1994
5%

Maternal Mortality

1990

PER 100,000
LIVE BIRTHS
570

World Farmers held in Bangalore on October 3 and 4, 1993, farmers declared that the 'seeds, plants, biological material and wealth of the Third World form part of the Collective Intellectual Property of the peoples of the Third World'. They pledged to develop these rights in the face of the private patenting system which encourages the spread of monoculture and threatens biodiversity.

[38] Despite the violence among religious communities, protests against the economic reforms and natural disasters - an earthquake killed over 10,000 people in September 1993 - the Government was optimistic in early 1994. However, differences between the states were growing. In the north, Utta Pradesh, home to over 140 million people, showed figures of social development far below the national average. The male population outnumbered that of females - 882 women for every 1,000 men in 1995 - figures which can indicate both female infanticide and reduced nutrition/ health care for girls and women. In the southern state of Kerala, where a Communist government had been in power for some years, beggars were less common. In addition, 90 per cent of the State's population could read and write and infant mortality (17 per 1,000) was closer to that of Latvia (16 per 1,000) instead of the rest of India (79 per 1,000).

[39] In 1994, the Supreme Court of India declared that state governments could lose some powers if they did not enforce religious freedom, which was stipulated in the Constitution. Conflicts between Hindus and Muslims continued in Karnataka. In December, three Cabinet members resigned after being involved in corruption cases related to public security.

[40] That year India signed two agreements with China: the first one stated a reduction of military troops stationed along the 4,000 km of common borders between the two countries while the other encouraged trade relations. When former Pakistani prime minister Nawaz Sharif claimed his country had nuclear weapons, relations between New Delhi and Islamabad were strained. Pakistan closed its consulate in Bombay.

[41] During 1995, Prime Minister Narasimha Rao changed his cabinet three times. Elections in several states revealed an increasingly weakened Congress Party, with several internal schisms, and growing support for the Hindu nationalist party Bharatiya Janata (BJP). The new BJP

Government in the state of Maharashtra decided to change the name of Bombay to Mumbai.

[42] Economic stability and assistance schemes announced by Rao, which included a school dinners plan for 110 million children and the construction of 10 million rural homes, were not enough to stop his popularity from plummeting. Rao resigned on May 10 1996, following his party's defeat in the general elections held between April 27 and May 7. The BJP, in alliance with other minor parties, took 187 seats in the lower house, while the Congress Party took 138 and the National Front - Left Front, which changed its name to the United Front, took 117.

[43] The BJP did not get a big enough parliamentary majority to govern. The new Prime Minister, Atal Bihari Vajpayee, resigned on May 28, 12 days after taking office. President Shankar Dayal Sharma appointed HD Deve Gowda, leader of the United Front, to head the new Government, with Congress Party support.

[44] An agreement between India and China reduced the number of troops from both countries along the common border. In March 1997, Pakistan's Foreign Minister, Shamshad Ahmad, visited India to reopen negotiations to normalize relations between the two countries.

[45] Also in March, the Congress Party withdrew support from the Gowda Government, toppling the Prime Minister. Sitaram Kesri, the main force behind the break with the Left, was elected president of the Congress Party in June. Nearly a month after the fall of Gowda, Inder Kumar Gujral, also of the United Front, was appointed Prime Minister. In July, Vice-President KR Narayanan was elected President.

[46] The Congress Party withdrew its support from the Gujral Government in November when an official commission revealed alleged links between a governing coalition party, the Dravida Munnetra Kazagham (DMK), and Sri Lanka's Tamil guerrillas, a group involved in the murder of former prime minister Rajiv Gandhi. Gujral was forced to resign.

[47] The BJP triumphed in the February 1998 parliamentary elections. The Bharatiya Janata Party and their allies took 251 seats, followed by the Congress Party (166) and the United Front (96). For the second time in 22 months, Atal Bihari Vajpayee was designated Prime Minister. India's exploding of atomic devices in May caused upset and outrage, provoking threats of similar action by Pakistan.

support for the Kashmir independence movements. There were fears that, if both countries went to war, one of them could resort to nuclear weapons. In November, confrontations between Hindus and Muslims escalated amidst a general worsening of the economic crisis. Prime Minister Singh was replaced by Chandra Shekhar, also from the Janata Dal.

[29] An election campaign which claimed over 280 lives gave way to parliamentary elections which started on May 20 1991. The following day, they were adjourned following the assassination of Rajiv Gandhi, attacked by the Tamil liberation movement. A week later, Narasimha Rao was appointed Gandhi's successor as leader of the Congress Party. The elections, in which only 53 per cent of those registered voted and which were to become the most violent in India's independent history, were resumed between June 12 and 16. The Congress Party obtained 225 seats followed by the Bharatiya Janata Party with 119.

[30] In August 1991, the new government announced a drastic shift toward liberalism that would change the economic policy in force since independence. This change gave rise to criticism and protests. Already in September of the previous year, 70,000 representatives of tribal groups had met to halt dam constructions on the holy Narmada river, which threatened to flood ancient temples and ancestral lands belonging to the region's peasants. Over 200,000 people driven from their lands by the dams demonstrated their disagreement in 1991.

[31] This and other infrastructure projects formed part of a tradition of industrial modernization without weighing possible ecological consequences. Safety problems of the country's seven nuclear reactors remain unsolved and controls over companies which use or emit toxic substances are insufficient.

[32] Numerous acts of violence took place in 1992 by Hindu fundamentalists against the Islamic population in the northern cities

of Bombay and Ayodhya. According to Hindu tradition, in the latter - which had a mosque that was built in 1528 - the god Rama had been born. In December, Lal Krishnan Advani, leader of the BJP, ordered his followers to destroy the temple. The following clashes between the two communities left approximately 1,300 dead in several Indian cities and reached neighboring countries such as Pakistan and Bangladesh. In 1995, the Supreme Court was consulted about the possible existence of a Hindu temple in Ayodhya, before the (ruined) Babri mosque was built. The members of the Court unanimously declined to issue an opinion on the matter.

[33] The reforms planned by Prime Minister Rao, implemented by finance minister Manmohan Singh, included opening up India's market to foreign investment. The state gradually reduced its intervention in the economy, leaving the rupee to fluctuate freely against the dollar, and removing import controls.

[34] The outcome was reflected in the reduction of inflation (below 10 per cent in 1995) and the fiscal deficit while exports have grown steadily since 1992. The country continues to bear the burden of a foreign debt equal to 38 per cent of the GDP while the per capita income of its over 935 million inhabitants is one of Asia's lowest.

[35] Economic reforms have triggered protests from several sectors, especially from agriculture. Resistance to multinationals involved in fertilizers and seeds was very strong. As part of the 'green revolution' and a capital-intensive agriculture, the World Bank had granted significant loans during the 1960s and 1970s for the purchase of hybrid seeds while the government subsidized farmers.

[36] The Government proceeded to eliminate those subsidies following instructions from the World Bank's structural adjustment plan. The Farmers' Association of the State of Karnataka (KKRS) headed rural protests which were responsible for a number of direct attacks against representatives of multinational corporations since 1991.

[37] At the International Conference on Rights of Third

Indonesia

Indonesia

Population: 200,453,000 (1996)
Area: 1,904,569 SQ KM
Capital: Jakarta

Currency: Rupiah
Language: Bahasa Indonesia

Indonesia has some of the world's earliest homo sapiens remains. The ancestors of the present-day population were Malay immigrants who arrived on the islands of Java and Sumatra around 400 BC. They brought with them the cultural and religious influences of India. Indonesian civilization reached its height in the 15th century when the state of Mojopahit extended far east, beyond Java, Bali, Sumatra, and Borneo, becoming commercially and culturally linked with China.

2 At the end of the 13th century, through contact with Arab traders, Islamic beliefs were introduced, rapidly flourishing in the archipelago. These beliefs were not imposed through conversion campaigns, but were freely adopted because they represented a simple, egalitarian faith suited to local conditions.

3 When the Muslim traders sent Indonesian spices to Europe, the Europeans' interest was aroused, and they set their colonial sights on the region. In 1511, the Portuguese arrived in Melaka; in 1521, the Spanish reached the Moluccas and in 1595, private Dutch merchants organized their first expedition. The Netherlands had just won its independence from Spain and wanted to secure its own supply of spices. In 1602, the Dutch East India Company was founded, obtaining a trade monopoly, with a colonial mandate from the Governor of the region.

4 During the 17th and 18th centuries, Indonesia was fought over by Spain, Portugal, the Netherlands and Britain, the latter creating another private company. The Netherlands gained the upper hand and became the colonial power. Cash crops, coffee and sugar, were introduced, yielding excellent profits for the European investors but seriously upsetting the local socio-economic organization, which had remained intact until then but was virtually destroyed by the export economy. Anti-colonial revolts broke out. Towards the end of the 19th century, rubber, palm oil and tin became the main export products, though industry only began to develop during World War II, when the Netherlands was unable to meet its production needs at home.

5 In December 1916, nationalist pressure caused the formation of the *Volksraad* (People's Council), a body designed to defend the rights of the local population. Although its proposals were largely ignored, the council encouraged political participation among the local population.

6 In 1939, eight nationalist organizations formed a coalition called the Gabusan Politick Indonesia (GAPI), demanding democracy, autonomy and national unity within the framework of the antifascist struggle. GAPI adopted the red and white flag and Bahasa Indonesia as the national language.

7 After the outbreak of World War II, the Netherlands were invaded by Germany, and Indonesia by Japan in 1942. The Japanese, who claimed to be the "Asiatic brothers" of the Indonesians, freed nationalist leaders like Achmed Sukarno and Muhammad Hatta who had been imprisoned under Dutch rule. On August 11 1945, just four days prior to the Japanese surrender, they invested Sukarno and Hatta with full powers to establish an autonomous Indonesian government.

8 Indonesia proclaimed its independence on August 17 1945. The Dutch tried to recover the archipelago, forcing the Indonesians to fight back. The Arab and Indian communities actively supported the pro-independence guerrillas, while Britain backed the Netherlands. The US pressed for a negotiated settlement.

9 Unable to recover military control, the Netherlands was forced to surrender in 1949, although it retained partial control through a Dutch-Indonesian confederation.

10 In 1954, the Dutch-Indonesian Union, which was never fully implemented, was renounced by the Sukarno government, and the archipelago became fully independent. Sukarno's government soon began its own colonial policies in the region. In 1963, reacting to The Hague's refusal to withdraw from the island of New Guinea, Indonesia occupied West Irian (Irian Jaya), the former Dutch colony whose territory took up half of the island. The Indonesian independence process offered an important example for the other Third World countries. Together with other major events of the period - Indian and Pakistani independence, the Cuban Revolution, the nationalization of the Suez Canal in Egypt, and the French defeats in Vietnam and Algeria - it heralded the arrival of the South onto the international political scene. Sukarno was one of the main leaders of the pro-Third World movement, and in 1955, the Indonesian city of Bandung played host to a meeting of heads of government, giving rise to the Non-Aligned Movement.

11 The three-million strong Communist Party, the second most powerful in Asia after the Chinese, supported Sukarno. He launched nationalist development programs, aimed at raising the living standards of a population with one of the world's lowest per capita incomes. The country had sizeable petroleum reserves, which were banked on to spur economic development. Sukarno created a state petroleum company, PERTAMINA to break the domination of the Anglo-Dutch transnational, Royal Dutch Shell.

12 In 1965, the Indonesian oil deposits were nationalized. In October of that year, a small force of soldiers led by General Suharto seized power under the pretext of

Maternal Mortality

Food Dependency

PER 100,000
LIVE BIRTHS
650
1990

1970
12%

1994
6%

PROFILE

ENVIRONMENT

Indonesia is the largest archipelago-state in the world, made up of approximately 3,000 islands. The most important are Borneo (Kalimantan), Sumatra, Java, Celebes, Bali, the Moluccas, Western New Guinea and Timor. Lying on both sides of the equator, the island group has a tropical, rainy climate and dense rainforest vegetation. The population, the fourth largest in the world, is unevenly distributed: Java has one of the highest population densities in the world, 640 people per sq km, while Borneo has fewer than 10 people per sq km. Cash crops, mainly coffee, tea, rubber and palm oil are cultivated, along with subsistence crops, especially rice. Indonesia is the tenth largest oil producer and the third largest tin producer in the world. Like neighboring Malaysia, Indonesia has suffered deforestation due to the expansion of the paper and lumber-exporting industries.

SOCIETY

Peoples: 90 per cent of Indonesians are of Malay origin, half of whom belong to the Javanese ethnic group. There are also Chinese and Indian minorities.

Religions: Mainly Muslim (86 per cent); 10 per cent are Christian; 2 per cent Hindi; 1 per cent Buddhist.

Languages: Bahasa Indonesia (official), similar to Malay, is the official language. The Governments of Indonesia and Malaysia have agreed to gradual language unification based on Melayu, the common mother tongue. Javanese, native language to 60 million of the country's inhabitants. English, the language of business and commerce. 250 regional languages.

Political Parties: A presidential decree of January 1960 allows the President to dissolve any party whose ideology runs counter to official policies. The governing party, the Sekretariat Bersama Golongan Karya (Sekber Golkar Party), was created in 1971. Supported by the armed forces, the Sekber Golkar is a coalition of various professional and interest groups. Civil servants are mostly affiliated to the National Association of Civil Servants (KDRPR), part of Sekber Golkar. Opposition parties organized by the Government in 1973 include the United Development Party (PPP), conservative and Muslim-based, and the Indonesian Democratic Party (PDI), which caters to Christians and old nationalistic groups from the Sukarno era. The Communist Party of Indonesia (PKI) which, until the 1965 coup, was the third largest Communist party in the world, has been outlawed and since then has gone underground. In 1990, the Free Aceh Movement and the Aceh National Liberation Front, made up of insurgents from the northern region of the island of Sumatra, started attacks on the Government, but they were virtually crushed by the Army.

Social Organizations: All-Indonesian Union of Workers (SPSI), founded in 1973 and renamed in 1985.

THE STATE

Official Name: Republik Indonesia.

Administrative Divisions: 26 Provinces (excluding East Timor).

Capital: Jakarta, 13,900,000 people (1994 est).

Other cities: Surabaya, 2,500,000 people; Bandung, 2,000,000; Medan, 1,700,000 (1990).

Government: Jusuf Habibie, President since May 1998. Legislature, single-chamber, made up of 500 members, 400 elected by direct popular vote, and 100 designated by the President.

National Holiday: August 17, Independence Day (1945).

Armed Forces: 274,000 (1995).

Other: Police, 215,000, Auxiliary Police, (*Karma*), 1.5 million, Auxiliary Armed Force, in regional commands (*Wanra*).

stemming the "communist penetration." This bloody coup left nearly 700,000 dead, and some 200,000 political activists were imprisoned.

[13] Though deprived of any real power, Sukarno remained the nominal president until 1967, when Suharto was officially named head of state. Suharto opened the doors to foreign oil exploiting companies that wanted drilling rights. But with the rise in oil prices, the influx of capital, and a liberal economic policy, the Government also widened the gap between those with the highest and lowest incomes. Living conditions did not improve for millions of rural dwellers, many of whom had to leave their lands, joining the shantytowns in the country's large cities.

[14] In 1971, defying repression, students took to the streets in opposition to the "corrupt generals, Chinese merchants, and Japanese investors" controlling the nation. In an attempt to divert the attention of young officers and neutralize local dissent, Suharto invaded East Timor, on that country's independence from Portugal in 1975. US President Gerald Ford visited Jakarta a few hours before the invasion and apparently gave it his blessing. However, from the point of view of the Maubere people of Timor the Indonesians were not seen as liberators but as new colonists. The unyielding resistance on the island only deepened Indonesia's internal problems.

[15] In May 1977, when elections were held for a portion of the seats in the House of Representatives, discontent surfaced once again. Despite repression, the banning of leftist parties and press censorship, the official Sekber Golkar Party lost in Jakarta to a Muslim coalition which had campaigned against the rampant corruption. The governing party also lost ground in rural areas where it had always previously maintained effective political control.

[16] In the light of this setback, and to ensure victory in the election five years later, the regime clamped down on political activity and reorganized the electoral system, making it dependent on the Ministry of Home Affairs.

[17] On March 10 1983, in spite of growing opposition, the People's Consultative Assembly unanimously re-elected Suharto for a fourth 5-year presidential term.

[18] Indonesia adopted a birth control policy which has led to a reduction in the growth rate of its population. While figures for the 1984 census revealed an annual increase of 2.34 per cent, the average rate of growth between 1980 and 1990 was only 1.8 per cent. Even so, demographic pressure, particularly on the island of Java, together with the radical reorientation of the country's economy and commerce toward a world market, coupled with rapid industrialization, have all led to a deterioration in the quality of the environment and the depletion of agricultural lands. From 1979, the government reacted to this situation with a population transfer project known as "Transmigrasi", which involved transferring 2.5 million Javanese to other less populated islands, causing great social tension, and destroying the lifestyles of the peoples already resident on these islands.

[19] In the 1980s over 300 ethnic groups in the area have seen their standards of living drop sharply. The most energetic protests have been those of the inhabitants of Irian Jaya (West Irian) who demanded self-determination and freedom of movement to and from the neighboring territory of Papua New Guinea, with which they have a high degree of cultural and historical affinity.

[20] The continued Indonesian occupation of East Timor (see East Timor) has seriously damaged the Indonesian international image. In 1988 it caused the rejection of Indonesia's candidacy for the chair of the Non-Aligned Movement. Meanwhile, the European Parliament recognized East Timor's right to self-determination.

[21] Suharto was re-elected in 1988, in an election marked by unprecedented discussion of issues in the press.

[22] In 1991 the fighting between the army and the Aceh liberation movements in Sumatra became more acute when the commander of the army called for the

PER CAPITA

$644

84%

annihilation of the insurgents. In November in Dili, capital city of East Timor, Indonesian troops fired against 1,000 protesters, 185 of whom died. At the beginning of March, 1992, an armed offensive of several separatist groups was started in the Irian Jaya province. At the same time the US Government asked Congress to approve $2,300,000 for the training of the official security forces of Indonesia.

23 Before the parliamentary elections of 1992 PPP, the main opposition party reached an agreement with influential Muslim leaders. Meanwhile, the PDI had Sukarno's children appear on the political scene, with Guruh, a well-known author of popular songs. Nevertheless Golkar once again won, with 68 per cent of the votes. In March 1993 the Popular Consultative Assembly chose Suharto as President for the sixth time.

24 In the 1990s the exports of gas, oil, wood and the new industrial goods, as well as tourism, contributed to an annual rate of growth of six per cent to eight per cent. Nevertheless the foreign debt put 27 per cent of Indonesians under conditions of extreme poverty. The compulsive cutting of timber and the large infrastructural works resulted in the loss of fertile land and displacement of the peasant population.

25 The Muslim 90 per cent of the population increasingly protested against the privileges of Chinese and Christian minorities alike. In March 1994 a scandal exploded which implicated Chinese business people and official politicians. In June, the Government closed an opposition paper and two weekly magazines. The protests and demonstrations by artists and intellectuals did not receive media coverage.

26 During 1995 the technocrat middle class manifested a growing interest in political openness.

27 In August, Suharto liberated three political prisoners held in prison for 30 years for participating in the rebellion that eliminated Sukarno, and promised to remove the stigma of the identity cards from more than 1.3 million ex-political detainees. In May, he announced a plan to reduce the seats

assigned to the military in Parliament by 1997.

28 Two years before the campaign for the parliamentary elections of mid-1997, Suharto's minister of information, Harmoko, toured Indonesia in support of Golkar, the most important political organization of the country. The opposition accused the government of interfering in its activities. Particularly vocal was the PDI, headed by Megawati Sukarnoputri, daughter of Sukarno, the still-respected independence leader.

29 In March 1995 Harmoko arrested several members of the Alliance of Independent Journalists, a group formed after the closure of three publications. In September, the Government censored the publication of the memoirs of an ex-Sukarno-aide, as well as public appearances of several opposition leaders. In annexed East Timor the separatist movement was repressed by military forces. The armed forces investigated the death of civilians at the hands of its troops.

30 In 1996 the pre-election debates reached a new low when complaints about the illegal enrichment of the Suharto family and its circle grew. The military saw Islamic groups as well as Sukarnoputri and the PDI as the main threats to Suharto's power. The change of political climate was due partly to a wider circulation of information via the Internet as well as campaigning journalism, and vigorous protest about arms sales to Indonesia.

31 In spite of a climate of political uncertainty, the economy continued to prosperer and inflation was kept at bay. However, the trade surplus fell due to the reduction of key exports, such as textiles. Suharto, then 75, had to travel to Germany for a medical check-up, which increased doubts over his government.

32 In early 1997, the population reached 200 million. The Government announced it would continue its program to transfer the people from "over-populated" regions to less populated areas. Extended forest fires had a serious impact on the environment. Dense smog also affected other countries in the region, such as Malaysia and Singapore.

STATISTICS

DEMOGRAPHY
Population: 200,453,000 (1996) **Annual growth:** 1.8% (1980/1996) **Estimates for year 2000:** 212,600,000 **Annual growth to year 2000:** 1.5% (1994/2000) **Urban Population:** 36.4% (1996) **Urban growth:** 4.84% (1980/95) **Children per woman:** 2.7 (1996).

HEALTH
Life expectancy at birth: 64 years (1996) male: 62 years (1994) female: 65 years (1994) **Infant mortality:** 47 per 1,000 (1996) **Under-5 child mortality:** 71 per 1,000 (1996) **Calorie consumption:** 121% (1988/90) 7,143 **people per doctor** (1988/91) **Safe water:** 62% (1990/96).

EDUCATION
Literacy: 84% (1995) male : 90% (1995) female: 78% (1995) **School enrolment :** Primary total: 115% (1990/95) male : 117% (1990/95) female: 113% (1990/95) Secondary: male : 49% (1990/95) female: 41% (1990/95) Tertiary: 11% (1995) **Primary school teachers:** one for every 23 students (1995).

COMMUNICATIONS
20 **newspapers,** 148 **radios,** 150 **TV sets** and 13 **main telephone lines** per 1,000 people (1994) **Books:** 3 new titles per 100,000 people (1992/94).

ECONOMY
Per capita, GNP: $ 1,080 (1996) **Annual growth, GNP:** 5.8% (1995/96) **Annual inflation:** 8.8% (1985/95) **Consumer price index:** 139.9 (1994) **Currency:** 2,308 rupiahs = $ 1 (1995) **Cereal imports:** 5,113 metric tons (1994) **Food import dependency:** 6% (1994) **Fertilizer use:** 847 kgs per ha (1994) **Exports:** $ 49,727 million (1996) **Imports:** $ 42,925 million (1996) **External debt:** $ 129,033 million (1996) $ 644 **per capita:** (1996) **Debt service:** 36.8% of exports (1996) **Development aid received:** $ 1,389 million (1995) $ 7 per capita (1995) 0.8% of GNP (1994).

ENERGY
Consumption: 366.30 Kgs of Oil equivalent per capita yearly (1994) -119.61% imported (1994)

HDI (rank / value) 99 / 0.668 (1994).

33 The government party, Golongan Karya (Golkar) won the May 1997 parliamentary elections, obtaining 74 per cent of the vote (325 of 400 seats at stake). The new parliament included 12 of President Suharto's relatives - six children, two wives, two son-in-laws, one brother and one cousin - as well as many of the leader's trade partners or cronies. On March 10 1998, parliament re elected Suharto for a seventh 5 - year term.

34 A deep stock market crisis in April increased inflation and caused a risk of hyperinflation. The currency had lost 50 per cent of its value since mid-1997. The price rise affected mostly basic goods. Two million workers lost their

jobs between October 1997 and March 1998. Widespread social unrest followed, including the listing of shops and victimization of the Chinese community who were seen as wealthy and therefore supporters of the status quo. Student demonstrations calling for democracy met a brutal response, but Suharto stepped down on 21 May to be succeeded by his Vice President, Jusuf Habibie.

Iran

Iran

Population: 69,975,000 (1996)
Area: 1,633,188 SQ KM
Capital: Teheran (Tehran)

Currency: Rials
Language: Persian

Shortly before the 18th century BC, nations of the Indo-European area reached the plains of Iran, subduing the shepherds who inhabited the region. More of these people arrived up until the 10th century, contributing to the Mesopotamian cultural mix. They later became known by different names: Medes, from the name of the ruling group; Iranians, the name they adopted in Persia and India (from Sanskrit *ayriana* meaning nobles); Persians (a Greco-Latin term alluding to Perseus, the mythological ancestor that the Greeks foisted on Iranians), with its corrupted forms: Parsis, Farsis, Fars, or Parthians (according to the time and source). Whatever their names, they first won control of the mountainous region, then conquered the Mesopotamian plains under the reign of Ciaxares. During the rule of Ciro the Great (559-530 BC), this wave of expansion reached as far west as Asia Minor, and as far east as present-day Afghanistan. These borders were later extended as far as Greece, Egypt, Turkestan and part of India.

[2]   Towards the end of the 4th century BC, this vast empire fell into the hands of Alexander of Macedonia. Alexander's successors, the Seleucides and Romans (see Syria) lost their hold on the eastern part of the empire to the Persians, who recovered their independence with the Arsacid dynasty (2nd century BC to 3rd AD). They remained independent under the Sassanids until the 7th century, though constantly at war with the Romans and Byzantines.

[3]   After the Arab conquest reached the region in 641 (see

Saudi Arabia), Islamic thought and practices became dominant. Unlike the people in most other provinces of the Arab Empire, they retained their own language and distinctive styles in arts and literature. With the fall of the Caliphate of Baghdad, Persia attained virtual independence, first under the descendants of Tahir, the last Arab viceroy, and later under the Seleucidian Turks and the Persian dynasties. Despite political restlessness, the period was remarkably rich in cultural and scientific progress, personified by the poet, mathematician, philosopher and astronomer, Ummar al-Khayyam.

[4]   The Mongol invasion led by Hulagu Khan, that began in 1258, was an altogether different matter. Three centuries of Mongol domination brought dynastic strife between the descendants of Timur Lenk (Tamburlaine) and the Ottomans. The dispute paved the way for Persian Ismail Shah whose grandson Abbas I (1587-1629) succeeded in unifying the country. He expelled the Turks from the west, the Portuguese from the Ormuz region, and also conquered part of Afghanistan. For a short time Iran ruled a region extending from India to Syria.

[5]   The weakness of the Persian ruler or Shah during frequent Anglo-Russian interventions in Iran and Afghanistan encouraged a strong nationalist movement, ideologically influenced by Syrian Pan-Islamic intellectuals.

[6]   A 1909 treaty divided the country into two areas - one of Russian and the other of British economic influence. A British firm was given the opportunity to exploit Iranian petroleum fields. Military occupation by the two powers during World War I, in addition to government corruption and inefficiency, led to the 1921 revolution headed by journalist Sayyid Tabatabai and Reza Khan, commander of the national guard.

[7]   Reza, the revolution's war minister, became prime minister in 1923. Two years later, the National Assembly dismissed Tabatabai, and Reza ousted the shah, occupying the throne himself. Reza repealed all treaties granting extra-territorial rights to foreign powers, abolished the obligatory

use of the veil by women, reformed the education and health systems, and cancelled oil concessions that favored the British.

[8]   His attempt to establish a militarily strong, internationally neutral modern state, that became known as Iran in 1935, met with strenuous resistance from European powers. Reza Shah insisted in maintaining strict neutrality, rejecting a July 1941 ultimatum demanding passage for allied arms to the Soviet Union through Iranian territory. In August, British and Soviet forces invaded, forcing the Iranian army to surrender in September. The shah was overthrown and sent into exile after abdicating in favor of his son, Muhammad Reza Pahlevi. Educated in Europe and more amenable to European interests, the new ruler governed under Anglo-Soviet tutelage until the end of the war.

[9]   A 1949 constitution curtailed the Shah's authority, and progressive, nationalist forces won seats in parliament. With their support, Prime Minister Muhammad Mossadegh attempted to nationalize oil reserves and expropriate the Anglo-Iranian Oil Company.

[10]   Mossadegh maintained that it was 'better to be independent and produce only one ton of oil a year than produce 32 million tons and continue as slaves of England',

despite the fact that Britain had other sources of supply in the Arab states, Venezuela and the US, while Iran had no alternative market. Mossadegh's audacity was met in 1953 by an economic blockade and a coup backed by the US Central Intelligence Agency (CIA) which returned almost absolute power to the shah. This chain of events was accompanied by the killing of nationalists and left-wing activists. Thousands were imprisoned. Mossadegh remained in prison until his death in 1967.

[11]   The Shah's power depended principally on the oil economy. He encouraged multinational penetration of Iran, citing 'modernization' which effectively consisted of promoting Western consumer habits.

[12]   Westernization was resisted by Islamic clergy who feared encroaching secularism, and by those social sectors most affected, notably small farmers and the urban poor. By the end of the 1970s, the growing power of foreign enterprises in the domestic market, plus rapidly changing consumption patterns, had lost the Shah the sympathies of the powerful commercial and industrial elites known locally as the 'bazaar'.

[13]   Opposition groups included the National Front founded by Mossadegh, the Tudeh Communist Party, and Fedayin (Marxist) and Mujahedin (Islamic) guerrillas -

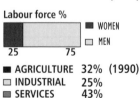

(1996)

Labour force %
- ■ WOMEN
- □ MEN

25   75

- ■ AGRICULTURE 32% (1990)
- □ INDUSTRIAL 25%
- ■ SERVICES 43%

Maternal Mortality

1990

PER 100,000
LIVE BIRTHS

120

Foreign Trade

MILLIONS $ 1996

IMPORTS
13,926

EXPORTS
22,102

Food Dependency

1970
7%

1994
16%

each using a different strategy. The most effective opposition was centered around the Muslim leader Ayatollah Ruhollah Khomeini, exiled in 1964. Khomeini was resident in Iraq for many years until the Shah, irritated by political ferment in Iranian mosques, pressured the Iraqi Government into deporting him to France.

[14] The recordings of Khomeini's preaching in Paris became well-known and encouraged the masses to organize. During 1977, demonstrations began in secondary schools and by 1978 became generalized. The Shah was forced to flee in January 1979 and Khomeini made a triumphant return to Iran. On February 11 1979 crowds invaded the imperial palace; the Shah's prime minister resigned, and a divided army accepted the new state of affairs. The Islamic Revolution, seen as a successful alternative to both socialist and capitalist Western models, was welcomed enthusiastically, not only in Iran but throughout the Muslim world.

[15] Prime Minister Mehdi Bazargan of the National Front sought to reconcile Muslim traditions with a model of progressive development permitting broad participation. However he was supported neither by the revolutionary left nor by the Muslim fundamentalists. The latter, bolstered by the 'revolutionary guards' and Khomeini's popularity, first excluded their former left-wing and right-wing allies and then proceeded to suppress them harshly.

[16] In early November 1979, a student group stormed the US embassy in Tehran, taking the diplomatic personnel hostage. Documents found inside provided evidence of CIA involvement in Iranian politics. In April 1980, a US attempt to rescue the hostages was unsuccessful.

[17] On July 17 1980, the shah died in Egypt and lengthy negotiations began for release of the hostages.

MILITARY EXPENDITURE

MILITARY (as % of health and education expenditures-1990/91) **38%**

This was finally accomplished on January 20 1981.

[18] In September 1980, Iran and Iraq went to war which lasted for eight years.

[19] The Islamic Revolutionary Party (IRP) won the presidential elections with more than 90 per cent of the vote in 1981. On August 30, violent incidents and bombings caused the death of 72 political leaders, among them President Muhammad Ali Rajai and Prime Minister Muhammad Javad Bahonar. A new president, Ali Khamenei, former secretary-general of the IRP, was elected.

[20] The clergy held a favored position, and the government made widespread use of imprisonment, exile and execution for both political opponents and common criminals. Government sources registered 500 executions in 1989 - mostly for drug trafficking.

[21] In 1985, the country made great commercial profits, despite the possibility of war with its neighbour. Their main clients were West Germany, Japan, Switzerland, Sweden, Italy and the Arab Emirates, with petroleum being the main export product, constituting 98 per cent of exports.

[22] Contrary to Western expectations, the death of Ayatollah Khomeini on June 3 1989 did not lead to widespread chaos and instability. As more than eight million, mostly poor mourners, gathered to bury Khomeini, President Ali Sayed Khameini was appointed Iran's spiritual leader by a vote of the Assembly of Experts.

[23] In August, new elections gave a landslide victory to Hojatoleslam Ali Akbar Hashemi Rafsanjani, ex-Speaker of Parliament, and now president. The new constitution enhanced the president's role and Rafsanjani took office as a fully empowered president rather than a ceremonial one. Iran's international image deteriorated when Khameini sentenced Indo-British writer, Salman Rushdie, to death, stating that the writer's book 'The Satanic Verses was blasphemous. Rushdie went into hiding, but in late 1990, he made a few public appearances, reconfirmed his Islamic faith and became reconciled with the main

PROFILE

ENVIRONMENT

Central Iran is a steppe-like plateau with a hostile climate, surrounded by deserts and mountains (the Zagros on the western border and the Elburz to the north). Underground water irrigates the oases where several varieties of grain and fruit trees are cultivated. The shores of the Caspian Sea are more humid and suited to tropical and subtropical crops (cotton, sugar cane and rice). Modern industries (petrochemicals, textiles, building) expanded during the time of Shah Pahlevi, but the industry of hand-made rugs and other materials remain an important activity. Deforestation is occuring in the last remaining forested areas along the Caspian Sea and in the western mountain region, the sea was heavily polluted during the Gulf War, threatening marine life, and there is air pollution from automobile exhaust emissions, industry and oil refineries, especially in urban areas.

SOCIETY

Peoples: The Persians 45 per cent, Azeris 16 per cent, Kurds 9 per cent, Gilakis 5 per cent, Luris 4 per cent, Mazandaranis 3.6%, Balochis 2.2 per cent, Arabs 2.2 per cent, Turkmenis 1.5 per cent, Armenians 0.5 per cent.
Religions: Mainly Islamic, with the Shi'a clearly predominant (93.4 per cent). Iran's Islamic constitution permits other Muslim groups (5.7 per cent), as well as Catholics (0.1 per cent), Jews (0.1 per cent) and Zoroastrians (0.1 per cent) to practice their religions. Members of the Bah'ai sect (0.6 per cent) suffered persecution in the early years of the Islamic revolution.
Languages: Persian (official), and languages of ethnic minorities.
Political Parties: Movement for the Liberation of Iran; Communist Party (Toudeh); National Front. The Revolutionary Council of the Resistance, People's Mujahedin Movement, Movement for the Independence of Kurdistan, and others.

THE STATE

Official Name: Dshumhurije Islâmije Irân.
Administrative divisions: 23 provinces, 472 towns and 499 municipalities.
Capital: Teheran (Tehran), 6,830,000 people (1995).
Other cities: Mashhad, 1, 760,000 people Isfahan, 1,128,000; Tabriz, 1,090,000 (1991).
Government: Presidential republic. Mohammad Khatami, President since May 1997. Religious power is exercised by Ali Sayed Khamenei. Legislature: Islamic Consultative Assembly (single-chamber), with 270 members elected by direct popular vote every four years. The members of parliament are elected by secret, universal ballot.
National Holiday: February 11, Revolution Day (1979).
Armed Forces: 513,000 (1995).
Other: BASIJ 'Popular Mobilization Army' volunteers, mostly youths: strength has been as high as 1 million during periods of offensive operations; Gendarmerie: (45,000 border guards).

Islamic authorities. However, the Iranian clergy have not lifted the death sentence (*fatwa*), and Rushdie remains in hiding.

[24] In 1990, Iran condemned the Iraqi invasion of Kuwait, taking advantage of the situation to negotiate previous border disputes. Iraq withdrew from 2,600 square kilometres of occupied Iranian territory, prisoners of war were exchanged, and the countries' sovereignty

over the Shatt-al Arab canal was divided. Iran remained neutral when hostilities broke out in 1991.

[25] The election of Rafsanjani to the country's presidency meant a strengthening of the "pro-Western" wing in the regime. According to the Iranian Constitution, religious and lay authorities share power. But, unlike his predecessor Ruholah Khomeini, Ali Khamenei was appointed supreme leader but not

PER CAPITA

$303

69%

STATISTICS

DEMOGRAPHY
Population: 69,975,000 (1996) **Annual growth:** 3.6% (1980/1996) **Estimates for year 2000:** 76,400,000 **Annual growth to year 2000:** 2.3% (1994/2000) **Urban Population:** 59.5% (1996) **Children per woman:** 4.9 (1996).

HEALTH
Life expectancy at birth: 69 years (1996) **Infant mortality:** 33 per 1,000 (1996) **Under-5 child mortality:** 37 per 1,000 (1996) **Calorie consumption:** 125% (1988/90) **Safe water:** 90% (1990/96).

EDUCATION
Literacy: 69% (1995) male : 78% (1995) female: 59% (1995) **School enrolment :** Primary total: 101% (1990/95) male : 104% (1990/95) female: 97% (1990/95) Secondary: male : 76% (1990/95) female: 62% (1990/95) Tertiary: 15% (1995) **Primary school teachers:** one for every 32 students (1995).

COMMUNICATIONS
20 **newspapers**, 237 **radios**, 120 **TV sets** and 66 **main telephone lines** per 1,000 people (1994) **Books:** 16 new titles per 100,000 people (1992/94).

ECONOMY
Annual growth, GNP: 0.6% (1995/96) **Consumer price index:** 236.0 (1994) **Currency:** 1,748 rials = $ 1 (1995) **Cereal imports:** 5,450 metric tons (1994) **Food import dependency:** 16% (1994) **Fertilizer use:** 561 kgs per ha (1994) **Exports:** $ 22,102 million (1996) **Imports:** $ 13,926 million (1996) **External debt:** $ 21,183 million (1996) $ 303 **per capita:** (1996) **Development aid received:** $ 183 million (1995) $ 3 per capita (1995) 0.2% of GNP (1994).

HDI (rank / value) 70 / 0.78 (1994)

Great Ayatollah. The old ayatollah, Araki, bore that responsibility.
[26] Sectors hostile to the West were pre-eminent, but did not have a two-thirds majority in the *Majlis* (Parliament), therefore having no power to change presidential resolutions. The Revolutionary Guards meanwhile were merged into the army, depriving the anti-West sectors of an important pressure group.
[27] Iranian neutrality during the Gulf War was designed to gain advantages over Baghdad, but also to gain acceptance in regional and international diplomacy. Diplomatic relations with Britain were renewed in 1990 and with Saudi Arabia in March 1991, during the Gulf War.
[28] This rapprochement with the West, and the refusal to openly support Iraq during the US offensive, affected relations with other Muslim groups in the region. Iran's lack of support to the Shi'a

rebellion in Iraq at the end of the War, disappointed those sectors which regarded Tehran as the capital of Shi'a expansion.
[29] In 1990, a five-year plan was approved to organize the country's economy and diversify its sources of foreign currency. Foreign investors were however wary of the revolutionary leadership and no foreign capital could be attracted to Iran. That year, the Government announced that foreign debt accounted for 12 per cent of the GDP in 1990.
[30] The much-desired normalization of relations between Iran and the West was hindered by the use of violence by groups linked to Tehran. The secretary of Chaput Bakhtiar, Shah Reza Pahlevi's former prime minister, was assassinated in April 1991. Bakhtiar himself was killed in May.
[31] With the disintegration of the Soviet Union, a new area of

influence lay open to Iran. In 1991, Tehran opened embassies in the Islamic republics of the Caucasus and Central Asia, signing trade and cultural agreements and opening new means of communications with its neighbors.
[32] Iran's biggest step taken in its rapprochement with the West was the release of ten hostages held by pro-Iranian forces in Lebanon, in a process which lasted throughout 1991. However, in early 1992, the upper echelons of the more than 2.000 revolutionary guards sent to Lebanon to organize the Hezbollah (Party of God), assured Iran would not cease its fight against the great enemy of the region, the US.
[33] Also in early 1992, the Rafsanjani government announced plans to privatize some major companies, previously nationalized by the Islamic revolution in 1979. This was seen as an attempt to attract foreign capital or Iranian investors abroad.
[34] On April 10 1992, legislative elections were held, with the "moderates" that supported President Rafsanjani winning a clear victory over the "radical" candidates.
[35] In July, Khamenei, Iran's spiritual leader, launched a campaign to "eradicate Western influence", clashing with Rafsanjani and his more moderate vision of Islam to such an extent that the president threatened to resign.
[36] However in June 1993, Rafsanjani was confirmed President by 63 per cent of the vote. The high rate of abstentions - 41 per cent of the country's 29 million voters - was read as a sign of discontent over corruption.
[37] In February 1994 - at a time of great tension among the different leading groups - a failed attempt was made on Rafsanjani's life during the celebration of the 15th anniversary of the Islamic Revolution. Disagreements with Saudi Arabia regarding the Muslim'annual pilgrimage to Mecca - Islam's main holy site, in Saudi territory -. affected relations with the government of King Fahd and reflected once more the struggle between the two states for the world leadership of Islamic states.
[38] In the economic field, the results did not turn out as expected. Oil sales between March

1994 and March 1995 amounted to $10.5 billion, compared to $17.7 billion in the previous year. Meanwhile, the Government stopped subsidizing 23 imported products, mostly food and medicine, which led to rising prices in Iran.
[39] Oil annual sales rose to $15 billion in March 1996, but was less than expected and less than the amount sold two years before. Inflation and the loss of purchasing power caused growing discontent in the population.
[40] In July, the US toughened its sanctions against Iran, blaming the country for terrorist actions. The measure proposed was challenged by the international community. At the time, unemployment in Iran reached 10 per cent of the working people.
[41] In the May 23 1997 elections, with a 90 per cent turnout of voters, the winner with 69 per cent of the vote was Mohammad Khatami, regarded as the most pro-Western candidate. A new government took over in August and Khatami announced it would open up the country to the West.
[42] The judicial decision to confiscate the property of influential ayatollah Hussein Ali Montazeri, a presidential ally and critic of Khamenei, revealed the power struggle between Montazeri's followers and those of the spiritual leader. Demonstrations of support were held in several Iranian cities for Khamenei, who was ratified in his position. Montazeri had criticized the leader's power, which interfered in State matters.
[43] Israel was criticized for its "expansionist policy" at the Islamic conference held in Teheran in December 1997. The declaration also condemned "terrorism", in what was regarded as a "favourable point" for Khatami in the power struggle within Iran.
[44] Masoume Ebtekar, vice-president of environmental affairs in Iran, denounced the oppressive conditions in which the women of Afghanistan were living under the Islamic regime of the Taliban. The statement took place on March 8 1998, International Women's Day. In Iran, in contrast with conservative Muslim countries, women have the right to vote and hold decision-making positions.

Iraq

'Iraq

Population: 20,607,000 (1996)
Area: 438,317 SQ KM
Capital: Baghdad

Currency: Dinars
Language: Arabic

1 Neutral Zone   Kurdistan   0   300 km

The territory of present-day Iraq was the cradle of the Sumerian civilization around 4000 BC. Over the centuries it was the home of a series of prestigious civilizations; the Akkad, Babylonian, and Assyrian or Chaldean. Known as Mesopotamia, from the Greek, 'between rivers', it was a crossroads for innumerable migrations and conquest expeditions; Hittites, Mitannians, Persians, Greeks, Romans and Byzantines all passed through the territory, leaving behind more destruction than cultural heritage.

2   In the 7th century the Arab conquest transformed Mesopotamia into the center of an enormous empire (see Saudi Arabia). A century later, the new Abbas dynasty decided to move the capital east from Damascus. Caliph al-Mansur built the new capital, Baghdad, on the banks of the Tigris and for three centuries the city of the 'thousand and one nights' was the center of a new culture.

3   This culture led to the greatest flourishing of the arts and sciences in the Mediterranean region since the days of the Greeks. The empire began to fall apart after the death of Harun al-Raschid. The African provinces were lost (see Tunisia: Islam in North Africa), and the region north and east of Persia won independence under the Tahiris (the Kingdom of Khorasan). The caliphs depended increasingly on armies of slaves or mercenaries (Sudanese or Turks) to retain their grip on an ever-shrinking empire. When the Mongols assassinated the last caliph in Baghdad in 1258, the title had already lost its political meaning. The conquests of Genghis Khan devastated the

region's agricultural economy, and the region was subsequently ruled in whole or part by Seleucids, Ottomans, Turks, Mongols, Turkomans, Tartars, and Kurds. The movement of steppe peoples (see Afghanistan), brought great instability to the fertile crescent, which finally achieved unification under the Ottoman Turks in the 16th century, having repelled an attack by Timur Lenk (Tamburlaine) in the 14th century.

4   A subsequent period of relative calm gave the people a chance to reorganize the economy. Irrigation systems were rebuilt and arable areas were expanded.

5   In the early 20th century, Arab Renaissance movements were active in Iraq, paving the way for the rebellion that rocked the Turkish realm during World War I (see Saudi Arabia, Jordan and Syria). The British already had a foothold in the region and were keen to expand their influence. With the defeat of the Turks, Iraq entertained hopes of independence. These however were dashed when the revolutionary Soviet government revealed the existence of the secret Sykes-Picot treaty (signed in 1916), whereby France and Britain divided the Arab territories between themselves. Faisal, son of the shereef Hussein, had proclaimed himself King of Syria and occupied Damascus. However, since this territory 'belonged' to the French, who had promised nothing to the Arabs, (see Saudi Arabia, Jordan and Syria), he was forcibly evicted. In 1920, Britain was awarded a mandate over Mesopotamia by the League of Nations, triggering a pro-independence rebellion.

6   In 1921, Emir Faisal ibn Hussain was appointed King of Iraq, in compensation for his previous bad treatment. In 1930, general Nuri as-Said was appointed Prime Minister, signing a treaty of alliance with the British, under which the country would become nominally independent on October 3 1932.

7   That year, the Baghdad Pact was founded, making Iraq part of a military alliance with Turkey, Pakistan, Iran, Britain and the US. This pact was resisted by all Iraqi nationalists. In July 1958, anti-imperialist agitation resulted in a

military coup led by Abdul Karim Kassim, bringing about the execution of the royal family.

8   In 1959 the regime tried to forge a union with Syria, but the Communist Party - one of the most important in the East - and the democrats, whose model was the European parliamentary system, opposed the move. In July, in an attempt to consolidate the regime, Kassim banned all political parties and proclaimed that the emirate of Kuwait belonged to Iraq. The Arab League, dominated by Egypt, authorized the deployment of British troops to protect the oil rich enclave.

9   Kassim's over-exaggerated ties with the Soviet Union and China fomented predictions that Iraq could become 'a new Cuba'. In the summer of 1960 the country suddenly moved towards the West. Steps toward economic change were taken, a land reform program was implemented, and the profits of the Iraq Petroleum Company were severely restricted. In 1963, Kassim was deposed by pan-Arabian sectors within the army. Several unstable governments ensued until July 17 1968, when a military coup placed the Ba'ath party in power.

10   Founded in 1947, the Arab Ba'ath Socialist Party (*ba'ath* meaning renaissance) was inspired

by the ideal of Pan-Arabism, regarding the Arab World as an indivisible political and economic unit' where no country 'can be self-sufficient'. The Ba'athists proclaim that 'socialism is a need which emerges from the very core of Arab nationalism. It is organized on a 'national' (Arab) level, having several 'regional' leaders in each country.

11   Iraq nationalized foreign companies, and Baghdad defended the use of oil as a 'political weapon in the struggle against imperialism and Zionism'. It insisted on protected prices and the consolidation of OPEC as an organization which would support the struggle of the Third World for the recovery and enhancement of its natural resources. A land reform program was decreed, and ambitious development plans encouraged the reinvestment of oil money into national industrialization.

12   In 1970, the Baghdad government gave the Kurdish language official status, and granted Kurdistan domestic autonomy. However, abetted by the Shah of Iran, and fearful of land reform, the traditional leaders rose in armed confrontation. In March 1975, the Iran-Iraq border agreement deprived the Kurds of their main foreign support and the rebels

PROFILE

ENVIRONMENT
The Mesopotamian region, between the rivers Tigris and Euphrates (Al-Furat) in the center of the country, is suitable for agriculture, and contains most of the population. In the mountainous areas in the north, in Kurdistan, there are important oil deposits. In Lower Mesopotamia, on the Shatt-al-Arab channel, where the Tigris and the Euphrates merge, 15 million palm trees produce 80 per cent of the world's dates which were sold worldwide, before the blockade. The war's devastation included the destruction of the major part of the country's infrastructure. Tank and troop movements caused profound damage to road surfaces and soil, especially in the environmentally sensitive area along the Saudi Arabian border.

SOCIETY
Peoples: Iraqis are mostly Arab; 20 per cent belong to a Kurdish minority living in the north.
Religions: Mainly Islamic. Most of the Shi'a Muslims (62 per cent) live in the south. In the center, Sunni Arabs predominate, and they share a common religion with the Kurds in the north. 35 per cent of Iraqi population is Sunni.
Languages: Arabic (official and predominant); in Kurdistan it is regarded as a second language, after Kurdish.
Political Parties: The Arab Ba'ath Socialist Party has been in power since 1968; the Kurdistan Democratic Party; the Kurdistan Fatherland Party.
Social Organizations: The General Federation of Trade Unions of Iraq.

THE STATE
Official Name: Al-Jumhuriyah al-'Iraqiyah.
Administrative divisions: 15 provinces and 3 autonomous regions.
Capital: Baghdad, 4,478,000 people (1995).
Other cities: Diyala, 961,073 people; Al-Basrah, 406, 296; Irbil, 485,968; Mosul, 664,221.
Government: Saddam Hussein, President since 1979 and Prime Minister since 1994.
National Holidays: July 14, Proclamation of the Republic (1958); July 17, Revolution Day (1968).
Armed Forces: There are no official figures.

STATISTICS

DEMOGRAPHY
Population: 20,607,000 (1996) **Annual growth:** 2.9% (1980/1996) **Estimates for year 2000:** 23,100,000 **Annual growth to year 2000:** 2.7% (1994/2000) **Urban population:** 75.0% (1996) **Children per woman:** 5.4 (1996).

HEALTH
Life expectancy at birth: 61 years (1996) male: 56 years (1994) female: 58 years (1994) **Infant mortality:** 94 per 1,000 (1996) **Under-5 child mortality:** 122 per 1,000 (1996) **Calorie consumption:** 128% (1988/90) 1,667 **people per doctor** (1988/91) **Safe water:** 78% (1990/96).

EDUCATION
Literacy: 58% (1995) male : 71% (1995) female: 45% (1995) **School enrolment :** Primary total: 91% (1990/95) male : 98% (1990/95) female: 83% (1990/95) Secondary: male : 53% (1990/95) female: 34% (1990/95) **Primary school teachers:** one for every 22 students (1995).

COMMUNICATIONS
30 **newspapers**, 218 **radios**, 70 **TV sets** and 34 **main telephone lines** per 1,000 people (1994).

ECONOMY
Currency: 0.31 dinars = $ 1 (1995) **Cereal imports:** 1,099 metric tons (1994) **Food import dependency:** 32% (1994) **Fertilizer use:** 653 kgs per ha (1994) **Exports:** $ 502 million (1996) **Imports:** $ 492 million (1996) **Development aid received** $ 326 million (1995) $ 16 per capita (1995) 1.6% of GNP (1994).

HDI (rank / value) 126 / 0.531 (1994)

---

were defeated. The Baghdad government decreed the teaching of Kurdish in local schools, greater state investment in the region, and the appointment of Kurds to key administrative positions.
[13] On July 16 1979, President Ahmed Hassan al-Bakr resigned because of ill-health. He was replaced by Vice-President Saddam Hussein.
[14] Saddam Hussein tried to establish himself as leader of the Arab world. He was one of the most outspoken critics of the 1979 Camp David agreements between Egypt, Israel and the US, but Iraqi relations with other Arab countries still worsened. A branch of the Ba'ath party took over power in Syria in 1970, but its discrepancies with Baghdad led to rivalry and some border disputes.
[15] These issues encouraged the Iraqi forces to wage attacks on Iranian positions. They were confident of a quick victory but in the event the war lasted for eight years.

[16] In 1981, claiming that Iraq intended to produce atomic weapons, Israeli planes bombed the nuclear power station at Tamuz, which had been built with French assistance.
[17] During the war, Saudis and Kuwaitis, who had benefited from Iraq acting as a bulwark against Iranian fundamentalism, granted Baghdad many loans, which were used both in the conflict and for strengthening the country's infrastructure. An oil pipeline was built through Turkey as an alternative to the one which crossed Syria to the Mediterranean; Syria had closed this in sympathy with Iran. The roads to Jordan were also improved.
[18] In November 1984, 17 years after they had broken off diplomatic relations, official links with the US were re-established. Despite American declarations of neutrality in the Iran-Iraq conflict, events disclosed the superpower's doublespeak. The 'Iran-contra' scandal made this clear.
[19] The 1988 armistice meant that Iraq retained 2,600 square kilometres of Iranian territory with its powerful and skilful army. Apart from refusing to establish export quotas, Kuwait also

extracted more oil than it was allowed to from deposits under the border. As the US declarations seemed to state that they would remain neutral in the event of conflict, Baghdad thought that it would be able to retaliate against the West by occupying the neighboring territory and exploiting its wealth. On August 2, Iraq invaded Kuwait and took thousands of foreign hostages.
[20] Four days later the UN decided on a total economic and military blockade until Iraq unconditionally retreated from the occupied territory. Withdrawal was rejected, but a proposal for an international conference to discuss the Middle East issue was submitted. When Iraq started to release the hostages and to make new attempts at negotiating, the US refused to talk and demanded an unconditional surrender.
[21] On January 17 1991, an alliance of 32 countries led by the US started attacks on Iraq. When the land offensive began in March, Saddam Hussein had already announced his unconditional

withdrawal. The Iraqi army did not resist the offensive and hardly attempted to stage an organized withdrawal, yet it suffered great losses. The war ended early in March, with the total defeat of the Iraqis.
[22] At the end of the offensive, the US encouraged an internal revolt of the southern Shi'a and of the northern Kurds so that Saddam Hussein would be deposed. However, the political differences between these factions made an alliance impossible, and Washington abandoned the rebels to their own devices, whereupon they were crushed by the still powerful Iraqi army. Over one million Kurds sought refuge in Iran and Turkey to escape the Baghdad forces, and thousands starved or froze to death when winter came.
[23] Between 150,000 and 200,000 people, mostly civilians, died in the war. As a result of the blockade - still in force - some 70,000 more may have died in the first year, among them 20,000 children. At the end of 1991, both the Turkish and Iraqi armies were continuing

to harass the Kurds in the border area.

24 According to documents captured after the war and publicized by human rights organization Middle East Watch, the Iraqi Government used chemical warfare against the Kurds in an attempt to exterminate them toward the end of the 1980s. Specific reference was made to the attack on Halabja in March 1988, in which 5,000 Kurdish civilians were killed.

25 The conditions stipulated for lifting sanctions became even more demanding with the increased determination on the part of the US Government to bring down Hussein. In addition, The New York Times and the Sunday Telegraph (London) reported that the United States had introduced huge amounts of counterfeit dinars (Iraq's currency), smuggled across the Jordanian, Saudi Arabian, Turkish and Iranian borders. Baghdad established the death penalty for anyone participating in these operations.

26 Toward the end of 1991, the Iraqi Government authorized UN inspections of military centres. In 1992, Iraq was found to have a uranium enrichment project, which had been developed using German technology. UN inspection teams destroyed 460 x 122mm warheads armed with sarin, a poisonous gas. They also dismantled the nuclear complex at al-Athir, the uranium enrichment installations at Ash-Sharqat and Tarmiuah, and the chemical weapons plant at Muthana.

27 In 1992 and 1993, the United States carried out several missile attacks on military targets and factories near Baghdad. They also bombed Iraqi troops along the border with Kuwait, recovering weapons abandoned by the retreating Iraqis. When Bill Clinton assumed the presidency of the United States, the Iraqi Government asked for a cease-fire. They put no conditions on further UN inspections.

28 During 1994, the pressure on Iraq continued in an attempt to force Baghdad to recognize the new frontier with Kuwait, amongst other things, but according to President Saddam Hussein this awarded a small part of Iraqi territory to the neighboring country.

29 This same year a frontier crossing was opened with Turkey to allow certain UN authorized foodstuffs and medicines to enter the country - the only exceptions to the trade embargo. However, a few months later, in March 1995, Turkish troops invaded Iraqi Kurdistan - under the military protection of 'allied' - basically US - troops to repress members of the Kurdish Workers' Party (PKK) which was launching attacks from there on Turkish troops stationed in Turkish Kurdistan.

30 The international isolation of Baghdad became even more serious in 1996, when Jordan distanced itself from Saddam's Government, as relations with Kuwait and Saudi Arabia improved. These two countries continued pressurising the United States not to lift the embargo on Iraq, amongst other reasons, because Saudi oil had replaced Iraqi's in several markets. However, the UN Security Council voted for the partial lifting of sanctions, allowing the controlled sale of crude oil, in order to buy the food and medicines needed by the Iraqi population.

31 In April 1997, a UN report revealed that the number of people dying from hunger as a result of the embargo had passed the million mark, and 570,000 of these were children. Meanwhile, UNICEF stated 25 per cent of children aged less than five years old were suffering from severe clinical malnutrition.

32 In October, Iraq was at the centre of a new crisis. The Security Council threatened to impose fresh sanctions if a new inspection were not authorised to verify the Saddam Government was not able to produce chemical and biological weapons. Iraq rejected the presence of US inspectors, which made Clinton dig in his heels. The agreements reached in Baghdad by UN Secretary-General Kofi Annan, in March 1998, reduced the tension, allowing fresh inspections to get underway.

Kurds: from nomadism to nationalism

The Kurds are an ethnic and linguistic group living mostly in the mountains of Taurus, in eastern Anatolia (Turkey), in the regions of Zagros and Khorasan (Iran), and in northern Iraq. It is estimated that, including the communities existing in Armenia, Georgia, Kazakhstan, Lebanon and Syria, they number more than 15 million people. For centuries they have been nomads in the Mesopotamian plains and the mountain regions of Iran and Turkey, raising sheep and goats. Exceptionally, they have also been farmers. After World War I, many were forced to live in urban areas, leaving their traditions behind.

Although the Kurds have lived in the same geographic region for a long time, they have never had a national state. The Treaty of Sèvres, which was concluded in 1920 and granted autonomy to Kurdistan, was never ratified. It was followed in 1923 by the Lausanne Treaty, which no longer mentioned Kurdistan nor the Kurds. After the war, the region was engulfed by violence, with the appearance of armed separatist movements .

For centuries, the Kurds had a form of social government which followed the rules of the tribe. The sheikh was the main authority. This holds true even today, although not as much in urban groups which have lost some of their tribal identity while adaptating to city life. In some cases, and even when the law does not allow it, as in Turkey, the Kurds practise polygamy.

In Turkey, Government discrimination against the Kurds is widespread. Their identity has been denied by calling them "mountain Turks", their language is banned (and regarded as a dialect derived from Turkish) as are some of their most typical customs. The Government repressed their political activity in the Eastern provinces and also encouraged their migration to urban areas in the west, in order to disperse Kurds concentrated in mountain areas.

In Iran they are subject to strong pressure by the Government to assimilate into the majority culture and religious persecution from the Shia majority.

In Iraq, when the monarchy was defeated in 1958, the Kurds expected their linguistic status would be acknowledged and thought they would receive more social benefits and greater participation in development projects. However, these expectations were not fulfilled. Instead, the Iraqi Government implemented a policy of displacement, promoted armed conflicts and, in the 1980s, used lethal chemical weapons against whole communities. Over a period of 15 years, more than 400,000 Kurds died in Iraq.

Kurdish nationalism has begun to appear not just as a response to these discriminatory conditions. Its late emergence can perhaps be attributed to their ancient nomadic lifestyle. In a way, this nationalism is prompted by certain Western influences (such as private property), the partition of the Kurdistan region into states, and the appearance of an urban intellectual minority. The interests of some Western countries in the Persian Gulf have played a part as well.

Ireland

Eire

Population:	3,554,000 (1996)
Area:	70,284 SQ KM
Capital:	Dublin
Currency:	Pounds
Language:	Irish and English

The religious tensions in Irish history date back to the 17th century when a large number of British Protestants (in particular, Scottish Presbyterians) were encouraged to settle in the province of Ulster in the northern part of the island by the English colonial rulers. They subjugated the native Catholic population, Celtic peoples who had been converted to Christianity in the early 5th century.

[2] By virtue of the 1800 Act of Union, Ireland was incorporated into the United Kingdom. During the 19th century most of the population outside the Protestant-dominated North-east supported independence, which led to the formation of a strong nationalist movement.

[3] In 1916, the republican Easter Rising in Dublin was crushed by the occupying forces but it marked the foundation of the Irish Republican Army (IRA) and the final stage of the long struggle for freedom.

[4] The IRA's campaign of guerrilla warfare forced the British in 1920 to grant independence to the 26 counties with Catholic majorities. Southern Ireland became a self-governing region within the UK. The remaining six north-eastern counties became Northern Ireland, with a devolved government in Belfast and representation in the British parliament in Westminster. In 1922 Southern Ireland had declared independence and become the Irish Free State, a dominion under the British crown. In 1949 the Free State became the Irish Republic, formally breaking its final links with the British commonwealth.

[5] The 1937 Irish Constitution considers Ireland to be a single country, where all the inhabitants - North and South - have citizenship rights.

[6] Supported by the Protestant majority, the Ulster Unionist Party always managed to retain control of the Parliament in Belfast. For 50 years, Northern Ireland was ruled exclusively by Unionists, led by the Provincial Prime Minister and a Governor acting as a representative of the British Crown.

[7] The Catholic minority in Northern Ireland was thus excluded from domestic political affairs, and many other fields. This led to the creation of an active civil rights movement in the 1960s.

[8] Although it was non-violent, the extremist Protestant groups considered the civil rights movement a threat to the region's status and their dominant position and they reacted to it with violence.

[9] In April 1969, amidst growing disturbances, the Northern Ireland government requested British troops to protect the region's strategic installations. In August, Belfast and London agreed that all the Province's security forces should come under British command.

[10] As a counterpart to the Provisional IRA, the "loyalists" (loyal to the British crown) formed a number of paramilitary organizations, including the Ulster Volunteer Force and the Ulster Defence Association. Between 1969 and the middle of 1994, more than 3,100 people died at the hands of the Protestant and Catholic paramilitaries, the British army and the Ulster police force, the Royal Ulster Constabulary (RUC). In 1972 political status was given to paramilitary prisoners, but this amendment was abolished in 1976.

[11] The growing violence provoked London to take over full responsibility for the maintenance of law and order in Northern Ireland. The government in Belfast was abolished and a system of "direct rule" from Westminster installed. In a plebiscite held in March 1973, 60 per cent of the population of Northern Ireland voted in favour of union with Britain.

[12] At the end of 1973, a Northern Irish Assembly and Executive was created in Belfast in which Protestant and Catholic representatives were supposed to share power.

[13] In December, the London and Dublin governments agreed on the establishment of an Irish Council. Both this agreement and the new power-sharing Assembly were bitterly opposed by most Protestants in Ulster. In 1974, the Protestant Ulster Workers' Council declared a general strike in Northern Ireland. This resulted in the resignation of the Executive and London took over direct government once more.

[14] In the 1973 election in the Irish Republic, Fianna Fáil - a conservative nationalist party which had been in power for 44 years - was defeated. A coalition between the conservative Fine Gael and the Labour Party took office. This new government was committed to power-sharing between the two communities in Ulster, but it rejected the immediate withdrawal of British troops from the region.

[15] In 1976, after the IRA murdered the British ambassador in Dublin, the Irish Government took stricter anti-terrorist measures. Fianna Fáil was elected in 1977 and it maintained the friendly relations with London established by the previous administration. Prime Minister Jack Lynch supported the creation of a devolved government in the North, instead of total unification.

PUBLIC EXPENDITURE

3%   61.6%
1995 ■ DEFENCE □ SOCIAL

In 1990/91 Military as % of health & education expenditure was 12%.

WORKERS

UNEMPLOYMENT 11.9% (1996)

Labour force %

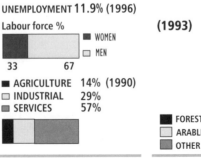

■ WOMEN
□ MEN

33   67

■ AGRICULTURE	14%	(1990)
□ INDUSTRIAL	29%	
■ SERVICES	57%	

LAND USE

(1993)

■ FOREST & WOODLAND	4.6%
□ ARABLE	13.1%
■ OTHER	82.3%

PER 100,000
LIVE BIRTHS

10

IMPORTS
35,750
EXPORTS
45,565

PROFILE

ENVIRONMENT
The country comprises most of the island of Ireland. The south is made up of rocky hills, none exceeding 1,000 meters in height. The central plain extends from east to west and is irrigated by many rivers and lakes. With a humid ocean climate and poor soil, much of the country is covered with grazing land. Farming is concentrated mainly along the eastern slopes of the hills and the Shannon valleys. The main agricultural products are wheat, barley, oats, potatoes and beet. Meat and milk processing are among the major local industrial activities.

SOCIETY
Peoples: The Irish comprise 94 per cent of the population, with a small English minority. The great famines which struck the island over the last two centuries, led to the emigration of about 4 million Irish people, especially to the US.
Religions: 91.6 per cent Catholic, 2.3 per cent Anglican, 0.4 per cent Presbyterian (1991).
Languages: Irish and English.
Political Parties: The conservative Fine Gael, linked to the rural population. The nationalist, conservative Fianna Fáil. The progressive Democrats. The center-leftist Labour Party; Sinn Féin, socialist and the political wing of the IRA; the Communist Party, and the Workers' Party, socialist.
Social Organizations: The Irish Congress of Trade Unions, with 600,000 members, amounts to 45 per cent of the economically active population.

THE STATE
Official Name: Poblacht na h'Eireann.
Administrative Divisions: 26 Counties.
Capital: Dublin, 1,021,449 people (city and county) (1991).
Other cities: Cork 127,024 people; Limerick 52,040; Galway 50,842; Waterford, 40,345 (1991).
Government: Mary McAleese, President since November 1997, elected through direct vote. Prime Minister Bertie Ahern, since June 1997. Bicameral parliament (*Oireachtas*); 166-member Chamber of Deputies (*Dail*), 60-member Senate (*Seanad*).
National Holiday: March 17 (St Patrick's Day).
Armed Forces: 12,900 (1995).

[16] In August 1979, Dublin agreed to increase border security after the murders, on the same day, of Lord Mountbatten (a prominent British public figure related to the Royal Family) in the Irish Republic, and 18 British soldiers in Warrenpoint, Northern Ireland. In December, Lynch resigned and was replaced by former prime minister Charles Haughey, who went back to the old idea of reunification with some form of autonomy in Ulster.

[17] The Irish Council of Womens' Affairs was created in 1972. The weight of Catholic tradition has been a hindrance to women's liberation. Women in both parts of Ireland had to travel to England to have an abortion, and in the Irish Republic the sale of contraceptives was limited to licensed outlets.

[18] In 1983, a controversial referendum in the Republic approved the outlawing of abortion under the Irish constitution. The law against divorce, in force for 60 years, was maintained in spite of the Government's proposal to revoke it.

[19] In 1980 there were talks between the heads of the Irish and British governments. This led to the formation of the Anglo-Irish Intergovernmental Council a year later, with the aim of holding ministerial level meetings.

[20] Discussions between the British and Irish governments finally led to the signing of the Anglo-Irish Agreement in 1985, under which the Dublin Government had some influence on the political, legal, security and border affairs of Northern Ireland. A majority of Protestants remained strongly opposed to the Agreement, although it guaranteed that the constitutional position of Northern Ireland was subject to the will of the majority of its population.

[21] In 1988, Dublin and London quarrelled over the British Government's refusal to investigate members of the RUC accused of shooting at terrorist suspects before attempting to arrest them.

[22] At the same time, an inquest was started in the Ulster Defence Regiment (UDR), a locally-recruited, part-time British Army regiment, which is dominated by Protestants, over the death of six IRA members in 1982.

[23] During the first months of 1989 a new wave of violence broke out. In April, three members of the paramilitary Ulster Defence Association were arrested in Paris together with a South African diplomat. Pretoria was supposedly supplying them with arms in exchange for secret British missile technology stolen from a Belfast arms production plant.

[24] In September 1989, the Irish Government demanded a complete review of the UDR, in particular of their links with the Protestant paramilitaries and the leaking of intelligence documents on Republican suspects. The United Kingdom accepted the Irish demands and as a result 94 UDR soldiers were arrested.

[25] In the Republic during the 1980s, unemployment ran high - an average of 16.4 per cent between 1983 and 1988 - and so did emigration. The country also faced spiralling inflation and industrial recession. A strict austerity program, implemented since 1987, brought about economic growth, and a significant decrease in inflation.

[26] In May 1987, Ireland reaffirmed its EC commitments through a national referendum. The Single Europe Act was approved by 69.9 per cent of the electorate.

[27] Since joining the EC in 1973, Community aid has played an important role in the economy of the Irish Republic, one of the poorest EC members.

[28] Irish women accounted for 38.5 per cent of the labour force in 1987; only one country in Western Europe had a smaller proportion of women in paid employment.

[29] In 1990, the General Synod of the Church of Ireland approved the ordination of female priests in the country. This decision placed the Church of Ireland ahead of most other Anglican churches.

[30] In November 1990, academic lawyer Mary Robinson was elected President of the Republic, the first-ever woman to be elected to this post. An independent candidate, supported by the Labour Party, the Political Association of Women and the trade unions, Robinson gained 52 per cent of the vote.

[31] In a country that is predominantly Catholic and overwhelmingly conservative, Mary Robinson has spoken out in defence of gay and womens' rights and the legal recognition of illegitimate children.

[32] In April 1991, multiparty negotiations began in Belfast, in another attempt to define Northern Ireland's political future. These were the first important talks to be held since 1974. Representatives of Ulster's main "constitutional" parties participated (Protestant Unionists, Catholic nationalists and the small non-sectarian Alliance Party), as did representatives of the government in London. Sinn Féin, the political wing of the Provisional IRA, which supported the immediate withdrawal of British troops, the disarming of the RUC and the reunification of Ireland, was excluded from the talks due to their refusal to condemn the IRA's campaign of violence.

[33] Opinion polls released in London at the time of the peace talks showed that most Britons favoured the withdrawal of British troops from Ulster.

[34] In January 1992, the IRA launched one of its major offensives, in Ulster and in England. In County Tyrone, Northern Ireland, the IRA killed seven Protestant construction workers, stating that, as they were working on British Army barracks, they were considered to be "collaborating with the occupiers". Republicans also carried out a series of arson attacks in Ulster on commercial establishments.

[35] From late 1991, there was a sharp increase in attacks on Catholics by Protestant paramilitary groups. These groups vowed to retaliate for each IRA attack with "an eye for an eye".

[36] In response to the demands of Protestant politicians and in order to confront the escalating violence, London sent several hundred military reinforcements to Ulster. They joined the 11,000 British troops already stationed there, as well as the 6,000 volunteers of the Ulster Defence Regiment, and the 12,000-strong police force.

[37] In March 1992, the issue of abortion hit the headlines. A 14 year-old girl who became pregnant as the result of a rape was forbidden by the High Court from travelling to England for an abortion. It was estimated that up to 4,000 Irish women per year have abortions in Britain as the operation is forbidden under the Irish constitution. The case of the 14 year-old girl went before the Supreme Court, provoking demonstrations from both pro-choice and anti-abortion groups, and calls for another referendum on abortion. The Supreme Court eventually overturned the High

STATISTICS

DEMOGRAPHY
Population: 3,554,000 (1996) **Annual growth:** 0.3% (1980/1996) **Estimates for year 2000:** 4,000,000 **Annual growth to year 2000:** 0.2% (1994/2000) **Urban Population:** 57.7% (1996) **Urban growth:** 0.48% (1980/95) **Children per woman:** 1.9 (1996).

HEALTH
Life expectancy at birth: 76 years (1996) male: 74 years (1994) female: 79 years (1994) **Infant mortality:** 6 per 1,000 (1996) **Under-5 child mortality:** 7 per 1,000 (1996) **Calorie consumption:** 157% (1988/90) 633 **people per doctor** (1988/91).

EDUCATION
School enrolment: Primary total: 104% (1990/95) male: 104% (1990/95) female: 104% (1990/95) Secondary: male: 110% (1990/95) female: 115% (1990/95) Tertiary: 37% (1995) **Primary school teachers:** one for every 23 students (1995).

COMMUNICATIONS
170 **newspapers**, 636 **radios**, 320 **TV sets** and 350 **main telephone lines** per 1,000 people (1994)

ECONOMY
Per capita, GNP: $ 17,110 (1996) **Annual growth, GNP:** 8.7% (1995/96) **Annual inflation:** 2.5% (1985/95) **Consumer price index:** 110.5 (1994) **Currency:** 0.62 pounds = $ 1 (1995) **Cereal imports:** 444 metric tons (1994) **Fertilizer use:** 5,717 kgs per ha (1994) **Exports:** $ 45,565 million (1996) **Imports:** $ 35,750 million (1996)

ENERGY
Consumption: 3,136.63 Kgs of Oil equivalent per capita yearly (1994) 68.48% imported (1994)

HDI (rank / value) 17 / 0.929 (1994)

Court decision, and the girl was allowed out of the country. The case raised important issues with regards to the relationship between the Irish constitution and European Community law, which guarantees the freedom of movement of EC citizens within member nations.

[38] In mid-July 1992, 69 per cent of the Irish population voted in favour of ratifying the Maastricht Treaty and the further integration of the European Community. This figure exceeded all expectations, with 57 per cent of the electorate participating in the vote.

[39] In January 1993, Albert Reynolds, of Fianna Fail, was confirmed as head of government, despite the fact that his party and the Fine Gael had lost seats to the Labour Party in the last election.

[40] In the meantime, a plebiscite was held on the abortion issue. Two-thirds of the voters pronounced themselves in favor of the right to have access to information on methods for interrupting pregnancy, as well as the right to travel abroad for an abortion. However, the electorate voted against legalizing abortion, except in cases where the mother's life is in danger.

[41] In 1993, with the reduction in workers in the rural and traditional industry sectors, unemployment reached 20 per cent, while the GDP grew due to an increase in exports, especially high-tech goods.

[42] The government lifted broadcasting restrictions on the Sinn Fein in early 1994. In August, the IRA declared a complete cessation of military operations, a gesture which enabled political talks to take place on the island.

[43] In November, the Reynolds administration collapsed after the Labour Party withdrew its support following a controversy over long delays in the extradition - to Northern Ireland - of a paedophile priest. Reynolds was succeeded as prime minister by John Bruton from Fine Gael, with support from the Labour Party and the democratic left.

[44] The government coalition achieved political and social stability in 1995. The February budget was advantageous for civil servants, small business and low-waged workers while economic growth amounted to 5.25 per cent.

[45] The Catholic Church continued to be the target of accusations regarding priests who molested children. In Dublin, the archbishop publicly confessed he had used part of the diocese's funds to pay off one of the clergy's victims. Meanwhile, the Supreme Court authorized doctors to inform women about abortion clinics abroad. In a close referendum, the Irish approved (with 50 per cent to 49 per cent of the vote) a constitutional reform which allowed the divorce of couples who have been separated for a period of 4 years.

[46] Bruton established an excellent relationship with British prime minister John Major, while also having close ties with Ulster's John Hume, SDLP leader, and Gerry Adams, president of Sinn Féin. Prince Charles' mid-year visit enhanced the need for links between England and Ireland. The opposition limited itself to staging peaceful demonstrations. Late in the year, the visit of United States president Bill Clinton had an encouraging effect on the parties to find a formula which would solve the armed conflict.

[47] The Prime Minister took part in a round of talks in Belfast in June 1996. Bruton supported Britain's initiative to exclude Sinn Féin representatives from the negotiations since both governments believed IRA behaviour - which in February had ended the unilateral truce observed since August 1994 with bombings in mainland UK - had made no contributions to peace.

[48] The Irish economy performed well this year, with an increase in consumption, sustained growth and the creation of jobs. The livestock sector was affected by the "mad cow" disease, BSE, which reduced exports to Russia and the Middle East.

[49] In April 1997, a series of attacks announced by the IRA against public thoroughfares, train stations and airports paralyzed the British transport system in the middle of the electoral period. Sinn Féin asked the IRA to call another cease-fire, which they did in July. In September, negotiations were restarted with the participation of Sinn Féin.

[50] The legislative election in June 1997 brought Bertie Ahern's Fianna Fáil to power, taking 77 of the 166 seats - followed by the Fine Gael with 54. The Labour Party took 17. The coalition with the Progressive Democrats (4 seats) did not provide the overall majority needed to constitute a centre-right government. Meanwhile, Sinn Féin gained one seat in a county in the north of the country. On June 26, Parliament named Ahern prime minister.

[51] In September, President Mary Robinson left her post to a presidential commission until a successor could be elected. On November 11, Mary McAleese of the Fianna Fáil took over the presidency. Four of the five contenders for the post were women. The economy continued to perform well this year, and the annual inflation rate was only 1 per cent, the lowest in the European Union.

[52] The abortion debate was reopened at the end of that year, following a ruling by a children's court allowing a girl to travel to Britain to terminate a pregnancy resulting from rape.

[53] On April 10 1998, following hard negotiations, Catholic separatists and Protestant unionists reached a peace agreement over Ulster in Belfast. The document, negotiated by eight political parties with the backing of London, Dublin and Washington, proposed limited autonomy for Northern Ireland with the creation of a legislative assembly and north-south co-operation bodies. The plan also stipulated the disarmament of the paramilitary organizations represented by political parties in the negotiations, and the freeing of prisoners.

[54] The majority of the political parties, including Sinn Féin, were in favour of the agreement in principle. The pact overcame a first obstacle when the Protestant Unionist leader, David Trimble, secured the agreement of his party, the Ulster Unionists. Only two extremist Protestant parties, the Reverend Ian Paisley's Democratic Unionist Party and Robert McCartney's UK Unionist Party, were opposed to the move.

[55] At the end of May a referendum ratified the agreement in both Ulster and Ireland. A month later, the first elections to integrate the Assembly were held, and in February 1999 the new institutions are to be established. The agreement left the door open for the Ulster people to decide the future of the Province in the polls - whether to reunite with Ireland or stay in the UK.

[56] In August 1998 a bomb in Omagh killed about 30 people, causing the fragile peace process to falter.

Israel

Yisra´el

Population: 5,664,000 (1996)
Area: 21,056 SQ KM
Capital: Jerusalem/Tel Aviv

Currency: New shekels
Language: Hebrew and Arabic

In 1896 Viennese journalist Theodor Herzl published a book entitled The Jewish State. Influenced by the European nationalism which had engendered the unification of Germany and the Italian Risorgimento, Herzl envisaged a Jewish nation-state which would put an end to anti-Semitic acts, like the Russian pogroms and the Dreyfus Affair (a spy case in France).

[2] This Jewish state was to be established in Palestine, then a Turkish colony. The name "Palestine" inspired the suffering Jews of Eastern Europe, who dreamed of the return to Zion, the land of the ancient kingdoms of Israel. Zion is the name of a hill in Jerusalem; by extension it became a synonym for Jerusalem itself and then for the whole of Palestine. But the Zionists, as Herzl's followers began to be called, preferred to ignore the fact that half a million Arabs had been living there for over 1,000 years, naturally becoming attached to their land and traditions.

[3] Zionism firmly pursued a policy of forming alliances with the great capitalist powers, denying the peoples of Palestine their national identity - the precise right the Jews claimed for themselves. This ideology was born out of the same Eurocentric womb that produced the English colonialist, explorer, and magnate Cecil Rhodes, French statesman and colonialist Jules Ferry, and Chancellor Otto von Bismarck, the godfather of German imperialism. Zionism has never been able to rid itself of this heritage, although it has always contained left wing and socialist sectors.

[4] During World War I, Britain and France agreed to divide up the remains of the Ottoman Empire in the Middle East. In 1917, British Foreign Secretary Arthur Balfour declared his support for the establishment of a national homeland for the Jewish people in Palestine, although Prime Minister in 1905 he had opposed Jewish immigration into Britain. The Balfour Declaration stated "that nothing shall be done which may prejudice the civil and religious rights of existing non-Jewish communities in Palestine"; these groups made up 90 per cent of the population.

[5] At the end of World War II, the French colonies of Syria and Lebanon and the British colonies of Iraq and Transjordan obtained their independence. But Britain retained control of Palestine, based on its commitment under the Balfour Declaration.

[6] Zionists regard Jews the world over to be exiles, and they organized migration to Israel from all corners of the globe. At the beginning of this century there were 500,000 Arabs and 50,000 Jews living in Palestine. By the 1930s, the number of Jews had risen to 300,000. The anti-Semitic persecutions in Nazi Germany raised immigration above the legally permitted quotas, alarming the British, who saw their power in Palestine threatened.

[7] In 1939 London declared that its aim was not to set up a Jewish state but an independent, binational Palestinian state with both peoples sharing government. Ships bringing refugees from Hitler's Europe were turned back from Palestinian ports. The Zionists organized acts of sabotage and terrorism, using force to hold Britain to its promise.

[8] Using donations from Jews all over the world, the Zionists purchased Arab lands from wealthy absentee owners living in Beirut or Paris, who cared little about the fate of their tenants, the Palestinian fellahin. The Jews then arrived, deeds in hand, to expel peasant families whose ancestors had lived there for untold generations. They set up agricultural colonies, kibbutzim, defended by armed Zionist militia.

[9] In February 1947, in view of intensified anti-British attacks, London submitted the Palestinian problem to the United Nations. A special committee recommended partition of the territory into two independent states; one Arab, the other Jewish. Jerusalem would remain under international administration.

[10] The Soviet Union preferred a Jewish state to continued British military presence, and its support was decisive in the creation of Israel. At the same time, London and Washington considered the partition unfeasible. US Secretary of Defense James Forrestal proposed that President Harry Truman send troops to impose a

OCCUPIED BY ISRAEL
1	Syria - Golan Heights - occupied in 1967
2	Southern Lebanon - occupied in 1983
3	West Bank - occupied in 1967
4	Gaza Strip - occupied in 1967
⊙	Recovered by Palestine from 1994: Gaza Strip, Jericho, Nablus, Ramallah

PUBLIC EXPENDITURE

19.4%   **57.5 %**
1995 ■ DEFENCE ☐ SOCIAL

In **1990/91** Military as % of health & education expenditure was 106%.

WORKERS

UNEMPLOYMENT 6.7% (1996)

Labour force %
■ WOMEN
☐ MEN
40   60

■ AGRICULTURE   4% (1990)
☐ INDUSTRIAL   29%
■ SERVICES   67%

IMPORTS
29,796
EXPORTS
20,504

PER 100,000
LIVE BIRTHS
7

PROFILE

ENVIRONMENT

Israel has 20,770 sq km, within the pre-1967 borders (see Palestine). These territories are currently occupied, both militarily and with settlements of Jewish colonists: Golan Heights (Syria) 1,150 sq km, West Bank 5,879 sq km, Gaza Strip 378 sq km, Greater Jerusalem 70 sq km The land comprises four natural regions: the coastal plains, with a Mediterranean climate, the country's agricultural center; a central hilly and mountainous region, stretching from Galilee to Judea; the western lowlands, bound on the north by the Jordan River, which flows into the Dead Sea; and the Negev Desert, to the south, which covers half of the total territory. The main agricultural products are citrus fruits for export, grapes, vegetables, cotton, beet, potatoes and wheat. There is considerable livestock production. Industrial production is growing rapidly and there are serious difficulties with water; the country has over 2,000 sq km of irrigated land - part of the Negev has been reclaimed through irrigation. Pollution, caused by both industrial and domestic waste, as well as pesticides, is also an important problem.

SOCIETY

Peoples: Jewish, 81.4 per cent; Arab and other, 18.6 per cent.
Religions: Judaism. Arabs are Moslem and Christian.
Languages: Hebrew and Arabic are official. English is used for business. Native languages of immigrants (notably Yiddish and Russian) are also spoken.
Political Parties: The Zionist left is made up of the Labor Party, and the Meretz (a front which includes three parties). The non-Zionist left is made up of Hadash (formerly Communist) and the Democratic Arab Party. The Zionist right is formed by Likud; the Tehiya (Renaissance); the Tsomet and the Moledet. The religious parties are: the Shas; the Agudat-Israel (the League of Israel); the National Religious Party and the Degel Hatora.
Social Organizations: The Histadrut Haoudim Haleumit (National Labor Federation) is the main trade union.

THE STATE

Official Name: Medinat Yisra'el (Hebrew); Isra'il (Arabic).
Administrative divisions: 6 districts, 31 municipalities, 115 local councils and 49 regional councils.
Capital: In 1980, Jerusalem (591,400 people in 1996) was proclaimed the "sole and indivisible" capital of Israel. The UN condemned this decision and most diplomatic missions are in Tel Aviv.
Other cities: Haifa, 252,300 people; Tel Aviv-Jaffa, 355,900; Holon, 163,900 (1996).
Government: Esser Weizman, President. Binyamin Netanyahu, Prime Minister since May 1996. Parliamentary system of government.
National Holiday: 7-V, Independence (1948).
Armed Forces: 175,000 (1996). **Other:** Border Police: 6,000; Coast Guard: 50.

UN trusteeship over the territory of Palestine.

[11] The UN General Assembly finally approved the partition plan in a 33 to 13 vote, there were 10 abstentions and the Arab countries and India voted against partition. Armed Zionist organizations seized control of major cities and towns and began to expel Palestinians en masse, alleging an imminent attack

by Arab armies. This policy culminated in a massacre at the village of Deir Yasin in April 1948, when its entire population was murdered by the Irgun, an extremist group led by Menachem Begin.

[12] On May 14, 1948, the British high commissioner withdrew from Palestine, and David Ben Gurion proclaimed the state of Israel. The

Jordanian, Egyptian, Syrian, Iraqi and Lebanese armies attacked immediately, and the governments of those countries urged the Palestinians to abandon their possessions and take refuge.

[13] The war ended with an armistice in January 1949, granting Israel 40 per cent more territory than it was due under the partition plan. Soviet weapons and aircraft, purchased in Czechoslovakia, proved decisive in the Israeli victory.

[14] Israel's government changed sides during the cold war and formed a permanent strategic alliance with the United States. This alliance was not forged easily nor immediately.

[15] In 1956, when Israeli troops, backed by France and Britain, invaded Egypt in response to the nationalization of the Suez Canal, the United States and the Soviet Union both firmly opposed the move, and the expeditionary force had to be withdrawn.

[16] The diaries of former Prime Minister Moshe Sharett, published posthumously, revealed that Israel used Zionist agents to sabotage Western targets in Cairo, forcing US President Dwight Eisenhower to opt for Tel Aviv and not Cairo as its principal Middle East ally. The episode is known as the Lavon affair.

[17] In the 1960s, Egyptian President Gamal Abdel Nasser was deprived of US credit and arms, and he turned to the Soviet Union. This was enough to produce closer relations between Israel and Washington.

[18] In the 1967 Six Day War, Israel carried out a lightning strike, using North American weaponry, and seizing the whole of Palestine, the Syrian Golan Heights and Egyptian Sinai.

[19] Paradoxically, this military victory undermined Israel's moral strength; the newborn state was transformed into an expansionist power in control of areas housing thousands of Palestinians.

[20] Resolution 242 of the UN Security Council, passed on November 22, 1967, called on Israel to withdraw from the occupied territories. Israel refused, claiming that it needed "secure borders" in order to resist Arab threats to its existence.

[21] Armed conflict broke out again in 1973, when Egyptian troops crossed the Suez Canal and ended the myth of Israeli military invincibility. In truth, by the time armistice was decreed, battlefield positions had hardly changed.

[22] In 1977, Menachem Begin was elected Prime Minister, breaking with the political and ideological continuity of the previous governments. For the first time in the history of the Israeli state, the Labor Party was not in power.

[23] Begin's victory resulted partly from growing social tension between Ashkenazim (economically and culturally privileged Jews of European origin who are traditionally Labor supporters) and Sephardim (Eastern Jews from Arab countries.

[24] The oriental Jews, who culturally had more in common with the Arabs than with European Jews, made up 55 per cent of the population, but their average income was just two-thirds that of the Ashkenazis. Their resentment of the Ashkenazim, aggravated to the point of fanaticism, provides the electoral basis for the political right.

[25] Begin completely rejected the idea of negotiating with the Palestine Liberation Organization (PLO) and expressed his intention to annex the West Bank. Meanwhile in 1977, the US persuaded Egyptian President Anwar Sadat to sign the Camp David Agreement, leading to peace between Cairo and Tel Aviv and the return of Sinai to Egypt.

[26] From then on, international attention gradually shifted from the issue of secure borders for Israel to the plight of the Palestinians. Changing tactics, the PLO gained sympathy and allies, so that when Jerusalem was declared the capital of Israel in 1980, the move was condemned as an arrogant gesture by many of Israel's supporters.

[27] In June 1982, the Israelis launched "Operation Peace for Galilee," invading Lebanon and devastating Beirut, under the pretext that these were manoeuvres to stop infiltration by Palestinian guerrilla groups. PLO combatants agreed to evacuate the city in exchange for the deployment of a joint force of Italians, French, and North Americans to guarantee the security of Palestinian civilians.

[28] In spite of the agreement, hundreds of Palestinians in the Sabra and Shatila refugee camps, in Israeli-controlled areas, were murdered by right-wing militia with Israeli complicity. The invasion of Lebanon fomented dissent in Israel, and 400,000 people attended a demonstration sponsored by the group Peace Now. Begin was forced to appoint a commission of inquiry which found Defense Minister Ariel Sharon and other military leaders "indirectly responsible" for the massacres.

[29] After the September 1984 elections, the Labor Party, headed by Shimon Peres, was able to form a government, though lacking an absolute majority. Its coalition included Likud, and the agreement stipulated that the leader of that party, Yitzhak Shamir, would assume the prime minister's post in 1986.

30 At the end of 1987, several young Palestinians were killed in a clash with Israeli military patrols in the occupied West Bank. The funerals turned into protest demonstrations and led to further confrontations, deaths, and general strikes - civil protests where people refuse to leave their homes. This marked the beginning of the intifada or uprising, and Middle Eastern politics were deeply disturbed from the least expected quarter: the unarmed grassroots. In 1989, during the last National Palestine Congress, the PLO recognized the State of Israel, accepting UN resolutions 242 and 338.

31 Images of young Palestinians, armed with slingshots, confronting the mighty Israeli army were televised worldwide, ruining Israel's international standing. This development came as quite a shock for a state founded on the basis of international solidarity.

32 The most apparent outcome of the questioning of Israeli credibility is that 250,000 young Israelis leave the country each year. Negative net migration throughout the 1980s was balanced only in 1989 with the massive immigration of Jews from the Soviet Union. Since its creation as a solution to the Jewish issue, the state of Israel has managed to attract only 20 per cent of the world's Jews.

33 According to US sources, their aid to Israel between 1949 and 1991 totalled $53 billion. In the 1979 Camp David Agreements, the figure reached $40 billion, 21.5 per cent of all US foreign aid.

34 In Israel military service is mandatory for both women (two years) and men (three years). All men up to the age of 51, and unmarried women up to age 24, belong to the reserve. The militarization of society also results in a high level of state interference in the economy and in an enormous weight of war industry on the country's production figures.

35 In its search for markets,

Israel has become an arms exporter involved in scandalous deals like the "Iran-Contras" scheme, supplying arms to Iran. It has also provided military training for Colombian drug militias.

36 Demographically, the Israeli idea of a stable Jewish nation state is contradicted by the government's expansionist practices. Successive territorial annexations have incorporated some two million Arabs into the present territory of Israel. By simple demographic progression, without including the Palestinians in exile, Arab inhabitants will outnumber the Jewish population by the end of the century.

37 In March 1990, these fundamental problems combined with other differences to produce a split in the Labor-Likud alliance.

38 Everything changed when Iraq invaded Kuwait, on August 2, 1990. Israel was excluded from the anti-Iraq coalition led by the United States, because if it had participated, the Arab countries would not have joined. Israel made preparations for war regardless, and a state of siege was declared in the occupied territories.

39 On January 17, in answer to the initiation of Allied bombing, Iraq launched several missile attacks against Israel. Their aim was to try and force Israel to enter the war. However, Israel did not join the war, leaving defence to Patriot anti-missile units manned by American troops. Israel's defence was out of its own hands for the first time in its history.

40 The Iraqis could not establish a direct link between a solution to their conflict and the larger Arab-Israeli question, but in March a joint Soviet-US statement expressed hope of finding a negotiated solution to the Arab-Israeli conflict. The terms of the statement were vague, however, and Israel harshly rejected it.

41 When the war ended in March 1991, the US presented diplomatic circles with a "land for peace" proposal. Two months later in Damascus, Syria and Lebanon signed a "brotherhood, co-operation and co-ordination" treaty. To Israel, this treaty constituted a military threat to the "water tank" of Israel; a region in the north containing many important water sources.

42 Israel asked the United States to approve loans of $10 billion to ease its economic difficulties, caused by the resettling of between 250,000 and 400,000 Soviet Jews from 1989 to 1991.

43 The Government began transferring immigrants to new settlements on the West Bank where, in 1991, unemployment

reached 11 per cent, despite efforts to create new jobs for immigrants.

44 Wishing to launch peace negotiations in the region, the US government imposed the condition that loans granted would not be invested in settlements in occupied territories.

45 The creation of Jewish settlements and the construction of new housing for Soviet Jews on the West Bank, became a double-edged sword for Shamir's government. The US loans and new settlements were vitally important, but Palestinians and other Arabs demanded that resettlement cease, in order for the peace talks to continue.

46 On October 30, 1991, a Middle-Eastern Peace Conference was held in Madrid, sponsored by the US and the former USSR. Shortly afterwards, hundreds of thousands of Israelis demonstrated, calling upon their government to maintain a dialogue with the Palestinians and Israel's Arab neighbors. Delegations from Jordan, Lebanon, Syria and Israel attended the conference; the Palestinians formed part of the Jordanian delegation, as Israel refused to negotiate directly with Palestinian representatives.

47 The Arab countries supported the "land for peace" scheme,

though it was rejected by Israel. Israel, in turn, showed itself willing to discuss limited self government by the Palestinian population in the occupied areas, as a provisional solution for a 5-year period. This offer triggered a crisis in the Likud's coalition government, when the Tehiya and Moladet (ultra-right-wing parties) walked out of the coalition, leaving Shamir without a parliamentary majority.

48 At the joint request of Israel and the US, the UN General Assembly did away with a 1975 resolution defining Zionism as "a form of racism and racial discrimination". In February 1992, Israel bombed Palestinian refugee camps in the south of Lebanon, killing Abas Musawi, the leader of Hezbollah, a pro-Iranian group.

49 This unleashed a new wave of violence along the northern border. Israeli soldiers received orders to shoot without warning at any Palestinian bearing weapons. The appearance of "death squads" in the occupied territories was attributed to the modification of the Penal Code, which granted immunity to members of these groups.

50 On June 23 1992, Labor won a decisive victory in the general elections and Yitzhak Rabin was nominated prime minister. Construction of housing in the occupied territories came to a

STATISTICS

DEMOGRAPHY
Population: 5,664,000 (1996) **Annual growth:** 2.4% (1980/1996) **Estimates for year 2000:** 6,000,000 **Annual growth to year 2000:** 2.1% (1994/2000) **Urban Population:** 90.8% (1996) **Children per woman:** 2.8 (1996).

HEALTH
Life expectancy at birth: 77 years (1996) male: 76 years (1994) female: 79 years (1994) **Infant mortality:** 8 per 1,000 (1996) **Under-5 child mortality:** 9 per 1,000 (1996) **Calorie consumption:** 125% (1988/90).

EDUCATION
Literacy: 95% (1995) male : 97% (1995) female: 93% (1995) **School enrolment** : Primary total: 95% (1990/95) male : 95% (1990/95) female: 95% (1990/95) Secondary: male : 83% (1990/95) female: 89% (1990/95) Tertiary: 41% (1995) **Primary school teachers:** one for every 16 students (1995).

COMMUNICATIONS
280 **newspapers**, 478 **radios**, 300 **TV sets** and 394 **main telephone lines** per 1,000 people (1994) **Books:** 86 new titles per 100,000 people (1992/94).

ECONOMY
Per capita, GNP: $ 15,870 (1996) **Annual inflation:** 17.11% (1985/95) **Consumer price index:** 166.1 (1994) **Currency:** 3.14 new shekels = $ 1 (1995) **Cereal imports:** 2,311 metric tons (1994) **Fertilizer use:** 2,390 kgs per ha (1994) **Exports:** $ 20,504 million (1996) **Imports:** $ 29,796 million (1996)

ENERGY
Consumption: 2,716.70 Kgs of Oil equivalent per capita yearly (1994) 96.36% imported (1994)

HDI (rank / value) 23 / 0.913 (1994)

LAND USE

IRRIGATED 51.4 % of arable

(1993)

■ FOREST & WOODLAND	6%
☐ ARABLE	16.6%
▨ OTHER	77.4%

sudden standstill, and as a result, the United States removed the embargo on loan guarantees for Israel.

[51] The Israeli Government proceeded to "settle accounts", attacking Hezbollah bases and the Popular Front for the Liberation of Palestine, in southern Lebanon by land, sea and air. In six days, 130 people were killed, 520 wounded, 15 towns destroyed and hundreds of thousands were left homeless.

[52] On September 13 1993, after months of secret negotiations in Oslo, Norway, Israeli authorities and PLO leaders signed the Declaration of the Principles of the Interim Self-government Agreement, in Washington. This agreement foresaw the installation of a limited autonomy system for Palestinians in the Gaza Strip and the city of Jericho, for a five-year period. This agreement would subsequently be extended to include all of the West Bank.

[53] Difficulties arose in the negotiations which followed in Cairo, due to differences of opinion over border station control and water access rights. In addition, the PLO demanded the release of 1,000 political prisoners.

[54] Hamas and the pro-Iranian Hezbollah questioned the agreement. Meanwhile, Jewish settlers in the occupied territories - who had been supplied with arms by the Government - rejected the agreement out of hand, as it provided for the withdrawal of settlers and the Israeli army.

[55] It was not long before this situation erupted in violence. On February 25 1994, Baruch Goldstein, a member of Kahane Kach's ultra-right-wing Jewish movement, entered the Tomb of the Patriarchs in Hebron, armed with an M-16 rifle and massacred several dozen Palestinians who were at prayer. He was subsequently beaten to death by Palestinians.

[56] The official investigation of the Hebron massacre revealed that soldiers in the occupied territories had been under orders not to shoot against armed settlers under any circumstances. According to the investigation,

several soldiers fired into the crowd, and doors were closed blocking the victims' escape. The PLO withdrew from the negotiations demanding that the settlers turn over their arms immediately, and that the United Nations issue an official condemnation. The latter approved a statement which categorically condemned the massacre and voted for a peacekeeping force to be sent to the occupied territories.

[57] In early May 1994, Israeli Prime Minister Yitzhak Rabin and PLO leader Yasser Arafat signed an agreement in Cairo granting autonomy to Gaza and Jericho. Late that month, the Israeli army withdrew from Gaza, ending 27 years of occupation (see Palestine).

[58] Negotiations with several Arab states progressed, especially with Jordan, which signed an agreement with Tel Aviv in July ending with the "state of aggression" between the two countries. However, disagreements with Syria carried on, among other things because Israel refused to accept a full evacuation of the Golan Heights, occupied since 1967.

[59] The new situation favoured economic expansion: in 1994, the GDP grew 7 per cent and investments 20 per cent while unemployment went from 11 per cent to 7.6 per cent. The following year, economic growth continued at 7 per cent and inflation fell from 14.5 per cent to 8.5 per cent.

[60] 1995 was marked by a growing division of Israeli society regarding the peace process with the Palestinians. Anti-Rabin demonstrations were frequent and led to the Prime Minister's assassination by a young Israeli member of the far right. Shimon Peres, also from the Labour Party, took Rabin's place but was defeated in the general elections of May 1996 by right-wing leader Binyamin Netanyahu.

[61] The return to power of the conservatives hindered negotiations with Palestine and heightened tensions, putting the country on the brink of a new war in September. In the middle of that month the Government authorised the opening of a

tunnel under the Al-Aqsa mosque, the third most sacred place of Islam, violating the status quo maintained since the signing of the peace agreements and provoking a Palestinian reaction. Several Israeli soldiers and dozens of Palestinians died during the disturbances.

[62] Netanyahu, harshly critical of Rabin for having held talks with Arafat and the PLO, ended up meeting with the Palestinian leader on repeated occasions in late 1996 and early 1997 to negotiate the complete withdrawal of Israeli troops from the city of Hebron in the West Bank.

[63] In March, the Government announced its plan to build a new settlement in the Har Homa hills, on the Palestinian outskirts of Jerusalem. The Palestine Authority and the United States rejected the project, considering it contrary to the spirit and letter of the Oslo agreements. Netanyahu's firm decision to go ahead with building the settlements stalled the negotiations.

[64] Ehud Barak, a retired general, replaced Peres as leader of the Labor Party and became leader of the opposition. Peres had shown himself party to an agreement with the Likud to form a unity Government which would allow for the reopening of the peace process, totally suspended in the early months of 1997.

[65] In November, the Israeli Supreme Court authorised the continued detention of 21 Lebanese prisoners, mostly members of Hezbollah, who had already completed their sentences, to be exchanged for Israelis kidnapped in Lebanon. Earlier on, "moderate physical force" had been authorised in the handling of prisoners during interrogation. Judge Aaron Barak even stated that the violation of human rights was "obligatory" in these cases.

[66] Also in November, a large crowd in Tel Aviv commemorated the second anniversary of the assassination of Rabin, calling for lasting peace with Palestine in the biggest demonstration since 1982. In December, both Arafat and Netanyahu warned of possible unilateral action if no progress were made in the negotiations

over land occupation on the West Bank.

[67] At the end of 1997, a three day strike, calling for reforms to the welfare system and government - planned privatizations, paralyzed the public sector, transport and financial activity.

[68] The resignation of Foreign Minister, David Levy, weakened Netanyahu. An Israeli proposal to maintain control over some areas of the West Bank - the area around Jerusalem, Jewish settlements, military bases, the highways and most important sources of water - was considered "imprecise" by the United States.

[69] In February 1998, Israel tightened its anti-Syrian and Iraqi military alliance with Turkey. In the same month, Lebanon rejected an offer from Netanyahu to negotiate the withdrawal of Israeli troops from Lebanese territory, considering this withdrawal should be made totally unconditionally.

[70] Mordechai Vanunu, the Israeli technician imprisonned for revealing Israel's nuclear secrets, was moved out of solitary confinment in March for the first time in 12 years. He was allowed to leave his cell and talk to other prisoners in the jail. The attitude was credited to international pressures in favour of Vanunu, who had been kidnapped by Israeli agents in London, in 1986, and condemned to 18 years of prison.

[71] The peace process reached its lowest point in June, when Israel decided to fill its Civil Guard in the occupied territories with Jewish settlers, who already armed themselves without any kind of restriction. The Labor leader Ehud Barak, alarmed because of the collapse of a mountain due to Israeli nuclear tests and Netanyahu's delays over the second withdrawal from occupied territory, warned the region was at the verge of a blood bath. As the Prime Minister refused to call a referendum to decide the issue of withdrawal, President Ezer Weizman urged him to bring forward the elections. This was also rejected by Netanyahu.

Italy

Italia

Population:	57,226,000 (1996)
Area:	301,268 SQ KM
Capital:	Rome (Roma)
Currency:	Lire
Language:	Italian

In the 13th century BC, ancient central European peoples occupied the northern part of what is now Italy.

[2] With the fall of the Hittite empire around 900 BC the Etruscans established themselves to the north of the Tiber River. Their influence extended throughout the Po valley until the end of the 6th century, when the Celts bore down on them, destroying their territorial unity.

[3] According to legend, Romulus founded the city of Rome upon the Palatine hill in the year 753 BC. During the following century, this settlement was united with those on the Quirinal, Capitoline and Esquiline hills. The first form of government was an elective monarchy. Its powers were limited by a senate and a people's assembly of clans which held the power of imperium, or mandate to govern.

[4] There were two social classes: the patricians, who could belong to the Senate, and the plebeians, who had to band together to protect themselves from the abuses of the large landowners.

[5] Under King Tarquinius Priscus (616-578), Rome entered the Latin League. The poverty of the plebeians and the system of debt-induced slavery led to the expulsion of the kings in 509. In the 5th century, the traditional laws were written down. This "Law of the Twelve Tables" extended to the plebeians, who after a lengthy struggle had managed to win some rights.

[6] The Punic Wars against Carthage in the 3rd century allowed Rome to increase its possessions once again; in the early 2nd century, after displacing the Macedonians, Greece became a "protectorate". Within a few years, Asia Minor, the northeast of Gaul, Spain, Macedonia and Carthage (including the northern part of Africa) had fallen into Roman hands.

[7] Toward the end of the 2nd century, the Gracchi brothers, Tiberius and Gaius - both Roman representatives - were assassinated by the nobles, along with 3,000 followers, for supporting the plebeians.

[8] The Roman Empire controlled the land from the Rhine in Germany to the north of Africa, and also included the entire Iberian Peninsula, France, Britain, Central Europe and the Middle East as far as Armenia. The 2nd century brought internal disputes which plunged Rome into chaos.

[9] In 330, the Emperor Constantine transferred the capital of the Empire to Byzantium - called New Rome - and converted to Christianity. In 364, the empire split into two parts: the Western and Eastern Roman Empires.

[10] The end of the 5th century was marked by the invasions of the Mongols and other northern tribes, and by the attempts of the Byzantine Empire to recover its lost territories. In the mid-6th century, Italy became a province once again, but the Lombards conquered the northern part of the peninsula.

[11] When the capital of the empire had been transferred to Byzantium, the bishops of Rome had presented themselves as an alternative to Byzantine power with a separate power base in Rome. When the Lombard kings began taking up arms in defence

of Christianity against Rome's enemies, the bishops broke the alliance, in order to maintain their temporal power.

[12] In 754, Pope Steven II asked for help from Pepin the Short, and in exchange, crowned him king of the Franks. After the defeat of the Lombards, Pepin turned over the center of the peninsula to the Pope. Charlemagne, Pepin's son, was crowned king and emperor of Rome in 800, but the Muslim invasions which took place mid-century once again left the region without government.

[13] Between the 9th and 10th centuries, the Church formed Pontifical States in the central region, including Rome itself. In the 12th century, self-government arose in some cities because of the lack of a centralized power.

[14] In the 14th century, when the struggle intensified between the Guelfs (those who favored the Pope) and the Ghibellines (the defenders of the German empire), the Holy See was transferred to Avignon, where it remained for the next seven

papacies. Two centuries later, the prosperity and stability of cities like Venice, Genoa, Florence and Milan produced the intellectual and artistic flowering or the Renaissance.

[15] In the early 16th century, the peninsula was attacked by the French, the Spanish and the Austrians, who all craved control of Italy. In 1794, Napoleon Bonaparte entered the country expelling the Austrians. Four years later, he occupied Rome and created the Roman Republic and the Parthenopean Republic, in Naples. Only the two Italian states of Sicily and Sardinia were not under Napoleon's control, as they were governed by Victor Emmanuel I. The French Emperor rescinded the temporal power of the popes and deported Pius VII to Savona.

[16] Before the fall of Napoleon in 1815, Victor Emmanuel II named Camillo Benso di Cavour president of the council of ministers. Cavour was to be the architect of Italian unification, forging a single kingdom of Italy from those of Sardinia and Piedmont, with only Rome and

WORKERS

UNEMPLOYMENT 12.1% (1996)

Labour force %

- ■ WOMEN
- □ MEN

38	62

- ■ AGRICULTURE 9% (1990)
- □ INDUSTRIAL 31%
- ▪ SERVICES 60%

LAND USE

IRRIGATED 30 % of arable

(1993)

- ■ FOREST & WOODLAND 22.5%
- □ ARABLE 30%
- ▪ OTHER 47.5%

PROFILE

ENVIRONMENT
The northern region of the country consists of the Po River plains, which extend as far as the Alps. It is the center of the country's economic activity, having the main concentration of industry and farming. Cattle are raised throughout the peninsula; important crops include olives and grapes, with vineyards extending along the southern coastal strip. The country includes not only the peninsula - which is divided by the Apennines - but also the islands of Sicily and Sardinia.

SOCIETY
Peoples: Italians 94 per cent. Others, particularly Sardinians and German on Alto Adige and immigrants from Africa.
Religions: Predominantly Catholic. Muslims are about 700,000.
Languages: Italian (official). Several regional languages, like Neapolitan and Sicilian, are widely spoken. French is spoken in Val d'Aosta and German in Alto Adige. Immigrants speak their own languages, particularly African languages.
Political Parties: L'Ulivo (Olive Tree), center-left electoral coallition, led by Romano Prodi, bringing together the Democratic Party of the Left (DPL, former Communist Italian Party), the Italian Party of the People (IPP, former Christian Democrats), Pact for Italy (PI), the Socialist Italian Party (SIP) and the Socialist Democratic Italian Party (SDIP); National Alliance; Forza Italia, led by Silvio Berlusconi; National Alliance, neo-fascist; League of the North, a regional xenophobic party; Recontructional Communists (RC); Liberal Party (PLI); Republican Party (PRI); Southern Tyrolean Popular Party; National Federation for the Green List, ecologists.
Social Organizations: Three central unions: the CGIL; the CISL and the UIL.

THE STATE
Official Name: Repubblica Italiana.
Administrative Divisions: 20 Regions divided into 95 Provinces.
Capital: Rome (Roma), 3,000,000 people (1994).
Other cities: Milan (Milano), 3,700,000 people; Naples (Napoli), 1,200,000; Palermo 734,000; Turin (Torino), 992,000 (1994).
Government: Oscar Luigi Scalfaro, President. Romano Prodi, Prime Minister, since April 1996. Bicameral parliamentary system.
National Holiday: June 2, Anniversary of the Republic (1946).
Armed Forces: 325,150 (1996).
Other: 111,800 Carabinieri.

Maternal Mortality
1990

PER 100,000
LIVE BIRTHS
12

Venice remaining outside the realm. In 1870, the Italians invaded Rome and, given Pope Pius IX's refusal to renounce his temporal power, they confined him to the Vatican, where his successors would remain until 1929. In 1878, the King, Humberto I brought Italy into the Triple Alliance with Austria-Hungary and Germany. Italy's colonial conquest of Eritrea and Somalia, in eastern Africa, also began.
[17] In 1872, influenced by the events of the Paris Commune, Italy's first socialist organization was formed, giving rise in 1892 to the Socialist Party (PSI). The encyclical Rerum Novarum (1891) oriented Catholics towards militant unionization and the union movement grew tremendously.
[18] When World War I broke out, Italy proclaimed its neutrality;

however, in the face of growing pressure from nationalist groups on the left, it ended up declaring war against its former allies of the Triple Alliance.
[19] Benito Mussolini, who had been expelled from the PSI for supporting Italy's entry into the war, was able to manipulate resentment over the poor outcome. Through a blend of nationalism and pragmatism, he called for the unions to work towards collaboration between capital and labor, in the name of "the interests of the nation". In 1921, a group headed by Amadeo Bordiga and Antonio Gramsci split off from the PSI to form the Communist Party (PCI), leaving the PSI without its radical wing.
[20] Having confronted one government crisis after another, and following Mussolini's impressive march on Rome, Victor Emmanuel III turned over the government to Mussolini. An electoral reform, giving Mussolini's Fascist Party a majority, was denounced by socialist leader Giacomo Matteotti, who was subsequently assassinated by followers of "Il Duce" Mussolini in 1924. A new constitution established

censorship of the press; in 1929 the Pact of Letran was signed with the Vatican, re-establishing the temporal power of the popes, and thereby gaining Catholic support for the Government.
[21] Mussolini's foreign policy was directed almost exclusively toward the acquisition of colonies. In 1936, Italy invaded Ethiopia, and a year later the Italian East African Empire was formed. During the Spanish Civil War, closer ties developed with Hitler's Germany, forming the basis for what was to become the Rome-Berlin axis. In April 1939, Italian troops took Albania.
[22] During World War II, Italy declared war on France and Britain. Not only did it lose its colonies at the end of the war, but the entire peninsula became a combat zone for Germans and Allies alike. In 1943, the latter defeated Hitler's troops, and Humberto II became king.
[23] Following a referendum at the end of the war (June 1946), the monarchy was abolished and the republic of Italy was formed. Under the leadership of Alcide de Gasperi, the Christian Democrats (DC) won a relative majority and formed a government. These first elections marked the beginning of the Christian Democrats' hold on power. In May 1948, Luigi Einaudi, also of the DC, was elected Italy's first President.
[24] The 1946 International Conference authorized Italy to continue administrating Somalia (known as Italian Somaliland), a situation which continued until 1960. During the 1950s, Italy participated in the reconstruction of Europe. In 1957, it became one of the charter members of the Common Market.
[25] At the same time that the socialists were seeking closer links with the Christian Democrats, the Communist Party (PCI) embarked upon a revision of its political base under the leadership of Palmiro Togliatti. The PCI reaffirmed its belief in a democratic means toward a socialist end. During this period, the Party's influence extended into the labor unions, shaping the power structure of the General

Union of Italian Workers (CGIL). The PCI, the country's second strongest electoral force, as well as the second largest Communist Party in the Western world, defined itself in terms of "Eurocommunism", that is, communism with a European face.
[26] After successive victories at the polls, in 1961 the DC began opening up toward the left, seeking alliances with the Socialists and Social Democrats. The powerful Communist Party, in spite of its strong electoral presence, was permanently excluded from the Cabinet. The economic and institutional crises which took place during that decade led radical groups from the right and left alike to turn to violence as a means of bringing about change. The far right organized bombings to draw attention to its demands, while the Red Brigades of the Left used political kidnapping as their main tool. In 1978, the kidnapping and assassination of former prime minister Aldo Moro sealed their isolation from mainstream politics.
[27] Between 1952 and 1962, the average income of Italians doubled, as a result of the development of industry, which had come to employ 38 per cent of the national workforce. At the same time, agricultural employment dropped by 11 per cent, triggering migrations from the countryside to the cities, and from the south to the north. The industrial triangle of Milan, Turin and Genoa attracted a concentration of millions of people, living in overcrowded conditions inferior to those of the rest of Europe.
[28] According to the 1948 constitution the president of the republic, elected every seven years, is the head of state. One of their duties is to select a head of the government, the Prime Minister, who will have the support of the bicameral parliament. Until 1978, when socialist Sandro Pertini was elected, all presidents had belonged to the DC. Francesco Cossiga, elected in 1985, returned Italy to the tradition of Christian Democrat presidents.
[29] Cabinets which take lengthy

Literacy 1995

98%

STATISTICS

DEMOGRAPHY
Population: 57,226,000 (1996) **Annual growth:** 0.1% (1980/1996) **Estimates for year 2000:** 57,300,000 **Urban Population:** 66.7% (1996) **Urban growth:** 6.34% (1980/95) **Children per woman:** 1.2 (1996).

HEALTH
Life expectancy at birth: 78 years (1996) male: 75 years (1994) female: 81 years (1994) **Infant mortality:** 6 per 1,000 (1996) **Under-5 child mortality:** 7 per 1,000 (1996) **Calorie consumption:** 139% (1988/90) 211 **people per doctor** (1988/91)

EDUCATION
Literacy: 98% (1995) male : 99% (1995) female: 98% (1995) **School enrolment :** Primary total: 98% (1990/95) male : 98% (1990/95) female: 99% (1990/95) Secondary: male : 81% (1990/95) female: 82% (1990/95) Tertiary: 41% (1995) **Primary school teachers:** one for every 11 students (1995).

COMMUNICATIONS
100 **newspapers**, 802 **radios**, 430 **TV sets** and 428 **main telephone lines** per 1,000 people (1994) **Books:** 57 new titles per 100,000 people (1992/94).

ECONOMY
Per capita, GNP: $ 19,880 (1996) **Annual growth, GNP:** 0.7% (1995/96) **Annual inflation:** 5.98% (1985/95) **Consumer price index:** 121.4 (1994) **Currency:** 1,585 lire = $ 1 (1995) **Cereal imports:** 6,014 metric tons (1994) **Fertilizer use:** 1,696 kgs per ha (1994) **Exports:** $ 250,718 million (1996) **Imports:** $ 202,908 million (1996)

ENERGY
Consumption: 2,706.58 Kgs of Oil equivalent per capita yearly (1994) 80.70% imported (1994)

HDI (rank / value) 21 / 0.921 (1994)

negotiations to form generally only manage to last a few months. Charges against Christian Democrat Arnaldo Forlani's government - linking his supporters and allies to an organization called "Propaganda Due"- brought the Government down in May 1981, giving way to just over a year of government led by Republican Giovanni Spadolini.

[30] The instability of the Government, coupled with astronomical fiscal deficits and the political influence of the Mafia and the "Camorra" led many to consider the need for constitutional reform.

[31] In February 1991, the last secretary-general of the PCI proposed that the old name be changed to the Democratic Party of the Left (PDS); immediately afterwards, the PDS sought admission into the Socialist International. The PDS also called for reunification with the PSI, hoping to heal the split which had taken place 70 years earlier. In December 1991, dissenters from the official party line decided to create the "Reformed" Communist Party (PRC), using the red flag, hammer and sickle as its symbols.

[32] By the end of 1991, confrontations between DC's Cossiga and the PDS leader, Achille Occhetto worsened. In February 1992, the President and the Prime Minister dissolved Parliament, bringing the legislative elections forward.

[33] In the April 1992 elections, the DC did not achieve a parliamentary majority, the first defeat of a Christian Democratic government since 1946. Days afterwards, Prime Minister Giulio Andreotti announced the dissolution of his government and President Cossiga resigned early. At the end of May, Judge Giovanni Falcone, enemy number one of the Mafia, was killed in Sicily. This allowed the election of former president of the chamber of deputies, Oscar Scalfaro.

[34] Two months after the assassination of Judge Falcone, the Mafia killed Paolo Borsellino, who had inherited the investigation against organized crime upon Falcone's death.

[35] In October 1992, the Government presented a series of economic adjustment measures. These gave rise to a general strike in protest against the measures, with 10 million workers participating.

[36] Attorney General Antonio di Pietro launched an investigation that revealed a complex system of illegal operations which included politicians of all persuasions, entrepreneurs and the mafia. During 1993, more than a thousand political and business leaders were tried under operation "Clean Hands", including former prime ministers Bettino Craxi and Giulio Andreotti.

[37] Between 1980 and 1992, corruption deprived State coffers of some $20 billion. Because of illegal payments to officials and politicians, Italian public investments were 25 per cent more expensive than in the rest of the European Community.

[38] In April 1993, former Central Bank president, Carlo Azeglio Ciampi, was designated Prime Minister. A few days later, a plebiscite was held on electoral reform according to which three quarters of the seats in the two chambers - Senate and Deputies - would be awarded by simple majority in the electoral districts. The remaining 25 per cent would be filled by proportional representation.

[39] For the March 1994 legislative elections, within a few months, media magnate, Silvio Berlusconi created the "Forza Italia" party which, allied with Umberto Bossi's federalist Northern League and the Gianfranco Fini's neo-fascist National Alliance (NA), won an absolute majority in Parliament.

[40] Berlusconi was appointed Prime Minister in June and consolidated his popularity when "Forza Italia" triumphed in the European elections. However, relations with the Northern League, which had persistently criticised Berlusconi, and the NA "fascists", started to complicate government action.

[41] In October, the unions opposed retirement pension reforms proposed by the Prime Minister as, in their view, the reforms limited benefits, increased contributions and

"privatized" part of the system. Following a large demonstration in Rome, attended by more than a million people, Berlusconi withdrew his reform bill. In December, Bossi - who despite a poor show in the election had nearly a fifth of the deputies behind him - withdrew his support for the Government and Berlusconi resigned.

[42] Scalfaro refused to hold fresh elections, naming Berlusconi's former finance minister Lamberto Dini Prime Minister. Counting on greater support in the international financial organizations than his predecessor - he had worked in the IMF years ago - Dini formed a government of supposedly "apolitical" technocrats.

[43] Support from the Left meant the new Prime Minister was able to reform the pensions system and reduce the public deficit. As occurred with Ciampi - another technocrat prime minister who governed between 1993 and 1994 - Dini formed an alliance with the PDS in order to impose economic austerity measures.

[44] On April 21 1996, the "L'Ulivo"(Olive tree) coalition led by former Democratic Christian Romano Prodi and supported by the PDS, triumphed in the legislative elections. Prodi was

named Prime Minister and formed a government made up of prominent PDS leaders as well as well-known independent conservative personalities, like Ciampi or Dini himself. The presence of former communists in the cabinet and the support offered to the Government by the Reconstructed Communists (RC) marked the new period.

[45] A serious crisis shook the Government in October 1997. The Communist Party threatened to withdraw support from Prodi and to block approval of the 1998 budget if the Government did not reduce the working week to 35 hours. Parliamentary negotiations ended with the Government committed to a reduction of the current 40 hours per week for companies with more than 15 employees from the year 2001.

[46] The triumph of the Olive Tree coalition in the municipal elections the following month consolidated the Government position.

[47] The proposed expansion of the Aviano base in southern Italy - the biggest NATO establishment in Europe - became highly controversial after a US plane flew too low and downed a cable car killing 20 people in February 1998.

Jamaica

Jamaica

Population: 2,491,000 (1996)
Area: 10,990 SQ KM
Capital: Kingston

Currency: Jamaica Dollar
Language: English

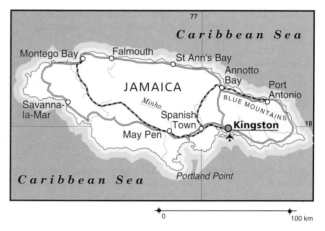

The name Jamaica apparently comes from the Arawak Indian name for the island - Xamayca. The Arawaks had pushed out the Guanahatabey, the original inhabitants, who had come from North America. The name Xamayca means "land of springs", a reference to the abundant waters of its luxuriant forests. The Arawaks lived in villages of houses made from palm branches and carried out farming and fishing activities.

[2] Columbus reached Jamaica on his second voyage to the New World in May 1494, but it was his son, Diego Colon, who conquered the island in 1509. From then on, the number of Arawaks decreased dramatically. Around 1545, Spanish historian Francisco López de Gomara wrote that "Jamaica resembles Haiti in all respects - here the Indians have also been wiped out." Some sources believe that prior to the Spanish Conquest, there may have been as many as 60,000 Arawaks.

[3] The Spanish, now absolute rulers of the island, began to plant sugar cane and cotton, and to raise cattle. There were incursions by the British in 1596 and 1636, and in 1655, 6,500 British soldiers under the command of William Penn dislodged the 1,500 Spaniards and Portuguese. Jamaica rapidly became a haven for pirates who ravaged Spanish trade in the Caribbean. The last important enemies that the English had to face on the island were the enclaves of rebel slaves or "quilombos", hidden in remote areas like the Blue Mountains. In 1760 a general rebellion in the colony was put down, and in 1795 a further revolution shook the island.

[4] By the late 19th century there were approximately 800 sugar mills and more than 1,000 cattle ranches in Jamaica. The economy was built on the labor of 200,000 slaves brought from Africa. Anti-slavery and anti-colonial rebellions of the 18th and 19th centuries were followed by labor union struggles in the first few decades of the 20th century. The two large contemporary political parties, the Labor Party and the People's National Party both grew out of workers' organizations. Independence was proclaimed in 1962, but successive Labor governments failed to rescue the economy from foreign hands.

[5] In 1942 rich deposits of bauxite were discovered, and the aluminium transnationals: ALCOA, ALCAN, Reynolds and Kaiser quickly established themselves on the island. The sugar industry was replaced by bauxite exploitation.

[6] The transnationals exploited Jamaica's bauxite by shipping the raw metal out of the country, making all the decisions on production, and paying minimal customs duties.

[7] After independence in 1962, a few plants were built to transform bauxite into aluminum, but the bulk of the mineral extracted continued to be shipped unprocessed to the US. In 1973, Jamaica was the second largest producer of bauxite in the world. The mineral accounted for half of the country's exports but employed only one per cent of the labor force. Transnationals' earnings were not reinvested in the country. Export and import duties were reduced as the transportation of the mineral was classified as an internal transfer, with preferential taxation rates.

[8] The People's National Party (PNP) won the 1972 elections and in 1974 the new Prime Minister, Michael Manley, raised the bauxite export tax. In addition, he began negotiations with the foreign companies to recover the third of the nation owned by them, and to assert greater control over their activities.

[9] At the same time, the PNP Government strongly supported Caribbean integration. A bi-national bauxite marketing company was created with Venezuela. Jamaica became a member of the Caribbean Multinational Merchant Fleet with Cuba and Costa Rica. Together, the associates devised ways to prevent penetration by US capital.

[10] These progressive measures were resisted by the mining companies and by local conservative forces who sought to upset the December 1976 elections. The PNP won anyway, with an overwhelming victory at the polls and an increased majority in parliament. Manley advocated socialism within the existing constitutional structure.

[11] Jamaica took active part in the Movement of Non-Aligned Countries. It also supported anti-colonial positions at all world forums and proclaimed its unconditional solidarity with all liberation movements, particularly those of southern Africa.

[12] This stand strained relations with the US. As a result, the transnational mining companies reduced their production, transferring operations to Guinea.

Export revenues fell, and with them, funding for government social programs.

[13] In 1979, the Government was forced to seek loans from the IMF, which imposed harsh conditions. In February 1980, Manley announced that he was suspending negotiations with the Fund since meeting its requirements would mean a drastic reduction in living standards for the population. That year elections were held ahead of schedule, in a climate of destabilization generated by the right-wing opposition, which finally won a landslide victory. The new Labor government, headed by Edward Seaga, expelled the Cuban ambassador and imposed neo-liberal economic policies, opening the country to unconditional foreign investment and even suggesting that it might request Jamaica's admittance to the United States. The results were counterproductive: between 1981 and 1983, unemployment increased, bauxite production continued to decline, inflation rose and the foreign debt doubled.

[14] In November 1983, Jamaica was one of the small group of Caribbean countries that gave diplomatic support and symbolic military assistance to the invasion of Grenada. A month later, taking advantage of the favourable political atmosphere, Seaga decided to call early parliamentary elections. The PNP boycotted the elections, accusing the Government of not having fulfilled a previous commitment to update the electoral register and reorganize the system of voter identification, so as to avoid rigging. Only the

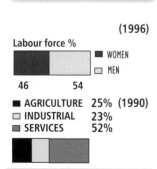

WORKERS

Labour force % (1996)

■ WOMEN
□ MEN

46   54

■ AGRICULTURE 25% (1990)
□ INDUSTRIAL 23%
■ SERVICES 52%

LAND USE

DEFORESTATION -5.3% annual (81/90)
IRRIGATED 22.6% of arable

(1993)

■ FOREST & WOODLAND 16.8%
□ ARABLE 14.1%
■ OTHER 69.1%

Maternal Mortality

1990

PER 100,000
LIVE BIRTHS

120

Food Dependency

1970

22%

1994

10%

STATISTICS

DEMOGRAPHY
Population: 2,491,000 (1996) **Annual growth:** 1% (1980/1996) **Estimates for year 2000:** 2,600,000 **Annual growth to year 2000:** 0.9% (1994/2000) **Urban Population:** 54.2% (1996) **Urban growth:** 2.2% (1980/95) **Children per woman:** 2.5 (1996).

HEALTH
Life expectancy at birth: 74 years (1996) male: 72 years (1994) female: 76 years (1994) **Infant mortality:** 10 per 1,000 (1996) **Under-5 child mortality:** 11 per 1,000 (1996) **Calorie consumption:** 114% (1988/90) 7,143 **people per doctor** (1988/91) **Safe water:** 86% (1990/96).

EDUCATION
Literacy: 85% (1995) male : 81% (1995) female: 89% (1995) **School enrolment :** Primary total: 109% (1990/95) male : 109% (1990/95) female: 108% (1990/95) Secondary: male : 62% (1990/95) female: 70% (1990/95) Tertiary: 6% (1995) **Primary school teachers:** one for every 37 students (1995).

COMMUNICATIONS
70 **newspapers**, 436 **radios**, 300 **TV sets** and 100 **main telephone lines** per 1,000 people (1994).

ECONOMY
Per capita, GNP: $ 1,600 (1996) **Annual growth, GNP:** -1.9% (1995/96) **Annual inflation:** 28.34% (1985/95) **Currency:** 39.62 Jamaica dollars = $ 1 (1995) **Cereal imports:** 335 metric tons (1994) **Food import dependency:** 10% (1994) **Fertilizer use:** 1,187 kgs per ha (1994) **Exports:** $ 1,347 million (1996) **Imports:** $ 2,916 million (1996) **External debt:** $ 4,041 million (1996) $ 1,622 **per capita:** (1996) **Debt service:** 18% of exports (1996) **Development aid received:** $ 108 million (1995) $ 43 per capita (1995) 2.7% of GNP (1994).

ENERGY
Consumption: 1,082.93 Kgs of Oil equivalent per capita yearly (1994) 99.63% imported (1994)

HDI (rank / value) 83 / 0.736 (1994)

PROFILE

ENVIRONMENT
Jamaica is the third largest of the Greater Antilles. A mountain range, occupying one third of the land area, runs across the island from East to West. A limestone plateau covered with tropical vegetation extends to the West. The plains are good for farming and the subsoil is rich in bauxite. The climate is rainy, tropical at sea level and temperate in the eastern highlands. Soil loss from deforestation and erosion reaches 80 million tons per year. In some metropolitan areas, the lack of sewerage and the dumping of industrial wastes have polluted drinking water supplies, threatening the urban population.

SOCIETY
Peoples: Most Jamaicans are of African descent. There are small Chinese, Indian, Arab and European minorities.
Religions: Protestants 56 per cent; Catholics 5 per cent, Rastafarians 5 per cent.
Languages: English (official). A dialect based on English is also spoken.
Political Parties: People's National Party (PNP); Jamaican Labor Party (JLP); National Democratic Movement; Workers' Party of Jamaica (JWP) .
Social Organizations: National Workers Union of Jamaica (NWUJ); Bustamante Industrial Trade Union (BITU).

THE STATE
Official Name: Jamaica.
Administrative Divisions: 13 Districts.
Capital: Kingston, 104,000 people (1991).
Other cities: Montego Bay, 83,500 people; Spanish Town, 92,000 people (1991).
Government: Parliamentary monarchy. Head of State: Elizabeth II of Britain. Prime Minister since March 1992: Percival J. Patterson. Bicameral Legislature: 21 member Senate, designated by the Governor General; Chamber of Deputies, 60 elected by direct popular vote every 5 years.
National Holiday: First Monday in August, Independence Day (1962).
Armed Forces: 3,350 troops.

MILITARY EXPENDITURE

MILITARY (as % of health and education expenditures-1990/91) **8%**

---

governing party nominated candidates, thereby winning all 60 seats.

[15] In 1984 the need to negotiate new loans with the IMF and the consequent cuts in public spending aggravated an already critical situation. Inflation soared from 4.7 per cent in 1981 to 32 per cent in 1984. In addition, in 1985 revenues from bauxite production fell and there was a 50 per cent decrease in tourism. Union federations announced that workers' living conditions were being allowed to deteriorate deliberately in order to attract transnationals to the Kingston "free zone" where workers' rights are not respected.

[16] 96 per cent of the workforce in the "Free Zone" were women who bore long working days in unhealthy conditions, with no security and low pay. This affected the situation of the children of Kingston, as 52 per cent of the heads of household were women.

[17] Between 1985 and 1987, the Labour Government adopted a campaign against drug trafficking, in agreement with the United States. Some $750 million worth of marijuana was estimated to enter the United States via Jamaica each year.

[18] In 1989, Michael Manley's PNP came to power again, strengthened by its triumph in the June 1986 municipal elections. He presented a very different programme from 1976, based on free enterprise and good relations with the United States. Manley re-established relations with Cuba and stated the agreements with the IMF would be respected, although he made it clear he would not accept conditions which would worsen the social inequalities. His aim was to maintain economic growth, but with better wealth distribution.

[19] In April 1992, Percival Patterson replaced Manley as Prime Minister, as the latter resigned from this post and the presidency of the PNP, following a long period of illness. Patterson, a well-known politician, former senator and minister of several PNP governments, was also elected party president.

[20] In 1992, promising labour guarantees, the Government started the privatization of around 300 State companies and public services classified as unproductive. This package included the entire sugar industry.

[21] In March 1993, the PNP took more than 60 per cent of the vote, confirming Patterson in the post of Prime Minister. The Labour Party - led once again by Edward Seaga - refused to participate in the partial elections in 1994 in order to show their disagreement with the electoral system and lobby for modifications. In October 1995, a group of Seaga's opponents within the Labour Party abandoned the group to found the National Democratic Movement.

[22] Prime Minister Patterson continued in 1995 with the economic and financial liberalization which, amongst other things, made Jamaica's financial sector one of the most prosperous in the country.

[23] In 1997, a committee of political parties, religious representatives and community groups was formed to seek solutions to the internal violence. Pressure from this committee contributed to Jamaica becoming the first country to abandon an agreement, within the framework of the United Nations International Convention on Civil and Political Rights, which made the death penalty more difficult to apply.

[24] The violence during the run-up to the December 18 1997 parliamentary elections led to the mass resignation of candidates. The National Democratic Movement had only 54 candidates for 60 seats. Following the election, the PNP retained the absolute majority, with 50 seats, while the Labour Party took 10.

Japan

Nihon

Population:	125,351,000 (1996)
Area:	377,801 SQ KM
Capital:	Tokyo
Currency:	Yen
Language:	Japanese

Earliest culture in Japan dates back 10,000 to 30,000 years ago to the Paleolithic Age, known as the Pre-Cambrian era. This was followed by the Jomon Neolithic culture, which lasted until 200-300 BC and extended throughout the Japanese archipelago.

[2] The Jomon culture was altered by the arrival of the Yayoi, who probably arrived from the continent at a time when Japan was still linked by land bridges across the straits of Korea, Tsushima, Soya and Tsugaru. The Yayoi introduced rice cultivation, horses and cows, the potter's wheel, weaving, and iron tools.

[3] According to Chinese chronicles, at the beginning of the Christian era the Wo region (Wa in Japanese) was divided into more than 100 states. During Himito's reign, some 30 of them were grouped together. The Wa people were divided into social classes and paid taxes, advanced building techniques were known and used, there were large markets and correspondence was exchanged with the continent.

[4] From the end of the civil war until Yamato's consolidation as emperor (266-413), the Wa territory was isolated. This led to the unification of the nation by the middle of the 4th century, a prerequisite for further expansion. In the year 369, Yamato subdued the Korean kingdoms of Paekche, Kaya and Sila and established military headquarters from which he could control the region.

[5] The Yamato empire suffered a rapid decline, due to both the resistance of its Korean subjects and to internal fighting within the court. During that period, between the years 538 and 552, Buddhism was introduced into the country, though initially it was merely an object of curiosity and admiration, due to its majestic temples and the magical powers that were attributed to it.

[6] The most important traces of Chinese presence in Japanese culture are the grid system for dividing the land, which dates back 1,500 years and is still visible today, the Chinese characters used in the writing system and the Buddhist religion.

[7] However, this cultural heritage underwent successive adaptations to the local weather, language, and habits, especially during the 17th and 18th centuries. This was particularly apparent in the architecture and the language, each of which shows evidence of very different local influences.

[8] Japan's first permanent capital was Nara, established in the year 710. In the 9th century, tribal chieftains were replaced by a permanent court with a hereditary right to title. The aristocracy made Buddhism a controlling force, which served to reinforce the power of the state. After several conflicts, Kammu (781-806) re-established the empire's independence and transferred the capital to Heian (Kyoto).

[9] In the new capital, the power of the Fujiwara family was consolidated. The Fujiwaras established the regent as the ruling figure, above and beyond the power of the emperor. With imperial approval, two new Buddhist sects - Tendai and Shingon - developed in Heian. They were both seen to be more closely identified with Japanese culture than the previous Buddhist sects, a fact which brought an end to Nara's religious hegemony.

[10] The imperial land tenure system also fell increasingly into private hands. The members of the aristocracy and the religious institutions began taking over large extensions of tax-free land (shoen). The nobility organized private armies for themselves, and a rural warrior class - the samurai - emerged.

[11] The Taira and Minamoto clans, who were prominent families and local leaders, became involved in a power struggle which led to a number of military confrontations between these two warlords. The Taira were in power from 1156 until their defeat in the Gempei War (1180-85). The shogun (general), Minamoto Yoritomo, founded the Kamakura shogunate, the first of a series of military regimes which ruled Japan until 1868.

[12] The Kamakura were put to the test during the Mongol invasions of 1274 and 1281. Aided by providential storms, which were called kamikaze (divine winds), the Japanese defeated the invaders. During this period, several new Buddhist sects emerged, such as Pure Land Buddhism, True Pure Land and Lotus.

[13] In the early 14th century, the Kamakura shogunate was destroyed, and Emperor Go-Daigo re-established his authority over the warlords in the Kemmu Restoration. However, a short while later he was expelled from Kyoto and replaced by a puppet emperor, who was controlled by the military clans. Go-Diago established his court in Yoshino, and for 56 years there were two imperial courts operating alongside each other.

PUBLIC EXPENDITURE

4.1%   n/a

1995 ■ DEFENCE □ SOCIAL

In **1990/91** Military as % of health & education expenditure was 12%.

WORKERS

UNEMPLOYMENT 3.4% (1996)

Labour force %

■ WOMEN
□ MEN
41   59

■ AGRICULTURE   7% (1990)
□ INDUSTRIAL   34%
□ SERVICES   59%

LAND USE

IRRIGATED 69.1% of arable

(1993)

■ FOREST & WOODLAND 66.4%
□ ARABLE   10.7%
■ OTHER   22.9%

14 The Onin War (1467-77), over succession within the Ashikaga shogunate, became a civil war which lasted a hundred years. New military chiefs emerged, independent of imperial or shogun authority. They established themselves and their vassals within fortified cities, leaving the surrounding villages to run themselves, and to pay tribute.

15 In the cities, trade and manufacturing ushered in a new way of life. Portugal began trading with Japan in 1545, and the missionary Francis Xavier introduced Catholicism to the Japanese in 1549. However, Christianity caused conflicts with feudal loyalties, and so it was proscribed in 1639. All of the Europeans in Japan, except for the Dutch, were banished from the country.

16 Toward the end of the 16th century, the Japanese warlords isolated themselves from the rest of society, pacifying and uniting the country around a single national authority. To achieve these objectives, the warlords made use of firearms and of military fortresses; in addition, they disarmed the peasants and achieved greater control over the land.

17 During the 17th century, the Tokugawa clan gained supremacy over the entire country. From the city-fortress of Edo (Tokyo), the Tokugawa shogunate governed Japan until 1867. A careful distribution of the land among their relatives and the local chieftains guaranteed them the control of the largest cities, Kyoto, Osaka and Nagasaki, as well as of the most important mines.

18 Local chieftains were compelled to spend half their time on the shogun's affairs while their families remained behind, as hostages. Transformed into military bureaucrats, the samurai were the highest level of a four-class system, followed by the peasants, artisans and traders.

19 A national market arose for textiles, food, handcrafts, books and other products. As of 1639, the Tokugawas implemented a policy of almost total isolation from the outside world. Nagasaki was the only exception; here, the Chinese and the Dutch were allowed to open trading posts, although the latter were restricted to a nearby island.

20 In the 19th century, the old economic and social order went into a state of collapse. Peasant revolts became more and more frequent, and the samurai and local chieftains found themselves heavily in debt with the traders. In 1840, the government tried to carry out a series of reforms, but these failed and weakness allowed the United States to prize open its ports.

21 Japan was forced out of its isolation by Commodore Matthew Perry, using cannon to persuade the Japanese to cooperate with him. The signing of unfavorable trade agreements with the United States and several European countries simply deepened the crisis within the shogunate. The samurai carried out several attacks against the foreigners and then turned against the shogun, forcing him to resign in 1867.

22 Imperial authority was restored with the young Meiji emperor, in 1868. During the Meiji Restoration, Japan's modernization process began, following the Western model. The United States exerted its influence, as did England, France and Germany, in the fields of education, the sciences, communication and Japanese cultural expression.

23 Within less than 50 years, Japan was transformed from a closed, feudal society into an industrialized world power. Western advisers and technology were brought in, for education, trade and industry. An army based on the draft replaced the military authority of the samurai, who were defeated when they tried to rebel, in 1877.

24 In 1889, succumbing to internal political pressure, the emperor approved a constitution which established a constitutional monarchy, with a bicameral legislature (Diet). However, only one per cent of the population was eligible for office, and the prime minister and his cabinet were responsible to the emperor who continued to be seen as a divine figure.

25 Japan defeated China in the war of 1894-95, and maintained control over Korea. Japan's victory in the Russo-Japanese War (1904-05) enabled it to annex the Sajalin Peninsula, with Korea being annexed a few years later (1910). Japan entered World War I as a British ally, as a treaty had been signed to that effect in 1902.

26 The war allowed Japan to gain control of several German possessions in East Asia, including the Chinese territory of Kiaochow. In 1915, Japan forced China to accept the extension of its influence over Manchuria and Inner Mongolia. In 1918, Hara Takashi became the head of the first government to have a parliamentary majority.

27 In 1921-22 Japan signed a naval arms limitation treaty with the US in Washington, replacing an agreement with Britain, and establishing a new balance of power in the Pacific.

28 The economic difficulties caused by the international depression of the 1930s gave the militarists the excuse they were seeking to attack the government. They proposed that the country's problems could only be solved by expanding its military power, and through the conquest of new markets for their products and as sources of raw materials.

29 Within this context, Japanese officers occupied Manchuria in 1931, without government authorization. Unable to deter the military, the government accepted the creation of the puppet state of Manchukuo, in February 1932. Three months later, the country's political leaders were forced to turn the government over to the militarists, who retained power until 1945.

30 In 1940, Japan invaded Indochina hoping to open up a passage through to Southeast Asia. The United States and Britain reacted by imposing a total embargo upon Japanese merchandise. The Japanese attack on Pearl Harbor, in Hawaii, and of the Philippines, Hong Kong and Malaysia, unleashed the war with the United States and opened up a new phase of World War II.

31 Japan surrendered on August 14 1945, after the US had dropped two atomic bombs on Hiroshima and Nagasaki on August 6 and 9. Japan was subsequently occupied by US troops who remained in the country between 1945 and 1952, and was governed by the Supreme Command of the Allied Powers (SCAP) under the leadership of General Douglas MacArthur. SCAP forced Japan to abandon the Meiji institutions, to renounce the

PROFILE

ENVIRONMENT

The country is an archipelago made up of 3,400 islands, the most important being Hokkaido, Honshu and Kyushu. The terrain is mountainous, dominated by the so-called Japanese Alps, which are of volcanic origin. Since 85 per cent of the land is taken up by high, uninhabitable mountains, 40 per cent of the population lives on only 1 per cent of the land area, in the narrow Pacific coastal plains, where demographic density exceeds 1,000 inhabitants per sq km. The climate is sub-tropical in the south, temperate in the center and cold in the north. Located where cold and warm ocean currents converge, Japanese waters have excellent fishing, and this activity is important to the country's economy. Japan's intensive and highly mechanized farming is concentrated along the coastal plains (rice, soybeans and vegetables). There are few mineral resources. Highly industrialized, the country's economy revolves around foreign trade, exporting manufactured products and importing raw materials. The major environmental problems are air pollution, especially in the major urban areas of Tokyo, Osaka and Yokohama, and acid rain in many parts of the country. One of the world's largest heavy industries has polluted many coastal areas.

SOCIETY

Peoples: The Japanese are culturally and ethnically homogeneous, having their origin in the migration of peoples from the Asian continent. There are Korean, Chinese, Ainu and Brazilian minorities.
Religions: Buddhism (38.3%) and Shintoism (51.3%). **Languages:** Japanese.
Political Parties: The Government coalition is made up of the Liberal Democratic Party (LDP), the Social Democratic Party of Japan (SPDJ) and the New Party Sakigake. The Shinshinto (Japan Renewal Party) has been in the opposition since 1994.
Social Organizations: The General Council of Japanese Trade Unions has 4,500,000 members.

THE STATE

Official Name: Nihon or Nippon
Capital: Tokyo, 11,771,819 people (1995).
Other cities: Yokohama, 3,307,408 people, Osaka, 2,602,352; Nagoya, 2,153,293; Kyoto, 1,463,601(1995).
Government: Parliamentary constitutional monarchy. Emperor Akihito has been Head of State since 1989, although his official coronation did not take place until November 12 1990. Keizo Obuchi Prime Minister and head of the Government since 1998. The Diet (Legislature) is bicameral: House of Representatives, made up of 512 members; House of Counsellors, with 252 members, elected by direct popular vote every 4 and 6 years, respectively.
National Holiday: January 1, New Year's Day. February 11, Founding of the Country (1889).
Armed Forces: 239,500 (including 8,000 women).
Other: 12,000 (non-combat Coast Guard, under the jurisdiction of the Ministry of Transport).

Maternal Mortality
1990

PER 100,000
LIVE BIRTHS
18

Foreign Trade
MILLIONS $ 1996

IMPORTS
347,496
EXPORTS
410,481

emperor's claim to divinity, and transfer the government to a parliament, which was charged with electing the prime minister and to establishing an independent judiciary.

[32] Although imposed upon the Japanese from the outside, the principles laid down in the 1947 constitution were accepted by all sectors of society and in 1952 the country recovered its independence. Japanese sovereignty was restored over the Tokara archipelago in 1951, over the Amami islands in 1953, over the Bonin islands in 1968, and over the rest of the Ryukyu, including Okinawa, in 1972.

[33] SCAP also took other measures to weaken the hierarchical model of the Meiji family-state. These ranged from giving tenants the right to purchase the land they lived on, and laws aimed at strengthening free trade and preventing the return of monopolies. However, the Japanese financial system remained intact and provided the basis for economic recovery at the end of the occupation.

[34] In 1955, opposing the country's conservative and nationalist sectors, which had supported the war policy, the Liberal Democratic Party (LDP) was formed. It was a center-right party, holding a majority in Parliament and has governed the country from its foundation to the present.

[35] The 1947 Constitution established restrictions upon the development of Japanese military power. During the postwar period, Japan bowed to US strategy for the region forming alliances with Taiwan and South Korea. In 1956 it joined the UN and re-established relations with the USSR.

[36] The return to independence found the Japanese economy in a state of growth and change. Farmers became unable to survive with the traditional methods of small-scale production and left the land in droves, leading to great urban migration. Industrialization and full employment triggered the need for technological innovation in the countryside to increase the food supply.

[37] During the 1960s, Japan specialized in the production of high technology products, which made it necessary to establish stable trade relations with more industrialized countries instead of its previous Asian partners. The oil crisis of 1973 did not halt the growth of the Japanese industry, which led the world in steel, ship building, electronics, and automobile manufacturing.

[38] Although Prime Minister Kakuei Tanaka's visit to Beijing in 1972 signalled Japanese recognition of the People's Republic of China, it damaged the country's relations with Taiwan. The scandal following the disclosure of the fact that Tanaka had been bribed by the Marubeni Corporation (a representative of the US Lockheed Aircraft Corporation), adversely affected the LDP's popularity and in 1976, for the first time in its history, it lost its absolute majority in parliament.

[39] During the 1960s and 1970s, there was a large trade surplus in Japan's favor in its trade with the US. During this period, Japan began ranking first or second with all its trading partners. With direct investment and the establishment of subsidiaries of Japanese companies, Japan expanded worldwide.

[40] The Japanese corporate world is dominated by the Sogo-Shosha system, huge conglomerates which commercialize virtually all kinds of raw material in almost every country in the world, by means of state-of-the-art information systems capable of supplying data for decision making instantaneously.

[41] The organization of Japanese corporations still maintains some principles which are the legacy of Japan's medieval tradition. The worker is bound to the corporation by an allegiance similar to that which bound the medieval peasant to his land and the local warlord. This often results in great company discipline and production efficiency.

[42] The impressive development of the Japanese economy is due not only to this efficiency but also to a policy of foreign investment in projects which quickly deplete non-renewable natural resources. This policy has caused irreversible damage to rainforests and serious alterations to the Third World ecosystem.

[43] Japan imports over 16 million cubic metres of tropical timber every year. This has caused a massive deforestation in Malaysia, Thailand, Indonesia, the Philippines, and Papua New Guinea. Japan has also become a consumer of endangered species and products derived from them, such as elephant tusks and tortoise shells.

[44] Japan makes direct investments in Third World countries and gives credits through its agencies to aid in building roads and in scientific research projects. As with all international aid this assistance is geared toward its own interest in gaining cheap, easy access to the raw materials of those countries.

[45] Throughout modern Japan, the pursuit of economic success has become people's main objective. Family, leisure, and individual ideals are sacrificed to the factory or the company. Within this system, women play a very subservient role as the pillar of the home and of the children's education.

[46] In Japan there is great social pressure for women to get married: 80 per cent of women are married by the age of 30 and 98 per cent are married, widowed, or divorced by the age of 50. Women may work outside the home, generally in second-rate, badly paid jobs.

[47] In spite of this age-old discrimination - a legacy of the country's traditional cultures - Japanese women are active in local movements against the pollution caused by industry and nuclear power plants. They also actively defend the quality of life and of consumer goods.

[48] The traditional full-employment situation in Japan was threatened by two factors: demographic growth and technological modernization which created a labor shortage. Japanese resistance to foreign immigrants and the progressively ageing profile of the population only intensified the problem. In June 1990, an immigration law went into effect opening up the Japanese labor market to foreign workers, for the first time ever.

[49] Although the United States continues to give military support to Japan, Washington started exerting pressure in 1982 so that the country would increase its military expenditure (around 0.9 per cent of its GDP) and assume greater responsibility in regional security in the Western Pacific.

[50] Since the early 1950s, Japan began demanding that the USSR return four small islands which Japan claimed belonged to the Kurile archipelago. Relations between the two countries entered a new era in 1986 with Minister of Foreign Affairs Eduard Shevardnadze's visit to Tokyo. This visit resulted in the decision to hold regular ministerial consultations, and to increase trade.

[51] Prime Minister Yasuhiro Nakasone travelled to Eastern Europe in 1987, in the first such visit by a Japanese head of government. Three years later, Prime Minister Toshiki Kaifu travelled to several European countries and declared his support of the liberalization of Eastern Europe.

[52] The economic and social stability of southeast Asia is of utmost importance for Japan because a growing part of its investments and a third of its foreign trade depends on this region, which provides the country with raw materials vital to its industry.

[53] The death of Emperor Hirohito in January 1989 brought to an end the Showa era, which had begun in 1926. The coronation of his successor, Akihito, in the traditional Japanese style, marked the beginning of the Heisei era (achievement of universal peace). The coronation ceremony was attended by more heads of state than had ever gathered together for any such event. The expense incurred generated internal protests.

[54] Japanese relations with the EC and the US have been strained at times, due to problems of protectionism and a trade imbalance (in Japan's favor). In 1987, Washington protested at Japan's sale of sophisticated submarine technology to the USSR, between 1982 and 1984. Nevertheless in 1989 Naboru Takeshita was the first head of government to be received by newly-elected US president, George Bush. Takeshita resigned in April, as a result of a real estate scandal. He was succeeded by Sosuke Uno, who was forced to resign after less than three months in office after admitting having sexual relations with a geisha woman.

55 At the end of the Cold War, Japan emerged as one of the three main world economic powers, together with the US and the EC. At present, it is the country with the largest overseas investment. It is a key participant in the world financial system, and is influential in the exchange of Third World debt funds.

56 On November 5 1991, Prime Minister Toshiki Kaifu presented his resignation, and was replaced by 72-year-old Kiichi Miyazawa who had been elected president of the Liberal Democratic Party nine days before. Kaifu had been elected in August 1989 because he was one of very few party members who had never been involved in a corruption scandal. His political career rapidly came to an end when he lost the support of the Takeshita clan, the most influential of the official party's five factions, and the one which had backed his election.

57 The Takeshita clan also backed the next prime minister, Miyazawa, even though he had been forced to resign as minister of finance in December 1988, because of his involvement in the Recruit scandal. (Recruit was a Japanese telecommunications firm that had made large financial contributions to many politicians in the hope of obtaining governmental favours.) In his inaugural speech, Miyazawa outlined the objectives he had set for his administration: to expand relations with, and aid to China; to negotiate with the United States and to normalize relations with the USSR. In addition, he announced his willingness to liberalize the rice market, making concessions similar to those already made by the EC and the United States, to ward off a failure of the Uruguay Round of the GATT.

58 The traditional leader of the PLD, 77-year-old Shin Kanemaru stated that despite his personal aversion to him, Miyazawa appeared to be the only politician which the party could back at the moment.

59 On November 23, US secretary of defense Richard Cheney called on Japan to play a more active role in the military and political aspects of world affairs. US military forces currently in Japan consist of three air bases, an aircraft carrier and some 56,000 troops, including a division of Marines.

60 On February 9 1992, Yukihise Yoshida, an opposition candidate supported by all four opposition parties, defeated the official candidate by 51 per cent to 37 per cent, in the western district of Nara. This outcome was attributed to popular disenchantment with the party in power, because endemic corruption was not only extant, but was very obviously on the increase. Prime Minister Kiichi

Miyazawa himself appeared to be entirely surrounded by people with a record of corruption.

61 On February 10 1992, it was revealed that the minister of postal services, Hideo Watanabe, had admitted to receiving a bribe greater than the $40,000 he had previously admitted to during the Recruit scandal of 1988. On February 14, four people were arrested with relation to another financial scandal, which involved more than 100 members of Miyazawa's government, as well as the mafia group known as Inagawagumi. It was revealed that billions of yen had been siphoned off from party donations making the new case, known as Kyubin, an even more serious breach of conduct than the Recruit scandal.

62 Toward the middle of the year, after heated debate, a law was passed authorizing troops to be sent abroad for the first time since World War II.

63 In early 1993, Miyazawa promised to broaden the scope of Japanese forces, both in terms of funding and personnel, within the framework of the UN peacekeeping missions.

64 Also in 1993 the Prime Minister was censured by the Diet for failing to carry out electoral reforms needed to end the endemic corruption in Japanese political life. The official party split, losing 54 seats, and elections were moved up to July.

65 The two dissident groups, led by Tsutomu Hata and Masayoshi Takemura, formed new parties; the Reformation Party and the Pioneer Party.

66 Debate intensified in April over whether Japanese troops should be sent abroad, after a civilian and a member of the Japanese police force were killed in Cambodia as members of the UN forces.

67 Diplomatic relations with the Russian Government improved slightly when Japan announced that, while not relinquishing its claim to the Kuril Islands, it would not allow its claim to the islands to prevent economic aid to Russia.

68 On July 18, general elections drew the lowest rate of voter participation since the war (67.3 per cent), a clear sign of the electorate's dissatisfaction with the corrupt state of Japan's political scene.

69 The LDP, in power since 1955, lost its majority in the Kokkai (Diet), obtaining only 228 of the 512 disputed seats in the House of Representatives, compared with 275 in the 1990 election. This result was significant enough to alter the balance of power which had been in effect since World War II.

70 Miyazawa, who had announced his decision to remain in office regardless of the election results, changed his mind. A few days later,

he resigned the party presidency, and assumed responsibility for the LDP's defeat. Yohei Kono was named party President.

71 In July, the "new majority" of the Socialist, Reformation, Komeito (Buddhist), Democratic Socialist, Unified Democratic Socialist and Pioneer parties, agreed to form a new Government, based upon a limited platform which would not attempt any profound changes.

72 Hosokawa, the former governor of the province of Kunamoto, was elected Prime Minister in August. Upon assuming office, he announced a far-reaching political-reform bill, aimed at fighting corruption, putting an end to the recession and modernizing the pension and health systems.

73 In his first speech before the Diet, Hosokawa referred to the aggression with which Japan had treated its Asian neighbors, from the 1930s until the end of World War II. On August 15, the 48th anniversary of Japan's surrender, Hosokawa offered condolences and apologies to the victims of Japanese colonialism.

74 In December 1993, the Japanese Government opened up the rice market, allowing up to 4 per cent of internal consumption, amounting to 10 million tons, to be imported. Many families tend to hoard domestic rice, and shopkeepers speculate with prices. The "Rice Lord", or kome, is a

sacred part in Japanese tradition, and is linked to the earth and the ancestors.

75 Japan's enormous trade surplus has been a source of constant tension on the international market, particularly with the United States. This surplus reached $107 billion in 1992, and $150 billion in 1993.

76 Beyond the problems caused by the surplus, the Japanese economy has also suffered the effects of world recession. The most apparent consequence being that of unemployment, which has been on the increase since mid-1992 and reached its peak in 1996 with 3.2 per cent.

77 A corruption scandal among top Government circles had been revealed in 1992 when Shin Kanemaru, historic LDP leader, admitted he had received bribes. Kanemaru was arrested in March 1993 and was granted an amnesty shortly afterward. When Hosokawa succeeded Miyazawa, the Confederation of Industries announced it would discontinue its "contributions" to the LDP. According to local press versions, these had amounted to $1 billion per year.

78 In August, 165 political leaders and 445 business people were arrested for irregularities committed during the July 1993 election campaign. 5,500 cases were brought to court to deal with

Japan's controversial plutonium programme

The development of 'supergenerators' – nuclear plants which work with plutonium-based fuel – in countries like France and Japan is considered far more dangerous than 'traditional' plants, which operate mainly on uranium-based power

"We don't want nuclear waste!" proclaimed the banners and slogans of hundreds of demonstrators in the port of Mutsu Ofawara in northern Japan, awaiting the arrival of the Pacific Teal on the morning of May 18 1997. The ship which was sailing under a British flag, came from France loaded with 20 tons of plutonium-derivative nuclear waste – a highly radioactive substance.

Long before the ship arrived, concern had been increasing following a decision to establish a temporary nuclear waste deposit in Rokkasho. The Pacific Teal followed in the wake of another nuclear cargo ship which in 1995 had sailed around South America en route to Japan.

The arrival of the Pacific Teal coincided with increasing demands in Japan for the plutonium programme to be cancelled. This programme had suffered serious problems in December 1995 when the Monju reactor developed a massive sodium leak. The government was forced to close the reactor that year, while industrialists tried, with all the means at their disposal, to prevent the true scale of the accident becoming known.

The Monju 'supergenerator' operates with plutonium-based fuel, unlike 'traditional' nuclear plants, which use uranium. Environmental organizations claim the technology of the supergenerators is even less controllable than that of the traditional plants. Hence,

Monju is potentially more dangerous than other reactors throughout the rest of the world. The trade in radioactive material between France and Japan is directly linked to the idea which led to the launch of the binational plutonium programme: in theory, the waste from supergenerators can be 'reprocessed' to be used again as fuel. Thus, the waste brought in by the controversial cargo ship actually started its working life in Monju, travelling to France and the United Kingdom to be 'reprocessed' into fuel before being sent back to Japan.

During its journey to Japan, the radioactive cargo of the Pacific Teal caused mass protests in several of the countries it passed. Some governments prevented the ship from coming within 200 miles of their coastlines. The protests led to the formation of an international campaign demanding Japan suspend its plutonium programme.

---

electoral fraud. In October, Shinji Kiyoyama - president of Kajima, the country's second largest construction firm - was arrested for paying a bribe in exchange for a building permit.

[79] Hosokawa's "romance" with public opinion, after reaching record levels of popularity, started to cool off in early 1994 as press reports became critical, accusing him of having received huge amounts of money in exchange for favors.

[80] Already in February 1994, the Prime Minister had been forced to abandon a scheme which he himself had sponsored, aimed at keeping the Government coalition intact. Worn out by the pressure, he had to issue a self-critique - unpleasant for a head of Government - explaining the reckless manner in which he had handled the situation.

[81] A new $140 billion plan to reactivate the economy also drew criticism. Its feasibility was questioned and the press stressed the plan did not address the problems posed by a rapidly ageing population.

[82] In March 1994, a summit meeting between Japan and the United States ended in failure. Although Hosokawa showed a willingness to accept opening up the Japanese automobile, telecommunications, medicine and insurance markets, he rejected the US scheme of mandatory quotas. Japanese businessmen disqualified Hosokawa and felt inclined to

wage a commercial war with the US before yielding to its pressures. The automobile industry employs 11 per cent of Japan's labor and contributes 30 per cent of the GDP.

[83] A new corruption case involved LDP member of parliament Nakamura, who was arrested for accepting bribes from Kajima and other construction firms. Hosokawa was unable to shake off accusations from the opposition about his own involvement in illicit business deals. In April he resigned and asked "sincerely for forgiveness from the people of Japan".

[84] Tsutomu Hata was nominated Prime Minister and on April 28, Japan's first minority Government in four decades was formed. The socialists had walked out of the Government coalition leaving the Government with only 182 of the 512 seats in the lower house.

[85] Hata made official visits to Europe aiming to establish closer trade links with the European Community. He also admitted that Japan's trade surplus had caused the trade crisis with the United States. After an initial agreement was reached between the two countries, Hata launched a scheme to promote economic deregulation.

[86] Socialist Tomiichi Murayama was elected Prime Minister on June 29 1994 and took office on July 18. His party, the Social Democratic Party of Japan (SDPJ) did not obtain a majority in

parliament but formed an alliance with its traditional rival, the LDP, and with a new party, the Sakigake.

[87] The opening of Kansai airport, located on an artificial island, led to a blossoming of island-city projects. The overpopulation of Japan's large cities has led to a real estate development, taking up what little space is available for construction.

[88] On January 17 1995, an earthquake hit the area of Hanshin. Over 6,000 died, 100,000 buildings were destroyed in the city of Kobe and over 300,000 were left homeless. The Government's delayed response to the disaster was harshly criticized. The lower house added $ 10 billion to the budget for the area's recovery.

[89] In March, a series of attacks with poisonous Sarin gas killed 12 people and affected 12,000 others in Tokyo's subways. A similar attack had taken seven lives in Matsumoto in June 1994. Shoko Asahara, the leader of a religious sect called Aum Shinriyko (Supreme Truth), was charged with the attack and arrested along with 16 other leaders from the movement.

[90] Murayama was defeated when Independent Yukio Aoshima was elected governor of Tokyo in the April 9 1995 elections. The Socialists did not obtain favorable returns at the July elections either, which renewed half of the upper house's seats and in which opposition party Sakigake had a significant growth.

[91] In January 1996, Ryutaro

Hashimoto (LDP president) replaced Murayama as Prime Minister. The new Head of Government called for general elections on October, in which his party won a relative majority in parliament. In November, Hashimoto formed a cabinet with only LDP members.

[92] In a referendum held in late 1997, slightly more than half of the Nago population, on Okinawa island, decided against the construction of a US heliport on the island. The United States had been stationed in Okinawa since the Japanese surrender in 1945 and had already built a sophisticated airbase with tens of thousands of soldiers. The Japanese and US governments claimed the construction of the heliport was a step towards the dismantling of the base which apparently did not convince the majority of Noga voters.

[93] The financial and economic crisis which struck Southeast Asia in 1997 also affected Japan, the second world power and first creditor of the world. On April 1998, the yen was at its lowest level in the last seven years and the Tokyo Stock Exchange had lost 6 per cent in three days. At an economic level, a reduction of the gross domestic product was expected. Hashimoto stated his country was facing an "extremely severe" situation, not seen since World War II.

Jordan

Urdunn

Population:	5,581,000 (1996)
Area:	97,740 SQ KM
Capital:	Amman
Currency:	Dinars
Language:	Arabic

OCCUPIED BY ISRAEL

1　Southern Lebanon - occupied in 1983
2　Syria - Golan Heights - occupied in 1967
3　West Bank - occupied in 1967 (some individual towns now have autonomy)

In biblical times, when it was divided among the Semitic nations of Gilead, Moab and Edom, the territory of present day Jordan was central to the development of the region's history. In classical times, the state of Petra was one of the "desert sentries" allies of the Roman Empire. In the 7th century it was the site of the battle of Yarmuk, in which the Arabs fought Byzantine Emperor Heraclius, winning access to the fertile crescent (see Saudi Arabia), and during the Crusades the western part of the territory served as the operational base to initiate warfare against the European strongholds.

[2] In the 16th century, Turkish domination made the territory part of the district of Damascus, and it remained so until the beginning of World War I in 1914.

[3] The Jordanians participated actively in the Arab rebellion against the Turkish Ottoman Empire. The secret 1916 Sykes-Picot Treaty between France and Britain, later formalized by the League of Nations, gave the French control of Lebanon and Syria and Britain a mandate over Iraq and Palestine (which included present-day Jordan). The British had promised Shereef Hussein of Mecca a unified Arab nation, including these territories, and the Arabian peninsula.

[4] The conflict with Faisal, the Shereef's son, in Syria (see Syria) and his expulsion by the French in 1920, led his brother Prince Abdullah to organize a support force of Jordanian Bedouin. The British persuaded Abdullah that he would be better off accepting the government of Trans-Jordan.

[5] With this, and the later

creation of the state of Iraq, which was granted to Faisal as compensation, Britain put Shereef Hussein in an awkward position; if he insisted on his Greater Arabia idea, his sons would lose their recently acquired positions as heads of state. Conversely, as Hussein controlled Hidjaz, three parts of the proposed nation were already in the hands of the family, making subsequent unification a possibility. This was not to happen, however. In 1924 the Shereef proclaimed himself Caliph. Emir Ibn Saud, King of Nejd, viewed this as a threat, so he invaded Hidjaz and drove Hussein out of Mecca (see Saudi Arabia).

[6] The emirate of Trans-Jordan remained under British mandate until 1928, when the borders with Palestine were established. Abdullah and his heirs were given legislative and administrative powers. Foreign and military affairs remained in British hands until May 1946, when the Emirate became the "Hashemite Kingdom of Trans-Jordan". After the Arab-Israeli War of 1948, King Abdullah annexed Palestinian territories on the West Bank of the Jordan River, calling the new nation Jordan. Palestinian refugees, the legal status of Jerusalem, and the doubling in length of the border with Israel were problems he had to face.

[7] In 1951, Abdullah was assassinated and his son Talal succeeded him. Talal appeared to harbour anti-British sentiments and promised a progressive government, but a year later he was deposed. In 1953, his 17-year-old son Hussein took over the throne.

[8] King Hussein managed to remain in power because of firm US support and the personal devotion of Bedouins, both essential to keep the army under control.

[9] For over 40 years, and particularly after Israel occupied the West Bank, Palestinian immigration has been large. First came those driven from their lands by Israeli occupation troops in 1948, then those expelled from refugee camps in 1967. Palestinians currently make up two-thirds of Jordan's population. Demographic pressure and Hussein's ambition to replace the PLO as

spokesperson for the Palestinians, were detonating factors in Black September, the 1970 Jordanian massacre of Palestinians.

[10] After the 1973 Arab-Israeli war, there was a startling change in Jordanian policy and the king re-established relations with the PLO in 1979.

[11] In 1984, Jordan reasserted its position against unilateral negotiations with Israel though closer links with Egypt began. In 1985, King Hussein and PLO leader Yasser Arafat announced a common diplomatic initiative for peace in the Middle East; this failed as Israel refused to negotiate.

[12] In July 1988, Hussein relinquished his claim on the West Bank, and made the PLO legally responsible for the territories under Israeli occupation.

[13] Most international currency came in remittances from migrant workers and the national budget depended on financial aid from Arab countries, estimated at $1 billion in 1989.

[14] A backlog of repayments, and a foreign debt that reached $6 billion in 1989, led the Government to turn to the IMF.

Price increases in consumer goods caused a popular revolt in April 1989.

[15] King Hussein gave parliament power over the monarchy, he freed political prisoners and called for democratic elections.

[16] The outbreak of the Gulf crisis, when Iraq invaded Kuwait in August 1990, found the King at the height of popularity, but his position was very difficult. He was surrounded by Israel and Iraq, most of his Palestinian subjects supported the Iraqi leader, Saddam Hussein. Jordan depended on Saudi Arabia financially, and on Baghdad for oil.

[17] Jordan joined the trade embargo on Iraq, while opposing the use of military force to enforce the resolutions of the Security Council. The country lost $570 million as a result of the embargo. It also received 40,000 Kurd refugees, more than a million Iraqis and some 300,000 Jordanians of Palestine origin expelled from Kuwait in reprisal for Jordan's support of Iraq.

[18] On June 9 1991, King Hussein and political representatives signed a new Constitution which legalized

WORKERS

(1996)

Labour force %

■ WOMEN
□ MEN

22　　78

■ AGRICULTURE 15% (1990)
□ INDUSTRIAL 23%
■ SERVICES 61%

PROFILE

ENVIRONMENT

75 per cent of the country is a desert plateau, 600 to 900 m. in altitude. The western part of this plateau has a series of cleavages at the beginning of the great Rift Fault, which crosses the Red Sea and stretches into east Africa. In the past, these fissures widened the Jordan River valley and formed the steep depression which is now the Dead Sea. As most of the country is made up of dry steppes, farming is limited to cereals (wheat and rye) and citrus fruits. Sheep and goats are also bred. The shortage of water is the chief environmental problem. Desertification and urban expansion have caused the loss of arable land near the Jordan River.

SOCIETY

Peoples: Most of the population is Palestinian, from Israeli post-war migrations. Native Jordanians are of the 20 large Bedouin ethnic groups of which about one third are still semi-nomadic. There is a Circassian minority from the Caucasus, who now play a major role in trade and administration.
Religions: 90 per cent of the population are Sunni Muslim but the Shiites are increasing rapidly. **Languages:** Arabic (official). English is often used. **Political Parties:** By March 1993, the Government recognized nine parties. The most important are: the Islamic Action Front, Shi'a oriented; the Jordanian Communist Party and the Socialist Arab Baas Party of Jordan.
Social Organizations: The most important labor union is the General Federation of Labor Unions of Jordan. The Union of Jordanian Women has participated in the democratization process and in the defence of the political rights of women.

THE STATE

Official Name: al-Mamlakah al-Urdunniya al-Hashimiyah.
Administrative divisions: 8 provinces.
Capital: Amman, 1,187,000 people (1995).
Other cities: az-Zarqa 344,500 people; Irbid 208,200; as-Salt 187,000; ar-Rusayfah 115,500 (1994).
Government: Hussein Ibn Talal, King since 1952. Abdul Salam Madjali, Prime Minister since 1997 (second time). Legislative branch: National Assembly (bicameral), with a 40 member Senate appointed by the king, and an 80 member Chamber of Deputies elected by direct popular vote; the latter can be dissolved by the king. **National Holiday:** May 25, Independence Day (1946). **Armed Forces:** 98,650 troops (1996). **Other:** 6,000 soldiers under the authority of the Department of Public Security; 200,000 militia in the "People's Army"; 3,000 Palestinians in the Palestinian Liberation Army, under the supervision of the Jordanian Army.

STATISTICS

DEMOGRAPHY

Population: 5,581,000 (1996) **Annual growth:** 4% (1980/1996) **Estimates for year 2000:** 6,300,000 **Annual growth to year 2000:** 3.5% (1994/2000) **Urban Population:** 72.0% (1996) **Urban growth:** 5.78% (1980/95) **Children per woman:** 5.3 (1996).

HEALTH

Life expectancy at birth: 69 years (1996) **Infant mortality:** 21 per 1,000 (1996) **Under-5 child mortality:** 25 per 1,000 (1996) **Calorie consumption:** 110% (1988/90) 649 **people per doctor** (1988/91) **Safe water:** 98% (1990/96).

EDUCATION

Literacy: 87% (1995) male : 93% (1995) female: 79% (1995) **School enrolment :** Primary total: 94% (1990/95) male : 94% (1990/95) female: 95% (1990/95) Secondary: male : 52% (1990/95) female: 54% (1990/95) **Primary school teachers:** one for every 21 students (1995).

COMMUNICATIONS

50 **newspapers**, 243 **radios**, 160 **TV sets** and 72 **main telephone lines** per 1,000 people (1994) **Books:** 10 new titles per 100,000 people (1992/94).

ECONOMY

Per capita, GNP: $ 1,650 (1996) **Annual growth, GNP:** 2.8% (1995/96) **Consumer price index:** 120.4 (1994) **Currency:** 0.71 dinars = $ 1 (1995) **Cereal imports:** 1,347 metric tons (1994) **Food import dependency:** 20% (1994) **Fertilizer use:** 345 kgs per ha (1994) **Exports:** $ 1,466 million (1996) Imports: $ 4,293 million (1996) **External debt:** $ 8,118 million (1996) $ 1,455 **per capita:** (1996) **Debt service:** 12.3% of exports (1996) **Development aid received:** $ 536 million (1995) $ 127 per capita (1995) 9.3% of GNP (1994).

ENERGY

Consumption: 1,067.16 Kgs of Oil equivalent per capita yearly (1994) 95.84% imported (1994)

HDI (rank / value) 84 / 0.73 (1994)

---

political parties and extended political rights to women.
[19] In the same month, Taher Al Masri was nominated Prime Minister, substituting Mudar Badram. Al Masri backed Jordanian participation in the Middle East Peace Conference and encouraged rapprochement with the US Bush administration. In November 1991, Taher Al Masri was removed from office following a vote of no confidence by the Islamic fundamentalist bloc in parliament. He was replaced by Sharif Zeid Ibn Shaker.
[20] The growth of the Islamic fundamentalist movement was less repressed here than in other countries of the region. The Muslim Brotherhood was authorized to function as a philanthropic organization. It gained prestige in the social welfare area, running hospitals, schools and various Islamic studies centres. The political wing of the Brotherhood was the Islamic Action Front (IAF). Both groups were opposed to Arab-Israeli dialogue. In November 1992, two IAF members of parliament were freed under an amnesty granted to 1,480 political and common prisoners.
[21] In May 1993, Abdul Salam Madjali, head of the Jordanian delegation in the peace talks with Israel, was appointed Prime Minister. In the first parliamentary elections in November, the television hostess Tuyan Faisal, became the first woman in the country to be elected to parliament.
[22] The difficult relations between Islamic groups and the throne obstructed the negotiations with Israel. It was not until July 1994, in Washington, that Jordan and Israel established a schedule to bring the 46 years of war to an end, including the repatriation of nearly 60,000 Palestinian refugees in Jordan.
[23] King Hussein and Israeli Prime Minister Yitzhak Rabin signed a bilateral peace treaty on October 26, 1994. Israel handed over 300 square kilometres of desert to Jordan and the frontier was established, but greater significance was given to King Hussein being given custody of the holy Islamic sites in Jerusalem. The Jordanian public was surprised by the speed of the peace agreement and the meagre economic benefits for their country.
[24] In November 1995, King Hussein visited Jerusalem for the first time since Israel had occupied the city in 1967, to attend the funeral of Yitzhak Rabin. Sharif Zaid ibn Saker, designated Prime Minister in January 1996, was replaced in February 1996 by Abdul Karim al-Kabariti, also foreign and defence minister.
[25] Despite its dependence on Iraqi oil (75,000 barrels at special prices), Jordan decided in 1996 to reduce trade with Baghdad. It dropped exports to that country by 50 per cent and it authorized the United States use of an air base in its territory. Two Iraqi diplomats were expelled from Jordan in August, accused of instigating uprisings following tension generated by the doubling of the cost of bread.
[26] Ahmed Yassine, the founder of Hamas (a Palestine resistance group) was freed on October 2, 1997, after serving eight an a half years in prison in Israel. Yassine created the organization in 1987 and had been sentenced to life imprisonment in 1989, for his part in numerous operations. His freedom was negotiated in exchange for two Israeli Mossad agents arrested in Amman after trying to murder a member of the Hamas political Bureau.
[27] Political support for King Hussein strengthened following the parliamentary elections of November 4 1997, where fewer voters turned out than in previous sessions. The so-called tribal chiefs - leaders of nomadic groups living in the desert -, mostly loyal to Hussein, took 68 of the 80 seats in the lower house. The other 12 went to traditionalist candidates. The elections were boycotted by the main fundamentalist group - the Islamic Action Front - protesting against restrictions on public freedoms, Hussein's economic policy and the peace agreement with Israel. Abdul Salam Madjali was designated Prime Minister for the second time.
[28] In the same month, the Jordanian Government announced it would offer Christian education in the State schools to the children wanting this.
[29] In February 1998, under the threat of a US bombardment of Iraq, Jordan prepared to receive a wave of refugees. During the 1991 Gulf War, more than a million Iraqis had sought refuge in Jordan. 150,000 were still in the country in 1998, although only 35,000 had legal residence.

Kanaky/New Caledonia

Population: 184,000 (1996)
Area: 18,575 SQ KM
Capital: Noumea

Currency: CFP francs
Language: French

Kanaky

New Caledonia (Kanaky) was populated by Melanesians (Kanaks) 3,000 years ago. The islands were named by Captain Cook in 1774, as the tree-covered hills reminded him of the Scottish - Caledonian - landscape.

[2] In 1853, the main island was occupied by the French Navy which organized a local guard to suppress frequent indigenous uprisings. Nickel and chrome mining attracted thousands of French settlers. The colonizers pushed out the original inhabitants, and traditional religions, crafts and social organizations were obliterated, and many landless natives were confined to "reservations", and the system of terraced fields were trodden over by cattle. The last armed rebellion, stifled in 1917, only accelerated European land appropriation.

[3] After Algerian independence, in July 1962, colonization increased with the arrival of pieds-noirs, the former French colonists in Algeria. By 1946, New Caledonia had become a French Overseas Territory, but the resulting political autonomy did not favour the Kanaks, now reduced to a minority group, in relation to the *caldoches* (descendants of Europeans who settled a century ago).

[4] The election of President Mitterrand in 1981 rekindled the hopes of the pro-independence parties. The French socialist leader was supported by most Kanaks, who saw independence as a way to end the unfair income distribution on the island. This stood at $7,000 per capita (the highest in the Pacific except for Nauru) but the vast majority of the money was concentrated in the hands of European - mostly French - business people, the *métros*, who enjoyed incredible fiscal benefits, and the caldoches who monopolized the most important official positions.

[5] Most of the Kanaks actively supported independence as the bulk of them lived in poverty, with high unemployment rates, and suffered educational discrimination.

[6] In the 1970s, discontent with the economic situation produced by colonial domination caused strikes, land invasions,

experiments in cooperative work, and a powerful campaign to restore traditional lands to the local groups. These had been totally occupied by settlers and used mostly as cattle pastures. The rescue of *coutume* (cultural traditions) and the Kanak identity became a priority, and the proposed luxury tourist Club Méditerranée camps were firmly rejected.

[7] Kanak claims were supported by other independent Melanesian countries (Fiji, Solomon, Papua New Guinea and above all Vanuatu), and were put forward at the South Pacific Forum in August 1981. A month later, pro-independence leader Pierre Declercq, a Catholic of European origin, was murdered at his home by right-wing extremists, changing the malaise to a fully-blown political crisis.

[8] Another strong reason why France is hesitant to grant Kanaky independence is that it has the world's second largest nickel deposits, and extensive reserves of other minerals including chrome, iron, cobalt, manganese, and polymetallic nodules, discovered recently on the ocean floor within territorial waters.

[9] Furthermore, the islands' strategic position is of great military value. Its ports, facilities and bases house 6,000 troops and a small war fleet (including a nuclear submarine), considered by the military command as a "vital point of support" for the French nuclear-testing site on Mururoa atoll.

[10] In July 1984, the French National Assembly passed special bills concerning the colony's autonomy, though it rejected amendments submitted by pro-independence parties, confirming Kanak fears that the socialist government of France had no intention of granting independence. In November, the main opposition force, the Socialist Kanak National Liberation Front (FLNKS) called for a boycott of local Territorial Assembly elections, which were sure to endorse the French government plan of postponing Kanak independence indefinitely.

[11] In December 1984, local government became fully

PROFILE

ENVIRONMENT
The territory consists of the island of New Caledonia (16,700 sq km), the Loyalty Islands (Ouvea, Lifou, Maré and Walpole), the archipelagos of Chesterfield, Avon, Huon, Belep, and the island of Noumea. The whole group is located in southern Melanesia, between the New Hebrides (Vanuatu) to the East and Australia to the West. Of volcanic origin, the islands are mountainous with coastal reefs. The climate is rainy, tropical, and suitable for agriculture. The vegetation is dense and the subsoil is rich in nickel deposits.

SOCIETY
Peoples: Indigenous New Caledonians are of Melanesian origin (the Kanaka group), 42.5 per cent; there are French and descendents of French (known as *caldoches*), 37.1 per cent; as well as Wallisian, 8.6 per cent, Vietnamese, Indonesian, Chinese and Polynesian minorities.
Religions: Roughly 60 per cent Catholic, 16 per cent Protestant and around 5 per cent Muslim.
Languages: French (official), Melanesian and Polynesian languages.
Political Parties: Rally for Caledonia within the Republic (RPCR); Kanak Liberation Party (PALIKA); Kanak Socialist National Liberation Front (FLNKS).
Social Organizations: The Caledonian Workers Confederation (CTC); the Federation of New Caledonian Miners' Unions (FSMNC); the New Caledonian Federation of Laborers' and Employees' Unions (USOENC); and the Union of Exploited Kanak Workers (USTKE).

THE STATE
Official Name: Territoire d'Outre-Mer de la Nouvelle-Calédonie.
Administrative divisions: Three provinces: Southern, Northern and Islands.
Capital: Noumea, 100,000 people (est. 1994).
Other Cities: Mont-Doré, 16,370 people; Dumbéa, 10,052; Poindimié; Koné (1989).
Government: Dominique Bur, High Commissioner named by Paris, since 1995. 54-member Territorial Assembly. The French President is Head of State.
Armed Forces: French troops; 3,700 (1993).

DEMOGRAPHY
Population: 184,000 (1996) **Urban population:** 62.4 % (1996).

ECONOMY
Cereal imports: 40 metric tons (1994) **Fertilizer use:** 1,230 kgs per ha (1994).

Melanesians - Survivors in the Pacific

The peoples of Melanesian origin (from the Greek: "melas" meaning black and "nesia", islands) are clustered in a group of South Pacific islands - New Guinea, Kanaky (New Caledonia), Vanuatu, Solomon, Fiji, Santa Cruz, in other smaller islands and in the Bismarck and Louisiade archipelagos. They are an anthropologically unique population.

Due to the dark colour of their skin and their curled hair, Melanesians were in the past included in the 'Negroid' group. However, recent studies link them human group to the Papuans and even to the aboriginal communities living in Australia. It is also now recognized that the peoples referred to as Melanesian actually include covered two distinct communities and cultures.

The first Melanesians arrived, probably from South Asia, some 40,000 years ago. About 9,000 years ago, these communities started growing crops such as sugarcane.

Later they also specialized in trade and shipbuilding, as well as in fishing. They travelled in small groups, living at certain sites depending the time cycle of crops.

Melanesians speak several languages, including some 400 dialects. The main one, used in Fiji, is spoken by some 334,000 people and used in press and official publications. Other dialects are Motu, Roviana, Bambatana, Tolai and Yabem.

Christianity gradually replaced traditional religions, although some communities still practise rites of cosmic initiation or sorcery.

Nowadays, Western culture has reached even the remotest villages, where it is possible to see certain types of entrepreneurial and capitalist organization, as well as dependence on imported products.

It is in the marginal areas that traditional culture survives and where resistance to the prevailing culture is greatest.

controlled by the caldoches with no indigenous Kanak representation, therefore, the FLNKS unilaterally declared New Caledonia independent, proclaiming a Kanak state. The resulting election boycott involved 80 per cent of the Kanak population, forcing the Government to call off the election, and prepare for negotiations.

[12] On December 5 1984 - immediately after the French Government announced its willingness to talk with the FLNKS - ten Kanak political activists were brutally murdered by right-wing caldoches. This incident led to widespread violence which continued throughout the following year, leaving a toll, among Kanak activists, of almost 40 dead and thousands wounded. Security forces sent in by the French Government, far from controlling the situation, were in fact linked to several of the crimes and violent incidents carried out against the independence movement.

[13] In December 1986, the United Nations General Assembly proclaimed the right of the Kanak people to self-determination and independence, proposing that the FLNKS be recognized as their legitimate representative.

[14] One year later a referendum was held to determine whether or not ties with France should be maintained. Voting was open to all residents of the island, even Europeans and immigrants who arrived as recently as three years and, for this reason, the FLNKS boycotted the referendum.

According to the opposition and the Australian and New Zealand/Aotearoan governments, the high abstention rate of around 41.5 per cent invalidated any claim to legitimacy for continued colonial domination.

[15] In May 1988, the FLNKS captured 22 French gendarmes and held them hostage on the island of Ouvea. Their objective was to negotiate their freedom in exchange for a post-electoral agreement with the French Government.

[16] When all attempts at negotiation failed for the Kanaks, the French attacked the island of Ouvéa, killing 19 people, most of whom were apparently executed rather than killed in combat.

[17] In June 1988, FLNKS leader, Jean-Marie Tjibaou, and Jacques Lafleur (leader of the Caledonian Popular Assembly for the Republic and strongly opposed to independence) signed Section I of the Matignon Accord, supported by the French prime minister Michel Rocard, in Paris. From July that year direct government over Kanaky was re-established from Paris. Section II of the Accord stipulated the adoption of preparatory measures for voting on self-determination in 1998 and the freezing of electoral roll, to prevent France increasing the number of voters by sending new colonists.

[18] The territory was divided into three regions, two with a majority of Kanak voters. One of the aims of this division was to create a Melanesian (Kanak) political and financial "elite", taking over power from the pro-

independence groups in most of the territory. Other clauses of the agreement planned greater financial support from Paris during the following ten years.

[19] In a first referendum that same year, the agreements were ratified. In May 1989, Tjibaou and another independence leader who supported the Matignon agreements were assassinated in Ouvéa.

[20] In 1991, the trade balance was affected by the fall in international prices for nickel and fish. In the two provinces controlled by the pro-independence parties, a new generation of leaders appeared, but the situation worsened for most of the Melanesian population. The imbalance of income became pronounced amongst the Kanaks and greater access to material goods distanced many Melanesians from their community structures and traditions.

[21] In the caldoche areas, mainly covering the capital Nouméa, social inequalities also increased, partly due to the arrival of Melanesian farmers who built shanty towns on the outskirts of the city, but also due to the impoverishment of some caldoches. In a context of increasing social tension, disturbances like those of March 1992 became more common.

[22] The political repercussions of these new social contradictions were reflected in the 1995 provincial elections. The Palika, one of the FLNKS groups, registered separately, criticising the leadership of the Front representatives in the two provinces controlled by the pro-

independence groups. Both political sectors obtained similar results.

[23] On the trade union front, the increasing inequalities showed themselves in the rising number of caldoches in the Union of Exploited Kanak Workers (USTKE). Furthermore, this union, the main "enemy" of the employers' groups, stepped up criticism of the "technocrats" leading the pro-independence provinces.

[24] Nickel exploitation by the pro-independence groups in the northern province gave outstanding results in the first years of their leadership, allowing them to form an association with the Canadian Falconbridge company. However, the pro-independence groups' attempts to establish a processing plant with the Canadian company were complicated by similar plans in the French State mining company, SLN-Eramet. FLNKS sympathizers protested, blocking access to the French-controlled installations.

[25] Negotiations for the independence of Kanaky changed direction in 1998. The FLNKS and Paris set the bases for a general agreement to replace the planned referendum. The co-existence of two different systems - one following the Kanaky tradition and the other imposed by France- was the aspect which provided most difficulties. The Kanaks wanted respect for their cultural roots and traditional civil organization.

Kazakhstan

Kazajstan

Population:	16,820,000 (1996)
Area:	2,717,300 SQ KM
Capitals:	Almaty and Aqmola
Currency:	Tengue
Language:	Kazakh

In the Bronze Age (about 2000 BC), the territory of Kazakhstan was inhabited by tribes who lived by farming and raising livestock. Around 500 BC, an alliance was formed among the Saka peoples and in the 3rd century BC, the Usune and Kangli tribes - who lived near the Uighur, Chechen and Alan - subdued the other tribes in the area. The region was subsequently occupied by Attila's Huns, until they were expelled by the Turks.

[2] In the mid-4th century, the Turkish *Kaganate* (Khanate or kingdom) was formed and later divided into Eastern and Western parts. In the 8th century two states emerged: a Turkish and a Karluk Kaganate. The Turkish conquerors built mosques and tried to impose Islam upon the local population. Over the following 300 years scholarship flourished in the area.

[3] Between the 9th and 12th centuries, the region was occupied by the Oghuz, Kimak, Kipchak and Karajanid tribes. The Kipchaks never achieved political unity and remained outside the realm of Islamic influence, which was concentrated in the cities along the Caspian Sea. Until the 13th century, successive waves of Seleucid, Kidan and Tatar invasions swept across the great steppes. Kipchak chiefs and Muscovite princes joined together to resist foreign domination, but did not achieve independence until the fall of the Mongols.

[4] Most of these peoples were nomads but gradually, settled groups of farmers and artisans were organized, and cities like Otrar, Suyab, Balasagun, Yanguikent, Sauran and Kulan arose. The Silk Road, uniting Byzantium, Iran and China, passed through Kazakhstan. Trade relations developed between the nomads of the steppes and the inhabitants of the oases, which extended as far as Western Europe, Asia Minor and the Far East.

[5] By the late 15th century, the khanate of Kazakh had been formed, disintegrating into three loosely allied but like-minded yuzos (hordes). By the 16th century, an ethnic identity had been forged among the Kazakhs. The khans of the Kazakh yuzos passed on their power to their heirs, who thought of themselves as descendants of Juchi, the eldest son of Genghis Khan. Below them were the sultans, with administrative and judicial power, who governed through the biy and the local chieftains.

[6] In the 17th century, the khanate of Dzhungar carried out successive raids in the Kazakh region, sometimes looting and other times remaining and occupying the area. Russian colonial expansion from the north began in the 18th century. The Russians built a line of forts and then began working their way southward, creating a line of defence against the Dzhungars. The two smaller hordes or yuzos fell under Russian protection eliminating their autonomy in the 1820s because of the frequent rebellions. With the defeat of the Great Horde, annexation of Kazakhstan to the Empire was completed.

[7] Russia installed its government institutions, collected taxes, established areas closed to the Kazakhs and built new cities, declaring the entire territory property of the State. As of 1868, there were six provinces under the control of governors general; the sultans and the biy became mere state officials. The conquest of Kazakhstan was a long process of wars against local tribes. The Cossack regiments were the vanguard of the Russian army and they overcame the khans of Khiva, Boukhara and Kokand, one by one, defeating the last of these in 1880.

[8] The Kazakhs were registered in the censuses as citizens of the State of Russia and were incorporated into the Russian army's foreign expeditions. Kazakhstan became a place to which Russian deportees were sent, including the Decembrists (aristocrats who had conspired against Czar Nikolai I in 1825), Polish and Ukrainian revolutionaries (including the Ukrainian hero, Taras Shevchenko) and the members of the St Petersburg "Petrashevski circle", which included the writer Feodor Dostoyevsky.

[9] In the late 19th century and early 20th century, Russia built huge railroads (the Trans-Caspian, the Trans-Aralian and the Trans-Siberian), which crossed the region, uniting it with distant urban centres and facilitating the exploitation of Kazakhstan's fabulous mineral wealth. A third of Russia's coal reserves, half its copper, lead and zinc reserves; strategic metals like tungsten and molybdenum; iron, and oil were found in Kazakhstan.

Agriculture remained stagnant and attempts to resettle farmers, after the abolition of feudal serfdom in Russia, met with limited success, although there was some development of cotton, wool and traditional Kazakh leather production.

[10] At the beginning of this century, a small nationalist movement emerged in Kazakhstan, and after the Russian Revolution of 1905 the Kazakhs had their own representatives to the first and second Duma (parliament) convened by the Czar. In 1916, when the czarist regime ordered the mobilization of all men between the age of 19 and 43 for auxiliary military service, the Kazakhs rebelled, led by Abdulghaffar and Amangeldy Imanov. The revolt was brutally crushed, but in November 1917, after the triumph of the Soviet revolution in Petrograd, the Kazakh nationalists demanded total autonomy for their country. In the early decades of this century, Kazakhstan received massive waves of Ukrainian, Belorusian, German, Bulgarian, Polish, Jewish and Tatar immigrants. A nationalist government was installed in Alma Ata (now Almaty) in 1918, but the country soon became a battleground.

[11] Fighting between the Red Army and the White Russians - the latter defending the Government that had been overthrown - lasted until 1920, when the counter-revolution was defeated. The Autonomous Soviet Socialist Republic (ASSR) of Kirghiz was formed, as a part of the Russian Federation; it later became known as the ASSR of Kazakhstan. In 1925, the revision of the borders

in Soviet central Asia was completed, and all Kazakh lands were unified. In 1936, Kazakhstan became one of the 15 republics of the USSR and the following year, the local Communist Party was founded.

[12] In addition to developing its industrial potential, the Soviet regime increased the amount of land under cultivation. Previously considered not very fertile (in 1913, only 4.2 million hectares were under cultivation), Kazakhstan increased the number of hectares of tilled land to 35.3 million, 15 per cent of all agricultural land in the USSR. Production included wheat, tobacco, mustard, fruit and cattle. Bringing virgin territory under cultivation was an achievement associated with Leonid Brezhnev, during his period as head of the Communist Party of Kazakhstan. Brezhnev replaced Nikita Khrushchev in 1964 as head of the Soviet Party until his death in 1982. Although he proclaimed an era of "developed socialism", the country's economic and political problems actually worsened during his administration.

[13] Until 1985, the person who wielded the power in Kazakhstan was Dinmujamed Kunaev, a member of the Politburo of the Soviet Communist Party Central Committee. In 1989, the forced resignation of Kunaev triggered student disturbances; the army resorted to violence in dealing with the demonstrators. That year, in mid-summer, a water shortage in the oil-producing city of Novy-Ouzen, on the Caspian Sea, led groups of city residents to launch an attack on the water distribution

PROFILE

ENVIRONMENT

Kazakhstan is bordered to the southeast by China; to the south by Kyrgyzstan; and to the north by the Russian Federation. In the western part of the country lie the Caspian and Turan plains; in the center, the Kazak plateau; and in the eastern and southeastern regions, the Altai, Tarbagatay, Dzhungarian Alatau and Tien Shan mountains. It has a continental climate, with average January temperatures of 18 degrees below zero in the north, and 3 below zero in the south. In July, the temperature varies from 19 degrees in the north, to 28 degrees in the south. Important rivers include the Ural, Irtysh, Syr Dar'ya, Chu and Ili. There is also Lake Balkhash and the Caspian and Aral Seas. The vegetation is characteristic of the steppes, but vast areas have come under cultivation (wheat, tobacco, etc) or are used for cattle-raising. The region's abundant mineral wealth includes coal, copper, semi-precious stones and gold.

SOCIETY

Peoples: Kazakhs, 46.5 per cent, Russians, 35 per cent, Ukrainians, 5 per cent, Uzbeks 2 per cent, Tatars 2 per cent.. **Religions:** Muslim and Christian Orthodox. **Languages:** Kazakh (official), Russian, German, Ugric, Korean, Tatar. **Political Parties:** Union of National Unity, President Nazarbayev's party, moderate; Socialist Party (which replaced the Communist Party); People's Congress; Republican Party, a nationalist party. **Social Organizations:** Independent labor unions are in the process of being formed. Birlik Movement, Zheltokso and Semipalatinsk-Nevada, an anti-nuclear movement.

THE STATE

Official Name: Respublika Kazajstan. **Administrative divisions:** 19 regions and 2 cities. **Capitals:** Almaty, 1,172,400 people (1995) and Aqmola. In 1991, the capital's name was changed from its Russian form, Alma-Ata, to its Kazakh form, Almaty. In 1994 the government decided to gradually transfer the national capital from Almaty to Aqmola in the following years. **Other cities:** Karaganda, 573,700 people, Semipalatinsk, 320,000 people, Pavlodar, 340,700 people, Kokchetav, 127,000 people (1995) **Government:** Nursultan Nazarbayev, President since December, 1991, confirmed in April, 1995. Nurlan Balgimbayev, Prime Minister since October 1997. Unicameral legislative power, with 360 members. **National Holiday:** December 16, Independence (1991). **Armed Forces:** 2 regiments of Russian Air Defence.

STATISTICS

DEMOGRAPHY

Population: 16,820,000 (1996) **Annual growth:** 0.7% (1980/1996) **Estimates for year 2000:** 17,000,000 **Annual growth to year 2000:** 0.1% (1994/2000) **Urban Population:** 60.0% (1996) **Urban growth:** 1.56% (1980/95) **Children per woman:** 2.4 (1996).

HEALTH

Life expectancy at birth: 68 years (1996) male: 63 years (1994) female: 72 years (1994) **Infant mortality:** 38 per 1,000 (1996) **Under-5 child mortality:** 45 per 1,000 (1996) **Safe water:** 93% (1990/96).

EDUCATION

Literacy: 100% (1995) male : 100% (1995) female: 99% (1995) **School enrolment :** Primary total: 87% (1990/95) male : 86% (1990/95) female: 86% (1990/95) Secondary: male : 89% (1990/95) female: 92% (1990/95) Tertiary: 33% (1995) **Primary school teachers:** one for every 20 students (1995).

COMMUNICATIONS

376 **radios**, 260 **TV sets** and 117 **main telephone lines** per 1,000 people (1994) **Books:** 7 new titles per 100,000 people (1992/94).

ECONOMY

Per capita, GNP: $1,350 (1996) **Annual growth, GNP:** 1.8% (1995/96) **Currency:** 59 tengue = $1 (1995) **Fertilizer use:** 34 kgs per ha (1994) **Exports:** $6,230 million (1996) **Imports:** $4,261 million (1996) **External debt:** $2,920 million (1996) $174 **per capita:** (1996) **Debt service:** 9.9% of exports (1996).

ENERGY

Consumption: 3,370.65 Kgs of Oil equivalent per capita yearly (1994) -25.03% imported (1994)

HDI (rank / value) 93 / 0.709 (1994)

---

company. The official version attributed the incident to a group of troublemakers but other sources claimed that the disturbances were more serious, and that they had religious and nationalistic connotations.

[14] After the transformations set in motion in the USSR by Mikhail Gorbachev, the republic of Kazakhstan declared independence. During this period two social movements arose - Birlik and Zheltoksan - as well as the anti-nuclear movement Semipalatinsk-Nevada. The main test-sites for Soviet nuclear weapons were situated in Kazakhstan, as is the Baykonur cosmodrome for launching Soviet space vehicles. After the failed coup against the Soviet President in August 1991, Nursultan Nazarbayev resigned as head of the Soviet Communist Party, of which he had been a member, in his capacity as president of a Soviet republic.

[15] In September, Kazakhstan presented a seven-point plan for the creation of a new union treaty, which was approved by Gorbachev and ten republics. On December 1 1991, Nazarbayev was elected the first president of an independent

Kazakhstan. The Communist Party became the Socialist Party of Kazakhstan. On December 21, in Almaty (Kazak form of Alma Ata), 11 republics signed an agreement which formally dissolved the USSR and created the new Commonwealth of Independent States, whose members will apply separately for admission to the UN. President Nazarbayev's foreign policy envisaged a privileged alliance with Russia and the Islamic republics of the region, as well as closer links with the West.

[16] In 1992, Nazarbayev let the Russian President Boris Yeltsin know that he would not allow the nuclear missiles - installed when Kazakhstan was still part of the USSR - to remain under the exclusive control of Moscow. In 1993, Almaty promised to dismantle these missiles in return for financial aid from the United States.

[17] This same year several political entities were created, like the Socialist Party, the Peoples Congress Party and the ruling Union of National Unity. Nazarbayev also undertook to bring in swiftly a series of privatizations and to stimulate foreign investment.

[18] In March 1994 the first multiparty legislative elections were held, and they were won by Nazarbayev's party. Shortly after the victory, a series of scandals over alleged corruption forced Prime Minister Sergey Tereschenko to resign. He was replaced by Akezhan Kazhegeldin, who immediately announced an acceleration of the economic liberalization process. The government resolved to transfer the national capital from Almaty to Aqmola over a period of several years.

[19] In April, Kazhegeldin launched a vast privatization plan, including 3,500 state enterprises, that is, 70 per cent of the public companies. The rapid introduction of the market economy and the natural riches of the country attracted a large number of foreign investors in 1995, but the economic liberalization also led to a fall in the standard of living for many Kazakhs.

[20] The Constitutional Court annulled the elections of the previous year and the President said he would govern by decree until new elections were held. Nazarbayev, concerned over widespread discontent and the risk of not being re-elected in elections with various candidates, took advantage of the political crisis suggesting his term be extended by referendum until the year 2000. The official results of this poll, carried out in April, gave the President almost unanimous support.

[21] In March 1996, a customs union was created between Kazakhstan, Kyrgyzstan, Belarus and the Russian Federation, aiming to form a common market for goods, capital and workers. The agreement also included possible integration of transport, energy and data systems.

[22] In April 1997, Kazakhstan, along with Kyrgyzstan and Tajikistan, signed an agreement to demilitarize the frontier and reduce the number of troops. This step followed the agreement between Russia and China, as part of a Russian policy of rapprochement with its Asian neighbours thought up in Gorbachev's time. At the end of this year, Kazakhstan signed an agreement for China to exploit some of its largest oil reserves. In October, the Government appointed Nurlan Balgimbayev Prime Minister, replacing Kazhegeldin.

[23] In March 1998, former deputy-prime minister, Kadyr Baikenov, was made head of Kazatomprom, the State atomic energy company, a move considered to mark the return to power of Nazarbayev's "old guard" as a consequence of the resignation of the "liberal" Kazhegeldin, the person behind the controversial privatizations. The latter, was made leader of the Industrial and Business Union and was expected to be a popular rival candidate for the general elections slated for 2000.

Kenya

Kenya

Population: 27,799,000 (1996)
Area: 580,367 SQ KM
Capital: Nairobi

Currency: Shilling
Language: English and Swahili

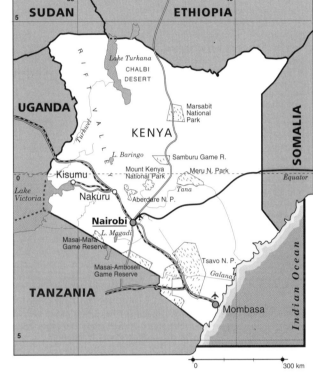

The prosperous city of Malindi was founded in the 10th century on the coast of what is now Kenya. It was the center of a rich African Arab culture (see Tanzania: The Zandj Culture), which was destroyed by a Portuguese armed occupation in the 16th century. When they were forced to withdraw in 1698, the Portuguese left behind only a few abandoned forts and economic ruin, ideal conditions for the slave and ivory trades managed by Shirazi merchants from Zanzibar.

[2] The inland peoples were mainly Bantu with Nilotic and Somalian groups also present. They did not develop material cultures comparable to those of the coast, nor did they evolve into organized states. It was only in the 19th century that the Masai, Nilotic shepherds, succeeded in establishing a certain degree of authority over other groups in the region. A few decades later when a bovine plague annihilated almost all of their herds and deprived them of their economic mainstay, their power base collapsed.

[3] At the end of the 19th century, the Berlin Conference and subsequent German-British agreements delimited spheres of European influence in East Africa. Zanzibar, Kenya and Uganda were assigned to the English who had already settled in Uganda, and who decided to build a railway line from this colony to the coast.

[4] White settlers occupied the lands which "became available" along the railway line after half the local population died in an epidemic of smallpox brought in with Indian labourers. As late as 1948, 4,200 sq km of the approximately 5,000 sq km of fertile land were held between 5,000 European planters, while one million Kikuyu occupied fewer than 1,000 sq km. There was no indemnity or compensation for this theft.

[5] In 1944, the Kenya African Union (KAU) was created to defend Kikuyu interests. Under the leadership of Jomo Kenyatta, KAU organized strikes, farmers' rallies and mass demonstrations.

[6] At almost the same time the Mau-Mau, a political and religious group organized as a secret society, launched its first offensive. The Mau-Mau program was both political and cultural. They demanded self-government, restitution of lands, and wage parity, while rejecting Christianity and other European influences in favor of traditional customs and beliefs.

[7] In 1952, in response to increased Mau-Mau attacks on settlers' lives and property, the colonial administration declared a state of emergency, arrested nationalist leaders (Kenyatta among them), dissolved political parties and imprisoned thousands of Kikuyu in concentration camps.

[8] After years of bitter repression and indiscriminate killing by colonial governments, KAU was legalized in 1960 as the Kenya African National Union (KANU).

[9] KANU found electoral support among leading urban and ethnic communities and, with British encouragement, was able to defeat tribal-based political movements. In 1961, Kenya was freed and in 1962 the Legislative Council was elected. After the May 1963 elections Kenya was granted autonomy. It achieved independence within the Commonwealth on December 12 1963. Kenyatta became Prime Minister, and when his country achieved full independence on December 12 1964, he was elected first president.

[10] However, Jomo Kenyatta, a nom de guerre meaning "Kenya's flaming spear", soon forgot his commitment to the nation as a whole, and began to favor his own ethnic group, the Kikuyu. His government encouraged private enterprise and transnational concerns. Farmers who had won back their lands lost them again under the burden of debt.

[11] A black bourgeoisie, largely Kenyatta's family and friends, took over where the former colonists had left off. KANU, once a model for other African parties in the struggle against foreign domination, succumbed to neo-colonialism. It even went so far as to admit British military forces to the port of Mombasa and allowed its own military installations to be used for the notorious Israeli raid on Entebbe, Uganda.

[12] This led to a breach of relations between Kenya and Uganda, and tension with Tanzania grew over differences in economic policies. The three countries were unable to consolidate 1967 plans for an East African Economic Community, and this ambitious integration project was finally dropped in 1977.

[13] Kenyatta died at the age of 85 in September 1978. He was succeeded by his vice-president, Daniel Arap Moi, a member of the smaller Kalenjin ethnic group.

[14] This might have soothed ethnic

PUBLIC EXPENDITURE

6.2% **27.1%**
1995 ■ DEFENCE □ SOCIAL

In 1990/91 Military as % of health & education expenditure was 24%.

WORKERS

(1996)

Labour force %
■ WOMEN
□ MEN
46   54

■ AGRICULTURE 80% (1990)
□ INDUSTRIAL 7%
■ SERVICES 13%

LAND USE

DEFORESTATION -0.6 % annual (81/90)
IRRIGATED 1.7 % of arable

(1993)

■ FOREST & WOODLAND 28.9%
□ ARABLE 6.9%
■ OTHER 64.2%

PROFILE

ENVIRONMENT

Kenya is located on the east coast of central Africa. There are four main regions, from east to west: the coastal plains with regular rainfall and tropical vegetation; a sparsely populated inland strip with little rainfall which extends towards the north and northwest; a mountainous zone linked to the eastern end of the Rift valley, with a climate tempered by altitude, and volcanic soil fit for agriculture (most of the population and the main economic activities are concentrated here); and the west which is covered by an arid plateau, part of which benefits from the moderating influence of Lake Victoria. The principal environmental problems are soil exhaustion, erosion and desertification; deforestation; pollution of drinking water supplies, especially near such large cities as Nairobi and Mombasa.

SOCIETY

Peoples: Kenyans are descended from the main African ethnic groups: Bantu, Nilo-Hamitic, Sudanese and Cushitic. Numerically and culturally, the most significant groups are the Kikuyu, the Luyia and the Luo. Others include the Kamba, Meru, Gusii and Embu. There are Indian and Arab minorities.
Religions: 73 per cent of the population are Christian, 6 per cent are Muslim and 20 per cent practice traditional religions.
Languages: English and Swahili are the official ones. The latter is the national language. Kikuyu and Kamba are also spoken.
Political Parties: Kenya African National Union (KANU) founded in 1943 by Jomo Kenyatta. A Constitutional reform allowed the formation of new parties in 1991. Forum for the Restoration of Democracy (FORD), split into two branches in 1992 (FORD-Asili and FORD-Kenya); Democratic Party (DP); Kenya Social Congress (KSC); Kenya National Congress (KNC).
Social Organizations: Central Organization of Trade Unions (COTU), founded by the Government in 1965.

THE STATE

Official Name: Jamhuri ya Kenya.
Capital: Nairobi, 2,079,000 people (1995).
Other cities: Mombasa, 465,000 people; Kisumu 185,100 people, Nakuru, 162,800 people; Machakos, 92,300 people (1989).
Government: Daniel Arap Moi, President since September 1978, re elected in 1993 and 1997. Legislature: National Assembly (single-chamber), with 202 members, elected every five years.
National Holiday: December 12, Independence Day (1963).
Armed Forces: 24,200 troops.
Other: 5,000.

Maternal Mortality
1990

PER 100,000 LIVE BIRTHS
650

Literacy
1995

78%

conflict in Kenya, but penetration by transnationals produced structural imbalances, worsening an already difficult economic situation and aggravating social tensions. Even before Kenyatta's death there was growing distrust between the urban consumer bourgeoisie and the larger rural population. The country people's whole way of life was being steadily degraded, as the market for cash crops undermined traditional communal self-sufficiency.

[15] Arap Moi was interim president from September 1978 until the general election of November. KANU was the only party authorized to run candidates, and Moi was confirmed as President.

[16] In early 1979, President Moi declared an amnesty for political prisoners and launched a campaign against corruption. The first measures of the new administration revealed a technocratic approach which deflated hopes of radical change. One of the outstanding

technocrats was Charles Njonjo, appointed minister of home affairs in June 1980.

[17] Njonjo played a key role in dissolving the ethnic-based organizations that arose in the early 1970s. The largest of these, GEMA (the Gikuyo, Embu and Meru Association), led by a millionaire, became a powerful pressure group for tribal leaders who were growing rich from business with British and US companies.

[18] GEMA opposed Moi's designation, and after the death of Jomo Kenyatta had been indirectly involved in a conspiracy to assassinate all top government officials.

[19] Droughts and crop changes led to a drop in the production of corn and other basic consumer goods. Credits supplied by multinational companies encouraged Kenyan farmers to grow flowers and to plant sugarcane, coffee and tea for export under the control of large North American and British firms. As a result, the government had to

import huge quantities of corn and wheat from the US and South Africa.

[20] These difficulties led President Moi to seek reconciliation with old political rivals who had been excluded from public life. It was a manoeuvre devised to neutralize potential opposition at a moment of great instability. Former vice-president Oginga Odinga, a veteran nationalist politician who had broken with Kenyatta in 1971 in disagreement with KANU's conciliatory policy, was one of the major beneficiaries of this relaxation of the regime. Odinga had lost his political rights after founding a dissident party, the Kenya Popular Union (KAPU). After 11 years of ostracism, he returned to parliament at the end of 1981.

[21] Despite all this reconciliation, the crisis erupted into violence in August 1982, in a military conspiracy that unleashed widespread rioting and looting of shops and public buildings in Nairobi. The coup attempt had been staged by members of the air force, leading to the disbanding of all airforce units after the army had suppressed the rebellion.

[22] Repression also affected the university, where dozens of professors and students were detained. Oginga Odinga was placed under house arrest and the university was closed down indefinitely. The frustrated coup precipitated profound changes in Kenyan politics and sowed distrust among the different political elements in KANU.

[23] In May 1983, President Moi denounced a conspiracy involving minister Charles Njonjo, supported by Israel and South Africa. In the midst of the confusion, President Moi decided to call general elections, in which his followers won a landslide victory, while Njonjo and his supporters were overwhelmingly defeated.

[24] Moi's administration reopened the border with Tanzania in November 1983, after a summit meeting in Arusha with Tanzania's Julius Nyerere and Uganda's Milton Obote. The meeting was a point of departure for gradually renewing economic co-operation between Kenya, Tanzania and Uganda after the failure of the

East African Economic Community in 1977.

[25] President Arap Moi had extended the executive's jurisdiction to the detriment of the parliament. He made it compulsory for civil servants to join KANU, and replaced secret voting in internal party elections with a public vote making intimidation easier. The moderate women's opposition group, Mandeleo Ya Wanawake, was taken over by the Government in 1986.

[26] Reports backed by Amnesty International and other groups implicated the government in torture and the murder of opposition members, especially the "subversive" Mwakenya group.

[27] During October and November 1987, Muslim demonstrations in Mombasa served to justify a further wave of repression in which Nairobi University was once again closed. In December, a series of frontier skirmishes with Uganda, plus the expulsion of Libyan diplomats accused of encouraging civil disorder, seemed to herald new disturbances.

[28] Despite harsh "restructuring" policies imposed by the IMF and World Bank, elections in March 1988 consolidated the position of Moi's followers within both KANU and the Government. By August, Moi had completed his authoritarian reorganization by placing the judiciary directly under his command. He prolonged the period for which detainees may be held without notifying a judge from 24 hours to 14 days.

[29] In the years that followed, cases of corruption and human rights violations became more widespread. In April 1989 Vice-President Josephat Karanja lost the confidence of parliament, accused of furthering his interests and those of his own tribe. After he resigned, Karanja was expelled from KANU.

[30] Robert Ouko, the Foreign Affairs minister and a harsh critic of corruption in the cabinet was murdered in February 1990. An inquest carried out by Scotland Yard disclosed that the culprits were close advisers of the President. This triggered a new wave of popular anti-government protests.

Food Dependency

1970
6 %

1994
15%

External Debt

1996

PER CAPITA
$248

STATISTICS

DEMOGRAPHY
Population: 27,799,000 (1996) **Annual growth:** 3.2% (1980/1996) **Estimates for year 2000:** 30,300,000 **Annual growth to year 2000:** 2.3% (1994/2000) **Urban Population:** 29.5% (1996) **Urban growth:** 7% (1980/95) **Children per woman:** 5 (1996).

HEALTH
Life expectancy at birth: 54 years (1996) male: 52 years (1994) female: 55 years (1994) **Infant mortality:** 61 per 1,000 (1996) **Under-5 child mortality:** 90 per 1,000 (1996) **Calorie consumption:** 89% (1988/90) 20,000 **people per doctor** (1988/91) **Safe water:** 53% (1990/96).

EDUCATION
Literacy: 78% (1995) male : 86% (1995) female: 70% (1995) **School enrolment :** Primary total: 91% (1990/95) male : 92% (1990/95) female: 91% (1990/95) Secondary: male : 28% (1990/95) female: 23% (1990/95) **Primary school teachers:** one for every 31 students (1995).

COMMUNICATIONS
10 **newspapers,** 88 **radios,** 20 **TV sets** and 9 **main telephone lines** per 1,000 people (1994).

ECONOMY
Per capita, GNP: $ 320 (1996) **Annual growth, GNP:** 3.1% (1995/96) **Annual inflation:** 13.02% (1985/95) **Consumer price index:** 290.6 (1994) **Currency:** 55.85 shillings = $ 1 (1995) **Cereal imports:** 622 metric tons (1994) **Food import dependency:** 15% (1994) **Fertilizer use:** 305 kgs per ha (1994) **Exports:** $ 2,203 million (1996) **Imports:** $ 3,480 million (1996) **External debt:** $6,893 million (1996) $ 248 **per capita:** (1996) **Debt service:** 27.5% of exports (1996) **Development aid received:** $ 707 million (1995) $ 42 per capita (1995) 3.9% of GNP (1994).

ENERGY
Consumption: 110.38 Kgs of Oil equivalent per capita yearly (1994) 83.00% imported (1994).

HDI (rank / value) 134 / 0.463 (1994)

[31] Through the active preaching of the Catholic and Protestant churches, democratization demands spread throughout the country.

[32] Kenya's diplomatic isolation became more marked during the 1980s, but it decreased after the Gulf war. Kenya's strict alignment with the interests of the US-led coalition enabled the country to receive economic aid from Britain, and military support from Washington.

[33] The permanent deterioration in the human rights situation, however, led to the severing of diplomatic relations with Norway in 1991, and relations with Sudan, Ethiopia, and Uganda also became tense. The governments of Kenya and Sudan accused each other of protecting rebel groups, hostile to Nairobi and Khartoum, operating in the neighboring country. Political differences between Uganda and Kenya have caused permanent conflict since 1986.

[34] The economy has been incapable of achieving growth rates like those of the past decade. According to official estimates, inflation in 1990 amounted to 15 per cent, but all independent sources indicate it was very near to 30 per cent. As a result of the Gulf war oil import expenditure was a great deal higher than expected, and this had a negative effect on the trade balance.

[35] Tourism dropped sharply, and the servicing of the foreign debt accounted for 30 per cent of 1990 exports. Like other countries in the region, Kenya implemented cuts in public expenditure, which included privatizing state-run companies and not filling vacancies in the public sector. Kenya's economy is heavily dependent on foreign aid.

[36] The KANU called the party Council to discuss the introduction of democratic reforms, including authorization for several national opposition parties. Lobbying groups such as the Forum for the Restoration of Democracy (FORD), led by Oginga Odinga, and the Moral Alliance for Peace (MAP), became fully-fledged parties.

[37] In order to keep the situation under control, the Government continued to imprison opposition leaders. Early in 1992, lawyer James Orengo and environmentalist Wangari Maathai were arrested and accused of "spreading malicious rumours" that President Moi planned to interrupt the democratization process started in 1991.

[38] In February, 1992, the Democratic Party (PD) was created. It was a new opposition group which proposed the creation of a multiparty democratic system. Meanwhile, women's groups demanded greater participation in politics; they constituted 53 per cent of the electoral roll and 80 per cent of the work force in agriculture, the country's main production sector. That same month a march organized by FORD rallied over 100,000 people in Nairobi demanding the end of repression and press censorship, and a definite date for elections. This was the first authorized anti-government march in the country's 22 years of independent life.

[39] Several Government ministers had resigned in January to form new political parties, and in March, a general strike called by wives of political prisoners was crushed by the government. Further violence occurred in April, when clashes broke out between various tribes in the western part of the country. The Government banned all political meetings and began censoring the press. Nevertheless, the general strike called by the opposition constituted a setback for President Arap Moi.

[40] General elections were held in December. President Arap Moi was re-elected amidst accusations of fraud. His party obtained 95 seats with 36 per cent of the vote, while the opposition had only 88 seats with 60 per cent of the returns.

[41] In February 1993, the IMF considered Kenya's plan to privatize and liberalize foreign trade was insufficient. In April, Sheik Khaled Balala from the opposition's Islamic Party was arrested on charges for the murder of three policemen. In November, international finance organizations lifted the boycott imposed in February, since the government promised to fight against corruption and remove several restrictions on free trade.

[42] Liberalization continued in 1994: Nairobi eliminated exchange controls to attract private investors from Kenya and abroad. An extended drought hit several provinces especially in the eastern side of the country and in the Rift Valley which led the Government to grant urgent assistance to the affected regions. The forced relocation of some 2,000 Kikuyu farmers from the Rift Valley caused serious riots and confrontation with police.

[43] In December, financial organizations and Kenya's creditor countries expressed their satisfaction with the country's economic policy and the introduction of a multiparty system by Nairobi. In 1995, the Government announced the partial privatization of the national airline and other major state companies. However, despite some isolated progress in the field, organizations such as Amnesty International continued to accuse Arap Moi of human rights violations.

[44] In March 1996 the World Bank approved a $115 million loan for road reconstruction. A month later, the IMF paid a $214 million loan, blocked since 1994. Kenya signed an economic cooperation agreement with China and Iran offered its assistance in energy, industry and crops.

[45] Thousands of people were displaced in 1997 due to floods in the northeast. Social and political tension grew significantly throughout the year. In February, thousands of students protested for the murder of a student leader. In late October, an opposition candidate was killed in a shootout between the police and criminals. The Government and part of the opposition initiated talks in Nairobi about the elections.

[46] In November, President Daniel Arap Moi dissolved Parliament and, on December 29, was re-elected by 40.1 per cent of the vote. His ruling party obtained 109 of the 202 seats at the National Assembly. In January 1998, the controversial President appointed a new cabinet.

[47] In August around 250 people were killed and many injured in a car-bomb explosion outside the US embassy. It was thought to be linked to the global World Islam Front network of Saudi Osama bin Laden.

Kiribati

Kiribati

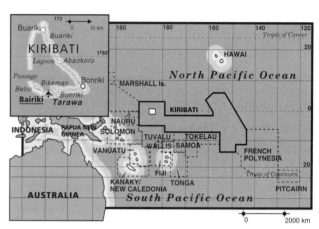

Population:	80,000 (1996)
Area:	726 SQ KM
Capital:	Bairiki on the island of Tarawa
Currency:	Australian dollars
Language:	Kiribati and English

The islands that make up the Republic of Kiribati (formerly known as Gilbert Islands) are inhabited by Micronesian people. In 1764 these islands were visited by and named after British explorer Gilbert.

[2] Missionaries arrived in 1857, and three years later, trade in palm oil and copra began. In 1892 the island became a British protectorate. In 1915 the islands were annexed to the neighboring Ellice archipelago (now Tuvalu), to form the colony of the Gilbert and Ellice Islands.

[3] In 1916 Banaba Island became part of the colony. At that time, there were large deposits of guano on the island which were exploited by the British Phosphate Commission from 1920, and exported to Australia and New Zealand. The Banabans were evacuated during World War II and resettled on the island of Rabi, 2,600 km from Fiji. They were unable to return to their island because the open-cast mining of guano had made the island uninhabitable.

[4] After discussing different alternatives in 1981 the Banabans obtained an indemnity of £19 million from the British Government. In 1957 Britain, as part of its nuclear armament program, detonated three hydrogen bombs near Christmas Island.

[5] The Polynesian population of the Ellice Islands obtained administrative separation in 1975, arguing that the ethnic, historical and cultural differences between them and the Melanesian majority of the Gilbert Islands made secession necessary. Under the name of the Territory of Tuvalu these islands gained independence in 1978.

[6] The inhabitants of the Gilbert Islands proclaimed independence on July 12 1979 adopting the name: Republic of Kiribati (the equivalent of "Gilbert" in Gilbertan).

[7] As the soil is not suitable for large-scale cultivation, copra and fish are the main exports. Copra production is in the hands of small landowners, while the exportation of the product is handled exclusively by the national trading company. Problems facing copra production include abrupt variations in price. Fishing is carried out primarily under agreements with Japanese, US, Korean and Taiwanese fishing fleets.

[8] Kiribati also hopes to exploit deep-sea mineral deposits. The manganese discovered is considered the highest-grade deposit of its kind in the world.

[9] In 1986 Kiribati began negotiations with the IMF and was recognized by the UN as one of the world's poorest countries, a fact which gives it access to certain credit and trade advantages.

[10] A 1989 UN report on global warming and the possible rise in sea level said that Kiribati could disappear under the rising sea.

[11] In the 1991 elections, Teatao Teannaki won with 46 per cent of the vote, producing the first change in president since independence.

[12] In a regional meeting attended by representatives of the Asian-Pacific nations in 1993, the Bairiki delegate asked for detailed studies of global warming. Australia promised aid to create a natural disasters prevention centre in Kiribati.

[13] In May 1994, the government of President Teannaki - accused of poor administration of public funds - lost a vote of confidence in Parliament and was forced to stand down. In July, the opposition coalition Maneaba Te Mauri won a parliamentary majority and in the September presidential elections, Teburoro Tito took over as national leader.

[14] The new president abandoned the privatization of State enterprises started by his predecessors, and in 1995 he announced his intention to increase the prices paid to the copra producers and the salaries of civil servants. The Tito government also expressed concern at the passage of Japanese plutonium-loaded vessels through the region and criticized French nuclear tests in the Pacific.

[15] In 1996 the Government proposed a balanced budget, including a 1.7 per cent rise in public spending. Part of the funds still came out of a reserve fund established from the payment of rights over phosphate mining on the island of Banaba, a resource depleted since 1979.

[16] Also in 1996, Kiribati signed a trade agreement with China, in order to increase commerce between both countries.

[17] In December, at the Conference for an Independent and Nuclear Energy-Free Pacific Ocean, in Fiji, Tito supported this country's proposal intended to definitely ban nuclear weapon tests in the world.

[18] In August 1997, Kiribati signed a friendship treaty with Tuvalu. In September, the Government of Japan contributed $40 million to build the Betio port, one of Kiribati's largest.

PROFILE

ENVIRONMENT
33 islands and coral atolls scattered over 5 thousand million sq km in Micronesia. The climate is tropical and rainy, tempered by the effect of sea winds. The country's large phosphate deposits are now virtually exhausted. Fishing and underwater mineral deposits make up Kiribati's major economic potential.

SOCIETY
Peoples: The population is mostly of Micronesian descent. Kiribati 97.4 per cent; mixed (Kiribati and other) 1.5 per cent; Tuvaluan 0.5 per cent; European 0.2 per cent; other 0.4 per cent. **Languages:** Kiribati and English. **Political Parties:** National Progressive Party and the Maneaban te Mauri. **Social Organizations:** Kiribati General Labor Confederation.

THE STATE
Official Name: Republic of Kiribati.
Capital: Bairiki on the island of Tarawa, 26,000 people (1994).
Other cities: Abaiang, 5,314 people; Tarawa, 28,802; Tabiteuea, 4,600. **Government:** Teburoro Tito, President since 1994. Parliament is made up of 39 members, elected by direct popular vote, plus one representative of Banaba Island.
National Holiday: July 12, Independence Day (1979).

DEMOGRAPHY
Population: 80,000 (1996) **Annual growth:** 1.7 % (1980/1996) **Urban population:** 36.0 % (1996)

HEALTH
Life expectancy at birth: 58 years (1996) **Infant mortality:** 56 per 1,000 (1996) **Under-5 child mortality:** 76 per 1,000 (1996) **Safe water:** 100 % (1990/96)

EDUCATION
Literacy: 93 % (1995) female: 92 % (1995) **School enrolment:** Primary total: 91 % (1990/95)

ECONOMY
Currency: 1.34 Australian dollars = $ 1 (1995) **Cereal imports:** 8 metric tons (1994)

Korea

North Korea
South Korea
(see history and
statistics on the
following pages)

The Korean peninsula lies between China and Japan, and this position has shaped the nation's history, and the character of its people. The territory has frequently been the arena of struggles between armies from China, Mongolia and Japan. The peninsula was first inhabited by tribes of the Tungu language which emigrated to Siberia. Between the 10th and 8th centuries BC several tribal states were established, of which the most complex was the one known as Old Choson, in the Taedong river basin. Towards the 4th century BC, Choson developed into a league of tribes grouped between the basins of the Liao and Taedong rivers. At this time, Choson inhabitants used weapons made of iron, harnesses for horses and war carriages. In 108 BC, the Chinese empire defeated the kingdom of Choson and replaced it with four Chinese colonies. During the height of Old Choson, other tribal states flourished in the peninsula: Puyo, in the Manchurian region of the Sungari river basin, and Chin, which during the 2nd century BC appeared to the south of the Han river and was later divided into three tribal states (Mahan, Chinhan and Pyonhan).

2   The different leagues expanded through the peninsula which, as of the 1st century BC, was divided into the rival kingdoms of Koguryo, Paekche and Silla. Koguryo (which in the 6th century covered an area similar to the present North Korea) was founded by Chu-mong in 37 BC; Paekche was founded by Onjo in 19 BC, and Silla by Pak Hyokkose in 57 BC. These three states were consolidated by king Taejo (53-146) in Koguryo, king Koi (204-286) in Paekche and king Naemul (356-402) in Silla. The three kingdoms developed into states through successive wars which led to the organization of centralized military and administrative systems. A powerful aristocracy grew up in all of them, comprised of tribal chiefs from the respective capitals. Another common feature of these kingdoms was that they developed highly sophisticated cultures and produced their own historiographies in order to strengthen the authority of the state.

3   With the support of the T'ang Chinese dynasty, Silla conquered Paekche in the year 660 and Koguryo in 668. However, the survivors of the defeated Koguryo, led by general Tae Cho-yang, established the kingdom of Perhae to the north of present Manchuria and soon, impeded by China from integrating with the other Korean kingdom, entered into direct confrontation with Silla. The peninsula was divided into two states, one in the north and one in the south, both paying taxes to China. Perhae became a very sophisticated state, called "the prosperous state of the East" by the Chinese, but after it fell into the hands of the Khitan, a nomad people from the north, its territory no longer came into the history of Korea.

4   United Silla became an absolute monarchy, which minimized the influence of the aristocracy. The Chinese variant of Avatamsaka Buddhism offered the ideological base for the monarchy and the aristocracy, while the underprivileged were attracted to Pure Land Buddhism, which promised redemption in the next world. In the capital (current Kyongju, in South Korea), the monarchs built giant palaces and royal tombs, while the state's administration was divided, following China's example, into provinces, prefectures and counties.

5   The decline of Silla began towards the end of the 8th century, as a result of peasant uprisings and conflicts with the aristocracy, which had abolished royal despotism. A new system was established which increased the power of some landlords. Two provincial leaders, Konhwon and Kungye, established the kingdoms of Late Koguryo and Late Paechke respectively. During this period, known as the Three Late Kingdoms, Zen Buddhism was the most popular religion, with emphasis on individual fulfilment through contemplation. This doctrine was much less hierarchical than that of Avatamsaka Buddhism, and favoured individual autonomy.

6   In 918, Wang Kong founded Songak (today's Kaesong, in North Korea) and in 936 he united the peninsula once more, incorporating the survivors of Late Paechke, devastated by the Khitan. Wang Kong proclaimed himself the legitimate succesor of Koguryo and repeatedly confronted the Khitan, expanding Koguryo's territory up to the Yalu river. Wang Kong was the founder of the Koryo dynasty, from which the western name Korea derives. The ruling class of Koryo was made up mainly of provincial lords, owners of castles, and by Silla's old aristocracy. Koryo was ruled by a Supreme State Council, formed by aristocrats, who adopted Buddhism as a religion to achieve spiritual goals and personal happiness, while they practised the political principles and ethical values of Confucianism.

7   In spite of the practical need to have a strong defensive system, the military were not well treated. This led to a coup in 1170 and, taking advantage of the subsequent chaos, one of the generals, Ch'oe Ch'ung-hon, established a military regime from 1197 to 1258. The Koryo dynasty stayed in power because the Ch'oe family preferred to rule behind the scenes and did not overtake the throne. In the 13th. century, Koryo was repeatedly invaded by the Mongols, who came to have great influence in the court. In 1392, Confucian master Yi song-gye overthrew the tottering dynasty and founded the Choson (Yi) dynasty, which would last until 1910. In 1394, Yi Song-gye founded Seoul and turned it into the capital of the kingdom.

8   The territory controlled by the Yi dynasty came to be known as Choson, with the approval of the emperor of China. The Confucian ethical system was officially adopted and replaced Buddhism, which had become corrupt. Choson was dominated by an hereditary aristocratic class, called yangban, which devoted itself to the study of neo-Confucian doctrines. During the kingdom of Sejo, the seventh monarch, a government structure emerged, led by the yangban ideology. The country was divided into eight provinces and the central government appointed the

administrative chiefs of the state. Legal codes were written and the State Council took charge of the administration. During the 15th century many teachers were recruited to serve the government. They criticized the bureaucracy and recommended several radical measures to implement the ideas of Confucius. However, these teachers had to leave the administration due to strong pressures.

9   In 1597, Toyotomi Hideyoshi, a Japanese military leader who had just reunited his country, invaded Shohon with the excuse of invading China. The national crisis made people from all spheres of life, including Buddhist monks, to join in the struggle against the invaders. In 1598, with China's help, the Koreans forced the retreat of the aggressors, but most of Shohon was devastated. Many palaces, public buildings and homes were burnt, numerous national treasures destroyed and a large number of craftsmen and experts were kidnapped and taken to Japan. In the beginning of the 17th century, nomad Manchurians invaded Shohon, took over the northern part of the territory, and captured Seoul in 1636, demanding the unconditional surrendering of the king. In 1640, the Manchurians overthrew the Ming dynasty in China and replaced it with the Ch'ing dynasty. The taxes Korea paid to the Ming went to the Ch'ing.

10   During the second half of the 17th century and throughout the 18th century, the Korean society underwent great changes. Rice became widespread and irrigation systems were improved. Agricultural production was increased and the peasants standard of living improved. Tobacco and gingseng crops encouraged domestic and foreign trade, thus intensifying contacts with European tradesmen and Catholic priests. Meanwhile, radical ideological changes were taking place in Korea, since many teachers no longer concerned themselves only with theoretical speculation but also with matters of practical importance. This gave birth to *silhak* or education based on pragmatism, which urged the government to undergo changes. Also, a school of silhak devoted itself to the study of the Korean language and history and facilitated, jointly with the development of popular art, the access of the people to written texts. To the end of the 18th century some teachers of silhak had converted to Catholicism, followed by members of the aristocracy. Large sectors of the population, encouraged by the hope of finding equality before God after death, were seduced by the new religion which expanded itself rapidly.

11   The decline of the Yi dynasty was characterized by economic and religious factors, added to outside pressures. The yangban or aristocracy had appropriated public lands and did not pay taxes, which led the government to increase the taxes on the poor, who could not pay and lost their lands. When the famines came, the government did not have enough money to alleviate the situation. Also, the state banned Christianity due to its incompatibility with Confucianism. During the persecutions of 1801, 1839 and 1866, the converted teachers were forced to die or fall into apostasy, while foreign missionaries were beheaded. At the same time, Japan pressed Korea to open its foreign trade and China increased its interference in the peninsula to counterbalance the Japanese influence. In 1860, the scholar Ch'oe-u founded a popular religion called *Tonhak* (oriental teachings) which combined elements of Confucianism, Christianity, Shamanism and Buddhism. Soon, these new teachings, in the name of resistance against foreigners and corruption, gained a large following among peasants and, by 1893, had turned into a political movement. In May 1893, the Tonhak followers took the city of Chonju, in the southwest and the two intervening powers, China and Japan, sent troops to crush them.

12   To justify their military presence in the peninsula, Japan proposed that China carry out a joint reform in Korea, but China's negative reply led to a military conflict which ended with a Japanese victory. Emboldened by the victory over China in 1895, Japan occupied Korea in 1905 and in 1910 the country was formally annexed, putting an end to the Yi dynasty.

13   With the defeat of Japan in World War II, Korea was occupied on each side of the 38th parallel: the northern part by Soviet troops and the southern by the United States. Korean hopes for a united, independent country seemed on the verge of being realized but a complex struggle of interests between the two powers did not make it possible. The Soviet Union maintained its influence and did not allow general elections in the north of the peninsula. In the south, under the supervision of a United Nations Temporary Commission, elections were held in May 1948 and Syngman Rhee was elected first president of the Republic of Korea, whose capital was established in Seoul. Meanwhile, the Supreme Assembly of the People of North Korea wrote a new constitution, which came into effect in August 1948. Kim Il-Sung was appointed prime minister and on September 9 the People's Republic of Korea was proclaimed, with its capital in Pyŏngyang.

14   On October 12, the Soviet Union recognized this state as the only legitimate government of Korea. In December, the General

Assembly of the United Nations recognized the exclusive sovereignty of the southern Republic of Korea. Most foreign troops left both countries the following year but US troops remained in the south under the UN flag, then dominated by the United States.

15   In June 1950, North Korea launched a carefully planned offensive against South Korea. The United Nations convened all of its members, to put a stop to the invasion. In the meantime, US President Truman called out his army to assist South Korea, without asking Congress to declare war.

16   Likewise, Truman failed to seek UN permission before sending the US Fleet to the Strait of Formosa to protect one of the US Army's flanks, and also to come to the assistance of Chiang Kai Shek's anti-communist Chinese regime, which had established itself on the island of Formosa (Taiwan). This, in turn, gave rise to fears in Peking of a nationalist invasion of "continental" China.

17   In the meantime, the military campaign on the Korean peninsula was turning into a disaster for the South Koreans and US troops, who had arrived hurriedly and poorly equipped, and were forced to retreat nearly as far as Pusan, on the southern coast.

18   Defeat was narrowly avoided by the action of General Douglas MacArthur, who landed some 160 km south of the 38th parallel and managed to divide and defeat North Korean troops.

19   China, concerned over the advancing allied troops, warned that the presence of the US in North Korea would force it to enter the war. MacArthur ignored the warning and in November launched his "Home by Christmas" offensive.

20   However, China sent 180,000 troops to Korea and by mid-December it had driven US troops back, south of the 38th parallel. On December 31 1951, China launched a second offensive against South Korea, subsequently taking up positions along the former border.

21   After differences of opinion on military strategy, MacArthur was relieved of his command by Truman. It was later revealed that MacArthur had outlined plans to use nuclear weapons against Chinese cities, advocating full-scale war with China.

22   The battle continued up and down the peninsula and the city of Seoul changed hands several times. The conflict lasted for 17 months and left four million dead.

23   After renewed fighting in June 1953, an armistice went into effect the following month. From that time on, Korea was officially separated by the 38th parallel.

24   On August 8 1990, the UN Security Council unanimously approved the admission of both Koreas. On December 13 1991, Prime Ministers Yon Kyong Muk (North Korea) and Chong Won Shik (South Korea) signed a "Reconciliation, Non-Aggression, Exchange, and Cooperation Agreement". This has been the most important step towards reunification since 1972. The Korean peninsula is in a strategic region located between the three large powers of Russia, China and Japan. There are currently intense negotiations underway to solve the nuclear question.

North Korea

Choson Minjujuui In´min

Population:	22,466,000 (1996)
Area:	120,538 SQ KM
Capital:	P'yongyang
Currency:	Won
Language:	Korean

On February 16 1948, the People's Republic of Korea was proclaimed in Pyongyang and Kim Il Sung, leader of the Korean Workers Party was elected Prime Minister.

[2] The kingdom of Koguryo, the equivalent in the 7th century of the present North Korea, had a special way of treating foreign enemies. It avoided direct confrontation and maintained an impressive military capacity within the cities (see history of Korea). North Korea also had a similar strategy since it limited its outer contact and devoted its efforts to achieve considerable military strength. Despite its geographical proximity to the People's Republic of China, North Korea tried to remain neutral in the Sino-Soviet conflict.

[3] The Korean Workers Party (KWP) has enjoyed uninterrupted power for five decades. The party's philosophy is called Juche, a blend of self-reliance, nationalism and centralized control of the economy.

[4] With the establishment of a socialist regime, agrarian reform was carried out, with part of the country's agriculture being collectivized. Industrialization had begun during Japanese occupation, and large textile, chemical and hydroelectric plants were established.

[5] With the war behind it (1950-53, see Korea), and armistice signed in Panmunjon, North Korea devoted all its efforts to the reconstruction of the country, which had been devastated by the War. When Syngman Rhee was ousted from office in South Korea (1960), North Korea attempted rapprochement with its neighbor. However, when the military took power in Seoul these overtures were interrupted.

[6] The development of industry, expanding rapidly after 1958, was aided by the availability of rich mineral deposits. The Yalu River Hydroelectric Plant was built in conjunction with China.

[7] Korea adopted a socialist economy with central planning; 90 per cent of the national industry was in the hands of the State with the remaining 10 per cent organized in cooperatives.

[8] Between 1954 and 1961, North Korea signed military assistance treaties with China and the USSR. In 1972, a new constitution was approved, making Kim Il Sung President as well as Prime Minister.

[9] Kim Jong Il, Kim Il Sung's son, was named head of the government in 1980. In 1984, North Korea provided relief to flood victims in South Korea. That same year, the formation of mixed enterprises was authorized in the construction, technology and tourist sectors.

[10] In 1988, North Korea began "ideological rectification" in direct contrast to the Soviet liberalization process introduced by Gorbachev.

[11] In 1990, there were massive demonstrations in support of the regime, on Kim Il Sung's 78th birthday; he was re-elected in May 1991. During this period, North and South Korea intensified their efforts toward warmer relations, with an eye to eventual reunification.

[12] According to North Korea, any possibility of reunification was to be preceded by a formal peace treaty with the US and removal of their troops from Korean soil. In 1990, North Korea submitted a proposal for denuclearization to the International Agency for Atomic Energy, subject to guarantees from the US that it would not use the 1,000 nuclear bombs it has in South Korea against them.

[13] In 1991, the USSR cut Korea's oil quota by half. Signs of the regime's growing economic difficulties began to show. From 1992, Kim Jong Il assumed responsibility for the formulation of the country's foreign policy.

[14] In mid-1992, the Government issued a report on the country's nuclear installations, including its Yongbyon plant, to the International Atomic Energy Agency (IAEA). However, in February 1993, North Korea refused to allow the IAEA inspection access sparking a serious crisis with the West. South Korea denounced the danger posed by North Korean possession of nuclear weapons. Negotiations between the two Koreas came to a halt.

[15] Kim Il Sung's death at 82 - officially announced on July 7 1994 - once again complicated talks with the United States and deferred the summit planned between the two Koreas. Kim Jong Il succeeded his father without having the same real power as the historical leader of North Korean communism, which gave way for a fight for power among leading cadres.

[16] In 1995, widespread floods affected some five million people. One consequence was the loss of the harvests. These losses were calculated at 1.9 million tons of crops, which led the North Korean Government to make an uncommon appeal for foreign aid. Japan, one of its main capitalist trade partners, donated 300,000 tons of rice and South Korea 150,000 tons.

[17] The United States decided to lift the trade embargo and a delegation of US investors visited the country, while Pyongyang reported it no longer opposed the presence of US troops in South Korea.

[18] The food shortage became more serious in 1996, reaching famine proportions in some areas. North Koreans continued to flee to South Korea seeking asylum. The defection of Worker'Party secretary, Huang Yang Yop, in February 1997, caused a new political crisis. Huang sought asylum in the South Korean embassy in Beijing, when returning from a tour of Japan and China. Two days later, Prime Minister Kang Song Dan was forced to resign and was replaced by Hong Song Nam. In October, Kim Jong Il, the de facto ruler following the death of his father, was officially designated head of the Worker'Party. However, due to internal rivalries, he was not formally designated president of the country.

[19] In late 1997, the Government proposed tripartheid negotiations between Pyongyang, Seoul and Washington for a definitive peace agreement on the peninsula. In 1998, it was estimated some 100,000 people had died of cold, hunger and the lack of medical attention since 1995.

[20] The UN World Food Programme (WFP) reported the per person daily ration of rice was only 100 grams. The situation turned critical due to the drought which followed the floods, but despite this Pyongyang did not weaken before political pressure from Seoul. In early 1998, international aid was insufficient. In March, the Government imposed the measures of a "war economy."

PROFILE

SOCIETY
Political Parties: The Korean Workers' Party (KWP), founded in 1945 with Marxist-Leninist orientation, is the dominant political organization. The Democratic People's Republic of Korea is a virtual one-party state, but smaller parties do exist: the Korean Social Democratic Party and the Chondokio Chong-u party, the first being affiliated to the KWP in a National Front for the Reunification of Korea, created in June 1945. Youth and women are organized as the Union of Young Socialist Workers and the Democratic Women's Union. **Social Organizations:** The General Federation of Trade Unions is the only workers' organization, while the union of Agricultural Workers is a peasants' association.

THE STATE
Official Name: Tschosson Mintschutschui Inmin Konghwaguk. **Administrative Divisions:** 9 Provinces, 1 District. **Capital:** Pyongyang 2,355,000 people (1987). **Other cities:** Hamhung, 701,000 people, Chongjin, 520,000, Sinudji, 330,000, Kaesong, 310,000 (1987). **Government:** Kim Jong Il, President of the Republic since July 1994. The supreme body of the state is the People's Assembly, with 541 members. **National Holiday:** September 9, Republic Day (1948). **Armed Forces:** 1,054,000 (1994). **Other:** 3,800,000 Peasant Red Guard, 115,000 Security Troops, of the Ministry of Public Security.

DEMOGRAPHY
Population: 22,466,000 (1996) **Annual growth:** 1.5 % (1980/1996) **Estimates for year 2000:** 23,900,000. **Annual growth to year 2000:** 1.6 % (1994/2000) **Urban population:** 61.5 % (1996) **Children per woman:** 2.1 (1996).

HEALTH
Life expectancy at birth: 72 years (1996) **Infant mortality:** 23 per 1,000 (1996) **Under-5 child mortality:** 30 per 1,000 (1996) **Calorie consumption:** 121 % (1988/90) **Safe water:** 81 % (1990/96).

EDUCATION
School enrolment : Primary total: 104 % (1990/95) male : 108 % (1990/95) female: 101% (1990/95)

South Korea

Taehaen – Min `Guk

Population: 45,314,000 (1996)
Area: 99,274 SQ KM
Capital: Seoul
Currency: Won
Language: Korean

On August 15 1948, a Republic was established in the southern part of the Korean peninsula, with its capital in Seoul (see Korea). Syngman Rhee was named its first president and, supported by US military, economic and political advisors, he ruled the southern portion of Korea for 14 years. Through constitutional laws giving him indefinite power, he ruled as a constitutional dictator. All opposition forces were controlled by charging them with cooperating with the North at the first signs of dissent.

[2] The US advisers convinced the Rhee regime of the need for a thorough land reform program. They were very much aware of events in China, where the nationalist Kuomintang had been defeated by the communists who promised rural peoples "land to the tiller". The US scheme in South Korea allowed for compensation, and land redistribution limited to three hectares per person; former Japanese-owned land was also redistributed. Many of the previous land-owners moved to the cities.

[3] Despite the introduction of a draconian National Security Law in 1958, when many political dissidents were jailed, the regime was unable to suppress opposition completely. Rhee was re-elected in 1952, 1956 and in 1960. The results of the last election were not accepted by the opposition, who claimed there had been fraud. There were protests in Seoul, which were repressed harshly by Government forces. Growing opposition and the danger of a revolution extending to the rest of the country, led Syngman Rhee to resign on April 27 1960. He was succeeded by Huh Chung Tok as interim President.

[4] New elections were held, and Po Sun Yun, a member of the Democratic Party, was elected president. John Chang, who had been named head of the government, attempted to lead the country toward effective economic development and put an end to the corruption and waste which had characterized the previous regime. Some members of his cabinet were in favor of warmer relations with North Korea.

[5] In May 1961 a military coup ousted Chang; a military junta was installed, presided over by General Chan Yung. In July, General Chung Hee Park took command of the junta and proceeded to suspend all democratic freedoms and imprison all members of the previous regime.

[6] The new regime initiated a National Reconciliation policy, including a planned strategy against communism and corruption, and promised a return to civilian government after completion of these "revolutionary tasks".

[7] In March 1962, Park took the presidency from Po Sun Yun. In late 1963, Park was confident of power and held elections. He won by a mere 1.4 per cent despite suppression of the opposition. The protests that followed led him to declare martial law, the military retained their political domination and a long, harsh dictatorship ensued.

[8] The military regime established strong centralized economic planning and, with the help of western technocrats, Korea became a full example of export-oriented development. Imports and exports, domestic prices and access to credit were used as levers to control and guide the economy. Restrictive laws were established governing the right to strike, organize or allow collective bargaining.

[9] From a war-torn, mainly rural, indebted economy, South Korea developed into an industrial economy, dominated by large, Korean-owned transnational corporations producing steel, ships, cars and electronics goods.

[10] Villagers, affected by low grain prices, were forced into cities and the urban labor pool, contributing to the "Korean miracle". Some of the world's lowest wages, longest hours and most unsafe working conditions are the norm for Korean workers.

[11] Eighteen years after taking power, Park was still president, having won four fraudulent elections.

[12] In October 1979, Park was killed; shot by the director of the hated Korean Central Intelligence Agency, Kim Jae Kiu, in unclarified circumstances.

[13] Before the end of 1979, General Chun Doo Hwan, head of military intelligence, decided to secure his position and arrested rival generals; on May 17 1980, martial law was once again established and civilian politicians were arrested.

[14] The following day, citizens in the southern city of Kwangju took control in protest against the military regime, and particularly the arrest of Kim Daw Jung, a leading opposition figure and a native of Kwangju. The Korean army suppressed the citizens with extreme brutality and "hundreds lost their lives" with the knowledge and agreement of US military commanders stationed in the country. Although the protest had been carried out as a public reaction to the arrest of Kim Daw Jung, this fact was ignored and Daw Jung was sentenced to life imprisonment, charged with "instigating" the uprising. The Kwangju incident was used by the military as justification for seizing power and questions were raised as to whether the whole event had been deliberately provoked by the military.

[15] Chun launched a "purification campaign" of public and private sectors, even setting quotas for singling out the corrupt and "subversives". In the same manner as his predecessor, Chun Doo Hwan held elections in an attempt to legitimize and civilianize his rule; he won the elections in 1981.

[16] In October 1983, several members of the South Korean cabinet were killed by a bomb at the Martyrs' Mausoleum in Burma during a state visit; arriving late, President Chun escaped the bomb blast. The Burmese, claiming proof of North Korean involvement, broke off diplomatic relations and rescinded their recognition of the North Korean government.

[17] Opposition to Chun's regime continued to grow as repression, reminiscent of Park's worst excesses, escalated. The US withdrew their support of the Marcos regime in the Philippines, after claims of election fraud and

human rights abuses, and a worried Korean regime instituted some reforms. Censorship was lifted somewhat and Kim Daw Jung released from house arrest.

[18] During 1987, hundreds of thousands of Korean workers joined in strikes and factory occupations in an unprecedented wave of protests. Korean workers demanded the right to form democratic unions independent of the government-run Federation of Korean Trade Unions, higher wages, an end to forced overtime and, in general, a larger share of the benefits of the nation's spectacular growth.

[19] In July 1987, Chun stepped down and designated Roh Tae Woo both as his successor and as president of the official Democratic Justice Party. Demonstrations followed amid protests that Roh would continue the dictatorship as a close military colleague of Chun. Demands that Chun face trial for his part in the Kwangju massacre were also voiced.

[20] Faced with the possibility of larger street demonstrations and concern over its international image (South Korea was host of the Olympic Games in 1988) political restrictions were eased during the December, 1987 election campaign.

[21] Polls showed government candidates trailing badly in late November when a Korean Airways passenger jet disappeared near Thailand with 118 passengers aboard. North Korea was again suspected, as in the Burma bombing, but Pyongyang denied any involvement.

[22] In the elections, the newly-freed opposition together polled a majority, but failed to unite the two factions, led by Kim Yong Sam of the Reunification Democratic Party and Kim Dae Jung of the Party for Peace and Democracy. The split enabled the incumbent government, under Roh Tae Woo, to secure power with a majority of 42 per cent.

[23] In January 1990, the most conservative opposition groupings formed a merger with the official Democratic Justice Party, and became the Democratic Liberal Party, controlling 220 seats in the 298-member National Assembly. The Party for Peace and Democracy remained the only real parliamentary opposition.

[24] In the spring of 1990, a new offensive against independent trade unions and labor rights resulted in the arrest of the movement's leaders. In April, police stormed the Hyundai shipyards and arrested over 600 union activists, ending a 72-hour worker occupation protesting the arrest of union leaders. A few days later, 400 striking workers occupying the Korean Broadcasting System's headquarters were also arrested. The resulting nationwide protests precipitated the biggest drop in the history of the Korean stock market.

[25] In September 1991, US President George Bush made the decision to withdraw tactical nuclear weapons from South Korea, and in November this was accomplished. This significant step met one of the requirements of North Korea and was necessary for inspections of their territory to be made.

[26] In December of that year, Seoul and Pyongyang signed a "Reconciliation, Non-aggression, Exchange and Cooperation Accord", affecting bilateral relations (see Korea).

[27] In the legislative elections of March 1992, both the pro-government groups and the left suffered a serious setback. The Democratic Liberal Party won 149 of the 299 seats, one short of the majority. The Democratic Party (DP) came in second with 30 per cent, followed by the Party of National Unification with 17.4 per cent and 31 seats, a new grouping led by a former corporate leader. The left-wing People's Party (PP) won 1.4 per cent of the vote and no seats.

[28] In May, President Roh Tae Woo named Kim Young Sam, who had obtained 41.4 per cent of the returns in the December presidential election, as his successor. Kim's election coincided with a weakening opposition, worsened by the resignation in February 1993 of Chung Ju-Yung, leader of the United People's Party, charged with having accepted illegal contributions from a major corporation during the electoral campaign.

[29] Corruption scandals also reached the government. Choi Ki Son, a close aide of president Kim, admitted he had embezzled $1 million in public funds. Furthermore, Suh Eui Hyun, leader of the country's largest Buddhist order, was accused of accepting $10 million from a businessman to hand them over to Kim Young Sam. This accusation caused confrontations among Buddhist monks which led to 134 arrests.

[30] In 1995, two former presidents, Chun Doo Hwan (1979-1988) and Roh Tae Woo (1988-1993), were arrested for their role in the coup which brought Chun to power in December 1979, accused of treason and making illicit wealth. In June of this year, the governing party was defeated in the first local and provincial elections not controlled by the government since 1961. The collapse of the department store Sampoong in Seoul, killing more than 500 people, brought the issue of corruption back to the fore, when it became known local authorities had approved the construction of the fifth floor after being paid hidden commissions.

[31] In April 1996, the governing New Korea Party took 139 of the 299 seats in contention. Meanwhile the National Congress for a New Policy took 79 seats and the United Liberal Democrats 50. In December, the Seoul courts sentenced former defence minister Lee Yang-Ho to four years imprisonment for accepting illegal commissions from the Daewoo company, the fourth biggest concern in the country.

[32] In December 1997, Kim Dae Jung, opposition Democratic Party candidate, was elected President. Two days later, and two months before assuming office, he agreed to free Chun Doo Hwan and Roh Tae Woo and announced an amnesty for political prisoners.

[33] In March 1998, the new president was sworn in. Kim Jong Pil became the new Prime Minister. The risks of hyperinflation and increasing unemployment in South Korea became bigger following the stock market crisis in several Southeast Asian nations.

Maternal Mortality

1990

PER 100,000 LIVE BIRTHS

130

Literacy

1995

98%

STATISTICS

DEMOGRAPHY
Population: 45,314,000 (1996) **Annual growth:** 1.1% (1980/1996) **Estimates for year 2000:** 46,900,000 **Annual growth to year 2000:** 0.9% (1994/2000) **Urban Population:** 82.5% (1996) **Urban growth:** 3.52% (1980/95) **Children per woman:** 1.7 (1996).

HEALTH
Life expectancy at birth: 72 years (1996) male: 68 years (1994) female: 75 years (1994) **Infant mortality:** 6 per 1,000 (1996) **Under-5 child mortality:** 7 per 1,000 (1996) **Calorie consumption:** 120% (1988/90) 1,205 **people per doctor** (1988/91) **Safe water:** 93% (1990/96).

EDUCATION
Literacy: 98% (1995) male : 99% (1995) female: 97% (1995) **School enrolment** : Primary total: 95% (1990/95) male : 95% (1990/95) female: 96% (1990/95) Secondary: male : 100% (1990/95) female: 99% (1990/95) Tertiary: 52% (1995) **Primary school teachers:** one for every 32 students (1995).

COMMUNICATIONS
400 **newspapers**, 1,017 **radios**, 320 **TV sets** and 396 **main telephone lines** per 1,000 people (1994) **Books**: 77 new titles per 100,000 people (1992/94).

ECONOMY
Per capita, GNP: $ 10,610 (1996) **Annual growth, GNP:** 5.6% (1995/96) **Annual inflation:** 6.7% (1985/95) **Consumer price index:** 129.3 (1994) **Currency:** 774.7 won = $ 1 (1995) **Cereal imports:** 11,936 metric tons (1994) **Food import dependency:** 4% (1994) **Fertilizer use:** 4,671 kgs per ha (1994) **Exports:** $ 124,404 million (1996) **Imports:** $ 144,724 million (1996) **Development aid received:** $ 58 million (1995) $ 1 per capita (1995).

ENERGY
Consumption: 2,981.53 Kgs of Oil equivalent per capita yearly (1994) 85.62% imported (1994).

HDI (rank / value) 32 / 0.89 (1994)

Kuwait

Kuwayt

Population:	1,687,000 (1996)
Area:	17,818 SQ KM
Capital:	Kuwait (Al-Kuwayt)
Currency:	Dinar
Language:	Arabic

In the history of navigation, the voyage of Nearco, one of Alexander of Macedonia's admirals, was a milestone; he sailed from the Indo River to the farthest end of the Gulf of Arabia, ending his voyage in the port of Diridotis, in present-day Kuwait. This was not, however, the first contact between India and Kuwait, which had already been an active trade center for almost 2,000 years. The fate of the country was always intimately linked to that of the Mesopotamian civilizations (see Iraq) but, beginning in the 13th century, after the Mongol invasion caused collapse of the Caliphate, the region entered into a long period of isolation.

[2] After this, new Arab groups began to settle there. In the 18th century, although nominally subject to the Ottoman Empire, the settlements were virtually independent; they decided to elect a shaij (sheikh) to conduct sporadic negotiations with the Turks. In 1756, the leader of the Anaiza tribe, Abdul Rahim al-Sabah, founder of the reigning dynasty, was designated for this task.

[3] At that time, the place, formerly known as the Qurain (horn) began to be called Kuwait, a diminutive for al-Kout, which is a local Arabic term to describe the fortified houses on the coast.

[4] The weakness of Turkish sultans and the growing British influence in the region were two fundamental factors that encouraged the formation of proto-states, of which the emirate of Najd (see Saudi Arabia) was the most dynamic.

[5] In order to avoid absorption by the Wahabites, the emirs of Kuwait requested support from the British who had moved the East India Company's overland mail terminal

from Basra to Kuwait in 1779. The British sent Indian troops to guarantee the autonomy of the Emirate, an initiative which the Turks were helpless to stop. For decades Kuwait was the most prosperous and peaceful part of a region peppered by constant disputes.

[6] In 1892, with Turkish support, the Emir of Najd was deposed and was granted asylum in Kuwait. Sheikh Mubarak al Sabah allowed the territory to be used as a base for their raids against the pro-Turkish Rashidis. Since this implied great risks, a treaty was signed with Britain in 1899, whereby the Sheikh undertook not to cede any part of the territory to another country without British consent; in exchange, Britain guaranteed Kuwait's territorial integrity. This treaty, and the subsequent British military presence in the region, frustrated Turkish attempts to expand the Berlin-Baghdad railway to reach the Gulf through Kuwaiti territory.

[7] At the end of World War I, France and Great Britain split the remains of the Ottoman Empire. Kuwait was now considered a British protectorate, separate from the newly-created kingdom of Iraq, which claimed it as a province, alleging the historical subjection of the region to the government of Baghdad.

[8] In 1938, oil began to flow from the Burgan wells. Ahmad Jabir al-Sabah, the crown prince, opposed the exploitation of the extensive deposits, arguing that a high income and high salaries resulting from the new activity would ruin pearl fishing, until then the country's main economic activity, employing 10,000 sailors as deep-sea divers. After the impasse created by World War II, the emir granted the concession to

1 Neutral Zone

0   100 km

the Kuwait Oil Company, owned by British BP and US Gulf, with oil first exported in 1946. The large-scale exploitation of these reserves soon turned the small port into a large trading center.

[9] In 1961, independence was negotiated, within the British policy of gradual decolonization. Sheikh Sabah proclaimed himself Emir and took up full powers. Iraq refused to recognize the new state, claiming that it was an artificial creation of the British to maintain access to oil. Consequently, the British troops remained to defend the emirate until they were replaced by the troops of the Arab League.

[10] In 1962 a Constitution was enforced creating a National Assembly of 50 members, elected individually by male citizens aged over 21, whose fathers or grandfathers had resided in Kuwait before 1920. None of the candidates belonged to a political party, as these had been made illegal. Thus, out of the 826,500 Kuwaitis who lived in the country in 1990, a minority of the population - only 85,000 - would have been entitled to vote if elections had been called.

[11] In 1966, Kuwait and Saudi Arabia solved their ancient border disputes, and the "neutral zone" which existed between both countries was divided equally. In 1969 the Central Bank of Kuwait was created, and in 1976 a Social Security Law and a Law of Reserves for Future Generations were passed. The latter established that 10 per cent of the State

revenue was to be earmarked for an investment fund.

[12] In a few years, oil entirely changed the country. The Bedouins replaced their camels with luxurious air-conditioned cars. Pearl fishing disappeared. The entire population settled in brand new cities, where the stylized mosque towers stood side-by-side with shopping centres which replaced the old souks (markets). The population's educational standards and life expectancy rose. All manual labor and work in the oil industry was done by immigrant workers. In 1970 the number of migrants equalled the local population, and by 1985 this figure had almost doubled.

[13] Kuwaiti rulers became concerned that despite so much prosperity in such a poor area its legitimacy could be questioned. In 1961 the Arab Fund for Economic Development was created, in order to channel "soft" loans and donations to Third World countries. When the Organization of Petroleum Exporting Countries (OPEC) succeeded in raising prices in 1973, Kuwait increased its revenue immensely.

[14] Most of the Third World countries supported OPEC, hoping that they would receive help to establish a "New International Economic Order", by asking for better prices for the other raw materials that they supply to the Northern countries. However, instead of investing their oil revenues in their own countries or in other Third World nations, the

PUBLIC EXPENDITURE

25.5%   44.2%
1995 ■ DEFENCE □ SOCIAL

In 1990/91 Military as % of health & education expenditure was 88%.

WORKERS

(1996)

Labour force %
■ WOMEN
□ MEN
29   71

■ AGRICULTURE   1%   **(1990)**
□ INDUSTRIAL   25%
▨ SERVICES   74%

PROFILE

ENVIRONMENT
Nearly all of the land is flat, except for a few ranges of dunes. The inland is desert with only one oasis, the al-Jahrah. The coast is low and uniform. The city and port of Kuwait is located in the only deep-water harbor. The climate is tempered by ocean currents but the temperature is high in summer. Winters are warm with frequent dust and sand storms. Petroleum is the main economic resource, with three refineries in Shuaiba, Mina al-Ahmadi and Mina Abdulla. Tremendous environmental damage was caused by burning oil wells, as a result of the Gulf war in 1991. The country also suffers from a lack of water.

SOCIETY
Peoples: Kuwaitis, of Arab descent, account for less than half of the population, 60 per cent of which is made up of immigrant workers from Palestine, Egypt, Iran, Pakistan, India, Bangladesh, the Philippines and other countries.
Religions: Muslim 85 per cent, of which Sunni 45 per cent, Shi'ah 30 per cent; other Muslim 10 per cent; other (mostly Christian and Hindu) 15 per cent. **Languages:** Arabic (official).
Political Parties: Islamic Constitutional Movement, a moderate Sunni group; Kuwaiti Democratic Forum, liberal; Salafeen, a fundamentalist Sunni group.
Social Organizations: Federation of Unions.

THE STATE
Official Name: Dawlat al-Kuwayt.
Administrative divisions: 5 governances.
Capital: Kuwait (Al-Kuwayt), 1,090,000 people (1995).
Other cities: al-Jahra139,476 people; as-Salimiyah 116,104 ; Hawalli 84,478; al-Farwaniyah 47,106 (1993).
Government: Jaber al-Ahmad al Sabah, emir. Saad al-Abdullah as-Salim as-Sabah, Prime Minister. The National Assembly has 50 members. **National Holiday:** February 25, Independence Day (1961). **Armed Forces:** 15,300 (1996).
Other: The National Guard has 5,000 troops.

STATISTICS

DEMOGRAPHY
Population: 1,687,000 (1996) **Annual growth:** 1.3% (1980/1996) **Estimates for year 2000:** 2,000,000 **Annual growth to year 2000:** 1.9% (1994/2000) **Urban Population:** 97.1% (1996) **Urban growth:** 0.93% (1980/95) **Children per woman:** 2.9 (1996).

HEALTH
Life expectancy at birth: 76 years (1996) **male:** 74 years (1994) **female:** 78 years (1994) **Infant mortality:** 13 per 1,000 (1996) **Under-5 child mortality:** 14 per 1,000 (1996)

EDUCATION
Literacy: 79% (1995) **male :** 82% (1995) **female:** 75% (1995) **School enrolment :** Primary total: 69% (1990/95) **male :** 69% (1990/95) **female:** 69% (1990/95) Secondary: **male :** 65% (1990/95) **female:** 64% (1990/95) Tertiary: 25% (1995) **Primary school teachers:** one for every 15 students (1995).

COMMUNICATIONS
400 **newspapers**, 445 **radios**, 410 **TV sets** and 226 **main telephone lines** per 1,000 people (1994) **Books:** 11 new titles per 100,000 people (1992/94).

ECONOMY
Annual inflation: -0.47% (1985/95) **Currency:** 0.3 dinars = $ 1 (1995) **Cereal imports:** 455 metric tons (1994) **Food import dependency:** 14% (1994) **Fertilizer use:** 2,000 kgs per ha (1994) **Exports:** $ 13,420 million (1996) **Imports:** $ 8,113 million (1996) **External debt:** $ million (1996) **$ per capita:** (1996) **Debt service:**% of exports (1996) **Development aid received:** $ 6 million (1995) $ 4 per capita (1995).

ENERGY
Consumption: 8,622.22 Kgs of Oil equivalent per capita yearly (1994) -692.66% imported (1994).

HDI (rank / value) 53 / 0.844 (1994)

Gulf monarchs placed their fortunes in transnational banks. This further accentuated the excess of liquidity in transnational private banks, which started to grant loans to the Third World quite indiscriminately. This situation was one of the main factors that provoked the "debt crisis" in 1982.
[15] Within the Gulf area, however, Kuwait was generous with its wealth. By the end of the 1980s, Kuwait had the highest rate of official development assistance in the world, proportional to its gross national product.
[16] Unfortunately, prosperity did not prevent political conflicts. In August 1976, the National Assembly was dissolved by Sheikh Jabir al-Sabah, arguing that it had acted against national interests. In December 1977, the emir died and the Crown of Kuwait passed to Jabir Al-Sabah, who called national elections in February 1981. Over 500 candidates ran for the 50 seats in the National Assembly and 40 were won by Sunni candidates, loyal to the ruling family. Shi'a candidates won four seats, and Islamic fundamentalists won six. Only 6.4 per cent of the population was permitted to vote.
[17] When the Iran-Iraq war broke out in 1979, Kuwait officially remained neutral, but in fact supported Iraq with large donations and loans. Kuwait considered Iraq to be a "first line of defence" against the Iranian Islamic revolution.
[18] In 1985, the National Assembly began to disapprove of governmental measures such as press control, increases in the prices of public services and educational reforms, echoing other accusations that corruption existed within the ruling family. In August 1986, the Emir dissolved the Assembly and began to rule by decree.
[19] In the late 1980s, the Kuwait Investments Office (KIO) had capital assets outside the country estimated at $1 billion, which included hotels, art galleries, European and US real estate, and major shares in large transnational corporations: 10 per cent of British Petroleum, 23 per cent of Hoechst, 14 per cent of Daimler-Benz, and 11 per cent of the Midland Bank.
[20] In 1987, alleging that Iraq was using the port of Kuwait to export oil and import weapons, the Iranian navy attacked Kuwaiti merchant ships. In response, Kuwait requested and obtained permission from the major powers - US, France, Britain, and the USSR - to use their flags for the Kuwait merchant navy. The US and Britain sent their navies to protect Kuwaiti ships in the Gulf.
[21] Once the war between Iran and Iraq ended in 1988, tensions between Kuwait and Iraq started to mount. Kuwait demanded the payment of $15 billion on account of war loans, which Iraq refused to return, alleging that those sums had been used to protect Kuwait. Iraq accused Kuwait of 'stealing' their country's oil, by extracting large amounts of oil from the common deposits which stretch along the border. Iraq claimed that the Emirate was pumping out much more oil than its entitlement, and demanded $2.4 billion in compensation.
[22] In spite of repeated attempts at mediation by Palestinian leader Yasser Arafat, tension mounted. On August 2 1990, Iraq invaded Kuwait quickly and decisively. Emir al-Sabah and his family took refuge in Saudi Arabia. Nearly 300,000 Kuwaitis fled the country, to join the other 100,000 who were abroad on their summer vacation. The occupation forces encouraged the exodus, perhaps to "de-Kuwaitize" the country. A pro-Iraqi provisional government, led by Al Hussein Ali, requested the total fusion of Iraq and Kuwait. A few days later the Emirate was declared an Iraqi province.
[23] Iraq had expected understanding from the US, in exchange for assured oil supplies, but the US reacted very harshly to the invasion and promoted a series of extremely tough measures from the UN Security Council. On August 6, the trading, financial, and military boycott of Iraq was voted through, and on November 29, the use of force against Iraq was approved if the country refused to withdraw from Kuwait before January 15 1991. Only Cuba and Yemen abstained from voting.
[24] When the Emir went into exile in Saudi Arabia he was pressured by the US to promise democratic elections once the country was liberated.
[25] The war devastated the country, not so much in terms of lives lost, for most of the fighting was done on Iraqi territory, but the bombings and forced withdrawal of the occupation troops left most of the country's oil wells burning and the country was unable to produce any oil until 1992.
[26] The war also turned Kuwait into an environmental disaster area. The black cloud formed by some 50 burning oil wells, and gigantic oil spills along the coast produced profound degradation of the air, marine resources and soil. An enormous mass of oil lined the coasts, posing a threat to birds and other animals. The Gulf's ecosystem was seriously affected, especially fish species which form a staple of the local diet.
[27] It was estimated that the clean-up and reconstruction will cost between $150 and 200 billion. On January 9 1991, Britain committed itself to grant a loan of $950 million

earmarked for reconstruction. Kuwait's debts to allied countries, arising from war costs, rose to more than $22 billion.

[28] After the War was over more than 1,300 people were killed by mines which were laid during the conflict.

[29] On March 18 1991, Amnesty International in London denounced the arbitrary detention and torture of Palestinians residing in Kuwait, carried out by Kuwaiti civilians and military.

[30] Also in March 1991, while US Secretary of State James Baker was visiting Kuwait, the prince and premier Sheikh Saad al-Abdallah promised to lead the Emirate towards democracy and to reinstate parliament.

[31] On April 1 1991 a group of Kuwaiti citizens demanded freedom of the press, independence of the judiciary, the legalization of political parties, and the implementation of measures to fight corruption.

[32] In June 1991, Sheikh Jabir al-Sabah called a National Council to discuss the elections, and female and foreign suffrage. The opposition was still demanding the re-establishment of the 1962 constitution and the formation of a democratically elected parliament, though no opposition leaders would be allowed in the Council. Over a thousand people demonstrated in the streets after the Emir made his announcement. Although street demonstrations are illegal in Kuwait, the Government made no attempt to stop the march.

[33] When the war ended, the Emir launched the slogan of "re-Kuwaitizing" Kuwait. The plan included a drastic reduction in the number of foreigners in the country. Over 800,000 people had to leave the country, to comply with the Sheikh's measure. A small number of foreigners were deported, but most are forced to leave when they fail to find jobs and schools for their children.

[34] In mid-December 1991, Saudi Arabia, the United Arab Emirates, Oman, Qatar, Bahrain, and Kuwait held a summit meeting aimed at creating a collective security mechanism, and establishing a new defensive framework for the region which holds 40 per cent of the world's oil reserves.

[35] After renewing oil production, Kuwait initially accepted the OPEC quota of two million barrels per day. However, in February, it confronted OPEC's other members and unilaterally decided to raise daily production to 2.16 million barrels. The Oil Minister explained that the country had confirmed the existence of new deposits of crude oil in what was formally a "neutral zone" along the border with Saudi Arabia.

[36] In January, press censorship was lifted. Demonstrations were organized by women's groups demanding the right to vote. Elections for the National Assembly were finally held on October 5, with independent opposition groups winning 31 seats, the fundamentalists 19 and the liberals 12. For the first time ever, the cabinet contained several Members of Parliament elected by direct popular vote.

[37] In early 1993, a financial scandal broke involving the Kuwait Investment Office (KIO), and two members of the royal family were found to have been involved. The personal holdings of high-ranking KIO officials were frozen when $5 billion were discovered to be missing. $1 billion had been diverted to Torras, a Spanish business consortium.

[38] As a result, the Government prohibited the publication of any information on government corruption, without prior official consent. Months later, the British newspaper, "The Financial Times", accused the KIO of having used $300 million to win the support of several UN diplomats in the military operation against Iraq.

[39] In 1993 the UN finally determined the frontier with Iraq, despite protests by Baghdad. As a response to supposed incursions by Iraqi troops, the US bombed Iraq repeatedly (see Iraq). Washington decided to install missiles in Kuwait and it began building a wall 130 kms long equipped with 1.3 million mines along the new frontier.

[40] In August the ex-chief of the Temporary Free Government imposed by Baghdad, Al-Hussein Ali, was condemned to death, as well as five Kuwaitis and 10 Jordanians accused of collaborating with the Iraqi occupation.

[41] In 1995, the Government, with the aid of numerous Kuwaiti investors, pursued the privatization of State companies and carried out major investments in arms.

[42] In February 1996, Amnesty International denounced summary executions, torture and expulsions without trial. In October, the Government obtained 30 of 50 seats in the National Assembly election. In the same year the economy grew due to the rise of international crude oil prices and new investments, both in the construction and oil sectors.

[43] In November 1997, the Emir ordered the closure of borders with Iraq and bolstered surveillance in several border points, due to the new crisis which erupted between Washington and Baghdad. Kuwait was the only Arab country which supported the US plan to promote a new armed intervention against its neighbor country.

[44] In March 1998, the Emir formed a new government and replaced his Finance minister.

Islamic civilization:

The Arab peninsula, inhabited during the first centuries of the Christian Era by nomad or semi-sedentary Bedouins, was the geographical and human context where Islamic culture and civilization emerged. It is said that it was in Mecca, a center of pilgrimage, a city of caravans, and a trade centre of the Medieval world, that Muhammad was born. There truth was revealed to him and there he began his preaching of Islam until in the year 622 - the origin of the Hejira - he sought refuge under menace of death in the city of Medina. The 30 years that followed Muhammad's death (632-661, during which period the four orthodox caliphs, who accompanied him in his preaching, governed) are considered by the Muslims as the "golden age" of Islam. Sustained by the inner belief in its message and by the overwhelming strength of the Arabic armies, Islamic expansion defeated the Sasanid and Byzantine empires, as well as the ancient Roman West and built a Muslim Empire which headed world trade and structured a web of major cities.

Islamic City and Religious Institutions

The Islamic city is a community of people who practise the Islamic religion. It constitutes the "umma", or nation, in which each Muslim person is included, whether he lives alone or as part of a group, whether peasant or citizen, nomad or settled. A much quoted expression defines it as "Dar al-Islam", 'the home of Islam', and it limits it to the countries or urban groups which obey the Islamic canonical law, and where its traditional lifestyles are practised. Islam, which signifies 'submission to God', comprises three basic religious institutions: the Koran, the Tradition of the Prophet (sunna), and the written and oral teachings of the jurists. Through the double testimony of the faith - "There is no more God than the One and Only" (Allah); "Muhammad is the messenger of God" - which declaration confers the condition of Muslim to every person of good will - the Koran proclaims its essential message, "al-tawhid" or 'Divine Unity', which establishes the rights of the Creator above all contingencies of our earthly existence and which achieves itself in the individual life of everyone who places his/her thoughts and actions nearest to God. With that purpose people are urged to read the Koran, to invoke the names of God, and to fulfill the obligatory practices of prayer, fasting, alms giving, and pilgrimage to Mecca, at least once in a lifetime. The Prophet, providentially 'chosen' in order to communicate Muslim law ("sharia"), became the most exalted person in the Islamic world. His sayings and advice, his acts and gestures, were gathered during the third century of Hejira, in the "hadits" or traditions, with the purpose of making the knowledge and transmission of them easier for the community of followers. Neither the Koran nor the Sunna were then elaborated as bodies of law. It was a later task of the learned men of Islam to formulate the juridical system that rules and divides the actions of the believers and makes them either compelling, recommended, permissible, damnable or prohibited. Its development led to a divergence between the "sunni" jurisprudence, which does not approve of personal reflection, or of the law being adaptable, or of its possible evolving into something else, and the "shii" jurisprudence, which approves of these things. A wisdom such as the Muslim, which tends to introduce the religious dimension in all aspects of life, takes this divergence as a difference of interpretation which derives, ultimately, from the kindness of God. "The disagreements between learned men - one of its proverbs declares - are a gift."

Society, community, and individual

The essential thing about the Islamic city is the "durable combination of the effort by every man in order to submit to the will of the divine legislator within the communal framework which is the help and support of his effort". In Islam, the link between the individual and the social whole is so strong that the task of individual salvation "includes ipso facto the sacralization of the social". The salvation of a single man depends on the people who surround him, as well as on favorable or unfavorable circumstances. Tradition assumes that it was Muhammad himself who formulated the principle of "iyma" or consensus of believers, which becomes concrete in Muslim law through the form of a collective statute called the 'duty

origins and foundations

of sufficiency'. It would exonerate a Muslim person of any compelling legal duty provided a sufficient number of followers would exonerate him of it. The individual, nevertheless, is not lost in the communal. Islamic law supposes that a person compromises only him/herself through his/her behavior and that, on the day, s/he alone will appear before the Supreme Judge to account for her/his behavior. The fact of all people being equal before God, and being also equally dependent on Him/Her, and compelled to obey the law, has given place to the definition of the Muslim community as 'equable theocracy'. The strong sense of social cohesion which accompanied the high degree of integration of traditional Muslim societies is due in a great degree to the socio-religious values which guided the life of its individuals and communities.

Government and Politics: the Islamic Community

The community established in Medina in the first century of Hejira (the 7th century AD), was the prime model of institutional religious organization which ruled in all traditional Muslim societies. Its name being Yatrib before that date, its new name, al-Madina ("the city by excellence"), designated its condition as a center of "umma" and a siege of authority and justice. The caliph or iman, a successor of the Prophet, united in his person the spiritual and the secular authority, and was the supreme chief of the city. He was in charge of creating the conditions for the application of Koranic law, of directing the Holy War (jihad), of organizing the army, and of assuring an orderly administration and the security of the countries under its dominion. The caliph designated also, in each city, the ministers or vizirs, the governors, the army chiefs, the tax collectors, and even the police corps ("surta") that maintained order and protected the city from enemies.

Justice in the traditional Islamic society was derived from divine mandate. It refers to an original pact through which God designated the people who exer-cise authority. These must protect the followers, and the followers must obey the authorities. The Platonic ideal of justice and Islam are synonomous: the order decreed by God will only prevail where virtuous people rule, who are capable of uniting their deep

knowledge of the divinity to a high moral quality. They have in their hands "the task of making people, in this life and in this milieu enjoy a maximum of happiness, and also of making them reach the joys of a future life through communal institutions based on justice and brotherhood" (al-Farabi, 4th century of Hejira). Despite the fact that the juridical order of traditional Islamic cities lacked the local and municipal autonomy enjoyed by medieval European cities, its institutions, guided by values that negated racial, religious, or social discrimination, nevertheless stimulated the high degree of integration shared by all cities of the Muslim world from al-Andalus to India. Muslim jurists accepted through the centuries, as source of legislation, the local customs and habits of the different cities. This shows their flexibility and democratic inclinations.

The Economy in Medieval Society

The economy of traditional Muslim cities was ruled by a corporate system which integrated the people dedicated to production, distribution, and services. Whether they were proprietors, employees, home servants, independent workers or government employees, whether they were "people of high or low condition, Muslim, Christian, or Jew, native or foreign residents, they all belonged to the corporate system". In the corporations the urban population was gathered according to the profession of each individual; there were artisan, merchant, auctioneer, lender, musician, singer, storyteller, transport, and sailor groups. The members of each corporation were considered also members of the community of believers to which service was specially credited the contribution of each profession and trade. These were learnt through hard work supervised by a master ("sayj") connected to a chain of corporation masters, linked as well to other corporations, to the Holy Patrons, and even to the Prophet. The corporations were structured according to a conceptual and ritual system transmitted orally from generation to generation and linked to the sufi orders (Islamic loggias). At the acceptance of a young person as an apprentice in a workshop there followed the recitation of the first "azora" (chapter) of the Koran before the masters of the corporation, and a period of years of work with low remuneration or none at all,

compensated by the notion that this was the way of learning and of becoming gradually integrated to the rest of the community. A branch of sweet basil was given on behalf of the master to the young apprentice, signalling the beginning of his initiation. The ceremony, celebrated in the house of a master or in some city garden, was attended by a large group of noble people, who undertook religious and ceremonial rites. At the end of these the young person became a member of the brotherhood, with a ritual expression of joy in which several traditions coincided: "God bless Jesus, Moses, and the ones who embellish their eyes with antimonium (*), so that no one can harm us". The initiation ended with a simple meal called "tamliha" (salad) in memory of the double value of salt, a link between those who share it, and also symbol of craftspeople themselves (known as "the salt of bazaars" for being seen as the nucleus of people who make a life out of sweat and patience). The initiate entered his own corporation, and through it, the umma. After some years, the execution of a masterpiece as a proof of his refined abilities could elevate the artisan to the position of a master. We should mention in passing that, for Islamic sufism, craftsmanship was synonymous with art and at the same time, it was considered a means of spiritual evolution. In this sense, it was "an image of the task a man must undertake on himself and on his soul if he aspires to the contemplation of the divine realities; he is compared to a rough material, without order or form, but potentially noble".

Education and Religious Instruction

Muslim education, initiated at the time of the Prophet in Mecca, was fundamentally given through the mosque, and its content was the "sharia" or Islamic law, whose learning was a 'duty of sufficiency' for the Islamic community. The highest distinction in Islam was to acquire the 'knowledge' - al-'ilm - or the knowledge of revealed law. Memory was a praised gift, and the title of 'hafiz' was granted to the person who knew the Koran by heart. Religious instruction was one of the key elements in order to assure the survival of Islamic civilization. A citizen of average education could be a consultant inside the community, as well as conduct the prayers, and practice the Koran law. At the beginning, religious instruction and overall

education were the same, but latterly there were differences between the two. The first century of Hejira, dedicated to military conquest and to the establishment of political authority in Islam, did not produce a noticeable development of Islamic education. But from the second century onwards (during which the institution of the mosque developed among the conquered territories) and above all from the third century onwards (in which a generation of jurists, theologians, and linguists sought to preserve the language and the traditions of a civilization which had spread through very diverse cultural areas) education became a foremost preoccupation. During the third and the fourth centuries the mosque was a virtual public university, a center of worship and also a center for social gatherings. But it was then also that the elementary school ("kultab") appeared, as well as the 'houses of wisdom' or of 'science', exclusively for academic activities. In the fifth century appeared the high school or "madrasa", fostered by the Government, which was from then on the highest centre of learning in the Muslim world. Towards the ninth century, it was necessary to have finished studies in a madrasa in order to occupy a position in government. It was not only the acquisition of knowledge - which is the means of distinguishing between the prohibited and the praiseworthy - but its transmission also, which became a religious obligation in Islam, anticipating thus the historical effort in order to democratize teaching. "Islamic society repudiates the 'alim' (learned person) who does not transmit his learning to others."

Islam has defended the freedom of thought, and has recognized the limits of reason. It can doubt neither divine unity nor the truth of Muhammad's message. From the point of view of Islam, reason can be either inborn - when it is a divine gift, or acquired - when it is the result of individual effort and experience. A valuable contribution of Islam is its recognition of the practical nature of thought and education, evident through a tradition attributed to the Prophet: "You should acquire all the wisdom of which you are capable! But God will not reward you for all that you have learned until you translate it into actions!"

(*) The custom of painting the eyes with antimonium which distinguished the Arabs.

Kyrgyzstan

Kirguizstan

Population:	4,469,000 (1996)
Area:	198,500 SQ KM
Capital:	Pishpek (Bishkek)
Currency:	Som
Language:	Kyrgyz

In the Bronze Age (2000 years BC), the present Kyrgyzstan was inhabited by tribes who farmed and raised livestock. Between the 7th and the 3rd centuries BC, the Saks settled in the area, and between the 3rd and 2nd centuries BC, a group of Usun tribes.

[2] From the 1st century BC to the 4th century AD, Kyrgyzstan was a part of the state of Kushan, which disappeared after the nomadic Eufalites invaded. Toward the end of the 4th century, Kyrgyzstan became part of the western region of the Turkish *Kaganate* (Khanate), governed by the brothers Tumin and Istemi.

[3] In the 7th century, Kyrgyz territory was occupied by the Turguesh (under the chieftain Moje-Dajan); between the 8th and 10th centuries it came under the Karluks who were replaced by the Karahanyds between the 10th and 12th centuries. From the 12th to the 14th century, the Turkish peoples of Kyrgyzstan were absorbed as part of the Mongol Empire, in the ulus (province) of the Chagatai khan.

[4] During this period, Kipchak-Kyrguish tribes in the area between the Irtysh and Yenisey rivers migrated to Tian Shan, where they mixed with the Mongols and local Turkish tribes. In the 15th and 16th centuries, the Kyrgyz people were formed. The Kyrgyz Khanate was established in Tian Shan by Khan Ajmet.

[5] The distinguishing feature of Kyrgyz social organization was the lack of a ruling class of princes or nobles, with authority exercised instead by the *manaps* (elders), whose leadership depended on their personal prestige. The tribes maintained a high degree of cohesion because they were constantly at war against neighbouring peoples.

[6] Between the 16th and 18th centuries, the Kyrgyz were subdued by the Oirat-Yungars. In the mid-18th century the Oirat-Yungar State was conquered by Chinese troops. Kyrgyzstan became a protectorate of the Tsin (Chin) Empire. In the early 19th century, Russia began to show interest in the region, which had been conquered by Khan Madali of Kokand.

[7] In 1862, Russian troops supported the Kyrgyz rebellion against the Khanate of Kokand, and took Pishpek. The following year, Kyrgyz representatives from central Tian Shan surrendered to Russia, in the city of Verni (today Alma-Ata). In 1864, Northern Kyrgyzstan joined the Russian Empire, as part of the region of Semirechensk.

[8] In 1867, Czar Alexander II created the Regional Government of Turkistan. Russian colonists began arriving by the thousands, and the Kyrgyz saw their best lands confiscated, and turned over to immigrants for agricultural use.

[9] In 1875 there was an uprising against Khan Jodoyar of Kokand. The Russian Empire leapt in to annex the Khanate of Kokand and Southern Kyrgyzstan. Despite the fact that the major part of its population was Uzbek, the region of Fergana was formed as part of the Province of Turkistan. Kyrgyzstan was divided into three regions - Semirechensk, Syr Darya and Fergana - within the province of Turkistan, with Tashkent as its center.

[10] Friction between the various ethnic groups periodically flared up over the issue of land ownership and mandatory military service, finally triggering a major revolt by the Kyrgyz, which was brutally put down by the czarist regime.

[11] Soviet power was established in the district of Pishpek in December 1917, though there was strong opposition from guerrilla groups in the rest of the country. In 1921 and 1922, agrarian and water reforms were carried out.

[12] In 1924 the Autonomous Region of Kara-Kirghiz was formed, as a part of the Russian Federation. In 1925, its name was changed to the Autonomous Region of Kirghizia, becoming, in 1926, an "Autonomous Soviet Socialist Republic". In December 1936, Kyrgyzstan became a federated republic of the Soviet Union (USSR).

[13] Under socialism the Kyrgyz had to change their nomadic way of life radically, joining the new agricultural cooperatives or working in the industries created by the State (textile, leather, tobacco, lumber, metal and hydroelectric power). They also had to change "Pishpek" to "Frunze", the name of a famous Red Army general, and the USSR continued to recruit a major part of its soldiers from among the Kyrgyz.

[14] As a part of the pre-World War II five-year development plans, the USSR built large plants in Kyrgyzstan for the extraction of antimony, as well as the processing of its agricultural products. The first metal-processing plants and modern blast furnaces were set up during this period.

[15] During the War and in the decades which followed, the region's industry underwent further expansion, producing machinery, building materials and electric power.

[16] From 1961 until the end of the Brezhnev era, Turdakun Usubaliev was first secretary of the Kyrgyzstan Communist Party, which functioned as a branch of the CP of the Soviet Union. Kyrgyz writer Chingiz Aytmatov achieved international fame during the 1970s, as the author of a play dealing with the moral compromises made under Stalinism.

[17] From 1986, with the changes put in motion in the USSR by Mikhail Gorbachev, an independence movement developed in Kyrgyzstan. After the failed coup against Gorbachev in August 1991, the republic of Kyrgyzstan decided to separate from the USSR.

[18] On August 31 1991, Kyrgyzstan's Soviet declared the new republic a democratic and independent state. On that occasion, a statement was made in recognition of the three new Baltic states of Estonia, Latvia and Lithuania.

[19] In Kyrgyzstan's first presidential elections, held in October of that year, Askar Akaev, former president of the Academy of Sciences and a physicist of international renown, ran unopposed and was elected. Akaev was among the few leaders - along with Russian President, Boris

WORKERS

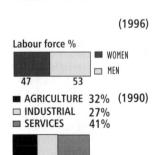

(1996)

Labour force %
- ■ WOMEN
- □ MEN

47   53

- ■ AGRICULTURE 32% (1990)
- □ INDUSTRIAL 27%
- ■ SERVICES 41%

LAND USE

IRRIGATED of arable (1993) 64.3%

- ■ FOREST & WOODLAND (1993) 3.5%
- □ ARABLE (1993) 7.1%
- ■ OTHER (1993) 89.4%

Maternal Mortality
1990

PER 100,000
LIVE BIRTHS
110

External Debt
1996

PER CAPITA
$177

Foreign Trade
MILLIONS $ 1996

IMPORTS
838

EXPORTS
507

PROFILE

ENVIRONMENT
Located in the northeastern part of Central Asia, Kyrgyzstan lies in the heart of the Tian Shan mountain range. It is bounded by China and Tajikistan in the south, Kazakhstan in the north, Uzbekistan in the west, the Pamir and Altai mountain ranges in the southwest and the Tian Shan range in the northeast. It has plateaus and valleys: in the north, the Chu and Talas valley; in the south, the Alai Valley; and in the southwest, the Fergana Valley. The climate is continental, with sharp contrasts between day and night temperatures. The eastern part of Tian Shan is dry, while the southwestern slopes of the Fergana range are rainy. The main rivers are the Narym and the Kara-Suu. Lake Issyk-Kul is the most important of the country's lakes. In the mountains there are forests and meadows, while desert and semi-desert vegetation abounds at lower altitudes. Metal deposits include lead and zinc; in addition, there are large coal reserves and some oil and natural gas deposits. Water pollution is a serious problem, since one third of the population obtains its water from rivers, streams, or wells.

SOCIETY
Peoples: Kyrgyz, 52.4 per cent; Russians, 21.5 per cent; Uzbeks, 12.9 per cent; Ukrainians, 2.5 per cent, Germans 2.4 per cent. **Religions:** Islam (Sunni) and Christian (Russian Orthodox Church). **Languages:** Kyrgyz (official), Russian, Uzbek. **Political Parties:** Democratic Movement of Kyrgyzstan, Erkin Kyrgyzstan Democratic Party, Communist Party.

THE STATE
Official Name: Respublika Kyrguyzstan.
Capital: Pishpek (Bishkek), 631,000 people (1991).
Other cities: Os, 218,700 people; Tokmok, 71,200; Kara-Köl 64,300 (1991).
Government: Askar Akaev, President since October 1991, re-elected in 1995. Apas Jumagulov, Prime Minister since 1993.
National Holiday: December 15, Independence (1991).
Armed Forces: 7,000.

STATISTICS

DEMOGRAPHY
Population: 4,469,000 (1996) **Annual growth:** 1.3% (1980/1996) **Estimates for year 2000:** 5,000,000 **Annual growth to year 2000:** 0.3% (1994/2000) **Urban Population:** 39.0% (1996) **Urban growth:** 1.64% (1980/95) **Children per woman:** 3.3 (1996).

HEALTH
Life expectancy at birth: 68 years (1996) male: 63 years (1994) female: 72 years (1994) **Infant mortality:** 39 per 1,000 (1996) **Under-5 child mortality:** 50 per 1,000 (1996) **Safe water:** 71% (1990/96).

EDUCATION
Literacy: 97% (1995) male : 99% (1995) female: 95% (1995) **School enrolment** : Primary total: 111% (1990/95) male : 110% (1990/95) female: 111% (1990/95) Secondary: male : 84% (1990/95) female: 89% (1990/95) Tertiary: 14% (1995) **Primary school teachers:** one for every 20 students (1995).

COMMUNICATIONS
10 **newspapers, radios,** 240 **TV sets** and 73 **main telephone lines** per 1,000 people (1994) **Books:** 7 new titles per 100,000 people (1992/94).

ECONOMY
Per capita, GNP: $ 550 (1996) **Annual growth, GNP:** 4.1% (1995/96) **Consumer price index:** 4,947.9 (1994) **Currency:** 11 som = $ 1 (1995) **Fertilizer use:** 197 kgs per ha (1994) **Exports:** $ 507 million (1996) Imports: $ 838 million (1996) **External debt:** $ 789 million (1996) $ 177 **per capita:** (1996) **Debt service:** 9.2% of exports (1996)

ENERGY
Consumption: 615.91 Kgs of Oil equivalent per capita yearly (1994) 47.36% imported (1994).

HDI (rank / value) 107 / 0.635 (1994)

Yeltsin - who personally resisted the failed coup in August, at the Parliament in Moscow.
[20] Akaev was the first head of state in the former Soviet Union to ban the Communist Party and to proclaim the independence of his republic. In December, Kyrgyzstan signed the founding charter of the Commonwealth of Independent States (CIS) with 10 other ex-Soviet republics
[21] In December 1991, President Akaev had to exercise his veto power over a law approved by the Parliament, establishing the exclusive right of the Kyrgyz to the land. He thus avoided inflaming aggression between the native population and the Uzbeks of Fergana, which could have turned into an even greater conflict with the neighboring republic of Uzbekistan. The previous year, in the region of Os, in the western part of the country, more than 200 Uzbeks

were assassinated by bands of young Kyrgyz, manipulated, it was claimed at the time, by agents of the former Soviet secret police (KGB).
[22] Kyrgyzstan started to create a National Guard of a thousand troops, and asked CIS forces to remain in its territory. This military presence was justified, for "security reasons", until the republic was ready for full membership of the international community.
[23] In March 1992, Akaev reaffirmed his intention to maintain a strict neutrality, in spite of the attempts of Muslim states like Pakistan, Saudi Arabia or Iran to have closer ties. However, the President of Kyrgyzstan stated he was willing to cultivate closer relations with Turkey.
[24] In May 1993, a new constitution was approved while controversies and disagreements between Akaev and parliament

continued, as parliament was opposed to his economic reform policies. A national currency, the *som,* was introduced that month. In the midst of growing tensions, many Kyrgyz of Russian origin, mainly intellectuals and engineers, began to flee the country.
[25] In 1994, Akaev continued his reforms policy recommended by the IMF. After the som's introduction, inflation fell from 40 and 50 per cent per month to 4 per cent, among the lowest in the former Soviet Union. At the same time, national production fell 19 per cent in 1992 and 16 per cent in 1993, imports - especially from Turkey and China - grew rapidly and social inequality was increased.
[26] In February 1995, legislative elections did not significantly modify Parliament's opposition to Akaev's economic liberalization policy. The President tried to

extend his term through a referendum, but Parliament decided to hold presidential elections in December, which were won by Akaev with 60 per cent of the vote.
[27] In February 1996, Akaev held a referendum on constitutional changes giving him greater powers, and most of his proposals were approved. Opponents of the Government, like journalists who criticised Akaev's policies, were persecuted, imprisoned on charges of slander and even mistreated, something which was denounced by Amnesty International in its 1997 report.
[28] The role played by Kyrgyzstan in the production and trafficking of drugs in the region changed substantially during 1997, going from a country of transit to a nation with an increasing number of processing laboratories.

Laos

Lao

Population: 5,035,000 (1996)
Area: 236,800 SQ KM
Capital: Vientiane (Viangchan)

Currency: New Kip
Language: Lao

In the 14th century Sam Sen Tal, a Burmese ruler united the present northeast Thailand with most of the modern day territory of Laos, founding the flourishing state of Lang Xang, the "Land of a Million Elephants". In the late 18th century, the country split into three parts: Champassac, Vientiane and Luang Prabang.

2   By the 19th century, the Thais had established dominion over the land and Tiao Anuvong, Prince of Vientiane, led an ill-fated nationalist rebellion in 1827. In 1892, the French invaded and by 1893 had established a protectorate over Luang Praband, with the rest of the country becoming part of French Indochina.

3   During World War II, Japan occupied Laos and a pro-independence movement arose in Vientiane, led by three native princes, Petsarath, Suvana Fuma, leader of the National Progressive Party, and his half-brother, Tiao Sufanuvong, head of the Neo Lao Issara (Laos National United Front). In September 1945, Sufanuvong set up a provisional government, declaring independence and promulgating the constitution of "independent Laos", in spite of protests from King Sisavang Vong, reigning since 1904.

4   In early 1946, the country was again under French occupation. The Pathet Lao provisional government sought refuge in Bangkok, where the Pathet leaders organized the anti-colonialist struggle through the Lao Issara or "free Laos" movement.

5   On July 19 1949, the Franco-Laotian Convention recognized Laotian independence "as part of the French Union". The Pathet Lao leaders saw this as mere formal independence and refused to

recognize it. Suvana Fuma opted for negotiation, but the opposition coalition decided on active resistance; the military victories led to a new treaty in 1953.

6   Differences between the Katay Sasorith, Suvana Fuma government, and the Pathet Lao were reconciled in November 1957. An agreement was reached, whereby the latter would participate in the political life of the country under the name "Neo Lao Haksat" (Laotian Patriotic Front), led by Tiao Sufanuvong.

7   The May 1958 elections were won by the left, worrying the US. Suvana Fuma's ruling party joined forces with the Independent Party to form the so-called Laotian People's Demonstration, together achieving a small majority. They formed a center-left coalition government, led by "neutralist" Suvana Fuma, with Sufanuvong as planning minister.

8   The US was strongly opposed and threatened to cut economic aid. This destabilized the Government, and in August the leaders of the Committee for the Defence of National Interests took over. A military offensive against the Pathet Lao drove Sufanuvong from the capital, forcing him into guerrilla action in the forests.

9   In 1959, the army gained control, while the Pathet Lao controlled the strategic northern provinces and the central plain of Jars.

10   General Fumi Nosavang, the former defence minister, and his troops seized Vientiane on December 13 1960, driving out Pathet Lao troops. A massive air raid left 1,500 dead and forced Vientiane to surrender.

11   The Thai and US supported Revolutionary Anti-Communist Committee, headed by Fumi Nosavang and Prince Bun Um claimed legitimacy to govern. On December 20 1960, however, Princes Suvana Fuma and Sufanuvong declared their intention of forming a national unity government.

12   The "neutralists" joined forces with the Pathet Lao and launched successful joint military campaigns.

13   In 1961 in Geneva, Britain and the Soviet Union initiated negotiations for a peaceful solution, and on January 19 1962, a

final agreement was signed for a national unity government.

14   Growing US intervention resulted in the internationalization of the Vietnam war. Air raids on Laotian territory increased to 500 missions per day by 1970 and in nine years Laos was subjected to a greater number of bombings than the whole of Europe during World War II.

15   The Pathet Lao declared an armistice in 1973, and the Vientiane Government formed a new cabinet, including Pathet Lao members, with a Council of Ministers headed by Suvana Fuma. After the US defeat in Vietnam, right-wing groups lost the support they had been getting from the US. In 1975, the national unity cabinet gave way to a majority of Neo Lao Haksat ministers, and on December 1, a peaceful movement put an end to the monarchy. A People's Democratic Republic was proclaimed with Sufanuvong as President, led by the Lao People's Revolutionary Party (PPRL). Entrepreneurs and state bureaucrats left the country en masse, ruining the economy and crippling public administration.

16   The Government nationalized banks and reorganized the public sector. Rice production rose from 700,000 tons in 1976 to 1,200,000 in 1981, when grain self-sufficiency was achieved. For access to the sea and to reduce dependence on

Thailand, a road was constructed to the Vietnamese port of Danang, and an oil pipeline to Vietnam's refineries.

17   In 1986, Phumi Vengvichit became President. In November, Kaysone Phomvihane was re-elected secretary general of the PPRL, subsequently becoming prime minister.

18   A bloody border war with Thailand, at the end of 1987 resulted in a great loss of life, but ended rapidly in a cease-fire.

19   In 1988 diplomatic relations were renewed with China, and in early 1989 cooperation agreements were signed with the US, which granted a symbolic $10 million to combat the cultivation and trafficking of opium.

20   The changes in Eastern Europe resulted in the suspension of all Soviet economic aid to Laos, and trade fell by 50 per cent.

21   In 1991, the poor economic situation was exacerbated by floods and pest infestations in a quarter of the country's farmlands. Consequently, over 200,000 tons of rice were imported to feed the population.

22   Also in 1991, Thailand and Laos agreed to a repatriation plan for 60,000 Laotian refugees by 1994, also signing a Cooperation and Security Treaty. Thai investments were meanwhile concentrated in banking and trade. Laos has also

PROFILE

ENVIRONMENT

Laos is the only landlocked country in Indochina. The territory is mountainous and covered with rainforests. The Mekong river valley, stretching down the country from north to south, is suited to agriculture, basically rice. It is estimated that 40 per cent of the arable land was left barren as a result of the 25-year war. The climate is tropical and the lowlands are prone to disasters such as the 1978 drought and the 1988 flood. The main environmental problem is intense logging and as a result of the this, dwindling water supplies and a loss of 70 per cent of natural habitats.

SOCIETY

Peoples: 60 per cent of Laotians are descendants of the Lao ethnic groups who inhabit the western valleys. The inhabitants of the mountains account for more than one-third of the total population, while 5 per cent are of Chinese and Vietnamese origin. **Religions:** Buddhist 57.8 per cent; traditional religions 33.6 per cent; Christian 1.8 per cent, of which Roman Catholic 0.8 per cent, Protestant 0.2 per cent; Muslim 1.0 per cent; atheist/no religion 4.8 per cent; Chinese folk-religions 0.9 per cent. **Languages:** Lao (official); minor ethnic group languages, and French. **Political Parties:** The Lao People's Revolutionary Party (PPRL), Marxist-Leninist, is in power. It originated in the old Neo Laotian Haksat. **Social Organizations:** The Patriotic Youth and the Association of Patriotic Women. The National Liberation Front, based in the Meo ethnic minority, wages guerrilla warfare and is accused of receiving Chinese support.

THE STATE

Official Name: Sathalanalat Paxathipatai Paxaxon Lao. **Administrative divisions:** 16 provinces, sub-divided into municipalities. **Capital:** Vientiane (Viangchan), 442,0000 people (1990). **Other cities:** Savannakhét 96,652 people; Louangphrabang 68,399. **Government:** Khamtay Siphandon, President since February 1998. Sisavat Keobunphan, Prime Minister since August 1998. Legislature: Supreme Assembly of the People. **National Holiday:** December 2, Proclamation of the Republic 1975. **Armed Forces:** 37,000 troops (conscripts) (1996). **Other:** 100,000 members of the Self-defence Militia Forces.

STATISTICS

DEMOGRAPHY

Population: 5,035,000 (1996) **Annual growth:** 2.8% (1980/1996) **Estimates for year 2000:** 5,700,000 **Annual growth to year 2000:** 3.1% (1994/2000) **Urban Population:** 21.2% (1996) **Urban growth:** 6.3% (1980/95) **Children per woman:** 6.7 (1996).

HEALTH

Life expectancy at birth: 53 years (1996) male: 50 years (1994) female: 53 years (1994) **Infant mortality:** 102 per 1,000 (1996) **Under-5 child mortality:** 128 per 1,000 (1996) **Calorie consumption:** 111% (1988/90) 4,545 **people per doctor** (1988/91) **Safe water:** 44% (1990/96).

EDUCATION

Literacy: 57% (1995) male : 69% (1995) female: 44% (1995) **School enrolment :** Primary total: 107% (1990/95) male : 123% (1990/95) female: 92% (1990/95) Secondary: male : 31% (1990/95) female: 19% (1990/95) Tertiary: 2% (1995) **Primary school teachers:** one for every 30 students (1995).

COMMUNICATIONS

0 **newspapers**, 127 **radios**, 10 **TV sets** and 4 **main telephone lines** per 1,000 people (1994) **Books:** 1 new title per 100,000 people (1992/94).

ECONOMY

Per capita, GNP: $ 400 (1996) **Annual growth, GNP:** 4% (1995/96) **Annual inflation:** 22.59% (1985/95) **Currency:** 923 new kips = $ 1 (1995) **Cereal imports:** 22 metric tons (1994) **Food import dependency:** 4% (1994) **Fertilizer use:** 23 kgs per ha (1994) **Exports:** $ 334 million (1996) **Imports:** $ 642 million (1996) **External debt:** $ 2,263 million (1996) $ 449 **per capita:** (1996) **Debt service:** 6.3% of exports (1996) **Development aid received:** $ 311 million (1995) $ 66 per capita (1995) 20.3% of GNP (1994).

ENERGY

Consumption: 38.33 Kgs of Oil equivalent per capita yearly (1994) -18.13% imported (1994).

HDI (rank / value) 136 / 0.459 (1994)

---

put a lot of effort into establishing closer ties with China.

[23] In September 1991, 70-year-old Kaysone Phomvihane was named President. Upon his death a year later, Prime Minister Khamtay Sifandon assumed interim presidency of the country and the party (PPRL).

[24] In December 1992, legislative elections were called; only the PPRL and a few independent government-authorized candidates took part. This essentially represented a continuation of the one-party system. Anti-government demonstrations were banned, and scores of government opponents were imprisoned.

[25] The Supreme Assembly of the People met in February 1993, and named Nouhak Phumsavanh president of the republic, and Khamtai Siphandon leader of the PPRL.

[26] Major free-market oriented reforms were introduced, but without drastically changing the political system. In 1993, Prince Suvana Fuma was authorized to return to the country in an unofficial capacity to represent foreign companies.

[27] Following IMF-proposed strategies, the country managed to bring down the inflation rate - averaging 46 per cent in the 1980s - to an annual rate of 10 per cent, meanwhile the GDP grew by 7 per cent. It is estimated that part of that economic "growth" resulted from the introduction into the market of products and activities previously not accounted for, and not from an actual increase in production.

[28] The United States Agency for International Development (USAID) approved a $9.7 million loan to build roads in several regions of the country, arguing that access to markets would improve living conditions.

[29] Deforestation became a serious environmental problem. The timber felled increased from 6,000 cubic meters in 1964 to over 600,000 in 1993. That year, the government began to restrict timber exports.

[30] As a result of this, there was an increase in the illegal felling of trees, and in 1993, half of all timber was logged illegally. In March 1994, the World Bank extended a loan given to Laos for reforestation, at an initial value of $8.7 million. A number of international environmental organizations have criticized the project, as it gave the funds directly to the Government, with little or no participation from the local communities and for placing emphasis on commercial tree plantations, an activity that could further endanger the forests and the livelihood of its inhabitants.

[31] On April 8 1994, the "Friendship Bridge" over the Mekong was opened, uniting Laos and Thailand. For Laos this reconciliation represented a distancing from Vietnam and marked the way for economic and cultural integration with Thailand - a more prosperous nation. The Thai banks, communication networks, transport companies and factories soon dominated investment in the Laos economy, which had now lost its socialist principles.

[32] A law approved in March of that year had established the rules for foreign investment, eliminating the remnants of the planned economic system. Another law guaranteed union rights and updated the labor legislation. Political liberalization, however, was not included in this reform: the Government was determined to maintain its communist identity.

[33] In mid-1995, Laos expressed its desire to become a full member of the Association of South East Asian Nations (ASEAN) within two years. This more liberal attitude was also reflected in the ratification of a border treaty with Myanmar. The United States lifted a veto on the country limiting US economic aid in place since the Vietnam war.

[34] In March 1996, at the Sixth Congress of the Lao People's Revolutionary Party (PPRL), Prime Minister Siphandon confirmed the single party rule, while also insisting on economic liberalisation, efficiency and growth.

[35] In December 1997, the PPRL retained its dominion in the parliamentary elections for the 99 posts in the General Assembly. The result, however, was no surprise, as only four of the 159 individuals standing were from outside the single party.

[36] The stock exchange crisis affecting several countries of the region also struck the economy of Laos. Its indirect effects included increased prices on imports and higher prices for consumers, particularly on the basic basket of foodstuffs.

[37] In February 1998, the Supreme Assembly of the People made Prime Minister Siphandon the new President. Sisavat Keobounphan became the new Prime Minister in August. Amnesty International appealed to Laos to release several prisoners of conscience, but one of these, Thongsouk Saysangkhi, died in prison.

Latvia

Latvija

Population: 2,504,000 (1996)
Area: 64,600 SQ KM
Capital: Riga

Currency: Lat
Language: Latvian

The first inhabitants of present-day Latvia were nomadic tribes of hunters, fishers and gatherers who migrated to the forests along the Baltic coast, after the last glaciers had retreated. Around 2,000 BC, these groups were replaced by the Baltic peoples, Indo-European tribes who began farming and established permanent settlements in Latvia, Lithuania and eastern Prussia.

2   The ancient Baltic peoples had come into contact with the Roman Empire through the amber trade. This activity, which reached its peak during the first two centuries of the Christian era, was brought to a halt by Slav expansion toward central and eastern Europe. At this time, the Balts' trade and cultural relations turned northward, to their Scandinavian neighbors.

3   The Danes used the Dvina and Dnepr rivers in their expansion toward the steppes north of the Black Sea, and therefore crossed Latvian territory. The Swedes and the Russians both claimed these lands during the 10th and 11th centuries and in the 12th century, German warriors and missionaries came to the Latvian coast. As it was inhabited at the time by the Livs, the Germans called it Livonia. In 1202, the bishop of the region, under authorization from Rome, established the Order of the Knights of the Sword.

4   Before becoming the Knights of the Teutonic Order, in 1237, the Germans had subdued and converted the tribal groups of Latvia and Estonia to Christianity. The Teutonic Knights created the so-called Livonian Confederation, consisting of areas controlled by the Church, free cities and regions governed by knights. In the mid-16th century, rivalries within Livonia became more pronounced with the expansion of Protestantism and discontent among the peasants.

5   During this period, Latvians benefited from Riga's participation in the Hanseatic League, a German mercantile society which attained a high level of prosperity. Nevertheless the Latvians were treated by the Germans like any vanquished people: the local nobility was done away with, and the peasants were forced to pay tithes and taxes, paying with labor when unable to pay otherwise. After being defeated by Lithuania and Poland, the power of the Teutonic Order declined. However, as the knights' power diminished, their exploitation of the Latvians actually increased.

6   When Russia invaded the region in 1558, to halt Polish-Lithuanian expansion, the Order fell apart and Livonia was partitioned. At the end of the Livonian War, in 1583, Lithuania annexed the area north of the Dvina river, the south remained in Polish hands and Sweden kept the north of Estonia. In 1621, Sweden occupied Riga and Jelgava; Estonia and the northern part of Latvia were subsequently ceded to Sweden by the Truce of Altmark (1629).

7   The region west of Riga, on the Baltic Sea, was organized into the Duchy of Courland, becoming a semi-independent vassal of Poland. In the mid-17th century, Courland became known as a major naval and trade center for northern Europe, and even had colonial aspirations. Duke Jacob led a brief Latvian occupation of Tobago, in the Caribbean, and of another island in the Gambia River delta in Africa. The name Great Courland Bay, in Tobago, dates back to this time.

8   Sweden kept these territories until the Great Northern War, when it was forced to cede them to Russia under the Peace of Nystad. In 1795, after the three partitions of Poland, Livonia was finally subdivided into three regions within Russia: Estonia (the northern part of Estonia); Livonia (the south of Estonia and north of Latvia) and Courland. The Russian Revolution of 1905 gave rise to the first instances of Latvian national reaffirmation.

9   The peasants revolted against their German feudal lords, and the Russian rulers. Although the rebellion was put down by czarist troops, this uprising set the stage for the war of independence 13 years later. After the Russian Revolution of 1917, the Latvian People's Council proclaimed the country's independence on November 18 1918. A government led by the leader of the Farmers' Union, Karlis Ulmanis, was formed.

10   Far from having its desire for independence and sovereignty respected, Latvia was attacked by German troops and by the Red Army. Only in 1920 was Latvia able to sign a peace treaty with the USSR, by means of which the latter renounced its territorial ambitions. In 1922, a constituent assembly established a parliamentary republic. The international economic crisis of the 1930s, and the polarization of socialists and Nazi sympathizers led to the collapse of the Latvian Government. In 1934, Prime Minister Ulmanis suspended parliament and governed under a state of emergency until 1938.

11   With the outbreak of World War II, according to the secret Russo-German pact, Latvia remained within the USSR's sphere of influence. In 1939, Latvia was forced to sign a treaty permitting the Soviets to install troops and bases on its soil. In 1940, it was invaded by the Red Army, and a new government was formed, which subsequently requested that the republic be admitted to the USSR.

12   During the German offensive against the USSR, between 1940 and 1944, Latvia was annexed to the German province of Ostland, and its Jewish population was practically exterminated. The liberation of Latvia by the Red Army meant the re-establishment of Soviet Government. Before the Soviet forces arrived, 65,000 Latvians fled to Western Europe.

13   In 1945 and 1946, about 105,000 Latvians were deported to Russia, and the far northeastern corner of Latvia - with its predominantly Russian population - was taken away from Latvia to form part of the USSR. In 1949, forced collectivization of agriculture triggered a mass deportation of Latvians, with about 70,000 being sent to Russia and Siberia. In 1959 the President of Latvia's Supreme Soviet, Karlis Ozolins, was dismissed because of his nationalist tendencies.

14   Armed Latvian resistance to the Soviet regime was finally put down, in 1952. All symbols of Latvian independence - the national anthem, the flag, and national monuments and history - were banned or adapted to the new regime. Russian became the official language, and massive immigration of Russians and other nationalities began. To the nationalists, this was taken to be a deliberate colonization policy, aimed at diminishing the influence of the indigenous population.

15   Until the 1980s, Latvian resistance was expressed in isolated actions by political and religious dissidents, which were systematically repressed by the regime; in addition, some nationalist campaigns were carried out by exiles. From 1987,

PUBLIC EXPENDITURE

2.6%   63.7%

■ DEFENCE
□ SOCIAL   (1995)

WORKERS

UNEMPLOYMENT 18.3% (1996)

Labour force %

■ WOMEN
□ MEN

50   50

■ AGRICULTURE 16% (1990)
□ INDUSTRIAL   40%
■ SERVICES   44%

PROFILE

Environment
Latvia's terrain is characterized by softly rolling hills (highest point: Gaizins, 310 m), and by the number of forests, lakes and rivers, which empty into the Baltic Sea and the Gulf of Riga, in the northeastern part of the country. Latvia has a 494 km coastline, with important ports and attractive beaches. The country's most fertile lands lie in the Zemgale Plain, which is known as the country's breadbasket. The plain is located in the south, extending as far as the Lithuanian border. The Highlands, which make up 40 per cent of the land, lie in the western and northern parts of the country, crossing over into Estonia. The climate is humid and cold, due to masses of cold air coming from the Atlantic. Summers are short and rainy, with an average temperature of 17 degrees C; winters last from December to March, with temperatures below zero, sometimes as low as -40 degrees C. Two-thirds of all arable land is used for grain production, and the rest for pasture. The main industries are metal engineering (ships, automobiles, railway passenger cars and agricultural machinery), followed by the production of motorcycles, electrical appliances and scientific instruments. Industrial wastes and the pollution of the country's rivers and lakes are problems which remain to be solved.

SOCIETY
Peoples: Latvians and Lithuanians constitute the two main branches of the Baltic Indo-European peoples, with a distinct language and culture that sets them apart from the Germans and Slavs. Ethnic Latvians make up 52 per cent of the country's population, followed by Russians, 34 per cent; Poles, Belarusians, Ukrainians, Lithuanians and Estonians account for the remaining 14 per cent. Religions: The majority is Protestant (Lutheran), followed by Catholics. Languages: Latvian (official); Russian and Polish. Political Parties: National Bloc; National Conciliation Bloc; Communist Party; Fatherland and Freedom movement.

THE STATE
Official Name: Latvijas Republika. Capital: Riga, 839,670 people (1995). Other cities: Daugavpils 120,152 people; Liepaja 100,271; Jelgava 71,129; Jurmala 59,247. Government: Parliamentary republic. Guntis Ulmanis, President, re-elected by parliament in June, 1996. Single-chamber parliament (Saeima), made up of 201 members, elected by direct vote. National holiday: November 18, Independence (1918).

STATISTICS

DEMOGRAPHY
Population: 2,504,000 (1996) Annual growth: -0.1% (1980/1996) Estimates for year 2000: 2,000,000 Annual growth to year 2000: -1.2% (1994/2000) Urban Population: 73.1% (1996) Urban growth: 0.46% (1980/95) Children per woman: 1.5 (1996).

HEALTH
Life expectancy at birth: 68 years (1996) male: 62 years (1994) female: 74 years (1994) Infant mortality: 16 per 1,000 (1996) Under-5 child mortality: 20 per 1,000 (1996)

EDUCATION
Literacy: 100% (1995) male : 100% (1995) female: 100% (1995) School enrolment : Primary total: 83% (1990/95) male : 85% (1990/95) female: 81% (1990/95) Secondary: male : 84% (1990/95) female: 89% (1990/95) Tertiary: 26% (1995) Primary school teachers: one for every 14 students (1995).

COMMUNICATIONS
230 newspapers, 662 radios, 470 TV sets and 258 main telephone lines per 1,000 people (1994) Books: 65 new titles per 100,000 people (1992/94).

ECONOMY
Per capita, GNP: $ 2,300 (1996) Annual growth, GNP: 3.5% (1995/96) Annual inflation: 72.45% (1985/95) Consumer price index: 2,989.0 (1994) Currency: 0.54 lat = $ 1 (1995) Cereal imports: 65 metric tons (1994). Fertilizer use: 547 kgs per ha (1994) Exports: $ 1,443 million (1996) Imports: $ 2,319 million (1996) External debt: $ 472 million (1996) $ 188 per capita: (1996) Debt service: 2.3% of exports (1996)

ENERGY
Consumption: 1,569.05 Kgs of Oil equivalent per capita yearly (1994) 89.69% imported (1994).

HDI (rank / value) 92 / 0.711 (1994)

the policy of glasnost (openness) initiated by Mikhail Gorbachev in the USSR, gave hope to Latvian aspirations, permitting public political demonstrations, and the reinstatement of the national symbols.

[16] In June 1987, some 5,000 people gathered in front of the Monument to Liberty, in Riga, to honour the victims of the 1941 Soviet deportations. This marked the beginning of increasingly important political agitation, in which independence began to be discussed openly once again. In 1988, the National Independence Movement of Latvia (LNNK) demanded an end to the Russification of the country, and called for freedom of the press and for the formation of independent political parties.

[17] In September 1988, the Environmental Protection Club of Latvia (VAK) organized an ecology-awareness rally, in which 30,000 people joined hands all along a stretch of the Baltic Sea coast. The following month, the Latvian Communist Party renewed its leadership, incorporating politicians who were identified with the reforms and who had broad popular support. The national flag was legalized, and Latvian was adopted as the country's official language.

[18] In October 1988, close to 150,000 people gathered to celebrate the founding of the Popular Front of Latvia (LTF), which brought together all of Latvia's recently formed social and political groups, as well as militant communists. A month later, for the first time since Soviet occupation, hundreds of thousands of Latvians commemorated the anniversary of the 1918 declaration of independence. The LTF began to have influence with the local government, and with the Moscow authorities.

[19] A year later, the LTF Congress endorsed the country's political and economic independence from the Soviet Union. Despite Moscow's resistance to Latvia's secession, the LTF's policy of carrying out changes peacefully met with widespread popular support, from citizens of Russian or other origins. The LTF program for non-violent change included public demonstrations, free elections and change through parliamentary procedure. Latvia's 1938 constitution went into effect once again, for the first time since the 1940 Soviet occupation.

[20] May 4 1990 marked the Declaration of the Re-establishment of Independence, as well as the reinstatement of the 1922 constitution. In September 1991, the new Council of State of the USSR, in its inaugural session, formally recognized the independence of the Baltic republics. They were also immediately recognized by a number of countries, and admitted as new members to the UN in the General Assembly session held that same month. The three Baltic States initiated negotiations with the European Community (EC), in the areas of trade and financial assistance. In February 1992, Latvia and Russia signed an agreement on the withdrawal of the former USSR's troops, stationed within Latvian territory.

[21] On June 1993 a new parliament was chosen which appointed Guntis Ulmanis as President. The beginning of an economic liberalization process caused a sharp rise of unemployment. In 1994, foreign investment grew but the economy was still dependant on Russia, its main supplier of fuel and its first exporting market. Also, in spite of the massive privatization of state companies, the budget deficit persisted, as that of the trade balance.

[22] In 1995, a lack of control over commercial banks led to the bankruptcy of several financial institutions. The September legislative elections did not reveal any clear winner since nine parties obtained between 5 per cent and 16 per cent of the vote. An agreement between the conservative National Block and two left-wing parties led to Andris Skele being appointed Prime Minister in December.

[23] In June 1996, Parliament re-elected Guntis Ulmanis as President, with 53 votes in 100. Throughout that year, relations with Russia improved slightly. However, Latvia still demanded a boundaries treaty between both countries.

[24] On July 1997, Guntars Krast became the new Prime Minister, in place of Andris Skele, who resigned after being charged with corruption. In November, Russia insisted on its opposition to Latvia's possible joining of the North Atlantic Treaty Alliance (NATO). Although Riga was not included in the list of candidates which would join NATO, the Latvian Government had stated on several occasions its intention of joining.

[25] In February 1998, Latvia adopted a law which would grant passports to those foreigners who had lived in the country permanently since 1991, in a new attempt to reduce tensions within the Russian minority.

Lebanon

Lubnan

Population:	3,084,000 (1996)
Area:	10,400 SQ KM
Capital:	Beirut (Bayrut)
Currency:	Pound
Language:	Arabic

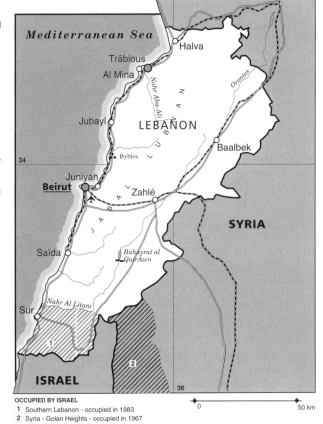

OCCUPIED BY ISRAEL
1 Southern Lebanon - occupied in 1983
2 Syria - Golan Heights - occupied in 1967

Much of present-day Lebanon corresponds to the ancient land of the Phoenicians, who probably arrived in the region in about 3000 BC. Commercial and religious connections were established with Egypt after about 2613 BC and continued until the end of the Egyptian Old Kingdom and the invasion of Phoenicia by the Amorites (c2200 BC). Other groups invading and periodically controlling Phoenicia included the Hyksos (18th century BC), the Egyptians of the New Kingdom (16th century BC), and the Hittites (14th century BC). Seti I (1290-79 BC) of the New Kingdom reconquered most of Phoenicia, but Ramses III (1187-56 BC) lost it to invaders from Asia Minor and Europe. Between the withdrawal of Egyptian rule and the western advance of Assyria (10th century BC), the history of Phoenicia is primarily the history of Tyre. This city-state rose to hegemony among Phoenician states and founded colonies throughout the Mediterranean region. The Achaemenians, an Iranian dynasty under the leadership of Cyrus II, conquered the area in 538 BC. Sidon, 20 miles (32 km) north of Tyre, became a principal coastal city of this empire. In 332 BC Tyre capitulated to the army of Alexander the Great after resisting for eight months. This event marked the demise of Tyre as a great commercial city, as its inhabitants were sold into slavery. In 64 BC Phoenicia was incorporated into the Roman province of Syria.

[2] Emperors embracing Christianity protected the area during the later Roman and Byzantine periods (c.AD 300-634). A 6th-century Christian group fleeing persecution in Syria settled in what is now northern Lebanon, absorbed the native population, and founded the Maronite Church. In the following century, Arab tribes settled in southern Lebanon after the Muslim conquest of Syria. Four hundred years later, many of this Arab group coalesced their beliefs into the Druze faith. In the coastal towns the population became mainly Sunni Muslim. By the end of the 11th century Lebanon had become part of the crusader states, and it later became part of the Mamluk state of Syria and Egypt. Lebanon was able to evolve a social and political system of its own between the 15th and the 18th century. Throughout this period European, particularly French, influence was growing. In 1516 the Ottoman Turks replaced the Mamluks. The social system came under severe strain as the Christian population grew.

[3] Around 1831 the vigorous Egypt of Muhammed Ali extended its influence northwards undermining the decadent Turkish empire. The European powers did not want the Turkish Empire to crumble until Europe was in a position to carry off the spoils. They conveniently decided that Christians anywhere in the world could be equated with Europeans, meriting their protection, and they began to support the Maronite Arab Christians against Egypt. Between 1831 and 1834, five powers intervened in the 'Syrian question'. Russia and Austria devoted their efforts exclusively to the Balkans, and France and Britain were left to dispute domination of the Arab countries, laboriously shunting Prussia aside. The Ottoman Turks ended the local rule of the Druze Shihab princes in 1842, exacerbating already poor relations between the Maronites and the Druze. These relations reached a low ebb with the massacre of Maronites by Druze in 1860.

[4] The French intervened on behalf of the Christians, forcing the Ottoman Sultan to form an autonomous province within the Ottoman Empire for the mountainous Christian area, known as Mount Lebanon. In 1919, Syria and Lebanon became French protectorates, while Britain took Egypt, Jordan and Iraq. For administrative purposes, France separated Lebanon from Syria and when the army pulled out in 1947, they left behind two separate states.

[5] Camille Chamoun was elected president of Lebanon in 1952, following a clearly pro-Western foreign policy. The 1957 parliamentary elections were marked by Muslim demonstrations and riots, demanding closer alignment with Egypt and Syria, and rejecting re-election for the Maronite president.

[6] By the following year the rioting had grown into full scale insurrection, pitting Muslims against Christians in a bloody civil war. In July 1958, President Chamoun allowed 10,000 US Marines to disembark in order to 'pacify' the country. The foreign troops remained in Beirut (Bayrut) and in other strategically important Lebanese cities until October of that year.

[7] By the early 1970s, the population had become mostly Muslim, and they began to question the traditional political system which required a Christian president and a Sunni Muslim prime minister in order to maintain a balance between the two communities. The Shi'as had no specified role.

[8] Differences between the various religious and ethnic communities were combined with an eminently unjust social and economic system. Predatory colonial exploitation had exhausted the traditional cedars of Lebanon, leaving the land barren and farmers impoverished. The new distribution of labor and wealth kept trade control for the Maronites, while the Muslims worked as artisans, laborers and farm workers.

[9] These tensions erupted in civil war again, when the Christian right wing used the 'Palestinian problem' as a pretext for conflict in 1975. Lebanon, which had remained neutral in the 1973 Arab-Israeli War, granted refuge to 300,000 Palestinians in the southern part of

WORKERS

(1996)

Labour force %

■ WOMEN
□ MEN

28 72

■ AGRICULTURE	7%	(1990)
□ INDUSTRIAL	31%	
■ SERVICES	62%	

PROFILE

Environment
One of the smallest Middle East countries, Lebanon has a fertile coastal plain where most of the population lives, with a mild Mediterranean climate making it rainy in the winter; two parallel mountain ranges, the Lebanon Mountains (whose highest peak is Sauda, at 3,083 m) and the Anti-Lebanon Mountains, with temperate forests on their slopes, and between the ranges, the fertile Bekaa Valley. The soil is very fertile because of rich alluvial deposits. Along the coast, a dry bush known as the *maquis* is grown, while vinyards, and wheat, olives, and oranges are cultivated. Cedar has become a national symbol. This wood was used to build the Phoenician fleet and temples. Nowadays there are little over 400 cedars left, ranging in age between 200 and 800 years old. The war has had disastrous consequences, causing a loss of vegetation and soil erosion.

SOCIETY
Peoples: Mostly Arab. There are also small Armenian, European, Syrian and Kurdish minorities, and a large group of Palestinian refugees.
Religions: 75 per cent are Muslim, with the traditionally powerful Sunni now being challenged by the militant Shiites. There is also a large Druze population. 25 per cent are Christian, mostly Maronites. There are also Catholics and Orthodox Christians.
Languages: Arabic (official and predominant). French is widely spoken, Armenian and English are less common.
Political Parties: There are innumerable political, political-military, political-religious factions and militia in Lebanon. The National Front is an alliance of groups from the left, especially Muslims. The Lebanese Phalange is the most important Maronite Christian party. The Progressive Socialist Party is primarily Druzian. The political-military Shi'a organization Amal ("Hope"), pro-Syria. Hezbollah ("party of God"), Shi'a guerrilla group, pro-Iran.

THE STATE
Official Name: al-Jumhouriyah al-Lubnaniyah.
Administrative divisions: 6 governmental divisions.
Capital: Beirut (Bayrut) 1,100,000 people (1991).
Other cities: Tripoli (Trâblous) 240,000 people; Juniyah 100,000; Zahlah 45,000 (1991). **Government:** Elias Hrawi, President since November 1989. Rafiq al-Hariri, Prime Minister since October 1992. **National Holiday:** November 22, Independence Day (1943).
Armed Forces: 44,300 troops (1995). **Other:** External Security Forces: UN peacekeeping forces 5,000; Syrian army 35,000. Civilian militias: Party of God 3,000; South Lebanese Army 2,500.

its territory. Israel used this fact to justify frequent incursions and bombings against civilians. Meanwhile, the Lebanese Christian Phalange militia unleashed its power on the Palestinian refugee camps.
[10] In 1976, Syrian troops, part of an Arab-League peace force, put a stop to the fighting and guaranteed national unity. The underlying causes of the civil war persisted, and Israeli attacks continued. In 1981, Israeli artillery, together with a unit of the former Lebanese commander Saad Haddad, bombarded the cities of Tyre and Sidon (Saida), while Syrian troops installed anti-aircraft missiles in the Bekaa Valley. That July, Israeli jets launched a number of attacks against Palestinian positions, including a wave of air raids on western Beirut; they left 166 dead and 600 wounded.
[11] In June 1982, Israeli troops invaded Lebanon by land, sea and air. Tyre and Sidon were quickly overrun, and Nabataea and Tripoli (Tarabulus) were devastated by bombings. This marked the beginning of Israel's Peace for Galilee operation.
[12] Beirut, the most important political and cultural capital in the Arab world, was virtually destroyed. Thousands of civilians were killed. Bridges, oil pipelines, airports, hospitals, schools, major buildings and modest homes, factories and museums were razed.
[13] Eight thousand Palestinians and Lebanese were captured and held in deplorable prison camps under suspicion of having belonged to the resistance. Israeli army officers and Mossad secret service agents ransacked the Palestine Liberation Organization's (PLO) Center for Palestinian Studies, where 80 scholars had spent 17 years studying Palestinian history and culture, and transferred the research material to an unknown destination.
[14] The PLO finally agreed to pull out of Beirut, providing that the evacuation was carried out under international supervision. US, French and Italian soldiers provided the necessary protection, and the people of western Beirut gave a heroes' farewell to the freedom fighters, who went to seven other Arab countries.
[15] On August 23 1982, what was left of the Lebanese Congress named Israel's nominee, Bashir Gemayel, the only candidate, to succeed President Elias Sarkis. The Maronite leader did not live to take office, however. He died on September 14 in a dynamite attack on the Phalange's eastern Beirut command headquarters. No one accepted responsibility for the act.
[16] The following day, Beirut was occupied by Israeli troops. On September 16 1982, a militia group led by former commander Haddad burst into the Palestinian refugee camps of Sabra and Chatila and assassinated hundreds of unarmed civilians, including old people, women and children.
[17] Later investigations left no doubt as to Israel's responsibility for the killings, as Israeli officers had encouraged the right-wing militia to act.
[18] While Israeli troops still held half of Lebanon, Amin Gemayel was elected president under the same conditions as his younger brother Bashir.
[19] The new president was unable to eliminate distrust among the various communities of Lebanon. A majority of the governing Phalange party sought to replace the 1943 National Alliance with a new constitutional dictate to divide the state into districts under a central federal government. This raised the prospect of Lebanon's political division into several religious mini-states. Sunni and Shiite leaders favored administrative (but not political) decentralization, and the Druze community wanted greater autonomy.
[20] In May 1983 Israel and Lebanon signed an agreement to cease hostilities. Israel promised to withdraw from Lebanese territory, along with the other foreign troops. Lebanon in turn promised not to harbour any armed groups, organizations, bases, offices or structures with the aim of 'carrying out raids on the other party's territory'.
[21] In July 1984 the Lebanese currency, which had remained relatively stable since the beginning of the war in 1975, slumped abruptly, producing unprecedented inflation.
[22] Recession in the Gulf constituted the death blow to Beirut's economy which was already severely weakened by the withdrawal of foreign currency. This caused a balance of payments deficit of over $1.5 billion in 1984.
[23] Before the Israeli army officially withdrew from Lebanon in 1985, it ensured that the Christian militia had displaced the Muslims from southern Lebanon guaranteeing a 'friendly' civilian population in the 10-kilometre security zone they imposed.
[24] In September 1988, pro-Israeli Maronite General Michel Aoun took over the presidency, which had been vacant since Amin Gemayel's constitutional mandate was truncated in a palace coup. The country was now governed by two rival administrations - Aoun's, and that of Muslim Prime Minister Selim al-Hoss.
[25] In October 1989, Lebanon's single chamber parliament met, for the first time since independence, outside the country and under the auspices of the Arab League. The league includes Saudi Arabia, Algeria and Morocco, who acted as intermediaries in negotiations between the Lebanese factions. The meeting in Taif sealed the peace and laid down an alternative to the political system that had been in place since 1943. Under a new constitution, the next president would be elected indirectly by the parliament.
[26] On October 12, Christian and Muslim Lebanese legislators announced a national reconciliation agreement, granting greater power to Muslims and providing for the withdrawal of Syrian troops from Lebanon. General Aoun rejected the agreement because it was instituted by Saudi Arabia, and he considered it a 'Syrian trap'.
[27] On November 5 1989, René Moawad, a Maronite Christian sympathetic to Muslim causes, was unanimously elected president. Moawad was killed by a car-bomb scarcely 17 days before taking office.
[28] On November 24 1989, Elias Hrawi, another Maronite Christian, was elected president by a meeting of the parliament at Zahle, in Syrian-controlled territory. General Aoun immediately rejected the election of a new president in an area

outside the Christian enclave under his control.

[29] In October, 1990, taking advantage of the new situation created by the Iraqi invasion of Kuwait, the Syrian-backed forces started an offensive against Aoun. Lacking international support, as Syria belonged to the anti-Iraq coalition, Aoun was soon defeated and he sought asylum in France.

[30] In December 1990, a national unity government was formed, for the first time since the beginning of the war. It incorporated the Lebanese Forces (Christian), the Amal (Shi'a), the PSP (Druze), and the pro-Syrian parties.

[31] On May 22 1991, the presidents of Lebanon and Syria signed a Brotherhood, Co-operation and Co-ordination Agreement in Damascus, the Syrian capital. Syria recognized Lebanon as a separate and independent state. The agreement established Syrian-Palestinian co-operation in military, security, cultural and economic matters, and it was ratified by the majority of the Lebanese parliament. The Israeli Government, the Phalangist party and the Lebanese Forces militia (both Christian and traditionally anti-Syrian), opposed the treaty as they believed that it gave Syria control over Lebanon's domestic matters.

[32] Early in July, 6,000 soldiers of the Lebanese army took over the territories occupied by the PLO around the port of Sidon, in the south of the country. This offensive forced the PLO out of its main operations base for campaigns against Israel. On July 7, in spite of the apparent defeat of the PLO, Israel stated that it would not withdraw its forces from the security zone.

[33] In November, Israel increased its offensive on the security zone, demanding that the Lebanese army should leave the territories within 12 hours. These actions caused the massive exodus of nearly 100,000 Shi'a Muslims.

[34] In December, 1991, Lebanon was granted loans amounting to $700 million, to be used over the next three years for the rehabilitation and reconstruction of the country.

[35] On February 16 1992 - eight days before peace talks between Arabs and Israelis were due to resume - an Israeli air raid killed Sheikh Abbas Mussawi, head of the Hezbollah (Iranian-backed Islamic group). Six days later, the Shi'a guerrillas suspended attacks against Israel as the result of an agreement between the Hezbollah, Amal (another Islamic grouping) and the representatives of Syrian and Lebanese forces. The Israeli defence minister said his country would retaliate against any attacks from that organization. The United Nations Security Council

condemned the use of violence in the region, at the request of the Lebanese ambassador.

[36] In March, an intense Israeli mobilization at the border caused combats with the pro-Iranian Muslim guerrillas. In April, Israel shelled several Shiite Muslim villages in the Bekaa Valley.

[37] A general strike against the government's economic policy, accompanied by violent public demonstrations brought about the fall of the pro-Syrian Omar Karame government. President Elias Hrawi designated Rashid Al Sohl, a moderate Sunni, as the new head of government. He formed his cabinet with an equal number of Christians and Muslims. The August parliamentary elections were boycotted by the Christians. The new parliament included Hezbollah and Amal representatives. In October, Rafiq al-Hariri, a nationalized Saudi Arabian millionaire, was named prime minister.

[38] In 1993, the World Bank granted a loan for reconstruction and education projects. The currency regained 10 per cent of its value and the country began receiving more foreign investment. The gap between rich and poor widened.

[39] Israel continued to bomb Palestinian refugee camps and PLO bases. In August, Lebanese authorities rejected an Israeli proposal for total withdrawal since Israel demanded Hezbollah's total disarmament.

[40] Although political violence continued to destabilize domestic political consensus, progress toward a definite peace was made. The economy grew by six per cent and banks from the Netherlands, United Kingdom and France returned to Beirut after 20 years of absence.

[41] Among other terrorist incidents, a bomb killed a top Hezbollah leader, 21 Israeli soldiers died and - on the domestic side - Christian churches were shelled causing dozens of deaths. In March, the Government suspended private radio and television broadcasting until a new press law had been enacted while it reinstated the death penalty for political murders or crimes.

[42] During 1995, government attention was focused on finding a solution to the armed conflict and the reconstruction of Beirut. In January, the UN Security Council decided to extend its intervention in the country. At the beginning of talks between Israel and Palestine in Oslo, Norway, the Hezbollah and Southern Lebanon Army resumed their attacks in order to displace Israeli troops and defer negotiations with Syria.

[43] The Palestinians' fate in Lebanon was uncertain. The UN

estimated the government had refused to acknowledge civilian rights to 338,000 Palestinians.

[44] On June 24, former Maronite leader Samir Geagea was sentenced to life imprisonment for the murders of his rival Dany Chamoun and his family. Political balance shifted toward the Muslims.

[45] Prime Minister al-Hariri promoted the 'Horizon 2000' scheme to deal with Beirut's urban renovation and a constitutional reform which would extend the presidential term from 6 to 9 years to achieve the necessary stability to carry out his project. His goal of reinstating Lebanon as a central financial centre in the Middle East, made progress. A plan to reconstruct Beirut's business and residential area was delayed by the discovery of archaeological remains, which led to a debate about their rescue and effect on the costs of urban renovation.

[46] The economic situation changed significantly from 1992 to 1996. This was evident among other things, in the reduction of annual inflation from 170 per cent to 10 per cent and in the 200-per-cent increase of foreign currency reserves.

[47] In 1997, fighting was renewed

between the Lebanese guerrillas and the Israeli army, which still occupied what Tel Aviv called a "security zone", an area covering 850 square kilometers in southern Lebanon. Israel lost 39 soldiers that year, the highest number since 1985. The rise of the number of victims inreased the pressure of Israeli public opinion on its government to put an end to the war.

[48] In February 1998, Beirut rejected a proposal from Tel Aviv to start negotiations on an eventual withdrawal of Israeli troops from its territory and demanded the unconditional end of the occupation, based on resolution 425 of the UN Security Council. Israel wanted, in exchange for its withdrawal, a bilateral agreement that would put an end to guerrilla attacks on its territory. However, an agreement between both countries was hardly imaginable without Syria's consent, which seemed hard to obtain. It was thought Damascus preferred the conflict in southern Lebanon to continue in order to strengthen its own position in the negotiations with Tel Aviv to recover the strategic region of the Golan Heights.

Lesotho

Lesotho

Population: 2,078,000 (1996)
Area: 30,355 SQ KM
Capital: Maseru

Currency: Maloti
Language: Sotho and English

For most African states, national unity is a task still to be accomplished. In some cases, however, the nation existed before the political state. Lesotho and Swaziland are both examples of this.

2 The Zulu conquests, begun in 1818 by Shaka, affected a large number of Bantu nations, among them the North Sotho or Pedi who occupied a vast area in present-day Transvaal. While some withdrew northwards, the head of the Bakwena tribe, Moshoeshoe, brought other Sotho tribes and groups of dissident Zulus together under his command, retreating with them towards the Drakensberg mountains. The lengthy war of resistance fought first against the Zulus, and then against the expansionist Boers, consolidated the bonds between these groups of diverse origin who gave Moshoeshoe the title of "Great Leader of the Mountain", and called themselves Basothos.

3 The Boers, the Dutch colonizers, tried to use the Basothos as labour. But they soon admitted defeat declaring that "these savages prefer liberty to slavery". Some Basothos refused to work on the Europeans' farms, saying "God created animals to feed men and not men to feed animals".

4 Until 1867, Dutch colonization in South Africa was tenuous. Then diamonds were discovered. Soon afterwards gold was found, and along with its discovery the British came up from the Cape. In 1868, British missionaries persuaded the Basotho traditional leader Moshoeshoe, that only the "protection" of the British Crown could save the people from subjection by the Boers. The territory became a protectorate, administered separately from South Africa even after the Boer War of 1899-1902, when the British took control of the whole country.

5 Britain had promised the South African Government that Basotholand (Lesotho), Bechuanaland (Botswana) and Swaziland, which were all in similar situations, would eventually be integrated into South Africa. However, when the South African Union broke all ties with London in 1961, consolidating its racist policy of apartheid, the British left those countries independent. In 1965, a constitution was promulgated in Basotholand and in 1966 the country proclaimed independence under the name of Lesotho.

6 However, as an enclave within South Africa. Lesotho depended on the surrounding country as an outlet for its products of wheat, asbestos, cattle, and diamonds. The currency was the South African rand and South African companies controlled its economy and communications.

7 Foreign trade was extremely unbalanced, with imports ten times higher than exports. The difference is offset by money that the migrant workers send home. Some 45 percent of the labor force works in the South African gold mines.

8 The difficult economic situation enabled the opposition Congress Party to win a victory in the legislative elections of 1970. Prime Minister Leabua Jonathan engineered a coup, dissolved parliament, and sent King Moshoeshoe into exile. He was allowed to return on the promise that he would refrain from any political activity.

9 After the 1976 student uprising which took place in Soweto, South Africa, Lesotho opened its doors to thousands of young South Africans refugees despite the tremendous economic sacrifice this implied for such a poor country. When South Africa began its «Bantustan» policy, Lesotho, in compliance with the UN resolution condemning this new form of apartheid, refused to recognize the puppet state in Transkei. In early 1977, South Africa closed the Lesotho border in retaliation. This economic aggression endangered the country's survival. Lesotho made dramatic appeals for international solidarity, requesting aid to resist the blockade.

10 After Zimbabwean independence, Lesotho joined the economic integration project promoted by the Front Line states, strengthening relations with Mozambique.

11 South Africa retaliated by supporting of groups opposed to the Jonathan government. This led the leader to seek help from the United Nations and the European Economic Community. The official Basotho National Party (BNP) also had to face the opposition of groups linked to the founder of the Basotho Congress Party (BCP), led by Ntsu Mokhele.

12 Most of the incidents were really caused by South African military groups interested in preventing the anti-apartheid refugees of the African National Congress (ANC) from organizing in Maseru (see South Africa). The most important of these attacks took place in December 1982, when a South African military air raid killed 45 people, 12 of them children, in the outskirts of Maseru. During the attack, three ANC leaders were killed, but the other victims were all bystanders.

13 In 1982, the Government imposed an emergency law allowing the arrest of anyone suspected of illegal activities, without any previous judicial process. The army and the police were reinforced and a paramilitary group known as Koeko violently suppressed BCP supporters in the Drakensberg mountains.

14 In March 1983, there was a border incident between Lesothan and South African troops, when saboteurs tried to enter the country to destroy the principal electric power plant. There was growing South African pressure to sign a non-aggression treaty with Pretoria, similar to the agreements that the apartheid regime had signed with Swaziland and Mozambique. The Prime Minister, Leabua Jonathan was against the treaty, but due to Lesotho's economic dependence on South Africa he was forced to be more flexible.

15 Towards the end of 1984, the South African Government began to prevent products from getting to Lesotho, particularly weapons purchased in Europe, and to delay the remittances sent by almost 400,000 migrant workers. They also delayed plans to build a dam on the Sengu River, on the border between the two countries. South African pressures were directed at intimidating the Lesotho electorate and strengthening

WORKERS

(1996)

Labour force %
- ■ WOMEN
- □ MEN

37   63

- ■ AGRICULTURE 40% (1990)
- □ INDUSTRIAL 28%
- ▨ SERVICES 32%

PROFILE

ENVIRONMENT

This small country is an enclave in the foothills of the Drakensberg mountains in southern Africa. Landlocked and mountainous, its only fertile land is located in the west where corn, sorghum and wheat are grown. In the rest of the country cattle is raised. Except for small diamond deposits, there are no mineral resources. Soil erosion is a serious problem.

SOCIETY

Peoples: Ethnically homogeneous, the country is inhabited by the Basotho (or Sotho) people, of Bantu origin (85 per cent) and a Zulu minority (15 per cent). There are small communities of Asian and European origin. **Religions:** Mainly Christian. Also traditional African beliefs are held. **Languages:** Sotho and English (officials). **Political Parties:** The Basotho Congress Party (BCP), founded in 1952; the Basotho National Party (BNP), founded in 1958; the Lesotho Communist Party (LCP), founded in 1962; the Maremattou Liberation Party, founded in 1962; the National Independence Party (NIP), Christian; and the People's Front for Democracy (PFD), which emerged from a split in the Lesotho Communist Party (LCP); the Kopanang of Basotho Party, Founded in 1992, leading campaigns for women's rights. **Social Organizations:** The Lesotho General Workers' Union (LGWU), founded in 1954 and led by L. Hamatsoso, is the only central labor organization.

THE STATE

Official Name: Kingdom of Lesotho. **Administrative Divisions:** 10 Districts. **Capital:** Maseru, 150,000 people (1994). **Other cities:** Mafeteng 12,667 people; Maputsoe 20,000 (1986). **Government:** King Moshoeshoe II, Chief of State since 1990. Ntsu Mokhelele, Prime Minister since 1994. Parliamentary Monarchy. **National Holiday:** October 4, Independence Day (1966). **Armed Forces:** 2,000 troops (1995).

STATISTICS

DEMOGRAPHY

Population: 2,078,000 (1996) **Annual growth:** 2.6% (1980/1996) **Estimates for year 2000:** 2,300,000. **Annual growth to year 2000:** 2.5% (1994/2000) **Urban Population:** 24.8% (1996) **Urban growth:** 6.53% (1980/95) **Children per woman:** 5 (1996).

HEALTH

Life expectancy at birth: 58 years (1996) male: 57 years (1994) female: 59 years (1994) **Infant mortality:** 96 per 1,000 (1996) **Under-5 child mortality:** 139 per 1,000 (1996) **Calorie consumption:** 93% (1988/90) 25,000 **people per doctor** (1988/91) **Safe water:** 62% (1990/96).

EDUCATION

Literacy: 71% (1995) male: 81% (1995) female: 62% (1995) **School enrolment :** Primary total: 99% (1990/95) male : 93% (1990/95) female: 104% (1990/95) Secondary: male : 23% (1990/95) female: 34% (1990/95) Tertiary: 2% (1995) **Primary school teachers:** one for every 49 students (1995).

COMMUNICATIONS

10 **newspapers**, 33 **radios**, 10 **TV sets** and 8 **main telephone lines** per 1,000 people (1994).

ECONOMY

Per capita, GNP: $ 660 (1996) **Annual growth, GNP:** 6.7% (1995/96) **Annual inflation:** 13.42% (1985/95) **Consumer price index:** 168.9 (1994) **Currency:** 3.65 malotis = $ 1 (1995) **Cereal imports:** 99 metric tons (1994) **Food import dependency:** 12% (1994) **Fertilizer use:** 187 kgs per ha (1994) **External debt:** $ 654 million (1996) $ 315 **per capita:** (1996) **Debt service:** 6.1% of exports (1996) **Development aid received:** $ 114 million (1995) $ 57 per capita (1995) 8.4% of GNP (1994).

HDI (rank / value) 137 / 0.457 (1994)

---

opposition to the BNP, the conservative Basotho Democratic Party (BDA) and the (ANC-aligned) BCP.

[16] But even these tough measures did not satisfy Pretoria and on January 20 1986, a military coup toppled Leabua Jonathan, and General Justin Lekhanya, head of Lesotho's paramilitary forces, led the Military Committee that replaced him.

[17] In 1988, workers residing in South Africa sent remittances totalling more than $350 million to Lesotho, that is 500 per cent of the total value of the country's exports.

[18] In March 1990, the military regime exiled King Moshoeshoe, accusing him of being a hindrance to the country's democratization program. His son Bereng Mohato Siisa replaced him as Letsie III. On April 30 1991, the armed forces went on strike for higher salaries, and a bloodless military coup deposed Lekhanya's government, setting up a Council chaired by Colonel Elias P Ramaema.

[19] The South African Government blocked remittances from emigrant workers in 1991. In May, a demonstration against foreign interference in the economy ended with 34 people dead and 425 arrests.

[20] A new constitution designated the King head of state in 1993, without giving him either legal or executive powers. The July legislative elections gave all the

seats to the BCP. In August the privatization of six state businesses was started with a loan from the IMF.

[21] Erosion affected 58 per cent of the low lying soils. Two thirds of all farming land belonged to emigrant workers, but was worked by their wives and families. Plans were developed to make use of the water from the highlands - the main natural resource of the country - through a hydroelectric project which will change the course of several rivers to feed water to South Africa in return for electricity.

[22] During 1994, the low salaries led to armed confrontations between rival military factions. The government plan to integrate the armed wing of the BCP into the army led to the kidnapping and murder of the finance minister by disgruntled soldiers.

[23] The king dissolved the government and Parliament. Protests outside the palace were put down by soldiers and police, with at least four people killed. The internal republican opposition and international pressure forced Letsie III to abdicate in favor of his father, King Moshoeshoe II, who was formally restored to the throne in January 1995.

[24] During 1995, the tunnel under the mountains, which will supply water to the Vaal river valley in South Africa, was completed.

[25] In March 1995, members of the National Security Forces

kidnapped several high-ranking officers, demanding their immediate withdrawal from the army for their part in assassinations and various sorts of corruption.

[26] In January 1996, the King died in a road accident. The Assembly designated his son Letsie III as his replacement.

[27] The Government picked up plans to use the water from the mountains again in 1998, and inaugurated the first stretch, including a dam, in April. The project had been suspended in 1997 following protests from the displaced local populations and accusations of corruption from the opposition. Non-governmental organizations in Italy accused the World Bank of violating the human rights of the communities and damaging the environment by funding the construction of hydroelectric dams in Lesotho.

[28] In early 1998, the Catholic Church protested over the

inclusion of introduction to Islam, Hinduism, Buddhism and Judaism courses, in schools controlled by Cahtolics. The Government quashed their complaint saying the Constitution authorised religious diversity.

[29] On March 8, hundreds of women called for tougher punishment for rapists. Official estimates said that on average, five women and girls were raped each day in Lesotho. A report from the Southern Africa Development Community stressed that in the majority of its 14 member nations - including Lesotho - the legislation on violence against women was not fulfilled.

[30] That same month, a new political party, the Democratic Christian Party (DCP), was born of a split in the National Progress Party.

The Origins of Yoruba Culture

In the 5th century, iron working rural communities settled in the forest region of the coastal strip which stretches between Volta and Cameroon, establishing an organized agricultural economy with advanced and stable ways of life. Amongst the largest, and seemingly oldest, of these were the Yoruba communities, found in the Ife, Ilesha and Ekiti regions.

In around the 13th century, a movement outwards by the groups which imposed economic, political and political supremacy on the weaker communities led to the creation of the Yoruba kingdoms. But the idea of a 'kingdom' associated with the traditional African societies is far from the Western view of, for example, the kingdom of Louis XVI.

The Yoruba kingdoms or states

The Yoruba kingdoms - south of modern-day Nigeria - owe their linguistic and cultural homogeneity to this ethnic group, recognizing their roots in these ancestors. The splendor accomplished by the Ife and Oyo kingdoms spread to the traditions of the other areas and overshadowed their own origins.

There is one belief structure which is based on the myth of Ife who created the world in the city of Ife-Ife, and another which attributes the creation to Oyo and says the Yoruba have their origins in a migration movement which came from the east. What is certain, however, is that the life of these kingdoms led to the spread of their institutions and practices amongst the local populations, and that the execution of complex functions - extensive agriculture, long-distance trade, tax systems, military expansion, citizen policies - were possible because of the well-planned and organized states.

Although each king aimed to leave his successor an even bigger kingdom, a policy of tolerance encouraged a certain level of interchange which led to the cultural enrichment of both the stronger communities and those they absorbed. It was this exchange which ultimately explained the heterogeneity of Yoruba civilization: a single culture expressed through differences.

The economic life of the Yoruba kingdoms

The Yoruba states were generally of a modest size, sometimes covering only a single city and the surrounding villages. The kingdom of Oyo was one important exception, spreading over a vast area and acquiring imperial status in the 17th century. The more typical kingdoms consisted of a compact town surrounding the compound of the kings and elders in an area contained by a wall marking the edge of the kingdom. Resources produced from agriculture, and a certain amount of mining and craftwork were taken to local markets organized on alternate days in order to prevent competition between markets. However, luxury articles - like the gold paid in tax in the courts, marble, art objects, nuts and others - were the main object of long distance trade, like that with the Hausa states of the eastern zones, to the benefit of the richest strata of society - the kings and their courts, officials, merchants and professionals. In the more developed communities slave ownership was common as a result of crimes or debts, and these people worked as domestic servants or agricultural laborers on the common lands. There was no slave trade amongst the early traditional Yoruba societies. Historical reports tell of a slave trade which probably began in the 15th century under the kings of Benin, by which time this kingdom had become a powerful expansionist state.

The Yoruba cosmovision

An ancient myth, revealing how mythical time is transposed over historical time, explains how the grandchildren of the mythical founder of Ife - the sacred city - spread out into the surrounding area establishing and naming the first generation of Yoruba states: Owu, Ketu, Benin, Illa, Dave, Popo and Oyo.

The Yoruba belief system is based on the idea of a superior entity made up of three divinities, Olofi, Oloddumare and Olorun. The first of these created the world, which was initially only populated by orixas, or saints. The power, or *ache* was later divided between the orixas, who from then on were empowered to intervene in human affairs and to represent people to Olofi through the mediation of the supreme judge or main messenger, Obbatala.

As in most of the languages of Black Africa, "the power" is expressed amongst the Yoruba through the word "ache" which means "the force," not in the sense of violence, but as a vital energy which creates a multiplicity of processes and determines everything from physical and moral integrity to luck.

The Yoruba cosmovision is prevalent in all the cultural creations of this group of people. As is generally the case with peoples where every action is carried out, interpreted and lived as part of an organic belief system which is not precisely religious, this cosmology includes the idea that the order of the cosmic forces can be upset by immoral actions which have the effect of unbalancing and damaging humanity, nature and the perpetrators themselves.

The unity between nature and ethics in these cultures constitutes a cosmic determinism, and along with it, a principle for the exercising of power, a condition for its beneficent application.

Community life

The community was of great value in the traditional Yoruba societies. It defined the conception of history - identified with the life of the group in continuous change, and time - conceived of as the social time, lived by the group, which transcends the time of the individual. It is, at the same time, the dimension where people can, and must, incessantly play out their fight against decadence and for the enrichment of their vital energy.

The Yoruba believed that throughout the history lived by the group a certain *ache* was accumulated, incarnated in objects. These objects were sent from the ancestors down through the successive generations via their patriarchs or kings, who were intermediaries between the transcendental and visible worlds, as gifts from the orixas.

Although they were headed by kings, the communities were led by governing councils made up of men of varied standing, where the elders enjoyed their deserved dignity. The Yoruba, as in the majority of traditional African societies, were societies of public opinion, where the conduct of the authorities was monitored, spied on, and the violations of the principles which ruled the community life were always denounced through persistent verbal criticism and rumors which were so wearing that, in time, the subject of these was forced either to explain their actions or stand down.

Women also had a great deal of authority in other aspects of community life.

The Yoruba religion

The religion of the traditional Yoruba societies is characterized by the cult of God and a group of intermediary divinities, whose intervention and wills rule human life. The orixas were ancestors who accumulated power and knowledge over the forces of nature and humanity during their lifetimes, by virtue of which they one day changed from people into gods.

Each one personifies certain forces of nature and is associated with a cult which obliges believers to offer food, sacrifices and prayers in order to escape their wrath and attract their favor.

The Yoruba gods and goddesses occasionally take possession of the faithful, and when this happens the god dances with his devotees in a friendly manner and sometimes speaks, offers advice or gives prophecies. The most well known orixas include: Eleggua, the god who opens paths and is found behind the doors of Yoruba homes; Oggun, the inventor of the forge, god of the minerals and the mountains; Oxosi, the god of hunting; Xango, the god of fire and war; Oxun, the goddess of fresh water, love and all tenderness and Iemanya, the queen of the sea.

Yoruba art

The art in the most ancient Yoruba communities was distinguished by its sculptures, metalwork and ceramics. Bas-reliefs, woodworking, masks and human heads created by the lost-wax method were jealousy guarded as divine heirlooms. However, Yoruba art is definitely dominated by music. Though this has a profane meaning, as an art form music is inseparably united to the Yoruba religious cults and liturgy.

The most characteristic musical tradition is the predominance of the drums and especially the presence of the "bata" (family) drums, an exclusive creation of the Yoruba people. This is an orchestra of three drums - "Iya" (the mother), "Itotele" and "Okongolo" played together by three drummers. For the Yoruba "the batas speak" and each of their blows - be they of the sacred bata or the non-sacred bembe - are inspired by legends attributed to the orixas.

The sound and symphonic integrity of the bata (the vegetable sound of the wood of the drums, the animal sound of the skins, and the mineral for the accompanying bells and rattles), along with human voices, obey a magical call through which the Yoruba invoke the cosmic powers.

Liberia

Liberia

Population: 2,245,000 (1996)
Area: 111,369 SQ KM
Capital: Monrovia

Currency: Liberian Dollar
Language: English

¹ The present Liberia was formerly known as the Grain Coast, and was inhabited by 16 different ethnic groups. The Kru speakers lived in the southwest, and the Mande speaking peoples, including the Mandingo, lived in the east and northeast. After the arrival of the Portuguese, Mandingo traders and artisans played an important role as they spread throughout the territory, becoming the principal propagators of Islam.

² Some people are unaware that the US also shared in the spoils of African colonization. Emancipated blacks posed a social problem to US southern slaveholders, long before US President Abraham Lincoln freed the slaves in 1865, during the US civil war. As a solution to the "problem" some were "repatriated." On the assumption that blacks would be at home in any part of Africa, it was planned to ship them to the British colony of Sierra Leone.

³ In 1821, the American Colonization Society purchased a portion of Sierra Leone and founded a city which was named Monrovia after James Monroe, President of the United States.

⁴ Only 20,000 US blacks returned to Africa. The native population distrusted these settlers whose language and religion were those of the colonizers. Supported by US Navy firepower, the newcomers settled on the coast and occupied the best lands. For a long time, they refused to mix with the "junglemals," whom they considered "savages." Even today only 15 per cent of the population speak English and practise Christianity.

⁵ In 1841, the US Government approved a constitution for the African territory. It was written by Harvard academics, who called the country Liberia. Washington also appointed Liberia's first African governor: Joseph J Roberts. In July 1847, a Liberian Congress representing only the repatriates from the US, proclaimed independence. Roberts was appointed President and the Harvard-made constitution was kept, along with a flag which resembled that of the United States.

⁶ The emblem on the Liberian coat of arms reads: "Love of liberty brought us here." However, independence brought little freedom for the original population. For a long time, only landowners were able to vote. Today, the 45,000 descendants of the former US slaves form the core of the local ruling class and are closely linked with transnational capital. One of the principal exports, rubber, is controlled by Firestone and Goodrich under 99-year concessions granted in 1926. The same is true of oil, iron ore and diamonds. Resistance to this situation has been suppressed on several occasions by US Marine interventions to "defend democracy."

⁷ The discovery of extensive mineral deposits, and the use of the Liberian flag by US ships, fanned a period of economic growth beginning in 1960. This was instantly dubbed an "economic miracle", but this so-called miracle only reached the American-Liberian sector of the population, who secured significant increases in income during this period.

⁸ The political establishment was shaken in 1979, when the increase in the price of rice triggered demonstrations and unrest. A year later, Sergeant Samuel Doe overthrew the regime of William Tolbert, who was executed, along with other members of his government. These disturbances led to the suspension of the Constitution and the banning of all political parties. In 1980, the beginning of a democratization process was announced, followed by the signing of the first agreement with the International Monetary Fund.

⁹ Falling exports, increasing unemployment, the reduction of salaries in both public and private sectors, and spiralling foreign debt threw the country into a crisis of substantial proportions.

¹⁰ Popular discontent increased. Between 1980 and 1989 Doe's administration uncovered many new anti-government conspiracies.

¹¹ Elections were held in 1985. With any viable political opposition banned, and accusations of fraud and imprisonment of opposition leaders abounding, Doe obtained 50.9 per cent of the vote. The Liberian People's Party (LPP) and United People's Party (UPP), which represented the major opposition forces, were not authorized to participate.

¹² In 1987, most Government financing came directly from the US, a fact related to the vast North American business interests in Liberia. These included $450 million of investments, military bases, a regional Voice of America station, and a communications center for all US diplomatic missions in Africa.

¹³ In May 1990, the National Patriotic Front of Liberia (NPFL) launched an attack against the city of Gbarnga, 120 km from the capital. The guerrilla movement rapidly took over several parts of the country.

¹⁴ In June, an NPFL victory, under the leadership of former civil servant Charles Taylor, seemed imminent. However, in July, when the battle to take Monrovia was just underway, the rebel front split, with one faction forming the Independent Patriotic Front (INPFL), led by Prince Johnson.

¹⁵ On July 31, 200 civilians, who had sought refuge in a Lutheran mission, were massacred by Government soldiers.

¹⁶ In September 1990, President Samuel Doe was assassinated by Johnson's troops. In the mêlée which followed, Johnson, Taylor, Amos Sawyer (a civil servant in Doe's government) and Raleigh Seekie (head of the Presidential Guard) all proclaimed themselves "Interim President".

¹⁷ In November 1990, Sawyer formed a provisional government, with the support of Cote d'Ivoire, Gambia, Nigeria, Burkina Faso and Togo, the five West African countries that had made up a peacekeeping force.

¹⁸ In 1992, Taylor turned down the vice-presidency which Sawyer had offered him. The NPFL controlled most of the country, through the Government of the Patriotic National Assembly of Reconstruction. In August, 2,000 NPFL troops were killed in an attack upon Tubmanburg, north of Monrovia by United Liberian forces (ULIMO).

¹⁹ ULIMO split into two factions in November. Alhaji Kromah,

PER 100,000
LIVE BIRTHS
560

38%

PROFILE

Environment
The country is divided into three geographic regions: the coastal plain contains most of the population, and is low and swampy; the central plateau, crossed by numerous valleys and covered by dense tropical forests; and the mountainous inland along the border with Guinea. In the fertile coastal areas, rice, coffee, sugarcane, cocoa and palm oil are produced. American companies own large rubber plantations. Liberia is also the leading African iron ore producer. War, the loss of biodiversity and erosion are the main threats to the environment.

SOCIETY
Peoples: Most Liberians belong to the Mende, Kwa and Vai groups, which are split into nearly 30 ethnic sub groups. Of these, the most significant are the Mandingo, Kpelle, Mendo, Kru, Gola and Bassa (the Vai are renowned for having created one of the few African written languages). The descendants of "repatriated" US slaves control business and politics, though they constitute only 5 per cent of the population.
Religions: The majority profess traditional African religions. About 15 per cent are Muslim, and slightly fewer Christian. The State, however, is officially Christian.
Languages: English is the official language, though it is spoken by only 15 per cent of the population. The rest speak local languages.
Political Parties: National Patriotic Front of Liberia (NPFL); United Liberation Movement for Democracy in Liberia (Ulimo); Liberia Peace Council (LNC); Ulimo-J and Ulimo-K (both created after the division of the United Liberian Independence Movement).

THE STATE
Official Name: Republic of Liberia.
Administrative divisions: 11 Counties and 2 Territories.
Capital: Monrovia, 720,000 people (1994).
Other cities: Harbel 60,000; Gbarnga 30,000; Buchanan 25,000; Yekepa 16,000 (1985).
Government: Charles Taylor, President since July 1997.
National Holiday: August 26, Independence Day (1846).
Armed Forces: 3,000 (1996).

STATISTICS

DEMOGRAPHY
Population: 2,245,000 (1996) **Annual growth:** 1.1% (1980/1996) **Urban Population:** 45.5% (1996) **Children per woman:** 6.5 (1996).

HEALTH
Life expectancy at birth: 48 years (1996) **Infant mortality:** 157 per 1,000 (1996) **Under-5 child mortality:** 235 per 1,000 (1996) **Calorie consumption:** 98% (1988/90) **Safe water:** 46% (1990/96).

EDUCATION
Literacy: 38% (1995) male : 54% (1995) female: 22% (1995) **School enrolment** : Primary total: 35% (1990/95).

ECONOMY
Currency: 1 Liberian dollars = $ 1 (1995) **Cereal imports:** 121 metric tons (1994)

accused of being overly-friendly toward Muslim groups and the Libyan Government, became the leader of the faction that established its headquarters in Tubmanburg. Raleigh Seekie became the leader of the Sierra Leone faction.
[20] In June 1993, ULIMO attacked a refugee camp in Kata. According to the United Nations High Commissioner for Refugees, during the attack 450 people were killed and many of the victims' bodies were mutilated.
[21] US support for an increased UN role in the conflict gave the Security Council the go-ahead to demand a cease-fire and decree an arms embargo, amongst other measures.
[22] The military stalemate and UN participation led to a peace

agreement being signed in Geneva, on July 17 1993. The two main armed forces and the provisional Sawyer government agreed a cease-fire in seven months and the calling of general elections.
[23] The NPFL made several protests about ULIMO attacks. The civil war worsened. The UN embargo and the consequent food shortages caused a wave of guerrilla attacks against civilian targets.
[24] In August, following the timetable established in Geneva, a transitional Council of State was established with representatives of the NPFL, ULIMO and Sawyer's government.
[25] By 1993, the total of civil war victims had risen to 150,000. Nearly a million Liberians, out of a

total population of 2.4 million, had been displaced to another part of the country, or were living as refugees in neighboring countries.
[26] In March 1994, the Council of State took power, but the formation of a new government was delayed until May due to disagreements between the NPFL, ULIMO and Sawyer's representatives. Meanwhile, the fighting between rival armed groups and the skirmishes between some of them and the recently deployed Economic Community of the West African States (ECOWAS) peace troops continued.
[27] In December, the seven warring groups agreed a cease-fire. In 1995, negotiations between the various bands continued. The composition of the Council of State was broadened, with the entry of Charles Taylor, and a new government was formed.
[28] Civil war broke out again in 1996 with violent clashes, particularly in Monrovia. In September, Ruth Perry took over leadership of the Council of State, with ECOWAS support. The war had seriously affected essential services. In August, the main leaders agreed a new truce. ECOWAS deployed more troops to guarantee the fulfilment of the agreements signed in 1995.
[29] In November, the peace forces started to disarm the rival

factions. The war had caused around 200,000 deaths and made hundreds of thousands of people into refugees.
[30] In July 1997, Charles Taylor won the presidential and parliamentary elections with 75.3 per cent of the vote, taking over as President a month later. Taylor's National Patriotic Front took 21 of the 26 posts in the Senate and 49 of the 64 seats in the Chamber of Representatives.
[31] The President approved a law to defend human rights and appointed a commission to monitor the situation. However, Amnesty International called for an impartial tribunal to investigate human rights violations committed during the civil war.
[32] In March 1998, some 480,000 Liberian refugees, in various African countries, started registering for voluntary repatriation. However, the plan ran into serious problems due to the lack of funds promised by donor organisations. The programme had also planned to help 220,000 Liberians displaced within national territory.

Libya

Libiya

Population: 5,593,000 (1996)
Area: 1,759,540 SQ KM
Capital: Tripoli (Tarabulus)

Currency: Dinar
Language: Arabic

The Socialist People's Libyan Arab Jamahiriya (known as Libya) has always been torn between the different political and economic centers of North Africa. Bordering pharaonic Egypt, Libya shared its culture and two Libyan dynasties ruled Egypt between the 10th and 8th centuries BC. However such influences did not lead to a unified state. The Carthaginian and Roman empires on the western border further stressed this division. After the Arab conquest in the 7th century, Tunisia, Morocco and Egypt became the new power centres.

[2] The development of maritime trade and the ensuing piracy turned Tripoli into one of the major Mediterranean ports, bringing European intervention which caused further intervention by the Turkish Sultan. In 1551, Suleiman the Magnificent annexed the region to the Ottoman Empire. A weakened central authority gave increasing autonomy to the governors precipitating independence movements. The beginning of the 19th century saw piracy again on Libya's shores; this was used as a pretext for US military intervention and in 1804 US forces attacked Tripoli.

[3] In 1837, Muhammad al-Sanussi founded a clandestine Muslim brotherhood (the Sanussi religious sect) which promoted resistance to Turkish domination, though the Italians really posed a greater threat. With the decline of the Ottoman Empire, Italy declared war on Turkey in 1911 and seized the Libyan coast, the northernmost Turkish possession in Africa. With the outbreak of World War I, the Italian presence was confined to Tripoli and Homs

(Al-Khums) while the rest of the territory remained autonomous. At the end of the War Italy attempted to recover control of the territory but faced resistance for 20 years by Sidi Omar al-Mukhtar's forces. In 1931, al-Mukhtar was captured and executed and the Italians formally annexed the territory.

[4] From Egypt and Tunisia, the Sanussi brotherhood remained active and co-operated with the Allies in World War II. Muhammad Idris al-Sanussi, leader of the brotherhood, was recognized as Emir of Cyrenaica by the British. At the end of the conflict, the country was divided into an British zone (Tripolitania and Cyrenaica) and a French (Fezzan) governed from Chad. In 1949, a UN resolution restored legitimate union to the region and established the independent nation of Libya, with Idris al-Sanussi as leader for his religious authority.

[5] Idris consolidated his position with support from the powerful Turkish-Libyan families, military advisers from the US and Britain and transnational oil companies. In 1960, foreigners settled in the country, as the oil began to flow in great quantities.

[6] In 1966, Muammar al-Khaddafi, the son of Bedouin nomads, founded the Union of Free Officials in London, where he was studying. He returned to Libya and, on September 1 1969, he led an insurrection in Sabha overthrowing the King.

[7] Khaddafi's Revolutionary Council proclaimed itself Muslim, Nasserist and socialist, beginning to eliminate all US and British military bases in Libya, and imposing severe limitations on transnationals operating in the country. The production of petroleum and its derivatives was placed under state control but the government kept some ties with the foreign companies.

[8] Khaddafi began an ambitious modernization program, with special emphasis on agricultural development. Each rural family was allotted 10 hectares of land, a tractor, a house, tools, and irrigation facilities. Over 1,500 artesian wells were drilled and two million hectares of desert were irrigated and turned into fertile farmland.

WORKERS

(1996)

Labour force %
- ■ WOMEN
- □ MEN

21 / 79

- ■ AGRICULTURE 11% (1990)
- □ INDUSTRIAL 23%
- ■ SERVICES 66%

Area claimed by Chad

0 — 300 km

[9] Rapid growth meant that immigrant workers and experienced technicians from other Arab countries were needed. In 1973 following publication of his Green Book a complex structure of popular participation was created through people's committees and a People's General Congress.

[10] In the cities, a social security system was created, with free medical assistance and family allowances to encourage large families. Industrial workers were granted 25 per cent participation in the profits of the companies. Industrial investment was 11 times greater than during the monarchy and agricultural investment was 30 times greater. This massive oil-financed reform transformed Libya into the North African Nation with the highest per-capita income on the continent, at $4,000 a year.

[11] In 1977, the country changed its name to the Socialist People's Libyan Arab Jamahiriya (meaning mass state in Arabic). But while Khaddafi achieved ample positive results internally, external relations were dismal. Attempts to unite with Syria and Egypt met with failure, and overtures towards Tunisia came to nothing. Khaddafi became the main critic of

the diplomatic rapprochement between Egypt and Israel; he clashed with the Saudi monarchy and the Emirates, and maintained his long-standing antagonism with King Hassan of Morocco. In OPEC, Libya opposed the moderate stand of Saudi Arabia and the Emirates on oil prices, and firmly resisted the pressures and manoeuvres of transnational corporations.

[12] From 1980, Libya became diplomatically active in Sub-Saharan Africa and Latin America. The Government supported the Polisario Front and participated directly in the civil war in Chad, defending the Transitional Government of National Union, led by Goukouni Oueddei.

[13] US President Reagan undertook a huge international campaign to link the Libyan leader with world terrorism. In August 1981 in the Gulf of Sidra two Libyan planes were shot down by the US Sixth Fleet. Khaddafi skilfully avoided any violent response to the provocation, winning the sympathy of the conservative Arab regimes which had, until then, been hostile to his government.

[14] In 1983 Libya attempted a resumption of friendly relations with Morocco, a move which met

PROFILE

ENVIRONMENT
Most of the country is covered by desert. The only fertile lands are located along the temperate Mediterranean coast, where most of the population live. There are no perennial rivers and rain is scarce. The country has major oil reserves. Water is scarce, with most of the supply pumped from underground reserves. The air is polluted by gases given off in the oil refining process and desertification, erosion and the destruction of vegetation are rapidly advancing.

SOCIETY
Peoples: Arabs and Berbers account for 79 per cent of the population. There are Tunisian, Egyptian, Greek and Italian and Chadian minorities (21 per cent).
Religions: Islam (official), mainly Sunni. There is a small Christian minority.
Languages: Arabic (official) is predominant. English and Italian are also spoken.
Political Parties: Socialist People's Libyan Arab Jamahiriya.
Social Organizations: There are mass organizations of workers, peasants, students and women.

THE STATE
Official Name: al-Jamahiriyah al-'Arabiyah al-Libiyah ash-Sha'biyah al-Ishtirakiyah.
Administrative divisions: 3 provinces, 10 counties and 1,500 communes.
Capital: Tripoli (Tarabulus) 1,500,000 people (1994).
Other cities: Benghazi 750,000 people; Misratah 360,000; az-Zawiyah 300,000 (1994)..
Government: The People's General Congress is the highest Government body. Col. Muammar Khaddafi, leader of the Revolution and commander-in-chief of the People's Armed Forces, is the Head of State since 1969.
National Holiday: September 1, Revolution Day (1969).
Armed Forces: 80,000.
Other: Revolutionary Guards, 3000.

STATISTICS

DEMOGRAPHY
Population: 5,593,000 (1996) **Annual growth:** 3.8% (1980/1996) **Estimates for year 2000:** 6,400,000 **Annual growth to year 2000:** 3.4% (1994/2000) **Urban Population:** 85.9% (1996) **Children per woman:** 6.1 (1996).

HEALTH
Life expectancy at birth: 65 years (1996) male: 62 years (1994) female: 66 years (1994) **Infant mortality:** 50 per 1,000 (1996) **Under-5 child mortality:** 61 per 1,000 (1996) **Calorie consumption:** 140% (1988/90) 962 **people per doctor** (1988/91) **Safe water:** 97% (1990/96).

EDUCATION
Literacy: 76% (1995) male : 88% (1995) female: 63% (1995) **School enrolment :** Primary total: 110% (1990/95) male : 110% (1990/95) female: 110% (1990/95) Secondary: male : 95% (1990/95) female: 95% (1990/95) Tertiary: 16% (1995).

COMMUNICATIONS
10 **newspapers**, 226 **radios**, 100 **TV sets** and 51 **main telephone lines** per 1,000 people (1994).

ECONOMY
Currency: 0.35 dinars = $ 1 (1995) **Cereal imports:** 1,790 metric tons (1994) **Food import dependency:** 19% (1994) **Fertilizer use:** 306 kgs per ha (1994) **Exports:** $ 10,126 million (1996) Imports: $ 5,191 million (1996) **Development aid received:** $ 7 million (1995) $ 1 per capita (1995)% of GNP (1994).

ENERGY
n/a

HDI (rank / value) 64 / 0.801 (1994)

---

with success in August 1984 when an agreement was signed. Most North African nations were surprised at the pact, for Moroccans and Libyans held opposite views on practically all political issues. However, the rapprochement could be regarded as a consequence of increasing cooperation between the Algerian, Tunisian and Mauritanian governments. Moreover, Morocco aimed at neutralizing Libyan support of the Polisario Front, while Libya sought to cut off Moroccan aid to Habre's regime in Chad.

[15] In January 1986, the US imposed an economic embargo on Libya, and on April 14 American war planes bombed Tripoli and Benghazi, leaving dozens of civilians dead. Subsequent information revealed the main objective had been to eliminate Colonel Khaddafi.

[16] In November, 1991, US and British courts blamed the Khaddafi Government for the bombing of two aeroplanes: a Pan Am flight in Britain, with 270 deaths, 17 of whom were US citizens and a

MILITARY EXPENDITURE

MILITARY (as % of health and education expenditures-1990/91) **71%**

UTA flight in Nigeria, with 170 casualties. Interpol issued an international arrest warrant on two people accused of the bombings. In January 1992, Libya expressed willingness to cooperate with the UN in the clarification of both attacks.

[17] Nevertheless Khaddafi rejected a UN extradition order, unsuccessfully proposing that the trial be held in Tripoli.

[18] Libyan inflexibility simply strengthened UN determination; in February and March the extradition of the accused Libyan agents was again demanded. The UN demanded that Libya explicitly renounce terrorism, setting April 15 as the deadline and threatening sanctions, a blockade and even military measures should the ultimatum not be met.

[19] Libya passed the deadline, invoking economic sanctions from the EC and the seven most industrialized countries. Khaddafi took the decision to the International Court of Justice.

[20] In August, when the embargo was renewed, Khaddafi decided on a change of foreign policy and designated as chancellor a "moderate", able to negotiate Libyan and US positions. In 1993 Tripoli continued a policy of economic liberalization, initiated in 1989, when it broke off relations with Iran.

[21] Libya's isolation increased in 1994. The UN intensified the embargo despite Khaddafi's concessions. In the end he accepted that the two accused men be tried in Scotland. Inside the country, the difficult situation made him more popular since at least a section of public opinion made the US responsible for the scarcity of goods and related problems.

[22] Nevertheless, some concessions awoke resistance: in the southern region of Fezzan the population protested when the area of Aouzou was given to Chad following a decision of the International Court of The Hague. On the other hand Tripoli made progress towards achieving an old project by signing an agreement for the building of an aqueduct that will allow water to come from other countries.

[23] In 1995 the country remained isolated despite the ongoing Libyan proposals for a dialogue with the West. This fact did not counter either the growth of the private sector or foreign investment. Several international firms were willing to participate in new projects to exploit oil resources.

[24] In the second half of 1996, the Libyan economy continued to benefit from the near 40 per cent increase in international oil prices despite the embargo. In the same

year, part of an aqueduct designed to supply water to isolated desert settlements was opened.

[25] In 1997, Libya began to emerge from international isolation fighting to get the embargo lifted. Three Security Council member countries, Egypt, Guinea-Bissau and Kenya, asked for a mission to be sent to Tripoli to evaluate the situation for the first time. The Movement of Non-Aligned Nations and the Organization of African Unity backed a Libyan request for the two men suspected of blowing up a passenger aeroplane over Lockerbie, Scotland in 1988 to be tried in a neutral country.

[26] In October, South Africa formally appealed to the UN to end the embargo, following President Nelson Mandela's visit to Libya, in an attempt to mediate on the conflict. Mandela said he supported the Libyan position, but that he would not ask for an "unconditional" lifting of sanctions. However, the Security Council renewed the measures in November.

[27] In March 1998, Libya saw its first international legal victory when the United Nations Court of Justice declared the plea for removal of the economic embargo valid. The decision caused conflict between the Security Council and the Court within the UN.

Lithuania

Lietuva

Population: 3,728,000 (1996)
Area: 65,200 SQ KM
Capital: Vilnius

Currency: Lit
Language: Lithuanian

Lithuanians have lived along the shores of the Baltic Sea since long before the Christian era. Protected by the forests, Lithuanian tribes fiercely resisted German efforts to subdue them in the 13th century, and united under the leadership of Mindaugas, who was crowned king by Pope Innocent IV in 1253.

[2] In the 14th century, Lithuania began its eastward and southern expansion, going into Belarusian lands. Gediminas built the Grand Duchy of Lithuania, which extended from the Baltic Sea to the Black Sea, with its capital at Vilnius. In 1386, Jagiello, Gediminas's grandson, married the Queen of Poland, thus uniting the two kingdoms.

[3] Lithuania withstood a series of attacks from the Teutonic Order, who continued to combat the Lithuanian-Polish union - despite the fact that the latter were Christian - until the Battle of Tannenberg in 1410, in which they suffered a crushing defeat. This defeat was a harsh blow to German supremacy in the Baltic region. A new pact between Lithuania and Poland, signed in 1413, reaffirmed the principle of union, while respecting the autonomy of both States.

[4] With the coronation of Ivan III of Muscovy, as the sovereign of all Russia, a new and greater threat emerged for historic Lithuania. Nevertheless, the Lithuanian-Polish union reached its peak in the 16th century, when it was unrivalled in Europe as a political system (see Poland), only to fall in the 17th century, in the course of a series of devastating wars with Sweden, Russia and Turkey and the peasant rebellions within.

[5] In the 1772 and 1793 partitions of Poland among Russia, Prussia and Austria, Russia kept

only Belarus. But the Polish state disappeared in 1795, and all of Lithuania was in Russian hands by 1815. The Congress of Vienna granted the Russian Emperor the additional titles of king of Poland and grand prince of Lithuania.

[6] Lithuanians were harshly suppressed by the Russians. The czarist regime treated Lithuania as though it were a part of Russia, calling it the Northwest Territory after 1832. Between 1864 and 1905, Russification extended to all aspects of life: books which were printed in Lithuanian had to use the Cyrillic alphabet, and Catholics were persecuted.

[7] With the Revolution of 1905, the peoples of the Russian Empire were granted freedom of speech. A congress with some 2,000 delegates called for the demarcation of Lithuania's borders, territorial autonomy and the election of a parliament by democratic means.

[8] During World War I, Germany occupied a major part of Lithuania. In 1915, a congress - authorized by the occupying Germans - elected the 20-member Council of Lithuania. The 214 delegates to the congress called for the creation of an independent Lithuanian state within its "ethnic borders" and with Vilnius as its capital. On February 16 1918, the Council declared Lithuania's independence and terminated all political ties with other nations.

[9] In 1919, the Red Army entered Vilnius and formed a communist government, but the Allied powers forced it to withdraw. The new head of the Polish State, Josef Pilsudski, tried to re-establish the former union, but failed due to the resistance of the Lithuanians, Ukrainians and Belarusians. In the end, the League of Nations and the

European powers agreed to the separation of Poland and Lithuania in 1923, but Lithuania refused to recognize the line of demarcation (with Poland) which had been established by these powers.

[10] In 1926, Lithuania and the Soviet Union signed a non-aggression treaty. A treaty of good will and cooperation was signed in Geneva in 1934 by Lithuania, Latvia and Estonia. As of 1938, relations with Warsaw became tense, due to Poland's claim of sovereignty over Vilnius. Tension increased when a group of Nazis came to power in Klaipeda; they demanded the ceding of that city, which meant the loss of Lithuania's only port on the Baltic.

[11] In September 1939, a secret German-Soviet non-aggression treaty brought Lithuania within the USSR's sphere of influence. In October, a mutual assistance treaty was signed in Moscow; according to its terms, Lithuania was forced to accept the installation of Soviet garrisons and air bases on its soil. In 1940, the Soviet Army occupied Lithuania and a number of local

political leaders were arrested and deported, while others fled toward Western Europe.

[12] The new prime minister, Justas Paleckis, and parliament asked to be admitted to the USSR, a request which was immediately granted by the Supreme Soviet. Lithuania thereby became a constituent republic of the USSR in August 1940. After German occupation in 1941, the Baltic Sates and Belarus became the German province of Ostland.

[13] During German occupation, 190,000 Jews were sent to concentration camps. A hundred thousand residents of Vilnius - a third of that city's population, most of them Jews - were killed. Vilnius was known as the "Jerusalem of Lithuania" and had been considered to be one of the most important centres of Jewish culture in the world. Many non-Jewish Lithuanians throughout the rest of the country were killed, and tens of thousands of young people were sent to Germany to work.

[14] Vilnius was reconquered by the Red Army in 1944. Lithuania was once again occupied by the Soviets and a new period of Sovietization began. This included religious persecution and wide-scale deportations to northern Russia and Siberia, amid the forced collectivization of agriculture.

[15] Religious persecution continued even after Stalin's death in 1953; thus, the resistance of the Catholic Church became identified with the nationalist movement. In 1972, the "Lithuanian Catholic Church Chronicle" (banned by the Government) was published by the

PUBLIC EXPENDITURE

1.9%   53.2%
■ DEFENCE
□ SOCIAL   (1995)

WORKERS

(1996)

Labour force %
■ WOMEN
□ MEN
48   52

■ AGRICULTURE   18% (1990)
□ INDUSTRIAL   41%
■ SERVICES   41%

LAND USE

(1993)

■ FOREST & WOODLAND   30.7%
□ ARABLE   34.6%
■ OTHER   34.7%

PROFILE

ENVIRONMENT
On the eastern coast of the Baltic Sea, Lithuania is characterized by gently rolling hills and flat plains. The largest of the Baltic "mini-States", it has more than 700 rivers and streams, many forests and around 3,000 lakes. The Nemunas river, which crosses the country from east to west, is the country's largest river. It is lined with castles built centuries ago and it is still an important shipping route. Lithuania's climate is moderate because of its proximity to the sea: in summer, the average temperature is around 18 degrees C and there is heavy rainfall; in the winter, it is often cold and foggy, with the temperature often falling below zero. 49 per cent of the land is arable; the chief crops are grain, potatoes and vegetables. There are large numbers of livestock. Among the country's most important industries are the food and machine manufacturing industries, as well as the export of energy. Most of the country's energy comes from Ignalina, a nuclear plant of the same type as that of Chernobyl, Ukraine, site of the nuclear accident in 1986. Since the 1980s, there has been an increase in pollution, especially bacterial pollution of rivers and lakes; the latter has been linked to the increase in infectious childhood diseases, particularly in the first few years of life

SOCIETY
Peoples: 83 per cent of the population is Lithuanian; the rest of the population includes Russians, 8.4 per cent, Poles, 7 per cent, Belarussians, 1.5 per cent Germans, Jews, Latvians and Tatars. **Religion:** Catholic majority (80 per cent); there are Protestant minorities. **Languages:** Lithuanian (official); Russian, Polish. **Political Parties:** Lithuanian Democratic Labor Party; Homeland Union. Demochristian Party, Conservative Party, Social Democrat Party, Liberal Union, Young Lithuania National Party, Lithuanian Women.

THE STATE
Official Name: Lietuvos Respublika. **Administrative Division:** 44 Districts. **Capital:** Vilnius, 575,000 people (1995). **Other cities:** Kaunas, 423,000 people; Klaipeda , 205,000; Siauliai, 149,000; Panevezys, 131,000 **Government:** Parliamentary republic, Valdas Adamkus, President, since January 1998. Gediminas Vagnorius, Prime Minister since December 1996. Single-chamber parliament (Seimas) made up of 141 members. **National Holiday:** February 16, Independence (1918). **Armed Forces:** 5,100 (1996). **Other:** Coast Guard, 5,000.

STATISTICS

DEMOGRAPHY
Population: 3,728,000 (1996) **Annual growth:** 0.5% (1980/1996) **Estimates for year 2000:** 3,700,000 **Annual growth to year 2000:** -0.2% (1994/2000) **Urban Population:** 72.6% (1996) **Urban growth:** 1.78% (1980/95) **Children per woman:** 1.6 (1996).

HEALTH
Life expectancy at birth: 70 years (1996) male: 64 years (1994) female: 76 years (1994) **Infant mortality:** 14 per 1,000 (1996) **Under-5 child mortality:** 18 per 1,000 (1996).

EDUCATION
Literacy: 99% (1995) male : 100% (1995) female: 99% (1995) **School enrolment :** Primary total: 96% (1990/95) male : 97% (1990/95) female: 95% (1990/95) Secondary: male : 80% (1990/95) female: 84% (1990/95) Tertiary: 28% (1995) **Primary school teachers:** one for every 17 students (1995).

COMMUNICATIONS
140 **newspapers**, 387 **radios**, 340 **TV sets** and 241 **main telephone lines** per 1,000 people (1994) **Books:** 77 new titles per 100,000 people (1992/94).

ECONOMY
Per capita, GNP: $ 2,280 (1996) **Annual growth, GNP:** 2.7% (1995/96) **Consumer price index:** 31,155.6 (1994) **Currency:** 4 lit = $ 1 (1995) **Cereal imports:** 19 metric tons (1994) **Fertilizer use:** 124 kgs per ha (1994) **Exports:** $ 3,356 million (1996) **Imports:** $ 4,559 million (1996) **External debt:** $ 1,286 million (1996) $ 345 **per capita:** (1996) **Debt service:** 2.9% of exports (1996).

ENERGY
Consumption: 2,030.36 Kgs of Oil equivalent per capita yearly (1994) 70.16% imported (1994).

HDI (rank / value) 76 / 0.762 (1994)

Lithuanian Movement for Human Rights. That year, a young man set fire to himself; his funeral triggered violent clashes in which 15 people were killed and 3,000 were arrested.

[16] With the democratization process initiated by Mikhail Gorbachev in the USSR, Lithuania began a period of intense political agitation. In June, the Lithuanian Movement to Support Perestroika (restructuring) was founded; its Executive Committee adopted the name *Sejm* (the name of the Lithuanian parliament at the time of independence) and is known by the name "Sajudis". The Sajudis installed a kind of "shadow" government, and demanded a return to the peace treaties which recognized the country's independence, stating that Lithuania's admission to the USSR was the result of a secret agreement and therefore had no legal value.

[17] In July, the Lithuanian Freedom League (LFL) emerged from underground activity. The LFL, which dates back to 1978, called for immediate withdrawal of Soviet troops from the country, and the independence of Lithuania. Police brutality toward participants of a demonstration sponsored by the LFL triggered joint protest actions by members of the League and the Sajudis, and led to a crisis within the Lithuanian Communist Party leadership.

[18] One of the main worries of Lithuanians, Latvians and Swedes was the nuclear plant at Ignalina with four reactors similar to those at Chernobyl. In 1988, after massive public protest, authorities closed down the second reactor, and suspended construction on the third and fourth reactors.

[19] The Lithuanian Government opted not to follow the example set by Estonia's Supreme Soviet, which had made a unilateral decision on the question of sovereignty. Instead, Lithuanian authorities began making concessions to local movements, legalizing the use of the flag and the national anthem, designating Independence Day as a holiday and authorizing public commemoration of that day. In addition, Lithuanian was adopted as the country's official language, and the Vilnius Cathedral and other churches were reopened.

[20] In February 1989, the first secretary of the CP and the Sajudis attended the official commemoration of the country's 1918 independence, side by side. In December, Lithuania's Supreme Soviet did away with the article of the constitution which assigned the CP a leading role; the first decision of its kind within the USSR.

[21] In January 1990, Gorbachev announced in Vilnius that the details of a future relation with the Union would be established through legislation. In March, the Lithuanian Parliament proclaimed the nation's independence, to be effected immediately. In September 1991, the new Council of State of the USSR accepted the independence of the three Baltic States, which were immediately recognized by several countries and by the UN.

[22] In August 1991, after the failed coup against Gorbachev in the USSR, the Lithuanian Parliament banned the Communist Party, the Democratic Workers' Party and the Lithuanian Communist Youth organization. The following month, President Vytautas Landsbergis issued a call, before the United Nations, for the withdrawal of 50,000 Soviet troops from Lithuania; they had been stationed in Vilnius since January of that year.

[23] The new constitution was approved by a referendum on October 25 1992. That year, the GNP diminished by 35 per cent and inflation soared to 1,150 per cent.

[24] On February 14 1993, the leader of the former Communist Party, Algirdas Brazauskas, was elected President with 60 per cent of the vote. In 1993 and 1994, Brazauskas continued with the transition policy toward a market economy.

[25] In 1995, around 80 per cent of Lithuanians were estimated to be "poor," 15 per cent "middle class," and 5 per cent "rich." The accentuation of social inequalities was seen as the key factor in the ruling party defeat in local elections this year.

[26] The 1996 parliamentary elections brought the opposition to power, allowing Landsbergis to become head of parliament. This cohabiting with the former Communists ended with the 1997-1998 elections, when Valdas Adamkus was elected President in the second round, with a narrow margin of votes above his rival, the former Communist Arturas Paulaskas. Adamkus, a 71 year-old who had lived more than forty years in the United States, had been a member of the Conservative Party. His campaign was based on the consolidation of a market economy, closer relations with the United States and NATO membership for Lithuania.

Luxembourg

Luxembourg

Population:	412,000 (1996)
Area:	2,586 SQ KM
Capital:	Luxembourg
Currency:	Luxembourg Franc
Language:	French and German

Luxembourg, Belgium, the Netherlands, and part of northern France constitute the Low Countries, and until 1579 they shared a common history (see the Netherlands).

[2] In the war of the Low Countries against Spain, Luxembourg sided with the southern provinces, acknowledging the authority of Philip II. Luxembourg was conquered by France in 1684, but returned to Spain 13 years later, under the Treaty of Rijswijk. In 1713, the Austrian Hapsburgs took control of the country until the Napoleonic invasion in 1795, when the country was annexed to the French Empire.

[3] In 1815, after the defeat of Napoleon, the Congress of Vienna handed over the Duchy of Luxembourg to William of Orange. William incorporated the Duchy as his kingdom's eighteenth province. After the Belgian revolt in 1831, Luxembourg was divided again: the largest section given to Belgium, and the smallest was handed over to William as the Grand Duchy of Luxembourg, which he finally accepted in 1839. Thereafter the Duchy was administered independently until 1867. In 1866, the German Confederation was dissolved, the Treaty of London guaranteed the neutrality of the grand duchy giving control to the House of Nassau.

[4] Germany invaded the country twice, in 1914 and again during World War II. After the War productivity increased when the country formed an economic alliance with Belgium and the Netherlands called the Benelux, later becoming a member of the EEC.

[5] The Christian Social Party, a centre-right party, maintained a majority in Parliament from 1919 until 1974. Afterwards a centre-left coalition of the Socialist Workers' Party and the Democratic Party took office. The Christian Social Party recovered its majority in 1979, forming alliances with the Parti Socialist Workers' Party and the Democratic Party.

[6] In 1949 Luxembourg became a founder member of NATO. In 1986, women were admitted to the armed forces.

[7] Women were granted the right to vote in 1919. The female presence in the registered workforce was 25.2 per cent in 1979, increasing to 34 per cent by 1988. In Luxembourg women occupy 74.8 per cent of posts in education, the highest percentage in the European Community.

[8] In 1988, the metal, iron and steel industries accounted for 31 percent of the workforce and 32 percent of the country's GNP. The whole sector is dominated by the transnational corporation ARBED in Germany and Belgium.

[9] The June 1989 legislative elections reaffirmed the dominance of the Social Christians and Socialists.

[10] In 1990, border controls were abolished with Belgium, France, Germany and the Netherlands.

[11] In 1993, Josée Jacobs became the first woman to hold a cabinet position in the history of the nation, becoming minister of agriculture and viniculture. In 1994, the PCS and the POS, who had governed the country together since 1984, were returned to power in the general elections, allowing Jacques Santer to continue as prime minister.

[12] On an internal front, the hostility of many of the local people to foreign workers, who made up 50 per cent of the working population of the country in 1994, began to be expressed openly.

[13] In 1995, Santer became president of the European Union Commission and was replaced as prime minister by Jean-Claude Juncker. Luxembourg established itself as one of the main financial markets of the world, especially in the administration of social funds - like pension funds - with an estimated worth of $356 billion.

[14] In May 1996, the European Union announced Luxembourg and France were the only countries eligible to adopt the EU single currency in 1999.

[15] As with the rest of the Union, unemployment rates increased in late 1997, although it continued to be the lowest of the 15 member states (3.7per cent). In November, some 30,000 people from various European countries demonstrated in Luxembourg for a Europe "serving employment".

[16] In March 1998, the Government announced it would increase its funding for the plan to extend the track for the high speed train (TGV) - initially developed in France - to the east, in order to intensify exchange with Eastern Europe.

PROFILE

ENVIRONMENT
Located on the southeastern side of the Ardennes, Luxembourg has two natural regions: the north with valleys and woods, and a maximum altitude of 500 meters, is sparsely populated with potato and grain farming; the south (Gutland) is a low plain and the country's main demographic corridor, with most of the population and cities and major industries (iron, steel and mining), including the capital.

SOCIETY
Peoples: Luxemburger 67.4 per cent; Portuguese 12.1 per cent; Italian 4.8 per cent; French 3.5 per cent; Belgian 2.8 per cent; German 2.3 per cent; other 7.1 per cent. **Religions:** Majority Catholic. (94.9 per cent) **Languages:** Luxemburgian, French, German, Portuguese. **Political Parties:** Christian Social People's Party; Socialist Workers' Party; Liberal Party; Democratic Party; Communist Party; Green Alternative Party and Ecological Initiative. **Social Organizations:** Luxembourg National Workers' Confederation; National Council of Unions.

THE STATE
Official Names, Grand-Duché de Luxembourg; Grossherzogtum Luxemburg; Groussherzogtum Lëtzebuerg. **Administrative divisions:** 12 cantons. **Capital:** Luxembourg, 76,446 people (1996). **Other cities:** Esch-sur-Alzette 24,255 people; Dudelange 15,883; Differdange 16,950 (1995). **Government:** Constitutional monarchy. Multi-party parliamentary system. Grand Duke Jean, head of State; Jean-Claude Juncker, Prime Minister and Chief of Government since 1995. Single-chamber legislature: Chamber of Deputies, with 60 members elected by direct popular vote, every 5 years. **National holiday:** June 23 (National day). **Armed Forces:** 800. **Other:** 560 (Gendarmes).

STATISTICS
Population: 412,000 (1996). **Annual growth:** 0.8 % (1980/1996). **Urban population:** 89.5 % (1996). **Children per woman:** 1.7 (1996) **Life expectancy at birth:** 76 years (1996). **Male:** 73 years (1994). **Female:** 79 years (1994). **Infant mortality:** 7 per 1,000 (1996). **Under-5 child mortality:** 7 per 1,000 (1996) **School enrolment :** Primary total: 91 % (1990/95) male : 88 % (1990/95) female: 94 % (1990/95) Secondary: male : 78 %(1990/95) female: 78 % (1990/95) 380 **newspapers,** 636 **radios,** 340 **TV sets** and 553 **main telephone lines** per 1,000 people (1994) **Books:** 169 new titles per 100,000 people (1992/94) **Consumer price index:** 112.6 (1994) **Currency:** 29.42 Luxembourg francs = $ 1 (1995) **HDI** (rank / value) 27 / 0.899 (1994)

Macedonia

Makedonija

Population: 2,174,000
(1996)
Area: 25,713 SQ KM
Capital: Skopje

Currency: Denar
Language: Macedonian

Macedonia's ancient cultural history is linked to that of Greece and Anatolia. According to archaeological studies, the ancestors of the Macedonians can be identified in the early Bronze Age. In the year 700 BC, a people calling themselves "Macedonian" migrated toward the east from their native lands on the banks of the Aliakmon River. Aegae was the capital of the kingdom which, during the reign of Amyntas I, extended to the Axios River and beyond, as far as the Chalcidice Peninsula.

2 Macedonia reached a position of power and influence within Greece during the reign of Philip II (359-336 BC). Warriors had the power to choose a new king, and also to try cases of high treason. Alexander "the Great", Philip's son and a student of Aristotle, defeated the Persian Empire and led the Macedonian armies to northern Africa and the Arabic peninsula, crossing Mesopotamia and reaching as far east as India.

3 The Macedonian Empire, built up over 11 years, contributed to the propagation of Greek culture in the Orient. Alexander the Great founded a large number of cities and was responsible for the fusion of Greek culture with the cultures of the peoples he conquered, giving rise to what is known as Hellenism. His death in 323 BC was followed by a period of internal struggles, though Macedonia maintained the unity of the empire.

4 Around the year 280 BC, groups of Galatian marauders invaded Macedonia, killing the king. Three years later, Antigonus II defeated the Galatians and was crowned king by an army from Macedonia. Most of the population were farmers, except in urban areas like Beroea and Pella, and the Greek settlements along the coast. The King held exclusive rights to the mines and forests.

5 During the reign of Philip V (221-179), Macedonia conquered Rome's client-states in Illyria and subsequently turned eastward and to the northeast, subduing the cities of Rhodes and Pergamum. Rome responded by going to war and defeated Philip in 197 adding Macedonia to its kingdom and taking Thessaly away from Macedonia. Philip collaborated

with the Romans and consolidated his power. This was a prosperous period for Macedonia, which also managed to recover Thessaly.

6 From 168 to 146 BC, Macedonia was a Roman province, with four independent administrative sections. Macedonia supervised the Greeks for Rome, keeping watch for rebellions and invasion attempts across the northern border. In the year 27, Macedonia became a senatorial province separate from Greece. By the 4th century AD, most Macedonians had adopted Christianity.

7 The ethnic composition of the Macedonians was not significantly affected by the Goth, Hun and Avar invasions. However, when Slavs arrived in the Balkans, they established permanent settlements throughout Macedonia. Between the 7th and the 14th centuries, Macedonia was successively subdued by the Bulgarian, Byzantine and Latin empires until they were almost completely dominated by the Serbs, except in the Greek region of Salonika.

8 Towards the end of the 14th century, Turkey began invading the Balkans. By 1371, it had conquered most of Macedonia and in 1389, inflicted a decisive defeat upon the Serbian Empire at Kosovo. The Ottomans seized the best lands for themselves and established a feudal system. Christian peasants either became vassals of Muslim lords, to whom they paid a tithe, or were driven onto the less fertile lands.

9 In 1864, the Ottoman Empire divided Macedonia into three provinces: Salonika, Monastir, including parts of Albania, and Kosovo, which extended into "Old Serbia". In 1878, Russia forced Turkey into accepting the creation of Bulgaria, which included most of Macedonia, but the other European powers returned this territory to the Ottomans. During the ensuing years, Bulgaria, Serbia and Greece all continued to lay claim to Macedonia.

10 Towards the end of the 19th century, a strong nationalist movement emerged in Macedonia. Macedonian Slavs created the VMRO (Vatreshna Makedonska Revolutsionna Organizatsia) in 1893, with the slogan "Macedonia for the Macedonians". At the same

time, Bulgaria and Greece began sending guerrillas into Macedonia, provoking the Greco-Turkish War of 1897. Turkey supported the Serbs to offset the influence of the VMRO and Bulgarians.

11 By 1903, the increase in opposition activities by Bulgarians, Greeks, Serbs and Macedonians led Russia and Austria-Hungary to demand that an inspector general be appointed, and that the police force be reorganized. Turkey agreed to meet the demands, but in August there was a general uprising, apparently initiated by Bulgaria. It was ruthlessly put down by the Turks, who destroyed 105 Macedonian-Slavonic villages.

12 In 1908, after the fall of the Ottoman Empire, with the "Young Turks" rebellion, the clamour to divide up Ottoman-Turkish territories in the region culminated in the two Balkan Wars of 1912 and 1913. Bulgaria and Serbia signed a Mutual Assistance Treaty, with Greece and Montenegro subsequently joining the alliance. Russia supported the Balkan League, because of its interest in halting the southeasterly advance of the Austro-Hungarian Empire.

13 After defeating Turkey in the first war, the allies turned against each other. Bulgaria provoked the second Balkan War, confronting both Greece and Serbia. Romania and Turkey then allied themselves with Greece and Serbia to defeat Bulgaria. The Treaty of Bucharest gave Greece Salonika and most of the Macedonian coastal area, while Serbia was given the center and

the northern parts of the territory.

14 When World War I broke out, Bulgaria saw a chance to reassert its territorial claims over Macedonia. Sofia joined the Central Powers (Austria-Hungary, Germany and Turkey), and occupied all of Serbian Macedonia and also a part of Serbia. The victorious allied powers left the Greco-Macedonian borders as they were, and Yugoslav Macedonia was incorporated into the new Serbian, Croat and Slovenian kingdom.

15 In the inter-war period, Serbian domination deepened Yugoslav inter-ethnic conflicts. King Alexander, who assumed dictatorial powers in 1929, was assassinated in Marseilles in 1934 by Croatian nationalists. At the beginning of World War II, when Germany invaded Yugoslavia, these internal divisions meant that the invaders met little resistance.

16 The Yugoslav nationalist struggle intensified during the following years. Guerrillas led by the Yugoslav Communist League (YCL) seized power in May 1945, later proclaiming the Socialist Federal Republic of Macedonia. Yugoslav Macedonia joined the new state as one of its six constituent republics.

17 In 1947, Yugoslavia declared that Macedonia was the country's least developed region. The federal government subsequently began earmarking funds for industrialization projects, especially in steel, chemical and textile production.

PROFILE

ENVIRONMENT
In the south-central part of the Balkan Peninsula, Macedonia, which has no maritime coast, is bounded in the north by Serbia and Kosovo, in the east by Bulgaria, in the south by Greece and in the west by Albania. Two mountain ranges cross the region, the Pindo (a continuation of the Alps) and the Rodope, in the center and the east. With a continental climate, the average temperature in the capital is 1°C in winter, and 24°C in summer. The country's main agricultural activity is centered in the Vardar River basin. In the mountain region, sheep and goats are raised. There are some copper, iron and lead deposits.

SOCIETY
Peoples: Macedonians 66.4 per cent; Albanians 23.1 per cent, Turks 3.9 per cent, Gypsies 2.3 per cent, Serbs 1.9 per cent, other 2.3 per cent (1994).
Religions: Christian Orthodox (majority); Muslim.
Languages: Macedonian (official), Albanian.
Political Parties: Macedonias's Alliance, a coalition of the Democrat Alliance of Macedonia, liberal, the Socialist Party and the Albanese Party for Democratic Prosperity. The Alliance was founded in 1994 and is in power since that date.

THE STATE
Official Name: Republika Makedonija.
Administrative divisions: 30 districts.
Capital: Skopje, 440,557 people (1994).
Other cities: Bitolj (Bitola) 75,386 people; Prilep 67,371; Kumanovo 66,237; Tetovo 50,376.
Government: President: Kiro Gligorov, re-elected in October 1994. Prime Minister: Branko Crvenkovski since August 1992.
National Holiday: September 8, Independence (1991).
Armed Forces: 10,400 (8,000 conscripts).
Other: 7,500 (police).

STATISTICS

DEMOGRAPHY
Population: 2,174,000 (1996) **Annual growth:** 1.2% (1980/1996) **Estimates for year 2000:** 2,200,000 **Annual growth to year 2000:** 0.7% (1994/2000) **Urban population:** 60.3% (1996) **Urban growth:** 1.46% (1980/95) Children per woman: 2 (1996).

HEALTH
Life expectancy at birth: 72 years (1996) male: 69 years (1996) female: 74 years (1996) Infant mortality: 26 per 1,000 (1996) **Under-5 child mortality:** 30 per 1,000 (1996)

EDUCATION
Primary total: 87% (1990/95) male : 88% (1990/95) female: 87% (1990/95) **Secondary: male** : 55% (1990/95) female: 56% (1990/95) **Tertiary:** 18% (1995) **Primary school teachers:** one for every 20 students (1995).

COMMUNICATIONS
20 **newspapers**, 182 **radios**, 160 **TV sets** and 161 **main telephone lines** per 1,000 people (1994) **Books:** 31 new titles per 100,000 people (1992/94).

ECONOMY
Per capita, GNP: $ 990 (1996) **Annual growth, GNP:** 0.6% (1995/96) **Currency:** 38.8 denars = $ 1 (1995) **Cereal imports:** 133 metric tons (1994) **Fertilizer use:** 226 kgs per ha (1996) Exports: $ 1,119 million (1996) **Imports:** $ 1,941 million (1996) **External debt:** $ 1,659 million (1996) $ 763 per capita: (1996) **Debt service:** 3.9% of exports (1996)

ENERGY
Consumption: 1,279.25 Kgs of Oil equivalent per capita yearly (1994) 43.52% imported (1994).

HDI (rank / value) 80 / 0.748 (1994)

---

[18] In January, 1990, a special YCL Congress decided to adopt a multiparty system, and eliminate the leadership role which the constitution assigned to the party. However, the motion to grant greater autonomy to YCL branches in the republics was not accepted. After the Congress, the Communist Leagues of Slovenia, Croatia and Macedonia decided to separate from the YCL, and call themselves by a new name, the Democratic Renewal Party.

[19] On September 8 1991, in the midst of fighting between the new separate republics of Croatia and Slovenia, and the federal army, a plebiscite was held in which Macedonians pronounced themselves in favor of separation from the former Yugoslav Federation. All Macedonian political parties, except for the Albanian ethnic minority, favored independence.

[20] In early 1992, when several countries recognized Croatia and Slovenia, Greece blocked recognition of Macedonia, considering the use of that name to be a usurpation of Greek history and culture.

[21] On January 20 1992, Greek and Bulgarian representatives held an informal meeting. Sofia had recognized Macedonia five days previously. From Skopje, the newspaper "Nova Makedonika" accused the Greek and Bulgarian governments of entertaining territorial designs upon their country.

[22] In a plebiscite held on January 12, Macedonia's Albanian minority voted in favor of having an independent State, but on April 3, 1992, the Independent Republic of Ilirida (the republic of the Albanian residents of Yugoslavia) was proclaimed, within Macedonian territory.

[23] The new Yugoslav Federation withdrew its troops from the country. In July, the Cabinet resigned en masse and international recognition was not received. In August, Parliament rejected the EEC proposal to change the country's name.

[24] Social Democrat Branko Crvenkovski became Prime Minister that month, gaining official recognition of the new Macedonian state from Russia, Albania, Bulgaria and Turkey.

[25] In April 1993, the UN Security Council recommended that the country be admitted to the General Assembly, with the provisional name of "The Former Yugoslav Republic (TFYR) of Macedonia".

[26] Greece withheld official recognition, fearing Macedonia's growing territorial ambitions on the Greek province of Macedonia.

[27] Athens did everything within its power to complicate Skopje's foreign relations, campaigning to change the country's official name, and to alter Macedonia's "expansionist" constitution. Athens also pressured Macedonia to adopt a new flag, as the emblem, the Vergina star - associated with Alexander the Great - is revered by the Greeks as a symbol of their own Hellenic culture.

[28] After Macedonia's admittance to the UN, negotiations with Greece began, mediated by Lord Owen (British) and Thornvald Stoltenberg (Swedish), both of whom were already conversant with Balkan politics. Andreas Papandreou's victory in the October 1993 Greek elections helped cool the debate.

[29] The Balkan War seriously affected the Macedonian economy. Although it maintained international sanctions on the former Yugoslavia, Kiro Gligorov's government was forced to allow trucks to cross its territory, transporting goods to Belgrade. Likewise, the oil-transporting Athens-Belgrade railway continued to operate.

[30] In early 1994, the IMF and the World Bank approved a plan for economic reforms, backed by US and EU financial aid.

[31] On February 16 1994, over two years after Macedonia independence, Greece decided on a total economic blockade of the country. Greece did not recognize the adoption of the Greek name "Macedonia". The North frontier and the port of Salonica, through which 80 per cent of Macedonian exports, plus all of its oil, went abroad, were closed. The Greek Government was denounced before the European Court of Justice in April, but the blockade continued.

[32] Gligorov was re-elected in October 1994 receiving 52.4 per cent of the votes. The Social Democratic Alliance of Macedonia (ASDM), headed by Prime Minister Branko Crvenkovski decided on a coalition government with the liberals, the Socialist Party, and the Party of Democratic Prosperity, the main Albanian political group. This coalition was called Alliance of Macedonia (AM).

[33] In October 1995, a bomb exploded in Gligorov's car. The President survived and remained in power. That same month, negotiations with Greece led to the lifting of the trade embargo.

[34] In 1996, a privatization plan caused a split in the governing coalition. Crvenkovski sacked four liberal ministers and reformed his cabinet.

[35] The country was in a difficult economic and social situation. In 1997, Macedonia was considered one of the poorest countries in Europe.

[36] The Albanian minority make up more than 20 per cent of the population. Albanian activists continued to campaign for the recognition of their language and culture. Some of these wanted the regions with an Albanian majority to be transferred to Albania.

Madagascar

Madagasikara

Population: 15,353,000 (1996)
Area: 587,041 SQ KM
Capital: Antananarivo

Currency: Franc
Language: Malagasy and French

About 2,000 years ago, Malay-Polynesian navigators reached the African coast in canoes, voyage which was frequently repeated between the 1st and 5th centuries.
[2] Towards the 14th century, groups of Comoran traders established a series of ports in the northern region. These ports were destroyed by the Portuguese in 1506-1507.
[3] When the Portuguese found no gold, ivory or spices, they lost interest in the territory. By this time the Europeans had introduced firearms to the island in exchange for slaves.
[4] In the 16th century the Sakalawas on the west coast and the Betsilios on the east coast established the first monarchies. In the 17th century the state of Merina or Imerina came into being on the eastern edge of the central plateau. A century later it was the Merinas, under their leader Nampoina, who initiated the process of unification which was completed later by Nampoina's son Radama I (1810-1828).
[5] Contact with the Arabs and Europeans became more frequent. Radama adopted the Latin alphabet for the Malagasy language. He also used their help to create a modern army. However, the untimely death of the ruler and the ensuing conflicts over succession paved the way for European occupation of the island by the end of the century.
[6] The colonials cleared the virgin forests to make way for sugar-cane, cotton, and coffee plantations. They seized the best lands and the peasants were forced to work in conditions of semi-slavery. The struggle for political rights and economic improvement led to a great

uprising from 1947 to 1948, and this was ruthlessly put down by the French army with the loss of thousands of lives.
[7] The failure of the insurrection enabled the colonial administration to control the transition to autonomy. Independence was finally proclaimed in 1960. In the following September the country held it's first elections and the Social Democratic Party (PSD) won by a large margin. Its leader, Philibert Tsiranana, became the Republic's first President, an office to which he was re-elected in 1965 and 1972.
[8] In May 1972, after a series of serious disturbances, Tsiranana was forced to resign; he turned over full presidential powers to General Ramanantsoa, who suspended the National Assembly and the Senate. He also eliminated the presidency and abolished the 1959 Constitution, giving a military government both executive and legislative power, and creating Institutional and National Councils. In October, he had these measures approved by referendum.
[9] A year later, France decided to withdraw its troops, and the succeeding three years of instability ended in June 1975, when Cdr D Ratsiraka became Prime Minister. He adopted socialist policies, and called a referendum on December 21 1975. His nomination as head of state was overwhelmingly approved, and the Charter of the Madagascan Socialist Revolution was adopted as the basis for a new constitution. On December 30 1975 the State changed the country's name to the

"Democratic Republic of Madagascar".
[10] In June 1976, the new power structure was put into operation, with a 12-member Supreme Council of the Revolution and the Government, which was presided over by Col J Rakotomalala. When he died in an airplane accident in July 1976, he was replaced by Justin Rakotoniaina. The legislative function was placed in the hands of a 144-member National Council.
[11] The progressive Malgache parties joined together to form the National Revolutionary Front. AREMA (the Malagasy Revolutionary Vanguard) was the leading party of the Front, and was created in 1975 in support of Ratsiraka's renewal program. The Supreme Council of the Revolution was made up primarily of AREMA members, with members of five other parties ranging in their views from Marxist/Leninist to Christian Democrat. In 1977, Désiré Rakotoarijaona became Prime Minister.
[12] In 1980, the fall in price of the main export commodities caused a crisis which forced Ratsiraka to impose austerity measures. The Government acted repressively displeasing some social sectors and imprisoning opponents. At the same time, it attempted to diversify foreign trade, to reach

reconciliation with France and to renew negotiations with the IMF. That year, the foreign debt reached $700 million.
[13] In 1982, the President was re-elected by 80 per cent of the vote while the radical sector - represented by MONIMA - obtained the remaining 20 per cent.
[14] Madagascar has unique ecological characteristics. Plant and animal species extinct in other parts of the world are found here. The island possesses 3 per cent of the world's flora varieties, 53 per cent of the bird species, and 80 per cent of the reptile and amphibian families present on Earth. But this enormous biological reserve is in danger of extinction. Small-scale farmers, pressured by the lack of land, add to the deforestation process by burning pieces of land for cultivation at a greater rate than ever before. Although this form of land-clearing has been practised for centuries, the forest is now being destroyed faster than it can regenerate.
[15] In 1988, Lt-Col Victor Ramahatra succeeded Raotoarijaona as Prime Minister. AREMA, the party in power, won the 1989 elections; Didier Ratsiraka was re-elected President, with 67.2 per cent of the vote. His presidency was characterized by reform, with the restoration of a

WORKERS

(1996)

Labour force %

45	55

■ WOMEN
□ MEN

■ AGRICULTURE 78% (1990)
□ INDUSTRIAL 7%
■ SERVICES 15%

LAND USE

DEFORESTATION -0.8 % annual (81/90)
IRRIGATED 42.1% of arable

(1993)

■ FOREST & WOODLAND	39.5%
□ ARABLE	4.4%
■ OTHER	56.1%

1990

PER 100,000
LIVE BIRTHS

490

1970

12%

1994

14%

STATISTICS

DEMOGRAPHY
Population: 15,353,000 (1996) **Annual growth:** 3.3% (1980/1996)
Estimates for year 2000: 17,400,000 **Annual growth to year
2000:** 3.2% (1994/2000) **Urban Population:** 27.0% (1996) **Urban
growth:** 5.73% (1980/95) **Children per woman:** 5.8 (1996).

HEALTH
Life expectancy at birth: 58 years (1996) male: years (1996) **Infant
mortality:** 100 per 1,000 (1996) **Under-5 child mortality:** 164 per
1,000 (1996) **Calorie consumption:** 95% (1988/90) 8,333 **people
per doctor** (1988/91) **Safe water:** 34% (1990/96).

EDUCATION
Literacy: 46% (1995) male : 60% (1995) female: 32% (1995) **School
enrolment :** Primary total: 73% (1990/95) male : 75% (1990/95)
female: 72% (1990/95) Secondary: male : 14% (1990/95) female:
14% (1990/95) Tertiary: 3% (1995) **Primary school teachers:** one
for every 40 students (1995).

COMMUNICATIONS
192 **radios**, 20 **TV sets** and 3 **main telephone lines** per 1,000
people (1994) **Books:** 1 new title per 100,000 people (1992/94).

ECONOMY
Per capita, GNP: $ 250 (1996) **Annual growth, GNP:** 0.5% (1995/
96) **Annual inflation:** 18.41% (1985/95) **Consumer price index:**
190.1 (1996) **Currency:** 3,423 francs = $ 1 (1995) **Cereal imports:**
140 metric tons (1994) **Food import dependency:** 14% (1994)
Fertilizer use: 36 kgs per ha (1994) **Exports:** $ 616 million (1996)
Imports: $ 671 million (1996) **External debt:** $ 4,175 million (1996)
$ 272 **per capita:** (1996) **Debt service:** 9.4% of exports (1996)
Development aid received: $ 301 million (1995) $ 23 per capita
(1995) 16.4% of GNP (1994).

ENERGY
Consumption: 36.15 Kgs of Oil equivalent per capita yearly (1994)
82.67% imported (1994).

HDI (rank / value) 152 / 0.35 (1994)

PROFILE

ENVIRONMENT
Madagascar is one of the world's largest islands, separated from
the African continent by the Mozambique Channel. The island has
an extensive central plateau of volcanic origin which overhangs
the hot and humid coastal plains. These are covered with dense
rainforest to the east and grasslands to the west. The eastern side
of the island is very rainy, but the rest has a dry, tropical climate.
The population is concentrated on the high central plateau. Rice
and export products (sugar, coffee, bananas, and vanilla) are
cultivated on the coast. Cattle-raising is also important
throughout the island. The major mineral resources are graphite,
chrome and phosphate. Deforestation is one of the major
environmental problems, it is estimated that the destruction of
forests affects up to 75 per cent of the island. Only 10 per cent
of the rural population has assured access to drinking water. The
lack of sewage facilities and concentration of organic wastes have
led to the pollution of many watercourses.

SOCIETY
Peoples: Malagasy 98.9 per cent, French 0.2 per cent, Indian 0.2
per cent, Chinese 0.1 per cent.
Religions: Christian 51 per cent (of which Roman Catholic 26 per
cent, Protestant 22.8 per cent); traditional beliefs 47.0 per cent;
Muslim 1.7 per cent.
Languages: Malagasy and French. Hovba and other local dialects
are also spoken. **Political Parties:** Committee of Living Forces, an
alliance of 16 groups; Militant pro-Socialist Movement.
Social Organizations: Confederation of Malagasy Workers
(FMM); Christian Confederation of Trade Unions (SEKRIMA);
Federation of Autonomous Trade Unions of Madagascar (USAM);
Federation of Workers' Unions of Madagascar (FISEMA).

THE STATE
Official Name: Repoblikan'i Madagasikara. République
Démocratique de Madagascar.
Administrative Divisions: 6 provinces, 10 districts, 1,252 sub-
districts, and 11,333 towns.
Capital: Antananarivo, 1,500,000 people (1994).
Other cities: Toamasina, 127,000 people; Mahajanga (Majunga),
100,000; Fianarantsoa, 99,000 (1993)
Government: Parliamentary republic. Didier Ratsiraka, President
since 1997; Pascal Rakotomavo, Prime Minister since 1997.
Bicameral Legislature-Senate (2/3 selected by an Electoral College
and 1/3 selected by the president) and a National Assembly,
whose members are elected directly.
National Holiday: July 26, Independence Day (1960).
Armed Forces: 21,000 (1996)
Other: Gendarmerie, 7,500.

multiparty system and the
inclusion in his cabinet of several
members of the opposition by
March 1990.
[16] In 1991, the opposition united
around the Committee of Living
Forces, made up of 16
organizations. A series of street
demonstrations and the taking of
the National Radio, led the
Government to declare a state of
emergency. The Committee called
for Ratsiraka's resignation and, in
July, nominated a transition
government.
[17] In August, following the

detention of two ministers from
the transition cabinet, 400,000
people took to the streets and
repeated the demand for
Ratsiraka's resignation. The
demonstration was brutally put
down, with 31 people killed and
more than 200 injured.
[18] In March 1992, a multiparty
forum was created to draw up a
new constitution and presidential
elections were set for August. In
this month, the new document was
approved and Albert Zafy was
elected President with 66.2 per
cent of the vote to Ratsiraka's 33.8.

[19] The economic and social
situation of the country, one of
the poorest in the world, was
considered disastrous. Per capita
income barely increased between
1976 and 1992, going from $200
to $230 per year, while calorie
consumption went from 108 per
cent of those required in 1964-66,
to 95 per cent in 1988-90.
[20] In March 1994, the
Government introduced a series
of austerity measures
recommended by the International
Monetary Fund, which increased
the social tensions even further. At
the end of that year, massive
demonstrations were held in
opposition to these policies. In
January 1995, the governor of the
Central Bank abandoned his post
on request from the IMF and the
World Bank.
[21] In September, the Malagasy
people approved increased
powers for Zafy in a referendum.
The debate over structural
adjustment coincided with
disagreements over the use of the
nation's natural resources, when
the mining transnational RTZ
proposed opening a mine on the
southern coast of the island to
extract titanium dioxide. The
project caused harsh protests by
militant ecologists, convinced the
project would destroy unique

species of the Madagascar flora
and fauna.
[22] In May 1996, the National
Assembly approved a vote of no
confidence in the Government,
leading to the formation of a new
cabinet. The motion was partly
caused by comments made by the
IMF director, Michel Camdessus,
who said the lack of governmental
cohesion meant agreements with
the body were not guaranteed.
[23] President Zafy resigned in
September, accused of violating
the Constitution. In the
presidential elections organized
at the end of this year, Didier
Ratsiraka became the new
President, taking 65 per cent of
the votes.
[24] In 1997, the social and health
situation of the nation
deteriorated. Illnesses like malaria
increased amongst the poorer
people. According to the FAO,
three quarters of the population
were malnourished.
[25] A new constitution, approved
by referendum in 1998, gave the
President greater powers and
conferred greater economic
independence onto the six
provinces. The opposition
Committee of Living Forces
boycotted the elections saying
the government had dictatorial
aims.

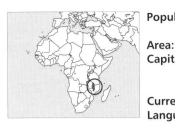

Malawi

Malawi

Population: 9,845,000 (1996)
Area: 118,484 SQ KM
Capital: Lilongwe

Currency: Kwacha
Language: Chewa

The state of Kitwara was part of a small country on the coast of Lake Malawi (previously Nyasa), and had been part of a series of nations related to gold production and ruled by the Monomotapa of Zimbabwe (see Zimbabwe). The decline of this power center allowed the Chewa to enlarge their territory, only to see it reduced again when the Changamira Rotsi restored the predominance of Zimbabwe. Around 1835, Zulu expansion (see South Africa) pushed the Ngoni-Ndwande to the shores of the lake, leading to 60 years of war between the Ngoni and the Chewa and Yao allies.

[2] The country was explored by Livingston in 1859 and it suffered a Portuguese attempt at colonization in 1890 which was ended by an ultimatum from the British Government. Britain wanted to keep the territory which would eventually serve as a link in a continuous chain of colonies joining South Africa to Egypt. In 1891, Cecil Rhodes' British South African Company negotiated the Protectorate of what became Nyasaland.

[3] The British idea was to create a Central African Federation embracing present-day Zimbabwe, Malawi and Zambia, regions linked by climatic similarities, plains, plateaus, dry forests and by common Bantu tribal ties. Politically this would have meant the extension of a Rhodesian-style white-racist domination to the entire Federation.

[4] The Malawi Congress Party (MCP), and the UNIP of Zambia, favored a pro-independence stance. They were strongly influenced by Dr Hastings Kamuzu Banda, a doctor who had studied in the United States and who was presented as the "nation's saviour".

[5] Banda's demands for greater power within the party were granted to prevent internal division. When the colony became independent in 1964, Banda seized control of the MCP and the country. The President established close economic and diplomatic relations with the racist governments of South Africa and Rhodesia, and with the colonial administration in Mozambique.

[6] South Africa became Malawi's main tea and tobacco purchaser while South African investors built roads, railways and a new capital city. South African managers took charge of the airline, information and development agencies and a large part of the state administration.

[7] In 1975, Mozambican independence radically changed Banda's situation. He had actively cooperated with the Portuguese in their struggle against FRELIMO. The closing of Mozambique's border with Rhodesia led to a drastic reduction in Malawi's trade with Rhodesia, depriving Ian Smith's racist government of an escape route from the international blockade.

[8] In June 1978, Banda held the first election in 17 years. All the candidates had to be MCP members and pass an English test, which immediately excluded the 90 per cent of the population who do not speak English.

[9] After 1980, Zimbabwe's independence changed the economic and political situation of Malawi. Banda lost direct communication with South Africa, and was therefore deprived of major support. Consequently the Government drew closer to the Front Line states, joining the SADCC association because of Malawi's dependence on the railway lines that run through Mozambique and Zimbabwe.

[10] The success of neighboring socialist governments strengthened the Socialist League of Malawi (LESOMA) which favored breaking economic and political ties with South Africa, putting an end to Banda's dictatorship and fully re-democratizing the country. In 1980, this party created a guerrilla force. The Malawi Freedom Movement (MAFREMO), led by Orton Chirwa, also gained strength.

[11] In 1983, Chirwa and Attati Mpakati, a LESOMA leader, were accused of conspiracy and sentenced to death. Shortly thereafter, Mpakati was assassinated by South African agents while visiting Harare. Chirwa and his wife were kidnapped in Zambia, where they lived as exiles, and imprisoned in Blantyre.

[12] Banda created a secret police force, called the Special Branch, with South African and Israeli advisers. The president-for-life also personally controlled the economy, owning 33 per cent of all businesses.

[13] Between 1987 and 1988, the country received 600,000 refugees from Mozambique, in whose civil war Malawi had supported the counter-revolutionaries of the National Resistance Movement. This support was discontinued in 1988, after the visit which Banda received from President Chissano of Mozambique.

[14] Also in 1988, Amnesty International denounced the imprisonment of well-known scholars and writers, among them Jack Mapanje, the country's foremost poet. The United States announced the cancellation of $40 million of foreign debt in November 1989.

PROFILE

Environment
The terrain and the climate are extremely varied. The major geological feature is the great Rift fault that runs through the country from north to south. Part of this large depression is filled by Lake Malawi, which takes up one fifth of the land area. The rest is made up of plateaus of varying altitudes. The most temperate region is the southern part, which is also the highest, containing most of the population and economic activities (basically farming). The lowlands receive heavy rainfall and are covered by grasslands, forests or rainforests, depending on the amount of rainfall they receive. The degradation of the soil and deforestation are the main environmental problems.

SOCIETY
Peoples: Maravi (including Nyanja, Chewa, Tonga, and Tumbuka) 58.3 per cent; Lomwe 18.4 per cent; Yao 13.2 per cent; Ngoni 6.7 per cent.
Religions: Many people follow traditional religions, but they also belong to Christian (64.5 per cent) and Muslim (16.2 per cent) communities.
Languages: Chewa (official) and English; several Bantu languages - other than Chewa - are spoken by their respective ethnic groups.
Political Parties: United Democratic Front (UDF); Alliance for Democracy (Aford); Malawi Congress Party (MCP).
Social Organizations: Trade Union Congress of Malawi.

THE STATE
Official Name: Republic of Malawi.
Administrative divisions: 24 districts.
Capital: Lilongwe, 395,000 people (1994).
Other cities: Blantyre 446,800 people; Mzuzu 62,700 (1994).
Government: Presidential republic. Bakili Muluzi, President since May 1994. Legislature: single-chamber: National Assembly, made up of 177 members.
National Holiday: July 6, Independence Day (1964).
Armed Forces: 9,800 (1996).
Other: 1,500.

Maternal Mortality
1990
PER 100,000 LIVE BIRTHS
560

Literacy
1995
56%

STATISTICS

DEMOGRAPHY
Population: 9,845,000 (1996) **Annual growth:** 2.9% (1980/1996) **Estimates for year 2000:** 11,000,000 **Annual growth to year 2000:** 2.3% (1994/2000) **Urban Population:** 13.8% (1996) **Urban growth:** 5.96% (1980/95) **Children per woman:** 6.8 (1996).

HEALTH
Life expectancy at birth: 41 years (1996) male: 41 years (1994) female: 42 years (1994) **Infant mortality:** 137 per 1,000 (1996) **Under-5 child mortality:** 217 per 1,000 (1996) **Calorie consumption:** 88% (1988/90) 50,000 **people per doctor** (1988/91) **Safe water:** 37% (1990/96).

EDUCATION
Literacy: 56% (1995) male : 72% (1995) female: 42% (1995) **School enrolment** : Primary total: 120% (1990/95) male : 126% (1990/95) female: 114% (1990/95) Secondary: male : 6% (1990/95) female: 4% (1990/95) Tertiary: 2% (1995) **Primary school teachers:** one for every 62 students (1995).

COMMUNICATIONS
226 **radios** and 3 **main telephone lines** per 1,000 people (1994) **Books:** 3 new titles per 100,000 people (1992/94).

ECONOMY
Per capita, GNP: $ 180 (1996) **Annual growth, GNP:** 13% (1995/96) **Annual inflation:** 22.05% (1985/95) **Currency:** 15.3 kwacha = $ 1 (1995) **Cereal imports:** 506 metric tons (1994) **Food import dependency:** 35% (1994) **Fertilizer use:** 214 kgs per ha (1994) **Exports:** $ 501 million (1996) **Imports:** $ 687 million (1996) **External debt:** $ 2,312 million (1996) $ 235 **per capita:** (1996) **Debt service:** 18.6% of exports (1996) **Development aid received:** $ 429 million (1995) $ 40 per capita (1995) 34.1% of GNP (1994).

ENERGY
Consumption: 38.97 Kgs of Oil equivalent per capita yearly (1994) 58.91% imported (1994).

HDI (rank / value) 161 / 0.32 (1994)

---

[15] The implementation of an IMF adjustment program led to a reduction in inflation and in the balance of payments deficit, as well as an increase in investments. However, it also aggravated the situation faed by the poorest sectors of the population.

[16] In 1990 and 1991, earthquakes and floods exacerbated food shortages among the rural population, 90 per cent of the country's total population. The privatization of the maize/corn market benefited a few producers at the expense of the poorest rural sectors.

[17] Despite the constant denunciations of human rights violations, US Vice-President Dan Quayle reaffirmed his government's support for the Banda regime.

[18] For the first time since independence, the Catholic Church wrote a pastoral letter criticizing the human rights situation, and calling for greater political freedom. This letter was followed by a popular uprising in Blantyre, which was harshly repressed by government forces.

[19] In April 1992, opposition leader Chafuka Chihana of the Alliance for Democracy was caught trying to return to the country, and imprisoned. An international campaign prevented him from being executed.

[20] During the Cold War, Banda was a staunch ally of the West, but the constant human rights violations of his government led to several countries cutting aid to Malawi.

[21] In May, a general strike called by textile workers was brutally put down, with 38 deaths and hundreds of injuries. In reprisal, the World Bank discontinued part of its financial aid.

[22] The ruling Congress Party of Malawi, the only party to participate in the June general elections, obtained 114 seats in the National Assembly.

[23] In late 1992, news was received of the death of Orton Chirwa of the Malawi Freedom Movement (MAFREMO). He had been in prison since 1983, and died under torture. To keep popular indignation from turning violent, Banda announced that a referendum would be held on opening up the political system.

[24] The referendum took place in June 1993. Two thirds of voters chose a multiparty system. That month, Banda promised presidential elections would be held in 1994 and released Vera Chirwa, widow of the assassinated dissident and who by that time had served the longest prison term for political reasons in Africa.

[25] Opposition member Bakili Muluzi was elected president in May 1994. His party, the United Democratic Front (UDF), won 84 of the 177 seats at stake in the legislative elections. In September, having won only 55 seats, Banda decided to retire from political activity.

[26] Malawi suffered the consequences of an intensive drought, in 1994, which led to a food shortage. In the midst of a growing difficult social situation, the government went ahead with its IMF-sponsored policy to cut back public spending. In January 1995, ex-president Banda was arrested, charged with the murder of three former ministers. The alleged violation of human rights by Muluzi's government was frequently denounced by opposition members throughout the year.

[27] In January 1996, Malawi entered negotiations to form a free trade area, along with another eleven Southern African nations. The Government announced it would revoke the laws affecting foreign investors in rural areas.

[28] In 1997, the United States started to train Malawi troops with a view to creating an African peace keeping force.

[29] The dry season, which affected vast regions of Africa, almost totally dried up the Shire river in Malawi, one of the country's main water courses. International experts recommended a reduction in the amount of water used in agriculture through the importing of food, and the progressive industrialization of the economy. In 1998, it was estimated the underground water reserves of the region would take 1,400 years to recover.

Malaysia

Malaysia

Population:	20,581,000 (1996)
Area:	329,758 SQ KM
Capital:	Kuala Lumpur
Currency:	Ringgit
Language:	Malay

The Malay Peninsula and the Borneo states of Sarawak and Sabah were originally inhabited by native aboriginal peoples, living in the forests.

2   In the second millennium BC, there was migration from the south of present-day China to present-day Malaysia, Indonesia and the Philippines. Over the millennia, metal-working techniques and agriculture were introduced. Rice farming was not developed until the first millennium AD. Indian influence was all pervasive, bringing religion, political systems and the Sanskrit language.

3   The Indianized kingdom of Funan was founded in the Mekong river area in the 1st century AD and Buddhist states eventually developed in the east, trading with China. In the 15th century, the port of Melaka (Malacca) was founded; its rulers were the first in the region to convert to Islam. Trade with Islamic merchants brought prosperity to Melaka. The new faith spread across the rest of present-day Malaysia and Indonesia, replacing Buddhism. At the beginning of the 16th century, Melaka, attracted the Portuguese, who were competing with Arab merchants for the Indian Ocean trade routes.

4   In 1511 the Portuguese viceroy of India, Alfonso de Albuquerque, seized the port by force. It was of vital strategic importance in the Portuguese struggle to maintain their monopoly on the spice-trade from the Moluccas Islands. These spices were exchanged for Indian textiles and Chinese silk and porcelain. In the 17th century, the Dutch formed an alliance with the Sultan of Johor to drive the Portuguese out of Melaka. This alliance between Johor and the Dutch was established in Batavia (present-day Jakarta) and it succeeded in eliminating European and Asian competition for a hundred years.

5   Meanwhile, the British began to set up back-up points for their trade with China in northern Borneo (Kalimantan), and in 1786 founded the port of Georgetown, on the island of Penang (Pulau-Pinang), off the western coast. The British model of free trade proved more successful than the Dutch trade monopoly and Penang attracted a cosmopolitan population of Malays, Sumatrans, Indians and Chinese. In 1819, the British founded Singapore, but at the time they were more interested in safeguarding shipping than in the local spice trade, as their imports from China were being paid for with opium from India. Nevertheless, the Dutch and the British found it difficult to coexist in the region; a treaty drawn up in 1824 granted control of Indonesia to the Dutch, while Malaya was left in British hands.

6   The colonies of Penang, Melaka and Singapore became the key points of the British colony. The British encouraged Chinese (and to a lesser degree, Indian) immigration to the ports along the straits, and large numbers of Chinese arrived to work the tin mines and service the urban ports. The Malay peasants and fishing people continued their traditional activities. From 1870, the British began to sign protectorate agreements with the sultans and in 1895 they encouraged them to form a federation, with Kuala Lumpur as its capital. The sultanates of northern Borneo (Brunei, Sabah and Sarawak, the latter ruled by James Brooke, and his heirs) also became British protectorates, administered from Singapore, but without any formal ties with the peninsula.

7   Towards the end of the 19th century, the British introduced rubber with *Hevea* seeds smuggled from Brazil, so bringing about an end to the rubber boom in the South American

PUBLIC EXPENDITURE

12.7%   48%

1995 ■ DEFENCE □ SOCIAL

In 1990/91 Military as % of health & education expenditure was 38%.

WORKERS

(1996)

Labour force %

■ WOMEN
□ MEN

37   63

■ AGRICULTURE   27% (1990)
□ INDUSTRIAL   23%
■ SERVICES   50%

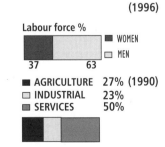

LAND USE

DEFORESTATION -1.8% annual (81/90)
IRRIGATED 32.7% of arable

(1993)

■ FOREST & WOODLAND 67.6%
□ ARABLE 3.2%
■ OTHER 29.2%

Food Dependency

Foreign Trade

1970

22%

1994

4%

MILLIONS $ 1996

IMPORTS
76,082

EXPORTS
78,151

PROFILE

ENVIRONMENT

The Federation of Malaysia is made up of Peninsular Malaysia (131,588 sq km), and the states of Sarawak (124,450 sq km) and Sabah (73,711 sq km) in northern Borneo (Kalimantan), 640 km from the peninsula in the Indonesian archipelago. Thick tropical forests cover more than 70 per cent of the mainland area, and a mountain range stretches from north to south across the peninsula. Coastal plains border the hills on both sides. In Sabah and Sarawak, coastal plains ascend to the mountainous interior. There is heavy annual rainfall. Malaysia's economy is export orientated. Tin and rubber, the traditional export products have recently been replaced by petroleum and manufactured goods. Indiscriminate logging and the use of highly toxic herbicides worries ecologists who fear irreparable damage to native species, and the destruction of the few surviving native cultures.

SOCIETY

Peoples: Malays (or Bumiputeras) 60 per cent, Chinese 33 per cent, Indians 10 per cent.
Religions: Islam, the official religion, is practised by 54 per cent of the populations. Buddhist 17 per cent, Taoist 22 per cent, Hindu, 7 per cent, Christians 7 per cent.
Languages: Malay is the official language, the common language, and the main language of education. Chinese dialects, Tamil and English are also used.
Political parties: Barisan Nasional (National Front), Democratic Action Party (DAP); People's Party (Parti Rakyat).
Social Organizations: The leading labor organization is the Congress of Malaysia's Unions.

THE STATE

Official Name: Persekutan Tanah Malaysia.
Capital: Kuala Lumpur, 3,030,000 people (1994).
Other cities: Ipoh, 382,633 people; Johor Baharu 328,646; Melaka 295,999; Petaling Jaya 254,849; Georgetown (Penang), 250,000 (1991).
Government: Constitutional, parliamentary and federal monarchy. Tuanku Ja'afar ibni al-Marhum Tuanku Abdul Rahman is the current king or *yang di-pertuan agong* (sovereign). The sovereign is elected every five years from among the nine regents (sultans), and only the sultans can vote. Datuk Seri Mahathir bin Mohamad, Prime Minister since 1981. Central bicameral parliament, 69-member senate, 192- member chamber of deputies, with a constitution and a legislative assembly for every state.
National Holiday: August 31, Independence Day (1957).
Armed Forces: 114,500 (1995).
Other: 21,500 Police, Regular, Sea and Air, Auxiliaries.

Amazon. They encouraged Tamil immigration from southern India, to get workers for the rubber plantations which faced growing demand from the incipient automobile industries.

[8] The colonial administration set up a three band education system that differed for Malays, Indians and Chinese. In the economy, the Malays stayed mainly in rural agriculture, the Chinese worked in tin mines and the urban service sectors, and the Indians worked on the

rubber estates. In the first decades of the 20th century, the Malays joined the Islamic reform movements of the Middle East, the Indians supported the struggles of Mahatma Gandhi, and the Chinese were ideologically influenced first by the nationalism of Sun Yat-Sen and then by the Communist Party.

[9] In 1942, during World War II, the country was occupied by the Japanese. The Japanese tried to form alliances with local

Southeast Asian nationalist movements to gain support against the European powers. The greatest resistance came from the Chinese, especially the Malayan Communist Party, which organized guerrillas to oppose the invading forces.

[10] At the end of the war it was clear that British domination could not persist without changes, but the difficulties of diverse ethnic interests, 'protected' sultanates and ports under direct colonial administration, made it difficult to find a suitable political system. The British proposed a Malayan Union with equal citizenship for all. This threatened the position of the Malays, and Malay nationalists gathered around the symbolic figure of the sultans founding the United Malays' National Organization (UMNO), controlled by the dominant class but with popular support.

[11] In 1948, there was a communist led insurrection that was suppressed by British forces. Its failure was partly due to the view of many poor Malays and Indians that the revolt was a Chinese effort and not the action of a unifying, anti-colonial progressive movement. The Marxist parties were outlawed and their leaders jailed. From 1948 until 1960, the Communist Party waged guerrilla warfare in the northern Malayan Peninsula and in Borneo.

[12] Journalist and activist Dato Onn made a new attempt at creating a pan-ethnic party. He left UMNO to found the Malayan Independence Party. He was defeated in the 1952 municipal elections by an alliance of UMNO and the Malayan Chinese Association. The alliance was later broadened to include the Indian Malayan Congress, winning nationwide elections, except for Singapore, where Lee Kuan Yew's socialists were victorious.

[13] Faced with the threat of an armed communist insurrection, the British decided to negotiate. This resulted in Malayan independence in 1957. Tunku Abdul Rahman, a prince who led the independence movement, became the first prime minister. A federation of 11 states was established with a parliamentary

system and a monarch chosen every five years from among nine state sultans. A constitutional bargain was struck by the three communities: citizenship was granted to the non-Malays, but the Malays were recognized as indigenous people. They were accorded special privileges in education and public-sector employment and Malay would be the official language. The country adopted the free market system and a reliance on foreign capital, which had been established under colonialism, remained dominant. Malaya was politically pro-Western.

[14] In 1963, the British colonial states of Singapore (south of Malaya), Sabah and Sarawak obtained independence and joined Malaya to form the Federation of Malaysia. There were major disagreements over ethnic policy and Singapore was expelled from the federation in 1965 becoming an independent republic.

[15] The conservative Alliance Party ruled with a large majority from 1957, but in the 1969 elections it lost many seats to the Islamic PAS Party, Gerakan and - mostly - to the Chinese-based Democratic Action Party (DAP). Tensions escalated into widespread riots and unrest, largely blamed by the authorities on 'Communist Terrorists'. The parliamentary system was suspended and the country was ruled for two years by a National Operations Council. The Malay population were dissatisfied with their share of corporate equity, because in 1970 they made up over 50 per cent of the population, but had only one per cent of the income. A new economic policy was formulated to deal with this. It set targets to increase the Malay and other 'Bumiputera' ('sons-of-the-soil' or indigenous people) share to 30 per cent by 1990, while the foreign share would drop from 70 to 30 per cent and the non-Bumiputera (mainly Chinese and Indian) share would be 40 per cent.

[16] This policy dominated internal economic policy for the next two decades. The Bumiputera equity share rose to almost 20 per cent by 1989

PER 100,000
LIVE BIRTHS
80

84%

PER CAPITA
$1,933

STATISTICS

DEMOGRAPHY
Population: 20,581,000 (1996) **Annual growth**: 2.5% (1980/1996) **Estimates for year 2000**: 22,300,000. **Annual growth to year 2000**: 2.1% (1994/2000) **Urban Population**: 54.4% (1994) **Urban growth**: 4.28% (1980/95) **Children per woman**: 3.4 (1996).

HEALTH
Life expectancy at birth: 72 years (1996) male: 69 years (1994) female: 74 years (1994) **Infant mortality**: 11 per 1,000 (1996) **Under-5 child mortality**: 13 per 1,000 (1996) **Calorie consumption**: 120% (1988/90) 2,564 **people per doctor** (1988/91) **Safe water**: 78% (1990/96).

EDUCATION
Literacy: 84% (1995) male : 89% (1995) female: 78% (1995) **School enrolment** : Primary total: 93% (1990/95) male : 93% (1990/95) female: 94% (1990/95) Secondary: male : 58% (1990/95) female: 64% (1990/95) Tertiary: 11% (1995) **Primary school teachers**: one for every 20 students (1995).

COMMUNICATIONS
140 **newspapers**, 432 **radios**, 230 **TV sets** and 147 **main telephone lines** per 1,000 people (1994) **Books**: 21 new titles per 100,000 people (1992/94).

ECONOMY
Per capita, GNP: $ 4,370 (1996) **Annual growth, GNP**: 5.8% (1995/96) **Annual inflation**: 3.27% (1985/95) **Consumer price index**: 117,4 (1994) **Currency**: 2.54 ringgits = $ 1 (1995) **Cereal imports**: 3,509 metric tons (1994) **Food import dependency**: 4% (1994) **Fertilizer use**: 1,586 kgs per ha (1994) **Exports**: $78,151 million (1996) **Imports**: $ 76,082 million (1996) **External debt**: $ 39,777 million (1996) $ 1,933 **per capita**: (1996) **Debt service**: 8.2% of exports (1996) **Development aid received**: $114 million (1995) $ 6 per capita (1995) 0.2% of GNP (1994).

ENERGY
Consumption: 1,698.64 Kgs of Oil equivalent per capita yearly (1996) -70.64% imported (1994).

HDI (rank / value) 60 / 0.832 (1994)

whilst foreign ownership fell below 40 per cent. Because of these policies, Malaysians of Chinese descent claimed that they faced discrimination at work, in education and elsewhere.

[17] Communist guerrilla warfare gradually died out, and the National Front won over two-thirds of the parliamentary seats in elections during the 1970s and 1980s. The present prime minister, Mahathir Mohamad, took office in 1981, and started to develop Malaysia's industry. In the late 1980s he faced increasing challenges to his leadership from UMNO (the Front's main party). Some of his

opponents left to form a new opposition party, Semangat 46. In 1990 they formed a loose opposition coalition with the Islamic PAS, the DAP and the small left-wing People's Party.

[18] The Internal Security Act allowed detention without trial for two years. Under Mahathir, the number of political prisoners declined from over 1,000 to a few hundred. In 1987 a major crackdown led to 150 more detentions, including opposition politicians and leaders of social groups, all of whom were released by 1990.

[19] In 1988, the chief judge and three other Supreme Court judges were sacked following a

dispute between the judiciary and the executive. Lawyers and critics accused the Government of threatening the judiciary's independence. There are currently serious limits imposed on the freedom of press and of assembly; permits are required for both newspapers and public meetings.

[20] Malaysian foreign policy has moved from its pro-western position in the 1960s through non-alignment in the 1970s to a pro-Third World stance in the 1980s. In 1990, Kuala Lumpur hosted the inaugural summit meeting of 15 Third World countries (including India, Brazil, Indonesia, Mexico, Venezuela, Tanzania and Senegal) aimed at fostering concrete South-South co-operation projects and aiming to reduce Northern dominance of Southern economies. It played a major role in the South Commission and actively supports the Palestine Liberation Organization and South Africa's African National Congress. Mahathir was internationally recognized as a pro-South leader.

[21] There has been a growth of activity and influence of civic organizations, including consumer, environmental and human rights groups. The Consumers Association of Penang has spearheaded actions on food safety, tenancy rights and business malpractice.

[22] The Sahabat Alam (Friends of the Earth) Malaysia assisted indigenous groups in Sarawak to defend their forest from loggers in a widely-publicized campaign. The natives (especially nomadic Penan) staged blockades on timber roads to prevent logs leaving the forest. In August 1991 a judge in Sarawak condemned eight protest leaders to nine months in prison.

[23] Malaysia is the major world exporter of tropical wood with a growing demand in the industrialized countries, especially Japan. In 1989 its timber exports earned $ 2.6 billion. More than 80 per cent of this timber comes from Sarawak and Sabah, in Borneo. It is estimated that out of the previous 305,000 square kilometres (sq km) of tropical forests, only 157,000 sq km are

left, and the country loses 5,000 sq km of tropical forest each year. Environmental organizations accuse several companies of destroying vast areas of forest, and of causing huge fires to create new areas for cultivation. Alternative development models based on satisfying basic needs and living in harmony with nature are increasingly advocated by social and ecological groups.

[24] In 1991, construction plans were approved for a hydroelectric dam on the Pergau River, north of Kelantan, the country's poorest state. The project was financed by Britain at a cost of $350 million and was tied to British arms purchases amounting to $1.5 billion. The dam would cause a damage to the environment which has met with opposition. A similar project in 1995 was also criticized for its anticipated social and ecological impact. Thousands of peasants were forced to leave forested areas which would later be flooded.

[25] The rapid growth of high-tech industries has led to a shortage of skilled and semi-skilled labour. Wages in the industrial sector have had a significant raise which led to increase social differences.

[26] In April 1994, Tuanku Ja'afar ibni al-Marhum Tuanku Abdul Rahman was elected sovereign of Malaysia. The support for Prime Minister Mohamad was made clear in 1995, when his coalition, the National Front, took 162 of the 192 seats in the Chamber of Representatives, and 84 per cent of the vote.

[27] Economic growth continued until 1997, when an unprecedented stock exchange crisis hit the region. The devaluation of the Malaysian currency coincided with a deterioration in the social situation. In early 1998, unemployment already topped a million. The Government tightened up migration policies. In the first three months of that year, 19,000 undocumented foreign workers without papers were expelled. The Government revealed a plan to expel a total of 200,000 people, approximately 10 per cent of the foreign workers living in the country.

Maldives

Population: 263,000 (1996)
Area: 298 SQ KM
Capital: Male

Currency: Rufiyaa
Language: Dhivehi

The Republic of the Maldives consists of an archipelago of more than 1,000 coral islands in the Indian Ocean, southwest of India and Sri Lanka, of which only 192 are permanently inhabited. Maldivans are excellent sailors and fishing people and have always had close contact with the mainland of Asia. It was through this connection that Arab and Muslim influence reached them in the 12th century; the islanders converted to Islam and their ruler took the title of Sultan.

[2] European colonizers came to the Maldives quite early on, as it was a compulsory stopover on the way to the Far East. The natives put up tenacious resistance to foreign domination, forcing the Portuguese to seek alternative harbours; hence the foundation of Goa on the west coast of India.

[3] Eventually, the Sultan of the Maldives gave in to the enticing offers of the agents of British imperialism and, in 1887, he agreed to place his islands under British "protection". The economy was makeshift based on the production of coconut oil, fishing and the cultivation of tropical fruits. On the other hand, the Maldives possessed great strategic value, which was enhanced on the opening of the Suez Canal.

[4] A naval base was set up on Gan Island, on the equator, which became a link in the safety chain that protected navigation from Gibraltar to Hong Kong, via Aden and Singapore.

[5] The local population was of no interest to the authorities even as a source of labor, so very little was done for their education, health or welfare. Even today the country has only one teacher for every 2,000 people and one doctor for every 15,000, it also has one of the world's lowest per capita incomes.

[6] This neglect stimulated rebellion against the Sultan, whose position as an intermediary between his people and the colonial capital made him the only person to benefit from this contact. In 1952, a popular revolt overthrew the ruler and a republic was proclaimed. British troops intervened to "restore order", putting the Sultan back on the throne two years later. In 1957, Britain requested permission to enlarge the Gan naval base and install facilities for fighter planes to land there. The proposal aroused fierce opposition and pro-British Prime Minister Ibrahim Ali Didi was forced to resign. His successor, Amir Ibrahim Nasir, refused permission to build the new facilities claiming that such a project would violate the country's neutrality.

[7] In 1959, rebellion broke out in the southern Maldives, which decided to break away under the name of the Republic of Suvadiva. This autonomy was short-lived, and in 1960, the 20,000 Suvadivan republicans were restored to the sultanate with British help. The colonialists took the opportunity of signing a new agreement with the sultan extending the protectorate, and maintaining and enlarging the bases.

[8] This time the British paid nothing towards them, only the pay due to the British soldiers and the cost of the ammunition used to stifle the rebellion in the south.

[9] The British Empire was by now in decline. During the 1960s, the British finally decided to withdraw from their strategic positions "east of Suez", making sure that their interests would continue to be defended by the United States. In 1965, the Maldives chose to become independent, receiving immediate recognition from the United Nations.

[10] The Sultan was unable to survive the withdrawal of foreign support and, in 1968, a plebiscite was held which favored the establishment of a republic. Amir Ibrahim Nasir, the prime minister, now became president.

[11] The Gan naval base remained in British hands until 1975, when the building of modern US military installations on the neighboring island of Diego Garcia rendered it obsolete.

[12] In March 1975, President Nasir announced that he had uncovered a conspiracy led by Prime Minister Ahmed Zaki; Zaki was exiled to a desert island along with some of his supporters. Nasir's proposal to rent the unused installations on Gan Island to transnational enterprises was rejected by the Majilis (legislative council). Realizing that he had lost support, Nasir ended his second presidential term in 1978, without standing for re-election. The Majilis appointed Maumoon Gayoom, an Islamic intellectual of international prestige, to replace him.

[13] The new president concerned himself with the serious difficulties of the fishing community and set up a state fisheries corporation to control the country's main economic resource from catch to marketing. Gayoom founded schools in 19 of the major atolls and opened up the archipelago to the rest of the world, personally travelling to Europe, the Middle East and the Sixth Summit Conference of the Non-Aligned Movement.

[14] In May 1980, he officially announced that his government had crushed an attempted mercenary invasion of the islands, organized from abroad by Ibrahim Nasir. Nasir's extradition from Singapore was immediately requested.

[15] The Republic of Maldives supported Islamic solidarity, non-alignment, Palestine, the New International Economic Order, disarmament, African solidarity, and demilitarization of the Indian Ocean. In spite of its size, population and resources, its strategic location gave it considerable bargaining power for the country and an independent position in foreign policy. In addition, non-aligned foreign policy provided the basis for assistance and support from all, without sacrificing too much freedom of action.

[16] In April 1980, the Maldives signed a scientific and

Map

Indian Ocean

Ihavandiffulu Atoll
Tiladunmati Atoll
Makunudu Atoll
Miladunmadulu Atoll
North Malosmadulu Atoll
Fadippolu Atoll
Male Atoll
South Malosmadulu Atoll
MALDIVES — Kardiva Channel
Male Atoll
Ari Atoll
South Male Atoll
North Nilandu Atoll
Felidu Atoll
South Nilandu Atoll
Mulaku Atoll
Kolumadulu Atoll
Veimandu Channel
Haddunmati Atoll
Addu Atoll
Huvadu Atoll
Equator
Gan
Addu Atoll

LAND USE

(1993)

■ FOREST & WOODLAND	3.3%
□ ARABLE	10%
▨ OTHER	86.7%

PROFILE

ENVIRONMENT
There are nearly 1,200 coral islets in this archipelago, where the land is never more than 3.5 meters above sea level. Vegetation is sparse except for coconut palms which are plentiful. A tropical monsoon climate prevails. There are no mineral or energy resources. Fishing is the economic mainstay.

SOCIETY
Peoples: The population of the archipelago came from migrations of Dravidian, Indo-Arian and Sinhalese peoples from India, later followed by Arab peoples.
Religions: Islam (official and proclaimed universal).
Languages: Dhivehi (official), an Indo-Arian language related to Sinhala, English and Arabic are also spoken.
Political Parties: There are no political parties. The Majlis, or parliament, is elected by direct vote, and in turn proposes a president whose candidacy is submitted to a plebiscite.

THE STATE
Official Name: Divehi Jumhuriyya (Republic of Maldives).
Administrative divisions: 20 districts.
Capital: Male, 63,000 people (1995).
Government: Presidential republic. Maumoon Abdul Gayoom, President since 1978, re-elected in 1993. Legislative Power; the Citizens' Council, with 48 members, 8 of whom are elected by the President.
National Holiday: July 26, Independence Day (1965).
Armed forces: About 1,000. The force performs both army and police functions.

STATISTICS

DEMOGRAPHY
Population: 263,000 (1996) **Annual growth:** 3.2% (1980/1996) **Estimates for year 2000:** 300,000 **Annual growth to year 2000:** 3.5% (1994/2000) **Urban Population:** 27.1% (1996) **Children per woman:** 6.8 (1996).

HEALTH
Life expectancy at birth: 64 years (1996) male: 64 years (1996) female: 62 years (1996) **Infant mortality:** 54 per 1,000 (1996) **Under-5 child mortality:** 76 per 1,000 (1996) **Safe water:** 96% (1990/96).

EDUCATION
Literacy: 93% (1995) male: 93% (1995) female: 93% (1995) **School enrolment :** Primary total: 134% (1990/95) male : 136% (1990/95) female: 133% (1990/95) Secondary: male : 49% (1990/95) female: 49% (1990/95).

COMMUNICATIONS
10 **newspapers,** 118 **radios,** 40 **TV sets** and 48 **main telephone lines** per 1,000 people (1994)

ECONOMY
Currency: 11.77 rufiyaa = $ 1 (1995) **Cereal imports:** 22 metric tons (1994) **Development aid received:** $ 55 million (1995) $220 per capita (1995) 22.1% of GNP (1994).

HDI (rank / value) 111 / 0.611 (1994)

---

technological cooperation agreement with the Soviet Union, and in April 1981, a trade agreement with India, which is the country's closest cooperator in the region. In July, 1981, Chinese foreign minister Huang Hua visited Male and signed a technical cooperation agreement.

[17] In July 1982, the Government achieved a major diplomatic victory when the Maldives became the 47th member of the British Commonwealth. This was the second major achievement of Gayoom's government since 1979, when the Maldives had joined the Non-Aligned Movement. The Maldives have, however, refused to join ASEAN as this organization tends to act on bloc decisions agreed by a majority.

[18] Being the country closest to the US naval base at Diego Garcia in the Indian Ocean, Maldivan developments have attracted the interest of other countries. In a referendum held in 1983, Gayoom was elected for another five-year period, with 95.5 per cent of the vote.

[19] In August 1988, three months before being elected president for the third time, Maumoon Gayoom frustrated another coup attempt,

allegedly promoted by Amir Nasir. Seventy-five people were arrested, most of them Sri Lankans, of whom 16 were sentenced to death, and 59 were given prison sentences.

[20] In 1985, there was a 37 per cent increase in tourism over the 1984 figure, coinciding with the virtual closing down of the Maldivan docks, as a result of the drastic reduction of its imports and the loss of important international markets. In 1986, tourism maintained its economic importance, generating $42 million per year, close to 17 per cent of the GDP, and in 1991, the Maldives had 200,000 tourists, who brought $80 million into the country. Fishing continued to be the main activity, employing 45 per cent of the country's workforce and generating 24 per cent of the GDP.

[21] The local environmental effects of industrial activity in developed countries, is a major issue to Maldivans. In March, 1990, thousands of schoolchildren demonstrated in the streets of the capital, voicing their concern over the rising sea levels around their tiny archipelago. This phenomenon is attributed to the "greenhouse effect" which is producing global warming, that will lead to the melting of the polar ice caps, causing the sea level to rise. According to scientific predictions, if present trends continue most of the islands will disappear over the next hundred years.

[22] To counteract the sea rise, large retaining walls were built around the islands. In 1987, gigantic waves flooded two-thirds

of the capital, Male, causing damage estimated at $40 million. In June 1991, heavy rainfalls destroyed the homes of over 10 per cent of the population, causing damage for $30 million worth of damage.

[23] Twenty-eight tons of garbage are collected daily in Male, generating serious environmental problems, given the island's small surface area. A UN body determined that the garbage should not be recycled, but should be taken instead to a neighboring island, to be used as filling material to gain land from the sea.

[24] The Government of Maldives denied Amnesty International access to prisoners held in the Dhoonidhoo detention center and the Gamadhoo prison, where there had been reports of inhumane treatment. Most political prisoners were sent there under the Prevention of Terrorism Act which, among other measures, authorizes detention without trial for up to 45 days.

[25] In 1993 and 1994, the Maldives went through an economic crisis caused by the 1991 monsoons and a chronic trade deficit dating from 1992. The Government sold 25 per cent of the Bank of Maldives' shares and applied a free market economy to all sectors except frozen fish exports.

[26] President Maumoon Abdul Gayoom began his fourth term in government in 1993 and remained as head of the ministries of defence, national security and finance. 27 per cent of the budget was turned over to

education, health and social security. The fishing sector received 30 per cent since it employs one fourth of the working population.

[27] $113 million in tourism revenues from 1994 helped in the recovery of the archipelago's economy in 1995.

[28] Although there are no political parties or an organized opposition allowed, young Maldivans educated abroad have shown signs of rejecting the system imposed by the President. The spread of religious radicalism throughout the islands is another reason for concern of Maumoon Abdul Gayoom's government.

[29] The Maldives experienced slow but firm economic progress in 1996, and industrial production increased 10 per cent. Education spending increased to 9.2 per cent of the national budget.

[30] In May 1997, the Southeast Asian Co-operation Association, meeting in Male, approved initiatives to eradicate poverty and, on the basis of studies proving sea level rise around Maldives, decided to protect the environment. At the end of the year, Gayoom transmitted this concern to United Nations delegates and Commonwealth Governors.

[31] In its 1997 annual report, Amnesty International said there were at least a dozen political prisoners in Maldives, detained for showing opposition to the Gayoom regime. Many of them had been imprisoned without trial or even charges filed against them.

Mali

Mali

Population: 11,134,000 (1996)
Area: 1,240,192 SQ KM
Capital: Bamako

Currency: CFA Franc
Language: French

The empire of Mali, one of the great cultural and commercial centres of Africa was occupied by the French in 1850. Together with what are now Burkina Faso (Upper Volta), Benin and Senegal it was renamed the French Sudan, and later, French West Africa.

[2] Domination brought about considerable changes. Trade, which traditionally flowed towards the Mediterranean, was turned back towards the Atlantic where Dakar had become the official trade center of the colony. This in turn caused the decline of the trans-Saharan trade routes. After 1945 the anti-colonial feelings of French Sudan were expressed in the formation of the African Democratic Assembly (RDA), at a conference in Bamako encouraged by the democratic atmosphere that prevailed after World War II. Under the impact of the Dien Bien Phu defeat of French colonialism in Vietnam and the Algerian revolution, Paris embarked on a policy of gradual concessions that would lead to Mali's independence in 1960.

[3] Aware of their limitations, the newly formed states formed the Federation of Mali, but their differences soon caused the federation to collapse. French Sudan then severed its last remaining ties with France, becoming the Republic of Mali, with Modibo Keita as its first president.

[4] Together with Senghor from Senegal and Houphouet-Boigny from Cote d'Ivoire, Keita belonged to a generation of African leaders educated in France and inspired by social democracy. Unlike his neighbors, the president of Mali did not accept neocolonialism. Instead he pushed for reforms and economic development under the banner of African socialism; moving closer to the views held by Guinea's Sekou Touré and Nkrumah of Ghana.

[5] The economy was nationalized, industrialization stimulated and the proportion of children in school rose from 4 to 20 per cent. His struggle for Pan-Africanism, non-alignment and independent foreign policy earned Keita a good reputation among progressive forces throughout the continent. He was, however, unable to build a strong political structure and there was a successful coup against him in November 1968.

[6] The Military Committee for National Liberation (CMLN) took over, headed by Moussa Traoré. The Committee promised to straighten out the economy and fight corruption, but the results were exactly the opposite. Grain, which had been produced in sufficient quantities to provide a surplus for export, began to be rationed in the 1970s.

[7] Economic dependence and agricultural intensification geared towards a world market caused a large foreign debt for Mali during this decade.

[8] In 1974 seeking to gain political support, the CMLN held a referendum on a new constitution. With the opposition banned and the followers of Keita imprisoned, the Government won a 99.8 per cent majority, too large to be believed. On May 16 1977 Modibo Keita died somewhere in the desert where he had been held prisoner since 1968. The official cause of death was food poisoning, but this was commonly re-interpreted as simply poisoning. In the largest mass demonstration ever seen in Bamoko, the people followed Keita's body to the cemetery in open defiance of the military regime.

[9] In 1979, President Moussa Traoré embarked upon an austerity program drawn up by the IMF and the international creditor banks. This naturally stirred up social unrest. In November 1979 students and teachers took to the streets staging rallies and demonstrations which lasted for over a month. Teachers also went on strike. The Government reacted violently. Thirteen students were tortured to death and around 100 were arrested.

[10] After 1983 Mali also drew closer to France. At the same time Traoré distanced himself from the Soviet Union after having received economic and educational aid during the 1970s.

[11] Key sectors, such as agriculture, continued to decline. A prolonged drought drastically reduced Mali's livestock.

[12] In June 1985, President Traoré was re-elected for a further six years. As the official party's only candidate he received 99.94 per cent of the vote.

[13] In 1988 students, teachers and public employees took to the streets once again. The Government was reorganised and a Social and Economic Council was created, headed by General Amadou Baba Diarra.

[14] The Government faced a foreign debt which amounted to 125 per cent of its GDP, with the servicing of the debt exceeding a quarter of the income earned from exports. Negotiations for an economic adjustment program began with the IMF in 1988. The privatization of Mali's banking system was initiated, financed by an 8,000,000 CFA franc loan from France. At the same time the Government announced a reduction in their number of employees, and the decision to sell off state enterprises.

[15] On April 10 1991, a popular and military revolt against the Traoré regime carried Lt-Col Amadou Toumani Touré to power. He was the leader of the Council of Transition for the Salvation of the People (CTSP), which promised to transfer government to civilians early in 1992.

[16] The CTSP contained many cadres from the previous military dictatorship. Popular distrust of the military led to violent action by student organizations, as buildings associated with the old dictatorial regime were raided.

[17] Old political parties reorganized and new ones appeared. Social organizations demonstrated in favour of several issues, including pay increases, and against the privatization of public companies in the telecommunication, railroad, textile, pharmaceutical and cement sectors.

[18] In June, the rising of the Tuaregs in the north and the Moors in the east increased the state of social unrest. The new president met with his colleagues in Algeria and Mauritania to deal with the Tuareg question.

[19] An attempted coup by some of the armed forces initially led Toumani Touré to grant a salary increase of 70 per cent to the armed forces and civil servants in an effort to avert unrest.

[20] In December 1991, talks were renewed between Mali's authorities and the Tuareg rebels, who accepted a cease-fire in order for prisoners to be exchanged.

[21] In March the next year, with Algerian mediation, the Government of Mali and the

(1996)

Labour force %
- ■ WOMEN
- □ MEN

46   54

- ■ AGRICULTURE 86% (1990)
- □ INDUSTRIAL 2%
- ▨ SERVICES 12%

PROFILE

ENVIRONMENT
There are three distinct regions: the northern region which is part of the Sahara desert; the central region which consists of the Sahel grasslands, subject to desertification, and finally, the southern region, with humid savannah vegetation, most of the population, and the two major rivers: the Senegal and the Niger. The shortage of water and the over use of forest resources have given rise to further aridity.

SOCIETY
Peoples: There are many ethnic groups, the largest being the Bambara. Other important groups are the Malinke, Songhai, Peul-Fulani, Dogon, Tuareg and Moor. 10 per cent of the population are nomads; they are the most affected by drought. **Religions:** the majority, 90 per cent, is Muslim, 9 per cent practice traditional African religions and there is a small Christian minority. **Languages:** French (official). Of the African languages, Bambara is the most widely spoken. Arabic and Tuareg are also spoken in the north. **Political Parties:** Alliance for Democracy in Mali (ADEMA); National Committee for Democratic Initiative (CNID); Sudanese Union-African Democratic Group (US-RDA); National Renaissance Party (PRN); Unified Movements and Fronts of Azawad (MFUA). **Social Organizations:** Workers' Union of Mali; Union of Malian Women (UNFM); National Union of Malian Youth (UNJM); Association of Pupils and Students of Mali (AEEM).

THE STATE
Official Name: République du Mali. **Administrative divisions:** 8 regions and the district of Bamako. **Capital:** Bamako, 840,000 people (1994). **Other cities:** Ségou 88,877 people; Mopti 73,979; Sikasso 73,050; Gao 54,874 (1987). **Government:** Parliamentary republic, with strong head of State. Alpha Oumar Konaré, President since April 1992, re elected in May 1997. Legislature: single-chamber: National Assembly, with 129 members, elected every 5 years. **National Holiday:** September 22, Independence Day (1960). **Armed Forces:** 7,350. **Other:** 7,350 (Gendarmes, Republican Guard, Militia and National Police).

STATISTICS

DEMOGRAPHY
Population: 11,134,000 (1996) **Annual growth:** 3% (1980/1996) **Estimates for year 2000:** 12,600,000 **Annual growth to year 2000:** 3.1% (1994/2000) **Urban Population:** 27.5% (1996) **Urban growth:** 5.32% (1980/95) **Children per woman:** 6.8 (1996).

HEALTH
Life expectancy at birth: 47 years (1996) male: 45 years (1994) female: 48 years (1994) **Infant mortality:** 134 per 1,000 (1996) **Under-5 child mortality:** 220 per 1,000 (1996) **Calorie consumption:** 96% (1988/90) 20,000 **people per doctor** (1988/91) **Safe water:** 66% (1990/96).

EDUCATION
Literacy: 31% (1995) male : 39% (1995) female: 23% (1995) **School enrolment :** Primary total: 32% (1990/95) male : 39% (1990/95) female: 25% (1990/95) Secondary: male : 11% (1990/95) female: 6% (1990/95) **Primary school teachers:** one for every 66 students (1995).

COMMUNICATIONS
44 **radios,** 10 **TV sets** and 2 **main telephone lines** per 1,000 people (1994)

ECONOMY
Per capita, GNP: $ 240 (1996) **Annual growth, GNP:** 1.2% (1995/96) **Annual inflation:** 4.57% (1985/95) **Currency:** 490 CFA francs = $ 1 (1995) **Cereal imports:** 70 metric tons (1994) **Food import dependency:** 15% (1994) **Fertilizer use:** 83 kgs per ha (1994) **Exports:** $ 288 million (1996) **Imports:** $ 1,159 million (1996) **External debt:** $ 3,020 million (1996) $ 271 **per capita:** (1996) **Debt service:** 17.9% of exports (1996) **Development aid received:** $ 542 million (1995) $ 57 per capita (1995) 29.6% of GNP (1994).

ENERGY
Consumption: 21.56 Kgs of Oil equivalent per capita yearly (1996) 79.51% imported (1994).

HDI (rank / value) 171 / 0.229 (1994)

Tuaregs reached a new peace agreement. In April a final peace settlement was signed with the Azawad Unified Front and Movements, an organization of four Tuareg opposition groups.

[22] In the March 1992 municipal and legislative elections, the Alliance for Democracy in Mali (ADEMA) won 76 of the 116 seats. The rest were divided up among other political alliances and representatives of the expatriate Mali community.

[23] The Malian Government and the Tuareg rebels in the north ratified a "national peace pact" in April 1992, putting an end to almost two years of armed conflict.

[24] On April 26, Alpha Oumar Konaré, leader of ADEMA, was elected President in the first multiparty elections since the country's independence in 1960. His main rival was Tieoule Mamadou Konaté, head of the Sudanese Union-African Democratic Group (US-RDA).

[25] Konaré, a teacher by profession, had played a key role in ousting Moussa Traoré's regime in 1991.

[26] Konaré and Konaté called for a second ballot, as neither had won an absolute majority in the initial round of voting on April 12, although seven candidates were eliminated in this first round. Both rounds of voting were characterized by a very low voter turnout (only 21 per cent of the voters participated in the second ballot).

[27] Most political parties boycotted the parliamentary election and challenged the electoral procedures, this perhaps accounted for the high rate of absenteeism.

[28] In its annual report for 1992, Amnesty International condemned the imprisonment of several opposition figures without charges or trial. Fourteen death sentences had also been passed, although these were later commuted to life sentences. Finally, according to the report, several dozen members of the Tuareg community had been executed without trial by the army.

[29] A group of students occupied the state radio station in March 1993, and massive demonstrations were held against the Government's economic policy in April. However, with support from international financial organizations, Konare consolidated the economic liberalization begun by Traoré. The President reformed the tax system, reduced public spending, privatized state companies and eliminated price controls.

[30] In February 1994, new demonstrations were staged against the government, and all the education centres except primary schools were closed. Some observers indicated the appearance of underground armed groups determined to attack properties belonging to Mali's major creditor countries.

[31] The Government signed an agreement with the MFUA, one of the main groups representing Tuareg rebels. But violent incidents continued to take place and on one occasion, some 200 people, including many women and children, died due to police repression in the cities of Gao and Beher.

[32] In 1995, the Government pursued negotiations with other Tuareg rebel groups - likewise with neighbouring countries - to organize the relocation of 120,000 Tuareg refugees from Algeria, Burkina Faso, Mauritania and Niger. A three year repatriation scheme was launched in October.

[33] The IMF approved the third annual structural adjustment plan after it considered Mali's economic results were good. At the same time, many foreign investors showed a renewed interest in Mali after new gold fields were found in the south.

[34] A new peace agreement, signed on March 27 1996, put an end to the conflict with the Tuareg. The Government arranged the return of some 25,000 refugees from Niger. The agreement also included the demobilisation of some 2,700 guerrillas.

[35] In May 1997, Alpha Oumar Konaré was re-elected President with 95.9 per cent of the valid votes. In the legislative elections of July and August, the governmental Alliance for Democracy (ADEMA) took 130 seats in the new parliament. In both cases, the opposition boycotted the elections and there was only a minimal turn-out.

[36] The opposition boycott coincided with increased violence in the streets, leading to the resignation of Prime Minister Keita and his government in late 1997. A group of intellectuals called for the liberation of various opposition leaders to ease the situation. However, the president confirmed the prime minister in his post and the latter designated a new government.

[37] In March 1998, the Government indefinitely postponed local elections planned for April 19. According to the Government, this measure was imposed to allow the political parties time to prepare, given the announcement of a further boycott by the opposition.

MILITARY EXPENDITURE

MILITARY (as % of health and education expenditures-1990/91) **53%**

Malta

Malta

Population:	369,000 (1996)
Area:	316 SQ KM
Capital:	Valletta
Currency:	Liri
Language:	Maltese and English

For territorial expansionists, Malta's most valuable asset is probably its geographic location which made it the historical focus of every conflict for domination of the Mediterranean. In ancient times, Phoenicians, Greeks, Carthaginians, Romans and Saracens successively occupied the island.

[2] In 1090, the Normans conquered the island and 300 years later it fell to the Spanish Kingdom of Aragon. In the 16th century, the defence of the island was entrusted to the ancient order of the Knights of St John of the Hospital. Renamed the Knights of Malta, they remained there for another three centuries, until they were driven out by the French in 1798. The Congress of Vienna granted Britain sovereignty over the island, in 1815.

[3] After a popular rebellion in 1921, London agreed to a certain degree of internal autonomy for the islands, revoked at the beginning of World War II.

[4] During World War II, Malta suffered greatly; it was used as a base for the Allied counter-offensive against Italy. The heroic struggle of the Maltese raised their national consciousness and in 1947, London restored autonomy to the island.

[5] Independence was formally declared on September 8 1964, but Britain assumed responsibility for defence and financial support. In 1971, Dominic Mintoff's government established relations with Italy, Tunisia, the USSR and Libya, from whom it received substantial financial assistance. NATO forces left in 1971, and Malta joined the Movement of Non-Aligned Countries two years later. In December 1974, the Republic of Malta was proclaimed.

[6] In 1980, tensions developed in Malta's relations with Libya, primarily over oil explorations. The conflict was eventually turned over to the International

Court of Justice in the Hague, and relations returned to normal.

[7] From the beginning of the Labour administration, measures to reduce the Church's power had been introduced. The bishops owned 80 per cent of all real estate on the island and virtually controlled education. In July 1983, the Government expropriated all Church properties and made secular education obligatory in primary schools. In 1985, the Government and the Church signed an agreement providing for a gradual transition to secular education at the secondary level.

[8] In May 1987, the Liberal Prime Minister, Dr Fenech Adami, initiated a policy of rapprochement towards US policies, favoring EEC membership.

[9] Forecasts of a falling birth rate and the increase in people aged over 60 forced the Government to draw up plans to deal with the problems of the elderly. At present 7 per cent of those over 65 live in hospitals.

[10] There was a certain amount of tension with the United States in 1993, when President Bill Clinton accused Malta of violating the UN trade embargo on the Yugoslav Federation.

[11] Tourism was the country's chief economic activity, with one-third of the workforce in this sector and more than one million visitors per year.

[12] In 1993, the EU declared that Malta's democratic stability and its human rights policy were acceptable for its incorporation into the Union. However, its economic structures were considered "archaic" and the implementation of "fundamental economic reforms" was advised.

[13] On January 1 1995 a Value Added Tax came into effect, under criticism from labour unions and shopkeepers.

[14] In the October 1996 elections, the Labour Party took 50.7 per cent of the vote, while the National Party took 47.8 per cent. Alfred Sant became Prime Minister.

[15] Following the elections, the new government withdrew Malta from NATO. Sant said his country would use its constitutional neutrality to promote the stability and security of the

Mediterranean region. He also put the brakes on the programme for entry to the European Union and announced he would be seeking more gradual entry through co-operation or free trade agreements.

[16] The 1997 budget deficit, added to the increased unemployment, and forced the Government to plan austerity measures for 1998.

PROFILE

ENVIRONMENT
Includes five islands, two of which are uninhabited. The inhabited islands are the three largest ones: Malta, where the capital is located, 246 sq km; **Gozo**, 67 sq km; and **Comino**, 3 sq km. The archipelago is located in the Central Mediterranean Sea, south of **Sicily**, east of **Tunis** and north of **Libya**. The coast is high and rocky, with excellent natural harbors. The islands' environmental problems are concentrated precisely in these areas. The problems are caused by the encroachment of civilization, the **development** of tourism, the gradual abandonment of lands devoted to agriculture and the increase in waste. The coastal areas are also polluted by industrial activity.

SOCIETY
Peoples: The Maltese (95.7 per cent) come from numerous ethnic combinations, with strong **Phoenician**, Arab, **Italian** and British roots. There is a small British minority (2.1 per cent).
Religions: mainly **Catholic**.
Languages: Maltese and English, both official.
Political Parties: The **Nationalist** Party (NP); the Labour Party (LP); **Democratic** Alternative.
Social Organizations: The Confederation of Trade Unions.

THE STATE
Official Name: Repubblika ta'Malta.
Capital: Valletta, 9,130 people (1995).
Other cities: Birkirkara, 21,770 people; Qormi 19,904; Hamrun 13,654; **Sliema**, 13,514 (1994).
Government: Ugo Mifsud Bonnici, President since 1994. **Alfred Sant**, Prime Minister since October 1996. Parliamentary Republic.
National Holiday: September 8, Independence day (1964).
Armed Forces: 1,950 troops (1996).

Marshall Islands

Marshall Islands

Population: 57,000 (1996)
Area: 181 SQ KM
Capital: Majuro

Currency: US Dollars
Language: Marshallese and English

The Kwajalein and Bikini atolls of the Marshall Islands were thrust into modern history in February 1944 when heavy bombing by combined US naval and air force units hit the islands. This was followed by a prolonged and bloody battle which ended with the defeat of the Japanese and the occupation of the islands. Countless lives were lost but the military command considered it was a fair price to pay for the islands given their strategic position.

2 In 1979, the US proposed to make an Associated Free State with the four administrative units of the region; the Kwajalein and Bikini atolls, plus the Mariana and Caroline islands which were also trust territories. The Marshall Islands were granted jurisdiction over local and foreign affairs but the US declared the islands military territory for specific use.

3 In 1961, Kwajalein became the Pacific experimental missile target area, especially for intercontinental ballistic missiles launched from California, and early in the 1980s the US chose the atoll as a testing site for its new MX missiles. The local population was totally evicted and entry was forbidden to civilians.

4 Twenty-three nuclear tests were performed there between 1946 and 1958, including the detonation of the first H-bomb. Despite the legacy of cancer, thyroid diseases and leukaemia left behind by the bomb, the inhabitants of the atoll insisted on returning to their homeland after having been transferred to the Rongerik atoll. In 1979, testing revealed that 139 of the total 600 inhabitants living on the Bikini atoll had extremely dangerous levels of plutonium in their bodies.

5 The inhabitants of Bikini, together with those living on Rongelap (also exposed to the radioactivity of the H-bomb dropped on Bikini) sued the US Government for $450 million. Abnormalities already existed in children under 10 years of age and could not be eliminated. The charges were filed together with reports compiled by US Government agencies proving that natives had been intentionally exposed to radioactivity in 1954 in order to study the effects of the bomb on human beings. Reports revealed by the US Government in 1995 proved the dangers of

exposure were known but this had never been passed on to the Marshall Islands population.

6 In April 1990, the US announced that it would use the area to destroy all the nerve gas supplies which had been installed in Europe to date. Environmentalists denounced plans to dispose of 25 million tons of toxic waste on the atoll, between 1989 and 1994.

7 In October 1986, the US and the Marshall Islands signed a pact, whereby the latter became a Free Associated State, responsible for its own internal politics. According to the pact, the US would be responsible for the defence of the new state for a period of 15 years, which would enable the US to have an air base on the island, and the island is also entitled to US financial aid.

8 In the first elections of the new state, held in 1986, Amata Kabua was elected President.

9 In the years following independence, the Marshall Islands attempted to consolidate diplomatic and commercial relations with most of the neighboring states. In 1988 they were admitted in the South Pacific Agreement on Economic Cooperation and Regional Trade, and in 1989 set up diplomatic relations with Japan and Taiwan.

10 On September 17 1990, during the 46th UN General Assembly, held in New York, the Marshall Islands were accepted as a member state of the organization.

11 Foreign affairs minister Tony de Brun founded the Ralik Ratak Democratic Party in June 1991, after becoming estranged from president Kabua. In the November elections, Kabua was re-elected for his fourth consecutive term.

12 That year, a Hawaiian court ordered the suspension of missile testing until the operations' effects on the environment had been assessed. Two years later, local environmentalists protested against an «alternative energy» project based on the burning of discarded tires, considering it a source of atmospheric contamination.

13 The controversy over the use of the Islands resurfaced in 1995 when the Government announced plans to install a nuclear waste dump on Bikini, even though atomic explosions between 1946 and 1958 had made it uninhabitable for a period of 10,000 years.

14 In December 1996, President

Amata Kabua died. In January 1997, Parliament made Imata Kabua, cousin of the late leader, the new President.

15 Opposition from the United States and ecologist organisations finally led the project to store nuclear waste being suspended in June 1997. The Government announced the construction of a massive hotel and casino complex, funded by South Korean capital.

16 This same month, in Majuro, 24 Pacific countries, including the

Marshall Islands, signed an agreement to conserve fishery resources.

17 In February 1998, the Asian Banks said they were satisfied with the government's reforms which had included a reduction in public spending and a 25 per cent drop in the number of state employees. The Government said the measures were related to the ending of its Free Associate State status in 2001, which would mean no more financial aid from the United States.

PROFILE

ENVIRONMENT
A total of 1,152 islands grouped in 34 atolls and 870 reefs. The land area covers 180 sq km, but the islands are scattered over a million sq km in the Pacific. The atolls of Mili, Majuro, Maloelap, Wotje and Likiep lie to the north-east. The south-west atolls are: Jaluit, Kwajalein, Rongelap, Bikini and Enewetak among others. The northern islands receive less rainfall than the southern atolls.

SOCIETY
Peoples: Sixty per cent of the population lives on Majuro and Kwajalein. A large part of Kwajalein's residents consist of US military personnel. **Religions:** Protestant 90.1 per cent; Roman Catholic 8.5 per cent; other 1.4 per cent. **Languages:** Marshallese (kajin-majol), English. **Political Parties:** Ralik Ratak Democratic Party, opposition.

THE STATE
Official Name: Major (Republic of the Marshall Islands) **Administrative divisions:** 25 districts. **Capital:** Majuro, 14,649 people (1988). **Other cities:** Ebeye, 8,324 people (1988). **Government:** Parliamentary Republic. Imata Kabua, President of the local Government since January 1997. A High Commissioner (Janet Mc Coy) is the US Government delegate and handles security, defence and foreign affairs. The constitution provides for a 33-member parliament which appoints the local President. **National Holiday:** December 22.

DEMOGRAPHY
Population: 57,000 (1996) **Annual growth:** 3 % (1980/1996) **Urban population:** 69.6 % (1996).

HEALTH
Infant mortality: 63 per 1,000 (1996) **Under-5 child mortality:** 92 per 1,000 (1996) **Safe water:** 74 % (1990/96).

EDUCATION
Literacy: 91 % (1995) female: 90 % (1995) **School enrolment:** Primary total: 95 % (1990/95)

Martinique

Martinique

Population: 384,000 (1996)
Area: 1,102 SQ KM
Capital: Fort-de-France

Currency: French Francs
Language: French

The Carib indians migrated throughout the central and northern parts of the South American continent, and from there to the nearby islands in the Caribbean. They called the largest of the Lesser Antilles "Madinina", becoming known as Martinique in the colonial period.

[2] The Caribs were primarily hunter-gatherers and banded together to form a small group on the island. The French occupied it in 1635, but economic development did not occur until a century and a half later.

[3] Late in the 17th century, sugar cultivation transformed the natural and economic landscape of the island, ending the indians' lifestyle. The system of production changed on the sugar cane plantations. The indigenous population was replaced by African slaves, brought to the island by slave-traders. This monoculture has since dominated Martinique's economy, reinforcing the colonial ties with France.

[4] A minority of 12,000 European land, sugar mill and business owners dominated 93,000 slave labourers, an imbalance that gave rise to countless uprisings, known as *Marronuage* - meaning collective rebellions of slaves. Accounts written in those days recall the existence of quilombos (see Quilombos in Brazil) on the island in 1811, 1822 and 1833; years when rebellions shook Martinique

[5] In the early 19th century, unprecedented social disturbances occurred as the traditional plantation system was abandoned without investment in industrialization.

[6] In 1937 the formation of Martinique's Central Labor Union, prompted social mobilization.

[7] In 1946, the French Government revised its approach to colonial relations, creating the Overseas Departments in 1948. At first, the Martinican middle class had hoped to have the same rights as French citizens, but lack of consensus within the anti-colonial movement hampered the achievement of this goal.

[8] In the March 1986 elections, the left-wing parties obtained 21 of the 41 seats on the Regional Council. Aimé Césaire, representing the leftist coalition, was re-elected president of the Council. Rodolphe Désiré became Martinique's first left-wing party (PPM) representative in the French Senate.

[9] In 1992, the establishment of a single European market worsened the island's economic situation. In the elections that year there was a tied vote between the Right on the one side and the pro-independence and Left parties on the other. In the plebiscite to ratify the Maastricht Treaty, the abstention rate was 75 per cent, showing hostility or at least a passive approach toward a deeper integration of the island into the European Union (EU).

[10] Other signs of hostility toward the EU were the demonstrations of banana producers, who protested against the opening of the European market to imports from Africa and Latin America, where fruits are cheaper than in the "French" Antilles. The crisis worsened in 1994 with a 20 per cent increase in unemployment and a noticeable drop in corporate investments.

[11] The future of the island caused disagreements between the various Martinique parties and was the object of intense debate during 1995 and 1996. While the Communist Party proposed greater autonomy without attempting to gain independence, the Martinique Independence Movement (MIM) called for negotiations for sovereignty.

[12] In 1997, the US continued to favour Central American banana production over than of the Caribbean producers, including the most important groups of Martinique and Guadeloupe, called on the European Union to revise its prices in line with increasing production costs.

[13] Social tension increased in early 1998. Unemployment affected 40 per cent of the active population, the highest level in national history. Strikes and demonstrations, mainly in the health and transport sectors, followed one after another, calling for employment, pay increases and better working conditions.

[14] Claude Lise, of the Progressive Party of Martinique, was re-elected in March 1998 to lead the General Council, one of the nation's two assemblies. However, the elections showed increased support for the MIM, which became the dominant force in the Council.

PROFILE

Environment
Martinique is a volcanic island, one of the Windward Islands of the Lesser Antilles. Mount Pelée, whose eruption in 1902 destroyed the city of Saint Pierre is a dominant feature of the mountainous terrain. The fertile land is suitable for agriculture, especially sugar cane. The tropical, humid climate is tempered by sea winds.

Society
Peoples: Descendants of former enslaved Africans (90 per cent). There is a minority made up of people of European origin (5 per cent), Indian, Lebanese and Chinese (5 per cent). **Religions:** Catholic (95 per cent) and traditional African rites (5 per cent). **Languages:** French (official), and Creole. **Political Parties:** Communist Party of Martinique, (PCM); Progressive Party of Martinique (PPM); Union of Martinican Democrats, (UDM); Socialist Party (SP); National Martinican Front for Autonomoy; Democrat Union of Martinique (DUM); Socialist Revolution Group; Martinican Independence Movement (MIM). **Social Organizations:** General Confederation of Workers

The State
Official Name: Département d'Outre-Mer de la Martinique. **Capital:** Fort-de-France, 101,540 people (1990). **Other cities:** Le Marin; La Trinité. **Government:** Jean François Cordet French appointed commissioner. Claude Lise, re-elected in 1998 as General Council President. The Council's 36 members are elected through universal suffrage for 6-year terms.

STATISTICS

DEMOGRAPHY
Population: 384,000 (1996) **Urban population:** 93.7 % (1996).

ECONOMY
Consumer price index: 113.3 (1994) **Cereal imports:** 66 metric tons (1994) **Fertilizer use:** 7,777 kgs per ha (1994).

Mauritania

Mauritanie

Population: 2,333,000 (1996)
Area: 1,025,520 SQ KM
Capital: Nouakchott

Currency: Ouguiya
Language: Arabic and French

The process of desertification that turned fertile plains into the Sahara desert, would have separated southern Berbers from the Mediterranean coast if camels had not been introduced into the area. The groups that migrated southward in search of pastures kept in touch with their native culture, and later shared the benefits of the Islamic civilization, which flourished along the Mediterranean coast.

[2] The southern part of present-day Mauritania was the setting for one of the most peculiar African civilizations. But the Almoravid conquest and later the Fulah migrations stimulated the integration and unification of the population.

[3] In the 14th century, the Beni Hilal, who had invaded North Africa three centuries before, reached Mauritania. For over 200 years, they plundered the region and warred with the Berbers throughout an area including present-day southern Algeria and Sahara. In 1644, all the Berber groups in the region joined to fight the Arabs, but the resulting conflict, the Cherr Baba War, ended 30 years later with the defeat of the Berbers. The Arabs became a warrior caste, known as the Hassani, monopolizing the use of weapons, while trade, education and other civilian activities were left in the hands of the local population. Beneath these two groups came the haratan, African shepherds from the south, kept as semi-serfs. Though this rigid social stratification weakened with time, it is still intact among the Arab-Berbers, the Fulah and Soninke.

[4] Towards the end of the 17th century various emirates arose. These were unable to achieve the political organization of the country, due to their internal rivalries and dynastic quarrels. Nevertheless, they provided a minimal degree of order within the region which led, in turn, to a small revival of trade caravans. These efforts were supported by the cultural unification being carried out by the zuaias. These Berber-Marabouts devised a simple system of Arabic writing, propagating it along with their religious teachings.

[5] In the 19th century, growing trade coincided with a French project to transfer Sudanese commercial activities to Senegal (see Mali), requiring the elimination of trans-Saharan trade and the frequent robberies in Senegal. The French therefore invaded Mauritania in 1858, under General Faidherbe, and the fighting continued until the 20th century. The resistance initially met in the emirates of Trarza and Brakna continued with the Sheikh Ma al-Aini (see Sahara), with his sons and later his cousin, Muhammad al-Mamun, the emir of Adrar. Pursued by the French almost a 1,000 km into the Sahara, Muhammad al-Mamun died in combat in 1934.

[6] After World War II, Mauritania became a French Overseas Province, sending deputies to the French Parliament. Ten years later internal autonomy was granted and in 1960 independence was gained. Lacking infrastructure and administrative capacities, the potential government officials were five university graduates and fifteen students.

[7] A French transnational company, MIFERMA, was more powerful than the Government. MIFERMA's iron ore mines supplied 80 per cent of the country's exports and employed one in four salaried workers.

[8] The progressive PPM wing gradually gained ground and created a desire for true independence. In 1965 Mauritania withdrew from OCAM (the Common Afro-Mauritanian Organization), created to maintain French control over their former colonies.

[9] In 1966, the Government set up a state company, SOMITEX, with a monopoly on sugar, rice and tea imports, and a campaign was launched to rekindle the Arab culture. Mauritania set up its own customs system independent from Senegal; the Arab-Mauritanian Bank was granted the monopoly on foreign trade and the country began to issue its own currency.

[10] In 1974 the iron mines were nationalized. The country started to replace French influence by closer links with Muslim countries, and finally became a member of the Arab League. Saudi Arabia, Kuwait, and Morocco supplied economic assistance.

[11] In 1975 Mauritania, fulfilling an old ambition to annex part of Sahara, joined Morocco in an attempt to divide the Spanish possession. With logistic and military support from France, 3,000 Mauritanian soldiers and 10,000 Moroccan troops occupied Sahara.

[12] Ould Haidalla's government paid an extremely high price for this aggression. Mauritania soon became the target of violent reprisals by the Polisario Front (see Sahara-Western) and was virtually occupied by Moroccan troops.

[13] Economic hardships aroused widespread popular unrest leading to protest rallies and street fighting. Opposition groups condemned Mauritanian interference in the Saharan liberation war.

[14] The crisis exploded in 1978 and over the next six years there were five coups. An attempt was made to Arabize the whole population, ignoring the African population (20 per cent), living in the southern part of the country.

[15] Ould Haidalla's government ended the Arabization process of total and also relinquished Mauritania's claim to the Sahara, making peace with the Polisario Front in August 1979. With the

PER 100,000
LIVE BIRTHS
930

38%

PROFILE

ENVIRONMENT

Two thirds of the country are occupied by the Sahara Desert. The terrain consists of rocky, dry plateaus and vast expanses of dunes where extremely dry climate prevails. The desert region reaches into the southern part of the country, the Sahel grasslands, with some rainfall and sparse vegetation. The southwestern region receives slightly more rain and is irrigated by a tributary of the Senegal river. This region holds most of the population and the main economic activities. Nomadic shepherds are scattered throughout the country. Desertification is a serious problem for Mauritania.

SOCIETY

Peoples: Three-fourths of all Mauritanians are descendents of the Moors; a mixture of Arab, Berber and African peoples, nomadic shepherds of north-west Africa. The other 25 per cent are from African groups in the south, the most important being the Peul and the Soninke. There are small groups of Wolof and Bambara.
Religions: Muslim 99.5 percent (official and predominant), Catholics 0.2 per cent.
Languages: Arabic and French (official). The Moors speak Bassanya, an Arab dialect. In southern Mauritania, Peul-Fulani and Sarakole (of the Soninke) are also spoken.
Political Parties: Democratic and Social Republican Party; Union of Democratic Forces-New Era (UDF-EN); Union for Democracy and Progress (UDP); Movement of Independent Democrats.
Social Organizations: Workers' Union of Mauritania.

THE STATE

Official Name: al-Jumhuriyah al-Islamiyah al-Muritaniyah
Administrative divisions: 12 regions and the district of Nouakchott.
Capital: Nouakchott, 500,800 people (1994).
Other cities: Nouadhibou 72,305; Kaédi 35,241; Kiffa 29,300; Rosso 27,783 (1992).
Government: Maawiya Ould Sid'Ahmed Taya, President since 1984, re elected in December 1997. Mohamed Lemine Ould Guig, Prime Minister since December, 1997.
National Holiday: November 28, Independence Day (1960).
Armed Forces: 15,600.
Other: 6,000 (National Guard and Gendarmes).

support of young officers and intellectuals from the left, a decree was signed abolishing slavery in Mauritania.
[16] A coup occurred on December 11 1984. Maawiya Ould Sid'Ahmed Taya, an army colonel and chief of staff, ousted Haidallah. The first measures of the new administration were the recognition of the Democratic Saharawi Arab Republic (Western Sahara) and steps to

MILITARY EXPENDITURE

MILITARY (as % of health and education expenditures-1990/91) **40%**

dismantle a growing "clandestine economy" (only 50 per cent of the firms operating in the country kept legal accounting records).
[17] In April 1985 the IMF announced that a $12 million standby credit had been granted to Mauritania under an agreement to restructure foreign debt. Conditions were particularly harsh for a country with a depleted agrarian economy affected by a persistent process of desertification and an annual grain deficit of 12,000 tons.
[18] The economic and social outlook deteriorated; the southern farming and grazing lands reduced as the desert

expanded, and the impoverished nomadic people were driven to the cities.
[19] In the fishing sector the Government adopted a long-term strategy, with two objectives: on the one hand, to save resources, and on the other, to integrate the fishing industry into the rest of the economy. No new licences are being given to foreign fishing fleets.
[20] Since 1987, a number of incidents have occurred between farmers and cattle herders in the border area along the Senegal River. In Nouakchott, many angry Mauritanians attacked hundreds of unarmed Senegalese with sticks and stones in 1989. In Dakar, Senegalese returning from Mauritania reported assassinations and mutilations of their compatriots in Mauritania. Scores of furious Senegalese reacted by murdering Mauritanian shop-keepers, and looting their shops. Within the country, there have been instances of violence between African Mauritanians from the south and Arabs and Berbers from the rest of the country. Throughout these events, the army supported the Arabs and Berbers, killing hundreds of African Mauritanians.
[21] Repeated border incidents with Senegal, leading to hundreds of victims on both sides, prompted Senegal to break diplomatic relations in August 1989. Thousands of refugees returned to their country of origin: 170,000 returned to Mauritania.
[22] In July 1991, the Mauritanians approved a referendum that recognized a multi-party system and established a democratic government. The opposition, concentrated in the United Democratic Front (FDU) exerted pressure on the Government to achieve this objective, but by early 1991 the only response from the Government had been increased repression. In spite of the constitutional reform, social tensions caused by the crisis did not decrease. A period of great social conflict ensued, and the majority of the population went on strike.
[23] Six months later, in January

1992, President Maawiya Ould Sid Ahmed Taya was re-elected, in the first multiparty elections to be held. The opposition and numerous international observers suspected a fraud. Taya defeated his main rival, Ahmed Ould Daddah, winning 63 per cent of the vote to Daddah's 33. In March, after two rounds of voting in the legislative election, the DSRP (the official party) achieved an absolute majority in the National Assembly, winning 67 of the 79 disputed seats.
[24] Six opposition groups boycotted the voting and denounced there had been a fraud in the elections. In April, Mauritania re-established diplomatic relations with Senegal and Mali. This allowed to resume negotiations on pending border disputes and to find a possible solution for the situation of Mauritanian refugees in both neighbouring countries.
[25] Foreign aid granted by China and France gave new impetus to Taya's discredited government, accused of electoral fraud and of being responsible for the country's difficult social conditions. The application of an IMF-sponsored adjustment plan further aggravated mounting tensions, peaking in October when the prices of basic consumer goods were increased.
[26] Protest demonstrations were widespread and harshly quelled by the police. In early 1993, Interior minister Ba Aliu Ibra Hasni Uld Dudi was forced to resign and was replaced by a "moderate" official. In January 1994, the ruling party won the local elections, also considered a fraud by opposition members. In May, the Government tried to prevent Le Calame newspaper from being issued since it included a report on Mauritania by the Human Rights International Association.
[27] Sixty Islamic leaders were arrested in October, on charges of creating an atmosphere of fear. Afterward, the Government ordered all "fundamentalist" militants to cease political activity.
[28] In January 1995, thousands of demonstrators rocked Nouakchott, setting cars on fire and looting shops after a new

DEMOGRAPHY
Population: 2,333,000 (1996) **Annual growth:** 2.6% (1980/1996) **Estimates for year 2000:** 2,600,000 **Annual growth to year 2000:** 2.6% (1994/2000) **Urban Population:** 52.7% (1996) **Urban growth:** 6.83% (1980/95) **Children per woman:** 5.1 (1996).

HEALTH
Life expectancy at birth: 53 years (1996) male: 51 years (1996) female: 54 years (1996) **Infant mortality:** 124 per 1,000 (1996) **Under-5 child mortality:** 183 per 1,000 (1996) **Calorie consumption:** 106% (1988/90) 16,667 **people per doctor** (1988/91) **Safe water:** 74% (1990/96).

EDUCATION
Literacy: 38% (1995) male : 50% (1995) female: 26% (1995) **School enrolment :** Primary total: 74% (1990/95) male : 81% (1990/95) female: 66% (1990/95) Secondary: male : 19% (1990/95) female: 11% (1990/95) Tertiary: 4% (1995) **Primary school teachers:** one for every 52 students (1995).

COMMUNICATIONS
147 **radios**, 40 **TV sets** and 4 **main telephone lines** per 1,000 people (1994).

ECONOMY
Per capita, GNP: $ 470 (1996) **Annual growth, GNP:** 1.8% (1995/96) **Annual inflation:** 6.93% (1985/95) **Currency:** 137.11 ouguiyas = $ 1 (1995) **Cereal imports:** 206 metric tons (1994) **Food import dependency:** 49% (1994) **Fertilizer use:** 192 kgs per ha (1994) **Exports:** $ 574 million (1996) **Imports:** $ 616 million (1996) **External debt:** $ 2,363 million (1996) $ 1,013 **per capita:** (1996) **Debt service:** 21.7% of exports (1996) **Development aid received:** $ 220 million (1995) $ 99 per capita (1995) 22.6% of GNP (1994).

ENERGY
Consumption: 103.32 Kgs of Oil equivalent per capita yearly (1994) 100.00% imported (1994).

HDI (rank / value) 150 / 0.355 (1994)

Food Dependency

1970
23%

1994
49%

External Debt

1996

PER CAPITA
$1,013

valued added tax caused a rise in prices. In June, Mauritania's creditors accepted a renegotiation of the public debt which was then partially cancelled.

[29] In January 1996, President Taya made El Afia Ould Mohamed Khouna, the fisheries minister, Prime Minister. Most of the opposition boycotted the April elections for a new Senate. The Democratic and Social Republican Party (PRSD), won the majority of the disputed seats in the Senate and, in the October legislative elections, took 71 of the 79 seats in the National Assembly.

[30] In June 1996, an agreement with the European Union gave Mauritania access to set figure credits for five years, in return for permission to fish its national waters, considered the richest in the world. International bodies said the nation's macroeconomic performance improved. However, it continued to rank amongst the poorest nations of the world in its social indicators.

[31] In December 1997, President Taya was re-elected with nearly 90 per cent of the vote, making Mohamed Lemine Ould Guig prime minister.

[32] In April 1998, Human Rights organizations appealed for an end to slavery in Mauritania. Three human rights activists were imprisoned for denouncing cases of practices of slavery.

Fishing: end of the line?

Four of the 15 main fishing regions of the world have already been decimated, and nine are well on the way to becoming exhausted. The Food and Agriculture Organization (FAO) warns that this crisis is a direct consequence of the over-exploitation of marine resources at the hands of the fishing industry

Marine fishing has shot up in the last 50 years. In 1952, 18.5 million tons of fish were extracted, but by the late 1980s this figure had risen to 89 million tons.

The commercialization of sea products which has led to this over-exploitation, is threatening to do away with certain species, like Canadian cod, forever.

Marine diversity is threatened by this relentless race to satisfy increasing world demand. In the United States alone, according to official figures, 80 per cent of the marine population (of more than 100 species) are in danger of extinction.

Millions of people whose way of life depends on fishing (both commercialized and subsistence) are today up against the exhaustion of these resources and extremely unequal competition with an industry supplied by the great fishing fleets.

Commercial competition made the fishing industries increase the volume of catches using equipment so indiscriminate that it kills many species which are not even eaten. Furthermore, enormous drag nets damage the sea bed, destroying marine habitats and coral reefs.

The FAO has forecast that if this situation continues, marine resources will soon be insufficient to meet human needs.

This threat is especially worrying for the millions of people living along the rivers of the Third World, for whom fish is the main source of protein.

Mauritius

Mauritius

Population: 1,129,000 (1996)
Area: 2,040 SQ KM
Capital: Port Louis

Currency: Rupee
Language: English

According to Portuguese accounts, the island of Mauritius was deserted when they first explored it in the 16th century. The island was immediately coveted by the imperial powers, who fought over it ceaselessly by both diplomatic and military means. Between 1598 and 1710, the Dutch, attracted by the island's ebony, installed themselves and named it Mauritius. In 1715, it was recolonized by the French Bourbons, who renamed it Ile de France. When rivalry between France and Britain recurred over the control of India, the island of Mauritius constituted an important strategic base. The island was used in trade with India, and treaties were signed with Madagascar and Mozambique to use their coasts to expand sugar cane plantations.

[2] During the French Revolution, Mauritius acquired a certain degree of autonomy but in 1810, it fell into British hands. In 1815, after Napoleon's defeat, the Treaty of Paris recognized the status of the island as a British colony. The British introduced sugar cane which became the island's main economic resource right up until the present.

[3] In the 19th century, sugar plantations expanded considerably, but in 1835 the emancipation of slaves, who constituted 70 per cent of the population, caused a serious labor shortage. Emancipation was opposed by the European landowners, who tried to alleviate the situation by importing over 450,000 Indian indentured "hired" workers over the next 100 years. With the passage of time, the Indians became an increasingly important

sector of the Mauritian social and economic structure, and today their descendants constitute the majority of the Mauritian population. Local culture however still bears the mark of French influence.

[4] In 1936, the Labor Party was organized but a series of strikes were brutally repressed, causing the death, imprisonment or exile of most party leaders. Seewooagur Ramgoolam, a doctor, started his political career as the leader of the Advance group. In the late 1940s, encouraged by the colonial administration, he became leader of the Labor Party of Mauritius (PLM).

[5] During World War II, the British were unable to guarantee the security of their colonial dominions, which encouraged the emergence of claims for independence. At the same time, US political and military influence increased. The inhabitants of Mauritius fought for and achieved representation within British colonial government. In 1957, a new government structure was created, giving Mauritius its own prime minister. In 1959, the first elections with universal suffrage brought the PLM to power, making Seewooagur Ramgoolam prime minister in 1961.

[6] From Mauritius, the British administration ran the islands of Rodrigues, Cargados-Carajos and the Chagos archipelago. In 1965, with the approval of Ramgoolam, Chagos and other islands became the British Indian Ocean Territories, and the United States established a major naval base on one of its islands, Diego García.

[7] The local population was secretly transferred to Mauritius, a move that caused a scandal in

Congress when it was later made public. However, the island was not returned to Mauritius and its inhabitants were not granted permission to return home.

[8] Mauritius became independent in 1968, after a long decolonization process. Britain expected the process to end with the granting of a very limited autonomy for the island, allowing it merely to solve its domestic affairs. The 1958 Constitution, which is still in force, was created by the Colonial Office following the usual model used in the Commonwealth. Mauritius was a monarchy, ruled by Elizabeth II, and the sovereign was represented by a Governor-General and a High Commissioner. In 1964, the Council of Ministers and the Legislative Assembly were created. The latter appoints the Prime Minister (head of government) and the rest of the ministerial cabinet.

[9] On independence there was an established two-party system in the country. The Labor Party, supported by the Indian population, was the majority party until 1958. That year, the French-Mauritians and Creoles gathered in the Social Democratic Party of Mauritius (PSDM), and Muslim groups founded the Muslim Action Committee. During the 1960s, the common struggle for independence drew the Indian Labor groups and Muslims

together, and in 1967 they formed an alliance which took them to power. Sir Seegwooagur Ramgoolam was re-elected Prime Minister, and Gaetan Duval, the leader of the PSDM, led the group which opposed independence. In 1969, a coalition government was formed with the Labor Party and the PSDM. Duval, the representative of the French elite and the main opponent to independence, became foreign minister, showing that the British-granted independence was a mere formality.

[10] Internally, the government was tainted by electoral fraud and trade union repression, and in foreign affairs, it established close links with Israel and South Africa. Pretoria had a free zone in Port Louis which enabled it to trade with the EEC, thus evading international sanctions.

[11] In the 1970s a new opposition group emerged, called the Militant Mauritian Movement (MMM). It denounced the alliance between the Labor Party and the former French settlers. The growth of the MMM and the general deterioration of the political environment led to the legislative elections scheduled for 1972, being postponed until 1976. The MMM was the best supported party in the 1976 elections, but the Labor party succeeded in forming weak alliances with

WORKERS

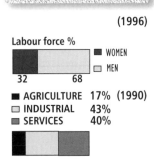

(1996)

Labour force %

■ WOMEN
□ MEN

32   68

■ AGRICULTURE 17% (1990)
□ INDUSTRIAL 43%
▪ SERVICES 40%

LAND USE

IRRIGATED 17% % of arable

(1993)

▪ FOREST & WOODLAND 21.6%
□ ARABLE 49%
▪ OTHER 29.4%

PROFILE

ENVIRONMENT

This island, located in the Indian Ocean, 800 sq km east of Madagascar, is 53 km wide and 72 km long. Mauritius also controls several dependencies: Rodrigues Island, 104 sq km with 23,000 inhabitants who farm and fish; Agalega, 69 sq km with 400 inhabitants, producing copra; and Saint Brandon, 22 small islands inhabited by people who fish and collect guano. The islands are of volcanic origin, surrounded by coral reefs. The terrain climbs from a coastal lowland to a central plain enclosed by mountains. Heavy rainfall contributes to the fertility of the red tropical soils. Sugar cane is the main crop. The degradation of the soil, due to monoculture and use of pesticides, and water pollution are the most serious environmental problems.

SOCIETY

Peoples: Indo-Pakistani 68.0 per cent; Creole (mixed Caucasian, Indo-Pakistani, and African) 27.0 per cent; Chinese 3.0 per cent.
Religions: 50.6 per cent Hindu; 27.2 per cent Christian (mostly Catholic, with an Anglican minority); 16.3 per cent Muslim; 0.3 per cent Buddhist; 2 per cent other.
Languages: English (official) 29.1 per cent. Creole 21.6 per cent. Hindi 18.6 per cent. Bhojpuri (a Hindi dialect), Urdu, Hakka, French, Chinese, Tamil, Arabic, Marati, Telegu, and other languages are also spoken.
Political Parties: Mauritian Social Democratic Party (PMSD). Mauritian Socialist Movement (MSM); Militant Mauritian Movement (MMM); Mauritian Militant Renaissance (RMM); **Social Organizations:** General Workers' Federation (GWF); Mauritian Women's Committee.

THE STATE

Official Name: State of Mauritius.
Administrative divisions: 4 islands and 9 districts.
Capital: Port Louis, 144,776 people (1994).
Other cities: Rose Hill, 96,621 people; Curepipe, 76,610 people; Quatre Bornes, 73,500 (1994).
Government: Parliamentary republic. Cassam Uteem, President since 1992, re-elected in June 1997. Navin Ramgoolam, Prime Minister since December 1995. Legislature: single-chamber: National Assembly, with 72 members, elected every 5 years.
National Holiday: March 12, Independence Day (1968).
Armed Forces: non-existent.
Other: 1,300 elite forces.

STATISTICS

DEMOGRAPHY

Population: 1,129,000 (1996) **Annual growth:** 1% (1980/1996) **Estimates for year 2000:** 1,200,000 **Annual growth to year 2000:** 1.1% (1994/2000) **Urban Population:** 40.6% (1996) **Urban growth:** 0.61% (1980/95) **Children per woman:** 2.3 (1996).

HEALTH

Life expectancy at birth: 71 years (1996) male: 67 years (1994) female: 74 years (1994) **Infant mortality:** 20 per 1,000 (1996) **Under-5 child mortality:** 23 per 1,000 (1996) **Calorie consumption:** 128% (1988/90) 1,176 **people per doctor** (1988/91) **Safe water:** 98% (1990/96).

EDUCATION

Literacy: 83% (1995) male : 87% (1995) female: 79% (1995) **School enrolment :** Primary total: 106% (1990/95) male : 107% (1990/95) female: 106% (1990/95) Secondary: male : 58% (1990/95) female: 60% (1990/95) Tertiary: 6% (1995) **Primary school teachers:** one for every 22 students (1995).

COMMUNICATIONS

70 **newspapers,** 367 **radios,** 190 **TV sets** and 117 **main telephone lines** per 1,000 people (1994) **Books:** 8 new titles per 100,000 people (1992/94).

ECONOMY

Per capita, GNP: $ 3,710 (1996) **Annual growth, GNP:** 4.5% (1995/96) **Annual inflation:** 8.83% (1985/95) **Consumer price index:** 132.8 (1994) **Currency:** 17.66 rupee = $ 1 (1995) **Cereal imports:** 255 metric tons (1994) **Food import dependency:** 12% (1994) **Fertilizer use:** 2,754 kgs per ha (1994) **Exports:** $ 1,699 million (1996) **Imports:** $ 2,255 million (1996) **External debt:** $ 1,818 million (1996) $ 1,610 **per capita:** (1996) **Debt service:** 7.2% of exports (1996) **Development aid received:** $ 23 million (1995) $ 21 per capita (1995) 0.7% of GNP (1994).

ENERGY

Consumption: 387.24 Kgs of Oil equivalent per capita yearly (1996) 92.11% imported (1994).

HDI (rank / value) 61 / 0.831 (1994)

---

certain minority groups, managing to stay in power. The workers' demonstrations and the social unrest caused by unemployment increased, reaching their peak in 1979.
[12] In the 1982 elections, the MMM, allied with the Socialist Party of Mauritius (PSM) and won with a landslide majority. This gave them control of 62 of the 66 seats and full control of the Government. Aneerood Jugnauth became Prime Minister. The government program of the MMM-PSM alliance promised to increase job opportunities and salaries, nationalize key sectors in the economy, reduce economic links with South Africa, and demand the return of Diego Garcia from the US.
[13] The increase in the price of oil, coupled with the drop in the world price of sugar, caused a deficit in the balance of payments equal to 12 percent of the gross domestic product. The Government was forced to turn to the IMF which approved five stand-by loans between 1979 and 1985.
[14] To receive these loans, the Government had to agree to a series of conditions imposed by the IMF; to adopt austerity measures, to postpone part of the planned salary increase and job creation programs, to relinquish part of its control over public expenditure, to cut subsidies on basic foods and to devalue the Mauritian rupee.
[15] All these measures led to clashes between the MMM and the socialists, a situation which eventually led to a call for early elections, in August of that year. The MMM was defeated and a new coalition was formed including labor, socialists and Duval's social-democrats. However, this apparent political stability was very weak and was followed by a series of governmental alliances which did not consolidate the coalition's position. Majority parties underwent serious divisions, giving rise to new political groups such as the Mauritius Socialist Movement (MSM), a splinter of the PSM, led by the current president Aneerood Jugnauth.
[16] The main economic potential lies in manufacture, in particular in textiles. The industrial free zones employ 90,000 people, around 10 per cent of the population, and the per capita income of the population in Mauritius is three or four times higher than the average for other African countries, though inflation is increasing at an annual rate of 16 per cent. The lack of skilled labor on Mauritius could bring a new migratory wave from Madagascar, India, and Kenya.
[17] In 1988, in agreement with the Organization of African Unity

Maternal Mortality
1990
PER 100,000 LIVE BIRTHS
120

Literacy
1995
83%

External Debt
1996
PER CAPITA
$1,610

(OAU), Mauritius again demanded the devolution of the island of Tromelin, administered by France, and of the Chagos archipelago, along with the demilitarization of the Indian Ocean, which is used for manoeuvres by the superpowers. Their claims are supported by environmentalist groups, because of the proliferation of nuclear weapons in the claimed territories.
[18] In the legislative elections of December, 1987, the coalition of MSM, PSDM and Labor won a very narrow victory, giving it a majority in parliament. Aneerood Jugnauth was re-elected prime minister, and the MMM became the main opposition force.
[19] In the legislative elections held in September 1991 the governing MSM succeeded in maintaining Jugnauth in the post of Prime Minister, by reinforcing the traditional alliance with the MMM. In March 1992, Mauritius changed from a constitutional monarchy to a republic, and in June Cassam

Uteem became the first President of the country.
[20] In August 1993, the Foreign Minister Paul Bérenger, of the MMM, withdrew from the cabinet, leaving Jugnauth without an absolute majority. In 1994, the island's economic results were still regarded as satisfactory by international agencies such as the World Bank. The foreign debt accounted for 25 per cent of the GDP and the per capita income was 2,740 dollars.

[21] In January 1995, Jugnauth included representatives of the right-wing Social Democratic Party of Mauritius in his government. In the legislative elections of December, an opposition coalition (the Militant Mauritian Movement-Labour Party) led by Paul Bérenger and Nuvin Rangoolam took two thirds of the seats. Rangoolam became Prime Minister.
[22] The social indicators in Mauritius improved in 1996. Life expectancy reached an average of 70 years and literacy reached 81.7 per cent. Most of the population had access to healthcare, and 99 per cent to clean drinking water and drainage.
[23] In June 1997, the MMM left the governing coalition. Rangoolam took over the functions of foreign minister when Bérenger abandoned the post. A few days later, Parliament re-elected Cassam Uteem president.

Diego García

Population: 1,000 (1996)
Area: 52 SQ KM

The settlement of Diego García began in 1776, when the French Viscount de Souillac sent a ship there from Mauritius, trying to establish French presence before the English could get there. French entrepreneurs obtained permission to exploit all of the island's riches; coconuts (for coconut oil), giant tortoises, fish and birds, and they established a leper colony on the island. With the defeat of Napoleon in 1815, the island passed into the hands of the British Crown, together with Mauritius's other dependencies. During the 19th century, many workers came from India and Africa. The risk of catching leprosy, especially among men, and the demanding nature of their work, gave rise to a matriarchal family organization.
[2] Around 1900, there were approximately 500 inhabitants, but the population increased radically over the next decades, with the arrival of Africans, Madagascans and Indians. Once they had settled, they developed a culture of their own. They spoke creole, a mixture of their local languages and they took part in the Tamul rituals (of Madagascan origin) even though they were mostly Roman Catholic. The indigenous Chagos community, the Ilois, had lived in their traditional manner, and this remained practically unchanged until the 1960s.
[3] In 1965, Britain decided to

remove Diego García from Mauritian jurisdiction, annexing it to the BIOT (British Indian Ocean Territory). Although this change was condemned by the UN, the British and Mauritian governments made a deal where a large sum changed hands. Two years later, Britain ceded the island to the United States for 50 years, in exchange for a discount on its purchase of nuclear arms. To make way for the construction of important air and naval bases, the Ilois were deported to Mauritius, in the early 1970s.
[4] The 2,000 or so Ilois were abandoned as soon as they arrived in the port of Mauritius, finding themselves in a situation of total indigence; they had not been allowed to keep a single belonging and they suffered the effects of being uprooted. Many died of despair or hunger, and to this day they lack the basic human right of having a nationality. The British Government does not recognize them as subjects, and the Mauritian Government does not consider them to be citizens. Ilois attempts to return to their land became increasingly numerous, as did their demands for a solution to their problems, and they began to receive the support of international opinion. The declarations of this situation reached the United States Senate in 1975, but to this day, both the US and British governments

have continued to ignore the real problem, each blaming the other for the situation and both spending intermittent sums of money, which do nothing more than temporarily alleviate the severity of the problem. A report issued by the Mauritian Government in 1981 revealed that 77 per cent of the Ilois wished to return to their homeland.
[5] In the meantime, the Government of Mauritius has decided to stop shipping foodstuffs and supplies to Diego García, by

way of reiterating its desire to recover the islands.
[6] Between 1992 and 1993, the Government issued repeated claims to the Chagos archipelago, including Diego García, before the UN and the International Court of Justice. In reprisal, Britain cut economic aid to the country.
[7] In July 1997, just as Britain turned Hong Kong over to Chinese control, Mauritius demanded that the British Prime Minister, Tony Blair, return Diego García to Mauritius.

PROFILE

ENVIRONMENT
The Chagos Archipelago is located some 1,600 km southwest of India, in the middle of the Indian Ocean. The main islands are Diego García (8 km long by 6 km wide), Chagos, Peros, Banhaus and Solomon. The islands are made up of coral formations and are flat; they have a large number of coconut trees, which grow well here because of the tropical climate and year-round rain.

SOCIETY
Peoples: All of the inhabitants are American or British military personnel.
Social Organizations: Lalit, local movement that demands the de-militarization of all the archipelago's islands and the devolution of Diego Garcia to Mauritius.

THE STATE
Government: It is nominally exercised by an English commissioner from the Foreign Office in London.
Armed Forces: 25-strong Royal Navy detachment.

Mexico

México

Population: 92,718,000 (1996)
Area: 1,958,201 SQ KM
Capital: Mexico City

Currency: New Peso
Language: Spanish

The 20,000-year history of the present Mexican territory includes only 2,000 years of urban life. Over this period, meso-American peoples developed advanced civilizations such as the Olmeca, Teotihuacan, Maya and Mexica. These cultures had complex political and social organizations, and they had advanced artistic, scientific, and technological skills.

[2] When the Spaniards arrived, Moctezuma II, Emperor of the Aztecs, ruled over an empire the size of modern Italy, with the capital, Tenochtitlan, under the present Mexico City. The conquest was completed in 1521, when Spanish explorer Hernan Cortes took advantage of internal strife between the ruling Aztecs and other native peoples who paid them tribute. Cortes succeeded in imposing Spanish domination over the local armies and, from then on, the colonials initiated Christianization and Hispanization of the indigenous inhabitants.

[3] In the 17th century, the major economic structures of the so-called 'New Spain' were laid down. The *hacienda*, a landed estate, emerged as the basic production unit, and mining became the basis of a colonial economy conceived to meet the gold and silver needs of the Spanish motherland. The American indian population was over-exploited and decimated by hard labor and disease. By 1800, Mexico had become one of the world's richest countries, a nation of great wealth and great poverty.

[4] After almost three centuries of colonial domination, in 1810 the struggle for independence began, led by *criollos* (Mexicans of Spanish descent) such as Miguel Hidalgo

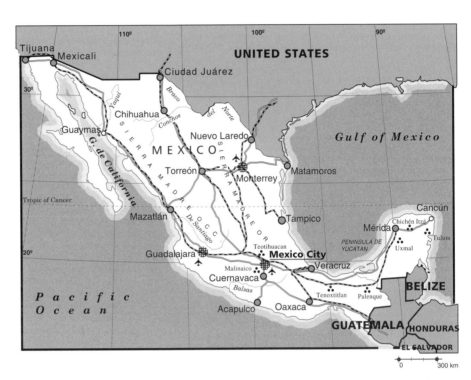

and José Maria Morelos, two priests. The struggle became a broad-based national movement as indians and mestizos (people of mixed European and indian descent) joined its ranks, but the rebels were soon crushed by the royal army. The liberal revolution in Spain radically changed the situation. Afraid to lose their privileges, the Spanish residents and the conservative clergy came to an agreement with the surviving revolutionaries. This pact became known as the Iguala Plan: trading independence for a guaranteed continuation of Spanish dominance. In 1821 General Iturbide proclaimed

himself Emperor, but was rapidly replaced by General Antonio López de Santa Anna.

[5] At the time, Mexico was the most extensive Spanish American country, covering 4.6 million square kilometres, including the Central American provinces, but it was also stricken by economic, political and social problems. In 1824, a Constitution was approved establishing a federal republic, made up of 19 states, four regions and a federal district. In 1836, Santa Anna, elected President three years previously, passed a new Constitution which did away with all vestiges of federalism and the Mexican state of Texas, which had been settled by some 30,000 US citizens, called on the United States for support and protection. Santa Anna led his army to victory against the Texans that year at the Alamo, but was defeated by US troops which took him prisoner later releasing for a large ransom.

[6] In 1845, the United States annexed Texas, which led to a break in diplomatic relations with Mexico, as well as causing a frontier conflict, as the United States claimed the southern border of Texas was on the Rio Bravo, not the Rio Nueces, as was commonly accepted, considerably

further north. In 1846, the US president James Polk tried to force through a frontier agreement and buy the state of California, both of which moves were rejected by Mexico. Polk ordered the US army to occupy the disputed lands between the two rivers, causing a war which lasted two years and was won by the United States. The victors annexed all Mexican territory north of the Rio Bravo, paying 15 million dollars and taking responsibility for a further three and a half million corresponding to US citizens' claims against the Mexican government. More than half of the Mexican territory was controlled by United States at the end of the war.

[7] Between 1821 and 1850, the country had 50 different governments. The first election did not produce stability. As with many other Latin American states, the Mexican bourgeoisie adhered to two political parties: the liberals and the conservatives. At the end, a brief and minor conflict between Mexico and France (known as the Pastry War) arose in 1838-39 from the claim of a French pastry cook living in Tacubaya, near Mexico City, that some Mexican army officers had damaged his

WORKERS

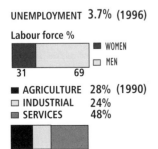

UNEMPLOYMENT 3.7% (1996)

Labour force %
- ■ WOMEN
- □ MEN

31   69

- ■ AGRICULTURE 28% (1990)
- □ INDUSTRIAL 24%
- ■ SERVICES 48%

LAND USE

DEFORESTATION -1.2% annual (81/90)
IRRIGATED 26.3 % of arable

(1993)

- ■ FOREST & WOODLAND 24.9%
- □ ARABLE 11.8%
- ■ OTHER 63.3%

PROFILE

ENVIRONMENT

The country occupies the southern portion of North America. It is mostly mountainous, with the Western Sierra Madre range on the Pacific side, the Eastern Sierra Madre on the Gulf of Mexico, the Southern Sierra Madre and the Sierra Neovolcánica Transversal along the central part of the country. The climate varies from dry desert wasteland conditions in the north to rainy tropical conditions in southeastern Mexico, with a mild climate in the central plateau, where the majority of the population live. Due to its geological structure, Mexico has abundant hydrocarbon reserves, both on and off shore. The great climatic diversity leads to very varied vegetation. The rainforests in the southeastern zone and the temperate forests on the slopes of the Sierra Neovolcánica are strategic economic centers. The river system is scanty and unevenly distributed throughout the country. Air, water and soil pollution levels are high in industrial areas. Deforestation affects 6,000 sq km per year. Mexico City and its surrounding area suffers from high levels of smog and atmospheric pollution.

SOCIETY

Peoples: Mexicans are the result of cultural and ethnic integration between predominant Meso-American native groups and Spanish colonizers. Of the 56 native American groups that live in Mexico today, the most important are the Tarahumara, Nahua, Huichole, Purepecha, Mixteco, Zapoteca, Lacandone, Otomie, Totonaca and Maya. Approximately seven million Mexicans live in the south of the United States.

Religions: Mainly Catholic.

Languages: Spanish (official). One million Mexicans speak indigenous languages.

Political Parties: The Institutional Revolutionary Party (PRI), in power since its foundation in 1929; the National Action Party (PAN), conservative, founded in 1939; the Democratic Revolution Party, led by Cuauhtémoc Cárdenas; the Party of the Cardenista Front for National Reconstruction (PFCRN); the Authentic Party of the Mexican Revolution (PARM); the People's Socialist Party (PPS); the Zapatista National Liberation Front (FZLN) arose in 1994, in the state of Chiapas, as a political-civic alternative promoted by the Zapatista National Liberation Army; the Revolutionary People's Democratic Party, of the Revolutionary People's Army (PDPR-EPR), underground.

Social Organizations: The Labor Congress is a congregation of 34 large union organizations serving as a basic labor support for the PRI Government. Altogether they represent nearly 8 million workers. The National Peasants' Front, also official, was created in 1983 in a merger of the National Confederation of Farmers (CNC), the General Union of Workers and Farmers of Mexico (UGOCM), the National Confederation of Small Landowners (CNPP) and the Independent Farmers' Central Union (CCI).

THE STATE

Official Name: Estados Unidos Mexicanos.

Administrative Divisions: 31 states and a federal district.

Capital: Mexico City, 15,643,000 people (1995).

Other cities: Guadalajara 1,650,000 people; Netzahualcóyotl 1,250,500; Monterrey 1,069,000; Puebla 1,007,200; Ciudad Juárez 789,500 (1990).

Government: Ernesto Zedillo President since December 1994. The system is both federal and presidential. Congress of the Union: Chamber of Senators (128), Deputies (500).

National Holiday: September 16, Independence Day (1810).

Armed Forces: 175,000 troops (include 60,000 conscripts), and 300,000 reserves (1996). **Other:** 14,000 Rural Defense Militia.

restaurant. A number of foreign powers had pressed the Mexican government without success to pay for losses that some of their nationals claimed they had suffered during several years of civil disturbances. France decided to back up its demand for $600,000 by sending a fleet to Veracruz and after occupying the city, the French won a guarantee of payment through the good offices of Britain and withdrew their fleet. The most important result of this conflict was the further enhancement of the prestige and influence of political dictator Antonio Lope de Santa Anna, who lost a leg in the fighting.

[8] The Liberal victory of 1857 led by Benito Juárez, tried to strengthen the republic, instituting a free market economy, prescribing individual rights and guarantees, and expropriating the wealth of the clergy. Juárez, a Zapotec indian educated as a middle-class liberal, and his party, sought to give a juridical base for their reforms by drafting a new constitution. The Constitution of 1857 prohibited slavery and restrictions on freedom of speech or the press. It abolished special courts and prohibited civil and ecclesiastical corporations from owning property, except buildings in use; it eliminated monopolies and prescribed that Mexico was to be a representative, democratic, republican nation. Neither the religious community nor the military accepted this constitution, and both inveighed against the reform, calling for retention of 'religion and *fueros*' (Religion and Privileges). The church excommunicated all civil officials who swore to support the constitutioin; civil war erupted and foreign powers became involved in the Mexican struggle. On April 6 1859, the United States recognized the Juárez government, permitted war supplies to be shipped to the liberal forces and encouraged its citizens to serve the liberal cause as volunteers; while Spain, Britain and France favoured the conservatives.

[9] President Benito Juárez was succesfull in re-establishing national unity in January, 1861. He was however faced with many serious problems: the opposition's forces still remained intact, the new Congress distrusted its president, and the treasury was virtually empty. As a solution to this latter problem Juárez decided in July 1861, to suspend payment on all foreign debts for two years. France, Britain and Spain invaded Mexico in January, 1862, landing with their troops in Veracruz. But when Britain and Spain realized that Napoleon III intended to conquer Mexico and control it thorugh a puppet, Maximilian of Austria, they withdrew their troops. Despite a major defeat at Puebla on May 5 1862, reinforcements enabled the French to occupy Mexico City in June 1863, and Maximilian - crowned Emperor of Mexico - soon followed to take control of the government. Forced to leave the capital again, Juárez kept himself and his government alive by a long series of retreats that ended only at Ciudad Juárez, on the Mexican-US border. Early in 1867, as a result of continued Mexican resistance, increased US pressure and criticism at home, Napoleon decided to withdraw his troops. Soon afterward, Mexican forces captured Maximilian and executed him.

[10] In 1871, Juan de Wata Rivera started the newspaper The Socialist. On September 10, this newspaper published the general statutes of the 1st Marxist International for the first time in Latin America. General Porfirio Diaz, who fought with the Liberals against French intervention, became president in 1876 and remained so until 1911. During the 35 years of his dictatorship, the country opened its doors to foreign investment, the economy was modernized and social inequalities increased.

[11] In 1910, Francisco Madero led the Mexican Revolution under the slogan 'effective suffrage, no re-election'. This was the first popular Latin American revolution of the century. In 1913, US ambassador Henry Lane Wilson participated in a conspiracy, resulting in the assassination of Madero. The people responded by taking up arms more vigorously than before. Peasants joined the revolt, led by Emiliano Zapata and Francisco (Pancho) Villa. The principles of this Revolution were set out in the Constitution of 1917, promulgated by Venustiano Carranza. It was the most socially-advanced constitution of its time and many of the principles are still in force today. However, conflict between the various revolutionary factions continued, resulting in the deaths of the major leaders.

[12] In 1929, under President Plutarco Elias Calles, these factions joined to form the National Revolutionary Party. In 1934, General Lázaro Cárdenas took office. He embodied the continuation of the revolutionary process, and was one of the main driving forces behind its accomplishments. The major reforms included land reform, the nationalization of oil (the founding PEMEX), the expropriation of oil refineries, incentives for new industries, and a national education system. The 'No re-election' principle became inscribed forever in the Mexican Constitution. When Cárdenas was asked to amend the constitution

90%

PER CAPITA
$1,695

STATISTICS

DEMOGRAPHY
Population: 92,718,000 (1996) **Annual growth:** 2% (1980/1996) **Estimates for year 2000:** 98,900,000 **Annual growth to year 2000:** 1.7% (1994/2000) **Urban Population:** 73.6% (1996) **Urban growth:** 3.05% (1980/95) **Children per woman:** 2.9 (1996).

HEALTH
Life expectancy at birth: 72 years (1996) male: 69 years (1994) female: 75 years (1994) **Infant mortality:** 27 per 1,000 (1996) **Under-5 child mortality:** 32 per 1,000 (1996) **Calorie consumption:** 131% (1988/90) 621 **people per doctor** (1988/91) **Safe water:** 83% (1990/96).

EDUCATION
Literacy: 90% (1995) male : 92% (1995) female: 87% (1995) **School enrolment :** Primary total: 111% (1990/95) male : 114% (1990/95) female: 110% (1990/95) Secondary: male : 57% (1990/95) female: 58% (1990/95) Tertiary: 14% (1995) **Primary school teachers:** one for every 29 students (1995).

COMMUNICATIONS
110 **newspapers,** 256 **radios,** 190 **TV sets** and 93 **main telephone lines** per 1,000 people (1994).

ECONOMY
Per capita, GNP: $ 3,670 (1996) **Annual growth, GNP:** 4.7% (1995/96) **Annual inflation:** 36.66% (1985/95) **Consumer price index:** 166.3 (1996) **Currency:** 7.64 new pesos = $ 1 (1995) **Cereal imports:** 8,100 metric tons (1994) **Food import dependency:** 9% (1994) **Fertilizer use:** 620 kgs per ha (1994) **Exports:** $ 95,199 million (1996) **Imports:** $ 97,630 million (1996) **External debt:** $ 157,125 million (1996) $ 1,695 **per capita:** (1996) **Debt service:** 35.4% of exports (1996) **Development aid received:** $ 379 million (1995) $ 4 per capita (1995) 0.1% of GNP (1994).

ENERGY
Consumption: 1,561.46 Kgs of Oil equivalent per capita yearly (1994) -48.11% imported (1994).

HDI (rank / value) 50 / 0.853 (1994)

for his own re-election, he refused. The National Revolutionary Party became the Institutional Revolutionary Party (PI) and the deeply rooted revolutionary socialist principles were gradually abandoned.

[13] Conditions created by World War II accelerated the first phase of Mexico's industrialization which reached its peak during Miguel Aleman's term of office (1946-1952). The changes that took place during this period altered the former social balance. Mexico's population still remained predominantly rural, with only 40 per cent in the cities, but this rapid development was not able to absorb the quickly growing population. Communal land ownership, which had stimulated solidarity and revolutionary feeling among peasants in the 19th century, was gradually replaced by a new type of individual land tenure causing the formation of large estates or *latifundios*. The socialist Mexico planned by the revolutionary prophets of 1910 had thus developed into Latin America's most successful post-war capitalist nation.

[14] During the following decade, Cárdenas' successors, though not always loyal to his principles, stabilized the system by reinforcing those factors responsible for its success in a continent generally afflicted by underdevelopment and stagnation. Strong governmental influence, involving substantial public investment, kept the economy strong. A reasonable balance was maintained between heavy and light industry, tourism was encouraged and a stable government, seeming to satisfy the people's demands, was in power.

[15] Against the backdrop of the 1968 Mexico Olympics, the students' movement organized protests against the true social situation in the country. A student rally held on the Plaza de las Tres Culturas was dispersed by the army. The order to shoot to kill was given without warning, and hundreds of people died or were injured in the 'Tlatelolco Massacre'.

[16] During the presidency of José Lopez Portillo (1976-1982), important oil deposits were discovered. This bound Mexico

more closely to the US, as its prime oil supplier.

[17] In 1982, Miguel de la Madrid assumed the presidency implementing an IMF economic adjustment plan. Subsidy and public spending cuts, changes in the pattern of public investment, and a dual currency exchange rate, caused public discontent and the PRI's first electoral defeat since its foundation.

[18] Under the pressure of foreign debt the trends of 1983 continued: growing inflation; losses in real wages; reductions of public spending; falls in production, and rising unemployment.

[19] In 1985, direct foreign investment increased by $1.5 billion, 66 per cent coming from American investors. However, export profits also increased, totalling $344 million in the first nine months. The $96 billion foreign debt continued to be the main problem, as it required an average annual servicing of $12 billion.

[20] The devastating earthquake of September 1986, which buried more than 20,000 people alive, further aggravated an already critical situation. The reduction in the oil quota by the US made it necessary to generate alternative sources of income. One of these was tourism, and another was the *maquiladoras* - foreign companies on the border with the US which are exempt from taxes and from paying their workers social insurance, disposing of the goods they produce on the vast domestic market.

[21] US Senator Helms led a defamation campaign against the Mexican Government, accusing it of sponsoring illegal immigration into the United States, and of having links with the drug mafia.

[22] Although the trade surplus and the accumulation of reserves grew in 1987, industrial employment fell by 7 per cent during the first quarter, and inflation - which stood at 106 per cent in 1986 - was 134 per cent higher by August 1987.

[23] The internal situation became more difficult for the PRI and it was accused of rigging the 1986 municipal elections. The formation of an independent Labor Union Negotiation Board posed a threat to the labor wing of the PRI, which

had traditionally formed a bloc within the Labor Congress, the largest co-ordinating board of labor federations.

[24] On July 6 1988, several parties gained a significant vote in the national elections, something which had not happened since 1910. Carlos Salinas de Gortari, the PRI candidate, won the ballot with - according to official figures - 50 per cent of the vote (the lowest percentage in party history). The left emerged for the first time as a real alternative to the PRI. Cuauhtemoc Cárdenas , the son of President Cárdenas , led a coalition of groups operating as a single party, the FDN, representing the masses and opposing the Institutional Revolutionary Party. Cárdenas took second place in an election marked by accusations of fraud and irregularities, obtaining more votes than the conservative PAN (National Action Party. The abstention rate was 49.72 per cent.

[25] In 1989, the FDN split, and Cárdenas founded the Democratic Revolution Party, made up of former members of the PRI, communists and members of smaller organizations. In the meantime, the People's Socialist Party (PPS), the Authentic Party of

the Mexican Revolution (PARM) and the Party of the Cardenista Front for National Reconstruction (PFCRN) continued as autonomous organizations which voted with the PRI in Congress.

[26] The PRI administration resolved to open up the country to foreign investment, and also announced a series of measures aimed at controlling inflation. Both these decisions were welcomed by the US Government. Mexico made overtures to the US to sign a free trade agreement, coinciding with Mexico's entry into GATT and the legal authorization for foreign investment in Mexican enterprises to go above the previously stipulated 49 per cent. In May 1990, President Salinas de Gortari privatized the banking system, which had been nationalized eight years earlier.

[27] On August 18 1991, elections were held for the following posts: 500 Congressional representatives, 32 senators, 6 state governors and 66 city council members (for Mexico City). Amid opposition accusations of widespread fraud, the PRI proclaimed itself the winner, with 61.4 per cent of the vote. This gave the PRI control of the Chamber of Deputies, and power to carry out constitutional reforms.

Aztec poetry

Many Aztec prophets had predicted the end of the Fifth Sun and with it the end of the Aztec civilization. The ephemeral quality of life was expressed in Náhuatl poetry:

"Even jade breaks,
Even gold decays,
Even the feathers of the quetzal end up in tatters.
One doesn't live forever on this Earth:
We only last an instant!"
Netzahualcoyotl, Poet King of Texcoco.

(Source: Rivera, Miguel and M° Cristina Lorenzo 1992. *Arqueología Americana*)

---

[28] On November 8 1991 an Agrarian Reform was presented by the President. Approved in December, it granted property rights to *campesinos* (peasants) who farm state lands known as *ejidos* (co-operative farms ceded by the Zapata Revolution in 1917). According to the PRI, the new system was designed to reduce the on an annual 10 million tons of imported food. According to the opposition, the reform - which allows campesinos to sell their lands - will bring about a transfer of small landholdings to larger investors.

[29] On December 17, 1992, the Mexican, U S and Canadian governments signed the North American Free Trade Association (NAFTA) Treaty. (See box in Canada).

[30] During the Salinas administration, inflation was reduced from three-digit figures to a rate of 9 per cent in 1993. Between the end of 1988 and mid-1993, the State received some $21 billion from the privatization of state interests. Private foreign debt increased by $11 billion in 1993, to an accumulated total of $34.265 billion.

[31] In the first quarter of 1994 - as the NAFTA treaty went into effect - trade with the US increased at an unprecedented rate. Mexican sales increased by 22.5 per cent, while US exports to Mexico were up 15.7 per cent on the preceding quarter.

[32] The high interest rates stifled the small and middle-sized businesses. Unemployment and under-employment affected 5 and 12 million people respectively, mostly indigenous people working as street vendors and domestic servants.

[33] On January 1 1994, the previously unknown Zapatista National Liberation Army (EZLN) took three towns in the southern state of Chiapas, declaring them a freed zone. Chiapas was the region where the paramilitary guards contracted by the landowners to expel the indigenous people from their land acted with most impunity. It is one of the states with the largest Maya population, mostly from the Tzotzil group. It also has the highest level of Spanish language illiteracy and the lowest incomes. However, it also has large oil and gas reserves - 21 per cent of the nation's crude oil is extracted in Chiapas.

[34] The government initially refused to accept the importance of the uprising which spread rapidly, increasing the size of the area under their control, with the rural public and workers of other areas taking up the cause. As a result, a fifth of the army was deployed to the region. When the number of dead rose above a thousand and the complaints of summary executions continued, the Government - on the insistence of Catholic Bishop Samuel Ruiz - agreed to negotiate.

[35] In February, a cease-fire was agreed and negotiations began in San Cristobal de las Casas - the city in the center of the Zapatista area - with the rebels demanding electoral reforms, the creation of new municipal areas, ethnic representation in Congress and the government of Chiapas, schooling in the native languages, health and education infrastructure, along with modifications to the Penal Code and land ownership. The Government accepted half the Zapatista claims, but after consulting with the indigenous communities, the rebels rejected the agreement.

[36] The PRI presidential candidate Luis Donaldo Colosio was murdered on March 23 in Tijuana. Three members of his bodyguard were involved. The PRI nominated Ernesto Zedillo as his replacement for the August 21 elections, and Zedillo was voted in by 49 per cent of the electorate. Both the PRD and the EZLN accused the Government of electoral fraud.

[37] In September, PRI secretary-general Jose Ruiz Massieu was assassinated, and in November his brother Mario resigned from his post as attorney general as he believed Party officials were blocking the criminal investigation. His brother's death increased suspicions that leading PRI figures, and perhaps the drug mafia, were also involved in the murders.

[38] The economy continued to grow until on December 20, due to an acceleration of capital flight, the new government abandoned the policy of gradually depreciating the currency. By the end of the year, the peso had lost 42 per cent of its value, with its plunge causing the stock market to collapse in an event which came to be known as 'the Tequila effect'.

[39] The Zedillo Government took until March 1995 to put an austerity plan into action, gaining the support of the United States and the IMF, which provided loans helping the nation to confront the financial crisis. The conditions attached to the international aid provoked a harsh recession.

[40] In order to alleviate the effects of the austerity plan on the poorer sectors, the Government increased the minimum wage by 10 per cent and extended free health care for the unemployed from two to six months.

[41] During the course of the year, millions of Mexicans joined spontaneous protest movements, like 'El Barzon'. Many of these protests, by the middle classes and the small business sector, were prompted by the increase in debts caused by the devaluation. In August, President Zedillo approved a relief plan which benefited 7.5 million debtors.

[42] In January, Zedillo attempted to achieve a quick, peaceful solution to the situation in Chiapas. Following the failure of his initiative, in February, he launched a military offensive. The investigations of the Colosio and Ruiz Massieu murders had still got nowhere.

[43] Raul Salinas de Gortari, brother of the former president, was arrested in February accused of masterminding the Ruiz Massieu killing. At the same time, the Government called for the extradition of Mario Ruiz Massieu from the United States, on charges of hampering the investigation into his brother's death. Raul Salinas's wife was arrested in Switzerland in November when using false documents to carry out a banking transaction. Mrs Salinas was attempting to transfer funds - presumably from the laundering of drug money - from her husband's account. The former president Carlos Salinas said he was astonished by his brother's illegal wealth.

[44] The PRI and the two leading opposition parties agreed an electoral reform in December, which included establishing an independent control commission and limiting campaign expenditure.

[45] In September 1996, the peace negotiations came to a halt after 16 months when the Zapatistas accused the Government of being arrogant and racist, and insensitive to their claims. Meanwhile, the interior minister declared there was no reason for suspending the talks.

[46] Cuahutémoc Cárdenas was elected the new mayor of Mexico City in July 1997, while in the same elections the PRD became the opposition party with most seats in the chamber of deputies, outdoing the PAN. These two parties, along with the Greens and the Workers Party, announced the creation of an opposition alliance against the PRI, from September 1.

[47] On December 22, in Acteal, Chiapas, 45 Tzotzil indigenous people of the "Las Abejas" (the bees) pacifist group were massacred by paramilitaries with the compliance of the public security forces. Acting governor of the state, Julio Ruiz Ferro, and his secretary, Emilio Chuayffet were forced to resign. The Attorney General initiated a federal investigation of the event.

[48] Even though investigators claimed that Mexico had overtaken Colombia as the main headquarters of the drug cartels, the United States certified the nation, meaning it was still able to receive US loans and facilities. This measure revived controversy over this unilateral and paradoxical qualification.

[49] On April 11 1998, on the orders of the new governor of Chiapas, Roberto Albores (appointed by Zedillo following Ruiz Ferro's resignation), hundreds of police officers and soldiers burst into the community of Taniperlas. This had been established the day before as capital of the Ricardo Flores Magón independent municipality to celebrate the 79th anniversary of the death of Zapata. Although the San Andrés agreements were not yet legally applicable, the National Indigenous Congress called for the creation of new municipalities throughout the republic.

[50] Accused of encouraging the creation of parallel authorities, and therefore interfering in Mexican politics, 12 foreigners found operating as observers in Taniperlas were deported under article 33 of the Constitution. This action earned Mexico criticism in both diplomatic circles and from national and international civil society.

Micronesia

Micronesia

Population: 126,000 (1996)
Area: 702 SQ KM
Capital: Palikir
Currency: US Dollar
Language: Kosrean, Yapese, Pohnpeian and Trukese

The name Micronesia is derived from the Greek, meaning small islands. It refers to the Marshall Islands, the Marianas (including Guam) and the Caroline Islands.

[2] In 1531, Ferdinand Magellan named them the Islands of Thieves, but they were later renamed after Queen Mariana of Austria, Spanish regent.

[3] In 1885, the Germans tried to impose a protectorate on the islands, but the Spaniards appealed to the Vatican and managed to keep the islands. Guam was annexed to the United States by the Treaty of Paris of December 12 1898, and the rest of the Marianas were sold to Germany.

[4] In 1914 Micronesia was occupied by the Japanese who were negotiating the demilitarization of the region with the US. The accord was broken in 1935, and the Japanese launched the attack on Pearl Harbor from Micronesia on December 7 1941, bringing World War II to the Pacific.

[5] In 1947, an agreement between the United Nations Security Council and the US Government assigned the islands to Washington as a trust territory.

[6] A UN mandate obliged the US to develop national consciousness and promote an economy enabling the native population to exercise their right to self determination.

[7] This 'Free Associated State' system allowed Washington to keep military bases in such countries, while handling their defence and foreign affairs. In 1975, the Northern Marianas voted for Free Associated State status, and in February 1978, the islands became part of the United States under a trusteeship agreement.

[8] In 1978, another plebiscite led to the creation of the Federated States of Micronesia. Four districts supported the motion, but Palau and the Marshall Islands decided to continue as autonomous states.

[9] Before World War II the major Micronesian economic activities were fishing and coconut plantations. After the War, the population increase made this economic base insufficient.

[10] Bikini and Eniwetok atolls, where the first hydrogen bomb was tested in 1954, were used as sites for nuclear experiments and the people displaced from these islands have not been able to return. In 1968 the Bikini atoll and 34 neighbouring islands were declared suitable for human inhabitation, but tests carried out in 1977 revealed that water, fruit, and vegetables were still too radioactive for consumption.

[11] Several countries dump radioactive waste in the Pacific, turning the ocean into a lethal sewer for industries and nuclear power stations. This situation has drawn strong protests from the local population, who have already had to suffer the consequences of nuclear waste, and displacement from atolls used for US navy and air force target practice.

[12] In October 1982, the US signed a Free Association agreement with the Marshall Islands and the Federated States of Micronesia. This meant that all the islands, including the Northern Marianas would manage their own internal affairs, while the US would be responsible for defence and security.

[13] On September 17 1990, the 46th UN General Assembly approved the admission of Micronesia and other six countries, increasing the number of member states from 159 to 166.

[14] Toward the end of the year, Hurricane Owen hit the islands, leaving 4,500 people homeless and destroying 90 per cent of subsistence crops.

[15] In the March 1991 legislative elections, President John Haglelgam was defeated, and in May, Bailey Olter was elected President.

[16] The Government decreed a state of emergency in April, 1992 to try to counteract the consequences of a severe drought. In June 1993 Micronesia joined the IMF which according to Olter was part of a scheme to solve the country's problems caused by the drought.

[17] The President called a national conference in 1994 to analyze the long-term possibilities of the Micronesian economy. One of the matters touched on was the country's dependence on the United States, whose aid equals about two thirds of the GDP. The participants also referred to problems dealing with fishing, tourism and the country's small industrial sector.

[18] In March 1995 Olter won the presidential elections. The President began his second term taking no heed of the pressures in favour of establishing a rotating presidency which would allow representatives from different regions of the country to become president.

[19] In late 1995, some 500 delegates of the Federated States of Micronesia met to continue discussing economic relations with the United States, with a view to the creation of a free association agreement in 2001. The summit proposed fiscal measures and the promotion of the private sector. They decided to apply greater fiscal discipline.

[20] In December 1996, a typhoon caused extensive damage to private homes and state dependencies, and also ruined the harvests. US President Bill Clinton declared a state of emergency in the region and decided to send aid.

[21] In November, President Bailey Olter was replaced by an interim leader, Jacob Nena, who was sworn in as president in May 1997. In the March 1997 elections, the ten seats members of Congress who had finished their terms were all re-elected.

[22] The economic difficulties continued all year. The Government tried to produce incentives to encourage 20 per cent of civil servants to retire.

PROFILE

ENVIRONMENT
Covers an area of 2,500 sq km, more than half of which is taken up by the island of Pohnpei (called Ponape until 1984). The terrain is mountainous, with tropical climate and heavy rainfall. The Federation is made up of four states, including the Caroline islands, except Palau: Yap,119 sq km; Chuuk, called Truk before 1990, 127 sq km; Pohnpei, 345 sq km; and Kosrae, 100 sq km

SOCIETY
Peoples: Trukese 41.1 per cent; Pohnpeian 25.9 per cent; Mortlockese 8.3 per cent; Kosraean 7.4 per cent; Yapese 6.0 per cent; Ulithian, or Woleaian, 4.0 per cent; Pingelapese, or Mokilese, 1.2 per cent; Western Trukese 1.0 per cent; Palauan 0.4 per cent; Filipino 0.2 per cent. **Religions:** Christianity is the predominant religious tradition, with the Kosraeans, Pohnpeians, and Trukese being mostly Protestant and the Yapese mostly Roman Catholic. **Languages:** Kosrean, Yapese, Pohnpeian and Trukese. English is a common language.

THE STATE
Official Name: Federated States of Micronesia. **Administrative Divisions:** 4 States. **Capital:** Palikir, on the island of Pohnpei, 5,000 people in 1983. **Other cities:** Weno (Moen) 15,253 people; Tol 6,705; Kolonia 6,169 (1989). **Government:** Jacob Nena, President since May 1997. Legislature, single-chamber: Congress, with 14 members (10 on 2-year terms, 4 on 4-year terms).

DEMOGRAPHY
Population: 126,000 (1996) **Annual growth:** 2.6 % (1980/1996) **Urban population:** 28.0 % (1996).

HEALTH
Infant mortality: 21 per 1,000 (1996) **Under-5 child mortality:** 27 per 1,000 (1996) **Safe water:** 100 % (1990/96).

EDUCATION
Literacy: 81 % (1995) female: 79 % (1995).

Moldova

Moldova

Population:	4,444,000 (1996)
Area:	33,700 SQ KM
Capital:	Chisinau
Currency:	Lei
Language:	Moldovan

Moldovans are descended from the peoples of the southern part of Eastern Europe who had been subdued, and culturally influenced, by the Roman Empire. The Vlachs were mentioned in Byzantine chronicler, John Skilitsa's, writings (976 AD) as the forebears of the Moldovan people. In the mid-14th century, Vlach tribes from the northeast formed their own state, independent of the Hungarian Kingdom, in the territory of South Bukovina. The first *gospodar* (governor) of the Moldovan Principality was Bogdan (1356-1374), although according to legend, it was Dragos who founded the principality.

2 During the second half of the 14th century, the Moldovans freed themselves from Hungarian domination, and of the Tatar khans. By the early 15th century, Moldova's borders were the Dnestr River (to the west), the Black Sea and the Danube (to the south) and the Carpathian mountains (to the west).

3 This small principality found itself subject to the influence and interest of the larger states: Hungary, Poland, the Grand Principality of Lithuania, Turkey and the Crimean Khanate. The principality was alternately a vassal of Hungary, Poland and the Ottoman Empire. The Christian Orthodox Church was the official church, and the country's language - known as Ecclesiastical Slav - was used for church liturgy, for official documents and education. The principality's first capitals were Baya, Stret and Suchava. The main economic activities were livestock herding and agriculture, especially wheat and vineyards.

4 The Moldovan Principality achieved its greatest political and economic success under the gospodars Alexander the Good (1400-1432) and Stephen the Great (1457-1504). During this period, Moldova warred against Hungary, Poland and the Crimean Khanate, but its main threat came from the Turks. Turkish expansionism posed a constant danger, Moldova also had to pay tribute to the Porte (the Ottoman government in Turkey). In 1475, the Turkish army invaded Moldova, suffering a resounding defeat at the Battle of Vaslui. Nevertheless, the Moldovans were no match for the Turks numerically, and in 1484 the Turks stripped Moldova of its territories. The Turks surrounded the fortresses at Kilia and Belgorod and gave them the Turkish name Akkerman; and the *raya* - enclaves ruled over by the Turks - were created.

5 In the early 16th century, Moldova lost its independence as a state, being forced to recognize the power of the Turkish sultan (although still maintaining considerable autonomy within the Ottoman Empire). Turkish domination over Bukovina lasted until 1775, when the latter was incorporated into the Austrian Empire. Bessarabia was under Turkish control until 1812, and the rest of the Moldovan Principality until 1878. Turkey seized one Moldovan territory after another; by the mid-18th century, Moldova had lost half of its lands between the Prut and the Dnestr rivers.

6 Anti-Turkish sentiment increased because of Moldova's territorial losses, by the increase in the tributes paid to the sultans, and invasions by Turkish and Tatar troops, who devastated Moldovan cities and towns. Gospodars Petra Rares (1527-38, 1541-46), Ioann Voda Liuti (1572-74) and Dmitri Kantemir (1710-11) all turned against Turkey. In 1711, Dmitri Liuti and his Moldovan army joined forces with Russian czar, Peter the Great. In its struggle against the Ottomans, Moldova was forced to ally itself with the large powers which had opposed Turkey, signing pacts with Hungary, Austria and Poland. From the end of the 18th century, Moldova began developing closer relations with Russia.

7 All the wars between Russia and Turkey in the 18th and 19th centuries included Moldova in some way. The Prut expedition undertaken by Peter the Great in 1711 was a failure for Russia and its ally, Moldova, but it demonstrated Moldova's intention of achieving independence by relying upon Russian aid. Distrusting the Moldovans, the Ottomans began putting Greek Phanariotes (from Phanar, a suburb of Istanbul), on the Moldovan throne. They continued to rule over Bessarabia until the beginning of the 19th century, and over the rest of the Moldovan Principality until 1821. There were bloody Russo-Turkish wars on Moldovan soil (1735-39; 1768-74; 1787-91), with a considerable number of Moldovan volunteers fighting against the Turks in Russian ranks.

8 Under the Treaty of Jassy (1792), the Russians obtained the left bank of the Dnestr, south of the Yagolik River. During the second partition of Poland between Russia, Prussia and Austria in 1793, Russia obtained the other part of the left bank of the Dnestr. After the Russo-Turkish War of 1806-1812 and the Peace of Bucharest, Russia seized the territory between the Prut and the Dnestr rivers calling it all Bessarabia. The Muslim population was deported, thus putting an end to the Turkish invasions of Bessarabia. At first, this territory was an autonomous region within Russia, with Kishinev (Kisinov) as its capital. However, in 1873 it became a Russian province, subject to all the laws of the Russian Empire.

9 During the 19th century, the population of Bessarabia grew from 250,000 to 2,500,000, and by the end of the century, Moldovans made up half of the province's population. There were also a significant number of Ukrainians and Russians, as well as Bulgarians, Germans, Jews and Gagauz (Muslims). In 1812, Kishinev had 7,000 inhabitants; by 1897, it had 109,000. During the Russian-Turkish wars of 1828-29, 1877-78 and the Crimean War (1853-56), Bessarabia acted as a rearguard for the Russian army. Under the Treaty of Paris (1856), the part of Southern Bessarabia next to the Danube and the Black Sea was incorporated into the Moldovan Principality, which joined Walachia in 1859 to form the State of Romania. In 1878, the Treaty of Berlin returned this territory to Russia.

10 Moldovan schools began to be closed in the 1840s, and as of 1866 the Moldovan language was no longer taught. After the Russian Revolution of 1905, the teaching of Moldovan was once again authorized. On December 2, 1917, the People's Republic of Moldova was proclaimed. Romanian troops entered Bessarabia and ousted local Soviet authorities. Between

(1996)

Labour force %

49	51	■ WOMEN □ MEN

- ■ AGRICULTURE 33% (1990)
- □ INDUSTRIAL 30%
- ■ SERVICES 37%

PROFILE

ENVIRONMENT
Located south of Russia, Moldova is bounded in the west by Romania and the east by Ukraine. Moldova lies at the foot of the Carpathian mountains, and is made up of plateaus of relatively low altitude. The region is drained by the Dnestr and the Prut rivers. The soil is black and very fertile. Average temperature in summer is 19-22 o C, and in winter, -3 to -5 o C. The country's main economic activities are livestock raising and agriculture - especially vinyards, sugar beets, fruits and vegetables. 40 per cent of the underground waters are contaminated with bacteria and 45 per cent of watercourses and lakes are contaminated with chemicals.

SOCIETY
Peoples: Moldovans, 64.5 per cent; Russians, 13 per cent; Ukrainians, 13.8 per cent; Gagauz, 3.5 per cent; Bulgarians, 1.5 per cent.
Religions: Christian Orthodox.
Languages: Moldovan (official), Russian, Ukrainian, Gagauz.
Political Parties: Communist Party; Democratic Convention; Movement for a Democratic and Prosperous Moldova, Party of Democratic Forces.

THE STATE
Official Name: Republica Moldova.
Capital: Chisinau 780,000 people (1994).
Other cities: Tiraspol 186,000 people; Bel'cy 165,000.
Government: President, Petru Lucinschi, elected in December 1996. Prime Minister, Ion Ciubuc, since January 1997.
National Holiday: August 27 Independence Day.
Armed Forces: 11,900 (1996).
Other: Internal Troops (Ministry of Interior): 2,500.

STATISTICS

DEMOGRAPHY
Population: 4,444,000 (1996) **Annual growth:** 0.6% (1980/1996) **Estimates for year 2000:** 5,000,000 **Annual growth to year 2000:** 0.1% (1994/2000) **Urban Population:** 52.3% (1996) **Urban growth:** 2.35% (1980/95) **Children per woman:** 1.9 (1996).

HEALTH
Life expectancy at birth: 68 years (1996) male: 63 years (1994) female: 72 years (1994) **Infant mortality:** 26 per 1,000 (1996) **Under-5 child mortality:** 32 per 1,000 (1996) **Safe water:** 55% (1990/96).

EDUCATION
Literacy: 99% (1995) male : 98% (1995) female: 99% (1995) **School enrolment :** Primary total: 94% (1990/95) male : 95% (1990/95) female: 94% (1990/95) Secondary: male : 71% (1990/95) female: 74% (1990/95) Tertiary: 25% (1995) **Primary school teachers:** one for every 23 students (1995).

COMMUNICATIONS
20 **newspapers**, 679 **radios**, 280 **TV sets** and 126 **main telephone lines** per 1,000 people (1994) **Books:** 18 new titles per 100,000 people (1992/94).

ECONOMY
Per capita, GNP: $ 590 (1996) **Annual growth, GNP:** -9.7% (1995/96) **Consumer price index:** 135,087.0 (1994) **Currency:** 4.5 moldovan lei = $ 1 (1995) **Cereal imports:** 120 metric tons (1994) **Fertilizer use:** 527 kgs per ha (1994) **Exports:** $ 1,104 million (1996) **Imports:** $ 1,522 million (1996) **External debt:** $ 834 million (1996) $ 188 **per capita:** (1996) **Debt service:** 6.2% of exports (1996).

ENERGY
Consumption: 1,094.86 Kgs of Oil equivalent per capita yearly (1994) 99.49% imported (1994).

HDI (rank / value) 110 / 0.612 (1994)

December 1917 and January 1918, first the Soviets and then the Romanians gained control over Moldova. Toward the end of January, the independent Moldovan Republic was proclaimed.

[11] In the 1920s and 1930s, the territory of modern Moldova was divided into two unequal parts. Bessarabia was part of the Romanian Kingdom, while the left bank of the Dnestr belonged to the USSR. On October 12 1924, the Autonomous Republic of Moldova was formed, in Ukraine. Its first capital was Balta, and after 1929, Tiraspol, Moldova made certain gains in industrial and cultural development, while Bessarabia, as part of Romania, remained at a standstill.

[12] On June 28 1940 - with World War II already underway - the Soviet Government issued an ultimatum whereby Romania was forced to accept Soviet annexation of Bessarabia. On August 2, the Federated Republic of Moldavia (now Moldova) was founded as a part of the USSR, uniting the central part of Bessarabia and the Autonomous Republic of Moldova. The northern and southern parts of Bessarabia, and the eastern region of the Autonomous Republic of Moldova, remained within Ukraine. In June 1941, Nazi troops invaded the USSR. Romania made an alliance with Hitler and recovered all of Bessarabia, as far as the Dnestr and Odessa. Three years later, the Red Army took on a weakened Germany, recovering Bessarabia and northern Bucovina.

[13] Leonid Brezhnev's political career began in Moldova, where he was leader of the local Communist Party. He was later to become Secretary General of the Communist Party of the Soviet Union (CPSU) and President of the USSR, positions which he held simultaneously until 1983.

[14] After the liberalization process initiated by Soviet president, Mikhail Gorbachev, in 1985, political and ethnic problems began to emerge in Moldova. In 1988, the Democratic Movement in Support of Perestroika (restructuring) began demanding the return to the use of the Latin alphabet instead of the Cyrillic alphabet for writing the Moldovan language. Moldovan nationalists called for an end to the political and economic privileges which Russian residents enjoyed, stating that if they could not do without them, they should return to their native land. In July 1989, a violent confrontation was barely avoided between Moldovan nationalists and Russians, who make up 14.2 per cent of the population. In August, some 300,000 Moldovans carrying Romanian flags, demonstrated in Kishinev in favor of Moldovan independence.

[15] On November 10 1989, Parliament approved the Official Language Law, which established Moldovan as the country's official language for political, economic, social and cultural affairs, with Russian to be used only in the press and other means of communication. There was an outbreak of nationalist protests, and a strike by

some 80,000 Russian workers. In the meantime, separatist activity increased in the Dnestr region, where a large proportion of the population is Russian, and the Gagauz Muslim region.

[16] On August 27 1991, Moldova declared its independence from the USSR. A month later, Dnestr and Gagauz - opposing both Moldova's independence and the possibility of union with Romania - declared themselves independent republics.

[17] After the failed coup against Gorbachev in Moscow in August 1991, the Moldovan Government arrested the leaders of the local separatist movements. In December, the country's first presidential elections were held, with Mircea Snegur winning the election. A few days later, 13 people were killed in violent clashes between Moldovan soldiers and members of the Russian minority, in Dnestr. On March 2 1992, Moldova was admitted to the UN as a new member. Given the continued fighting in Dnestr, President Snegur declared a state of emergency on March 16, and ordered the elimination of the opposition forces fighting in the region.

[18] In June 1992, fighting broke out between the pro-Russian Pridnestrovie government in the Dnestr river basin and the Moldovan army. Pridnestrovie

managed to maintain its independence.

[19] In Moldova, the Government's refusal to use force to resolve the conflict marked an important change in policy. The political scene was divided in two camps, one pro-unification with Romania, and the other pro-sovereignty and independence.

[20] In the parliamentary elections, independent parties received widespread support and confirmed Andrei Sangheli as Prime Minister. In August, the new Constitution came into force, declaring the state independent and democratic. Two months later, an agreement was signed with Moscow to begin the withdrawal of Russian troops.

[21] In 1995, Chisinau intensified the privatizations of public enterprises and facilitated the entrance of foreign investment. President Snegur failed to gather much support for his policies and was defeated by Petru Lucinschi in the November-December 1996 elections.

[22] Lucinschi continued economic reforms but the Communists' victory, with 30.7 per cent of the vote in the March 1998 parliamentary elections, was considered a rebuff of the Government. The Communist Party still advocated state centralism and questioned the privatization program.

Mongolia

Mongol Ard Uls

Population: 2,515,000 (1996)
Area: 1,566,500 SQ KM
Capital: Ulaanbaatar (Ulan Bator)
Currency: Tughrik
Language: Khalkha Mongolian

The Mongols constitute one of the principal ethnic groups of northern and eastern Asia, linked by cultural ties and a common language. Dialects vary from one part of the region to another, but few cannot be understood by a Mongolian.

[2] Direct lineage from a male ancestor gives the family or clan its name, though there was an earlier tradition of female lineages. Intermarriage between members of the same clan was forbidden; so there was great need for establishing alliances between clans, who formed tribal groups.

[3] The Mongols were mostly nomadic, with the movement of livestock and campsites determined by pasturage needs throughout the year. Animals were owned individually, while the grazing lands were collective property.

[4] The most powerful clans tended to control the tribal groups' activities. The weakest families maintained their own authority and their ownership of the animals, but they were obliged to pay tribute to the dominant clan. They moved, camped, grazed their livestock and went to war under that clan's orders.

[5] Political and military organization was adapted to the needs of each clan or tribe. A person capable of handling a weapon could be a chief or a soldier, according to the needs of the moment. Capturing livestock, women or prisoners from other tribes was a common means of acquiring wealth.

[6] When a tribal group became very powerful, as with that of Genghis Khan in the 13th century, it organized itself in groups of 10, 100, 1,000 or 10,000 soldiers. The leaders of large units were assigned a territory where they could collect tribute and recruit warriors for the supreme leader.

[7] The Siung-nu, or Huns, were the earliest inhabitants of the Selenga valleys, joining Siberia to the heart of Asia, and they are thought to have been settled in this region by 400 BC.

[8] The Huns created a great tribal empire in Mongolia when China was undergoing unification as an imperial state under the Ch'in and Han dynasties (221 BC-220 AD). The Hun Empire warred against China for centuries, until it disintegrated - perhaps due to internal conflicts - around the 4th century.

[9] Some of the southern tribes surrendered to China and settled in Chinese territory, where they were eventually absorbed by the Chinese, while others migrated westward. In the 5th century, Attila's Huns conquered almost all of Europe, reaching Gaul and the Italian peninsula.

[10] The Huns were subsequently displaced by the Turks, who established themselves throughout the region. The major Hun chieftains set up general headquarters, surrounded by cultivated lands where they bred larger, stronger horses, capable of carrying a warrior in armour.

[11] This led to a differentiation between aristocrats and traditional tribal archers, who rode smaller horses. Agriculture also became more important to the economy. The Uigurs, who came to occupy the Orhon valley after the Turks, developed a settlement around an oasis, where agriculture was possible.

[12] The term "Mongol" first appeared in records of different tribes which were written during the T'ang Chinese dynasty. It then disappeared until the 11th century, when the Kidan became the rulers of Manchuria and northern China, controlling almost all of present day Mongolia.

[13] The Kidan established the Liao dynasty in China (907-1125) and ruled Mongolia, fostering division between the different tribes. Historical records mention the existence of a single Mongol nation, although it did not include all Mongolian-speaking peoples.

[14] The Kidan were succeeded by the Juchen, who were in turn succeeded by the Tatars, before the era of Genghis Khan (Temujin). Born in 1162, Temujin was the grandson of Qabul (Kublai Khan), who had been the Mongols' greatest leader to date. Temujin inherited several fiefdoms that had been seized from his family.

[15] In 1206, because of his political and military prowess, Temujin was recognized as leader of all the Mongols, and given the title of Genghis Khan. His armies invaded northern China, reaching Beijing. By 1215, the Mongolian Empire extended as far as Tibet and Turkistan.

[16] Upon Genghis Khan's death in 1227 disputes among his successors caused the Mongolian Empire to disintegrate, until the Chinese throne was left in the hands of the Ming dynasty in 1368. China invaded Mongolia and destroyed Karakorum, the former imperial capital by fire, though it was unable to bring the territory under control.

[17] In the 15th and 16th centuries, controlling the areas beyond the Great Wall of China demanded military mobilization. In addition, cities were needed, to act as centers of trade and serve as a market place for food produced by local peasants.

[18] From far-away western Mongolia, the Oyrat began gaining control of the territory. They added their own mercantile and administrative expertise to the Mongols' tribal organization.

[19] The separation of the Oyrat from the Jaljas began during this period, with the latter forming the core of what was later to become Outer Mongolia. A tribal league was formed between the Khalkhas in the north and the Chahars in the south, while the leadership passed over to the Ordos, during the reign of Altan Khan (1543-83).

[20] To keep their hold on power, the Mongolian princes thought it useful to be backed up by a religious ideology. They adopted the Tibetan Buddhist religion as Tibet posed no cultural threat, and the Tibetan script was easy to use.

[21] Altan Khan proceeded to invite a Tibetan prelate, whom the Mongols called "Dalai Lama" to lead the state religion. The merging of religious interests with those of the State was accomplished by claiming that an heir to the

PUBLIC EXPENDITURE

11.5% DEFENCE
38.8% SOCIAL
(1995)

WORKERS

(1996)

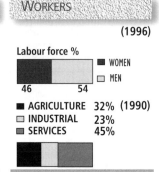

Labour force %
■ WOMEN
□ MEN
46   54

■ AGRICULTURE 32% (1990)
□ INDUSTRIAL 23%
■ SERVICES 45%

LAND USE

IRRIGATED 5.7% of arable

(1993)

■ FOREST & WOODLAND 8.8%
□ ARABLE 0.9%
■ OTHER 90.3%

Khalkhas clan was the first "reincarnation" of the Living Buddha of Urga.

[22] In 1644, after consolidating their power in Manchuria, the Manchus seized the Chinese throne, with the help of Mongolian tribes from the far east. Before occupying Beijing, the Manchus took control of southern Mongolia, which was henceforth known as Inner Mongolia.

[23] It took China almost a century to conquer Outer Mongolia. Meanwhile, Inner Mongolia became a part of China, and the Khalkhas' desire to retain power in the south prevented the Oyrats from attaining reunification.

[24] This was the final stage of the great wars among the Mongols; ending in their overall dispersal. Several groups of Khalkhas remained in the south; some Chahars settled in Sinkiang and the Oyrat dispersed in different directions, including czarist Russia.

[25] In the Russo-Japanese War of 1904-05, both armies used Mongolian troops and staff. This served Japanese interests well as a resurgence of Mongolian nationalism could weaken both Russia and China. At the end of the war, Russia secretly recognized Inner Mongolia as belonging to Japan's sphere of influence.

[26] With the outbreak of the Chinese Revolution in 1911, there was a pervading malaise in Mongolia. Until then, the region had been nothing more than an object of disputes between Russia and Japan. However, the Mongolians' social and political discontent was directed against the Manchus and the local government.

[27] Led by their Buddhist leader, Mongolia proclaimed independence from China and sought Russian support. However, because of its secret treaties with Japan and England, Russia could offer nothing more than mere "autonomy". After lengthy negotiations, this status was granted to Outer Mongolia.

[28] This situation continued until the Russian Revolution in 1917. China sent in troops and made the Mongolians sign a request for aid from Beijing. But the region was invaded by retreating czarist troops, who expelled the Chinese and mistreated the Mongolians.

[29] With the traditional leaders discredited because of their poor handling of the Chinese and White Russian interventions, some groups of Mongolian revolutionaries sought help from the Bolsheviks. Russian and Mongolian troops took the capital, Urga, in July 1921.

[30] This was the beginning of the republic, although the first monarchy had the Living Buddha as puppet king, only authorized to endorse the new regime's proposals. Upon his death in 1924, the People's Republic of Mongolia was proclaimed.

[31] The People's Revolutionary Party (PRP), made up of conservatives and revolutionary nationalists, wavered between Beijing and Moscow until the defeat of the Chinese Revolution, at the hands of Chiang Kai-shek. At this time, Mongolia began to fall increasingly under the influence of the USSR, and Joseph Stalin.

[32] The new republic proclaimed the right for women to vote. The efforts to impose socialism upon Mongolia, which was still feudal in many ways, were marked by even greater excesses than were committed in other republics.

[33] Following the Soviet model, the PRP Government tried to collectivize the economy in order to break the power of the feudal lords and the Buddhist priests. Between 1936 and 1938, the Mongolian regime purged the party and the army, executing many leaders.

[34] In the 1930s, the PRP destroyed 750 monasteries and killed over a thousand monks. Mongolia's demographic level had been unchanged for hundreds of years, as a large part of the male population became Buddhist monks.

[35] In 1939, Japan invaded northeastern Mongolia, along the Siberian border. With Soviet help Japan was defeated; a blow to the Axis powers in Berlin and Tokyo. Mongolia and the USSR fought together in the Inner Mongolian and Manchurian campaign, two weeks before the end of World War II.

[36] As part of the Yalta agreement, Chiang Kai-shek agreed to hold a plebiscite in Mongolia. Although the result overwhelmingly favored independence, Mongolia failed to receive diplomatic recognition because of an unresolved territorial dispute. In 1961, Mongolia was admitted to the UN.

[37] In 1960, Government officials in Ulaanbaatar accused the Chinese Government of mistreating Mongolian citizens and of seeking territorial expansion, at Mongolia's expense. In the early 1970s, there were a number of incidents along the border between the two countries, and 2,000 Chinese immigrants were expelled from Mongolia.

[38] Friction continued until 1986, when the Chinese Deputy Minister of the Council of Ministers visited Mongolia and re-established consular and commercial relations. In 1987, the Soviet Government announced the withdrawal of part of its military forces, as a goodwill gesture aimed at stabilizing the region.

[39] In March 1988, China and Mongolia signed the first treaty ever, aimed at defining the 4,655 km border between the two countries. A year later, during Mongolian premier Tserenpylium Gombasuren's visit, the first in 40 years, relations between the two countries were returned to normal.

PROFILE

ENVIRONMENT

Comprises the northern section of Mongolia, also known as "Outer Mongolia" (the southern part, "Inner Mongolia", is part of the Chinese territory under the name of Inner Mongolian Autonomous Region). At the center of the country, lies the wide Gobi desert which is bordered north and south with steppes where there is extensive nomadic sheep, horses and camel raising. The Altai mountain region, in west Mongolia, is rich in mineral resources: copper, tin, phosphates, coal and oil. Desertification is aggravated by an arid climate and fragile soils. Water is a limited resource, especially in areas bordering the Gobi Desert.

SOCIETY

Peoples: Khalkha Mongol 78.8 per cent; Kazakh 5.9 per cent; Dörbed Mongol 2.7 per cent; Bayad 1.9 per cent; Buryat Mongol 1.7 per cent; Dariganga Mongol 1.4 per cent; other 7.6 per cent.
Religions: Buddhism.
Languages: Khalkha Mongolian.
Political Parties: Mongolian People's Revolutionary Party (MPRP); Mongolian National Democratic Party (MNDP); Mongolian Social Democratic Party (SDP); Mongolian Democratic Renewal Party.
Social Organizations: Central Council of Mongolian Unions; "Blue Mongolia"; Mongolian Confederation of Free Unions.

THE STATE

Official Name: Bügd Nairamdach Mongol Ard Uls.
Administrative divisions: 18 provinces and 1 municipality (**Ulan Bator**).
Capital: Ulaanbaatar (Ulan Bator), 680,000 people (1994).
Other cities: Darhan 85,800 people; Erdenet 63,000; Choybalsan 46,000; Ölgiy 29,400 (1994).
Government: Parliamentary republic. Natsagiyn Bagabandi, President since May, 1997; Mendsayhany Enkhsaikhan, Prime Minister. Legislature: single-chamber Assembly with 76 members elected every 4 years.
National Holiday: July 11.
Armed Forces: 21,100 (1996).
Other: 10,000 (internal security and border guards).

[40] In 1989, within the framework of Soviet *perestroika* (restructuring), Moscow announced that three-quarters of its troops would be withdrawn in 1990. Shortly afterwards, both governments agreed to the complete withdrawal of all Soviet military personnel and equipment from Mongolian territory, by the end of 1992.

[41] At the same time, the PRP leadership admitted that social and economic reforms were not having satisfactory results. The official party adopted changes in its internal elections, making them more democratic, and rehabilitated some figures who had been purged during the 1930s.

[42] In 1989 and 1990, several opposition groups emerged. One of the most active, the Democratic Union of Mongolia, was officially recognized in January 1990. In March of that year, increasingly frequent public demonstrations against the Government triggered a new crisis within the PRP.

[43] The National Assembly approved a constitutional amendment withdrawing the reference to the PRP as society's "prime moving force" and approving new electoral legislation; however, no changes were made with relation to political party activity.

[44] Toward the end of March, demonstrators in the streets of Ulaanbaatar clamoured for the dissolution of the National Assembly. Leaders of the opposition stated that the changes which had been proposed were insufficient, and called for legislation allowing all parties to present candidates.

[45] Rich in oil, minerals, livestock, lumber and wool, what Mongolia currently lacks is the money, machinery and specialized personnel to exploit these

STATISTICS

DEMOGRAPHY
Population: 2,515,000 (1996) **Annual growth:** 2.6% (1980/1996) **Estimates for year 2000:** 2,700,000 **Annual growth to year 2000:** 2.1% (1994/2000) **Urban Population:** 61.3% (1996) **Urban growth:** 3.63% (1980/95) **Children per woman:** 3.4 (1996).

HEALTH
Life expectancy at birth: 65 years (1996) male: 63 years (1994) female: 66 years (1994) **Infant mortality:** 55 per 1,000 (1996) **Under-5 child mortality:** 71 per 1,000 (1996) **Calorie consumption:** 97% (1988/90) 389 **people per doctor** (1988/91) **Safe water:** 40% (1990/96).

EDUCATION
Literacy: 83% (1995) male : 89% (1995) female: 77% (1995) **School enrolment :** Primary total: 84% (1990/95) male : 82% (1990/95) female: 87% (1990/95) Secondary: male : 50% (1990/95) female: 70% (1990/95) Tertiary: 15% (1995) **Primary school teachers:** one for every 25 students (1995).

COMMUNICATIONS
90 **newspapers**, 136 **radios**, 60 **TV sets** and 29 **main telephone lines** per 1,000 people (1994) **Books:** 12 new titles per 100,000 people (1992/94).

ECONOMY
Per capita, GNP: $ 360 (1996) **Annual growth, GNP:** -0.1% (1995/96) **Annual inflation:** 51.57% (1985/95) **Currency:** 473.62 tughrik = $ 1 (1995) **Cereal imports:** 63 metric tons (1994) **Food import dependency:** 23% (1994) **Fertilizer use:** 41 kgs per ha (1994) **Exports:** $ 424 million (1996) **Imports:** $ 451 million (1996) **External debt:** $ 524 million (1996) $ 208 **per capita:** (1996) **Debt service:** 9.7% of exports (1996) **Development aid received:** $ 208 million (1995) $ 88 per capita (1995) 28.8% of GNP (1994).

ENERGY
Consumption: 1,058.12 Kgs of Oil equivalent per capita yearly (1994) 15.01% imported (1994).

HDI (rank / value) 101 / 0.661 (1994)

resources, particularly after the loss of Soviet subsidies and withdrawal of 50,000 Soviet technicians and government advisers.

[46] The legendary figure of Genghis Khan, whose name was forbidden for many years, has begun to be rehabilitated as an authentic expression of Mongolian pride and tradition, sentiments which until recently were condemned as being an expression of a narrow-minded "nationalism".

[47] In spite of 65 years of Soviet aid, Mongolia has an economy that maintains vestiges of nomadism. Urbanization is just beginning, and half of Ulaanbator's population lives in tents, with rudimentary electric and water supplies.

[48] In the first trimester of 1991, Mongolia registered a substantial reduction in its foreign trade. Its balance of payments deficit reached $250 million. Shortages of food, medicine and fuel became more acute. The currency suffered devaluation, from 7.1 to 40 tughrik per US dollar, and Government income declined sharply, while expenditure steadily increased.

[49] Prime Minister Dashiun Byambasuren announced a new economic policy which included incentives to attract foreign investment, the establishment of a national stock exchange, the sale of two-thirds of the state's capital goods, deregulation of prices and changes in the banking system. The Government warned that the reform is very complex and will take time to implement.

[50] The life of the Mongolians, whose median income is $100 per year, has become even harder than before. The population is not only anxious to see the results of the changes announced by the Government, but is also worried about the scandals which have affected this administration.

[51] After an official investigation, the president of the Central Bank of Mongolia, Zhargalsaikhan, together with a group of new investors, were arrested in December 1991, for a $82 million fraud, money which they had invested in business deals that went wrong. As a result, the country lost the major part of its reserves. At the same time, the deputy prime minister, Cabaadorjiyn Ganbold - the highest ranking reform figure in a government dominated by former communists - was accused of secretly authorizing the transfer of 4,400 kg of gold to a branch of Goldman Sachs - a British merchant bank. The gold was collateral for a $46 million loan, apparently earmarked for covering losses. The reform sector said that the minister of finance would try to cover the losses, and accused the former communists of using such denunciations to try to discredit the transition toward a market economy.

[52] In January 1992, the National Assembly approved a proposed constitutional reform presented to the Government, adopting the official name "Republic of Mongolia", and dropping the term "People's". The reform also established a pluralistic democratic system, replacing the socialist system in effect until the present.

[53] The governing People's Revolutionary Party gained more than 70 of the 76 Mongolian parliamentary seats in the June 1992 legislative elections. The opposition democratic coalition only obtained three or four seats according to the Electoral Commission which supervised the count. Over 90 per cent of the electorate voted.

[54] In October 1992, after being defeated in the June elections, the Mongolian National Democratic Party (MNDP) became an opposition party. The Social Democrats preferred to remain independent.

[55] In November 1992, the scheme implemented for privatizing 80 per cent of State enterprises involved distributing bonds for the purchase of shares to all of the country's inhabitants. However, it seems that the scheme was not explained fully enough to the largely nomadic population. They appeared not to understand it, and most of the bonds were sold on the black market.

[56] In 1992, the withdrawal of Russian troops - begun in 1987 - was completed. Meanwhile, Otchirbat had a rapprochement with the NMDP and the SDP to prepare the presidential elections in June 1993. Thanks to the two groups, which had been previous members of the opposition, the president was re-elected with almost 58 per cent of the vote and announced the "westernization" of economy.

[57] However, disagreements between Otchirbat and the former communist majority in parliament were frequent. Poverty and unemployment kept growing and, according to official estimations, 26.5 per cent of the population did not earn the minimum income to subsist.

[58] Meanwhile, for the first time since the collapse of the Communist regime, Mongolia yielded a 2.5 per cent economic growth in 1994. Differences between the parliament majority and the opposition NMDP and SDP groups diminished, which enabled a deal in 1995 to modify the election system. Thus, it was decided that 24 of the 76 members of parliament would be elected by proportional vote and the majority system would continue for the remaining seats.

[59] In the economic field, several international organizations criticized Mongolia's apparent sluggishness in liberalizing its economy and promote the private sector's development.

[60] The June 1996 elections marked the end of communist dominion, with victory of the Democratic Alliance (DA), a coalition formed by the Social Democratic party and the Mongolian National Democratic Party. The DA took 50 of the 76 seats, while the former communist bloc shrank from 70 to 25 seats. In July, Parliament accepted Mendsayhany Enkhsaikhan as Prime Minister.

[61] Once the election was over, the Government went ahead with reforms intending to introduce the market economy as fast as possible. This process had a high social cost, increasing unemployment and poverty. This situation added to the damage caused by the lack of technical and economic assistance following the disappearance of the Soviet Union. Around 19.6 per cent of the population were living below the poverty line.

[62] In May 1997, Natsagiyn Bagabandi, of the Mongolian People's Revolutionary Party, won the presidential election with 60.8 per cent of the vote. President Punsalmaagiyn Otchirbat, the AD re-election candidate, took 29.8 per cent. The result was interpreted as a reaction against the "shock therapy" applied in order to reach a liberal economy.

[63] The FAO estimated Mongolia would need 90,000 tons of aid to overcome a food crisis which threatened to turn into widespread famine in 1998.

Montserrat

Montserrat

Population: 11,000 (1996)
Area: 102 SQ KM
Capital: Plymouth

Currency: E.C. Dollar
Language: English

Montserrat was first inhabited by Carib Indians but after being sighted by Columbus in 1493, it shared the history of the other Lesser Antilles.

[2] The island was colonized by Irish people, driven out from neighboring St Kitts. Owing to its barren nature and unsuitable coastline, it was never really coveted by Europeans, and apart from sugar cane and cotton, no crops were grown in the Island. In the mid-19th century it had a population of about 10,000 people, including 9,000 slaves.

[3] Montserrat was a member of the Federation of the Leeward Islands and later of the West Indies Federation, until the latter was dissolved in 1962. Since 1960 Montserrat's colonial statute has ensured a rather autonomous political organization. The Progressive Democratic Party (PDP) founded by William Bramble and later headed by his son, Austin Bramble, refused to change this situation when the group of Associated States of the Antilles was formed in 1967 as a preliminary step towards total independence.

[4] Despite its isolation the island felt the influence of the decolonization process. Bramble's party lost all its parliamentary seats in November 1973, driven out by the new People's Liberation Movement (PLM). In 1979, Montserrat's Prime Minister John Osborne announced that the island would attain full independence in 1982, a promise that failed to materialize.

[5] Barely a quarter of the country's surface area is agricultural land, and the population density on those lands is very high. Half of the island is suitable for cattle raising, which has been a major source of export for some time. Montserrat has one of the highest swimming-pool counts per capita in the world: 2 per inhabitant. Tourist activity has developed since 1979, largely because of US immigration. Another source of income is international radio stations; Radio Antilles, and the Voice of Germany both broadcast from the island.

[6] In August 1987, 11 months late, Osborne called elections. The PLM won four of the seven elective seats, the National Development Party (NDP) two and the PDP one.

[7] Tourism revenues and pay sent home from Montserrat workers abroad are insufficient to cover the enormous balance of payments deficit. At the moment, Britain makes up the balance, and this is the main sustaining argument of those who stand against independence.

[8] Relations between the Government and the United Kingdom are not good. By early 1989, Montserrat was the accommodation address for 347 offshore banks, though the Government only receives about five per cent of the sale of licences. The lack of control over banking has given rise to accusations that the island has been used in fraud and in laundering drug money. Since 1990, the island's new governor, David Pendleton, has encouraged stiffer regulations for offshore companies.

[9] In 1989, Hurricane Hugo devastated Montserrat. The British granted $35 million for reconstruction on the island to revive the economy. The tourism sector was one of those which grew most.

[10] During 1991, new legislation permitted the re-establishment of the offshore financial activities. Systematic investigations of banking operations in 1992 led the United Kingdom to close 90 per cent of commercial banks and offshore concerns as they were involved in illegal transactions and money laundering of money from drug trafficking. Frank Savage was appointed Governor in February 1993.

[11] From 1995 and throughout 1996, the Chances Peak volcano continually spewed out ash. The resulting uncertainty seriously weakened the economy. Prime Minister Bertrand Osborne resigned in August 1997 after residents protested over how the population had been evacuated.

Morocco

Magreb

Population: 27,021,000 (1996)
Area: 446,550 SQ KM
Capital: Rabat

Currency: Dirham
Language: Arabic

Morocco was the cradle of the two North African empires that dominated the Iberian peninsula (see Almoravids and Almohads p.404). It became one of the power centers of the region because of its geographic location: it was close to Spain, and at the northern end of the trans-Saharan trade routes. Although neither Fez nor Marrakesh achieved the academic prestige of Cairo, their political influence was felt as far as Timbuktu and Valencia. Their close ties with Spain were culturally enriching during the Cordovan Caliphate, but they brought negative consequences to Morocco in the final stages of the 'Reconquest'. The war moved into Africa and the Spanish seized strongholds on the coast (Ceuta in 1415, and Tangier in 1471). European naval dominance blocked Mediterranean and Atlantic routes to Morocco causing a decline in trade.

[2] Unlike Algeria and Tunisia, Morocco was not formally annexed to the Ottoman empire, but it did benefit from the presence of Turkish corsairs who hampered Luso-Spanish expansion. This precarious balance allowed the sultans to remain autonomous until the 20th century. France's policy of economic penetration meant that France was supervising Moroccan finances, aiming to guarantee repayment of the Moroccan foreign debt, while France argued with Germany over who should have political sway over the area. The French finally won, securing agreements with Spain over the borders of the Spanish Sahara, and Sultan Muley Hafid ended his support of the Saharan rebels (see Sahara, Western). In 1912, an agreement between France, Spain and Britain transformed

Morocco into a French protectorate, giving Spain the Rif region, to the north (where Ceuta and Melilla are located), and the Ifni region to the south, near the Sahara. In exchange, Britain obtained French consent for its policies in Egypt and Sudan. The city of Tangier was declared an international free port and the sultan became a figurehead.

[3] The areas under Spanish control became sanctuaries for the nationalists who disagreed with European domination. In 1921, it was on Spanish territory that the Berber revolt led by Emir Abdel Krim (Abd al-Karim al-Khattab) began. Backed by the Third International and the Pan-Islamic Movement, he proclaimed the Republic of the Confederated Tribes of the Rif, induced the inland peoples to rebel, and put Spain on the defensive. The French intervened causing the rebellion to spread throughout the entire country. It took them until 1926 to force the Emir to surrender.

[4] In the south, Spanish rule was nominal, and French pressures to close down this 'sanctuary' for Algerian, Moroccan, Saharan and Mauritanian rebels failed (see Sahara, Western).

[5] During World War II, there was sustained nationalist agitation. Demands for liberation were so pressing that Sultan Muhammad V himself became the spokesperson for the cause. To calm the people, the French thought they could rely on the prestige of the elderly Emir Abdel Krim who had been deported to Reunion. Unfortunately for them, the veteran fighter took advantage of a stopover in Egypt to escape from the ship seeking refuge in Cairo, where he died in 1963. Growing tension led the French to

depose Muhammad V in 1953, but this only succeeded in making the nationalist movement more radical. The nationalists raised an army and fought until they achieved Muhammad's return to power. In 1956, the French were forced to acknowledge the total independence of Morocco.

[6] On April 7 1956, Morocco recovered Tangier, as well as the 'special zones' of Ceuta and Melilla, although the ports of these two cities still remain under Spanish control. Ifni was not returned to Morocco until 1969.

[7] The goal set by Muhammad V was 'to move forward slowly' gradually modernizing the country's economic and political structures. But his son, Hassan II, who succeeded him in 1961, had more conservative ideas. His family came from the lineage of Muhammad, the prophet, and his theocratic regime, based on a paternalistic system of favors and duties prevented the development of authentic national commerce. The King also encouraged foreign investment to exploit the nation's natural resources, especially from France.

[8] In 1965, Ben Barka, leader of the powerful National Union of Popular Forces (NUPF) was assassinated on the orders of Hassan II. The NUPF

worked for the social and economic welfare of workers and peasants.

[9] The death of Ben Barka in Paris was followed by a crackdown on popular organizations. The NUPF split and Ben Barka's followers were banned. Meanwhile, another NUPF faction, headed by Abderrahim Bouabid, changed its name to the Socialist Union and traded Ben Barka's principles for a minority place in parliament. The Istiqlal, who were originally anti-colonialist, became supporters of right-wing nationalist expansionism, fully backing Hassan's dream of restoring 'Greater Morocco' through the annexation of the Western Sahara and, if possible, Mauritania.

[10] In 1975, the conflicts underlying Moroccan society surfaced when King Hassan ordered the occupation of Sahara, unleashing a war that has brought about important political changes in North Africa (see Sahara, Western).

[11] Funds for the military campaign, the fall in the price of phosphates on the international market, and the loss of financial aid from Saudi Arabia - in retaliation for Hassan's support of the Camp David agreements between Israel and Egypt - deepened the economic crisis. The political consequences of the crisis soon appeared; in 1979,

WORKERS

(1996)

Labour force %

■ WOMEN	
□ MEN	

35 / 65

■ AGRICULTURE 45% (1990)
□ INDUSTRIAL 25%
▨ SERVICES 31%

LAND USE

DEFORESTATION 0.7% annual (81/90)
IRRIGATED 13.6% of arable

(1993)

■ FOREST & WOODLAND 20.1%
□ ARABLE 20.7%
▨ OTHER 59.2%

Maternal Mortality	Literacy	Food Dependency	External Debt
1990	1995	1970 **21%**	1996
PER 100,000 LIVE BIRTHS **610**	**44%**	1994 **11%**	PER CAPITA **$806**

PROFILE

ENVIRONMENT
The country has a long, 800-km coastline influenced by the ocean. In the eastern part there are two mountain ranges (Atlas and Rif), covered with a barren steppe and inhabited by nomadic Berbers. In the foothills lie irrigated plains where citrus fruit, vegetables and grain are cultivated. On the western slopes of the Atlas Mountains (Grand Atlas and Anti-Atlas), cattle are raised and there are phosphate, zinc and lead mines. Along the coastal plains, grapes and citrus fruit are grown. Fishing is important, though mainly exploited by foreign fleets. In the cities, many run-down neighborhoods have been occupied by the homeless, turning them into shanty towns. Some 700,000 people live as squatters in 12 such shanty towns in historic zones. This type of housing increased by 10 per cent per annum between 1971 and 1982. The lack of any kind of planned development in the countryside - which has a high agricultural potential - has led to depletion of the soil.

SOCIETY
Peoples: Arab 70 per cent; Berber 30 per cent.
Religions: Mainly Sunni Muslim (98.7 per cent). There are Christian (1.1 per cent) and Jewish minorities. (Many members of the Jewish community have emigrated since 1975).
Languages: Arabic (official), is spoken by most of the population. Berber, French and Spanish are also spoken. **Political Parties:** The Independence Party (Istiqlal) founded in 1943; the Constitutional Union (UC) founded in 1983 by former Prime Minister Maait Buabid. The Socialist Union of Popular Forces (USFP), progressive. The Independence National Union (RNI), moderate. The Popular Movement, Berberist. The National Union of Popular Forces (UNFP), founded by Mehdi Ben Barka. The Party of Progress and Socialism, communist. **Social Organizations:** Moroccan Workers' General Union (UGTM); Moroccan Labor Union; Democratic Labor Confederation, 1979.

THE STATE
Official Name: al-Mamlakah al-Maghribiyah.
Administrative divisions: 30 provinces and two municipalities, Casablanca and Rabat. **Capital:** Rabat, 1,386,000 people (1996). **Other cities:** Casablanca (Dar-el-Beida), 2,941,000 people; Marrakesh, 1,517,000; Fez, 510,000 (1994). **Government:** Hassan II, King since 1961. Abederrahmane El Youssoufi, Prime Minister since February 1998. In September 1996, constitutional reform inaugurated a bicameral legislative regime. House of Deputies, Majkis an-Nawbab, with 325 members elected by direct vote for a 5-years term. The 270 members of the Senate, Majlis ash-Shura, an advisory body, are elected by non direct vote. **National Holiday:** March 3, Independence Day (1956).
Armed Forces: 194,000 (1996). **Other:** 40,000: Gendarmerie Royale: 10,000; Force Auxiliaire: 30,000.

STATISTICS

DEMOGRAPHY
Population: 27,021,000 (1996) **Annual growth:** 2.1% (1980/1996) **Estimates for year 2000:** 29,000,000 **Annual growth to year 2000:** 1.8% (1994/2000) **Urban Population:** 52.6% (1996) **Urban growth:** 3.32% (1980/95) **Children per woman:** 3.3 (1996).

HEALTH
Life expectancy at birth: 66 years (1996) male: 64 years (1996) female: 67 years (1996) **Infant mortality:** 64 per 1,000 (1996) **Under-5 child mortality:** 74 per 1,000 (1996) **Calorie consumption:** 125% (1988/90) **Safe water:** 65% (1990/96).

EDUCATION
Literacy: 44% (1995) male : 57% (1995) female: 31% (1995) **School enrolment :** Primary total: 80% (1990/95) male : 92% (1990/95) female: 68% (1990/95) Secondary: male : 43% (1990/95) female: 32% (1990/95) Tertiary: 11% (1995) **Primary school teachers:** one for every 28 students (1995).

COMMUNICATIONS
10 **newspapers**, 219 **radios**, 70 **TV sets** and 38 **main telephone lines** per 1,000 people (1994) **Books:** 1 new title per 100,000 people (1992/94).

ECONOMY
Per capita, GNP: $ 1,290 (1996) **Annual growth, GNP:** 10.4% (1995/96) **Annual inflation:** 4.84% (1985/95) **Consumer price index:** 126.3 (1994) **Currency:** 8.47 dirhams = $ 1 (1995) **Cereal imports:** 1,678 metric tons (1994) **Food import dependency:** 11% (1994) **Fertilizer use:** 312 kgs per ha (1994) **Exports:** $ 4,742 million (1996) **Imports:** $ 8,254 million (1996) **External debt:** $ 21,767 million (1996) $ 806 **per capita:** (1996) **Debt service:** 27.7% of exports (1996) **Development aid received:** $ 494 million (1995) $ 19 per capita (1995) 1.7% of GNP (1994).

ENERGY
Consumption: 326.68 Kgs of Oil equivalent per capita yearly (1994) 94.55% imported (1994).

HDI (rank / value) 119 / 0.566 (1994)

---

students and workers held massive street demonstrations. The withdrawal of Mauritania from the Sahara war, in July 1980, constituted a serious blow to the Moroccan Government, which now bore sole responsibility for carrying on the fight.
[12] Severe drought in 1980 and 1981 drastically reduced food supplies, forcing the government to increase food imports. This sent the country's foreign debt soaring to intolerable levels. The IMF assisted

the monarchy with emergency loans which carried a condition eliminating subsidies on food and housing, a measure which increased the hardships faced by the working classes. The Government failed to achieve their ambitious development aims, and the export of unemployed workers was limited by French immigration restrictions.
[13] The situation worsened when several moderate opposition parties decided to break the tacit

political truce. The Socialist Union of Popular Forces (USFP) staged anti-government street demonstrations. In June 1981, Casablanca was the scene of bloody repression which left 60 dead, according to official reports, or 637, according to the opposition. Two thousand people were arrested. This 'Casablanca massacre' led to an open conflict between the King and the leftist parties over the high cost of the Sahara war which was swallowing more than $1 million a day.
[14] The stalemate on the battlefield caused conflict within the Moroccan armed forces, and in early 1983, they began to show signs of internal dissent. This tension became evident with the assassination of General Ahmed Dlimi, the supreme

commander of the Royal Armed Forces, who was killed in mysterious circumstances after having secret meetings with European countries over ending the Sahara war.
[15] On June 10 1983, the Moroccans went to the polls to elect their 15,492 municipal councillors. The results were very controversial as international observers believed that figures had been tampered with by the government. The opposition denounced the electoral fraud, and

Almoravids and Almohads

Around 1030 AD, as frequently occurred in Islamic history, Abdallah Ibn Yassin and some Moroccan Berbers launched a religious campaign, hiding political aims beneath theological demands for greater doctrinal purity. The campaign was really intended to recover the influence the Berber had lost as Arab-influenced Moroccans had gained ground. Finding little support in their own country, they emigrated to what they called "Bilad as-Sudan" (the land of the Negro) setting up a religious center on an island of the Senegal river. By 1042 they had recruited thousands of followers, Berber from the south and other Islamized African natives, with this following they launched a holy war or "Jihad". 20 years later they had won control of all the territory between Senegal and the Mediterranean. This empire, with its capital in Marrakesh, lasted for a hundred years and was known as, Almoravid, derived from al-Murabitum, meaning the predestined or devout.

[2] In 1076, the Berbers, headed by Ysuf ibn Tashfin, conquered the ancient Sudanese state of Ghana-Uagadu (see Mauritania), introducing Islam to central Africa. They did not succeed in dominating the gold producing region and only made small profits from the gold trade. In 1086 the Almoravids left Ghana, concentrating their forces on the invasion of Spain. They did succeeded at this, claiming to be allies of "the Taifa kingdoms", the states which had emerged after the fragmentation of the Cordovan Caliphate. Within a few years, the Almoravid had managed to dominate all the Muslim states except Valencia, which was conquered by "El Cid", Lord Rodrigo. They added the European possessions to their African empire.

[3] This created a joint Spanish -Arab -African culture, which proved to be extremely rich and creative, in spite of intense political activity: in 1125 the Almohad, the "unitarian" Berber of the central atlas, raised an army under the leadership of Muhammad Ibn Tumart, who proclaimed himself "Mahdi". He accused the Almoravid of drifting towards polytheism and neglecting the Koran. The conflict lasted for 20 years, until the last Almoravid sultan was defeated and killed near Oran.

[4] Abd al-Munin, the first Almohad Sultan, consolidated his power over the African part of the empire, including Algeria, Tunisia, an eastern section of Libya, and part of southern Mauritania. In 1165, his successor crossed the Mediterranean easily dominating the Almoravid Emirs who failed to present a united defence. At its height, the empire extended from Senegal to the Ebro river, and from the Atlantic Ocean to Libya. Its "achilles heel" was the Spanish section, where Christian troops were constantly pressing during the "Reconquest" campaign. In 1212, in Navas de Tolosa, the Almohad suffered their first important defeat. The need to concentrate troops on the European front weakened their African rearguard, enabling other native groups to grow powerful and dispute their supremacy. As a result they gradually lost ground on both continents. In 1269, the Marini, eastern Berbers, occupied Marrakesh, delivering the coup de grace to the empire and ending the unification of the Magreb.

[5] Ten years later, the death of the Berber leader, and the need to strengthen the invasion force in Spain, forced the Berbers to retreat. They left Islam in their wake, far into Central Africa, giving the region distinct cultural characteristics.

[6] The Almoravids had succeeded in controlling the gold bearing region of Bambuk, at the foot of the Futa Djalon massif, north of present-day Guinea (see Mali - map), separating it from its trade center. They had also seized control of the western desert route (Sidjilmasa-Audaghost-Koumbisaleh) interrupting the gold and salt trade, causing it to be re-organized along a more central route running from Tuat (southern Algeria) to Gao or Tombouctou, on the Niger river, passing through the Tilemsi valley.

[7] The small states that arose, or rather re-emerged, in the region: Diara, in southwestern Mali; Tekrour, valley of Senegal; Ghana, southern Mauritania ; Djénne, on the Bani, a branch of the Niger River; Sosso, southeastern Mali; and Niani, northern Guinea, including the Bambuk, were too small to keep the trading territory together, so trade was suspended for the following 150 years.

accused King Hassan II of ignoring the will of the people.

[16] In 1984, the Saharan Arab Democratic Republic (RASD), proclaimed by the Polisario Front's fighters in the territory of the former Spanish Saharan colony, was recognized as a full member of the Organization of African Unity (OAU). Morocco reacted by withdrawing from the pan-African organization.

[17] In his capacity as religious leader, the Moroccan king became worried about the current of Islamic fundamentalism on the increase throughout the Arab world. For this reason, Hassan II improved administrative measures for reinforcing the power of the ulemas (priests) and other religious representatives.

[18] In 1987, the Moroccan monarch suggested to King Juan Carlos of Spain that both governments form a study group designed to consider the future of Ceuta and Melilla (see boxes). The proposal was not well received in Spain, as there was an insistence on the 'historical nature' of Spain's presence in Ceuta and Melilla.

[19] In May 1988, after 12 years of tension, Morocco and Algeria re-established diplomatic relations, through the mediation of Saudi Arabia and Tunisia. The cause of the disruption in their relations had been the war in the Sahara, as Algeria had openly supported the Saharan nationalists from the very beginning.

[20] Better relations between Algeria and Morocco meant that a gas pipeline was built across the Strait of Gibraltar joining the two countries to Europe. From 1995, an Algerian-Moroccan firm based in Rabat will transport between 10 and 15 billion cubic meters of Algerian gas via the line.

[21] Unemployment in Morocco is on the increase. Urban migration of a million people per year has exacerbated the urban housing situation, putting a strain on sanitation, water and other services.

In October 1992, 800 Moroccans were arrested in Tarifa, in the south of Spain, trying to enter the country illegally, while another 35 failed to make it to Spain, drowning in the Mediterranean.

[22] In March 1992, the Paris Club of creditor nations signed an agreement with Morocco, renegotiating its foreign debt of $21.3 billion. Development credits were renegotiated for 20 years, while other types of credit were extended to 15 years. The country's economy has been undergoing adjustment. The state deficit was reduced from 10 per cent in the early 1980s to 3.2 per cent in 1992. The balance of payments has

improved and the country's net reserves have increased.

[23] The United Nations International Council for the Control of Narcotics, condemned the fact that many farmers in countries like Morocco have been pressured into cultivating opium and coca, respectively the raw materials for the production of heroin and cocaine.

[24] In Western Sahara, a UN peace plan announced in 1991 resulted in a cease-fire and plans for a referendum in which Saharans would choose either independence or integration with Morocco. But the referendum process fell apart over disagreements as to who should be able to vote - Morocco wished 120,000 extra votes to be identified so as to increase its chances of victory However, the cease-fire held and the UN presence remained (see Sahara, Western).

[25] Torture and disappearances are common both in Sahara and in Morocco itself. In February 1993, the Moroccan Human Rights Association announced the existence of 750 political prisoners - Nubier Amau', secretary general of the Democratic Confederation of Labor, was sentenced to two years imprisonment, for 'defaming' the regime. He was released a few months later, after the opposition triumph in Parliament.

[26] In August 1992, King Hassan II dismissed Prime Minister Azedine Laraki and his fellow ministers, replacing the entire executive branch. Mohamed Karim Lamrani became prime minister; having already held that office from 1971 to 1983. A government referendum approved a new constitution designed to extend parliament's powers, though the king retained the power to choose the prime minister.

[27] The opposition triumphed in the first parliamentary elections following the reform, in June 1993, winning 99 of the 222 seats, while the ruling party won only 74. Two months later, Hassan held a spectacular inauguration ceremony in the biggest mosque in the world, built in Casablanca at a cost of $536 million.

[28] Despite the constitutional reform, the King continued to dominate national politics, and in May 1994, he designated one of his relations by marriage, Abd al-Latif Filali as prime minister. In August, the King issued a surprise call for the integration of Berber culture an language into national life.

[29] The economic situation of the country worsened abruptly in 1995, due largely to the lack of rains, meaning harvests dropped to a sixth of the previous year's figures. The GDP, which had grown 12 per cent in 1994, fell 4 per cent in 1995. Following tough negotiations, Morocco and the European Union signed a new association agreement in November.

[30] In early 1996, the Government announced it would submit a group of proposals for constitutional reform to referendum. The changes, which basically aimed toward the formation of a bicameral legislative, were approved in September. The King still had the right to dissolve the chambers. The privatisation policies continued that year with the sale of several companies.

[31] In 1997 Morocco was forced by UN and US pressure to agree to a series of direct meetings with the Polisario Front which resulted in an agreement to relaunch the peace plan in Western Sahara (see Sahara, Western). The long-postponed referendum offering self-determination for the Saharan people was set for December 1998 and a clear timetable laid down for the release of prisoners and return of refugees.

[32] In the November 1997 legislative elections, an opposition coalition made up of four political parties took 102 of the 325 seats in parliament. The block included the Socialist Union of Popular Forces, which took 57 seats and the Independence Party, with 32. The right-wing and pro-Government Wifaq alliance took 100 seats (including the Constitutional Union, with 50) and its centre allies, 97, (including the National Union of Independents, with 46), providing the Government broad parliamentary support.

[33] In February 1998, King Hassan II made the leader of the Socialist Union of Popular Forces, Abderrahmane El Youssoufi, Prime Minister, appointing a new cabinet in March.

Ceuta

Population:	71,000 (1994)
Area:	19 SQ KM
Currency:	Pesetas

This is an enclave on the Mediterranean coast of Morocco facing Gibraltar (Spain). The climate is Mediterranean with hot summers and moderate winters. There is sparse rainfall in winter.

[2] Occupied by troops of Portuguese King John in 1415, Ceuta was transferred to Spain in 1688 and retained by the Spanish after Moroccan independence in 1956. Despite many UN backed claims and negotiations, before the United Nations Decolonization Committee, this port is still in Spanish hands. It is used as a harbor, but two thirds of the territory is reserved exclusively for military purposes.

SOCIETY
Peoples: 80 per cent of the population is Spanish . Minorities include Arabs, 10 per cent and others (according to November 1991 census taken by the Ceuta municipal goverment).
Religions: Catholic (majority), Muslim and others.
Languages: Arabic and Spanish.

THE STATE
Government: Civil authority is exercised by a representative of the Spanish Home Affairs Ministry, who administers it as part of Cádiz Province. Military authority lies in the hands of a General Commander. The territory has one representative in the Spanish parliament.

Melilla

Population:	58,000 (1994)
Area:	12 SQ KM
Currency:	Pesetas

Melilla is a small peninsula on the Mediterranean coast of Morocco with two adjacent island groups. The climate is similar to that of Ceuta. Melilla is an ancient walled town built upon a hill with a modern European-style city on the plain. It is an important port which, like Ceuta, hopes to be a tourist attraction.

[2] Founded by Phoenicians and successively held by Romans, Goths and Arabs, Melilla was occupied by Spain in 1495. It was repeatedly besieged by the Riffs, a Berber group that opposed French and Spanish domination, most recently in 1921. Like Ceuta, it has been claimed by Morocco and it also is a port and a military base; more than half of the territory is used for military purposes.

[3] On the northern Moroccan coast the Spanish also hold Peñón (rock) de Vélez de la Gomera, which had 60 inhabitants in 1982; Peñón de Alhucemas with 61 inhabitants in 1982; (with the islets of Mar and Tierra) and the Chafarinas Archipelago (Islands of Congreso, Isabel II and Rey), 1 sq km in area and with a population of 191 inhabitants in 1982.

SOCIETY
Peoples, languages, religions and other features of the population are similar to those of Ceuta.

THE STATE
Government: A representative of the Spanish Government is responsible for administrating the territory's civilian affairs. There is a military command in charge of military affairs. Like Ceuta, Melilla has a representative in Cortes, the traditional Spanish parliament.

Mozambique

Moçambique

Population:	17,796,000 (1996)
Area:	801,590 SQ KM
Capital:	Maputo
Currency:	Meticais
Language:	Portuguese

The city of Sofa was founded by Shirazis towards the end of the 10th century. It became a point of contact between two of the most flourishing developed cultures in Africa: the commercial, Muslim cultures of the east coast and the metallurgical, animist culture of Zimbabwe.

[2] As with other civilizations on the continent, the Portuguese presence on the coast of present-day Mozambique was fatal; they planned to seize control of the Eastern trade which had nourished the two civilizations for centuries. This led to the destruction of the ports and the stifling of Zimbabwean gold exports.

[3] The Portuguese were never able to re-establish this trade to their own benefit, nor were they able to achieve their other goals. The Monomotapa (leaders of the Karanga) became Portuguese subjects in 1629, but these authorities were insignificant figureheads on the coast, and the way to the gold mines was still closed by the Changamiras of Zimbabwe.

[4] When Zanzibar expelled the Portuguese from their area of influence, the colonists turned to the slave trade as a profitable business. Attempts at connecting Mozambique and Angola by land failed repeatedly and European control was confined to a coastal strip where their entire "administration" was limited to granting *prazos*, concessions of huge areas of land, to Portuguese and Indian adventurers who either plundered the land or searched for natives to enslave. These *prazeiros* became virtually independent of the Portuguese authorities.

[5] In 1890, the English questioned Portuguese control over these lands and threatened to occupy them. The Portuguese Government underwent a long, hard struggle to forcibly subdue the *prazeiros*, and prove their authority over the region. The conquest of the interior, however, was only completed around 1920 when they finally defeated the ruler, Mokombe, in the Tete region.

[6] Mozambique started to supply South African gold mines with migrant workers (up to one million every year) and its ports were open to South African and Rhodesian foreign trade.

[7] Portuguese colonialism controlled the country as an "Overseas Province", encouraging local group rivalries to prevent nationalist feelings from developing. Split into several movements, the nationalists staged strikes and demonstrations in their struggle for independence.

[8] In 1960, a spontaneous and peaceful demonstration in Mueda was fiercely repressed, leaving over 500 people dead. This convinced many Mozambicans that any peaceful negotiations with colonialism were doomed to failure.

[9] The following year, Eduardo Mondlane, then a United Nations official, visited his home country and persuaded the struggling pro-independence groups that their unity was essential. This was finally achieved on July 25 1962, in Tanzania, with the creation of FRELIMO (the Front for the Liberation of Mozambique). FRELIMO was made up of individuals and organizations from all regions and ethnic groups of Mozambique.

[10] On December 25, 1964, after

two years of underground activity, FRELIMO started guerrilla warfare to win "total and complete independence". By the end of 1965, FRELIMO controlled some areas in Mozambique and by 1969, one-fifth of the country's territory was under their control.

[11] In February of that year, Mondlane was assassinated by colonialist agents. Differences of opinion developed within FRELIMO about the desired form of independence; some wanting a mere "Africanization" of the established system and others seeking to create a new popular democratic society.

[12] The second faction dominated FRELIMO's second congress, held in the liberated areas, and Samora Machel was elected to be president of the organization. From then on, the fighting intensified and spread to other areas. The impossibility of winning the colonial wars in Africa led to a military uprising in Lisbon on April 25 1974, ending Salazar and Caetano's regime.

[13] A transitional government was established in Mozambique and on June 25 1975, the People's Republic of Mozambique was formed, with Samora Machel announcing that "the struggle will continue" in solidarity with the freedom fighters in Zimbabwe and South Africa.

[14] On the domestic front, the FRELIMO Government nationalized education, health care, foreign banks and several transnational corporations. The Government promoted communal villages, bringing together the scattered rural population and organizing collective production methods.

[15] In 1977, FRELIMO held its third congress in Maputo. Marxist-Leninism was announced as the Front's ideology.

[16] Mozambique supported Zimbabwe's struggle, blockading the imports and exports of Ian Smith's racist regime despite severe repercussions on the Mozambican economy. Zimbabwean freedom fighters were given permission to set up bases within Mozambican

WORKERS

(1996)

Labour force %
- ■ WOMEN
- □ MEN

48%　52%

- ■ AGRICULTURE 83% (1990)
- □ INDUSTRIAL 8%
- ■ SERVICES 9%

LAND USE

DEFORESTATION - 0.7% annual (81/90)
IRRIGATED 4% of arable

(1993)

- ■ FOREST & WOODLAND 17.5%
- □ ARABLE 3.7%
- ■ OTHER 78.8%

PER 100,000
LIVE BIRTHS
1,500

40%

PROFILE

ENVIRONMENT
The wide coastal plain, wider in the south, gradually rises to relatively low inland plateaus. The Tropic of Capricorn runs across the country and the climate is hot and dry. Two major rivers cross the country: the Zambeze in the center and the Limpopo in the south. Due to its geographic location, the country's ports are the natural ocean outlets for Malawi, Zimbabwe and part of South Africa. However, trade has been hampered by wars during the past two decades. Mineral resources are important though scarcely exploited. The war devastated the country's entire productive structure, especially in the agricultural sector. The use of its mangrove forests for firewood has caused deforestation.

SOCIETY
Peoples: The Mozambican population is made up of a variety of ethnic groups, mainly of Bantu origin. The main groups are: Makua (47 per cent); Tsonga (23.3 per cent); Malawi (12 per cent); (Shona 11.3 per cent); Yao (3.8 per cent); Swahili (9.8 per cent); Makonde (0.6 per cent).
Religions: The rural population practise traditional religions. Most of the urban population is Christian or Muslim. Islam prevails in the north.
Languages: Portuguese (official). Most of the population speak Bantu languages, the main ones being Swahili and Macoa-Lomne.
Political Parties: Mozambique Liberation Front (FRELIMO); National Resistance of Mozambique (RENAMO); Liberal and Democratic Party of Mozambique (PALMO); National Union of Mozambique (UNAMO).
Social Organizations: Organization of Mozambican Women; Mozambican Youth Organization was formed.

THE STATE
Official Name: República de Moçambique.
Administrative divisions: 10 provinces and 1 city (Maputo).
Capital: Maputo- Matola conurbation, 1,300,000 est (1994).
Government: Joaquim Chissano, President since November 1986, re elected in October 1994. The People's Assembly is the main political body.
National Holiday: June 25, Independence Day (1975).
Armed Forces: 50,000 (1993).

MILITARY EXPENDITURE

MILITARY (as % of health and education expenditures-1990/91) **121%**

---

territory, which was retaliated by the white minority regimes with air raids and invasions.

[17] Zimbabwe finally gained independence in 1980, altering the political outlook of the region, tightening the circle around apartheid and allowing Mozambique to revitalize its economy through the economic integration of the Front-Line nations (Tanzania, Zambia, Angola and Botswana) and with Zimbabwe, Malawi, Lesotho and Swaziland.

[18] In March 1980 President Samora Machel launched a political campaign aimed at eliminating corruption, inefficiency and the increasing bureaucracy of state agencies and companies. A ten-year program for economic development was implemented, calling for investments of $1 billion in agriculture, transport and industry, and the political organization of the country was improved by consolidating FRELIMO, which decided to implement a more rational distribution of political leaders between the Government and the Front.

[19] All of these projects were affected by the increasing deterioration of relations with South Africa. In 1981 they invaded Mozambique territory, attacking the Maputo suburb of Matola. They also backed the anti-Government Movement of National Resistance (RENAMO), made up of former Salazar followers and mercenaries. South Africa's terrorism was aimed at their anti-racist refugees living in Mozambique, while RENAMO aimed to sabotage economic objectives and intimidate the rural population.

[20] At the end of 1982, the Government cracked down on the black market and launched a major offensive against RENAMO in the Gorongoza region, where RENAMO's armed bands were attacking the communal villages of the interior.

[21] At the fourth congress of FRELIMO in April 1983, deep changes in the Government's economic program were discussed. One of the main subjects under debate was a proposed reduction in the emphasis given to large agricultural projects to provide greater incentives for smaller projects.

[22] Debate of the "eight points" of the fourth congress resulted in the wider participation of party members who were called in to supervise the behaviour of Government officials more directly. This initiative to re-furbish the links between the party leadership and its rank and file, brought about a complete change in the constitution of the delegation attending the congress. The overwhelming majority became rural workers and the number of women delegates had more than doubled since the third FRELIMO congress in 1977.

[23] The emphasis given to small-scale agriculture and industry was the result of a major reappraisal of all the large state-run farms. These were charged with excessive centralization, bureaucracy and economic inefficiency.

[24] 1985 marked the beginning of a critical period for Mozambique, with RENAMO terrorist attacks, on the one hand, and a severe drought, on the other. The drought decimated cattle, causing a 70 per cent drop in production, and was also responsible for a 25 per cent reduction in grain production.

[25] President Samora Machel denounced South Africa's covert support of RENAMO, saying that it was a violation of the Nkomati agreements of March 1984, when the two countries had signed a treaty of non-aggression.

[26] Already tense economic and defence situations were compounded by the death of President Samora Machel on October 19 1986; his plane crashed while returning from a high-level conference in Zambia. At that conference, presidents Kenneth Kaunda of Zambia, Mobutu Sese Seko of Zaire, José Eduardo Dos Santos of Angola and Samora himself had debated joining forces to confront South Africa's growing aggression toward the independent countries of southern Africa. They wanted to end South African support of UNITA and RENAMO in Angola and Mozambique. It has never yet been established whether the plane crash in which Machel died was an accident or an act of sabotage.

[27] On November 3, the Central Committee of the FRELIMO Party met in a special session where they elected Joaquim Chissano (minister of Foreign Relations) as the new president and Commander-in-Chief of the Armed Forces.

[28] In the following year, the Government began to reconsider the economic strategy it had adopted on independence, in 1975. A more flexible foreign investment policy was adopted and local producers were encouraged to invest more. This was the first step toward the establishment of a mixed economy, a concept adopted by the FRELIMO Congress in July 1989. The party dropped all references to its Marxist-Leninist orientation.

[29] Peace negotiations between RENAMO and the Government in Maputo began in 1990. These negotiations were made easier as the new constitution had recently brought in a multi-party system. The continuation of the single-party system had been one of the arguments used by the rebels to justify their terrorist activity.

[30] In October 1991 the authorities of Manica province, one of the most fertile regions of the country, declared a state of emergency because of the drought which destroyed most of the

External Debt
1996
PER CAPITA
$328

Food Dependency
1994
16%

Foreign Trade
MILLIONS $ 1996
IMPORTS
783
EXPORTS
226

STATISTICS

DEMOGRAPHY
Population: 17,796,000 (1996) **Annual growth:** 2.4% (1980/1996) **Estimates for year 2000:** 19,600,000 **Annual growth to year 2000:** 2.7% (1994/2000) **Urban Population:** 35.2% (1996) **Urban growth:** 8.52% (1980/95) **Children per woman:** 6.2 (1996).

HEALTH
Life expectancy at birth: 47 years (1996) male: 45 years (1994) female: 48 years (1994) **Infant mortality:** 133 per 1,000 (1996) **Under-5 child mortality:** 214 per 1,000 (1996) **Calorie consumption:** 77% (1988/90) 33,333 **people per doctor** (1988/91) **Safe water:** 63% (1990/96).

EDUCATION
Literacy: 40% (1995) male : 58% (1995) female: 23% (1995) **School enrolment :** Primary total: 65% (1990/95) male : 75% (1990/95) female: 54% (1990/95) Secondary: male : 10% (1990/95) female: 6% (1990/95) Tertiary: 1% (1995) **Primary school teachers:** one for every 58 students (1995).

COMMUNICATIONS
10 **newspapers,** 37 **radios** and 3 **main telephone lines** per 1,000 people (1994).

ECONOMY
Per capita, GNP: $ 80 (1996) **Annual growth, GNP:** 5% (1995/96) **Annual inflation:** 52.24% (1985/95) **Currency:** 10,890 meticais = $ 1 (1995) **Cereal imports:** 496 metric tons (1994) **Food import dependency:** 16% (1994) **Fertilizer use:** 22 kgs per ha (1994) **Exports:** $ 226 million (1996) **Imports:** $ 783 million (1996) **External debt:** $ 5,842 million (1996) $ 328 **per capita:** (1996) **Debt service:** 32.3% of exports (1996) **Development aid received:** $ 1,102 million (1995) $ 66 per capita (1995) 90.4% of GNP (1994).

ENERGY
Consumption: 39.75 Kgs of Oil equivalent per capita yearly (1994) 73.99% imported (1994).

HDI (rank / value) 166 / 0.281 (1994).

crops. It was considered the worst drought to have affected the area in the last forty years causing enormous shortages for the 300,000 local inhabitants. Faced with this situation, Joaquím Chissano's government requested international aid of more than a million tons of food to prevent starvation of a large part of the population.

[31] In Rome, in November 1991, a peace protocol was signed by the Government of Mozambique and RENAMO. It foresaw the recognition of the rebel movement as a legal political party. This protocol was considered the forerunner to a peace agreement.

[32] In addition to the new laws regulating the political parties, this agreement guaranteed freedom of information, expression and association, and pledged that elections would be held.

[33] The refinancing of the $1.6 billion foreign debt was contingent upon the success of the peace accord. Prime Minister Machungo explained that his country was suffering badly from the effects of the cessation of aid from the former USSR and the Eastern European countries.

[34] When RENAMO activities continued, the elections scheduled for 1991 were postponed. In May 1991, a new opposition party, the Liberal and Democratic Party of

Mozambique, was created. The following month, a coup attempt by those opposed to peace negotiations ended in failure.

[35] In August, Chissano was re-elected during FRELIMO's 6th Congress, and Feliciano Salamao was named secretary general.

[36] In early 1992, the new political party regulations became one of the major hindrances to peace negotiations in Mozambique. The Chissano Government initially offered RENAMO a special status, guaranteeing their members political rights but the rebels turned down the offer. The armed opposition also refused to accept the terms which stated that they would have to have a minimum of a hundred registered members in each province, as well as in the capital, to qualify as a *bona fide* political party.

[37] On October 4 1992, with Italy as mediator, Chissano and Alfonso Dhlakama (of RENAMO) signed a peace agreement in Rome, putting an end to 16 years of conflict which had caused over a million deaths, and five million refugees..

[38] According to the terms of the agreement, RENAMO and Government troops were confined to pre-established areas, and weapons were to be turned over to UN soldiers charged with disarming both sides within a six-month period.

[39] Zimbabwean troops, who controlled the corridors linking that country with Mozambique's ports, were to be withdrawn. The agreement also provided for the creation of an army of both Government and guerrilla forces.

[40] Discrepancies between the two parties led to direct UN Security Council intervention, in December 1992. The Peace Plan approved civilian observers and 7,500 troops being sent into Mozambique. The first contingent, under the command of a Brazilian general, reached Maputo in February 1993, and the remaining 4,700 troops arrived in May, including troops from Bangladesh, Italy, Uruguay, Argentina, India, Japan and Portugal.

[41] In February and March 1993, FRELIMO participated in joint military manoeuvres with the United States. This change of attitude was interpreted as an

attempt at rapprochement with the West, a source from which Mozambique hopes to obtain foreign aid.

[42] The UN decided to postpone elections until October 1994, hoping to overcome the stalemate in which the peace process had fallen.

[43] After several comings and goings, the RENAMO agreed to take part of the elections. Chissano was re-elected with over 53 per cent of the vote and in parliamentary elections, the FRELIMO won with 44.3 per cent followed by the RENAMO with 37.7 per cent.

[44] In March 1995, the Paris Club promised to give Maputo $780 billion for the country's reconstruction. Social conditions after the civil war were disastrous, among other things because Mozambique, one of the poorest countries in the world, came out of the strife with a dismantled agriculture sector and a large part of its fields ridden with mines.

[45] During 1996, the Government managed to restore old trade links between Johannesburg and Maputo. Investments were crucially needed to revive the ailing economy. An agreement between Chissano and his peer Nelson Mandela allowed thousands of South African farmers of European origin to settle in 200,000 hectares in the North of the country, as part of a process resisted by the opposition.

[46] The heavy rains of 1997 displaced thousands of people, most of whom sought refuge in Malawi. This water, however, helped maintain cereal production, a family subsistence and main export product.

[47] The Government privatization programme went ahead. By mid-year, more than 900 of the 1,200 State companies had been sold. Inflation reached 5.8 per cent this year, the lowest figure since the World Bank and IMF began to supervise the national economy.

[48] In early 1998, a cholera epidemic killed more than 800 people. The illness spread mostly in the south and the central provinces.

Myanmar/Burma

Myanmar/Burma

Population: 45,922,000 (1996)
Area: 676,578 SQ KM
Capital: Yangon (Rangoon)

Currency: Kyat
Language: Burmese

Inscriptions dating from the 6th century BC testify to the very early establishment of advanced civilizations in Burma. Migrations occurred frequently from north to south and from the mountains to the coast. The people intermingled and occasionally engaged in battles until the 11th century when Burmese conquered the southern Hmong and the northern Kadu, establishing the state of Pagan.

2   The following two centuries were a golden age in Burmese thought and architecture. The Mongols attacked from the North, with aid from the Great Khan in Beijing. In 1283, the Mongol invasion ended the Pagan state and the Mongols remained in power until 1301. Marco Polo, in the service of Kublai Khan, participated in the invasion and is thought to have been the first European to visit the country.

3   Burma remained divided into small ethnic states until the 16th century when Toungoo local leaders reunified the territory. The second of these rulers, Bayinnaung, extended his domain to parts of present-day Laos and Thailand.

4   Extravagance undermined the agricultural foundations of the economy, resulting in an exodus of peasants to neighboring states. The process of fragmentation was hastened by the presence of early European traders and their consequent rivalries.

5   In 1740, a Toungoo ruler again achieved unification, with the help of the British. But when his successors continued the project of national reconstruction, they clashed with British interests in Assam, India, and a confrontation resulted with their former European allies. The Burmese fought three wars against the British throughout the 19th century, in 1820-26, 1852-53 and 1885-86. During the last war, King Thibaw was taken prisoner and Burma was annexed to the British viceroyalty of India.

6   The 1930s began with a rising tide of nationalist movements; that of the Buddhist monk, U Ottama, inspired by Gandhi; Saya San's attempt to restore the monarchy; and uprisings organized by the University of Rangoon, bringing together Buddhists and Marxists. In 1936, a student demonstration became an anti-British national protest, led by Aung San.

7   The anti-colonial movement was not restricted to the urban elites. Heavy taxes and the collapse of the world rice market in 1930 forced thousands of small farmers into debt and ruin at the hands of British banks and Indian moneylenders. Discontent expressed itself as a generalized xenophobia, leading to popular rebellions in 1938 and 1939.

8   When World War II broke out, a group of militant anti-colonialists in Bangkok, known as "the 30 comrades", including members from the newly-created Communist Party, formed the Burma Independence Army (BIA). They joined the Japanese against the British and invaded the capital on 7 March 1942. Minority groups of Karen, Kachin and Chin organized guerrilla groups to combat both the BIA and the Japanese.

9   The Japanese granted Burma independence on August 1 1943, appointing Ba Maw head of state. The "national" army was placed under the command of Ne Win. However, friction soon developed between the Japanese and the socialist wing of the "30 comrades". On March 27 1945, the BIA declared war on Japan and was recognized by the British as the Patriotic Burmese Forces. On May 30, they captured Rangoon, this time with the help of the British. Aung San organized a transition government, and in 1947, a constitution was drafted. On July 19, a military commando assassinated Aung San and several aides in the palace, and U Nu stepped in as premier. On January 4 1948, independence was proclaimed.

10   Several challenges faced the new government: ethnic minorities rebelled; recently-defeated Chinese Kuomintang forces moved into Shan state, where they were also involved in drug trafficking, and Aung San's army, renamed the People's Volunteer Organization and linked to the Communist Party, mounted a further armed insurrection.

11   On May 2 1962, General Ne Win overthrew U Nu, who had been very successful in the 1960 elections. Burma had peacefully settled its border conflicts with India and China, and throughout the war in Southeast Asia Rangoon maintained a policy of non-alignment. Ne Win nationalized the banks, the rice industry (which accounted for 70 per cent of foreign earnings), and the largely Indian controlled trade.

12   In 1972, a new constitution confirmed the governing Burma Socialist Program Party (BSSP) as the only legal political organization.

13   Ne Win's regime declined after the 1973 economic crisis and opponents emphasized the ambiguity of his "Burmese Socialism".

14   In 1979, Burma withdrew from the Non-Aligned Movement. In 1981, the National Congress named San Yu as successor to Ne Win, who resigned the presidency but continued as party chairperson and thus maintained control of the country.

15   At the end of 1987, the social and economic situation worsened. In August, Ne Win admitted making mistakes in the economic policy of the previous 25 years. A BSPP ruling congress appointed Sein Lwin as head of state, triggering a new wave of protests. Hundreds of students and Buddhist monks died in the streets, and Lwin - nicknamed 'the butcher of Rangoon' was forced to resign after 17 days, replaced by Dr Maung Maung.

16   The opposition organized for the multiparty elections scheduled for May 1990. The Government changed the country's name to Union of Myanmar and dropped the term "Socialist".

17   The National League for

WORKERS

(1996)

Labour force %

■ WOMEN
□ MEN

43   57

■ AGRICULTURE 73% **(1990)**
□ INDUSTRIAL 10%
■ SERVICES 17%

ENVIRONMENT

The country lies between the Tibetan plateau and the Malayan peninsula. Mountain ranges to the east, north and west surround a central valley where the Irrawaddy, Sittang and Salween rivers flow. Most of the population are concentrated in this area where rice is grown. The climate is tropical with monsoon rains between May and October. Rainforests extend over most of the country. Deforestation has been responsible for the destruction of two-thirds of the country's tropical forest.

SOCIETY

Peoples: Burmese (69 per cent); Shan (8.5 per cent); Karen (6.2 per cent), Rakhine (4.5 per cent); Mon (2.4 per cent), Chin (2.2 per cent); Kachin (1.4 per cent)
Religions: Bhuddist, 89.1 per cent, Christian 4-9 per cent, Muslim 3.8 per cent; other 2.2 per cent.
Languages: Burmese (official) and the languages of the ethnic groups. **Political Parties:** National League for Democracy (NLD), League of Shan Nationalities for Democracy; Arakan League for Democracy; the National Unity Party (NUP).
Social Organizations: The Workers' Organization of Burma; the Peasants' Organization.

THE STATE

Official Name: Pyidaungzu Myanma Naingngnandaw.
Capital: Yangón (Rangoon) 3,851,000 people (1995).
Other cities: Mandalay 533,000 people; Moulmein 220,000; Pegu 150,000; Bassein, 144,100 (1983). **Government:** General Than Shué, President, Head of state and Government since April 1992. Legislature: suspended since 1988. **National Holiday:** January 4, Independence Day (1948).
Armed Forces: 286,000 (1995).
Other: 85,000 (People's Police, People's Militia).

DEMOGRAPHY

Population: 45,922,000 (1996) **Annual growth:** 1.9% (1980/1996) **Estimates for year 2000:** 49,300,000. **Annual growth to year 2000:** 1.8% (1994/2000) **Urban Population:** 26.2% (1996) **Children per woman:** 3.4 (1996).

HEALTH

Life expectancy at birth: 59 years (1996) male: 57 years (1994) female: 60 years (1994) **Infant mortality:** 105 per 1,000 (1996) **Under-5 child mortality:** 150 per 1,000 (1996) **Calorie consumption:** 114% (1988/90) 12,500 **people per doctor** (1988/91) **Safe water:** 60% (1990/96).

EDUCATION

Literacy: 83% (1995) male : 89% (1995) female: 78% (1995) **School enrolment :** Primary total: 100% (1990/95) male : 112% (1990/95) female: 108% (1990/95) Secondary: male : 23% (1990/95) female: 23% (1990/95) Tertiary: 5% (1995) **Primary school teachers:** one for every 48 students (1995).

COMMUNICATIONS

20 **newspapers**, 82 **radios**, 80 **TV sets** and 3 **main telephone lines** per 1,000 people (1994) **Books:** 8 new titles per 100,000 people (1992/94).

ECONOMY

Consumer price index: 264.0 (1994) **Currency:** 5.78 kyats = $ 1 (1995) **Cereal imports:** 49 metric tons (1994) **Food import dependency:** 15% (1994) **Fertilizer use:** 171 kgs per ha (1994) **Exports:** $ 1,187 million (1996) **Imports:** $ 2,524 million (1996) **External debt:** $ 5,184 million (1996) $ 113 **per capita:** (1996) **Development aid received:** $ 152 million (1995) $ 3 per capita (1995) 0.2% of GNP (1994).

HDI (rank / value) 131 / 0.475 (1994)

Democracy (NLD) won 80 per cent of the vote, while the ruling National Unity Party (ex-BSPP) retained only 10 of the 485 seats. The election results were ignored by the Government who banned opposition activities, imprisoned or banished its leaders, and harshly repressed street demonstrations.
[18] In July 1989, the leader of the NLD, Aung San Suu Kyi, the daughter of anti-colonial hero Aung San, was sentenced to house arrest and held incommunicado. She received the Nobel Peace Prize in 1991.
[19] The opposition was reinforced by agreements between students, Buddhist monks and some minorities. In March 1992, the UN High Commission for Refugees denounced the massacres carried out against ethnic minorities. All political parties were dissolved or banned.
[20] In April, General Than Shué took power releasing 200 dissidents and permitting 31 universities and schools to reopen. Myanmar returned to the Movement of Non-Aligned Nations. In September, martial law was suspended, but Amnesty International reported the continued use of torture.
[21] In January 1993, the military invoked a National Convention to draw up a new constitution. At the end of that year, Amnesty International denounced the imprisonment of over 1,550 opposition figures.
[22] An article of the new 1994 constitution stipulated presidential candidates could neither be married to foreigners nor bear children under foreign citizenship and they should have been residing in Myanmar for the last 20 consecutive years. The regulation was custom-made for Suu Kyi who is married to a British subject and lived several years abroad. The military junta met with her in September 1994 for the first time since she was arrested. No agreement was reached regarding the new constitution.
[23] In July 1995, Suu Kyi was released from house arrest and called on the State Law and Order Restoration Council (SLORC) to hold a dialogue. The SLORC refused, jailed dozens of dissidents and maintained the ban on political debates.
[24] The headquarters of the rebel minority in Manerplaw was taken by the SLORC in January. The fall of Manerplaw was an important defeat for the opposition since it was also an important base for undercover organizations belonging to the rebel armies and democrat activists. In January 1996 through a secret accord the Government achieved the surrender of Khun Sa, known as the "opium king" and leader of a Shan force.
[25] Huge crowds - some of them with up to 10,000 followers - periodically gathered to express support at the door of Suu Kyi's home in May and June 1996 but these demonstrations lost strength due to government repression. In June, the SLORC banned statements against the Government and threatened with a complete prohibition of the NLD's activities and the arrest of its members for unlawful association. In July, Amnesty International denounced the Government of Myanmar for arresting hundreds of NLD members, in some cases for watching videos of Suu Kyi's speeches in their own homes.
[26] Taking advantage of the NLD's weakness, the military held monthly press conferences both for the local and foreign press, which shortly before they had considered biased. The SLORC declared 1996 as year of tourism. It promoted the development of public works and the real estate sector - a base for drug money laundering - with strong participation by the state and foreign investors.
[27] In 1996, the military junta ordered the arrest of some 250 members of the NLD, who had planned to celebrate the anniversary of their victory in the 1990 parliamentary elections. The regime also approved a law banning NLD political meetings.
[28] However, thousands of Suu Kyi's followers once again congregated around her house. The NLD managed to establish the foundations of a new Constitution based on the non-participation of the armed forces in government.

The military junta rejected attempts at dialogue demanding the armed forces be in charge of the political affairs of the nation.
[29] Arrests of members of the NLD continued to be arrested in 1996. The Government restricted Suu Kyi's freedom, to the point of banning her use of the telephone.
[30] The SLORC, submitted to increasing international pressure, above all from the United States and the European Union, made some concessions in 1997. In September, it allowed the NLD to hold its first congress in seven years, although it only authorised the attendance of half its 600 delegates. Amnesty International called on the UN to press the regime into freeing 90 prisoners of conscience and some 1,200 political prisoners.
[31] In an attempt at renovation, toward the end of 1997, the military junta dissolved itself appointing a State Peace and Development Council (SPDC) in its place. In July of that year, Burma became a member of the Association of Southeast Asian Nations (ASEAN).
[32] In early 1998, inflation increased as a consequence of the stock exchange crisis in Southeast Asia. The harvest of rice, one of the main products for internal consumption and export, was far smaller than expected.

Namibia

Nammibia

Population:	1,575,000 (1996)
Area:	824,292 SQ KM
Capital:	Windhoek
Currency:	Rands
Language:	English

Southwestern Africa was occupied by Khoikhoi and San peoples, Ovambo in the north, the Bantu-speaking Herero. In the late 1480s Portuguese navigators explored the coastal regions and during the 17th, 18th and early 19th centuries the Dutch and English explored the coast and limited inland areas. In the 1840s the German connection with the territory began with the arrival of the Rhenish Missionary Society. In the 1860s tribal wars prompted missionaries, settlers, and the German Government to offer the British territorial sovereignty in exchange for protection. Each request was denied by the British, until, in 1876, the British Government agreed only to annex Walvis Bay and some adjacent territory.

[2] Finally, in 1884, Germany´s chancellor, Otto von Bismarck annexed the region to Germany. In their determination to take full possession of the territory the Germans massacred the Hereros and Nama in the 1904-7 colonial wars.

[3] This large, arid and sparsely populated country acquired greater strategic value when rich deposits of iron ore, lead, zinc, copper and diamonds were found. More recently metals with military applications including manganese, tungsten, vanadium, cadmium and large quantities of uranium were discovered.

[4] When conflicts between imperialist powers led to the outbreak of World War I, South African troops invaded Namibia and took over.

[5] At the end of the war, Namibia became a League of Nations trust territory, assigned to the Union of South African as "a sacred trust in the name of civilization" to "promote to the utmost the material and moral well-being of its inhabitants."

[6] After overcoming their initial differences, the South African Boers and the German colonists of Namibia soon discovered a common interest, namely the exploitation of the local population whose well-being they were supposed to be promoting.

[7] In 1947, after World War II, South Africa formally announced to the United Nations its intention to annex the territory. The UN, which had inherited responsibility for League of Nations trust territories, opposed the plan, arguing that "the African inhabitants of South-West Africa have not yet achieved political autonomy". Until 1961, the UN insisted on this point, year after year, and was systematically ignored by South Africa's apartheid regime.

[8] Between 1961 and 1968, the UN tried to annul its trusteeship and establish Namibian independence. Legal pressure was ineffective and the Namibian people, led by the South West African People's Organization (SWAPO) chose to fight for their freedom. The first clashes occurred on August 26 1966. Most fighting took place in Ovamboland on the Angolan border area.

[9] In 1968, the UN finally declared the South African occupation of the country, now internationally known as Namibia, to be illegal. A UN Council for Namibia was established to give the territory legal representation until its people achieved sovereignty. However, efforts by the majority of the UN General Assembly to reinforce this condemnation with economic sanctions were routinely vetoed by the Western powers.

[10] Angolan independence, in 1975, radically changed the Namibian struggle for freedom, as it provided SWAPO with a friendly rearguard. The guerrilla war was stepped up in spite of South African pressure on Angola, and the Western powers began to urge Pretoria to seek a "moderate" settlement to prevent a revolutionary regime from coming to power.

[11] In December 1978, South Africa held elections in Namibia to establish an autonomous government the first step towards independence. But these elections lacked credibility as United Nations observers were denied access, apartheid troops were occupying the territory and SWAPO was excluded.

[12] South African economic concerns wield great influence in Namibia. Foreign interests are concentrated in the three key sectors of the Namibian economy; mining, agriculture and fishing.

[13] Transnationals increased their presence in the economy through investments in mining, which was controlled by British, North American, German and South African companies. The Consolidated Diamond Mines company, a subsidiary of the transnational Anglo-American, contributed 40 per cent of South Africa's administrative budget for Namibia in mining taxes.

[14] In Swakopmund, the Rossing uranium mine, the largest open-pit mine in the world, produces over 5,000 tons of uranium dioxide a year. This mine is controlled by a British transnational, the RTZ (Rio Tinto Zinc) corporation. Two other transnationals, the French Elf-Aquitaine and Anglo-American (South Africa), also hold uranium concessions in Namibia.

[15] US firms AMEX and Newmont are associated with the Tsumeb Mining Company, which operates copper and pyrites mines in Otjihase. All of these companies benefited from the extremely generous facilities granted to foreign firms by the South African administration in Namibia.

[16] The South African-controlled administration in Windhoek operated along traditional colonial lines. The country produced what it did not consume, and imported everything it needed, especially food. Namibia still exports maize, meat and fish, especially to South Africa, and imports rice and wheat. It exports minerals and raw materials, and, having few

WORKERS

(1996)

Labour force %

■ WOMEN	□ MEN
41%	59%

■ AGRICULTURE	49%	(1990)
□ INDUSTRIAL	15%	
▨ SERVICES	36%	

LAND USE

DEFORESTATION -0.3 % annual (81/90)
IRRIGATED 0.9 % of arable

(1993)

■ FOREST & WOODLAND	21.8%
□ ARABLE	0.8%
▨ OTHER	77.4%

Maternal Mortality

1990

PER 100,000
LIVE BIRTHS
370

Literacy

1995

76%

PROFILE

ENVIRONMENT

Mainly made up of plateaus in the desert region along the Tropic of Capricorn. The Namib desert, along the coast, contains rich diamond deposits and is only populated because of mining activities. To the east, the country shares the Kalahari desert with Botswana, an area populated by shepherds and hunters. The population is densest in the north, and in the central plateau, where rainfall is heaviest. There is a coastal fishing industry which, together with cattle raising, was the mainstay of the economy before mining began in the 1960s. The country has important reserves of copper, lead, zinc, cadmium and uranium.

SOCIETY

Peoples: Ovambo 47.4 per cent; Kavango 8.8 per cent; Herero 7.1 per cent; Damara 7.1 per cent; Nama 4.6 per cent; Hererp 7-1 per cent; There is a European minority (4.6 per cent).
Religions: Many people practise traditional African religions although there are a large number of Christians (Lutheran 51.2 per cent, Catholics 19.8 per cent, Anglican 5 per cent).
Languages: English (official), Khoisan, Bantu, German and Afrikaans.
Political Parties: Southwest African People's Organization (SWAPO); Southwest African People's Organization for Justice (SWAPO for Justice); Democratic Turnhalle Alliance (DTA); United Democratic Front; National Christian Action.
Social Organizations: National Union of Workers of Namibia.

THE STATE

Official Name: Republic of Namibia.
Administrative divisions: 13 districts.
Capital: Windhoek, 150,000 people (1994).
Other cities: Walvis Bay, 45,000 people; Swakopmund 15,500; Rundu 15,000; Rehoboth 15,000; Keetmanshoop 25,000.
Government: Sam Nujoma, President since March, 1990. Hage Geingob, Prime Minister since 1990. The Constitution established a presidential regime and a multiparty system.
National Holiday: March 21 (Independence).
Armed Forces: 8,100.

industries, imports manufactured goods. Ninety per cent of consumer goods in Namibia come from South Africa.

[17] Until 1990, the system of privilege continued. Indigenous Africans, 90 per cent of the population, consumed 12.8 per cent of the GDP while the Europeans, 10 per cent of the population, consumed 81.5 per cent of the GDP. When independence was declared, three-quarters of agrarian and livestock production belonged to farmers of European descent.

[18] Average per capita income in Namibia was one of the highest in Africa: $1,410, but this figure concealed enormous inequalities. While the average salary of whites is $1,880, an African would not earn more than $108.

[19] South Africa not only refused to seek a negotiated settlement for the independence of Namibia, but also increased its military budget by 30 per cent to pay for a campaign against the Popular Liberation Army of Namibia, an affiliate of SWAPO.

[20] During late 1982 and early 1983, fighting intensified along the border between Namibia and Angola. It also spread to the south, with SWAPO forces staging daring attacks within the "iron triangle", close to the city of Grootfontein, where the main South African military forces were concentrated.

[21] On the diplomatic front, the failure of the five-point plan proposed by the Contact Group (France, United States, Britain, West Germany and Canada) brought the issue of Namibian independence to a deadlock. South Africa bound any accord to the withdrawal of Cuban troops from Angola and demanded guarantees that its investments in Namibia would not be affected.

[22] SWAPO refused to agree to special benefits for the European population, nor would it accept limitations, suggested by the Contact Group, for constitutional change after independence. Pretoria also baulked at SWAPO demands for elections with UN supervision.

[23] In 1983, the interim Democratic Turnhalle Alliance (DTA) government in Namibia was ousted by the South African government when its leaders began to take critical stands on apartheid issues despite the party's strong links with Pretoria.

[24] This attempt to gain some popular support failed, and the Government of Namibia was handed over to a colonial administrator appointed directly by Prime Minister Botha. France immediately withdrew from the Contact Group arguing that its efforts had been frustrated by Pretoria's delaying tactics.

[25] In February, 1984, Angolan and South African government representatives met in the Zambian capital, Lusaka, for peace negotiations. They agreed on a South African troop withdrawal from southern Angola in exchange for a ceasefire.

[26] In May of the same year, SWAPO delegates and other Namibian political party leaders met with a South African representative, but Pretoria's uncompromising attitude dashed the hopes of any agreement. South African troops failed to withdraw from Namibia on schedule and the deadlock continued.

[27] In June, Botha appointed an "interim government" based on a Multiparty Conference (MPC) of six multiracial and white groups, including a section of the ruling National Party. The new regime was to have limited authority in domestic matters while South Africa would control foreign affairs and military matters. SWAPO was excluded.

[28] From 1987, all the states directly or indirectly involved in the conflict began to recognize the need to end this long drawn out confrontation, though negotiations were laborious due to the complexity of the economic and political interests at stake.

[29] There were many reasons for this sudden turnaround; after 14 years of uninterrupted war, Angola's economy was on the brink of collapse, and the Angola/Namib war is calculated to have cost the country $13 billion.

[30] Pretoria's permanent harassment of Angola and occupation of Namibia were costing the regime dearly both economically and diplomatically. Its final drive to set up its counter-revolutionary protégé UNITA (National Union for the Total Independence of Angola) in government over the "liberated territory" was defeated by joint Angolan and Cuban forces in the battle of Cuito-Cananale (April 1988).

[31] In December, 1988, after prolonged US-mediated negotiations, South Africa, Angola and Cuba reached an agreement whereby South African troops would leave Namibia, and Cuba would gradually withdraw its 50,000 soldiers.

[32] Throughout 1989, thousands of exiles began to flood back into the country and many political prisoners were released. In September, 60-year-old SWAPO leader Sam Nujoma returned from 30 years in exile to lead his organization into the elections two months later. SWAPO, which had not been party to the peace accord and did not feel bound by it, attempted to infiltrate from Angolan territory with large numbers of troops. These were detected and neutralized by South African troops, causing heavy losses.

[33] The liberation movement in exile was shaken by two scandals. It was discovered that political commissars at refugee camps had tortured alleged dissidents, and that the number of exiles had been wildly exaggerated in order to obtain greater international food assistance.

[34] In November 1989 more than 710,000 Namibians voted for the members of the National Assembly who would draft the country's first constitution. Ten parties contested the elections, supervised throughout by the UN. SWAPO won a resounding victory with over 60 per cent of the vote. This ensured control of the constituent assembly and the appointment of Sam Nujoma as Namibia's first President.

[35] Independence was proclaimed on March 21 1990. The presidential guard of honor included SWAPO and the South West Africa Territorial Force fighters. The latter had protected the South African-backed regime and was to be integrated into the new National Army of Namibia.

[36] The Government of independent Namibia has had to deal with many social injustices and inequalities inherent in the apartheid system imposed by South African domination, especially in the health and education spheres. In the territories which used to be reserved for whites there is an acceptable infrastructure for education and good sanitation, but in the areas where the blacks live, in particular in the north of the country, there are inadequate schooling and health facilities and few well-qualified staff.

Food Dependency

1994
9%

STATISTICS

DEMOGRAPHY
Population: 1,575,000 (1996). **Annual growth:** 2.7% (1980/1996). **Estimates for year 2000:** 1,700,000 **Annual growth to year 2000:** 2.5% (1994/2000). **Urban Population:** 37.0% (1996). **Urban growth:** 6.24% (1980/95). **Children per woman:** 5 (1996).

HEALTH
Life expectancy at birth: 56 years (1996). **Infant mortality:** 60 per 1,000 (1996). **Under-5 child mortality:** 77 per 1,000 (1996).4,545 **people per doctor** (1988/91). **Safe water:** 57% (1990/96).

EDUCATION
Literacy: 76% (1995). male : 78% (1995). female: 74% (1995). **School enrolment :** Primary total: 137% (1990/95). male : 136% (1990/95). female: 138% (1990/95). Secondary: male : 57% (1990/95). female: 69% (1990/95). Tertiary: 8% (1995). **Primary school teachers:** one for every 32 students (1995).

COMMUNICATIONS
100 **newspapers**, 139 **radios**, 30 **TV sets** and 47 **main telephone lines** per 1,000 people (1996).

ECONOMY
Per capita, GNP: $ 2,250 (1996). **Annual growth, GNP:** 0.3% (1995/96). **Annual inflation:** 10.35% (1985/95). **Consumer price index:** 159.3 (1994). **Currency:** 3.65 rands = $ 1 (1995) **Cereal imports:** 112 metric tons (1994). **Food import dependency:** 9% (1994). **Development aid received:** $ 188 million (1995). $ 125 per capita (1995). 6.4% of GNP (1994).

HDI (rank / value) 118 / 0.57 (1994)

[37] On independence, Namibia adopted English as its official language, replacing Afrikaans. The Government set up an informal department of education to teach women to read. The body's initial work, which had UNICEF support, showed that Namibian women would have to be taught how to read in their own languages, before they could English. As for health, a main concern of the Government is the fate of some 40,000 disabled people, mostly victims of the 23-year-long guerrilla warfare.

[38] The UN's Development Program considered land reform to be Namibia's most pressing issue. This belief was based on the fact that 65 per cent of the land is owned by people of European origin, many of whom were absentee landlords.

[39] In mid-February 1991, the civil servants, the town hall workers, and the Namibian Parastatal Corporation went on strike demanding higher salaries, labor legislation, and protesting against alleged government racism. The Government responded by accusing the workers of attempted economic sabotage of the administration.

[40] The inequality in Namibian incomes has led economic analysts from various international organizations to call the country a "dual economy nation". Seventy per cent of the inhabitants live in Third World conditions, 25 per cent live in a transition economy, and only 5 percent benefit from the economic conditions of development.

[41] Its economy is heavily dependent on mining and imports of manufactured consumer goods. Over 70 per cent of the population depends directly or indirectly from agriculture, but this sector represents only 10 per cent of Namibia's GNP.

[42] Namibia has been expanding its fishing industry, but one of the main problems with this is that its territorial waters are frequently invaded by fishing boats from other countries. This friction over territorial waters has aggravated a dispute with South Africa over the sovereignty of territorial waters, a dispute that is difficult to solve, because Namibia lacks military power.

[43] In 1991, the Nujoma Government reached an agreement with the US to start a military education and training program, under which Namibian Defence Force officers will receive free professional military training. In December of that same year, the defence minister, Peter Muesiniange, travelled to Brazil to be advised on the establishment of a modern air force.

[44] Early in 1991, the Namibian President, ready to play a leading role in southern Africa, donated a million rand to the African National Congress (ANC), then the main African opposition to the minority government in South Africa. The money was given to ANC leader Nelson Mandela when he visited Namibia on January 31. Democracy in South Africa and lasting peace in Angola, which shares an economic identity with Namibia along their common border, would enable Namibia to achieve significant economic development.

[45] In September 1991, an agreement was reached with South Africa over joint administration of the port at Walvis Bay. The agreement also established the middle of the Orange River as the country's southern border, which should reduce armed confrontations between the two countries in that region.

[46] The following month, Namibia announced the opening of a commercial office in Pretoria. In November the Government set up control posts along the border with Zambia to fight smuggling and drug trafficking.

[47] That same month, the Government set up a commission to investigate charges that anti-independence Namibian parties were being financed by Pretoria. The ensuing scandal made it impossible for the opposition Turnhalle Democratic Alliance, which was under suspicion in the affair, to become a unified party under the leadership of Mishae Muyongo.

[48] On December 11 1991, the first legal SWAPO congress established the need to promote political and economic relations with the world community, particularly with Third World countries. During the congress,

Nujoma was re-elected president of SWAPO.

[49] In 1992, Namibia and South Africa agreed to return the port of Walvis Bay to Windhoek in 1994. A year later, the National Council, the upper chamber of parliament, went into operation. In 1994, the government approved a land law which aimed, amongst other things, to limit the concentration of property, as it was already estimated that 1 per cent of the population owned 75 per cent of the national land area.

[50] In December of that year, Sam Nujoma was re-elected President with 70 per cent of the vote. However, in May 1995, SWAPO - the President's party - split, leading to the creation of SWAPO for Justice.

[51] After achieving 5 per cent growth in 1994, the Government predicted economic growth of 3 per cent for 1995, while unemployment affected some 38 per cent of the active population.

[52] In 1996, the Government agreed the elimination of its pre-independence debt with South Africa. In return, Nujoma committed himself to investments in southern South Africa. In view of the trade imbalance, the President aimed his economic policy at revitalising exports, economic diversification and the creation of new jobs.

[53] In mid-1997, a SWAPO congress proclaimed Nujoma President of Namibia for a third term. In the same year, the

Government refused to open investigations into the crimes committed in the pre-independence period. This decision created tension with South Africa.

[54] Social protests, above all over unemployment, were ignored by the Government. Many of the former SWAPO army members were still unemployed.

[55] Environmental and human rights groups opposed the construction of a hydroelectric dam on the Kunene river in the north of the country. They said the dam would displace the Himba, a large semi-nomadic tribe, and cause other damage.

[56] The number of HIV-positive individuals and people with AIDS increased alarmingly. In 1997, the illness caused 1,539 deaths, taking the number of casualties registered since 1988 to 3,677. A total of 40,629 registered AIDS cases were registered that year.

[57] The fishing industry gave signs of recovery in 1998. The Government started the year promoting Namibia as a tourist destination - a sector never really developed before.

Nauru

Nauru

Population: 11,000 (1996)
Area: 21 SQ KM
Currency: Australian Dollar
Language: English

Nauru, which lies in the central Pacific, was populated by migrating Polynesian, Micronesian and Melanesian people. The British sailor John Fearn was the first European to visit the island, which he named Pleasant Island. Whaling ships often called at Nauru during the 19th century, until it was annexed by the German Second Reich in 1888.

2 In 1899, Nauru was found to have phosphate-rich rock which made it one of the wealthiest countries in the world. In 1905, an Anglo-German company began mining on the island.

3 At the beginning of World War I, Nauru came under Australian trusteeship and during World War II, under Japanese control with thousands of Nauruans sent to forced labor camps on the island of Truk (in present-day Micronesia). At the end of the war, only 700 came back alive. Australia recovered the island, and mining was continued by British, Australian and Aotearoan/New Zealand transnational consortium.

4 The Nauruans did not adjust well to mining and were soon replaced by immigrants, mostly Chinese. Immigrant workers became so numerous that in 1964, the Australian government officially suggested that they should accept resettlement on a different island or elsewhere in Australia. Nauruans rejected this, deciding to stay on their island and seek autonomy.

5 The mining sector was nationalized in 1967, which meant a large increase in per capita income. In 1992, the minimum annual salary was $6,500. Nauru declared independence on January 31 1968, rejecting Australian attempts at domination. A year later it became a member of the Commonwealth. It is still the smallest republic in the world.

6 Government expenses and public investment are paid out of a huge legal fund fed by phosphate revenues. Education, medical care and housing are free.

7 Hammer de Roburt dominated the political scene, and as the first President, he governed continuously until 1976 when he lost the majority to Bernard Dowiyogo, of the Nauru Party. Two years later, De Roburt once again obtained the majority, holding office from 1978 to 1986. In the general election that year a woman was elected to parliament for the first time since independence.

8 Bernard Dowiyogo returned to the presidency in 1989. His government started a court case against the Australian state for the indiscriminate exploitation of the phosphate mines during the last 50 years. In 1991, Australia recognized Nauru's right to claim compensation. Britain and Aotearoa promised to collaborate with Australia in the payment of $100 million to Nauru.

9 This year the economy of Nauru registered a budget deficit for the first time in its history. It is estimated that if mining continues at the same rate until the year 2000, the phosphate resources of the island could be exhausted. The current dependence on phosphate exports has forced islanders to think of conversion. The only apparent viable alternative is fishing, as the land is not fit for agriculture. The production of vegetables and tropical fruits is enough to meet domestic needs.

10 The Government, led by Lagumot Harris from 1995, invested in developing the nation's air and fishing fleets. Harris aimed to correct the deficit, reducing spending and increasing taxes, freezing pay for two years, closing some consulates abroad and privatizing some State dependencies.

11 Falling international phosphate prices, the high maintenance costs of the airline, and unprofitable investments, pushed the economy into serious difficulties.

12 On February 13 1997, Parliament made Kinza Godfrey Clodumar the new President, the fourth in only four months. One of his first policies was to try to attract foreign investors, above all Australians. In December, Nauru re-established diplomatic relations with France, suspended since 1995 in protest over the nuclear tests in French Polynesia.

13 In late 1997, Clodumar called on the world for drastic reductions in the production of greenhouse gases. The leader stressed that Nauru could disappear under the sea as an indirect consequence of global warming.

PROFILE

ENVIRONMENT
Nauru is a coral island, 6 km long by 4 km wide, located in Micronesia just south of the Equator. With sandy beaches and a thin belt of fertile land (300 meters wide), the island has a 60-meter high central plateau of guano, rich in phosphoric acid and nitrogen.

SOCIETY
Peoples: Nauruans, are descendents of Polynesian, Micronesian and Melanesian immigrants. There are also Australian, Aotearoan, Chinese, European minorities, and workers from Tuvalu, Kiribati and other neighboring islands. There are two men to every woman.
Religions: Christian. **Languages:** English (official) and Nauruan.
Political Parties: Nauru Party (NP). Democratic Party of Nauru.
Social Organizations: There are two organizations: the Nauru Workers Organization (NWO), founded in 1974 and affiliated to the NP; and the Phosphate Workers' Organization (PWO), founded in 1953.

THE STATE
Official Name: Republic of Nauru. **Capital:** There are no population centers and so the island has no formal capital. The Government buildings are located opposite the airport in the Yaren district.
Administrative Divisions: 14 districts.
Government: Kinza Godfrey Clodumar, President since February 1997. One-chamber parliament of 18 deputies.
National Holiday: January 31, Independence Day (1968).

DEMOGRAPHY
Population: 11,000 (1996). **Annual growth:** 2.8 % (1980/1996).
Urban population: 100.0 % (1996).

HEALTH
Infant mortality: 25 per 1,000 (1996). **Under-5 child mortality:** 31 per 1,000 (1996).

Nepal

Nepal

Population:	22,021,000 (1996)
Area:	147,181 SQ KM
Capital:	Kathmandu
Currency:	Rupees
Language:	Nepali

Nepal is a landlocked country in the central Himalayas between two of the world's most densely populated countries; India and China. References to Nepal Valley and Nepal's lower hill areas are found in the ancient Indian classics, suggesting that the Central Himalayan hills were closely connected culturally and politically to the Gangetic Plain at least 2,500,000 years ago. Lumbini, Gautama Buddha's birthplace in southern Nepal, and Nepal Valley also figure prominently in Buddhist accounts. There is substantial archaeological evidence of an early Buddhist influence in Nepal, including a famous column inscribed by Ashoka (Emperor of India, 3rd century BC) at Lumbini and several shrines in the valley.

[2] Although there are gaps, the sequence of the Nepal Valley's history can be traced along with the rise of the Licchavi dynasty in the 4th or 5th century AD. While the earlier Kirati dynasty had claimed the status of the Kshatriya caste of rulers and warriors, the Licchavis were probably the first ruling family in that area of plain Indian origin. This set a precedent for what became the normal pattern thereafter - Hindu kings claiming high-caste Indian origin ruling over a population much of which was neither Indo-Aryan nor Hindu.

[3] The Licchavi dynastic chronicles, supplemented by numerous stone inscriptions, are particularly full from AD 500 to 700; a powerful, unified kingdom also emerged in Tibet during this period, and the Himalayan passes to the north of the valley were opened. Extensive cultural, trade and political relations developed across the Himalayas, transforming the valley from a relatively remote backwater into the major intellectual and commercial centre between South and Central Asia. Nepal's contacts with China began in the mid-7th century with the exchange of several missions. But intermittent warfare between Tibet and China terminated this relationship; and while there were briefly renewed contacts in subsequent centuries, these were re-established on a continuing basis only in the late 18th century.

[4] The middle period in Nepalese history is usually considered synonymous with the rule of the Malla dynasty (10th-18th century) in Nepal Valley and surrounding areas. Although most of the Licchavi kings were devout Hindus, they did not impose Brahmanic social codes or values on their non-Hindu subjects; the Mallas perceived their responsibilities differently, however, and the great Malla ruler Jaya Sthiti (reigned c. 1832-95) introduced the first legal and social code strongly influenced by contemporary Hindu principles. His successor Yaksa Malla (reigned 1429-1482) divided his kingdom among his three sons, thus creating the independent principalities of Kathmandu, Patan, and Bhaktpur (Bhagdaon) in the valley. Each of these states controlled territory in the surrounding hill areas, with particular importance attached to the trade routes northward to Tibet and southward to India that were vital to the valley's economy. There were also numerous small principalities in the western and eastern hill areas, whose independence was sustained through a delicate balance of power based upon traditional inter-relationships and, in some cases, common ancestral origins among the ruling families.

[5] In the 16th century virtually all these principalities were ruled by dynasties claiming high-caste Indian origin whose members had left the hills in the wake of Muslim invasions of Northern India. In the early 18th century the principality of Gorkha (also spelled Gurkha) began to assert a predominant role in the hills and even to pose a challenge to Nepal Valley. The Mallas, weakened by familial dissent and widespread social and economic discontent, were no match for the great Gorkha ruler Prithvi Narayan Shah, who conquered the valley in 1769 and moved his capital to Kathmandu shortly thereafter, providing the foundation of the modern state of Nepal.

[6] The Shah (or Sah) rulers faced tremendous and persistent problems in trying to centralize an area long characterized by extreme diversity and ethnic and regional parochialism. They absorbed dominant regional and local elites into the central administration of Kathmandu, thus neutralizing potentially disintegrative political forces and involving them in national politics. However, this also severely limited the centre's authority in outlying areas because local administration was based upon a compromise division of responsibilities between the local elites and the central administration.

[7] The British conquest of India in the 19th century posed a serious threat to Nepal and left the country with no real alternative but to seek an accommodation with the British to preserve its independence. This was accomplished by the Rana family regime after 1860. Under this de facto alliance, Kathmandu permitted the recruitment of highly valued Gurkha units for the British Indian Army and also accepted British 'guidance' on foreign policy. In exchange, the British guaranteed the Rana regime protection against both foreign and domestic enemies and allowed it virtual autonomy in domestic affairs. Nepal, was also careful to maintain a friendly relationship with China and Tibet, for economic reasons.

[8] When the British withdrew from India in 1947, the Ranas were deprived of a vital external source of support and the regime was exposed to new dangers. Anti-Rana forces, composed mainly of Nepalese residents in India who had served their political apprenticeship in the Indian nationalist movement, formed an alliance with the Nepalese royal family, led by the king. A tripartite agreement between Nepal, India and the UK was signed in Kathmandu in November 1947, and Gurkha troops were used by India in the war against China, in 1961-62;

Pakistan in 1965 and 1971, and by the UK against Argentina in 1982.

[9] In February 1951, the Nepalese Congress succeeded in overthrowing the Rana regime with support from King Tribhuvan Bir Bikram Shah Deva. From this time to December 1960 a series of democratic experiments took place in Nepal; political parties were legalized and a general election was held in 1959, based on the Constitution approved by King Mahendra Bir Bikran Shah Deva. On December 15 1960, the first elected prime minister, B P Koirala, was arrested. Parliament was dissolved and most of the provisions of the Constitution were suspended. Political parties were outlawed and a non-party system or Panchayat was introduced in December 1962.

[10] Nepal became a member of the United Nations in 1955, and it has been an active member of the Non-Aligned Movement since the days of the Bandung Conference. By July 1986, some 75 countries, including the major powers, endorsed a proposal by King Birendra Bir Birkram Shah Dev that Nepal should be declared a peace zone. All of its neighbors except India and Bhutan endorsed the proposal.

[11] India is Nepal's major trading partner, and they have signed several treaties on trade and transit routes since 1950. The last treaty expired in 1989, and the two countries became locked in an undeclared trade war. Nepal had earlier antagonized India by importing arms from China, and India had suspended trade with Nepal, closing 19 of the 21 transit routes from March 1989, seriously

PROFILE

ENVIRONMENT

Nepal is a landlocked country in the Himalayas with three distinct geographical regions: the fertile, tropical plains of Terai, the central plateaus, covered with rainforest, and the Himalayan mountains, where the world's highest peaks are located. The climate varies according to altitude, from rainy and tropical, to cold in the high mountains. This diversity allows for the cultivation of rice, sugarcane, tobacco, jute and cereals. Livestock is also important; sheep and buffalo. Mineral and hydroelectric resources are as yet unexploited. Wood provides 90 per cent of the energy consumed, resulting in deforestation and soil erosion. Air and water pollution especially affect urban areas. The lack of sewerage systems in the most important cities has also contributed to the deterioration of the environment.

SOCIETY

Peoples: The Nepalese are descended from Indian, Tibetan and Mongolian migrants. Nepalese 53.2 per cent; Bihari (including Maithili and Bhojpuri) 18.4 per cent; Tharu 4.8 per cent; Tamang 4.7 per cent; Newar 3.4 per cent; Magar 2.2 per cent; Abadhi 1.7 per cent; other 11.6 per cent
Religions: Hinduism 86.2 per cent (official), Buddhism 7,8 per cent, Muslim 3.8 per cent, Christian 0.2 per cent; Jain 0.1 per cent; other 2 per cent. **Languages:** Nepali (official) is spoken by only half the population; many other languages are spoken, corresponding to the different cultural communities, with Tibetan being the second most common. **Political Parties:** The Nepalese Congress Party (NCP); United Communist Party of Nepal (UCPN); National Democratic Party (NDM), the Communist Party of Nepal-Maoist (CPNM); Sadbhavana Party and a Peoples' front, the Sumukta Jan Morcha (SJM).

THE STATE

Official Name: Sri Nepála Sarkár. **Administrative divisions:** 75 districts. **Capital:** Kathmandu, 660,000 people (1994 est). **Other cities:** Biratnagar 130,129 people; Lalitpur 117,203; Pokhara 95,311; Birganj 68,764 (1991). **Government:** Birendra Bir Bikram Shah Deva, King since 1972. Girija Prasad Koirala, Prime Minister and Chief of Government since April 1998. The House of Representatives has 205 members. **National Holidays:** February 15 (Constitution) and February 18 (Fatherland). **Armed Forces:** 35.000 (1994). **Other:** 28.000 (Police Forces).

STATISTICS

DEMOGRAPHY

Population: 22,021,000 (1996). **Annual growth:** 2.6% (1980/1996). **Estimates for year 2000:** 24,300,000 **Annual growth to year 2000:** 2.6% (1994/2000). **Urban Population:** 10.6% (1996). **Urban growth:** 7.77% (1980/95). **Children per woman:** 5.1 (1996).

HEALTH

Life expectancy at birth: 56 years (1996). male: 56 years (1994). female: 55 years (1994). **Infant mortality:** 82 per 1,000 (1996). **Under-5 child mortality:** 116 per 1,000 (1994). **Calorie consumption:** 100% (1988/90). 16,667 **people per doctor** (1988/91). **Safe water:** 63% (1990/96).

EDUCATION

Literacy: 28% (1995). male : 41% (1995). female: 14% (1995). **School enrolment :** Primary total: 109% (1990/95). male : 129% (1990/95). female: 88% (1990/95). Secondary: male : 46% (1990/95). female: 23% (1990/95). Tertiary: 5% (1995). **Primary school teachers:** one for every 39 students (1995).

COMMUNICATIONS

10 **newspapers**, 35 **radios**, and 4 **main telephone lines** per 1,000 people (1994).

ECONOMY

Per capita, GNP: $ 210 (1996). **Annual growth, GNP:** 1.8% (1995/96). **Annual inflation:** 11.64% (1985/95). **Consumer price index:** 157.6 (1994). **Currency:** 56 rupees = $ 1 (1995) **Cereal imports:** 62 metric tons (1994). **Food import dependency:** 9% (1996). **Fertilizer use:** 383 kgs per ha (1994). **Exports:** $ 358 million (1996). **Imports:** $ 664 million (1996). **External debt:** $ 2,414 million (1994). $ 110 **per capita:** (1994). **Debt service:** 7.7% of exports (1996). **Development aid received:** $ 430 million (1995). $ 21 per capita (1995).

ENERGY

Consumption: 27.81 Kgs of Oil equivalent per capita yearly (1994). 87.62% imported (1994).

HDI (rank / value) 154 / 0.347 (1994)

---

affecting the Nepalese economy. Nepal claimed that transit was a basic right for a landlocked country and that India had accepted trade as a separate issue in previous treaties they had agreed on. India threatened to withdraw all special trade facilities and suspended the supply of petroleum products and other essentials.

[12] In 1979, student protest movements emerged in Kathmandu and other cities, challenging the system. King Birendra responded by holding a plebiscite to choose between a multiparty system or a reformed Panchayat. The 1980 referendum frustrated the hopes of a return to a multiparty system as 55 per cent of the electorate voted for continued, reformed, Panchayat rule. The transition to parliamentary democracy with a constitutional monarchy was proclaimed by royal decree in April 1990.

[13] The Birendra monarchy was accused of having one of Asia's worst human rights records. In mid-1989 more than 300 political prisoners were held in Nepalese jails. The king has even passed laws that contradict the human rights provisions of the country's 1962 constitution.

[14] On April 12 1991, the first free elections were held in Nepal after 32 years of semi-monarchic rule. The Communist Party of Nepal and the Nepalese Congress allied for the elections, and other groups joined them. The communists obtained 4 of the 5 seats in the capital, but the national majority went to the Nepalese Congress Party.

[15] In 1991, the Nepali and Indian governments signed two treaties on trade and transit, both subject to parliamentary approval. The major criticism, from the left and the right alike, was the fact that the 1950 Friendship Treaty was not revised or abrogated. Critics considered it to be a threat to the country's sovereignty, in that it expressly forbid the acquisition of military equipment from countries other than India.

[16] Escaping from the ethnic conflict in Bhutan, 22,000 Bhutanese people of Nepalese origin entered the country in 1992. One month later, a general strike against corruption and price increases paralyzed the nation. The repression of the demonstrations left many people dead.

[17] Girija Prasad Koirala, prime minister and secretary general of the Congress Party, announced the convertibility of the rupee to stimulate foreign investment, and new trade agreements were signed with India. Two thirds of the Nepalese budget was funded by foreign aid.

[18] From 1994 onwards, the Government decided to charge $50,000 to any expedition planning to climb Mount Everest. The rivers flowing from the Himalayas potentially make Nepal one of the world's richest countries; however, the full exploitation of this resource for energy production, flood control and irrigation has been deterred by the lack of agreement between Nepal and India on sharing dam construction costs.

[19] Koirala was unsuccessful in his fight against poverty and illiteracy. The loss of parliamentary support and infighting in the monarchist Nepalese Congress Party (NCP) forced him to resign on July 10 1994. In the November elections, the United Communist Party took 88 seats in the Chamber of Representatives, surpassing the NCP who had 83. Man Mohan Adhikari was nominated prime minister. When unable to gain majority political support for his leadership in September 1995, the Communist prime minister handed over control to NCP leader, Sher Bahadur Deuba.

[20] Nepal is one of the poorest countries in the world. The annual per capita income stood at $250 in 1995, infant mortality was around 165 per thousand live births, and 71 per cent of the population lived below the poverty line. Living conditions in Kathmandu and the provinces are very different, for while life expectancy is 71 years in the capital, in rural areas the average drops to 34.

[21] In early 1996, guerrilla groups describing themselves as Maoist started campaigns to "eradicate feudalism." In its 1997 report, Amnesty International denounced the abuses committed, mainly by the Government forces, in armed confrontations with the guerrillas.

[22] In March 1997, Bahadur Deuba resigned and Lokendra Kahadur Chand took over with support from a coalition, including the pro-monarchy Sadbhavana Party of Nepal (SPN) and the United Communist Party (UCPN). In October, Surya Bahadur Thapa took over as Prime Minister, with the support of another fragile coalition, similar to that which had designated his predecessor. In April 1998, the Nepalese Congress withdrew their support, forcing him to stand down and pushing through the nomination of Koirala as the new Head of Government

Netherlands

Nederland

Population:	15,575,000 (1996)
Area:	40,844 SQ KM
Capital:	Amsterdam
Currency:	Guilder
Language:	Dutch

The Netherlands, Belgium, Luxembourg and the northern part of France constitute the region once known as the Low Countries. The first inhabitants of these lands arrived at the end of the last Ice Age. They changed over thousands of years from hunting and gathering groups to the more elaborate and hierarchical cultures which the Romans encountered.

2 When the Romans reached the area in the 1st century BC it was inhabited by Celts and Germanic people. The Empire never managed to occupy the land of the Frisians, in the north above the Rhine, so the Romans settled in the southern delta, where they created the provinces of Belgica and lesser Germanica.

3 The Frisians lived by fishing and raising cattle, while in the south, agriculture was practised around the villages and towns. By the second half of the 3rd century, the encroaching sea had drastically altered the economic basis of the region.

4 The strengthening of the Germanic tribes forced Rome to grant them custody of the Empire's borders, as it did with the Franks in Toxandria and Brabant. The line between the Romance and Germanic languages ran across the middle of the Low Countries, coinciding with the borders of the Roman Empire.

5 The Frisians remained independent until the 7th century, when the Franks and the Catholic Church started a strong offensive. By the end of the century, the region had been subdued by the Franks, under the Pepin and Carolingian dynasties.

6 The decline of the Carolingian Empire led to a period of instability during the 10th century. Several principalities were formed, with feudal ties to the kingdoms of Germany and France. The Frisians still remained free of sovereign authorities.

7 The secular principalities of Flanders (Vlaanderen), Hainaut, Namur, Loon, Holland, Zeeland, Guelders, and the duchies of Brabant and Limburg were formed. In the principalities of Utrecht and Liege, the secular and ecclesiastic authorities shared power.

8 The principalities worked towards greater freedom from royal authority. Flanders was the first to establish an efficient administration, followed by Brabant, Hainaut, and Namur. The designation of their own bishops marked the end of German influence, and the establishment of closer links between the principalities.

9 France tried to subdue Flanders but was defeated in the Battle of the Spurs in 1302. In general, France and Britain kept a balance of power, a situation that contributed to preserving the autonomy of the region.

10 Population pressure led to the creation of new farmlands. On the coast, the Cistercian and Premonstratensian monks (an order founded by St Norbert) constructed many dykes. These were initially built to defend people from the high tides, but they later served to reclaim land.

11 From the 11th century onwards, the Frisians developed a drainage system which removed the sea-water, providing land for pasturage and arable fields. During the 12th and 13th centuries, a vast peat bog in the Netherlands and Utrecht was reclaimed for agriculture.

12 This area of polders on the coast of Flanders and Friesland, became economically very significant. Between the 12th and 14th centuries, the struggle against the sea and inland water became so important that water authorities were created to organize the construction of dikes and the use of water.

13 This increase in arable land and population brought about growth, not only in agriculture, but also in industry and commerce. The new towns gave birth to new social classes who sought autonomy. Merchants in the towns had to swear an oath of co-operation; promising that they would keep law and order.

14 The towns gradually became independent centres, having the power to sign commercial, political, and military agreements, with other towns or with the Prince. The town owned the land within its boundaries and the inhabitants did not rely on any external authorities.

15 During the second half of the 14th century, the dukes of Burgundy from the French royal house of Valois, ruled over most of the Low Countries where they tried to create a centralized state. There was a movement to prevent this centralization, in 1477, but the accession of the Habsburgs interrupted it.

16 The fate of the Low Countries depended on the outcome of the House of Austria's struggle for European domination. Centralization was on the increase and the Church was no exception. A Papal Bull was issued, creating a Rome-based administration, with three archbishops and 15 bishops. This was deeply resented by the local nobility.

17 The Lutheran and Anabaptist faiths had difficulty gaining converts in the Low Countries, while Calvinism quickly gained acceptance among the lower classes and the intellectuals. Repression drove many Calvinists into exile, but they still had influence in the 1567 anti-absolutism rebellion.

18 Popular unrest and the nobility and urban gentry's desire for autonomy led to a successful rebellion in Holland. After the defeat of the Spanish troops, the rebellion extended to all the provinces, ending with the Treaty of Ghent in 1576.

19 Three years later, for geographic, economic, political, and religious reasons, this union dissolved. The Union of Arras was founded in the south, and the Union of Utrecht in the north, both of these being within the boundaries of a larger unit led by the States-General.

20 In 1581, the States-General passed an Act of Abjuration making the Union of Utrecht into a State, seizing sovereignty from Philip II. The Netherlands was the largest economic and political power within the union, so all of the union's inhabitants became known as Netherlanders.

21 During the Twelve Years' Truce with Spain, 1609-21, controversies within the Union grew. The collaboration between the province of Holland and the House of Orange during the war gave way to a growing rivalry. This situation was antagonized by the dispute over Church-State relations.

22 In 1618, Maurice of Orange, supported by the States-General, executed the leader of the main party in the Netherlands. When war against Spain resumed in 1621, the French and Dutch rivals were forced to reunite until the signing of the Treaty of Utrecht in 1713.

23 The 17th century is called the golden age in Dutch history, because the country was the center of attention, and it established relations with the great powers of the time. This was viewed as the birth of a great nation, a fact that was only called into question at the end of the 17th century.

24 Dutch prosperity was not only the result of continental trade, but also of its colonial

PROFILE

ENVIRONMENT

The country is a vast plain and 38 per cent of its territory is below sea level. Intensive agriculture and cattle raising produce high priced milk products and crops (particularly flowers). Population density is amongst the highest in the world. Highly industrialized, the country is the world's third largest producer of natural gas, and is a dominant influence in petroleum activity. It has large refineries in the Antilles and Rotterdam, the world center of the free, or "spot", crude oil market. As a result of the massive use of pesticides, underground water supplies contain high levels of nitrates. Similarly, the country's main rivers are filled will all kinds of organic and industrial wastes, which often originate in other European countries.

SOCIETY

Peoples: Dutch 95 per cent; Turks 1.3 per cent; Moroccans 1 per cent; Germans 0.3 per cent.
Religions: 31 per cent Catholic, Dutch Reformed Church 14 per cent; Calvinist 8 per cent; Muslim 3.9 per cent; other 4.1 per cent; no religion 39 per cent.
Languages: Dutch (official), Turkish, Arab.
Political Parties: Christian Democratic Appeal; People's Party for Freedom and Democracy, liberal; Democrats 66, liberal; Labour Party, affiliated to the Socialist International; among the minor parties are three religious (protestant) parties; Green Left, the Socialist Party .
Social Organizations: There are two large central unions: the Federation of Dutch Trade Unions and the Christian National Trade Union.

THE STATE

Official Name: Koninkrijk der Nederlanden.
Administrative Divisions: 12 Provinces.
Capital: Greater Amsterdam, 1,100,000 people (1994). Although the Government has its seat in The Hague, Amsterdam is still considered the capital.
Other cities: Rotterdam, 599,521 people; The Hague (s'-Gravenhage), 442,105 people; Utrecht, 235,357 people, Eindhoven, 197,055 (1995).
Government: Constitutional and parliamentary monarchy. Queen Beatrix, Head of State; Wim Kok, Prime Minister since 1994, re-elected August 1998. Bicameral parliament, with 75 members elected by regional parliaments, and 150-member second chamber
National Holiday: April 30.
Armed Forces: 74,400 (1995).
Other: 3,600 Royal Military Corps.
Dependencies: See "Netherlands" Antilles and Aruba.

power. In 1602, the East India Company was created, with bases in South Africa, Ceylon, India and Indonesia. The Netherlands had sovereign powers in these colonies, as did the British and French in theirs.

[25] At first the Company only held coastal trading bases, but later on, it started to occupy the hinterland controlling the region and certain commodities. The colonial administration was autonomous, as the Dutch preferred governing through agreements with local leaders.

[26] In 1621, the West Indies Company was founded. It made the bulk of its profits from the slave trade and privateering, it also operated outside Zeeland, especially against Spanish ships. The Netherlands dominated the slave trade during the 17th century.

[27] In 1648, the Dutch had three large settlements in the Americas: one in the north, for the fur trade; another on the Atlantic coast, with outposts for the slave trade and smuggling with Spanish colonies; and another in what is now Brazil and Suriname, formerly Dutch Guyana. By 1700, they were left with only the trading outposts in Curaçao, St Eustacius and St Martin, the plantations in Guyana, and the slave port of Elmina.

[28] Dutch maritime power weakened in the 18th century, especially after the war against Britain (1708-84). The country used up a portion of its capital to buy bonds in foreign governments. The bankers in Amsterdam were among the most powerful in Europe.

[29] The 1750s saw the emergence of the Patriot movement, a group of factions who had been overlooked in governmental policies: they ranged from bankers and simple artisans, to dissident Protestants and Catholics, unhappy with monarchic abuse of power.

[30] The Patriots had to go into exile during the Prussian invasion of 1786. Their hopes were rekindled with the French Revolution, but it was not until 1794 that France managed effective opposition to Britain and Prussia, who supported William V. They proclaimed the Batavian Republic and started the process of political modernization.

[31] The new republic declared equality among its citizens and changed the institutional framework. It replaced the assembly of States-General for a National Assembly with direct electoral representation, and executive power was separated from the legislative and the judicial.

[32] In 1806, France annexed the state to the Empire, under the name of the Napoleonic Kingdom of the Netherlands. Five years later, Bonaparte incorporated the Netherlands into France, until the fall of the Empire. In 1814, King William I of Orange was chosen by the Dutch leaders, and he restored the monarchy.

[33] In the Congress of Vienna, the victorious powers gave William I sovereignty over the whole of the Low Countries. The Belgian revolution of 1830 broke out during his reign. His successors, William II and William III made the final move towards parliamentary monarchy.

[34] Universal male suffrage was approved in 1917; women were granted the vote in 1922. After decades of debate over the school system, Protestants and Catholics allied themselves against the liberals and, in 1888, the first private denominational schools were opened.

[35] New political parties were founded, based on the religious ideas and ideologies of the time. To the Liberal, Protestant and Catholic parties were added the Protestant Conservative, the Socialist and the Communist parties. As none could obtain a majority, coalitions became commonplace.

[36] During World War I, the Netherlands declared its neutrality, and political parties agreed on a truce in order to devote themselves to the domestic economy and trade. The merchant navy had recovered and industry grew, in particular textiles, electronics, and chemicals.

[37] During the postwar period, the Netherlands was a member of the League of Nations, but it re-affirmed its neutrality. Symbolically, The Hague became the seat of the International Court of Justice. During the Versailles negotiations, Belgium tried unsuccessfully to revive an old territorial claim against the Netherlands.

[38] During World War II, Hitler attacked France through the Netherlands, and Queen Wilhelmina formed a government in exile in London. All political factions took part in anti-Nazi resistance. German repression was harsh, and by the end of the war the country was on the verge of famine.

[39] In 1945, an agreement was signed by the Government, companies and trade unions. It lasted 20 years and was aimed at controlling prices and salaries. Indonesia became independent soon afterwards, while Suriname had to wait until 1975. The Netherlands underwent a rapid industrialization process, in particular in the fields of steel production, electronics, and petrochemicals.

[40] Dutch capital controls some large transnational corporations, such as Royal Dutch Shell, the oil company (jointly a British company). Unilever, the world's largest food and soap manufacturer, has branches all over the world and its products

are used by companies everywhere. Other Dutch transnationals include Philips electronics, AKZO, a chemical manufacturer, DSM, Hoogoven Groep and Heineken.

[41] In the postwar period, the Government was composed of Labor party (the former socialists) and Catholic coalitions. The Netherlands gave up neutrality, becoming a member of NATO and of the European Economic Community. Also, together with Belgium and Luxembourg it formed an economic alliance known as the Benelux.

[42] During the 1960s, youth demonstrations developed into violent riots, the royal marriages also became the subject of public controversy and ideological and religious questioning occurred in all Dutch institutions.

[43] In the 1970s, voters favored the center and the left, while the Government reformed the tax system and redistributed income. The most controversial subjects were the defence budget and the installation of NATO atomic missiles within the country.

[44] The Netherlands is one of the few OECD countries giving over 0.7 per cent of its GNP for aid to the Third World. It has also maintained a coherent policy on the defence of human rights and against apartheid in South Africa, though links with Israel have tended to estrange it from some Arab countries.

[45] In 1989 the Government approved a 0.6 per cent increase in the defence budget for 1990 and 1991, to be followed by a budget suspension until 1995 and the withdrawal of 750 Dutch soldiers posted in West Germany. This Dutch resolution caused much malaise within NATO.

[46] In the Netherlands there are some 100,000 farms, with around 4,500,000 head of cattle. The cost to the country of raising and feeding each cow is $2,000 per year, a sum which is higher than the per capita income of many Third World countries. The Dutch export dairy products and flowers, but also import a great amount of raw materials for their agro-industry. Fifteen million hectares of land in other countries

STATISTICS

DEMOGRAPHY
Population: 15,575,000 (1996). **Annual growth**: 0.6 % (1980/1996). **Estimates for year 2000**: 16,000,000 **Annual growth to year 2000**: 0.5 % (1994/2000). **Urban population**: 89.0 % (1996). **Urban growth**: 0.64 % (1980/95). **Children per woman**: 1.6 (1996).

HEALTH
Life expectancy at birth: 78 years (1996). male: 74 years (1994) female: 80 years (1994) **Infant mortality**: 5 per 1,000 (1996) **Under-5 child mortality**: 6 per 1,000 (1996) **Calorie consumption**: 114 % (1988/90) 398 **people per doctor** (1988/91)

EDUCATION
School enrolment : Primary total: 97 % (1990/95) male : 96 % (1990/95) female: 98 % (1990/95) Secondary: male : 129 % (1990/95) female: 118 % (1990/95) Tertiary: 49 % (1995) **Primary school teachers**: one for every 19 students (1995)

COMMUNICATIONS
330 **newspapers**, 909 **radios**, 490 **TV sets** and 511 **main telephone lines** per 1,000 people (1994) **Books**: 222 new titles per 100,000 people (1992/94)

ECONOMY
Per capita, GNP: $ 25,940 (1996) **Annual growth, GNP**: 3.9 % (1995/96) **Annual inflation**: 1.69 % (1985/95) **Consumer price index**: 112.2 (1994) **Currency**: 1.6 guilders = $ 1 (1995) **Cereal imports**: 6,676 metric tons (1994). **Fertilizer use**: 5,453 kgs per ha (1994) **Exports**: $ 177,228 million (1996) **Imports**: $ 160,700 million (1996)

ENERGY
Consumption: 4,579.63 Kgs of Oil equivalent per capita yearly (1994) 6.62 % imported (1994)

HDI (rank / value) 6 / 0.94 (1994)

(including 5 million in the Third World) is under production for Dutch needs. This is mainly because much of the soya and tapioca that their farm animals eat comes from other countries, mainly Brazil and Thailand. Only 20 per cent of the vegetable protein fed to animals is converted to animal protein. The rest produces 110 million tons of manure a year, of which only half is used in agriculture. The other half ends up polluting the soil, drinking water and the air, where it adds to industrial emissions to cause acid rain. Over 40 per cent of Holland's trees have been irreversibly damaged by acid rain and the country has exceptionally high levels of contamination.

[47] Dutch agriculture is also characterized by a high energy consumption (in heated greenhouses to produce summer crops in winter) and the intensive use of pesticides, at a rate of about 20 kg per hectare per year. These seep into underground water reserves, contaminating drinking water supplies. Likewise, the high level of industrialization and population density have given rise to the presence of heavy metals, nitrates and other organic wastes in the Maas, Rhine and Waal rivers.

[48] Due to the high level of consumption which characterizes Dutch society, each person produces an estimated 3,000 kg of refuse per year. In Amsterdam and other cities many apartment buildings are inhabited by people who live alone, a fact which

increases the demand for housing.

[49] Taking advantage of the fact that the Netherlands was occupying the EU presidency at the time, the Dutch Parliament exhorted EU heads of state and governments, to condemn all forms of racism in Maastricht in December 1991. In addition, they urged the adoption of legislation prohibiting xenophobic acts throughout Europe.

[50] Despite this official position, the country was beset by growing racism, although to a lesser degree than other European countries. In September 1993 the Netherlands adopted legislation restricting the admission of immigrants from outside the European Union.

[51] Government agencies devised economic indicators capable of assessing environmental damage, and methods for calculating national income. In 1992, the Central Office of Statistics announced the "green gross national product" (GGNP). This indicator evaluates losses in natural resources, according to the capacity for regeneration, and the effect on local communities.

[52] The government coalition parties suffered a serious setback in the March 1994 local elections, which showed the growth of the anti-immigration far right. On August 22, Wim Kok became Prime Minister.

[53] In 1995, for the second year in a row, the complex hydraulic system failed, causing flooding of vast areas in the south and centre.

[54] In late 1996, the unemployment rate fell to 6.6 per cent. The GDP grew 2.7 per cent as a result of, among other things, the rise of exports and the recovery of local demand.

[55] In March 1998, the European Union demanded "considerable efforts" - ie, economic "austerity" policies - from the Netherlands and five more countries to allow for the introduction the European single currency.

[56] The May 1998 elections resulted in the first-ever left-wing majority in Parliament.

Netherlands Antilles

Population: 195,000 (1996)
Area: 800 SQ KM
Capital: Willemstad

Currency: NA guilders
Language: Dutch

The Coquette were the original inhabitants of what today are the islands of Aruba, Bonaire and Curaçao. Soon after the arrival of the Spaniard Alonso de Ojeda in 1499, these local people were enslaved and taken to Hispaniola (present-day Haiti and Dominican Republic). The indians that Columbus found on the "S Islands" (the Windward Islands) in 1493 met a similar fate.

2   The conquistadors attached little importance to these islands because they lacked readily exploitable natural resources. However, the Windward Islands (particularly St Martin Island) acquired strategic importance as a port of entry into the Caribbean and also became important for their salt deposits. Ports on the Iberian Peninsula were closed to Holland after the war with Spain and Portugal, so the Dutch were forced to seek alternative sources of salt in the Antilles.

3   In 1606, the Spanish Crown decided to put a halt to this intense traffic, and prohibited Dutch shipping in the Antilles. Holland retaliated by creating the West Indies Company, which was charged with establishing, managing and defending the colonies. Thus the theft of Spanish ships became one of the main sources of income.

4   Although salt and Brazilwood were important products, the slave trade became the principal economic activity. In 1634, the stockholders of the Company in Amsterdam decided to invade Curaçao. The Spaniards offered no resistance and Curaçao became a major international slave-trading center.

5   In 1648, after three centuries of conflict, the Treaty of Westphalia was signed, granting Holland control over these small islands in the Antilles. The native populations - particularly those of Curaçao and Bonaire - were replaced by African slaves to meet the needs of new agricultural operations, and thus became a minority on these islands. As in the rest of the Antilles, slave rebellions were frequent, culminating in the 18th century with a massacre at the hands of colonial troops.

6   During the Napoleonic wars, at the beginning of the 19th century, the three islands passed into British hands on two different occasions; however, the change failed to produce any improvement in the lives of the local inhabitants. Although the slave trade had been prohibited in 1814, it was not abolished in the Dutch colonies until 1863. Even then, although the slaves were "free", their lives did not change substantially. Many migrated to the Dominican Republic, Panama, Venezuela and Cuba.

7   Once slavery was abolished, interest in the islands lagged. In 1876, the Dutch parliament proposed to sell them to Venezuela, but negotiations fell through. With the rise of the oil industry at the beginning of the 20th century, refineries were installed here because of the proximity of the islands to Lake Maracaibo. From the 1920s onward, this new activity radically changed the colony. The plantations were abandoned and the demand for labour attracted thousands of immigrants from Venezuela, Suriname and the British West Indies.

8   However, this boom dwindled over time, as automation significantly reduced the number of jobs. On May 30 1969, when unemployment stood at 20 per cent, police broke up a labor demonstration. This sparked large-scale riots which were quelled only by the joint intervention of 300 Dutch marines and some US marines from the American fleet, which happened to be anchored in the archipelago. As a result of these disturbances, parliament was dissolved.

9   The islands have been more politically active since 1937 when the first local parties were founded. However, they have only existed as states since 1948, when the new post-war Dutch constitution renamed what had been known as "Curaçao and dependencies" as the "Netherlands Antilles".

10   The issue of independence has long been at the center of local political life. In 1954, a new law established the islands' autonomy over their internal affairs. Nevertheless, the People's Electoral Movement (PEM), founded in 1971 in Aruba, maintains that, as the islands are

no longer "Dutch", they have nothing in common (not even a name, because "Antilles" is the generic designation of the whole region) and each island should be free to choose its own constitution and set itself up as an autonomous republic. Secessionist feeling was strong in Aruba, where a referendum carried out in 1977 for consultation purposes only (ie, not politically binding), showed that the majority wished to separate from the other islands.

11   The Netherlands however preferred to maintain the political unity of the islands, arguing that this would ensure better economic prospects for the whole group and, above all, more political stability in the turbulent Caribbean region. This difference of opinion, together with the diversity of views held by the local parties on the matter, delayed negotiations for independence.

12   The delay radicalized the electorate and in 1979 the New Antilles Movement (MAN) achieved a parliamentary majority in Curaçao (7 out of 12 seats). In coalition with the PEM and the UPB (Bonaire Patriotic

Union) it formed the first left-of-center government in the history of the islands. The MAN favoured a federal formula with considerable autonomy for each of the islands but the PEM insisted on the total separation of Aruba.

[13] In 1980 it was agreed to set independence for 1990, on the condition that each of the six islands submitted the issue to a referendum as soon as possible. Aruba chose to become an individual associated state, breaking away from the federation in January 1986 (see Aruba).

[14] The Netherlands Antilles became modern trading posts, totally dependent on transnational oil companies. Exxon and Royal Dutch Shell (an Anglo-Dutch consortium), maintained a monopoly on all oil refining and processing. They also controlled the petrochemical fertilizer industry and all transportation and sales. These powerful companies, linked

> The Netherlands Antilles became modern trading posts, totally dependent on transnational oil companies. Exxon and Royal Dutch Shell (an Anglo-Dutch consortium), maintained a monopoly on all oil refining and processing.

financially and commercially to branches of approximately 2,500 foreign firms registered on the islands, have an impact on 85 per cent of the total imports, 99 per cent of the exports and 50 per cent of the islands' net income.

[15] Despite modest industrial growth and a booming tourist industry, the economy was fragile. This was clearly demonstrated towards the end of 1984, when the transnational oil companies announced their withdrawal from the islands and spread panic among the people and local political leaders. The conflict was partially resolved in

October 1985, with the purchase of the Curaçao refinery by the Antilles Government, which in turn rented the facility to Petroleos de Venezuela SA., an oil company owned by the Venezuelan Government. The deal did not include the Exxon plant on Aruba, which closed down.

[16] The separation of Aruba favored the 1984 victory of a right-of-center coalition headed by Maria Liberia Peters of the National People's Party (PNP). This coalition was unable to sustain the minimum consensus necessary to stay in power. Therefore in January 1986, MAN leader, Domenico Martina, became Prime Minister once again. Two years later, Maria Liberia Peters returned to power.

[17] In 1990 the Government renewed its contracts with the Venezuelan oil company and introduced a series of austerity measures designed to cover the deficit generated by the Aruban withdrawal from the federation.

[18] The election of the Island Councils in 1991 was marked by the defeat of the Democratic Party as a result of internal divisions and financial irregularities committed by the administration.

[19] The Netherlands requested that each island make a separate proposal for constitutional reform in 1993. Accordingly, Curaçao received special status, St Martin was made independent, while Bonaire, Saba and St Eustatius continued under Dutch control. The constitution also dictated that the Treaty of Strasburg, which predicted complete independence for 1999, would not be applied in the islands.

[20] In a plebiscite held in 1994, the constituent members of the Netherlands Antilles voted to preserve their federation.

[21] This same year, Miguel Pourier was appointed Prime Minister. In 1996, the structural adjustment programme caused tensions in the Government, which led to the resignation of the labour minister, Jeffrey Corion. The legislative elections of January 1998, confirmed Pourier in his post.

PROFILE

ENVIRONMENT

The Netherlands Antilles are made up of two Caribbean island groups. The main group is composed of Bonaire (288 sq km) and Curaçao (444 sq km). Located near the coast of Venezuela, they are known (together with Aruba) as the "Dutch Leeward Islands" or the "ABC Islands". The smaller group is made up of three small islands of volcanic origin: Saint Eustatius (21 sq km), Saba (13 sq km) and Saint Martin (34 sq km -the southern part of which is a dependency of the French island of Guadeloupe). These are known as the "S Islands" or the "Dutch Windward Islands", although in fact they are part of the Leeward group of the Lesser Antilles. In general the climate is tropical, moderated by ocean currents. There is little farming. One of the largest oil refineries in the world is located on Curaçao; it is leased to a Venezuelan oil company. The coastal areas of the islands have suffered the consequences of economic development. The soil has been polluted, and waste disposal poses a serious problem. Curaçao is the most polluted of the islands.

SOCIETY

Peoples: Most of the population descend from African slaves. There are also Carib indians and descendants of Europeans and Asians.

Religions: Mainly Catholic.

Languages: Dutch (official). The most widely spoken language - in Curaçao and Bonaire - is *papiamento*, a local dialect based on Spanish with elements of Dutch, Portuguese, English and some African languages. In Saint Eustatius, Saba and Saint Martin, English is the main language. Spanish is also spoken and many claim that it should be taught as a second language (instead of English) to facilitate integration with Latin America.

Political Parties: National People's Party (NVP); Antilles Re-Structure Movement (MAN); Patriotic Union of Bonaire (UPB); Democratic Party (DP); Labour Party (LP); Democratic Party (DP); Antiyas Nobo Movement (ANM).

Social Organizations: National Confederation of Curaçao Trade Unions (AVVC); General Workers' Union (CGT); Bonaire Labor Federation (FEDEBON); General Worker's Federation (GWF).

THE STATE

Capital: Willemstad, 50,000 people (1981).

Government: Jaime M Saleh, Governor appointed by the Dutch Government since 1989. Miguel Pourier, Prime Minister since 1994, re elected in January 1998. There is an Advisory Council and a Council of Ministers, responsible to the Staten (Legislature) composed of 22 elected members. Defense and foreign relations are handled by the Dutch crown.

National Holiday: May 30, Anti-colonial Movement (1969).

DEMOGRAPHY
Population: 195,000 (1996). **Urban population:** 69.4 % (1996).

ECONOMY
Consumer price index: 109.5 (1994). **Currency:** 1.79 NA guilders = $ 1 (1995) **Cereal imports:** 60 metric tons (1994).

Nicaragua

Nicaragua

Population: 4,238,000 (1996)
Area: 130,000 SQ KM
Capital: Managua

Currency: Córdobas
Language: Spanish

W hat today is Nicaragua was in pre-Colombian times an area of influence for the Chibcha (see Colombia) and the Maya. The Caribbean coast was inhabited by the Miskito and was visited by Christopher Columbus in 1502. By converting local leaders Nicoya and Nicarao to Christianity and crushing the resistance of Diriangen's armies, the conquistadors Gil Gonzales Dávila and Andrés Nino consolidated Spain's hold over the territory. In 1544 it was incorporated into the Captaincy-General of Guatemala.

2 In 1821 Nicaragua became independent, together with the rest of Central America, joining the Mexican Empire but subsequently withdrawing in 1824 to form the Federation of the United Provinces of the Center of America.

3 Nicaragua left the Federation in 1839, declaring itself an independent state. The country was divided between wo groups: the coffee and sugar oligarchies, and the artisans and small landowners. The former would become the conservatives, and the latter, the liberals who favored free trade.

4 In 1856, 120 soldiers landed in Nicaragua under the command of William Walker, an American mercenary. With Washington's tacit support, he proclaimed himself President of Nicaragua. His purpose was to find new territories for slavery which was on the point of being abolished in the Union. Walker was defeated by the allied armies of Central America in 1857, and later executed. Nicaragua's ports were occupied by Germany in 1875 and Britain in 1895. Britain commandeered Nicaragua's

Customs in order to collect on unpaid debts.

5 After 30 years of conservative rule the Liberal Party came to power in 1893, and José Santos Zelaya became President. The liberals refused to comply with demands made by the United States so in 1912 the US invaded. After killing the Liberal Party leader, Benjamin Zeledón, the US Marine force remained in Nicaragua until 1925. In 1926 they returned to protect president Adolfo Díaz, who was about to be overthrown.

6 This second US occupation was resisted by Augusto C Sandino, who raised and commanded a popular army of about 3,000 troops. For more than six years they held out against 12,000 US marines who were supported by the airforce and ground troops of the local oligarchy. Sandino promised that he would lay down arms when the last marine left Nicaragua. He carried out his promise in 1933, but was assassinated by US-backed Anastasio Somoza García who, after seizing power, ruled despotically until he was killed by the patriot Rigoberto López Pérez in 1956.

7 During two decades of dictatorship, Somoza had achieved almost absolute control of the nation's economy. He was succeeded by his son, engineer Luis Somoza Debayle, who in turn handed the government on to his son, Anastasio, a West Point graduate.

8 Anastasio Somoza outlawed all trade unions, massacred members of peasant movements and banned all opposition parties. In the 1960s the Sandinista National Liberation Front was founded. This organized

and developed the guerrilla warfare which lasted for 17 years. When opposition leader Pedro Joaquín Chamorro, editor of the daily La Prensa, was assassinated on Somoza's orders in January 1978, a nationwide strike was called and there were massive protest demonstrations.

9 By March 1979, the Sandinista Front had united its three factions and began to lead the political opposition, the 'Patriotic Front'. In May 1979 the Front launched the "final offensive", combining a general strike, a popular uprising, armed combat, and intense diplomatic activity abroad. On July 17, Somoza fled the country, bringing an end to a dynasty that had killed 50,000 people. The Junta for National Reconstruction, created a few weeks before in Costa Rica, was installed in Managua two days later.

10 The victorious revolutionaries nationalized the Somozas' lands

and industrial properties, which constituted 40 per cent of the economic resources of Nicaragua. They also replaced the defeated National Guard with the Sandinista Popular Army. The revolutionary government implemented a literacy campaign and began the reconstruction of the devastated economy. Other important policies were non-alignment, a mixed economy, political pluralism, and respect for individual rights and liberties.

11 In May 1980 two non-Sandinista members of the Junta, Violeta Barrios de Chamorro and Alfonso Robelo, resigned. The Government avoided a crisis by replacing them with Rafael Córdoba and Arturo Cruz, two "moderate" anti-Somoza activists.

12 In 1981, US President Ronald Reagan announced his aim of destroying the Sandinistas. Between April and July 1982 deputy interior minister, Edén Pastora ("Commander Zero"), deserted and announced from Costa Rica that he would drive the Sandinista Front's National Directorate out "at gunpoint". Some 2,500 former National Guardsmen, supported by the US, invaded Nicaragua from Honduras. From then on Nicaragua was harassed without respite, forcing the authorities to extend the state of emergency, to institute compulsory military service and to ban pro-American political declarations.

13 In 1983, President Reagan

PUBLIC EXPENDITURE

n/a	

63.5%
1995 ■ DEFENCE □ SOCIAL

In 1990/91 Military as % of health & education expenditure was 97%.

WORKERS

(1996)

Labour force %
■ WOMEN
□ MEN
36%   64%

■ AGRICULTURE 28% (1990)
□ INDUSTRIAL 26%
■ SERVICES 46%

LAND USE

DEFORESTATION -1.7% annual (81/90)
IRRIGATED 8 % of arable

(1993)

■ FOREST & WOODLAND 24.6%
□ ARABLE 8.5%
■ OTHER 66.9%

PER 100,000
LIVE BIRTHS
160

66%

admitted the existence of secret funds destined for covert CIA operations against Nicaragua. The funds were also used to aid counter-revolutionaries or contras operating from Honduran territory. Reagan referred to the contras as "freedom fighters".

[14] Concerned at the serious threat of a war that might escalate throughout Central America, the governments of Colombia, Mexico, Panama and Venezuela began to seek a negotiated settlement to the conflict. As the "Contadora Group", these countries' foreign ministers advanced peace plans which won great diplomatic support and prevented an imminent invasion by US forces.

[15] Contra attacks intensified steadily with open US backing. Elections were held in November 1984. Candidates were drawn from the Sandinista National Liberation Front (FSLN), the Democratic Conservative Party, the Independent Liberal Party, the Popular Social Christian Party, the Communist Party, the Socialist Party and the Marxist-Leninist People's Action Movement. Over 80 per cent of Nicaragua's 1.5 million registered voters went to the polls and the Sandinista Front Government led by Daniel Ortega obtained 67 per cent of the vote. In November Reagan was re-elected and in April 1985 he declared a trade embargo against Nicaragua and seized its assets.

[16] In 1986, the Assembly discussed the details of a new Constitution, which went into effect in January 1987. It provided for a presidential system, with a president elected by direct vote for a six-year term. Legislators would be elected on the basis of proportional representation.

[17] In 1987, with UN and OAS participation, the Central American presidents met for negotiations in Esquipulas, Guatemala. The Esquipulas II accords stipulated an end to external support for armed opposition groups; the opening of internal dialogue in each of the countries, mediated by the Catholic Church; and an amnesty for those who lay down their arms, with guarantees of political representation.

[18] In Nicaragua a National Reconciliation Commission was formed. Among its most spectacular achievements was the return of contra leader Fernando Chamorro from exile. He was granted an amnesty after he renounced violence. Press censorship was lifted and Violeta Chamorro's opposition daily La Prensa reappeared. On October 7, a unilateral cease-fire went into effect in several parts of the country, although contra leaders announced that they would continue hostilities.

[19] Throughout 1988, as US pressure increased the economic situation worsened. A monetary reform and a 10 per cent reduction in the government budget in February were insufficient to halt spiralling inflation.

[20] In July 1988, the US ambassador to Managua was expelled on the accusation of encouraging anti-Sandinista activities. The US Government responded by expelling Nicaragua's representative in Washington.

[21] The Esquipulas II accords seemed to be doomed to oblivion, but when the five Central American presidents met at Costa del Sol, El Salvador, in February 1989, President Daniel Ortega embarked on fresh negotiations. The Sandinista proposal was to bring the elections forward to February 1990 and to accept proposed modifications to the 1988 electoral law. The condition was that the contras dismantle their bases in Honduras within three months of an agreement. The US however insisted that the contras continue in Honduras, and George Bush persuaded Congress to award them $40 million in "humanitarian aid".

[22] Daniel Ortega was the FSLN presidential candidate. The National Opposition Union (UNO), a 14-party coalition, presented Pedro Joaquín Chamorro's widow, Violeta Barrios de Chamorro. Unexpectedly, the UNO won the elections with 55 per cent of the vote against the FSLN's 41 per cent. The Sandinistas accepted defeat and ascribed it to the Nicaraguan people's desperate desire for peace, the dire state of the economy and FSLN overconfidence that victory was assured.

[23] On April 25, before she took office, the President and the FSLN signed a "Transition Protocol". This included respecting the standing Constitution and the social achievements of the revolution, and supporting disarmament of the contras. The new president announced that she would personally assume the defence portfolio and maintain the Sandinista General Humberto Ortega as commander of the armed forces. She also indefinitely suspended compulsory military service.

[24] The UNO's Vice-President, Virgilio Godoy, and other members of the coalition withdrew from the government accusing Chamorro of betraying pre-election agreements by keeping Humberto Ortega in office.

[25] In May 1990, public employees went on strike for wage increases of up to 200 per cent. The Government declared the strike illegal, and revoked the civil service law (under which civil servants cannot be fired without

PROFILE

ENVIRONMENT

Nicaragua has both Pacific and Caribbean coastlines. It is crossed by two important mountain ranges: the Central American Andes, running from northwest to southeast, and a volcanic chain with several active volcanoes along the western coast. The Managua and Nicaragua lakes lie between the two ranges. On the eastern slopes, the climate is tropical with abundant rainfall, while it is drier on the western side where the population is concentrated. Cotton is the main cash crop in the mountain area, while bananas are grown along the Atlantic coast. Changes in water and soil have affected approximately 40 per cent of the country's territory.

SOCIETY

Peoples: Over 70 per cent of Nicaraguans are mixed descendents of American natives and Spanish colonizers; there are minorities of Europeans, Miskitos, Sunos and Ramas, and African descendents.
Religion: Mainly Catholic.
Languages: Spanish (official and predominant). Miskito, Suno and English are spoken on the Atlantic coast.
Political Parties: Sandinista Front for National Liberation (FSLN); Political Opposition Alliance, formerly the National Union of the Opposition (UNO), made up of: Democratic Party of National Confidence (PDCN), National Conservative Party (PNC), Conservative Popular Alliance Party (PAPC), Independent Liberal Party (PLI), Social Democratic Party (PSD), Liberal Constitutionalist Party (PLC). Other parties include: Nicaraguan Socialist Party (PSN); Communist Party of Nicaragua (PCdeN); Neoliberal Party (PAL); Nicaraguan Democratic Movement (MDN); National Action Party (PAN); Central American Integrationist Party (PIAC); National Conservative Alliance Party (PANC); People's Social Christian Party (PPSC); Yatama Indigenous Movement; Yatama Social Christian Party (PSC); United Revolutionary Movement (MRU); Party of the Nicaraguan Resistance (PRN).
Social Organizations: The Sandinista Labor Confederation (CST); the General Labor Confederation (Independent) (CGT-I); the Nicaraguan Labor Confederation (CTN); the Labor Unity and Action Confederation (CAUS); the Rural Workers' Association (ATC); the Workers' Front (FO); the Unified Labor Confederation (CUS); the National Employees Union (UNE); the National Confederation of Professionals (CONAPRO).

THE STATE

Official Name: República de Nicaragua.
Administrative Division: 16 Departments.
Capital: Managua, 819,731 people (1995).
Other cities: León, 124,117 people; Masaya, 101,900; Chinandega; 84,281; Matagalpa, 95,300; Granada, 74,300 (1995).
Government: President, Arnoldo Alemán, elected in October 1996.
National Holidays: September 15, Independence Day (1821); July 19, Sandinista Revolution Day (1979).
Armed Forces: 17,000 troops (1996).

Food Dependency

1970
10%

1994
19%

Foreign Trade

MILLIONS $ 1996

IMPORTS
1,076

EXPORTS
653

STATISTICS

DEMOGRAPHY
Population: 4,238,000 (1996). **Annual growth:** 2.6% (1980/1996). **Estimates for year 2000:** 4,700,000 . **Annual growth to year 2000:** 2.7% (1994/2000). **Urban Population:** 62.7% (1996). **Urban growth:** 3.94% (1980/95). **Children per woman:** 4 (1996).

HEALTH
Life expectancy at birth: 68 years (1994). male: 65 years (1994). female: 70 years (1994). **Infant mortality:** 44 per 1,000 (1996). **Under-5 child mortality:** 57 per 1,000 (1996). **Calorie consumption:** 99% (1988/90). 2,000 **people per doctor** (1988/91). **Safe water:** 61% (1990/96).

EDUCATION
Literacy: 66% (1995). male : 65% (1995). female: 67% (1995). **School enrolment :** Primary total: 104% (1990/95). male : 102% (1990/95). female: 105% (1990/95). Secondary: male : 40% (1990/95). female: 47% (1990/95). Tertiary: 9% (1995). **Primary school teachers:** one for every 38 students (1995).

COMMUNICATIONS
30 **newspapers**, 262 **radios**, 150 **TV sets** and 20 **main telephone lines** per 1,000 people (1994).

ECONOMY
Per capita, GNP: $ 380 (1996). **Annual growth, GNP:** 4.2% (1995/96). **Annual inflation:** 961.58% (1985/95). **Currency:** 7.97 córdobas = $ 1 (1995) **Cereal imports:** 174 metric tons (1994). **Food import dependency:** 19% (1994). **Fertilizer use:** 244 kgs per ha (1994). **Exports:** $ 653 million (1996). **Imports:** $ 1,076 million (1996). **External debt:** $ 5,929 million (1996). $ 1,399 **per capita:** (1996). **Debt service:** 24.2% of exports (1996). **Development aid received:** $ 662 million (1995). $ 155 per capita (1995). 48.1% of GNP (1994).

ENERGY
Consumption: 299.71 Kgs of Oil equivalent per capita yearly (1996). 62.60% imported (1994).

HDI (rank / value) 127 / 0.53 (1996)

---

just cause) as well as the agrarian reform law passed by the Sandinista Government. Workers responded by extending the strike over the whole country. After a week, the Government partially gave in to the workers' demands, and the strike ended.

[26] In mid-1990, the Government received several offers from international consortia interested in carrying out projects in northern Nicaragua. This area comprises some 270,000 hectares of tropical rain forests, occupying more than half of the country's total land area. The proposals ranged from the creation of landfills for toxic waste, to the exploitation of the region's vast fishing, mineral and forestry resources.

[27] When the Government was accused of carrying out secret negotiations with a Taiwanese enterprise, the existence of large mineral deposits was inadvertently revealed. These include gold, silver, copper, tungsten and Central America's largest deposits of calcium carbonate, a raw material used in cement production.

[28] A partial disarming of the contras was carried out, at the same time that significant reductions in army personnel were announced. In October 1991, a number of former contra commanders founded the Nicaraguan Resistance Party. This new political group rejected the return to violence by other contras - some 600, in all - in the northern part of the country, where civilians were being killed, and farms as well as farm cooperatives were being burned.

[29] In 1991, President Chamorro agreed with the FSLN to recognize agrarian reform and to set aside for the workers at least 25 per cent of shares in state enterprises slated for privatization.

[30] Inflation fell from 7,000 per cent in 1990 to 3.8 per cent in 1992 due to an IMF and World Bank-sponsored adjustment program. Productive investments and spending in education and health were reduced. Unemployment rose to 60 per cent.

[31] Differences between the President and the UNO led them to break in 1993 after which Chamorro received support from the Sandinistas and the UNO's Center Group. The following month, the UNO expelled that group and changed its name to Political Opposition Alliance (APO).

[32] Parliamentary debate on constitutional reform caused the FSLN's orthodox sector, led by former president Daniel Ortega, to exclude former Vice-President Sergio Ramirez, head of the Sandinista parliamentary bloc, from the Front. By-passing the party's leadership, the parliamentary bloc presented its own bill against nepotism which banned presidential re-election and prohibited relatives of the current president from running for president. This clause put an end to the political aspirations of Chamorro's son-in-law, minister Antonio Lacayo.

[33] The economic crisis was intensified by a drought which led to the loss of 80,000 hectares of crops and left 200,000 farmers without food. Child malnutrition has affected 300,000 children and some have been blinded by a lack of vitamin A.

[34] In January 1994, the UNO, with less than half its founders and unable to obtain the support to set up a constituent assembly, put an end to a year of boycotting the National Assembly. Violence continued between the army, gangs of criminals and small guerrilla groups.

[35] General Humberto Ortega confirmed he would resign after a new military law had been passed. In August the Assembly passed the law which aimed at eliminating political involvement by the Sandinista Popular Army and increasing its dependence on civilian authority, although the power was actually left in the hands of a military council.

[36] The Government signed a 3-year agreement with the IMF which opened the possibility of renegotiating public debt. Unemployment was estimated between 43 per cent and 60 per cent. The per capita GDP dropped for the eleventh year in a row.

[37] Debate on constitutional reform prevailed in 1995. In February, the Assembly proposed to change the army's name, ban compulsory military service and grant guarantees to private property. These measures were supported by President Chamorro but she did not agree with the shift of power from the executive to the legislative branch, regarding the right to raise taxes. The Assembly published the reforms unilaterally in February and began to implement them.

[38] In June, an agreement was reached on a general law for constitutional reforms which stated these had to be supported by a majority of 60 per cent in the Assembly before being signed by the President, who concluded the agreement in July. The National Assembly ratified its choice of judges for the Supreme Court of Justice and a new Supreme Electoral Tribunal was appointed.

[39] The approval of the nepotism law was deferred. President Chamorro's son-in-law remained in the Government, although he announced his resignation to launch his presidential campaign.

[40] Conservative Arnoldo Aleman, ex-mayor of Managua, obtained 49 per cent of the vote in the October 1996 elections. The electoral law established that if any of the candidates obtains more than 45 per cent of the vote, there is no need for a second vote, thus leaving Sandinista ex President Daniel Ortega (with 39 per cent) out of the race. The FSLN suspected a fraud but the Supreme Electoral Court named Alemán president.

[41] On assuming the presidency, Alemán promised to create 500,000 new jobs and launched a plan to relieve the debt of the agricultural sector, estimated at 1$50 million.

[42] In April 1997, the Government and opposition accused each other of arming and training paramilitaries. Despite negotiations, no understanding was reached and relations between the ruling party and the Sandinistas remained tense.

[43] In August, the Government announced it would not pass goods confiscated by the Sandinistas in 1979 on to Anastasio Somoza's heirs, in answer to a lawsuit filed by Lilian Somoza, the former dictator's daughter.

[44] According to estimates made in early 1998, the United States had once again become Managua's main trade partner. Nicaraguan exports to this country were worth $375 million in 1997, 30 per cent up on two years previously.

Niger

Niger

Population: 9,465,000 (1996)
Area: 1,267,000 SQ KM
Capital: Niamey
Currency: CFA francs
Language: French

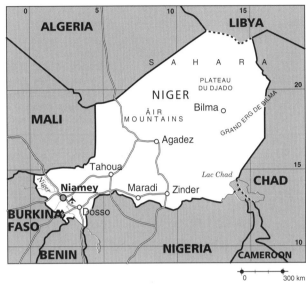

Fossil remains found in the Niger region indicate that it was inhabited in prehistoric times and later populated by many different nomadic and trading peoples. The Nok Empire, reaching its peak in present-day Nigeria between the 15th century BC and the 5th century AD (see Nigeria) left its mark on this neighboring region.

[2] During the 7th century AD, the western side of the country became part of the Songhai Empire created by the Berber, who were important propagators of Islam from the 11th century onwards.

[3] Between the 14th and 19th centuries the eastern part of the territory belonged to the Kanem-Bornu State, hich had been founded by the Kurani in the 8th century. Meanwhile, during the 19th century, the Haussa states flourished in the south (see Nigeria), until conquered by the Fulani.

[4] Throughout the 19th century, the French colonized the territory, making Niger an official French colony in 1922. Traditional subsistence crops were replaced by cash crops like peanuts and cotton, which were grown for export, causing endemic food shortages in Niger.

[5] In the 1950s, Niger launched its own independence movement, led by Hamani Diori. In 1960, the country's first constitution was approved and Niger became an independent state.

[6] When it broke its colonial ties, Niger was the poorest country in French West Africa, with 80 per cent of the population living in rural areas with persistent drought, soil erosion and population pressure which threaten the country's agriculture and ecology.

[7] In the new republic's first election the Progressive Party's candidate, Hamani Diori, was elected president. The new government maintained deep economic and political ties with France, to the point of allowing French troops to remain within its territory. In the first years of his presidency, Diori banned the Sawaba party, forcing its leader, Djibo Bakari into exile. The Government was accused of corruption and of the harsh repression of the growing political opposition.

[8] In the early 1970s, the drought which hit the Sahel region meant that the army was charged with distributing food among the peasants. This brought them into contact with the needs of the rural people for the first time. On April 13 1974, a Supreme Military Committee took power, naming Seyni Kuntch'e as President. Price controls were set on agricultural products, salaries were raised, nepotism was eliminated, investments were reoriented and education and health services were planned. An attempt was made to access underground water sources and incentives were given to set up farming cooperatives.

[9] The new government tried out new ways of organizing the youth to establish the political base which the country lacked. It also expelled Djibo Bakari, who had returned from exile to lend his support to the regime, and signed bilateral agreements with France. These agreements allowed neocolonialism to focus greater attention on the exploitation of Niger's mineral wealth than on traditional colonial products.

[10] During the 1970s the country experienced an economic boom, based on an increase in the international price of uranium. This mineral accounted for 90 per cent of the country's exports in 1980, when the so-called "miracle" came to an abrupt end.

[11] The foreign debt was $207 million in 1977, and by 1983 it had increased to $1 billion, forcing Kuntch'e to introduce an IMF supervised structural adjustment program, in an attempt to turn the economy around. The hoped-for return of favourable uranium prices did not materialize and, between 1984 and 1985, the perennial drought in the Sahel region worsened. The Government also confronted political challenges on different fronts: in 1983, it put down an attempted coup by former members of the secret police and it also engaged in combat with the Tuareg, an ethnic group which had resorted to guerrilla warfare.

[12] The economic crisis worsened when Nigeria closed its borders between April 1984 and March 1986 halting traffic between the two countries, including the transportation of cattle and basic foodstuffs. The decision to close the borders was made by authorities in Lagos to carry out a readjustment of their monetary system. An exception was made in 1985, allowing fuel to be transported across the border.

[13] In 1985 there was no change in the situation: the price of uranium fell an additional four points, there was a deficit of 400,000 tons of grain, a growing foreign debt and the increasing cost of servicing this debt

[14] In 1986 the Government tried changing its policies, but General Kuntch'e had a cerebral haemorrhage, dying in a Paris military hospital 11 months later. The Supreme Military Committee designated Ali Seibou as his successor. Among his first measures as President was the appointment of 10 new ministers, and the declaration of an amnesty which provided for the return of political exiles, including Djibo Bakari and Hamani Diori, who were personally welcomed by the President and were allowed to return to political activity. In April 1989, Diori died in Rabat, Morocco.

[15] In 1988, Seibou was faced with 3,000 protesting students, who boycotted classes for 22 days, until their demands were finally met.

[16] On August 2, the National Movement for a Developing Society (MNSD) was formed as the only government authorized

WORKERS

(1996)

Labour force %

■ WOMEN
□ MEN

44   56

■ AGRICULTURE 90% (1990)
□ INDUSTRIAL   4%
▨ SERVICES   6%

LAND USE

IRRIGATED 1.8 % of arable

(1993)

■ FOREST & WOODLAND   2%
□ ARABLE   2.8%
▨ OTHER   95.2%

Tuareg:
children of the wind and sand

The Tuareg people were originally settled farmers and came from North Africa - the Libya and Algeria of today. This is discovered from fragments of 'tifinar' writing - a style with a Tuareg alphabet differing from the Arabic - dating back to 130 BC. The Tuareg belong to the group of Berber speaking peoples, who number around 12 million in total.

The Tuareg were forced to take up a nomadic lifestyle when they were expelled into the Sahara by the Hilaliana and Arab invasions of the 12th century AD. They adopted some of the ideas of Islam, but only to a degree which suited them - maintaining their original common law and justice system intact, surviving, and eventually getting rich by trading camels and zebu with other peoples of the region.

Their fame as fearless warriors, better armed and trained than any other, stemmed from their systematic sacking of farming settlements and caravans for food and slaves. This plunder allowed them to survive in the Sahara, maintaining a rigid caste structure with separate groups of

nobles, clergy, free men and artisans. The political structure consisted of families, councils and heads of councils. Inheritance went down the female line, in the Berber tradition, although daily life was organized in a patriarchal system. Household chores were the mainly in charge of servants, and women spent their time on crafts or composing poetry, whilst the men gained prestige and power within the group in the battles and raids.

For centuries the Tuareg confederations - Ahaggar (also called Hoggar), Azjer (Ajjer), Asben (A´r Tuareg), Ifora, Itesan (Kel Geres), Aulliminden and Kel Tademaket - dominated trade and trade routes. The Tuareg established themselves as the great lords of the desert and savannah. However, the arrival of French colonists in the early 19th century, began to rapidly erode their culture. They made their living by carrying merchandise from west to east, from the Atlantic Ocean to the Mediterranean Sea, and trading or exchanging spices from group to group, travellingin caravans of hundreds of camels.

Once independent from France, newly formed states like Mali, Niger,

Mauritania and Chad found their Tuareg inhabitants demanding independence and the return of lands taken by the colonists. However, the governments' need to exploit the large petrol, gold and uranium reserves on these lands to pay off debts to the IMF led to years of battles, persecution and expulsions.

These events led to the appearance of Tuareg guerrilla groups. The civil wars added to the misery of the famines of the 1970s and 1980s forcing many Tuareg to flee to refugee camps in neighbouring countries like Burkina Faso, or to urban centres where they settled and took on different values and cultures. The men no longer use the traditional blue veil in front of women, foreigners or the courts - the only known instance of such a practice in the Islamic world. At the same time, the introduction of new means of transport and communication led to the decline of the camel and the Tuareg role as expert guides on the sands of the Sahara. The Tuareg population is currently estimated at around 900,000.

---

party, and the National Development Council drew up a new constitution, put to the vote and approved by plebiscite in 1989. In December, Seibou was elected President of the Republic by universal suffrage, in the first elections to be held since independence in 1960.
[17] The drought in the Sahel forced the Government to give special attention to agricultural production and to the inhabitants of the country's rural areas. During the 1980-90 period it invested 32 per cent of the national budget in agriculture. A fundamental part of the environmental problem was that 98 per cent of people use firewood for cooking. In a country facing deforestation and almost permanent drought, this almost exclusive use of wood for household energy is dangerously destructive. Facing the problem head-on, the Government had solar and wind-powered generators installed, developed electric energy and sponsored the manufacture of low-cost energy-saving stoves. With wood

consumption at close to two million tons per year, the Government proposed six-fold increases in the cost of wood-cutting permits, in the hope that this would put an end to further deforestation.
[18] The new president has a favourable economic outlook on his side, as there was a grain surplus of 200,000 tons in 1989. He promised that he would initiate a true democratization process, but this did not occur and throughout 1990 there was intense opposition from the political sector, the labor unions and the students, demanding salary increases, the enactment of educational reforms, and the establishment of a multiparty system. Strikes and massive protest demonstrations were organized in support of these demands and these were harshly suppressed by the police.
[19] In 1990, the country's agricultural production dropped by more than 70 per cent, while the population continued to increase at 3 per cent per year. Despite doubling the amount of

arable land, food production rose by only one per cent, and the land has lost its fertility through phosphate and nitrogen depletion.
[20] To confront the crisis the Government launched another structural adjustment plan, imposed by the World Bank and the IMF. A two-year freeze on the salaries of public employees was announced as part of the plan. Workers and students reacted by calling a new series of strikes and holding more demonstrations. In late 1990, Seibou publicly announced his commitment to leading the country towards a multiparty democratic system and he created the National Conference, which was charged with organizing the political transformation.
[21] After four months, the National Conference decided to form a transitional government, headed by a new Prime Minister, Amadou Cheffou. André Salifou was named president of the High Council of the Republic, the body holding legislative power

during the transition period. However, the country's situation had never been more critical. The state was bankrupt; there was no money to pay the salaries of the public employees, and students did not receive money for their grants.
[22] The economic disaster and its accompanying social crisis can be traced back to the end of the uranium boom; in 1989, this mineral cost Fr30,000,000 per kilo, dropping to Fr19,000,000 per kilo in 1991.
[23] In February 1992, Tuareg guerrillas rose up in arms against the government once more. In December, the new constitution was approved with nearly 90 per cent of the votes in a referendum, but two months later in February 1993 the ruling party was defeated in the legislative elections.
[24] In April, Mahamane Ousmane became the first President of Niger, with 55.4 per cent of the vote in the second round. The efforts to reach an agreement to end the insurrection of the Tuareg guerrillas in the north of

Maternal Mortality	Literacy	Food Dependency	External Debt
1990	1995	1970	1996
PER 100,000 LIVE BIRTHS **1,200**	**14%**	**14%** 1994 **22%**	PER CAPITA **$165**

PROFILE

ENVIRONMENT

Most of this land-locked country is made up of a plateau at an average altitude of 350 m. The north is covered by the Sahara desert and the south by savannas. There are uranium, iron, coal and tin deposits, and possibly oil. 80 per cent of the population lives in rural areas. There are nomadic shepherds in the center of the country, and peanut, rice and cotton farming in the south. 85 per cent of all energy is provided by firewood. This region is affected by marked desertification. There is also considerable erosion, produced by strong winds. There is air and water pollution primarily in densely populated urban areas.

SOCIETY

Peoples: Among the shepherds of the central steppe, ethnic origins vary from the Berber Tuareg, to the Fulah, including the Tibu (Tubu). In the south there are western African ethnic groups; the Haussa, Djerma (Zarma), Songhai and Kamuri.
Religions: mostly Muslim; in the south there are traditional African religions and a Christian minority.
Languages: French (official) and 'several local languages.
Political Parties: National Movement for a Developing Society (MNSD); Alliance for Democracy and Progress (AFC).
Social Organizations: Nigerien National Workers Union (UNTN).

THE STATE

Official Name: République du Niger.
Administrative Divisions: 7 Departments.
Capital: Niamey, 392,000 people (1988).
Other cities: Zinder, 120,000 people (1981); Maradi, 104,000; Tahoua, 50,000 (1988).
Government: Ibrahim Baré Mainassara, President since July, 1996. Ibrahim Hassane Mayaki, Prime Minister since November, 1997. Legislative power. National Assembly, with 883 members.
National Holiday: August 3, Independence (1960).
Armed Forces: 5,300.
Other: 5,400 Gendarmes, Republican Guards and National Police.

STATISTICS

DEMOGRAPHY

Population: 9,465,000 (1996). **Annual growth:** 3.3% (1980/1996). **Estimates for year 2000:** 10,800,000. **Annual growth to year 2000:** 3.4% (1994/2000). **Urban Population:** 18.6% (1996). **Urban growth:** 7.2% (1980/95). **Children per woman:** 7.2 (1996).

HEALTH

Life expectancy at birth: 48 years (1996). male: 46 years (1994). female: 49 years (1994). **Infant mortality:** 191 per 1,000 (1996). **Under-5 child mortality:** 320 per 1,000 (1996). **Calorie consumption:** 95% (1988/90). 50,000 **people per doctor** (1988/91). **Safe water:** 48% (1990/96).

EDUCATION

Literacy: 14% (1995). male : 21% (1995). female: 7% (1995). **School enrolment :** Primary total: 30% (1990/95). male : 35% (1990/95). female: 21% (1990/95). Secondary: male : 9% (1990/95). female: 5% (1990/95). **Primary school teachers:** one for every 37 students (1995).

COMMUNICATIONS

61 **radios**, 20 **TV sets** and 1 **main telephone line** per 1,000 people (1994).

ECONOMY

Per capita, GNP: $ 200 (1996). **Annual growth, GNP:** -0.1% (1995/96). **Annual inflation:** 1.28% (1985/95). **Currency:** 490 CFA francs = $ 1 (1995) **Cereal imports:** 155 metric tons (1994). **Food import dependency:** 22% (1994). **Fertilizer use:** 3 kgs per ha (1994). **Exports:** $ 79 million (1996). **Imports:** $ 567 million (1996). **External debt:** $ 1,557 million (1996). $ 165 **per capita:** (1996). **Debt service:** 17.3% of exports (1996). **Development aid received:** $ 268 million (1995). $ 30 per capita (1995). 17.8% of GNP (1994).

ENERGY

Consumption: 37.48 Kgs of Oil equivalent per capita yearly (1996). 83.18% imported (1994).
HDI (rank / value) 173 / 0.206 (1996)

the country continued throughout the year and lasted for most of 1994.
[25] The fighting continued - in May 1994, 40 people were killed in confrontations between the rebel and Government forces - but the main guerrilla group, the Coordination of Armed Resistance and the Government managed to seal an agreement. Thus, in June, Niamey granted independence to part of the country inhabited by some 750,000 Tuaregs.
[26] Amidst student protests calling for, amongst other things, the payment of money owed in grants, the Government arrested 91 members of the opposition. In September, Prime Minister Mahamadou Issoufou resigned

after his party, the Nigerien Party for Democracy and Socialism, withdrew from the Government coalition, leaving it without an absolute majority in Parliament.
[27] In January 1995, an opposition coalition triumphed in the legislative elections and immediately replaced the prime minister, Boubacar Cissé Amadou with Hama Amadou. The latter announced that his first move would be to bring in an economic austerity plan, reaching an agreement for settling the payment of overdue civil service salaries.
[28] Tension continued to mount between the new government and the President. In January 1996, a military coup toppled

Ousmane, who was replaced by the National Salvation Council, headed by Colonel Ibrahim Baré Mainassara, who designated Boukary Adji as Prime Minister. In July, Mainassara was elected President with 52 per cent of the vote. The new "strongman" dissolved the Independent National Electoral Commission, leading the main opposition parties to boycott the November legislative elections. In December, following the victory of Mainassara's supporters, Boubacar Cissé was made Prime Minister.
[29] In October 1997, Ali Sabo, campaign co-ordinator of the Front for the Restoration and Defence of Democracy, made up of eight opposition parties, was

imprisoned for making declarations hostile to Mainassara. In November 1997, Ibrahim Hassane Mayaki was made Prime Minister replacing Cissé. A month later, in Algiers, a ceasefire was agreed between the Government and the Tuareg guerrillas.
[30] In early 1998, Mainassara ordered the arrest of various opposition figures, including Amadou, accused of conspiracy. The MNSD denied the accusation, saying it was a manoeuvre to distract national and international public from the Government's failure to resolve crucial problems like hunger, falling levels of pay and the insecurity.

Nigeria

Nigeria

Population: 115,020,000 (1996)
Area: 923,768 SQ KM
Capital: Abuja

Currency: Naira
Language: English

A s heirs to the ancient Nok civilization, the Yoruba lived in walled cities with broad avenues. As early as the 11th century they developed a democratic system of urban administration, also producing beautiful ceramics and bronze sculptures (see The origins of the Yoruba culture).

[2] Between the 10th and 11th centuries, Ife, Oyo, Ilorin and Benin (not the present-day nation) were loosely confederated city-states extending their influence from the Niger River in the east to present-day Togo.

[3] Ife always enjoyed a reputation as the main religious center of the nation, and the Oni of Ife is still the High Priest of all Yorubans, whether Nigerian or not.

[4] The city of Oyo, strengthened since the 16th century by the slave trade, had a higher status as a political and economic center, through the Alafin (ruler). The dependence on slavery caused its downfall when that institution was abolished.

[5] The northern part of the country held the Haussa states and was the center of a different culture. A similar group of active Ibo traders emerged in the southeast, but they did not develop urban civilizations like the Yoruba.

[6] The British colonial system disregarded these differences, forcing all the territories under a single administration in 1914, creating an artificial state that has not attained national unity. British interests focused on the exploitation of tin and agricultural and timber resources.

[7] British administration in northern Nigeria was indirect, based on traditional Muslim emirs who acted as middlemen.

Consequently this area, populated by Haussa and Peul, enjoyed greater political autonomy than the other regions.

[8] Independence in 1960 brought the Northern People's Congress to power, in an alliance with the National Council of Nigerian Citizens, an Ibo organization. The country had been divided into a federal structure of four states, and a two-chamber parliament was established, based on the British model.

[9] These political imports proved to be poorly suited to local conditions. Regional governors acquired more power than the President Nnambi Azikiwe. Progressive parties were pushed aside in a succession of electoral frauds, while political leaders lost their national outlook, encouraging ethnic rivalries.

[10] After months of infighting, the military chose General Yacuba Gowon as President. About this time the oil industry began to develop, just as France was inciting the separatist movement among the Ibo, provoking a three-year secessionist civil war in Biafra.

[11] Nigeria became the world's 8th largest oil producer, and Gowon expropriated 55 per cent of the transnational petroleum operations, creating financing for local entrepreneurs.

[12] Real power was vested in the nationalist Supreme Military Council, with different leaders acting as President. The council closed US military and espionage installations. During Olusegun Obasanjo's presidency, Barclays Bank and British Petroleum assets were nationalized as these companies were violating economic sanctions against South Africa.

[13] In 1978, constitutional reform was proposed, calling for elections and a return to civilian government. The Federal Election Commission authorized only five parties, all representing the traditional financial and political elite. Parties with socialist or revolutionary perspectives were barred from the electoral process, under the pretext of avoiding political fragmentation.

[14] The National Party of Nigeria (NPN) won the election, with 25 per cent of the vote, and the Unity Party of Nigeria (UPN) came second, with 20 per cent.

[15] The inauguration of Shagari, who lacked majorities in both legislative chambers, ended 13 years of military rule. He launched a capitalist development plan based exclusively on petrodollars, to transform Nigeria into the development hub of sub-Saharan Africa. His promises included constructing a new capital, doubling primary school attendance and achieving self-sufficiency in food production via controversial "green revolution" methods.

[16] None of these proposals came to anything. Contraband, large urban concentrations of immigrants and poor peasants, unemployment and poverty all increased.

[17] The International Monetary Fund demanded the refinancing of the foreign debt putting the country under further pressure. Shagari announced new elections, and took part as the NPN candidate. He was re-elected, amidst accusations of electoral fraud and military conspiracies.

[18] On January 1 1984, Muhamad Buhari staged the fourth coup in the country's republican history. The new leaders accused their predecessors of corruption in the petroleum sector, accounting for 95 per cent of export earnings. Hundreds of people were arrested, and all civilian government officials were replaced by military personnel.

[19] However, the crisis was not checked, and the price of rice quadrupled in a single year. Repression extended to foreigners and 600,000 were expelled, classed as illegal immigrants. These events set the stage for another coup, the country's sixth, on August 26 1985. General Ibrahim Babangida became the new President. That year, the foreign debt reached $15 billion.

[20] In December 1987, local elections were held with 15,000 unaffiliated candidates taking part. A National Election Commission had been appointed to oversee the voting and ensure that the

WORKERS

(1996)

Labour force %
- ■ WOMEN
- □ MEN

36 — 64

- ■ AGRICULTURE 43% (1990)
- □ INDUSTRIAL 7%
- ▨ SERVICES 50%

LAND USE

DEFORESTATION -0.7% annual (81/90)
IRRIGATED 3.2 % of arable

(1993)

- ■ FOREST & WOODLAND 12.2%
- □ ARABLE 32.3%
- ▨ OTHER 55.5%

Maternal Mortality	Literacy	Food Dependency	External Debt
1990	1995	1970	1996
PER 100,000 LIVE BIRTHS **1,000**	**57%**	**8%** 1994 **13%**	PER CAPITA **$273**

PROFILE

ENVIRONMENT

The country's extensive river system includes the Niger and its main tributary, the Benue. In the north, the "harmattan", a dry wind from the Sahara, creates a drier region made up of plateaus and grasslands where cotton and peanuts are grown for export. The central plains are also covered by grasslands, and are sparsely populated. The southern lowlands receive more rainfall, they have dense tropical forests and most of the country's population lives there. Cocoa and oil-palms are grown in this area. The massive delta of the Niger River divides the coast into two separate regions. In the east, oil production is concentrated around Port Harcourt, the homeland of the Ibo, who converted to Christianity and fought to establish an independent Biafra. To the west, the industrial area is concentrated around Lagos and Ibadan. Yoruba are the predominant western ethnic group, and some of them have converted to Islam. Nigeria has lost between 70 and 80 per cent of its original forests.

SOCIETY

Peoples: Nigeria has the largest population in Africa. The 250 or so ethnic groups can be divided into four main groups: the Haussa and Fulani in the north; the Yoruba in the southwest; and the Ibo in the southeast.
Religions: The north is predominantly Muslim, while Christians form the majority in the southeast; Muslims, Christians and followers of traditional African religions can be found in the southwest.
Languages: English (official). Each region has a main language depending on the predominant ethnic group, Hausa, Ibo or Yoruba.
Political Parties: the United Nigerian Congress Party; the Committee for National Consensus; the National Central Party of Nigeria; the Democratic Party of Nigeria and the "Grassroots" Democratic Movement
Social Organizations: Unified Federation of Nigerian Unions.

THE STATE

Official Name: Federal Republic of Nigeria.
Administrative Divisions: 30 States.
Capital: Abuja, 40,000 people (1995 est.)
Other cities: Lagos, 5,6000,000 people (1995); Ibadan, 1,295,000; Ogbomosho, 660,000; Kano, 700,000 (1992).
Government: General Abdulsalam Abubakar, President since June 9 1998.
National Holiday: October 1, Independence Day (1960).
Armed Forces: 77,100 troops (1995).
Other: 7,000 National Guard, 2,000 Port Security Police.

STATISTICS

DEMOGRAPHY

Population: 115,020,000 (1996). **Annual growth:** 2.9% (1980/1996). **Estimates for year 2000:** 128,800,000. **Annual growth to year 2000:** 2.9% (1994/2000). **Urban Population:** 40.5% (1996). **Urban growth:** 5.58% (1980/95). **Children per woman:** 6.1 (1996).

HEALTH

Life expectancy at birth: 52 years (1996). male: 50 years (1994). female: 53 years (1994). **Infant mortality:** 114 per 1,000 (1996). **Under-5 child mortality:** 191 per 1,000 (1996). **Calorie consumption:** 93% (1988/90). 5,882 **people per doctor** (1988/91). **Safe water:** 50% (1990/96).

EDUCATION

Literacy: 57% (1995). male : 67% (1995). female: 47% (1995). **School enrolment :** Primary total: 89% (1990/95). male : 100% (1990/95). female: 79% (1990/95). Secondary: male : 33% (1990/95). female: 28% (1990/95). Tertiary: 4% (1995). **Primary school teachers:** one for every 37 students (1995).

COMMUNICATIONS

20 **newspapers**, 196 **radios**, 40 **TV sets** and 3 **main telephone lines** per 1,000 people (1994). **Books:** 1 new title per 100,000 people (1992/94).

ECONOMY

Per capita, GNP: $ 240 (1996). **Annual growth, GNP:** 1.9% (1995/96). **Annual inflation:** 32.98% (1985/95). **Consumer price index:** 403.2 (1994). **Currency:** 21.89 nairas = $ 1 (1995) **Cereal imports:** 1,078 metric tons (1994). **Food import dependency:** 13% (1994). **Fertilizer use:** 120 kgs per ha (1994). **Exports:** $ 15,610 million (1996). **Imports:** $ 6,433 million (1996). **External debt:** $ 31,407 million (1996). $ 273 **per capita:** (1996). **Debt service:** 16% of exports (1996). **Development aid received:** $ 208 million (1995). $ 2 per capita (1995). 0.6% of GNP (1994).

ENERGY

Consumption: 162.04 Kgs of Oil equivalent per capita yearly (1996). -483.54% imported (1994).

HDI (rank / value) 141 / 0.393 (1994)

---

election was clean and free of coercion. The lack of proper preparation for the voting itself, however, led to acts of violence, confusion and subsequent accusations of fraud. The election was finally annulled.
[21] On December 7 1989, the military government announced that the elections, originally scheduled for the end of the month, would be postponed until December 1990. Six months later, President Babangida announced that the ban on political activism had been lifted, in an attempt to monitor the transition from

military to civilian government in 1992.
[22] In May 1990, Babangida visited Britain; one outcome of the visit was a treaty between the two countries granting Nigeria $100 million in aid. Most of its trade is with the United States, the United Kingdom and France, though it sought more balanced international relations by maintaining relations with all the countries in the world.
[23] Nigeria saw its fortunes rise and fall with the fluctuations in oil prices. In 1990 the foreign debt reached $30 billion, and to service

its debt, the Government had to carry out constant negotiations with international agencies.
[24] In April and June 1990, news services announced a failed coup attempt, put down by forces loyal to the Government.
[25] Between August and October, the creation of nine new states to separate hostile ethnic groups generated protests which were repressed by the army, causing some 300 deaths according to unofficial figures. The Government imposed a curfew.
[26] Toward the end of 1991, the Government invalidated the allegedly fraudulent internal party elections, held to select government candidates. In November, a new census eliminated 20 million non-existent

voters from the electoral register. On December 14, governmental elections were held; the Social Democratic Party (SDP) won in 16 states, and the National Republican Convention (NRC) in 14.
[27] The opposition were granted a general amnesty, and 11 dissidents were freed. A law prohibiting former Government officials from running for office was revoked.
[28] In early 1992, the imprisonment of 263 Muslim militants, caused protests in the state of Katsina. During this period, there was also an escalation of inter-ethnic conflict between Haussa and Kataj in the state of Kaduna, and territorial conflict between Tiv and Jukin in the Taraba.

The Creation of Africa

African peoples have an array of creation myths, stories about the origins of life and the universe. Creation myths provide the model for other stories that refer to the origins of cultural practices

Konos from Guinea believe the initial force of the world, prior even to God, was Death. The Pangwa from Tanzania claim the world was created out of ant excrement and the Yorubas from Nigeria think God was intoxicated with wine when he created disabled people and albinos.

For the herding tribes of the Peules or Fulanis from Mali, milk is the centre of creation. In the beginning there was a huge drop of milk.

Then Doondari came and created the stone, then the stone created steel, and steel created fire, and fire created water, and water created the air. Then Doondari came down for a second time. He took the five elements and with them created man. But man was proud. Then Doondari created blindness and blindness humbled man. But when blindness became too proud, Doondari created dreams, and dreams humbled blindness; but when dreams became too proud, Doondari created grief, and grief humbled dreams, and when grief became too proud, Doondari created death, and death humbled grief, but when death became too proud, Doondari came down for a third time. And he came as Gueno the Eternal. And Gueno conquered death.

[29] On December 5, Nigeria recovered its position in the International Court of Justice, after the UN Security Council and the General Assembly voted to fill the vacancy left by the death of Nigerian Judge Taslim Elias. The Nigerian general prosecutor and minister of justice, Ola Ajibola, won over the Ghanaian, Kenyan, and Ugandan candidates.

[30] Nigeria received $240 million in aid from the European Community to be used in agricultural, health, telecommunication, road building, and conservation projects.

[31] In July 1992, legislative elections were held, but the National Assembly did not convene until December. The SDP obtained 52 seats in the Senate, and 314 in the Chamber of Representatives. The National Republican Convention obtained 37 seats in the Senate, and 275 in the Chamber of Representatives. Nigeria subsequently began the transition to civilian government, after 23 years of military regimes.

[32] In October, presidential primary elections were held, with candidates from the two main parties, the SDP (left-of-center) and the RNC (right-of-center). Both parties were created by the regime, with nearly indistinguishable manifestos. Another 23 candidates also took part. President Babangida invalidated the election, claiming fraud, stripped the candidates of their authority and ousted the leadership of the SDP and RNC. Later that month, the military government suspended all political activity. These developments halted the democratic transition process, jeopardizing the possibility of a transfer to civilian government in early 1993.

[33] In November Babangida announced that elections slated for January 1993 had been postponed until June. He also ratified the proscription of the 23 1992 presidential candidates. Finally, he postponed the transfer to a democratic regime until August.

[34] On June 12, the first presidential elections since 1983 were held. The military government did not divulge election results until it had concluded an investigation of alleged fraud. The main contest was between the NCR and SDP candidates, who had been authorized to take part in the election, although the original candidates continued in proscription.

[35] Babangida invalidated the election results on June 23, accusing SDP and NCR candidates of "buying votes". Chief Moshood Abiola, a wealthy Muslim who was the SDP candidate and who had apparently won the June election, left for London to campaign for international condemnation of the Babangida regime.

[36] The United States and the United Kingdom suspended their economic aid and training of Nigerian military personnel. Abiola launched a civil disobedience campaign and massive protests broke out in the streets of Lagos, where at least 25 people were killed by federal troops.

[37] Clashes continued, and on August 26, Babangida resigned, leaving the provisional command of the country in the hands of Chief Ernest Shonekan, who promised to hold new elections.

[38] The following month, Abiola returned to London and labor unions called a general strike, demanding he be recognized as Nigerian president. Toward the end of 1993 the minister of defence, General Sani Abacha, overthrew Shonekan, dissolved Parliament and banned all political activity.

[39] This new "strongman" had been a very influential member of the previous military regime and a key figure in the military coup that had ousted the Government in 1983. In one of his first statements, Abacha announced he would abandon some liberal economic reforms adopted in the 1980s.

[40] The interest rates went down and a new foreign exchange control was established, at a time in which any possibility of reaching an agreement with the IMF was increasingly remote. Popular support for Abiola mounted; in June 1994, the political leader was arrested, which triggered a 10-day-strike by oil workers, the most important sector in the country.

[41] Abacha did not give in despite all the pressures for Abiola's release. In April 1995, Archbishop Desmond Tutu - on behalf of South African President Nelson Mandela - travelled to Nigeria in support of Abiola's liberation. Despite Abiola's agreement to accept the annulment of the 1993 election, the Nigerian President refused to free him.

[42] In November, the execution of nine members of the Movement for the Survival of the Ogoni People, resulted in the isolation of the military regime. Several countries, including the United States, withdrew their ambassadors from Nigeria.

[43] In February 1996, the human rights organization, Amnesty International, stated its concern for the situation of other Ogoni activists arrested.

[44] In June on the basis of a register of political parties drawn up by the National Electoral Commission, Abacha and his military council legalised in June five political groups: the United Nigerian Congress Party, the Committee for National Consensus, the National Central Party of Nigeria, the Democratic Party of Nigeria and the "Grassroots" Democratic Movement.

[45] An increase in oil prices stimulated economic growth in 1997. On several occasions, the government confirmed that this increase had led to improvements in the difficult social situation of the country. However, official data indicated that 80 per cent of the population was living in poverty.

[46] In April 1998, Abacha announced that the August elections were to be substituted by a plebiscite that would have had to determine if he was to continue in power. The sudden death of the dictator, on June 8, led to massive expressions of happiness and generated expectations of political changes. Abacha's demise was soon followed by the equally unexpected death of Abiola. General Abdulsalam Abubakar, appointed by the military junta as new President in June 9, committed to respect the democratic transition, but he did not modify the proposal for referendum.

Northern Marianas

Population:	49,000 (1996)
Area:	464 SQ KM
Capital:	Saipan
Currency:	US Dollar
Language:	English

Northern Marianas

1 In Saipan, the largest island of the Mariana archipelago, evidence has been found of human habitation from 1500 BC.

2 During his first expedition around the world, the Portuguese navigator Ferdinand Magellan first sighted the islands in 1521 and claimed them for the Spanish Crown. They were held by the Spanish until being ceded to Germany in 1899 as the Spanish empire declined.

3 During World War I the islands came under the control of Japan, which had an alliance with Britain since 1902. The Japanese occupied the islands until World War II.

4 In June 1944, after fierce fighting, the US took Saipan and Tinian from the Japanese due to their strategic location in the North Pacific, on the route between Hawaii and the Philippines. They finally came to form part of the Trust Territory of the Pacific Islands in 1947.

5 The islands continued in this situation until they became a Free Associated State under a referendum held in 1975. In 1977, US President Jimmy Carter approved the constitution of the Northern Mariana islands. At the end of the year this new constitution brought about elections for posts in the bicameral legislative.

6 In 1978, the islands began to be administered autonomously. Washington developed a project to turn two-thirds of Tinian into a military air base and an alternative center for the storage of nuclear weapons. Negotiations with Tinian landowners have been under way since 1984.

7 When news leaked out that cement deposits containing radioactive waste from Japanese nuclear plants - cobalt 60, strontium 90 and caesium 137 - had been dumped in this part of the Pacific, the alarm was sounded on similar US projects that would directly affect the Mariana Islands.

8 In 1984 US President Ronald Reagan granted some civil and political rights to the islands' residents, such as equal employment opportunities in the federal Government, the civil service and the US armed forces.

9 The Northern Marianas were formally admitted to the Commonwealth of the United States in 1986. Mariana inhabitants were granted US citizenship but not the right to vote in presidential elections. They have a representative in the US Congress with no voting rights.

10 The main economic activities of the country are fishing, agriculture - concentrated in smallholdings - and tourism which employs about 10 per cent of the workforce. Some of these activities have been affected often by the typhoons which the islands suffer in the rainy season: in January 1988 Rota Island was devastated by a typhoon which forced the US to declare a state of emergency there. Two years later, the Koryn typhoon struck the archipelago in January 1990 .

11 In the local elections held in 1989, Republicans retained the governorship, ousting the Democrat representative from Washington. Larry Guerrero was elected governor after Pedro Tenorio had decided to stand down.

12 The termination of UN Security Council trusteeship of the islands was approved in 1990. Thus, the Northern Marianas became an independent state, associated to the United States.

13 The Republican Party won the November 1991 legislative elections by a wide margin. Given this majority, it hoped to modify the islands' status with relation to the United States, in order to guarantee control over a 200-mile exclusive economic zone.

14 In 1992, the US Supreme Court ratified the property ownership system, whereby only nationals can own land. In 1994, Froilan C Tenorio was re-elected governor.

15 In 1995, there were some 22,600 foreign workers in the country, three times the number of Marianan workers. Unemployment amongst the latter stood at 15 per cent.

16 In January 1998, Pedro P Tenorio was elected governor. His victory was questioned by opposition groups, as it was his third period in office following previous terms in 1982 and 1986.

PROFILE

ENVIRONMENT

The Marianas archipelago, located in Micronesia, east of the Philippines and south of Japan consists of 16 islands (excluding the island of Guam), of which only six are inhabited. The most important in size and population are: Saipan (122 sq km), Tinian (101 sq km) and Rota (85 sq km). Of volcanic origin, the islands are generally mountainous. The climate is tropical, with rain forest vegetation. In the northernmost islands, however, these conditions shade gradually into a more temperate climate and brush-like, herbaceous vegetation.

SOCIETY

Peoples: The population is mostly indigenous, of Chamorro origin. There are also Japanese, Chinese, Korean, European and Micronesian minorities.
Religions: Catholic.
Languages: English (official), 55 per cent speak Chamorro.
Political Parties: Republican Party; Democratic Party.

THE STATE

Official Name: Commonwealth of the Northern Mariana Islands.
Capital: Saipan, 28,000 people (est. 1994).
Other islands: Rota, 2,295 people; Tinian, 2,118 people (1990).
Government: By virtue of the US Commonwealth status, the President of the United States is the Head of State. Froilan C Tenorio, Governor by direct election, since January 1998. There is a two-chamber legislature with 9 senators and 18 representatives .
National Holiday: Commonwealth Day, January 8 (1986).
Armed forces: The US is in charge of defense affairs.

DEMOGRAPHY

Population: 49,000 (1996). **Urban population:** 53.8 % (1996).

Norway

Norge

Population: 4,348,000 (1996)
Area: 323,877 SQ KM
Capital: Oslo

Currency: Kroner
Language: Norwegian

The earliest traces of humans in Norway correspond to the period between the 9th and the 7th millennia BC. Germanic tribes are thought to have emigrated to these areas when glaciers receded from the northern European coasts and mountains. Cave drawings show that navigation was already known to the peoples of the time, as were something like skis, designed for gliding over the snow.

[2] Historians believe that Norwegian nationality and conversion to Christianity began between 800 and 1030 AD. These dates also correspond to the rise of the Vikings, the name given to Scandinavian seafarers, merchants, and above all, raiders, who dominated the northern seas for 200 years. Harald Harfagre is considered to be the founder of the nation, a feat which he accomplished after defeating his rivals in a naval battle at Hafrsfjord, near the city of Stavanger. After this victory, a large part of the country came under his control.

[3] Viking expeditions expanded the Norwegian Empire, reaching Greenland to the west, and Ireland to the south. According to official history, in 1002, the Norwegian Leif Erikson and his followers were the first Europeans to cross the Atlantic and reach North America, which they named Vinland.

[4] At the end of the Viking era, Norway was an independent kingdom in which four regional peasant assemblies (lagting) elected the monarch. Legitimate and illegitimate children of the king had equal rights to succession before the lagtings. In the 10th and 12th centuries it was common for

two kings to govern simultaneously without any conflict arising between them.

[5] King Magnus III Barfot (1093-1103) conquered the Scottish Orkney and Hebrides Islands. His three sons governed together: they imposed a tithe, founded the first monasteries and built cathedrals. At the beginning of the 12th century, a hundred-year civil war broke out, as a result of the increased power of the monarchy and also of disputes between the monarchy and the church.

[6] This war continued until the coronation of Haakon IV in 1217. The new king reorganized public administration, imposing a hereditary monarchy. Haakon signed a treaty with Russia over the country's northern border. Greenland and Iceland agreed to a union with the King; thus, with the Scottish islands and the Faeroes, the Norwegian Empire attained its maximum extension.

[7] The Black Death killed close to 50 per cent of Norway's population between 1349 and 1350. The upper classes were decimated; Danes and Swedes were hired to fill the positions left vacant in the higher levels of the Government and the church. However, the King lost control over his dominions and isolated regions organized autonomous administrations.

[8] The ascent of Queen Margaret of Denmark to the throne in 1387 paved the way for the union of the Scandinavian countries. In 1389, she was crowned Queen of Sweden and in 1397, her adopted nephew, Erik, was elected king of all Scandinavia in Kalmar, Sweden. With the Kalmar union, Norway was gradually subordinated, ultimately becoming a province of

Denmark, a situation which lasted for more than 400 years.

[9] After 1523, Norway's administrative council tried to obtain greater independence from Denmark. However, the fact that power lay in the hands of the Catholic bishops made it difficult to obtain Swedish support. At the end of the civil war, between 1533 and 1536, the council was abolished. In 1537, the Danish King made the Lutheran religion the country's official religion; the

Norwegian Church has been a State church ever since.

[10] During this period, social conditions in Norway were better than in Denmark. There was a class of rich landlords in the countryside which exploited the regional timber resources, as well as a large group of rural wage-earners. Most of Norway's population were peasants and fishing people. Cities were limited to fewer than 15,000 inhabitants.

[11] At the end of the Napoleonic wars, Denmark unilaterally surrendered control of Norway to Sweden. In 1814, Norway's constituent assembly proclaimed national independence. Sweden re-established its dominance over Norway by force, but this union was dissolved once again without bloodshed in 1905, with Norway regaining its sovereignty and with its full previous territories intact.

[12] In spite of its subordination to Sweden, the majority of the laws enacted in 1814 remained in force during this period. The Norwegian constitution is one of the oldest in the world, second only to that of

PUBLIC EXPENDITURE

n/a

51.1%
1995 ■ DEFENCE □ SOCIAL

In 1990/91 Military as % of health & education expenditure was 22%.

WORKERS

UNEMPLOYMENT 4.9% (1996)

Labour force %

■ WOMEN
□ MEN

46   54

■ AGRICULTURE   6%   (1990)
□ INDUSTRIAL   25%
■ SERVICES   68%

LAND USE

IRRIGATED   10.9 % of arable

(1993)

■ FOREST & WOODLAND   25.7%
□ ARABLE   2.7%
■ OTHER   71.6%

PROFILE

ENVIRONMENT
The Scandinavian mountain range runs north-south along the coast of the country. On the western side, glacier erosion has gouged out deep valleys that are way below actual sea level, resulting in the famous "fjords", narrow, deep inlets walled in by steep cliffs. Maritime currents produce humid, mild winters and cool summers. The population is concentratred in the south, especially round Oslo. Nine tenths of the territory is uninhabited.

SOCIETY
Peoples: Norwegians 96.3 per cent, Dannish 0.4 per cent, British 0.3 per cent, Paquistanis 0.2 per cent, Iranians 0.2 per cent, others (including 40,000 Sami, an indigenous people who live chiefly in the northern province of Lapland) 1.9 per cent.
Religions: 88 per cent of the population belongs to the Church of Norway (Lutheran), there are Evangelical and Catholic minorities.
Languages: Two forms of Norwegian are officially recognized; 80 per cent of school children learn the old form "Bokmal", and 20 per cent learn the neo-Norwegian "Landsmal". In the north, the Sami speak their own language.
Political Parties: Labor Party; Conservative Party; Progress Party; Party of the Socialist Left; Christian Democratic Party, Center Party.
Social Organizations: Norwegian Federation of Unions; Organization of Academics (AF); Organization of Trades (YS).

THE STATE
Official Name: Kongeriket Norge.
Administrative divisions: 19 provinces (Fylker).
Capital: Oslo, 487,908 people (1996).
Other cities: Bergen, 223,000 people; Trondheim, 143,746; Stavanger 104,000 (1996).
Government: Parliamentary constitutional monarchy since 1884; Harald V, king since January 17 1991. Prime Minister: Kjell Magne Bondevik, since October 1997. Legislative power resides in the Storting, the 165-member unicameral parliament.
National Holiday: May 17, Constitution Day (1814).
Armed Forces: 29,000 (1995).

STATISTICS

DEMOGRAPHY
Population: 4,348,000 (1996). **Annual growth:** 0.4% (1980/1996). **Estimates for year 2000:** 4,400,000. **Annual growth to year 2000:** 0.4% (1994/2000). **Urban Population:** 73.4% (1996). **Urban growth:** 0.66% (1980/95). **Children per woman:** 1.9 (1996).

HEALTH
Life expectancy at birth: 77 years (1996). male: 75 years (1994). female: 80 years (1994). **Infant mortality:** 5 per 1,000 (1996). **Under-5 child mortality:** 6 per 1,000 (1996). **Calorie consumption:** 120% (1988/90). 309 **people per doctor** (1988/91).

EDUCATION
School enrolment : Primary total: 99% (1990/95). male : 99% (1990/95). female: 99% (1990/95). Secondary: male : 118% (1990/95). female: 114% (1990/95). Tertiary: 55% (1995). **Primary school teachers:** one for every 9 students (1995).

COMMUNICATIONS
610 **newspapers**, 799 **radios**, 430 **TV sets** and 550 **main telephone lines** per 1,000 people (1994). **Books:** 159 new titles per 100,000 people (1992/94).

ECONOMY
Per capita, GNP: $ 34,510 (1996). **Annual growth, GNP:** 4.6% (1995/96). **Annual inflation:** 3.02% (1985/95). **Consumer price index:** 109.8 (1994). **Currency:** 6.32 kroner = $ 1 (1995) **Cereal imports:** 668 metric tons (1994). **Fertilizer use:** 2,297 kgs per ha (1994). **Exports:** $ 48,922 million (1996). **Imports:** $ 34,290 million (1996).

ENERGY
Consumption: 5,317.52 Kgs of Oil equivalent per capita yearly (1994). -637.85% imported (1994).

HDI (rank / value) 3 / 0.943 (1994)

---

the United States. It is based on the principles of national sovereignty, the separation of powers and the inviolability of human rights.

[13] Under a constitutional amendment in 1884, Norway adopted a parliamentary monarchy as its system of government. The Danish Prince Carl was elected king of Norway, under the name Haakon VII, in 1905. Up until 1914, the country experienced rapid economic expansion, with the hydroelectric wealth of the region allowing large-scale industrial development.

[14] The sale of a large number of Norwegian water courses with hydroelectric power-generating potential, to foreigners, caused great concern among the population. In 1906, 75 per cent of Norway's hydroelectric dams belonged to foreign investors. In 1909, Parliament passed laws for the protection of the country's natural resources.

[15] Universal suffrage, a term which applied to men only when it was passed in 1898, was extended to women by reforms approved in 1907 and 1913. One consequence of industrialization and universal suffrage was the growth of the Labor Party (LP).

[16] During World War I, Norway tried to remain neutral, but was obliged by the other powers to cut trade with Germany. Anti-German feeling was strong, particularly because of the various accidents caused by German war submarines. Price increases provoked by the conflict hit the workers hardest.

[17] Unlike other Western European social democracies, Norway's LP (in which the left-wing formed the majority) decided to join the Third Communist International in 1918. However, the Norwegian LP could not agree with the centralization applied by the Soviet Communist Party, and cut its ties with the Comintern in 1923.

[18] Despite economic difficulties and serious labor conflicts (with unemployment reaching 20 per cent in 1938), Norway underwent vigorous industrial expansion in the inter-war years. Moreover, the Government extended social legislation to include old-age pensions, mandatory leave for workers and unemployment benefits.

[19] In 1940, at the beginning of World War II, Norway was invaded by Germany, which seized control of the country after two months of fighting. King Haakon and the Government went into exile in London, co-ordinating the resistance from there. Norway was liberated in 1945. Haakon died in 1957 and was succeeded by his son Olaf V.

[20] The LP governed continuously between 1935 and 1965, except for a brief one-month period in 1963. In 1965, the LP lost its parliamentary majority and Per Borten, the leader of the Center Party, was named Prime Minister. However, he resigned in 1971 when it was revealed that he had leaked confidential information during EC negotiations.

[21] After the War, Norway abandoned its neutrality policy, joining NATO in 1949. This membership was encouraged by the fear of Soviet expansionism and the unsuccessful attempt to establish a Scandinavian military alliance between Norway, Denmark and Sweden. However, in 1952, the Scandinavian countries established the Nordic Council to deal with their common interests. Norway has been a member of the Nordic Council since 1952, and of EFTA since 1960. By 1972, the idea of joining the EC had been proposed. The issue divided the population and a plebiscite

was held to decide the question; 53 per cent voted against, while 47 per cent were in favor.

[22] Trygve Bratteli, the Labor Prime Minister resigned and a new government was formed by Lars Korvald of the Christian People's Party, to negotiate a trade agreement with the EEC. After this the Labor Party formed a minority cabinet under Oddvar Nordli, who served until 1981, when the LP appointed Gro Harlem Brundtland, the first woman Prime Minister.

[23] In 1977, Norway extended its territorial waters to 200 miles and designated a protected fishing zone in its territory of Svalbard.

[24] In 1986, the Labor Party formed a minority government, once more under Gro Harlem Brundland, who appointed 8 women to her 18-member cabinet.

[25] Trade conflicts between Norway and the US have frequently occurred. In 1987, the state-owned Kongsberg Vapenfabrik exported advanced automated machinery to the Soviet Union, violating NATO sales restrictions to Warsaw Pact and Third World countries.

[26] There were also problems with 'heavy water' exports.

Maternal Mortality	Foreign Trade
1990	MILLIONS $ 1996

PER 100,000
LIVE BIRTHS
6

IMPORTS
34,290
EXPORTS
48,922

The Sami culture

The Sami are descendants of nomadic tribes which travelled throughout northern Scandinavia for thousands of years. Presently settled in Norway, they are a small community of some 40,000 people, living in the centre and north of the country (the province of Lapland). Some Sami also live in Russia, Sweden and Finland.

Their origins are uncertain and lost in time. Some claim they are linked to Siberian peoples, others to Alpine communities from Central Europe. The reindeer formed the basis of their economy until a few years ago. However, a more settled existence has substantially altered their traditions.

The last remaining Sami herders accompany the reindeer through valleys with grasslands, while their families live in modern homes. Through the years, their survival has now come to depend on fishing and agriculture.

The use of the Sami language was banned for a long time in schools in Norway. It is composed of three basic dialects: each one with several subtypes and local variations. The number of Sami has increased since the last century, but the number of those who speak the language has decreased.

Romania and West Germany, had re-sold some to India, but later pledged not to re-sell the material for weapons production without Norwegian authorization. The dispute was not properly resolved until Norway prohibited all 'heavy water' exports in 1988.

[27] In 1988, US threats to impose sanctions were dropped after Norway agreed to limit its whaling quota to scientific studies. In 1990, however, the Government announced its intention to return to the whaling tradition.

[28] In 1986, the pollution of rivers and lakes in southern Norway was attributed to acid rain coming from the United Kingdom. The British Government announced its intention to reduce emissions by 14 per cent by 1997, but the Norwegians considered this measure to be insufficient. A 60 per cent reduction of emissions within the country since the early 1980s has been insufficient to stop the environmental damage.

[29] The vulnerability of the Norwegian environment to events beyond national borders was underscored in April 1986 when a fire broke out in the Chernobyl nuclear power plant, in the Ukraine. The high levels of radioactivity released into the atmosphere most seriously affected the Sami population in the northern part of the country, and over 70 per cent of all reindeer meat had to be destroyed.

[30] Since the early 1970s, Norway and the former USSR have been at odds over rights to large parts of the Barents Sea. A temporary agreement signed in 1978 defined a 'grey area' for the joint management of fishing. The unresolved questions continued to create tension until early 1989, when the USSR proposed that they begin negotiations.

[31] Protests have been triggered by acid rain emanating from industries on the Kola Peninsula to the east of Norway. Since the fall of the communist regime this situation has changed, and there is growing trade across the border. Norway, Sweden and Finland have joined forces to help Russia solve the immense environmental problems in the area.

[32] Towards the end of 1986, Norway suffered a recession, immediately following a veritable consumer boom which had transformed Norway into the Scandinavian country with the highest standard of living. There was a large devaluation that year, tax reforms were carried out, and unemployment increased. The Government responded by implementing a harsh austerity plan.

[33] Norway is the world's sixth largest producer of natural gas and crude oil, and the third largest oil exporter. Operating outside the OPEC system, oil concessions have always been handled as an economic and political weapon. Although drilling rights are granted to foreign companies, the state looks after its own interests by requiring 50 per cent participation by Statoil, the national oil company, in all operations.

[34] In January 1992, Norway's mission in South Africa was upgraded from a consulate to an embassy, and in the course of 1993, Norwegian diplomacy gained a great deal of prestige when the minister of foreign affairs, Johan Juergen Holst served as an intermediary in the Israeli-PLO negotiations.

[35] In 1993 the economy picked up, although unemployment remained at 6 per cent. Oil, fishing (with 25,000 employed), the merchant marine (with 1,059 ships and a capacity of 36 million tons) and agriculture play important roles in the country's economy. The Norwegian agricultural system is one of the most heavily subsidized in Europe, but while the country must import fruit, vegetables and cereals, it is self-sufficient in animal products.

[36] Despite serious disagreements between the various sectors of Norwegian society, Oslo sought entry to the European Union (EU) in late 1992. The unions considered that joining the former European Community would threaten national sovereignty, while many entrepreneurs - particularly in the export sector - wanted full access to the EU market.

[37] However, for entry to be effective it had to be approved by a referendum, and a date was set for November 1994. The campaign for this vote largely dominated political life for two years and revolved around three main issues: oil exploitation, the regional policy and the fishing policy.

[38] The social democrats and conservatives supported joining the EU, while all the other opposed the move, leading to an extremely close outcome: 52.4 per cent of the electorate voted against integration, blocking Norway's membership of the bloc.

[39] In 1994, the economy continued to expand and unemployment to fall. In 1995, unemployment reached 4.8 per cent and the trend was expected to continue.

[40] In October 1996, Labor party's Thorbjorn Jagland became head of government after Gro Harlem Brundland resigned.

[41] Following the September 1997 elections, Jagland was forced to stand down. The ruling Labor party took 35 per cent of the votes and 65 seats out of the total 165 in play. The Prime Minister had announced he would stand down if the party could not equal the 36.9 per cent it had achieved in 1993.

[42] Christian Democrat, Kjell Magne Bondevik was appointed his successor. A coalition of three "centre" parties took control. These parties held only 43 votes in Parliament. Bondevik started by earmarking part of the oil income for investments in health and education.

[43] In 1997, the economy expanded for the fifth year running. However in early 1998, Norway (one of the world's largest oil exporters) started to suffer the consequences of falling international crude oil prices, following the stock exchange crash in Southeast Asia - the biggest oil importing market in the world.

[44] The 1998 wage settlements were expected to result in an average increase of 6-8 per cent, well above the Government's fiscal plan figure of 3.5 per cent. With inflation at 2.5 per cent, further expansion of the economy was expected.

Oman

'Uman

Population: 2,302,000 (1996)
Area: 212,457 SQ KM
Capital: Muscat (Masqat)

Currency: Omani rials
Language: Arabic

Sumerian clay tablets from the third century BC mention Oman as one of the outstanding markets in the economy of the Mesopotamian cities. Omani navigators became the lords of the Indian Ocean, connecting the Gulf to India, Indonesia and Indochina. In the 7th century they also played a major role in the peaceful propagation of Islam. Around 690 AD Abd Al-Malik decided to control the expansion of dissident sects. Consequently, some defeated leaders were forced to abandon the country. One of them, Prince Hamza, emigrated to Africa where he founded Zanzibar (see Tanzania: The Zandj Culture) beginning a relationship between Oman and the African coast which would last until the 19th century.

[2] Persecution only served to further reinforce Sharite "heresy". Towards 751, Oman took advantage of the dynastic strife in Damascus to elect an imam who gradually evolved from a spiritual leader to a temporal sovereign. Omani wealth gave the imam considerable power in the entire Gulf region, but also made Oman the object of successive invasions by the caliphs of Baghdad, the Persians, the Mongols and the local groups of central Arabia. The Portuguese arrived from 1507, destroying the fleet and coastal fortifications, opening the way for the occupation of the principal cities and the control of the Straits of Hormuz. The Portuguese held control of the region for almost 150 years, suffocating the Gulf's trade.

[3] In 1630, Imam Nasir bin Murshid launched an inland struggle against the invaders. His son, Said, concluded this endeavour in 1650 with the expulsion of the

Portuguese from Muscat (Musqat) and the recovery of Zanzibar and the African coast of Mombasa in 1698. Thus a powerful state was created which obtained the political unification of the African and Asian territories where a common culture and economy had developed.

[4] Sultan Said expanded the African territories and moved the capital to Zanzibar in 1832. At the time of his death in 1856, the British presence was already being strongly felt on both continents. Said's sons argued and as a result, the African and Asian parts of the state were separated: the elder son, Thuwaini, kept the sultanate of Oman while his brother Majid took control of Zanzibar. The 1891 Canning Agreement virtually made Oman a British protectorate.

[5] In 1913, inland peoples elected their own imam in opposition to the sultan's hereditary rule. The struggle came to an end only in 1920, when a treaty was signed acknowledging the country's division in two: the Sultanate of Muscat and the Imamate of Oman.

[6] Muscat is an extremely poor country, where arable lands account for less than one per cent of the total territory. Between 1932 and 1970, it suffered the despotic rule of Sultan Said bin Taimur, who fanatically opposed any foreign influence in the country, even in education and health. This did not prevent him from granting control over the country's oil deposits to Royal Dutch Shell.

[7] Imam Ghaleb bin Alim, elected in 1954, proclaimed independence and announced his intention to join the Arab League. In 1955 the British reunified Oman. Since then, a liberation movement has stubbornly put up resistance,

especially in the southern province of Dhofar.

[8] Taimur was overthrown by his own son Qabus on July 23 1970. Those who expected the young, Oxford-educated monarch to introduce modernizing changes soon realized that British domination was only being replaced by US domination. The US became a net importer of oil and began to develop an active interest in the area.

[9] Oil has been produced commercially since 1967. It provides more than half of the Gross Domestic Product. However more than half of Oman's labour force remain involved in agriculture, in the thin coastal strip that contains the country's only arable land.

[10] With US assistance, Qabus organized a mercenary army but when this force proved incapable of smashing the Popular Front for the Liberation of the Gulf, he signed an agreement with Shah Reza Pahlevi to secure Iranian intervention in the conflict.

[11] The guerrilla fighters were

forced to retreat under the superior firepower of Iranian troops. Iranians also placed the Strait of Hormuz under their jurisdiction.

[12] Upon the Shah's downfall, Iranian soldiers were quickly replaced by Egyptian commandos and troops. The Sultan decided to give the US the Masira island air base, and later the air bases at Ihamrit and Sib and the naval bases at Matrah and Salalah. Two-thirds of the national budget are committed to defence, while the people continue to suffer acute poverty and widespread illiteracy.

[13] Oman's strategic importance, with a geographic position giving the country full control over oil routes, led the US to concentrate on the sultanate in efforts to settle in the area.

[14] The country's isolation gradually came to an end during the first part of Qabus' rule, but a massive "opening" towards foreign capital, followed by insignificant action in the education and cultural fields, did not end the extremely

PUBLIC EXPENDITURE

36.5%   26.3%
1995 ■ DEFENCE □ SOCIAL

In 1990/91 Military as % of health & education expenditure was 293%.

WORKERS

(1996)

Labour force %

■ WOMEN
□ MEN

15   85

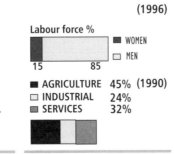

■ AGRICULTURE 45% (1990)
□ INDUSTRIAL 24%
▨ SERVICES 32%

Food Dependency	Foreign Trade	Maternal Mortality	External Debt
1970 **2%** 1994 **13%**	MILLIONS $ 1996 IMPORTS **4,610** EXPORTS **6,395**	1990 PER 100,000 LIVE BIRTHS **190**	1996 PER CAPITA **$1,483**

PROFILE

ENVIRONMENT
With its 2,600 km coastline, Oman occupies a strategic position on the southeastern edge of the Arabian Peninsula and flanking the Gulf of Oman, where oil tankers leave the Persian Gulf. It is separated from the rest of the peninsula by the Rub al Khali desert which stretches into the center of the country. Local nomadic groups now live with petroleum and natural gas exploitation. Favored by ocean currents, the coastal regions enjoy a better climate. Monsoon summer rains fall in the north.

SOCIETY
Peoples: Omani Arab 73.5 per cent; Pakistani (mostly Baluchi) 18.7per cent; other 5.5 per cent.
Religions: Muslim 86 per cent; Hindu 13 per cent; other 1 per cent.
Languages: Arabic, official and predominant, English, Baluchi and Urdu are also spoken.
Political Parties: There are no legal political parties.

THE STATE
Official Name: Saltanat 'Uman (Sultante of Oman).
Administrative divisions: 59 Districts.
Capital: Muscat (Masqat), 51,969 people (1990).
Other cities: Nizwa 62,880; Sama'il 44,721; Salalah 10,000.
Government: Qabus ibn Said, Sultan in power since July, 1970.
National Holiday: November 19. The Sultan's birthday.
Armed Forces: 43,500 (1996).
Other: 3,900.

STATISTICS

DEMOGRAPHY
Population: 2,302,000 (1996). **Annual growth:** 4.4% (1980/1996). **Estimates for year 2000:** 2,700,000. **Annual growth to year 2000:** 4.2% (1994/2000). **Urban Population:** 77.7% (1996). **Urban growth:** 8.57% (1980/95). **Children per woman:** 7.2 (1996).

HEALTH
Life expectancy at birth: 70 years (1996). **Infant mortality:** 15 per 1,000 (1996). **Under-5 child mortality:** 18 per 1,000 (1996). **Safe water:** 82% (1990/96).

EDUCATION
Literacy: 59% (1995), male : 71% (1995). female: 46% (1995). **School enrolment :** Primary total: 83% (1990/95). male : 85% (1990/95). female: 80% (1990/95). Secondary: male : 67% (1990/95). female: 61% (1990/95). Tertiary: 5% (1995). **Primary school teachers:** one for every 26 students (1995).

COMMUNICATIONS
30 **newspapers**, 583 **radios**, 730 **TV sets** and 76 **main telephone lines** per 1,000 people (1994). **Books:** 1 new title per 100,000 people (1992/94).

ECONOMY
Annual inflation: -0.21% (1985/95). **Currency:** 0.38 Omani rials = $ 1 (1995) **Cereal imports:** 460 metric tons (1994). **Food import dependency:** 13% (1994). **Fertilizer use:** 1,587 kgs per ha (1994). **Exports:** $ 6,395 million (1994). **Imports:** $ 4,610 million (1996). **External debt:** $ 3,415 million (1996). $ 1,483 **per capita:** (1996). **Debt service:** 9.9% of exports (1996). **Development aid received:** $ 59 million (1995). $ 29 per capita (1995). 0.6% of GNP (1994).

ENERGY
Consumption: 2,391.80 Kgs of Oil equivalent per capita yearly (1994). -786.96% imported (1994).

HDI (rank / value) 88 / 0.718 (1994)

---

authoritarian features of the traditional social system. The only real opposition is the People's Front for the Liberation of Oman (PFLO), which dropped the armed struggle, to create a broad based democratic front. The organization's objectives were to form an alliance with the Arab nationalists, especially the Palestinians, and to expel the foreign troops.
[15] During the Iran-Iraq war, US presence grew in Oman; 10,000 soldiers were stationed in different bases, mainly on the Masira Island base, equipped with atomic weapons and where the Rapid Intervention Force has operated since 1984 despite violent protests. Subsequently Oman purchased two F-16 combat aircraft squads with sophisticated equipment.
[16] In June 1989, the Petroleum Development of Oman announced the discovery of the most important natural gas deposits found within the last 20 years.
[17] In March, Oman adopted a conciliation policy toward Iran, which included an economic cooperation agreement, though this aid was contingent upon efforts to

achieve political stability in the Gulf region.
[18] In March 1991, after the Iraqi invasion of Kuwait, a member of the Gulf Cooperation Council, Oman suspended all aid to Jordan and the PLO.
[19] In 1991, the Foreign Ministers of Egypt, Syria and the six Arab member States of the Cooperation Council signed an agreement with the United States in Riyadh, the capital of Saudi Arabia, aimed at maintaining the region's security.
[20] Later that year, the Government announced that the democratization process was underway; this included the creation of a parliament directly elected by the country's citizens.
[21] Anticipating a depletion of oil reserves before the year 2010, Sultan Qabus launched a plan to diversify the economy, aiming to develop fishing, agriculture and tourism, among other sectors.
[22] During the summer of 1994, some 500 dissidents were arrested, including several senior officials and well-known business people, charged with trying to topple the Government "using Islam as a cover". The fiscal deficits accumulated by the Government

since 1981, regarded as excessive, led the World Bank to warn that the level of State expenditure was "unsustainable".
[23] Taking heed of the international financial organization's stand, the Sultan announced in 1995 a programme of reforms which included a reduction of state spending, a series of privatizations and measures to attract foreign investment.
[24] In 1996, the Government announced a five-year plan to balance the budget by 2000. The project, aiming to free the economy from oil dependence, included privatizations and stimuli to increase foreign investment.
[25] That same year, the Sultan established a new sucession mechanism. This meant that, if the royal family could not reach agreement on the appointment of a

sucessor within three days of his death, the candidate chosen by the Sultan himself would be accepted.
[26] Oman became one of the first Arab countries to establish diplomatic and trade relations with Israel in January 1997. A month later, the rapprochement process came to a halt, when the Arab League questioned the Israeli decision to build new settlements in eastern Jerusalem.
[27] In early 1998, Oman, along with all the other Gulf Co-operation Council (GCC) member nations, debated the possibility of freeing its currency from the dollar to prevent the loss of income on oil sales. The six GCC nations controlled 45 per cent of the world's crude oil reserves, but were losing millions of dollars per year due to falling international exchange rates on the US currency.

Pakistan

Pakistan

Population:	139,973,000 (1996)
Area:	796,095 SQ KM
Capital:	Islamabad
Currency:	Rupees
Language:	Urdu

Pakistan means the land of the pure, as it was religion (Islam) that bound together the people of different ethnic communities and languages. Poet-philosopher Mohammed Iqbal articulated the concept of Pakistan in its basic form in 1931 when he proposed a separate state for the Muslims in India.

[2] The first Muslims to arrive in the Indian subcontinent were the traders from Arabia and Persia. A permanent Muslim foothold was achieved with Mohammed bin Qasim's conquest of Sind in 711 AD. It was in the early 13th century that the foundations of Muslim rule in India were laid, establishing borders and a capital in Delhi. The region including the present territory of Pakistan was subsequently ruled by several Muslim dynasties, finishing with the Mughals.

[3] The question of Muslim identity emerged alongside the decline of Muslim power and the rise of the Hindu middle class during British colonialism. In the early years of the 20th century, Muslim leaders became convinced of the need for effective political organization. A delegation of Muslim leaders met the viceroy (the chief representative of the British imperial government in India) in October 1906, demanding the status of a separate electorate for the Muslims. The All India Muslim League (ML) was founded in Dhaka that year with the objective of defending the political rights and interests of Indian Muslims. The British conceded the status of a separate electorate in the Government of India Act of 1909, confirming the ML's status as the representative organization of Indian Muslims.

[4] In the 1930s there was a growing awareness of a separate Muslim identity and a greater desire to preserve it within separate territorial boundaries. Under the leadership of Mohammed Ali Jinnah, ML continued its campaign for Pakistan; a separate homeland in British India. After the general election of April 1946, ML called a convention of the newly-elected ML parliamentarians in Delhi. A motion by Hussain Shaheed Suhrawardi, then chief minister of Bengal, reiterated the demand for Pakistan in no uncertain terms.

[5] The Hindu-Muslim relationship had been seriously affected by communal tensions and riots in different parts of India. This convinced the leadership of the Indian National Congress (representing mainly the nationalists) to accept Pakistan as a solution for the communal problem. A Partition Plan for transfer of power was announced on June 3 1947. Both the ML and the Congress accepted the Plan and on August 14 1947, the new state of Pakistan was born comprising West Punjab, Sind, Baluchistan, North-West Frontier Province and East Bengal.

[6] Pakistan has suffered numerous political crises. The first constitution was adopted on March 23 1956, but the civilian government was deposed in a coup on October 7 1958. Martial law was proclaimed and the constitution abrogated. On October 27 1958, General Ayub Khan emerged as the new leading force. He introduced 'basic democracy', a system of local self-government and indirect presidential elections. Martial law was withdrawn in 1962 and a new

1 Claimed by India
2 Claimed by Pakistan

0   300 km

constitution, granting absolute power to the president, was instituted, with Pakistan being declared an Islamic Republic. Ayub Khan was forced to resign on March 25, 1969, following a popular uprising. Martial law was promulgated again and General Yahya Khan became president.

[7] A general election was held at the end of 1970, the first ever in Pakistan under neutral administration. Two political parties, the Awami League (AL) and the Pakistan People's Party (PPP) emerged victorious in East and West Pakistan, respectively. However, the AL won an absolute majority in the parliamentary election on an all-Pakistan basis, forming the federal government. However, the parliamentary session was postponed, and the people of East Pakistan began the movement for an independent Bangladesh under the leadership of the AL in March 1971. The AL was banned and its leader Sheikh Mujibur Rahman was arrested. A civil war broke out, leading the AL to form a government in exile in India. The Indian army intervened and on December 16 1971, Bangladesh became independent.

[8] Zulfiqar Ali Bhutto, the leader of the PPP, formed a civilian government in 1972 following the resignation of General Yahya Khan. He encouraged strong public sector participation in the economy, followed a non-aligned foreign policy and approved radical land reforms. The PPP was victorious again in the general election of 1977, but the results were rejected by opposition political parties who accused the PPP of vote-rigging. Against this backdrop of political unrest, General Zia-ul Haq ousted the Bhutto government and proclaimed martial law. Bhutto was arrested and later sentenced to death on charge of conspiring to murder an opposition political leader.

[9] General Zia accelerated the process of Islamicization in all spheres of political and social life. Many political opponents were harassed and detained. A general election on a non-party basis was held in February 1985 under martial law, and a pro-Zia government was formed. Zia was killed in a mysterious air crash in August 1988. In the general election of November 1988, the PPP were victorious and a government was formed under

WORKERS

(1996)

Labour force %

■ WOMEN
□ MEN

27   73

■ AGRICULTURE 52% (1990)
□ INDUSTRIAL 19%
■ SERVICES 30%

LAND USE

DEFORESTATION -2.9% annual (81/90)
IRRIGATED 82.3% of arable

(1993)

■ FOREST & WOODLAND 4.4%
□ ARABLE 26.1%
■ OTHER 69.5%

1970

21%

1994

11%

IMPORTS
11,812

EXPORTS
9,266

1996

PROFILE

ENVIRONMENT
Pakistan is mountainous and semi-arid, with the exception of the Indus River basin in the east. This is virtually the only irrigated zone in the country, suitable for agriculture and vital to the local economy. The Indus rises in the Himalayas in the disputed province of Kashmir and flows into the Arabian Sea. The majority of the population live along its banks. The main agricultural products are wheat and cotton, grown under irrigation. The country's main industry is the manufacture of cotton goods. Pakistan suffers from water shortage, soil depletion and deforestation.

SOCIETY
Peoples: Pakistan has a complex ethnic and cultural composition, basically Indo-European combined with Persian, Greek and Arab in the Indus Valley, plus Turkish and Mongolian in the mountainous areas. Much Indian immigration has occurred in recent years.
Religions: Islam is the official religion followed by 97 per cent of the population (most belong to the Sunni sect); 2 per cent are Christian; 1.6 per cent are Hindu; the remainder belong to other smaller sects.
Languages: Urdu (official, although it is spoken by only 9 per cent of the population). Other languages are Punjabi, Sindhi, Pashto, Baluchi, English and several dialects.
Political Parties: The Pakistan People's Party (PPP); the Pakistan Muslim League (IJI or IDA).
Social Organizations: The National Pakistan Federation of Unions.

THE STATE
Official Name: Islam-i Jamhuriya-e Pakistan.
Administrative divisions: 4 Provinces.
Capital: Islamabad, 340,000 people (1994).
Other cities: Karachi, 8,800,000 people (1994); Lahore, 2,952,689; Faisalabad 1,104,209 (1981).
Government: Mohammad Rafiq Tarar, President and Head of State since 1998. Nawaz Sharif, Prime Minister and Head of Government since 1997. Legislature: bicameral. 87-member Senate; 217-member National Assembly, elected every 6 and 5 years, respectively.
National Holidays: August 14, Independence Day (1947); March 23, Proclamation of the Republic (1956).
Armed Forces: 587,000 (1996).
Other: 275,000 (National Guard, Border Corps, Maritime Security, Mounted Police).

the leadership of Bhutto's daughter Benazir Bhutto. The democratic system was brought back after an 11 year absence.
[10] Bhutto became the first woman to serve as head of state of a predominantly Islamic country. One of her first moves was to release all female prisoners charged with crimes other than murder. Many of these had been imprisoned under discriminatory 'Black Laws' passed during Zia's term in office. They include the law of evidence, under which the declaration of one man is given more weight than that of two women in legal proceedings. Zia left a legacy of such laws in the form of constitutional amendments, which required a virtually politically-impossible two-thirds majority to overturn.
[11] The army has always been a strong institution in Pakistan. The country became a member of the Southeast Asian Treaty Organization (SEATO) in 1954 and the Central Treaty Organization (CENTO) in 1955, two strong military alliances led by the United States. Although Pakistan later withdrew from these alliances, bilateral relations with the US have been fluent. Pakistan has received military and economic aid from the US.
[12] Relations with India have always been strained. The two countries both have territorial claims over the state of Kashmir. India treats it as an integral part of the country, while Pakistan has been demanding a plebiscite there to allow the people of Kashmir to decide their own fate. After wars in 1948, 1965 and 1971, the two states agreed on a cease-fire zone on both sides of the Kashmir border. This meant not only a division of land, but also a separation of the local population. Since then, Kashmiri nationalist groups have demanded the creation of an independent state in the region.
[13] Throughout the 1980s, Pakistan was very vocal in its opposition to the Soviet intervention in Afghanistan (started in December 1979). Pakistan also supported the Mujahedin, Afghan resistance groups based in Pakistan, in their fight against the pro-Soviet regime in Kabul. During the Soviet intervention in Afghanistan, the US used Pakistani territory to supply arms to the rebel groups. This turned Pakistan into a key ally for the US regional policy, and resulted in the granting of significant economic assistance to the country. There were about three million Afghan refugees living in Pakistan in mid-1990.
[14] On August 6 1990, President Ghulam Ishaq Khan dissolved the government of Prime Minister Benazir Bhutto, charging her administration with nepotism and corruption. The President suspended the National Assembly and named Ghulam Mustafa Jatoi, leader of the Combined Opposition Parties (COP) coalition, head of the interim government.
[15] Elections were held on October 24. Nawaz Sharif was elected Prime Minister, with the support of the Muslim League, the main party in the coalition opposing Bhutto. Benazir Bhutto also put forward her candidacy, but her Peoples Party of Pakistan claimed the elections had been rigged and started an intense opposition campaign.
[16] After the Iraqi invasion of Kuwait when the war broke out in the Persian Gulf, Pakistan quickly aligned with the US and sent troops to Saudi Arabia. Surveys showed that the population had strong pro-Iraqi tendencies, but the government announced that the country's forces would only defend Islamic holy places, and would not take part in combat or go into Iraqi territory.
[17] Shortly after taking office, Prime Minister Nawaz Sharif, who belongs to a family of Pakistani industrialists, implemented an economic reform plan, aimed at encouraging private investment. The plan includes a far-reaching privatization process which was strongly resisted by the 300,000 workers in the state-run companies.
[18] Apart from the economic reforms, Sharif's government promoted a strongly-resisted process of Islamic reinforcement. The plan included the introduction of Sharia or Islamic law. In the Sharif's opinion, Benazir Bhutto's term was a period of religious regression. The enforcement of Sharia immediately resulted in obvious setbacks of women's social and legal status. The Government banned the media from making any reference to a woman's right to divorce. The main leaders of the women's movements, who demanded the end of discrimination against women, were harassed by security forces, and some were kidnapped and raped.
[19] On November 22 1990, a serious political and administrative scandal broke out. The opposition accused Nawaz Sharif of embezzling public funds. Sharif was responsible for the bankruptcy of several cooperative credit institutions. Only the unconditional support of President Ishaq Khan prevented the fall of the prime minister and the matter was referred to the judiciary. The scandal triggered a wave of demonstrations led by the PPP, and the Government responded with increased repression.
[20] In 1991, there were increased accusations of human rights violations levelled against the Pakistani Government. In November, Amnesty International demanded the suspension of the sentences on 20 people on death row. According to Amnesty

STATISTICS

DEMOGRAPHY
Population: 139,973,000 (1996). **Annual growth:** 3.1% (1980/1996). **Estimates for year 2000:** 156,000,000. **Annual growth to year 2000:** 2.7% (1994/2000). **Urban Population:** 34.8% (1996). **Urban growth:** 4.55% (1980/95). **Children per woman:** 5.2 (1996).

HEALTH
Life expectancy at birth: 63 years (1996). male: 61 years (1996). female: 63 years (1994). **Infant mortality:** 95 per 1,000 (1996). **Under-5 child mortality:** 136 per 1,000 (1996). **Calorie consumption:** 99% (1988/90). 2,000 **people per doctor** (1988/91). **Safe water:** 74% (1990/96).

EDUCATION
Literacy: 38% (1995). male: 50% (1995). female: 24% (1995). **School enrolment :** Primary total: 69% (1990/95). male : 94% (1990/95). female: 42% (1990/95). Secondary: male : 33% (1990/95). female: 17% (1990/95). Tertiary: 3% (1995).

COMMUNICATIONS
20 **newspapers**, 88 **radios**, 20 **TV sets** and 15 **main telephone lines** per 1,000 people (1996).

ECONOMY
Per capita, GNP: $ 480 (1996). **Annual growth, GNP:** 0.3% (1995/96). **Annual inflation:** 9.16% (1985/95). **Consumer price index:** 150.6 (1994). **Currency:** 34.25 rupees = $ 1 (1995) **Cereal imports:** 1,916 metric tons (1994). **Food import dependency:** 11% (1994). **Fertilizer use:** 1,023 kgs per ha (1994). **Exports:** $ 9,266 million (1994). **Imports:** $ 11,812 million (1996). **External debt:** $ 29,901 million (1996). $ 214 **per capita:** (1996). **Debt service:** 27.4% of exports (1996). **Development aid received:** $ 805 million (1995). $ 6 per capita (1995). 1.5% of GNP (1994).

ENERGY
Consumption: 254.25 Kgs of Oil equivalent per capita yearly (1994). 39.53% imported (1994).

HDI (rank / value) 139 / 0.445 (1994)

[26] President Ishaq Khan accused Prime Minister Mohammed Nawaz Sharif of poor administration, corruption and nepotism, forcing him to resign in April 1993. The National Assembly was dissolved and elections were announced for July. Sharif appealed to the Supreme Court and was reinstated in May. The dissolution of the Assembly was revoked and the call for elections cancelled.

[27] Sharif's return aggravated the conflict with President Ishaq Khan. Both leaders resigned in July. The interim president, Moin Kureishi, a former World Bank and IMF official, took unprecedented measures: he abolished the old system whereby members of parliament had received funds for investment in their own districts, a source of endless corruption, and also taxed large property units.

[28] Traditionally, powerful landowners had dominated Pakistan's economy and political system and had exempted themselves from paying taxes. Only one per cent of the country's 130 million inhabitants paid their taxes, but charges of tax evasion had never been filed.

[29] Benazir Bhutto returned to power with the October 6 elections. The PPP won 86 of the Assembly's 217 seats, against 72 obtained by Sharif. Bhutto received the support of minor parties and was confirmed with 121 votes. Her position was strengthened with the election of Faruk Ahmed Leghari (also from the PPP) as president in November.

[30] The Prime Minister tried to activate the economy and avoided confrontation with the conservative clergy. However, Islamic fundamentalists put a price on the head of the justice minister, who supported a proposal to modify Pakistan's laws on blasphemy. The modification included making false charges of blasphemy as an offence.

[31] Bhutto's efforts to bring democracy and equal rights to her country were tainted by political and ethnic violence in 1994 and 1995, the bloodiest years since 1971 when Bangladesh separated. Karachi and the northern separatist areas were the center of disputes. Over 3,500 people

died in confrontations between August 1994 and October 1995.

[32] An attempted coup led by fundamentalist military officials was put down by the Government in late 1995.

[33] In June 1996, hundreds of people protesting against the proscription of pro-independence candidates in local elections in Azad, Jammu and Kashmir were arrested.

[34] One of Benazir Bhutto's main political rivals, her brother Murtaza, died in a confrontation with police on September 20 1996. Murtaza commanded a guerrilla group demanding the prime minister's resignation. The Bhuttos had been rivals since their father was overthrown in 1977.

[35] In November 1996, Bhutto was forced to leave her position as Prime Minister, charged with corruption, and new parliamentary elections were held. The Pakistan People's Party was defeated, receiving only 19 seats out of the 217 at stake, compared to the 136 won by the followers of former prime minister Nawaz Sharif. Miraj Khalid led the Government as Deputy Prime Minister until Sharif came to office once again in early 1997.

[36] A 1997 report by Amnesty International claimed there were political prisoners in Pakistan, subject to torture and ill-treatment. A list of "disappeared" people was also reported, including summary executions.

[37] The military confrontations between India and Pakistan continued in Kashmir. Talks held between New Delhi and Islamabad were at a standstill: while India claimed sovereignty over the region and stated its future was "non-negotiable", the Sharif administration demanded a referendum on self-determination.

International, the people sentenced to capital punishment were denied the most basic legal rights.

[21] Apart from the disputes between the government and the opposition, Pakistan has been periodically shaken by inter-ethnic violence, in particular between the Sindhis and the Muhajirs (former Indian refugees). Violence has particularly affected the Sind region and the city of Karachi, the country's main industrial center.

[22] The end of Soviet intervention in Afghanistan placed Pakistan in a difficult position. From the US viewpoint, Pakistan had lost the key position that it had held during the years of Soviet military intervention. The Islamicization process started by Sharif was also unacceptable to the US, because of the implication of greater cooperation with other Islamic regimes in the area.

[23] In February 1992, the ancient dispute over the border territory of Kashmir brought Pakistan and India to the brink of a new armed conflict. The Jammu and Kashmir Liberation Front, a Muslim group which demands the creation of an independent state in this borderline region, staged a protest

march along the line that divides the country between Pakistan and India. The organizers encouraged thousands of demonstrators on both sides to cross the border. The Pakistani government ordered the army to shoot at the demonstrators in order to stop the separatist march. Five people died and fifty were injured.

[24] Amidst the tension created by the Kashmir border crisis, the differences between Washington and Islamabad became more obvious. When Pakistan announced their nuclear weapon construction project was well under way, the US began to exert pressure on the country. This resulted in the virtual suspension of US economic assistance and arms sales to Pakistan. As a response to the US measures, Pakistan announced that China had guaranteed economic and technological support to continue the nuclear research program.

[25] In November 1992, Benazir Bhutto led an opposition march from Rawalpindi to Islamabad, demanding Sharif's resignation. The Government arrested 1,600 people, including Bhutto, who was held for 30 days in a Karachi prison.

Palau

Palau

Population: 17,000 (1996)
Area: 459 SQ KM
Capital: Koror

Language: English

Five thousand years ago, sailors from Formosa and China peopled the islands of Micronesia, forming highly stratified societies where age, sex and military prowess defined rank, and wealth.

[2] European colonization in the 19th century, did not totally eliminate the indigenous peoples of Palau as it had on other islands.

[3] In 1914, the Japanese took the islands from Germany, who had bought them from Spain in 1899. During World War II, Japan installed its main naval base in Palau and it soon became the scene of fierce combat when the US recognized its strategic position in relation to the Philippines.

[4] By the end of World War II, the indigenous population of Palau had been reduced from 45,000 to 6,000. Micronesia became a US trust territory. The US used the islands as nuclear testing grounds and reneged on promises of self-government, instead fostering economic dependence.

[5] In 1978, at the beginning of the transition to self-government, the archipelago opted for separation from Micronesia. In January 1979, the new constitution banned all nuclear weapons installations, nuclear waste storage, and foreign land ownership. A further amendment established a 200-mile area of territorial waters under the UN-approved Law of the Sea, which the US tried to veto.

[6] The new constitution received majority approval of assembly members, but the US put pressure on the local parliament to change provisions which would frustrate their attempts to use Palau as a military base. In July 1979, a referendum showed 92 per cent support for an unamended constitution. Bending to US pressure, the local Supreme Court annulled the referendum and entrusted Palau's parliament to draft a "revised" constitution. In October 1979, this document was rejected by 70 per cent of the voters, and In July 1980, a third referendum ratified the original document by a 78 per cent majority.

[7] US Ambassador Rosemblat declared the Constitution "incompatible with the system of Free Association" in effect since November 1980 "because it impedes (the US) from exercising its responsibility of defending the territory".

[8] In 1981, International Power Systems (IPESCO) scheduled the installation of a 16-megawatt nuclear power plant in Palau; the scheme was to be financed by the US, subject to amendments to the anti-nuclear constitution.

[9] President Haruo Remliik was persuaded to hold another plebiscite to decide on the IPESCO plan and a "Compact of Free Association" with the US. The Compact received majority support, but failed to achieve the 75 per cent needed to override the constitution. In 1983, despite this ambiguous ballot, the President signed agreements for a loan totalling $37.5 million. UN intervention was immediately called for by the opposition.

[10] In 1984, the power plant was built and the following year, Remliik refused to call a third plebiscite when the US proposed to revoke the historic anti-nuclear constitution. A few days later he was assassinated.

[11] The Palau Congress amended the constitution by a referendum requiring a simple majority, and on August 21 1987, a further plebiscite approved the Compact. However, in April 1988, the constitutional amendment was invalidated by the Supreme Court, stating the 75 per cent majority requirement.

[12] In August 1988, then President Salii was found dead with a bullet in his head and a pistol at his side. His death was officially described as suicide.

[13] A new referendum held in February 1989 again did not gain the necessary majority for approval. Moreover, to restrain constant violations of its territorial waters by Indonesian vessels, in early 1992 Palau requested Japanese assistance in monitoring the area, in exchange for fishing rights.

[14] Towards the end of that year, Kuniwo Nakamura was elected president by a narrow margin. At the same time, a plebiscite was supported by 62 per cent of the electorate to reduce the percentage needed to approve the status of Free Associated State of the US to a simple majority in a new referendum.

[15] This eighth referendum on the same issue was held in July 1993. No special majority was required, and therefore the Free Associated State system was approved by the favourable vote of 68 per cent of the electorate.

[16] Palau became a Free Associated State as of October 1994, when the new status - so many times postponed due to the controversial storage of nuclear materials in the island - came into effect.

[17] Nakamura tightened links with Japan and increased trade and tourism exchange between the two countries. He visited Tokyo in April 1995, stopping over in Taiwan.

[18] In November 1996, the first presidential elections since independence were held. Nakamura became President elect. Despite Chinese opposition, Palau decided to establish diplomatic relations with Taiwan and to open a consulate in Taipei.

[19] In 1997, the Government of Palau designed an economic plan to diversify income and reduce dependence on tourism.

Palestine

Palestine

Population:	2,761,000 (1997)
Area:	6,220 SQ KM
Capital:	Jerusalem (Al-Quds Ash Sharif)
Language:	Arabic

Around 4000 BC, the Canaanites, a Semitic people from the inner Arabian peninsula, settled in the land which became known as Canaan and later, Palestine. The Jebusites, one of the Canaanite tribes, built a settlement which they called Urusalim (Jerusalem), meaning "the city of peace".

[2] The Egyptian Pharaohs occupied part of Canaan in 3,200 BC, building fortresses to protect their trade routes, but the country kept its independence. Around 2000 BC, another Semitic people, Abraham's Hebrews, passed through Palestine on their way south. Seven centuries later, twelve Hebrew tribes returned from Egypt, following Moses. There was fierce fighting over possession of the land. The Bible records that "The sons of Judah were unable to exterminate the Jebusites that dwell in Jerusalem" (Joshua 15, 63).

[3] Four centuries later, Isaac's son David managed to defeat the Jebusites and unite the Jewish nation. After the death of his son Solomon the Hebrews split into two states, Israel and Judah. These later fell into the hands of the Assyrians, in 721 BC, and Chaldeans, in 587 BC. It was in 587 that Nebuchadnezzar destroyed Jerusalem and took the Jews into captivity in Babylon.

[4] In 332 BC, Alexander the Great conquered Palestine, but the territory returned to the Egyptian Empire of the Ptolemies soon after his death. The country was subdued by the Seleucids from Syria before a rebellion, headed by Judas Maccabeus, restored the Jewish state in 67 BC.

[5] In 63 BC, the Roman Empire seized Jerusalem, placing the city under its domination. Maccabeans, Zealots and other Jewish tribes resisted the invaders but were

▨	Jewish State, UN Plan, 1947
☐	Arab State, UN Plan, 1947
1	West Bank

▨	Jewish State, UN Plan, 1947
▨	Annexed to Israel in the 1948 war
2	Gaza Strip

▨	Israel's pre-1967 borders
▨	Occupied by Israel in 1967
◻	Recovered by Palestine from 1994: Gaza Strip, Jericho, Nablus, Ramallah

fiercely subdued. Solomon's temple was demolished around 70 AD, and the Jews were expelled from Jerusalem around 135 AD.

[6] The Romans gave Palestine its present name, and Roman domination was followed by that of the Byzantine Empire (the Roman Empire in the East), which lasted until 611 when the province was invaded by the Persians. The Arabs, a Semitic people from the inner peninsula, conquered Palestine in 634, and, according to legend, it was in Jerusalem that the prophet Muhammad rose to the heavens. As a result, the city became a holy place for all three monotheistic religions.

[7] The Islamic faith and the Arabic language united all the Semitic peoples except for the Jews. With short intervals of partial domination by the Christian Crusaders and the Mongols in the 11th, 12th and 13th centuries, Palestine had Arab rulers for almost 1,000 years and Islamic governments for 15 centuries.

[8] In 1516, Jerusalem was conquered by the Ottoman Empire

which maintained power until the end of World War I. During this conflict, the British promised Shereef Hussein the independence of the Arab lands in exchange for his cooperation in the struggle against the Turks. At the same time, in 1917, British Foreign Secretary Lord Balfour promised the Zionist Movement the establishment of a "Jewish National Homeland" in Palestine.

[9] Britain had no power at all over the area, either de facto or de jure, but it soon obtained this right by defeating the Turks, with the help of Arab allies, with a League of Nations mandate in 1922. Massive immigration raised the Jewish population of Palestine from 50,000 at the beginning of the century to 300,000 prior to World War II (see Israel).

[10] The Palestinians staged a general strike in April 1936, in protest against this immigration, which they saw as a threat to their rights. The British put forward a plan for the partition of Palestine into three states: Jewish in the north, Arab in the south, and a

third section under British administration in the Jerusalem-Jaffa (Tel Aviv) corridor. The Arabs rejected the plan and rebellion broke out, lasting until 1939, when London gave up the idea and set limits to immigration.

[11] Once World War II was over, Britain handed the problem over to the newly-established United Nations.

[12] When the UN General Assembly approved a new partition plan (1947) 749,000 Arabs and 9,250 Jews lived in the territory where the Arab State would be set up, while 497,000 Arabs and 498,000 Jews lived in the part which was to become the Jewish state.

[13] To drive the Palestinians from their land, a detachment of the Irgun organization commanded by Menahem Begin raided the village of Deir Yasin on April 9 1948, killing 254 civilians. 10,000 terrified Palestinians left the country.

[14] On May 14 1948, Israel unilaterally proclaimed itself an independent country. Neighboring Arab armies immediately attacked,

84%

but were unable to prevent the consolidation of the Jewish State. On the contrary, the latter emerged from the 1949 war with a land area larger than that proposed by the United Nations.

[15] More than half of Palestine's inhabitants had abandoned their homes: most of them lived as refugees on the West Bank, a territory which had been annexed by the Hashemite kingdom of Transjordan, and in the Gaza Strip, which was under Egyptian administration.

[16] In the eyes of the United Nations, and therefore, of international law, the Palestinians were not a people, but simply refugees, a "problem" to be solved.

[17] Political decisions about the Palestinian cause were left entirely in the hands of the Arab governments, who even had the right to appoint the Palestinian representative to the Arab League. At the 1964 Arab summit, Egyptian leader, Gamal Abdel Nasser, asked the League to take on the task of forging a unified Palestinian organization.

[18] In Jerusalem, on May 27, the Palestine National Council met for the first time. There were 422 participants, including personalities, business leaders, representatives of the refugee camps, the trade-union organizations, and the young people's and women's groups; they founded the Palestine Liberation Organization (PLO).

[19] Palestinian groups already operating secretly, such as Al Fatah, were wary of this Arab promoted organization as they distrusted its emphasis on using diplomatic channels for its struggle. They were convinced that their land could only be recovered by military force.

[20] On January 1 1965, the first armed operation took place in Israel. The attacks intensified during the following months, until the outbreak of the Six Day War in 1967, when Israel occupied all of Jerusalem, Syria's Golan Heights, Egypt's Sinai Peninsula, the Palestinian territories of the West Bank and the Gaza strip. The defeat of the regular Arab armies strengthened the conviction that guerrilla warfare was the only path.

[21] In March 1968, during a battle in the village of Al-Karameh, Palestinians forced the Israelis to withdraw. The event passed into

PROFILE

ENVIRONMENT

In terms of international law "Palestine" is the 27,000 sq km territory west of the Jordan River which the League of Nations handed over to Great Britain's "mandatory" power in 1918. This territory comprises: the area occupied by Israel before 1967, 20,073 sq km; Jerusalem and its surroundings, 70 sq km; the West Bank area, 5,879 sq km and the Gaza Strip, 378 sq km. It is a land of temperate Mediterranean climate, fertile on the coast and in the Jordan Valley. It is surrounded in the south and the northeast by the Sinai and Syrian deserts respectively. The Gaza region suffer from a severe scarcity of water. The accumulation of waste waters and refuse convert the refugee camps into highly contaminated areas. Soil erosion and deforestation are also serious problems.

SOCIETY

Peoples: Palestinians are an Arab people. In 1997 estimations were of near seven million Palestinians living in Palestine and abroad. There are 700,000 in Israel; 1,500,000 on the West Bank; 800,000 in the Gaza Strip, and the rest spread in Middle Eastern and European countries. 33 per cent of the inhabitants of the occupied territories live in refugee camps. There are large Palestinian populations in US, Chile, Brazil and other countries. **Religions:** Most are Muslim (97 per cent), but there are a large number of Christians. **Languages:** Palestinians speak Arabic and often also use Hebrew in the occupied territories, a language with the same Semite root which is more similar to Arabic than to the European languages of immigrants. **Political Parties:** The main political organization represented in the PLO is the Al-Fatah National Liberation Movement, founded in 1965 by Yasser Arafat. The Popular Front for the Liberation of Palestine (PFLP), the second party in number, founded in 1967 by George Habash, with a Marxist-Leninist self-definition, like the Democratic Front for the Liberation of Palestine (DFLP), led by Nayef Hawatmeth. Al-Saika, led by Zuheir Moshen, gathers since 1967 the Palestinians who support the Sirian Baas Party; the Arab Liberation Front, of Abder Rahin Ahmed, hold close links with the Iraqui Baas Party; the General Command-DFLP, a split of the DFLP, led by Ahmed Yabril. The Hamas (Islamic Resistance Movement), with great influence in West Bank and the Gaza Strip, opposes autonomy arrangements.

THE STATE

Official name: State of Palestine. Capital: Jerusalem (Al-Quds Ash Sharif) has traditionally been the capital of Palestine; the Palestine National Authority (PNA) is in Jericho, 16,000 people (1993). **Government:** Yasser Arafat, President of the Palestine National Authority since July 1994, re-elected in January 1996. The Autonomous Council acts as a Parliament. Armed Forces: there are no official data available.

folk history as the first victory of the Palestinian force.

[22] With their prestige thus restored, the various armed groups joined the PLO and obtained the support of the Arab governments. In February 1969, Yasser Arafat was elected chairman of the organization.

[23] The growing political and military strength of the Palestinians was seen as a threat by King Hussein of Jordan, who had acted as their representative and spokesman. Tension mounted between the King and the Palestinians eventually reaching explosive proportions. In September 1970, after much bloody fighting, the PLO was expelled from Jordan to set up its headquarters in Beirut.

[24] This new exile reduced the possibility of armed attacks on targets inside Israel, and new radical groups such as "Black September" directed their efforts towards Israeli institutions and businesses in Europe and other parts of the world. Palestinians,

until then regarded by world opinion purely as refugees, quickly came to be identified by some as terrorists.

[25] PLO leaders promptly realized the need to change their tactics and, without abandoning armed struggle, launched a large-scale diplomatic offensive, starting to devote much of their energy to consolidating Palestinian unity and identity. The Algiers Conference of Non-Aligned Countries (1973) identified the Palestine problem, and not Arab-Israeli rivalry, as the key to the conflict in the Middle East for the first time.

[26] In 1974, an Arab League summit conference recognized the PLO as "the only legitimate representative of the Palestinian people". In October of the same year the PLO was granted observer status in the UN General Assembly, which recognized the right of the Palestinian people to self-determination and independence, and condemned Zionism as "a form of racism".

[27] The PLO program proposes to

set up "a secular and independent state in the whole of the Palestinian territory, where Muslims, Christians and Jews can live in peace, enjoying the same rights and duties". This necessarily implies the end of the present state of Israel. Without giving up this ultimate goal, the PLO has gradually come to accept the "temporary solution" of setting up an independent Palestinian state "in any part of the territory that might be liberated by force of arms, or from which Israel may withdraw".

[28] In 1980, the Likud prime minister, Menahem Begin and Egyptian president Anwar Sadat signed a peace accord at Camp David, with US mediation. Shortly afterwards, Begin began officially to annex the Arab part of Jerusalem, proclaiming it the "sole and indivisible capital" of Israel. Jewish settlements on the West Bank multiplied, using Palestinian lands and increasing tension in the occupied territories. Successive United Nations votes against these measures, or for any action against Israel, were stripped of any practical value by the US using its veto in the Security Council.

[29] In July 1982, in an attempted "final settlement" of the Palestine issue, Israeli forces invaded Lebanon. The intention, as it later became clear, was to destroy the PLO's military structure, capture the greatest possible number of its leaders and combatants, annex the southern part of Lebanon and set up a puppet government in Beirut. Surrounded in Beirut, the Palestinian forces only agreed to withdraw after receiving guarantees of protection for civilians under a French-Italian-North American international peace-keeping force.

[30] The massacres that took place at the refugee camps of Sabra and Chatila showed the ineffectiveness of international protection, but the PLO managed to transform what seemed a final defeat into a political and diplomatic victory. The headquarters of the organization were moved to Tunis and Yasser Arafat toured Europe receiving the honors due a head of state in various countries, most notably in the Vatican.

[31] The PLO quietly initiated talks with Israeli leaders receptive to a negotiated settlement with the Palestinians. With the invasion of Lebanon, small but active peace groups emerged in Israel, demanding the initiation of a dialogue with the PLO. Palestinian radicals called these overtures into question, breaking with Yasser Arafat's policies. This division of the PLO put its factions at odds with each other, sometimes causing violent confrontations.

[32] In 1987, after several years of internal difficulties, the Palestine

Palestinians: still wandering

The recent history of Palestinians, especially since the 1940s, has been marked by confrontations, enforced segregation, overcrowding and massive geographic displacement throughout several Middle East regions.

Many Palestinians have emigrated to countries such as Iraq, Syria, Lebanon, and several states of the Persian Gulf region in search of better livng conditions. Victims of discrimination and police surveillance, few have been granted citizenship in these countries.

Their history has been different in Jordan, where they make up two-thirds of the total population. In the late1940s, the Jordanian monarchy granted them citizenship, in order to carry out its expansionist goals. There were serious confrontations with the recently created state of Israel, which occupied the West Bank and exerted its control over this Palestinian region. The Jordanian authorities carried out a policy of influence and control to manage the political future of the Palestinians.

In May 1950, the United Nations, which had already set up an agency to assist Palestinian refugees, reported the existence of 53 refugee camps in Jordan, the Gaza Strip, Syria and Lebanon. Over 600,000 refugees lived there in difficult conditions, in tents shared by several families, receiving some basic services like water, health and education, but unable to overcome poverty.

The limited avenues of employment open to them depended on the efforts of the United Nations' agency, which attempted to integrate them in countries of the region.

The government of Egypt controlled the Gaza Strip from 1948 to 1967 with repressive and violent policies, denying citizen status to the Palestinians and only granting them a small share of power in the local administration. However, Palestinians were not prevented from attending Egyptian universities.

Presently, most of the territory's inhabitants live in poverty. The area is regarded as one of the most densely populated in the world. The unemployment rate is very high and the refugee camps are overcrowded. The land is depleted due to over-cropping and is completely useless for agricultural purposes.

Arab Israelis - some 150,000 people who, in 1948, chose not to emigrate from the newly created state of Israel - account for one-eighth of the Palestinian diaspora. Since many of their lands had been confiscated, they had to move to towns in Western Galilee and were forced to became unskilled workers - most had been farmers - hired by Israeli construction companies and industries.

In the Sixties, Palestinians witnessed the erosion of some of their traditions due to the exodus towards urban areas. The social system based on a clan led by an elder could not survive these changes.

Palestinians living in Israel have been subject to the restraints of a military jurisdiction since 1966. They live under a very severe regime of restrictions which not only hampers political activity, but also harms civil rights and freedom of worship.

Even under these conditions, a number of Palestinians are politically neutral, while others accept the situation taking part in elections, education and the economy. Israeli policies have been aimed at preventing the development of a Palestinian national identity.

National Council met in Algiers, with representatives from all Palestinian organizations, except those groups that favored direct action, and the internal structure of the PLO was rebuilt.

[33] In November 1987, several Palestinian laborers were run over by a military truck in the Gaza Strip. In protest, Palestinian businesses closed down and the people took to the streets.

[34] The official answer to the Arab protests was to increase the repression. But unlike what had happened on other occasions, this time the military intervention only managed to increase the number of women, elderly people and children taking part in the demonstrations. The more civilian casualties there were, the greater the hatred grew and the more demonstrations, strikes, and closures occurred. Funerals transformed into acts of open political defiance. This marked the beginning of the intifada or rebellion.

[35] During the first few months of 1988 a great many Palestinians with Israeli citizenship participated in the strikes called by the so-called "Unified Direction of the Popular Uprising in the Occupied Territories". This was the first instance of their joint political expression with the Palestinians of the occupied territories.

[36] In July 1988, King Hussein of Jordan announced that all economic and political links were being broken with the inhabitants of the West Bank. From that moment on, the PLO assumed sole responsibility for the territory's inhabitants.

[37] At a meeting in Algeria on November 15 1988, the Palestine National Council proclaimed an independent Palestinian state in the occupied territories, citing Jerusalem as its capital. It also approved UN resolutions 181 and 242, which in effect meant accepting Israel's right to exist. Within the next 10 days, 54 countries around the world recognized the new state.

[38] Arafat, elected president, was received in Geneva by the UN General Assembly, which had called a special session in order to hear him. The Palestinian leader repudiated terrorism, accepted the existence of Israel and asked that international forces be sent to the occupied territories. As a result of his speech, US president Reagan decided to initiate talks with the PLO.

[39] The Security Council met in Geneva, at the bidding of the Arab countries, to listen to Arafat discuss violence in the occupied territories. The Palestinian leader exhorted the UN to call an urgent international conference on peace in the Middle East.

[40] When tensions began between Iraq and Kuwait, in the second half of 1990, Arafat tried unsuccessfully to start negotiations between the countries. After the invasion, the Palestinian position seemed to

strengthen when a parrallel could be drawn between Kuwait and Palestine; if Iraq could be forced to submit to UN resolutions, then so could Israel.

[41] When the war broke out, it was clear that the Palestine people were pro-Iraqi. This support deprived the PLO of the financial support of the rich Gulf monarchies, who were opposed to the Iraqi regime. When Iraq was defeated in March 1991, the situation in the occupied territories was very volatile.

[42] In September 1991, in the closing session of the Palestine National Council, Yasser Arafat was confirmed as President of Palestine and of the PLO. The body accepted the resignation of Abu Abbas, the leader of the Palestine Liberation Front. Abbas had been given a life sentence in absentia by an Italian tribunal, for the hijacking of the "Achille Lauro" liner in 1985.

[43] Between October 30 and November 4 1991, the first Peace Conference for the Middle East was held in Madrid, with support from the US and the former USSR. The Arab delegations unanimously demanded that the negotiations should be based on resolutions 242 and 338 of the UN Security Council. These resolutions forbid the acquisition of territories by force and recommend the granting of territories in exchange for peace agreements.

[44] The Conference for the Middle East continued in Washington in December. No progress was made as far as the Palestinian issue was concerned, as Israel reaffirmed the validity of its own interpretations of the UN resolutions. At the end of the Conference, the Israeli delegation left satisfied because UN resolution 3379, defining Zionism as a form of racism, had been eliminated.

[45] Following the Israeli elections of June 1992, the Labor leader and new prime minister Yitzak Rabin froze the settlement of new colonies in the Gaza strip and on the West Bank. However, it was difficult to restart negotiations which had been interrupted by the expulsion of 415 Palestinians from the Hamas group to Lebanon.

[46] Secret negotiations between the PLO and Israel, with the active participation of Norwegian diplomats, resulted in mutual

recognition in September 1993. The Declaration of Principles on the autonomy of the occupied territories granted limited autonomy to Palestinians in the Gaza strip and the city of Jericho in the West Bank. This autonomy will be extended to the rest of the West Bank and, five years later, a definite status will be negotiated for the occupied territories and the part of Jerusalem occupied by Israel since 1967.

[47] Hamas and Hezbollah on the Palestinian side, as well as settlers in the occupied territories and far-right parties on the Israeli side, opposed the agreement. In a climate of hostility, Israeli military withdrawal from Gaza and Jericho anticipated for December 13 was postponed.

[48] In May, 1994 Rabin and Arafat signed the "Gaza and Jericho first" autonomy agreement, while Israeli withdrawal continued, enabling the return of several contingents of the Palestinian Liberation Army exiled in Egypt, Yemen, Libya, Jordan or Algeria.

[49] Arafat arrived in Gaza in July and took office as head of the Palestine National Authority's Executive Council. The struggle between the PLO leader and his fundamentalist rivals became increasingly violent. After the death of Islamic Jihad leader Hani Abed, allegedly by Israeli secret services, three Israeli soldiers were murdered in November 1994. A week later, the recently created Palestinian police shot a group of people outside a mosque regarded as a sacred place for fundamentalist activists. 13 people were killed.

[50] Once again, Gaza was on the brink of civil war in April 1995 when an explosion destroyed a building, killing 7 people, including Kamal Kaheil, one of the leaders of the Ezzedin-El-Kassam brigades. In retaliation, suicide attacks by Hamas and Islamic Jihad caused the death of 7 Israeli soldiers and a US tourist, leaving 40 wounded. The Jihad's military wing said the attempt was a "heroic suicide operation" and a "gift for the soul of the criminal massacre's martyrs" - referring to the building's explosion.

[51] Tension continued, as well as negotiations between Islamic fundamentalists and PLO leaders. Among other things, Arafat wanted Hamas to participate in the

Palestinian general elections of January 1996, which would have legitimated his leadership. After comings and goings, the fundamentalists decided to boycott the elections. Arafat was elected president with 87 per cent of the vote and government candidates won 66 out of the 88 seats.

[52] Binyamin Netanyahu's election as Israeli prime minister (see Israel) in May 1996 aggravated tension between both countries. This led to new confrontations such as the controversial opening of a tunnel below El-Aqsa mosque in Jerusalem by Israeli authorities in September. Dozens of Palestinians and Israelis died in the riots and the critical situation had to be discussed in a summit meeting between Arafat and Netanyahu with the participation of United States president Bill Clinton.

[53] The difficult negotiations which finally brought about the withdrawal of Israeli troops from the city of Hebron gave a new support to the government led by Yasser Arafat. In January 1997, the Palestinian President highlighted again that the subject of Jerusalem's status was still pending and that, together with the formation of the Palestinian state, both were the next issues of the political agenda.

[54] The Israeli decision to build a new settlement in the Har Homa hills, within the Palestinian sector in Jerusalem, was firmly rejected by the PNA and Western diplomats. The works started in March 1997, and led to harsh confrontations between Palestinians and the Army and stalled the peace process. At the same time, the Israeli Government announced that it was going to return only 2 per cent of the West Bank to the PNA. Israeli

President Ezer Weizman met Arafat as a token of good will, but he could not change Netanyahu's attitude nor the violent reaction of Palestinians. Soon afterwards, the PNA decided to apply capital punishment to those citizens who sold lands or houses to Israelis.

[55] In November 1997, the commemoration of the second anniversary of the assassination of prime minister Yitzhak Rabin led to the biggest pro-peace with Palestine demonstration in recent years. In February 1998, some 50 campaigners from the left-wing Israeli "Peace Now" gathered in the Israeli settlement of Kyriat Arba, on the outskirts of Hebron, to protest against the erection of a monument to Baruch Goldstein - a man who had killed 29 Palestinians in this city four years earlier.

[56] Arafat and Netanyahu met in London in May 1998 on the invitation of British Prime Minister, Tony Blair, and in the presence of US Secretary of State Madeleine Albright, in an attempt to re-establish the peace process, but negotiations floundered on the issue of the occupied West Bank. The West Bank had been divided into three zones under previous treaties: Zone A - covering three per cent of the territory, and administered by Palestinians; Zone B, with large Palestinian contingents, 24 per cent - an area which would become administered jointly; and Zone C, covering 73 per cent of the total, which was entirely occupied by Israel. The week before the meeting, the United States had proposed - with Arafat's approval, as a sign of goodwill - that Israel returned 13 per cent of Zone C and 14 per cent of B, but Netanyahu refused to accept more than 9 per cent.

Panama

Panamá

Population: 2,677,000 (1996)
Area: 75,517 SQ KM
Capital: Panama City

Currency: Balboa
Language: Spanish

The Chibcha civilization (see Colombia: muisca) was one of America's great cultures, which developed in the Isthmus of Panama. They had a highly stratified society, developed elaborate architecture, crafted gold and had a wide scientific knowledge.

[2] In 1508, Diego de Nicuesa was given the task of colonizing what was known as the Gold Coast, present day Panama and Costa Rica. The enterprise ended in complete failure. In 1513, Vasco Nuñez de Balboa, was sent to look for what was assumed to be a "South Sea", and on the 25th of September he found the Pacific.

[3] The isthmus soon acquired great geopolitical importance. Panama became an important commercial center with merchandise distributed throughout America from San Francisco to Santiago. The Peruvian gold followed the opposite route, and the Ecuadorian straw hats are still called Panama hats because they were transported from there. The concentration of riches attracted English pirates and buccaneers; Francis Drake razed Portobelo in 1596 and Henry Morgan set fire to Panama in 1671.

[4] Panama was dependent upon the viceroyalty of Peru until 1717, when the Bourbons transferred it to the new viceroyalty of Granada, this was later to be a part of Greater Colombia when the country became independent from Spain in 1821.

[5] In 1826, Panama was selected by Simón Bolívar as the site of the Congressional Assembly which was to seal the continent's unity. But the economic decadence of the end of the 18th century, coupled with the change in commercial routes meant that Panama did not maintain its strategic importance after breaking with Spain, and did not become an independent nation with the disintegration of Greater Colombia in 1830.

[6] In 1831 Panama seceded from New Granada for a year, with the intention of forming a Colombian Confederation while maintaining autonomy. The state of Panama was created in 1855 within the Federation of New Granada (present-day Colombia).

[7] The first direct reference to the United States' "right" of military intervention in Panama, is the Mallarino-Bidlak treaty of 1864 signed by the governments of Washington and Bogota. The document authorized the United States to obtain a faster means of uniting the east coast with the west and to build a railroad across the isthmus; the Atlantic terminal was the Island of Manzanillo in the Bay of Limón. With the railway the US tried to offset British presence in the area, especially in Nicaragua.

[8] On January 1 1880, a French company started to build the Panama Canal. In 1891, the company was accused of fraud in its dealings, causing its eventual bankruptcy, though 33 km of the project had already been completed.

[9] In 1844 the New Panama Canal Company was formed to complete the canal project.

[10] In 1902, the United States bought out the French company, and in January 1903, the Hay-Herran Treaty was signed with a representative of the Colombian Government. The treaty spelled out the terms of the construction and administration of the canal, granting the United States the right to rent a 9.5 km-wide strip across the isthmus in perpetuity. The Colombian Senate rejected the treaty unanimously, considering it improper and an affront to Colombia's sovereignty, and only a revolution allowed the United States to remain. The "revolutionaries", supported by US marines, declared Panama's independence in November 1903, and the US recognized the new state within three days. While Theodore Roosevelt was President, the "Big Stick" policy of sending troops into Central American states was common practice.

[11] A new treaty, the Hay-Buneau Varilla Treaty, granted the United States full authority over a 16 km-wide strip and the waters at either end of the canal in perpetuity. Buneau Varilla, a former shareholder of the canal company and a French citizen, signed as the official representative of Panama. He received payment for his services in Washington, and did not return to Panama. The canal, covering a distance of 82 km, was officially dedicated on August 15 1914, and from then on was administrated and governed by the United States.

[12] The Canal Zone brought incalculable wealth to the United States, not so much in toll fees but in time and distance saved by vessels travelling between California and the East coast. US military bases in Panama functioned as an effective means of control over Latin America. Against the backdrop of the Cold War, American military instructors lectured Latin American military officers on the National Security Doctrine, a politico-military system which guaranteed loyalty to the US, including when necessary ousting legally constituted governments and replacing them with military dictators. Also, the financial center created in the isthmus became an initial foothold for the expansion of US transnational corporations and money laundering.

[13] In January 1964, 21 students died in an attempt to raise Panama's flag in the Canal Zone, under US jurisdiction The sacrifice of these young Panamanian lives transformed them into national martyrs.

[14] The demand for full sovereignty over the Zone was taken up by the government of General Torrijos. He rose to power in 1969, upon the

PUBLIC EXPENDITURE

5.4%   69.6%
1995 ■ DEFENCE □ SOCIAL

In 1990/91 Military as % of health & education expenditure was 34%.

WORKERS

UNEMPLOYMENT 13.9% (1996)

Labour force %

■ WOMEN
□ MEN

34   66

■ AGRICULTURE   26% (1990)
□ INDUSTRIAL   16%
■ SERVICES   58%

LAND USE

DEFORESTATION annual (81/90) **-1.7%**
IRRIGATED of arable (1993) **6.4%**

■ FOREST & WOODLAND (1993)   43.2%
□ ARABLE (1993)   6.6%
■ OTHER (1993)   50.2%

PROFILE

ENVIRONMENT
The country is bordered by the Caribbean in the north and the Pacific in the south. A high mountain range splits the country into two plains, a narrow one covered by rain-forests along the Atlantic slopes and a wider one with forests on the Pacific slopes. Panamanians generally say that their main resource is their geographic location, since the canal and the trade activities connected to it constitute the main economic resource of the country. Tropical products are cultivated and copper is mined at the large Cerro Colorado mines. Air and water pollution in both urban and rural areas is significant. 40 million tons of raw sewage are pumped into Panama Bay each year.

SOCIETY
Peoples: 64 per cent of the inhabitants are the result of integration between native Americans and European colonist immigrants. 14 per cent are African descendents and mulattos. The three main native groups are the Cunas on the island of San Blas in the Caribbean, the Chocoles in the province of Darien and the Guaymies, in the provinces of Chiriqui, Veraguas and Bocas del Toro.
Religions: 80 per cent Catholic, 10 per cent Protestant, 5 per cent Muslim, 1 per cent Baha'i, 0.3 per cent Jews.
Languages: Spanish, official and spoken by the majority.
Political Parties: Democratic Revolutionary Party (PRD), founded by Omar Torrijos, Liberal Republican Party, Labor Party, Nationalist Republican Liberal Movement, Christian Democrat Party, Authentic Liberal Party.
Social Organizations: The National Council of Workers' Organizations (CONATO); Ishtmenian Central of Workers (CIT)

THE STATE
Official Name: República de Panamá.
Capital: Panama City, 948,000 people (1995).
Other cities: San Miguelito, 293, 564 people; Colón, 54,654; David, 50,000 (1990).
Government: Ernesto Pérez Balladares, President since May 8, 1994. Single-chamber parliament: Legislative Assembly, made up of 67 members, elected every 5 years by direct vote.
National Holiday: November 3, Independence (1903).
Armed Forces: The National Guard was declared illegal in June 1991. US forces stationed in the former Canal Zone amount to 9,100 (1995).
Other: 11,000 National Police.

dissolution of a three member Military Junta which had overthrown President Arnulfo Arias in 1968. The diplomatic battle against the colonial enclave was waged in all the international forums and gained the support of the Latin American countries, the Movement of Non-Aligned Countries and the United Nations.

[15] The struggle for sovereignty drew Panamanians closer together stimulating nationalistic feelings submerged by decades of foreign cultural penetration. At the same time, the Torrijos government initiated a process of transformation aimed at establishing a more equitable social order. The outstanding reforms included agriculture, education, and the exploitation of copper on a nationalized basis. The "banana war" was also waged against transnational fruit companies like the United Fruit Company to obtain fairer prices.

[16] The US finally agreed to open negotiations in favour of a new canal treaty, as the Panama issue was damaging its image in Latin America. The 1977 Torrijos-Carter Treaty abrogated the previous one and provided for a Panamanian canal from the year 2,000. Amendments introduced by the US Senate, however, added provisions to the treaty that were contrary to Panamanian sovereignty. The United States retained the right to intervene "in defence of the Canal" even after expiration of the treaty, scheduled for December 31 1999.

[17] On July 31 1981 General Omar Torrijos died in a suspicious airplane accident. Unconfirmed reports suggested that the plane's instruments were interfered with from the ground. President Aristides Royo, who succeeded Torrijos in 1978, lost the support of the National Guard and was forced to resign by his new commander-in-chief, Ruben Paredes. He started realigning the country's policies, adopting a pro-US stance.

[18] The role of the United States in the Malvinas (Falklands) War and the Contadora Group, (a meeting of South American heads of states seeking peace in Central America) of which Panama was the first host, led to new friction in the relations between the nations. The island of Contadora had already gained a certain notoriety as the hiding place chosen by the US for the exiled shah of Iran, Reza Pahlevi, after he was overthrown.

[19] In 1983, Paredes was replaced as commander-in-chief of the National Guard by General Manuel Noriega. Presidential and legislative elections were narrowly won by Nicolas Barletta, the candidate of the Democratic Revolutionary Party, which was founded by Torrijos and supported by the armed forces. The opposition, led by veteran politician Arnulfo Arias brought accusations of fraud. Barletta encountered growing opposition to his economic policies, and resigned toward the end of 1985.

[20] He was succeeded by Eric del Valle, but the leading force continued to be General Noriega, who was singled out as a target for the United States to oust. As an former protegé of the American Government, they could not forgive his lack of collaboration with its plans to invade Nicaragua. A "settling of accounts" began, in which Noriega was accused of links with drug traffickers and other crimes. The opposition united behind the National Civil Crusade, made up of parties of the right and center with broad support of the business community.

[21] In 1987 the United States withdrew its economic and military aid. In 1988, it froze Panama's assets in the United States and imposed economic sanctions, including the cessation of payments for Canal operations. In March all the Panamanian banks closed for several weeks, provoking a financial crisis. American military presence increased. Del Valle ousted Noriega, but the National Assembly backed the commander-in-chief and removed the President, replacing him with the Minister of Education, Manuel Solis Palma.

[22] Elections were called for May 5 1989. The official candidate was Carlos Duque and the opposition, the so-called Democratic Alliance of Civilian Opposition, put forward Guillermo Endara. Amid interference from the White House, which discredited the electoral process and its results even before it had taken place, the results of the ballot were kept secret for several days and, because they favored the opposition, the election was declared null and void.

[23] Solis declared that the United States' objective was to set up a puppet government regardless of the election results and retain control of the Canal Zone, going back on the commitments it had assumed through the Torrijos-Carter treaty.

[24] An anti-Noriega uprising by a group of young officers failed in October 1989, and as the climax of a series of economic sanctions which destroyed the country's economy, the United States invaded Panama. The attack began at dawn on December 20 1989, the attack began, without prior declaration of war, and Endara was installed as president at Fort Clayton, the American base, at the start of the invasion.

[25] This was the largest American military operation since the Vietnam War (1964-1973), with the mobilization of 26,000 troops. Indiscriminate bombing damaged heavily-populated neighbourhoods. The invaders withheld all information concerning the number of people killed or injured, as well as figures for property damage. The number of dead is estimated at between 4,000 and 10,000, and the Chamber of Commerce estimated losses at more than $2 billion.

[26] Panamanian resistance proved to be stronger than the invaders had anticipated, and prolonged the military undertaking. Noriega, who took refuge within the Vatican Embassy, was later arrested and transferred to the United States. About 5,000 Panamanians were arrested and temporarily imprisoned.

[27] The new government of Guillermo Endara eliminated the National Defence Force and replaced it with a minor police agency, called the Public Force. In order to disarm the population, $150 was paid for each weapon that was turned in. American economic aid, which the new

Panama

DEMOGRAPHY
Population: 2,677,000 (1996). **Annual growth:** 2% (1980/1996). **Estimates for year 2000:** 2,900,000. Annual growth to year 2000: 1.7% (1994/2000). **Urban Population:** 56.0% (1996). **Urban growth:** 2.75% (1980/95). **Children per woman:** 2.7 (1996).

HEALTH
Life expectancy at birth: 74 years (1996). male: 71 years (1994). female: 75 years (1994). **Infant mortality:** 18 per 1,000 (1996). **Under-5 child mortality:** 20 per 1,000 (1996). **Calorie consumption:** 98% (1988/90). 562 **people per doctor** (1988/91). **Safe water:** 93% (1990/96).

EDUCATION
Literacy: 91% (1995). male : 91% (1995). female: 90% (1995). **School enrolment :** Primary total: 106% (1990/95). male : 108% (1990/95). female: 104% (1990/95). Secondary: male : 60% (1990/95). female: 65% (1990/95). Tertiary: 30% (1995).

COMMUNICATIONS
60 **newspapers**, 227 **radios**, 170 **TV sets** and 111 **main telephone lines** per 1,000 people (1994).

ECONOMY
Per capita, GNP: $ 3,080 (1996). **Annual growth, GNP:** 4.1% (1995/96). **Annual inflation:** 1.66% (1985/95). **Consumer price index:** 104.9 (1994). **Currency:** 1 balboas = $ 1 (1995) **Cereal imports:** 273 metric tons (1994). **Food import dependency:** 8% (1994). **Fertilizer use:** 480 kgs per ha (1994). **Exports:** $ 558 million (1996). **Imports:** $ 2,778 million (1996). **External debt:** $ 6,990 million (1996). $ 2,611 **per capita:** (1996). **Debt service:** 10.7% of exports (1996). Development aid received: $ 50 million (1995). $ 19 per capita (1995). 0.8% of GNP (1994).

ENERGY
Consumption: 618.27 Kgs of Oil equivalent per capita yearly (1994). 87.10% imported (1994).

HDI (rank / value) 45 / 0.864 (1994)

government had counted on, did not materialize and Endara himself began a hunger strike in order to get it. The Government had to accept the presence of US "supervisors" in the ministries and the actions of the South Commando troops outside the canal zone in order to fight drug trafficking and Colombian guerrilla warfare.

[28] Washington's interest in the region waned after the defeat of the Sandinistas in Nicaragua, so the economic crisis in Panama at the time of the invasion was never overcome. Independent sources put unemployment at 20 per cent in 1991.

[29] The Organization of American States called the invasion "deplorable" and called for a vote on the withdrawal of troops, there were 20 votes in favor, one against (the United States) and six abstentions. Britain supported the invasion and France vetoed the UN Security Council denunciation. In Latin America, only El Salvador supported the US invasion.

[30] In spite of this, control of the canal was given to Panama. In March 1991, a Panamanian took over the administration of the canal for the first time.

[31] In April 1991, Endara announced the end of his alliance with the Christian Democrat Party (PDC), dismissing five of their ministers. The Government's precarious stability was shaken by five coup attempts during its first two years. The Democratic Revolutionary Party (PRD), which won a significant victory in the by-elections of January 1991, called for general elections.

[32] In the course of General Noriega's trial, which started late in 1991 in Miami, it was disclosed that the former leader had close connections with the Drug Enforcement Agency (DEA) and the CIA. That same year it was discovered that President Endara's legal office had connections with 14 companies which laundered drug money. The DEA also disclosed that drug dealings had increased since the American invasion. In June 1992, Noriega was sentenced to 40 years in prison.

[33] The Government suffered a serious setback when, in a plebiscite on constitutional reform on November 15 1992, the people rejected the formal abolition of the Defence Force by 63.5 to 31.5 per cent. The Government was further weakened when the deputy vice-president, Christian Democrat Ricardo Arias Calderón, resigned on December 17 after accusing Endara of failing to deal with the social crisis.

[34] Foreign Minister Julio Linares was forced to resign in August 1993 as he had been involved in the sale of weapons to Serbian forces in Bosnia through the consulate in Barcelona.

[35] Economist Ernesto Perez Balladares, former minister and admirer of Omar Torrijos, was elected President in 1994 with 34 per cent of the vote. Balladares ran as candidate for the social democratic alliance Pueblo Unido (United People), made up of the PRD, the Liberal Republican Party and the Labour Party. Mireya Moscoso, from the right-wing Democratic Alliance, had 29 per cent and salsa singer Ruben Blades, from the Papa Egoro Movement, had 17 per cent. These were the first general elections held after the US invasion.

[36] In June 1994, the Kuna and Embera indigenous groups rejected the construction of a road through their autonomous territory. They were supported by environmentalist groups and the Catholic Church. The highway was to have crossed the 550,000 hectare rainforest called "Darien's Stopper", declared a universal heritage by the UNESCO. The 108-km highway would link Panama with Colombia. For years, this forest has endured illegal logging of oak, cedar and mahogany. Likewise, the area has been devoted to coca cultivation and arms smuggling.

[37] A plan to assassinate Pérez Balladares and several cabinet members was uncovered in January 1995. Ten National Police members were arrested on charges of conspiracy but the investigation was shelved for lack of evidence.

[38] The country continued to have an active role in arms and drug traffic as well as money laundering. The explosion of a package during a routine drug inspection killed three officials and injured 25. The explosives, grenades and ammunitions, were being sent to Ecuador, supposedly to guerrilla groups. Two arms deposits were found in the capital, belonging to a Colombian citizen.

[39] The reform of the labor code, aimed at attracting foreign investment, led to an atmosphere of social violence and strikes, since it would reduce labor security and the freedom to unionize and negotiate collectively. Confrontations between workers and students with the police left 4 dead and 86 injured in August. However, the law was passed.

[40] Talks with the United States over the transfer of the sovereignty of the Canal from 1999 seemed to point to the continuation of some form of US presence in Panama. In July 1996, President Pérez Balladares announced that the Howard US Air Force Base would remain, in order to keep drug trafficking under control. The US army spent $319 million in Panama that year (5 per cent of the country's GDP).

[41] The announcement that US troops would remain in Panama was made after it became known Balladares had received money from the Columbian Cali cartel to fund his 1994 election campaign. The President admitted the fact but denied having known of the origin of the funds. This scandal was followed by the forced closure of the Agro-Industrial and Commercial Bankdue to its excessive debts and drug money laundering activities.

[42] In March 1997, the Government decreed price freezes on various products like school books, milk, gas, sugar and medicines. The measure was designed to counteract the indiscriminate price increases complained of by the Free Competition Commission.

[43] In September, after 80 years' presence in Panama's territory, the Southern Command headquarters returned to the US, in Miami. The Government released statements guaranteeing that the operation of the Panama Canal would not be affected by its return to national ownership. It also announced plans for building a third set of lock gates in early 2000, due to the increase in traffic and the tonnage of the ships.

Papua New Guinea

Papua-New Guinea

Population: 4,400,000 (1996)
Area: 462,840 SQ KM
Capital: Port Moresby

Currency: Kina
Language: English

Papua New Guinea (PNG) has been inhabited by Melanesian peoples since 3,000-2,000 BC. Traditionally, its population lived in groups scattered throughout the dense tropical jungle, cut off from the outside world. As a result, over 700 dialects are spoken on the New Guinean island and the smaller islands of the republic. One third of the population lives in the highlands, and many communities there knew neither the wheel, iron implements nor Europeans until the 1930s.

[2] In a short time, PNG has passed from the stone age into the plastic age, and it currently faces an economic boom based on the exploitation of non-renewable natural resources (copper, gold, oil and hardwoods).

[3] The present state of Papua New Guinea was formed when the Territory of Papua, a British protectorate, under Australian administration since 1906, was joined with New Guinea, a German colony until World War I, later administered by Australia under mandate, first from the League of Nations and then the United Nations.

[4] The process leading to self-government really began in 1964 and culminated in the proclamation of independence in 1975. That same year, there was an unsuccessful attempt at secession by the island of Bougainville. This island has rich deposits of copper and gold and the population is ethnically closer to the Solomon Islanders than to the Papuans. Australia maintains a strong presence in the PNG, providing considerable

investment in business, and military and financial assistance.

[5] Papua New Guinea's system of government is currently parliamentary. There have been four prime ministers since independence, backed by shifting party alliances. Each government enjoys a six-month truce period after which it has to submit its actions to parliamentary approval. Political parties form around personalities and regional groups rather than ideological differences. Although this might suggest a tendency to instability, the fact that no single group is dominant has produced a government of political consensus, which in itself has a stabilizing influence.

[6] Papua New Guinea has strong links with Australia and, in turn, exercises a degree of leadership among South Pacific states. Its military contributed to suppressing a secession attempt by the island of Espiritu Santo (Vanuatu) in 1979, led by Jemmy Stevens, and backed by French authorities and US economic interests.

[7] In May 1988, Papua New Guinea together with Vanuatu and the Solomon Islands, signed an agreement to defend and preserve traditional Melanesian cultures. It also expressed support for Kanaky's (New Caledonia) independence. Relations with the Government of Indonesia, which occupies the western portion of the island, Irian Jaya, are troubled. The Free Papua independence movement operates in this province, and Indonesian military operations here in 1984 led 12,000

inhabitants to seek refuge in Papua New Guinea.

[8] The country's peculiar personality has been caricatured by a North American economist who said "Papua New Guinea is a mixture between a political system *a la italiana*, an economic policy worthy of a West German *bundesbank* (for its fiscal and monetary discipline), and African infrastructure". The labor market is much like Australia's, with minimum wages renegotiated every three years, and index-linked to inflation. Indigenous communities own 98 per cent of the land, but as the economy is increasingly open to foreign penetration, the exploitation of natural resources has reached proportions that are seriously damaging the environment.

[9] Two thirds of the population are subsistence agriculturalists,

and the 0.3 per cent that work with mining concerns generate 66 per cent of export earnings. Mines at Bougainville and Ok Tedi boasted the largest copper deposits in the world and also produce gold. The Porgera gold mine went into production in 1990, and will soon be the largest in the world outside South Africa. Another on the island of Lihir may be even larger. The mines are exploited by transnationals, some of them Australian. Sizeable oil deposits have also been found and will be exploited only after a 175-mile oil pipeline is built, at a cost of $1 billion.

[10] In 1989, Papua New Guinea strengthened its ties with Southeast Asia, signing a friendship and co-operation treaty with ASEAN and opening negotiations with Malaysia. At the same time, it granted the Soviets permission to open an embassy in Port Moresby. In December, a maritime agreement was signed with the Federated States of Micronesia which allowed PNG to take advantage of an existing multilateral fishing agreement between the South Pacific and the US.

[11] Parliament reinstated the death penalty in August 1991 34 years after it had been abolished. This move was denounced by Christian movements, feminists and human rights organizations. The National Council of Women feared that the reinstatement of the death penalty might lead to a

PUBLIC EXPENDITURE

3.3% 30.5%
1995 ■ **DEFENCE** □ **SOCIAL**

In **1990/91** Military as % of health & education expenditure was 41%.

WORKERS
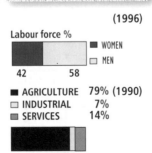

(1996)

Labour force %
■ WOMEN
□ MEN
42   58

■ AGRICULTURE   79% (1990)
□ INDUSTRIAL   7%
▪ SERVICES   14%

LAND USE

DEFORESTATION annual (81/90) **-0.3%**

■ FOREST & WOODLAND (1993)   90.7%
□ ARABLE (1993)   0.1%
▪ OTHER (1993)   9.2%

Maternal Mortality	Literacy	Food Dependency	Foreign Trade
1990	1995	1970	MILLIONS $ 1996
PER 100,000 LIVE BIRTHS		24%	IMPORTS
930	72%	1994 14%	1,866 EXPORTS 2,554

PROFILE

ENVIRONMENT

Located east of Indonesia, just south of the Equator, the country is made up of the eastern portion of the island of New Guinea (the western part is the Indonesian territory of Irian Jaya) plus a series of smaller islands; New Britain, New Ireland and Manus, in the Bismarck archipelago; Bougainville, Buka and Nissau, which form the northern part of the Solomon Islands; the Louisiade and Entrecasteaux archipelagos; and the islands of Trobriand and Woodlark, southeast of New Guinea. The terrain is volcanic and mountainous, except for the narrow coastal plains. The climate is tropical and the vegetation is equatorial rain forest. The country suffers from deforestation, due to large-scale indiscriminate felling.

SOCIETY

Peoples: Papuans 85 per cent; Melanesians 15 per cent.
Religions: Many people practise local traditional religions but they also belong to Catholic (32.8 per cent) and Protestant (58.4 per cent) communities.
Languages: English (official). A local Pidgin, with many English words and Melanesian grammar is widely spoken, as well as 700 other local languages.
Political Parties: Popular Democratic Movement (PDM); Pangu Pati (PP); Popular Action Party; Popular Progressive Party (PPP).

THE STATE

Official Name: Independent State of Papua New Guinea.
Administrative Divisions: 20 Provinces.
Capital: Port Moresby, 220,000 people (1994).
Other cities: Lae, 80,655 people; Madang, 27,057; Wewak, 23,224; Goroka, 17,855 (1990).
Government: Queen Elizabeth II, Head of State, represented by Governor General Silas Atopare. Bill Skate, Prime Minister and Head of the Government since 1997. Single-chamber legislature: Parliament, with 109 members.
National Holiday: September 16, Independence Day (1975).
Armed Forces: 3,700 troops (1996).

STATISTICS

DEMOGRAPHY

Population: 4,400,000 (1996). **Annual growth:** 2.2% (1980/1996). **Estimates for year 2000:** 4,800,000. **Annual growth to year 2000:** 2.3% (1994/2000). **Urban Population:** 16.3% (1996). **Urban growth:** 3.62% (1980/95). **Children per woman:** 4.8 (1996).

HEALTH

Life expectancy at birth: 57 years (1996). male: 56 years (1994). female: 57 years (1994). **Infant mortality:** 79 per 1,000 (1996). **Under-5 child mortality:** 112 per 1,000 (1996). **Calorie consumption:** 114% (1988/90). **Safe water:** 28% (1990/96).

EDUCATION

Literacy: 72% (1995). male : 81% (1995). female: 63% (1995). **School enrolment :** Primary total: 82% (1990/95). male : 88% (1990/95). female: 75% (1990/95). Secondary: male : 17% (1990/95). female: 11% (1990/95). Tertiary: 3% (1995). **Primary school teachers:** one for every 33 students (1995).

COMMUNICATIONS

20 **newspapers**, 76 **radios**, 170 **TV sets** and 9 **main telephone lines** per 1,000 people (1994).

ECONOMY

Per capita, GNP: $ 1,150 (1996). **Annual growth, GNP:** -2.4% (1995/96). **Annual inflation:** 4.46% (1985/95). **Consumer price index:** 120.4 (1994). **Currency:** 1.34 kina = $ 1 (1995) **Cereal imports:** 275 metric tons (1994). **Food import dependency:** 14% (1994). **Fertilizer use:** 313 kgs per ha (1994). **Exports:** $ 2,554 million (1996). **Imports:** $ 1,866 million (1996). **External debt:** $ 2,359 million (1996). $ 536 **per capita:** (1996). **Debt service:** 12.6% of exports (1996). Development aid received: $ 372 million (1995). $ 88 per capita (1995). 7.4% of GNP (1994).

ENERGY

Consumption: 235.57 Kgs of Oil equivalent per capita yearly (1994). -149.69% imported (1994).

HDI (rank / value) 128 / 0.525 (1994)

---

return of 'bounty' payments in assassination cases, as was traditional in Papua New Guinean culture.
[12] Prime Minister Palas Wingti launched a fight against corruption in July 1992, through a public accountability campaign for those holding public office. Several governors were forced to resign.
[13] In June, the Justice Department brought corruption charges against former prime minister Namaliu and his minister of finance, Paul Pora.
[14] Wingti has pledged to increase the country's participation in joint ventures with foreign capital. This triggered an angry reaction from PJV, an Anglo-Austro-Canadian consortium which controls 90 per cent of Porgera, the country's largest gold mine.

[15] Wingti was replaced in August 1994 by Julius Chan. That year, the Government recovered the copper mine on Bougainville island, but an explosion in the Porgera gold mine interrupted extraction works.
[16] Chan harshly denounced the new series of French nuclear tests in the Pacific. After the second atomic test was carried out in October 1995, the Prime Minister of Papua New Guinea suspended talks between France and the South Pacific Forum, acting as president of the regional organization.
[17] The conflict in Bougainville worsened when Theodore Miriung was assassinated in 1996. He had been the main transitional authority on the island and had promoted a peace agreement. The Prime Minister was accused by a military leader of contracting

international mercenaries to quash the secessionist forces, and, consequently, representatives of the armed forces called for Chan to be sacked. In June 1996 a settlement was reached between an Australian mining company (BHP) and villagers represented by an Australian law firm which provided financial compensation for environmental damage caused by the Ok Tedi mine.
[19] Despite having parliamentary backing, the Prime Minister resigned in March 1997, and was replaced by an interim ruler, John Giheno. A few weeks later, Parliament designated Bill Skate as Head of Government.
[20] In July 1997, in Aotearoa, the Government and secessionist rebels brought an end to the Bougainville crisis signing a definitive peace agreement, including the demilitarisation of

the island and the deployment of UN peace-keeping troops. Australia promised funds for the rebuilding of Bougainville.
[21] In late 1997, the Government began mining in Bougainville again. The drought in other parts of the country caused extensive fires and also affected coffee production.
[22] In February 1998, thirteen forestry companies closed down as an indirect effect of the stock market and financial crisis in other Southeast Asian countries in 1997 and 1998, causing the loss of 4,000 jobs.

Paraguay

Paraguay

Population: 4,957,000 (1996)
Area: 406,752 SQ KM
Capital: Asunción

Currency: Guaraní
Language: Spanish and Guaraní

There were three ethnic groups in the Paraguay River basin in the 16th century: the Guaranís, in the center, and the Guaycurús and Payaguás, in the Chaco region to the south. The Guaranís cultivated cassava, squash, sweet potatoes and corn. They were settled agriculturalists, organized in villages headed by a *tubichá* (chief).

[2] The Payaguás and Guaycurús were nomadic hunters and fishers. They periodically attacked the Guaraní plantations, leading the Guaranís to aid the Spaniards in the conquest of the Chaco area.

[3] Spanish conquistadors sailed up the Paraná River in the mid-16th century, searching for the mythical silver mountains that gave the Rio de la Plata (silver river) region its name. In 1537, Juan de Salazar founded the fort of Nuestra Señora de Asunción. This tiny settlement grew and became capital of the Rio de la Plata Province for over a century.

[4] Having failed to find precious metals in these "worthless lands", it was only much later that Spanish colonizers were attracted by the wild cattle herds that prospered on the fertile plains of the Banda Oriental (today's Uruguay) and the humid Argentinean Pampas. A powerful oligarchy of trade merchants developed in the ports of Buenos Aires and Montevideo, and the former provincial capital, Asunción declined.

[5] A pre-capitalist system of large landed estates grew up around Buenos Aires and Montevideo. Meanwhile, in what is now Paraguay, the Jesuits organized a system of agricultural colonies in which the indigenous population worked the land and produced handicrafts on a communal basis. Private interests and the Government both resented this system, and the Society of Jesus was finally expelled in 1767. The natives either became slaves on Brazilian sugar cane plantations or peasant labourers on large cattle ranches.

[6] Although the Paraguayan province did not initially join the 1810 Liberal Revolution, the Asunción oligarchy ousted the Spanish Governor Velazco on May 14 1811, demanding free trade for yerba *mate* (a local tea) and tobacco.

[7] This rebellion began a process which concentrated all the power in the hands of Gaspar Rodríguez de Francia. He was supported by the peasants, owners of small and medium-sized plots who wanted order and feared the "anarchy" that was affecting the other provinces of the old viceroyalty. The oligarchy in Asunción, the new system's only enemy, was eliminated, and Paraguay withdrew into itself. Stimulated by public investment, industry began to develop, laying the foundations for Paraguay's future economic strength.

[8] Paraguay continued to develop under the patriarchal governments of Gaspar Rodríguez de Francia (El Supremo), Carlos Antonio López and his son, Francisco Solano López. It remained cut off from the rest of the world for decades and was untouched by the British influence that was so greatly felt in the other newly independent Rio de la Plata provinces. Left to develop alone, the State assumed an important role in the country's economy, controlling agricultural production (yerba *mate* tea and high quality timber), and the first railroads, telegraph system and steel furnaces in South America.

[9] The leaders of Brazil, Argentina, and Uruguay - Pedro II, Mitre and Venancio Flores respectively - signed the Triple Alliance. In 1865, with the support of the British Empire and the Baring Brothers' Bank, they began a war to eliminate Paraguay on the pretext of frontier disputes (see The Triple Alliance war).

[10] Sixty-two years later, Paraguay fought a second fratricidal war, this time against Bolivia, orchestrated by rival oil multinationals of the "Seven Sisters" group. The Chaco War (1932-1935) was won, but it cost Paraguay 50,000 lives.

[11] In 31 years, there were 22 presidents, until the 1954 coup which brought General Alfredo Stroessner to power. Descended from Germans, and an admirer of Nazism, he gave refuge to war criminals fleeing Europe. Stroessner had himself re-elected seven times, the last time in February 1988. He allowed only a legal "opposition", whose leaders he often appointed himself.

[12] By the mid-1980s, the Stroessner regime was showing clear signs of weakening. Democratization processes elsewhere in Latin America doubtless contributed to this. Internal opposition was growing in a variety of forms: an Inter-Union Labor Movement; a Permanent Assembly of Landless Rural Workers (APCT); indigenous peoples' organizations; and the Rural Women's Co-ordination Group. The Catholic church, through the Paraguayan clergy, began to voice the need for change.

[13] On February 3 1989, General Stroessner was overthrown by a coup headed by his son's father-in-law, army commander General Andrés Rodríguez, who immediately called free elections

PUBLIC EXPENDITURE

10.7%   54.1%
1995 ■ DEFENCE □ SOCIAL

In 1990/91 Military as % of health & education expenditure was 42%.

WORKERS

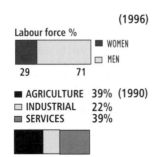

(1996)

Labour force %
■ WOMEN
□ MEN

29   71

■ AGRICULTURE 39% (1990)
□ INDUSTRIAL   22%
■ SERVICES   39%

LAND USE

DEFORESTATION -2.4% annual (81/90)
IRRIGATED 3.1%   of arable

(1993)

■ FOREST & WOODLAND 31.6%
□ ARABLE   5.4%
■ OTHER   63%

PROFILE

ENVIRONMENT

A landlocked country in the heart of the Río de la Plata basin, Paraguay is divided into two distinct regions by the Paraguay River. To the east lie fertile plains irrigated by the tributaries of the Paraguay and Paraná rivers, and covered with rainforest; this is the main farming area, producing soybeans (the major export crop), wheat, corn and tobacco. The western region or Northern Chaco is dry savannahs, producing cotton and cattle. Farmers, especially those linked to large agricultural operations, have felled large areas of forest, destroying habitats in the process. Indiscriminate hunting, combined with deforestation, have resulted in 14 species of mammals, 11 birds and 2 reptiles now being in danger of extinction. Large amounts of industrial and domestic waste are dumped into watercourses, and untreated sewage from the capital city flows directly into the Bay of Asunción.

SOCIETY

Peoples: 90 per cent of Paraguayans are of mixed descent from indigenous peoples and Spanish colonizers. The native Guaraní people currently account for only 5 per cent of the population and are threatened with the loss of their cultural identity. There are German, Italian, Argentinian and Brazilian minorities. This last group is expanding along the border between the two countries. One million Paraguayans live abroad, some 200,000 having migrated for political reasons.
Religions: Mainly Catholic, official.
Languages: Spanish and Guaraní (both official); most Paraguayans are bi-lingual.
Political Parties: Colorado Party. Electoral Alliance, an electoral coalition composed of the parties led by Laíno and Filizzola (Authentic Radical Liberal Party and National Encounter; the "Febrerista" Revolutionary Party; Colorado Popular Movement (MOPOCO) - which grew from a split within the Colorado Party, in 1959. Christian Democratic Party. Communist Party.
Social Organizations: The Paraguayan Labor Confederation; the United Workers' Center (CUT) founded in 1990, uniting labor unions and the powerful rural workers' movement; the Paraguayan Women's Union.

THE STATE

Official Name: República del Paraguay.
Administrative Divisions: 19 departments.
Capital: Asunción, 502,400 people (1992).
Other cities: Ciudad del Este, 133,900 people (1995); Pedro Juan Caballero, 80,000; Encarnación, 31,445; Pilar, 26,352; Concepción, 25,607 (1984).
Government: Presidential republic. Raúl Cubas, President since May 10 1998.
National Holiday: May 14, Independence Day (1811).
Armed Forces: 20,200 (1996).

STATISTICS

DEMOGRAPHY
Population: 4,957,000 (1996). **Annual growth:** 2.9% (1980/1996). **Estimates for year 2000:** 5,500,000. **Annual growth to year 2000:** 2.6% (1994/2000). **Urban Population:** 53.2% (1996). **Urban growth:** 4.65% (1980/95). **Children per woman:** 4.3 (1996).

HEALTH
Life expectancy at birth: 69 years (1996). male: 67 years (1994). female: 71 years (1994). **Infant mortality:** 28 per 1,000 (1996). **Under-5 child mortality:** 34 per 1,000 (1996). **Calorie consumption:** 116% (1988/90). 1,587 **people per doctor** (1988/91). **Safe water:** 60% (1990/96).

EDUCATION
Literacy: 92% (1995). male : 94% (1995). female: 91% (1995). **School enrolment :** Primary total: 109% (1990/95). male : 111% (1990/95). female: 108% (1990/95). Secondary: male : 38% (1990/95). female: 40% (1990/95). Tertiary: 10% (1995). **Primary school teachers:** one for every 24 students (1995).

COMMUNICATIONS
40 **newspapers**, 172 **radios**, 70 **TV sets** and 31 **main telephone lines** per 1,000 people (1994). **Books:** 3 new titles per 100,000 people (1992/94).

ECONOMY
Per capita, GNP: $ 1,850 (1996). **Annual growth, GNP:** -1.5% (1995/96). **Annual inflation:** 24.89% (1985/95). **Consumer price index:** 204.0 (1994). **Currency:** 1,995 guaraníes = $ 1 (1995) **Cereal imports:** 31 metric tons (1994). **Food import dependency:** 7% (1994). **Fertilizer use:** 100 kgs per ha (1994). **Exports:** $ 1,043 million (1996). **Imports:** $ 3,107 million (1996). **External debt:** $ 2,141 million (1996). $ 432 **per capita:** (1996). **Debt service:** 5.5% of exports (1996). Development aid received: $ 146 million (1995). $ 30 per capita (1995). 1.9% of GNP (1994).

ENERGY
Consumption: 298.69 Kgs of Oil equivalent per capita yearly (1994). -123.25% imported (1994).

HDI (rank / value) 94 / 0.706 (1994)

---

for the following May to elect a government and legislators to see out Stroessner's term.
[14] The elections, held on May 1 1989, were open to all political parties except the still-banned Communist Party. General Rodríguez was elected President with 68 per cent of the vote. The principal opposition group, the Authentic Radical Liberal Party, led by Domingo Laíno, took 21 per cent. Despite the presence of foreign observers, voting was plagued by countless irregularities, attributed to the Colorado Party which was leaving power.
[15] Nevertheless, opposition groups still considered the election to be the start of a democratization process, which was to be completed by 1993, with a Constituent Assembly convened, and a new constitution in place.
[16] Transnationals became involved in the production of

soybeans and cotton. At that time, 2 per cent of all landholders had 85 per cent of the land. Most of the companies and foreign settlers congregated along the border with Brazil on a strip of land 2000 km long and 65 km wide. The main language was Portuguese, and the Brazilian cruzeiro wsa common currency. Between 300,000 and 400,000 Brazilians lived in the border districts.
[17] The World Bank-supported Caazapa and Caaguazu rural development projects involve the settlement and ranching of indigenous lands in eastern Paraguay. The indians find themselves restricted to tiny pockets of their former territories. Twelve indigenous communities asked the Unitary Workers' Center (CUT) to represent them in the National Constitutional Assembly. In December 1991, in the first round of elections to designate

representatives to this Assembly, the CUT gave its support to the "Constitution for All" Movement.
[18] When the huge Itaipú hydroelectric plant, on the border with Brazil, went into operation, economic ties between the two countries increased.
[19] The first free municipal elections, held in June 1991, were marked by the emergence of the independent Asuncion for All movement in the capital. Led by Carlos Filissola, a 31 year-old doctor, the movement counted on the support of the United Workers Center and various social groups, and was elected with more than 35 per cent of the vote.
[20] In the elections for the National Constituent Assembly in

December, the Colorado Party took 60 per cent of the vote. The Authentic Liberal Radical Party (PLRA) of Domingo Laíno came second with 29 per cent and the Constitution for All Movement, led by Filizzola, came third.
[21] The Constitution of June 1992 replaced the one brought in by Stroessner in 1967. The presidents of the Republic, the Supreme Court and Congress did not take part in the public meeting held to announce the new constitution, which included broad dispensations for the protection of human rights and banned the death penalty for common crimes.
[22] The repeated accusations of widespread corruption within the armed forces, including drug trafficking, led to investigations.

PER 100,000
LIVE BIRTHS
160

92%

Warrants were issued for the arrest of leading generals, including the commander in chief of the army.

[23] In December 1992, Paraguay signed an agreement for the constitution of a common market. The Mercosur, which would come into operation in 1995, with Argentina, Brazil and Uruguay (see box in Brazil).

[24] In an atmosphere tempered by the danger of fraud and declarations from the army that it would keep the Colorado Party in power, the ruling party candidate, Juan Carlos Wasmosy took 40 per cent of the vote in the May 1993 elections. Some 75 per cent of the 1.7 million eligible adults voted. However, troops positioned on the borders prevented the entry of citizens resident in Argentina and Brazil. The PLRA took 33 per cent of the vote, and the National Encounter, a pro-business coalition, 25 per cent.

[25] When Wasmosy took over the presidency in August, he became the first elected civilian president in the 182 years since national independence. Congress granted civilian power the control over the military.

[26] In September, the World Jewish Congress asked President Wasmosy for access to the government archives in order to locate Nazis who took refuge in Paraguay following World War II.

[27] Parliament voted in a law banning members of the military from party politics in May. The Government and the high command immediately started action to declare this law unconstitutional. This attitude led the opposition to abandon the cooperation pact with the Colorados.

[28] Under pressure from the United States, Wasmosy nominated General Ramón Rozas Rodríguez leader of the war on drugs. Rozas was assassinated in 1994, when he was to have presented a report on corruption involving the military hierarchy, including General Lino Oviedo.

[29] Violent confrontations between rural people and the police affected several regions of the nation. A hundred demonstrators blocking the access to Asunción were injured by rubber bullets. The farmers were supported by church organizations, unions and opposition parties. A general strike was declared in May to press for pay rises and protest against the privatization of State companies. The Government admitted that purchasing power had fallen by 42 per cent in the last five years and upped salaries by 35 per cent. In December, all timber exports were suspended with the aim of halting deforestation.

[30] In January 1995, the National Human Rights Commission said many of the crimes from the time of Stroessner had gone unpunished and that rural people continued to be murdered.

[31] The President forced a group of eight high-ranking army officers to retire in April 1996. General Lino Oviedo resisted the order and occupied army barracks along with a group of young officers. Wasmosy took refuge in the US embassy, from where he appointed Oviedo Defence Minister in order to quell the crisis, later revoking the decision. In May, the Colorado Party and the opposition agreed to ban the serving military from political activity.

[32] In the Colorado Party internal elections in September 1997, Lino Oviedo was elected presidential candidate with 36.8 per cent of the vote, to the 35 of Luis María Argaña and the 22.5 of Wasmosy's favourite, Carlos Facetti. Oviedo was arrested on sedition charges in October.

[33] Oviedo was sentenced to ten years' imprisonment by a military tribunal in April 1998, sparking rumours of a coup and the postponement of the presidential election. The political uncertainty compounded the nation's economic crisis, reflected in a 35 per cent drop in value of the national currency, the *guarani*, against the US dollar in only four months.

[34] In the May 10 elections, with Oviedo in prison, 46.8 per cent of the vote went to the Colorado Party's Raúl Cubas-Luis María Argaña partnership, compared with 38.2 per cent to the Democratic Alliance of Laíno and Filizzola.

The Tupi and the Guaraní

The Tupi were an indigenous people who lived mainly in southern Amazonia, the most extensive rainforest region of the world. They were farmers and fishers, speaking languages which stemmed from a common root. Today, many of these languages, like Guaraní, are still in use in Amazonia.

Using their canoeing expertize the Tupi travelled the intricate network of rivers and streams to expand their settlements into the interior of the continent.. Their society was based on the extended family unit, with parents, children, their offspring and relations in general living together in large, common houses.

The Guaraní lived mainly towards the east of Paraguay, but also in the neighbouring areas of Brazil and Argentina. Some communities are still settled in the tropical forests of north-east Paraguay.

The Guaraní were used as slave workers by the Spanish conquistadors in gold and silver mines and building works.

In the 18th century, the Jesuits established missions in eastern Paraguay, bringing the indigenous populations together and protecting them. However, in 1767, the evangelization process was brought to an abrupt end with the expulsion of the Jesuits, the dispersal of these communities and the confiscation of lands occupied by the indigenous people. Contemporary Paraguay is attempting to keep the customs of the Guarani alive.

The Tupi legacy is scattered among various indigenous groups - the Potiguara, Caeté, Tupinamba, Ttupinikin and some Guarani - who are collectively known as Tupinamaba and who speak Tupi languages, in Brazil's Ceará state, as also among the Kawaib of Mato Grosso and the Siriono of eastern Bolivia.

Peru

Perú

Population: 23,944,000 (1996)
Area: 1,285,216 SQ KM
Capital: Lima

Currency: New Sol
Language: Spanish, Aymara and Quechua

Caves near Ayacucho revealed evidence that human beings had lived in Peru for more than 15 thousand years. For millennia complex cultures had settled in the Andean zone. The Chavin civilization excelled at urban planning, reaching its apogee between 1400 and 200 BC. The cultures which followed inherited its knowledge. The Paraca (700 to 100 BC) were the first to carry out brain surgery. The Mochica built great adobe temples in the Mocha valley, and it is thought their direct descendants were the Chimu (1000 to 1400 AD) who were great metalworkers. The Nazca culture (200 BC to 800 AD) developed agriculture with large-scale irrigation systems and built great calendars which can still be seen from the heights. The Tiahuanaco-Huari culture (600 BC to 1000 AD), based in what is now Bolivia, expanded into the Peruvian highlands.

2   The 12th century marked the beginning of the rise of the Incas, who were united the various cultures and languages of the region. As with the rest of the Andean civilizations, the Incas' cultural legacy was preserved down the generations by oral tradition and texts written after the Spanish conquest. According to tradition, the founders of the Inka dynasty, Manco Capac and Mama Oclo, established their tribe in Cuzco, which remained the capital from then on. Up until the 14th century, little distinguished the Incas from the rest of the cultures dominating small territories in the Andes. It was during this century, under the reign of the fourth Emperor (or Inca) Mayta Capac, that the Incas began to attack the neighbouring populations.

3   The next in the dynastic line, Capac Yupanqui, was the first to extend the influence of the Inkas beyond the Cuzco valley. With the eighth emperor, Viracocha Inca, the empire began a programme of permanent conquest, establishing garrisons amongst the settlements of the conquered peoples. In 1438, Pachacuti Inca Yupanqui, one of the sons of Viracocha Inca, usurped the throne from his brother Inca Urcon and the empire expanded beyond lake Titicaca, subjugating powerful peoples like the Chanca, Quechua and the Chimu and taking over the kingdom of the Shiri in Quito.

4   The Incas began a policy of forced resettlement, thereby assuring the political stability of the Empire. Great contingents of subjects were taken from their place of origin and redistributed to other points within the Empire. They were forced to live and work alongside other ethnic groups, in order to make the organization of uprisings against the seat of power in Cuzco difficult. Quechua was imposed as the common language across the Empire and during the reign of Topa Inca Yupanqui (1471-1493) the Inkas extended their power southwards, towards what is now central Chile. On the death of Topa Inca a war of succession broke out, which was won by Huayna Capac (1493-1525). He extended the northern frontier up to the river Ancasmayo (the current frontier between Ecuador and Colombia) before dying. On his death, Tahuantisuyu, as the Inca state was known, imposed its government over more than 12 million people.

5   The death of Huayna Capac caused a new war of succession between Huáscar, who governed in Cuzco, and his younger brother Atahualpa, who was a son of Huayna Capac and a Shiri princess, who ruled the northern part of the empire from Quito. In 1532, the scales were tipped in favour of Atahualpa when a group of 180 Spaniards, led by Francisco Pizarro and his lieutenant Diego de Almagro disembarked in Tumbes. The Spanish interfered in the civil war, killing those loyal to Atahualpa but at the same time recognizing him as the legitimate governor of the Empire until they were able to meet him in Cajamarca, kidnap him and demand a large ransom in silver and gold. During his time in captivity, Atahualpa arranged for Huáscar to

be killed, before being strangled himself in 1533. The news of the death of Atahualpa paralysed the forces of the Empire, allowing the Spanish to reach Cuzco, where they crowned Topa Hualpa, an ally of Huáscar. This put the Europeans, who wanted to reign through an Inka emperor, in a difficult situation, as they found themselves committed to the faction they initially did not want to support.

6   Topa Hualpa died some months later and the Spanish reinforced their alliance with the pro-Huáscar faction by putting his brother Manco Capac on the throne and helping him to disperse the last of Atahualpa's army. In 1535, Pizarro prohibited Manco Capac from re-establishing control over the dominions along the coast and in the north, which were either still loyal to Atahualpa or lacked central control. Manco Capac then understood that the Spanish were a far greater threat than any of Atahualpa's followers and in 1536 he besieged Cuzco for a year. But his forces were finally disbanded by Diego de Almagro,

returning from an expedition to Chile.

7   After his defeat, Manco Capac founded an independent Inka state in the Amazon regions which lasted until 1572, with the death by poisoning of Titu Cusi Yupanqui, the last Inca. The days of the Tahuantisuyu were numbered from the moment Pizarro founded Lima in 1535 on the coast, operating as the centre of Spanish power. The Spanish administration radically changed the property and land-use rules; the payment of tributes and forced labour broke up the bases of the old society and the old gods were officially replaced with Catholicism. Even though the official Inka religion was suppressed, an incalculable number of cults survived amongst the people. Similarly, regions and cities of the old Empire survived beyond the reach of the Spanish Crown for centuries. The most notable example of this was the fortress of Macchu Pichu, 80 kilometres north-east of Cuzco which was only re-discovered in 1911 by Hiram Bingham, a Yale University professor.

WORKERS

UNEMPLOYMENT 7% (1996)

Labour force %

	■ WOMEN
	□ MEN
29	71

- ■ AGRICULTURE 36% (1990)
- □ INDUSTRIAL 18%
- ■ SERVICES 46%

PROFILE

ENVIRONMENT

The Andes divide the country into three regions. The desert coastal area, with large artificially irrigated plantations and some natural valleys has historically been the most modern and westernized. Half of the populaton live in the *Sierra* (highlands), between two ranges of the Andes. Numerous peasants here are still organized into *ayllus* (communities) with Incan roots. Subsistence farming of corn and potatoes is practised, the traditional raising of llamas and alpacas having been forced onto the higher slopes due to the incursions of mining and sheep rearing. The eastern region, comprising the Amazon lowlands, with tropical climate and rainforests, is sparsely populated. Perú is one of the largest producers of coca, a medicinal and energizing plant. Coca - traditionally consumed among indians who chew its leaves - once chemically refined and developed into a different substance, becomes the basis of cocaine. The country suffers from soil depletion, on soils which are poor to begin with. Indiscriminate fishing has endangered some species. The coastal area has been polluted by both industrial and household waste.

SOCIETY

Peoples: Nearly half of all Peruvians are of indigenous American origin, mostly from the Quechua and Aymara ethnic groups living on the *Sierra*. Along the coast, most of the population are mixed descendents of native Indians and Spaniards. There are several indigenous groups in the East Amazon jungle.
Religions: Catholic (official), with syncretic expressions related to Indian beliefs..
Languages: Spanish and Quechua, Aymara (all official). **Political Parties:** The Change 90-New Majority, founded in 1989 by Alberto Fujimori. In the1995 elections none of the traditional parties reached 5 per cent of the vote; for this reason, those parties must obtain their registration by collecting signatures in order to participate in future elections. The most important traditional parties were: Popular Action (AP), led by Fernando Belaúnde Terry; the Peruvian "Aprista" Party, founded in 1930; the Christian Popular Party; the United Left (IU), an alliance of the National Workers' and Campesinos' (Farmers') Front, the Peruvian Communist Party and the Union of the Revolutionary Left; the Socialist Left, of Alfonso Barrantes, withdrew from the IU in the 1990 elections. **Social Organizations:** The Peruvian Workers', General Central Union (CGTP), founded in 1928 and predominantly Communist. The Peruvian Workers' Central Union (CTP), founded in 1944, linked to the APRA. The independent National Worker's Confederation (CNT), founded in 1971. The Workers' Central of the Peruvian Revolution, founded in 1972 by Velasco. In March, 1991, the four trade union federations (CGTP, CTP, CTRP, and CNT) created the national Coordinating Body of Trade Union Federations, as a step towards the creation of a single federation. There are two rural organizations: the National Agrarian Confederation (CNA), founded in 1972, and the Peruvian *Campesino* Confederation (CCP), founded in 1974.

THE STATE

Official Name: República del Perú.
Administrative divisions: 25 Departments, 155 Provinces and 1,586 Districts. **Capital:** Lima, 6,022,213 people (1995). **Other cities:** Arequipa, 726,000 people; Callao, 684,000; Trujillo, 627,000; Chiclayo, 411,500 (1995).
Government: Alberto Fujimori, President since July 28 1990, re-elected in April 1995.
National Holiday: July 28, Independence (1821). **Armed Forces:** 115,000 troops (65,000 conscripts). 188,000 reserves.
Other: National Police: 60,000 members. Coast Guard: 600 members. Campesino Rounds: the campesino self-defense forces, made up of 2,000 groups mobilized within emergency zones.

[8] Conflicts between the conquistadores (the Spanish conquerors) meant that the Crown of the King of Spain could not fully establish its authority for decades. Almagro, disillusioned by losing his chances to conquer lands in Chile, besieged Cuzco until he was beaten and executed in 1538. His allies continued conspiring with Almagro's son and they attacked Pizarro's palace. Pizarro died in 1541. The Spanish Crown refused to recognize the young Almagro, who was captured and executed in 1542. But the conquistadores, led by Francisco Pizarro's brother Gonzalo, unhappy with the Spanish King's new laws (aiming to impede feudalism, and thereby threatening their wealth and power) rebelled again in 1542, remaining independent from Spanish power to all intents and purposes until 1544, when Gonzalo Pizarro was defeated and executed.

[9] It was only with the appointment of Viceroy Francisco de Toledo in 1569 that Spain consolidated its dominion over the region. The Andeans' institutions were adapted to the ends of the Spanish authority and for a long time the chiefs of the various Andean nations administered the interests of their communities while taking on responsibility for the collection of tributes and the provision of an indigenous workforce for the mines. In any case, Toledo did not trust the Andeans and when the son of Manco Capac, Tupac Amaru, led the indigenous rural population in an uprising, the Spanish authority had him executed in 1571.

[10] Once Toledo's administration was over, the Viceroyalty in Peru assumed the form it maintained until the 18th century, including all of South America except Venezuela and Brazil. The discovery of the silver mines in Potosí in 1545 was followed by those of Huancavelica in 1563. With the exception of the gold from New Granada (Colombia), mineral production was concentrated in Peru itself, or in Upper Peru (Bolivia). The Spanish Crown prioritized these areas, which became the most developed and rich parts of the continent.

[11] During the 16th and 17th centuries, Lima was the centre of power and wealth for all of Spanish-controlled South America. Based on the labour of the indigenous workforce, the Court of Lima - where the King's justice was meted out - attracted not only the rich and powerful but also religious orders, intellectuals and artists. It was in Lima that the tribunals of the Inquisition worked most avidly and cruelly. With the advent of the Bourbon dynasty in 1700, replacing the Hapsburgs as rulers of Spain, measures were taken to promote the development of the colonies and to achieve better government of the continent, something which severely affected Peru. The creation of the Viceroyalty of New Granada meant the Viceroyalty of Peru lost control over the port of Quito as well as the territory constituting modern day Colombia. The creation of the Viceroyalty of the River Plate in 1777 also removed control over Upper Peru and what are today Argentina, Paraguay and Uruguay. Chile, meanwhile, became an independent Captaincy of the Viceroy of Peru.

[12] Reforms to the mercantile system, allowing the Pacific and Atlantic ports to trade directly with Spain, weakened the condition of the Viceroyalty even further. In 1780, the *cacique* (indigenous leader) José Gabriel Condorcanqui had a *corregidor* (chief magistrate) arrested on charges of cruelty. He led a general uprising of indigenous people against the authority of the Viceroyalty in 1781 under the name of Tupac Amaru II,

even gaining the support of some *criollos* (descendants of the Spanish). The rebellion, which spread to Bolivia and Argentina lost support when it turned into a violent battle between the indigenous people and the whites. Tupac Amaru II was captured in 1781 and taken to Cuzco where, after being forced to witness the execution of his wife and children, he was quartered and beheaded. The revolution continued, however, until the Spanish Government approved a general pardon for the insurgents.

[13] The effective suppression of the indigenous uprisings, the presence of numerous Spaniards, the concentration of the Crown's military power in Lima and the conservative attitude of the local oligarchy, meant that Peru remained loyal to Spain when the rest of the Hispanic colonies in South America began the fight for independence between 1810 and 1821. The forces which finally expelled the Spanish came from beyond Peruvian borders. General José de San Martín freed Chile in 1818 and used it as a base to attack Peru by sea with the aim of securing control over the mines of Upper Peru and of assuring independence for the Argentine provinces. In September 1820, San Martín's forces occupied the port of Pisco and the Viceroy withdrew his troops into the interior of the country. San Martín entered Lima and declared independence on July 18 1821.

[14] Lacking sufficient forces to attack the large Spanish contingents in the interior of Peru, San Martín asked for the help of Venezuela's Simón Bolívar, who had liberated the northern part of South America, but Bolívar would not agree to share the leadership. Hence, San Martín withdrew and Bolívar took over in Peru in order to continue the fight. In the battles of Junín and Ayacucho, in August and December 1824, the Spanish were defeated and effectively Peru became politically independent.

[15] The first years of independence were spent in constant battles between the conservative oligarchy, yearning for the times of the viceroyalty, and the liberals. The wars with Colombia, in 1827, and Bolivia took place against that backdrop. The unification of Peru with Bolivia, attempted by Bolivian President Andrés Santa Cruz in 1835, failed both socially and economically

[16] Marshal Ramón Castilla, who ruled the country from 1845 to 1862, shaped the modern Peru, after abolishing slavery and proclaiming the Constitution.

[17] In 1864, Spain attempted to establish enclaves on the Peruvian coast. Peru, Chile, Bolivia and Ecuador declared war on the country. The Spanish fleet bombarded Valparaíso, Chile, and

El Callao in Peru, before being defeated in 1866.

[18] From 1845, with the silver mines exhausted, guano - bird faeces used as fertilizer - became Peru's main export product. When the guano "boom" was over it was replaced by saltpetre from the southern deserts. The potential wealth to be made from this product brought about the Pacific War (1879-1883). Peru and Bolivia joined forces against Chile, which exploited the saltpetre, with the support of British companies. Peru and Bolivia lost the war and with it the provinces of Arica, Tarapacá and Antofagasta.

[19] The early decades of the 20th century marked the beginning of large-scale copper mining, particularly by the North American Cerro de Pasco Copper Corporation. Foreign capital was also involved in oil exploitation in the north, and sugar cane and cotton in the north and centre. The anachronistic agrarian structures, however, continued unchanged.

[20] Within this context, the APRA (American Popular Revolutionary Alliance), a Marxist-inspired party committed to Latin Americanism, achieved widespread support. Victor Haya de la Torre, its main leader, was in favour of merging class boundaries and debated with José Carlos Mariátegui, founder of the Peruvian Communist Party (PC). Triumphant in several elections, APRA never actually came to power as it was always prevented by military coups.

[21] APRA dissidents and sectors of the revolutionary left unsuccessfully attempted guerrilla warfare in the 1960s.

[22] In 1968, a military faction headed by General Juan Velasco Alvarado ousted President Fernando Belaúnde Terry and started a process of change by nationalizing oil production. This also included recovery of the natural resources and fishing, co-operative based agrarian reform, worker participation in company ownership, the creation of socially-owned enterprises, the expropriation of the press - planning to hand this over to organised social sectors - and an independent non-aligned foreign policy.

[23] An ailing Velasco gradually lost control over the process and the trust of his allies. He was overthrown by his Prime Minister, General Francisco Morales Bermúdez, in August 1975. Under pressure from the IMF and an oligarchy keen on regaining power, Morales called elections in 1978. APRA, the Left and the Christian People's Party - the traditional right - took almost equal seats in the Constituent Assembly.

[24] Belaunde's Acción Popular (AP), which had boycotted the constituent elections, triumphed in 1980 presidential elections. Its economic policy followed IMF guidelines with disastrous results: unemployment grew, income became even more concentrated and an unregulated informal economy developed with no social benefits. In 1980, fighting broke out with the Shining Path guerrillas and the Tupac Amaru Revolutionary Movement (MRTA) in 1984.

[25] The United Left (IU), a parliamentary coalition of left-wing parties, won the mayoralty of Lima in the 1982 elections. Faced with increased guerrilla action, the provinces most affected were placed under military control, with a state of emergency declared in 1983.

[26] In the 1985 elections, the APRA candidate Alan García came in first with 46 per cent. When García took power in July 1985, the foreign debt stood at $14 billion, with annual servicing of $3.5 billion. García announced he would limit payments to 10 per cent of the annual export income and would negotiate directly with the creditors, without IMF mediation.

[27] In the second half of 1988, international reserves hit rock bottom and amidst growing inflation and recession the Government began an economic adjustment policy.

[28] In the 1989 general elections, the Democratic Front (FREDEMO) with Mario Vargas Llosa as its candidate stood against APRA's Luis Alva Castro, the Left with the "United" Henry Pease and the "Socialist" Alfonso Barrantes, and Change 90 (Cambio 90), with the unknown outsider, Alberto Fujimori. Fujimori was elected with 56.4 per cent of the vote.

[29] On assuming power in July 1990, Fujimori implemented a severe anti-inflationary plan, or "fujishock," which dropped the standard of living of all Peruvians, leaving more than half in extreme poverty. The four union groups convened a "march against hunger," and later united to form the National Co-ordination. When parliamentary opposition got in his way, Fujimori began to govern by decree.

[30] On April 5 1992, Fujimori led a coup claiming that Parliament was corrupt and inoperative and that the judicial system was obstructing national reconstruction.

[31] The United States suspended economic and military aid to Peru, but soon restarted negotiations. In late April, the IMF approved the Peruvian Government's economic and structural reform programme.

[32] In September, the imprisonment of Abimael Guzmán, founder and leader of the Shining Path, dealt a hard blow to the guerrilla group, which said it was prepared to start peace negotiations. In the election for the Democratic Constituent Congress in November, Fujimori's party took the absolute majority,

STATISTICS

DEMOGRAPHY
Population: 23,944,000 (1996). **Annual growth:** 2% (1980/1996). **Estimates for year 2000:** 25,700,000. **Annual growth to year 2000:** 1.8% (1994/2000). **Urban Population:** 71.3% (1996). **Urban growth:** 2.86% (1980/95). **Children per woman:** 3.1 (1996).

HEALTH
Life expectancy at birth: 68 years (1996). male: 65 years (1994). female: 70 years (1994). **Infant mortality:** 45 per 1,000 (1996). **Under-5 child mortality:** 58 per 1,000 (1996). **Calorie consumption:** 87% (1988/90). 1,031 **people per doctor** (1988/91). **Safe water:** 67% (1990/96).

EDUCATION
Literacy: 89% (1995). male : 95% (1995). female: 83% (1995). **School enrolment :** Primary total: 123% (1990/95). Tertiary: 31% (1995). **Primary school teachers:** one for every 28 students (1995).

COMMUNICATIONS
90 **newspapers,** 255 **radios,** 100 **TV sets** and 33 **main telephone lines** per 1,000 people (1994). **Books:** 9 new titles per 100,000 people (1992/94).

ECONOMY
Per capita, GNP: $ 2,420 (1996). **Annual growth, GNP:** 0% (1995/96). **Annual inflation:** 398.52% (1985/95). **Consumer price index:** 1,625.5 (1994). **Currency:** 2,310 new soles = $ 1 (1995) **Cereal imports:** 2,289 metric tons (1994). **Food import dependency:** 13% (1994). **Fertilizer use:** 504 kgs per ha (1994). **Exports:** $ 5,226 million (1996). **Imports:** $ 7,947 million (1996). **External debt:** $ 29,176 million (1996). $ 1,219 **per capita:** (1996). **Debt service:** 35.4% of exports (1996). **Development aid received:** $ 428 million (1995). $ 18 per capita (1995). 0.9% of GNP (1994).

ENERGY
Consumption: 366.54 Kgs of Oil equivalent per capita yearly (1994). 0.46% imported (1994).

HDI (rank / value) 89 / 0.717 (1994)

with the absence of the traditional parties.

[33] The economy grew by 6.5 per cent on income from fishing, construction, manufactured goods and the informal economy. Peruvian reticence over the removal of tariffs obstructed the creation of a common Andean market with Colombia, Venezuela and Bolivia, planned for 1995.

[34] In early 1995, Peru and Ecuador fought an undeclared war on their common frontier in the Condor mountains. The peace negotiations were held under the patronage of the Rio Protocol, with Argentina, Brazil, Chile and the United States as guarantors.

[35] In the April elections, Fujimori was re-elected in a resounding victory. Javier Pérez de Cuéllar, former UN Secretary General, did not get enough votes to enter the second round.

[36] That year, Fujimori granted an amnesty to all military and police personnel convicted for human rights violations during fighting with the guerrillas since 1980. The so-called "faceless judges", who maintained anonymity during the trials, sentenced more than 2,000 people between 1992 and 1995.

[37] In December 1996, a MRTA group took over the Japanese ambassador's residence in Lima, during a reception for 450 guests, causing national and international commotion. Negotiations led to the freeing of successive groups of hostages. On April 22, 126 days later, a group of army commandos stormed the building. The death toll included 14 MRTA members, one of the remaining 72 hostages, and two soldiers. Fujimori's popularity soared to 65 per cent approval in the polls.

[38] In May 1997 members of the Constitutional Tribunal were sacked after it ruled that Fujimori's standing for re-election would be unconstitutional.

[39] Amnesty International reported some 5,000 Peruvians were arrested and imprisoned under the anti-terrorist laws in the last five years. Some 1,400 of these had been unjustly detained, and 600 were still in prison at the close of 1997.

[40] Defence Minister, César Saucedo, stated in November 1997 that, so far that year, the MRTA and the Shining Path had carried out 534 attacks, compared with 660 the previous year, and 4,467 in 1992 - the peak year for guerrilla action in the country. A month later, the Shining Path declared it still maintained the offer of peace made to the Fujimori Government in 1993.

Philippines

Pilipinas

Population:	69,282,000 (1996)
Area:	300,000 SQ KM
Capital:	Manila
Currency:	Peso
Language:	Filipino

The Philippine archipelago was first inhabited in Palaeolithic times, and the Neolithic culture on the islands began around 900 BC with metal working beginning in about the 15th century. Native peoples, such as the Aeta and the Igorot, probably subsisted without being assimilated by the later groups of migrants.

[2] Between the 2nd and 15th centuries AD, migrants from Indonesia and Malaysia settled on the islands, gathering in clans. Unlike the rest of the Malays, they were virtually uninfluenced by the classical Indian culture. Between the 11th and 13th centuries the coastal areas were raided by Muslim, Japanese, and Chinese merchant ships, bringing traders and craftsmen to the islands. The southern islands adopted Islam and sultanates soon appeared.

[3] The archipelago was only 'discovered' by Ferdinand Magellan in 1521 when it was named after the Spanish king Felipe. The explorer was killed on one of its beaches and Spanish possession of the islands, which were also coveted by the British and the Dutch, was not secured until 1564. The Igorot of the Cordillera region and the Islamic population of Mindanao were never fully incorporated by European colonization, and most of the rural population preserved their subsistence economy, never even paying tribute to the Europeans. Several uprisings by these communities and the Chinese were repressed by the Spaniards.

[4] Spanish colonization in the Philippines followed similar patterns to that in America. However, the Philippines had two distinguishing features; they were located on the oceanic trading routes, in a position that received merchandise from all over Southeast Asia on its way to Europe, and they were ruled by the Viceroyalty of Mexico.

[5] Late in the 19th century, a local independence movement developed, led by the native bourgeoisie, who wanted the political power which was barred to them. They were soon followed by the other oppressed sectors. Anti-colonial revolution erupted in 1896 and independence was proclaimed on July 12th. However, the US was attracted by the archipelago's strategic position and vulnerability, and it immediately stepped in to seize control. This resulted in the signing of the Treaty of Paris, on December 10 1898, ending the Spanish-US war (see history of Cuba and Puerto Rico). In meetings, which barred Filipino delegates, Spain decided to cede the archipelago to the US in exchange for compensation.

[6] Between 1899 and 1911, more than 500,000 Filipinos died in the struggle against occupying troops commanded by US general Arthur MacArthur. During World War II, the archipelago was occupied by Japan and the Huk Movement, peasant-based and socialist inspired, emerged during the struggle against the invaders. In 1946, after the war had ended, occupation troops returned led by Douglas MacArthur, son of the earlier General MacArthur. The archipelago was eventually granted formal independence but the Philippines have remained under US economic domination ever since.

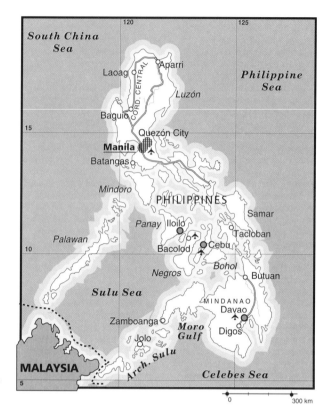

[7] Nor did independence bring about any social changes. The hacienda system still persists in the country, where large estates are farmed by sharecroppers. More than half the population are peasants, and 20 per cent of the population own 60 per cent of the land. Although the sharecropper is supposed to receive half of the harvest, most of the peasant's actual income goes to paying off the debts incurred with the *cacique*, the landowner. There is almost 9 per cent unemployment and the country suffers from the consequences of a balance of trade deficit, typical of a producer of agricultural commodities.

[8] The Nationalist Party, a conservative party of landowners, was in power until 1972 when Ferdinand Marcos, president since 1965, declared Martial Law. In 1986 a coalition of opposition forces rebelled against the continuous abuses of Ferdinand Marcos. During his presidency repression grew both against armed movements (the Muslim independent groups of Mindanao and the New People's Army led by the Maoist Communist Party), and against political and trade union opposition. This repression often had the military support of the US.

[9] Due to its long presence in the country, the Catholic Church is deeply rooted in Filipino society. This is reflected in the fact that 75 per cent of Filipinos over the age of 10 have learnt to read in institutions dependent on the Church. The Church played an active role in the denunciation of fraud when the 1976 referendum supported the invocation of martial law. Five years later, 45 political and trade union organizations united to boycott the fraudulent and unconstitutional elections that Marcos used to stay in power. In September 1981 thousands of people demonstrated in Manila, demanding the end of dictatorship and the withdrawal of the US military bases. Since the 19th century, the US army has had its two largest foreign bases in the Philippines.

[10] On August 21 1983,

PUBLIC EXPENDITURE

10.6%   26.3%
1995 ■ DEFENCE □ SOCIAL

In **1990/91** Military as % of health & education expenditure was 41%.

WORKERS

UNEMPLOYMENT 7.4% (1996)

Labour force %

■ WOMEN
□ MEN

37   63

■ AGRICULTURE	46%	(1990)
□ INDUSTRIAL	15%	
■ SERVICES	39%	

Food Dependency

Foreign Trade

MILLIONS $
1970

11%

1994

6%

1996

IMPORTS

34,663

EXPORTS

20,328

opposition leader Benigno Aquino was murdered at Manila airport as he stepped down from the commercial flight that had brought him back to his country after prolonged exile in the US, a murder which was attributed to Marcos. More than 500,000 mourners followed his coffin to the cemetery, blaming Marcos for the crime. The crowds flooded the streets refusing to go home until the dictator was ousted.

[11] In the May 14 1984 by-elections, the opposition made important progress; for though it lost the elections, it won 78 of the 183 parliamentary seats. In April 1985, the 'Reform of the Army Movement' (RAM) was formed by officers who were opposed to Marcos' interventions in the army.

[12] Amidst a scenario of increased violence and repression, compared by the Church with the dirty war of Argentina in the 1970s, a large section of the population put pressure on Marcos, demanding early elections in 1986, and supporting the candidacy of Corazon Aquino, widow of the assassinated leader.

[13] Elections were held in February 1986, but widespread fraud prevented Cory Aquino from winning, and she subsequently called for civil disobedience. Marcos' minister of defence, Juan Ponce Enrile, attempted a coup against the dictator, but failed. A million supporters surrounded the rebels, led by Enrile, in the field where they had taken refuge. The air force refused to bombard their comrades-in-arms and the people who supported them, so Marcos opted for exile and Corazon Aquino assumed the presidency with Enrile as her minister of defence.

[14] Aquino faced various attempts at ousting her; the most threatening of which took place in November 1986 and September 1987, both ending in cabinet reshuffles. After the first attempt, Enrile resigned from his post. The breach with the more conservative figures had to be balanced by the removal of several front-line advisors who were directly involved in grassroots movements and the defence of human rights.

[15] The new constitution was approved by a large majority in the February 1987 plebiscite. The charter granted autonomy to the Mindanao and Cordillera regions, thus paving the way for a truce with guerrilla groups operating in those areas. The New People's Army representatives soon left the negotiating table, after several acts of provocation against mass organizations and attempts on the lives of civilian leaders. Agrarian reform, which should have been the cornerstone of the government's plan for social transformation, was diluted after going through a legislature where many of the members are landowners. The debate over the future of the Clark and Subic Bay American military bases began in April 1988, as the contracts were due to expire in 1991.

[16] In 1990, 39 per cent of the Filipino population was under the age of 14, and in spite of NGO efforts to alleviate their suffering, only a third of their basic needs were met. A number of government 'internal refugee' camps were created to provide basic assistance to some 1,250,000 homeless people.

[17] The UN has recorded a total of 110 regional and ethnic groups in the Philippines. During 1991 increasing pressure from these groups, the urgent need for better land and wealth distribution and, possibly, the approaching presidential elections of May 1992, led Corazon Aquino to create a Bureau of Northern Communities. The bureau was concerned with the mountain tribes and ethnic groups, particularly in Luzon. There was also a Bureau of Southern Cultural Communities, excluding the Muslims. The staff of those bureaux were recruited from among the communities concerned.

[18] In the Mindanao region there has been a Bureau of Muslim Affairs since 1987. Conflict was brewing there, as the 20,000-strong Moro Liberation Front considers that the government has not respected conditions set out in the 1987 Constitution.

[19] In June 1991, the eruption of Mount Pinatubo shook the country, claiming the lives of over 700 Filipinos, flattening entire villages, forcing the evacuation of over 300,000 people, and

PROFILE

ENVIRONMENT
Of the 7,000 islands that make up the archipelago, spread over 1,600 km. from north to south, eleven account for 94 per cent of the total area and house most of the population. Luzon and Mindanao are the most important. The archipelago is of volcanic origin, forming part of the "Ring of Fire of the Pacific". The terrain is mountainous with large coastal plains where sugar cane, hemp, copra and tobacco are grown. The climate is tropical with heavy rainfall and dense rainforests. The country is the main producer of iron ore in Southeast Asia, there are chrome, copper, nickel, cobalt, silver and gold deposits. Like other countries in the region, it is suffering the effects of rapid deforestation.

SOCIETY
Peoples: Most of the population migrated from Malaysia and Indonesia between the 24th century BC and the 11th. century AD. Native peoples such as the Aetas and the Igorots may have subsisted without being assimilated into the other ethnic groups. In the 15th century, when Islamic communities arrived from Borneo, some 200,000 Chinese traders were already established on the islands. The Spanish arrived in 1521, evangelizing much of the population as they conquered. Some peoples of Malay extraction, were not converted. Finally, from 1898 onwards, US colonization influenced Filipino culture and society. **Religions**: Catholics 83 per cent; Protestants 8 per cent, Muslims 5 per cent, Anglipayans (Independent Filipino Church), 3 per cent; Animists and Buddhists. **Languages**: The Philippines presents a complex linguistic map. 55 per cent of the population speaks Filipino (official), based on Tagalog, a language of Malaysian origin. English, spoken by 45 per cent, is obligatory in schools. 90 per cent of the population speaks one of the following: Cebuano (6 million); Hiligayano (3 million); Bikolano (2 million); Waray-Waray (1 million). Spanish and Chinese are minority languages.
Political Parties: Lakas ñg Bansa (The People's Struggle); the Laban Party (The People's Power Movement), founded in 1988 by Benigno Aquino, the Democratic Christian Party; the BISIG, socialist movement of Tagalog speakers; the People's Reform Party founded in 1991; the Liberal Party; the right-wing Nationalist Party. The main leftist opposition force is the National Democratic Front (NDF) which includes mass organizations, religious and cultural groups led by the Philippine Communist Party (PKP) and its military wing, the New People's Army (NPA). In the Cordillera region, an NPA splinter group, the Cordillera People's Liberation Army (CPLA) organized the Cordillera Bodong Association (CBA) which demands full autonomy for the north. In the southern Muslim areas, the Moro National Liberation Front also demands autonomy. Kababaihan Para Sa Inang Bayan (Women for the Motherland), created in 1986, the first party exclusively for women; the Mindanao Alliance, regional. Social Organizations: Labor is divided between the left-wing Kihusan Mayo Uno (May Day Confederation) and the Trade Union Congress of the Philippines (TUCP), affiliated with AFL-CIO. The Philippines has 720 voluntary organizations and church groups, gathered in the "Green Forum".

THE STATE
Official Name: Republika ñg Pilipinas. Capital: Metro Manila, 9,280,000 people (1995). **Other cities**: Quezon City, 1,627,900 people; Davao 867,800; Cebu 641,000; Calaocan 629,500; Zamboanga 453,200 (1991). Government: Presidential republic, Joseph Estrada, President since May 1998. Bicameral Legislative: Chamber of Deputies (Congress) 250 members, 200 elected by general vote, 50 chosen by the President, and a 24-member Senate. **Administrative Divisions**: 3 regions, 73 provinces. **National Holiday**: July 12th, Independence Day (1946). Armed Forces: 106,500 troops (1995). **Other**: 40,500 National Police (Ministry of the Interior), 2,000 Coastguards.

PER 100,000
LIVE BIRTHS

280

95%

PER CAPITA

$595

STATISTICS

DEMOGRAPHY
Population: 69,282,000 (1996). **Annual growth:** 2.3% (1980/1996). **Estimates for year 2000:** 75,000,000. **Annual growth to year 2000:** 2.1% (1994/2000). **Urban Population:** 55.0% (1996). **Urban growth:** 4.87% (1980/95). **Children per woman:** 3.7 (1996).

HEALTH
Life expectancy at birth: 68 years (1996). male: 65 years (1994). female: 69 years (1994). **Infant mortality:** 32 per 1,000 (1996). **Under-5 child mortality:** 38 per 1,000 (1996). **Calorie consumption:** 104% (1988/90). 8,333 **people per doctor** (1988/91). **Safe water:** 84% (1990/96).

EDUCATION
Literacy: 95% (1995). male : 95% (1995). female: 94% (1995). **School enrolment :** Primary total: 111% (1990/95). male : 110% (1990/95). female: 111% (1990/95). Tertiary: 27% (1995). **Primary school teachers:** one for every 35 students (1995).

COMMUNICATIONS
70 **newspapers,** 144 **radios,** 120 **TV sets** and 17 **main telephone lines** per 1,000 people (1994). **Books:** 2 new titles per 100,000 people (1992/94).

ECONOMY
Per capita, GNP: $ 1,160 (1996). **Annual growth, GNP:** 4.5% (1995/96). **Annual inflation:** 9.81% (1985/95). **Consumer price index:** 151.7 (1994). **Currency:** 26.21 pesos = $ 1 (1995) **Cereal imports:** 2,219 metric tons (1994). **Food import dependency:** 6% (1994). **Fertilizer use:** 654 kgs per ha (1994). **Exports:** $ 20,328 million (1996). **Imports:** $ 34,663 million (1996). **External debt:** $ 41,214 million (1996). $ 595 **per capita:** (1996). **Debt service:** 13.7% of exports (1996). **Development aid received:** $ 884 million (1995). $ 109 per capita (1995). 23.8% of GNP (1994).

ENERGY
Consumption: 316.22 Kgs of Oil equivalent per capita yearly (1994). 71.31% imported (1994).

HDI (rank / value) 98 / 0.672 (1994)

---

completely burying the evacuated Clark US airforce base under the ashes.
[20] With its airbase completely unusable, and swamped with difficult negotiations as the contract approached their expiry dates, the US opted to abandon the base of its own accord. On November 26 1991, Clark airbase was formally abandoned. It had employed over 6,000 US military, and over 40,000 Filipinos, most of whom had carried out the menial work. The Aetan people claimed the territory they had been deprived of when the base was installed, and the Philippines Government made plans to build an airport there.
[21] The issue of closing the Subic Bay naval base, with the relocation or loss of around 12,000 personnel, resulted in unease in the Senate because of the economic implications. In October, the Senate voted not to renew the bases' agreement.
[22] The evacuation of Clark base and its relocation on a nearby island outside Filipino sovereignty worried local and international environmental movements. They were concerned that the constant circulation of nuclear weapons may pose a threat to the area.
[23] The forest, which covered 75 per cent of the land in the 1950s, was reduced to 42 per cent by 1990. The effect of natural disasters like typhoon Uring which killed 8,000 in 1991, was magnified by the lack of trees.
[24] Of the 32 million Filipinos entitled to vote, 25 million took part in the May 1992 elections which were considered the calmest and cleanest in the country's history. The winner was Fidel Ramos, former minister of defence in the Aquino administration. In September, the United States left its naval base at Subic Bay with an infrastructure worth $8 billion. Thousands of rural women who had worked as prostitutes were left unemployed.
[25] In 1993 the Government and Congress tightened their links with Muslim secessionists and the guerrillas in northern Luzon. At the same time, the authorities were charged with torture and 'disappearances'.
[26] In 1994, the Ramos government had to turn to the opposition's support to control evasion of the 10 per cent VAT tax. This measure won him the IMF's support - including a loan - and enabled a five per cent growth of the GNP. The campaign against crime, now headed by Vice-President Estrada, implicated two per cent of police forces - who were discharged - in criminal activities, while another 5 per cent was kept under investigation. The NPA communist guerrillas lost strength due to an amnesty for its members and to internecine conflicts regarding the amnesty.
[27] In 1995 Imelda Marcos won the elections in the Chamber of Deputies, in spite of being accused of many corruption charges. Swiss banks returned $475 million to the country deposited by Marcos during the dictatorship, but the Government is convinced billions remain in other accounts.
[28] The elimination of restrictions to investments, the reduction in customs barriers and the presence of educated and cheap labour, attracted investors which led to a six-per-cent growth of the GNP. Remittances totalling $2 billion from 4.2 million workers living abroad - mainly housemaids - came into the country in 1995.
[29] In late 1995, there was an unprecedented food crisis, with a 70 per cent increase in rice prices. More than two thirds of the population were estimated to be living below the poverty line. The farmers organizations blamed the government for their incoherent and corrupt agricultural policy, calling for agrarian reform, including the industrialisation of rural activity, food self-sufficiency and protection of the environment.
[30] Despite protests from representatives of the Christian Filipinos, who make up the majority of the nation, the Government continued negotiations with the Muslim guerrillas, offering its leaders presence in Congress, the Supreme Court and the cabinet, while incorporating the guerrillas into the army and police force. The government objective was to pacify the country in order to impose economic reforms and put it in a position to compete with its partners in the Association of Southeast Asian Nations (ASEAN).
[31] On September 30, 1996, the government and the Muslim guerrillas signed a peace agreement. Nur Misuari, leader of the Moro National Liberation Front, became governor of Mindanao, an independent region which covers around a quarter of the national territory. The Christian opposition organised a referendum in 1998 against this agreement. President Ramos also started negotiations with the Communist Party, whose armed wing, the New People's Army, continued to operate in cities and rural towns. In August 1997, Ramos accepted the resignation of his defence minister Renato de Villa.
[32] In January 1998, thousands of children from various countries marched through the streets of Manila in protest against exploitative child labour. This sparked a world-wide campaign for better conditions for the world's 250 million working children, employed despite international agreements banning this. 63 per cent of the exploited children are estimated to be living in Asia.
[33] Following a formal protest from the Chinese government, Ramos denied having negotiated with the Taiwanese prime minister. That month, the Swiss Supreme Court agreed to transfer the bulk of the fortune of former dictator Ferdinand Marcos to Filipino banks. In May, Vice President Joseph Estrada was elected President with 37 per cent of the vote.

Pitcairn

Pitcairn

Population: 70 (1996)
Area: 5 SQ KM
Capital: Adamstown

Currency: NZ Dollar
Language: English

Like most of the islands of the region, Pitcairn's first settlers were Polynesians. The first European to visit the island was the English seaman Robert Pitcairn who sailed along its coasts in 1767.

2 In 1789, part of the crew of HMS Bounty mutinied on their return to Britain from six months in Tahiti. The captain and the rest of the crew were given a small boat and the other men returned to Tahiti. They stayed there a short time and then transferred to Pitcairn Island.

3 The group, led by Fletcher Christian, was made up of eight crew members, six Tahitian men and twelve women. Ten years later, only one of the mutineers, John Evans, was still alive, with eleven women and 23 children. Purportedly guided by "apparitions", Adams christened the children and peopled Pitcairn, which later became a British colonial dependency.

4 The population reached 200 inhabitants in 1937, but decreased in recent times as young islanders emigrated to Aotearoa/New Zealand in search of work.

5 Pitcairn was under the jurisdiction of the Governor of Fiji between 1952 and 1970. At this time, it became a dependency of the British High Commissioner in Aotearoa, who assumed the functions of a governor, in consultation with the island's Administrative Council.

6 The island's communications with the outside world are limited to a radio and boats that occasionally anchor off the coast.

7 Despite the lack of communications, education in the islands is important and primary school is compulsory for all children between the ages of 5 and 15. A New Zealand teacher is appointed for a period of two years, and is also responsible for publishing the Pitcairn Miscellany, a four-page bulletin.

8 The island's Administrative Council is made up of 11 representatives, only 5 of which are chosen from inhabitants over the age of 18 who have lived on the island at least 3 years.

9 The only national celebration is the Queen's birthday, which is celebrated on the second Saturday in June. The Queen is the Head of State.

10 The inhabitants work almost exclusively at subsistence fishing and farming. The fertile valleys produce a wide variety of fruit and vegetables, including citrus, sugar cane, watermelons, bananas, potatoes, and beans. However, the island's main source of income is the export of postage stamps for sale to stamp collectors.

11 The reforestation plan carried out in 1963 increased plantations of the miro tree, which provides a kind of wood that can be used for many kinds of handcrafts.

12 Since 1987 the Japanese Tuna Fisheries Cooperative Association fleet has been allowed to operate within Pitcairn's 200-mile Exclusive Economic Zone, which ended in 1990.

13 That same year, the British High Commissioner in Fiji - representing Pitcairn, the United Kingdom's last possession in the South Pacific - met representatives of the United States, France, Aotearoa/New Zealand, and six other states of the region, to sign a Regional Convention of the South Pacific for the Protection of the Environment. The aim of this agreement was to put an end to the dumping of nuclear waste in the region.

14 In 1989, Henderson island, located 68 kilometres northeast of Pitcairn, was listed among the UK property to be preserved as a natural bird reserve. It is the home of five unique species. In early 1992, deposits of manganese, iron, copper, zinc, silver and gold were identified in underwater volcanoes within the island's territorial waters.

15 In 1995, Robert John Alston became the new Governor, replacing David Moss.

16 The population of Pitcairn has been continuously shrinking in recent years. In January 1998, there were just 30 people, only eight of whom were working. Ten had emigrated the year before.

17 The survival of the island, the last British colony in the Pacific, is dependent on the boats which ship in the necessary goods, as there is no airstrip. The lack of crews for the boats could accelerate depopulation. London aimed to avoid this happening by building an emergency air strip.

PROFILE

ENVIRONMENT
Four islands of volcanic origin, of which only Pitcairn is inhabited. The others are: Henderson, Ducie and Oeno. The group is located in the eastern extreme of Polynesia, slightly south of the Tropic of Capricorn, east of French Polynesia. The economy is based on subsistence agriculture, fishing, handicrafts, and there are very few export products. The rainy, tropical climate is tempered by sea winds. The islands are subject to typhoons between November and March.

SOCIETY
Peoples: The population consists of descendants of mutineers from HMS Bounty and Polynesian women from Tahiti.
Religion: Seventh Day Adventist (100 per cent).
Languages: English (official). **Political Parties:** None.

THE STATE
Official Name: Pitcairn, Henderson, Ducie and Oeno Islands.
Capital: Adamstown.
Government: Robert John Alston, British high comissioner in Aotearoa, acting governor of the islands since 1995. Jay Warren, magistrate and president of the Council since 1993. The Council is made up of ten members. In addition to the magistrate who presides over it, one member functions as the Council's secretary. Five members are elected every year and three are named by the Government for a one-year period.

Poland

Polska

Population: 38,601,000 (1996)
Area: 323,250 SQ KM
Capital: Warsaw (Warzawa)

Currency: Zloty
Language: Polish

The name Poland comes from a Polanian tribe, the Poles, who tilled the soil in the Warta basin region. A region later known as Greater Poland. Their chiefs belonged to the Piast dynasty, descendants of a legendary ancestor, and they lived in the town of Gniezno.

2 During the 10th century, the Polanians subdued the Kujavians, the Mazovians, the Ledzians, the Pomeranians, the Vistulans, and the Silesians. Mieszko I (960-992) duke of the Piast, founded the first Polish State when he united neighboring tribes under a common state structure. Mieszko was christened in the year 966 establishing the Christian influence in the area.

3 Poland was a hereditary monarchy until the 12th century. The duke and a group of noblemen held power, supported by an army of elite warriors. Free peasants, who constituted the largest and poorest group, were mobilized as they were needed, and paid taxes to support the system.

4 The greatest dilemma for Poland was what stance to take towards the German Empire and the Pope. As the empire expanded, Mieszko submitted, in exchange for an acknowledgement of his sovereignty. As compensation, he appealed for Papal protection and in 1,000 AD he founded the first Polish ecclesiastical city state.

5 From then on, the Roman Catholic Church became a crucial element in the political structure of the Polish State. Poland alternated phases of independence and annexation until the 12th century, when the State started to split up.

6 During the feudal period, Poland was subdivided into several duchies, led by the Piasts and some 20 overlords. The nobility and the Church became increasingly autonomous as the central power and the dukes lost strength. This was also a period of great demographic growth.

7 The arrival of German settlers created a new ethnic situation in the country, for up to then the population had been of Slavic stock. From the 13th century, the population of the towns became increasingly German and Jewish. Immigrants brought in their own legal systems, their capital, their crafts and their agricultural skills.

8 Under the reign of Casimir the Great (1333-70), Poland became a monarchy divided into estates, with the king acting as an arbiter between the nobility, the clergy, the bourgeoisie, and the peasants. The State ceased to be royal property and in 1399 the monarchy became elective.

9 Through a royal marriage in 1386, Poland joined with Lithuania, and they adopted an organization which respected the differences between the two countries. In 1409, the Teutonic Order attempted to stop Polish-Lithuanian expansion, but it was defeated at Grunwald. The Peace of Torun, in 1411, did not stop the conflict, and the power of the Order suffered a setback.

10 In 1466, after a new victory over the Teutons, Poland recovered Pomerania of Gdansk and Malbork, Elblag, and the Land of Chelm; it also gained the territory of Warmia. In recognition of their assistance during the war, Poland granted autonomy to Pomerania and some privileges to the towns. A period of economic prosperity and cultural renaissance began.

11 During the 15th century the General Diet (parliament) of Poland and Lithuania was created. It had two houses: a lower house, constituted by members of the nobility, and an upper house, or royal council, presided over by the king. The two states shared the king, the diet, and the management of foreign affairs, while administration, justice, finance and the army remained separate.

12 The 16th or "Golden" century is also known as the period of the Royal Republic, for the king had to consult the noblemen before fixing taxes or declaring war. The reduction of the rights of the bourgeoisie and the peasantry in favor of the nobility and the clergy modified the original monarchy of divided estates.

13 In 1573, with the end of the Jagiellon dynasty, the Diet approved the free election of the king and guaranteed religious tolerance, which was exceptional in a time when Europe was being shaken by religious wars. King Stephen Bathory (1576-86) gave up arbitration, and the nobility started to elect their own courts.

14 During the 17th century, international developments were unfavorable for Poland and Lithuania. Sweden fought against Poland over the control of the Baltic, and Russia entered into conflict with Lithuania. Turkish and Austrian ambitions in central Europe also exerted pressure on Poland.

15 On the lower Dnepr, on the border with the Ukraine, free peasants and impoverished noblemen became the first cossacks, warriors who lived by pillaging. In 1648, the cossacks and the Ukranian peasants started a national revolt. The king made unsuccessful attempts to reach an agreement with the rebels, whose victories weakened the Polish republic.

16 The cossacks formed occasional alliances with the Turks and the Russians. In 1654, Russian troops entered Polish territory, and Sweden invaded the rest of the country a year later. King John Casimir fled to Silesia, and Poland was aided by Austria, while the peasants in the provinces organized the first large-scale armed resistance.

17 The Swedes and the Turks were expelled from the country and the cossacks were defeated. Russia kept Smolensk and the Ukraine, the left bank of the Dnepr and the city of Kiev. The wars devastated the land, decimated the population and split the republic.

18 In 1772, Russia, Prussia, and

WORKERS

UNEMPLOYMENT 12.3% (1996)

Labour force %

- ■ WOMEN
- □ MEN

46   54

- ■ AGRICULTURE 27% (1990)
- □ INDUSTRIAL 36%
- ■ SERVICES 37%

LAND USE

IRRIGATED of arable (1993) **0.7%**

- ■ FOREST & WOODLAND (1993) 28.1%
- □ ARABLE (1993) 45.7%
- ■ OTHER (1993) 26.2%

Austria agreed on the territorial partition of Poland. A second partition followed in 1793, after a fresh Russian invasion annulled the 1791 Constitution and put an end to a new Polish attempt to reorganise the State.

[19] A patriotic insurrection was crushed in 1794, and was followed a year later by the third partition of Poland. The Polish State disappeared from the map, but the Polish people retained a feeling of national identity.

[20] During the 19th century, the Poles made several attempts to free their motherland. National conscience and Catholicism, both under persecution, became stronger. New political parties appeared; a peasants', a workers', and a national party, and resistance was expressed through culture.

[21] The consolidation of the Russian revolution in 1917 brought Poland the support of western powers. In 1918 a provisional government was created, led by Jozef Pilsudski. It established an eight-hour working day and equal rights for men and women.

[22] Boundaries could not be moved back, as a national sense of identity had emerged in the Ukraine, Lithuania and Belarus. The creation of a federation failed with the counteroffensive of the Soviet army. The Peace of Riga, signed in 1921, guaranteed the independence of the Baltic states and fixed the eastern border of Poland at Zbrucz.

[23] The 1921 Constitution adopted a parliamentary system. During the years that followed, the government had to resort to coalitions, generally between the National and Social Christian parties, which were both conservative, or the Peasants' party, which was moderate.

[24] Political instability, a tariff war against Germany, unemployment and social unrest benefited the Communist Party, which had been banned in 1923. Their main military leader, Jozef Pilsudski, staged a coup in 1926, but the ensuing prosperity was ended by the effects of the 1929 Wall Street crash.

[25] The growing power of Germany and the USSR became a threat to Poland, and Britain and France only gave the country

PROFILE

ENVIRONMENT

On the extensive northern plains, crossed by the Vistula (Wisla), Warta and Oder (Odra) rivers, there are coniferous woodlands, rye, potato and linen plantations. The fertile soil of Central Poland's plains and highlands yield a considerable agricultural production of beet and cereals. The southern region, on the northern slopes of the Carpathian Mountains, is less fertile. Poland has large mineral resources: coal in Silesia (the world's fourth largest producer); sulphur in Tarnobrzeskie (the world's second largest producer); copper; zinc and lead. Major industries are steel, chemicals and shipbuilding. The country has high levels of air pollution; due to its geographical location in the center of Europe, it absorbs polluted water and air "in transit" from other countries. Soil depletion has caused extensive erosion, due to the excessive deforestation that has accompanied intensive agriculture.

SOCIETY

Peoples: Polish, 98.7 per cent; Ukrainian, 0.6 per cent; other (Belarusian, German), 0.7 per cent.
Religions: Catholic, 90.7 per cent; Orthodox, 1.4 per cent. Other (7.9 per cent).
Languages: Polish.
Political Parties: Solidarity Electoral Action (SEA); Polish Peasant Party (PPP); Democratic Left Alliance (DLA); Work Union; Reform Support Block; Movement for the Reconstruction of Poland (MRP).
Social Organizations: Central Council of Trade Unions; Central Union of Agricultural Groups; Solidarity.

THE STATE

Official Name: Polska Rzeczpospolita.
Administrative Divisions: 49 provinces.
Capital: Warsaw (Warzawa), 1,638,300 people (1996).
Other cities: Lódz, 825,000 people; Kraków, 745,000; Wroclaw, 643,600; Poznan, 589,700 (1996).
Government: Aleksander Kwasniewski, Head of State and President since 1995. Jerzy Buzec, Prime Minister since 1997. Legislature, bicameral: Senate and *Sejm*, whose members are elected every four years.
National Holiday: July 22.
Armed Forces: 248,600 (1996).
Other: 23,400 Border Guard, Police, Coast Guard.

formal support. In a secret agreement, the USSR and Germany divided the Polish territory once more. On September 1 1939, Germany invaded Poland.

[26] Britain and France declared war on Germany. On September 17, the USSR also invaded Poland. In the occupied territories millions of Poles died, especially Jews, some of whom were taken to German concentration camps, many others starved or were executed.

[27] The Polish government-in-exile led the resistance. A military contingent fought on the western front, while the Home Army staged subversive acts. After the German invasion, the USSR

accepted the creation of a Polish army under its jurisdiction.

[28] The Soviet counter-offensive modified relations with Poland. The government-in-exile demanded an inquiry into the murders of Polish officers, and the USSR broke diplomatic relations. The Red Army invaded Poland and re-established military occupation.

[29] After the defeat of Germany, the allies gathered at Malta and agreed on a Provisional Polish Government of National Unity (made up by representatives from pro-Soviet and exile groups) which was to call elections. The government was dominated by the Polish Workers' Party.

[30] In 1945 the provisional

government and the USSR signed an agreement establishing the Polish eastern border, along the Curso line. The same year, the allies fixed the eastern border, along the Oder-Neisse line of Lusetia.

[31] The Polish Workers' Party and the Socialist Party of Poland constituted the Polish United Workers' Party (PUWP). The Polish Peasants' Party disintegrated, and elections were postponed.

[32] The PUWP governed the country, modelling itself on the Soviet Communist Party (CPSU) in the USSR. Industry and commerce were nationalized, the State built great steel and metal works, and forcibly collectivized agriculture. Women were incorporated into the workforce.

[33] The denunciation of Stalin's crimes during the 20th Congress of the CPSU, in 1956, had repercussions on the PUWP. In November of that year Wladyslaw Gomulka was elected party first secretary and promised to take a "Polish path towards socialism". Gomulka freed Cardinal Stefan Wyszynski, who was the head of the Catholic Church, and stirred up popular expectations.

[34] In 1968, action taken by an anti-Semitic group within the PUWP forced Jewish groups to leave the country. In a treaty signed in 1970, West Germany recognized the Polish borders established after the war. East Germany had done so in 1950.

[35] In 1970, strikes broke out because of a staggering increase in prices. The government ordered the army to open fire on the workers and started another crisis within the PUWP. Gomulka was replaced by Edward Gierek, but the regime underwent renewed crises, over corruption charges and internal fights within the party.

[36] In 1976, new strikes broke out, and this time they were repressed not by the use of firearms but by long prison sentences. In 1979, the Polish pope John Paul II visited his native land rekindling the hopes of the population, who welcomed him at massive gatherings.

[37] The 1980 strike at Gdansk's Lenin Dockyard was led by Lech Walesa. It turned into a general strike and the government had to negotiate with the strikers. Two

STATISTICS

DEMOGRAPHY
Population: 38,601,000 (1996). **Annual growth:** 0.5% (1980/1996). **Estimates for year 2000:** 39,000,000. **Annual growth to year 2000:** 0.1% (1994/2000). **Urban Population:** 64.0% (1996). **Urban growth:** 1.24% (1980/95). **Children per woman:** 1.7 (1996).

HEALTH
Life expectancy at birth: 71 years (1996). male: 67 years (1994). female: 76 years (1994). **Infant mortality:** 12 per 1,000 (1996). **Under-5 child mortality:** 14 per 1,000 (1996). **Calorie consumption:** 131% (1988/90). 467 **people per doctor** (1988/91).

EDUCATION
Literacy: male: 99% (1995). female: 98% (1995). **School enrolment:** Primary total: 99% (1990/95). male: 100% (1990/95). female: 98% (1990/95). Secondary: male: 95% (1990/95). female: 96% (1990/95). Tertiary: 27% (1995). **Primary school teachers:** one for every 16 students (1995).

COMMUNICATIONS
140 **newspapers**, 441 **radios**, 300 **TV sets** and 131 **main telephone lines** per 1,000 people (1994). **Books:** 28 new titles per 100,000 people (1992/94).

ECONOMY
Per capita, GNP: $ 3,230 (1996). **Annual growth, GNP:** 6.2% (1995/96). **Annual inflation:** 91.77% (1985/95). **Consumer price index:** 435.6 (1994). **Currency:** 2.47 zlotys = $ 1 (1995) **Cereal imports:** 505 metric tons (1994). **Food import dependency:**% (1994). **Fertilizer use:** 975 kgs per ha (1994). **Exports:** $ 24,387 million (1996). Imports: $ 37,092 million (1996). **External debt:** $ 40,895 million (1996). $ 1,059 **per capita:** (1996). **Debt service:** 6.4% of exports (1996). Development aid received: $ million (1995). $ per capita (1995).% of GNP (1994).

ENERGY
Consumption: 2,400.83 Kgs of Oil equivalent per capita yearly (1994). -2.05% imported (1994).

HDI (rank / value) 58 / 0.834 (1994)

Foreign Trade
MILLIONS $ 1996
IMPORTS
37,092
EXPORTS
24,387

External Debt
1996
PER CAPITA
$1,059

[45] In December 1990, the first direct presidential elections were held, and Lech Walesa was elected head of State with 75 per cent of the vote. In August 1991, new prime minister Jan Krysztof Bielecki resigned, upsetting the precarious balance of political transition. The former Communist party and a small peasant party were ready to accept his resignation, but Walesa backed the prime minister and insisted on giving him special powers, by threatening to dissolve the Diet.

[46] In December 1991, the new Diet appointed Jan Olszewski as Prime Minister. He was accepted by President Walesa three days later, but the cabinet was not ratified by the Diet until December 23, and then only by a narrow margin of 17 votes.

[47] As of November 1991, Poland has been the twenty-sixth member country of the European Council, a Western European organization which also includes Turkey, Czechoslovakia, and Hungary.

[48] On January 13 1992, there was a general strike; it lasted for one hour and was the first since the non-Communist Government took office. Solidarity called the strike to protest against the non negotiated rises in the price of electricity, gas, and municipal heating.

[49] At the end of May, President Walesa asked the Sjem to form a new Government because of a lack of confidence in Olszewski. In mid-July Parliament accepted Walesa's proposal and appointed Hanna Suchocka Prime Minister, supported by a 7 party coalition.

[50] Suchocka applied strict monetary controls and promoted the privatization of approximately 600 state enterprises with a privatizations act in August 1992. Meanwhile, in February 1993 Walesa made the provocative decision to revoke, under pressure from the Church, the law which instituted the right to abortion.

[51] Dissatisfied with Suchocka's social policies, Solidarity sponsored a motion censuring the government, finally passed by a one-vote difference, forcing the prime minister to call early legislative elections.

[52] Elections were held in September and led to the return to power of the political sectors which had supported the communist regime: the Democratic Left Alliance (SLD) and the Polish Peasants' Party (PSL), winning 73 of the 100 seats.

[53] Initially refusing to acknowledge the defeat, Walesa appointed PSL leader Waldemar Pawlack as Prime Minister. Although 1994 featured constant conflicts between the President and the Government, the latter did not significantly modify the economic liberalization policy, despite its attempt to slow the pace of some reforms in order to reduce its social impact.

[54] The former communists' return to power was concluded in November 1995 when Aleksander Kwasniewski defeated Walesa in the second round of presidential elections, with 52 per cent of the vote. The outgoing president had based his election campaign on anti-communism and the support of "Christian values", insisting on the need to maintain the ban on abortion.

[55] At first, the government of Prime Minister Josef Olesky, which replaced Pawlak, was not modified. However, in January 1996, Olesky (former Communist), was forced to resign after the Interior minister accused him of having been a collaborator of Soviet KGB. The following month, Olesky was replaced by Wlodzimierz Cimoszweicz.

[56] Right-wing factions of several parties, unified by the notion of a conservative social policy and anti-communism, formed a coalition headed by Marian Krzaklewski, called Solidarity Electoral Action (SEA).

[57] In the 1997 parliamentary elections, the SEA defeated the ruling Democratic Left Alliance, with 33.8 per cent of the vote. Jerzy Buzek, a chemical engineer from Silesia, who designed the SEA's economic program, was named Prime Minister.

[58] Although in 1997 the economy grew (7 per cent) for sixth year in a row, it was estimated the expansion of local demand was due to a proliferation of credit agencies.

[59] Poland's intention to join the European Union was debated during 1998, especially regarding the modernization of agriculture (one of the EU's requirements), and the use that would be given to the subsidies received.

months later, the government was forced to recognize Solidarity, a workers' union with 10 million members. Rural Solidarity was created, to represent three million peasants.

[38] The PUWP suffered other crises that led to the appointment of Wojciech Jaruzelski, the then prime minister, to the post of party first secretary. In December 1981, Jaruzelski declared martial law, Solidarity was banned and its leaders went underground.

[39] Martial law was lifted in 1983, but the Constitution was modified to include a state of emergency. With the Catholic Church acting as a mediator, the government and Solidarity representatives went back to negotiations in 1989, while the USSR was starting its "perestroika" (restructuring).

[40] In the elections in June of that year, the PUWP only obtained the fixed number of representatives that had been agreed on during the negotiations with the opposition. Solidarity rejected General Jaruzelski's proposal to share government with the PUWP. Tadensz Mazowiecki, a journalist and a moderate member of Solidarity, was appointed the first president of a non-communist government in the East European bloc.

[41] Poland re-established diplomatic relations with the Vatican and with Israel. The United States and Germany committed themselves to financial assistance. German reunification caused some alarm, but the Four-Plus-Two negotiations (see Germany) ratified the postwar Polish borders.

[42] In December 1989, the National Assembly approved the reinstating of the name, the Republic of Poland. In January 1990, the PUWP was dissolved to create another party, but it later split into the Social Democracy of the Republic of Poland and the Polish Social Democratic Union.

[43] In January 1990, the government started an economic adjustment programme agreed to with the International Monetary Fund. Poland requested its incorporation to the Council of Europe and established relations with the European Economic Community. The United States and the Council of Europe made entry to NATO dependent on the results of the economic reforms under way.

[44] On May 10 1990, the first strike was held against Mazowiecki's government. This exercise of power hastened the fragmentation of Solidarity. The union became a political party in July 1990, and later divided into several factions.

Portugal

Portugal

Population: 9,808,000 (1996)
Area: 91,982 SQ KM
Capital: Lisbon

Currency: Escudo
Language: Portuguese

In ancient times Portugal was inhabited by Lusitanians, an Iberian tribe whose cultural influence extended over a vast area including the whole western shore of the Iberian Peninsula. This area was successively conquered by several Middle Eastern peoples, who only occupied the coastal areas.

2   During the 2nd century BC the Romans settled in the territory, ruling over it until the fall of the Empire around the 5th century AD. Like the rest of Europe, Portugal was invaded by Northern European peoples, generically called Barbarians, who raided the Roman dominions. Among these peoples were the Visigoths. They had a developed culture and settled on the Iberian Peninsula dividing the territory into various kingdoms, and spreading the Christian faith. Their domination over the whole region lasted for nearly six centuries.

3   In the 8th century AD Arab peoples invaded the region imposing their political and cultural domination in spite of resistance from the earlier inhabitants.

4   During the 11th century the reconquest of the Lusitanian territory started, ending with the expulsion of the Arabs a hundred years later. With Muslim domination over, the territory was politically unified and Portugal entered a period of great economic prosperity. This reached its height during the 15th and 16th centuries, with great maritime expeditions and conquests of vast territories in America, Africa, and the Far East.

5   Its maritime superiority enabled Portugal to develop active worldwide trade and achieve a privileged economic position within Europe. A long time elapsed before other nations like Britain and the Netherlands were in a position to threaten Portugal's naval supremacy.

6   Following a series of dynastic stuggles, the country was made subject to Philip II, King of Spain. The two kingdoms remained united until 1688 when Portugal succeeded in having its independence recognized in the Treaty of Lisbon. Unity with Spain brought the decline of Portugal's power. Most of the maritime empire collapsed, besieged by the British and the Dutch, who started to control most of the trading routes and outposts.

7   By the time Portugal recovered its independence, it had been devastated by three decades of war against Spain. The country was forced to look on while the new maritime powers seized most of its colonies in Africa and Asia. Brazil meanwhile remained under Portuguese rule. The position of Britain as the leading maritime power became painfully obvious when Portugal was forced to sign the Treaty of Methuen, which established Portugal's political and economic dependence on the British. Pombal, an adviser of Jose I, carried out economic reforms. Like the Spanish Bourbons, Pombal had been influenced by the ideas of the French Enlightment and he changed colonial management. The discovery and exploitation of gold mines in Brazil enabled the country to enjoy a period of great economic prosperity. But in spite of Pombal, Portugal finally went into decline.

8   Dependence on Britain was further consolidated when Portugal was forced to seek support to end Napoleonic occupation, which lasted from 1807 to 1811 French domination led to the independence of Brazil; the Portuguese court had fled there in exile. Brazil had enjoyed a significant expansion in trade, in particular with Britain. At the end of the Napoleonic period in Europe, the rising Brazilian bourgeoisie was not ready to be displaced, so in 1821 Brazil declared independence. Meanwhile a civil war broke out in Portugal between those who wanted the restoration of absolutism and liberal groups preferring greater political participation.

9   The economy of the country maintained its traditional agrarian structure. Other countries were embarking on an accelerated industrialization process which would quickly give them economic eminence. Portugal reached the end of the 19th century economically stagnant, deprived of the richest and largest part of its colonial empire, and suffering from acute internal political crisis.

10   The monarchy was incapable of ensuring the stability needed to start economic recovery, and was definitively overthrown by liberal opposition forces in 1910. This started the Republican period. Once they had attained their objective, the alliance of Liberal and Republican groups started to fragment and internal differences prevented them from achieving a common governmental agenda. One of the few things they shared was active opposition to the Church, which had been a traditional ally of the ancien regime and had important privileges and powers, including the control of education. The inefficiency of the Liberals, together with the ruthless persecution of representatives of the ancien regime, encouraged the formation of a vast opposition movement.

11   Portugal sided with Britain in World War I. This only deepened the economic crisis and

UNEMPLOYMENT 7.2% (1996)

Labour force %

■ WOMEN
□ MEN

43   57

■ AGRICULTURE   18% (1990)
□ INDUSTRIAL   34%
■ SERVICES   48%

LAND USE

IRRIGATED 26.7% of arable

(1993)

■ FOREST & WOODLAND 35.7%
□ ARABLE   25.5%
■ OTHER   38.8%

IMPORTS
33,979
EXPORTS
23,184

PER 100,000
LIVE BIRTHS

15

PROFILE

ENVIRONMENT
The country includes the Iberian continental territory and the islands of the Azores and Madeira archipelagos. The Tagus, the country's largest river, divides the continental region into two separate areas. The northern region is mountainous, with abundant rains and intensive agriculture: wheat, corn, vines and olives are grown. In the valley of the Douro, the major wine-growing region in the country, large vinyards extend in terraces along the valley slopes. The city of Oporto is the northern economic center. The South, Alentejo, with extensive low plateaus and a very dry climate, has large wheat and olive plantations and sheep farming. The cork tree woods, which made Portugal a great cork producer, are found here. Fishing and shipbuilding are major contributors to the country's economy. Mineral resources include pyrite, tungsten, coal and iron. The effects of erosion are accentuated by the poor quality of the soil. Air pollution levels are significant in urban areas, or near cellulose and cement factories.

SOCIETY
Peoples: The Portuguese (99.5 per cent) came from the integration of various ethnic groups: Celts, Arabs, Berbers, Phoenicians, Carthaginians and others. Immigrants come from Africa (0.2 per cent) and America (Brazilians 0.1 per cent, US Americans 0.1 per cent). There is a great migration of Portuguese towards richer countries in the continent.
Religions: Mainly Catholic.
Language: Portuguese.
Political Parties: The center-right Social Democratic Party; the center-left Socialist Party; the Communist Party; the Center Democratic Party, affiliated to the European Union of Christian Democrats. **Other minor parties:** the right Popular Party; the National Solidarity Party, the Revolutionary Socialist Party; the Greens, ecological; the People's Monarchist Party; and the Democratic Renewal Party.
Social Organizations: The General Confederation of Portuguese Workers (CGTP), a nation-wide multi-union organization with 287 union members (represents 80 per cent of the organized workers); the General Union of Portuguese Workers (UGTP), which combines 50 unions.

THE STATE
Official Name: República Portuguesa.
Administrative Divisions: 18 districts, 2 autonomous regions.
Capital: Lisbon, 2,300,000 people (1994).
Other cities: Oporto 309,500 people; Vila Nova de Gaia 247,500; Amadora 176,100 (1991).
Government: Jorge Sampaio, President of the Republic since March 1996. Antonio Guterres, Prime Minister since 1995. Legislative power is exercised by a unicameral Assembly, made up of 230 members elected for 4-year terms, through universal suffrage.
National holiday: April 25, Liberty Day. December 1, Restoration of Independence.
Armed Forces: 54,200 (1995). **Other:** 20,900 Republican National Guard; 20,000 Public Security Police; 8,900 Border Security Guard.

increased popular discontent. Political instability and economic stagnation are the most salient features of the period. In 1926 this led to a coup bringing a right-wing military group to power. They set up an authoritarian corporatist regime which they called the "New State". With a few changes, it was to rule the country for over 40 years. Political opposition was proscribed, with major figures imprisoned or exiled. Trade unions were dissolved and replaced by corporatist organizations similar to those in fascist Italy.

[12] The most significant figure of this period and the true ruler behind the military was economist Antonio de Oliveira Salazar, who occupied various positions and dominated Portuguese political and economic life. The country remained neutral during the Spanish Civil War and World War II which could both have jeopardized the country's barely stable economy.

[13] The agricultural system remained unchanged throughout the whole period, causing much migration towards the major cities of Portugal and Europe. During the 1950s the decolonization movement started, and the country was faced with the possibility of losing its last dominions in Africa. From that moment on, Salazar's regime fought against the liberation movements emerging in the Portuguese colonies, becoming increasingly isolated from other countries and unpopular at home.

[14] The human and economic cost of these colonial wars accelerated the internal attrition of Salazar's government. Repressive measures had to be increased to halt the growing opposition. Salazar's death in 1970 and the deepening of the economic crisis showed that the end of the regime was close at hand.

[15] In 1974, amidst the opposition of many social groups and political parties, a significant number of dissatisfied army officers gathered under the Armed Forces Movement (Movimento das Forças Armadas-MFA). In April, they staged a coup intending to end the wars in Africa and start the democratization process.

[16] The military government which emerged from the «Revolution of the Carnations» or «Captains' Revolution» had vast popular support. This support came out as active encouragement of the progressive tendencies within the MFA. The new government quickly decolonized Angola, Mozambique, and Guinea-Bissau. Meanwhile it actively sought international recognition and attempted to improve the country's image abroad. It legalized left-wing political parties, decreed an amnesty for political prisoners, and passed a series of land laws aiming at breaking up large rural estates and modernizing agricultural production.

[17] The Socialist and Communist parties were the main supporters of the new regime, but after a year in office, their alliance began to break up. This slowed down the political democratization of the country which had been started in April 1974. In the 1976 general elections, the Socialist Party led by Mario Soares won the majority vote to become Portugal's first democratic constitutional government in the 20th century.

[18] The continuing economic crisis, together with strong political and trade union opposition, wore the Socialist Government down very quickly. This situation was aggravated by Mario Soares' harsh economic adjustment programme.

[19] During the 1980s the transition process continued. The electorate approved a new constitution and eliminated all the special bodies created under military rule. Portugal's foreign policy changed, and the country underwent speedy economic and political integration with Europe, including incorporation in NATO and the EEC, in 1986. That year, the Socialist Party lost power again, this time to its one-time ally the centre-left Social Democratic Party (PSD).

[20] By the end of the 1980s the country was experiencing significant economic growth, but still far below the average level for the rest of Europe. Changes accelerated after the electoral victory of the PSD, which used its ample parliamentary majority to liberalize the economy. The new economic policy received strong opposition, particularly from the workers in the public sector, who make up 5 per cent of the country's active labour force and who saw the PSD's reforms as a threat to their jobs.

[21] The trade union movement brought the country to a complete or partial standstill on several occasions. It opposed the privatization of public companies, the elimination of labor legislation enacted during the 1974 revolution, and the attempt

to repeal the 1974 land reform legislation. In 1984 an extreme left-wing group, called the Popular Forces of April 25 (FP-25), also started to take action against these measures. The group, which had been very active in recent years, demanded that the parties in power respect the achievements of the «Revolution of the Carnations».

[22] In April 1987, the governments of Portugal and the People's Republic of China signed an agreement charging Portugal with the administration of Macau until 1999. Sovereignty is then transferred to China, under the "one country, two systems" principle (see Macau).

[23] In 1988, after over a month of negotiations, the PSD and the Socialist Party agreed to modify the constitution to allow the re-privatization of various companies nationalized during the "Revolution of the Carnations" and to further reduce presidential powers. President Mario Soares, former leader of the Socialist Party, opposed these reforms.

[24] Portuguese politics became polarized between the ruling PSD and the PS. The latter was a more viable left-wing alternative after the collapse of real socialism. However, in the October 1991 parliamentary elections, the PSD won over 50 per cent of the vote while the PS did not reach 30 per cent. Cavaco Silva's political victory was due to the social democratic slant with which he disguised his orthodox liberal economic orientation. The right-wing Social Democratic Center received a mere four per cent which led its leader Diego Freitas do Amaral to resign. Support for the Communist Party dropped 3 per cent since 1987.

[25] In January 1992, Portugal took over the presidency of the European Community. The new President, Luis Mira de Amaral, Portuguese minister of industry and energy, announced he would promote industrial cooperation with Latin America, Africa and central Europe. Another of his priorities was the signing of the Maastricht Treaty which entailed political, economic and monetary union between the members of the Community.

[26] In August 1993, the Assembly restricted the right to seek asylum and enabled the expulsion of foreigners from the country. The legislation was based on the defence of the job market and was opposed by President Soares. Unemployment reached eight per cent but it was set to increase with the privatization or closing of state-run airlines, shipyards and steel industries.

[27] Meanwhile a plan financed by the European Union was approved for the 1993-1997 period for the poorest members, including Portugal, providing investment in education, transport, industrial reconversion and job creation.

[28] Portugal's population numbered 10 million in 1993, with 4 million workers abroad.

[29] Portuguese politics were rocked by intense student protests against the cost and quality of education, and by strikes for higher wages in the public sector. The 50 per cent increase in the toll charged at Lisbon's access bridge cause several blockades by transport workers. The Government justified the raise citing the need to finance a new bridge for the last World Expo of the century, to be held in 1998.

[30] The equilibrium between socialist President Mario Soares and centre-right Prime Minister Cavaco Silva was broken. Soares denounced the excessive power in the hands of the Prime Minister and warned about the dangers of a "dictatorship of the majority". Prior to the elections, the PSD privatized 28 per cent of Portugal Telecom and 40 per cent of Portucel Industrial.

[31] The October 1995 general elections were won by the Socialist Party which gained an absolute majority at the Assembly. Antonio Guerres was appointed Prime Minister, replacing Anibal Cavaco. After 10 years of PSD dominance, oriented toward European integration and economic liberalism, the PS capitalized on domestic discontent with education and health and assured the financial market it would not interfere with the goals regarding monetary union and privatization.

STATISTICS

DEMOGRAPHY
Population: 9,808,000 (1996). **Annual growth:** 0% (1980/1996). **Estimates for year 2000:** 9,800,000. **Annual growth to year 2000:** -0.1% (1994/2000). **Urban Population:** 36.0% (1996). **Urban growth:** 1.29% (1980/95). **Children per woman:** 1.5 (1996).

HEALTH
Life expectancy at birth: 75 years (1996). male: 71 years (1994). female: 78 years (1994). **Infant mortality:** 7 per 1,000 (1996). **Under-5 child mortality:** 7 per 1,000 (1996). **Calorie consumption:** 136% (1988/90). 352 **people per doctor** (1988/91).

EDUCATION
Literacy: 90% (1995). male : 92% (1995). female: 87% (1995). **School enrolment :** Primary total: 117% (1990/95). male : 122% (1990/95). female: 118% (1990/95). Secondary: male : 63% (1990/95). female: 74% (1990/95). Tertiary: 34% (1995). **Primary school teachers:** one for every 12 students (1995).

COMMUNICATIONS
40 **newspapers**, 233 **radios**, 230 **TV sets** and 348 **main telephone lines** per 1,000 people (1994). **Books:** 68 new titles per 100,000 people (1992/94).

ECONOMY
Per capita, GNP: $ 10,160 (1996). **Annual growth, GNP:** 2.4% (1995/96). **Annual inflation:** 11.23% (1985/95). **Consumer price index:** 122.1 (1994). **Currency:** 149.41 escudos = $ 1 (1995) **Cereal imports:** 2,351 metric tons (1994). **Fertilizer use:** 875 kgs per ha (1994). **Exports:** $ 23,184 million (1996). **Imports:** $ 33,979 million (1996).

ENERGY
Consumption: 1,826.90 Kgs of Oil equivalent per capita yearly (1994). 88.39% imported (1994).

HDI (rank / value) 31 / 0.89 (1994)

[32] The Socialist Jorge Sampaio took over the presidency of the country in March 1996, after winning the elections with 54 per cent of the vote, against the 46 per cent of former prime minister Cavaco Silva. The Government brought in an economic plan in line with European Union demands, particularly regarding to the budget deficit.

[33] A successful campaign against tax evasion meant increased spending on health, education and social policies. The privatisation programme was intensified, selling shares in telecommunications, electricity and roads. Unemployment fell to 6.7 per cent of the active population.

[34] The Socialist Party triumphed in the December 1997 municipal elections, maintaining control over the main cities, Lisbon and Oporto, and beating the conservative Social Democratic Party by an overall margin of five points (38.2 to 33.1 per cent).

[35] In February 1998, Parliament approved a law legalizing abortion for up to 10 weeks of pregnancy. Various estimates showed there were around 16,000 illegal abortions carried out each year.

Puerto Rico

Puerto Rico

Population: 3,736,000 (1996)
Area: 8,897 SQ KM
Capital: San Juan

Currency: US Dollar
Language: Spanish and English

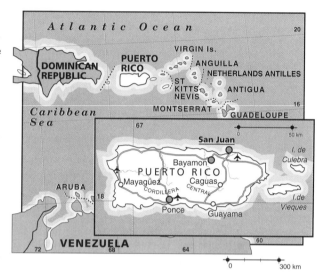

In 1508, fifteen years after Christopher Columbus had arrived on the Caribbean island of Borinquen, that territory came under colonial domination, a status which remains unchanged to this day. Due to its strategic location at the entrance of the Caribbean - Puerto Rico is the easternmost of the Greater Antilles - the island suffered 400 years of Spanish rule, as it also reeled under repeated attacks of pirates and regular naval forces, whether British, Dutch or French, plus US administration after the Spanish-American War of 1898.

[2] In the first few decades of the 16th century, a sugar-based economy began to take shape. By some estimates, by 1560 there were already 15,000 slaves on the island. This was however a short-lived period in the island's history: in the latter part of the century leather became the principal product, a repetition of what had occurred some time before in Santo Domingo.

[3] As in neighboring islands, the native Taino people were exterminated by war, disease and overwork. African slaves were brought in to take their place in the fields where most food supplies for Spanish expeditions into the mainland were produced. Thus, Puerto Rican culture is a blend of its African and Spanish heritage.

[4] Spanish rule was continually challenged by external attacks and rebellions by both the Tainos and enslaved African workers. The latter rebelled successively in 1822, 1826, 1843, and 1848. The struggle for independence in the rest of Latin America had its counterpart in Puerto Rico's struggle for administrative reform (1812-1840), but Spanish troops ruthlessly stifled the uprising.

[5] In 1868, five years before slavery was finally abolished, a group of patriots led by Ramón Emeterio Betances moved things a step nearer to liberation. In the town of Lares they proclaimed Puerto Rico's independence and took up arms to free the island. Despite their defeat, the Lares revolt signalled the birth of the Puerto Rican nation.

[6] The independence movement continued to gain strength in the following years. In 1897, the Cubans were already up in arms led by José Martí in a movement that reached Puerto Rico. US military intervention in the war against Spain, in 1898 hastened European defeat but for Puerto Rico it only meant the imposition of a new ruler.

[7] US colonial administrations, first military and then civilian, imposed English as the official language and attempted to turn the island into a sugar plantation and a military base. Puerto Ricans were made US citizens in 1917, though they were given no participation in the island's government. As a result, resistance to colonial rule continued to increase in strength. In 1922 the pro-independence Nationalist Party (PN) was founded. PN-led uprisings in 1930 and 1950 were fiercely put down.

[8] The PN leader from 1930 until his death in 1965 was Pedro Albizu Campos, who suffered exile and imprisonment for his anticolonial activities.

[9] In 1947, intense internal and international pressure forced the US to allow Puerto Rico to elect its own governor. The 1948 elections gave the post to Luis Muñoz Marín, leader of the Popular Democratic Party (PPD), who favored turning the country into a self-governing, commonwealth, or free associated state. The US Government authorized the drafting of a constitution in 1959, which was approved by a plebiscite and later ratified by the US. Muñoz Marín's program was thus sanctioned.

[10] Commonwealth status, still in effect today, leaves defence, financial affairs and foreign relations to Washington, while maintaining common citizenship and currency, as well as free access to the US for Puerto Ricans and vice versa.

[11] With the institution of Commonwealth status, US administrations were freed from the obligation of reporting on Puerto Rico's status to the UN Decolonization Committee. Moreover, in this way the UN tacitly endorsed the arrangement declaring the "end" of colonial rule. Nevertheless, in September 1978, the Decolonization Commission reconsidered the situation, and in December of the same year a UN General Assembly resolution defined Puerto Rico as a colony once again and demanded self-determination for its people.

[12] During World War II, Puerto Rico was again turned into a military garrison for controlling the Caribbean. The US built seven bases on the island.

[13] Muñoz Marín promoted industrialization on the island, through massive US private investment enticed by government tax incentives. During the 1960s, Puerto Rican agriculture was destroyed and farmers uprooted by an influx of US products, resulting in over 50 per cent of the island's food being imported. The newly-formed labor reserve was more than enough to supply cheap hands for the growing US corporate community, and Puerto Ricans soon began migrating en masse to the US, and especially to New York in search of work. The 1980 US census registered over two million Puerto Ricans living in the United States.

[14] With the great social upheavals of the 1960s, the struggle for independence flowered anew on the island. Despite the revival of the independence movement, a 1967 plebiscite confirmed the Commonwealth. Moreover, elections the following year gave the governorship to the New Progressive Party (PNP) which favored making the island the 51st state of the US. Nevertheless after the 1972 elections the PPD returned to power led by Rafael Hernández Colón. In 1976, supporters of the US statehood option returned to the governorship. Carlos Romero Barceló announced that if he was re-elected for a second term, he would call a pro-statehood referendum. Barceló went on to win in 1980, but by such a slim margin that plans for a statehood plebiscite were abandoned, despite encouragement from President Reagan.

[15] Puerto Rico has one representative in the US Congress, but with no voting rights other than in committees. US citizenship only gave Puerto Ricans the right to participate in the 1980 presidential elections, although residents in the US are able to vote in all elections.

[16] Rafael Hernández Colón was

WORKERS

UNEMPLOYMENT 13.4% (1996)

Labour force %

■ WOMEN
□ MEN

36   64

PROFILE

ENVIRONMENT

The smallest and easternmost island of the Greater Antilles. A central mountain range, covered with rainforests, runs across the island. In the highlands, subsistence crops are grown (corn, manioc); on the western slopes there are large coffee plantations and in the central region small tobacco farms. On the northern slopes citrus and pineapples are grown, exported to the United States. The main crop is sugar cane which uses the best farmlands along the coastline. The islands of Vieques (43 sq km), Mona (40 sq km) and Culebra also belong to Puerto Rico.

SOCIETY

Peoples: Most Puerto Ricans are descendants of African slave workers (20 per cent) and Spanish colonizers (80 per cent). In addition, about 3 million Puerto Ricans have emigrated to the United States to escape unemployment and poverty.
Religions: No official religion. Catholics (85.3 per cent), Protestants (4.7 per cent), others (10 per cent).
Languages: Spanish and English (both official); with the United States, English is used. Compulsory introduction of English in education, administration and communications was supported when in 1993 it was declared joint official language together with Spanish.
Political Parties: the New Progressive Party (PNP), led by Pedro Rosselló, advocates total integration to the United States as the 51st state of the Union; the Democratic People's Party (PPD), founded in 1938 by Luis Muñoz Marín, supports the current "Commonwealth" status; the Puerto Rican Renewal Party (PRP), a split of the PNP; the Puerto Rican Independence Party (PI), founded in 1946 from a breakup of the PPD, Social-democrat; the Communist Party (PC), founded in 1934, had intense activity which lost momentum following a strong repression in the 1950s; Puerto Rican Socialist Party (PSP), founded in 1971.

THE STATE

Official Name: Estado Libre Asociado de Puerto Rico.
Capital: San Juan, 1,085,000 people (1980).
Other cities: Ponce, 159,151 people; Bayamon, 196,206; Caguas, 92,429 (1990).
Government: Pedro Rosselló, Governor, in office January 1993, re-elected in January 1997.
National Holiday: September 23, the Battle of Grito de Lares (start of the anti-colonial armed revolt in 1868).
Armed Forces: 3.518 troops of the US Army (1992).

STATISTICS

DEMOGRAPHY
Population: 3,736,000 (1996)
Urban population: 73.7 % (1996)

ECONOMY
Consumer price index: 113.0 (1994)

In 1989 the Special United Nations Decolonization Committee expressed its wish that the people of Puerto Rico exercise their right to self-determination and independence.

elected President on November 6 1984. He promised a "four-year term of struggle against corruption and unemployment". He renewed Puerto Rico's Commonwealth status thus rejecting his predecessor's intention to integrate into the Union.

[17] Hernández Colón was re-elected in November 1988, with 48.7 per cent of the vote, against 45.8 per cent for those in favor of annexation by the United States, and 5.3 per cent for those who favored independence.

[18] In 1989 the Special United Nations Decolonization Committee expressed its wish that the people of Puerto Rico exercise their right to self-determination and independence. The resolution stressed the "clearly Latin American character and identity of Puerto Rico's people and culture".

[19] In April 1991, Governor Hernández Colón passed a law granting official status for the Spanish language. A few weeks later, the Puerto Rican people were granted the Prince of Asturias award by the Spanish crown, "in recognition of the country's efforts to defend the Spanish language".

[20] In the plebiscite carried out late in 1991, various strategies were proposed to promote development on the island. The governor succeeded in rallying moderate nationalists and supporters of independence, who campaigned together. They were in favor of self-determination, the end of subjection to US jurisdiction, the affirmation of Puerto Rican identity, regardless of any future referendum decisions, and the maintenance of US citizenship. However, all this effort came to nothing in the polls, when 55 per cent of the voters supported the PNP's position that a break with Washington had to be avoided.

[21] Given this result, Hernández's position within his party was weakened, strengthening the hand of more pro-independence sectors and Hernández finally resigned the Popular Democratic Party leadership.

[22] Pedro Rosselló, a supporter of Puerto Rico's annexation by the United States, was elected governor in 1992. His plan to transform English into the only official language on the island - replacing Spanish - caused massive protest demonstrations. Finally in 1993 English was made an official language alongside Spanish.

[23] In November, a referendum was held to decide on the political future of the island. Those wanting to maintain the "free associated state" status won a narrow victory, with 48.4 per cent of the vote, while the group supporting the transformation of Puerto Rico into the 51st US state took 46.2 per cent. Independence supporters had a mere 4 per cent.

[24] Some pro-independence supporters had agreed to collaborate - in sectors like culture - with the "pro-annexation" cabinet led by the present governor. However, when Rosselló sacked the director of the Puerto Rico Institute of Culture, Awilda Palau, in May 1995, the possibilities of collaboration were reduced.

[25] In 1996, opposition continued to the US Congress decision to grant tax exemptions to companies established in Puerto Rico, as this was the main fiscal instrument for development on the island.

[26] In January 1997, Rosselló was elected for a second term. In a message for the occasion, US President Bill Clinton promised to promote legislation in Congress allowing Puerto Rico to hold a referendum on its future political status.

[27] In February 1998, Clinton went even further, openly supporting a plebiscite for Puerto Rico, allowing the nationals to choose between total incorporation to the United States, independence or maintaining the island as an associated state.

Qatar

Qatar

Population:	558,000 (1996)
Area:	11,000 SQ KM
Capital:	Doha (Ad-Dawhah)
Currency:	Riyals
Language:	Arabic

In a small desert country without a single river, 400 farms are now producing almost all the foodstuffs required for domestic consumption. The miracle that changed the desert into a kitchen garden was the advent of oil revenues. Half a million barrels of oil per day, and the successful policies of Amir Khalifa bin Ath-Thani's government, have helped bring about these achievements.

[2] Like the neighboring island of Bahrain, the Qatar peninsula has participated from ancient times in the active Gulf trade between Mesopotamia and India. Islamized in the 7th century (see Saudi Arabia), at the time of the Caliphate of Baghdad, Qatar had already obtained autonomy which was maintained until 1076 when it was conquered by the Emir of Bahrain.

[3] From the 16th century, after a brief period of Portuguese occupation, the country lived in great prosperity due to the development of pearl fishing attracting immigrants. Settled on the coasts, under the leadership of the Al-Thani family, these settlers succeeded in politically unifying the country in the 18th century, though it remained subject to Bahrain's sovereignty. The process of independence, begun in 1815 by Sheikh Muhammad and his son Jassim, culminated in 1868 with the mediation of the English; the Al-Thanis agreed to end the war in exchange for guaranteed territorial integrity.

[4] The Turkish sultans, nominal sovereigns of the entire Arabian peninsula since the 16th century, did not look favorably upon increasing British penetration in the Gulf. Consequently, they named the reigning sheikh (Jassim Al-Thani) governor of the "province" of Qatar as a pretext to establishing a small military garrison in Dawhah (Doha).

WORKERS

- ■ **AGRICULTURE** 3% (1990)
- ☐ **INDUSTRIAL** 32%
- ▥ **SERVICES** 65%

Neither the Qataris nor the British concerned themselves over this formal affirmation of sovereignty and the garrison remained until World War I without the slightest effect on British influence in the region.

[5] In 1930, the price of pearls dropped with the Japanese flooding the market with a cheaper version of cultivated pearls. Consequently Sheikh Abdullah sold all the country's oil prospecting and exploitation rights, and granted a 75-year lease on its territorial waters, for £400,000. The Anglo-Iranian Oil Co. discovered oil in 1939 but actual production only began after World War II, attracting other companies who purchased parts of the original concession. The immense wealth obtained by the Royal Dutch Shell did not seem to concern Sheikh Ahmad bin Ali Al-Thani as oil and tariff revenues increased his personal fortune by £15 million.

[6] Shortly thereafter, Ahmad was ousted by his own family, who replaced him with his cousin Khalifa, giving him the task of "removing any elements which are opposed to progress and modernization".

[7] Sheikh Khalifa created a Council of Ministers and an Advisory Council to share the responsibilities of his absolute power and promised "a new era of enlightened government, social justice and stability". Redistributing the oil revenues, he exempted all inhabitants from taxation and provided free education and medical attention. His greatest achievement has perhaps been the subsidizing and promotion of productive activities not connected with oil prospecting, activities which were symbolically expressed by the first tomato exports at the beginning of his mandate.

[8] To reduce Qatar's dependency on a single product, the fishing industry was revitalized, industrialization was accelerated with new cement and fertilizer plants, plus iron and steel mills being built. The country took advantage of its strategic position to provide commercial and financial services to the economies of the entire region. In addition, a large part of the country's financial surplus was invested abroad (in Europe and the US). In 1980, estimated income from this "exportation of capital" will eventually equal all oil revenues. In this way Qatar seeks to ensure its future when the oil wells run dry.

[9] As an indispensable element of control, a state oil company, the Qatar Petroleum Producing Authority (QPPA), was set up in 1972 and by February 1977, all foreign oil installations had been expropriated.

[10] Qatar's economic expansion required the large-scale immigration of foreign technical experts and workers (the former being European and American; the latter Iranian, Pakistani, Indian and Palestinian). Estimates as to the actual number of immigrant workers vary widely, since surveys are not taken, but the figure is believed to be approximately 150,000 people, or about 60 per cent of the total population.

[11] To avoid any profound transformation of the local culture, the Government prefer and promote immigration from other Arab countries. Nevertheless, the advanced systems of social security also protect foreign workers. The local Iranian community lived in better conditions than in any other Gulf emirate and, because of this, Qatar had fewer conflicts with the Khomeini regime than any other country in the region.

[12] Adhering to OPEC policy, in 1982 the country decreased crude oil production by 25 per cent. Consequently exports decreased, reflected in a considerable reduction in volume of petrodollars invested in the West, in public spending and in industrial expansion. Nevertheless, Qatar has the infrastructure to face the change. In the industrial center of Umm Said the iron and steel plant was producing 450,000 tons a year at the beginning of the decade. A liquid gas plant is also in full operation and the Government decided to go ahead with a six-billion-dollar natural gas project for use in its energy and desalinization programs.

PROFILE

ENVIRONMENT
The country consists of the Qatar Peninsula, on the eastern coast of the Arabian Peninsula in the Persian Gulf. The land is flat and the climate is hot and dry. Farming is possible only along the coastal strip. The country's main resource is its fabulous oil wealth on the western coast. Qatar suffered the negative effects of the burning oil wells during the Gulf War.

SOCIETY
Peoples: The native Qatari Arab inhabitants account for 20 per cent of the population. Arabs, though, are a majority thanks to Palestinian, Egyptian and Yemenite immigrants, who account for 25 per cent of the population. The remaining 55 per cent are immigrants, mostly from Pakistan, India and Iran.
Religions: Muslim (official and predominant). The majority are Sunni, with Iranian immigrants mainly Shi'a. There are also Christian and Hindu minorities.
Languages: Arabic (official and predominant). Urdu is spoken by Pakistani immigrants, and Farsi by Iranians. English is the business language.
Political Parties: There are no organized political parties.

THE STATE
Official Name: Dawlat Qatar.
Capital: Doha (Ad-Dawhah), 236,131 people (1987).
Other cities: Rayyan, 100,000 people; Wakrah, 26,000; Umm Salal, 12,100 (1987).
Government: Hamad ibn Khalifa ath-Thani, Emir and Head of State since June 1995. Sheikh Abdullah ibn Khalifa ath-Thani, Prime Minister since October 1997. Legislative Power: a Consultative Council with 30 members appointed by the Emir to 3 year-terms.
National Holiday: September 3, Independence Day (1971).
Armed Forces: 11,800 (1996)

STATISTICS

DEMOGRAPHY
Population: 558,000 (1996). **Annual growth**: 5.6% (1980/1996). **Estimates for year 2000**: 600,000. **Annual growth to year 2000**: 1.8% (1994/2000). **Urban Population**: 91.6% (1996). **Urban growth**:% (1980/95). **Children per woman**: 3.9 (1996).

HEALTH
Life expectancy at birth: 71 years (1996). male: 69 years (1994). female: 75 years (1994). **Infant mortality**: 17 per 1,000 (1996). **Under-5 child mortality**: 21 per 1,000 (1996).

EDUCATION
Literacy: 79% (1995). male: 79% (1995). female: 80% (1995). **School enrolment** : Primary total: 87% (1990/95). male : 89% (1990/95). female: 84% (1990/95). Secondary: male : 82% (1990/95). female: 82% (1990/95).

COMMUNICATIONS
150 **newspapers**, 428 **radios**, 430 **TV sets** and 215 **main telephone lines** per 1,000 people (1994). **Books**: 69 new titles per 100,000 people (1992/94).

ECONOMY
Currency: 3.64 riyals = $ 1 (1995) **Cereal imports**: 142 metric tons (1994). **Food import dependency**: 12% (1994). **Fertilizer use**: 7,500 kgs per ha (1994). **Development aid received**: $ 3 million (1995). $ 6 per capita (1995).

ENERGY
Consumption:

HDI (rank / value) 55 / 0.84 (1994)

---

[13] Qatar's geographical position has brought the country both economic benefits and geopolitical worries. Israeli aggression against Lebanon, Syria and Iraq, the lack of solutions to the Palestinian problem, the war between Iran and Iraq and the Reagan administration's frightening interest in the region's "military security" all helped to convince Qatar's rulers of the need to enter new alliances with their neighbors on the Arabian Gulf.

[14] Since 1981, together with Bahrain, Kuwait, Oman, the United Arab Emirates and Saudi Arabia, Qatar has participated in the Gulf Cooperation Council, an organization designed to coordinate the area's policies in political, economic, social, cultural and military issues. Qatar strongly supported Saudi Arabia's stand regarding the need to reduce and, if possible, eliminate US troops stationed in the region, mainly in Oman.

[15] In April 1986, tensions flared between Bahrain and Qatar over the artificial island of Fasht ad-Dibal. This conflict was resolved through negotiations sponsored by members of the Gulf Cooperation Council. In November 1987, the Government renewed diplomatic relations with Egypt.

[16] In March 1991, after the Iraqi invasion of Kuwait, the Gulf Cooperation Council, to which Kuwait and Qatar belong, suspended all economic aid to Jordan and the PLO.

[17] Also in March 1991, the Foreign Ministers of Egypt, Syria, and the six Arab countries which belonged to the Cooperation Council gathered in Riyadh, the capital of Saudi Arabia, to sign an agreement with the US to preserve security in the region. The plan included four points; a common military strategy between the US and the Arab countries in the anti-Iraqi coalition; mechanisms to avoid arms proliferation; acceptance of a peace treaty by Israel; and a new economic program for the development of the region.

[18] During the Gulf War, oil wells set ablaze in Kuwait and Saudi Arabia filled the air over Qatar with thick smoke. Estimated pollution problems include acid rain and climatic disturbances in the area. Health experts stated that burning oil wells cause a high concentration of sulphur dioxide and soot particles that cause asthma and bronchitis, and increase the risk of cancer.

[19] In September 1991, private European companies began exploiting huge gas deposits along the coasts of Qatar.

[20] In December, a group of 53 people, among them some government officials, drew up and signed a petition addressed to the Emir of Qatar, asking for free parliamentary elections, a written constitution and increased personal and political freedoms. As a result, several citizens were arrested and detained in the Doha Central Prison; they were eventually released several months later.

[21] Toward the end of 1992, Qatar and Bahrain became involved in another territorial dispute over several small islands off the coast of the two emirates: Howard Island, and more especially, underground rights to Dibval and Qitat, both potentially rich in oil. Growing tension between the two countries prompted Saudi Arabia to step in and mediate the conflict.

[22] In 1993, the fall in the price of oil in the international market triggered an almost 20 per cent decrease in fiscal income. Furthering his program to develop alternative income sources, in 1994 Doha negotiated new agreements with several Asian companies for the exploitation of natural gas.

[23] In June 1995, heir to the throne Hamad ibn Khalifah ath-Thani overthrew his father to become Emir of Qatar. The new sovereign promised to step up efforts to resolve the territorial disputes with Saudi Arabia and Bahrain. Qatar's membership of the Gulf Cooperation Council was thrown into doubt when its delegation withdrew from a Council meeting in December.

[24] In April 1996, Qatar and Saudi Arabia resolved their territorial disputes on the basis of a previous treaty. A similar dispute between Qatar and Bahrain came to an end in March 1997, when both nations agreed to deal with the issue in the International Courts.

[25] In 1997, Qatar froze relations with Israel, applying the Arab League decision to reactivate the boycott on this country, but offered its capital, Doha, to host the Economic Conference of the Middle East and North Africa, to be held in November, as part of the peace process. In October, Sheikh Abdullah ibn Khalifa ath-Thani was appointed Prime Minister, a post occupied up until then by Emir Hamad.

[26] On March 17 1998, the 25th Conference of Foreign Ministers of the of the Islamic Conference Organization (ICO) closed in Doha. Its resolutions included a call to the Arab states to reconsider relations with Israel. Qatar gratefully received the agreement between Saudi Arabia, Venezuela and Mexico to reduce their respective oil production limits, undertaking to do the same during that year.

[27] In the same month, Qatar and France held joint naval manoeuvres under the title "Pearl Collection II". In April, the Emir signed a military co-operation agreement with Russia, including the exchange of specialists and military training projects.

Réunion

Réunion

Population:	664,000
	(1996)
Area:	2,510 SQ KM
Capital:	Saint Denis
Currency:	French Franc
Language:	French

The island of Réunion was uninhabited until the beginning of the 17th century when Arab explorers arrived and called it Diva Margabin. The Portuguese renamed it Ilha Santa Apolonia and the French settlers called it Bourbon, and after the French Revolution it was given its current name: Réunion.

[2] The island's four renamings reflect the struggle between the colonial powers for possession of this strategically important point in the Indian Ocean. After decades of fighting, the French finally retained colonial rights over Réunion.

[3] The colonial regime replaced subsistence farming with the export commodities of sugar cane and coffee, and the island's fishing resources were depleted because of the over-exploitation of several species.

[4] Since March 1946, Réunion has been considered an Overseas Department by the French Government. The local middle-class and the French colonists supported the integration of the island into French territory. Later, conservative political changes in France brought realignment of political forces on the island.

[5] While sectors tied to colonial interests defended the Department status, the Réunion Communist Party (PCR) changed its stance, and in 1959 campaigned for partial autonomy. The PCR suffered the consequences of its about-face, and for ten years was the sole supporter of gradual independence.

[6] In July 1978, the UN Decolonization Committee issued a pronouncement in favor of full independence for Réunion. The question of independence was now transformed into an international issue.

[7] In 1978, the independence movement made important international contacts in a meeting with other anti-imperialist and anti-colonialist organizations in the Indian Ocean area. At this meeting, a Permanent Liaison Committee was formed in a joint effort against foreign domination. In June 1979, during elections for the European Parliament, Paul Vergés raised the issue of double colonialism, charging that Réunion Island was not only dominated by the French, but forced to serve the interests of the entire European Community.

[8] The production crisis and unemployment were not due to unfavourable climatic conditions (extensive drought, cyclones, etc.) but to the structure of the economy itself. The situation was worsened by the demographic explosion on the island, as the population increased 20 per cent in the last decade.

[9] Disturbances became more frequent, as the social situation deteriorated. In 1991, eight people died in clashes with police, in protest over the closure of the pirate television station Tele Free-DOM, directed by the popular Camille Sudre. Sudre, a Frenchman settled in Reunion, formed a political list in record time and won the regional elections in 1992. Support from the CPR enabled him to become leader of the region, one of the two main executive authorities of the island.

[10] However, the main French administrative tribunal annulled the elections for alleged irregularities and banned Sudre from standing again. In fresh regional elections in 1993, the Free-DOM party, led by Marguerite Sudre, Camille's wife, won again. The brand-new leader formed links with the French right and was appointed minister in the cabinet of the conservative, Edouard Balladur (1993-1995), in Paris.

[11] Unemployment soared in 1996 to an all time high of 40 per cent, and it was estimated to be even higher amongst the young. In 1997, the tension and social discontent erupted in constant demonstrations.

[12] In March 1998, Paul Vergés, the CPR leader was elected head of the Regional Council by 24 votes to the 20 of the right wing Union for French Democracy candidate, Jean-Paul Virapoullé. The outcome was due to the support Marguerite Sudre gave Vergés, who had not achieved the 23 vote majority needed for him to stand in the first round.

PROFILE

ENVIRONMENT
Located in the Indian Ocean, 700 km east of Madagascar, Réunion is a volcanic, mountainous island with a tropical climate, heavy rainfall and numerous rivers. These conditions favor the growth of sugar cane, the main economic activity.

SOCIETY
Peoples: Mostly of African descent (63.5 per cent): Europeans 2.2 per cent; Chinese 2.2 per cent; Indian 28.3 per cent..
Religions: Mainly Catholic (94 per cent). Muslim, Hindu and Buddhist minorities.
Languages: French (official) and Creole.

Political Parties: Free-DOM Movement; Communist Party of Reunion; Union for the Republic (RPR); Union for French Democracy (UDF); Socialist Party.

THE STATE
Official Name: Département d'Outre-Mer de la Réunion.
Administrative Divisions: 5 Arrondisements.
Capital: Saint Denis, 104,454 people (1994).
Other cities: St Paul, 72,000 people, St Pierre 59,000; Le Tampon, 27,300; St. André, 25,237 (1994).
Government: Robert Pommies, Prefect appointed by the French Government in 1996. There are two local councils: the 47-member General Council, and the 45-member Regional Council. The island has 5 representatives and 3 senators in the French parliament.
National Holiday: December 20, Abolition of slavery (1848).
Armed Forces: 4,000 French troops.

DEMOGRAPHY
Population: 664,000 (1996) **Urban population:** 68.3% (1996)

ECONOMY
Consumer price index: 113.5 (1994)
Cereal imports: 189 metric tons (1994)
Fertilizer use: 3,673 kgs per ha (1994)

Romania

România

Population:	22,655,000 (1996)
Area:	238,391 SQ KM
Capital:	Bucharest
Currency:	Lei
Language:	Romanian

The earliest inhabitants of Romania included the Thracians, whose descendants, known as the Getae, established contact with Greek colonies that appeared on the shore of the Black Sea in the 7th century BC. Together with the Dacians, a related people living in the Carpathian Mountains and in Transylvania, the Getae established a distinct society by the 4th century BC.

2   In the first century BC, the Geto-Dacians bitterly resisted conquest by the Romans, who were interested in the region's mineral wealth. Rome finally triumphed over the powerful Dacian kingdom in 106 AD, putting its inhabitants to death or expelling them to the north. According to some Roman sources, most of the males of the conquered area who could not run were put to death or brought to Rome as slaves. However many Dacians ran away from the center of the former kingdom, into vast areas that belonged to the so-called free Dacians, in the north, east and north-east of the Roman province of Dacia.

3   The province was then subdivided into Dacia Superior, Dacia Inferior and Dacia Porolissensis. Emperor Marcus Aurelius abandoned Dacia Superior and Inferior during the period between 271-275. Unwilling to acknowledge before the Senate that he withdrew from such important provinces, he reorganized the province of Moesia Superior at the south of Danube into Dacia Ripensis and Dacia Mediterranea (to keep the name Dacia). The center and east of present Walachia, southern Moldova and Dobrudja were at that time part of the Roman province of Moesia Inferior, which he still occupied. Roman rule left an

enduring legacy on the Romanian language which is derived from Latin. This rule continued in the territory of present Romania until the 7th century, when the Byzantine Empire lost its last northern Danubian strongholds to the migratory peoples.

4   Between the 3rd to the 12th century, the region underwent successive invasions by Germanic peoples, Slavs, Avars, and others. Roman Christianity was brought by Romans during the 2nd and 3rd centuries and spread to the whole region by the 4th century. The Romanian-Bulgarian Empire, which lasted over 200 years, introduced Greek Orthodox Christianity. The Romanian Church adopted the Slavonic language as a result of Bulgarian influence. Towards the end of the 9th century, the Bulgarians were expelled by the Magyars from the Pannonic plains (now Hungary) though they remained in what is today Romania.

5   Transylvania, the cradle of the Romanian nation, was conquered by Hungary during the 10th - 12th century. According to Hungarian sources (Gesta Hungarorum) the existing feudal states in Transylvania put up fierce resistance. The Vlachs from Transylvania reappeared in the 13th century to the south of the Carpathian Mountains, in two separate regions, Walachia and Moldova. Inlanders immediately accepted the newcomers as people with the same origins. The Tatar-Mongol invasion of 1241 produced big losses among the Romanians.

6   The first Romanian state, Walachia, was established south of the Carpathians during the early 14th century and a second, Moldova, was founded in 1349 east of the Carpathians in the Spruth River valley.

7   The principalities of Walachia and Moldova fought for their independence from Hungary, which after conquering Transylvania, tried unsuccessfully to conquer them also. This struggle ended in the first half of the 14th century, when Hungarian invaders were defeated both in Walachia and Moldova. By the 15th century the Ottoman Empire began to be a greater threat.

8   After defeating the Serbs in Kosovo in 1389, the Ottoman Empire began closing in on Walachia, with pressure intensifying after the fall of Bulgaria in 1393. Walachia became a vassal state of Sultan Mehmed I, in 1417, though Prince Mircea maintained the claim to the throne and the Christian religion remained intact. In 1455 Moldova also became a vassal state.

9   King Mircea's death in 1418 was followed by a rapid succession of princes, until the Turks appointed a Romanian prince of their choice to the throne. Walachia put up resistance, but after the Hungarian defeat at the battle of Mohacs in 1526, Turkish domination became inevitable. The Hungarian kingdom disappeared and was transformed by the Ottomans into a Pashalic. The three Romanian principalities, Walachia, Moldova and Transylvania entered into the sphere of influence of the Ottomans, but kept some indigence by paying a tribute in money.

10   In 1594, the Turkish inhabitants of Walachia were massacred by Prince Michael in alliance with Moldova. He went on to invade Turkish territory, taking several key sites along the banks of the Danube. Faced with the collapse of his

counter-offensive, the Sultan had no choice but to recognize the sovereignty of Walachia, which subsequently became linked to Transylvania.

11   In 1600, Michael conquered Moldova, proclaiming himself regent. The Austrian Emperor Rudolf II recognized the claim, although he later tried to take over Transylvania and Moldova. Michael the Brave is a national hero because he was the first and the last to unite the Romanians until the modern reunification in 1918.

12   In the 17th and 18th centuries, Walachia and Moldova fell under Turkish rule again. The sultans did not trust the native Romanian princes, so they named either Greek princes from Romania, or Romanian princes from the Greek quarter in Istanbul, Fanar, to rule Walachia and Moldova. Russia occupied the region in 1769, but Austria forced Russia to return the principalities to the sultan in 1774.

13   Under the Treaty of Bucharest in 1812, Russia retained the southeastern part of Moldova - Bessarabia.

14   The Sultan managed to divide the Romanians and the Greeks by allowing the principalities to pass laws in their own languages and elect native-born princes. Ion Sandu Sturza and Grigore IV Ghica assumed control of the Government of Moldova and Walachia, respectively, and both moved closer to Greece and Russia.

15   Another war broke out between Russia and Turkey in 1828. The following year, the Treaty of Adrianopolis maintained the principalities as tributaries of the

6.2%   54.8%
1995 ■ **DEFENCE** □ **SOCIAL**

In 1990/91 Military as % of health & education expenditure was 25%.

UNEMPLOYMENT 6.7% (1996)

Labour force %

■ WOMEN
□ MEN

44   56

■ AGRICULTURE 24% (1990)
□ INDUSTRIAL 47%
■ SERVICES 29%

PROFILE

ENVIRONMENT

The country is crossed from north to center by the Carpathian Mountains, the western part of which are known as the Transylvanian Alps. The Transylvanian plateau is contained within the arc formed by the Carpathian Mountains. The Moldavian plains extend to the east, while the Walachian plains stretch to the south, crossed by the Danube, which flows into a large delta on the Black Sea. The mountain forests supply raw material for a well developed timber industry. With abundant mineral resources (oil, natural gas, coal, iron ore and bauxite), Romania has begun extensive industrial development. Its economy still depends to a great extent on the export of raw materials and agricultural products. Romania defines itself as a "developing country", and is attuned with Third World demands. It is also one of Europe's largest oil producers. Copsa Mica, in the center of Romania, is considered to be one of the areas with the highest levels of industrial pollution in Europe.

SOCIETY

Peoples: Romanian 89.4 per cent; Hungarian 9 per cent; German 0.5 per cent; Ukrainian, Turkish, Greek and Croatian. These official data do not include Romani, which represented between 5 and 10 per cent of the population, but who usually are considered as Romanian in the census. **Religions:** Mainly Romanian-Orthodox (86.8 per cent). There are Catholic (5 per cent) and Protestant (3.5 per cent) minorities. **Languages:** Romanian (official language, spoken by the majority); ethnic minorities often speak their own languages, particularly Hungarian and Romany. **Political Parties:** Democratic Convention; Social Democrat Union; Hungarian Democratic Union of Romania Party of Social Democracy in Romania. **Social Organizations:** General Confederation of Trade Unions.

THE STATE

Official Name: România. **Administrative Divisions:** 40 Districts and the Municipality of Bucharest. **Capital:** Bucharest, 2,080,000 people (1994). **Other cities:** Timisoara, 327,830 people; Constanza, 348,000; Iasi, 339,889 (1994). **Government:** Emil Constantinescu, President and Head of State since November 1996. Victor Ciorbea, Prime Minister and Head of Government since 1996. Legislature, bicameral: Senate, 143 members; Deputies, 341 members, 13 representing ethnic minorities. **National Holiday:** November 1 Union (1947) **Armed Forces:** 228,400 (1996). **Other:** 43,000 Border Guard, Gendarmes, Construction Troops.

Sultan, but under Russian occupation. Russian troops remained in the region, and the princes began to be named for life.

[16] The local nobility drew up a constitution known as the "Reglement organique", which was passed in Walachia in 1831 and in Moldova in 1832. This established administrative and legislative bodies made up of natives of the principalities. In 1834, after the Sultan's approval of the "Reglement", Russia withdrew.

[17] During the European revolutions of 1848, nationalist sentiment in Moldova and Walachia was stimulated by peasant rebellions. These reached a climax in May with the protests at Blaj, which were put down by Turkish and Russian troops, restoring the "Reglement organique". The revolutions were defeated with foreign aid, Ottoman in Walachia, Russian in Moldova, and Austrian and Russian in Transylvania.

[18] During the Crimean War, the three Romanian principalities were occupied alternately by Ottoman, Russian and Austrian troops. The Treaty of Paris, 1856, maintained the ancient statutes of the principalities until its revision by a European

commission in Bucharest in 1857, with delegates representing the sultan and both principalities.

[19] The local delegates made the following proposals: that the provinces be autonomous, joining together under the name "Romania"; that a foreign king be elected, with the right to hereditary succession; and that the country be neutral. In August 1858, despite the sultan's opposition, the Treaty of Paris created a commission to carry out the unification process.

[20] In 1859, the principalities elected a single prince, Alexandru Ion Cuza, who was recognized by the major powers and by the Sultan in 1861. The Constitution of 1864 established a bicameral legislative body, granting property holders greater electoral power.

[21] When the war between Russia and Turkey resumed in 1877, Romania authorized the transit of Russian troops through its territory in April. Moscow declared war on Turkey in May. After suffering heavy losses at Pevna, the Russians asked Prince Carol I of Romania for military support. Romanian troops contributed to the Russian victory against the Turks.

[22] The 1878 Treaty of Berlin respected Romania's independence, but failed to return Bessarabia to Romania, instead giving it Dobrudja - without its southern part - and the Danube Delta. In 1881 Romania became a kingdom.

[23] When the Balkan War broke out in 1912, tension from territorial disputes in past wars, persisted between Romania and its neighbors. After the first few battles, Bucharest demanded a ratification of its borders in Dobrudja. The St Petersburg Conference of 1913 gave Romania Silistra, much to Bulgaria's displeasure.

[24] Romania took advantage of the second Balkan War of 1913 to shore up its position. The Treaty of Bucharest gave Romania the southern part of Dobrudja, which was occupied by Romanian troops. At the beginning of World War I, Romania wavered between taking Bessarabia or Transylvania, finally opting for the latter.

[25] In 1916, Romania allied itself with Britain, France, Russia and Italy, declaring war on Austria and Hungary. After the occupation of Bucharest, King Ferdinand and the Romanian Government and army took refuge in Moldova. The defeat of the Central Powers in 1918 made it possible for Romania to double its size, since Transylvania, Bessarabia, Bucovina and Banat expressed their will to belong to Romania through referendums.

[26] In 1918 the King approved electoral reforms making voting obligatory for men over the age of 21, and introducing the secret ballot. At the time the peasants made up 80 per cent of the population, and they had their own political party. Conservatives found their position weakened because of having supported Germany, liberals included only people linked to professional and commercial activity, and the socialists carried little weight.

[27] Social upheaval, and the landowners' fear of having their lands expropriated, led General Averescu (the hero of two wars and now the head of the government) to take harsh measures. The general strike of 1920 was put down and the Communist Party was declared illegal in 1924.

[28] In the 1928 election, the National Peasant Party (NPP) obtained 349 of 387 seats. The government abolished martial law and press censorship, also decentralizing public administration, an issue supported by the ethnic minorities. It also authorized the sale of land and foreign investment in the country.

[29] The council of regency, which had been formed upon Ferdinand's death, was dissolved when King Carol assumed the throne in 1930, a succession agreed on by the major political parties. The economic crisis

led to the displacement of the NPP, and the King took advantage of the emergence of the Iron Guard, a fascist Moldovan group similar to those that existed in Germany and Italy, to weaken the traditional parties.

[30] In 1938, after a fraudulent plebiscite, Carol passed a new corporative constitution. Seeking closer ties with Germany, he met Hitler in November 1938. Upon his return, he had 13 officials of the Iron Guard assassinated, along with its leader, and Carol founded his own party, the National Renaissance Front (NRF).

[31] Carol assured the other powers that he was acting under pressure from Hitler, obtaining French and German assurances of the country's territorial integrity. When Germany and the USSR invaded Poland in 1939, Romania not only renounced the mutual defence treaty which it had signed with Warsaw, but also detained Polish authorities as they fled across Romanian territory.

[32] Between June and September of 1940, Romania was forced to turn Bessarabia and Bucovina over to the USSR, north-east Transylvania over to Hungary, and southern Dobrudja to Bulgaria. Because of his disastrous foreign policy, Carol had no choice but to abdicate in September, leaving his son Michael on the throne and turning over the government of the country to General Antonescu. Romania was occupied by 500,000 German troops, and was proclaimed a "national legionary state".

[33] Romanian troops cooperated with the abortive German offensive against the USSR, but when the counter-offensive was mounted by the Red Army, Bucharest abruptly changed sides. In June 1944, the Peasant, Liberal, Social Democratic and Communist Parties created the National Bloc and in August, King Michael ousted Antonescu and declared war on Germany.

[34] In September, with the major part of its territory occupied since mid-August by Soviet troops, Romania signed an armistice with the Allies. After three short-lived military governments, the USSR intervened in the naming of a new prime minister, Petru Groza, leader of the Ploughers' Front, a leftist party which was not a part of the National Bloc.

[35] At the Potsdam Conference, the Allies decided to resume relations with Romania, provided its government was "recognized and democratic". The USSR granted it immediate recognition while the United States and Britain adopted a "wait-and-see" attitude. In the 1946 election, the party in power was re-elected, with 71 per cent of the vote.

[36] The Government initiated a series of detentions, summary trials and life sentences against the leaders and members of the Social

Democratic, the National Liberal and National Peasant parties. In 1947, King Michael was forced to abdicate.

[37] In 1948, the Communists and some Social Democrats formed the Romanian Workers' Party (RWP) which joined the Ploughers' Front and the Hungarian People's Union to form the People's Democratic Front (PDF). In the March election that year, the PDF won 405 of the 414 seats of the National Assembly.

[38] On December 30 1947, the People's Republic of Romania was proclaimed, and a soviet style socialist constitution was adopted. In April, the government adopted centralized economic planning.

[39] Between 1948 and 1949, Bucharest signed friendship and cooperation treaties with the European socialist bloc, and joined the Council for Mutual Economic Assistance (CMEA). In 1955, Romania joined the Warsaw Pact, but in 1963 it began to drift away from the Soviet fold.

[40] In 1951 the First Five Year Plan was started, aimed at socialist industrialization of steel, coal, and oil. In 1952, the new regime started to consolidate under President Groza and Prime Minister Gheorghiu-Dej, head of state from 1961.

[41] Gheorghe Maurer was appointed Prime Minister in 1961, while Gheorghiu-Dej was President of the republic. Maurer tried to achieve greater economic and political independence, so Romania did not take sides in the Sino-Soviet dispute. In 1962 the economy underwent a series of reforms. The land collectivization policy was finished, and trade with the US, France, and Germany began.

[42] In 1965, when Gheorghiu-Dej died, Nicolae Ceausescu was elected First Secretary of the RWP, which subsequently changed its name to the "Romanian Communist Party" (RCP). The constitution was reformed, and the name of the country was changed to "the Socialist Republic of Romania", by the National Assembly. In 1967, Ceausescu was elected president of the State Council.

[43] On the diplomatic front, Ceausescu placed some distance between his country and the USSR. In 1966, he affirmed that his country was continuing its struggle for independence. Romania established diplomatic relations with West Germany and, unlike other members of the Warsaw Pact, it did not break off relations with Israel in 1967, nor intervene over the Soviet invasions of Czechoslovakia in 1968.

[44] Reaffirming Romania's independence from the USSR but not renouncing communism, Ceausescu modified the structure of the RCP and the State.

[45] In the 1970s and early 1980s, Ceausescu was re-elected several times, in apparently free elections, as secretary general of the RCP and as president of the country. Despite numerous government reorganizations, economic hardships, accentuated by administrative corruption, led to growing discontent.

[46] From 1987, difficult living and labor conditions triggered marches and strikes. These were put down by the security forces. In 1988 and 1989, several government scandals broke out; various cabinet ministers and government authorities were subsequently tried and dismissed.

[47] Towards the end of 1989, confrontations between civilians and the army in Timisoara left many dead or injured, the international press spoke of hundreds of deaths, and the news had strong repercussions within Romania.

[48] The Government declared a state of emergency, but a faction within the regime carried out a coup with massive popular support. Accused of "genocide, corruption and destruction of the economy", Ceausescu and his wife were secretly executed by army soldiers. The National Salvation Front (NSF) assumed control of the government.

[49] The leaders of the NSF came under suspicion. Resistance towards the new government increased, leading to violent confrontations in the streets. In the May 1990 election, the NSF claimed 85 per cent of the vote; but charges of election rigging were confirmed by international observers.

[50] In December 1991, 77 per cent of the electorate approved the new constitution which turned Romania into a multiparty presidentialist democracy. In Transylvania, however, the new constitution received scant support.

[51] On January 1 1992, the cooperative farming system created by the Ceausescu regime ceased to exist legally, but in fact it was still operating. In the municipal elections of February 1992, incidents occurred in Transylvania when the Magyar Democratic Union candidate was barred from participation.

[52] One month before the elections, a new opposition party, the Democratic Convention, was created. It obtained 24.3 per cent of the vote, against the 33.6 per cent of the FSN. Opposed to the First Minister Petre Roman's re-election as party president, Ion Iliescu's faction withdrew from the FSN in March, founding the FSN/22nd of December Group, changing its name in April to the Democratic Front for National Salvation (FDSN).

[53] Also in January, Romania and Germany signed a Friendship and Cooperation Treaty. In the meantime, the United States included Romania on the list of "Most Favored Nations" (MFN), granting preferential treatment in trade. The State privatized 6,000 enterprises in June, selling 30 per cent of the shares to the general public.

[54] The World Bank and the IMF granted Romania loans of $400 million for economic reforms. Iliescu won the September and October general elections, but in Parliament, the FDSN obtained a mere 28 per cent of the seats.

[55] Western countries and international financial organizations continued to voice their discontent to the Government for its alleged sluggishness in implementing economic reforms. One of the features criticized was land ownership, since 30 per cent still belonged to the State in 1994.

[56] 1995 was also dominated by disagreement between Bucharest and some of its trade partners, such as the European Union, on the pace of the reforms. Finally, in June, after two years of deliberation, Bucharest passed in June the law to privatize state enterprises.

[57] Human rights organizations, such as Amnesty International, also criticized Romania especially for the violence and discrimination often practised against the approximately 500,000 to 2,000,000 Romanian gypsies.

[58] After years of attempts, Bucharest and Budapest signed a treaty in September 1996 regarding the 1.6 million Hungarians living in Romania. Hungary had to agree to a commitment to "guarantee the rights of the minority", leaving aside its demand of "autonomy" for Transylvanian hungarians. Although relations with Hungary (which opened a consulate in Cluj, capital of Transylvania) improved after ultranationalist tendencies diminished with the defeat of Iliescu in the November elections, problems arose again when the Romanian senate voted against a university education project for the minorities.

[59] The new government of Emil Constantinescu, the President elected in November 1996, announced it would attack corruption and organized crime. Prime minister Victor Ciorbea implemented an economic and structural adjustment program inspired in IMF prescriptions: balanced state finance, increased privatizations and descentralization of the administration.

[60] Constant friction between parties of the ruling coalition delayed reforms and the adoption of laws in Parliament. Social unrest with government policies led to a wave of demonstrations which climaxed in October 1997.

[61] One of the main goals of Romanian foreign policy in 1998 was to speed up the incorporation into NATO and the European Union.

STATISTICS

DEMOGRAPHY
Population: 22,655,000 (1996). **Annual growth:** 0.1% (1980/1996). **Estimates for year 2000:** 22,500,000. **Annual growth to year 2000:** -0.2% (1994/2000). **Urban Population:** 56.3% (1996). **Urban growth:** 0.98% (1980/95). **Children per woman:** 1.4 (1996).

HEALTH
Life expectancy at birth: 70 years (1996). male: 66 years (1994). female: 73 years (1994). **Infant mortality:** 21 per 1,000 (1996). **Under-5 child mortality:** 25 per 1,000 (1996). **Calorie consumption:** 116% (1988/90). 552 **people per doctor** (1988/91).

EDUCATION
Literacy: 98% (1995). male : 99% (1995). female: 97% (1995). **School enrolment :** Primary total: 94% (1990/95). male : 94% (1990/95). female: 93% (1990/95). Secondary: male : 77% (1990/95). female: 78% (1990/95). Tertiary: 18% (1995). **Primary school teachers:** one for every 20 students (1995).

COMMUNICATIONS
300 **newspapers**, 204 **radios**, 200 **TV sets** and 123 **main telephone lines** per 1,000 people (1994). **Books:** 18 new titles per 100,000 people (1992/94).

ECONOMY
Per capita, GNP: $ 1,600 (1996). **Annual growth, GNP:** 4.7% (1995/96). **Annual inflation:** 68.68% (1985/95). **Consumer price index:** 2,617.1 (1994). **Currency:** 2,578 lei = $ 1 (1995) **Cereal imports:** 529 metric tons (1994). **Fertilizer use:** 389 kgs per ha (1994). **Exports:** $ 8,084 million (1996). **Imports** $ 11,435 million (1996). **External debt:** $ 8,291 million (1996). $ 366 **per capita:** (1996).

ENERGY
Consumption: 1,732.77 Kgs of Oil equivalent per capita yearly (1994). 26.82% imported (1994).

HDI (rank / value) 79 / 0.748 (1994)

Russia

Rossiya

Population: 148,126,000 (1996)
Area: 17,075,400 SQ KM
Capital: Moscow (Moskva)

Currency: Rouble
Language: Russian

Before the Slavs appeared on the historical scene, the European territory of the present Russian Federation, Belarus and Ukraine was inhabited by different peoples, and underwent successive invasions by the Huns, Avars, Goths and Magyars. The first mention of the Slavs dates back to the 6th century. Byzantine writers wrote of several Slavic peoples: the Polians (based in Kiev), Drevlians, Dregoviches, Kriviches, Viatiches, Meria and others.

[2] In the 9th century, the first Russian State was formed, known as the "Ancient Rus" or "Kievan Rus". The latter emerged from the struggle against the Khazars of the south, and the Varangians (Scandinavians) of the north. In the 9th century, the route between the Baltic and Black seas, down the Dnepr river, "the route of the Varangians and the Greeks", became important for European trade.

[3] In 882, Prince Oleg of Novgorod conquered Kiev and transferred the center of the Russian State there. In the year 907, Oleg signed a treaty which was to be beneficial for the Rus. During the reign of Sviatoslav, Oleg's grandson, the struggle between Byzantium and Bulgaria intensified. Vladimir (980-1015), Sviatoslav's son and successor, consolidated the judicial, dynastic and territorial organization of the Russian State. To overcome the isolation of the "pagan" Rus vis-á-vis a monotheistic Europe, Vladimir made Christianity the state religion in 988, adopting the ornate Byzantine ritual.

[4] At the end of Vladimir's reign, strong separatist tendencies were evident within the Principality of Novgorod. Svyatopolk, Vladimir's successor, killed three of his brothers in order to consolidate his own power, but Yaroslav, the fourth brother and prince of Novgorod, ousted Svyatopolk and assumed power in Kiev, granting Novgorod several benefices. After his death, the feudal republic of Novgorod was formed, along with the principalities of Vladimir-Suzdal, Galich-Volin and others. Muscovy (the principality of Rostov-Suzdal) is first mentioned in historical chronicles in 1147.

[5] In 1237, the troops of the Tatar Khan Batu, the grandson of Genghis Khan, invaded the principalities of Riazan and Vladimir, taking Moscow and other Russian cities. From 1239-40, the conquest of Russian principalities continued, followed by two and half centuries of Tatar rule. Apart from the Mongols in the East, the Teutons and the Swedes posed an additional danger in the West. In 1242, Prince Alexander of Novgorod defeated the Teutons in the famous "battle on ice" on Lake Chudskoye, near the Neva River, obtaining the title "Prince of Nevsky" as a result of this victory.

[6] The Mongols governed through local princes or Turkish chieftains and Muslim merchants, who were given the authority (*yarlik*) to govern. In the early 14th century, Tver, Moscow, Riazan and Novgorod were the main principalities. Dmitry, grand prince of Moscow began uniting forces in order to expel the Tatars, but ran up against the opposition of the princes of Tver, Nizhni-Novgorod and Riazan. In 1378, the Mamai Khan led an expedition aimed at conquering Russia, but was defeated.

[7] In 1380, Dmitry defeated Mamai in the battle of Kulikov, near the Don river, marking the beginning of Russian liberation from the Tatars. The struggle for liberation lasted a century, and ended in 1480, when Ajmat, the last of the Golden Horde's khans, retreated from a confrontation with the troops of Prince Ivan III, at the Ugra river.

[8] In 1547, Ivan "the Terrible" came to the throne. In 1552, Ivan IV took Kazan, and annexed the territory of the middle course of the Volga river, inhabited by Tatars, Chuvashes, Mari, Morduins and Udmurts. In 1556, he

PUBLIC EXPENDITURE

16.4% 34.6%
1995 ■ DEFENCE ☐ SOCIAL

In **1990/91** Military as % of health & education expenditure was 132%.

WORKERS

UNEMPLOYMENT 9.3% (1996)

Labour force %

■ WOMEN
☐ MEN

49   51

■ AGRICULTURE **14%** (1990)
☐ INDUSTRIAL **42%**
▨ SERVICES **45%**

PROFILE

ENVIRONMENT

The largest country in the world, Russia is divided into five vast regions: the European region, the Ural area, Siberia, Caucasia and the Central Asian region. The European region is the richest of the Russian Federation, and lies between Russia's western border and the Ural Mountains (the conventional boundary between Europe and Asia); it is a vast plain crossed by the Volga, Don and Dnepr rivers. The Urals, which extend from north to south, have important mineral and oil deposits in their outlying areas. The third region, Siberia, lies between the Urals and the Pacific coast. It is rich in natural resources, but sparsely populated because of its rigorous climate. Caucasia is an enormous steppe which extends northward from the mountains of the same name, between the Black and Caspian Seas. Finally, the Central Asian region is an enormous depression of land made up of deserts, steppes and mountains. Grain, potatoes and sugar beet are grown on the plains; cotton and fruit in Central Asia; tea, grapes and citrus fruit in the subtropical Caucasian and Black Sea regions. The country's vast mineral resources include oil, coal, iron, copper, zinc, lead, bauxite, manganese and tin, found in the Urals, Caucasia and Central Siberia. Chelyabinsk, a city which lies south of the Ural Mountains, has high levels of radioactivity, due to leaks in its plutonium plant. Pollution, caused by the dumping of industrial wastes, threatens Lake Baikal. Heavy industry and mining have contributed to increasing contamination of the country's main rivers, air and soil. Other contributing factors include the dependence upon coal in electrical generating plants, defects in nuclear reactors and the abuse of agrochemical products. Deforestation and soil erosion also threaten large areas of the countryside.

SOCIETY

Peoples: Russians, 81.5 per cent; Tatars, 3.8 per cent; Ukrainians, 3 per cent; over 100 other nationalities (1996). **Religions**: Christian Orthodox is the main one. There are also Muslim, Protestant and Jewish minorities. **Languages**: Russian (official). **Political Parties**: Russia Our Home and Option of Russia, both neo-liberal, are Yeltsin's support; the Liberal Democratic Party, Nationalist conservative; Communist Party; Democratic Agrarian Party; Yabloko; Congress of Russian Communities. **Social Organizations**: Federation of Independent Labor Unions of Russia (FNPR), with more than 40 million workers; Sotsprof Labor Union Association, with one million affiliates.

THE STATE

Official Name: Rossiyskaya Federatsiya.

Administrative divisions: The federation is made up of 26 autonomous republics: the republics of Bashkortostan (formerly Bashkir), Chechen-Ingush, Chuvash, Dagestan, Kabardino-Balkar, Kalmykia, Komi, Mari, Mordovia, North Ossetia, Tatar, Tuva and Saja (formerly Yakut); the regions of Adigueya, Gorno-Altai, Hebrea and Karachai-Cherkessk; and the territories of Buryat-Aguin, Buryat-Ust-Ordin, Chukchi, Dolgano-Neneos of Taimir, Evenkos, Janti and Mansi, Koriakos, Neneos and Yamalo-Neneos. **Capital**: Moscow (Moskva), 8,400,000 people (1996).

Other cities: St Petersburg, 4,200,000 peope; Nizhny-Novgorod, 1,424,600; Novosibirsk, 1,418,200; Ekaterinburg (former Sverdlovsk), 1,347,000; Samara, 1,522,500; Omsk, 1,116,200; Chelyabinsk, 1,124,500; Kazan, 1,092,300; Ufa, 1,091,800; Perm, 1,086,100; Rostov-na-Donu, 1,023,200 (1994). **Government**: Boris Yeltsin, President since 1991 (re-elected in 1996); Yevgeny Primakov, elected Prime Minister in September 1998. Parliamentary republic. Legislature, bicameral: Congress of People's Deputies, with 1,068 members elected by direct popular vote; Supreme Soviet, with 252 members appointed from the members of the Congress. **National Holiday**: June 12.
Armed Forces: 1,270,000 (1996).
Other: 220,000.

---

occupied Astrakhan, while the west continued to war against the Polish-Lithuanian State, trying to gain an outlet to the Baltic Sea. Serfdom was established, with peasants losing the right to leave without the feudal lord's permission. Ivan IV established absolute power by eliminating several upper nobility, boyar clans.

[9] Upon the death of Ivan IV, he was succeeded by his mentally ill son Fyodor in 1584 and power passed to the boyar Boris Godunov. Godunov conducted a short war against Sweden, signed an alliance with Georgia - which became a Russian protectorate - and annexed the principality of Siberia. On Fyodor's death in 1598, the Council of Territories (Zemski Sodor) elected Boris Godunov as czar. However, the boyar clans of older lineage felt they had a greater claim to the throne, and a period of intrigue and conflict over succession began.

[10] In 1601-2, in the Ukrainian territory - which belonged to Poland - an impostor calling himself "Prince Dmitry" appeared, claiming to have escaped an attempt on his life by Boris Godunov. Amassing an army, he moved towards Moscow, managing to gain a following among the disaffected members of the population, and eventually seizing the throne. In 1606, the boyars killed the "False Dmitry" but in 1607 another impostor - a second False Dmitry - appeared, supported by Poles, Lithuanians and Swedes. Polish troops occupied Moscow with the help of turncoat boyar. The Poles were finally expelled from Moscow, and in 1613 the Zemsky

Sodor elected Michael Romanov as the new Czar. Between 1654 and 1667, Russia warred against the kingdoms of Sweden and Poland, managing in the process to annex eastern Ukraine.

[11] Under the Romanovs, the Russian State became an absolute monarchy, administrated by an efficient bureaucracy and an oligarchy (made up of nobles, merchants and bishops) which was integrated into the government structure. The church was reformed and the bible translated into cyrillic script, causing a schism in the Russian church. During the 17th century the economy grew rapidly, as a result of territorial expansion, and the exploitation of Siberia's natural resources. A market also developed for Russia's forest products and semi-manufactured goods, primarily in Britain and Holland.

[12] In 1694, after the accession of Peter I, the Muscovite kingdom became known as the Russian Empire. Peter turned to the West to secure its scientific and technical advances, especially in order to develop the Russian Navy. Allied with Denmark and Poland, Russia successfully intervened in the Great Northern War (1700-21). In 1703, he founded St Petersburg, transferring the capital of his empire there and organizing the Government along a set of strict regulations.

[13] Peter established what amounted to a caste system, as well as an espionage network within his own administration, essential for maintaining his strict autocracy. He

put down the boyar in Moscow, and had his own son, Alexei, tortured and executed for joining them.

[14] In 1721, by the Treaty of Nystad, Russia obtained control of the Gulf of Finland and the provinces along the east coast of the Baltic Sea. After winning the war against Persia, Peter extended Russia's southern borders as far as the Caspian Sea. The territorial, economic and commercial expansion which characterized this period made Russia one of the major European powers but also created a mosaic of ethnic and cultural groups which could not easily be assimilated into a single unit.

[15] Peter's sudden death in 1725 ushered in a period of instability, until the accession of Catherine II, in 1762. The Empire's conquests continued, with the occupation of Belarus and the part of Ukraine east of the Dnepr; the partition of Poland between Russia and Prussia; and the annexation of Lithuania and Crimea. Russia also gained control of the northern coast of the Black Sea, penetrating the steppes beyond the Urals and all along the coast, they began exercising an ever-increasing influence over the Balkans.

[16] In the meantime, the impoverishment of the peasants increased. The military democracy of the Ukrainian Cossacks was abolished, and the nationalist sentiment of the subdued peoples began to cause friction.

[17] Toward the end of the 18th century the French Revolution and the fight against absolutism influenced the Russian intelligentsia,

which began rebelling against existing social conditions. The accession of Alexander I to the throne brought with it radical changes in the policies of the Russian Empire.

[18] Although Alexander sought peace, Napoleon declared war in 1805, and defeated Russia at Austerlitz. In 1812, Napoleon's troops invaded Russia. The "War for the Motherland" in which peasant fighters were also involved, ended with the triumph of the Russian army commanded by Marshall Kutuzov. This victory transformed Russia into the continent's major power. In December 1825, after the death of Alexander I, a group of aristocrats later known as "the Decembrists" attempted a coup in the Senate Square in St Petersburg. When the 1848 revolutions shook Europe, Russia - governed by Nikolai I - remained untouched and used its army to subdue the Hungarians in Transylvania, though it was defeated in the Crimean War against Britain and France (1853-56).

[19] In 1861, Czar Alexander II abolished serfdom. However, freedom was not "free", as the peasants had to pay their former landlords for the land which they farmed. A system of elected local assemblies was also established, with peasant representation, though the landowners maintained control.

[20] In the 1860s-70s, radical groups emerged whose aims ranged from demanding a constituent assembly to calling for insurrection. Socialist ideas influenced students and intellectuals, who saw in the peasants a revolutionary class. In

1996

PER CAPITA

$842

1990

PER 100,000
LIVE BIRTHS

75

1861-62, several different revolutionary groups created an underground association in St Petersburg, called "Land and Freedom", which existed until 1864. The Polish uprising of 1863 and a failed attempt on the Czar's life in 1866 deepened government repression.

[21] The intellectuals reached the conclusion that they would have to "go to the people" in order to explain to them who their enemies were. In 1876, another "Peace and Freedom" underground movement was established. Three years later the group split into three, including the "People's Will", which assassinated Alexander II in 1881, and whose main leaders were hanged. Alexander III did away with his predecessor's reforms, and increased the power of the autocracy.

[22] In the early 20th century, Russian socialism had two main currents. The socialist revolutionaries promoted the socialization of the land in peasant communities, while the social democrats based socialism upon industrialization and the working class. Within the Social Democratic Worker's Party of Russia (SDWPR), the Bolsheviks, led by Vladimir Ilich Ulyanov (known as "Lenin") defended the idea of a workers' revolt, while the Mensheviks shared the idea of an evolutionary socialism, put forward by Europe's other social democratic parties.

[23] Russian expansionism in Eastern Asia led to a war with Japan in 1904. The violent repression of a demonstration in Moscow in 1905 unleashed a revolt in both capitals, which was only brought under control by the October 17 Manifesto: the Czar's promise to convene a national parliament (Duma). The Bolsheviks boycotted the elections. The first Duma's majority was in the hands of constitutional democrats who were moderate liberals.

[24] The Duma's demands for agrarian reform, equal rights for members of all religions (Russian Orthodoxy was the official religion), an amnesty for political prisoners, and autonomy for Poland were unacceptable to the Czar. The Duma was dissolved and the regime put down the revolt after a long and bloody struggle. In 1907, the second Duma was elected, with the presence of the SDWPR. Both the

left and the right wings were reinforced, and the main political issue continued to be land. Prime Minister Stolipin promoted an agrarian reform, in order to create a class of land-owning peasants and put an end to the traditional communal use of the land. However, he was unsuccessful and was assassinated. The second Duma was also dissolved. An electoral reform guaranteed that the Duma committees which followed also had a conservative majority.

[25] Russia's entry into World War I precipitated a crisis within the regime. The losses brought about by war, and the lack of food, simply deepened popular discontent. In January 1917, in Petrograd, a Council (Soviet) elected by workers, soldiers and members of the Duma formed a government. In February, Nicholas II abdicated and the Duma committee established a new Provisional Government, while local soviets multiplied. The German Government authorized a group of Bolsheviks, led by Lenin, to pass through German territory, hoping to destabilize the enemy's internal situation. The Bolsheviks returned to Russia in a sealed railway car. Their influence within the soviets began to grow, and a power split emerged between the councils and Alexander Kerensky's Government.

[26] The Bolsheviks launched the slogans "Peace, land and bread" and "All power to the soviets", exhorting the people to "turn the world war into a civil war". On November 7, Lenin led the uprising which brought down the Government, and the first socialist republic was established. In early 1918, the Bolsheviks dissolved the Constituent Assembly, in which the revolutionary socialists held a majority.

[27] The Soviet Government (Council of People's Commissars) approved a peace "without annexation or indemnities", the abolition of private ownership of the land and its being turned over to the peasants and the nationalization of the banking system. Other measures were approved, including the control of factories by their workers, the creation of a militia and of revolutionary tribunals, the abolition of the privileges associated with class and of the right of inheritance, the separation

of Church and State and equal rights for men and women.

[28] Following Russia's unilateral peace settlement in 1918, Germany, France and Britain sent expeditionary forces to Russia (their former ally), to support the "White Russians" - the former regime's army forces - and bring down the revolutionary government. This foreign intervention force was ousted in 1920, and two years later the civil war ceased, with the triumph of the Red Army. During this period, the Soviet Government's policy of "war communism" resulted in a maximum centralization of power and a near-collapse of the monetary system.

[29] In December 1922, the Russian Federation, Ukraine, Belarus and the Transcaucasian Federation (Azerbaijan, Armenia and Georgia) established the Union of Soviet Socialist Republics (USSR). During the civil war, the regime had become the official preserve of the Russian (Bolshevik) Communist Party, or R(B)CP.

[30] In 1921, the R(B)CP - faced with the danger of an imminent economic collapse - was forced to do away with its "war communism" policy, and adopt a New Economic Policy (NEP). This consisted of a return to the laws of a market system and private ownership of small business, while the State took care of infrastructure, heavy industry and general planning. In 1924, the NEP was interrupted by Lenin's death; internal disputes within the R(B)CP came to an end with the triumph of Joseph Stalin, who had become secretary general of the Party in 1922. Trotsky (Lenin's close associate) went into exile and was assassinated under Stalin's orders, in Mexico in 1940.

[31] Stalin re-established the system of centralized planning of the economy, and forcibly imposed the collectivization of agriculture. Opposition figures and dissidents were eliminated through summary trials, like the Great Purge of 1935-38. Official plans cited huge figures for grain harvests as well as the production of electricity and steel, while the secret police held almost absolute power.

[32] At the beginning of World War II, by means of a secret agreement with Germany (the Molotov-Ribbentrop Pact), the USSR occupied part of Poland, as well as Romania, Estonia, Latvia and Lithuania. In 1941, Hitler launched a massive attack against Moscow, sending in thousands of troops, as well as German air power. At a cost of some 20 million lives, the Soviets were able to repel the German attack, and the Red Army liberated several countries, finally taking Berlin in May 1945.

[33] In 1945, at the Yalta conference, the Western powers and the USSR

"carved up" their respective areas of influence. In those countries occupied by the Red Army (Bulgaria, Hungary, Romania, Czechoslovakia, Poland and East Germany), the Communists took power and proclaimed first "people's republics", then socialist republics, following the model of the Communist Party of the Soviet Union (CPSU).

[34] In 1956, at the 20th Party Congress of the CPSU, Nikita Krushchev began a de-Stalinization process, which abruptly came to an end when Leonid Brezhnev ousted Krushchev in October 1964. Despite difficulties of implementation, "developed socialism" was proclaimed.

[35] The strategy of the Cold War devised by the United States in the post-war period fuelled the arms race. A by-product of the Cold War was the creation of the Warsaw Pact between the USSR and its Eastern European allies in 1955. The East-West confrontation eventually included nuclear weapons and the control of outer space, where the United States and the USSR actively pursued their own space programs in the 1960s and 1970s, with neither one actually taking a lead.

[36] In 1985, Mikhail Gorbachev became Secretary General of the CPSU and initiated drastic changes to avert a social and economic crisis. Glasnost (transparency) and perestroika (restructuring) - geared to carrying out a series of transformations within the country - unleashed forces which had long been repressed, and brought out into the open the issue of the autonomy of different ethnic groups and nationalities. Changes within the USSR set in motion similar processes in other nations throughout Eastern Europe.

[37] In April 1986, there was a serious accident in one of the reactors of the nuclear power plant at Chernobyl in the Ukraine. Some 135,000 people were evacuated and by 1993 7,000 people had died (see Ukraine).

[38] Gorbachev initiated internal reforms and also made other initiatives in the area of foreign policy, such as the withdrawal of Soviet troops from Afghanistan (where the Soviet army had been involved in a war since 1979). In addition, he was responsible for accords leading to the reduction of nuclear weapons in Europe, and also accepted the reunification of Germany. In 1990, he proposed that the Warsaw Pact and NATO be phased out gradually.

[39] Economic reform, the opening of the country to foreign capital and a return to a free-market economy were all slow in being implemented due to the resistance of the CPSU leadership. After a failed coup, in August, the CPSU was dissolved after 70 years in power. Gorbachev resumed his duties as Soviet

president, but his position had by now been irrevocably weakened. In June 1991, Boris Yeltsin was elected president of Russia.

[40] Trouble broke out in the Chechen-Ingush region (Northern Caucasia). Toward the end of October, parliamentary and presidential elections were held there. General Dzhojar Dudaev, leader of the Chechen nationalist movement, seized power. In early November he proclaimed the independence of the Chechen Republic. An economic embargo was promptly announced by Moscow.

[41] On October 6, 1991, Yegor Gaidar was named Deputy Prime Minister, and he launched liberal economic reforms, dubbed "shock therapy". On December 8, Boris Yeltsin (Russia), Stanislav Shushkevich (Belarus) and Leonid Kravchuk (Ukraine) revoked the 1922 treaty under which the USSR had been founded, proclaiming the Commonwealth of Independent States (CIS) to take its place (see box on CIS). Russia assumed the formal representation of the former USSR in foreign affairs. Latvia, Estonia and Lithuania withdrew and were recognized as separate countries by the UN.

[42] In early 1992, there was a growing rivalry between the two most important members of the CIS, Russia and Ukraine, revolving around the issue of who controlled the nuclear weapons and navy which had belonged to the former USSR. Relations between them were further complicated by the issue of Crimea's sovereignty. President Yeltsin declared that the United States was no longer a "strategic rival", and continued the reform of the economy that Gorbachev had begun, including the liberalization of prices, and the privatization of industry, agriculture and trade.

[43] On February 23 1992, violent confrontations broke out between communist and nationalist protesters, and the militia, with several people being killed by the police.

[44] On March 13, the autonomous republics associated to Russia signed the Federation Treaty, except for the Tatar and Chechen republics. A week later, in a referendum in the Tatar republic, the population voted in favor of state sovereignty and the termination of the bilateral treaty with Moscow.

[45] In April 1992, Yeltsin managed to maintain control of his reformist government, despite attacks from the 6th Congress of People's Deputies. In June he threatened to dissolve parliament, which opposed his reforms. In the meantime, the Constitutional Court declared that Yeltsin's decree banning the Communist Party was illegal. On June 12 and 22 there were further

clashes between opposition members and the police.

[46] On October 31 a territorial dispute broke out in Northern Caucasia between Ossetia and Ingushetia over part of North Ossetia which had previously been part of Ingushetia. Moscow declared a state of emergency in the region, and after several days, the rebellion was put down.

[47] In early December 1992, the 7th Congress of People's Deputies refused to ratify Boris Yeltsin's choice for Prime Minister, Yegor Gaidar. After exchanging recriminations, the President and Congress agreed to ratify Victor Chernomyrdin in the position.

[48] The "arm wrestling" between the President and Parliament continued. In March 1993, Congress opposed a referendum proposed by Yeltsin and tried unsuccessfully to limit the powers of the leader. Following further disagreements, Yeltsin took all the power from Parliament, which ousted the President and substituted him with Alexandr Rutskoi. On the same day, September 22, the police surrounded the seat of the legislative power.

[49] The tension continued to increase and on October 4 Parliament was taken by force after having been attacked with tanks. Several opposition leaders, like Rutskoi, vice-president of Congress, and its leader, Ruslan Khasbulatov, were arrested. A few days later, Yeltsin called for new elections and organized a referendum to increase his own powers.

[50] The December elections marked the defeat of those sectors faithful to Yeltsin, but 60 per cent of the voters approved the constitutional reform which granted him greater powers. In February 1994, a bilateral agreement was signed with the Russian republic of Tartarstan and a similar document was expected to be signed with Chechnya. However, the tension between Moscow and the pro-independence groups of this mostly Muslim republic, which had declared independence in 1991, became more serious and in December 1994, Yeltsin ordered military intervention.

[51] Despite protests both within Russia and abroad, the president maintained the military attacks on Grozny, the Chechen capital, which was almost totally destroyed in 1995. In December of that year, the Communist Party led by Zyuganov won the legislative elections with 22.3 per cent, followed by the ultra-right and xenophobic Liberal Democratic Party of Vladimir Zhirinovski, with 11.8 per cent and the Russia Our Home of Prime Minister Victor Chernomyrdin, with 10.1 per cent.

[52] Fearful of defeat in the July 1996 presidential elections, Yeltsin tried to

modify his policies, stopping the privatizations and nominating Evguenni Primakov - a diplomat from the Soviet era who was an ally of Gorbachev - as foreign minister. In the electoral campaign all the opposition candidates from Gorbachev to the Communists, criticized the unlimited financial speculation, corruption and "clanishness" of Yeltsin and his allies.

[53] In the second round of the July elections, Yeltsin took 53.8 per cent of the vote and Zyuganov only 40 per cent (4.8 per cent of the voters voted against both). The outgoing president was able to win through an unexpected alliance with Alexandr Lebed, an opposition candidate who had received 11 million votes.

[54] Appointed State security adviser, Lebed immediately started action to end the war in Chechnya, which he stated had caused the deaths of 80,000 people. When it was announced Yeltsin would be undergoing surgery in September, Lebed and Prime Minister Chernomyrdin became the alternative, and opposed, choices should there be a power vacuum.

[55] Yeltsin returned in March 1997, following a long absence. He reformed his cabinet and launched a far-reaching plan to cut back State spending, and privatizations. The

living conditions of the population continued to fall. The chaotic change to a market economy damaged the production mechanisms, dismantled the social protection systems, and fed the rise of the mafias. In that year 73 per cent of the banking sector was under mafia control, and one of their most lucrative lines was the trafficking of nuclear material.

[56] On May 12, Yeltsin signed an agreement with Chechnya granting it wide-ranging autonomy. The same day, the Russian Central Bank made an agreement with the Chechen bank similar to that between the US State Bank and the Panamanian bank: Chechnya would provisionally maintain the rouble as its currency, but Moscow would no longer control its bank.

[57] An explosion in the Zeryanovoskaja coal mine in December killed more than 60 people exposing the dreadful safety conditions common in this sector. Some 1,720 miners had died in the five years up to this date.

[58] In 1998 Chernomyrdin was re-instated as Prime Minister in August after the devaluation of the rouble. In September he was replaced by Yevgeny Primakov. The State backlog in salaries and pensions broke the record level set the previous year. This led to mass protests.

STATISTICS

DEMOGRAPHY
Population: 148,126,000 (1996). **Annual growth:** 0.4% (1980/1996). **Estimates for year 2000:** 146,000,000. **Annual growth to year 2000:** -0.3% (1994/2000). **Urban Population:** 76.3% (1996). **Urban growth:** 0.8% (1980/95). **Children per woman:** 1.4 (1996).

HEALTH
Life expectancy at birth: 65 years (1996). male: 59 years (1994). female: 72 years (1994). **Infant mortality:** 20 per 1,000 (1996). **Under-5 child mortality:** 25 per 1,000 (1996).

EDUCATION
Literacy: 99% (1995). male : 100% (1995). female: 99% (1995). **School enrolment :** Primary total: 109% (1990/95). male : 109% (1990/95). female: 108% (1990/95). Secondary: male : 84% (1990/95). female: 91% (1990/95). Tertiary: 43% (1995). **Primary school teachers:** one for every 20 students (1995).

COMMUNICATIONS
270 **newspapers**, 339 **radios**, 380 **TV sets** and 162 **main telephone lines** per 1,000 people (1994). **Books:** 20 new titles per 100,000 people (1992/94).

ECONOMY
Per capita, GNP: $ 2,410 (1996). **Annual growth, GNP:** -5% (1995/96). **Annual inflation:** 148.85% (1985/95). **Consumer price index:** 64,688.2 (1994). **Currency:** 4,640 roubles = $ 1 (1995). **Cereal imports:** metric tons (1994). **Food import dependency:**% (1994). **Fertilizer use:** 116 kgs per ha (1994). **Exports:** $ 81,438 million (1996). **Imports:** $ 43,318 million (1996). **External debt:** $ 124,785 million (1996). $ 842 **per capita:** (1996). **Debt service:** 6.6% of exports (1996).

ENERGY
Consumption: 4,013.75 Kgs of Oil equivalent per capita yearly (1994). -52.93% imported (1994).

HDI (rank / value) 67 / 0.792 (1994)

National Conflicts in the former USSR

Conflicts among different national groups in the former Soviet Union – that gained new strength by its dissolution – are the result, among other things, of the expansionist policy of the Czarist regime begun in the 18th century and continued by its Soviet successors.

At the time of its break-up in October 1991 the USSR was a vast conglomerate of numerous ethnic groups. This was the result of a long historical process of Czarist expansion which since the 18th century had transformed Russia. The Czarist regime implemented a systematic policy of "Russianisation", with the absolute pre-eminence of the Russian language and of the Orthodox Church, as well as obedience to a central power embodied in the Czar. During the civil wars that followed the October 1917 revolution, the various republics were federated to form the Union of Soviet Socialist Republics.

Soviet policy, unlike the Czarist one, sought, at least in name, to grant equal rights to the different ethnic groups and political divisions in the State. This implied giving primacy to the central power of the Soviet over land and ethnic conflicts between different regions, the forceful "sedentarization" of nomadic peoples (such as in Kyrgysztan) and initiatives to fight ethnic divisions which consisted mostly of huge forced migrations from one region to another. The Baltic republics were annexed to the USSR in 1940, in accordance with a secret agreement signed by Stalin and Hitler in 1939, jointly with the German-Soviet pact signed before World War II. Bukovina and Besarabia were confiscated from Romania in 1944, which, together with the Autonomous Republic of Moldavia, in Ukranian territory, made up the Socialist Republic of Moldavia (now Moldova).

The USSR consisted of 15 Soviet socialist republics, which were further subdivided into 20 autonomous Soviet socialist republics, 8 autonomous regions (smaller and less populated than the republics) and 10 autonomous districts (for small ethnic groups, mostly nomadic, from Siberia and the Far East).

In 1986, with Mikhail Gorbachev in the Presidential seat, it was clear that the tensions had only been muted (and in some cases increased) by the administrative initiatives of the Communist regime. Several republics demanded their independence, which led to the dissolution of the USSR. Several regions and districts also demanded their autonomy, leading to armed conflicts. In 1998, some new republics which had declared their sovereignty had not yet resolved their status. These were the Transnitrian Republic of Moldavia (known as Transnitria), the Republic of South Ossetia, the Republic of Nagorno-Karabakh and the People's Republic of Abkhazia.

Transnitria

The 1989 census revealed that the population of Transnitria was still mostly Slavic (28 per cent Ukranians, 24 per cent Russians), while Moldavians amounted to 40 per cent. However, that year, the Government of Moldavia declared Moldavian as the Republic's sole official language, which led to strikes and social unrest. From January to October 1990, the population of Transnitria organized referenda which decided the creation of the Autonomous Republic of Transnitria. But the Supreme Soviet of the USSR declared these referenda illegal and refused to grant the territory autonomy. In December 1991, after the dissolution of the Soviet Union, Igor Smirnov was chosen first President of Transnitria and a new referendum declared independence. Moldavian police clashed with Transnitrian militias and, in 1992, the Russian Federation and Moldavia signed an agreement to re-establish peace in the region. In 1994, Transnitria and Moldavia re-established economic relations and 100,000 refugees returned to their homes, although in 1998 the political situation remained uncertain.

South Ossetia

Ossetians came to the Caucasus territory in the 13th century. In 1774, Russia annexed the territories held by the Ossetians and, in 1918, created the Autonomous Republic of Ossetia (in the present Federated Republic of Russia). In 1922, the autonomous region of South Ossetia was created in Georgia. In the Eighties, when several movements for self-determination appeared in various parts of the Soviet Union, the idea of joining the Autonomous Republic of Ossetia started to grow in South Ossetia. In September 1990, South Ossetia proclaimed itself a sovereign republic. In December 1990, the parliament of Georgia repealed the status of autonomous region in South Ossetia and declared a state of emergency in the territory, which led to the beginning of armed confrontations. A Russian-Georgian-Ossetian peace force succeeded in putting an end to the fighting in 1992. In 1994, L Chibirov was elected president of the parliament in South Ossetia and, in 1996, became President of the territory. Since then, several meetings between Georgian and Ossetians authorities failed to reach an agreement on the political status of South Ossetia.

Nagorno-Karabakh

Since May 1918, when Moscow's authority was established over Nagorno-Karabakh, it was discussed whether the region, mostly populated by Armenians, should belong to Armenia or Azerbaijan. In 1923 the territory became a province of Azerbaijan. The strikes of 1988 in Nagorno-Karabakh were one of the first signs of instability due to nationalist demands in the Soviet Union. In 1991, the Nagorno-Karabakh parliament not only declared the region's independence, but also annexed the district of Shaumia. Three months later, the majority of the population voted for independence. By then, a full-blown war had erupted between the Karabakhs (supported by Armenia) and Azerbaijan, in which 4,600 Karabakhs and some 30,000 Azerbaijanis died.

In 1994, Azerbaijan and Nagorno-Karabakh signed an armistice. The first elections of Nagorno-Karabakh elected Robert Kocharian President in December 1996. In 1997, Kocharian was appointed Prime Minister of Armenia and left Karabakh, being replaced by Arcady Gukassian. In 1998, the creation of Nagorno-Karabakh was still in process and negotiations with Azerbaijan progressed slowly.

Rwanda

Rwanda

Population: 5,397,000 (1996)
Area: 26,338 SQ KM
Capital: Kigali

Currency: Francs
Language: Rwanda, English and French

[1] Inhabited since ancient times by the Hutu (Bantus) and Twa (pygmy) ethnic groups, Rwanda's highlands were invaded in the 15th century by the Tutsis (or Watutsis) from Ethiopia. After subduing the local population, the Tutsis set up a stratified society. This social and political organization remained basically unchanged even after German colonization started in the region in 1897. The territory became part of German East Africa, which also included Burundi.

[2] After World War I, the territory named Rwanda-Urundi was placed under Belgian custody and administered by them from the Congo (today's DR Congo, formerly Zaire). Of the three groups which inhabit the region, the minority - made up of the pastoralist and warrior Tutsis - consolidated its control over the agricultural Hutu and artisan Twa. In 1959, farm workers organized by the Parmehutu (Party of the Hutu Emancipation Movement) revolted against Tutsi rule. A bloody civil war ensued and the Belgian colonial government chose to abandon the territory. The Parmehutu won elections supervised by the United Nations in 1961 and proclaimed a Republic in 1962, autonomous from neighboring Burundi.

[3] The power structure favoring Tutsi rulers was abolished and land distributed on the capitalist basis of private ownership. However, this did not lead to true national unity, nor did it settle controversies between ethnic groups. The following year, civil war broke out again. Approximately 20,000 people died and 160,000 Tutsis were expelled from the country.

[4] Lacking other patterns, the Parmehutu reorganized society according to ethnic group interests: the Twa (40,000 in all) were assigned the crafts industry; the Tutsis, cattle-raising, and land ownership was reserved for the Hutus. The system virtually ignored the possibility of urban development, a fact evidenced by the tiny size of the capital city of Kigali. In order to set an example, President Gregory Kayibanda worked his own piece of land. As a result agriculture was almost entirely reduced to subsistence farming, with little surplus left over for the market.

[5] In the late 1960s, attempts to increase market production saw a revival of the coffee plantations, burnt down in 1959, in protest against colonial despotism. The new policy however did not solve Rwanda's economic problems but rather exacerbated social tensions as a new group of landowners arose, adding complexity to existing ethnic conflicts, and giving rise to new and violent outbreaks.

[6] Faced with the threat of a new civil war, Colonel Juvenal Habyarimana overthrew Kayibanda on July 5 1973. Habyarimana, previously defence minister, dissolved the Parmehutu, jailed Kayibanda (who died shortly afterwards) and launched a diplomatic offensive successfully dealing with conflicts which had arisen between Rwanda and neighboring countries during the previous regime.

[7] The close relationship between Habyarimana and France, and with Zaire's President Mobutu caused disagreements within the governing party, the National Revolutionary Movement for Development (MRND). Progressive factions criticized the situation and Habyarimana's liberal policies. During the 1980 party congress they were expelled. Their leader, labor minister Alexis Kanyarengwe, went into exile in Tanzania to escape prison. Resolutions by the party congress endorsed "planned liberalism", which resulted in an open-door policy for foreign investments.

[8] In 1982, Uganda expelled large numbers of Rwandan exiles, who were not allowed back into their own country. Whole towns were burned down by Ugandan troops leaving at least 10,000 people homeless and without food.

[9] In 1986, the new president of Uganda, Museveni, announced that Rwandans who had lived in the country for more than ten years would automatically receive citizenship. Relations improved between the two countries; in 1988, both presidents signed a declaration confirming progress in their international policies.

[10] President Habyarimana changed his policies and took firm steps towards establishing a democracy. Initially he set up a National Development Council in an attempt to draw up national policies taking into consideration the country's different social and economic realities. Later, he executed an austerity program, which yielded some positive economic results, he released more than 1,000 political prisoners, and implemented measures to ensure respect for human rights in the prisons.

[11] Habyarimana was re-elected in 1988. On December 26 that year, elections were held to renew one-third of the 70 deputies. Of these, eleven women, but only two Tutsis, were elected. 60,000 Hutu refugees from Burundi, entered the country in the course of the year.

[12] On September 30 1990, Fred Rwigyema, an important government official belonging to the Tutsi ethnic group, led an uprising, entering Rwanda from Uganda. President Habyarimana requested help from Belgium, France and Zaire, whose troops played a decisive role in repelling the rebel offensive, although there was also fighting in the capital. In October, a cease-fire was reached between the two parties, through the intervention of Belgian Prime Minister, Wilfried Martens.

[13] At the end of January 1991, some 600 troops belonging to the Rwandan People's Front entered the country from Uganda. In March, a cease-fire was signed. Among its provisions were the liberation of political prisoners and prisoners of war, and a commitment by President Habyarimana to initiate negotiations establishing a more open political atmosphere. In June of that year, the President signed the new constitution, which provided for a multi-party system,

WORKERS

(1996)

Labour force %
- WOMEN
- MEN

49   51

- ■ AGRICULTURE 92% (1990)
- □ INDUSTRIAL 3%
- ■ SERVICES 5%

LAND USE

DEFORESTATION -0.2% annual (81/90)
IRRIGATED 0.5% of arable

(1993)

- ■ FOREST & WOODLAND 20.9%
- □ ARABLE 32.5%
- ■ OTHER 46.6%

PER CAPITA
$192

61%

PROFILE

ENVIRONMENT

Known as the country of a thousand hills on account of its geographical location between two mountain ranges, Rwanda lies in the heart of the African continent. The terrain is mountainous and well irrigated by numerous rivers and lakes supporting varied wild life. The population is concentrated in the highlands where the economic mainstay is subsistence agriculture. The lowlands have been eroded and their natural vegetation is disappearing as a result of excessive grazing. 90 per cent of the energy consumed by Rwandans is derived from natural resources, consequently leading to deforestation and erosion.

SOCIETY

Peoples: Rwanda's ethnic composition is the result of close integration between successive migrations and the original pygmy population. Today, 84 per cent are Hutu (a branch of Bantu people), 15 per cent Tutsi (Hamitic) and 1 per cent Twa (descendants of the pygmies). There is a minority of European origin most of whom are Belgian.
Religions: There is no official religion. Most of the population (69 per cent) profess traditional African religions, 20 per cent are Catholic, 10 per cent Protestant and 1 per cent Muslim.
Languages: Rwanda, English and French (the three of them official).
Political Parties: Rwandan Patriotic Front (FPR); National Revolutionary Movement for Development (MRND); Republican Democratic Movement (MDR); Liberal Party (PL).

THE STATE

Official Names: Republika y'u Rwanda; République Rwandaise; Republic of Rwanda.
Capital: Kigali, 238,000 people (1991)
Other cities: Butare, 29,000 people; Ruhengeri, 30,000; Gisenyi, 22,000 (1991).
Government: Pasteur Bizimungu, President in transition. Pierre-Celestin Rwigema, Prime Minister since 1996.
National Holiday: July 1, Independence Day (1962).
Armed Forces: 33,000 (1996).

STATISTICS

DEMOGRAPHY

Population: 5,397,000 (1996). **Annual growth**: 0.3% (1980/1996). **Estimates for year 2000**: 7,700,000. **Annual growth to year 2000**: 6.4% (1994/2000). **Urban Population**: 5.8% (1996). **Urban growth**: 4.66% (1980/95). **Children per woman**: 6.2 (1996).

HEALTH

Life expectancy at birth: 36 years (1996). **Infant mortality**: 105 per 1,000 (1996). **Under-5 child mortality**: 170 per 1,000 (1996). **Calorie consumption**: 82% (1988/90). 25,000 **people per doctor** (1988/91).

EDUCATION

Literacy: 61% (1995). male : 70% (1995). female: 52% (1995). **School enrolment** : Primary total: 77% (1990/95). male : 78% (1990/95). female: 76% (1990/95). Secondary: male : 11% (1990/95). female: 9% (1990/95).

COMMUNICATIONS

67 **radios**, **TV sets** and 2 **main telephone lines** per 1,000 people (1994).

ECONOMY

Per capita, GNP: $ 190 (1996). **Annual growth, GNP**: 7.8% (1995/96). **Annual inflation**: 10.84% (1985/95). **Consumer price index**: (1994). **Currency**: 299.81 francs = $ 1 (1995) **Cereal imports**: 97 metric tons (1994). **Food import dependency**: 25% (1994). **Fertilizer use**: 8 kgs per ha (1994). **Exports**: $ 168 million (1996). **Imports**: $ 385 million (1996). **External debt**: $ 1,034 million (1996). $ 192 **per capita**: (1996). **Debt service**: 20.3% of exports (1996). **Development aid received**: $ 711 million (1995). $ 92 per capita (1995). 122.8% of GNP (1994).

ENERGY

Consumption: 33.54 Kgs of Oil equivalent per capita yearly (1994). 77.99% imported (1994).

HDI (rank / value) 174 / 0.187 (1994)

---

creating the post of Prime Minister, guaranteeing freedom of the press, limiting the presidential term to two five-year periods with no further re-election, and establishing a separation of the powers of the state.
[14] In March 1992, at least 300 members of the Tutsi ethnic minority were assassinated, and another 15,000 were forcibly relocated to the region of Bugesera. The leaders of the two principal opposition parties, the Republican Democratic

Movement (MDR) and the Liberal Party (PL), blamed the Government for the violence, and especially a militia made up of young Hutus belonging to the MRND.
[15] In early 1993, President Habyarimana rejected the agreement signed in Arusha between the Rwandan delegation - led by Prime Minister Dismas Nsengiyaremye, of the Republican Democratic Movement - and the rebels of the Rwandan Patriotic Front (FPR), led by Alex Kanyarengue, made up of Tutsi exiles who had been questioning the Hutu domination of their community.
[16] The President refused any form of power-sharing with the FPR, which had demanded five cabinet positions, the incorporation of its soldiers into

the regular army and the repatriation of Tutsi refugees from Uganda and Tanzania.
[17] Although both bands had respected the cease-fire which had been in effect since August 1992, the FPR broke off negotiations in February, launching a new offensive which enabled them to gain control over most of the country's territory, and prepare an advance upon the capital.
[18] The death of Presidents of Rwanda, Juvenal Habyarimana, and Burundi, Cyprien Nyataryamira, in an attack on the aeroplane carrying them to Kigali after attending a peace conference in Tanzania on April 6 1994, initiated a new bloodbath which cost the lives of 800,000 people in three months. Both presidents were Hutu.

[19] Given the worsening of the civil war, France, the United States and Belgium decided in April to send in troops to "guarantee security and evacuate the foreigners." French troops took control of Kigali airport to oversee the repatriation of 600 French citizens resident in the capital.
[20] The new government tried to revive the Rwandan economy and organize trials for those guilty of what the UN described as "genocide". However, the Government did not receive the aid expected from the Western countries and many members of the militias responsible for the massacres continued to operate from their refuge in Zaire (now DR Congo).
[21] During 1995 and 1996 further mass graves were discovered

nearly every week, while the violence of the new Rwandan army - formed around a core of FPR fighters - and the militias led to more deaths. Many of the victims of the militias had been witnesses of events in 1994, along with Hutu public officials, accused of "collaboration".

[22] Increasing tensions in eastern Zaire and the mass deportations of refugees made attacks on human rights more serious. In February 1997, Amnesty International denounced the death of dozens of civilians, both Tutsi and Hutu, and the murder of four UN officials in the city of Cyangugu.

[23] In April 1998, despite the call for clemency made by Pope John Paul II and UN Secretary-General Kofi Annan, 22 of those responsible for the genocide were executed in strategically chosen places, where the largest massacres had taken place. The four executed in Kigali, included Silas Munyagishali (assistant district attorney in Kigali), Froduald Karamira (former vice president of the MDR) and Elie Nhimiyimana (organizer of the massacre in the Gikondo neighbourhood of the capital). Amnesty International classed the executions as "a brutal parody of justice which jeopardises any hope of reconciliation in Rwanda following the genocide and which will perpetuate the cycle of violence".

[24] Rwandan President, Pasteur Bizimungu, told the press; "We have no rancour for the Europeans, but I cannot fail to point out it was precisely they who were responsible for the chaos in this region," adding to the criticism and denunciations of human rights groups which accused France, Belgium and the United States of being responsible for the genocide, either by action or oversight.

Siblings, ethnic groups and classes

The peoples who traditionally inhabited the territory encompassing what is now Rwanda and its neighboring equatorial African countries, have a common ancestry. The Banyarwanda included the Hutu, the Tutsi and the Twa. They speak Kinyarwanda, and are related to the Bayakole and the Bakiga of Uganda, and the Barundi of Burundi.

[2] In addition to a common language, these groups also share the same territory, the same traditional political institutions and identical physical characteristics.

[3] Up until the fall of the monarchy, the kingdom of Rwanda was a highly organized society, with a rigid system of social stratification. The posts of nobility and upper echelons of the army - and nearly all the country's livestock - were almost exclusively in hands of the Tutsi, while the Twa were traditionally hunters and potters, and the Hutu, agriculturalists.

[4] By the mid-20th century, the population break-down was as follows: Hutu, 84 per cent; Tutsi, 14 per cent, and Twa, 1 per cent. However, contrary to popular belief, not all Tutsi were members of the governing or privileged classes.

[5] At the time of independence, all 43 chieftains and 549 of the 559 sub-chieftains in Rwanda-Burundi were Tutsi, and around 80 percent of positions in the judicial branch of the government were held by members of that ethnic group.

[6] The hold which the Tutsis were able to maintain over the Hutu majority until the dawn of independence was based upon their almost exclusive monopoly of livestock ownership. In traditional times, the distribution of cattle was carried out through a social mechanism known as "ubuhake". This system meant that a person of lower prestige and wealth - generally a Hutu- offered his services to another - generally a Tutsi - in exchange for access to the produce of one or more animals.

[7] The Tutsis also maintained their esprit de corps and their sense of superiority, by dominating the military, membership of which was barred to members of other ethnic groups.

[8] Social cohesion was guaranteed by a series of hierarchical structures (territorial, military, mutual solidarity, etc.) to which every inhabitant belonged, with the king overseeing them all.

[9] European colonization resulted in massive changes in these ethnic relationships, and began undermining some aspects of the country's social structure. While the Rwanda-Burundi region was still under Belgian control, a movement giving voice to Hutu demands began to emerge in 1957. Two years later, the mysterious death of King Mutara, a reformist who lived in Bujumbura - now the capital of Burundi - marked the beginning of a bloody civil war. By 1962, 22,000 Tutsis had been displaced, within the country's borders.

[10] The Hutus, who came to power in Rwanda through the electoral process, never managed to establish ethnic harmony between the different groups which share the same geographical space. Violent rivalries erupted periodically, affecting both Burundi (which was governed until only a few years ago mostly by Tutsis) and its neighbors to the north.

[11] Fearing for their lives, close to 60 per cent of Rwanda's Tutsis left the country between 1959 and 1964, heading mostly for Burundi. In 1966, ethnic violence once again took a heavy toll. In Burundi, in turn, violence between the two groups erupted in 1965, 1966, 1969, 1972 and 1988.

[12] The last episodes in this chain of violence began in Rwanda in the early 1990s when the government headed a movement appealing to the Hutu primacy. This campaign had its climax during 1994's genocide, which cost at least 500,000 lives and affected mostly but not only Tutsis. Confrontations between both groups continued in Burundi, and the 1996 coup made thousands of Burundans seek asylum in Zaire (now DR Congo).

Western Sahara

Sahara Occidental

Population: 1,000.000
Area: 266,000 SQ KM (1996)
Capital: L'ayoun

Language: Arabic and Spanish

From the 5th century, the far west of the Sahara has been populated by Moors, Tuaregs and Tubus. The presence of these peoples is documented by the Tassili stone carvings and other sources. But successive waves of migration and conquest have swept across the region over the centuries, as Arabs collided and intermarried with Berbers and with black Africans from south of the Sahara. Around the 13th century there was a major migration of people into the area of people from beyond Africa, in Yemen.

[2] By the eighteenth century this particular mix of peoples and cultures had blended into something distinct: a group of nomadic tribes called the Ahl Essahel who shared the same branch of Arabic, Hassania, and the same mild, tolerant form of Sunni Islam.

[3] Spanish occupation of the Saharan coast was carried out mainly for strategic reasons: to cover the flank of the Canary Islands. The occupation was practically limited to Villa Cisneros (present-day Dakhla) until 1884, when Madrid proclaimed the coastal area between Cape Blanc and Cape Boujdour a "protectorate", determined that this "empty space" would not fall to another power.

[4] The borders of the Spanish Sahara were established by agreement with France in 1904 but the local inhabitants, the Saharawis, refused to relinquish their nomadic lifestyle and put up stiff resistance.

[5] In 1895, Sheikh Ma al-Aini founded the Smara citadel and, with the support of the Sultan of Morocco, continued fighting the Franco-Spanish presence until 1910. Under French pressure, the Sultan of Morocco finally suspended assistance to the rebels, who enlarged their field of action to include Morocco and even threatened Marrakesh. A French counter-attack invaded "Spanish" territory and occupied Smara in 1913, though resistance continued until 1920.

[6] In 1933 Muhammad al Mamún, the Emir of Adrad and Ma al-Aini's cousin, defeated the French, forcing a change of tactics. France occupied the rebel base at the Tindouf oasis and advanced into Algeria, Mauritania and Morocco, while Spanish troops took Smara, overcoming the rebels and instituting full colonial rule in 1936.

[7] Even then Spain showed little interest in developing the colony until the natural resources of the territory (mainly its phosphates) became evident. It then developed a new capital, L'ayoun, from which phosphates from the mine at Boucraa were exported. The phosphate deposits have been estimated at 1.7 billion tons in the Boucraa area, but there are thought to be another 10 billion tons in other parts of the territory.

[8] The Franco Government, in close association with transnational companies, invested more than $160 million in Sahara, transforming the country, particularly the population distribution. In 1959, L'ayoun had 6,000 inhabitants; in 1974 there were 28,000, while the percentage of nomads decreased from 90 to 16 per cent.

[9] With the progressive abandonment of the traditional nomadic way of life, tribal ties and relationships began to weaken. Over the years, however, a new national identity has slowly been forged, transcending traditional divisions.

[10] In 1966 the UN General Assembly called on Spain to organize a referendum in which Saharawis could exercise their right to self-determination. Locally the Movement for the Liberation of the Sahara was formed in 1967 and organized huge demonstrations before being savagely put down and banned on 17 June 1970.

[11] The repression only increased nationalist aspirations and the Polisario Front (the Popular Front for the Liberation of Saguia el Hamra and Rio de Oro) was formed on 10 May 1973, led by Elwali Mustafa Sayed. This began as a vanguard group committed to armed struggle against colonialism but very quickly became a mass movement.

[12] Spain reluctantly organized a census of the colony in preparation for a referendum on self-determination. The census showed that there were 73,497 Saharawis, 20,126 Europeans and 1,396 other Africans living in Western Sahara.

[13] Morocco, however, also claimed sovereignty over Western Sahara. As a result of such claims, the International Court of Justice in The Hague ruled in October 1975 that there were no historic legal ties with Morocco that debarred Western Sahara from decolonization and self-determination.

[14] King Hassan II of Morocco, increasingly beleaguered by bread riots and assassination attempts, seized his chance to unify the nation and organized the so-called "Green March", a propaganda move which mobilized 350,000 Moroccans to march southward into the Sahara. They crossed the border on November 6 1975.

[15] On November 14, as General Franco lay on his deathbed, Spain signed a secret agreement which handed over the territory to Morocco and Mauritania. A Polisario force which at this stage numbered no more than about 5,000 had no chance against a Moroccan Army which could call in total on 65,000 soldiers.

[16] The Moroccan occupation was already well established by the time the Spanish officially withdrew on February 27 1976, though on the same day Polisario declared the independence of the Saharawi Arab Democratic Republic (SADR).

[17] Thousands of ordinary Saharawis fled the Moroccan invaders into the desert, setting up their own makeshift refugee camps. Many, like the 25,000 which gathered at Guelta Zemmour, were determined to stay on Western Saharan territory but were repeatedly bombed by Moroccan planes which the Red Cross confirmed were using napalm.

[18] In the face of this onslaught, the refugees had to walk hundreds of kilometres across the desert to the Algerian town of Tindouf. Here the Algerian Government ceded control over a portion of its own territory to Polisario, which built and administered its own refugee camps..

[19] Polisario was faced with war on two fronts: against Morocco in the north and Mauritania in the south. The relative weakness of the Mauritanian Army made it the more sensible target and Polisario mounted raids deep into Mauritanian territory, one of which cost the life of the movement's inspirational young leader, Wali Mustafa Sayed.

[20] But on the whole the attacks

were successful and in 1979 Mauritania, on the verge of bankruptcy, signed a peace treaty with Polisario. But as Mauritania withdrew Moroccan troops moved in to take over the south, including the city of Dakhla.

[21] The Polisario Front's military victories led to a diplomatic triumph at the June 1980 conference of the Organization for African Unity (OAU) in Freetown. Twenty-six African nations officially recognized the RASD as the legitimate title for Western Sahara, and four months later the UN issued a resolution requesting Moroccan withdrawal.

[22] Still vastly outnumbered, Polisario had no chance of regaining and holding major towns by military force. Instead it concentrated on lightning strikes by highly mobile guerrilla units, not least on the longest conveyor belt in the world which carries phosphates from the Boucraa mine to the sea .

[23] The Moroccan response from 1980 onwards was to build a fortified wall or berm, protected by minefields and artillery. By 1982 the first of these walls was complete, stretching from the border right past Smara to meet the sea south of Boujdour.

[24] In the ensuing years further walls were built until by the late 1980s the Wall stretched a full 2,500 kilometres across the desert from the Moroccan border in the north to near the Mauritanian border in the south. The Wall is a vast drain on the Moroccan economy but it now encloses fully three-quarters of Western Sahara.

[25] Militarily Morocco was digging in, with significant aid from both France and the US. But in international diplomacy it was losing ground: in 1985 the RASD was welcomed into the Organization of African Unity, prompting Morocco to leave, and by the end of 1986, 67 countries had recognized the independent Western Saharan state.

[26] Through the 1980s Morocco steadfastly refused to debate the issue of Western Sahara in any international forum. But by 1990 diplomatic pressure on Morocco led to a UN peace plan aimed at holding a referendum in which Saharawis could decide their

own future. There was to be a cease-fire, repatriation of refugees and the new UN Mission for the Referendum in Western Sahara (MINURSO) would identify legitimate voters. The electoral roll was to be based on the 1974 Spanish census.

[27] On April 29 1991, the UN Security Council approved the peace plan. The cease-fire was enforced on September 6, and the referendum was scheduled for January 1992.

[28] In the following months, the Moroccan Government settled thousands of Moroccan citizens in the Saharan territory, to ensure their voter eligibility; furthermore, the cease-fire was ignored, and journalists were hindered. They also banned international observers as repression against the Saharans mounted.

[29] The UN Special Representative for the Western Sahara, Johannes Manz, resigned in December 1991, protesting not only at these Moroccan tactics but also at UN Secretary-General Javier Pérez de Cuellar's appeasement of them. The result was stalemate and a vastly expensive UN operation which failed to make Morocco comply with the peace plan

[30] Faced with criticism in the US Congress, the UN began to talk about winding up MINURSO and Polisario began to prepare for a return to war. The stalling of the referendum was felt to favour Moroccan authority.

[31] At the beginning of 1997, UN withdrawal and a resume of war seemed inevitable. The new UN Secretary-General, Kofi Annan, sought US support for a last attempt to rescue the peace plan and appointed former US Secretary of State James Baker as his Personal Envoy.

[32] Baker visited the region then initiated a series of direct talks in Lisbon and London between the Moroccan Government and Polisario - these had never taken place before since Morocco felt they would legitimize Polisario's cause.

[33] On September 16 1997 the two parties signed an agreement which established guidelines for voter identification, repatriation

of refugees, release of prisoners, troop withdrawal and a code of conduct for the referendum campaign. Voter identification was to be concluded in the first half of 1998 and the referendum to take place on December 7 1998.

[34] Polisario's Defence Minister, Brahim Gali, and Foreign Minister, Bachir Mustafa Sayed (director of the diplomacy of the past 15 years), were replaced in January 1998. This move was attributed to the Government's need to keep its hands free for negotiating the last phase of the referendum.

[35] RASD President Muhammad Abdelaziz said that if Polisario Front won the referendum, Moroccan citizens could remain in the territory provided they were not "related to the occupation and annexation".

[36] On 13 April 1998 the UN Secretary-General reported to the Security Council that the identification process was being seriously hampered by Morocco's insistence that an

extra 12,000 individuals be accepted as voters while only presenting 1,500 of them for identification. Kofi Annan expressed his concern also about the continuing propaganda against MINURSO in the Moroccan press.

[37] A letter from Moroccan Minister Driss Basri, written on January 22 1998, was leaked to the international community in April. It advised Moroccan local-government officials on how to coach individuals so as to persuade the identification commission that they are Saharawi. The letter stated that the results of identification have "so far fallen far short of the necessary level" partly due "to the manifestly insufficient preparation of our applicants".

[38] The continuing problems over voter identification and human-rights abuses in the occupied territories made increasingly unlikely that the referendum would take place at the end of 1998.

St Helena

St Helena

Population: 6,000 (1996)
Area: 122 SQ KM
Capital: Jamestown

Currency: Pound Sterling
Language: English

St Helena was uninhabited when Portuguese navigators arrived in 1502. In 1659 an outpost of the British East Indies Company was established on the islands, and since then St Helena has been an English colony. Of scant economic interest, the island acquired notoriety as the location of Napoleon's second exile, from 1815 until his death in 1821. The Malvinas War put it back on the map, a century and a half later.

[2] An English representative stated: "It was only with the help of Ascension and the labor force provided by St Helena, that we could recover the Falklands". This may justify the expensive maintenance of this British enclave through the Administration for Overseas Development. The British could have a shared base like Ascension Island which is a US base and a bridgehead of the Royal Air Force, or they could simply transfer the territory to the US, as they did with Diego Garcia.

[3] The United Nations supports all nation's rights to self-determination and independence, and in December 1984, the UN General Assembly urged Britain to bolster the fishing industry, handicrafts and reforestation on the island and to foster awareness of the right to independence. Washington and London both voted against the resolution. The UN also questioned the existence of the military base in Ascension since there should not be any base in non-autonomous territories.

[4] On January 1, 1989, a new constitution was instituted conferring greater powers on the members of the Legislative Council and enabling civil servants to become election candidates with the approval of the governor. The new constitution also reduced the voting age to 18.

[5] The island's only export is fish, but in the last few years, there has been a sudden decline in the total catch: 27.2 tons in 1985, and a mere 9.2 tons in 1990.

[6] St. Helena is of scientific interest because of the its rare flora and fauna. The island has some 40 plant species unknown in the rest of the world.

PROFILE

ENVIRONMENT
Located in the South Atlantic some 2,000 km from the coast of Angola (West Africa), slightly west of the Greenwich meridian. Of volcanic origin, the island is mountainous, has no mineral reserves and industries and the only productive activities are subsistence agriculture and fishing.

SOCIETY
Peoples: The island's population is largely of African descent. Some 6,000 natives of St. Helena have emigrated to South Africa and Great Britain.
Religions: Protestant, Anglicane, Baptist, Seventh-Day Adventists, and also Roman Catholic.
Languages: English (official).
Political Parties: St Helena Progressive Party (SHPP), the St. Helena Labor Party (SHLP), both inactive since 1976.

THE STATE
Official Name: St Helena Colony with Dependencies.
Capital: Jamestown, 1,744 people in 1989. Inland is Longwood, where Napoleon Bonaparte was exiled
Government: David Leslie Smallman, Governor appointed by the British Crown in 1995. There is an Executive Council and a Legislative Council of 15 seats: twelve members elected by popular vote for a four-year term, the governor and two former officers.
Armed Forces: Security is the responsibility of the United Kingdom.

DEMOGRAPHY
Population: 6,000 (1996) **Urban population:** 64.5% (1996)

ECONOMY
Consumer price index: 122.8 (1994)

Tristan da Cunha

The most important of a group of South Atlantic islands 2,400 km west of Cape Town, South Africa, under the administration of St Helena. The islands total 201 sq km (Tristan da Cunha 98 sq km; Inaccessible island 10 sq km, 32 km west of Cunha; Nightingale Islands 25 sq km, 32 km south of Cunha, and Diego Alvarez or Gough Island 91 sq km, 350 km south of Cunha).

[2] The 306 inhabitants (1988) are concentrated in Tristan da Cunha, the majority employed by the Government and in a lobster processing factory. There were volcanic eruptions in 1961 and the island was evacuated, though the population returned in 1963. On Diego Alvarez there is a small weather station run by the South African Government. The main religion is Protestant and the official language is English. There is an administrator, R Perrys, who represents the Government of St Helena and an advisory council with executive and legislative duties, comprising 8 elected and 3 appointed members.

[3] A 10-year contract to operate Tristan's lucrative lobster-fishing concession, which was awarded in 1996 to a South African firm, went into effect on January 1. The 300 residents of Tristan da Cunha - as those of St Helena did - demanded British citizenship during the annual visit by St Helena's Governor.

Ascension Island

Ascension Island is of volcanic origin, covering 88 sq km. Its importance derives from its strategic location in the South Atlantic, 1,200 km northwest of St Helena. It is a communication relay center between South Africa and Europe, and the United States maintains a missile tracking station - Wideawake Airfield - there under an accord with Britain. The islands naval installation and airbase were vital to Britain during the Malvinas Islands (Falklands) war (April-June 1982) and afterwards as a base for the ships and planes that continue to supply the British troops occupying the islands which are claimed by Argentina.

[2] There is no indigenous population on Ascension Island, and the majority are employees of the St Helena Government. In 1988, of 1,099 inhabitants, 765 were from St Helena, 222 were British, 102 were American, and 10 were of other nationalities. These figures do not include British military personnel. The main religion is Protestant and the official language is English. The island's administrator, Brian Connelly, represents the Government of St Helena.

St Kitts-Nevis

Saint Kitts-Nevis

Population:	41,000 (1996)
Area:	261 SQ KM
Capital:	Basseterre
Currency:	E.C. Dollar
Language:	English

The island of Liamuiga, or "fertile land" in the language of the Carib Indians who originally lived there, was renamed St Christopher by Columbus on his second voyage to America, in 1493. It was not colonized by Europeans until 1623, when adventurer Thomas Walker established the first English settlement in the Caribbean. The neighboring island of Nevis was colonized five years later. After the rapid extermination of the Caribs, the English started to grow plantation crops, especially sugar cane, for which they used slaves from Africa.

[3] In the 20th century, the decolonization process following World War II gave the islands total internal autonomy, while foreign relations and defence were left to the colonial capitals. These islands joined the Associate States of the West Indies. In 1980, Anguilla formally separated from St Kitts and Nevis (see Anguilla), and the islands were then governed by a prime minister and a parliament, both elected by universal suffrage.

[4] The Labour Party had been in office since 1967, but suffered a major defeat in the 1980 election, at the hands of an opposition coalition of the People's Action Movement (PAM) and the Nevis Reformation Party (NRP). Kennedy Alphonse Simmonds became Prime Minister. The opposition victory meant that independence, planned for June 1980, had to be postponed as the NRP was opposed to a post-independence federation with St Kitts. The 1976 plebiscite showed that 99.4 per cent of the population of Nevis favoured separation, but the secessionist unrest on Nevis appeared to ease after the NRP joined the government.

[6] In the 1984 elections, Kennedy Simmonds and his government increased their parliamentary representation. Simmonds was re-elected in March 1989, in line with the US interests in the region.

[7] In 1990, strikes broke out among agricultural workers who had been refused a 10 per cent wage increase. Sugar companies responded by hiring close to 1,000 workers from St Vincent and the Grenadines, to cut sugar-cane. Nevis Prime Minister Daniel Simeon promised that Nevis would secede from St Kitts by the end of 1992.

[8] In June 1992, the Concerned Citizens' Movement, in opposition, won the election in Nevis, obtaining three seats in the Nevis Assembly, ousting the Nevis Reformation Party (NRP) led by Daniel Simeon. Together with the People's Action Movement, the NRP made up the main coalition. Weston Paris, Governor-General Sir Clement Athelston's representative on Nevis, died in unclarified circumstances.

[9] The November 1993 election was inconclusive. Further elections were held in July 1995 in which the St Kitts-Nevis Labour Party, led by Denzil Douglas, came to power.

[10] In mid-1996, a new constitutional crisis broke out in regard to the secession of Nevis. Vance Amory, the Premier of Nevis, declared he had started the legal process for secession from the federation. Douglas warned him they were running the risk of "fragmentation".

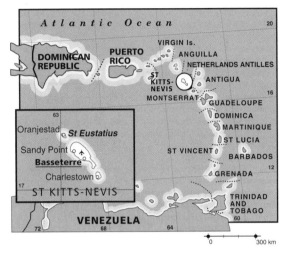

STATISTICS

DEMOGRAPHY
Population: 41,000 (1996). **Annual growth:** -0.4 % (1980/1996). **Urban population:** 33.9 % (1996).

HEALTH
Life expectancy at birth: 69 years (1996). **Infant mortality:** 31 per 1,000 (1996). **Under-5 child mortality:** 38 per 1,000 (1996). **Safe water:** 100 % (1990/96).

EDUCATION
Literacy: 90 % (1995).

COMMUNICATIONS
666 **radios**, 220 **TV sets** and 332 **main telephone lines** per 1,000 people (1994).

ECONOMY
Currency: 2.7 E.C. dollars = $ 1 (1995) **Fertilizer use:** 928 kgs per ha (1994). **Development aid received:** $4 million (1995). $ 100 **per capita** (1995). 2.1 % of GNP (1994)

HDI (rank / value) 49 / 0.853 (1994)

PROFILE

ENVIRONMENT
The territory is divided between St Kitts, 168.4 sq km, and Nevis, 93.2 sq km. The two islands are in the Windward Islands of the Lesser Antilles. They are of volcanic origin, hilly, with a rainy tropical climate, tempered by sea winds which make the land fit for plantation crops, especially sugar cane.

SOCIETY
Peoples: 95 per cent of the population are African descendants and people descended from the integration of African slaves and European colonizers (mulattos). There is a British minority.
Religions: Mainly Protestant (76.4 per cent, of which Anglican 32.3 per cent, Methodist 32.3 per cent); Roman Catholic 10.7 per cent; other 12.9 per cent.
Languages: English (official).
Political Parties: The People's Action Movement (PAM); the Nevis Reformation Party (NRP); the Labour Party (Workers' League); the United National Movement (UNM); and the Concerned Citizens' Movement.

THE STATE
Official Name: Federation of St Christopher (St Kitts) and Nevis.
Capital: Basseterre, 18,000 people (1995).
Government: Denzil Douglas, Prime Minister since July 1995; Cuthbert Montroville-Sebastian, Governor-General appointed by the British Crown in 1996. There is a Parliament with 11 members chosen by universal suffrage (8 representatives of St Kitts and 3 of Nevis), and 3 appointed senators.
National Holiday: September 19, Independence (1983).

St Lucia

St Lucia

Population: 144,000 (1996)
Area: 622 SQ KM
Capital: Castries
Currency: E.C. Dollar
Language: English

Before Christopher Columbus named it Santa Lucia in 1502, the island had already been conquered by the Caribs who had expelled the Arawak indians.

[2] Neither the Spaniards nor the British succeeded in defeating local resistance, and in 1660 the French settled on the island, starting a dispute with Britain which was to last for 150 years. Over this period, the flag of St Lucia changed 14 times.

[3] In 1814, the Treaty of Paris transferred the island from France to Britain, which kept it until 1978. France left the legacy of patois, a pidgin language of mixed African and French.

[4] Under British rule, St Lucia became one big sugarcane plantation populated by African slave labourers. Agriculture is still the main economic resource but 20 years ago sugar gave way to banana cultivation.

[5] The island was part of the Colony of the Windward Islands, and between 1959 and 1962 St Lucia belonged to the West Indies Federation. In 1967 the island became more autonomous and was granted a new constitution as one of the Federate States of the Antilles.

[6] In the first elections held as an independent nation, in July 1979, Prime Minister John G M Compton and his United Workers Party (UWP), who had governed the island since 1964, were beaten. The progressive St Lucia Labor Party (SLP) won.

[7] The new prime minister, Allen Louisy, promised to help workers and peasants and to encourage small business as a means of curbing unemployment. George Odlum was Deputy Prime Minister and minister of trade, industry, tourism and foreign affairs. He was also leader of the predominant SLP's "new left" wing, and he promoted the

> The increase in exports and tourism revenues was not enough to leave economic crisis behind, which continued through the 1990s.

country's entry to the Non-Aligned Movement and established diplomatic relations with Cuba and North Korea. He also adopted a policy of close collaboration with the neighboring island of Grenada, which had launched its own revolutionary process some months before.

[8] After repeated political crisis, the United Workers' Party won the 1982 and 1987 elections. Compton returned to power with a conservative platform, favouring a market economy and proposing adjustment measures recommended by the IMF. The increase in exports and tourism revenues was not enough to leave economic crisis behind, which continued through the 1990s.

[9] The years 1994 and 1995 were marked by protests from workers on banana plantations - the island's main export - and also by dock employees, demanding higher wages. In 1996, Vaughn Allen Lewis was elected President.

[10] In May 1997, the Labor Party won the elections with 61.3 per cent of the vote. Kenny Anthony took over as Prime Minister. One of his first measures was to form a commission to investigate corruption during the UWP administration.

LAND USE

IRRIGATED 20% of arable

(1993)

■ FOREST & WOODLAND	12.9%
□ ARABLE	8.1%
▨ OTHER	79%

PROFILE

ENVIROMENT
One of the volcanic Windward Islands of the Lesser Antilles, south of Martinique and north of St. Vincent. The climate is tropical with heavy rainfall, tempered by ocean currents. The soil is fertile, bananas, cocoa, sugar cane and coconuts are grown.

SOCIETY
Peoples: Most inhabitants are descended from the integration of African slave laborers and European colonists.
Religions: Roman Catholic 79 per cent; Protestant 15.5 per cent, of which Seventh-day Adventist 6.5 per cent, Pentecostal 3 per cent; other 5.5 per cent.
Languages: English (official) and a local dialect (Patois) derived from French and African elements.
Political Parties: The St Lucia Labor Party. The United Workers' Party (UWP). Progressive Labor Party (PLP). The Citizens' Democratic Party.

THE STATE
Official name: St Lucia. **Capital:** Castries, 53,933 people (1990).
Government: W George Mallet, Governor-General appointed by the British Crown in 1996. Kenny Anthony, Prime Minister since May, 1997. **National Holiday:** 13 December, Independence Day (1978), and Discovery by Christopher Columbus.

DEMOGRAPHY
Population: 144,000 (1996) **Annual growth:** 1.4 % (1980/1996) **Estimates for year 2000:** 200,000 (1997) **Annual growth to year 2000:** 1.3 % (1994/2000) **Urban population:** 37.2 % (1996)

HEALTH
Life expectancy at birth: 71 years (1996) **Infant mortality:** 18 per 1,000 (1996) **Under-5 child mortality:** 22 per 1,000 (1996)

EDUCATION
School enrolment: Primary total: 95 % (1990/95)

COMMUNICATIONS
764 **radios,** 250 **TV sets** and 172 **main telephone lines** per 1,000 people (1994)

ECONOMY
Consumer price index: 115.3 (1994) **Currency:** 2.7 E.C. dollars = $ 1 (1995) **Fertilizer use:** 3,888 kgs per ha (1994) **Development aid received:** $ 47 million (1995) $ 313 per capita (1995) 9.6 % of GNP (1994)

HDI (rank / value) 56 / 0.838 (1994)

St Vincent

St Vincent

Population: 110,000 (1996)
Area: 388 SQ KM
Capital: Kingstown

Currency: E.C. Dollar
Language: English

The first inhabitants were Arawaks who were displaced by the Caribs, the island's inhabitants when Columbus arrived in 1498.

[2] In 1783, St Vincent became a British colony. However, the local people resisted European conquest; the former slaves who had rebelled on the neighboring islands and those who took refuge in St Vincent joined the Caribs to oppose the invaders. In 1796, they were defeated and exterminated or deported.

[3] A plantation economy developed, using slave labor, the chief crops being sugar cane, cotton, coffee and cocoa. In 1833, St Vincent became part of the Windward Islands colony. In 1960, together with the Grenadine Islands, it was granted a new constitution with substantial internal autonomy. It also participated in the West Indies Federation until its dissolution in 1962.

[4] St Vincent became a self-governing state in association with the UK in 1969. The post of head minister - equivalent to that of prime minister, but with more limited powers - was held then by Milton Cato, together with the pro US St Vincent Labor Party (SVLP). Defence and foreign relations continued to be controlled by Britain, but independence was declared in October 1979.

[5] The elections in December 1979 reinforced the predominance of the SVLP, and the opposition PPP received only 2.4 percent of the vote.

[6] The new government faced an armed rebellion of Rastafarians led by Lennox "Bumba" Charles on Union Island. This rebellion was quickly put down by troops from Barbados.

[7] In the early 1980s, the Government faced a serious socio-economic crisis, enabling the popular movements to gain ground. In May 1981, the national Committee in Defence of Democracy was formed, supported by several opposition parties, the labor unions and other organizations. Several days later, the Government attempted to impose repressive legislation designed to maintain "public order", triggering mass protests.

[8] Cato's government supported the US invasion in Grenada and sent a police detachment to join the occupation forces (see Grenada). Cato called early elections, but the economic crisis and the SVLP's tax policies meant the New Democratic Party (NDP) won the election, while the left found its vote reduced by half, to 7.2 per cent.

[9] In the May 1989 election, James Mitchell (NDP) was re-elected, going on to sign an agreement with the prime ministers of Dominica, St Lucia, and Grenada to create a new state of the four islands in 1990 (see Dominica).

[10] In February 1992, the Government of St Vincent adopted the Tlatelolco Treaty to ban nuclear weapons in Latin America and the Caribbean.

[11] Given the Grenadians' secessionist feelings, which had already erupted in violence in 1980, Mitchell created a Ministry of Grenadine Affairs and named Herbert Young, a Grenadian, as Minister of Foreign Affairs.

[12] The SVLP took three of the fifteen seats in Parliament in the early elections held in February 1994, becoming the official opposition to the NDP Government. In August, Mitchell survived a motion of no confidence. The opposition blamed him for the failure to fight the crisis and the fall in banana exports. This product brought in 80 per cent of the income of St Vincent.

[13] Three men accused of murder were hanged in February 1995. The suspension of the moratorium on hanging, in place for many years, was condemned by Amnesty International.

[14] In 1996, Saint Vincent signed an agreement with the United States allowing the US coastguard to pursue drug traffickers through the island's territorial waters. This co-operation agreement was reinforced in August with an extradition treaty facilitating the transferral of drug-trafficker suspects to the United States.

PROFILE

ENVIRONMENT
Comprises the island of St Vincent (345 sq km) and the northern part of the Grenadines (43 sq km) including Bequia, Canouan, Mustique, Matreau, Quatre, Savan and Union. They are part of the Windward islands of the Lesser Antilles. Of volcanic origin, the islands have fertile rolling hills. The climate, tropical with heavy rainfall and tempered by ocean currents, is fit for plantation crops. St Vincent is a leading arrowroot producer, a plant with starch-rich rhizomes, used in the manufacture of a type of paper used in electronics. The population is concentrated on the island of St Vincent.

SOCIETY
Peoples: Descendants of African slaves 82 per cent, mixed 14 per cent; there are also European, Asian, and Indigenous minorities. **Religions:** Anglican, Catholic and other Protestant **Languages:** English (official); also a local dialect. **Political Parties:** The New Democratic Party (NDP). The St. Vincent Labour Party (SVLP); 2. The National Unity Movement (MNV); the United People's Movement (UPM).

THE STATE
Official name: Commonwealth of St Vincent and the Grenadines **Capital:** Kingstown, 15,824 people in 1993. **Government:** Charles Antrobus, Governor General appointed by Britain, since 1996. James Fitz-Allen Mitchell, Prime Minister and Head of State since 1984. There are 13 elected representatives in Parliament and a Senate with 6 members. **National Holiday:** October 27, Independence Day (1979).

DEMOGRAPHY
Population: 113,000 (1996) **Annual growth:** 0.9 % (1980/1996) **Estimates for year 2000:** 100,000 (1997) **Annual growth to year 2000:** 0.9 % (1994/2000) **Urban population:** 49.5 % (1996)

HEALTH
Life expectancy at birth: 72 years (1996) **Infant mortality:** 19 per 1,000 (1996) **Under-5 child mortality:** 23 per 1,000 (1996) **Safe water:** 89 % (1990/96)

EDUCATION
Literacy: 82% (1995) **Primary total:** 95% (1990/95)

COMMUNICATIONS
667 **radios,** 230 **TV sets** and 155 **main telephone lines** per 1,000 people (1994)

ECONOMY
Consumer price index: 115.1 (1994) **Currency:** 2.7 E.C. dollars = $ 1 (1995) **Fertilizer use:** 2,727 kgs per ha (1994) **Development aid received:** $ 47 million (1995) $ 427 per capita (1995) 20.5 % of GNP (1994)

HDI (rank / value) 57 / 0.836 (1994)

Samoa

Samoa

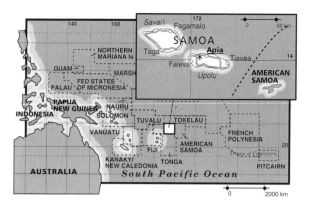

Population:	166,000 (1996)
Area:	2,831 SQ KM
Capital:	Apia
Currency:	Tala
Language:	Samoan and English

The archipelago of Samoa has been inhabited since at least 1,000 BC. The people developed a complex social structure. Four of these local groups still hold a privileged position: the Malietoa, the Tamasese, the Mataafa and the Tuimalealiifano.

2   The Dutch were the first Europeans to visit the islands in 1722, but colonization did not begin until the end of the 19th century.

3   In 1855, Germany finally occupied the islands. German merchants bought copra with Bolivian and Chilean currency valued at 10 times its real worth. In 1889 a new treaty recognized the US rights over the part of Samoa located east of meridian 171; "rights" which the US still retains. The western half remained under German rule.

4   In 1914, upon the outbreak of World War I, New Zealand occupied the German part of the island, which was later granted to Aotearoa (New Zealand) by the League of Nations as a trust territory.

5   In 1920, an influenza epidemic killed 25 per cent of the population. At about the same time, the 'Mau' movement began to spread throughout the archipelago, preaching resistance to the foreign governments. Samoans carried out a nine-year-long civil disobedience campaign, which eventually became a vigorous pro-independence movement.

6   In 1961 after intense protests and pressure from the UN, a plebiscite was held for Samoans to vote on independence. This was achieved the following year, with a Constitution based largely on the traditional social structure and the executive power in the hands of two rulers, Tupua Tamasase Meoble and Malietoa Tanumafili. Only the leading group (*matai*), around 8,500 in all, are eligible to vote.

7   After being elected prime minister in 1970, Tupua Tamasese Lealofi launched a battle against the matai. He also backed the establishment of foreign corporations on the archipelago, despite strong opposition.

8   The 1976 elections were won by the opposition. Tupuola Tais became prime minister. In 1979

he retained office by only one vote in parliament. The price of cocoa and copra fell, further aggravating the economic and financial situation, making it necessary for 2,000 Samoans to emigrate each year.

9   In February 1982, Va'al Kolone, leader of the Party for the Protection of Human Rights, came to power. In September he was removed from government, amid accusations of corruption and abuse of power.

10   In April 1988, Tofilau Eti Alesana came to power; his political party won an absolute majority in the legislative in the 1985 elections, when it obtained 31 of the 47 seats.

11   Malnutrition is on the increase; one in six pre-school children and 11 per cent of all primary school children are undernourished. The islands have 200,000 hectares of arable land but less than a third of this is cultivated.

12   The 1991 constitutional reform extended the parliamentary term from three to five years, and increased the number of seats from 47 to 49. Fiame Naomi became minister of education that year, the first woman to be appointed to the cabinet.

13   Exports suffered a sharp reduction in 1993 and 1994. In that year, the country's exports amounted to only 4 per cent of the imports. Remittances from Samoan workers living abroad partially compensated for the gap.

14   Following recommendations from the United States, Samoa opened up to foreign investment with major tourist development projects, which implied the construction of hotels and airports.

15   A new tax on goods and services passed in 1995 and a 15 per cent cut of state services funds caused widespread rejection among the population.

16   In the 1996 elections, the party of Prime Minister Tofilau Eti Alesana lost most of its support. Even so, it was able to stay in power due to an alliance with independent groups.

17   The economic situation deteriorated and demonstrations increased. In December 1997, there were protests against the rise of prices.

PROFILE

ENVIRONMENT
Includes the islands of Savai'i, 1,690 sq km, 40,000 people; Upolu, 1,100 sq km, 110,000 people, Manono and Apolina, in Polynesia, northeast of Fiji. The eastern portion of the Samoa archipelago is under US administration. The islands are of volcanic origin, mountainous, with fertile soil in the lowland areas. The climate is tropical, tempered by sea winds.

SOCIETY
Peoples: Samoans are mostly Polynesian (92.6 per cent). "Euronesians" (a result of European and Polynesian integration) make up 10 per cent of the population. There are Europeans and Pacific islanders.
Religions: Congregational 47.2 per cent; Roman Catholic, 22.3 per cent; Methodist, 15.1 per cent; Mormon, 8.6 per cent; other, 6.8 per cent.
Languages: Samoan and English are the official languages.
Political Parties: The Human Rights Protection Party (HRPP); the Samoa National Development Party.

THE STATE
Official Name: Samoa i Sisifo.
Capital: Apia, 40,000 people (1994).
Government: Malietoa Tanumafili II, Head of State for life. Tofilau Eti Alesana, Prime Minister since 1988. By the 1991 constitutional reform, 2 of the 49 representatives are elected by universal suffrage while the rest are chosen by the Heads of the Samoan clans and families. After the death of Tanumafili II, the president will be elected by direct vote.
National Holiday: June 10, Independence Day (1962).

DEMOGRAPHY
Population: 166,000 (1996) **Annual growth:** 0.4 % (1980/1996) **Urban population:** 21.1 % (1996) **Children per woman:** 3.9 (1996)

HEALTH
Life expectancy at birth: 69 years (1996) **Infant mortality:** 42 per 1,000 (1996) **Under-5 child mortality:** 53 per 1,000 (1996) **Safe water:** 82 % (1990/96)

EDUCATION
Literacy: 98 % (1995) **female:** 98 % (1995) **School enrolment: Primary total:** 100 % (1990/95)

COMMUNICATION
462 **radios.**

ECONOMY
Consumer price index: 128.9 (1994) **Currency:** 2.53 tala = $ 1 (1995) **Development aid received:** $ 43 million (1995) $ 253 per capita (1995) 24.3 % of GNP (1994)

HDI (rank / value) 96 / 0.684 (1994)

American Samoa

Population: 56,000 (1996)
Area: 199 SQ KM
Capital: Pago Pago

Currency: US Dollar
Language: Samoan and English

American Samoa

In the 18th century, 150 years after the Europeans had reached the islands, the colonial interests of Germany, Britain and North America disputed the possession. The 1899 treaty settled the conflict, granting the United States the seven islands east of Meridian 171. Traditional social structures were maintained but agriculture was not stimulated so the population became totally dependent on the external colonial economy. This situation resulted in the increasing number of emigrants; over half of the Samoan population currently lives in Hawaii and other parts of the United States.

[2] On December 5 1984, the UN General Assembly considered Eastern Samoa's right to self-determination and independence. A unanimous vote reiterated that factors such as territory, geographic location, population and meagre resources should not hinder independence. The United States, in its role as administrative power, was urged to implement an educational program to assure Samoans' full awareness of their rights, to hasten the decolonization process. The islanders, however, seem to be content with their present state, which allows them to emigrate to the United States without restrictions. There are no organized pro-independence groups.

[3] In 1984, Governor Coleman (elected in the first elections for governor held in 1977) submitted proposals for a new Constitution in American Samoa for ratification by the US Congress. The proposals were withdrawn in May of the same year, because it was feared that they would be harmful to the interests of US citizens. In November, A P Lutali was elected Governor and Faleomavaega Eni Hunkin became Vice-Governor.

[4] In July 1988, the delegate to the US house of representatives, Fofo Sunia, announced that he would not stand for re-election because he was going to be subjected to official investigations after accusations of financial mismanagement. In October, he was sentenced to a 5 to 15 week term in prison for fraud. Hence, Eni Hunkin replaced Sunia. In November, Coleman was re-elected for his third term and Galeani Poumele replaced Hunkin as Vice-Governor.

[5] In the second half of 1986, the governments of American Samoa and Samoa signed an agreement to create a permanent committee for the development of both countries in tourism, transport, and fishing.

[6] Economic development is dependent on the 90 per cent of Samoan foreign trade going to the US. Tuna fishing and tuna processing plants are the backbone of the private sector economy, with the canneries as the second-largest employers, exceeded only by the Government.

[7] Despite reforms to the 1967 constitution during the 1980s,

---

The projected social security reform in the United States and its dependencies led to a debate in the second half of 1996 about the consequences for the inhabitants of American Samoa.

---

proposed changes were not ratified by the United States Congress. According to the constitution currently in effect, in addition to a governor, who is elected for a four-year term, there is also a legislature, or "Fono" with an 18-member Senate elected every four years by the Matai, or clan heads. There is also a 20-member House of Representatives elected by direct popular vote for two-year terms. Women do not have the right to vote.

[8] After his re-election for governor in 1992, Lutali took measures to cut public spending, especially by reducing the number of government employees. The projected social security reform in the United States and its dependencies led to a debate in the second half of 1996 about the consequences for the inhabitants of American Samoa.

[9] Figures from the archipelago expressed the concern for the

PROFILE

ENVIRONMENT
The island occupies 197 sq km of the eastern part of the Samoan archipelago, located in Polynesia, slightly to the east of the International Date Line, northwest of the Fiji islands. The most important islands are Tutuila (where the capital is located), Tau, Olosega, Ofu, Annuu, Rose and Swains. Of volcanic origin, the islands are mountainous with fertile soil on the plains. The climate is rainy and tropical, tempered by sea winds. There is dense, woody vegetation and major streams of shallow waters. The main export product is fish, especially tuna.

SOCIETY
Peoples: Samoans are mostly Polynesians (89 per cent); Tongans 4 per cent; other 5 per cent.
Religions: Christian (Protestant 50 per cent, Catholic 20 per cent); others 30 per cent.
Languages: Samoan, predominant, and English are the official languages.

THE STATE
Official Name: Territory of American Samoa.
Capital: Pago Pago, on Tutuila, 9,000 people (1994 est).
Government: William Clinton, US President is Head of State. Tauese P Sunia, Governor since January 1997. There is a bicameral Legislative Power. Samoans are considered US "nationals", but without the right to vote in presidential elections while living on the islands.

DEMOGRAPHY
Population: 56,000 (1996) **Estimates for year 2000:** 200,000 **Annual growth to year 2000:** 1.1% (1994/2000) **Urban population:** 50.8% (1996)

reform's effects on American Samoan residents - regarded as US "nationals" but with fewer rights than the "citizens" of that country - and on immigrants, specifically those from other Polynesian territories.

[10] In November 1996, Tauese Pita Sunia was elected Governor with 51 per cent of the vote, to substitute AP Lutali. Togiola Tulafono became Vice-Governor. Both took office in January 1997.

[11] In November 1997, after expressing concern over a supposed crime wave, the Government imposed a curfew in Pago Pago between nine at night and six in the morning.

[12] In February 1998, a high ranking official in the Education Ministry accused the Governor of using funds for improving schools to build a sauna in his official residence.

Population: 135,000 (1996)
Area: 964 SQ KM
Capital: São Tomé

Currency: Dobras
Language: Portuguese

São Tomé e Príncipe

São Tomé island was probably uninhabited when it was first visited by European navigators in the1470s. Thereafter, the Portuguese began to settle convicts and exiled Jews on the island and established sugar plantations there, using slave labor from the African mainland. Strategically located 300 kms off the African coast, the islands' natural ports were used by the Portuguese as "supply stops for ships" in the 15th century. Dutch, French, Spanish, British and Portuguese slave traders bought enslaved African laborers to be sold in the American colonies. Some of those slaves remained on the islands, which later became the leading African producers of sugarcane

[2] Rebellion soon broke out and after the failure of an insurrection headed by Yoan Gato, a slave named Amador led a revolt that succeeded in controlling two-thirds of the island of São Tomé, where he proclaimed himself ruler.

[3] Soon defeated, the rebels hid in quilombos (guerrilla shelters in the forest) after burning their crops. The lndlords who moved to Brazil with their enslaved workers took with them the seed of insurrection which quickly produced quilombos in Brazil, some of which, such as the Palmares quilombo, became true republics and held out for nearly a century.

[4] In São Tomé and Príncipe, agriculture disappeared for three centuries. In the 17th century the island was held briefly by the Dutch. After a period of decline, the colony recovered its prosperity in the late 19th century with the cultivation of cocoa.

[5] Even after abolition was declared in 1869, slavery continued in a disguised manner ("free" workers signed contracts for nine years at fixed salaries), leading to revolts and an international boycott against the "cocoa slavery" of the Portuguese colony in the early 20th century.

[6] This neo-slave system continued until the mid-1900s. A Society for Immigration of São Tomé organized the modern slave trade, "hiring" plantation workers in other Portuguese colonies: Angola, Cape Verde, Guinea and Mozambique. This flow "re-Africanized" the country as the "filhos da terra" (sons of the earth), the result of several centuries of integration between the natives and the Portuguese, mixed with the African immigrants. During the colonial regimes of Salazar and Caetano, repression was particularly harsh. In February 1953, over 1,000 people were killed in Batepá in less than a week.

[7] This massacre revealed the need for the rebels to join forces, and in 1969 the Movement for the Liberation of São Tomé and Príncipe (MLSTP) was founded, with two main objectives: independence and land reform.

[8] Foreign companies owned 90 per cent of the land of São Tomé and despite the fertile soil, most food was imported due to the island's monoculture policy. Rural workers were and still are one of the major pillars of the MLSTP, as shown by a 24-hour strike in August 1963, which paralyzed all the plantations.

[9] As the island's terrain did not favor guerrilla warfare, the MLSTP launched an intensive underground political campaign that resulted in its recognition by the OAU and the Non-Aligned Nations. Together with the MPLA of Angola, the PAIGC of Guinea and Cape Verde, and FRELIMO of Mozambique, the MLSTP joined the Conference of National Organizations of the Portuguese Colonies. It was the only legitimate group in existence when, after the 1974 revolution, Portugal began to free its colonies.

[10] The MLSTP joined a transition government in 1974 and in the following year declared independence. Its accomplishments were impressive: banks and farms were nationalized, medicine was socialized, a national currency was created, a major administrative reform was launched to reorganize public administration, and numerous centers of popular culture, based on the culture-building educational methods of Brazilian

57%

Paulo Freire, were created as part of a literacy campaign.
[11] Opposing these reforms was a rightist faction led by Health Minister Carlos da Graca, who fled to Gabon to plot a mercenary invasion of the islands in early 1978. The thwarted conspiracy consolidated the unity of the MLSTP, which held its first congress in August 1978. Mass organizations to defend the revolution were fostered and a People's Militia was formed. Miguel Trovoada, Prime Minister since independence, was removed, thus strengthening the more progressive trends of the Party Co-ordinating Committee.
[12] In March 1986, two opposition groups based outside the country - the São Tomé e Príncipe Independent Democratic Union (UDISTP) and the more radical São Tomé e Príncipe National Resistance Front (FRNSTP), founded by Carlos da Graça- announced the formation of an alliance called the Democratic Opposition Coalition. The aim of this coalition was to put pressure on the Government to hold free elections. A month later, a fishing vessel with 76 members of the FRNSTP on board arrived in Walvis Bay, the South African enclave in Namibia. They asked the Pretoria Government to supply military aid needed to destabilize the São Tomé Government. These events led to Carlos de Graca's resignation as president of the FRNSTP. In May, he announced his willingness to cooperate with the Government, on the condition that Cuban and

---

Gradually, the State relinquished economic control, previously heavily dependent upon such key products as cocoa, coffee and bananas.

Angolan troops stationed in the country be withdrawn.
[13] In 1985, in the midst of the worst drought in the country's history, the Government sought to open up the economy: new legislation was designed to promote foreign investment and privatize the so-called "people's stores". Gradually, the State relinquished economic control, previously heavily dependent upon such key products as cocoa, coffee and bananas. The Government sought ways to attract foreign capital to the agricultural, fishing and tourist sectors. In 1989 there was a 20 per cent devaluation of the nation's currency (the dobra) which triggered a steep increase in basic commodity prices.
[14] Late in 1989, the MLSTP leadership discussed reform of the party statutes and of the national constitution. In March 1990, the People's National Assembly approved amendments to the Charter, later to be submitted to a referendum. These changes made possible a move to a multi-party system. Independent candidates were admitted in the legislative elections, and the tenure of the President was limited to no longer than two five-year terms.
[15] The first parliamentary elections after independence were held in January 1991. The opposition Democratic Convergence of Leonel d'Alva was voted into power. In March, the former prime minister Miguel Trovoada returned from exile and was unopposed in the presidential elections.
[16] The heads of state of São Tomé and Principe, Cape Verde, Guinea-Bissau, Mozambique and Angola - all former Portuguese colonies - met in February 1992. After being organized under single party systems, the five countries experienced rapid political change and economic liberalization processes.
[17] The social and economic situation of the country worsened in recent years as the result of an IMF and World Bank imposed austerity plan. Public sector salaries were frozen, a third of all civil servants were dismissed and the local currency was devalued by 80 per cent.

STATISTICS

DEMOGRAPHY
Population: 135,000 (1996). **Annual growth:** 2.3% (1980/1996). **Estimates for year 2000:** 100,000. **Annual growth to year 2000:** 2% (1994/2000). **Urban Population:** 43.7% (1996).

HEALTH
Life expectancy at birth: 69 years (1996). **Infant mortality:** 62 per 1,000 (1996). **Under-5 child mortality:** 80 per 1,000 (1996). **Safe water:** 82% (1990/96).

EDUCATION
Literacy: 57% (1995). male : 73% (1995). female: 42% (1995).

COMMUNICATIONS
270 **radios**, **TV** sets and 20 **main telephone lines** per 1,000 people (1994).

ECONOMY
Currency: dobras = $ 1 (1995) **Cereal imports:** 11 metric tons (1994). **Development aid received:** $ 78 million (1995). $ 600 per capita (1995). 339.1% of GNP (1994).

HDI (rank / value) 125 / 0.534 (1994)

The social and economic situation of the country worsened in recent years as the result of an IMF- and World Bank-imposed austerity plan.

While inflation fell, the price of basic foodstuffs quadrupled and unemployment reached 30 per cent.
[18] The island of Principe declared independence on April 29 1995 and established a five-member regional government.
[19] In August, a group of army officers took power in a bloodless coup. Negotiations led to the immediate re-establishment of the legal government.
[20] The General Assembly censured Prime Minister Armindo Vaz D'Almeida, in power since December 31 of the previous year, for "bad management, inefficiency, incompetence and corruption."
[21] Miguel Trovoada was re-elected in the July 1996 elections and in November, he nominated Raul Bragança Neto as Prime Minister.
[22] The economy of São Tome was sustained by international aid in 1997: 60 per cent of the budget was funded by contributions, particularly from Europe. The European Development Fund funded a programme to create jobs, set up medical care centres and supply medical equipment.

Saudi Arabia

'Arabiyah as-Sa'udiyah

Population:	18,836,000 (1996)
Area:	2,149,690 SQ KM
Capital:	Riyadh (Ar-Riyad) (royal capital)
Currency:	Saudi Arabian riyals
Language:	Arabic

Arabia was drawn into the orbit of western Asiatic civilization toward the end of the 3rd millennium BC. Caravan trade between south Arabia and the Fertile Crescent began about the middle of the 2nd millennium BC. The domestication of the camel around the 12th century BC made desert travel easier and gave rise to a flourishing society in South Arabia, centred around the state of Saab (Sheila). In eastern Arabia the island of Dolman (Bahrain) had become a thriving entrepot between Mesopotamia, South Arabia, and India as early as the 24th century BC. The discovery by the Mediterranean peoples of the monsoon winds in the Indian Ocean made possible flourishing Roman and Byzantine suborn trade between the northern Red Sea ports and South Arabia, extending to India and beyond. In the 5th and 6th centuries AD, successive invasions of the Christian Ethiopians and the counter-invasion of the Sasanian kings disrupted the states of South Arabia.

[2] In the 6th century Quraysh - the noble and holy house of the confederation of the Hejaz controlling the sacred enclave of Mecca - contrived a series of agreements with the northern and southern tribes. Under this aegis, caravans moved freely from the southern Yemen coast to Mecca and thence northward to Byzantium or eastward to Iraq. Furthermore, members of the Quraysh house of 'Abd Manaf concluded pacts with Byzantium, Persia, and rulers of Yemen and Ethiopia, promoting commerce outside Arabia. The 'Abd Manaf house could effect such agreements because of Quraysh's superior position with the tribes.

WORKERS

(1996)

Labour force %

■ WOMEN
□ MEN

14   86

■ AGRICULTURE 19% (1990)
□ INDUSTRIAL 20%
■ SERVICES 61%

Quraysh had some sanctity as lords of the Meccan temple (the Ka'bah) and were themselves known as the Protected Neighbors of Allah. The tribes on pilgrimage to Mecca were called the Guests of Allah.

[3] In its enclave Quraysh was secure from attack; it arbitrated in tribal disputes, attaining thereby at least a local pre-eminence and seemingly a kind of loose hegemony over many Arabian tribes. The Ka'bah, through the additions of other cults, developed into a pantheon, the cult of other gods perhaps being linked with political agreements between Quraysh - worshippers of Allah - and the tribes.

[4] Mohammed was born in 570 of the Hashimite branch of the noble house of 'Abd Manaf; though orphaned at an early age and in consequence with little influence, he never lacked protection by his clan. Marriage to a wealthy widow improved his position as a merchant, but he began to make his mark in Mecca by preaching the oneness of Allah. Rejected by the Quraysh lords, Mohammed sought affiliation with other groups; he was unsuccessful until he managed to negotiate a pact with the tribal chiefs of Medina, whereby he obtained their protection and became theocratic head and arbiter of the Medinan tribal confederation (*ummah*). Those Quraysh who joined him there were known as muhajirun (refugees or emigrants), while his Medinan allies were called *ansar* (supporters). The Muslim era dates from the *hijrah* (hegira) - Mohammed's move to Medina in AD 622.

[5] Mohammed's supporters attacked a Quraysh caravan in AD 624, thus breaking the vital security system established by the 'Abd Manaf house, and hostilities broke out against his Mecca kin. In Medina two problems confronted him - the necessity to enforce his role as arbiter and to raise supplies for his moves against Quraysh. He overcame internal opposition, removing in the process three Jewish tribes, whose properties he distributed among his followers. Externally, his rising power was demonstrated following Quraysh's failure to overrun Medina, when he declared it his own sacred enclave. Mohammed foiled Quraysh

offensives and marched back to Mecca. After taking Mecca in AD 630 he became lord of the two sacred enclaves; however, even though he broke the power of some Quraysh lords, his policy thenceforth was to conciliate his Quraysh kin.

[6] After Mohammed's entry into Mecca the tribes linked with Quraysh came to negotiate with him and to accept Islam; this meant little more than giving up their local deities and worshipping Allah alone. They had to pay the tax, but this was not novel because the tribal chiefs had already been taxed to protect the Meccan enclave. Many tribes probably waited to join the winner. From then on Islam was destined for a world role. Under Mohammed's successors the expansionist urge of the tribal groups, temporarily united around the nucleus of the two sacred enclaves, coincided with the weakness of Byzantium and Sasanian Persia. Tribes summoned to the banners of Islam launched a career of conquest that promised to satisfy the mandate of their new faith as well as the desire for booty and lands. With families and flocks, they left the peninsula. Population movements of such magnitude affected all of Arabia; in

Hadhramaut they possibly caused neglect of irrigation works, resulting in erosion of fertile lands. In Oman, too, when Arabs evicted the Persian ruling class, its complex irrigation system suffered. Many Omani Arabs about the mid-7th century left for Basra (in Iraq) and formed the influential Azd group there. Arabian Islam replaced Persian influence in the Bahrain district and Al-Hasa province in the northeast, and in Yemen.

[7] As the conquests far beyond Arabia poured loot into the Holy Cities (Mecca and Medina), they became wealthy centres of a sophisticated Arabian culture. Medina became a centre for Qur'anic (Koran) study, the evolution of Islamic law, and historical record. Under the caliphs - Mohammed's successors - Islam began to assume its characteristic shape. Paradoxically, outside the cities it made little difference to Arabian life for centuries. After the Prophet's death, Omar, the second caliph, led the Arab conquest. Within ten years the Arabs occupied Syria, Palestine, Egypt and Persia. With Muawiya, the caliphate became hereditary in the family of the Ummaias and the Arabs became a privileged caste which ruled over the conquered nations.

8 In the 8th century, the borders of the Arabian Empire reached from North Africa and Spain to the west, to Pakistan and Afghanistan in the east. Upon moving the capital to Damascus, Syria became the cultural, political and economic center of the Empire, and it was in Damascus that the foundations of a new culture were laid. Greco-Roman, Persian and Indian components blended into an original combination in which science played an important role. Contrary to Mohammed's expectations, the Arabian peninsula was to remain on the sidelines within the enormous empire, except in religious matters. Mecca, although failing to match Baghdad or Damascus in socio-economic and cultural importance, continued to be the center of Islam and the destination of multitudinous pilgrimages that came from all over the world.

9 This situation remained unchanged for centuries. The empire split up; the capital moved to Baghdad and the power of the caliphs passed over to the viziers, while culturally Arabic civilization attained the highest standards in all fields of knowledge and artistic creation. Arabic became the language of scholars, from Portugal to India. But little changed in the land that gave birth to all this civilization. Nomadic groups continued to shepherd their flocks; the settled population kept up their commerce, and rivalries between the two were frequently settled through war. As in Mohammed's time, demographic growth was channelled towards conquest, with the emigration of whole communities, such as the Been Hills in the 11th century. Trading caravans carrying supplies to Mecca and stopping points along the way, became much more frequent, while the ports became more active as a result of trade with Africa (see box in Tanzania: The Zandj culture). The peninsula was governed from Egypt, first by Saladin and later by the Mamelukes. The Turks ruled from the 16th century to the 20th century, without introducing any major changes in the socio-economic pattern of the Arab nation.

10 Under Turkish rule the provinces of Hidjaz and Asir, on the Red Sea, had a reasonable degree of autonomy due to the religious prestige of the shereefs of Mecca, descendents of Mohammed. The interior, with Riyadh as the main urban center, became the Emirate of Najd at the end of the 18th century, through the efforts of the Saud family supported by the Wahabite sect (known as the Islamic Puritans). In the 19th century, with Turkish assistance, the Rated clan forced Abd al-Rah man bin Saud out of power; the ousted

leader sought exile in Kuwait. In 1902, his son Abd al-Aziz, again with the support of the Wahabites, organized a religious-military sect, the Ikhwan, in which he enlisted nearly 50,000 Bedouins in order to reconquer Najd. Twelve years later the Saudis defeated the Rachidis and added the Al-Hasa region on the Gulf until then under direct control of the Turks, against whom the Saudi forces fought during World War I. At the end of the conflict, Britain, the predominant power in the area, faced a difficult situation. In exchange for Abd al-Aziz' continued anti-Turk campaign, Britain had promised to guarantee the integrity of his state. But for the same reason, it had also promised to make Hussein bin Ali (the shereef of Mecca) king of a nation that would encompass Palestine, Jordan, Iraq and the Arabian peninsula.

11 The Emir of Najd waited for some time. It seemed clear to him that Britain would not keep its word to Hussein: such a powerful kingdom, ruled by the Prophet's family with the capital in the holy city, would alter the regional balance of power. But in 1924 Hussein proclaimed himself caliph (see Jordan). Abd al-Aziz invaded his territory immediately, despite English opposition and in January 1926 was declared King of Hidjaz and Sultan of Nadj in the great mosque of Mecca. Six years later the 'Kingdom of Hidjaz, of Nedj and its dependencies' was formally unified under the name of Saudi Arabia.

12 In 1930, the monarch gave US companies permission to drill for oil. When he died in 1953, his son Saud squandered all the revenues paid into the Kingdom's treasury by the Arab-American Oil Company (Aramco), on palaces, harems, fancy cars and casinos on the French Riviera. In 1964 the country was on the verge of bankruptcy when Saud was ousted by his brother Faisal, an able diplomat who had also proved a valiant soldier in the wars. Monogamous, deeply religious and austere to the point of asceticism, Faisal gave new life to the country's economy and began to invest petrodollars in ambitious development programs, though maintaining the traditional feudal structure headed by the autocratic ruler.

13 Faisal's religious views led him to bluntly reject the Soviet Union and any other system linked with atheism, including Nasser's nationalism in Egypt, as well as Iraqi or Syrian Ba'athism. His strategic alliance with the United States was seen as 'natural', but was disturbed by US support of Israel after the war of 1967. (Faisal used to say that his only dream was to be able to pray one day in Omar's mosque, in a freed Jerusalem) and rivalries

with neighboring Iran, which under the Shah Pahlevi also played watchdog to Washington's interests in the Gulf.

14 During the 1973 Arab-Israeli war, Faisal supported an oil embargo on the countries backing Israel, including the US. The sudden oil shortage allowed OPEC countries to increase oil prices in a short space of time, heralding a new era in international relations. On March 25 1975, Faisal was murdered by an apparently insane nephew. His brother Khaled, almost paralyzed by a rheumatic illness, was named as his successor. However, due to his paralysis, the governing duties in an era of superabundance fell to his brother, Crown Prince Fahd ibn Abd al-Aziz.

15 The oil revenue, which amounted to $500 million a year when Faisal was crowned in 1964, had gone up to almost $30 billion when he died. That same year the Bank of America closed its balance with assets of $57.5 billion, and West Germany's exports amounted to $90 billion. These figures reveal that, when compared

with other major economic powers, Saudi economic power has been overrated. These were staggering figures for the Third World: three times the income of Egypt, whose population was eight times bigger.

16 New cities, universities, hospitals, freeways and mosques sprouted up everywhere. Yet there was surplus money available. Instead of planning oil production to meet the country's needs, which would have avoided the fall in prices and the weakening of OPEC during the 1980s, fortunes accumulated in western banks. Thus, Saudi Arabia tied its future more closely with the industrialized capitalist world. In addition it created a surplus of money in circulation, which the banks lent to Third World countries in some irresponsible ventures. This gave rise to the 1984-85 foreign debt crisis, with a rise in interest rates.

17 The Muslim fundamentalist groups denounced the Saudi dynasty for allegedly betraying Islam, leading to several violent confrontations with government

forces. The theological basis which legitimised the ruling autocracy may be undermined by the progressive rise to power of new members of the ruling family, trained in European and US universities and military academies, rather than in the traditional desert-tent Koranic schools.

[18] After the overthrow of the Shah of Iran, the Saudi government drew closer to the US. With King Khaled's death, on June 13 1982, his brother Fahd - the architect of Saudi Arabia's foreign policy - became king.

[19] The year before, the new monarch had created a peace plan for the Middle East which had been approved by several Arab countries, the PLO and the United States, though the plan collapsed in August, 1981 due to Israeli opposition. This plan proposed the creation of a Palestinian State, with Jerusalem as its capital, the withdrawal of Israel from the occupied Arab territories, and the dismantling of the Jewish colonies set up in 1967, as well as the recognition of the right of every State in the area to live peacefully. On September 26 1982, during the Haj or pilgrimage to Mecca, the King condemned Israeli intervention in Lebanon, which he called criminal aggression. He also criticized Soviet intervention in Afghanistan, accused Ayatollah Khomeini of attempting to destabilize the regime through sabotage, and generally condemned the 'influence of great powers' in the Muslim world.

[20] Naval bases in Jubail and Jeddah were built under the supervision of the US Army. Also, investments and bank deposits by the Saudi State and nobility were closely linked with the performance of the US economy: two-thirds of the huge amount of Saudi petrodollars invested abroad have gone into corporation stocks, treasury bonds and bank deposits in the US.

[21] The official development plans established an industrial policy to reduce dependency from oil resources. Priority was given to the petrochemical industry, and there was a proliferation of steel mills, mechanical manufacturing plants, heavy industry, and others.

[22] The industrial infrastructure is concentrated in two new cities: Jubail, on the shores of the Gulf, and Yanbu, on the Red Sea. They are connected with the eastern hydrocarbon deposits through gas and oil pipelines.

[23] The 1985-89 five-year plan promised a 'wide income redistribution'. Yet, that intention coincided with the first signs of economic trouble in the Kingdom. In 1984, due to another drop in the price of crude, the official budget closed with a deficit for the first time. The Minister of Industry, Ghazi Al Gosaibi, was forced to

resign after writing a poem which made reference to corruption.

[24] Million-dollar investments in all kinds of mainly US weapons continued, aiming to secure the Gulf coast against the potential Iranian aggression and satisfying the ambitions of an increasingly powerful and influential army.

[25] During the Iran-Iraq war, Saudi Arabia backed Iraq financially, afraid that the Iranian Islamic revolution might spread over the Gulf. Fahd changed his title of King to Guardian of the Holy Sites, but every year the pious pilgrims to Mecca protested more loudly, angry about the alliance between Riyadh and Washington and by what they considered a commercialization and westernization of the sacred places, surrounded today by shopping centers, highways and other symbols of transnational culture. On August 1 1987, a march by Iranian women and maimed war veterans in Mecca was fired upon by Saudi police. Hundreds of pilgrims were killed. In retaliation, the embassies of Saudi Arabia and Kuwait in Tehran were attacked and burned, and the relations between both countries grew very tense.

[26] In early 1990 Amnesty International disclosed "a clear pattern of human rights violations, including torture" of political opposition and labor leaders, belonging primarily to the Shi'a sect.

[27] After the Iraqi invasion of Kuwait, in August 1990, Saudi Arabia was the scene of a huge military deployment by a multinational coalition led by the United States. Apart from the loss of human lives, the war caused a huge ecological disaster. Since the end of the war, Saudi Arabia has spent some $14 billion on US weapons.

[28] In March 1992, King Fahd issued several decrees aimed at decentralizing political power. This legislation, of 83 articles, is called 'The Basic System of Government'. Amongst other amendments, it established an Advisory Council, which has the right to review all matters of national policy. However, the ultimate decision-making power always belongs to the King.

[29] The royal decrees also created the mutawein, religious police, whose mandate is to ensure the observance of Islamic customs. The home is defined as a sacred place, and therefore the state (the religious police) may enter without legal authorization. This situation has led to the detention of several alleged violators of the law.

[30] The Iraqi invasion of Kuwait, and the subsequent crisis in the Persian Gulf, exposed the Kingdom's political and military dependence upon the United States. It also served as a catalyst

for political reform within Saudi Arabia itself.

[31] In 1992, Fahd confirmed his brother Abdullah ibn Abd al-Aziz al-Saud as heir to the throne. Human rights organizations, such as Amnesty International, expressed their concern throughout 1993 over the arbitrary arrest of mainly Christians and Shi'a Muslims, but also Sunnis.

[32] In the economic field, Fahd announced in May 1994 his goal to implement a program to privatize large state enterprises, such as the national airline and telephone companies. Despite a small rise in the price of oil in 1995, the King decreed significant reductions of public spending, which amounted to 20 per cent in the education sector.

[33] According to several observers, growing social differentiation aggravated tensions among Saudis themselves, regarded as privileged compared to the millions of foreign workers living in the country. The attempt against the offices of US advisers in Riyadh, in November, killing at least 6 people, was seen as proof of those tensions.

[34] Fahd's illness became more serious toward the end of 1995, and he was forced to withdraw

from the political scene until the second half of 1996. Hostility toward the United States became stronger in one part of the population, reaching crisis point with the attack on the US El Khobar base on June 25 1996. A 2,200 kilogram bomb left 19 soldiers dead and hundreds injured. The United States applied extreme security measures and demanded investigations to find those responsible, as it feared violence would break out again.

[35] This same year, Saudi Arabia was highlighted as one of the world's biggest arms purchasers. Internal battles over who would succeed the 70-year-old king continued in the heart of the royal family, while the social crisis led to the radicalisation of Islamic sectors hostile to Fahd's pro-United States policy.

[36] In 1997, tension between Washington and Baghdad weakened the alliance with the US. Saudi Arabia warned President Bill Clinton the contrast between its "hard line" policy against Iraq and to the "soft" policy with Israel, could exasperate the region's Arab population. At the end of this year, 2,000 immigrants without papers were expelled, marking a U-turn in migration policy.

Senegal

Sénégal

Population: 8,532,000 (1996)
Area: 196,722 SQ KM
Capital: Dakar

Currency: CFA francs
Language: French

The banks of the Senegal River have been inhabited for many centuries by peoples who had been Islamicized through contact with neighboring Arab countries. This group of countries make up the region known as the Sahel. The Wolof (who constitute more than a third of the population), Fulani, Pulaar and other peoples, all lived within the area of modern Senegal.

2   When the French occupied the area during the 17th century, they incorporated it into the triangular world trade pattern of the time: European manufactured goods were exchanged for slaves, sold in the Antilles, where colonial European powers produced rum and sugar, which were sold back in Europe.

3   After slavery was abolished by the French revolution of 1848, the Senegalese became "second class citizens" of the French Empire, with one political representative in Paris. At this time Senegal exported thousands of tons of peanuts per year and supplied the French army with soldiers.

4   During the second half of the 19th century, there were frequent rebellions among the Muslim leaders, and it was only in 1892 that the French managed to fully "pacify" the country.

5   The pan-African movement inspired Senegalese Leopold Sédar Senghor and Martinique's Aimé Césaire, and together in Paris, they created the concept of *négritude,* an idea first presented to public opinion in 1933. Négritude stood against the imposition of French cultural patterns, which were enforced throughout the colonies. The concept was designed to serve as "an effective liberation tool". In Senghor's view, it had to escape "peculiarism" and find a place within contemporary movements of

solidarity, that is, to achieve a definite political profile.

6   Senghor had been a member of the French *maquis* (resistance) during World War II, he had fought against fascism and was elected representative to the French National Assembly in 1945. Three years later, he brought about the foundation of the Senegalese Progressive Union, which demanded greater autonomy for the colonies, though not independence.

7   Finally, on April 4 1960, Senegal declared independence, and on September 5 adopted a republican system. Senghor was elected President and through successive re-elections he stayed in power for two decades. He was finally replaced by Abdou Diouf on January 1 1981.

8   The ideology of African socialism promoted by Senghor was based on the premise that traditional African agrarian society had always been essentially collectivist. Senghor believed that socialism already existed on the continent and therefore did not need to be imposed. This "collectivism" actually mainly served to provide cheap labor for the export-oriented production of peanuts and cotton. 82 per cent of the nation's industry was French-controlled.

9   In an effort to keep up with political changes in France, Senghor requested membership of the Socialist International. To this end he pushed through a constitutional reform restricting political representation to three political parties: a "liberal democratic" party (the Senegalese Democratic Party), a Marxist-Leninist party (the African Party for Independence) and a "social democratic" party (his own, renamed the Senegalese Socialist Party).

10   In the 1980s Diouf brought flexibility to the rigid political system he inherited from his predecessor. This prevented the major political adversary Abdoulaye Wade's Democratic Party of Senegal (PDS), from uniting all the government opposition forces. In 1982, in the southern province of Casamance, on the border with Guinea-Bissau, there was a resurgence of separatist activity, leading to the creation of the Casamance Movement of Democratic Forces (MFDC) led by an abbot, Austin Diamacoune Senghor. The people of Casamance are primarily from the Diole ethnic group, animists who have prided themselves on their independence and resistance to the Islamic hierarchical societies of the north. In December 1983, after successive confrontations with the Senegalese police forces, many leaders of the MFDC were detained, among them Abbot Diamacoune.

11   The country faced a series of serious droughts over the last 20 years. These are seen as part of the desertification process caused by climatic conditions and the French-imposed substitution of export crops for traditional food crops,. In the early 1980s the Government gave in to pressure from the US, France, the World Bank and the IMF to accept a structural adjustment plan. The elimination of agricultural subsidies triggered a rise in production costs and the prices of basic consumer goods.

12   The drought afflicting the country since 1983 ruined peanut production (peanuts represent over one third of total exports), and the

food deficit required the import of 400,000 tons of rice.

13   In 1988 the Socialist Party (PS) won another victory in the national elections, obtaining 72.3 per cent of the vote, while the Senegalese Democratic Party (PDS) won only 25.8 per cent. After the legitimacy of the election was called into question by various groups, government troops were mobilized to keep the peace. In the aftermath, hundreds of people were arrested, and the PDS candidate, Abdoulaye Wade, was forced to go into exile, only returning to Senegal in March 1989.

14   A month later a border conflict broke out with Mauritania triggered by violent altercations between peasants and farmers, causing hundreds of casualties and forcing some 70,000 refugees to enter Senegal.

15   In January 1991, Amnesty International accused the Senegalese Government of human rights violations, on account of the tortures and murders committed in the Casamance region. Late in May, the Government announced its intention to free political prisoners, including MFDC leader, Abbot Diamacoune Senghor as part of an amnesty settlement.

16   This conflict affected the planned Senegambian integration, as Diouf criticized Gambian tolerance of the Casamance guerrillas and the signing of a mutual defence treaty with Nigeria.

17   In July 1991, Diouf was elected president of the ECOWAS (Economic Community of the Western African States), which

WORKERS

(1996)

Labour force %

■ WOMEN
□ MEN

43   57

■ AGRICULTURE 77% (1990)
□ INDUSTRIAL   8%
■ SERVICES   16%

LAND USE

DEFORESTATION annual (81/90) **-0.6%**
IRRIGATED of arable (1993) **3%**

■ FOREST & WOODLAND (1993)   **53.1%**
□ ARABLE (1993)   **11.8%**
■ OTHER (1993)   **35.1%**

The Fulah states

This African nation of shepherds (according to different sources, known as Fulah, Fulani, Peul, and also "nations of the western group"), were nomads in some cases and migrants in others. Throughout their history these peoples developed certain traits that explain the peculiar role they played in the area known as Sahel - south of the Sahara desert.

[2] Their nomadic condition allowed them to interact with the sophisticated cultures of the north as well as the rudimentary local societies of the south, giving the Fulani a particular cultural flexibility. Pastoralists in hostile lands, they quickly became excellent warriors. Their traditional social system, hierarchically graded to an extent reminiscent of feudal echelons, favored a rapid emergence and concentration of centralized power among the Fulani.

[3] In the ninth century, emigration led people out of present-day Mauritania, towards the south and the east, in search of better pastures. Most of their tribes were early converts to Islam; the Fulani became true travelling religious promoters making a significant contribution to the spread of Islam.

[4] Futa Toro (present-day north Senegal) was the first state they established in the 10th century. Initially they paid tribute to Ghana but later became allies of the Almoravid and eventually extending their domination over Tekrour, central Senegal. The Fulani successively fell under Mali and Songhai rule but following the crisis of this empire, the Koli dynasty was extended to Futa Djalon (north Guinea), where it remained in control until the 18th century. In the 15th century, Fulah groups settled in Massina, in the Niger valley, north of Djénne, and their leader was appointed local ruler by the Sultan of Mali. Since the Fulani knew the area, and other nations had no connection with the sedentary population, Fulah leaders frequently served as local administrators and intermediaries of established states. Whether under Mali, Songhai or Bambar sovereignty, which they accepted equally, the Fulani of Massina maintained their local autonomy until the 19th century.

[5] In the 16th century, other groups of the same nation settled in Liptako, in similar conditions. The need to defend the territory from the bold, neighboring Mossi (inhabitants of present-day Burkina Faso) allowed leader Ibrahima Faidu to claim greater autonomy. Though formally a subject of the Songhai empire, he set up a practically independent state that survived until 1810. Later, other Fulah groups settled among the Haussa in present-day Nigeria and in the north-central part of what is now Cameroon.

[6] In the 18th century a revival of religious fervor among the Fulani, within the context of an Islamic rebirth, led to the rise of Mahdism (see Sudan) and had major political consequences throughout the area.

[7] In Tekrour and Futa Toro, religious leader Abdel Kader Torodo succeeded in displacing the Koli dynasty, and in 1776 adopted the title of Almamy (variant of the Arabic al-Imam which means prayer leader), establishing a virtual theocracy.

[8] A similar process occurred in Futa Djalon, led by two religious leaders Ibrahima Sory and Karamoko Alfa; however this situation was threatened by ensuing rivalries. In 1784, the two families came up with the Solomonic and original solution of "alternate theocracy". In effect, an Almamy from the Sory family ruled the country for two years and then "switched" power over to an Almamy from the Alfa family who undertook to return office to the Sory family two years later; a system that was in effect until 1848.

[9] In the south of present day Niger, consolidation of the Fulah community was stimulated by Osman Dan Fodio's preachings. Born in 1754 and with a widespread reputation for holiness, he spoke in favor of the regeneration of Islam. The Hausa rulers became aware of the danger and tried to control the movement. Osman called for a holy war, seized the state of Gobir in 1801 and proclaimed himself Sheikh and then Commander of the Believers. Within a short time, he had captured all the Hausa states except Bornu, where Ali Kaneime's troops fought off the Islamic crusaders. From the capital in Sokoto, Dan Fodio ruled over a large portion of today's Niger and Nigeria until his death in 1818. His successors held power as emirs of Sokoto until 1917.

[10] One of Osman's disciples, Adama, assumed the leadership of the Fulani of the Benue Valley in north central Cameroon. In 1810, this relationship matured leading to the creation of the Emirate of Adamaua ruled by Adama's descendants until the German invasion of 1910.

[11] In Massina, Hamadu Bari preached similarly and in 1816 his followers succeeded in overthrowing the Fulah local officials and the Bambar ruler of Ségou. Bari's Sheikdom gained recognition from Osman Dan Fodio, considered by the Fulani as their spiritual leader. His troops went on to seize Djene and Timbuktu (Tombouctou), and founded a state that survived until the 1860s.

[12] Omar Saidu Tall (1797-1864), known as El Hadj Omar for his pilgrimage to Mecca, was Dan Fodio's last disciple. In 1848 Omar organized an army in Futa Djalon and set out to enlarge its boundaries. His troops overran the Bambar domain of Kaarta but failed in their attempt to recover Futa Toro, occupied by the French in 1860. Turning to the east, Omar's army seized all the area from Massina to Timbuktu and the emir (grandson of Hamadu Seku) was executed for his leniency towards Europeans. Omar Saidu Tall died in combat in 1864. His son Ahmadu, who succeeded "El Hadj", was left simultaneously confronting both the heirs of the emir and the French who gradually seized control of the region between 1889 and 1893.

Maternal Mortality

1990

PER 100,000
LIVE BIRTHS

1,200

Literacy

1995

33%

STATISTICS

DEMOGRAPHY
Population: 8,532,000 (1996). **Annual growth:** 2.7% (1980/1996). **Estimates for year 2000:** 9,500,000. **Annual growth to year 2000:** 2.7% (1994/2000). **Urban Population:** 44.3% (1996). **Urban growth:** 4.03% (1980/95). **Children per woman:** 5.8 (1996).

HEALTH
Life expectancy at birth: 51 years (1996). male: 49 years (1994). female: 51 years (1994). **Infant mortality:** 74 per 1,000 (1996). **Under-5 child mortality:** 127 per 1,000 (1996). **Calorie consumption:** 98% (1988/90). 16,667 **people per doctor** (1988/91). **Safe water:** 63% (1990/96).

EDUCATION
Literacy: 33% (1995). male : 43% (1995). female: 23% (1995). **School enrolment :** Primary total: 60% (1990/95). male : 68% (1990/95). female: 51% (1990/95). Secondary: male : 21% (1990/95). female: 11% (1990/95). Tertiary: 3% (1995). **Primary school teachers:** one for every 58 students (1995).

COMMUNICATIONS
10 **newspapers,** 117 **radios,** 40 **TV sets** and 9 **main telephone lines** per 1,000 people (1994).

ECONOMY
Per capita, GNP: $ 570 (1996). **Annual growth, GNP:** 3.2% (1995/96). **Annual inflation:** 3.72% (1985/95). **Consumer price index:** 128.9 (1994). **Currency:** 490 CFA francs = $ 1 (1995) **Cereal imports:** 579 metric tons (1994). **Food import dependency:** 29% (1994). **Fertilizer use:** 85 kgs per ha (1994). **Exports:** $ 655 million (1996). **Imports:** $ 1,672 million (1996). **External debt:** $ 3,663 million (1996). $ 429 **per capita:** (1996). **Debt service:** 15.9% of exports (1996). **Development aid received:** $ 663 million (1995). $ 82 per capita (1995). 17.9% of GNP (1994).

ENERGY
Consumption: 97.17 Kgs of Oil equivalent per capita yearly (1994). 100.00% imported (1994).

HDI (rank / value) 160 / 0.326 (1994)

PROFILE

ENVIRONMENT
Located on the west coast of Africa, its northern border formed by the Senegal River, the country's population is concentrated in the less arid western part, close to Dakar. The Senegal Valley is still under-populated as a result of slave trade which was very intense in this region. Senegal is undergoing an acute deforestation and desertification process. A project which is currently underway for building a hydroelectric dam in the Senegal River valley in the north poses a threat to the local environment.

SOCIETY
Peoples: Wolof, 42 per cent; Peul- (Fulani-) Tukulor, 9.3 per cent; Serer, 14.9 per cent; Diola, 5.3 per cent; Malinke (Mandingo), 3.6 per cent. Approximately 3 per cent are immigrants from non African countries, basically France, Lebanon and Syria.
Religions: 94 per cent Muslim, 5 per cent Christian, traditional African religions and others 1 per cent.
Languages: French (official). The most widely spoken indigenous languages are Wolof, Peul and Ful.
Political Parties: Socialist Party; Senegalese Democratic Party. There are several other minor parties and a coalition of oppositional groups, the Coordination of Democratic Forces.
Social Organizations: National Federation of Senegalese Workers (CNTS); Union of Free Senegalese Workers (UTLS).

THE STATE
Official Name: République du Sénégal.
Administrative Divisions: 10 Districts.
Capital: Dakar, 1,986,000 people (1995).
Other cities: This, '216,400 people; Kaolack, 193,115; Ziguinchor, 161,680; Saint-Louis, 132,444 (1994).
Government: Abdou Diouf, President since January 1, 1981. Habib Thiam, Prime Minister since April 1991. 120-member single-chamber Legislative Power.
National Holiday: April 4, Independence Day (1960).
Armed Forces: 13,400, and 1,200 French troops.

included 16 countries of the region.

[18] In September, the US Government cancelled $42 million of the Senegalese debt as a recognition of the country's support to the allies during the Gulf War and to its contribution to the "peace troops" stationed in Liberia. The IMF approved a fresh $57.2 million loan.

[19] In 1991, a series of political and institutional changes was launched. The office of prime minister was restored and members of opposition parties were named to two cabinet posts. In September 1991, after three months of negotiations with opposition parties, a consensus was reached for

MILITARY EXPENDITURE

MILITARY (as % of health and education expenditures-1990/91) **33%**

reforming the electoral laws. The conflict with the Casamance separatist movement (MFDC) resumed in 1992, after a truce which had been in effect since February 21.

[20] On February 21 1993, amid denunciations of widespread fraud, President Diouf won the presidential elections on the first ballot, with 58.4 per cent of the vote. In the May legislative elections, his PSS party maintained control of the National Assembly, with 84 of the 120 seats. The main opposition party - the PDS - won 27 seats.

[21] The economic and financial situation of Senegal became more difficult during 1993, amongst other things because the international prices of the Senegalese export products fell considerably. This made the trade deficit worse, which was compensated by new loans which took the foreign debt to $3.5 billion, more than 60 per cent of the GDP.

[22] The 100 per cent devaluation of the CFA franc decided by France and the IMF accentuated the social tensions in early 1994. The opposition Coordination of Democratic Forces organized an anti-government demonstration on February 16, which ended in confrontations with the police. Six police officers died and dozens of people were injured.

[23] Some 180 people were arrested with supposed responsibility for the disturbances, including the opposition leaders, Abdoulaye Wade and Landing Savané, who were declared innocent and freed in July. The repressive policy of the Senegalese Government was criticized by the human rights organizations, the European Parliament and US Congress.

[24] Wade began negotiations with the Government, which led to him entering Diouf's cabinet in March 1995. The President received the clear support of the international funding organizations, when he announced legislative modifications to encourage foreign investment and accelerate privatization.

[25] Despite support from Paris and Washington, the Government offensives did not achieve any

decisive advantage over the Casamance guerrillas. According to some observers, the popularity of the MFDC amongst the Casamance youth, along with the geography of the region, ruled out any possibility of military victory for Dakar. The adoption of a "regionalization" project in the nation, in 1996, did not produce any political solution to the conflict either.

[26] Following relative calm, in 1997 fresh guerrilla action led to the mobilisation of 2,500 soldiers against the MFDC bases, along the frontier with Guinea-Bissau.

[27] In March, Senegal extended its protocol with the European Union for four more years, under which it would receive nearly $11 million per year in compensation, an increase of 33 per cent.

[28] In early 1998, Amnesty International denounced the reigning "terror" in Casamance, due to conflict which was decimating a population mainly made up of farmers and ruining an area considered prosperous before the outbreak of war.

[29] During his visit to Dakar in April 1998, US President Bill Clinton proposed the creation of a continental "African peace maintaining force".

Seychelles

Seychelles

Population: 74,000 (1996)
Area: 455 SQ KM
Capital: Victoria

Currency: Rupees
Language: English and French

During the 18th century, the French and British colonists fought violently over this Indian Ocean colony. After expelling the French in 1794, the British paid little attention to it, and it was governed from the island of Mauritius until 1903. During the world wars, the Seychelles archipelago gained strategic significance.

[2] The Seychelles People's United Party (SPUP) founded in 1964 gave the local population - most of them descendants of enslaved Africans and Indian workers - a new sense of nationalism. The party proved its strength during the general strikes of 1965 and 1966, and in the mass demonstrations of 1972. The colonial interests were opposed to the SPUP and independence, and they organized themselves into the Seychelles' Taxpayers Association. It was later renamed the Seychelles Democratic Party, led by James Mancham.

[3] In the legislative elections of April 1974, the SPUP won 47.6 per cent of the vote. However, the peculiar colonial "democratic" system awarded the party only 2 of the 15 seats and Mancham remained the prime minister. In spite of this, it was too late to stem the tide of nationalism and, in 1976, Mancham agreed to the British Foreign Office's suggestion that he become the first president of the Republic of Seychelles. Shortly before independence, he had agreed to "return" the strategic British Indian Ocean Territory (BIOT) islands to Britain; they had been administered from Mahé since 1967. The British in turn passed them on to the United States which built the important Diego Garcia naval base there.

[4] Aware that the people would not accept this deal, Mancham postponed the elections until 1979, arguing that they were not necessary as all of the parties were in favor of independence.

[5] Mancham's foreign policy was directed at cementing a strong alliance with South Africa, the source of most of the tourists, while domestic policy destroyed tea and coconut plantations to make room for new five-star

hotels, owned by foreign companies. Entire islands were sold off to foreigners like Harry Oppenheimer, the South African gold magnate, and the actor Peter Sellers.

[6] In 1977, while Mancham was manoeuvering to postpone the elections yet again, the SPUP took over the country "with the collaboration of the local police force" while Mancham was out of the country. Accused of "leading a wasteful life while his people worked hard", Mancham was replaced by SPUP leader Albert René.

[7] René renewed his support for the Non-Aligned Movement, which had recognized the SPUP as the country's sole legitimate liberation movement prior to independence. He also strengthened the Seychelles' ties with left-wing countries and movements around the Indian Ocean. The new government turned to socialism, promising to reorganize tourism, give priority to self-sufficiency in agriculture and fishing, increase education, and cut the high level of unemployment; which was affecting nearly half of the working population.

[8] In mid-1978, in order to meet the new political situation, the SPUP became the Seychelles People's Progressive Front (SPPF). In June 1979, the SPPF won the national elections with 98 per cent of the vote, in elections where the abstention rate was a mere 5 per cent. After the victory, President René announced his decision to close down the American satellite tracking station on the archipelago and demanded that the US base on Diego Garcia be closed, with the island returning to Mauritius.

[9] In August 1978, he launched a land reform program calling for the expropriation of all uncultivated land. He also nationalized the water and electricity services, the construction industry and transportation. Controls were placed on food prices and an obligatory literacy program was introduced. These measures led to a rapid economic recovery in the Seychelles, and by 1979-80, on account of mineral and

petroleum wealth, they had the largest per capita income of any of the islands in the region. The national currency was also revalued, something virtually unheard of in the Third World.

[10] This economic growth was encouraged and supported by tourism and effective administration. The Seychelles receive an average of 80,000 tourists a year. Under the Mancham Government, most of them were South Africans, but after René took over more Europeans came, especially British. The Seychelles received funding for the expansion of several quays from the African Development Bank, aiming to increase the country's fishing activity.

[11] The opponents of Albert René, mainly the South African Government, did not give up their efforts to overthrow the socialist government of the Seychelles. In November 1981, a group of 45 mercenaries led by former colonel Mike Hoare tried to invade the island and oust the government. The plot had been hatched in London by former president Mancham, with South African assistance. The attempted coup failed and the mercenaries had to hijack an Indian airliner to escape to South Africa. After the unsuccessful invasion, the

Seychelles Government declared a state of emergency and imposed a curfew. The popular militia proved effective in neutralizing conspiracies and tightening controls on all foreigners.

[12] The failed invasion and the economic recession in Europe caused tourism to decline by approximately 10 per cent. In August 1982, the situation deteriorated further when military personnel plotted an unsuccessful rebellion, strengthening rumours of another approaching mercenary conspiracy, and European conservative groups organized a smear campaign to support these rumours. In June 1984, Albert René was re-elected with 93 per cent of the vote, and the last political prisoner was released immediately after the elections. The country's greater political stability allowed the President to adopt a more pragmatic policy.

[13] In 1986, the Seychelles and the United States renegotiated their treaty, originally signed in 1976 and renewed in 1981, allowing a US satellite tracking station to be stationed on Mahé.

[14] In September 1986, there was another coup attempt. Albert René, who was in Zimbabwe participating in a Non-Aligned Countries summit conference,

84%

PROFILE

ENVIRONMENT

An archipelago composed of 92 islands. Mahé, Praslim, and La Digue are the largest islands, and are granite islands; the rest are coralloid. The climate is tropical with plentiful vegetation and heavy rainfall. Only the largest islands are inhabited, but some economic use is made of the other islands.

SOCIETY

Peoples: Most residents of the Seychelles are mulattos; descendants of mixed African and European origin and most of them live on the island of Mahé. There are minorities of European, Chinese and Indian origin.
Religions: Roman Catholic, 88.6 per cent; other Christian (mostly Anglican), 7.7 per cent; Hindu, 0.7 per cent; other, 3 per cent (1996).
Languages: English and French (official); most of the population speak Creole, a local dialect with European and African influences.
Political Parties: The People's Progressive Front of Seychelles (FPPS; Seychelle Movement for Democracy; Christian Democratic Party/Encounter of the People of Seychelles for Democracy.
Social Organizations: The National Workers' Union.

THE STATE

Official Name: Repiblik Sesel.
Capital: Victoria, 24,325 people (1987).
Government: France-Albert René, President since 1977. Legislature, single-chamber: National Assembly, with 33 members.
National Holiday: June 28, Independence Day (1976).
Armed Forces: 800 (1994).
Other: 1,300 National Guard.

STATISTICS

DEMOGRAPHY
Population: 74,000 (1996). **Annual growth:** 1% (1980/1996). **Estimates for year 2000:** 100,000. **Annual growth to year 2000:** 0.9% (1994/2000). **Urban Population:** 55.3% (1996).

HEALTH
Life expectancy at birth: 72 years (1996). male: years (1994). female: years (1994). **Infant mortality:** 15 per 1,000 (1996). **Under-5 child mortality:** 19 per 1,000 (1996).

EDUCATION
Literacy: 84% (1995). male : 83% (1995). female: 86% (1995). **School enrolment :** Primary total: 102% (1990/95).

COMMUNICATIONS
40 **newspapers**, 490 **radios**, 320 **TV sets** and 170 **main telephone lines** per 1,000 people (1994).

ECONOMY
Per capital, GNP: $6,620 (1995) **Consumer price index:** 108.7 (1994). **Currency:** 4.86 rupees = $ 1 (1995) **Cereal imports:** 11 metric tons (1994). **Development aid received:** $ 13 million (1995). $ 186 per capita (1995). 2.8% of GNP (1994).

HDI (rank / value) 52 / 0.845 (1994)

---

returned immediately and put down the rebellion. Most of those responsible for the coup were arrested, among them the main leader of the conspiracy, Minister of Defence Colonel Ogilvy Berlouis.
[15] The Seychelles Government promoted the creation of a peace zone in the Indian Ocean. It required all warships wanting to call at its ports to be "nuclear-free", and for this reason, the United States and United Kingdom naval fleets have stopped calling at the archipelago. The Seychelles established diplomatic relations with Comoros and Mauritius in 1988, and with Morocco and Côte d'Ivoire in 1989.
[16] In the presidential elections of June 1989, Albert René was the only candidate and was re-elected for a third term, with 96 per cent of the vote, according to final election returns. After the election, the President announced that he was reorganizing his cabinet. He personally took charge of the ministry of industry and

amalgamated the ministries of planning, foreign affairs, finance and tourism into a single cabinet post.
[17] In September 1989, Indian President Ramaswamy Venkataraman carried out a three-day visit to Victoria, signing a cultural exchange agreement. In January 1990, the Seychelles established diplomatic relations with Kenya.
[18] The opposition forced President René to accept a multiparty system. The first experiment was carried out in July 1992, when a commission was elected to draw up the new constitution. The People's Progressive Front of Seychelles (FPPS), the ruling party, took 13 of the 23 seats. The Democratic Party (PD) of former president Mancham won eight seats.
[19] The Government continued its authoritarian ways. The PD soon withdrew from the commission and the first draft constitution was rejected. The project was suspended until the PD returned to the commission in June 1993, and the text was

> Tourism continued to be the main source of income for the nation. The annual number of visitors was higher than the national population in 1993 and 1994.

written with support from both parties; 73.6 per cent of the voters approved the new constitution.
[20] This document made official the multiparty system, the 33-member National Assembly and a five year presidential term. The President can be re-elected twice. René won the July 1993 elections and his party took the absolute majority in the National Assembly.
[21] Tourism continued to be the main source of income for the nation. The annual number of visitors was higher than the

national population in 1993 and 1994. Oil derivatives and tinned tuna made up more than 80 per cent of the islands' exports during this period. Despite unemployment running at 22 per cent, the gross national product of the Seychelles reached $6,680 per head in 1994. Nearly all have access to drinking water and 100 per cent can meet their basic nutritional needs.
[22] There was moderate economic growth during 1995 and 1996. Various projects were funded with international aid which totalled $13 million in 1996, especially focusing on the preservation of the environment and improvements to the road infrastructure.
[23] In 1997, only one per cent of the budget was dependent on international contributions, although some forms of technical assistance were maintained.

Sierra Leone

Sierra Leone

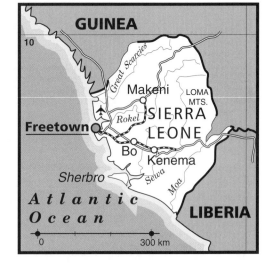

Population:	4,297,000 (1996)
Area:	71,740 SQ KM
Capital:	Freetown
Currency:	Leones
Language:	English

The Temne and Mende ethnic groups constitute the majority of the population of Sierra Leone. Minority groups of Lokko, Sherbo, Limba, Sussu Fulani, Kono, and Krio also exist.

[2] When Britain faced a "demographic problem" with runaway slaves in the 1800s, the Government decided to "return" them to Africa. They had come to London hoping to benefit from a court ruling that had abolished slavery in the city of London. Abolitionist leader Granville Sharp purchased an area of 250 sq km for £60 from the local rulers, organizing an agricultural society based on democratic principles. However, this society was quickly transformed into a colonial company involved in the British conquest of the entire country.

[3] Tossed into a land where they had no roots, the "creoles" sought to copy European culture, and considered themselves superior to the "savages" of the inland, acting as brokers for British colonialism.

[4] Yet, the "savages" resisted strongly and in 1898, Bai Buré, rallied most of the inland people, already angered by a British tax on their dwellings. However, after nearly a year of resistance, British military superiority overwhelmed and stifled the opposition.

[5] In 1960, the British wanted to withdraw from Sierra Leone, and an agreement was negotiated with the traditional leaders to protect their interests. In 1961, Sir Milton Margai, secretary general of Sierra Leone People's Party (SLPP), became the first prime minister of an independent Sierra Leone.

[6] The creoles, together with British and Syrian-Lebanese merchants, held the colony's economic power. Although removed from political power, they maintained significant influence over the Margai Government.

[7] When Margai died in 1964, he was succeeded by his brother Albert and the situation quickly deteriorated. Corruption and gambling became so widespread that it was compared to the Batista period in Cuba. The diamond trade gave birth to a chain of smuggling operations and crime became a main source of income.

[8] In 1967 the All People's Congress (APC), party led by Syaka Stevens won the elections, signalling the possibility for change; however, the conservative creoles, the traditional leaders, and the neo-colonialist British united to prevent Stevens from taking control of the country as they considered him "dangerously progressive". As a result, Stevens was overthrown by a military coup and forced into exile in Conakry (Guinea).

[9] In April 1968, a group of low-ranking officers took power through the so-called Sergeants' Revolt. They brought back Stevens who in 1971 broke all ties with Britain and declared Sierra Leone a republic, becoming its first President.

[10] Important goals were achieved in the first years: the lumber industry was nationalized and the state seized majority control of the mining firm, which controlled the diamond trade. To protect the prices of iron ore and bauxite, Sierra Leone joined the associations of iron and bauxite producing countries.

[11] In 1978, Stevens called for a plebiscite to establish a one-party system, in an attempt to appease the opposition. Stevens' proposal was approved and the APC incorporated prominent members of the SLPP within its ranks, granting them posts within the Government.

[12] In 1979, President Stevens' popularity began to ebb as a result of worsening living conditions, growing inflation, authoritarian measures, government corruption, a fall in exports and the increasing foreign debt.

[13] Popular unrest reached its climax in September 1981, when the Sierra Leone Labor Congress (SLLC) declared a general strike, demanding immediate changes in economic policy. The strike spread throughout the country and nearly toppled the Government, which had to make several concessions.

[14] In urban areas, the scarcity of staple foods, particularly rice, as well as periodic fuel shortages became chronic. Inflation and the high cost of living reduced the purchasing power of salaried workers by 60 per cent, and the late payment of salaries became normal. Members of parliament were paid with sacks of rice which were later sold on the black market at a large profit.

[15] The powerful Lebanese trade clique controlled the unofficial market, and more than 70 per cent of the country's exports. Gold and diamond smuggling was estimated at nearly $150 million per year while official exports dropped from $80 million to barely $14 million between 1980 and 1984.

[16] After several postponements and an alleged coup attempt, the 1982 elections took place amid serious outbreaks of violence. The Liberian Government was forced to accept refugees, and the following year they announced the presence of 4,000 refugees from Sierra Leone, living in their country.

[17] In November 1985, Syaka Stevens handed over the presidency to Joseph Momoh, a member of his cabinet, changing nothing in the political and social condition of the country.

[18] The dimensions of the crisis culminated in the government declaration of a state of economic emergency in 1987. This measure included granting the State the sole right to commercialize gold and diamonds, a 15 per cent surcharge on imports, and the reduction of salaries of public employees.

[19] In March 1991, rebel forces operating from Liberia occupied two border towns. Guerrilla groups from Burkina Faso, Liberia, and Sierra Leone joined them, occupying one third of the country.

[20] On April 13 1991, President Joseph Momoh announced that Nigeria and Guinea had deployed troops in his country to help repel the rebel incursions from Liberia. Sierra Leone, Guinea, and Nigeria are members of the West African Economic Community, an organization which had signed a peace agreement with Liberia in August 1990.

[21] In August 1991, a referendum approved a new constitution establishing a multiparty system. However, the economic crisis continued alongside ever increasing corruption.

[22] In 1992, the Government launched a structural adjustment

WORKERS

(1996)

Labour force %

- ■ WOMEN
- □ MEN

36   64

- ■ AGRICULTURE 67% (1990)
- □ INDUSTRIAL 15%
- ■ SERVICES 17%

LAND USE

DEFORESTATION -6 % annual (81/90)
IRRIGATED 6 % of arable

(1993)

- ■ FOREST & WOODLAND 28.4%
- □ ARABLE 6.8%
- ■ OTHER 64.8%

PROFILE

ENVIRONMENT

The country is divided into three regions. The coastal strip, with a width of nearly 100 kilometers, is a swampy plain that includes the island of Sherbro. Several rivers drain the inner tropical forest, mostly cleared for agricultural exploitation. The eastern plateau contains the country's diamond mines. Deforestation is very severe, 85 per cent of all natural habitat has been destroyed.

SOCIETY

Peoples: The Temne and Mende ethnic groups account for nearly one-third of the population. Lokko, Sherbo, Limba, Sussu, Fulah, Kono and Krio are other important groups. The Krio are descendants of African slaves freed in the 19th century who settled in Freetown (Krio is a corruption of the English word creole). There is also an Arab minority.
Religions: Most of the people profess traditional African religions; nearly one third are Muslims, concentrated in the north; the Christian minority is located in the capital.
Languages: English (official). The most widely spoken native languages are Temne, Mende and Krio. The latter serves as the commercial language in the capital.
Political Parties: All Peoples' Congress (APC); Sierra Leone's People Party (SLPP); United Political Movements Front; Revolutionary United Front (RUF).
Social Organizations: Sierra Leone Labor Congress.

THE STATE

Official Name: Republic of Sierra Leone.
Capital: Freetown, 469,776 people (1985).
Other cities: Koidu, 80,000 people; Bo, 26,000; Kenema, 13,000 (1985).
Government: Ahmad Tejan Kabbah, President elected in March 1996 was ousted by Major General Paul Koroma in May 1997 and re-installed in Government after UN-Ecomog forces seized control of Sierra Leone in February 1998.
National Holiday: April 19, Republic Day (1971).
Armed Forces: 13,000 troops (1995).

STATISTICS

DEMOGRAPHY

Population: 4,297,000 (1996). **Annual growth:** 1.8% (1980/1996). **Estimates for year 2000:** 4,900,000. **Annual growth to year 2000:** 2.8% (1994/2000). **Urban Population:** 33.9% (1996). **Urban growth:** 4.92% (1980/95). **Children per woman:** 6.2 (1996).

HEALTH

Life expectancy at birth: 37 years (1996). male: 32 years (1994). female: 35 years (1994). **Infant mortality:** 164 per 1,000 (1996). **Under-5 child mortality:** 284 per 1,000 (1996). **Calorie consumption:** 83% (1988/90). **Safe water:** 34% (1990/96).

EDUCATION

Literacy: 31% (1995). male : 45% (1995). female: 18% (1995). **School enrolment** : Primary total: 51% (1990/95). male : 60% (1990/95). female: 42% (1990/95). Secondary: male : 22% (1990/95). female: 12% (1990/95).

COMMUNICATIONS

233 **radios**, 10 **TV** sets and 3 **main telephone lines** per 1,000 people (1994).

ECONOMY

Per capita, GNP: $ 200 (1996). **Annual growth, GNP:** 7.6% (1995/96). **Annual inflation:** 61.58% (1985/95). **Consumer price index:** (1994). **Currency:** 943.4 leones = $ 1 (1995) **Cereal imports:** 141 metric tons (1994). **Food import dependency:** 57% (1994). **Fertilizer use:** 55 kgs per ha (1994). **Exports:** $ 214 million (1996). **Imports:** $ 334 million (1996). **External debt:** $ 1,167 million (1996). $ 272 **per capita:** (1996). **Debt service:** 52.6% of exports (1996). **Development aid received:** $ 205 million (1995). $ 45 per capita (1995). 27.7% of GNP (1994).

ENERGY

Consumption: 77.22 Kgs of Oil equivalent per capita yearly (1994). 100.00% imported (1994).

HDI (rank / value) 175 / 0.176 (1994)

---

program which had been imposed by the International Monetary Fund. James Funa, a former World Bank executive, was named minister of finance. He implemented monetary control, incentives for natural resource exploration by foreign companies, widespread privatization, an overhaul of the State apparatus, and a purge on the widespread corruption.

[23] On April 29, Captain Valentine Strasser seized power through a coup and, after suspending the constitution, created the National Provisional Governing Council, prohibiting all political activity and confirmed the Minister of Finance in his post. In June, all civilian members of the Governing Council were expelled, and its name was changed to "Supreme Council of State". Press censorship began.

[24] The eastern part of the country was occupied at the time by the United Movement for Liberian Liberation and Democracy, which used Sierra Leone as a base from which to carry out attacks against Charles Taylor's forces (see Liberia). In the meantime, the Revolutionary United Front of Sierra Leone was operating in the southeast.

[25] The regions affected by warfare also happened to be the country's richest, where gold and diamond deposits and the main agricultural production area were located.

Guerrilla activity led to an abrupt decline in mining activity; the percentage represented by diamonds in the country's exports dropped from 54.7 per cent in 1987 to a mere 7 per cent in 1990. The per capita GDP dropped from $320 in 1980 to $210 in 1991.

[26] More than a million people were displaced as a result of the war. Some fled to more secure areas within the country, while others sought refuge in neighboring Guinea and Liberia.

[27] On December 1 1993, British pressure forced the Government to decree a unilateral cease-fire, promising to grant an amnesty to all rebels who lay down their arms. The RUF refused to accept the proposal.

[28] Extreme poverty gave rise to the trafficking of children and young people. According to the terms of an unusual sort of contract, Lebanese traders in Sierra Leone took the daughters of poor families to Lebanon to work as household servants for five-year periods. However, the traders frequently failed to keep their part of the bargain, and the girls never returned.

[29] Those who managed to escape from the system described the verbal and physical abuse to which they were subjected. Although it was estimated that hundreds of girls and children were involved, no government action was taken

against the influential Lebanese community.

[30] The Government promise to organize elections did not convince the RUF, which continued with the armed struggle. The rebels had a series of military victories in early 1994, which left a total of 150 civilians dead.

[31] The World Bank expressed its "satisfaction" with the economic policies of the country, which amongst other things had managed to reduce inflation from 120 per cent in 1991 to 15 per cent in 1994.

[32] In early 1995 the war extended over nearly all the country. The governmental forces recovered the Sierra Rutile titanium mine, which produced 50 per cent of Freetown's foreign trade. However, despite dedicating 75 per cent of the national budget to the war, and having increased the size of the army to 13,000 troops, the Government did not appear in a position to defeat the guerrillas.

[33] In January 1996, following a bloodless coup, Strasser was substituted by a close former ally, Brigadier General Julius Maada Bio. The presidential elections held in February as planned were won by Ahmad Tejan Kabbah of the Sierra Leone People's Party (SLPP) in the second round with nearly 60 per cent of the vote.

[34] The war caused 10,000 deaths

between 1991 and 1996, forcing two million people to flee the combat zone and take refuge in neighbouring countries or other areas within Sierra Leone.

[35] Rebel troops led by Major General Johnny Paul Koroma ousted President Ahmad Tejan Kabbah on May 25. The Organisation of African Unity, meeting in Namibia, criticised the coup and began negotiations to make the leaders abandon power.

[36] In September 1997, former president Tejan Kabbah asked the UN's General Assembly for help to re-establish his government. Kabbah recalled that the Security Council had, a month earlier, promised to force Koroma to hand back power to the elected authorities.

[37] In February 1998, the UN ECOWAS troops, paradoxically mostly Nigerians - then governed by the dictator Sani Abacha (see Nigeria) - took the main cities and regions of Sierra Leone, forcing out Koroma and his military junta. Kabbah's return to government was not seen as a guarantee of the rapid re-establishment of peace in a country riddled with corruption.

[38] In March 1998, the Kabbah Government ordered a halt to the gold and diamond mining in foreign hands for the last 60 years, granting exemptions to Sierra Leone citizens with valid mining licences.

Singapore

Singapore

Population: 3,384,000 (1996)
Area: 618 SQ KM
Capital: Singapore

Currency: Singapore dollars
Language: Malay, English

Singapore's original name was Temasek, meaning "people of the sea" in Sanskrit. Later on, the city was named Singa-Pura, the "city of the lion", after a visiting prince experienced a vision.

[2] Singapore was founded in 1297 and destroyed 100 years later. From 1819 onwards, it became an extremely important base for the British; Sir Thomas Stamford Raffles established the local headquarters of the British East India Company there.

[3] In 1824, the island of Singapore and the small adjacent islets were purchased as a single lot by Raffles from the Sultan of Johore (see Malaysia). The Company appointed Prince Hussein as the new ruler of Singapore. In gratitude, he granted the Company royal authorization to improve the port. Chinese immigrants soon constituted the majority of the local population.

[4] Singapore was part of the British colony called "the Straits Settlements", together with the ports of Penang and Melaka (Malacca). In 1946, Penang and Melaka joined the Malayan Union and Singapore became a crown colony.

[5] At one point during World War II the Japanese dominated the whole of southeast Asia. They conquered Singapore in 1942 but were later defeated. Their defeat was partly due to a strong internal resistance group, organized by a revolutionary movement and led by the Communist Party of Malaya (CPM). The name Malaya included both Singapore and the Malay peninsula; the separation of the latter was always questioned by the Left.

[6] Once the war was over, the Malay sultanates and the former Straits Settlements attempted to

form a union or federation, with a view to attaining independence for the territory. However, the conflicting interests of the Chinese and Malay communities, and the conservative and progressive forces, made progress difficult. In January 1946, the Singapore Labor Union declared a general strike and in 1948 the Communist Party led an anti-colonial uprising which failed, as it failed to gain the support of the Malays and the poorer sectors of the Indian population. Marxist parties were outlawed and had to move into the forests, where they resorted to guerrilla warfare.

[7] As the first step towards the self-government of the city-state, municipal elections were held in 1949. Only English-speaking people were allowed to vote until 1954, when the People's Action Party (PAP) was founded. The anti-imperialism advocated by the PAP brought citizens of British and Chinese backgrounds together for the first time. In 1959, the Chinese were allowed to vote; full internal autonomy was granted, and the PAP obtained an overwhelming victory. Lee Kuan Yew, founder of the party, became Prime Minister, campaigning on a platform of social reforms and independence. He planned a federation with Malaya, which had been independent since 1957.

[8] The PAP split into a socialist faction, led by Lim Chin Siong, and the "moderates" of Lee Kuan Yew, who encouraged the promotion of private enterprise and foreign investment

[9] In 1961, the left wing of the PAP founded Barisan Sosialis (the Socialist Front), which opposed the prospect of uniting Singapore and Malaya under British control. In September 1963, the Federation of Malaysia, consisting of Singapore, the Malay peninsula, Sarawak and Sabah (both in the north and northeast of Borneo) was set up, after those opposed to the Federation had been conveniently purged.

[10] As a Federation member, Singapore depended heavily on the peninsula; even its water supply came from there. Integration at that time was not feasible because of profound disagreements between Singapore's Chinese community and the Malay

community of the rest of the Federation. On August 9 1965, after several ethnic conflicts, Prime Minister Lee decided to withdraw from the Federation.

[11] In 1965, serious internal conflicts were caused by the mistreatment of the Malay population and other ethnic minorities. There were also intense struggles with the left-wing opposition, which the Government classified as "communist subversives". The island became an independent republic, and a Commonwealth member. A mutual assistance and defence treaty was signed with Malaysia, and on October 15 of the same year Singapore became a member of the United Nations.

[12] The first years of independence witnessed substantial economic growth. The island was turned into an "enclave" for the export of products manufactured by transnationals, and into an international financial center which controlled the regional economy.

[13] The situation turned gloomy in 1974, when the oil crisis upset Singapore's export scheme. Singapore was the fourth largest port in the world, with the second highest per capita income in Asia, after Japan. The ensuing economic deterioration brought about public demonstrations by students

and workers. These protests were fiercely controlled, reaching such proportions that the Socialist International expelled the PAP from its ranks in 1975.

[14] In order to placate criticism from the opposition, the regime approved a reform which allowed the entering of two representatives of the Worker's Party and the Democratic Party of Singapore, respectively.

[15] Despite the sustained economic growth since 1987, the Government expelled thousands of Thai and Filipino workers blaming them for taking over the jobs of the natural citizens.

[16] The decision to prohibit the circulation of foreign publications judged detrimental by the Government, the imprisonment of opposition members and a Security Law that allows indefinite imprisonment without trial for two renewable years each time, raised countless denunciations of violations of human rights.

[17] In the 1988 elections the opposition vote grew, but due to the mechanisms of the electoral system its parliamentary representation diminished. In 1991, the PAP again won an overwhelming majority of seats. In November, Goh Chok Tong replaced Lee Kuan Yew as Prime Minister, but the latter nevertheless retained considerable political weight. At his initiative,

PUBLIC EXPENDITURE

37.4% **48.5%**
1995 ■ DEFENCE □ SOCIAL

In 1990/91 Military as % of health & education expenditure was 129%.

Maternal Mortality	Literacy	Food Dependency	Foreign Trade
1990	1995	1970	MILLIONS $ 1996
PER 100,000 LIVE BIRTHS		16%	IMPORTS
10	91%	1994	131,083
		3%	EXPORTS 124,794

PROFILE

ENVIRONMENT

Singapore consists of one large island and 54 smaller adjacent islets. The country is connected to Malaysia by a causeway across the Johore Strait. The terrain, covered by swampy lowlands, is not conducive to farming and the population traditionally works in business and trade. The climate is tropical with heavy rainfall. In its strategic geographical location, central to the trade routes between Africa, Asia and Europe, the island has become a flourishing commercial center. Economically, the main resources of the country have been its port, the British naval base and, more recently, industrial activity; textiles, electronic goods and oil refining. Industrialization has caused severe air and water pollution.

SOCIETY

Peoples: 76 per cent of Singaporeans are of Chinese origin. Malaysians account for 15 per cent and 6 per cent are from India and Sri Lanka. **Religions**:Buddhism, 28 per cent; Christian, 19 per cent; Islam 13 per cent; Taoism, 13 per cent; Hinduism, 5 per cent. There are Sikh and Jewish minorities. **Languages**: Bahasa Malaysia, English, Chinese (Mandarin) and Tamil are the official languages. Bahasa Malaysia is viewed as the national language, but English is spoken in the public administration and serves as a unifying element for the communities. Various Chinese dialects are spoken, with Punjabi, Hindi, Bengali, Telegu and Malayalam in the Indian communities. **Political Parties**: The People's Action Party (PAP; Singapore Democratic Party; the Workers' Party; Barisan Sosialis (the Socialist Front); the Singapore Justice Party; the United People's Front and the Singapore United Front. **Social Organizations**: The major national trade union is the Congress of Singapore Labor Unions.

THE STATE

Official Name: Hsin-chia-p'o Kung-ho-kuo (Mandarin); Republik Singapura (Bahasa Malaysia); Singapore Kudiyarasu (Tamil);Republic of Singapore. **Capital**: Singapore, 2,848,000 people (1995). **Government**: Parliamentary republic. Ong Teng Cheong, President elected on August 29, 1993, by direct popular vote. Goh Chok Tong, Prime Minister since November 1991. Legislature, single-chamber, made up of 81 members, dominated since independence by the offical Popular Action Party, which obtained 77 seats in 1991. **National Holiday**: August 9, Independence Day (1965). **Armed Forces**: 55,500, inc. 34,800 conscripts. **Other**: 11,600 Police and Maritime Police (estimate). 100,000 Civil Defence Force.

STATISTICS

DEMOGRAPHY

Population: 3,384,000 (1996). **Annual growth**: 2.1% (1980/1996). **Estimates for year 2000**: 3,600,000. **Annual growth to year 2000**: 1.6% (1994/2000). **Urban Population**: 100.0% (1996). **Urban growth**: 1.79% (1980/95). **Children per woman**: 1.8 (1996).

HEALTH

Life expectancy at birth: 77 years (1996). male: 75 years (1994). female: 79 years (1994). **Infant mortality**: 4 per 1,000 (1996). **Under-5 child mortality**: 4 per 1,000 (1996). **Calorie consumption**: 136% (1988/90). 725 **people per doctor** (1988/91). **Safe water**: 100% (1990/96).

EDUCATION

Literacy: 91% (1995). male : 96% (1995). female: 86% (1995). **School enrolment** : Primary total: 107% (1990/95). male : 109% (1990/95). female: 107% (1990/95). Secondary: male : 69% (1990/95). female: 71% (1990/95). Tertiary: 34% (1995).

COMMUNICATIONS

360 **newspapers**, 645 **radios**, 380 **TV sets** and 455 **main telephone lines** per 1,000 people (1994).

ECONOMY

Per capita, GNP: $ 30,550 (1996). **Annual growth, GNP**: 5.6% (1995/96). **Annual inflation**: 3.87% (1985/95). **Consumer price index**: 111.5 (1994). **Currency**: 1.41 Singapur dollars = $ 1 (1995) **Cereal imports**: 776 metric tons (1994). **Food import dependency**: 3% (1994). **Fertilizer use**: 48,000 kgs per ha (1994). **Exports**: $ 124,794 million (1996). **Imports**: $ 131,083 million (1996). **Development aid received**: $ 16 million (1995). $ 6 per capita (1995).% of GNP (1994).

ENERGY

Consumption: 8,103.41 Kgs of Oil equivalent per capita yearly (1994). 100.00% imported (1994).

HDI (rank / value) 26 / 0.9 (1994)

Singapore offered Washington the possibility of installing bases in the country when the Filipino Congress decided to close US military installations in the Philippines.

[18] As an exporter of high technology goods, industry was only marginally affected by the recession of its main partners, the US, Japan, and the European Union. In order to expand its activity, the Government started a policy of "regionalization" increasing its investments in Indonesia and Malaysia. The investments in China surpassed $1 billion per year, and Singapore became the main commercial partner of Vietnam. From 1993 on, annual growth was over eight per cent.

[19] Between 1994 and 1995 relations were strained between the Government and the US, Philippines, and Holland. The hanging of a Dutch engineer accused of heroin trafficking, the sentencing of a young US citizen to be hit with a rattan cane for vandalism, and the execution of a Filipino maid accused of murdering a fellow servant were the reasons for this diplomatic stress. In the case of the maid, the crime was proved and diplomatic relations were re-established. Concerning the young American, the number of blows and months in prison were reduced at the behest of President Clinton.

[20] On domestic affairs, an employee, two economists, and two journalists were sent to prison for violating a law which protects state secrets. Their crime was to publish the economic growth forecast before its official publication.

[21] In June 1996, the "Speak Mandarin Campaign" was challenged by the ethnic minorities, concerned by the fact that this language became a requirement when applying for a job. The Government - while exhorting the Chinese to have more children - responded that minorities have to be tolerant with the population's majority.

[22] Droughts and changes in wind systems caused by the "El Niño" climatic phenomenon in late 1997 led to serious losses in agriculture and tourism. The winds carried dense clouds of smoke from the forest fires in the neighbouring Indonesia, affecting the health of the population, forcing schools and businesses to close and flights to be cancelled.

[23] In January 1998, the depreciation of the Singapore dollar against the US currency continued in free fall as part of the Asian financial crisis. In April, Singapore took part in a meeting in Washington, organized by President Clinton, along with the Group of Seven and some Southeast Asian, Latin American and Southern African nations, in an attempt to "strengthen the international financial system".

WORKERS

UNEMPLOYMENT 3% (1996)

Labour force %

38	62

■ WOMEN □ MEN

Slovakia

Slovenska

Population: 5,347,000 (1996)
Area: 43,035 SQ KM
Capital: Bratislava

Currency: Slovak Koruna
Language: Slovak

Between the years 500 and 100 BC, a Celtic tribe from western Europe, the Cotini, settled in the territory of present-day Slovakia. Later, from the year 100 BC to 400 AD, the Quadi, a Germanic tribe, formed satellite states of the Roman Empire north of the Danube (the "Limes Romanum"). Both the Hadi and the Marcomani, their Germanic neighbours in Bohemia, were pushed out by the Huns led by Attila.

[2] The Slovaks, a Slav tribe from the eastern region of the Vistula and closely related to the Czechs, started to settle in the territory between the sixth and seventh centuries. They soon had to defend themselves from the Avars, nomads from lower Panonia, until the Frankish trader Samo united the Slav tribes and was chosen as their King. In 805, the Frankish King Charlemagne, expanding his Christian empire, formed an alliance with the Czech leaders of Bohemia and Moravia to defeat the Avars once and for all. In return for their help, Charlemagne distributed dukedoms amongst the Czechs, who took control over the regions of Moravia, Bohemia and Slovakia. The kingdom of Moravia, which included Bohemian and Slovakian territories, was thus established. The first Moravian monarch, Mojmir I, ruled from 830 to 846, and Christianity was adopted under his rule.

[3] The nephew who succeeded him, Rotislav I (ruling from 846 to 870), expanded the kingdom to include all of Bohemia and founded Great Moravia, unifying the Slav territories of the region for the first time. Rotislav consolidated relations with the

Frankish Empire, which answered to Rome, and maintained constant contact with the Byzantine Empire. In 863, answering a request from Rotislav, the Byzantine Emperor sent Constantine and Methodius, leading a group of missionaries. The monks translated the gospels and designed the first Slav alphabet (see Czech Republic).

[4] During the reign of Svatopluc (870-894) the Moravian frontiers extended to include the western part of present-day Hungary and southern Poland. Svatopluc abandoned relations with the Byzantine Emperor, and Methodius' disciples were forced to abandon the kingdom and take refuge in the Balkans.

[5] Great Moravia came to an end in 906, when it was destroyed by the German king Arnulf in alliance with the Magyars, a nomadic tribe from the Upper Volga who controlled most of the territories of modern-day Hungary. The western part of the old kingdom remained in the possession of the Czech dukes of Bohemia, while the area between the Carpathians and the Danube - the Slovakia of today - was occupied by the Magyars. Despite repeated attempts to take control of Slovak territory by the dukes of Bohemia, it continued as a dependency of the Hungarian Kings for ten centuries.

[6] The Slovaks never lost their language and cultural characteristics, retaining their links with the Czechs. During the 15th century, the University of Prague exercised considerable influence over the Slovaks. The Hussites of Bohemia repeatedly invaded Hungary, bringing the custom of reciting the liturgy in

the national language instead of Latin to Slovakia.

[7] The Hussite incursions prepared the ground for the later reception of Protestantism, based on the teaching of the Kralice Bible translated by the Bohemian Brethren. In the early 16th century most of the Slovaks had adopted Calvinism. However, when Hungary was invaded by the Ottoman Empire in 1525, Slovakia was governed by the House of Austria, which strengthened the Counter-reformation throughout the region. This dependence on the House of Austria Germanized Slovak culture to a large extent.

[8] In 1620, the Czech nobles were beaten by the Magyars, and Slovakia once again formed part of the Kingdom of Hungary. The conquest of central Hungary by the Ottoman Empire increased Magyar influence in Slovakia. Hungarian nobles fleeing Turkish power settled in Slovak villages and initiated Hungarian customs.

[9] In the 17th century Turkish dominion in Hungary was replaced by the House of Hapsburg. At the end of the 18th century the Emperor Joseph II changed the Kingdom of Hungary by Germanizing the bureaucracy and limited the power of the Hungarian authorities. This helped the Slovaks hark back to their Slav origin and their cultural links with the Czechs.

[10] The nationalist fever which ran across Europe following the Napoleonic Wars also reached the territories dominated by the Austrian Crown. Slovak and Hungarian nationalism came into

conflict. In 1834, Magyar replaced Latin as the legal language. In 1848, the Slovaks, allied with Czechs and German Republicans rose up in arms against the Magyars, who had in turn rebelled against the Austrians. Within this period, the Slovaks took over control of their secondary education and founded their first scientific society, the Matica Slovaka.

[11] In the late 19th century, the Hungarian authorities banned the Slovak language from public life, replacing it with Magyar. Slovak leaders, especially editors of journals, were persecuted and many were imprisoned. In 1907, the Appony law made Slovak-speaking primary schools adopt Magyar.

[12] In 1914, World War I presented the Slovaks with the chance to embrace the cause of the Allies fighting the Austro-Hungarian Empire. Tens of thousands of Slovak soldiers forced to serve in the Hungarian army joined the Allies. In 1915, the Czech Alliance and the Slovak League (of the United States) reached an agreement in Cleveland proclaiming the liberation of the Czech and Slovak nations and their federate union, with complete independence for Slovakia. It would have its own parliament and administration with Slovak as its official State language.

[13] Once the War had ended with the Allied victory in 1918, the nationalist efforts of the Slovak doctor Thomas G Masaryk (the son of a Slovak coachman and a German-Moravian mother), the

WORKERS

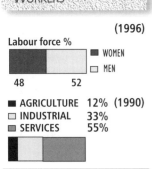

(1996)

Labour force %

■ WOMEN
□ MEN

48   52

■ AGRICULTURE   12% (1990)
□ INDUSTRIAL   33%
■ SERVICES   55%

LAND USE

IRRIGATED 5.4% of arable

(1993)

■ FOREST & WOODLAND   40.6%
□ ARABLE   30.3%
■ OTHER   29.1%

PROFILE

ENVIRONMENT

The terrain is mountainous, dominated by the Carpathian Mountain range. Mountainous areas are covered by forests which supply an important timber industry. Agriculture is concentrated in the fertile plains of the Danube and Uh rivers. There are abundant mineral resources, including copper, zinc, lead and mercury, as well as oil and natural gas deposits. Industrial pollution and sulphur emissions in the atmosphere constitute the country's main environmental problem.

SOCIETY

Peoples: Slovak, 85.7 per cent; Hungarian, 10.7 per cent; Romany, 1.6 per cent; Czech, 1.1 per cent; Ruthenian, 0.3 per cent; Ukrainian, 0.3 per cent; German, 0.1 per cent; other, 0.3 per cent (1994).
Religions: Roman Catholic, 60.3 per cent; non-religious and atheist, 9.7 per cent; Protestant, 7.9 per cent, of which Slovak Evangelical, 6.2 per cent and Reformed Christian, 1.6 per cent; Greek Catholic, 3.4 per cent; Eastern Orthodox, 0.7 per cent; other, 18 per cent.
Languages: Slovak is the official language; Hungarian is also spoken.
Political parties: Movement for a Democratic Slovakia, led by Vladimir Meciar; Party of the Democratic Left, successor to the Communist Party of Slovakia; Christian Democratic Movement; Slovakian National Party; Alternative for a Real Democracy. "Coexistence" is a coalition made up of the Hungarian Christian Democratic Movement; the Hungarian People's Party and the group known as Coexistence. Social Organizations: The Confederation of Slovakian Labor Unions, led by Alojs Englis.

THE STATE

Official Name: Slovenska Republika.
Administrative divisions: 4 regions divided into 38 municipalities.
Capital: Bratislava, 450,776 people (1994).
Other cities: Kosice, 239,927 people; Presov, 92,013; Nitra, 87,127; Zilina, 8,373; Banská Bystrica 84,741 (1995).
Government: Parliamentary republic, according to the constitution effective since January 1 1993. Michal Kovac, President elected in February 1993. Vladimir Meciar, Prime Minister since October, 1994, for the second time. One legislative house, National Council, 150 members. **Armed Forces**: 47,000 (1995).
Other: Border Guards:600; Internal Security Forces: 250; Civil Defence Troops: 3,100.

scientist Milan Stefanik (a Slovak living abroad), and the Czech Eduard Benes, working with the opposition forces in Czech and Slovak lands, led to the creation of the Republic of Czecho-Slovakia on October 28 of that year.

[14] In November, Masaryk, who had promised to respect the rights of the Germanic and Hungarian minorities, was elected President of the new Republic, a position he was to maintain until 1935 (see Czech Republic). During all of his term in government, and also that of his successor, Benes, the Slovaks felt they were relegated within a State controlled by the Czechs, without fair participation.

[15] The German occupation of the Sudetenland in 1938 forced Benes into exile in London, and the occupation of Czechoslovakia by Nazi troops in 1939 put the history of the Republic on hold. Czechoslovakia was dismembered. Bohemia became a German province and Carpathian Russia was taken by the Hungarians. In March 1939, Slovak independence was proclaimed, making it a free state on paper,

with Hitler's puppet President Joseph Tiso in power.

[16] After the allied victory in 1945, with the support of Soviet presence in the territory, the Czecho-Slovak republic returned to its former shape. The exiled Eduard Benes returned from abroad and continued in power. The integrity of the Republic was guaranteed by its membership of the Soviet bloc until, in 1991, with the fall of the Soviet regime and the system of alliances, the Czech and Slovak peoples divided to develop separate political lives.

[17] On February 15 1993 Michal Kovac was elected President of the new Republic of Slovakia. Vladimir Meciar, leader of the Movement for a Democratic Slovakia (MED) and the architect of Czechoslovakian separation, was named Prime Minister.

[18] Meciar's administration was marked by controversy and accusations of authoritarianism, from the opposition. He re-nationalized the newspaper Smena, and created a compulsory television slot for the broadcasting of government news and propaganda.

[19] Separation from the Czech

Republic proved detrimental to the Slovakian economy, which lost nearly $1 billion in bilateral trade. The country suffered more severely than the Czech Republic, because of dependence upon the Socialist bloc. In the first half of 1993, according to the Organization for Economic Co-operation and Development, 500,000 jobs were lost and inflation rose by 18 per cent.

[20] There was also a substantial loss of foreign reserves. Economic reforms and privatizations came to an almost complete standstill. In order to reduce the budget deficit, which in the first eight months of 1993 amounted to some $280 million - 6 per cent of the GDP - the Government cut subsidies and social programmes.

[21] In April, the Confederation of Slovakian Labour Unions mobilized a demonstration of workers through the streets of the capital, to protest the lack of any concrete action on the part of Government authorities.

[22] Pressure from environmental groups forced Hungarian authorities to abandon plans for an important binational hydroelectric plant, which had been approved and signed in conjunction with the former Czechoslovakia. This project would have constructed two large dams, diverting the Danube River. The decision led to a distinct cooling of relations between the two governments.

[23] Another cause of friction was the treatment of the Hungarian minority in Slovakia, which was demanding greater cultural autonomy. While in June the Slovakian Parliament approved a law allowing the Hungarian language to be taught in schools, Meciar also called for the enforcement of an old law, which had fallen into disuse, making it mandatory for Hungarian women to add the Slav feminine suffix "-ova" to their last names.

[24] By the end of 1993, more than half of all industries had recorded losses and the construction industry had suffered a 60 per cent reduction. Slovakia had received an IMF loan, but was experiencing difficulties in reducing the deficit and implementating privatization programmes. In January, Slovakia applied for full membership of NATO.

[25] Jozef Moravcik was named Prime Minister in March 1994, after long negotiations between the parties which had ousted the regime of Vladimir Meciar. Moravcik announced the formation of a government of national salvation and urgent economic measures.

[26] The new government, with the participation of the

Democratic Left Party and Alternative for Real Democracy (both consisting of former MED allies) and the right-wing Christian Democratic Movement was built upon two objectives: to keep Meciar out of power and to accept the general principles of European democracy. The internal differences in the coalition weakened the government and made it impracticable as a long-term alternative.

[27] Meciar won 35 per cent of the vote in the 1994 elections. The coalition parties suffered a tough defeat and the parties of the Hungarian minorities formed a coalition which emerged as the third force in Parliament. Meciar became Prime Minister again and immediately put the privatization initiative, started by his predecessor, into reverse, stressing nationalism.

[28] President Kovac had played an active part in ousting Meciar, and as a result, the Prime Minister was tireless in his efforts to topple him. The pressure from Parliament was increased by the issue of a warrant for the arrest of Kovac's son by the German authorities in connection with a corruption scandal. In the autumn of 1995, the son was kidnapped by Slovak intelligence agents and abandoned in Austrian territory, where he was arrested and extradited to Germany.

[29] The Meciar Government took various measures to limit the rights of the Hungarians, without those supporting a more open policy towards minorities being able to prevent him. A campaign to avoid Slovak being imposed as the only official language of the country did not get sufficient support. The United States and the European Union warned Meciar his nationalist policy could lead the country into isolation.

[30] Despite falling inflation and unemployment, Slovakia left the list of countries with the greatest chances of entering the European Union and NATO in 1997. In May, a referendum on joining NATO was boycotted by 90 per cent of the electorate, after an opposition proposal to consult voters on the issue of direct presidential elections via the same ballot papers was turned down.

[31] The opposition to Meciar continued efforts at organization throughout the year. The new Democratic Slovak Coalition (SDK), formed by five parties opposed to the governing MED, signed an agreement with the Coexistence coalition. President Kovac, already involved in tense relations with Meciar, added to the criticism of the Prime Minister, urging him to improve relations with the United States and the European Union in 1998.

Slovenia

Slovenija

Population: 1,924,000 (1996)
Area: 20,256 SQ KM
Capital: Ljubljana

Currency: Tolar
Language: Slovene

One of the southern Slav groups, the Slovenes occupied what is now Slovenia, and the land to the north of this region, in the 6th century AD. Subdued by the Bavarians around the year 743, they were later incorporated into the Frankish Empire of the Carolingians.

2   With the division of the Empire in the 9th century, the region was given to the Germans. The Slovenes were reduced to serfdom and the region north of the Drava River was completely Germanized.

3   The Slovene people preserved their cultural identity because of the educational efforts of their native intelligentsia who were mostly Catholic monks and priests. The House of Austria gradually established itself in the region, from the latter part of the 13th century onwards.

4   Between the 15th and 16th centuries, the Slovenes participated in several peasant revolts - some, like the 1573 revolt, in conjunction with the Croats - leading the Hapsburgs to improve the system of land tenure.

5   After 1809, a large part of Slovene territory fell within the Napoleonic Empire's Illyrian provinces. After Napoleon's defeat in 1814, Hapsburg (House of Austria) rule was restored within the region. With the 1848 Revolution, the Slovenes called for the creation of a unified Slovene province within the Austrian Empire. The first glimmer of hope for a union of southern Slavs (Slavs, Serbs and Croats) emerged in the 1870s.

6   In the 1890s, the Slovene People's Party (Catholic), and the Progressive (Liberal) and Socialist parties were formed. Members of the Catholic clergy also promoted a large-scale organization of peasants and artisans into cooperatives.

7   In 1917 the Austrian Parliament, representing Slovenes and other southern Slav peoples, defended the unification of these territories into a single autonomous political entity, within the Hapsburg realm.

8   At the end of World War I, amid widespread enthusiasm over the fall of the Austro-Hungarian Empire, Slovene leaders supported the creation of a kingdom of Serbs, Croats and Slovenes. In 1919, the new state adopted the name Yugoslavia (land of the southern Slavs). Nevertheless, at the Paris Peace Conference, the victorious powers handed Gorica to Italy despite the presence of a large Slovene population.

9   The St Germain Treaty, signed between the victorious powers and Austria, gave Yugoslavia only a small part of southern Carintia. Two plebiscites were announced, to define the future of the rest of Carintia. However, when the southern region opted to join Austria in 1920, the second plebiscite was not held, and both regions remained part of Austria.

10   Serbian hegemony within the Yugoslav kingdom gave rise to a certain resentment among Slovenes. This feeling never reached the extremes that characterized Croat feelings and which led to a strong anti-Serbian movement there.

11   In World War II, Slovenia was partitioned between Italy (the southwest), Germany (the northeast) and Hungary (a small area north of the Mura River). The most prominent group within the Slovene resistance movement was the Liberation Front, led by the Communists.

12   The communist guerrillas fought on two fronts at the same time: against the foreign invaders and against their internal enemies (especially groups belonging to the Slovene People's Party). The occupiers, in turn, organized anti-communist military units, with the participation of the local population. After the defeat of the Axis (Germany, Italy and Japan), the major part of old Slovenia was returned to Yugoslavia.

13   Upon the foundation of the Federated People's Republic of Yugoslavia, in 1945, Slovenia became one of the Federation's six republics, with its own governing and legislative bodies. Legislative power was made up of a republican council, elected by all citizens, and the council of producers, elected from among Slovenian industrial workers and officials.

14   Although such entities did not add up to an autonomous government, Slovenia managed to maintain a high degree of cultural and economic independence through this self-management brand of socialism (led by the Yugoslav League of Communists). In

1974, changes in the Yugoslavian federal constitution made Slovenia a Socialist Republic.

15   Slovenia became one of the most industrialized of the Federation's republics, especially in the area of steel production and the production of heavy equipment. Yugoslavia's first nuclear power plant was completed in 1981 in Krsko, with the assistance of a private US firm.

16   During the socialist period, Slovenia was first or second among the Yugoslav republics with regard to family income, leading the table for economically active population outside the rural sector. Slovenia produces both agricultural produce and cattle.

17   In the late 1980s, influenced by the changes in Eastern Europe, Slovenia evolved toward a multiparty political system. In January 1989, the Slovene League of Social Democrats was founded, the country's first legal opposition party, and in October Slovenia's National Assembly approved a constitutional amendment permitting Slovenia to secede from Yugoslavia.

18   The Slovene League of Communists left the Yugoslav League in January 1990, becoming the Democratic Renewal Party. In April, in the first multiparty elections to be held in Yugoslavia since World War II, the Demos coalition came out victorious. This coalition's members represent a broad political spectrum - including several communists - united in

their aim of achieving Slovenian separation from the federation.

19   Slovenia and Croatia declared their independence on June 25, 1991. In the hours which followed, central government tanks flocked to Slovenia's Austrian, Hungarian and Italian borders; 20,000 federal troops stationed within the republic were mobilized. After fierce fighting and the bombing of the Ljubljana airport, Belgrade announced that it controlled the federation's borders.

20   A cease-fire went into effect on July 7 1991, following negotiations held on the Yugoslav island of Brioni between federal and Slovene authorities, with the mediation of the European Community. The agreement resulting from the negotiations reaffirmed the sovereignty of Yugoslav peoples and postponed Slovenian independence for a three-month period. At the same time, the federal president's authority over the army was recognized, and the Slovene police authority over Slovenia's borders.

21   According to Brioni's compromise, customs tariffs along Slovenia's borders remained in the hands of Slovene police, although the income generated was to go into a joint account belonging to the various Yugoslav republics. The federal army was to remain in the green area (free of border controls) during the three-month period established for jurisdiction to be turned over to Slovene authorities.

22   In order for the cease-fire to be

PROFILE

ENVIRONMENT

Bordered in the west by Italy, in the north by Austria, in the northeast by Hungary and in the south and southeast by Croatia, Slovenia is characterized by mountains, forests and deep, fertile valleys. The Sava River flows from the Julian Alps (highest peak: Mt. Triglav, 2,864 meters), in the northwest of the country, to the southeast, crossing the coal-mining region. The Karavanke mountain range is located along the northern border. The region lying between the Mura, Drava, Savinja and Sava rivers is known for its vineyards and wine production. To the west and southwest of Ljubljana, all along the Soca river (known as "Isonzo" on the Italian side), the climate is less continental, and more Mediterranean. The capital has an average annual temperature of 9°C, with an average of -1°C in the winter and 19°C in summer. The country's main mineral resources are coal and mercury, which contribute to the country's high level of industrialization.

SOCIETY

Peoples: Slovene, 87.8 per cent; Croat, 2.8 per cent; Serb, 2.4 per cent; Bosnian, 1.4 per cent; Magyar, 0.4 per cent; other, 5.2 per cent. **Religions**: Mostly Catholic (83.6 per cent); Traditional Catholic Slovene Church and Orthodox 16.4 per cent.
Languages: Slovene, official; Serbo-Croat.
Political Parties: Demos, a right-of-center coalition. Slovene League of Social Democrats. Party of Democratic Renewal (formerly the Slovene League of Communists). People's Party (right wing, conservative).

THE STATE

Official Name: Republika Slovenija.
Administrative Divisions: 62 Districts. **Capital**: Ljubljana, 276,119 people (1995)
Other cities: Maribor, 139,979 people; Celje, 50,155 people; Kranj, 51,602 people; Velenje, 33,436 people (1995).
Government: President, Milan Kucan, since April 1990, re-elected in November 1997. Janez Drnovsek, Prime Minister since April 22, 1992, re-elected in January 1997. Bicameral legislature:90-member National Assembly, and 40-member National Council.
National Holiday: June 25, Independence (1991).
Armed Forces: 9,550 (1996). Other:4,500 Police (1994).

STATISTICS

DEMOGRAPHY

Population: 1,924,000 (1996). **Annual growth**: 0.3% (1980/1996). **Estimates for year 2000**: 2,000,000. **Annual growth to year 2000**: -0.1% (1994/2000). **Urban Population**: 51.5% (1996). **Urban growth**: 2.17% (1980/95). **Children per woman**: 1.3 (1996).

HEALTH

Life expectancy at birth: 73 years (1996). male: 68 years (1994). female: 78 years (1994). **Infant mortality**: 6 per 1,000 (1996). **Under-5 child mortality**: 6 per 1,000 (1996).

EDUCATION

Literacy: 99% (1995). male : 100% (1995). female: 99% (1995). **School enrolment** : Primary total: 100% (1990/95). male : 100% (1990/95). female: 100% (1990/95). Secondary: male : 89% (1990/95). female: 91% (1990/95). Tertiary: 32% (1995). **Primary school teachers**: one for every 14 students (1995).

COMMUNICATIONS

180 **newspapers**, 378 **radios**, 300 **TV sets** and 287 **main telephone lines** per 1,000 people (1994). **Books**: 151 new titles per 100,000 people (1992/94).

ECONOMY

Per capita, GNP: $ 9,240 (1996). **Annual growth, GNP**: 3.2% (1995/96). **Consumer price index**: 494.2 (1994). **Currency**: 125.99 tolar = $ 1 (1995) **Cereal imports**: 512 metric tons (1994). **Food import dependency**:% (1994). **Fertilizer use**: 2,860 kgs per ha (1994). **Exports**: $ 8,308 million (1996). **Imports**: $ 9,412 million (1996). **External debt**: $ 4,031 million (1996). $ 2,095 **per capita**: (1996). **Debt service**: 8.7% of exports (1996).

ENERGY

Consumption: 2,611.99 Kgs of Oil equivalent per capita yearly (1994). 51.18% imported (1994).

HDI (rank / value) 35 / 0.886 (1994)

---

enforced, the agreement established an unconditional return of federal army units to army barracks, and the demobilization of the Slovene territorial defence forces. Likewise, directives were established for clearing the highways and freeing prisoners on both sides.

[23] Within the following three months, Slovenia strengthened its separatist resolve, while federal troops gradually withdrew from the territory. Only hours before the three-month period was to expire, Slovene authorities announced the creation of a new national currency, the *tolar*, which was to replace the Yugoslavian *dinar*. On October 8 1991, Slovenia's declaration of independence went into effect.

[24] When it was part of Yugoslavia, the population of Slovenia was only 8 per cent of the total (approx. 1.9 million inhabitants). Yet its industrial production accounted for 25 per cent.

[25] Between 1991 and January 1992, the EC countries recognized Slovenia and Croatia as independent states, although civil war continued in the latter. The EC threatened to apply economic sanctions to Belgrade unless fighting stopped. The homogeneity

of the Slovenian population made its secession the least painful in the Yugoslavian dissolution process.

[26] Slovenia's recognition was also one of the most clear-cut cases for the international community, as it controlled its own borders, maintained its own armed forces, and had already issued its own currency. After the withdrawal of Yugoslavian troops, the Government, headed by Milan Kucan, undertook the task of economic reconstruction, with practically no interference from the former Yugoslav government.

[27] Between 1991 and 1992, the independence process was marked by two years of steady decline in economic activity. During this period, inflation climbed to more than 200 per cent annually, and unemployment to over 13 per cent. By the beginning of 1993, the foreign debt totalled $1.764 billion. Even so, Slovenia maintained an annual per capita income of over $6,000 - higher than that of any other former Yugoslav republic.

[28] In April 1992, the centre candidate Janez Drnovsek was appointed Prime Minister. In the December elections, the majority was taken by the Liberal Democratic Party, led by Drnovsek, which formed a coalition

government with the Democratic Christians, the second biggest political force in the nation.

[29] Slovenia began to define itself as a "European, not Balkan" State in 1993. Good trade relations with the European Union (EU) and the Slovenian authorities' willingness to open up markets led the country to seek association into the EU. The growth of tourism and the tolar's stability - convertible since September 1995 - enabled Slovenia's exports and gross domestic product to increase.

[30] Italy opposed Slovenia's association with the EU. Italian authorities demanded compensation for the nationalization of property belonging to 150,000 Italians between 1945 and 1972. The Catholic Church also demanded the return of property which had been nationalized by the communist regime.

[31] The European Commission approved Slovenia's request in May 1995 but Italian opposition continued. In late 1995, Croatia and Slovenia had not reached an agreement regarding the sovereignty of the waters of Piran bay. The destination of Croatian funds deposited in Slovenia's main bank, the Ljubljanska Banka, prior to the break-up of former Yugoslavia, was also discussed.

[32] In June 1996, Slovenia signed an association agreement with the EU, as a formal step to becoming a full member in 2001. One of the preconditions imposed by the EU - particularly Italy - was the inclusion of a clause in the country's constitution allowing foreigners to acquire property in Slovenia. The economic policy took the new EU demands into account, particularly on the budgetary level.

[33] In the November legislative elections, Drnovsek's centre Liberal Democratic Party maintained its small majority, taking 25 of the 90 disputed seats. After difficult preliminary negotiations, the conservative Popular Party, which had taken 19 seats, entered the new government led by the outgoing prime minister.

[34] In January 1997, Parliament officially re-elected Janez Drnovsek Prime Minister with 46 votes to 44. In November that year, former communist Milan Kucan was re-elected for a second term with 55.6 per cent of the vote. His closest rival, Janez Pidobnik, took 18.4 per cent.

[35] In early 1998, the Slovene economy was considered one of the most suitable for entry into the EU by several Western European countries, unlike those of the poorer countries like Romania.

Solomon Islands

Solomon Islands

Population: 391,000 (1996)
Area: 28,896 SQ KM
Capital: Honiara
Currency: Solomon Is. Dollar
Language: English

The Solomon Islands have been inhabited by Melanesians since at least 2000 BC. The Islands have a complex social organization based on the *wantok* or extended family system

[2] The Spaniard Alvaro de Mendaña arrived in 1567, searching for El Dorado - land of gold. In the 18th and 19th centuries, the islands were used as a source of slave labor for the sugar plantations of Fiji and Australia.

[3] After World War I, Britain colonized the archipelago, which was taken over by the Japanese in 1942. After World War II, the archipelago was recovered and divided in two. The northern part, some 14,000 sq km, was placed under Australian administration, and later annexed to Papua New Guinea.

[4] On May 21 1975, Britain agreed to independence claims. The Islands were granted internal autonomy in 1976, and independence was finally declared on July 7 1978.

[5] The financial system and the Solomons' land holdings, the main center of production, are under foreign control. Although efforts have been made at economic diversification, the Solomon Islands continue to depend almost entirely on external markets.

[6] Solomon Mamaloni was elected prime minister in August 1981, after the Islands' parliament censured Kenilorea. He banned atomic-powered ships and planes, or those carrying nuclear arms, from the Islands' territorial waters and air space.

[7] In the 1984 election, a coalition worked together to achieve the re-election of Kenilorea as Prime Minister. He patched up relations with the United States and in 1986, named Ezequiel Alebua as his successor. After taking office, Alebua followed Kenilorea's policies faithfully.

[8] In 1989, Mamaloni was re-elected Prime Minister. In 1991 the Islands turned down a proposal by an American company to dispose of industrial waste on their territory. The environmental organization Greenpeace revealed that within the last 20 years, there had been close to 20 similar proposals.

[9] Mamaloni's government was subjected to parliamentary investigation in 1992 because of irregularities in the sale of the National Fishing Development Company, a Canadian enterprise. The Government's image was tarnished even though it was not found directly responsible. On another front, the Government's development plan included the creation of 21 rural training centres to modernize agriculture, and incentives to increase tourism.

[10] The Islands' relations with Papua New Guinea deteriorated as a result of the conflict in the secessionist island of Bougainville. Two Solomon Islanders had been killed in an armed confrontation there in September 1992. In April 1993, after attempts at defusing the situation, Papuan troops carried out several incursions into Solomon Island territory (see Papua New Guinea).

[11] Francis Billy Hilly was elected Prime Minister in June 1994 but on October 31 was forced to step down after a vote of no confidence from Parliament. Billy Hilly denounced accusations that the logging industry was a source of government corruption. The new Prime Minister, Mamaloni, did not pursue the conservationist policy. In 1995, the Government ordered the felling of all the trees on Pavuvu island and its inhabitants were transferred to other islands.

[12] In September 1997 Bartholomew Ulufa'alu was appointed Prime Minister. The new government announced the nationalization of the logging industry and ordered an investigation into the use of development funds by the previous administration. In December, the national currency was devalued by 20 per cent and commodity prices rose.

PROFILE

ENVIRONMENT

Comprises most of the island group of the same name, except for those in the northwest which belong to Papua-New Guinea, the archipelago of Ontong Java (Lord Howe Atoll), the Rennell Islands and the Santa Cruz Islands. The Solomon Islands are part of Melanesia, east of New Guinea.

The major islands, of volcanic origin, are: Guadalcanal (with the capital), Malaita, Florida, New Georgia, Choiseul, Ysabel and Makira. The land is mountainous and there are several active volcanoes.

Fishing and subsistence agriculture are the traditional economic activities. Ninety per cent of Solomon Islanders live as subsistence farmers in village communities of 100 to 1,000 people. Deforestation is severe. Heavy rains cause soil erosion, particularly in exposed areas.

SOCIETY

Peoples: Most of the population is of Melanesian origin (94 per cent). There are also Polynesians (4 per cent), Micronesians (1.4 per cent) and some Chinese and Europeans. **Religions:** Christian, 96.7 per cent, of which Protestant account for 77.5 per cent and Roman Catholic for 19.2 per cent; Baha'i, 0.4 per cent; traditional beliefs, 0.2 per cent; other and no religion, 2.7 per cent. **Languages:** English (official), Pidgin (local dialect derived from English) and over 80 dialects. **Political Parties:** Solomon Islands National Unity, Reconciliation and Progressive Party (SINURPP) - formerly party for the Alliance of the People; People's Alliance Party; National Action Party of the Solomon Islands; Solomon Islands Labor Party; United Party. **Social Organizations:** The Solomon Islands Council of Trade Unions (SICTU), formed in 1986, made up of 6 trade unions.

THE STATE

Official Name: Solomon Islands. **Administrative Divisions:** 7 Provinces and the Capital. **Capital:** Honiara, 35,288 people (1994). **Other cities:** Gizo, 3,727 people; Auki, 3,262; Kira Kira, 2,585; Buala, 1,913. **Government:** Moses Pitakaka, Governor-General since June 1994, appointed by the British Government. Barholomew Ulufa alu, Prime Minister since September 1997. **National Holiday:** July 7, Independence Day (1978).

DEMOGRAPHY

Population: 391,000 (1996) **Annual growth:** 3.4 % (1980/1996) **Estimates for year 2000:** 400,000 **Annual growth to year 2000:** 3.3 % (1994/2000) **Urban population:** 17.5 % (1996) **Children per woman:** 5.1 (1996)

HEALTH

Life expectancy at birth: 71 years (1996) **Infant mortality:** 24 per 1,000 (1996) **Under-5 child mortality:** 29 per 1,000 (1996)

EDUCATION

Literacy: 62 % (1995) female: 56 % (1995) **School enrolment:** Primary total: 97 % (1990/95) male : 104 % (1990/95) female: 90 % (1990/95) Secondary: male: 21 % (1990/95) female: 14 % (1990/95)

COMMUNICATIONS

122 **radios**, 20 **TV sets** and 15 **main telephone lines** per 1,000 people (1994)

ECONOMY

Consumer price index: 155.9 (1994) **Currency:** 3.48 Solomon Is. dollars = $ 1 (1995) **Food import dependency:** 14 % (1994) **Development aid received:** $ 47 million (1995) $ 127 per capita (1995) 15.1 % of GNP (1994)

HDI (rank / value) 122 / 0.556 (1994

Somalia

Somaliya

Population: 9,822,000 (1996)
Area: 637,657 SQ KM
Capital: Mogadishu (Muqdisho)

Currency: Shillings
Language: Somali and Arabic

The region of Somalia, called "the land of Punt" by the Egyptians thousands of years ago, was an Egyptian trading partner. Centuries later, the Romans called it "the land of aroma" because of the incense produced there.

[2] This ancient commercial tradition took on new dimensions from the eighth century when Arab refugees founded a series of commercial settlements on the coast.

[3] In the 13th century, Islamicized and led by Yemeni immigrants, Somalians founded a state which they called Ifat, with its principal center in Zeila. Tribute was initially paid to the Ethiopian Empire but Ifat quickly entered into conflict with the Abyssinians and succeeded in consolidating its independence. New territories were annexed and a new name adopted: the Sultanate of Adal.

[4] Ties established with Arab markets and the southern part of the coast of Zandj contributed to develop intense commercial activity. At the same time, the sultans tried to enlarge their dominion, at the expense of the none too stable Ethiopian Empire.

[5] However, it was not until 1541 that the Portuguese Government, having acquired a clearer knowledge of Indian Ocean trade, sent its fleet. Backed up by the Ethiopian army, the latter razed the city of Zeila, going on to destroy Mogadishu (Muqdisho), Berbera and Brava.

[6] The Portuguese destroyed but did not occupy the area, though the presence of their armada hindered economic reconstruction. Adal declined, and was divided into a series of minor sultanates, the northern ones controlled by the Ottoman Empire, while the ones in the south accepted the sovereignty of the Sultan of Zanzibar after the expulsion of the Portuguese in 1698.

[7] The Suez Canal gave new strategic value to the region. In 1862, the French bought the port of Obock, leading to the creation of present-day Djibouti and in 1869 the Italians settled in Aseb and later extended their control over Eritrea.

[8] In 1885 the British, who had already occupied Aden on the Arabian peninsula, took the Egyptian settlements in Zeila and Berbera. In 1906, in compensation for their defeat in Ethiopia, the Italians obtained Somalia's southern coast.

[9] The British colony was the leading centre of resistance to foreign domination. Sheikh Muhammad bin Abdullah Hassan organized an Islamic revolutionary movement, which defeated the British troops on four occasions between 1900 and 1904. The British finally gained control of the territory in 1920.

[10] On July 1 1960, with decolonization in Africa underway, the British and Italian regions became independent and were merged as the Republic of Somalia. The new republic adopted a parliamentary system, until October 21 1969, when a group of officers led by General Said Barre seized power and proclaimed a socialist regime.

[11] In July 1976, the Front for the Liberation of Western Somalia initiated a military offensive in the Ogaden supported by the Somali Government. The invasion was repelled by the Ethiopian army, supported by Cuban troops and backed by most African nations who opposed changes in colonial frontiers. The country broke off relations with Cuba and ended its military agreements with the Soviet Union.

[12] The war against Ethiopia caused serious difficulties to Somalia's fragile economy; prices of fuel and grain increased and a severe drought affected most of the country in 1978-79, bringing the Barre government to the brink of collapse. A group of army officers unsuccessfully attempted to overthrow the government, in April 1978. In October 1980 Barre declared a state of emergency and reinstated the Supreme Revolutionary Council which had ceased functioning in 1976.

[13] The northeastern province of Kenya has historically been claimed by Somalia, but relations with Kenya have improved since 1984, through commercial and technical cooperation agreements.

[14] Problems with Ethiopia recurred sporadically because of the dispute over the Ogaden plains and the steady flow of Ethiopian refugees into Somali camps. In 1988 alone the number of refugees was estimated at 840,000.

[15] Said Barre was re-elected in December 1986 by 99 per cent of the vote. In February 1989, he sent Prime Minister Ali Samater to London and Washington, to announce the amnesty and commuting of sentences for 400 political prisoners.

[16] Western credits and investments were drastically reduced and exports to Saudi Arabia, the principal market for its cattle, stopped almost completely.

[17] In January 1991, the opposition formed the United Somali Congress (USC) and ousted the President, replacing him with Ali Mahdi Mohammed, leader of the USC and representing business interests.

[18] After bloody confrontations between the two factions of the USC, President Mahdi fled Mogadishu in November 1991. The capital remained in the hands of General Mohamed Farah Aideed, leader of the military wing of the USC.

[19] The two rival factions of the United Somali Congress were made up of members of different sub-groups of the Hawiye clan, led by Farah Aideed and Ali Mahdi, respectively.

[20] Since the beginning of the war between the rival clans, 300,000 Somali children have died, and 1.5 million inhabitants - a quarter of the total population - have left the country.

[21] On March 9 1991, taking advantage of a cease-fire, 100,000 women and children held a peaceful march through Mogadishu. Nine tribal leaders of the Hiraan region met to discuss how to bring about peace in their country. It was the first meeting of *ugas* or kings in more than a hundred years.

[22] In 1993, after two years of civil war and total anarchy, Somalia still had no central governmental structures. The traditional authorities, unable to

PER 100,000
LIVE BIRTHS
1,600

24%

PROFILE

ENVIRONMENT
Somalia is a semi-desert country with a large population of nomads. The north is mountainous, descending gradually from the Galia-Somali plateau to the coastal strip bathed by the Gulf of Aden. The south is almost entirely desert with the exception of a fertile area crossed by two rivers originating in Ethiopia, the Juba and Shebeli. Drought, endemic in this region, has been exacerbated by overpasturing. A drastic increase in livestock has led to desertification. Fishing using explosive charges has damaged coral reefs and aquatic vegetation. The destruction of these fish habitats may have put stocks and future catches of many species at risk. There are 74 endangered species, including mammals, plants and birds.

SOCIETY
Peoples: The Somalian people are Hamitic and the most important ethnic groups (Isaq, Dir and Digil) have linguistic and cultural unity, a relatively unusual situation in Africa.
Religions: Islam (official), mostly the orthodox Sunni version. There are a few Christians in Mogadishu.
Languages: Somali and Arabic (official).

Political Parties: Therere is confrontation between rival factions of the various clans. Major groupings of clans include the United Somali Congress (USC), the Somali Salvation Alliance (SSA) and the Somali National Alliance (SNA). The United Somali Congress (USC), created in 1991, led by Osman Ali Atto. The Somali National Alliance (SNA), made up of Siad Barre's former troops, (formerly loyal to Farah Aideed, but ousted him in 1995). The USC and SNA then formed an alliance. The Somali Salvation Alliance (SSA), Ali Mahdi Mohammed's party. The Somali Patriotic Movement (SPM, Darod clan). The Somali Salvation Democratic Front (SSDF, Majertein clan) in the south. The Somali Democratic Alliance (SDA, Gadabursi clan) and the United Somali Front (USF, Issa clan) in the north.
Social Organizations: The General Federation of Somali Trade Unions, created in 1977.

THE STATE
Official Name: Jamhuriaydda Soomaliya.
Administrative divisions: Somalia is divided into 18 regions or provinces.
Capital: Mogadishu, 750,000 people (1994).
Government: Neither the Government nor the public administration have functioned since November 1991, when Ali Mahdi Mohammed fled the capital.
National Holiday: July 1, Independence Day (1960).
Armed Forces: Regular armed forces have not existed since rebel forces ousted the government in 1991.

STATISTICS

DEMOGRAPHY
Population: 9,822,000 (1996). **Annual growth**: 2.4 % (1980/1996). **Urban population**: 26.0 % (1996). **Children per woman**: 7 (1996).

HEALTH
Life expectancy at birth: 48 years (1996). **Infant mortality**: 125 per 1,000 (1996). **Under-5 child mortality**: 211 per 1,000 (1996). **Calorie consumption**: 81 % (1988/90). **Safe water**: 31% (1990/96).

EDUCATION
Literacy: 24 % (1995). male : 36 % (1995). female : 14 % (1995). **School enrolment** : Primary total: 11 % (1990/95).

ECONOMY
Currency: shillings = $ 1 (1995) **Cereal imports**: 129 metric tons (1994).

handle these unprecedented conditions, had abandoned their normal functions, leaving clans and sub-clans unrestrained. In some regions, though, the local population still respected the traditional authority of the tribal elders. However, in the vacuum created by the absence of central administration, power remained in the hands of the warlords and of heavily armed bands of looters.
[23] Under pressure from the United States, the UN sent 28,000 troops to assist. This was the first time the world organization had intervened militarily in the internal affairs of a nation.
[24] At the suggestion of the UN, in March 1993 military chiefs, councils of elders and prominent citizens agreed to create a provisional government and a National Transition Council. Aideed's forces confronted the UN blue helmets with losses on both sides. The elite US Rangers failed in their attempt to capture Aideed. In March 1994, the UN withdrew 10,000 European troops, leaving 19,000, mostly Africans and Indians. The peace efforts did not prosper, despite a meeting organized in Nairobi, Kenya, between the main opponents: Aideed and Ali Mahdi. The last contingent of UN troops left the country in March, protected by a force of 1,800 marines. And even though the regional conflicts continued, the civil war did not spread and economic life seemed to recover.
[25] The Republic of Somaliland broke away from Somalia and declared independence in 1994. The fledgling republic - comprising about 30 per cent of Somalia's territory - is not officially recognized. The port of Berbere, on the Gulf of Aden, forms its economic base. With the economy in ruins, it sheltered a million people displaced from the southern zone (Somalia).
[26] Divided and still without international recognition, the Republic of Somaliland continued to function in 1995. In Somalia the factions regrouped around the Somali Salvation Front (SSF), of Ali Mahdi Mohamed, and the Somali National Alliance (SNA) led by Farah Aideed, both self-proclaimed governments. Farah Aideed died from gunshot wounds in August 1996 and was succeeded by his son Hussein. Osman Hassan Ali ("Ato"), Farah's former right hand man, emerged as a new force, but in association with Ali Mahdi.
[27] In January 1997, in Sodere, Ethiopia, 26 political leaders associated to the SSF, with the support of the Organization of African Unity, decided to establish a National Salvation Council empowered to organize a transition Government. Hussein Aideed and Mohammed Ibrahim Egal, re-elected President of Somaliland in March, refused to recognize this decision.
[28] The floods of November and December 1997 left 230,000 Somalis stranded in the southern regions of the nation. The UN began a refugee aid programme air dropping tons of food over the Garbahari and Gedo districts, alongside the Juba river.
[29] In April 1998, at fresh meetings in Nairobi, Kenya, the military chiefs - Ali Mahdi Mohammed, Hussein Aideed, Osman Hassan Ali and Mohamed Kanyere - declared their commitment to peace for the Somali people. Meanwhile, the devastated economy suffered another downturn following a ban on imports of Somali livestock imposed by Saudi Arabia.

South Africa

South Africa

Population: 42,393,000 (1996)
Area: 1,221,037 SQ KM
Capital: Pretoria
Currency: Rands
Language: Afrikaans, English + 9 African languages

The first Dutch settlers arrived in Cape Town in 1652, more than 150 years after the voyage around the Cape of Good Hope by the Portuguese navigator Vasco da Gama. The Portuguese had focused their attention on India and showed little desire to challenge the Khoikhoi people, who had been established in the region for more than a thousand years, and were hostile to foreign navigators.

2 Jan Van Riebeeck was the first of the Dutch to challenge the Khoikhoi. In Cape Town he founded a colony where vegetables were cultivated and animals raised to supply the ships en route to Indonesia. By 1688, about 600 farmers had already settled in Cape Town, dividing their time between farming and fighting the war against the Khoikhoi. Being in such a tiny minority, the first Dutch settlers were fiercely united and aggressive, two characteristics which were to become striking features of the whole Boer (farmer) society in South Africa.

3 The Dutch increased the areas under their control to gain greater security, but they were not typical colonists. They were not allowed to trade with local people and they had to hand over everything they produced to the Dutch East India Company's ships. This arrangement finally led them into conflict with their overseas employers. In this dispute, the Boers slowly gained ground and by the end of the 17th century, the so-called free settlers, the burghers, were already in a majority. The population of European origin split into two groups; those linked to foreign trade and settled agriculture and those (pastoralists) who moved deeper inland in search of new territories.

4 Between 1770 and 1840, there were seven large wars against the Xhosa. In 1806, with the weakening of the Dutch colonial empire, the British installed themselves in Cape Town. The British established a system which would enable them to exchange merchandise, incorporate African leaders as intermediaries and end slavery. This quickly led to a clash with the Boers, who began calling themselves Afrikaners to distinguish themselves from the more recently arrived colonists. In 1834 close to 14,000 Boers migrated inland, initiating the Great Trek which would take them to what is now Gantery, the Free State and KwaZulu-Natal. Objecting to outside interference, the Afrikaners established the states of Transvaal in 1852 and the Orange Free State in 1854. These regions were already occupied by African people who fiercely resisted the new settlers.

5 The British recognized the independence of both regions, as European occupation of the new lands contributed to Cape Town's security. The Boers had no choice but to trade through the ports which were held by the British. Although official history minimizes the African resistance, it was extremely strong and organized and caused many casualties within the native population. In their expansion northward, the Afrikaners confronted the Xhosa and the Zulu. The latter had been led by Shaka, a military genius, who died in 1828. The resistance blocked the colonists' advance over a period of 50 years. Shaka had become the head of a huge empire which crumbled shortly before the Great Trek, not because of external pressure, but due to internal problems linked to the issue of royal succession.

6 Conflict between the Boers and the British Crown erupted in the late 19th century when rich gold and diamond deposits were discovered in the interior. The realization that the area had great strategic importance led the British to propose a federation between the Cape Colony, the Transvaal (South African Republic), Natal and the Orange Free State. The proposal was rejected by the Boers and later, in 1899, war broke out. Britain had the backing of most of its colonies while the Boers had the support of Germany. After three years of war, in which about 50,000 people died and 100,000 were confined to British concentration camps, the Boers surrendered and accepted British domination in exchange for certain concessions in regional autonomy. The British victory in the Boer or South African War signalled the end of the controlling power of landed Boer farmers in the Orange Free State and the Transvaal, and the beginning of the pre-eminence of mining in the economy.

7 For the Boer settlers, local people were nothing but savages who had to be tamed by force. White supremacy and racial segregation were established to justify the subjugation of the black population, and to guarantee a supply of cheap farm labor from tenants. Boer farms in the interior were backward and unprofitable in comparison with the farming practised in the Cape and Natal.

8 The British focus on trade and liberalism led them to consider slavery a restraint on the creation of consumer markets. This view did not prevent them from erecting rigid barriers to exclude South African black people from economic and social gains. Labor laws imposed severe controls on worker mobility. The 1843 Master and Servant Act, along with later decrees, made it a criminal act to break a work contract.

9 In the 19th century the British also hired black workers in the territories now called Mozambique, Lesotho and Botswana, as well as Indians. No 'imported' worker was allowed to bring any members of his or her family; they received only a minimum salary and were obliged to return to their own country if they lost their job. Both in the Cape and Natal hut and poll taxes were introduced, designed to force local people to work for far lower wages than workers of

WORKERS

Labour force % (1996)

■ WOMEN
□ MEN

37   63

■ AGRICULTURE 14% (1990)
□ INDUSTRIAL 32%
■ SERVICES 55%

LAND USE

DEFORESTATION annual (81/90) **6.7 %**
IRRIGATED of arable (1993) **10.3%**

■ FOREST & WOODLAND (1993) 6.7%
□ ARABLE (1993) 10.1%
■ OTHER (1993) 83.2%

European descent. In this way, the traditional African ways of life were destroyed and at the same time, wages were kept low.

[10] When the gold and diamond mines came into operation, the large European interests which controlled them had to rely on white workers who had some training and educational background. Many of them were former Boer farmers who had lost out in the war, and others came from Europe, attracted by the gold rush. Both groups, used to the workings of the industrial capitalist system, demanded economic rewards and labor rights. This situation was ably manipulated by the mining companies, who promised benefits to the white workers provided that they become accomplices in the exploitation of the black labor force. The so-called colour bar was established throughout the mining sector and in major urban centres. In 1910, the Constitution of the Union of South Africa (a federation of Cape Province, Natal, the Orange Free State and the Transvaal) deprived most black people of the right to vote or to own land.

[11] After 1910, segregationist legislation gradually increased. The Natives Land Act of 1913 set aside 7 per cent of the nation's land for blacks as reserves, which became home to 35-40 per cent of the country's population. Much of the remaining land was reserved for ownership by whites, who represented only 20 per cent of the population. On the overpopulated black reservations, subsistence agriculture predominated. The rest - belonging to whites - was intensively farmed with the reservations functioning as a permanent source of cheap labor. The 1923 Native Urban Act tightly regulated blacks' lives in cities which were considered to be white strongholds.

[12] Until 1984, political participation was limited very largely to whites. Most Black Africans, comprising almost 66 per cent of the country's population, were still deprived of the right to vote.

[13] From colonial times, power was monopolized by the white minority. At the outset of World War I, the white economy was based on mining and intensive farming. The post-war recession made it necessary for the large mining companies to hire blacks, leading to racial confrontations among the workers. The Rand strike in 1922, was harshly put down by the government. Most of the strikers were poor whites, descendants of both English and Boers. Frustrated over having lost the war, over the loss of their lands and over the difficulty of gaining access to the country's incipient industrial structure, Afrikaners were attracted by the ultra-nationalistic propaganda of the extreme right. The Nationalists, who won the 1924 election together with their English-speaking allies, broke with the tradition of liberal economic policies, and imposed protectionist measures instead. These affected the large mining companies and were aimed at initiating a process of internal industrialization.

[14] The emergence of state capitalism promoted by the Nationalists, enabled the country to achieve impressive growth rates, classified by many as an 'economic miracle'. But at the end of the 1920s, euphoria gave way to a new crisis: the Great Depression. The Nationalists were forced into another alliance in order to survive. This time they joined forces with traditionally despised foreign capital, keeping the system of racial segregation, which guaranteed a supply of cheap labor. The industrial development which followed brought with it an increase in the number of blacks employed in industry, and an increase in racial conflict. The Afrikaner BroederBond or Brotherhood emerged; it was a secret society, which became the bastion of white right-wing politics.

[15] The recession that followed World War II, again led to the 'poor whites' rebelling when faced with the possibility of losing their jobs. Racism once again flourished, under the slogan Gevaar KKK (beware of blacks, Indians and communism - Kafir, Koelie, Komunism). Predictably enough, the Nationalists formed a government by themselves in 1948 and imposed even harsher restrictions on black people.

[16] The first national political organization of South African blacks appeared in 1912. The African National Congress (ANC) was created by a group of former students from schools run by missionaries. Among its founders were several people who had studied or gained degrees in American or European universities. The first ANC leaders believed that the Afrikaners could be persuaded of the injustice of its segregationist laws. They also believed that Anglophile liberals would accept black participation in politics. These high hopes were dashed in 1920, when the black mine workers strike was crushed and segregation entrenched.

[17] In the 1940s the ANC adopted a strategy of non-violent resistance against segregationist laws. In 1955 the anti-racist front was broadened with the so-called Freedom Charter, proclaimed at a multi-racial gathering in Kliptown.

Food Dependency
1970
5%
1994
5%

Foreign Trade
MILLIONS $ 1996
IMPORTS
26,861
EXPORTS
18,132

The Charter contained a vehement denunciation of apartheid (separateness) and called for its abolition and a redistribution of wealth.

[18] Beginning in 1943, the Youth League branch of the ANC launched a more aggressive program. Its leaders, Nelson Mandela and Oliver Tambo, gradually attained positions of leadership within the ANC. In 1958, sectors of the ANC that did not agree with the multi-racial policy of the movement created the Pan-Africanist Congress (PAC). In 1960, the PAC organized a demonstration in the town of Sharpeville to protest against the pass law which restricted the movement of black workers in areas reserved for whites. The demonstration was brutally repressed by the police and 70 people were killed. Immediately after this Sharpeville Massacre, the PAC, the ANC and the Communist Party were outlawed and the anti-racist struggle underwent a radical change. The African National Congress created an armed movement, *Umkhonto we Sizwe* (Spear of the Nation) while the PAC organized another guerrilla group, *Poqo* (Only us). In 1963, the main ANC leaders were arrested. Nelson Mandela was sentenced to life imprisonment and Oliver Tambo, who went into exile, took over leadership of the movement. The government's repressive violence, and the lack of supply bases in neighboring countries which were under regimes allied with the Afrikaners, kept the guerrillas from making the progress necessary to attract massive numbers of recruits.

[19] In 1964, any South African who was not white could not vote, had to use passes, could not leave certain areas, could be arrested arbitrarily, could not belong to a union nor support a strike, could not go to schools or universities with whites, could be transferred to other areas against their will, did not have access to public services, and could not participate in public demonstrations against segregation. The survival of the racist system depended, to a large extent, on international capitalist investment in the region, attracted by the availability of a large pool of cheap labor. Foreign investment, especially from America, quintupled in value between 1958 and 1967. The Afrikaners' protectionist policies created the infrastructure necessary for large industries to move there, with the long-term objective of creating an industrial development zone capable of supplying all southern Africa.

[20] The 1960s witnessed an increase in the migration of black farm workers to the cities. The massive exodus was fuelled by a number of factors: the misery of the 'Homelands', or Bantustans, with poor quality of the soil, which was incapable of producing very much, and the absence of social services. This migration affected the expectations of other urban sectors, like the coloured people, who saw their hopes of integration in the white economy dashed. In 1976 the black community in the suburbs of Johannesburg rebelled. The rebellion by the young people of SOWETO (South Western Township) made whites realize that the crisis had reached their own cities, where they had once felt safe. In 1970, 75 per cent of all those who worked in agriculture, mining or services were black, and the participation of non-whites in specialized jobs had tripled within the last 20 years, though blacks earned 5 to 10 times less than whites for equal work. The ruling white minority were dependent upon black labour, and they proposed a few reforms to apartheid, aimed at preventing new social crises among workers who had migrated to the cities. The Pretoria regime declared four Bantustans, Transkei, Ciskei, Venda and Bophuthatswana, independent States, in an attempt to prevent further urban migration by the unemployed. Eight million people were thus deprived of their South African citizenship, though few countries in the world recognized these newly independent states.

[21] The situation in southern Africa was radically modified by the independence of Angola and Mozambique in 1975, and Zimbabwe in 1980. The African National Congress found the support bases it desperately needed, in these, and the other Front Line States of Botswana, Tanzania and Zambia. South Africa,

with an economy three times greater than that of these independent countries combined, initiated a destabilisation campaign which included economic pressure, sabotage, support of rebel movements and invasion. All these measures were designed to force these governments to deny support to the anti-apartheid movement, and block attempts by newly independent countries to escape South African domination.

[22] One of the main scenes of conflict in southern Africa was Namibia, a former German colony which South Africa had occupied during World War I. In 1966 the UN determined that South Africa should grant Namibia its independence. This proposal was taken up by the OAU and the Front Line countries, despite the delaying tactics adopted by South Africa and the Western powers. The independence of Namibia did not actually occur until March 21 1990.

[23] For South Africa to be able to impose its power throughout the southern part of Africa, the support which it received from Europe and the United States was essential. Approximately 400 US companies had interests in South Africa; US capital and technology were vital for South African industrial development and for maintaining its military might. South Africa is also the world's major exporter of platinum, gold, manganese, chrome and vanadium; the second largest exporter of antimony, diamonds, fluoride and asbestos; and the third, of titanium, uranium and zirconium. Also, its geographical location is strategic: ships carrying 70 per cent of the oil destined for Europe, and 30 per cent of the oil destined for the United States, navigate its waters.

[24] During the Reagan era, the United States used all its economic and military leverage to avoid revolutionary change in southern Africa. On the domestic front, South African Prime Minister PW Botha (in office 1978-1989) began reforming the segregationist system. Between 1982 and 1984, a constitutional reform went into effect whereby Indians and coloured people were given the right to vote through the creation of two more chambers in the legislature for these racial groups. Blacks continued to be excluded, limiting their participation to the local level. Many non-white citizens boycotted the reform, abstaining from voting. The South African economy went into recession in 1983, due to the fall in the international price of gold, its main export product. The economic difficulties affected the white middle class, which until then had been largely impervious to economic troubles. Given this

situation, the racist parties of the extreme right attracted more votes.

[25] The gradual liberalization of apartheid promised by Botha found many opponents. Repression against blacks did not diminish; it was merely complicated by inter-tribal confrontations, and conflict between opposing parties. In July 1985 the government declared a state of emergency in 36 districts. By the end of 1986, more than 750 people had been killed and thousands of the government's opponents had been arrested.

[26] In the United States and western Europe the anti-apartheid campaign grew over the next few years. Public pressure forced Western governments and a growing number of companies and banks to limit their activities in South Africa. The US Congress lifted the veto imposed by President Reagan on economic sanctions, bringing about a change in the policy of constructive engagement in the area. Within South Africa, internal political opposition led to the creation of the United Democratic Front (UDF), which brought together more than 600 organizations working together within the law.

[27] From the beginning of 1988, the Government showed greater intransigence toward the opposition, to the point of declaring all opposition illegal in February of that year. Religious leaders opposed to apartheid were briefly detained, among them black Archbishop Desmond Tutu, who had won the Nobel Peace Prize for his activity against racial segregation. Labour unions, led by the Congress of South African Trade Unions (COSATU), founded in 1985, were suppressed as subversive. In August 1989, Botha was faced with an internal crisis within his own party which had been in power for the past 41 years, and he resigned. He was succeeded by FW De Klerk, who was aware of the need to change the image of the South African government in the eyes of international public opinion, and he came out in favour of a change in the racist system. In 1990, South Africa had to refinance part of its $12 billion foreign debt, and changes in its system of segregation would help in its negotiations with international agencies.

[28] In September 1989, parliamentary elections were held within the state of emergency which had been in effect since 1986. The Mass Democratic Movement (MDM) an anti-apartheid coalition of legal organizations, called a general strike. Despite police round-ups and threats, three million South African blacks interrupted their

work in the largest protest in the country's history. The growing momentum was accompanied by repression and killings. But by now an increasing number of the white minority was joining the protests, making the situation even more difficult to subdue.

[29] In February 1990, De Klerk legalized the African National Congress and other opposition groups. After several announcements, and an equal number of delays, Nelson Mandela, the country's most famous political prisoner was freed on the 11 of that month. He had served the longest prison sentence of all political prisoners; 27 years. A period of negotiation began. Upon being freed, Mandela, acclaimed by multitudes, took up his role as leader of the black majority. Being in a position of leadership was not

altogether without its difficulties, however: one of these was the confrontation between the ANC and members of the Zulu nationalist organization Inkatha, which had not been fighting apartheid.

[30] ANC leaders maintained that the conflict lay between those who wanted a united, democratic and non-racist South Africa, and those who would only accept changes based on the preservation of privileges. The ultra-right, playing on the fears of the poor whites, defended racial segregation. In May 1990, after three days of meetings between the ANC and the Government, Mandela announced an agreement to put an end to violence and begin a normal political life. He called on the international community to maintain economic

Maternal Mortality
1990

PER 100,000
LIVE BIRTHS

230

Literacy
1995

82%

sanctions and other forms of pressure on the South African government. Some opposition groups on the left were against talks with the government, claiming that these would only postpone the struggle and the radical change which they demanded. The police, whose terrible repressive habits had not been modified, were linked to the formation of death squads, adding to the uncertainty of a peaceful end to apartheid. In May 1990, the Government renounced the policy of creating Bantustans (ten had been established), and abolished racial segregation in hospitals. In December, ANC president Oliver Tambo returned to the country, after more than 30 years in exile.

[31] In mid-April 1991, the European Community began studying the possibility of lifting the economic blockade, and set June 30 as a deadline for beginning the democratization of the country. At the same time, the government did away with the Population Registration Act and the Land Acts, whereby blacks were forbidden to own land. De Klerk promised to begin negotiations for a new constitution. The United States went ahead and lifted the blockade, while the EC, though intending to lift it, got caught up in internal debates. In the end, Denmark and Spain, which had just hosted a visit from Mandela, vetoed the move.

[32] While these developments were taking place, the 'Inkathagate' scandal broke out. This was chiefly about state money being given to the Inkatha Freedom Party (IFP) for their activities, many of which were aimed at opposing the ANC. Given the fact that friction between the ANC and Inkatha had claimed 5,000 lives since 1986, these revelations cast doubt on the government's intentions. The ANC had suspended hostilities in August 1990, but the confrontations became more violent after June 1991. In late June, De Klerk replaced the ministers of defence and of the interior. In October, despite an agreement between the two groups and the government, signed the previous month, more than 50 deaths were reported.

[33] In addition to these confrontations, crime was on the rise, as a result of the economic recession. For the third consecutive year, the GDP dropped by 0.6 per cent in 1991, and unemployment reached almost 40 per cent of the economically active population.

[34] In August 1991, Mandela reiterated his demands: an interim government, the election of a Constituent Assembly, the release of all political prisoners and the principle of one person, one vote. In November, negotiations between the government and 20 political organizations led to the establishment of the Convention for Democracy in South Africa (CODESA), which would discuss the new constitution. Groups which excluded themselves by choice from these talks included the ultra-right white Conservative Party, the National Reform Party, the Afrikaner Resistance Movement (AWB) and black groups including: the Pan-Africanist Congress (PAC) and the extreme left Azanian People's Organization (Azapo). In December, CODESA met for the first time, but Mandela insisted that the economic blockade be maintained.

[35] In February 1992, the National Party lost the by-election at Potchefstroom, a small university city located west of the capital. The Conservative Party took advantage of the election results to claim that De Klerk did not have a mandate to negotiate within CODESA. De Klerk immediately announced a referendum among South African whites, to decide whether the government should continue the negotiations. The ANC and the labour organization COSATU rejected the referendum, claiming that the country's destiny must not depend exclusively on the opinion of the whites. The conservatives, however, took up De Klerk's challenge. On March 17 almost 70 per cent of the white population voted 'yes' to the transition envisaged by De Klerk.

[36] Death squad activity continued. In June, the massacre of 46 people in the township of Boipatong brought talks between the ANC and the government to a halt.

[37] In September 1992, with the resumption of the negotiations, a Protocol of Understanding was signed between President De Klerk and ANC leaders. This document established the guidelines for the transition, including the creation of a joint committee charged with preparing elections for a Constitutional Assembly, as well as a multiracial transitional government. In addition, it provided for the release of all political prisoners. The agreement was rejected by Inkatha and extreme right-wing groups. Armed confrontations broke out between Inkatha and the ANC, especially in Natal Province, where the government doubled the number of troops. The ANC's regional representative from Natal, Reggie Hadebe, was shot dead when he was returning from a meeting in which peace in the region was being discussed.

[38] Russia re-established diplomatic relations with Pretoria, followed shortly by Côte d'Ivoire. A few days later, De Klerk made an official visit to Nigeria, where he expressed South Africa's desire to join the Organization of African Unity (OAU).

[39] Difficulties continued to mount on the economic front. By the end of 1992, the nation's GNP had fallen by 5.7 per cent, the highest figure in recent years, due to a decrease in agricultural production, brought on in part by drought but also affected by the lack of investment and capital flight.

[40] The Executive Committee of the ANC, meeting on November 25, recognized the necessity of forming a 'government of national unity'. The Government set the date for elections for April 1994. For their contributions to the dismantling of apartheid, the Swedish Academy gave the 1993 Nobel Peace Prize to Nelson Mandela and FW De Klerk.

[41] The progress made by the political leadership did not put an end to the violence. In January 1993, the Independent Human Rights Commission set the number of violent deaths of the previous year at 3,499, of which 299 were members of the security forces and 123 were civilians killed in police custody. The ANC denounced the formation of a new group of armed whites, made up of members and former members of the South African Defence Forces.

[42] In April 1993 talks resumed in a new forum - the Council of Multiparty Negotiation - which replaced the defunct CODESA, suspended in June 1992.

[43] However, yet another act of violence threatened to derail the talks definitively. On April 10, Chris Hani, Secretary General of the Communist Party, member of the Executive Committee of the ANC, was assassinated. He had a wide following and respect, especially among the most radical sections of the ANC, and was thought by many to be the likely successor to Mandela. A large number of ANC youth reacted to Hani's death by calling for a return to armed conflict. Several members of the Conservative Party were implicated in the conspiracy which had led to Hani's death. The weeks which followed were marked by numerous protest demonstrations.

[44] In May, another plot was uncovered - this time to assassinate Joe Slovo, former Secretary General of the Communist Party. In October, Janusz Walus, a South African citizen of Polish origin, and Clive Derby-Lewis, a former Conservative Party MP and presidential adviser, were found guilty of assassinating Hani and sentenced to death.

[45] The mobilization of the ultra-right parties reached its peak during this period, when a conference of 21 racist groups was convened. These included the neo-Nazi Afrikaner Resistance Movement (AWB) led by Eugene Terreblanche, the Reformed National Party; the Afrikaner National Union, as well as white labor unions and organizations representing agribusiness. The main outcome of this meeting was the formation of the Afrikaner National Front (NFA), led by General Viljoen.

[46] The NFA attempted to build an independent white state. In January, some 3,000 armed militants from the AWB deployed their forces at the World Trade Centre, where the negotiating talks were being held.

[47] A Human Rights Commission report registered 9,352 deaths in the period from 1990 to 1993 as a result of political violence.

[48] Maintaining a distance from the talks on the provisional constitution, the Inkatha Freedom Party (IFP), the NFA and the Conservative Party decided to boycott the electoral process. Bophuthatswana president Lucas Mangope declared he would join the boycott, in the midst of a civil servants' strike. Street protests immediately ensued. Simultaneously, neo-Nazi leader Terreblanche ordered his followers from the Afrikaner Resistance Movement to invade Bophuthatswana, and come to Mangope's aid. Resistance from black civilians and local forces made them withdraw. Mangope was deposed and the South African army seized control. 50 dead and 300 wounded was the outcome. A few days later, Terreblanche decided to participate in the electoral process

through the recently created Freedom Front.

[49] In the meantime, Inkatha boycotted ANC activities and had severe confrontations with Mandela's followers, particularly in the Inkatha stronghold of KwaZulu-Natal. Buthelezi finally agreed to participate in the elections after the constitution finally recognized his nephew Goodwill Zwelethini as king of the Zulus.

[50] In October, the UN agreed to lift sanctions against the South African regime. The US immediately lifted its financial restrictions.

[51] The provisional Constitution formed a 400-member National Assembly and a 90-member Senate. The president, with less powers than the prime minister, would be elected by the Assembly for a 5-year term. The territory was divided differently, with nine provinces, each with its own governor and legislature; the ten bantustans were abolished as such and incorporated into the provinces.

[52] The South African National Defence Force (SANDF) was created which brought together the South Africa Defence Force and some ANC and PAC guerrillas.

[53] The first multi-ethnic elections in South Africa were held between April 26-29, 1994 and 87 per cent of those registered to vote took part. The ANC obtained 63 per cent of the vote, De Klerk's NP 20 per cent and Inkatha 10 per cent. The far right, represented by the Freedom Front, won 2 per cent.

[54] The Government of National Unity included NP and IFP members as well as the ANC majority. The minister of finance and the governor of the South African Reserve Bank from the previous government remained in their posts.

[55] Although the barriers of apartheid were removed, economic and cultural obstacles remain. Black workers earn far less than whites and unemployment is far higher respectively. The overall infant mortality rate for the country is 50 per 1,000 (1998) but this disguises the fact that the rate is much higher among the black population that the white.

[56] The May 1994 constitution was radical in tone. Among the measures to be implemented by his government, Mandela proposed free health care for children under 6 and pregnant women, the launching of a basic dietary plan for schoolchildren and provision of electricity for 350,000 homes. He pledged to create 2.5 million jobs and build a million homes for 1999.

[57] The implementation of the Reconstruction and Development Program progressed slowly in 1995 as a result of financial and bureaucratic limitations. A law set a new structure for education. In October it was announced 3.5 million would have access to water services in the following 18 months. The first full budget by the Government of National Unity allocated 47 per cent to social services and 26 per cent to education, investment in housing was doubled and military expenditures were reduced. An ambitious agrarian reform program was put into effect by minister Derek Hanekom, a farmer. A labor relations act was passed which guaranteed the right to strike and formed forums of discussion at workplaces. South Africa registered a lower number of strikes than in previous years.

[58] In January, the ANC withdrew the immunity it had guaranteed prior to the elections to two former Cabinet members and 3,500 police members, who were under investigation. The trial of a former police colonel charged with 121 murders, kidnappings and fraud brought forth new evidence regarding police incitement of political violence during the previous regime. Prominent Inkatha leaders were implicated in payoffs to security police. A report by the Goldstone Commission sent to President De Klerk in 1994 was published, listing all these charges. In June an IFP under-secretary was arrested for murders committed in 1987.

[59] Strikes and accusations of racism among the police led to the resignation of the force's chief. His successor, George Fivaz, proposed demilitarization of the force, among other reforms. Although there was a growing concern over the increase of crime, the new Constitutional Court abolished the death penalty.

[60] The Government of National Unity had internal tensions, especially as the November local elections grew nearer. Inkatha withdrew from parliament and the constitutional assembly as a result of what it believed was the ANC's intention to establish complete dominance. The ANC accused the IFP of promoting KwaZulu-Natal secession, threatened to cut the supply of funds to the area and sent military and police forces to the province. Overall, political violence in Natal was reduced: in mid-1995 there were 70 deaths per month while before the elections the number had been 300.

[61] The November 1995 elections favoured the ANC throughout the country. In May 1996, the NP left the government and joined the opposition, for the first time since 1948.

[62] The National Assembly passed a new Constitution which, according to the Government, would consolidate transition toward democracy. While the new text was being drafted, a clause which granted employers the right to close their factories was taken out of the final text after thousands of workers and shopowners held demonstrations against it.

[63] In 1996, the Government passed a law which allowed abortion up to the 12th week of pregnancy.

[64] Also that year the Truth and Reconciliation Comission was set up, chaired by Nobel peace prize Desmond Tutu. The Commission started to hear testimony on human rights abuses committed between 1960 and 1993. During the investigations, numerous crimes came out in the open. Several police officers admitted the use of torture and hired assassins during the 1980s. Those responsible could benefit from an amnesty, as long as they recognized their involvement in the abuse.

[65] The Government announced a new macroeconomic strategy which sought to create 800,000 jobs by the year 2000. The aim was to reduce the fiscal deficit and attract foreign investment. The plan was opposed by business associations, which considered it "neoliberal". Mandela admitted privatization was a basic tool of his economic policy.

[66] Throughout 1996, the GDP grew 3 per cent. Late that year, unemployment was estimated in 32.6 per cent. By late November, some two million hectares of land had been redistributed under the Government's land reform program.

[67] In October, Mandela visited Libya to mediate in the conflict between Tripoli, Washington and London over the bombing of an aeroplan over Lockerbie, Scotland, which led to an embargo against that country as of 1992 (see history of Libya). Mandela supported Libya's request to hold a trial in a neutral country, although adding he did not ask for an unconditional lifting of the embargo.

[68] Because of the rise in crime, in April 1998 Mandela suggested the possibility of declaring a curfew in some regions of the country to maintain law and order.

STATISTICS

DEMOGRAPHY
Population: 42,393,000 (1996). **Annual growth:** 2.3% (1980/1996). **Estimates for year 2000:** 46,300,000. **Annual growth to year 2000:** 2.2% (1994/2000). **Urban Population:** 49.5% (1996). **Urban growth:** 2.73% (1980/95). **Children per woman:** 3.9 (1996).

HEALTH
Life expectancy at birth: 65 years (1996) male: 61 years (1994) female: 67 years (1994) **Infant mortality:** 50 per 1,000 (1996). **Under-5 child mortality:** 66 per 1,000 (1996). **Calorie consumption:** 128% (1988/90). **Safe water:** 99% (1990/96).

EDUCATION
Literacy: 82% (1995). male : 82% (1995) female: 82% (1995) **School enrolment:** Primary total: 117% (1990/95) male : 119% (1990/95) female: 115% (1990/95). Secondary: male: 76% (1990/95) female: 88% (1990/95). Tertiary: 17% (1995). **Primary school teachers:** one for every 37 students (1995).

COMMUNICATIONS
30 **newspapers,** 314 **radios,** 100 **TV sets** and 91 **main telephone lines** per 1,000 people (1994). **Books:** 11 new titles per 100,000 people (1992/94).

ECONOMY
Per capita, GNP: $ 3,520 (1996). **Annual growth, GNP:** 1% (1995/96). **Annual inflation:** 13.86% (1985/95). **Consumer price index:** 157.0 (1994). **Currency:** 3.65 rands = $ 1 (1995) **Cereal imports:** 913 metric tons (1994). **Food import dependency:** 5% (1994). **Fertilizer use:** 631 kgs per ha (1994). **Exports:** $ 18,132 million (1996). **Imports:** $ 26,861 million (1996). **External debt:** $ 23,590 million (1996). $ 556 **per capita:** (1996). **Debt service:** 11.1% of exports (1996). **Development aid received:** $ 384 million (1995). $ 10 per capita (1995). % of GNP (1994).

ENERGY
Consumption: 2,145.95 Kgs of Oil equivalent per capita yearly (1994). -35.28% imported (1994).

HDI (rank / value) 90 / 0.716 (1994)

Spain

España

Population: 39,674,000 (1996)
Area: 505,992 SQ KM
Capital: Madrid

Currency: Peseta
Language: Spanish

Between the 9th and the 8th century BC Celtic peoples started to settle in the center and west of the Iberian peninsula. Later, during the 6th and 5th centuries BC, the Iberian culture developed in the south of the peninsula. The fusion of these two cultures gave rise to what is known as the Celt-Iberian peoples. The peninsula was colonized by the Phoenicians, the Greeks, and the Romans in succession.

[2] The fall of the Roman Empire coincided with the spread of Christianity and, more importantly, with the invasion of the northern peoples who raided Europe. The Iberian peninsula was occupied by the Visigoths who ruled over the area for 300 years.

[3] In 700 AD the peninsula was invaded by Arabs who defeated Rodrigo, the last Visigoth king, thus starting a period of Muslim domination. The descendants of the Visigoths lived in the north of the territory and set up kingdoms like Castille, Catalonia, Navarre, Aragon, Leon and Portugal. Over the centuries they underwent a slow unification process, which consolidated when they started fighting against the Arabs.

[4] The Arabs called the lands in the south of the Iberian peninsula Al-Andalus, a region that reached its peak during the 10th century. In contrast with the rest of impoverished rural Europe, its cities - and Cordoba in particular - prospered through active trade with the East. Religious tolerance enabled Muslims, Jews, and Christians to live side by side, and science, medicine, and philosophy developed. Copies and translations of the Greek classics were made, paving the way for the 15th century European Renaissance.

[5] In 1492, a triple process of national unification took place in Spain, through the marriage of Isabel of Castille and Fernando of Aragon, the expulsion of the Moors, and the conquest and subsequent colonization of the new American territories. The unification of the country's political power and the creation of the Kingdom of Spain were carried out at the expense of the Jews (and members of other cultures) who were expelled from Spain after having lived there for many centuries. Both the Inquisition and centralized power were institutionalized under the new system, while the new American colonies supplied precious metals, sustaining three centuries of economic bonanza. The indigenous people in America had Christianity imposed upon them by the Crown, and the exploitation they were subject to through forced labor was responsible for decimating many of their populations.

[6] The economic prosperity provided by the colonies was reflected in a period of great cultural development in Spain. Literature in particular developed extensively during the 16th and 17th centuries, which were dubbed the Spanish Golden Age.

[7] In the 18th century, the Bourbons came to the Spanish throne. They reorganized domestic and colonial administration, ruling in accordance with the principles of Enlightenment, as the liberal ideas of the French Revolution spread throughout Europe and America. Combined with Napoleonic expansion, this view contributed to the disintegration of the Spanish colonies after the wars of independence.

[8] At the end of the Napoleonic era, there was great conflict between the liberal sectors seeking political and economic modernization, and the absolutists who wished to preserve the traditional order. The disputes between groups weakened the power of the Empire, making way for revolutions in Spanish America.

[9] By the end of the 19th century Spain had renounced its last American territories and had come to terms with the loss of its privileges.

[10] At the beginning of the 20th century, Spain was plunged into a deep political, social, and economic crisis, exacerbated by World War I. Within an atmosphere of extreme polarization, Primo de Rivera's dictatorship which resulted from the 1923 coup attempted to halt any further increase in demands from workers or regional groups seeking autonomy. The Government, closely resembling the Italian fascist model, retained power until 1931. Its eventual loss of power was a result of existing contradictions within the Church, the armed forces and industry, who were all fascist supporters, and not to the continuous opposition from political and labor organizations. The end of the dictatorship marked the end of the monarchy, and the dawn of a new republican era.

[11] The "Second Republic" was born in the midst of a series of extremely complex political and economic difficulties. In 1936, after two moderate governments, the People's Front, formed with socialists, republicans, communists and anarchists, gained a narrow electoral triumph, causing much friction with their political opponents.

[12] Immediately after the elections, the army, the Church, and powerful sectors of the Spanish economy started to plot the overthrow of the Government. The deep contradictions within the Front and the incessant opposition led to the rise of an important faction of the army, led by Francisco Franco, which provoked the Spanish Civil War lasting for three years. The republican government waited in vain for assistance from the European democracies, but they had decided not to intervene in the conflict. The Soviet Union was the only state which provided material support to the republican government, while a large number of volunteers from America and Europe also joined the republican army.

[13] Franco won in March 1939, assisted by internal divisions within the republican forces, the military superiority of the troops loyal to him, and German and Italian support.

PUBLIC EXPENDITURE

6.8% **54%**
1995 ■ DEFENCE □ SOCIAL

In **1990/91** Military as % of health & education expenditure was 18%.

WORKERS

UNEMPLOYMENT 22.2% (1996)
Labour force %

■ WOMEN
□ MEN

36 **64**

■ AGRICULTURE 12% (1990)
□ INDUSTRIAL 33%
■ SERVICES 55%

PER 100,000
LIVE BIRTHS
7

97%

IMPORTS
122,842
EXPORTS
101,417

[14] When the civil war ended, Franco became head of the new Spanish state. He set up an authoritarian regime along fascist lines, with a corporatist state, a personality cult, and extreme nationalism. Franco ruled over a deeply divided society and an economy that had been virtually devastated by the civil war.

[15] From the beginning of the Cold War, the US tried to secure Spanish support and Spain became a member of the United Nations in 1955, confirming a change in Franco's foreign policy, which was becoming preoccupied with improving the international image.

[16] In the 1960s, Franco opened parliament to other groups and movements. During those years key figures of the Opus Dei, an ultra-conservative Catholic movement, occupied important posts in government and changed the country's economic policies.

[17] Spain rid itself of economic isolation and liberalized its economy by eliminating many mechanisms of state control. The urban middle classes enjoyed a substantial improvement in their standard of living, which allowed a significant political relaxation. However, the peasants were still extremely poor and many emigrated to the major Spanish and European cities.

[18] Franco died in 1975, and power was handed to his successor, the heir to the Spanish throne, Juan Carlos I of Bourbon. The new monarch immediately started negotiations with the political opposition to re-establish the democratic system overthrown in 1939.

[19] Between 1976 and 1981 Adolfo Suarez, the leader of the Center Democratic Union (UCD), was Prime Minister. In December 1978, while he was in office, a plebiscite was held, turning Spain into a parliamentary monarchy, re-establishing political freedom, and guaranteeing the right of autonomy to some Spanish regions. Several politicians, intellectuals, and artists were able to return to the country, after up to 40 years in exile.

[20] In February 1981, a group of Civil Guard officers took the Cortes (parliament) by force. The firm reaction of all the democratic political groups and in particular of King Juan Carlos, who had the support of the army, guaranteed the failure of the plan and the consolidation of the democratization process.

[21] The Spanish Socialist Workers' Party (PSOE) won the October 1982 elections, with a solid majority in the Cortes. Felipe González became President of the Government, the equivalent of Prime Minister in other countries. He was subsequently re-elected in 1988 and 1993.

[22] Despite some setbacks, the parliamentary majority of the PSOE was able to enforce an ambitious adjustment and growth plan which has deeply transformed the Spanish economy and given vast social sectors access to unprecedented levels of consumption. However, this modernization resulted in high unemployment and tensions which led to a split between the government and the UGT, the trade union which had supported the PSOE.

[23] ETA, the Basque separatist group which many times has used violent means to achieve its political goals, suffered serious setbacks in 1993. Co-operation between French and Spanish security forces led to the arrest of some of its leaders, and the discovery in Bayonne, France, of the organization's main weapons deposit.

[24] The Spanish Government has been very active in international affairs, joining the European Economic Community and NATO in 1986. Membership of NATO had been opposed by the PSOE while it was in the opposition, but once in power the party defended the decision and confirmed it through consultation with the people.

[25] Spain has maintained a long-standing dispute with Britain over the possession of Gibraltar, which has been under British control since 1704; it maintains control of Ceuta and Melilla, which are claimed by Morocco.

[26] In 1990, Felipe Gonzalez' government started negotiations with the US to reduce US military presence in Spain. Despite the agreements, some of the B-52 bombers that raided Iraqi territory during the Gulf War took off from the US air bases in Spain.

[27] In 1992 Spain spent $10 billion on the celebration to mark the 500

PROFILE

ENVIRONMENT
Spain comprises 82 per cent of the Iberian Peninsula; and includes the Balearic and Canary Islands. The center of the country is a plateau which rises to the Pyrenees in the north, forming a natural border with France. The Betica mountain ranges extend to the South. Inland the Central Sierras separate the plateaus of Nueva and Vieja Castilla. In the Ebro River basin, to the north, lie the prairies of Cataluña, Valencia, and Murcia, and the Guadalquivir River basin, to the south, forms the plains of Andalucia. The climate is moderate and humid in the north and northwest, where there are many woodlands. In the interior, the climate is dry in the south and east. 40 per cent of the land is arable. Approximately 5 per cent of the total land area is under environmental protection. Natural resources include coal, some oil and natural gas, uranium and mercury. Industry is concentrated in Catalonia and the Basque Provinces. Per capita emissions of air and water pollutants exceed Western European averages. Since 1970, the use of nitrogen fertilizers has doubled. Nitrate concentrations in the Guadalquivir River are 25 per cent above 1975 levels. The percentage of the population serviced by sewage systems rose from 14 per cent in 1975, to 48 per cent in the late 1980s. This fact, together with industrial wastes from oil refining plants and natural gas production, has raised the level of pollution of the Mediterranean. The Government has implemented a reforestation program to increase production of timber and prevent further erosion. Many seedlings have been lost in recent years to forest fires. An additional problem is the fact that the large-scale planting of single species, such as eucalyptus, does not take biodiversity into account. Approximately 22 per cent of Spain's forests have suffered some degree of defoliation.

SOCIETY
Peoples: Castillians, Asturians, Andalucians and Valencians, Catalans, Basques and Galicians, descended from a fusion of the Iberian people of the Mediterranean, the Celts of Central Europe and the Arabs of North Africa.
Religion: Catholicism is the religion of the vast majority of the Spanish people (95.2 per cent). Muslims 1.2 per cent.
Languages: Spanish or Castillian (official national); there are also official regional languages, such as Basque, Catalan, Valencian and Galician. **Political Parties:** Peoples' Party, rightist. Spanish Socialist Workers' Party (PSOE); United Left; Convergence and Union; Basque Nationalist Party, as well as other regionalist parties. **Social Organizations:** There are several national workers' organizations: the General Union of Workers (socialist tendency); the Workers' Commissions (communist tendency); the National Confederation of Labor (anarchist tendency); the Workers' Trade Union (of social democratic tendency).

THE STATE
Official Name: Estado Español. **Administrative Divisions:** Spain is divided into 17 autonomous regions: the Basque Country, Catalonia, Galicia, Andalucia, the Principality of Asturias, Cantabria, La Rioja, Murcia, Valencia, Aragon, Castilla, La Mancha, the Canaries, Navarre, Extremadura, the Balearic Islands, Madrid and Castilla León. Each one has its own institutional system, a local leader in executive power and a unicameral legislative.
Capital: Madrid, 4,600,000 people (1994).
Other cities: Barcelona, 4,000,000 people (1994); Valencia, 777,427; Seville, 704,857; Zaragoza, 622,371 (1991).
Government: Hereditary monarchy, with King Juan Carlos I de Borbon y Borbon as Head of State. Prime Minister: José María Aznar since April 1996. The parliament, las Cortes, consists of two bodies: the Senate, with 255 members, and the Chamber of Deputies with 350 members elected by proportional representation. **National Holiday:** October 12 **Armed Forces:** 206,000 (1995). **Other:** Guardia Civil: 66,000 (3,000 conscripts); Guardia del Mar: 340.

DEMOGRAPHY
Population: 39,674,000 (1996). **Annual growth:** 0.3% (1980/ 1996). **Estimates for year 2000:** 40,000,000. **Annual growth to year 2000:** 0.1% (1994/2000). **Urban Population:** 76.7% (1996). **Urban growth:** 0.61% (1980/95). **Children per woman:** 1.2 (1996).

HEALTH
Life expectancy at birth: 78 years (1996) male: 74 years (1994) female: 81 years (1994). **Infant mortality:** 5 per 1,000 (1996). **Under-5 child mortality:** 5 per 1,000 (1996). **Calorie consumption:** 141% (1988/90). 262 **people per doctor** (1988/91).

EDUCATION
Literacy: 97% (1995) male: 98% (1995) female: 96% (1995). **School enrolment:** Primary total: 104% (1990/95). male: 104% (1990/95) female: 105% (1990/95). Secondary: male: 107% (1990/95) female: 120% (1990/95). Tertiary: 46% (1995). **Primary school teachers:** one for every 18 students (1995).

COMMUNICATIONS
100 **newspapers**, 312 **radios**, 430 **TV sets** and 375 **main telephone lines** per 1,000 people (1994). **Books:** 112 new titles per 100,000 people (1992/94).

ECONOMY
Per capita, GNP: $ 14,350 (1996). **Annual growth, GNP:** 1.6% (1995/96). **Annual inflation:** 6.31% (1985/95). **Consumer price index:** 122.9 (1994). **Currency:** 121.41 pesetas = $ 1 (1995) **Cereal imports:** 5,047 metric tons (1994). **Fertilizer use:** 916 kgs per ha (1994). **Exports:** $ 101,417 million (1996). **Imports:** $ 122,842 million (1996).

ENERGY.
Consumption: 2,457.65 Kgs of Oil equivalent per capita yearly (1994) 69.38% imported (1994).

HDI (rank / value) 11 / 0.934 (1994)

Gibraltar

A peninsula on the southern coast of Spain, only 32 km from Morocco, Gibralter's strategic position allows it to control maritime trade between the Mediterranean and the Atlantic ocean.

[2] Gibraltar was occupied by England in 1704 and ceded by Spain in 1714, following the Treaty of Utretcht. Since 1964 Spain has tried to regain political control of the area. In 1967, a plebiscite opted for continued colonial dependency. In 1968 the UN voted in favor of the Spanish re-incorporation of Gibraltar. Since 1972, the two countries have started negotiations several times, but no significant progress has yet been made.

PROFILE

Peoples: Most of the permanent population is of British origin. The non-permanent population are mainly Spanish workers.
Religions: Anglican and Catholic.
Languages: English (official) and Spanish.
Official Name: Gibraltar.
Government: Non-autonomous territory, subject to UN control.
Administrative power: United Kingdom. Governor named by the British crown: Admiral Sir Richard Luce, since February 1997. Chief minister: Peter Caruana, since 17 May 1996, appointed by the 15-member advisory council. In the council's last election, held in May 1996, the Social Democrat Party obtained 53 per cent of the vote, while the second political force, the Socialist Labor Party, was supported by 42 per cent of the electorate. Britain has made Gibraltarian independence dependent upon an agreement with Spain. In September 1996, the NATO Headquarters aknowledged that in the future the military control over the peninsula would be exercised by Spain.

STATISTICS

DEMOGRAPHY
Population: 28,000 (1996)
Urban population: 100.0 % (1996)

ECONOMY
Consumer price index: 121.4 (1994)

---

years since the conquest of Latin America. At the same time the country made political moves towards Europe. The demands of the European policy resulted in a weakening of Spain's traditional links with Latin America.
[28] The will to align the country with European standards led the Government to carry out cutbacks in defence, public spending and subsidies for the industrial sector. In November, Parliament ratified the Maastricht treaty. The legal proposal to facilitate the dismissal and redeployment of workers caused a general strike in January 1994, but this was approved anyway with the argument that it was necessary to make the nation competitive. Unemployment reached 22 per cent, the highest level in the European Union.
[29] Many of the Socialist Party leaders were implicated in fraud investigations. The former governor of the Bank of Spain was imprisoned along with the former director of the Madrid Exchange Reserve, and the financier Mario Conde, who had supervised the sale of the Spanish Credit Bank (Banesto).
[30] Due to the numerous scandals, the Socialist Government lost a key part of its parliamentary support in 1995. The Catalan nationalist group Convergence and Union withdrew their support in July and voted in the budget with the right-wing People's Party (PP). Whilst defending his action and that of his government, Gonzalez moved the elections forward a year.
[31] The imminent electoral success of the right led ETA to change its strategy: in January they assassinated the PP leader in the province of Guipuzcoa, and in April tried to kill the PP candidate for prime minister, Jose Maria Aznar. In the May regional elections, the PP comfortably won 10 of the 13 areas at stake.
[32] A former security chief and a socialist official were tried for their connections with the anti-terrorist Liberation Groups (GALs), which legal investigations had linked to the security forces. One of them told the Court that Felipe Gonzalez had been responsible for the GALs, which had killed 27 people on the frontier with France in the so-called "dirty war" against ETA. A former interior minister was also investigated for paying French officials to collaborate in the persecution of the Basque separatists.
[33] Fishing conflicts set Spain at odds with Canada and Morocco. Both ended with the European Union mediating in agreements limiting their action in the territorial waters of the other nations. Spain took over the presidency of the European Union from July 1 1995, and held several international summits. The opposition, however, questioned the government's ability to fulfil the necessary requirements for integration to European Monetary Union planned for 1997.
[34] The People's Party won the March 1996 parliamentary elections with 38.9 per cent of the vote. The PSOE came second with 37.5 per cent. The IU (Izquierda Unida, United Left) took 10.6 per cent. On April 5, PP leader José Maria Aznar became Prime Minister.
[35] At an international level, the Aznar administration decided to bolster Cuba's isolation, by proposing that the EU place sanctions on island, and suspending the loans Spain had promised to the Castro government.
[36] In August 1997, ETA kidnapped Miguel Angel Blanco, PP supporter and councillor of a small town in the Basque Country. The organization announced his execution in 48 hours if the Spanish Government did not order the concentration of guerrilla prisoners in basque jails. Once the time was up, Blanco was murdered, which unleashed immediate protests throughout the country. The Government and the opposition, excluding the Herri Batasuna political group linked to ETA, signed an agreement against violence, while millions of people marched on the streets to repudiate the murder. The demonstrations were attended by more people than at any other Spanish political event in the second half of the century.
[37] On December 1 1997, the Spanish Supreme Court sentenced 23 Herri Batasuna leaders to seven years in prison for "collaborating" in the broadcast of an ETA television commercial during the electoral campaign in 1996. In early 1998, new trials were begun against former Socialist ministers José Barrionuevo and Rafael Vera, for their supposed connections to the GAL.

Sri Lanka

Sri Lanka

Population:	18,100,000 (1996)
Area:	65,610 SQ KM
Capital:	Colombo
Currency:	Rupees
Language:	Sinhalese

The island of Ceylon was populated by the Vedda in ancient times, it was then successively invaded by the Sinhalese, Indo-Europeans and Tamils, who laid the foundations of an advanced civilization. When the Portuguese arrived in 1505, the island was divided into seven autonomous local societies.

2   The Dutch expelled the Portuguese from their coastal trading posts 150 years later, but it was the British, who had already taken possession of neighboring India, who finally made the island a colony in 1796. Even then, it took them until 1815 to subdue all the local governments, as they fought hard to remain autonomous. The British then introduced new export crops such as coffee and tea, products which gave Ceylon a worldwide reputation, because of their excellent quality.

3   In the 20th century, a strong nationalist movement developed in Ceylon. In 1948, independence was achieved and Ceylon became a member of the British Commonwealth. Under the leadership of Sir John Kotelawala and Prime Minister Bandaranaike, Ceylon pursued a vigorous anti-colonial foreign policy. In August 1954, Bandaranaike met in Colombo with India's Nehru, Muhammad Ali of Pakistan, U Nu of Burma and Indonesia's Sastroamidjojo. The meeting was of great political importance as it led to the 1955 summit conference of Afro-Asian countries in Bandung, heralding the Movement of Non-Aligned Countries.

4   In the late 1950s, the Tamil minority staged a series of secessionist uprisings and in September 1959 the Prime Minister was assassinated. His widow

Sirimavo Bandaranaike led the Sri Lanka Freedom Party to electoral victory at the beginning of 1960, although she had no previous political experience. Sirimavo Bandaranaike became the first woman in the world to head a government. Governing in coalition with the Communist and Trotskyist parties, in 1962 she nationalized various US oil and other companies. In 1965, she was defeated by a right-wing coalition but regained power in 1970, in a landslide election victory.

5   She was faced with a "Guevarist" (after Che Guevara) guerrilla uprising which she had forcibly crushed. She never gave up her anti-imperialist stand and in 1972 declared Sri Lanka a republic, cutting all ties with the British Empire.

6   A land reform program nationalized British-owned plantations but had little effect on the standard of living of the bulk of the rural population.

7   Conflict between the Sinhalese majority and the Tamil minority, who are descended from the Dravidians of South India, has persisted throughout most of the island's known history. The Sinhalese account for 74 per cent of the country's population, while the Tamils comprise 22 per cent and are divided into two groups: the Sri Lanka Tamils and the Indian Tamils. The Sri Lanka Tamils reached the island approximately 2,000 years ago and settled principally in the northern and eastern provinces, while the Indian Tamils are more recent immigrants. Both groups possess common ethnic characteristics and seek regional autonomy or even the formation of a separate Tamil nation. The Tamil United Liberation Front (TULF)

founded on May 4 1972, resulted from the fusion of three Tamil parties: the Federal Party, the Tamil Congress and the pro-Indian Ceylon Workers Congress.

8   Bandaranaike's main achievement was probably her appointment as president of the Non-Aligned Movement in 1976, at the Conference in Colombo. However, accusations of nepotism, and reaction from the country's intellectuals to the censorship of the press and to emergency security measures in force since 1971, caused Bandaranaike to lose the July 1977 election.

9   The United National Party, led by Junius Jayewardene, won a comfortable parliamentary majority, with the Tamil Liberation Front coming in second. In spite of his socialist leanings, the new prime minister's economic policy exposed the country to transnational capital.

10   A constitutional reform, which went into effect in 1978, made Jayewardene Sri Lanka's first president. In November 1980, a series of IMF approved economic measures started to be applied, with disastrous consequences for the country. A month earlier, Bandaranaike had been expelled from Parliament and deprived of her political rights for seven years. A presidential commission had found her guilty of "abuse of authority" during her coalition government, between 1970 and July 1977.

11   An International Monetary Fund "package" of measures went into effect. There was a general strike against the measures and the new economic policy, and 44,000 civil servants lost their jobs in the summer of 1980. In 1981 the Government received substantial US aid, supplied with the alleged purpose of stabilizing the region same argument was put forth to justify increasingly frequent visits by US naval ships to the port of Colombo.

12   Sri Lanka's first presidential election in October 1982, gave Jayewardene a clear victory, with 52.5 per cent of the vote. His campaign was backed by the state apparatus and benefited from the division and internal strife of the Freedom Party. In some parts of the country, the political upheaval meant that elections had to be carried out under "state of emergency" conditions.

PUBLIC EXPENDITURE

2.6%   46.2%
1995 ■ DEFENCE □ SOCIAL

In 1990/91 Military as % of health & education expenditure was 107%.

WORKERS

UNEMPLOYMENT 11.3% (1996)

Labour force %

■ WOMEN
□ MEN

35   65

■ AGRICULTURE   48% (1990)
□ INDUSTRIAL   21%
■ SERVICES   31%

LAND USE

DEFORESTATION -1.3% annual (81/90)
IRRIGATED 59.1% of arable

(1993)

■ FOREST & WOODLAND   32%
□ ARABLE   14.2%
■ OTHER   53.8%

Food Dependency

1970
47%

1994
7%

External Debt

1996

PER CAPITA
$442

Foreign Trade

1996

MILLIONS $

IMPORTS
5,028

EXPORTS
4,097

PROFILE

ENVIRONMENT

An island in the Indian Ocean, southeast of India, separated from the continent by the Palk Channel. The land is flat, except for a central mountainous region. These mountains divide the island into two distinct regions and also block the monsoon winds which are responsible for the tropical climate. The southwest area receives abundant rainfall, and the remainder of the island is drier. Large tea plantations cover the southern mountain slopes, and other major crops are rice, for domestic consumption, and rubber, coconuts and cocoa, for export. Deforestation and soil erosion are important environmental problems. Likewise, air pollution is on the increase, due to industrial gas emissions.

SOCIETY

Peoples: 82.7 per cent of Sri Lankans are Sinhalese; Tamils are the largest minority group, 8.9 per cent, and there is a small Arab minority (7.7 per cent). **Religions:** 69 per cent Buddhist; 15 per cent Hindu; 8 per cent Christian; 7 per cent Muslim; and 1 per cent other religions. **Languages:** Sinhalese (official). Also Tamil and English. **Political Parties:** The United National Party (Siri Kotha; the Sri Lanka Freedom Party; the United Democratic National Front; the Tamil United Liberation Front (TULF); the Communist Party; the Equal Society Party (Lanka Sama Samaja); the People's Democratic Party (Mahajana Prajathantra); the People's Liberation Front (Janata Vimuktui Peramuna); and the Popular Alliance coalition. **Social Organizations:** Workers' Congress; Trade Union Federation; Trade Union Council; the Labor Federation.

THE STATE

Official Name: Sri Lanka Prajathanthrika Samajavadi Janarajaya. **Administrative Divisions:** 9 Provinces, 24 Districts. **Capital** Colombo, 3,620,000 people (1994). **Other cities:** Dehiwala-Mount Lavina, 196,000 people; Moratuwa, 170,000; Jaffna, 151,000; Kandy, 122,000 (1994). **Government:** Chandrika Kumaratunga Bandaranaike, President and Head of State since November 1994. Sirimavo Bandaranaike, Prime Minister since 1994. Unicameral Parliament with 225 members. **National Holiday:** February 4, Independence Day (1948). **Armed Forces:** 126,000 (1994) **Other:** 70,000 Police Force, National Guard, Private Guard.

---

[13] The project to turn Sri Lanka into an "export center" like Hong Kong or Taiwan led to the creation of a free zone in Latunyabe where foreign investment has been steadily on the increase since 1978.

[14] In early 1982, in spite of earlier denials and the government's outspoken commitment to non-alignment, the US Navy was granted permission to use Sri Lanka's refuelling facilities in Trincomalee, a vital spot linking eastern and western sea routes through the Suez Canal.

[15] Early in 1983, the ethnic conflict worsened. It reached crisis point in July and August, leaving hundreds dead and wounded and thousands more homeless. More than 40,000 Sri Lankan Tamils fleeing the conflict sought refuge in Tamil Nadu. President Jayewardene's refusal to negotiate with the Tamil minority led the Indian Government to withdraw its attempts at mediation.

[16] In 1984, Jayewardene made overtures toward the Israeli Government, which had offered him support to bring the rebel minorities under control. A diplomatic mission was set up in Colombo with the support of the US embassy. However, Secretary of State Douglas Liyanage was forced to resign in September 1984, after violent protest demonstrations following a government visit to Tel Aviv. The protesters were mainly from the Muslim community.

[17] The "ethnic war", turned more bitter during 1985, discouraging foreign investors. Tourism is still one of the main sources of income of this "fiscal paradise".

[18] Military operations also seriously affected agriculture in the northern and eastern provinces, where rice farming covers more than 200,000 hectares. The Government had to import 150,000 tons of Chinese rice to stabilize the prices.

[19] Peace negotiations between the Tamils and Sinhalese, took place throughout 1986. The efforts included a meeting of the leaders of seven southeast Asian countries in Bangalore, India, all of whom were concerned about the civil war that had shaken Sri Lanka. The Freedom Party, the main opposition group, demanded that elections be called in advance and that the Government disclose how people felt about the ethnic conflict. The Government chose to ignore them. In a gesture, aimed at diffusing internal opposition, Jayewardene promised to restore former prime minister Sirimavo Bandaranaike's political rights.

[20] In late July 1987, in Colombo, presidents Rajiv Gandhi (of India) and Junius Jayewardene finally signed an accord granting a certain autonomy to the Tamil minority of the northern and eastern provinces of Sri Lanka. The accord provided for the merger of the two provinces under a single government, and gave Tamil the status of a national language. India guaranteed the agreement and sent troops - the India Peace Keeping Force - to ensure that its terms were complied with. These terms were to be ratified by the parliaments of India and Sri Lanka, and approved by the main guerrilla group, the Liberation Tigers of Tamil Eelam (LTTE) known as the Tamil Tigers.

[21] These efforts did not manage to pacify the country, and the Indian military presence, far from guaranteeing peace, became a further cause for irritation and renewed confrontations. Inter-ethnic violence worsened as the Tamil Tigers' rejected the 1987 accords.

[22] In November 1988, the official party's hold on power was ratified by 50.4 per cent of the votes. Jayewardene, at the age of 82, ceded his post to Ranasinghe Premadasa, the former prime minister. Political violence was so pervasive that only 53 per cent of the electorate actually went to the polling stations to vote. Elections were boycotted, by both the Tamil guerrillas and the Popular Liberation Front (made up of Sinhalese who were violently opposed to any kind of concessions to ethnic minorities). Political opposition to the Government increased, partly fuelled by a strong student movement which the Government eventually put down in early 1989, using extremely harsh repressive measures.

[23] In early 1990, the Indian Government withdrew the last of its 60,000 peacekeeping force, which had been stationed in Sri Lanka since 1987. More than 1,000 troops had died on the island. Amnesty International announced that, in 1990, the Government had killed thousands of civilians in the region.

[24] In May 1991, the Tamil Tigers were accused of murdering Rajiv Gandhi in a suicide mission. Rajiv had become an enemy of the Tigers after the Indian peace forces in Sri Lanka had attacked the rebels. The Tigers, however, denied any involvement in the attempt. Their guerrilla group was considered the most efficient and best armed in the world. It was financed by expatriate Tamils who make annual donations of millions of dollars. The guerrilla leader, Velupillai Prabhakaran, had his general headquarters in the north of the country, hidden in the jungle.

[25] The next stage of the war against the Tigers started in June 1991, when the Tigers broke off after 13 months of talks with the Government. Since then, thousands more people have died in combat, and many civilians have taken refuge in the south or in India. In August, according to official estimates, over 2,000 guerrillas and 170 Sri Lankan soldiers died in an attack in the strategic "Pass of the Elephant", which was under government control. This was deemed to be the most important battle of the decade, and as yet, a peace agreement seems unlikely.

[26] In spite of the war, the country was visited by some 300,000 tourists in 1990. In some western countries the island is promoted for its countless brothels. The number of prostitutes in the capital is put at 50,000, with over 10,000 young boys and girls in the business. One reason for the extremely high number of prostitutes is that half of the population in the country live in extreme poverty.

[27] Nearly two decades after the large tea plantations were nationalized, the Government decided to hand management over to private companies, while maintaining state ownership. It was estimated that the state companies which managed these plantations, employing over 400,000 people (mostly Tamil), had accumulated debts of $128.1 million by the end of 1989. Agriculture continues to be the main source of revenue, with 36.3 per cent of the exports coming from tea, rubber, and coconuts.

PER 100,000
LIVE BIRTHS

140

90%

[28] In August 1991, President Premadasa, who had been accused of violating the constitution and other crimes - such as treason, embezzlement, corruption, abuse of power, and moral depravity - suspended parliamentary sessions to avoid being censured. He also faced serious confrontations within his party and the hostility of the opposition, led by Sirimavo Bandaranaike, who demanded democratization and the end of the presidential system.

[29] In February 1992, in negotiations observed by the UN, the LTTE supremo, Velupillai Prabhakaran declared his desire for a peaceful end to the conflict. Prabhakaran stated that he wanted an agreement based on the recognition of a degree of autonomy for the northern and eastern provinces, where most of the Tamils live. President Premadasa expressed an interest in the proposed solution.

[30] In February 1993, the leader of the LTTE expressed his willingness to accept a negotiated settlement, in resolving the federalist issue. The Government rejected Prabhakran's request for a lifting of the economic blockade of the Tamil region of Jaffna (decreed in February 1992 and subsequently extended in January 1993); nevertheless, parliament began discussing the terms of such an agreement.

[31] The issue of human rights violations by both sides complicated the negotiations. In October 1992, the Tamil Tigers had massacred 170 Muslims in the village of Polonnrua, in the northeastern part of the country. The following month, a car-bomb had killed a high-ranking naval officer in Colombo. In April 1993, the Government required that all property owners in the capital provide a list of tenants, as a way of monitoring activist movement. That same month former cabinet minister Lalith Athulatmudali, president of the United National Democratic Front (split from the UNP in 1991) was assassinated.

[32] On May 1 1993, during the Labor Day parade in Colombo, President Ranasinghe Premadasa was assassinated by a suicide attacker, who threw himself upon the presidential entourage with a bomb tied to his body. The Government accused the Tamil separatists of carrying out the assassination, but spokespersons for the rebels denied responsibility for the attack. Thousands of Tamils fled the capital, fearing government reprisals.

[33] On May 7, Prime Minister Dingiri Banda Wijetunge was named president. Wijetunge promised to continue the political agenda established by his predecessor. A few days later, police identified the presidential assassin as a Tamil, from Jaffna.

[34] The UNP won the May 17 elections, which took place in an atmosphere of relative calm, with a majority in six of the seven provinces. In August, Velupillai accused his vice-president of negotiating with the government and gave him the sack. The possibilities of a peace agreement appeared very remote.

[35] The confrontations left the economy of the north and eastern regions of the island devastated and thousands of people were forced to emigrate.

[36] In the November 1994 presidential elections, the Popular Alliance candidate, Chandrika Bandaranaike Kumaratunga, won with 63 per cent of the vote. Kumaratunga had been designated Prime Minister following the parliamentary elections in August and now became the first woman president of Sri Lanka. Her mother, Sirimavo Bandaranaike succeeded her as Prime Minister.

[37] The government and the Tigers agreed to start negotiations in January 1995, but the pact was broken by the Tamils. The guerrillas initiated a new series of attacks against the government forces in April.

[38] Kumaratunga presented a plan for state reform in August. The proposal, which was supported by the Tamil parliamentarians, included transforming Sri Lanka into a federation of eight regions. The central government was to keep control over defence, foreign relations and international economic relations.

[39] This project required the support of two-thirds of Parliament followed by approval by referendum before it could come into action. The negotiations between the various parties were slow and the increasing military action prevented it being completed.

[40] The city of Jaffna, on the peninsula of the same name, was at the center of the fighting from October 1995. The government forces occupied the city on December 5. Only 400 of the 140,000 people who lived there stayed throughout the fighting. By mid-1996, half of the Tamil population of the peninsula had returned to their homes.

[41] An attack on the Central Bank, in the centre of Colombo, killed 84 people in February 1996. This led to fears of a more widespread inter-ethnic conflict. The Tigers' attacks continued in the streets and trains of Colombo.

[42] In early 1997, the Tigers destroyed an army garrison in Paranthan, in the north of the country, killing all the military personnel, an estimated 1,200 troops. The Government land and air response led to great losses for the LTTE.

[43] In May, the army deployed some 20,000 troops in the biggest offensive since the outbreak of war. The government forces were able to capture strategic positions and roads, pushing the guerrilla into the jungle. The LTTE, however, responded with a series of bomb attacks in the main tourist centres.

[44] The government offensive affected international rice prices, as it destroyed a large proportion of Sri Lanka's paddy fields, forcing the country to start importing this product. The social situation on the island worsened during the years of conflict. One example of this was that very young people were involved in prostitution. According to United Nations estimates, around two thirds of all prostitutes were under the age of consent.

[45] The Government offered to suspend the military offensive and discuss proposals to increase the autonomy of regional councils administered by Tamils and Muslims. However, it continued to demand the surrender of the LTTE as a pre-condition for negotiations, something the guerrilla considered unacceptable. In April, the Government and the main opposition group, the United National Party, agreed to present a common front in any negotiations with the LTTE.

[46] Despite efforts at mediation, the civil war worsened in March 1998, with dozens of dead on both sides. In April, the Government promised to publish the outcome of investigations into the disappearance of some 700 people reported in Jaffna, in the north of the country. An estimated 50,000 people have died since war broke out.

STATISTICS

DEMOGRAPHY
Population: 18,100,000 (1996). **Annual growth:** 1.3% (1980/1996). **Estimates for year 2000:** 18,800,000. **Annual growth to year 2000:** 1% (1994/2000). **Urban Population:** 22.3% (1996). **Urban growth:** 1.62% (1980/95). **Children per woman:** 2.1 (1996).

HEALTH
Life expectancy at birth: 73 years (1996) male: 70 years (1994) female: 75 years (1994). **Infant mortality:** 17 per 1,000 (1996). **Under-5 child mortality:** 19 per 1,000 (1996). **Calorie consumption:** 101% (1988/90). 7,143 **people per doctor** (1988/91). **Safe water:** 57% (1990/96).

EDUCATION
Literacy: 90% (1995) male : 93% (1995) female: 87% (1995). **School enrolment:** Primary total: 105% (1990/95) male : 106% (1990/95) female: 104% (1990/95). Secondary: male : 71% (1990/95) female: 79% (1990/95). Tertiary: 5% (1995). **Primary school teachers:** one for every 28 students (1995).

COMMUNICATIONS
30 **newspapers**, 201 **radios**, 70 **TV sets** and 10 **main telephone lines** per 1,000 people (1994). **Books:** 17 new titles per 100,000 people (1992/94).

ECONOMY
Per capita, GNP: $ 740 (1996). **Annual growth, GNP:** 0.5% (1995/96). **Annual inflation:** 11.77% (1985/95). **Consumer price index:** 151.4 (1994). **Currency:** 54.05 rupees = $ 1 (1995) **Cereal imports:** 927 metric tons (1994). **Food import dependency:** 7% (1994). **Fertilizer use:** 1,131 kgs per ha (1994). **Exports:** $ 4,097 million (1996). **Imports:** $ 5,028 million (1996). **External debt:** $ 7,995 million (1996). $ 442 **per capita:** (1996). **Debt service:** 7.3% of exports (1996). **Development aid received:** $ 553 million (1995). $ 31 per capita (1995). 48% of GNP (1994)

ENERGY
Consumption: 96.72 Kgs of Oil equivalent per capita yearly (1994). 79.62% imported (1994).

HDI (rank / value) 91 / 0.711 (1994)

Sudan

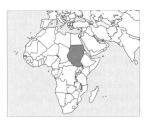

Sudan

Population: 27,291,000 (1996)
Area: 2,505,813 SQ KM
Capital: Khartoum (Al-Khartum)

Currency: Pound
Language: Arabic

Around 3000 BC, the region called Kush by the Egyptians and Nubia by the Greeks, received its influence from Pharaonic Egypt, a fact which considerably delayed the formation of an organized state. Pharaohs favored disparate groups under their rule. Consequently, the state of Napata did not come into being until the 8th century when Egypt's decline gave foreign dynasties the opportunity to take over the country. The last of these was Sudanese. The rulers of Napata conquered Egypt in 730 BC and governed as pharaohs until the Assyrian conquest in 663 BC, when the ruling family was ousted. The country disintegrated, though it was not occupied. Shortly afterwards, the three "waterfall states", which would last over 20 centuries, rose in its place: Nobatia, Dongola and Alodia.

[2] While Egypt was ruled by Persians, Greeks, Romans and Arabs in succession, the waterfall states maintained their political and cultural autonomy. This was due to their position as trade intermediaries between the Mediterranean market and the sources of slaves, ivory, furs, and other goods in equatorial Africa. They were converted to Christianity in the 6th century under Ethiopian influence. A century later, the Arabs invaded forcing the ruler of Dongola to give financial aid to Arab merchants and to allow Muslim preaching in exchange for preservation of the territorial integrity of Dongola and Alodia. This treaty remained in effect for over 600 years.

[3] Egyptian Mamelukes destroyed Dongola and Alodia in the 14th century. Raids grew more frequent despite the emergence of new Islamic states: Sennar, on the Blue Nile; Kordofan to the west, and Darfur in the middle of the desert.

[4] Intent on exterminating Egyptian soldiers, Pasha Muhammad Ali (see: Egypt) entered Sudan in 1820. The Egyptian forces set up permanent quarters in Khartoum, holding control of the entire country by 1876. Foreign military occupation brought about radical changes: the country was unified, limiting the autonomy of various small local governments; the introduction of foreign religious rites (even within the predominant Orthodox Sunni religion) upset established religious communities. Under British pressure, slavery was abolished, undermining the influence of powerful slave dealers. Additionally, the burden of heavy taxes, particularly for farmers and cattle raisers, contributed to a general atmosphere of discontent.

[5] In 1881, Muhammad Ahmad proclaimed himself Mahdi, meaning saviour or redeemer, and launched a crusade to restore Islam. He rapidly gained support, especially among the Arabized population in the North. The British, having occupied Egypt in 1882, intervened militarily but were unable to change the course of the conflict. In 1885 Mahdi occupied Khartoum, defeated General Gordon's troops, and established the first national government, which was to last 13 years. The existence of the state threatened the British plan to unify all the territory from Cairo to Cape Town under their rule. In 1898, Egyptian troops moved in from Uganda and Kenya, attacking Mahdi from both fronts.

[6] The French, with their own east-west transcontinental designs, were also interested in Sudan, and sent troops into the area. This three pronged attack defeated Mahdi in September 1898. The colonial armies met in Fachoda, with small skirmishes between the French and British, but France finally recognized British predominance over the Nile basin. In 1899, Sudan was jointly administered by Britain and Egypt.

[7] Egypt sought to achieve unity of the Nile by joining Cairo and Khartoum politically, and Britain was determined to prevent this.

The Empire threatened to grant "federated independence" to the southern population, who were animists and Christians, but not to the Arabic and Muslim north. To make their threat effective, the British started a policy of "closed districts", which prevented any contact between north and south.

[8] A self-governing statute obtained by Sudan in 1953 was followed by the election of an all-Sudanese parliament in 1955 and the declaration of independence on January 1 1956. However, southerners charged that they had been politically marginalized, and five months before independence a civil war broke out, which continued for 16 years.

[9] In 1969, General Gaafar al-Nimeiry seized power through a coup. He dissolved Parliament, proclaimed the creation of the Sudanese Democratic Republic, and set up a one-party system, the Sudanese Socialist Union. The new government promised to support reconstruction and the development of the southern territories, offering them a certain degree of administrative autonomy.

[10] After coming to power, Nimeiry changed course; he broke with the Sudanese Socialist Union and drew closer to conservative Arab regimes, never fulfilling his promise of greater autonomy for the South.

[11] Nimeiry was forced to sign an agreement with the guerrillas in 1972. This agreement granted autonomy to the southern provinces, while the guerrillas were incorporated into the regular army.

[12] In May 1977, Nimeiry was re-elected for a six-year term. Shortly afterwards the Government announced a "national reconciliation" process which enabled exiled political leaders to return and paved the way for the rehabilitation of former opponents of the ruling Umma Party. However, the Sudanese Communist Party and the National Front, formed by former Finance Minister Shereef al-Hindi, were ignored.

[13] In 1976, Sudan signed a mutual defence pact with Egypt and initially the Nimeiry government backed the Camp David accords

WORKERS

(1996)

Labour force %
- ■ WOMEN
- □ MEN

29   71

- ■ AGRICULTURE 69% (1990)
- □ INDUSTRIAL 8%
- ■ SERVICES 22%

PROFILE

ENVIRONMENT

The largest African country, Sudan has three distinct geographic regions:the barren deserts of Libya and the Sahara in the north, the flatlands of the central region and the dense rainforests of the south. Most of the population lives along the Nile, where cotton is grown. Port Sudan, on the Red Sea, handles all of the country's foreign trade. Desertification has affected nearly 60 per cent of the territory. Industrial waste has contaminated coastal areas and some rivers.

SOCIETY

Peoples: The country has a wide ethnic spectrum with over 570 groups. Arabs, who live in the center and north of the country, together with Nubians, account for nearly half of the population. Among the other groups, the most important are the Nilote, Nilo-Hamitic and a few Bantu groups. In the south there are nearly 400,000 refugees from neighboring nations (Chad, Uganda, Ethiopia and Eritrea).
Religions: Islam is the predominant religion among Arabs and Nubians with a majority of Sunni Muslims. In the south, traditional African religions are practised and there are Christian communities in both north and south.
Languages: Arabic (official and spoken by most of the population); the different ethnic groups speak over 100 different languages.
Political parties: Political parties were dissolved after the 1989 coup. The leading parties based on the 1986 electoral results were:the Umma Party; the Democratic Unionist Party (DUP); the National Islamic Front. Opposition separatist movements in the south include the Sudan People's Liberation Movement (SPLM).

THE STATE

Official Name: Jumhuriyat as-Sudan.
Administrative Divisions: 9 states, 66 Provinces and 281 Local Government Areas.
Capital: Khartoum (Al-Khartum), 2,492,000 people (1995).
Other cities: Kassala, 234,270 people; Port Sudan (Bur Sudan), 305,385 people (1993).
Government: General Omar al-Bashir, Head of State since June 30, 1989, re-elected in March 1996.
National Holiday: January 1, Independence Day (1956).
Armed Forces: 118,500 (1995).
Other: 30,000-50,000 People's Defence Force.

STATISTICS

DEMOGRAPHY

Population: 27,291,000 (1996). **Annual growth:** 2.4% (1980/1996). **Estimates for year 2000:** 29,800,000. **Annual growth to year 2000:** 2.2% (1994/2000). **Urban Population:** 32.3% (1996). **Urban growth:**% (1980/95). **Children per woman:** 4.7 (1996).

HEALTH

Life expectancy at birth: 54 years (1996) male: 50 years (1994) female: 52 years (1994). **Infant mortality:** 73 per 1,000 (1996). **Under-5 child mortality:** 116 per 1,000 (1996). **Calorie consumption:** 87% (1988/90). **Safe water:** 50% (1990/96).

EDUCATION

Literacy: 46% (1995) male: 58% (1995) female: 35% (1995). **School enrolment:** Primary total: 55% (1990/95) male: 61% (1990/95) female: 48% (1990/95). Secondary: male: 24% (1990/95) female: 19% (1990/95). **Primary school teachers:** one for every 36 students (1995).

COMMUNICATIONS

20 **newspapers**, 258 **radios**, 80 **TV sets** and 2 **main telephone lines** per 1,000 people (1994).

ECONOMY

Cereal imports: 1,022 metric tons (1994). **Food import dependency:** 22% (1994). **Fertilizer use:** 55 kgs per ha (1994). **Exports:** $ 468 million (1996). **Imports:** $ 1,439 million (1996). **External debt:** $ 16,972 million (1996). $ 622 **per capita:** (1996). **Debt service:** 5% of exports (1996). **Development aid received:** $ 225 million (1995). $ 8 per capita (1995).

HDI (rank / value) 158 / 0.333 (1994)

---

signed between Egypt, Israel and the US. However when it became clear that this position would isolate Sudan from the Arab world, Nimeiry distanced himself from Cairo and grew closer to Saudi Arabia. Nimeiry stressed the Islamic nature of his regime, arousing opposition in the non-Muslim south.

[14] Nimeiry's weakness became apparent in March 1981 when he was barely able to stave off the 12th plot against his government. In October 1981, in an effort to neutralize his opponents and secure a new term in office, he dissolved the National Assembly and the Regional Assembly of the South, promising to hold new elections. This move coincided with growing unrest among southerners who charged that Nimeiry made no effort to develop their region and, in fact, transferred the region's scant resources to the north.

MILITARY (as % of health and education expenditures-1990/91) **44%**

[15] Nimeiry was re-elected to a third six-year term in 1983, amid widespread accusations of electoral fraud. In September, Nimeiry suddenly imposed Islamic law (the Sharia) on the entire national territory on the advice of Saudi Arabia, and in order to obtain economic assistance. This measure triggered a general protest among the animists and Christians in the north, and recharged the guerrilla movement.

[16] A revolt broke out in the city of Bor, where the Sudanese Popular Liberation Movement (SPLM) arose. This political and military organization gave the southern guerrilla movement a new ideological foundation, with the objectives of achieving national unity and establishing socialism, while respecting southern autonomy and religious freedom.

[17] In the north, Nimeiry was severely criticized by the Muslim Brotherhood and opposition parties for using Muslim law as a tool of repression against dissidents. The financial community also exerted pressure on the Sudanese president to limit the application of the Sharia in business as it stood in opposition to IMF policies.

[18] Sudan's external debt rapidly rose to $8 billion. Debt servicing was systematically delayed until early 1984, with the country considered bankrupt on at least two occasions.

[19] In 1985 the US suspended all credit and the IMF forced the Government to raise food prices. Rebellion broke out, quickly reaching to the capital. Nimeiry visited the US in search of backing, but was unable to return as Abdul Rahman Suwar al-Dahab, minister of defence and army chief of staff, had seized power in his absence.

[20] The coup did not have much of an effect on the political scenario. The Islamic bourgeoisie in the north made deals with the Government, while the SPLM continued its activities in the south, as the political and economic discrimination against the region continued. Political parties were dissolved and the previous government's subdivision of the south was revoked. The new government promised to review the application of the Sharia, and Dahab promised elections in 1986.

[21] The elections were held in April 1986, and Sadiq al-Mahdi was elected Prime Minister. His Party of the People (UMMA), based on the Koran and on Islamic tradition, obtained 99 seats, while the Democratic Unionist Party (DUP) won 64. The UMMA had 8 ministers, the DUP, six, and other minor parties, 4. A ruling coalition was thus established based on

agreements which had led to the approval of a new Constitution in 1985.

[22] Thirty-seven representatives were not elected because of the war in the southern provinces. The SPLM's 12,000 guerrillas besieged government garrisons in the southern provinces, practically splitting Sudan in two, and the south suffered from food shortages as a result of an insurgent blockade. However, the guerrillas agreed to let through airborne food and medical supplies sent by the UN to besieged cities.

[23] In June, 1989 the war between the SPLM and the army continued, the foreign debt reached $12 billion and the social tension increased, exacerbated by price increases. In February of that year, Major-General Omar al-Bashir ousted the President, blaming his government for the political and economic crisis. Bashir dissolved political parties and created a 15-member military junta, promising to bring the war to an end.

[24] Ten months after the military government took office, there was a coup attempt by a faction of army officials. Ethiopia, Kenya, Uganda, Zaire (now DR Congo), and the US all attempted mediation and all failed. Peace negotiations failed, and southern people continued to suffer at the hands of government troops and Arab paramilitary groups financed by Bashir. These armed groups harassed the southern African

Kanem-Bornu

Where the Bilma trade route neared Lake Chad, there lived, according to oral tradition, communities of "small red men" who must have given rise, between the first and fifth centuries of our era, to the so-called Civilization of Chad, known for its high-quality artistic and metallurgical production. The Sao probably arrived towards the 10th century. They were a Nilotic nation, noted for their great size. They exterminated the "little red men" and established a confederation of groups to the southeast of the lake. On the other side of the lake, communities of shepherds related to the Tibu (autochthonous nomads from the Tibesti mountains) had settled around the eighth century. These shepherds were the Kanuri who, after subduing the local population, set up the state of Kanema, ruled by a military caste. Converted to Islam in the 11th century, they cultivated close ties with the Arab world, based on the slave trade.

2   The capture of slaves frequently took the Kanuri to Sao territory which they eventually conquered. Thereafter, the Saif (Kanuri ruling family) came to be called "the rulers of Kanem, the masters of Bornu" and their nation was known by this compound name.

3   The most outstanding period was during Dunama Dibalim's rule. Between 1220 and 1260 Dibalim ruled over the territory that extended from the banks of Lake Chad to Fezzan (Libya) in the north, and from the Haussa states in the west to Ouaddai (border of present-day Sudan) in the east.

4   The flourishing traffic allowed him to maintain a standing army of 30,000 horsemen. He also built a large residence in Cairo (Al Qahirah) for the young Kanuri who studied at the famous Al Azhar University.

5   However, total dominion over the other nations did not occur: the Sao, Tibu and Bulala (to the southeast) shook the 14th and 15th centuries with frequent rebellions, forcing the Saifs to leave Kanem and to move their capital.

6   Idris Alaoma (1571-1603) decided to solve these problems drastically; he bought muskets, hired instructors in Tunis and modernized the army to confront his enemies one by one.

7   The Sao, long considered rebellious, were completely exterminated in a campaign that razed all their towns. The Tibu were forced to abandon their mountains and settle in Bornu where they were easier to control. To subdue the Bulala he had to conquer the north of what is now Cameroon.

8   Paradoxically, this "putting things in order" did not benefit the Kanuri economically. Although the Haussa merchants yielded to Idris' military drive, and eventually paid tribute to the Kanem-Bornu rulers, they succeeded in gaining control of the slave trade, thus benefitting from the "peace" obtained with so much blood.

9   This situation remained more or less stable until the 19th century, when the Fulani invasion forced the king of Bornu to turn for help to Mahamad Al-Kanemi, a military chieftain. Al-Kanemi repulsed the invaders, but stayed and became the real power behind the throne, even though the crisis was over. This dual situation lasted until 1846, when the last of the Saifs, Ibrahim, was executed by Omar, al-Kanemi's son.

10   In 1893, Omar's successor was deposed by Rabah, a Sudanese guerrilla who had fought alongside the Mahdi (see Sudan). The new ruler extended the boundaries of Kanem-Bornu to Sudan. After several years of fighting against the French who wanted to seize control of the territory, Rabah was defeated by the joint action of three colonial armies coming from Algeria, Congo and Mali. His death signalled the end of resistance to colonial penetration.

---

peoples and forced them from their lands.

25   On February 4 1991, the Government established a federal system in the country. According to the decree, Sudan would be divided into nine states, each administered by a governor and a ministerial cabinet. On January 31 of that year, the Government of general Omar Bashir also signed a new criminal code based on the Sharia, only to be implemented in the north of the country, where Islam is predominant.

26   In March the army launched a military offensive against the Sudan People's Liberation Army (SPLA), supported by Ethiopia, Iran and Libya. Government forces recaptured the city of Bor in the south which had been a symbol to the rebel movement.

27   With the People's Liberation Army, led by John Garang, operating in the south, and the Nasir rebel group - a splinter group of the SPLA led by Riak Mashar - operating in the north, the Government lost control. This led to violent government repression against its opponents in urban areas, and against rural communities which supported the guerrillas in the countryside.

28   Negotiations in May 1992, sponsored by the President of Nigeria, in Abuja, Nigeria, ended in June with the issuing of an ambiguous communiqué. International pressure forced Omar Bashir to revoke the ban on airplane movements to the south of the country, which had kept food and medicine from being transported. It was estimated that some 9 million people were on the verge of starvation; this, in addition to the 60,000 people who had already died of hunger in Parayang, 800 kilometers southeast of Khartoum.

29   In January 1993, disagreements among high-ranking members of the Government led to a cabinet shake-up, aimed at bringing the Government's policies into line with the IMF and World Bank objectives. However, both international agencies found the reforms insufficient; especially as the debt had not been serviced. The financing for infrastructure projects was consequently

discontinued in April. In the meantime, $2 million a day was being spent on defence.

30   In February 1993, the SPLA and the Government resumed negotiations in Entebbe, Uganda. These were boycotted by Mashar, who was in Nairobi trying to speed up negotiations to merge with another SPLA splinter group, led by William Nyuon. This alliance, signed in April, paved the way for a cease-fire agreement with the government, and the promise to carry on with the talks initiated in Nigeria. Disagreements between Garang and Bashir, in Abuja, over the devolution of power to the provinces, caused the talks to founder in June 1993, and the impasse remained until the end of the year.

31   In May 1994, the Government signed a protocol for humanitarian aid with both rebel factions in order to provide relief for villages cut off by the conflict. Their situation continued to worsen and humanitarian organizations voiced their concerns. In July 1995, African Rights charged Khartoum with responsibility for the "genocide" of the Nubian ethnic group.

32   In the March 1996 elections, Bashir was re-elected with 76 per cent of the vote. The possibilities of coexistence between the "theocrats" of the north and the rebels of the south appeared increasingly smaller. The twelve years of war left a million dead and three million refugees.

33   In November 1997, disputes with Egypt over administration of the Halaib triangle - rich in phosphates, manganese and, supposedly, oil - led to Sudan asking for intervention from the Arab League. Under an agreement made in 1899, Halaib belonged to Egypt, but under a newer agreement of 1905, it had been awarded to Sudan.

34   In January 1998, the United States announced an economic embargo on Sudan, alleging it had supported international terrorism, training opposition groups from neighbouring countries in order to destabilise them, and lacking respect for human rights.

35   A month later, the UN appealed to the international community for more than $100 million to aid 4 million victims of war and drought in Sudan.

36   The Sudanese guerrillas vindicated the air attack which had killed Vice-President Al Zubair Mohammed Saleh in February. According to observers, the Christian PLA rebels had been given US support in return for collaboration with Uganda, Ethiopia and Eritrea. The Catholic Church of Sudan decided to take part in peace talks between the Islamic Government and the military Sudanese Peoples Liberation Army faction prepared for dialogue.

37   In August 1998, the Shifa pharmaceutical plant was destroyed by US missiles in retaliation for the bombing of US embassies in Kenya and Tanzania. The factory was said to be linked with the World Islam Front led by Saudi millionaire and former US ally against communism, Osama bin Laden.

Suriname

Population: 432,000 (1996)
Area: 163,265 SQ KM
Capital: Paramaribo

Currency: Guilder
Language: Dutch and Spanish

Suriname

The Caribs settled along the Atlantic coasts of Central and South America. The original groups gradually dispersed; some inland, and others to the islands that lie off the coast of the continent. They lived in small communities where they existed by hunting, fishing and small-scale farming. They were also able warriors.

[2] In the early 17th century Dutch colonists founded a settlement in Guyana and began to trade in slaves.

[3] In 1863, when slavery was abolished in Dutch territories it was replaced by another source of cheap labor, Asian Indian and Javanese immigrants. This gave rise to a complex ethnic structure in the Guyana region. Asian Indians formed one of the largest groups, the most resistant to intermarriage and most strongly attached to their cultural heritage. Then came the Creoles or Afro-Americans, the Javanese, the "bush people" whose ancestors had rebelled against slavery and fled the plantations, indigenous people and a small European minority.

[4] These ethnic, cultural and linguistic differences hindered the development of a national identity. Political movements tended to represent individual ethnic communities, especially as these broadly corresponded to social divisions. The Creoles formed the NPK (National Party Combination), a coalition of four center-left parties, and they led the fight for independence after World War II. Jaggernauth Lachmon's Vatan Hitakarie represented the Indian population of shop owners and business people, and they sought to postpone independence.

[5] Since 1954, local government had enjoyed a degree of autonomy and, in October 1973, the independence faction won the legislative elections. Liberal Hanck Arron, NPS (National Surinamese Party) leader was appointed prime minister.

[6] Arron and Lachmon reached an agreement, and independence was finally proclaimed in 1975. Many middle-income Surinamese took advantage of their status as Dutch citizens to emigrate to the ex-colonial power. Nearly a third of the population, mostly Asian Indian, left the country, causing a serious shortage of technical, professional and administrative personnel. The country lost much-needed qualified labor with only SURALCO and Billiton, the two transnationals which monopolize local bauxite mining, surviving the exodus. Economic activity decreased and agriculture declined to dangerous levels. In this difficult situation, Arron and his group of politicians were repeatedly accused of corruption and complicity with foreign companies.

[7] On February 25 1980, the premier was overthrown by a coup which had begun as a protest by the sergeants' union for better working conditions. The National Military Council (NMC) summoned opposition leaders to form a government and several leftwing politicians accepted cabinet posts.

[8] The Military Council, led by Lt-Colonel Desi Bouterse, took power from the politicians on February 4 1981, accusing the administration of corruption and underhand dealings with the Netherlands and the United States. This new government established relations with Cuba, in the face of opposition from the major internal parties, from the United States and from the Netherlands. Brazil came to its aid on more than one occasion.

[9] In January 1983, Bouterse formed a new government, which appointed Errol Halibux, a nationalist and member of the Farmers' and Labor Union, as Prime Minister. After the American invasion of Grenada, the Suriname Government did an about-face in its relations with Cuba, asking Havana to recall its ambassador

PROFILE

ENVIRONMENT
The coastal plain, low and subject to floods, is suitable for agriculture. Rice, sugar and other crops are grown. Land has been reclaimed from the sea through drainage and dykes. Inland, the terrain is hilly with dense tropical vegetation, rich in bauxite deposits. Year-round heavy rainfall feeds an important system of rivers, some of which are used to generate hydro-electric power for the aluminum industry.

SOCIETY
Peoples: Suriname Creole 30 per cent; Indo-Pakistani 33 per cent; Javanese 16 per cent; "Bush Negro" 10 per cent; Amerindian 3 per cent; other 3 per cent. **Religions:** Christian 44 per cent (21.6 per cent Catholic, 18 per cent Protestant); Muslim 18.6 per cent; Hinduism 26 per cent; other 15.8 per cent.
Languages: Dutch(official). English (for business), Hindi, Javanese, and a form of Creole are spoken. The Creole, called either Taki-Taki or Senango-Tongo, is based on African languages mixed with Dutch, Spanish and English.

Political Parties: New Front for Democracy and Development (NF) comprised of four parties: Progressive Reform Party (VHP), Suriname National Party (NPS), Javanese Farmers' Party (KPTI) and the National Democratic Party NPD), Democratic Alternative, Jungle Commando, Angola, Mandela Liberation Movement, Tucaya.
Social Organizations: Suriname Trade Union Federation; Central Organization of Civil Servants.

THE STATE
Official Name: Republiek Suriname.
Administrative Divisions: 9 Districts.
Capital: Paramaribo, 200,000 people.
Other cities: Nieuw Nickerie 6,078 people; Meerzorg 5,355; Marienburg 3,633.
Government: Parliamentary Republic. President, Jules Wijdenmbosch since September 1996. Prime Minister, Pretaapnarian Radhakishun since September 1996. 51-member unicameral parliament.
National Holiday: November 25, Independence Day (1975).
Armed forces: 1,800 (1996).

Food Dependency

1994
13%

Literacy

1995

93%

and suspending all agreements for cooperation between the countries.

[10] In late 1983 and early 1984, there was a series of strikes by bauxite workers - a product which accounted for 80 per cent of the country's exports - who were joined by power, water and transport workers. Bouterse attributed it to errors by the Prime Minister and the entire cabinet automatically resigned. Bouterse proceeded to eliminate all fiscal restrictions by presidential decree, and appointed two union leaders to the new cabinet.

[11] An effort was made to reduce Suriname's isolation and diversify its foreign relations, which were excessively dependent on Holland. To accelerate this process, the Government began to pursue a more aggressive foreign policy, joining CARICOM (Caribbean Community and Common Market) as an observer and establishing relations with Cuba, Grenada, Nicaragua, Brazil and Venezuela. It also became a member of SELA (Latin American Economic System), the OAS (Organization of American States) and the Amazon Pact.

[12] In mid-1986, former soldier Ronnie Brunswijk, aided by foreign mercenaries and funded by the Netherlands, began a campaign of harassment from bases in French Guyana.

[13] In April 1987, the 33-member National Assembly (of whom 11 are labor union representatives) unanimously approved a draft constitution providing for a return to institutional government. The

draft was supported by the three main political parties.

[14] The coalition United Front for Democracy and Development won. On July 21 1989, President Ramsewak Shankar granted an amnesty to the still-active guerrilla movement, allowing them to hold on to their weapons as long as they were in the forests. Bouterse and the NDP opposed this agreement, arguing that it legalized an autonomous military force and encouraged the division.

[15] In December 1990, another coup deposed Ramsewak Shankar, who had been the constitutional president since January 1988. Colonel Desi Bouterse, who had resigned a week prior to the coup, resumed his leadership of the army on December 30. The National Assembly, which had been set up in September 1987 for a period of five years appointed the NPS's Johan Draag as provisional president.

[16] During 1991, Dutch and US sources accused the top military echelons of Bouterse's regime of being involved in drug trafficking.

[17] The May elections were held to choose the National Assembly, and the New Front (NF) won; they are a broad coalition of civilian parties and ethnic groups who oppose the military government. The NF proposed the re-establishment of relations with the Dutch Government and the tightening of economic and political links with the former colonizer.

[18] Fresh elections in May 1991 elected a new government to begin ruling in September. Spokespeople in The Hague and Washington independently announced their intentions of carrying out a military intervention in the country "should the new government request it". International observers warned about the threat implicit in these announcements, in the light of the recent experiences in Grenada and Panama.

[19] In September, Ronald Venetiaan of the NF was elected President. The new head of state launched a 50 per cent cut in defence spending and a peace process, including a UN-

sponsored guerrilla disarmament, under the supervision of Brazil and Guyana. In June 1992, a cooperation agreement was signed with the Netherlands, and a year later, a severe structural adjustment program was adopted, which gave rise to discontent among the population.

[20] Poverty and unemployment in the rural agricultural communities formed the background for the occupation of the Afobakka dam, 100 kilometres south of Paramaribo, in March 1994. The rebels, who called for the resignation of the government, were expelled by government troops, after a four-day occupation. Another important movement took place in rural areas in 1995, when representatives of Indians and Bush *Negroes* (runaway slaves living in the forest in their own communities) gathered to protest for the environmental damage caused by a Canadian mining company and an Indonesian timber company.

[21] In September 1996, the Parliament elected Jules

Wijdenbosch as president, thus blocking Venetiaan's re-election.

[22] In April 1997, the Netherlands issued an international warrant on former dictator Besi Bouterse, suspected of links with drug-trafficking. In response, Wijdenbosch appointed the former dictator State councillor, granting him diplomatic immunity.

[23] Toward the end of that year, a failed coup d'état ended in the arrest of 17 low-ranking officers. The army called for better pay and greater investment in equipment and weapons. The strength of the army had fallen since the late 1980s when the Bouterse regime had fought the guerrilla groups. The coup attempt was related to the working conditions of the troops, which had deteriorated, with low salaries and outdated equipment.

WORKERS

- ■ AGRICULTURE **21%** (1990)
- □ INDUSTRIAL **18%**
- ■ SERVICES **61%**

MILITARY EXPENDITURE

MILITARY (as % of health and education expenditures-1990/91) **27%**

STATISTICS

DEMOGRAPHY
Population: 432,000 (1996). **Annual growth:** 1.2% (1980/1996). **Estimates for year 2000:** 500,000. **Annual growth to year 2000:** 1.1% (1994/2000). **Urban Population:** 49.7% (1996). **Children per woman:** 2.5 (1996).

HEALTH
Life expectancy at birth: 71 years (1996). **Infant mortality:** 25 per 1,000 (1996). **Under-5 child mortality:** 31 per 1,000 (1996).

EDUCATION
Literacy: 93% (1995) male: 95% (1995) female: 91% (1995). **School enrolment:** Primary total: 127% (1990/95) male: 129% (1990/95) female: 125% (1990/95). Secondary: male: 50% (1990/95) female: 58% (1990/95).

COMMUNICATIONS
100 **newspapers**, 680 **radios**, 150 **TV sets** and 120 **main telephone lines** per 1,000 people (1994).

ECONOMY
Consumer price index: 2,065.0 (1994). **Currency:** 407 guilders = $ 1 (1995) **Cereal imports:** 36 metric tons (1994). **Food import dependency:** 13% (1994). **Fertilizer use:** 632 kgs per ha (1994). **Development aid received:** $ 77 million (1995). $ 183 per capita (1995). 27.6% of GNP (1994)

HDI (rank / value) 66 / 0.792 (1994)

Swaziland

Swaziland

Population:	881,000 (1996)
Area:	17,364 SQ KM
Capital:	Mbabane
Currency:	Emalangeni
Language:	English

Like Lesotho, (see Lesotho) Swaziland achieved centralized administration when groups of very different origins joined to form a nation. The danger posed by Zulu expansion, (see South Africa) led Sobhuza, head of the Dlamini local groups, to bring together the remains of several groups split apart by Shaka, including Zulu deserters and Bushmen or San who remained in the region. They became a powerful force in the northeastern part of the present-day South African province of Natal. Sobhuza died shortly after the Zulu defeat by the Boers (1839) leaving his son, Mswati, the task of keeping the nation together, in the face of constant threats from the Afrikaners. The nation was named after its king who led the nation in 30 years of resistance - aside from a period of alliance with the Boers against the Pedi - allying with the British shortly before his death so as to avoid defeat by the Boers.

2   In 1867, Swaziland formally became a British protectorate, like Basutoland (Lesotho) and Bechuanaland (Botswana).

3   When Britain defeated the Boers and imposed its dominion over the whole of South Africa, these countries remained under separate colonial administrations, though South African settlers attempted to establish claims over the territories. Native authorities were formally recognized according to British criterion of making use of "local" intermediaries to facilitate colonial administration.

4   In 1961, when the Union of South Africa broke relations with Britain and toughened racial segregation policies, London accelerated the decolonization process in the region. Swaziland was granted internal autonomy in 1967 and formal independence the following year. Sobhuza II was recognized as head of state and governed with two legislative

chambers. On April 12, 1973, he dissolved Parliament, claiming that it contained "destructive elements" and proclaimed himself absolute monarch, banning all political parties and activities.

5   In the event, Sobhuza II placed himself in the service of the South African colonizers against whom his grandfather had fought. Communications, the postal service, transport, currency and the Bank of Swaziland all became completely dependent on South Africa. South African companies exploited the country's asbestos and iron ore and South African experts ran the state's public administration - guaranteeing efficient control - and supervised agricultural production. Cotton, the main export product, was marketed by South African merchants and white South Africans opened brothels and cabarets which the strict "puritanical" official morality prohibited in their own country.

6   Due to the lack of job opportunities, thousands of workers emigrate every year to work in the South African gold mines. The money they send home to their families accounts for 25 per cent of Swaziland's foreign currency earnings. In October 1977, teachers went on strike for better salaries and were supported by students. The following year, the Swazi Liberation Movement (Swalimo) was founded, led by Dr Swane, who managed to escape from prison in the capital, Mbabane. The strengthening of the opposition was accompanied by a rapid growth of the armed forces, from 1,000 in 1975 to more than 5,000 in 1979, and the police force was considerably reinforced.

7   Mounting opposition inside the country was encouraged by the consolidation of a socialist regime in Mozambique, amongst other things. Increasing tension in Swaziland also led the government to develop closer military relations with South Africa and Israel; Sobhuza II was one of only three African rulers who never broke diplomatic relations with the government of Tel Aviv.

8   After the 1977 strikes, the government severely repressed all opposition, invoking a special law allowing detention without charges for up to 60 days.

9   The Constitution was suspended in 1973 and a reformed version was introduced in 1978 without approval from or consultation with the electorate. Following tribal rules, the process of approval consisted of consultation with the heads of the 40 clans a fortnight before the enactment of the new constitutional draft. It banned the existence of opposition parties and established a parliament with little decision-making power.

10   After 1980, the economic situation in Swaziland was affected by the world recession. The post-independence boom period came to an end with an increase in the prices of imported goods and a drop in prices for corn, sugar and wood exports. Inflation climbed, and a deficit appeared in the balance of payments, the rate of investment fell radically, and the GNP dropped by 4 per cent. Mineral exports fell from 40 per cent of total exports to only 10 per cent due to the depletion of iron ore reserves. Various new coal deposits were discovered in 1980 but their exploitation has been slow due to legal difficulties and the lack of adequate transport facilities.

11   In August 1982, King Sobhuza died at the age of 83 when his successor, Prince Makhosetive was

only 15 years old. The lack of effective government sparked a power struggle between several princes and Prince Mabandla Dlamini was deposed from his position as prime minister. He was succeeded by Bhekimpi Dlamini, a pro-South African conservative, who began his reign by persecuting South African refugees.

12   In August 1983, Ntombi, one of Sobhuza's widows, overthrew the reigning Queen and took power, strengthening the conservative faction. Two months later, 200,000 of the country's 760,000 inhabitants voted for a new parliament through a complicated indirect electoral system called tinkhundla. As expected, Prince Bhekimpi Dlamini was successful in an electoral contest where no political parties participated.

13   The election resulted in closer ties with South Africa. The repression of anti-apartheid militants increased in 1984, with detention and return to the Pretoria government becoming the norm.

14   During the second half of 1984, a student protest led the government to close down the university. Prime Minister Bhekimpi Dlamini's authoritarianism stimulated the revival of the Swazi Liberation

WORKERS

- ■ AGRICULTURE 39% (1990)
- □ INDUSTRIAL 22%
- ▦ SERVICES 38%

STATISTICS

DEMOGRAPHY
Population: 881,000 (1996). **Annual growth:** 2.8% (1980/1996). **Estimates for year 2000:** 1,000,000. **Annual growth to year 2000:** 2.8% (1994/2000). **Urban Population:** 32.0% (1996). **Children per woman:** 4.6 (1996).

HEALTH
Life expectancy at birth: 59 years (1996). male: 56 years (1994). female: 61 years (1994). **Infant mortality:** 68 per 1,000 (1996). **Under-5 child mortality:** 97 per 1,000 (1996). 9,091 **people per doctor** (1988/91). **Safe water:** 60% (1990/96).

EDUCATION
Literacy: 77% (1995) male : 78% (1995) female: 76% (1995). **School enrolment:** Primary total: 122% (1990/95) male : 125% (1990/95) female: 119% (1990/95). Secondary: male: 53% (1990/95) female: 51% (1990/95).

COMMUNICATIONS
10 **newspapers**, 163 **radios**, 70 **TV sets** and 20 **main telephone lines** per 1,000 people (1994).

ECONOMY
Consumer price index: 156.8 (1994). **Currency:** 3.65 emalangeni = $ 1 (1995) **Cereal imports:** 75 metric tons (1994). **Food import dependency:** 8% (1994). **Fertilizer use:** 696 kgs per ha (1994). (1996). **Development aid received:** $ 54 million (1995). $ 59 per capita (1995). 5.6% of GNP (1994)

HDI (rank / value) 114 / 0.582 (1994)

PROFILE

ENVIRONMENT
The country is divided into three distinct geographical regions known as the high, middle and low "veld" (fields) all approximately the same size. The western region is mountainous with a central plateau and flatlands to the east. The main crops are sugar cane, citrus fruits and rice (irrigated), cotton, corn (the basic foodstuff), sorghum and tobacco. In the lower veld, infections caused by polluted water are responsible for the high mortality rate. Wildlife was exterminated by European hunters in the first half of this century.

SOCIETY
Peoples: 84.3 per cent of the population belong to the Swazi ethnic group. Zulu account for 9.9 per cent; Tonga and Shangaan another 3 per cent; there are Indian (0.8 per cent), Pakistani (0.8 per cent) and Portuguese (0.2 per cent) minorities. **Religions:** 77 per cent of the population are Christian, the rest follow traditional African religions. **Languages:** Swazi and English (official); ethnic minorities speak their own languages. **Political Parties:** Popular United Democratic Movement (PUDEMO); Swaziland Democratic Alliance; National Congress of Ngwane Liberation.
Social Organizations: Swaziland Federation of Trade Unions (SFTU); Swaziland Youth Congress.

THE STATE
Official Name: Umbuso weSwatini. Administrative Divisions: 210 Tribal Areas, including 40 traditional communities. **Capital:** Mbabane, 46,000 people (1990). **Other cities:** Manzini, 53,000 people (1990). **Government:** King Mswati III, crowned on April 25, 1986. **Prime Minister:** Barnabas Sibusiso Dlamini since July 1996. **National holiday:** September 6 (Independence Day). **Armed Forces:** 2,657 (1983).

Movement, which resumed its activities in January 1985. This movement was led by Prince Clement Dumisa Dlamini, who was the former secretary-general of the Progressive Party and a well-known nationalist leader. He was later exiled to England.

[15] On April 25 1986, Prince Makhosetive was crowned, taking the name King Mswati III. His inaugural address reflected his conservative stance. In May he dissolved the Liqoqo (an assembly of local group leaders acting as Supreme State Council), consolidating his power and that of his ministers. Prime Minister Bhekimpi was relieved of his post and replaced by Sotsha Dlamini. In September 1987, King Mswati dissolved Parliament, announcing elections for November, a year ahead of schedule. The 40 members of Parliament and 10 senators were elected by an electoral college. The King however disputed the election of the senators, demanding that the

process be repeated in a more satisfactory manner.

[16] Relations with South Africa did not change with the change of king. The Government condemned economic sanctions against the Pretoria regime and continued to harass anti-apartheid militants.

[17] Since the late 1980s the country's economic situation had improved noticeably. The economy grew and foreign investment continued. A significant part of the food produced was sold to the European Community. This improvement, a direct consequence of trade sanctions against South Africa, allowed the manufacturing sector to increase - contributing 20 per cent of the GDP by 1991 - and helped the country raise its economic growth rate to 3.5 per cent per year.

[18] In 1992, a significant part of the opposition joined the Popular United Democratic Movement (PUDEMO) and lobbied for the king to accept a multiparty system. Discontent mounted in

1993, as a prolonged drought destroyed the corn crop and generated further unemployment.

[19] According to some studies carried out in 1994, even though calorie consumption was slightly higher than the necessary minimum, the country still had a high child mortality rate - 107 per 1,000 - and only 30 per cent of the population had access to drinking water. Moreover, Swaziland was still dependent on South Africa, the source of 90 per cent of imports.

[20] Protests against Mswati III continued. After the deliberate fire of February 1995 in the seat of parliament, for which the Swaziland Youth Congress claimed responsibility, 40,000 people took part in a demonstration in support of a two-day general strike. South Africa pressed the King, and in February 1996 he expressed his willingness to authorize political parties.

[21] South Africa put pressure on the King, who in February 1996 said he was prepared to authorize political parties, amidst rumours of possible intervention from the South African army. The Swaziland Federation of Trade Unions called for an end to the absolute monarchy and the establishment of a multiparty regime. Violent clashes between demonstrators and the security forces caused at least three deaths.

[22] Mid-year, the King called for an end to the upheaval, repeating he would reconsider the banning of the political parties.

Furthermore, he said the citizens would be given the opportunity to participate in drawing up a new Constitution. In May, he sacked Prime Minister Mbilini Dlamini and appointed Barnabas Sibusiso Dlamini as his replacement in July.

[23] The political situation did not vary substantially in 1997. In March the King let down the opposition by not sending delegates to the agreed negotiations. In July, he created a 30-member committee, charged with drafting a Constitution, asking for all related initiatives be referred to this body.

[24] These delaying tactics intensified the protests. The King reacted, ordering the security forces to fire live ammunition on demonstrators. The clashes produced large numbers of wounded and several union leaders were arrested. In October 1997, fresh strikes broke out in strategic areas, like the sugar sector. The unions also called for the Constitutional Revision Committee to be dissolved.

[25] In April 1998, the King put and "environmental conservation" plan into action, with public and private sector participation. Five critical areas were identified. At the same time, bidding was opened on large-scale public works projects including bridges, the re-routing of major water courses, and irrigation structures for vast areas hit by drought.

Sweden

Sverige

Population: 8,819,000 (1996)
Area: 449,964 SQ KM
Capital: Stockholm

Currency: Kronor
Language: Swedish

According to archaeological research, the first inhabited area in Sweden is thought to have been the southern part of the country, with occupation dating back to 10,000 years BC. Between 8,000 and 6,000 BC, the region was inhabited by peoples who made a living by hunting and fishing, using simple stone tools. The Bronze Age (1,800- 500 BC) brought with it cultural development, reflected in particular in the richness of the tombs of that period.

2 In 500 AD, in Lake Malaren valley, the Sveas created the first important center of political power. From the 6th century BC until the year 800 the population went through a migration period, later becoming settled, with agriculture becoming the basis of economic and social activities.

3 Between the 9th and 11th centuries, the Swedish vikings, on trade expeditions, as well as pirate raids, reached the Baltic shores and also went as far as what is now Russia, reaching the Black and Caspian Seas. There they established relations with the Byzantine and Arab empires.

4 Between the 9th and 11th centuries, Christian missions from the Carolingian empire (led by the missionary, Ansgar) converted most of Sweden. However, the gods of the ancient local mythologies survived into the 12th century. Sweden had its first archbishop in 1164.

5 From the middle of the 12th century, Sverker and Erik's respective fiefdoms fought against each other to gain control of the Swedish kingdom, alternating in power between 1160 and 1250. The feudal chieftains remained relatively autonomous until the

second half of the 13th century, when the King enforced nationwide laws and annexed Finland.

6 The Black Death brought the country's growth to a standstill in 1350, and it remained so until the second half of the 15th century. In that period the foundries in the central region became important. During the 15th and 16th centuries the German Hanseatic League dominated Swedish commerce and encouraged the foundation of several cities.

7 In 1397, the royal power of Norway, Sweden and Denmark was handed over to the Danish queen Margaret, who proclaimed the Union of Kalmar. The ensuing conflicts between the central Danish power and the rebellious Swedish nobility, townspeople and peasants ended in 1523, with the accession of Gustav Vasa to the throne of Sweden.

8 Under the reign of Vasa, the monarchy ceased to be elected by the nobility and became hereditary. A German administrative model was adopted and the foundations were laid for a nation state. The possessions of the Church went to the state, with the Protestant Reformation following hot on its heels. From then on, Sweden aspired to becoming the main power in the Baltic region.

9 In 1630, after intervening successfully in the Thirty Years' War, Sweden waged two more wars to conquer the Danish regions of Skane, Halland, Blekinge, and the Baltic island of Gotland, as well as the Norwegian islands of Bohuslan, Jamtland, and Harjedalen.

10 Sweden thus became a great power in northern Europe, as it

now ruled over Finland, several northern German provinces, and the Baltic provinces of Estonia, Latvia and Lithuania. However, the country was still basically rural and lacked resources to maintain that position indefinitely.

11 After its defeat in the Great Northern War (1700-21), the Swedish empire lost most of the provinces to the south and east of the Gulf of Finland. It was reduced to the territories roughly corresponding to modern Sweden and Finland, with Finland being ceded to Russia during the Napoleonic Wars.

12 In 1718, after the death of Charles XII, a parliament (*Riksdag*) made up of nobles did away with the monarchy, assuming power itself. However, the new king Gustav II staged a coup in 1772, gradually claiming more and more power, and finally re-establishing full monarchic powers in 1789.

13 In compensation for the losses incurred during the Napoleonic Wars, Norway was ceded to King Charles XIV John, who had become king in 1810. After a short war, it was forced to join Sweden in 1814. Nevertheless, after a series of conflicts, the union dissolved peacefully in 1905.

14 In the second half of the 19th century, Sweden continued to be a poor country, with 90 per cent of the population engaged in agriculture. At this point, a great emigration movement began: one million out of a total of 5 million Swedes left, mainly for North America.

15 During this period the liberal majority in parliament, supported by King Oscar I, established universal education (1842), the free enterprise system and the liberalization of foreign trade (1846). Legislation was also passed

WORKERS

UNEMPLOYMENT 8% (1996)
Labour force %

■ WOMEN
□ MEN

48   52

■ **AGRICULTURE** 4% (1990)
□ **INDUSTRIAL** 30%
■ **SERVICES** 66%

LAND USE

IRRIGATED 4.1 % of arable

(1993)

■ **FOREST & WOODLAND** 62.2%
□ **ARABLE** 6.2%
■ **OTHER** 31.6%

establishing sexual equality in inheritance law (1845), the rights of unmarried women (1858), and religious freedom (1860).

[16] Important social movements such as the temperance league, free churches, women's advancement, and especially the workers' movement emerged, growing with industrialization and influencing the government through social democracy.

[17] From 1890 onwards, with the support of foreign capital, the process of industrialization accelerated in Sweden. The country had one of the most thriving economies in that part of Europe. Finished products using Swedish technical innovations quickly became the country's main exports.

[18] Universal male suffrage has been operating since 1908, a state old-age pension system was adopted in 1913, and in 1918 the 8-hour working day was established by law. That same year, the vote was extended to women.

[19] The parliamentary system has been in effect since 1918. The Social Democrats came to power in 1932; their policies fostered understanding between workers and industrialists, which was enshrined in the 1938 Pact of Salsboejaden.

[20] Sexual equality has been achieved to a greater extent in Sweden than in other industrialized countries, through the efforts of feminists and state campaigns against social and sexual prejudice.

[21] The country's educational system - from primary onwards - seeks to eliminate sexist conditioning by teaching both girls and boys how to keep house, take care of a newborn baby, do woodwork and metalwork.

[22] Abortion is available on demand to women up to the third month of pregnancy. The law concerning rape states that there are no extenuating circumstances to be considered in the man's case, and there are also stiff sentences for rape within marriage.

[23] Women can take on any profession, with the exception of the army. However, the female population is still concentrated in the lowest income groups. In general their earnings are 20 per cent lower than those of their male counterparts for similar jobs. In 1981, over 50 per cent of all married women had a professional activity outside the home.

[24] Within the civil service, there is an official position of Ombudsman, whose role is to investigate cases of abuse of authority, breach of ethics, and ethnic or sexual discrimination in state agencies and private companies.

[25] Since World War I, Sweden has

refused to take part in peacetime alliances in order to stay neutral in times of war. This policy relies on Sweden's strong defence system and compulsory male national service.

[26] Trade routes were disrupted during the war, which caused serious food shortages in the country. For security reasons Sweden is almost self-sufficient, with up to 80 per cent of its agricultural produce produced internally. The Government maintains a protectionist policy on agricultural imports, which means that food prices are higher than those on the international market.

[27] Sweden favored a thaw in East-West relations during the Cold War, and worked actively for international disarmament. One of the cornerstones of its foreign policy is its support for the UN.

[28] During four decades in power, from 1932 to 1976, under the leadership of Tage Erlander, the Social Democrats established conditions which made it possible to combine rapid economic and industrial growth with a redistribution of wealth through direct taxation. Thus, a costly social welfare system was established, using the framework of a capitalist economy with strong state intervention.

[29] There are a number of Swedish corporations among the largest transnationals in the world, including Volvo, Stora Kopparbergs, Skf, Trelleborg, Ikea, Aga, Procordia,

Modo, Sandvik, Esselte, Saab and Svensk Stål.

[30] However, during the 1970s, there was a slow-down of economic growth, due partly to the increasing cost of oil imports to satisfy half the country's energy needs. Of the other 50 per cent 15 came from nuclear reactors and 7 per cent from coal and coke. After a plebiscite held in 1980, Parliament decided that until the year 2010, the 12 nuclear reactors which were already in operation would remain closed.

[31] From 1981 onwards, relations between Sweden and the USSR were affected by the incursion of Soviet submarines into Swedish waters and the effects of the Chernobyl disaster.

[32] Atomic radiation from the Soviet Chernobyl nuclear plant affected northern and central Sweden as well as the south of Lapland in 1986. The two main subsistence activities of the Sami people there, reindeer-herding and fishing, were badly affected by radiation, which contaminated all animal life in the area.

[33] Sweden was the first Western state to officially recognize North Vietnam (1969). The country's Prime Minister Olof Palme also acted as a mediator in the conflict between Iran and Iraq in 1982, and in 1988 Sweden sponsored a meeting between Palestinians and American Jews in 1988.

[34] After the 1976 elections, amid an incipient economic crisis, the

moderate, liberal and conservative parties formed a coalition. Six years later, the Social Democrats returned to power. In 1986, charismatic leader Olof Palme was shot dead in a murder case that has still not been solved. Ingvar Carlsson succeeded him as prime minister.

[35] In the years that followed, parliament investigated an alleged case of bribery - involving the Government and Bofors, an arms manufacturing company - with relation to the sale of weapons to the Middle East and India. The country's laws forbid such conduct, as well as trade with areas where there are military tensions or with countries that are at war.

[36] In spite of this scandal, the population was more concerned with the economy and the environment. Two accidents attributed to toxic substances destroyed the ecological balance along the west coast, and a virus killed off much of the fauna in the Baltic and North Seas.

[37] Gas emissions from Soviet industries increased the fall of acid rain and polluted snow in northern Scandinavia. In 1989, the USSR committed itself to a 40 per cent reduction in emissions before 1993.

[38] The social service and welfare system established in Sweden by the Social Democrats was aimed at ensuring a minimum level of assistance and a more egalitarian wealth redistribution, through graduated taxation of the highest income groups.

[39] In spite of the important benefits obtained by the Swedish population, the largest taxpayers managed to evade taxation. On Carlsson's initiative, parliament approved a fiscal reform in 1989, but it was considered too liberal and divided the Social Democrats.

[40] Under this new law, citizens with incomes below a certain level would pay the same rate of tax, at 30 per cent. The rate for incomes above this limit went down from 72 to 50 per cent, while capital started to be taxed directly.

[41] Toward the end of the 1980s, the prospect of the European Union rekindled debate in Sweden over relations with its main trading partners. Until that time, Sweden had been a member of OECD, the Council of Europe and EFTA (European Free Trade Association). It was also on the Nordic Council, which had created a common labor market and had achieved a high degree of uniformity in legislation among the five member countries.

[42] In 1990 negotiations were held in order to create a "European economic space" and in June 1991 Sweden - represented by the

Carlsson government - applied for entry to the EC.

[43] In the September 1991 elections, the Social Democrats lost their parliamentary majority. A coalition of the Moderate, Liberal, Center, and Christian Democratic parties appointed Carl Bildt, the leader of the Moderates, as prime minister. The new government promised to speed up the union of Sweden with the EC, and the liberalization of the country's economy.

[44] In the last three elections, three new political parties have entered the Swedish Parliament: the Green Party, which had seats in 1988 but lost them in 1991; the Christian Democrats, in the new government coalition, and the New Democracy, a right-wing party. Both of the latter gained their first seats in 1991.

[45] By the end of 1991, unemployment in Sweden hit a record 160,000 workers, doubling figures for the previous year. An additional 83,000 people were receiving vocational training, and 14,000 had been absorbed by government unemployment schemes.

[46] In 1991 and 92, the economic crisis served as the background for a wave of xenophobia and attacks perpetrated against foreigners, phenomena which had previously been non-existent in a country that had had liberal immigration and asylum policies throughout the 1960s and 1970s.

[47] The government budget for the 1992-93 fiscal year involved serious cutbacks in public spending. This refuelled the controversy over the Swedish model, whose main features are a strong public sector and heavy taxation. In late January, for the first time in 35 years, thousands of Swedish construction workers held demonstrations, demanding jobs.

[48] The president of the trade union confederation, Stig Malm, considered the government plan a declaration of war. However, because of the high unemployment rate, trade unions were in a weak position to use confrontational tactics. Bildt had the support of employers, but his parliamentary majority depended on the vote of the New Democracy, which was not its unconditional ally.

[49] On August 26 1993, the King opened a new parliament for the Sami population of Lapland. There are currently 17,000 Sami in Lapland, of a total population of 60,000 living in Norway (40,000), Finland, Russia and Sweden. Most of the people by herd reindeer, with 10 per cent living by hunting deer. A major dispute with the government is in process over the abolition of the Sami's exclusive hunting rights over their lands.

[50] Sami children are given two weeks off in the autumn and two weeks in the spring, in order for them to learn about pasturing reindeer. In 1971, the law regulating reindeer-raising recognized special Sami rights over the lands and watercourses where this is practised.

[51] Unemployment rose significantly during 1993, and in 1994 it reached a record 13 per cent of the active population. Also in 1994, GDP increased for the first time since 1990, while fiscal deficit remained higher than in many European countries: 13 per cent of the gross product.

[52] After a contentious electoral campaign, in a referendum held in November, 52 per cent of voters approved Sweden's entry into the European Union (EU). A significant part of the political establishment and a number of entrepreneurs supported entry, while left-wing groups and environmentalists were against it. There were also "geographical" disagreements, since the majority of southern urban population voted for it and rural and northern inhabitants voted against it.

[53] The referendum was an acid test for Social Democrats - who had returned to power that same year, after obtaining a small majority in parliament in the general elections - because their party did not succeed in reaching an agreement and had a divided opinion on the EU issue. Entry into the former European Community came into force on January 1 1995. In September, the disappointment of many Swedes became evident in the European elections. Groups against entry took 30 per cent of the vote, doubling the percentage of the general election of the previous year. The turnout for the elections was only 41 per cent.

STATISTICS

DEMOGRAPHY
Population: 8,819,000 (1996). **Annual growth:** 0.4% (1980/1996). **Estimates for year 2000:** 9,000,000. **Annual growth to year 2000:** 0.3% (1994/2000). **Urban Population:** 83.1% (1996). **Urban growth:** 0.42% (1980/95). **Children per woman:** 1.9 (1996).

HEALTH
Life expectancy at birth: 78 years (1996) male: 76 years (1994) female: 81 years (1994). **Infant mortality:** 4 per 1,000 (1996). **Under-5 child mortality:** 4 per 1,000 (1996). **Calorie consumption:** 111% (1988/90). 395 **people per doctor** (1988/91).

EDUCATION
School enrolment: Primary total: 100% (1990/95) male: 100% (1990/95) female: 100% (1990/95). Secondary: male: 99% (1990/95) female: 100% (1990/95). Tertiary: 43% (1995). **Primary school teachers:** one for every 11 students (1995).

COMMUNICATIONS
480 **newspapers**, 879 **radios**, 470 **TV sets** and 683 **main telephone lines** per 1,000 people (1994). **Books:** 158 new titles per 100,000 people (1992/94).

ECONOMY
Per capita, GNP: $ 25,710 (1996). **Annual growth, GNP:** 0.8% (1995/96). **Annual inflation:** 5.48% (1985/95). **Consumer price index:** 119.7 (1994). **Currency:** 6.66 kronor = $ 1 (1995) **Cereal imports:** 211 metric tons (1994). **Fertilizer use:** 1,148 kgs per ha (1994). **Exports:** $ 82,704 million (1996). **Imports:** $ 63,970 million (1996).

ENERGY
Consumption: 5,722.77 Kgs of Oil equivalent per capita yearly (1994). 37.63% imported (1994).

HDI (rank / value) 10 / 0.936 (1994)

[54] Relations with France, one of the 15 members of the EU, became complicated because Stockholm openly criticized Paris' decision to hold further nuclear tests in late 1995 and 1996. In the domestic field, Social Democrats continued their policy of reducing public deficit, by increasing taxes and reducing state expenditure, which brought about the confidence of the so-called "international financial markets".

[55] In May 1996, Minister of Finance Göran Persson replaced Carlsson and became head of a government that included 11 women and 10 men.

[56] Once in power, Persson made an effort to ease the budget deficit through tax increases. Meanwhile, unemployment continued to affect 13 per cent of the active population.

[57] In September, the Prime Minister announced measures aimed to make the labour market more "flexible". The powerful Confederation of Swedish Unions considered the proposals an attack on worker security. Furthermore, it accused the Government of "swerving to the right" and threatened to withhold its annual contribution to the governing Social Democratic Party funds.

[58] In January 1997, Persson announced the formation of a new cabinet. Defence Minister Thage Peterson was replaced by Björn von Sydow. The Government announced the budget would be balanced in 1998.

[59] In August it was revealed that some 60,000 people, mostly women, had been sterilised between 1935 and 1976, as part of a government plan aiming to prevent "inferior human beings from multiplying". The concept of the "purity" of the Swedish race had been defined in 1922 by the Uppsala Institute of Racial Biology. The Government authorized a parliamentary investigation into the issue.

[60] At the end of the year, with a healthier economic situation - with lower unemployment (achieved, some believed, by government short-term programs which masked the real situation) the Government announced it would not be participating in monetary union with other EU nations, saying the project was "highly dubious".

Switzerland

Schweiz / Confederatio Helvetica

Population: 7,224,000 (1996)
Area: 41,84 SQ KM
Capital: Bern

Currency: Swiss franc
Language: German, French and Italian

Some Celtic tribes occupied the territory of Switzerland before Roman colonization. The most important of these were the Helvetians, who settled in the Alps and the Jura mountains. The area was strategically important for Rome, with access to its dominions. Consequently, the Alpine valleys north of the Italian peninsula were conquered by Julius Caesar in 58 BC.

[2] The Germanic tribes north of the Rhine invaded from the year 260 onwards. Between the 5th and 6th centuries the Germans established permanent settlements in the region east of the Aar river, together with Burgundian and Frankish groups. By 639 they had founded the kingdoms that would later become France.

[3] The Christian survivors from Roman times had completely disappeared when St Columba and St Gall arrived in the 6th century. These missionaries created the dioceses of Chur, Sion, Basel, Constance and Lausanne. Monasteries were built, in Saint-Gall, Zurich, Disentis and Romainmotier.

[4] Until the partition of Verdun, in 843, these territories belonged to Charlemagne's empire. Thereafter, the region west of the Aar was allotted to Lothair, while the east remained in the hands of Louis the German. The French and German influence formed a peculiar blend with the Latin tradition of the Roman Catholic Church.

[5] Around 1033, for dynastic and political reasons, Helvetia became a part of the Holy Roman Empire, remaining so during the Middle Ages. In the 11th century the region was divided after the re-establishment of imperial authority and its disputes with the Papacy. Dukes, counts, and bishops exerted virtually autonomous local power.

[6] Walled cities served as administrative and commercial centres, and protected powerful families seeking to expand their possessions through wars against other lords and kingdoms. In the 13th century, Rudolf IV of Hapsburg conquered most of the territories of Kyburg and became the most powerful lord in the region.

[7] In the cities independence gradually developed in opposition to the nobility. Meanwhile the peasant communities, in the most inaccessible valleys, practised economic cooperation to survive the harsh conditions, rejecting forced labor and payment of tithes in cash or kind.

[8] In 1231 Uri fell under the authority of the Holy Roman Empire, and in 1240 Schwyz and Nidwald were subjected to Emperor Frederick II, although retaining the right to choose their own magistrates.

[9] The Hapsburg overlords questioned this freedom and uncertainty remained until Rudolf of Hapsburg was crowned king of Germany, in 1273. He exerted his imperial rights in Uri and inherited rights over Schwytz and Unterwald until his death in 1291. These regions, thereafter constituted the Perpetual League.

[10] As with other circumstantial alliances among the regions, the Perpetual League constituted an agreement for dispute arbitration, putting law above armed strength. The honorary magistrates had to be residents of those cantons.

[11] The league of the Uri, Schwyz, and Unterwald cantons was joined by the city of Zurich, constituting the first historic antecedent of the Swiss Confederation. This confederation was consolidated with the victory of Margarten in 1315, defeating an army of knights sent to impose imperial law in the region by the Hapsburgs.

[12] The Confederation was supported by new alliances. In 1302 the League signed a pact with the city of Luzern, previously dependent on Vienna. In 1315 Zurich reaffirmed its union and in 1353 it was joined by Bern. The Glarus and Zug cantons joined later, forming the core of an independent state within the Germanic Empire.

[13] During the second half of the 14th century, the rural oligarchy was defeated, and their lands and laws given over to city councils. This democratic rural movement gave birth to the "Landesgemeinde", a sovereign assembly of canton inhabitants and a similar movement was led by the city guilds.

[14] The Confederation soon launched into territorial conquest. During the 15th century the union grew to 13 cantons, it made alliances with other states, and the institution of government known as the Diet was formed where each canton was represented by two seats and one vote.

[15] In 1516, after the defeat of the Helvetians, the King of France forced a peace treaty with the cantons. In 1521 an alliance gave France the right to recruit Swiss soldiers. Only Zurich refused to sign this alliance, maintaining military and economic links with the Old Confederation until its end in 1798.

[16] The Reformation came to Switzerland with Huldrych Zwingli, a priest who preached against the mercenary service and the corruption and power of the clergy. Popular support for Zwingli strengthened the urban bourgeoisie. The Reformation became more radical in rural areas where harsh repression re-established the domination of cities over peasants.

[17] Zwingli's attempt to alter the federal alliance to benefit the reformed cities was frustrated by the military victory of the Catholic rural areas. The second national peace of Kappel, signed in

PUBLIC EXPENDITURE

15.2% **75.2%**
1995 ■ DEFENCE □ SOCIAL

In 1990/91 Military as % of health & education expenditure was 14%.

WORKERS

UNEMPLOYMENT 3.7% **(1996)**
Labour force %

■ WOMEN
□ MEN

40   60

■ AGRICULTURE	6%	(1990)
□ INDUSTRIAL	35%	
■ SERVICES	60%	

LAND USE

IRRIGATED **6.3%** of arable

(1993)

■ FOREST & WOODLAND	30.3%
□ ARABLE	9.6%
■ OTHER	60.1%

Foreign Trade

MILLIONS $ 1996

IMPORTS
79,192
EXPORTS
80,756

Maternal Mortality

1990

PER 100,000
LIVE BIRTHS
6

PROFILE

ENVIRONMENT

A small landlocked state in continental Europe, Switzerland is a mountainous country made up of three natural regions. To the northwest, on the French border, are the massive Jura mountains, an agricultural and industrial (watchmaking) area. Industry is concentrated in the Mitteland, a sub-Alpine depression between the Jura and the Alps, with numerous lakes of glacial origin. It is also an agricultural and cattle-raising region. The Alps cover more than half of the territory and extend in a west-east direction with peaks of over 4,000 meters. The main activities of this region are dairy farming and tourism. The country's ecosystem is currently threatened by acid rain.

SOCIETY

Peoples: Two-thirds of the population are of German origin, while 18 per cent and 13 per cent are French and Italian, respectively. 17.1 per cent of the country's citizens or permanent residents are Italian, Yugoslav, Portuguese, German, Turkish or other nationalities. **Religions:** 47.6 per cent Catholic, 44.3 per cent Protestant, 2.2 per cent Muslim, 1 per cent Orthodox Christian. **Languages:** German, French and Italian. A very small minority (0.4 per cent) in certain parts of the Grisons canton to the east speak Rhaeto-Romanic (or Romansch), of Latin origin. **Political Parties:** Major political parties are: the Social Democrats; the center-right Radical Party; the center-right Christian Democratic Party; the center-left Swiss People's Party; the center-left Socialist Party; the Democratic Union of the Centre, the right-wing Liberal Party; the Independent Party; and the leftist Labor Party. The ecologist Greens. **Social Organizations:** The Swiss Federation of Trade Unions, with 480,000 members; the Confederation of Christian Trade Unions, with 110,000 members; the Federation of Swiss Employees' Societies with 160,000 members.

THE STATE

Official Name: Confoederatio Helvetica (Romansche); Schweizerische Eidgenossenschaft (German); Confédération Suisse (French); Confederazione Svizzera (Italian). Administrative Divisions: 20 Cantons, 6 Sub-Cantons. **Capital:** Bern (administrative), 128,422 people; Lausanne (judicial) 117,.553 (1995). **Other cities:** Zurich, 342,872 people; Basel, 175,561; Geneva 172,737; Lausanne, 117,153 (1995). **Government:** Arnold Koller, President since 1997. Parliamentary republic with strong direct democracy. The legislative power is exercised by a federal assembly, with two bodies: the State Council, with 46 members, and the National Council, with 200 members. The executive power is in the hands of the Federal Council, with 7 members elected by parliament for 4-year terms. **National Holiday:** August 1. **Armed Forces:** 3,400 regular troops (1995) 28,000 annual conscripts (15 week courses). **Other:** 480,000 Civil Defence.

1531 gave the Catholic minority advantages over the Protestant majority.

[18] The areas where both religions coexisted were subject to constant tension, but cooperation was required to preserve the union of the federation. In Catholic regions agriculture prevailed, while in Protestant areas trade and industry flourished, aided by French, Italian and Dutch refugees.

[19] Popular consultation disappeared in the 17th century. The power of the cities caused uprisings, such as the great peasant revolt of 1653, which were harshly repressed. Three years later when a further war ensued the prerogatives of the Catholic cantons were re-established.

[20] During the European conflicts of the 17th and 18th centuries Switzerland remained neutral because of its religious division and its mercenary armies. Neutrality became a condition for the Confederation's existence. The policy of armed neutrality, which still holds, was first formulated by the Diet in 1674.

[21] In 1712 the Protestant victory in the second battle of Villmergen ended religious struggles, ensuring the hegemony of cities which were undergoing industrial expansion. Switzerland became the most industrialized country in Europe. Industry was based on labor at home, completely transforming work in the countryside.

[22] Throughout the 18th century, a series of popular revolts against the urban oligarchy called for the reform of the Swiss Constitution. In March 1798, the Old Confederation fell under pressure from Napoleon's army. The Helvetic Republic was proclaimed, "whole and indivisible", with sovereignty for the people.

[23] Between the unitary Republic and the 1848 Federal Constitution, Switzerland was shaken by coups, popular revolts, and civil wars. The new federal pact marked a final victory for liberalism in the country. Two legislative bodies were established guaranteeing the rights of the small Catholic cantons.

[24] A state monopoly was created for custom duties and coin minting, while weights and measures were unified, so satisfying the industrial and commercial bourgeoisie's economic requirements. The 1848 Constitution thus removed the obstacles to capitalist expansion.

[25] Nepotism and the concentration of capital benefited only the few and fuelled growing opposition to the institutional system. The 1874 Constitution partially addressed these issues, and introduced the mechanism of referendum as an element of direct democracy.

[26] Expansion of the home labor system delayed organization of the Swiss workers' movement in relation to the country's industrialization. The Swiss Workers' Federation, created in 1873 had only 3,000 members, and the Swiss Workers' Union, which replaced it in 1880, only exceeded this figure ten years later.

[27] The first achievement of the workers' movement was factory legislation, passed by parliament in 1877. The working day was limited to 11 hours with improved working conditions. In 1888 the Socialist Party was formed to give workers a political voice.

[28] In 1910, 15 per cent of the workers in Switzerland were foreign. Many were anarchists and socialists who had suffered persecution in their own countries and they consequently encouraged radical positions in the workers' movement. The Swiss Workers' Union took up a platform of "proletarian class struggle", and the Socialist Party was inspired by the Second International's Marxism.

[29] World War I brought great internal tensions to Switzerland, especially between the French- and German-speaking regions. Under the leadership of Ulrich Wile, the Swiss army cooperated with Germany. Tension only decreased after the French victory, when Switzerland formally approached the allies and became a member of the League of Nations.

[30] Clashes between trade unions and employers echoed the tensions between the different language regions. The 1918 general strike, although lifted three days later under pressure from the armed forces, led the bourgeoisie to form an anti-Socialist bloc. That year proportional representation was introduced.

[31] The elections in 1919 marked the end of the liberal hegemony, in place since 1848. The Socialists obtained 20 per cent of the vote, leading liberals to ally with the peasants who had 14 per cent, while the conservatives became the second power in the Federal Council.

[32] These changes produced noticeable consequences during the following years. The 48-hour week was included in factory legislation, while in 1925 an article on old-age pensions was added to the constitution. Assistance to the unemployed improved and collective work contracts became more common.

[33] In the years before World War II, the Socialist Party was threatened by foreign and national fascism, and a sector split to form the Communist Party. The socialists were forced to include formal recognition of the state and national defence in their policies.

[34] During World War II, European powers recognized Swiss armed neutrality, but the country still suffered strong pressure from Nazi Germany. Throughout the war Switzerland maintained a delicate balance between accepting Hitler's advances and defending its independence; a strategy that kept them out of the conflict.

[35] After the war, the West resented Switzerland's relations with Germany, and the USSR refused to re-establish diplomatic relations, broken off 1918. However, the country's financial power paved the way for its return to the international community. During the Cold War, Switzerland sided with the West but did not join the UN, in order to preserve its neutrality.

[36] The Swiss economy expanded greatly during the postwar period. The chemical, food, and machinery exporting industries became great transnational corporations. In 1973 Switzerland was placed fourth in direct foreign capital

investments, after the US, France, and Britain.

[37] Switzerland's main transnational corporation, the food and babymilk manufacturer Nestlé AG, had 196,940 workers worldwide and sales worth $29.36 billion in 1989.

[38] The Swiss economic expansion attracted workers from Italy, Spain and other southern European countries. Between 1945 and 1974 the number of immigrants rose from 5 to 17 per cent. Several referenda called for an end to immigration and the 1974-76 crisis forced thousands of people back to their countries.

[39] Due to its political neutrality, Switzerland did not join the European Economic Community in 1957. However, it has been a member of EFTA (European Free Trade Association) since 1960. In 1983 Swiss development aid constituted only five per cent of the total capital invested in poor countries.

[40] In 1959, after 10 years of voluntary absence, the socialists joined the Federal Council with two representatives. The Executive consisted of two Radicals, two Christian Democrats, two Socialists, and a peasants' representative. This meant that 80 per cent of the electorate was represented in government.

[41] Women gained the right to vote in 1971, but some cantons retained male-only suffrage until 1985. In 1984, the first woman minister was elected when Elisabeth Kopp was made minister for justice and police.

[42] Switzerland is governed by consensus, but the population has increasingly abstained in referendums. In the 1979 elections participation was lower than 50 per cent for the first time.

[43] New economic and social phenomena have occurred. The labor structure has become more differentiated and minorities (women, young and old people, immigrants) are still subject to discrimination, bringing the institutional system into question.

[44] During the 1980s new opposition groups appeared, some feminist, some opposed to nuclear plants, and some youth groups fighting against the consumer society. A referendum in 1981 added a clause on equal rights to the Constitution.

[45] According to 1981 statistics, male students outnumber female by three to one in Switzerland. Women accounted for no more than 32.5 per cent of the economically active population, while men made up 63.9 per cent.

[46] Since 1986 environmental problems have become more serious and the Government has taken measures to curb pollution, especially acid rain and pollution of the Rhine. In 1987 France, Germany and the Netherlands received compensation for damage caused by an accident in the Swiss chemical industry.

[47] Another serious problem is the damage to the Alpine ecosystem. The rapid growth of cities in this area, and the increased transit of heavy trucks, have contributed to regional desertification. As a direct result, so-called natural disasters, such as floods and avalanches of rock, mud and snow have increased; events that would be less likely to occur if the area still had the protection offered by its natural tree coverage.

[48] The Chernobyl disaster greatly concerned the Swiss population and in 1989, a series of demonstrations took place. A referendum proposed the gradual elimination of existing nuclear power plants, and the Federal Parliament cancelled the construction of a sixth nuclear station.

[49] Increasing social problems and the presence of immigrants have given encouragement to the Swiss extreme right. Although being small, the Swiss Democratic Party and the Party of Drivers, xenophobic and opposed to social security policies, have both gained support since the fall of the Berlin Wall.

[50] Switzerland's integration into the IMF was approved by a plebiscite in May 1992. In June 1993, Parliament approved the incorporation of Swiss troops into the United Nations peacekeeping forces. This represented an important change in Switzerland's traditional policy of neutrality. However, most of the Swiss voted against this proposal in a referendum in 1994.

[51] One of the main obstacles to Swiss integration into the

European Union was the objection to the free movement of workers between countries. A referendum in the same year approved an anti-racism law which punished discrimination while another granted the police powers to use greater "harshness" against illegal immigrants committing crimes within the country. This measure was widely criticized and considered a violation of the Swiss Constitution and the European Human Rights Convention.

[52] In the general elections of October 22 1995, the Social Democrats took 54 seats, the Radicals 45, the Christian Democrats, 34, the Swiss People's Party 29 and the Greens 9.

[53] A government study on unemployment forecast a substantial reduction by the year

2000. If annual growth in GDP did not fall below 2.25 per cent, unemployment would only claim 60,000 people in that year, compared with 192,000 in 1996.

[54] In July 1997, Swiss banks - sued internationally by individuals - released a list of names of account-holders with funds untouched since World War II. Most of these were Jews later exterminated by the Nazis. The World Jewish Congress, the main plaintiff, said this presentation was a mere symbolic gesture, as the banks had taken advantage of the funds for over 50 years.

[56] In September 1997, 50.8 per cent of voters in a referendum rejected the reduction in unemployment benefit proposed by the Government. Observers claimed this could complicate the planned economic austerity measures.

STATISTICS

DEMOGRAPHY
Population: 7,224,000 (1996). **Annual growth:** 0.8% (1980/1996). **Estimates for year 2000:** 7,400,000. **Annual growth to year 2000:** 0.7% (1994/2000). **Urban Population:** 61.3% (1996). **Urban growth:** 1.17% (1980/95). **Children per woman:** 1.5 (1996).

HEALTH
Life expectancy at birth: 78 years (1996) male: 75 years (1994) female: 82 years (1994). **Infant mortality:** 5 per 1,000 (1996). **Under-5 child mortality:** 5 per 1,000 (1996). **Calorie consumption:** 130% (1988/90). 585 **people per doctor** (1988/91).

EDUCATION
School enrolment: Primary total: 101% (1990/95) male: 100% (1990/95) female:102% (1990/95). Secondary: male: 93% (1990/95) female: 89% (1990/95). Tertiary: 32% (1995). **Primary school teachers:** one for every 12 students (1995).

COMMUNICATIONS
410 **newspapers**, 841 **radios**, 400 **TV sets** and 597 **main telephone lines** per 1,000 people (1994). **Books:** 217 new titles per 100,000 people (1992/94).

ECONOMY
Per capita, GNP: $ 44,350 (1996). **Annual growth, GNP:** -1.2% (1995/96). **Annual inflation:** 3.37% (1985/95). **Consumer price index:** 114.8 (1994). **Currency:** 1.15 swiss francs = $ 1 (1995) **Cereal imports:** 380 metric tons (1994). **Fertilizer use:** 3,364 kgs per ha (1994). **Exports:** $ 80,756 million (1996). **Imports:** $ 79,192 million (1996).

ENERGY
Consumption: 3,628.82 Kgs of Oil equivalent per capita yearly (1994). 56.54% imported (1994).

HDI (rank / value) 16 / 0.93 (1994)

Syria

Suriyah

Population:	14,574,000 (1996)
Area:	185,180 SQ KM
Capital:	Damascus (Dimashq)
Currency:	Pound
Language:	Arabic

Syria was once the name for the entire region between the peninsulas of Anatolia (Turkey) and Sinai. Ancient civilizations coveted the territory: the Egyptians wanted it as a port, while the Persians considered the region a bridge to their plans of a universal empire.

2 Between the 12th and 7th centuries BC, the Phoenician civilization developed on the central coastal stretch of the territory; a society of sailors and traders without expansionist aims. Phoenician cities were always independent, although some exercised temporary hegemony over others, and they developed the world's first commercial economy.

3 The Phoenicians invented the alphabet, constructed ocean-going ships, practised large-scale ceramic and textile manufacturing, expanded and systematized geography, sailing around the coast of Africa. The propagation of these throughout the Mediterranean helped form what would be later called "Western civilization," of which the Greeks were the main exponents.

4 The territory came under the control of Alexander of Macedonia (also known as Alexander the Great) during the 4th century BC. After Alexander's death, his vast empire was divided and Syria became the center of a Seleucidan state (named for Seleucus Nicator, one of Alexander's generals) that initially stretched as far as India. The eastern part was later lost to the Parthians. In the Roman era the province of Syria was a border zone constantly shaken by fierce local wars and resistance. One example of the latter was Queen

Zenobia, whom the Romans finally managed to defeat in 272 AD.

5 The Arabization of the territory was carried out by the Ummaia Caliphs, who, between the years 650 and 750, turned Damascus (Dimashq) into the capital of the empire (see Saudi Arabia), and fostered a strong national spirit. When the Ummaias were defeated by the Abbas, the capital was transferred to Baghdad, where the new caliphs enjoyed greater support. Although still economically and culturally important, the loss of political power proved significant: in the 11th century when Europeans invaded during the Crusades, the caliphs of Baghdad reacted with indifference. Local emirs were left to their own resources, and disagreements among them allowed a small Christian force to conquer the area, leading to 200-years of occupation.

6 The Egyptians initiated the process to drive out the Europeans. One result was that Syria became a virtual Egyptian province and center stage for a confrontation with Mongol invaders. In the 16th century, the country became a part of the Ottoman Empire.

7 The Crusaders left behind a significant Christian community, especially with the Maronites, serving as sufficient cause for European interference from the 17th century onwards. The Egyptian Khedive Muhammad (Mehemet) Ali conquered Syria in 1831, and heavy taxes and compulsory military service provoked revolt among both Christian and Muslim communities. The European powers, concerned with propping

OCCUPIED BY ISRAEL	1	Southern Lebanon 1983
	2	Syria - Golan Heights 1967
	3	West Bank 1967 (some towns now have autonomy)

up the Turkish Empire to stave off the potential emergence of a more aggressive power like Egypt, used the repression of Christians as an excuse for intervention. Ali's offensive was suppressed and the "protection of Syrian Christians" was entrusted to the French. A withdrawal of Egyptian troops took place in 1840, along with the restoration of Ottoman domination and the establishment of Christian missions and schools subsidized by Europeans.

8 However, the scene was set for confrontation and in 1858, Maronite Christians gathered in the mountainous region between Damascus and Jerusalem rebelled against the ruling class and eliminated the traditional system of land ownership. Their Muslim neighbors, particularly the Druze,

moved to repress the movement before it spread further, triggering a conflict that culminated in the deaths of a large number of Christians in June 1860.

9 A month later, French troops disembarked in Beirut, ostensibly to protect the Christian community, and forcing the Turkish Government to create a separate province called "Little Lebanon." This was to be governed by a Christian appointed by the Sultan but with the approval of the European powers, with its own police force, and traditional privileges were abolished in the territory. The social conflict thus became a confrontation between confessional groups with the Christians in "Little Lebanon" placed in a position of superiority over the local Muslim population, providing firm roots for the politico-religious conflict that has marked Lebanese history ever since.

10 When an Arab rebellion broke out during World War I (see Saudi Arabia, Jordan and Iraq), Emir Faisal was proclaimed king of Syria. At the time French and British intentions were unknown, but the Sykes-Picot agreement divided the fertile crescent giving Syria (with Lebanon) to France, and Palestine (including Jordan) and Iraq to Britain.

11 In 1920 France occupied Syria forcing Faisal to retreat. Two

PUBLIC EXPENDITURE

28.2%   **26.8%**

1995 ■ **DEFENCE** □ **SOCIAL**

In **1990/91** Military as % of health & education expenditure was 373%.

WORKERS

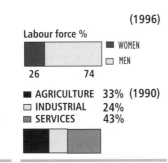

(1996)

Labour force %

■ WOMEN
□ MEN

26   74

■ AGRICULTURE 33% (1990)
□ INDUSTRIAL 24%
■ SERVICES 43%

LAND USE

DEFORESTATION -2.8% annual (81/90)
IRRIGATED 17.7 % of arable

(1993)

■ FOREST & WOODLAND 3.5%
□ ARABLE 27.6%
■ OTHER 68.9%

PER 100,000
LIVE BIRTHS
180 71%

PROFILE

ENVIRONMENT
To the west, near the sea, lies the Lebanon mountain range. To the south there are semi-desert plateaus and to the north low plateaus along the basin of the Euphrates River. Farming -grains, grapes and fruit- is concentrated in the western lowlands that receive adequate rainfall. In the south, the volcanic plateaus of the Djebel Druze are extremely fertile farmlands, some as the oases surrounding the desert, the main one being that of Damascus. Cotton and wool are exported. Exploitation of oil fields is the country's chief industry. The dumping of toxic substances from the extraction of crude is responsible for the high levels of pollution of Syria's waters.

SOCIETY
Peoples: Syrians are mostly Arabs, with minority ethnic groups in the north: Kurds, Turks and Armenians. There are few statistics on the number of Palestinian refugees (they were around 200,000 in 1977), and the Jewish population was authorized to emigrate in 1992.
Religions: Mainly Muslims, mostly Sunni, followed by Alamites, Shiites and Ismailites. Also minor communities of eastern Christian religions.
Languages: Arabic (official). Minority groups speak their own languages. **Political Parties:** The Ba'ath Arab Socialist Party, founded in Damascus in 1947 by Michel Aflaq, including the National Progressive Front and other minor parties. The armed political-religious opposition is represented by the Muslim Brotherhood, a fundamentalist Sunni sect. **Social Organizations:** The General Federation of Labor Unions unites ten workers' federations representing different sectors of the economy.

THE STATE
Official Name: Al-Jumhouriya al Arabiya as-Suriya. **Administrative Divisions:** 14 Districts. **Capital:** Damascus (Dimashq), 1,591,400 people (1995). **Other cities:** Aleppo (Halab), 1,591,000 people; Homs (Hims), 644,000; Latakia, 306,500; Hamah, 229,000 (1994). **Government:** Hafez al-Assad, President since 1970, reelected in 1971, 1978, 1985 and 1991; Mahmoud Az Zoubi, Prime Minister. The People's Council (a unicameral legislature) has 195 members. **National Holidays:** April 17, Independence Day (1946); November 16, Revolution Day (1978). **Armed Forces:** 421, 000 troops (1996). **Other:** 8,000 Gendarmes.

months later, Syria was divided into five states: Greater Lebanon (adding other regions to the province of "Little Lebanon"), Damascus, Aleppo, Djabal Druza and Alawis (Latakia). The latter four were reunified in 1924.
[12] Throughout 1932, Syria experienced a period of relative stability, and independence seemed imminent. A Syrian president and parliament were elected that year, but France made it clear that autonomy was unacceptable. This attitude engendered political agitation and confrontation, which only ended with a 1936 agreement with the French. France recognized certain Syrian demands, chiefly reunification with Lebanon. However, the French Government never ratified the

agreement, and this led to new waves of violence, which culminated in the 1939 resignation of the Syrian President and a French order to suspend the 1930 constitution that governed both Syria and Lebanon.
[13] In 1941, French and British troops occupied the region to flush out Nazi collaborators. In 1943 Chikri al-Quwatli was elected president of Syria, and Bechara al-Kuri, president of Lebanon. Bechara al-Kuri proposed elimination of the mandate provisions from the constitution; however, he and his cabinet members were imprisoned by the ever-present French troops. Violent demonstrations followed in both Lebanon and Syria, and the British pressed for withdrawal of the French. In March 1946, the

United Nations finally ordered the European forces to withdraw. This was completed in 1947 and the end of the French mandate was officially declared.
[14] In 1948 Syrian troops fought to prevent the partition of Palestine, and in 1956 joined Egypt in the battle against Israeli, French and British aggression. This aggression was the answer to Egyptian President Gamal Abdel Nasser's decision to nationalize the Suez Canal.
[15] In 1958, Syria joined Egypt in founding the United Arab Republic, but Nasser's ambitious integration project collapsed in 1961. Ten years later the scheme was reactivated, with greater flexibility and the Federation of Arab Republics was created including Libya.
[16] In 1963, after a revolution, the Ba'ath Arab Socialist Party came to power. Their main tenet was that the Arab countries were merely "regions" of a larger Arab Nation. In November 1970, General Hafez al-Assad became president. He launched a modernization campaign, including a series of social and economic changes. The subsequent party congress named Assad party leader and proposed "accelerating the stages towards socialist transformation of different sectors." This guideline was adopted, and became part of the new constitution which was approved in 1973.
[17] Syria took an active part in the Arab-Israeli wars of 1967 and 1973, during which Israeli troops occupied the Golan Heights. Syria also resisted US efforts to impose a "settlement" in the Middle East, together with Algeria, Iraq, Libya, Yemen and the Palestine Liberation Organization (PLO). They also opposed the Camp David agreement (see Egypt).
[18] Syrian troops formed a major part of the Arab Deterrent Force that intervened in Lebanon in 1976 to prevent partition of the country by right-wing Lebanese factions allied with Israel.
[19] In 1978, the Syrian and Iraqi branches of the Ba'ath Party drew closer, but negotiations for creation of a single state disintegrated. In late 1979, at the congress of the Syrian branch of the Ba'ath Party, the Muslim

Brotherhood (a right-wing Islamic movement) was harshly censured and were labelled "zionist agents".
[20] In 1980, the Government set a September deadline giving brotherhood members the opportunity to surrender before capital punishment was enforced for acts of sabotage.
[21] Brotherhood attacks continued. In 1982 the army launched a full offensive which resulted in thousands of casualties. The Syrian Government blamed Iraq for arming the rebels, and closed the border between the two countries in April 1982. Iraq retaliated by closing the oil pipeline connecting Kirkuk, Iraq, to the Syrian port of Banias.
[22] The virtual alliance formed in 1980 between Saudi Arabia, Iraq and Jordan and tensions between those three countries and Syria were exacerbated by the outbreak of the Iran-Iraq War. Assad charged Iraq as the aggressor and diverted attention from what he called the major regional issue - the Palestinian question. Toward the end of the year, Syrian accusations of Jordanian support for the Brotherhood brought the two countries to the verge of war. The mediation of Saudi prince Abdalla Ibn Abdul-Aziz averted armed conflict.
[23] In 1981 the "missile crisis" broke out in Syria, when the Christian Phalangist Movement sought to extend their area of authority to include the area around the Lebanese city of Zahde. An Arab Deterrent Force, organized and commanded by Syria, attempted to prevent the advance. Syria installed Soviet surface-to-air SAM-9 missiles, triggering an Israeli reaction. The crisis was finally averted, but in 1982 Israel invaded Lebanon, and destroyed the bases of Syrian missiles.
[24] In mid-1983 there was a crisis between the Syrian authorities and the PLO leadership. This encouraged Syria to support the Palestinian groups opposed to Yasser Arafat's leadership, until the division ended in 1987. The fall in oil prices further aggravated the economic problems caused by the war and the Government set up strict austerity measures in 1984: financial activities were tightly controlled, borders were closed to the illegal trafficking of

Food Dependency

1970
21%

1994
10%

External Debt

1996

PER CAPITA
$1,470

Foreign Trade

MILLIONS $ 1996

IMPORTS
6,399
EXPORTS
3,980

STATISTICS

DEMOGRAPHY
Population: 14,574,000 (1996). **Annual growth:** 3.2% (1980/ 1996). **Estimates for year 2000:** 16,100,000. **Annual growth to year 2000:** 2.6% (1994/2000). **Urban Population:** 52.7% (1996). **Urban growth:** 4.13% (1980/95). **Children per woman:** 4.2 (1996).

HEALTH
Life expectancy at birth: 68 years (1996) male: 66 years (1994) female: 70 years (1994). **Infant mortality:** 28 per 1,000 (1996). **Under-5 child mortality:** 34 per 1,000 (1996). **Calorie consumption:** 126% (1988/90). 1,220 **people per doctor** (1988/ 91). **Safe water:** 86% (1990/96).

EDUCATION
Literacy: 71% (1995) male: 86% (1995) female: 56% (1995). **School enrolment:** Primary total: 103% (1990/95). male: 108% (1990/95) female: 97% (1990/95). Secondary: male: 50% (1990/ 95) female: 41% (1990/95). Tertiary: 18% (1995). **Primary school teachers:** one for every 24 students (1995).

COMMUNICATIONS
20 **newspapers,** 257 **radios,** 80 **TV sets** and 48 **main telephone lines** per 1,000 people (1994). **Books:** 4 new titles per 100,000 people (1992/94).

ECONOMY
Per capita, GNP: $ 1,160 (1996). **Annual growth, GNP:** 0.6% (1995/96). **Annual inflation:** 15.97% (1985/95). **Consumer price index:** 158.0 (1994). **Currency:** 11.23 pounds = $ 1 (1995) **Cereal imports:** 952 metric tons (1994). **Food import dependency:** 10% (1994). **Fertilizer use:** 635 kgs per ha (1994). **Exports:** $ 3,980 million (1996). **Imports:** $ 6,399 million (1996). **External debt:** $ 21,420 million (1996). $ 1,470 **per capita:** (1996). **Debt service:** 3.8% of exports (1996). **Development aid received:** $ 347 million (1995). $ 25 per capita (1995).

ENERGY
Consumption: 997.17 Kgs of Oil equivalent per capita yearly (1994). -130.15% imported (1994).

HDI (rank / value) 78 / 0.755 (1994)

merchandise, previously tolerated, and public expenditure was substantially reduced. Smuggling from Lebanon was reduced by 90 per cent, and the balance of payments deficit halted.

[25] In 1985, President Assad won a new seven-year term. In 1987, Prime Minister Abdul Rauf al-Kassem was forced to resign amid charges of corruption, following the resignation of four other ministers. In November 1987, Mahmoud Az-Zoubi, president of the People's Assembly, was chosen as Prime Minister.

[26] In April 1987, at a summit meeting of Arab countries, most nations sought alignment with Syria, in exchange for economic assistance, and condemned Iranian prolongation of the war. Syria maintained its position on Iran, and vetoed the motion for Egypt's re-entry into the Arab League.

[27] In October 1986, the British Government accused Syria of supporting a terrorist attempt against an Israeli plane at London airport. In November most of the EEC countries broke diplomatic relations with Syria, although there were disagreements from some countries. In July 1987 all the EEC countries except for Britain re-established relations with Syria, when the Syrian Government withdrew support of the Al-Fatah Revolutionary Council, a Palestinian organization which opposed Yasser Arafat. In May 1990, Syria finally re-established diplomatic relations with Egypt.

[28] When Iraq invaded Kuwait, Syria immediately sided with the anti-Iraqi alliance and sent troops to Saudi Arabia. Diplomatic relations with the US improved noticeably. During the crisis Syria increased its influence over Lebanon and strengthened the allied government in that country; they were also successful in disarming most of the autonomous militias.

[29] On April 29 1991, Syrian President Hafez Assad met in Damascus with Iranian President Akbar Ashemi Rafsanjani, and announced his country's military presence would be maintained in Lebanon. He thereby gained the support of the Hezbollah (Party of God), and of the Revolutionary Guards (fundamentalist Iranians).

[30] In April 1991, Syria took part in the Middle East Peace Conference, held in Madrid with US and USSR support. Syria supported the proposal of negotiating with Israel on the basis of UN declarations 242 and 338, which condemned the occupation of territories by Israel. The Arab countries supported the motto "peace for territories", which was rejected by Israel.

[31] In May 1991 Syria and Lebanon signed a cooperation agreement whereby Syria recognized Lebanon as an independent and separate state, for the first time since both countries gained independence from France.

[32] In December 1991, al-Assad was re-elected for the fourth time, by 99.98 per cent of the vote, in elections which had him as sole candidate. That month, the Government announced the pardon of 2,800 political prisoners, members of the Muslim Brotherhood.

[33] In 1992, the Government abolished the death penalty and allowed the emigration of 4,000 Jews. At the economic level, the GNP grew 7 per cent and exports of oil and its by-products amounted to $2 billion. New legislation favored investments in the private sector, which had a significant growth between 1991 and 1993.

[34] Syria stayed away from the first stages of the regional peace process, which enabled the establishment of a limited autonomy for Palestine and the signing of agreements between Israel and Jordan in July 1994. In January, a "historic" meeting took place between US President Bill Clinton and Assad in Geneva and in September, the Syrian minister of foreign affairs was interviewed for the first time on Israeli television. However, Damascus maintained its refusal to negotiate officially with Israel, due to the murder of 29 Palestinians in Hebron, committed by an Israeli settler in February.

[35] In the domestic field, the death of Basel al-Assad, eldest son and supposed successor of the Syrian President, increased uncertainty regarding the country's political future. In August, the ruling National Progressive Front won the general elections but only 49 per cent of registered voters took part.

[36] In June 1995, official negotiations with Israel failed to return of the Golan Heights to Syria as Tel Aviv wanted to maintain limited military presence in the region indefinitely. In October, a Hezbollah ambush of Israeli troops in southern Lebanon complicated negotiations again. In mid 1996, al-Assad participated in a meeting of Arab countries to co-ordinate a common strategy for negotiation with Israel.

[37] As part of a policy to stimulate the Syrian economy private sector, key State sectors, including electricity generation, cement production and pharmaceuticals were opened up to private capital.

[38] In November 1997, Damascus unexpectedly strengthened relations with Baghdad on the threat of fresh US military intervention in Iraq - a strategy designed to work against the rapidly consolidating Turkish-Israeli alliance. Given the situation of the Golan Heights, militarily, Syria would remain in the middle of this new bloc. If Iraq were to be beaten, new States could emerge on the basis of linguistic or religious criteria, with Turkey possibly gaining control of the oil fields of Iraqi Kurdistan.

[39] The threat presented by the Turkish-Israeli military bloc - which planned to produce a thousand new tanks for its armed forces - forced Iran to join the Syrian-Iraqi negotiations on security issues in April 1998.

Tajikistan

Tadzhikistan

Population: 5,935,000 (1996)
Area: 143,100 SQ KM
Capital: Dushanbe (Dusanbe)
Currency: Rouble
Language: Tajik

Around 500 BC, Central Asia and southern Siberia's first centers of settled civilization arose in what is now Tajikistan. The Bactrian State was located in the upper tributaries of the Amu Darya. Likewise, in the Zeravshan river basin and the Kashkadarya river valley lay the nucleus of another State, Sogdiana. The inhabitants of these early civilizations built villages, with adobe and stone houses, all along the rivers, which they used for irrigating their crops. These included wheat, barley and millet, and a variety of fruits. Navigation was well developed and the cities which lay along the route of the caravans uniting Persia, China and India became important trading centers.

[2] In the 6th century BC these lands were annexed by the Persian Achaemenid empire. In the 4th century BC, Alexander the Great conquered Bactria and Sogdiana. With the fall of his empire in the 3rd century, the Greco-Bactrian State and the Kingdom of Kushan emerged, and subsequently fell to the onslaught of the advancing steppe Yuechzhi and Tojar tribes. In the 4th and 5th centuries AD, Sogdiana and its surrounding regions were invaded by the Eftalites, and in the 6th and 7th centuries, by Central Asian Turkish peoples. In the 7th century, Tajikistan became a part of the Arab Caliphate, along with other Central Asian regions. After its demise, the region was incorporated into the Tahirid and Samanid kingdoms. In the 9th and 10th centuries, the Tajik people emerged as an identifiable ethnic group.

[3] From the 10th to the 13th centuries AD, Tajikistan formed part of the Gaznevid and Qarakhanid empires, as well as the realm of the Shah of Khwarezm. In the early 13th century, Tajikistan was conquered by Genghis Khan's Mongol Tatars. In 1238, Tarabi, a Tajik artisan, led a popular revolt. From the 14th to the 17th centuries, the Tajiks were under the control of the Timurids and the Uzbek Shaybanid dynasty. From the 17th to the 19th centuries, there were small fiefdoms throughout Tajikistan whose chieftains alternately submitted to or revolted against the khans of Bukhara.

[4] In the 1860s and 1870s, the Russian Empire conquered Central Asia, and the northern part of

Tajikistan was annexed by Russia. The Khanate of Bukhara however maintained a relation of sovereignty rather than annexation, with Russia. The Tajik population of Kuliab, Guissar, Karateguin and Darvaz was incorporated into the khanate as the province of Eastern Bukhara. Oppression by the Russian bureaucracy and the local feudal lords triggered a wave of peasant revolts toward the end of the 19th century and beginning of the 20th century. The most important of these was the 1885 uprising led by Vose.

[5] In 1916, during World War I, the native populations of Central Asia and Kazakhstan revolted over the mobilization of their people for rearguard duty with the retreating Russian army. After the triumph of the Bolshevik revolution in St Petersburg in October 1917, Soviet power was established in Northern Tajikistan. In April 1918, this territory became a part of the Autonomous Soviet Socialist Republic of Turkistan. Nevertheless, a massive number of Tajiks remained under the power of the Emirate of Bukhara, which existed until 1921. In early 1921, the Red Army took Dushanbe, but in February it was forced to withdraw from Eastern Bukhara.

[6] Having broken Alim Khan's resistance in 1921-22, Soviet power was proclaimed throughout the entire territory of Tajikistan. In 1924, the Soviet Socialist Republic of Uzbekistan was formed, of which the Autonomous Soviet Socialist Republic of Tajikistan was a part. In January 1925, the Autonomous Region of Gorno-Badakhshan was established, high up in the Pamir range. On November 16 1929, Tajikistan became a federated republic of the Soviet Union. In the 1920s and 1930s, land and water reforms were carried out. The collectivization of agriculture was followed by industrialization, and the so-called 'cultural revolution' campaign.

[7] After World War II, the Soviet regime carried out a series of large construction projects, including a system of canals and reservoirs linking up with water projects in the neighboring republic of Uzbekistan. The purpose of this irrigation network was to develop the region's agricultural potential, especially for the cultivation of

cotton. In the 1970s and 1980s, the effects of mismanagement and economic stagnation were felt in Tajikistan, one of the poorest regions in the USSR, with a high rate of unemployment, especially among the young, who make up most of the population.

[8] From 1985 onwards, the changes promoted by President Mikhail Gorbachev made the democratization process possible, which in turn gave way to the expression of long-suppressed ethnic and religious friction in Tajikistan. In February 1990, there were violent incidents between Tajiks and Russians in the capital, with more than 30 people killed and scores injured. The government decreed a state of emergency, which remained in effect during that year's Supreme Soviet (Parliament) elections, in which the Communist Party won 90 per cent of the available seats. The opposition attributed the February events to provocation by the former Soviet secret police (KGB), aimed at discrediting Gorbachev's reforms and suppressing nationalist tendencies. Muslims and Democrats called for the dissolution of the Soviet, because the elections had been held while a state of emergency was in effect.

[9] After the February 1990 events in Dushanbe, there was an exodus of Russian and Ukrainian technicians, which triggered the closure of half the country's hospitals, schools and factories, further aggravating its social and economic problems. In

late August, Parliament passed a vote of no-confidence on President Majkamov, accusing him of supporting those responsible for the Moscow coup, and forcing him to resign. He was succeeded by Kadridin Aslonov as interim president of the republic.

[10] Aslonov's decision to ban the Communist Party (CP) of Tajikistan, announced after the coup attempt against Gorbachev in August 1991, was not supported by parliament. Dominated by hardline communists, they forced Aslonov to resign, naming Rajmon Nabiev to take his place as interim president. Nabiev had been First Secretary of the local CP until ousted by Gorbachev in 1985. In mid-September 1991, Parliament approved the Declaration of Independence and the new constitution, decreeing a state of emergency and banning the Islamic Renaissance Party.

[11] Tajikistan's religious revival has been stronger than in the rest of the former Soviet Union republics. In the early 1980s, there were 17 mosques; 10 years later, as a result of the liberalization promoted by Moscow, there were 128 large mosques, 2,800 places of prayer, an Islamic institute and five centers offering religious instruction. According to unofficial estimates, between 60 and 80 per cent of the population are practising Muslims. The Islamic Renaissance Party, created within the past few years, has proposed that the state allow political and religious freedom, but that it be based on Islam, with sharia

PROFILE

ENVIRONMENT

The Tian Shan, Guissaro-Alai and Pamir mountains occupy more than 90 per cent of Tajikistan's territory. This republic is located in the southeastern part of Central Asia between the Syr Darya River and the Fergana Valley in the north, the Pamir and Paropaniz mountain ranges in the south, the Karakul lake and the headwaters of the Murgab in the east, and the Guissar and Vakhsh valleys in the southwest. The Turkistan, Alai and Zeravshan mountains cross Tajikistan from north to south, joining the Pamir plateau. The highly cultivated valleys (lying at an altitude of 1000-2000 meters) have a warm, humid climate. Lower mountains and valleys, located in northern and southeastern Tajikistan, have an arid climate. It is bounded by Kyrgyzstan in the north, Uzbekistan in the west, China in the southeast and Afghanistan in the southwest. Abundant mineral resources include iron, lead, zinc, antimony and mercury, as well as important uranium deposits. Since 1960, land under irrigation has increased by 50 per cent, but as in other countries where cotton is the sole crop, the salinity of the soil has increased. Due to the lack of adequate sewage systems, and insufficient supplies of drinking water, a high proportion of Tajik infants suffer from diarrhea, the main cause of the country's high infant mortality rate.

SOCIETY

Peoples: Tajik, 63.8 per cent; Uzbek, 24.0 per cent; Russian, 6.5 per cent; Tatar, 1.4 per cent; Kyrgyz, 1.3 per cent; Ukrainian, 0.7 per cent; German, 0.3 per cent; other, 2.0 per cent.
Religions: Muslim (Sunni 80 per cent; Shi'a (5 per cent).
Languages: Tajik (official), Uzbek, Russian.
Political Parties: Communist Party; Socialist Party; Rastokhez People's Movement; Islamic Renaissance Party; Democratic Party.
Social Organizations: Union Federation of Tajikistan.

THE STATE

Official Name: Yumhuri Tochikiston. **Administrative Divisions:** 3 Regions, 57 Districts. **Capital:** Dushanbe (Dusanbe), 720,000 people (1994). **Other cities:** Khujand (formerly Leninabad) 164,500 people; Kulob 79,300; Qurghonteppa 58,400; Urateppa 47,700 **Government:** Imomali Rakhmonov, President since 1994. Yakhyo Azimov, Prime Minister since February, 1996. **National Holiday:** September 9, Independence (1991). **Armed Forces:** 7,000; 6,000 Russian troops (1996).

STATISTICS

DEMOGRAPHY

Population: 5,935,000 (1996). **Annual growth:** 2.5% (1980/1996). **Estimates for year 2000:** 6,000,000. **Annual growth to year 2000:** 1.9% (1994/2000). **Urban Population:** 32.3% (1996). **Children per woman:** 4 (1996).

HEALTH

Life expectancy at birth: 67 years (1996) male: 64 years (1994) female: 70 years (1994). **Infant mortality:** 56 per 1,000 (1996). **Under-5 child mortality:** 76 per 1,000 (1996). **Safe water:** 60% (1990/96).

EDUCATION

Literacy: 100% (1995) male: 100% (1995) female: 100% (1995). **School enrolment:** Primary total: 89% (1990/95) male: 91% (1990/95) female: 88% (1990/95). Secondary: male: 83% (1990/95) female: 75% (1990/95). Tertiary: 20% (1995). **Primary school teachers:** one for every 23 students (1995).

COMMUNICATIONS

10 **newspapers, radios,** 190 **TV sets** and 45 **main telephone lines** per 1,000 people (1994). **Books:** 4 new titles per 100,000 people (1992/94).

ECONOMY

Per capita, GNP: $ 340 (1996). **Annual growth, GNP:** -8.4% (1995/96). **Currency:** 291 ruble = $ 1 (1995) **Fertilizer use:** 813 kgs per ha (1994). **Exports:** $ 770 million (1996). **Imports:** $ 668 million (1996). **External debt:** $ 707 million (1996). $ 119 **per capita:** (1996). **Debt service:** 0.1% of exports (1996).

HDI (rank / value) 115 / 0.58 (1994)

(Islamic law) as the law of the land. In 1991, the Tajik Government instituted the celebration of several important Muslim holy days.
[12] The mobilization of pro-Islamic forces, on the one hand, and mediation by Moscow, on the other, led to the state of emergency and the Communist Party ban being lifted in early October. Two months later, in its first presidential elections in November 1991, Nabiev was confirmed in his post by 58 per cent of the voters. According to official tallies, Davlav Khudonazarov, a former member of the CP Central Committee and president of the Soviet Film Actors Union, and a candidate supported by Muslims and democrats, came in second with 38 per cent of the vote.
[13] On December 21 Tajikistan entered the Commonwealth of Independent States (CIS). At the same time, the Autonomous Region of Gorno-Badakhshan, high in the Pamir mountains, asked to be granted the status of an autonomous republic. Like neighboring Afghanistan, the majority of this region's inhabitants are Shi'a Muslims.
[14] During his visit to Dushanbe, in February 1992, US Secretary of State James Baker expressed the West's concern over the region's

uranium deposits. Tajikistan, together with Turkmenistan and Uzbekistan, have important deposits of this mineral, which is crucial to the development of nuclear weapons.
[15] In April and May 1992, there were a number of confrontations, leading to the resignation of the president of parliament, Kendzhaev. On May 7, a coalition government was formed, with government and opposition representatives.
[16] Outside Dushanbe, however, there was violence from both pro-government and opposition forces, causing a conflict of civil-war proportions. Another protest demonstration against Nabiev led to his resignation on September 8. A private pro-communist army in the northern part of the country, far from accepting this state of affairs, launched a major offensive. The attack ended in December, with the fall of the capital and the formation of a new government controlled by the Popular Front.
[17] Some 300,000 people fled to other CIS republics and Afghanistan. As of February 1993, the persecution and massacre of members of the opposition began to diminish.
[18] The Russian Government of President Boris Yeltsin was the first

to recognize the new regime, led by Imamali Rajmonov, whom Yeltsin considered ideal for keeping the Islamic groups under control. In March, bombing started from Afghanistan, followed by incursions of opposition troops across the Russian-controlled frontier.
[19] Following nine months of confrontations, in April 1994, representatives of the government and the Islamic and liberal opposition met in Moscow, at a time when Tajikistan was more dependent than ever on Russian aid, both military and economic. Rajmonov proposed a new constitution, approved in November by referendum. The outgoing president was also re-elected in the presidential elections which accompanied the referendum, but the Islamic opposition accused the government of fraud.
[20] The exiled opposition representatives did not recognize the validity of the February 1995 parliamentary elections either, and sporadic armed confrontations continued to affect the country. On an economic front, the war-devastated Tajikistan could not convince Russia to form a monetary union between the two nations.
[21] In February 1996, prime minister Jamshed Karimov resigned and was replaced by Yakhyo Azimov. Two ceasefires, sponsored by the United Nations, and an agreement signed in Moscow, late that year, failed to stop the fighting. Also, the

Government was weakened after the rebellion of two of its main military leaders. The crisis was settled after a compromise was reached with both.
[22] The civil war ended officially on June 27, 1997 with the signing in Moscow of a peace agreement between the Government and the opposition, grouped in the so-called Tajik Opposition Union (TOU). The agreement secured 30 per cent of cabinet positions for the opposition, places in the justice system and an amnesty for those accused of war crimes.
[23] The agreement failed to stop the violence or the activity of armed bands in major cities. An attack in the capital against a presidential office confirmed the fragility of the pact. The Islamic opposition blamed the attack on TOU splinter groups. Various smaller armed groups, excluded from the peace process, made their presence felt with attacks against the Government and the opposition.
[24] In February 1998, the Government announced the intensification of a privatization program to attract investments. The four year war had taken the lives of tens of thousands and more than 600,000 were displaced within the country, while another 300,000 fled to Afghanistan, Russia and other CIS countries. The conflict also greatly damaged the economy, making Tajikistan into the poorest CIS country. In 1997, cotton production amounted to 60 per cent of the expected total.

Tanzania

Tanzania

Population: 30,799,000 (1996)
Area: 883,749 SQ KM
Capital: Dodoma

Currency: Shillings
Language: Swahili and English

The oldest fossils of the human race were found in the Olduvai gorge, in the north of Tanzania. These remains date from millions of years ago, yet little is known about life on most of modern Tanzania's mainland before the 7th century.

[2] A mercantile civilization, heavily influenced by Arab culture, flourished in this region between 695 and 1550 (See The Zandj Culture in East Africa) but it was eventually destroyed by Portuguese invaders. One hundred and fifty years later, under the leadership of the Sultan of Oman, the Arabs succeeded in driving out the remaining Lusitanians, but the rich cultural and commercial life of past times did not return. As the slave trade grew, Kilwa and Zanzibar became the leading trade centres.

[3] Between 1698 and 1830, Zanzibar and the coast were under the rule of the Oman Sultanate, with the Sultan living in Zanzibar. His sons, under British pressure, later split the inherited domain, dividing the old Sultanate in two.

[4] At the end of the 19th century a German adventurer, claiming rights over Tanzania, based on «treaties» signed by local Tanganyika leaders set up a company which immediately received imperial endorsement, leasing out the mainland coastal strip to the sultan of Zanzibar. The British had also made a similar deal, so the Berlin Conference, where the European powers distributed Africa among themselves, was obliged to recognize the claims of both powers. The European powers eventually agreed upon the «cession of German rights» in favor of Britain.

[5] The areas of influence were delimited in 1886. Tanganyika, Rwanda and Burundi were recognized as German possessions while Zanzibar formally became a British protectorate in 1890. German troops and British warships joined efforts to stifle a Muslim rebellion on the coast of Tanganyika in 1905.

[6] After the defeat of Germany in World War I, the League of Nations placed Tanganyika under British mandate, while Rwanda-Burundi was handed over to the Belgians.

[7] Nationalist feelings were channelled into TANU (Tanganyikan African National Union), a party founded in 1954 by Julius Nyerere, a primary school teacher known by the people as Mwalimu, the teacher.

[8] After seven years of organizing and fighting against racial discrimination and the appropriation of lands by European settlers, independence was achieved in 1961, and Nyerere became president, elected by an overwhelming majority.

[9] Meanwhile, in Zanzibar, two nationalist organizations, which had been active sporting and cultural institutions since the 1930s, merged to form the Afro-Shirazi Party in February 1957. In December 1963, the British transferred power to the Arab minority, and a month later this government was overthrown by the Afro-Shirazi. In April, Tanganyika and Zanzibar formed the United Republic of Tanzania, though the island maintained some autonomy.

[10] Under Nyerere's leadership, Tanzania based its foreign policy on non-alignment, standing for African unity, providing unconditional support to liberation movements, particularly FRELIMO in neighboring Mozambique.

[11] In February 1967, TANU issued the Arusha Declaration proclaiming socialism as its objective. The declaration lays down the principle of self-sufficiency and gives top priority to the development of agriculture, on the basis of communal land ownership, a traditional system known in Swahili as ujamaa, which means community.

[12] Ten years later TANU and the Afro-Shirazi Party merged into the Chama Cha Mapinduzi (CCM), which officially incorporated the aim of «building socialism on the basis of self-sufficiency».

[13] In October 1978, Tanzania was invaded by Ugandan troops in an obvious attempt by dictator Idi Amin to distract attention from his internal problems. At the same time he sought to divert Tanzanian energies from supporting the liberation struggles in Southern Africa. The aggression was repelled in a few weeks, and Tanzanian troops co-operated closely with the Ugandan National Liberation Front to overthrow Idi Amin.

[14] The cost of mobilizing the army and maintaining troops to prevent chaos in Uganda weighed heavily on the State budget, which was facing serious difficulties by the end of the 1970s. The falling price of Tanzania's main exports; coffee, spices, cotton, pyrethrum and cashew nuts, plus the growing cost of imported products, caused serious financial imbalances and forced cutbacks in the program to expand the *ujamaa* (community) villages.

[15] These villages were conceived as the nucleus of the Tanzanian economy and were designed to be self-sufficient. To achieve autonomy, they received sizeable initial investments from the Government. Despite Nyerere's enormous efforts, various factors hindered the progress of ujamaa which grew slowly when compared with small and medium-sized private farms. They continued to depend upon imported foodstuffs and as the government aid was cut, many of them collapsed.

[16] At the end of 1982, the CCM held its second general congress. A new generation of young leaders, most of them strongly committed to the development of the socialist project were appointed to key posts within both the Government and the party.

[17] Edward Sokoine was appointed prime minister and immediately launched a campaign against corruption while adopting a more flexible policy towards foreign investment. Sokoine also arranged for Tanzania and Kenya to resume relations which had broken down in 1977 when the East African Economic Community of Tanzania, Kenya and Uganda was dissolved.

[18] After his death, his successor Salim Ahmed Salim from

LAND USE

DEFORESTATION -1.1% annual (81/90)
IRRIGATED 5 % of arable

(1993)

■ FOREST & WOODLAND	35.4%
☐ ARABLE	3.2%
▨ OTHER	61.4%

PROFILE

ENVIRONMENT

The country is made up of the former territory of Tanganyika plus the islands of Zanzibar and Pemba. The offshore islands are made of coral. The coastal belt, where a large part of the population live, is a flat lowland along the Indian Ocean with a tropical climate and heavy rainfall. To the west lies the central plateau, dry and riddled with tsetse flies. The north is a mountainous region with slopes suited for agriculture. Around Lake Victoria, a heavily populated area, there are irrigated farmlands. Large plantations of sisal and sugar cane stretch along the coastal lowlands. Mount Kilimanjaro, the highest peak in Africa at 6,000 m is located in the northern highlands. The need to increase exports has led to intensification of agricultural production in semi-arid areas, leading, in turn, to further soil erosion. Indiscriminate cutting of forests has continued.

SOCIETY

Peoples: Most Tanzanians are of Bantu origin, split into around 120 ethnic groups. In the western region of the mainland there are Nilo-Hamites; in Zanzibar there is a Shirazi minority, of Persian origin. In both regions there are small groups of Arabs, Asians and Europeans. **Religions:** Muslim, 35 per cent; traditional religions, 35 per cent; Christian, 30 per cent. **Languages:** Swahili and English are the official ones. Several local languages are spoken. **Political Parties:** Revolutionary Party of Tanzania (CCM-Chama Cha Mapinduzi); Party for Democracy and Progress (CHADEMA); Civic United Front (CUF); National Convention for Construction and Reform-Mageuzi (NCCR-Mageuzi); Movement for a Democratic Alternative (MDA), of Zanzibar. **Social Organizations:** Union of Tanzanian Workers (JUWATA), Youth League (VIJANZ), Union of Women of Tanzania (UWT), Co-operative Union of Tanzania (WASHIRICA).

THE STATE

Official Name: Jamhuri ya Muungano wa Tanzania. **Administrative Divisions:** 25 Divisions. **Capital:** Dodoma, 120,000 people (1994). **Other cities:** Dar es Salaam, 1,540,000 people; Mwanza, 1,700,000; Tanga, 187,000; Zanzibar and Pemba, 680,189 (1994). **Government:** Benjamin Mkapa, President, and Frederick Sumaye, Prime Minister, since October 1995. Unicameral Legislature: 291-member Assembly, 216 elected by direct popular vote. **National Holiday:** April 26, Union Day (1964). **Armed Forces:** 34,600 (1996). Other: 1,400 Rural Police, 85,000 Militia.

STATISTICS

DEMOGRAPHY

Population: 30,799,000 (1996). **Annual growth:** 3.2% (1980/1996). **Estimates for year 2000:** 33,700,000. **Annual growth to year 2000:** 2.4% (1994/2000). **Urban Population:** 25.0% (1996). **Urban growth:** 6.68% (1980/95). **Children per woman:** 5.6 (1996).

HEALTH

Life expectancy at birth: 51 years (1996) male: 49 years (1994) female: 52 years (1994). **Infant mortality:** 93 per 1,000 (1996). **Under-5 child mortality:** 144 per 1,000 (1996). **Calorie consumption:** 95% (1988/90). **Safe water:** 38% (1990/96).

EDUCATION

Literacy: 68% (1995) male: 79% (1995) female: 57% (1995). **School enrolment:** Primary total: 70% (1990/95) male: 71% (1990/95) female: 69% (1990/95). Secondary: male: 6% (1990/95) female: 5% (1990/95). Tertiary: 1% (1995). **Primary school teachers:** one for every 37 students (1995).

COMMUNICATIONS

10 **newspapers**, 26 **radios** and 3 **main telephone lines** per 1,000 people (1994).

ECONOMY

Per capita, GNP: $ 170 (1996). **Annual growth, GNP:** 1.7% (1995/96). **Annual inflation:** 32.27% (1985/95). **Consumer price index:** 254.1 (1994). **Currency:** 550.36 shillings = $ 1 (1995) **Cereal imports:** 195 metric tons (1994). **Food import dependency:** 8% (1994). **Fertilizer use:** 114 kgs per ha (1994). **Exports:** $ 828 million (1996). **Imports:** $ 1,642 million (1996). **External debt:** $ 7,412 million (1996). $ 241 **per capita:** (1996). **Debt service:** 18.7% of exports (1996). **Development aid received:** $ 875 million (1995). $ 30 per capita (1995).

ENERGY

Consumption: 33.87 Kgs of Oil equivalent per capita yearly (1994). 83.07% imported (1994).

HDI (rank / value) 149 / 0.357 (1994)

Zanzibar continued along the same lines.

[19] A national debate was organized to discuss constitutional reform to reorganize the executive power, grant greater political

WORKERS

Labour force %

	WOMEN
	MEN

49   51

participation to women, strengthen democracy along CCM lines and prohibit more than two successive presidential re-elections.

[20] On November 5 1985, after 24 years as head of state, President Julius Nyerere passed power on to Ali Hassan Mwinyi, winner of the October 27 election, gaining 92.2 per cent of the vote.

MILITARY EXPENDITURE

MILITARY (as % of health and education expenditures-1990/91) **77%**

Nyerere took on a new post, presiding over the South-South Commission, an organization based in Geneva, working to strengthen Third World unity and its negotiating capacity with the North.

[21] In 1986, an economic recovery plan went into effect. It was designed by the government of Ali Hassan Mwinyi, following IMF and World Bank guidelines. The measures emphasized the reduction of tariff barriers which stifle imports and included incentives for private capital.

[22] Agricultural production improved and some industrial enterprises increased their profits.

[23] In the meantime, the crisis surrounding the ujamaa model intensified, partly due to its poor results and partly to the growing resistance of the population towards the resettlement of entire villages, especially when carried out by force. The recovery of the economy as a whole now depended on the credit promised by international agencies, which would only be granted when the required structural modifications have been introduced.

[24] The development of private capital and incentives to create such capital have caused new problems. According to UNICEF studies, half the children in the country are malnourished. Tanzania remained among the 30 poorest countries in the world, although it has managed to escape the famine which has hit other Central African nations.

The Zandj culture

The eastern coast of Africa, south of the "horn" of Somalia, was known to Mediterranean navigators in ancient times but it was only between the 4th and 5th centuries AD that trade began to develop in the area. In the 7th century, this activity became extremely important when links were established with Arabia, and then with Persia.

[2] For political or religious reasons, small groups of Arabian dissidents subsequently left their homeland to settle in eastern Africa: in 695, Prince Hamza of Oman went to Zanzibar with a handful of followers; in 740, fugitives from Mecca founded Maqdishu (Mogadishu); in 834, the survivors of a frustrated rebellion in Basrah became prosperous pirates with headquarters in Socotra; and in 920, a group of Omanians conquered Mogadishu, driving its founders into the interior where they created caravans. Around 975, Ali bin Sultan al Hassan, prince of Shiraz was driven out of his country; when he reached Africa with his family he built the ports of Kilua, Pemba, Manisa (later, Mombasa) and Sofala (near present-day Beira in Mozambique). His descendants, and by extension, the whole mestizo population of the coast, called themselves the "Shirazis", a generic term still in use today.

[3] The Arabs called the whole region "the country of the Zandj" or the country of the Blacks (Zandj-bar, meaning "coast of the Blacks") since the small white contingent soon merged totally with the Somalians and Bantus of the coast. Their contribution was formative, both economically and culturally. They brought a form of writing which supplemented the Swahili language (the most widespread of the Bantu languages), supplying an essential element for forming cultural unity from Mogadishu to Sofala. This gave the Zandj access to Arabian civilization and to the appropriate markets for their products.

[4] Direct trade was established, first with Arabia and Persia, and then with India, Siam (Thailand) and even China. In 1415, an official mission from China arrived in Zandj, escorted by a fleet headed by the first admiral of the Ming Empire. The main African export products included excellent steel from Malindi and Manisa later used in Syria (or India) to manufacture the famous swords of Damascus, and ivory of a quality that surpassed Indian ivory. They also exported furs from the savannas, gold from Zimbabwe (through Sofala) and, of course, slaves. All these were in high demand internationally.

[5] In exchange, the Zandj received cloth, books, jewels, pearls and porcelain; even today, archaeologists are amazed at the enormous amount of Chinese pottery found in the region.

[6] This chain of city-ports, though independent, maintained intense exchange and close cooperation between themselves. With houses built of stone or coral blocks, in the Arabian style, and large public spaces where poets and minstrels recited epics and poems in front of large audiences, these cities contributed to building a common culture. Though heavily influenced by Arabian culture, the newborn nation had genuine local roots which was perfectly evident at the most sophisticated levels of artistic and intellectual creation.

[7] In 1498, when the Portuguese reached Zandj on their way to India, they were impressed by the size and cleanliness of the cities, the quality of the houses, the luxurious good taste with which they were decorated and the beauty and elegance of the women who were active participants in society.

[8] However, since the main goal of the Portuguese was trading with India and later establishing a trade monopoly, they viewed Zandj cities as a frightening source of competition that had to be destroyed. In 1500 they attacked and ruined Mozambique, continuing their devastating work with such application that, within 50 years, they had destroyed all the cities on the eastern coast. Their target was to transfer all this thriving business to their own trading posts. Not only did they fail in their efforts, but their action caused long-lasting economic and cultural damage to all the peoples involved.

[25] Agricultural tasks have traditionally been carried out chiefly by women. While nearly half the work force in the economy as a whole is made up of women, 85 per cent of all agricultural work is performed by women. In the outlying areas around the major cities, the female population is increasingly opting for work in the underground economy.

[26] Economic data for 1989 revealed that the agricultural sector accounts for 51 per cent of the GDP, industry 10.2 per cent, trade 13.3 per cent and services 25 per cent. With only 10 per cent of the employed work force, the latter is the most competitive sector; agriculture, in turn, is the least capital-intensive but the most labor-intensive, with 85.6 per cent of the total work force.

[27] At the beginning of 1990, former president Julius Nyerere said that he was not opposed to a multi party democracy in his country. According to Nyerere, the absence of an opposition party contributed to the fact that the CCM had abandoned its program and its commitments, straying from its commitment to the masses.

[28] In February 1991, under the leadership of Abdullah Fundikira, a commission was formed to oversee the country's transition period.

[29] In its 1991 report, Amnesty International disclosed the existence of 120 prisoners on the island of Zanzibar, of which at least 40 are presumed to be political prisoners. Mwinyi's government denied that any political arrests had been made, and invited the human rights organization to prove its charges.

[30] In March 1991, the Tanzanian Workers' Organization (JUWATA) broke its ties with the CCM.

[31] In December, after a 23-year exile in England, opposition leader Oscar Kambona announced his plan to return to Tanzania and lead the fight for a multi party system.

[32] The opposition leader announced the founding of the Democratic Alliance of Tanzania party. However, the national elections held in April 1993 confirmed yet again the predominance of the Chama Cha Mapinduzi, the party in power, which obtained 89 per cent of the vote.

[33] The Government pledged to the IMF it would implement a harsh program of economic adjustment which, among other measures, included the elimination of 20,000 public sector jobs and a reduction of the budget deficit. It thus reduced the education budget which went from 30 per cent in 1960 to 5 per cent of total public expenditure and in February 1994, authorized a 68 per cent raise in electricity bills and 233 per cent increase of several local taxes.

[34] In March, the World Bank praised Tanzania considering it the second-best African «student» after Ghana. The country's harsh social conditions were aggravated by a massive influx of Rwandan refugees, fleeing from massacres which killed over 500,000 in the neighboring state.

[35] 1995 was dominated by the multiparty legislative and presidential elections held in October, where the CCM triumphed again due to Nyerere's support. Benjamin Mkapa became the new President and appointed Frederick Sumaye Prime Minister.

[36] In December 1996, the Government decided to expel the majority of the 540,000 Rwandan refugees from the country. Most of them were forced to their deaths, coming up against the same conflicts they had fled three years previously. Tanzania still has 230,000 Hutu refugees from Burundi, and some 50,000 from the Democratic Republic of Congo (former Zaire).

[37] Production of the nation's leading exports: coffee and cotton, fell again in 1997. Benjamin Mkapa called for international aid, stating that thirteen of the nation's twenty productive zones were unable to meet the basic needs of the population due to the destructive effects of the El Niño phenomenon.

[38] In 1998, Tanzania's parliament began discussion of the Sexual Offences Law, proposing harsher sentences for sexual abuses committed against children aged under 18 years old. Poverty, child abuse and sex tourism were considered the main causes of the increase in child prostitution in the country.

[39] A bomb at the US embassy in Dar es Salaam killed several people in August. It was thought to be linked with the global Islam network of Osama bin Laden, based in Afghanistan.

Thailand

Prathet Thai

Population:	58,703,000 (1996)
Area:	513,115 SQ KM
Capital:	Bangkok (Krung Thep)
Currency:	Baht
Language:	Thai or Siamese

Archaeological evidence indicates almost continuous human occupation of Thailand for the last 20,000 years. Thai-speaking peoples migrated southward from China around the 10th century AD. During the 13th century two Thai states emerged. The Sukhothai Kingdom was founded about 1220 after a successful revolt against the Khmer kingdom. Chiang Mai was founded in 1296. In 1350 the Thai kingdom of Aytthaya succeeded the state of Sukhotai and devastated the declining Khmer kingdom.

2 The Myanmar (Burmese) were the most powerful rival of the Aytthaya kingdom, and in 1569 they defeated Aytthayan forces, occupied their capital, and ruled the kingdom for 15 years. In 1767 the Myanmar again occupied the Thai capital and ended the Ayutthayan rule.

3 In 1782, Rama I founded the Chakri dynasty that still rules the country, with its capital in Bangkok (Krung Thep). Rama III extended the Thai Empire south along the Malay Peninsula, north into Laos and southeast into Cambodia.

4 Throughout the 19th century, Siam (as Thailand was called) was disputed by the French and the British. In 1896, the two powers agreed to leave the state formally independent, but continued to compete for control over flourishing agricultural resources. In World War I, Siam fought alongside the Allies and later joined the League of Nations.

5 On June 24 1932, a coup curtailed the power of the monarchy, creating a parliament elected by universal suffrage. The democratic experience was short-lived and in 1941, during World War II, the Bangkok Government allowed Japan to use its territory, becoming a virtual satellite of that country. During the conflict, Siamese troops occupied part of Malaysia, but was forced to abandon it in 1946, after the allied victory.

6 In June of that year, King Ananda Mahidol was assassinated in mysterious circumstances. US manoeuvring succeeded in putting his brother, Rama IX, into power. Born in the United States, the new king had never hidden his pro-US leanings. Since then, Thailand has remained under Washington's patronage.

7 US interests in Thailand are essentially strategic as its geographical location and plans for a projected channel through the Kra Isthmus made the country critical to US military policy in the area. In 1954, the Southeast Asian Treaty Organization (SEATO), a military pact designed to counterbalance the growing power of revolutionary forces in the region, established its headquarters in Bangkok.

8 In 1961, large numbers of US troops entered the country in reaction to an insurrection in Laos. The US military maintained its presence in Thailand for 14 years, resulting in strong ties being forged between the Thai and US armed forces. In exchange for their participation in the anti-communist struggle, the Thai military enjoyed greater political influence and impunity from their corrupt activities, which included control of the drug trade from the famous "golden triangle" in the north.

9 Between 1950 and 1975, US support of military regimes in Thailand cost it over $2 billion. On October 14 1973, a popular uprising by students brought down the government, and as a result, in 1975 the first civilian government in 20 years was formed. Elections

brought Prince Seni Pramoj to power. He demanded the immediate withdrawal of US troops, the dismantling of military bases and an improvement of relations with neighboring revolutionary governments.

10 The Thai military disagreed with the new government, and in October 1976, Pramoj was overthrown in a bloody coup plotted by right-wing navy officers. Thousands of students and intellectuals joined a guerrilla struggle led by the Communist Party in the rural areas, and Thai relations with neighbors became extremely tense. Finally, in October 1977, a second coup brought the "civilized right wing" of the military to power, taking a liberal line in policy-making, as they were eager to attract new transnational investments. In 1979, Thailand granted asylum to Cambodian refugees. Refugee camps along the border became the rearguard of Cambodian strong man Pol Pot's Khmer Rouge guerrillas; a large part of international humanitarian aid was unwittingly channelled to them. Thailand thus served US interests in the region, as a base for new attacks against communist Vietnam which was supported the anti-Khmer forces.

11 On April 1 1981, another military coup shook Bangkok. This

PUBLIC EXPENDITURE

n/a	
57.7%	
1995 ■ DEFENCE □ SOCIAL	

In 1990/91 Military as % of health & education expenditure was 71%.

WORKERS

(1996)

Labour force %

■ WOMEN
□ MEN

46   54

■ AGRICULTURE	64% (1990)
□ INDUSTRIAL	14%
■ SERVICES	22%

LAND USE

DEFORESTATION -2.9% annual (81/90)
IRRIGATED 25 % of arable

(1993)

■ FOREST & WOODLAND	26.3%
□ ARABLE	34.3%
■ OTHER	39.4%

time it was led by General Sant Chitpatima with the support of young middle-ranking officers demanding institutional democracy and social change. The King and Prime Minister General Prem had been asked to lead the coup and had apparently accepted. However, they finally opposed the uprising, and it was put down after three days of great tension. The young officers' revolt, rooted within the military establishment, was at base a reaction to government measures bringing in forced retirement for certain senior generals. Nevertheless, the short-lived coup gained unusually strong support from trade unions and student groups - and this support in itself was extraordinary since the coup was instigated by the military.

[12] At the same time, the left-wing opposition was severely weakened by an internal split in the Communist Party into the pro-Vietnamese and pro-Chinese factions.

[13] On April 20 1983, elections were held and General Prem Tinsulanonda was appointed Prime Minister for a second successive term.

[14] Towards the end of 1984, the currency was sharply devalued, sparking discontent from General Arthit Kamlang-Ek and other hardline generals, who threatened to withdraw military support for Prem. Some timely political manoeuvring by the prime minister, offering incentives to the officers for their support, allowed Prem to isolate Arthit. After a further coup attempt in September 1985, Prem relieved Arthit of his command and designated General Chaovalit Yongchaiyut as the head of the armed forces.

[15] Political instability continued in Bangkok, with several cabinet changes and requests for early legislative elections on two separate occasions. In May 1986, the Democrat Party obtained enough of a majority to form a coalition, presided over once again by General Prem as Prime Minister. While General Chaovalit's stature continued to grow, enhanced by his harsh attacks on corruption, the Government called for early elections in April 1988, to avoid the censure of Prem. The main criticisms of his administration were his questionable management of public funds and overall incompetence, particularly in the handling of the border war with Laos several months earlier, which had escalated from a dispute over the control of three villages.

[16] In the first general election since 1976, amid massive vote-buying campaigns (a practice considered normal by almost all candidates), the Thai Nation Party won the election. King Bhumibol Adulyahed asked General Chatichai

Choonhavan to form a new government, which he did by arranging a six-party coalition.

[17] Thailand's new leading force and a successful entrepreneur, Chatichai introduced important policy changes, breaking with the traditional focus on internal affairs and security. His main idea was to convert what had once been the Indochinese battlefield into a huge regional market. Tempted by the possibility of Cambodia and Laos opening up their markets, he invested considerably in those countries. This formula further fuelled the Thai economy, and in 1989 the growth rate exceeded 10 per cent. Thailand then challenged Western Europe and its subsidy policies for agricultural export products. There were also disagreements with the United States over Bangkok's refusal to accept North American trade criteria on intellectual property, especially with regard to computer programs.

[18] Chatichai's government made foreign policy one of its main priorities, while failing to pay sufficient attention to serious domestic problems such as the deterioration and pollution of the environment, and the extreme poverty of the majority of the population. In 1989, rapid deforestation contributed to serious flooding, as the regulatory effect of the forests on the water cycle was altered and trees had been removed from river banks, where they had formed natural dikes. To avoid more serious damage in the future, the Government was forced to prohibit further logging. Peasants have also resisted the massive eucalyptus plantation projects promoted by the Government and the World Bank. The natural forests have been transformed into private commercial plantations for urban industrial use without considering the local people and their traditional use of forest products.

[19] Charges of corruption and nepotism levelled against the Chatichai government grew as quickly as the economy. General Chaovalit, a political "rising star," was named minister of defence in 1990, in order to lend an image of honesty to the government.

[20] In March 1991, the military carried out another coup led by General Sunthorn Kongsompong, who presented King Bhumibol Adulyahed with a draft for a new constitution. The latter approved the draft, and justified the military coup on the grounds of "growing corruption" within the civilian government. The King also agreed with the military on the need for calling new elections. As an indirect result of the military coup in Thailand, peace negotiations in neighboring Cambodia came to a

standstill, with the Cambodian Government denouncing Thailand for its renewed support of the Cambodian armed opposition.

[21] Throughout 1991, Thailand remained under the command of the Council for the Maintenance of National Peace (NPKC), a body of the military commanded by Sunthorn. In December, the King approved the new constitution which stipulated that elections to replace the NPKC Government would be held within 120 days. However, the military junta reserved the right to directly designate 270 senators out of a total of 360, giving them total control over the new government.

[22] In elections held on March 22 1992, the majority of votes went to the opposition. There were 15 parties, with a total of 2,740 candidates, and 32 of 57 million Thais turned out to vote. In early April, General Suchinda Kraprayoon, commander in chief of the army at the time, became Prime Minister, backed by a small majority made up of five pro-military parties. On his 49-member cabinet, Suchinda included 11 former ministers who had been accused of embezzlement during Chatichai's government. A few weeks later,

50,000 people attended a demonstration held by four opposition parties, demanding that the head of the government resign. In the meantime, political leader Chamlong Srimuang and 42 militants from opposition parties began a hunger strike.

[23] At the end of May, what began as an anti-government demonstration ended in a massacre, with hundreds of people killed and injured. Army troops fired into a crowd gathered at the Democracy Monument. The protests continued until an unexpected television appeal for national reconciliation from the Thai king. Suchinda, in the meantime, announced his support of a constitutional amendment whereby the Prime Minister would have to be an elected member of Parliament, a clause which would disqualify even Suchinda himself from holding the post. Srimuang was subsequently freed, and an amnesty announced for those who had been arrested. With a curfew still in effect in Bangkok, parliament initiated discussion of the constitutional amendment and the King appointed General Pren Tinsulanonda to supervise the process.

[24] On May 24, Suchinda resigned and his Vice President, Mitchai

STATISTICS

DEMOGRAPHY
Population: 58,703,000 (1996). **Annual growth:** 1.4% (1980/ 1996). **Estimates for year 2000:** 60,500,000. **Annual growth to year 2000:** 0.8% (1994/2000). **Urban Population:** 20.2% (1996). **Urban growth:** 2.6% (1980/95). **Children per woman:** 1.8 (1996).

HEALTH
Life expectancy at birth: 69 years (1996) male: 67 years (1994) female: 72 years (1994). **Infant mortality:** 31 per 1,000 (1996). **Under-5 child mortality:** 38 per 1,000 (1996). **Calorie consumption:** 103% (1988/90). 4,762 **people per doctor** (1988/ 91). **Safe water:** 89% (1990/96).

EDUCATION
Literacy: 94% (1995) male: 96% (1995) female: 92% (1995). **School enrolment:** Primary total: 87% (1990/95) male: 98% (1990/95) female: 97% (1990/95). Secondary: male: 38% (1990/95) female: 37% (1990/95). Tertiary: 20% (1995). **Primary school teachers:** one for every 20 students (1995).

COMMUNICATIONS
50 **newspapers**, 190 **radios**, 250 **TV sets** and 47 **main telephone lines** per 1,000 people (1994). **Books:** 13 new titles per 100,000 people (1992/94).

ECONOMY
Per capita, GNP: $ 2,960 (1996). **Annual growth, GNP:** 4.4% (1995/ 96). **Annual inflation:** 5.01% (1985/95). **Consumer price index:** 119.5 (1994). **Currency:** 24.9 baht = $ 1 (1995) **Cereal imports:** 740 metric tons (1994). **Food import dependency:** 2% (1994). **Fertilizer use:** 615 kgs per ha (1994). **Exports:** $ 55,789 million (1996). **Imports:** $ 73,289 million (1996). **External debt:** $ 90,824 million (1996). $ 1,547 **per capita:** (1996). **Debt service:** 11.5% of exports (1996). **Development aid received:** $ 863 million (1995). $ 15 per capita (1995). 0.6% of GNP (1994)

ENERGY
Consumption: 769.41 Kgs of Oil equivalent per capita yearly (1994). 60.89% imported (1994).

HDI (rank / value) 59 / 0.833 (1994)

Maternal Mortality
1990

PER 100,000 LIVE BIRTHS

200

Literacy
1995

94%

Ruchuphan, became interim president. Constitutional amendments approved in June reduced military participation in the government. In the first week of June, after the amendment had been passed by Parliament, King Bhumibol named Anand Panyarachun Prime Minister. Panyarachun, who enjoyed a great deal of prestige in Thailand, had been prime minister after the 1991 military coup.

[25] Parliament accepted the King's nomination of Panyarachun, who named a number of technocrats to cabinet positions and requested the resignations of the 12 military officers responsible for the May massacre.

[26] On June 29, he dissolved parliament and announced elections for September. The Democratic Party (DP) won the election, obtaining 79 seats in the Chamber of Representatives. On September 23, a parliamentary majority made up of the DP, the Palang Dharma (PD) and the Party of New Aspirations emerged, holding 177 seats, and anti-military political leader Chuan Leekpai was elected Prime Minister. Shortly afterwards, the pro-military Social Action Party joined the coalition.

[27] Prime Minister Chuan Leekpai

announced an economic program on January 19 1993, which aimed at winning back the foreign investment which had been scared off by political instability. Thailand's main attraction is that it has the cheapest workforce in the region.

[28] Finance minister Tarrin Nimmanahaeminda's plan included financial incentives to attract migration from other parts of the country to rural areas. In addition, it was designed to stimulate a return to the provinces by the urban unemployed, in an effort to check Bangkok's spiralling demographic growth. The 1993 budget deficit ($22 billion), equal to 0.9 per cent of the GDP, was justified by the Government by the need to invest in infrastructure, given its goal of transforming Thailand into a "bridge" for companies investing in Laos, Vietnam or Cambodia.

[29] Nevertheless, many obstacles remained in Thailand, among the most important was that 15 per cent of the population lived in extreme poverty. Also of major concern was the proliferation of AIDS in a country which has been a center for prostitution for many years. The opposition accused Prime Minister Chuan Leekpai of being slow and inefficient at a time when the country's problems

demanded urgent attention. Between June 10 and 12, 1993, a motion to censure Leekpai was put before parliament; his coalition managed to defeat the motion by 204 votes to 153.

[30] Although Leekpai's personal honesty was not called into question, some members of his cabinet were linked to illegal behaviour. The most upsetting element for the opposition was the interruption of the case against Montri Pongpanich. As a leader of the Social Action Party and a member of the government coalition, Pongpanich had legal immunity.

[31] Several violent incidents motivated by religious sensitivities took place in 1993. Concerned with his country's role in the region, Chuan reinforced ties with China and Indonesia and in October officially terminated the support which Thailand had provided to Cambodia's Khmer Rouge since 1979. Cambodian authorities accused Thailand of supporting the "Pol Potists" after 14 Thais were arrested during a thwarted coup attempt in Phnom Penh. Toward the end of the year, Thailand and Brazil were involved in intense diplomatic negotiations to extradite Brazilian financier Paulo César Farias, arrested in Bangkok in November 1993. After the extradition, Farias was killed in mid-1996, in a Brazilian seaside resort.

[32] The Government approved a reform to liberalize the banking system in January 1994. Among other things, the reform permitted the opening of branches of foreign banks in various Thai cities.

[33] A proposal for a constitutional reform generated a long debate in Parliament. The new project envisaged a reduction of the size and power of the Senate and lowered the voting age to 18 years. The subject remained unsettled due to mutual accusations by the different parties and the parliamentary changes which took place in 1995.

[34] Although in 1994 the economy of Thailand was among those that grew most, its economic stability did not reach the political sphere. The first parliamentary session of 1995 brought an exchange of accusations and the tense political atmosphere led to the dissolution of Parliament. On July 2 early

elections took place. The Thai Nation Party obtained 25 per cent of the seats and the Democrats 22 per cent. Banham Silapa-archa, leader of the winning party, formed a government supported by several small parties.

[35] The cabinet selected by Silapa-archa was severely criticized by the press, since some of its members had been investigated for their links with the state coup of 1991. The Prime Minister's response to the military insinuations of a coup was made public through a radio program. He said that coups were "obsolete".

[36] In 1995, inflation reached 6.5 per cent. It was considered "manageable" by the Central Bank. With an annual population growth of 1.5 per cent and a growth in the economy of over 8 per cent, Thailand remained on the list of countries with sustained economic success.

[37] In November 1996, Chavalit Yonchaiyudh (NAP) was elected new Prime Minister, with 125 of the 393 seats in the Chamber of Representatives. Chuan Leekpai's DP, took 123 seats. A coalition with the Chart Pattana (52), Social Action (20), Prachakorn Thai (18) plus two minor parties, allowed Chavalit to obtain the majority weeks later.

[38] Thailand was hit by a financial crisis in 1997, exacerbated by scandals and attempts to salvage the banks - leading to the resignation of the economy minister and the closure of businesses - and by Chavalit's proposal for constitutional reform in order to lift a vote of no confidence lodged by the opposition.

[39] In August 1997, the constitutional reform project was completed. It aimed to limit corruption, put citizens rights into the legislation and eliminate army influence from the Senate. Alarmed by the envisaged loss of power, the governing parties initially rejected this project, but they were forced to accept it given the agreement between the army and King Bhumibol. The new Constitution was passed in a General Assembly on October 11.

[40] When the new Prime Minister Chuan Leekpai took office, in November 1997, the Thai currency, the baht had lost 37 per cent of its value.

Togo

Togo

Population: 4,201,000 (1996)
Area: 56,785 SQ KM
Capital: Lomé

Currency: CFA Franc
Language: French

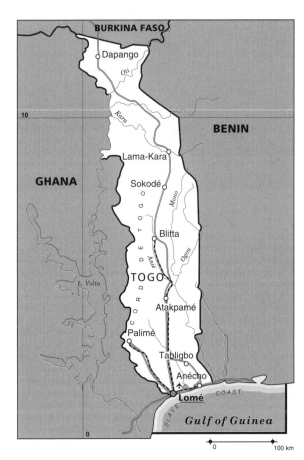

Togo was peopled by the Ewe (of the same origin as the Ibo and Yoruba of Nigeria and the Ashanti of Ghana), who still make up a third of its population. The Ewe were a relatively poor and peaceful people with simple social structures like the Dagomba kingdoms in the north.

[2] The slave trade gave the region the name of Slave Coast, and millions of people were shipped to slavery in the US between the 16th and 19th centuries.

[3] Togo became a German colony in 1884 under "treaties" signed with local chieftains. Occupied by Anglo-French troops during World War I, the territory was divided between the two powers with the endorsement of the League of Nations. The western part was annexed to Ghana in 1956, after a British-organized plebiscite, while the eastern part remained under French rule.

[4] In 1958, Sylvanus Olympio, (a member of the Togolese Unity party) won the elections. His program was pro-independence, but moderate. The 1960 proclamation of independence seemed to overlook a contract signed in 1957 with the Benin Mines Company, in which the French consortium had seized control of Togo's phosphate reserves, its main natural resource, thus compromising independence. When Olympio confronted this situation in 1963, proposing a series of basic reforms - doubtlessly influenced by Nkrumah's radical pro-independence program in neighboring Ghana - he was assassinated in a military revolt, allegedly involving a young military officer, Eyadéma.

[5] Olympio's successor, the neo-colonialist Nicholas Grunitzky, from the opposition Togolese Progress Party, was overthrown by a further coup, led by General Gnassingbé Eyadéma, who became the new head of state.

[6] In 1969, Eyadéma's Togo Peoples' Group (RPT) brought in a one-party system. In 1972 a law gave the state 35 per cent of shares of the mining company, which was raised to 51 per cent in 1975 and in 1976 the production and export of phosphate was nationalized.

[7] On December 30 1979, a constitution was approved and Eyadéma was re-elected President for a seven-year term. His government was confident of improving the economy, basing its optimism on tourism, oil and a rise in world phosphate prices. However in 1981 phosphate prices dropped by 50 per cent and a worldwide economic recession reduced the number of European tourists. A serious balance of payments deficit increased the foreign debt to $1 billion.

[8] In June 1984 a refinancing agreement with stringent conditions, was reached with the Paris Club and the IMF. Consequently, there were salary freezes, reduction of government investments and high taxes levied to increase government funds, including a so-called "solidarity tax" which took 5 per cent of the population's incomes.

[9] In January 1985 the Lomé III agreements were signed in Togo, regulating cooperation between ACP (Africa, Caribbean and Pacific) countries and the EEC.

[10] In January 1986 Eyadéma was re-elected for 7 years, with 99.95 per cent of the vote. Consultation with the IMF resumed and new agreements were planned in 1988. In 1990, adjustment programs were initiated, including denationalization, on account of trade deficits and a public deficit of $1.27 billion. Meanwhile food production rose slightly.

[11] In 1991, more than 10,000 peasants in the northern district of Keran Oti lost their lands to create an 80 sq km game reserve for hunting.

[12] In early April 1991, there were protest demonstrations throughout the country, and on April 8 more than a thousand people took over one of Lomé's neighbourhoods, setting up barricades and demanding Eyadéma's resignation. The police reacted violently, killing more than thirty people and injuring many more. However on April 12, opposition parties were legalized and Eyadéma announced an amnesty for political prisoners, and liberalization of the political system.

[13] On August 28 1991, a National Conference named Kokou Koffigoh - president of Togo's Bar Association and a recognized human rights leader - as provisional prime minister. A legislative assembly was established which ousted Eyadéma as head of the armed forces and blocked his candidacy in the upcoming 1992 elections.

[14] The dissolution of the RPT on November 26 1991, caused a military coup. Two days later, the armed forces took over the government, dissolved the legislative assembly and kidnapped Koffigoh for several hours. The perpetrators of the coup claimed that the legislative assembly was made up of extremists, whose aim was to "disrupt the army and discredit the military regime and its achievements". Political parties and other opposition organizations cooperated together within the framework of the National Resistance Committee, and encouraged people to resist a return to dictatorship.

[15] Togo's complicated political

WORKERS

Labour force %

■ WOMEN	
□ MEN	

40   60

■ AGRICULTURE	66% (1990)
□ INDUSTRIAL	10%
▨ SERVICES	24%

LAND USE

DEFORESTATION -1.4% annual (81/90)
IRRIGATED 0.3 % of arable

(1993)

■ FOREST & WOODLAND	15.8%
□ ARABLE	36.5%
▨ OTHER	47.7%

Maternal Mortality	Literacy	Food Dependency	External Debt
1990	1995	1970	1996
PER 100,000 LIVE BIRTHS 640	52%	23% 1994 10%	PER CAPITA $348

PROFILE

ENVIRONMENT

The country is a long, narrow strip of land with distinct geographical regions. In the South, a low coastline with lakes, typical of the Gulf of Guinea; a highly populated plain where manioc, corn, banana and palm oil are grown. In the North, subsistence crops are gradually giving way to coffee and cocoa plantations. The Togo Mountains run through the country from Northeast to Southwest.

SOCIETY

Peoples: The prevailing ethnic groups are the Ewe (43.1 per cent), Kabye (26.7 per cent), Gurma (16.1 per cent), Kebu (3.8 per cent) and Ana (Yoruba, 3.2 per cent). The descendants of formerly enslaved Africans who returned to Togo from Brazil are called Brazilians. They form a caste with great economic and political influence. The small European minority (0.3 per cent) is concentrated in the capital. **Religions:** The majority profess traditional African religions (50 per cent). There are Christian (35 per cent) and Muslim (15 per cent) minorities. **Languages:** French (official). The main local languages are Ewe, Kabye, Twi and Hausa. **Political Parties:** Rally of the Togolese People; Union for Justice and Democracy; Action Committee for Renewal. **Social Organizations:** National Confederation of Togolese Workers (CNT).

THE STATE

Official Name: République Togolaise. **Administrative Divisions:** 5 Regions and 21 Prefectures. **Capital:** Lomé, 600,000 people (1989). **Other cities:** Sokodé, 48,098 people; Kpalimé, 27,700 people (1983). **Government:** Gnassingbé Eyadema, President since January 1967; Kwassi Klutse, Prime Minister since August 1996. Unicameral 79-member Legislative Assembly. **National Holiday:** April 27, Independence Day (1960). **Armed Forces:** 6,950 (1997). **Other:** 750 Gendarmes.

STATISTICS

DEMOGRAPHY

Population: 4,201,000 (1996). **Annual growth:** 3% (1980/1996). **Estimates for year 2000:** 4,700,000. **Annual growth to year 2000:** 2.8% (1994/2000). **Urban Population:** 31.2% (1996). **Urban growth:** 5.05% (1980/95). **Children per woman:** 6.2 (1996).

HEALTH

Life expectancy at birth: 50 years (1996) male: 49 years (1994) female: 52 years (1994). **Infant mortality:** 78 per 1,000 (1996). **Under-5 child mortality:** 125 per 1,000 (1996). **Calorie consumption:** 99% (1988/90). 11,111 **people per doctor** (1988/91). **Safe water:** 55% (1990/96).

EDUCATION

Literacy: 52% (1995) male : 67% (1995) female: 37% (1995). **School enrolment:** Primary total: 102% (1990/95) male : 122% (1990/95) female: 81% (1990/95). Secondary: male: 34% (1990/95). female: 12% (1990/95). Tertiary: 3% (1995). **Primary school teachers:** one for every 51 students (1995).

COMMUNICATIONS

212 **radios**, 10 **TV sets** and 5 **main telephone lines** per 1,000 people (1994).

ECONOMY

Per capita, GNP: $ 300 (1996). **Annual growth, GNP:** 4.3% (1995/96). **Currency:** 490 CFA francs = $ 1 (1995) **Cereal imports:** 69 metric tons (1994). **Food import dependency:** 10% (1994). **Fertilizer use:** 45 kgs per ha (1994). **Exports:** $ 363 million (1996). **Imports:** $ 1,032 million (1996). **External debt:** $ 1,463 million (1996). $ 348 per capita (1996). **Debt service:** 10.8% of exports (1996). **Development aid received:** $ 188 million (1995). $ 47 per capita (1995). 20.2% of GNP (1994)

ENERGY

Consumption: 46.11 Kgs of Oil equivalent per capita yearly (1994). 100.00% imported (1994).

HDI (rank / value) 147 / 0.365 (1994

scenario was compounded by economic, social and ethnic problems. Eyadéma belongs to the southern Kabye group, which provided the majority of the country's 12,000 troops. Meanwhile, Koffigoh is a member of the Ewe tribe. Negotiations have begun between those who favor the military regime and the opposition. The negotiations hoped to precipitate the transition to civilian government by 1992. That year, a timetable was established for a return to democracy, and all citizens were re-registered to vote.

[16] In June, opposition leader Tavio Komlavi was assassinated. After an attempt upon the life of Mining Minister Joseph Yao Amefia, Eyadéma took advantage of the incident to have his powers restored by the High Council of the Republic (the interim legislature). Eyadéma proceeded to pack the cabinet with his supporters. In the face of widespread protests from the opposition, the Government postponed elections indefinitely. The unions, in reprisal, called a long-term general strike.

[17] The opposition split from Koffigoh in January 1993, after which they met in Benin and nominated a government in exile. In this same month the presidential guard killed around a hundred demonstrators in Lomé, which led to thousands of people fleeing to Ghana and Benin.

[18] Eyadéma agreed to organize elections for August. In an atmosphere of civil war, he won with 96.5 per cent of the vote, in a poll classed as "fraudulent" by the opposition. The protests in the streets intensified, and in January 1994, Eyadéma was unharmed in a foiled assassination attempt - carried out by around a hundred armed attackers - which left 67 people dead.

[19] The opposition won the February legislative elections, but Eyadéma did not allow one of its leaders, Edem Kodjo, to form a government without members of the ruling parties. The Action Committee for Renewal, which included the opposition groups, decided to boycott Parliament, paralyzing government for a large part of the year.

[20] On another front, widespread floods in Lomé left 150,000 people homeless in July. In September three weeks of heavy rains destroyed whole villages, roads and bridges, particularly in the northern and central regions of the nation, leaving 21,000 people destitute.

[21] In August 1996, Kodjo resigned from the post of prime minister and was substituted by Kwassi Klutse, from the Rally of the Togolese People (RTP).

[22] In July 1997, the opposition increased efforts to become unified managing to defeat Eyadema. The President, in power since 1967, was even up against pressure to liberalise the political system from within the military itself.

[23] The European Union agreed to provide the government with $30 million in aid for public health, education and the building of rural roads.

[24] In 1998, the legislative assembly approved new laws on the press, banning the arbitrary arrest of journalists and other police abuses, like their midnight "visits" to private houses without a legal authorisation.

MILITARY (as % of health and education expenditures-1990/91) **39%**

Tonga

Tonga

Population: 101,000 (1996)
Area: 699 SQ KM
Capital: Nukualofa

Currency: Pa'anga
Language: Tongan and English

The native inhabitants of Tonga, which means "south" in several Polynesian languages, immigrated from Fiji and Samoa over 1,000 years ago. Tongans developed a complex social organization, with a traditional leader in charge. According to oral tradition, the first Tui Tonga (ruler, Son of the Creator) of the islands was Aholitu in the second half of the 10th century. Towards the 15th century, religious and social roles were assigned to different leaders and this system of double leadership had continued until the Dutch came to the islands in 1616. English explorer Captain James Cook, visited them in 1775 and named them the "Friendly Islands".

[2] The archipelago only achieved political reunification in the mid-19th century, in a civil war, under the leadership of Taufa'ahau Tupou, ruler of the island of Haapai from 1820 onwards. Converted to Christianity and subsequently backed by European missionaries, Taufa'ahau Tupou seized Vavau and Tongatopu, securing control over the whole of the territory which he ruled under the Christian name of George I until 1893. The King introduced a parliamentary system including the local leaders, and an agrarian reform which granted each adult male in the country 3.3 ha of arable land. This ensured social stability and agricultural self-sufficiency. This system is still used but since the population has grown very quickly, there are not so many fertile plots left and families have to share them.

[3] In 1889, Britain and Germany signed a treaty which gave Britain a free hand in its relations with Tonga. The following year the archipelago was made a "protectorate" of the British crown, though the monarchy was kept with limited powers.

[4] Queen Salote, great-grand-daughter of George I was crowned in 1918. In 1960, she gave women the right to vote in legislative elections.

[5] The British transformed the country's agriculture, which was reoriented towards the export crops of copra and bananas.

[6] Present King Taufa'ahau Tupou IV was crowned in 1967, and three years later Tonga obtained independence. The high international market prices for copra and bananas helped Tonga to develop a wide-ranging social security system which included free education and medical services for all the inhabitants of the islands.

[7] In the mid-1970s welfare programs suffered because of the drop in fruit prices, and about 10,000 Tongans emigrated to Aotearoa/New Zealand.

[8] In February 1990, the proponents of the reform were re-elected and they announced the creation of the first political party in the Kingdom. The King accused the leader of the movement, Akalisi Pohiva, of Marxist tendencies.

[9] The UN questioned Tonga about the absence of trade unions in the country, in spite of there being over 3,000 civil servants. The Government of Tonga explained that there were no trade unions because they were unnecessary. The UN dismissed the Tongan response.

[10] The Crown Prince and Prime Minister since 1965, Fatafehi Tu'ipelehake, was replaced by Baron Vaea in 1991. In 1992, opposition groups founded the Pro-Democracy Movement which won 6 of the 9 seats in the National Assembly in the February 1993 elections.

[11] However, power continued to be controlled by the King, subjects named by him to high posts in the government and a small group belonging to the royalty. In September 1994, the Pro-Democracy Movement became the Tonga Democratic Party, led by 'Akilisi Pohiva.

[12] The King continued to promote a multiparty system but did not modify his quasi-monopolistic grip on power. As tourism had a significant growth of 11.3 per cent in 1994, Tonga refused to authorize Tokyo's request to fish for whales in its territorial waters.

[13] Along with other countries from the South Pacific Forum, Nukualofa harshly denounced French nuclear testing in the Polynesian atolls of Mururoa and Fangataufa in 1995 and 1996.

[14] Protests against the regime and in favour of political liberalisation continued in 1997. Several political leaders and journalists were arrested this year.

[15] In March 1998, Land Minister Fakafanua, the King's brother-in-law, was arrested. He had been accused of mishandling public funds and accepting bribes. The court did not pass a custodial sentence and he was freed a few days later, although he was barred from leaving the country.

PROFILE

ENVIRONMENT
This archipelago is also known as "Friendly Isles" and is located in western Polynesia, east of the Fiji Islands, slightly north of the Tropic of Capricorn. It comprises approximately 169 islands, only 36 of which are permanently inhabited. It includes three main groups of islands: yTongatapu, the southernmost group where more than half of the population live; Vavau, to the north, and Haapai in between. The volcanic islands are mountainous while the coral ones are flat. The climate is mild and rainy with very hot summers. The fertile soil is suitable for growing banana, copra and coconut trees.

SOCIETY
Peoples: Tongans are Polynesian people. It is estimated that 20 per cent of them now live abroad.
Religions: Free Wesleyan, 43.6 per cent; Roman Catholic, 16.0 per cent; Mormon, 12.1 per cent; Free Church of Tonga, 11.0 per cent.
Languages: Tongan and English are official.
Political Parties: Tonga Democratic Party.

THE STATE
Official Names: Pule'anga Fakatu'i 'o Tonga. Kingdom of Tonga.
Administrative Divisions: 23 Districts.
Capital: Nuku'alofa, 32,000 people (1994)
Other cities: Neiafu 15,170 people; Haveluloto 3,070; Vaini 2,697; Tofoa-Koloua 2,298. **Government:** Taufa'ahau Tupou IV, King since 1967; Baron Vaea, Prime Minister, since 1991. **National Holiday:** June 4, Independence Day (1970). **Armed Forces:** There is no army in Tonga. 300 National Police (1991)

DEMOGRAPHY
Population: 98,000 (1996) **Annual growth:** 0.4% (1980/1996) **Urban population:** 42.1% (1996)

HEALTH
Life expectancy at birth: 69 years (1996) **Infant mortality:** 19 per 1,000 (1996) **Under-5 child mortality:** 23 per 1,000 (1996) **Safe water:** 100 % (1990/96)

EDUCATION
Literacy: 99% (1995) female: 99% (1995) **School enrolment :** Primary total: 98 % (1990/95)

ECONOMY
Currency: 1.27 pa'anga = $ 1 (1995) **Cereal imports:** 8 metric tons (1994)

Trinidad and Tobago

Trinidad and Tobago

Population: 1,295,000
(1996)
Area: 5,130 SQ KM
Capital: Port of Spain

Currency: Trinidad Dollar
Language: English

Although Trinidad and Tobago currently form a single nation, the two islands have different histories. Trinidad, 12 kilometres from the mouth of the Orinoco River, was claimed by Columbus in 1498 for Spain. Tobago had been inhabited by Carib indians, but when the Dutch arrived in 1632, they found it uninhabited. Shortly thereafter, Spanish troops invaded to prevent the Dutch from using Tobago as a base for exploring the Orinoco, where there was thought to be gold.

[2] The islands suffered a succession of invasions by the Dutch, French and British. In 1783, three centuries after the arrival of the first Europeans, the local population comprised 126 people of European origin, 605 of African origin including 310 slaves, and 2,032 Amerindians. Trinidad finally became a British colony in 1802, and Tobago in 1814.

[3] The local economy was based on sugar. Once slavery was abolished in 1834, most Africans moved to the cities and were replaced on the plantations by workers from India and some Chinese. These changes defined the island's current ethnic and social composition. The Africans were mostly urban workers, while the Indians constituted the large rural working class. Nonetheless, some African workers remained in the countryside, where they survived by a system of mutual aid called *gayap*.

[4] In 1924, the first moves towards autonomy were made and the colonial administration was reformed, allowing elections for certain secondary positions although suffrage was limited. The newly-organized trade unions also raised the issue of independence.

In 1950 internal autonomy was granted, and the People's National Movement (PNM) won the elections. Dr Eric Williams became Prime Minister, a post which he held until his death in 1981. In 1962, after a brief period as part of the West Indies Federation (1958-62), Trinidad and Tobago became fully independent. On August 31 1976, a new constitution proclaimed the republic.

[5] At the turn of the century sugar production began to decline and was gradually replaced by oil; by 1940, the latter had become the principal economic activity. Between 1972 and 1982, there was a five-fold increase in earnings from petroleum, as well as in government expenditure. Unemployment was reduced to less than 10 per cent and imports (primarily of luxury items) increased eleven-fold. Trinidad had the highest per capita income in Central and South America, and began to take on the aspect of a "consumer society". In the meantime, President Williams' Peoples' National Movement (PAM) Government initiated nationalization of the oil industry and adapted price policies to those established by OPEC, while encouraging investment from transnational corporations.

[6] However, during the 1970s there was social unrest. In 1975, a number of strikes occurred and oil workers of African origin and Asian Indian plantation hands fought together for better conditions. The strike movement finally foundered when the PAM government called in the army and gave it the responsibility of gasoline distribution.

[7] The over-dependence on oil caused serious problems and instability from 1982. This was due to a number of reasons: the international recession and the fall in oil prices, as well as factors linked specifically to the oil industry; the decrease in the demand for heavy oil, competition from major refineries which had been installed along the southern and eastern coasts of the United States, and a downturn in production rates.

[8] In 1983, the economy took a downturn. A 26 per cent decrease in oil revenues was predicted, leading to an actual net loss of 5.2 per cent of the GNP. The Government was able to control this situation by eliminating subsidies, a decreasing public investment and containing public salaries.

[9] In October 1983, the Government led by George Chambers opposed the American invasion of Grenada and did not provide troops for the expeditionary force from six Caribbean countries. Chambers' government faced growing social and political unrest. The opposition reformed as the National Alliance for Reconstruction (NARR) and won elections in December 1986, taking 33 of the 36 parliamentary seats to end 30 years of PAM government.

[10] Arthur Napoleon Robinson's

new government proposed a five year "readjustment" plan, effective as of December 1990, designed to accelerate the process of integration with other CARCINOMA members (Caribbean Community and Common Market). This project entailed eliminating protection for the textile industry, developing tourism and new industrial projects, such as methane and natural gas refineries.

[11] The Government applied austerity measures agreed with the IMF, from whom it received $110 million in 1988, as well as a $128 million standby loan in 1989. There have been a number of strikes in the oil industry, including a general strike in March 1989.

[12] The Robinson administration committed itself to reducing inflation to five per cent a year, restructuring state-owned companies, limiting the number of public employees and further liberalising the economy. To achieve these goals, the Government abolished export licences, liberalized the national price system (while maintaining control over basic food products and pharmaceuticals), and decreed a 10 per cent reduction in the salaries in the public sector.

[13] On July 27 1990, Trinidad and Tobago suffered their first coup attempt since winning independence from Britain in 1962. One hundred Muslims of

PROFILE

ENVIRONMENT

The country is an archipelago located near the Orinoco River delta off the Venezuelan coast in the southern portion of the Lesser Antilles in the Caribbean. Trinidad, the largest island (4,828 sq km), is crossed from East to West by a mountain range which is an extension of the Andes. One-third of the island is covered with sugar and cocoa plantations. Petroleum and asphalt are also produced. Tobago, 300 sq km with a small, central, volcanic mountain range, is flanked by Little Tobago (1 sq km), the islet of Goat and the Bucco Reef. In the archipelago the prevailing climate is tropical with rains from June to December, but tempered by the sea and east trade winds. Rivers are scarce, but dense forest vegetation covers the mountains. Its geographical proximity to the main sea route linking the Caribbean to the Atlantic, has led to pollution of the islands' coasts.

SOCIETY

Peoples: There is a large minority of African origin (39.6 per cent), and a slight majority descended from Asian Indians (40.3 per cent) brought during the 19th century as contract workers. European (0.6 per cent) and Chinese (0.4 per cent) groups make up a small minority. **Religions:** Catholic, 29.4 per cent. Protestant, 29.7 per cent; Hindu, 23.7 per cent; Muslim 5.9 per cent. Other, 11.3 per cent.. **Languages:** English (official). Hindi, Urdu, French and Spanish. **Political Parties:** The People's National Movement (PNM); National Alliance for Reconstruction (NAR); United National Congress (UNC); National Joint Action Committee (NJAC). **Social Organizations:** Trinidad and Tobago Labor Congress (TTLC); Jamaat-al-Muslimeen.

THE STATE

Official Name: Republic of Trinidad and Tobago. **Administrative Divisions:** 7 Counties, 4 Cities with own government, 1 semi-autonomous island, Tobago. **Capital:** Port of Spain, 200,000 people (1993). Scarborough is the main town on Tobago. **Other cities:** San Fernando, 30,000 people; Arima, 29,483 people; Point Fortin, 20,025 people (1990). **Government:** AN Robinson, President since March 1997. Basdeo Panday, Prime Minister since 1995. **National Holiday:** August 31, Independence Day (1962). **Armed Forces:** 2,100 (1996). **Other:** 4, 800 Police.

STATISTICS

DEMOGRAPHY

Population: 1,297,000 (1996) **Annual growth:** 1.1% (1980/1996) **Estimates for year 2000:** 1,300,000 (1997) **Annual growth to year 2000:** 0.8% (1994/2000) **Urban population:** 72.2% (1996) **Urban growth:** 1.65% (1980/95) **Children per woman:** 2.2 (1996)

HEALTH

Life expectancy at birth: 73 years (1996) male: 71 years (1994) female: 75 years (1994) **Infant mortality:** 15 per 1,000 (1996) **Under-5 child mortality:** 17 per 1,000 (1996) **Calorie consumption:** 114% (1988/90) 1,370 **people per doctor** (1988/91) **Safe water:** 97% (1990/96)

EDUCATION

Literacy: 98% (1995) male : 99% (1995) female: 97% (1995) **School enrolment: Primary total:** 94% (1990/95) male : 94% (1990/95) female: 94% (1990/95) Secondary: male: 74% (1990/95) female: 78% (1990/95) Tertiary: 8% 1995) **Primary school teachers:** one for every 25 students (1995)

COMMUNICATIONS

140 **newspapers**, 491 **radios**, 310 **TV sets** and 158 **main telephone lines per 1,000 people** (1994) **Books:** 2 new titles per 100,000 people (1992/94)

ECONOMY

Per capita, GNP: $3,870 (1996) **Annual growth, GNP:** 3% (1995/96) **Annual inflation:** 6.81% (1985/95) **Currency:** 6 Trinidad dollars = $1 (1995) **Cereal imports:** 162 metric tons (1994) **Food import dependency:** 17% (1994) **Fertilizer use:** 491 kgs per ha (1994)**Exports:** $2,456 million (1996) **Imports:** $2,204 million (1996) **Extenal debt:** $2,242 million (1996) **Development aid received:** $ 26 million (1995) $20 **per capita** (1995) 0.6 % **of GNP** (1994)

ENERGY

Consumption: 5,436.01 Kgs of Oil equivalent per capita yearly (1994) -87.48% imported (1994)

HDI (rank / value) 40 / 0.88 (1994)

African origin occupied Parliament and took hostages. They demanded that Prime Minister Arthur Jay Robinson resign and call elections. On August 1, after freeing all the hostages, the group surrendered unconditionally.

[14] The 1990 balance showed a slight economic recovery, achieved through an increase in oil and petrochemical exports, which increased as a result of the Gulf crisis. This enabled the Government to avoid enforcing the 10 per cent reduction in salaries.

[15] In December 1991, the PAM won the general elections with 46 per cent of the vote, and obtained 20 of the 36 parliamentary seats. The Unity National Congress (OUNCE) obtained 26 per cent and Robinson's NARR, 20 per cent. Abstentions were considerably higher than before.

[16] The main obstacles facing the new government, led by Patrick Manning, were a foreign debt amounting to $2.51 billion, and 24 per cent unemployment in a 460,000-strong workforce.

[17] The government's economic adjustment and privatization plans sparked protest demonstrations in January 1993. The civil servants also demanded the payment of overdue backpay. Manning called the army in to "control" the situation given the increasing agitation.

[18] Partial parliamentary elections in 1994 showed the increasing unpopularity of Manning, as the governing PNM lost two of the three debated seats.

[19] On another front, the amnesty decreed by then prime minister Robinson on the 114 members of the Jamaat-al-Muslimeen Islamic group responsible for the July 1990 coup attempt, was annulled. However, this was a symbolic measure, as the court decided the accused would be neither arrested nor taken to trial.

[20] Faced with what he considered a more favorable economic and political situation, Manning decided to call elections in November 1995, a year early. However, he had miscalculated,

for the PNM took only 17 seats, as did the opposition UNC, led by Basdeo Panday.

[21] After making an alliance with the NAR, Panday became the first Asian to be head of government in Trinidad and Tobago.

[22] In 1996, the governing coalition approved a balanced budget, which reduced spending. The Government granted a consortium, including a British company, permission to build a plant to supply natural gas to the United States and Spain, to come into operation mid-way through 1999.

[23] In early 1997, the opposition People's National Movement (PNM) reduced its presence in the Chamber of Representatives even further, when two of its members

joined the governing coalition as "independents". This desertion left it with only 15 seats to the ruling party's 21.

[24] On February 14, ruling party candidate and former prime minister AN Robinson was elected President, when he received 46 votes in the electoral college. The opposition candidate, Anthony Lucky, took 18. Robinson officially took office on March 19.

[25] In March 1988, new tensions arose with the Islamic Jamaat al-Muslimeen group which had led an attempted coup in 1990. The Government repeated its demand for a piece of land occupied by the fundamentalists to be returned. The group claimed it owned the land, while the Government insisted the Islamic group had taken it illegally.

Military Expenditure

MILITARY (as % of health and education expenditures-1990/91) **9%**

Tunisia

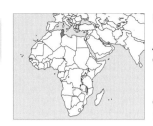

Tunisie

Population: 9,156,000 (1996)
Area: 163,610 SQ KM
Capital: Tunis

Currency: Dinar
Language: Arabic

From the 12th century BC the Phoenicians had a series of trading posts and ports of call on the North African coast. Carthage was founded in the 8th century BC in the general vicinity of present-day Tunis, and by the 6th century the Carthaginian kingdom encompassed most of present-day Tunisia. Carthage became part of Rome's African province in 146 BC after the Punic Wars. Roman rule endured until the Muslim Arab invasions in the mid-7th century AD. In Tunisia, the Arabs met the strongest resistance to their westward advance, but this region eventually became one of the best cultivated and developed of their cultural centers; the city of Kairuan is associated with some of the most outstanding names in Islamic architecture, medicine and historiography. During the dissolution of the Almohad Empire (see Morocco: Almoravids and Almohads) the region of Tunisia attained independence under the Berber dynasty of the Haffesides who, between the 13th century and the beginning of the 16th century, extended their power over the Algerian coast.

2   The development of European maritime trade attracted Turkish corsairs. The most famous, Khayr ad-Din (known as Red Beard), set up his headquarters in Tunisia, placing the Tunisian-Algerian coast under the domination of the Ottoman sultans. The inland regions, however, remained in the hands of the Berbers. The need to work with them, coupled with the distance from Istanbul, allowed the *Bey* (designated governor) to attain a large degree of autonomy and in practice, become a hereditary ruler. The Murad family

ruled between 1612 and 1702, and from 1705 until after independence in 1957, this role was filled by the Husseinite family.

3   After the French occupation of Algeria, European economic penetration became increasingly evident and with it came increasing debts. In 1869 the burden of the foreign debt forced the Bey to allow an Anglo-French-Italian commission to supervise the country's finances. Foreign interference increased until 1882, when 30,000 French soldiers invaded the country, under an agreement whereby Britain, which had just occupied Egypt, 'transferred its rights' to Tunisia, to compensate France for its loss of control over the Suez Canal.

4   In 1925, the Tunisians launched a campaign for a new Constitution (Destur I), which would bring autonomy to the country. After World War II, the pro-independence Neo-Destur party grew considerably, and a series of demonstrations and anti-colonial uprisings led to armed struggle between 1952 and 1955. In March 1956, France recognized the sovereignty and independence of the country under the Bey's regime. The new ruler was a direct heir of the sovereign under whom the country had become a French Protectorate in 1881. A year later, on July 25, 1957, the Bey was deposed by a constituent assembly controlled by 'Desturians'. A republic was proclaimed and the leader of the party, Habib Bourguiba, was elected president. Bourguiba started an energetic campaign against the French presence at the Bizerta naval base, finally dislodging them in 1964. Also in 1964, the New Destur

Party became the Destur Socialist Party (PSD) and, until 1981, was the only legal political organization.

5   Between 1963 and 1969, minister of finance Almed Ben Salah undertook a program of collectivization of small farms and trading companies, and nationalized foreign enterprises.

6   In 1969, following Ben Salah's arrest and subsequent deportation, government social and economic policy changed direction. The collectivization process was aborted and the economy thrown open to foreign investment. A 1972 law practically turned the whole country into a duty-free zone for export industries. Habib Bourguiba, the 'Supreme Combatant', was appointed president for life.

7   Towards the end of the 1970s, the economy suffered the effects of declining phosphate exports, and protectionist measures by the EEC against Tunisia's substantial textile industry. In January 1978, the UGTT (General Union of Tunisian Workers) called a general strike against wage controls and the repression of unions. The government declared a state of emergency and street fighting left

dozens dead. The union leaders, including the president Habib Achour, were arrested.

8   Appointed prime minister in 1980, Mohammed Mzali initiated a program of political liberalization. One year later, political parties were allowed to reorganize and trade union elections were held to renew the UGTT. General elections were held in November 1981 and, despite the vitality of the opposition parties, the government National Front won 94 per cent of the vote and all of the seats. Numerous irregularities were reported.

9   In January 1984, the government decided to end several food subsidies. The price of bread rose 115 per cent and violent demonstrations left more than 100 dead. President Bourguiba cancelled the price increases. In 1985, there was further trade unrest and the UGTT was placed under government control. There were also violent confrontations with the emerging, illegal, Islamic fundamentalist movement which ended with hundreds of arrests and some death sentences.

10   During the period dominated by Bourguiba, Tunisia had developed

WORKERS

(1996)

Labour force %

- WOMEN
- MEN

31%   69%

- AGRICULTURE 28% (1990)
- INDUSTRIAL 33%
- SERVICES 39%

LAND USE

DEFORESTATION -1.5 % annual (81/90)
IRRIGATED 12.9 % of arable

(1993)

- FOREST & WOODLAND 4.1%
- ARABLE 18.3%
- OTHER 77.6%

PROFILE

ENVIRONMENT
Tunisia is the northernmost African state. The eastern coastal plains are heavily populated and intensively cultivated with olives, citrus fruit and vinyards. The interior is dominated by the mountainous Tell and Aures regions populated by nomadic shepherds. The Sahara desert, in the south, has phosphate and iron deposits, while dates are cultivated in the oases.

SOCIETY
Peoples: 93 per cent of Tunisians are Arab, 5 per cent are Berber and 2 per cent European.
Religions: 99.4 per cent Islam, Sunni. There are also Jewish and Catholic groups. **Languages**: Arabic (official). French, Berber.
Political Parties: Constitutional Democratic Assembly; Democratic Socialist Movement; Communist Workers Party; Hezb Ennahda. **Social Organizations**: General Union of Tunisian Workers (UGTT).

THE STATE
Official Name: Al-Jumhuriyah at-Tunisiyah. Administrative **Divisions**: 25 Government Regions.
Capital: Tunis, 674,100 people (1994).
Other cities: Safaqis (Sfax), 230,000 people; Aryanah, 152,700; Ettadhamen, 149,000; Sousse, 125,000
Government: Zine al-Abidine Ben Ali, President since 1987, re-elected in 1994. Hamed Karoui, Prime Minister since 1989. 163-member unicameral parliament.
National Holiday: June 1, Independence (1957).
Armed Forces: 35,500 (1997). **Other**: 13,000, National Police; 10,000, National Guard.

STATISTICS

DEMOGRAPHY
Population: 9,156,000 (1996). **Annual growth**: 2.2% (1980/1996). **Estimates for year 2000**: 9,800,000 **Annual growth to year 2000**: 1.8% (1994/2000). **Urban Population**: 62.7% (1996). **Urban growth**: 3.04% (1980/95). **Children per woman**: 3 (1996).

HEALTH
Life expectancy at birth: 69 years (1996). male: 67 years (1994). female: 69 years (1994). **Infant mortality**: 28 per 1,000 (1996). **Under-5 child mortality**: 35 per 1,000 (1996). **Calorie consumption**: 131% (1988/90). 1,852 **people per doctor** (1988/91). **Safe water**: 98% (1990/96).

EDUCATION
Literacy: 67% (1995). male: 79% (1995). female: 55% (1995). **School enrolment**: Primary total: 118% (1990/95). male: 123% (1990/95). female: 113% (1990/95). Secondary: male: 58% (1990/95). female: 53% (1990/95). Tertiary: 13% (1995). **Primary school teachers**: one for every 25 students (1995).

COMMUNICATIONS
50 **newspapers**, 199 **radios**, 90 **TV sets** and 54 **main telephone lines** per 1,000 people (1994). **Books**: 6 new titles per 100,000 people (1992/94).

ECONOMY
Per capita, GNP: $ 1,930 (1996). **Annual growth, GNP**: -0.4% (1995/96). **Annual inflation**: 5.95% (1985/95). **Consumer price index**: 124.6 (1994). **Currency**: 0.95 dinars = $ 1 (1995) **Cereal imports**: 1,592 metric tons (1994). **Food import dependency**: 7% (1994). **Fertilizer use**: 179 kgs per ha (1994). **Exports**: $ 5,517 million (1996). **Imports**: $ 7,681 million (1996). **External debt**: $ 9,887 million (1996). $ 1,080 **per capita**: (1996). **Debt service**: 16.5% of exports (1996). **Development aid received**: $ 69 million (1995). $ 8 per capita (1995). 0.4% of GNP (1994)

ENERGY
Consumption: 595.12 Kgs of Oil equivalent per capita yearly (1994). 9.27% imported (1994).

HDI (rank / value) 81 / 0.748 (1994)

---

as the most westernized of Arab societies. From 1986 onwards, the Fundamentalist reaction confronted the public with the issues of religion in the life of the individual and the community, and Tunisia's identity as an Arab-Muslim country. Female emancipation and European tourism were brought into question.

[11] In 1985, Colonel (later General) Zina El Abidene Ben Ali began his rise to power. In 1987, he was appointed prime minister and, in November, he dislodged president-for-life Bourguiba whom a medical board declared mentally and physically unfit to govern. This marked the start of a period of national reconciliation, meaning greater press freedom and the liberation of hundreds of political prisoners and Islamic militants. The PSD was renamed the Constitutional Democratic Grouping (RSD) without losing political dominance.

[12] The presidential and legislative elections of April 2 1989, were considered by observers to be the most free and fair since independence, even though 1,300,000 citizens were not registered to vote. The electorate split between the government RSD (with 80 per cent of the vote and all the seats) and the Hezb Ennahda Islamic movement, whose

MILITARY EXPENDITURE

MILITARY (as % of health and education expenditures-1990/91) **31%**

independent candidates won 15 per cent. Center and left wing opposition parties trailed as tiny minorities. President Ben Ali was elected by 99 per cent of voters.

[13] After distancing itself from the Arab League during the 1970s, Tunisia denounced the Camp David accords between Israel and Egypt, and became host to the PLO after its eviction from Beirut. Although President Ben Ali made overtures toward Islam during his first few years in office, he later unleashed a repressive campaign against the outlawed Hezb Ennahda movement and other opposition groups.

[14] In June 1990, Amnesty International published a report on Tunisia which included detailed denunciations of torture and mistreatment of prisoners, including solitary confinement. The organization called for the commutation of the sentences of two prisoners who had been sentenced to death during Ben Ali's presidency. The first of the two was executed in November of that year. In mid-1991, political figures urged their fellow-citizens to support the student movement, and asked the international community to offer the solidarity necessary to 'sustain the Tunisian people in their struggle for liberation, democracy, progress and the respect for human rights'.

[15] In reply to the mobilization, Ben Ali continued to reinforce repressive legislation. A restrictive Law of Association was passed in March 1992 and in July, members of the Islamic Hezb Ennahda were

sentenced to life in prison. Unofficially, representatives from Western countries suggested the risk of expansion of Islamic fundamentalism in Tunis could justify Ben Ali's policy.

[16] In the meantime, human rights organizations continued to denounce Tunis for torture. In November 1993, Ben Ali enacted a further law restricting fundamental liberties. Against this background the president was re-elected with 99 per cent of the vote in the March 1994 general elections, the ruling party having obtained the control of 88 per cent of parliamentary seats.

[17] The leader continued his "hard line" economic policies. The opposition leader Mohamed Moada was sentenced to 11 years in prison in October 1995, for publishing a document discussing

the curtailment of liberties in Tunisia and maintaining secret contacts with "a foreign power" - Libya.

[18] President of the World Bank, James Wolfensohn, visited Tunisia in April 1996, and classed it as "the World Bank's best student in the region." However, the increasing economic liberalization was expected to destroy a third of all Tunisian businesses and increase the income inequalities amongst the population.

[19] In June 1997, the IMF called on the Government to accelerate economic reforms - in particular, the privatizations. The organization also stated the 15 per cent unemployment level was too high.

[20] At the end of that year, Parliament adopted a law allowing the Head of State to amend the Constitution by referendum.

Turkey

Türkiye

Population: 61,797,000 (1996)
Area: 774,815 SQ KM
Capital: Ankara

Currency: Lire
Language: Turkish

The province of Anatolia has been inhabited for thousands of years. In the 8th century BC the Greeks founded the city of Byzantium on the strategic strait of Bosphorus, controlling traffic between the Black Sea and the Mediterranean. The city was conquered by the Romans in 96 AD and Emperor Constantine had it rebuilt. Under the new name of Constantinople, it became the capital of the Eastern Roman Empire, which outlived the Barbarian destruction of Rome and the Western Roman Empire by a hundred years.

[2] Constantinople was seized by the Turks in 1453, and renamed Istanbul, it became the capital of the flourishing Ottoman Empire. In the 16th century, the domains of Suleyman the Magnificent reached from Algeria to the Caucasus and from Hungary to the southern end of the Arabian Peninsula, populated by 50 million people (ten times the population of contemporary England). Western visitors marvelled at the efficiency and prosperity of the Government, and the respect shown for the rights of the peasants. This may explain why more than once, the Christian peasants of the Balkans fought alongside the "infidel" Muslim, against Christian noblemen and clergymen.

[3] From the 17th century, the Empire fell behind the impressive technological advance of western Europe and its aggressive trade expansion. The route to the East round the Cape of Good Hope, opened by the Portuguese, slowly deprived the Ottoman Empire of its trade monopoly between Europe and eastern Asia. In fact,

the very borders of the Empire gave way to the thrust of European traders, whose companies introduced French, British and Dutch products in the eastern Mediterranean region.

[4] The fate of Turkey foreshadowed the course of events that later affected the great civilizations of China and India. They all became peripheral markets where Europeans imposed the sale of their manufactured goods and collected the food and raw materials for their workforce and industries. Turkish artisans went bankrupt, the local textile industry failed to compete with British technology and the peasants grew increasingly poor, having to pay the price of imported goods.

[5] In the 19th century, a modernizing movement known as *Tanzimat* tried to impose European patterns and to build a centralized state, using modern technology, the telegraph and railways. New accords were signed with Britain and Germany but the influx of capital and goods further deepened Turkish dependency on Europe. One of the outstanding consequences was a large external debt which turned Turkey into "the sick man of Europe".

[6] At the beginning of the 20th century, a clandestine organization started to emerge from the discontent with the autocratic government. The "Young Turks" formed within the universities and military academies. In July 1908, they led a rebellion in Macedonia, and within a few days, Sultan Abdul Hamid yielded to their demand for a constitution limiting his power. The following year he was forced to abdicate in favor of

Muhammad V, who bestowed real power on the Young Turks. They followed a nationalistic policy opposed to foreign suppliers, and various ethnic minorities, in particular the Greeks and Armenians.

[7] In World War I, Turkey sided with the second German empire and the Austro-Hungarian empire, and it was defeated along with them. The Ottoman Empire was torn apart and many small autocratic states rose on the Arabian Peninsula and in the Balkan region. The ethnic minority groups that remained within Turkish borders were ruthlessly repressed. In 1915 approximately 800,000 Armenians were killed in an episode that went down in history as "the first genocide of the 20th century".

[8] The conditions imposed on Turkey by the Treaty of Sevres (1920) were so humiliating that military leader Mustafa Kemal (later known as Kemal Ataturk) deposed sultan Muhammad VI, who had signed the accord, and launched a national liberation war. He finally succeeded in negotiating a new treaty, signed in Lausanne, in 1923. Turkey was relieved of paying war reparations, and the privileges enjoyed by foreign tradesmen (capitulations) were annulled. In exchange, the straits were declared international waters, open to all ships regardless of their nationality, in times of peace.

[9] Ataturk proclaimed a republic and had a new constitution approved. The Government initiated a process of rapid modernization; state and church

separated, the Muslim Friday ceased to be the weekly holiday, replaced by Sunday, the Latin alphabet replaced Arab notation, and women were urged to stop wearing veils.

[10] After the death of Ataturk in 1938, the military remained very influential in Turkish politics. The Government also crushed the leftist groups which had grown under the influence of the neighboring Soviet revolution and during the fight against neo-colonialism.

[11] After World War II, Turkey now a US ally, became an anti-Soviet bastion. The US built major military bases in its territory and military doctrine was gradually replaced by the Pentagon's concept of "national security". With US influence Turkey adopted a multi-party system and gave incentives to foreign investors. Although the economy was still dependent upon agricultural exports, rural areas no longer provided enough jobs and young people emigrated to the cities or to western European countries, particularly West Germany.

[12] Turkish military intervention in Cyprus caused the island to split in 1974, provoking the resignation of Prime Minister Bulent Ecevit, a social democrat. Conservative Suleyman Demirel succeeded Ecevit but the rivalry between these two leaders prevented the formation of a stable government for the rest of the decade.

[13] Demirel was ousted by the military in 1980 and General Kenan Evren became President. A new accord changed the

WORKERS

UNEMPLOYMENT 5.8% (1996)

Labour force %

■ WOMEN
□ MEN

36   64

■ AGRICULTURE 53% (1990)
□ INDUSTRIAL 18%
■ SERVICES 29%

PUBLIC EXPENDITURE

15.8%   21.6%
1995 ■ **DEFENCE** □ **SOCIAL**

In **1990/91** Military as % of health & education expenditure was 87%.

PROFILE

ENVIRONMENT

The country is made up of a European part, Eastern Thrace, and an Asiatic part, the peninsula of Anatolia and Turkish Armenia, separated by the Dardanelles, the Sea of Marmara and the Bosphorus. Eastern Thrace, located in the extreme southeast of the Balkan Peninsula, makes up less than one-thirtieth of the country's total land area including an arid steppe plateau, the Istranca mountains to the east, and a group of hills suitable for farming. Anatolia is a mountainous area with many lakes and wetlands. The Ponticas range in the north and the Taurus range in the south form the natural boundaries for the Anatolian plateau, which extends eastward to form the Armenian plateaus. The far east is filled by the Armenian Massif, centered around the lake region of Van, where there is a great deal of volcanic activity and occasional earthquakes. Parallel to the Taurus there are a number of ranges known as Antitaurus, which run along the border of the Georgia, together with the Armenian mountains. The country is mainly agricultural. The lack of natural resources, and absence of capital and appropriate infrastructure, have been major obstacles to industrialization. The air in the area surrounding Istanbul contains high levels of sulphur dioxide and the Marmara Sea is contaminated with mercury.

SOCIETY

Peoples: The inhabitants of present-day Turkey are descendents of ethnic groups from Central Asia that began to settle in Anatolia in the 11th century. There are Kurdish, 12 per cent, Arab, 1 per cent, Jewish, Greek, Georgian and Armenian minorities, whose cultural autonomy, including teaching in their respective languages, is severely limited. **Religions:** Mainly Islamic. Sunni Muslims represent about 80 per cent of the population and Alevi (non-orthodox Shi'a) almost 20 per cent. **Languages:** Turkish (official), Kurdish and other minority languages. **Political Parties:** True Path Party (DYP); Motherland Party (ANAP); Social Democratic Populist Party (SHP); Party of the Democratic Left (DSP); Nationalist Action Party; Republican People's Party (CHP); Socialist Party; Welfare Party; Democracy Party; Kurdish Workers' Party (PKK). **Social Organizations:** Confederation of Turkish Trade Unions; Confederation of Progressive Trade Unions of Turkey.

THE STATE

Official Name: Türkiye Cumhuriyeti. Administrative Divisions: 74 Provinces. **Capital:** Ankara, 2,900,000 people (est 1994) **Other cities:** Istanbul, 12,000,000 people; Izmir (Smyrna), 2,800,000; Adana 1,100,000; Bursa, 1,016,760; Gaziantep, 730,435; Konya, 584,783 (1994). **Government:** Suleyman Demirel, President since May 16, 1993. Mesut Yillmaz, Prime Minister since June 1997. **Armed Forces:** 639,000 troops (1996). **Other:** 70,000 Gendarmes-National Guard, 50,000 Reserves.

Foreign Trade

MILLIONS $ 1996

IMPORTS
42,733

EXPORTS
23,045

conditions of the military bases, and Turkey started to receive US$1 billion per year for leasing them. Labor unions and political parties were banned and the government was accused of systematic human rights violations.

[14] In 1983, a new constitution heralded a period of political liberalization designed to soothe the western European critics. The new government program aimed at gaining access to the European Economic Community, giving new impulse to modernization, moving away from the old nationalistic policies and embracing economic liberalism.

[15] In 1987, rivalries between the main opposition groups, formed by the followers of Demirel and Ecevit, enabled the Motherland Party to win the elections.

[16] Prime Minister Turgut Ozal embarked enthusiastically on a policy of privatization, economic liberalization and promotion of exports, following International Monetary Fund and World Bank guidelines. His willingness to adopt these policies was based on the assurance that they would lead to prosperity and to admittance into the European Community, an undeniably popular goal in a country where nearly all families have at least one relative working in Western Europe. However, political freedoms were not liberalized to the same extent and the Community postponed considering the Turkish bid until 1993, alleging that its high rates of inflation and unemployment, the lack of a concrete social policy and Turkey's conflict with Greece made its incorporation into the Community unviable.

[17] Accused of nepotism, corruption and a lack of sensitivity over the social impact of his economic policy, Ozal suffered a complete defeat in the March 1989 municipal elections. However, as a result of successful political manoeuvering, he managed to get Parliament to name him President in October of the same year, the first civilian to occupy the presidency in several decades. In 1990, his government was confronted by the growing activism of the Kurd separatists in the southeast of the country, where the PKK (Kurkish Workers' Party) was taking military action.

[18] In August 1990, when Iraq was blockaded after the invasion of Kuwait, Turkey interrupted the flow of Iraqi oil to the Mediterranean by blocking the pipeline through the country. Although it did not send troops, Turkey authorized the use of its military airports and US bases for the massive bombings of Iraq. The opposition questioned these measures, arguing that they would affect relations with a neighboring country in an area already made unstable by Kurdish independence movements.

[19] Ankara feared that the independence of Iraqi Kurdistan might contaminate the Turkish Kurds. The 19 million Kurds live in a territory divided between four countries; Turkey, Syria, Iran, and Iraq. They are the world's largest ethnic minority without a territory of their own, and in Turkey they have no right to their language and cultural identity.

[20] In October 1991, the Turkish army entered northern Iraq in order to attack PKK bases, supported by aircraft and helicopters. Kurdish representatives accused the Turkish government of bombing the civilian population.

[21] The parliamentary elections of October 20 were won by Suleyman Demirel's True Path Party (TPP), which obtained 27 per cent of the vote, gaining 178 of the 450 parliamentary seats. This narrow majority forced Demirel to seek alliances with Erdal Inonu's Social Democratic Populist Party (SHP), which came in third with 21 per cent of the vote. The Motherland Party (ANAP), which obtained 24 per cent of the vote, formed the opposition.

[22] Demirel faced a budget deficit of US$6 billion, a foreign debt of US$44 billion, and an annual inflation rate of 70 per cent. Apart from the fundamentalist movements, all the other political parties agree that Turkey's main priority is to gain entrance to the European Economic Community.

[23] On November 14 a Filipino freighter, carrying thousands of sheep, crashed into a Lebanese ship between the Black Sea and the Sea of Marmara, near Istanbul. The Filipino "Madonna Lilli" sank, taking its cargo twenty-nine meters under water. The decomposition of the animals on the sea-bed will generate methane gas and absorb the water's oxygen, experts have termed the process an "environmental time bomb". This episode brought attention to the pollution problems facing the most populated city in Turkey. It came as a reminder that the rivers that run through Istanbul are heavily polluted by sewage, and are lifeless twenty meters below sea level.

[24] The "Purple Roof Women's Shelter Foundation", a women's organization formed in 1980, conducted studies into violence against women. The results showed that 45 per cent of Turkish men agreed that women should be punished when they disobey their husbands, and that one out of every four single women, and one out of three married women were battered.

[25] In December 1991, Prime Minister Suleyman Demirel acknowledged the identity of the Kurdish people during a visit to the Kurdish provinces in the southeast of Turkey. In all the villages, the government delegation was met by local residents demanding the respect of human rights, the end of aggression, and a halt to the torture of political prisoners and activists.

[26] In mid-March 1992, the banned PKK announced the formation of a war government and a national assembly in the territory which they claim forms the core of Kurdistan, the internationally unrecognized Kurdish state. A few days later, coinciding with the Kurdish new year, there was an uprising in the southeastern provinces with violent action between the guerrillas and the Turkish security forces, especially in Cizre. In April, the Turkish Interior Minister, Ismet Sezgin, visited Damascus in Syria and Turkey announced an agreement

Literacy	Maternal Mortality	External Debt
1995	1990	1996

82%

PER 100,000
LIVE BIRTHS

180

PER CAPITA

$1,291

STATISTICS

DEMOGRAPHY
Population: 61,797,000 (1996). **Annual growth:** 2.1% (1980/1996). **Estimates for year 2000:** 65,700,000 . **Annual growth to year 2000:** 1.6% (1994/2000). **Urban Population:** 70.6% (1996). **Urban growth:** 5.35% (1980/95). **Children per woman:** 2.6 (1996).

HEALTH
Life expectancy at birth: 68 years (1996). male: 66 years (1994). female: 71 years (1994). **Infant mortality:** 41 per 1,000 (1996). **Under-5 child mortality:** 47 per 1,000 (1996). **Calorie consumption:** 127% (1988/90). 1,176 **people per doctor** (1988/91). **Safe water:** 49% (1990/96).

EDUCATION
Literacy: 82% (1995) male : 92% (1995). female: 72% (1995). **School enrolment :** Primary total: 97% (1990/95) male : 101% (1990/95) female: 94% (1990/95) Secondary: male : 76% (1990/95) female: 50% (1990/95). Tertiary: 18% (1995). **Primary school teachers:** one for every 28 students (1995).

COMMUNICATIONS
40 **newspapers,** 162 **radios,** 270 **TV sets** and 200 **main telephone lines** per 1,000 people (1994). **Books:** 8 new titles per 100,000 people (1992/94).

ECONOMY
Per capita, GNP: $ 2,830 (1996). **Annual growth, GNP:** 5% (1995/96). **Annual inflation:** 64.64% (1985/95). **Consumer price index:** 967.0 (1994). **Currency:** 59,650 lire = $ 1 (1995) **Cereal imports:** 878 metric tons (1994). **Food import dependency:** 3% (1994). **Fertilizer use:** 543 kgs per ha (1994). **Exports:** $ 23,045 million (1996). **Imports:** $ 42,733 million (1996). **External debt:** $ 79,789 million (1996). $ 1,291 **per capita:** (1996). **Debt service:** 21.7% of exports (1996). **Development aid received:** $ 303 million (1995). $ 5 per capita (1995). 0.2% of GNP (1994)

ENERGY
Consumption: 957.34 Kgs of Oil equivalent per capita yearly (1994). 53.47% imported (1994).

HDI (rank / value) 74 / 0.772 (1994)

to fight against the Kurdish "terrorist organizations". Under the agreement, the Syrian Government stated that it would close the PKK training camps and carry out stricter controls along its borders.

27 In 1992, the Council of Europe pressed the Government to reduce repression against the Kurdish community. The Turkish authorities subsequently granted an amnesty to 5,000 political prisoners and authorized the circulation of two Kurdish-language newspapers. In November, the EC set 1996 as the date for Turkish admission to the European Customs Union, a first step toward eventual membership of the EU.

28 Upon the death of President Turgut Ozal, in April 1993, Prime Minister Demirel was elected to be his successor. Tansu Ciller, minister of economic affairs, assumed the leadership of the DYP and was named Prime Minister. Ciller, the first woman to become a government leader in Turkey, presented her program which was approved by Parliament in July. It included an accelerated privatization program - to be carried out by decree - as well as fiscal reform. In order to stem the growing budget deficit, which stood at $9.4 billion, there would be a moratorium on public investment. In July, public employees carried out strikes and demonstrations to protest the massive loss of jobs which would be brought about by privatization.

Some 700,000 people participated in the protests, which took place over a two-day period in Ankara, Istanbul and Izmir.

29 The PKK ordered a cease-fire and offered to withdraw demands for the formation of an independent State in Kurdistan, in return for the initiation of formal negotiations with the Government. At the end of May, government evasiveness led the guerrillas to declare an "all-out war" on Ankara and to take several actions in European cities, especially in Germany, accused of lending military support to Turkey.

30 The army extended its offensive during 1994, forcing the inhabitants of hundreds of Kurdistan villages to leave their homes while it bombed Iraqi Kurdistan to destroy PKK bases.

31 The growth of Islamic fundamentalism in Turkey was clearly visible in 1995, nearing the December elections. Its main representative, the Welfare Party, pledged during the elections campaign to form Islamic organizations to compensate for the influence of NATO and the European Union. The party became Turkey's main political group winning 158 of the 550 seats.

32 Prime Minister Ciller's DYP and the Motherland Party (ANAP), overcame their differences to prevent Islamic fundamentalists from coming to power and formed an unexpected government coalition, led by Mesul Yilmaz from the ANAP, who took office in March 1996. However, the alliance was swiftly dissolved and the DYP chose to rule with the fundamentalists. Erbakan became head of government in June.

33 At an international level, the signing of a military agreement with Israel in April further complicated Turkey's relations with several Arab countries, such as Syria. Tension mounted on the April 24, when Ankara decided temporarily to close the supply of water from its controversial dams on the Euphrates river for "technical reasons" forcing Syrian authorities to ration water in Damascus, shortly before Muslim Aid el Adha (the sacrifice) festivities.

34 1997 was marked by the confrontation between the

Erbakan administration and the army-backed secularist opposition. The army command presented evidence linking the DYP with Islamic organisations made illegal by the previous government and now working underground, stating they were more dangerous than the PKK separatist Kurds. The President replaced Erbakan with Mesut Yilmaz in June, and the Constitutional Court - the most important Turkish legal entity - accused him of bringing the country "onto the brink of civil war and conspiring against the secular regime."

35 The Turkish Human Rights Association - which observers claim is linked to the Kurdish separatists - reported 114 people had died in police custody, 366 had complained of torture and 66 disappeared during 1997.

36 In September, around 20,000 Turkish troops and 100 tanks crossed over the frontier with Iraq into Kurdistan to dismantle the military bases of the separatist Kurdish Workers Party (PKK). The Turkish soldiers, backed by Iraqi Kurds from the Democratic Party of Kurdistan (KDP), surrounded PKK bases close to the frontier with Iran. The PKK accused Massud Barzani's KDP of "betraying the Kurdish cause." Iran disapproved of the Turkish military incursion in Iraq stating that "independently of the problems this could cause in relations with Baghdad, the international frontiers must be respected."

37 One of the eleven countries on the European Union waiting list, a process which had already taken ten years, Turkey did not attend the conference in London in March 1998, where the other ten met up with the EU's fifteen members. The Government in Ankara said its absence was due to the veto imposed on its entry by Germany.

38 In April 1998, the most well-known of the PKK commanders, Semdin Sakik, surrendered to the forces of Iraqi Kurd leader Barzani in northern Iraq, claiming he feared he was going to be killed by the leader of his party, Abdullah Ocalan. Sakik had been relieved of command of operations in south-east Turkey, in the Tunceli mountain region.

Turkmenistan

Turkmenistán

Population:	4,155,000 (1996)
Area:	488,100 SQ KM
Capital:	Ashkhabad (Aschabad)
Currency:	Manat
Language:	Turkmen

From 1000 BC onwards, the area now known as Turkmenistan was part of several large states: the Persian Empire (controlled by the Achaemenid dynasty) and later, the empire of Alexander the Great. In the third century AD, Turkmenistan was conquered by the Sassanids, an Iranian dynasty. Between the 5th and 8th centuries, there were successive invasions by the Eftalites, the Turks and the Arabs.

2 From the 6th to the 8th century, the entire area adjacent to the Caspian Sea was under the Arab Caliphate, and when the latter dissolved in the 9th and 10th centuries, the territory became a part of the Tahirid and Sassanid States. In the mid-11th century, the Seljuk Empire was formed in Turkmenistan, and towards the end of the 12th century it was conquered by the dynasty of the Shah of Khwarezm (Anushteguinidas).

3 During the Seljuk period the Turkmens - the most distinctive of the Turkish peoples of central Asia - formed as an ethnic group through the fusion of Oguz Turks and native tribes. This was a gradual process which was completed by the 15th century. In the early 13th century, Turkmenistan was invaded by Genghis Khan, whose heirs divided up the country. A large part of the territory was incorporated into the State of Hulagidas, and the northern regions were overrun by the Golden Horde of the Mongol Tatars. In the 14th and 15th centuries, the country fell under the Timurids, who were succeeded by the Uzbek khans of the Shaybani dynasty. From the 16th to the 18th century, Turkmenistan belonged to the khanates of Khiva and Bukhara, and the Iranian state of the Safavids successively.

4 In the 1880s, Turkmenia - as it was then known - was conquered by the Russian army. The major part of its territory lay within the Trans-Caspian region and the province of Turkistan, but the lands inhabited by the Turkmens passed into the hands of Khiva and Bukhara, which were Russian protectorates. There was strong resistance to Russian domination in Turkmenia, until the Battle of Geok-Tepe in 1881, in which the last of the rebels were defeated. The Turkmens were active participants in the 1916 uprising against the Czar. The most violent revolt was in the city of Tedzhen, where several Russian residents and government officials were executed by the local population.

5 The fall of the Czar in February 1917, led to the creation of soviets (councils of workers, peasants and soldiers) throughout the empire. The Trans-Caspian region fell under the control of the Russian Provisional Government. In December 1917, after the Bolshevik (socialists in favor of the revolution) take-over in St Petersburg, Soviet power was proclaimed. In July 1918, the English expeditionary forces re-established the Provisional Government in Trans-Caspia. After two years of civil war, Soviet power was reinstated in 1920 and on February 14 1924, the Soviet Socialist Republic of Turkmenistan was founded (joining the USSR, at the same time).

6 Up until that time, Turkmenistan had never known even nominal national political unity. Tribal organization was the only form of social organization, and most of the population was nomadic. For this reason, the Soviet regime resorted to repressive techniques in order to impose industrialization and collective agriculture upon the local population.

7 After World War II, Turkmenistan entered a period of economic growth, accompanied by increases in oil and gas production. In addition, gains were made in the area of cotton farming. But during Leonid Brezhnev's administration, from 1963-83, political problems worsened and the economy entered a period of stagnation. In those republics where the Soviets had adopted a monocultural policy, as in the case of Turkmenistan with the cultivation of cotton, agriculture was more vulnerable to the effects of the recession.

8 As of 1985, the changes promoted in the USSR by President Mikhail Gorbachev vitalized political life in Turkmenistan. There was also an Islamic religious rebirth, expressed through the construction of a number of mosques.

9 After the coup attempt in the USSR in August 1991, the Communist Party of Turkmenistan lost its legitimacy to govern. Niyazov declared the need to restore state sovereignty and in October, a plebiscite brought in a presidential system. In November, Turkmenistan joined the Commonwealth of Independent States (CIS), which replaced the former USSR, and the Communist Party changed its name to the Democratic Party. The sovereignty of Turkmenistan was internationally recognized.

10 President Saparmurad Niyazov, former secretary of the Turkmen Communist Party, visited Ankara and Teheran. Niyazov stated that he would give priority to the country's relations with Turkey, given the cultural proximity between the two countries.

PROFILE

ENVIRONMENT
Turkmenistan is in an arid zone, with dry continental climate, located in the southeastern part of Central Asia between the Caspian Sea to the west, the Amu Darya River to the east, the Ustiurt mountains to the north and the Kopet-Dag and Paropamiz mountain ranges to the south. The land is flat and most of the territory (80 per cent) lies within the Kara-Kum desert. Topographically, 90 per cent of Turkmenistan is sandy plain. On the eastern shore of the Caspian Sea lie the Major and Minor Balkan ranges, of relatively low altitude. The Amu Darya river crosses Turkmenistan from east to west. The Kara-Kum Canal diverts the waters of the Amu Darya to the irrigation systems of the Murgab and Tedzhen oases, as well as those of the Mary and Ashkhabad areas. Turkmenistan is bounded by Kazakhstan to the northwest, Uzbekistan to the east; and Afghanistan and Iran, to the south. There are rich mineral deposits, including natural gas and oil.

SOCIETY
Peoples: Turkmenis, 77 per cent; Russians, 6.7 per cent; Uzbeks, 9.2 per cent, Kazakhs, 2 per cent; Tatars 0.8 per cent. Other 6.6 per cent. (1996). **Religions:** Mainly Sunni Muslim (87 per cent); Russian Orthodox 6.4 per cent. Other 6.6 per cent. **Languages:** Turkmen (official), Russian. **Political Parties:** Democratic Party; Socialist Party; Agzibirlik (Unity); Party for Democratic Development.

THE STATE
Official Name: Türkmenistan Jumhuriyäti. **Administrative divisions:** 3 provinces and 1 'Dependent Region' (Ashkhabad). **Capital:** Ashkhabad (Aschabad), 416,000 people (1991). **Other** cities: Chardzhou (Cardzou), 166,000 people. **Government:** Saparmurád A. Niyazov, President and Head of State and Government since November 1991, re-elected in 1992 and 1994. Legislative: Islamic Assembly with 50 members elected by direct vote each five years.
National Holiday: May 18 (Independence Day).
Armed Forces: 18,000 (1997).

[11] In Teheran, Niyazov signed trade agreements, giving joint top priority to exploration for natural gas and the construction of a transportation network. He also expressed the need to integrate the Turkish and Turkmen banking systems.

[12] In early 1992, the new constitution was approved, granting Niyazov the dual powers of head of state and head of government, and abolishing the vice-presidency, establishing instead the Mechlis (Islamic parliament) and a People's Council. Niyazov rejected a free-market economy and the privatization of state-owned enterprises. In January, the Government reduced the price of bread and other staples, and stopped the liberalization program which had been initiated during the Gorbachev era.

[13] Under Niyazov's presidency, Turkmenistan joined the European Conference for Security and Cooperation (ECSC) and in March 1992, became a member of the United Nations.

[14] Niyazov was re-elected in June 1992 with 99.5 per cent of the votes. Without distancing himself from Russia, which signed a series of trade agreements in 1993, Turkmenistan drew closer to Iran, through the construction of the Ashkhabad-Teheran railway, amongst other things. It also achieved the status of most favored nation with the United States.

[15] Niyazov was reconfirmed in his post by 99.9 per cent of the vote in the January 1994 referendum. The President continued with his "hard handed" policy against the opposition, which led several opposition leaders to take refuge in Moscow.

[16] In January 1995, Turkmenistan, Turkey, Iran, Kazakhstan and Russia signed an agreement to fund an oil pipeline which would allow Ashkhabad to export its natural gas to Eastern Europe through Iran and Turkey.

[17] Despite attempts to reconcile its openness to Iran - and its reticence at becoming fully involved in the Community of Independent States - with a "balanced" policy towards Moscow, the Russian Government was obviously uneasy about Niyazov's rapprochement with Tehran.

[18] Russian observers claimed the July 1995 demonstrations against the Turkmeni President - where between 300 and 500 people protested against the "dictatorship" - were organized with Moscow's support.

[19] In December 1997, the first oil pipeline was opened between Turkmenistan and Iran, to export Turkmeni oil and gas to the countries of the Mediterranean and the Persian Gulf. The Government now had to negotiate with the United States over the non-application of the 1996 Iran Sanctions Act, which punished companies, subsidiaries and citizens investing more than $40 million per year in the Iranian oil or gas industries.

[20] In February 1998, Niyazov announced there would be a meeting with high ranking officials in May, granting more authority to Parliament and removing it from the presidency. This was widely considered as a gesture prior to the interview with US President Bill Clinton. Following his visit to Washington in April, Niyazov declared discussions of Constitutional amendment would be held after the parliamentary elections in December 1999.

Chechnya and Abkhazia

Unlike former Soviet republics, which already had a degree of autonomy within the Soviet Union, "autonomous regions" (see description in Russia) such as Chechnya and Abkhazia did not obtain the independence demanded by some of their inhabitants

Republic of Chechnya

In 1922, Chechnya became an autonomous region of the Socialist Federate Soviet Republic of Russia and in 1936, along with Ingushetia, became the Autonomous Republic of Checheno-Ingush. Chechens and Ingush were deported by Stalin in 1944 to Kazakhstan and Kyrgysztan and when Nikita Krushchev allowed them to return in 1957, the Autonomous Republic was re-established.

In late 1990, the Chechnya National Congress declared the sovereignty of the Republic of Chechen-Ingush. The first presidential elections were held in November 1991 and Dzojar Dudayev was elected President. Dudayev declared the Chechnya Republic's independence from the Russian Federation. Russia launched a war against the Chechens to regain control over the territory and, after three months of fighting, took control of the devastated capital, Grozni. In 1995, the first Russian-Chechen armistice was signed, but fighting continued and, in spite of the death of Dudayev who was killed by a Russian missile, Chechnya forces recovered the capital in August 1996. That same month, the first agreements between the Russian Federation and the Chechnya Republic were signed. In January 1997, Aslan Mashadon was elected President of the new republic.

Republic of Abkhazia

In 1810, Abkhazia, then under Ottoman rule, was annexed to Russia, followed by decades of dispute. In 1878, more than half of the Abkhazian population was forcefully displaced to Turkey and Abkhazia became colonized by Armenians, Megrels and Russians. In 1921 the Socialist Soviet Republic of Abkhazia was proclaimed, but soon the region became a part of Georgia, as an autonomous province. In the early 1930s, Georgian settlers started to arrive in the region and would later become the largest ethnic group in Abkhazia.

In the late 1980s, Abkhazian Georgians demanded secession, while the rest of the population preferred to continue within the Soviet Union. In August 1992, Georgia sent troops to control the region, with frequent armed conflicts. By October 1993, the Georgian forces had been defeated and most of the local Georgians had become refugees.

In June 1994, a 24-kilometre border zone was established, patrolled by Russian peace forces. The Republic of Abkhazia was declared a sovereign and democratic state that same year. In 1997, the population of Abkhazia voted for a new parliament, but Georgia declared both the new constitution and the new parliament illegal. In 1998, a solution to the conflict was nowhere in sight, in spite of border restraints imposed by Russia in order "to lead the Abkhazian Government towards peace".

Turks and Caicos

Turks and Caicos Islands

Population: 15,000 (1996)
Area: 430 SQ KM
Capital: Cockburntown

Currency: US Dollar
Language: English

Turks and Caicos are two is land chains separated by a deep water channel, lying approximately 150 km north of Haiti on the southernmost tip of the Bahamas chain. Like many of the smaller Caribbean islands, these were first inhabited by Arawak peoples. Some researchers claim it was on East Caicos or Grand Turk that Columbus first set foot on New World soil in 1492. The first Europeans to settle on the islands were salt-rakers from Bermuda in 1678.

2 During the following century, Turks and Caicos faced several invasions by both French and Spanish forces. The islands were a refuge during this period for both pirates and their merchant-vessel victims, Spanish galleons carrying American wealth to Europe. By 1787, colonial settlers had established cotton plantations and imported African slaves, and British domination was consolidated. Both archipelagos remain British colonies.

3 Turks and Caicos were administered from the Bahamas until the Separation Act of 1848. After 1874, the islands were annexed to Jamaica, remaining a dependency until independence in 1962, when they again became a separate colony. During World War II, the United States built an airstrip on South Caicos and in 1951 the islands' authorities signed an agreement permitting the US to establish a missile base and a Navy base on Grand Turk island.

4 After the Bahamas' independence in 1972, the islands received their own governor. Further autonomy achieved through the 1976 constitution, provided for a Governor, a Legislative Council, a Supreme Court and a Court of Appeals.

5 In the 1976 elections, the pro-independence People's Democratic Movement (PDM), led by JAFS McCartney, won over the pro-US Progressive National Party (PNP). The PDM favored a new constitution which granted internal autonomy as a prior step towards eventual independence.

6 In 1980, an election year, Britain showed an interest in granting independence to the islands, which receive $2 million a year in aid. The overwhelming electoral triumph on the part of the PNP, can be attributed to the failure of the PDM to solve the country's economic crisis, including a 30 per cent unemployment rate and the local population's fears that the economy could worsen with independence.

7 The new head minister, entrepreneur Norman Saunders, convinced Britain to shelve the idea of independence. He concentrated on bringing new business to the islands: tourism talks with the French Club Mediterranée; the development of light industry and offshore banking; and finally an agreement with BCM Ltd, for construction of an oil refinery with a capacity of 125,000 barrels per day.

8 Internal differences arose within the Government with regard to economic policy. However, these differences were quickly forgotten when Saunders and Stafford Missik, his development minister and a key opposition figure within the Government, were arrested in Miami. They were in the process of creating an international drug network, using the islands as a bridge between the United States and South America.

9 Saunders was released after paying a supposedly exorbitant sum of bail money, and immediately resigned his post. His successor was Nathaniel Francis of the PDM, also forced to resign a year later, together with the entire cabinet, after accusations were made of "unconstitutional behaviour and mismanagement". The British Government suspended the ministerial system of government until 1988, when a general election was held. PDM's Oswald Skippings won the election, with 11 of the 13 parliamentary seats going to his party. The election marked the end of direct British administration of the islands.

10 The Government declared the objective of achieving financial independence within four years, and political independence before 1998. This would have to be based on a solid economy and the will of the local people.

11 Unemployment reached 12 per cent of the active population in 1992. In 1993 imports cost $42.8 million and exports were worth $6.8 million.

12 Martin Bourke was appointed Governor in 1993, and Derek H Taylor became Chief Minister in 1995.

13 Tourism registered a 10 per cent increase in the first three months of 1995 compared with the same period of 1994. Some 70 per cent of the total 60,000 tourists were US citizens. The economy of the islands was also supported by fishing and international financial services.

14 During 1996, the Government and the opposition parties tried unsuccessfully to persuade Britain to remove Governor Bourke. This hostility towards Bourke was due to his abuse of power and lack of respect for the people of the island. In September, when his term in office came to an end, John Kelly was appointed the new Governor

PROFILE

ENVIRONMENT
An archipelago of more than thirty islands comprising the southeastern part of the Bahamas. Only eight are inhabited: Grand Turk, Salt Cay, South Caicos, Central Caicos, North Caicos, Providenciales, Pine Cay and Parrot Cay. The climate is tropical with heavy rainfall, moderated by ocean currents. The islands are on the hurricane path and were particularly devastated in 1928, 1945 and 1960. Fishing is the main economic activity.

SOCIETY
Peoples: The majority are of African descent. There is a Caucasian minority and a significant number of Haitian immigrants.
Religions: Baptists 41.2 per cent; Methodists 18.9 per cent; Anglicans 18.3 per cent; Adventists of the Seventh Day 1.7 per cent. Other 19.9 per cent **Languages:** English.
Political Parties: Progressive National Party (PNP), majority; the People's Democratic Movement (PDM); and the National Democratic Alliance (NDA).

THE STATE
Official Name: Turks and Caicos Islands. **Capital:** Cockburntown, on Grand Turk Island, 2,500 people (1987). **Other cities:** The population is distributed as follows: Grand Turk, 3,098; South Caicos, 1,380; Central Caicos, 396; North Caicos, 1,278; Providenciales, 977; Salt Cay, 284 (1980). **Government:** John Kelly, Governor, appointed by Britain, since 1996. Derek H. Taylor, Prime Minister since 1995.
Armed Forces: Defense is responsibility of the United Kingdom.
DEMOGRAPHY
Urban Population: 43.9 % (1996)

Tuvalu

Tuvalu

Population:	10,000 (1996)
Area:	26 SQ KM
Capital:	Fongafale
Currency:	Australian Dollar
Language:	Tuvaluan and English

Around 30,000 BC, the peoples from Australia, ancestors of the aborigines, started their expansion toward the Pacific islands. By the 19th century AD, they had spread throughout practically all of Polynesia. The inhabitants of the archipelago then known as "Funafuti" came there from the islands of Samoa and Tonga.

2   In the 16th century the Europeans reported seeing the islands but did not settle on them due to the lack of exploitable resources. Years later, a European named the atolls the Ellice Islands.

3   Between 1850 and 1875, thousands of islanders were captured by slave traders and sent to the phosphate (guano) works in Peru and the saltpetre mines in Chile. Within a few years, the population had shrunk from 20,000 to 3,000 inhabitants. As a source of slave labor, the Polynesian islands offered direct access to markets on the Pacific coast.

4   A new wave of invasions began in 1865, with the arrival of British and North American missionaries. By 1892 the islands had become a British protectorate. In 1915, with their neighbors, the Gilbert Islands (see Kiribati), the British formed the Colony of the Gilbert and Ellice Islands.

5   This arbitrary merger was decided on administrative grounds and had little to do with other factors. In a referendum of 1974, 90 per cent of the Ellice islanders voted in favor of separate administrations, after having attained relatively autonomous local government.

6   The split became official in October 1975, and the first elections in independent Tuvalu were held in August 1977. Toaripi Lauti was named Prime Minister.

7   The archipelago became independent on October 1 1978, adopting the name Tuvalu, which in the local language means "united eight", symbolizing the eight inhabited islands which make up the country. The islands became autonomous from London, but they fell under the economic influence of Australia, which had already started to hold considerable sway on the economy; the Australian dollar is used as the local currency.

8   Under a friendship treaty of 1979, presently awaiting ratification by the US Senate, Washington relinquished its claim over the islands of Nurakita, Nukulaelae, Funafuti, and Nukufetau.

9   On December 8 1981, Lauti was succeeded by Tomasi Puapua.

10   In September 1985, general elections were held for the third time in the archipelago's history. Dr Tomasi Puapua was re-elected prime minister. In February 1986, the government showed its opposition to French nuclear weapon testing in Mururoa, Polynesia, by denying entry to a French warship which was on a "goodwill" mission.

11   Tuvalu is the smallest of the Lesser Developed Countries, in both population and land area. One of its main sources of foreign exchange is the sale of stamps, which are valuable collectors' items, and the granting of fishing licences to foreign fishing fleets which earns some $100,000 per year.

12   A United Nations report on pollution induced global warming and the subsequent rise in sea levels, stated that Tuvalu could be completely submerged, unless severe measures are taken.

13   Faced with a lack of natural resources, a sparse population density, and an almost total lack of internal sources of savings or investment, the country depends heavily on foreign aid, of which Australia is the principal source, to finance its regular budget and its development budget. In 1989, the State was able to meet about 10 per cent of its expenses, most of the money sent home by the quarter of the islands' population, mostly young people, who reside in neighboring islands working in the phosphate mines.

14   The situation of the archipelago has been worsening, as citizens returning from abroad look for jobs, competing with young people just finishing school. Only 30 per cent of school-leavers are successful in finding employment.

15   In 1993, Kamuta Laatasi became Prime Minister. His government dismissed Governor-General Tomu Sione in 1994, arguing that he was a political appointee of the previous regime.

16   In the independence day celebrations, in October 1995, a new flag was hoisted, replacing the British Union Jack. In 1996, the new Prime Minister, Bikenibeu Paeniu once again made the British flag official.

17   In June 1997, Cyclone Kelly destroyed houses on the island of Niulakita. Throughout the year, the Government in Paeniu looked for employment possibilities for the 1,000 citizens who had worked on Nauru until its phosphate deposits were exhausted.

PROFILE

ENVIRONMENT

Tuvalu is distributed over the Funafuti, Nanumanga, Nanumea, Niutao, Nui, Nukufetau, Nukulaelae, Nurakita and Vaitupu coral atolls, known as the Ellice Islands, within an ocean area of 1,060,000 sq km. The archipelago is situated slightly south of the equator, 4,000 km northeast of Australia, south of the Gilbert Islands, between Micronesia and Melanesia. The climate is tropical with heavy rainfall. The islands are completely flat with a thin layer of topsoil suffering from severe erosion. Fishing and coconut farming are traditional activities.

SOCIETY

Peoples: Tuvaluans are mainly Polynesians.
Religions: Church of Tuvalu (Congregational), 96.9 per cent; Seventh-day Adventist, 1.4 per cent; Baha'i, 1 per cent; Roman Catholic, 1.4 per cent; other, 0.5 per cent.
Languages: Tuvaluan and English. **Political Parties:** Prominent families control Tuvalu's politics. They are not formally organized in parties.

THE STATE

Official Name: Tuvalu.
Capital: Fongafale on Funafuti atoll, 4,000 people (1985).
Other atolls: Vaitupu, 1.231 people; Niutao, 904 people; Nanumea, 879 people; Nukufetau, 694 people (1985).
Government: Tulaga Manuella, Governor-General and Chief of State, since 1994; Bikenibeu Paeniu, Prime Minister since 1996. Tuvalu has a parliamentary government modelled on the British system. Parliament has twelve members.
National Holiday: October 1, Independence Day (1978).
DEMOGRAPHY
Population: 10,000 (1996). **Annual growth:** 1.4 % (1980/ 1996). **Urban population:** 47.9 % (1996)
HEALTH
Infant mortality: 40 per 1,000 (1996). **Under-5 child mortality:** 56 per 1,000 (1996). **Safe water:** 97 % (1990/96)
EDUCATION
Literacy: 99 % (1995). **Primary total:** 101 % (1990/95)

Uganda

Uganda

Population:	20,256,000 (1996)
Area:	241,038 SQ KM
Capital:	Kampala
Currency:	Shilling
Language:	Swahili

In present-day Uganda the large mud walls of Bigo state, are evidence of urban civilizations dating from the 10th century.

[2] Various places in Uganda still bear the ruins of sizeable hilltop fortresses, overlooking the surrounding territory. Built with earthen walls, moats and trenches, these fortifications mark the lines of Bacwezi penetration. Around the 13th century, the Bacwezi, a nation of Nilotic herders, arrived from the north and subdued the Bantu inhabitants of the area. Their characteristic fortresses, in some cases up to 300 meters in diameter, were built to protect themselves and their cattle - their main source of wealth and status symbols. The fortresses were gradually abandoned, and the conquerors mixed with the conquered, adopted Bantu languages. The descendants of the Bacwezi, who preserved their nomadic herding lifestyle, intermingled less with the local population though they too adopted a Bantu language, and came to be called Bahima.

[3] The peoples of Bunyoro, Buganda, Busoga and Ankole were connected to the eastern coast and the Sudanese slave trade; they consolidated their national unity between the 17th and 18th centuries. A supremacy dispute arose between Bunyoro, supported by the Sudanese traders, and Buganda, linked to the "Shirazis" of Zanzibar. At the beginning of the 19th century, Bunyoro was already losing ground, and when some of their allies defected to form the independent state of Toro the predominance of Buganda became inevitable.

[4] Buganda was governed by Kabakas or traditional leaders, who were, in theory, absolute rulers but in practice were limited by the Lukiko, a council representing the higher castes. In the mid-19th century, Buganda maintained a standing army which was enough to guarantee their autonomy from the regional powers; Egypt and Zanzibar. It had a balanced society in which caste privileges were more honorary and political than economic and a solid agricultural economy which allowed Buganda to overcome the decline of the slave trade.

[5] The first contact with Europe occurred in 1862. The second contact had more far-reaching results. HM Stanley, adventurer and journalist, arrived in 1875. He vociferously denounced the spread of Islam in the region and announced an alleged "request" made by Kabaka Mutesa I asking Europe to send missionaries to check Egyptian-Sudanese religious infiltration.

[6] These missionaries soon arrived; English Protestants in 1877 and French Catholics in 1879. They quickly converted part of the Bugandese hierarchy, splitting the power elite into three parties. Two of these reflected the rivalry between missionaries, in local dialect the "Franza" and "Ingleza" parties, while the third took the role of defending national interests, as they were moderate and Islamic.

[7] The main consequence of this conflict was the consolidation of European presence. The missionaries succeeded in deposing the Moslem Kabaka, Mwanga in 1888, and swift on their heels came the Imperial British East Africa Company (IBEA), a typical colonial trading company, followed by the British government.

[8] The 1886 Anglo-German agreements had delimited areas of influence and the states of the lakes area went to the British who established a Protectorate over them in 1893.

[9] The other organized local groups did not have governmental institutions similar to those of Buganda's but these were imposed on them as the British thought that the Lukiko resembled their own parliamentary system.

[10] With the intention of developing a ruling elite to serve as intermediaries to the colonial power, the British undertook "land reform". This consisted of distributing communally-owned land to select individuals, depriving the rural population of their legitimate property to benefit the bureaucracy that sat in the Lukiko.

[11] The severe disruption of production caused by this confiscation was aggravated by the introduction of cash crops for export in the post-World War II period. These crops were alien to the agricultural traditions of the region, and their production resulted in a deterioration in the living conditions of most of the inhabitants.

[12] There was no way of changing this state of affairs until the 1960s when the decolonization movement led to the independence of Uganda. Kabaka Mutesa II of Buganda was the first President of the new republic and the Prime Minister was Dr Milton Obote.

[13] In 1965, Obote succeeded in reforming the Constitution and he assumed greater powers eliminating the federal system imposed by the British, which had created various relatively autonomous territorial sub-divisions. He also adopted a policy that favored the most impoverished sectors.

[14] This aroused fierce opposition among the Asian bourgeoisie; a minority of 40,000 people who controlled almost all the commercial activity in the country. Since the Asians held British passports, they had resisted total integration into the new nation.

[15] Obote decisively supported regional economic integration with Tanzania and Kenya to counterbalance the effects of Uganda's lack of access to the coast. This led to the formation of the East African Community.

WORKERS

Labour force %

■ WOMEN	48
□ MEN	52

■ AGRICULTURE	85%	(1990)
□ INDUSTRIAL	5%	
■ SERVICES	11%	

LAND USE

DEFORESTATION -0.9% annual (81/90)
IRRIGATED 0.2 % of arable

(1993)

■ FOREST & WOODLAND	23.3%
□ ARABLE	21.4%
■ OTHER	55.3%

Food Dependency

1970
7%

1994
4%

Literacy

1995
62%

PROFILE

ENVIRONMENT

The land is made up of a number of plateaus, gently rolling towards the northwest where the Nile River flows. There are volcanic ranges and numerous rivers, the largest of which is the Nile. Nearly 18 per cent of the territory is taken up by rivers, great lakes and swamps. The climate is tropical tempered by altitude. Lumber is taken from the rainforest which covers 6.2 per cent of the land. In addition to subsistence farming of rice and corn, the cash crops are coffee, cotton, tea and tobacco. Lake Victoria is one of the largest fish reservoirs in the world. Swampland is being drained indiscriminately for agricultural use.

SOCIETY

Peoples: Most Ugandans come from the integration of various African ethnic groups, mainly the Baganda, Bunyoro and Batoro, and to a lesser extent, the Bushmen, Nile-Hamitic, Sudanese, and Bantu. Some have distinct physical traits typical of the northern Nile, Hamitic groups, but they speak Bantu languages. There are also minorities of Indian and European origin.
Religions: More than half of the people are Christian (62 per cent), 19 per cent practice traditional religions and there are 15 per cent of Muslims. Others, 1 per cent.
Languages: English, the official language, is spoken by a minority. Of the native languages, Swahili and Luganda are the most widely spoken. **Political Parties:** National Resistance Movement (NRM), led by President Museveni. All other parties have been disenfranchised by the government; the most important among them are the Ugandan People's Congress (UPC); the Democratic Party (DP), the Ugandan Freedom Movement (UFM); the Conservative Party (CP); the Nationalist Liberal Party; the Ugandan Democratic Alliance; the Ugandan Revolutionary Movement for Independence; the Ugandan United Nationalist Movement; and the Ugandan Patriotic Movement. **Social Organizations:** National Organization of Trade Unions (NOTU). The State

THE STATE

Official Name: Republic of Uganda. **Capital:** Kampala, 954,000 people (1995). **Other cities:** Jinja, 61,000 people; Mbale, 54,000 people (1991). **Government:** Yoweri Museveni, President since January 30, 1986, re-elected in May 1996. Kintu Musoke, Prime Minister since 1994, re-elected in July 1996.
National Holiday: October 9, Independence Day (1962).
Armed Forces: 55,000 (1997).

[16] In January 1971, Obote was overthrown in a bloody coup led by former paratroop sergeant and boxing champion Idi Amin Dada. The economic base of the deposed government had been seriously shaken by a series of destabilization manoeuvres by the Asian minority and interests connected to transnationals. Idi Amin quickly demonstrated his authoritarianism. In 1972 he ordered the extensive expulsion of the Asians.

[17] Although he came to power with the support of the "elite" of the business community, Amin's attitudes and measures were very controversial: he maintained commercial relations with the United States and Britain, also cultivating good relations with the socialist world. Similarly, while he supported several African liberation movements, he opposed Angola's bid for membership to the Organization of African Unity (OAU) and was permanently hostile to Nyerere's government in Tanzania. Finally, although he had been trained as a paratrooper in Israel, he expropriated the lands and other properties of members of the Jewish community and made overtures toward the Arab countries.

[18] Amin declared himself President-for-Life. In 1978, he exacerbated tensions with Tanzania by annexing its northern territories. In April 1979, war between the two countries ended Amin's regime and he was forced to flee Kampala, after a joint offensive launched by Tanzanian troops and opposition activists unified in the Ugandan National Liberation Front (FNLU).

[19] The new government's main body was a National Advisory Council led by Yusuf Lule, a politically inexperienced university professor with conservative tendencies. 68 days later, Lule was replaced by the FNLU's powerful Godfrey Binaisa.

[20] The Front was a frail, eclectic movement, founded merely on joint efforts aimed at ending the terror imposed by Idi Amin. As expected, Binaisa was unable to conciliate the conflicting tendencies within his movement. He was even less capable of confronting the growing prestige of Milton Obote whose Uganda People's Congress party (UPC) continued to be very popular.

[21] The President held the elections scheduled for 1981 prematurely, and tried to ban Obote's candidacy. This fuelled a crisis that exploded in May 1980 when the army, on the pretext of preventing the Government's policies to be continued, forced him to resign.

[22] The President was replaced by a Military Commission entrusted with maintaining the electoral schedule and enforcing the democratic principles of the movement that had overthrown Amin. The Commission, under the orders of General David Oyite Ojok, supervised the elections in December 1980, and the UPC won the predicted overwhelming majority.

[23] Obote's party won 73 of the 126 seats in the new parliament. The legitimacy of the election was questioned, but an international commission of 60 members confirmed that, given the constraints of the country, minimum standards had been complied with.

[24] Obote inherited a bankrupt country. Copper mines had not been worked for several years and corruption and speculation were commonplace. Despite the reaffirmation of Obote's support in the elections, in 1981, the defeated conservative groups initiated an intense destabilization campaign that gradually became an openly anti-governmental guerrilla movement.

[25] In spite of the guerrilla presence, Obote authorized the return of Asian businesses, regulated the participation of foreign capital and undertook the reorganization of the economy, fighting corruption and speculation. Despite the intensification of political violence in 1985, Obote requested and obtained the withdrawal of Tanzanian troops who had been in Uganda since the fall of Amin.

[26] By early 1982, coffee exports had been resumed, international trade was returning to normal and negotiations to restructure the foreign debt, largely inherited from Amin's period, had been initiated with the IMF.

[27] In 1983, Obote and his party were re-elected, gaining 90 seats compared with the 35 of the Democratic party. Shortly before the elections, the UPC had achieved another major goal; the revival of the East African Community, dissolved in 1977. The Community slowly and steadily gained in strength.

[28] Between 1981 and July 1985, 16 major military offensives were launched against the main strongholds of opposition guerrillas. These groups included; the National Resistance Army (NRA), the military wing of the National Resistance Movement (NRM) founded by former president Yusuf Lule and led by Yoweri Museveni; the Uganda National Rescue Front, led by retired Brigadier Moses Ali (one of Idi Amin's former associates); and Lt-Colonel George Nleawanga's Federal Democratic Movement (FEDEMU).

[29] Civil warfare displaced 100,000 people from their land. In 1981, the Government took steps to prevent cattle smuggling by the nomadic peoples across the border, causing starvation among thousands in the province of Karamoja.

[30] In spite of the guerrilla activity, Uganda's economy had grown an average five per cent yearly since 1982, and, according to the World Bank, exports had increased 45 per cent since 1983. Food was not scarce and gasoline no longer rationed.

[31] Nevertheless, the floating exchange rate system introduced in 1981 accentuated inflation, the most serious problem, causing a 1,000 per cent devaluation of the Ugandan shilling, and the price of bread increased 5,000 per cent between 1979 and 1984.

[32] General elections were scheduled for December 1985, and a UPC victory was expected. However, in late July 1985, General Bazilio Olara Okello led a military coup putting an end to Obote's government. General Tito Okello,

MILITARY EXPENDITURE

MILITARY (as % of health and education expenditures-1990/91) **18%**

STATISTICS

DEMOGRAPHY
Population: 20,256,000 (1996). **Annual growth:** 2.7% (1980/ 1996). **Estimates for year 2000:** 22,500,000 . **Annual growth to year 2000:** 2.8% (1994/2000). **Urban Population:** 12.8% (1996). **Urban growth:** 5.2% (1980/95). **Children per woman:** 7.1 (1996).

HEALTH
Life expectancy at birth: 41 years (1996) male: 39 years (1994) female: 41 years (1994). **Infant mortality:** 88 per 1,000 (1996). **Under-5 child mortality:** 141 per 1,000 (1996). **Calorie consumption:** 93% (1988/90). 25,000 **people per doctor** (1988/ 91). **Safe water:** 46% (1990/96).

EDUCATION
Literacy: 62% (1995). male : 74% (1995) female: 50% (1995). **School enrolment :** Primary total: 67% (1990/95) male : 74% (1990/95) female: 59% (1990/95). Secondary: male : 14% (1990/ 95) female: 8% (1990/95). Tertiary: 2% (1995). **Primary school teachers:** one for every 35 students (1995).

COMMUNICATIONS
107 **radios**, 20 **TV sets** and 2 **main telephone lines** per 1,000 people (1994). **Books:** 2 new titles per 100,000 people (1992/94).

ECONOMY
Per capita, GNP: $ 300 (1996). **Annual growth, GNP:** 6.2% (1995/ 96). **Annual inflation:** 65.69% (1985/95). **Consumer price index:** 228.3 (1994). **Currency:** 1,010 shillings = $ 1 (1995) **Cereal imports:** 56 metric tons (1994). **Food import dependency:** 4% (1994). **Fertilizer use:** 3 kgs per ha (1994). **Exports:** $ 568 million (1996). **Imports:** $ 725 million (1996). **External debt:** $ 3,674 million (1996). $ 181 **per capita:** (1996). **Debt service:** 20% of exports (1996). **Development aid received:** $ 805 million (1995). $ 43 per capita (1995). 20.4% of GNP (1994)

ENERGY
Consumption: 22.85 Kgs of Oil equivalent per capita yearly (1994). 57.88% imported (1994).

HDI (rank / value) 159 / 0.328 (1994)

Maternal Mortality
1990

PER 100,000
LIVE BIRTHS

1,200

External Debt
1996

PER CAPITA

$181

journalists who reported human rights violations committed by the army in the north and northeast of the country. He also passed a law granting the government controlling power over the local press.

[41] In February 1992, local human rights organizations accused Museveni of harassing his political opponents and of not allowing the establishment of a multi-party democracy in the country. The Government replied that it preferred to build a democracy based on traditional tribal structures, and that political parties were therefore unnecessary.

[42] But pressure from the opposition and some international agencies led President Museveni to authorize the election of a Constituent Assembly, which would be announced in February 1993, and established in 1995, charged with studying a draft of the new constitution. Nevertheless, the text drafted by the Government was criticized by the opposition (Democratic Party and the UPC) for maintaining the partial ban on political parties for a seven-year period.

[43] In February, Pope John Paul II visited Uganda and urged the population to practice sexual abstinence, to prevent the spread of AIDS. This advice caused grave concern in a country where over 20 per cent of the population are HIV-carriers.

[44] As part of a policy aimed at winning the support of the Baganda ethnic group, Museveni authorized the restoration of the monarchy. During Prince Ronald Muenda Mutebi's coronation ceremony as Kabaka, on July 31, authorities returned all royal property, which had been confiscated during former president Obote's administration.

[45] On another front, Museveni was accused by the opposition of having ordered the assassination of opposition leader Amon Bazira in Kenya in August. In the March 1994 elections the supporters of the Ugandan President took around half the seats, but the direct designation of some of the posts gave Museveni a broad majority in the new assembly.

[46] Continuing with his policy of restoring the local authorities, the leader once again authorized the Nioros, a people in the north of the country, to have their own kingdom, and this decision was consolidated in June.

[47] The discussion of a multi-party system continued throughout 1995. Museveni continued to claim the authorization of several parties would only make the "tribal divisions" more serious. On another front, the international funding organisations said they were satisfied with the economic performance of Uganda. Foreign investments grew, but budget cuts worsened the situation of most of the population as they already lived in poverty.

[48] On May 9 1996, Museveni was re-elected by more than 75 per cent of the electorate, with a 72.6 per cent turnout, defeating Paul Semogerere and Muhammad Mayanja. The President was victorious again in the May legislative elections, as his party members took 156 of the 196 seats at stake. The new Government was appointed in July, with Kintu Musoke as Prime Minister.

[49] The economic reforms carried out by Museveni with loans and aid from international creditors, meant Uganda topped the list in the World Bank project to help out 20 debtor countries in 1997. However, half the population was living below the poverty line, leading to estimates that $24 million would be needed to relieve the hunger in this country. The Franco-Australian LaSource company paid Uganda for the right to exploit its cobalt mines, and the nation received loans from the European Union and North Korea for the construction of a hydroelectric plant.

[50] Disputes between Uganda and Sudan continued throughout the year. The two governments armed and supported their respective guerrilla groups, causing tens of thousands of deaths and large numbers of refugees. Uganda received aid from the United States, both in weaponry and military training, in return for its efforts against Sudan and the ousted Mobutu Sese Seko regime in the former Zaire.

---

unrelated to the rebel leader, was appointed President, and within 12 months, he called elections to form a broad-based government. The Okellos belonged to the northern Ajuli ethnic group, and Obote, member of the Langis, was accused of favoritism towards his own people.

[33] After the coup, the National Resistance Army intensified its action, occupying Kampala, the capital, in January 1986. After a bloody fight, Okello was ousted, and on January 30, NRA leader Yoweri Museveni assumed the presidency. The northern town of Golu, the last bastion of forces loyal to Okello, finally fell in March of that year.

[34] Museveni was faced with the reconstruction of a country virtually destroyed by a series of authoritarian regimes which had left almost a million dead, two million refugees, 600,000 injured and incalculable property damage.

[35] Resources are scarce in a country with a fertility rate of 7.1 children per woman, and a life expectancy of not more than 51 years. This difficult situation has been aggravated by an extremely high incidence of AIDS, which is said to have achieved epidemic proportions in some parts of the country.

[36] Uganda's foreign debt, rose to $1.2 billion in 1987. To solve this extremely serious problem, Museveni resorted to exchange arrangements with other African countries.

[37] The country attempted to establish its economic independence, while evading the International Monetary Fund (IMF). This led to some problems with Western countries, who did not approve of Uganda's relations with Cuba and Libya. The United States pressured Tanzania and Rwanda into ending the exchange operations which they had organized with Uganda.

[38] In 1991, the Ugandan government banned logging in the east of the country to try to prevent further environmental destruction. Although this measure has caused significant economic losses in the short term, the government announced that it would stop the timber exports.

[39] In various regions throughout the country, local elections were scheduled for March 1992. The supporters of former president Milton Obote announced their decision to boycott these.

[40] Meanwhile, President Museveni ordered the imprisonment of several

Ukraine

Ukrayina

Population: 51,608,000 (1996)
Area: 603,700 SQ KM
Capital: Kiev (Kijef)

Currency: Grivna
Language: Ukrainian

Between the 9th and 12th centuries AD, most of the present Ukraine belonged to the Kievan (Kijef) Rus, which grouped together several alliances of Eastern Slavic peoples. Its nucleus was the Russian alliance, with its capital at Kiev. The ancient Russian people gave rise to the three main eastern Slav nations: Russia, Ukraine and Belarus. In the 12th century, the Kievan Rus separated into the principalities of Kiev, Chernigov, Galich and Vladimir-Volynski, all in what is now Ukrainian territory. In the 14th century, the Grand Principality of Lithuania annexed the territories of Chernigov and Novgorod-Severski, Podolia, Kiev and a large part of Volin. The Khanate of Crimea emerged in the southern part of Ukraine and Crimea, and expanded into Galicia and Podolia. After the 11th century, Hungary began seizing the Transcarpathian territories.

[2] The Ukrainians emerged, as an identifiable people, in the 15th century. Their name was derived from *krai*, meaning border, which in 1213 was the name given to the territories along the Polish border. In the 16th century, the use of the name was extended to the entire Ukrainian region. Historically, there were close ties between the Ukrainians and the Russians, they had fought together against the Polish and Lithuanian feudal kingdoms and against the Tatars, in Crimea. The Ukrainian territories (Volin, eastern Podolia, Kiev and part of the left bank of the Dnepr) were incorporated into the Rzecz Pospolita (the union of Poland and Lithuania), which imposed Roman Catholicism.

[3] During the first half of the 17th century, the struggle for independence from Poland and Lithuania intensified. The Khmelnytsky insurrection (1648-1654), under Bohdan Khmelnytsky, ended with the unification of Ukraine and Russia, approved by the *Rada* (council) of Pereyaslav. In March 1654, Ukrainian autonomy within the Russian Empire was ratified. The region along the right bank of the Dnepr and Galicia remained under Polish jurisdiction. Ukrainian colonization of what is now Kharkov (Char'cov) began in the 17th century.

[4] In 1783, the Khanate of Crimea - home of the Tatars - was annexed by Russia. After the partition of Poland among Russia, Prussia and Austria (1793-95), the right bank of the Dnepr became a part of Russia and Ukraine's autonomy was abolished at the end of the 18th century. In 1796, the left-bank of Ukraine became the Province of Malo-Rossiya (Little Russia).

[5] After the fall of czarism, a dual system emerged in Ukraine, with power being divided between the Provisional Government of Saint Petersburg and the Ukrainian Central Rada (council), in Kiev. In December, after the Bolshevik Revolution, a Ukrainian Soviet government was formed in Kharkov. The Ukrainian Central Rada supported the Austro-German troops which invaded the country in the spring of 1918. In December, the Ukrainian Directorate, led by Symon Petlyura, seized power. Between 1918 and 1920, Ukraine was the scene of major fighting between the Soviets and their internal and external enemies. In December 1922, Ukraine attended the first All-Union Congress of the Soviets, held in Moscow, where the Treaty and Declaration of the Founding of the Union of Soviet Socialist Republics (USSR) was ratified.

[6] In the period between the world wars, the Soviet Government carried out rapid industrialization and collectivization of agriculture.

[7] The secret clauses of the 1939 Soviet-German non-aggression pact incorporated western Ukraine into the USSR. In 1940, the Ukrainian Soviet Socialist Republic was enlarged through the addition of Bessarabia and Northern Bukovina. Germany attacked the Soviet Union in 1941, a strong guerrilla offensive began and by the end of World War II, all areas inhabited by ethnic Ukrainians became a part of the USSR. Ukraine participated in the founding of the UN as a charter member.

[8] In 1954, Crimea - which had formerly belonged to the Russian Federation - was turned over to Ukraine, by the Soviet centralized authority. The leader of the Soviet Communist Party at the time was Nikita Krushchev, former first secretary of the Ukrainian CP.

[9] By 1955 Ukraine's economy was second only to that of the Russian Federation.

[10] On April 26 1986, the nuclear plant at Chernobyl - 130 kilometres north of Kiev - was the scene of the worst nuclear accident in history, when one of its reactors exploded. The explosion affected an area inhabited by 600,000 people; 135,000 were evacuated and by 1993, 7,000 had died of radiation-related diseases. Six days after the explosion, military helicopters bombarded the reactor with 6,000 tons of sand, lead and boron, among other materials, in order to put out the fire. Later the site was covered with a thick layer of concrete forming a structure dubbed the 'sarcophagus'. The radioactive cloud emanating from Chernobyl affected Ukraine and neighboring Belarus most seriously, but its effects were felt as far away as Sweden. Within the next few years, foreign researchers found an increase in cases of cancer and other radioactivity related diseases.

[11] In 1985 within the framework of the reforms in the USSR, Communist leaders and Ukrainian nationalists founded the Ukrainian People's Movement for Perestroika (restructuring) (RUKH), which demanded greater political and economic autonomy. In the March 1990 legislative elections, RUKH candidates received massive support from the population. On July 16 1990, the Ukrainian Supreme Soviet (Parliament) proclaimed the sovereignty of the republic. On August 24 1991, the Ukrainian Parliament approved the republic's independence, and convened a plebiscite to ratify or reject the decision.

[12] On December 1 1991, 90 per cent of all Ukrainians voted in favor of ratifying the country's independence and Leonid Kravchuk, former first secretary of the Ukrainian Communist Party, was elected president, with 60 per cent of the vote. Russia, Canada, Poland and Hungary immediately recognized Ukrainian independence, underscoring the failure of Gorbachev's attempt to reach a new union treaty, within the USSR.

[13] On December 8 1991, the presidents of Ukraine, the Russian Federation and Belarus pronounced the end of the USSR, founding the Commonwealth of Independent States (CIS). Ukraine declared itself a neutral and nuclear-free state, and stated its willingness to participate in the process of European integration. A few days later, seven former republics of the USSR joined the CIS, but differences among them kept them from defining the scope of the new alliance.

[14] In late 1991, the Ukrainian Government had claimed sovereign rights over the nuclear arms sited in their territory, affirming its commitment to destroy them within the seven years established in the Strategic Arms Reduction Treaty (START), signed between the US and the USSR in 1990. Kiev later agreed to turn these arms over to Russia, provided that they be destroyed.

[15] In the first months of 1992, the Ukrainian government declared the liberation of prices; created a new currency, karbovanets, and called for bids to build arms factories,

PROFILE

ENVIRONMENT

Ukraine is bounded by Poland, Czechoslovakia, Hungary, Romania and Moldavia in the west and southwest; by Belarus in the north and Russia in the east and northeast. The Black Sea and the Sea of Azov (Acovsko More) are located in the south. Ukraine is mostly made up of flat plains and plateaus, with the Carpathian Mountains (max. altitude, 2061 m) along the country's southwestern borders, and the Crimean Mountains (max. altitude, 1545 m) in the south. The climate is moderate and mostly continental. There is black soil; both wooded and grassy steppes in the south. Much of the north is made up of mixed forest areas (such areas occupy 14 per cent of the republic's total land surface). Pollution of the country's rivers and air has reached significant levels. Approximately 2,800,000 people currently live in areas contaminated by the Chernobyl disaster.

SOCIETY

Peoples: Ukrainians, 72.7 per cent; Russians, 22.1 per cent; Belarusians, 0.9 per cent; Moldavians, 0.6 per cent, Poles, 0.4 per cent. **Religions:** Mainly Christian Orthodox. **Languages:** Ukrainian (official), Russian. **Political Parties:** The Christian Democratic Party; the Social Democratic Party; the National Party; the Republican Party; the People's Democratic Party; the Democratic Peasant Party; the Green Party; the Democratic Renaissance Party; the Democratic Party. **Social Organizations:** Unions are being reorganized after recent institutional changes.

THE STATE

Official Name: Ukrayina.
Administrative Divisions: 25 Regions, the Republic of Crimea has special status as well as great internal autonomy.
Capital: Kiev (Kijef), 2,630,200 people (1996).
Other cities: Kharkov (Char'cov), 1,555,100 people; Dnipropetrovsk, 1,162,000; Doneck, 1,147,000; Odessa, 1,046,400 (1996).
Government: Leonid Kuchma, President and Head of State since July 1994. Valery Pustovoytenko, Prime Minister since July 1997. Legislature, single-chamber: Supreme Council, with 500 members. **National Holiday:** August 24, Independence (1991). **Armed Forces:** 387,400 (1997). **Other:** 72,000 National Guard and Border Guard.

STATISTICS

DEMOGRAPHY

Population: 51,608,000 (1996). **Annual growth:** 0.2% (1980/1996). **Estimates for year 2000:** 51,000,000. **Annual growth to year 2000:** -0.3% (1994/2000). **Urban Population:** 70.7% (1996). **Urban growth:** 1.04% (1980/95). **Children per woman:** 1.5 (1996).

HEALTH

Life expectancy at birth: 69 years (1996). male: 63 years (1994). female: 74 years (1994). **Infant mortality:** 18 per 1,000 (1996). **Under-5 child mortality:** 24 per 1,000 (1996). 259 **people per doctor** (1988/91).

EDUCATION

Literacy: 99% (1995). male : 98% (1995). female: 99% (1995). **School enrolment:** Primary total: 87% (1990/95). male : 87% (1990/95). female: 87% (1990/95). Secondary: male: 88% (1990/95). female: 95% (1990/95). Tertiary: 41% (1995).

COMMUNICATIONS

120 **newspapers**, 812 **radios**, 230 **TV sets** and 157 **main telephone lines** per 1,000 people (1994). **Books:** 10 new titles per 100,000 people (1992/94).

ECONOMY

Per capita, GNP: $ 1,200 (1996). **Annual growth, GNP:** -8.5% (1995/96). **Currency:** 179,400 grivna = $ 1 (1995) **Cereal imports:** metric tons (1994). **Fertilizer use:** 349 kgs per ha (1994). **Exports:** $ 16,040 million (1996). **Imports:** $ 24,042 million (1996). **External debt:** $ 9,335 million (1996). $ 181 **per capita:** (1996). **Debt service:** 6.1% of exports (1996).

ENERGY

Consumption: 3,180.44 Kgs of Oil equivalent per capita yearly (1994). 47.92% imported (1994).

HDI (rank / value) 95 / 0.689 (1994)

---

announcing incentives for attracting foreign investment.

[16] On May 5, Crimea declared independence, but it was vetoed by the Ukrainian Parliament. Crimea yielded, and withdrew the declaration. Russia reacted to the situation in June, annulling the 1954 decree by which it had ceded Crimea to Ukraine, demanding that it be returned. Kiev refused, but granted Crimea economic autonomy. After the dissolution of the USSR, Crimea became one of the chief sources of conflict between the Kiev and Moscow governments.

[17] In March 1993, Ukraine suspended the transfer of tactical nuclear weapons to the Russian Federation, claiming there were no guarantees that these would actually be destroyed.

[18] The four CIS States with nuclear arms (Russia, Ukraine, Belarus and Kazakhstan) subsequently agreed to form an international commission to supervise the withdrawal and destruction of the nuclear weapons sited on Ukrainian soil.

[19] Tension surrounding the 'ownership' of the Black Sea fleet

came to a head in April, with both the Russian and Ukrainian governments claiming sovereignty over the powerful former-Soviet navy. Nevertheless, they subsequently agreed to initiate negotiations to settle the issue.

[20] Prime Minister Vitold Fokin resigned in September over the failure of his economic policies. He was replaced by Leonid Kuchma, former president of the Union of Industrialists and Entrepreneurs.

[21] The liberal policies of the new government and its privatization scheme soon came up against the dual obstacles of the Supreme Council - dominated by former communists- and worker resistance. Kuchma presented his resignation on May 21, but it was not accepted.

[22] In June, in a direct challenge to Kravchuk's moderate foreign policy, the Supreme Council announced the appropriation of the entire ex-USSR nuclear arsenal in Ukraine. With the disintegration of the Soviet Union, Ukraine became the world's third most important nuclear power.

[23] Finding himself politically vulnerable, in September 1993

Kravchuk ceded the part of the Black Sea fleet belonging to Ukraine to Russia, in compensation for debts incurred through oil and gas purchases from Moscow. In addition, he accepted help from Russia in dismantling the 46 powerful intercontinental SS24 missiles which Ukraine had wanted to keep, as a last bastion against any possible future expansionist schemes on the part of Russia. However, opposition in Kiev led to the invalidation of the agreement.

[24] In the meantime, the economy went out of control altogether - with inflation reaching 100 per cent per month and Kuchma resigned.

[25] In November 1993, the Council ratified the START-1 strategic weapons limitation treaty, and agreed to the gradual dismantling of 1656 nuclear warheads.

[26] The first presidential elections of the post-soviet era took place in June and July 1994. The former prime minister Leonid Kuchma defeated the outgoing president with 52 per cent of the vote, after which he declared his intention to tighten links with Russia and enter fully into the Commonwealth of Independent States (CIS).

[27] The economic and social situation continued to worsen in 1994 and 1995. The GDP fell by more than 20 per cent in 1994 and more than 12 per cent in 1995, while the constantly falling standard

of living worsened poverty in the country.

[28] The tenth anniversary of the Chernobyl accident, in April 1996, fired an international campaign against the nuclear plants of the former soviet countries. According to studies, a million people were directly affected by the radiation, 2.4 million lived within affected regions and 12 per cent of the farming land in the country was contaminated.

[29] 1997 was a year marked by accusations of corruption against the Prime Minister, Pavlo Lazarensko, who resigned from his post and was substituted by Valery Pustovoytenko on July 16. Meanwhile, the President and Parliament were at odds over slow progress on a law concerning access to and the composition of Parliament. The law finally approved stipulated the body should have a total of 500 deputies, 250 elected by territorial districts and the other 250 designated by the party blocs.

[30] In September 1997, the United States, Belarus, Russia, Kazakhstan and Ukraine signed disarmament agreements which would bring an end to the suspension of the nuclear arms reduction treaty, Start 2, signed in 1993.

[31] The rehabilitation of a reactor in the Chernobyl nuclear plant was announced in April 1998.

United Arab Emirates

Ittihad al-Imarat al-´Arabiyah

Population: 2,260,000 (1996)
Area: 83,600 SQ KM
Capital: Abu Dhabi (Abu Zaby)

Currency: Dirham
Language: Arabic

In the southeastern corner of the Arab peninsula, between the Jabal Ajdar mountain range in Oman and the rocky steppe of Najd extending from the center of the peninsula to the Gulf shores (al-Hasa), is the Rub al-Khali desert taking up part of the territory of present-day Saudi Arabia and almost the entire United Arab Emirates.

2   Toward the 6th century the oases which were spread over the land supplied enough water to the small stable population, enabling them to farm regular crops. The residents of the area spoke different Arabian dialects and shared diverse lifestyles. Some were grain growers, others were merchants or craftspeople from small villages and others still, usually known as "Bedouins", were nomads who raised camels, sheep and goats, making the most of the desert's scant water resources. Along with these activities, the coastal peoples also fished in Gulf waters.

3   Despite being a minority, the nomads - taking advantage of their condition as a mobile and armed group - and together with the merchants, dominated farmers and craftspeople. Gathered around relatively stable family chiefs, they had a typically tribal organization.

4   Among shepherds and farmers, religion had become another type of social control but it appeared not to have a defined form. Local gods were identified with the heavenly bodies and could incarnate into rocks, trees or animals. Some families, claiming they had the power to understand the language of the gods, managed to control the others.

5   Until the 7th century, Byzantine and Sassanid empires waged a long

(1996)

Labour force %

■ WOMEN
□ MEN

14   86

■ AGRICULTURE   8%   (1990)
□ INDUSTRIAL   27%
■ SERVICES   65%

war with constant comings and goings which involved the peninsula, although not directly the land of the present-day Emirates. Likewise, such activity and opening of trade routes brought immigrants (mostly merchants, dealers and craftspeople) who shared their culture and knowledge of the foreign world.

6   Islam was peacefully adopted in the area during Muhammad's lifetime. Tribal chiefs secured their power but the lifestyle of the few inhabitants was not significantly modified.

7   Upon the Prophet's death, various groups appeared which disputed his spiritual inheritance. One of them, the Ibadis (who claimed to descend straight from Muhammad), created the Uman (Oman) imanate in mid-8th century. It lasted up to the 9th century when it was suppressed by the Abassids, caliphs who claimed a universal authority and whose main capital was in Baghdad.

8   After the 11th century, the Sunni form of Islam gradually went on from being the ruling groups' religion to reach the population at large. Likewise, the Ibadis communities continued to exist until the 15th century, exerting strong religious authority.

9   The Gulf ports were already of significant importance for the traffic of commodities which came from China (textiles, glass, porcelain and spices), being transported to the Red Sea through an oasis chain.

10   During the 17th and 18th centuries, the Ottoman Empire occupied a large area of the peninsula but had not reached the Gulf coast in the southeastern region. The Ibadis had reinstated their imanate under a Yaribi dynasty. Further to the north, Bahrain was under Iranian domain.

11   Beyond the reach of the Ottomans (occupied with constant fights in Europe, Africa and Asia), the southeastern region of the peninsula thrived on trade. Ruling families linked directly with merchants appeared and piracy developed, benefiting from the natural advantages of the indented coasts. The area came to be known as "Pirate coast".

12   An important change was introduced when European fleets increasingly used the maritime

route through the Cape. British influence grew gradually, since they used the Gulf ports as a stop on the way to India, and helped to combat piracy.

13   At the beginning of the 19th century, Britain held complete control over the region, obtained through agreements reached with the local chiefs and small governors of the ports. Since then, the Pirate Coast was to be known as the "Trucial States", which included Abu Dhabi, Dubai and Sharja. Relations with Britain were conducted in the same way until the first decades of the 20th century.

14   Around 1914, the Saudi state re-emerged as a great force in Central Arabia, becoming a threat even for the Ottoman power. Russia, France and Germany also sought to intensify their presence in the area. This led the British to formalize relations with the Trucial States of Bahrain, Oman and Kuwait, which let the government in London handle their affairs with the rest of the world.

15   World War I, which led to the end of the Ottoman Empire and the independence of several Arab peninsula states, did not alter the relations between Britain and the Trucial States. London was the real power behind the puppet Abd al-Aziz in the new kingdom of Saudi Arabia, who controlled the southern and southeastern coasts of the peninsula. Furthermore, air routes were beginning to develop and the Gulf's airfields along with those in Egypt, Palestine and Iraq,

had an important role in the Middle East.

16   During the period between the world wars, England focused its attention onto Egypt and Iraq (where oil fields were already being exploited). After World War II, relations among Arab countries changed. The League of Arab States was formed in 1945 by those countries which had some form of independence.

17   At the beginning of the 1960s, the Middle East's oil deposits were known to be among the largest in the world. The United States joined Britain in keeping their control over the Gulf States, which received almost 100 per cent of their revenues from oil.

18   The growing influence of Gamal Abdel Nasser in the Arab world led Britain to allow greater local participation in the governments of several states of the protectorate. In 1968, it decided to withdraw all its military force from the region. That same year, the OPEAC was created - a branch of OPEC - formed exclusively by oil-exporting Arab states.

19   In 1971, upon Britain's definite withdrawal, Abu Dhabi began a large-scale exploitation of its oil wells. Thus, the clear setting of borders within the territories became indispensable. Under British influence, the United Arab Emirates were created that year without participation of Qatar or Bahrain.

20   Immediately after its formation, the new state had to face a conflict with Iran which, claiming historical

PROFILE

ENVIRONMENT

Located in the southeastern part of the Arabic peninsula, stretching from the Qatar peninsula toward the strait of Hormuz, the land is mostly desert with few oases and wadis (dry and rocky river beds). The coastal areas are very hilly lowlands with coral islands offshore and sand dunes. Most of the oil fields are located in these areas.

SOCIETY:

Peoples: Arabs 25 per cent, of which 13 per cent come from other Arab countries (mainly Egypt) and 12 per cent from the Emirates themselves. Population includes large immigrant component. From Bangladesh, India, Pakistan, Sri Lanka (45 per cent), Iran (17 per cent) and other Asian and African countries 8 per cent (1993). Europeans and US 5 per cent. 80 per cent live in Dubai, attracted by the oil wealth. **Religions:** Muslim 94,9 per cent (Sunni 80 per cent, Shi'a 20 per cent); Christian 3,8 per cent; others 1,3 per cent. **Languages:** Arabic (official). English is used among immigrants and in business. **Political Parties:** There are neither political parties nor trade unions.

THE STATE

Official name: Daulat al-Imarat al-'Arabiyah al-Muttahidah. **Administrative divisions:** 7 emirates Abu Dhabi, Dubai, Sharjah, Ras al-Khaimah, Ajman, Fujairah and Umm al-Qaiwain. **Capital:** Abu Dhabi (Abu Zaby), 363,432 people (1990). **Other cities:** Dubayy, 585,189 people; Al-'Ayn 176,411; Ash-Shariqah 125,000; Ra's al-Khaymah 42,000 (1989). **Government:** Parliamentary Republic with a president of the federation as a Head of State (Sheikh Zaid ibn Sultan al-Nuhayyan, Emir of Abu Dhabi, since 1971); a Vice President and Prime Minister (Sheikh Rashid ibn Said al-Maktum, Emir of Dubai, since 1990) and a National Federal Council with 40 members appointed by the emirs, serves as the legislative body. **National Holiday:** December 1. Proclamation of the Union (1971) **Armed Forces:** 70,000 (1995)

STATISTICS

DEMOGRAPHY

Population: 2,260,000 (1996). **Annual growth:** 5% (1980/1996). **Estimates for year 2000:** 2,400,000. **Annual growth to year 2000:** 2.1% (1994/2000). **Urban Population:** 84.3% (1996). **Urban growth:** 5.75% (1980/95). **Children per woman:** 3.6 (1996).

HEALTH

Life expectancy at birth: 75 years (1996) male: 73 years (1994) female: 76 years (1994). **Infant mortality:** 15 per 1,000 (1996). **Under-5 child mortality:** 18 per 1,000 (1996). 1,042 **people per doctor** (1988/91). **Safe water:** 95% (1990/96).

EDUCATION

Literacy: 79% (1995) male: 79% (1995) female: 80% (1995). **School enrolment**: Primary total: 110% (1990/95) male : 112% (1990/95). female: 108% (1990/95). Secondary: male : 88% (1990/95) female: 97% (1990/95). Tertiary: 9% (1995). **Primary school teachers:** one for every 17 students (1995).

COMMUNICATIONS

160 **newspapers**, 312 **radios**, 290 **TV sets** and 276 **main telephone lines** per 1,000 people (1994). **Books:** 14 new titles per 100,000 people (1992/94).

ECONOMY

Currency: 3.67 dirhams = $ 1 (1995) **Cereal imports:** 759 metric tons (1994). **Food import dependency:** 6% (1994). **Fertilizer use:** 9,076 kgs per ha (1994). **Exports:** $ 28,096 million (1996). **Imports:** $ 30,374 million (1996). **Development aid received:** $ 8 million (1995). $ 4 per capita (1995).

ENERGY

Consumption: 10,530.79 Kgs of Oil equivalent per capita yearly (1994). -454.42% imported (1994).

HDI (rank / value) 44 / 0.866 (1994)

---

reasons, occupied the islands of Abu Mussa, Tunb al-Cubra and Tunb al-Sughra on the strait of Ormuz. During the first decade, oil production had constant growth, mainly in the three most important emirates: Abu Dhabi with 79 per cent of the total, Dubai and Sharjah. National participation in the control of oil exploitation also grew.

[21] When the oil-exporting countries, through OPEC, decided in 1973 to raise the price of the barrel by 70 per cent and reduce supply by 5 per cent, a new era in the relations with the industrialized world had begun. The results of this policy were explosive. From the rock-bottom price of $1.50 a barrel of crude oil in the early 1960s, it rose to $10 in 1973 and to $34 between 1979 and 1980. The Emirates' annual growth rate in the 1970s was over 10 per cent due to the revenues obtained.

[22] This led to two immediate effects: a rapid growth of cities with state-of-the-art highways, oil pipelines and banks, and a large influx of immigrants attracted by the region's economic possibilities. Little was left of the ancient peoples' pursuits of fishing or collecting of pearls in the coast.

[23] The 1980s began with the Iran-Iraq war. Although the Emirates maintained an apparently neutral stand, they gave economic support to Iraq to avoid a possible "Iranization" of the region. Once the conflict had ended, the Arab Emirates had become the Middle East's third biggest oil producer, after Saudi Arabia and Libya.

[24] Although since 1981 the Government has tried to develop other industrial fields, technological differences with other countries and a limited domestic market make difficult a possible industrial diversification which would diminish dependence on oil production.

[25] The UAE has been a member of the Non-Aligned Movement and has supported Palestinian claims. In late 1986, diplomatic relations were established with the Soviet Union and the People's Republic of Benin. In 1987, relations with Egypt were reinstated, broken after the Camp David agreements with Israel.

[26] During the Gulf War, the Emirates made financial contributions to the fight against Iraq. Once the conflict had ended, the policy to diversify the economy seemed to gather strength when the free port of Jabel Ali was opened to over 260 foreign companies.

[27] In March 1991, the Gulf Cooperation Council signed an agreement with the US to preserve security in the region, which includes a common military strategy and mechanisms to prevent arms proliferation, among other items.

[28] In 1992, with Syrian mediation, Iran restricted the claims it had over the islands of the Strait of Ormuz, occupied since the 1970s. Tehran claims sovereignty over Abu Mussa and has allowed expelled Arab residents to return. The conflict is, by pressure from the Emirates, under international arbitration.

[29] Successive immigration waves have formed a very heterogeneous population. According to 1993 figures, the Arab population in the country amounts to barely one quarter, half of it coming from other countries (mainly Egypt). The rest of the population is made up by immigrants from Bangladesh, Pakistan, Sri Lanka, Iran and other Asian or African states.

[30] Everything indicates that the influence of Islamic fundamentalism has grown in the Emirates between 1993 and 1996. Sheikh Zaid, President of the Union, has often made it understood - as in a speech at the end of Ramadan in 1993 - that official circles were concerned about the spread of Muslim "radicalism". In February 1994, Zaid decided to extend Islamic law to many criminal cases which had been dealt with by civil courts up to then.

[31] In 1995, new talks were held in an attempt to solve the dispute with Iran over the Strait of Hormuz islands, without any results. In 1997, in view of the United States' threat of an armed intervention in Iraq, Sheik Zaid stated that the Iraqi people deserved a "new chance". Afterwards, he added that a measure of this type would be "unacceptable and loathsome".

[32] At a domestic level, the Head of State carried on with an economic liberalization policy which led in 1998, among other things, to the creation of a free trade area in the city of Ra's al-Khaymah, the first in the Middle East. Meanwhile, reports of human rights violations continued while the Government increasingly curtailed the rights of foreigners, in a country where three quarters of the population is made up of immigrants.

United Kingdom

United Kingdom

Population: 58,144,000 (1996)
Area: 244,100 SQ KM
Capital: London

Currency: Pound Sterling
Language: English

The first known inhabitants of the island of Britain were paleolithic hunters, following herds of wild animals. After the final ice age, agriculturalists began to settle on the island. Over thousands of years, these people, and the many others who migrated from the continent, evolved increasingly complex social systems. By the final millennium BC, Britain was dominated by Celtic tribes who used iron tools and had extensive contact with the European mainland.

[2] In 44 AD the Romans invaded southern Britain. In 90 AD they created the province of Britannia, and between 70 and 100 AD, founded London. In the early 5th century, they abandoned the island, leaving it largely defenceless against the raids of Angles, Saxons and Jutes. These Germanic peoples pushed the Celts westwards, taking over the southern part of the island and establishing Anglo-Saxon kingdoms.

[3] During the 5th century, the inhabitants of Ireland and Wales adopted Christianity. In the 7th century, the British church came under the power of Rome.

[4] During the 7th and 9th centuries Danish invaders overran the eastern part of England. In the 11th century, the Normans, led by William the Conqueror, invaded England and secured the throne. Successive Anglo-Norman kings maintained their power by establishing various forms of vassalage over the feudal lords.

[5] The prestige which Richard the Lion-Heart (1189-99), one of the leaders of the Third Crusade, gained for the English Crown was lost under the reign of his successor, King John (1199-1216). Under John, England lost its French territories, and the barons, in alliance with the clergy, were able to restrict the power of the monarchy through the Magna Carta, signed in 1215.

[6] The Magna Carta laid the foundations for the British parliamentary system. It also marked the beginning of a continuous power struggle between the monarchy and the nobility. The growing power of the land-owning class and later the bourgeoisie, eventually led to the consolidation of a parliamentary monarchy.

[7] Frequent dynastic conflicts, disputes over territories in France belonging to the English Crown, commercial rivalry between England and France in Flanders, and French aid to Scotland in its wars with England paved the way for the Hundred Years' War (1337-1453), which culminated in the loss of the English possessions on the continent.

[8] The negative effects of the War increased the unpopularity of the monarchy, which was faced, at the same time, with an anti-Papal movement led by the followers of Wycliffe (a precursor of Luther) and a peasant rebellion. The peasants, led by Wat Tyler, rose up against the payment of tribute and the power of the feudal lords. In 1381, Tyler and his followers managed to enter London and negotiate directly with the King. The Peasants' Revolt was unsuccessful, however, and Tyler was later executed.

[9] The period following the Hundred Years' War was dominated by a long struggle for control of the throne between the Houses of Lancaster and of York. This finally led to the War of the Roses which ended with the coming to power of the Welsh House of Tudor in 1485. The Tudor period is considered the beginning of the modern British state. One of the Tudor kings, Henry VIII (1509-47) broke away from the Church of Rome, confiscating all its monasteries and founding the Anglican Church. The desire to extend English authority and the religious Reformation to Ireland led to the subjugation of Ulster by Henry's successor Elizabeth I (1558-1603). Tudor involvement in Ireland laid the foundations of centuries of religious and political conflict in the country.

[10] Under the reign of Elizabeth I (1558-1603), poetry and the theatre flourished with playwrights such as Ben Jonson, Marlowe, and Shakespeare. Industry and trade developed, and the country embarked upon its "colonial adventure", the beginning of its future empire. After defeating the Spanish fleet, the "Invincible Armada" in 1588, the British Navy "ruled the waves", with no other fleet capable of opposing it.

[11] British merchant ships involved in the slave trade, or laden with colonists or belonging to pirates and privateers sailed the oceans freely. Markets multiplied, demand grew rapidly, and producers were forced to seek new techniques in order to accelerate production. It was a prelude to the industrial revolution which was to arise in the country at the beginning of the 18th century.

[12] In 1603, the crowning of James I (James VI of Scotland) put an end to the independent Scottish monarchy. The religious intolerance of James' son Charles I, led to a Scottish uprising and increasing discontent in England. The deteriorating political situation led to the Puritans forming an army supported by Parliament; led by Oliver Cromwell, they defeated the royal forces in 1642. In 1649, Parliament sentenced the king to death and proclaimed Cromwell "Lord Protector", establishing a republic known as the Commonwealth. After his death, in 1658, the monarchy was restored with Charles II.

[13] The priorities of the new regime were the colonization of North America and trade with America, the Far East and the

PROFILE

ENVIRONMENT
The country consists of Britain (England, Scotland and Wales), Northern Ireland, and several smaller islands. The center of Britain is occupied by the Pennines low mountains. The Grampian mountains are located in Scotland and the Cambrian mountains in Wales. The largest plains are in the southeast, around London. The climate is temperate. Farming is highly mechanized and is now a secondary activity. The huge coal and iron ore deposits, which made the Industrial Revolution possible, have nearly run out, but recent gas and oil finds in the North Sea have turned the United Kingdom into an exporter of these products. The country is highly industrialized and environmental pollution, especially air pollution, poses a serious problem. A nuclear reprocessing plant on the Irish Sea appeared to be linked to the high incidence of leukaemia in areas along both coastlines.

SOCIETY
Peoples: English, Scots, Welsh and Irish. Minorities: Pakistani, 0.9 per cent, Indian, 1.5 per cent, and Afro-Caribbean, 0.8 per cent, among others. **Religions:** Protestant, 53.4 per cent (Anglican 43.5 per cent; Presbyterian 4.5 per cent; Methodist 2.2 per cent); Roman Catholic 9.8 per cent; Orthodox 1 per cent; other Christians 1.7 per cent; Islam 2.6 per cent; Hindu 0.6 per cent, Sikh 0.5 per cent; Jewish 0.5 per cent; other/no religion 29.9 per cent. **Languages:** English (official), Welsh and Gaelic. **Political Parties:** Labour Party (social democrat), led by Tony Blair, in government. Conservative Party in opposition. Liberal Democrat Party, centre. Green Party. The Republican Party Sinn Fein in Northern Ireland gained two seats in the last elections. **Social Organizations:** Trade Union Congress (TUC), with 12 million affiliates.

THE STATE
Official Name: United Kingdom of Great Britain and Northern Ireland. **Administrative Divisions:** 39 Counties and 7 Metropolitan Districts. **Capital:** London, 7,007,100 people (1995). **Other cities:** Birmingham, 1,017,500 people; Leeds, 725,000; Glasgow, 674,800; Sheffield, 528,500; Bradford, 482,700; Liverpool, 470,800; Edinburgh, 447,600; Manchester, 432,600; Bristol, 400,700 (1995). **Government:** Queen Elizabeth II, Head of State. Tony Blair, Prime Minister since May 2 1997. Parliamentary monarchy. Legislative Power: House of Lords, with 1,197 life members, and a House of Commons, with 659 members elected every five years. **Armed Forces:** 213,800 (1996). **Dependencies:** See Gibraltar (Spain), Malvinas (Argentina), Montserrat, Virgin Islands, Cayman Islands, Turks and Caicos, Bermuda, St Helena, British Indian Ocean Territories (Mauritius), and Pitcairn (Oceania).

Maternal Mortality
1990

PER 100,000
LIVE BIRTHS

9

Foreign Trade
MILLIONS $ 1996

IMPORTS
283,682
EXPORTS
259,039

Smith. The liberal doctrine provided the political ideology for British imperialism, which used the concept of "free trade" as a justification for forcing open the ports and markets of the Third World, often with the use of naval force. Perhaps the most notorious examples of this were the Opium Wars fought against China in the mid-19th century.

[18] After the crushing of a nationalist rebellion in Ireland in 1798, the United Kingdom of Great Britain and Ireland was created in 1801 with the dissolution of the Irish Parliament.

[19] The 18th century gave rise to the agricultural "revolution", which introduced important innovations in farming techniques, as well as major changes in land tenure. The large landowners enclosed their properties, eliminating communal lands which had hitherto been used by small farmers, and introducing a more capitalist agricultural economy.

[20] At the same time, the industrial revolution began, with the textile manufacturers being the first to confront the problem of meeting a growing demand for fabric overseas. The introduction of machinery changed the way in which work was done, and the medieval shop was replaced by the factory. On the heels of the textile industry came mining and metallurgy. The mechanization process was consolidated with the invention of the steam engine, the use of coal as a fuel and the substitution of first iron, then steel, for wood in construction.

[21] This period was characterized by population growth (going from 10,900,000 in 1801 to 21,000,000 in 1850), increasing demand and expanding trade, improvements in the transport system, capital accumulation, the creation of a vast colonial empire, scientific advances and the golden age of the bourgeoisie. Britain became the world's number one manufacturing nation. Its colonial policy helped to prevent competition with its factories; for example it established regulations which destroyed the Indian textile industry.

[22] The United Kingdom obtained new territories from its different wars with France, and its triumph over Napoleon at Waterloo (1815).

[23] One result of the industrial revolution was growing discontent among the rapidly increasing working class, due to low salaries, unhealthy working conditions, unsatisfactory housing, malnutrition, job insecurity and the long and tiring working days to which men, women and children were subjected. In many cases, popular uprisings were characterized by violence, and were met with equally violent repression.

[24] In the early stages of the industrial revolution, spontaneous movements arose, like the "Luddites", textile workers who destroyed machinery to prevent it from destroying their cottage-industry. Trade unions began to appear later.

[25] In 1819 a demonstration in Manchester was violently put down, and repressive legislation followed, limiting the right of association and freedom of the press. Nevertheless, resistance movements continued their activity. One of the main movements of this period was the nationalist Irish Association led by Daniel O'Connell.

[26] The most important of the mass movements was the Chartist Movement, made up primarily of workers. It took its name from the People's Charter, published in 1838 at a mass assembly in Glasgow, Scotland. This movement brought a number of issues to the forefront, both political: universal suffrage, use of the secret ballot, reform of voting registers; and social: better salaries and better working conditions. After its demonstrations and strikes, "Chartism" faded away; however, it had a far-reaching influence and its grievances were subsequently taken up by some members of parliament.

[27] Robert Owen (1771-1858), considered to be the founder of socialism and the English co-operative movement, argued that the predominance of individual interests led to the impoverishment of the masses. From 1830 on, he devoted himself to the establishment of co-operatives and the organization of labour into trade unions.

Mediterranean. The slave trade, the kidnapping, trafficking and selling of slaves from Africa to buyers in America and other places, initiated in the 16th century, became one of the main sources of income for the empire.

[14] The absolutism of James II and his espousal of Catholicism were opposed by the Protestant Parliament which deposed James through the "Glorious Revolution". Parliament invited the Dutch prince William of Orange to assume the English throne. William was forced to sign the Declaration of Rights (1689), limiting royal powers and guaranteeing the supremacy of Parliament.

[15] In this period John Locke summarized revolutionary ideals, proposing that human beings have basic natural rights: to property, life, liberty and personal security. Government, created by society to protect these rights, must fulfil its mission; if it fails to do so, the people have the right to resist its authority.

[16] In 1707, the parliaments of Scotland and England were joined together, creating the United Kingdom of Great Britain. Britain intervened in the war of succession in Spain, obtaining Minorca, Gibraltar and Nova Scotia through the Treaty of Utrecht (1713). In 1765, increased taxes imposed by the Stamp Act triggered the rebellion and secession of the American colonies, who declared their independence in 1776.

[17] During this period, the two large traditional political parties were formed: the Conservatives (Tories), representing the interests of the large landowners, and the Liberals (Whigs), representing the merchant class. The ideas forming the basis of economic liberalism were developed at this time by Adam

28 During the long reign of Queen Victoria (1837-1901), the traditional nobility strengthened its alliance with the industrial and mercantile bourgeoisie. Trade unions were legalized in 1871, and shortly afterwards, some labour legislation was approved.

29 Beginning in 1873, the rising population numbers led to a food shortage, making imports necessary. At the same time industry began to feel the competition from the US and Germany. Britain increased its imperial activities in Africa, Asia and Oceania, not only for economic reasons, but also because of the political ambition to build a great empire. The Boer or South African War (1899-1902), fought to secure control over southern Africa, was the most expensive regional conflict of the 19th century.

30 The first quarter of the 20th century saw the birth of the women's liberation movement. The militancy of the suffragettes led to some women obtaining the right to vote in 1917. The most famous example of their militancy was the suicide of Emily Davison, who threw herself in front of the King's horse during a race in 1913.

31 In Ireland, the majority Catholic population were stripped of their lands, restricted in their civil rights because of their religion, and deprived of their political autonomy. Millions emigrated, and political unrest periodically resulted in violent uprisings. Not until 1867 were the privileges of the Anglican Church eliminated; at the same time, measures were taken to improve the situation of the peasants. The 1916 Easter Rising in Dublin was ruthlessly put down by the British, but the Crown forces were unable to win the ensuing guerrilla war which began in 1918, and Britain finally granted Ireland independence in 1921. Six counties in the north-east, with Protestant majorities, remained under British control with a devolved administration in Belfast.

32 Economic and political rivalry between the European powers led to the outbreak of World War I (1914-18). The Central Powers of Austro-Hungary and Germany, joined subsequently by Turkey and Bulgaria, fought against the Allied powers of France, Britain, Russia, Serbia and Belgium, with Italy, Japan, Portugal, Romania, the United States and Greece joining during the course of the war.

33 Despite its victory, Britain emerged from the War weakened. It had invested $40 billion in military expenditure, mobilized 7,500,000 troops, suffered a loss of 1,200,000 soldiers and acquired an enormous foreign debt. The deep economic depression in the post-War years led to renewed unrest among workers, which reached its height in the General Strike of 1926. The Conservative Government declared the strike illegal, but did not take any measures to revive British industry. In the elections of 1929, the Labour Party, formed in 1924, came to power for the first time.

34 The United Kingdom supported the US proposal to create the League of Nations. In 1931, the British Community of Nations (Commonwealth) was established under the Statute of Westminster. This formally recognized the independence of Canada, Australia, New Zealand and South Africa.

35 On September 3 1939, Britain declared war on Germany, marking the beginning of its participation in World War II (1939-45). In May 1940 a coalition cabinet was formed, with Winston Churchill as Prime Minister. From 1939 to 1941, Britain and France were ranged against Germany, which was joined by Italy in 1940. Hungary, Romania, Bulgaria and Yugoslavia participated in the war as "lesser" allies of the Nazis.

36 In 1941, the Soviet Union, Japan and the US entered the conflict. On May 8 1945, Germany surrendered. The UK, US and the USSR emerged as the major victors from the war. However, the British Empire was eclipsed by the rising power of the US, which became the undisputed economic, technological and military leader.

37 In May 1945, the Labour Government of Clement Attlee, who won the elections with the slogan "We won the war, now we will win the peace", nationalized the coal mines, the Bank of England and the iron and steel industries.

38 Pakistan was formed and India became independent in 1947, although both remained members of the British Commonwealth. During the following decade, most of Britain's overseas colonies obtained their independence. Britain was a founder member of NATO in 1949.

39 The Franco-British military intervention in the Suez Canal Zone in 1956, which failed due to a lack of US support, was met by strong criticism from both inside and outside Britain (see Egypt). The following year, the United Kingdom set off its first hydrogen bomb in the Pacific Ocean.

40 The general election of 1964 was won by the Labour Party under the leadership of Harold Wilson. His government faced serious problems, such as the declaration of independence by Southern Rhodesia (today Zimbabwe), and the breaking of diplomatic relations with nine other African countries.

41 In 1967, having been denied entry to the Common Market, and faced with rapidly increasing unemployment, Wilson withdrew British troops from South Yemen, evacuated all bases located east of Suez except for Hong Kong, discontinued arms purchases from the US and implemented a savage austerity budget.

42 In Northern Ireland in 1969, the latent conflict erupted. A number of people were killed and wounded in riots between Catholics and Protestants. The Catholics demanded equal political rights, and better access to housing, schools and social security. The Protestant-controlled Northern Irish Government responded by sending in their armed police reserves against the Catholic demonstrators. The British Government sent in their troops to separate the two sides and took control of police and reserve forces away from the Belfast Government.

43 In August 1971, the prime minister of Northern Ireland, Brian Faulkner, opened internment camps and authorized the detention of suspects without

PUBLIC EXPENDITURE

n/a

54.5%

1995 ■ DEFENCE □ SOCIAL

In 1990/91 Military as % of health & education expenditure was 40%.

WORKERS

UNEMPLOYMENT 8.2% (1996)

Labour force %

■ WOMEN
□ MEN

43   57

■ AGRICULTURE 2% (1990)
□ INDUSTRIAL 29%
■ SERVICES 69%

trial. Protests against these measures resulted in more than 25 deaths. On January 30 1972, "Bloody Sunday", British soldiers opened fire on a peaceful protest march in Derry (Londonderry), killing 13 Catholics and injuring hundreds more. The Irish Republican Army (IRA) responded with numerous assassinations.

44 In March 1973, the people of Northern Ireland voted in a referendum to remain within the United Kingdom rather than join a united Ireland. Voting was characterized by a high rate of abstentions of 41.4 per cent, and the Protestant majority voted to stay in the UK.

45 In the 1970s, social conflict in Britain intensified, and Edward Heath's Conservative Government was faced with strikes in key public enterprises. The dockers, coal miners and railway workers all went on strike. Inability to deal with this labor unrest led to his resignation in 1974, and the Labour Party won the following elections. Amid a complex situation on the domestic front, in January 1973, a majority of the electorate voted in favor of entering the EEC. A policy of progressive integration with Europe began, as well as a search for new markets for ailing British industry.

46 A new divorce law was passed in 1975. The same year, feminists campaigned successfully against restrictions being added to the 1967 abortion law.

47 In 1979, voters in Scotland and Wales turned down autonomy for their regions in referenda organized by James Callaghan's Labour Government.

48 In May of that year, after the "winter of discontent", characterized by strikes, the Conservative Party won the election, with Margaret Thatcher as its leader. The new prime minister brought in a severe monetarist policy to bring down inflation. She began to reverse the nationalization process carried out under Labour, and returned to a free market policy.

49 In 1981, a group of IRA prisoners began a hunger strike as part of their campaign to win recognition as political prisoners. The Government refused to accept the prisoners demands. The strike resulted in 12 deaths.

50 In April 1982, Thatcher sent a Royal Navy force, including aircraft carriers and nuclear submarines, to the Malvinas islands (Falklands) which had been occupied by troops from the military junta in Argentina. After 45 days of fighting the British recovered the islands for the Crown (see Argentina).

51 In October 1983, the British Government decided to withdraw its troops from Belize. The following year, in agreement with a treaty dating back to the First Opium War, Britain ceded sovereignty over Hong Kong to the People's Republic of China, with effect from June 1997.

52 During the Thatcher administration, the trade union movement suffered serious setbacks, with the loss of local affiliates in the industrial sector, itself in decline. The 1984/85 miners' strike culminated in defeat for the union after a year of violent internal strife and confrontation with the police.

53 In 1987, Thatcher was elected to her third consecutive term in office. She continued her policies as before: radical economic liberalization, privatization of state corporations, and opposition to union demands. In foreign affairs, Britain opposed greater European Community integration and continued to align itself closely with the US.

54 In mid-1989, after several years of growth, inflation reached high levels, unemployment continued to rise steeply, productive investments fell and the balance of payments deficit grew. At the same time, the introduction of a new Poll Tax and other projected reforms produced strong popular resistance.

55 In February 1990, the United Kingdom and Argentina renewed diplomatic relations, and their representatives met in Madrid to negotiate the issue of the return of the Malvinas.

56 In November 1990 Thatcher was replaced as head of the government and Tory leader by her former minister, John Major. Upon taking office, Major declared himself to be in favor of capitalism with a human face, thus setting himself apart from the reality of the "Iron Lady's" harsh capitalism.

57 In 1991, Major announced that the Poll Tax would be replaced, and promoted the adoption of a bill of rights for the sick, for working women, the consumer and the family, among other social categories. However, Major continued most of Thatcher's reforms, including that of the health system and the selling-off of nationalized industries such as the railways.

58 In European affairs, the Prime Minister distanced himself from his predecessor. In 1991, London gave its backing to European agreements on monetary union. However, the fidelity which British diplomacy showed towards the United States, remained unaltered, as proved by British aid to the US in the Gulf War.

59 The Government managed to bring down inflation (which dropped from 10 per cent to 3.8 per cent between 1990 and 1991) and interest rates (which decreased from 15 per cent to 9.5 per cent), but economic activity remained stagnant. In 1991, industrial production declined and numerous small businesses failed. Unemployment, in turn, continued to rise (over 9 per cent by late 1991), and started affecting white-collar workers and professionals, groups which had supported Thatcher's neo-liberal policies.

60 Within this context, Major's personal popularity (the highest in British history since Winston Churchill) did not translate itself into a similar level of support for his party. In the local elections held at the end of April 1991, the Tories lost 800 council seats and several of its traditional districts, while Labour gained more than 400 council seats. In these elections, the Liberal Democratic Party also made important gains.

61 In September 1991, frustration with high unemployment and cuts in social spending erupted in a wave of urban violence not seen since 1976. Demonstrations - specially by young people - took place in cities as far apart as Cardiff, Newcastle, Birmingham and Oxford. At the same time, racist violence had significantly increased, according to Scotland Yard.

62 In 1992, the Conservatives won parliamentary elections for the fourth consecutive time with 336 seats out of 651 giving them an overall majority. Shortly after the voting in which Gerry Adams, president of Sinn Fein - the political wing of the Irish Republican Army (IRA) - lost his seat, several high-powered bombs went off in London.

63 As of 1993, the Conservatives suffered a series of setbacks at the polls in local elections, in the middle of an economic recession and high unemployment affecting some 3 million. On December 15, London signed a joint declaration with Dublin regarding the situation in Northern Ireland, which paved the way for peace talks (see Ireland).

64 In spite of a more favorable economic context, the Conservative government was not able to recover its popularity during 1994. The GDP grew 3 per cent and unemployment went down to 2.5 million (9 per cent of the working population), but a series of scandals, such as the illegal financing of a dam in Malaysia, further tarnished the Tories' image. Meanwhile, Parliament decided to lower the legal age of consent for homosexual intercourse from 21 to 18, refusing to put it on the same level as heterosexual intercourse, where the age of consent is 16.

65 The Labour Party, led by Tony Blair since July 1994, pursued its "modernization" program, eliminating Clause Four of the Party's constitution which aimed at "the common ownership of the means of production, distribution and exchange".

66 Labour won a landslide victory in the May 1997 general elections, and Tony Blair took office as Prime Minister. The Conservatives suffered a crushing defeat, taking only 30 per cent of the vote to Labour's 43.1 - a difference unprecedented so far this century - forcing through changes in leadership in the former party. However, the new government kept to spending limits planend by the Conservatives, keeping nurses and other public-sector workers on their low pay. The Government also adopted right-of-centre policies on law and order, defence and social welfare.

67 In June, Blair announced the preparation of a new round of negotiations on Northern Ireland. The Prime Minister gave Sinn Fein permission to participate, once the IRA had called a cease-fire. This happened on July 20 and Sinn Fein joined talks opening on September 15.

68 Finance Minister Gordon Brown told Parliament the country would not be adopting the Euro (common currency unit within the EU) in January 1999, but would reserve judgement on joining until after the next general election. Denmark and the United Kingdom were the only European countries granted a special clause exempting them from the monetary union.

69 Two referenda held in Wales and Scotland in 1997 approved greater autonomy and an elected assembly for each region. In early 1998, negotiations on Northern Ireland ended with a new peace formula. Approval of the agreements exceeded 70 per cent in Northern Ireland when this was submitted to a referendum in May.

70 Under these agreements, Northern Ireland would have a directly-elected legislative assembly, with safeguards against domination by one population group. Simultaneously, a referendum held in Ireland won 95 per cent approval, ending its territorial claim over the North.

United States

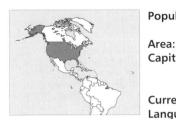

United States

Population: 269,444,000 (1996)
Area: 9,363,520 SQ KM
Capital: Washington

Currency: Dollar
Language: English

IRRIGATED **11.1%** of arable

(1993)

■ FOREST & WOODLAND	29.2%
□ ARABLE	18.9%
▨ OTHER	51.9%

The continental territory occupied by the United States was inhabited 30,000 years before the arrival of the Europeans by peoples who came from the northwest, probably from Asia across the Bering Strait. Among the most important peoples were those who became the Apache, Arapaho, Cherokee, Cheyenne, Chippewa, Crow, Comanche, Hopi, Iroquois, Lakota, Navajo, Nez Perce, Oglala Sioux, Pawnee, Pueblo, Seminole, Shawnee, Shoshone and the Ute.

2   In the deserts and on the plains, they were primarily hunters and gatherers, living in small tribes with a simple social structure. Where the lands were more fertile, agriculture developed and relatively large towns were established. The first and largest of these, Cahokia, close to what is now St Louis, is thought to have had a population of 40,000 in the year 1000 AD.

3   The religious beliefs of these peoples were rooted in a cosmic conception of the Earth - that as it belongs to the Universe, it belongs to no one. The Earth is considered to be a living being, with both material and spiritual powers. American Indian religious leaders or shamans have the power to call upon the forces of this sacred Universe, either to fortell the future, to lead their people, or to heal the sick.

4   The first Europeans to come to America were Viking sailors from Greenland, but they did not settle permanently in the region. After the voyage of Christopher Columbus, in 1492, the Spaniards established the colonies of Saint Augustine in Florida, and Santa Fe in New Mexico; in addition, they explored both Texas and California. After the Spaniards came the British, French and Dutch, all bent on territorial conquest.

5   In 1540, Hernando De Soto wrote in his journals of having found among the Cherokee an advanced agricultural society, linked to the peoples of the Ohio, the Mississippi and even the Aztecs. Europeans introduced not only firearms, but also the concept of killing (the enemy) as the objective of warfare: both significantly altered life among the American peoples, and ultimately established domination by white people.

6   There were an estimated 1,500,000 Native Americans in the 15th century. Two centuries later, the large plantations of the South began buying slaves, and by 1760 there was a total of 90,000 Africans, twice the number of whites in that part of the country. The total number of British settlers on the Atlantic coast at the time was 300,000, greatly exceeding the French in the Mississippi Valley.

7   Most British immigrants left their country fleeing from poverty, religious persecution and political instability. Yet the birth of the colonies was marked by war against the native peoples, whose culture and way of life were systematically destroyed, and against other European colonists. By 1733, there were 13 English colonies, whose chief economic activities were agriculture, fishing and trade.

8   In 1763, with the 17th and 18th century European imperial wars behind them, France ceded its colonies east of the Mississippi to Britain, while its possessions west of that river went to Spain.

PROFILE

ENVIRONMENT

There are four geo-economic regions. The East includes New England, the Appalachian Mountains and part of the Great Lakes and the Atlantic coast, a sedimentary plain which stretches from the mouth of the Hudson River to the peninsula of Florida. To the west are the Appalachian mountains, where mineral deposits (iron ore, and coal) abound. This is the most densely populated and industrialized area, where the country's largest steelmaking plants are located. A highly technological agriculture provides food for the large cities. The Midwest stretches from the western shores of Lake Erie to the Rocky Mountains, also including the middle Mississippi. Formed by the grasslands of the central plain, the Midwest is the country's largest agricultural area; horticulture and milk production predominate in the north, while wheat, corn and other cereals are cultivated in the south, side by side with cattle ranches where oxen and pigs are raised. Major industrial centers are located near the Great Lakes, near the area's agricultural production and large iron ore and coal deposits. The South is a subtropical flatland area, comprising the south of the Mississippi plain, the peninsula of Florida, Texas and Oklahoma. Large plantations (cotton, sugarcane, rice) predominate here, while there is extensive cattle-raising in Texas. The region is also rich in mineral deposits (oil, coal, aluminum, etc.). The West is a mountainous, mineral-rich area (oil, copper, lead, zinc). A sizeable horticultural production exists along the fertile valleys of the Sacramento and San Joaquin rivers in California. Large industrial centers are located along the Pacific coast. In addition, the US has two states outside its original contiguous area: Alaska, on the continent's northwest where Mt. McKinley is located (Mt. «Denali», in the indigenous Atabasco language), the highest peak in North America, and Hawaii, an archipelago in the Pacific Ocean. The United States is the main producer of gases - principally carbon dioxide - which are responsible for the greenhouse effect.

SOCIETY

Peoples: There are 1.9 million Native Americans, half of whom live in 300 reservations. The white population came originally from immigrant Europeans including English, Germans, Irish, Russian and Italian, now mixed with immigrants from all parts of the world. The largest minorities are of African origin, 11 per cent of the total population; Hispanic, 10 per cent; and Asian, 8 per cent.
Religions: There is a Protestant majority (58 per cent), which encompasses several denominations. There are also a considerable number of Catholics (21 per cent. Other Christians, 6.4 per cent, Jewish 2 per cent, Muslims, 2 per cent.
Languages: English; Spanish; Native American Languages and those of each immigrant group.
Political Parties: Democratic Party; Republican Party.
Social Organizations: The American Federation of Labor-Congress of Industrial Organizations (AFL-CIO) is the country's largest workers' organization, with 13,500,000 members. Many of the country's rural laborers, especially those of Mexican origin, are organized in the United Farm Workers (UFW) labor union, founded by César Chávez.

THE STATE

Official Name: United States of America. **Administrative Divisions:** Federal State, 50 States and 1 Federal District, Columbia. **Capital:** Washington, DC, 606,900 people (1990). **Other cities:** New York, 7,333,300 people; Los Angeles, 3,448,600; Chicago, 2,731,700; Houston, 1,702,100; Philadelphia, 1,524,200 (1994). **Government:** William Clinton, President since 1992, re-elected in 1996. Presidential government, federal system (50 states). There is a bicameral Congress where each state has two senators and a number of representatives proportional to its population. **National Holiday:** July 4, Independence (1776). **Armed Forces:** 1,547,300 (1995). **Other:** 68,000 Civil Air Control.

[9] War with England broke out in 1775. The Declaration of Independence, which marked the birth of the United States, was signed on July 4 1776. The war continued, but in the end the United States won (aided by its ally, France), with American sovereignty finally being recognized by England in 1783.
[10] In 1787, the Philadelphia Constitutional Convention drew up the first federal constitution, which went into effect the following year. George Washington, commander of the Continental Army, was elected president in April 1789. In 1791, ten amendments dealing with individual freedoms and "states' rights" were added to the original constitution.
[11] The prime attraction of the West was the possibility of acquiring land and wealth without previous ownership, simply by staking a claim. The presidents in power at the time justified this "Empire of Freedom": it was the United States' "Manifest Destiny" to occupy the entire continent, in order to become a great nation.
[12] In 1803, the Louisiana purchase doubled the size of the Union. Between 1810 and 1819, the US went to war against Spain in order to annex Florida. In 1836, the Texans rebelled against Mexico and set up a republic, subsequently joining the Union in 1845. The United States declared war on Mexico, taking over vast areas of Mexican territory. California became a state in 1850, and Oregon in 1853.
[13] Westward expansion meant not only a change of "ownership", but also still another tragedy for the original inhabitants of the region, decimated by successive waves of land and gold fever. Treaties were signed then ignored as thousands of new settlers poured onto native lands. On occasion new treaties were imposed by force. In 1838, 14,000 Cherokee people were forced off their lands by the army, 4,000 perishing in a march to their new territory.
[14] The Civil War (or War of Secession), from 1861-65 revolved around the question of the preservation of slavery, but it was in fact a struggle between the two economic systems prevailing in the country. While the industrial North sought to free an important source of labor, and protect the domestic market, the slave-owning and agricultural South's interest was to maintain its cheap force of labour and continue to enjoy free access to foreign markets.
[15] In 1850, of the 6 million inhabitants of European origin in the South, only 345,525 were slave owners; nevertheless, most whites were pro-slavery, remembering the slave rebellions which had taken place in South Carolina (1822) and Virginia (1800 and 1831).
[16] The election of Abraham Lincoln in 1860 precipitated the conflict: before he had even been inaugurated as president, the Southern states seceded. Committed to preserving the Union, and with a superior industrial base and superior weapons, the North finally triumphed over the South, although a million people were killed on both sides. Slavery was abolished, but ill-feeling between the two regions continued to exist.
[1] After the Civil War, the Native Americans of the Great Plains, especially the Sioux, launched repeated wars of defence. The

Foreign Trade

MILLIONS $ 1996

IMPORTS
814,888
EXPORTS
575,477

treaties of 1851 and 1868, which had granted them sovereignty over their tribal lands were ignored after the discovery of gold in the area. The gradual occupation of their territory was completed by 1890, when the Sioux were defeated for the last time.
[18] In the 1880s, the remaining Native Americans were confined to reservations most of which were on arid, barren lands. Years later, when uranium, coal, oil, natural gas and other minerals were discovered on some of the reservations, mining companies became interested in developing these mineral resources. This triggered the question of "rights" to the land on which the reservations were located.
[19] Between 1870 and 1920, the population of the United States grew from 38 to 106 million, and the number of states increased from 37 to 48. It was a period of rapid capitalist expansion, triggered by the growth of the railroads as huge companies. By the turn of the century, what had been essentially an agrarian country had been transformed into an industrial society.
[20] By the end of the 19th century, a two-party system of government had been established, with the Republican and Democratic parties alternately in power. Despite their different traditions, both parties have historically maintained a large degree of consensus on major national and international issues, a fact which led to a highly coherent foreign policy. The long struggle for women's suffrage began in 1889, being achieved in 1920.
[21] Having dealt with its principal domestic problems, the US ventured onto the international scene. The Spanish-American War in 1898, fought in Cuba and the Philippines, marked the beginning of a US imperial era. The occupation of Panama, and subsequent construction of the Panama Canal and a series of military bases turned Central America - an area of "vital security interest" to the US - into a kind of protectorate.
[22] The United States justified its interventions with the Monroe Doctrine, and former-President Monroe's slogan "America for the Americans". France was forced to withdraw its troops from Mexico

(where they were protecting Emperor Maximilian) and Britain had to drop a territorial dispute with Venezuela. In 1890, the first Pan-American conference was held, paving the way for the inter-American system later set up.

23 When World War I broke out in 1914, the United States declared its neutrality. However in 1917 it declared war on Germany, Austria and Turkey. In 1918, President Woodrow Wilson was one of the architects of the Treaty of Versailles, which established the framework for a new European peace. However in 1920 US entry into the League of Nations was blocked by Congress.

24 The United States emerged from the War more powerful than ever, but the Great Crash on Wall Street (the US Stock Exchange) shook the country in 1929. In its wake, many banks failed, industry and trade were severely affected and unemployment figures rose to 11 million. Under Franklin Roosevelt's presidency (1933-45), the Government managed to bring the financial crisis under control.

25 While Europe headed steadily toward another war, Congress passed a law in 1935 proclaiming US neutrality. However, when war broke out, Roosevelt introduced amendments to that law in order to allow arms shipments to France and Britain. In 1941, the Japanese attack on the US military base at Pearl Harbor in Hawaii precipitated the US entry into the World War II.

26 The War acted as a dynamo for the entire American economy. With 15 million Americans at the front, employment grew from 45,500,000 to 53,000,000, as workers churned out more supplies and arms for the war effort. To meet the demand for workers, six million people migrated from the countryside to the cities. On the labor front, in spite of a labor "truce" in support of the war effort, there were 15,000 strikes during the War, a fact which led Congress to pass a law limiting the right to strike.

27 With Germany defeated on the European front, President Harry Truman (who had assumed the presidency upon Roosevelt's

death) unleashed the United States' new military might upon Japan. On August 6 and 9, 1945 he gave the order for history's first atomic bombs to be dropped on the cities of Hiroshima and Nagasaki, wiping them out. That same year, at Yalta and Potsdam, Britain, the United States and the Soviet Union spelled out the terms for peace, and divided up the areas which would come under their respective spheres of influence.

28 Truman presided over the opening of the United Nations in 1945, and was re-elected President in 1948. As the number one Western power, the United States was in firm opposition to the USSR and its communist system. Soon a 'Cold War' developed as the two superpowers confronted each other in Eastern Europe and jousted for allies throughout the Third World. Within this framework, the Inter-American Treaty of Reciprocal Assistance was signed, and the North Atlantic Treaty Organization (NATO) was created.

29 The United States took it upon itself to safeguard the global capitalist system, with the support of such international institutions as the World Bank and the IMF, as well as armed intervention by its troops all around the world.

30 In 1952, General Dwight Eisenhower, commander-in-chief of American forces in Europe during the War and head of NATO, was elected President of the United States. The events of this period - the Korean War (1950-53), the partition of Germany, popular uprisings in Poland and Hungary, the delicate balance of nuclear weapons between the super powers and the space race - all served to maintain the tension in US-Soviet relations. In 1960, a summit meeting between Eisenhower and Soviet leader Khrushchev had to be called off when an American U-2 spy plane flying over Soviet territory was brought down.

31 In the 1950s, the US economy grew steadily, as did its population, leading to a sense of over-all prosperity and contentment. The

"American way of life" was exported to the rest of the world, hand-in-hand with American investments abroad. In 1956, the US offered South Vietnam's puppet government military support. Labor conflict increased; in 1959, Congress passed a law aimed at curbing corruption in the labor unions.

32 The election of Democrat presidential candidate John F Kennedy in 1960 reflected the US people's desire for relief from domestic and foreign tensions. However, the President supported the abortive Bay of Pigs invasion of Cuba in 1961, initiated the economic blockade of Cuba and presided over the Cuban Missile Crisis. In 1963, the assassination of President Kennedy in Dallas, Texas, underscored the violence in American society.

33 With regard to Latin America, President Kennedy had launched the Alliance for Progress in Uruguay in 1961, in an attempt to stem the influence of the Cuban Revolution throughout the hemisphere. However, the funds earmarked for this project were insufficient to effect real change, serving merely to expose the region's problems. Faced with growing guerrilla activity in the region, the United States decided to support official regional armies.

34 Lyndon Johnson, elected in 1964, launched the "Great Society". However, the country was brought face to face with new frustrations. The war in Vietnam escalated and then came to a stalemate, unleashing a wave of protests throughout the US. This led the Government to initiate a withdrawal from Vietnam, a blow to the American psyche. Racial segregation led to increasing confrontation. In 1968, violent protests in black neighborhoods in urban areas were sparked off by the assassination of black Civil Rights leader, Revd Martin Luther King.

35 That same year, the American Indian Movement (AIM) was founded by two Chippewa leaders. In 1969, AIM occupied the abandoned prison on Alcatraz Island in San Francisco to call attention to its demands and denounce the mistreatment of their people, which was followed by similar actions elsewhere in the country.

36 Richard Nixon was re-elected President in 1972 and visited Moscow and Beijing in 1973. In 1974, he signed the final withdrawal of US troops from Vietnam but he was forced to resign that same year, after the discovery that Republicans had spied on the Democrat

PUBLIC EXPENDITURE

18.1% 55%
1995 ■ DEFENCE □ SOCIAL

In 1990/91 Military as % of health & education expenditure was 46%.

WORKERS

UNEMPLOYMENT 5.4% (1996)
Labour force %

■ WOMEN
□ MEN

46   54

■ AGRICULTURE 3% (1990)
□ INDUSTRIAL 26%
■ SERVICES 71%

Maternal Mortality

1990

PER 100,000
LIVE BIRTHS

12

Literacy

1995

99%

U.S Dependencies

JOHNSTON:
Coral atoll of 2.6 sq km, made up of the Johnston island and the Sand, East and North islets, located approximately 1,150 km west-southwest of Honolulu (Hawaii). With an Air Force base the population (all military) is approximately 1,000. The atoll was uninhabited when it was discovered by British Captain Johnston in 1807. In 1858, Hawaii claimed sovereignty, but that same year US companies started exploitation of phosphate. Since 1934, the atoll has been administered by the US Navy. Civilians are not admitted.

MIDWAY:
A round atoll which comprises two islands: Sand and Eastern, with 5 sq km of total area and 2,300 inhabitants (1985) almost exclusively military. In 1867, they were annexed by the US and are currently administered by its Navy. The islands are used for military purposes and operate as a refuelling base for trans-Pacific flights. In 1942, during World War II, an important sea battle took place here.

WAKE:
Together with neighboring Wilkes and Peale, they make up an atoll with an area of 6.5 sq km and an estimated population of 1,600 inhabitants, mainly military effectives. Located between Midway and Guam, the island was seized by the United States during the 1898 war with Spain. It has a large airport which used to be a stopover for trans-Pacific flights, but nowadays it is not used for business purposes. Since 1972 it has been administered by the Air Force which now uses it as a missile testing station.

HOWLAND, JARVIS & BAKER:
Located in central Polynesia, in the Equatorial Pacific they were occupied by the US in the middle of the 19th century. Uninhabited since the end of World War II as major phosphate deposits had been depleted. There is a lighthouse in Howland. The islands are administered by the US Fishing and Wild Life Service.

PALMIRA & KINGMAN:
The northernmost islands of the Line archipelago. Palmira is an atoll surrounded by more than fifty coral islets covered with exuberant tropical vegetation. It was annexed in 1898 during the war with Spain and is now a private property, dependent on the US Department of the Interior. Kingman is a reef, located north of Palmira, annexed by the US in 1922. The total area of both islands is 7 sq km. Although uninhabited, the US-Japanese project to turn them into deposits of radioactive waste raised protests throughout the Pacific region in the 1980s.

headquarters located in the Watergate Hotel.

[37] In 1978, thousands of Native Americans demanding action on their grievances, carried out "The Longest March", descending on Washington DC from the official "Indian reservations" throughout the country. In 1982, AIM occupied the Black Hills in South Dakota, a site sacred to the Sioux, to protest against the mining operations of some 30 multinational companies, in that area.

[38] In the post-war period, the economy expanded as American transnational companies spread around the world. These companies included Ford and General Motors (with more than a million workers combined), the oil companies Exxon and Mobil Oil, International Business Machine (IBM), ITT, General Electric and Philip Morris, amongst others.

[39] The conservative Republican government of Ronald Reagan (1980-88) reduced taxes on wealth and state social assistance, while increasing defence expenditure. The military-industrial complex energized the whole economy and partly made up for lagging behind Japan and Western Europe on other fronts.

[40] The Hispanic proportion of the population increased by 53 per cent in the 1980s, reaching more than 22 million in total. The proportion of Asian-Americans grew even more.

[41] In the 1980s the United States emitted 25 per cent of the world total of carbon dioxide, (compared with the 13 per cent for the European Community which had a similar sized industrial sector) and refused to establish a deadline for reducing this. In 1991, the United States was the biggest user of most forms of energy. It was also number one producer of nuclear energy and liquid gas, the number two producer of coal, hydroelectric power and natural gas, and the third largest oil producer. It was also the main consumer.

[42] In February 1991, the United States led the multinational force which confronted Iraq. The Gulf War demonstrated US military supremacy and allowed President George Bush to propose a new world order under the hegemony of his country.

[43] In 1991, 15 per cent of the population lived below the poverty line. Those most affected were the US citizens of African (33 per cent) and Latin American (29 per cent) origins.

[44] Bill Clinton, Governor of Arkansas, was elected President in November 1992, and the Democratic Party also gained the majority in the House of Representatives. Clinton promised to concentrate on domestic problems, to move the greatest income tax burden on to the richer sectors, and to meet the health needs of all citizens. The health system reform, conducted by the nation's First Lady Hillary Clinton in 1994, was rejected by Congress.

[45] The North American Free Trade Agreement (NAFTA) with Mexico and Canada went into operation in January 1994. The measures tending towards the globalization of the economy were criticized for giving other countries the jobs lost internally, both in the public and private sectors. The feeling of rejection grew amongst the immigrant workers, especially when California approved a state law taking away the right to education from immigrants' children.

[46] Although the crime rate fell, the US citizens called for increasingly tougher punishment for offenders. The prisons overflowed as the number of inmates doubled and even tripled the figures of 10 years earlier. In 1994, civilians were banned from using assault weapons, a measure which was questioned by gun rights advocates.

[47] The summit between Clinton and Russian president Boris Yeltsin in Moscow in January that year marked the end of the threat of nuclear war between the two superpowers.

[48] The economy recovered and unemployment fell. Consumption remained high despite increased credit card interest rates, only falling towards the end of the year. The social security reform included cuts in benefits and aggressive worker training programs.

[49] The Democrats lost the majority in the House of Representatives in the mid-term elections of 1994, for the first time in 40 years. The discontent also showed in 1995 with the formation of right-wing paramilitary organizations who refused to recognize federal authority. In one extreme case two Gulf War veterans exploded a car bomb outside a federal office in Oklahoma.

[50] Relying on foreign policy which bolstered his image as world leader, in the year before the elections Clinton pushed a military intervention in Bosnia-Herzegovina and set the Dayton (Ohio) Accords in November 1995. In October 1996 he sponsored a round of Israeli-Palestinian talks in Washington. In November, he was reelected by 49.2 per cent of the vote.

[51] In May 1997, the administration obtained one of its most significant diplomatic victories after signing an agreement with Russia on the expansion of NATO into Eastern Europe.

[52] At home, the enforcement of Affirmative Action laws aiming to place visible minorities in decision-making positions was restricted in Texas and California. Over 80 prisoners were executed in 1997 - the highest number since the death penalty was reinstated in 1976.

[53] In October 1997, Resolution 1134 of the UN Security Council threatened to impose new sanctions on Iraq if Baghdad did not authorize the inspection of all potential weapons-manufacturing facilities. President Clinton then tried to reorganize the multinational alliance (which in 1991 had confronted the Iraqi Government) to carry out a new attack against Iraq. However, in November, the Security Council dismissed a new armed intervention which allowed for negotiations. In February 1998, thousands of US residents demonstrated against Clinton's policy: "We don't want your racist war", said the banners. The CIA spent over $100 million in a period of six years in attempts to oust Iraqi president Saddam Hussein.

Uruguay

Uruguay

Population: 3,204,000 (1996)
Area: 177,414 SQ KM
Capital: Montevideo

Currency: Peso
Language: Spanish

The range lands and forests of the eastern shore of the Uruguay River have been inhabited for at least 10,000 years. By the beginning of the 16th century there were three major cultural groups: the Charrúa, the Chaná and the Guarani. The Charrúa were hunters, while the Chaná developed a rudimentary form of agriculture along the banks of the Uruguay River. Eventually, the Guarani, developed some agricultural skills, mastered ceramics and navigation of the river in canoes.

[2] In 1527, Sebastián Cabot was the first European to sail up the rivers Paraná and Uruguay, where he established the first Spanish settlement in the territory. The settlers ignored the east bank of the Uruguay river for over a century, until cattle were brought in by the governor of Asunción, Hernando Arias de Saavedra (Hernandarias) in 1611.

[3] Good pasture and a moderate climate were conducive to large-scale cattle rearing. This attracted the "faeneros", the Río de la Plata equivalent of cowboys, from Brazil and Buenos Aires. The indian culture was totally transformed by the introduction of beef in their diet, and the horse as a means of obtaining it. Through intermarriage with the indians these "cowboys" - hunters of wild cattle, and not cattle tenders - gave rise to the "gaucho". Not all the gauchos were mestizos (people of mixed European and Indian ancestry) but sometimes were white, black, or "mulatto" (of mixed black and white ancestry). In the 18th century, cattle-raising led to the extinction of some indigenous mammals, a reduction of plant diversity and soil degradation. The

American indians who could not adapt to this new life were displaced and moved to the Jesuit missions further north, or exterminated by the mid-19th century.

[4] In search of cattle and to gain control of the rivers which led to the interior regions of the Río de la Plata basin, the Portuguese advanced on the Banda Oriental (East Bank), an area approximately equivalent to that of present-day Uruguay, and founding Colonia del Sacramento on the shore opposite Buenos Aires in 1680. This settlement caused constant friction between Portugal and Spain. In 1724, Spain ordered the Governor of Buenos Aires, Bruno Mauricio de Zabala, to cross the Río de la Plata and establish a fort in the Bay of Montevideo.

[5] Montevideo depended on the Viceroyalty of Peru until 1776, as did Buenos Aires. That year, the Bourbon reforms decreed the creation of the Viceroyalty of the Río de la Plata, with Buenos Aires as the capital, and Montevideo as a naval station.

[6] The May Revolution which broke out in Buenos Aires in 1810 was rejected by the Montevideans, who profited from the monopoly on trade with Spain. But it found support in the countryside among small and medium-scale producers and the landless masses, led by the popular caudillo (leader) José Artigas. A Federal League was created with what is now Uruguay and the Argentine provinces of Cordoba, Corrientes, Entre Ríos, Misiones and Santa Fe.

[7] Uruguay was invaded by the Portuguese in 1816, with the tacit approval of Buenos Aires, whose government was alarmed by events known as the "Artigan

chaos". In 1820, Artigas fought his way to Paraguay, where he remained until his death in 1850. Portugal ruled over the Uruguayan territory until 1823 when Brazil became independent. Uruguay became the Brazilian Cisplatine Province. In 1825 the "orientales" renewed their campaign against the Brazilian Empire was renewed, and one of its objectives was to return to the United Provinces of the Río de la Plata. On August 25 1825, independence was declared and the decision made to reunite with the territories of the former Viceroyalty.

[8] The country was eventually

granted its independence in 1828, through an agreement between Buenos Aires and Brazil mediated by Britain. The 1830 Constitution created a republic for the elite: only independently wealthy males of European origin could vote or be eligible for office. The 19th century was shaken by civil wars and witnessed the formation of two political parties: the Blanco (White) or National Party, linked to Argentine leader Juan Manuel de Rosas, and the Colorado (Red but not communist), linked to European capital and liberal ideas.

[9] In 1865, Colorado dictator Venancio Flores signed an agreement with Brazil and Argentina and created the Triple Alliance, breaking Paraguayan isolation, with European support, forcing the country to open its borders to foreign trade (see Paraguay).

[10] Between 1876 and 1879, under the dictator of Colonel Lorenzo Latorre, the countryside was enclosed by fences. The implications of this event were far-reaching: the land was completely appropriated by the private sector, production was geared to the capitalist market (over which

PUBLIC EXPENDITURE

7.3%   **79.8%**
1995 ■ **DEFENCE** □ **SOCIAL**

In **1990/91** Military as % of health & education expenditure was **38%**.

WORKERS

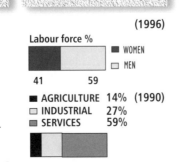

(1996)
Labour force %
■ WOMEN
□ MEN
41   **59**

■ AGRICULTURE **14%** (1990)
□ INDUSTRIAL **27%**
■ SERVICES **59%**

LAND USE

DEFORESTATION **-0.2%** annual (81/90)
IRRIGATED **11.1%** of arable

(1993)

■ FOREST & WOODLAND **5.2%**
□ ARABLE **7.1%**
■ OTHER **87.7%**

PROFILE

ENVIRONMENT
Uruguay has a gently rolling terrain, crossed by characteristic low hills - an extension of Brazil's southern plateau - belonging to the old Guayanic-Brazilian massif. Its average altitude is 300 meters above sea level. This, together with its location and latitude, determines its temperate, subtropical, semi-humid weather, with rainfall throughout the year. The vegetation is made up almost entirely of natural grasslands, suitable for cattle and sheep raising. The territory is well irrigated by many rivers, and has over 1,100 km of navigable waterways, in particular on the rivers Negro and Uruguay, and on the Plata estuary. The coast is made up of many sandy beaches which attract tourists from the neighboring countries. There is increasing pollution in the northern departments as a result of emissions from a thermoelectric plant in Candiota (Brazil), while rivers and streams suffer from the use of poisonous agricultural chemicals. A growing loss of ecosystems on the plains and in the eastern wetlands has been observed, due to monoculture of wood and rice, respectively. Large infrastructure projects (e.g. the Buenos Aires-Colonia bridge, and connecting highway to Sao Paulo, Brazil) pose an additional threat to the environment.

SOCIETY
Peoples: Most Uruguayans are descendants of Spanish, Italian and other European immigrants. The native population was annihilated in the mid-19th century. Afro-American descendants make up about 8 per cent of today's population. **Religions**: Catholics 66 per cent; Protestans 2 per cent. Afro-Brazilian cults are also practised. **Languages**: Spanish. **Political Parties**: Colorado (Red) Party; National (White) Party; The Broad Front (Frente Amplio); the "New Space" (Nuevo Espacio). **Social Organizations**: PIT-CNT (Inter-Union Workers' Bureau - National Workers' Convention). FUCVAM (Uruguayan Federation of Housing Construction by Mutual Help). Federation of University Students (FEUU).

THE STATE
Official Name: República Oriental del Uruguay.
Administrative Divisions: 19 Departments **Capital**: Montevideo, 1,378,707 people (1996).
Other cities: Salto, 81,600 people, Paysandú, 79,100; Las Piedras, 68,400; Rivera, 59,700; Maldonado, 40,700.
Government: Julio María Sanguinetti, President since November, 1994. Presidential system, with a bicameral legislature. A 99-member House of Representatives and a 30-member House of Senators, chosen by proportional representation. Vice-president Hugo Batalla chairs the Senate.
National Holidays: August 25, Independence (1825); July 18, Constitution (1830). **Armed Forces**:25,600 (1994). **Other**: 700 Metropolitan Guard, 500 Republican Guard.

Britain held undisputed control) and the countryside was "organized" leaving no space for the lifestyle of the gaucho, who was transformed into a hired hand.
[11] In 1903 the Colorado José Batlle y Ordoñez assumed the presidency. The following year he fought and defeated Aparicio Saravia - the last rural caudillo of the Blancos. With the ideological influence of European social-democracy, and the support of immigrants, Batlle laid the foundations for the modern Uruguayan state. The high rate of productivity of extensive cattle-raising generated such a surplus that, without changing the land structure of large units in the hands of a few, the State was able to redistribute the wealth in the form of welfare, education, and protection of local industry oriented toward domestic consumption.
[12] The country underwent rapid urbanization. Commerce and services expanded quickly, with the State as the main employer. A large liberal middle-class developed, educated in State schools with Europeanized curricula.
[13] The Church and the State were separated and divorce was legalized. A collegiate system of government was introduced in 1917 to avoid power accumulation. Urban migration and European immigration enlarged the cities, but the birth-rate dropped. Abortion was the major birth-control technique, becoming so common that it was legal between 1933 and 1935, although illegalized again after political negotiations with Catholic authorities. In 1934, women were granted the right to vote. This open legislation earned the country the title "the Switzerland of South America".
[14] Uruguayan exports grew during both world war periods. Meat and its products were supplied first to the Allies, who were fighting against Nazism and Fascism in Europe, and later to US troops fighting in Korea.
[15] Trade balance surpluses secured the country large foreign currency reserves. The welfare policy of subsidies encouraged the emergence of relatively strong import-substitution industries. Meanwhile, a prosperous building industry contributed to maintaining a high rate of employment.
[16] Instead of reinvesting their profits, land owners invested capital abroad, engaging in financial speculation and superfluous consumption. This inevitably led to inflation, corruption and the exacerbation of social conflict. In the mid-1950s, the industrial sector stagnated, a situation that proved impossible to reverse.
[17] The first Blanco government of the century, which came to power in 1959, accepted IMF economic guidelines which accelerated the recession causing a strong reaction among workers. The situation became critical in 1968 when Jorge Pacheco Areco's government, yielding to IMF prescriptions, curtailed the purchasing power of wage-earners and aimed to eliminate the bargaining power of trade unions.

The National Workers' Convention and the student organizations opposed such policies. At the same time the Tupamaro (MLN) guerrilla movement were active throughout the country. In 1971 the Broad Front (Frente Amplio), a left-wing coalition, was founded. It promoted a progressive government program, and nominated a retired general, Liber Seregni, in the presidential elections of that year.
[18] Juan Maria Bordaberry, the Colorado and country nominee, won the elections, which the Blanco National Party denounced as fraudulent. During that regime, the military took up the fight against the guerrilla movement, with the backing of a parliamentary declaration of a state of civil war. In 1972 the Tupamaros were defeated. A campaign including the systematic use of torture rapidly dismantled the clandestine organization. On June 27 1973, President Bordaberry and the armed forces staged a coup. Parliament was dissolved, and a civilian-military government was formed. Local trade unions resisted the coup with a 15-day strike.
[19] The Uruguayan military set up a regime based on the National Security Doctrine, a system learnt in US training academies. Economically, the neo-liberal theories of US Professor Milton Freedman were applied, favouring the concentration of wealth in transnational corporations. Salaries lost 50 per cent of their purchasing power, while the foreign debt reached $5 billion. During this period, all public and private institutions, political parties and unions were banned, people disappeared and torture and arbitrary detentions were commonplace.
[20] The economic situation deteriorated and the civilian population systematically rebuffed efforts to legalize the police state, voting overwhelmingly against the draft of a new constitution that would support this. The Uruguayan generals had no alternative but to work out a timetable for reinstating an institutionally legitimate government.

97%

PER CAPITA
$1,841

STATISTICS

DEMOGRAPHY
Population: 3,204,000 (1996). **Annual growth:** 0.6% (1980/1996). **Estimates for year 2000:** 3,300,000. **Annual growth to year 2000:** 0.6% (1994/2000). **Urban Population:** 90.5% (1996). **Urban growth:** 0.96% (1980/95). **Children per woman:** 2.3 (1996).

HEALTH
Life expectancy at birth: 73 years (1996) male: 69 years (1994) female: 76 years (1994). **Infant mortality:** 20 per 1,000 (1996). **Under-5 child mortality:** 22 per 1,000 (1996). **Calorie consumption:** 101% (1988/90).

EDUCATION
Literacy: 97% (1995). male : 97% (1995) female: 98% (1995). **School enrolment :** Primary total: 109% (1990/95) male : 110% (1990/95) female: 109% (1990/95). Secondary: male : 74% (1990/95). female: 88% (1990/95). Tertiary: 27% (1995). **Primary school teachers:** one for every 20 students (1995).

COMMUNICATIONS
240 **newspapers,** 606 **radios,** 520 **TV sets** and 184 **main telephone lines** per 1,000 people (1994).

ECONOMY
Per capita, GNP: $ 5,760 (1996). **Annual growth, GNP:** 6.8% (1995/96). **Annual inflation:** 70.71% (1985/95). **Consumer price index:** 758.9 (1994). **Currency:** 7.11 pesos = $ 1 (1995) **Cereal imports:** 277 metric tons (1994). **Food import dependency:** 8% (1994). **Fertilizer use:** 828 kgs per ha (1994). **Exports:** $ 2,391 million (1996). **Imports:** $ 3,322 million (1996). **External debt:** $5,899 million (1996). $ 1,841 **per capita:** (1996). **Debt service:** 15.6% of exports (1996). **Development aid received:** $ 81 million (1995). $ 26 per capita (1995). 0.5% of GNP (1994)

ENERGY
Consumption: 622.35 Kgs of Oil equivalent per capita yearly (1994). 67.42% imported (1994)

HDI (rank / value) 37 / 0.883 (1994)

[21] In April 1983, the Inter-union Plenary of Workers (PIT) was formed and May Day was celebrated for the first time since the coup. The three political parties recognized as legal by the military government took up the banner for the labor movement and the causes espoused prior to the dictatorship. They also demanded the release of all political prisoners. The Broad Front, whose president had been in prison since 1973, was excluded from political activity.

[22] Protests against the military regime intensified as a result of the break-down in negotiations. Women's groups defied the Government's prohibition of street demonstrations. After a successful 24-hour general strike called by the PIT, talks between the political parties and the military were re-initiated in January 1984, this time with the participation of representatives of the Broad Front.

[23] The National Party leader Wilson Ferreira Aldunate was arrested on his return to the country after an 11-year exile. He was not permitted to run as a candidate in the 1984 election. General Liber Seregni and hundreds of others were also proscribed as candidates.

[24] Under the slogan of "cambios en paz" (changes without conflict), the leader of the Colorado Party, Julio Maria Sanguinetti, won the national election. During the new government's first month in power, an amnesty law was approved whereby all political prisoners were freed.

[25] President Sanguinetti supported many international diplomatic moves in Latin America. The first two years of his term coincided with a favorable international situation, but he returned to the neo-liberal policies of the previous government, which were strongly resisted by the population.

[26] In 1986, under pressure from the President and the armed forces, Parliament approved an amnesty to military personnel accused of violations of human rights, by 3 to 1. A referendum in April 1988 ratified the law, with 56 per cent in favor, with 42 per cent wanting to try the military for their crimes.

[27] In May 1989, the Government signed a secret structural adjustment agreement with the World Bank, in exchange for rescheduling Uruguay's debt. The Government committed itself to reduce expenditure on social security; to privatize bankrupt banks absorbed by the State; and to reform public companies, making them profitable and attractive for privatization.

[28] In the November 1989 election the Blanco/National Party under Luis Alberto Lacalle inflicted a severe electoral defeat upon the Colorado Party, taking 17 of the country's 19 departments. The Broad Front won in Montevideo with its candidate Tabaré Vázquez. The Left assumed responsibility for municipal administration for the first time in the history of the country. Six women were elected to the Chamber of Deputies and another seven to the Municipal Council (legislative) of the capital.

[29] The associations of pensioners succeeded in bringing about constitutional reform - contra to the agreement with the World Bank - and pensions were readjusted, in line with the salaries of civil servants. This legislation was approved in a referendum.

[30] Lacalle carried out his neo-liberal policy: taxes were increased and the privatization of state-run companies was encouraged. Salaries lost over 15 per cent of their purchasing power during the first year of his term, while inflation mounted from 90 to 130 per cent at the end of his term. In March 1991, Argentina, Brazil and Paraguay approved the Mercosur agreement (see box in Brazil).

[31] A commission convened by the labor union movement, constituted by members of several parties, presented a petition requesting a plebiscite on a privatization law. In December 1992, 72 per cent of the population voted to repeal the law. However, the Government continued trying to privatize certain state enterprises, including the national airline, the gasworks and the sugar cane plantations in the north of the country. The latter caused several demonstrations, including a cane workers' march on Montevideo.

[32] The mayor of Montevideo had approval ratings higher than the electoral support which he had received during his first four years in office. He decentralized the departmental government into 18 zones, within which local voters could elect their own representatives.

[33] In the general and regional elections of November 27 1994, Colorado Party candidate Julio Maria Sanguinetti was elected once again by a small majority.

[34] The Progressive Encounter - made up of the Broad Front, the Christian Democrats and other sectors which had split from the traditional parties - won the mayoralty of the capital for the second consecutive

[35] Sanguinetti took office on March 1 1995, two months after Mercosur came into force, and proposed political and economic reforms. The fall in inflation and the loss of jobs - mainly among the construction and industrial sectors - were the outcome of austerity measures implemented by Economy Minister Luis Mosca.

[36] In October, Uruguay became the first country officially to receive Cuban President Fidel Castro in two decades. Sanguinetti rejected Castro's invitation to visit Cuba in September 1996, considering the time was not right.

[37] The wife of former President Lacalle and several of his closest aides were involved in accusations of corruption which rocked the foundations of the political parties in mid-1996. A system of social security by savings accounts was implemented that year, in line with reforms previously carried out in Argentina and Chile.

[38] In late 1996, Parliament discussed a constitutional reform which entailed difficult political negotiations. The main goal of the reform was the electoral system. In his last trips abroad - Malaysia, Chile, Mexico - Sanguinetti travelled with business people who promoted the country as a financial center fit for investments as the future capital of Mercosur.

[39] The Gross Domestic Product grew 4.9 percent in the 1996, while unemployment reached 11 per cent. Unemployment continued to rise during the first seven months of 1997, reaching 12 per cent.

[40] Uruguay ran into problems with Brazil in 1997, due to the latter's unilateral decision to restrict imports. Montevideo claimed this contravened the Mercosur Treaty.

Uzbekistan

Uzbekistan

Population: 23,209,000 (1996)
Area: 447,400 SQ KM
Capital: Tashkent

Currency: Som-Kupon
Language: Uzbek

Several ancient agricultural centers developed in what is now Uzbekistan, including Khwarezm, Ma Wara an-Nahr and the Fergana Valley. The population and the languages of the first states to emerge in the 10th century BC were Indo-European. Between the 6th and 7th centuries AD, these states formed part of the Persian Achaemenid empire, the empire of Alexander the Great, the Greco-Bactrian kingdoms, and that of Kusha, the white Hun or Eftalite state.

[2] Turkish nomads defeated the Eftalites and brought the major part of Central Asia into their empire, the Turkish *kaganate* (khanate), between the 6th and 8th centuries. During this period, Turkish-speaking peoples began coming to the region and integrating with the local population. In the mid-8th century, the country was conquered by the Arabs. Islam spread quickly, particularly in the cities.

[3] When the power of the Arab caliphs declined, during the reign of the local Samanid and Karajanid dynasties, and under the shahs of Khwarezm (9th to early 13th centuries), an Islamic civilization developed. Agriculture was its main activity, made possible by a highly developed irrigation system; this culture was also noted for its artisans. The cities of Bukhara, Samarkand and Urgenca became prosperous trading centers for the caravans that crossed the Great Silk Route, from China to Byzantium.

[4] From 1219-1221, the state ruled over by the shahs of Khwarezm was overrun by the Tatars, and completely devastated. Khwarezm was turned over to the Golden Horde, under the leadership of Genghis Khan's oldest son. Ma Wara an-Nahr and Fergana went to the second son, Chagatai; the inhabitants of the area began calling themselves Chagatais. Turkish and Mongol tribes moved into the steppes, and in the second half of the 14th century, Timur, the head of one of these tribes, settled in Ma Wara an-Nahr, making Samarkand the capital of his empire. Later, Samarkand became the residence of Ulug Beg, the grandson of Timur Lenk (Tamburlaine), a khan and an astronomer.

[5] The union of nomad tribes who called themselves Uzbeks was achieved in the 15th century, in Central Kazakhstan. During the second half of the century, the great

Uzbek poet and thinker Ali Shir Navai, who lived at the court of one of Timur's descendents, became a world-renowned figure. The leader of the Uzbeks, Muhammad Shaybani, conquered Ma Wara an-Nahr at the beginning of the 16th century, and the Uzbek immigrants gave their name to all the country's inhabitants. After dissolving the State of Shaybani, Uzbek khanates emerged in the region. In 1512, the Khanate of Khiva was formed; its military elite belonged to the Kungrats, an Uzbek people. In 1806 Muhammad Amin, head of the Kungrats, founded the dynasty which was to rule over Khiva until 1920.

[6] The khanate of Bukhara was formed in the mid-16th century, Its military elite belonged to the Uzbek Manguite people. Muhammad Rajim, leader of the Manguites, founded his dynasty in 1753; it also lasted until 1920. The khanate of Bukhara reached its apogee at the time of Nasrula, a khan who ruled from 1826-1860. In the early 19th century, the emirs of Fergana (of the Ming dynasty) created the khanate of Kokand. These feudal theocracies were populated by Uzbeks, as well as Turkmens, Tajiks, Kyrgyz and Karakalpaks, who were in constant conflict.

[7] None of these states had definite boundaries, nor were they capable of exacting absolute fidelity from their chieftains. The emirs of Khiva and Bukhara exercised only nominal sovereignty over the Turkmen tribes of the Kara Kum Desert, who were slave traders in Iranian territory. Although the three Uzbek khanates reached their highest level of organization during this period, they were not prepared to face the imminent European expansion. In Central Asia, Russian and British colonial interests clashed over the cotton market.

[8] In 1860, the Russian offensive against the khanates began, though it was impeded by their geographical isolation, particularly in the case of Khiva, which was surrounded by desert. In 1867, the Czar created the province of Turkistan, with its center in Tashkent. Although it belonged to Kokand, it was officially annexed in 1875. By the end of the 19th century, the province included the regions of Samarkand, Syr Darya and Fergana. On August 12 1873, the Khan of Khiva signed a peace treaty with Russia, accepting protectorate status, as did the khan of Bukhara in September of the

same year. The difficult living conditions imposed on the people by czarist Russia triggered several uprisings, like Andizhan in 1898, and Central Asia in 1916.

[9] With the fall of the Czar in February 1917, power was shared by the committee of the Provisional Government, and the Soviets (councils) of workers and soldiers. After the triumph of the October Revolution in St Petersburg power was concentrated in the hands of the Tashkent Soviet. In 1918, Red Army units crushed both the attempt to form an autonomous Muslim government in Kokand and an anti-Bolshevik uprising in Turkistan. The Red Army occupied Khiva in April 1920, and entered Bukhara in September. Land and water reform began in spring 1921, with military operations continuing until mid-1922, when the implementation of the reforms left the rebels without a cause.

[10] In 1924, the Soviet Government reorganized Central Asian borders along ethnic lines, and proclaimed the Soviet Socialist Republic (SSR) of Uzbekistan. In May 1925, Uzbekistan became a federated republic of the Soviet Union. The Autonomous Soviet Socialist Republic of Tajikistan was a part of Uzbekistan until 1929, when it joined the USSR. In Moscow, during the Great Purge of 1937-38, a number of Uzbeks, including the prime minister, Fayzullah Khodzhayev and the first secretary of the Uzbek Communist Party, Akmal Ikramov, were sentenced to death. In 1953, both leaders were rehabilitated.

[11] The socialist reforms were aimed primarily at taking advantage of the region's agricultural potential. Huge mechanized irrigation systems, including the Great Fergana, North Fergana and Tashkent canals, were

constructed by the State, as were reservoirs like the Kattakurgan on the Zeravshan River (the Uzbek Sea), the Kuyumazar and the Akhangaran (the Tashkent Sea). Between 1956 and 1983, when Sharaf Rashidov was first secretary of the Communist Party, the republic's economy revolved around cotton and the national industry was geared toward producing machines and heavy equipment for cotton cultivation, harvesting and processing. Uzbekistan became the USSR's largest cotton producer and the third largest in the world.

[12] In the 1940s, the population increased, Kurds and Mesketian Turks, who had been deported from the Caucasus, came to Uzbekistan, and all was stable until the 1980s. When Leonid Brezhnev became head of the Communist Party of the USSR in 1983 he changed the Uzbek authorities. The new first secretary of the local CP, Inamjon Ousmankhodjaev, revealed that official cotton production statistics had been systematically falsified by his predecessor.

[13] The Uzbek corruption case was the biggest scandal in the Soviet Union at the time, and triggered large amounts of arrests, lawsuits against 4,000 civil servants and expulsions from the party. However, this turned out to be just another political purge, as it did not bring about any substantial changes.

[14] From 1985 onward, the changes initiated by President Mikhail Gorbachev, the deterioration of the economic situation and the weakening of the Soviet Communist Party's centralized authority gave rise to increased ethnic and religious conflicts in Uzbekistan. The Uzbeks, predominantly Sunni Muslims, resisted the Party's anti-clerical campaigns.

[15] The USSR's intervention in

PROFILE

ENVIRONMENT

Uzbekistan is bounded in the north and northwest by Kazakhstan, in the southeast by Tajikistan, in the northeast by Kyrgyzstan and in the south by Afghanistan. Part of its terrain is flat, while the rest is mountainous. There are two main rivers and more than 600 streams, some of which are diverted for irrigation, while others are utilized for hydroelectric projects. The plains are located in the northwest and the center (the Ustyurt Plateau, the Amu Darya Valley and the Kyzylkum desert), while the mountains are in the southeast (the Tien-Shan and Gissar and Alay ranges). It has a hot, dry climate on the plains, and is more humid in the mountains. There are large deposits of natural gas, oil and coal. Among the most pressing environmental problems are the salinization of the soil as a result of monoculture, desertification, drinking water and air contamination.

SOCIETY

Peoples: Uzbeks, 75.8 per cent; Russians, 6 per cent; Tajiks, 4.8 per cent; Kazakhs, 4.1 per cent, Kyrghizs, 0.9 per cent; Ukranians, 0.6 per cent; Turks 0.6 per cent. Other, 7.2 per cent (1995). **Religions:** Muslim (Sunni), 88 per cent: Orthodox, 1 per cent. Other (mostly non religious), 11 per cent. **Languages:** Uzbek (official), Russian, Tajik. **Political Parties:** People's Democratic Party; National Progress Party; Birlik Democratic Party; Islamic Renaissance Party.

THE STATE

Official Name: Uzbekistan Jumhuriyati. **Capital:** Tashkent, 2,107,000 people (1995). **Other cities:** Samarkand, 362,000 people; Namangan, 333,000; Andizhan, 313,000; Bukhara, 235,000 (1995). **Government:** Islam Karimov, President since December, 1991. Otkir Sultonov, Prime Minister since 1995. Legislature: Supreme Assembly, (single-chamber), with 150 members elected by direct popular vote every five years.
National Holiday: September 1, Independence (1991).
Armed Forces: 65,000 (1995). **Other:** (National Guard) 700.

STATISTICS

DEMOGRAPHY

Population: 23,209,000 (1996). **Annual growth:** 2.3% (1980/1996). **Estimates for year 2000:** 25,000,000. **Annual growth to year 2000:** 1.9% (1994/2000). **Urban Population:** 41.3% (1996). **Urban growth:** 2.5% (1980/95). **Children per woman:** 3.6 (1996).

HEALTH

Life expectancy at birth: 68 years (1996) male: 64 years (1994) female: 71 years (1994). **Infant mortality:** 46 per 1,000 (1996). **Under-5 child mortality:** 60 per 1,000 (1996). **Safe water:** 62% (1990/96).

EDUCATION

Literacy: 100% (1995) male : 100% (1995) female: 100% (1995). **School enrolment :** Primary total: 77% (1990/95) male : 78% (1990/95) female: 76% (1990/95). Secondary: male : 99% (1990/95). female: 87% (1990/95). Tertiary: 32% (1995). **Primary school teachers:** one for every 21 students (1995).

COMMUNICATIONS

10 **newspapers**, 81 **radios**, 180 **TV sets** and 69 **main telephone lines** per 1,000 people (1994). **Books:** 6 new titles per 100,000 people (1992/94).

ECONOMY

Per capita, GNP: $ 1,010 (1996). **Annual growth, GNP:** -0.8% (1995/96). **Consumer price index:** (1994). **Currency:** 32.2 som-kupon = $ 1 (1995) **Cereal imports:** metric tons (1994). **Food import dependency:** % (1994). **Fertilizer use:** 1,073 kgs per ha (1994). **Exports:** $ 2,671 million (1996). **Imports:** $ 4,761 million (1996). **External debt:** $ 2,319 million (1996). $ 100 **per capita:** (1996). **Debt service:** 8.1% of exports (1996).

ENERGY

Consumption: 1,869.02 Kgs of Oil equivalent per capita yearly (1994). -0.16% imported (1994).

HDI (rank / value) 100 / 0.662 (1994)

Afghanistan against fellow-Sunni Muslims only worsened the situation, and all of these factors combined to create a hostile climate toward Moscow and the Russian minority residing in Uzbekistan. The most serious consequence was the conflict in the region of Fergana in June 1989, and conflicts in Namangan, in December 1990.
[16] In August 1991, the Uzbek Soviet (Parliament) approved the Law of Independence. On December 12, in Alma Ata, the Uzbek delegation signed the agreement creating the Commonwealth of Independent States (CIS), which marked the end of the USSR.
[17] On the 29th of the same month, presidential elections were held with a referendum supporting independence. Islam Karimov, the former first secretary of the Uzbek Communist Party, was elected president.
[18] In January 1992, students demonstrating in Tashkent against the shortage of bread and the high price of staple goods were fired upon by police; six people were killed and many were injured. The Uzbekistan Government has gradually started to liberalize the economy by deregulating some prices, following the example of other former Soviet republics. In an attempt to reduce the tension, authorities announced an increase in student grants.
[19] At the same time, a leadership struggle in the upper echelons of the religious (Islamic) hierarchy,

reinforced the secular power of the president.
[20] Karimov imposed a harsh, authoritarian style in an attempt to maintain the country's political stability. When the deregulation of prices resulted in student protests, the government responded with severe repressive measures. One such demonstration resulted in two students being killed and several injured.
[21] In March, arrests were made in the city of Namangan, a bastion of Muslim opposition. The Islamic center was attacked; with several leaders of the Birlik Democratic Party and other religious leaders being arrested.
[22] In March 1992, the presidents of the parliaments of seven member republics of the CIS - Armenia, Belarus, Kazakhstan, Kyrgyzstan, the Russian Federation, Tajikistan and Uzbekistan - agreed to create an inter-parliamentary assembly, for consultation and coordination. That same month Uzbekistan was admitted to the UN as a new member.
[23] In June, Karimov defined a new economic course for Uzbekistan, based upon the Southeast Asian development model: eliminating dissidence and modernizing the economy by adopting free-market policies. The opposition went underground.
[24] The deregulation of prices, privatization and financial and fiscal reforms which have been implemented since 1992, have been far less drastic in Uzbekistan

than in other former Soviet republics.
[25] During 1993, Uzbekistan tightened political links with other former soviet republics in Central Asia, establishing diplomatic relations with Hungary and signing bilateral agreements with Turkey, Afghanistan and Pakistan.
[26] Criticized for the apparent slowness of his economic reforms, Karimov decided to launch a privatization plan in January 1994, announcing price increases of basic goods and energy of around 300 per cent.
[27] Several countries of Central Asia tried to design a program to defend the environment in the region of the Aral Sea. However, one of the conditions needed to prevent the drying of the lake, according to Western experts, would mean reducing the irrigation of cotton crops in Uzbekistan.
[28] On a diplomatic front, the country aimed to contain the Russian and Iranian influences in the region, particularly from 1995 onwards. Karimov actively supported the US embargo on Iran calling for the creation of a common Turkmenistan between the nations of the region, making it understood that it was threatened by the 'imperialist' tendencies of Russia.
[29] In 1996, for the first time, the parliament admitted human rights

abuses had been committed in the past approving new legislation on the issue. Two official visits by the Uzbek President, to France and the United States, in April and June respectively, ratified Uzbekistan's rapprochement to the Western countries.
[30] In 1997, media censorship continued. The proclaimed economic success, making the nation one of the most prosperous in central Asia, was achieved with soaring inflation and heavy restrictions on imports, severely affecting the standard of living of the population.
[31] In June, Uzbekistan refused to sign a peace agreement formally putting an end to the civil war in Tajikistan, stating this would provoke political instability, as the process overlooked several of the warring groups.
[32] In late 1997, Uzbekistan - along with Israel and the United States - objected to lifting the economic embargo on Cuba in the UN General Assembly. A majority of 143 countries voted in favour of the resolution.
[33] In early 1998, Tashkent expressed its concern over the advance of the Islamic fundamentalists in Tajikistan and the action of the "Wahhabi" sect in the Fergana valley, a densely populated area belonging to Uzbekistan, Tajikistan and Kyrgyzstan.

Vanuatu

Vanatu

Population:	174,000 (1996)
Area:	12,189 SQ KM
Capital:	Vila
Currency:	Vatu
Language:	Bislama, English and French

The first colonization of Polynesia is still a mystery to anthropologists and historians. Thor Heyerdahl's highly publicized Kon Tiki expedition tried to demonstrate that people could have reached the South Pacific islands from America. But linguistic, cultural and agricultural similarities relate Melanesians to Indonesians.

[2] Sailing westwards, Polynesians reached Vanuatu around 1400 BC. These navigators crossed and populated the entire Pacific Ocean from Antarctica to Hawaii and as far as Easter Island on the eastern edge of the Pacific Ocean. Their culture was highly developed, Polynesians domesticated animals and developed some subsistence crops; they manufactured ceramics and textiles, organized their societies with a caste system and, in some cases, possessed a historical knowledge which had been orally transmitted down the generations for centuries.

[3] On April 29 1605 the Portuguese-Spanish navigator, Pedro Fernandez de Quiros, was the first European to sight mountains which he believed to be part of the Great Southern Continent for which he was searching; he named the place, Tierra del Espíritu Santo (Land of the Holy Spirit). A century and a half later, Frenchman Louis Antoine de Bougainville, sailed around the region and demonstrated that it was not part of Australia but rather a series of islands. In 1774, James Cook drew the first map of the archipelago, calling it the New Hebrides after the Scottish Hebrides Islands.

[4] Shortly thereafter traders arrived and felled all the aromatic sandalwood forests. Lacking other

attractive natural resources, the islands became the source of a semi-enslaved labor force. The workers were either taken by force or purchased from local leaders in exchange for tobacco, mirrors and firearms. In the 19th century, the Civil War in the United States created an increase of international cotton prices and Indochina's plantations became so lucrative that the slave trade continued long after slavery had been officially abolished.

[5] Popular resentment of this plundering caused the murders of more European missionaries in the New Hebrides than in any other area of the Pacific.

[6] During almost all of the 19th century, the archipelago was on the dividing line between the French (in New Caledonia) and British (in the Solomon islands) zones of influence, and these nations finally decided to share the islands instead of fighting over them. In 1887, a Joint Naval Commission was established, and in 1906, the Condominium was formalized. The native islanders soon referred to it as the "pandemonium".

[7] The formula of shared domination envisaged the joint upkeep of some basic services; the post, radio, customs, public works, but left each power free to develop other services. Consequently, there were two police forces, two monetary systems, two independent health services and two school systems ruled by two representatives on the islands.

[8] Melanesians were relegated to being "stateless" in their own country, and they were not considered citizens until a legislative assembly was established in the territory in 1974. Until then only British or French people were entitled to citizenship or land ownership.

[9] Most of the neighboring archipelagos achieved independence in the 1970s. This encouraged the foundation of the National Party of the New Hebrides (today the Vanuatu Party) in 1971. The Party organized grassroots groups on all of the islands on the basis of the Protestant parochial structure. The Party became the country's leading political force and

demanded total independence, in opposition to various "moderate" pro-French parties that preferred to maintain the colonial situation. When the Party won two-thirds of the vote in 1979, this convinced the British that independence could no longer be postponed. They also carried out a strong anti-nuclear policy and turned Vanuatu into the only nation among the Pacific islands to become a member of the Non-Aligned Movement.

[10] During that period French agents and US business encouraged the growth of the Na Griamel separatist group in Espíritu Santo. This group began as a popular protest movement against the sale of property to North American hotels. The group's leader, Jimmy Stevens, received $250,000, arms and a radio from the Phoenix Foundation, an ultra-right US organization, in return for concessions to install a casino and, presumably, cover for illicit activities from Stevens' "Republic of Vemarana".

[11] Stevens visited France to obtain the support of President Giscard d'Estaing, and the French police did nothing to prevent the rebellion and expulsion of Vanuatu Party followers from the island. Meanwhile francophone support of the other islands encouraged small "moderate" pro-French parties to oppose the Government of Walter Lini, who

was accused of being authoritarian, too centralist and too close to Britain and Australia.

[12] Finally, Lini, supported by forces from Papua New Guinea, managed to disarm the separatists, deporting Stevens and his followers, who were granted asylum in Kanaky/New Caledonia.

[13] Vanuatan independence was declared on July 30 1980. Measures were immediately taken to return the land held by foreigners to the Melanesians; the school system was unified and a national army was created.

[14] In February 1981, the newly-arrived itinerant ambassador of Vanuatu, Barak Sope, was refused entry at the Noumea airport by the French Government, to prevent his participation in the Melanesian Independence Front Congress in New Caledonia. Retaliation was immediate; Lini's government declared the French ambassador persona non grata and requested that the French diplomatic mission be reduced to five members. This incident delayed the cooperation program between the governments.

[15] Government revenues depend heavily on foreign aid and the country's exports cover only half of the cost of its imports. Since the country is a tax haven with more than 60 banks established in Vila, the capital, and over 1,000 absentee firms in the territory, there is no solid strategy to ensure provision of finances for

LAND USE

(1993)

■ FOREST & WOODLAND	75%
□ ARABLE	1.6%
■ OTHER	23.4%

PROFILE

ENVIRONMENT

Vanuatu is a Melanesian archipelago, of volcanic origin, comprising more than 70 islands and islets many of them uninhabited. It stretches for 800 km, in a north-south direction in the South Pacific about 1,200 km east of Australia. Major islands are: Espiritu Santo, Malekula, Epi, Pentecost, Aoba, Maewa, Paama, Ambrym, Efate, Erromango, Tanna and Aneityum. Active volcanoes are found in Tanna, Ambrym and Lopevi and the area is subject to earthquakes. The land is mountainous and covered with dense tropical forests. The climate is tropical with heavy rainfall, moderated by the influence of the ocean. The subsoil of Efate is rich in manganese and the soil is suitable for farming. Fishing is a traditional economic activity. The land tenure system has contributed to general soil depletion (deforestation, erosion). Rising sea levels - a 20 cm increase in Vanuatu's tides has been estimated for the next four decades - will affect both inhabited and uninhabited coastal areas. There is also a risk that salt water (from rising tides) will seep into ground water, threatening water supplies

SOCIETY

Peoples: The people are basically Melanesian (98 per cent), with 1 per cent European (British and French) and smaller groups from Vietnam, China and other Pacific islands.
Religions: Mainly Christian (77 per cent).
Languages: Bislama, English and French are official. Other Melanesian languages are also spoken.
Political Parties: Union of Moderate Parties; National United Party; People's Democratic Party; Unity Front; Tan Union, Frei Melanesio and Na Griamel. Social Organisations: Vanuatu Trade Union Congress (VTUC).

THE STATE

Official Name: Ripablik blong Vanuatu. République de Vanuatu, Republic of Vanuatu.
Capital: Vila, on Efate Island, 30,000 people (1992).
Other cities: Luganville (Santo), 6,900 people; Port Olry, 884; Isangel, 752 (1989).
Administrative Divisions: 11 Government Regions, 2 Municipalities.
Government: Jean-Marie Leye, President since 1994; Serge Vohor, Prime Minister since 1996. The unicameral Representative Assembly is made up of 46 representatives elected every 4 years.
National Holiday: July 30, Independence Day (1980).

STATISTICS

DEMOGRAPHY
Population: 174,000 (1996). **Annual growth**: 2.5% (1980/1996). **Estimates for year 2000**: 200,000. **Annual growth to year 2000**: 2.6% (1994/2000). **Urban Population**: 19.1% (1996). **Children per woman**: 4.5 (1996).

HEALTH
Life expectancy at birth: 67 years (1996) male: years (1994) female: years (1994). **Infant mortality**: 41 per 1,000 (1996). **Under-5 child mortality**: 53 per 1,000 (1996). **Safe water**: 87% (1990/96).

EDUCATION
Literacy: 64% (1995) male :% (1995) female: 60% (1995). **School enrolment**: Primary total: 106% (1990/95) male : 105% (1990/95). female: 107% (1990/95). Secondary: male : 23% (1990/95) female: 18% (1990/95).

COMMUNICATIONS
294 **radios**, 10 **TV sets** and 27 **main telephone lines** per 1,000 people (1994).

ECONOMY
Consumer price index: 117.4 (1994). **Currency**: 113.74 vatu = $1 (1995) **Cereal imports**: 11 metric tons (1994). **Development aid received**: $ 46 million (1995). $ 288 per capita (1995). 24.5% of GNP (1994).

HDI (rank / value) 124 / 0.547 (1994)

---

the Public Treasury. One proposed project calls for opening the country to international maritime registration under Vanuatu's flag.
[16] In February 1984, President Ati George Sokomanu resigned. He justified his action by claiming that the constitution did not adequately protect the head of state or his ministers, or guarantee "coherent management". However, after this governmental crisis, the resigning president agreed to participate in the March 1984 elections, and was re-elected.
[17] The second Vanuatu Development Plan (1987-1991) was effected to achieve the following goals: to ensure balanced regional and rural development, to take better advantage of the country's natural resources, to provide for the faster development of human resources and to promote development of the private sector. The plan suffered a serious set-back in February 1987, with Hurricane Ulna, which caused an estimated $36 million damage and

affected about 34 per cent of the population.
[18] In the December 1987 elections, Lini won over Barak Sope, who attempted an unsuccessful challenge for the party leadership. Barak Sope accepted the cabinet post of minister of tourism and immigration, but in May 1988 he was relieved of his responsibilities by Lini, due to violent demonstrations by his followers. Finally, Sope split from the ruling party and founded his own political group, the Melanesian Progressive Party.
[19] In 1988, former president Sokomau, together with Barak Sope, tried unsuccessfully to oust Prime Minister Walter Lini. They were both arrested and imprisoned. Fred Timakata was appointed the new president.
[20] On August 7 1991, the ruling party of Vanuatu voted in favor of deposing Walter Lini as prime minister. The minister of foreign affairs, Donald Kalpokas, was appointed to this post.
[21] In October, Walter L ini founded the United National Party.

The Union of Moderate Parties, led by Maxime Carlot Korman, won the elections held on December 2.
[22] In January 1992, Carlot Korman formed a coalition with the UNP. Lini's sister Hilda was named minister of health, occupying the cabinet position to which the UNP - as a member of the coalition - was entitled. At this time, French was re-established as an official language. Minister of Finance Willy Jimmy's economic plan established a series of priorities, including exports, foreign investment, agrarian reform and free primary education.
[23] Carlot Korman launched a program to diversify agriculture in 1993, a year after Hurricane Betsy had destroyed 30 per cent of the harvest. In 1994, the Government decided to eliminate 200 of the 4,800 posts in the existing public service. One of the arguments for this was the disproportionate increase of state employees since 1985, when there had been 3,300.

[24] On the international front, Vanuatu was the only country of the South Pacific Forum which did not join this organisation's protest against French nuclear tests in Polynesia, in September 1995.
[25] Carlot Korman was forced to resign in February 1996 and Serge Vohor became Prime Minister. In August 1996, the Vanuatu Mobile Force (VMF), a paramilitary group, declared a strike over unpaid wages. Three months later, its officers were arrested by the police and freed once they had sworn their loyalty.
[26] In 1997, against a background of political instability, caused partly by constant rumours of a new VMF uprising, the Asian Development Bank agreed a $14 million loan for the economic reform programme brought in by the Government.
[27] In early 1998, the Court of Appeal confirmed the dissolution of Parliament called for by President Jean-Marie Leye.

Venezuela

Venezuela

Population:	22,311,000 (1996)
Area:	912,050 SQ KM
Capital:	Caracas
Currency:	Bolívar
Language:	Spanish

Cumanagotos, Tamaques, Maquiritares, Arecunas, and other Carib groups inhabited the northern tip of South America when Christopher Columbus arrived on these shores in 1498. Local buildings, constructed on poles, reminded the Spaniards of the appearance of Venice, so they named the country Venezuela.

[2] During the colonial period, Venezuela was organized as a Captaincy General of the Viceroyalty of New Granada, and in the 18th century it became the most important farming colony, producing mainly cocoa. A local aristocracy of "mantuanos" developed, a landowning class of European extraction, who used African slave labor on their plantations. The "pardos" (blacks) who constitute the overwhelming majority of the population are descended from the slaves.

[3] Two of the greatest leaders of the Latin American independence movement were born in the Captaincy: Francisco de Miranda and Simón Bolívar. On April 19 1810, the wars of independence broke out after the constitution of a Cabildo or Assembly. Miranda became the commander of the army, envisaging a vast American Confederacy to be known as Colombia, which would crown an Inka emperor. His dreams did not however come to fruition as he was captured by the Spaniards in 1811, and later died in prison.

[4] Bolívar took up Miranda's project for American liberation and was backed, in principle, by the mantuano oligarchy. In a swift campaign (1812-13) he took over the country, and was able to install a government in Caracas. His plans for independence did not include changes in social structure, and he was not supported by the masses who lived in the plains (llaneros), most of whom were mulattos living under the severe repression of white creole masters who they hated. Their liberation movement was led by the Spanish loyalist General José Tomás Boves, who defeated Bolívar in 1814. Boves abolished slavery and redistributed the land among the people.

[5] Having lost the first republic, Bolívar went into exile, working closely with the Haitian President, Alexandre Sabés Petión, who helped him to add a social dimension to his American revolutionary project. Bolívar returned to Venezuela and, championing popular demands, he won mass support.

[6] Accompanied by other important military leaders like Antonio José de Sucre, Mariño, José A Páez and Arismendi, he carried out successful military campaigns in the northern half of the continent. He subsequently founded Bolivia in what had hitherto been known as "Upperu".

[7] In 1819, the Angostura Congress created the new republic of "Gran Colombia", uniting Colombia, Ecuador, Panama and Venezuela. In 1830, after Bolívar's death, General José Antonio Páez declared Venezuela's secession from Gran Colombia, establishing it as an independent nation.

[8] For decades, Venezuelan politics revolved around the caudillo, or leader, Páez. His political successor, Antonio Guzmán Blanco, was determined to modernize Venezuela. He carried out the aim to a certain extent, introducing new technology, new means of communication, and reforming the country's legal code.

[9] Juan Vicente Gómez took power in 1908 ruling for 17 years, and his government made an attempt to eliminate the caudillo system. He gave free access to the multinational oil companies, which set up oil extracting operations primarily on the Lake Maracaibo oil fields.

[10] In 1935 his former aide, General Eleazar López Contreras, took office. He was succeeded in 1941, by General Isaías Medina Angarita, who laid the foundations for freer political activity by legalizing the Democratic Action Party (AD).

[11] It was a long time before majority demands were met, however, and this situation was aggravated by the unrest within the army. A civilian-military movement took power, led by Rómulo Betancourt, the leader of AD, and general Marcos Pérez Jiménez, and they held the country's first free elections in 1947. The writer Rómulo Gallegos, of the AD, was elected President only to be overthrown in 1948 by yet another military coup, installing the harsh dictatorship of Marcos Pérez Jiménez.

[12] Ten years later, in January 1958, Pérez Jiménez was overthrown by a popular revolt and he fled the country. Venezuela then entered a stable democratic period under a coalition government formed by Democratic Action, COPEI (the Christian Democrats) and the

Republican Democratic Union (URD). This stability was largely achieved because of the influx of massive oil revenues, improved relations with the US, and expanded political rights. Unfortunately, the ensuing economic growth brought little change to the lives of the poor majority, with popular discontent resulting in guerrilla warfare led by the Communist Party, the Movement of the Revolutionary Left (which split from AD), and other left-wing groups.

[13] In 1960, Venezuela sponsored the formation of the Organization of Petroleum Exporting Countries (OPEC). Sixteen years later, during the presidency of social democrat Carlos Andrés Pérez, Venezuelan reserves of oil and iron were nationalized. Pérez also supported the creation of the Latin American Economic System (SELA) and argued in favor of a New International Economic Order.

[14] The Christian Democrats were returned to power in the December 1978 elections, but the administration of President Luis Herrera Campins brought no substantial change to reformist policy.

[15] Venezuela was the world's third largest oil exporter and it received its highest prices during the governments of Pérez and Herrera. At this time, Venezuela

Military Expenditure

MILITARY (as % of health and education expenditures-1990/91) **33%**

Workers

(1996)

Labour force %

33	67
■ WOMEN	□ MEN

Land Use

DEFORESTATION -1.2% annual (81/90)
IRRIGATED 5.9% of arable

(1993)

■ FOREST & WOODLAND	32.9%
□ ARABLE	3.5%
■ OTHER	63.6%

Literacy
1995

91%

Food Dependency
1970
10%
1994
11%

PROFILE

ENVIRONMENT

The country comprises three main regions. In the north and west, the Andes and other mountain chains, and high mountains to the south. The central Orinoco Plains are a livestock farming area. In the southeast, highlands of ancient rock and sandstone extend to the borders with Brazil and Guyana, forming Venezuelan Guyana. It is a sparsely inhabited area with thick forests, savannas, rivers, and some peculiar features: the "tepuyes" or plateau mountains, and the rare Sarisarinama depths. Most of the population lives in the hilly north. The oil-rich Maracaibo lowlands and Gulf of Paria are on the coast. The country produces oil, iron ore, manganese, bauxite, tungsten and chrome, gold and diamonds. Among the country's most important environmental problems are deforestation and the degradation of the soil. In addition, the lack of sewage treatment facilities in the main urban and industrial centers has increased pollution in the country's rivers and the Caribbean Sea.

SOCIETY

Peoples: Venezuelans come from the integration of indigenous peoples, Afro-Caribbeans and European settlers. Today, indigenous peoples and Afro-Caribbeans each account for less than 7 per cent of the population. In recent times, Venezuela has received more immigrants than any other South American country.
Religions: Mainly Catholic, 92.7 per cent.
Languages: Spanish, official and predominant; 31 native languages are spoken.
Political Parties: Democratic Action (AD), member of the Socialist International; the Social Christian Party (COPEI), a member of the Christian Democrat International; the Movement Toward Socialism (MAS), founded in 1970; Radical Cause; Convergence, created in 1993 by Christian Democratic splinter groups; the People's Electoral Movement (MEP); the Venezuelan Communist Party (PCV); the New Democratic Generation, linked to the Liberal International; Intergration, Representation, New Hope (IRENE), founded in 1997 by independent mayor of Chacao, Irene Saez.
Social Organizations: The Venezuelan Confederation of Workers (CTV) is the main trade union, and is controlled by AD. There are other trade unions which are clearly linked to political parties.

THE STATE

Official Name: República de Venezuela.
Administrative divisions: 21 states with partial autonomy (including the Federal District), 2 Federal territories.
Capital: Caracas, 2,959,000 people (1995).
Other cities: Maracaibo 1,249,670 people; Valencia 1,034,033 people; Barquisimeto 692,600 people; Guyana City 523,580 people (1990).
Government: Rafael Caldera, President since February 1994. Presidential system, Congress with Chamber of Deputies and Senate (201 and 49 members respectively).
National Holiday: July 5, Independence Day (1811).
Armed Forces: 79,000, including 18,000 conscripts (1997).
Other: Cooperation Army, 23,000.

had the highest per capita income in Latin America, but the Government was unable to manage the enormous amounts of money coming into the country. Huge state-run companies were created for the manufacture of iron ore, aluminium, cement, and for hydroelectric power, while most private companies were being subsidized. Today, the Venezuelan state still generates 95 per cent of the country's exports and is by far its largest business owner.

[16] Long-standing border disputes between Venezuela and its neighbors flared up again in 1981 and 1982. Disputes with Colombia over the Guajira peninsula, and with Guyana over the Essequibo region, continued. Meanwhile, after holding many conferences to discuss the issue of national waters, Venezuela established its territorial rights over huge areas of the Caribbean sea.

[17] In 1982, a sharp decrease in oil revenues, foreign debt, and a massive flight of private capital abroad, forced the Government to take control of exchange rates and foreign trade. The foreign debt grew, while inflation, unemployment, and housing shortages started to mount, and critical poverty rose.

[18] Charges of government corruption contributed to the victory of the AD's Jaime Lusinchi in the December 1983 elections, where he gained 56 per cent of the vote, defeating COPEI's Rafael Caldera.

[19] The population continued to support Lusinchi for some time, but when the June 1983 economic collapse proved impossible to halt, Venezuela had to suspend $5 billion in service payments on its $37 billion debt, and the ensuing difficulties resulted in a drop in his popularity.

[20] In reaction to the economic problems, Lusinchi's policy comprised an austerity plan which gave meagre results, and a flawed "social pact" between employers and unions and, towards the end of his term, increasing state control over the economy.

[21] In its foreign relations, Venezuela resumed its active role in the Contadora Group, but dealt with the IMF and US in a "traditional" way. In January 1986,

Venezuela rescheduled nearly two thirds of its foreign debt over ten years, but falling oil prices forced the Government to renegotiate a year later. Before leaving office, Lusinchi announced a moratorium to obtain a further rescheduling.

[22] The AD's candidate for the December 1988 elections was former president Carlos Andrés Pérez. Backed by the Confederation of Venezuelan Workers (CTV), he took 54.5 per cent of the vote, and Eduardo Fernández, the COPEI candidate, took 41.7 per cent.

[23] Increasing social tension could not be halted and 25 days later the most underprivileged sectors of the population responded with a wave of riots and looting. Police repression left more than 1,000 dead (246 according to the government), and 2,000 wounded or jailed.

[24] The populist tone was dropped, and IMF-backed economic restructuring measures were initiated. In December 1989, these policies were blamed for abstention rates of nearly 70 per cent and broad gains by the Christian Democrats and left-wing parties, when Venezuelans elected their 20 state governors and 369 mayors for the first time.

[25] Ten AD governors were elected, and COPEI had four with the AD losing seats in many of its traditional strongholds. Most remarkable, however, were the left-wing victories in three states: in Bolívar, the trade union leader Andrés Velázquez of the Popular Cause party was elected; in Aragua, the Movement To Socialism (MAS) won an easy victory; and Anzoátegui elected a leader of the People's Electoral Movement (MEP).

[26] In the early 1990s, Venezuela's indigenous population totalled around 200,000 - approximately one per cent of the population, but their future survival is threatened. Despite the fact that the Government has clearly recognized Yanomami land rights, there has not been adequate protection of the indigenous population. They have continued to suffer persecution from landowners, farmers and government officials, while Brazilian miners continue to invade their land prospecting for gold within Venezuelan territory.

[27] The immigration rate has fallen, but between 1950 and 1980 it was immense. The Government is bringing in selection methods, admitting mainly Eastern Europeans. Most of the present immigrants are from Colombia and there are smaller numbers of Ecuadorans, Peruvians, and Dominicans.

[28] Early in 1992, the popularity of the Pérez Government was at its lowest ebb, with the AD party distancing itself from imposing further economic measures. The Congress exercised its controlling function by investigating crimes, but due to the corruption and inefficiency of the Judiciary these investigations very rarely led to prosecutions.

[29] On February 4 1992, a group of lieutenant-colonels staged a coup against President Carlos Andrés

Pérez. The group was led by Francisco Arias and while the attempt failed, it re-emphasized the fact that administrative corruption and the economic crisis were the causes of instability. Arias and parachute commander Hugo Chavez, both belonging to the Bolívar-200 Military Movement, were arrested.

[30] This coup attempt had caused several dozen civilian and military casualties. The defence minister Fernando Ochoa officially stated that 51 military personnel had been injured, 19 had died, and an indeterminate number of soldiers had been arrested.

[31] On the day of the attempted coup, the Venezuelan President suspended all constitutional rights. This emergency measure, ratified by Congress, banned meetings, limited the freedom of

Maternal Mortality
1990

PER 100,000 LIVE BIRTHS

120

External Debt
1996

PER CAPITA

$1,584

STATISTICS

DEMOGRAPHY
Population: 22,311,000 (1996). **Annual growth:** 2.4% (1980/1996). **Estimates for year 2000:** 24,200,000. **Annual growth to year 2000:** 2.1% (1994/2000). **Urban Population:** 86.2% (1996). **Urban growth:** 3.26% (1980/95). **Children per woman:** 3.1 (1996).

HEALTH
Life expectancy at birth: 72 years (1996) male: 69 years (1994) female: 75 years (1994). **Infant mortality:** 24 per 1,000 (1996). **Under-5 child mortality:** 28 per 1,000 (1996). **Calorie consumption:** 99% (1988/90). **Safe water:** 79% (1990/96).

EDUCATION
Literacy: 91% (1995) male : 92% (1995) female: 90% (1995). **School enrolment :** Primary total: 94% (1990/95) male : 93% (1990/95) female: 96% (1990/95). Secondary: male : 29% (1990/95) female: 41% (1990/95). Tertiary: 29% (1995). **Primary school teachers:** one for every 23 students (1995).

COMMUNICATIONS
20 **newspapers**, 443 **radios**, 180 **TV sets** and 108 **main telephone lines** per 1,000 people (1994). **Books:** 17 new titles per 100,000 people (1992/94).

ECONOMY
Per capita, GNP: $ 3,020 (1996). **Annual growth, GNP:** -3.7% (1995/96). **Annual inflation:** 37.62% (1985/95). **Consumer price index:** 392.0 (1994). **Currency:** 290 bolívares = $ 1 (1995) **Cereal imports:** 2,015 metric tons (1994). **Food import dependency:** 11% (1994). **Fertilizer use:** 613 kgs per ha (1994). **Exports:** $ 22,633 million (1996). **Imports:** $ 8,902 million (1996). **External debt:** $ 35,344 million (1996). $ 1,584 **per capita:** (1996). **Debt service:** 16.8% of exports (1996). **Development aid received:** $81 million (1995). $4 per capita (1995). 0.1% of GNP (1994).

ENERGY
Consumption: 2,186.33 Kgs of Oil equivalent per capita yearly (1994). -269.49% imported (1994).

HDI (rank / value) 47 / 0.861 (1994)

---

press and movement and made it possible to arrest citizens without a warrant. An agreement was reached with the teachers' trade unions, putting an end to a fortnight of strikes and police repression of students and teachers.

[32] On February 12, a military judge started to investigate the charges against the 13 officers and nearly a thousand soldiers who had staged the coup. The lieutenant- colonels who had led the insurrection were detained in the San Carlos barracks, awaiting sentence. Two days later Pérez lifted the emergency measures.

[33] Political and military tension increased again in early March with more trouble from the army. The President was asked to resign, it was reported that weapons had been stolen and

military units were confined to barracks.

[34] On March 5 1992, in the light of the impending crisis, Pérez announced a popular referendum to reform the Constitution, the creation of a national unity cabinet, a reform of the judiciary, and a "change of direction" in the economic policy instigating a further economic austerity program.

[35] In early April, a "National Civic Strike" was organized by students, labor unions and other organizations, to put pressure on the president to resign. The strike's organizers also demanded the release of the military officers who had been arrested for participating in the February 4 coup attempt.

[36] While protest demonstrations against Carlos Andrés Pérez continued to

increase throughout the country, the party in power (Democratic Action) and COPEI reached an agreement in late May, deciding to form an alliance which they believed would reinforce the stability of Venezuela's democratic system.

[37] Another coup attempt took place on November 27 1992. The air force played a key role in controlling the rebels. The ruling party only won in 7 of the 22 states where elections for governors, mayors, regional legislative assemblies and municipal councils were held.

[38] President Carlos Andres Pérez was suspended from office on May 21 1993, charged with the misappropriation of funds. He was provisionally replaced by Ramón Velázquez.

[39] Rafael Caldera, president between 1969 and 1974 from the Social Christian Party, won the general elections on December 5 1993. He was supported by a wide range of sectors and political parties, with the backing of Convergencia and MAS being the most important factors in his success. Abstention reached 40 per cent as few over five million voters actually exercised their right to vote.

[40] According to official statistics, the annual rate of inflation reached nearly 40 per cent in 1993 and almost half of the population was living below the poverty line.

[41] Another source of social unrest was the repeated violation of human rights, both of ethnic minorities and of inmates in several prisons. On August 21 the murder of 16 Yanomami close to the Brazilian border at the hands of the "garimpeiros" - Brazilian gold prospectors - was reported. Several members of the Yupca indigenous tribe were murdered by landowners in the state of Zulia.

[42] The repression of a riot in a Maracaibo jail by the security forces caused 122 deaths on January 3 1994. Built to accommodate 1,500, the prison housed 2,500 inmates.

[43] Because of age - over 75 - former president Carlos Andrés Pérez was sentenced to house arrest. In his opulent residence overlooking Caracas, Pérez concluded his sentence in September 1996 and returned to the political scene, affirming he would be president once more. During his "confinement", Pérez was accused of having travelled abroad.

[44] At the end of the 1980s, Caracas turned into one of Latin America's most violent cities. A feeling of insecurity prevailed as the number of murders rose. In

1995 it was estimated that 10 per cent of Caracas residents carried a weapon.

[45] The economic crisis worsened after 1994. The banks' collapse began in February 1993 with the fall of the Banco Latino, the country's second commercial bank. In August 1995, 18 out of the 41 private banks had been investigated and 70 per cent of the deposits were being managed by the government.

[46] President Caldera suspended constitutional guarantees regarding real estate, private property and business. He also restricted trips abroad, meetings and the immunity against arbitrary arrests. Despite the Congress's vote to reinstate these rights, the president restricted them once more to prevent speculation and capital flight.

[47] Efforts to attract foreign investors failed in 1995 and the Government decided to offer equal opportunities both to nationals and foreigners for the prospecting and exploitation of oil for the first time since the oil industry's nationalization in 1976.

[48] In September 1995 and March 1996 fuel prices doubled, producing significant increases in other branches of consumption, especially in the basic necessities.

[49] In April 1996, Caldera announced new liberalizing economic measures that enabled him to release a $1.4 billion loan from the IMF, suspended since July 1995.

[50] In 1997 the divisions both between and within the political parties interrupted parliamentary analysis of the "Agenda Venezuela" reform project promoted by the Government. This was to include privatization of the electricity, aluminium and iron industries; reform of the judicial system and the reorganization of public finances. With less than 10 per cent of the seats, Caldera's party had to seek alliances in various sectors in order to get the reforms approved. Democratic Action demanded a greater economic liberalization in return for its support.

[51] In March 1998, Venezuela made an agreement with Saudi Arabia and Mexico to reduce daily oil production, in an attempt to increase the international price per barrel, which had seen a significant drop since the Organization of Petroleum Exporting Countries decided to increase its production by 10 per cent in November 1997. The agreement signed in Riyadh, the Saudi capital, came into effect for the whole year on April 1.

Vietnam

Viêt-nam

Population: 75,181,000 (1996)
Area: 331,689 SQ KM
Capital: Hanoi

Currency: Dong
Language: Vietnamese

The Vietnamese nation was established after centuries of struggle against more powerful peoples. In the ninth century, they defeated the Chinese Han dynasty, ending nearly a thousand years of subjugation. In the 11th and 12th centuries, the Vietnamese succeeded in fighting off the Chams. They repulsed Genghis Khan, his Mongol hordes, and later his grandson Kublai Khan, when these were conquering the Asian world in the 18th century. In the 15th and 18th centuries the Vietnamese were victorious over the Ming and Ching Chinese dynasties, and in the 18th century they drove back the Khmers.

[2] In 1860, the French began to occupy Indochina, meeting with spontaneous, disorganized and badly armed resistance which, nonetheless, took them three decades to overcome. By 1900 the French had consolidated their domination over the region. Vietnam was divided into three parts: Tonkin in the north, Annam in the center and Cochinchina in the south. To eliminate Chinese cultural influence, the French taught Quoc Ngu, a Romanized writing script of the Vietnamese language. The French did not intend to help Vietnam's nationalists in the renewal and dissemination of national culture, but this system of notation facilitated reading and lowered printing costs when compared with the formerly used Chinese ideograms.

[3] In the 1920s, the first nationalist organizations were created. Marxist-Leninist parties appeared in different parts of Vietnam in 1929, achieving unity as the following year. This was founded by a patriot called Nguyen Ai Quoc, who adopted the name Ho Chi Minh. The party later decided that it would be more effective if it was split into three different national sections, for Cambodia, Laos and Vietnam respectively. The latter was known as the Workers' Party until its 4th Congress in 1976, when it became the Communist Party of Vietnam once again.

[4] During World War II, the country was occupied by Japan. Vietnam's communists organized the resistance from the start, cooperating with the allies but staying true to their intent to defeat colonialism. In 1941, Ho Chi Minh founded the Viet Minh or League for the Independence of Viet Nam, conceived as a broad unity front to include workers, peasants, the petty-bourgeoisie and the nationalist bourgeoisie. By the time of the Japanese surrender, the Viet Minh army had become a powerful force with widespread popular support in the northern part of the country. On August 18 1945, Ho Chi Minh launched a general insurrection in the north. Within two weeks the revolutionary forces took control of the entire country, and an independent republic was declared. Emperor Bao Dao abdicated and offered to cooperate in advising the new regime.

[5] Negotiations between the French - who seized the southern part known as Cochinchina - and Ho Chi Minh led to an agreement in March 1946 that appeared to promise a peaceful solution. Under the agreement France would recognize the Viet Minh government and give Vietnam the status of a free state within the French Union. However, the French meant to re-establish colonial rule, while Hanoi wanted total independence. Georges-Thierry d'Angelieu, the High Commissioner for Indochina, proclaimed Cochinchina as an autonomous republic in June 1946. The French reunited Cochinchina with the rest of Vietnam in 1949 and proclaimed the Associated State of Vietnam, appointing former emperor Bao Dao as chief of state. The Viet Minh did not surrender and waged an increasingly successful guerrilla war, aided after 1949 by the new Communist Government of China. After nine years of fighting, the Vietnamese were finally victorious when they captured the garrison of Dien Bien Phu, in the north, on May 7 1954.

[6] The 1954 Geneva Agreements stipulated the withdrawal of the French and directed the Vietnamese to hold general elections in 1956. Viet Minh troops were to withdraw north of the 17th parallel. The United States set up the Ngo Dinh Diem regime in Saigon (present-day Ho Chi Minh), dividing the country and violating the Geneva agreements, as elections were prevented. In 1960, the organizations hostile to Diem's regime (democratic, socialist, nationalist and Marxist forces), became the National Liberation Front, led by lawyer Nguyen Huu Tho. The 'second resistance' was then launched, this time against the successive military governments based in Saigon and, above all, against the United States, the true supporter, arms-supplier and policy-maker. US aid was initially limited to a handful of advisors; then troops were sent, a process that escalated until, by 1969, 580,000 US troops were in Vietnam. A larger tonnage of bombs was dropped in Vietnam than

WORKERS

Labour force % **(1996)**

- ■ WOMEN
- □ MEN

49 51

- ■ AGRICULTURE 71% (1990)
- □ INDUSTRIAL 14%
- ■ SERVICES 15%

LAND USE

DEFORESTATION -1.4 % annual (81/90)
IRRIGATED 33.8 % of arable

(1993)

- ■ FOREST & WOODLAND 29.1%
- □ ARABLE 16.6%
- ■ OTHER 54.3%

during the whole of World War II, and terrible chemical and biological weapons were used.

[7] The US spent $150 billion in Vietnam, destroyed 70 per cent of the northern villages and left 10 million hectares of productive land barren. Despite their efforts, Saigon was finally liberated by the Viet Cong on April 30 1975. On July 2 1976, Vietnam was reunified under the name of the Socialist Republic of Vietnam.

[8] Since then Vietnam has not enjoyed stable peace. In January 1979, it went to war against Pol Pot's regime in Cambodia; Pol Pot had claimed vast portions of Vietnamese territory. No sooner had the Cambodian regime been overthrown, than China invaded Vietnam on its northern border (see Cambodia) as a punitive measure. China, in the meantime, had been a staunch ally of the ousted Cambodian regime. Subsequent clashes along the border in 1980 underscored the military superiority of the Vietnamese, but the border between the two countries remained unchanged.

[9] Vietnam considered Cambodia's union with the other Indochinese states to be essential for its security. Vietnam's support of the Heng Samrin Government against the Khmer Rouge, Prince Sihanouk, and the National Liberation Front entailed costly military efforts and a drain on Vietnam's resources, particularly in terms of food, which was already scarce. China launched a brief but fierce punitive invasion along the Sino-Vietnamese border in early 1979 in response to Vietnamese actions in Cambodia. During the month-long war the Chinese destroyed major Vietnamese towns and inflicted heavy damage in the frontier zone, but also suffered heavy casualties from the Vietnamese defenders. Also, from 1978 to 1981, Vietnam suffered floods, typhoons and droughts.

[10] After 1981, Vietnam faced active hostility from the Reagan administration, which stopped grain shipments provided by an American charitable association and blocked a Vietnamese aid program organized by the United Nations Development Program (UNDP).

[11] The 6th Congress confirmed that self-sufficiency was the aim in some key sectors. The agricultural sector planned to produce 20 million tons of cereal, and energy self-sufficiency was to be achieved with the construction of steam power plants and a new contract for oil prospecting with the USSR.

[12] In April 1985, several political prisoners were freed, and diplomatic ties with ASEAN countries and the United States were intensified in an effort to reach negotiated settlements for Indochina. Arrangements were made to cooperate with the US to search for the corpses of missing soldiers as well as to allow people loyal to the former government to leave the country, and to permit the exit of children of US servicemen.

[13] Le Duan, Secretary-General of the Communist Party of Vietnam since 1969 and a close collaborator of Ho Chi Minh, died on July 11 1986. The Congress designated 71 year-old Nguyen Van Linh, a former Viet Cong strategist, as the new Secretary-General.

[14] Van Linh proposed a "complete and radical renovation" of the political and economic system, the government was renewed and restructured, and a series of economic reforms was announced, loosening restrictions governing the commercializing of agricultural products and the establishment of private businesses. Laws were also passed to attract foreign investment and guarantee that foreign enterprises would not be nationalized.

[15] Toward the end of 1988, the government adopted austerity measures to combat inflation, including a marked devaluation of the dong (national currency), in relation to the dollar. In the process, many businesses were forced to close down, and the already high unemployment rate reached almost 30 per cent, while lack of food led to popular protests.

[16] However, a good rice harvest in 1988-89 resulted in a slight improvement in the living conditions of the population, as well as Vietnam's admission to the group of rice-exporting countries. By the end of 1989, they had exported around 1 millon tons of rice, valued at $250 million. Most of the rice was exported to western Africa, the Philippines, India, Sri Lanka and China.

[17] The political changes in Eastern Europe at the end of the 1980s were not well-received by Vietnamese communists since these had local repercussions, specifically growing demands for a multiparty political system. In the absence of such a system, dissenting voices sought expression within the Vietnamese Communist Party (VCP) itself. Some sectors of the party demanded change toward a multiparty, parliamentary political system.

[18] Another group, calling itself the "Resistance Fighters' Group" made up of southern revolutionaries who had fought against the French and the Americans for the country's independence, voiced its disagreement, in particular with the government's economic and political policies. This Group which described itself as a pressure group within the party urged its leaders to speed up the pace of reforms and the granting of political freedoms. The

ENVIRONMENT
A long and narrow country covering the eastern portion of Indochina along the Gulf of Tongkin and the South China Sea. The monsoon influenced climate is hot and rainy. Rainforests predominate and there is a well-supplied river system. The northern region is comparatively higher. There are two river deltas: the Song Koi in the north, and the Mekong in the south. Most of the population are farmers, and rice is the main crop. The north is rich in anthracite, lignite, coal, iron ore, manganese, bauxite and titanium. Textile manufacture, food products and mining are the major economic activities. The felling of trees for domestic use (firewood) and construction have contributed to deforestation. However, the most significant losses - particularly in the northern part of the country - are a result of the Vietnam War, specifically from the use of such chemical defoliants like "Agent Orange". Vietnamese Government policy - started after 1975 and reaching its peak in the mid-1980s - that moved millions of Northern Vietnamese to what was thought to be the relatively underpopulated central highlands took a terrible toll on the environment, including massive deforestation on the highlands.

SOCIETY
Peoples: Most are native Vietnamese. Mountain groups of different ethnic origins from southern Asia - Tho, Hoa, Tai, Khmer, Muong, Nung - and descendants of the Chinese form the rest of the population.
Religions: Mainly Buddhist; traditional religions. There are some 2 million Catholics and 3 million followers of the Hoa-Hao and Cao-Dai sects.
Languages: Vietnamese (official) and languages of the ethnic minorities.
Political Parties: The Vietnamese Communist Party (Dan Cong San Vietnam), according to the constitution "the leading organization of society", founded by Ho Chi Minh in 1931; the Democratic Party and the Socialist Party of Vietnam, founded respectively in 1944 and 1946, organized intellectuals and the national bourgeoisie for the anti-colonialist struggle.
Social Organizations: The Federation of Unions of Vietnam (Tong Cong Doan Vietnam), founded in 1946, is the only union confederation and a WFTU member; the Vietnamese Women's Union, founded in 1930.

THE STATE
Official Name: Nu'ó'c Công Hòa Xã; Hôi Chu' Nghî'a Viêt Nam.
Administrative Divisions: 39 Provinces, including the urban areas of Hanoi, Haiphong and Ho Chi Minh City.
Capital: Hanoi (Hanoi), 2,154,900 people (1993).
Other cities: Ho Chi Minh City (formerly Saigon), 3,555,000 people (1995); Haiphong, 1,573,000; Da-Nang, 381,410 (1993).
Government: Tran Duc Luong, President and Head of State, elected in September 1997. Phan Van Khai, Prime Minister and Head of Government, elected in September 1997. The National Assembly is made up of 496 members elected by universal suffrage; it elects the members of the Council of State. The Executive Power is exercised by a Council of Ministers.
National Holiday: September 2, Independence Day (1945).
Armed Forces: 572,000 troops (1995).
Other: 5,000,000 (Urban Defence Units, Rural Defence Units).

appearance of this group shed light upon the country's economic and social reality, characterized by the most dynamic economic center being in the surroundings of Ho Chi Minh City.

[19] In August, the Central Committee of the VCP accused the West of trying to destroy the socialist world. Nguyen Van Linh urged his fellow-citizens to reject bourgeois liberalization, multiparty politics and opposition parties, whose aims were to make them renounce socialism. Even so, the participation of non-communist candidates was authorized in the 1989 National Assembly elections, and a year later, the government authorized the formation of the Vietnam Veterans Association. However, this liberalization was accompanied by a reaffirmation of the dominant role of the VCP, with the arrest of a number of campaigners for multiparty politics, and the dismissal of 18,000 public employees accused of corruption.

[20] During the 1980s, "illegal emigration" - the flight of Vietnamese toward neighboring countries - continued. The reluctance of Western countries to receive them has indefinitely prolonged their stays in overpopulated refugee centers. This has been especially true in Hong Kong; the British government began deporting them from there in December 1989, though this

operation was later suspended because of international pressure.

[21] The 8th VCP Congress, held in June 1991, agreed to continue the process of building socialism, a path considered to be "the only correct choice". Van Linh was replaced as the party's general secretary by Du Muoi, who continued with the renewal process which had been initiated in 1986 (called Doi Moi). Tron My Moa, the first woman to be a part of the country's new leadership, became a member of the 9-member Secretariat of the Central Committee.

[22] The VCP confirmed the continued existence of a single-party system. The first step toward renewal and reform was a more flexible economic policy, specifically, a change to a mixed economy. This implied allowing private enterprise and foreign investment within pre-established parameters.

[23] In October 1991, the initiation of negotiations between the four Cambodian factions opened the way for the normalization of Sino-Vietnamese relations.

[24] In November 1991, the British government with the support of the US, began the forcible repatriation of 64,000 Vietnamese exiles from refugee camps within Hong Kong, a British dependency.

[25] The new constitution approved in April 1992 authorized independent candidates to run for election, but in the July legislative elections, 90 per cent of the candidates belonged to the VCP. In September, the new Assembly elected General Le Duc Anh president, known ally of Prime Minister Vo Van Kiet. In November, a commission of US senators visited the country to discuss the issue of the missing remains of over 2,000 US military killed in action.

[26] At the beginning of the 1990s Vietnam appeared to be ready for economic takeoff, following the example of its neighbors, the so-called "Asian tigers". Privatization and the liberalization of foreign investment led to an 8.3 per cent increase in the GDP in 1992. For 1993 and 1994, 8 and 9 per cent increases are expected respectively. In the meantime, the volume of exports has risen 20 per cent per year since 1991. However, the 'economic takeoff' had also brought a number of negative impacts. The Vietnamese workers are among the lowest paid in Asia, while economic growth put growing pressure on the environment, particularly in the cities.

[27] As for foreign trade, Vietnam depends primarily on two products: rice and, to a lesser extent, oil. Since 1989, Vietnam has become the world's third largest exporter of rice, after Thailand and the United States. However, this dependence upon a single product - until oil production increases to the point

where it can be considered an important export product - makes the country vulnerable to the vagaries of the international market. This problem is compounded by falling rice prices, and the loss of part of the rice crop each year because of a lack of storage facilities.

[28] According to Vietnamese standards, a poor family is one that can not afford 13 kg of rice person each month. A hungry family is one that can not afford 8 kg of rice person each month.

[29] The south has been the main beneficiary of the rice production and export boom in the Mekong delta. This has underscored the structural inequality between the two parts of the country. With more than five million inhabitants - almost double the size of Hanoi, the capital city - Ho Chi Minh City is the country's economic capital, adapting itself far better to the new era than the north.

[30] This expansion of trade is taking place in what is primarily an agricultural country. Around 57 million of the 70 million Vietnamese depend upon agriculture, the backbone of the economy and of Vietnamese society. As a result, the Government has granted a number of benefits to farmers, such as loans and long-term land leases, tax cuts and the right to inherit up to three hectares of land. However, total private land ownership has not yet been authorized (for instance, farmers enjoy what is called Land Use Rights, under which they can sell, transfer or will land).

[31] The effects of several decades of war are still evident, especially in the economic structure which was tailored to the demands of war. The devastation remains visible in a large part of the country, as a result of the use of lethal weapons like napalm or Agent Orange, a powerful defoliant. The country's infrastructure, in telecommunications, highways and energy production, slowly began to recover as a result of projects financed by the World Bank and Asian Development Bank loans.

[32] In 1993, the per capita GDP was among the lowest in Asia. Between $230 and $350 per year, it was roughly equivalent to one-sixth of Thailand's GDP, and one-twentieth of South Korea's. Unemployment and underemployment, taken together, continue to stand at 30 per cent, while the underground economy and contraband are on the increase.

[33] The US embargo of Vietnam began to be lifted in January 1993, when a US Senate commission concluded that there was no evidence of US prisoners of war in Vietnam. In February 1994, US President Clinton announced the end of the trade embargo, which had lasted 19 years.

[34] By adapting to international

STATISTICS

DEMOGRAPHY
Population: 75,181,000 (1996). **Annual growth:** 2.1% (1980/1996). **Estimates for year 2000:** 80,500,000. **Annual growth to year 2000:** 1.8% (1994/2000). **Urban Population:** 19.4% (1996). **Urban growth:** 2.67% (1980/95). **Children per woman:** 3.1 (1996).

HEALTH
Life expectancy at birth: 67 years (1996) male: 64 years (1994) female: 68 years (1994). **Infant mortality:** 33 per 1,000 (1996). **Under-5 child mortality:** 44 per 1,000 (1996). **Calorie consumption:** 103% (1988/90). 247 **people per doctor** (1988/91). **Safe water:** 43% (1990/96).

EDUCATION
Literacy: 94% (1995) male: 97% (1995) female: 91% (1995). **School enrolment :** Primary total: 114% (1990/95). Tertiary: 4% (1995). **Primary school teachers:** one for every 34 students (1995).

COMMUNICATIONS
10 **newspapers,** 104 **radios,** 110 **TV sets** and 6 **main telephone lines** per 1,000 people (1994). **Books:** 8 new titles per 100,000 people (1992/94).

ECONOMY
Per capita, GNP: $ 290 (1996). **Annual growth, GNP:** 7.3% (1995/96). **Annual inflation:** 88.34% (1985/95). **Cereal imports:** 387 metric tons (1994). **Food import dependency:** 5% (1994). **Fertilizer use:** 1,745 kgs per ha (1994). **Exports:** $ 7,016 million (1996). **Imports:** $ 13,910 million (1996). **External debt:** $ 26,764 million (1996). $ 356 **per capita:** (1996). **Debt service:** 3.5% of exports (1996). **Development aid received:** $ 826 million (1995). 5.3% of GNP (1994).

ENERGY
Consumption: 100.87 Kgs of Oil equivalent per capita yearly (1994). -54.83% imported (1994).

HDI (rank / value) 121 / 0.557 (1994)

competition, it is likely that ecological damage will increase. Even today, the intensification of agriculture, particularly the intensive cultivation of rice, and the felling of trees for construction or timber exports have become serious environmental problems.

[35] The Communist Party continued to oppose political liberalization, and is cautious in on economic liberalization, fearing a massive return of emigrants and the ensuing Western influence. However, Prime Minister Vo Van Kiet forced his government officials to learn foreign languages, especially English.

[36] Vietnam and the United States established formal diplomatic relations in August 1995. President Clinton stated his concern for the 2,200 US soldiers still considered to be lost in action in Southeast Asia.

[37] The rapprochement between the governments of Hanoi and Washington did not lead to a massive arrival of US firms, although many multinational corporations showed their interest in the Vietnamese economy, in anticipation of the consolidation of economic liberalization.

[38] Systematic complaints from the rural population over the increasing impoverishment and the effects of

the monetary crisis occurring in the neighbouring countries of Southeast Asia, marked the socio-economic life of Vietnam in 1997, making way for official measures toward containing possible social uprisings.

[39] In September, Tran Duc Luong and Phan Van Khai, were elected as new President and Prime Minister, respectively. Observers said the former would maintain his predecessor's economic policy and "rejuvenate" the party leadership. In December, the CPV Central Committee decided to replace three of its leading figures. Former president Le Duc Anh and former prime minister Vo Van Kiet went and the civilian Le Kha Phieu was appointed Secretary General, replacing veteran leader Du Muoi.

[40] In April 1998, the drought which had affected the southern province since January destroyed some 7,000 hectares of coffee plantations, while a further 40,000, out of a total of 160,000, were threatened if the rainy season delayed any longer. Vietnam had increased its plantations from 15,000 to 260,000 hectares throughout the country since the economic liberalization of the 1980s, exporting the product mainly to Europe and the United States.

Virgin Is. (US)

Virgin Islands

Population: 106,000 (1996)
Area: 347 SQ KM
Capital: Charlotte Amalie

Currency: US Dollar
Language: English

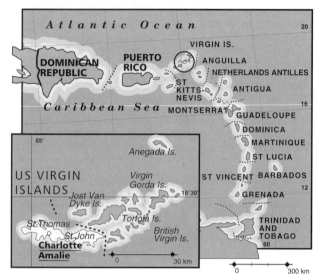

A s is the case in other Caribbean islands, the Virgin Islands were originally inhabited by Carib and Arawak Indians. The only gold on the islands was seen in the ornaments worn by the inhabitants and was of little economic interest. From the time of Columbus' arrival in 1493 onwards, the local population was persecuted and massacred until they were all destroyed by the second half of the 16th century.

[2] The western part of the archipelago was claimed by other countries after the departure of the Spaniards. The Netherlands gained control in the 18th century and organized crop cultivation; first of sugar cane and then of cotton. With this in mind, they imported African slaves, as in many other parts of Latin America and the Caribbean. At the height of Dutch colonization, there were 40,000 African slaves on the islands.

[3] During Abraham Lincoln's second presidential term, the United States failed to acquire the islands. But in 1917, after World War I when the US wanted to consolidate its presence in the area, $25 million was paid to the Danes for the islands and the 26,000 African former slaves who inhabited them.

[4] From that time on, the US initiated a series of changes in the territorial administration, ranging from the continuation of the legislation established by the Danes, to the new law approved in 1969. This instituted the election of a Governor and Vice-Governor, the election of a non-voting Congressional delegate and the right of its inhabitants to vote in American elections. In a 1981 plebiscite, a proposed Constitution was voted against by 50 per cent of the registered voters. In December 1984, the UN General Assembly reiterated the right of the islands to self-determination, and urged the local population to exercise their right to independence.

[5] The local economy is totally dependent upon the United States. It revolves, to a great extent, around an oil refinery owned by US-Ameranda Hess Corporation on the island of St Croix. Today the refinery is the largest of its kind in the world producing over 700,000 barrels of oil per day. The company's influence on local politics is very important, as it has 1,300 permanent and 1,700 temporary employees. The corporation also supplies all the islands' energy needs. In spite of this, tourism is still the island's main source of income.

[6] A referendum scheduled for November 1989 was to decide the future status of the islands. However, it was not held because in September 1989 the islands were severely damaged by Hurricane Hugo. According to official estimates, 80 per cent of the buildings were destroyed. The disaster caused an outburst of looting and unrest. Armed bands wandered the streets; some members of the police and National Guard also took part in the pillaging. The US sent more than 1,000 troops to the area; however, the disturbances had virtually ceased by the time they arrived and in the words of the locals, there was nothing left to steal.

[7] The US Government declared the islands a disaster area and granted $500 million in humanitarian aid. However, damages were estimated at $1 billion.

[8] An aluminium oxide plant, which had been closed in 1985, was purchased in 1989 by an international group trading in raw materials. The plant has a capacity for an annual production of 700,000 metric tons. Shipments to the US and Europe began in 1990.

[9] Alexander A Farrelly, who had governed the islands since 1987, left his post in 1995 and was replaced by Roy L Schneider.

Virgin Is. (British)

British Virgin Islands

Population: 19,000 (1996)
Area: 153 SQ KM
Capital: Road Town

Currency: US Dollar
Language: English

The Virgin Islands, were named by Christopher Columbus in 1493 in honour of St Ursula. At that time the islands were inhabited by Caribs and Arawaks, but by the mid-16th century they had all been exterminated by the Europeans.

[2] In the 18th century, the English gained control of the easternmost islands of the archipelago and, using African slave labor, they began cultivating sugar cane, indigo and cotton. By the mid-18th century, the islands' slave population had reached 7,000, outnumbering the European colonists 6 to 1. Slavery was eventually abolished in the islands in the 1830s.

[3] From 1872 the islands joined the British colony of the Leeward Islands, which were administered under a federal system. This federation was dissolved in July 1956, but the Governor of the Leeward Islands continued to be responsible for the administration of the Virgin Islands until 1960. In that year direct control over the islands passed into the hands of an administrator designated by the British Crown. Unlike the Leeward Islands, the British Virgin Islands did not belong to the East Indies Federation, which existed between 1958 and 1962, preferring to develop links with the American Virgin Islands, under US control.

[4] Constitutional reform required elections to fill the seats of the Legislative Council. They were held in November 1979, and independent candidates won five of the nine disputed seats and the Virgin Islands Party (VIP) won the four remaining seats. Five years later, the independent candidates only retained one seat; however, by forming an alliance with the United Party (UP), they managed to have one of their members appointed prime minister.

[5] The colony has been governed under several constitutions this century, and the ministerial form of government began in 1967 with the first open elections. In 1977 the Constitution was modified, granting greater self-government and carrying out changes in the electoral system. The responsibility for defence, internal security and foreign affairs remains in the hands of the British-appointed governor.

[6] Tourism accounts for 45 per cent of the national income, while fishing is the traditional economic activity. Gravel and sand are important exports, and a "tax-haven" banking facility has been established. The mineral potential of the islands is being examined in the hope of finding deposits that can be exploited.

[7] In August 1986, the British Government dissolved the Legislative Council, calling a new election several days after the opposition presented a vote of no-confidence in the Prime Minister. In September the VIP won 5 of the 9 seats and the UP won 2. Lavity Stott, the VIP leader, was named chief minister.

[8] In March 1988, Prime Minister Omar Hodge resigned under accusations of corruption, being replaced by Ralph O'Neal. Hodge denied the charges against him, and in March 1989 he created a new party, the Independent People's Movement and in early 1990 was cleared of the charges against him.

[9] In the November elections, the VIP increased its majority to 6 seats, while the IPM obtained 1 seat, and the independents 2. Stott maintained his post as head minister, and O'Neal was re-elected prime minister.

[10] Due to the increase in drug trafficking, and following recommendations by the British Government, legislation was introduced to control operations of international financial companies. These would need a licence to operate on the islands and their activities would be subject to periodic inspections, as the authorities believed most of the investments were coming from the drug trade.

[11] In October 1991, Peter Alfred Penfold was named Governor.

[12] As a result of tourism activities in coastal areas, environmental degradation grew, particularly in coral reefs.

[13] In the legislative elections of February 1995, the VIP took six seats, the IPM three, the Movement of Concerned Citizens (CCM) took two, as did the UP. On May 15 1995, following the death of H Lavity Stoutt, Ralph O'Neal took over as chief minister. In June 1995, David Mackilligin was appointed the new governor.

[14] In 1995, unemployment affected three per cent of the population, growth reached four per cent and per capita annual income stood at $10,200.

[15] In July 1997, the Government approved a three year development plan, which included a $2 million plan to extend the port and the construction of two tourist centres.

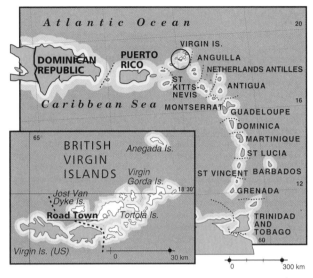

PROFILE

ENVIRONMENT
The eastern portion of the Virgin Islands comprises 36 islands and reefs, 16 of which are inhabited. The larger ones are Tortola, Anegada, Virgin Gorda and Jost Van Dyke, which hold most of the population. The islands' rolling terrain is of volcanic origin. Agricultural production is limited to fruit and vegetables as a result of erratic rainfall. The major economic activities are fishing and tourism. The coral reefs are threatened by tourist activities.

SOCIETY
Peoples: Most are descendants of African slaves. There is also a small British minority. 86 per cent of the population are concentrated on Tortola Island, 9 per cent live on Virgin Gorda, 3 per cent on Anegada and 2 per cent on Jost Van Dyke.
Religions: Mainly Protestant (45 per cent Methodist, 21 per cent Anglican, 7 per cent Church of God, 5 per cent Adventist of the Seventh Day, 4 per cent Baptist, 2 per cent Witnesses of Jehova, 2 per cent others), 6 per cent Roman Catholic, 6 per cent others (1981).
Languages: English (official).
Political Parties: The Virgin Islands Party (VIP), of Ralph T O'Neal; the Independent People's Movement (IPM), of Omar Hodge and Allen O'Neal; the United Party (UP), of Conrad Maduro; the Concerned Citizens Movement (CCM), of E Walwyln Brewley.

THE STATE
Official Name: British Virgin Islands.
Capital: Road Town, 6,000 people (1994).
Government: David Mackilligin, British-appointed Governor since June 1995. Ralph O'Neal is the Chief Minister since May 1995. There is a Legislative Council of 9 elected and 4 appointed members.
Armed Forces: The United Kingdom is responsible for defence.
DEMOGRAPHY
Population: 19,000 (1996). **Urban population:** 57.1 % (1996)

Yemen

Yaman

Population: 15,678,000 (1996)
Area: 527,968 SQ KM
Capital: Political Capital: San'a

Currency: Rials
Language: French

When the Cretan civilization reached its highest point, another trade culture was flourishing on the Arabian peninsula which rapidly led to the appearance of numerous cities. Ma'in, Marib, Timna, and Najzan were the principle cities of the interior, along the caravan routes that brought aromatic fragrances from Dhufar (presently part of Oman) and Punt (Somalia). These extensive trade routes continued along the coast of the Red Sea as far as the Mediterranean markets, and from Taima on towards Mesopotamia.

[2] These cities were united and ruled by whichever trade center held greatest power at the time, first Mina and later the better-known Saba, cited in the Bible. The latter's ties with the African coast dated from the founding of the Ethiopian state of Axum (see Ethiopia).

[3] In spite of the rudimentary state of their fleet, Saban merchants kept close links with Africa for centuries, and as a result Christianity was propagated among the Yemenis through the teachings of Ethiopian preachers during the fourth century. Shortly thereafter, the Himyarites (a Hebrew sect) took control in Southern Arabia, establishing Judaism as the official religion and provoking a series of conflicts between the groups.

[4] Ethiopians conquered the country in 525 AD and were driven out by the Persians in 570. At this time the Persians established their first contact with southern African trade, which was renewed centuries later when the Persians settled in Africa (see Tanzania: The Zandj Culture in East Africa).

[5] By the time of Muhammad and the ensuing Arab unification, the region had suffered almost three centuries of conflict and invasions, resulting in the loss of much of its splendour. Even the Marib Dam, a monumental construction forming the center of the agricultural irrigation system, had collapsed from lack of maintenance. The downfall of this civilization triggered great population migrations towards Africa and the eastern part of the peninsula.

[6] By the end of the 8th century the borders of the Arabian Empire reached from north Africa and Spain in the west, to Pakistan and Afghanistan in the east. Damascus in Syria became the capital of the empire, where the foundations of a new culture were laid. Greco-Roman, Persian and Indian components blended to form the new dominant culture, with the Arabs reaching high levels of scholarship and philosophy. The Arabs formed the social elite, the ruling class, though little changed in the lives of the Yemenis and other subject peoples.

[7] Then, in the 16th century, the Ottoman expansion started. The Turks occupied a few of the coastal areas of the Red Sea, leaving inland areas and the southern coast independent, governed by an *imam* (priest).

[8] In 1618, the British arrived in the area and established the East India Company in the port of Mukha (Mocha: origin of the name for a type of coffee).

[9] In the 19th century they expanded their presence. As a consequence of Muhammad Ali's conquest of the country, the British occupied the entire extreme south-western region (see Egypt) and took Aden, the best harbour in the region, to discreetly monitor Turkish activities. Meanwhile the Turks consolidated their inland dominion, which was finally achieved in 1872. Concessions were made to allow the imam to retain his position and also make the post hereditary rather than elective.

[10] Towards 1870, with the opening of the Suez Canal and the consolidation of Turkish domination over the northern part of Yemen, the Aden settlement acquired new importance in British global strategy; it was a key port on the Red Sea and ultimately gave them access to the new canal. Friendship and protectorate treaties were gradually signed with local leaders, but it was a slow process, only completed in 1934 when the British gained control of the entire territory, as far as the border with Oman.

[11] In 1911, Imam Yahya Ad-Din led a nationalist rebellion; and two years later the Turks recognized the imam's full authority over the territory in exchange for the formal acceptance of Turkish sovereignty. After World War I Yahya proclaimed himself independent sovereign of the whole of Yemen. Whereafter, conflicts arose with the Saudi Emir of Najd and with the British, in Aden.

[12] After uniting Hidjaz with his nation, Ibn Saud launched a rapid

military offensive against Yahya. In the 1934 peace treaty, Yahya accepted the loss of territory in the northern part of the country in return for the cessation of aggression. The British stopped before the actual declaration of war, but internal rivalries were fuelled and groups actively opposed to the imam were encouraged; the imam was assassinated in 1948.

[13] In 1958, his successor, Ahmad, joined the United Arab Republic formed by Egypt and Syria, but he later withdrew in 1961. He was succeeded in 1962 by his son Muhammad Al Badr, who was later deposed by the Nasserist military, in September of that year. The former imam received both Saudi and British support, initiating a long civil war against the republican government, which lasted until 1970.

[14] The conflict was settled when a coup, staged by a group of the republican faction, put the moderate Al Iryani in power. In 1967, in South Yemen, the National Liberation Front, formed in 1963, took the port of Aden and declared independence and the completion of a socialist revolution.

[15] The new People's Democratic Republic of Yemen closed all the British bases in 1969, nationalized the banking system, took charge of foreign trade and the shipbuilding industry and initiated agrarian reform. In efforts to isolate the

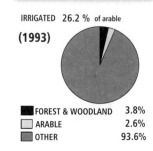

PER 100,000
LIVE BIRTHS

1,400

PROFILE

ENVIRONMENT

The Republic of Yemen is formed by the union of Democratic and Arab Yemen. North Yemen has the most fertile lands of the Arabian Peninsula. For that reason the country, together with the Hadhramaut Valley, used to be called "Happy Arabia". Beyond a semi-desert coastal strip along the Red Sea, lies a more humid mountainous region where the agricultural lands are found (sorghum is grown for internal consumption and cotton for export). The traditional coffee crop has been replaced by qat, a narcotic herb. The climate is tropical with high temperatures especially in Tihmah -where rainfall is heavy- and in the eastern region. The country has no mineral resources. The southern territory is dry, mountainous and lacks permanent rivers. Two-thirds of its land area is either desert or semi-desert. Agriculture is concentrated in the valleys and oases (1.2 per cent of the territory). Fishing is an important commercial activity. The country's boundaries include the island of Socotra, which due to its location at the entrance to the Gulf of Aden, has important strategic value. This island, which became part of South Yemen in 1967, has 17,000 inhabitants spread over 3,626 sq.km. The use of ground water beyond its capacity to regenerate has caused a decline in its levels.

SOCIETY

Peoples: Nearly all Arab. A small Persian minority lives along the sea coast.
Religions: Islam, official (Shi'a, 53 per cent and Sunni, 46.9 per cent).
Languages: Arabic, official.
Political Parties: General Congress of the People; the Yemenite Socialist Party; the Islah Party.

THE STATE

Official Name: Al-Jumhouuriya al-Jamaniya. **Administrative Divisions:** 16 Provinces. **Political Capital:** San'a, 972,000 people (1992). **Other cities:** Aden, 562,000 people; Al-Hudaydah (Hodeida), 246,000; Taiz, 290,107 (1995). **Government:** Since unification of the Yemen Arab Republic (North) and the People's Democratic Republic of Yemen (South) in May 1990, Presidential Council made up of 5 members (3 from the North, 2 from the South). Faraj Said ibn Ghanem, Prime Minister since May, 1997. Single-chamber Parliament, with 301 members (159 northern deputies, 111 from the south, 31 non-elected members). **National Holiday:** May 22, unification (1990). **Armed Forces:** 66,300 (1997). **Other:** 20,000 (Central Organization for Security); 20,000 (tribal forces)

"Cuba of the Middle East", Saudi Arabia concluded that Al Iryani was the lesser of several possible evils.

[16] In October 1972, despite ideological and political differences between North and South Yemen, Al Iryani signed a treaty with the revolutionary government of the People's Democratic Republic of Yemen (South Yemen) for a future merger of the two States.

[17] This ran counter to Saudi strategy and, in June 1974, Colonel Ibrahim al-Hamadi forced Al Iryani to resign and installed himself as ruler in San'a. Although initially accepted by Saudi's King Faisal, the young officer made a powerful enemy when he challenged the landlords of the north in an effort to centralize power. He survived three assassination attempts, but was finally killed on October 11 1977, together with his brother, Lt-Colonel Abdallah Muhammad al Hamdi.

[18] A junta led by Lt-Colonel Ahmed al-Gashmi, with Prime Minister Abdelaziz Abdul Ghani and Major Abdul al-Abdel Aalim, took power vowing to continue their predecessor's policies. This action cost al-Gashmi his life as he died in a bomb attack in June 1978.

[19] In October 1978, with the help of a Congress that was well supported by the people, the NLF founded the Yemeni Socialist Party. In December, the first free elections since independence were held to choose the 111 members of the People's Revolutionary Council from the 175 candidates. Abdel Fattah Ismail, secretary general of the Party, was named head of state, but resigned in April 1980 and was replaced by Prime Minister Ali Nasser Mohammed, one of the founders of the National Liberation Front.

[20] When South Yemen claimed territorial rights over the areas where the Algerian state-owned oil enterprise had discovered large deposits, Saudi Arabia intensified hostilities and the US military presence in Saudi Arabia added to tensions in the area.

[21] Major Ali Abdullah Saleh was appointed President in 1978 but was unable to prevent internal dissent from leading to armed conflict in January 1979. The National Democratic Front, which included the nation's progressive sectors, was on the brink of taking power, so with Saudi provocation the conflict was diverted into a war with Democratic Yemen. Syria, Iraq and Jordan intervened and their mediation led to a cease-fire and negotiations for the unification of the two Yemeni states, which had been suspended since 1972.

[22] In February 1985, the People's Supreme Council made President Ali Nasser Muhammad step down from the office of prime minister, appointing Haider Abu Bakr Al-Atlas - linked to Fattah Ismail - as his successor. Nasser Muhammad resented the loss of power and conspired to recover his position. On January 13, a counter-coup unleashed a brief but intense armed confrontation leaving 10,000 dead, including Fattah Ismail. Nasser Muhammad was ousted and Haider Abu Bakr Al-Atlas was appointed president. The new head of state pledged to maintain the alliance with Ethiopia and Syria.

[23] In May 1981, both countries agreed to draw up a more accurate inventory of their mineral wealth. In 1985, the discovery of significant oil deposits on both sides of the border helped to establish close links between the governments. These deposits have turned Yemen into one of the main oil producers in the Arab world.

[24] President Saleh's successful efforts to balance internal and external pressures resulted in more favourable conditions for rapid reunification.

[25] Finally, on May 22 1990, the Republic of Yemen was proclaimed, with the political capital in San'a (former capital of the Arab Republic of Yemen) and the economic capital in Aden (former capital of the Democratic Republic of Yemen).

[26] In a joint session of the Legislative Assemblies of the two states, held in Aden, a Presidential Council was elected, made up of General Ali Abdullah Saleh (ex-president of North Yemen), Kadi Abdul Karim al-Arshi, Salem Saleh Mohammed and Abdul Aziz Abdel Ghani. The members of the Council elected Ali Abdullah Saleh president of the united republic. Ali Al Beid was vice-president and General Haidar Abu Bakr Al-Atlas, ex-president of South Yemen, was also given a post in the new government.

[27] In May 1991, the Constitution was ratified in a national referendum: an overwhelming majority voted for freedom of expression and political pluralism. Islamic fundamentalist groups opposed to unification called for a boycott, finding the absence of the principles of *sharia* (law based on the Koran) unacceptable, including, among other things, the introduction of voting rights for women.

[28] The new constitution caused immediate changes. Some 53 political parties and 85 daily newspapers and periodicals have appeared throughout the country, political prisoners have been released and the freedom of expression is being fully taken advantage of.

[29] The unification of Yemen was an important step in the development of the region. In spite of the political turmoil experienced between British colonization and reunification, the Yemenis have always shared the common denominator of Islamic religion.

[30] As a consequence of the Gulf

Food Dependency

1970

63%

1994

25%

Literacy

1995

33%

External Debt

1996

PER CAPITA

$405

War, a million Yemenis were expelled from Saudi Arabia and other countries of the region in retaliation for Yemen's pro-Iraqi stance during the Gulf War. However, Yemen made proposals to Saudi Arabia to settle border disputes, which had existed since 1930 when Saudi Arabia had annexed three Yemeni provinces.

[31] At the same time, another million Yemenis returned to the country from Africa, mainly from Somalia. The sudden arrival of such a large number of people from abroad had a negative effect on the economic situation within Yemen. Unemployment currently stands at over two million in a total population of ten and a half million. The returning workers, especially from Saudi Arabia, also deprived Yemen of an important source of foreign currency which came from the money sent home by these migrant workers.

[32] In response to the measures adopted by Saudi Arabia, the Yemeni Government withdrew the contracts of thousands of foreign employees, including approximately ten thousand Arabian citizens employed as teachers. This economic crisis resulted in spiralling inflation and the rapid growth of the black market.

[33] After unification, in the middle of the crisis triggered by the Gulf War, the San'a Government was not able to begin the project to convert the old capital of South Yemen into a center of economic development. Strikes and demonstrations are symptomatic of increasing social tension which the government has tried to control under the conviction that stability would bring about an immediate increase in foreign investment.

[34] The War also resulted in the suspension of petrol refining in the Yemeni industrial processing plants in Aden, as the crude oil they normally worked with came from Iraq and Kuwait. US economic aid dropped from $22 million to $2.9 million. Saudi Arabia was even harsher on the country, simply suspending their grant of $70 million to the Yemeni Government.

[35] In late 1991, Yemen was exporting around 300,000 barrels of crude oil per day and hoped to increase this figure. However, in 1992, oil production fell to 200,000 barrels, although it rose back once again the following year. Activity by local rebel groups and Saudi Arabia's territorial claims prevented exploitation of new oil deposits along border areas.

[36] Thirty-six per cent unemployment and price rises of basic consumer goods, led to a series of protest demonstrations in late 1992 and early 1993. At the same time, Islamic fundamentalism, strongly supported by the poorest sectors of the population, was blamed for a series of attacks against politicians from South Yemen.

[37] In March 1993, Saleh's General Congress of the People won the elections and obtained 122 seats, followed by the fundamentalist Reform (Islah) Party, with 62. The Socialist Party of then vice-president Salem El Baidh came in third place, with 56 seats. In order to weaken unified Yemen, a hypothetical "bad example" to the region's monarchies, Saudi Arabia supported the fight for secession led by El Baidh.

[38] In May 1994, once again secessionists proclaimed the creation of a southern Yemen democratic republic and requested diplomatic support from Saudi Arabia and the Gulf states. However, they were defeated by forces loyal to the Government. In July, the council of ministers adopted a plan of general amnesty in order to protect political pluralism. Furthermore, the Government named Aden as the country's economic capital, which was regarded as a gesture towards southern Yemenites.

[39] In September, Socialist Party members were forced to leave the government, while Islah obtained six new places in the cabinet. The Constitution was modified, stating that sharia law would be the source of all Yemenite legislation.

[40] In February 1995, 11 parties formed a new alliance, the Opposing Democratic Coalition, seeking to obtain the power. The Government signed an agreement draft with Saudi Arabia in which both states express their will to set permanent common borders and promote bilateral relations.

[41] In December, the landing of Eritrean forces on the Hanish Islands in the Red Sea, was considered an act of aggression by the Yemeni Government, causing a war. Egypt's President Hosni Mubarak offered to mediate, and in March 1996, Yemen and Eritrea accepted international arbitration to resolve the disagreement. At the end of that year, however, the key points had still not been resolved.

[42] On April 27 1997, the GCP won the parliamentary elections, taking 187 of the 301 seats, followed by the Islamic Islah party, with 53. The Socialist Party, after extensive internal debate, boycotted the elections.

[43] On May 15, the new Prime Minister, Faraj Said Ibn Ghanem formed a 28-member government, including 24 GCP representatives. That year the Government implemented a structural adjustment plan to revive an economy suffering the effects of civil war and the reduction of aid from many Western and Arab nations. The economic reforms, especially the privatizations, earned the Government funding from the World Bank and the International Monetary Fund.

[44] According to Amnesty International, Yemen was one of the five countries still applying the death penalty to offending minors in 1998, along with Iran, Pakistan, Saudi Arabia and the United States.

STATISTICS

DEMOGRAPHY
Population: 15,678,000 (1996) **Annual growth:** 4% (1980/1996) **Estimates for year 2000:** 18,100,000. **Annual growth to year 2000:** 4% (1994/2000) **Urban Population:** 34.4% (1996) **Urban growth:** 7.64% (1980/95) **Children per woman:** 7.6 (1996).

HEALTH
Life expectancy at birth: 57 years (1996) male: 56 years (1994) female: 57 years (1994) **Infant mortality:** 78 per 1,000 (1996) **Under-5 child mortality:** 105 per 1,000 (1996). 4,348 **people per doctor** (1988/91) **Safe water:** 61% (1990/96).

EDUCATION
Literacy: 33% (1995) male : 53% (1995) female: 26% (1995) **School enrolment** : Primary total: 83% (1990/95) male : 118% (1990/95) female: 47% (1990/95) Secondary: male : 37% (1990/95) female: 9% (1990/95) Tertiary: 4% (1995) **Primary school teachers:** one for every students (1995).

COMMUNICATIONS
20 **newspapers,** 32 **radios,** 270 **TV sets** and 12 **main telephone lines** per 1,000 people (1994)

ECONOMY
Per capita, GNP: $ 380 (1996) **Annual growth, GNP:** -7.8% (1995/96) **Currency:** 50.04 rials = $ 1 (1995). **Food import dependency:** 25% (1994) **Fertilizer use:** 74 kgs per ha (1994) **Exports:** $ 4,538 million (1996) **Imports:** $ 3,443 million (1996) **External debt:** $ 6,356 million (1996) $ 405 **per capita:** (1996) **Debt service:** 2.4% of exports (1996) **Development aid received:** $ 173 million (1995) $ 13 per capita (1995) 4.7% of GNP (1994).

ENERGY
Consumption: 205.88 Kgs of Oil equivalent per capita yearly (1994) -463.33% imported (1994)

HDI (rank / value) 148 / 0.361 (1994).

Yugoslavia Fed. Rep.

Yugoslavija

Population:	10,294,000 (1996)
Area:	102,173 SQ KM
Capital:	Belgrade
Currency:	New Dinar
Language:	Serb

In the 4th century BC, the Balkan Peninsula and the Adriatic coast were inhabited by Illyrian, Thracian and Panonian tribes, and they were also the site of Greek colonies. In the mid-2nd century, Rome defeated the alliance of the Illyrian peoples and began colonizing the new province of Illyria. Important Roman cities developed, such as Emona (now Ljubljana), Mursa (Osijek) and Singidunum (Belgrade). When the Roman Empire split into Eastern and Western regions, the border between the two ran straight through what is now Yugoslavian territory. Towards the end of Roman domination, Christianity was established in the region.

2   In the 5th and 6th centuries AD, these territories were invaded by a number of nomadic tribes: Visigoths, Huns, Ostrogoths, Avars, Bulgars and Slavs. They imposed their own religious beliefs upon the people, but Christianity gradually took hold again, between the 9th and 11th centuries. From the 7th to the 13th centuries there were several feudal states. The Serbs were separate from these states, although they were unable to resist external pressure. Bosnia was subdued by Hungary, and the rest of the territory, as far as the state of Ducla, by Byzantium. Macedonia was divided up between Byzantium and Bulgaria (see Bosnia and Herzegovina, and Croatia).

3   In the mid-11th century, under the reign of Stephen Nemanja (1168-1196), Serbia freed itself from Byzantine domination. The Serbian rulers of the Nemanja dynasty fought against the non-Christian religions which had been spread by the Bulgars. They received a royal title from the Pope in 1217, but the hoped-for propagation of the Catholic faith did not follow. In 1219, the Serbian Orthodox Church was founded, and mass began to be celebrated in Serbian. Under the reign of Stefan Dusan (1331-1355) the

medieval Serbian State reached its apogee when it occupied Albania and Macedonia.

4   The Ottoman Empire began its conquest of the Balkans in the mid-14th century, after the Battle of Kosovo in 1389. In the 14th and 15th centuries, the first of a series of migrations began, from Serbia and Bosnia to neighboring Slav regions and ultimately to Russia. In 1395, all of Macedonia came under the Ottoman Empire, and Bosnia, which had been a part of the Hungarian kingdom since the 12th century, was conquered in 1463. The Slav population of Bosnia became Muslim within a relatively short period of time. In 1465, the Turks occupied Herzegovina. By this time, Venetia had annexed the territories of Neretva and Zetina, along the coast. The city-state of Dubrovnik came under Hungarian control, and then, after 1526, became a part of the Ottoman Empire for 489 years.

5   Between the 16th and 18th centuries, all of Yugoslavia's territories had been divided up. Serbia, Bosnia, Herzegovina, Montenegro and Macedonia belonged to the Ottoman Empire; Croatia, Slovenia, Slavonia, part of Dalmatia and Vaivodina belonged to the Hapsburgs; and Istria and Dalmatia belonged to the Venetian Republic. After the 1690 revolution was put down in Old Serbia, some 70,000 people took refuge in the Hapsburg Empire. The Ottoman Empire transferred Albanian Muslims to the abandoned territories of Kosovo and Motojia.

6   After the Russo-Turkish war of 1768-74, Russia obtained the right to sponsor the Orthodox population of the Ottoman Empire, through the Treaty of Kuchuk-Kainardzhi. Austria seized the Balkans in 1797, as a result of the Napoleonic Wars, The Balkan pashalik (the north of Serbia), which belonged to the Ottoman Empire after the first Serbian uprising (1804-13), the Russo-Turkish war (1806-12) and the second Serbian uprising (1815), was granted internal autonomy. The political and military leaders Gueorgui Cherny (Karadjordje) and Milos Obrenovic founded Serbia's ruling dynasties. In 1829, Serbia became an independent principality within the Ottoman Empire, with Milos Obrenovic as its prince.

7   In the 1878 Congress of Berlin, the Great Powers recognized the full independence of Serbia and Montenegro, which became kingdoms in 1882 and 1905, respectively. In the first Balkan war in 1912, Serbia, Montenegro, Greece, Romania and Bulgaria formed an alliance. In the second, in 1913, they warred against each other over the Ottoman Empire's domains. The end result was Macedonia's partition between Serbia, Greece and Bulgaria, while Serbia and Montenegro expanded their territories.

8   Serbian resistance to the Austro-Hungarian Empire led to the assassination of the Austrian archduke Franz Ferdinand in 1914, in Sarajevo, the event that marked the beginning of World War I. After the war, which put an end to Austria-Hungary's empire, a kingdom of Serbs, Croats and Slovenes was founded, including Serbia, Montenegro and the territories of Slovenia, Croatia, Slavonia, Bosnia and Herzegovina.

9   In 1929, the nation began to be called Yugoslavia: the land of the southern Slavs. The Government remained in the hands of Serbians, and under the reign of Alexandr Karagueorgevich, it became an absolute monarchy. The regime's exclusivist policies gave rise to a strong anti-Serbian movement

among Croats and other ethnic minorities, which led to the king's assassination in Marseilles, in 1934.

10   At the beginning of World War II, Yugoslavia was neutral. In 1941, when Hitler attacked Yugoslavia, the country was so divided internally that it was easily subdued within a few days. The King and the members of the government fled the country, and the German Command carried out a policy of extermination against the Serbian and Muslim population.

11   Two groups which were hostile towards each other launched the resistance movement: the nationalists loyal to the king - called 'chetniks'- led by Draza Mihajlovic, and the partisans, under the leadership of Josip Brozxz, a Croat better known by his nom de guerre, Tito. This group was made up of communists in favor of a unified Yugoslavia, and anti-Nazi forces from all the republics with the exception of Serbia; it later became the Yugoslavian League of Communists (YLC).

12   After bloody fighting against occupation troops and the Croatian 'ustasha' (fascist) movement allied to the Germans, Tito emerged victorious. After the liberation of the country in May 1945, a Provisional Government was formed, led by Tito and

(1996)

Labour force %

■ WOMEN
□ MEN

42   58

PROFILE

ENVIRONMENT

Most of the country is taken up by mountain ranges, leaving one important plain north of the Sava River, a tributary of the Danube, where agricultural activities are concentrated. The climate is continental in this area, and Mediterranean along the coast. Rich deposits of bauxite, coal, lead, copper and zinc in the mountains, together with tourism in the Adriatic coast of Montenegro are major sources of income.

SOCIETY

Peoples: Thirteen distinct ethnic groups are represented in the Yugoslav population. The major ones are Serbs and Montenegrans. In Kosovo, up to 90 per cent of the population is of Albanian origin. **Religions:** 65 per cent Serb-Orthodox, 19 per cent Muslim, 4 per cent Catholic. **Languages:** Serb (official), Albanian, Montenegran, Hungarian.
Political Parties: Socialist Party of Serbia (SPS), nationalist, led by Serbian President S Milosevic; Serbian Radical Party; Reformist Party, neoliberal, led by former prime minister A Markovic; Democratic Movement of Serbia; Socialist Party of Voivodina; Hungarian Democratic League of Voivodina; Green Party, among others. **Social Organizations:** League of Unions.

THE STATE

Official name: Savezna Republika Jugoslavija (Federal Republic of Yugoslavia). **Capital:** Belgrade, 1,470,000 people (1995). **Other cities:** Novi Sad, 179,626 people; Nis, 175,391; Krusevac, 146,607; Pristina, 108,020; Subotica, 100,386 (1991).
Government: Federal parliamentary republic, made up of the republics of Serbia and Montenegro. President, Zoran Lillic, since June 1993; Prime Minister, Radoje Kontic, since February 1993. Parliament, bicameral: citizens' assembly, with 138 members (Serbia:108, Montenegro:30), and assembly of the republics, with 40 members (20 from each republic). President of Serbia, Slobodan Milosevic; President of Montenegro, Momir Bulatovic. Kosovo and Voivodina are provinces within Serbia that were autonomous until 1990 and 1989, respectively. The government and parliament of Kosovo have been operating since 1991 and 1992, respectively, but are not recognized by Serbia.
National Holiday: November 29, Proclamation of the Republic (1945).
Armed Forces: 126,500 (60,000 recruits) (1995).

supported by the Soviet Union and Britain.

[13] During the war 2,000,000 Yugoslavians were killed and 3,500,000 were left homeless. When the war finally ended, the country was in ruins.

[14] On November 29 1945, a Constituent Assembly abolished the monarchy, proclaiming a federation of six republics: Slovenia and Croatia in the North, Serbia in the East, Bosnia-Herzegovina and Montenegro at the center, and Macedonia in the South. It also founded two autonomous provinces:Voyvodina and Kosovo, to the northeast and southeast of Serbia, respectively.

[15] The YLC joined the Cominform (Communist and Workers' Parties' Information Bureau) in 1947, but withdrew in the Spring of 1948 over disagreements with the Soviet CP. leadership. The USSR initiated an embargo against Yugoslavia, which led to the strengthening of its ties with the West and the Third World.

[16] After a phase of economic centralization including the forced collectivization of agriculture, in 1950, Tito introduced the concept of 'self-management'. Its goals were to ensure workers direct democratic participation in all decision-making processes concerning their living and working conditions, and to protect social democracy against the distortions and abuses of 'Statism', bureaucracy and technocracy. The system was based on social (not state) ownership of the means of production and natural resources, managed directly by workers in their own and the community's interest. Similar forms of self-management were developed for trade and services.

[17] Tito was one of the founders of the Non-Aligned Movement. The Yugoslav leader defined non-alignment as the process whereby countries which were not linked to political or military blocs could take part in international issues, without being satellites of the major powers.

[18] The Yugoslavian leadership was charged with revisionism and isolated from the international Communist movement because of its neutral foreign policy and heterodox model of social and economic organization. Relations with the USSR slowly returned to normal after Stalin's death in 1953.

[19] That same year, an Agrarian Reform Law was approved authorizing private farming, and 80 per cent of the land returned to private hands. The combination of private economic activity and the self-management system led to average annual GNP growth rates of 8.1 per cent, between 1953 and 1965. In 1968, industrial production was 12 times greater than in 1950, the year in which the self-management system was first introduced. Likewise, industrial production was three times as important as agricultural production, in its impact upon the national economy. As a result, Yugoslavia's social and economic model was of great interest to the European left.

[20] The country's growth rate declined slightly toward the end of the 1960s. Even so, until the end of the 1970s, the annual growth rate exceeded 5 per cent.

[21] President Tito was aware of the inter-ethnic tensions in the Yugoslavia of his day, as well as the sharp contrasts between the socio-economic situation of the industrialized north, and that of the underdeveloped south. In 1970, President Tito announced that after he stepped down, the country's leadership should be exercised by a body made up of the federated republics and the autonomous provinces.

[22] In 1971 and 1972, ethnic conflicts worsened, especially between Serbs and Croats, and Croatia presented a formal complaint against the confederated system. After 1974, there was an increase in separatist activity by Kosovo's Albanian majority.

[23] After Tito's death in April 1980, the executive power was vested in a collective presidential body, made up of a representative of each republic and autonomous province, and the president of the YLC with a rotating annual presidency. The new regime ratified Tito's policies of self-management socialism and non-alignment.

[24] Despite a strong economic position during the 1960s, both Serbia and Croatia became exporters of labor. Yugoslavia continued to export workers, and cash remittances from Yugoslavian workers in Western Europe, together with revenues from tourism, constituted an essential source of foreign currency to improve the balance of payments. This became more important in 1980 when the economic situation worsened.

[25] In March and April 1981, in the autonomous province of Kosovo, (bordering on Albania), there were riots, which recurred in 1988 and 1990. In Kosovo, 90 per cent of the population (1.9 million) is of Albanian origin. It is the poorest region of Yugoslavia, with unemployment reaching 50 per cent in 1990, with a per capita GNP of $730 while Serbia's was $2,200.

[26] According to the federal government, Kosovo housed nationalist forces and separatist extremists inspired and instigated from abroad, whose final objective was secession from Serbia and Yugoslavia. Many Serbs and Montenegrins left the area. Repression of the uprisings in Kosovo, that left a number of people dead and injured, led to mutual diplomatic recrimination between Belgrade and Tirana and the resignation of Kosovo's governor, Jusuf Zejnullahu, in March 1990. There was also tension in other republics due to the growth of militant Muslim and Catholic groups.

[27] Ethnic conflicts - coupled with inflation, which reached 90 per cent in 1986 and four figures in 1989 - were considered by the central committee of the Communist League to be rooted in deeper contradictions. During these years, several lawsuits dealing with government corruption exposed

Gypsies and the World

According to Iranian historiography, the true legend of the old Gypsy homeland was only known by Gypsies living on the island of Leinos in the Aegean Sea. The same sources claim the Gypsies - now known derogatively as 'lurios' or 'nutters' in Iran - came to Persia in the third century AD and were known as 'Sindis' or 'Hindis' after the river which gave its name to India, the original homeland of the Gypsies.

Gypsies reached the Mediterranean and Greece in the 11th century, where they were known as 'Egyptians' - as they were believed to have come from Egypt - a term which later became 'Gypsies.' They have been present in Macedonia, Croatia and Romania since the 14th century and in Slovenia and Ireland since the 15th. Dispersed across Asia, Europe and even South America (where their presence has been recorded since 1581), these nomadic peoples have been given endless names. In Turkey, Macedonia and Russia, they are known as 'Cigani', in Kurdistan as 'Luri' and in India as 'Banjar'. Depending on the country or the tasks they carry out, they are also known as 'Farao Nerek', 'Bohemians', 'Gypsy', 'Romany', 'Manush', 'Sinti', 'Kale', 'Kalderash', 'Burugoti', and by several other names.

But despite the varied names, one common feature in Europe is that throughout history they have almost always been discriminated against and persecuted. This reached an extreme with the systematic extermination of Gypsies under the Nazi regime during World War II, but the limitation of the rights of Gypsies dates back much further. There was active persecution in France, Spain, the Netherlands and Germany in the 16th century. In the 17th century, a law was passed in England saying it was a serious crime to come into contact with Gypsies, and similar laws came into being in Switzerland at around the same time. In the first half of this century of 'enlightenment', in Austria and Germany alone, 68 laws were passed to persecute Gypsies. In Ireland, legal discrimination began in 1541 - in 1596, a group of 198 Gypsies were sentenced to death for being 'unemployed' - and the persecution continued without a break until the 18th century.

The quest for rights

There are far too many examples of persecution to list, and even though active persecution has reduced, Gypsy rights have not improved greatly during the 20th century. The progress which has been made, however limited, has been the fruit of hard work by international organizations lobbying for the rights of Gypsies within countries in which they live or travel, and the efforts of the Gypsy communities themselves which, in recent decades have tried to recover their cultural values and identity.

In the 1970s, organizations came into being to defend the political rights of Gypsies. In London, the first Gypsy Congress in 1971 established a Gypsy anthem and flag. The first International Gypsy Festival took place in India in 1976. In 1977, following an Indian proposal, the United Nations commissions for the Prevention of Discrimination and the Protection of Minorities issued a call asking all countries with Gypsy populations to respect their rights.

In 1978, the Second Gypsy World Congress was held in Genoa (followed by a third in Sweden in 1981, and a fourth in Poland in 1990). Apart from strengthening the ethnic and cultural identity of the Gypsies in the countries where they live, these Congresses also tried to support their access to education. In present-day Europe, Gypsies have political parties in the Czech Republic, Croatia and Yugoslavia, and there are important institutions working to improve the legal, economic, cultural and social rights of Gypsies in other countries (like France, Britain, Hungary, Italy and India). In Macedonia, they have three political parties, two representatives in Parliament, one mayor, and radio and television channels in their language. ❑

---

the fact that the system was crumbling. The Communist parties of Slovenia and Croatia announced their withdrawal from the YLC. In its January 1990 congress, the Yugoslavian League of Communists renounced its constitutional single-party role, and called on the parliament to draft a new constitution, eliminating the leading role assigned to the League in all spheres of Yugoslav life.

[28] In April of the same year, in the first multiparty elections to be held in Yugoslavia since World War II, nationalist groups demanding either secession or a confederated structure won in all of the republics except Serbia and Montenegro.

[29] In 1989, Yugoslavia's last socialist prime minister, Ante Markovic - a Croat and a neo-liberal - launched a series of structural reforms in order to put an end to the crisis. The country eliminated customs duties on 90 per cent of its imports. As a result, imports increased by 11.9 per cent, while exports increased at a slower rate. There was minimal growth of the country's GDP and of its industrial production. Agricultural production increased by 5.2 per cent, and real income grew an average 26.6 per cent. Retail prices rose by percentages of 1,255 in 1989, and 586.6 in 1990.

[30] Yugoslavia had hoped that all the new attention on the part of Western Europe toward the countries of Eastern Europe would lead to a liberalization of its economy. However, in all of 1989, Yugoslavia did not receive a single dollar in foreign aid, and paid, during the same period between $3.7 and $3.8 billion to its creditors.

[31] As of 1990, the situation began to deteriorate even further, with the exception of foreign trade which began registering negative figures a year later. Industrial production fell by 18-20 per cent in Serbia and 13 in Montenegro - while the gross foreign debt of the entire Federation reached $16.295 million. Of this, more than $5.5 million corresponded to Serbia and Montenegro.

[32] With mounting social pressures because of the economic situation and the disintegrating state, Yugoslavian politics were polarized by two fundamentally opposed concepts. Kucan in Slovenia argued for decentralization to relieve the wealthier regions of the obligation to subsidize the more backward areas, while Slobodan Milosevic, charismatic president of the Serbian Communist League, proposed greater centralization and solidarity in the Federation.

[33] In December 1990, the Croatian parliament adopted a new constitution, which established the right to withdraw from the Federation. At the same time, a plebiscite in Slovenia endorsed independence. In the following months, disagreement over the reform of the federal system and the designation of the presidency gave rise to an insoluble crisis within Yugoslavia's collective leadership.

[34] On September 8 1991, Croatia and Slovenia declared their independence from the Federation, and the Serbian population of Croatia declared its intention of separating from this country. The federal army, whose officials answered primarily to Serbia, intervened in Slovenia and Croatia, stating that separation was a threat to Yugoslavia's integrity. War broke out, with many victims on both sides (see Bosnia and Herzegovina).

[35] War led to the destruction by federal troops of entire cities - like Osijek, Vukovar and Karlovac - as well as the occupation of nearly a fourth of Croat's total land area. Areas affected included the territories of West and East Slavonia, as well as the area known as Krajina, which toward the end of 1991 proclaimed itself the 'Republic of Serbian Krajina'.

[36] In December, both the president of the governing council, Stjepan Mesic, and Prime Minister Markovic resigned, the last representatives of a unified

government. Markovic - like Mesic, a Croat - was unwilling to present the preliminary legislation for the 1992 budget, believing it to be biased against Croatia (81 per cent of the projected budget was earmarked for the federal army). By the end of 1991, there was a total of 550,000 refugees, 300,000 of them from occupied areas of Croatia.

[37] In 1992, within the territory which still defined itself as Yugoslavia, Serbian president Milosevic shored up his position by retiring 70 generals and admirals of the federal armed forces who were not definitely loyal to him. He also won Montenegrin support for his plan to establish a unified Yugoslavia with its capital in Belgrade, through a plebiscite in that republic. The March 1 plebiscite was boycotted by the opposition.

[38] On January 15 1992, the European Community recognized Croatia and Slovenia as sovereign states. On April 27, the parliament of Serbian and Montenegran deputies announced the foundation of the new Federal Republic of Yugoslavia, a federation between Serbia and Montenegro with a parliamentary system of government.

[39] In the meantime, fighting continued in the regions characterized by inter-ethnic strife. Since April 1992, the heart of the fighting had been the republic of Bosnia-Herzegovina, which was recognized by the EC on April 7. In order to divest itself of responsibility for the aggression in Croatia and Bosnia-Herzegovina, in early May Belgrade announced that it was no longer in control of troops from what had formerly been the federal army, now fighting in the independent republics. Far from having the desired effect, Serbia's position led the EC to declare a trade embargo against Yugoslavia on May 28.

[40] However, the general elections held in the new federation on May 31 served to further strengthen Slobodan Milosevic's position. His Socialist Party won 70.6 per cent of the vote in Serbia, while the Socialist Democratic Party of Montenegro won 76.6 per cent. The democratic opposition, as well as the Albanian minorities and the Muslims of Sandchak, boycotted the elections; only 56 per cent of the electorate participated.

[41] With the election of Dobrica Cosic, a writer, as federal president on June 15, and Milan Panic, a businessman, as prime minister on July 14 Serbia's leaders projected an image of a greater willingness to negotiate. Unlike Milosevic, Panic agreed with the London peace proposals of August 26 and 27. Nevertheless, this new development did not prevent the intensification of Serbian aggression in Bosnia.

[42] In the presidential elections held in Serbia on December 20, Panic was defeated by Milosevic, and Radoje Kontic succeeded Panic as prime minister on February 9. A series of purges began within Serbian government institutions, in which more than a thousand state radio and television employees - as well as dissident intellectuals and professors - lost their jobs. Finally, on June 25 federal president Cosic was replaced by Zoran Lilic, a member of Milosevic's inner circle.

[43] The intransigence of the Serbian government was evident in Kosovo, where any attempt at independence was met with repression, within the framework of a policy of cultural annihilation. Serbia has refused to recognize Kosovo's parliament and its provincial government, which have been operating since May 24 1992. In 1993, Serbian police violently broke up a meeting in memory of Albanians who had been killed; in addition, they arrested several political party leaders and closed the Kosovo Academy of Sciences.

[44] As Milosevic and the ruling SPAS party grew more authoritarian, international pressure increased and the social and economic crisis deepened. In 1993, 80 per cent of the federal budget was earmarked for the armed forces, and 20 per cent of the country's GNP went to supporting the Serbs in Bosnia and Croatia. During the first nine months of the year, industrial-activity dropped 39 per cent in relation to 1992, and the GNP decreased from $25 billion in 1991, to $10 billion, 2 years later.

[45] Consequently, by the end of 1993, unemployment had reached 50 per cent. Given the fact that 80 per cent of the country's public spending was being financed by uncontrolled printing of currency, inflation shot up from 100 per cent in January to 20,190 per cent in November. The monthly minimum wage was approximately $1.50, enough to feed a family of four for 3 days.

[46] In the autumn, the government introduced the rationing of basic foodstuffs, sugar, flour and oil, and in December the first electricity cuts occurred. In early 1996, the income of 78 per cent of the families in the federation was no higher than $235 per month.

[47] The power of the Socialist Party of Serbia, led by Milosevic, grew from 1994 onwards. After the parliamentary elections of December 1993 they held 123 of the 250 seats in the Assembly and had formalized alliances with eight opposition deputies, gaining the majority in the chamber. Milosevic

imprisoned his most important political rivals and tried to take a less central role in the war. This line of action included selective collaboration with the war crimes trials in The Hague.

[48] Milosevic's main aim was that the UN should suspend its sanctions on Yugoslavia from May 1992. On September 24 1994, the international organization decided to partially lift the measures for 100 days, allowing international flights, and cultural and sporting exchanges. This diplomatic coup by Milosevic - who was previously accused of being the main instigator of the war in the Balkans - contributed to his increasing popularity in the Federation.

[49] The Yugoslav President continued to play an important role in the peace process in Bosnia-Herzegovina during 1995. The political distancing between Yugoslavia and the Bosnian Serb leaders Radovan Karadzic and Ratko Mladic was at odds with the attitude adopted on the military front. The bloody conquest of Srebrenica and Zepa by the Bosnian Serbs in July contributed to the marginalization of the opposition practised by Milosevic.

[50] Belgrade continued to supply arms and troops to the Serbian Republic of Krajina in Croatia, during the first half of the year. However, Yugoslavia did not intervene when the Croats invaded the territory of Krajina in August. Some Serbian refugees were authorized to enter Yugoslavia and were housed in the province of Kosovo, amongst a majority Albanian population, along with groups of Hungarians and Croats expelled from Vojvodina.

[51] The popularity of Milosevic soared again following the signing of the peace agreement in Dayton, Ohio, though his major triumph came on December 14, 1995, when the United States suspended the sanctions on Yugoslavia as a result of the signing of the Paris agreement. During the embargo, per capita income had fallen to half the previous amount and more than one and a half million people were unemployed.

[52] In August 1996, a month before the elections in Bosnia, 220,640 Bosnian refugees had registered to vote in the territories of Serbia and Montenegro.

[53] 1997 was marked by confrontations between the federal army and the population of Kosovo (90 per cent of Albanian origin). Milosevic called a referendum, in all of Serbia, on the need for foreign mediation on this conflict. This move was rejected by 75 per cent of the voters (with a boycott by the Albanian-speaking population of Kosovo).

[54] In April 1998, Yugoslav army soldiers killed two Albanian citizens trying to enter the federation, claiming they were "terrorists". This aggravated tension between Yugoslavia and Albania - accused by Belgrade of arming Kosovan independence rebels.

[55] A week later, members of the "contact group", the United States, France, Italy, Germany, Russia and Britain, meeting in Rome to agree a common stance, confirmed they would seek dialogue between the parts. The US stated its support for a fresh embargo on Belgrade if Milosevic refused dialogue, including a ban on weapons deliveries and a ban on investments. This proposal was not accepted by Russia.

[56] Further killings in Kosovo in June 1998 led to a call by Britain and other countries for NATO to become involved in the region.

Zambia

Zambia

Population:	8,275,000 (1996)
Area:	752,618 SQ KM
Capital:	Lusaka
Currency:	Kwacha
Language:	English

Archaeological evidence suggests that early humans roamed present-day Zambia between 2,000,000 and 1,000,000 years ago. Stone Age sites and artefacts are found in many areas. Early Iron Age peoples settled in the region with their agriculture and domesticated animals about 2,000 years ago. Ancestors of the modern Tonga tribe reached the region early in the 2nd millennium AD, but other modern peoples reached the country only in the 17th and 18th centuries from Zaire and Angola. Portuguese trading missions were established early in the 18th century at the confluence of the Zambezi and Luangwa rivers. The mighty state of Lunda began to lose power towards the end of the 18th century. The slave trade declined in the 19th century, weakening the authority of the Mwata Yambo (traditional Lunda leaders). This, coupled with the growing autonomy of Kazembes (provincial governors), gave rise to small local autocratic states. In 1835 a group of Bantu-speaking Ngoni settled in the Lake Nyasa-Luangwa watershed. The Sotho people, the Kololo (Makololo), crossed the upper Zambezi and in 1835 took control of what became Barotseland.

[2] In 1851, David Livingstone, a British missionary, followed the Zambezi river as far as Victoria Falls. Later came merchants and explorers in the service of British-born millionaire Cecil Rhodes, who owned a vast fortune in South Africa and wanted to expand northwards. In 1889 the British Crown granted Rhodes, and his British-South Africa Company exclusive rights to establish a mining and trade

monopoly in the Katanga area in present day Zaire. A year later Cecil Rhodes signed a treaty with the Barotse ruler Lewanika and this protectorate was soon followed by colonial domination which created Northern Rhodesia.

[3] The British-South Africa Company kept control of this territory in order to prevent the Portuguese from achieving their plan of joining Angola and Mozambique. In 1909, a railway line was built to the coast of the Indian Ocean and in 1924, Britain assumed direct control of the region, developing arable and livestock farms along the railway. South African and US mining companies increased their investment in copper, and 13 years later nearly 40,000 Africans worked in the mines which made massive profits as the labor came cheap. The miserable conditions of the miners led to protest campaigns and stimulated the formation of workers unions; the North Rhodesia African National Congress (NRANC), linked to South Africa's African National Congress (ANC), was born in this era. In 1952, Kenneth Kaunda, a primary school teacher, became NRANC secretary-general with Harry Nkumbula as president. Kaunda was to be Zambia's main leader in the independence struggle.

[4] In 1953, the British engineered a federation which threatened to serve white settler interests alone. The Federation comprised Northern Rhodesia (Zambia), Southern Rhodesia (Zimbabwe) and Nyasaland (Malawi), assigning Zambia mining production and Zimbabwe, agricultural. The ANC had just launched its struggle for independence and against racial

discrimination. When Nkumbula hesitated before a constitutional project designed to institutionalize European domination, Kaunda chose to leave the NRANC, founding the African National Council of Zambia (ANCZ) and boycotting the elections.

[5] The ANCZ was promptly outlawed and Kaunda was arrested in 1959. Undaunted, his followers created the United National Independence Party (UNIP), which Kaunda chaired when he was released in 1960.

[6] The UNIP was outlawed a few months later, when the British recognized the existence of massive popular support for the party's nationalist platform. In 1961, repression and marginalization of the majority led to an outbreak of violence in

Zambia. By October 1964, the federation was dissolved, UNIP candidates had won the general election and proclaimed independence.

[7] Zambia actively supported liberation movements in Angola and Mozambique. It nationalized its copper reserves, acted as a founding member of OCEC, sometimes referred to as the "copper OPEC", and served as host for the 3rd Summit Meeting of the Non-Aligned Countries Movement in 1970.

[8] In 1974, with the inauguration of the Tan-Zam Railway, Zambia gained access to an ocean outlet not dominated by colonial forces. In the same year, Angolan and Mozambican independence brought about a complete turnaround in the regional balance of power.

[9] Zimbabwean independence in 1980 was welcomed by Zambia. However, forces from the South African army made incursions into Zambia, attacking Namibian refugee camps. In October, a coup against Kaunda, supported by the South African regime, failed.

[10] The situation forced the government to decree a state of emergency and curfew.

[11] President Kaunda tried to surround himself with former comrades-at-arms, generating friction with the younger sectors,

PUBLIC EXPENDITURE

n/a

59%
1995 ■ DEFENCE □ SOCIAL

In 1990/91 Military as % of health & education expenditure was 63%.

WORKERS

(1996)

Labour force %

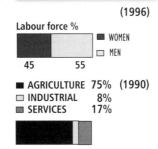

■ WOMEN
□ MEN

45   55

■ AGRICULTURE 75% (1990)
□ INDUSTRIAL   8%
■ SERVICES   17%

LAND USE

DEFORESTATION -1 % annual (81/90)
IRRIGATED 0.9 % of arable

(1993)

■ FOREST & WOODLAND 38.1%
□ ARABLE   7%
■ OTHER   54.9%

PROFILE

ENVIRONMENT

A high plateau extends from Malawi on the east to the swamp region along the border with Angola in the west. The Zambezi River flows from north to south and provides hydroelectric power at the Kariba Dam. The climate is tropical, tempered by altitude. Mining is the main economic activity, as there are large copper deposits. Mining has had a bad effect upon the environment. Soil erosion and loss of fertility are associated with the overuse of fertilizers. Shanty towns account for 45 per cent of the housing in Lusaka, linked with problems like the lack of drinking water and adequate health care, factors which contributed to the 1990 and 1991 cholera epidemics. Wildlife is threatened by poaching, and a lack of resources with which to maintain wildlife reserves.

SOCIETY

Peoples: 98 per cent of Zambians are descendants of successive waves of Bantu migrants, currently divided into 73 ethnic groups. There are approximately 70,000 inhabitants of European descent and 15,000 Asians. **Religions:** Traditional African religions are practised. There are Christians and Muslim and Hindu minorities. **Languages:** English (official). Of the many Bantu languages, five are officially used in education and administration; Nyanja, Bemba, Lozi, Luvale and Tonga. **Political Parties:** The United National Independence Party (UNIP), was the sole party until 1991. In the 1991 elections, the Movement for a Multiparty Democracy (MMD) won 81 per cent of the votes and 125 of the 150 contested parliamentary seats; UNIP obtained 25 seats. **Social organizations:** The Trade Union Congress of Zambia comprises 16 unions. The newly-created Workers Trade Union has 2 million members.

THE STATE

Official Name: Republic of Zambia. **Capital:** Lusaka, 1,327,000 people (1997). **Other cities:** Ndola, 376,300 people; Kitwe, 348,600; Mufulira, 175,000 (1990). **Government:** Frederick Chiluba, President, re-elected November 1996. Legislative power: National Assembly, single-chamber, with 150 members, of which 10 are appointed directly by the President. **National Holiday:** October 24, Independence Day (1964). **Armed Forces:** 21,600 (1997). **Other:** Police Mobile Unit (PMU): 700; Police Paramilitary Unit (PPMU): 700.

STATISTICS

DEMOGRAPHY

Population: 8,275,000 (1996) **Annual growth:** 2.3 % (1980/1996) **Estimates for year 2000:** 9,100,000. **Annual growth to year 2000:** 2.5 % (1994/2000) **Urban population:** 43.3 % (1996) **Urban growth:** 3.96 % (1980/95) **Children per woman:** 5.6 (1996)

HEALTH

Life expectancy at birth: 43 years (1996) male: 42 years (1994) female: 43 years (1994) **Infant mortality:** 112 per 1,000 (1996) **Under-5 child mortality:** 202 per 1,000 (1996) **Calorie consumption:** 87 % (1988/90) 11,111 people per doctor (1988/91) **Safe water:** 27 % (1990/96)

EDUCATION

Literacy: 78 % (1995) male : 86 % (1995) female: 71 % (1995) **School enrolment** : Primary total: 82 % (1990/95) male : 85 % (1990/95) female: 79 % (1990/95) Secondary: male : 31 % (1990/95) female: 19 % (1990/95) Tertiary: 3 % (1995) **Primary school teachers:** one for every 39 students (1995)

COMMUNICATIONS

10 **newspapers,** 83 **radios,** 30 **TV sets** and 9 **main telephone lines** per 1,000 people (1994)

ECONOMY

Per capita, GNP: $ 360 (1996) **Annual growth, GNP:** 3.4 % (1995/96) **Annual inflation:** 91.51 % (1985/95) **Currency:** 1,000 kwacha = $ 1 (1995) **Cereal imports:** 35 metric tons (1994) **Food import dependency:** 3 % (1994) **Fertilizer use:** 111 kgs per ha (1994) **Exports:** $ 1,020 million (1996) **Imports:** $ 1,106 million (1996) **Extenal debt:** $ 7,113 million (1996) $ 860 **per capita:** (1996) **Debt service:** 24.6 % of exports (1996) **Development aid received:** $ 2,029 million (1995) $ 221 **per capita** (1995) 62.9 % of GNP (1994)

ENERGY

Consumption: 148.53 Kgs of Oil equivalent per capita yearly (1994) 31.32 % imported (1994)

HDI (rank / value) 143 / 0.369 (1994)

---

who felt that after Zimbabwe's independence, they no longer needed to live in a climate of war. They even questioned the one-party system. This inter-generational conflict diminished after the October 1983 election, where President Kenneth Kaunda won 93 per cent of the votes, 10 per cent more than in 1978.

[12] In 1984, Zambia faced drought, the worsening of the economic crisis, and trade union demands for wage-increases. Severe food shortages affected 300,000 people. The constant deterioration of world copper prices led the Government to announce a price rise of up to 70 per cent on basic foodstuffs in July 1984 as part of an IMF-adjustment-programme..

[13] The rising cost of living has led Zambian trade unions to protest against IMF impositions. Various strikes broke out in early 1985 and were suppressed by security forces.

[14] Toward the end of that year, IMF conditions for a $200 million credit for the 1986-87 period, led to a decision to increase the price of corn meal. This caused violent protests in the mining region, in the northern part of the country. Three days of protests and looting left 15 people dead and $90 million of damage done. In May 1987, Kaunda changed his policy towards the IMF, and limited debt servicing to 10 per cent of the country's foreign exchange.

[15] With 45 per cent abstention, Kaunda was re-elected in 1988. The following elections were moved forward two years to 1991, because of the critical economic situation. This time, Kaunda was defeated by Frederick Chiluba, a former labor union leader who gained 81 per cent of the vote, and 125 of the 150 seats in Parliament. Kaunda resigned as UNIP party leader in January 1992.

[16] The new government restructured the economy, privatized state enterprises and doubled the price of corn meal and other basic consumer goods. In December 1992, the government adopted the IMF and the World Bank recommendations, devaluing the country's currency by 29 per cent, freeing the exchange market and deregulating foreign trade. In early 1992, southern Africa experienced the worst drought of the century, resulting in widespread food shortages.

[17] A meeting of Western countries called by the World Bank granted $400 million of food aid to Zambia, and the Paris Club agreed to restructure its debt.

[18] President Chiluba declared Christianity the official religion and banned the formation of a fundamentalist party. The Muslim religious authorities estimated there were around 1.2 million Shi'a believers and more than one million Sunnis in the country.

[19] In March 1993, a state of emergency was called in an attempt to undermine a campaign of civil disobedience. Several members of the UNIP - who admitted there had been a plot - were imprisoned. The state of emergency was lifted at the end of the month.

[20] Inflation reached 140 per cent in 1993. The Government had to reduce public spending, promote the privatization of companies and fight drug trafficking in order to get the aid asked of the Paris Club in 1994.

[21] The University of Zambia was closed in April 1994, when 300 teachers and researchers were dismissed for striking over pay claims. The reduction of spending on public schools led to constant teachers strikes.

[22] Accusations of corruption and of the lack of agricultural policy in 1995 led President Chiluba to ask his minister of lands to resign, and the others to declare their income. Shortly afterwards he ousted the governor of the Bank of Zambia, when the local currency, the kwacha, was suddenly devalued by 20 per cent. Chiluba attributed the crisis to the foreign debt, as the servicing of this ate up 40 per cent of GDP. The trade minister admitted in July that 5.5 of the 9.5 million Zambians live in extreme poverty.

[23] In March 1996, the Paris Club cancelled 67 per cent of Zambia's debt. The implementation of the structural adjustment programme dictated by the IMF and the World Bank in 1997 led to increased poverty amongst the rural population and redundancies for at least 150,000 workers with the privatization of the State companies.

[24] A controversial bill in May 1996, passed by the President, amended the Constitution to state that presidential candidates must be second-generation Zambians. Chiluba was re-elected in November 1996.

[25] In November 1997, a month after a failed coup attempt, several people - including Kaunda, disqualified from standing for re-election by the constitutional amendment - were arrested for alleged links with the rebel troops. Representatives of the opposition and human rights organizations said the failed coup became a pretext for summary arrests and torture.

Zimbabwe

Zimbabwe

Population:	11,439,000 (1996)
Area:	390,757 SQ KM
Capital:	Harare
Currency:	Zimbabwe Dollar
Language:	English

B etween the Zambezi and Limpopo rivers one can find, in the words of French historian Pierre Bertaux, "thousands of abandoned mines; cultivated terraces that covered entire mountains, irrigation canals, paths, and wells 12 meters deep excavated in rock...".

2   Among the ruins scattered over an extensive region including nearly 300 archaeological sites, the most important cities were Khami, Naletali, DhloDhlo, Mapungubwe and the better known Zimbabwe with its high-walled enclosure. The Karangas, members of the present-day Shona people built these walls in the 10th century.

3   The Bantu ironworkers who settled in the region in the 5th century also discovered gold, copper and tin deposits. In a few centuries they developed sophisticated techniques for working these metals. In the 8th century, the rise of Arab-influenced trade centres on the coast provided a market for their goods, and the growth of trade resulted in a great expansion of this culture. When the Shirazis founded Sofala (in present-day Mozambique) in the 10th century, the Karanga state acquired an export market for its mining production. The "Monomotapa", the Karanga leader, imposed a tributary relation on the neighboring Muslim nation as he had done with other minor cultures of the area. Thus, Karangan supremacy was established over a region including parts of present-day Malawi.

4   This civilization established important trading connections with Asia and continued to develop until the mid-15th century when the Rotsi, a

southern people belonging to the Shona, the same ethnic group as the Karanga, forced the Monomotapa to withdraw towards the north and the coast. The Zimbabwe citadel and palace were taken over by the Rotsi, whose Changamira (king) extended his control over the mining area. He did not however succeed in controlling an area as vast as the ancient Karanga had done.

5   Portuguese presence brought about the end of the prosperous trade with the east and a consequent economic decline. Also, in reaction to the Europeans' greed for gold, the Shona miners filled in their mines, keeping only their ironworks functioning.

6   In 1834, the Zulu devastated the region. The Rotsi emigrated westwards; cities and farmlands, palaces and irrigation canals were abandoned and grass began to grow over the ancient walls of Zimbabwe. In the first half of the 19th century, the territory was divided between the Shona peoples in the northeast, and the Zulu kingdom of Ndebele in the southeast. In 1889, Lobenguela, the Ndebele ruler, received a visit from Charles Rudd, envoy of the wealthy English adventurer-entrepreneur Cecil Rhodes. In exchange for arms and a life pension, Lobenguela granted exclusive rights for the exploitation of the country's mineral resources to Rhodes' British-South Africa Company (BSA).

7   The British Government gave the BSA control over trade, immigration, communications and the police in the Ndebele territory. Since Matabeleland, as the British called it, was an

independent state, the concession of these privileges granted by a foreign government, needed "formal and free" approval from ruler Lobenguela who lived in Bulawayo. After Rhodes took control, British settlers were established in the Shona territory. They were protected by 700 police officers and were authorized to live there, founding a fortified camp which they called Salisbury. The settlers had no legal title deeds to the land other than the backing of the British Government.

8   Lobenguela withheld his approval for the BSA's activities. So Rhodes's agents created conflictual situations with him to provide a "reason" to depose him. In 1895, under the pretext of arresting some Ndebele who had stolen cattle from the Shona, Rhodes's "police" attacked Bulawayo, capital of Lobenguela. The ruler was driven into the bush and his nation and the Shona territory fell under BSA domination, under the name of Southern Rhodesia.

9   In 1960, settlers of European origin accounted for hardly five per cent of the population but owned more than 70 per cent of the arable land. When the decolonization process began in Africa, Zambia and Malawi, formerly part of a federation with

Southern Rhodesia, resisted further European domination and gained independence in 1964. In Rhodesia, the African National Congress (ANC) also intensified the struggle for independence. The colonial government of Prime Minister Ian Smith reacted declaring a "state of emergency" in November 1965. The British Government urged Southern Rhodesia to transfer power gradually to the African native majority. Smith flatly refused and proclaimed independence on November 11 1965 in order to remain in power with his segregationist Rhodesian Front.

10   The rebel regime faced an embargo declared by the United Nations, though the blockade was systematically violated by the western powers. Guerrilla warfare organized by ZAPU (Zimbabwe African People's Union) and ZANU (Zimbabwe African National Union), was launched. The armed struggle grew increasingly intense and the Smith regime bombarded Zambia and Mozambique. These countries together with Angola, Botswana and Tanzania, formed the group of Front Line Countries to fight racism. In Zimbabwe, ZAPU and ZANU joined to form the Patriotic Front under the joint leadership of Joshua Nkomo and Robert Mugabe.

WORKERS

(1996)

Labour force %

■ WOMEN
□ MEN

44   56

■ AGRICULTURE 68%   (1990)
□ INDUSTRIAL   8%
■ SERVICES   24%

LAND USE

DEFORESTATION -0.6 % annual (81/90)
IRRIGATED   7 %   of arable

(1993)

■ FOREST & WOODLAND 22.5%
□ ARABLE   7%
■ OTHER   70.5%

85%

1994

3%

PROFILE

ENVIRONMENT
The country consists mainly of a high rolling plateau. Most of the urban population live in the High Veld, an area of fertile land, with moderate rainfall and mineral wealth. The climate is tropical, tempered by altitude. Soil depletion is very severe, above all on communal farms, where subsistence agriculture is practised.

SOCIETY
Peoples: The majority of Zimbabweans, 94 per cent, are of Bantu origin from the Shona (founders of the first nation in the region) and the Ndebele group (a Zulu people arrived in the 19th century).
Religions: Most of the population are Christian (45 per cent), predominantly Anglican. Also African traditional beliefs are followed.
Languages: English, official. Most of the people speak their own Bantu languages.
Political Parties: Zimbabwe African National Union-Patriotic Front (ZANU-PF), emerged from the fusion of the Zimbabwe African National Union (ZANU), led by Mugabe, and the Zimbabwe People's Union (ZAPU), led by Joshua Nkomo, in December 1987; Zimbabwe Unity Movement (ZUM), of Edgar Tekere; Regional ZANU-Ndonga party, of right-wing nationalist Ndabaningi Sithole; Emmanuel Magoche's Democratic Party split from the ZUM in 1991.
Social Organizations: Organization of Rural Associations for Progress (ORAP).

THE STATE
Official Name: Republic of Zimbabwe.
Administrative Divisions: 8 Provinces.
Capital: Harare 854,000 people (1995).
Other cities: Bulawayo, 620,900 people; Chitungwiza, 274,000; Mutare, 131,800; Gweru, 124,700 (1992).
Government: Robert Mugabe, President since 1987, re-elected in April 1996. There is a bicameral parliament with a 40-member Senate and a House of Assembly with 100 seats elected through universal suffrage.
National Holiday: April 18, Independence Day (1980).
Armed Forces: 39,000 (1997).
Other: 15,000 Republican Police Force, 2,000 Police Support Unit, 4,000 National Militia.

[11] In 1978 Smith and some African leaders opposed to the Patriotic Front signed an "internal agreement", which legalized their own political parties. In 1979, after fraudulent elections, Bishop Abel Muzorewa became premier and changed the name of the country to ZimbabweRhodesia. With the majority of parliamentary seats, the racist minority had the power to control the socio-economic and political system.

[12] However, guerrilla pressure was mounting, and finally the European government and its African allies were forced to negotiate. The British Government agreed to supervise free elections arranged for February 1980, when Robert Mugabe's ZANU party won a landslide victory. By the Lancaster House agreements, signed on April 18 1980, Britain held power temporarily before transferring to the ZANU Party. Although the Europeans maintained some economic and political privileges, they lost their veto over possible constitutional changes.

[13] Meanwhile, because of war, the country's cattle herd had shrunk to a third of its previous size; many roads had been rendered useless, and some schools had remained closed for seven years. The medical and sanitary systems were also in serious disrepair, and various diseases, such as malaria, were increasingly in evidence among the population.

[14] Prime Minister Robert Mugabe offered generous cabinet participation to the ZAPU leadership, also calling segregationist politicians to form the government team. These steps were aimed at preventing old rivalries from interfering with national reconstruction, especially the ambitious National Development Plan. The gross national product grew by seven per cent, farm production broke all records, and consumption reached higher levels than expected. However, Robert

Mugabe had to face two major difficulties: South Africa's blockade on Zimbabwe's agricultural exports and political dissent between ZANU and ZAPU. In 1981 this led the Prime Minister to remove Nkomo from the home affairs ministry, though maintaining his ministerial rank.

[15] Political differences intensified. In 1982, Nkomo's followers created an armed movement called "Super-ZAPU". Growing political tension coincided with the start of the great drought which was responsible for a drop in agricultural production.

[16] Pressure from African farmers, who had hoped for a true agrarian reform after independence, clashed with the limitations imposed by the Lancaster House agreement. This treaty impeded the expropriation of European land-holdings and the British and Americans avoided giving Zimbabwe the resources promised for the purchase and distribution of land. In Matabeleland, Nkomo's followers explained that the difficulties stemming from the drought and lack of funds were anti-Ndebele schemes of Mugabe's, aimed at repressing the country's second largest ethnic group after the Shona, and that they were all elements designed to create inter-tribal animosity.

[17] Towards the end of June 1985, Mugabe's Zimbabawe African National Union obtained a comfortable victory in parliamentary elections throughout the country, except in Matabeleland, while the majority of whites voted for the Rhodesian Front, created by Ian Smith, a fact which led the President to remind them that the privileges granted to former colonists under the Lancaster House agreement should not be considered unalterable.

[18] The political privileges enjoyed by whites were subsequently eliminated, though there were extensive privileges in other areas. These were evident by figures in a technical report on Zimbabwe's land tenure system: 4,500 farmers (most of them white) owned 50 per cent of the country's productive land while the 4.5 million peasants lived in communally-owned rural areas - known as "tribal lands",

where the black population were moved to during the colonial era.

[19] The Commercial Farmers' Union (CFU) of white farmers blocked many initiatives for rural relocation. They controlled 90 per cent of all agricultural production, paid a third of the country's salaries and exported 40 per cent of the country's goods. This situation existed despite the fact that a third of the properties belonging to members were not exploitable, and that productivity could be increased, and that the great efficiency of the farmers was due to state support rather than the managerial talent of the farmers themselves.

[20] Two constitutional reforms were carried out in September 1987. Previously, 20 seats of the Assembly and 10 in the Senate had been reserved for whites, but this practice was abolished. In addition, an executive authority was assigned to the president, elected by parliament for a six-year period.

[21] Mugabe played an important role in the summit of the Movement of Non-Aligned Countries held in September in Harare, where he enthusiastically promoted the widespread adoption of sanctions against South Africa. In addition, Zimbabwe supported the Government of Mozambique against

the counter-revolutionaries of the National Resistance of Mozambique (RENAMO). In May 1987, some 12,000 Zimbabwean troops were stationed in Mozambique, while RENAMO led incursions into Zimbabwean territory during 1987 and 1988.

[22] In December 1987, Mugabe and Nkomo reached reconciliation, and the two major political parties agree to unification. This agreement was ratified in April 1988 creating the Patriotic Front of the Zimbabwe African National Union (ZANU-PF). Subsequently, with the help of the alliance of several white deputies within ZANU, the country oriented itself, against the general trend in Africa, toward a one-party system.

[23] In the March 1990 elections, ZANU-PF obtained 116 of the 119 parliamentary seats. Mugabe interpreted the results as a mandate in favor of a one-party system. Nevertheless, only 54 per cent of the people went to the polls and the newly organized Zimbabwe Unity Movement obtained 15 per cent of the votes. In Harare and other urban centers, the opposition obtained almost 30 per cent of the votes, while ZAPU held its ground in rural areas.

[24] In an economy with an average annual growth of 4 per cent, the

STATISTICS

DEMOGRAPHY
Population: 11,439,000 (1996) **Annual growth:** 3 % (1980/1996) **Estimates for year 2000:** 12,400,000 **Annual growth to year 2000:** 2.2 % (1994/2000) **Urban population:** 32.5 % (1996) **Urban growth:** 5.65 % (1980/95) **Children per woman:** 4.8 (1996)

HEALTH
Life expectancy at birth: 49 years (1996) male: 48 years (1994) female: 50 years (1994) **Infant mortality:** 49 per 1,000 (1996) **Under-5 child mortality:** 73 per 1,000 (1996) **Calorie consumption:** 94 % (1988/90) 7,692 **people per doctor** (1988/91) **Safe water:** 79 % (1990/96)

EDUCATION
Literacy: 85 % (1995) male : 90 % (1995) female: 80 % (1995) **School enrolment :** Primary total: 115 % (1990/95) male : 119 % (1990/95) female: 111 % (1990/95) Secondary: male : 49 % (1990/95) female: 39 % (1990/95) Tertiary: 7 % (1995) **Primary school teachers:** one for every 39 students (1995)

COMMUNICATIONS
20 **newspapers,** 86 **radios,** 30 **TV sets** and 12 **main telephone lines** per 1,000 people (1994) **Books:** 2 new titles per 100,000 people (1992/94)

ECONOMY
Per capita, GNP: $ 610 (1996) **Annual growth, GNP:** 5.8 % (1995/96) **Annual inflation:** 20.93 % (1985/95) **Consumer price index:** 273.4 (1994) **Currency:** 9.31 Zimbabwe dollars = $ 1 (1995) **Cereal imports:** 100 metric tons (1994) **Food import dependency:** 3 % (1994) **Fertilizer use:** 593 kgs per ha (1994) **Exports:** $ 2,094 million (1996) **Imports:** $ 2,808 million (1996) **Extenal debt:** $ 5,005 million (1996) $ 438 per capita: (1996) **Debt service:** 21.2 % of exports (1996) **Development aid received:** $ 490 million (1995) $ 45 per capita (1995) 9.6 % of GNP (1994)

ENERGY
Consumption: 438.09 Kgs of Oil equivalent per capita yearly (1994) 24.46 % imported (1994)

HDI (rank / value) 129 / 0.513 (1994)

share of agriculture in the GNP was 14 per cent in 1980, and rose to 20 per cent in 1990. That same year, Parliament approved land reform authorizing the Government to expropriate land held by Europeans, at a price fixed by the State, and to redistribute it among the poor. The majority of the African population supported the law, deeming it an act of racial and economic justice. The white farmers, on the other hand, supported by legal experts, criticized it as a violation of the civil and human rights established under the Constitution.

[25] The Organization of Rural Associations for Progress (ORAP) was inaugurated after Zimbabwean independence aimed at preserving indigenous culture and social organization. In 1991, it had half a million members in 16 villages, covering 3.5 of the country's 5 provinces. The basic structure of the ORAP is the "Amalema", a neighbourhood association of 10 families, attempting to recreate the communal organization and production methods existing before colonization. ORAP operate under the hypothesis that the traditional lifestyles of the local population may

do more to solve the country's problems than the paternalistic models imported by European settlers.

[26] In June 1991, the ruling ZANU-PF decided to relinquish its Marxist-Leninist doctrine, eliminating all references to this and scientific socialism from its programme. ZANU-PF is still maintaining a socialist perspective for as long as it feels is appropriate for the Zimbabwean situation. Mugabe appealed for the doctrine of pure socialism to be abandoned, in favor of social democracy and a mixed economy.

[27] In October 1991, the Zimbabwean Unity Movement split, creating the Democratic Party, led by Emmanuel Magoche, the former president of the ZUM.

[28] Although Zimbabwe has a multiparty system, it operates similarly to a one-party regime. The absence of effective opposition to the ZANU-PF has meant that the ruling party has gradually come to control all state mechanisms, the police force, and the state administration. Although the ZANU-PF leadership reached a consensus decision to maintain the

regime, the emergence of movements in favor of a multiparty system in South Africa, Angola, Namibia, Mozambique, and Zambia pressured Zimbabwe into allowing the formal creation of several parties.

[29] In January 1992, the Government announced that a five-year reform plan would be implemented. Its aim would be to liberalize the economy, bring the budget deficit down to 5 per cent of the GNP, and to substantially increase job opportunities.

[30] One of the first measures adopted in January 1992 was the elimination of 32,000 public sector jobs. Under pressure from the IMF, Mugabe began reducing the number of ministries.

[31] Within the framework of public spending cuts, in May, the Government reduced the education budget and announced that tertiary education would no longer be free. As a result, massive student protests broke out, culminating in the expulsion of 10,000 students from the University of Zimbabwe in June. Demonstrations repudiating this measure were harshly repressed by the police. The Labor Union Congress declared a general strike, protesting the government's economic policies.

[32] A demonstration by students, women and children demanding better life conditions in the gold mines region, east of Harare, culminated with three deaths under police fire. US elite troops, acting together with Zimbabwe troops, undertook military manoeuvres. According to the government, these manoeuvres were intended to prepare the troops that would operate in Somalia under the UN, but according to the opposition the purpose was to train them for domestic repression.

[33] By the middle of 1993, the Union of Commercial Farmers, supported by minority parties of European origin, accused the government of expropriating unproductive land. Mugabe threatened them with deportation in case they did not accept the agrarian reform. Nevertheless, he did not ask them to assure minimal life conditions for the rural workers. In 1994, a rural worker earned $30 per month in the bigger properties.

[34] The countries that gave Zimbabwe economic assistance

gathered in Paris in March 1995, a month later than planned, because Mugabe's government did not have their finance books in good order. Despite some local fear of reprisals for not having carried on the financial reforms demanded by the IMF "in due time", the country received a bigger amount than the figure initially announced. The foreign debt of Zimbabwe was equal to the PBI, so that 23 per cent of the national budget was earmarked for servicing the debt.

[35] In October 1995, Ndabaningi Sithole, leader of the ZANU-Ndonga, and one of the two members of the Assembly not belonging to the ZANU-PF, was arrested for allegedly planning the assassination of the President. Mugabe's opponents attributed the arrest to Sithole's announcement of his candidacy for the presidency.

[36] With the abstention of 68 per cent of the voters, the April 1996 elections resulted in Mugabe's victory with 93 per cent of the votes. Several opposition parties boycotted the elections since they questioned the electoral procedures.

[37] In August a civil servants strike was declared as salaries had fallen 40 per cent in the last six years. The Government proposed a 9 per cent increase but the conflict did not come to an end until a 20 per cent increase was accepted. In 1997, 62 per cent of the population lived below the poverty line, compared with 25 per cent in the 1980s.

[38] In January 1998, a price increase in essential products led thousands of residents in the suburbs of the capital to raid shops and businesses, until the army was called in to recover order. The price increase was seen as a consequence of November's devaluation of the Zimbabwe dollar. However, Information Minister Chen Mutengwende accused traders of European origin of deliberately increasing prices to provoke an uprising against the government. Unemployment of more than 45 per cent of the active population had been feeding fears of a social explosion for some months.

[39] In the wake of the Indonesian students' protest in May 1998 which toppled President Suharto, Zimbabwean students called for Mugabe also to step down.

Bibliography

ABDEL-MALEK, A., ed.- Contemporary Arab Political Thought. London, Zed, 1983.

AGUILAR DERPICH, J.- Guyana: Otra vía al socialismo. Caracas, El ojo del camello, 1973.

ALGERIE: Guide economique et social. Dely, ANEP, 1987.

ALIANZAS políticas y procesos revolu-cionarios. Mexico, SEPLA, 1979.

ALMANAQUE BRASIL 1995/1996. Editora Terceiro Mundo, Rio de Janeiro, 1995.

AMARASINGAM, SP.- The Industrialized Nations of the West and the Third World. Colombo, Tribune, 1982.

AMIN, S., et al.- Nuevo Orden Internacional. Mexico, Nueva Política, 1977.

AMNESTY INTERNATIONAL.- Contra la pena de muerte. Madrid, 1992.

AMNESTY INTERNATIONAL.- Guía de la Carta Africana de los derechos humanos y de los pueblos. Madrid, 1991.

AMNESTY INTERNATIONAL.- Informes 1984-1996. Madrid, 1996.

AMNESTY INTERNATIONAL.- Reino Unido: desigualdad ante la ley. Madrid, 1991.

ANUARIO del Centro de Investigaciones para la Paz 1988/1989: Paz, militarización y conflictos. Madrid, IEPALA, 1989.

ANNUAIRE Geopolitique Mondial. Paris, Hachette, 1989. (Suppl. de Politique International.)

ARNOLD, M.- The Testimony of Steve Biko. Suffolk, Granada Publ., 1979.

ARRUDA, M., et al.- Transnational Corporations: A Challenge for Churches and Christians. Geneva, World Council of Churches, 1982.

ASIA 1990 Yearbook. Hong Kong, Dai Nippon, 1990.

ATLAS Barsa. Rio de Janeiro, Encyclopaedia Britannica, 1980.

ATLASECO du Monde 1997. Paris, Les Editions EOC, 1996.

ATLAS de L'humanité. Paris, Solar, 1983.

AZIZ, T.- Reflexions sur les relations Arabo-Iraniennes. Baghdad, 1980.

BARDINI, R.- Belice:historia de una nación en movimiento. Tegucigalpa, Universi-taria, 1978.

BARDINI, R.- El Frente Polisario y la lucha del pueblo saharaui. Tegucigalpa, CIPAAL, 1979.

BARRACLOUGH, G.- Introducción a la Historia Contemporánea. Barcelona, Anagrama, 1975.

BASSOLS BATALLA, A.- Geografía, sub-desarrollo y regionalización. Mexico, Nuestro Tiempo, 1976.

BASSOLS BATALLA, A.- Los recursos naturales. Mexico, Nuestro Tiempo, 1974.

BASTIDE, R.- Las Américas negras. Madrid, Alianza, 1969.

BECKFORD, G.- Persistent Poverty, Underdevelopment in the Plantations of the Third World. 2a.ed. London, 1983.

BEDJAQUI, M.- Towards a new International Economic Order. Paris, UNESCO, 1979.

BELFRACE, C & ARONSON, J.- Something to Guard. New York, Columbia Univ.Press, 1978.

BELLER, WS., ed.- Environmental and Economic Growth in the Smaller Caribbean Island. Washington, Department of State, 1979.

BENOT, I.- Ideologías de las independencias africanas. Barcelona, 1973.

BENZ, W.- El siglo XX: Problemas mundiales entre los dos bloques de poder. Madrid, Siglo XXI, 1984.

BERGER, J. & MOHR, J.- A seventh man. Middlesex, 1975.

BIANCO , L.- Asia contemporánea. Mexico, Siglo XXI, 1980.

BILAN Economique et Social 1984-1989-1991. Le Monde; Dossiers et Documents; Paris, 1992.

BOUSTANI, R & FARGUES, P.- Atlas du Monde Arabe. Géopolitique et Societé. Paris, Bordas, 1990.

BRANDT, W.et al.- Das Ueberleben sichern. Kiepenheur y Witsch, Koln, 1980.

BRITTAIN, V., & SIMMONS, M.- Third World Review. London, Guardian, 1987.

BROWN, L.- Food or Fuel: New Competition for the Worlds Cropland. Washington, Worldwatch Institute, 1980.

BRUBAKER, S.- Para vivir en la tierra. Mexico, Pax, 1973.

BRUHAT, J.- Historia de Indonesia. Buenos Aires, EUDEBA, 1964.

BUETTNER, T., et al.- Afrika: Geschichte von den Anfaengen bis zur Gegenwart. Koln, Pahl-Rugenstein, 1979.

BURCHETT, WG.- Otra vez Corea. Mexico, ERA, 1968.

BURGER, J.- The Gaia Atlas of first peoples. A future for the indigenous world. London, Gaia, 1990.

CALCAGNO, AE & JAKOBOWICZ, JM.- El monólogo Norte-Sur y la explotación de los países subdesarrollados. México, Siglo XXI, 1981.

CALCHI NOVATI, G.- La revolución argelina. Barcelona, Bruguera, 1970.

CALDWELL, M.- The Wealth of Some Nations. London, Zed, 1977.

CARATINI, R.- Dictionnaire des nationalités et des minorités en URSS. Paris, Larousse, 1990.

CARRERAS, J.- Historia de Jamaica. Havana, Ed.Ciencias Sociales, 1984.

CARTA africana de Derechos Humanos y de los pueblos. Nairobi, 1981. Adoptada por la Decimoctava Conferencia de Jefes de Estado y de Gobierno de la Organización de la Unidad Africana.

CASTRO, F.- La crisis económica y social del mundo. Havana, OPCE, 1983.

CAVALLA, A.- Geopolítica y Seguridad Nacional en América. Mexico, UNAM, 1979.

CEPAL.- Anuario estadístico de América Latina. Santiago de Chile, 1981.

CEPAL.- Estudio económico de América Latina y el Caribe. Santiago de Chile, 1984.

CEPAL.- Notas sobre la economía y el desarrollo. Santiago de Chile, 1985.

CEPAL.- La evolución de la economía de América Latina en 1983. Santiago de Chile, 1984.

CHALIAND, G.- Revolution in the Third World. Middlesex, Penguin, 1979.

CHEE, Y.- How big powers dominate the Third World. Penang, Third World Network, 1987.

CHOMSKY, N., STEELE, J. & GITTINGS, J.- Super Powers in Collision. Penguin, 1984.

CHRISTENSEN, Ch.- The Right to Food: how to guarantee. New York, 1978.

CINCO conferencias Cumbres de los Países No Alineados. Havana, 1979.

CIPOLLA, C.- La explosión demográfica (entrevista). Barcelona, Salvat, 1973.

CLAIRMONTE, FF & CAVANAGH, H.- Transnational Corporations and Services: The final frontier. Geneva, UNCTAD, 1984.

CLARK, C.- Crecimiento demográfico y utilización del suelo. Madrid, 1968.

COLCHESTER, M & LOHMANN, L.- The tropical forestry action plan;what progress? 1990.

COMANDANTE de los pobres: testimonios sobre Omar Torrijos. Madrid, Centro de Estudios Torrijistas, 1984.

COMISION INTERNACIONAL SOBRE PROBLEMAS DE LA COMUNICACION.- Un solo mundo, voces múltiples. Mexico, Fondo de Cultura, 1980.

CONNELL-SMITH, G.- Los Estados Unidos y la América Latina. Mexico, 1977.

CONSTANTINO, R.- The Philippines:A past revisited. Manila, 1975.

CONTRERAS, M.& SOSA, I.-Latinoamérica en el siglo XX. Mexico, UNAM, 1973.

CORDOVA, A., et alii.- El Imperialismo. Mexico, Nuestro Tiempo, 1979.

CORM, G.- Le Proche-Orient éclaté. Paris, La Découverte, 1983.

LE COURIER des Pays de l'est. Paris, 1986.

CUEVA, A.- El proceso de dominación política en el Ecuador. Quito, Critica, 1973.

DAVIDSON, B.- The Liberation of Guiné. Middlesex, Penguin, 1971.

DAWISHA, K.- Eastern Europe, Gorbachev and reform: the great challenge. 2a.ed. New York, Cambridge Univ., 1990.

DEBRAY, R.-La crítica de la armas. Madrid, Siglo XXI, 1975.

DECRAENE, P.- El Panafricanismo. Bs.As., EUDEBA, 1962.

DEGENHARDT, H, comp.- Political dissention international guide to dissent, extraparliamentary, guerrillas and illegal political movements. London, Longman, 1983.

DE LA COURT, T.; PICK, D & NORDQUIST, D.- The nuclear fix. A guide to nuclear activities in the Third World. Amsterdam, Wise, 1982.

DENVERS, A.- Points choc:l'environnement dans tous ses états. Editions 1, 1990.

DE SOUZA, M.- El capital mundial. Montevideo, CUI, 1987. v.1.

DER FISCHER WELT ALMANACH 1993. Fischer Taschenbuch Verlag. Bonn, 1992.

DIFRIERI, H., et al.- Geografía Universal. Bs.As., ANESA, 1971.

DORE, F.- Los regímenes políticos en Asia. Mexico, Siglo XXI, 1976.

DRECHSLER, H.-Africa del Sudoeste bajo la dominación colonial alemana. Berlin, Verlag, 1986.

DREIFUSS, R.-A Internacional capitalista. Rio de Janeiro, Espaço e Tempo, 1986.

ECE.- Economic Bulletin for Europe. New York, 1991.

ECE.- Economic Survey of Europe in 1988-1989. New York, 1989.

ECE.- Economic Survey of Europe in 1989-1990. New York, 1990.

ECE.- Economic Survey of Europe in 1990-1991. New York, 1991.

ECKHOLM, E.- The dippossessed of the earth:Land reform and Sustainable Development. Washington, Worldwatch Institute, 1979.

L'ECONOMIE de la drogue. Le Monde; Dossiers et Documents; Paris, feb.1990.

L'ECONOMIE de l'Espagne. Le Monde; Dossiers et Documents; Paris, Jan.1990.

ELLIOT, F.- A Dictionary of Politics. Middlesex, Penguin, 1974.

EMMANUEL, A., AMIN, S, et al.- Impe-rialismo y comercio Internacional.(El intercambio desigual). Madrid, Siglo XXI, 1977.

El EMPUJE del Islam. Madrid, IEPALA, 1989. (Africa Internacional, 7)

El SALVADOR. Alianzas políticas y proceso revolucionario. Mexico, SEPLA, 1979.

ENTRALGO, A., ed.- Africa. Havana, Ed.Ciencias Sociales, 1979.

ENZENSBERG, H.-Zur Kritik der politischen Okologie. Berlin, Kursbuch, 1973.

L'ETAT du Monde 1989-1990. Annuaire économique et géopolitique mondial. Paris, La Découverte, 1989.

L'ETAT des religions dans le Monde. Paris, La Découvert, 1987.

L'ETAT du Monde. Paris, La Découverte, 1996 and 1997.

L'ETAT du Tiers Monde. Paris, La Découverte, 1989.

The EUROPA Yearbook. London, Europa Pub., 1984.

FABER, G.- The Third World and the EEC. Netherlands, 1982.

FAHRNI, D.- Historia de Suiza. Ojeada a la evolución de un pequeño país desde sus orígenes hasta nuestros días. 2a.ed. Zurich, Pro Helvetia, 1984.

FALK, R & WAHL, P.- Befreiungsbewegungen in Afrika. Pahl-Rugenstein, Koln, 1980.

FANON, F.- Os condenados da Terra. Rio de Janeiro, Civilizaçao Brasileira, 1979.

FAO.- Estado mundial de la agricultura y la alimentación. Rome, 1983.

FAO.- Production Yearbook. Rome, 1993.

FERNANDEZ, W.- El gran culpable.La responsabilidad de los Estados Unidos en el proceso militar uruguayo. Montevideo, Atenea, 1986.

FIELDHOUSE, DK.- The Colonial Empires.A comparative survey from the eighteenth century. 2a.ed. London, MacMillan1982.

FIGUEROA ALCACES, E, ed.- Antología de geografía histórica moderna y contemporánea. Mexico, UNAM, 1974.

FISHLOW, A, et al.- Rich and Poor Nations in the World Economy. New York, McGraw Hill, 1978.

FORDHAM, P.- The geography of African Affairs. Middlesex, Penguin.

FOREST Resources crisis in the Third World, Malaysia, Sep.1986. Proceeding. Malaysia, 1987.

FRENTE POLISARIO.-VII Anniversaire du Declenchement de la Lutte de Liberation nationale. Dep. Informations, 1989.

FRETILIN Conquers the Right to Dialogue. London, 1978.

GALEANO, E.- As Véias Abertas de América Latina. Rio de Janeiro, Vozes, 1979.

GALTUNG, J. & O'BRIEN, P., et al.- Self-reliance. A Strategy for development. London, IDS, 1980.

GANDHI, MK.- An autobiography. Boston, Beacon Press, 1957.

GATT International trade 1981-1982. New York, 1982.

GAZOL SANTAGE, A.- Los países pobres. México, FCE, 1987.

GENOUD, R.- Sobre las revoluciones parciales del Tercer Mundo. Barcelona, Anagrama, 1974.

GEORGE, P.- Geografía económica. Barcelona, Ariel, 1976.

GEORGE, P.- Panorama del mundo actual. Barcelona, Ariel, 1970.

GEORGE, P.- Geografía y medio ambiente, población y economía. Mexico, UNAM, 1979.

GEORGE, S.- How the Other Half Dies. Middlesex, Penguin, 1980.

GEZE, F., et al.- L'Etat du Monde-1982. Paris, Maspero, 1982.

GOUROU, P.- L'Afrique. Paris, Hachette, 1970.

GRANT, JP.- Situaçao Mundial da Infancia. New York, UNICEF, 1984.

GREENBERG, S, ed.- Guinness book of Olympic Records. Bantam, 1988.

GREINER, B.- Amerikanische Aussenpolitik von Truman bis heute. Koln, Pahl-Rugenstein, 1980.

GROUSSET, R.- Historia de Asia. Buenos Aires, EUDEBA, 1962.

GUIA CIUDADANA sobre el Banco Mundial y el Banco Interamericano de Desarrollo, Red Bancos, Instituto del Tercer Mundo, Montevideo, 1996.

GRUNEBAM, GE, ed.- El Islam. Desde la caída de Constantinopla hasta neustros días. Mexico, Siglo XXI, 1975.

GUIM, JB.- Compendio de geografía Universal. Mexico, Bouret, 1875.

HALLIDAY, F.- Arabia without Sultans. Middlesex, Penguin, 1974.

HALPERIN DONGHI, T.- Historia contemporánea de América Latina. Madrid, Alianza, 1983.

HAMELINK, C.- The Corporate Village. Rome, IDOC, 1977.

HANDWÖRTERBUCH INTERANTIONALE POLITIK. Wichard Woyke (Hrsg.). Leske Budrich. 1993.

HAYES, MD.- Dimensiones de seguridad de los intereses de Estados Unidos en América Latina. Mexico, CIDE, 1981.

HERRERA, L & VAYRYNEN, R, ed.- Pace, development and New International Economic Order. Tampere, IPRA, 1979.

HUIZER, G.- El potencial revolucionario del campesino en América Latina. Mexico, Siglo XXI, 1974.

HUMAN Right Newsletter. 1991.

HUMANN, K. & BRODERSEN, I.- Welt Aktuell'86. Hamburg, Roro, 1985.

IBGE.- Tabulaçoes Avançadas do Censo Demográfico. Rio de Janeiro, 1982.

IDB.- External Debt and Economic Development in Latin America. Washington, 1984.

IDB.- Progreso económico y social en América Latina. Washington, 1984.

ILO.- Yearbook of Labour Statistics/Anuario de Estadísticas del Trabajo. Geneva, 1997.

IIED.- World Resources 1986. New York, 1986.

INDEX on Censorship. London. 1991-1992

INSTITUTE OF RACE RELATIONS.- Patterns of Racism. London, 1982.

INSTITUTO GEOGRAFICO DE AGOSTINI.- Atlas Universal Geo- económico. Barcelona, Teide, 1977.

INTERNATIONAL INSTITUTE FOR STRATEGIC STUDIES.- The Military Balance 1993-94. London, Brassey's, 1993.

INTERNATIONAL INSTITUTE FOR STRATEGIC STUDIES.- Strategic Survey 1982-1983. London, 1983.

INTERNATIONAL COMMISION OF JURISTS AND CONSUMERS'ASSOCIATION OF PENANG.- Rural development and Human Rights in South East Asia. Penang, 1982.

INTERNATIONAL MONETARY FUND.- Directory of Regional Economic Organizations and Intergovernmental Commodity Organizations. Washington, 1979.

INTERNATIONAL MONETARY FUND.- Estadísticas Financieras Internacionales. Washington, 1985.

JALEE, P.- El Tercer Mundo en la economía Mundial. Mexico, Siglo XXI, 1980.

JAULIN, R.- La des-civilización. Política y práctica del etnocidio. Mexico, Nueva Imagen, 1979.

JONAS, S.& TOBIS, D.-Guatemala. New York, NACLA, 1974.

JOYAUX, F.- L'année internationale 1990. Paris, Hachete, 1989. Annuaire géopolitique de la Revue Politique Internationale.

KAPLAN, L.- Revoluciones. Mexico, Extemporáneos, 1973.

KÄKÖNEN, J.- The Mechanics of Neo-Colonialism. Mänttä, Finnish Peace Research Association, 1974.

KENT, G.- Food Trade: The Poor Feed the Rich en the Ecologist Ecosystem. United Kingdom, 1985.

KETTANI, M.- Ali, the Muslim Minorities. Leicester, Islamic Foundation, 1979.

KHADAFI, M.- O livro verde. Tripoli, EPOEPD.

KHOR, K.P.- Recession and the Malaysian Economy. Penang, Masyarakat, 1983.

KIDROM, M & SEGAL, R.- The State of the World Atlas. London, Pan Books, 1981.

KINDER, H. & HILGEMANN, W.- The Penguin Atlas of World History. New York, 1978.

KI-ZERBO, J.- Historia del Africa Negra. Madrid, Alianza, 1981.

KLAINER, R, LOPEZ, D & PIERA, V.- Aprender con los chicos:propuesta para una tarea docente fundada en los Derechos Humanos. Buenos Aires, MEDH, 1988.

KLARE, M, et al.- Supplying Repression. Washington, IPS, 1981.

KUPER, L.- Genocide: Its political use in the Twentieth Century. Middlesex, Penguin, 1981.

LACOSTE, Y.-Geografía del subdesarrollo. Barcelona, Ariel, 1978.

LACOSTE, Y.-Los países subdesarrollados. Buenos Aires, EUDEBA, 1965.

LAINO, D.- Paraguai: Fronteiras e penetraçao brasileira. Sao Paulo, Global, 1979.

LEBEDEV, N.- La URSS en la política mundial. Moscow, Progreso, 1983.

LEGER SIVARD, R.- World Military and Social Expenditures 1986. Washington, 1986.

LEGER SIVARD, R.- World Military and Social Expenditures 1989. Washington, 1989.

LEWIS, DE.- Reform and revolution in Grenada:1950-1981. Havana, Casa de las Américas, 1984.

LEWYCKY, D.& WHITE, S.- An African abstract;Council for International Cooperation. Manitoba, 1979.

LICHTHEIM, G.- Imperialism. Middlesex, Penguin, 1974.

LINHARES, MY.- A luta contra a metrópole (Asia e Africa). Sao Paulo, Brasilense, 1981.

LINIGER GOUMAZ, M.- Guinée Equatoriale: de la dictadure des Colons á la Dictadure des Colonels. Geneva, Ed.Temps, 1982.

LINIGER GOUMAZ, M.- De la Guinée Equatoriale Nguemiste. Geneva, Ed.Temps, 1983.

LINTER, B.- OUTRAGE: Burma's struggle for democracy. Hong Kong, Review Publ., 1989.

LIPSCHUTZ, A.-El problema racial en la conquista de América. Mexico, Siglo XXI, 1963.

LUNA, J.-Granada, la nueva joya del Caribe. Havana, Ciencias Sociales, 1982.

McCOY, A.& JESUS, EDC.- Philippine Social History. Manila, ASSA, 1982.

McEVEDY, C.& JONES, R.-Atlas of world Population History. Kerala, 1986. Middlesex, Penguin, 1978

MAGDOFF, H.- La empresa multinacional en una perspectiva histórica. Barcelona, 1980.

MAHATHIR BIN MOHAMED.- The Malay dilema. Selangor, 1982.

MANORAMA Yearbook 1986. Kerala, 1986.

MASUREL, E.- L'année 1989 dans le Monde:les principaux evénements en France et a l'etranger. Paris, Gallinard, 1990.

MAX-NEEF, M.- La economía descalza. Lima, 1985.

MAYOBRE MACHADO, J.- Información dependencia y desarrollo;la prensa y el nuevo orden económico internacional. Caracas, Monte Avila, 1978.

MEILE, P.- Historia de la India. Buenos Aires, EUDEBA, 1962.

MEJIA RICART, T.- Breve historia dominicana. Santa Dominica, 1982.

MENENDEZ DEL VALLE, E.- Angola, imperialismo y guerra civil. Barcelona, Akal, 1976.

MICHELINI, Z.- Uruguay vencerá. Barcelona, Laja, 1978.

MOITA, L. Os Congressos da Frelimo do PAIGC e do MPLA, CIDAC. Lisbon, 1979.

MOORE LAPPE, F & COLLINS, J.-El hambre en el mundo. Diez mitos. Mexico, COPIDER/FONAPAS, 1980.

MOREIRA, N.- Modelo peruano. Rio de Janeiro, Paz e Terra, 1975.

MOREIRA, N.- El Nasserrismo y la revolución del Tercer Mundo. Montevideo, EBO, 1970.

MPLA.- Historia de Angola. Porto, Afron–tamento, 1975.

MYERS, N., ed.- The Gaia Atlas of Planet Management. London, Pan Books, 1985.

MYERS, N.- The Gaia Atlas of future worlds: challenge and opportunity in age of change. London, Gaia, 1990.

MYLLYMAKI, E.& DILLINGER, B.- Depen–dency and Latin American Development. Finnish Peace Research Asociation. Tampere, 1977.

El NACIMIENTO de una nación: la lucha por la liberación de Namibia. London, Zed, 1985.

NKRUMAH, K.- I Speak of Freedom. New York, Praeger, 1961.

NKRUMAH, K.- Africa debe unirse. Buenos Aires, EUDEBA, 1965

NEARING, S & FREEMAN, J.- La diplomacia del dólar. Mexico, SELFA, 1926.

NEDJATIGIL, ZM.- The Cyprus Conflict. Nicosia, A-Z Publ., 1981.

NYERERE, JK.- El reto del Sur; informe de la Comisión Sur.

NYERERE, JK.- Freedom and Socialism. London, Oxford Univ.Press, 1968.

NEWLAND, K.- The Sisterhood of Man. New York, WW Norton, 1979.

OECD.- Geographical Distribution of Financial Flows to Developing Countries. Paris, 1982.

OMAR TORRIJOS imágenes y voz. Panama, CET, 1985.

O MUNDO HOJE/93. Anuario Economico e Geopolitico Mundial. Ensaio, Sao Paulo, 1993.

ORTIZ MENA, A.-América Latina en desarrollo. Washington, IDB, 1980.

ORTIZ QUESADA, F.- Salud en la pobreza. Mexico, CEESTEM-Nueva Imagen, 1982.

OSBORNE, M.- Region of Revolt. Focus of Southeast Asia. Middlesex, Penguin, 1970.

OSMANCZYK, EJ.-Enciclopedia Mundial de relaciones internacionales y Naciones Unidas. Madrid, Fondo de Cultura, 1976.

PAIGC.- História da Guiné e Ilhas de Cabo Verde. Porto, Afrontamento, 1974.

PAISES NO ALINEADOS, Los. Mexico, Diogenes, 1979.

PAISES NO ALINEADOS, Los. Prague, Prensa Latina-Orbis, 1979.

PALOMINO, E.- Qosqo, Centro del Mundo, Perú, Municipalidad Provincial del Qosqo, 1993.

PAQUE, R., ed.- Afrika antwortet Europa. Berlin, Ullstein, 1976.

PEASE GARCIA, H., ed.- América Latina 80: Democracia y movimiento popular. Lima, DESCO, 1981.

PERROT, D.& PREISWEK, R.- Etnocentrismo e historia. Mexico, Nueva Imagen, 1979.

LE PETROLE, les matières de base et le développment. Algeria, Sonatrach, 1974.

PIACENTINI, P.- O Mundo do petróleo. Lisbon, Tricontinental, 1984.

PONCE SANGINES, C.- La cultura nativa en Bolivia, La Paz, Ed. Amigos del Libro, 1992.

PIERRE-CHARLES, G.- El caribe contemporáneo. Mexico, Siglo XXI, 1981.

PUTZGER, FW.- Historicher Weltatlas. Berlin, Velhagen, 1961.

QUALITY OF LIFE, from a common people's point of view, by PapyRossa Verlags GmbH & Co. KG, Köln & World Data Research Center, Ernst Fidel Fürntratt-Kloep, 1995, Hackås, Sweden.

QUIROGA SANTA CRUZ, M.- El saqueo de Bolivia. Buenos Aires, Crisis, 1973.

RAGHAVAN, Ch.- Un GATT sin cascabel. La Ronda Uruguay, una sigilosa reconquista del tercer Mundo. Montevideo, Red del Tercer Mundo, 1990

RAGHAVAN, Ch.- Recolonization. GATT, the Uruguay round and the Third World. Penang, Third World Network, 1990

RAHMAN, MA.- Grass-Roots Participation and self-reliance: experiences in South and South East. Asia, ILO, 1984.

RAMA, C.- Historia de América Latina. Barcelona, Bruguera, 1978.

REFORMS in foreigns economic relations of Eastern Europe and the Soviet Union. Proceedings. New York, ECE, 1991. (Economic Studies, 2)

RETURN to the good earth. Third World Network Dossier, Penang, 1983.

REYES MATTA, F, ed.- La noticia internacional. Mexico, ILET, 1977.

RIBEIRO, D.- Las Américas y la civilización. Buenos Aires, Centro Editor, 1973.

RIBEIRO, S.- Sobre a unidade no pensamento de Amilcar Cabral. Lisbon, Tricontinental, 1983.

RODNEY, W.- How Europe Underdeveloped Africa. Washington, Howard Univ., 1974.

RODRIGUEZ, M.- Haití, un pueblo rebelado. Mexico, 1982.

ROGER, M.- Timor - hier la colonisation portugaise, aujourd'hui la résistance. Paris, L'Harmattan, 1977.

SAID, E.- Orientalism. Middlesex, Penguin, 1985.

SALAS, RM.- Estado de la población mundial. Barcelona, FNUA, 1983.

SARKAR, S, - Modern India 1885-1947. Madras, McMillan India, 1985.

SCHLESINGER, R.-La Internacional Comunista y el Problema Colonial. Mexico, Pasado y Presente, 1974.

SCHMIEDER, O.- Geografía de América Latina. Mexico, FCE, 1975.

SCHUON, F.- Understanding Islam. London, Mandala Books, 1979.

SEAGER, J & OLSON, A.- Women in the world. An International Atlas. London, Pan Books, 1986.

SECRETARIA DE AGRICULTURA (MEXICO).- El desarrollo Agroindustrial y la Economía Internacional. 1979.

SEGAL, G.- The world affairs companion. New York, Touchstone, 1991.

SELSER, G.- Apuntes sobre Nicaragua. Mexico, CESTEM, 1981.

SERRYN, P.- le Monde d'aujourd'hui. Paris, Bordas, 1981.

SHINNIE, M.- Ancient African Kingdoms. New York, Mentor, 1980.

SHIVA, V.- The violence of the green revolution, ecological degradation and political conflict in Punjab. India, 1989.

SITUACION en el mundo 1991, La. Buenos Aires, Sudamericana, 1991.

SIVARD, RL.- World Military and Social Expeditures. Virginia, World Priorities, 1979.

SOCIAL WATCH - The Starting Point, Nº1 and Nº2, Instituto del Tercer Mundo, Montevideo, 1996, 1997 and 1998.

SOMALIA.MINISTRY OF INFORMATION.- The Arab World. Mogadishu, 1975.

SOY un soldado de América Latina. Panama, CET, 1981.

STANLEY, D.- Eastern Europe on a shoestring. Australia, Lonely Planet, 1989.

STANLEY, D.- South Pacific Handbook. Hong Kong, Moon Publ., 1982.

STATE OF THE WORLD 1991-1996. World Watch Institute, New York, Norton & Company, 1996.

STAVRIANOS, LS.- Global Rift.The Third World Comes of Age. New York, William Morow, 1981.

SUAREZ, L.- Los Países No Alineados. Mexico, FCE, 1975.

SUB-SHARAN AFRICA: From crisis to sustainable growth, a long-term perspective study. Washington, World Bank, 1989.

SUTER, K.- West Irian, East Timor and Indonesia. London, 1979.

SWEEZY, P.- Teoria do Desenvolvimento Capitalista. Sao Paulo, Abril, 1983.

TERRE DES FEMMES. Panorama de la situation des femmes dans le monde. Paris, La Découverte, 1982.

THE STATE of the World's Refugees 1995, United Nations High Commissioner for Refugees-UNHCR, New York, 1995.

THE UNIVERSAL ALMANAC 1994. Wright, John W. USA, 1993.

THIRD WORLD FOUNDATION.- Third World Affairs 1987. London, 1987.

THOMAS, EJ., ed.- Les travailleurs immigrés en Europe: quel status? Paris, UNESCO, 1981.

TIMERMAN, J.- Israel: La Guerra más larga. Madrid, Mochnik, 1983.

TITO, JB.- La misión histórica del Movimiento de No Alineación. Beograd, CAS, 1979.

TOMLINSON, A. & WHANNEL, G., ed.- Five-ring circus: Money, power and politics at the Olympic Games. London, Pluto Press, 1984.

TORRIELLO GARRIDO, G.- Tras la Cortina de Banano. Havana, Ciencias Sociales, 1979.

TORRIJOS, O.- La quinta frontera. Costa Rica, Ed.Univ.Centroamericana, 1981.

TORRIJOS, O.- Figura, tiempo, faena. Panama, Lotería Nacional, 1981.

TOWARDS Socialist Planning. Tanzania, UCHEMI, 1980.

TRIBUNAL PERMANENTE DOS POVOS. Sessao sobre Timor-Leste. Lisbon, 1981.

TURNBULL, M.- A Short History of Malaysia, Singapore and Brunei. Singapore, Graham Brash, 1980.

UL HAQ, M.- La cortina de la pobreza. Mexico, FCE, 1978.

UN.- ABC das Nacoes Unidas. New York, 1982.

UN.- Concise Report on the World Population situation. New York, 1979.

UN.- Demographic Yearbook. New York, 1984.

UN.- Efectos de la empresas multinacionales en el desarrollo. New York, 1974.

UN.- Final documents of the Eighth Conference of Heads of States or Government of Non-Aligned Countries. New York, 1986.

UN.- A guide to the New Law of the Sea. New York, 1979.

UN.- Informe del Comité Especial sobre descolonización. New York, 1975.

UN.- Monthly Bulletin of Statistics. New York.

UN.- Resolutions and Decisions. General Assembly. New York, 1995.

UN.- Resolutions on the Palestine question. Beirut

UN.- Statistical Yearbook, 41st issue. New York, 1997.

UN.- Statistical Yearbook for Asia and the Pacific. New York, 1980.

UN.- Terminology Bulletin. New York, 1979.

UN.- A trust betrayed: Namibia. New York, 1974.

UN.- UNCTAD VII. Actas. Geneva 1987.

UNCTAD.- Handbook of International Trade and Development Statistics 1995. New York, 1997.

UNESCO.- Geografía de América Latina. Barcelona, 1975.

UNESCO.- Historia General de Africa. UNESCO-Tecnos, 1987.

UNESCO.- Recherches en matière du relations raciales. Paris, 1965.

UNESCO.- Résumé statistique. Paris, 1982.

UNESCO.- Yearbook 1984. Paris, 1985.

UNDP- Human Development Reports 1980-1996. New York, 1996.

UNICEF.- The State of the World's Children Report 1998. New York 1998.

URSS Anuario 1991. Moscow, Novosti.

US ARMS CONTROL AND DISARMAMENNT AGENCY.- World Military Expenditure and Arms Transfer 1972-1982. Washington, 1982.

VALDES VIVO, R.- Etiopía: la Revolución desconocida. Havana, Ciencias Sociales, 1977.

VARELA BARRAZA, H.- Africa:Crisis del poder político. Mexico, CEESTEM, 1981.

VARGAS, JA.- Terminología sobre Derecho del Mar. Mexico, CEESTEM, 1979.

VENTURA, J.- El Poder Popular en El Salvador. Mexico, SALPRESS, 1983.

VERDIEU, E & BWATSHIA, K.- Les Eglises face au Nouvel Ordre Economique National e International. Quebec, CECI, 1980.

VERDIEU, E & BWATSHIA, K.- Cooperation Technique des Pays en Development;est-ce Possible? Quebec, CECI, 1980.

VERDIEU, E & BWATSHIA, K.- Liberation et Autonomie Collectives. Québec, CECI, 1980.

VERLAG DIE WIRTSHAFT.- Länder der Erde. Koln, Pahl- Rugenstein, 1982.

VIEL, B.- La explosión demográfica. Mexico, PAX, 1974.

VILLALOBOS, J.- Por qué lucha el FMLN. Radio Venceremos, 1983.

VILLEGAS QUIROGA, C & AGUIRRE BADANI, A.- Estudio de la crisis y la nueva política económica en Bolivia. Bolivia, Centro de Estudios para el Desarrollo Laboral y Agrario.

VISION de Belice. Havana, Casa de las América, 1982.

VIVO ESCOTO, JA.- Geografía Humana y Económica. Mexico, Patria, 1975.

WEISSMAN, S. et al.- The Trojan Horse. A radical Look at Foreign Aid. San Francisco, Ramparts, 1974.

WETTSTEIN, G.- Subdesarrollo y geografía. Mérida, Universida de los Andes, 1978.

WHANNEL, G.- Blowing the whistle: The politics of sport. London, Pluto, 1983.

WIENER, D.- Shalom, Israels Friedensbewegung. Hamburg, Rowohlt, 1984.

WILLIAMS, N.- Chronology of the modern World 1763-1965. Middlesex, Penguin, 1975.

WOLFE, A.et al.- La cuestión de la Democracia. Mexico, UILA, 1980.

WORLD DEBT TABLES 1996. External debt of developing countries. Washington, 1996.

WORLD BANK.- Atlas 1996. New York, 1996.

WORLD BANK.- Energy in the Developing Countries. Washington, 1980.

WORLD BANK.- World Development Indicators 1998. Washington, 1998.

WORLD FACTS and MAPS. Rand Mc Nally. USA, 1994.

WORLD Military Expenditure and Arms Transfer 1972-1982. Washington,1984.

WORLD RESOURCES INSTITUTE.- The Environmental Almanac 1993. Houghton Mifflin Company, Boston & New York, 1992.

WORLD RESOURCES INSTITUTE.- World Resources 1990-91. A guide to the global environment. New York, Oxford Univ., 1991.

WORLD RESOURCES INSTITUTE.- World Resources 1986. New York, Basic Books, 1986.

WORSLEY, P.- El tercer Mundo: una nueva fuerza en los asuntos internacionales. Mexico, Siglo XXI, 1978.

ZERAOUI, Z.- El mundo arabe: imperialismo y nacionalismo. Mexico, CEESTEM-Nueva Imágen, 1981.

ZERAOUI, Z.- Irán-Iraq: guerra política y sociedad. Mexico, Nueva Imágen, 1982.

ZIEGLER, J.- Main Basse sur l'Afrique. Paris, Du Seuil, 1978.

PERIODICALS

Africa News, Durham, NC, EUA
Afrique Mass-Media, Budapest, Hungary
Afrique Nouvelle, Dakar, Senegal
Afrique-Asie, Paris, France
ALAI, Montreal, Canada
ALDHU, Quito, Ecuador
Altercom, Mexico,
AMPO Japan-Asia Quarterly Review, Tokyo,
Análisis, Santiago de Chile,
APSI, Santiago de Chile, Chile
AQUI, La Paz, Bolivia
Barricada Internacional, Managua, Nicaragua
Bohemia, La Habana, Cuba
Boletín de Namibia, UNITED NATIONS, New York
Bulletin of Concerned African Scholars, Charlemont, MA, EUA
Caribbean Monthly, Río Piedras, Puerto Rico
CEAL, Brussels, Belgium
Central America Update, Toronto, Canada
CERES, Rome, Italy
CILA, Mexico
Comercio Exterior, Mexico,
Contextos, Mexico,
Counterspy, Washington, DC, EUA
CovertAction, Washington, EUA
CRIE, Mexico,
Cuadernos del Tercer Mundo, Brasil,
Descolonización, UNITED NATIONS, New York
Diálogo Social, Panama,
Documentos FIPAD, Ginebra, Switzerland
Economie et Politique, Paris, France
El Caribe Contemporáneo, Mexico,
Eritrea in Struggle, New York, EUA
Facts & Reports, Amsterdam, Netherlands
Far Eastern Economic Review, Asia 1990, Yearbook. Japan
Fortune International, Los Angeles, CA, EUA
Freedomways, New York, EUA
Gombay, Belize
IFDA, Nyon, Switzerland
Informe R - CEDOIN , Bolivia.
Indian and Foreign Review, New Delhi, India
Internews, Berkeley, EUA
Isis, Rome, Italy
Ko-Eyú, Caracas, Venezuela
L'Economiste du Tiers Monde, Paris, France
Lateinamerika Nachrichten, Berlin
Latin America Weekly Report, London, United Kingdom
Le Monde Diplomatique, Paris, France
Monthly Review, New York, US
Mujer-Fempress, Santiago, Chile.
Multinational Monitor, Washington, US
NACLA Report on the Americas, New York, US
New Outlook, Dar-es-Salaam, Tanzania
New Internationalist, Oxford, UK
Newsfront International, Oakland, US
Noticias Aliadas, Lima, Peru
Novembro, Luanda, Angola
O Correio da UNESCO, Paris-Rio de Janeiro,
Onze Wereld, Den Haag, Netherlands
Palestine, Beirut, Lebanon
Pensamiento Propio, Managua, Nicaragua
Philippine Liberation Courier, Oakland, US
Politica Internazionale, Rome, Italy
Política Internacional, Belgrade, Yugoslavia
Resister (Bulletin of the Committee on South African War Resistance), London, UK
Revista del Centro de Estudios del Tercer Mundo, Mexico.

Revista del Sur, ITeM, Montevideo, Uruguay.
Sharing, Geneva, Switzerland
SIAL, Italy
Soberanía, Managua, Nicaragua
Southern Africa, New York, US
Statesman's Yearbook, 1988-1989.
Tempo, Maputo, Mozambique
Tercer Mundo Económico, ITeM, Montevideo, Uruguay
The Black Scholar, Sausalito, CA, US
The Ecologist, United Kingdom.
The CTC Reporter, UNITED NATIONS, New York.
Third World Quarterly, London, United Kingdom.
Third World Resurgence, Penang, Malaysia.
Tiempos Nuevos, Moscow
Tigris, Madrid, Spain
Tribune, Sri Lanka
Tricontinental, Havana, Cuba
Two Thirds, A journal of underdevelopment studies, Toronto, Canada
WISE (World Information Service on Energy), Netherlands
YEKATIT Quarterly, Addis Ababa, Ethiopia

NEWS AGENCIES

Interpress - IPS, INA, WAFA, SALPRESS, ANN, Prensa Latina, Angop, AIM, Shihata.
ALAI (Agencia Latinoamericana de Información).
SEM (Servicio Especial de la Mujer).

ELECTRONIC SOURCES

Rulers: http://www.geocities.com/Athens/1058/rulers.html
Le Monde Diplomatique online: http://www.ina.fr/CP/MondeDiplo/Thesaurus/thesaurus.fr.html
Folha de São Paulo: http://www.uol.com.br/fsp/
OneWorld News Service: http://www.oneworld.org/news/index.html
Fourth World Documentation Project: http://www.halcyon.com/FWDP/fwdp.html
Banco Interamericano de Desarrollo: http://www.iadb.org/
OMRI Daily Digest: http://www.omri.cz/Publications/Digests/DigestIndex.html
Il Manifesto in Rete: http://www.mir.it/mani/index.html
Electric Library: http://www.elibrary.com/id/2525/
United Nations: http://www.un.org/
The Washington Report's Resources Page: http://www.washington-report.org/links.html
Foundation for Middle East Peace: http://www2.ari.net/fmep/
Institute of Latin American Studies: http://lanic.utexas.edu/
New Internationalist magazine: http://www.newint.org

Arron, Hank 525
arrowroot 487
Arroyo, Carlos Alberto 231
Arsacid dynasty 118, 308
Artashes 108
Arthur 53, 128, 151, 317, 327, 342, 456, 549, 550
Artigas, José Gervasio 575
Artois 131
Aruba 110, 418, 420, 421
Arusha 338, 480
asbestos 169, 513, 359, 527
ASEAN (Association of Southeast Asian Nations) 63, 64, 114, 155, 230, 353, 379, 410, 448, 458
Aseb 222, 243, 248, 509
Ashanti 271, 272, 546
Ashkenazim 318
Ashkhabad 556, 557
Ashoka 301, 415
Ash-Sharqat 313
Asir 493
Aslonov, Kadridin 538
Asmara 243, 247
Assad, Hafez al 536, 537
Assanga, Sigo 167
Assyrian 235, 311, 522
Astrakhan 474
Asturias 467, 517
Asua 252
Asuncion 103, 152, 450, 451, 452, 575
Atafu atoll 102
Atahualpa 231, 453
Ataturk, Kemal 24, 553
Athens 214, 274, 275, 276, 370
Ath-Thani 468
Athulatmudali 521
Atlas 91, 403, 591
atomic energy 60, 336
Atropatene 118
Atropates, general 118
Attila 156, 267, 335, 398, 504
Attlee, Clement 569
Attoumane 196
Aubame, Jean Hilaire 261
Auckland 99
Audaghost 404
Augsburg 267
Augustine, Saint 571
Augustus Caesar 255
Aung San Suu Kyi 409, 410
Aures 552
Austerlitz 475
Austin, Hudson 277, 278
Australia 22, 26, 79, 101, 111, 112, 113, 114, 146, 229, 230, 252, 258, 300, 333, 334, 340, 414, 448, 449, 508, 559, 569, 580, 581
Austria 37, 57, 60, 81, 115, 116, 117, 131, 156, 157, 208, 216, 217, 219, 249, 267, 268, 269, 270, 296, 297, 321, 356, 369, 392, 395, 396, 417, 460, 461, 472, 504, 507, 563, 573, 593, 595
Austrian Empire 116, 208, 396
Austro-Hungarian Empire 208, 217, 268, 296, 369, 504, 593
Avar 369
Avarua 100
Avon 333
Avril, Prosper 292
Awami League 124, 125, 437
Axios 369
Axum 246, 590
Ayacucho 453, 454
Aylwin, Patricio 181
Aymara 140, 141, 142, 181, 454
Ayodhya 304
Aytmatov 350
Azerbaijan 108, 109, 118, 119, 129, 265, 266, 476, 478
Azeri 108, 118, 119
Azikiwe, Nnambi 428
Aznar, José María 517, 518
Azores, archipelago 136, 137, 464
Azov Sea 564
Az-Zoubi, Mahmoud 537

B

Baba Diarra, Amadou 380
Babangida, Ibrahim 428, 429, 430
Babek 118
Babur 301
Bactrian State 538, 578
Bacwezi 560
Badr 590
Baganda 561, 562

Bagaza, Jean Baptiste 161
Baghdad 308, 310, 311, 312, 313, 331, 332, 346, 348, 435, 468, 493, 494, 535, 537, 555, 565, 574
Bagratids 108
Bagrianov 157
Bahamas 120, 121, 558
Bahonar, Javad 309
Bahrain 122, 123, 348, 468, 469, 492, 565
Bai 500
Baidh 592
Baikal lake 475
Bairiki 340
Bakari, Djibo 425
Baker, James 69, 199, 347, 483, 539
Bakili Muluzi 374
Baku 109, 118, 119
Balaguer, Joaquín 226, 227, 228
Balala 339
Balante 288
Balasagun 335
Balboa, Vasco Nuñez de 445
Balearic Islands 517
Balfour declaration 317, 441
Balgimbayev, Nurlan 336
Bali 305
Balkans 88, 156, 208, 210, 356, 369, 475, 504, 553, 593, 596
Balkhash 336
Balladur, Edouard 258, 470
Balmaceda, José M. 179
Balta 397
Baltic Sea 244, 245, 254, 268, 354, 355, 366, 367, 475
Baltic States 244, 245, 355, 367
Baluchistan 437
Bamako city 380, 381, 382
Bambar 496
Bambuk 285, 404
Banaba Island 340
Bandar Seri Begawan 155
Bandaranaike, Sirimavo 519, 520, 521
Bandung 236, 271, 305, 415, 519
Bangalore 302, 304, 520
Bangkok 165, 352, 409, 540, 541, 542, 543, 544, 545
Bangladesh 32, 46, 124, 125, 126, 301, 302, 304, 347, 408, 437, 439, 566
Bangui 175, 176, 177
Banhaus 390
Bani 404
Banja Luka 144
Banjul 263, 264
Bantu people 93, 94, 95, 161, 162, 166, 195, 200, 201, 242, 261, 262, 337, 338, 360, 373, 374, 407, 411, 412, 480, 490, 523, 542, 560, 561, 597, 598, 599, 600
Bantustans 512, 513, 514
Banyarwanda 481
Bao Dao, emperor 585
Baptist 97, 484, 588
Baptist, Leonard 225
Baranja 209
Barbados 96, 127, 128, 224, 277, 278, 383, 487
Barbuda 98
Barcelona 447, 517
Barents Sea 300, 434
Bari, Hamadu 496
Barka, Ben 402, 403
Barotseland 597
Barrientos, René 141
Barrow, Errol Warren 127, 128, 134
Basel 532, 533, 537
Bashir, Omar al 357, 523, 524
Basque 256, 517, 518
Basra 346, 492
Basrah 312, 542
Bassa 563
Bassein 410
Basseterre 485
Bastille 256
Bata 242
Batalla, Hugo 249, 576
Batavia 375
Bateman, Jaime 193
Bathory 460, 471
Bathsheba 128
Batista, Fulgencio 211, 500
Batoro 561
Battambang 163, 164

Batumi 265, 266
Baudouin 131, 132, 197
Baulé people 206
bauxite 112, 150, 256, 259, 272, 273, 285, 286, 289, 290, 292, 297, 324, 325, 472, 475, 500, 525, 526, 583, 586
Bavadra, Timoci 252
Bavaria 116, 217, 275
Baya 177, 396
Bayakole 481
Bayamon 467
Bayele 241
Bayinnaung 409
Bayonne 517
Bazargan, Mehdi 309
Bazin, Marc 293
BCCI (Bank of Credit and Commerce International) 174, 368
Beagle canal 106
Beatrix, Queen 418
Bechuanaland (Botswana) 146, 359, 527
Bédié, Henry Konan 207
Bedouin 331, 332, 364
Beg, Ulug 578
Begho 271
Begin, Menahem 318, 319, 441, 442
Beid 591
Beijing 32, 33, 77, 164, 183, 184, 186, 187, 188, 189, 190, 328, 343, 398, 399, 409, 574
Beira (Sofala) 542
Beirut 214, 317, 318, 356, 357, 358, 442, 535, 552
Bekaa Valley 357, 358
Belarus 129, 130, 336, 366, 461, 474, 475, 476, 477, 563, 564, 579
Belaunde Terry, Fernando 455
Belfast 314, 315, 316, 569
Belgium 26, 81, 92, 131, 132, 161, 173, 197, 198, 199, 255, 269, 368, 417, 418, 419, 479, 480, 481, 569
Belgorod 396
Belgrade 209, 210, 370, 593, 594, 595, 596
Belize 133, 134, 281, 282, 283, 570
Belmopan 134
Belo Horizonte 150
Ben Bella, Ahmed 91
Benelux 131, 368, 419
Bengal 124, 125, 437
Benhanzin 135
Benin 95, 135, 136, 195, 261, 361, 380, 428, 546, 547, 566
Benue 429, 496
Berber 91, 177, 178, 256, 385, 387, 402, 403, 404, 405, 425, 426, 427, 551, 552
Berbera 509
Berberati 177
Berbice 289
Bergen 433
Bering Strait 168, 571
Berisha, Sali 89
Berlin 78, 93, 117, 156, 166, 177, 197, 201, 257, 268, 269, 270, 293, 297, 322, 337, 346, 396, 399, 472, 476, 534, 593
Berlouis, Ogilvy 499
Berlusconi, Silvio 322, 323
Bermuda 137, 558, 568
Bermúdez, Juan 136
Bern 532, 533
Berov, Liuben 158
Bessarabia 396, 397, 472, 473, 563
Betances, Ramón Emeterio 466
Betancourt, Rómulo 582
Betancur, Belisario 192, 193
Betica mountain 517
Bfetislav I 216
Bogomils (or Cathari) 143
Bhindranwale, Jarnail Singh 303
Bhutan 138, 139, 415, 416
Bhutto, Benazir 437, 438, 439
Biafra 241, 428, 429, 490
Bignone, Reynaldo 105
Bigo 560
Bikini 383, 395
Bildt, Carl 531
Bilen 243
Bilma 524
Binaisa 561
Bioko 242
BIOT (British Indian Overseas Territory) 390, 498
Biratnagar 416
Bird, Vere 98
Birendra Bir Birkram Shah Dev 415, 416
Bisalanca 287
Bishkek 351
Bishop, Maurice 277, 278

Bismarck, Otto von 267, 268, 317, 334, 411, 449
Bissau 74, 93, 172, 264, 287, 288, 365, 491, 495, 497
Biya, Paul 166, 167
Bizerta 551
Bizimungu, Pasteur 480, 481
Black Hills 574
Black Sea 108, 156, 157, 266, 354, 366, 396, 471, 472, 475, 553, 554, 564
Blades, Ruben 447
Blair, Tony 390, 444, 568, 570
Blaize, Herbert 278
Blanco Party 575, 576, 577
Blanco, Antonio Guzmán 582
Blanco, Salvador Jorge 226, 227
Blantyre 373, 374
Blekinge 529
Bligh, William 251
Blue Mountains 324
Bluetooth, Harald 219
Boa Vista 172
Boat Peace, The 230
Bocas del Toro 446
Boer 146, 359, 511, 512, 569
Boganda, Barthelemy 175
Bogdan 396
Bogotazo 192
Bohemia 115, 116, 216, 217, 269, 296, 504, 505
Bohuslan 529
Boii 216
Boipatong 514
Bokassa, Jean-Bedel 175, 176
Bolger, Jim 101
Bolívar, Simón 140, 192, 193, 194, 231, 291, 445, 453, 582, 583, 584
Bolivia 20, 26, 103, 140, 141, 142, 150, 153, 179, 232, 233, 284, 450, 452, 453, 454, 455, 582
Bolkiah, Hassanal 155
Bolshevik 244, 253, 265, 476, 538, 556, 563, 578
Bombay 301, 302, 304
Bombom 490
Bonaire 110, 420, 421
Bonaparte, Napoleon 256, 291, 321, 418, 484
Bongo 178, 261, 262
Bonin Islands 328
Borballo, Ricardo 280
Bordaberry, Juan María 576
Bordiga, Amadeo 322
Borinquen 466
Boris III 157
Borja, Rodrigo 232
Borneo 154, 155, 305, 375, 376, 377, 457, 502
Bornhausen, Jorge 150
Bornu 177, 425, 496, 524
Boross, Peter 298
Borten, Per 433
Bosch, Juan 226, 227, 228
Boshilov 157
Bosna River 144
Bosnia-Herzegovina 78, 79, 89, 143, 144,145, 208, 209, 210, 296, 447, 574, 593, 595, 596
Bosphorus 553, 554
Bossi, Umberto 323
Botchwey, Kwesi 273
Botero, Fernando 194
Botha, Pieter Willem 412, 513
Botswana 146, 147, 407, 412, 511, 512, 527, 599
Bouabid, Maali 402
Bouar 175, 177
Bougainville, Louis Antoine de 107, 448, 449, 508, 580
Bourassa, Robert 170
Bourbons, The 231, 388, 445, 516
Bourguiba, Habib 551, 552
Bouterse, Desi 525, 526
Boves, José Tomás 582
Bowe, Nigel 121
Boyer, J.P. 291
Brabant 417
Brahmaputra 125
Braithwaite, Nicholas 225, 278
Brakna 385
Bramble, Austin 401
Branco 151, 172
Brandt, Willy 269, 270, 401
Brasilia 150
Bratislava 218, 505
Bratteli, Trygve 433
Brava 172, 509
Brazauskas, Algirdas 367

Elburz 309
Elchibei, Abulfaz 119
Electrolux 530
Elias, Taslim 430
Elizabeth I 567
Elizabeth II 98, 121, 134, 137, 325, 388, 449, 568
Ellacuria 239
Ellice 102, 340, 559
Elmina 418
Elobey 242
Eman, Herny 110
embargo 109, 141, 162, 185, 199, 204, 213, 215, 228, 292, 293, 313, 320, 327, 331, 343, 363, 365, 370, 382, 423, 477, 493, 515, 524, 579, 593, 596, 599
Embu 338
Endara, Guillermo 446, 447
energy 21, 35, 53, 56, 60, 61, 133, 135, 138, 139, 159, 160, 170, 184, 192, 200, 219, 245, 256, 264, 266, 270, 273, 288, 300, 336, 339, 361, 367, 379, 383, 416, 419, 426, 427, 442, 469, 480, 530, 574, 579, 588
Eni Hunkin, Faleomavaega 489
Eniwetok 395
Enkhsaikhan, Mendsayhany 400
Ennahda, Hezb 552
Enosis 214
Entebbe 337, 524
Entrecasteaux 449
environment 23, 35, 37, 45, 49, 52, 56, 62, 70, 76101, 111, 113, 121, 139, 161, 202, 209, 252, 254, 260, 266, 299, 300, 306, 307, 360, 363, 377, 379, 383, 388, 416, 434, 448, 458, 497, 499, 530, 541, 544, 576, 579, 586, 598
Epi 581
Erebuni 108
Erie, Lake 572
Erik of Scandinavia 432
Erik, fiefdom of 529
Erikson, Leif 432
Eritrea 222, 243, 246, 247, 248, 321, 509, 523, 524, 592
Erlander, Leif 530
Erromango 581
Ershad, Hussein Muhammad 124, 125, 126
Escobar, Pablo 194
Espinoza, Pedro 181
Esquiline 321
Esquivel, Manuel 133, 134
Esselte 530
Essequibo 289, 583, 290
Estonia 80, 244, 245, 266, 350, 354, 355, 366, 367, 476, 477, 529
Estrada Cabrera, Manuel 281
Estrada Rabago, Juan 203,
Estrada, Joseph 457, 458
Ethiopia 24, 80, 94, 161, 162, 213, 215, 221, 223, 243, 246, 247, 248, 322, 339, 492, 509, 510, 523, 524, 590, 591
EU 37, 213, 215, 221, 254, 368, 370, 382, 384, 419, 434, 462, 518, 531, 555, 570
Euondos 167
Euphrates 24, 25, 312, 536, 555
Euripides 275
Everest 416
Evita 104
Evren, Kenan 553
Ewe 135, 272, 546, 547
Extremadura 517
Exxon 110, 420, 421, 574

F

Fachoda 522
Faeroe Islands 219, 220
Fahd ibn Abdul Aziz 310, 493, 494
Faidherbe 385
Faidu, Ibrahima 496
Faisalabad 438
Fakaofo 102
Fala, Fenua 102
Falkland Islands see Malvinas
famine 172, 177, 178, 185
Fang 241, 242, 261, 262
Fangataufa 260, 548
Fanon, Franz 90
Fanti 271, 272
FAO 20, 21, 22, 97, 273, 283, 295, 372, 386, 400
Faraj Said ibn Ghanem 591, 594
Farnavaz 265
Farrapos War 149
Farrelly, Alexander 588
fascist 229, 322, 323, 472, 516, 517, 593
Fattah Ismail, Abdel 591

Febres Cordero, León 231, 232, 234
Fenech Adami, Edward 382
Ferdinand I 115, 217
Ferdinand II 116, 217
Ferdinand of Saxe-Coburg 156
Ferdinand, Franz 593
Fergana Valley 350, 351, 539, 578, 579
Fernandes, George 303
Fernández Reyna 227, 228
Fernández, Max 142
Fernando VII 103
Ferreira Aldunate, Wilson 577
Fez city 402, 403
Fezzan 177, 364, 365, 524
Figueiredo, Joao Baptista 151
Figueres, José 203, 204, 205
Fiji Island 251, 252, 257, 333, 334, 340, 459, 488, 489, 508, 548
Filali, al Latif 405
Filizzola, Carlos 451, 452
Fini, Gianfranco 323
Finland 22, 37, 61, 219, 245, 253, 254, 299, 434, 475, 529, 531
Finnbogadottir, Vigdis 299, 300
Finno-Ugric 244
Firestone 362
fishing 97, 102, 107, 111, 122, 125, 155, 167, 170, 171, 173, 174, 231, 234, 244, 245, 257, 289, 299, 300, 324, 327, 334, 340, 346, 375, 378, 379, 386, 395, 411, 412, 413, 414, 417, 424, 431, 432, 433, 434, 436, 440, 448, 455, 459, 468, 470, 483, 484, 489, 491, 498, 525, 529, 530, 558, 559, 566, 571, 588, 589
Flanders 131, 132, 149, 417, 567
Florence 321
Flores, Venancio 103, 450, 575
Florida 120, 212, 508, 571, 572
FMLN 238, 239, 240
Fodio, Osman Dan 496
Fogo (Leeward Is) 172
Fon people 135, 136
Ford, Gerald, 229, 306
Foreign Legion 177
Formosa 342, 440
Franca, Fernando 94
France 22, 26, 28, 30, 45, 48, 57, 58, 60, 61, 66, 74, 76, 77, 81, 90, 91, 92, 93, 101, 103, 107, 114, 131, 135, 136, 163, 164, 167, 168, 169, 175, 176, 177, 178, 195, 196, 198, 199, 200, 206, 217, 222, 223, 236, 241, 249, 255, 256, 257, 258, 259, 260, 261, 263, 267, 268, 269, 275, 277, 279, 285, 286, 288, 291, 292, 309, 311, 317, 318, 321, 322, 327, 330, 331, 333, 334, 346, 347, 356, 358, 368, 371, 380, 384, 385, 386, 388, 390, 392, 402, 412, 414, 417, 418, 425, 426, 428, 429, 447, 449, 459, 461, 470, 472, 473, 475, 476, 479, 480, 481, 482, 483, 486, 495, 499, 517, 518, 522, 531, 532, 534, 535, 536, 537, 551, 565, 567, 568, 569, 571, 572, 573, 579, 580, 595, 596
Francistown 147
Franco, Francisco 516
Franco, Itamar 152
Frank 101, 232, 234, 401
Frankish Empire 208, 216, 267, 504, 532
Frederick 115, 116, 137, 220, 224, 253, 272, 532, 598
Freetown 501
Frei, Eduardo 153, 180, 181, 234
Freire, Paulo 491
FRELIMO 373, 406, 407, 408, 490
Friedman, Milton, 81
Friendly Islands 548
Friesland 417
Frondizi, Arturo 104
Front Line States 512
Fru Ndi, John 167
Fujairah 566
Fujian 191
Fujimori, Alberto 142, 455
Fujiwara 326
Fulah 159, 166, 271, 285, 286, 287, 288, 385, 427, 496
Fulani 136, 206, 264, 288, 381, 382, 387, 425, 429, 495, 496, 497, 500, 524
Fulbes people 167
Funa, James 501
Funafuti 559
Funan 163, 375
Futa Djalon 285, 286, 404, 496
Futa people 264
Futa Toro 496, 560
Fyodor 475

G

Gabon 74, 135, 175, 178, 241, 242, 261, 262, 285, 490, 491
Gaborone 146, 147
Gairy, Eric Matthew 96, 277, 278
Galante, Marie 279
Galich-Volin, Principality of 474
Galicia 517, 563
Gallegos, Rómulo 582
Galtieri, Leopoldo F. 105
Gambia 263, 264, 354, 362
Gamsakhurdia, Zviad 266
Gan, Island 378
Gandhi, Indira 303
Gandhi, Rajiv 303, 304, 520
Ganges 125, 301, 302
Ganilau, Penaia 252
Gao 381, 382, 404
Garang, John 524
Garcia de Hurtado 179
Garcia Meza, Luis 141
Gashmi, Ahmed al 591
Gaspar de Espinosa 203
Gassner, Cornelia 249
GATT 64, 113, 153, 171, 213, 329, 393
Gaul 255, 267, 321, 398
Gaulle, Charles de 91, 257, 285
Gaviria, César 193, 194
Gayoom, Mohamoon Abdul 378, 379
Gaza strip 25, 236, 318, 320, 442, 443, 444
Gbadolite 96, 198, 199
Geba 287
Gediminas, Vagnorius 366, 367
Gempei War 326
Geneva 64, 86, 107,209, 210, 230, 352, 363, 366, 443, 533, 537
Genghis Khan 85, 183, 187, 335, 398, 400, 538, 556, 578
Genoa 321, 322, 595
Geoffrey, Henry 100
Geok-Tepe Battle of 556
George I 275, 548
George Town 174
Georgetown 290, 375, 376
Georgia 107, 108, 109, 118, 119, 129, 265, 266, 313, 475, 476, 478, 508, 554, 557
Georgiev, Kimon 157
Georgievsk, Treaty of 265
Germany 26, 38, 45, 52, 57, 61, 66, 69, 78, 79, 81, 82, 116, 117, 129, 131, 147, 151, 156, 157, 161, 164, 166, 170, 208, 209, 217, 218, 220, 241, 247, 250, 253, 256, 257, 267, 268, 269, 270, 297, 305, 307, 309, 317, 321, 322, 327, 366, 368, 369, 395, 397, 401, 402, 411, 412, 417, 419, 422, 431, 433, 434, 440, 461, 462, 472, 473, 476, 488, 489, 493, 505, 511, 532, 533, 534, 548, 553, 555, 563, 565, 569, 573, 595, 596
Gero, Erno 297
Ghana 95, 159, 271, 272, 273, 302, 380, 404, 496, 546, 547
Ghani, Abdelaziz Abdul 591
Ghent 131, 132, 417
Gheorghiu-Dej, Ghoerge 473
Ghezo 135
Gibraltar 378, 404, 405, 517, 568
Gierek, Edward 461
Gilbert Islands 102, 340, 559
Giscard D'Estaing, Valery 258, 261, 580
Gissar 579
Gitega 162
Glarus 532
glasnost 118, 130, 157, 158, 265, 355
Gligorov, Kiro 370
Gobir 496
Go-Daigo, Emperor 326
Godoy, Virgilio 423
Godunov, Boris 475
Goh Chok Tong 503
Gola people 363
Golan 24, 25, 236, 318, 320, 358, 442, 536, 537
Golkar, Sekber 306, 307
Golu town 562

Gomel 129, 130
Gomulka, Wladyslaw 461
Gondar 247
González, Felipe 517, 518
Goodrich 362
Goose Bay 171
Gorbachev, Mikhail 80, 118, 130, 213, 217, 244, 265, 299, 336, 343, 350, 355, 366, 367, 397, 476, 477, 478, 538, 556, 557, 563, 578
Gorda, Virgin 588
Goris 108
Gorm 219
Gorno-Badakhshan 538, 539
Gotland 529
Goulart, Joao 151
Gouled Aptidon, Hassan 222, 223
Goumba, Abel 175
Gowon, Yakubu 428
Graca, Carlos da 491
Gracchi, Gaius 321
Grain 256, 362, 380, 475
Gramsci, Antonio 322
Gran Malvina 105
Granada 192, 231, 423, 445, 454, 582
Grand Bahama 120, 121
Grand Mogul 301
Graz 116
Great Lakes 79, 162, 169, 572
Great Northern War 354, 475, 529
Great Purge 476, 578
Great Trek 511
Great War 103
Greece 88, 156, 157, 214, 215, 265, 269, 274, 275, 276, 298, 303, 308, 321, 369, 370, 472, 554, 569, 593, 595
Green 19, 20, 112, 116, 132, 172, 180, 219 254, 266, 277, 322, 364, 368, 418, 457, 482, 530, 531, 564, 568
greenhouse 21, 56, 102, 379, 414, 572
Greenland 169, 219, 221, 300, 432, 571
Greenpeace 35, 37, 114, 258, 260, 300, 508
Gregory the Illuminator 108
Grenada 96, 97, 127, 224, 225, 277, 278, 289, 324, 486, 487, 525, 526, 549
Grenadine Islands 278, 485, 487
Grib, Mercheslav 130
Grigore Ghica IV 472
Grodno 130
Group of Seven (G-7) 503
Groza, Petru 473
Grunitzky, Nicholas 546
Guadalajara 392
Guadalcanal 508
Guadalquivir 517
Guadeloupe 224, 225, 259, 279, 384, 401, 421
Guaira 149
Guajira 583
Guam 280, 395, 431
Guanahani Island 120
Guanahatabey 324
Guandong 188
guano 340, 389, 414, 454, 455, 559
Guantanamo military base 212, 293
Guarani 104, 140, 141, 142, 148, 149, 202 139, 140, 141, 147, 148, 259, 452, 575
Guatemala 26, 28, 133, 134, 203, 204, 205, 238, 281, 282, 283, 294, 422, 423
Guayaquil 232, 234
Guaycure 103
Gueiler, Lydia 141
Guerrero, Larry 431
guerrillas 23, 28, 86, 87, 92, 105, 117, 119, 140, 162, 164, 166, 177, 193, 194, 197, 199, 209, 211, 223, 239, 266, 275, 282, 283, 304, 305, 308, 358, 369, 375, 381, 416, 426, 427, 455, 458, 495, 497, 501, 512, 515, 520, 521, 522, 523, 524, 540, 543, 554, 555, 561
Guevara Arce, Walter 141
Guevara, Ernesto "Che" 141, 211, 519
Guinea 33, 74, 93, 111, 136, 159, 172, 206, 207, 241, 242, 264, 268, 271, 285, 286, 287, 288, 305, 306, 324, 328, 333, 334, 363, 365, 380, 404, 430, 448, 449, 490, 491, 495, 496, 497, 500, 501, 508, 547, 580
Guiteras, Antonio 211
Gulf and Western transational 226
Gulf War 106, 123, 126, 176, 215, 227, 309, 310, 312, 332, 469, 493, 497, 518, 566, 570, 574, 591, 592
Guliyev, Fulad 119
Gumbs, Emile 97
Gurion, Ben 318
Guseinov, Colonel 119
Gustav 166, 217, 268, 529
Gutierrez, Carl T.C. 280

Guyana 128, 259, 289, 290, 418, 525, 526, 583
Gypsies 209, 218, 370, 595
Gyula Horn 297, 298

H

Haakon IV 432, 433
Haapai Island 548
Habibie, JB 307
Habibur Rahman 126
Hadebe, Keggie 514
Hadhramaut valley 492, 591, 594
Hafrsfjord 432
Haglelgam, John 395
Haidallah, Khouna Ould 386
Haider, Joerg 117
Haifa 318
Hainaut 131, 417
Haiphong 586
Haiti 121, 170, 226, 228, , 291, 292, 293, 324, 420, 558
Haley, Alex 263
Halibux, Errol 525
Halland 529
Hallstat 115
Hamadou, Gourad 223
Hamas 91, 92, 320, 332, 444
Hamburg 268
Hamdi, Muhammad-al 591
Hamhung 343
Hamid, Abdul 553
Hamilton 99, 137
Hamza, Prince 435, 542
Han 184, 341, 398
Handal, Shafick 240
Hanekom, Derek 515
Hani Abed 444
Hani, Chris 514
Hannibalsson 300
Hanoi 165, 586
Hans Adam II 249
Hanseatic League 219, 529, 354
Hansen, Erik Ninn 221
Hapsburg 115, 116, 296, 504, 532, 593
Haq, Zia-ul 437
Harald Bluetoth 219
Harald Harfagre 432, 433
Harappa 301
Harare 196, 373, 600, 601
Harbel 363
Harcourt, Port 429
Hardie Boys, Michael 99
Hariri 357, 358
Harjedalen Island 529
Harmoko 307
Harris, Lagumoto 414
Harris, Robert 97
Hashimoto 327, 330
Hasina 125, 126
Hassan II 402, 403, 404, 405, 482
Hata, Tusmotu 329, 330
Hatta, Muhammad 305
Haughey, Charles 314
Hausa 246, 272, 425, 427, 428, 429
Havana 211, 212, 213, 228, 496, 524, 525
Havel, Vaclav 217, 218, 219
Hawaii 327, 431, 489, 572, 573, 580
Hawalli 347
Hawiye clan 509
Hawke, Robert 113, 114
Hayasa 108
Hayden, William George 114
Hay-Herran Treaty 445
Hebrides 252, 333, 432, 580
Hebron 320, 444, 537
Hedeby 219
Heian 326
Hekhmatyar, Gulbuddin 86, 87
Helms-Burton Act 213
Helsinki 88, 253, 254
Helvetia 532
Henry III 216
Henry VIII 567
Herder 267
Herero 411, 412
Hermannsson, Steingrimur 299, 300
Hernandarias (Hernando Arias de Saavedra) 575
Herrera Campins, Luis 583
Herzegovina 79, 89, 144, 209, 210, 574, 593, 595, 596
Herzl, Theodor 317
Herzog, Roman 268, 270
Hessen, Frederick Charles of 268
Heynes, Richard 128
Hezbollah 310, 320, 357, 358, 444, 537

Hidalgo, Miguel 391
Hidareb 243
Hidjaz 331, 493, 590
Hilal, Beni 385
Hilly, Francis Billy 508
Himalayas 187, 301, 302, 415, 416, 438
Himito 326
Hindenburg, Paul von 268, 269
Hindi 252, 290, 302, 389, 503, 522, 525, 550
Hinds 290
Hindus 126, 301, 302, 303, 304, 415
Hiraan 509
Hirohito, Emperor 328
Hiroshima 60, 61, 327, 573
Hispaniola 110, 226, 227, 292, 420
Hitler, Adolf 116, 117, 129, 209, 210, 217, 220, 268, 269, 317, 322, 397, 418, 472, 476, 478, 505, 533, 593
Ho Chi Minh 163, 164, 184, 345, 586
Hoare, Mike 498
Hodge, Omar 588, 589
Hoechst 347
Hogbonu 135
Hokkaido Island 327
Holland 99, 110, 131, 417, 419, 420, 475, 503, 526
Holon 318
Holst, Johan Juergen 434
Holstein, Duchies of 220, 268
Holy Roman Empire 131, 216, 267, 296, 532
Homs 364, 536
Honduras 20, 26, 29, 133, 134, 204, 205, 238, 240, 281, 294, 295, 422, 423
Honecker, Erich 269, 270
Hong Kong 64, 134, 155, 183, 184, 185, 186, 188, 189, 191, 222, 252, 327, 378, 390, 520, 569, 570
Hopi 571
Horthy, Milkos Admiral 297
Hosokawa, Morihiro 329, 330
Houphouet-Boigny, Felix 206, 207, 380
House of Nassau 368
House of Orange 417
Howard Island 469
Howard, John 112, 114
Howe atoll 508
Hoxha, Enver 88, 89
Hoyte, Desmond 289, 290
Hryb, Myachaslaw 130
Huanghe 183
Huaorani 232
Huascar 231, 284
Hubmaier 115
Hudaydah al 591, 594
Hudson Bay 169, 170
Hudson River 572
Huerpe 103
Hughes, Hubert 97
Hui 184, 187
Huichole 392
Huk Movement 456
Hulagidas 553
Hulagu Khan 308
human rights 33, 96 106, 113, 139, 150, 158, 165, 166, 180, 181, 190, 194, 197, 204, 223, 226, 228, 230, 231, 232, 238, 239, 240, 248, 257, 266, 273, 282, 283, 288, 290, 292, 293, 294, 298, 312, 320, 338, 339, 345, 360, 363, 374, 377, 382, 387, 413, 416, 419, 430, 433, 439, 448, 451, 455, 457, 479, 481, 494, 495, 497, 503, 515, 521, 524, 546, 552, 554, 562, 566, 577, 579, 584, 598, 601
Humboldt current 232
Hun 369 398
Hun Sen 88, 164, 165
Hungary 57, 80, 81, 114, 115, 116, 157, 208, 209, 216, 217, 270, 277, 296, 297, 298, 321, 369, 396, 462, 471, 472, 473, 476, 504, 507, 553, 563, 564, 569, 573, 579, 593, 595
Hunkanrin, Louis 135
Huon 333
Hurd, Douglas 107
Hurricane David 224
Hurricane Hugo 279, 401, 588
Hurricane Luis 97, 98
Hurtado, Osvaldo 231, 232
Husak, Gustav 217
Huss, John 216
Hussain Onn 154
Hussein, Prince 502
Hussein, Saddam 237, 311, 312, 313, 331, 574
Husseynov, Surat 119
Hutter, Jakob 115
Hutu 161, 162, 199, 479, 480, 481
Hyderabad 302

I

IAEA 343
Iala 288
Ibadan 429
Iberian 90, 149, 321, 402, 420, 464, 516, 517
Ibo 242, 428, 429, 546
Ibrahim al-Hamadi 591
Ibrahim Bare Mainassara 427
Ice Age 417
Iceland 219, 221, 299, 300, 432
Idris Mohamed Adem 243
Ifat 509
Ife 135, 361, 428
Ignalina 367
Ihamrit 435
Ikramov, Akmal 578
Ilich, Vladimir 476
Iliescu, Ion 298, 473
Ilirida, Republic of 370
Illyrian 143, 156, 593
Ilorin 428
Imanov, Amangledy 335
Imata Kabua 383
India 19, 23, 26, 46, 69, 76, 85, 122, 124, 125, 133, 138, 139, 148, 155, 164, 183, 187, 189, 246, 251, 252, 275, 301, 302, 303, 304, 305, 308, 318, 346, 347, 349, 369, 375, 376, 378, 379, 388, 389, 390, 408, 409, 415, 416, 418, 434, 435, 437, 438, 439, 468, 469, 492, 493, 503, 511, 519, 520, 530, 535, 538, 542, 549, 553, 565, 566, 569, 595
Indochina 164, 285, 327, 352, 353, 435, 544, 580, 586
Indonesia 22, 111, 114, 154, 155, 229, 230, 260, 278, 302, 305, 306, 307, 328, 375, 376, 418, 435, 448, 449, 456, 457, 503, 511, 519, 542, 545
Indus 85, 301, 438
inflation 89, 101, 106, 116, 119, 121, 127, 128, 130, 134, 136, 151, 152, 158, 171, 176, 187, 188, 189, 199, 205, 210, 221, 227, 232, 234, 272, 290, 297, 298, 299, 300, 304, 307, 315, 316, 320, 324, 339, 351, 353, 357, 358, 367, 374, 389, 393, 394, 410, 423, 434, 448, 455, 491, 500, 501, 505, 542, 545, 548, 549, 554, 561, 564, 570, 576, 577, 579, 583, 584, 592, 594, 596
Ingraham 121
Ingushetia 477, 557
Inka 140, 179, 231, 233, 284, 453, 454, 582
Innocent IV 366
Innu 169, 171
International Court of Justice 365, 382, 390, 418, 430, 482
International Monetary Fund 22, 63, 64, 69, 127, 136, 197, 204, 272, 278, 362, 372, 428, 462, 501, 519, 554, 562, 592
Inuit 168, 169, 170, 171, 221
Ionian Sea 275
Ioseliani, Dzhaba 266
Iqbal, Mohammad 437
IRA 314,-315, 316, 569, 570
Iran 53, 79, 85, 86, 87, 91, 108, 109, 118, 119, 122, 236, 265, 301, 308, 309, 310, 311, 312, 313, 319, 335, 339, 347, 351, 357, 365, 436, 446, 469, 493, 494, 524, 530, 536, 537, 554, 555, 556, 557, 565, 566, 579, 592, 595
Iraq 24, 53, 78, 79, 80, 106, 122, 123, 222, 230, 237, 280, 309, 310, 311, 312, 313, 317, 319, 331, 332, 346, 347, 348, 356, 358, 436, 443, 444, 469, 492, 493, 494, 530, 535, 536, 537, 554, 555, 565, 566, 574, 591, 592
Irbid 332
Ireland 21, 30, 66, 132, 314, 315, 316, 432, 449, 567, 568, 569, 570, 595
Irigoyen, Hipólito 104
iron 86, 91, 93, 94, 95, 100, 112, 115, 116, 119, 144, 146, 150, 157, 164, 166, 169, 184, 237, 241, 254, 256, 261, 262, 265, 274, 284, 285, 286, 296, 301, 302, 326, 333, 335, 341, 343, 361, 362, 363, 368, 370, 385, 411, 412, 427, 448, 457, 459, 464, 468, 472, 475, 500, 527, 530, 539, 552, 567, 568, 569, 572, 582, 583, 584, 586
Iroquois 571
Irtysh river 336, 350
Iryani, Abdel Karim al 590, 591
Isaac, Kendall 121
Isabel II 405
Isabel of Castille 516
Isfahan 309
Ishaq Kan 438, 439
Ishmael I 118

hydrogen bomb 340, 395, 569l

Islam 88, 89, 91, 108, 118, 125, 155, 177, 195, 222, 235, 301, 310, 320, 335, 348, 349, 351, 362, 365, 375, 376, 379, 404, 407, 425, 426, 429, 435, 436, 437, 438, 456, 482, 483, 492, 493, 494, 496, 503, 510, 522, 523, 524, 538, 552, 560, 565, 568, 578, 579, 591, 594
Islamabad 87, 304, 438, 439
Islamic 38, 79, 85, 86, 87, 91, 92, 104, 109, 118, 119, 122, 123, 125, 126, 154, 155, 164, 166, 177, 196, 223, 235, 236, 237, 251, 255, 263, 264, 301, 304, 305, 307, 308, 309, 310, 312, 332, 335, 336, 339, 347, 358, 375, 376, 378, 385, 386, 402, 404, 426, 437, 438, 439, 441, 442, 444, 456, 457, 469, 493, 494, 495, 509, 522, 523, 524, 536, 538, 539, 550, 551, 552, 554, 555, 556, 557, 560, 566, 578, 579, 591, 592
Ismailites 536
Israel 24, 25, 117, 123, 175, 182, 235, 236, 237, 246, 247, 298, 310, 311, 317, 318, 319, 320, 331, 332, 338, 357, 358, 364, 383, 388, 403, 419, 436, 441, 442, 443, 444, 462, 469, 473, 493, 494, 523, 527, 536, 537, 552, 555, 561, 566, 579
Issa 222, 223, 510
Issoufou, Mahamadou 427
Issyk-Kul 351
Istanbul 77, 156, 235, 396, 472, 551, 553, 554, 555
Istemi 350
Itaipu 170
Italian 37, 60, 88, 104, 132, 169, 200, 224, 243, 246, 249, 250, 256, 267, 268, 274, 302, 321, 322, 323, 357, 364, 365, 368, 398, 442, 444, 451, 507, 509, 516, 517, 532, 533, 551, 572, 576
Italy 37, 60, 66, 88, 92, 115, 117, 173, 217, 243, 250, 255, 260, 268, 269, 274, 297, 309, 321, 322, 323, 359, 364, 382, 391, 408, 472, 507, 534, 569, 595, 596
Iturbide 294, 391
Ivan Asen II 156
Ivan III 366, 474
Ivan IV 474, 475
Ivigtut 221
Izetbegovic, Alija 144, 210
Izmery, Antoine 293

J

Jaber, al-Ahmad al Sabah 347
Jacobs, José 368
Jaffa 318, 441
Jaffna 521
Jagan, Cheddi Sharat 289, 290
Jagiello 366
Jahrah 347
Jakarta 229, 230, 306, 375
Jaluit 383
Jamaica 133, 174, 204, 277, 324, 325, 558
James Bay Power Project 170
James II 568
James VI 567
Jammeh 264
Jammu 302, 439
Jamtland Island 529
Japan 26, 56, 57, 60, 61, 62, 63, 64, 66, 78, 79, 112, 126, 128, 139, 170, 183, 184, 189, 190, 196, 230, 260, 269, 280, 300, 305, 309, 326, 327, 328, 329, 330, 340, 341, 342, 343, 344, 352, 377, 383, 399, 408, 409, 431, 440, 456, 476, 502, 503, 540, 543, 569, 573, 574
Jaramillo, Bernardo 193
Jarpa, Onofre 180
Jaruzelski, Wojciech 462
Jassy 396
Java 111, 114, 163, 305, 306, 508
Jawara, Dawda 263, 264
Jaya, Irian 305, 306, 307, 376, 415, 448, 449
Jayewardene, Junius Richard 519, 520
Jeddah 493, 494
Jelgava 354, 355
Jelling 219
Jericho 320, 442, 444
Jerusalem 236, 317, 318, 320, 331, 332, 366, 436, 441, 442, 443, 444, 493, 494, 535
Jiang Qing 186
Jiang Zemin 184, 188, 189
Jinja 561
Jinnah, Mohammad Ali 33, 437
Joao VI 172, 287, 288
Jodoyar, khan of Kokand 350
Johnson, Lyndon 573
Johor Baharu 376
Johore 502, 503
Jomon 326

612

pesticides 26, 37, 42, 130, 187, 205, 266, 318, 389, 418, 419
Petain, Henri-Philippe 256
Peter I 475
Peter the Great 109, 396
Petite-Terre 279
Petlyura, Symon 563
Petra 331, 396
Petsarath 352
Peul 381, 382, 387, 428, 496, 497
Phidias 275
Philadelphia 572
Philip II 275, 368, 369, 417
Philip V 369
Philippines 155, 280, 327, 328, 345, 347, 375, 383, 431, 440, 456, 457, 458, 503, 572
Phillips Petroleum 230
Phnom Penh 164, 165, 545
Phoenician 356, 357, 535,
Phoenix Foundation 580
Phomvihane, Kaysone 352, 353
phosphate 101, 135, 164, 252, 340, 372, 403, 414, 426, 482, 483, 546, 551, 552, 559
Piast 460
Pichincha, Battle of 231
pieds-noirs 90, 257, 333
Pigalu 242
Pigs, Bay of 211, 573
Pilar 451
Pilsudski, Jozef 366, 461
Pinatubo 457
Pindling, Lynden Oscar 120, 121
Pindo 370
Pine Cay Island 558
Pinochet, César Augusto 180, 181, 182, 252
Pinsk 129
Pipile 238
piracy 107, 133, 364, 565
Pishpek 350, 351
Pitcairn 113, 459, 568
Pizarro, Carlos 193
Pizarro, Francisco 453, 454
Platt Amendments 211
Plovdiv 157
Plymouth 401
Po river 321, 322, 344
Po, Fernando 166
Podkrepa 158
Podolia 563
Pohiva, Akalisi 548
Pohnpei Island 395
Point Saline 277
Point Fortin 550
Point-a-Pitre 279
Pol Pot 164, 165, 540, 543
Poland 61, 80, 81, 115, 117, 129, 130, 216, 217, 244, 253, 256, 269, 296, 297, 298, 354, 366, 396, 460, 461, 462, 472, 475, 476, 504, 563, 564, 573, 595
Polisario Front 364, 365, 385, 404, 405, 482, 483
Polje, Krbavsko 208
Poll Tax 570
pollution 21, 45, 56, 81, 102, 119, 123, 125, 130, 132, 141, 144, 152, 157, 170, 177, 190, 191, 201, 215, 219, 227, 236, 252, 266, 268, 270, 286, 298, 309, 327, 328, 338, 344, 351, 355, 367, 372, 389, 392, 416, 427, 434, 446, 461, 464, 469, 472, 503, 505, 534, 536, 541, 544, 550, 554, 559, 568, 576, 583
Polotsk 129
Polynesia 99, 101, 102, 257, 260, 414, 459, 488, 489, 548, 559, 580, 581
Pomak community 157
Ponape 395
Ponce Enrile, Juan 457
Ponce, Emilio 240
Ponticas range 554
Pora, Paul 449
Porgera gold mine 448, 449
Porkkala 254
Port Louis 388, 389
Port Louis (Malvinas Islands) 107
Port of Spain 550
Portales 179
Porto Alegre 150
Porto Novo 136, 136
Portobelo 445
Portsmouth 225
Portugal 81, 93, 96, 103, 148, 149, 172, 189, 206, 229, 230, 241, 284, 287, 288, 305, 306, 326, 408, 420, 464, 490, 493, 516, 569, 575
Postdam 268, 573
Potsdam Conference 473
Poumele, Galeani 489

Poznan 461
Prague 216, 217, 219, 269, 296, 504
Praia 172
Pramoj, Seni 540, 543
Premadasa, Ramasinghe 520, 521
Pretoria 94, 96, 224, 315, 388, 411, 412, 413, 491, 512, 513, 514, 527, 528
Price, George 133, 134
Pridnestrovie 397
Primakov, Evgenni 477
Primo de Rivera, José Antonio 516
Primo de Rivera, Lieutenant 241
Prince Abdullah 331
Prince Johnson 362
prison 29, 45, 89, 92, 111, 113, 119, 126, 152, 165, 175, 186, 189, 194, 223, 224, 234, 240, 241, 242, 248, 278, 286, 307, 308, 332, 353, 357, 374, 377, 379, 439, 447, 452, 455, 461, 479, 489, 503, 513, 518, 527, 552, 574, 576, 582, 584
Prodi, Romano 322, 323
protest 86, 91, 114, 130, 132, 137, 157, 167, 205, 224, 225, 227, 230, 236, 238, 250, 260, 265, 266, 289, 290, 292, 297, 307, 319, 323, 344, 348, 367, 377, 385, 394, 409, 414, 416, 422, 426, 439, 441, 443, 444, 452, 458, 462, 467, 470, 479, 505, 512, 513, 514, 520, 523, 525, 526, 527, 539, 546, 550, 555, 569, 574, 580, 581, 584, 592, 597, 598, 601
Protestant 94, 99, 100, 101, 102, 104, 110, 113, 114, 115, 116, 134, 147, 169, 172, 174, 177, 180, 212, 217, 221, 224, 225, 239, 241, 243, 244, 249, 253, 260, 264, 267, 268, 278, 282, 290, 297, 314, 315, 316, 333, 339, 353, 355, 367, 372, 383, 395, 418, 446, 449, 472, 475, 480, 484, 485, 486, 487, 490, 505, 508, 525, 529, 533, 550, 568, 569, 570, 572, 580, 588
Prussia 220, 267, 296, 354, 356, 396, 418, 460, 475, 563
Prut 396, 397
Pskov 245
Ptolemies, Empire of 441
Puapua, Tomasi 559
Pueblo people 571
Puerto Argentino 107
Puerto Rico 228, 401, 456, 466, 467, 588
Punakha Treaty 138
Punic Wars 321, 551
Punjab 301, 303, 437
Punt 509, 590
Puntarenas 204
Punu 262
Purwanto, Coronel 229
Pusan 342, 344
Pushtus 86
Pyongyang 343, 345
Pyrenees 249, 517

Q
Qabul 398
Qabus bin Said 435, 436
Qasim, Mohammad bin 437
Qatar 122, 123, 348, 468, 469, 565, 566
Qian Quichen 185
Qin Shihuang 183
Qing 190
Qinghai 188
Quadros, Janio 151
Quebec 161, 168, 169, 170, 171
Quechua 104, 140, 141, 231, 232, 453
Queensland 112, 113, 114
Queme 136
quilombos 226, 324, 384, 490
Quirinal 321
Quisqueya Island 226, 291
Quito 231, 232, 234, 453, 454

R
Rabah 175, 524
Rabat 199, 403, 404, 425
Rabbani, Mohammad 87
Rabi Island 340
Rabikuna, Sitiveni 261
Rabin, Yitzak 320, 332, 444
Rabuka, Sitiveni 252
racism 93, 117, 137, 279, 288, 320, 413, 419, 442, 444, 515, 534, 599
Radama 371
Radic 209
Radimich 129
Raffles, Thomas Stanford 502
Rafsanjani, Ali Akbar Hashemi 537
Ragnar Grimsson, Olaftur 300
Rajai, Muhammad Ali 309

Rajim, Muhammad 578
Rajmonov, Imamali 539
Rakosi, Matyas 297
Rakotoarijaona, Desire 371
Rama dinasty 543
Rama, Rao 303, 304
Ramaema, Elias P. 360
Ramahatra, Víctor 371
Ramanantsoa, Gabriel 371
Ramos Horta, José 230
Ramos, Fidel 458
Rana family 415
Rangoon 409, 410
Rares, Petra 396
Rarotonga 100, 252
Rashaida 243
Rashidov, Sharaf 578
Rasmussen, Poul 219, 221
Ratsiraka, Ddier 371, 372
Rawlings, Jerry 272, 273
Razdan 108
Reagan, Ronald 45, 69, 105, 181, 198, 212, 231, 238, 299, 364, 395, 422, 423, 431, 443, 466, 469, 513, 574
Red Sea 222, 235, 243, 246, 247, 248, 332, 492, 493, 494, 523, 565, 590, 591, 592, 594
Redjambe 261
Redonda 98
refugees 28, 79, 80, 86, 87, 117, 121, 124, 126, 134, 139, 157, 161, 162, 171, 177, 197, 199, 204, 205, 209, 210, 221, 222, 243, 248, 254, 283, 286, 288, 293, 294, 297, 317, 331, 332, 352, 357, 359, 363, 373, 381, 386, 405, 407, 408, 438, 439, 442, 443, 478, 479, 480, 481, 482, 483, 492, 495, 500, 509, 523, 524, 527, 530, 533, 536, 540, 543, 557, 562, 595, 596
Rehuelche 103
Reich 117, 414
Reid, Michel 224, 225
Renaissance 30, 136, 144, 284, 311, 318, 321, 381, 382, 389, 472, 516, 538, 539, 564, 579
RENAMO 196, 407, 408, 600
René, Albert 498, 499
Renner, Karl 116
Reunion 91, 92, 196, 402, 470
Rex, Robert 101
Reykjavik 299, 300
Reyna, Fernández 227, 228
Reynolds and Kaiser 324
Reynolds, Albert 316
Rhee, Syngman 342, 343, 344
Rhine 249, 255, 267, 321, 417, 419, 532, 534
Rhodes city 369
Rhodes, Cecil 197, 317, 373, 597, 599
Rhodesia 96, 373, 569, 597, 599
rice 19, 89, 125, 141, 157, 163, 164, 165, 184, 191, 195, 204, 232, 236, 239, 259, 285, 286, 288, 290, 309, 326, 327, 329, 343, 344, 352, 353, 362, 363, 385, 409, 410, 411, 416, 427, 428, 458, 488, 495, 500, 520, 521, 528, 544, 561, 572, 576, 586
Richard the Lion-Heart 567
Rico, Aldo 106
Rif 402, 403
Riga 129, 354, 355
Rijeka 208, 209
Rijswijk, Treaty 368
Rio de Janeiro 19, 23, 62, 77, 149, 150, 151, 152
Río de la Plata 141, 450
Rioja, La 106, 517
Ríos Montt, Efraín 283
Ríos, Aldo 106
Riyadh 122, 123, 436, 469, 493, 494, 584
Robaina, Roberto 213, 225
Robelo, Alfonso 422
Roberts, Joseph J. 362
Robespierre 256
Robinson, AN 549, 550
Robinson, Mary 315
Roburt, Hammer de 414
Rocard, Michel 258, 334
Rocca, La 250
Rocha Vieira, Vasco 189
Rocky Mountains 572
Rodney, Walter 289
Rodrigo, El Cid don 404
Rodriguez Lara, Guillermo 231
Rodríguez, Andrés 153
Rodríguez, Miguel Angel 204, 205
Roh Tae Wo 345
Roman 58 88, 97, 108, 115, 131, 143, 144, 156, 169, 172, 177, 208, 209, 225, 227, 233, 235, 250, 255, 267, 268, 270, 275, 296, 297, 321, 331, 348, 353, 354, 356, 364, 369, 372, 383, 390, 395, 396, 417, 441, 460, 471, 473,

484, 485, 486, 488, 489, 490, 492, 493, 499, 504, 505, 508, 516, 532, 535, 548, 551, 553, 559, 563, 568, 588, 590, 593
Romania 156, 157, 269, 297, 298, 369, 396, 397, 434, 471, 472, 473, 476, 478, 564, 569, 593
Romanov, Michael (Czar) 475
Rome 77, 85, 92, 108, 156, 216, 233, 250, 255, 257, 265, 267, 269, 275, 296, 321, 322, 323, 354, 369, 408, 417, 471, 504, 532, 551, 553, 567, 593, 596
Romero Barceló, Carlos 466
Romero, Carlos Humberto 238
Romero, Oscar Arnulfo 238, 239
Rongelap 383
Rosario 104
Rosas, Juan Manuel de 103, 575
Rose 389
Roseau 225
Roskilde 219
Rostislav I 216
Rota Island 431
Rotsi 373, 599
Rotterdam 418
Royal Dutch Shell 154, 305, 420, 435, 468
Rozas Rodríguez, Ramón 452
rubber 152, 154, 164, 166, 175, 198, 200, 305, 362, 363, 375, 376, 452, 520, 544
Ruchuphan, Mitchai 541, 545
Rudd, Charles 599
Rudolf 42 115, 116, 217, 296, 471, 532
Ruiz Massieu, Mario 394
Russia (see also Soviet Union and USSR) 61, 78, 79, 80, 81, 85, 86, 87, 109, 116, 118, 119, 129, 130, 147, 156, 213, 214, 244, 245, 253, 254, 265, 266, 268, 275, 296, 300, 316, 329, 335, 336, 342, 350, 354, 355, 356, 366, 369, 370, 396, 397, 399, 432, 434, 460, 472, 474, 475, 476, 477, 478, 505, 514, 529, 531, 538, 539, 557, 563, 564, 565, 569, 574, 578, 579, 593, 595, 596
Russo-Turkish 396, 593
Rustavi 266
Ruth Perry 363
Rutskoi, Alexander 477
Ruvubu 162
Rwagasore, Louis 161
Rwanda 74, 80, 131, 161, 162, 199, 479, 480, 481, 562
Rwigema, Pierre Celestin 480
Ryswick Treaty 226, 291
Ryukyu 328

S
Saad al-Abdallah as-Salim as-Sabah 347, 357
Saba 421, 590
Sabah 154, 346, 347, 348, 375, 376, 377, 502
Sabra 319, 357, 442
Sacramento 572, 575
Sadat, Anwar 24, 236, 318, 442
Sahara 90, 91, 94, 95, 160, 166, 177, 178, 257, 381, 382, 385, 386, 387, 402, 403, 404, 405, 426, 427, 429, 482, 483, 496, 523, 552
Sahel 159, 160, 172, 177, 178, 381, 382, 387, 425, 426, 495, 496
Said al-Maktum, Rashid ibn 566
Said Barre,Muhammad 509
Saidu Tall, Omar 496
Saif, Ibrahim 524
Saiffudin, Omar Ali 154
Saifur Rahman 126
Saigon 163, 586
Saintes, Les 279
Saipan 431
Sajalin 327
Saka 335
Saks 350
Sal 172
Saladin 493
Salah, Ahmed Ben 551
Salalah 435, 436
Salifou, André 426
Salii, Lazarus 440
Salim 347
Salinas de Gortari, Carlos 393, 394
Salona 208
Salonika 369
Salote, Queen 548
Salsboejaden, Pact of 530
salt 97, 180, 302, 349, 404, 420, 558, 581
Salt Cay Island 558
Salto 576
Salvador, Jorge Blanco 226
Salween 410
Salzburg 115, 116

Sukarnoputri, Megawati 307
Sukhumi 266
Suleyman the Magnificent 553, 554
Sumatra 305, 306
Sumgait 118, 119
Sun 30, 140, 184, 233, 256, 344, 375, 394
Sunia, Fofo 489
Sunni 86, 123, 236, 312, 332, 347, 351, 356, 357, 358, 365, 403, 438, 469, 482, 493, 510, 522, 523, 536, 539, 552, 554, 556, 565, 566, 578, 579, 591, 594
Suriname 290, 418, 420, 525, 526
Sushkevich, Stanislav 130
Sussu 286, 500
Suu Kyi, Aung San 410
Suur Muna Magi 245
Suva 251, 252
Suvadiva, Republic of 378
Suvana Fuma 352, 353
Suyab 335
Svacic, Petar 208
Svoboda, Ludwik 217
Swahili 162, 195, 198, 338, 407, 542, 561
Swane, Ambrose 527
SWAPO 94, 411, 412, 413
Swaziland 359, 407, 527, 528
Sweden 22, 26, 37, 60, 61, 116, 219, 221, 244, 253, 299, 303, 309, 354, 366, 432, 433, 434, 460, 475, 529, 530, 531, 563, 595
Switzerland 66, 76, 107, 139, 174, 199, 249, 255, 300, 309, 394, 532, 533, 534, 595
Syaka Stevens 500
Sykes-Picot 311, 331, 535
Symonette, Roland 120
Syr Darya 336, 350, 539, 578
Syria 24, 25, 123, 236, 237, 257, 308, 311, 312, 313, 317, 318, 319, 320, 331, 356, 357, 358, 364, 436, 441, 442, 443, 469, 493, 497, 535, 536, 537, 542, 554, 555, 590, 591
Syrian 25, 98, 109, 236, 308, 318, 320, 356, 357, 358, 442, 493, 500, 535, 536, 537, 555, 566

T

Tabatabai, Sayyid 308
Tadjoura 222, 223
Taegu 344
Tahirid kingdom 538, 556
Tahiti 260, 459
Tahuantinsuyo 140, 233, 284
Taima 590
Taimur, Said bin 435
Taino 211, 226, 466
Taipei 190, 191, 440
Taiping 183
Taira 326
Tais, Tupuola 488
Taiwan 64, 184, 185, 186, 188, 189, 190, 191, 273, 280, 328, 342, 383, 440, 520
Tajidine Ben Said Massomde 195
Tajikistan 87, 336, 351, 538, 539, 578, 579
Takashi, Hara 327
Takemura, Masayoshi 329
Takeshita 328, 329
Taki, Mohammed 195, 196, 525
Talal, Hussein Ibn 331, 332
Talas 351
Taliban 79, 86, 87, 310
Tallinn 244, 245
Tamara, Queen 265
Tamasese 488
Tambo, Oliver 512, 514
Tamils 303, 519, 520, 521
Tampere 254
Tamuz 312
Tanaka, Kakuei 328
Tang 183
Tanna Island 581
Tanumafili, Malietoa 488, 489
Tan-Zam Railway 597
Tanzania 79, 161, 162, 186, 195, 246, 303, 337, 338, 376, 406, 407, 430, 435, 479, 480, 493, 512, 561, 562, 590, 599
Taraba 429
Tarabi 538
Tarahumara 392
Tarbagatay 336
Tarmiuah 313
Tarquinius Priscus 321
Tartu, Treaty of 245
Tashfin, Ysuf Ibn 404
Tashkent 350, 578, 579
Tasman, Abel 99
Tasmania Island 112, 113
Tassili 482

Tatar 335, 336, 396, 471, 475, 477, 539
Taveuni Island 252
Taya, Ahmed Sidi Ould 386, 387
Tbilisi 265, 266
tea 124, 183, 338, 373, 385, 450, 475, 498, 519, 520, 561
Teannaki, Teatao 340
Tedzhen 556
Teheran 309, 310, 556, 557
Tekrour 404, 496
Tel Aviv 247, 318, 320, 358, 441, 520, 527, 537
Temaru, Oscar 260
Temasek 502
Temne 500
Temuco 180
Temujin 398
Tenochtitlan 391
Tenorio 431
Teotihuacan 391
Terai 416
Ter-Petrosian, Levon 109
Terreblanche, Eugene 514
Tete 406
Tetovo 370
Teutonic Order 354, 366, 460
Texaco 231
Texas 174, 391, 571, 572, 573, 574
Thailand 20, 113, 155, 163, 165, 328, 345, 352, 353, 409, 419, 540, 541, 542, 543, 544, 545
Thakombau 251
Thatcher, Margaret 69, 181, 570
The Hague 178, 305, 365, 418, 482, 526, 596
Thessaloniki 275
Thessaly 274, 275, 369
Thiam, Habib 497
Thibaw 409
Thimbu 138
Third World 24, 26, 45, 46, 58, 61, 62, 69, 74, 77, 79, 133, 154, 170, 212, 221, 270, 276, 304, 305, 311, 328, 346, 376, 386, 413, 419, 433, 472, 493, 494, 498, 568, 573, 593
Thracia 156, 157
Thuwaini 435
Tiahuanaco 140, 202, 233, 284, 453
Tiananmen 78, 188
Tiber 250, 321
Tibesti 177, 178, 524
Tibet 138, 184, 187, 188, 398, 415
Tibu 427, 524
Tiflis 265
Tigranes 108
Tigre 243, 247
Tigrinya 243
Tigris 24, 311, 312
Tihmah 591, 594
Tilemsi 404
Timakata, Fred 581
timber 21, 94, 133, 148, 241, 261, 262, 273, 281, 289, 307, 328, 353, 377, 428, 432, 450, 452, 472, 505, 517, 526, 544, 562
Timbuktu 95, 402, 496
Timisoara 472, 473
Timna 590
tin 139, 140, 197, 198, 268, 305, 375, 427, 428, 475, 599
Tinian 431
Tinsulananonda, Prem 540, 541, 544
Tiradentes 149
Tirana 88, 89, 594
Tiraspol 397
Tisza 297
Titicaca Lake 140, 141, 233, 453
Tito, Josip Broz 88, 271, 302, 593, 594
Tito, Teburoro 340
Tiv 429
Tjibaou, Jean Marie 334
Tlatelolco Massacre 393
Tlatelolco Treaty 487
Toba 104
tobacco 66, 89, 108, 110, 127, 157, 177, 191, 192, 213, 335, 336, 350, 373, 416, 450, 451, 457, 467, 528, 561, 580
Tobago Island 354, 549, 550
Togo 268, 272, 362, 428, 546, 547
Tojar 538
Tokara 327
Tokugawas 327
Tokyo 64, 327, 328, 330, 399, 440, 548
Tolbert, William 362
Tomb Islands 320
Tombalbaye, Ngarta 177
Tonga 101, 251, 252, 374, 528, 548, 559, 597, 598
Tongatapu Islands 548

Tonton-Macoutes 277, 292, 293
Tordesillas Treaty 148, 149
Torodo, Abdel Kader 496
Toronto 169
Torres, Camilo 192
Torres, Juan José 141
Torrijos, Omar 445, 446, 447
torture 40, 90, 92, 105, 194, 210, 223, 242, 248, 283, 295, 338, 347, 348, 374, 410, 439, 458, 494, 515, 552, 554, 555, 576, 598
Tosco, Agustín 105
Totonaca 392
Toungoo 409
Touré, Samori 206
Tournai 131
Toxandria 417
toxic 54, 56, 60, 61, 81, 119, 142, 190, 245, 268, 300, 304, 376, 383, 424, 440, 530, 536
Transcaucasia 109, 118, 119, 265, 266
Transjordan 317, 442
Transkei 512
transnationals 20, 66, 67, 109, 118, 119, 206, 261, 281, 324, 325, 338, 364, 411, 419, 448, 502, 525, 530, 561
Transvaal 511, 512, 513
Transylvania 115, 296, 297, 471, 472, 473, 475
Trarza 385
Trejos, José Joaquín 204
Trelleborg 530
Trianon Treaty 297
Tribhuvan Bir Bikram Shah Deva 415
Trincomalee 520
Trinidad and Tobago 549, 550
Triple Alliance 103, 105, 150, 268, 321, 322, 450, 575
Tripoli 177, 357, 364, 365, 515
Tripolitza 275
Trobriand Island 33, 449
Tromelin Island 390
Troodos 215
Trotsky, Leon 476
Trovoada, Miguel 490, 491
Troy 274
Trucial states 565
Trudeau, Pierre 168, 169
Trujillo, Rafael Leonidas 226
Truman, Harry 317, 342, 573
Tsachila 232
Tsankov, Aleksandur 157
Tshisekedi, Etienne 198, 199
Tsiranana, Philbert 371
Tsonga 407, 513
Tsugaru 326
Tsumeb 411
Tsushima 326
Tswana 146, 147, 513
Tu 548
Tuanku Ja'afar ibni al-Marhum Tuanku Abdul Rahman 376, 377
Tuareg 91, 178, 380, 381, 382, 425, 426, 427
Tuat 404
Tubu 178, 427
Tudjman, Franco 209, 210
Tuimalealiifano 488
Tumart, Muhammad Ibn 404
Tumbuka 374
Tumin 350
Tungu 341, 343
Tunis 237, 442, 524, 551, 552
Tunisia 90, 257, 285, 364, 382, 402, 404, 551, 552
Tupac Amaru 454, 455
Tupac Katari 140, 141, 142
Tupamaros 576
Tupou IV, Taufa'ahau 548
Turbay Ayala, Julio César 192
Turkey 24, 33, 86, 108, 109, 118, 119, 156, 157, 214, 215, 223, 265, 266, 268, 269, 276, 311, 312, 313, 320, 351, 364, 366, 369, 370, 396, 462, 472, 535, 537, 553, 554, 555, 556, 557, 566, 573, 579, 595
Turkmenistan 119, 266, 539, 556, 557, 579
Turku 254
Turov 129
Tushpa 108
Tutsi 161, 162, 199, 479, 480, 481
Tutu, Desmond 430, 513, 515
Tuvalu 102, 257, 340, 414, 559
Tuzla 144
Twa 162, 479, 480, 481
Tyler, Wat 567
Tyre 356, 357
Tyrins 274
Tyrol 115, 116

U

Ubico, Jorge 281
Uganda 74, 76, 161, 162, 337, 338, 339, 479, 480, 481, 522, 523, 524, 560, 561, 562
Uighur 184, 335
UK 181, 273, 299, 314, 316, 415, 459, 487, 569, 570
Ukraine 60, 61, 129, 130, 208, 367, 397, 434, 460, 461, 474, 475, 476, 477, 563, 564
Ulan Bator 400
Ulate, Otilio 203
Ulivau, Na 251
Ulmanis, Karlis 354, 355
Ulna 581
Ummaia 535
UN 21, 60, 78, 79, 86, 87, 102, 105, 109, 114, 118, 123, 125, 130, 131, 138, 139, 147, 154, 155, 158, 162, 165, 169, 174, 176, 181, 190, 195, 199, 209, 210, 213, 215, 221, 222, 230, 236, 239, 240, 242, 243, 248, 252, 260, 280, 282, 283, 287, 288, 289, 292, 293, 295, 312, 313, 317, 318, 319, 320, 328, 329, 340, 342, 347, 348, 355, 357, 358, 363, 364, 365, 367, 370, 379, 382, 383, 390, 395, 397, 399, 405, 408, 410, 411, 412, 413, 423, 430, 431, 440, 441, 442, 443, 444, 447, 449, 455, 457, 466, 470, 477, 480, 481, 482, 483, 488, 489, 493, 501, 510, 513, 515, 521, 523, 524, 526, 530, 533, 537, 548, 563, 574, 579, 588, 596, 601
UNDP 79, 98, 167
UNESCO 58, 447
Ungo, Guillermo 239
UNHCR 79, 80
UNICEF 46, 79, 313, 413
UNITA 93, 94, 96, 186, 198, 407, 412
United Arab Emirates 122, 123, 348, 469, 565
United Brands 281, 294
United Provinces of Central America 203
United States 19, 26, 28, 29, 33, 37, 53, 54, 57, 58, 60, 61, 62, 66, 67, 69, 71, 74, 77, 78, 79, 80, 87, 89, 92, 96, 97, 101, 102, 103, 104, 105, 106, 113, 116, 117, 120, 121, 122, 123, 126, 127, 130, 132, 137, 142, 153, 165, 168, 169, 170, 171, 174, 176, 177, 185, 188, 189, 190, 193, 194, 198, 199, 200, 203, 209, 210, 211, 212, 213, 219, 220, 221, 228, 231, 232, 237, 245, 250, 256, 264, 269, 275, 276, 277, 278, 279, 280, 282, 290, 292, 293, 299, 300, 313, 316, 318, 319, 320, 324, 325, 327, 328, 329, 330, 332, 336, 342, 343, 353, 362, 367, 373, 374, 378, 382, 383, 386, 388, 390, 391, 392, 393, 394, 395, 408, 410, 412, 422, 424, 429, 430, 431, 433, 436, 438, 444, 445, 446, 447, 452, 455, 459, 462, 466, 467, 473, 476, 477, 480, 481, 484, 487, 488, 489, 493, 494, 498, 499, 504, 505, 508, 510, 513, 514, 524, 525, 540, 541, 543, 544, 549, 550, 557, 558, 561, 562, 564, 565, 566, 569, 570, 571, 572, 573, 574, 579, 580, 588, 592, 596
Upolu 488, 489
Upper Volta 159, 380
Uppsala 530, 531
Ural 336, 475
uranium 60, 112, 114, 161, 169, 175, 177, 178, 197, 198, 219, 234, 261, 262, 268, 289, 313, 330, 411, 412, 425, 426, 427, 513, 517, 539, 572
Uri 532
Uruguay 28, 56, 64, 103, 106, 113, 150, 153, 170, 181, 329, 408, 450, 452, 454, 573, 575, 576, 577
USSR 53, 61, 78, 80, 86, 88, 109, 118, 129, 130, 132, 157, 158, 175, 185, 213, 217, 220, 244, 245, 247, 253, 254, 265, 266, 269, 270, 297, 319, 328, 329, 335, 336, 343, 347, 350, 354, 355, 366, 367, 382, 397, 399, 408, 434, 444, 461, 462, 472, 473, 476, 477, 478, 530, 533, 537, 538, 556, 563, 564, 569, 573, 578, 579, 593, 594
Ustyurt 579
Usubaliev, Turdakun 350
Usune 335
Ute 571
Uteem, Cassam 389, 390
Utrecht 131, 417, 418, 568
Uvea Island 257
Uzbekistan 87, 130, 351, 538, 539, 556, 578, 579

V

Va 488
Vaea, Baron 548
Vaez de Torres 111
Vafiades, Marcos 275

INSTITUTO DEL TERCER MUNDO

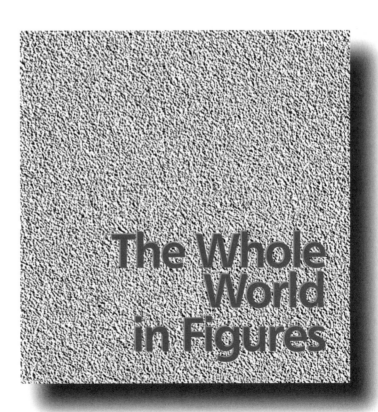

The Whole
World
in Figures

	Area (in sq km)	Total population (thousands) /4	Demographic growth to year 2000 (%)	Population estimate for year 2000 (millions)	Total fertility rate (children per woman)	Infant mortality rate (per 1,000 live births)	Under-5 mortality rate (per 1,000 live births)	Life expectancy at birth (years)	% of population with access to health services	Literacy (total adult literacy rate %)
	1994	1996	1994-2000		1996	1996	1996	1996	1990-1996	1995
Afghanistan	652,090	20,883	..	..	6.9	165	257	45	29	32
Albania	28,748	3,401	0.6	4.0	2.7	34	40	71	..	..
Algeria	2,381,741	28,784	2.4	31.6	4.0	34	39	68	98	62
Andorra	453	71	..	..	..	5	6	..	..	..
Angola	1,246,700	11,185	3.4	12.8	6.8	170	292	47	..	42
Anguilla	96	8	..	..	..	..	..	..	..	..
Antigua	442	66	0.8	0.1	..	18	22	75	..	95
Aotearoa/New Zealand	270,534	3,602	1.1	4.0	2.1	7	7	77	..	..
Argentina	2,791,810	35,219	1.3	37.0	2.7	22	25	73	71	96
Armenia	29,800	3,638	0.2	4.0	1.8	25	30	71	..	100
Aruba	193	71	..	..	..	..	..	..	..	..
Australia	7,741,220	18,053	1.1	19.0	1.9	6	6	78	..	..
Austria	83,859	8,106	0.6	8.3	1.4	5	6	77	..	..
Azerbaijan	86,600	7,594	0.8	8.0	2.4	34	44	71	..	100
Bahamas	13,878	284	1.6	0.3	2.0	19	23	73	..	98
Bahrain	694	570	2.2	0.6	3.1	18	22	73	..	85
Bangladesh	143,998	120,073	1.6	128.3	3.2	83	112	57	45	38
Barbados	430	261	0.2	0.3	1.7	11	12	76	..	97
Belarus	207,600	10,348	-0.1	10.0	1.5	14	18	70	..	99
Belgium	30,519	10,159	0.3	10.3	1.6	6	7	77	..	..
Belize	22,696	219	2.6	0.2	3.8	36	44	74	..	80
Benin	112,622	5,563	2.8	6.2	6.0	84	140	54	18	37
Bermuda	53	64	..	..	..	..	..	..	..	..
Bhutan	47,000	1,812	2.6	2.0	5.9	90	127	52	65	42
Bolivia	1,098,581	7,593	2.4	8.3	4.5	71	102	61	67	83
Bosnia-Herzegovina	51,129	3,628	..	..	1.4	15	17	73	..	..
Botswana	581,730	1,484	2.3	1.6	4.6	40	50	52	..	70
Brazil	8,511,965	161,087	1.3	169.2	2.3	44	52	67	..	83
Brunei	5,765	300	2.2	0.3	2.8	9	11	75	..	88
Bulgaria	110,912	8,468	-0.5	8.0	1.5	16	19	71	..	98
Burkina Faso	274,000	10,780	2.8	12.1	6.7	82	158	46	90	19
Burma (see Myanmar)	..	..	..	..	..	..	..	..	..	..
Burundi	27,834	6,221	2.7	7.0	6.4	106	176	46	80	35
Cambodia	181,035	10,273	2.3	11.2	4.6	108	170	53	53	65
Cameroon	475,442	13,560	2.8	15.1	5.4	63	102	56	80	63
Canada	9,970,610	29,680	0.9	31.0	1.6	6	7	79	..	97
Cape Verde	4,033	396	2.5	0.4	3.7	54	73	66	..	72
Cayman Is.	264	32	..	..	..	..	..	..	..	..
Central African Rep.	622,984	3,344	2.2	3.6	5.1	103	164	49	52	60
Ceuta	19	71*	..	..	..	..	..	..	..	..
Chad	1,284,000	6,515	2.8	7.3	5.6	92	149	47	30	48
Chile	756,626	14,421	1.4	15.2	2.5	11	13	75	97	95
China	9,562,036	1,232,083	0.9	1,276.3	1.8	38	47	69	88	82
Christmas Is.	135	0.9*	..	..	..	..	..	..	..	..
Cocos	14	0.6*	..	..	..	..	..	..	..	..
Colombia	1,138,914	36,444	1.7	38.9	2.8	26	31	71	81	91
Comoros	2,235	632	3.1	0.7	5.7	83	122	57	..	57
Congo D.R.	2,344,858	46,812	2.8	51.7	6.4	128	207	53	26	77
Congo R.	342,000	2,668	2.9	3.0	6.0	81	108	51	83	75
Cook Is.	236	19	..	..	..	26	30	..	..	99
Costa Rica	51,100	3,500	2.1	3.8	3.0	13	15	77	..	95
Côte d'Ivoire	322,463	14,015	2.2	15.1	5.3	90	150	51	..	40
Croatia	88,117	4,501	-0.1	4.5	1.6	10	11	72	..	98
Cuba	110,861	11,018	0.4	11.2	1.6	10	10	76	100	96
Cyprus	9,251	756	1.3	0.8	2.3	9	10	77	..	94
Czech Republic	78,864	10,251	-0.1	10.0	1.5	6	7	73	..	..
Denmark	43,094	5,237	0.2	5.3	1.8	6	6	75	..	..
Diego García	52	1*	..	..	..	..	..	..	..	..

	Primary pupil / teacher ratio	Newspapers, copies per 1,000 people	TVs per 1,000 people	Radios per 1,000 people	Book titles published per 100,000 people	GNP per capita (US$)	GNP per capita, annual growth %	Average Annual inflation (%)	Exports (million $)	Imports (million $)
	1995	1994	1994	1994	1992-1994	1996	1995-1996	1985-1995	1996	1996
Afghanistan	..	..	..	..	..	..	..	..	..	..
Albania	18	50	90	190	..	820	..	27.34	296	1,283
Algeria	27	50	70	236	1	1,520	1.8	22.94	12,609	8,372
Andorra	..	..	..	..	..	..	..	..	..	..
Angola	..	10	30	30	..	270	-1.7	169.46	4,472	2,039
Anguilla	..	..	..	..	..	..	..	..	..	..
Antigua	..	..	350	427	..	..	..	..	..	..
Aotearoa/New Zealand	18	300	510	991	..	15,720	-0.6	3.87	13,789	14,716
Argentina	..	140	320	673	26	8,380	2.7	255.62	23,810	23,762
Armenia	22	20	240	..	6	630	7.4	183.06	290	862
Aruba	..	..	..	..	..	..	..	..	..	..
Australia	16	260	480	1,291	61	20,090	2.6	3.73	53,252	60,897
Austria	12	470	480	619	100	28,110	1.0	3.19	57,822	67,142
Azerbaijan	20	30	210	..	5	480	-1.3	..	618	1,255
Bahamas	..	130	240	735	..	..	..	..	..	..
Bahrain	..	130	420	556	..	..	..	..	..	..
Bangladesh	..	10	10	47	..	260	3.8	6.41	3,297	6,898
Barbados	..	160	260	877	..	..	..	..	..	..
Belarus	20	190	260	285	32	2,070	2.9	..	5,122	6,778
Belgium	12	320	460	774	..	26,440	1.4	3.15	168,010	157,860
Belize	..	..	170	581	34	..	..	..	..	..
Benin	49	..	20	91	2	350	3.2	..	255	869
Bermuda	..	..	..	..	..	..	..	..	..	..
Bhutan	..	..	..	17	..	..	..	..	..	..
Bolivia	..	70	140	670	..	830	2.6	18.41	1,087	1,601
Bosnia-Herzegovina	..	..	..	..	..	..	..	..	..	..
Botswana	26	20	20	125	..	..	..	11.48	..	..
Brazil	23	50	250	393	14	4,400	6.7	875.31	47,164	53,736
Brunei	..	70	320	271	16	..	..	..	..	..
Bulgaria	17	210	260	454	69	1,190	-8.8	45.89	4,543	4,313
Burkina Faso	58	..	10	28	..	230	3.3	2.59	216	783
Burma (see Myanmar)	..	..	..	..	..	..	..	..	..	..
Burundi	65	..	10	64	..	170	-11.1	6.05	37	125
Cambodia	45	..	10	108	..	300	3.9	..	300	1,647
Cameroon	46	..	80	148	..	610	4.5	1.95	1,758	1,204
Canada	16	190	650	1,051	76	19,020	0.5	2.88	199,071	170,265
Cape Verde	..	..	..	176	..	..	..	..	..	..
Cayman Is.	..	..	..	..	..	..	..	..	..	..
Central African Rep.	..	..	10	73	..	310	-5.0	3.75	115	180
Ceuta	..	..	..	..	..	..	..	..	..	..
Chad	62	..	..	246	..	160	0.5	3.05	125	217
Chile	27	100	250	345	13	4,860	8.5	17.85	14,979	16,810
China	24	20	230	184	8	750	8.9	9.26	151,047	138,833
Christmas Is.	..	..	..	..	..	..	..	..	..	..
Cocos	..	..	..	..	..	..	..	..	..	..
Colombia	25	60	220	178	..	2,140	-0.5	25.17	10,976	13,863
Comoros	..	..	10	129	..	..	..	..	..	..
Congo D.R.	45	..	..	98	..	130	-0.1	..	1,461	1,331
Congo R.	70	10	10	115	..	670	4.7	2.21	1,833	1,590
Cook Is.	..	..	..	..	..	..	..	..	..	..
Costa Rica	31	100	220	260	29	2,640	-2.0	18.43	2,882	3,871
Côte d'Ivoire	45	10	60	143	..	660	4.6	4.01	4,996	2,909
Croatia	20	580	230	261	59	3,800	4.7	..	4,512	7,788
Cuba	14	120	190	347	9	..	..	..	1,834	3,004
Cyprus	..	110	160	300	142	..	..	..	..	..
Czech Republic	20	220	380	631	91	4,740	4.6	12.22	21,882	27,709
Denmark	10	360	540	1,036	230	32,100	1.8	2.84	48,868	43,093
Diego García	..	..	..	..	..	..	..	..	..	..

	Area (in sq km)	Total population (thousands) /4	Demographic growth to year 2000 (%)	Population estimate for year 2000 (millions)	Total fertility rate (children per woman)	Infant mortality rate (per 1,000 live births)	Under-5 mortality rate (per 1,000 live births)	Life expectancy at birth (years)	% of population with access to health services	Literacy (total adult literacy rate %)
	1994	1996	1994-2000		1996	1996	1996	1996	1990-1996	1995
Djibouti	23,200	617	2.7	0.7	5.5	112	157	50	..	46
Dominica	751	71	..	0.1	..	17	20	73	..	..
Dominican Republic	48,734	7,961	1.7	8.5	2.9	45	56	71	78	82
East Timor	14,874	829	..	..	4.9	149		45	..	..
Ecuador	283,561	11,699	2.0	12.6	3.2	31	40	70	..	90
Egypt	1,001,449	63,271	1.9	68.1	3.5	57	78	65	99	51
El Salvador	21,041	5,796	2.2	6.3	3.2	34	40	69	40	72
Equatorial Guinea	28,051	410	2.5	0.5	5.6	111	173	49	..	79
Eritrea	117,600	3,280	3.6	3.8	5.5	78	120	50	..	..
Estonia	45,100	1,471	-1.0	1.0	1.4	13	16	69	..	98
Ethiopia	1,104,300	58,243	3.2	66.2	7.0	113	177	49	46	36
Faeroe Is.	1,399	47	..	..	..	..	..	..	..	..
Fiji	18,274	797	1.6	0.8	2.8	20	24	72	..	92
Finland	338,145	5,126	0.3	5.2	1.8	4	4	76	..	..
France	551,500	58,333	0.3	59.0	1.7	5	6	79	..	..
French Guiana	90,000	153	..	..	..	..	..	..	..	..
French Polynesia	4,000	223	..	..	..	..	..	..	..	..
Gabon	267,668	1,106	2.8	1.2	5.3	87	145	55	..	63
Gambia	11,295	1,141	2.4	1.2	5.3	78	107	46	93	39
Georgia	69,700	5,442	-0.1	5.0	2.0	23	29	73	..	99
Germany	356,733	81,922	0.3	83.0	1.3	5	6	76	..	..
Ghana	238,533	17,832	2.8	19.9	5.4	70	110	57	60	65
Gibraltar	6	28	..	..	..	..	..	..	..	..
Greece	131,990	10,490	0.3	11.0	1.4	8	9	78	..	97
Greenland	2,175,600	58	..	..	..	..	..	..	..	..
Grenada	344	92	0.4	0.1	..	25	31	..	..	96
Guadeloupe	1,705	431	..	..	..	..	..	..	..	..
Guam	549	153	..	..	..	..	..	..	..	..
Guatemala	108,889	10,928	2.9	12.2	5.0	43	56	66	57	56
Guinea	245,857	7,518	1.7	7.9	6.7	130	210	46	80	36
Guinea-Bissau	36,125	1,091	2.0	1.2	5.5	132	223	44	40	55
Guyana	214,969	838	1.0	0.9	2.4	60	83	64	..	98
Haiti	27,750	7,259	1.9	7.8	4.7	94	134	54	60	45
Honduras	112,088	5,816	2.8	6.5	4.5	29	35	69	69	73
Hungary	93,032	10,049	-0.6	10.0	1.5	11	12	69	..	99
Iceland	103,000	271	1.0	0.3	2.2	5	5	79	..	..
India	3,287,590	944,580	1.6	1,006.8	3.2	73	111	62	85	52
Indonesia	1,904,569	200,453	1.5	212.6	2.7	47	71	64	93	84
Iran	1,633,188	69,975	2.3	76.4	4.9	33	37	69	88	69
Iraq	438,317	20,607	2.7	23.1	5.4	94	122	61	93	58
Ireland	70,284	3,554	0.2	4.0	1.9	6	7	76	..	..
Israel	21,056	5,664	2.1	6.0	2.8	8	9	77	..	95
Italy	301,268	57,226	..	57.0	1.2	6	7	78	..	98
Jamaica	10,990	2,491	0.9	2.6	2.5	10	11	74	90	85
Japan	377,801	125,351	0.2	126.0	1.5	4	6	80	..	..
Jordan	97,740	5,581	3.5	6.3	5.3	21	25	69	97	87
Kanaky/New Caledonia	18,575	184	..	..	..	..	..	..	..	..
Kazakhstan	2,717,300	16,820	0.1	17.0	2.4	38	45	68	..	100
Kenya	580,367	27,799	2.3	30.3	5.0	61	90	54	77	78
Kiribati	726	80	..	..	..	56	76	58	..	93
Korea, North	120,538	22,466	1.6	23.9	2.1	23	30	72	..	..
Korea, South	99,274	45,314	0.9	46.9	1.7	6	7	72	100	98
Kuwait	17,818	1,687	1.9	2.0	2.9	13	14	76	100	79
Kyrgyzstan	198,500	4,469	0.3	5.0	3.3	39	50	68	..	97
Laos	236,800	5,035	3.1	5.7	6.7	102	128	53	67	57
Latvia	64,600	2,504	-1.2	2.0	1.5	16	20	68	..	100
Lebanon	10,400	3,084	2.0	3.3	2.9	33	40	69	95	92
Lesotho	30,355	2,078	2.5	2.3	5.0	96	139	58	80	71
Liberia	111,369	2,245	..	..	6.5	157	235	48	39	38

	Primary pupil / teacher ratio	Newspapers, copies per 1,000 people	TVs per 1,000 people	Radios per 1,000 people	Book titles published per 100,000 people	GNP per capita (US$)	GNP per capita, annual growth %	Average Annual inflation (%)	Exports (million $)	Imports (million $)
	1995	1994	1994	1994	1992-1994	1996	1995-1996	1985-1995	1996	1996
Djibouti	..	..	50	81	..	..	..	..	..	..
Dominica	..	..	70	600	..	..	..	..	..	..
Dominican Republic	35	30	90	173	..	1,600	5.7	26.38	3,893	6,300
East Timor	..	..	..	..	..	..	..	..	..	..
Ecuador	26	70	130	327	..	1,500	1.2	45.52	4,762	3,733
Egypt	24	60	90	307	5	1,080	3.5	15.67	3,534	13,020
El Salvador	28	50	230	443	..	1,700	0.0	14.87	1,023	2,670
Equatorial Guinea	..	..	90	424	..	..	..	..	..	..
Eritrea	41	..	10	87	3	..	..	..	..	..
Estonia	17	240	360	467	152	3,080	5.2	77.18	2,074	3,196
Ethiopia	33	..	..	197	..	100	7.2	..	494	1,492
Faeroe Is.	..	..	..	..	..	..	..	..	..	..
Fiji	..	50	70	607	52	..	..	..	..	..
Finland	..	470	500	1,003	247	23,240	3.5	3.82	40,520	30,853
France	19	240	580	891	78	26,270	1.0	2.75	283,318	274,088
French Guiana	..	..	..	..	..	..	..	..	..	..
French Polynesia	..	..	..	..	..	..	..	..	..	..
Gabon	52	20	50	147	..	3,950	-1.2	5.01	3,146	898
Gambia	30	..	..	163	2	..	..	9.01	22	272
Georgia	16	..	220	550	6	850	..	310.04	261	884
Germany	18	320	550	935	87	28,870	0.9	..	511,728	443,043
Ghana	28	20	20	229	..	360	2.3	28.57	1,684	3,219
Gibraltar	..	..	..	..	..	..	..	..	..	..
Greece	16	160	210	418	..	11,460	2.2	15.38	9,558	26,881
Greenland	..	..	..	..	..	..	..	..	..	..
Grenada	..	..	160	595	..	..	..	..	..	..
Guadeloupe	..	..	..	..	..	..	..	..	..	..
Guam	..	..	..	..	..	..	..	..	..	..
Guatemala	34	20	50	68	..	1,470	8.6	18.64	2,031	3,146
Guinea	49	..	10	43	..	560	1.8	..	774	810
Guinea-Bissau	..	10	..	40	..	250	3.7	62.47	56	107
Guyana	..	100	40	491	4	..	..	..	..	..
Haiti	..	10	10	50	..	310	0.0	14.71	180	865
Honduras	35	40	80	408	..	660	-0.3	14.29	845	1,922
Hungary	11	230	520	625	100	4,340	2.6	19.88	13,138	16,207
Iceland	..	520	320	793	537	..	..	..	..	..
India	63	..	60	81	1	380	5.1	9.77	32,325	36,055
Indonesia	23	20	150	148	3	1,080	5.8	8.80	49,727	42,925
Iran	32	20	120	237	16	..	0.6	..	22,102	13,926
Iraq	22	30	70	218	..	..	..	..	502	492
Ireland	23	170	320	636	..	17,110	8.7	2.50	45,565	35,750
Israel	16	280	300	478	86	15,870	..	17.11	20,504	29,796
Italy	11	100	430	802	57	19,880	0.7	5.98	250,718	202,908
Jamaica	37	70	300	436	..	1,600	-1.9	28.34	1,347	2,916
Japan	18	580	620	912	28	40,940	3.6	1.37	410,481	347,496
Jordan	21	50	160	243	10	1,650	2.8	..	1,466	4,293
Kanaky/New Caledonia	..	..	..	..	..	..	..	..	..	..
Kazakhstan	20	..	260	376	7	1,350	1.8	..	6,230	4,261
Kenya	31	10	20	88	..	320	3.1	13.02	2,203	3,480
Kiribati	..	..	..	..	..	..	..	..	..	..
Korea, North	..	210	120	126	..	..	..	..	1,007	2,201
Korea, South	32	400	320	1,017	77	10,610	5.6	6.70	124,404	144,724
Kuwait	15	400	410	445	11	..	..	-0.47	13,420	8,113
Kyrgyzstan	20	10	240	..	7	550	4.1	..	507	838
Laos	30	..	10	127	1	400	4.0	22.59	334	642
Latvia	14	230	470	662	65	2,300	3.5	72.45	1,443	2,319
Lebanon	12	170	260	889	..	2,970	0.6	..	1,153	7,560
Lesotho	49	10	10	33	..	660	6.7	13.42	..	..
Liberia	..	..	..	..	..	..	..	..	..	..

	Area (in sq km)	Total population (thousands)	Demographic growth to year 2000 (%)	Population estimate for year 2000 (millions)	Total fertility rate (children per woman)	Infant mortality rate (per 1,000 live births)	Under-5 mortality rate (per 1,000 live births)	Life expectancy at birth (years)	% of population with access to health services	Literacy (total adult literacy rate %)
	1994	1996	1994-2000		1996	1996	1996	1996	1990-1996	1995
Libya	1,759,540	5,593	3.4	6.4	6.1	50	61	65	95	76
Liechtenstein	160	31	..	..	..	6	7	..	..	100
Lithuania	65,200	3,728	-0.2	3.7	1.6	14	18	70	..	99
Luxembourg	2,586	412	1.1	0.4	1.7	7	7	76	..	..
Macau	18	440	..	..	..	..	..	..	..	..
Macedonia, TFYR	25,713	2,174	0.7	2.2	2.0	26	30	72	..	..
Madagascar	587,041	15,353	3.2	17.4	5.8	100	164	58	38	46
Malawi	118,484	9,845	2.3	11.0	6.8	137	217	41	35	56
Malaysia	329,758	20,581	2.1	22.3	3.4	11	13	72	..	84
Maldives	298	263	3.5	0.3	6.8	54	76	64	..	93
Mali	1,240,192	11,134	3.1	12.6	6.8	134	220	47	40	31
Malta	316	369	0.6	0.4	..	10	11	77	..	91
Malvinas/Falkland Is.	11,410	2	..	..	..	..	..	..	..	..
Marshall Is.	181	57	..	..	..	63	92	..	..	91
Martinique	1,102	384	..	..	..	..	..	..	..	..
Mauritania	1,025,520	2,333	2.6	2.6	5.1	124	183	53	63	38
Mauritius	2,040	1,129	1.1	1.2	2.3	20	23	71	100	83
Mayotte	375	97*	..	..	..	..	..	..	..	..
Melilla	12	58*	..	..	..	..	..	..	..	..
Mexico	1,958,201	92,718	1.7	98.9	2.9	27	32	72	93	90
Micronesia	702	126	..	..	..	21	27	..	..	81
Moldova	33,700	4,444	0.1	5.0	1.9	26	32	68	..	99
Monaco	1	32	..	..	..	5	6	..	..	..
Mongolia	1,566,500	2,515	2.1	2.7	3.4	55	71	65	95	83
Montserrat	102	11	..	..	..	..	..	..	..	..
Morocco	446,550	27,021	1.8	29.0	3.3	64	74	66	70	44
Mozambique	801,590	17,796	2.7	19.6	6.2	133	214	47	39	40
Myanmar/Burma	676,578	45,922	1.8	49.3	3.4	105	150	59	60	83
Namibia	824,292	1,575	2.5	1.7	5.0	60	77	56	59	76
Nauru	21	11	..	..	..	25	31	..	..	..
Nepal	147,181	22,021	2.6	24.3	5.1	82	116	56	..	28
Netherlands	40,844	15,575	0.5	16.0	1.6	5	6	78	..	..
Netherlands Antilles	800	195	..	..	..	..	..	..	..	..
New Zealand (see Aotearoa)	..	..	..	..	..	..	..	..	..	..
Nicaragua	130,000	4,238	2.7	4.7	4.0	44	57	68	83	66
Niger	1,267,000	9,465	3.4	10.8	7.2	191	320	48	99	14
Nigeria	923,768	115,020	2.9	128.8	6.1	114	191	52	51	57
Niue	260	2	..	..	..	..	..	..	..	99
Norfolk Is.	36	/2 2.7	..	..	..	..	..	..	..	..
Northern Marianas	464	49	..	..	..	..	..	..	..	..
Norway	323,877	4,348	0.4	4.4	1.9	5	6	77	..	..
Oman	212,457	2,302	4.2	2.7	7.2	15	18	70	96	59
Pakistan	796,095	139,973	2.7	156.0	5.2	95	136	63	55	38
Palau	459	17	..	..	..	25	35	..	..	98
Palestine /1	6,220	2,761	..	..	6.1	30	36	..	..	84
Panama	75,517	2,677	1.7	2.9	2.7	18	20	74	70	91
Papua New Guinea	462,840	4,400	2.3	4.8	4.8	79	112	57	96	72
Paraguay	406,752	4,957	2.6	5.5	4.3	28	34	69	63	92
Peru	1,285,216	23,944	1.8	25.7	3.1	45	58	68	44	89
Philippines	300,000	69,282	2.1	75.0	3.7	32	38	68	71	95
Pitcairn	5	/3 0.07	..	..	..	..	..	..	..	..
Poland	323,250	38,601	0.1	39.0	1.7	12	14	71	..	..
Portugal	91,982	9,808	-0.1	9.8	1.5	7	7	75	..	90
Puerto Rico	8,897	3,736	..	..	..	..	..	..	..	..
Qatar	11,000	558	1.8	0.6	3.9	17	21	71	..	79
Reunion	2,510	664	..	..	..	..	..	..	..	..
Romania	238,391	22,655	-0.2	22.5	1.4	21	25	70	..	98
Russia	17,075,400	148,126	-0.3	146.0	1.4	20	25	65	..	99
Rwanda	26,338	5,397	6.4	7.7	6.2	105	170	36	80	61

	Primary pupil / teacher ratio	Newspapers, copies per 1,000 people	TVs per 1,000 people	Radios per 1,000 people	Book titles published per 100,000 people	GNP per capita (US$)	GNP per capita, annual growth %	Average Annual inflation (%)	Exports (million $)	Imports (million $)
	1995	1994	1994	1994	1992-1994	1996	1995-1996	1985-1995	1996	1996
Libya	..	10	100	226	..	..	..	..	10,126	5,191
Liechtenstein	..	..	..	..	..	..	..		..	..
Lithuania	17	140	340	387	77	2,280	2.7	..	3,356	4,559
Luxembourg	..	380	340	636	169	..	..	..	..	..
Macau	..	..	..	..	..	..	..	..	..	..
Macedonia, TFYR	20	20	160	182	31	990	0.6	..	1,119	1,941
Madagascar	40	..	20	192	1	250	0.5	18.41	616	671
Malawi	62	..	..	226	3	180	13.0	22.05	501	687
Malaysia	20	140	230	432	21	4,370	5.8	3.27	78,151	76,082
Maldives	..	10	40	118	..	..	..	..	..	..
Mali	66	..	10	44	..	240	1.2	4.57	288	1,159
Malta	..	180	410	530	115		..	..	..	..
Malvinas/Falkland Is.	..	..	..	..	..	..	..	..	..	..
Marshall Is.	..	..	..	..	..	..	..	..	..	..
Martinique	..	..	..	..	..	..	..	..	..	..
Mauritania	52	..	40	147	..	470	1.8	6.93	574	616
Mauritius	22	70	190	367	8	3,710	4.5	8.83	1,699	2,255
Mayotte	..	..	..	..	..	..	..	..	..	..
Melilla	..	..	..	..	..	..	..	..	..	..
Mexico	29	110	190	256	..	3,670	4.7	36.66	95,199	97,630
Micronesia	..	..	..	..	..	..	..	..	..	..
Moldova	23	20	280	679	18	590	-9.7	..	1,104	1,522
Monaco	..	..	..	..	..	..	..	..	..	..
Mongolia	25	90	60	136	12	360	-0.1	51.57	424	451
Montserrat	..	..	..	..	..	..	..	..	..	..
Morocco	28	10	70	219	1	1,290	10.4	4.84	4,742	8,254
Mozambique	58	10	..	37	..	80	5.0	52.24	226	783
Myanmar/Burma	48	20	80	82	8	..	..	..	1,187	2,524
Namibia	32	100	30	139	..	2,250	0.3	10.35	..	..
Nauru	..	..	..	..	..	..	..	..	..	..
Nepal	39	10	..	35	..	210	1.8	11.64	358	664
Netherlands	19	330	490	909	222	25,940	3.9	1.69	177,228	160,700
Netherlands Antilles	..	..	..	..	..	..	..	..	..	..
New Zealand (see Aotearoa)	..	..	..	..	..	..	..	..	..	..
Nicaragua	38	30	150	262	..	380	4.2	961.58	653	1,076
Niger	37	..	20	61	..	200	-0.1	1.28	79	567
Nigeria	37	20	40	196	1	240	1.9	32.98	15,610	6,433
Niue	..	..	..	..	..	..	..	..	..	..
Norfolk Is.	..	..	..	..	..	..	..	..	..	..
Northern Marianas	..	..	..	..	..	..	..	..	..	..
Norway	9	610	430	799	159	34,510	4.6	3.02	48,922	34,290
Oman	26	30	730	583	1	..	..	-0.21	6,395	4,610
Pakistan	..	20	20	88	..	480	0.3	9.16	9,266	11,812
Palau	..	..	..	..	..	..	..	..	..	..
Palestine/1	42	..	..	..	..	..	..	..	..	..
Panama	..	60	170	227	..	3,080	4.1	1.66	558	2,778
Papua New Guinea	33	20	170	76	..	1,150	-2.4	4.46	2,554	1,866
Paraguay	24	40	70	172	3	1,850	-1.5	24.89	1,043	3,107
Peru	28	90	100	255	9	2,420	0.0	398.52	5,226	7,947
Philippines	35	70	120	144	2	1,160	4.5	9.81	20,328	34,663
Pitcairn	..	..	..	..	..	..	..	..	..	..
Poland	16	140	300	441	28	3,230	6.2	91.77	24,387	37,092
Portugal	12	40	230	233	68	10,160	2.4	11.23	23,184	33,979
Puerto Rico	..	..	..	..	..	..	..	..	..	..
Qatar	..	150	430	428	69	..	..	..	..	..
Reunion	..	..	..	..	..	..	..	..	..	..
Romania	20	300	200	204	18	1,600	4.7	68.68	8,084	11,435
Russia	20	270	380	339	20	2,410	-5.0	148.85	81,438	43,318
Rwanda	..	..	..	67	..	190	7.8	10.84	168	385

	Area (in sq km)	Total population (thousands) /4	Demographic growth to year 2000 (%)	Population estimate for year 2000 (millions)	Total fertility rate (children per woman)	Infant mortality rate (per 1,000 live births)	Under-5 mortality rate (per 1,000 live births)	Life expectancy at birth (years)	% of population with access to health services	Literacy (total adult literacy rate %)
	1994	1996	1994-2000		1996	1996	1996	1996	1990-1996	1995
Sahara, Western	266,000	256	..	..	..	..	..	..	..	..
Samoa	2,831	166	1.1	0.2	3.9	42	53	69	..	98
Samoa, American	199	56	..	..	..	..	..	..	..	..
San Marino	61	25	..	..	..	12	13	..	..	..
São Tome and Principe	964	135	2.0	0.1	..	62	80	69	..	57
Saudi Arabia	2,149,690	18,836	3.4	21.7	6.0	25	30	71	97	63
Senegal	196,722	8,532	2.7	9.5	5.8	74	127	51	90	33
Seychelles	455	74	0.9	0.1	..	15	19	72	..	84
Sierra Leone	71,740	4,297	2.8	4.9	6.2	164	284	37	38	31
Singapore	618	3,384	1.6	3.6	1.8	4	4	77	..	91
Slovakia	49,012	5,347	0.2	5.4	1.6	10	11	71	..	..
Slovenia	20,256	1,924	-0.1	1.9	1.3	6	6	73	..	99
Solomon Is.	28,896	391	3.3	0.4	5.1	24	29	71	..	62
Somalia	637,657	9,822	..	..	7.0	125	211	48	..	24
South Africa	1,221,037	42,393	2.2	46.3	3.9	50	66	65	..	82
Spain	505,992	39,674	0.1	40.0	1.2	5	5	78	..	97
Sri Lanka	65,610	18,100	1.0	18.8	2.1	17	19	73	..	90
St Helena	122	6	..	..	..	..	..	..	..	..
St Kitts-Nevis	261	41	..	..	..	31	38	69	..	90
St Lucia	622	144	1.3	0.2	..	18	22	71	..	..
St Pierre and Miquelon	242	7	..	..	..	..	..	..	..	..
St Vincent	388	113	0.9	0.1	..	19	23	72	..	82
Sudan	2,505,813	27,291	2.2	29.8	4.7	73	116	54	70	46
Suriname	163,265	432	1.1	0.5	2.5	25	31	71	..	93
Swaziland	17,364	881	2.8	1.0	4.6	68	97	59	..	77
Sweden	449,964	8,819	0.3	9.0	1.9	4	4	78	..	..
Switzerland	41,284	7,224	0.7	7.4	1.5	5	5	78	..	..
Syria	185,180	14,574	2.6	16.1	4.2	28	34	68	90	71
Taiwan	36,960	21,035*	..	..	..	..	..	..	..	..
Tajikistan	143,100	5,935	1.9	6.0	4.0	56	76	67	..	100
Tanzania	883,749	30,799	2.4	33.7	5.6	93	144	51	42	68
Thailand	513,115	58,703	0.8	60.5	1.8	31	38	69	90	94
Togo	56,785	4,201	2.8	4.7	6.2	78	125	50	..	52
Tokelau	12	2	..	..	..	..	..	..	..	..
Tonga	747	98	..	..	..	19	23	69	..	99
Trinidad and Tobago	5,130	1,297	0.8	1.3	2.2	15	17	73	100	98
Tunisia	163,610	9,156	1.8	9.8	3.0	28	35	69	..	67
Turkey	774,815	61,797	1.6	65.7	2.6	41	47	68	..	82
Turkmenistan	488,100	4,155	1.9	5.0	3.7	57	78	65	100	98
Turks and Caicos	430	15	..	..	..	..	..	..	..	..
Tuvalu	26	10	..	..	..	40	56	..	..	99
Uganda	241,038	20,256	2.8	22.5	7.1	88	141	41	49	62
Ukraine	603,700	51,608	-0.3	51.0	1.5	18	24	69	..	99
United Arab Emirates	83,600	2,260	2.1	2.4	3.6	15	18	75	99	79
United Kingdom	244,100	58,144	0.1	58.4	1.7	6	7	77	..	..
United States	9,363,520	269,444	0.8	278.0	2.0	8	8	76	..	99
Uruguay	177,414	3,204	0.6	3.3	2.3	18	22	73	82	97
Uzbekistan	447,400	23,209	1.9	25.0	3.6	46	60	68	..	100
Vanuatu	12,189	174	2.6	0.2	4.5	41	53	67	..	64
Vatican	0.44	1	..	..	..	..	..	..	..	..
Venezuela	912,050	22,311	2.1	24.2	3.1	24	28	72	..	91
Vietnam	331,689	75,181	1.8	80.5	3.1	33	44	67	90	94
Virgin Is. (Am.)	347	106	..	..	..	..	..	..	..	..
Virgin Is. (Br.)	153	19	..	..	..	..	..	..	..	..
Wallis and Futuna	200	15	..	..	..	..	..	..	..	..
Yemen	527,968	15,678	4.0	18.1	7.6	78	105	57	38	33
Yugoslavia Fed. Rep.	102,173	10,294	..	..	1.8	19	22	72	..	98
Zambia	752,618	8,275	2.5	9.1	5.6	112	202	43	..	78
Zimbabwe	390,757	11,439	2.2	12.4	4.8	49	73	49	85	85

	Primary pupil / teacher ratio	Newspapers, copies per 1,000 people	TVs per 1,000 people	Radios per 1,000 people	Book titles published per 100,000 people	GNP per capita (US$)	GNP per capita, annual growth %	Average Annual inflation (%)	Exports (million $)	Imports (million $)
	1995	1994	1994	1994	1992-1994	1996	1995-1996	1985-1995	1996	1996
Sahara, Western	..	..	..	..	..	..	..	..	..	..
Samoa	..	..	..	462	..	..	..	..	..	..
Samoa, American	..	..	..	..	..	..	..	..	..	..
San Marino	..	..	..	..	..	..	..	..	..	..
São Tome and Principe	..	..	..	270	..	..	..	..	..	..
Saudi Arabia	13	50	250	294	..	..	..	2.80	58,117	27,764
Senegal	58	10	40	117	..	570	3.2	3.72	655	1,672
Seychelles	..	40	320	490	..	..	..	..	..	..
Sierra Leone	..	..	10	233	..	200	7.6	61.58	214	334
Singapore	..	360	380	645	..	30,550	5.6	3.87	124,794	131,083
Slovakia	24	260	280	568	65	3,410	6.3	10.56	8,824	10,924
Slovenia	14	180	300	378	151	9,240	3.2	..	8,308	9,412
Solomon Is.	..	..	20	122	..	..	..	..	..	..
Somalia	..	..	..	..	..	..	..	..	..	..
South Africa	37	30	100	314	11	3,520	1.0	13.86	18,132	26,861
Spain	18	100	430	312	112	14,350	1.6	6.31	101,417	122,842
Sri Lanka	28	30	70	201	17	740	0.5	11.77	4,097	5,028
St Helena	..	..	..	..	..	..	..	..	..	..
St Kitts-Nevis	..	..	220	666	..	..	..	..	..	..
St Lucia	..	..	250	764	..	..	..	..	..	..
St Pierre and Miquelon	..	..	..	..	..	..	..	..	..	..
St Vincent	..	..	230	667	..	..	..	..	..	..
Sudan	36	20	80	258	..	..	..	..	468	1,439
Suriname	..	100	150	680	..	..	..	..	..	..
Swaziland	..	10	70	163	..	..	..	..	..	..
Sweden	11	480	470	879	158	25,710	0.8	5.48	82,704	63,970
Switzerland	12	410	400	841	217	44,350	-1.2	3.37	80,756	79,192
Syria	24	20	80	257	4	1,160	0.6	15.97	3,980	6,399
Taiwan	..	..	..	..	..	..	..	..	115,646	101,338
Tajikistan	23	10	190	..	4	340	-8.4	..	770	668
Tanzania	37	10	..	26	..	170	1.7	32.27	828	1,642
Thailand	20	50	250	190	13	2,960	4.4	5.01	55,789	73,289
Togo	51	..	10	212	..	300	4.3	..	363	1,032
Tokelau	..	..	..	..	..	..	..	..	..	..
Tonga	..	..	..	..	..	..	..	..	..	..
Trinidad and Tobago	25	140	310	491	2	3,870	3.0	6.81	2,456	2,204
Tunisia	25	50	90	199	6	1,930	-0.4	5.95	5,517	7,681
Turkey	28	40	270	162	8	2,830	5.0	64.64	23,045	42,733
Turkmenistan	..	..	220	..	14	940	-4.3	..	1,693	1,313
Turks and Caicos	..	..	..	..	..	..	..	..	..	..
Tuvalu	..	..	..	..	..	..	..	..	..	..
Uganda	35	..	20	107	2	300	6.2	65.69	568	725
Ukraine	20	120	230	812	10	1,200	-8.5	..	16,040	24,042
United Arab Emirates	17	160	290	312	14	..	..	..	28,096	30,374
United Kingdom	19	350	450	1,429	164	19,600	2.3	5.07	259,039	283,682
United States	16	230	780	2,122	20	28,020	1.4	3.18	575,477	814,888
Uruguay	20	240	520	606	..	5,760	6.8	70.71	2,391	3,322
Uzbekistan	21	10	180	81	6	1,010	-0.8	..	2,671	4,761
Vanuatu	..	..	10	294	..	..	..	..	..	..
Vatican	..	..	..	..	..	..	..	..	..	..
Venezuela	23	20	180	443	17	3,020	-3.7	37.62	22,633	8,902
Vietnam	34	10	110	104	8	290	7.3	88.34	7,016	13,910
Virgin Is. (Am.)	..	..	..	..	..	..	..	..	..	..
Virgin Is. (Br.)	..	..	..	..	..	..	..	..	..	..
Wallis and Futuna	..	..	..	..	..	..	..	..	..	..
Yemen	..	20	270	32	..	380	-7.8	..	4,538	3,443
Yugoslavia Fed. Rep.	22	..	..	..	..	..	..	..	1,842	4,101
Zambia	39	10	30	83	..	360	3.4	91.51	1,020	1,106
Zimbabwe	39	20	30	86	2	610	5.8	20.93	2,094	2,808

Also from New Internationalist Publications

The A-Z of World Development

A major reference book on global issues for the new century.
by Andy Crump and Wayne Ellwood
The A-Z of World Development is a first-rate reference book on key themes and ideas of global development. The book combines the authority of a comprehensive reference work with the unique political and economic analysis for which the New Internationalist is famous.

◆ The book contains over 700 entries covering essential items as well as the eclectic. The listings vary in length from the short and snappy to longer definitions of a few hundred words.
◆ Entries are compiled in an alphabetical format but with a mix ranging from acronym, ideas and concepts through to individuals and events.
◆ Examples of listings include the UNITED NATIONS, STRUCTURAL ADJUSTMENT and ORAL REHYDRATION THERAPY but also include RASTAFARIANISM, INDIRA GANDHI and the CHIPKO MOVEMENT.
◆ Additional information to some of the main entries are in sidebars or boxes. These contain factual information or brief, colourful, atmospheric vignettes in the form of quotes or anecdotes.

The book is handsomely visual: three to four colour images per spread including colour photos, historical line-work drawings, colour illustrations, design motifs as well as charts, graphs and cartoons.

The A-Z of World Development book and accompanying CD-ROM is ideal for teachers and students at high school, college and university levels, as well as for home reference. It meets the strong public appetite for factual reference works and appeals to the many active supporters of human rights, social justice and Third World development organizations.

About the Authors:
Andy Crump has written *The Dictionary of Environment and Development* and works with the World Health Organization.
Wayne Ellwood is one of the most experienced staff editors of the New Internationalist magazine and works out of Toronto, Canada.

Format: Large paperback 274 mm x 216 mm (11" x 8 1/2 ") 294 pages, full colour throughout. Also available on CD-Rom.

Contact details:
New Internationalist Publications, 55 Rectory Road,
Oxford OX4 1BW, UK.
e-mail: jol@newint.org OR your national distributor.

'Thanks to the A-Z of World Development for guiding us on our way to better understanding the world. A rattling good book!'
Professor Norman Myers, Editor of The Gaia Atlas of Planet Management